iWorship
DAILY DEVOTIONAL BIBLE

iWorship
DAILY DEVOTIONAL BIBLE

NEW LIVING TRANSLATION®

INTEGRITY®

PUBLISHERS

Nashville

Contents

The Books of the Bible

CANONICAL LISTING OF THE BOOKS OF THE BIBLE

OLD TESTAMENT

New Testament

ALPHABETICAL LISTING OF THE BOOKS OF THE BIBLE

Contributors

DEVELOPMENT TEAM
Dr. Bruce B. Barton
Kirk Luttrell
Joey Paul
Betsy Todt Schmitt
David R. Veerman
Byron Williamson
Neil Wilson

SENIOR EDITORS
Betsy Todt Schmitt
David R. Veerman

COPY EDITORS
Mary Horner Collins
Linda Taylor

PRODUCTION AND TYPESETTING
Ashley Taylor
Kathleen Ristow
Thomas Ristow
Rosalie Krusemark

INTEGRITY PUBLISHERS CONTRIBUTORS
Byron Williamson
Joey Paul
Kris Bearss
Rob Birkhead
Amy Williams
Jacque Carrigan
Pete Sanchez

DESIGN
Cover design by The Office
of Bill Chiaravalle
Interior design by The Office
of Bill Chiaravalle

NOTES AND FEATURES

My Daily Worship
Greg Asimakoupoulos
Virginia Blackwell
Debbie Carsten
Katherine Cloyd
Susie Cross
Betsy Rossen Elliot
Kent Keller
Barbara Kois
Margaret Reneker
Marjorie Wallen Rowe
Eric Stanford
Linda Washington
Neil Wilson
Len Woods

Book Introductions
Dr. Mark Fackler
Mary Ann Lackland
Jan Harris
David Sanford
Len Woods

Words of Worship
Dr. Richard Leonard
Pete Sanchez

Worship Quotes
Peter Gregory, compiler

Indexes
Joanna Guest
Dr. Richard Leonard

Introduction to the iWorship

DAILY DEVOTIONAL BIBLE

The iWorship Daily Devotional Bible is just what the name implies—a special Bible devoted to helping readers develop a daily lifestyle of worship.

ELEVEN TRUTHS ABOUT
LIFESTYLE WORSHIP

✦**Truth #1:** In its purest sense, *worship* is simply assigning worth or value to someone or something. Did you know the word *worship* actually comes from the Old English term "worthship"—that is, the state of having worth or value?

✦**Truth #2:** Worship always involves the glad and lavish giving of our devotion. Did you ever notice that when a person views someone or something as valuable, he or she eagerly devotes time, allegiance, affection, emotional energy, material resources, and even praise to that person or object? Think of rabid football fans or young couples truly in love and this point will be obvious.

✦**Truth #3:** Everyone in the world is a worshiper. That is to say, we each have relationships or objects in our lives that we consider valuable, and usually *one* person or object we view as having supreme worth. The question is never "*Will* a person worship?" but rather, "*Who* or *what* will he or she worship?"

✦**Truth #4:** Not everyone in the world worships *God.* This statement needs—or *should* need—no explanation! Just look around today at the countless things people focus their lives on.

✦**Truth #5:** What a person truly worships can be easily discovered. Want to know what a person values above all else? Look at his calendar or schedule book, listen to her conversation, observe how he spends his money, and you will have a good indication of what that person considers as having the highest worth in life.

✦**Truth #6:** The Bible declares God, our Creator and Redeemer, to be *the* One who deserves our worship. He alone is truly worthy. (See Revelation 4:6, 8–11 and 7:9–12.)

✦**Truth #7:** God doesn't *need* our worship. He is complete, independent, and self-sufficient. It has been this way from eternity past and will ever remain so. Perfect and lacking nothing, the Lord is in no way diminished if human creatures refuse or fail to worship. The heavens themselves shout the glory of God (Psalm 19:1), and he is surrounded by angelic beings who forever praise him (Revelation 4:8). But God was complete even before the heavens were made or the angels existed!

✦**Truth #8:** Worshiping God leads to ultimate fulfillment; worshiping anything other than God is idolatry. The psalm writer boldly declared: "You will show me the way of life, granting me the joy of your presence and the pleasures of living with you forever" (Psalm 16:11). The theologian Augustine wisely observed: "You have made us for yourself, O God, and our hearts are restless until they find their rest in you."

✦**Truth #9:** Worship involves a sense of the presence of God. Whether it's bowing down *before* God (Psalm 95:6), searching *for* the Lord (Psalm 105:3–4), trusting *in* his holy name (Psalm 33:20–21), dwelling *in* his house (Psalm 84), lifting hands (Psalm 134:2) or shouting *to* him (Psalm 47:1), worship always involves a recognition that God is near.

✦**Truth #10:** Worship should be active, emotional, and enjoyable. The picture painted in Scripture is *not* of passive, sit-on-your-hands, dry, drab, going-through-the-motions worship. It is of enthusiastic celebration. The mood is one of gratitude and reverence, yet the worshipers seem genuinely excited (see 2 Samuel 6:–16).

✦**Truth #11** and the major point of The iWorship Daily Devotional Bible: Worship isn't merely something we do for ninety minutes in church on Sunday mornings. Worship is something we are. Worship isn't an activity. It is a lifestyle. Worship isn't just about singing or praying. Or reading the Bible. Or doing some other "religious" act. Worship is about life. And vice versa. When we finally understand that we have been created through God and for God (Colossians 1:16), when we truly grasp that God wants to receive glory in everything we do (1 Corinthians 10:31), then it begins to dawn on us that every place on earth can be a sanctuary and every act in life a sacrifice of praise. Name any responsibility, list every imaginable hobby, and that activity—no matter how mundane it may seem—can become a high and holy act. Even work. Even scrubbing the bathroom and walking the dog.

So go ahead and sing along with the choir or the praise band at your church. If your heart is right and your mind is focused on God, that is a wonderful act of worship. But the same can be true for mowing the yard, running errands, talking with a friend, paying bills, even fishing.

Right now you might be saying, "Sure, I'd like to live this lifestyle of praise and worship that you're talking about, but I don't know how. I'm not sure how to praise God—not the way you're talking about."

Most of us feel this way at the outset. Remember two facts. First, God created you to worship him; if you ask him to help you do it, he will. And second, you haven't any choice in the matter; he *commands* you to worship him. Philippians 4:4 says, "Always be full of joy in the Lord. I say it again—rejoice!" First Thessalonians 5:16–18 underscores this idea: "Always be joyful. Keep on praying. No matter what happens, always be thankful, for this is God's will for you who belong to Christ Jesus." You see? A worship-filled life is not an option. You were made to praise God, and you're commanded to bring glory to him.

How to Practice a Worship Lifestyle

1. Life a Life Full of Praise

Just imagine for a moment how you want your children to approach you. If you're a dad, do you want your children to throw a barrage of complaints and requests at you the moment you walk through the front door after a hard day's work? Which would you prefer to hear: "Joshua hit me with his lunchbox!" and "Can we go to the new frozen yogurt place after dinner?" Or would you rather hear, "Daddy! I'm so glad to see you!" followed by hugs and kisses? And how would you feel if every time your children came to you, they arrived with shame on their faces and fear in their hearts? Of course you'd be deeply grieved because you love them and you want them to be able to communicate freely and openly.

Your heavenly Father is no different. Before you hit him with a laundry list of problems, spend time telling him you're glad to be with him. The Lord's Prayer begins with praise: "Our Father in heaven, may your name be honored." The first request for something, "Give us our food for today," does not come until a number of verses later!

Thanksgiving

The place to start is with *thanksgiving*, which simply means to count your blessings and communicate verbally to God your gratitude for what he's already done. Even in the midst of difficulty, don't focus on the situation so much that you miss the opportunity to thank God. Thank him for the specific blessings he has poured on your life—for your health, for your family, for your job, for your relationship with him. Cultivate a thankful attitude and practice having a thankful heart. If you don't *feel* particularly thankful, that's fine. You are obeying the Word of God and giving thanks to his name. Just keep enumerating your blessings one by one and thanking God for them out loud. It will release something as you become aware how intimately God is involved with you.

Praise

After thanksgiving comes *praise*, which, like thanksgiving, is an act of your will and doesn't depend on how you feel. Here you begin to declare God's attributes and his great glory—praise him for his faithfulness, goodness, and mercy, for the way he has sustained and delivered you. Praise him for his great power, for his forgiveness, for his wondrous creation and all the works of his hands.

Worship

This will lead naturally into *worship*. Thanksgiving and praise are acts of your will, but worship is something God does. This is where he draws back the curtain and makes a way in the Spirit for you to draw very, very close to him. It's where he invites you into a place of adoration where you do less and he does more. Thanksgiving and praise are actions you initiate. But worship is a deep communion and fellowship with the Lord.

Remember: thanksgiving first, praise second, worship third.

2. Say God's Word in Every Situation

Another life-changing practice that you will learn in the *iWorship Daily Devotional Bible* is to *say God's Word back to him*. Readers will see that one of the best ways to praise God is to open the Bible to the book of Psalms and echo the words that David spoke to him. Read out loud the passages of Scripture that declare God's power and majesty.

Saying God's words back to him blesses his heart and moves us swiftly into a posture of praise. He anointed men and women of old to speak the truth and he anoints the expression of this truth today. When you say his Word back to him, you know you're on good ground.

3. Make Every Moment God-Centered

A third objective, at which we've already hinted, is that the *iWorship Daily Devotional Bible* is intended to help readers develop a 24/7 lifestyle of praise and worship. Whether it's your laundry room, your kitchen, your office, or your car, we want to help you make that place a place of praise and worship. You can do this by speaking or singing to God yourself, or you can join along with others worshiping God as you play praise and worship recordings.

These bedrock truths and other reminders and creative ideas for worship are what the *iWorship Daily Devotional Bible* is all about. Our desire is to launch you into a lifestyle of life-changing worship. Are you ready to make praise a daily discipline?

Michael Coleman
President, Integrity Worship Ministries

How to Use the iWorship

Daily Devotional Bible

Welcome to the *iWorship Daily Devotional Bible*—a Bible designed to help you develop and nurture an attitude and posture of worship that goes beyond Sunday morning and permeates your everyday life. The features and notes in this Bible can be used in a variety of ways. You can read through the entire Bible in a year, using the daily devotionals tied to each reading passage as part of your time with God. A One Year Daily Devotional Reading Plan is outlined for you in this section to help you keep track. Or you can choose whichever devotional topic is of most interest or need for you at a particular time by using the Topical Index to "My Daily Worship" Devotionals. Each devotional is listed once, so by working your way through each topic, you will have covered the entire Bible. You also may use the introductions to each Bible book as an entry point into the Bible. The introductions provide a unique overview of the book as it pertains to personal worship and offer key worship moments that can be found in each book.

"My Daily Worship" devotionals are designed to lead you into a daily personal worship experience. Each devotional is tied to a key verse within the daily reading passage that speaks to worship. The *i reflect* portion of the devotional expounds on that verse, providing a thought or action to take with you throughout the day. The focus may be on the importance of confessing sin to an intimate relationship with God or on how to worship

during difficult times. The devotional thought may simply point to our wonderfully awe-inspiring God. Each devotional has an *i pray* to guide your prayer time during personal worship, and then closes with an *i respond*—an activity or step that will help you develop worship as a lifestyle throughout the day, week, and month.

In addition, there are one hundred "Words of Worship" notes scattered throughout the Bible. These brief uplifting notes focus on words, names of God, attributes of God, and objects associated with worship. By reading these notes, you will gain insight into worship as experienced during Bible times and how it relates to your personal worship today. Use these notes as a reference point to further study or to dig deeper into particular passages.

Also included in this Bible are one hundred inspirational quotes from worship leaders, church fathers, theologians, and Christian authors from throughout history. These brief statements are designed to provoke thought about worship—from who we worship to why we worship to what life would be like without worship.

We pray that these features—the "My Daily Worship" devotionals, the "Words of Worship" and worship quotes—will enhance your own personal worship time and that the Bible will be a tool for you to utilize in developing a lifestyle of genuine intimate relationship with God.

One Year Daily Devotional Reading Plan

One Year Topical Devotional Reading Plan

Note to the Reader

Since its early years, Tyndale House Publishers has been committed to publishing editions of the Bible in the language of the people. With over forty million copies in print, *The Living Bible* represented this tradition well for more than thirty years. More recently, Tyndale has continued this tradition by commissioning ninety evangelical scholars to produce the *Holy Bible,* New Living Translation. This general-purpose translation is accurate and excellent for study, while also being easy to read. The NLT is helping many discover, and rediscover, the power of God's living Word.

The goal of any translation of the Scriptures is to convey the meaning of the ancient Hebrew and Greek texts as accurately as possible to the contemporary reader. The challenge for our translators was to create a text that would make the same impact in the lives of modern readers that the original text did in the lives of readers in its ancient context. In the New Living Translation, this has been accomplished by translating entire thoughts (rather than just words) into natural, everyday English. The end result is a translation that is easy to read and understand and that accurately communicates the meaning of the original texts.

We believe that the New Living Translation, which combines the latest in scholarship with the best in translation style, will speak to your heart. We publish it with the prayer that God will use it to speak his timeless truth to the church and to the world in a fresh and powerful way.

The Publishers
July 1996

Introduction to the New Living Translation

TRANSLATION PHILOSOPHY AND METHODOLOGY

There are two general theories or methods of Bible translation. The first has been called "formal equivalence." According to this theory, the translator attempts to render each word of the original language into the receptor language and seeks to preserve the original word order and sentence structure as much as possible. The second has been called "dynamic equivalence" or "functional equivalence." The goal of this translation theory is to produce in the receptor language the closest natural equivalent of the message expressed by the original-language text—both in meaning and in style. Such a translation attempts to have the same impact on modern readers as the original had on its own audience.

A dynamic-equivalence translation can also be called a thought-for-thought translation, as contrasted with a formal-equivalence or word-for-word translation. Of course, to translate the thought of the original language requires that the text be interpreted accurately and then be rendered in understandable idiom. So the goal of any thought-for-thought translation is to be both reliable and eminently readable. Thus, as a thought-for-thought translation, the New Living Translation seeks to be both exegetically accurate and idiomatically powerful.

In making a thought-for-thought translation, the translators must do their best to enter into the thought patterns of the ancient authors and to present the same ideas, connotations, and effects in the receptor language. In order to guard against personal biases and to ensure the accuracy of the message, a thought-for-thought translation should be created by a group of scholars who employ the best exegetical tools and who also understand the receptor language very well. With these concerns in mind, the Bible Translation Committee assigned each book of the Bible to three different scholars. Each scholar made a thorough review of the assigned book and submitted suggested revisions to the appropriate general reviewer. The general reviewer reviewed and summarized these suggestions and then proposed a first-draft revision of the text. This draft served as the basis for several additional phases of exegetical and stylistic committee review. Then the Bible Translation Committee jointly reviewed and approved every verse in the final translation.

A thought-for-thought translation prepared by a group of capable scholars has the potential to represent the intended meaning of the original text even more accurately than a word-for-word translation. This is illustrated by the various renderings of the Hebrew word *hesed*. This term cannot be adequately translated by any single English word because it can connote love, mercy, grace, kindness, faithfulness, and loyalty. The context—not the lexicon—must determine which English term is selected for translation.

The value of a thought-for-thought translation can be illustrated by comparing 1 Kings 2:10 in the King James Version, the *New International Version,* and the New Living Translation. "So David slept with his fathers, and was buried in the city of David" (KJV). "Then David rested with his fathers and was buried in the City of David" (NIV). "Then David died and was buried in the City of David" (NLT). Only the New Living Translation clearly translates the real meaning of the Hebrew idiom "slept with his fathers" into contemporary English.

WRITTEN TO BE READ ALOUD

It is evident in Scripture that the biblical documents were written to be read aloud, often in public worship (see Nehemiah 8; Luke 4:16-20;

1 Timothy 4:13; Revelation 1:3). It is still the case today that more people will hear the Bible read aloud in church than are likely to read it for themselves. Therefore, a new translation must communicate with clarity and power when it is read aloud. For this reason, the New Living Translation is recommended as a Bible to be used for public reading. Its living language is not only easy to understand, but it also has an emotive quality that will make an impact on the listener.

THE TEXTS BEHIND THE NEW LIVING TRANSLATION

The translators of the Old Testament used the Masoretic Text of the Hebrew Bible as their standard text. They used the edition known as *Biblia Hebraica Stuttgartensia* (1977) with its up-to-date textual apparatus, a revision of Rudolf Kittel's *Biblia Hebraica* (Stuttgart, 1937). The translators also compared the Dead Sea Scrolls, the Septuagint and other Greek manuscripts, the Samaritan Pentateuch, the Syriac Peshitta, the Latin Vulgate, and any other versions or manuscripts that shed light on textual problems.

The translators of the New Testament used the two standard editions of the Greek New Testament: the *Greek New Testament,* published by the United Bible Societies (fourth revised edition, 1993), and *Novum Testamentum Graece,* edited by Nestle and Aland (twenty-seventh edition, 1993). These two editions, which have the same text but differ in punctuation and textual notes, represent the best in modern textual scholarship.

TRANSLATION ISSUES

The translators have made a conscious effort to provide a text that can be easily understood by the average reader of modern English. To this end, we have used the vocabulary and language structures commonly used by the average person. The result is a translation of the Scriptures written generally at the reading level of a junior high school student. We have avoided using language that is likely to become quickly dated or that reflects a narrow subdialect of English, with the goal of making

the New Living Translation as broadly useful as possible.

But our concern for readability goes beyond the concerns of vocabulary and sentence structure. We are also concerned about historical and cultural barriers to understanding the Bible, and we have sought to translate terms shrouded in history or culture in ways that can be immediately understood by the contemporary reader. Thus, our goal of easy readability expresses itself in a number of other ways:

✦ Rather than translating ancient weights and measures literally, which communicates little to the modern reader, we have expressed them by means of recognizable contemporary equivalents. We have converted ancient weights and measures to modern English (American) equivalents, and we have rendered the literal Hebrew or Greek measures, along with metric equivalents, in textual footnotes.

✦ Instead of translating ancient currency values literally, we have generally expressed them in terms of weights in precious metals. In some cases we have used other common terms to communicate the message effectively. For example, "three shekels of silver" might become "three silver coins" or "three pieces of silver" to convey the intended message. Again, a rendering of the literal Hebrew or Greek is given in textual footnotes.

✦ Since the Hebrew lunar calendar fluctuates from year to year in relation to the solar calendar used today, we have translated Hebrew dates in a way that communicates with our modern readership. It was clear that we could not use the names of the Hebrew months, such as *Abib,* which are meaningless to the modern reader. Nor could we use a simple designation such as "first month," because the months of the Hebrew lunar calendar do not correspond with the months of our calendar. Thus, we have often used seasonal references to communicate the time of year when something happened. For example, "the first month" (which occurs in March and April) might be translated "early spring." Where it is possible to define a specific ancient date in terms of our modern calendar, we use modern dates in the text. Textual footnotes then give the literal Hebrew date and state the rationale for our rendering. For example, Ezra 7:9 pinpoints the date when Ezra arrived in Jerusalem: "the first day of the fifth month." This was during the seventh year of King Artaxerxes' reign (Ezra 7:7). We translate that lunar date as August 4, with a footnote giving the Hebrew and identifying the year as 458 B.C.

✦ Since ancient references to the time of day differ from our modern methods of denoting time, we used renderings that are instantly understandable to the modern reader. Accordingly, we have rendered specific times of day by using approximate equivalents in terms of our common "o'clock" system. On occasion, translations such as "at dawn the next morning" or "as the sun began to set" have been used when the biblical reference is general.

✦ Many words in the original texts made sense to the original audience but communicate something quite different to the modern reader. In such cases, some liberty must be allowed in translation to communicate what was intended. Places identified by the term normally translated "city," for example, are often better identified as "towns" or "villages." Similarly, the term normally translated "mountain" is often better rendered "hill."

✦ Many words and phrases carry a great deal of cultural meaning that was obvious to the original readers but needs explanation in our own culture. For example, the phrase "they beat their breasts" (Luke 23:48) in ancient times meant that people were very upset. In our translation we chose to translate this phrase dynamically: "They went home in deep sorrow." In some cases, however, we have simply illuminated the existing expression to make it immediately understandable. For example, we might have expanded the literal phrase to read "they beat their breasts in sorrow."

✦ Metaphorical language is often difficult for contemporary readers to understand, so at times we have chosen to translate or illuminate the metaphor. For example, the ancient poet writes, "Your eyes are doves" (Song of Songs 1:15). To help the modern reader, who might be confused or distracted by a literal visualization of this image, we converted the metaphor to a simile to make the meaning immediately clear: "Your eyes are soft like doves." Here we also added the modifier "soft" to help the modern reader catch the significance of the metaphoric expression. A few chapters later, the poet writes, "Your neck is like the tower of David" (Song of Songs 4:4). We rendered it "Your neck is as stately as the tower of David" to clarify the intended positive meaning of the metaphor.

✦ We did not feel obligated to display all Hebrew poetry in English poetic form. Only the book of Psalms is set entirely in poetic lines. Other books, though poetic in nature, are set in prose for the sake of easier reading. Nonetheless, these prose renderings reflect the poetic language of the original Hebrew. Where a portion of text is explicitly said to be a poem or song, however, it has usually been set as such.

✦ One challenge we faced was in determining how to translate accurately the ancient biblical text that was originally written in a context where male-oriented terms were used to refer to humanity generally. We needed to respect the nature of the ancient context while also trying to make the translation clear to a modern audience that tends to read male-oriented language as applying only to males. Often the original text, though using masculine nouns and pronouns, clearly intends that the message be applied to both men and women. One example is found in the New Testament epistles, where the believers are called "brothers" (adelphoi). Yet it is clear that these epistles were addressed to all the believers—male and female. Thus, we have usually translated this Greek word "brothers and sisters" in order to represent the historical situation more accurately.

We have also been sensitive to passages

where the text applies generally to human beings or to the human condition. In many instances we have used plural pronouns (they, them) in place of the masculine singular (he, him). For example, a traditional rendering of Proverbs 22:6 is: "Train up a child in the way he should go, and when he is old he will not turn from it." We have rendered it: "Teach your children to choose the right path, and when they are older, they will remain upon it." At times, we have also replaced third person pronouns with the second person to ensure clarity. A traditional rendering of Proverbs 26:27 is: "He who digs a pit will fall into it, and he who rolls a stone, it will come back on him." We have rendered it: "If you set a trap for others, you will get caught in it yourself. If you roll a boulder down on others, it will roll back and crush you." All such decisions were driven by the concern to reflect accurately the intended meaning of the original texts of Scripture.

We should emphasize, however, that all masculine nouns and pronouns used to represent God (for example, "Father") have been maintained without exception. We believe that essential traits of God's revealed character can only be conveyed through the masculine language expressed in the original texts of Scripture.

LEXICAL CONSISTENCY IN TERMINOLOGY

For the sake of clarity, we have maintained lexical consistency in areas such as divine names, synoptic passages, rhetorical structures, and nontheological technical terms (i.e., liturgical, cultic, zoological, botanical, cultural, and legal terms). For theological terms, we have allowed a greater semantic range of acceptable English words or phrases for a single Hebrew or Greek word. We avoided weighty theological terms that do not readily communicate to many modern readers. For example, we avoided using words such as "justification," "sanctification," and "regeneration." In place of these words (which are carryovers from Latin), we provided renderings such as "we are made right with God," "we are made holy," and "we are born anew."

THE SPELLING OF PROPER NAMES

Many individuals in the Bible, especially the Old Testament, are known by more than one name or by a number of variant names (e.g., Uzziah/Azariah). For the sake of clarity, we have tried to use a single spelling for any one individual, footnoting the literal spelling whenever we differ from it. This is especially helpful in delineating the kings of Israel and Judah. King Joash/Jehoash of Israel has been consistently called Jehoash, while King Joash/Jehoash of Judah is called Joash. A similar distinction has been used to distinguish between Joram/Jehoram of Israel and Joram/Jehoram of Judah. All such decisions were made with the goal of clarifying the text for the reader. When the ancient biblical writers clearly had a theological purpose in their choice of a variant name (e.g., Eshbaal/Ishbosheth), the different names have been maintained with an explanatory footnote.

THE RENDERING OF DIVINE NAMES

All appearances of 'el, 'elohim, or 'eloah have been translated "God," except where the context demands the translation "god(s)." We have rendered the tetragrammaton *(YHWH)* consistently as "the LORD," utilizing a form with small capitals that is common among English translations. This will distinguish it from the name 'adonai, which we render "Lord." When 'adonai and YHWH appear in conjunction, we have rendered it "Sovereign LORD." This also distinguishes 'adonai YHWH from cases where YHWH appears with 'elohim, which is rendered "LORD God." When YH (the short form of YHWH) and YHWH appear together, we have rendered it "LORD GOD." The Hebrew word 'adon is rendered "lord," or "master," or sometimes "sir."

In the New Testament, the Greek word *christos* has been translated as "Messiah" when the context assumes a Jewish audience. When a Gentile audience can be assumed, *christos* has been translated as "Christ." The Greek word *kurios* is consistently translated "Lord," except in four quotations of Psalm 110:1, where it is translated "Lᴏʀᴅ."

Textual Footnotes

The New Living Translation provides several kinds of textual footnotes:

✦ All Old Testament passages that are clearly quoted in the New Testament are identified in a textual footnote in the New Testament.

✦ Some textual footnotes provide cultural and historical information on places, things, and people in the Bible that are probably obscure to modern readers. Such notes should aid the reader in understanding the message of the text. For example, in Acts 12:1, "King Herod" is named in this translation as "King Herod Agrippa" and is identified in a footnote as being "the nephew of Herod Antipas and a grandson of Herod the Great."

✦ When various ancient manuscripts contain different readings, these differences are often documented in footnotes. For instance, textual variants are footnoted when the variant reading is very familiar (usually through the King James Version). We have used footnotes when we have selected variant readings that differ from the Hebrew and Greek editions normally followed.

✦ When the meaning of a proper name (or a wordplay inherent in a proper name) is relevant to the meaning of the text, it is illuminated with a textual footnote. For example, the footnote at Genesis 3:20 reads: "*Eve*" sounds like a Hebrew term that means "to give life." This wordplay in the Hebrew illuminates the meaning of the text, which goes on to say that Eve "would be the mother of all people everywhere." If the meaning of the name is more certain, it is stated more simply. For example, the footnote at Genesis 16:11 reads: "*Ishmael* means 'God hears.' " In this case, Hagar named her son Ishmael after realizing that God had heard her cry for help.

✦ When we translate the meaning of a place-name that is often simply transliterated from the Hebrew or Greek, we provide a textual footnote showing the transliteration that appears in many English translations. For example, the name usually transliterated "Havvoth-jair" in Judges 10:4 has been translated "the Towns of Jair," with a footnote that gives the traditional transliteration: "Hebrew *Havvoth-jair*."

✦ Textual footnotes are also used to show alternative renderings. These are prefaced with the word "Or." On occasion, we also provide notes on words or phrases that represent a translation that departs from long-standing tradition. These notes are prefaced with the words "traditionally rendered." For example, a footnote to the translation "contagious skin disease" at Leviticus 13:2 says, "Traditionally rendered *leprosy.*"

AS WE SUBMIT this translation of the Bible for publication, we recognize that any translation of the Scriptures is subject to limitations and imperfections. Anyone who has attempted to communicate the richness of God's Word into another language will realize it is impossible to make a perfect translation. Recognizing these limitations, we sought God's guidance and wisdom throughout this project. Now we pray that he will accept our efforts and use this translation for the benefit of the church and of all people.

We pray that the New Living Translation will overcome some of the barriers of history, culture, and language that have kept people from reading and understanding God's Word. We hope that readers unfamiliar with the Bible will find the words clear and easy to understand and that readers well versed in the Scriptures will gain a fresh perspective. We pray that readers will gain insight and wisdom for living but most of all that they will meet the God of the Bible and be forever changed by knowing him.

The Bible Translation Committee
July 1996

Holy Bible,
New Living Translation

BIBLE TRANSLATION TEAM

PENTATEUCH
Daniel I. Block, General Reviewer
The Southern Baptist Theological Seminary

GENESIS
Allan Ross, *Trinity Episcopal Seminary*
John Sailhamer, *Northwestern College*
Gordon Wenham, *The Cheltenham and Gloucester College of Higher Education*

EXODUS
Robert Bergen, *Hannibal-LaGrange College*
Daniel I. Block, *The Southern Baptist Theological Seminary*
Eugene Carpenter, *Bethel College, Mishawaka, Indiana*

LEVITICUS
David Baker, *Ashland Theological Seminary*
Victor Hamilton, *Asbury College*
Kenneth Mathews, *Beeson Divinity School, Samford University*

NUMBERS
Dale A. Brueggemann, *Assemblies of God Division of Foreign Missions*
Roland K. Harrison (deceased), *Wycliffe College*
Gerald L. Mattingly, *Johnson Bible College*

DEUTERONOMY
J. Gordon McConville, *The Cheltenham and Gloucester College of Higher Education*
Eugene H. Merrill, *Dallas Theological Seminary*
John A. Thompson, *University of Melbourne*

HISTORICAL BOOKS
Barry J. Beitzel, General Reviewer
Trinity Evangelical Divinity School

JOSHUA/JUDGES
Carl E. Armerding, *Schloss Mittersill Study Centre*
Barry J. Beitzel, *Trinity Evangelical Divinity School*
Lawson Stone, *Asbury Theological Seminary*

1 & 2 SAMUEL
Barry J. Beitzel, *Trinity Evangelical Divinity School*
V. Philips Long, *Covenant Theological Seminary*
J. Robert Vannoy, *Biblical Theological Seminary*

1 & 2 KINGS
Bill T. Arnold, *Asbury Theological Seminary*
William H. Barnes, *North Central University*
Frederic W. Bush, *Fuller Theological Seminary*

1 & 2 CHRONICLES
Raymond B. Dillard (deceased), *Westminster Theological Seminary*
David A. Dorsey, *Evangelical School of Theology*
Terry Eves, *Erskine College*

EZRA/NEHEMIAH/ESTHER/RUTH
William C. Williams, *Southern California College*
Hugh G. M. Williamson, *Oxford University*

POETRY
Tremper Longman III, General Reviewer
Westmont College

JOB
August Konkel, *Providence Theological Seminary*
Tremper Longman III, *Westmont College*
Al Wolters, *Redeemer College*

PSALMS 1–75
Mark D. Futato, *Westminster Theological Seminary in California*
Douglas Green, *Westminster Theological Seminary*
Richard Pratt, *Reformed Theological Seminary*

PSALMS 76–150
David M. Howard Jr., *Bethel Theological Seminary*
Raymond C. Ortlund Jr., *Trinity Evangelical Divinity School*
Willem VanGemeren, *Trinity Evangelical Divinity School*

PROVERBS
Ted Hildebrandt, *Grace College*
Richard Schultz, *Wheaton College*
Raymond C. Van Leeuwen, *Eastern College*

ECCLESIASTES/SONG OF SONGS
Daniel C. Fredericks, *Belhaven College*
David Hubbard (deceased), *Fuller Theological Seminary*
Tremper Longman III, *Westmont College*

PROPHETS
John N. Oswalt, General Reviewer
Wesley Biblical Seminary

ISAIAH
John N. Oswalt, *Wesley Biblical Seminary*
Gary Smith, *Bethel Theological Seminary*
John Walton, *Moody Bible Institute*

JEREMIAH/LAMENTATIONS
G. Herbert Livingston, *Asbury Theological
Seminary*
Elmer A. Martens, *Mennonite Brethren Biblical
Seminary*

EZEKIEL
Daniel I. Block, *The Southern Baptist Theological
Seminary*
David H. Engelhard, *Calvin Theological Seminary*
David Thompson, *Asbury Theological Seminary*

DANIEL/HAGGAI/ZECHARIAH/MALACHI
Joyce Baldwin Caine (deceased), *Trinity College,
Bristol*
Douglas Gropp, *Catholic University of America*
Roy Hayden, *Oral Roberts School of Theology*

HOSEA–ZEPHANIAH
Joseph Coleson, *Nazarene Theological Seminary*
Andrew Hill, *Wheaton College*
Richard Patterson, *Professor Emeritus, Liberty
University*

GOSPELS AND ACTS
Grant R. Osborne, General Reviewer
Trinity Evangelical Divinity School

MATTHEW
Craig Blomberg, *Denver Conservative Baptist
Seminary*
Donald A. Hagner, *Fuller Theological Seminary*
David Turner, *Grand Rapids Baptist Seminary*

MARK
Robert Guelich (deceased), *Fuller Theological
Seminary*
Grant R. Osborne, *Trinity Evangelical Divinity
School*

LUKE
Darrell Boch, *Dallas Theological Seminary*
Scot McKnight, *North Park College*
Robert Stein, *Bethel Theological Seminary*

JOHN
Gary M. Burge, *Wheaton College*
Philip W. Comfort, *Wheaton College*
Marianne Meye Thompson, *Fuller Theological
Seminary*

ACTS
D. A. Carson, *Trinity Evangelical Divinity School*
William J. Larkin, *Columbia Biblical Seminary*
Roger Mohrlang, *Whitworth College*

LETTERS AND REVELATION
Norman R. Ericson, General Reviewer
Wheaton College

ROMANS/GALATIANS
Gerald Borchert, *The Southern Baptist Theological
Seminary*
Douglas J. Moo, *Trinity Evangelical Divinity
School*
Thomas R. Schreiner, *Bethel Theological Seminary*

1 & 2 CORINTHIANS
Joseph Alexanian, *Trinity International University*
Linda Belleville, *North Park Theological Seminary*
Douglas A. Oss, *Central Bible College*
Robert Sloan, Baylor University

EPHESIANS–PHILEMON
Harold W. Hoehner, *Dallas Theological Seminary*
Moises Silva, *Gordon-Conwell Theological
Seminary*
Klyne Snodgrass, *North Park Theological Seminary*

HEBREWS/JAMES/1 & 2 PETER/JUDE
Peter Davids, *Canadian Theological Seminary*
Norman R. Ericson, *Wheaton College*
William Lane (deceased), *Seattle Pacific University*
J. Ramsey Michaels, *S.W. Missouri State University*

1–3 JOHN/REVELATION
Greg Beale, *Gordon-Conwell Theological Seminary*
Robert Mounce, *Whitworth College*
M. Robert Mulholland Jr., *Asbury Theological
Seminary*

SPECIAL REVIEWERS
F. F. Bruce (deceased), *University of Manchester*
Kenneth N. Taylor, *Tyndale House Publishers*

COORDINATING TEAM
Mark R. Norton, Managing Editor and O.T.
Coordinating Editor
Philip W. Comfort, N.T. Coordinating Editor
Ronald A. Beers, Executive Director and Stylist
Mark D. Taylor, Director and Chief Stylist
Daniel W. Taylor, Consultant

the Old Testament

Genesis

I am God Almighty; serve me faithfully and live a blameless life (17:1).

And So It Begins

Worship begins with God, and what better place to discover his character, his nature, and his heart than in Genesis, the book of beginnings. From the creation of the world to its destruction and restoration, from the men and women whom God called to serve and follow him, from the promises made and handed down through thousands of generations later, we encounter a God who longs to be intimately involved with humankind.

Consider the God who claims us as his own. He walked and talked with man and woman in the Garden, providing for them and then disciplining them for their disobedience. He visited his chosen leaders, declaring his promise to establish a people through whom the entire world would be blessed. He granted a child to an elderly Abraham and Sarah, despite their disbelief. He wrestled with Jacob, transforming his character and passing on a great blessing to him as the father of his holy people, Israel. Through Joseph and his brothers, we see a God active behind the scenes, working out his plan and purpose for his people. This is the God of Genesis, the God whom we serve and who calls us to worship him.

As you read through Genesis, allow the Spirit of Christ to guide you and introduce you in new and fresh ways to your Creator, your Provider, your Promise-keeper, and your Sustainer. Then respond to him with worship.

Worship Moments

- Cain and Abel presented the first offerings to God in worship. One brother brought "a gift of his farm produce," while the other brother selected "the best of his flock." Only one was acceptable before God (4:1–7).

- Abraham presented the first tithe to Melchizedek, the king of Salem and the first priest of the God Most High mentioned. Melchizedek responded with a blessing for Abraham (14:17–24).

- Abraham interceded for Sodom and discovered the greatness and depth of God's mercy and forgiveness for those who follow him (18:16–33).

- God's character is revealed through many names—*El Roi*, "the God who sees me," 16:13; *El Shaddai*, "God Almighty," 17:1—and in his relationship to his people, "the God of my grandfather Abraham, the awe-inspiring God of my father, Isaac" (31:42).

THE ACCOUNT OF CREATION

1 In the beginning God created* the heavens and the earth. ²The earth was empty, a formless mass cloaked in darkness. And the Spirit of God was hovering over its surface. ³Then God said, "Let there be light," and there was light. ⁴And God saw that it was good. Then he separated the light from the darkness. ⁵God called the light "day" and the darkness "night." Together these made up one day.

⁶And God said, "Let there be space between the waters, to separate water from water." ⁷And so it was. God made this space to separate the waters above from the waters below. ⁸And God called the space "sky." This happened on the second day.

⁹And God said, "Let the waters beneath the sky be gathered into one place so dry ground may appear." And so it was. ¹⁰God named the dry ground "land" and the water "seas." And God saw that it was good. ¹¹Then God said, "Let the land burst forth with every sort of grass and seed-bearing plant. And let there be trees that grow seed-bearing fruit. The seeds will then produce the kinds of plants and trees from which they came." And so it was. ¹²The land was filled with seed-bearing plants and trees, and their seeds produced plants and trees of like kind. And God saw that it was good. ¹³This all happened on the third day.

¹⁴And God said, "Let bright lights appear in the sky to separate the day from the night. They will be signs to mark off the seasons, the days, and the years. ¹⁵Let their light shine down upon the earth." And so it was. ¹⁶For God made two great lights, the sun and the moon, to shine down upon the earth. The greater one, the sun, presides during the day; the lesser one, the moon, presides through the night. He also made the stars. ¹⁷God set these lights in the heavens to light the earth, ¹⁸to govern the day and the night, and to separate the light from the darkness. And God saw that it was good. ¹⁹This all happened on the fourth day.

²⁰And God said, "Let the waters swarm with fish and other life. Let the skies be filled with birds of every kind." ²¹So God created great sea creatures and every sort of fish and every kind of bird. And God saw that it was good. ²²Then God blessed them, saying, "Let the fish multiply and fill the oceans. Let the birds increase and fill the earth." ²³This all happened on the fifth day.

²⁴And God said, "Let the earth bring forth every kind of animal—livestock, small animals, and wildlife." And so it was. ²⁵God made all sorts of wild animals, livestock, and small animals, each able to reproduce more of its own kind. And God saw that it was good.

²⁶Then God said, "Let us make people* in our image, to be like ourselves. They will be masters over all life—the fish in the sea, the birds in the sky, and all the livestock, wild animals,* and small animals."

²⁷ So God created people in his own image;
　　God patterned them after himself;
　　male and female he created them.

²⁸God blessed them and told them, "Multiply and fill the earth and subdue it. Be masters over the fish and birds and all the animals." ²⁹And God said, "Look! I have given you the seed-bearing plants throughout the earth and all the fruit trees for your food. ³⁰And I have given all the grasses and other green plants to the animals and birds for their food." And so it was. ³¹Then God looked over all he had made, and he saw that it was excellent in every way. This all happened on the sixth day.

2 So the creation of the heavens and the earth and everything in them was completed. ²On the seventh day, having finished his task, God rested from all his work. ³And God blessed the seventh day and declared it holy, because it was the day when he rested from his work of creation.

⁴This is the account of the creation of the heavens and the earth.

1:1 Or *In the beginning when God created,* or *When God began to create.*　1:26a Hebrew *man;* also in 1:27.　1:26b As in Syriac version; Hebrew reads *all the earth.*

The Man and Woman in Eden

When the LORD God made the heavens and the earth, ⁵there were no plants or grain growing on the earth, for the LORD God had not sent any rain. And no one was there to cultivate the soil. ⁶But water came up out of the ground and watered all the land. ⁷And the LORD God formed a man's body from the dust of the ground and breathed into it the breath of life. And the man became a living person.

⁸Then the LORD God planted a garden in Eden, in the east, and there he placed the man he had created. ⁹And the LORD God planted all sorts of trees in the garden—beautiful trees that produced delicious fruit. At the center of the garden he placed the tree of life and the tree of the knowledge of good and evil.

¹⁰A river flowed from the land of Eden, watering the garden and then dividing into four branches. ¹¹One of these branches is the Pishon, which flows around the entire land of Havilah, where gold is found. ¹²The gold of that land is exceptionally pure; aromatic resin and onyx stone are also found there. ¹³The second branch is the Gihon, which flows around the entire land of Cush. ¹⁴The third branch is the Tigris, which flows to the east of Asshur. The fourth branch is the Euphrates.

¹⁵The LORD God placed the man in the Garden of Eden to tend and care for it. ¹⁶But the LORD God gave him this warning: "You may freely eat any fruit in the garden ¹⁷except fruit from the tree of the knowledge of good and evil. If you eat of its fruit, you will surely die."

¹⁸And the LORD God said, "It is not good for the man to be alone. I will make a companion who will help him." ¹⁹So the LORD God formed from the soil every kind of animal and bird. He brought them to Adam* to see what he would call them, and Adam chose a name for each one. ²⁰He gave names to all the livestock, birds, and wild animals. But still there was no companion suitable for him. ²¹So the LORD God caused Adam to fall into a deep sleep. He took one of Adam's ribs* and closed up the place from which he had taken it. ²²Then the LORD God made a woman from the rib and brought her to Adam.

²³"At last!" Adam exclaimed. "She is part of my own flesh and bone! She will be called 'woman,' because she was taken out of a man." ²⁴This explains why a man leaves his father and mother and is joined to his wife, and the two are united into one. ²⁵Now, although Adam and his wife were both naked, neither of them felt any shame.

The Man and Woman Sin

3 Now the serpent was the shrewdest of all the creatures the LORD God had made. "Really?" he asked the woman. "Did God really say you must not eat any of the fruit in the garden?"

²"Of course we may eat it," the woman told him. ³"It's only the fruit from the tree at the center of the garden that we are not allowed to eat. God says we must not eat it or even touch it, or we will die."

⁴"You won't die!" the serpent hissed. ⁵"God knows that your eyes will be opened when you eat it. You will become just like God, knowing everything, both good and evil."

⁶The woman was convinced. The fruit looked so fresh and delicious, and it would make her so wise! So she ate some of the fruit. She also gave some to her husband, who was with her. Then he ate it, too. ⁷At that moment, their eyes were opened, and they suddenly felt shame at their nakedness. So they strung fig leaves together around their hips to cover themselves.

⁸Toward evening they heard the LORD God walking about in the garden, so they hid themselves among the trees. ⁹The LORD God called to Adam,* "Where are you?"

¹⁰He replied, "I heard you, so I hid. I was afraid because I was naked."

¹¹"Who told you that you were naked?" the

2:19 Hebrew *the man,* and so throughout this chapter.   2:21 Or *took a part of Adam's side.*   3:9 Hebrew *the man,* and so throughout this chapter.

My Daily Worship

— *January 1* —

FINE CRAFTSMANSHIP
GENESIS 1:1–3:24

Then God looked over all he had made, and he saw that
it was excellent in every way (1:31).

[i reflect]

Excellent in every way. That phrase sums up God's creative acts very well.

"Excellent" seems an apt description when we look up at the night sky and see the stars he hung there and knows by name. We easily see excellence in a sunset so brilliantly hued that it takes our breath away or in a pine tree stretching heavenward, its feathery branches moving with the breeze.

But what about when we look in the mirror? Or when we look across the breakfast table at family members? Or when you're across the desk from a superior at work? God also made people excellent in every way. Of course, we go astray, wandering from his loving care into sin and its consequences. (We need look no further than the third chapter of Genesis to discover that.) But in our essence—and in the character of every human no matter how far fallen—is excellence from God's hand, excellence that reflects his image.

We sing "I stand in awe of you," and other similar worship songs. Part of what inspires that wonder is God's creative abilities. Who else could have made the magnificent human body? Who but God could have invented the method whereby infants are conceived, grow, and make their dramatic entry into the world? Or fashioned a solar system in which each part functions in precise relationship to the others?

Do you stand in awe of God and his creative power? Do you thank him that you are "wonderfully complex" (Psalm 139:14) and made in his image? Is there someone you need to view differently, through the "excellent in every way" lens? Ask God to give you a new perspective on his excellent creation, then thank him for his awesome works.

[i pray]

> *Lord, I stand in awe of you and all you have done. Help me to see*
> *your glory in nature, in other people, and even in myself.*
> *Allow me to treat others by valuing their excellence, because you do.*

[i respond]

Reflect on what places or events prompt you to say, "God, your creation is excellent." As an act of worship, jot down six evidences of God's excellent creativity. Ask him to give you a new sense of appreciation for the excellence he has instilled in all facets of his creation throughout this day.

LORD God asked. "Have you eaten the fruit I commanded you not to eat?"

¹²"Yes," Adam admitted, "but it was the woman you gave me who brought me the fruit, and I ate it."

¹³Then the LORD God asked the woman, "How could you do such a thing?"

"The serpent tricked me," she replied. "That's why I ate it."

¹⁴So the LORD God said to the serpent, "Because you have done this, you will be punished. You are singled out from all the domestic and wild animals of the whole earth to be cursed. You will grovel in the dust as long as you live, crawling along on your belly. ¹⁵From now on, you and the woman will be enemies, and your offspring and her offspring will be enemies. He will crush your head, and you will strike his heel."

¹⁶Then he said to the woman, "You will bear children with intense pain and suffering. And though your desire will be for your husband,* he will be your master."

¹⁷And to Adam he said, "Because you listened to your wife and ate the fruit I told you not to eat, I have placed a curse on the ground. All your life you will struggle to scratch a living from it. ¹⁸It will grow thorns and thistles for you, though you will eat of its grains. ¹⁹All your life you will sweat to produce food, until your dying day. Then you will return to the ground from which you came. For you were made from dust, and to the dust you will return."

²⁰Then Adam named his wife Eve,* because she would be the mother of all people everywhere. ²¹And the LORD God made clothing from animal skins for Adam and his wife.

²²Then the LORD God said, "The people have become as we are, knowing everything, both good and evil. What if they eat the fruit of the tree of life? Then they will live forever!" ²³So the LORD God banished Adam and his wife from the Garden of Eden, and he sent Adam out to cultivate the ground from which he had been made. ²⁴After banishing them from the garden, the LORD God stationed mighty angelic beings* to the east of Eden. And a flaming sword flashed back and forth, guarding the way to the tree of life.

CAIN, ABEL, AND SETH

4 Now Adam* slept with his wife, Eve, and she became pregnant. When the time came, she gave birth to Cain,* and she said, "With the LORD's help, I have brought forth* a man!" ²Later she gave birth to a second son and named him Abel.

When they grew up, Abel became a shepherd, while Cain was a farmer. ³At harvesttime Cain brought to the LORD a gift of his farm produce, ⁴while Abel brought several choice lambs from the best of his flock. The LORD accepted Abel and his offering, ⁵but he did not accept Cain and his offering. This made Cain very angry and dejected.

⁶"Why are you so angry?" the LORD asked him. "Why do you look so dejected? ⁷You will be accepted if you respond in the right way. But if you refuse to respond correctly, then watch out! Sin is waiting to attack and destroy you, and you must subdue it."

⁸Later Cain suggested to his brother, Abel, "Let's go out into the fields."* And while they were there, Cain attacked and killed his brother.

⁹Afterward the LORD asked Cain, "Where is your brother? Where is Abel?"

"I don't know!" Cain retorted. "Am I supposed to keep track of him wherever he goes?"

¹⁰But the LORD said, "What have you done? Listen—your brother's blood cries out to me from the ground! ¹¹You are hereby banished from the ground you have defiled with your brother's blood. ¹²No longer will it yield abundant crops for you, no matter how hard you work! From now on you will be a homeless fugitive on the earth, constantly wandering from place to place."

3:16 Or *And though you may desire to control your husband.*   3:20 *Eve* sounds like a Hebrew term that means "to give life."   3:24 Hebrew *cherubim.*   4:1a Hebrew *the man.*   4:1b *Cain* sounds like a Hebrew term that can mean "bring forth" or "acquire."   4:1c Or *I have acquired.*   4:8 As in Samaritan Pentateuch, Greek and Syriac versions, Latin Vulgate; Masoretic Text lacks *"Let's go out into the fields."*

My Daily Worship

— January 2 —

ONLY MY BEST

GENESIS 4:1−5:32

The LORD accepted Abel and his offering, but he did not accept Cain and his offering.
This made Cain very angry and dejected (4:4–5).

[i reflect]

Jeff planned to make a large donation toward the costs of the addition to the church's Christian Education wing. As an insurance executive, he worked hard and he had the means to make a significant contribution. He expressed his desire to the pastor, who was, of course, grateful for Jim's generosity. But when Jim got a call the next week from Karen, head of children's ministries, asking him to be a Sunday school teacher in the nursery, he was miffed.

"I don't really have time," he told her.

"Oh, I'm sorry. Pastor Doug told me of your heart for children's ministries, and we really need teachers. I thought I'd ask if you'd be willing to serve." Jeff saw no connection between his willingness to give a donation for the Christian Education wing and the request to serve as a Sunday school teacher.

Like Cain, Jeff brought God what he wanted to bring, and he thought that was enough. Like Cain, he wanted to worship God in his own way, without considering what God wanted him to bring. In commenting on Cain's offering, Martin Luther wrote, "[Cain] brought his offering with an arrogant and overconfident attitude. He assumed that God would be pleased with his sacrifice for the simple reason that he was the firstborn. Because he lacked faith and didn't acknowledge his sinfulness, he felt no need to pray and didn't place his confidence in the mercy of God."

We act like that whenever we rely on our own efforts to earn God's approval. When we focus on the "good" that *we* can do in hopes of pleasing God rather than on *his* mercy and goodness, we miss the point of offering him our best.

The offering God wants most is the offering of our hearts, dedicated and fully turned toward him in a lifestyle of continual worship. As you pray today, release your gifts and talents and abilities to him and ask him what kind of a sacrifice he wants from you. The answer might surprise you.

[i pray]

God, I want to give you everything I have, but I find it difficult to do.
It's easy for me to give some things, much harder to give others.
Help me to be a cheerful giver, one who brings sacrifices that please you.

[i respond]

List the gifts of service that you have brought to God during the past month or so. Consider each one, asking the question, "Is this what you want me to bring to you?

¹³Cain replied to the LORD, "My punishment* is too great for me to bear! ¹⁴You have banished me from my land and from your presence; you have made me a wandering fugitive. All who see me will try to kill me!"

¹⁵The LORD replied, "They will not kill you, for I will give seven times your punishment to anyone who does." Then the LORD put a mark on Cain to warn anyone who might try to kill him. ¹⁶So Cain left the LORD's presence and settled in the land of Nod,* east of Eden.

¹⁷Then Cain's wife became pregnant and gave birth to a son, and they named him Enoch. When Cain founded a city, he named it Enoch after his son.

¹⁸ Enoch was the father of* Irad.

Irad was the father of Mehujael.

Mehujael was the father of Methushael.

Methushael was the father of Lamech.

¹⁹Lamech married two women—Adah and Zillah. ²⁰Adah gave birth to a baby named Jabal. He became the first of the herdsmen who live in tents. ²¹His brother's name was Jubal, the first musician—the inventor of the harp and flute. ²²To Lamech's other wife, Zillah, was born Tubal-cain. He was the first to work with metal, forging instruments of bronze and iron. Tubal-cain had a sister named Naamah.

²³One day Lamech said to Adah and Zillah, "Listen to me, my wives. I have killed a youth who attacked and wounded me. ²⁴If anyone who kills Cain is to be punished seven times, anyone who takes revenge against me will be punished seventy-seven times!"

²⁵Adam slept with his wife again, and she gave birth to another son. She named him Seth,* for she said, "God has granted me another son in place of Abel, the one Cain killed." ²⁶When Seth grew up, he had a son and named him Enosh. It was during his lifetime that people first began to worship the LORD.

FROM ADAM TO NOAH

5 This is the history of the descendants of Adam. When God created people,* he made them in the likeness of God. ²He created them male and female, and he blessed them and called them "human."*

³When Adam was 130 years old, his son Seth was born,* and Seth was the very image of his father.* ⁴After the birth of Seth,* Adam lived another 800 years, and he had other sons and daughters. ⁵He died at the age of 930.

⁶When Seth was 105 years old, his son Enosh was born. ⁷After the birth of Enosh, Seth lived another 807 years, and he had other sons and daughters. ⁸He died at the age of 912.

⁹When Enosh was 90 years old, his son Kenan was born. ¹⁰After the birth of Kenan, Enosh lived another 815 years, and he had other sons and daughters. ¹¹He died at the age of 905.

¹²When Kenan was 70 years old, his son Mahalalel was born. ¹³After the birth of Mahalalel, Kenan lived another 840 years, and he had other sons and daughters. ¹⁴He died at the age of 910.

¹⁵When Mahalalel was 65 years old, his son Jared was born. ¹⁶After the birth of Jared, Mahalalel lived 830 years, and he had other sons and daughters. ¹⁷He died at the age of 895.

¹⁸When Jared was 162 years old, his son Enoch was born. ¹⁹After the birth of Enoch, Jared lived another 800 years, and he had other sons and daughters. ²⁰He died at the age of 962.

²¹When Enoch was 65 years old, his son Methuselah was born. ²²After the birth of Methuselah, Enoch lived another 300 years in close fellowship with God, and he had other sons and daughters. ²³Enoch lived

---

4:13 Or *My sin.* **4:16** *Nod* means "wandering." **4:18** Or *the ancestor of,* and so throughout the verse. **4:25** *Seth* probably means "granted"; the name may also mean "appointed." **5:1** Hebrew *man.* **5:2** Hebrew *man.* **5:3a** Or *his son, the ancestor of Seth, was born;* similarly in 5:6, 9, 12, 15, 18, 21, 25. **5:3b** Hebrew *was in his own likeness, after his image.* **5:4** Or *After the birth of this ancestor of Seth;* similarly in 5:7, 10, 13, 16, 19, 22, 26.

365 years in all. [24]He enjoyed a close relationship with God throughout his life. Then suddenly, he disappeared because God took him.

[25]When Methuselah was 187 years old, his son Lamech was born. [26]After the birth of Lamech, Methuselah lived another 782 years, and he had other sons and daughters. [27]He died at the age of 969.

[28]When Lamech was 182 years old, his son Noah was born. [29]Lamech named his son Noah,* for he said, "He will bring us relief from the painful labor of farming this ground that the LORD has cursed." [30]After the birth of Noah, Lamech lived 595 years, and he had other sons and daughters. [31]He died at the age of 777.

[32]By the time Noah was 500 years old, he had three sons: Shem, Ham, and Japheth.

NOAH AND THE FLOOD

6 When the human population began to grow rapidly on the earth, [2]the sons of God saw the beautiful women of the human race and took any they wanted as their wives. [3]Then the LORD said, "My Spirit will not put up with humans for such a long time, for they are only mortal flesh. In the future, they will live no more than 120 years."

[4]In those days, and even afterward, giants* lived on the earth, for whenever the sons of God had intercourse with human women, they gave birth to children who became the heroes mentioned in legends of old.

[5]Now the LORD observed the extent of the people's wickedness, and he saw that all their thoughts were consistently and totally evil. [6]So the LORD was sorry he had ever made them. It broke his heart. [7]And the LORD said, "I will completely wipe out this human race that I have created. Yes, and I will destroy all the animals and birds, too. I am sorry I ever made them." [8]But Noah found favor with the LORD.

[9]This is the history of Noah and his family. Noah was a righteous man, the only blameless man living on earth at the time. He consis-

---

Words of Worship

GOD

God—Hebrew '*E-lo-him* "mighty one, deity"; Greek *the-os* "deity." These are the generic terms for a deity or god in Scripture. They are used both for false gods and the one God of Israel and the Christian community.

The Hebrew word means "strong one" and can also refer to angelic beings (Psalm 8:5) or even to powerful people (Psalm 82:6). It is not God's name, but his title or office. The word '*Elohim* is a plural form (there is a rare singular form, '*Eloah*), but when applied to the one God, it always takes a singular verb. It is a "plural of majesty," indicating God's greatness, not his number.

"In the beginning God" (Genesis 1:1). The Bible never offers us proof that God exists. His presence and power are simply assumed as facts of life. There is no atheism in Scripture; the fool who denies him (Psalm 53:1) is just refusing to take him into account and worship him. As Paul stated, from the existence of the universe itself, people "can clearly see his invisible qualities— his eternal power and divine nature. So they have no excuse whatsoever for not knowing God" (Romans 1:20). The writer to the Hebrews adds, "This is the God to whom we must explain all that we have done" (Hebrews 4:13). Come before him and worship.

---

tently followed God's will and enjoyed a close relationship with him. [10]Noah had three sons: Shem, Ham, and Japheth.

[11]Now the earth had become corrupt in God's sight, and it was filled with violence. [12]God observed all this corruption in the world, and he saw violence and depravity everywhere. [13]So God said to Noah, "I have decided to

---

5:29 *Noah* sounds like a Hebrew term that can mean "relief" or "comfort." 6:4 Hebrew *Nephilim*.

destroy all living creatures, for the earth is filled with violence because of them. Yes, I will wipe them all from the face of the earth!

¹⁴"Make a boat* from resinous wood and seal it with tar, inside and out. Then construct decks and stalls throughout its interior. ¹⁵Make it 450 feet long, 75 feet wide, and 45 feet high.* ¹⁶Construct an opening all the way around the boat, 18 inches* below the roof. Then put three decks inside the boat—bottom, middle, and upper—and put a door in the side.

¹⁷"Look! I am about to cover the earth with a flood that will destroy every living thing. Everything on earth will die! ¹⁸But I solemnly swear to keep you safe in the boat, with your wife and your sons and their wives. ¹⁹Bring a pair of every kind of animal—a male and a female—into the boat with you to keep them alive during the flood. ²⁰Pairs of each kind of bird and each kind of animal, large and small alike, will come to you to be kept alive. ²¹And remember, take enough food for your family and for all the animals."

²²So Noah did everything exactly as God had commanded him.

THE FLOOD COVERS THE EARTH

7 Finally, the day came when the LORD said to Noah, "Go into the boat with all your family, for among all the people of the earth, I consider you alone to be righteous. ²Take along seven pairs of each animal that I have approved for eating and for sacrifice, and take one pair of each of the others. ³Then select seven pairs of every kind of bird. There must be a male and a female in each pair to ensure that every kind of living creature will survive the flood. ⁴One week from today I will begin forty days and forty nights of rain. And I will wipe from the earth all the living things I have created."

⁵So Noah did exactly as the LORD had commanded him. ⁶He was 600 years old when the flood came, ⁷and he went aboard the boat to escape—he and his wife and his sons and their wives. ⁸With them were all the various kinds of animals—those approved for eating and sacrifice and those that were not—along with all the birds and other small animals. ⁹They came into the boat in pairs, male and female, just as God had commanded Noah. ¹⁰One week later, the flood came and covered the earth.

¹¹When Noah was 600 years old, on the seventeenth day of the second month, the underground waters burst forth on the earth, and the rain fell in mighty torrents from the sky. ¹²The rain continued to fall for forty days and forty nights. ¹³But Noah had gone into the boat that very day with his wife and his sons—Shem, Ham, and Japheth—and their wives. ¹⁴With them in the boat were pairs of every kind of breathing animal—domestic and wild, large and small—along with birds and flying insects of every kind. ¹⁵Two by two they came into the boat, ¹⁶male and female, just as God had commanded. Then the LORD shut them in.

¹⁷For forty days the floods prevailed, covering the ground and lifting the boat high above the earth. ¹⁸As the waters rose higher and higher above the ground, the boat floated safely on the surface. ¹⁹Finally, the water covered even the highest mountains on the earth, ²⁰standing more than twenty-two feet* above the highest peaks. ²¹All the living things on earth died—birds, domestic animals, wild

I need to know more about how to worship and to praise my Father, for it's the essential task that connects my temporal life with my eternal one.

DAVID JEREMIAH

6:14 Traditionally rendered *an ark.* 6:15 Hebrew *300 cubits* [135 meters] *long, 50 cubits* [22.5 meters] *wide, and 30 cubits* [13.5 meters] *high.* 6:16 Hebrew *1 cubit* [45 centimeters]. 7:20 Hebrew *15 cubits* [6.8 meters].

animals, all kinds of small animals, and all the people. [22]Everything died that breathed and lived on dry land. [23]Every living thing on the earth was wiped out—people, animals both large and small, and birds. They were all destroyed, and only Noah was left alive, along with those who were with him in the boat. [24]And the water covered the earth for 150 days.

THE FLOOD RECEDES

8 But God remembered Noah and all the animals in the boat. He sent a wind to blow across the waters, and the floods began to disappear. [2]The underground water sources ceased their gushing, and the torrential rains stopped. [3]So the flood gradually began to recede. After 150 days, [4]exactly five months from the time the flood began,* the boat came to rest on the mountains of Ararat. [5]Two and a half months later,* as the waters continued to go down, other mountain peaks began to appear.

[6]After another forty days, Noah opened the window he had made in the boat [7]and released a raven that flew back and forth until the earth was dry. [8]Then he sent out a dove to see if it could find dry ground. [9]But the dove found no place to land because the water was still too high. So it returned to the boat, and Noah held out his hand and drew the dove back inside. [10]Seven days later, Noah released the dove again. [11]This time, toward evening, the bird returned to him with a fresh olive leaf in its beak. Noah now knew that the water was almost gone. [12]A week later, he released the dove again, and this time it did not come back.

[13]Finally, when Noah was 601 years old, ten and a half months after the flood began,* Noah lifted back the cover to look. The water was drying up. [14]Two more months went by,* and at last the earth was dry! [15]Then God said to Noah, [16]"Leave the boat, all of you. [17]Release all the animals and birds so they can breed and reproduce in great numbers." [18]So Noah,

his wife, and his sons and their wives left the boat. [19]And all the various kinds of animals and birds came out, pair by pair.

[20]Then Noah built an altar to the LORD and sacrificed on it the animals and birds that had been approved for that purpose. [21]And the LORD was pleased with the sacrifice and said to himself, "I will never again curse the earth, destroying all living things, even though people's thoughts and actions are bent toward evil from childhood. [22]As long as the earth remains, there will be springtime and harvest, cold and heat, winter and summer, day and night."

GOD'S COVENANT WITH NOAH

9 God blessed Noah and his sons and told them, "Multiply and fill the earth. [2]All the wild animals, large and small, and all the birds and fish will be afraid of you. I have placed them in your power. [3]I have given them to you for food, just as I have given you grain and vegetables. [4]But you must never eat animals that still have their lifeblood in them. [5]And murder is forbidden. Animals that kill people must die, and any person who murders must be killed. [6]Yes, you must execute anyone who murders another person, for to kill a person is to kill a living being made in God's image. [7]Now you must have many children and repopulate the earth. Yes, multiply and fill the earth!"

[8]Then God told Noah and his sons, [9]"I am making a covenant with you and your descendants, [10]and with the animals you brought with you—all these birds and livestock and wild animals. [11]I solemnly promise never to send another flood to kill all living creatures and destroy the earth." [12]And God said, "I am giving you a sign as evidence of my eternal covenant with you and all living creatures. [13]I have placed my rainbow in the clouds. It is the sign of my permanent promise to you and to all the earth. [14]When I send clouds over the earth, the rainbow will be seen in the clouds,

---

8:4 Hebrew *on the seventeenth day of the seventh month;* see 7:11. **8:5** Hebrew *On the first day of the tenth month;* see 7:11 and note on 8:4. **8:13** Hebrew *on the first day of the first month;* see 7:11. **8:14** Hebrew *The twenty-seventh day of the second month arrived;* see note on 8:13.

¹⁵and I will remember my covenant with you and with everything that lives. Never again will there be a flood that will destroy all life. ¹⁶When I see the rainbow in the clouds, I will remember the eternal covenant between God and every living creature on earth." ¹⁷Then God said to Noah, "Yes, this is the sign of my covenant with all the creatures of the earth."

NOAH'S SONS

¹⁸Shem, Ham, and Japheth, the three sons of Noah, survived the Flood with their father. (Ham is the ancestor of the Canaanites.) ¹⁹From these three sons of Noah came all the people now scattered across the earth.

²⁰After the Flood, Noah became a farmer and planted a vineyard. ²¹One day he became drunk on some wine he had made and lay naked in his tent. ²²Ham, the father of Canaan, saw that his father was naked and went outside and told his brothers. ²³Shem and Japheth took a robe, held it over their shoulders, walked backward into the tent, and covered their father's naked body. As they did this, they looked the other way so they wouldn't see him naked. ²⁴When Noah woke up from his drunken stupor, he learned what Ham, his youngest son, had done. ²⁵Then he cursed the descendants of Canaan, the son of Ham:

"A curse on the Canaanites!
May they be the lowest of servants
   to the descendants of Shem and
   Japheth."

²⁶Then Noah said,

"May Shem be blessed by the LORD my God;
   and may Canaan be his servant.
²⁷ May God enlarge the territory of Japheth,
   and may he share the prosperity of Shem;*
   and let Canaan be his servant."

²⁸Noah lived another 350 years after the Flood. ²⁹He was 950 years old when he died.

10 This is the history of the families of Shem, Ham, and Japheth, the three sons of Noah. Many children were born to them after the Flood.

DESCENDANTS OF JAPHETH

²The descendants of Japheth were Gomer, Magog, Madai, Javan, Tubal, Meshech, and Tiras.
³The descendants of Gomer were Ashkenaz, Riphath, and Togarmah.
⁴The descendants of Javan were Elishah, Tarshish, Kittim, and Rodanim.* ⁵Their descendants became the seafaring peoples in various lands, each tribe with its own language.

DESCENDANTS OF HAM

⁶The descendants of Ham were Cush, Mizraim,* Put, and Canaan.
⁷The descendants of Cush were Seba, Havilah, Sabtah, Raamah, and Sabteca. The descendants of Raamah were Sheba and Dedan.

⁸One of Cush's descendants was Nimrod, who became a heroic warrior. ⁹He was a mighty hunter in the LORD's sight.* His name became proverbial, and people would speak of someone as being "like Nimrod, a mighty hunter in the LORD's sight." ¹⁰He built the foundation for his empire in the land of Babylonia,* with the cities of Babel, Erech, Akkad, and Calneh. ¹¹From there he extended his reign to Assyria, where he built Nineveh, Rehoboth-ir, Calah, ¹²and Resen—the main city of the empire, located between Nineveh and Calah.

¹³Mizraim was the ancestor of the Ludites, Anamites, Lehabites, Naphtuhites, ¹⁴Pathrusites, Casluhites, and the Caphtorites, from whom the Philistines came.* ¹⁵Canaan's oldest son was Sidon, the ancestor of the Sidonians. Canaan was also the ancestor of the Hittites, ¹⁶Jebusites,

9:27 Hebrew *may he live in the tents of Shem.*   10:4 As in some Hebrew manuscripts and Greek version (see also 1 Chr 1:7); most Hebrew manuscripts read *Dodanim.*   10:6 Or *Egypt;* also in 10:13.   10:9 Hebrew *a mighty hunter before the LORD;* also in 10:9b. 10:10 Hebrew *Shinar.*   10:14 Hebrew *Casluhites, from whom the Philistines came, Caphtorites.* Compare Jer 47:4; Amos 9:7.

My Daily Worship

— *January 3* —

GIVE ME A SIGN

GENESIS 6:1–9:17

It is the sign of my permanent promise to you and to all the earth. When I send clouds over the earth, the rainbow will be seen in the clouds, and I will remember my covenant with you and with everything that lives (9:13–15).

[i reflect]

Children delight in rainbows. They want to follow the rainbow to its end or run and jump through it if it appears in a spray of water. Parents enjoy telling their children the story of Noah and the first rainbow—a sign of God's lasting promise that he would never again destroy the earth. Sometimes, we see God's promises reflected in other ways.

Consider Becky, a single mom with two toddler girls. She received no child support or other assistance from her ex-husband, and while Becky had a hard time making ends meet, somehow they managed. When the week's groceries ran out a day early, a friend brought over a pizza. When she needed to pay a doctor's bill, her tax refund came a month early. When it looked as though her week's vacation would be spent at home with her two girls, a couple from church offered to let them stay in their cottage.

Becky saw God's faithfulness often—she didn't know how a need would be met, but it always was. For Becky, each met need was a rainbow—a sign from God of his faithfulness to her and of his provision and care.

What rainbows do you see? Where do you witness God's faithfulness to you? Look for it in the small needs he meets at just the right time. Credit his goodness when good fortune comes your way and when he's close to you in times of trouble.

Children delight in rainbows—looking for them after a summer rainstorm, drawing them with colorful chalk on the sidewalk, listening again and again to Noah's great adventure with God. What tangible sign or symbol can you place in your life to remind you of God's faithfulness? Make that your "rainbow," your sign of God's promise to care for you, your signal to worship him in gratitude and love.

[i pray]

God, thank you for your permanent promise to me. Thank you for all the countless ways I see you fulfill that promise, day in and day out, caring for me and mine in amazing ways.

[i respond]

List four or five ways God has provided for you unexpectedly. Ask him to help you keep watch for his work in your life, growing ever more grateful as you find him faithful again and again.

Amorites, Girgashites, [17]Hivites, Arkites, Sinites, [18]Arvadites, Zemarites, and Hamathites. [19]Eventually the territory of Canaan spread from Sidon to Gerar, near Gaza, and to Sodom, Gomorrah, Admah, and Zeboiim, near Lasha.

[20]These were the descendants of Ham, identified according to their tribes, languages, territories, and nations.

DESCENDANTS OF SHEM

[21]Sons were also born to Shem, the older brother of Japheth.* Shem was the ancestor of all the descendants of Eber. [22]The descendants of Shem were Elam, Asshur, Arphaxad, Lud, and Aram.

[23]The descendants of Aram were Uz, Hul, Gether, and Mash.

[24]Arphaxad was the father of Shelah,* and Shelah was the father of Eber. [25]Eber had two sons. The first was named Peleg—"division"—for during his lifetime the people of the world were divided into different language groups and dispersed. His brother's name was Joktan.

[26]Joktan was the ancestor of Almodad, Sheleph, Hazarmaveth, Jerah, [27]Hadoram, Uzal, Diklah, [28]Obal, Abimael, Sheba, [29]Ophir, Havilah, and Jobab. [30]The descendants of Joktan lived in the area extending from Mesha toward the eastern hills of Sephar.

[31]These were the descendants of Shem, identified according to their tribes, languages, territories, and nations.

[32]These are the families that came from Noah's sons, listed nation by nation according to their lines of descent. The earth was populated with the people of these nations after the Flood.

THE TOWER OF BABEL

11 At one time the whole world spoke a single language and used the same words. [2]As the people migrated eastward, they found a plain in the land of Babylonia* and settled there. [3]They began to talk about construction projects. "Come," they said, "let's make great piles of burnt brick and collect natural asphalt to use as mortar. [4]Let's build a great city with a tower that reaches to the skies—a monument to our greatness! This will bring us together and keep us from scattering all over the world."

[5]But the LORD came down to see the city and the tower the people were building. [6]"Look!" he said. "If they can accomplish this when they have just begun to take advantage of their common language and political unity, just think of what they will do later. Nothing will be impossible for them! [7]Come, let's go down and give them different languages. Then they won't be able to understand each other."

[8]In that way, the LORD scattered them all over the earth; and that ended the building of the city. [9]That is why the city was called Babel,* because it was there that the LORD confused the people by giving them many languages, thus scattering them across the earth.

FROM SHEM TO ABRAM

[10]This is the history of Shem's family.

When Shem was 100 years old, his son Arphaxad was born. This happened two years after the Flood. [11]After the birth of Arphaxad, Shem lived another 500 years and had other sons and daughters.

[12]When Arphaxad was 35 years old, his son Shelah was born.* [13]After the birth of

---

10:21 Or *Shem, whose older brother was Japheth.* 10:24 Greek version reads *Arphaxad was the father of Cainan, Cainan was the father of Shelah.* 11:2 Hebrew *Shinar.* 11:9 *Babel* sounds like a Hebrew term that means "confusion." 11:12 Or *his son, the ancestor of Shelah, was born;* similarly in 11:14, 16, 18, 20, 22, 24. 11:12-13 Greek version reads [12]*When Arphaxad was 135 years old, his son Cainan was born.* [13]*After the birth of Cainan, Arphaxad lived another 430 years and had other sons and daughters, and then he died. When Cainan was 130 years old, his son Shelah was born. After the birth of Shelah, Cainan lived another 330 years and had other sons and daughters, and then he died.*

My Daily Worship

— January 4 —

A Monumental Mistake

Genesis 9:18–11:32

Let's build a great city with a tower that reaches to the skies—a monument
to our greatness! This will bring us together and keep us
from scattering all over the world (11:4).

[i reflect]

Part of what it means to be created in the image of God (Genesis 1:27) is that we humans have the God-given capacity to make a difference. By dreaming and working, we really *can* change our world.

The problem is that our good desire to "leave a legacy" is easily twisted. We forget that God is the central point and that everything—including ourselves—has been created by him and for him. We exist to do his bidding—not the other way around.

The tower of Babel incident is a continuation of the ugly events begun in Eden. Can you hear the hissing of the serpent behind the scenes? "Fill the earth? Obey God? Don't be ridiculous! You're much better off serving your own desires! Can't you see how he's keeping good things from you? Your only hope for life is to throw off his oppressive rule and do your own thing."

Contrast a distrustful humanity's decision—"Let's do something to obtain fame and call attention to ourselves" with God's declaration to his trusting servant Abraham in the next chapter, "I will . . . make you famous." Consider the irony that while nobody remembers anyone who was part of the Babel debacle, Abraham is a household name.

It's easy to feel like the people of Babel and want to build a personal monument to ourselves through our families, our possessions, or our accomplishments. Every day we are confronted with opportunities to choose that way or Abraham's way.

Humble yourself today before God, knowing that he will exalt you at the proper time. Today, ask God to help you build monuments to his glory and not yourself.

[i pray]

Lord, teach me how to keep in step with the Spirit, acting only in your way and in your time,
relying on your infinite wisdom and power. May you receive glory,
and may I find deep satisfaction, as I walk with you.

[i respond]

Notice tall things today—trees, buildings, etc. In each instance let your gaze go even farther upward, so that your thoughts are of God and his lordship over the earth.

Shelah, Arphaxad lived another 403 years and had other sons and daughters.*

[14]When Shelah was 30 years old, his son Eber was born. [15]After the birth of Eber, Shelah lived another 403 years and had other sons and daughters.

[16]When Eber was 34 years old, his son Peleg was born. [17]After the birth of Peleg, Eber lived another 430 years and had other sons and daughters.

[18]When Peleg was 30 years old, his son Reu was born. [19]After the birth of Reu, Peleg lived another 209 years and had other sons and daughters.

[20]When Reu was 32 years old, his son Serug was born. [21]After the birth of Serug, Reu lived another 207 years and had other sons and daughters.

[22]When Serug was 30 years old, his son Nahor was born. [23]After the birth of Nahor, Serug lived another 200 years and had other sons and daughters.

[24]When Nahor was 29 years old, his son Terah was born. [25]After the birth of Terah, Nahor lived another 119 years and had other sons and daughters.

[26]When Terah was 70 years old, he became the father of Abram, Nahor, and Haran.

THE FAMILY OF TERAH

[27]This is the history of Terah's family. Terah was the father of Abram, Nahor, and Haran; and Haran had a son named Lot. [28]But while Haran was still young, he died in Ur of the Chaldeans, the place of his birth. He was survived by Terah, his father. [29]Meanwhile, Abram married Sarai, and his brother Nahor married Milcah, the daughter of their brother Haran. (Milcah had a sister named Iscah.) [30]Now Sarai was not able to have any children.

[31]Terah took his son Abram, his daughter-in-law Sarai, and his grandson Lot (his son Haran's child) and left Ur of the Chaldeans to go to the land of Canaan. But they stopped instead at the village of Haran and settled there. [32]Terah lived for 205 years* and died while still at Haran.

THE CALL OF ABRAM

12 Then the LORD told Abram, "Leave your country, your relatives, and your father's house, and go to the land that I will show you. [2]I will cause you to become the father of a great nation. I will bless you and make you famous, and I will make you a blessing to others. [3]I will bless those who bless you and curse those who curse you. All the families of the earth will be blessed through you."

[4]So Abram departed as the LORD had instructed him, and Lot went with him. Abram was seventy-five years old when he left Haran. [5]He took his wife, Sarai, his nephew Lot, and all his wealth—his livestock and all the people who had joined his household at Haran—and finally arrived in Canaan. [6]Traveling through Canaan, they came to a place near Shechem and set up camp beside the oak at Moreh. At that time, the area was inhabited by Canaanites.

[7]Then the LORD appeared to Abram and said, "I am going to give this land to your offspring.*" And Abram built an altar there to commemorate the LORD's visit. [8]After that, Abram traveled southward and set up camp in the hill country between Bethel on the west and Ai on the east. There he built an altar and worshiped the LORD. [9]Then Abram traveled south by stages toward the Negev.

ABRAM AND SARAI IN EGYPT

[10]At that time there was a severe famine in the land, so Abram went down to Egypt to wait it out. [11]As he was approaching the borders of Egypt, Abram said to Sarai, "You are a very beautiful woman. [12]When the Egyptians see you, they will say, 'This is his wife. Let's kill him; then we can have her!' [13]But if you say you are my sister, then the Egyptians will treat me well because of their interest in you, and they will spare my life."

11:32 Some ancient versions read *145 years*; compare 11:26; 12:4.   12:7 Hebrew *seed.*

¹⁴And sure enough, when they arrived in Egypt, everyone spoke of her beauty. ¹⁵When the palace officials saw her, they sang her praises to their king, the pharaoh, and she was taken into his harem. ¹⁶Then Pharaoh gave Abram many gifts because of her—sheep, cattle, donkeys, male and female servants, and camels.

¹⁷But the LORD sent a terrible plague upon Pharaoh's household because of Sarai, Abram's wife. ¹⁸So Pharaoh called for Abram and accused him sharply. "What is this you have done to me?" he demanded. "Why didn't you tell me she was your wife? ¹⁹Why were you willing to let me marry her, saying she was your sister? Here is your wife! Take her and be gone!" ²⁰Pharaoh then sent them out of the country under armed escort—Abram and his wife, with all their household and belongings.

ABRAM AND LOT SEPARATE

13 So they left Egypt and traveled north into the Negev—Abram with his wife and Lot and all that they owned, ²for Abram was very rich in livestock, silver, and gold. ³Then they continued traveling by stages toward Bethel, to the place between Bethel and Ai where they had camped before. ⁴This was the place where Abram had built the altar, and there he again worshiped the LORD.

⁵Now Lot, who was traveling with Abram, was also very wealthy with sheep, cattle, and many tents. ⁶But the land could not support both Abram and Lot with all their flocks and herds living so close together. There were too many animals for the available pastureland. ⁷So an argument broke out between the herdsmen of Abram and Lot. At that time Canaanites and Perizzites were also living in the land.

⁸Then Abram talked it over with Lot. "This arguing between our herdsmen has got to stop," he said. "After all, we are close relatives! ⁹I'll tell you what we'll do. Take your choice of any section of the land you want, and we will separate. If you want that area over there, then

I'll stay here. If you want to stay in this area, then I'll move on to another place."

¹⁰Lot took a long look at the fertile plains of the Jordan Valley in the direction of Zoar. The whole area was well watered everywhere, like the garden of the LORD or the beautiful land of Egypt. (This was before the LORD had destroyed Sodom and Gomorrah.) ¹¹Lot chose that land for himself—the Jordan Valley to the east of them. He went there with his flocks and servants and parted company with his uncle Abram. ¹²So while Abram stayed in the land of Canaan, Lot moved his tents to a place near Sodom, among the cities of the plain. ¹³The people of this area were unusually wicked and sinned greatly against the LORD.

¹⁴After Lot was gone, the LORD said to Abram, "Look as far as you can see in every direction. ¹⁵I am going to give all this land to you and your offspring* as a permanent possession. ¹⁶And I am going to give you so many descendants that, like dust, they cannot be counted! ¹⁷Take a walk in every direction and explore the new possessions I am giving you." ¹⁸Then Abram moved his camp to the oak grove owned by Mamre, which is at Hebron. There he built an altar to the LORD.

ABRAM RESCUES LOT

14 About this time war broke out in the region. King Amraphel of Babylonia,* King Arioch of Ellasar, King Kedorlaomer of Elam, and King Tidal of Goiim ²fought against King Bera of Sodom, King Birsha of Gomorrah, King Shinab of Admah, King Shemeber of Zeboiim, and the king of Bela (now called Zoar).

³The kings of Sodom, Gomorrah, Admah, Zeboiim, and Bela formed an alliance and mobilized their armies in Siddim Valley (that is, the valley of the Dead Sea*). ⁴For twelve years they had all been subject to King Kedorlaomer, but now in the thirteenth year they rebelled.

⁵One year later, Kedorlaomer and his allies arrived. They conquered the Rephaites in

13:15 Hebrew *seed.* 14:1 Hebrew *Shinar;* also in 14:9. 14:3 Hebrew *Salt Sea.*

Ashteroth-karnaim, the Zuzites in Ham, the Emites in the plain of Kiriathaim, ⁶and the Horites in Mount Seir, as far as El-paran at the edge of the wilderness. ⁷Then they swung around to En-mishpat (now called Kadesh) and destroyed the Amalekites, and also the Amorites living in Hazazon-tamar.

⁸But now the army of the kings of Sodom, Gomorrah, Admah, Zeboiim, and Bela (now called Zoar) prepared for battle in the valley of the Dead Sea* ⁹against King Kedorlaomer of Elam and the kings of Goiim, Babylonia, and Ellasar—four kings against five. ¹⁰As it happened, the valley was filled with tar pits. And as the army of the kings of Sodom and Gomorrah fled, some slipped into the tar pits, while the rest escaped into the mountains. ¹¹The victorious invaders then plundered Sodom and Gomorrah and began their long journey home, taking all the wealth and food with them. ¹²They also captured Lot— Abram's nephew who lived in Sodom—and took everything he owned. ¹³One of the men who escaped came and told Abram the Hebrew, who was camped at the oak grove belonging to Mamre the Amorite. Mamre and his relatives, Eshcol and Aner, were Abram's allies.

¹⁴When Abram learned that Lot had been captured, he called together the men born into his household, 318 of them in all. He chased after Kedorlaomer's army until he caught up with them in Dan. ¹⁵There he divided his men and attacked during the night from several directions. Kedorlaomer's army fled, but Abram chased them to Hobah, north of Damascus. ¹⁶Abram and his allies recovered everything—the goods that had been taken, Abram's nephew Lot with his possessions, and all the women and other captives.

MELCHIZEDEK BLESSES ABRAM

¹⁷As Abram returned from his victory over Kedorlaomer and his allies, the king of Sodom came out to meet him in the valley of Shaveh

(that is, the King's Valley). ¹⁸Then Melchizedek, the king of Salem and a priest of God Most High, brought him bread and wine. ¹⁹Melchizedek blessed Abram with this blessing:

"Blessed be Abram by God Most High,
　　Creator of heaven and earth.
²⁰ And blessed be God Most High,
　　who has helped you conquer your
　　enemies."

Then Abram gave Melchizedek a tenth of all the goods he had recovered.

²¹The king of Sodom told him, "Give back my people who were captured. But you may keep for yourself all the goods you have recovered."

²²Abram replied, "I have solemnly promised the LORD, God Most High, Creator of heaven and earth, ²³that I will not take so much as a single thread or sandal thong from you. Otherwise you might say, 'I am the one who made Abram rich!' ²⁴All I'll accept is what these young men of mine have already eaten. But give a share of the goods to my allies— Aner, Eshcol, and Mamre."

THE LORD'S COVENANT WITH ABRAM

15 Afterward the LORD spoke to Abram in a vision and said to him, "Do not be afraid, Abram, for I will protect you, and your reward will be great."

²But Abram replied, "O Sovereign LORD, what good are all your blessings when I don't even have a son? Since I don't have a son, Eliezer of Damascus, a servant in my household, will inherit all my wealth. ³You have given me no children, so one of my servants will have to be my heir."

⁴Then the LORD said to him, "No, your servant will not be your heir, for you will have a son of your own to inherit everything I am giving you." ⁵Then the LORD brought Abram

14:8 Hebrew in Siddim Valley; see 14:3.

My Daily Worship

— *January 5* —

HERE, THERE & EVERYWHERE
GENESIS 12:1–14:24

Blessed be Abram by God Most High, Creator of heaven and earth. And blessed be God Most High,
who has helped you conquer your enemies (14:19–20).

[i reflect]

Author A.W. Tozer once observed that what we think about God is the most important thing about us. And surely what we think of him is reflected in the various ways we describe him and in the assorted names or titles by which we address him.

In blessing Abram, Melchizedek, the mysterious king and priest of ancient Salem, spoke of "God Most High." In other words God is lofty and exalted. He sits enthroned above the heavens. He is, to use an old theological term, transcendent.

But he is not aloof. Notice that, in Melchizedek's words, he is also the God who intervenes, who injects himself into the mundane lives of his people. Scholars call this quality God's immanence. On this historical occasion, the Lord helped Abram conquer actual foes in a literal fight.

Amazing, isn't it? Our great Creator rules and reigns. But more than that, he sees and hears. Even better, he shows up, helping, delivering, always desiring to pour out blessings on his beloved servants.

Thomas Oliver, an evangelist and associate of John Wesley, captured this dual aspect of God's character in his well-known hymn "The God of Abraham Praise." In the second stanza, Oliver wrote, "The God of Abraham praise, at whose supreme command/ From earth we rise and seek the joys at his right hand./ We all on earth forsake its wisdom, fame, and power;/ And him our only portion make, our shield and tower." The words reveal our need for close, daily dependence on the One who is in command and who is our "shield and tower."

What God did for Abram he will also do for you. What is it that you need most? Protection, guidance, safekeeping? Bring your needs to God Most High. He promises to bless you.

[i pray]

God, the question is not will you show up today in my life, or will you be present, or will you
speak and work. No, the question is will I notice and praise you when you do all these things.
Grant that I, one with most low vision, might see you today, O Most High God.

[i respond]

Take a few minutes to record a great act of God in your life that you have experienced recently. Throughout this day and the remainder of the week, look for the numerous ways that God Most High intervenes on your behalf.

outside beneath the night sky and told him, "Look up into the heavens and count the stars if you can. Your descendants will be like that—too many to count!" [6]And Abram believed the LORD, and the LORD declared him righteous because of his faith. [7]Then the LORD told him, "I am the LORD who brought you out of Ur of the Chaldeans to give you this land."

[8]But Abram replied, "O Sovereign LORD, how can I be sure that you will give it to me?"

[9]Then the LORD told him, "Bring me a three-year-old heifer, a three-year-old female goat, a three-year-old ram, a turtledove, and a young pigeon." [10]Abram took all these and killed them. He cut each one down the middle and laid the halves side by side. He did not, however, divide the birds in half. [11]Some vultures came down to eat the carcasses, but Abram chased them away. [12]That evening, as the sun was going down, Abram fell into a deep sleep. He saw a terrifying vision of darkness and horror.

[13]Then the LORD told Abram, "You can be sure that your descendants will be strangers in a foreign land, and they will be oppressed as slaves for four hundred years. [14]But I will punish the nation that enslaves them, and in the end they will come away with great wealth. [15](But you will die in peace, at a ripe old age.) [16]After four generations your descendants will return here to this land, when the sin of the Amorites has run its course."

[17]As the sun went down and it became dark, Abram saw a smoking firepot and a flaming torch pass between the halves of the carcasses. [18]So the LORD made a covenant with Abram that day and said, "I have given this land to your descendants, all the way from the border of Egypt* to the great Euphrates River—[19]the land of the Kenites, Kenizzites, Kadmonites, [20]Hittites, Perizzites, Rephaites, [21]Amorites, Canaanites, Girgashites, and Jebusites."

THE BIRTH OF ISHMAEL

16 But Sarai, Abram's wife, had no children. So Sarai took her servant, an Egyptian woman named Hagar, [2]and gave her to Abram so she could bear his children. "The LORD has kept me from having any children," Sarai said to Abram. "Go and sleep with my servant. Perhaps I can have children through her." And Abram agreed. [3]So Sarai, Abram's wife, took Hagar the Egyptian servant and gave her to Abram as a wife. (This happened ten years after Abram first arrived in the land of Canaan.)

[4]So Abram slept with Hagar, and she became pregnant. When Hagar knew she was pregnant, she began to treat her mistress Sarai with contempt. [5]Then Sarai said to Abram, "It's all your fault! Now this servant of mine is pregnant, and she despises me, though I myself gave her the privilege of sleeping with you. The LORD will make you pay for doing this to me!*"

[6]Abram replied, "Since she is your servant, you may deal with her as you see fit." So Sarai treated her harshly, and Hagar ran away.

[7]The angel of the LORD found Hagar beside a desert spring along the road to Shur. [8]The angel said to her, "Hagar, Sarai's servant, where have you come from, and where are you going?"

"I am running away from my mistress," she replied.

[9]Then the angel of the LORD said, "Return to your mistress and submit to her authority." [10]The angel added, "I will give you more descendants than you can count." [11]And the angel also said, "You are now pregnant and will give birth to a son. You are to name him Ishmael,* for the LORD has heard about your misery. [12]This son of yours will be a wild one—free and untamed as a wild donkey! He will be against everyone, and everyone will be against him. Yes, he will live at odds with the rest of his brothers."

15:18 Hebrew *the river of Egypt,* referring either to an eastern branch of the Nile River or to the brook of Egypt in the Sinai (see Num 34:5). 16:5 Hebrew *Let the LORD judge between you and me.* 16:11 *Ishmael* means "God hears."

My Daily Worship

— January 6 —

EYES WIDE OPEN

GENESIS 15:1–17:27

Thereafter, Hagar referred to the LORD, who had spoken to her, as "the God who sees me,"
for she said, "I have seen the One who sees me!" (16:13).

[i reflect]

Peek a boo! This game is fun for kids because they know Mom and Dad won't disappear when they close their eyes. But early on, before infants reach the developmental stage called object permanence, young children think that if they can't see someone, the other person can't see them. The world literally vanishes behind their closed eyes.

As adults, we sometimes react to God like infants stuck before the object permanence phase. We become convinced that if we hide from him, he won't see our true identities. We even play this game with ourselves—"If I don't think about this problem, or talk to others about my sin, then it's not really there." Being seen can be scary.

God *saw* Hagar, and Hagar responded wisely. She was honest with God about what she was doing. She openly admitted, "I'm running away!" God already knew Hagar's heart, but blessed her for openly revealing herself to him. And when Hagar stopped getting in the way, her transparency allowed her to see God.

God blesses our open and transparent lives. When we're honest about ourselves, we'll start to see God for who he really is. Only when we see the true God can we worship him in truth.

It's time to stop burying secrets. There's nothing you can hide from God (even if you're already hiding certain sins from yourself). He *sees* you. And he's already chosen to love you. You have nothing to fear. Open your eyes and come into the light of God's love.

Tell him what's on your heart. Share your fears and concerns. Tell him. He knows.

[i pray]

Lord, it's difficult to let you inside the hidden places within me. But you've already seen those
places and love me anyway. I want to worship you in truth. Cleanse each part of me
and allow me to be more and more transparent with you.

[i respond]

What parts of your life have you tried to keep from God? Remember God's deep love for you. Picture the Lord entering into places of the heart you've never allowed anyone to go. Allow him to begin the process of healing and cleansing.

[13]Thereafter, Hagar referred to the LORD, who had spoken to her, as "the God who sees me,"* for she said, "I have seen the One who sees me!" [14]Later that well was named Beer-lahairoi,* and it can still be found between Kadesh and Bered.

[15]So Hagar gave Abram a son, and Abram named him Ishmael. [16]Abram was eighty-six years old at that time.

ABRAM IS NAMED ABRAHAM

17 When Abram was ninety-nine years old, the LORD appeared to him and said, "I am God Almighty; serve me faithfully and live a blameless life. [2]I will make a covenant with you, by which I will guarantee to make you into a mighty nation." [3]At this, Abram fell face down in the dust. Then God said to him, [4]"This is my covenant with you: I will make you the father of not just one nation, but a multitude of nations! [5]What's more, I am changing your name. It will no longer be Abram; now you will be known as Abraham,* for you will be the father of many nations. [6]I will give you millions of descendants who will represent many nations. Kings will be among them!

[7]"I will continue this everlasting covenant between us, generation after generation. It will continue between me and your offspring* forever. And I will always be your God and the God of your descendants after you. [8]Yes, I will give all this land of Canaan to you and to your offspring forever. And I will be their God.

THE SIGN OF CIRCUMCISION

[9]"Your part of the agreement," God told Abraham, "is to obey the terms of the covenant. You and all your descendants have this continual responsibility. [10]This is the covenant that you and your descendants must keep: Each male among you must be circumcised; [11]the flesh of his foreskin must be cut off. This will be a sign that you and they have accepted this covenant. [12]Every male child must be circumcised on the eighth day after his birth. This applies not only to members of your family, but also to the servants born in your household and the foreign-born servants whom you have purchased. [13]All must be circumcised. Your bodies will thus bear the mark of my everlasting covenant. [14]Anyone who refuses to be circumcised will be cut off from the covenant family for violating the covenant."

SARAI IS NAMED SARAH

[15]Then God added, "Regarding Sarai, your wife—her name will no longer be Sarai; from now on you will call her Sarah.* [16]And I will bless her and give you a son from her! Yes, I will bless her richly, and she will become the mother of many nations. Kings will be among her descendants!"

[17]Then Abraham bowed down to the ground, but he laughed to himself in disbelief. "How could I become a father at the age of one hundred?" he wondered. "Besides, Sarah is ninety; how could she have a baby?" [18]And Abraham said to God, "Yes, may Ishmael enjoy your special blessing!"

[19]But God replied, "Sarah, your wife, will bear you a son. You will name him Isaac,* and I will confirm my everlasting covenant with him and his descendants. [20]As for Ishmael, I will bless him also, just as you have asked. I will cause him to multiply and become a great nation. Twelve princes will be among his descendants. [21]But my covenant is with Isaac, who will be born to you and Sarah about this time next year."

[22]That ended the conversation, and God left Abraham. [23]On that very day Abraham took his son Ishmael and every other male in his household and circumcised them, cutting off their foreskins, exactly as God had told him. [24]Abraham was ninety-nine years old at that time, [25]and Ishmael his son was thirteen. [26]Both were circumcised the same day, [27]along with all the other men and boys of the household, whether they were born there or bought as servants.

16:13 Hebrew *El-roi.* **16:14** *Beer-lahairoi* means "well of the Living One who sees me." **17:5** *Abram* means "exalted father"; *Abraham* means "father of many." **17:7** Hebrew *seed;* also in 17:8. **17:15** *Sarah* means "princess." **17:19** *Isaac* means "he laughs."

A Son Promised to Sarah

18 The LORD appeared again to Abraham while he was camped near the oak grove belonging to Mamre. One day about noon, as Abraham was sitting at the entrance to his tent, ²he suddenly noticed three men standing nearby. He got up and ran to meet them, welcoming them by bowing low to the ground. ³"My lord," he said, "if it pleases you, stop here for a while. ⁴Rest in the shade of this tree while my servants get some water to wash your feet. ⁵Let me prepare some food to refresh you. Please stay awhile before continuing on your journey."

"All right," they said. "Do as you have said."

⁶So Abraham ran back to the tent and said to Sarah, "Quick! Get three measures* of your best flour, and bake some bread." ⁷Then Abraham ran out to the herd and chose a fat calf and told a servant to hurry and butcher it. ⁸When the food was ready, he took some cheese curds and milk and the roasted meat, and he served it to the men. As they ate, Abraham waited on them there beneath the trees.

⁹"Where is Sarah, your wife?" they asked him.

"In the tent," Abraham replied.

¹⁰Then one of them said, "About this time next year I will return, and your wife Sarah will have a son."

Now Sarah was listening to this conversation from the tent nearby. ¹¹And since Abraham and Sarah were both very old, and Sarah was long past the age of having children, ¹²she laughed silently to herself. "How could a worn-out woman like me have a baby?" she thought. "And when my master—my husband—is also so old?"

¹³Then the LORD said to Abraham, "Why did Sarah laugh? Why did she say, 'Can an old woman like me have a baby?' ¹⁴Is anything too hard for the LORD? About a year from now, just as I told you, I will return, and Sarah will have a son." ¹⁵Sarah was afraid, so she denied that she had laughed. But he said, "That is not true. You did laugh."

Abraham Intercedes for Sodom

¹⁶Then the men got up from their meal and started on toward Sodom. Abraham went with them part of the way.

¹⁷"Should I hide my plan from Abraham?" the LORD asked. ¹⁸"For Abraham will become a great and mighty nation, and all the nations of the earth will be blessed through him. ¹⁹I have singled him out so that he will direct his sons and their families to keep the way of the LORD and do what is right and just. Then I will do for him all that I have promised." ²⁰So the LORD told Abraham, "I have heard that the people of Sodom and Gomorrah are extremely evil, and that everything they do is wicked. ²¹I am going down to see whether or not these reports are true. Then I will know."

²²The two other men went on toward Sodom, but the LORD remained with Abraham for a while. ²³Abraham approached him and said, "Will you destroy both innocent and guilty alike? ²⁴Suppose you find fifty innocent people there within the city—will you still destroy it, and not spare it for their sakes? ²⁵Surely you wouldn't do such a thing, destroying the innocent with the guilty. Why, you would be treating the innocent and the guilty exactly the same! Surely you wouldn't do that! Should not the Judge of all the earth do what is right?"

²⁶And the LORD replied, "If I find fifty innocent people in Sodom, I will spare the entire city for their sake."

²⁷Then Abraham spoke again. "Since I have begun, let me go on and speak further to my Lord, even though I am but dust and ashes. ²⁸Suppose there are only forty-five? Will you destroy the city for lack of five?"

And the LORD said, "I will not destroy it if I find forty-five."

²⁹Then Abraham pressed his request further. "Suppose there are only forty?"

And the LORD replied, "I will not destroy it if there are forty."

³⁰"Please don't be angry, my Lord," Abraham

18:6 Hebrew *3 seahs*, about 15 quarts or 18 liters.

pleaded. "Let me speak—suppose only thirty are found?"

And the LORD replied, "I will not destroy it if there are thirty."

³¹Then Abraham said, "Since I have dared to speak to the Lord, let me continue—suppose there are only twenty?"

And the LORD said, "Then I will not destroy it for the sake of the twenty."

³²Finally, Abraham said, "Lord, please do not get angry; I will speak but once more! Suppose only ten are found there?"

And the LORD said, "Then, for the sake of the ten, I will not destroy it."

³³The LORD went on his way when he had finished his conversation with Abraham, and Abraham returned to his tent.

SODOM AND GOMORRAH DESTROYED

19 That evening the two angels came to the entrance of the city of Sodom, and Lot was sitting there as they arrived. When he saw them, he stood up to meet them. Then he welcomed them and bowed low to the ground. ²"My lords," he said, "come to my home to wash your feet, and be my guests for the night. You may then get up in the morning as early as you like and be on your way again."

"Oh no," they said, "we'll just spend the night out here in the city square."

³But Lot insisted, so at last they went home with him. He set a great feast before them, complete with fresh bread made without yeast. After the meal, ⁴as they were preparing to retire for the night, all the men of Sodom, young and old, came from all over the city and surrounded the house. ⁵They shouted to Lot, "Where are the men who came to spend the night with you? Bring them out so we can have sex with them."

⁶Lot stepped outside to talk to them, shutting the door behind him. ⁷"Please, my brothers," he begged, "don't do such a wicked thing. ⁸Look—I have two virgin daughters. Do with

them as you wish, but leave these men alone, for they are under my protection."

⁹"Stand back!" they shouted. "Who do you think you are? We let you settle among us, and now you are trying to tell us what to do! We'll treat you far worse than those other men!" And they lunged at Lot and began breaking down the door. ¹⁰But the two angels reached out and pulled Lot in and bolted the door. ¹¹Then they blinded the men of Sodom so they couldn't find the doorway.

¹²"Do you have any other relatives here in the city?" the angels asked. "Get them out of this place—sons-in-law, sons, daughters, or anyone else. ¹³For we will destroy the city completely. The stench of the place has reached the LORD, and he has sent us to destroy it."

¹⁴So Lot rushed out to tell his daughters' fiancés, "Quick, get out of the city! The LORD is going to destroy it." But the young men thought he was only joking.

¹⁵At dawn the next morning the angels became insistent. "Hurry," they said to Lot. "Take your wife and your two daughters who are here. Get out of here right now, or you will be caught in the destruction of the city."

¹⁶When Lot still hesitated, the angels seized his hand and the hands of his wife and two daughters and rushed them to safety outside the city, for the LORD was merciful. ¹⁷"Run for your lives!" the angels warned. "Do not stop anywhere in the valley. And don't look back! Escape to the mountains, or you will die."

¹⁸"Oh no, my lords, please," Lot begged. ¹⁹"You have been so kind to me and saved my life, and you have granted me such mercy. But I cannot go to the mountains. Disaster would catch up to me there, and I would soon die. ²⁰See, there is a small village nearby. Please let me go there instead; don't you see how small it is? Then my life will be saved."

²¹"All right," the angel said, "I will grant your request. I will not destroy that little village. ²²But hurry! For I can do nothing until you are there." From that time on, that village was known as Zoar.*

19:22 Zoar means "little."

My Daily Worship

— *January 7* —

RUGGED WORSHIP

GENESIS 18:1–20:18

The two other men went on toward Sodom, but the LORD remained with Abraham
for a while. Abraham approached him and said, "Will you destroy
both innocent and guilty alike?" (18:22–23).

[i reflect]

Call to mind a typical worshiper. He or she is smiling, right? Almost jaunty. Perhaps even clapping with a beatific look of bliss.

Now behold Abraham, the so-called "friend of God." God has just confided in his faithful follower that catastrophic judgment is coming soon to Sodom. No wonder Abraham is visibly upset. No wonder he wrings his hands. He has family in the doomed city.

Notice what Abraham doesn't do. He doesn't pout, or stew, or complain to friends. Instead, he takes his heavy heart straight to God himself. His questions aren't rhetorical. His words aren't self-talk. This is a desperate dialogue with the Divine. A crisis conversation with the Creator.

If worship is acknowledging God and turning to him, . . . if it is focusing on him and giving him our undivided attention, . . . then guess what? The care-worn, distraught Abraham is worshiping even at this sobering moment!

Martin Luther wrote, "In difficult times, we may not be able to believe God as strongly, praise him as wholeheartedly, and pray to him as sincerely as we do in good times. But at least we should believe and pray as much as we are able." Abraham understood this. Burdened with concern for the fate of his family, he did the best he could—he approached the One who was, and is, over all and spoke directly and honestly about what was on his heart.

Perhaps you are overwhelmed with worry and anxiety. Don't let these feelings keep you from God. Instead, worship him with your questions and doubts today. Then believe and pray as much as you are able.

[i pray]

Lord, give me the grace to cling to you. Make me a fully devoted worshiper in times
where I don't always understand what you are doing. Help me, like Abraham,
to bring my questions and concerns to you.

[i respond]

Read a psalm written by David during a time of stress, confusion, or trouble. You might want to read Psalm 13, Psalm 27, or Psalm 42. What strikes you about his attitude and response?

²³The sun was rising as Lot reached the village. ²⁴Then the LORD rained down fire and burning sulfur from the heavens on Sodom and Gomorrah. ²⁵He utterly destroyed them, along with the other cities and villages of the plain, eliminating all life—people, plants, and animals alike. ²⁶But Lot's wife looked back as she was following along behind him, and she became a pillar of salt.

²⁷The next morning Abraham was up early and hurried out to the place where he had stood in the LORD's presence. ²⁸He looked out across the plain to Sodom and Gomorrah and saw columns of smoke and fumes, as from a furnace, rising from the cities there. ²⁹But God had listened to Abraham's request and kept Lot safe, removing him from the disaster that engulfed the cities on the plain.

LOT AND HIS DAUGHTERS

³⁰Afterward Lot left Zoar because he was afraid of the people there, and he went to live in a cave in the mountains with his two daughters. ³¹One day the older daughter said to her sister, "There isn't a man anywhere in this entire area for us to marry. And our father will soon be too old to have children. ³²Come, let's get him drunk with wine, and then we will sleep with him. That way we will preserve our family line through our father." ³³So that night they got him drunk, and the older daughter went in and slept with her father. He was unaware of her lying down or getting up again.

³⁴The next morning the older daughter said to her younger sister, "I slept with our father last night. Let's get him drunk with wine again tonight, and you go in and sleep with him. That way our family line will be preserved." ³⁵So that night they got him drunk again, and the younger daughter went in and slept with him. As before, he was unaware of her lying down or getting up again. ³⁶So both of Lot's daughters became pregnant by their father.

³⁷When the older daughter gave birth to a son, she named him Moab.* He became the ancestor of the nation now known as the Moabites. ³⁸When the younger daughter gave birth to a son, she named him Ben-ammi.* He became the ancestor of the nation now known as the Ammonites.

ABRAHAM DECEIVES ABIMELECH

20 Now Abraham moved south to the Negev and settled for a while between Kadesh and Shur at a place called Gerar. ²Abraham told people there that his wife, Sarah, was his sister. So King Abimelech sent for her and had her brought to him at his palace.

³But one night God came to Abimelech in a dream and told him, "You are a dead man, for that woman you took is married."

⁴But Abimelech had not slept with her yet, so he said, "Lord, will you kill an innocent man? ⁵Abraham told me, 'She is my sister,' and she herself said, 'Yes, he is my brother.' I acted in complete innocence!"

⁶"Yes, I know you are innocent," God replied. "That is why I kept you from sinning against me; I did not let you touch her. ⁷Now return her to her husband, and he will pray for you, for he is a prophet. Then you will live. But if you don't return her to him, you can be sure that you and your entire household will die."

⁸Abimelech got up early the next morning and hastily called a meeting of all his servants. When he told them what had happened, great fear swept through the crowd. ⁹Then Abimelech called for Abraham. "What is this you have done to us?" he demanded. "What have I done to you that deserves treatment like this, making me and my kingdom guilty of this great sin? This kind of thing should not be done! ¹⁰Why have you done this to us?"

¹¹"Well," Abraham said, "I figured this to be a godless place. I thought, 'They will want my wife and will kill me to get her.' ¹²Besides, she is my sister—we both have the same father,

19:37 *Moab* sounds like a Hebrew term that means "from father." 19:38 *Ben-ammi* means "son of my people."

ALMIGHTY GOD

Almighty God—Hebrew *'El shad-dai,* "mighty God." *Shaddai* comes from a word meaning "mountain" and conveys the sense of a God of strength and majesty.

As a title for God, *'El shaddai* is associated with the Hebrew patriarchs, and is used often in the book of Job, which is set in the patriarchal period. As *'El shaddai,* God changes the names of both Abram (Genesis 17:5) and Jacob (Genesis 35:10–12), and reaffirms his promise to make of them a great people who will serve him.

The psalmist asks, "I look up to the mountains—does my help come from there?" (Psalm 121:1). His answer is that his help comes from the LORD. The mountain symbolizes so many things about God that cause us to rely on his help—his strength, his majesty, his eternity. Jesus urged his followers to "flee to the hills" (Luke 21:21) when unsettled and difficult times would come their way. As God's worshipers, we can always flee to Almighty God, "our refuge and strength" (Psalm 46:1).

though different mothers—and I married her. ¹³When God sent me to travel far from my father's home, I told her, 'Wherever we go, have the kindness to say that you are my sister.'"

¹⁴Then Abimelech took sheep and oxen and servants—both men and women—and gave them to Abraham, and he returned his wife, Sarah, to him. ¹⁵"Look over my kingdom, and choose a place where you would like to live," Abimelech told him. ¹⁶Then he turned to Sarah. "Look," he said, "I am giving your 'brother' a thousand pieces of silver* to compensate for any embarrassment I may have

caused you. This will settle any claim against me in this matter."

¹⁷Then Abraham prayed to God, and God healed Abimelech, his wife, and the other women of the household, so they could have children. ¹⁸For the LORD had stricken all the women with infertility as a warning to Abimelech for having taken Abraham's wife.

THE BIRTH OF ISAAC

21 Then the LORD did exactly what he had promised. ²Sarah became pregnant, and she gave a son to Abraham in his old age. It all happened at the time God had said it would. ³And Abraham named his son Isaac.* ⁴Eight days after Isaac was born, Abraham circumcised him as God had commanded. ⁵Abraham was one hundred years old at the time.

⁶And Sarah declared, "God has brought me laughter! All who hear about this will laugh with me. ⁷For who would have dreamed that I would ever have a baby? Yet I have given Abraham a son in his old age!"

HAGAR AND ISHMAEL SENT AWAY

⁸As time went by and Isaac grew and was weaned, Abraham gave a big party to celebrate the happy occasion. ⁹But Sarah saw Ishmael—the son of Abraham and her Egyptian servant Hagar—making fun of Isaac. ¹⁰So she turned to Abraham and demanded, "Get rid of that servant and her son. He is not going to share the family inheritance with my son, Isaac. I won't have it!"

¹¹This upset Abraham very much because Ishmael was his son. ¹²But God told Abraham, "Do not be upset over the boy and your servant wife. Do just as Sarah says, for Isaac is the son through whom your descendants will be counted. ¹³But I will make a nation of the descendants of Hagar's son because he also is your son."

¹⁴So Abraham got up early the next morning, prepared food for the journey, and strapped a container of water to Hagar's

20:16 Hebrew *1,000 shekels of silver,* about 25 pounds or 11.4 kilograms in weight.   **21:3** *Isaac* means "he laughs."

shoulders. He sent her away with their son, and she walked out into the wilderness of Beersheba, wandering aimlessly. ¹⁵When the water was gone, she left the boy in the shade of a bush. ¹⁶Then she went and sat down by herself about a hundred yards* away. "I don't want to watch the boy die," she said, as she burst into tears.

¹⁷Then God heard the boy's cries, and the angel of God called to Hagar from the sky, "Hagar, what's wrong? Do not be afraid! God has heard the boy's cries from the place where you laid him. ¹⁸Go to him and comfort him, for I will make a great nation from his descendants."

¹⁹Then God opened Hagar's eyes, and she saw a well. She immediately filled her water container and gave the boy a drink. ²⁰And God was with the boy as he grew up in the wilderness of Paran. He became an expert archer, ²¹and his mother arranged a marriage for him with a young woman from Egypt.

A TREATY WITH ABIMELECH

²²About this time, Abimelech came with Phicol, his army commander, to visit Abraham. "It is clear that God helps you in everything you do," Abimelech said. ²³"Swear to me in God's name that you won't deceive me, my children, or my grandchildren. I have been loyal to you, so now swear that you will be loyal to me and to this country in which you are living."

²⁴Abraham replied, "All right, I swear to it!" ²⁵Then Abraham complained to Abimelech about a well that Abimelech's servants had taken violently from Abraham's servants.

²⁶"This is the first I've heard of it," Abimelech said. "And I have no idea who is responsible. Why didn't you say something about this before?" ²⁷Then Abraham gave sheep and oxen to Abimelech, and they made a treaty. ²⁸But when Abraham took seven additional ewe lambs and set them off by themselves, ²⁹Abimelech asked, "Why are you doing that?"

³⁰Abraham replied, "They are my gift to you as a public confirmation that I dug this well." ³¹So ever since, that place has been known as Beersheba—"well of the oath"—because that was where they had sworn an oath. ³²After making their covenant, Abimelech left with Phicol, the commander of his army, and they returned home to the land of the Philistines. ³³Then Abraham planted a tamarisk tree at Beersheba, and he worshiped the LORD, the Eternal God, at that place. ³⁴And Abraham lived in Philistine country for a long time.

ABRAHAM'S OBEDIENCE TESTED

22 Later on God tested Abraham's faith and obedience. "Abraham!" God called.

"Yes," he replied. "Here I am."

²"Take your son, your only son—yes, Isaac, whom you love so much—and go to the land of Moriah. Sacrifice him there as a burnt offering on one of the mountains, which I will point out to you."

³The next morning Abraham got up early. He saddled his donkey and took two of his servants with him, along with his son Isaac. Then he chopped wood to build a fire for a burnt offering and set out for the place where God had told him to go. ⁴On the third day of the journey, Abraham saw the place in the distance. ⁵"Stay here with the donkey," Abraham told the young men. "The boy and I will travel a little farther. We will worship there, and then we will come right back."

⁶Abraham placed the wood for the burnt offering on Isaac's shoulders, while he himself carried the knife and the fire. As the two of them went on together, ⁷Isaac said, "Father?"

"Yes, my son," Abraham replied.

"We have the wood and the fire," said the boy, "but where is the lamb for the sacrifice?"

⁸"God will provide a lamb, my son," Abraham answered. And they both went on together.

⁹When they arrived at the place where God had told Abraham to go, he built an altar and placed the wood on it. Then he tied Isaac up

21:16 Hebrew *a bowshot.*

My Daily Worship

— January 8 —

No Rivals

GENESIS 21:1–23:20

Take your son, your only son—yes, Isaac, whom you love so much—
and go to the land of Moriah. Sacrifice him there as a burnt offering
on one of the mountains, which I will point out to you (22:2).

[i reflect]

It is one thing to sit in church and sing the old hymn, "Take My Life, and Let It Be"—to pledge your silver and gold, to offer God your hands and will.

It is another thing altogether to hear God say to you: "I want your only child. Take the joy of your life and give it to me."

This was Abraham's dilemma. God had given the old saint and his wife Sarah a miracle son. Now, a few years later comes the abrupt announcement from heaven, "I want the boy back." As Abraham begins his torturous walk up the mountain, imagine what he must have felt. Put yourself in his place.

This scene shocks us with its blunt and sobering truth: God will have no rivals. He must possess our souls, and he will ruthlessly take us to places where he can unveil what we value most. If the great treasure of our hearts is not himself, then God will demonstrate that he is all we need by making sure that he is all we have.

Ironically, it is in these darkest of moments—if we are at all perceptive—that we discover that he is what we hunger for most and that nothing else can ever truly satisfy. Then we can sing without hesitation: "Take my heart, it is Thine own; It shall be Thy royal throne."

What will it mean for you to make your heart God's royal throne? Take time to assess any activities or even relationships that may threaten to replace God as the top priority in your life. Offer these to God as an act of obedient sacrifice.

[i pray]

Make me willing, O great King of my soul, to turn my back on anything and
everything that threatens to displace you from the throne of my life.

[i respond]

Try a "fast" for twenty-four hours from your favorite hobby, possession, amusement, indulgence, or pleasure. Let those superficial longings point you to the deeper hunger of your heart.

and laid him on the altar over the wood. ¹⁰And Abraham took the knife and lifted it up to kill his son as a sacrifice to the LORD. ¹¹At that moment the angel of the LORD shouted to him from heaven, "Abraham! Abraham!"

"Yes," he answered. "I'm listening."

¹²"Lay down the knife," the angel said. "Do not hurt the boy in any way, for now I know that you truly fear God. You have not withheld even your beloved son from me."

¹³Then Abraham looked up and saw a ram caught by its horns in a bush. So he took the ram and sacrificed it as a burnt offering on the altar in place of his son. ¹⁴Abraham named the place "The LORD Will Provide."* This name has now become a proverb: "On the mountain of the LORD it will be provided."

¹⁵Then the angel of the LORD called again to Abraham from heaven, ¹⁶"This is what the LORD says: Because you have obeyed me and have not withheld even your beloved son, I swear by my own self that ¹⁷I will bless you richly. I will multiply your descendants into countless millions, like the stars of the sky and the sand on the seashore. They will conquer their enemies, ¹⁸and through your descendants,* all the nations of the earth will be blessed—all because you have obeyed me."

¹⁹Then they returned to Abraham's young men and traveled home again to Beersheba, where Abraham lived for quite some time.

²⁰Soon after this, Abraham heard that Milcah, his brother Nahor's wife, had borne Nahor eight sons. ²¹The oldest was named Uz, the next oldest was Buz, followed by Kemuel (the father of Aram), ²²Kesed, Hazo, Pildash, Jidlaph, and Bethuel. ²³Bethuel became the father of Rebekah. ²⁴In addition to his eight sons from Milcah, Nahor had four other children from his concubine Reumah. Their names were Tebah, Gaham, Tahash, and Maacah.

THE BURIAL OF SARAH

23 When Sarah was 127 years old, ²she died at Kiriath-arba (now called Hebron) in the land of Canaan. There Abra-

ham mourned and wept for her. ³Then, leaving her body, he went to the Hittite elders and said, ⁴"Here I am, a stranger in a foreign land, with no place to bury my wife. Please let me have a piece of land for a burial plot."

⁵The Hittites replied to Abraham, ⁶"Certainly, for you are an honored prince among us. It will be a privilege to have you choose the finest of our tombs so you can bury her there."

⁷Then Abraham bowed low before them and said, ⁸"Since this is how you feel, be so kind as to ask Ephron son of Zohar ⁹to let me have the cave of Machpelah, down at the end of his field. I want to pay the full price, of course, whatever is publicly agreed upon, so I may have a permanent burial place for my family."

¹⁰Ephron was sitting there among the others, and he answered Abraham as the others listened, speaking publicly before all the elders of the town. ¹¹"No, sir," he said to Abraham, "please listen to me. I will give you the cave and the field. Here in the presence of my people, I give it to you. Go and bury your dead."

¹²Abraham bowed again to the people of the land, ¹³and he replied to Ephron as everyone listened. "No, listen to me," he insisted. "I will buy it from you. Let me pay the full price for the field so I can bury my dead there."

¹⁴"Well," Ephron answered, ¹⁵"the land is worth four hundred pieces* of silver, but what is that between friends? Go ahead and bury your dead."

¹⁶So Abraham paid Ephron the amount he had suggested, four hundred pieces of silver, as was publicly agreed. ¹⁷He bought the plot of land belonging to Ephron at Machpelah, near Mamre. This included the field, the cave that was in it, and all the trees nearby. ¹⁸They became Abraham's permanent possession by the agreement made in the presence of the Hittite elders at the city gate. ¹⁹So Abraham buried Sarah there in Canaan, in the cave of Machpelah, near Mamre, which is at Hebron.

22:14 Hebrew *Yahweh Yir'eh*. 22:18 Hebrew *seed*. 23:15 Hebrew *400 shekels*, about 10 pounds or 4.6 kilograms in weight; also in 23:16.

²⁰The field and the cave were sold to Abraham by the Hittites as a permanent burial place.

ISAAC MARRIES REBEKAH

24 Abraham was now a very old man, and the LORD had blessed him in every way. ²One day Abraham said to the man in charge of his household, who was his oldest servant, ³"Swear* by the LORD, the God of heaven and earth, that you will not let my son marry one of these local Canaanite women. ⁴Go instead to my homeland, to my relatives, and find a wife there for my son Isaac."

⁵The servant asked, "But suppose I can't find a young woman who will travel so far from home? May I then take Isaac there to live among your relatives?"

⁶"No!" Abraham warned. "Be careful never to take my son there. ⁷For the LORD, the God of heaven, who took me from my father's house and my native land, solemnly promised to give this land to my offspring.* He will send his angel ahead of you, and he will see to it that you find a young woman there to be my son's wife. ⁸If she is unwilling to come back with you, then you are free from this oath. But under no circumstances are you to take my son there."

⁹So the servant took a solemn oath* that he would follow Abraham's instructions. ¹⁰He loaded ten of Abraham's camels with gifts and set out, taking with him the best of everything his master owned. He traveled to Aram-naharaim* and went to the village where Abraham's brother Nahor had settled. ¹¹There the servant made the camels kneel down beside a well just outside the village. It was evening, and the women were coming out to draw water.

¹²"O LORD, God of my master," he prayed. "Give me success and show kindness to my master, Abraham. Help me to accomplish the purpose of my journey. ¹³See, here I am, standing beside this spring, and the young women of the village are coming out to draw water. ¹⁴This is my request. I will ask one of them for a drink. If she says, 'Yes, certainly, and I will water your camels, too!'—let her be the one you have appointed as Isaac's wife. By this I will know that you have shown kindness to my master."

¹⁵As he was still praying, a young woman named Rebekah arrived with a water jug on her shoulder. Her father was Bethuel, who was the son of Abraham's brother Nahor and his wife, Milcah. ¹⁶Now Rebekah was very beautiful, and she was a virgin; no man had ever slept with her. She went down to the spring, filled her jug, and came up again. ¹⁷Running over to her, the servant asked, "Please give me a drink."

¹⁸"Certainly, sir," she said, and she quickly lowered the jug for him to drink. ¹⁹When he had finished, she said, "I'll draw water for your camels, too, until they have had enough!" ²⁰So she quickly emptied the jug into the watering trough and ran down to the well again. She kept carrying water to the camels until they had finished drinking. ²¹The servant watched her in silence, wondering whether or not she was the one the LORD intended him to meet. ²²Then at last, when the camels had finished drinking, he gave her a gold ring for her nose and two large gold bracelets* for her wrists.

²³"Whose daughter are you?" he asked. "Would your father have any room to put us up for the night?"

²⁴"My father is Bethuel," she replied. "My grandparents are Nahor and Milcah. ²⁵Yes, we have plenty of straw and food for the camels, and we have a room for guests."

²⁶The man fell down to the ground and worshiped the LORD. ²⁷"Praise be to the LORD, the God of my master, Abraham," he said. "The LORD has been so kind and faithful to Abraham, for he has led me straight to my master's relatives."

24:3 Hebrew *Put your hand under my thigh, and I will make you swear.* 24:7 Hebrew *seed.* 24:9 Hebrew *put his hand under the thigh of Abraham his master and swore an oath.* 24:10 *Aram-naharaim* means "Aram of the two rivers," thought to have been located between the Euphrates and Balih Rivers in northwestern Mesopotamia. 24:22 Hebrew *a gold nose-ring weighing a half shekel* [0.2 ounces or 6 grams] *and two gold bracelets weighing 10 shekels* [4 ounces or 114 grams].

²⁸The young woman ran home to tell her family about all that had happened. ²⁹Now Rebekah had a brother named Laban. ³⁰When he saw the nose-ring and the bracelets on his sister's wrists, and when he heard her story, he rushed out to the spring, where the man was still standing beside his camels. Laban said to him, ³¹"Come and stay with us, you who are blessed by the LORD. Why do you stand here outside the village when we have a room all ready for you and a place prepared for the camels!"

³²So the man went home with Laban, and Laban unloaded the camels, gave him straw to bed them down, fed them, and provided water for the camel drivers to wash their feet. ³³Then supper was served. But Abraham's servant said, "I don't want to eat until I have told you why I have come."

"All right," Laban said, "tell us your mission."

³⁴"I am Abraham's servant," he explained. ³⁵"And the LORD has blessed my master richly; he has become a great man. The LORD has given him flocks of sheep and herds of cattle, a fortune in silver and gold, and many servants and camels and donkeys. ³⁶When Sarah, my master's wife, was very old, she gave birth to my master's son, and my master has given him everything he owns. ³⁷And my master made me swear that I would not let Isaac marry one of the local Canaanite women. ³⁸Instead, I was to come to his relatives here in this far-off land, to his father's home. I was told to bring back a young woman from here to marry his son.

³⁹"'But suppose I can't find a young woman willing to come back with me?' I asked him. ⁴⁰'You will,' he told me, 'for the LORD, in whose presence I have walked, will send his angel with you and will make your mission successful. Yes, you must get a wife for my son from among my relatives, from my father's family. ⁴¹But if you go to my relatives and they refuse to let her come, you will be free from your oath.'

⁴²"So this afternoon when I came to the spring I prayed this prayer: 'O LORD, the God of my master, Abraham, if you are planning to make my mission a success, please guide me in a special way. ⁴³Here I am, standing beside this spring. I will say to some young woman who comes to draw water, "Please give me a drink of water!" ⁴⁴And she will reply, "Certainly! And I'll water your camels, too!" LORD, let her be the one you have selected to be the wife of my master's son.'

⁴⁵"Before I had finished praying these words, I saw Rebekah coming along with her water jug on her shoulder. She went down to the spring and drew water and filled the jug. So I said to her, 'Please give me a drink.' ⁴⁶She quickly lowered the jug from her shoulder so I could drink, and she said, 'Certainly, sir, and I will water your camels, too!' And she did. ⁴⁷When I asked her whose daughter she was, she told me, 'My father is Bethuel, the son of Nahor and his wife, Milcah.' So I gave her the ring and the bracelets.

⁴⁸"Then I bowed my head and worshiped the LORD. I praised the LORD, the God of my master, Abraham, because he had led me along the right path to find a wife from the family of my master's relatives. ⁴⁹So tell me— will you or won't you show true kindness to my master? When you tell me, then I'll know what my next step should be, whether to move this way or that."

⁵⁰Then Laban and Bethuel replied, "The LORD has obviously brought you here, so what can we say? ⁵¹Here is Rebekah; take her and go. Yes, let her be the wife of your master's son, as the LORD has directed."

⁵²At this reply, Abraham's servant bowed to the ground and worshiped the LORD. ⁵³Then he brought out silver and gold jewelry and lovely clothing for Rebekah. He also gave valuable presents to her mother and brother. ⁵⁴Then they had supper, and the servant and the men with him stayed there overnight. But early the next morning, he said, "Send me back to my master."

⁵⁵"But we want Rebekah to stay at least ten days," her brother and mother said. "Then she can go."

My Daily Worship

— *January 9* —

PRACTICING THE PRESENCE

GENESIS 24:1–25:18

Then I bowed my head and worshiped the LORD. I praised the LORD, the God of my master,
Abraham, because he had led me along the right path to find a wife
from the family of my master's relatives (24:48).

[i reflect]

The secular man or woman approaches each day armed with verbs and phrases like: "Get busy!" "Hurry up!" "Produce!" and "Make it happen!" They rush through life, checking off items on their "to do" lists.

The spiritual man or woman operates from a different vocabulary. "Lift up your eyes." "Listen." "Call unto me." "Ask." "Seek." "Knock." "Wait." "Trust."

A great illustration of this second, less common lifestyle is embedded in the story of Abraham's servant. Sent on a mission to find a wife for Isaac, Eliezer is wholly dependent on help from above. He is faithful, trustworthy, and deliberate. He prays nonstop, and his cries for direction and help are amazingly specific. When at last he senses clear leading from God, he erupts in praise. And at the end of the day, his mission is a great success. The Lord has gone before him and with him. The Lord has undergirded him and watched over him.

This God-drenched mindset is what Brother Lawrence called "practicing the presence of God." It is simply recognizing that God is ever with us. It is acknowledging him, leaning on him, calling on him, and rejoicing in his power and presence. It is the "secret"—if there is such a thing—to becoming a true 24/7 worshiper of God.

As you go through your daily routines, remember Eliezer's example. Slow down and take time to acknowledge God while going to the dry cleaners or preparing dinner. Ask him for guidance while interacting with clients. Thank him for his guidance while caring for your family. Trust him to lead you along the right path today.

[i pray]

Teach me to invite all that you are into all that I am about—and then to get out of the way
so that you can work . . . and so you can get maximum glory.

[i respond]

Today when you read the newspaper or watch a televised news report, turn each item into an object of prayer or praise. Make it your goal to include God in every detail of your life.

⁵⁶But he said, "Don't hinder my return. The LORD has made my mission successful, and I want to report back to my master."

⁵⁷"Well," they said, "we'll call Rebekah and ask her what she thinks." ⁵⁸So they called Rebekah. "Are you willing to go with this man?" they asked her.

And she replied, "Yes, I will go."

⁵⁹So they said good-bye to Rebekah and sent her away with Abraham's servant and his men. The woman who had been Rebekah's childhood nurse went along with her. ⁶⁰They blessed her with this blessing as she parted:

"Our sister, may you become
   the mother of many millions!
May your descendants overcome
   all their enemies."

⁶¹Then Rebekah and her servants mounted the camels and left with Abraham's servant.

⁶²Meanwhile, Isaac, whose home was in the Negev, had returned from Beer-lahairoi. ⁶³One evening as he was taking a walk out in the fields, meditating, he looked up and saw the camels coming. ⁶⁴When Rebekah looked up and saw Isaac, she quickly dismounted. ⁶⁵"Who is that man walking through the fields to meet us?" she asked the servant.

And he replied, "It is my master." So Rebekah covered her face with her veil. ⁶⁶Then the servant told Isaac the whole story.

⁶⁷And Isaac brought Rebekah into his mother's tent, and she became his wife. He loved her very much, and she was a special comfort to him after the death of his mother.

THE DEATH OF ABRAHAM

25 Now Abraham married again. Keturah was his new wife, ²and she bore him Zimran, Jokshan, Medan, Midian, Ishbak, and Shuah. ³Jokshan's two sons were Sheba and Dedan. Dedan's descendants were the Asshurites, Letushites, and Leummites. ⁴Midian's sons were Ephah, Epher, Hanoch, Abida, and Eldaah. These were all descendants of Abraham through Keturah.

⁵Abraham left everything he owned to his son Isaac. ⁶But before he died, he gave gifts to the sons of his concubines and sent them off to the east, away from Isaac.

⁷Abraham lived for 175 years, ⁸and he died at a ripe old age, joining his ancestors in death. ⁹His sons Isaac and Ishmael buried him in the cave of Machpelah, near Mamre, in the field of Ephron son of Zohar the Hittite. ¹⁰This was the field Abraham had purchased from the Hittites, where he had buried his wife Sarah. ¹¹After Abraham's death, God poured out rich blessings on Isaac, who settled near Beer-lahairoi in the Negev.

ISHMAEL'S DESCENDANTS

¹²This is the history of the descendants of Ishmael, the son of Abraham through Hagar, Sarah's Egyptian servant. ¹³Here is a list, by their names and clans, of Ishmael's descendants: The oldest was Nebaioth, followed by Kedar, Adbeel, Mibsam, ¹⁴Mishma, Dumah, Massa, ¹⁵Hadad, Tema, Jetur, Naphish, and Kedemah. ¹⁶These twelve sons of Ishmael became the founders of twelve tribes that bore their names, listed according to the places they settled and camped. ¹⁷Ishmael finally died at the age of 137 and joined his ancestors in death. ¹⁸Ishmael's descendants were scattered across the country from Havilah to Shur, which is east of Egypt in the direction of Asshur. The clans descended from Ishmael camped close to one another.*

THE BIRTHS OF JACOB AND ESAU

¹⁹This is the history of the family of Isaac, the son of Abraham. ²⁰When Isaac was forty years old, he married Rebekah, the daughter of Bethuel the Aramean from Paddan-aram and the sister of Laban. ²¹Isaac pleaded with the LORD to give Rebekah a child because she was childless. So the LORD answered Isaac's prayer, and his wife became pregnant with twins. ²²But the two children struggled with each other in her womb. So she went to ask the LORD about it. "Why is this happening to me?" she asked.

25:18 The meaning of the Hebrew is uncertain.

²³And the LORD told her, "The sons in your womb will become two rival nations. One nation will be stronger than the other; the descendants of your older son will serve the descendants of your younger son."

²⁴And when the time came, the twins were born. ²⁵The first was very red at birth. He was covered with so much hair that one would think he was wearing a piece of clothing. So they called him Esau.* ²⁶Then the other twin was born with his hand grasping Esau's heel. So they called him Jacob.* Isaac was sixty years old when the twins were born.

ESAU SELLS HIS BIRTHRIGHT

²⁷As the boys grew up, Esau became a skillful hunter, a man of the open fields, while Jacob was the kind of person who liked to stay at home. ²⁸Isaac loved Esau in particular because of the wild game he brought home, but Rebekah favored Jacob.

²⁹One day when Jacob was cooking some stew, Esau arrived home exhausted and hungry from a hunt. ³⁰Esau said to Jacob, "I'm starved! Give me some of that red stew you've made." (This was how Esau got his other name, Edom—"Red.")

³¹Jacob replied, "All right, but trade me your birthright for it."

³²"Look, I'm dying of starvation!" said Esau. "What good is my birthright to me now?"

³³So Jacob insisted, "Well then, swear to me right now that it is mine." So Esau swore an oath, thereby selling all his rights as the firstborn to his younger brother. ³⁴Then Jacob gave Esau some bread and lentil stew. Esau ate and drank and went on about his business, indifferent to the fact that he had given up his birthright.

ISAAC DECEIVES ABIMELECH

26 Now a severe famine struck the land, as had happened before in Abraham's time. So Isaac moved to Gerar, where Abimelech, king of the Philistines, lived.

²The LORD appeared to him there and said, "Do not go to Egypt. ³Do as I say, and stay here in this land. If you do, I will be with you and bless you. I will give all this land to you and your descendants, just as I solemnly promised Abraham, your father. ⁴I will cause your descendants to become as numerous as the stars, and I will give them all these lands. And through your descendants* all the nations of the earth will be blessed. ⁵I will do this because Abraham listened to me and obeyed all my requirements, commands, regulations, and laws."

⁶So Isaac stayed in Gerar. ⁷And when the men there asked him about Rebekah, he said, "She is my sister." He was afraid to admit that she was his wife. He thought they would kill him to get her, because she was very beautiful. ⁸But some time later, Abimelech, king of the Philistines, looked out a window and saw Isaac fondling Rebekah.

⁹Abimelech called for Isaac and exclaimed, "She is obviously your wife! Why did you say she was your sister?"

"Because I was afraid someone would kill me to get her from me," Isaac replied.

¹⁰"How could you treat us this way!" Abimelech exclaimed. "Someone might have taken your wife and slept with her, and you would have made us guilty of great sin." ¹¹Then Abimelech made a public proclamation: "Anyone who harms this man or his wife will die!"

CONFLICT OVER WATER RIGHTS

¹²That year Isaac's crops were tremendous! He harvested a hundred times more grain than he planted, for the LORD blessed him. ¹³He became a rich man, and his wealth only continued to grow. ¹⁴He acquired large flocks of sheep and goats, great herds of cattle, and many servants. Soon the Philistines became jealous of him, ¹⁵and they filled up all of Isaac's wells with earth. These were the wells that had been dug by the servants of his father, Abraham.

25:25 *Esau* sounds like a Hebrew term that means "hair." 25:26 *Jacob* means "he grasps the heel"; this can also figuratively mean "he deceives." 26:4 Hebrew *seed.*

¹⁶And Abimelech asked Isaac to leave the country. "Go somewhere else," he said, "for you have become too rich and powerful for us."

¹⁷So Isaac moved to the Gerar Valley and lived there instead. ¹⁸He reopened the wells his father had dug, which the Philistines had filled in after Abraham's death. Isaac renamed them, using the names Abraham had given them. ¹⁹His shepherds also dug in the Gerar Valley and found a gushing spring.

²⁰But then the local shepherds came and claimed the spring. "This is our water," they said, and they argued over it with Isaac's herdsmen. So Isaac named the well "Argument,"* because they had argued about it with him. ²¹Isaac's men then dug another well, but again there was a fight over it. So Isaac named it "Opposition."* ²²Abandoning that one, he dug another well, and the local people finally left him alone. So Isaac called it "Room Enough,"* for he said, "At last the LORD has made room for us, and we will be able to thrive."

²³From there Isaac moved to Beersheba, ²⁴where the LORD appeared to him on the night of his arrival. "I am the God of your father, Abraham," he said. "Do not be afraid, for I am with you and will bless you. I will give you many descendants, and they will become a great nation. I will do this because of my promise to Abraham, my servant." ²⁵Then Isaac built an altar there and worshiped the LORD. He set up his camp at that place, and his servants dug a well.

A TREATY WITH ABIMELECH

²⁶One day Isaac had visitors from Gerar. King Abimelech arrived with his adviser, Ahuzzath, and also Phicol, his army commander. ²⁷"Why have you come?" Isaac asked them. "This is obviously no friendly visit, since you sent me from your land in a most unfriendly way."

²⁸They replied, "We can plainly see that the LORD is with you. So we decided we should have a treaty, a covenant between us. ²⁹Swear that you will not harm us, just as we did not harm you. We have always treated you well, and we sent you away from us in peace. And now look how the LORD has blessed you!"

³⁰So Isaac prepared a great feast for them, and they ate and drank in preparation for the treaty ceremony. ³¹Early the next morning, they each took a solemn oath of nonaggression. Then Isaac sent them home again in peace. ³²That very day Isaac's servants came and told him about a well they had dug. "We've found water!" they said. ³³So Isaac named the well "Oath,"* and from that time to this, the town that grew up there has been called Beersheba—"well of the oath."

³⁴At the age of forty, Esau married a young woman named Judith, the daughter of Beeri the Hittite. He also married Basemath, the daughter of Elon the Hittite. ³⁵But Esau's wives made life miserable for Isaac and Rebekah.

JACOB STEALS ESAU'S BLESSING

27 When Isaac was old and almost blind, he called for Esau, his older son, and said, "My son?"

"Yes, Father?" Esau replied.

²"I am an old man now," Isaac said, "and I expect every day to be my last. ³Take your bow and a quiver full of arrows out into the open country, and hunt some wild game for me. ⁴Prepare it just the way I like it so it's savory and good, and bring it here for me to eat.

> *Worship does not satisfy our hunger for God—it whets our appetite.*
>
> EUGENE PETERSON

26:20 Hebrew *Esek*.   26:21 Hebrew *Sitnah*.   26:22 Hebrew *Rehoboth*.   26:33 Hebrew *Shibah*, which can mean "oath" or "seven."

Then I will pronounce the blessing that belongs to you, my firstborn son, before I die."

⁵But Rebekah overheard the conversation. So when Esau left to hunt for the wild game, ⁶she said to her son Jacob, "I overheard your father asking Esau ⁷to prepare him a delicious meal of wild game. He wants to bless Esau in the LORD's presence before he dies. ⁸Now, my son, do exactly as I tell you. ⁹Go out to the flocks and bring me two fine young goats. I'll prepare your father's favorite dish from them. ¹⁰Take the food to your father; then he can eat it and bless you instead of Esau before he dies."

¹¹"But Mother!" Jacob replied. "He won't be fooled that easily. Think how hairy Esau is and how smooth my skin is! ¹²What if my father touches me? He'll see that I'm trying to trick him, and then he'll curse me instead of blessing me."

¹³"Let the curse fall on me, dear son," said Rebekah. "Just do what I tell you. Go out and get the goats."

¹⁴So Jacob followed his mother's instructions, bringing her the two goats. She took them and cooked a delicious meat dish, just the way Isaac liked it. ¹⁵Then she took Esau's best clothes, which were there in the house, and dressed Jacob with them. ¹⁶She made him a pair of gloves from the hairy skin of the young goats, and she fastened a strip of the goat's skin around his neck. ¹⁷Then she gave him the meat dish, with its rich aroma, and some freshly baked bread. ¹⁸Jacob carried the platter of food to his father and said, "My father?"

"Yes, my son," he answered. "Who is it—Esau or Jacob?"

¹⁹Jacob replied, "It's Esau, your older son. I've done as you told me. Here is the wild game, cooked the way you like it. Sit up and eat it so you can give me your blessing."

²⁰Isaac asked, "How were you able to find it so quickly, my son?"

"Because the LORD your God put it in my path!" Jacob replied.

²¹Then Isaac said to Jacob, "Come over here. I want to touch you to make sure you really are Esau." ²²So Jacob went over to his father, and Isaac touched him. "The voice is Jacob's, but the hands are Esau's," Isaac said to himself. ²³But he did not recognize Jacob because Jacob's hands felt hairy just like Esau's. So Isaac pronounced his blessing on Jacob. ²⁴"Are you really my son Esau?" he asked.

"Yes, of course," Jacob replied.

²⁵Then Isaac said, "Now, my son, bring me the meat. I will eat it, and then I will give you my blessing." So Jacob took the food over to his father, and Isaac ate it. He also drank the wine that Jacob served him. Then Isaac said, ²⁶"Come here and kiss me, my son."

²⁷So Jacob went over and kissed him. And when Isaac caught the smell of his clothes, he was finally convinced, and he blessed his son. He said, "The smell of my son is the good smell of the open fields that the LORD has blessed. ²⁸May God always give you plenty of dew for healthy crops and good harvests of grain and wine. ²⁹May many nations become your servants. May you be the master of your brothers. May all your mother's sons bow low before you. All who curse you are cursed, and all who bless you are blessed."

³⁰As soon as Isaac had blessed Jacob, and almost before Jacob had left his father, Esau returned from his hunting trip. ³¹Esau prepared his father's favorite meat dish and brought it to him. Then he said, "I'm back, Father, and I have the wild game. Sit up and eat it so you can give me your blessing."

³²But Isaac asked him, "Who are you?"

"Why, it's me, of course!" he replied. "It's Esau, your older son."

³³Isaac began to tremble uncontrollably and said, "Then who was it that just served me wild game? I have already eaten it, and I blessed him with an irrevocable blessing before you came."

³⁴When Esau understood, he let out a loud and bitter cry. "O my father, bless me, too!" he begged.

³⁵But Isaac said, "Your brother was here, and he tricked me. He has carried away your blessing."

³⁶Esau said bitterly, "No wonder his name is Jacob,* for he has deceived me twice, first taking my birthright and now stealing my blessing. Oh, haven't you saved even one blessing for me?"

³⁷Isaac said to Esau, "I have made Jacob your master and have declared that all his brothers will be his servants. I have guaranteed him an abundance of grain and wine—what is there left to give?"

³⁸Esau pleaded, "Not one blessing left for me? O my father, bless me, too!" Then Esau broke down and wept.

³⁹His father, Isaac, said to him, "You will live off the land and what it yields, ⁴⁰and you will live by your sword. You will serve your brother for a time, but then you will shake loose from him and be free."

JACOB FLEES TO PADDAN-ARAM

⁴¹Esau hated Jacob because he had stolen his blessing, and he said to himself, "My father will soon be dead and gone. Then I will kill Jacob."

⁴²But someone got wind of what Esau was planning and reported it to Rebekah. She sent for Jacob and told him, "Esau is threatening to kill you. ⁴³This is what you should do. Flee to your uncle Laban in Haran. ⁴⁴Stay there with him until your brother's fury is spent. ⁴⁵When he forgets what you have done, I will send for you. Why should I lose both of you in one day?"

⁴⁶Then Rebekah said to Isaac, "I'm sick and tired of these local Hittite women. I'd rather die than see Jacob marry one of them."

28 So Isaac called for Jacob, blessed him, and said, "Do not marry any of these Canaanite women. ²Instead, go at once to Paddan-aram, to the house of your grandfather Bethuel, and marry one of your uncle Laban's daughters. ³May God Almighty bless you and give you many children. And may your descendants become a great assembly of nations! ⁴May God pass on to you and your descendants the blessings he promised to Abraham. May you own this land where we now are foreigners, for God gave it to Abraham."

⁵So Isaac sent Jacob away, and he went to Paddan-aram to stay with his uncle Laban, his mother's brother, the son of Bethuel the Aramean.

⁶Esau heard that his father had blessed Jacob and sent him to Paddan-aram to find a wife, and that he had warned Jacob not to marry a Canaanite woman. ⁷He also knew that Jacob had obeyed his parents and gone to Paddan-aram. ⁸It was now very clear to Esau that his father despised the local Canaanite women. ⁹So he visited his uncle Ishmael's family and married one of Ishmael's daughters, in addition to the wives he already had. His new wife's name was Mahalath. She was the sister of Nebaioth and the daughter of Ishmael, Abraham's son.

JACOB'S DREAM AT BETHEL

¹⁰Meanwhile, Jacob left Beersheba and traveled toward Haran. ¹¹At sundown he arrived at a good place to set up camp and stopped there for the night. Jacob found a stone for a pillow and lay down to sleep. ¹²As he slept, he dreamed of a stairway that reached from earth to heaven. And he saw the angels of God going up and down on it.

¹³At the top of the stairway stood the LORD, and he said, "I am the LORD, the God of your grandfather Abraham and the God of your father, Isaac. The ground you are lying on belongs to you. I will give it to you and your descendants. ¹⁴Your descendants will be as numerous as the dust of the earth! They will cover the land from east to west and from north to south. All the families of the earth will be blessed through you and your descendants.* ¹⁵What's more, I will be with you, and I will protect you wherever you go. I will someday bring you safely back to this land. I will be with you constantly until I have finished giving you everything I have promised."

¹⁶Then Jacob woke up and said, "Surely the

27:36 Jacob means "he grasps the heel"; this can also figuratively mean "he deceives." 28:14 Hebrew seed.

My Daily Worship

A BETTER PERSPECTIVE

GENESIS 25:19–28:9

"Look, I'm dying of starvation!" said Esau. "What good is my birthright to me now?"
So Jacob insisted, "Well then, swear to me right now that it is mine." So Esau swore an oath,
thereby selling all his rights as the firstborn to his younger brother (25:32–33).

[i reflect]

Most people see the world through eyes that see only what is happening to me or what is happening right *now.*

And the results of such a self-absorbed, impatient mindset? Not very pretty to look at. You end up with embarrassing episodes like the one cited above—Esau forfeiting enormous privilege and honor and essentially throwing away his prominent place in the eternal purposes of God. And for what? One big bowl of beans. How tragic!

How common.

The children of God take a different perspective. Rather than becoming obsessed with the small stories of their individual lives, they focus on God's big story. As they do, these worshiping saints remember the past faithfulness of God, even as they place their hope in his future promises.

The result is that the faithful live steadier lives. They are not so susceptible to whims and fads and sudden urges. Because they keep the big picture in view, they finish well. They're living for much more than a bowl of beans.

What are *you* living for today? What thoughts and desires fill your mind even now?

When we focus on the present and on our feelings, we can quickly lose sight of God's future and his truth. To put our hope and trust in God is to stand in awe of him and his power with the confidence that God will faithfully perform his Word.

Throughout your day, keep your focus on the One who has proven himself worthy of your trust.

[i pray]

Gracious Father, keep me from the foolish trap of living selfishly and living only
for the moment. Grant me an eternal perspective so that my heart, mind,
and will are captured by your noble purposes.

[i respond]

Make a mental list today of the trivial, physical (but not necessarily wrong) things that keep you from focusing on eternal, spiritual realities. What one change can you make in your schedule today to help you keep your focus on God?

LORD is in this place, and I wasn't even aware of it." ¹⁷He was afraid and said, "What an awesome place this is! It is none other than the house of God—the gateway to heaven!" ¹⁸The next morning he got up very early. He took the stone he had used as a pillow and set it upright as a memorial pillar. Then he poured olive oil over it. ¹⁹He named the place Bethel—"house of God"—though the name of the nearby village was Luz.

²⁰Then Jacob made this vow: "If God will be with me and protect me on this journey and give me food and clothing, ²¹and if he will bring me back safely to my father, then I will make the LORD my God. ²²This memorial pillar will become a place for worshiping God, and I will give God a tenth of everything he gives me."

JACOB ARRIVES AT PADDAN-ARAM

29 Jacob hurried on, finally arriving in the land of the east. ²He saw in the distance three flocks of sheep lying in an open field beside a well, waiting to be watered. But a heavy stone covered the mouth of the well. ³It was the custom there to wait for all the flocks to arrive before removing the stone. After watering them, the stone would be rolled back over the mouth of the well. ⁴Jacob went over to the shepherds and asked them, "Where do you live?"

"At Haran," they said.

⁵"Do you know a man there named Laban, the grandson of Nahor?"

"Yes, we do," they replied.

⁶"How is he?" Jacob asked.

"He's well and prosperous. Look, here comes his daughter Rachel with the sheep."

⁷"Why don't you water the flocks so they can get back to grazing?" Jacob asked. "They'll be hungry if you stop so early in the day."

⁸"We don't roll away the stone and begin the watering until all the flocks and shepherds are here," they replied.

⁹As this conversation was going on, Rachel arrived with her father's sheep, for she was a shepherd. ¹⁰And because she was his cousin, the daughter of his mother's brother, and because the sheep were his uncle's, Jacob went over to the well and rolled away the stone and watered his uncle's flock. ¹¹Then Jacob kissed Rachel, and tears came to his eyes. ¹²He explained that he was her cousin on her father's side, her aunt Rebekah's son. So Rachel quickly ran and told her father, Laban.

¹³As soon as Laban heard about Jacob's arrival, he rushed out to meet him and greeted him warmly. Laban then brought him home, and Jacob told him his story. ¹⁴"Just think, my very own flesh and blood!" Laban exclaimed.

JACOB MARRIES LEAH AND RACHEL

After Jacob had been there about a month, ¹⁵Laban said to him, "You shouldn't work for me without pay just because we are relatives. How much do you want?"

¹⁶Now Laban had two daughters: Leah, who was the oldest, and her younger sister, Rachel. ¹⁷Leah had pretty eyes,* but Rachel was beautiful in every way, with a lovely face and shapely figure. ¹⁸Since Jacob was in love with Rachel, he told her father, "I'll work for you seven years if you'll give me Rachel, your younger daughter, as my wife."

¹⁹"Agreed!" Laban replied. "I'd rather give her to you than to someone outside the family."

²⁰So Jacob spent the next seven years working to pay for Rachel. But his love for her was so strong that it seemed to him but a few days. ²¹Finally, the time came for him to marry her. "I have fulfilled my contract," Jacob said to Laban. "Now give me my wife so we can be married."

²²So Laban invited everyone in the neighborhood to celebrate with Jacob at a wedding feast. ²³That night, when it was dark, Laban took Leah to Jacob, and he slept with her. ²⁴And Laban gave Leah a servant, Zilpah, to be her maid.

29:17 Or *dull eyes.* The meaning of the Hebrew is uncertain.

My Daily Worship

— January 11 —

FAITH, NOT FEELINGS

GENESIS 28:10–30:43

Once again she became pregnant and had a son. She named him Judah,
for she said, "Now I will praise the LORD!" (29:35).

[i reflect]

If there were such a thing as a time machine and we could go back in history to the events described in Genesis 28–30, . . . if we could sit down with Leah and interview her, . . . if we could ask her what it was like—*really*—to be an unloved wife, . . . what would she tell us?

Surely she would describe feeling overlooked, or even feeling ugly. Perhaps she would tell of poignant moments of rejection, of tearful times of prayer, of wrestling with deep-seated jealousy, of heart-wrenching, unanswered questions.

All of this is, of course, speculation. What we know for sure is the little bit that God's Word tells us. Leah gave Jacob four sons. And in naming each one, Leah expressed her stubborn faith and desperate hope. First *Reuben*, meaning "Look, a son!" because she really trusted that God saw her situation; then *Simeon*, meaning "hearing," because she honestly believed that God had heard her plight; next, *Levi*, meaning "attachment," in the last-ditch hope that maybe, just maybe, Jacob would finally develop deep affection for her.

It didn't happen. Leah's younger sister Rachel remained the delight of Jacob's eyes. A bitter pill to swallow. A crushing blow. When you're reading this passage for the first time, you expect a kind of bitter resentment to begin to fill Leah's heart.

It doesn't. Shockingly, she gives birth to a fourth son and names him *Judah*, which means "Let him—God—be praised."

Living by faith isn't easy—certainly Leah must have struggled. But it's the only way to show that we believe God knows and wants only the best for us. Today when events or your feelings pull you toward fear and cynicism, remember Leah and choose faith.

[i pray]

O Father in heaven, give me Leah's brand of spiritual tenacity. When I want to lash out, help me to cry out instead. When I start to focus on my problems, move my heart to praise.

[i respond]

Take a few minutes to think back on an especially bitter or hard time in your life. Find something in that experience that you can make an occasion for true worship.

²⁵But when Jacob woke up in the morning—it was Leah! "What sort of trick is this?" Jacob raged at Laban. "I worked seven years for Rachel. What do you mean by this trickery?"

²⁶"It's not our custom to marry off a younger daughter ahead of the firstborn," Laban replied. ²⁷"Wait until the bridal week is over, and you can have Rachel, too—that is, if you promise to work another seven years for me."

²⁸So Jacob agreed to work seven more years. A week after Jacob had married Leah, Laban gave him Rachel, too. ²⁹And Laban gave Rachel a servant, Bilhah, to be her maid. ³⁰So Jacob slept with Rachel, too, and he loved her more than Leah. He then stayed and worked the additional seven years.

JACOB'S MANY CHILDREN

³¹But because Leah was unloved, the LORD let her have a child, while Rachel was childless. ³²So Leah became pregnant and had a son. She named him Reuben,* for she said, "The LORD has noticed my misery, and now my husband will love me." ³³She soon became pregnant again and had another son. She named him Simeon,* for she said, "The LORD heard that I was unloved and has given me another son." ³⁴Again she became pregnant and had a son. She named him Levi,* for she said, "Surely now my husband will feel affection for me, since I have given him three sons!" ³⁵Once again she became pregnant and had a son. She named him Judah,* for she said, "Now I will praise the LORD!" And then she stopped having children.

30 When Rachel saw that she wasn't having any children, she became jealous of her sister. "Give me children, or I'll die!" she exclaimed to Jacob.

²Jacob flew into a rage. "Am I God?" he asked. "He is the only one able to give you children!"

³Then Rachel told him, "Sleep with my servant, Bilhah, and she will bear children for me." ⁴So Rachel gave him Bilhah to be his wife, and Jacob slept with her. ⁵Bilhah became pregnant and presented him with a son. ⁶Rachel named him Dan,* for she said, "God has vindicated me! He has heard my request and given me a son." ⁷Then Bilhah became pregnant again and gave Jacob a second son. ⁸Rachel named him Naphtali,* for she said, "I have had an intense struggle with my sister, and I am winning!"

⁹Meanwhile, Leah realized that she wasn't getting pregnant anymore, so she gave her servant, Zilpah, to Jacob to be his wife. ¹⁰Soon Zilpah presented him with another son. ¹¹Leah named him Gad,* for she said, "How fortunate I am!" ¹²Then Zilpah produced a second son, ¹³and Leah named him Asher,* for she said, "What joy is mine! The other women will consider me happy indeed!"

¹⁴One day during the wheat harvest, Reuben found some mandrakes growing in a field and brought the roots to his mother, Leah. Rachel begged Leah to give some of them to her. ¹⁵But Leah angrily replied, "Wasn't it enough that you stole my husband? Now will you steal my son's mandrake roots, too?"

Rachel said, "I will let him sleep with you tonight in exchange for the mandrake roots."

¹⁶So that evening, as Jacob was coming home from the fields, Leah went out to meet him. "You must sleep with me tonight!" she said. "I have paid for you with some mandrake roots my son has found." So Jacob slept with her. ¹⁷And God answered her prayers. She became pregnant again and gave birth to her fifth son. ¹⁸She named him Issachar,* for she said, "God has rewarded me for giving my servant to my husband as a wife." ¹⁹Then she

---

29:32 *Reuben* means "Look, a son!" It also sounds like the Hebrew for "He has seen my misery." **29:33** *Simeon* probably means "one who hears." **29:34** *Levi* sounds like a Hebrew term that means "being attached" or "feeling affection for." **29:35** *Judah* sounds like the Hebrew term for "praise." **30:6** *Dan* is a play on the Hebrew term meaning "to vindicate" or "to judge." **30:8** *Naphtali* means "my struggle." **30:11** *Gad* means "good fortune." **30:13** *Asher* means "happy." **30:18** *Issachar* sounds like a Hebrew term that means "reward."

became pregnant again and had a sixth son. [20]She named him Zebulun,* for she said, "God has given me good gifts for my husband. Now he will honor me, for I have given him six sons." [21]Later she gave birth to a daughter and named her Dinah.

[22]Then God remembered Rachel's plight and answered her prayers by giving her a child. [23]She became pregnant and gave birth to a son. "God has removed my shame," she said. [24]And she named him Joseph,* for she said, "May the LORD give me yet another son."

JACOB'S WEALTH INCREASES

[25]Soon after Joseph was born to Rachel, Jacob said to Laban, "I want to go back home. [26]Let me take my wives and children, for I have earned them from you, and let me be on my way. You know I have fully paid for them with my service to you."

[27]"Please don't leave me," Laban replied, "for I have learned by divination that the LORD has blessed me because you are here. [28]How much do I owe you? Whatever it is, I'll pay it."

[29]Jacob replied, "You know how faithfully I've served you through these many years, and how your flocks and herds have grown. [30]You had little indeed before I came, and your wealth has increased enormously. The LORD has blessed you from everything I do! But now, what about me? When should I provide for my own family?"

[31]"What wages do you want?" Laban asked again.

Jacob replied, "Don't give me anything at all. Just do one thing, and I'll go back to work for you. [32]Let me go out among your flocks today and remove all the sheep and goats that are speckled or spotted, along with all the dark-colored sheep. Give them to me as my wages. [33]This will make it easy for you to see whether or not I have been honest. If you find in my flock any white sheep or goats that are not speckled, you will know that I have stolen them from you."

[34]"All right," Laban replied. "It will be as you have said." [35]But that very day Laban went out and removed all the male goats that were speckled and spotted, the females that were speckled and spotted with any white patches, and all the dark-colored sheep. He placed them in the care of his sons, [36]and they took them three days' distance from where Jacob was. Meanwhile, Jacob stayed and cared for Laban's flock.

[37]Now Jacob took fresh shoots from poplar, almond, and plane trees and peeled off strips of the bark to make white streaks on them. [38]Then he set up these peeled branches beside the watering troughs so Laban's flocks would see them as they came to drink, for that was when they mated. [39]So when the flocks mated in front of the white-streaked branches, all of their offspring were streaked, speckled, and spotted. [40]Jacob added them to his own flock, thus separating the lambs from Laban's flock. Then at mating time, he turned the flocks toward the streaked and dark-colored rams in Laban's flock. This is how he built his flock from Laban's. [41]Whenever the stronger females were ready to mate, Jacob set up the peeled branches in front of them. [42]But he didn't do this with the weaker ones, so the weaker lambs belonged to Laban, and the stronger ones were Jacob's. [43]As a result, Jacob's flocks increased rapidly, and he became very wealthy, with many servants, camels, and donkeys.

JACOB FLEES FROM LABAN

31 But Jacob soon learned that Laban's sons were beginning to grumble. "Jacob has robbed our father!" they said. "All his wealth has been gained at our father's expense." [2]And Jacob began to notice a considerable cooling in Laban's attitude toward him.

[3]Then the LORD said to Jacob, "Return to the land of your father and grandfather and to your relatives there, and I will be with you."

[4]Jacob called Rachel and Leah out to the field where he was watching the flocks, [5]so he

---

30:20 *Zebulun* probably means "honor."   **30:24** *Joseph* means "may he add."

could talk things over with them. "Your father has turned against me and is not treating me like he used to," he told them. "But the God of my father has been with me. ⁶You know how hard I have worked for your father, ⁷but he has tricked me, breaking his wage agreement with me again and again. But God has not allowed him to do me any harm. ⁸For if he said the speckled animals were mine, the whole flock began to produce speckled lambs. And when he changed his mind and said I could have the streaked ones, then all the lambs were born streaked. ⁹In this way, God has made me wealthy at your father's expense. ¹⁰During the mating season, I had a dream and saw that the male goats mating with the flock were streaked, speckled, and spotted. ¹¹Then in my dream, the angel of God said to me, 'Jacob!' And I replied, 'Yes, I'm listening!' ¹²The angel said, 'Look, and you will see that only the streaked, speckled, and spotted males are mating with the females of your flock. For I have seen all that Laban has done to you. ¹³I am the God you met at Bethel, the place where you anointed the pillar of stone and made a vow to serve me. Now leave this country and return to the land you came from.'"

¹⁴Rachel and Leah said, "That's fine with us! There's nothing for us here—none of our father's wealth will come to us anyway. ¹⁵He has reduced our rights to those of foreign women. He sold us, and what he received for us has disappeared. ¹⁶The riches God has given you from our father are legally ours and our children's to begin with. So go ahead and do whatever God has told you."

¹⁷So Jacob put his wives and children on camels. ¹⁸He drove the flocks in front of him—all the livestock he had acquired at Paddan-aram—and set out on his journey to the land of Canaan, where his father, Isaac, lived. ¹⁹At the time they left, Laban was some distance away, shearing his sheep. Rachel stole her father's household gods and took them with her. ²⁰They set out secretly and never told Laban they were leaving. ²¹Jacob took all his possessions with him and crossed the Euphrates River, heading for the territory of Gilead.

LABAN PURSUES JACOB

²²Laban didn't learn of their flight for three days. ²³But when he did, he gathered a group of his relatives and set out in hot pursuit. He caught up with them seven days later in the hill country of Gilead. ²⁴But the previous night God had appeared to Laban in a dream. "Be careful about what you say to Jacob!" he was told.

²⁵So when Laban caught up with Jacob as he was camped in the hill country of Gilead, he set up his camp not far from Jacob's. ²⁶"What do you mean by sneaking off like this?" Laban demanded. "Are my daughters prisoners, the plunder of war, that you have stolen them away like this? ²⁷Why did you slip away secretly? I would have given you a farewell party, with joyful singing accompanied by tambourines and harps. ²⁸Why didn't you let me kiss my daughters and grandchildren and tell them good-bye? You have acted very foolishly! ²⁹I could destroy you, but the God of your father appeared to me last night and told me, 'Be careful about what you say to Jacob!' ³⁰I know you feel you must go, and you long intensely for your childhood home, but why have you stolen my household gods?"

³¹"I rushed away because I was afraid," Jacob answered. "I said to myself, 'He'll take his daughters from me by force.' ³²But as for your household gods, let the person who has taken them die! If you find anything that belongs to you, I swear before all these relatives of ours, I will give it back without question." But Jacob didn't know that Rachel had taken them.

³³Laban went first into Jacob's tent to search there, then into Leah's, and then he searched the tents of the two concubines, but he didn't find the gods. Finally, he went into Rachel's tent. ³⁴Rachel had taken the household gods and had stuffed them into her camel saddle, and now she was sitting on them. So although Laban searched all the tents, he couldn't find them. ³⁵"Forgive my not getting up, Father,"

Rachel explained. "I'm having my monthly period." So despite his thorough search, Laban didn't find them.

[36]Then Jacob became very angry. "What did you find?" he demanded of Laban. "What is my crime? You have chased me as though I were a criminal. [37]You have searched through everything I own. Now show me what you have found that belongs to you! Set it out here in front of us, before our relatives, for all to see. Let them decide who is the real owner!

[38]"Twenty years I have been with you, and all that time I cared for your sheep and goats so they produced healthy offspring. In all those years I never touched a single ram of yours for food. [39]If any were attacked and killed by wild animals, did I show them to you and ask you to reduce the count of your flock? No, I took the loss! You made me pay for every animal stolen from the flocks, whether the loss was my fault or not. [40]I worked for you through the scorching heat of the day and through cold and sleepless nights. [41]Yes, twenty years—fourteen of them earning your two daughters, and six years to get the flock. And you have reduced my wages ten times! [42]In fact, except for the grace of God—the God of my grandfather Abraham, the awe-inspiring God of my father, Isaac—you would have sent me off without a penny to my name. But God has seen your cruelty and my hard work. That is why he appeared to you last night and vindicated me."

JACOB'S TREATY WITH LABAN

[43]Then Laban replied to Jacob, "These women are my daughters, and these children are my grandchildren, and these flocks and all that you have—all are mine. But what can I do now to my own daughters and grandchildren? [44]Come now, and we will make a peace treaty, you and I, and we will live by its terms."

[45]So Jacob took a stone and set it up as a monument. [46]He also told his men to gather stones and pile them up in a heap. Jacob and Laban then sat down beside the pile of stones to share a meal. [47]They named it "Witness Pile," which is Jegar-sahadutha in Laban's language and Galeed* in Jacob's.

[48]"This pile of stones will stand as a witness to remind us of our agreement," Laban said. [49]This place was also called Mizpah,* for Laban said, "May the LORD keep watch between us to make sure that we keep this treaty when we are out of each other's sight. [50]I won't know about it if you are harsh to my daughters or if you take other wives, but God will see it. [51]This heap of stones and this pillar [52]stand between us as a witness of our vows. I will not cross this line to harm you, and you will not cross it to harm me. [53]I call on the God of our ancestors—the God of your grandfather Abraham and the God of my grandfather Nahor—to punish either one of us who harms the other."

So Jacob took an oath before the awesome God of his father, Isaac, to respect the boundary line. [54]Then Jacob presented a sacrifice to God and invited everyone to a feast. Afterward they spent the night there in the hills. [55]Laban got up early the next morning, and he kissed his daughters and grandchildren and blessed them. Then he returned home.

JACOB SENDS GIFTS TO ESAU

32 As Jacob and his household started on their way again, angels of God came to meet him. [2]When Jacob saw them, he exclaimed, "This is God's camp!" So he named the place Mahanaim.*

[3]Jacob now sent messengers to his brother, Esau, in Edom, the land of Seir. [4]He told them, "Give this message to my master Esau: 'Humble greetings from your servant Jacob! I have been living with Uncle Laban until recently, [5]and now I own oxen, donkeys, sheep, goats, and many servants, both men and women. I have sent these messengers to inform you of my coming, hoping that you will be friendly to us.'"

31:47 *Jegar-sahadutha* means "witness pile" in Aramaic; *Galeed* means "witness pile" in Hebrew.   31:49 *Mizpah* means "watchtower."
32:2 *Mahanaim* means "two camps."

⁶The messengers returned with the news that Esau was on his way to meet Jacob—with an army of four hundred men! ⁷Jacob was terrified at the news. He divided his household, along with the flocks and herds and camels, into two camps. ⁸He thought, "If Esau attacks one group, perhaps the other can escape."

⁹Then Jacob prayed, "O God of my grandfather Abraham and my father, Isaac—O LORD, you told me to return to my land and to my relatives, and you promised to treat me kindly. ¹⁰I am not worthy of all the faithfulness and unfailing love you have shown to me, your servant. When I left home, I owned nothing except a walking stick, and now my household fills two camps! ¹¹O LORD, please rescue me from my brother, Esau. I am afraid that he is coming to kill me, along with my wives and children. ¹²But you promised to treat me kindly and to multiply my descendants until they become as numerous as the sands along the seashore—too many to count."

¹³Jacob stayed where he was for the night and prepared a present for Esau: ¹⁴two hundred female goats, twenty male goats, two hundred ewes, twenty rams, ¹⁵thirty female camels with their young, forty cows, ten bulls, twenty female donkeys, and ten male donkeys. ¹⁶He told his servants to lead them on ahead, each group of animals by itself, separated by a distance in between.

¹⁷He gave these instructions to the men leading the first group: "When you meet Esau, he will ask, 'Where are you going? Whose servants are you? Whose animals are these?' ¹⁸You should reply, 'These belong to your servant Jacob. They are a present for his master Esau! He is coming right behind us.' " ¹⁹Jacob gave the same instructions to each of the herdsmen and told them, "You are all to say the same thing to Esau when you see him. ²⁰And be sure to say, 'Your servant Jacob is right behind us.' " Jacob's plan was to appease Esau with the presents before meeting him face to face. "Perhaps," Jacob hoped, "he will be friendly to us." ²¹So the presents were sent on ahead, and Jacob spent that night in the camp.

JACOB WRESTLES WITH GOD

²²But during the night Jacob got up and sent his two wives, two concubines, and eleven sons across the Jabbok River. ²³After they were on the other side, he sent over all his possessions. ²⁴This left Jacob all alone in the camp, and a man came and wrestled with him until dawn. ²⁵When the man saw that he couldn't win the match, he struck Jacob's hip and knocked it out of joint at the socket. ²⁶Then the man said, "Let me go, for it is dawn."

But Jacob panted, "I will not let you go unless you bless me."

²⁷"What is your name?" the man asked.

He replied, "Jacob."

²⁸"Your name will no longer be Jacob," the man told him. "It is now Israel,* because you have struggled with both God and men and have won."

²⁹"What is your name?" Jacob asked him.

"Why do you ask?" the man replied. Then he blessed Jacob there.

³⁰Jacob named the place Peniel—"face of God"—for he said, "I have seen God face to face, yet my life has been spared." ³¹The sun rose as he left Peniel,* and he was limping because of his hip. ³²That is why even today the people of Israel don't eat meat from near the hip, in memory of what happened that night.

JACOB AND ESAU MAKE PEACE

33 Then, in the distance, Jacob saw Esau coming with his four hundred men. ²Jacob now arranged his family into a column, with his two concubines and their children at the front, Leah and her children next, and Rachel and Joseph last. ³Then Jacob went on ahead. As he approached his brother, he bowed low seven times before him. ⁴Then Esau ran to meet him and embraced him affectionately and kissed him. Both of them were in tears.

32:28 *Israel* means "God struggles" or "one who struggles with God." 32:31 Hebrew *Penuel*, a variant name for Peniel.

My Daily Worship

— January 12 —

NIGHTWRESTLING
GENESIS 31:1–36:43

Then the man said, "Let me go, for it is dawn." But Jacob panted,
"I will not let you go unless you bless me" (32:26).

[i reflect]

It sounds like the stuff of dreams: a man camping alone by a riverside who engages in a nightlong wrestling match with an angel of the Lord. Scripture paints an unusual portrait for us in this story of Jacob's sweaty struggle with God on the banks of the Jabbok, a struggle culminating in Jacob's receiving the name his people carry to this day.

Jacob, whose name means "grabber," was a man who always had been determined to do things his way—whether it was wresting control of his brother's birthright or Laban's flocks. After years of learning the hard way that his way wasn't God's way, he finally did something right. He seized an opportunity to grab on to God and hold on with all his might.

Worship is composed of familiar elements such as praise, adoration, confession, and intercession. Sometimes we forget, however, that worshiping God also involves persistence—pursuing hard after the one who is impossible to see, but never at a distance from us.

Worship doesn't always feel good; at times it resembles Jacob's struggle more than Sunday morning singing. Scripture reminds us that problems and trials are good for us because they help us learn to endure, and endurance produces the strength of character God longs to see in us (Romans 5:3–4).

Are you struggling with God right now and feeling frustrated? Take a lesson from Jacob and hold fast to the One who has promised to never let you go. Perhaps your wrestling match will leave you, like Jacob, with a "limp"—a perpetual reminder of your dependency on God. Praise him, then, for this reminder of his eternal sufficiency for you.

Got God? Then hold on!

[i pray]

Lord, you know that I'm really struggling right now. I never thought of it as wrestling with you, though. I'm hanging on to you, Lord. Bless me through the pain!

[i respond]

Identify those issues or struggles that are making worship difficult right now. Look for the ways that God is actually strengthening you through these circumstances. Take heart that wrestling with God brings you into intimate contact with him and that he is fighting on your side.

⁵Then Esau looked at the women and children and asked, "Who are these people with you?"

"These are the children God has graciously given to me," Jacob replied. ⁶Then the concubines came forward with their children and bowed low before him. ⁷Next Leah came with her children, and they bowed down. Finally, Rachel and Joseph came and made their bows.

⁸"And what were all the flocks and herds I met as I came?" Esau asked.

Jacob replied, "They are gifts, my lord, to ensure your goodwill."

⁹"Brother, I have plenty," Esau answered. "Keep what you have."

¹⁰"No, please accept them," Jacob said, "for what a relief it is to see your friendly smile. It is like seeing the smile of God! ¹¹Please take my gifts, for God has been very generous to me. I have more than enough." Jacob continued to insist, so Esau finally accepted them.

¹²"Well, let's be going," Esau said. "I will stay with you and lead the way."

¹³But Jacob replied, "You can see, my lord, that some of the children are very young, and the flocks and herds have their young, too. If they are driven too hard, they may die. ¹⁴So go on ahead of us. We will follow at our own pace and meet you at Seir."

¹⁵"Well," Esau said, "at least let me leave some of my men to guide and protect you."

"There is no reason for you to be so kind to me," Jacob insisted.

¹⁶So Esau started back to Seir that same day. ¹⁷Meanwhile, Jacob and his household traveled on to Succoth. There he built himself a house and made shelters for his flocks and herds. That is why the place was named Succoth.* ¹⁸Then they arrived safely at Shechem, in Canaan, and they set up camp just outside the town. ¹⁹Jacob bought the land he camped on from the family of Hamor, Shechem's father, for a hundred pieces of silver.* ²⁰And there he built an altar and called it El-Elohe-Israel.*

REVENGE AGAINST SHECHEM

34 One day Dinah, Leah's daughter, went to visit some of the young women who lived in the area. ²But when the local prince, Shechem son of Hamor the Hivite, saw her, he took her and raped her. ³But Shechem's love for Dinah was strong, and he tried to win her affection. ⁴He even spoke to his father about it. "Get this girl for me," he demanded. "I want to marry her."

⁵Word soon reached Jacob that his daughter had been defiled, but his sons were out in the fields herding cattle so he did nothing until they returned. ⁶Meanwhile, Hamor, Shechem's father, came out to discuss the matter with Jacob. ⁷He arrived just as Jacob's sons were coming in from the fields. They were shocked and furious that their sister had been raped. Shechem had done a disgraceful thing against Jacob's family,* a thing that should never have been done.

⁸Hamor told Jacob and his sons, "My son Shechem is truly in love with your daughter, and he longs for her to be his wife. Please let him marry her. ⁹We invite you to let your daughters marry our sons, and we will give our daughters as wives for your young men. ¹⁰And you may live among us; the land is open to you! Settle here and trade with us. You are free to acquire property among us."

¹¹Then Shechem addressed Dinah's father and brothers. "Please be kind to me, and let me have her as my wife," he begged. "I will give whatever you require. ¹²No matter what dowry or gift you demand, I will pay it—only give me the girl as my wife."

¹³But Dinah's brothers deceived Shechem and Hamor because of what Shechem had done to their sister. ¹⁴They said to them, "We couldn't possibly allow this, because you aren't circumcised. It would be a disgrace for her to marry a man like you! ¹⁵But here is a solution. If every man among you will be circumcised like we are, ¹⁶we will intermarry with you and live here and unite with you to

---

33:17 *Succoth* means "shelters." 33:19 Hebrew *100 kesitahs;* the value or weight of the kesitah is no longer known. 33:20 *El-Elohe-Israel* means "God, the God of Israel." 34:7 Hebrew *in Israel.*

Words of Worship

COVENANT

Covenant—Hebrew *be-rit* "covenant"; Greek *di-a-the-ke* "covenant, testament."

In the Old Testament, God grants covenants to his people through their representatives. In the covenants with Abraham and David, God promises them a benefit. The covenant with Israel, through Moses, has a fuller structure similar to that of a treaty, in which the people also take on obligations to God. In essence, the covenant creates a family with the Lord at the head. The covenant is renewed through Christ (Luke 22:20), and the names "New Testament" and "New Covenant" are translations of the same Greek word.

It's no fun to feel alone, misunderstood, and not cherished. The Lord wants more for us. Our heavenly Father has called all his worshipers into his covenant, a loving family. He promises, "I will be their God, and they will be my people" (Jeremiah 31:33).

In the Bible, a covenant is symbolized by the shedding of blood. We enter our new covenant family through the blood Jesus shed on the cross (Hebrews 12:24). In him, we have a family of brothers and sisters with whom we can share our lives at the deepest level. "Share each other's troubles and problems, and in this way obey the law of Christ" (Galatians 6:2).

become one people. ¹⁷Otherwise we will take her and be on our way."

¹⁸Hamor and Shechem gladly agreed, ¹⁹and Shechem lost no time in acting on this request, for he wanted Dinah desperately. Shechem was a highly respected member of his family, ²⁰and he appeared with his father before the town leaders to present this proposal. ²¹"Those men are our friends," they said. "Let's invite them to live here among us and ply their trade. For the land is large enough to hold them, and we can intermarry with them. ²²But they will consider staying here only on one condition. Every one of us men must be circumcised, just as they are. ²³But if we do this, all their flocks and possessions will become ours. Come, let's agree to this so they will settle here among us."

²⁴So all the men agreed and were circumcised. ²⁵But three days later, when their wounds were still sore, two of Dinah's brothers, Simeon and Levi, took their swords, entered the town without opposition, and slaughtered every man there, ²⁶including Hamor and Shechem. They rescued Dinah from Shechem's house and returned to their camp. ²⁷Then all of Jacob's sons plundered the town because their sister had been defiled there. ²⁸They seized all the flocks and herds and donkeys—everything they could lay their hands on, both inside the town and outside in the fields. ²⁹They also took all the women and children and wealth of every kind.

³⁰Afterward Jacob said to Levi and Simeon, "You have made me stink among all the people of this land—among all the Canaanites and Perizzites. We are so few that they will come and crush us. We will all be killed!"

³¹"Should he treat our sister like a prostitute?" they retorted angrily.

JACOB'S RETURN TO BETHEL

35 God said to Jacob, "Now move on to Bethel and settle there. Build an altar there to worship me—the God who appeared to you when you fled from your brother, Esau."

²So Jacob told everyone in his household, "Destroy your idols, wash yourselves, and put on clean clothing. ³We are now going to Bethel, where I will build an altar to the God who answered my prayers when I was in distress. He has stayed with me wherever I have gone."

⁴So they gave Jacob all their idols and their earrings, and he buried them beneath the tree near Shechem. ⁵When they set out again, terror from God came over the people in all the towns of that area, and no one attacked them. ⁶Finally, they arrived at Luz (now called Bethel) in Canaan. ⁷Jacob built an altar there and named it El-bethel,* because God had appeared to him there at Bethel when he was fleeing from Esau.

⁸Soon after this, Rebekah's old nurse, Deborah, died. She was buried beneath the oak tree in the valley below Bethel. Ever since, the tree has been called the "Oak of Weeping."*

⁹God appeared to Jacob once again when he arrived at Bethel after traveling from Paddan-aram. God blessed him ¹⁰and said, "Your name is no longer Jacob; you will now be called Israel."* ¹¹Then God said, "I am God Almighty. Multiply and fill the earth! Become a great nation, even many nations. Kings will be among your descendants! ¹²And I will pass on to you the land I gave to Abraham and Isaac. Yes, I will give it to you and your descendants." ¹³Then God went up from the place where he had spoken to Jacob.

¹⁴Jacob set up a stone pillar to mark the place where God had spoken to him. He then poured wine over it as an offering to God and anointed the pillar with olive oil. ¹⁵Jacob called the place Bethel—"house of God"—because God had spoken to him there.

THE DEATHS OF RACHEL AND ISAAC

¹⁶Leaving Bethel, they traveled on toward Ephrath (that is, Bethlehem). But Rachel's pains of childbirth began while they were still some distance away. ¹⁷After a very hard delivery, the midwife finally exclaimed, "Don't be afraid—you have another son!" ¹⁸Rachel was about to die, but with her last breath she named him Ben-oni; the baby's father, how-

ever, called him Benjamin.* ¹⁹So Rachel died and was buried on the way to Ephrath (that is, Bethlehem). ²⁰Jacob set up a stone monument over her grave, and it can be seen there to this day.

²¹Jacob* then traveled on and camped beyond the tower of Eder. ²²While he was there, Reuben slept with Bilhah, his father's concubine, and someone told Jacob about it.

These are the names of the twelve sons of Jacob:

²³The sons of Leah were Reuben (Jacob's oldest son), Simeon, Levi, Judah, Issachar, and Zebulun.
²⁴The sons of Rachel were Joseph and Benjamin.
²⁵The sons of Bilhah, Rachel's servant, were Dan and Naphtali.
²⁶The sons of Zilpah, Leah's servant, were Gad and Asher.

These were the sons born to Jacob at Paddan-aram.

²⁷So Jacob came home to his father Isaac in Mamre, which is near Kiriath-arba (now called Hebron), where Abraham had also lived. ²⁸Isaac lived for 180 years, ²⁹and he died at a ripe old age, joining his ancestors in death. Then his sons, Esau and Jacob, buried him.

DESCENDANTS OF ESAU

36 This is the history of the descendants of Esau (also known as Edom). ²Esau married two young women from Canaan: Adah, the daughter of Elon the Hittite; and Oholibamah, the daughter of Anah and granddaughter of Zibeon the Hivite. ³He also married his cousin Basemath, who was the daughter of Ishmael and the sister of Nebaioth. ⁴Esau and Adah had a son named Eliphaz. Esau and Basemath had a son named Reuel. ⁵Esau and Oholibamah had sons

35:7 El-bethel means "the God of Bethel." 35:8 Hebrew Allon-bacuth. 35:10 Jacob means "he grasps the heel"; this can also figuratively mean "he deceives"; Israel means "God struggles" or "one who struggles with God." 35:18 Ben-oni means "son of my sorrow"; Benjamin means "son of my right hand." 35:21 Hebrew Israel; also in 35:22a.

named Jeush, Jalam, and Korah. All these sons were born to Esau in the land of Canaan.

6Then Esau took his wives, children, household servants, cattle, and flocks—all the wealth he had gained in the land of Canaan—and moved away from his brother, Jacob. 7There was not enough land to support them both because of all their cattle and livestock. 8So Esau (also known as Edom) settled in the hill country of Seir.

9This is a list of Esau's descendants, the Edomites, who lived in the hill country of Seir.

10Among Esau's sons were Eliphaz, the son of Esau's wife Adah; and Reuel, the son of Esau's wife Basemath.
11The sons of Eliphaz were Teman, Omar, Zepho, Gatam, and Kenaz. 12Eliphaz had another son named Amalek, born to Timna, his concubine. These were all grandchildren of Esau's wife Adah.
13The sons of Reuel were Nahath, Zerah, Shammah, and Mizzah. These were all grandchildren of Esau's wife Basemath.
14Esau also had sons through Oholibamah, the daughter of Anah and granddaughter of Zibeon. Their names were Jeush, Jalam, and Korah.

15Esau's children and grandchildren became the leaders of different clans.

The sons of Esau's oldest son, Eliphaz, became the leaders of the clans of Teman, Omar, Zepho, Kenaz, 16Korah, Gatam, and Amalek. These clans in the land of Edom were descended from Eliphaz, the son of Esau and Adah.
17The sons of Esau's son Reuel became the leaders of the clans of Nahath, Zerah, Shammah, and Mizzah. These clans in the land of Edom were descended from Reuel, the son of Esau and Basemath.
18The sons of Esau and his wife Oholibamah became the leaders of the clans of Jeush, Jalam, and Korah. These are the clans descended from Esau's wife Oholibamah, the daughter of Anah.

19These are all the clans descended from Esau (also known as Edom).

ORIGINAL PEOPLES OF EDOM

20These are the names of the tribes that descended from Seir the Horite, one of the families native to the land of Seir: Lotan, Shobal, Zibeon, Anah, 21Dishon, Ezer, and Dishan. These were the Horite clans, the descendants of Seir, who lived in the land of Edom.

22The sons of Lotan were Hori and Heman. Lotan's sister was named Timna.
23The sons of Shobal were Alvan, Manahath, Ebal, Shepho, and Onam.
24The sons of Zibeon were Aiah and Anah. This is the Anah who discovered the hot springs in the wilderness while he was grazing his father's donkeys.
25The son of Anah was Dishon, and Oholibamah was his daughter.
26The sons of Dishon* were Hemdan, Eshban, Ithran, and Keran.
27The sons of Ezer were Bilhan, Zaavan, and Akan.
28The sons of Dishan were Uz and Aran.

29So the leaders of the Horite clans were Lotan, Shobal, Zibeon, Anah, 30Dishon, Ezer, and Dishan. The Horite clans are named after their clan leaders, who lived in the land of Seir.

A private relationship
of worshiping
God is the greatest essential element
of spiritual fitness.

OSWALD CHAMBERS

36:26 Hebrew *Dishan,* a variant name for Dishon; compare 36:21, 28.

RULERS OF EDOM

³¹These are the kings who ruled in Edom before there were kings in Israel*:

³²Bela son of Beor, who ruled from his city of Dinhabah.

³³When Bela died, Jobab son of Zerah from Bozrah became king.

³⁴When Jobab died, Husham from the land of the Temanites became king.

³⁵When Husham died, Hadad son of Bedad became king and ruled from the city of Avith. He was the one who destroyed the Midianite army in the land of Moab.

³⁶When Hadad died, Samlah from the city of Masrekah became king.

³⁷When Samlah died, Shaul from the city of Rehoboth on the Euphrates River* became king.

³⁸When Shaul died, Baal-hanan son of Acbor became king.

³⁹When Baal-hanan died, Hadad* became king and ruled from the city of Pau. Hadad's wife was Mehetabel, the daughter of Matred and granddaughter of Me-zahab.

⁴⁰These are the leaders of the clans of Esau, who lived in the places named for them: Timna, Alvah, Jetheth, ⁴¹Oholibamah, Elah, Pinon, ⁴²Kenaz, Teman, Mibzar, ⁴³Magdiel, and Iram. These are the names of the clans of Esau, the ancestor of the Edomites, each clan giving its name to the area it occupied.

JOSEPH'S DREAMS

37 So Jacob settled again in the land of Canaan, where his father had lived.

²This is the history of Jacob's family. When Joseph was seventeen years old, he often tended his father's flocks with his half brothers, the sons of his father's wives Bilhah and Zilpah. But Joseph reported to his father some of the bad things his brothers were doing. ³Now Jacob* loved Joseph more than any of his other children because Joseph had been born to him in his old age. So one day he gave Joseph a special gift—a beautiful robe.* ⁴But his brothers hated Joseph because of their father's partiality. They couldn't say a kind word to him.

⁵One night Joseph had a dream and promptly reported the details to his brothers, causing them to hate him even more. ⁶"Listen to this dream," he announced. ⁷"We were out in the field tying up bundles of grain. My bundle stood up, and then your bundles all gathered around and bowed low before it!"

⁸"So you are going to be our king, are you?" his brothers taunted. And they hated him all the more for his dream and what he had said.

⁹Then Joseph had another dream and told his brothers about it. "Listen to this dream," he said. "The sun, moon, and eleven stars bowed low before me!"

¹⁰This time he told his father as well as his brothers, and his father rebuked him. "What do you mean?" his father asked. "Will your mother, your brothers, and I actually come and bow before you?" ¹¹But while his brothers were jealous of Joseph, his father gave it some thought and wondered what it all meant.

¹²Soon after this, Joseph's brothers went to pasture their father's flocks at Shechem. ¹³When they had been gone for some time, Jacob said to Joseph, "Your brothers are over at Shechem with the flocks. I'm going to send you to them."

"I'm ready to go," Joseph replied.

¹⁴"Go and see how your brothers and the flocks are getting along," Jacob said. "Then come back and bring me word." So Jacob sent him on his way, and Joseph traveled to Shechem from his home in the valley of Hebron.

¹⁵When he arrived there, a man noticed him wandering around the countryside. "What are you looking for?" he asked.

¹⁶"For my brothers and their flocks," Joseph replied. "Have you seen them?"

36:31 Or *before an Israelite king ruled over them.*   **36:37** Hebrew *the river.*   **36:39** As in some Hebrew manuscripts, Samaritan Pentateuch, and Syriac version (see also 1 Chr 1:50); most Hebrew manuscripts read *Hadar.*   **37:3a** Hebrew *Israel;* also in 37:13.   **37:3b** Traditionally rendered *a coat of many colors.* The exact meaning of the Hebrew is uncertain.

¹⁷"Yes," the man told him, "but they are no longer here. I heard your brothers say they were going to Dothan." So Joseph followed his brothers to Dothan and found them there.

JOSEPH SOLD INTO SLAVERY

¹⁸When Joseph's brothers saw him coming, they recognized him in the distance and made plans to kill him. ¹⁹"Here comes that dreamer!" they exclaimed. ²⁰"Come on, let's kill him and throw him into a deep pit. We can tell our father that a wild animal has eaten him. Then we'll see what becomes of all his dreams!"

²¹But Reuben came to Joseph's rescue. "Let's not kill him," he said. ²²"Why should we shed his blood? Let's just throw him alive into this pit here. That way he will die without our having to touch him." Reuben was secretly planning to help Joseph escape, and then he would bring him back to his father.

²³So when Joseph arrived, they pulled off his beautiful robe ²⁴and threw him into the pit. This pit was normally used to store water, but it was empty at the time. ²⁵Then, just as they were sitting down to eat, they noticed a caravan of camels in the distance coming toward them. It was a group of Ishmaelite traders taking spices, balm, and myrrh from Gilead to Egypt.

²⁶Judah said to the others, "What can we gain by killing our brother? That would just give us a guilty conscience. ²⁷Let's sell Joseph to those Ishmaelite traders. Let's not be responsible for his death; after all, he is our brother!" And his brothers agreed. ²⁸So when the traders* came by, his brothers pulled Joseph out of the pit and sold him for twenty pieces* of silver, and the Ishmaelite traders took him along to Egypt.

²⁹Some time later, Reuben returned to get Joseph out of the pit. When he discovered that Joseph was missing, he tore his clothes in anguish and frustration. ³⁰Then he went back to his brothers and lamented, "The boy is gone! What can I do now?"

³¹Then Joseph's brothers killed a goat and dipped the robe in its blood. ³²They took the beautiful robe to their father and asked him to identify it. "We found this in the field," they told him. "It's Joseph's robe, isn't it?"

³³Their father recognized it at once. "Yes," he said, "it is my son's robe. A wild animal has attacked and eaten him. Surely Joseph has been torn in pieces!" ³⁴Then Jacob tore his clothes and put on sackcloth. He mourned deeply for his son for many days. ³⁵His family all tried to comfort him, but it was no use. "I will die in mourning for my son," he would say, and then begin to weep.

³⁶Meanwhile, in Egypt, the traders sold Joseph to Potiphar, an officer of Pharaoh, the king of Egypt. Potiphar was captain of the palace guard.

JUDAH AND TAMAR

38 About this time, Judah left home and moved to Adullam, where he visited a man named Hirah. ²There he met a Canaanite woman, the daughter of Shua, and he married her. ³She became pregnant and had a son, and Judah named the boy Er. ⁴Then Judah's wife had another son, and she named him Onan. ⁵And when she had a third son, she named him Shelah. At the time of Shelah's birth, they were living at Kezib.

⁶When his oldest son, Er, grew up, Judah arranged his marriage to a young woman named Tamar. ⁷But Er was a wicked man in the LORD's sight, so the LORD took his life. ⁸Then Judah said to Er's brother Onan, "You must marry Tamar, as our law requires of the brother of a man who has died. Her first son from you will be your brother's heir."

⁹But Onan was not willing to have a child who would not be his own heir. So whenever he had intercourse with Tamar, he spilled the semen on the ground to keep her from having a baby who would belong to his brother. ¹⁰But the LORD considered it a wicked thing for Onan to deny a child to his dead brother. So the LORD took Onan's life, too.

¹¹Then Judah told Tamar, his daughter-in-law,

37:28a Hebrew *Midianites;* also in 37:36. **37:28b** Hebrew *20 shekels,* about 8 ounces or 228 grams in weight.

not to marry again at that time but to return to her parents' home. She was to remain a widow until his youngest son, Shelah, was old enough to marry her. (But Judah didn't really intend to do this because he was afraid Shelah would also die, like his two brothers.) So Tamar went home to her parents.

¹²In the course of time Judah's wife died. After the time of mourning was over, Judah and his friend Hirah the Adullamite went to Timnah to supervise the shearing of his sheep. ¹³Someone told Tamar that her father-in-law had left for the sheep-shearing at Timnah. ¹⁴Tamar was aware that Shelah had grown up, but they had not called her to come and marry him. So she changed out of her widow's clothing and covered herself with a veil to disguise herself. Then she sat beside the road at the entrance to the village of Enaim, which is on the way to Timnah. ¹⁵Judah noticed her as he went by and thought she was a prostitute, since her face was veiled. ¹⁶So he stopped and propositioned her to sleep with him, not realizing that she was his own daughter-in-law.

"How much will you pay me?" Tamar asked.

¹⁷"I'll send you a young goat from my flock," Judah promised.

"What pledge will you give me so I can be sure you will send it?" she asked.

¹⁸"Well, what do you want?" he inquired.

She replied, "I want your identification seal, your cord, and the walking stick you are carrying." So Judah gave these items to her. She then let him sleep with her, and she became pregnant. ¹⁹Afterward she went home, took off her veil, and put on her widow's clothing as usual.

²⁰Judah asked his friend Hirah the Adullamite to take the young goat back to her and to pick up the pledges he had given her, but Hirah couldn't find her. ²¹So he asked the men who lived there, "Where can I find the prostitute* who was sitting beside the road at the entrance to the village?"

"We've never had a prostitute here," they replied. ²²So Hirah returned to Judah and told him that he couldn't find her anywhere and that the men of the village had claimed they didn't have a prostitute there.

²³"Then let her keep the pledges!" Judah exclaimed. "We tried our best to send her the goat. We'd be the laughingstock of the village if we went back again."

²⁴About three months later, word reached Judah that Tamar, his daughter-in-law, was pregnant as a result of prostitution. "Bring her out and burn her!" Judah shouted.

²⁵But as they were taking her out to kill her, she sent this message to her father-in-law: "The man who owns this identification seal and walking stick is the father of my child. Do you recognize them?"

²⁶Judah admitted that they were his and said, "She is more in the right than I am, because I didn't keep my promise to let her marry my son Shelah." But Judah never slept with Tamar again.

²⁷In due season the time of Tamar's delivery arrived, and she had twin sons. ²⁸As they were being born, one of them reached out his hand, and the midwife tied a scarlet thread around the wrist of the child who appeared first, saying, "This one came out first." ²⁹But then he drew back his hand, and the other baby was actually the first to be born. "What!" the midwife exclaimed. "How did you break out first?" And ever after, he was called Perez.* ³⁰Then the baby with the scarlet thread on his wrist was born, and he was named Zerah.*

JOSEPH IN POTIPHAR'S HOUSE

39 Now when Joseph arrived in Egypt with the Ishmaelite traders, he was purchased by Potiphar, a member of the personal staff of Pharaoh, the king of Egypt. Potiphar was the captain of the palace guard.

²The LORD was with Joseph and blessed him greatly as he served in the home of his Egyptian master. ³Potiphar noticed this and realized that the LORD was with Joseph, giving

38:21 Hebrew *shrine prostitute*; also in 38:21b, 22.   38:29 *Perez* means "breaking out."   38:30 *Zerah* means "scarlet" or "brightness."

My Daily Worship

— *January 13* —

It's the Pits

Genesis 37:1–41:57

*He took Joseph and threw him into the prison where the king's prisoners were held. But the LORD
was with Joseph there, too, and he granted Joseph favor with the chief jailer (39:20–21).*

[i reflect]

What a story! Aren't you glad it's Joseph's story and not yours? Or is it?

- A teen is wrongly incriminated by a friend at school who is hiding his own guilt. The teen is suspended.
- A pastor spurns the attentions of a woman in his congregation only to be falsely accused of harassment.
- A manager shares her faith at work only to be charged with religious discrimination by a disgruntled employee.

Believers in Christ are not exempt from unjust accusations. How, then, do we worship in the midst
of such awful circumstances?

The key is found in today's verse: *the Lord was with Joseph there*. God could have chosen to keep
Joseph out of prison. Instead he did something far better; he accompanied him there.

When God is with us, even a prison cell can become a place of worship. Regardless of our circumstances, we can take comfort in the fact that God has promised to stay close by our side.
Remember his promise to Moses? *"I will be with you."* To Gideon? *"I will be with you."* And to
Paul? *"I will be with you."*

Corrie ten Boom, who herself was in a Nazi prison for hiding Jews during World War II, often said,
"There is no pit so deep that Jesus is not deeper still." No pit, no prison, and no person's accusations can keep you apart from the One who made you and who loves you.

Worship need not take place in a sanctuary or even in the comfort of home. Learn to welcome
those times when life's unfairness draws you closest to the One who has promised never to leave
you. He already is there, waiting.

[i pray]

*Dear Father, you know how painful my personal situation has become. I feel imprisoned
by my own bitterness towards those who have misunderstood me. Forgive me, Lord,
and help me to rejoice in the knowledge of your presence.*

[i respond]

Are you locked in a prison of your own making, imprisoned by painful memories or the sting of
unjust accusations? Praise holds the key that can unlock the doors of your cell and set you free.
Pause and consider those circumstances that threaten to imprison you. Pray about each one.

him success in everything he did. ⁴So Joseph naturally became quite a favorite with him. Potiphar soon put Joseph in charge of his entire household and entrusted him with all his business dealings. ⁵From the day Joseph was put in charge, the LORD began to bless Potiphar for Joseph's sake. All his household affairs began to run smoothly, and his crops and livestock flourished. ⁶So Potiphar gave Joseph complete administrative responsibility over everything he owned. With Joseph there, he didn't have a worry in the world, except to decide what he wanted to eat!

Now Joseph was a very handsome and well-built young man. ⁷And about this time, Potiphar's wife began to desire him and invited him to sleep with her. ⁸But Joseph refused. "Look," he told her, "my master trusts me with everything in his entire household. ⁹No one here has more authority than I do! He has held back nothing from me except you, because you are his wife. How could I ever do such a wicked thing? It would be a great sin against God."

¹⁰She kept putting pressure on him day after day, but he refused to sleep with her, and he kept out of her way as much as possible. ¹¹One day, however, no one else was around when he was doing his work inside the house. ¹²She came and grabbed him by his shirt, demanding, "Sleep with me!" Joseph tore himself away, but as he did, his shirt came off. She was left holding it as he ran from the house.

¹³When she saw that she had his shirt and that he had fled, ¹⁴she began screaming. Soon all the men around the place came running. "My husband has brought this Hebrew slave here to insult us!" she sobbed. "He tried to rape me, but I screamed. ¹⁵When he heard my loud cries, he ran and left his shirt behind with me."

¹⁶She kept the shirt with her, and when her husband came home that night, ¹⁷she told him her story. "That Hebrew slave you've had around here tried to make a fool of me," she said. ¹⁸"I was saved only by my screams. He ran out, leaving his shirt behind!"

JOSEPH PUT IN PRISON

¹⁹After hearing his wife's story, Potiphar was furious! ²⁰He took Joseph and threw him into the prison where the king's prisoners were held. ²¹But the LORD was with Joseph there, too, and he granted Joseph favor with the chief jailer. ²²Before long, the jailer put Joseph in charge of all the other prisoners and over everything that happened in the prison. ²³The chief jailer had no more worries after that, because Joseph took care of everything. The LORD was with him, making everything run smoothly and successfully.

JOSEPH INTERPRETS TWO DREAMS

40 Some time later, Pharaoh's chief cup-bearer and chief baker offended him. ²Pharaoh became very angry with these officials, ³and he put them in the prison where Joseph was, in the palace of Potiphar, the captain of the guard. ⁴They remained in prison for quite some time, and Potiphar assigned Joseph to take care of them.

⁵One night the cup-bearer and the baker each had a dream, and each dream had its own meaning. ⁶The next morning Joseph noticed the dejected look on their faces. ⁷"Why do you look so worried today?" he asked.

⁸And they replied, "We both had dreams last night, but there is no one here to tell us what they mean."

"Interpreting dreams is God's business," Joseph replied. "Tell me what you saw."

⁹The cup-bearer told his dream first. "In my dream," he said, "I saw a vine in front of me. ¹⁰It had three branches that began to bud and blossom, and soon there were clusters of ripe grapes. ¹¹I was holding Pharaoh's wine cup in my hand, so I took the grapes and squeezed the juice into it. Then I placed the cup in Pharaoh's hand."

¹²"I know what the dream means," Joseph said. "The three branches mean three days. ¹³Within three days Pharaoh will take you out of prison and return you to your position as

UNFAILING LOVE

Unfailing Love—Hebrew *che-sed* "unfailing love, steadfast love, kindness, mercy." This important and rich word occurs more than 175 times in the Old Testament to denote God's unswerving faithfulness to his worshipers.

The Lord loves his people, and they love him in return. Every page of Scripture proclaims that truth. But with human beings, *love* can have many different meanings. The love the Bible reveals is based on the Hebrew word *chesed*, which refers to a special kind of love—God's steadfast loyalty to those who have accepted his covenant. God loves all he has made, but his *unfailing love* is reserved for members of his family.

When, as God's children and servants, we run into difficulties, we can ask for his help. We appeal to him not on the basis of how much we deserve, but on the basis of his faithfulness: "Save us because of your unfailing love" (Psalm 44:26). To everyone who worships the Lord with a loyal and sincere heart, his promise is clear: "I will not fail you or abandon you" (Joshua 1:5). You are Lord!

his chief cup-bearer. ¹⁴And please have some pity on me when you are back in his favor. Mention me to Pharaoh, and ask him to let me out of here. ¹⁵For I was kidnapped from my homeland, the land of the Hebrews, and now I'm here in jail, but I did nothing to deserve it."

¹⁶When the chief baker saw that the first dream had such a good meaning, he told his dream to Joseph, too. "In my dream," he said, "there were three baskets of pastries on my head. ¹⁷In the top basket were all kinds of bakery goods for Pharaoh, but the birds came and ate them."

¹⁸"I'll tell you what it means," Joseph told him. "The three baskets mean three days. ¹⁹Three days from now Pharaoh will cut off your head and impale your body on a pole. Then birds will come and peck away at your flesh."

²⁰Pharaoh's birthday came three days later, and he gave a banquet for all his officials and household staff. He sent for his chief cup-bearer and chief baker, and they were brought to him from the prison. ²¹He then restored the chief cup-bearer to his former position, ²²but he sentenced the chief baker to be impaled on a pole, just as Joseph had predicted. ²³Pharaoh's cup-bearer, however, promptly forgot all about Joseph, never giving him another thought.

PHARAOH'S DREAMS

41 Two years later, Pharaoh dreamed that he was standing on the bank of the Nile River. ²In his dream, seven fat, healthy-looking cows suddenly came up out of the river and began grazing along its bank. ³Then seven other cows came up from the river, but these were very ugly and gaunt. These cows went over and stood beside the fat cows. ⁴Then the thin, ugly cows ate the fat ones! At this point in the dream, Pharaoh woke up.

⁵Soon he fell asleep again and had a second dream. This time he saw seven heads of grain on one stalk, with every kernel well formed and plump. ⁶Then suddenly, seven more heads appeared on the stalk, but these were shriveled and withered by the east wind. ⁷And these thin heads swallowed up the seven plump, well-formed heads! Then Pharaoh woke up again and realized it was a dream.

⁸The next morning, as he thought about it, Pharaoh became very concerned as to what the dreams might mean. So he called for all the magicians and wise men of Egypt and told them about his dreams, but not one of them could suggest what they meant. ⁹Then the king's cup-bearer spoke up. "Today I have

been reminded of my failure," he said. ¹⁰"Some time ago, you were angry with the chief baker and me, and you imprisoned us in the palace of the captain of the guard. ¹¹One night the chief baker and I each had a dream, and each dream had a meaning. ¹²We told the dreams to a young Hebrew man who was a servant of the captain of the guard. He told us what each of our dreams meant, ¹³and everything happened just as he said it would. I was restored to my position as cup-bearer, and the chief baker was executed and impaled on a pole."

¹⁴Pharaoh sent for Joseph at once, and he was brought hastily from the dungeon. After a quick shave and change of clothes, he went in and stood in Pharaoh's presence. ¹⁵"I had a dream last night," Pharaoh told him, "and none of these men can tell me what it means. But I have heard that you can interpret dreams, and that is why I have called for you."

¹⁶"It is beyond my power to do this," Joseph replied. "But God will tell you what it means and will set you at ease."

¹⁷So Pharaoh told him the dream. "I was standing on the bank of the Nile River," he said. ¹⁸"Suddenly, seven fat, healthy-looking cows came up out of the river and began grazing along its bank. ¹⁹But then seven other cows came up from the river. They were very thin and gaunt—in fact, I've never seen such ugly animals in all the land of Egypt. ²⁰These thin, ugly cows ate up the seven fat ones that had come out of the river first, ²¹but afterward they were still as ugly and gaunt as before! Then I woke up.

²²"A little later I had another dream. This time there were seven heads of grain on one stalk, and all seven heads were plump and full. ²³Then out of the same stalk came seven withered heads, shriveled by the east wind. ²⁴And the withered heads swallowed up the plump ones! I told these dreams to my magicians, but not one of them could tell me what they mean."

²⁵"Both dreams mean the same thing," Joseph told Pharaoh. "God was telling you what he is about to do. ²⁶The seven fat cows and the seven plump heads of grain both represent seven years of prosperity. ²⁷The seven thin, ugly cows and the seven withered heads of grain represent seven years of famine. ²⁸This will happen just as I have described it, for God has shown you what he is about to do. ²⁹The next seven years will be a period of great prosperity throughout the land of Egypt. ³⁰But afterward there will be seven years of famine so great that all the prosperity will be forgotten and wiped out. Famine will destroy the land. ³¹This famine will be so terrible that even the memory of the good years will be erased. ³²As for having the dream twice, it means that the matter has been decreed by God and that he will make these events happen soon.

³³"My suggestion is that you find the wisest man in Egypt and put him in charge of a nationwide program. ³⁴Let Pharaoh appoint officials over the land, and let them collect one-fifth of all the crops during the seven good years. ³⁵Have them gather all the food and grain of these good years into the royal storehouses, and store it away so there will be food in the cities. ³⁶That way there will be enough to eat when the seven years of famine come. Otherwise disaster will surely strike the land, and all the people will die."

JOSEPH MADE RULER OF EGYPT

³⁷Joseph's suggestions were well received by Pharaoh and his advisers. ³⁸As they discussed who should be appointed for the job, Pharaoh said, "Who could do it better than Joseph? For he is a man who is obviously filled with the spirit of God." ³⁹Turning to Joseph, Pharaoh said, "Since God has revealed the meaning of the dreams to you, you are the wisest man in the land! ⁴⁰I hereby appoint you to direct this project. You will manage my household and organize all my people. Only I will have a rank higher than yours."

⁴¹And Pharaoh said to Joseph, "I hereby put you in charge of the entire land of Egypt." ⁴²Then Pharaoh placed his own signet ring on Joseph's finger as a symbol of his authority. He dressed him in beautiful clothing and

placed the royal gold chain about his neck. [43]Pharaoh also gave Joseph the chariot of his second-in-command, and wherever he went the command was shouted, "Kneel down!" So Joseph was put in charge of all Egypt. [44]And Pharaoh said to Joseph, "I am the king, but no one will move a hand or a foot in the entire land of Egypt without your approval."

[45]Pharaoh renamed him Zaphenath-paneah* and gave him a wife—a young woman named Asenath, the daughter of Potiphera, priest of Heliopolis.* So Joseph took charge of the entire land of Egypt. [46]He was thirty years old when he entered the service of Pharaoh, the king of Egypt. And when Joseph left Pharaoh's presence, he made a tour of inspection throughout the land.

[47]And sure enough, for the next seven years there were bumper crops everywhere. [48]During those years, Joseph took a portion of all the crops grown in Egypt and stored them for the government in nearby cities. [49]After seven years, the granaries were filled to overflowing. There was so much grain, like sand on the seashore, that the people could not keep track of the amount.

[50]During this time, before the arrival of the first of the famine years, two sons were born to Joseph and his wife, Asenath, the daughter of Potiphera, priest of Heliopolis. [51]Joseph named his older son Manasseh,* for he said, "God has made me forget all my troubles and the family of my father." [52]Joseph named his second son Ephraim,* for he said, "God has made me fruitful in this land of my suffering."

[53]At last the seven years of plenty came to an end. [54]Then the seven years of famine began, just as Joseph had predicted. There were crop failures in all the surrounding countries, too, but in Egypt there was plenty of grain in the storehouses. [55]Throughout the land of Egypt the people began to starve. They pleaded with Pharaoh for food, and he told them, "Go to Joseph and do whatever he tells you." [56]So with severe famine everywhere in the land, Joseph opened up the storehouses and sold grain to the Egyptians. [57]And people from surrounding lands also came to Egypt to buy grain from Joseph because the famine was severe throughout the world.

JOSEPH'S BROTHERS GO TO EGYPT

42 When Jacob heard that there was grain available in Egypt, he said to his sons, "Why are you standing around looking at one another? [2]I have heard there is grain in Egypt. Go down and buy some for us before we all starve to death." [3]So Joseph's ten older brothers went down to Egypt to buy grain. [4]Jacob wouldn't let Joseph's younger brother, Benjamin, go with them, however, for fear some harm might come to him. [5]So Jacob's* sons arrived in Egypt along with others to buy food, for the famine had reached Canaan as well.

[6]Since Joseph was governor of all Egypt and in charge of the sale of the grain, it was to him that his brothers came. They bowed low before him, with their faces to the ground. [7]Joseph recognized them instantly, but he pretended to be a stranger. "Where are you from?" he demanded roughly.

"From the land of Canaan," they replied. "We have come to buy grain."

[8]Joseph's brothers didn't recognize him, but Joseph recognized them. [9]And he remembered the dreams he had had many years before. He said to them, "You are spies! You have come to see how vulnerable our land has become."

[10]"No, my lord!" they exclaimed. "We have come to buy food. [11]We are all brothers and honest men, sir! We are not spies!"

[12]"Yes, you are!" he insisted. "You have come to discover how vulnerable the famine has made us."

[13]"Sir," they said, "there are twelve of us brothers, and our father is in the land of Canaan. Our youngest brother is there with

41:45a *Zaphenath-paneah* probably means "God speaks and lives." 41:45b Hebrew *of On;* also in 41:50. 41:51 *Manasseh* sounds like a Hebrew term that means "causing to forget." 41:52 *Ephraim* sounds like a Hebrew term that means "fruitful." 42:5 Hebrew *Israel's.*

our father, and one of our brothers is no longer with us."

[14]But Joseph insisted, "As I said, you are spies! [15]This is how I will test your story. I swear by the life of Pharaoh that you will not leave Egypt unless your youngest brother comes here. [16]One of you go and get your brother! I'll keep the rest of you here, bound in prison. Then we'll find out whether or not your story is true. If it turns out that you don't have a younger brother, then I'll know you are spies."

[17]So he put them all in prison for three days. [18]On the third day Joseph said to them, "I am a God-fearing man. If you do as I say, you will live. [19]We'll see how honorable you really are. Only one of you will remain in the prison. The rest of you may go on home with grain for your families. [20]But bring your youngest brother back to me. In this way, I will know whether or not you are telling me the truth. If you are, I will spare you." To this they agreed.

[21]Speaking among themselves, they said, "This has all happened because of what we did to Joseph long ago. We saw his terror and anguish and heard his pleadings, but we wouldn't listen. That's why this trouble has come upon us."

[22]"Didn't I tell you not to do it?" Reuben asked. "But you wouldn't listen. And now we are going to die because we murdered him."

[23]Of course, they didn't know that Joseph understood them as he was standing there, for he had been speaking to them through an interpreter. [24]Now he left the room and found a place where he could weep. Returning, he talked some more with them. He then chose Simeon from among them and had him tied up right before their eyes.

[25]Joseph then ordered his servants to fill the men's sacks with grain, but he also gave secret instructions to return each brother's payment at the top of his sack. He also gave them provisions for their journey. [26]So they loaded up their donkeys with the grain and started for home.

[27]But when they stopped for the night and one of them opened his sack to get some grain to feed the donkeys, he found his money in the sack. [28]"Look!" he exclaimed to his brothers. "My money is here in my sack!" They were filled with terror and said to each other, "What has God done to us?" [29]So they came to their father, Jacob, in the land of Canaan and told him all that had happened.

[30]"The man who is ruler over the land spoke very roughly to us," they told him. "He took us for spies. [31]But we said, 'We are honest men, not spies. [32]We are twelve brothers, sons of one father; one brother has disappeared, and the youngest is with our father in the land of Canaan.' [33]Then the man, the ruler of the land, told us, 'This is the way I will find out if you are honest men. Leave one of your brothers here with me, and take grain for your families and go on home. [34]But bring your youngest brother back to me. Then I will know that you are honest men and not spies. If you prove to be what you say, then I will give you back your brother, and you may come as often as you like to buy grain.' "

[35]As they emptied out the sacks, there at the top of each one was the bag of money paid for the grain. Terror gripped them, as it did their father. [36]Jacob exclaimed, "You have deprived me of my children! Joseph has disappeared, Simeon is gone, and now you want to take Benjamin, too. Everything is going against me!"

[37]Then Reuben said to his father, "You may kill my two sons if I don't bring Benjamin back to you. I'll be responsible for him."

[38]But Jacob replied, "My son will not go down with you, for his brother Joseph is dead, and he alone is left of his mother's children. If anything should happen to him, you would bring my gray head down to the grave in deep sorrow."

THE BROTHERS RETURN TO EGYPT

43 But there was no relief from the terrible famine throughout the land. [2]When the grain they had brought from Egypt

was almost gone, Jacob said to his sons, "Go again and buy us a little food."

³But Judah said, "The man wasn't joking when he warned that we couldn't see him again unless Benjamin came along. ⁴If you let him come with us, we will go down and buy some food. ⁵But if you don't let Benjamin go, we may as well stay at home. Remember that the man said, 'You won't be allowed to come and see me unless your brother is with you.'"

⁶"Why did you ever tell him you had another brother?" Jacob* moaned. "Why did you have to treat me with such cruelty?"

⁷"But the man specifically asked us about our family," they replied. "He wanted to know whether our father was still living, and he asked us if we had another brother so we told him. How could we have known he would say, 'Bring me your brother'?"

⁸Judah said to his father, "Send the boy with me, and we will be on our way. Otherwise we will all die of starvation—and not only we, but you and our little ones. ⁹I personally guarantee his safety. If I don't bring him back to you, then let me bear the blame forever. ¹⁰For we could have gone and returned twice by this time if you had let him come without delay."

¹¹So their father, Jacob, finally said to them, "If it can't be avoided, then at least do this. Fill your bags with the best products of the land. Take them to the man as gifts—balm, honey, spices, myrrh, pistachio nuts, and almonds. ¹²Take double the money that you found in your sacks, as it was probably someone's mistake. ¹³Then take your brother and go back to the man. ¹⁴May God Almighty give you mercy as you go before the man, that he might release Simeon and return Benjamin. And if I must bear the anguish of their deaths, then so be it."

¹⁵So they took Benjamin and the gifts and double the money and hurried to Egypt, where they presented themselves to Joseph. ¹⁶When Joseph saw that Benjamin was with them, he said to the manager of his household, "These men will eat with me this noon.

43:6 Hebrew *Israel;* also in 43:11.

Take them inside and prepare a big feast." ¹⁷So the man did as he was told and took them to Joseph's palace.

¹⁸They were badly frightened when they saw where they were being taken. "It's because of the money returned to us in our sacks," they said. "He plans to pretend that we stole it. Then he will seize us as slaves and take our donkeys."

> *Worship is transcendent wonder.*
>
> THOMAS CARLYLE

A FEAST AT JOSEPH'S PALACE

¹⁹As the brothers arrived at the entrance to the palace, they went over to the man in charge of Joseph's household. ²⁰They said to him, "Sir, after our first trip to Egypt to buy food, ²¹as we were returning home, we stopped for the night and opened our sacks. The money we had used to pay for the grain was there in our sacks. Here it is; we have brought it back again. ²²We also have additional money to buy more grain. We have no idea how the money got into our sacks."

²³"Relax. Don't worry about it," the household manager told them. "Your God, the God of your ancestors, must have put it there. We collected your money all right." Then he released Simeon and brought him out to them.

²⁴The brothers were then led into the palace and given water to wash their feet and food for their donkeys. ²⁵They were told they would be eating there, so they prepared their gifts for Joseph's arrival at noon.

²⁶When Joseph came, they gave him their gifts and bowed low before him. ²⁷He asked them how they had been getting along, and then he said, "How is your father—the old man you spoke about? Is he still alive?"

²⁸"Yes," they replied. "He is alive and well." Then they bowed again before him.

²⁹Looking at his brother Benjamin, Joseph asked, "Is this your youngest brother, the one you told me about? May God be gracious to you, my son." ³⁰Then Joseph made a hasty exit because he was overcome with emotion for his brother and wanted to cry. Going into his private room, he wept there. ³¹Then he washed his face and came out, keeping himself under control. "Bring on the food!" he ordered.

³²Joseph ate by himself, and his brothers were served at a separate table. The Egyptians sat at their own table because Egyptians despise Hebrews and refuse to eat with them. ³³Joseph told each of his brothers where to sit, and to their amazement, he seated them in the order of their ages, from oldest to youngest. ³⁴Their food was served to them from Joseph's own table. He gave the largest serving to Benjamin—five times as much as to any of the others. So they all feasted and drank freely with him.

JOSEPH'S SILVER CUP

44 When his brothers were ready to leave, Joseph gave these instructions to the man in charge of his household: "Fill each of their sacks with as much grain as they can carry, and put each man's money back into his sack. ²Then put my personal silver cup at the top of the youngest brother's sack, along with his grain money." So the household manager did as he was told.

³The brothers were up at dawn and set out on their journey with their loaded donkeys. ⁴But when they were barely out of the city, Joseph said to his household manager, "Chase after them and stop them. Ask them, 'Why have you repaid an act of kindness with such evil? ⁵What do you mean by stealing my master's personal silver drinking cup, which he

uses to predict the future? What a wicked thing you have done!'"

⁶So the man caught up with them and spoke to them in the way he had been instructed. ⁷"What are you talking about?" the brothers responded. "What kind of people do you think we are, that you accuse us of such a terrible thing? ⁸Didn't we bring back the money we found in our sacks? Why would we steal silver or gold from your master's house? ⁹If you find his cup with any one of us, let that one die. And all the rest of us will be your master's slaves forever."

¹⁰"Fair enough," the man replied, "except that only the one who stole it will be a slave. The rest of you may go free."

¹¹They quickly took their sacks from the backs of their donkeys and opened them. ¹²Joseph's servant began searching the oldest brother's sack, going on down the line to the youngest. The cup was found in Benjamin's sack! ¹³At this, they tore their clothing in despair, loaded the donkeys again, and returned to the city. ¹⁴Joseph was still at home when Judah and his brothers arrived, and they fell to the ground before him.

¹⁵"What were you trying to do?" Joseph demanded. "Didn't you know that a man such as I would know who stole it?"

¹⁶And Judah said, "Oh, my lord, what can we say to you? How can we plead? How can we prove our innocence? God is punishing us for our sins. My lord, we have all returned to be your slaves—we and our brother who had your cup in his sack."

¹⁷"No," Joseph said. "Only the man who stole the cup will be my slave. The rest of you may go home to your father."

JUDAH SPEAKS FOR HIS BROTHERS

¹⁸Then Judah stepped forward and said, "My lord, let me say just this one word to you. Be patient with me for a moment, for I know you could have me killed in an instant, as though you were Pharaoh himself.

¹⁹"You asked us, my lord, if we had a father

or a brother. [20]We said, 'Yes, we have a father, an old man, and a child of his old age, his youngest son. His brother is dead, and he alone is left of his mother's children, and his father loves him very much.' [21]And you said to us, 'Bring him here so I can see him.' [22]But we said to you, 'My lord, the boy cannot leave his father, for his father would die.' [23]But you told us, 'You may not see me again unless your youngest brother is with you.' [24]So we returned to our father and told him what you had said. [25]And when he said, 'Go back again and buy us a little food,' [26]we replied, 'We can't unless you let our youngest brother go with us. We won't be allowed to see the man in charge of the grain unless our youngest brother is with us.' [27]Then my father said to us, 'You know that my wife had two sons, [28]and that one of them went away and never returned—doubtless torn to pieces by some wild animal. I have never seen him since. [29]If you take away his brother from me, too, and any harm comes to him, you would bring my gray head down to the grave in deep sorrow.'

[30]"And now, my lord, I cannot go back to my father without the boy. Our father's life is bound up in the boy's life. [31]When he sees that the boy is not with us, our father will die. We will be responsible for bringing his gray head down to the grave in sorrow. [32]My lord, I made a pledge to my father that I would take care of the boy. I told him, 'If I don't bring him back to you, I will bear the blame forever.' [33]Please, my lord, let me stay here as a slave instead of the boy, and let the boy return with his brothers. [34]For how can I return to my father if the boy is not with me? I cannot bear to see what this would do to him."

JOSEPH REVEALS HIS IDENTITY

45 Joseph could stand it no longer. "Out, all of you!" he cried out to his attendants. He wanted to be alone with his brothers when he told them who he was. [2]Then he broke down and wept aloud. His sobs could be heard throughout the palace, and the news was quickly carried to Pharaoh's palace.

[3]"I am Joseph!" he said to his brothers. "Is my father still alive?" But his brothers were speechless! They were stunned to realize that Joseph was standing there in front of them. [4]"Come over here," he said. So they came closer. And he said again, "I am Joseph, your brother whom you sold into Egypt. [5]But don't be angry with yourselves that you did this to me, for God did it. He sent me here ahead of you to preserve your lives. [6]These two years of famine will grow to seven, during which there will be neither plowing nor harvest. [7]God has sent me here to keep you and your families alive so that you will become a great nation. [8]Yes, it was God who sent me here, not you! And he has made me a counselor to Pharaoh—manager of his entire household and ruler over all Egypt.

[9]"Hurry, return to my father and tell him, 'This is what your son Joseph says: God has made me master over all the land of Egypt. Come down to me right away! [10]You will live in the land of Goshen so you can be near me with all your children and grandchildren, your flocks and herds, and all that you have. [11]I will take care of you there, for there are still five years of famine ahead of us. Otherwise you and your household will come to utter poverty.'"

[12]Then Joseph said, "You can see for yourselves, and so can my brother Benjamin, that I really am Joseph! [13]Tell my father how I am honored here in Egypt. Tell him about everything you have seen, and bring him to me quickly." [14]Weeping with joy, he embraced Benjamin, and Benjamin also began to weep. [15]Then Joseph kissed each of his brothers and wept over them, and then they began talking freely with him.

PHARAOH INVITES JACOB TO EGYPT

[16]The news soon reached Pharaoh: "Joseph's brothers have come!" Pharaoh was very happy to hear this and so were his officials.

[17]Pharaoh said to Joseph, "Tell your brothers to load their pack animals and return

quickly to their homes in Canaan. ¹⁸Tell them to bring your father and all of their families, and to come here to Egypt to live. Tell them, 'Pharaoh will assign to you the very best territory in the land of Egypt. You will live off the fat of the land!' ¹⁹And tell your brothers to take wagons from Egypt to carry their wives and little ones and to bring your father here. ²⁰Don't worry about your belongings, for the best of all the land of Egypt is yours."

²¹So the sons of Jacob* did as they were told. Joseph gave them wagons, as Pharaoh had commanded, and he supplied them with provisions for the journey. ²²And he gave each of them new clothes—but to Benjamin he gave five changes of clothes and three hundred pieces* of silver! ²³He sent his father ten donkeys loaded with the good things of Egypt, and ten donkeys loaded with grain and all kinds of other food to be eaten on his journey. ²⁴So he sent his brothers off, and as they left, he called after them, "Don't quarrel along the way!" ²⁵And they left Egypt and returned to their father, Jacob, in the land of Canaan.

²⁶"Joseph is still alive!" they told him. "And he is ruler over all the land of Egypt!" Jacob was stunned at the news—he couldn't believe it. ²⁷But when they had given him Joseph's messages, and when he saw the wagons loaded with the food sent by Joseph, his spirit revived.

²⁸Then Jacob said, "It must be true! My son Joseph is alive! I will go and see him before I die."

JACOB'S JOURNEY TO EGYPT

46 So Jacob* set out for Egypt with all his possessions. And when he came to Beersheba, he offered sacrifices to the God of his father, Isaac. ²During the night God spoke to him in a vision. "Jacob! Jacob!" he called.

"Here I am," Jacob replied.

³"I am God," the voice said, "the God of your father. Do not be afraid to go down to Egypt, for I will see to it that you become a

great nation there. ⁴I will go with you down to Egypt, and I will bring your descendants back again. But you will die in Egypt with Joseph at your side."

⁵So Jacob left Beersheba, and his sons brought him to Egypt. They carried their little ones and wives in the wagons Pharaoh had provided for them. ⁶They brought their livestock, too, and all the belongings they had acquired in the land of Canaan. Jacob and his entire family arrived in Egypt—⁷sons and daughters, grandsons and granddaughters—all his descendants.

⁸These are the names of the Israelites, the descendants of Jacob, who went with him to Egypt:

Reuben was Jacob's oldest son. ⁹The sons of Reuben were Hanoch, Pallu, Hezron, and Carmi.

¹⁰The sons of Simeon were Jemuel, Jamin, Ohad, Jakin, Zohar, and Shaul. (Shaul's mother was a Canaanite woman.)

¹¹The sons of Levi were Gershon, Kohath, and Merari.

¹²The sons of Judah were Er, Onan, Shelah, Perez, and Zerah. (But Er and Onan had died in the land of Canaan.) The sons of Perez were Hezron and Hamul.

¹³The sons of Issachar were Tola, Puah,* Jashub,* and Shimron.

¹⁴The sons of Zebulun were Sered, Elon, and Jahleel.

¹⁵These are the sons of Jacob who were born to Leah in Paddan-aram, along with their sister, Dinah. In all, Jacob's descendants through Leah numbered thirty-three.

¹⁶The sons of Gad were Zephon,* Haggi, Shuni, Ezbon, Eri, Arodi, and Areli.

¹⁷The sons of Asher were Imnah, Ishvah, Ishvi, and Beriah. Their sister was named

---

45:21 Hebrew *Israel;* also in 45:28.   45:22 Hebrew *300 shekels,* about 7.5 pounds or 3.4 kilograms in weight.   46:1 Hebrew *Israel;* also in 46:30.   46:13a As in Syriac version and Samaritan Pentateuch (see also 1 Chr 7:1); Hebrew reads *Puvah.*   46:13b As in some Greek manuscripts and Samaritan Pentateuch (see also Num 26:24; 1 Chr 7:1); Hebrew reads *Iob.*   46:16 As in Greek version and Samaritan Pentateuch (see also Num 26:15); Hebrew reads *Ziphion.*

My Daily Worship

— *January 14* —

RESTORED RELATIONSHIPS

GENESIS 42:1–45:28

Then Joseph kissed each of his brothers and wept over them,
and then they began talking freely with him (45:15).

[i reflect]

Sorrow. Joy. Expressions of deep affection. The flow of earnest conversation.

Today's passage captures the dynamics of a human family. All families experience ups and downs. They can have the potential to bring us some of the greatest happiness we can experience on this side of eternity. They also can cause us the deepest pain.

Families function in very different ways, but by any comparison, Joseph's family was far from typical. He was the favored son out of twelve brothers, and his preferred status created jealousy so intense that his siblings sold him into slavery. Later, after God had brought Joseph into prominence as a ruler in Egypt, he had his brothers at his mercy. He could either pay them back for the years of pain they had caused him, or he could forgive them and restore their shattered family relationship. Joseph chose to forgive.

What kind of selflessness does it take to return good for evil? Where did Joseph find the strength of character to tearfully embrace the very ones who had once left him for dead?

Only a soul refined in the fires of adversity can react in such a way. Throughout the years of slavery, and later imprisonment, Joseph found solace and strength in his relationship with the one family member who never left his side—his heavenly Father. Joseph spent so much time *with* God that the supernatural love *of* God changed him from the inside out. When opportunity came to bless or curse those who had wronged him, Joseph chose blessing.

Look at your personal family relationships in the light of Scripture. Have you allowed old grievances to separate you from the very people you care for most deeply? Spend time *with* God, like Joseph, and allow God's love to change your heart.

[i pray]

Lord, you know I love my family. But I see wounds from family friction that continue to fester.
Show me how I can become an instrument of your peace within my family.

[i respond]

What family member comes to mind when you think of restored relationships? Today, call, write, or e-mail that person who needs to receive God's love and your forgiveness.

Serah. Beriah's sons were Heber and Malkiel.

[18]These sixteen were descendants of Jacob through Zilpah, the servant given to Leah by her father, Laban.

[19]The sons of Jacob's wife Rachel were Joseph and Benjamin.
[20]Joseph's sons, born in the land of Egypt, were Manasseh and Ephraim. Their mother was Asenath, daughter of Potiphera, priest of Heliopolis.*
[21]Benjamin's sons were Bela, Beker, Ashbel, Gera, Naaman, Ehi, Rosh, Muppim, Huppim, and Ard.

[22]These fourteen were the descendants of Jacob and his wife Rachel.

[23]The son of Dan was Hushim.
[24]The sons of Naphtali were Jahzeel, Guni, Jezer, and Shillem.

[25]These seven were the descendants of Jacob through Bilhah, the servant given to Rachel by her father, Laban.

[26]So the total number of Jacob's direct descendants who went with him to Egypt, not counting his sons' wives, was sixty-six. [27]Joseph also had two sons* who had been born in Egypt. So altogether, there were seventy* members of Jacob's family in the land of Egypt.

JACOB'S FAMILY ARRIVES IN GOSHEN

[28]Jacob sent Judah on ahead to meet Joseph and get directions to the land of Goshen. And when they all arrived there, [29]Joseph prepared his chariot and traveled to Goshen to meet his father. As soon as Joseph arrived, he embraced his father and wept on his shoulder for a long time. [30]Then Jacob said to Joseph, "Now let me die, for I have seen you with my own eyes and know you are still alive."

[31]And Joseph said to his brothers and to all their households, "I'll go and tell Pharaoh that you have all come from the land of Canaan to join me. [32]And I will tell him, 'These men are shepherds and livestock breeders. They have brought with them their flocks and herds and everything they own.' [33]So when Pharaoh calls for you and asks you about your occupation, [34]tell him, 'We have been livestock breeders from our youth, as our ancestors have been for many generations.' When you tell him this, he will let you live here in the land of Goshen, for shepherds are despised in the land of Egypt."

JACOB BLESSES PHARAOH

47 So Joseph went to see Pharaoh and said, "My father and my brothers are here from Canaan. They came with all their flocks and herds and possessions, and they are now in the land of Goshen."

[2]Joseph took five of his brothers with him and presented them to Pharaoh. [3]Pharaoh asked them, "What is your occupation?"

And they replied, "We are shepherds like our ancestors. [4]We have come to live here in Egypt, for there is no pasture for our flocks in Canaan. The famine is very severe there. We request permission to live in the land of Goshen."

[5]And Pharaoh said to Joseph, "Now that your family has joined you here, [6]choose any place you like for them to live. Give them the best land of Egypt—the land of Goshen will be fine. And if any of them have special skills, put them in charge of my livestock, too."

[7]Then Joseph brought his father, Jacob, and presented him to Pharaoh, and Jacob blessed Pharaoh. [8]"How old are you?" Pharaoh asked him.

[9]Jacob replied, "I have lived for 130 hard years, but I am still not nearly as old as many of my ancestors." [10]Then Jacob blessed Pharaoh again before he left.

[11]So Joseph assigned the best land of

46:20 Hebrew *of On.*   **46:27a** Greek version reads *nine sons,* probably including Joseph's grandsons through Ephraim and Manasseh (see 1 Chr 7:14-20).   **46:27b** Greek version reads *seventy-five;* see note on Exod 1:5.

Egypt—the land of Rameses to his father and brothers, just as Pharaoh had commanded. [12]And Joseph furnished food to his father and brothers in amounts appropriate to the number of their dependents.

JOSEPH'S LEADERSHIP IN THE FAMINE

[13]Meanwhile, the famine became worse and worse, and the crops continued to fail throughout Egypt and Canaan. [14]Joseph collected all the money in Egypt and Canaan in exchange for grain, and he brought the money to Pharaoh's treasure-house. [15]When the people of Egypt and Canaan ran out of money, they came to Joseph crying again for food. "Our money is gone," they said, "but give us bread. Why should we die?"

[16]"Well, then," Joseph replied, "since your money is gone, give me your livestock. I will give you food in exchange." [17]So they gave their livestock to Joseph in exchange for food. Soon all the horses, flocks, herds, and donkeys of Egypt were in Pharaoh's possession. But at least they were able to purchase food for that year.

[18]The next year they came again and said, "Our money is gone, and our livestock are yours. We have nothing left but our bodies and land. [19]Why should we die before your very eyes? Buy us and our land in exchange for food; we will then become servants to Pharaoh. Just give us grain so that our lives may be saved and so the land will not become empty and desolate."

[20]So Joseph bought all the land of Egypt for Pharaoh. All the Egyptians sold him their fields because the famine was so severe, and their land then belonged to Pharaoh. [21]Thus, all the people of Egypt became servants to Pharaoh.* [22]The only land he didn't buy was that belonging to the priests, for they were assigned food from Pharaoh and didn't need to sell their land.

[23]Then Joseph said to the people, "See, I have bought you and your land for Pharaoh. I will provide you with seed, so you can plant the fields. [24]Then when you harvest it, a fifth of your crop will belong to Pharaoh. Keep four-fifths for yourselves, and use it to plant the next year's crop and to feed yourselves, your households, and your little ones."

Words of Worship

ADORE, ADORATION

Adore, Adoration—These English words come from the Latin *adorare*, to honor or pay homage to a divinity. No biblical word specifically means "adore," although translators might use a form of the English word as a synonym for another expression of worship, such as the lifting up of praise (1 Chronicles 29:11).

When the Lord touches our lives in a deeply personal way, our response can also be deeply personal. Life may seem hopeless, the future uncertain. We may be fighting what seems like a losing battle with guilt, with emotional or even physical pain. Suddenly, with a touch from God or from his Word, everything changes. Or maybe we simply come to a point in life's journey where the goodness and love of God opens up in a new way, and we realize how great he is. Life is renewed.

At such times, we respond with adoration, a worship of special intensity. Like the woman who anointed Jesus' feet because she knew her sins were forgiven (Luke 7:38), we're overwhelmed with thanksgiving and love for our Redeemer. We find ourselves, as the hymn says, "lost in wonder, love, and praise." The greater our need, the more we adore God when he meets us and sets us free.

47:21 As in Greek version and Samaritan Pentateuch; Hebrew reads *He moved the people into the towns throughout the land of Egypt.*

²⁵"You have saved our lives!" they exclaimed. "May it please you, sir, to let us be Pharaoh's servants." ²⁶Joseph then made it a law throughout the land of Egypt—and it is still the law—that Pharaoh should receive one-fifth of all the crops grown on his land. But since Pharaoh had not taken over the priests' land, they were exempt from this payment.

²⁷So the people of Israel settled in the land of Goshen in Egypt. And before long, they began to prosper there, and their population grew rapidly. ²⁸Jacob lived for seventeen years after his arrival in Egypt, so he was 147 years old when he died. ²⁹As the time of his death drew near, he called for his son Joseph and said to him, "If you are pleased with me, swear most solemnly that you will honor this, my last request: Do not bury me in Egypt. ³⁰When I am dead, take me out of Egypt and bury me beside my ancestors." So Joseph promised that he would. ³¹"Swear that you will do it," Jacob insisted. So Joseph gave his oath, and Jacob* bowed in worship as he leaned on his staff.*

JACOB BLESSES MANASSEH AND EPHRAIM

48 One day not long after this, word came to Joseph that his father was failing rapidly. So Joseph went to visit him, and he took with him his two sons, Manasseh and Ephraim. ²When Jacob heard that Joseph had arrived, he gathered his strength and sat up in bed to greet him.

³Jacob said to Joseph, "God Almighty appeared to me at Luz in the land of Canaan and blessed me. ⁴He said to me, 'I will make you a multitude of nations, and I will give this land of Canaan to you and your descendants as an everlasting possession.' ⁵Now I am adopting as my own sons these two boys of yours, Ephraim and Manasseh, who were born here in the land of Egypt before I arrived. They will inherit from me just as Reuben and Simeon will. ⁶But the children born to you in the future will be your own.

> We are called to an everlasting preoccupation with God.
>
> A.W. TOZER

The land they inherit will be within the territories of Ephraim and Manasseh. ⁷As I was returning from Paddan, Rachel died in the land of Canaan. We were still on the way, just a short distance from Ephrath (that is, Bethlehem). So with great sorrow I buried her there beside the road to Ephrath."

⁸Then Jacob* looked over at the two boys. "Are these your sons?" he asked.

⁹"Yes," Joseph told him, "these are the sons God has given me here in Egypt."

And Jacob said, "Bring them over to me, and I will bless them."

¹⁰Now Jacob was half blind because of his age and could hardly see. So Joseph brought the boys close to him, and Jacob kissed and embraced them. ¹¹Then Jacob said to Joseph, "I never thought I would see you again, but now God has let me see your children, too."

¹²Joseph took the boys from their grandfather's knees, and he bowed low to him. ¹³Then he positioned the boys so Ephraim was at Jacob's left hand and Manasseh was at his right hand. ¹⁴But Jacob crossed his arms as he reached out to lay his hands on the boys' heads. So his right hand was on the head of Ephraim, the younger boy, and his left hand was on the head of Manasseh, the older.

¹⁵Then he blessed Joseph and said, "May God, the God before whom my grandfather Abraham and my father, Isaac, walked, the God who has been my shepherd all my life,

---

47:31a Hebrew *Israel.*   47:31b As in Greek version; Hebrew reads *bowed in worship at the head of his bed.*   48:8 Hebrew *Israel;* also in 48:10, 11, 13, 14, 21.

¹⁶and the angel who has kept me from all harm—may he bless these boys. May they preserve my name and the names of my grandfather Abraham and my father, Isaac. And may they become a mighty nation."

¹⁷But Joseph was upset when he saw that his father had laid his right hand on Ephraim's head. So he lifted it to place it on Manasseh's head instead. ¹⁸"No, Father," he said, "this one over here is older. Put your right hand on his head."

¹⁹But his father refused. "I know what I'm doing, my son," he said. "Manasseh, too, will become a great people, but his younger brother will become even greater. His descendants will become a multitude of nations!" ²⁰So Jacob blessed the boys that day with this blessing: "The people of Israel will use your names to bless each other. They will say, 'May God make you as prosperous as Ephraim and Manasseh.' " In this way, Jacob put Ephraim ahead of Manasseh.

²¹Then Jacob said to Joseph, "I am about to die, but God will be with you and will bring you again to Canaan, the land of your ancestors. ²²And I give you an extra portion* beyond what I have given your brothers—the portion that I took from the Amorites with my sword and bow."

Jacob Blesses His Sons

49 Then Jacob called together all his sons and said, "Gather around me, and I will tell you what is going to happen to you in the days to come.

² "Come and listen, O sons of Jacob;
   listen to Israel, your father.

³ "Reuben, you are my oldest son,
   the child of my vigorous youth.
   You are first on the list in rank and honor.
⁴ But you are as unruly as the waves of the
      sea,
   and you will be first no longer.

For you slept with one of my wives;
   you dishonored me in my own bed.

⁵ "Simeon and Levi are two of a kind—
   men of violence.
⁶ O my soul, stay away from them.
   May I never be a party to their wicked
      plans.
For in their anger they murdered men,
   and they crippled oxen just for sport.
⁷ Cursed be their anger, for it is fierce;
   cursed be their wrath, for it is cruel.
Therefore, I will scatter their descendants
   throughout the nation of Israel.

⁸ "Judah, your brothers will praise you.
   You will defeat your enemies.
   All your relatives will bow before you.
⁹ Judah is a young lion
      that has finished eating its prey.
Like a lion he crouches and lies down;
   like a lioness—who will dare to rouse
      him?
¹⁰ The scepter will not depart from Judah,
   nor the ruler's staff from his descen-
      dants,
until the coming of the one to whom it
      belongs,*
   the one whom all nations will obey.
¹¹ He ties his foal to a grapevine,
   the colt of his donkey to a choice vine.
He washes his clothes in wine
   because his harvest is so plentiful.
¹² His eyes are darker than wine,
   and his teeth are whiter than milk.

¹³ "Zebulun will settle on the shores
      of the sea
   and will be a harbor for ships;
   his borders will extend to Sidon.

¹⁴ "Issachar is a strong beast of burden,
   resting among the sheepfolds.*
¹⁵ When he sees how good the countryside is,
   how pleasant the land,

48:22 Or *give you the ridge of land.* The meaning of the Hebrew is uncertain. 49:10 Or *until tribute is brought to him and the peoples obey;* traditionally rendered *until Shiloh comes.* 49:14 Or *saddlebags,* or *hearths.*

he will bend his shoulder to the task
and submit to forced labor.

16 "Dan will govern his people
like any other tribe in Israel.
17 He will be a snake beside the road,
a poisonous viper along the path,
that bites the horse's heels
so the rider is thrown off.
18 I trust in you for salvation, O LORD!

19 "Gad will be plundered by marauding
bands,
but he will turn and plunder them.

20 "Asher will produce rich foods,
food fit for kings.

21 "Naphtali is a deer let loose,
producing magnificent fawns.

22 "Joseph is a fruitful tree,
a fruitful tree beside a fountain.
His branches reach over the wall.
23 He has been attacked by archers,
who shot at him and harassed him.
24 But his bow remained strong,
and his arms were strengthened
by the Mighty One of Jacob,
the Shepherd, the Rock of Israel.
25 May the God of your ancestors help you;
may the Almighty bless you
with the blessings of the heavens above,
blessings of the earth beneath,
and blessings of the breasts and womb.
26 May the blessings of your ancestors
be greater than the blessings of the
eternal mountains,
reaching to the utmost bounds of the
everlasting hills.
These blessings will fall on the head of
Joseph,
who is a prince among his brothers.

27 "Benjamin is a wolf that prowls.
He devours his enemies in the morning,

and in the evening he divides the
plunder."

28 These are the twelve tribes of Israel, and
these are the blessings with which Jacob*
blessed his twelve sons. Each received a blessing that was appropriate to him.

JACOB'S DEATH AND BURIAL

29 Then Jacob told them, "Soon I will die. Bury
me with my father and grandfather in the cave
in Ephron's field. 30 This is the cave in the field
of Machpelah, near Mamre in Canaan, which
Abraham bought from Ephron the Hittite for
a permanent burial place. 31 There Abraham
and his wife Sarah are buried. There Isaac and
his wife, Rebekah, are buried. And there I
buried Leah. 32 It is the cave that my grandfather Abraham bought from the Hittites."
33 Then when Jacob had finished this charge to
his sons, he lay back in the bed, breathed his
last, and died.

50 Joseph threw himself on his father and
wept over him and kissed him. 2 Then
Joseph told his morticians to embalm the
body. 3 The embalming process took forty
days, and there was a period of national
mourning for seventy days. 4 When the period
of mourning was over, Joseph approached Pharaoh's advisers and asked them to speak to
Pharaoh on his behalf. 5 He told them, "Tell
Pharaoh that my father made me swear an
oath. He said to me, 'I am about to die; take
my body back to the land of Canaan, and bury
me in our family's burial cave.' Now I need to
go and bury my father. After his burial is complete, I will return without delay."

6 Pharaoh agreed to Joseph's request. "Go
and bury your father, as you promised," he
said. 7 So Joseph went, with a great number of
Pharaoh's counselors and advisers—all the
senior officers of Egypt. 8 Joseph also took his
brothers and the entire household of Jacob.
But they left their little children and flocks
and herds in the land of Goshen. 9 So a great

49:28 Hebrew *Israel.*

My Daily Worship

— January 15 —

SITUATION UNDER CONTROL

GENESIS 46:1–50:26

As far as I am concerned, God turned into good what you meant for evil. He brought me
to the high position I have today so I could save the lives of many people (50:20).

[i reflect]

The world seems so out of control—careening through the corridors of time, a colossal accident looking for a time and place to finally happen. Do you get this same feeling when reading the morning paper or watching a nightly newscast?

And don't our individual lives often feel the same way? An unexpected pink slip. A spouse announcing his or her intention to leave. A child in trouble. A job transfer. A heart-stopping lab result. A church split. Events like these suddenly sweep us up and carry us along, and God only knows where we'll end up.

This is the lesson of Joseph's life. And it is the message of Joseph's lips. Sold into slavery as a teenager by his jealous brothers. Taken to a foreign land. Falsely accused of attempted rape. Thrown into an Egyptian dungeon. Forgotten. Can it get any worse? Why? Where is God in all this chaos and injustice?

Answer: He's watching. Working. Writing a masterpiece. Weaving all these jumbled, seemingly random events together into a purposeful, beautiful whole. And just when we think evil really has won, God orchestrates the ultimate plot twist. Joseph is inexplicably rescued from the depths and set in a position where he is able to save his speechless brothers and devastated father.

Our great challenge today and every day is to look beyond and behind events to the One who controls all things. As you listen, read, or watch the news today, use it as a springboard to worship. Thank God that in the reports of chaos and evil, he is working out his good purposes in the world and in your life.

[i pray]

Lord, grant that, regardless of my circumstances, I might truly believe that you are in control,
and further, that I might trust you—in your way and your time—
to give meaning and purpose to my pain.

[i respond]

Grab a hymnbook and your journal. Go to a quiet, lonely place. Once there, lift up your biggest, current crisis to God in prayer. And then, by faith (regardless of your feelings), commit to worship God. Thank God in prayer. Worship him in song. Record your "worship service" in your journal.

number of chariots, cavalry, and people accompanied Joseph.

[10]When they arrived at the threshing floor of Atad, near the Jordan River, they held a very great and solemn funeral, with a seven-day period of mourning for Joseph's father. [11]The local residents, the Canaanites, renamed the place Abel-mizraim,* for they said, "This is a place of very deep mourning for these Egyptians." [12]So Jacob's sons did as he had commanded them. [13]They carried his body to the land of Canaan and buried it there in the cave of Machpelah. This is the cave that Abraham had bought for a permanent burial place in the field of Ephron the Hittite, near Mamre.

JOSEPH REASSURES HIS BROTHERS

[14]Then Joseph returned to Egypt with his brothers and all who had accompanied him to his father's funeral. [15]But now that their father was dead, Joseph's brothers became afraid. "Now Joseph will pay us back for all the evil we did to him," they said. [16]So they sent this message to Joseph: "Before your father died, he instructed us [17]to say to you: 'Forgive your brothers for the great evil they did to you.' So we, the servants of the God of your father, beg you to forgive us." When Joseph received the message, he broke down and wept. [18]Then his

brothers came and bowed low before him. "We are your slaves," they said.

[19]But Joseph told them, "Don't be afraid of me. Am I God, to judge and punish you? [20]As far as I am concerned, God turned into good what you meant for evil. He brought me to the high position I have today so I could save the lives of many people. [21]No, don't be afraid. Indeed, I myself will take care of you and your families." And he spoke very kindly to them, reassuring them.

THE DEATH OF JOSEPH

[22]So Joseph and his brothers and their families continued to live in Egypt. Joseph was 110 years old when he died. [23]He lived to see three generations of descendants of his son Ephraim and the children of Manasseh's son Makir, who were treated as if they were his own.

[24]"Soon I will die," Joseph told his brothers, "but God will surely come for you, to lead you out of this land of Egypt. He will bring you back to the land he vowed to give to the descendants of Abraham, Isaac, and Jacob."

[25]Then Joseph made the sons of Israel swear an oath, and he said, "When God comes to lead us back to Canaan, you must take my body back with you." [26]So Joseph died at the age of 110. They embalmed him, and his body was placed in a coffin in Egypt.

50:11 *Abel-mizraim* means "mourning of the Egyptians."

Exodus

I am the LORD your God, who rescued you from slavery in Egypt.

Do not worship any other gods besides me (20:2–3).

"Let My People Go!"

Exodus (which means "to go forth" or "to depart") is the story of a people rescued through the blood of a sacrificial lamb, breaking the bonds of slavery to worship the God who rescued them, and then being taught how to worship him. It is a book detailing some of the essential elements of worship: trusting, leaving, listening, and obeying. The Israelites had to trust both Moses, their leader, and their God, to lead them safely out of Egypt. Once out, they had to leave their old ways and adopt the Lord's ways. They had to listen to God's instructions about how to live and worship. And, finally, they had to obey.

Throughout their journey—from experiencing the first Passover, to witnessing the incredible power of a God who could part the seas, to seeing his daily provision of food and water—the Israelites witnessed many miracles. Worship flowed out of their experiences, until the next crisis came along and they had forgotten who had provided for them.

We are no different from the Israelites. We get engrossed in our own concerns and forget what God has done for us, just as they did. God had to constantly remind them to seek his presence (16:9). He even gave them specific ways to help them worship him: a weekly holy day (16:5; 20:8–10); a covenant making them his holy nation (19:5); holy laws to live by (chapters 20–23); a holy place to worship (chapters 35–39), and special people—priests—were set apart to serve God (28:2–43).

Exodus is filled with detailed instructions about worship. All these details show us that God desires worship from us; worship that can be as diverse in its expression as the various talents each one of us brings to that worship.

Worship Moments

- Moses led the Israelites in a song praising God for rescuing them from slavery and from the pursuing Egyptian army (15:1–18). Miriam then took a tambourine and led the women in rhythm and dance as she sang a song of praise to the Lord (15:20–21).

- Recognizing God's awesome power is an essential element of worship (20:20).

- The Lord descended in a cloud, stood with Moses, and then passed before him, identifying himself as "the LORD." Moses fell to the ground in worship (34:5–7).

- God's character is revealed through his many names: "I AM WHO I AM" or "I WILL BE WHAT I WILL BE" (3:14); "The LORD Is My Banner"—*Yahweh Nissi* (17:5); "I am the merciful and gracious God" (34:6).

THE ISRAELITES IN EGYPT

1 These are the sons of Jacob* who went with their father to Egypt, each with his family: ²Reuben, Simeon, Levi, Judah, ³Issachar, Zebulun, Benjamin, ⁴Dan, Naphtali, Gad, and Asher. ⁵Joseph was already down in Egypt. In all, Jacob had seventy* direct descendants.

⁶In time, Joseph and each of his brothers died, ending that generation. ⁷But their descendants had many children and grandchildren. In fact, they multiplied so quickly that they soon filled the land. ⁸Then a new king came to the throne of Egypt who knew nothing about Joseph or what he had done. ⁹He told his people, "These Israelites are becoming a threat to us because there are so many of them. ¹⁰We must find a way to put an end to this. If we don't and if war breaks out, they will join our enemies and fight against us. Then they will escape from the country."

¹¹So the Egyptians made the Israelites their slaves and put brutal slave drivers over them, hoping to wear them down under heavy burdens. They forced them to build the cities of Pithom and Rameses as supply centers for the king. ¹²But the more the Egyptians oppressed them, the more quickly the Israelites multiplied! The Egyptians soon became alarmed ¹³and decided to make their slavery more bitter still. ¹⁴They were ruthless with the Israelites, forcing them to make bricks and mortar and to work long hours in the fields.

¹⁵Then Pharaoh, the king of Egypt, gave this order to the Hebrew midwives, Shiphrah and Puah: ¹⁶"When you help the Hebrew women give birth, kill all the boys as soon as they are born. Allow only the baby girls to live." ¹⁷But because the midwives feared God, they refused to obey the king and allowed the boys to live, too.

¹⁸Then the king called for the midwives. "Why have you done this?" he demanded. "Why have you allowed the boys to live?"

¹⁹"Sir," they told him, "the Hebrew women are very strong. They have their babies so quickly that we cannot get there in time! They are not slow in giving birth like Egyptian women."

²⁰So God blessed the midwives, and the Israelites continued to multiply, growing more and more powerful. ²¹And because the midwives feared God, he gave them families of their own.

²²Then Pharaoh gave this order to all his people: "Throw all the newborn Israelite boys into the Nile River. But you may spare the baby girls."

THE BIRTH OF MOSES

2 During this time, a man and woman from the tribe of Levi got married. ²The woman became pregnant and gave birth to a son. She saw what a beautiful baby he was and kept him hidden for three months. ³But when she could no longer hide him, she got a little basket made of papyrus reeds and waterproofed it with tar and pitch. She put the baby in the basket and laid it among the reeds along the edge of the Nile River. ⁴The baby's sister then stood at a distance, watching to see what would happen to him.

⁵Soon after this, one of Pharaoh's daughters came down to bathe in the river, and her servant girls walked along the riverbank. When the princess saw the little basket among the reeds, she told one of her servant girls to get it for her. ⁶As the princess opened it, she found the baby boy. His helpless cries touched her heart. "He must be one of the Hebrew children," she said.

⁷Then the baby's sister approached the princess. "Should I go and find one of the Hebrew women to nurse the baby for you?" she asked.

⁸"Yes, do!" the princess replied. So the girl rushed home and called the baby's mother.

⁹"Take this child home and nurse him for me," the princess told her. "I will pay you for your help." So the baby's mother took her baby home and nursed him.

1:1 Hebrew *Israel*.   1:5 Dead Sea Scrolls and Greek version read *seventy-five*; see notes on Gen 46:27.

[10]Later, when he was older, the child's mother brought him back to the princess, who adopted him as her son. The princess named him Moses,* for she said, "I drew him out of the water."

MOSES ESCAPES TO MIDIAN

[11]Many years later, when Moses had grown up, he went out to visit his people, the Israelites, and he saw how hard they were forced to work. During his visit, he saw an Egyptian beating one of the Hebrew slaves. [12]After looking around to make sure no one was watching, Moses killed the Egyptian and buried him in the sand.

[13]The next day, as Moses was out visiting his people again, he saw two Hebrew men fighting. "What are you doing, hitting your neighbor like that?" Moses said to the one in the wrong.

[14]"Who do you think you are?" the man replied. "Who appointed you to be our prince and judge? Do you plan to kill me as you killed that Egyptian yesterday?"

Moses was badly frightened because he realized that everyone knew what he had done. [15]And sure enough, when Pharaoh heard about it, he gave orders to have Moses arrested and killed. But Moses fled from Pharaoh and escaped to the land of Midian.

When Moses arrived in Midian, he sat down beside a well. [16]Now it happened that the priest of Midian had seven daughters who came regularly to this well to draw water and fill the water troughs for their father's flocks. [17]But other shepherds would often come and chase the girls and their flocks away. This time, however, Moses came to their aid, rescuing the girls from the shepherds. Then he helped them draw water for their flocks.

[18]When the girls returned to Reuel, their father, he asked, "How did you get the flocks watered so quickly today?"

[19]"An Egyptian rescued us from the shepherds," they told him. "And then he drew water for us and watered our flocks."

[20]"Well, where is he then?" their father asked. "Did you just leave him there? Go and invite him home for a meal!"

[21]Moses was happy to accept the invitation, and he settled down to live with them. In time, Reuel gave Moses one of his daughters, Zipporah, to be his wife. [22]Later they had a baby boy, and Moses named him Gershom,* for he said, "I have been a stranger in a foreign land."

[23]Years passed, and the king of Egypt died. But the Israelites still groaned beneath their burden of slavery. They cried out for help, and their pleas for deliverance rose up to God. [24]God heard their cries and remembered his covenant promise to Abraham, Isaac, and Jacob. [25]He looked down on the Israelites and felt deep concern for their welfare.

MOSES AND THE BURNING BUSH

3 One day Moses was tending the flock of his father-in-law, Jethro,* the priest of Midian, and he went deep into the wilderness near Sinai,* the mountain of God. [2]Suddenly, the angel of the LORD appeared to him as a blazing fire in a bush. Moses was amazed because the bush was engulfed in flames, but it didn't burn up. [3]"Amazing!" Moses said to himself. "Why isn't that bush burning up? I must go over to see this."

[4]When the LORD saw that he had caught Moses' attention, God called to him from the bush, "Moses! Moses!"

"Here I am!" Moses replied.

[5]"Do not come any closer," God told him. "Take off your sandals, for you are standing on holy ground." [6]Then he said, "I am the God of your ancestors—the God of Abraham, the God of Isaac, and the God of Jacob." When Moses heard this, he hid his face in his hands because he was afraid to look at God.

[7]Then the LORD told him, "You can be sure I have seen the misery of my people in Egypt.

2:10 Moses sounds like a Hebrew term that means "to draw out." 2:22 Gershom sounds like a Hebrew term that means "a stranger there." 3:1a Moses' father-in-law went by two names, Jethro and Reuel. 3:1b Hebrew *Horeb,* another name for Sinai.

I have heard their cries for deliverance from their harsh slave drivers. Yes, I am aware of their suffering. [8]So I have come to rescue them from the Egyptians and lead them out of Egypt into their own good and spacious land. It is a land flowing with milk and honey—the land where the Canaanites, Hittites, Amorites, Perizzites, Hivites, and Jebusites live. [9]The cries of the people of Israel have reached me, and I have seen how the Egyptians have oppressed them with heavy tasks. [10]Now go, for I am sending you to Pharaoh. You will lead my people, the Israelites, out of Egypt."

[11]"But who am I to appear before Pharaoh?" Moses asked God. "How can you expect me to lead the Israelites out of Egypt?"

[12]Then God told him, "I will be with you. And this will serve as proof that I have sent you: When you have brought the Israelites out of Egypt, you will return here to worship God at this very mountain."

[13]But Moses protested, "If I go to the people of Israel and tell them, 'The God of your ancestors has sent me to you,' they won't believe me. They will ask, 'Which god are you talking about? What is his name?' Then what should I tell them?"

[14]God replied, "I AM THE ONE WHO ALWAYS IS.* Just tell them, 'I AM has sent me to you.' " [15]God also said, "Tell them, 'THE LORD,* the God of your ancestors—the God of Abraham, the God of Isaac, and the God of Jacob—has sent me to you.' This will be my name forever; it has always been my name, and it will be used throughout all generations.

[16]"Now go and call together all the leaders of Israel. Tell them, 'The LORD, the God of your ancestors—the God of Abraham, Isaac, and Jacob—appeared to me in a burning bush. He said, "You can be sure that I am watching over you and have seen what is happening to you in Egypt. [17]I promise to rescue you from the oppression of the Egyptians. I will lead you to the land now occupied by the Canaanites, Hittites, Amorites, Perizzites, Hivites, and Jebusites—a land flowing with milk and honey." '

[18]"The leaders of the people of Israel will accept your message. Then all of you must go straight to the king of Egypt and tell him, 'The LORD, the God of the Hebrews, has met with us. Let us go on a three-day journey into the wilderness to offer sacrifices to the LORD our God.'

[19]"But I know that the king of Egypt will not let you go except under heavy pressure. [20]So I will reach out and strike at the heart of Egypt with all kinds of miracles. Then at last he will let you go. [21]And I will see to it that the Egyptians treat you well. They will load you down with gifts so you will not leave empty-handed. [22]The Israelite women will ask for silver and gold jewelry and fine clothing from their Egyptian neighbors and their neighbors' guests. With this clothing, you will dress your sons and daughters. In this way, you will plunder the Egyptians!"

SIGNS OF THE LORD'S POWER

4 But Moses protested again, "Look, they won't believe me! They won't do what I tell them. They'll just say, 'The LORD never appeared to you.' "

[2]Then the LORD asked him, "What do you have there in your hand?"

"A shepherd's staff," Moses replied.

[3]"Throw it down on the ground," the LORD told him. So Moses threw it down, and it became a snake! Moses was terrified, so he turned and ran away.

[4]Then the LORD told him, "Take hold of its tail." So Moses reached out and grabbed it, and it became a shepherd's staff again.

[5]"Perform this sign, and they will believe you," the LORD told him. "Then they will realize that the LORD, the God of their ancestors—the God of Abraham, the God of Isaac, and the God of Jacob—really has appeared to you."

[6]Then the LORD said to Moses, "Put your

3:14 Or I AM WHO I AM, or I WILL BE WHAT I WILL BE.   3:15 Hebrew Yahweh; traditionally rendered Jehovah.

My Daily Worship

— January 16 —

LOOKING FOR HOLY GROUND?

EXODUS 1:1–4:31

When the LORD saw that he had caught Moses' attention, God called to him from the bush,
"Moses! Moses!" "Here I am!" Moses replied. "Do not come any closer," God told him.
"Take off your sandals, for you are standing on holy ground" (3:4–5).

[i reflect]

Moses wasn't looking for God in the wilderness. He wouldn't have known what to look for. God found *him*. In fact, it took a huge flashing spectacle just to catch Moses' attention. God's gesture gave Moses a gateway to step into a place of true worship. Thankfully, in today's world where our jobs and families, the phone and TV, battle for our time, God still seeks to gain our attention.

We often think that if God is present, believers should notice him. Moses should have sensed he was on holy ground, right? But the act of "coming into God's presence" doesn't mean discerning God's specific location. We take the first step towards worship each time we become aware that God constantly surrounds us.

Moses' sudden awareness of God's presence *preceded* his training in worship. Out of our desire to worship, we often rush to manufacture forms and feelings of worship. We're missing out on the real thing. Our "It's Sunday, let's worship" attitude skips an important step. Like Moses, our worship only begins after we recognize God and attune our hearts to listen.

Looking for holy ground? God will direct you to that place of worship in the most unexpected times. Be ready to turn your attention to him. Let him change the way you look at your surroundings and the task at hand. You'll see things you might have missed. When you allow God to pervade your office, your car, your daily routine, you'll realize that you've been occupying God's ground the whole time—a place that he's already sanctified for his work.

[i pray]

Throughout my day, Lord, help me to keep watch for your guiding hand. When you do display yourself,
let me be as courageous as Moses in coming into your presence, shouting "Here I am!"

[i respond]

What specific things move your attention away from worshiping God? In what ways can you prepare yourself to meet him during the week? If you struggle to find true worship, take a step back and listen for God's direction.

hand inside your robe." Moses did so, and when he took it out again, his hand was white as snow with leprosy.* ⁷"Now put your hand back into your robe again," the LORD said. Moses did, and when he took it out this time, it was as healthy as the rest of his body.

⁸"If they do not believe the first miraculous sign, they will believe the second," the LORD said. ⁹"And if they do not believe you even after these two signs, then take some water from the Nile River and pour it out on the dry ground. When you do, it will turn into blood."

¹⁰But Moses pleaded with the LORD, "O Lord, I'm just not a good speaker. I never have been, and I'm not now, even after you have spoken to me. I'm clumsy with words."

¹¹"Who makes mouths?" the LORD asked him. "Who makes people so they can speak or not speak, hear or not hear, see or not see? Is it not I, the LORD? ¹²Now go, and do as I have told you. I will help you speak well, and I will tell you what to say."

¹³But Moses again pleaded, "Lord, please! Send someone else."

¹⁴Then the LORD became angry with Moses. "All right," he said. "What about your brother, Aaron the Levite? He is a good speaker. And look! He is on his way to meet you now. And when he sees you, he will be very glad. ¹⁵You will talk to him, giving him the words to say. I will help both of you to speak clearly, and I will tell you what to do. ¹⁶Aaron will be your spokesman to the people, and you will be as God to him, telling him what to say. ¹⁷And be sure to take your shepherd's staff along so you can perform the miraculous signs I have shown you."

MOSES RETURNS TO EGYPT

¹⁸Then Moses went back home and talked it over with Jethro, his father-in-law. "With your permission," Moses said, "I would like to go back to Egypt to visit my family. I don't even know whether they are still alive."

"Go with my blessing," Jethro replied.

¹⁹Before Moses left Midian, the LORD said to him, "Do not be afraid to return to Egypt, for all those who wanted to kill you are dead."

²⁰So Moses took his wife and sons, put them on a donkey, and headed back to the land of Egypt. In his hand he carried the staff of God.

²¹Then the LORD reminded him, "When you arrive back in Egypt, go to Pharaoh and perform the miracles I have empowered you to do. But I will make him stubborn so he will not let the people go. ²²Then you will tell him, 'This is what the LORD says: Israel is my firstborn son. ²³I commanded you to let him go, so he could worship me. But since you have refused, be warned! I will kill your firstborn son!'"

²⁴On the journey, when Moses and his family had stopped for the night, the LORD confronted Moses* and was about to kill him. ²⁵But Zipporah, his wife, took a flint knife and circumcised her son. She threw the foreskin at Moses' feet and said, "What a blood-smeared bridegroom you are to me!" ²⁶(When she called Moses a "blood-smeared bridegroom," she was referring to the circumcision.) After that, the LORD left him alone.

²⁷Now the LORD had said to Aaron, "Go out into the wilderness to meet Moses." So Aaron traveled to the mountain of God, where he found Moses and greeted him warmly. ²⁸Moses then told Aaron everything the LORD had commanded them to do and say. And he told him about the miraculous signs they were to perform.

²⁹So Moses and Aaron returned to Egypt and called the leaders of Israel to a meeting. ³⁰Aaron told them everything the LORD had told Moses, and Moses performed the miraculous signs as they watched. ³¹The leaders were soon convinced that the LORD had sent Moses and Aaron. And when they realized that the LORD had seen their misery and was deeply concerned for them, they all bowed their heads and worshiped.

4:6 Or *with a contagious skin disease.* The Hebrew word used here can describe various skin diseases. 4:24 Or *confronted Moses' son;* Hebrew reads *confronted him.*

MOSES AND AARON SPEAK TO PHARAOH

5 After this presentation to Israel's leaders, Moses and Aaron went to see Pharaoh. They told him, "This is what the LORD, the God of Israel, says: 'Let my people go, for they must go out into the wilderness to hold a religious festival in my honor.'"

²"Is that so?" retorted Pharaoh. "And who is the LORD that I should listen to him and let Israel go? I don't know the LORD, and I will not let Israel go."

³But Aaron and Moses persisted. "The God of the Hebrews has met with us," they declared. "Let us take a three-day trip into the wilderness so we can offer sacrifices to the LORD our God. If we don't, we will surely die by disease or the sword."

⁴"Who do you think you are," Pharaoh shouted, "distracting the people from their tasks? Get back to work! ⁵Look, there are many people here in Egypt, and you are stopping them from doing their work."

MAKING BRICKS WITHOUT STRAW

⁶That same day Pharaoh sent this order to the slave drivers and foremen he had set over the people of Israel: ⁷"Do not supply the people with any more straw for making bricks. Let them get it themselves! ⁸But don't reduce their production quotas by a single brick. They obviously don't have enough to do. If they did, they wouldn't be talking about going into the wilderness to offer sacrifices to their God. ⁹Load them down with more work. Make them sweat! That will teach them to listen to these liars!"

¹⁰So the slave drivers and foremen informed the people: "Pharaoh has ordered us not to provide straw for you. ¹¹Go and get it yourselves. Find it wherever you can. But you must produce just as many bricks as before!" ¹²So the people scattered throughout the land in search of straw.

¹³The slave drivers were brutal. "Meet your daily quota of bricks, just as you did before!" they demanded. ¹⁴Then they whipped the Israelite foremen in charge of the work crews. "Why haven't you met your quotas either yesterday or today?" they demanded.

¹⁵So the Israelite foremen went to Pharaoh and pleaded with him. "Please don't treat us like this," they begged. ¹⁶"We are given no straw, but we are still told to make as many bricks as before. We are beaten for something that isn't our fault! It is the fault of your slave drivers for making such unreasonable demands."

¹⁷But Pharaoh replied, "You're just lazy! You obviously don't have enough to do. If you did, you wouldn't be saying, 'Let us go, so we can offer sacrifices to the LORD.' ¹⁸Now, get back to work! No straw will be given to you, but you must still deliver the regular quota of bricks."

¹⁹Since Pharaoh would not let up on his demands, the Israelite foremen could see that they were in serious trouble. ²⁰As they left Pharaoh's court, they met Moses and Aaron, who were waiting outside for them. ²¹The foremen said to them, "May the LORD judge you for getting us into this terrible situation with Pharaoh* and his officials. You have given them an excuse to kill us!"

²²So Moses went back to the LORD and protested, "Why have you mistreated your own people like this, Lord? Why did you send me? ²³Since I gave Pharaoh your message, he has been even more brutal to your people. You have not even begun to rescue them!"

PROMISES OF DELIVERANCE

6 "Now you will see what I will do to Pharaoh," the LORD told Moses. "When he feels my powerful hand upon him, he will let the people go. In fact, he will be so anxious to get rid of them that he will force them to leave his land!"

²And God continued, "I am the LORD. ³I appeared to Abraham, to Isaac, and to Jacob

---

5:21 Hebrew *for making us a stench in the nostrils of Pharaoh.*

as God Almighty,* though I did not reveal my name, the LORD,* to them. 4And I entered into a solemn covenant with them. Under its terms, I swore to give them the land of Canaan, where they were living. 5You can be sure that I have heard the groans of the people of Israel, who are now slaves to the Egyptians. I have remembered my covenant with them.

6"Therefore, say to the Israelites: 'I am the LORD, and I will free you from your slavery in Egypt. I will redeem you with mighty power and great acts of judgment. 7I will make you my own special people, and I will be your God. And you will know that I am the LORD your God who has rescued you from your slavery in Egypt. 8I will bring you into the land I swore to give to Abraham, Isaac, and Jacob. It will be your very own property. I am the LORD!'"

9So Moses told the people what the LORD had said, but they wouldn't listen anymore. They had become too discouraged by the increasing burden of their slavery.

10Then the LORD said to Moses, 11"Go back to Pharaoh, and tell him to let the people of Israel leave Egypt."

12"But LORD!" Moses objected. "My own people won't listen to me anymore. How can I expect Pharaoh to listen? I'm no orator!"

13But the LORD ordered Moses and Aaron to return to Pharaoh, king of Egypt, and to demand that he let the people of Israel leave Egypt.

THE ANCESTORS OF MOSES AND AARON

14These are the ancestors of clans from some of Israel's tribes:

The descendants of Reuben, Israel's oldest son, included Hanoch, Pallu, Hezron, and Carmi. Their descendants became the clans of Reuben.
15The descendants of Simeon included Jemuel, Jamin, Ohad, Jakin, Zohar, and Shaul (whose mother was a Canaanite).

Their descendants became the clans of Simeon.
16These are the descendants of Levi, listed according to their family groups. In the first generation were Gershon, Kohath, and Merari. (Levi, their father, lived to be 137 years old.)
17 The descendants of Gershon included Libni and Shimei, each of whom is the ancestor of a clan.
18 The descendants of Kohath included Amram, Izhar, Hebron, and Uzziel. (Kohath lived to be 133 years old.)
19 The descendants of Merari included Mahli and Mushi.

These are the clans of the Levites, listed according to their genealogies.

20Amram married his father's sister Jochebed, and she bore him Aaron and Moses. (Amram lived to be 137 years old.)
21The descendants of Izhar included Korah, Nepheg, and Zicri.
22The descendants of Uzziel included Mishael, Elzaphan, and Sithri.
23Aaron married Elisheba, the daughter of Amminadab and sister of Nahshon, and she bore him Nadab, Abihu, Eleazar, and Ithamar.
24The descendants of Korah included Assir, Elkanah, and Abiasaph. Their descendants became the clans of Korah.
25Eleazar son of Aaron married one of the daughters of Putiel, and she bore him Phinehas.

These are the ancestors of the Levite clans, listed according to their family groups.

26The Aaron and Moses named in this list are the same Aaron and Moses to whom the LORD said, "Lead all the people of Israel out of the land of Egypt, division by division." 27They are the ones who went to Pharaoh to ask permission to lead the people from the land of Egypt.

6:3a Hebrew El Shaddai.　6:3b Hebrew Yahweh; traditionally rendered Jehovah.

My Daily Worship

— January 17 —

WHERE'S YOUR FOCUS?

EXODUS 5:1–7:13

I will make you my own special people, and I will be your God. And you will know
that I am the LORD your God who has rescued you from your slavery in Egypt.
I will bring you into the land I swore to give to Abraham, Isaac, and Jacob.
It will be your very own property. I am the LORD! (6:7–8).

[i reflect]

We praise people for what they do. Advance the company—receive a promotion. Make high grades—get on the honor roll. Rarely does someone become famous based on lofty character traits alone. They have to publish, score, sell, win, or record. And then *maybe*, if they're in the right place at the right time, they'll get recognized.

This method of praising others is often what we use to praise God. Our first question is, "What has God done to benefit me?" The quality of his blessing equals the quality of our thanks. With this standard, Pharaoh might not have had much to say in reply. God unleashed terror upon terror on Pharaoh's country for holding the Israelites. Did that exempt him from worshiping God?

God tells us a lot about himself in the Scriptures. He also proclaims that he *does* many things: "I fulfill my oath," "I am mighty to save." He *should* be praised for these deeds. But when our worship becomes contingent on God doing things for us, we walk on dangerous ground. God will not be managed or manipulated. Like us, Pharaoh still had an obligation to worship God for who God is.

In his reintroduction to this band of Israelites, God begins and ends his address with the declaration, "I am the LORD!" In fact, he repeats this phrase over 130 times in the Old Testament when addressing Israel. God wanted his people to know him. He expected that worship would be the by-product of that relationship. Our worship of God must center on a clear knowledge of who he is, not what he does. Take time right now to worship the God that *you* know.

[i pray]

Forgive me, Lord, for forgetting to praise you when things aren't going my way.
I want to know you as you know me. Especially when my spirit falls, let me
still praise you for who you are, not what you can do for me.

[i respond]

Do you find yourself waiting for God's next blessing to motivate you to worship? Do you blame God for your bad days, and forget to praise him when things turn around? Make worship a daily habit focused on God, not yourself.

²⁸At that time, the LORD had said to them, ²⁹"I am the LORD! Give Pharaoh the message I have given you." ³⁰This is the same Moses who had argued with the LORD, saying, "I can't do it! I'm no orator. Why should Pharaoh listen to me?"

AARON'S STAFF BECOMES A SNAKE

7 Then the LORD said to Moses, "Pay close attention to this. I will make you seem like God to Pharaoh. Your brother, Aaron, will be your prophet; he will speak for you. ²Tell Aaron everything I say to you and have him announce it to Pharaoh. He will demand that the people of Israel be allowed to leave Egypt. ³But I will cause Pharaoh to be stubborn so I can multiply my miraculous signs and wonders in the land of Egypt. ⁴Even then Pharaoh will refuse to listen to you. So I will crush Egypt with a series of disasters, after which I will lead the forces of Israel out with great acts of judgment. ⁵When I show the Egyptians my power and force them to let the Israelites go, they will realize that I am the LORD."

⁶So Moses and Aaron did just as the LORD had commanded them. ⁷Moses was eighty years old, and Aaron was eighty-three at the time they made their demands to Pharaoh.

⁸Then the LORD said to Moses and Aaron, ⁹"Pharaoh will demand that you show him a miracle to prove that God has sent you. When he makes this demand, say to Aaron, 'Throw down your shepherd's staff,' and it will become a snake."

¹⁰So Moses and Aaron went to see Pharaoh, and they performed the miracle just as the LORD had told them. Aaron threw down his staff before Pharaoh and his court, and it became a snake. ¹¹Then Pharaoh called in his wise men and magicians, and they did the same thing with their secret arts. ¹²Their staffs became snakes, too! But then Aaron's snake swallowed up their snakes. ¹³Pharaoh's heart, however, remained hard and stubborn. He still refused to listen, just as the LORD had predicted.

Words of Worship

GOD MOST HIGH, HIGHEST GOD

God Most High, Highest God—Hebrew *'El 'el-yon* "God most high"; Greek *hu-psis-tos* "highest one." Authorities are unsure whether *'El* is a shortened form of *'Elohim* or is another word entirely, but it conveys the same sense of a mighty one to be feared and worshiped.

'El 'elyon appears in connection with worship at Salem, a pre-Israelite name for Jerusalem (Genesis 14:18–20). The Israelite sanctuary would be erected there, on Mount Zion, and in the psalms *'El 'elyon* is usually associated with Zion. Ancient sanctuaries were often placed on a hill, the intersection of heaven and earth. The word *'elyon* may relate to the verb *'alah*, "go up," because God was worshiped at a high place. But the Greek term for "the Highest" shows that God himself was known to be above all things.

In the era of satellites, orbiters, and space probes, the idea that God is high might seem less impressive. But presuming to reach God's altitude is as old as the Tower of Babel (Genesis 11:4) and as dangerous as ever. To worship God Most High is to admit we can never fully comprehend him or penetrate his being. He is "over us all and in us all and living through us all" (Ephesians 4:6).

A PLAGUE OF BLOOD

¹⁴Then the LORD said to Moses, "Pharaoh is very stubborn, and he continues to refuse to let the people go. ¹⁵So go to Pharaoh in the morning as he goes down to the river. Stand on the riverbank and meet him there. Be sure to take along the shepherd's staff that turned

into a snake. ¹⁶Say to him, 'The LORD, the God of the Hebrews, has sent me to say, "Let my people go, so they can worship me in the wilderness." Until now, you have refused to listen to him. ¹⁷Now the LORD says, "You are going to find out that I am the LORD." Look! I will hit the water of the Nile with this staff, and the river will turn to blood. ¹⁸The fish in it will die, and the river will stink. The Egyptians will not be able to drink any water from the Nile.' "

¹⁹Then the LORD said to Moses: "Tell Aaron to point his staff toward the waters of Egypt—all its rivers, canals, marshes, and reservoirs. Everywhere in Egypt the water will turn into blood, even the water stored in wooden bowls and stone pots in the people's homes."

²⁰So Moses and Aaron did just as the LORD had commanded them. As Pharaoh and all of his officials watched, Aaron raised his staff and hit the water of the Nile. Suddenly, the whole river turned to blood! ²¹The fish in the river died, and the water became so foul that the Egyptians couldn't drink it. There was blood everywhere throughout the land of Egypt. ²²But again the magicians of Egypt used their secret arts, and they, too, turned water into blood. So Pharaoh's heart remained hard and stubborn. He refused to listen to Moses and Aaron, just as the LORD had predicted. ²³Pharaoh returned to his palace and put the whole thing out of his mind. ²⁴Then the Egyptians dug wells along the riverbank to get drinking water, for they couldn't drink from the river. ²⁵An entire week passed from the time the LORD turned the water of the Nile to blood.

A PLAGUE OF FROGS

8 Then the LORD said to Moses, "Go to Pharaoh once again and tell him, 'This is what the LORD says: Let my people go, so they can worship me. ²If you refuse, then listen carefully to this: I will send vast hordes of frogs across your entire land from one border to the other. ³The Nile River will swarm with them. They will come up out of the river and into your houses, even into your bedrooms and onto your beds! Every home in Egypt will be filled with them. They will fill even your ovens and your kneading bowls. ⁴You and your people will be overwhelmed by frogs!' "

⁵Then the LORD said to Moses, "Tell Aaron to point his shepherd's staff toward all the rivers, canals, and marshes of Egypt so there will be frogs in every corner of the land." ⁶Aaron did so, and frogs covered the whole land of Egypt! ⁷But the magicians were able to do the same thing with their secret arts. They, too, caused frogs to come up on the land.

⁸Then Pharaoh summoned Moses and Aaron and begged, "Plead with the LORD to take the frogs away from me and my people. I will let the people go, so they can offer sacrifices to the LORD."

⁹"You set the time!" Moses replied. "Tell me when you want me to pray for you, your officials, and your people. I will pray that you and your houses will be rid of the frogs. Then only the frogs in the Nile River will remain alive."

¹⁰"Do it tomorrow," Pharaoh said.

"All right," Moses replied, "it will be as you have said. Then you will know that no one is as powerful as the LORD our God. ¹¹All the frogs will be destroyed, except those in the river."

¹²So Moses and Aaron left Pharaoh, and Moses pleaded with the LORD about the frogs he had sent. ¹³And the LORD did as Moses had promised. The frogs in the houses, the courtyards, and the fields all died. ¹⁴They were piled into great heaps, and a terrible stench filled the land. ¹⁵But when Pharaoh saw that the frogs were gone, he hardened his heart. He refused to listen to Moses and Aaron, just as the LORD had predicted.

A PLAGUE OF GNATS

¹⁶So the LORD said to Moses, "Tell Aaron to strike the dust with his staff. The dust will turn into swarms of gnats throughout the

land of Egypt." [17]So Moses and Aaron did just as the LORD had commanded them. Suddenly, gnats infested the entire land, covering the Egyptians and their animals. All the dust in the land of Egypt turned into gnats. [18]Pharaoh's magicians tried to do the same thing with their secret arts, but this time they failed. And the gnats covered all the people and animals.

[19]"This is the finger of God!" the magicians exclaimed to Pharaoh. But Pharaoh's heart remained hard and stubborn. He wouldn't listen to them, just as the LORD had predicted.

A PLAGUE OF FLIES

[20]Next the LORD told Moses, "Get up early in the morning and meet Pharaoh as he goes down to the river. Say to him, 'This is what the LORD says: Let my people go, so they can worship me.' [21]If you refuse, I will send swarms of flies throughout Egypt. Your homes will be filled with them, and the ground will be covered with them. [22]But it will be very different in the land of Goshen, where the Israelites live. No flies will be found there. Then you will know that I am the LORD and that I have power even in the heart of your land. [23]I will make a clear distinction between your people and my people. This miraculous sign will happen tomorrow.'"

[24]And the LORD did just as he had said. There were terrible swarms of flies in Pharaoh's palace and in every home in Egypt. The whole country was thrown into chaos by the flies.

[25]Pharaoh hastily called for Moses and Aaron. "All right! Go ahead and offer sacrifices to your God," he said. "But do it here in this land. Don't go out into the wilderness."

[26]But Moses replied, "That won't do! The Egyptians would detest the sacrifices that we offer to the LORD our God. If we offer them here where they can see us, they will be sure to stone us. [27]We must take a three-day trip into the wilderness to offer sacrifices to the LORD our God, just as he has commanded us."

[28]"All right, go ahead," Pharaoh replied. "I will let you go to offer sacrifices to the LORD your God in the wilderness. But don't go too far away. Now hurry, and pray for me."

[29]"As soon as I go," Moses said, "I will ask the LORD to cause the swarms of flies to disappear from you and all your people. But I am warning you, don't change your mind again and refuse to let the people go to sacrifice to the LORD."

[30]So Moses left Pharaoh and asked the LORD to remove all the flies. [31]And the LORD did as Moses asked and caused the swarms to disappear. Not a single fly remained in the land! [32]But Pharaoh hardened his heart again and refused to let the people go.

A PLAGUE AGAINST LIVESTOCK

9 "Go back to Pharaoh," the LORD commanded Moses. "Tell him, 'This is what the LORD, the God of the Hebrews, says: Let my people go, so they can worship me. [2]If you continue to oppress them and refuse to let them go, [3]the LORD will send a deadly plague to destroy your horses, donkeys, camels, cattle, and sheep. [4]But the LORD will again make a distinction between the property of the Israelites and that of the Egyptians. Not a single one of Israel's livestock will die!'"

[5]The LORD announced that he would send the plague the very next day, [6]and he did it, just as he had said. The next morning all the livestock of the Egyptians began to die, but the Israelites didn't lose a single animal from their flocks and herds. [7]Pharaoh sent officials to see whether it was true that none of the Israelites' animals were dead. But even after he found it to be true, his heart remained stubborn. He still refused to let the people go.

A PLAGUE OF BOILS

[8]Then the LORD said to Moses and Aaron, "Take soot from a furnace, and have Moses toss it into the sky while Pharaoh watches. [9]It will spread like fine dust over the whole land of Egypt, causing boils to break out on people and animals alike."

[10]So they gathered soot from a furnace and

went to see Pharaoh. As Pharaoh watched, Moses tossed the soot into the air, and terrible boils broke out on the people and animals throughout Egypt. [11]Even the magicians were unable to stand before Moses, because the boils had broken out on them, too. [12]But the LORD made Pharaoh even more stubborn, and he refused to listen, just as the LORD had predicted.

A PLAGUE OF HAIL

[13]Then the LORD said to Moses, "Get up early in the morning. Go to Pharaoh and tell him, 'The LORD, the God of the Hebrews, says: Let my people go, so they can worship me. [14]If you don't, I will send a plague that will really speak to you and your officials and all the Egyptian people. I will prove to you that there is no other God like me in all the earth. [15]I could have killed you all by now. I could have attacked you with a plague that would have wiped you from the face of the earth. [16]But I have let you live for this reason—that you might see my power and that my fame might spread throughout the earth. [17]But you are still lording it over my people, and you refuse to let them go. [18]So tomorrow at this time I will send a hailstorm worse than any in all of Egypt's history. [19]Quick! Order your livestock and servants to come in from the fields. Every person or animal left outside will die beneath the hail.'"

[20]Some of Pharaoh's officials believed what the LORD said. They immediately brought their livestock and servants in from the fields. [21]But those who had no respect for the word of the LORD left them out in the open.

[22]Then the LORD said to Moses, "Lift your hand toward the sky, and cause the hail to fall throughout Egypt, on the people, the animals, and the crops." [23]So Moses lifted his staff toward the sky, and the LORD sent thunder and hail, and lightning struck the earth. The LORD sent a tremendous hailstorm against all the land of Egypt. [24]Never in all the history of Egypt had there been a storm like that, with such severe hail and continuous lightning. [25]It left all of Egypt in ruins. Everything left in the fields was destroyed—people, animals, and crops alike. Even all the trees were destroyed. [26]The only spot in all Egypt without hail that day was the land of Goshen, where the people of Israel lived.

[27]Then Pharaoh urgently sent for Moses and Aaron. "I finally admit my fault," he confessed. "The LORD is right, and my people and I are wrong. [28]Please beg the LORD to end this terrifying thunder and hail. I will let you go at once."

[29]"All right," Moses replied. "As soon as I leave the city, I will lift my hands and pray to the LORD. Then the thunder and hail will stop. This will prove to you that the earth belongs to the LORD. [30]But as for you and your officials, I know that you still do not fear the LORD God as you should."

[31]All the flax and barley were destroyed because the barley was ripe and the flax was in bloom. [32]But the wheat and the spelt were not destroyed because they had not yet sprouted from the ground.

[33]So Moses left Pharaoh and went out of the city. As he lifted his hands to the LORD, all at once the thunder and hail stopped, and the downpour ceased. [34]When Pharaoh saw this, he and his officials sinned yet again by stubbornly refusing to do as they had promised. [35]Pharaoh refused to let the people leave, just as the LORD had predicted.

A PLAGUE OF LOCUSTS

10 Then the LORD said to Moses, "Return to Pharaoh and again make your demands. I have made him and his officials stubborn so I can continue to display my power by performing miraculous signs among them. [2]You will be able to tell wonderful stories to your children and grandchildren about the marvelous things I am doing among the Egyptians to prove that I am the LORD."

[3]So Moses and Aaron went to Pharaoh and said, "This is what the LORD, the God of the

Hebrews, says: How long will you refuse to submit to me? Let my people go, so they can worship me. ⁴If you refuse, watch out! For tomorrow I will cover the whole country with locusts. ⁵There will be so many that you won't be able to see the ground. They will devour everything that escaped the hailstorm, including all the trees in the fields. ⁶They will overrun your palaces and the homes of your officials and all the houses of Egypt. Never in the history of Egypt has there been a plague like this one!" And with that, Moses turned and walked out.

⁷The court officials now came to Pharaoh and appealed to him. "How long will you let these disasters go on? Please let the Israelites go to serve the LORD their God! Don't you realize that Egypt lies in ruins?"

⁸So Moses and Aaron were brought back to Pharaoh. "All right, go and serve the LORD your God," he said. "But tell me, just whom do you want to take along?"

⁹"Young and old, all of us will go," Moses replied. "We will take our sons and daughters and our flocks and herds. We must all join together in a festival to the LORD."

¹⁰Pharaoh retorted, "The LORD will certainly need to be with you if you try to take your little ones along! I can see through your wicked intentions. ¹¹Never! Only the men may go and serve the LORD, for that is what you requested." And Pharaoh threw them out of the palace.

¹²Then the LORD said to Moses, "Raise your hand over the land of Egypt to bring on the locusts. Let them cover the land and eat all the crops still left after the hailstorm."

¹³So Moses raised his staff, and the LORD caused an east wind to blow all that day and through the night. When morning arrived, the east wind had brought the locusts. ¹⁴And the locusts swarmed over the land of Egypt from border to border. It was the worst locust plague in Egyptian history, and there has never again been one like it. ¹⁵For the locusts covered the surface of the whole country,

making the ground look black. They ate all the plants and all the fruit on the trees that had survived the hailstorm. Not one green thing remained, neither tree nor plant, throughout the land of Egypt.

¹⁶Pharaoh quickly sent for Moses and Aaron. "I confess my sin against the LORD your God and against you," he said to them. ¹⁷"Forgive my sin only this once, and plead with the LORD your God to take away this terrible plague."

¹⁸So Moses left Pharaoh and pleaded with the LORD. ¹⁹The LORD responded by sending a strong west wind that blew the locusts out into the Red Sea.* Not a single locust remained in all the land of Egypt. ²⁰But the LORD made Pharaoh stubborn once again, and he did not let the people go.

A PLAGUE OF DARKNESS

²¹Then the LORD said to Moses, "Lift your hand toward heaven, and a deep and terrifying darkness will descend on the land of Egypt." ²²So Moses lifted his hand toward heaven, and there was deep darkness over the entire land for three days. ²³During all that time the people scarcely moved, for they could not see. But there was light as usual where the people of Israel lived.

²⁴Then Pharaoh called for Moses. "Go and worship the LORD," he said. "But let your flocks and herds stay here. You can even take your children with you."

To worship in spirit is to draw near to God with an undivided heart.

ERWIN LUTZER

10:19 Hebrew *sea of reeds.*

²⁵"No," Moses said, "we must take our flocks and herds for sacrifices and burnt offerings to the LORD our God. ²⁶All our property must go with us; not a hoof can be left behind. We will have to choose our sacrifices for the LORD our God from among these animals. And we won't know which sacrifices he will require until we get there."

²⁷So the LORD hardened Pharaoh's heart once more, and he would not let them go. ²⁸"Get out of here!" Pharaoh shouted at Moses. "Don't ever let me see you again! The day you do, you will die!"

²⁹"Very well," Moses replied. "I will never see you again."

DEATH FOR EGYPT'S FIRSTBORN

11 Then the LORD said to Moses, "I will send just one more disaster on Pharaoh and the land of Egypt. After that, Pharaoh will let you go. In fact, he will be so anxious to get rid of you that he will practically force you to leave the country. ²Tell all the Israelite men and women to ask their Egyptian neighbors for articles of silver and gold."

³(Now the LORD had caused the Egyptians to look favorably on the people of Israel, and Moses was considered a very great man in the land of Egypt. He was respected by Pharaoh's officials and the Egyptian people alike.)

⁴So Moses announced to Pharaoh, "This is what the LORD says: About midnight I will pass through Egypt. ⁵All the firstborn sons will die in every family in Egypt, from the oldest son of Pharaoh, who sits on the throne, to the oldest son of his lowliest slave. Even the firstborn of the animals will die. ⁶Then a loud wail will be heard throughout the land of Egypt; there has never been such wailing before, and there never will be again. ⁷But among the Israelites it will be so peaceful that not even a dog will bark. Then you will know that the LORD makes a distinction between the Egyptians and the Israelites. ⁸All the officials of Egypt will come running to me, bowing low. 'Please leave!' they will beg. 'Hurry! And

take all your followers with you.' Only then will I go!" Then, burning with anger, Moses left Pharaoh's presence.

⁹Now the LORD had told Moses, "Pharaoh will not listen to you. But this will give me the opportunity to do even more mighty miracles in the land of Egypt." ¹⁰Although Moses and Aaron did these miracles in Pharaoh's presence, the LORD hardened his heart so he wouldn't let the Israelites leave the country.

THE FIRST PASSOVER

12 Now the LORD gave the following instructions to Moses and Aaron while they were still in the land of Egypt: ²"From now on, this month will be the first month of the year for you. ³Announce to the whole community that on the tenth day of this month each family must choose a lamb or a young goat for a sacrifice. ⁴If a family is too small to eat an entire lamb, let them share the lamb with another family in the neighborhood. Whether or not they share in this way depends on the size of each family and how much they can eat. ⁵This animal must be a one-year-old male, either a sheep or a goat, with no physical defects.

⁶"Take special care of these lambs until the evening of the fourteenth day of this first month. Then each family in the community must slaughter its lamb. ⁷They are to take some of the lamb's blood and smear it on the top and sides of the doorframe of the house where the lamb will be eaten. ⁸That evening everyone must eat roast lamb with bitter herbs and bread made without yeast. ⁹The meat must never be eaten raw or boiled; roast it all, including the head, legs, and internal organs. ¹⁰Do not leave any of it until the next day. Whatever is not eaten that night must be burned before morning.

¹¹"Wear your traveling clothes as you eat this meal, as though prepared for a long journey. Wear your sandals, and carry your walking sticks in your hands. Eat the food quickly, for this is the LORD's Passover. ¹²On that night I will pass through the land of Egypt and kill

all the firstborn sons and firstborn male animals in the land of Egypt. I will execute judgment against all the gods of Egypt, for I am the LORD! ¹³The blood you have smeared on your doorposts will serve as a sign. When I see the blood, I will pass over you. This plague of death will not touch you when I strike the land of Egypt.

¹⁴"You must remember this day forever. Each year you will celebrate it as a special festival to the LORD. ¹⁵For seven days, you may eat only bread made without yeast. On the very first day you must remove every trace of yeast from your homes. Anyone who eats bread made with yeast at any time during the seven days of the festival will be cut off from the community of Israel. ¹⁶On the first day of the festival, and again on the seventh day, all the people must gather for a time of special worship. No work of any kind may be done on these days except in the preparation of food.

¹⁷"Celebrate this Festival of Unleavened Bread, for it will remind you that I brought your forces out of the land of Egypt on this very day. This festival will be a permanent regulation for you, to be kept from generation to generation. ¹⁸Only bread without yeast may be eaten from the evening of the fourteenth day of the month until the evening of the twenty-first day of the month. ¹⁹During those seven days, there must be no trace of yeast in your homes. Anyone who eats anything made with yeast during this week will be cut off from the community of Israel. These same regulations apply to the foreigners living with you, as if they had been born among them. ²⁰I repeat, during those days you must not eat anything made with yeast. Wherever you live, eat only bread that has no yeast in it."

²¹Then Moses called for the leaders of Israel and said, "Tell each of your families to slaughter the lamb they have set apart for the Passover. ²²Drain each lamb's blood into a basin. Then take a cluster of hyssop branches and dip it into the lamb's blood. Strike the hyssop against the top and sides of the doorframe, staining it with the blood. And remember, no one is allowed to leave the house until morning. ²³For the LORD will pass through the land and strike down the Egyptians. But when he sees the blood on the top and sides of the doorframe, the LORD will pass over your home. He will not permit the Destroyer to enter and strike down your firstborn.

²⁴"Remember, these instructions are permanent and must be observed by you and your descendants forever. ²⁵When you arrive in the land the LORD has promised to give you, you will continue to celebrate this festival. ²⁶Then your children will ask, 'What does all this mean? What is this ceremony about?' ²⁷And you will reply, 'It is the celebration of the LORD's Passover, for he passed over the homes of the Israelites in Egypt. And though he killed the Egyptians, he spared our families and did not destroy us.'" Then all the people bowed their heads and worshiped.

²⁸So the people of Israel did just as the LORD had commanded through Moses and Aaron. ²⁹And at midnight the LORD killed all the firstborn sons in the land of Egypt, from the firstborn son of Pharaoh, who sat on the throne, to the firstborn son of the captive in the dungeon. Even the firstborn of their livestock were killed. ³⁰Pharaoh and his officials and all the people of Egypt woke up during the night, and loud wailing was heard throughout the land of Egypt. There was not a single house where someone had not died.

ISRAEL'S EXODUS FROM EGYPT

³¹Pharaoh sent for Moses and Aaron during the night. "Leave us!" he cried. "Go away, all of you! Go and serve the LORD as you have requested. ³²Take your flocks and herds, and be gone. Go, but give me a blessing as you leave." ³³All the Egyptians urged the people of Israel to get out of the land as quickly as possible, for they thought, "We will all die!"

³⁴The Israelites took with them their bread dough made without yeast. They wrapped their kneading bowls in their spare clothing and carried them on their shoulders. ³⁵And the people of Israel did as Moses had instructed

My Daily Worship

— *January 18* —

REMEMBER YOUR PASSOVER

EXODUS 7:14–12:30

The blood you have smeared on your doorposts will serve as a sign. When I see the blood,
I will pass over you. This plague of death will not touch you when I strike the land of Egypt.
You must remember this day forever. (12:13–14).

[i reflect]

For nearly 3,500 years, the Jews have been remembering the Lord's "pass over" since the time of their exodus from Egypt. God instituted the Passover celebration as an integral part of Israel's law. It's a good thing, too. Not long after their deliverance from slavery, the Israelites' praise seemed to be drowned out by mounting complaints.

Sound familiar? So often we forget God's blessings the next day, never mind reflecting upon his interaction with past generations. Do you know in what specific ways he blessed your great grand-parents? Have you told your children about God's blessings in your life? There's value in both look-ing back and passing on a record of God's work. Worshiping God becomes more and more natural when we take time to remember *why* we worship.

The recent fascination with family ancestry demonstrates the value of remembering. Struggling families find comfort in knowing their ancestors built themselves up from nothing after they immi-grated to a new land. For Christians, remembering God's past blessings helps us trust him with our future.

When you begin to complain, sit down and literally count your blessings! You will never come to the end of God's good deeds. Remember that you also have a Passover to celebrate. First Corinthians reveals, "Christ, our Passover Lamb, has been sacrificed for us" (5:7b). The penalty of your sin has "passed over" you and has been placed on Jesus. *Don't forget*. You have the respon-sibility of passing on this great act of God, and his many other good works, to younger generations. What can you pass on about God's greatness to someone today?

[i pray]

Shield me, Lord, from participating in the complaining all around me.
Give me eyes to see your blessings everyday and the courage to share them with others.
Let my life be a celebration of your Passover.

[i respond]

Have your parents or relatives shared specific experiences of God's blessing? Write them down. For your own children, start a journal where you record your prayers and God's answers. Your own faith will be strengthened as you remember and retell.

and asked the Egyptians for clothing and articles of silver and gold. ³⁶The LORD caused the Egyptians to look favorably on the Israelites, and they gave the Israelites whatever they asked for. So, like a victorious army, they plundered the Egyptians!

³⁷That night the people of Israel left Rameses and started for Succoth. There were about 600,000 men, plus all the women and children. And they were all traveling on foot. ³⁸Many people who were not Israelites went with them, along with the many flocks and herds. ³⁹Whenever they stopped to eat, they baked bread from the yeastless dough they had brought from Egypt. It was made without yeast because the people were rushed out of Egypt and had no time to wait for bread to rise.

⁴⁰The people of Israel had lived in Egypt for 430 years. ⁴¹In fact, it was on the last day of the 430th year that all the LORD's forces left the land. ⁴²This night had been reserved by the LORD to bring his people out from the land of Egypt, so this same night now belongs to him. It must be celebrated every year, from generation to generation, to remember the LORD's deliverance.

INSTRUCTIONS FOR THE PASSOVER

⁴³Then the LORD said to Moses and Aaron, "These are the regulations for the festival of Passover. No foreigners are allowed to eat the Passover lamb. ⁴⁴But any slave who has been purchased may eat it if he has been circumcised. ⁴⁵Hired servants and visiting foreigners may not eat it. ⁴⁶All who eat the lamb must eat it together in one house. You must not carry any of its meat outside, and you may not break any of its bones. ⁴⁷The whole community of Israel must celebrate this festival at the same time.

⁴⁸"If there are foreigners living among you who want to celebrate the LORD's Passover, let all the males be circumcised. Then they may come and celebrate the Passover with you.

They will be treated just as if they had been born among you. But an uncircumcised male may never eat of the Passover lamb. ⁴⁹This law applies to everyone, whether a native-born Israelite or a foreigner who has settled among you."

⁵⁰So the people of Israel followed all the LORD's instructions to Moses and Aaron. ⁵¹And that very day the LORD began to lead the people of Israel out of Egypt, division by division.

DEDICATION OF THE FIRSTBORN

13 Then the LORD said to Moses, ²"Dedicate to me all the firstborn sons of Israel and every firstborn male animal. They are mine."

³So Moses said to the people, "This is a day to remember forever—the day you left Egypt, the place of your slavery. For the LORD has brought you out by his mighty power. (Remember, you are not to use any yeast.) ⁴This day in early spring* will be the anniversary of your exodus. ⁵You must celebrate this day when the LORD brings you into the land of the Canaanites, Hittites, Amorites, Hivites, and Jebusites. This is the land he swore to give your ancestors—a land flowing with milk and honey. ⁶For seven days you will eat only bread without yeast. Then on the seventh day, you will celebrate a great feast to the LORD. ⁷Eat only bread without yeast during those seven days. In fact, there must be no yeast in your homes or anywhere within the borders of your land during this time.

⁸"During these festival days each year, you must explain to your children why you are celebrating. Say to them, 'This is a celebration of what the LORD did for us when we left Egypt.' ⁹This annual festival will be a visible reminder to you, like a mark branded on your hands or your forehead. Let it remind you always to keep the LORD's instructions in your minds and on your lips. After all, it was the LORD who rescued you from Egypt with great power.

13:4 Hebrew *in the month of Abib.* This month of the Hebrew lunar calendar usually occurs in March and April.

¹⁰"So celebrate this festival at the appointed time each year. ¹¹And remember these instructions when the LORD brings you into the land he swore to give your ancestors long ago, the land where the Canaanites are now living. ¹²All firstborn sons and firstborn male animals must be presented to the LORD. ¹³A firstborn male donkey may be redeemed from the LORD by presenting a lamb in its place. But if you decide not to make the exchange, the donkey must be killed by breaking its neck. However, you must redeem every firstborn son.

¹⁴"And in the future, your children will ask you, 'What does all this mean?' Then you will tell them, 'With mighty power the LORD brought us out of Egypt from our slavery. ¹⁵Pharaoh refused to let us go, so the LORD killed all the firstborn males throughout the land of Egypt, both people and animals. That is why we now offer all the firstborn males to the LORD—except that the firstborn sons are always redeemed.' ¹⁶Again I say, this ceremony will be like a mark branded on your hands or your forehead. It is a visible reminder that it was the LORD who brought you out of Egypt with great power."

ISRAEL'S WILDERNESS DETOUR

¹⁷When Pharaoh finally let the people go, God did not lead them on the road that runs through Philistine territory, even though that was the shortest way from Egypt to the Promised Land. God said, "If the people are faced with a battle, they might change their minds and return to Egypt." ¹⁸So God led them along a route through the wilderness toward the Red Sea,* and the Israelites left Egypt like a marching army.

¹⁹Moses took the bones of Joseph with him, for Joseph had made the sons of Israel swear that they would take his bones with them when God led them out of Egypt—as he was sure God would.

²⁰Leaving Succoth, they camped at Etham on the edge of the wilderness. ²¹The LORD guided them by a pillar of cloud during the day and a pillar of fire at night. That way they could travel whether it was day or night. ²²And the LORD did not remove the pillar of cloud or pillar of fire from their sight.

14 Then the LORD gave these instructions to Moses: ²"Tell the people to march toward Pi-hahiroth between Migdol and the sea. Camp there along the shore, opposite Baal-zephon. ³Then Pharaoh will think, 'Those Israelites are confused. They are trapped between the wilderness and the sea!' ⁴And once again I will harden Pharaoh's heart, and he will chase after you. I have planned this so I will receive great glory at the expense of Pharaoh and his armies. After this, the Egyptians will know that I am the LORD!" So the Israelites camped there as they were told.

THE EGYPTIANS PURSUE ISRAEL

⁵When word reached the king of Egypt that the Israelites were not planning to return to Egypt after three days, Pharaoh and his officials changed their minds. "What have we done, letting all these slaves get away?" they asked. ⁶So Pharaoh called out his troops and led the chase in his chariot. ⁷He took with him six hundred of Egypt's best chariots, along with the rest of the chariots of Egypt, each with a commander. ⁸The LORD continued to strengthen Pharaoh's resolve, and he chased after the people of Israel who had escaped so defiantly. ⁹All the forces in Pharaoh's army—all his horses, chariots, and charioteers—were used in the chase. The Egyptians caught up with the people of Israel as they were camped beside the shore near Pi-hahiroth, across from Baal-zephon.

¹⁰As Pharaoh and his army approached, the people of Israel could see them in the distance, marching toward them. The people began to panic, and they cried out to the LORD for help.

¹¹Then they turned against Moses and complained, "Why did you bring us out here to die

---

13:18 Hebrew *sea of reeds.*

in the wilderness? Weren't there enough graves for us in Egypt? Why did you make us leave? ¹²Didn't we tell you to leave us alone while we were still in Egypt? Our Egyptian slavery was far better than dying out here in the wilderness!"

¹³But Moses told the people, "Don't be afraid. Just stand where you are and watch the LORD rescue you. The Egyptians that you see today will never be seen again. ¹⁴The LORD himself will fight for you. You won't have to lift a finger in your defense!"

ESCAPE THROUGH THE RED SEA

¹⁵Then the LORD said to Moses, "Why are you crying out to me? Tell the people to get moving! ¹⁶Use your shepherd's staff—hold it out over the water, and a path will open up before you through the sea. Then all the people of Israel will walk through on dry ground. ¹⁷Yet I will harden the hearts of the Egyptians, and they will follow the Israelites into the sea. Then I will receive great glory at the expense of Pharaoh and his armies, chariots, and charioteers. ¹⁸When I am finished with Pharaoh and his army, all Egypt will know that I am the LORD!"

¹⁹Then the angel of God, who had been leading the people of Israel, moved to a position behind them, and the pillar of cloud also moved around behind them. ²⁰The cloud settled between the Israelite and Egyptian camps. As night came, the pillar of cloud turned into a pillar of fire, lighting the Israelite camp. But the cloud became darkness to the Egyptians, and they couldn't find the Israelites.

²¹Then Moses raised his hand over the sea, and the LORD opened up a path through the water with a strong east wind. The wind blew all that night, turning the seabed into dry land. ²²So the people of Israel walked through the sea on dry ground, with walls of water on each side! ²³Then the Egyptians—all of Pharaoh's horses, chariots, and charioteers— followed them across the bottom of the sea. ²⁴But early in the morning, the LORD looked down on the Egyptian army from the pillar of fire and cloud, and he threw them into confusion. ²⁵Their chariot wheels began to come off, making their chariots impossible to drive. "Let's get out of here!" the Egyptians shouted. "The LORD is fighting for Israel against us!"

²⁶When all the Israelites were on the other side, the LORD said to Moses, "Raise your hand over the sea again. Then the waters will rush back over the Egyptian chariots and charioteers." ²⁷So as the sun began to rise, Moses raised his hand over the sea. The water roared back into its usual place, and the LORD swept the terrified Egyptians into the surging currents. ²⁸The waters covered all the chariots and charioteers—the entire army of Pharaoh. Of all the Egyptians who had chased the Israelites into the sea, not a single one survived.

²⁹The people of Israel had walked through the middle of the sea on dry land, as the water stood up like a wall on both sides. ³⁰This was how the LORD rescued Israel from the Egyptians that day. And the Israelites could see the bodies of the Egyptians washed up on the shore. ³¹When the people of Israel saw the mighty power that the LORD had displayed against the Egyptians, they feared the LORD and put their faith in him and his servant Moses.

A SONG OF DELIVERANCE

15 Then Moses and the people of Israel sang this song to the LORD:

"I will sing to the Lord, for he has
    triumphed gloriously;
    he has thrown both horse and rider into
      the sea.
² The LORD is my strength and my song;
    he has become my victory.
He is my God, and I will praise him;
    he is my father's God, and I will exalt
      him!
³ The LORD is a warrior;
    yes, the LORD is his name!
⁴ Pharaoh's chariots and armies,
    he has thrown into the sea.

My Daily Worship
— January 19 —

MY BEST DEFENSE
EXODUS 12:31–15:21

But Moses told the people, "Don't be afraid. Just stand where you are and watch the LORD rescue you. The Egyptians that you see today will never be seen again. The LORD himself will fight for you. You won't have to lift a finger in your defense!" (14:13–14).

[i reflect]

From the corner of your eye, you catch sight of a huge dog. Turning, you watch as it charges towards you. A mental sign lights up: "DON'T MOVE!" It's unlikely, however, that this advice corresponds with your pounding fight-or-flight instincts. Standing still can be the hardest thing to do in a threatening situation. It feels as if you are doing nothing to defend yourself.

We take our defense seriously. Having a good defense means winning a case or triumphing over an opponent. We naturally connect defending ourselves with *action*. With this mindset, Moses' instruction for the people to not "lift a finger" sounds wimpy, or at best, risky.

The dog is still closing in. Time to take the law into our own hands? If you decide to stand still, you'll have to trust, in this case, the advice. For the Israelites facing the rushing Egyptian army, standing still tested and demonstrated their trust in God. And that's when the people ceased standing still and started standing firm in their faith.

We also have someone defending us. While our instincts may scream for us to be proactive, these impulses are repeatedly driven by fear and pride. We will all face circumstances which threaten our security. Having an attitude of expectant stillness during these intimidating experiences opens the door for us to trust and worship God.

Although you feel trapped, just wait a little longer. Remember the words of the psalmist, "But you, O LORD, are a shield around me, my glory, and the one who lifts my head high" (3:3). Stand firm and worship the One who is already fighting for you.

[i pray]

Lord, I often feel my situation won't improve unless I step in and take over.
Please help me to trust in your timing and intervention. Give me peace
to stand firm when my problems rush to overtake me.

[i respond]

What's your general course of action when you feel trapped by a situation? What emotions trigger those actions? Believe that the Lord yearns to defend and deliver you. Be humble enough to accept his rescuing.

The very best of Pharaoh's officers
    have been drowned in the Red Sea.*
5 The deep waters have covered them;
    they sank to the bottom like a stone.

6 "Your right hand, O LORD,
    is glorious in power.
Your right hand, O LORD,
    dashes the enemy to pieces.
7 In the greatness of your majesty,
    you overthrew those who rose against you.
Your anger flashed forth;
    it consumed them as fire burns straw.
8 At the blast of your breath, the waters
        piled up!
    The surging waters stood straight like a
        wall;
    in the middle of the sea the waters
        became hard.

9 "The enemy said, 'I will chase them,
    catch up with them, and destroy them.
I will divide the plunder,
    avenging myself against them.
I will unsheath my sword;
    my power will destroy them.'
10 But with a blast of your breath,
    the sea covered them.
They sank like lead
    in the mighty waters.

11 "Who else among the gods is like you,
        O LORD?
Who is glorious in holiness like you—
    so awesome in splendor,
    performing such wonders?
12 You raised up your hand,
    and the earth swallowed our enemies.

13 "With unfailing love you will lead
    this people whom you have ransomed.
You will guide them in your strength
    to the place where your holiness dwells.
14 The nations will hear and tremble;
    anguish will grip the people of Philistia.
15 The leaders of Edom will be terrified;

the nobles of Moab will tremble.
All the people of Canaan will melt with fear;
16   terror and dread will overcome them.
Because of your great power,
    they will be silent like a stone,
until your people pass by, O LORD,
    until the people whom you purchased
        pass by.
17 You will bring them in and plant them on
        your own mountain—
    the place you have made as your home,
        O LORD,
    the sanctuary, O Lord, that your hands
        have made.
18 The LORD will reign forever and ever!"

19 When Pharaoh's horses, chariots, and charioteers rushed into the sea, the LORD brought the water crashing down on them. But the people of Israel had walked through on dry land! 20 Then Miriam the prophet, Aaron's sister, took a tambourine and led all the women in rhythm and dance. 21 And Miriam sang this song:

"I will sing to the LORD, for he has
    triumphed gloriously;
he has thrown both horse and rider into
    the sea."

BITTER WATER AT MARAH

22 Then Moses led the people of Israel away from the Red Sea, and they moved out into the Shur Desert. They traveled in this desert for three days without water. 23 When they came to Marah, they finally found water. But the people couldn't drink it because it was bitter. (That is why the place was called Marah, which means "bitter.")

24 Then the people turned against Moses. "What are we going to drink?" they demanded.

25 So Moses cried out to the LORD for help, and the LORD showed him a branch. Moses took the branch and threw it into the water. This made the water good to drink.

It was there at Marah that the LORD laid before them the following conditions to test

15:4 Hebrew *sea of reeds*; also in 15:22.

their faithfulness to him: [26]"If you will listen carefully to the voice of the LORD your God and do what is right in his sight, obeying his commands and laws, then I will not make you suffer the diseases I sent on the Egyptians; for I am the LORD who heals you."

[27]After leaving Marah, they came to Elim, where there were twelve springs and seventy palm trees. They camped there beside the springs.

MANNA AND QUAIL FROM HEAVEN

16 Then they left Elim and journeyed into the Sin* Desert, between Elim and Mount Sinai. They arrived there a month after leaving Egypt.* [2]There, too, the whole community of Israel spoke bitterly against Moses and Aaron.

[3]"Oh, that we were back in Egypt," they moaned. "It would have been better if the LORD had killed us there! At least there we had plenty to eat. But now you have brought us into this desert to starve us to death."

[4]Then the LORD said to Moses, "Look, I'm going to rain down food from heaven for you. The people can go out each day and pick up as much food as they need for that day. I will test them in this to see whether they will follow my instructions. [5]Tell them to pick up twice as much as usual on the sixth day of each week."

[6]Then Moses and Aaron called a meeting of all the people of Israel and told them, "In the evening you will realize that it was the LORD who brought you out of the land of Egypt. [7]In the morning you will see the glorious presence of the LORD. He has heard your complaints, which are against the LORD and not against us. [8]The LORD will give you meat to eat in the evening and bread in the morning, for he has heard all your complaints against him. Yes, your complaints are against the LORD, not against us."

[9]Then Moses said to Aaron, "Say this to the entire community of Israel: 'Come into the

LORD's presence, and hear his reply to your complaints.'" [10]And as Aaron spoke to the people, they looked out toward the desert. Within the guiding cloud, they could see the awesome glory of the LORD.

[11]And the LORD said to Moses, [12]"I have heard the people's complaints. Now tell them, 'In the evening you will have meat to eat, and in the morning you will be filled with bread. Then you will know that I am the LORD your God.'"

[13]That evening vast numbers of quail arrived and covered the camp. The next morning the desert all around the camp was wet with dew. [14]When the dew disappeared later in the morning, thin flakes, white like frost, covered the ground. [15]The Israelites were puzzled when they saw it. "What is it?" they asked.

And Moses told them, "It is the food the LORD has given you. [16]The LORD says that each household should gather as much as it needs. Pick up two quarts* for each person."

[17]So the people of Israel went out and gathered this food—some getting more, and some getting less. [18]By gathering two quarts for each person, everyone had just enough. Those who gathered a lot had nothing left over, and those who gathered only a little had enough. Each family had just what it needed.

[19]Then Moses told them, "Do not keep any of it overnight." [20]But, of course, some of them didn't listen and kept some of it until morning. By then it was full of maggots and had a terrible smell. And Moses was very angry with them.

[21]The people gathered the food morning by morning, each family according to its need. And as the sun became hot, the food they had not picked up melted and disappeared. [22]On the sixth day, there was twice as much as usual on the ground—four quarts* for each person instead of two. The leaders of the people came and asked Moses why this had happened. [23]He

---

16:1a Not to be confused with the English word *sin*.   16:1b Hebrew *on the fifteenth day of the second month*. The Exodus had occurred on the fourteenth day of the first month (see 12:6).   16:16 Hebrew *1 omer* [2 liters]; also in 16:18, 32, 33.   16:22 Hebrew *2 omers* [4 liters].

replied, "The LORD has appointed tomorrow as a day of rest, a holy Sabbath to the LORD. On this day we will rest from our normal daily tasks. So bake or boil as much as you want today, and set aside what is left for tomorrow."

²⁴The next morning the leftover food was wholesome and good, without maggots or odor. ²⁵Moses said, "This is your food for today, for today is a Sabbath to the LORD. There will be no food on the ground today. ²⁶Gather the food for six days, but the seventh day is a Sabbath. There will be no food on the ground for you on that day."

²⁷Some of the people went out anyway to gather food, even though it was the Sabbath day. But there was none to be found. ²⁸"How long will these people refuse to obey my commands and instructions?" the LORD asked Moses. ²⁹"Do they not realize that I have given them the seventh day, the Sabbath, as a day of rest? That is why I give you twice as much food on the sixth day, so there will be enough for two days. On the Sabbath day you must stay in your places. Do not pick up food from the ground on that day." ³⁰So the people rested on the seventh day.

³¹In time, the food became known as manna.* It was white like coriander seed, and it tasted like honey cakes.

³²Then Moses gave them this command from the LORD: "Take two quarts of manna and keep it forever as a treasured memorial of the LORD's provision. By doing this, later generations will be able to see the bread that the LORD provided in the wilderness when he brought you out of Egypt."

³³Moses said to Aaron, "Get a container and put two quarts of manna into it. Then store it in a sacred place* as a reminder for all future generations." ³⁴Aaron did this, just as the LORD had commanded Moses. He eventually placed it for safekeeping in the Ark of the Covenant.* ³⁵So the people of Israel ate manna for forty years until they arrived in the land of Canaan, where there were crops to eat.

³⁶(The container used to measure the manna was an omer, which held about two quarts.)*

WATER FROM THE ROCK

17 At the LORD's command, the people of Israel left the Sin* Desert and moved from place to place. Eventually they came to Rephidim, but there was no water to be found there. ²So once more the people grumbled and complained to Moses. "Give us water to drink!" they demanded.

"Quiet!" Moses replied. "Why are you arguing with me? And why are you testing the LORD?"

³But tormented by thirst, they continued to complain, "Why did you ever take us out of Egypt? Why did you bring us here? We, our children, and our livestock will all die!"

⁴Then Moses pleaded with the LORD, "What should I do with these people? They are about to stone me!"

⁵The LORD said to Moses, "Take your shepherd's staff, the one you used when you struck the water of the Nile. Then call some of the leaders of Israel and walk on ahead of the people. ⁶I will meet you by the rock at Mount Sinai.* Strike the rock, and water will come pouring out. Then the people will be able to drink." Moses did just as he was told; and as the leaders looked on, water gushed out.

⁷Moses named the place Massah—"the place of testing"—and Meribah—"the place of arguing"—because the people of Israel argued with Moses and tested the LORD by saying, "Is the LORD going to take care of us or not?"

ISRAEL DEFEATS THE AMALEKITES

⁸While the people of Israel were still at Rephidim, the warriors of Amalek came to fight against them. ⁹Moses commanded Joshua, "Call the Israelites to arms, and fight the army of Amalek. Tomorrow, I will stand at

---

16:31 Manna means "What is it?" See 16:15. **16:33** Hebrew *before the LORD.* **16:34** Hebrew *in front of the Testimony.* **16:36** Hebrew *An omer is one tenth of an ephah.* **17:1** Not to be confused with the English word *sin.* **17:6** Hebrew *Horeb,* another name for Sinai.

My Daily Worship

— *January 20* —

GIVING AN ASSIST

EXODUS 15:22 – 18:27

Moses built an altar there and called it
"The LORD Is My Banner" (17:15).

[i reflect]

Winning battles typically involves superior weapons, larger forces, or a better strategy. But when God is Commander-in-Chief, all rules of war are thrown out. Consider how various people participated in winning this particular battle (Exodus 17:8–16): Joshua fought, Moses prayed, Aaron and Hur assisted, and the Lord God, *Yahweh Nissi,* was the rallying point—the banner lifted high that carried them to victory.

As long as Moses kept his eyes focused on God and his arms lifted to him, the Israelites prevailed. But as he grew tired and his arms sagged, the enemy advanced. Aaron and Hur saw Moses' problem, helped him sit, and then physically assisted Moses to keep his arms raised over the battlefield.

How true that is in our lives as well. When we are focused on God, recalling that he is our banner, our victory, and our only hope, we are able to overcome the obstacles and conflicts in life. But when we tire and allow fatigue and weariness of spirit to distract us from spending time with God in worship and prayer, the enemy advances and overtakes us. If we insist on solitary worship and obedience, we will fail. We need other believers to come alongside and assist us to persevere.

Let the examples of Aaron and Hur remind you of an important asset when it comes to your faith walk. Look for opportunities where you can join with others in prayer, encouragement, and worship. Identify those fellow believers who can come alongside you and hold up your hands.

Begin your day as Joshua did, fighting in God's name. Raise your hands to God in constant prayer as Moses did. And look for those Aarons and Hurs who can assist you throughout the day to persevere, keeping your eyes on the Lord, your banner lifted high.

[i pray]

Thank you, Jesus, for the Aarons and Hurs in my life, who come alongside and help.
We lift each other's arms in encouragement and endurance that you provide through one another.
We salute you as Yahweh Nissi *our banner of victory.*

[i respond]

Who are those one or two friends who act as your Aarons and Hurs? Take time to write them a note of thanks, pointing out specifically the ways in which they have assisted you to persevere in the faith. Pledge to them your assistance in return.

the top of the hill with the staff of God in my hand."

[10]So Joshua did what Moses had commanded. He led his men out to fight the army of Amalek. Meanwhile Moses, Aaron, and Hur went to the top of a nearby hill. [11]As long as Moses held up the staff with his hands, the Israelites had the advantage. But whenever he lowered his hands, the Amalekites gained the upper hand. [12]Moses' arms finally became too tired to hold up the staff any longer. So Aaron and Hur found a stone for him to sit on. Then they stood on each side, holding up his hands until sunset. [13]As a result, Joshua and his troops were able to crush the army of Amalek.

[14]Then the LORD instructed Moses, "Write this down as a permanent record, and announce it to Joshua: I will blot out every trace of Amalek from under heaven." [15]Moses built an altar there and called it "The LORD Is My Banner."* [16]He said, "They have dared to raise their fist against the LORD's throne, so now* the LORD will be at war with Amalek generation after generation."

JETHRO'S VISIT TO MOSES

18 Word soon reached Jethro, the priest of Midian and Moses' father-in-law, about all the wonderful things God had done for Moses and his people, the Israelites. He had heard about how the LORD had brought them safely out of Egypt.

[2]Some time before this, Moses had sent his wife, Zipporah, and his two sons to live with Jethro, his father-in-law. [3]The name of Moses' first son was Gershom,* for Moses had said when the boy was born, "I have been a stranger in a foreign land." [4]The name of his second son was Eliezer,* for Moses had said at his birth, "The God of my fathers was my helper; he delivered me from the sword of Pharaoh." [5]Jethro now came to visit Moses, and he brought Moses' wife and two sons with him. They arrived while Moses and the people were camped near the mountain of God.

[6]Moses was told, "Jethro, your father-in-law, has come to visit you. Your wife and your two sons are with him."

[7]So Moses went out to meet his father-in-law. He bowed to him respectfully and greeted him warmly. They asked about each other's health and then went to Moses' tent to talk further. [8]Moses told his father-in-law about everything the LORD had done to rescue Israel from Pharaoh and the Egyptians. He also told him about the problems they had faced along the way and how the LORD had delivered his people from all their troubles. [9]Jethro was delighted when he heard about all that the LORD had done for Israel as he brought them out of Egypt.

[10]"Praise be to the LORD," Jethro said, "for he has saved you from the Egyptians and from Pharaoh. He has rescued Israel from the power of Egypt! [11]I know now that the LORD is greater than all other gods, because his people have escaped from the proud and cruel Egyptians."

[12]Then Jethro presented a burnt offering and gave sacrifices to God. As Jethro was doing this, Aaron and the leaders of Israel came out to meet him. They all joined him in a sacrificial meal in God's presence.

JETHRO'S WISE ADVICE

[13]The next day, Moses sat as usual to hear the people's complaints against each other. They were lined up in front of him from morning till evening.

[14]When Moses' father-in-law saw all that Moses was doing for the people, he said, "Why are you trying to do all this alone? The people have been standing here all day to get your help."

[15]Moses replied, "Well, the people come to me to seek God's guidance. [16]When an argument arises, I am the one who settles the case. I inform the people of God's decisions and teach them his laws and instructions."

[17]"This is not good!" his father-in-law

17:15 Hebrew *Yahweh Nissi.*   **17:16** Or *Hands have been lifted up to the LORD's throne, and now.*   **18:3** Gershom sounds like a Hebrew term that means "a stranger there."   **18:4** Eliezer means "God is my helper."

exclaimed. [18]"You're going to wear yourself out—and the people, too. This job is too heavy a burden for you to handle all by yourself. [19]Now let me give you a word of advice, and may God be with you. You should continue to be the people's representative before God, bringing him their questions to be decided. [20]You should tell them God's decisions, teach them God's laws and instructions, and show them how to conduct their lives. [21]But find some capable, honest men who fear God and hate bribes. Appoint them as judges over groups of one thousand, one hundred, fifty, and ten. [22]These men can serve the people, resolving all the ordinary cases. Anything that is too important or too complicated can be brought to you. But they can take care of the smaller matters themselves. They will help you carry the load, making the task easier for you. [23]If you follow this advice, and if God directs you to do so, then you will be able to endure the pressures, and all these people will go home in peace."

[24]Moses listened to his father-in-law's advice and followed his suggestions. [25]He chose capable men from all over Israel and made them judges over the people. They were put in charge of groups of one thousand, one hundred, fifty, and ten. [26]These men were constantly available to administer justice. They brought the hard cases to Moses, but they judged the smaller matters themselves.

[27]Soon after this, Moses said good-bye to his father-in-law, who returned to his own land.

The Lord Reveals Himself at Sinai

19 The Israelites arrived in the wilderness of Sinai exactly two months after they left Egypt.* [2]After breaking camp at Rephidim, they came to the base of Mount Sinai and set up camp there.

[3]Then Moses climbed the mountain to appear before God. The LORD called out to him from the mountain and said, "Give these instructions to the descendants of Jacob, the people of Israel: [4]'You have seen what I did to the Egyptians. You know how I brought you to myself and carried you on eagle's wings. [5]Now if you will obey me and keep my covenant, you will be my own special treasure from among all the nations of the earth; for all the earth belongs to me. [6]And you will be to me a kingdom of priests, my holy nation.' Give this message to the Israelites."

[7]Moses returned from the mountain and called together the leaders of the people and told them what the LORD had said. [8]They all responded together, "We will certainly do everything the LORD asks of us." So Moses brought the people's answer back to the LORD.

[9]Then the LORD said to Moses, "I am going to come to you in a thick cloud so the people themselves can hear me as I speak to you. Then they will always have confidence in you."

Moses told the LORD what the people had said. [10]Then the LORD told Moses, "Go down and prepare the people for my visit. Purify them today and tomorrow, and have them wash their clothing. [11]Be sure they are ready on the third day, for I will come down upon Mount Sinai as all the people watch. [12]Set boundary lines that the people may not pass. Warn them, 'Be careful! Do not go up on the mountain or even touch its boundaries. Those who do will certainly die! [13]Any people or animals that cross the boundary must be stoned to death or shot with arrows. They must not be touched by human hands.' The people must stay away from the mountain until they hear one long blast from the ram's horn. Then they must gather at the foot of the mountain."

[14]So Moses went down to the people. He purified them for worship and had them wash their clothing. [15]He told them, "Get ready for an important event two days from now. And until then, abstain from having sexual intercourse."

[16]On the morning of the third day, there was a powerful thunder and lightning storm, and

19:1 Hebrew *in the third month . . . on the very day,* i.e., two lunar months to the day after leaving Egypt. This day of the Hebrew lunar calendar occurs in late May or early June; compare note on 13:4.

a dense cloud came down upon the mountain. There was a long, loud blast from a ram's horn, and all the people trembled. ¹⁷Moses led them out from the camp to meet with God, and they stood at the foot of the mountain. ¹⁸All Mount Sinai was covered with smoke because the LORD had descended on it in the form of fire. The smoke billowed into the sky like smoke from a furnace, and the whole mountain shook with a violent earthquake. ¹⁹As the horn blast grew louder and louder, Moses spoke, and God thundered his reply for all to hear. ²⁰The LORD came down on the top of Mount Sinai and called Moses to the top of the mountain. So Moses climbed the mountain.

²¹Then the LORD told Moses, "Go back down and warn the people not to cross the boundaries. They must not come up here to see the LORD, for those who do will die. ²²Even the priests who regularly come near to the LORD must purify themselves, or I will destroy them."

²³"But LORD, the people cannot come up on the mountain!" Moses protested. "You already told them not to. You told me to set boundaries around the mountain and to declare it off limits."

²⁴But the LORD said, "Go down anyway and bring Aaron back with you. In the meantime, do not let the priests or the people cross the boundaries to come up here. If they do, I will punish them."

²⁵So Moses went down to the people and told them what the LORD had said.

THE TEN COMMANDMENTS

20 Then God instructed the people as follows:

²"I am the LORD your God, who rescued you from slavery in Egypt.

³"Do not worship any other gods besides me.

⁴"Do not make idols of any kind, whether in the shape of birds or animals or fish. ⁵You must never worship or bow down to them, for I, the LORD your God, am a jealous God who will not share your affection with any other god! I do not leave unpunished the sins of those who hate me, but I punish the children for the sins of their parents to the third and fourth generations. ⁶But I lavish my love on those who love me and obey my commands, even for a thousand generations.

⁷"Do not misuse the name of the LORD your God. The LORD will not let you go unpunished if you misuse his name.

⁸"Remember to observe the Sabbath day by keeping it holy. ⁹Six days a week are set apart for your daily duties and regular work, ¹⁰but the seventh day is a day of rest dedicated to the LORD your God. On that day no one in your household may do any kind of work. This includes you, your sons and daughters, your male and female servants, your livestock, and any foreigners living among you. ¹¹For in six days the LORD made the heavens, the earth, the sea, and everything in them; then he rested on the seventh day. That is why the LORD blessed the Sabbath day and set it apart as holy.

¹²"Honor your father and mother. Then you will live a long, full life in the land the LORD your God will give you.

¹³"Do not murder.

¹⁴"Do not commit adultery.

¹⁵"Do not steal.

¹⁶"Do not testify falsely against your neighbor.

¹⁷"Do not covet your neighbor's house. Do not covet your neighbor's wife, male or female servant, ox or donkey, or anything else your neighbor owns."

¹⁸When the people heard the thunder and the loud blast of the horn, and when they saw the lightning and the smoke billowing from the mountain, they stood at a distance, trembling with fear.

¹⁹And they said to Moses, "You tell us what God says, and we will listen. But don't let God speak directly to us. If he does, we will die!"

²⁰"Don't be afraid," Moses said, "for God has

My Daily Worship

— *January 21* —

UNNOTICED IDOLS EVERYWHERE?

EXODUS 19:1–21:36

"I am the LORD your God, who rescued you from slavery in Egypt.
Do not worship any other gods besides me. Do not make idols of any kind,
whether in the shape of birds or animals or fish" (20:2–4).

[i reflect]

In 1964, three thousand screaming fans greeted the Beatles as they stepped off the plane for their first United States tour. Their television appearances attracted millions of viewers. Although numerous "teen idols" existed before this group, the Beatles symbolize the invasion of "teen idols" and "rock gods" into the media. "Worshiping idols" sounds absurd to us today. On the other hand, becoming a star's number one fan is accepted, and is almost a rite of adolescence.

As adults, we convince ourselves that we have overcome this teen idol phase. All the while, our real idols go unnoticed and unchecked. In the name of "trying to get ahead," we might worship money and success. Our idolization of outward beauty may translate in our minds as merely a "healthy" quest to look our best.

We're not carving statues, you say. So what?! Our tendency to turn away from God echoes the Israelites' selfishness. We naturally find it easier to dedicate our time, money, love, and strength on the things we *think* we control. And there's the trap. Idols always end up controlling us. Even the words we use to talk about our idols reveal their suffocating effect: We get wrapped up in work or addicted to shopping.

In contrast, worshiping God always has a liberating effect. He asks for your total dedication to *free* you from bondage. God knows our great temptation to worship idols. That's why he highlighted the importance of proper worship from the beginning of his relationship with Israel.

God spoke about faithfulness in his very first commandment to the Israelites. Your desensitization to idols does not excuse your actions. Today, God still asks for your wholehearted devotion. Is there some "idol" in your life right now that is preventing you from wholehearted devotion? Ask God to reveal that to you, and then takes steps to remove it.

[i pray]

I love you Lord. I don't want to share my affection for you with idols. Search my heart
and free me from spiritual bondage and addictions. Forgive me for
devoting my time and energy to worshiping false gods.

[i respond]

A good indication of what or who you serve can be found in your checkbook and date book. Take a minute to go over the last month's entries. How do you spend your time and money? Identify things or activities that have become idols. Ask God to renew your devotion to him.

come in this way to show you his awesome power. From now on, let your fear of him keep you from sinning!"

²¹As the people stood in the distance, Moses entered into the deep darkness where God was.

Proper Use of Altars

²²And the LORD said to Moses, "Say this to the people of Israel: You are witnesses that I have spoken to you from heaven. ²³Remember, you must not make or worship idols of silver or gold.

²⁴"The altars you make for me must be simple altars of earth. Offer on such altars your sacrifices to me—your burnt offerings and peace offerings, your sheep and goats and your cattle. Build altars in the places where I remind you who I am, and I will come and bless you there. ²⁵If you build altars from stone, use only uncut stones. Do not chip or shape the stones with a tool, for that would make them unfit for holy use. ²⁶And you may not approach my altar by steps. If you do, someone might look up under the skirts of your clothing and see your nakedness.

Fair Treatment of Slaves

21 "Here are some other instructions you must present to Israel:

²"If you buy a Hebrew slave, he is to serve for only six years. Set him free in the seventh year, and he will owe you nothing for his freedom. ³If he was single when he became your slave and then married afterward, only he will go free in the seventh year. But if he was married before he became a slave, then his wife will be freed with him.

⁴"If his master gave him a wife while he was a slave, and they had sons or daughters, then the man will be free in the seventh year, but his wife and children will still belong to his master. ⁵But the slave may plainly declare, 'I love my master, my wife, and my children. I would rather not go free.' ⁶If he does this, his master must present him before God.* Then

his master must take him to the door and publicly pierce his ear with an awl. After that, the slave will belong to his master forever.

⁷"When a man sells his daughter as a slave, she will not be freed at the end of six years as the men are. ⁸If she does not please the man who bought her, he may allow her to be bought back again. But he is not allowed to sell her to foreigners, since he is the one who broke the contract with her. ⁹And if the slave girl's owner arranges for her to marry his son, he may no longer treat her as a slave girl, but he must treat her as his daughter. ¹⁰If he himself marries her and then takes another wife, he may not reduce her food or clothing or fail to sleep with her as his wife. ¹¹If he fails in any of these three ways, she may leave as a free woman without making any payment.

Cases of Personal Injury

¹²"Anyone who hits a person hard enough to cause death must be put to death. ¹³But if it is an accident and God allows it to happen, I will appoint a place where the slayer can run for safety. ¹⁴However, if someone deliberately attacks and kills another person, then the slayer must be dragged even from my altar and put to death.

¹⁵"Anyone who strikes father or mother must be put to death.

¹⁶"Kidnappers must be killed, whether they are caught in possession of their victims or have already sold them as slaves.

¹⁷"Anyone who curses father or mother must be put to death.

¹⁸"Now suppose two people quarrel, and one hits the other with a stone or fist, causing injury but not death. ¹⁹If the injured person is later able to walk again, even with a crutch, the assailant will be innocent. Nonetheless, the assailant must pay for time lost because of the injury and must pay for the medical expenses.

²⁰"If a male or female slave is beaten and dies, the owner must be punished. ²¹If the slave recovers after a couple of days, however,

21:6 Or *before the judges.*

then the owner should not be punished, since the slave is the owner's property.

²²"Now suppose two people are fighting, and in the process, they hurt a pregnant woman so her child is born prematurely. If no further harm results, then the person responsible must pay damages in the amount the woman's husband demands and the judges approve. ²³But if any harm results, then the offender must be punished according to the injury. If the result is death, the offender must be executed. ²⁴If an eye is injured, injure the eye of the person who did it. If a tooth gets knocked out, knock out the tooth of the person who did it. Similarly, the payment must be hand for hand, foot for foot, ²⁵burn for burn, wound for wound, bruise for bruise.

²⁶"If an owner hits a male or female slave in the eye and the eye is blinded, then the slave may go free because of the eye. ²⁷And if an owner knocks out the tooth of a male or female slave, the slave should be released in payment for the tooth.

²⁸"If a bull gores a man or woman to death, the bull must be stoned, and its flesh may not be eaten. In such a case, however, the owner will not be held liable. ²⁹Suppose, on the other hand, that the owner knew the bull had gored people in the past, yet the bull was not kept under control. If this is true and if the bull kills someone, it must be stoned, and the owner must also be killed. ³⁰However, the dead person's relatives may accept payment from the owner of the bull to compensate for the loss of life. The owner will have to pay whatever is demanded.

³¹"The same principle applies if the bull gores a boy or a girl. ³²But if the bull gores a slave, either male or female, the slave's owner is to be given thirty silver coins* in payment, and the bull must be stoned.

³³"Suppose someone digs or uncovers a well and fails to cover it, and then an ox or a donkey falls into it. ³⁴The owner of the well must pay in full for the dead animal but then gets to keep it.

³⁵"If someone's bull injures a neighbor's bull and the injured bull dies, then the two owners must sell the live bull and divide the money between them. Each will also own half of the dead bull. ³⁶But if the bull was known from past experience to gore, yet its owner failed to keep it under control, the money will not be divided. The owner of the living bull must pay in full for the dead bull but then gets to keep it.

PROTECTION OF PROPERTY

22 "A fine must be paid by anyone who steals an ox or sheep and then kills or sells it. For oxen the fine is five oxen for each one stolen. For sheep the fine is four sheep for each one stolen.

²"If a thief is caught in the act of breaking into a house and is killed in the process, the person who killed the thief is not guilty. ³But if it happens in daylight, the one who killed the thief is guilty of murder.

"A thief who is caught must pay in full for everything that was stolen. If payment is not made, the thief must be sold as a slave to pay the debt. ⁴If someone steals an ox or a donkey or a sheep and it is recovered alive, then the thief must pay double the value.

⁵"If an animal is grazing in a field or vineyard and the owner lets it stray into someone else's field to graze, then the animal's owner must pay damages in the form of high-quality grain or grapes.

⁶"If a fire gets out of control and goes into another person's field, destroying the sheaves or the standing grain, then the one who started the fire must pay for the lost crops.

⁷"Suppose someone entrusts money or goods to a neighbor, and they are stolen from the neighbor's house. If the thief is found, the fine is double the value of what was stolen. ⁸But if the thief is not found, God* will determine whether or not it was the neighbor who stole the property.

⁹"Suppose there is a dispute between two people as to who owns a particular ox,

---

21:32 Hebrew *30 shekels of silver,* about 12 ounces or 342 grams in weight 22:8 Or *the judges.*

Bow

Bow—Hebrew *hish-tach-e-vah* [from *shachah*], "bow down, prostrate oneself"; *ka-ra'* "bow down"; *qa-dad* "bow low"; Greek *pros-ku-ne-o* "bow down, prostrate oneself."

The Bible has a concrete way of expressing things. It doesn't go in for grand abstractions but looks at the specific action associated with a spiritual truth. For one thing, it doesn't have an abstract word for *worship*. Both the Greek and Hebrew words translated *worship* mean, literally, to bow down or fall prostrate.

Bowing is a gesture of humility before someone who is greater than us. It conveys the respect a servant has for his master. To "give your bodies to God," Paul says, is a mark of our worship (Romans 12:1). If the Lord is our Master, we might look for some way in our prayer and devotion to symbolize that relationship—not just in our heads or in our spirits but with our bodies as well. Whether we fall on our faces or our knees, or find some other way to bow before the Lord, our action is a reminder that worship is a down-to-earth activity.

donkey, sheep, article of clothing, or anything else. Both parties must come before God* for a decision, and the person whom God declares* guilty must pay double to the other.

¹⁰"Now suppose someone asks a neighbor to care for a donkey, ox, sheep, or any other animal, but it dies or is injured or gets away, and there is no eyewitness to report just what happened. ¹¹The neighbor must then take an oath of innocence in the presence of the LORD. The owner must accept the neighbor's word, and no payment will be required. ¹²But if the animal or property was stolen, payment must be made to the owner. ¹³If it was attacked by a wild animal, the carcass must be shown as evidence, and no payment will be required.

¹⁴"If someone borrows an animal from a neighbor and it is injured or killed, and if the owner was not there at the time, the person who borrowed it must pay for it. ¹⁵But if the owner is there, no payment is required. And no payment is required if the animal was rented because this loss was covered by the rental fee.

SOCIAL RESPONSIBILITY

¹⁶"If a man seduces a virgin who is not engaged to anyone and sleeps with her, he must pay the customary dowry and accept her as his wife. ¹⁷But if her father refuses to let her marry him, the man must still pay the money for her dowry.

¹⁸"A sorceress must not be allowed to live.

¹⁹"Anyone who has sexual relations with an animal must be executed.

²⁰"Anyone who sacrifices to any god other than the LORD must be destroyed.

²¹"Do not oppress foreigners in any way. Remember, you yourselves were once foreigners in the land of Egypt.

²²"Do not exploit widows or orphans. ²³If you do and they cry out to me, then I will surely help them. ²⁴My anger will blaze forth against you, and I will kill you with the sword. Your wives will become widows, and your children will become fatherless.

²⁵"If you lend money to a fellow Hebrew in need, do not be like a money lender, charging interest. ²⁶If you take your neighbor's cloak as a pledge of repayment, you must return it by nightfall. ²⁷Your neighbor will need it to stay warm during the night. If you do not return it and your neighbor cries out to me for help, then I will hear, for I am very merciful.

²⁸"Do not blaspheme God* or curse anyone who rules over you.

²⁹"Do not hold anything back when you give me the tithe of your crops and your wine.

22:9a Or *before the judges.*   **22:9b** Or *whom the judges declare.*   **22:28** Or *Do not revile your judges.*

"You must make the necessary payment for redemption of your firstborn sons.

[30]"You must also give me the firstborn of your cattle and sheep. Leave the newborn animal with its mother for seven days; then give it to me on the eighth day.

[31]"You are my own holy people. Therefore, do not eat any animal that has been attacked and killed by a wild animal. Throw its carcass out for the dogs to eat.

A CALL FOR JUSTICE

23 "Do not pass along false reports. Do not cooperate with evil people by telling lies on the witness stand.

[2]"Do not join a crowd that intends to do evil. When you are on the witness stand, do not be swayed in your testimony by the opinion of the majority. [3]And do not slant your testimony in favor of a person just because that person is poor.

[4]"If you come upon your enemy's ox or donkey that has strayed away, take it back to its owner. [5]If you see the donkey of someone who hates you struggling beneath a heavy load, do not walk by. Instead, stop and offer to help.

[6]"Do not twist justice against people simply because they are poor.

[7]"Keep far away from falsely charging anyone with evil. Never put an innocent or honest person to death. I will not allow anyone guilty of this to go free.

[8]"Take no bribes, for a bribe makes you ignore something that you clearly see. A bribe always hurts the cause of the person who is in the right.

[9]"Do not oppress the foreigners living among you. You know what it is like to be a foreigner. Remember your own experience in the land of Egypt.

[10]"Plant and harvest your crops for six years, [11]but let the land rest and lie fallow during the seventh year. Then let the poor among you harvest any volunteer crop that may come up. Leave the rest for the animals to eat. The same applies to your vineyards and olive groves.

[12]"Work for six days, and rest on the seventh. This will give your ox and your donkey a chance to rest. It will also allow the people of your household, including your slaves and visitors, to be refreshed.

[13]"Be sure to obey all my instructions. And remember, never pray to or swear by any other gods. Do not even mention their names.

THREE ANNUAL FESTIVALS

[14]"Each year you must celebrate three festivals in my honor. [15]The first is the Festival of Unleavened Bread. For seven days you are to eat bread made without yeast, just as I commanded you before. This festival will be an annual event at the appointed time in early spring,* for that is the anniversary of your exodus from Egypt. Everyone must bring me a sacrifice at that time. [16]You must also celebrate the Festival of Harvest,* when you bring me the first crops of your harvest. Finally, you are to celebrate the Festival of the Final Harvest* at the end of the harvest season. [17]At these three times each year, every man in Israel must appear before the Sovereign LORD.

[18]"Sacrificial blood must never be offered together with bread that has yeast in it. And no sacrificial fat may be left unoffered until the next morning.

[19]"As you harvest each of your crops, bring me a choice sample of the first day's harvest. It must be offered to the LORD your God.

"You must not cook a young goat in its mother's milk.

A PROMISE OF THE LORD'S PRESENCE

[20]"See, I am sending my angel before you to lead you safely to the land I have prepared for you. [21]Pay attention to him, and obey all of his instructions. Do not rebel against him, for he will not forgive your sins. He is my

---

23:15 Hebrew *in the month of Abib.* This month of the Hebrew lunar calendar usually occurs in March and April. **23:16a** Or *Festival of Weeks.* **23:16b** This was later called the Festival of Shelters; see Lev 23:33-36.

representative—he bears my name. [22]But if you are careful to obey him, following all my instructions, then I will be an enemy to your enemies, and I will oppose those who oppose you. [23]For my angel will go before you and bring you into the land of the Amorites, Hittites, Perizzites, Canaanites, Hivites, and Jebusites, so you may live there. And I will destroy them. [24]Do not worship the gods of these other nations or serve them in any way, and never follow their evil example. Instead, you must utterly conquer them and break down their shameful idols.

[25]"You must serve only the LORD your God. If you do, I will bless you with food and water, and I will keep you healthy. [26]There will be no miscarriages or infertility among your people, and I will give you long, full lives.

[27]"I will send my terror upon all the people whose lands you invade, and they will panic before you. [28]I will send hornets ahead of you to drive out the Hivites, Canaanites, and Hittites. [29]But I will not do this all in one year because the land would become a wilderness, and the wild animals would become too many to control. [30]I will drive them out a little at a time until your population has increased enough to fill the land. [31]And I will fix your boundaries from the Red Sea to the Mediterranean Sea,* and from the southern deserts to the Euphrates River.* I will help you defeat the people now living in the land, and you will drive them out ahead of you.

[32]"Make no treaties with them and have nothing to do with their gods. [33]Do not even let them live among you! If you do, they will infect you with their sin of idol worship, and that would be disastrous for you."

ISRAEL ACCEPTS THE LORD'S COVENANT

24 Then the LORD instructed Moses: "Come up here to me, and bring along Aaron, Nadab, Abihu, and seventy of Israel's leaders. All of them must worship at a distance. [2]You alone, Moses, are allowed to come near to the LORD. The others must not come too close. And remember, none of the other people are allowed to climb on the mountain at all."

[3]When Moses had announced to the people all the teachings and regulations the LORD had given him, they answered in unison, "We will do everything the LORD has told us to do."

[4]Then Moses carefully wrote down all the LORD's instructions. Early the next morning he built an altar at the foot of the mountain. He also set up twelve pillars around the altar, one for each of the twelve tribes of Israel. [5]Then he sent some of the young men to sacrifice young bulls as burnt offerings and peace offerings to the LORD. [6]Moses took half the blood from these animals and drew it off into basins. The other half he splashed against the altar.

[7]Then he took the Book of the Covenant and read it to the people. They all responded again, "We will do everything the LORD has commanded. We will obey."

[8]Then Moses sprinkled the blood from the basins over the people and said, "This blood confirms the covenant the LORD has made with you in giving you these laws."

[9]Then Moses, Aaron, Nadab, Abihu, and seventy of the leaders of Israel went up the mountain. [10]There they saw the God of Israel. Under his feet there seemed to be a pavement of brilliant sapphire, as clear as the heavens. [11]And though Israel's leaders saw God, he did not destroy them. In fact, they shared a meal together in God's presence!

[12]And the LORD said to Moses, "Come up to me on the mountain. Stay there while I give you the tablets of stone that I have inscribed with my instructions and commands. Then you will teach the people from them." [13]So Moses and his assistant Joshua climbed up the mountain of God.

[14]Moses told the other leaders, "Stay here and wait for us until we come back. If there are any problems while I am gone, consult with Aaron and Hur, who are here with you." [15]Then Moses went up the mountain, and

---

23:31a Hebrew *from the sea of reeds to the sea of the Philistines.*   23:31b Hebrew *the river.*

My Daily Worship

— *January 22* —

Is Your God Awesome?

EXODUS 22:1–24:18

The Israelites at the foot of the mountain saw an awesome sight.
The awesome glory of the LORD on the mountaintop
looked like a devouring fire (24:17).

[i reflect]

"That's totally awesome!" we say. Of all God's attributes, his *awesomeness* has taken the largest verbal mangling by the younger generation. Around your home or on TV, this word has probably been hurled at you more than once. It's overused and is applied to anything. (A new car? *Awesome!*) The time has come to reclaim this word, because in all seriousness, God *is* totally awesome.

To be awesome is to command both fear and adoration. In the Bible, God chose certain situations to highlight different parts of his character, including his awesomeness. With Moses and seventy other leaders perched on Mount Sinai, God chose to demonstrate this characteristic in the hearts of the people standing below.

At the time, the Israelites fully understood God's greatness as he seemingly torched the mountain. Sadly, a month later the people were bowing down to a golden cow. Apparently, asking for signs and proof of God's awesomeness did not guarantee they would worship him.

Experiencing God's awesomeness moves us one step closer to knowing him. So, how do you get to the place where you personally recognize and respond to God's greatness? Does simply singing the words, "Our God is an awesome God!" help you experience fear and adoration in his presence?

Instead of attempting to force a respectful response in worship, begin by looking inward. Seeing God's awesomeness also means acknowledging the truth about yourself—seeing your own frailty and dependence on him for *everything*. Picture yourself standing before God, insignificant in the light of his glory. Let God's greatness resonate in your spirit and change your posture. God yearns to greatly impact and work in the lives of those who humble themselves in this way.

[i pray]

Forgive me, Lord, for puffing up my status and importance instead of acknowledging
your awesome glory. Teach me to view myself honestly. I depend on you
for my daily needs, and I give you the praise for my successes.

[i respond]

When you think of God, what characteristics immediately come to mind? Do these attributes reflect one side of God's personality (loving, kind), while ignoring others (holy, truthful)? Just as no one can define you with a few words, don't limit God to a narrow definition or picture in your mind.

the cloud covered it. [16]And the glorious presence of the LORD rested upon Mount Sinai, and the cloud covered it for six days. On the seventh day the LORD called to Moses from the cloud. [17]The Israelites at the foot of the mountain saw an awesome sight. The awesome glory of the LORD on the mountaintop looked like a devouring fire. [18]Then Moses disappeared into the cloud as he climbed higher up the mountain. He stayed on the mountain forty days and forty nights.

OFFERINGS FOR THE TABERNACLE

25 The LORD said to Moses, [2]"Tell the people of Israel that everyone who wants to may bring me an offering. [3]Here is a list of items you may accept on my behalf: gold, silver, and bronze; [4]blue, purple, and scarlet yarn; fine linen; goat hair for cloth; [5]tanned ram skins and fine goatskin leather; acacia wood; [6]olive oil for the lamps; spices for the anointing oil and the fragrant incense; [7]onyx stones, and other stones to be set in the ephod and the chestpiece.

[8]"I want the people of Israel to build me a sacred residence where I can live among them. [9]You must make this Tabernacle and its furnishings exactly according to the plans I will show you.

PLANS FOR THE ARK

[10]"Make an Ark of acacia wood—a sacred chest 3¾ feet long, 2¼ feet wide, and 2¼ feet high.* [11]Overlay it inside and outside with pure gold, and put a molding of gold all around it. [12]Cast four rings of gold for it, and attach them to its four feet, two rings on each side. [13]Make poles from acacia wood, and overlay them with gold. [14]Fit the poles into the rings at the sides of the Ark to carry it. [15]These carrying poles must never be taken from the rings; they are to be left there permanently. [16]When the Ark is finished, place inside it the stone tablets inscribed with the terms of the covenant,* which I will give to you.

[17]"Then make the Ark's cover—the place of atonement—out of pure gold. It must be 3¾ feet long and 2¼ feet wide. [18]Then use hammered gold to make two cherubim, and place them at the two ends of the atonement cover. [19]Attach the cherubim to each end of the atonement cover, making it all one piece. [20]The cherubim will face each other, looking down on the atonement cover with their wings spread out above it. [21]Place inside the Ark the stone tablets inscribed with the terms of the covenant, which I will give to you. Then put the atonement cover on top of the Ark. [22]I will meet with you there and talk to you from above the atonement cover between the gold cherubim that hover over the Ark of the Covenant.* From there I will give you my commands for the people of Israel.

PLANS FOR THE TABLE

[23]"Then make a table of acacia wood, 3 feet long, 1½ feet wide, and 2¼ feet high. [24]Overlay it with pure gold and run a molding of gold around it. [25]Put a rim about three inches* wide around the top edge, and put a gold molding all around the rim. [26]Make four gold rings, and put the rings at the four corners by the four legs, [27]close to the rim around the top. These rings will support the poles used to carry the table. [28]Make these poles from acacia wood and overlay them with gold. [29]And make gold plates and dishes, as well as pitchers and bowls to be used in pouring out drink offerings. [30]You must always keep the special Bread of the Presence on the table before me.

PLANS FOR THE LAMPSTAND

[31]"Make a lampstand of pure, hammered gold. The entire lampstand and its decorations will be one piece—the base, center stem, lamp cups, buds, and blossoms. [32]It will have six branches, three branches going out from each

25:10 Hebrew *2½ cubits* [1.1 meters] *long, 1½ cubits* [0.7 meters] *wide, and 1½ cubits high.* In this chapter, the distance measures are calculated from the Hebrew cubit at a ratio of 18 inches or 45 centimeters per cubit. 25:16 Hebrew *place inside it the Testimony;* also in 25:21. 25:22 Or *Ark of the Testimony.* 25:25 Hebrew *a handbreadth* [8 centimeters].

My Daily Worship

— January 23 —

GOD'S MOBILE HOME

EXODUS 25:1–27:21

I want the people of Israel to build me a sacred residence
where I can live among them (25:8).

[i reflect]

When men and women venture into the wilderness, they often carry their homes on their backs. Lightweight tents provide shelter from wind and rain, yet can be folded up and packed to the next campsite. Though thin walls and a simple framework can't pass for bricks and beams, a tent creates a special place of protection, warmth, unity, and fellowship. Tents enclose those who enter. When God commissioned the Israelites to build him a moveable home, he obviously wasn't asking them for protection from the rain. He's *God*. Like a backpacking tent, the Tabernacle served much greater purposes. It invited God's people to meet him.

In all of its grandeur, the Tabernacle never came close to the complexity and wonder of the birth of a single baby. The structure would always be man-made. The Tabernacle was important for its ability to teach the Israelites about their Lord. The Holy Place and Most Holy Place declared God's perfect holiness and purity. The Tabernacle's detailed instructions proclaimed God's creative genius. And finally, the Tabernacle's portable nature told a migrant people that their God would always be with them.

For us, the Tabernacle is merely a copy of what's awaiting us in heaven—an eternal communion in God's presence. Throughout the Bible, from the Tabernacle to the Temple to the birth of Jesus Christ, God has shown himself as our Immanuel, "God with us."

Wherever you go, God is with you. You don't have to make a pilgrimage to worship God. He goes with you and "lives among you." You don't have to reach up to the heavens. God is with you right now. Come into his presence and worship.

[i pray]

Even though I often forget about you, you still promise never to leave me or abandon me.
You are my Immanuel! You want to be with me just as I am. I will praise you, Lord.
Walk beside me and teach me your holiness.

[i respond]

Do you always talk with God in a certain location? Expand your comfort zone by reaching out to him in new or unusual places. Since God is always with you, recognizing his presence in each corner of your life will point out areas you still need to give him.

side of the center stem. ³³Each of the six branches will hold a cup shaped like an almond blossom, complete with buds and petals. ³⁴The center stem of the lampstand will be decorated with four almond blossoms, complete with buds and petals. ³⁵One blossom will be set beneath each pair of branches where they extend from the center stem. ³⁶The decorations and branches must all be one piece with the stem, and they must be hammered from pure gold. ³⁷Then make the seven lamps for the lampstand, and set them so they reflect their light forward. ³⁸The lamp snuffers and trays must also be made of pure gold. ³⁹You will need seventy-five pounds* of pure gold for the lampstand and its accessories.

⁴⁰"Be sure that you make everything according to the pattern I have shown you here on the mountain.

PLANS FOR THE TABERNACLE

26 "Make the Tabernacle from ten sheets of fine linen. These sheets are to be decorated with blue, purple, and scarlet yarn, with figures of cherubim skillfully embroidered into them. ²Each sheet must be forty-two feet long and six feet wide.* All ten sheets must be exactly the same size. ³Join five of these sheets together into one set; then join the other five sheets into a second set. ⁴Put loops of blue yarn along the edge of the last sheet in each set. ⁵The fifty loops along the edge of one set are to match the fifty loops along the edge of the other. ⁶Then make fifty gold clasps to fasten the loops of the two sets of sheets together, making the Tabernacle a single unit.

⁷"Make heavy sheets of cloth from goat hair to cover the Tabernacle. There must be eleven of these sheets, ⁸each forty-five feet long and six feet wide. All eleven of these sheets must be exactly the same size. ⁹Join five of these together into one set, and join the other six into a second set. The sixth sheet of the second set is to be doubled over at the entrance

of the sacred tent. ¹⁰Put fifty loops along the edge of the last sheet in each set, ¹¹and fasten them together with fifty bronze clasps. In this way, the two sets will become a single unit. ¹²An extra half sheet of this roof covering will be left to hang over the back of the Tabernacle, ¹³and the covering will hang down an extra eighteen inches on each side. ¹⁴On top of these coverings place a layer of tanned ram skins, and over them put a layer of fine goatskin leather. This will complete the roof covering.

¹⁵"The framework of the Tabernacle will consist of frames made of acacia wood. ¹⁶Each frame must be 15 feet high and 2¼ feet wide. ¹⁷There will be two pegs on each frame so they can be joined to the next frame. All the frames must be made this way. ¹⁸Twenty of these frames will support the south side of the Tabernacle. ¹⁹They will fit into forty silver bases—two bases under each frame. ²⁰On the north side there will also be twenty of these frames, ²¹with their forty silver bases, two bases for each frame. ²²On the west side there will be six frames, ²³along with an extra frame at each corner. ²⁴These corner frames will be connected at the bottom and firmly attached at the top with a single ring, forming a single unit. Both of these corner frames will be made the same way. ²⁵So there will be eight frames on that end of the Tabernacle, supported by sixteen silver bases—two bases under each frame.

²⁶"Make crossbars of acacia wood to run across the frames, five crossbars for the north side of the Tabernacle ²⁷and five for the south side. Also make five crossbars for the rear of the Tabernacle, which will face westward. ²⁸The middle crossbar, halfway up the frames, will run all the way from one end of the Tabernacle to the other. ²⁹Overlay the frames with gold and make gold rings to support the crossbars. Overlay the crossbars with gold as well.

³⁰"Set up this Tabernacle according to the design you were shown on the mountain.

25:39 Hebrew *1 talent* [34 kilograms]. 26:2 Hebrew *28 cubits* [12.6 meters] *long and 4 cubits* [1.8 meters] *wide.* In this chapter, the distance measures are calculated from the Hebrew cubit at a ratio of 18 inches or 45 centimeters per cubit.

³¹"Across the inside of the Tabernacle hang a special curtain made of fine linen, with cherubim skillfully embroidered into the cloth using blue, purple, and scarlet yarn. ³²Hang this inner curtain on gold hooks set into four posts made from acacia wood and overlaid with gold. The posts will fit into silver bases. ³³When the inner curtain is in place, put the Ark of the Covenant* behind it. This curtain will separate the Holy Place from the Most Holy Place.

³⁴"Then put the Ark's cover—the place of atonement—on top of the Ark of the Covenant inside the Most Holy Place. ³⁵Place the table and lampstand across the room from each other outside the inner curtain. The lampstand must be placed on the south side, and the table must be set toward the north.

³⁶"Make another curtain from fine linen for the entrance of the sacred tent, and embroider exquisite designs into it, using blue, purple, and scarlet yarn. ³⁷Hang this curtain on gold hooks set into five posts made from acacia wood and overlaid with gold. The posts will fit into five bronze bases.

PLANS FOR THE ALTAR OF BURNT OFFERING

27 "Using acacia wood, make a square altar 7½ feet wide, 7½ feet long, and 4½ feet high.* ²Make a horn at each of the four corners of the altar so the horns and altar are all one piece. Overlay the altar and its horns with bronze. ³The ash buckets, shovels, basins, meat hooks, and firepans will all be made of bronze. ⁴Make a bronze grating, with a metal ring at each corner. ⁵Fit the grating halfway down into the firebox, resting it on the ledge built there. ⁶For moving the altar, make poles from acacia wood, and overlay them with bronze. ⁷To carry it, put the poles into the rings at two sides of the altar. ⁸The altar must be hollow, made from planks. Be careful to build it just as you were shown on the mountain.

PLANS FOR THE COURTYARD

⁹"Then make a courtyard for the Tabernacle, enclosed with curtains made from fine linen. On the south side the curtains will stretch for 150 feet. ¹⁰They will be held up by twenty bronze posts that fit into twenty bronze bases. The curtains will be held up with silver hooks attached to the silver rods that are attached to the posts. ¹¹It will be the same on the north side of the courtyard—150 feet of curtains held up by twenty posts fitted into bronze bases, with silver hooks and rods. ¹²The curtains on the west end of the courtyard will be 75 feet long, supported by ten posts set into

---

Words of Worship

MERCY

Mercy, Have Mercy—Hebrew *cha-nan* "show mercy, favor"; *chen* "mercy, favor"; Greek *e-le-e-o* "have mercy"; *e-le-os* "mercy."

Our worship of our Creator is a response to his greatness. Confronted by his awesome power, we can only bow humbly before him. But our worship is also a response to his mercy. Overwhelmed by a sense of our unworthiness, we praise God for the help and forgiveness he extends to us. "For he understands how weak we are; he knows we are only dust" (Psalm 103:14).

Jesus told of a tax collector who cried out, "O God, be merciful to me, for I am a sinner" (Luke 18:13). This is also our prayer. But our worship doesn't stop with this plea because we have the assurance of God's mercy to everyone who comes to him through the cross of Christ. With Paul, we rejoice in God's mercy: "But God showed his great love for us by sending Christ to die for us while we were still sinners" (Romans 5:8).

26:33 Or *Ark of the Testimony*; also in 26:34. **27:1** Hebrew *5 cubits* [2.3 meters] *wide, 5 cubits long, and 3 cubits* [1.4 meters] *high*. In this chapter, the distance measures are calculated from the Hebrew cubit at a ratio of 18 inches or 45 centimeters per cubit.

ten bases. [13]The east end will also be 75 feet long. [14]The courtyard entrance will be on the east end, flanked by two curtains. The curtain on the right side will be 22½ feet long, supported by three posts set into three bases. [15]The curtain on the left side will also be 22½ feet long, supported by three posts set into three bases.

[16]"For the entrance to the courtyard, make a curtain that is 30 feet long. Fashion it from fine linen, and decorate it with beautiful embroidery in blue, purple, and scarlet yarn. It will be attached to four posts that fit into four bases. [17]All the posts around the courtyard must be connected by silver rods, using silver hooks. The posts are to be set in solid bronze bases. [18]So the entire courtyard will be 150 feet long and 75 feet wide, with curtain walls 7½ feet high, made from fine linen. The bases supporting its walls will be made of bronze.

[19]"All the articles used in the work of the Tabernacle, including all the tent pegs used to support the Tabernacle and the courtyard curtains, must be made of bronze.

[20]"Tell the people of Israel to bring you pure olive oil for the lampstand, so it can be kept burning continually. [21]The lampstand will be placed outside the inner curtain of the Most Holy Place in the Tabernacle.* Aaron and his sons will keep the lamps burning in the LORD's presence day and night. This is a permanent law for the people of Israel, and it must be kept by all future generations.

CLOTHING FOR THE PRIESTS

28 "Your brother, Aaron, and his sons, Nadab, Abihu, Eleazar, and Ithamar, will be set apart from the common people. They will be my priests and will minister to me. [2]Make special clothing for Aaron to show his separation to God—beautiful garments that will lend dignity to his work. [3]Instruct all those who have special skills as tailors to make the garments that will set Aaron apart from

everyone else, so he may serve me as a priest. [4]They are to make a chestpiece, an ephod, a robe, an embroidered tunic, a turban, and a sash. They will also make special garments for Aaron's sons to wear when they serve as priests before me. [5]These items must be made of fine linen cloth and embroidered with gold thread and blue, purple, and scarlet yarn.

DESIGN OF THE EPHOD

[6]"The ephod must be made of fine linen cloth and skillfully embroidered with gold thread and blue, purple, and scarlet yarn. [7]It will consist of two pieces, front and back, joined at the shoulders with two shoulder-pieces. [8]And the sash will be made of the same materials: fine linen cloth embroidered with gold thread and blue, purple, and scarlet yarn. [9]Take two onyx stones and engrave on them the names of the tribes of Israel. [10]Six names will be on each stone, naming all the tribes in the order of their ancestors' births. [11]Engrave these names in the same way a gemcutter engraves a seal. Mount the stones in gold settings. [12]Fasten the two stones on the shoulder-pieces of the ephod as memorial stones for the people of Israel. Aaron will carry these names before the LORD as a constant reminder. [13]The settings are to be made of gold filigree, [14]and two cords made of pure gold will be attached to the settings on the shoulders of the ephod.

DESIGN OF THE CHESTPIECE

[15]"Then, with the most careful workmanship, make a chestpiece that will be used to determine God's will. Use the same materials as you did for the ephod: fine linen cloth embroidered with gold thread and blue, purple, and scarlet yarn. [16]This chestpiece will be made of two folds of cloth, forming a pouch nine inches* square. [17]Four rows of gemstones* will be attached to it. The first row will contain a red carnelian, a chrysolite, and an emerald. [18]The second row will contain a turquoise, a sapphire, and a white moonstone.

27:21 Hebrew *in the Tent of Meeting, outside of the inner curtain, in front of the Testimony.* 28:16 Hebrew *1 span* [23 centimeters]. 28:17 The identification of some of these gemstones is uncertain.

¹⁹The third row will contain a Jacinth, an agate, and an amethyst. ²⁰The fourth row will contain a beryl, an onyx, and a jasper. All these stones will be set in gold. ²¹Each stone will represent one of the tribes of Israel, and the name of that tribe will be engraved on it as though it were a seal.

²²"To attach the chestpiece to the ephod, make braided cords of pure gold. ²³Then make two gold rings and attach them to the top corners of the chestpiece. ²⁴The two gold cords will go through the rings on the chestpiece, ²⁵and the ends of the cords will be tied to the gold settings on the shoulder-pieces of the ephod. ²⁶Then make two more gold rings, and attach them to the two lower inside corners of the chestpiece next to the ephod. ²⁷And make two more gold rings and attach them to the ephod near the sash. ²⁸Then attach the bottom rings of the chestpiece to the rings on the ephod with blue cords. This will hold the chestpiece securely to the ephod above the beautiful sash. ²⁹In this way, Aaron will carry the names of the tribes of Israel on the chestpiece over his heart when he goes into the presence of the LORD in the Holy Place. Thus, the LORD will be reminded of his people continually. ³⁰Insert into the pocket of the chestpiece the Urim and Thummim, to be carried over Aaron's heart when he goes into the LORD's presence. Thus, Aaron will always carry the objects used to determine the LORD's will for his people whenever he goes in before the LORD.

ADDITIONAL CLOTHING FOR THE PRIESTS

³¹"Make the robe of the ephod entirely of blue cloth, ³²with an opening for Aaron's head in the middle of it. The opening will be reinforced by a woven collar* so it will not tear. ³³Make pomegranates out of blue, purple, and scarlet yarn, and attach them to the hem of the robe, with gold bells between them. ³⁴The gold bells and pomegranates are to alternate all the way around the hem. ³⁵Aaron will wear

this robe whenever he enters the Holy Place to minister to the LORD, and the bells will tinkle as he goes in and out of the LORD's presence. If he wears it, he will not die.

³⁶"Next make a medallion of pure gold. Using the techniques of an engraver, inscribe it with these words: SET APART AS HOLY TO THE LORD. ³⁷This medallion will be attached to the front of Aaron's turban by means of a blue cord. ³⁸Aaron will wear it on his forehead, thus bearing the guilt connected with any errors regarding the sacred offerings of the people of Israel. He must always wear it so the LORD will accept the people.

³⁹"Weave Aaron's patterned tunic from fine linen cloth. Fashion the turban out of this linen as well. Also make him an embroidered sash.

⁴⁰"Then for Aaron's sons, make tunics, sashes, and headdresses to give them dignity and respect. ⁴¹Clothe Aaron and his sons with these garments, and then anoint and ordain them. Set them apart as holy so they can serve as my priests. ⁴²Also make linen underclothes for them, to be worn next to their bodies, reaching from waist to thigh. ⁴³These must be worn whenever Aaron and his sons enter the Tabernacle* or approach the altar in the Holy Place to perform their duties. Thus they will not incur guilt and die. This law is permanent for Aaron and his descendants.

DEDICATION OF THE PRIESTS

29 "This is the ceremony for the dedication of Aaron and his sons as priests: Take a young bull and two rams with no physical defects. ²Then using fine wheat flour and no yeast, make loaves of bread, thin cakes mixed with olive oil, and wafers with oil poured over them. ³Place these various kinds of bread in a single basket, and present them at the entrance of the Tabernacle, along with the young bull and the two rams.

⁴"Present Aaron and his sons at the entrance of the Tabernacle,* and wash them

28:32 The meaning of the Hebrew is uncertain. 28:43 Hebrew *Tent of Meeting.* 29:4 Hebrew *Tent of Meeting;* also in 29:10, 11, 30, 32, 42, 44.

with water. ⁵Then put Aaron's tunic on him, along with the embroidered robe of the ephod, the ephod itself, the chestpiece, and the sash. ⁶And place on his head the turban with the gold medallion. ⁷Then take the anointing oil and pour it over his head. ⁸Next present his sons, and dress them in their tunics ⁹with their woven sashes and their headdresses. They will then be priests forever. In this way, you will ordain Aaron and his sons.

¹⁰"Then bring the young bull to the entrance of the Tabernacle, and Aaron and his sons will lay their hands on its head. ¹¹You will then slaughter it in the LORD's presence at the entrance of the Tabernacle. ¹²Smear some of its blood on the horns of the altar with your finger, and pour out the rest at the base of the altar. ¹³Take all the fat that covers the internal organs, also the long lobe of the liver and the two kidneys with their fat, and burn them on the altar. ¹⁴Then take the carcass (including the skin and the dung) outside the camp, and burn it as a sin offering.

¹⁵"Next Aaron and his sons must lay their hands on the head of one of the rams ¹⁶as it is slaughtered. Its blood will be collected and sprinkled on the sides of the altar. ¹⁷Cut up the ram and wash off the internal organs and the legs. Set them alongside the head and the other pieces of the body, ¹⁸and burn them all on the altar. This is a burnt offering to the LORD, which is very pleasing to him.

¹⁹"Now take the other ram and have Aaron and his sons lay their hands on its head ²⁰as it is slaughtered. Collect the blood and place some of it on the tip of the right earlobes of Aaron and his sons. Also put it on their right thumbs and the big toes of their right feet. Sprinkle the rest of the blood on the sides of the altar. ²¹Then take some of the blood from the altar and mix it with some of the anointing oil. Sprinkle it on Aaron and his sons and on their clothes. In this way, they and their clothing will be set apart as holy to the LORD.

²²"Since this is the ram for the ordination of Aaron and his sons, take the fat of the ram,

> *Sing lustily and with a good courage.*
> *Beware of singing as if you were*
> *half dead, or half asleep; but lift up*
> *your voice with strength.*
>
> JOHN WESLEY

including the fat tail and the fat that covers the internal organs. Also, take the long lobe of the liver, the two kidneys with their fat, and the right thigh. ²³Then take one loaf of bread, one cake mixed with olive oil, and one wafer from the basket of yeastless bread that was placed before the LORD. ²⁴Put all these in the hands of Aaron and his sons to be lifted up as a special gift to the LORD. ²⁵Afterward take the bread from their hands, and burn it on the altar as a burnt offering that will be pleasing to the LORD. ²⁶Then take the breast of Aaron's ordination ram, and lift it up in the LORD's presence as a special gift to him. Afterward keep it for yourself.

²⁷"Set aside as holy the parts of the ordination ram that belong to Aaron and his sons. This includes the breast and the thigh that were lifted up before the LORD in the ordination ceremony. ²⁸In the future, whenever the people of Israel offer up peace offerings or thanksgiving offerings to the LORD, these parts will be the regular share of Aaron and his descendants.

²⁹"Aaron's sacred garments must be preserved for his descendants who will succeed him, so they can be anointed and ordained in them. ³⁰Whoever is the next high priest after Aaron will wear these clothes for seven days before beginning to minister in the Tabernacle and the Holy Place.

³¹"Take the ram used in the ordination ceremony, and boil its meat in a sacred place. ³²Aaron and his sons are to eat this meat, along

with the bread in the basket, at the Tabernacle entrance. ³³They alone may eat the meat and bread used for their atonement in the ordination ceremony. The ordinary people may not eat them, for these things are set apart and holy. ³⁴If any of the ordination meat or bread remains until the morning, it must be burned. It may not be eaten, for it is holy.

³⁵"This is how you will ordain Aaron and his sons to their offices. The ordination ceremony will go on for seven days. ³⁶Each day you must sacrifice a young bull as an offering for the atonement of sin. Afterward make an offering to cleanse the altar. Purify the altar by making atonement for it; make it holy by anointing it with oil. ³⁷Make atonement for the altar every day for seven days. After that, the altar will be exceedingly holy, and whatever touches it will become holy.

³⁸"This is what you are to offer on the altar. Offer two one-year-old lambs each day, ³⁹one in the morning and the other in the evening. ⁴⁰With one of them, offer two quarts of fine flour mixed with one quart of olive oil; also, offer one quart of wine* as a drink offering. ⁴¹Offer the other lamb in the evening, along with the same offerings of flour and wine as in the morning. It will be a fragrant offering to the LORD, an offering made by fire.

⁴²"This is to be a daily burnt offering given from generation to generation. Offer it in the LORD's presence at the Tabernacle entrance, where I will meet you and speak with you. ⁴³I will meet the people of Israel there, and the Tabernacle will be sanctified by my glorious presence. ⁴⁴Yes, I will make the Tabernacle and the altar most holy, and I will set apart Aaron and his sons as holy, that they may be my priests. ⁴⁵I will live among the people of Israel and be their God, ⁴⁶and they will know that I am the LORD their God. I am the one who brought them out of Egypt so that I could live among them. I am the LORD their God.

PLANS FOR THE INCENSE ALTAR

30 "Then make a small altar out of acacia wood for burning incense. ²It must be eighteen inches square and three feet high,* with horns at the corners carved from the same piece of wood as the altar. ³Overlay the top, sides, and horns of the altar with pure gold, and run a gold molding around the entire altar. ⁴Beneath the molding, on opposite sides of the altar, attach two gold rings to support the carrying poles. ⁵The poles are to be made of acacia wood and overlaid with gold. ⁶Place the incense altar just outside the inner curtain, opposite the Ark's cover—the place of atonement—that rests on the Ark of the Covenant.* I will meet with you there.

⁷"Every morning when Aaron trims the lamps, he must burn fragrant incense on the altar. ⁸And each evening when he tends to the lamps, he must again burn incense in the LORD's presence. This must be done from generation to generation. ⁹Do not offer any unholy incense on this altar, or any burnt offerings, grain offerings, or drink offerings. ¹⁰"Once a year Aaron must purify the altar by placing on its horns the blood from the offering made for the atonement of sin. This will be a regular, annual event from generation to generation, for this is the LORD's supremely holy altar."

MONEY FOR THE TABERNACLE

¹¹And the LORD said to Moses, ¹²"Whenever you take a census of the people of Israel, each man who is counted must pay a ransom for himself to the LORD. Then there will be no plagues among the people as you count them. ¹³His payment to the LORD will be one-fifth of an ounce* of silver. ¹⁴All who have reached their twentieth birthday must give this offering to the LORD. ¹⁵When this offering is given to the LORD to make atonement for yourselves, the rich must not give more, and the poor must not give less. ¹⁶Use this money for

---

29:40 Hebrew *¹/₁₀ of an ephah* [2 liters] *of fine flour . . . ¹/₄ of a hin* [1 liter] *of olive oil . . . ¹/₄ of a hin of wine.* **30:2** Hebrew *1 cubit* [45 centimeters] *square and 2 cubits* [90 centimeters] *high.* **30:6** Or *Ark of the Testimony;* also in 30:26, 36. **30:13** Hebrew *half a shekel* [6 grams], *according to the sanctuary shekel, 20 gerahs to each shekel.*

the care of the Tabernacle.* It will bring you, the Israelites, to the LORD's attention, and it will make atonement for your lives."

PLANS FOR THE WASHBASIN

[17]And the LORD said to Moses, [18]"Make a large bronze washbasin with a bronze pedestal. Put it between the Tabernacle and the altar, and fill it with water. [19]Aaron and his sons will wash their hands and feet there [20]before they go into the Tabernacle to appear before the LORD and before they approach the altar to burn offerings to the LORD. They must always wash before ministering in these ways, or they will die. [21]This is a permanent law for Aaron and his descendants, to be kept from generation to generation."

THE ANOINTING OIL

[22]Then the LORD said to Moses, [23]"Collect choice spices—12½ pounds of pure myrrh, 6¼ pounds* each of cinnamon and of sweet cane, [24]12½ pounds of cassia, and one gallon* of olive oil. [25]Blend these ingredients into a holy anointing oil. [26]Use this scented oil to anoint the Tabernacle, the Ark of the Covenant, [27]the table and all its utensils, the lampstand and all its accessories, the incense altar, [28]the altar of burnt offering with all its utensils, and the large washbasin with its pedestal. [29]Sanctify them to make them entirely holy. After this, whatever touches them will become holy. [30]Use this oil also to anoint Aaron and his sons, sanctifying them so they can minister before me as priests. [31]And say to the people of Israel, 'This will always be my holy anointing oil. [32]It must never be poured on the body of an ordinary person, and you must never make any of it for yourselves. It is holy, and you must treat it as holy. [33]Anyone who blends scented oil like it or puts any of it on someone who is not a priest will be cut off from the community.'"

THE INCENSE

[34]These were the LORD's instructions to Moses concerning the incense: "Gather sweet spices—resin droplets, mollusk scent, galbanum, and pure frankincense—weighing out the same amounts of each. [35]Using the usual techniques of the incense maker, refine it to produce a pure and holy incense. [36]Beat some of it very fine and put some of it in front of the Ark of the Covenant, where I will meet with you in the Tabernacle. This incense is most holy. [37]Never make this incense for yourselves. It is reserved for the LORD, and you must treat it as holy. [38]Those who make it for their own enjoyment will be cut off from the community."

CRAFTSMEN: BEZALEL AND OHOLIAB

31 The LORD also said to Moses, [2]"Look, I have chosen Bezalel son of Uri, grandson of Hur, of the tribe of Judah. [3]I have filled him with the Spirit of God, giving him great wisdom, intelligence, and skill in all kinds of crafts. [4]He is able to create beautiful objects from gold, silver, and bronze. [5]He is skilled in cutting and setting gemstones and in carving wood. Yes, he is a master at every craft!

[6]"And I have appointed Oholiab son of Ahisamach, of the tribe of Dan, to be his assistant. Moreover, I have given special skill to all the naturally talented craftsmen so they can make all the things I have instructed you to make: [7]the Tabernacle itself; the Ark of the Covenant;* the Ark's cover—the place of atonement; all the furnishings of the Tabernacle; [8]the table and all its utensils; the gold lampstand with all its accessories; the incense altar; [9]the altar of burnt offering with all its utensils; the washbasin and its pedestal; [10]the beautifully stitched, holy garments for Aaron the priest, and the garments for his sons to wear as they minister as priests; [11]the anointing oil; and the special incense for the Holy

30:16 Hebrew *Tent of Meeting;* also in 30:18, 20, 26, 36.   30:23 Hebrew *500 shekels* [5.7 kilograms] *of pure myrrh, 250 shekels* [2.9 kilograms].   30:24 Hebrew *500 shekels* [5.7 kilograms] *of cassia, according to the sanctuary shekel, and 1 hin* [3.8 liters].
31:7 Hebrew *the Tent of Meeting; the Ark of the Testimony.*

My Daily Worship

— *January 24* —

CLEAN UP YOUR ACT, WILL YOU?

EXODUS 28:1–30:38

*Aaron and his sons will wash their hands and feet there before they go into the Tabernacle
to appear before the LORD and before they approach the altar
to burn offerings to the LORD. (30:19–20).*

[i reflect]

"I can't come to church with you—there are issues, habits in my life that God would not approve of."

"I'm not the kind of person you want in your church. You don't know what I've done, where I've been."

"Thanks for inviting me, . . . but I need to clean up my act a bit before I go to a worship service of any kind."

Maybe a friend or acquaintance has said something like that to you—or perhaps you have said those words. That kind of thinking is based on the idea that we have to "clean up our act" *before* we can come to God. The truth is actually the very opposite: We *cannot* clean up our act. We must come to God *first*, acknowledge our utter unworthiness, and allow *him* to do the cleaning.

Our Old Testament forebears had to go through elaborate cleansing rituals before they entered God's presence, or they would die. We who live on this side of the Incarnation and cross of Christ have a great advantage: Jesus has opened for us a "new, life-giving way," and we "have been sprinkled with Christ's blood to make us clean" (Hebrews 10:19–22). We don't go through complex purification rites involving water and basins; Jesus has made us clean by his own body and blood. And we don't need any other person to represent us before the Lord; Jesus himself is our High Priest, and he has made us a kingdom of priests (1 Peter 2:9).

What thought pattern, habit, or activity is making you feel like you are too dirty to enter God's presence, either individually or in a corporate worship setting? Don't try to clean up your act. Instead, take time to thank God that you already have been made clean by the blood of his Son.

[i pray]

*Father, I thank you that I don't have to jump through any elaborate hoops or
observe intricate ceremonies to have access to you. Through Jesus, you have provided
the cleansing I need in his blood, and because of him, I am clean in your eyes.*

[i respond]

Using a pencil, write down several habits, thoughts, or actions that you know would not meet God's approval. Now erase each item, one at a time. As you do, thank God that he has cleansed you through the blood of Christ.

Place. They must follow exactly all the instructions I have given you."

INSTRUCTIONS FOR THE SABBATH

[12]The LORD then gave these further instructions to Moses: [13]"Tell the people of Israel to keep my Sabbath day, for the Sabbath is a sign of the covenant between me and you forever. It helps you to remember that I am the LORD, who makes you holy. [14]Yes, keep the Sabbath day, for it is holy. Anyone who desecrates it must die; anyone who works on that day will be cut off from the community. [15]Work six days only, but the seventh day must be a day of total rest. I repeat: Because the LORD considers it a holy day, anyone who works on the Sabbath must be put to death. [16]The people of Israel must keep the Sabbath day forever. [17]It is a permanent sign of my covenant with them. For in six days the LORD made heaven and earth, but he rested on the seventh day and was refreshed."

[18]Then as the LORD finished speaking with Moses on Mount Sinai, he gave him the two stone tablets inscribed with the terms of the covenant,* written by the finger of God.

THE CALF OF GOLD

32 When Moses failed to come back down the mountain right away, the people went to Aaron. "Look," they said, "make us some gods who can lead us. This man Moses, who brought us here from Egypt, has disappeared. We don't know what has happened to him."

[2]So Aaron said, "Tell your wives and sons and daughters to take off their gold earrings, and then bring them to me."

[3]All the people obeyed Aaron and brought him their gold earrings. [4]Then Aaron took the gold, melted it down, and molded and tooled it into the shape of a calf. The people exclaimed, "O Israel, these are the gods who brought you out of Egypt!"

[5]When Aaron saw how excited the people were about it, he built an altar in front of the calf and announced, "Tomorrow there will be a festival to the LORD!"

[6]So the people got up early the next morning to sacrifice burnt offerings and peace offerings. After this, they celebrated with feasting and drinking, and indulged themselves in pagan revelry.

[7]Then the LORD told Moses, "Quick! Go down the mountain! The people you brought from Egypt have defiled themselves. [8]They have already turned from the way I commanded them to live. They have made an idol shaped like a calf, and they have worshiped and sacrificed to it. They are saying, 'These are your gods, O Israel, who brought you out of Egypt.'"

[9]Then the LORD said, "I have seen how stubborn and rebellious these people are. [10]Now leave me alone so my anger can blaze against them and destroy them all. Then I will make you, Moses, into a great nation instead of them."

[11]But Moses pleaded with the LORD his God not to do it. "O LORD!" he exclaimed. "Why are you so angry with your own people whom you brought from the land of Egypt with such great power and mighty acts? [12]The Egyptians will say, 'God tricked them into coming to the mountains so he could kill them and wipe them from the face of the earth.' Turn away from your fierce anger. Change your mind about this terrible disaster you are planning against your people! [13]Remember your covenant with your servants—Abraham, Isaac, and Jacob.* You swore by your own self, 'I will make your descendants as numerous as the stars of heaven. Yes, I will give them all of this land that I have promised to your descendants, and they will possess it forever.'"

[14]So the LORD withdrew his threat and didn't bring against his people the disaster he had threatened.

[15]Then Moses turned and went down the mountain. He held in his hands the two stone tablets inscribed with the terms of the covenant.* They were inscribed on both sides,

---

31:18 Hebrew *the Testimony.* 32:13 Hebrew *Israel.* 32:15 Hebrew *the Testimony.*

front and back. [16]These stone tablets were God's work; the words on them were written by God himself.

[17]When Joshua heard the noise of the people shouting below them, he exclaimed to Moses, "It sounds as if there is a war in the camp!"

[18]But Moses replied, "No, it's neither a cry of victory nor a cry of defeat. It is the sound of a celebration."

[19]When they came near the camp, Moses saw the calf and the dancing. In terrible anger, he threw the stone tablets to the ground, smashing them at the foot of the mountain. [20]He took the calf they had made and melted it in the fire. And when the metal had cooled, he ground it into powder and mixed it with water. Then he made the people drink it.

[21]After that, he turned to Aaron. "What did the people do to you?" he demanded. "How did they ever make you bring such terrible sin upon them?"

[22]"Don't get upset, sir," Aaron replied. "You yourself know these people and what a wicked bunch they are. [23]They said to me, 'Make us some gods to lead us, for something has happened to this man Moses, who led us out of Egypt.' [24]So I told them, 'Bring me your gold earrings.' When they brought them to me, I threw them into the fire—and out came this calf!"

[25]When Moses saw that Aaron had let the people get completely out of control—and much to the amusement of their enemies— [26]he stood at the entrance to the camp and shouted, "All of you who are on the LORD's side, come over here and join me." And all the Levites came.

[27]He told them, "This is what the LORD, the God of Israel, says: Strap on your swords! Go back and forth from one end of the camp to the other, killing even your brothers, friends, and neighbors." [28]The Levites obeyed Moses, and about three thousand people died that day.

[29]Then Moses told the Levites, "Today you have been ordained for the service of the LORD, for you obeyed him even though it

Words of Worship

PRESENCE

Presence—Hebrew *lif-nei* "to the face of"; Greek *en-o-pi-on* "in the face of"; *pro-so-pon* "face." The abstract concept of "presence" is conveyed through the concrete image of facing another.

Being out of touch with the Lord is like living in a remote desert, isolated from a companionship dear to us. With the psalmist we cry, "I thirst for God, the living God. When can I come and stand before him?" (Psalm 42:2). Sensing God's presence again—in prayer, praise, worship—we're restored to wholeness and free communication with One we love.

Scripture speaks of the Lord's presence in down-to-earth-terms. The biblical expressions for entering his presence mean, literally, to come *before his face*. We see him and he sees us because we're in each other's face! We can't know his presence as uninvolved spectators. We can only know it when, like Moses, we speak with him "face to face, as a man speaks to his friend" (Exodus 33:11).

meant killing your own sons and brothers. Because of this, he will now give you a great blessing."

MOSES INTERCEDES FOR ISRAEL

[30]The next day Moses said to the people, "You have committed a terrible sin, but I will return to the LORD on the mountain. Perhaps I will be able to obtain forgiveness for you."

[31]So Moses returned to the LORD and said, "Alas, these people have committed a terrible sin. They have made gods of gold for themselves. [32]But now, please forgive their sin—and if not, then blot me out of the record you are keeping."

33The LORD replied to Moses, "I will blot out whoever has sinned against me. 34Now go, lead the people to the place I told you about. Look! My angel will lead the way before you! But when I call the people to account, I will certainly punish them for their sins."

35And the LORD sent a great plague upon the people because they had worshiped the calf Aaron had made.

33 The LORD said to Moses, "Now that you have brought these people out of Egypt, lead them to the land I solemnly promised Abraham, Isaac, and Jacob. I told them long ago that I would give this land to their descendants. 2And I will send an angel before you to drive out the Canaanites, Amorites, Hittites, Perizzites, Hivites, and Jebusites. 3Theirs is a land flowing with milk and honey. But I will not travel along with you, for you are a stubborn, unruly people. If I did, I would be tempted to destroy you along the way."

4When the people heard these stern words, they went into mourning and refused to wear their jewelry and ornaments. 5For the LORD had told Moses to tell them, "You are an unruly, stubborn people. If I were there among you for even a moment, I would destroy you. Remove your jewelry and ornaments until I decide what to do with you." 6So from the time they left Mount Sinai,* the Israelites wore no more jewelry.

7It was Moses' custom to set up the tent known as the Tent of Meeting far outside the camp. Everyone who wanted to consult with the LORD would go there. 8Whenever Moses went out to the Tent of Meeting, all the people would get up and stand in their tent entrances. They would all watch Moses until he disappeared inside. 9As he went into the tent, the pillar of cloud would come down and hover at the entrance while the LORD spoke with Moses. 10Then all the people would stand and bow low at their tent entrances. 11Inside the Tent of Meeting,

the LORD would speak to Moses face to face, as a man speaks to his friend. Afterward Moses would return to the camp, but the young man who assisted him, Joshua son of Nun, stayed behind in the Tent of Meeting.

MOSES SEES THE LORD'S GLORY

12Moses said to the LORD, "You have been telling me, 'Take these people up to the Promised Land.' But you haven't told me whom you will send with me. You call me by name and tell me I have found favor with you. 13Please, if this is really so, show me your intentions so I will understand you more fully and do exactly what you want me to do. Besides, don't forget that this nation is your very own people."

14And the LORD replied, "I will personally go with you, Moses. I will give you rest—everything will be fine for you."

15Then Moses said, "If you don't go with us personally, don't let us move a step from this place. 16If you don't go with us, how will anyone ever know that your people and I have found favor with you? How else will they know we are special and distinct from all other people on the earth?"

17And the LORD replied to Moses, "I will indeed do what you have asked, for you have found favor with me, and you are my friend."

18Then Moses had one more request. "Please let me see your glorious presence," he said.

19The LORD replied, "I will make all my goodness pass before you, and I will call out my name, 'the LORD,' to you. I will show kindness to anyone I choose, and I will show mercy to anyone I choose. 20But you may not look directly at my face, for no one may see me and live." 21The LORD continued, "Stand here on this rock beside me. 22As my glorious presence passes by, I will put you in the cleft of the rock and cover you with my hand until I have passed. 23Then I will remove my hand, and you will see me from behind. But my face will not be seen."

33:6 Hebrew *Horeb,* another name for Sinai.

A New Copy of the Covenant

34 The LORD told Moses, "Prepare two stone tablets like the first ones. I will write on them the same words that were on the tablets you smashed. ²Be ready in the morning to come up Mount Sinai and present yourself to me there on the top of the mountain. ³No one else may come with you. In fact, no one is allowed anywhere on the mountain. Do not even let the flocks or herds graze near the mountain."

⁴So Moses cut two tablets of stone like the first ones. Early in the morning he climbed Mount Sinai as the LORD had told him, carrying the two stone tablets in his hands.

⁵Then the LORD came down in a pillar of cloud and called out his own name, "the LORD," as Moses stood there in his presence. ⁶He passed in front of Moses and said, "I am the LORD, I am the LORD, the merciful and gracious God. I am slow to anger and rich in unfailing love and faithfulness. ⁷I show this unfailing love to many thousands by forgiving every kind of sin and rebellion. Even so I do not leave sin unpunished, but I punish the children for the sins of their parents to the third and fourth generations."

⁸Moses immediately fell to the ground and worshiped. ⁹And he said, "If it is true that I have found favor in your sight, O Lord, then please go with us. Yes, this is an unruly and stubborn people, but please pardon our iniquity and our sins. Accept us as your own special possession."

¹⁰The LORD replied, "All right. This is the covenant I am going to make with you. I will perform wonders that have never been done before anywhere in all the earth or in any nation. And all the people around you will see the power of the LORD—the awesome power I will display through you. ¹¹Your responsibility is to obey all the commands I am giving you today. Then I will surely drive out all those who stand in your way—the Amorites, Canaanites, Hittites, Perizzites, Hivites, and Jebusites.

¹²"Be very careful never to make treaties with the people in the land where you are going. If you do, you soon will be following their evil ways. ¹³Instead, you must break down their pagan altars, smash the sacred pillars they worship, and cut down their carved images. ¹⁴You must worship no other gods, but only the LORD, for he is a God who is passionate about his relationship with you.

¹⁵"Do not make treaties of any kind with the people living in the land. They are spiritual prostitutes, committing adultery against me by sacrificing to their gods. If you make peace with them, they will invite you to go with them to worship their gods, and you are likely to do it. ¹⁶And you will accept their daughters, who worship other gods, as wives for your sons. Then they will cause your sons to commit adultery against me by worshiping other gods. ¹⁷You must make no gods for yourselves at all.

¹⁸"Be sure to celebrate the Festival of Unleavened Bread for seven days, just as I instructed you, at the appointed time each year in early spring,* for that was when you left Egypt.

¹⁹"Every firstborn male belongs to me—of both cattle and sheep. ²⁰A firstborn male donkey may be redeemed from the LORD by presenting a lamb in its place. But if you decide not to make the exchange, you must kill the donkey by breaking its neck. However, you must redeem every firstborn son. No one is allowed to appear before me without a gift.

²¹"Six days are set aside for work, but on the Sabbath day you must rest, even during the seasons of plowing and harvest. ²²And you must remember to celebrate the Festival of Harvest* with the first crop of the wheat harvest, and celebrate the Festival of the Final Harvest* at the end of the harvest season. ²³Three times each year all the men of Israel must appear before the Sovereign LORD, the God of Israel. ²⁴No one will attack and conquer your land when you go to appear before

---

34:18 Hebrew *in the month of Abib.* This month of the Hebrew lunar calendar usually occurs in March and April. **34:22a** Or *Festival of Weeks.* **34:22b** This was later called the Festival of Shelters; see Lev 23:33-36

the LORD your God those three times each year. I will drive out the nations that stand in your way and will enlarge your boundaries.

25"You must not offer bread made with yeast as a sacrifice to me. And none of the meat of the Passover lamb may be kept over until the following morning. 26You must bring the best of the first of each year's crop to the house of the LORD your God.

"You must not cook a young goat in its mother's milk."

27And the LORD said to Moses, "Write down all these instructions, for they represent the terms of my covenant with you and with Israel."

28Moses was up on the mountain with the LORD forty days and forty nights. In all that time he neither ate nor drank. At that time he wrote the terms of the covenant—the Ten Commandments—on the stone tablets.

29When Moses came down the mountain carrying the stone tablets inscribed with the terms of the covenant,* he wasn't aware that his face glowed because he had spoken to the LORD face to face. 30And when Aaron and the people of Israel saw the radiance of Moses' face, they were afraid to come near him.

31But Moses called to them and asked Aaron and the community leaders to come over and talk with him. 32Then all the people came, and Moses gave them the instructions the LORD had given him on Mount Sinai. 33When Moses had finished speaking with them, he put a veil over his face. 34But whenever he went into the Tent of Meeting to speak with the LORD, he removed the veil until he came out again. Then he would give the people whatever instructions the LORD had given him, 35and the people would see his face aglow. Afterward he would put the veil on again until he returned to speak with the LORD.

INSTRUCTIONS FOR THE SABBATH

35 Now Moses called a meeting of all the people and told them, "You must obey these instructions from the LORD. 2Each week,

work for six days only. The seventh day is a day of total rest, a holy day that belongs to the LORD. Anyone who works on that day will die. 3Do not even light fires in your homes on that day."

GIFTS FOR THE TABERNACLE

4Then Moses said to all the people, "This is what the LORD has commanded. 5Everyone is invited to bring these offerings to the LORD: gold, silver, and bronze; 6blue, purple, and scarlet yarn; fine linen; goat hair for cloth; 7tanned ram skins and fine goatskin leather; acacia wood; 8olive oil for the lamps; spices for the anointing oil and the fragrant incense; 9onyx stones, and other stones to be set in the ephod and the chestpiece.

10"Come, all of you who are gifted craftsmen. Construct everything that the LORD has commanded: 11the entire Tabernacle, including the sacred tent and its coverings, the clasps, frames, crossbars, posts, and bases; 12the Ark and its poles; the Ark's cover—the place of atonement; the inner curtain to enclose the Ark in the Most Holy Place; 13the table, its carrying poles, and all of its utensils; the Bread of the Presence; 14the lampstand and its accessories; the lamp cups and the oil for lighting; 15the incense altar and its carrying poles; the anointing oil and fragrant incense; the curtain for the entrance of the Tabernacle; 16the altar of burnt offering; the bronze grating of the altar and its carrying poles and utensils; the large washbasin with its pedestal; 17the curtains for the walls of the courtyard; the posts and their bases; the curtain for the entrance to the courtyard; 18the tent pegs of the Tabernacle and courtyard and their cords; 19the beautifully stitched clothing for the priests to wear while ministering in the Holy Place; the sacred garments for Aaron and his sons to wear while officiating as priests."

20So all the people left Moses and went to their tents to prepare their gifts. 21If their hearts were stirred and they desired to do so, they brought to the LORD their offerings of

34:29 Hebrew the Testimony.

My Daily Worship

— January 25 —

SHOCK AND AWE

EXODUS 31:1–34:35

I am the LORD, I am the LORD, the merciful and gracious God.
I am slow to anger and rich in unfailing love and faithfulness (34:6).

[i reflect]

God never repeats himself unless he wants to make a point. Divine repetition doesn't result from lack of clarity on his part, but inattentiveness on our part.

When God said "I am the LORD" twice, he pointed out the failure we make when we try to divide or isolate part of God's character, such as his mercy and grace or his justice and holiness. God will not have his character "averaged out" to a dull in-between. God will not submit to any taming and dulling definition. Whatever aspect of his awesome character we may choose to consider, the effect on us will be shocking. If it isn't, that simply means we weren't truly thinking about God.

We can never put God in a neat little package. We can try to define him as a benign and loving old man, or vilify him as a power-hungry warlord. Neither description fits the God who is beyond comprehension. We grow to know God the same way Moses did—by listening to what God tells us about his character.

Still, we will never reach an end point in our understanding of God. That's OK! If we could grasp all of God's motives and deeds, then God would cease to be God. The very fact that God is greater than we can imagine also signifies his ability to save and protect us from overpowering evil.

The more we know about God, the more we'll be moved to praise him, and the more we will be in shock and awe. Thankfully, he keeps telling us about himself. Moses was shown God and instantly responded in worship. Our response should be the same.

There will always be something new to learn about God's character. Feeling bored or complacent in worship shows you're not paying attention. God continually reveals himself to you. Look for him. Get to know him. Never expect to reach the end of that journey.

[i pray]

Help me, Lord, to respond to you with the same spirit as Moses. Forgive me for simplifying
and shaping your character to fit my needs and desires. Please shape my life instead.
As you reveal yourself to me, teach me to worship you in truth.

[i respond]

God revealed many of his attributes to Moses. Do you connect with some of God's attributes more easily than others? Why? Make a list of each characteristic and identify how God has shown himself to you in each of these ways.

materials for the Tabernacle* and its furnishings and for the holy garments. ²²Both men and women came, all whose hearts were willing. Some brought to the LORD their offerings of gold—medallions, earrings, rings from their fingers, and necklaces. They presented gold objects of every kind to the LORD. ²³Others brought blue, purple, and scarlet yarn, fine linen, or goat hair for cloth. Some gave tanned ram skins or fine goatskin leather. ²⁴Others brought silver and bronze objects as their offering to the LORD. And those who had acacia wood brought it.

²⁵All the women who were skilled in sewing and spinning prepared blue, purple, and scarlet yarn, and fine linen cloth, and they brought them in. ²⁶All the women who were willing used their skills to spin and weave the goat hair into cloth. ²⁷The leaders brought onyx stones and the other gemstones to be used for the ephod and the chestpiece. ²⁸They also brought spices and olive oil for the light, the anointing oil, and the fragrant incense. ²⁹So the people of Israel—every man and woman who wanted to help in the work the LORD had given them through Moses—brought their offerings to the LORD.

³⁰And Moses told them, "The LORD has chosen Bezalel son of Uri, grandson of Hur, of the tribe of Judah. ³¹The LORD has filled Bezalel with the Spirit of God, giving him great wisdom, intelligence, and skill in all kinds of crafts. ³²He is able to create beautiful objects from gold, silver, and bronze. ³³He is skilled in cutting and setting gemstones and in carving wood. In fact, he has every necessary skill. ³⁴And the LORD has given both him and Oholiab son of Ahisamach, of the tribe of Dan, the ability to teach their skills to others. ³⁵The LORD has given them special skills as jewelers, designers, weavers, and embroiderers in blue, purple, and scarlet yarn on fine linen cloth. They excel in all the crafts needed for the work.

36 "Bezalel, Oholiab, and the other craftsmen whom the LORD has gifted with wisdom, skill, and intelligence will construct and furnish the Tabernacle, just as the LORD has commanded."

²So Moses told Bezalel and Oholiab to begin the work, along with all those who were specially gifted by the LORD. ³Moses gave them the materials donated by the people for the completion of the sanctuary. Additional gifts were brought each morning. ⁴But finally the craftsmen left their work to meet with Moses. ⁵"We have more than enough materials on hand now to complete the job the LORD has given us to do!" they exclaimed.

⁶So Moses gave the command, and this message was sent throughout the camp: "Bring no more materials! You have already given more than enough." So the people stopped bringing their offerings. ⁷Their contributions were more than enough to complete the whole project.

BUILDING THE TABERNACLE

⁸The skilled weavers first made ten sheets from fine linen. One of the craftsmen then embroidered blue, purple, and scarlet cherubim into them. ⁹Each sheet was exactly the same size—forty-two feet long and six feet wide.* ¹⁰Five of these sheets were joined together to make one set, and a second set was made of the other five. ¹¹Fifty blue loops were placed along the edge of the last sheet in each set. ¹²The fifty loops along the edge of the first set of sheets matched the loops along the edge of the second set. ¹³Then fifty gold clasps were made to connect the loops on the edge of each set. Thus the Tabernacle was joined together in one piece.

¹⁴Above the Tabernacle, a roof covering was made from eleven sheets of cloth made from goat hair. ¹⁵Each sheet was exactly the same size—forty-five feet long and six feet wide. ¹⁶The craftsmen joined five of these sheets together to make one set, and the six remain-

35:21 Hebrew *Tent of Meeting.* **36:9** Hebrew *28 cubits* [12.6 meters] *long and 4 cubits* [1.8 meters] *wide.* In this chapter, the distance measures are calculated from the Hebrew cubit at a ratio of 18 inches or 45 centimeters per cubit.

ing sheets were joined to make a second set. [17]Then they made fifty loops along the edge of the last sheet in each set. [18]They also made fifty small bronze clasps to couple the loops, so the two sets of sheets were firmly attached to each other. In this way, the roof covering was joined together in one piece. [19]Then they made two more layers for the roof covering. The first was made of tanned ram skins, and the second was made of fine goatskin leather.

[20]For the framework of the Tabernacle, they made frames of acacia wood standing on end. [21]Each frame was 15 feet high and 2¼ feet wide. [22]There were two pegs on each frame so they could be joined to the next frame. All the frames were made this way. [23]They made twenty frames to support the south side, [24]along with forty silver bases, two for each frame. [25]They also made twenty frames for the north side of the Tabernacle, [26]along with forty silver bases, two for each frame. [27]The west side of the Tabernacle, which was its rear, was made from six frames, [28]plus an extra frame at each corner. [29]These corner frames were connected at the bottom and firmly attached at the top with a single ring, forming a single unit from top to bottom. They made two of these, one for each rear corner. [30]So for the west side they made a total of eight frames, along with sixteen silver bases, two for each frame.

[31]Then they made five crossbars from acacia wood to tie the frames on the south side together. [32]They made another five for the north side and five for the west side. [33]The middle crossbar of the five was halfway up the frames, along each side, running from one end to the other. [34]The frames and crossbars were all overlaid with gold. The rings used to hold the crossbars were made of pure gold.

[35]The inner curtain was made of fine linen cloth, and cherubim were skillfully embroidered into it with blue, purple, and scarlet yarn. [36]This curtain was then attached to four gold hooks set into four posts of acacia wood. The posts were overlaid with gold and set into four silver bases.

[37]Then they made another curtain for the entrance to the sacred tent. It was made of fine linen cloth and embroidered with blue, purple, and scarlet yarn. [38]This curtain was connected by five hooks to five posts. The posts with their decorated tops and bands were overlaid with gold. The five bases were molded from bronze.

BUILDING THE ARK

37 Next Bezalel made the Ark out of acacia wood. It was 3¾ feet long, 2¼ feet wide, and 2¼ feet high.* [2]It was overlaid with pure gold inside and out, and it had a molding of gold all the way around. [3]Four gold rings were fastened to its four feet, two rings at each side. [4]Then he made poles from acacia wood and overlaid them with gold. [5]He put the poles into the rings at the sides of the Ark to carry it.

[6]Then, from pure gold, he made the Ark's cover—the place of atonement. It was 3¾ feet long and 2¼ feet wide. [7]He made two figures of cherubim out of hammered gold and placed them at the two ends of the atonement cover. [8]They were made so they were actually a part of the atonement cover—it was all one piece. [9]The cherubim faced each other as they looked down on the atonement cover, and their wings were stretched out above the atonement cover to protect it.

BUILDING THE TABLE

[10]Then he made a table out of acacia wood, 3 feet long, 1½ feet wide, and 2¼ feet high. [11]It was overlaid with pure gold, with a gold molding all around the edge. [12]A rim about 3 inches* wide was attached along the edges of the table, and a gold molding ran around the rim. [13]Then he cast four rings of gold and attached them to the four table legs [14]next to

37:1 Hebrew 2½ cubits [1.1 meters] long, 1½ cubits [0.7 meters] wide, and 1½ cubits high. In this chapter, the distance measures are calculated from the Hebrew cubit at a ratio of 18 inches or 45 centimeters per cubit. 37:12 Hebrew a handbreadth [8 centimeters].

the rim. These were made to hold the carrying poles in place. [15]He made the carrying poles of acacia wood and overlaid them with gold. [16]Next, using pure gold, he made the plates, dishes, bowls, and pitchers to be placed on the table. These utensils were to be used in pouring out drink offerings.

BUILDING THE LAMPSTAND

[17]Then he made the lampstand, again using pure, hammered gold. Its base, center stem, lamp cups, blossoms, and buds were all of one piece. [18]The lampstand had six branches, three going out from each side of the center stem. [19]Each of the six branches held a cup shaped like an almond blossom, complete with buds and petals. [20]The center stem of the lampstand was also decorated with four almond blossoms. [21]One blossom was set beneath each pair of branches, where they extended from the center stem. [22]The decorations and branches were all one piece with the stem, and they were hammered from pure gold. [23]He also made the seven lamps, the lamp snuffers, and the trays, all of pure gold. [24]The entire lampstand, along with its accessories, was made from seventy-five pounds* of pure gold.

BUILDING THE INCENSE ALTAR

[25]The incense altar was made of acacia wood. It was eighteen inches square and three feet high, with its corner horns made from the same piece of wood as the altar itself. [26]He overlaid the top, sides, and horns of the altar with pure gold and ran a gold molding around the edge. [27]Two gold rings were placed on opposite sides, beneath the molding, to hold the carrying poles. [28]The carrying poles were made of acacia wood and were overlaid with gold.

[29]Then he made the sacred oil, for anointing the priests, and the fragrant incense, using the techniques of the most skilled incense maker.

BUILDING THE ALTAR OF BURNT OFFERING

38 The altar for burning animal sacrifices also was constructed of acacia wood. It was 7½ feet square at the top and 4½ feet high.* [2]There were four horns, one at each of the four corners, all of one piece with the rest. This altar was overlaid with bronze. [3]Then he made all the bronze utensils to be used with the altar—the ash buckets, shovels, basins, meat hooks, and firepans. [4]Next he made a bronze grating that rested on a ledge about halfway down into the firebox. [5]Four rings were cast for each side of the grating to support the carrying poles. [6]The carrying poles themselves were made of acacia wood and were overlaid with bronze. [7]These poles were inserted into the rings at the side of the altar. The altar was hollow and was made from planks.

BUILDING THE WASHBASIN

[8]The bronze washbasin and its bronze pedestal were cast from bronze mirrors donated by the women who served at the entrance of the Tabernacle.*

BUILDING THE COURTYARD

[9]Then he constructed the courtyard. The south wall was 150 feet long. It consisted of curtains made of fine linen. [10]There were twenty posts, each with its own bronze base, and there were silver hooks and rods to hold up the curtains. [11]The north wall was also 150 feet long, with twenty bronze posts and bases and with silver hooks and rods. [12]The west end was 75 feet wide. The walls were made from curtains supported by ten posts and bases and with silver hooks and rods. [13]The east end was also 75 feet wide.

[14]The courtyard entrance was on the east side, flanked by two curtains. The curtain on the right side was 22½ feet long and was supported by three posts set into three bases.

37:24 Hebrew *1 talent* [34 kilograms].   38:1 Hebrew *5 cubits* [2.3 meters] *square at the top, and 3 cubits* [1.4 meters] *high.* In this chapter, the distance measures are calculated from the Hebrew cubit at a ratio of 18 inches or 45 centimeters per cubit.   38:8 Hebrew *Tent of Meeting;* also in 38:30.

My Daily Worship

— *January 26* —

SPECTATOR OR PARTICIPANT?

EXODUS 35:1–40:38

The craftsmen joined five of these sheets together to make one set,
and the six remaining sheets were joined to make a second set. (36:16).

[i reflect]

How many people does it take to make a worship service happen? The preacher, probably an instrumentalist or two, a vocal leader, and maybe a choir or ensemble. Just add a congregation and . . . wait a minute.

Does your church have a bulletin? Somebody typed, printed, and copied it. Did someone hand you that bulletin? How about the people who took up the offering, or greeted you as you entered? Is your church air conditioned or heated? Someone made sure that was turned on, as well as the lights and sound system, and someone paid the electric bill. Does your church have a children's service? How about Christian education classes, youth ministry, prayer groups, nursery, etc.?

The point is, a lot more people serve on the worship team than the small handful of folks you see up front in the service. And consider the architects, builders, carpenters, painters, maintenance crew, lawn crew, and a myriad other "behind the scenes" workers, doing tasks that practically nobody sees. All of these tasks, carefully and meticulously done, are acts of worship, yet they don't necessarily happen on a Sunday.

What gifts or talents do you have that could be utilized in assisting with worship, or serving the Lord in some other way? Before you say, "I don't have anything to contribute," consider the passage before us. The craftsmen Moses called to do the work in the Temple were charged with fairly unspectacular "behind the scenes" tasks—making curtains, clasps, coverings, frames, bases—and yet these tasks were deemed important enough to be recorded in the very Word of God. Worship in the Tabernacle would have been greatly diminished—and also much less than what God wanted it to be—without their seemingly insignificant contributions.

Even today, look for ways you can use your particular gifts and abilities as an act of worship to God.

[i pray]

Father, I feel so inadequate and unworthy to be involved in offering you the worship you deserve.
I cannot imagine what I could do or say that would bring you pleasure,
but if you have something you want me to do, please reveal it to me.

[i respond]

Have you ever considered what your spiritual gift(s) might be? Ephesians 4:11–13 says all Christians are gifted and equipped for ministry. If you don't know what your gift is, talk with your pastor or another trusted Christian friend and ask how you go about discerning it.

¹⁵The curtain on the left side was also 22½ feet long and was supported by three posts set into three bases. ¹⁶All the curtains used in the courtyard walls were made of fine linen. ¹⁷Each post had a bronze base, and all the hooks and rods were silver. The tops of the posts were overlaid with silver, and the rods to hold up the curtains were solid silver.

¹⁸The curtain that covered the entrance to the courtyard was made of fine linen cloth and embroidered with blue, purple, and scarlet yarn. It was 30 feet long and 7½ feet high, just like the curtains of the courtyard walls. ¹⁹It was supported by four posts set into four bronze bases. The tops of the posts were overlaid with silver, and the hooks and rods were also made of silver.

²⁰All the tent pegs used in the Tabernacle and courtyard were made of bronze.

INVENTORY OF MATERIALS

²¹Here is an inventory of the materials used in building the Tabernacle of the Covenant.* Moses directed the Levites to compile the figures, and Ithamar son of Aaron the priest served as recorder. ²²Bezalel son of Uri, grandson of Hur, of the tribe of Judah, was in charge of the whole project, just as the LORD had commanded Moses. ²³He was assisted by Oholiab son of Ahisamach, of the tribe of Dan, a craftsman expert at engraving, designing, and embroidering blue, purple, and scarlet yarn on fine linen cloth.

²⁴The people brought gifts of gold totaling about 2,200 pounds,* all of which was used throughout the Tabernacle.

²⁵The amount of silver that was given was about 7,545 pounds.* ²⁶It came from the tax of one-fifth of an ounce of silver* collected from each of those registered in the census. This included all the men who were twenty years old or older, 603,550 in all. ²⁷The 100 bases for the frames of the sanctuary walls and for the posts supporting the inner curtain required 7,500 pounds of silver, about 75 pounds for each base.* ²⁸The rest of the silver, about 45 pounds,* was used to make the rods and hooks and to overlay the tops of the posts.

²⁹The people also brought 5,310 pounds* of bronze, ³⁰which was used for casting the bases for the posts at the entrance to the Tabernacle, and for the bronze altar with its bronze grating and altar utensils. ³¹Bronze was also used to make the bases for the posts that supported the curtains around the courtyard, the bases for the curtain at the entrance of the courtyard, and all the tent pegs used to hold the curtains of the courtyard in place.

CLOTHING FOR THE PRIESTS

39 For the priests, the craftsmen made beautiful garments of blue, purple, and scarlet cloth—clothing to be worn while ministering in the Holy Place. This same cloth was used for Aaron's sacred garments, just as the LORD had commanded Moses.

MAKING THE EPHOD

²The ephod was made from fine linen cloth and embroidered with gold thread and blue, purple, and scarlet yarn. ³A skilled craftsman made gold thread by beating gold into thin

> *Worship is the act of magnifying God. Enlarging our vision of him. Stepping into the cockpit to see where he sits and observe how he works.*
>
> MAX LUCADO

38:21 Hebrew *the Tabernacle, the Tabernacle of the Testimony.* **38:24** Hebrew *29 talents* [2,175 pounds or 986 kilograms] *and 730 shekels* [18.3 pounds or 8.3 kilograms], *according to the sanctuary shekel.* **38:25** Hebrew *100 talents* [7,500 pounds or 3,400 kilograms] *and 1,775 shekels* [44.4 pounds or 20.2 kilograms], *according to the sanctuary shekel.* **38:26** Hebrew *1 beka* [6 grams] *per person, that is, half a shekel, according to the sanctuary shekel.* **38:27** Hebrew *100 talents* [3,400 kilograms] *of silver, 1 talent* [34 kilograms] *for each base.* **38:28** Hebrew *1,775 shekels* [20.2 kilograms]. **38:29** Hebrew *70 talents* [5,250 pounds or 2,380 kilograms] *and 2,400 shekels* [60 pounds or 27.4 kilograms].

sheets and cutting it into fine strips. He then embroidered it into the linen with the blue, purple, and scarlet yarn.

⁴They made two shoulder-pieces for the ephod, which were attached to its corners so it could be tied down. ⁵They also made an elaborate woven sash of the same materials: fine linen cloth; blue, purple, and scarlet yarn; and gold thread, just as the LORD had commanded Moses. ⁶The two onyx stones, attached to the shoulder-pieces of the ephod, were set in gold filigree. The stones were engraved with the names of the tribes of Israel, just as initials are engraved on a seal. ⁷These stones served as reminders to the LORD concerning the people of Israel. All this was done just as the LORD had commanded Moses.

MAKING THE CHESTPIECE

⁸The chestpiece was made in the same style as the ephod, crafted from fine linen cloth and embroidered with gold thread and blue, purple, and scarlet yarn. ⁹It was doubled over to form a pouch, nine inches* square. ¹⁰Four rows of gemstones* were set across it. In the first row were a red carnelian, a chrysolite, and an emerald. ¹¹In the second row were a turquoise, a sapphire, and a white moonstone. ¹²In the third row were a jacinth, an agate, and an amethyst. ¹³In the fourth row were a beryl, an onyx, and a jasper. Each of these gemstones was set in gold. ¹⁴The stones were engraved like a seal, each with the name of one of the twelve tribes of Israel.

¹⁵To attach the chestpiece to the ephod, they made braided cords of pure gold. ¹⁶They also made two gold rings and attached them to the top corners of the chestpiece. ¹⁷The two gold cords were put through the gold rings on the chestpiece, ¹⁸and the ends of the cords were tied to the gold settings on the shoulder-pieces of the ephod. ¹⁹Two more gold rings were attached to the lower inside corners of the chestpiece next to the ephod. ²⁰Then two gold rings were attached to the ephod near the

sash. ²¹Blue cords were used to attach the bottom rings of the chestpiece to the rings on the ephod. In this way, the chestpiece was held securely to the ephod above the beautiful sash. All this was done just as the LORD had commanded Moses.

ADDITIONAL CLOTHING FOR THE PRIESTS

²²The robe of the ephod was woven entirely of blue yarn, ²³with an opening for Aaron's head in the middle of it. The edge of this opening was reinforced with a woven collar,* so it would not tear. ²⁴Pomegranates were attached to the bottom edge of the robe. These were finely crafted of blue, purple, and scarlet yarn. ²⁵Bells of pure gold were placed between the pomegranates along the hem of the robe, ²⁶with bells and pomegranates alternating all around the hem. This robe was to be worn when Aaron ministered to the LORD, just as the LORD had commanded Moses.

²⁷Tunics were then made for Aaron and his sons from fine linen cloth. ²⁸The turban, the headdresses, and the underclothes were all made of this fine linen. ²⁹The sashes were made of fine linen cloth and embroidered with blue, purple, and scarlet yarn, just as the LORD had commanded Moses. ³⁰Finally, they made the sacred medallion of pure gold to be worn on the front of the turban. Using the techniques of an engraver, they inscribed it with these words: SET APART AS HOLY TO THE LORD. ³¹This medallion was tied to the turban with a blue cord, just as the LORD had commanded Moses.

MOSES INSPECTS THE WORK

³²And so at last the Tabernacle* was finished. The Israelites had done everything just as the LORD had commanded Moses. ³³And they brought the entire Tabernacle to Moses: the sacred tent with all its furnishings, the clasps, frames, crossbars, posts, and bases; ³⁴the layers of tanned ram skins and fine goatskin leather;

39:9 Hebrew *1 span* [23 centimeters]. 39:10 The identification of some of these gemstones is uncertain. 39:23 The meaning of the Hebrew is uncertain. 39:32 Hebrew *the Tabernacle, the Tent of Meeting;* also in 39:40.

the inner curtain that enclosed the Most Holy Place; [35]the Ark of the Covenant* and its carrying poles; the Ark's cover—the place of atonement; [36]the table and all its utensils; the Bread of the Presence; [37]the gold lampstand and its accessories; the lamp cups and the oil for lighting; [38]the gold altar; the anointing oil; the fragrant incense; the curtain for the entrance of the sacred tent; [39]the bronze altar; the bronze grating; its poles and utensils; the large washbasin and its pedestal; [40]the curtains for the walls of the courtyard and the posts and bases holding them up; the curtain at the courtyard entrance; the cords and tent pegs; all the articles used in the operation of the Tabernacle; [41]the beautifully crafted garments to be worn while ministering in the Holy Place—the holy garments for Aaron the priest and for his sons to wear while on duty.

[42]So the people of Israel followed all of the LORD's instructions to Moses. [43]Moses inspected all their work and blessed them because it had been done as the LORD had commanded him.

THE TABERNACLE COMPLETED

40 The LORD now said to Moses, [2]"Set up the Tabernacle* on the first day of the new year.* [3]Place the Ark of the Covenant* inside, and install the inner curtain to enclose the Ark within the Most Holy Place. [4]Then bring in the table, and arrange the utensils on it. And bring in the lampstand, and set up the lamps.

[5]"Place the incense altar just outside the inner curtain, opposite the Ark of the Covenant. Set up the curtain made for the entrance of the Tabernacle. [6]Place the altar of burnt offering in front of the Tabernacle entrance. [7]Set the large washbasin between the Tabernacle* and the altar and fill it with water. [8]Then set up the courtyard around the outside of the tent, and hang the curtain for the courtyard entrance.

[9]"Take the anointing oil and sprinkle it on the Tabernacle and on all its furnishings to make them holy. [10]Sprinkle the anointing oil on the altar of burnt offering and its utensils, sanctifying them. Then the altar will become most holy. [11]Next anoint the large washbasin and its pedestal to make them holy.

[12]"Bring Aaron and his sons to the entrance of the Tabernacle, and wash them with water. [13]Clothe Aaron with the holy garments and anoint him, setting him apart to serve me as a priest. [14]Then bring his sons and dress them in their tunics. [15]Anoint them as you did their father, so they may serve me as priests. With this anointing, Aaron's descendants are set apart for the priesthood forever, from generation to generation."

[16]Moses proceeded to do everything as the LORD had commanded him. [17]So the Tabernacle was set up on the first day of the new year.* [18]Moses put it together by setting its frames into their bases and attaching the crossbars and raising the posts. [19]Then he spread the coverings over the Tabernacle framework and put on the roof layers, just as the LORD had commanded him.

[20]He placed inside the Ark the stone tablets inscribed with the terms of the covenant,* and then he attached the Ark's carrying poles. He also set the Ark's cover—the place of atonement—on top of it. [21]Then he brought the Ark of the Covenant into the Tabernacle and set up the inner curtain to shield it from view, just as the LORD had commanded.

[22]Next he placed the table in the Tabernacle, along the north side of the Holy Place, just outside the inner curtain. [23]And he arranged the Bread of the Presence on the table that stands before the LORD, just as the LORD had commanded.

[24]He set the lampstand in the Tabernacle across from the table on the south side of the Holy Place. [25]Then he set up the lamps in the LORD's presence, just as the LORD had com-

---

39:35 Or Ark of the Testimony. 40:2a Hebrew the Tabernacle, the Tent of Meeting; also in 40:6, 29. 40:2b Hebrew the first day of the first month. This day of the Hebrew lunar calendar occurs in March or early April. 40:3 Or Ark of the Testimony; also in 40:5, 21. 40:7 Hebrew Tent of Meeting; also in 40:12, 22, 24, 26, 30, 32, 34, 35. 40:17 Hebrew the first day of the first month, in the second year. See note on 40:2b. 40:20 Hebrew the Testimony.

manded. ²⁶He also placed the incense altar in the Tabernacle, in the Holy Place in front of the inner curtain. ²⁷On it he burned the fragrant incense made from sweet spices, just as the LORD had commanded.

²⁸He attached the curtain at the entrance of the Tabernacle, ²⁹and he placed the altar of burnt offering near the Tabernacle entrance. On it he offered a burnt offering and a grain offering, just as the LORD had commanded.

³⁰Next he placed the large washbasin between the Tabernacle and the altar. He filled it with water so the priests could use it to wash themselves. ³¹Moses and Aaron and Aaron's sons washed their hands and feet in the basin. ³²Whenever they walked past the altar to enter the Tabernacle, they were to stop and wash, just as the LORD had commanded Moses.

³³Then he hung the curtains forming the courtyard around the Tabernacle and the altar. And he set up the curtain at the entrance of the courtyard. So at last Moses finished the work.

THE LORD'S GLORY FILLS THE TABERNACLE

³⁴Then the cloud covered the Tabernacle, and the glorious presence of the LORD filled it. ³⁵Moses was no longer able to enter the Tabernacle because the cloud had settled down over it, and the Tabernacle was filled with the awesome glory of the LORD.

³⁶Now whenever the cloud lifted from the Tabernacle and moved, the people of Israel would set out on their journey, following it. ³⁷But if the cloud stayed, they would stay until it moved again. ³⁸The cloud of the LORD rested on the Tabernacle during the day, and at night there was fire in the cloud so all the people of Israel could see it. This continued throughout all their journeys.

As you worship, so you serve.

THOMAS L. JOHNS

Leviticus

I will show myself holy among those who are near me (10:3).

Read the Instructions First!

Nearly every parent can relate to the joy that lights up a child's face at Christmas upon seeing the box holding the new bike or the new computer game. And nearly every parent can relate to the feelings of frustration when hours later the chain on the new bike falls off, or the new computer game fails to run as promised.

That's when the truth hits: "When all else fails, read the instructions."

The book of Leviticus is God's instruction manual for his people. Ignoring instructions for building a train set can yield frustration, but skipping over God's rules and regulations can be hazardous to a person's spiritual *and* physical well-being.

The book reads as a "how-to" for worship—the rituals, who was in charge, the system of sacrifice, the holy celebrations—as well as a primer on holy living. Leviticus introduces the group of men wholly responsible for leading God's people in worship—the priests from the tribe of Levi. But at the heart of worship is the principle that God's people were set apart for his service. God told the people, "You must be holy because I, the LORD your God, am holy" (19:2).

Leviticus contains detailed instructions on a variety of issues involved with holy living, from confessing unintentional sin (5:5) to the difference between clean and unclean animals (chapter 11), to dealing with skin diseases and contaminated houses (chapters 12–15). The duties of the high priest are detailed in anticipation of the perfect work of Jesus, the High Priest who atoned for sin once for all. The book ends with a list of blessings for obedience—and the consequences for disobedience.

Because it is an instruction manual, Leviticus is a tough read. But buried within its pages are unexpected clues to the character of God—a God who engages our heads, hearts, and hands in worship. Look for the different ways God enjoins us to worship him. Then come before him as one set apart for his service and his love.

Worship Moments

- The newly ordained priests discover that worship and obedience go hand in hand when Moses and Aaron tell them that they must "stay at the entrance of the Tabernacle day and night for seven days" (8:35).

- God's character is revealed through his laws; he repeatedly reminds the Israelites that "you were once foreigners in the land of Egypt." For this reason, the way to treat foreigners is to "love them as you love yourself" (19:34).

- God identifies himself throughout this book as the LORD—*He Who Is;* as holy—*set apart* (19:2); and as God—*object of worship* (19:4).

PROCEDURES FOR THE BURNT OFFERING

1 The LORD called to Moses from the Tabernacle* and said to him, ²"Give the following instructions to the Israelites: Whenever you present offerings to the LORD, you must bring animals from your flocks and herds.

³"If your sacrifice for a whole burnt offering is from the herd, bring a bull with no physical defects to the entrance of the Tabernacle so it will be accepted by the LORD. ⁴Lay your hand on its head so the LORD will accept it as your substitute, thus making atonement for you. ⁵Then slaughter the animal in the LORD's presence, and Aaron's sons, the priests, will present the blood by sprinkling it against the sides of the altar that stands in front of the Tabernacle. ⁶When the animal has been skinned and cut into pieces, ⁷the sons of Aaron the priest will build a wood fire on the altar. ⁸Aaron's sons will then put the pieces of the animal, including its head and fat, on the wood fire. ⁹But the internal organs and legs must first be washed with water. Then the priests will burn the entire sacrifice on the altar. It is a whole burnt offering made by fire, very pleasing to the LORD.

¹⁰"If your sacrifice for a whole burnt offering is from the flock, bring a male sheep or goat with no physical defects. ¹¹Slaughter the animal on the north side of the altar in the LORD's presence. Aaron's sons, the priests, will sprinkle its blood against the sides of the altar. ¹²Then you must cut the animal in pieces, and the priests will lay the pieces of the sacrifice, including the head and fat, on top of the wood fire on the altar. ¹³The internal organs and legs must first be washed with water. Then the priests will burn the entire sacrifice on the altar. It is a whole burnt offering made by fire, very pleasing to the LORD.

¹⁴"If you bring a bird as a burnt offering to the LORD, choose either a turtledove or a young pigeon. ¹⁵The priest will take the bird to the altar, twist off its head, and burn the head on the altar. He must then let its blood drain out against the sides of the altar. ¹⁶The priest must remove the crop and the feathers* and throw them to the east side of the altar among the ashes. ¹⁷Then, grasping the bird by its wings, the priest will tear the bird apart, though not completely. Then he will burn it on top of the wood fire on the altar. It is a whole burnt offering made by fire, very pleasing to the LORD.

PROCEDURES FOR THE GRAIN OFFERING

2 "When you bring a grain offering to the LORD, the offering must consist of choice flour. You are to pour olive oil on it and sprinkle it with incense. ²Bring this offering to one of Aaron's sons, and he will take a handful of the flour mixed with olive oil, together with all the incense, and burn this token portion on the altar fire. It is an offering made by fire, very pleasing to the LORD. ³The rest of the flour will be given to Aaron and his sons. It will be considered a most holy part of the offerings given to the LORD by fire.

⁴"When you present some kind of baked bread as a grain offering, it must be made of choice flour mixed with olive oil but without any yeast. It may be presented in the form of cakes mixed with olive oil or wafers spread with olive oil. ⁵If your grain offering is cooked on a griddle, it must be made of choice flour and olive oil, and it must contain no yeast. ⁶Break it into pieces and pour oil on it; it is a kind of grain offering. ⁷If your offering is prepared in a pan, it also must be made of choice flour and olive oil.

⁸"No matter how a grain offering has been prepared before being offered to the LORD, bring it to the priests who will present it at the altar. ⁹The priests will take a token portion of the grain offering and burn it on the altar as an offering made by fire, and it will be very pleasing to the LORD. ¹⁰The rest of the grain offering will be given to Aaron and his

---

1:1 Hebrew *Tent of Meeting;* also in 1:3, 5.   1:16 Or *the crop and its contents.* The meaning of the Hebrew is uncertain.

sons as their food. It will be considered a most holy part of the offerings given to the LORD by fire.

[11]"Do not use yeast in any of the grain offerings you present to the LORD, because no yeast or honey may be burned as an offering to the LORD by fire. [12]You may add yeast and honey to the offerings presented at harvesttime, but these must never be burned on the altar as an offering pleasing to the LORD. [13]Season all your grain offerings with salt, to remind you of God's covenant. Never forget to add salt to your grain offerings.

[14]"If you present a grain offering to the LORD from the first portion of your harvest, bring kernels of new grain that have been roasted on a fire. [15]Since it is a grain offering, put olive oil on it and sprinkle it with incense. [16]The priests will take a token portion of the roasted grain mixed with olive oil, together with all the incense, and burn it as an offering given to the LORD by fire.

PROCEDURES FOR THE PEACE OFFERING

3 "If you want to present a peace offering from the herd, use either a bull or a cow. The animal you offer to the LORD must have no physical defects. [2]Lay your hand on the animal's head, and slaughter it at the entrance of the Tabernacle.* Aaron's sons, the priests, will then sprinkle the animal's blood against the sides of the altar. [3]Part of this peace offering must be presented to the LORD as an offering made by fire. This includes the fat around the internal organs, [4]the two kidneys with the fat around them near the loins, and the lobe of the liver, which is to be removed with the kidneys. [5]The sons of Aaron will burn these on the altar on top of the burnt offering on the wood fire. It is an offering made by fire, very pleasing to the LORD.

[6]"If you present a peace offering to the LORD from the flock, you may bring either a goat or a sheep. It may be either male or female, and it must have no physical defects. [7]If you bring a sheep as your gift, present it to the LORD [8]by laying your hand on its head and slaughtering it at the entrance of the Tabernacle. The sons of Aaron will then sprinkle the sheep's blood against the sides of the altar. [9]Part of this peace offering must be presented to the LORD as an offering made by fire. This includes the fat of the entire tail cut off near the backbone, the

3:2 Hebrew *Tent of Meeting;* also in 3:8, 13.

fat around the internal organs, [10]the two kidneys with the fat around them near the loins, and the lobe of the liver, which is to be removed with the kidneys. [11]The priest will burn them on the altar as food, an offering given to the LORD by fire.

[12]"If you bring a goat as your offering to the LORD, [13]lay your hand on its head, and slaughter it at the entrance of the Tabernacle. Then the sons of Aaron will sprinkle the goat's blood against the sides of the altar. [14]Part of this offering must be presented to the LORD as an offering made by fire. This part includes the fat around the internal organs, [15]the two kidneys with the fat around them near the loins, and the lobe of the liver, which is to be removed with the kidneys. [16]The priest will burn them on the altar as food, an offering made by fire; these will be very pleasing to the LORD. Remember, all the fat belongs to the LORD.

[17]"You must never eat any fat or blood. This is a permanent law for you and all your descendants, wherever they may live."

PROCEDURES FOR THE SIN OFFERING

4 Then the LORD said to Moses, [2]"Give the Israelites the following instructions for dealing with those who sin unintentionally by doing anything forbidden by the LORD's commands.

[3]"If the high priest sins, bringing guilt upon the entire community, he must bring to the LORD a young bull with no physical defects. [4]He must present the bull to the LORD at the entrance of the Tabernacle,* lay his hand on the bull's head, and slaughter it there in the LORD's presence. [5]The priest on duty will then take some of the animal's blood into the Tabernacle, [6]dip his finger into the blood, and sprinkle it seven times before the LORD in front of the inner curtain of the Most Holy Place. [7]The priest will put some of the blood on the horns of the incense altar that stands in the LORD's presence in the Tabernacle. The

rest of the bull's blood must be poured out at the base of the altar of burnt offerings at the entrance of the Tabernacle. [8]The priest must remove all the fat around the bull's internal organs, [9]the two kidneys with the fat around them near the loins, and the lobe of the liver. [10]Then he must burn them on the altar of burnt offerings, just as is done with the bull or cow sacrificed as a peace offering. [11]But the rest of the bull—its hide, meat, head, legs, internal organs, and dung—[12]must be carried away to a ceremonially clean place outside the camp, the place where the ashes are thrown. He will burn it all on a wood fire in the ash heap.

[13]"If the entire Israelite community does something forbidden by the LORD and the matter escapes the community's notice, all the people will be guilty. [14]When they discover their sin, the leaders of the community must bring a young bull for a sin offering and present it at the entrance of the Tabernacle. [15]The leaders must then lay their hands on the bull's head and slaughter it there before the LORD. [16]The priest will bring some of its blood into the Tabernacle, [17]dip his finger into the blood, and sprinkle it seven times before the LORD in front of the inner curtain. [18]He will then put some of the blood on the horns of the incense altar that stands in the LORD's presence in the Tabernacle. The rest of the blood must then be poured out at the base of the altar of burnt offerings at the entrance of the Tabernacle. [19]The priest must remove all the animal's fat and burn it on the altar, [20]following the same procedure as with the sin offering for the priest. In this way, the priest will make atonement for the people, and they will be forgiven. [21]The priest must then take what is left of the bull outside the camp and burn it there, just as is done with the sin offering for the high priest. This is a sin offering for the entire community of Israel.

[22]"If one of Israel's leaders does something forbidden by the LORD his God, he will be guilty even if he sinned unintentionally. [23]When he becomes aware of his sin, he must

4:4 Hebrew *Tent of Meeting*; also in 4:5, 7, 14, 16, 18.

bring as his offering a male goat with no physical defects. ²⁴He is to lay his hand on the goat's head and slaughter it before the LORD at the place where burnt offerings are slaughtered. This will be his sin offering. ²⁵Then the priest will dip his finger into the blood of the sin offering, put it on the horns of the altar of burnt offerings, and pour out the rest of the blood at the base of the altar. ²⁶He must burn all the goat's fat on the altar, just as is done with the peace offering. In this way, the priest will make atonement for the leader's sin, and he will be forgiven.

²⁷"If any of the citizens of Israel* do something forbidden by the LORD, they will be guilty even if they sinned unintentionally. ²⁸When they become aware of their sin, they must bring as their offering a female goat with no physical defects. It will be offered for their sin. ²⁹They are to lay a hand on the head of the sin offering and slaughter it at the place where burnt offerings are slaughtered. ³⁰The priest will then dip his finger into the blood, put the blood on the horns of the altar of burnt offerings, and pour out the rest of the blood at the base of the altar. ³¹Those who are guilty must remove all the goat's fat, just as is done with the peace offering. Then the priest will burn the fat on the altar, and it will be very pleasing to the LORD. In this way, the priest will make atonement for them, and they will be forgiven.

³²"If any of the people bring a sheep as their sin offering, it must be a female with no physical defects. ³³They are to lay a hand on the head of the sin offering and slaughter it at the place where the burnt offerings are slaughtered. ³⁴The priest will then dip his finger into the blood, put it on the horns of the altar of burnt offerings, and pour out the rest of the blood at the base of the altar. ³⁵Those who are guilty must remove all the sheep's fat, just as is done with a sheep presented as a peace offering. Then the priest will burn the fat on the altar on top of the offerings given to the LORD by fire. In this way, the priest will make atonement for them, and they will be forgiven.

4:27 Hebrew *people of the land.*

SINS REQUIRING A SIN OFFERING

5 "If any of the people are called to testify about something they have witnessed, but they refuse to testify, they will be held responsible and be subject to punishment.

²"Or if they touch something that is ceremonially unclean, such as the dead body of an animal that is ceremonially unclean—whether a wild animal, a domesticated animal, or an animal that scurries along the ground—they will be considered ceremonially unclean and guilty, even if they are unaware of their defilement.

³"Or if they come into contact with any source of human defilement, even if they don't realize they have been defiled, they will be considered guilty as soon as they become aware of it.

⁴"Or if they make a rash vow of any kind, whether its purpose is for good or bad, they will be considered guilty even if they were not fully aware of what they were doing at the time.

⁵"When any of the people become aware of their guilt in any of these ways, they must confess their sin ⁶and bring to the LORD as their penalty a female from the flock, either a sheep or a goat. This will be a sin offering to remove their sin, and the priest will make atonement for them.

⁷"If any of them cannot afford to bring a sheep, they must bring to the LORD two young turtledoves or two young pigeons as the penalty for their sin. One of the birds will be a sin offering, and the other will be a burnt offering. ⁸They must bring them to the priest, who will offer one of the birds as the sin offering. The priest will wring its neck but without severing its head from the body. ⁹Then he will sprinkle some of the blood of the sin offering against the sides of the altar, and the rest will be drained out at the base of the altar. ¹⁰The priest will offer the second bird as a whole burnt offering, following all the procedures that have been prescribed. In this way, the

My Daily Worship

— January 27 —

THE SACRIFICE THAT COSTS NOTHING

LEVITICUS 1:1–4:35

*If any of the citizens of Israel do something forbidden by the LORD, they will be guilty
even if they sinned unintentionally. When they become aware of their sin,
they must bring . . . [an] offering (4:27–28).*

[i reflect]

We often forget that the Israelite worship center was a slaughterhouse. It was a place where birds were torn apart with bare hands, where the plunge of knives turned livestock into dead-stock, where blood flowed in trenches, and the odor of charred flesh filled the nostrils of worshipers. Death was ever present in the house of God—a reminder of the consequences of sin.

We are spared the necessity of such a messy corollary to our worship. Christ's death on the cross is the only sacrifice we need to escape the penalty due our sin, becoming effective for us when we put our faith in him. Nothing we can do will either earn or add to our acceptance by God through Christ.

Yet there is this: God desires the free offering of our worship. "With Jesus' help, let us continually offer our sacrifice of praise to God by proclaiming the glory of his name" (Hebrews 13:15). It pleases God when we praise him, not in the hope of receiving anything in return, but just because we love him for all he is and all he has done.

Our worship is always a response to God giving to us. And as his mercy and grace are infinite, so our worship must be never ending, daily, even moment by moment. Death will only modulate our singing of "Holy, holy, holy" upward to richer chords of praise.

Such worship resounds with goodness. In this sense, it is no "sacrifice" at all; it takes nothing away from us but only gives. Worship is a circular system of blessings. God is the source and we are the happy participants.

[i pray]

*Lord, may my praise to you flow more freely than the blood of bulls in temple days.
I worship you for your great goodness to me.*

[i respond]

Before your next time of individual worship, take a pen and paper and list twenty-five examples of how God has been good to you. Allow these benefits to help motivate your "sacrifice of praise."

priest will make atonement for those who are guilty, and they will be forgiven.

[11]"If any of the people cannot afford to bring young turtledoves or pigeons, they must bring two quarts* of choice flour for their sin offering. Since it is a sin offering, they must not mix it with olive oil or put any incense on it. [12]They must take the flour to the priest, who will scoop out a handful as a token portion. He will burn this flour on the altar just like any other offering given to the LORD by fire. This will be their sin offering. [13]In this way, the priest will make atonement for those who are guilty, and they will be forgiven. The rest of the flour will belong to the priest, just as with the grain offering."

PROCEDURES FOR THE GUILT OFFERING

[14]Then the LORD said to Moses, [15]"If any of the people sin by unintentionally defiling the LORD's sacred property, they must bring to the LORD a ram from the flock as their guilt offering. The animal must have no physical defects, and it must be of the proper value in silver as measured by the standard sanctuary shekel.* [16]They must then make restitution for whatever holy things they have defiled by paying for the loss, plus an added penalty of 20 percent. When they give their payments to the priest, he will make atonement for them with the ram sacrificed as a guilt offering, and they will be forgiven.

[17]"If any of them sin by doing something forbidden by the LORD, even if it is done unintentionally, they will be held responsible. When they become aware of their guilt, [18]they must bring to the priest a ram from the flock as a guilt offering. The animal must have no physical defects, and it must be of the proper value. In this way, the priest will make atonement for those who are guilty, and they will be forgiven. [19]This is a guilt offering, for they have been guilty of an offense against the LORD."

SINS REQUIRING A GUILT OFFERING

6 And the LORD said to Moses, [2]"Suppose some of the people sin against the LORD by falsely telling their neighbor that an item entrusted to their safekeeping has been lost or stolen. Or suppose they have been dishonest with regard to a security deposit, or they have taken something by theft or extortion. [3]Or suppose they find a lost item and lie about it, or they deny something while under oath, or they commit any other similar sin. [4]If they have sinned in any of these ways and are guilty, they must give back whatever they have taken by theft or extortion, whether a security deposit, or property entrusted to them, or a lost object that they claimed as their own, [5]or anything gained by swearing falsely. When they realize their guilt, they must restore the principal amount plus a penalty of 20 percent to the person they have harmed. [6]They must then bring a guilt offering to the priest, who will present it before the LORD. This offering must be a ram with no physical defects or the animal's equivalent value in silver.* [7]The priest will then make atonement for them before the LORD, and they will be forgiven."

FURTHER INSTRUCTIONS FOR THE BURNT OFFERING

[8]Then the LORD said to Moses, [9]"Give Aaron and his sons the following instructions regarding the whole burnt offering. The burnt offering must be left on the altar until the next morning, and the altar fire must be kept burning all night. [10]The next morning, after dressing in his special linen clothing and undergarments, the priest on duty must clean out the ashes of the burnt offering and put them beside the altar. [11]Then he must change back into his normal clothing and carry the ashes outside the camp to a place that is ceremonially clean. [12]Meanwhile, the fire on the altar must be kept burning; it must never go out. Each morning the priest will add fresh

---

5:11 Hebrew *1/10 of an ephah* [2 liters]. 5:15 Each sanctuary shekel was about 0.4 ounces or 11 grams in weight. 6:6 Or *and the animal must be of the proper value;* Hebrew lacks *in silver;* compare 5:15.

My Daily Worship

— *January 28* —

MAKE IT RIGHT—RIGHT AWAY

LEVITICUS 5:1–7:3

When any of the people become aware of their guilt in any of these ways,
they must confess their sin and bring to the LORD as their penalty
a female from the flock, either a sheep or a goat (5:5–6).

[i reflect]

Why is it that at times we feel so dry, like our inner spirit has shriveled up?

If you're going through a period of spiritual dryness, when worship becomes something you must force or fake, it could be you are experiencing what certain mystics called "the dark night of the soul"—a period in which God removes the sense of his presence in the process of raising a Christian to a higher level of devotion. Or it could be much simpler than that. You could just have unconfessed sin in your life.

The practical religion of the Hebrews made provision for confession, restitution, and atonement in its sacrificial system. We're not governed by the same Old Testament laws. But we, too, have to do something about our sin if the kinks pinching off our connection with God are to be straightened out. We have to admit our sin to ourselves, then to others (God and other people affected), and finally make whatever amends are appropriate.

Jesus advised his listeners that if they were waiting to offer a sacrifice at the temple and remembered that another person had something against them, they should leave the temple immediately and be reconciled with the other. Afterward, they could return to the temple and complete the sacrifice (Matthew 5:23–24). The principle? Confession first, then worship.

Mature Christians tell us that we do ourselves a favor when we confess our sin right away. Mature worshipers assure us that confession of sin can actually enhance worship by peeling back the covering from the nerve in us that senses God's astounding mercy.

Before you leave this place and time, consider the state of your own conscience. Is there some unconfessed sin that is preventing you from enjoying God's presence? Take time right now to bring that before God.

[i pray]

I am weak and I fail, Lord; I know it. Help me to settle my accounts
with all so that I may enjoy unclouded fellowship with you.

[i respond]

Write a note of confession to God. Tell him what's interfering with your worship life. Ask God to show you what needs to be done to reconnect with him.

wood to the fire and arrange the daily whole burnt offering on it. He must then burn the fat of the peace offerings on top of this daily whole burnt offering. [13]Remember, the fire must be kept burning on the altar at all times. It must never go out.

FURTHER INSTRUCTIONS FOR THE GRAIN OFFERING

[14]"These are the instructions regarding the grain offering. Aaron's sons must present this offering to the LORD in front of the altar. [15]The priest on duty will take a handful of the choice flour that has been mixed with olive oil and sprinkled with incense. He will burn this token portion on the altar, and it will be very pleasing to the LORD. [16]After burning this handful, the rest of the flour will belong to Aaron and his sons for their food. It must, however, be baked without yeast and eaten in a sacred place within the courtyard of the Tabernacle.* [17]Remember, this flour may never be prepared with yeast. I have given it to the priests as their share of the offerings presented to me by fire. Like the sin offering and the guilt offering, it is most holy. [18]Any of Aaron's male descendants, from generation to generation, may eat of the grain offering, because it is their regular share of the offerings given to the LORD by fire. Anyone or anything that touches this food will become holy."

PROCEDURES FOR THE ORDINATION OFFERING

[19]And the LORD said to Moses, [20]"On the day Aaron and his sons are anointed, they must bring to the LORD a grain offering of two quarts* of choice flour, half to be offered in the morning and half to be offered in the evening. [21]It must be cooked on a griddle with olive oil, and it must be well mixed and broken* into pieces. You must present this grain offering, and it will be very pleasing to the LORD. [22]As the sons of the priests replace their fathers, they will be inducted into office by offering this same sacrifice on the day they are anointed. It is the LORD's regular share, and it must be completely burned up. [23]All such grain offerings of the priests must be entirely burned up. None of the flour may be eaten."

FURTHER INSTRUCTIONS FOR THE SIN OFFERING

[24]Then the LORD said to Moses, [25]"Give Aaron and his sons these further instructions regarding the sin offering. The animal given as a sin offering is most holy and must be slaughtered in the LORD's presence at the place where the burnt offerings are slaughtered. [26]The priest who offers the sacrifice may eat his portion in a sacred place within the courtyard of the Tabernacle. [27]Anything or anyone who touches the sacrificial meat will become holy, and if the sacrificial blood splatters anyone's clothing, it must be washed off in a sacred place. [28]If a clay pot is used to boil the sacrificial meat, it must be broken. If a bronze kettle is used, it must be scoured and rinsed thoroughly with water. [29]Only males from a priest's family may eat of this offering, for it is most holy. [30]If, however, the blood of a sin offering has been taken into the Tabernacle to make atonement in the Holy Place for the people's sins, none of that animal's meat may be eaten. It must be completely burned up.

> *In commanding us*
> *to glorify Him,*
> *God is inviting us*
> *to enjoy Him.*
>
> C. S. LEWIS

6:16 Hebrew *Tent of Meeting;* also in 6:26, 30. 6:20 Hebrew *1/10 of an ephah* [2 liters]. 6:21 The meaning of this Hebrew term is uncertain.

FURTHER INSTRUCTIONS FOR THE GUILT OFFERING

7 "These are the instructions for the guilt offering, which is most holy. ²The animal sacrificed as a guilt offering must be slaughtered where the burnt offerings are slaughtered, and its blood sprinkled against the sides of the altar. ³The priest will then offer all its fat on the altar, including the fat from the tail, the fat around the internal organs, ⁴the two kidneys with the fat around them near the loins, and the lobe of the liver, which is to be removed with the kidneys. ⁵The priests will burn these parts on the altar as an offering to the LORD made by fire. It is a guilt offering. ⁶All males from a priest's family may eat the meat, and it must be eaten in a sacred place, for it is most holy.

⁷"For both the sin offering and the guilt offering, the meat of the sacrificed animal belongs to the priest in charge of the atonement ceremony. ⁸In the case of the whole burnt offering, the hide of the sacrificed animal also belongs to the priest. ⁹Any grain offering that has been baked in an oven, prepared in a pan, or cooked on a griddle belongs to the priest who presents it. ¹⁰All other grain offerings, whether flour mixed with olive oil or dry flour, are to be shared among all the priests and their sons.

FURTHER INSTRUCTIONS FOR THE PEACE OFFERING

¹¹"These are the instructions regarding the different kinds of peace offerings that may be presented to the LORD. ¹²If you present your peace offering as a thanksgiving offering, the usual animal sacrifice must be accompanied by various kinds of bread—loaves, wafers, and cakes—all made without yeast and soaked with olive oil. ¹³This peace offering of thanksgiving must also be accompanied by loaves of yeast bread. ¹⁴One of each kind of bread must be presented as a gift to the LORD. This bread will then belong to the priest who sprinkles the altar with blood from the sacrificed animal. ¹⁵The animal's meat must be eaten on the same day it is offered. None of it may be saved for the next morning.

¹⁶"However, if you bring an offering to fulfill a vow or as a freewill offering, the meat may be eaten on that same day, and whatever is left over may be eaten on the second day. ¹⁷But anything left over until the third day must be completely burned up. ¹⁸If any of the meat from this peace offering is eaten on the third day, it will not be accepted by the LORD. It will have no value as a sacrifice, and you will receive no credit for bringing it as an offering. By then, the meat will be contaminated; if you eat it, you will have to answer for your sin.

¹⁹"Meat that touches anything ceremonially unclean may not be eaten; it must be completely burned up. And as for meat that may be eaten, it may only be eaten by people who are ceremonially clean. ²⁰Anyone who is ceremonially unclean but eats meat from a peace offering that was presented to the LORD must be cut off from the community. ²¹If anyone touches anything that is unclean, whether it is human defilement or an unclean animal, and then eats meat from the LORD's sacrifices, that person must be cut off from the community."

THE FORBIDDEN BLOOD AND FAT

²²Then the LORD said to Moses, ²³"Give the Israelites these instructions: You must never eat fat, whether from oxen or sheep or goats. ²⁴The fat of an animal found dead or killed by a wild animal may never be eaten, though it may be used for any other purpose. ²⁵Anyone who eats fat from an offering given to the LORD by fire must be cut off from the community. ²⁶Even in your homes, you must never eat the blood of any bird or animal. ²⁷Anyone who eats blood must be cut off from the community."

A PORTION FOR THE PRIESTS

²⁸Then the LORD said to Moses, ²⁹"Give these further instructions to the Israelites: When you present a peace offering to the LORD, bring part of it as a special gift to the LORD. ³⁰Present it to him with your own hands as an

offering given to the LORD by fire. Bring the fat of the animal, together with the breast, and present it to the LORD by lifting it up before him. ³¹Then the priest will burn the fat on the altar, but the breast will belong to Aaron and his sons. ³²You are to give the right thigh of your peace offering to the priest as a gift. ³³The right thigh must always be given to the priest who sprinkles the blood and offers the fat of the peace offering. ³⁴For I have designated the breast and the right thigh for the priests. It is their regular share of the peace offerings brought by the Israelites. ³⁵This is their share. It has been set apart for Aaron and his descendants from the offerings given to the LORD by fire from the time they were appointed to serve the LORD as priests. ³⁶The LORD commanded that the Israelites were to give these portions to the priests as their regular share from the time of the priests' anointing. This regulation applies throughout the generations to come."

³⁷These are the instructions for the whole burnt offering, the grain offering, the sin offering, the guilt offering, the ordination offering, and the peace offering. ³⁸The LORD gave these instructions to Moses on Mount Sinai when he commanded the Israelites to bring their offerings to the LORD in the wilderness of Sinai.

ORDINATION OF THE PRIESTS

8 The LORD said to Moses, ²"Now bring Aaron and his sons, along with their special clothing, the anointing oil, the bull for the sin offering, the two rams, and the basket of unleavened bread ³to the entrance of the Tabernacle.* Then call the entire community of Israel to meet you there."

⁴So Moses followed the LORD's instructions, and all the people assembled at the Tabernacle entrance. ⁵Moses announced to them, "The LORD has commanded what I am now going to do!" ⁶Then he presented Aaron and his sons and washed them with water. ⁷He clothed Aaron with the embroidered tunic and tied

the sash around his waist. He dressed him in the robe of the ephod, along with the ephod itself, and attached the ephod with its decorative sash. ⁸Then Moses placed the chestpiece on Aaron and put the Urim and the Thummim inside it. ⁹He placed on Aaron's head the turban with the gold medallion at its front, just as the LORD had commanded him.

¹⁰Then Moses took the anointing oil and anointed the Tabernacle and everything in it, thus making them holy. ¹¹He sprinkled the altar seven times, anointing it and all its utensils and the washbasin and its pedestal, making them holy. ¹²Then he poured some of the anointing oil on Aaron's head, thus anointing him and making him holy for his work. ¹³Next Moses presented Aaron's sons and clothed them in their embroidered tunics, their sashes, and their turbans, just as the LORD had commanded him.

¹⁴Then Moses brought in the bull for the sin offering, and Aaron and his sons laid their hands on its head ¹⁵as Moses slaughtered it. Moses took some of the blood, and with his finger he put it on the four horns of the altar to purify it. He poured out the rest of the blood at the base of the altar. In this way, he set the altar apart as holy and made atonement for it.* ¹⁶He took all the fat around the internal organs, the lobe of the liver, and the two kidneys and their fat, and he burned them all on the altar. ¹⁷The rest of the bull, including its hide, meat, and dung, was burned outside the camp, just as the LORD had commanded Moses.

¹⁸Then Moses presented the ram to the LORD for the whole burnt offering, and Aaron and his sons laid their hands on its head ¹⁹as Moses slaughtered it. Then Moses took the ram's blood and sprinkled it against the sides of the altar. ²⁰Next he cut the ram into pieces and burned the head, some of its pieces, and the fat on the altar. ²¹After washing the internal organs and the legs with water, Moses burned the entire ram on the altar as a whole burnt offering. It was an offering given to the

8:3 Hebrew *Tent of Meeting;* also in 8:4, 31, 33, 35. 8:15 Or *that atonement may be made on it.*

LORD by fire, very pleasing to the LORD. All this was done just as the LORD had commanded Moses.

[22]Next Moses presented the second ram, which was the ram of ordination. Aaron and his sons laid their hands on its head [23]as Moses slaughtered it. Then Moses took some of its blood and put it on the lobe of Aaron's right ear, the thumb of his right hand, and the big toe of his right foot. [24]Next he presented Aaron's sons and put some of the blood on the lobe of their right ears, the thumb of their right hands, and the big toe of their right feet. He then sprinkled the rest of the blood against the sides of the altar.

[25]Next he took the fat, including the fat from the tail, the fat around the internal organs, the lobe of the liver, and the two kidneys with their fat, along with the right thigh. [26]On top of these he placed a loaf of unleavened bread, a cake of unleavened bread soaked with olive oil, and a thin wafer spread with olive oil. All these were taken from the basket of bread made without yeast that was placed in the LORD's presence. [27]He gave all of these to Aaron and his sons, and he presented the portions by lifting them up before the LORD. [28]Moses then took all the offerings back and burned them on the altar on top of the burnt offering as an ordination offering. It was an offering given to the LORD by fire, very pleasing to the LORD. [29]Then Moses took the breast and lifted it up in the LORD's presence. This was Moses' share of the ram of ordination, just as the LORD had commanded him.

[30]Next Moses took some of the anointing oil and some of the blood that was on the altar, and he sprinkled them on Aaron and his clothing and on his sons and their clothing. In this way, he made Aaron and his sons and their clothing holy.

[31]Then Moses said to Aaron and his sons, "Boil the rest of the meat at the Tabernacle entrance, and eat it along with the bread that is in the basket of ordination offerings, just as I commanded you. [32]Any meat or bread that is left over must then be burned up. [33]Do not leave the Tabernacle entrance for seven days, for that is the time it will take to complete the ordination ceremony. [34]What has been done today was commanded by the LORD in order to make atonement for you. [35]Remember, you must stay at the entrance of the Tabernacle day and night for seven days, doing everything the LORD requires. If you fail in this, you will die. This is what the LORD has said." [36]So Aaron and his sons did everything the LORD had commanded through Moses.

THE PRIESTS BEGIN THEIR WORK

9 After the ordination ceremony, on the eighth day, Moses called together Aaron and his sons and the leaders of Israel. [2]He said to Aaron, "Take a young bull for a sin offering and a ram for a whole burnt offering, both with no physical defects, and present them to the LORD. [3]Then tell the Israelites to take a male goat for a sin offering for themselves and a year-old calf and a year-old lamb for a whole burnt offering, each with no physical defects. [4]Also tell them to take a bull* and a ram for a peace offering and flour mixed with olive oil for a grain offering. Tell them to present all these offerings to the LORD because the LORD will appear to them today."

[5]So the people brought all of these things to the entrance of the Tabernacle,* just as Moses had commanded, and the whole community came and stood there in the LORD's presence. [6]Then Moses told them, "When you have followed these instructions from the LORD, the glorious presence of the LORD will appear to you."

[7]Then Moses said to Aaron, "Approach the altar and present your sin offering and your whole burnt offering to make atonement for yourself. Then present the offerings to make atonement for the people, just as the LORD has commanded."

[8]So Aaron went to the altar and slaughtered the calf as a sin offering for himself. [9]His sons brought him the blood, and he dipped his

9:4 Or *cow*; also in 9:18, 19. 9:5 Hebrew *Tent of Meeting*; also in 9:23.

finger into it and put it on the horns of the altar. He poured out the rest of the blood at the base of the altar. [10]Then he burned on the altar the fat, the kidneys, and the lobe of the liver from the sin offering, just as the LORD had commanded Moses. [11]The meat and the hide, however, he burned outside the camp.

[12]Next Aaron slaughtered the animal for the whole burnt offering. His sons brought him the blood, and he sprinkled it against the sides of the altar. [13]They handed the animal to him piece by piece, including the head, and he burned each part on the altar. [14]Then he washed the internal organs and the legs and also burned them on the altar as a whole burnt offering.

[15]Next Aaron presented the sacrifices for the people. He slaughtered the people's goat and presented it as their sin offering, just as he had done previously for himself. [16]Then he brought the whole burnt offering and presented it in the prescribed way. [17]He also brought the grain offering, burning a handful of the flour on the altar, in addition to the regular morning burnt offering.

[18]Then Aaron slaughtered the bull and the ram for the people's peace offering. His sons brought him the blood, and he sprinkled it against the sides of the altar. [19]Then he took the fat of the bull and the ram—the fat from the tail and from around the internal organs—along with the kidneys and the lobe of the liver. [20]He placed these fat parts on top of the breasts of these animals and then burned them on the altar. [21]Aaron then lifted up the breasts and right thighs as an offering to the LORD, just as Moses had commanded.

[22]After that, Aaron raised his hands toward the people and blessed them. Then, after presenting the sin offering, the whole burnt offering, and the peace offering, he stepped down from the altar. [23]Next Moses and Aaron went into the Tabernacle, and when they came back out, they blessed the people again, and the glorious presence of the LORD appeared to the whole community. [24]Fire blazed forth from the LORD's presence and consumed the burnt offering and the fat on the altar. When the people saw all this, they shouted with joy and fell face down on the ground.

THE SIN OF NADAB AND ABIHU

10 Aaron's sons Nadab and Abihu put coals of fire in their incense burners and sprinkled incense over it. In this way, they disobeyed the LORD by burning before him a different kind of fire than he had commanded. [2]So fire blazed forth from the LORD's presence and burned them up, and they died there before the LORD.

[3]Then Moses said to Aaron, "This is what the LORD meant when he said,

'I will show myself holy
    among those who are near me.
I will be glorified
    before all the people.'"

And Aaron was silent.

[4]Then Moses called for Mishael and Elzaphan, Aaron's cousins, the sons of Aaron's uncle Uzziel. He said to them, "Come and carry the bodies of your relatives away from the sanctuary to a place outside the camp." [5]So they came forward and carried them out of the camp by their tunics as Moses had commanded.

[6]Then Moses said to Aaron and his sons Eleazar and Ithamar, "Do not mourn by letting your hair hang loose* or by tearing your clothes. If you do, you will die, and the LORD will be angry with the whole community of Israel. However, the rest of the Israelites, your relatives, may mourn for Nadab and Abihu, whom the LORD has destroyed by fire. [7]But you are not to leave the entrance of the Tabernacle,* under penalty of death, for the anointing oil of the LORD is upon you." So they did as Moses commanded.

10:6 Or *by uncovering your heads.*   10:7 Hebrew *Tent of Meeting;* also in 10:9.

My Daily Worship
— January 29 —

I WOULD NEVER HAVE DREAMED
LEVITICUS 8:1–10:20

*Fire blazed forth from the LORD's presence and consumed the burnt offering
and the fat on the altar. When the people saw all this, they shouted
with joy and fell face down on the ground (9:24).*

[i reflect]

Who is this God we worship? How nearly do our ideas about him approximate the reality? Are we ever guilty of forming a tamed and manageable deity and placing him within a cage in our minds?

C. S. Lewis wrote, "[God] must constantly work as the iconoclast. Every idea of him we form, he must, in mercy, shatter. The most blessed result of prayer would be to rise thinking, *But I never knew before. I never dreamed . . .*"

From time to time, people in Scripture got a glimpse of the real God. And as at the inauguration of the Tabernacle, they responded with powerful emotions such as joy and fear. No tame God here. No deity-masters are we.

Does your worship generate a thrill in touching something of the real God—at least from time to time? If you experience a conflict of emotions, such as awe and delight, do not worry about that. But if spending time in the presence of God is always comfortable, never anything that would make you fall on your face in reverence, know you have further to go.

Scripture says we have God as our friend if we are Christ's partisans. In a sense we can grow comfortable with God, as with a friend. But this familarity in no way changes his holiness—which is brighter than a flame, his power that is mightier than a lightning bolt and, his utter and most glorious otherness—the very reason for which we worship him.

As you go through the day, take with you a sense of his majesty, his power, his awesome presence. Fire blazes forth from the presence of the Lord. Feel the heat.

[i pray]

*It scares me to say this, great God, and yet I say it anyway:
Show me the real you in all the fullness I can bear.*

[i respond]

Undertake a Bible study designed to reveal the many facets of God's nature. Make this not a mere intellectual exercise but a means of learning more ways in which to experience God in worship.

INSTRUCTIONS FOR PRIESTLY CONDUCT

[8]Then the LORD said to Aaron, [9]"You and your descendants must never drink wine or any other alcoholic drink before going into the Tabernacle. If you do, you will die. This is a permanent law for you, and it must be kept by all future generations. [10]You are to distinguish between what is holy and what is ordinary, what is ceremonially unclean and what is clean. [11]And you must teach the Israelites all the laws that the LORD has given through Moses."

[12]Then Moses said to Aaron and his remaining sons, Eleazar and Ithamar, "Take what is left of the grain offering after the handful has been presented to the LORD by fire. Make sure there is no yeast in it, and eat it beside the altar, for it is most holy. [13]It must be eaten in a sacred place, for it has been given to you and your descendants as your regular share of the offerings given to the LORD by fire. These are the commands I have been given. [14]But the breast and thigh that were lifted up may be eaten in any place that is ceremonially clean. These parts have been given to you and to your sons and daughters as your regular share of the peace offerings presented by the people of Israel. [15]The thigh and breast that are lifted up must be lifted up to the LORD along with the fat of the offerings given by fire. Then they will belong to you and your descendants forever, just as the LORD has commanded."

[16]When Moses demanded to know what had happened to the goat of the sin offering, he discovered that it had been burned up. As a result, he became very angry with Eleazar and Ithamar, Aaron's remaining sons. [17]"Why didn't you eat the sin offering in the sanctuary area?" he demanded. "It is a holy offering! It was given to you for removing the guilt of the community and for making atonement for the people before the LORD. [18]Since the animal's blood was not taken into the Holy Place, you should have eaten the meat in the sanctuary area as I ordered you."

[19]Then Aaron answered Moses on behalf of his sons. "Today my sons presented both their sin offering and their burnt offering to the LORD," he said. "This kind of thing has also happened to me. Would the LORD have approved if I had eaten the sin offering today?" [20]And when Moses heard this, he approved.

CEREMONIALLY CLEAN AND UNCLEAN ANIMALS

11 Then the LORD said to Moses and Aaron, [2]"Give the following instructions to the Israelites: The animals you may use for food [3]include those that have completely divided hooves and chew the cud. [4]You may not, however, eat the animals named here* because they either have split hooves or chew the cud, but not both. The camel may not be eaten, for though it chews the cud, it does not have split hooves. [5]The same is true of the rock badger* [6]and the hare, so they also may never be eaten. [7]And the pig may not be eaten, for though it has split hooves, it does not chew the cud. [8]You may not eat the meat of these animals or touch their dead bodies. They are ceremonially unclean for you.

[9]"As for marine animals, you may eat whatever has both fins and scales, whether taken from fresh water or salt water. [10]You may not, however, eat marine animals that do not have both fins and scales. You are to detest them, [11]and they will always be forbidden to you. You must never eat their meat or even touch their dead bodies. [12]I repeat, any marine animal that does not have both fins and scales is strictly forbidden to you.

[13]"These are the birds you must never eat because they are detestable for you: the eagle, the vulture, the osprey, [14]the buzzard, kites of all kinds, [15]ravens of all kinds, [16]the ostrich, the nighthawk, the seagull, hawks of all kinds, [17]the little owl, the cormorant, the great owl, [18]the white owl, the pelican, the carrion vulture, [19]the stork, herons of all kinds, the hoopoe, and the bat.

11:4 The identification of some of the animals, birds, and insects in this chapter is uncertain. 11:5 Or *coney,* or *hyrax.*

My Daily Worship

— *January 30* —

WEARING OUR SPIRITUAL ATTIRE

LEVITICUS 11:1–14:57

I, the LORD, am your God. You must be holy
because I am holy (11:44).

[i reflect]

A wedding invitee was digging postholes on his ranch when he suddenly remembered the wedding, which was to begin in less than half an hour. He hopped into his pickup truck and raced off to the church. At first congratulating himself on managing to slip into a pew before the bride began her procession, he soon noticed other guests casting glances his way. This was a formal wedding—and he was in dirty work clothes! He was mortified.

To borrow some biblical imagery, we must be clothed in righteousness by washing our robes in the blood of the Lamb if we are to worship him who dwells in unapproachable light.

The lyric to an angelic praise chorus begins this way: "Holy, holy, holy is the Lord God Almighty" (Revelation 4:8). The triple use of "holy" indicates complete holiness. God is not somewhat holy or essentially holy, but wholly holy.

Singing such a song is all well and good for angels who have never sinned. But what about us? How can we, who swim in the sin-polluted pool known as humanity, presume to come near to God and declare his holiness? Our clothes have a lust smudge here, a bitterness stain there, and a self-ishness tear at the hem.

God chooses to see us as righteous if we ask to be clothed in Christ's righteousness and washed in his blood. And he wants us, in addition, to do our best at bringing our actual behavior in line with our granted position before God. Do a mental assessment of your spiritual attire. What is preventing you from worshiping him "in the splendor of his holiness" (Psalm 29:2)?

[i pray]

O Lord, help me to see how the sin I play with is not a toy but a weapon
turned upon me. Make my feet swift as I flee sin.

[i respond]

Who is the holiest person you know? Get together with him or her and ask to hear the hard-earned lessons this person must have learned about climbing the stairway of sanctification.

²⁰"You are to consider detestable all swarming insects that walk along the ground. ²¹However, there are some exceptions that you may eat. These include insects that jump with their hind legs: ²²locusts of all varieties, crickets, bald locusts, and grasshoppers. All these may be eaten. ²³But you are to consider detestable all other swarming insects that walk or crawl.

²⁴"The following creatures make you ceremonially unclean. If you touch any of their dead bodies, you will be defiled until evening. ²⁵If you move the dead body of an unclean animal, you must immediately wash your clothes, and you will remain defiled until evening.

²⁶"Any animal that has divided but unsplit hooves or that does not chew the cud is unclean for you. If you touch the dead body of such an animal, you will be defiled until evening. ²⁷Of the animals that walk on all fours, those that have paws are unclean for you. If you touch the dead body of such an animal, you will be defiled until evening. ²⁸If you pick up and move its carcass, you must immediately wash your clothes, and you will remain defiled until evening.

²⁹"Of the small animals that scurry or creep on the ground, these are unclean for you: the mole, the mouse, the great lizard of all varieties, ³⁰the gecko, the monitor lizard, the common lizard, the sand lizard, and the chameleon. ³¹All these small animals are unclean for you. If you touch the dead body of such an animal, you will be defiled until evening. ³²If such an animal dies and falls on something, that object, whatever its use, will be unclean. This is true whether the object is made of wood, cloth, leather, or sackcloth. It must be put into water, and it will remain defiled until evening. After that, it will be ceremonially clean and may be used again.

³³"If such an animal dies and falls into a clay pot, everything in the pot will be defiled, and the pot must be smashed. ³⁴If the water used to cleanse an unclean object touches any food, all of that food will be defiled. And any beverage that is in such an unclean container will be defiled. ³⁵Any object on which the dead body of such an animal falls will be defiled. If it is a clay oven or cooking pot, it must be smashed to pieces. It has become defiled, and it will remain that way.

³⁶"However, if the dead body of such an animal falls into a spring or a cistern, the water will still be clean. But anyone who removes the dead body will be defiled. ³⁷If the dead body falls on seed grain to be planted in the field, the seed will still be considered clean. ³⁸But if the seed is wet when the dead body falls on it, the seed will be defiled.

³⁹"If an animal that is permitted for eating dies and you touch its carcass, you will be defiled until evening. ⁴⁰If you eat any of its meat or carry away its carcass, you must wash your clothes. Then you will remain defiled until evening.

⁴¹"Consider detestable any animal that scurries along the ground; such animals may never be eaten. ⁴²This includes all animals that slither along on their bellies, as well as those with four legs and those with many feet. All such animals are to be considered detestable. ⁴³Never defile yourselves by touching such animals. ⁴⁴After all, I, the LORD, am your God. You must be holy because I am holy. So do not defile yourselves by touching any of these animals that scurry along the ground. ⁴⁵I, the LORD, am the one who brought you up from the land of Egypt to be your God. You must therefore be holy because I am holy.

⁴⁶"These are the instructions regarding the land animals, the birds, and all the living things that move through the water or swarm over the earth, ⁴⁷so you can distinguish between what is unclean and may not be eaten and what is clean and may be eaten."

PURIFICATION AFTER CHILDBIRTH

12 The LORD said to Moses, "Give these instructions to the Israelites: ²When a woman becomes pregnant and gives birth to a son, she will be ceremonially unclean for

seven days, just as she is defiled during her menstrual period. ³On the eighth day, the boy must be circumcised. ⁴Then the woman must wait for thirty-three days until the time of her purification from the blood of childbirth is completed. During this time of purification, she must not touch anything that is holy. And she must not go to the sanctuary until her time of purification is over. ⁵If a woman gives birth to a daughter, she will be ceremonially defiled for two weeks, just as she is defiled during her menstrual period. She must then wait another sixty-six days to be purified from the blood of childbirth.

⁶"When the time of purification is completed for either a son or a daughter, the woman must bring a year-old lamb for a whole burnt offering and a young pigeon or turtledove for a purification offering. She must take her offerings to the priest at the entrance of the Tabernacle.* ⁷The priest will then present them to the LORD and make atonement for her. Then she will be ceremonially clean again after her bleeding at childbirth. These are the instructions to be followed after the birth of a son or a daughter.

⁸"If a woman cannot afford to bring a sheep, she must bring two turtledoves or two young pigeons. One will be for the whole burnt offering and the other for the purification offering. The priest will sacrifice them, thus making atonement for her, and she will be ceremonially clean."

CONTAGIOUS SKIN DISEASES

13 The LORD said to Moses and Aaron, ²"If some of the people notice a swelling or a rash or a shiny patch on their skin that develops into a contagious skin disease,* they must be brought to Aaron the priest or to one of his sons. ³The priest will then examine the affected area of a person's skin. If the hair in the affected area has turned white and appears to be more than skin-deep, then it is a contagious skin disease, and the

priest must pronounce the person ceremonially unclean.

⁴"But if the affected area of the skin is white but does not appear to be more than skin-deep, and if the hair in the spot has not turned white, the priest will put the infected person in quarantine for seven days. ⁵On the seventh day the priest will make another examination. If the affected area has not changed or spread on the skin, then the priest will put the person in quarantine for seven more days. ⁶The priest will examine the skin again on the seventh day. If the affected area has faded and not spread, the priest will pronounce the person ceremonially clean. It was only a temporary rash. So after washing the clothes, the person will be considered free of disease. ⁷But if the rash continues to spread after this examination and pronouncement by the priest, the infected person must return to be examined again. ⁸If the priest notices that the rash has spread, then he must pronounce this person ceremonially unclean, for it is a contagious skin disease.

⁹"Anyone who develops a contagious skin disease must go to the priest for an examination. ¹⁰If the priest sees that some hair has turned white and an open sore appears in the affected area, ¹¹it is clearly a contagious skin disease, and the priest must pronounce that person ceremonially unclean. In such cases, the person need not be quarantined for further observation because it is clear that the skin is defiled by the disease.

¹²"Now suppose the priest discovers after his examination that a rash has broken out all over someone's skin, covering the body from head to foot. ¹³In such cases, the priest must examine the infected person to see if the disease covers the entire body. If it does, he will pronounce the person ceremonially clean because the skin has turned completely white. ¹⁴But if any open sores appear, the infected person will be pronounced ceremonially unclean. ¹⁵The priest must make this pronouncement as

12:6 Hebrew *Tent of Meeting.*   13:2 Traditionally rendered *leprosy.* The Hebrew word used throughout this passage is used to describe various skin diseases.

soon as he sees an open sore because open sores indicate the presence of a contagious skin disease. [16]However, if the open sores heal and turn white like the rest of the skin, the person must return to the priest. [17]If, after another examination, the affected areas have indeed turned completely white, then the priest will pronounce the person ceremonially clean.

[18]"If anyone has had a boil on the skin that has started to heal, [19]but a white swelling or a reddish white spot remains in its place, that person must go to the priest to be examined. [20]If the priest finds the disease to be more than skin-deep, and if the hair in the affected area has turned white, then the priest must pronounce that person ceremonially unclean. It is a contagious skin disease that has broken out in the boil. [21]But if the priest sees that there is no white hair in the affected area, and if it doesn't appear to be more than skin-deep and has faded, then the priest is to put the person in quarantine for seven days. [22]If during that time the affected area spreads on the skin, the priest must pronounce the person ceremonially unclean, because it is a contagious skin disease. [23]But if the area grows no larger and does not spread, it is merely the scar from the boil, and the priest will pronounce that person ceremonially clean.

[24]"If anyone has suffered a burn on the skin and the burned area changes color, becoming either a shiny reddish white or white, [25]then the priest must examine it. If the hair in the affected area turns white and the problem appears to be more than skin-deep, a contagious skin disease has broken out in the burn. The priest must then pronounce that person ceremonially unclean, for it is clearly a contagious skin disease. [26]But if the priest discovers that there is no white hair in the affected area and the problem appears to be no more than skin-deep and has faded, then the priest is to put the infected person in quarantine for seven days. [27]If at the end of that time the affected area has spread on the skin, the priest must pronounce that person ceremonially

unclean, for it is clearly a contagious skin disease. [28]But if the affected area has not moved or spread on the skin and has faded, it is simply a scar from the burn. The priest must then pronounce the person ceremonially clean.

[29]"If anyone, whether a man or woman, has an open sore on the head or chin, [30]the priest must examine the infection. If it appears to be more than skin-deep and fine yellow hair is found in the affected area, the priest must pronounce the infected person ceremonially unclean. The infection is a contagious skin disease of the head or chin. [31]However, if the priest's examination reveals that the infection is only skin-deep and there is no black hair in the affected area, then he must put the person in quarantine for seven days. [32]If at the end of that time the affected area has not spread and no yellow hair has appeared, and if the infection does not appear to be more than skin-deep, [33]the infected person must shave off all hair except the hair on the affected area. Then the priest must put the person in quarantine for another seven days, [34]and he will examine the infection again on the seventh day. If it has not spread and appears to be no more than skin-deep, the priest must pronounce that person ceremonially clean. After washing clothes, that person will be clean. [35]But if the infection begins to spread after the person is pronounced clean, [36]the priest must do another examination. If the infection has spread, he must pronounce the infected person ceremonially unclean, even without checking for yellow hair. [37]But if it appears that the infection has stopped spreading and black hair has grown in the affected area, then the infection has healed. The priest will then pronounce the infected person ceremonially clean.

[38]"If anyone, whether a man or woman, has shiny white patches on the skin, [39]the priest must examine the affected area. If the patch is only a pale white, this is a harmless skin rash, and the person is ceremonially clean.

[40]"If a man loses his hair and his head becomes bald, he is still ceremonially clean. [41]And if he loses hair on his forehead, he sim-

ply has a bald forehead; he is still clean. [42]However, if a reddish white infection appears on the front or the back of his head, this is a contagious skin disease. [43]The priest must examine him, and if he finds swelling around the reddish white sore, [44]the man is infected with a contagious skin disease and is unclean. The priest must pronounce him ceremonially unclean because of the infection.

[45]"Those who suffer from any contagious skin disease must tear their clothing and allow their hair to hang loose.* Then, as they go from place to place, they must cover their mouth and call out, 'Unclean! Unclean!' [46]As long as the disease lasts, they will be ceremonially unclean and must live in isolation outside the camp.

TREATMENT OF CONTAMINATED CLOTHING

[47]"Now suppose an infectious mildew* contaminates some woolen or linen clothing, [48]some woolen or linen fabric, the hide of an animal, or anything made of leather. [49]If the affected area in the clothing, the animal hide, the fabric, or the leather has turned bright green or a reddish color, it is contaminated with an infectious mildew and must be taken to the priest to be examined. [50]After examining the affected spot, the priest will put it away for seven days. [51]On the seventh day the priest must inspect it again. If the affected area has spread, the material is clearly contaminated by an infectious mildew and is unclean. [52]The priest must burn the linen or wool clothing or the piece of leather because it has been contaminated by an infectious mildew. It must be completely destroyed by fire.

[53]"But if the priest examines it again and the affected spot has not spread in the clothing, the fabric, or the leather, [54]the priest will order the contaminated object to be washed and then isolated for seven more days. [55]Then the priest must inspect the object again. If he sees that the affected area has not changed appearance after being washed, even if it did not spread, the object is defiled. It must be completely burned up, whether it is contaminated on the inside or outside. [56]But if the priest sees that the affected area has faded after being

---

Words of Worship

SACRIFICE

Sacrifice—Hebrew *za-vach* "to slaughter," *ze-vach* "a slaughter"; Greek **thu-o** "to smoke, sacrifice," *thu-si-a* "a sacrifice."

In Israel's worship, animals from the herd or flock were slaughtered and then consumed by fire (in whole or part) on the altar after their blood was poured out. The animal's life was considered to be in the blood, and the release of life was intended to secure the Lord's favor on the worshiper.

Only the best, most costly gift was worthy to be offered to God. By this sacrifice, the worshiper believed he could maintain his relationship with the Lord and receive forgiveness. But those sacrifices weren't enough. Only the offering of God's own Son, the most perfect Lamb of God, could remove the barrier between God's holiness and our disobedience. Jesus offered that sacrifice on the cross (1 Corinthians 5:7).

That which costs little or nothing is no sacrifice, only a hollow gesture. Jesus' sacrifice cost him everything. We're also asked to make a sacrifice. Ours can't compare with that of Jesus, but in a way it's costly also. It's a sacrifice of worship when we acknowledge that God is in charge of our lives—not us or our own wants and desires. "With Jesus' help, let us continually offer our sacrifice of praise to God by proclaiming the glory of his name" (Hebrews 13:15).

13:45 Or *and uncover their heads.* **13:47** Traditionally rendered *leprosy.* The Hebrew term used throughout this passage is the same term used for the various skin diseases described in 13:1-46.

washed, he is to cut the spot from the clothing, the fabric, or the leather. [57]If the spot reappears at a later time, however, the mildew is clearly spreading, and the contaminated object must be burned up. [58]But if the spot disappears after the object is washed, it must be washed again; then it will be ceremonially clean.

[59]"These are the instructions for dealing with infectious mildew in woolen or linen clothing or fabric, or in anything made of leather. This is how the priest will determine whether these things are ceremonially clean or unclean."

CLEANSING FROM SKIN DISEASES

14 And the LORD said to Moses, [2]"The following instructions must be followed by those seeking purification from a contagious skin disease.* Those who have been healed must be brought to the priest, [3]who will examine them at a place outside the camp. If the priest finds that someone has been healed of the skin disease, [4]he will perform a purification ceremony, using two wild birds of a kind permitted for food, along with some cedarwood, a scarlet cloth, and a hyssop branch. [5]The priest will order one of the birds to be slaughtered over a clay pot that is filled with fresh springwater. [6]He will then dip the living bird, along with the cedarwood, the scarlet cloth, and the hyssop branch, into the blood of the slaughtered bird. [7]The priest will also sprinkle the dead bird's blood seven times over the person being purified, and the priest will pronounce that person to be ceremonially clean. At the end of the ceremony, the priest will set the living bird free so it can fly away into the open fields.

[8]"The people being purified must complete the cleansing ceremony by washing their clothes, shaving off all their hair, and bathing themselves in water. Then they will be ceremonially clean and may return to live inside the camp. However, they must still remain outside their tents for seven days. [9]On the seventh day, they must again shave off all their hair, including the hair of the beard and eyebrows, and wash their clothes and bathe themselves in water. Then they will be pronounced ceremonially clean.

[10]"On the next day, the eighth day, each person cured of the skin disease must bring two male lambs and one female year-old lamb with no physical defects, along with five quarts* of choice flour mixed with olive oil and three-fifths of a pint* of olive oil. [11]Then the officiating priest will present that person for cleansing, along with the offerings, before the LORD at the entrance of the Tabernacle.* [12]The priest will take one of the lambs and the olive oil and offer them as a guilt offering by lifting them up before the LORD. [13]He will then slaughter the lamb there in the sacred area at the place where sin offerings and burnt offerings are slaughtered. As with the sin offering, the guilt offering will be given to the priest. It is a most holy offering. [14]The priest will then take some of the blood from the guilt offering and put it on the tip of the healed person's right ear, on the thumb of the right hand, and on the big toe of the right foot.

[15]"Then the priest will pour some of the olive oil into the palm of his own left hand. [16]He will dip his right finger into the oil and sprinkle it seven times before the LORD. [17]The priest will then put some of the oil remaining in his left hand on the tip of the healed person's right ear, on the thumb of the right hand, and on the big toe of the right foot, in addition to the blood of the guilt offering. [18]The oil remaining in the priest's hand will then be poured over the healed person's head. In this way, the priest will make atonement before the LORD for the person being cleansed. [19]"Then the priest must offer the sin offering and again perform the atonement ceremony for the person cured of the skin disease. After that, the priest will slaughter the whole burnt offering [20]and offer it on the altar along

---

14:2 Traditionally rendered *leprosy.* See note at 13:2.   14:10a Hebrew ³/₁₀ *of an ephah* [5.4 liters].   14:10b Hebrew *1 log* [0.3 liters]; also in 14:21.   14:11 Hebrew *Tent of Meeting;* also in 14:23.

with the grain offering. In this way, the priest will make atonement for the person being cleansed, and the healed person will be ceremonially clean.

²¹"But anyone who cannot afford two lambs must bring one male lamb for a guilt offering, along with two quarts* of choice flour mixed with olive oil as a grain offering and three-fifths of a pint of olive oil. The guilt offering will be presented by lifting it up, thus making atonement for the person being cleansed. ²²The person being cleansed must also bring two turtledoves or two young pigeons, whichever the person can afford. One of the pair must be used for a sin offering and the other for a whole burnt offering. ²³On the eighth day, the person being cleansed must bring the offerings to the priest for the cleansing ceremony to be performed in the LORD's presence at the Tabernacle entrance. ²⁴The priest will take the lamb for the guilt offering, along with the olive oil, and lift them up before the LORD as an offering to him. ²⁵Then the priest will slaughter the lamb for the guilt offering and put some of its blood on the tip of the person's right ear, on the thumb of the right hand, and on the big toe of the right foot.

²⁶"The priest will also pour some of the olive oil into the palm of his own left hand. ²⁷He will dip his right finger into the oil and sprinkle some of it seven times before the LORD. ²⁸The priest will then put some of the olive oil from his hand on the lobe of the person's right ear, on the thumb of the right hand, and on the big toe of the right foot, in addition to the blood of the guilt offering. ²⁹The oil that is still in the priest's hand will then be poured over the person's head. In this way, the priest will make atonement for the person being cleansed.

³⁰"Then the priest will offer the two turtledoves or the two young pigeons, whichever the person was able to afford. ³¹One of them is for a sin offering and the other for a whole burnt offering, to be presented along with the grain offering. In this way, the priest will make atonement before the LORD for the person being cleansed. ³²These are the instructions for cleansing those who have recovered from a contagious skin disease but who cannot afford to bring the sacrifices normally required for the ceremony of cleansing."

TREATMENT OF CONTAMINATED HOUSES

³³Then the LORD said to Moses and Aaron, ³⁴"When you arrive in Canaan, the land I am giving you as an inheritance, I may contaminate some of your houses with an infectious mildew.* ³⁵The owner of such a house must then go to the priest and say, 'It looks like my house has some kind of disease.' ³⁶Before the priest examines the house, he must have the house emptied so everything inside will not be pronounced unclean. Then the priest will go in and inspect the house. ³⁷If he finds bright green or reddish streaks on the walls of the house and the contamination appears to go deeper than the wall's surface, ³⁸he will leave the house and lock it up for seven days. ³⁹On the seventh day the priest must return for another inspection. If the mildew on the walls of the house has spread, ⁴⁰the priest must order that the stones from those areas be removed. The contaminated material will then be thrown into an area outside the town designated as ceremonially unclean. ⁴¹Next the inside walls of the entire house must be scraped thoroughly and the scrapings dumped in the unclean place outside the town. ⁴²Other stones will be brought in to replace the ones that were removed, and the walls will be replastered.

⁴³"But if the mildew reappears after all these things have been done, ⁴⁴the priest must return and inspect the house again. If he sees that the affected areas have spread, the walls are clearly contaminated with an infectious mildew, and the house is defiled. ⁴⁵It must be torn down, and all its stones, timbers, and plaster must be carried out of town to the

---

14:21 Hebrew ¹/₁₀ of an ephah [2 liters]. **14:34** Traditionally rendered leprosy. See note at 13:47.

place designated as ceremonially unclean. [46]Anyone who enters the house while it is closed will be considered ceremonially unclean until evening. [47]All who sleep or eat in the house must wash their clothing.

[48]"But if the priest returns for his inspection and finds that the affected areas have not reappeared after the fresh plastering, then he will pronounce the house clean because the infectious mildew is clearly gone. [49]To purify the house the priest will need two birds, some cedarwood, a scarlet cloth, and a hyssop branch. [50]He will slaughter one of the birds over a clay pot that is filled with fresh springwater. [51]Then he will dip the cedarwood, the hyssop branch, the scarlet cloth, and the living bird into the blood of the slaughtered bird, and he will sprinkle the house seven times. [52]After he has purified the house in this way, [53]he will release the living bird in the open fields outside the town. In this way, the priest will make atonement for the house, and it will be ceremonially clean.

[54]"These are the instructions for dealing with the various kinds of contagious skin disease* and infectious mildew,* [55]whether in clothing, in a house, [56]in a swollen area of skin, in a skin rash, or in a shiny patch of skin. [57]These instructions must be followed when dealing with any contagious skin disease or infectious mildew, to determine when something is ceremonially clean or unclean."

BODILY DISCHARGES

15 The LORD said to Moses and Aaron, [2]"Give these further instructions to the Israelites: Any man who has a genital discharge* is ceremonially unclean because of it. [3]This defilement applies whether the discharge continues or is stopped up. In either case the man is unclean. [4]Any bedding on which he lies and anything on which he sits will be defiled.

[5]"So if you touch the man's bedding, you will be required to wash your clothes and

> True worship is a gift that blesses rather than a chore that we wearily fulfill.
>
> JACK HAYFORD

bathe in water, and you will remain ceremonially defiled until evening. [6]If you sit where the man with the discharge has sat, you will be required to wash your clothes and bathe in water. You will then remain defiled until evening. [7]The same instructions apply if you touch the man who has the unclean discharge. [8]And if he spits on you, you must undergo the same procedure. [9]Any blanket on which the man rides will be defiled. [10]If you touch or carry anything that was under him, you will be required to wash your clothes and bathe in water, and you will remain defiled until evening. [11]If the man touches you without first rinsing his hands, then you will be required to wash your clothes and bathe in water, and you will remain defiled until evening. [12]Any clay pot touched by the man with the discharge must be broken, and every wooden utensil he touches must be rinsed with water.

[13]"When the man's discharge heals, he must count off a period of seven days. During that time, he must wash his clothes and bathe in fresh springwater. Then he will be ceremonially clean. [14]On the eighth day he must bring two turtledoves or two young pigeons and present himself to the LORD at the entrance of the Tabernacle* and give his offerings to the priest. [15]The priest will present the offerings there, one for a sin offering and the other for a whole burnt offering. In this way, the priest will make atonement for the man before the LORD for his discharge.

14:54 Traditionally rendered *leprosy.* See notes at 13:2 and 13:47. 15:2 Hebrew *a discharge from his flesh;* also in 15:32. 15:14 Hebrew *Tent of Meeting;* also in 15:29.

16"Whenever a man has an emission of semen, he must wash his entire body, and he will remain ceremonially defiled until evening. 17Any clothing or leather that comes in contact with the semen must be washed, and it will remain defiled until evening. 18After having sexual intercourse, both the man and the woman must bathe, and they will remain defiled until evening.

19"Whenever a woman has her menstrual period, she will be ceremonially unclean for seven days. If you touch her during that time, you will be defiled until evening. 20Anything on which she lies or sits during that time will be defiled. 21If you touch her bed, you must wash your clothes and bathe in water, and you will remain defiled until evening. 22The same applies if you touch an object on which she sits, 23whether it is her bedding or any piece of furniture. 24If a man has sexual intercourse with her during this time, her menstrual impurity will be transmitted to him. He will remain defiled for seven days, and any bed on which he lies will be defiled.

25"If the menstrual flow of blood continues for many days beyond the normal period, or if she discharges blood unrelated to her menstruation, the woman will be ceremonially unclean as long as the discharge continues. 26Anything on which she lies or sits during that time will be defiled, just as it would be during her normal menstrual period. 27If you touch her bed or anything on which she sits, you will be defiled. You will be required to wash your clothes and bathe in water, and you will remain defiled until evening.

28"When the woman's menstrual discharge stops, she must count off a period of seven days. After that, she will be ceremonially clean. 29On the eighth day, she must bring two turtledoves or two young pigeons and present them to the priest at the entrance of the Tabernacle. 30The priest will offer one for a sin offering and the other for a whole burnt offering. In this way, the priest will make atonement for her

before the LORD for her menstrual discharge. 31"In this way, you will keep the people of Israel separate from things that will defile them, so they will not die as a result of defiling my Tabernacle that is right there among them. 32These are the instructions for dealing with a man who has been defiled by a genital discharge or an emission of semen; 33for dealing with a woman during her monthly menstrual period; for dealing with anyone, man or woman, who has had a bodily discharge of any kind; and for dealing with a man who has had intercourse with a woman during her period."

THE DAY OF ATONEMENT

16 The LORD spoke to Moses after the death of Aaron's two sons, who died when they burned a different kind of fire than the LORD had commanded.* 2The LORD said to Moses, "Warn your brother Aaron not to enter the Most Holy Place behind the inner curtain whenever he chooses; the penalty for intrusion is death. For the Ark's cover—the place of atonement—is there, and I myself am present in the cloud over the atonement cover.

3"When Aaron enters the sanctuary area, he must follow these instructions fully. He must first bring a young bull for a sin offering and a ram for a whole burnt offering. 4Then he must wash his entire body and put on his linen tunic and the undergarments worn next to his body. He must tie the linen sash around his waist and put the linen turban on his head. These are his sacred garments. 5The people of Israel must then bring him two male goats for a sin offering and a ram for a whole burnt offering.

6"Aaron will present the bull as a sin offering, to make atonement for himself and his family. 7Then he must bring the two male goats and present them to the LORD at the entrance of the Tabernacle.* 8He is to cast sacred lots to determine which goat will be sacrificed to the LORD and which one will be the scapegoat.* 9The goat chosen to be sacrificed to the LORD

16:1 Hebrew when they approached the LORD's presence; compare 10:1.   16:7 Hebrew Tent of Meeting; also in 16:16, 17, 20, 23, 33.   16:8 Hebrew azazel, which in this context means "the goat of removal"; also in 16:10, 26.

will be presented by Aaron as a sin offering. [10]The goat chosen to be the scapegoat will be presented to the LORD alive. When it is sent away into the wilderness, it will make atonement for the people.

[11]"Then Aaron will present the young bull as a sin offering for himself and his family. After he has slaughtered this bull for the sin offering, [12]he will fill an incense burner with burning coals from the altar that stands before the LORD. Then, after filling both his hands with fragrant incense, he will carry the burner and incense behind the inner curtain. [13]There in the LORD's presence, he will put the incense on the burning coals so that a cloud of incense will rise over the Ark's cover—the place of atonement—that rests on the Ark of the Covenant.* If he follows these instructions, he will not die. [14]Then he must dip his finger into the blood of the bull and sprinkle it on the front of the atonement cover and then seven times against the front of the Ark.

[15]"Then Aaron must slaughter the goat as a sin offering for the people and bring its blood behind the inner curtain. There he will sprinkle the blood on the atonement cover and against the front of the Ark, just as he did with the bull's blood. [16]In this way, he will make atonement for the Most Holy Place, and he will do the same for the entire Tabernacle, because of the defiling sin and rebellion of the Israelites. [17]No one else is allowed inside the Tabernacle while Aaron goes in to make atonement for the Most Holy Place. No one may enter until he comes out again after making atonement for himself, his family, and all the Israelites.

[18]"Then Aaron will go out to make atonement for the altar that stands before the LORD by smearing some of the blood from the bull and the goat on each of the altar's horns. [19]Then he must dip his finger into the blood and sprinkle it seven times over the altar. In this way, he will cleanse it from Israel's defilement and return it to its former holiness.

[20]"When Aaron has finished making atonement for the Most Holy Place, the Tabernacle, and the altar, he must bring the living goat forward. [21]He is to lay both of his hands on the goat's head and confess over it all the sins and rebellion of the Israelites. In this way, he will lay the people's sins on the head of the goat; then he will send it out into the wilderness, led by a man chosen for this task. [22]After the man sets it free in the wilderness, the goat will carry all the people's sins upon itself into a desolate land.

[23]"As Aaron enters the Tabernacle, he must take off the linen garments he wore when he entered the Most Holy Place, and he must leave the garments there. [24]Then he must bathe his entire body with water in a sacred place, put on his garments, and go out to sacrifice his own whole burnt offering and the whole burnt offering for the people. In this way, he will make atonement for himself and for the people. [25]He must also burn all the fat of the sin offering on the altar.

[26]"The man chosen to send the goat out into the wilderness as a scapegoat must wash his clothes and bathe in water. Then he may return to the camp.

[27]"The bull and goat given as sin offerings, whose blood Aaron brought into the Most Holy Place to make atonement for Israel, will be carried outside the camp to be burned. This includes the animals' hides, the internal organs, and the dung. [28]The man who does the burning must wash his clothes and bathe himself in water before returning to the camp.

[29]"On the appointed day in early autumn,* you must spend the day fasting and not do any work. This is a permanent law for you, and it applies to those who are Israelites by birth, as well as to the foreigners living among you. [30]On this day, atonement will be made for you, and you will be cleansed from all your sins in the LORD's presence. [31]It will be a Sabbath day of total rest, and you will spend the day in fasting. This is a permanent law for

16:13 Hebrew *on the Testimony,* referring to the terms of God's covenant with Israel, which were kept in the Ark. 16:29 Hebrew *On the tenth day of the seventh month.* This day of the Hebrew lunar calendar occurs in September or early October.

My Daily Worship

— *January 31* —

THE DRIPPING CROSS

LEVITICUS 15:1–17:16

The life of any creature is in its blood. I have given you the blood
so you can make atonement for your sins. It is the blood,
representing life, that brings you atonement (17:11).

[i reflect]

Those of us who attend churches where the old hymns are still sung can find ourselves singing some pretty gruesome lines:

• "There is a fountain filled with blood drawn from Emmanuel's veins."

• "What can wash away my sin? Nothing but the blood of Jesus."

• "In the old rugged cross, stained with blood so divine, a wondrous beauty I see."

Gruesome, yes, but maybe the old hymns have gotten something right. Worship is not solely about focusing on the pleasant aspects of the Christian faith. After all, the book of Psalms—Israel's hymnbook—includes songs of lament and sorrow over sin, as well as uplifting praises of thanksgiving and gratitude.

The blood-splatter of Old Testament sacrifices was like graffiti spelling out, "Death is the only currency that can pay for sin!" And then Christ's death, in the ultimate way, fulfilled God's teaching—that atonement comes by blood. There is life in the blood of Christ yet. Oh yes, there is.

Instructive for our worship is the way the old hymns (as well as many newer praise songs) treat solemnly the death of Christ while still finding joy in it. This is a biblical attitude, of course. Christ's gift of the Lord's Supper—our regular mental turning back to the Cross—is a solemn and joyful occasion. Easter comes through Good Friday.

O bless the Lord for the atoning blood of Christ! May our worship never forget the blood. Rejoice today in the blood of the Lamb.

[i pray]

I slump in wondering awe, Lord, when I contemplate the death of your Beloved. I weep, I shout
with joy! May the bloodstained beams of the cross form the very intersection of my being.

[i respond]

Turn to any one of the Gospels and read about the suffering of Christ, or what is known as his "Passion." Ponder how you can work themes you find there into a passionate and creative form of worship. A prayer-poem? A painting? A new song?

you. [32]In future generations, the atonement ceremony will be performed by the anointed high priest who serves in place of his ancestor Aaron. He will put on the holy linen garments [33]and make atonement for the Most Holy Place, the Tabernacle, the altar, the priests, and the entire community. [34]This is a permanent law for you, to make atonement for the Israelites once each year."

Moses followed all these instructions that the LORD had given to him.

PROHIBITIONS AGAINST EATING BLOOD

17 Then the LORD said to Moses, [2]"Give Aaron and his sons and all the Israelites these commands from the LORD: [3]If any Israelite sacrifices a bull* or a lamb or a goat anywhere inside or outside the camp [4]and does not bring it to the entrance of the Tabernacle* to present it as an offering to the LORD, that person will be guilty of a capital offense.* Such a person has shed blood and must be cut off from the community. [5]This rule will stop the Israelites from sacrificing animals in the open fields. It will cause them to bring their sacrifices to the priest at the entrance of the Tabernacle, so he can present them to the LORD as peace offerings. [6]That way the priest will be able to sprinkle the blood and burn the fat on the LORD's altar at the entrance of the Tabernacle, and it will be very pleasing to the LORD. [7]The people must no longer be unfaithful to the LORD by offering sacrifices to evil spirits* out in the fields. This is a permanent law for them, to be kept generation after generation.

[8]"Give them this command as well, which applies both to Israelites and to the foreigners living among you. If you offer a whole burnt offering or a sacrifice [9]and do not bring it to the entrance of the Tabernacle to offer it to the LORD, you will be cut off from the community.

[10]"And I will turn against anyone, whether an Israelite or a foreigner living among you, who eats or drinks blood in any form. I will cut off such a person from the community, [11]for the life of any creature is in its blood. I have given you the blood so you can make atonement for your sins. It is the blood, representing life, that brings you atonement. [12]That is why I said to the Israelites: 'You and the foreigners who live among you must never eat or drink blood.'

[13]"And this command applies both to Israelites and to the foreigners living among you. If you go hunting and kill an animal or bird that is approved for eating, you must drain out the blood and cover it with earth. [14]The life of every creature is in the blood. That is why I have told the people of Israel never to eat or drink it, for the life of any bird or animal is in the blood. So whoever eats or drinks blood must be cut off.

[15]"And this command also applies both to Israelites and the foreigners living among you. If you eat from the carcass of an animal that died a natural death or was killed by a wild animal, you must wash your clothes and bathe yourselves in water. Then you will remain ceremonially unclean until evening; after that, you will be considered clean. [16]But if you do not wash your clothes and bathe, you will be held responsible."

FORBIDDEN SEXUAL PRACTICES

18 Then the LORD said to Moses, [2]"Say this to your people, the Israelites: I, the LORD, am your God. [3]So do not act like the people in Egypt, where you used to live, or like the people of Canaan, where I am taking you. You must not imitate their way of life. [4]You must obey all my regulations and be careful to keep my laws, for I, the LORD, am your God. [5]If you obey my laws and regulations, you will find life through them. I am the LORD.

[6]"You must never have sexual intercourse with a close relative, for I am the LORD. [7]Do not violate your father by having sexual intercourse with your mother. She is your mother; you must never have intercourse with her. [8]Do

17:3 Or cow.   17:4a Hebrew Tent of Meeting; also in 17:5, 6, 9.   17:4b Hebrew blood guilt.   17:7 Or goat idols.

not have sexual intercourse with any of your father's wives, for this would violate your father.

⁹"Do not have sexual intercourse with your sister or half sister, whether she is your father's daughter or your mother's daughter, whether she was brought up in the same family or somewhere else.

¹⁰"Do not have sexual intercourse with your granddaughter, whether your son's daughter or your daughter's daughter; that would violate you. ¹¹Do not have sexual intercourse with the daughter of any of your father's wives; she is your half sister. ¹²Do not have intercourse with your aunt, your father's sister, because she is your father's close relative. ¹³Do not have sexual intercourse with your aunt, your mother's sister, because she is your mother's close relative. ¹⁴And do not violate your uncle, your father's brother, by having sexual intercourse with his wife; she also is your aunt. ¹⁵Do not have sexual intercourse with your daughter-in-law; she is your son's wife. ¹⁶Do not have intercourse with your brother's wife; this would violate your brother.

¹⁷"Do not have sexual intercourse with both a woman and her daughter or marry both a woman and her granddaughter, whether her son's daughter or her daughter's daughter. They are close relatives, and to do this would be a horrible wickedness.

¹⁸"Do not marry a woman and her sister because they will be rivals. But if your wife dies, then it is all right to marry her sister.

¹⁹"Do not violate a woman by having sexual intercourse with her during her period of menstrual impurity.

²⁰"Do not defile yourself by having sexual intercourse with your neighbor's wife.

²¹"Do not give any of your children as a sacrifice to Molech, for you must not profane the name of your God. I am the LORD.

²²"Do not practice homosexuality; it is a detestable sin.

²³"A man must never defile himself by having sexual intercourse with an animal, and a woman must never present herself to a male

animal in order to have intercourse with it; this is a terrible perversion.

²⁴"Do not defile yourselves in any of these ways, because this is how the people I am expelling from the Promised Land have defiled themselves. ²⁵As a result, the entire land has become defiled. That is why I am punishing the people who live there, and the land will soon vomit them out. ²⁶You must strictly obey all of my laws and regulations, and you must not do any of these detestable things. This applies both to you who are Israelites by birth and to the foreigners living among you.

²⁷"All these detestable activities are practiced by the people of the land where I am taking you, and the land has become defiled. ²⁸Do not give the land a reason to vomit you out for defiling it, as it will vomit out the people who live there now. ²⁹Whoever does any of these detestable things will be cut off from the community of Israel. ³⁰So be careful to obey my laws, and do not practice any of these detestable activities. Do not defile yourselves by doing any of them, for I, the LORD, am your God."

HOLINESS IN PERSONAL CONDUCT

19 The LORD also said to Moses, ²"Say this to the entire community of Israel: You must be holy because I, the LORD your God, am holy. ³Each of you must show respect for your mother and father, and you must always observe my Sabbath days of rest, for I, the LORD, am your God. ⁴Do not put your trust in idols or make gods of metal for yourselves. I, the LORD, am your God.

⁵"When you sacrifice a peace offering to the LORD, offer it properly so it will be accepted on your behalf. ⁶You must eat it on the same day you offer it or on the next day at the latest. Any leftovers that remain until the third day must be burned. ⁷If any of the offering is eaten on the third day, it will be contaminated, and I will not accept it. ⁸If you eat it on the third day, you will answer for the sin of profaning

what is holy to the LORD and must be cut off from the community.

⁹"When you harvest your crops, do not harvest the grain along the edges of your fields, and do not pick up what the harvesters drop. ¹⁰It is the same with your grape crop—do not strip every last bunch of grapes from the vines, and do not pick up the grapes that fall to the ground. Leave them for the poor and the foreigners who live among you, for I, the LORD, am your God.

¹¹"Do not steal.

"Do not cheat one another.

"Do not lie.

¹²"Do not use my name to swear a falsehood and so profane the name of your God. I am the LORD.

¹³"Do not cheat or rob anyone.

"Always pay your hired workers promptly.

¹⁴"Show your fear of God by treating the deaf with respect and by not taking advantage of the blind. I am the LORD.

¹⁵"Always judge your neighbors fairly, neither favoring the poor nor showing deference to the rich.

¹⁶"Do not spread slanderous gossip among your people.*

"Do not try to get ahead at the cost of your neighbor's life, for I am the LORD.

¹⁷"Do not nurse hatred in your heart for any of your relatives.

"Confront your neighbors directly so you will not be held guilty for their crimes.

¹⁸"Never seek revenge or bear a grudge against anyone, but love your neighbor as yourself. I am the LORD.

¹⁹"You must obey all my laws.

"Do not breed your cattle with other kinds of animals. Do not plant your field with two kinds of seed. Do not wear clothing woven from two different kinds of fabric.

²⁰"If a man has sexual intercourse with a slave girl who is committed to become someone else's wife, compensation must be paid. But since she had not been freed at the time, the couple will not be put to death. ²¹The man, however, must bring a ram as a guilt offering and present it to the LORD at the entrance of the Tabernacle.* ²²The priest will then make atonement for him before the LORD with the sacrificial ram of the guilt offering, and the man will be forgiven.

²³"When you enter the land and plant fruit trees, leave the fruit unharvested for the first three years and consider it forbidden.* ²⁴In the fourth year the entire crop will be devoted to the LORD as an outburst of praise. ²⁵Finally, in the fifth year you may eat the fruit. In this way, its yield will be increased. I, the LORD, am your God.

²⁶"Never eat meat that has not been drained of its blood.

"Do not practice fortune-telling or witchcraft.

²⁷"Do not trim off the hair on your temples or clip the edges of your beards.

²⁸"Never cut your bodies in mourning for the dead or mark your skin with tattoos, for I am the LORD.

²⁹"Do not defile your daughter by making her a prostitute, or the land will be filled with promiscuity and detestable wickedness.

³⁰"Keep my Sabbath days of rest and show reverence toward my sanctuary, for I am the LORD.

³¹"Do not rely on mediums and psychics, for you will be defiled by them. I, the LORD, am your God.

³²"Show your fear of God by standing up in the presence of elderly people and showing respect for the aged. I am the LORD.

³³"Do not exploit the foreigners who live in your land. ³⁴They should be treated like everyone else, and you must love them as you love yourself. Remember that you were once foreigners in the land of Egypt. I, the LORD, am your God.

³⁵"Do not use dishonest standards when measuring length, weight, or volume. ³⁶Your scales and weights must be accurate. Your

19:16 Hebrew *Do not act as a merchant toward your own people.* **19:21** Hebrew *Tent of Meeting.* **19:23** Hebrew *consider it uncircumcised.*

containers for measuring dry goods or liquids must be accurate.* I, the LORD, am your God, who brought you out of the land of Egypt. ³⁷You must be careful to obey all of my laws and regulations, for I am the LORD."

PUNISHMENTS FOR DISOBEDIENCE

20 The LORD said to Moses, ²"Give the Israelites these instructions, which apply to those who are Israelites by birth as well as to the foreigners living among you. If any among them devote their children as burnt offerings to Molech, they must be stoned to death by people of the community. ³I myself will turn against them and cut them off from the community, because they have defiled my sanctuary and profaned my holy name by giving their children to Molech. ⁴And if the people of the community ignore this offering of children to Molech and refuse to execute the guilty parents, ⁵then I myself will turn against them and cut them off from the community, along with all those who commit prostitution by worshiping Molech.

⁶"If any among the people are unfaithful by consulting and following mediums or psychics, I will turn against them and cut them off from the community. ⁷So set yourselves apart to be holy, for I, the LORD, am your God. ⁸Keep all my laws and obey them, for I am the LORD, who makes you holy.

⁹"All who curse their father or mother must be put to death. They are guilty of a capital offense.

¹⁰"If a man commits adultery with another man's wife, both the man and the woman must be put to death. ¹¹If a man has intercourse with his father's wife, both the man and the woman must die, for they are guilty of a capital offense. ¹²If a man has intercourse with his daughter-in-law, both must be put to death. They have acted contrary to nature and are guilty of a capital offense.

¹³"The penalty for homosexual acts is death to both parties. They have committed a detestable act and are guilty of a capital offense. ¹⁴If a man has intercourse with both a woman and her mother, such an act is terribly wicked. All three of them must be burned to death to wipe out such wickedness from among you.

¹⁵"If a man has sexual intercourse with an animal, he must be put to death, and the animal must be killed. ¹⁶If a woman approaches a male animal to have intercourse with it, she and the animal must both be put to death. Both must die, for they are guilty of a capital offense.

¹⁷"If a man has sexual intercourse with his sister, the daughter of either his father or his mother, it is a terrible disgrace. Both of them must be publicly cut off from the community. Since the man has had intercourse with his sister, he will suffer the consequences of his guilt. ¹⁸If a man has intercourse with a woman suffering from a hemorrhage,* both of them must be cut off from the community, because he exposed the source of her flow, and she allowed him to do it.

¹⁹"If a man has sexual intercourse with his aunt, whether his mother's sister or his father's sister, he has violated a close relative. Both parties are guilty of a capital offense. ²⁰If a man has intercourse with his uncle's wife, he has violated his uncle. Both the man and woman involved are guilty of a capital offense and will die childless. ²¹If a man marries his brother's wife, it is an act of impurity. He has violated his brother, and the guilty couple will remain childless.

²²"You must carefully obey all my laws and regulations; otherwise the land to which I am bringing you will vomit you out. ²³Do not live by the customs of the people whom I will expel before you. It is because they do these terrible things that I detest them so much. ²⁴But I have promised that you will inherit their land, a land flowing with milk and honey. I, the LORD, am your God, who has set you apart from all other people.

²⁵"You must therefore make a distinction

19:36 Hebrew *Use an honest ephah* [a dry measure] *and an honest hin* [a liquid measure]. 20:18 Or *a woman who is menstruating.*

between ceremonially clean and unclean animals, and between clean and unclean birds. You must not defile yourselves by eating any animal or bird or creeping creature that I have forbidden. [26]You must be holy because I, the LORD, am holy. I have set you apart from all other people to be my very own.

[27]"Men and women among you who act as mediums or psychics must be put to death by stoning. They are guilty of a capital offense."

INSTRUCTIONS FOR THE PRIESTS

21 The LORD said to Moses, "Tell the priests to avoid making themselves ceremonially unclean by touching a dead relative [2]unless it is a close relative—mother or father, son or daughter, brother [3]or virgin sister who was dependent because she had no husband. [4]As a husband and among his relatives,* he must not defile himself.

[5]"The priests must never shave their heads, trim the edges of their beards, or cut their bodies. [6]They must be set apart to God as holy and must never dishonor his name. After all, they are the ones who present the offerings to the LORD by fire, providing God with his food, and they must remain holy.

[7]"The priests must not marry women defiled by prostitution or women who have been divorced, for the priests must be set apart to God as holy. [8]You must treat them as holy because they offer up food to your God. You must consider them holy because I, the LORD, am holy, and I make you holy. [9]If a priest's daughter becomes a prostitute, defiling her father's holiness as well as herself, she must be burned to death.

[10]"The high priest, who has had the anointing oil poured on his head and has been ordained to wear the special priestly garments, must never let his hair hang loose* or tear his clothing. [11]He must never defile himself by going near a dead person, even if it is his father or mother. [12]He must not desecrate the sanctuary of his God by leaving it to attend his parents' funeral, because he has been made holy by the anointing oil of his God. I am the LORD.

[13]"The high priest must marry a virgin. [14]He must not marry a widow, a divorced woman, or a woman defiled by prostitution. She must be a virgin from his own clan, [15]that he may not dishonor his descendants among the members of his clan, because I, the LORD, have made him holy."

[16]Then the LORD said to Moses, [17]"Tell Aaron that in all future generations, his descendants who have physical defects will not qualify to offer food to their God. [18]No one who has a defect may come near to me, whether he is blind or lame, stunted or deformed, [19]or has a broken foot or hand, [20]or has a humped back or is a dwarf, or has a defective eye, or has oozing sores or scabs on his skin, or has damaged testicles. [21]Even though he is a descendant of Aaron, his physical defects disqualify him from presenting offerings to the LORD by fire. Since he has a blemish, he may not offer food to his God. [22]However, he may eat from the food offered to God, including the holy offerings and the most holy offerings. [23]Yet because of his physical defect, he must never go behind the inner curtain or come near the altar, for this would desecrate my holy places. I am the LORD who makes them holy."

[24]So Moses gave these instructions to Aaron and his sons and to all the Israelites.

22 The LORD said to Moses, [2]"Tell Aaron and his sons to treat the sacred gifts that the Israelites set apart for me with great care, so they do not profane my holy name. I am the LORD. [3]Remind them that if any of their descendants are ceremonially unclean when they approach the sacred food presented by the Israelites, they must be cut off from my presence. I am the LORD!

[4]"If any of the priests have a contagious skin disease* or any kind of discharge that makes them ceremonially unclean, they may not eat the sacred offerings until they have been pronounced clean. If any of the priests become

---

21:4 The meaning of the Hebrew is uncertain. 21:10 Or *uncover his head.* 22:4 Traditionally rendered *leprosy.* See note at 13:2.

My Daily Worship

— *February 1* —

SEPARATED FOR WORSHIP
LEVITICUS 18:1–23:44

Set yourselves apart to be holy, for I, the LORD, am your God.
Keep all my laws and obey them, for I am the LORD,
who makes you holy (20:7–8).

[i reflect]

What does it take to create an elite group—whether it's soldiers, athletes, or scholars? The elite in any discipline develop through separation. Their appearance may not change, but their internal orientation and purpose become radically different. Elite troops, athletes, or scholars have to commit to being isolated, often physically, in order to properly train for their tasks. Separation enhances focus and change.

God gave the ancient Israelites marks to set them apart—marks ranging from peculiar food choices to a unique ethical system. They were to be his elite group, his chosen people. We, also, are to be different from unredeemed humanity, in our focus, our values, and our lifestyle. Adopting worship as a lifestyle means accepting an identity as something of a holy oddball, for unlike most others, our first motivation in life is to know God. We are choosing to be separate *from* others in certain ways so that we may be separated *to* God. Under God's instructions, this actually makes us treat others much more lovingly than when we leave God out of the picture.

As we write the scripts of our daily lives, let us separate ourselves so that we can conform to the nature of Christ rather than to any other pattern set before us. Let us say, "Father, your will be done today" and then live that prayer. Let us entrust our spirits to God in life as in death. Let us be separated unto God so that others may actually be drawn to him.

A worshipful life should make us separated in regard to the world. In fact, it could not be otherwise as we worship a God who is so "other" in relation to sinful humankind. But we'll find that the mold Christ shapes us into is our right shape.

[i pray]

Father, help me as I seek to follow your higher ways and comprehend your higher thoughts,
regardless of how it may make me appear to others. Make me like Christ.

[i respond]

Cast your mind back over the past week and consider if at any point you allowed the expectations of others or your own sinful impulses to interfere with your pursuit of God. What can you learn about your worship from this self-examination?

Words of Worship

F E A R

Fear—Hebrew *ya-re'* "to fear"; *yir'ah* "fear"; Greek *pho-be-o-mai* "to fear." In the New Testament, Gentile worshipers of the Lord in the synagogues are called *phoboumenoi*, "fearers" of God.

God is our close and dear friend. We know we can approach him with every concern and every need. But can we become too casual in the way we relate to him? He is the Creator and Ruler of all. Our response to him must also be one of awe, of fear and trembling before the mystery of his presence.

The Bible doesn't often mention *religion*. Instead, it prefers to speak of the *fear of the Lord*. To fear the Lord means we live with reverence for his name and respect for his ways. We don't cower before him, because we know he loves us; Jesus made that clear when he died to reconcile us to his Father. But we can't presume on God's love and do whatever we like. The way to life is his way, not ours. The fear of the Lord is where the wise life begins (Proverbs 9:10). Our God is awesome.

unclean by touching a corpse, or are defiled by an emission of semen, ⁵or by touching a creeping creature that is unclean, or by touching someone who is ceremonially unclean for any reason, ⁶they will remain defiled until evening. They must not eat any of the sacred offerings until they have purified their bodies with water. ⁷When the sun goes down, they will be clean again and may eat the sacred offerings. After all, this food has been set aside for them. ⁸The priests may never eat an animal that has died a natural death or has been torn apart by wild animals, for this would defile them. I am the LORD. ⁹Warn all the priests to follow these instructions carefully;

otherwise they will be subject to punishment and die for violating them. I am the LORD who makes them holy.

¹⁰"No one outside a priest's family may ever eat the sacred offerings, even if the person lives in a priest's home or is one of his hired servants. ¹¹However, if the priest buys slaves with his own money, they may eat of his food. And if his slaves have children, they also may share his food. ¹²If a priest's daughter marries someone outside the priestly family, she may no longer eat the sacred offerings. ¹³But if she becomes a widow or is divorced and has no children to support her, and she returns to live in her father's home, she may eat her father's food again. But other than these exceptions, only members of the priests' families are allowed to eat the sacred offerings.

¹⁴"Anyone who eats the sacred offerings without realizing it must pay the priest for the amount eaten, plus an added penalty of 20 percent. ¹⁵No one may defile the sacred offerings brought to the LORD by the Israelites ¹⁶by allowing unauthorized people to eat them. The negligent priest would bring guilt upon the people and require them to pay compensation. I am the LORD, who makes them holy."

WORTHY AND UNWORTHY OFFERINGS

¹⁷And the LORD said to Moses, ¹⁸"Give Aaron and his sons and all the Israelites these instructions, which apply to those who are Israelites by birth as well as to the foreigners living among you. If you offer a whole burnt offering to the LORD, whether to fulfill a vow or as a freewill offering, ¹⁹it will be accepted only if it is a male animal with no physical defects. It may be either a bull, a ram, or a male goat. ²⁰Do not bring an animal with physical defects, because it won't be accepted on your behalf.

²¹"If you bring a peace offering to the LORD from the herd or flock, whether to fulfill a vow or as a freewill offering, you must offer an animal that has no physical defects of any kind. ²²An animal that is blind, injured, mutilated,

or that has a growth, an open sore, or a scab must never be offered to the LORD by fire on the altar. ²³If the bull* or lamb is deformed or stunted, it may still be offered as a freewill offering, but it may not be offered to fulfill a vow. ²⁴If an animal has damaged testicles or is castrated, it may never be offered to the LORD. ²⁵You must never accept mutilated or defective animals from foreigners to be offered as a sacrifice to your God. Such animals will not be accepted on your behalf because they are defective."

²⁶And the LORD said to Moses, ²⁷"When a bull or a ram or a male goat is born, it must be left with its mother for seven days. From the eighth day on, it will be acceptable as an offering given to the LORD by fire. ²⁸But you must never slaughter a mother animal and her offspring on the same day, whether from the herd or the flock. ²⁹When you bring a thanksgiving offering to the LORD, it must be sacrificed properly so it will be accepted on your behalf. ³⁰Eat the entire sacrificial animal on the day it is presented. Don't leave any of it until the second day. I am the LORD.

³¹"You must faithfully keep all my commands by obeying them, for I am the LORD. ³²Do not treat my holy name as common and ordinary. I must be treated as holy by the people of Israel. It is I, the LORD, who makes you holy. ³³It was I who rescued you from Egypt, that I might be your very own God. I am the LORD."

The Appointed Festivals

23 The LORD said to Moses, ²"Give the Israelites instructions regarding the LORD's appointed festivals, the days when all of you will be summoned to worship me. ³You may work for six days each week, but on the seventh day all work must come to a complete stop. It is the LORD's Sabbath day of complete rest, a holy day to assemble for worship. It must be observed wherever you live. ⁴In addition to the Sabbath, the LORD has established festivals, the holy occasions to be observed at the proper time each year.

Passover and the Festival of Unleavened Bread

⁵"First comes the LORD's Passover, which begins at twilight on its appointed day in early spring.* ⁶Then the day after the Passover celebration,* the Festival of Unleavened Bread begins. This festival to the LORD continues for seven days, and during that time all the bread you eat must be made without yeast. ⁷On the first day of the festival, all the people must stop their regular work and gather for a sacred assembly. ⁸On each of the next seven days, the people must present an offering to the LORD by fire. On the seventh day, the people must again stop all their regular work to hold a sacred assembly."

The Festival of Firstfruits

⁹Then the LORD told Moses ¹⁰to give these instructions to the Israelites: "When you arrive in the land I am giving you and you harvest your first crops, bring the priest some grain from the first portion of your grain harvest. ¹¹On the day after the Sabbath, the priest will lift it up before the LORD so it may be accepted on your behalf. ¹²That same day you must sacrifice a year-old male lamb with no physical defects as a whole burnt offering to the LORD. ¹³A grain offering must accompany it consisting of three quarts* of choice flour mixed with olive oil. It will be an offering given to the LORD by fire, and it will be very pleasing to him. Along with this sacrifice, you must also offer one quart* of wine as a drink offering. ¹⁴Do not eat any bread or roasted grain or fresh kernels on that day until after you have brought this offering to your God. This is a permanent law for you, and it must be observed wherever you live.

22:23 Or *cow;* also in 22:27.   23:5 Hebrew *on the fourteenth day of the first month.* This day of the Hebrew lunar calendar occurs in late March or early April.   23:6 Hebrew *On the fifteenth day of the same month.*   23:13a Hebrew ²⁄₁₀ *of an ephah* [3.6 liters]; also in 23:17. 23:13b Hebrew ¼ *of a hin* [1 liter].

THE FESTIVAL OF HARVEST

[15]"From the day after the Sabbath, the day the bundle of grain was lifted up as an offering, count off seven weeks. [16]Keep counting until the day after the seventh Sabbath, fifty days later, and bring an offering of new grain to the LORD. [17]From wherever you live, bring two loaves of bread to be lifted up before the LORD as an offering. These loaves must be baked from three quarts of choice flour that contains yeast. They will be an offering to the LORD from the first of your crops. [18]Along with this bread, present seven one-year-old lambs with no physical defects, one bull, and two rams as burnt offerings to the LORD. These whole burnt offerings, together with the accompanying grain offerings and drink offerings, will be given to the LORD by fire and will be pleasing to him. [19]Then you must offer one male goat as a sin offering and two one-year-old male lambs as a peace offering.

[20]"The priest will lift up these offerings before the LORD, together with the loaves representing the first of your later crops. These offerings are holy to the LORD and will belong to the priests. [21]That same day, you must stop all your regular work and gather for a sacred assembly. This is a permanent law for you, and it must be observed wherever you live.

[22]"When you harvest the crops of your land, do not harvest the grain along the edges of your fields, and do not pick up what the harvesters drop. Leave it for the poor and the foreigners living among you. I, the LORD, am your God."

THE FESTIVAL OF TRUMPETS

[23]The LORD told Moses [24]to give these instructions to the Israelites: "On the appointed day in early autumn,* you are to celebrate a day of complete rest. All your work must stop on that day. You will call the people to a sacred assembly—the Festival of Trumpets—with loud blasts from a trumpet. [25]You must do no regular work on that day. Instead, you are to present offerings to the LORD by fire."

THE DAY OF ATONEMENT

[26]Then the LORD said to Moses, [27]"Remember that the Day of Atonement is to be celebrated on the ninth day after the Festival of Trumpets.* On that day you must humble yourselves, gather for a sacred assembly, and present offerings to the LORD by fire. [28]Do no work during that entire day because it is the Day of Atonement, when atonement will be made for you before the LORD your God, and payment will be made for your sins. [29]Anyone who does not spend that day in humility will be cut off from the community. [30]And I will destroy anyone among you who does any kind of work on that day. [31]You must do no work at all! This is a permanent law for you, and it must be observed wherever you live. [32]This will be a Sabbath day of total rest for you, and on that day you must humble yourselves. This time of rest and fasting will begin the evening before the Day of Atonement* and extend until evening of that day."

THE FESTIVAL OF SHELTERS

[33]And the LORD said to Moses, [34]"Tell the Israelites to begin the Festival of Shelters on the fifth day after the Day of Atonement.* This festival to the LORD will last for seven days. [35]It will begin with a sacred assembly on the first day, and all your regular work must stop. [36]On each of the seven festival days, you must present offerings to the LORD by fire. On the eighth day, you must gather again for a sacred assembly and present another offering to the LORD by fire. This will be a solemn closing assembly, and no regular work may be done that day.

[37]"These are the LORD's appointed annual festivals. Celebrate them by gathering in sacred assemblies to present all the various offerings to the LORD by fire—whole burnt

---

23:24 Hebrew *On the first day of the seventh month.* This day of the Hebrew lunar calendar occurs in September or early October. 23:27 Hebrew *on the tenth day of the seventh month;* see 23:24 and the note there. 23:32 Hebrew *the evening of the ninth day of the month;* see 23:24, 27 and the notes there. 23:34 Hebrew *on the fifteenth day of the seventh month;* see 23:24, 27 and the notes there.

offerings and grain offerings, sacrificial meals and drink offerings—each on its proper day. ³⁸These festivals must be observed in addition to the LORD's regular Sabbath days. And these offerings must be given in addition to your personal gifts, the offerings you make to accompany your vows, and any freewill offerings that you present to the LORD.

³⁹"Now, on the first day of the Festival of Shelters,* after you have harvested all the produce of the land, you will begin to celebrate this seven-day festival to the LORD. Remember that the first day and closing eighth day of the festival will be days of total rest. ⁴⁰On the first day, gather fruit from citrus trees,* and collect palm fronds and other leafy branches and willows that grow by the streams. Then rejoice before the LORD your God for seven days. ⁴¹You must observe this seven-day festival to the LORD every year. This is a permanent law for you, and it must be kept by all future generations. ⁴²During the seven festival days, all of you who are Israelites by birth must live in shelters. ⁴³This will remind each new generation of Israelites that their ancestors had to live in shelters when I rescued them from the land of Egypt. I, the LORD, am your God."

⁴⁴So Moses gave these instructions regarding the annual festivals of the LORD to the Israelites.

PURE OIL AND HOLY BREAD

24 The LORD said to Moses, ²"Command the people of Israel to provide you with pure olive oil for the lampstand, so it can be kept burning continually. ³Aaron will set it up outside the inner curtain of the Most Holy Place in the Tabernacle* and must arrange to have the lamps tended continually, from evening until morning, before the LORD. This is a permanent law for you, and it must be kept by all future generations. ⁴The lamps on the pure gold lampstand must be tended continually in the LORD's presence.

⁵"You must bake twelve loaves of bread

> *God is not moved or impressed with our worship until our hearts are moved and impressed by Him.*
>
> KELLY SPARKS

from choice flour, using three quarts* of flour for each loaf. ⁶Place the bread in the LORD's presence on the pure gold table, and arrange the loaves in two rows, with six in each row. ⁷Sprinkle some pure frankincense near each row. It will serve as a token offering, to be burned in place of the bread as an offering given to the LORD by fire. ⁸Every Sabbath day this bread must be laid out before the LORD on behalf of the Israelites as a continual part of the covenant. ⁹The loaves of bread belong to Aaron and his male descendants, who must eat them in a sacred place, for they represent a most holy portion of the offerings given to the LORD by fire."

AN EXAMPLE OF JUST PUNISHMENT

¹⁰One day a man who had an Israelite mother and an Egyptian father got into a fight with one of the Israelite men. ¹¹During the fight, this son of an Israelite woman blasphemed the LORD's name. So the man was brought to Moses for judgment. His mother's name was Shelomith. She was the daughter of Dibri of the tribe of Dan. ¹²They put the man in custody until the LORD's will in the matter should become clear.

¹³Then the LORD said to Moses, ¹⁴"Take the blasphemer outside the camp, and tell all those who heard him to lay their hands on his head. Then let the entire community stone

23:39 Hebrew *on the fifteenth day of the seventh month;* see 23:24 and the note there. 23:40 Or *fruit from majestic trees.* 24:3 Hebrew *the curtain of the Testimony in the Tent of Meeting.* 24:5 Hebrew *2/10 of an ephah* [3.6 liters].

him to death. [15]Say to the people of Israel: Those who blaspheme God will suffer the consequences of their guilt and be punished. [16]Anyone who blasphemes the LORD's name must be stoned to death by the whole community of Israel. Any Israelite or foreigner among you who blasphemes the LORD's name will surely die.

[17]"Anyone who takes another person's life must be put to death.

[18]"Anyone who kills another person's animal must pay it back in full—a live animal for the animal that was killed.

[19]"Anyone who injures another person must be dealt with according to the injury inflicted—[20]fracture for fracture, eye for eye, tooth for tooth. Whatever anyone does to hurt another person must be paid back in kind. [21]"Whoever kills an animal must make full restitution, but whoever kills another person must be put to death.

[22]"These same regulations apply to Israelites by birth and foreigners who live among you. I, the LORD, am your God."

[23]After Moses gave all these instructions to the Israelites, they led the blasphemer outside the camp and stoned him to death, just as the LORD had commanded Moses.

THE SABBATH YEAR

25 While Moses was on Mount Sinai, the LORD said to him, [2]"Give these instructions to the Israelites: When you have entered the land I am giving you as an inheritance, the land itself must observe a Sabbath to the LORD every seventh year. [3]For six years you may plant your fields and prune your vineyards and harvest your crops, [4]but during the seventh year the land will enjoy a Sabbath year of rest to the LORD. Do not plant your crops or prune your vineyards during that entire year. [5]And don't store away the crops that grow naturally or process the grapes that grow on your unpruned vines. The land is to have a year of total rest. [6]But you, your male and female slaves, your hired servants, and any foreigners who live with you may eat the produce that grows naturally during the Sabbath year. [7]And your livestock and the wild animals will also be allowed to eat of the land's bounty.

THE YEAR OF JUBILEE

[8]"In addition, you must count off seven Sabbath years, seven years times seven, adding up to forty-nine years in all. [9]Then on the Day of Atonement of the fiftieth year,* blow the trumpets loud and long throughout the land. [10]This year will be set apart as holy, a time to proclaim release for all who live there. It will be a jubilee year for you, when each of you returns to the lands that belonged to your ancestors and rejoins your clan. [11]Yes, the fiftieth year will be a jubilee for you. During that year, do not plant any seeds or store away any of the crops that grow naturally, and do not process the grapes that grow on your unpruned vines. [12]It will be a jubilee year for you, and you must observe it as a special and holy time. You may, however, eat the produce that grows naturally in the fields that year. [13]In the Year of Jubilee each of you must return to the lands that belonged to your ancestors.

[14]"When you make an agreement with a neighbor to buy or sell property, you must never take advantage of each other. [15]When you buy land from your neighbor, the price of the land should be based on the number of years since the last jubilee. The seller will charge you only for the crop years left until the next Year of Jubilee. [16]The more the years, the higher the price; the fewer the years, the lower the price. After all, the person selling the land is actually selling you a certain number of harvests. [17]Show your fear of God by not taking advantage of each other. I, the LORD, am your God.

[18]"If you want to live securely in the land, keep my laws and obey my regulations. [19]Then the land will yield bumper crops, and you will eat your fill and live securely in it. [20]But you might ask, 'What will we eat during the seventh year, since we are not allowed to plant or

---

25:9 Hebrew *on the tenth day of the seventh month, on the Day of Atonement;* see 23:27 and the note there.

harvest crops that year?' ²¹The answer is, 'I will order my blessing for you in the sixth year, so the land will produce a bumper crop, enough to support you for three years. ²²As you plant the seed in the eighth year, you will still be eating the produce of the previous year. In fact, you will eat from the old crop until the new harvest comes in the ninth year.' ²³And remember, the land must never be sold on a permanent basis because it really belongs to me. You are only foreigners and tenants living with me.

REDEMPTION OF PROPERTY

²⁴"With every sale of land there must be a stipulation that the land can be redeemed at any time. ²⁵If any of your Israelite relatives go bankrupt and are forced to sell some inherited land, then a close relative, a kinsman redeemer, may buy it back for them. ²⁶If there is no one to redeem the land but the person who sold it manages to get enough money to buy it back, ²⁷then that person has the right to redeem it from the one who bought it. The price of the land will be based on the number of years until the next Year of Jubilee. After buying it back, the original owner may then return to the land. ²⁸But if the original owner cannot afford to redeem it, then it will belong to the new owner until the next Year of Jubilee. In the jubilee year, the land will be returned to the original owner.

²⁹"Anyone who sells a house inside a walled city has the right to redeem it for a full year after its sale. During that time, the seller retains the right to buy it back. ³⁰But if it is not redeemed within a year, then the house within the walled city will become the permanent property of the buyer. It will not be returned to the original owner in the Year of Jubilee. ³¹But a house in a village—a settlement without fortified walls—will be treated like property in the open fields. Such a house may be redeemed at any time and must be returned to the original owner in the Year of Jubilee.

³²"The Levites always have the right to redeem any house they have sold within the cities belonging to them. ³³And any property that can be redeemed by the Levites—all houses within the Levitical cities—must be returned in the Year of Jubilee. After all, the cities reserved for the Levites are the only property they own in all Israel. ³⁴The strip of pastureland around each of the Levitical cities may never be sold. It is their permanent ancestral property.

REDEMPTION OF THE POOR AND ENSLAVED

³⁵"If any of your Israelite relatives fall into poverty and cannot support themselves, support them as you would a resident foreigner and allow them to live with you. ³⁶Do not demand an advance or charge interest on the money you lend them. Instead, show your fear of God by letting them live with you as your relatives. ³⁷Remember, do not charge your relatives interest on anything you lend them, whether money or food. ³⁸I, the LORD, am your God, who brought you out of Egypt to give you the land of Canaan and to be your God.

³⁹"If any of your Israelite relatives go bankrupt and sell themselves to you, do not treat them as slaves. ⁴⁰Treat them instead as hired servants or as resident foreigners who live with you, and they will serve you only until the Year of Jubilee. ⁴¹At that time they and their children will no longer be obligated to you, and they will return to their clan and ancestral property. ⁴²The people of Israel are my servants, whom I brought out of the land of Egypt, so they must never be sold as slaves. ⁴³Show your fear of God by treating them well; never exercise your power over them in a ruthless way.

⁴⁴"However, you may purchase male or female slaves from among the foreigners who live among you. ⁴⁵You may also purchase the children of such resident foreigners, including those who have been born in your land. You may treat them as your property, ⁴⁶passing them on to your children as a permanent inheritance. You may treat your slaves like

this, but the people of Israel, your relatives, must never be treated this way.

⁴⁷"If a resident foreigner becomes rich, and if some of your Israelite relatives go bankrupt and sell themselves to such a foreigner, ⁴⁸they still retain the right of redemption. They may be bought back by a close relative—⁴⁹an uncle, a nephew, or anyone else who is closely related. They may also redeem themselves if they can get the money. ⁵⁰The price of their freedom will be based on the number of years left until the next Year of Jubilee—whatever it would cost to hire a servant for that number of years. ⁵¹If many years still remain, they will repay most of what they received when they sold themselves. ⁵²If only a few years remain until the Year of Jubilee, then they will repay a relatively small amount for their redemption. ⁵³The foreigner must treat them as servants hired on a yearly basis. You must not allow a resident foreigner to treat any of your Israelite relatives ruthlessly. ⁵⁴If any Israelites have not been redeemed by the time the Year of Jubilee arrives, then they and their children must be set free at that time. ⁵⁵For the people of Israel are my servants, whom I brought out of the land of Egypt. I, the LORD, am your God.

BLESSINGS FOR OBEDIENCE

26 "Do not make idols or set up carved images, sacred pillars, or shaped stones to be worshiped in your land. I, the LORD, am your God. ²You must keep my Sabbath days of rest and show reverence for my sanctuary. I am the LORD.

³"If you keep my laws and are careful to obey my commands, ⁴I will send the seasonal rains. The land will then yield its crops, and the trees will produce their fruit. ⁵Your threshing season will extend until the grape harvest, and your grape harvest will extend until it is time to plant grain again. You will eat your fill and live securely in your land.

⁶"I will give you peace in the land, and you will be able to sleep without fear. I will remove the wild animals from your land and protect you from your enemies. ⁷In fact, you will chase down all your enemies and slaughter them with your swords. ⁸Five of you will chase a hundred, and a hundred of you will chase ten thousand! All your enemies will fall beneath the blows of your weapons.

⁹"I will look favorably upon you and multiply your people and fulfill my covenant with you. ¹⁰You will have such a surplus of crops that you will need to get rid of the leftovers from the previous year to make room for each new harvest. ¹¹I will live among you, and I will not despise you. ¹²I will walk among you; I will be your God, and you will be my people. ¹³I, the LORD, am your God, who brought you from the land of Egypt so you would no longer be slaves. I have lifted the yoke of slavery from your neck so you can walk free with your heads held high.

PUNISHMENTS FOR DISOBEDIENCE

¹⁴"However, if you do not listen to me or obey my commands, ¹⁵and if you break my covenant by rejecting my laws and treating my regulations with contempt, ¹⁶I will punish you. You will suffer from sudden terrors, with wasting diseases, and with burning fevers, causing your eyes to fail and your life to ebb away. You will plant your crops in vain because your enemies will eat them. ¹⁷I will turn against you, and you will be defeated by all your enemies. They will rule over you, and you will run even when no one is chasing you!

¹⁸"And if, in spite of this, you still disobey me, I will punish you for your sins seven times over. ¹⁹I will break down your arrogant spirit by making the skies above as unyielding as iron and the earth beneath as hard as bronze. ²⁰All your work will be for nothing, for your land will yield no crops, and your trees will bear no fruit.

²¹"If even then you remain hostile toward me and refuse to obey, I will inflict you with seven more disasters for your sins. ²²I will release wild animals that will kill your children and destroy your cattle, so your numbers will dwindle and your roads will be deserted.

My Daily Worship

— *February 2* —

A VACATION WITH GOD

LEVITICUS 24:1—27:34

This year will be set apart as holy, a time to proclaim release for all
who live there. It will be a jubilee year for you (25:10).

[i reflect]

A common complaint today is that people are too busy. Busyness is the plague of our day and an enemy of true spirituality. Tired, stressed-out people are hobbled in their ability to enjoy the presence of God. It's time for a change.

The year of jubilee was a time to get off the hamster wheel of moneymaking and trust in God's provision. It was a time to relax and let life flow back into the mold God had made for it. Longer than a Sabbath, longer even than a religious festival, jubilee was an extended period in which to gaze on the face of God until that face came clear, in all its loveliness, through the haze of everyday concerns. What freedom! Is it any wonder that jubilee was the theme of many a slave?

And who among us could not benefit from an extended period in which to put down our tools and spend our time gazing on God? If it's true that we become like what we choose to focus on, then there's no more direct pathway to holiness, to mercy, to love.

The word *jubilee* comes from the name of the ram's horn used in Israelite worship. Our own jubilee experiences can be times when worship goes from being an interlude to being the permanent cast of our nature. We'll learn what it means to keep in step with the Spirit and pray without ceasing.

You don't need to wait for an extended period of time to experience jubilee. Make a point to schedule a time of "mini-jubilee" today. Shorten your lunch break and spend the time in communion with God. Instead of watching your favorite TV show, use it as a time to focus on God.

And when our jubilee time is over, we'll be changed. We'll each be a "human being" instead of a "human doing."

[i pray]

Lord, I don't want the hubbub of the voices around me or the humdrum of my daily routine
to drown out your still, small voice. Meet me! And help me to meet you!

[i respond]

Want to take a "jubilee vacation"? Grab your calendar and schedule it! Where will you go (or will you stay at home)? Who will you take with you, if anybody? How will you incorporate prayer, meditation, singing, and so on?

[23]"And if you fail to learn a lesson from this and continue your hostility toward me, [24]then I myself will be hostile toward you, and I will personally strike you seven times over for your sins. [25]I will send armies against you to carry out these covenant threats. If you flee to your cities, I will send a plague to destroy you there, and you will be conquered by your enemies. [26]I will completely destroy your food supply, so the bread from one oven will have to be stretched to feed ten families. They will ration your food by weight, and even if you have food to eat, you will not be satisfied.

[27]"If after this you still refuse to listen and still remain hostile toward me, [28]then I will give full vent to my hostility. I will punish you seven times over for your sins. [29]You will eat the flesh of your own sons and daughters. [30]I will destroy your pagan shrines and cut down your incense altars. I will leave your corpses piled up beside your lifeless idols, and I will despise you. [31]I will make your cities desolate and destroy your places of worship, and I will take no pleasure in your offerings of incense. [32]Yes, I myself will devastate your land. Your enemies who come to occupy it will be utterly shocked at the destruction they see. [33]I will scatter you among the nations and attack you with my own weapons. Your land will become desolate, and your cities will lie in ruins. [34]Then at last the land will make up for its missed Sabbath years as it lies desolate during your years of exile in the land of your enemies. Then the land will finally rest and enjoy its Sabbaths. [35]As the land lies in ruins, it will take the rest you never allowed it to take every seventh year while you lived in it.

[36]"And for those of you who survive, I will demoralize you in the land of your enemies far away. You will live there in such constant fear that the sound of a leaf driven by the wind will send you fleeing. You will run as though chased by a warrior with a sword, and you will fall even when no one is pursuing you. [37]Yes, though no one is chasing you, you will stumble over each other in flight, as though fleeing in battle. You will have no power to stand before your enemies. [38]You will die among the foreign nations and be devoured in the land of your enemies. [39]Those still left alive will rot away in enemy lands because of their sins and the sins of their ancestors.

[40]"But at last my people will confess their sins and the sins of their ancestors for betraying me and being hostile toward me. [41]Finally, when I have given full expression to my hostility and have brought them to the land of their enemies, then at last their disobedient hearts will be humbled, and they will pay for their sins. [42]Then I will remember my covenant with Jacob, with Isaac, and with Abraham, and I will remember the land. [43]And the land will enjoy its years of Sabbath rest as it lies deserted. At last the people will receive the due punishment for their sins, for they rejected my regulations and despised my laws.

[44]"But despite all this, I will not utterly reject or despise them while they are in exile in the land of their enemies. I will not cancel my covenant with them by wiping them out. I, the LORD, am their God. [45]I will remember my ancient covenant with their ancestors, whom I brought out of Egypt while all the nations watched. I, the LORD, am their God."

[46]These are the laws, regulations, and instructions that the LORD gave to the Israelites through Moses on Mount Sinai.

REDEEMING GIFTS OFFERED TO THE LORD

27 The LORD said to Moses, [2]"Give the following instructions to the Israelites: If you make a special vow to dedicate someone to the LORD by paying the value of that person, [3]here is the scale of values to be used. A man between the ages of twenty and sixty is valued at fifty pieces of silver*; [4]a woman of that age is valued at thirty pieces of silver.

27:3 Hebrew *50 shekels of silver, according to the standard sanctuary shekel,* each about 0.4 ounces or 11 grams in weight. The term *shekels* also appears in 27:4, 5, 6, 7, 16.

⁵A boy between five and twenty is valued at twenty pieces of silver; a girl of that age is valued at ten pieces of silver. ⁶A boy between the ages of one month and five years is valued at five pieces of silver; a girl of that age is valued at three pieces of silver. ⁷A man older than sixty is valued at fifteen pieces of silver; a woman older than sixty is valued at ten pieces of silver. ⁸If you desire to make such a vow but cannot afford to pay the prescribed amount, go to the priest and he will evaluate your ability to pay. You will then pay the amount decided by the priest.

⁹"If your vow involves giving a clean animal—one that is acceptable as an offering to the LORD—then your gift to the LORD will be considered holy. ¹⁰The animal should never be exchanged or substituted for another—neither a good animal for a bad one nor a bad animal for a good one. But if such an exchange is in fact made, then both the original animal and the substitute will be considered holy. ¹¹But if your vow involves an unclean animal—one that is not acceptable as an offering to the LORD—then you must bring the animal to the priest. ¹²He will assess its value, and his assessment will be final. ¹³If you want to redeem the animal, you must pay the value set by the priest, plus 20 percent.

¹⁴"If you dedicate a house to the LORD, the priest must come to assess its value. The priest's assessment will be final. ¹⁵If you wish to redeem the house, you must pay the value set by the priest, plus 20 percent. Then the house will again belong to you.

¹⁶"If you dedicate to the LORD a piece of your ancestral property, its value will be assessed by the amount of seed required to plant it—fifty pieces of silver for an area that produces* five bushels* of barley seed. ¹⁷If the field is dedicated to the LORD in the Year of Jubilee, then the entire assessment will apply. ¹⁸But if the field is dedicated after the Year of Jubilee, the priest must assess the land's value in proportion to the years left until the next Year of Jubilee. ¹⁹If you decide to redeem the dedicated field, you must pay the land's value as assessed by the priest, plus 20 percent. Then the field will again belong to you. ²⁰But if you decide not to redeem the field, or if the field is sold to someone else by the priests, it can never be redeemed. ²¹When the field is released in the Year of Jubilee, it will be holy, a field specially set apart* for the LORD. It will become the property of the priests.

²²"If you dedicate to the LORD a field that you have purchased but which is not part of your ancestral property, ²³the priest must assess its value based on the years until the next Year of Jubilee. You must then give the assessed value of the land as a sacred donation to the LORD. ²⁴In the Year of Jubilee the field will be released to the original owner from whom you purchased it. ²⁵All the value assessments must be measured in terms of the standard sanctuary shekel.*

²⁶"You may not dedicate to the LORD the firstborn of your cattle or sheep because the firstborn of these animals already belong to him. ²⁷However, if it is the firstborn of a ceremonially unclean animal, you may redeem it by paying the priest's assessment of its worth, plus 20 percent. If you do not redeem it, the priest may sell it to someone else for its assessed value.

²⁸"However, anything specially set apart by the LORD—whether a person, an animal, or an inherited field—must never be sold or redeemed. Anything devoted in this way has been set apart for the LORD as holy. ²⁹A person specially set apart by the LORD for destruction cannot be redeemed. Such a person must be put to death.

³⁰"A tenth of the produce of the land, whether grain or fruit, belongs to the LORD and must be set apart to him as holy. ³¹If you want to redeem the LORD's tenth of the fruit or grain, you must pay its value, plus 20 percent.

27:16a Or requires. 27:16b Hebrew 1 homer [182 liters]. 27:21 The Hebrew term used here refers to the complete consecration of things or people to the LORD, either by destroying them or by giving them as an offering; also in 27:28, 29. 27:25 Hebrew measured according to the sanctuary shekel, 20 gerahs to each shekel. Each sanctuary shekel was about 0.4 ounces or 11 grams in weight.

[32]The LORD also owns every tenth animal counted off from your herds and flocks. They are set apart to him as holy. [33]The tenth animal must not be selected on the basis of whether it is good or bad, and no substitutions will be allowed. If any exchange is in fact made, then both the original animal and the substituted one will be considered holy and cannot be redeemed."

[34]These are the commands that the LORD gave to the Israelites through Moses on Mount Sinai.

Numbers

The LORD is slow to anger and rich in unfailing love, forgiving every kind of sin (14:18).

The Picture of Patience

Remember teaching a child how to ride a bike, or coaching a youth soccer team, or mentoring a young person spiritually? Each one is a picture of patience—coming alongside a younger person, offering encouragement, providing instruction, and helping that person master the goal. Now imagine that same young charge totally disregarding your instructions, or even worse, constantly complaining about the job you were doing.

That's the kind of picture we encounter in Numbers—a God who repeatedly showed his love, his patience, his power, and his faithfulness to his children, and a people who consistently complained, grumbled, and whined the moment that they felt discomfort or uncertainty. "Trust me," said God. "Not yet," said the people. For their lack of faith, they were sentenced to wandering another forty years in the desert.

As God responded to his children's unfaithfulness, he taught them two principles of worship. First, God *requires* our worship. We see in Numbers how God chose and set apart the Levites for serving him in his holy Tabernacle (chapter 3). We see how God ordered worship by delegating the various duties and assignments (chapter 4). The proper offerings were outlined and the rules establishing order and holy living were reviewed.

Second, God *requests* our worship. We see a God who is worthy of our worship because we are his covenant people—bought and paid for by his own blood. He gives us opportunities to serve him out of love, not just obligation. We freely offer him praise and thanksgiving as we acknowledge his unfailing love, his forgiveness of every sin, and his patience with a people who are prone to complain and wander.

As you read through Numbers, consider the God you worship and your relationship to him. What complaints are you harboring? Trust in his patience and his provision. Have you wandered from him? Turn to his unfailing love right now.

Worship Moments

- God gives Aaron a special blessing for the people of Israel (6:22–26)—one that is probably familiar to us.

- Whenever "the glorious presence of the LORD appeared" (16:19, 42; 20:6), Moses and Aaron fell face down in response (16:22, 45; 20:6).

- Moses asks God to appoint a leader to succeed him. God chooses Joshua, upon whom Moses lays hands, transferring his authority to him, and publicly commissioning him (27:16–23).

ISRAEL'S FIRST CENSUS

1 One day in midspring,* during the second year after Israel's departure from Egypt, the LORD spoke to Moses in the Tabernacle* in the wilderness of Sinai. He said, [2]"Take a census of the whole community of Israel by their clans and families. List the names of all the men [3]twenty years old or older who are able to go to war. You and Aaron are to direct the project, [4]assisted by one family leader from each tribe."

[5]These are the tribes and the names of the leaders chosen for the task:

Tribe	Leader
Reuben	Elizur son of Shedeur
[6] Simeon	Shelumiel son of Zurishaddai
[7] Judah	Nahshon son of Amminadab
[8] Issachar	Nethanel son of Zuar
[9] Zebulun	Eliab son of Helon
[10] Ephraim son of Joseph	Elishama son of Ammihud
Manasseh son of Joseph	Gamaliel son of Pedahzur
[11] Benjamin	Abidan son of Gideoni
[12] Dan	Ahiezer son of Ammishaddai
[13] Asher	Pagiel son of Ocran
[14] Gad	Eliasaph son of Deuel
[15] Naphtali	Ahira son of Enan

[16]These tribal leaders, heads of their own families, were chosen from among all the people.

[17]Now Moses and Aaron and the chosen leaders [18]called together the whole community of Israel on that very day.* All the people were registered according to their ancestry by their clans and families. The men of Israel twenty years old or older were registered, one by one, [19]just as the LORD had commanded Moses. So Moses counted the people there in the wilderness of Sinai.

[20-21]This is the number of men twenty years old or older who were able to go to war, each listed according to his own clan and family*:

Tribe	Number
Reuben (Jacob's* oldest son)	46,500
[22-23] Simeon	59,300
[24-25] Gad	45,650
[26-27] Judah	74,600
[28-29] Issachar	54,400
[30-31] Zebulun	57,400
[32-33] Ephraim son of Joseph	40,500
[34-35] Manasseh son of Joseph	32,200
[36-37] Benjamin	35,400
[38-39] Dan	62,700
[40-41] Asher	41,500
[42-43] Naphtali	53,400

[44]These were the men counted by Moses and Aaron and the twelve leaders of Israel, all listed according to their ancestral descent. [45]They were counted by families—all the men of Israel who were twenty years old or older and able to go to war. [46]The total number was 603,550.

[47]But this total did not include the Levites. [48]For the LORD had said to Moses, [49]"Exempt the tribe of Levi from the census; do not include them when you count the rest of the Israelites. [50]You must put the Levites in charge of the Tabernacle of the Covenant,* along with its furnishings and equipment. They must carry the Tabernacle and its equipment as you travel, and they must care for it and camp around it. [51]Whenever the Tabernacle is moved, the Levites will take it down and set it up again. Anyone else who goes too near the Tabernacle will be executed. [52]Each tribe of Israel will have a designated camping area with its own family banner. [53]But the Levites will camp around the Tabernacle of the Covenant to offer the people of Israel protection from the LORD's fierce anger. The Levites are responsible to stand guard around the Tabernacle."

[54]So the Israelites did everything just as the LORD had commanded Moses.

ORGANIZATION FOR ISRAEL'S CAMP

2 Then the LORD gave these instructions to Moses and Aaron: [2]"Each tribe will be assigned its own area in the camp, and the

---

1:1a Hebrew *On the first day of the second month.* This day of the Hebrew lunar calendar occurs in April or early May. 1:1b Hebrew *Tent of Meeting.* 1:18 Hebrew *on the first day of the second month;* see 1:1. 1:20-21a In the Hebrew text, *number of men . . . family* is repeated in 1:22, 24, 26, 28, 30, 32, 34, 36, 38, 40, 42. 1:20-21b Hebrew *Israel's.* 1:50 Or *Tabernacle of the Testimony;* also in 1:53.

various groups will camp beneath their family banners. The Tabernacle* will be located at the center of these tribal compounds.

³⁻⁴"The divisions of Judah, Issachar, and Zebulun are to camp toward the sunrise on the east side of the Tabernacle, beneath their family banners. These are the names of the tribes, their leaders, and the number of their available troops:

	Tribe	Leader	Number
	Judah	Nahshon son of Amminadab	74,600
5-6	Issachar	Nethanel son of Zuar	54,400
7-8	Zebulun	Eliab son of Helon	57,400

⁹So the total of all the troops on Judah's side of the camp is 186,400. These three tribes are to lead the way whenever the Israelites travel to a new campsite.

¹⁰⁻¹¹"The divisions of Reuben, Simeon, and Gad are to camp on the south side of the Tabernacle, beneath their family banners. These are the names of the tribes, their leaders, and the number of their available troops:

	Tribe	Leader	Number
	Reuben	Elizur son of Shedeur	46,500
12-13	Simeon	Shelumiel son of Zurishaddai	59,300
14-15	Gad	Eliasaph son of Deuel*	45,650

¹⁶So the total of all the troops on Reuben's side of the camp is 151,450. These three tribes will be second in line whenever the Israelites travel.

¹⁷"Then the Levites will set out from the middle of the camp with the Tabernacle. All the tribes are to travel in the same order that they camp, each in position under the appropriate family banner.

¹⁸⁻¹⁹"The divisions of Ephraim, Manasseh, and Benjamin are to camp on the west side of the Tabernacle, beneath their family banners. These are the names of the tribes, their leaders, and the number of their available troops:

	Tribe	Leader	Number
	Ephraim	Elishama son of Ammihud	40,500
20-21	Manasseh	Gamaliel son of Pedahzur	32,200
22-23	Benjamin	Abidan son of Gideoni	35,400

²⁴So the total of all the troops on Ephraim's side of the camp is 108,100, and they will follow the Levites in the line of march.

²⁵⁻²⁶"The divisions of Dan, Asher, and Naphtali are to camp on the north side of the Tabernacle, beneath their family banners. These are the names of the tribes, their leaders, and the number of their available troops:

	Tribe	Leader	Number
	Dan	Ahiezer son of Ammishaddai	62,700
27-28	Asher	Pagiel son of Ocran	41,500
29-30	Naphtali	Ahira son of Enan	53,400

³¹So the total of all the troops on Dan's side of the camp is 157,600. They are to bring up the rear whenever the Israelites move to a new campsite."

³²In summary, the troops of Israel listed by their families totaled 603,550. ³³The Levites were exempted from this census by the LORD's command to Moses. ³⁴So the people of Israel did everything just as the LORD had commanded Moses. Each clan and family set up camp and marched under their banners exactly as the LORD had instructed them.

LEVITES APPOINTED FOR SERVICE

3 This is the family line of Aaron and Moses as it was recorded when the LORD spoke to Moses on Mount Sinai: ²Aaron's sons were Nadab (the firstborn), Abihu, Eleazar, and Ithamar. ³They were anointed and set apart to minister as priests. ⁴But Nadab and Abihu died in the LORD's presence in the wilderness of Sinai when they burned before the LORD a different kind of fire than he had commanded. Since they had no sons, this left only Eleazar and Ithamar to serve as priests with their father, Aaron.

⁵Then the LORD said to Moses, ⁶"Call forward the tribe of Levi and present them to Aaron the priest as his assistants. ⁷They will serve Aaron and the whole community, performing their sacred duties in and around the

2:2 Hebrew *Tent of Meeting;* also in 2:17.   2:14-15 As in many Hebrew manuscripts, Samaritan Pentateuch, and Latin Vulgate (see also 1:14); most Hebrew manuscripts read *son of Reuel.*

Tabernacle.* ⁸They will also maintain all the furnishings of the sacred tent,* serving in the Tabernacle on behalf of all the Israelites. ⁹Assign the Levites to Aaron and his sons as their assistants. ¹⁰Appoint Aaron and his sons to carry out the duties of the priesthood. Anyone else who comes too near the sanctuary must be executed!"

¹¹And the LORD said to Moses, ¹²"I have chosen the Levites from among the Israelites as substitutes for all the firstborn sons of the people of Israel. The Levites are mine ¹³because all the firstborn sons are mine. From the day I killed all the firstborn sons of the Egyptians, I set apart for myself all the firstborn in Israel of both men and animals. They are mine; I am the LORD."

THE CENSUS OF THE LEVITES

¹⁴The LORD spoke again to Moses, there in the wilderness of Sinai. He said, ¹⁵"Take a census of the tribe of Levi by its families and clans. Count every male who is one month old or older." ¹⁶So Moses counted them, just as the LORD had commanded.

¹⁷Levi had three sons, who were named Gershon, Kohath, and Merari.
¹⁸The clans descended from Gershon were named for two of his descendants, Libni and Shimei.
¹⁹The clans descended from Kohath were named for four of his descendants, Amram, Izhar, Hebron, and Uzziel.
²⁰The clans descended from Merari were named for two of his descendants, Mahli and Mushi.

These were the Levite clans, listed according to their family groups.

²¹The descendants of Gershon were composed of the clans descended from Libni and Shimei. ²²There were 7,500 males one month old or older among these Gershonite clans.

²³They were assigned the area to the west of the Tabernacle for their camp. ²⁴The leader of the Gershonite clans was Eliasaph son of Lael. ²⁵These two clans were responsible to care for the tent of the Tabernacle with its layers of coverings, its entry curtains, ²⁶the curtains of the courtyard that surrounded the Tabernacle and altar, the curtain at the courtyard entrance, the cords, and all the equipment related to their use.

²⁷The descendants of Kohath were composed of the clans descended from Amram, Izhar, Hebron, and Uzziel. ²⁸There were 8,600* males one month old or older among these Kohathite clans. They were responsible for the care of the sanctuary. ²⁹They were assigned the area south of the Tabernacle for their camp. ³⁰The leader of the Kohathite clans was Elizaphan son of Uzziel. ³¹These four clans were responsible for the care of the Ark, the table, the lampstand, the altars, the various utensils used in the sanctuary, the inner curtain, and all the equipment related to their use. ³²Eleazar the priest, Aaron's son, was the chief administrator over all the Levites, with special responsibility for the oversight of the sanctuary.

³³The descendants of Merari were composed of the clans descended from Mahli and Mushi. ³⁴There were 6,200 males one month old or older among these Merarite clans. ³⁵They were assigned the area north of the Tabernacle for their camp. The leader of the Merarite clans was Zuriel son of Abihail. ³⁶These two clans were responsible for the care of the frames supporting the Tabernacle, the crossbars, the pillars, the bases, and all the equipment related to their use. ³⁷They were also responsible for the posts of the courtyard and all their bases, pegs, and cords.

³⁸The area in front of the Tabernacle in the east toward the sunrise* was reserved for the tents of Moses and of Aaron and his sons, who had the final responsibility for the sanctuary on behalf of the people of Israel. Anyone

---

3:7 Hebrew *around the Tent of Meeting, doing service at the Tabernacle.* 3:8 Hebrew *Tent of Meeting.* 3:28 Some Greek manuscripts read 8,300; see total in 3:39. 3:38 Hebrew *toward the sunrise, in front of the Tent of Meeting.*

My Daily Worship

— *February 3* —

NAME YOUR GIFT
NUMBERS 1:1–4:49

Then the LORD said to Moses, "Call forward the tribe of Levi and present them to Aaron
the priest as his assistants. They will serve Aaron and the whole community,
performing their sacred duties in and around the Tabernacle" (3:5–7).

[i reflect]

Larry was a recovering alcoholic. This construction worker's thirst for booze had been replaced by a thirst for Jesus. With a mouth that used to spew profanities, he now sang praise to God. He asked his pastor one Sunday if he could gather with the staff and members of the worship team for prayer. Pastor Greg was willing.

Standing in a circle, each person took a turn seeking the Lord's blessing on the church service. When it was Larry's turn, he talked to Jesus with confidence and sincerity. Though his language wasn't eloquent, it was clear he knew who he was talking to. As those who would lead worship prepared to leave for the sanctuary, Larry wrapped his huge arms around them and said, "Go give 'em heaven, you guys!"

The next week Pastor Greg asked Larry if he'd be willing to attend the pre-service prayer gathering again. Larry had found a place of ministry. For the next five years he joined Pastor Greg each Sunday to seek the Lord's anointing on the worship team. Based on the vibrant worship that filled the sanctuary each week, it was clear Larry was playing a meaningful part.

Just as the Levites were set apart to use their gifts and abilities in corporate worship in Moses' day, so you have been gifted too. Be encouraged by Larry's example. He was affirmed as an intercessor and encourager. And that's not all. As he grew in his faith he discovered he had the gift of evangelism. Five years after beginning his weekly prayer ministry with the staff, he and his wife, Linda, joined Wycliffe Bible Translators as missionaries in South America.

You have been gifted by God to contribute uniquely to building his kingdom. Name and celebrate your gifts. Then worship the Giver today by using them for his glory.

[i pray]

Lord, thank you for how you are able to use me to build your kingdom.
Bring to mind the unique way you have gifted me, and show me throughout
this day how I can worship you by using these gifts. Amen.

[i respond]

Jot down a list of three ways you can use your gifts to worship God. Ask God to provide you with an opportunity today to accomplish at least one of those ways.

other than a priest or Levite who came too near the sanctuary was to be executed.

[39]So among the Levite clans counted by Moses and Aaron at the LORD's command, there were 22,000 males one month old or older.

REDEEMING THE FIRSTBORN SONS

[40]Then the LORD said to Moses, "Now count all the firstborn sons in Israel who are one month old or older, and register each name. [41]The Levites will be reserved for me as substitutes for the firstborn sons of Israel; I am the LORD. And the Levites' livestock are mine as substitutes for the firstborn livestock of the whole nation of Israel."

[42]So Moses counted the firstborn sons of the people of Israel, just as the LORD had commanded. [43]The total number of firstborn sons who were one month old or older was 22,273.

[44]Now the LORD said to Moses, [45]"Take the Levites in place of the firstborn sons of the people of Israel. And take the livestock of the Levites as substitutes for the firstborn livestock of the people of Israel. The Levites will be mine; I am the LORD. [46]To redeem the 273 firstborn sons of Israel who are in excess of the number of Levites, [47]collect five pieces of silver for each person, each piece weighing the same as the standard sanctuary shekel.* [48]Give the silver to Aaron and his sons as the redemption price for the extra firstborn sons."

[49]So Moses collected redemption money for the firstborn sons of Israel who exceeded the number of Levites. [50]The silver collected on behalf of these firstborn sons of Israel came to about thirty-four pounds in weight.* [51]And Moses gave the redemption money to Aaron and his sons as the LORD had commanded.

DUTIES OF THE KOHATHITE CLAN

4 Then the LORD said to Moses and Aaron, [2]"Take a census of the clans and families of the Kohathite division of the Levite tribe.

[3]Count all the men between the ages of thirty and fifty who qualify to work in the Tabernacle.*

[4]"The duties of the Kohathites at the Tabernacle will relate to the most sacred objects. [5]When the camp moves, Aaron and his sons must enter the Tabernacle first to take down the inner curtain and cover the Ark of the Covenant* with it. [6]Then they must cover the inner curtain with fine goatskin leather, and the goatskin leather with a dark blue cloth. Finally, they must put the carrying poles of the Ark in place.

[7]"Next they must spread a blue cloth over the table, where the Bread of the Presence is displayed, and place the dishes, spoons, bowls, cups, and the special bread on the cloth. [8]They must spread a scarlet cloth over that, and finally a covering of fine goatskin leather on top of the scarlet cloth. Then they must insert the carrying poles into the table.

[9]"Next they must cover the lampstand with a dark blue cloth, along with its lamps, lamp snuffers, trays, and special jars of olive oil. [10]The lampstand with its utensils must then be covered with fine goatskin leather, and the bundle must be placed on a carrying frame.

[11]"Aaron and his sons must also spread a dark blue cloth over the gold altar and cover this cloth with a covering of fine goatskin leather. Then they are to attach the carrying poles to the altar. [12]All the remaining utensils of the sanctuary must be wrapped in a dark blue cloth, covered with fine goatskin leather, and placed on the carrying frame.

[13]"The ashes must be removed from the altar, and the altar must then be covered with a purple cloth. [14]All the altar utensils—the firepans, hooks, shovels, basins, and all the containers—are to be placed on the cloth, and a covering of fine goatskin leather must be spread over them. Finally, the carrying poles must be put in place. [15]When Aaron and his sons have finished covering the sanctuary

---

3:47 Hebrew 5 shekels [2 ounces or 57 grams] apiece, according to the sanctuary shekel, 20 gerahs to each shekel. 3:50 Hebrew 1,365 shekels [15.5 kilograms], according to the sanctuary shekel. 4:3 Hebrew Tent of Meeting; also in 4:4, 15, 23, 25, 28, 30, 31, 33, 35, 37, 39, 41, 43, 47. 4:5 Or Ark of the Testimony.

and all the sacred utensils, the Kohathites will come and carry these things to the next destination. But they must not touch the sacred objects, or they will die. So these are the objects of the Tabernacle that the Kohathites must carry.

¹⁶"Eleazar son of Aaron the priest will be responsible for the oil of the lampstand, the fragrant incense, the daily grain offering, and the anointing oil. In fact, the supervision of the entire Tabernacle and everything in it will be Eleazar's responsibility."

¹⁷Then the LORD said to Moses and Aaron, ¹⁸"Don't let the Kohathite clans be destroyed from among the Levites! ¹⁹This is what you must do so they will live and not die when they approach the most sacred objects. Aaron and his sons must always go in with them and assign a specific duty or load to each person. ²⁰Otherwise they must not approach the sanctuary and look at the sacred objects for even a moment, or they will die."

DUTIES OF THE GERSHONITE CLAN

²¹And the LORD said to Moses, ²²"Take a census of the clans and families of the Gershonite division of the tribe of Levi. ²³Count all the men between the ages of thirty and fifty who are eligible to serve in the Tabernacle.

²⁴"The duties of the Gershonites will be in the areas of general service and carrying loads. ²⁵They must carry the curtains of the Tabernacle, the Tabernacle itself with its coverings, the outer covering of fine goatskin leather, and the curtain for the Tabernacle entrance. ²⁶They are also to carry the curtains for the courtyard walls that surround the Tabernacle and altar, the curtain across the courtyard entrance, the necessary cords, and all the altar's accessories. The Gershonites are responsible for transporting all these items. ²⁷Aaron and his sons will direct the Gershonites regarding their duties, whether it involves moving or doing other work. They must assign the Gershonites the loads they are to carry. ²⁸So these are the duties assigned to the Gershonites at the Tabernacle. They will

be directly responsible to Ithamar son of Aaron the priest.

DUTIES OF THE MERARITE CLAN

²⁹"Now take a census of the clans and families of the Merarite division of the Levite tribe. ³⁰Count all the men between the ages of thirty and fifty who are eligible to serve in the Tabernacle.

³¹"Their duties at the Tabernacle will consist of carrying loads. They will be required to carry the frames of the Tabernacle, the crossbars, the pillars with their bases, ³²the posts for the courtyard walls with their bases, pegs, cords, accessories, and everything else related to their use. You must assign the various loads to each man by name. ³³So these are the duties of the Merarites at the Tabernacle. They are directly responsible to Ithamar son of Aaron the priest."

THE CENSUS OF THE LEVITES

³⁴So Moses, Aaron, and the other leaders of the community counted the Kohathite division by its clans and families. ³⁵The count included all the men between thirty and fifty years of age who were eligible for service in the Tabernacle, ³⁶and the total number came to 2,750. ³⁷So this was the total of all those from the Kohathite clans who were eligible to serve at the Tabernacle. Moses and Aaron counted them, just as the LORD had commanded through Moses.

³⁸The Gershonite division was also counted by its clans and families. ³⁹The count included all the men between thirty and fifty years of age who were eligible for service in the Tabernacle, ⁴⁰and the total number came to 2,630. ⁴¹So this was the total of all those from the Gershonite clans who were eligible to serve at the Tabernacle. Moses and Aaron counted them, just as the LORD had commanded.

⁴²The Merarite division was also counted by its clans and families. ⁴³The count included all the men between thirty and fifty years of age who were eligible for service in the

Tabernacle, ⁴⁴and the total number came to 3,200. ⁴⁵So this was the total of all those from the Merarite clans who were eligible for service. Moses and Aaron counted them, just as the LORD had commanded through Moses.

⁴⁶So Moses, Aaron, and the leaders of Israel counted all the Levites by their clans and families. ⁴⁷All the men between thirty and fifty years of age who were eligible for service in the Tabernacle and for its transportation ⁴⁸numbered 8,580. ⁴⁹Each man was assigned his task and told what to carry, just as the LORD had commanded through Moses.

And so the census was completed, just as the LORD had commanded Moses.

PURITY IN ISRAEL'S CAMP

5 The LORD gave these instructions to Moses: ²"Command the people of Israel to remove anyone from the camp who has a contagious skin disease* or a discharge, or who has been defiled by touching a dead person. ³This applies to men and women alike. Remove them so they will not defile the camp, where I live among you." ⁴So the Israelites did just as the LORD had commanded Moses and removed such people from the camp.

⁵Then the LORD said to Moses, ⁶"Give these instructions to the people of Israel: If any of the people—men or women—betray the LORD by doing wrong to another person, they are guilty. ⁷They must confess their sin and make full restitution for what they have done, adding a penalty of 20 percent and returning it to the person who was wronged. ⁸But if the person who was wronged is dead, and there are no near relatives to whom restitution can be made, it belongs to the LORD and must be given to the priest, along with a ram for atonement. ⁹All the sacred gifts that the Israelites bring to a priest will belong to him. ¹⁰Each priest may keep the sacred donations that he receives."

PROTECTING MARITAL FAITHFULNESS

¹¹And the LORD said to Moses, ¹²"Say to the people of Israel: 'Suppose a man's wife goes astray and is unfaithful to her husband. ¹³Suppose she sleeps with another man, but there is no witness since she was not caught in the act. ¹⁴If her husband becomes jealous and suspicious of his wife, even if she has not defiled herself, ¹⁵the husband must bring his wife to the priest with an offering of two quarts* of barley flour to be presented on her behalf. Do not mix it with olive oil or frankincense, for it is a jealousy offering—an offering of inquiry to find out if she is guilty.

¹⁶"'The priest must then present her before the LORD. ¹⁷He must take some holy water in a clay jar and mix it with dust from the Tabernacle floor. ¹⁸When he has presented her before the LORD, he must unbind her hair and place the offering of inquiry—the jealousy offering—in her hands to determine whether or not her husband's suspicions are justified. The priest will stand before her, holding the jar of bitter water that brings a curse to those who are guilty. ¹⁹The priest will put the woman under oath and say to her, "If no other man has slept with you, and you have not defiled yourself by being unfaithful, may you be immune from the effects of this bitter water that causes the curse. ²⁰But if you have gone astray while under your husband's authority and defiled yourself by sleeping with another man"—²¹at this point the priest must put the woman under this oath—"then may the people see that the LORD's curse is upon you when he makes you infertile.* ²²Now may this water that brings the curse enter your body and make you infertile.*" And the woman will be required to say, "Yes, let it be so." ²³Then the priest will write these curses on a piece of leather and wash them off into the bitter water. ²⁴He will then make the woman drink the bitter water, so it may bring

5:2 Traditionally rendered *leprosy*. The Hebrew word used here describes various skin diseases. 5:15 Hebrew *1/10 of an ephah* [2 liters]. 5:21 Hebrew *when he causes your thigh to waste away and your abdomen to swell*. 5:22 Hebrew *enter your body so that your abdomen swells and your thigh wastes away*.

on the curse and cause bitter suffering in cases of guilt.

[25] " 'Then the priest will take the jealousy offering from the woman's hand, lift it up before the LORD, and carry it to the altar. [26]He will take a handful as a token portion and burn it on the altar. Then he will require the woman to drink the water. [27]If she has defiled herself by being unfaithful to her husband, the water that brings the curse will cause bitter suffering. She will become infertile,* and her name will become a curse word among her people. [28]But if she has not defiled herself and is pure, she will be unharmed and will still be able to have children.

[29] " 'This is the ritual law for dealing with jealousy. If a woman defiles herself by being unfaithful to her husband, [30]or if a man is overcome with jealousy and suspicion that his wife has been unfaithful, the husband must present his wife before the LORD, and the priest will apply this entire ritual law to her. [31]The husband will be innocent of any guilt in this matter, but his wife will be held accountable for her sin.' "

NAZIRITE LAWS

6 Then the LORD said to Moses, "Speak to the people of Israel and give them these instructions: [2]If some of the people, either men or women, take the special vow of a Nazirite, setting themselves apart to the LORD in a special way, [3]they must give up wine and other alcoholic drinks. They must not use vinegar made from wine, they must not drink other fermented drinks or fresh grape juice, and they must not eat grapes or raisins. [4]As long as they are bound by their Nazirite vow, they are not allowed to eat or drink anything that comes from a grapevine, not even the grape seeds or skins.

[5]"They must never cut their hair throughout the time of their vow, for they are holy and set apart to the LORD. That is why they must let their hair grow long. [6]And they may not go near a dead body during the entire period of their vow to the LORD, [7]even if their own father, mother, brother, or sister has died. They must not defile the hair on their head, because it is the symbol of their separation to God. [8]This applies as long as they are set apart to the LORD.

[9]"If their hair is defiled because someone suddenly falls dead beside them, they must wait for seven days and then shave their heads. Then they will be cleansed from their defilement. [10]On the eighth day they must bring two turtledoves or two young pigeons to the priest at the entrance of the Tabernacle.* [11]The priest will offer one of the birds for a sin offering and the other for a burnt offering. In this way, he will make atonement for the guilt they incurred from the dead body. Then they must renew their vow that day and let their hair begin to grow again. [12]The days of their vow that were completed before their defilement no longer count. They must rededicate themselves to the LORD for the full term of their vow, and each must bring a one-year-old male lamb for a guilt offering.

[13]"This is the ritual law of the Nazirites. At the conclusion of their time of separation as Nazirites, they must each go to the entrance of the Tabernacle [14]and offer these sacrifices to the LORD: a one-year-old male lamb without defect for a burnt offering, a one-year-old female lamb without defect for a sin offering, a ram without defect for a peace offering, [15]a basket of bread made without yeast—cakes of choice flour mixed with olive oil and wafers spread with olive oil—along with their prescribed grain offerings and drink offerings. [16]The priest will present these offerings before the LORD: first the sin offering and the burnt offering; [17]then the ram for a peace offering, along with the basket of bread made without yeast. The priest must also make the prescribed grain offering and drink offering.

[18]"Then the Nazirites will shave their hair at the entrance of the Tabernacle and put it on the fire beneath the peace-offering sacrifice. [19]After each Nazirite's head has been shaved,

---

5:27 Hebrew *Her body will swell and her thigh will waste away.* 6:10 Hebrew *Tent of Meeting;* also in 6:13, 18.

the priest will take for each of them the boiled shoulder of the ram, one cake made without yeast, and one wafer made without yeast, and put them all into the Nazirite's hands. ²⁰The priest will then lift the gifts up before the LORD in a gesture of offering. These are holy portions for the priest, along with the breast and thigh pieces that were lifted up before the LORD. After this ceremony the Nazirites may again drink wine.

²¹"This is the ritual law of the Nazirites. If any Nazirites have vowed to give the LORD anything else beyond what is required by their normal Nazirite vow, they must fulfill their special vow exactly as they have promised."

THE PRIESTLY BLESSING

²²Then the LORD said to Moses, ²³"Instruct Aaron and his sons to bless the people of Israel with this special blessing:

²⁴ 'May the LORD bless you
　　and protect you.
²⁵ May the LORD smile on you
　　and be gracious to you.
²⁶ May the LORD show you his favor
　　and give you his peace.'

²⁷This is how Aaron and his sons will designate the Israelites as my people,* and I myself will bless them."

OFFERINGS OF DEDICATION

7 On the day Moses set up the Tabernacle, he anointed it and set it apart as holy, along with all its furnishings and the altar with its utensils. ²Then the leaders of Israel—the tribal leaders who had organized the census—came and brought their offerings. ³Together they brought six carts and twelve oxen. There was a cart for every two leaders and an ox for each leader. They presented these to the LORD in front of the Tabernacle.

⁴Then the LORD said to Moses, ⁵"Receive their gifts and use these oxen and carts for the work of the Tabernacle.* Distribute them among the Levites according to the work they have to do." ⁶So Moses presented the carts and oxen to the Levites. ⁷He gave two carts and four oxen to the Gershonite division for their work, ⁸and four carts and eight oxen to the Merarite division for their work. All their work was done under the leadership of Ithamar son of Aaron the priest. ⁹But he gave none of the carts or oxen to the Kohathite division, since they were required to carry the sacred objects of the Tabernacle on their shoulders.

¹⁰The leaders also presented dedication gifts for the altar at the time it was anointed. They each placed their gifts before the altar. ¹¹The LORD said to Moses, "Let each leader bring his gift on a different day for the dedication of the altar."

¹²On the first day Nahshon son of Amminadab, leader of the tribe of Judah, presented his offering.

¹³The offering consisted of a silver platter weighing about 3¼ pounds and a silver basin of about 1¾ pounds.* These were both filled with grain offerings of choice flour mixed with olive oil. ¹⁴He also brought a gold container weighing about four ounces,* which was filled with incense. ¹⁵He brought a young bull, a ram, and a one-year-old male lamb as a burnt offering; ¹⁶a male goat for a sin offering; ¹⁷and two oxen, five rams, five male goats, and five one-year-old male lambs for a peace offering. This was the offering brought by Nahshon son of Amminadab.

¹⁸On the second day Nethanel son of Zuar, leader of the tribe of Issachar, presented his offering.

¹⁹The offering consisted of a silver platter weighing about 3¼ pounds and a silver basin of about 1¾ pounds. These were both filled with grain offerings of choice

6:27 Hebrew *will put my name on the people of Israel.* 7:5 Hebrew *Tent of Meeting;* also in 7:89. 7:13 Hebrew *silver platter weighing 130 shekels* [1.5 kilograms] *and a silver basin weighing 70 shekels* [0.8 kilograms], *according to the sanctuary shekel;* also in 7:19, 25, 31, 37, 43, 49, 55, 61, 67, 73, 79, 85. 7:14 Hebrew *10 shekels* [114 grams]; also in 7:20, 26, 32, 38, 44, 50, 56, 62, 68, 74, 80, 86.

My Daily Worship

— *February 4* —

GOD IS SMILING AT YOU

NUMBERS 5:1–7:89

Then the LORD said to Moses, "Instruct Aaron and his sons to bless the people of Israel with this special blessing: May the LORD bless you and protect you. May the LORD smile on you and be gracious to you. May the LORD show you his favor and give you his peace" (6:22–26).

[i reflect]

Being validated by a father or a mother is critical. Sons and daughters who have not received their parents' blessing in some shape or form often struggle with self-doubt and feelings of inferiority. They can lose their spiritual moorings and even drift away from worship.

Our heavenly Father's heart beats with concern for those in need of validation. It always has. It's significant in this passage that the Lord is the one who takes the initiative. He told Moses to tell Aaron and his sons to speak words of encouragement and blessing on his behalf. It wasn't Moses' idea. It wasn't Aaron's idea. It was God's idea that his people have the assurance that he was smiling on them. He desired to shower them with protection, grace, favor, and peace.

The good news is that he still desires to do that for us today. His heart is one of compassion, care . . . and JOY! And he wants to bestow upon you this day his blessing, his protection, and yes, even his smile. Think about it. Right where you are—whether it's in your office, at the kitchen table, sitting outside on a park bench—God the Creator is smiling at you. Reflect on that image and thank God for his love . . . then smile back!

From the beginning of time God has used all sorts of ways to make sure his people know that they are loved, accepted, and forgiven. Out of that assurance, draw near to him now, and worship him in spirit and in truth.

[i pray]

Father, I am overwhelmed with gratitude knowing all the good you desire for me.
I know I don't deserve all that you promise, but I long to know that I have been accepted
by you. Although I have not always known the blessing of those who raised me,
my heart leaps with joy to know you are smiling at me. Amen.

[i respond]

Think about what it means that the Lord is capable of smiling on you. After reflecting on the delight he feels claiming you as his own, return his smile with a song of praise as you sit in your easy chair or commute to work.

flour mixed with olive oil. ²⁰He also brought a gold container weighing about four ounces, which was filled with incense. ²¹He brought a young bull, a ram, and a one-year-old male lamb as a burnt offering; ²²a male goat for a sin offering; ²³and two oxen, five rams, five male goats, and five one-year-old male lambs for a peace offering. This was the offering brought by Nethanel son of Zuar.

Words of Worship

ANOINTING

Anointing—Hebrew *ma-shach* "apply oil, anoint"; *ma-shi-ach* "oiled, anointed"; Greek *chris-ma* "anointing." Oil was applied to a person or object to set them apart for sacred use.

Fragrant oil, poured on the head, is a biblical symbol of favor and honor (Psalm 23:5). Priests and sacred objects were consecrated for God's use through anointing with oil. The king of Judah was commissioned to rule by anointing. He was called *mashiach,* the Lord's anointed (Psalm 2:2). After Jesus rose from the dead, his disciples understood that he was their long-awaited King—Messiah, the Christ. When he poured out his Holy Spirit on them, they told this good news to everyone who would listen (Acts 2:36). Oil became a symbol of the Spirit, and the life and healing he imparts.

Sometimes it's hard to believe, but we, too, are anointed. As worshipers of Christ, we know he has poured his anointing on us, to commission us as his witnesses and to heal our wounds. That's Jesus' gift to all his worshipers. As John said, "You have received the Holy Spirit"—the anointing—"and he lives within you" (1 John 2:27).

²⁴On the third day Eliab son of Helon, leader of the tribe of Zebulun, presented his offering. ²⁵The offering consisted of a silver platter weighing about 3¼ pounds and a silver basin of about 1¾ pounds. These were both filled with grain offerings of choice flour mixed with olive oil. ²⁶He also brought a gold container weighing about four ounces, which was filled with incense. ²⁷He brought a young bull, a ram, and a one-year-old male lamb as a burnt offering; ²⁸a male goat for a sin offering; ²⁹and two oxen, five rams, five male goats, and five one-year-old male lambs for a peace offering. This was the offering brought by Eliab son of Helon.

³⁰On the fourth day Elizur son of Shedeur, leader of the tribe of Reuben, presented his offering. ³¹The offering consisted of a silver platter weighing about 3¼ pounds and a silver basin of about 1¾ pounds. These were both filled with grain offerings of choice flour mixed with olive oil. ³²He also brought a gold container weighing about four ounces, which was filled with incense. ³³He brought a young bull, a ram, and a one-year-old male lamb as a burnt offering; ³⁴a male goat for a sin offering; ³⁵and two oxen, five rams, five male goats, and five one-year-old male lambs for a peace offering. This was the offering brought by Elizur son of Shedeur.

³⁶On the fifth day Shelumiel son of Zurishaddai, leader of the tribe of Simeon, presented his offering. ³⁷The offering consisted of a silver platter weighing about 3¼ pounds and a silver basin of about 1¾ pounds. These were both filled with grain offerings of choice flour mixed with olive oil. ³⁸He also brought a gold container weighing about four ounces, which was filled with incense. ³⁹He brought a young bull, a ram, and a one-year-old male lamb as a burnt offer-

ing; ⁴⁰a male goat for a sin offering; ⁴¹and two oxen, five rams, five male goats, and five one-year-old male lambs for a peace offering. This was the offering brought by Shelumiel son of Zurishaddai.

⁴²On the sixth day Eliasaph son of Deuel, leader of the tribe of Gad, presented his offering.

⁴³The offering consisted of a silver platter weighing about 3¼ pounds and a silver basin of about 1¾ pounds. These were both filled with grain offerings of choice flour mixed with olive oil. ⁴⁴He also brought a gold container weighing about four ounces, which was filled with incense. ⁴⁵He brought a young bull, a ram, and a one-year-old male lamb as a burnt offering; ⁴⁶a male goat for a sin offering; ⁴⁷and two oxen, five rams, five male goats, and five one-year-old male lambs for a peace offering. This was the offering brought by Eliasaph son of Deuel.

⁴⁸On the seventh day Elishama son of Ammihud, leader of the tribe of Ephraim, presented his offering.

⁴⁹The offering consisted of a silver platter weighing about 3¼ pounds and a silver basin of about 1¾ pounds. These were both filled with grain offerings of choice flour mixed with olive oil. ⁵⁰He also brought a gold container weighing about four ounces, which was filled with incense. ⁵¹He brought a young bull, a ram, and a one-year-old male lamb as a burnt offering; ⁵²a male goat for a sin offering; ⁵³and two oxen, five rams, five male goats, and five one-year-old male lambs for a peace offering. This was the offering brought by Elishama son of Ammihud.

⁵⁴On the eighth day Gamaliel son of Pedahzur, leader of the tribe of Manasseh, presented his offering.

⁵⁵The offering consisted of a silver platter weighing about 3¼ pounds and a silver basin of about 1¾ pounds. These were both filled with grain offerings of choice flour mixed with olive oil. ⁵⁶He also brought a gold container weighing about four ounces, which was filled with incense. ⁵⁷He brought a young bull, a ram, and a one-year-old male lamb as a burnt offering; ⁵⁸a male goat for a sin offering; ⁵⁹and two oxen, five rams, five male goats, and five one-year-old male lambs for a peace offering. This was the offering brought by Gamaliel son of Pedahzur.

⁶⁰On the ninth day Abidan son of Gideoni, leader of the tribe of Benjamin, presented his offering.

⁶¹The offering consisted of a silver platter weighing about 3¼ pounds and a silver basin of about 1¾ pounds. These were both filled with grain offerings of choice flour mixed with olive oil. ⁶²He also brought a gold container weighing about four ounces, which was filled with incense. ⁶³He brought a young bull, a ram, and a one-year-old male lamb as a burnt offering; ⁶⁴a male goat for a sin offering; ⁶⁵and two oxen, five rams, five male goats, and five one-year-old male lambs for a peace offering. This was the offering brought by Abidan son of Gideoni.

⁶⁶On the tenth day Ahiezer son of Ammishaddai, leader of the tribe of Dan, presented his offering.

⁶⁷The offering consisted of a silver platter weighing about 3¼ pounds and a silver basin of about 1¾ pounds. These were both filled with grain offerings of choice flour mixed with olive oil. ⁶⁸He also brought a gold container weighing about four ounces, which was filled with incense. ⁶⁹He brought a young bull, a ram, and a one-year-old male lamb as a burnt offering; ⁷⁰a male goat for a sin offering; ⁷¹and two oxen, five rams, five male goats, and five one-year-old male lambs for a peace offering. This was the offering brought by Ahiezer son of Ammishaddai.

⁷²On the eleventh day Pagiel son of Ocran, leader of the tribe of Asher, presented his offering.

⁷³The offering consisted of a silver platter weighing about 3¼ pounds and a silver basin of about 1¾ pounds. These were both filled with grain offerings of choice flour mixed with olive oil. ⁷⁴He also brought a gold container weighing about four ounces, which was filled with incense. ⁷⁵He brought a young bull, a ram, and a one-year-old male lamb as a burnt offering; ⁷⁶a male goat for a sin offering; ⁷⁷and two oxen, five rams, five male goats, and five one-year-old male lambs for a peace offering. This was the offering brought by Pagiel son of Ocran.

⁷⁸On the twelfth day Ahira son of Enan, leader of the tribe of Naphtali, presented his offering.

⁷⁹The offering consisted of a silver platter weighing about 3¼ pounds and a silver basin of about 1¾ pounds. These were both filled with grain offerings of choice flour mixed with olive oil. ⁸⁰He also brought a gold container weighing about four ounces, which was filled with incense. ⁸¹He brought a young bull, a ram, and a one-year-old male lamb as a burnt offering; ⁸²a male goat for a sin offering; ⁸³and two oxen, five rams, five male goats, and five one-year-old male lambs for a peace offering. This was the offering brought by Ahira son of Enan.

⁸⁴So this was the dedication offering for the altar, brought by the leaders of Israel at the time it was anointed: twelve silver platters, twelve silver basins, and twelve gold incense containers. ⁸⁵In all, the silver objects weighed about 60 pounds,* about 3¼ pounds for each platter and 1¾ pounds for each basin. ⁸⁶The weight of the donated gold came to about three pounds,* about four ounces for each of the gold containers that were filled with incense. ⁸⁷Twelve bulls, twelve rams, and twelve one-year-old male lambs were donated for the burnt offerings, along with their prescribed grain offerings. Twelve male goats were brought for the sin offerings. ⁸⁸Twenty-four young bulls, sixty rams, sixty male goats, and sixty one-year-old male lambs were donated for the peace offerings. This was the dedication offering for the altar after it was anointed.

⁸⁹Whenever Moses went into the Tabernacle to speak with the LORD, he heard the voice speaking to him from between the two cherubim above the Ark's cover—the place of atonement—that rests on the Ark of the Covenant.* The LORD spoke to him from there.

PREPARING THE LAMPS

8 The LORD said to Moses, ²"Tell Aaron that when he sets up the seven lamps in the lampstand, he is to place them so their light shines forward." ³So Aaron did this. He set up the seven lamps so they reflected their light forward, just as the LORD had commanded Moses. ⁴The entire lampstand, from its base to its decorative blossoms, was made of beaten gold. It was built according to the exact design the LORD had shown Moses.

THE LEVITES DEDICATED

⁵Then the LORD said to Moses, ⁶"Now set the Levites apart from the rest of the people of Israel and make them ceremonially clean. ⁷Do this by sprinkling them with the water of purification. And have them shave their entire body and wash their clothing. Then they will be ceremonially clean. ⁸Have them bring a young bull and a grain offering of choice flour mixed with olive oil, along with a second young bull for a sin offering. ⁹Then assemble the whole community of Israel and present the Levites at the entrance of the Tabernacle.* ¹⁰When you bring the Levites before the LORD, the people of Israel must lay their hands on them. ¹¹Aaron must

---

7:85 Hebrew *2,400 shekels* [27.4 kilograms]. 7:86 Hebrew *120 shekels* [1.4 kilograms]. 7:89 Or *Ark of the Testimony.* 8:9 Hebrew *Tent of Meeting;* also in 8:15, 19, 22, 24, 26.

present the Levites to the LORD as a special offering from the people of Israel, thus dedicating them to the LORD's service.

[12]"Next the Levites will lay their hands on the heads of the young bulls and present them to the LORD. One will be for a sin offering and the other for a burnt offering, to make atonement for the Levites. [13]Then have the Levites stand in front of Aaron and his sons, and present them as a special offering to the LORD. [14]In this way, you will set the Levites apart from the rest of the people of Israel, and the Levites will belong to me. [15]After this, they may go in and out of the Tabernacle to do their work, because you have purified them and presented them as a special offering.

[16]"Of all the people of Israel, the Levites are reserved for me. I have claimed them for myself in place of all the firstborn sons of the Israelites; I have taken the Levites as their substitutes. [17]For all the firstborn males among the people of Israel are mine, both people and animals. I set them apart for myself on the night I killed all the firstborn sons of the Egyptians. [18]Yes, I claim the Levites in place of all the firstborn sons of Israel. [19]And of all the Israelites, I have assigned the Levites to Aaron and his sons. They will serve in the Tabernacle on behalf of the Israelites and make atonement for them so no plague will strike them when they approach the sanctuary."

[20]So Moses, Aaron, and the whole community of Israel dedicated the Levites, carefully following all the LORD's instructions to Moses. [21]The Levites purified themselves and washed their clothes, and Aaron presented them to the LORD as a special offering. He then performed the rite of atonement over them to purify them. [22]From then on the Levites went into the Tabernacle to perform their duties, helping Aaron and his sons. So they carried out all the commands that the LORD gave Moses concerning the Levites.

[23]The LORD also instructed Moses, [24]"This is the rule the Levites must follow: They must begin serving in the Tabernacle at the age of twenty-five, [25]and they must retire at the age of fifty. [26]After retirement they may assist their fellow Levites by performing guard duty at the Tabernacle, but they may not officiate in the service. This is how you will assign duties to the Levites."

THE SECOND PASSOVER

9 The LORD gave these instructions to Moses in early spring,* during the second year after Israel's departure from Egypt, while he and the rest of the Israelites were in the wilderness of Sinai: [2]"Tell the Israelites to celebrate the Passover at the proper time, [3]at twilight on the appointed day in early spring.* Be sure to follow all my laws and regulations concerning this celebration."

[4]So Moses told the people to celebrate the Passover [5]in the wilderness of Sinai as twilight fell on the appointed day.* And they celebrated the festival there, just as the LORD had commanded Moses. [6]But some of the men had been ceremonially defiled by touching a dead person, so they could not offer their Passover lambs that day. So they came to Moses and Aaron that day [7]and said, "We have become ceremonially unclean by touching a dead person. But why should we be excluded from presenting the LORD's offering at the proper time with the rest of the Israelites?"

[8]Moses answered, "Wait here until I have received instructions for you from the LORD."

[9]This was the LORD's reply: [10]"Say to the Israelites: 'If any of the people now or in future generations are ceremonially unclean at Passover time because of touching a dead body, or if they are on a journey and cannot be present at the ceremony, they may still celebrate the LORD's Passover. [11]They must offer the Passover sacrifice one month later,* at twilight on the appointed day. They must eat

9:1 Hebrew *in the first month.* This month of the Hebrew lunar calendar usually occurs in March and April. 9:3 Hebrew *on the fourteenth day of the first month.* This day of the Hebrew lunar calendar occurs in late March or early April. 9:5 Hebrew *on the fourteenth day of the first month;* see note on 9:3. 9:11 Hebrew *on the fourteenth day of the second month.* This day of the Hebrew lunar calendar occurs in late April or early May.

the lamb at that time with bitter herbs and bread made without yeast. [12]They must not leave any of the lamb until the next morning, and they must not break any of its bones. They must follow all the normal regulations concerning the Passover.

[13]"'But those who are ceremonially clean and not away on a trip, yet still refuse to celebrate the Passover at the regular time, will be cut off from the community of Israel for failing to present the LORD's offering at the proper time. They will suffer the consequences of their guilt. [14]And if foreigners living among you want to celebrate the Passover to the LORD, they must follow these same laws and regulations. The same laws apply both to you and to the foreigners living among you.'"

THE FIERY CLOUD

[15]The Tabernacle was set up, and on that day the cloud covered it.* Then from evening until morning the cloud over the Tabernacle appeared to be a pillar of fire. [16]This was the regular pattern—at night the cloud changed to the appearance of fire. [17]When the cloud lifted from over the sacred tent, the people of Israel followed it. And wherever the cloud settled, the people of Israel camped. [18]In this way, they traveled at the LORD's command and stopped wherever he told them to. Then they remained where they were as long as the cloud stayed over the Tabernacle. [19]If the cloud remained over the Tabernacle for a long time, the Israelites stayed for a long time, just as the LORD commanded. [20]Sometimes the cloud would stay over the Tabernacle for only a few days, so the people would stay for only a few days. Then at the LORD's command they would break camp. [21]Sometimes the cloud stayed only overnight and moved on the next morning. But day or night, when the cloud lifted, the people broke camp and followed. [22]Whether the cloud stayed above the Tabernacle for two days, a month, or a year, the

people of Israel stayed in camp and did not move on. But as soon as it lifted, they broke camp and moved on. [23]So they camped or traveled at the LORD's command, and they did whatever the LORD told them through Moses.

THE SILVER TRUMPETS

10 Now the LORD said to Moses, [2]"Make two trumpets of beaten silver to be used for summoning the people to assemble and for signaling the breaking of camp. [3]When both trumpets are blown, the people will know that they are to gather before you at the entrance of the Tabernacle.* [4]But if only one is blown, then only the leaders of the tribes of Israel will come to you.

[5]"When you sound the signal to move on, the tribes on the east side of the Tabernacle will break camp and move forward. [6]When you sound the signal a second time, the tribes on the south will follow. You must sound short blasts to signal moving on. [7]But when you call the people to an assembly, blow the trumpets using a different signal. [8]Only the priests, Aaron's descendants, are allowed to blow the trumpets. This is a permanent law to be followed from generation to generation.

[9]"When you arrive in your own land and go to war against your enemies, you must sound the alarm with these trumpets so the LORD your God will remember you and rescue you from your enemies. [10]Blow the trumpets in times of gladness, too, sounding them at your annual festivals and at the beginning of each month to rejoice over your burnt offerings and peace offerings. The trumpets will remind the LORD your God of his covenant with you. I am the LORD your God."

THE ISRAELITES LEAVE SINAI

[11]One day in midspring,* during the second year after Israel's departure from Egypt, the cloud lifted from the Tabernacle of the Covenant.* [12]So the Israelites set out from the wilderness of Sinai and traveled on in

---

9:15 Hebrew *covered the Tabernacle, the Tent of the Testimony.* 10:3 Hebrew *Tent of Meeting.* 10:11a Hebrew *On the twentieth day of the second month.* This day of the Hebrew lunar calendar occurs in late April or early May. 10:11b Or *Tabernacle of the Testimony.*

My Daily Worship

— *February 5* —

THEY'RE PLAYING OUR SONG

NUMBERS 8:1–10:36

Blow the trumpets in times of gladness, too, sounding them at your annual festivals and at the beginning of each month to rejoice over your burnt offerings and peace offerings. The trumpets will remind the LORD your God of his covenant with you. I am the LORD your God (10:10).

[i reflect]

In spring 1863, the Confederate and Union armies confronted each other at Spotsylvania, Virginia, on the banks of the Rappanhannock River. One night, the two army bands began to play music.

First, the Union band struck up with its melodies, such as "The Star Spangled Banner," "Hail Columbia," and other northern favorites. From across the river came the sounds of the Confederate tunes "Dixie" and "Bonnie Blue Flag." At the conclusion of their particular songs, the armies would whoop and cheer loudly.

It went on into the night, until one band began playing the sweet plaintive notes of "Home Sweet Home." Soon the other band joined in, and together they played. At the conclusion, both sides erupted in cheers. A chord had been struck which caused both sides to play in unison.

Music has the amazing ability to rouse an army, to inspire an emotion, to touch a memory, to unify a people. God knew this when he ordered the use of trumpets as the signal for times of battle and times of gladness. Centuries later, the psalm writer reminded the people, "Sound the trumpet for a sacred feast. . . . For this is required by the laws of Israel; it is a law of the God of Jacob" (Psalm 81:3–4).

But note, too, that the rich triumphant blasts of the trumpet would also serve as a reminder to the Lord of his covenant with the people. Incredible! Music served as a reminder *to God* of his relationship and his promises with his people.

Take a bit of worship with you as you commute to work, work around the house, or do errands. Plug in a worship-oriented Christian CD, or tune into a Christian radio station, and let God's gift of music fill you and refresh you—and remind you of his promises!

[i pray]

I want to thank you, Lord, for the beautiful sounds that emanate from those who praise you
with lips pressed against mouthpieces and fingers pounding on keys or plucking strings.
In the cacophony of sounds my spirit is motivated to sing with joy and strength.
It is all because of the gifts you've given, and I thank you.

[i respond]

Try your hand at writing a few lines of verse that will remind you of God's rich promises and blessings to you. Let this be a work in progress, adding lines as God's blessings are shown to you.

stages until the cloud stopped in the wilderness of Paran.

¹³When the time to move arrived, the LORD gave the order through Moses. ¹⁴The tribes that camped with Judah headed the march with their banner, under the leadership of Nahshon son of Amminadab. ¹⁵The tribe of Issachar was led by Nethanel son of Zuar. ¹⁶The tribe of Zebulun was led by Eliab son of Helon.

¹⁷Then the Tabernacle was taken down, and the Gershonite and Merarite divisions of the Levites were next in the line of march, carrying the Tabernacle with them. ¹⁸Then the tribes that camped with Reuben set out with their banner, under the leadership of Elizur son of Shedeur. ¹⁹The tribe of Simeon was led by Shelumiel son of Zurishaddai. ²⁰The tribe of Gad was led by Eliasaph son of Deuel.

²¹Next came the Kohathite division of the Levites, carrying the sacred objects from the Tabernacle. When they arrived at the next camp, the Tabernacle would already be set up at its new location. ²²Then the tribes that camped with Ephraim set out with their banner, under the leadership of Elishama son of Ammihud. ²³The tribe of Manasseh was led by Gamaliel son of Pedahzur. ²⁴The tribe of Benjamin was led by Abidan son of Gideoni.

²⁵Last of all, the tribes that camped with Dan set out under their banner. They served as the rear guard for all the tribal camps. The tribe of Dan headed this group, under the leadership of Ahiezer son of Ammishaddai. ²⁶The tribe of Asher was led by Pagiel son of Ocran. ²⁷The tribe of Naphtali was led by Ahira son of Enan.

²⁸This was the order in which the tribes marched, division by division.

²⁹One day Moses said to his brother-in-law, Hobab son of Reuel the Midianite, "We are on our way to the Promised Land. Come with us and we will treat you well, for the LORD has given wonderful promises to Israel!"

³⁰But Hobab replied, "No, I will not go. I must return to my own land and family."

³¹"Please don't leave us," Moses pleaded. "You know the places in the wilderness where we should camp. ³²Come, be our guide and we will share with you all the good things that the LORD does for us."

³³They marched for three days after leaving the mountain of the LORD, with the Ark of the LORD's covenant moving ahead of them to show them where to stop and rest. ³⁴As they moved on each day, the cloud of the LORD hovered over them. ³⁵And whenever the Ark set out, Moses would cry, "Arise, O LORD, and let your enemies be scattered! Let them flee before you!" ³⁶And when the Ark was set down, he would say, "Return, O LORD, to the countless thousands of Israel!"

THE PEOPLE COMPLAIN TO MOSES

11 The people soon began to complain to the LORD about their hardships; and when the LORD heard them, his anger blazed against them. Fire from the LORD raged among them and destroyed the outskirts of the camp. ²The people screamed to Moses for help; and when he prayed to the LORD, the fire stopped. ³After that, the area was known as Taberah—"the place of burning"—because fire from the LORD had burned among them there.

⁴Then the foreign rabble who were traveling with the Israelites began to crave the good things of Egypt, and the people of Israel also began to complain. "Oh, for some meat!" they exclaimed. ⁵"We remember all the fish we used to eat for free in Egypt. And we had all the cucumbers, melons, leeks, onions, and garlic that we wanted. ⁶But now our appetites are gone, and day after day we have nothing to eat but this manna!"

⁷The manna looked like small coriander seeds, pale yellow in color.* ⁸The people gathered it from the ground and made flour by grinding it with hand mills or pounding it in mortars. Then they boiled it in a pot and made it into flat cakes. These cakes tasted like they had been cooked in olive oil. ⁹The manna

11:7 Hebrew *the color of gum resin.*

My Daily Worship

— *February 6* —

No Power Shortage Here!

NUMBERS 11:1–14:45

Then the LORD said to Moses, "Is there any limit to my power?
Now you will see whether or not my word comes true!" (11:23).

[i reflect]

Before Lloyd John Ogilvie was appointed chaplain of the United States Senate, he served as the senior minister at First Presbyterian Church of Hollywood, California. Wearing a royal blue liturgical robe with red piping, he stood before the congregation of that historic church each Sunday prior to the start of the service.

Smiling yet reverent, he called the people to worship by referencing the power of God available to them. With his deep signature bass voice, Dr. Ogilvie would say, "The living Lord is here to meet you at the point of your deepest need. People of God, come. Let us worship him!" For Lloyd Ogilvie, every Sunday was Easter Sunday. The power that emptied the tomb of its weekend tenant could be expected to accomplish great and mighty things.

Similarly, the Lord announced to Moses that there was no power shortage in the wilderness. "Is there any limit to my power?" The Lord knew the people were beginning to doubt his ability to care for them en route to the Promised Land. Time and time again he demonstrated the degree to which he was in control. It saddened him to see the children of Israel act like children, throwing tantrums instead of allowing their experience of God's power to motivate their desire for him.

Yet, don't we do the same when we resort to complaining instead of praising, worrying instead of depending, shrinking in fear instead of going boldly in God's power? Like the Israelites, we need to pause and remember how God has demonstrated—time and time again—his power in our lives.

Look around you and then inside—where do you see God at work, using his awesome power to change lives? Whisper your acknowledgment and gratitude to the One who is limitless in power.

[i pray]

Awesome God, I thank you for the way you display your power in my life. Time and time again you invade circumstances that seem impenetrable. As I contemplate the powerful way you provide for my needs, I can't help but lift my heart in worship.

[i respond]

Jot down on a sheet of paper ways your current situation is like the wilderness. Then describe ways God has eased the challenge of hard times by making himself available to you. What has God provided for you that would be equivalent to manna and quail?

came down on the camp with the dew during the night.

[10]Moses heard all the families standing in front of their tents weeping, and the LORD became extremely angry. Moses was also very aggravated. [11]And Moses said to the LORD, "Why are you treating me, your servant, so miserably? What did I do to deserve the burden of a people like this? [12]Are they my children? Am I their father? Is that why you have told me to carry them in my arms—like a nurse carries a baby—to the land you swore to give their ancestors? [13]Where am I supposed to get meat for all these people? They keep complaining and saying, 'Give us meat!' [14]I can't carry all these people by myself! The load is far too heavy! [15]I'd rather you killed me than treat me like this. Please spare me this misery!"

MOSES CHOOSES SEVENTY LEADERS

[16]Then the LORD said to Moses, "Summon before me seventy of the leaders of Israel. Bring them to the Tabernacle* to stand there with you. [17]I will come down and talk to you there. I will take some of the Spirit that is upon you, and I will put the Spirit upon them also. They will bear the burden of the people along with you, so you will not have to carry it alone.

[18]"And tell the people to purify themselves, for tomorrow they will have meat to eat. Tell them, 'The LORD has heard your whining and complaints: "If only we had meat to eat! Surely we were better off in Egypt!" Now the LORD will give you meat, and you will have to eat it. [19]And it won't be for just a day or two, or for five or ten or even twenty. [20]You will eat it for a whole month until you gag and are sick of it. For you have rejected the LORD, who is here among you, and you have complained to him, "Why did we ever leave Egypt?" ' "

[21]But Moses said, "There are 600,000 foot soldiers here with me, and yet you promise them meat for a whole month! [22]Even if we butchered all our flocks and herds, would that satisfy them? Even if we caught all the fish in the sea, would that be enough?"

[23]Then the LORD said to Moses, "Is there any limit to my power? Now you will see whether or not my word comes true!"

[24]So Moses went out and reported the LORD's words to the people. Then he gathered the seventy leaders and stationed them around the Tabernacle.* [25]And the LORD came down in the cloud and spoke to Moses. He took some of the Spirit that was upon Moses and put it upon the seventy leaders. They prophesied as the Spirit rested upon them, but that was the only time this happened.

[26]Two men, Eldad and Medad, were still in the camp when the Spirit rested upon them. They were listed among the leaders but had not gone out to the Tabernacle, so they prophesied there in the camp. [27]A young man ran and reported to Moses, "Eldad and Medad are prophesying in the camp!" [28]Joshua son of Nun, who had been Moses' personal assistant since his youth, protested, "Moses, my master, make them stop!"

[29]But Moses replied, "Are you jealous for my sake? I wish that all the LORD's people were prophets, and that the LORD would put his Spirit upon them all!" [30]Then Moses returned to the camp with the leaders of Israel.

THE LORD SENDS QUAIL

[31]Now the LORD sent a wind that brought quail from the sea and let them fall into the camp and all around it! For many miles in every direction from the camp there were quail flying about three feet above the ground.* [32]So the people went out and caught quail all that day and throughout the night and all the next day, too. No one gathered less than fifty bushels*! They spread the quail out all over the camp. [33]But while they were still eating the meat, the anger of the LORD blazed against the people, and he caused a severe plague to break out among them. [34]So that

11:16 Hebrew *Tent of Meeting.* 11:24 Hebrew *the tent;* also in 11:26. 11:31 Or *there were quail 3 feet* [2 cubits or 90 centimeters] *deep on the ground.* 11:32 Hebrew *10 homers* [1.8 kiloliters].

place was called Kibroth-hattaavah "the graves of craving"—because they buried the people there who had craved meat from Egypt. [35]From there the Israelites traveled to Hazeroth, where they stayed for some time.

THE COMPLAINTS OF MIRIAM AND AARON

12 While they were at Hazeroth, Miriam and Aaron criticized Moses because he had married a Cushite woman. [2]They said, "Has the LORD spoken only through Moses? Hasn't he spoken through us, too?" But the LORD heard them.

[3]Now Moses was more humble than any other person on earth. [4]So immediately the LORD called to Moses, Aaron, and Miriam and said, "Go out to the Tabernacle,* all three of you!" And the three of them went out. [5]Then the LORD descended in the pillar of cloud and stood at the entrance of the Tabernacle.* "Aaron and Miriam!" he called, and they stepped forward. [6]And the LORD said to them, "Now listen to me! Even with prophets, I the LORD communicate by visions and dreams. [7]But that is not how I communicate with my servant Moses. He is entrusted with my entire house. [8]I speak to him face to face, directly and not in riddles! He sees the LORD as he is. Should you not be afraid to criticize him?"

[9]The LORD was furious with them, and he departed. [10]As the cloud moved from above the Tabernacle, Miriam suddenly became white as snow with leprosy.* When Aaron saw what had happened, [11]he cried out to Moses, "Oh, my lord! Please don't punish us for this sin we have so foolishly committed. [12]Don't let her be like a stillborn baby, already decayed at birth."

[13]So Moses cried out to the LORD, "Heal her, O God, I beg you!"

[14]And the LORD said to Moses, "If her father had spit in her face, wouldn't she have been defiled for seven days? Banish her from the camp for seven days, and after that she may return."

[15]So Miriam was excluded from the camp for seven days, and the people waited until she was brought back before they traveled again. [16]Then they left Hazeroth and camped in the wilderness of Paran.

TWELVE SCOUTS EXPLORE CANAAN

13 The LORD now said to Moses, [2]"Send men to explore the land of Canaan, the land I am giving to Israel. Send one leader from each of the twelve ancestral tribes." [3]So Moses did as the LORD commanded him. He sent out twelve men, all tribal leaders of Israel, from their camp in the wilderness of Paran. [4]These were the tribes and the names of the leaders:

Tribe	Leader
Reuben	Shammua son of Zaccur
[5]Simeon	Shaphat son of Hori
[6]Judah	Caleb son of Jephunneh
[7]Issachar	Igal son of Joseph
[8]Ephraim	Hoshea son of Nun
[9]Benjamin	Palti son of Raphu
[10]Zebulun	Gaddiel son of Sodi
[11]Manasseh son of Joseph	Gaddi son of Susi
[12]Dan	Ammiel son of Gemalli
[13]Asher	Sethur son of Michael
[14]Naphtali	Nahbi son of Vophsi
[15]Gad	Geuel son of Maki

[16]These are the names of the men Moses sent to explore the land. By this time Moses had changed Hoshea's name to Joshua.*

[17]Moses gave the men these instructions as he sent them out to explore the land: "Go northward through the Negev into the hill country. [18]See what the land is like and find out whether the people living there are strong or weak, few or many. [19]What kind of land do they live in? Is it good or bad? Do their towns have walls or are they unprotected? [20]How is the soil? Is it fertile or poor? Are there many trees? Enter the land boldly, and bring back samples of the crops you see." (It happened to be the season for harvesting the first ripe grapes.)

12:4 Hebrew *Tent of Meeting.* 12:5 Hebrew *the tent;* also in 12:10. 12:10 Or *with a contagious skin disease.* The Hebrew word used here can describe various skin diseases. 13:16 *Hoshea* (see 13:8) means "salvation"; *Joshua* means "The LORD is salvation."

²¹So they went up and explored the land from the wilderness of Zin as far as Rehob, near Lebo-hamath. ²²Going northward, they passed first through the Negev and arrived at Hebron, where Ahiman, Sheshai, and Talmai—all descendants of Anak—lived. (The ancient town of Hebron was founded seven years before the Egyptian city of Zoan.) ²³When they came to what is now known as the valley of Eshcol, they cut down a cluster of grapes so large that it took two of them to carry it on a pole between them! They also took samples of the pomegranates and figs. ²⁴At that time the Israelites renamed the valley Eshcol—"cluster"—because of the cluster of grapes they had cut there.

> You have made us for yourself,
> and our heart is restless
> until it rests in you.
>
> AUGUSTINE

THE SCOUTING REPORT

²⁵After exploring the land for forty days, the men returned ²⁶to Moses, Aaron, and the people of Israel at Kadesh in the wilderness of Paran. They reported to the whole community what they had seen and showed them the fruit they had taken from the land. ²⁷This was their report to Moses: "We arrived in the land you sent us to see, and it is indeed a magnificent country—a land flowing with milk and honey. Here is some of its fruit as proof. ²⁸But the people living there are powerful, and their cities and towns are fortified and very large. We also saw the descendants of Anak who are living there! ²⁹The Amalekites live in the Negev, and the Hittites, Jebusites, and Amorites live in the hill country. The Canaanites live along the coast of the Mediterranean Sea* and along the Jordan Valley."

³⁰But Caleb tried to encourage the people as they stood before Moses. "Let's go at once to take the land," he said. "We can certainly conquer it!"

³¹But the other men who had explored the land with him answered, "We can't go up against them! They are stronger than we are!" ³²So they spread discouraging reports about the land among the Israelites: "The land we explored will swallow up any who go to live there. All the people we saw were huge. ³³We even saw giants* there, the descendants of Anak. We felt like grasshoppers next to them, and that's what we looked like to them!"

THE PEOPLE REBEL

14 Then all the people began weeping aloud, and they cried all night. ²Their voices rose in a great chorus of complaint against Moses and Aaron. "We wish we had died in Egypt, or even here in the wilderness!" they wailed. ³"Why is the LORD taking us to this country only to have us die in battle? Our wives and little ones will be carried off as slaves! Let's get out of here and return to Egypt!" ⁴Then they plotted among themselves, "Let's choose a leader and go back to Egypt!"

⁵Then Moses and Aaron fell face down on the ground before the people of Israel. ⁶Two of the men who had explored the land, Joshua son of Nun and Caleb son of Jephunneh, tore their clothing. ⁷They said to the community of Israel, "The land we explored is a wonderful land! ⁸And if the LORD is pleased with us, he will bring us safely into that land and give it to us. It is a rich land flowing with milk and honey, and he will give it to us! ⁹Do not rebel against the LORD, and don't be afraid of the people of the land. They are only helpless prey to us! They have no protection, but the LORD is with us! Don't be afraid of them!"

¹⁰But the whole community began to talk about stoning Joshua and Caleb. Then the

13:29 Hebrew *the sea*.   13:33 Hebrew *nephilim*.

glorious presence of the LORD appeared to all the Israelites from above the Tabernacle.* [11]And the LORD said to Moses, "How long will these people reject me? Will they never believe me, even after all the miraculous signs I have done among them? [12]I will disown them and destroy them with a plague. Then I will make you into a nation far greater and mightier than they are!"

Moses Intercedes for the People

[13]"But what will the Egyptians think when they hear about it?" Moses pleaded with the LORD. "They know full well the power you displayed in rescuing these people from Egypt. [14]They will tell this to the inhabitants of this land, who are well aware that you are with this people. They know, LORD, that you have appeared in full view of your people in the pillar of cloud that hovers over them. They know that you go before them in the pillar of cloud by day and the pillar of fire by night. [15]Now if you slaughter all these people, the nations that have heard of your fame will say, [16]'The LORD was not able to bring them into the land he swore to give them, so he killed them in the wilderness.'

[17]"Please, Lord, prove that your power is as great as you have claimed it to be. For you said, [18]'The LORD is slow to anger and rich in unfailing love, forgiving every kind of sin and rebellion. Even so he does not leave sin unpunished, but he punishes the children for the sins of their parents to the third and fourth generations.' [19]Please pardon the sins of this people because of your magnificent, unfailing love, just as you have forgiven them ever since they left Egypt."

[20]Then the LORD said, "I will pardon them as you have requested. [21]But as surely as I live, and as surely as the earth is filled with the LORD's glory, [22]not one of these people will ever enter that land. They have seen my glorious presence and the miraculous signs I performed both in Egypt and in the wilderness, but again and again they tested me by refusing to listen. [23]They will never even see the land I swore to give their ancestors. None of those who have treated me with contempt will enter it. [24]But my servant Caleb is different from the others. He has remained loyal to me, and I will bring him into the land he explored. His descendants will receive their full share of that land. [25]Now turn around and don't go on toward the land where the Amalekites and Canaanites live. Tomorrow you must set out for the wilderness in the direction of the Red Sea.*"

The Lord Punishes the Israelites

[26]Then the LORD said to Moses and Aaron, [27]"How long will this wicked nation complain about me? I have heard everything the Israelites have been saying. [28]Now tell them this: 'As surely as I live, I will do to you the very things I heard you say. I, the LORD, have spoken! [29]You will all die here in this wilderness! Because you complained against me, none of you who are twenty years old or older and were counted in the census [30]will enter the land I swore to give you. The only exceptions will be Caleb son of Jephunneh and Joshua son of Nun.

[31]" 'You said your children would be taken captive. Well, I will bring them safely into the land, and they will enjoy what you have despised. [32]But as for you, your dead bodies will fall in this wilderness. [33]And your children will be like shepherds, wandering in the wilderness forty years. In this way, they will pay for your faithlessness, until the last of you lies dead in the wilderness.

[34]" 'Because the men who explored the land were there for forty days, you must wander in the wilderness for forty years—a year for each day, suffering the consequences of your sins. You will discover what it is like to have me for an enemy.' [35]I, the LORD, have spoken! I will do these things to every member of the community who has conspired against me. They will all die here in this wilderness!"

14:10 Hebrew *Tent of Meeting.* **14:25** Hebrew *sea of reeds.*

³⁶Then the ten scouts who had incited the rebellion against the LORD by spreading discouraging reports about the land ³⁷were struck dead with a plague before the LORD. ³⁸Of the twelve who had explored the land, only Joshua and Caleb remained alive.

³⁹When Moses reported the LORD's words to the Israelites, there was much sorrow among the people. ⁴⁰So they got up early the next morning and set out for the hill country of Canaan. "Let's go," they said. "We realize that we have sinned, but now we are ready to enter the land the LORD has promised us."

⁴¹But Moses said, "Why are you now disobeying the LORD's orders to return to the wilderness? It won't work. ⁴²Do not go into the land now. You will only be crushed by your enemies because the LORD is not with you. ⁴³When you face the Amalekites and Canaanites in battle, you will be slaughtered. The LORD will abandon you because you have abandoned the LORD."

⁴⁴But the people pushed ahead toward the hill country of Canaan, despite the fact that neither Moses nor the Ark of the LORD's covenant left the camp. ⁴⁵Then the Amalekites and the Canaanites who lived in those hills came down and attacked them and chased them as far as Hormah.

Laws concerning Offerings

15 The LORD told Moses to give these instructions to the people of Israel: ²"When you finally settle in the land I am going to give you, ³and you want to please the LORD with a burnt offering or any other offering given by fire, the sacrifice must be an animal from your flocks of sheep and goats or from your herds of cattle. When it is an ordinary burnt offering, a sacrifice to fulfill a vow, a freewill offering, or a special sacrifice at any of the annual festivals, ⁴whoever brings it must also give to the LORD a grain offering of two quarts* of choice flour mixed with one quart* of olive oil. ⁵For each lamb offered as a whole burnt offering, you must also present one quart of wine for a drink offering.

⁶"If the sacrifice is a ram, give three quarts* of choice flour mixed with two and a half pints* of olive oil, ⁷and give two and a half pints of wine for a drink offering. This sacrifice will be very pleasing to the LORD.

⁸"When you present a young bull as a burnt offering or a sacrifice in fulfillment of a special vow or as a peace offering to the LORD, ⁹then the grain offering accompanying it must include five quarts* of choice flour mixed with two quarts* of olive oil, ¹⁰plus two quarts of wine for the drink offering. This will be an offering made by fire, very pleasing to the LORD.

¹¹"These are the instructions for what is to accompany each sacrificial bull, ram, lamb, or young goat. ¹²Each of you must do this with each offering you present. ¹³If you native Israelites want to present an offering by fire that is pleasing to the LORD, you must follow all these instructions. ¹⁴And if any foreigners living among you want to present an offering by fire, pleasing to the LORD, they must follow the same procedures. ¹⁵Native Israelites and foreigners are the same before the LORD and are subject to the same laws. This is a permanent law for you. ¹⁶The same instructions and regulations will apply both to you and to the foreigners living among you."

¹⁷The LORD also said to Moses at this time, ¹⁸"Give the people of Israel the following instructions: When you arrive in the land where I am taking you, ¹⁹you will eat from the crops that grow there. But you must set some aside as a gift to the LORD. ²⁰Present a cake from the first of the flour you grind and set it aside as a gift, as you do with the first grain from the threshing floor. ²¹Throughout the generations to come, you are to present this offering to the LORD each year from the first of your ground flour.

²²"But suppose some of you unintentionally

15:4a Hebrew *1/10 of an ephah* [2 liters]. **15:4b** Hebrew *1/4 of a hin* [1 liter]; also in 15:5. **15:6a** Hebrew *2/10 of an ephah* [3.6 liters]. **15:6b** Hebrew *1/3 of a hin* [1.3 liters]; also in 15:7. **15:9a** Hebrew *3/10 of an ephah* [5.4 liters]. **15:9b** Hebrew *1/2 of a hin* [2 liters]; also in 15:10.

fail to carry out all these commands that the LORD has given you through Moses. ²³And suppose some of your descendants in the future fail to do everything the LORD has commanded through Moses. ²⁴If the mistake was done unintentionally, and the community was unaware of it, the whole community must present a young bull for a burnt offering. It will be pleasing to the LORD, and it must be offered along with the prescribed grain offering and drink offering and with one male goat for a sin offering. ²⁵With it the priest will make atonement for the whole community of Israel, and they will be forgiven. For it was an unintentional sin, and they have corrected it with their offering given to the LORD by fire and by their sin offering. ²⁶The whole community of Israel will be forgiven, including the foreigners living among you, for the entire population was involved in the sin.

²⁷"If the unintentional sin is committed by an individual, the guilty person must bring a one-year-old female goat for a sin offering. ²⁸The priest will make atonement for the guilty person before the LORD, and that person will be forgiven. ²⁹This same law applies both to native Israelites and the foreigners living among you.

³⁰"But those who brazenly violate the LORD's will, whether native Israelites or foreigners, blaspheme the LORD, and they must be cut off from the community. ³¹Since they have treated the LORD's word with contempt and deliberately disobeyed his commands, they must be completely cut off and suffer the consequences of their guilt."

PENALTY FOR BREAKING THE SABBATH

³²One day while the people of Israel were in the wilderness, they caught a man gathering wood on the Sabbath day. ³³He was apprehended and taken before Moses, Aaron, and the rest of the community. ³⁴They held him in custody because they did not know what to do with him. ³⁵Then the LORD said to Moses, "The man must be put to death! The whole community must stone him outside the camp." ³⁶So the whole community took the man outside the camp and stoned him to death, just as the LORD had commanded Moses.

TASSELS ON CLOTHING

³⁷And the LORD said to Moses, ³⁸"Say to the people of Israel: 'Throughout the generations to come you must make tassels for the hems of your clothing and attach the tassels at each corner with a blue cord. ³⁹The tassels will remind you of the commands of the LORD, and that you are to obey his commands instead of following your own desires and going your own ways, as you are prone to do. ⁴⁰The tassels will help you remember that you must obey all my commands and be holy to your God. ⁴¹I am the LORD your God who brought you out of the land of Egypt that I might be your God. I am the LORD your God!' "

KORAH'S REBELLION

16 One day Korah son of Izhar, a descendant of Kohath son of Levi, conspired with Dathan and Abiram, the sons of Eliab, and On son of Peleth, from the tribe of Reuben. ²They incited a rebellion against Moses, involving 250 other prominent leaders, all members of the assembly. ³They went to Moses and Aaron and said, "You have gone too far! Everyone in Israel has been set apart by the LORD, and he is with all of us. What right do you have to act as though you are greater than anyone else among all these people of the LORD?"

⁴When Moses heard what they were saying, he threw himself down with his face to the ground. ⁵Then he said to Korah and his followers, "Tomorrow morning the LORD will show us who belongs to him and who is holy. The LORD will allow those who are chosen to enter his holy presence. ⁶You, Korah, and all your followers must do this: Take incense burners, ⁷and burn incense in them tomorrow before the LORD. Then we will see whom the LORD chooses as his holy one. You Levites are the ones who have gone too far!"

[8]Then Moses spoke again to Korah: "Now listen, you Levites! [9]Does it seem a small thing to you that the God of Israel has chosen you from among all the people of Israel to be near him as you serve in the LORD's Tabernacle and to stand before the people to minister to them? [10]He has given this special ministry only to you and your fellow Levites, but now you are demanding the priesthood as well! [11]The one you are really revolting against is the LORD! And who is Aaron that you are complaining about him?"

[12]Then Moses summoned Dathan and Abiram, the sons of Eliab, but they replied, "We refuse to come! [13]Isn't it enough that you brought us out of Egypt, a land flowing with milk and honey, to kill us here in this wilderness, and that you now treat us like your subjects? [14]What's more, you haven't brought us into the land flowing with milk and honey or given us an inheritance of fields and vineyards. Are you trying to fool us? We will not come."

[15]Then Moses became very angry and said to the LORD, "Do not accept their offerings! I have not taken so much as a donkey from them, and I have never hurt a single one of them." [16]And Moses said to Korah, "Come here tomorrow and present yourself before the LORD with all your followers. Aaron will also be here. [17]Be sure that each of your 250 followers brings an incense burner with incense on it, so you can present them before the LORD. Aaron will also bring his incense burner."

[18]So these men came with their incense burners, placed burning coals and incense on them, and stood at the entrance of the Tabernacle* with Moses and Aaron. [19]Meanwhile, Korah had stirred up the entire community against Moses and Aaron, and they all assembled at the Tabernacle entrance. Then the glorious presence of the LORD appeared to the whole community, [20]and the LORD said to Moses and Aaron, [21]"Get away from these people so that I may instantly destroy them!"

[22]But Moses and Aaron fell face down on the ground. "O God, the God and source of all life," they pleaded. "Must you be angry with all the people when only one man sins?"

[23]And the LORD said to Moses, [24]"Then tell all the people to get away from the tents of Korah, Dathan, and Abiram."

[25]So Moses got up and rushed over to the tents of Dathan and Abiram, followed closely by the Israelite leaders. [26]"Quick!" he told the people. "Get away from the tents of these wicked men, and don't touch anything that belongs to them. If you do, you will be destroyed for their sins." [27]So all the people stood back from the tents of Korah, Dathan, and Abiram. Then Dathan and Abiram came out and stood at the entrances of their tents with their wives and children and little ones.

[28]And Moses said, "By this you will know that the LORD has sent me to do all these things that I have done—for I have not done them on my own. [29]If these men die a natural death, then the LORD has not sent me. [30]But if the LORD performs a miracle and the ground opens up and swallows them and all their belongings, and they go down alive into the grave, then you will know that these men have despised the LORD."

[31]He had hardly finished speaking the words when the ground suddenly split open beneath them. [32]The earth opened up and swallowed the men, along with their households and the followers who were standing with them, and everything they owned. [33]So they went down alive into the grave, along with their belongings. The earth closed over them, and they all vanished. [34]All of the people of Israel fled as they heard their screams, fearing that the earth would swallow them, too. [35]Then fire blazed forth from the LORD and burned up the 250 men who were offering incense.

[36]And the LORD said to Moses, [37]"Tell Eleazar son of Aaron the priest to pull all the incense burners from the fire, for they are holy. Also tell him to scatter the burning incense [38]from the burners of these men who have sinned

16:18 Hebrew *Tent of Meeting;* also in 16:19, 42, 43, 50.

My Daily Worship

— February 7 —

WHOSE SERVICE IS IT, ANYWAY?

NUMBERS 15:1–18:32

*The tassels will remind you of the commands of the LORD,
and that you are to obey his commands instead of following your own desires
and going your own ways, as you are prone to do (15:39).*

[i reflect]

How often do we leave a time of worship, whether corporate or personal, thinking about what's next on the agenda, or what someone said the day before that has left a lingering hurt, or even how that particular devotion or sermon just left us flat? Too often, we tend to rush through a time of worship, forgetting not only *who* we're worshiping, but *whose* worship it is. Worship almost becomes a time about "me" rather than God.

In ordering the priests to wear tassels on their clothing, God gave them a physical reminder that they were not to seek after their own desires, but rather to seek him and obey him. The tassels were a constant admonition of what worship was truly all about.

Former Archbishop of Canterbury William Temple said worship is:
- to quicken the conscience by the holiness of God;
- to feed the mind with the truth of God;
- to purge the imagination by the beauty of God;
- to open the heart to the love of God;
- to devote the will to the purpose of God.

In other words, worship is a fully engaged activity—one that should focus on God rather than our own desires as we are prone to do.

The word *worship* is an abbreviation for "worth-ship." Thus, worship is the act of *ascribing worth to God,* declaring his glory, honor, majesty, holiness, and *worth*iness. That's why we worship: to declare the goodness of our God. Worship is first and foremost for God's pleasure—it's what we offer up to him. That's why we call it a worship *service.*

The Israelites were commanded to wear tassels as a reminder that they belonged to God by covenant and were to place his honor above all else, including their own desires and preferences. It's not a bad idea. Today, choose a symbol you can adopt as a reminder of the One you worship.

[i pray]

*Father, forgive me for thinking worship is about me and what I want, instead of you
and what pleases you. Help me think more in terms of giving "my utmost
for your highest" than just getting blessings for myself.*

[i respond]

Re-read William Temple's definition of worship. Evaluate your own time spent in worship. How have you specifically engaged those faculties in your adoration of our awesome God? Work through each one as you spend time with God today.

at the cost of their lives. He must then hammer the metal of the incense burners into a sheet as a covering for the altar, for these burners have become holy because they were used in the LORD's presence. The altar covering will then serve as a warning to the people of Israel."

³⁹So Eleazar the priest collected the 250 bronze incense burners that had been used by the men who died in the fire, and they were hammered out into a sheet of metal to cover the altar. ⁴⁰This would warn the Israelites that no unauthorized man—no one who was not a descendant of Aaron—should ever enter the LORD's presence to burn incense. If anyone did, the same thing would happen to him as happened to Korah and his followers. Thus, the LORD's instructions to Moses were carried out.

⁴¹But the very next morning the whole community began muttering again against Moses and Aaron, saying, "You two have killed the LORD's people!" ⁴²As the people gathered to protest to Moses and Aaron, they turned toward the Tabernacle and saw that the cloud had covered it, and the glorious presence of the LORD appeared.

⁴³Moses and Aaron came and stood at the entrance of the Tabernacle, ⁴⁴and the LORD said to Moses, ⁴⁵"Get away from these people so that I can instantly destroy them!" But Moses and Aaron fell face down on the ground.

⁴⁶And Moses said to Aaron, "Quick, take an incense burner and place burning coals on it from the altar. Lay incense on it and carry it quickly among the people to make atonement for them. The LORD's anger is blazing among them—the plague has already begun."

⁴⁷Aaron did as Moses told him and ran out among the people. The plague indeed had already begun, but Aaron burned the incense and made atonement for them. ⁴⁸He stood between the living and the dead until the plague was stopped. ⁴⁹But 14,700 people died in that plague, in addition to those who had died

in the incident involving Korah. ⁵⁰Then because the plague had stopped, Aaron returned to Moses at the entrance of the Tabernacle.

THE BUDDING OF AARON'S STAFF

17 Then the LORD said to Moses, ²"Take twelve wooden staffs, one from each of Israel's ancestral tribes, and inscribe each tribal leader's name on his staff. ³Inscribe Aaron's name on the staff of the tribe of Levi, for there must be one staff for the leader of each ancestral tribe. ⁴Put these staffs in the Tabernacle in front of the Ark of the Covenant,* where I meet with you. ⁵Buds will sprout on the staff belonging to the man I choose. Then I will finally put an end to this murmuring and complaining against you."

⁶So Moses gave the instructions to the peo-

Words of Worship

SHOUT

Shout—Hebrew *ru-a'* "to shout, *te-ru-'ah* "a shout." The words signify a war shout, or a trumpet blast rallying fighters in battle.

Normally you're a quiet person, not given to loud talk. Then you find yourself in the stands at a football game, shouting at the top of your lungs! A "battle" is being waged, and you and the other fans are filling the air with noise, doing your part for the victory of your team.

The psalmist urges us to "shout to God with joyful praise" (Psalm 47:1), using the Hebrew word that refers to a war cry. Worship is a form of warfare in the spirit, and sometimes it's appropriate to raise that war cry. A battle is being waged for our souls, and you just want to shout—not because it feels good, but because God is winning!

17:4 Hebrew *in the Tent of Meeting before the Testimony.*

ple of Israel, and each of the twelve tribal leaders, including Aaron, brought Moses a staff. [7]Moses put the staffs in the LORD's presence in the Tabernacle of the Covenant.* [8]When he went into the Tabernacle of the Covenant the next day, he found that Aaron's staff, representing the tribe of Levi, had sprouted, blossomed, and produced almonds!

[9]When Moses brought all the staffs out from the LORD's presence, he showed them to the people. Each man claimed his own staff. [10]And the LORD said to Moses: "Place Aaron's staff permanently before the Ark of the Covenant* as a warning to rebels. This should put an end to their complaints against me and prevent any further deaths." [11]So Moses did as the LORD commanded him.

[12]Then the people of Israel said to Moses, "We are as good as dead! We are ruined! [13]Everyone who even comes close to the Tabernacle of the LORD dies. We are all doomed!"

DUTIES OF PRIESTS AND LEVITES

18 The LORD now said to Aaron: "You, your sons, and your relatives from the tribe of Levi will be held responsible for any offenses related to the sanctuary. But you and your sons alone will be held liable for violations connected with the priesthood. [2]"Bring your relatives of the tribe of Levi to assist you and your sons as you perform the sacred duties in front of the Tabernacle of the Covenant.* [3]But as the Levites go about their duties under your supervision, they must be careful not to touch any of the sacred objects or the altar. If they do, both you and they will die. [4]The Levites must join with you to fulfill their responsibilities for the care and maintenance of the Tabernacle,* but no one who is not a Levite may officiate with you.

[5]"You yourselves must perform the sacred duties within the sanctuary and at the altar. If you follow these instructions, the LORD's anger will never again blaze against the people of Israel. [6]I myself have chosen your fellow Levites from among the Israelites to be your special assistants. They are dedicated to the LORD for service in the Tabernacle. [7]But you and your sons, the priests, must personally handle all the sacred service associated with the altar and everything within the inner curtain. I am giving you the priesthood as your special gift of service. Any other person who comes too near the sanctuary will be put to death."

SUPPORT FOR THE PRIESTS AND LEVITES

[8]The LORD gave these further instructions to Aaron: "I have put the priests in charge of all the holy gifts that are brought to me by the people of Israel. I have given these offerings to you and your sons as your regular share. [9]You are allotted the portion of the most holy offerings that is kept from the fire. From all the most holy offerings—including the grain offerings, sin offerings, and guilt offerings—that portion belongs to you and your sons. [10]You must eat it as a most holy offering. All the males may eat of it, and you must treat it as most holy.

[11]"All the other offerings presented to me by the Israelites by lifting them up before the altar also belong to you as your regular share. Any member of your family who is ceremonially clean, male and female alike, may eat of these offerings.

[12]"I also give you the harvest gifts brought by the people as offerings to the LORD—the best of the olive oil, wine, and grain. [13]All the firstfruits of the land that the people present to the LORD belong to you. Any member of your family who is ceremonially clean may eat this food.

[14]"Whatever is specially set apart for the LORD* also belongs to you.

[15]"The firstborn of every mother, whether human or animal, that is offered to the LORD

17:7 Or *Tabernacle of the Testimony;* also in 17:8. **17:10** Hebrew *before the Testimony.* **18:2** Or *Tabernacle of the Testimony.*
18:4 Hebrew *Tent of Meeting;* also in 18:6, 21, 22, 23, 31. **18:14** The Hebrew term used here refers to the complete consecration of things or people to the LORD, either by destroying them or by giving them as an offering.

will be yours. But you must always redeem your firstborn sons and the firstborn males of ritually unclean animals. [16]Redeem them when they are one month old. The redemption price is five pieces of silver, each piece weighing the same as the standard sanctuary shekel.*

[17]"However, you may not redeem the firstborn of cattle, sheep, or goats. They are holy and have been set apart for the LORD. Sprinkle their blood on the altar, and burn their fat as an offering given by fire, very pleasing to the LORD. [18]The meat of these animals will be yours, just like the breast and right thigh that are presented by lifting them up before the altar. [19]Yes, I am giving you all these holy offerings that the people of Israel bring to the LORD. They are for you and your sons and daughters, to be eaten as your regular share. This is an unbreakable covenant* between the LORD and you and your descendants."

[20]And the LORD said to Aaron, "You priests will receive no inheritance of land or share of property among the people of Israel. I am your inheritance and your share. [21]As for the tribe of Levi, your relatives, I will pay them for their service in the Tabernacle with the tithes from the entire land of Israel.

[22]"From now on, Israelites other than the priests and Levites are to stay away from the Tabernacle. If they come too near, they will be judged guilty and die. [23]The Levites must serve at the Tabernacle, and they will be held responsible for any offenses against it. This is a permanent law among you. But the Levites will receive no inheritance of land among the Israelites, [24]because I have given them the Israelites' tithes, which have been set apart as offerings to the LORD. This will be the Levites' share. That is why I said they would receive no inheritance of land among the Israelites."

[25]The LORD also told Moses, [26]"Say this to the Levites: 'When you receive the tithes from the Israelites, give a tenth of the tithes you receive—a tithe of the tithe—to the LORD as a gift. [27]The LORD will consider this to be your harvest offering, as though it were the first grain from your own threshing floor or wine from your own winepress. [28]You must present one-tenth of the tithe received from the Israelites as a gift to the LORD. From this you must present the LORD's portion to Aaron the priest. [29]Be sure to set aside the best portions of the gifts given to you as your gifts to the LORD.'

[30]"Also say to the Levites: 'When you present the best part, it will be considered as though it came from your own threshing floor or winepress. [31]You Levites and your families may eat this food anywhere you wish, for it is your compensation for serving in the Tabernacle. [32]You will not be considered guilty for accepting the LORD's tithes if you give the best portion to the priests. But be careful not to treat the holy gifts of the people of Israel as though they were common. If you do, you will die.' "

THE WATER OF PURIFICATION

19 The LORD said to Moses and Aaron, [2]"Here is another ritual law required by the LORD: Tell the people of Israel to bring you a red heifer that has no physical defects and has never been yoked to a plow. [3]Give it to Eleazar the priest, and it will be taken outside the camp and slaughtered in his presence. [4]Eleazar will take some of its blood on his finger and sprinkle it seven times toward the front of the Tabernacle.* [5]As Eleazar watches,

> *If God were small enough*
> *to be understood,*
> *He would not be big enough*
> *to be worshiped.*
>
> EVELYN UNDERHILL

18:16 Hebrew 5 shekels [about 2 ounces or 57 grams] of silver, according to the sanctuary shekel, 20 gerahs to each shekel.
18:19 Hebrew a covenant of salt.   19:4 Hebrew Tent of Meeting.

the heifer must be burned—its hide, meat, blood, and dung. ⁶Eleazar the priest must then take cedarwood, a hyssop branch, and scarlet thread and throw them into the fire where the heifer is burning.

⁷"Then the priest must wash his clothes and bathe himself in water. Afterward he may return to the camp, though he will remain ceremonially unclean until evening. ⁸The man who burns the animal must also wash his clothes and bathe in water, and he, too, will remain unclean until evening. ⁹Then someone who is ceremonially clean will gather up the ashes of the heifer and place them in a purified place outside the camp. They will be kept there for the people of Israel to use in the water for the purification ceremony. This ceremony is performed for the removal of sin. ¹⁰The man who gathers up the ashes of the heifer must also wash his clothes, and he will remain ceremonially unclean until evening. This is a permanent law for the people of Israel and any foreigners who live among them.

¹¹"All those who touch a dead human body will be ceremonially unclean for seven days. ¹²They must purify themselves on the third and seventh days with the water of purification; then they will be purified. But if they do not do this on the third and seventh days, they will continue to be unclean even after the seventh day. ¹³All those who touch a dead body and do not purify themselves in the proper way defile the LORD's Tabernacle and will be cut off from the community of Israel. Since the water of purification was not sprinkled on them, their defilement continues.

¹⁴"This is the ritual law that applies when someone dies in a tent: Those who enter that tent, and those who were inside when the death occurred, will be ceremonially unclean for seven days. ¹⁵Any container in the tent that was not covered with a lid is also defiled. ¹⁶And if someone outdoors touches the corpse of someone who was killed with a sword or who died a natural death, or if someone touches a human bone or a grave, that person will be unclean for seven days.

¹⁷"To remove the defilement, put some of the ashes from the burnt purification offering in a jar and pour fresh water over them. ¹⁸Then someone who is ceremonially clean must take a hyssop branch and dip it into the water. That person must sprinkle the water on the tent, on all the furnishings in the tent, and on anyone who was in the tent, or anyone who has touched a human bone, or has touched a person who was killed or who died naturally, or has touched a grave. ¹⁹On the third and seventh days the ceremonially clean person must sprinkle the water on those who are unclean. Then on the seventh day the people being cleansed must wash their clothes and bathe themselves, and that evening they will be cleansed of their defilement.

²⁰"But those who become defiled and do not purify themselves will be cut off from the community, for they have defiled the sanctuary of the LORD. Since the water of purification has not been sprinkled on them, they remain defiled. ²¹This is a permanent law. Those who sprinkle the water of purification must afterward wash their clothes, and anyone who touches the water of purification will remain defiled until evening. ²²Anything and anyone that a defiled person touches will be ceremonially defiled until evening."

MOSES STRIKES THE ROCK

20 In early spring* the people of Israel arrived in the wilderness of Zin and camped at Kadesh. While they were there, Miriam died and was buried.

²There was no water for the people to drink at that place, so they rebelled against Moses and Aaron. ³The people blamed Moses and said, "We wish we had died in the LORD's presence with our brothers! ⁴Did you bring the LORD's people into this wilderness to die, along with all our livestock? ⁵Why did you make us leave Egypt and bring us here to this terrible place? This land has no grain, figs,

20:1 Hebrew *In the first month.* This month of the Hebrew lunar calendar usually occurs in March and April.

grapes, or pomegranates. And there is no water to drink!"

⁶Moses and Aaron turned away from the people and went to the entrance of the Tabernacle,* where they fell face down on the ground. Then the glorious presence of the LORD appeared to them, ⁷and the LORD said to Moses, ⁸"You and Aaron must take the staff and assemble the entire community. As the people watch, command the rock over there to pour out its water. You will get enough water from the rock to satisfy all the people and their livestock."

⁹So Moses did as he was told. He took the staff from the place where it was kept before the LORD. ¹⁰Then he and Aaron summoned the people to come and gather at the rock. "Listen, you rebels!" he shouted. "Must we bring you water from this rock?" ¹¹Then Moses raised his hand and struck the rock twice with the staff, and water gushed out. So all the people and their livestock drank their fill.

¹²But the LORD said to Moses and Aaron, "Because you did not trust me enough to demonstrate my holiness to the people of Israel, you will not lead them into the land I am giving them!" ¹³This place was known as the waters of Meribah,* because it was where the people of Israel argued with the LORD, and where he demonstrated his holiness among them.

EDOM REFUSES ISRAEL PASSAGE

¹⁴While Moses was at Kadesh, he sent ambassadors to the king of Edom with this message:

"This message is from your relatives, the people of Israel: You know all the hardships we have been through, ¹⁵and that our ancestors went down to Egypt. We lived there a long time and suffered as slaves to the Egyptians. ¹⁶But when we cried out to the LORD, he heard us and sent an angel who brought us out of Egypt. Now we are camped at Kadesh, a town on the border of your land. ¹⁷Please let us pass through your country. We will be careful not to go through your fields and vineyards. We won't even drink water from your wells. We will stay on the king's road and never leave it until we have crossed the opposite border."

¹⁸But the king of Edom said, "Stay out of my land or I will meet you with an army!"

¹⁹The Israelites answered, "We will stay on the main road. If any of our livestock drinks your water, we will pay for it. We only want to pass through your country and nothing else."

²⁰But the king of Edom replied, "Stay out! You may not pass through our land." With that he mobilized his army and marched out to meet them with an imposing force. ²¹Because Edom refused to allow Israel to pass through their country, Israel was forced to turn around.

THE DEATH OF AARON

²²The whole community of Israel left Kadesh as a group and arrived at Mount Hor. ²³Then the LORD said to Moses and Aaron at Mount Hor on the border of the land of Edom, ²⁴"The time has come for Aaron to join his ancestors in death. He will not enter the land I am giving the people of Israel, because the two of you rebelled against my instructions concerning the waters of Meribah. ²⁵Now take Aaron and his son Eleazar up Mount Hor. ²⁶There you will remove Aaron's priestly garments and put them on Eleazar, his son. Aaron will die there and join his ancestors."

²⁷So Moses did as the LORD commanded. The three of them went up Mount Hor together as the whole community watched. ²⁸At the summit, Moses removed the priestly garments from Aaron and put them on Eleazar, Aaron's son. Then Aaron died there on top of the mountain, and Moses and Eleazar went back down. ²⁹When the people realized that Aaron had died, all Israel mourned for him thirty days.

20:6 Hebrew *Tent of Meeting.* 20:13 *Meribah* means "arguing."

My Daily Worship

— *February 8* —

WHAT'S MISSING?

NUMBERS 19:1–21:35

"Assemble the people, and I will give them water." There the Israelites sang this song:
"Spring up O well! Yes, sing about it! Sing of this well, which princes dug, which
great leaders hollowed out with their scepters and staffs" (21:16–18).

[i reflect]

What's missing? We're Christians, and we're supposed to be experiencing "life in all its fullness" (John 10:10), and yet . . . something's not quite right.

We read the books, go to the seminars, listen to the tapes or watch the videos of those who say they have the missing ingredient, and, for a while, our spiritual walk does go better. But then, inevitably, sooner or later we're back where we were before, searching . . . for what?

Augustine, the great Christian thinker and church leader of the fourth and fifth centuries, summed it up this way: "Thou hast made us for thyself, O God, and our hearts are restless until they find their rest in thee." What many of us experience is nothing more nor less than the universal cry of the soul for God. We are thirsty for the living water that only *he* can give.

Moses and the people of Israel experienced a foretaste of this in the wilderness at Beer, where God provided water for them from a well their princes had dug in years gone by. It was cause for great celebration and song. It also is a wonderful word picture of what we read in John 4:10, where Jesus promises the Samaritan woman "living water," and John 7:37–39, where he tells the crowds that for whoever comes to him in faith, "rivers of living water will flow out from within."

We are all thirsty for life. Some will find the well of living water; some will find only lesser substitutes, temporary "fixes" that anesthetize but do not quench. Don't settle for anything less than the genuine article: a vital, life-giving relationship with the One who alone gives living water.

As you satisfy your thirst today, remember the source of your "living water." Use these times of thirst-quenching to give thanks to the Lord who ultimately satisfies your spiritual thirst.

[i pray]

Lord, life is so hectic, and often I look for the shortcut, the easy way, the "microwave formula"
for spirituality. Help me not to settle for anything less than a genuine, open, and sincere
relationship with you, and help me drink deeply from the well of living water.

[i respond]

Name specifically what you feel is missing in your life—whether spiritually, physically, or emotionally. Offer that list to God in prayer. Throughout the day, ask God to refresh your soul and to satisfy those inner longings.

VICTORY OVER THE CANAANITES

21 The Canaanite king of Arad, who lived in the Negev, heard that the Israelites were approaching on the road to Atharim. So he attacked the Israelites and took some of them as prisoners. ²Then the people of Israel made this vow to the LORD: "If you will help us conquer these people, we will completely destroy* all their towns." ³The LORD heard their request and gave them victory over the Canaanites. The Israelites completely destroyed them and their towns, and the place has been called Hormah* ever since.

THE BRONZE SNAKE

⁴Then the people of Israel set out from Mount Hor, taking the road to the Red Sea* to go around the land of Edom. But the people grew impatient along the way, ⁵and they began to murmur against God and Moses. "Why have you brought us out of Egypt to die here in the wilderness?" they complained. "There is nothing to eat here and nothing to drink. And we hate this wretched manna!"

⁶So the LORD sent poisonous snakes among them, and many of them were bitten and died. ⁷Then the people came to Moses and cried out, "We have sinned by speaking against the LORD and against you. Pray that the LORD will take away the snakes." So Moses prayed for the people.

⁸Then the LORD told him, "Make a replica of a poisonous snake and attach it to the top of a pole. Those who are bitten will live if they simply look at it!" ⁹So Moses made a snake out of bronze and attached it to the top of a pole. Whenever those who were bitten looked at the bronze snake, they recovered!

ISRAEL'S JOURNEY TO MOAB

¹⁰The Israelites traveled next to Oboth and camped there. ¹¹Then they went on to Iye-abarim, in the wilderness on the eastern border of Moab. ¹²From there they traveled to the valley of Zered Brook and set up camp. ¹³Then they moved to the far side of the Arnon River, in the wilderness adjacent to the territory of the Amorites. The Arnon is the boundary line between the Moabites and the Amorites. ¹⁴For this reason *The Book of the Wars of the LORD* speaks of "the town of Waheb in the area of Suphah, and the ravines; and the Arnon River ¹⁵and its ravines, which extend as far as the settlement of Ar on the border of Moab."

¹⁶From there the Israelites traveled to Beer,* which is the well where the LORD said to Moses, "Assemble the people, and I will give them water." ¹⁷There the Israelites sang this song:

"Spring up, O well!
    Yes, sing about it!
¹⁸ Sing of this well,
    which princes dug,
  which great leaders hollowed out
    with their scepters and staffs."

Then the Israelites left the wilderness and proceeded on through Mattanah, ¹⁹Nahaliel, and Bamoth. ²⁰Then they went to the valley in Moab where Pisgah Peak overlooks the wasteland.*

VICTORY OVER SIHON AND OG

²¹The Israelites now sent ambassadors to King Sihon of the Amorites with this message:

²²"Let us travel through your land. We will stay on the king's road until we have crossed your territory. We will not trample your fields or touch your vineyards or drink your well water."

²³But King Sihon refused to let them cross his land. Instead, he mobilized his entire army and attacked Israel in the wilderness, engaging them in battle at Jahaz. ²⁴But the Israelites slaughtered them and occupied their land from the Arnon River to the Jabbok River.

21:2 The Hebrew term used here refers to the complete consecration of things or people to the LORD, either by destroying them or by giving them as an offering; also in 21:3. **21:3** *Hormah* means "destruction." **21:4** Hebrew *sea of reeds.* **21:16** *Beer* means "well." **21:20** Or *overlooks Jeshimon.*

They went only as far as the Ammonite border because the boundary of the Ammonites was fortified.*

²⁵So Israel captured all the towns of the Amorites and settled in them, including the city of Heshbon and its surrounding villages. ²⁶Heshbon had been the capital of King Sihon of the Amorites. He had conquered a former Moabite king and seized all his land as far as the Arnon River. ²⁷For this reason the ancient poets wrote this about him:

"Come to Heshbon, city of Sihon!
    May it be restored and rebuilt.
²⁸ A fire flamed forth from Heshbon,
    a blaze from the city of Sihon.
It burned the city of Ar in Moab;
    it destroyed the rulers of the Arnon
        heights.
²⁹ Your destruction is certain, O people of
        Moab!
    You are finished, O worshipers of
        Chemosh!
Chemosh has left his sons as refugees,
    and his daughters as captives of Sihon,
        the Amorite king.
³⁰ We have utterly destroyed them,
    all the way from Heshbon to Dibon.
We have completely wiped them out
    as far away as Nophah and Medeba.*"

³¹So the people of Israel occupied the territory of the Amorites. ³²After Moses sent men to explore the Jazer area, they captured all the towns in the region and drove out the Amorites who lived there. ³³Then they turned and marched toward Bashan, but King Og of Bashan and all his people attacked them at Edrei. ³⁴The LORD said to Moses, "Do not be afraid of him, for I have given you victory over Og and his entire army, giving you all his land. You will do the same to him as you did to King Sihon of the Amorites, who ruled in Heshbon." ³⁵And Israel was victorious and killed King Og, his sons, and his subjects; not

a single survivor remained. Then Israel occupied their land.

BALAK SENDS FOR BALAAM

22 Then the people of Israel traveled to the plains of Moab and camped east of the Jordan River, across from Jericho. ²Balak son of Zippor, the Moabite king, knew what the Israelites had done to the Amorites. ³And when they saw how many Israelites there were, he and his people were terrified. ⁴The king of Moab said to the leaders of Midian, "This mob will devour everything in sight, like an ox devours grass!"

So Balak, king of Moab, ⁵sent messengers to Balaam son of Beor, who was living in his native land of Pethor* near the Euphrates River.* He sent this message to request that Balaam come to help him:

"A vast horde of people has arrived from
Egypt. They cover the face of the earth and
are threatening me. ⁶Please come and
curse them for me because they are so
numerous. Then perhaps I will be able to
conquer them and drive them from
the land. I know that blessings fall on the
people you bless. I also know that the
people you curse are doomed."

⁷Balak's messengers, officials of both Moab and Midian, set out and took money with them to pay Balaam to curse Israel. They went to Balaam and urgently explained to him what Balak wanted. ⁸"Stay here overnight," Balaam said. "In the morning I will tell you whatever the LORD directs me to say." So the officials from Moab stayed there with Balaam.

⁹That night God came to Balaam and asked him, "Who are these men with you?"

¹⁰So Balaam said to God, "Balak son of Zippor, king of Moab, has sent me this message: ¹¹'A vast horde of people has come from Egypt and has spread out over the whole land. Come at once to curse them. Perhaps then I

21:24 Or because the terrain of the Ammonite frontier was rugged; Hebrew because the boundary of the Ammonites was strong. 21:30 Or until fire spread to Medeba. The meaning of the Hebrew is uncertain. 22:5a Or who was at Pethor in the land of the Amavites. 22:5b Hebrew the river.

will be able to conquer them and drive them from the land.' "

¹²"Do not go with them," God told Balaam. "You are not to curse these people, for I have blessed them!"

¹³The next morning Balaam got up and told Balak's officials, "Go on home! The LORD will not let me go with you."

¹⁴So the Moabite officials returned to King Balak and reported, "Balaam refused to come with us." ¹⁵Then Balak tried again. This time he sent a larger number of even more distinguished officials than those he had sent the first time. ¹⁶They went to Balaam and gave him this message:

"This is what Balak son of Zippor says: Please don't let anything stop you from coming. ¹⁷I will pay you well and do anything you ask of me. Just come and curse these people for me!"

¹⁸But Balaam answered them, "Even if Balak were to give me a palace filled with silver and gold, I would be powerless to do anything against the will of the LORD my God. ¹⁹But stay here one more night to see if the LORD has anything else to say to me."

²⁰That night God came to Balaam and told him, "Since these men have come for you, get up and go with them. But be sure to do only what I tell you to do."

BALAAM AND HIS DONKEY

²¹So the next morning Balaam saddled his donkey and started off with the Moabite officials. ²²But God was furious that Balaam was going, so he sent the angel of the LORD to stand in the road to block his way. As Balaam and two servants were riding along, ²³Balaam's donkey suddenly saw the angel of the LORD standing in the road with a drawn sword in his hand. The donkey bolted off the road into a field, but Balaam beat it and turned it back onto the road. ²⁴Then the angel of the LORD stood at a place where the road narrowed between two vineyard walls. ²⁵When the donkey saw the angel of the LORD standing there, it tried to squeeze by and crushed Balaam's foot against the wall. So Balaam beat the donkey again. ²⁶Then the angel of the LORD moved farther down the road and stood in a place so narrow that the donkey could not get by at all. ²⁷This time when the donkey saw the angel, it lay down under Balaam. In a fit of rage Balaam beat it again with his staff.

²⁸Then the LORD caused the donkey to speak. "What have I done to you that deserves your beating me these three times?" it asked Balaam.

²⁹"Because you have made me look like a fool!" Balaam shouted. "If I had a sword with me, I would kill you!"

³⁰"But I am the same donkey you always ride on," the donkey answered. "Have I ever done anything like this before?"

"No," he admitted.

³¹Then the LORD opened Balaam's eyes, and he saw the angel of the LORD standing in the roadway with a drawn sword in his hand. Balaam fell face down on the ground before him.

³²"Why did you beat your donkey those three times?" the angel of the LORD demanded. "I have come to block your way because you are stubbornly resisting me. ³³Three times the donkey saw me and shied away; otherwise, I would certainly have killed you by now and spared the donkey."

³⁴Then Balaam confessed to the angel of the LORD, "I have sinned. I did not realize you were standing in the road to block my way. I will go back home if you are against my going."

³⁵But the angel of the LORD told him, "Go with these men, but you may say only what I tell you to say." So Balaam went on with Balak's officials. ³⁶When King Balak heard that Balaam was on the way, he went out to meet him at a Moabite town on the Arnon River at the border of his land.

³⁷"Did I not send you an urgent invitation? Why didn't you come right away?" Balak asked Balaam. "Didn't you believe me when I said I would reward you richly?"

³⁸Balaam replied, "I have come, but I have no power to say just anything. I will speak only the messages that God gives me." ³⁹Then Balaam accompanied Balak to Kiriath-huzoth, ⁴⁰where the king sacrificed cattle and sheep. He sent portions of the meat to Balaam and the officials who were with him. ⁴¹The next morning Balak took Balaam up to Bamoth-baal. From there he could see the people of Israel spread out below him.

Balaam Blesses Israel

23 Balaam said to King Balak, "Build me seven altars here, and prepare seven young bulls and seven rams for a sacrifice." ²Balak followed his instructions, and the two of them sacrificed a young bull and a ram on each altar.

³Then Balaam said to Balak, "Stand here by your burnt offerings, and I will go to see if the LORD will respond to me. Then I will tell you whatever he reveals to me." So Balaam went alone to the top of a hill, ⁴and God met him there. Balaam said to him, "I have prepared seven altars and have sacrificed a young bull and a ram on each altar."

⁵Then the LORD gave Balaam a message for King Balak and said, "Go back to Balak and tell him what I told you."

⁶When Balaam returned, the king was standing beside his burnt offerings with all the officials of Moab. ⁷This was the prophecy Balaam delivered:

"Balak summoned me to come from Aram;
the king of Moab brought me from the
eastern hills.
'Come,' he said, 'curse Jacob for me!
Come and announce Israel's doom.'
⁸ But how can I curse
those whom God has not cursed?
How can I condemn
those whom the LORD has not
condemned?
⁹ I see them from the cliff tops;
I watch them from the hills.
I see a people who live by themselves,
set apart from other nations.
¹⁰ Who can count Jacob's descendants, as
numerous as dust?
Who can count even a fourth of Israel's
people?
Let me die like the righteous;
let my life end like theirs."

¹¹Then King Balak demanded of Balaam, "What have you done to me? I brought you to curse my enemies. Instead, you have blessed them!"

¹²But Balaam replied, "Can I say anything except what the LORD tells me?"

Balaam's Second Prophecy

¹³Then King Balak told him, "Come with me to another place. There you will see only a portion of the nation of Israel. Curse at least that many!" ¹⁴So Balak took Balaam to the plateau of Zophim on Pisgah Peak. He built seven altars there and offered a young bull and a ram on each altar.

¹⁵Then Balaam said to the king, "Stand here by your burnt offering while I go to meet the LORD."

¹⁶So the LORD met Balaam and gave him a message. Then he said, "Go back to Balak and give him this message."

¹⁷So Balaam returned to the place where the king and the officials of Moab were standing beside Balak's burnt offerings. "What did the LORD say?" Balak asked eagerly.

¹⁸This was the prophecy Balaam delivered:

"Rise up, Balak, and listen!
Hear me, son of Zippor.
¹⁹ God is not a man, that he should lie.
He is not a human, that he should
change his mind.
Has he ever spoken and failed to act?
Has he ever promised and not carried it
through?
²⁰ I received a command to bless;
he has blessed, and I cannot reverse it!
²¹ No misfortune is in sight for Jacob;
no trouble is in store for Israel.

For the LORD their God is with them;
    he has been proclaimed their king.
²² God has brought them out of Egypt;
    he is like a strong ox for them.
²³ No curse can touch Jacob;
    no sorcery has any power against Israel.
For now it will be said of Jacob,
    'What wonders God has done for Israel!'
²⁴ These people rise up like a lioness;
    like a majestic lion they stand.
They refuse to rest
    until they have feasted on prey,
    drinking the blood of the slaughtered!"

²⁵Then Balak said to Balaam, "If you aren't going to curse them, at least don't bless them!"

²⁶But Balaam replied, "Didn't I tell you that I must do whatever the LORD tells me?"

BALAAM'S THIRD PROPHECY

²⁷Then King Balak said to Balaam, "Come, I will take you to yet another place. Perhaps it will please God to let you curse them from there."

²⁸So Balak took Balaam to the top of Mount Peor, overlooking the wasteland.* ²⁹Balaam again told Balak, "Build me seven altars and prepare me seven young bulls and seven rams for a sacrifice." ³⁰So Balak did as Balaam ordered and offered a young bull and a ram on each altar.

24 By now Balaam realized that the LORD intended to bless Israel, so he did not resort to divination as he often did. Instead, he turned and looked out toward the wilderness, ²where he saw the people of Israel camped, tribe by tribe. Then the Spirit of God came upon him, ³and this is the prophecy he delivered:

"This is the prophecy of Balaam son of Beor,
    the prophecy of the man whose eyes see clearly,
⁴ who hears the words of God,
    who sees a vision from the Almighty,

who falls down with eyes wide open:
⁵ How beautiful are your tents, O Jacob;
    how lovely are your homes, O Israel!
⁶ They spread before me like groves of palms,
    like fruitful gardens by the riverside.
They are like aloes planted by the LORD,
    like cedars beside the waters.
⁷ Water will gush out in buckets;
    their offspring are supplied with all they need.
Their king will be greater than Agag;
    their kingdom will be exalted.
⁸ God brought them up from Egypt,
    drawing them along like a wild ox.
He devours all the nations that oppose him,
    breaking their bones in pieces,
    shooting them with arrows.
⁹ Like a lion, Israel crouches and lies down;
    like a lioness, who dares to arouse her?
Blessed is everyone who blesses you,
    O Israel,
    and cursed is everyone who curses you."

¹⁰King Balak flew into a rage against Balaam. He angrily clapped his hands and shouted, "I called you to curse my enemies! Instead, you have blessed them three times. ¹¹Now get out of here! Go back home! I had planned to reward you richly, but the LORD has kept you from your reward."

¹²Balaam told Balak, "Don't you remember what I told your messengers? I said, ¹³'Even if Balak were to give me a palace filled with silver and gold, I am powerless to do anything against the will of the LORD.' I told you that I could say only what the LORD says! ¹⁴Now I am returning to my own people. But first let me tell you what the Israelites will do to your people in the future."

BALAAM'S FINAL PROPHECIES

¹⁵This is the prophecy Balaam delivered:

"This is the message of Balaam son of Beor,
    the prophecy of the man whose eyes see clearly,

23:28 Or *overlooking Jeshimon.*

My Daily Worship

— *February 9* —

FAR AND NEAR

NUMBERS 22:1–25:18

God is not a man, that he should lie. He is not a human,
that he should change his mind. Has he ever spoken and failed to act?
Has he ever promised and not carried it through? (23:19).

[i reflect]

In some very important ways God is intimately involved in his creation—he personally cares for us and loves us; he even has created us in his own image with the ability to think, feel, and create. We refer to these attributes as God's *imminence.*

In other, equally important ways God is radically different from us. He is distinctly separate from his creation, sovereign over all he has made. In that sense, God is all-powerful, all-present, all-knowing, and unchangeable; he's perfectly holy, just, loving, wise, and trustworthy. We refer to these characteristics by the term, God's *transcendence.*

This passage emphasizes God's *transcendence*—as even Balaam pointed out in this prophecy given to the pagan King Balak, God is "not a man." Some people who are drawn to this aspect of who God is will see him as high and lifted up, like Isaiah's vision in Isaiah 6. They want to engage in worship that emphasizes his majesty, sovereignty, and kingly rule. These people focus on this aspect of who God is because it is reverent and respectful, and it does "give to the LORD the glory he deserves" (Psalm 96:8).

Others, however, like this aspect of God because it keeps him at a safe distance—way up there or out there, where he won't meddle in my life, won't invade my space. A nice, safe, *distant* deity.

Transcendence and *imminence*. Both are realities; both need to be kept in balanced perspective. He is the all-powerful, all-present, all-knowing, and unchangeable King of the universe, . . . and he's also our heavenly Father.

Today find ways to worship God as your personal heavenly Father and as your sovereign King.

[i pray]

Lord God Almighty, help me remember who you are and who I am before you:
a rebel who has been granted pardon by the mercy of a King, and
an orphan who has been adopted by the love of a Father.

[i respond]

As you study the Bible, try keeping a journal of the characteristics of God as they are presented in various passages. Divide them under the two headings of Transcendence and Imminence. Which aspect of God's character do you think is highlighted more prominently throughout the Scriptures?

[16] who hears the words of God,
who has knowledge from the Most High,
who sees a vision from the Almighty,
who falls down with eyes wide open:
[17] I see him, but not in the present time.
I perceive him, but far in the distant
future.
A star will rise from Jacob;
a scepter will emerge from Israel.
It will crush the foreheads of Moab's
people,
cracking the skulls of the people of Sheth.
[18] Edom will be taken over,
and Seir, its enemy, will be conquered,
while Israel continues on in triumph.
[19] A ruler will rise in Jacob
who will destroy the survivors of Ir."

[20]Then Balaam looked over at the people of
Amalek and delivered this prophecy:

"Amalek was the greatest of nations,
but its destiny is destruction!"

[21]Then he looked over at the Kenites and
prophesied:

"You are strongly situated;
your nest is set in the rocks.
[22] But the Kenites will be destroyed
when Assyria* takes you captive."

[23]Balaam concluded his prophecies by saying:

"Alas, who can survive when God does this?
[24] Ships will come from the coasts of
Cyprus*;
they will oppress both Assyria and Eber,
but they, too, will be utterly destroyed."

[25]Then Balaam and Balak returned to their
homes.

MOAB SEDUCES ISRAEL

25 While the Israelites were camped at
Acacia,* some of the men defiled
themselves by sleeping with the local Moabite
women. [2]These women invited them to
attend sacrifices to their gods, and soon the
Israelites were feasting with them and worshiping the gods of Moab. [3]Before long Israel
was joining in the worship of Baal of Peor,
causing the LORD's anger to blaze against his
people.

[4]The LORD issued the following command
to Moses: "Seize all the ringleaders and execute them before the LORD in broad daylight,
so his fierce anger will turn away from the
people of Israel." [5]So Moses ordered Israel's

Words of Worship

GLADNESS

Gladness, Be Glad—Hebrew *sa-me-ach* "be
joyful"; *sim-chah* "joy"; *gil* "to dance" (in
a circle); Greek *chai-ro* "rejoice"; *cha-ra*
"joy." The same words are used for joy and
rejoicing.

We could be glad about a lot of things. Life
is going well—a problem situation has taken
a turn for the better, or we've received some
good news—and we're glad. Even if everything isn't wonderful, when we're in the presence of the Lord, we're glad. But who would
know it, unless we show our gladness?

The Bible often refers to being glad because
of what the Lord has done for us, and
because we're coming into his presence.
"Worship the LORD with gladness," the
psalmist cries (Psalm 100:2) This kind of
gladness isn't just a feeling of satisfaction or
a contented thought. The Hebrew word for
gladness is usually associated with festivity,
even lavish celebration. And the early
Christians seem to have understood it in
much the same way. When we're glad in the
Lord, it's like having a party! Celebrate!
Rejoice! Be glad!

24:22 Hebrew *Asshur;* also in 24:24. 24:24 Hebrew *Kittim.* 25:1 Hebrew *Shittim.*

judges to execute everyone who had joined in worshiping Baal of Peor.

⁶Just then one of the Israelite men brought a Midianite woman into the camp, right before the eyes of Moses and all the people, as they were weeping at the entrance of the Tabernacle.* ⁷When Phinehas son of Eleazar and grandson of Aaron the priest saw this, he jumped up and left the assembly. Then he took a spear ⁸and rushed after the man into his tent. Phinehas thrust the spear all the way through the man's body and into the woman's stomach. So the plague against the Israelites was stopped, ⁹but not before 24,000 people had died.

¹⁰Then the LORD said to Moses, ¹¹"Phinehas son of Eleazar and grandson of Aaron the priest has turned my anger away from the Israelites by displaying passionate zeal among them on my behalf. So I have stopped destroying all Israel as I had intended to do in my anger. ¹²So tell him that I am making my special covenant of peace with him. ¹³In this covenant, he and his descendants will be priests for all time, because he was zealous for his God and made atonement for the people of Israel."

¹⁴The Israelite man killed with the Midianite woman was named Zimri son of Salu, the leader of a family from the tribe of Simeon. ¹⁵The woman's name was Cozbi; she was the daughter of Zur, the leader of a Midianite clan.

¹⁶Then the LORD said to Moses, ¹⁷"Attack the Midianites and destroy them, ¹⁸because they assaulted you with deceit by tricking you into worshiping Baal of Peor, and because of Cozbi, the daughter of a Midianite leader, who was killed on the day of the plague at Peor."

ISRAEL'S SECOND CENSUS

26 After the plague had ended, the LORD said to Moses and to Eleazar son of Aaron, the priest, ²"Take a census of all the men of Israel who are twenty years old or older, to find out how many of each family are of military age." ³At that time the entire nation of Israel was camped on the plains of Moab beside the Jordan River, across from Jericho.

So Moses and Eleazar the priest issued these census instructions to the leaders of Israel: ⁴"Count all the men of Israel twenty years old and older, just as the LORD commanded Moses." This is the census record of all the descendants of Israel who came out of Egypt.

THE TRIBE OF REUBEN

⁵These were the clans descended from Reuben, Jacob's* oldest son:

The Hanochite clan, named after its ancestor Hanoch.

The Palluite clan, named after its ancestor Pallu.

⁶ The Hezronite clan, named after its ancestor Hezron.

The Carmite clan, named after its ancestor Carmi.

⁷The men from all the clans of Reuben numbered 43,730.

⁸Pallu was the ancestor of Eliab, ⁹and Eliab was the father of Nemuel, Dathan, and Abiram. This Dathan and Abiram are the same community leaders who conspired with Korah against Moses and Aaron, defying the LORD. ¹⁰But the earth opened and swallowed them with Korah, and 250 of their followers were destroyed that day by fire from the LORD. This served as a warning to the entire nation of Israel. ¹¹However, the sons of Korah did not die that day.

THE TRIBE OF SIMEON

¹²These were the clans descended from the sons of Simeon:

The Nemuelite clan, named after its ancestor Nemuel.

The Jaminite clan, named after its ancestor Jamin.

The Jakinite clan, named after its ancestor Jakin.

25:6 Hebrew *Tent of Meeting.* 26:5 Hebrew *Israel's.*

¹³ The Zerahite clan, named after its ancestor Zerah.

The Shaulite clan, named after its ancestor Shaul.

¹⁴The men from all the clans of Simeon numbered 22,200.

THE TRIBE OF GAD

¹⁵These were the clans descended from the sons of Gad:

The Zephonite clan, named after its ancestor Zephon.

The Haggite clan, named after its ancestor Haggi.

The Shunite clan, named after its ancestor Shuni.

¹⁶ The Oznite clan, named after its ancestor Ozni.

The Erite clan, named after its ancestor Eri.

¹⁷ The Arodite clan, named after its ancestor Arodi.*

The Arelite clan, named after its ancestor Areli.

¹⁸The men from all the clans of Gad numbered 40,500.

THE TRIBE OF JUDAH

¹⁹Judah had two sons, Er and Onan, who had died in the land of Canaan. ²⁰But the following clans descended from Judah's surviving sons:

The Shelanite clan, named after its ancestor Shelah.

The Perezite clan, named after its ancestor Perez.

The Zerahite clan, named after its ancestor Zerah.

²¹These were the subclans descended from the Perezites:

The Hezronites, named after their ancestor Hezron.

The Hamulites, named after their ancestor Hamul.

²²The men from all the clans of Judah numbered 76,500.

THE TRIBE OF ISSACHAR

²³These were the clans descended from the sons of Issachar:

The Tolaite clan, named after its ancestor Tola.

The Puite clan, named after its ancestor Puah.*

²⁴ The Jashubite clan, named after its ancestor Jashub.

The Shimronite clan, named after its ancestor Shimron.

²⁵The men from all the clans of Issachar numbered 64,300.

THE TRIBE OF ZEBULUN

²⁶These were the clans descended from the sons of Zebulun:

The Seredite clan, named after its ancestor Sered.

The Elonite clan, named after its ancestor Elon.

The Jahleelite clan, named after its ancestor Jahleel.

²⁷The men from all the clans of Zebulun numbered 60,500.

THE TRIBE OF MANASSEH

²⁸Two clans were descended from Joseph through Manasseh and Ephraim.

²⁹These were the clans descended from Manasseh:

The Makirite clan, named after its ancestor Makir.

The Gileadite clan, named after its ancestor Gilead, Makir's son.

³⁰These were the subclans descended from the Gileadites:

The Iezerites, named after their ancestor Iezer.

26:17 As in Samaritan Pentateuch and Syriac version (see also Gen 46:16); Hebrew reads *Arod*.   **26:23** As in Samaritan Pentateuch, Greek and Syriac versions, and Latin Vulgate (see also 1 Chr 7:1); Hebrew reads *The Punite clan, named after its ancestor Puvah.*

The Helekites, named after their ancestor Helek.

[31] The Asrielites, named after their ancestor Asriel.

The Shechemites, named after their ancestor Shechem.

[32] The Shemidaites, named after their ancestor Shemida.

The Hepherites, named after their ancestor Hepher.

[33] Hepher's son, Zelophehad, had no sons, but his daughters' names were Mahlah, Noah, Hoglah, Milcah, and Tirzah.

[34]The men from all the clans of Manasseh numbered 52,700.

THE TRIBE OF EPHRAIM

[35]These were the clans descended from the sons of Ephraim:

The Shuthelahite clan, named after its ancestor Shuthelah.

The Bekerite clan, named after its ancestor Beker.

The Tahanite clan, named after its ancestor Tahan.

[36]This was the subclan descended from the Shuthelahites:

The Eranites, named after their ancestor Eran.

[37]The men from all the clans of Ephraim numbered 32,500.

These clans of Manasseh and Ephraim were all descendants of Joseph.

THE TRIBE OF BENJAMIN

[38]These were the clans descended from the sons of Benjamin:

The Belaite clan, named after its ancestor Bela.

The Ashbelite clan, named after its ancestor Ashbel.

The Ahiramite clan, named after its ancestor Ahiram.

[39] The Shuphamite clan, named after its ancestor Shupham.*

The Huphamite clan, named after its ancestor Hupham.

[40]These were the subclans descended from the Belaites:

The Ardites, named after their ancestor Ard.*

The Naamites, named after their ancestor Naaman.

[41]The men from all the clans of Benjamin numbered 45,600.

THE TRIBE OF DAN

[42]These were the clans descended from the sons of Dan:

The Shuhamite clan, named after its ancestor Shuham.

[43]All the clans of Dan were Shuhamite clans, and the men from these clans numbered 64,400.

THE TRIBE OF ASHER

[44]These were the clans descended from the sons of Asher:

The Imnite clan, named after its ancestor Imnah.

The Ishvite clan, named after its ancestor Ishvi.

The Beriite clan, named after its ancestor Beriah.

[45]These were the subclans descended from the Beriites:

The Heberites, named after their ancestor Heber.

The Malkielites, named after their ancestor Malkiel.

[46]Asher also had a daughter named Serah.

26:39 As in some Hebrew manuscripts, Samaritan Pentateuch, Greek and Syriac versions, and Latin Vulgate; most Hebrew manuscripts read *Shephupham.*   26:40 As in Samaritan Pentateuch, some Greek manuscripts, and Latin Vulgate; Hebrew lacks *named after their ancestor Ard.*

⁴⁷The men from all the clans of Asher numbered 53,400.

THE TRIBE OF NAPHTALI

⁴⁸These were the clans descended from the sons of Naphtali:

The Jahzeelite clan, named after its ancestor Jahzeel.

The Gunite clan, named after its ancestor Guni.

⁴⁹ The Jezerite clan, named after its ancestor Jezer.

The Shillemite clan, named after its ancestor Shillem.

⁵⁰The men from all the clans of Naphtali numbered 45,400.

THE CENSUS RESULTS

⁵¹So the total number of Israelite men counted in the census numbered 601,730.

⁵²Then the LORD said to Moses, ⁵³"Divide the land among the tribes in proportion to their populations, as indicated by the census. ⁵⁴Give the larger tribes more land and the smaller tribes less land, each group's inheritance reflecting the size of its population. ⁵⁵Make sure you assign the land by lot, and define the inheritance of each ancestral tribe by means of the census listings. ⁵⁶Each inheritance must be assigned by lot among the larger and smaller tribal groups."

THE TRIBE OF LEVI

⁵⁷This is the census record for the Levites who were counted according to their clans:

The Gershonite clan, named after its ancestor Gershon.

The Kohathite clan, named after its ancestor Kohath.

The Merarite clan, named after its ancestor Merari.

⁵⁸The Libnites, the Hebronites, the Mahlites, the Mushites, and the Korahites were all subclans of the Levites.

Now Kohath was the ancestor of Amram, ⁵⁹and Amram's wife was named Jochebed. She also was a descendant of Levi, born among the Levites in the land of Egypt. Amram and Jochebed became the parents of Aaron, Moses, and their sister, Miriam. ⁶⁰To Aaron were born Nadab, Abihu, Eleazar, and Ithamar. ⁶¹But Nadab and Abihu died when they burned before the LORD a different kind of fire than he had commanded.

⁶²The men from the Levite clans who were one month old or older numbered 23,000. But the Levites were not included in the total census figure of the people of Israel because they were not given an inheritance of land when it was divided among the Israelites.

⁶³So these are the census figures of the people of Israel as prepared by Moses and Eleazar the priest on the plains of Moab beside the Jordan River, across from Jericho. ⁶⁴Not one person that was counted in this census had been among those counted in the previous census taken by Moses and Aaron in the wilderness of Sinai. ⁶⁵For the LORD had said of them, "They will all die in the wilderness." The only exceptions were Caleb son of Jephunneh and Joshua son of Nun.

THE DAUGHTERS OF ZELOPHEHAD

27 One day a petition was presented by the daughters of Zelophehad—Mahlah, Noah, Hoglah, Milcah, and Tirzah. Their father, Zelophehad, was the son of Hepher, son of Gilead, son of Makir, son of Manasseh, son of Joseph. ²These women went and stood before Moses, Eleazar the priest, the tribal leaders, and the entire community at the entrance of the Tabernacle.* ³"Our father died in the wilderness without leaving any sons," they said. "But he was not among Korah's followers, who rebelled against the LORD. He died because of his own sin. ⁴Why should the name of our father disappear just because he had no sons? Give us property along with the rest of our relatives."

27:2 Hebrew *Tent of Meeting.*

[5]So Moses brought their case before the LORD. [6]And the LORD replied to Moses, [7]"The daughters of Zelophehad are right. You must give them an inheritance of land along with their father's relatives. Assign them the property that would have been given to their father. [8]Moreover announce this to the people of Israel: 'If a man dies and has no sons, then give his inheritance to his daughters. [9]And if he has no daughters, turn his inheritance over to his brothers. [10]If he has no brothers, give his inheritance to his father's brothers. [11]But if his father has no brothers, pass on his inheritance to the nearest relative in his clan. The Israelites must observe this as a general legal requirement, just as the LORD commanded Moses.'"

JOSHUA CHOSEN TO LEAD ISRAEL

[12]One day the LORD said to Moses, "Climb to the top of the mountains east of the river,* and look out over the land I have given the people of Israel. [13]After you have seen it, you will die as Aaron your brother did, [14]for you both rebelled against my instructions in the wilderness of Zin. When the people of Israel rebelled, you failed to demonstrate my holiness to them at the waters." (These are the waters of Meribah at Kadesh* in the wilderness of Zin.)

[15]Then Moses said to the LORD, [16]"O LORD, the God of the spirits of all living things, please appoint a new leader for the community. [17]Give them someone who will lead them into battle, so the people of the LORD will not be like sheep without a shepherd."

[18]The LORD replied, "Take Joshua son of Nun, who has the Spirit in him, and lay your hands on him. [19]Present him to Eleazar the priest before the whole community, and publicly commission him with the responsibility of leading the people. [20]Transfer your authority to him so the whole community of Israel will obey him. [21]When direction from the LORD is needed, Joshua will stand before

> *If there is one characteristic more than others that contemporary public worship needs to recapture, it is this awe before the surpassingly great and gracious God.*
>
> HENRY SLOANE COFFIN

Eleazar the priest, who will determine the LORD's will by means of sacred lots.* This is how Joshua and the rest of the community of Israel will discover what they should do."

[22]So Moses did as the LORD commanded and presented Joshua to Eleazar the priest and the whole community. [23]Moses laid his hands on him and commissioned him to his responsibilities, just as the LORD had commanded through Moses.

THE DAILY OFFERINGS

28 The LORD said to Moses, [2]"Give these instructions to the people of Israel: The offerings you present to me by fire on the altar are my food, and they are very pleasing to me. See to it that they are brought at the appointed times and offered according to my instructions.

[3]"Say to them: When you present your daily whole burnt offerings to the LORD, you must offer two one-year-old male lambs with no physical defects. [4]One lamb will be sacrificed in the morning and the other in the evening. [5]With each lamb you must offer a grain offering of two quarts* of choice flour mixed with one quart* of olive oil. [6]This is the regular burnt offering ordained at Mount Sinai, an offering made by fire, very pleasing to the LORD. [7]Along with it you must present the proper drink offering, consisting of one quart of fermented drink with each lamb, poured

27:12 Hebrew *the mountains of Abarim.* 27:14 Hebrew *waters of Meribath-kadesh.* 27:21 Hebrew *of the Urim.* 28:5a Hebrew 1/10 of an ephah [2 liters]; also in 28:13, 21, 29. 28:5b Hebrew 1/4 of a hin [1 liter]; also in 28:7.

out in the Holy Place as an offering to the LORD. [8]Offer the second lamb in the evening with the same grain offering and drink offering. It, too, is an offering made by fire, very pleasing to the LORD.

THE SABBATH OFFERINGS

[9]"On the Sabbath day, sacrifice two one-year-old male lambs with no physical defects. They must be accompanied by a grain offering of three quarts* of choice flour mixed with olive oil, and a drink offering. [10]This is the whole burnt offering to be presented each Sabbath day, in addition to the regular daily burnt offering and its accompanying drink offering.

THE MONTHLY OFFERINGS

[11]"On the first day of each month, present an extra burnt offering to the LORD of two young bulls, one ram, and seven one-year-old male lambs, all with no physical defects. [12]These will be accompanied by grain offerings of choice flour mixed with olive oil—five quarts* with each bull, three quarts with the ram, [13]and two quarts with each lamb. This burnt offering must be presented by fire, and it will be very pleasing to the LORD. [14]You must also give a drink offering with each sacrifice: two quarts* of wine with each bull, two and a half pints* for the ram, and one quart* for each lamb. Present this monthly burnt offering on the first day of each month throughout the year.

[15]"Also, on the first day of each month you must offer one male goat for a sin offering to the LORD. This is in addition to the regular daily burnt offering and its accompanying drink offering.

OFFERINGS FOR THE PASSOVER

[16]"On the appointed day in early spring,* you must celebrate the LORD's Passover. [17]On the following day a joyous, seven-day festival will begin, but no bread made with yeast may be eaten. [18]On the first day of the festival you must call a sacred assembly of the people. None of your regular work may be done on that day. [19]You must present as a burnt offering to the LORD two young bulls, one ram, and seven one-year-old male lambs, all with no physical defects. [20]These will be accompanied by grain offerings of choice flour mixed with olive oil—five quarts with each bull, three quarts with the ram, [21]and two quarts with each of the seven lambs. [22]You must also offer a male goat as a sin offering, to make atonement for yourselves. [23]You will present these offerings in addition to your regular morning sacrifices. [24]On each of the seven days of the festival, this is how you will prepare the food offerings to be presented by fire, very pleasing to the LORD. These will be offered in addition to the regular whole burnt offerings and drink offerings. [25]On the seventh day of the festival you must call another holy assembly of the people. None of your regular work may be done on that day.

OFFERINGS FOR THE FESTIVAL OF HARVEST

[26]"On the first day of the Festival of Harvest,* when you present the first of your new grain to the LORD, you must call a holy assembly of the people. None of your regular work may be done on that day. [27]A special whole burnt offering will be offered that day, very pleasing to the LORD. It will consist of two young bulls, one ram, and seven one-year-old male lambs. [28]These will be accompanied by grain offerings of choice flour mixed with olive oil—five quarts with each bull, three quarts with the ram, [29]and two quarts with each of the seven lambs. [30]Also, offer one male goat to make atonement for yourselves. [31]These special burnt offerings, along with their drink offerings, are in addition to the regular daily burnt offering and its accompanying grain offering. Be sure that all the animals you sacrifice have no physical defects.

28:9 Hebrew *2/10 of an ephah* [3.6 liters]; also in 28:12, 20, 28. **28:12** Hebrew *3/10 of an ephah* [5.4 liters]; also in 28:20, 28. **28:14a** Hebrew *½ of a hin* [2 liters]. **28:14b** Hebrew *1/3 of a hin* [1.3 liters]. **28:14c** Hebrew *¼ of a hin* [1 liter]. **28:16** Hebrew *On the fourteenth day of the first month.* This day of the Hebrew lunar calendar occurs in late March or early April. **28:26** Or *Festival of Weeks.*

29 "The Festival of Trumpets will be cele- brated on the appointed day in early autumn* each year. You must call a solemn assembly of all the people on that day, and no regular work may be done. ²On that day you must present a burnt offering, very pleasing to the LORD. It will consist of one young bull, one ram, and seven one-year-old male lambs, all with no physical defects. ³These must be accompanied by grain offerings of choice flour mixed with olive oil—five quarts* with the bull, three quarts* with the ram, ⁴and two quarts* with each of the seven lambs. ⁵In addition, you must sacrifice a male goat as a sin offering, to make atonement for your- selves. ⁶These special sacrifices are in addition to your regular monthly and daily burnt offerings, and they must be given with their prescribed grain offerings and drink offer- ings. These offerings are given to the LORD by fire and are very pleasing to him.

OFFERINGS FOR THE DAY OF ATONEMENT

⁷"Ten days later,* you must call another holy assembly of all the people. On that day, the Day of Atonement, the people must go with- out food, and no regular work may be done. ⁸You must present a burnt offering, very pleasing to the LORD. It will consist of one young bull, one ram, and seven one-year-old male lambs, all with no physical defects. ⁹These offerings must be accompanied by the prescribed grain offerings of choice flour mixed with olive oil—five quarts of choice flour with the bull, three quarts of choice flour with the ram, ¹⁰and two quarts of choice flour with each of the seven lambs. ¹¹You must also sacrifice one male goat for a sin offering. This is in addition to the sin offering of atonement and the regular daily

burnt offering with its grain offering, and their accompanying drink offerings.

OFFERINGS FOR THE FESTIVAL OF SHELTERS

¹²"Five days later,* you must call yet another holy assembly of all the people, and on that day no regular work may be done. It is the beginning of the Festival of Shelters, a seven- day festival to the LORD. ¹³That day you must present a special whole burnt offering by fire, very pleasing to the LORD. It will consist of thirteen young bulls, two rams, and fourteen one-year-old male lambs, all with no physical defects. ¹⁴Each of these offerings must be accompanied by a grain offering of choice flour mixed with olive oil—five quarts for each of the thirteen bulls, three quarts for each of the two rams, ¹⁵and two quarts for each of the fourteen lambs. ¹⁶You must also sacrifice a male goat as a sin offering, in addition to the regular daily burnt offering with its accom- panying grain offering and drink offering.

¹⁷"On the second day of this seven-day fes- tival, sacrifice twelve young bulls, two rams, and fourteen one-year-old male lambs, all with no physical defects. ¹⁸Each of these offer- ings of bulls, rams, and lambs must be accom- panied by the prescribed grain offering and drink offering. ¹⁹You must also sacrifice a male goat as a sin offering, in addition to the regu- lar daily burnt offering with its accompanying grain offering and drink offering.

²⁰"On the third day of the festival, sacrifice eleven young bulls, two rams, and fourteen one-year-old male lambs, all with no physical defects. ²¹Each of these offerings of bulls, rams, and lambs must be accompanied by the prescribed grain offering and drink offering. ²²You must also sacrifice a male goat as a sin offering, in addition to the regular daily burnt offering with its accompanying grain offering and drink offering.

²³"On the fourth day of the festival, sacrifice

29:1 Hebrew *on the first day of the seventh month.* This day of the Hebrew lunar calendar occurs in September or early October. 29:3a Hebrew ³/₁₀ *of an ephah* [5.4 liters]; also in 29:9, 14. 29:3b Hebrew ²/₁₀ *of an ephah* [3.6 liters]; also in 29:9, 14. 29:4 Hebrew ¹/₁₀ *of an ephah* [2 liters]; also in 29:10, 15. 29:7 Hebrew *On the tenth day of the seventh month;* see 29:1 and the note there. 29:12 Hebrew *On the fifteenth day of the seventh month;* see 29:1, 7 and the notes there.

ten young bulls, two rams, and fourteen one-year-old male lambs, all with no physical defects. ²⁴Each of these offerings of bulls, rams, and lambs must be accompanied by the prescribed grain offering and drink offering. ²⁵You must also sacrifice a male goat as a sin offering, in addition to the regular daily burnt offering with its accompanying grain offering and drink offering.

²⁶"On the fifth day of the festival, sacrifice nine young bulls, two rams, and fourteen one-year-old male lambs, all with no physical defects. ²⁷Each of these offerings of bulls, rams, and lambs must be accompanied by the prescribed grain offering and drink offering. ²⁸You must also sacrifice a male goat as a sin offering, in addition to the regular daily burnt offering with its accompanying grain offering and drink offering.

²⁹"On the sixth day of the festival, sacrifice eight young bulls, two rams, and fourteen one-year-old male lambs, all with no physical defects. ³⁰Each of these offerings of bulls, rams, and lambs must be accompanied by the prescribed grain offering and drink offering. ³¹You must also sacrifice a male goat as a sin offering, in addition to the regular daily burnt offering with its accompanying grain offering and drink offering.

³²"On the seventh day of the festival, sacrifice seven young bulls, two rams, and fourteen one-year-old male lambs, all with no physical defects. ³³Each of these offerings of bulls, rams, and lambs must be accompanied by the prescribed grain offering and drink offering. ³⁴You must also sacrifice one male goat as a sin offering, in addition to the regular daily burnt offering with its accompanying grain offering and drink offering.

³⁵"On the eighth day of the festival, call all the people to another holy assembly. You must do no regular work on that day. ³⁶You must present a burnt offering, very pleasing to the LORD. It will consist of one young bull, one ram, and seven one-year-old male lambs, all with no physical defects. ³⁷Each of these offerings must be accompanied by the prescribed

grain offering and drink offering. ³⁸You must also sacrifice one male goat as a sin offering, in addition to the regular daily burnt offering with its accompanying grain offering and drink offering.

³⁹"You must present these offerings to the LORD at your annual festivals. These are in addition to the sacrifices and offerings you present in connection with vows, or as freewill offerings, burnt offerings, grain offerings, drink offerings, or peace offerings."

⁴⁰So Moses gave all of these instructions to the people of Israel, just as the LORD had commanded him.

LAWS CONCERNING VOWS

30 Now Moses summoned the leaders of the tribes of Israel and told them, "This is what the LORD has commanded: ²A man who makes a vow to the LORD or makes a pledge under oath must never break it. He must do exactly what he said he would do.

³"If a young woman makes a vow to the LORD or a pledge under oath while she is still living at her father's home, ⁴and her father hears of the vow or pledge but says nothing, then all her vows and pledges will stand. ⁵But if her father refuses to let her fulfill the vow or pledge on the day he hears of it, then all her vows and pledges will become invalid. The LORD will forgive her because her father would not let her fulfill them.

⁶"Now suppose a young woman takes a vow or makes an impulsive pledge and later marries. ⁷If her husband learns of her vow or pledge and raises no objections on the day he hears of it, her vows and pledges will stand. ⁸But if her husband refuses to accept her vow or impulsive pledge on the day he hears of it, he nullifies her commitments, and the LORD will forgive her. ⁹If, however, a woman is a widow or is divorced, she must fulfill all her vows and pledges no matter what.

¹⁰"Suppose a woman is married and living in her husband's home when she makes a vow or pledge. ¹¹If her husband hears of it and does nothing to stop her, her vow or pledge will

My Daily Worship

— *February 10* —

PARTY ON!

NUMBERS 26:1–31:54

You must present these offering to the LORD at your annual festivals. These are in addition to the sacrifices and offerings you present in connection with vows, or as freewill offerings, burnt offerings, grain offerings, drink offerings, or peace offerings (29:39).

[i reflect]

An oldie-but-goodie song often heard at karaoke sing-a-longs is "Celebrate Good Times, Come On!" No, it's not a Christian song, but it calls attention to the inherent desire people have to party. There is something deep inside us that longs to dress up and sit down at a fancy table. Kicking up our heels comes naturally. We were born to celebrate!

Judging from what we read in Numbers, our inclination to throw confetti has a place. The Lord established a rhythm of celebration for the Israelites that called for special festivals over and above the regular worship observances that punctuated their calendars. You can't look at the worship life of the people of God without seeing the trappings of ceremony and pageantry. It's everywhere.

Worshipping the Lord was not a casual "oh, by the way, let's pray and be done with it" sort of thing. The worship of God was an event. Think about it. There were scads of people, adults and kids. There were animals. There was fire and food, tents and music . . . and time. The festivals, sacrifices, and offerings took time.

The Creator called his people then (and still does) to take time in his presence, fix their thoughts on him, and feast on good food. He wanted them to have a good time doing it, but he also wanted them not to rush. Plenty of parties was part of God's original design. How sad that people with so few reasons to celebrate know how to party better than those who have every reason to rejoice and celebrate with gusto!

Since he loves being the object of our celebration, he reminds us to celebrate often. And to help us do the very thing he wants, he gave us hearts that love to do that very thing. You can worship while you eat or while you're at a party. Celebrate *his* good times, come on!

[i pray]

Lord, as I come into your presence each day, help me not to be so time-conscious. As I think about the festivals of the Old Testament, there is a longing within me to be more creative in my expressions of praise. Inspire me to make my personal worship times a celebration.

[i respond]

Color outside the lines when it comes to thinking of ways to encounter the Lord during the week. Use your boombox. Use a sketchpad. Light a candle. Plan to have a good time!

stand. [12]But if her husband refuses to accept it on the day he hears of it, her vow or pledge will be nullified, and the LORD will forgive her. [13]So her husband may either confirm or nullify any vows or pledges she makes to deny herself. [14]But if he says nothing on the day he hears of it, then he is agreeing to it. [15]If he waits more than a day and then tries to nullify a vow or pledge, he will suffer the consequences of her guilt."

[16]These are the regulations the LORD gave Moses concerning relationships between a man and his wife, and between a father and a young daughter who still lives at home.

CONQUEST OF THE MIDIANITES

31 Then the LORD said to Moses, [2]"Take vengeance on the Midianites for leading the Israelites into idolatry. After that, you will die and join your ancestors."

[3]So Moses said to the people, "Choose some men to fight the LORD's war of vengeance against Midian. [4]From each tribe of Israel, send one thousand men into battle." [5]So they chose one thousand men from each tribe of Israel, a total of twelve thousand men armed for battle. [6]Then Moses sent them out, a thousand men from each tribe, and Phinehas son of Eleazar the priest led them into battle. They carried along the holy objects of the sanctuary and the trumpets for sounding the charge. [7]They attacked Midian just as the LORD had commanded Moses, and they killed all the men. [8]All five of the Midianite kings—Evi, Rekem, Zur, Hur, and Reba—died in the battle. They also killed Balaam son of Beor with the sword.

[9]Then the Israelite army captured the Midianite women and children and seized their cattle and flocks and all their wealth as plunder. [10]They burned all the towns and villages where the Midianites had lived. [11]After they had gathered the plunder and captives, both people and animals, [12]they brought them all to Moses and Eleazar the priest, and to the whole community of Israel, which was camped on the plains of Moab beside the Jordan River, across from Jericho. [13]Moses, Eleazar the priest, and all the leaders of the people went to meet them outside the camp. [14]But Moses was furious with all the military commanders* who had returned from the battle.

[15]"Why have you let all the women live?" he demanded. [16]"These are the very ones who followed Balaam's advice and caused the people of Israel to rebel against the LORD at Mount Peor. They are the ones who caused the plague to strike the LORD's people. [17]Now kill all the boys and all the women who have slept with a man. [18]Only the young girls who are virgins may live; you may keep them for yourselves. [19]And all of you who have killed anyone or touched a dead body must stay outside the camp for seven days. You must purify yourselves and your captives on the third and seventh days. [20]Also, purify all your clothing and everything made of leather, goat hair, or wood."

[21]Then Eleazar the priest said to the men who were in the battle, "The LORD has given Moses this requirement of the law: [22]Anything made of gold, silver, bronze, iron, tin, or lead—[23]that is, metals that do not burn—must be passed through fire in order to be made ceremonially pure. These metal objects must then be further purified with the water of purification. But everything that burns must be purified by the water alone. [24]On the seventh day you must wash your clothes and be purified. Then you may return to the camp."

DIVISION OF THE SPOILS

[25]And the LORD said to Moses, [26]"You and Eleazar the priest and the family leaders of each tribe are to make a list of all the plunder taken in the battle, including the people and animals. [27]Then divide the plunder into two parts, and give half to the men who fought the battle and half to the rest of the people. [28]But first give the LORD his share of the captives,

31:14 Hebrew *the commanders of thousands, and the commanders of hundreds;* also in 31:48, 52, 54.

cattle, donkeys, sheep, and goats that belong to the army. Set apart one out of every five hundred as the LORD's share. ²⁹Give this share of their half to Eleazar the priest as an offering to the LORD. ³⁰Also take one of every fifty of the captives, cattle, donkeys, sheep, and goats in the half that belongs to the people of Israel. Give this share to the Levites in charge of maintaining the LORD's Tabernacle." ³¹So Moses and Eleazar the priest did as the LORD commanded Moses.

³²The plunder remaining from the spoils that the fighting men had taken totaled 675,000 sheep, ³³72,000 cattle, ³⁴61,000 donkeys, ³⁵and 32,000 young girls.

³⁶So the half of the plunder given to the fighting men totaled 337,500 sheep, ³⁷of which 675 were the LORD's share; ³⁸36,000 cattle, of which 72 were the LORD's share; ³⁹30,500 donkeys, of which 61 were the LORD's share; ⁴⁰16,000 young girls, of whom 32 were the LORD's share. ⁴¹Moses gave all the LORD's share to Eleazar the priest, just as the LORD had directed him.

⁴²The half of the plunder belonging to the people of Israel, which Moses had separated from the half belonging to the fighting men, ⁴³amounted to 337,500 sheep, ⁴⁴36,000 cattle, ⁴⁵30,500 donkeys, ⁴⁶and 16,000 young girls. ⁴⁷From the half-share given to the people, Moses took one of every fifty prisoners and animals and gave them to the Levites who maintained the LORD's Tabernacle. All this was done just as the LORD had commanded Moses.

⁴⁸Then all the military commanders came to Moses ⁴⁹and said, "Sir, we have accounted for all the men who went out to battle under our command; not one of us is missing! ⁵⁰So we are presenting the items of gold we captured as an offering to the LORD from our share of the plunder—armbands, bracelets, rings, earrings, and necklaces. This will make atonement for our lives before the LORD."

⁵¹So Moses and Eleazar the priest received the gold from all the military commanders, all

kinds of jewelry and crafted objects. ⁵²In all, the gold that the commanders presented as a gift to the LORD weighed about 420 pounds.* ⁵³All the fighting men had taken some of the plunder for themselves. ⁵⁴So Moses and Eleazar the priest accepted the gifts from the military commanders and brought the gold to the Tabernacle* as a reminder to the LORD that the people of Israel belong to him.

Words of Worship

LIFTING THE HANDS

Lifting the Hands—Hebrew *na-sa' ya-dai* "lift the hands"; *na-sa' kap-pai* "lift the palms"; *pe-ras ya-dai* "spread out the hands"; Greek *e-pai-ro chei-ras* "lift up hands." Other expressions are found.

Why might we lift our hands? To reach for what is high, to project something forward, to seek recognition from the leader of a gathering we're part of? All of these might suggest why lifting our hands could be part of our worship of the Lord. But in another time, outside of worship, we have seen people lifting their hands—in the courtroom or an inauguration ceremony, taking an oath. When we lift our hands to the Lord, we're pledging ourselves to his truth and affirming our loyalty to him.

Lifting the hand is an ancient gesture of fidelity to a ruler. The Lord wants our gifts and service but he wants our hearts' devotion even more. As Paul suggests, lifting hands from a life consecrated to him goes along with prayer (1 Timothy 2:8). It symbolizes our desire to be faithful to God. "Accept my prayer as incense offered to you, and my upraised hands as an evening offering" (Psalm 141:2).

31:52 Hebrew *16,750 shekels* [191 kilograms]. 31:54 Hebrew *Tent of Meeting.*

32 Now the tribes of Reuben and Gad owned vast numbers of livestock. So when they saw that the lands of Jazer and Gilead were ideally suited for their flocks and herds, [2]they came to Moses, Eleazar the priest, and the other leaders of the people. They said, [3]"Ataroth, Dibon, Jazer, Nimrah, Heshbon, Elealeh, Sebam, Nebo, and Beon—[4]the LORD has conquered this whole area for the people of Israel. It is ideally suited for all our flocks and herds. [5]If we have found favor with you, please let us have this land as our property instead of giving us land across the Jordan River."

[6]"Do you mean you want to stay back here while your brothers go across and do all the fighting?" Moses asked the Reubenites and Gadites. [7]"Are you trying to discourage the rest of the people of Israel from going across to the land the LORD has given them? [8]This is what your ancestors did when I sent them from Kadesh-barnea to explore the land. [9]After they went up to the valley of Eshcol and scouted the land, they discouraged the people of Israel from entering the land the LORD was giving them. [10]Then the LORD was furious with them, and he vowed, [11]'Of all those I rescued from Egypt, no one who is twenty years old or older will ever see the land I solemnly promised to Abraham, Isaac, and Jacob, for they have not obeyed me completely. [12]The only exceptions are Caleb son of Jephunneh the Kenizzite and Joshua son of Nun, for they have wholeheartedly followed the LORD.'

[13]"The LORD was furious with Israel and made them wander in the wilderness for forty years until the whole generation that sinned against him had died. [14]But here you are, a brood of sinners, doing exactly the same thing! You are making the LORD even angrier with Israel. [15]If you turn away from him like this and he abandons them again in the wilderness, you will be responsible for destroying this entire nation!"

[16]But they responded to Moses, "We simply want to build sheepfolds for our flocks and fortified cities for our wives and children. [17]Then we will arm ourselves and lead our fellow Israelites into battle until we have brought them safely to their inheritance. Meanwhile, our families will stay in the fortified cities we build here, so they will be safe from any attacks by the local people. [18]We will not return to our homes until all the people of Israel have received their inheritance of land. [19]But we do not want any of the land on the other side of the Jordan. We would rather live here on the east side where we have received our inheritance."

[20]Then Moses said, "If you keep your word and arm yourselves for the LORD's battles, [21]and if your troops cross the Jordan until the LORD has driven out his enemies, [22]then you may return when the land is finally subdued before the LORD. You will have discharged your duty to the LORD and to the rest of the people of Israel. And the land on the east side of the Jordan will be your inheritance from the LORD. [23]But if you fail to keep your word, then you will have sinned against the LORD, and you may be sure that your sin will find you out. [24]Go ahead and build towns for your families and sheepfolds for your flocks, but do everything you have said."

[25]Then the people of Gad and Reuben replied, "We are your servants and will follow your instructions exactly. [26]Our children, wives, flocks, and cattle will stay here in the towns of Gilead. [27]But, sir, all who are able to bear arms will cross over to fight for the LORD, just as you have said."

[28]So Moses gave orders to Eleazar, Joshua, and the tribal leaders of Israel. [29]He said, "If all the men of Gad and Reuben who are able to fight the LORD's battles cross the Jordan with you, then when the land is conquered, you must give them the land of Gilead as their property. [30]But if they refuse to cross over and march ahead of you, then they must accept land with the rest of you in the land of Canaan."

[31]The tribes of Gad and Reuben said again,

"Sir, we will do as the LORD has commanded! ³²We will cross the Jordan into Canaan fully armed to fight for the LORD, but our inheritance of land will be here on this side of the Jordan."

³³So Moses assigned to the tribes of Gad, Reuben, and half the tribe of Manasseh son of Joseph the territory of King Sihon of the Amorites and the land of King Og of Bashan—the whole land with its towns and surrounding lands.

³⁴The people of Gad built the towns of Dibon, Ataroth, Aroer, ³⁵Atroth-shophan, Jazer, Jogbehah, ³⁶Beth-nimrah, and Beth-haran. These were all fortified cities with sheepfolds for their flocks.

³⁷The people of Reuben built the towns of Heshbon, Elealeh, Kiriathaim, ³⁸Nebo, Baal-meon, and Sibmah. They changed the names of some of the towns they conquered and rebuilt.

³⁹Then the descendants of Makir of the tribe of Manasseh went to Gilead and conquered it, and they drove out the Amorites, who were living there. ⁴⁰So Moses gave Gilead to the Makirites, descendants of Manasseh, and they lived there. ⁴¹The people of Jair, another clan of the tribe of Manasseh, captured many of the towns in Gilead and changed the name of that region to the Towns of Jair.* ⁴²Meanwhile, a man named Nobah captured the town of Kenath and its surrounding villages, and he renamed that area Nobah after himself.

REMEMBERING ISRAEL'S JOURNEY

33 This is the itinerary the Israelites followed as they marched out of Egypt under the leadership of Moses and Aaron. ²At the LORD's direction, Moses kept a written record of their progress. These are the stages of their march, identified by the different places they stopped along the way.

³They set out from the city of Rameses on the morning after the first Passover celebration in early spring.* The people of Israel left defiantly, in full view of all the Egyptians. ⁴Meanwhile, the Egyptians were burying all their firstborn sons, whom the LORD had killed the night before. The LORD had defeated the gods of Egypt that night with great acts of judgment!

⁵After leaving Rameses, the Israelites set up camp at Succoth.

⁶Then they left Succoth and camped at Etham on the edge of the wilderness.

⁷They left Etham and turned back toward Pi-hahiroth, opposite Baal-zephon, and camped near Migdol.

⁸They left Pi-hahiroth and crossed the Red Sea* into the wilderness beyond. Then they traveled for three days into the Etham wilderness and camped at Marah.

⁹They left Marah and camped at Elim, where there are twelve springs of water and seventy palm trees.

¹⁰They left Elim and camped beside the Red Sea.*

¹¹They left the Red Sea and camped in the Sin* Desert.

¹²They left the Sin Desert and camped at Dophkah.

¹³They left Dophkah and camped at Alush.

¹⁴They left Alush and camped at Rephidim, where there was no water for the people to drink.

¹⁵They left Rephidim and camped in the wilderness of Sinai.

¹⁶They left the wilderness of Sinai and camped at Kibroth-hattaavah.

¹⁷They left Kibroth-hattaavah and camped at Hazeroth.

¹⁸They left Hazeroth and camped at Rithmah.

¹⁹They left Rithmah and camped at Rimmon-perez.

32:41 Hebrew *Havvoth-jair.* 33:3 Hebrew *on the fifteenth day of the first month.* This day of the Hebrew lunar calendar occurs in late March or early April. 33:8 Hebrew *the sea.* 33:10 Hebrew *sea of reeds;* also in 33:11. 33:11 Not to be confused with the English word *sin.*

²⁰They left Rimmon-perez and camped at Libnah.

²¹They left Libnah and camped at Rissah.

²²They left Rissah and camped at Kehelathah.

²³They left Kehelathah and camped at Mount Shepher.

²⁴They left Mount Shepher and camped at Haradah.

²⁵They left Haradah and camped at Makheloth.

²⁶They left Makheloth and camped at Tahath.

²⁷They left Tahath and camped at Terah.

²⁸They left Terah and camped at Mithcah.

²⁹They left Mithcah and camped at Hashmonah.

³⁰They left Hashmonah and camped at Moseroth.

³¹They left Moseroth and camped at Bene-jaakan.

³²They left Bene-jaakan and camped at Hor-haggidgad.

³³They left Hor-haggidgad and camped at Jotbathah.

³⁴They left Jotbathah and camped at Abronah.

³⁵They left Abronah and camped at Ezion-geber.

³⁶They left Ezion-geber and camped at Kadesh in the wilderness of Zin.

³⁷They left Kadesh and camped at Mount Hor, at the border of Edom.

³⁸While they were at the foot of Mount Hor, Aaron the priest was directed by the LORD to go up the mountain, and there he died. This happened on a day in midsummer,* during the fortieth year after Israel's departure from Egypt. ³⁹Aaron was 123 years old when he died there on Mount Hor.

⁴⁰It was then that the Canaanite king of Arad, who lived in the Negev in the land of Canaan, heard that the people of Israel were approaching his land.

⁴¹Meanwhile, the Israelites left Mount Hor and camped at Zalmonah.

⁴²Then they left Zalmonah and camped at Punon.

⁴³They left Punon and camped at Oboth.

⁴⁴They left Oboth and camped at Iye-abarim on the border of Moab.

⁴⁵They left Iye-abarim* and camped at Dibon-gad.

⁴⁶They left Dibon-gad and camped at Almon-diblathaim.

⁴⁷They left Almon-diblathaim and camped in the mountains east of the river,* near Mount Nebo.

⁴⁸They left the mountains east of the river and camped on the plains of Moab beside the Jordan River, across from Jericho. ⁴⁹Along the Jordan River they camped from Beth-jeshimoth as far as Abel-shittim on the plains of Moab.

⁵⁰While they were camped near the Jordan River on the plains of Moab opposite Jericho, the LORD said to Moses, ⁵¹"Speak to the Israelites and tell them: 'When you cross the Jordan River into the land of Canaan, ⁵²you must drive out all the people living there. You must destroy all their carved and molten images and demolish all their pagan shrines. ⁵³Take possession of the land and settle in it, because I have given it to you to occupy. ⁵⁴You must distribute the land among the clans by sacred lot and in proportion to their size. A larger inheritance of land will be allotted to each of the larger clans, and a smaller inheritance will be allotted to each of the smaller clans. The decision of the sacred lot is final. In this way, the land will be divided among your ancestral tribes. ⁵⁵But if you fail to drive out the people who live in the land, those who remain will be like splinters in your eyes and

---

33:38 Hebrew *on the first day of the fifth month.* This day of the Hebrew lunar calendar occurs in July or early August. **33:45** As in 33:44; Hebrew reads *Iyim,* another name for Iye-abarim. **33:47** Hebrew *the mountains of Abarim;* also in 33:48.

My Daily Worship

— *February 11* —

MILESTONES & MILEPOSTS

NUMBERS 32:1–36:13

At the LORD's direction, Moses kept a written record of their progress. These are the stages
of their march, identified by the different places they stopped along the way (33:2).

[i reflect]

For as long as she could remember, Star A. had kept a journal. In addition to charting mundane trivia like weather and what she accomplished each day, she maintained a list of details that might prove helpful in the future.

For example, if she entertained houseguests on a given day, she'd record the menu she prepared (so not to repeat the same recipe each time). But Star's journal was more than facts and figures. It also chronicled her faith. Significant milestones of God's intervention—times of unexpected blessing, documentations of answered prayer. From time to time, she would pick up one of her completed journals and reflect on God's faithfulness.

As Star entered her eighth decade of life and began to struggle with short-term memory loss, she wondered if she would fall prey to the same monster that had destroyed her mother's mind. Tests for Alzheimer's disease were negative, but the fear of what might still happen motivated Star to maintain her daily routine of making journal entries before going to bed. "Even if I am spared from coming down with that dreaded disease," she said, "at least I will have a thorough record of my life to pass on to my children and grandchildren."

This grandmother discovered on her own the very blessing God gave the Israelites. He commanded them to keep a written record of their progress prior to reaching the Promised Land. The discipline of looking back helps you come to terms with the distance you've come by faith. Can you think of some pivotal mileposts along the way? Allow those to prompt you to look up in worship today.

[i pray]

Lord, it troubles me how easy it is to forget the times you've answered my prayers.
I'm memory-challenged! Looking back where I was when I first started walking with you,
I'm amazed at how far you've brought me, and I'm grateful.

[i respond]

Journaling doesn't have to be a time-consuming exercise. It doesn't have to be a "guilt-producer" either. Carry a small spiral notebook with you. A couple of times a week record answers to prayer or other "God-sightings."

thorns in your sides. They will harass you in the land where you live. [56]And I will do to you what I had planned to do to them.' "

BOUNDARIES OF THE LAND

34 Then the LORD said to Moses, [2]"Give these instructions to the Israelites: When you come into the land of Canaan, which I am giving you as your special possession, these will be the boundaries. [3]The southern portion of your country will extend from the wilderness of Zin, along the edge of Edom. The southern boundary will begin on the east at the Dead Sea.* [4]It will then run south past Scorpion Pass* in the direction of Zin. Its southernmost point will be Kadesh-barnea, from which it will go to Hazar-addar, and on to Azmon. [5]From Azmon the boundary will turn toward the brook of Egypt and end at the Mediterranean Sea.*

[6]"Your western boundary will be the coastline of the Mediterranean Sea.

[7]"Your northern boundary will begin at the Mediterranean Sea and run eastward to Mount Hor, [8]then to Lebo-hamath, and on through Zedad [9]and Ziphron to Hazar-enan. This will be your northern boundary.

[10]"The eastern boundary will start at Hazar-enan and run south to Shepham, [11]then down to Riblah on the east side of Ain. From there the boundary will run down along the eastern edge of the Sea of Galilee,* [12]and then along the Jordan River to the Dead Sea. These are the boundaries of your land."

[13]Then Moses told the Israelites, "This is the territory you are to divide among yourselves by sacred lot. The LORD commands that the land be divided up among the nine and a half remaining tribes. [14]The families of the tribes of Reuben, Gad, and half the tribe of Manasseh have already received their inheritance of land [15]on the east side of the Jordan River, across from Jericho."

LEADERS TO DIVIDE THE LAND

[16]And the LORD said to Moses, [17]"These are the men who are to divide the land among the people: Eleazar the priest and Joshua son of Nun. [18]Also enlist one leader from each tribe to help them with the task. [19]These are the tribes and the names of the leaders:

Tribe	Leader
Judah	Caleb son of Jephunneh
[20] Simeon	Shemuel son of Ammihud
[21] Benjamin	Elidad son of Kislon
[22] Dan	Bukki son of Jogli
[23] Manasseh son of Joseph	Hanniel son of Ephod
[24] Ephraim son of Joseph . . .	Kemuel son of Shiphtan
[25] Zebulun	Elizaphan son of Parnach
[26] Issachar	Paltiel son of Azzan
[27] Asher	Ahihud son of Shelomi
[28] Naphtali	Pedahel son of Ammihud

[29]These are the men the LORD has appointed to oversee the dividing of the land of Canaan among the Israelites."

TOWNS FOR THE LEVITES

35 While Israel was camped beside the Jordan on the plains of Moab, across from Jericho, the LORD said to Moses, [2]"Instruct the people of Israel to give to the Levites from their property certain towns to live in, along with the surrounding pasturelands. [3]These towns will be their homes, and the surrounding lands will provide pasture for their cattle, flocks, and other livestock. [4]The pastureland assigned to the Levites around these towns will extend 1,500 feet* from the

---

If we don't worship God, we'll worship something or someone else.

JOHN WIMBER

34:3 Hebrew *Salt Sea;* also in 34:12.   34:4 Hebrew *the ascent of Akrabbim.*   34:5 Hebrew *the sea;* also in 34:6, 7.   34:11 Hebrew *sea of Kinnereth.*   35:4 Hebrew *1,000 cubits* [450 meters].

town walls in every direction. ⁵Measure off 3,000 feet* outside the town walls in every direction—east, south, west, north—with the town at the center. This area will serve as the larger pastureland for the towns.

⁶"You must give the Levites six cities of refuge, where a person who has accidentally killed someone can flee for safety. In addition, give them forty-two other towns. ⁷In all, forty-eight towns with the surrounding pastureland will be given to the Levites. ⁸These towns will come from the property of the people of Israel. The larger tribes will give more towns to the Levites, while the smaller tribes will give fewer. Each tribe will give in proportion to its inheritance."

CITIES OF REFUGE

⁹And the LORD said to Moses, ¹⁰"Say this to the people of Israel: 'When you cross the Jordan into the land of Canaan, ¹¹designate cities of refuge for people to flee to if they have killed someone accidentally. ¹²These cities will be places of protection from a dead person's relatives who want to avenge the death. The slayer must not be killed before being tried by the community. ¹³Designate six cities of refuge for yourselves, ¹⁴three on the east side of the Jordan River and three on the west in the land of Canaan. ¹⁵These cities are for the protection of Israelites, resident foreigners, and traveling merchants. Anyone who accidentally kills someone may flee there for safety.

¹⁶" 'But if someone strikes and kills another person with a piece of iron, it must be presumed to be murder, and the murderer must be executed. ¹⁷Or if someone strikes and kills another person with a large stone, it is murder, and the murderer must be executed. ¹⁸The same is true if someone strikes and kills another person with a wooden weapon. It must be presumed to be murder, and the murderer must be executed. ¹⁹The victim's nearest relative is responsible for putting the murderer to death. When they meet, the avenger must execute the murderer. ²⁰So if

in premeditated hostility someone pushes another person or throws a dangerous object and the person dies, it is murder. ²¹Or if someone angrily hits another person with a fist and the person dies, it is murder. In such cases, the victim's nearest relative must execute the murderer when they meet.

²²" 'But suppose someone pushes another person without premeditated hostility, or throws something that unintentionally hits another person, ²³or accidentally drops a stone on someone, though they were not enemies, and the person dies. ²⁴If this should happen, the assembly must follow these regulations in making a judgment between the slayer and the avenger, the victim's nearest relative. ²⁵They must protect the slayer from the avenger, and they must send the slayer back to live in a city of refuge until the death of the high priest.

²⁶" 'But if the slayer leaves the city of refuge, ²⁷and the victim's nearest relative finds him outside the city limits and kills him, it will not be considered murder. ²⁸The slayer should have stayed inside the city of refuge until the death of the high priest. But after the death of the high priest, the slayer may return to his own property. ²⁹These are permanent laws for you to observe from generation to generation, wherever you may live.

³⁰" 'All murderers must be executed, but only if there is more than one witness. No one may be put to death on the testimony of only one witness. ³¹Also, you must never accept a ransom payment for the life of someone judged guilty of murder and subject to execution; murderers must always be put to death. ³²And never accept a ransom payment from someone who has fled to a city of refuge, allowing the slayer to return to his property before the death of the high priest. ³³This will ensure that the land where you live will not be polluted, for murder pollutes the land. And no atonement can be made for murder except by the execution of the murderer. ³⁴You must not defile the land where you are going to live,

35:5 Hebrew *2,000 cubits* [900 meters].

for I live there myself. I am the LORD, who lives among the people of Israel.'"

WOMEN WHO INHERIT PROPERTY

36 Then the heads of the clan of Gilead—descendants of Makir, son of Manasseh, son of Joseph—came to Moses and the family leaders of Israel with a petition. ²They said, "Sir, the LORD instructed you to divide the land by sacred lot among the people of Israel. You were told by the LORD to give the inheritance of our brother Zelophehad to his daughters. ³But if any of them marries a man from another tribe, their inheritance of land will go with them to the tribe into which they marry. In this way, the total area of our tribal land will be reduced. ⁴Then when the Year of Jubilee comes, their inheritance of land will be added to that of the new tribe, causing it to be lost forever to our ancestral tribe."

⁵So Moses gave the Israelites this command from the LORD: "The men of the tribe of Joseph are right. ⁶This is what the LORD commands concerning the daughters of Zelo-

phehad: Let them marry anyone they like, as long as it is within their own ancestral tribe. ⁷None of the inherited land may pass from tribe to tribe, for the inheritance of every tribe must remain fixed as it was first allotted. ⁸The daughters throughout the tribes of Israel who are in line to inherit property must marry within their tribe, so that all the Israelites will keep their ancestral property. ⁹No inheritance may pass from one tribe to another; each tribe of Israel must hold on to its allotted inheritance of land."

¹⁰The daughters of Zelophehad did as the LORD commanded Moses. ¹¹Mahlah, Tirzah, Hoglah, Milcah, and Noah all married cousins on their father's side. ¹²They married into the clans of Manasseh son of Joseph. Thus, their inheritance of land remained within their ancestral tribe.

¹³These are the commands and regulations that the LORD gave to the people of Israel through Moses while they were camped on the plains of Moab beside the Jordan River, across from Jericho.

Deuteronomy

You must fear the LORD your God and worship him (10:20).

A Time to Remember

"Never doubt in the darkness what God has shown you in the light"—Dr. V. Raymond Edman.

That statement, made first to assembled students of Wheaton College by their president decades ago, highlights two truths: first, darkness will come; second, in the darkness, remember the light.

Darkness can immobilize—we stay still, afraid to stub or stumble. Darkness can frighten—we imagine all sorts of terrors. Darkness can breed doubt—we wonder about what's really there.

That's when we must remember.

Darkness comes in many forms; shadows of persecution, sickness, worry, opposition, and other enemies move close and hinder our sight. That's when we must remember . . . the fact that God loves us, the promise of his presence, and the reality of his past deliverance.

The book of Deuteronomy is about remembering. As the people stood poised at long last to enter the land that God had promised them, Moses reviewed their history, their laws, and, most importantly, their relationship with the Holy One of Israel. He knew dark days would come, challenges from without and within. So they needed to remember their history and their God.

The stories were familiar, but Moses also gave the story behind the story—his perspective as one who knew he was deeply loved by God. The book ends with a profoundly beautiful praise song expressing Moses' deep gratitude to the "Rock of their salvation" (32:15).

As you read, consider the ways that God has shown his deep love for you—remember—and then respond with praise words or songs as Moses did.

Worship Moments

- Moses asks for a wholehearted commitment to the Lord's commands, and suggests ways for Israel to remain constantly aware of them: "Repeat them. . . . Talk about them. . . . Tie them to your hands, . . . wear them. . . . Write them on the doorposts" (6:7–9).

- Worship is to be the first act Israel performs after entering Canaan: "When you cross the Jordan River and enter the land, . . . build an altar there to the LORD your God, . . . and feast there with great joy" (27:2, 5, 7).

- Moses established the reading of the law during worship: "At the end of every seventh year, . . . you must read this law to all the people" (31:10–11).

THE COMMAND TO LEAVE SINAI

1 This book records the words that Moses spoke to all the people of Israel while they were in the wilderness east of the Jordan River. They were camped in the Jordan Valley* near Suph, between Paran on one side and Tophel, Laban, Hazeroth, and Di-zahab on the other. [2]Normally it takes only eleven days to travel from Mount Sinai* to Kadesh-barnea, going by way of Mount Seir. [3]But forty years after the Israelites left Mount Sinai, on a day in midwinter,* Moses gave these speeches to the Israelites, telling them everything the LORD had commanded him to say. [4]This was after he had defeated King Sihon of the Amorites, who had ruled in Heshbon, and King Og of Bashan, who had ruled in Ashtaroth and Edrei.

[5]So Moses addressed the people of Israel while they were in the land of Moab east of the Jordan River. He began to explain the law as follows: [6]"When we were at Mount Sinai, the LORD our God said to us, 'You have stayed at this mountain long enough. [7]It is time to break camp and move on. Go to the hill country of the Amorites and to all the neighboring regions—the Jordan Valley, the hill country, the western foothills,* the Negev, and the coastal plain. Go to the land of the Canaanites and to Lebanon, and all the way to the great Euphrates River. [8]I am giving all this land to you! Go in and occupy it, for it is the land the LORD swore to give to your ancestors Abraham, Isaac, and Jacob, and to all their descendants.'

MOSES APPOINTS LEADERS FROM EACH TRIBE

[9]"At that time I told you, 'You are too great a burden for me to carry all by myself. [10]The LORD your God has made you as numerous as the stars! [11]And may the LORD, the God of your ancestors, multiply you a thousand times more and bless you as he promised! [12]But how can I settle all your quarrels and problems by myself? [13]Choose some men from each tribe who have wisdom, understanding, and a good reputation, and I will appoint them as your leaders.'

[14]"You agreed that my plan was a good one. [15]So I took the wise and respected men you had selected from your tribes and appointed them to serve as judges and officials over you. Some were responsible for a thousand people, some for a hundred, some for fifty, and some for ten. [16]I instructed the judges, 'You must be perfectly fair at all times, not only to fellow Israelites, but also to the foreigners living among you. [17]When you make decisions, never favor those who are rich; be fair to lowly and great alike. Don't be afraid of how they will react, for you are judging in the place of God. Bring me any cases that are too difficult for you, and I will handle them.' [18]And at that time I gave you instructions about everything you were to do.

SCOUTS EXPLORE THE LAND

[19]"Then, just as the LORD our God directed us, we left Mount Sinai and traveled through the great and terrifying wilderness, which you yourselves saw, and headed toward the hill country of the Amorites. When we arrived at Kadesh-barnea, [20]I said to you, 'You have now reached the land that the LORD our God is giving us. [21]Look! He has placed it in front of you. Go and occupy it as the LORD, the God of your ancestors, has promised you. Don't be afraid! Don't be discouraged!'

[22]"But you responded, 'First, let's send out scouts to explore the land for us. They will advise us on the best route to take and decide which towns we should capture.' [23]This seemed like a good idea to me, so I chose twelve scouts, one from each of your tribes. [24]They crossed into the hills and came to the valley of Eshcol and explored it. [25]They picked some of its fruit and brought it back to us. And they reported that the land the LORD our God had given us was indeed a good land.

1:1 Hebrew *the Arabah;* also in 1:7.   1:2 Hebrew *Horeb,* another name for Sinai; also in 1:6, 19.   1:3 Hebrew *on the first day of the eleventh month.* This day of the Hebrew lunar calendar occurs in January or early February.   1:7 Hebrew *the Shephelah.*

Israel Rebels against the Lord

²⁶"But you rebelled against the command of the Lord your God and refused to go in. ²⁷You murmured and complained in your tents and said, 'The Lord must hate us, bringing us here from Egypt to be slaughtered by these Amorites. ²⁸How can we go on? Our scouts have demoralized us with their report. They say that the people of the land are taller and more powerful than we are, and that the walls of their towns rise high into the sky! They have even seen giants there—the descendants of Anak!'

²⁹"But I said to you, 'Don't be afraid! ³⁰The Lord your God is going before you. He will fight for you, just as you saw him do in Egypt. ³¹And you saw how the Lord your God cared for you again and again here in the wilderness, just as a father cares for his child. Now he has brought you to this place.' ³²But even after all he did, you refused to trust the Lord your God, ³³who goes before you looking for the best places to camp, guiding you by a pillar of fire at night and a pillar of cloud by day.

³⁴"When the Lord heard your complaining, he became very angry. So he solemnly swore, ³⁵'Not one of you from this entire wicked generation will live to see the good land I swore to give your ancestors, ³⁶except Caleb son of Jephunneh. He will see this land because he has followed the Lord completely. I will give to him and his descendants some of the land he walked over during his scouting mission.'

³⁷"And the Lord was also angry with me because of you. He said to me, 'You will never enter the Promised Land! ³⁸Instead, your assistant, Joshua son of Nun, will lead the people into the land. Encourage him as he prepares to enter it. ³⁹I will give the land to your innocent children. You were afraid they would be captured, but they will be the ones who occupy it. ⁴⁰As for you, turn around now and go on back through the wilderness toward the Red Sea.*'

⁴¹"Then you confessed, 'We have sinned against the Lord! We will go into the land and fight for it, as the Lord our God has told us.' So your men strapped on their weapons, thinking it would be easy to conquer the hill country.

⁴²"But the Lord said to me, 'Tell them not to attack, for I will not go with them. If they do, they will be crushed by their enemies.' ⁴³This is what I told you, but you would not listen. Instead, you again rebelled against the Lord's command and arrogantly went into the hill country to fight. ⁴⁴But the Amorites who lived there came out against you like a swarm of bees. They chased and battered you all the way from Seir to Hormah. ⁴⁵Then you returned and wept before the Lord, but he refused to listen. ⁴⁶So you stayed there at Kadesh for a long time.

Remembering Israel's Wanderings

2 "Then we turned around and set out across the wilderness toward the Red Sea,* just as the Lord had instructed me, and we wandered around Mount Seir for a long time. ²Then at last the Lord said to me, ³'You have been wandering around in this hill country long enough; turn northward. ⁴Give these orders to the people: "You will be passing through the country belonging to your relatives the Edomites, the descendants of Esau, who live in Seir. The Edomites will feel threatened, so be careful. ⁵Don't bother them, for I have given them all the hill country around Mount Seir as their property, and I will not give you any of their land. ⁶Pay them for whatever food or water you use. ⁷The Lord your God has blessed everything you have done and has watched your every step through this great wilderness. During these forty years, the Lord your God has been with you and provided for your every need so that you lacked nothing." ' ⁸So we went past our relatives, the descendants of Esau, who live in Seir, and avoided the road through the Arabah Valley that comes up from Elath and Ezion-geber.

"Then as we traveled northward along the

1:40 Hebrew *sea of reeds.*   2:1 Hebrew *sea of reeds.*

desert route through Moab, ⁹the LORD warned us, 'Do not bother the Moabites, the descendants of Lot, or start a war with them. I have given them Ar as their property, and I will not give you any of their land.' "

¹⁰(A numerous and powerful race of giants called the Emites had once lived in the area of Ar. They were as tall as the Anakites, another race of giants. ¹¹Both the Emites and the Anakites are often referred to as the Rephaites, but the Moabites called them Emites. ¹²In earlier times the Horites had lived at Mount Seir, but they were driven out and displaced by the descendants of Esau. In a similar way the peoples in Canaan were driven from the land that the LORD had assigned to Israel.)

¹³Moses continued, "Then the LORD told us to cross Zered Brook, and we did. ¹⁴So thirty-eight years passed from the time we first arrived at Kadesh-barnea until we finally crossed Zered Brook! For the LORD had vowed that this could not happen until all the men old enough to fight in battle had died in the wilderness. ¹⁵The LORD had lifted his hand against them until all of them had finally died.

¹⁶"When all the men of fighting age had died, ¹⁷the LORD said to me, ¹⁸'Today you will cross the border of Moab at Ar ¹⁹and enter the land of Ammon. But do not bother the Ammonites, the descendants of Lot, or start a war with them. I have given the land of Ammon to them as their property, and I will not give you any of their land.' "

²⁰(That area, too, was once considered the land of the Rephaites, though the Ammonites referred to them as Zamzummites. ²¹They were a numerous and powerful race, as tall as the Anakites. But the LORD destroyed them so the Ammonites could occupy their land. ²²He had similarly helped the descendants of Esau at Mount Seir, for he destroyed the Horites so they could settle there in their place. The descendants of Esau live there to this day. ²³A similar thing happened when the Caphtorites

from Crete* invaded and destroyed the Avvites, who had lived in villages in the area of Gaza.)

²⁴Moses continued, "Then the LORD said, 'Now cross the Arnon Gorge! Look, I will help you defeat Sihon the Amorite, king of Heshbon, and I will give you his land. Attack him and begin to occupy the land. ²⁵Beginning today I will make all people throughout the earth terrified of you. When they hear reports about you, they will tremble with dread and fear.'

VICTORY OVER SIHON OF HESHBON

²⁶"Then from the wilderness of Kedemoth I sent ambassadors to King Sihon of Heshbon with this proposal of peace: ²⁷'Let us pass through your land. We will stay on the main road and won't turn off into the fields on either side. ²⁸We will pay for every bite of food we eat and all the water we drink. All we want is permission to pass through your land. ²⁹The descendants of Esau at Mount Seir allowed us to go through their country, and so did the Moabites, who live in Ar. Let us pass through until we cross the Jordan into the land the LORD our God has given us.' ³⁰But King Sihon refused to allow you to pass through, because the LORD your God made Sihon stubborn and defiant so he could help you defeat them, as he has now done.

³¹"Then the LORD said to me, 'Look, I have begun to hand King Sihon and his land over to you. Begin now to conquer and occupy his land.' ³²Then King Sihon declared war on us and mobilized his forces at Jahaz. ³³But the LORD our God handed him over to us, and we crushed him, his sons, and all his people. ³⁴We conquered all his towns and completely destroyed* everyone—men, women, and children. Not a single person was spared. ³⁵We took all the livestock as plunder for ourselves, along with anything of value from the towns we ransacked.

2:23 Hebrew *from Caphtor.* 2:34 The Hebrew term used here refers to the complete consecration of things or people to the LORD, either by destroying them or by giving them as an offering.

[36]"The LORD our God helped us conquer Aroer on the edge of the Arnon Gorge, the town in the gorge, and the whole area as far as Gilead. No town had walls too strong for us. [37]However, we stayed away from the Ammonites along the Jabbok River and the towns in the hill country—all the places the LORD our God had commanded us to leave alone.

VICTORY OVER OG OF BASHAN

3 "Next we headed for the land of Bashan, where King Og and his army attacked us at Edrei. [2]But the LORD told me, 'Do not be afraid of him, for I have given you victory over Og and his army, giving you his entire land. Treat him just as you treated King Sihon of the Amorites, who ruled in Heshbon.' [3]So the LORD our God handed King Og and all his people over to us, and we killed them all. [4]We conquered all sixty of his towns, the entire Argob region in his kingdom of Bashan. [5]These were all fortified cities with high walls and barred gates. We also took many unwalled villages at the same time. [6]We completely destroyed* the kingdom of Bashan, just as we had destroyed King Sihon of Heshbon. We destroyed* all the people in every town we conquered—men, women, and children alike. [7]But we kept all the livestock for ourselves and took plunder from all the towns.

[8]"We now possessed all the land of the two Amorite kings east of the Jordan River—from the Arnon Gorge to Mount Hermon. [9](Mount Hermon is called Sirion by the Sidonians; the Amorites call it Senir.) [10]We had now conquered all the cities on the plateau, and all Gilead and Bashan as far as the towns of Salecah and Edrei, which were part of Og's kingdom in Bashan. [11](Incidentally, King Og of Bashan was the last of the giant Rephaites. His iron bed was more than thirteen feet long and six feet wide.* It can still be seen in the Ammonite city of Rabbah.)

LAND DIVISION EAST OF THE JORDAN

[12]"When we took possession of this land, I gave the territory beyond Aroer along the Arnon Gorge, plus half of the hill country of Gilead with its towns, to the tribes of Reuben and Gad. [13]Then I gave the rest of Gilead and all of Bashan—Og's former kingdom—to the half-tribe of Manasseh. (The Argob region of Bashan used to be known as the land of the Rephaites. [14]Jair, a leader from the tribe of Manasseh, acquired the whole Argob region in Bashan all the way to the borders of the Geshurites and Maacathites. Jair renamed this region after himself, calling it the Towns of Jair,* as it is still known today.) [15]I gave Gilead to the clan of Makir. [16]And to the tribes of Reuben and Gad I gave the area extending from Gilead to the middle of the Arnon Gorge, all the way to the Jabbok River on the Ammonite frontier. [17]They also received the Jordan Valley, including the Jordan River and its eastern banks, all the way from the Sea of Galilee down to the Dead Sea,* with the slopes of Pisgah on the east.

[18]"At that time I gave this command to the tribes that will live east of the Jordan: 'Although the LORD your God has given you this land as your property, all your fighting men must cross the Jordan, armed and ready to protect your Israelite relatives. [19]Your wives, children, and numerous livestock, however, may stay behind in the towns I have given you. [20]When the LORD has given security to the rest of the Israelites, as he has to you, and when they occupy the land the LORD your God is giving them across the Jordan River, then you may return here to the land I have given you.'

MOSES FORBIDDEN TO ENTER THE LAND

[21]"At that time I said to Joshua, 'You have seen all that the LORD your God has done to these

3:6 The Hebrew term used here refers to the complete consecration of things or people to the LORD, either by destroying them or by giving them as an offering. 3:11 Hebrew 9 cubits [4.1 meters] long and 4 cubits [1.8 meters] wide. 3:14 Hebrew Havvoth-jair. 3:17 Hebrew from Kinnereth to the sea of the Arabah, the Salt Sea.

two kings. He will do the same to all the kingdoms on the west side of the Jordan. ²²Do not be afraid of the nations there, for the LORD your God will fight for you.'

²³"At that time I pleaded with the LORD and said, ²⁴'O Sovereign LORD, I am your servant. You have only begun to show me your greatness and power. Is there any god in heaven or on earth who can perform such great deeds as yours? ²⁵Please let me cross the Jordan to see the wonderful land on the other side, the beautiful hill country and the Lebanon mountains.'

²⁶"But the LORD was angry with me because of you, and he would not listen to me. 'That's enough!' he ordered. 'Speak of it no more. ²⁷You can go to Pisgah Peak and view the land in every direction, but you may not cross the Jordan River. ²⁸But commission Joshua and encourage him, for he will lead the people across the Jordan. He will give them the land you now see before you.' ²⁹So we stayed in the valley near Beth-peor.

MOSES URGES ISRAEL TO OBEY

4 "And now, Israel, listen carefully to these laws and regulations that I am about to teach you. Obey them so that you may live, so you may enter and occupy the land the LORD, the God of your ancestors, is giving you. ²Do not add to or subtract from these commands I am giving you from the LORD your God. Just obey them. ³You saw what the LORD did to you at Baal-peor, where the LORD your God destroyed everyone who had worshiped the god Baal of Peor. ⁴But all of you who were faithful to the LORD your God are still alive today.

⁵"You must obey these laws and regulations when you arrive in the land you are about to enter and occupy. The LORD my God gave them to me and commanded me to pass them on to you. ⁶If you obey them carefully, you will display your wisdom and intelligence to the surrounding nations. When they hear about these laws, they will exclaim, 'What other nation is as wise and prudent as this!' ⁷For

what great nation has a god as near to them as the LORD our God is near to us whenever we call on him? ⁸And what great nation has laws and regulations as fair as this body of laws that I am giving you today?

⁹"But watch out! Be very careful never to forget what you have seen the LORD do for you. Do not let these things escape from your mind as long as you live! And be sure to pass them on to your children and grandchildren. ¹⁰Tell them especially about the day when you stood before the LORD your God at Mount Sinai,* where he told me, 'Summon the people before me, and I will instruct them. That way, they will learn to fear me as long as they live, and they will be able to teach my laws to their children.' ¹¹You came near and stood at the foot of the mountain, while the mountain was burning with fire. Flames shot into the sky, shrouded in black clouds and deep darkness. ¹²And the LORD spoke to you from the fire. You heard his words but didn't see his form; there was only a voice. ¹³He proclaimed his covenant, which he commanded you to keep—the Ten Commandments—and wrote them on two stone tablets. ¹⁴It was at that time that the LORD commanded me to issue the laws and regulations you must obey in the land you are about to enter and occupy.

A WARNING AGAINST IDOLATRY

¹⁵"But be careful! You did not see the LORD's form on the day he spoke to you from the fire at Mount Sinai. ¹⁶So do not corrupt yourselves by making a physical image in any form—whether of a man or a woman, ¹⁷an animal or a bird, ¹⁸a creeping creature or a fish. ¹⁹And when you look up into the sky and see the sun, moon, and stars—all the forces of heaven—don't be seduced by them and worship them. The LORD your God designated these heavenly bodies for all the peoples of the earth. ²⁰Remember that the LORD rescued you from the burning furnace of Egypt to become his own people and special possession; that is what you are today.

4:10 Hebrew *Horeb,* another name for Sinai; also in 4:15.

My Daily Worship

— February 12 —

NEARER MY GOD TO ME

DEUTERONOMY 1:1–4:31

For what great nation has a god as near to them as the LORD
our God is near to us whenever we call on him? (4:7).

[i reflect]

At the age of 120, Moses had a definite perspective on God's nearness. He was about to review for the people of Israel all the amazing reasons why they should never lose sight of God's closeness nor wander from his instructions. Unlike the distant, silent, impotent gods other cultures claimed, Israel's God, the Lord God, was never far away, uncaring, or powerless. He had traveled with them through the wilderness en route to the Promised Land, repeatedly demonstrating his closeness through anger and grace.

Israel was surrounded with visual reminders of God's nearness: the Tabernacle, the daily manna, the pillar of cloud and fire. The people carried God's stone-written commandments. They traveled under his direction. Yet none of these factors mattered without heartfelt obedience.

External reminders of God's nearness today aren't nearly so obvious. But he's here. In fact, your heart is God's tabernacle. And in that place, God accepts the sacrifices you willingly present—your pride, your worries, your sin. You don't need to wait for church on Sunday to connect with him. Obviously, being in a place of tangible worship and teaching has advantages. But you can engage God at the moment you need him, right where you are, no matter what you are doing.

When the cares of the world have you wandering and wondering about God's nearness, remember that he's committed to being close. Just recognize your dependence on him, and call out his name, with a cry or a whisper, with a song or a prayer. God is listening for those who want to access the "privilege of proximity." Asking God to draw near is simply a way of recognizing his closeness. As a way to remember that God is always near, include small "God-breaks" during your day—times when you specifically focus on him, praying for your needs, and offering praises.

[i pray]

I love it, Father, that I can call on you wherever I am, no matter what time of day it is.
Even better, I love the fact that you want me to do that. You take delight in my dependence.
In a strange sort of way, my prayers for help are actually a way of praising you.

[i respond]

Write down today's key verse on several index cards. Place them around your house, in your work space, or even in your car, as a daily reminder that the One we worship is always near.

²¹"But the LORD was very angry with me because of you. He vowed that I would never cross the Jordan River into the good land the LORD your God is giving you as your special possession. ²²Though you will cross the Jordan to occupy the land, I will die here on this side of the river. ²³So be careful not to break the covenant the LORD your God has made with you. You will break it if you make idols of any shape or form, for the LORD your God has absolutely forbidden this. ²⁴The LORD your God is a devouring fire, a jealous God.

²⁵"In the future, when you have children and grandchildren and have lived in the land a long time, do not corrupt yourselves by making idols of any kind. This is evil in the sight of the LORD your God and will arouse his anger.

²⁶"Today I call heaven and earth as witnesses against you. If you disobey me, you will quickly disappear from the land you are crossing the Jordan to occupy. You will live there only a short time; then you will be utterly destroyed. ²⁷For the LORD will scatter you among the nations, where only a few of you will survive. ²⁸There, in a foreign land, you will worship idols made from wood and stone, gods that neither see nor hear nor eat nor smell. ²⁹From there you will search again for the LORD your God. And if you search for him with all your heart and soul, you will find him.

³⁰"When those bitter days have come upon you far in the future, you will finally return to the LORD your God and listen to what he tells you. ³¹For the LORD your God is merciful—he will not abandon you or destroy you or forget the solemn covenant he made with your ancestors.

THERE IS ONLY ONE GOD

³²"Search all of history, from the time God created people on the earth until now. Then search from one end of the heavens to the other. See if anything as great as this has ever happened before. ³³Has any nation ever heard the voice of God* speaking from fire—as you did—and survived? ³⁴Has any other god taken one nation for himself by rescuing it from another by means of trials, miraculous signs, wonders, war, awesome power, and terrifying acts? Yet that is what the LORD your God did for you in Egypt, right before your very eyes.

³⁵"He showed you these things so you would realize that the LORD is God and that there is no other god. ³⁶He let you hear his voice from heaven so he could instruct you. He let you see his great fire here on earth so he could speak to you from it. ³⁷Because he loved your ancestors, he chose to bless their descendants and personally brought you out of Egypt with a great display of power. ³⁸He drove out nations far greater than you, so he could bring you in and give you their land as a special possession, as it is today. ³⁹So remember this and keep it firmly in mind: The LORD is God both in heaven and on earth, and there is no other god! ⁴⁰If you obey all the laws and commands that I will give you today, all will be well with you and your children. Then you will enjoy a long life in the land the LORD your God is giving you for all time."

EASTERN CITIES OF REFUGE

⁴¹Then Moses set apart three cities of refuge east of the Jordan River, ⁴²where anyone who had accidentally killed someone without having any previous hostility could flee for safety. ⁴³These were the cities: Bezer on the wilderness plateau for the tribe of Reuben; Ramoth in Gilead for the tribe of Gad; Golan in Bashan for the tribe of Manasseh.

INTRODUCTION TO THE LAW

⁴⁴This is the law that Moses handed down to the Israelites. ⁴⁵These are the stipulations, laws, and regulations that Moses gave to the people of Israel when they left Egypt, ⁴⁶and as they camped in the valley near Beth-peor east of the Jordan River. (This land was formerly occupied by the Amorites under King Sihon of Heshbon. He and his people had been

---

4:33 Or *voice of a god.*

destroyed by Moses and the Israelites as they came up from Egypt. ⁴⁷Israel conquered his land and that of King Og of Bashan—the two Amorite kings east of the Jordan. ⁴⁸So Israel conquered all the area from Aroer at the edge of the Arnon Gorge to Mount Sirion,* also called Mount Hermon. ⁴⁹And they took the eastern bank of the Jordan Valley as far south as the Dead Sea,* below the slopes of Pisgah.)

THE TEN COMMANDMENTS

5 Moses called all the people of Israel together and said, "Listen carefully to all the laws and regulations I am giving you today. Learn them and be sure to obey them! ²"While we were at Mount Sinai,* the LORD our God made a covenant with us. ³The LORD did not make this covenant long ago with our ancestors, but with all of us who are alive today. ⁴The LORD spoke to you face to face from the heart of the fire on the mountain. ⁵I stood as an intermediary between you and the LORD, for you were afraid of the fire and did not climb the mountain. He spoke to me, and I passed his words on to you. This is what he said:

⁶"'I am the LORD your God, who rescued you from slavery in Egypt.

⁷"'Do not worship any other gods besides me.

⁸"'Do not make idols of any kind, whether in the shape of birds or animals or fish. ⁹You must never worship or bow down to them, for I, the LORD your God, am a jealous God who will not share your affection with any other god! I do not leave unpunished the sins of those who hate me, but I punish the children for the sins of their parents to the third and fourth generations. ¹⁰But I lavish my love on those who love me and obey my commands, even for a thousand generations.

¹¹"'Do not misuse the name of the LORD your God. The LORD will not let you go unpunished if you misuse his name.

¹²"'Observe the Sabbath day by keeping it holy, as the LORD your God has commanded you. ¹³Six days a week are set apart for your daily duties and regular work, ¹⁴but the seventh day is a day of rest dedicated to the LORD your God. On that day no one in your household may do any kind of work. This includes you, your sons and daughters, your male and female servants, your oxen and donkeys and other livestock, and any foreigners living among you. All your male and female servants must rest as you do. ¹⁵Remember that you were once slaves in Egypt and that the LORD your God brought you out with amazing power and mighty deeds. That is why the LORD your God has commanded you to observe the Sabbath day.

¹⁶"'Honor your father and mother, as the LORD your God commanded you. Then you will live a long, full life in the land the LORD your God will give you.

¹⁷"'Do not murder.

¹⁸"'Do not commit adultery.

¹⁹"'Do not steal.

²⁰"'Do not testify falsely against your neighbor.

²¹"'Do not covet your neighbor's wife. Do not covet your neighbor's house or land, male or female servant, ox or donkey, or anything else your neighbor owns.'

²²"The LORD spoke these words with a loud voice to all of you from the heart of the fire, surrounded by clouds and deep darkness. This was all he said at that time, and he wrote his words on two stone tablets and gave them to me. ²³But when you heard the voice from the darkness, while the mountain was blazing with fire, all your tribal leaders came to me. ²⁴They said, 'The LORD our God has shown us his glory and greatness, and we have heard his voice from the heart of the fire. Today we have seen God speaking to humans, and yet we live!

4:48 As in Syriac version (see also 3:9); Hebrew reads *Mount Sion*. 4:49 Hebrew *took the Arabah on the east side of the Jordan as far as the sea of the Arabah.* 5:2 Hebrew *Horeb*, another name for Sinai.

²⁵But now, why should we die? If the LORD our God speaks to us again, we will certainly die and be consumed by this awesome fire. ²⁶Can any living thing hear the voice of the living God from the heart of the fire and yet survive? ²⁷You go and listen to what the LORD our God says. Then come and tell us everything he tells you, and we will listen and obey.'

²⁸"The LORD heard your request and said to me, 'I have heard what the people have said to you, and they are right. ²⁹Oh, that they would always have hearts like this, that they might fear me and obey all my commands! If they did, they and their descendants would prosper forever. ³⁰Go and tell them to return to their tents. ³¹But you stay here with me so I can give you all my commands, laws, and regulations. You will teach them to the people so they can obey them in the land I am giving to them as their inheritance.'"

³²So Moses told the people, "You must obey all the commands of the LORD your God, following his instructions in every detail. ³³Stay on the path that the LORD your God has commanded you to follow. Then you will live long and prosperous lives in the land you are about to enter and occupy.

A CALL FOR WHOLEHEARTED COMMITMENT

6 "These are all the commands, laws, and regulations that the LORD your God told me to teach you so you may obey them in the land you are about to enter and occupy, ²and so you and your children and grandchildren might fear the LORD your God as long as you live. If you obey all his laws and commands, you will enjoy a long life. ³Listen closely, Israel, to everything I say. Be careful to obey. Then all will go well with you, and you will have many children in the land flowing with milk and honey, just as the LORD, the God of your ancestors, promised you.

⁴"Hear, O Israel! The LORD is our God, the LORD alone.* ⁵And you must love the LORD your God with all your heart, all your soul,

and all your strength. ⁶And you must commit yourselves wholeheartedly to these commands I am giving you today. ⁷Repeat them again and again to your children. Talk about them when you are at home and when you are away on a journey, when you are lying down and when you are getting up again. ⁸Tie them to your hands as a reminder, and wear them on your forehead. ⁹Write them on the doorposts of your house and on your gates.

¹⁰"The LORD your God will soon bring you into the land he swore to give your ancestors Abraham, Isaac, and Jacob. It is a land filled with large, prosperous cities that you did not build. ¹¹The houses will be richly stocked with goods you did not produce. You will draw water from cisterns you did not dig, and you will eat from vineyards and olive trees you did not plant. When you have eaten your fill in this land, ¹²be careful not to forget the LORD, who rescued you from slavery in the land of Egypt. ¹³You must fear the LORD your God and serve him. When you take an oath, you must use only his name.

¹⁴"You must not worship any of the gods of neighboring nations, ¹⁵for the LORD your God, who lives among you, is a jealous God. His anger will flare up against you and wipe you from the face of the earth. ¹⁶Do not test the LORD your God as you did when you complained at Massah. ¹⁷You must diligently obey the commands of the LORD your God—all the stipulations and laws he has given you. ¹⁸Do what is right and good in the LORD's sight, so all will go well with you. Then you will enter and occupy the good land that the LORD solemnly promised to give your ancestors. ¹⁹You will drive out all the enemies living in your land, just as the LORD said you would.

²⁰"In the future your children will ask you, 'What is the meaning of these stipulations, laws, and regulations that the LORD our God has given us?' ²¹Then you must tell them, 'We were Pharaoh's slaves in Egypt, but the LORD brought us out of Egypt with amazing power. ²²Before our eyes the LORD did miraculous

6:4 Or *The LORD our God is one LORD*, or *The LORD our God, the LORD is one*, or *The LORD is our God, the LORD is one.*

My Daily Worship

THE HEART OF WORSHIP

DEUTERONOMY 4:32–6:25

Hear O Israel! The LORD is our God, the LORD alone. And you must love the LORD your God with all your heart, all your soul, and all your strength (6:4–5).

[i reflect]

Matt Redman knows what worship is all about. As an anointed songwriter, performer, and worship leader in England, he is committed to helping Christians worship better. One thing is for sure. As far as Matt is concerned, it has more to do with what's in our hearts than the kind of songs we sing or how we feel singing them.

Several years ago the pastor at Matt's church sensed that the praise music and instrumentation had lost its focus and authenticity. The congregation was not entering into worship with their entire selves. In a radical departure from the norm, the minister banned the band. For several months praise was led with only an acoustic guitar or acappella voices.

Interestingly, the essence of dynamic worship returned. The heart of worship had little to do with keyboards, drums, and electric guitars or new and improved lyrics. It was all about encountering the living Lord and loving him. Deeply moved by what he experienced during the "music moratorium," Matt Redman was inspired to write "The Heart of Worship." In this song, he describes what happens when the music fades and all the periphery is stripped away. His song brings into focus what the Lord desired Moses to teach the Israelites. When we understand who God is, the only appropriate response is to come into his presence and offer ourselves. The variety of worship styles, lyrics, and instruments isn't all that important, nor whether we stand, sit, or raise our arms. The pressure of performance is gone.

Today, offer yourself to God. Your mind. Your attitudes. Your thoughts. Your feelings. Your heart. Lay it all before him, then worship *him* for loving you because he chooses to, not because of your performance.

[i pray]

Take my life, Lord. Take my heart, soul, and strength. I give them all to you. Although I am tempted at times to devote myself to secondary allurements, I know that my life is all about you. Increase my desire to worship you and you alone.

[i respond]

What might be keeping you from pure and undefiled worship? Take a "fast" from those comfortable (and enjoyable) routines that only serve to distract you from the object of your personal worship.

signs and wonders, dealing terrifying blows against Egypt and Pharaoh and all his people. [23]He brought us out of Egypt so he could give us this land he had solemnly promised to give our ancestors. [24]And the LORD our God commanded us to obey all these laws and to fear him for our own prosperity and well-being, as is now the case. [25]For we are righteous when we obey all the commands the LORD our God has given us.'

THE PRIVILEGE OF HOLINESS

7 "When the LORD your God brings you into the land you are about to enter and occupy, he will clear away many nations ahead of you: the Hittites, Girgashites, Amorites, Canaanites, Perizzites, Hivites, and Jebusites. These seven nations are all more powerful than you. [2]When the LORD your God hands these nations over to you and you conquer them, you must completely destroy* them. Make no treaties with them and show them no mercy. [3]Do not intermarry with them, and don't let your daughters and sons marry their sons and daughters. [4]They will lead your young people away from me to worship other gods. Then the anger of the LORD will burn against you, and he will destroy you. [5]Instead, you must break down their pagan altars and shatter their sacred pillars. Cut down their Asherah poles and burn their idols. [6]For you are a holy people, who belong to the LORD your God. Of all the people on earth, the LORD your God has chosen you to be his own special treasure.

[7]"The LORD did not choose you and lavish his love on you because you were larger or greater than other nations, for you were the smallest of all nations! [8]It was simply because the LORD loves you, and because he was keeping the oath he had sworn to your ancestors. That is why the LORD rescued you with such amazing power from your slavery under Pharaoh in Egypt. [9]Understand, therefore, that the LORD your God is indeed God. He is

the faithful God who keeps his covenant for a thousand generations and constantly loves those who love him and obey his commands. [10]But he does not hesitate to punish and destroy those who hate him. [11]Therefore, obey all these commands, laws, and regulations I am giving you today.

[12]"If you listen to these regulations and obey them faithfully, the LORD your God will keep his covenant of unfailing love with you, as he solemnly promised your ancestors. [13]He will love you and bless you and make you into a great nation. He will give you many children and give fertility to your land and your animals. When you arrive in the land he swore to give your ancestors, you will have large crops of grain, grapes, and olives, and great herds of cattle, sheep, and goats. [14]You will be blessed above all the nations of the earth. None of your men or women will be childless, and all your livestock will bear young. [15]And the LORD will protect you from all sickness. He will not let you suffer from the terrible diseases you knew in Egypt, but he will bring them all on your enemies!

[16]"You must destroy all the nations the LORD your God hands over to you. Show them no mercy and do not worship their gods. If you do, they will trap you. [17]Perhaps you will think to yourselves, 'How can we ever conquer these nations that are so much more powerful than we are?' [18]But don't be afraid of them! Just remember what the LORD your God did to Pharaoh and to all the land of Egypt. [19]Remember the great terrors the LORD your God sent against them. You saw it all with your own eyes! And remember the miraculous signs and wonders, and the amazing power he used when he brought you out of Egypt. The LORD your God will use this same power against the people you fear. [20]And then the LORD your God will send hornets* to drive out the few survivors still hiding from you!

[21]"No, do not be afraid of those nations, for the LORD your God is among you, and he is a

---

7:2 The Hebrew term used here refers to the complete consecration of things or people to the LORD, either by destroying them or by giving them as an offering; also in 7:26. 7:20 Or *will spread panic,* or *will send a plague.* The meaning of the Hebrew is uncertain.

My Daily Worship

A Little Picture of God's Greatness

DEUTERONOMY 7:1–10:22

The LORD did not choose you and lavish his love on you because you were larger or greater than other nations, for you were the smallest of the nations! It was simply because the LORD loves you, and because he was keeping the oath he had sworn to your ancestors (7:7–8).

[i reflect]

It must be a God thing! What other explanation can there be? The tiny nation of Israel has survived three thousand years of religious conflict, horrific attempts at ethnic cleansing, and continual border disputes.

Have you ever considered the disproportional influence Israel has had in history, given its geographic size? If you look at a map of the world in an encyclopedia, you'll likely need a magnifying glass to locate it. The "Promised Land" is dwarfed by huge continents like Africa and Europe. Once you located Israel on the coast of the Mediterranean Sea near Egypt and Saudi Arabia, you're amazed to see that she's only about 150 miles long by 75 miles wide. All that considered, Israel is the focus of world attention, not to mention biblical prophecy.

It's obvious that God has had his hand on this stretch of real estate. But then again, Scripture is clear that, from the beginning, the vulnerability and insignificant size of Israel was a means by which God was making a point. There would be no way the people of God could take credit for what they had accomplished. They were too small and too weak. That way, God would get the credit. And seeing that it was God who was choreographing their success, his people were brought to their knees in humble worship.

Paul, in a letter to the early Christians in Corinth, would later pick up on this principle, when he said that through weakness, God's glory is more apparent (2 Corinthians 12:9). This truth should be the principle that propels us into heartfelt worship each day.

Recognize your insignificance and unworthiness as you come into his presence today. Be encouraged by what he has accomplished on your behalf *in spite of* yourself. Then worship him.

[i pray]

Lord, I can't take the credit for the way you have sustained my faith or strengthened my resolve.
Like the nation of Israel, I am the picture of insignificance. May I never get over the fact
that you have fixed your love on me because of your divine choice. Amen.

[i respond]

Locate Israel on a world map. Compare it to the large nations that surround it. Allow this study in contrast to encourage you as you deal with feelings of inferiority or low self-esteem.

great and awesome God. ²²The LORD your God will drive those nations out ahead of you little by little. You will not clear them away all at once, for if you did, the wild animals would multiply too quickly for you. ²³But the LORD your God will hand them over to you. He will throw them into complete confusion until they are destroyed. ²⁴He will put their kings in your power, and you will erase their names from the face of the earth. No one will be able to stand against you, and you will destroy them all.

²⁵"You must burn their idols in fire, and do not desire the silver or gold with which they are made. Do not take it or it will become a snare to you, for it is detestable to the LORD your God. ²⁶Do not bring any detestable objects into your home, for then you will be set apart for destruction just like them. You must utterly detest such things, for they are set apart for destruction.

A CALL TO REMEMBER AND OBEY

8 "Be careful to obey all the commands I am giving you today. Then you will live and multiply, and you will enter and occupy the land the LORD swore to give your ancestors. ²Remember how the LORD your God led you through the wilderness for forty years, humbling you and testing you to prove your character, and to find out whether or not you would really obey his commands. ³Yes, he humbled you by letting you go hungry and then feeding you with manna, a food previously unknown to you and your ancestors. He did it to teach you that people need more than bread for their life; real life comes by feeding on every word of the LORD. ⁴For all these forty years your clothes didn't wear out, and your feet didn't blister or swell. ⁵So you should realize that just as a parent disciplines a child, the LORD your God disciplines you to help you.

⁶"So obey the commands of the LORD your God by walking in his ways and fearing him. ⁷For the LORD your God is bringing you into a good land of flowing streams and pools of water, with springs that gush forth in the val-

leys and hills. ⁸It is a land of wheat and barley, of grapevines, fig trees, pomegranates, olives, and honey. ⁹It is a land where food is plentiful and nothing is lacking. It is a land where iron is as common as stone, and copper is abundant in the hills. ¹⁰When you have eaten your fill, praise the LORD your God for the good land he has given you.

¹¹"But that is the time to be careful! Beware that in your plenty you do not forget the LORD your God and disobey his commands, regulations, and laws. ¹²For when you have become full and prosperous and have built fine homes to live in, ¹³and when your flocks and herds have become very large and your silver and gold have multiplied along with everything else, ¹⁴that is the time to be careful. Do not become proud at that time and forget the LORD your God, who rescued you from slavery in the land of Egypt. ¹⁵Do not forget that he led you through the great and terrifying wilderness with poisonous snakes and scorpions, where it was so hot and dry. He gave you water from the rock! ¹⁶He fed you with manna in the wilderness, a food unknown to your ancestors. He did this to humble you and test you for your own good. ¹⁷He did it so you would never think that it was your own strength and energy that made you wealthy. ¹⁸Always remember that it is the LORD your God who gives you power to become rich, and he does it to fulfill the covenant he made with your ancestors.

¹⁹"But I assure you of this: If you ever forget the LORD your God and follow other gods, worshiping and bowing down to them, you will certainly be destroyed. ²⁰Just as the LORD has destroyed other nations in your path, you also will be destroyed for not obeying the LORD your God.

VICTORY BY GOD'S GRACE

9 "Hear, O Israel! Today you are about to cross the Jordan River to occupy the land belonging to nations much greater and more powerful than you. They live in cities with walls that reach to the sky! ²They are strong

and tall—descendants of the famous Anakite giants. You've heard the saying, 'Who can stand up to the Anakites?' ³But the LORD your God will cross over ahead of you like a devouring fire to destroy them. He will subdue them so that you will quickly conquer them and drive them out, just as the LORD has promised.

⁴"After the LORD your God has done this for you, don't say to yourselves, 'The LORD has given us this land because we are so righteous!' No, it is because of the wickedness of the other nations that he is doing it. ⁵It is not at all because you are such righteous, upright people that you are about to occupy their land. The LORD your God will drive these nations out ahead of you only because of their wickedness, and to fulfill the oath he had sworn to your ancestors Abraham, Isaac, and Jacob. ⁶I will say it again: The LORD your God is not giving you this good land because you are righteous, for you are not—you are a stubborn people.

REMEMBERING THE GOLD CALF

⁷"Remember how angry you made the LORD your God out in the wilderness. From the day you left Egypt until now, you have constantly rebelled against him. ⁸Remember how angry you made the LORD at Mount Sinai,* where he was ready to destroy you. ⁹That was when I was on the mountain receiving the tablets of stone inscribed with the covenant that the LORD had made with you. I was there for forty days and forty nights, and all that time I ate nothing and drank no water. ¹⁰The LORD gave me the covenant, the tablets on which God himself had written all the words he had spoken to you from the fire on the mountain.

¹¹"At the end of the forty days and nights, the LORD handed me the two stone tablets with the covenant inscribed on them. ¹²Then the LORD said to me, 'Go down immediately because the people you led out of Egypt have become corrupt. They have already turned

from the way I commanded them to live and have cast an idol for themselves from gold.'

¹³"The LORD said to me, 'I have been watching this people, and they are extremely stubborn. ¹⁴Leave me alone so I may destroy them and erase their name from under heaven. Then I will make a mighty nation of your descendants, a nation larger and more powerful than they are.'

¹⁵"So I came down from the fiery mountain, holding in my hands the two stone tablets of the covenant. ¹⁶There below me I could see the gold calf you had made in your terrible sin against the LORD your God. How quickly you had turned from the path the LORD had commanded you to follow! ¹⁷So I raised the stone tablets and dashed them to the ground. I smashed them before your very eyes. ¹⁸Then for forty days and nights I lay prostrate before the LORD, neither eating bread nor drinking water. I did this because you had sinned by doing what the LORD hated, thus making him very angry. ¹⁹How I feared for you, for the LORD was ready to destroy you. But again he listened to me. ²⁰The LORD was so angry with Aaron that he wanted to destroy him. But I prayed for Aaron, and the LORD spared him. ²¹I took your sin—the calf you had made— and I melted it in the fire and ground it into fine dust. I threw the dust into the stream that cascades down the mountain.

²²"You also made the LORD angry at Taberah,* Massah,* and Kibroth-hattaavah.* ²³And at Kadesh-barnea the LORD sent you out with this command: 'Go up and take the land I have given you.' But you rebelled against the command of the LORD your God and refused to trust him or obey him. ²⁴Yes, you have been rebelling against the LORD as long as I have known you.

²⁵"That is why I fell down and lay before the LORD for forty days and nights when he was ready to destroy you. ²⁶I prayed to the LORD and said, 'O Sovereign LORD, do not destroy your own people. They are your special possession,

---

9:8 Hebrew *Horeb,* another name for Sinai. 9:22a *Taberah* means "place of burning." See Num 11:1-3. 9:22b *Massah* means "place of testing." See Exod 17:1-7. 9:22c *Kibroth-hattaavah* means "graves of craving." See Num 11:31-34.

redeemed from Egypt by your mighty power and glorious strength. ²⁷Overlook the stubbornness and sin of these people, but remember instead your servants Abraham, Isaac, and Jacob. ²⁸If you destroy these people, the Egyptians will say, "The LORD destroyed them because he wasn't able to bring them to the land he had sworn to give them." Or they might say, "He destroyed them because he hated them; he brought them into the wilderness to slaughter them." ²⁹But they are your people and your special possession, whom you brought from Egypt by your mighty power and glorious strength.'

NEW TABLETS OF STONE

10 "At that time the LORD said to me, 'Prepare two stone tablets like the first ones, and make a sacred chest of wood to keep them in. Return to me on the mountain, ²and I will write on the tablets the same words that were on the ones you smashed. Then place the tablets in the sacred chest—the Ark of the Covenant.'

³"So I made a chest of acacia wood and cut two stone tablets like the first two, and I took the tablets up the mountain. ⁴The LORD again wrote the terms of the covenant—the Ten Commandments—on them and gave them to me. They were the same words the LORD had spoken to you from the heart of the fire on the mountain as you were assembled below. ⁵Then I came down and placed the tablets in the Ark of the Covenant, which I had made, just as the LORD commanded me. And the tablets are still there in the Ark.

⁶"The people of Israel set out from the wells of the people of Jaakan* and traveled to Moserah, where Aaron died and was buried. His son Eleazar became the high priest in his place. ⁷Then they journeyed to Gudgodah, and from there to Jotbathah, a land with brooks of water. ⁸At that time the LORD set apart the tribe of Levi to carry the Ark of the LORD's covenant, to minister before the LORD, and to pronounce blessings in his name.

These are still their duties. ⁹That is why the Levites have no share or inheritance reserved for them among the other Israelite tribes. The LORD himself is their inheritance, as the LORD your God told them.

¹⁰"As I said before, I stayed on the mountain in the LORD's presence for forty days and nights, as I had done the first time. And once again the LORD yielded to my pleas and didn't destroy you. ¹¹But the LORD said to me, 'Get up and lead the people into the land I swore to give their ancestors, so they may take possession of it.'

A CALL TO LOVE AND OBEDIENCE

¹²"And now, Israel, what does the LORD your God require of you? He requires you to fear him, to live according to his will, to love and worship him with all your heart and soul, ¹³and to obey the LORD's commands and laws that I am giving you today for your own good. ¹⁴The highest heavens and the earth and everything in it all belong to the LORD your God. ¹⁵Yet the LORD chose your ancestors as the objects of his love. And he chose you, their descendants, above every other nation, as is evident today. ¹⁶Therefore, cleanse your sinful hearts and stop being stubborn.

¹⁷"The LORD your God is the God of gods and Lord of lords. He is the great God, mighty and awesome, who shows no partiality and takes no bribes. ¹⁸He gives justice to orphans and widows. He shows love to the foreigners living among you and gives them food and clothing. ¹⁹You, too, must show love to foreigners, for you yourselves were once foreigners in the land of Egypt. ²⁰You must fear the LORD your God and worship him and cling to him. Your oaths must be in his name alone. ²¹He is your God, the one who is worthy of your praise, the one who has done mighty miracles that you yourselves have seen. ²²When your ancestors went down into Egypt, there were only seventy of them. But now the LORD your God has made you as numerous as the stars in the sky!

10:6 Or *set out from Beeroth of Bene-jaakan.*

11 "You must love the LORD your God and obey all his requirements, laws, regulations, and commands. ²Listen! I am not talking now to your children, who have never experienced the discipline of the LORD your God or seen his greatness and awesome power. ³They weren't there to see the miraculous signs and wonders he performed in Egypt against Pharaoh and all his land. ⁴They didn't see what the LORD did to the armies of Egypt and to their horses and chariots—how he drowned them in the Red Sea* as they were chasing you, and how he has kept them devastated to this very day! ⁵They didn't see how the LORD cared for you in the wilderness until you arrived here. ⁶They weren't there to see what he did to Dathan and Abiram (the sons of Eliab, a descendant of Reuben) when the earth opened up and swallowed them, along with their households and tents and every living thing that belonged to them. ⁷But you have seen all the LORD's mighty deeds with your own eyes!

THE BLESSINGS OF OBEDIENCE

⁸"Therefore, be careful to obey every command I am giving you today, so you may have strength to go in and occupy the land you are about to enter. ⁹If you obey, you will enjoy a long life in the land the LORD swore to give to your ancestors and to you, their descendants—a land flowing with milk and honey! ¹⁰For the land you are about to enter and occupy is not like the land of Egypt from which you came, where you planted your seed and dug out irrigation ditches with your foot as in a vegetable garden. ¹¹It is a land of hills and valleys with plenty of rain—¹²a land that the LORD your God cares for. He watches over it day after day throughout the year!

¹³"If you carefully obey all the commands I am giving you today, and if you love the LORD your God with all your heart and soul, and if you worship him, ¹⁴then he will send the rains in their proper seasons so you can harvest crops of grain, grapes for wine, and olives for oil. ¹⁵He will give you lush pastureland for your cattle to graze in, and you yourselves will have plenty to eat.

¹⁶"But do not let your heart turn away from the LORD to worship other gods. ¹⁷If you do, the LORD's anger will burn against you. He will shut up the sky and hold back the rain, and your harvests will fail. Then you will quickly die in that good land the LORD is now giving you. ¹⁸So commit yourselves completely to these words of mine. Tie them to your hands as a reminder, and wear them on your forehead. ¹⁹Teach them to your children. Talk about them when you are at home and when you are away on a journey, when you are lying down and when you are getting up again. ²⁰Write them on the doorposts of your house and on your gates, ²¹so that as long as the sky remains above the earth, you and your children may flourish in the land the LORD swore to give your ancestors.

²²"Be careful to obey all the commands I give you; show love to the LORD your God by walking in his ways and clinging to him. ²³Then the LORD will drive out all the nations in your land, though they are much greater and stronger than you. ²⁴Wherever you set your feet, the land will be yours. Your frontiers will stretch from the wilderness in the south to Lebanon in the north, and from the Euphrates River in the east to the Mediterranean Sea in the west.* ²⁵No one will be able to stand against you, for the LORD your God will send fear and dread ahead of you, as he promised you, wherever you go in the whole land.

²⁶"Today I am giving you the choice between a blessing and a curse! ²⁷You will be blessed if you obey the commands of the LORD your God that I am giving you today. ²⁸You will receive a curse if you reject the commands of the LORD your God and turn from his way by worshiping foreign gods.

²⁹"When the LORD your God brings you into the land to possess it, you must pronounce a blessing from Mount Gerizim and a curse

---

11:4 Hebrew *sea of reeds.* 11:24 Hebrew *to the western sea.*

from Mount Ebal. [30](These two mountains are west of the Jordan River in the land of the Canaanites who live in the Jordan Valley,* near the town of Gilgal. They are located toward the west, not far from the oaks of Moreh.) [31]For you are about to cross the Jordan to occupy the land the LORD your God is giving you. When you are living in that land, [32]you must be careful to obey all the laws and regulations I am giving you today.

THE LORD'S CHOSEN PLACE FOR WORSHIP

12 "These are the laws and regulations you must obey as long as you live in the land the LORD, the God of your ancestors, is giving you.

[2]"When you drive out the nations that live there, you must destroy all the places where they worship their gods—high on the mountains, up on the hills, and under every green tree. [3]Break down their altars and smash their sacred pillars. Burn their Asherah poles and cut down their carved idols. Erase the names of their gods from those places!

[4]"Do not worship the LORD your God in the way these pagan peoples worship their gods. [5]Rather, you must seek the LORD your God at the place he himself will choose from among all the tribes for his name to be honored. [6]There you will bring to the LORD your burnt offerings, your sacrifices, your tithes, your special gifts, your offerings to fulfill a vow, your freewill offerings, and your offerings of the firstborn animals of your flocks and herds. [7]There you and your families will feast in the presence of the LORD your God, and you will rejoice in all you have accomplished because the LORD your God has blessed you.

[8]"Today you are doing whatever you please, but that is not how it will be [9]when you arrive in the place of rest the LORD your God is giving you. [10]You will soon cross the Jordan River and live in the land the LORD your God is giving you as a special possession. When he gives you rest and security from all your ene-

mies, [11]you must bring everything I command you—your burnt offerings, your sacrifices, your tithes, your special gifts, and your offerings to fulfill a vow—to the place the LORD your God will choose for his name to be honored. [12]You must celebrate there with your sons and daughters and all your servants in the presence of the LORD your God. And remember the Levites who live in your towns, for they will have no inheritance of land as their own. [13]Be careful not to sacrifice your burnt offerings just anywhere. [14]You may do so only at the place the LORD will choose within one of your tribal territories. There you must offer your burnt offerings and do everything I command you.

[15]"But you may butcher animals for meat in any town, wherever you want, just as you do now with gazelle and deer. You may eat as many animals as the LORD your God gives you. All of you, whether ceremonially clean or unclean, may eat that meat. [16]The only restriction is that you are not to eat the blood. You must pour it out on the ground like water.

[17]"But your offerings must not be eaten at home—neither the tithe of your grain and new wine and olive oil, nor the firstborn of your flocks and herds, nor an offering to fulfill a vow, nor your freewill offerings, nor your special gifts. [18]You must eat these in the presence of the LORD your God at the place he will choose. Eat them there with your children, your servants, and the Levites who live in your towns, celebrating in the presence of the LORD your God in all you do. [19]Be very careful never to forget the Levites as long as you live in your land.

[20]"When the LORD your God enlarges your territory as he has promised, you may eat meat whenever you want. [21]It might happen that the place the LORD your God chooses for his name to be honored is a long way from your home. If so, you may butcher any of the cattle or sheep the LORD has given you, and you may eat the meat at your home as I have commanded you. [22]Anyone, whether

11:30 Hebrew *the Arabah.*

My Daily Worship

— *February 15* —

FROM GENERATION TO GENERATION

DEUTERONOMY 11:1 – 15:23

*Rather, you must seek the LORD your God at the place he himself will choose from among
all the tribes for his name to be honored. . . . You must celebrate there with your sons
and daughters and all your servants in the presence of the LORD your God (12:5, 12).*

[i reflect]

How important is it for a young person to have his or her parents involved in a local church?
Consider these statistics from a recent study:

- If both Mom and Dad attend church regularly, 72 percent of their children remain faithful.
- If only Dad attends, 55 percent remain faithful.
- If only Mom attends, it drops off to 15 percent.
- If neither attend regularly, only 6 percent remain faithful.

These statistics illustrate the critical role that parents play in their children's spiritual upbringing,
especially fathers. In fact, the likelihood of a young person ever being involved in the church without any parental role model to follow is only *6 percent*.

God's laws placed a heavy emphasis on family worship. That's what this passage is all about.
Whether offering sacrifices or attending a festival, the family was together. This practice helped
develop heathy attitudes toward worship within young people and instilled within them a foundation of faith that they could pass on to their children.

If your parents raised you in the church, thank God for them and the godly heritage they passed
on to you. If they didn't, start that tradition with *your* children, if you have any. If you have no children of your own, or yours are already grown, perhaps you can help someone else's child(ren)
become active in your church.

The greatest legacy a person can leave behind is to have godly sons and daughters who follow
Jesus and actively participate in worship. Pray specifically for the children you know—your own,
grandchildren, nephews and nieces—that they would faithfully follow Christ.

[i pray]

*Father, remind me of my need for communion with you, and of the importance of the example I set
for others—good or bad—and especially children. Above all else, on those days when my will to obey
is weak, remind me what it cost your Son to make it possible for me to come into your presence.*

[i respond]

Write a "faith will" to a family member. Tell them the importance of worship as a discipline for
you. Write some suggestions—such as journaling, daily prayer time, listening to a favorite Christian
song—that will help them carry on your legacy.

ceremonially clean or unclean, may eat that meat, just as you do now with gazelle and deer. ²³The only restriction is never to eat the blood, for the blood is the life, and you must not eat the life with the meat. ²⁴Instead, pour out the blood on the ground like water. ²⁵Do not eat the blood; then all will go well with you and your children, because you will be doing what pleases the LORD. ²⁶Take your sacred gifts and your offerings given to fulfill a vow to the place the LORD chooses to dwell. ²⁷You must offer the meat and blood of your burnt offerings on the altar of the LORD your God. The blood of your other sacrifices must be poured out beside the altar of the LORD your God, but you may eat the meat. ²⁸Be careful to obey all my commands so that all will go well with you and your children, because you will be doing what pleases the LORD your God.

²⁹"When the LORD your God destroys the nations and you drive them out and occupy their land, ³⁰do not be trapped into following their example in worshiping their gods. Do not say, 'How do these nations worship their gods? I want to follow their example.' ³¹You must not do this to the LORD your God. These nations have committed many detestable acts that the LORD hates, all in the name of their gods. They have even burned their sons and daughters as sacrifices to their gods. ³²Carefully obey all the commands I give you. Do not add to them or subtract from them.

A WARNING AGAINST IDOLATRY

13 "Suppose there are prophets among you, or those who have dreams about the future, and they promise you signs or miracles, ²and the predicted signs or miracles take place. If the prophets then say, 'Come, let us worship the gods of foreign nations,' ³do not listen to them. The LORD your God is testing you to see if you love him with all your heart and soul. ⁴Serve only the LORD your God and fear him alone. Obey his commands, listen to

his voice, and cling to him. ⁵The false prophets or dreamers who try to lead you astray must be put to death, for they encourage rebellion against the LORD your God, who brought you out of slavery in the land of Egypt. Since they try to keep you from following the LORD your God, you must execute them to remove the evil from among you.

⁶"Suppose your brother, son, daughter, beloved wife, or closest friend comes to you secretly and says, 'Let us go worship other gods'—gods that neither you nor your ancestors have known. ⁷They might suggest that you worship the gods of peoples who live nearby or who come from the ends of the earth. ⁸If they do this, do not give in or listen, and have no pity. Do not spare or protect them. ⁹You must put them to death! You must be the one to initiate the execution; then all the people must join in. ¹⁰Stone the guilty ones to death because they have tried to draw you away from the LORD your God, who rescued you from the land of Egypt, the place of slavery. ¹¹Then all Israel will hear about it and be afraid, and such wickedness will never again be done among you.

¹²"Suppose you hear in one of the towns the LORD your God is giving you ¹³that some worthless rabble among you have led their fellow citizens astray by encouraging them to worship foreign gods. ¹⁴In such cases, you must examine the facts carefully. If you find it is true and can prove that such a detestable act has occurred among you, ¹⁵you must attack that town and completely destroy* all its inhabitants, as well as all the livestock. ¹⁶Then you must pile all the plunder in the middle of the street and burn it. Put the entire town to the torch as a burnt offering to the LORD your God. That town must remain a ruin forever; it may never be rebuilt. ¹⁷Keep none of the plunder that has been set apart for destruction. Then the LORD will turn from his fierce anger and be merciful to you. He will have compassion on you and make you a great

13:15 The Hebrew term used here refers to the complete consecration of things or people to the LORD, either by destroying them or by giving them as an offering; also in 13:17.

nation, just as he solemnly promised your ancestors.

[18]"The LORD your God will be merciful only if you obey him and keep all the commands I am giving you today, doing what is pleasing to him.

CEREMONIALLY CLEAN AND UNCLEAN ANIMALS

14 "Since you are the people of the LORD your God, never cut yourselves or shave the hair above your foreheads for the sake of the dead. [2]You have been set apart as holy to the LORD your God, and he has chosen you to be his own special treasure from all the nations of the earth.

[3]"You must not eat animals that are ceremonially unclean. [4]These are the animals* you may eat: the ox, the sheep, the goat, [5]the deer, the gazelle, the roebuck, the wild goat, the ibex, the antelope, and the mountain sheep.

[6]"Any animal that has split hooves and chews the cud may be eaten, [7]but if the animal doesn't have both, it may not be eaten. So you may not eat the camel, the hare, or the rock badger.* They chew the cud but do not have split hooves. [8]And the pig may not be eaten, for though it has split hooves, it does not chew the cud. All these animals are ceremonially unclean for you. You may not eat or even touch the dead bodies of such animals.

[9]"As for marine animals, you may eat whatever has both fins and scales. [10]You may not, however, eat marine animals that do not have both fins and scales. They are ceremonially unclean for you.

[11]"You may eat any bird that is ceremonially clean. [12]These are the birds you may not eat: the eagle, the vulture, the osprey, [13]the buzzard, kites of all kinds, [14]ravens of all kinds, [15]the ostrich, the nighthawk, the seagull, hawks of all kinds, [16]the little owl, the great owl, the white owl, [17]the pelican, the carrion vulture, the cormorant, [18]the stork, herons of all kinds, the hoopoe, and the bat.

[19]"All flying insects are ceremonially unclean for you and may not be eaten. [20]But you may eat any winged creature that is ceremonially clean.

[21]"Do not eat anything that has died a natural death. You may give it to a foreigner living among you, or you may sell it to a foreigner. But do not eat it yourselves, for you are set apart as holy to the LORD your God.

"Do not boil a young goat in its mother's milk.

Words of Worship

OBEY

Obey—Hebrew *sha-ma'* "to hear"; Greek *hu-pa-kou-o* "to listen intently." In both the Old Testament and New Testament, translators bring out the full meaning of these words by rendering them as "obey."

Reading the Bible we often find an admonition such as, "Obey the LORD your God by keeping all these commands and laws that I am giving you today" (Deuteronomy 27:10). Or, "We know we love God's children if we love God and obey his commandments" (1 John 5:2). We get a new insight on statements like this when we understand that the words for *obey* are actually the words that mean *hear* or *listen*.

At worship, we hear what the Lord is saying to us—especially when reading from the Scripture is an important part of our worship. But if we aren't obeying God, we haven't really heard him. Jesus warned that hearing his words without doing them makes for a life on a shaky foundation (Matthew 7:24–27). Obeying the Son of God is a key to experiencing eternal life (John 3:36). Worship isn't just listening to the truth, it's *doing* the truth (James 1:22).

14:4 The identification of some of the animals and birds listed in this chapter is uncertain. 14:7 Or *coney,* or *hyrax.*

THE GIVING OF TITHES

22"You must set aside a tithe of your crops—one-tenth of all the crops you harvest each year. 23Bring this tithe to the place the LORD your God chooses for his name to be honored, and eat it there in his presence. This applies to your tithes of grain, new wine, olive oil, and the firstborn males of your flocks and herds. The purpose of tithing is to teach you always to fear the LORD your God. 24Now the place the LORD your God chooses for his name to be honored might be a long way from your home. 25If so, you may sell the tithe portion of your crops and herds and take the money to the place the LORD your God chooses. 26When you arrive, use the money to buy anything you want—an ox, a sheep, some wine, or beer. Then feast there in the presence of the LORD your God and celebrate with your household. 27And do not forget the Levites in your community, for they have no inheritance as you do.

28"At the end of every third year bring the tithe of all your crops and store it in the nearest town. 29Give it to the Levites, who have no inheritance among you, as well as to the foreigners living among you, the orphans, and the widows in your towns, so they can eat and be satisfied. Then the LORD your God will bless you in all your work.

RELEASE FOR DEBTORS

15 "At the end of every seventh year you must cancel your debts. 2This is how it must be done. Creditors must cancel the loans they have made to their fellow Israelites. They must not demand payment from their neighbors or relatives, for the LORD's time of release has arrived. 3This release from debt, however, applies only to your fellow Israelites—not to the foreigners living among you. 4There should be no poor among you, for the LORD your God will greatly bless you in the land he is giving you as a special possession. 5You will receive this blessing if you carefully obey the commands of the LORD your God that I am giving you today. 6The LORD your God will

bless you as he has promised. You will lend money to many nations but will never need to borrow! You will rule many nations, but they will not rule over you!

7"But if there are any poor people in your towns when you arrive in the land the LORD your God is giving you, do not be hard-hearted or tightfisted toward them. 8Instead, be generous and lend them whatever they need. 9Do not be mean-spirited and refuse someone a loan because the year of release is close at hand. If you refuse to make the loan and the needy person cries out to the LORD, you will be considered guilty of sin. 10Give freely without begrudging it, and the LORD your God will bless you in everything you do. 11There will always be some among you who are poor. That is why I am commanding you to share your resources freely with the poor and with other Israelites in need.

RELEASE FOR HEBREW SLAVES

12"If an Israelite man or woman voluntarily becomes your servant and serves you for six years, in the seventh year you must set that servant free.

13"When you release a male servant, do not send him away empty-handed. 14Give him a generous farewell gift from your flock, your threshing floor, and your winepress. Share with him some of the bounty with which the LORD your God has blessed you. 15Remember that you were slaves in the land of Egypt and the LORD your God redeemed you! That is why I am giving you this command. 16But suppose your servant says, 'I will not leave you,' because he loves you and your family, and he is well off with you. 17In that case, take an awl and push it through his earlobe into the door. After that, he will be your servant for life.

"You must do the same for your female servants.

18"Do not consider it a hardship when you release your servants. Remember that for six years they have given you the services worth double the wages of hired workers, and the LORD your God will bless you in all you do.

SACRIFICING FIRSTBORN MALE ANIMALS

¹⁹"You must set aside for the LORD your God all the firstborn males from your flocks and herds. Do not use the firstborn of your herds to work your fields, and do not shear the firstborn of your flocks. ²⁰Instead, you and your family must eat these animals in the presence of the LORD your God each year at the place he chooses. ²¹But if this firstborn animal has any defect, such as being lame or blind, or if anything else is wrong with it, you must not sacrifice it to the LORD your God. ²²Instead, use it for food for your family at home. Anyone may eat it, whether ceremonially clean or unclean, just as anyone may eat a gazelle or deer. ²³But do not eat the blood. You must pour it out on the ground like water.

PASSOVER AND THE FESTIVAL OF UNLEAVENED BREAD

16 "In honor of the LORD your God, always celebrate the Passover at the proper time in early spring,* for that was when the LORD your God brought you out of Egypt by night. ²Your Passover sacrifice may be from either the flock or the herd, and it must be sacrificed to the LORD your God at the place he chooses for his name to be honored. ³Eat it with bread made without yeast. For seven days eat only bread made without yeast, as you did when you escaped from Egypt in such a hurry. Eat this bread—the bread of suffering—so that you will remember the day you departed from Egypt as long as you live. ⁴Let no yeast be found in any house throughout your land for seven days. And do not let any of the meat of the Passover lamb remain until the next morning.

⁵"The Passover must not be eaten in the towns that the LORD your God is giving you. ⁶It must be offered at the place the LORD your God will choose for his name to be honored. Sacrifice it there as the sun goes down on the anniversary of your exodus from Egypt.

⁷Roast the lamb and eat it in the place the LORD your God chooses. Then go back to your tents the next morning. ⁸For the next six days you may not eat bread made with yeast. On the seventh day the people must assemble before the LORD your God, and no work may be done on that day.

THE FESTIVAL OF HARVEST

⁹"Count off seven weeks from the beginning of your grain harvest. ¹⁰Then you must celebrate the Festival of Harvest* to honor the LORD your God. Bring him a freewill offering in proportion to the blessings you have received from him. ¹¹It is a time to celebrate before the LORD your God at the place he chooses for his name to be honored. Celebrate with your whole family, all your servants, the Levites from your towns, and the foreigners, orphans, and widows who live among you. ¹²Remember that you were slaves in Egypt, so be careful to obey all these laws.

THE FESTIVAL OF SHELTERS

¹³"Another celebration, the Festival of Shelters, must be observed for seven days at the end of the harvest season, after the grain has been threshed and the grapes have been pressed. ¹⁴This festival will be a happy time of rejoicing with your family, your servants, and with the Levites, foreigners, orphans, and widows from your towns. ¹⁵For seven days celebrate this festival to honor the LORD your

> *God is to be praised with the voice, and the heart should go therewith in holy exultation.*
>
> CHARLES H. SPURGEON

16:1 Hebrew *in the month of Abib.* This month of the Hebrew lunar calendar usually occurs in March and April.   16:10 Or *Festival of Weeks;* also in 16:16.

God at the place he chooses, for it is the LORD your God who gives you bountiful harvests and blesses all your work. This festival will be a time of great joy for all.

¹⁶"Each year every man in Israel must celebrate these three festivals: the Festival of Unleavened Bread, the Festival of Harvest, and the Festival of Shelters. They must appear before the LORD your God at the place he chooses on each of these occasions, and they must bring a gift to the LORD. ¹⁷All must give as they are able, according to the blessings given to them by the LORD your God.

JUSTICE FOR THE PEOPLE

¹⁸"Appoint judges and officials for each of your tribes in all the towns the LORD your God is giving you. They will judge the people fairly throughout the land. ¹⁹You must never twist justice or show partiality. Never accept a bribe, for bribes blind the eyes of the wise and corrupt the decisions of the godly. ²⁰Let true justice prevail, so you may live and occupy the land that the LORD your God is giving you.

²¹"You must never set up an Asherah pole beside the altar of the LORD your God. ²²And never set up sacred pillars for worship, for the LORD your God hates them.

17 "Never sacrifice a sick or defective ox or sheep to the LORD your God, for he detests such gifts.

²"Suppose a man or woman among you, in one of your towns that the LORD your God is giving you, has done evil in the sight of the LORD your God and has violated the covenant ³by serving other gods or by worshiping the sun, the moon, or any of the forces of heaven, which I have strictly forbidden. ⁴When you hear about it, investigate the matter thoroughly. If it is true that this detestable thing has been done in Israel, ⁵then that man or woman must be taken to the gates of the town and stoned to death. ⁶But never put a person to death on the testimony of only one witness. There must always be at least two or three witnesses. ⁷The witnesses must throw the first

stones, and then all the people will join in. In this way, you will purge all evil from among you.

⁸"Suppose a case arises in a local court that is too hard for you to decide—for instance, whether someone is guilty of murder or only of manslaughter, or a difficult lawsuit, or a case involving different kinds of assault. Take such cases to the place the LORD your God will choose, ⁹where the Levitical priests and the judge on duty will hear the case and decide what to do. ¹⁰The decision they make at the place the LORD chooses will always stand. You must do exactly what they say. ¹¹After they have interpreted the law and reached a verdict, the sentence they impose must be fully executed; do not modify it in any way. ¹²Anyone arrogant enough to reject the verdict of the judge or of the priest who represents the LORD your God must be put to death. Such evil must be purged from Israel. ¹³Then everyone will hear about it and be afraid to act so arrogantly.

GUIDELINES FOR A KING

¹⁴"You will soon arrive in the land the LORD your God is giving you, and you will conquer it and settle there. Then you may begin to think, 'We ought to have a king like the other nations around us.' ¹⁵If this happens, be sure that you select as king the man the LORD your God chooses. You must appoint a fellow Israelite, not a foreigner. ¹⁶The king must not build up a large stable of horses for himself, and he must never send his people to Egypt to buy horses there, for the LORD has told you, 'You must never return to Egypt.' ¹⁷The king must not take many wives for himself, because they will lead him away from the LORD. And he must not accumulate vast amounts of wealth in silver and gold for himself.

¹⁸"When he sits on the throne as king, he must copy these laws on a scroll for himself in the presence of the Levitical priests. ¹⁹He must always keep this copy of the law with him and read it daily as long as he lives. That way he will learn to fear the LORD his God by obeying

all the terms of this law. ²⁰This regular reading will prevent him from becoming proud and acting as if he is above his fellow citizens. It will also prevent him from turning away from these commands in the smallest way. This will ensure that he and his descendants will reign for many generations in Israel.

GIFTS FOR THE PRIESTS AND LEVITES

18 "Remember that the Levitical priests and the rest of the tribe of Levi will not be given an inheritance of land like the other tribes in Israel. Instead, the priests and Levites will eat from the offerings given to the LORD by fire, for that is their inheritance. ²They will have no inheritance of their own among the Israelites. The LORD himself is their inheritance, just as he promised them.

³"These are the parts the priests may claim as their share from the oxen and sheep that the people bring as offerings: the shoulder, the cheeks, and the stomach. ⁴You must also give to the priests the first share of the grain, the new wine, the olive oil, and the wool at shearing time. ⁵For the LORD your God chose the tribe of Levi out of all your tribes to minister in the LORD's name forever.

⁶"Any Levite who so desires may come from any town in Israel, from wherever he is living, to the place the LORD chooses. ⁷He may minister there in the name of the LORD his God, just like his fellow Levites who are serving the LORD there. ⁸He may eat his share of the sacrifices and offerings, even if he has a private source of income.

A CALL TO HOLY LIVING

⁹"When you arrive in the land the LORD your God is giving you, be very careful not to imitate the detestable customs of the nations living there. ¹⁰For example, never sacrifice your son or daughter as a burnt offering.* And do not let your people practice fortune-telling or sorcery, or allow them to interpret omens, or engage in witchcraft, ¹¹or cast spells, or func-

tion as mediums or psychics, or call forth the spirits of the dead. ¹²Anyone who does these things is an object of horror and disgust to the LORD. It is because the other nations have done these things that the LORD your God will drive them out ahead of you. ¹³You must be blameless before the LORD your God. ¹⁴The people you are about to displace consult with

---

Words of Worship

THANKSGIVING

Thanksgiving, Give Thanks—Hebrew *ho-dah* "give thanks, make confession"; *to-dah* "thanksgiving"; Greek *eu-cha-ri-**ste**-o* "give thanks"; *eu-cha-ris-**ti**-a* "thanksgiving."

It's so easy to notice what other people possess that we don't have. Left to ourselves, we might be tempted into a bitter and grasping approach to life. Fortunately, we have the Scriptures to remind us to be satisfied with what we have (Hebrews 13:5), and to maintain a constant attitude of thankfulness (Ephesians 5:20). What Jesus has done for us, in rescuing us from sin, outweighs any cause for ingratitude.

The Bible, however, presents another side to thanksgiving. It's not just gratitude for the blessings God provides. When the psalmist invites us to "give thanks to him" (Psalm 100:4), he uses a Hebrew word derived from the word for *hand*. To give thanks is to lift the hand, as if to take an oath of loyalty. Biblical thanksgiving is a way of saying, "Lord, you are my God and I commit my life to you." The service of the Lord's Table is traditionally called the *Eucharist* because receiving the Lord's Supper is a way of pledging our commitment to the Lord. We're thankful not only that God is our provider, but that he calls us to serve him.

18:10 Or *never make your son or daughter pass through the fire.*

sorcerers and fortune-tellers, but the LORD your God forbids you to do such things.

TRUE AND FALSE PROPHETS

15"The LORD your God will raise up for you a prophet like me from among your fellow Israelites, and you must listen to that prophet. 16For this is what you yourselves requested of the LORD your God when you were assembled at Mount Sinai.* You begged that you might never again have to listen to the voice of the LORD your God or see this blazing fire for fear you would die.

17"Then the LORD said to me, 'Fine, I will do as they have requested. 18I will raise up a prophet like you from among their fellow Israelites. I will tell that prophet what to say, and he will tell the people everything I command him. 19I will personally deal with anyone who will not listen to the messages the prophet proclaims on my behalf. 20But any prophet who claims to give a message from another god or who falsely claims to speak for me must die.' 21You may wonder, 'How will we know whether the prophecy is from the LORD or not?' 22If the prophet predicts something in the LORD's name and it does not happen, the LORD did not give the message. That prophet has spoken on his own and need not be feared.

CITIES OF REFUGE

19 "The LORD your God will soon destroy the nations whose land he is giving you, and you will displace them and settle in their towns and homes. 2Then you must set apart three cities of refuge in the land the LORD your God is giving you to occupy. 3Divide the land the LORD your God is giving you into three districts, with one of these cities in each district. Keep the roads to these cities in good repair so that anyone who has killed someone can flee there for safety.

4"If someone accidentally kills a neighbor without harboring any previous hatred, the slayer may flee to any of these cities and be safe. 5For example, suppose someone goes into the forest with a neighbor to cut wood. And suppose one of them swings an ax and the ax head flies off the handle, killing the other person. In such cases, the slayer could flee to one of the cities of refuge and be safe. 6If the distance to the nearest city of refuge was too far, an enraged avenger might be able to chase down and kill the person who caused the death. The slayer would die, even though there was no death sentence and the first death had been an accident. 7That is why I am commanding you to set aside three cities of refuge.

8"If the LORD your God enlarges your territory, as he solemnly promised your ancestors, and gives you all the land he promised them, 9you must designate three additional cities of refuge. (He will give you this land if you obey all the commands I have given you—if you always love the LORD your God and walk in his ways.) 10That way you will prevent the death of innocent people in the land the LORD your God is giving you as a special possession, and you will not be held responsible for murder.

11"But suppose someone hates a neighbor and deliberately ambushes and murders that neighbor and then escapes to one of the cities of refuge. 12In that case, the leaders of the murderer's hometown must have the murderer brought back from the city of refuge and handed over to the dead person's avenger to be killed. 13Do not feel sorry for that murderer! Purge the guilt of murder from Israel so all may go well with you.

CONCERN FOR JUSTICE

14"When you arrive in the land the LORD your God is giving you as a special possession, never steal someone's land by moving the boundary markers your ancestors set up to mark their property.

15"Never convict anyone of a crime on the testimony of just one witness. The facts of the case must be established by the testimony of two or three witnesses. 16If a malicious witness

18:16 Hebrew *Horeb*, another name for Sinai.

My Daily Worship

— *February 16* —

WHEN YOU FEEL LIKE A LOSER

DEUTERONOMY 16:1–20:20

[The priest] will say, "Listen to me, all you men of Israel!
Do not be afraid as you go out to fight today! Do not lose heart or panic.
For the LORD your God is going with you! He will fight for you
against your enemies, and he will give you victory!" (20:3–4).

[i reflect]

Some days feel like we are losing the battle. We fight to keep our heads above water financially. We struggle with depression or a sense of failure. We can't seem to win a battle against an addiction. We wonder if we will ever find another job. We wrestle with a troubled relationship. Everyone's battle is different, but we all have them.

"Do not be afraid," God tells us. "Do not lose heart or panic." God is fighting with us. We are not in charge; God is. We're not fighting our battles alone. It is not up to us. "What can we say about such wonderful things as these? If God is for us, who can ever be against us? . . . Overwhelming victory is ours through Christ, who loved us. . . . Our fears for today, our worries about tomorrow, and even the powers of hell can't keep God's love away" (Romans 8:31, 37–38).

What defines a win for our battles? Sometimes we think we know the right answer, the best outcome, the terms of surrender for our "enemy." We pray only for the outcome we want. But God may fight the battle very differently than we can, and his victory may not look like what we envisioned. But we can be certain that God's victory is the right one, and his timing will be perfect.

What battle are you fighting? Give the battle to God, and claim victory! Then move ahead without fear, certain that God is by your side. Praise him for fighting for you, and for the victory which will certainly come. Claim victory, *his* victory, and feel his presence with you throughout this day.

[i pray]

Forgive me, Lord, for thinking I'm in charge of fighting my battles.
Help me to remember that you are with me, fighting for me because of your great love.
Help me to claim victory because of you.

[i respond]

What battle within do you need to turn over to God and let him fight for you? Tell God you need his help and that the terms of victory are his alone.

comes forward and accuses someone of a crime, [17]then both the accuser and accused must appear before the priests and judges who are on duty before the LORD. [18]They must be closely questioned, and if the accuser is found to be lying, [19]the accuser will receive the punishment intended for the accused. In this way, you will cleanse such evil from among you. [20]Those who hear about it will be afraid to do such an evil thing again. [21]You must never show pity! Your rule should be life for life, eye for eye, tooth for tooth, hand for hand, foot for foot.

REGULATIONS CONCERNING WAR

20 "When you go out to fight your enemies and you face horses and chariots and an army greater than your own, do not be afraid. The LORD your God, who brought you safely out of Egypt, is with you! [2]Before you go into battle, the priest will come forward to speak with the troops. [3]He will say, 'Listen to me, all you men of Israel! Do not be afraid as you go out to fight today! Do not lose heart or panic. [4]For the LORD your God is going with you! He will fight for you against your enemies, and he will give you victory!'

[5]"Then the officers of the army will address the troops and say, 'Has anyone just built a new house but not yet dedicated it? If so, go home! You might be killed in the battle, and someone else would dedicate your house! [6]Has anyone just planted a vineyard but not yet eaten any of its fruit? If so, go home! You might die in battle, and someone else would eat from it! [7]Has anyone just become engaged? Well, go home and get married! You might die in the battle, and someone else would marry your fiancée.' [8]Then the officers will also say, 'Is anyone terrified? If you are, go home before you frighten anyone else.' [9]When the officers have finished saying this to their troops, they will announce the names of the unit commanders.

[10]"As you approach a town to attack it, first offer its people terms for peace. [11]If they accept your terms and open the gates to you, then all the people inside will serve you in forced labor. [12]But if they refuse to make peace and prepare to fight, you must attack the town. [13]When the LORD your God hands it over to you, kill every man in the town. [14]But you may keep for yourselves all the women, children, livestock, and other plunder. You may enjoy the spoils of your enemies that the LORD your God has given you. [15]But these instructions apply only to distant towns, not to the towns of nations nearby.

[16]"As for the towns of the nations the LORD your God is giving you as a special possession, destroy every living thing in them. [17]You must completely destroy* the Hittites, Amorites, Canaanites, Perizzites, Hivites, and Jebusites, just as the LORD your God has commanded you. [18]This will keep the people of the land from teaching you their detestable customs in the worship of their gods, which would cause you to sin deeply against the LORD your God.

[19]"When you are besieging a town and the war drags on, do not destroy the trees. Eat the fruit, but do not cut down the trees. They are not enemies that need to be attacked! [20]But you may cut down trees that you know are not valuable for food. Use them to make the equipment you need to besiege the town until it falls.

CLEANSING FOR UNSOLVED MURDER

21 "Suppose someone is found murdered in a field in the land the LORD your God is giving you, and you don't know who committed the murder. [2]In such cases, your leaders and judges must determine which town is nearest the body. [3]Then the leaders of that town must select a young cow that has never been trained or yoked to a plow. [4]They must lead it to a valley that is neither plowed nor planted with a stream running through it. There they must break the cow's neck. [5]The

---

20:17 The Hebrew term used here refers to the complete consecration of things or people to the LORD, either by destroying them or by giving them as an offering.

Levitical priests must go there also, for the LORD your God has chosen them to minister before him and to pronounce blessings in the LORD's name. And they are to decide all lawsuits and punishments.

6"The leaders of the town nearest the body must wash their hands over the young cow whose neck was broken. 7Then they must say, 'Our hands did not shed this blood, nor did we see it happen. 8O LORD, forgive your people Israel whom you have redeemed. Do not charge your people Israel with the guilt of murdering an innocent person.' Then they will be absolved of the guilt of this person's blood. 9By following these instructions and doing what is right in the LORD's sight, you will cleanse the guilt of murder from your community.

MARRIAGE TO A CAPTIVE WOMAN

10"Suppose you go to war against your enemies and the LORD your God hands them over to you and you take captives. 11And suppose you see among the captives a beautiful woman, and you are attracted to her and want to marry her. 12If this happens, you may take her to your home, where she must shave her head, cut her fingernails, 13and change all her clothes. Then she must remain in your home for a full month, mourning for her father and mother. After that you may marry her. 14But if you marry her and then decide you do not like her, you must let her go free. You may not sell her or treat her as a slave, for you have humiliated her.

RIGHTS OF THE FIRSTBORN

15"Suppose a man has two wives, but he loves one and not the other, and both have given him sons. And suppose the firstborn son is the son of the wife he does not love. 16When the man divides the inheritance, he may not give the larger inheritance to his younger son, the son of the wife he loves. 17He must give the customary double portion to his oldest son, who represents the strength of his father's manhood and who owns the rights of the firstborn son, even though he is the son of the wife his father does not love.

DEALING WITH A REBELLIOUS SON

18"Suppose a man has a stubborn, rebellious son who will not obey his father or mother, even though they discipline him. 19In such cases, the father and mother must take the son before the leaders of the town. 20They must declare: 'This son of ours is stubborn and rebellious and refuses to obey. He is a worthless drunkard.' 21Then all the men of the town must stone him to death. In this way, you will cleanse this evil from among you, and all Israel will hear about it and be afraid.

VARIOUS REGULATIONS

22"If someone has committed a crime worthy of death and is executed and then hanged on a tree, 23the body must never remain on the tree overnight. You must bury the body that same day, for anyone hanging on a tree is cursed of God. Do not defile the land the LORD your God is giving you as a special possession.

22 "If you see your neighbor's ox or sheep wandering away, don't pretend not to see it. Take it back to its owner. 2If it does not belong to someone nearby or you don't know who the owner is, keep it until the owner comes looking for it; then return it. 3Do the same if you find your neighbor's donkey, clothing, or anything else your neighbor loses. Don't pretend you did not see it.

4"If you see your neighbor's ox or donkey lying on the road, do not look the other way. Go and help your neighbor get it to its feet!

5"A woman must not wear men's clothing, and a man must not wear women's clothing. The LORD your God detests people who do this.

6"If you find a bird's nest on the ground or in a tree and there are young ones or eggs in it with the mother sitting in the nest, do not take the mother with the young. 7You may take the young, but let the mother go, so you may prosper and enjoy a long life.

⁸"Every new house you build must have a barrier around the edge of its flat rooftop. That way you will not bring the guilt of bloodshed on your household if someone falls from the roof.

⁹"Do not plant any other crop between the rows of your vineyard. If you do, you are forbidden to use either the grapes from the vineyard or the produce of the other crop.

¹⁰"Do not plow with an ox and a donkey harnessed together.

¹¹"Do not wear clothing made of wool and linen woven together.

¹²"You must put tassels on the four corners of your cloaks.

REGULATIONS FOR SEXUAL PURITY

¹³"Suppose a man marries a woman and, after sleeping with her, changes his mind about her ¹⁴and falsely accuses her of having slept with another man. He might say, 'I discovered she was not a virgin when I married her.' ¹⁵If the man does this, the woman's father and mother must bring the proof of her virginity to the leaders of the town. ¹⁶Her father must tell them, 'I gave my daughter to this man to be his wife, and now he has turned against her. ¹⁷He has accused her of shameful things, claiming that she was not a virgin when he married her. But here is the proof of my daughter's virginity.' Then they must spread the cloth before the judges. ¹⁸The judges must then punish the man. ¹⁹They will fine him one hundred pieces of silver,* for he falsely accused a virgin of Israel. The payment will be made to the woman's father. The woman will then remain the man's wife, and he may never divorce her.

²⁰"But suppose the man's accusations are true, and her virginity could not be proved. ²¹In such cases, the judges must take the girl to the door of her father's home, and the men of the town will stone her to death. She has committed a disgraceful crime in Israel by being promiscuous while living in her par-ents' home. Such evil must be cleansed from among you.

²²"If a man is discovered committing adultery, both he and the other man's wife must be killed. In this way, the evil will be cleansed from Israel.

²³"Suppose a man meets a young woman, a virgin who is engaged to be married, and he has sexual intercourse with her. If this happens within a town, ²⁴you must take both of them to the gates of the town and stone them to death. The woman is guilty because she did not scream for help. The man must die because he violated another man's wife. In this way, you will cleanse the land of evil.

²⁵"But if the man meets the engaged woman out in the country, and he rapes her, then only the man should die. ²⁶Do nothing to the

---

Words of Worship

ETERNAL GOD

Eternal God—Hebrew *'El 'o-lam* "eternal God." The word *'olam* refers to continuous or long duration, in the past as well as the future.

Adrift in a world of "here today, gone tomorrow," we seek that which endures. Only a God who is forever, and from forever, can satisfy our quest. In the Lord, Abraham found and worshiped the eternal God, and the children of Abraham have sought him ever since.

We can trust the stability of the universe, for the eternal God sustains his creation. And as his worshipers, we trust him to guarantee his covenant with us. The God who swears, "as surely as I live" (Deuteronomy 32:40), will uphold his everlasting covenant (Hebrews 13:20). Joyfully we bow before "the one who is, who always was, and who is still to come" (Revelation 1:4).

22:19 Hebrew *100 shekels of silver,* about 2.5 pounds or 1.1 kilograms in weight.

young woman; she has committed no crime worthy of death. This case is similar to that of someone who attacks and murders a neighbor. ²⁷Since the man raped her out in the country, it must be assumed that she screamed, but there was no one to rescue her.

²⁸"If a man is caught in the act of raping a young woman who is not engaged, ²⁹he must pay fifty pieces of silver* to her father. Then he must marry the young woman because he violated her, and he will never be allowed to divorce her.

³⁰"A man must not have intercourse with his father's wife, for this would violate his father.

Regulations concerning Worship

23 "If a man's testicles are crushed or his penis is cut off, he may not be included in the assembly of the LORD.

²"Those of illegitimate birth and their descendants for ten generations may not be included in the assembly of the LORD.

³"No Ammonites or Moabites, or any of their descendants for ten generations, may be included in the assembly of the LORD. ⁴These nations did not welcome you with food and water when you came out of Egypt. Instead, they tried to hire Balaam son of Beor from Pethor in Aram-naharaim* to curse you. ⁵(But the LORD your God would not listen to Balaam. He turned the intended curse into a blessing because the LORD your God loves you.) ⁶You must never, as long as you live, try to help the Ammonites or the Moabites in any way.

⁷"Do not detest the Edomites or the Egyptians, because the Edomites are your relatives, and you lived as foreigners among the Egyptians. ⁸The third generation of Egyptians who came with you from Egypt may enter the assembly of the LORD.

Miscellaneous Regulations

⁹"When you go to war against your enemies, stay away from everything impure.

¹⁰"Any man who becomes ceremonially defiled because of a nocturnal emission must leave the camp and stay away all day. ¹¹Toward evening he must bathe himself, and at sunset he may return to the camp.

¹²"Mark off an area outside the camp for a latrine. ¹³Each of you must have a spade as part of your equipment. Whenever you relieve yourself, you must dig a hole with the spade and cover the excrement. ¹⁴The camp must be holy, for the LORD your God moves around in your camp to protect you and to defeat your enemies. He must not see any shameful thing among you, or he might turn away from you.

¹⁵"If slaves should escape from their masters and take refuge with you, do not force them to return. ¹⁶Let them live among you in whatever town they choose, and do not oppress them.

¹⁷"No Israelite man or woman may ever become a temple prostitute. ¹⁸Do not bring to the house of the LORD your God any offering from the earnings of a prostitute, whether a man or a woman, for both are detestable to the LORD your God.

¹⁹"Do not charge interest on the loans you make to a fellow Israelite, whether it is money, food, or anything else that may be loaned with interest. ²⁰You may charge interest to foreigners, but not to Israelites, so the LORD your God may bless you in everything you do in the land you are about to enter and occupy.

²¹"When you make a vow to the LORD your God, be prompt in doing whatever you promised him. For the LORD your God demands that you promptly fulfill all your vows. If you don't, you will be guilty of sin. ²²However, it is not a sin to refrain from making a vow. ²³But once you have voluntarily made a vow, be careful to do as you have said, for you have made a vow to the LORD your God.

²⁴"You may eat your fill of grapes from your neighbor's vineyard, but do not take any away in a basket. ²⁵And you may pluck a few heads of your neighbor's grain by hand, but you may not harvest it with a sickle.

22:29 Hebrew *50 shekels of silver,* about 1.25 pounds or 570 grams in weight.   23:4 *Aram-naharaim* means "Aram of the two rivers," thought to have been located between the Euphrates and Balih Rivers in northwestern Mesopotamia.

24 "Suppose a man marries a woman but later discovers something about her that is shameful. So he writes her a letter of divorce, gives it to her, and sends her away. [2]If she then leaves and marries another man [3]and the second husband also divorces her or dies, [4]the former husband may not marry her again, for she has been defiled. That would be detestable to the LORD. You must not bring guilt upon the land the LORD your God is giving you as a special possession.

[5]"A newly married man must not be drafted into the army or given any other special responsibilities. He must be free to be at home for one year, bringing happiness to the wife he has married.

[6]"It is wrong to take a pair of millstones, or even just the upper millstone, as a pledge, for the owner uses it to make a living.

[7]"If anyone kidnaps a fellow Israelite and treats him as a slave or sells him, the kidnapper must die. You must cleanse the evil from among you.

[8]"Watch all contagious skin diseases* carefully and follow the instructions of the Levitical priests; obey the commands I have given them. [9]Remember what the LORD your God did to Miriam as you were coming from Egypt.

[10]"If you lend anything to your neighbor, do not enter your neighbor's house to claim the security. [11]Stand outside and the owner will bring it out to you. [12]If your neighbor is poor and has only a cloak to give as security, do not keep the cloak overnight. [13]Return the cloak to its owner by sunset so your neighbor can sleep in it and bless you. And the LORD your God will count it as a righteous act.

[14]"Never take advantage of poor laborers, whether fellow Israelites or foreigners living in your towns. [15]Pay them their wages each day before sunset because they are poor and are counting on it. Otherwise they might cry out to the LORD against you, and it would be counted against you as sin.

[16]"Parents must not be put to death for the

> *Glory is what God looks like*
> *when for the time being*
> *all you have to look at him with*
> *is a pair of eyes.*
>
> FREDERICK BUECHNER

sins of their children, nor the children for the sins of their parents. Those worthy of death must be executed for their own crimes.

[17]"True justice must be given to foreigners living among you and to orphans, and you must never accept a widow's garment in pledge of her debt. [18]Always remember that you were slaves in Egypt and that the LORD your God redeemed you. That is why I have given you this command.

[19]"When you are harvesting your crops and forget to bring in a bundle of grain from your field, don't go back to get it. Leave it for the foreigners, orphans, and widows. Then the LORD your God will bless you in all you do. [20]When you beat the olives from your olive trees, don't go over the boughs twice. Leave some of the olives for the foreigners, orphans, and widows. [21]This also applies to the grapes in your vineyard. Do not glean the vines after they are picked, but leave any remaining grapes for the foreigners, orphans, and widows. [22]Remember that you were slaves in the land of Egypt. That is why I am giving you this command.

25 "Suppose two people take a dispute to court, and the judges declare that one is right and the other is wrong. [2]If the person in the wrong is sentenced to be flogged, the judge will command him to lie down and be beaten in his presence with the number of lashes appropriate to the crime. [3]No more

24:8 Traditionally rendered *leprosy.* The Hebrew word used here can describe various skin diseases.

than forty lashes may ever be given; more than forty lashes would publicly humiliate your neighbor.

⁴"Do not keep an ox from eating as it treads out the grain.

⁵"If two brothers are living together on the same property and one of them dies without a son, his widow must not marry outside the family. Instead, her husband's brother must marry her and fulfill the duties of a brother-in-law. ⁶The first son she bears to him will be counted as the son of the dead brother, so that his name will not be forgotten in Israel. ⁷But if the dead man's brother refuses to marry the widow, she must go to the town gate and say to the leaders there, 'My husband's brother refuses to preserve his brother's name in Israel—he refuses to marry me.' ⁸The leaders of the town will then summon him and try to reason with him. If he still insists that he doesn't want to marry her, ⁹the widow must walk over to him in the presence of the leaders, pull his sandal from his foot, and spit in his face. She will then say, 'This is what happens to a man who refuses to raise up a son for his brother.' ¹⁰Ever afterward his family will be referred to as 'the family of the man whose sandal was pulled off'!

¹¹"If two Israelite men are fighting and the wife of one tries to rescue her husband by grabbing the testicles of the other man, ¹²her hand must be cut off without pity.

¹³"You must use accurate scales when you weigh out merchandise, ¹⁴and you must use full and honest measures. ¹⁵Yes, use honest weights and measures, so that you will enjoy a long life in the land the LORD your God is giving you. ¹⁶Those who cheat with dishonest weights and measures are detestable to the LORD your God.

¹⁷"Never forget what the Amalekites did to you as you came from Egypt. ¹⁸They attacked you when you were exhausted and weary, and they struck down those who were lagging behind. They had no fear of God. ¹⁹Therefore, when the LORD your God has given you rest from all your enemies in the land he is giving

you as a special possession, you are to destroy the Amalekites and erase their memory from under heaven. Never forget this!

HARVEST OFFERINGS AND TITHES

26 "When you arrive in the land the LORD your God is giving you as a special possession and you have conquered it and settled there, ²put some of the first produce from each harvest into a basket and bring it to the place the LORD your God chooses for his name to be honored. ³Go to the priest in charge at that time and say to him, 'With this gift I acknowledge that the LORD your God has brought me into the land he swore to give our ancestors.' ⁴The priest will then take the basket from your hand and set it before the altar of the LORD your God. ⁵You must then say in the presence of the LORD your God, 'My ancestor Jacob was a wandering Aramean who went to live in Egypt. His family was few in number, but in Egypt they became a mighty and numerous nation. ⁶When the Egyptians mistreated and humiliated us by making us their slaves, ⁷we cried out to the LORD, the God of our ancestors. He heard us and saw our hardship, toil, and oppression. ⁸So the LORD brought us out of Egypt with amazing power, overwhelming terror, and miraculous signs and wonders. ⁹He brought us to this place and gave us this land flowing with milk and honey! ¹⁰And now, O LORD, I have brought you a token of the first crops you have given me from the ground.' Then place the produce before the LORD your God and worship him. ¹¹Afterward go and celebrate because of all the good things the LORD your God has given to you and your household. Remember to include the Levites and the foreigners living among you in the celebration.

¹²"Every third year you must offer a special tithe of your crops. You must give these tithes to the Levites, foreigners, orphans, and widows so that they will have enough to eat in your towns. ¹³Then you must declare in the presence of the LORD your God, 'I have taken

the sacred gift from my house and have given it to the Levites, foreigners, orphans, and widows, just as you commanded me. I have not violated or forgotten any of your commands. [14]I have not eaten any of it while in mourning; I have not touched it while I was ceremonially unclean; and I have not offered any of it to the dead. I have obeyed the LORD my God and have done everything you commanded me. [15]Look down from your holy dwelling place in heaven and bless your people Israel and the land you have given us—a land flowing with milk and honey—just as you solemnly promised our ancestors.'

A CALL TO OBEY THE LORD'S COMMANDS

[16]"Today the LORD your God has commanded you to obey all these laws and regulations. You must commit yourself to them without reservation. [17]You have declared today that the LORD is your God. You have promised to obey his laws, commands, and regulations by walking in his ways and doing everything he tells you. [18]The LORD has declared today that you are his people, his own special treasure, just as he promised, and that you must obey all his commands. [19]And if you do, he will make you greater than any other nation. Then you will receive praise, honor, and renown. You will be a nation that is holy to the LORD your God, just as he promised."

THE ALTAR ON MOUNT EBAL

27 Then Moses and the leaders of Israel charged the people as follows: "Keep all these commands that I am giving you today. [2]When you cross the Jordan River and enter the land the LORD your God is giving you, set up some large stones and coat them with plaster. [3]Then write all the terms of this law on them. I repeat, you will soon cross the river to enter the land the LORD your God is giving you, a land flowing with milk and honey, just as the LORD, the God of your ancestors, promised you. [4]When you cross the Jordan, set up these stones at Mount Ebal and coat them with plaster, as I am commanding you today. [5]Then build an altar there to the LORD your God, using natural stones. [6]Do not shape the stones with an iron tool. On the altar you must offer burnt offerings to the LORD your God. [7]Sacrifice peace offerings on it also, and feast there with great joy before the LORD your God. [8]On the stones coated with plaster, you must clearly write all the terms of this law."

[9]Then Moses and the Levitical priests addressed all Israel as follows: "O Israel, be quiet and listen! Today you have become the people of the LORD your God. [10]So obey the LORD your God by keeping all these commands and laws that I am giving you today."

CURSES FROM MOUNT EBAL

[11]That same day Moses gave this charge to the people: [12]"When you cross the Jordan River, the tribes of Simeon, Levi, Judah, Issachar, Joseph, and Benjamin must stand on Mount Gerizim to proclaim a blessing over the people. [13]And the tribes of Reuben, Gad, Asher, Zebulun, Dan, and Naphtali must stand on Mount Ebal to proclaim a curse. [14]Then the Levites must shout to all the people of Israel:

[15]"Cursed is anyone who carves or casts idols and secretly sets them up. These idols, the work of craftsmen, are detestable to the LORD.'
And all the people will reply, 'Amen.'

[16]"Cursed is anyone who despises father or mother.'
And all the people will reply, 'Amen.'

[17]"Cursed is anyone who steals property from a neighbor by moving a boundary marker.'
And all the people will reply, 'Amen.'

[18]"Cursed is anyone who leads a blind person astray on the road.'
And all the people will reply, 'Amen.'

My Daily Worship

IS THAT YOUR BEST OFFER?

DEUTERONOMY 21:1–26:19

*When you arrive in the land the LORD your God is giving you as a special possession
and you have conquered it and settled there, put some of the first produce
from each harvest into a basket and bring it to the place the LORD
your God chooses for his name to be honored (26:1–2).*

[i reflect]

What is in the basket you bring to God? What do you give that brings honor to his holy name? The Israelites brought baskets overflowing with vegetables, fruits, and grains. Their gifts provided food for the priests, who were chosen by God to serve the people rather than spending their time tilling the soil and growing their own food. For us as Christians, our financial gifts support those who teach and serve in our churches and provide for others who need extra help. Next time you write a check for your tithe, picture yourself carrying a basket of food to someone in need—that's really what you are doing!

But giving back to God is not limited to tithes and offerings. You can give "first produce" every day. Your gift of time can encourage someone who's ill, or cheer a homebound elderly person. You can offer a gift of service by nurturing the budding faith of a child or providing a meal for someone who's hungry. The list of ways we can give is as endless as the joy that follows after obeying God.

How will you honor God's name today? What "first produce" can you give him? Wherever you are, in your home or running errands, in the office or at school, this is the place God has chosen for you to be this day. Think about what you have to accomplish and offer those tasks to God as an act of worship. Fill your basket with your best efforts, kind words, a helping hand, a grateful heart, a song of praise, and offer these gifts to your heavenly Father.

[i pray]

*Thank you for the privilege of giving my "first produce." Thank you for your gift to me,
your Son, Jesus. His love encourages me to follow his example of giving to others.*

[i respond]

Are you following the command to give first to God? What do you hold back for yourself—money, time, talents—that God may need? What new "first produce" might you give today in honor of God's holy name?

¹⁹"Cursed is anyone who is unjust to foreigners, orphans, and widows.'

And all the people will reply, 'Amen.'

²⁰"Cursed is anyone who has sexual intercourse with his father's wife, for he has violated his father.'

And all the people will reply, 'Amen.'

²¹"Cursed is anyone who has sexual intercourse with an animal.'

And all the people will reply, 'Amen.'

²²"Cursed is anyone who has sexual intercourse with his sister, whether she is the daughter of his father or his mother.'

And all the people will reply, 'Amen.'

²³"Cursed is anyone who has sexual intercourse with his mother-in-law.'

And all the people will reply, 'Amen.'

²⁴"Cursed is anyone who kills another person in secret.'

And all the people will reply, 'Amen.'

²⁵"Cursed is anyone who accepts payment to kill an innocent person.'

And all the people will reply, 'Amen.'

²⁶"Cursed is anyone who does not affirm the terms of this law by obeying them.'

And all the people will reply, 'Amen.'

BLESSINGS FOR OBEDIENCE

28 "If you fully obey the LORD your God by keeping all the commands I am giving you today, the LORD your God will exalt you above all the nations of the world. ²You will experience all these blessings if you obey the LORD your God:

³ You will be blessed in your towns and in the country.

⁴ You will be blessed with many children and productive fields.

You will be blessed with fertile herds and flocks.

⁵ You will be blessed with baskets overflowing with fruit, and with kneading bowls filled with bread.

⁶ You will be blessed wherever you go, both in coming and in going.

⁷"The LORD will conquer your enemies when they attack you. They will attack you from one direction, but they will scatter from you in seven!

⁸"The LORD will bless everything you do and will fill your storehouses with grain. The LORD your God will bless you in the land he is giving you.

⁹"If you obey the commands of the LORD your God and walk in his ways, the LORD will establish you as his holy people as he solemnly promised to do. ¹⁰Then all the nations of the world will see that you are a people claimed by the LORD, and they will stand in awe of you.

¹¹"The LORD will give you an abundance of good things in the land he swore to give your ancestors—many children, numerous livestock, and abundant crops. ¹²The LORD will send rain at the proper time from his rich treasury in the heavens to bless all the work you do. You will lend to many nations, but you will never need to borrow from them. ¹³If you listen to these commands of the LORD your God and carefully obey them, the LORD will make you the head and not the tail, and you will always have the upper hand. ¹⁴You must not turn away from any of the commands I am giving you today to follow after other gods and worship them.

CURSES FOR DISOBEDIENCE

¹⁵"But if you refuse to listen to the LORD your God and do not obey all the commands and laws I am giving you today, all these curses will come and overwhelm you:

¹⁶ You will be cursed in your towns and in the country.

My Daily Worship

— February 18 —

HOW TO BE BLESSED BY GOD

DEUTERONOMY 27:1–30:20

You will be blessed wherever you go, both in coming and in going. . . . If you obey
the commands of the LORD your God and walk in his ways, the LORD will
establish you as his holy people as he solemnly promised to do (28:6, 9).

[i reflect]

Just as the Israelites were God's holy people of the Old Testament, we believers are God's holy people of the New Testament. If we follow the example of Jesus, we can claim the same promise given the Israelites: "You will be blessed wherever you go, both in coming and in going." What a wonderful promise! In coming and in going, from our birth to our death, from awaking each morning to when we go to sleep at night, his love and mercy are always available to us.

For the Israelites, who had been living in tents for forty years in the wilderness, God's blessings included a land of their own, security and prosperity, the joy of raising a family, and having plenty to eat. How wonderful those promised blessings must have seemed to those homeless wanderers! Yet God had blessed them throughout the forty years of wandering, too. He kept them safe, gave them manna from heaven to eat, and quenched their thirst with water from a rock. He forgave them again and again when they complained and turned against him.

When things are going well for us, it's easy to recognize his blessing and respond with joy and thanksgiving. But how do we respond when trouble strikes or when we are suffering? The truth is, God still is present with us, no matter what we're facing. If you feel more like complaining than praising today, ask God to forgive you and remind you of the blessings he has already bestowed upon you. As you open your heart to his presence, he will help you see the blessings in your life, not just the difficulties.

[i pray]

I want to be a part of your holy people, Lord. Help me to follow your teachings and to experience
the joy of your blessings in my life. Thank you for your wonderful promises to me.

[i respond]

Are you able to recognize and thank God for his blessings to you? Can you rejoice and praise him for whatever circumstances you face? Do you have blessings you have not recognized for which you can praise him today?

¹⁷ You will be cursed with baskets empty of fruit, and with kneading bowls empty of bread.

¹⁸ You will be cursed with few children and barren fields.

You will be cursed with infertile herds and flocks.

¹⁹ You will be cursed wherever you go, both in coming and in going.

²⁰"The LORD himself will send against you curses, confusion, and disillusionment in everything you do, until at last you are completely destroyed for doing evil and forsaking me. ²¹The LORD will send diseases among you until none of you are left in the land you are about to enter and occupy. ²²The LORD will strike you with wasting disease, fever, and inflammation, with scorching heat and drought, and with blight and mildew. These devastations will pursue you until you die. ²³The skies above will be as unyielding as bronze, and the earth beneath will be as hard as iron. ²⁴The LORD will turn your rain into sand and dust, and it will pour down from the sky until you are destroyed.

²⁵"The LORD will cause you to be defeated by your enemies. You will attack your enemies from one direction, but you will scatter from them in seven! You will be an object of horror to all the kingdoms of the earth. ²⁶Your dead bodies will be food for the birds and wild animals, and no one will be there to chase them away.

²⁷"The LORD will afflict you with the boils of Egypt and with tumors, scurvy, and the itch, from which you cannot be cured. ²⁸The LORD will strike you with madness, blindness, and panic. ²⁹You will grope around in broad daylight, just like a blind person groping in the darkness, and you will not succeed at anything you do. You will be oppressed and robbed continually, and no one will come to save you.

³⁰"You will be engaged to a woman, but another man will ravish her. You will build a house, but someone else will live in it. You will plant a vineyard, but you will never enjoy its fruit. ³¹Your ox will be butchered before your eyes, but you won't get a single bite of the meat. Your donkey will be driven away, never to be returned. Your sheep will be given to your enemies, and no one will be there to help you. ³²You will watch as your sons and daughters are taken away as slaves. Your heart will break as you long for them, but nothing you do will help. ³³A foreign nation you have never heard about will eat the crops you worked so hard to grow. You will suffer under constant oppression and harsh treatment. ³⁴You will go mad because of all the tragedy around you. ³⁵The LORD will cover you from head to foot with incurable boils.

³⁶"The LORD will exile you and the king you crowned to a nation unknown to you and your ancestors. Then in exile you will worship gods of wood and stone! ³⁷You will become an object of horror, a proverb and a mockery among all the nations to which the LORD sends you.

³⁸"You will plant much but harvest little, for locusts will eat your crops. ³⁹You will plant vineyards and care for them, but you will not drink the wine or eat the grapes, for worms will destroy the vines. ⁴⁰You will grow olive trees throughout your land, but you will never use the olive oil, for the trees will drop the fruit before it is ripe. ⁴¹You will have sons and daughters, but you will not keep them, for they will be led away into captivity. ⁴²Swarms of insects will destroy your trees and crops. ⁴³The foreigners living among you will become stronger and stronger, while you become weaker and weaker. ⁴⁴They will lend money to you, not you to them. They will be the head, and you will be the tail!

⁴⁵"If you refuse to listen to the LORD your God and to obey the commands and laws he has given you, all these curses will pursue and overtake you until you are destroyed. ⁴⁶These horrors will serve as a sign and warning among you and your descendants forever. ⁴⁷Because you have not served the LORD your God with joy and enthusiasm for the abun-

dant benefits you have received, [48]you will serve your enemies whom the LORD will send against you. You will be left hungry, thirsty, naked, and lacking in everything. They will oppress you harshly until you are destroyed.

[49]"The LORD will bring a distant nation against you from the end of the earth, and it will swoop down on you like an eagle. It is a nation whose language you do not understand, [50]a fierce and heartless nation that shows no respect for the old and no pity for the young. [51]Its armies will devour your livestock and crops, and you will starve to death. They will leave you no grain, new wine, olive oil, calves, or lambs, bringing about your destruction. [52]They will lay siege to your cities until all the fortified walls in your land—the walls you trusted to protect you—are knocked down. They will attack all the towns in the land the LORD your God has given you. [53]The siege will be so severe that you will eat the flesh of your own sons and daughters, whom the LORD your God has given you. [54]The most tenderhearted man among you will have no compassion for his own brother, his beloved wife, and his surviving children. [55]He will refuse to give them a share of the flesh he is devouring—the flesh of one of his own children—because he has nothing else to eat during the siege that your enemy will inflict on all your towns. [56]The most tender and delicate woman among you—so delicate she would not so much as touch her feet to the ground—will be cruel to the husband she loves and to her own son or daughter. [57]She will hide from them the afterbirth and the new baby she has borne, so that she herself can secretly eat them. She will have nothing else to eat during the siege and terrible distress that your enemy will inflict on all your towns.

[58]"If you refuse to obey all the terms of this law that are written in this book, and if you do not fear the glorious and awesome name of the LORD your God, [59]then the LORD will overwhelm both you and your children with indescribable plagues. These plagues will be intense and without relief, making you miserable and unbearably sick. [60]He will bring against you all the diseases of Egypt that you feared so much, and they will claim you. [61]The LORD will bring against you every sickness and plague there is, even those not mentioned in this Book of the Law, until you are destroyed. [62]Though you are as numerous as the stars in the sky, few of you will be left because you would not listen to the LORD your God.

[63]"Just as the LORD has found great pleasure in helping you to prosper and multiply, the LORD will find pleasure in destroying you, until you disappear from the land you are about to enter and occupy. [64]For the LORD will scatter you among all the nations from one end of the earth to the other. There you will worship foreign gods that neither you nor your ancestors have known, gods made of wood and stone! [65]There among those nations you will find no place of security and rest. And the LORD will cause your heart to tremble, your eyesight to fail, and your soul to despair. [66]Your lives will hang in doubt. You will live night and day in fear, with no reason to believe that you will see the morning light. [67]In the morning you will say, 'If only it were night!' And in the evening you will say, 'If only it were morning!' You will say this because of your terror at the awesome horrors you see around you. [68]Then the LORD will send you back to Egypt in ships, a journey I promised you would never again make. There you will offer to sell yourselves to your enemies as slaves, but no one will want to buy you."

29 These are the terms of the covenant the LORD commanded Moses to make with the Israelites while they were in the land of Moab, in addition to the covenant he had made with them at Mount Sinai.*

MOSES REVIEWS THE COVENANT

[2]Moses summoned all the Israelites and said to them, "You have seen with your own eyes everything the LORD did in Egypt to Pharaoh

29:1 Hebrew *Horeb,* another name for Sinai.

and all his servants and his whole country—
³all the great tests of strength, the miraculous
signs, and the amazing wonders. ⁴But to this
day the LORD has not given you minds that
understand, nor eyes that see, nor ears that
hear! ⁵For forty years I led you through the
wilderness, yet your clothes and sandals did
not wear out. ⁶You had no bread or wine or
other strong drink, but he gave you food so
you would know that he is the LORD your
God. ⁷When we came here, King Sihon of
Heshbon and King Og of Bashan came out to
fight against us, but we defeated them. ⁸We
took their land and gave it to the tribes of
Reuben and Gad and to the half-tribe of
Manasseh as their inheritance.

⁹"Therefore, obey the terms of this
covenant so that you will prosper in everything you do. ¹⁰All of you—your tribal leaders,
your judges, your officers, all the men of
Israel—are standing today before the LORD
your God. ¹¹With you are your little ones, your
wives, and the foreigners living among you
who chop your wood and carry your water.
¹²You are standing here today to enter into a
covenant with the LORD your God. The LORD
is making this covenant with you today, and
he has sealed it with an oath. ¹³He wants to
confirm you today as his people and to confirm that he is your God, just as he promised
you, and as he swore to your ancestors
Abraham, Isaac, and Jacob. ¹⁴But you are not
the only ones with whom the LORD is making
this covenant with its obligations. ¹⁵The LORD
your God is making this covenant with you
who stand in his presence today and also with
all future generations of Israel.

¹⁶"Surely you remember how we lived in the
land of Egypt and how we traveled through
the lands of enemy nations as we left. ¹⁷You
have seen their detestable idols made of wood,
stone, silver, and gold. ¹⁸The LORD made this
covenant with you so that no man, woman,
family, or tribe among you would turn away
from the LORD our God to worship these gods
of other nations, and so that no root among
you would bear bitter and poisonous fruit.

¹⁹Let none of those who hear the warnings of
this curse consider themselves immune,
thinking, 'I am safe, even though I am walking
in my own stubborn way.' This would lead to
utter ruin! ²⁰The LORD will not pardon such
people. His anger and jealousy will burn
against them. All the curses written in this
book will come down on them, and the LORD
will erase their names from under heaven.
²¹The LORD will separate them from all the
tribes of Israel, to pour out on them all the
covenant curses recorded in this Book of
the Law.

²²"Then the generations to come, both your
own descendants and the foreigners who
come from distant lands, will see the devastation of the land and the diseases the LORD will
send against it. ²³They will find its soil turned
into sulfur and salt, with nothing planted and
nothing growing, not even a blade of grass. It
will be just like Sodom and Gomorrah, Admah
and Zeboiim, which the LORD destroyed in his
anger. ²⁴The surrounding nations will ask,
'Why has the LORD done this to his land? Why
was he so angry?'

²⁵"And they will be told, 'This happened
because the people of the land broke the
covenant they made with the LORD, the God
of their ancestors, when he brought them out
of the land of Egypt. ²⁶They turned to serve
and worship other gods that were foreign to
them, gods that the LORD had not designated
for them. ²⁷That is why the LORD's anger
burned against this land, bringing down on it
all the curses recorded in this book. ²⁸In great
anger and fury the LORD uprooted his people
from their land and exiled them to another
land, where they still live today!'

²⁹"There are secret things that belong to the
LORD our God, but the revealed things belong
to us and our descendants forever, so that we
may obey these words of the law.

A CALL TO RETURN TO THE LORD

30 "Suppose all these things happen to
you—the blessings and the curses I
have listed—and you meditate on them as you

are living among the nations to which the LORD your God has exiled you. [2]If at that time you return to the LORD your God, and you and your children begin wholeheartedly to obey all the commands I have given you today, [3]then the LORD your God will restore your fortunes. He will have mercy on you and gather you back from all the nations where he has scattered you. [4]Though you are at the ends of the earth, the LORD your God will go and find you and bring you back again. [5]He will return you to the land that belonged to your ancestors, and you will possess that land again. He will make you even more prosperous and numerous than your ancestors!

[6]"The LORD your God will cleanse your heart and the hearts of all your descendants so that you will love him with all your heart and soul, and so you may live! [7]The LORD your God will inflict all these curses on your enemies and persecutors. [8]Then you will again obey the LORD and keep all the commands I am giving you today. [9]The LORD your God will make you successful in everything you do. He will give you many children and numerous livestock, and your fields will produce abundant harvests, for the LORD will delight in being good to you as he was to your ancestors. [10]The LORD your God will delight in you if you obey his voice and keep the commands and laws written in this Book of the Law, and if you turn to the LORD your God with all your heart and soul.

THE CHOICE OF LIFE OR DEATH

[11]"This command I am giving you today is not too difficult for you to understand or perform. [12]It is not up in heaven, so distant that you must ask, 'Who will go to heaven and bring it down so we can hear and obey it?' [13]It is not beyond the sea, so far away that you must ask, 'Who will cross the sea to bring it to us so we can hear and obey it?' [14]The message is very close at hand; it is on your lips and in your heart so that you can obey it.

[15]"Now listen! Today I am giving you a choice between prosperity and disaster, between life and death. [16]I have commanded you today to love the LORD your God and to keep his commands, laws, and regulations by walking in his ways. If you do this, you will live and become a great nation, and the LORD your God will bless you and the land you are about to enter and occupy. [17]But if your heart turns away and you refuse to listen, and if you are drawn away to serve and worship other gods, [18]then I warn you now that you will certainly be destroyed. You will not live a long, good life in the land you are crossing the Jordan to occupy.

[19]"Today I have given you the choice between life and death, between blessings and curses. I call on heaven and earth to witness the choice you make. Oh, that you would choose life, that you and your descendants might live! [20]Choose to love the LORD your God and to obey him and commit yourself to him, for he is your life. Then you will live long in the land the LORD swore to give your ancestors Abraham, Isaac, and Jacob."

JOSHUA BECOMES ISRAEL'S LEADER

31 When Moses had finished saying* these things to all the people of Israel, [2]he said, "I am now 120 years old and am no longer able to lead you. The LORD has told me that I will not cross the Jordan River. [3]But the LORD your God himself will cross over ahead

> *Our heavenly Father loves us with an extravagant abandon. Passionate, undignified worship is our only reasonable response.*
>
> MATT REDMAN

31:1 As in Dead Sea Scrolls and Greek version; Masoretic Text reads *Moses went and spoke.*

of you. He will destroy the nations living there, and you will take possession of their land. Joshua is your new leader, and he will go with you, just as the LORD promised. ⁴The LORD will destroy the nations living in the land, just as he destroyed Sihon and Og, the kings of the Amorites. ⁵The LORD will hand over to you the people who live there, and you will deal with them as I have commanded you. ⁶Be strong and courageous! Do not be afraid of them! The LORD your God will go ahead of you. He will neither fail you nor forsake you."

⁷Then Moses called for Joshua, and as all Israel watched he said to him, "Be strong and courageous! For you will lead these people into the land that the LORD swore to give their ancestors. You are the one who will deliver it to them as their inheritance. ⁸Do not be afraid or discouraged, for the LORD is the one who goes before you. He will be with you; he will neither fail you nor forsake you."

PUBLIC READING OF THE LAW

⁹So Moses wrote down this law and gave it to the priests, who carried the Ark of the LORD's covenant, and to the leaders of Israel. ¹⁰Then Moses gave them this command: "At the end of every seventh year, the Year of Release, during the Festival of Shelters, ¹¹you must read this law to all the people of Israel when they assemble before the LORD your God at the place he chooses. ¹²Call them all together—men, women, children, and the foreigners living in your towns—so they may listen and learn to fear the LORD your God and carefully obey all the terms of this law. ¹³Do this so that your children who have not known these laws will hear them and will learn to fear the LORD your God. Do this as long as you live in the land you are crossing the Jordan to occupy."

ISRAEL'S DISOBEDIENCE PREDICTED

¹⁴Then the LORD said to Moses, "The time has come for you to die. Call Joshua and take him

with you to the Tabernacle,* and I will commission him there." So Moses and Joshua went and presented themselves at the Tabernacle. ¹⁵And the LORD appeared to them in a pillar of cloud at the entrance to the sacred tent.

¹⁶The LORD said to Moses, "You are about to die and join your ancestors. After you are gone, these people will begin worshiping foreign gods, the gods of the land where they are going. They will abandon me and break the covenant I have made with them. ¹⁷Then my anger will blaze forth against them. I will abandon them, hiding my face from them, and they will be destroyed. Terrible trouble will come down on them, so that they will say, 'These disasters have come because God is no longer among us!' ¹⁸At that time I will hide my face from them on account of all the sins they have committed by worshiping other gods.

¹⁹"Now write down the words of this song, and teach it to the people of Israel. Teach them to sing it, so it may serve as a witness against them. ²⁰For I will bring them into the land I swore to give their ancestors—a land flowing with milk and honey. There they will become prosperous; they will eat all the food they want and become well nourished. Then they will begin to worship other gods; they will despise me and break my covenant. ²¹Then great disasters will come down on them, and this song will stand as evidence against them, for it will never be forgotten by their descendants. I know what these people are like, even before they have entered the land I swore to give them." ²²So that very day Moses wrote down the words of the song and taught it to the Israelites.

²³Then the LORD commissioned Joshua son of Nun with these words: "Be strong and courageous! You must bring the people of Israel into the land I swore to give them. I will be with you."

²⁴When Moses had finished writing down this entire body of law in a book, ²⁵he gave these instructions to the Levites who carried

31:14 Hebrew *Tent of Meeting;* also in 31:14b.

the Ark of the LORD's covenant: ²⁶"Take this Book of the Law and place it beside the Ark of the Covenant of the LORD your God, so it may serve as a witness against the people of Israel. ²⁷For I know how rebellious and stubborn you are. Even now, while I am still with you, you have rebelled against the LORD. How much more rebellious will you be after my death! ²⁸Now summon all the leaders and officials of your tribes so that I can speak to them and call heaven and earth to witness against them. ²⁹I know that after my death you will become utterly corrupt and will turn from the path I have commanded you to follow. In the days to come, disaster will come down on you, for you will make the LORD very angry by doing what is evil in his sight."

THE SONG OF MOSES

³⁰So Moses recited this entire song to the assembly of Israel:

32 ¹"Listen, O heavens, and I will speak!
Hear, O earth, the words that I say!
² My teaching will fall on you like rain;
my speech will settle like dew.
My words will fall like rain on tender grass,
like gentle showers on young plants.
³ I will proclaim the name of the LORD;
how glorious is our God!
⁴ He is the Rock; his work is perfect.
Everything he does is just and fair.
He is a faithful God who does no wrong;
how just and upright he is!

⁵ "But they have acted corruptly toward him;
when they act like that, are they really his children?*
They are a deceitful and twisted generation.
⁶ Is this the way you repay the LORD,
you foolish and senseless people?
Isn't he your Father who created you?

Has he not made you and established you?
⁷ Remember the days of long ago;
think about the generations past.
Ask your father and he will inform you.
Inquire of your elders, and they will tell you.
⁸ When the Most High assigned lands to the nations,
when he divided up the human race,
he established the boundaries of the peoples
according to the number of angelic beings.*
⁹ For the people of Israel belong to the LORD;
Jacob is his special possession.

¹⁰ "He found them in a desert land,
in an empty, howling wasteland.
He surrounded them and watched over them;
he guarded them as his most precious possession.*
¹¹ Like an eagle that rouses her chicks
and hovers over her young,
so he spread his wings to take them in
and carried them aloft on his pinions.
¹² The LORD alone guided them;
they lived without any foreign gods.
¹³ He made them ride over the highlands;
he let them feast on the crops of the fields.
He nourished them with honey from the cliffs,
with olive oil from the hard rock.
¹⁴ He fed them curds from the herd and milk from the flock,
together with the fat of lambs and goats.
He gave them choice rams and goats from Bashan,
together with the choicest wheat.
You drank the finest wine,
made from the juice of grapes.

32:5 The meaning of the Hebrew is uncertain. **32:8** As in Dead Sea Scrolls, which read *of the sons of God,* and Greek version, which reads *of the angels of god;* Masoretic Text reads *of the sons of Israel.* **32:10** Hebrew *as the apple of his eye.*

15 But Israel* soon became fat and unruly;
the people grew heavy, plump, and
stuffed!
Then they abandoned the God who had
made them;
they made light of the Rock of their
salvation.
16 They stirred up his jealousy by worshiping
foreign gods;
they provoked his fury with detestable
acts.
17 They offered sacrifices to demons, non-
gods,
to gods they had not known before,
to gods only recently arrived,
to gods their ancestors had never feared.
18 You neglected the Rock who had fathered
you;
you forgot the God who had given you
birth.

19 "The LORD saw this and was filled with
loathing.
He was provoked to anger by his own
sons and daughters.
20 He said, 'I will abandon them;
I will see to their end!
For they are a twisted generation,
children without integrity.
21 They have roused my jealousy by worshiping non-gods;
they have provoked my fury with useless
idols.
Now I will rouse their jealousy by blessing
other nations;
I will provoke their fury by blessing the
foolish Gentiles.
22 For my anger blazes forth like fire
and burns to the depths of the grave.*
It devours the earth and all its crops
and ignites the foundations of the
mountains.
23 I will heap disasters upon them
and shoot them down with my arrows.
24 I will send against them wasting famine,

burning fever, and deadly disease.
They will be troubled by the fangs of wild
beasts,
by poisonous snakes that glide in the
dust.
25 Outside, the sword will bring death,
and inside, terror will strike
both young men and young women,
both infants and the aged.
26 I decided to scatter them,*
so even the memory of them would
disappear.
27 But I feared the taunt of the enemy,
that their adversaries might
misunderstand and say,
"Our power has triumphed!
It was not the LORD who did this!"'

28 "Israel is a nation that lacks sense;
the people are foolish, without
understanding.
29 Oh, that they were wise and could understand this!
Oh, that they might know their fate!
30 How could one person chase a thousand of
them,
and two people put ten thousand to
flight,
unless their Rock had sold them,
unless the LORD had given them up?
31 But the rock of our enemies is not like our
Rock,
as even they recognize.*
32 Their vine grows from the vine of Sodom,
from the vineyards of Gomorrah.
Their grapes are poison,
and their clusters are bitter.
33 Their wine is the venom of snakes,
the deadly poison of vipers.

34 " 'I am storing up these things,
sealing them away within my treasury.
35 I will take vengeance; I will repay those
who deserve it.
In due time their feet will slip.

32:15 Hebrew *Jeshurun,* a term of endearment for Israel.   32:22 Hebrew *of Sheol.*   32:26 As in Greek version; the meaning of the Hebrew
is uncertain.   32:31 The meaning of the Hebrew is uncertain. Greek version reads *our enemies are fools.*

Their day of disaster will arrive,
  and their destiny will overtake them.'

³⁶ "Indeed, the LORD will judge his people,
  and he will change his mind about* his
    servants,
when he sees their strength is gone
  and no one is left, slave or free.
³⁷ Then he will ask, 'Where are their gods,
  the rocks they fled to for refuge?
³⁸ Where now are those gods,
  who ate the fat of their sacrifices
  and drank the wine of their offerings?
Let those gods arise and help you!
  Let them provide you with shelter!
³⁹ Look now; I myself am he!
  There is no god other than me!
I am the one who kills and gives life;
  I am the one who wounds and heals;
  no one delivers from my power!
⁴⁰ Now I raise my hand to heaven
  and declare, "As surely as I live,
⁴¹ when I sharpen my flashing sword
  and begin to carry out justice,
I will bring vengeance on my enemies
  and repay those who hate me.
⁴² I will make my arrows drunk with blood,
  and my sword will devour flesh—
the blood of the slaughtered and the
    captives,
  and the heads of the enemy leaders." '

⁴³ "Rejoice with him, O heavens,
  and let all the angels of God worship
    him,*
  for he will avenge the blood of his
    servants.
He will take vengeance on his enemies
  and cleanse his land and his people."

⁴⁴So Moses came with Joshua* son of Nun
and recited all the words of this song to the
people. ⁴⁵When Moses had finished reciting
these words to Israel, ⁴⁶he added: "Take to
heart all the words I have given you today.
Pass them on as a command to your children
so they will obey every word of this law.
⁴⁷These instructions are not mere words—
they are your life! By obeying them you will
enjoy a long life in the land you are crossing
the Jordan River to occupy."

MOSES' DEATH FORETOLD

⁴⁸That same day the LORD said to Moses, ⁴⁹"Go
to Moab, to the mountains east of the river,*
and climb Mount Nebo, which is across from
Jericho. Look out across the land of Canaan,
the land I am giving to the people of Israel as
their own possession. ⁵⁰Then you must die
there on the mountain and join your ancestors, just as Aaron, your brother, died on
Mount Hor and joined his ancestors. ⁵¹For
both of you broke faith with me among the
Israelites at the waters of Meribah at Kadesh*
in the wilderness of Zin. You failed to demonstrate my holiness to the people of Israel
there. ⁵²So you will see the land from a distance, but you may not enter the land I am
giving to the people of Israel."

MOSES BLESSES THE PEOPLE

33 This is the blessing that Moses, the
man of God, gave to the people of
Israel before his death:

² "The LORD came from Mount Sinai
  and dawned upon us* from Mount Seir;
he shone forth from Mount Paran
  and came from Meribah-kadesh
  with flaming fire at his right hand.*
³ Indeed, you love the people;
  all your holy ones are in your hands.
They follow in your steps
  and accept your instruction.
⁴ Moses charged us with the law,
  the special possession of the assembly of
    Israel.*
⁵ The LORD became king in Israel* —

32:36 Or will take revenge for.   32:43 As in Dead Sea Scrolls and Greek version; Masoretic Text reads Rejoice with his people, O nations.
32:44 Hebrew Hoshea, a variant name for Joshua.   32:49 Hebrew the mountains of Abarim.   32:51 Hebrew waters of Meribath-kadesh.
33:2a As in Greek and Syriac versions; Hebrew reads upon them.   33:2b Or came from myriads of holy ones, from the south, from his
mountain slopes. The meaning of the Hebrew is uncertain.   33:4 Hebrew of Jacob.   33:5 Hebrew in Jeshurun, a term of endearment for Israel.

when the leaders of the people
    assembled,
    when the tribes of Israel gathered."

⁶Moses said this about the tribe of Reuben:*

"Let the tribe of Reuben live and not die
    out,
    even though their tribe is small."

⁷Moses said this about the tribe of Judah:

"O LORD, hear the cry of Judah
    and bring them again to their people.
Give them strength to defend their cause;
    help them against their enemies!"

⁸Moses said this about the tribe of Levi:

"O LORD, you have given the sacred lots*
    to your faithful servants the Levites.
You put them to the test at Massah
    and contended with them at the waters
        of Meribah.
⁹ The Levites obeyed your word
    and guarded your covenant.
They were more loyal to you
    than to their parents, relatives, and
        children.
¹⁰ Now let them teach your regulations to
        Jacob;
    let them give your instructions to Israel.
They will present incense before you
    and offer whole burnt offerings on the
        altar.
¹¹ Bless the Levites, O LORD,
    and accept all their work.
Crush the loins of their enemies;
    strike down their foes so they never rise
        again."

¹²Moses said this about the tribe of Benjamin:

"The people of Benjamin are loved by the
    LORD

and live in safety beside him.
He surrounds them continuously
    and preserves them from every harm."

¹³Moses said this about the tribes of Joseph:

"May their land be blessed by the LORD
    with the choice gift of rain from the
        heavens,
    and water from beneath the earth;
¹⁴ with the riches that grow in the sun,
    and the bounty produced each month;
¹⁵ with the finest crops of the ancient
        mountains,
    and the abundance from the everlasting
        hills;
¹⁶ with the best gifts of the earth and its
        fullness,
    and the favor of the one who appeared
        in the burning bush.
May these blessings rest on Joseph's head,
    crowning the brow of the prince among
        his brothers.
¹⁷ Joseph has the strength and majesty of a
        young bull;
    his power is like the horns of a wild ox.
He will gore distant nations,
    driving them to the ends of the earth.
This is my blessing for the multitudes of
        Ephraim
    and the thousands of Manasseh."

¹⁸Moses said this about the tribes of Zebulun
and Issachar*:

"May the people of Zebulun prosper in
    their expeditions abroad.
May the people of Issachar prosper at
    home in their tents.
¹⁹ They summon the people to the mountain
    to offer proper sacrifices there.
They benefit from the riches of the sea
    and the hidden treasures of the sand."

²⁰Moses said this about the tribe of Gad:

33:6 Hebrew lacks *Moses said this about the tribe of Reuben.*   **33:8** Hebrew *given your Thummim and Urim.* See Exod 28:30.
33:18 Hebrew lacks *and Issachar.*

My Daily Worship

— February 19 —

USING GOD'S ARM OF PROTECTION

DEUTERONOMY 31:1–34:12

The eternal God is your refuge, and his everlasting
arms are under you (33:27).

[i reflect]

A child cries. We reach out and cradle him in our arms for comfort. Someone we love learns she has a life-threatening illness. We put our arms around her and hold her close. Someone we love dies. We welcome the arms that enfold and comfort us. We all need human touch. No matter how old we are, we all long for someone to hold and protect us when we are troubled, afraid, or sorrowing. Here we have the promise that the eternal God holds us in his arms. What a wonder-filled, healing image!

Take a moment and imagine yourself wrapped in the arms of God. Sink into his protection and love and give all your cares to him. God is not distant or unapproachable. He wants to comfort you as a father comforts his child. He wants to protect you like a mother hen who gathers her chicks beneath her wings (Luke 13:34). He will provide sanctuary for you when troubles come. With his everlasting arms, he will place you out of reach on a high rock (Psalm 27:5). When you lean on God's everlasting arms, you are safe, secure, protected, loved.

When you are afraid or troubled or grieving, having someone you care about hold you in their arms does indeed give comfort, strength, and courage. How much more powerful is the refuge and comfort available to you from our heavenly Father! He will provide the strength to accept the life-threatening illness, the courage to go on living when someone you love dies, the energy and compassion to comfort others, the joy of knowing you are loved by the eternal God. Feel his arms around you today. Draw strength from his presence with you.

[i pray]

Dear Father, thank you for the wonder of being able to lean on your everlasting
arms and experience your refuge. I praise you for the strength your comfort
gives me and the joy of knowing you will always be with me.

[i respond]

Are you able to experience the comfort of God's everlasting arms? Or does he seem far away and unapproachable? What burden do you have that you can ask him to carry for you? He will. You can trust his promises.

"Blessed is the one who enlarges Gad's
territory!
Gad is poised there like a lion
to tear off an arm or a head.
²¹ The people of Gad took the best land for
themselves;
a leader's share was assigned to them.
When the leaders of the people were
assembled,
they carried out the LORD's justice
and obeyed his regulations for Israel."

²²Moses said this about the tribe of Dan:

"Dan is a lion's cub,
leaping out from Bashan."

²³Moses said this about the tribe of Naphtali:

"O Naphtali, you are rich in favor
and full of the LORD's blessings;
may you possess the west and the south."

²⁴Moses said this about the tribe of Asher:

"May Asher be blessed above other sons;
may he be esteemed by his brothers;
may he bathe his feet in olive oil.
²⁵ May the bolts of your gates be of iron and
bronze;
may your strength match the length of
your days!"

²⁶ "There is no one like the God of Israel.*
He rides across the heavens to help you,
across the skies in majestic splendor.
²⁷ The eternal God is your refuge,
and his everlasting arms are under you.
He thrusts out the enemy before you;
it is he who cries, 'Destroy them!'
²⁸ So Israel will live in safety,
prosperous Jacob in security,
in a land of grain and wine,
while the heavens drop down dew.
²⁹ How blessed you are, O Israel!

Who else is like you, a people saved by
the LORD?
He is your protecting shield
and your triumphant sword!
Your enemies will bow low before you,
and you will trample on their backs!"

THE DEATH OF MOSES

34 Then Moses went to Mount Nebo
from the plains of Moab and climbed
Pisgah Peak, which is across from Jericho. And
the LORD showed him the whole land, from
Gilead as far as Dan; ²all the land of Naphtali;
the land of Ephraim and Manasseh; all the
land of Judah, extending to the Mediterranean Sea*; ³the Negev; the Jordan Valley
with Jericho—the city of palms—as far as
Zoar. ⁴Then the LORD said to Moses, "This is
the land I promised on oath to Abraham,
Isaac, and Jacob, and I told them I would give
it to their descendants. I have now allowed
you to see it, but you will not enter the land."

⁵So Moses, the servant of the LORD, died
there in the land of Moab, just as the LORD
had said. ⁶He was buried* in a valley near
Beth-peor in Moab, but to this day no one
knows the exact place. ⁷Moses was 120 years
old when he died, yet his eyesight was clear,
and he was as strong as ever. ⁸The people of
Israel mourned thirty days for Moses on the
plains of Moab, until the customary period of
mourning was over.

⁹Now Joshua son of Nun was full of the
spirit of wisdom, for Moses had laid his hands
on him. So the people of Israel obeyed him
and did everything just as the LORD had commanded Moses.

¹⁰There has never been another prophet like
Moses, whom the LORD knew face to face.
¹¹The LORD sent Moses to perform all the
miraculous signs and wonders in the land of
Egypt against Pharaoh, all his servants, and
his entire land. ¹²And it was through Moses
that the LORD demonstrated his mighty power
and terrifying acts in the sight of all Israel.

33:26 Hebrew *of Jeshurun,* a term of endearment for Israel. **34:2** Hebrew *the western sea.* **34:6** Hebrew *He buried him,* that is, "The
LORD buried him." Samaritan Pentateuch and some Greek manuscripts read *They buried him.*

Joshua

Every promise of the LORD your God has come true (23:14b).

The Power of the Promise

A s children, the words flowed easily. "I'll do it—I promise," we would say, pledging to clean the room, improve the grades, change an attitude, or make any number of personal adjustments. Promises were cheap. But as we grew older, we began to realize the power of a promise. And we came to understand that the people we can truly count on are those who keep their word, like our friends. We trust them to do what they say they will; we believe that they will keep their commitments. When they promise us that they will be there, we know they will keep their word.

The book of Joshua tells of promises—promises made and promises kept. As the Israelites are about to enter the Promised Land, God says, "I promise you what I promised Moses: . . . No one will be able to stand their ground against you as long as you live. For I will be with you as I was with Moses. I will not fail you or abandon you" (1:3, 5).

Powerful words, powerful promises! Throughout the book, we see God keep his words as the Israelites cross the Jordan River (3:14–17) and begin their campaign to conquer the land. Then, in grateful response, Joshua leads the people in worship. In the closing days of his life, Joshua urges the nation to worship God alone and always trust his good promises (21:43–45; 23:1–16; 24:14–28, 31).

God's faithful character and the power behind his word are interwoven throughout Joshua. Use these exciting stories to remind you of God's faithfulness to you. And then, like Joshua, respond in worship.

Worship Moments

- When God stopped the Jordan River so the Israelites could safely enter the land, Joshua set up two memorials. Why? So that the future generations would remember what God had done and worship him (4:1–24).

- After Joshua publicly worshiped God and asked for a miracle, the earth's rotation appeared to stop until Joshua's army won a strategic battle (10:12–14).

- In this book God is praised as "the supreme God of the heavens above and the earth below" (2:11); "the living God" (3:10); "the Lord of the whole earth" (3:11; cf. 3:13); "Sovereign LORD" (7:7); and "a holy and jealous God" (24:19).

THE LORD'S CHARGE TO JOSHUA

1 After the death of Moses the LORD's servant, the LORD spoke to Joshua son of Nun, Moses' assistant. He said, ²"Now that my servant Moses is dead, you must lead my people across the Jordan River into the land I am giving them. ³I promise you what I promised Moses: 'Everywhere you go, you will be on land I have given you—⁴from the Negev Desert in the south to the Lebanon mountains in the north, from the Euphrates River on the east to the Mediterranean Sea* on the west, and all the land of the Hittites.' ⁵No one will be able to stand their ground against you as long as you live. For I will be with you as I was with Moses. I will not fail you or abandon you.

⁶"Be strong and courageous, for you will lead my people to possess all the land I swore to give their ancestors. ⁷Be strong and very courageous. Obey all the laws Moses gave you. Do not turn away from them, and you will be successful in everything you do. ⁸Study this Book of the Law continually. Meditate on it day and night so you may be sure to obey all that is written in it. Only then will you succeed. ⁹I command you—be strong and courageous! Do not be afraid or discouraged. For the LORD your God is with you wherever you go."

JOSHUA'S CHARGE TO THE ISRAELITES

¹⁰Joshua then commanded the leaders of Israel, ¹¹"Go through the camp and tell the people to get their provisions ready. In three days you will cross the Jordan River and take possession of the land the LORD your God has given you."

¹²Then Joshua called together the tribes of Reuben, Gad, and the half-tribe of Manasseh. He told them, ¹³"Remember what Moses, the servant of the LORD, commanded you: 'The LORD your God is giving you rest and has given you this land.' ¹⁴Your wives, children, and cattle may remain here on the east side of the Jordan River, but your warriors, fully armed, must lead the other tribes across the Jordan to help them conquer their territory. Stay with them ¹⁵until the LORD gives rest to them as he has given rest to you, and until they, too, possess the land the LORD your God is giving them. Only then may you settle here on the east side of the Jordan River in the land that Moses, the servant of the LORD, gave you."

¹⁶They answered Joshua, "We will do whatever you command us, and we will go wherever you send us. ¹⁷We will obey you just as we obeyed Moses. And may the LORD your God be with you as he was with Moses. ¹⁸Anyone who rebels against your word and does not obey your every command will be put to death. So be strong and courageous!"

RAHAB PROTECTS THE SPIES

2 Then Joshua secretly sent out two spies from the Israelite camp at Acacia.* He instructed them, "Spy out the land on the other side of the Jordan River, especially around Jericho." So the two men set out and came to the house of a prostitute named Rahab and stayed there that night.

²But someone told the king of Jericho, "Some Israelites have come here tonight to spy out the land." ³So the king of Jericho sent orders to Rahab: "Bring out the men who have come into your house. They are spies sent here to discover the best way to attack us."

⁴Rahab, who had hidden the two men, replied, "The men were here earlier, but I didn't know where they were from. ⁵They left the city at dusk, as the city gates were about to close, and I don't know where they went. If you hurry, you can probably catch up with them." ⁶(But she had taken them up to the roof and hidden them beneath piles of flax.) ⁷So the king's men went looking for the spies along the road leading to the shallow crossing places of the Jordan River. And as soon as the king's men had left, the city gate was shut.

⁸Before the spies went to sleep that night, Rahab went up on the roof to talk with them.

1:4 Hebrew *the Great Sea.* 2:1 Hebrew *Shittim.*

My Daily Worship

— *February 20* —

THE FEAR FACTOR

JOSHUA 1:1–3:17

No one will be able to stand their ground against you as long as you live. For I will be
with you as I was with Moses. I will not fail you or abandon you (1:5).

[i reflect]

Joshua had good reason to be afraid. He had just been given the assignment to lead God's people across the Jordan into the land promised to them. He must have been inwardly terrified to suddenly be responsible for the fate of over a million people. But did you notice the factor that changed everything? The Lord God promised to be with him at all times, in all circumstances, and in every place.

A recent advertising campaign proclaimed the slogan, "No Fear." Wouldn't it be fantastic to never experience a moment of anxiety or doubt simply by buying a product, or hiring a bodyguard, or installing a security system? But we know better. Fear seems to haunt us—fear of the future, fear of a doctor's report, fear of a failed relationship.

What fears do you face? Name them. What personal battles do you have to fight, or what strange land are you about to enter? As God promised Joshua, so he extends the same promise to you: "I will be with you wherever you go." There is no place you can go that God is not, and nothing he will ask you to do that he will not first prepare you for. When you accept that as truth, you can worship him with a thankful heart no matter what your situation.

"I will be with you." What an incredible statement! Wherever you are right now, in whatever circumstance, the holy God of Israel is with you. Let that truth build your confidence today. Turn your fear into faith.

[i pray]

Lord, how often I allow my fears to overwhelm me! I'm afraid of heartbreak, of loss,
of failure. Help me to embrace the promise of your presence in every moment of
my day and to celebrate the fact that everywhere I go, you have gone before.

[i respond]

What responsibilities or tasks cause you to fear the possibility of failure? Remember that Joshua drew strength not from his own physical or emotional resources but rather from the promise of the presence of God. Review today's key verse again. This time, substitute your own name when "you" is used. Rest in those promises today.

9"I know the LORD has given you this land," she told them. "We are all afraid of you. Everyone is living in terror. 10For we have heard how the LORD made a dry path for you through the Red Sea* when you left Egypt. And we know what you did to Sihon and Og, the two Amorite kings east of the Jordan River, whose people you completely destroyed.* 11No wonder our hearts have melted in fear! No one has the courage to fight after hearing such things. For the LORD your God is the supreme God of the heavens above and the earth below. 12Now swear to me by the LORD that you will be kind to me and my family since I have helped you. Give me some guarantee that 13when Jericho is conquered, you will let me live, along with my father and mother, my brothers and sisters, and all their families."

14"We offer our own lives as a guarantee for your safety," the men agreed. "If you don't betray us, we will keep our promise when the LORD gives us the land."

15Then, since Rahab's house was built into the city wall, she let them down by a rope through the window. 16"Escape to the hill country," she told them. "Hide there for three days until the men who are searching for you have returned; then go on your way."

17Before they left, the men told her, "We can guarantee your safety 18only if you leave this scarlet rope hanging from the window. And all your family members—your father, mother, brothers, and all your relatives—must be here inside the house. 19If they go out into the street, they will be killed, and we cannot be held to our oath. But we swear that no one inside this house will be killed—not a hand will be laid on any of them. 20If you betray us, however, we are not bound by this oath in any way."

21"I accept your terms," she replied. And she sent them on their way, leaving the scarlet rope hanging from the window.

22The spies went up into the hill country and stayed there three days. The men who were chasing them had searched everywhere along the road, but they finally returned to the city without success. 23Then the two spies came down from the hill country, crossed the Jordan River, and reported to Joshua all that had happened to them. 24"The LORD will certainly give us the whole land," they said, "for all the people in the land are terrified of us."

THE ISRAELITES CROSS THE JORDAN

3 Early the next morning Joshua and all the Israelites left Acacia* and arrived at the banks of the Jordan River, where they camped before crossing. 2Three days later, the Israelite leaders went through the camp 3giving these instructions to the people: "When you see the Levitical priests carrying the Ark of the Covenant of the LORD your God, follow them. 4Since you have never traveled this way before, they will guide you. Stay about a half mile* behind them, keeping a clear distance between you and the Ark. Make sure you don't come any closer."

5Then Joshua told the people, "Purify yourselves, for tomorrow the LORD will do great wonders among you."

6In the morning Joshua said to the priests, "Lift up the Ark of the Covenant and lead the people across the river." And so they started out.

7The LORD told Joshua, "Today I will begin to make you great in the eyes of all the Israelites. Now they will know that I am with you, just as I was with Moses. 8Give these instructions to the priests who are carrying the Ark of the Covenant: 'When you reach the banks of the Jordan River, take a few steps into the river and stop.' "

9So Joshua told the Israelites, "Come and listen to what the LORD your God says. 10Today you will know that the living God is among you. He will surely drive out the Canaanites, Hittites, Hivites, Perizzites, Girgashites,

2:10a Hebrew sea of reeds. 2:10b The Hebrew term used here refers to the complete consecration of things or people to the LORD, either by destroying them or by giving them as an offering. 3:1 Hebrew Shittim. 3:4 Hebrew about 2,000 cubits [900 meters].

Amorites, and Jebusites. ¹¹Think of it! The Ark of the Covenant, which belongs to the Lord of the whole earth, will lead you across the Jordan River! ¹²Now choose twelve men, one from each tribe. ¹³The priests will be carrying the Ark of the LORD, the Lord of all the earth. When their feet touch the water, the flow of water will be cut off upstream, and the river will pile up there in one heap."

¹⁴When the people set out to cross the Jordan, the priests who were carrying the Ark of the Covenant went ahead of them. ¹⁵Now it was the harvest season, and the Jordan was overflowing its banks. But as soon as the feet of the priests who were carrying the Ark touched the water at the river's edge, ¹⁶the water began piling up at a town upstream called Adam, which is near Zarethan. And the water below that point flowed on to the Dead Sea* until the riverbed was dry. Then all the people crossed over near the city of Jericho. ¹⁷Meanwhile, the priests who were carrying the Ark of the LORD's covenant stood on dry ground in the middle of the riverbed as the people passed by them. They waited there until everyone had crossed the Jordan on dry ground.

MEMORIALS TO THE JORDAN CROSSING

4 When all the people were safely across the river, the LORD said to Joshua, ²"Now choose twelve men, one from each tribe. ³Tell the men to take twelve stones from where the priests are standing in the middle of the Jordan and pile up at the place where you camp tonight."

⁴So Joshua called together the twelve men ⁵and told them, "Go into the middle of the Jordan, in front of the Ark of the LORD your God. Each of you must pick up one stone and carry it out on your shoulder—twelve stones in all, one for each of the twelve tribes. ⁶We will use these stones to build a memorial. In the future, your children will ask, 'What do these stones mean to you?' ⁷Then you can tell them, 'They remind us that the Jordan River stopped flowing when the Ark of the LORD's covenant went across.' These stones will stand as a permanent memorial among the people of Israel."

⁸So the men did as Joshua told them. They took twelve stones from the middle of the Jordan River, one for each tribe, just as the LORD had commanded Joshua. They carried them to the place where they camped for the night and constructed the memorial there.

⁹Joshua also built another memorial of twelve stones in the middle of the Jordan, at the place where the priests who carried the Ark of the Covenant were standing. The memorial remains there to this day.

¹⁰The priests who were carrying the Ark stood in the middle of the river until all of the LORD's instructions, which Moses had given to Joshua, were carried out. Meanwhile, the people hurried across the riverbed. ¹¹And when everyone was on the other side, the priests crossed over with the Ark of the LORD. ¹²The armed warriors from the tribes of Reuben, Gad, and the half-tribe of Manasseh led the Israelites across the Jordan, just as Moses had directed. ¹³These warriors—about forty thousand strong—were ready for battle, and they crossed over to the plains of Jericho in the LORD's presence.

¹⁴That day the LORD made Joshua great in the eyes of all the Israelites, and for the rest of his life they revered him as much as they had revered Moses.

¹⁵The LORD had said to Joshua, ¹⁶"Command the priests carrying the Ark of the Covenant* to come up out of the riverbed." ¹⁷So Joshua gave the command. ¹⁸And as soon as the priests carrying the Ark of the LORD's covenant came up out of the riverbed, the Jordan River flooded its banks as before.

¹⁹The people crossed the Jordan on the tenth day of the first month—the month that marked their exodus from Egypt.* They

3:16 Hebrew *the sea of the Arabah, the Salt Sea.* 4:16 Hebrew *Ark of the Testimony.* 4:19 Hebrew *the tenth day of the first month.* This day of the Hebrew lunar calendar occurs in late March or early April.

camped at Gilgal, east of Jericho. ²⁰It was there at Gilgal that Joshua piled up the twelve stones taken from the Jordan River. ²¹Then Joshua said to the Israelites, "In the future, your children will ask, 'What do these stones mean?' ²²Then you can tell them, 'This is where the Israelites crossed the Jordan on dry ground.' ²³For the LORD your God dried up the river right before your eyes, and he kept it dry until you were all across, just as he did at the Red Sea* when he dried it up until we had all crossed over. ²⁴He did this so that all the nations of the earth might know the power of the LORD, and that you might fear the LORD your God forever."

5 When all the Amorite kings west of the Jordan and all the Canaanite kings who lived along the Mediterranean coast* heard how the LORD had dried up the Jordan River so the people of Israel could cross, they lost heart and were paralyzed with fear.

ISRAEL REESTABLISHES COVENANT CEREMONIES

²At that time the LORD told Joshua, "Use knives of flint to make the Israelites a circumcised people again." ³So Joshua made flint knives and circumcised the entire male population of Israel at Gibeath-haaraloth.*

⁴Joshua had to circumcise them because all the men who were old enough to bear arms when they left Egypt had died in the wilderness. ⁵Those who left Egypt had all been circumcised, but none of those born after the Exodus, during the years in the wilderness, had been circumcised. ⁶The Israelites wandered in the wilderness for forty years until all the men who were old enough to bear arms when they left Egypt had died. For they had disobeyed the LORD, and the LORD vowed he would not let them enter the land he had sworn to give us—a land flowing with milk and honey. ⁷So Joshua circumcised their sons

who had not been circumcised on the way to the Promised Land—those who had grown up to take their fathers' places. ⁸After all the males had been circumcised, they rested in the camp until they were healed.

⁹Then the LORD said to Joshua, "Today I have rolled away the shame of your slavery in Egypt." So that place has been called Gilgal* to this day.

¹⁰While the Israelites were camped at Gilgal on the plains of Jericho, they celebrated Passover on the evening of the fourteenth day of the first month—the month that marked their exodus from Egypt.* ¹¹The very next day they began to eat unleavened bread and roasted grain harvested from the land. ¹²No manna appeared that day, and it was never seen again. So from that time on the Israelites ate from the crops of Canaan.

THE LORD'S COMMANDER CONFRONTS JOSHUA

¹³As Joshua approached the city of Jericho, he looked up and saw a man facing him with sword in hand. Joshua went up to him and asked, "Are you friend or foe?"

¹⁴"Neither one," he replied. "I am commander of the LORD's army."

At this, Joshua fell with his face to the ground in reverence. "I am at your command," Joshua said. "What do you want your servant to do?"

¹⁵The commander of the LORD's army replied, "Take off your sandals, for this is holy ground." And Joshua did as he was told.

THE FALL OF JERICHO

6 Now the gates of Jericho were tightly shut because the people were afraid of the Israelites. No one was allowed to go in or out. ²But the LORD said to Joshua, "I have given you Jericho, its king, and all its mighty warriors. ³Your entire army is to march around the city once a day for six days. ⁴Seven priests will walk

---

4:23 Hebrew *sea of reeds*. 5:1 Hebrew *along the sea*. 5:3 Gibeath-haaraloth means "hill of foreskins." 5:9 *Gilgal* sounds like the Hebrew word *galal*, meaning "to roll." 5:10 Hebrew *the fourteenth day of the first month.* This day of the Hebrew lunar calendar occurs in late March or early April.

My Daily Worship

— February 21 —

Do You Remember When?

JOSHUA 4:1–6:27

Then you can tell them, "They remind us that the Jordan River stopped flowing when
the Ark of the LORD's covenant went across." These stones will stand
as a permanent memorial among the people of Israel (4:7).

[i reflect]

When you hear the word *memorial*, what comes to mind? Perhaps a marble statue erected in memory of a famous citizen or a tall obelisk of granite in honor of a hero stretching into the sky. Cities and towns have numerous memorial buildings, parks, cemeteries, and statues to help us remember.

God gave Joshua directions for building a very specific memorial: a monument of twelve stones that would stand as a permanent reminder of the people's miraculous crossing of the Jordan on dry ground. God wanted his people to remember and to worship.

As God's people today, we often enter times of worship with our minds fixed on things far away. Today we also need memorials—"stones of remembrance"—that continually remind us of what God has done.

A church on Cape Cod recently named its office building "Riverstone" because of the miracle God worked in its purchase. A Christian family in Connecticut christened their home "Gracehaven" to commemorate the presence of grace in their lives. You may not have a building to name or a home to christen, but you will discover countless rock-solid reasons to praise God once you begin remembering all he has done for you in the past.

Drive or walk through your old neighborhood or another area of past victories. Look for "memorials" and use each one as a cause for praise and prayer.

[i pray]

You've done so much for me in the past, Lord, but in the press of the present I tend to forget that.
Help me to give thanks with a grateful heart for the things you have done.

[i respond]

Think of the miracles that you have seen in your own life—the close calls, the unexpected provisions, the answered prayers. Find someone today with whom you can share this memory. Use those memories as a springboard for praise.

ahead of the Ark, each carrying a ram's horn. On the seventh day you are to march around the city seven times, with the priests blowing the horns. ⁵When you hear the priests give one long blast on the horns, have all the people give a mighty shout. Then the walls of the city will collapse, and the people can charge straight into the city."

⁶So Joshua called together the priests and said, "Take up the Ark of the Covenant, and assign seven priests to walk in front of it, each carrying a ram's horn." ⁷Then he gave orders to the people: "March around the city, and the armed men will lead the way in front of the Ark of the LORD."

⁸After Joshua spoke to the people, the seven priests with the rams' horns started marching in the presence of the LORD, blowing the horns as they marched. And the priests carrying the Ark of the LORD's covenant followed behind them. ⁹Armed guards marched both in front of the priests and behind the Ark, with the priests continually blowing the horns. ¹⁰"Do not shout; do not even talk," Joshua commanded. "Not a single word from any of you until I tell you to shout. Then shout!" ¹¹So the Ark of the LORD was carried around the city once that day, and then everyone returned to spend the night in the camp.

¹²Joshua got up early the next morning, and the priests again carried the Ark of the LORD. ¹³The seven priests with the rams' horns marched in front of the Ark of the LORD, blowing their horns. Armed guards marched both in front of the priests with the horns and behind the Ark of the LORD. All this time the priests were sounding their horns. ¹⁴On the second day they marched around the city once and returned to the camp. They followed this pattern for six days.

¹⁵On the seventh day the Israelites got up at dawn and marched around the city as they had done before. But this time they went around the city seven times. ¹⁶The seventh time around, as the priests sounded the long blast on their horns, Joshua commanded the people, "Shout! For the LORD has given you the city! ¹⁷The city and everything in it must be completely destroyed* as an offering to the LORD. Only Rahab the prostitute and the others in her house will be spared, for she protected our spies. ¹⁸Do not take any of the things set apart for destruction, or you yourselves will be completely destroyed, and you will bring trouble on all Israel. ¹⁹Everything made from silver, gold, bronze, or iron is sacred to the LORD and must be brought into his treasury."

²⁰When the people heard the sound of the horns, they shouted as loud as they could. Suddenly, the walls of Jericho collapsed, and the Israelites charged straight into the city from every side and captured it. ²¹They completely destroyed everything in it—men and women, young and old, cattle, sheep, donkeys—everything.

²²Then Joshua said to the two spies, "Keep your promise. Go to the prostitute's house and bring her out, along with all her family."

²³The young men went in and brought out Rahab, her father, mother, brothers, and all the other relatives who were with her. They moved her whole family to a safe place near the camp of Israel.

²⁴Then the Israelites burned the city and everything in it. Only the things made from silver, gold, bronze, or iron were kept for the treasury of the LORD's house. ²⁵So Joshua spared Rahab the prostitute and her relatives who were with her in the house, because she had hidden the spies Joshua sent to Jericho. And she lives among the Israelites to this day.

²⁶At that time Joshua invoked this curse:

"May the curse of the LORD fall on anyone
who tries to rebuild the city of Jericho.
At the cost of his firstborn son,
he will lay its foundation.
At the cost of his youngest son,
he will set up its gates."

6:17 The Hebrew term used here refers to the complete consecration of things or people to the LORD, either by destroying them or by giving them as an offering; also in 6:18, 21.

²⁷So the LORD was with Joshua, and his name became famous throughout the land.

AI DEFEATS THE ISRAELITES

7 But Israel was unfaithful concerning the things set apart for the LORD.* A man named Achan had stolen some of these things, so the LORD was very angry with the Israelites. Achan was the son of Carmi, of the family of Zimri,* of the clan of Zerah, and of the tribe of Judah.

²Joshua sent some of his men from Jericho to spy out the city of Ai, east of Bethel, near Beth-aven. ³When they returned, they told Joshua, "It's a small town, and it won't take more than two or three thousand of us to destroy it. There's no need for all of us to go there."

⁴So approximately three thousand warriors were sent, but they were soundly defeated. The men of Ai ⁵chased the Israelites from the city gate as far as the quarries,* and they killed about thirty-six who were retreating down the slope. The Israelites were paralyzed with fear at this turn of events, and their courage melted away.

⁶Joshua and the leaders of Israel tore their clothing in dismay, threw dust on their heads, and bowed down facing the Ark of the LORD until evening. ⁷Then Joshua cried out, "Sovereign LORD, why did you bring us across the Jordan River if you are going to let the Amorites kill us? If only we had been content to stay on the other side! ⁸Lord, what am I to say, now that Israel has fled from its enemies? ⁹For when the Canaanites and all the other people living in the land hear about it, they will surround us and wipe us off the face of the earth. And then what will happen to the honor of your great name?"

¹⁰But the LORD said to Joshua, "Get up! Why are you lying on your face like this? ¹¹Israel has sinned and broken my covenant! They have stolen the things that I commanded to be set apart for me. And they have not only stolen them; they have also lied about it and hidden the things among their belongings. ¹²That is why the Israelites are running from their enemies in defeat. For now Israel has been set apart for destruction. I will not remain with you any longer unless you destroy the things among you that were set apart for destruction.

¹³"Get up! Command the people to purify themselves in preparation for tomorrow. For this is what the LORD, the God of Israel, says: Hidden among you, O Israel, are things set apart for the LORD. You will never defeat your enemies until you remove these things. ¹⁴In the morning you must present yourselves by tribes, and the LORD will point out the tribe to which the guilty man belongs. That tribe must come forward with its clans, and the LORD will point out the guilty clan. That clan will then come forward, and the LORD will point out the guilty family. Finally, each member of the guilty family must come one by one. ¹⁵The one who has stolen what was set apart for destruction will himself be burned with fire, along with everything he has, for he has broken the covenant of the LORD and has done a horrible thing in Israel."

ACHAN'S SIN

¹⁶Early the next morning Joshua brought the tribes of Israel before the LORD, and the tribe of Judah was singled out. ¹⁷Then the clans of Judah came forward, and the clan of Zerah was singled out. Then the families of Zerah came before the LORD, and the family of Zimri was singled out. ¹⁸Every member of Zimri's family was brought forward person by person, and Achan was singled out.

¹⁹Then Joshua said to Achan, "My son, give glory to the LORD, the God of Israel, by telling the truth. Make your confession and tell me what you have done. Don't hide it from me."

²⁰Achan replied, "I have sinned against the LORD, the God of Israel. ²¹For I saw a beautiful

---

7:1a The Hebrew term used here refers to the complete consecration of things or people to the LORD, either by destroying them or by giving them as an offering; also in 7:11, 12, 13, 15. **7:1b** As in Greek version (see also 1 Chr 2:6); Hebrew reads *Zabdi*. Also in 7:17, 18. **7:5** Or *as far as Shebarim*.

robe imported from Babylon,* two hundred silver coins,* and a bar of gold weighing more than a pound.* I wanted them so much that I took them. They are hidden in the ground beneath my tent, with the silver buried deeper than the rest."

²²So Joshua sent some men to make a search. They ran to the tent and found the stolen goods hidden there, just as Achan had said, with the silver buried beneath the rest. ²³They took the things from the tent and brought them to Joshua and all the Israelites. Then they laid them on the ground in the presence of the LORD.

²⁴Then Joshua and all the Israelites took Achan, the silver, the robe, the bar of gold, his sons, daughters, cattle, donkeys, sheep, tent, and everything he had, and they brought them to the valley of Achor. ²⁵Then Joshua said to Achan, "Why have you brought trouble on us? The LORD will now bring trouble on you." And all the Israelites stoned Achan and his family and burned their bodies. ²⁶They piled a great heap of stones over Achan, which remains to this day. That is why the place has been called the Valley of Trouble* ever since. So the LORD was no longer angry.

THE ISRAELITES DEFEAT AI

8 Then the LORD said to Joshua, "Do not be afraid or discouraged. Take the entire army and attack Ai, for I have given to you the king of Ai, his people, his city, and his land. ²You will destroy them as you destroyed Jericho and its king. But this time you may keep the captured goods and the cattle for yourselves. Set an ambush behind the city."

³So Joshua and the army of Israel set out to attack Ai. Joshua chose thirty thousand fighting men and sent them out at night ⁴with these orders: "Hide in ambush close behind the city and be ready for action. ⁵When our main army attacks, the men of Ai will come out to fight as they did before, and we will run away from them. ⁶We will let them chase us until they have all left the city. For they will say, 'The Israelites are running away from us as they did before.' ⁷Then you will jump up from your ambush and take possession of the city, for the LORD your God will give it to you. ⁸Set the city on fire, as the LORD has commanded. You have your orders."

⁹So they left that night and lay in ambush between Bethel and the west side of Ai. But Joshua remained among the people in the camp that night. ¹⁰Early the next morning Joshua roused his men and started toward Ai, accompanied by the leaders of Israel. ¹¹They camped on the north side of Ai, with a valley between them and the city. ¹²That night Joshua sent five thousand men to lie in ambush between Bethel and Ai, on the west side of the city. ¹³So they stationed the main army north of the city and the ambush west of the city. Joshua himself spent that night in the valley.

¹⁴When the king of Ai saw the Israelites across the valley, he and all his army hurriedly went out early the next morning and attacked the Israelites at a place overlooking the Jordan Valley.* But he didn't realize there was an ambush behind the city. ¹⁵Joshua and the Israelite army fled toward the wilderness as though they were badly beaten, ¹⁶and all the men in the city were called out to chase after them. In this way, they were lured away from the city. ¹⁷There was not a man left in Ai or Bethel* who did not chase after the Israelites, and the city was left wide open.

¹⁸Then the LORD said to Joshua, "Point your spear toward Ai, for I will give you the city." Joshua did as he was commanded. ¹⁹As soon as Joshua gave the signal, the men in ambush jumped up and poured into the city. They quickly captured it and set it on fire.

²⁰When the men of Ai looked behind them, smoke from the city was filling the sky, and they had nowhere to go. For the Israelites who had fled in the direction of the wilderness now turned on their pursuers. ²¹When Joshua

---

7:21a Hebrew *Shinar.* 7:21b Hebrew *200 shekels of silver,* about 5 pounds or 2.3 kilograms in weight. 7:21c Hebrew *50 shekels,* about 20 ounces or 570 grams in weight. 7:26 Hebrew *valley of Achor.* 8:14 Hebrew *the Arabah.* 8:17 Some manuscripts lack *or Bethel.*

My Daily Worship

— *February 22* —

CONFESS IT AND COME CLEAN

JOSHUA 7:1–11:23

Then Joshua said to Achan, "My son, give glory to the LORD, the God of Israel, by telling the truth. Make your confession and tell me what you have done. Don't hide it from me" (7:19).

[i reflect]

When we consider what it means to give glory to God, we usually think in terms of praise. Nothing feels better than singing or even shouting our thanks aloud to the Lord as we celebrate his goodness and his activity on our behalf. When we express our gratitude to God in passionate praise, it *feels* like worship, doesn't it?

Sometimes, however, the most critical component of worship is one that doesn't feel pleasant. When we allow sinful attitudes or actions to infiltrate our lives, our ability to worship God becomes severely compromised. We may continue to observe the public forms of worship—church attendance, public prayer, perhaps even Scripture reading—but inwardly we know that we are far from God. Sin separates us from the One who is absolutely holy, and the chasm between us grows steadily wider the longer we allow our sin to remain unconfessed.

Achan's sin not only brought shame and ruin upon his own family but also judgment on the entire nation. He attempted to hide his actions, but in so doing he caused the nation itself to suffer severe losses. Rather than come willingly, Achan had to be confronted by the leaders and asked to confess his sin and deceit.

If we want to be worshipers who are in continual communion with God, we need to make confession a regular part of our daily experience. Only when we humble ourselves before God can we once again experience the unhindered joy of being in a right relationship with him.

Don't wait for God to call you on the carpet, or for a close friend to pull you aside to confront you with "hidden" sin. Reflect on what might be hindering your relationship with God. Confess it, and come clean.

[i pray]

Lord, I know I have done what I ought not to have done, or failed to do what I should. At times I have tried to bury my sin like Achan. Today I choose to turn away from it and accept your forgiveness.

[i respond]

Remember when you were a child and your mom reminded you to wash your hands before coming to the table? Do a mental inventory today and ask God to cleanse you of everything that contradicts what you know to be true in his Word. Experience the joy of coming clean!

and the other Israelites saw that the ambush had succeeded and that smoke was rising from the city, they turned and attacked the men of Ai. ²²Then the Israelites who were inside the city came out and started killing the enemy from the rear. So the men of Ai were caught in a trap, and all of them died. Not a single person survived or escaped. ²³Only the king of Ai was taken alive and brought to Joshua.

²⁴When the Israelite army finished killing all the men outside the city, they went back and finished off everyone inside. ²⁵So the entire population of Ai was wiped out that day— twelve thousand in all. ²⁶For Joshua kept holding out his spear until everyone who had lived in Ai was completely destroyed.* ²⁷Only the cattle and the treasures of the city were not destroyed, for the Israelites kept these for themselves, as the LORD had commanded Joshua. ²⁸So Ai* became a permanent mound of ruins, desolate to this very day.

²⁹Joshua hung the king of Ai on a tree and left him there until evening. At sunset the Israelites took down the body and threw it in front of the city gate. They piled a great heap of stones over him that can still be seen today.

THE LORD'S COVENANT RENEWED

³⁰Then Joshua built an altar to the LORD, the God of Israel, on Mount Ebal. ³¹He followed the instructions that Moses the LORD's servant had written in the Book of the Law: "Make me an altar from stones that are uncut and have not been shaped with iron tools." Then on the altar they presented burnt offerings and peace offerings to the LORD. ³²And as the Israelites watched, Joshua copied the law of Moses onto the stones of the altar.*

³³Then all the Israelites—foreigners and citizens alike—along with the leaders, officers, and judges, were divided into two groups. One group stood at the foot of Mount Gerizim, the other at the foot of Mount Ebal. Each group faced the other, and between them stood the Levitical priests carrying the Ark of the LORD's covenant. This was all done according to the instructions Moses, the servant of the LORD, had given for blessing the people of Israel.

³⁴Joshua then read to them all the blessings and curses Moses had written in the Book of the Law. ³⁵Every command Moses had ever given was read to the entire assembly, including the women and children and the foreigners who lived among the Israelites.

THE GIBEONITES DECEIVE ISRAEL

9 Now all the kings west of the Jordan heard about what had happened. (These were the kings of the Hittites, Amorites, Canaanites, Perizzites, Hivites, and Jebusites, who lived in the hill country, in the western foothills,* and along the coast of the Mediterranean Sea* as far north as the Lebanon mountains.) ²These kings quickly combined their armies to fight against Joshua and the Israelites.

³But when the people of Gibeon heard what had happened to Jericho and Ai, ⁴they resorted to deception to save themselves. They sent ambassadors to Joshua, loading their donkeys with weathered saddlebags and old patched wineskins. ⁵They put on ragged clothes and worn-out, patched sandals. And they took along dry, moldy bread for provisions. ⁶When they arrived at the camp of Israel at Gilgal, they told Joshua and the men of Israel, "We have come from a distant land to ask you to make a peace treaty with us."

⁷The Israelites replied to these Hivites, "How do we know you don't live nearby? For if you do, we cannot make a treaty with you."

⁸They replied, "We will be your servants."

"But who are you?" Joshua demanded. "Where do you come from?"

⁹They answered, "We are from a very distant country. We have heard of the might of the LORD your God and of all he did in Egypt.

8:26 The Hebrew term used here refers to the complete consecration of things or people to the LORD, either by destroying them or by giving them as an offering. 8:28 Ai means "ruin." 8:32 Or onto stones. 9:1a Hebrew the Shephelah. 9:1b Hebrew the Great Sea.

LEAD, LEADERSHIP

Lead, Leadership—In the Bible the worship of the Lord was a concern of all community leaders, so it has no word that specifically means "leader" in this context. The Hebrew *menatseach* is used with fifty-five of the psalms, apparently designating the director of music, but not elsewhere. According to the *First Apology* of Justin Martyr (around A.D. 150), the Christian worship assembly was led by a *proestotes*, or president of the congregation, but the word is not used in this sense in the New Testament.

When God's people gather to worship, visible leadership is needed so that "everything is done properly and in order" (1 Corinthians 14:40). The Bible offers numerous examples of people who take the lead in the worship of the faithful—heads of families, elders, prophets, priests, and kings. All these roles are summed up in Jesus Christ. Yet apostles like Paul and James offer practical direction for the church's worship life, and prophets in the church speak the word of encouragement and thanksgiving. In Revelation we see the elders of God's people taking the lead in the worship of the Lord (Revelation 4:9–11). Their actions reveal the most important role of the worship leader—to be first of all a *worshiper*, leading by example.

¹⁰We have also heard what he did to the two Amorite kings east of the Jordan River—King Sihon of Heshbon and King Og of Bashan (who lived in Ashtaroth). ¹¹So our leaders and our people instructed us, 'Prepare for a long journey. Go meet with the people of Israel and declare our people to be their servants, and ask for peace.'

¹²"This bread was hot from the ovens when we left. But now, as you can see, it is dry and moldy. ¹³These wineskins were new when we filled them, but now they are old and cracked. And our clothing and sandals are worn out from our long, hard trip."

¹⁴So the Israelite leaders examined their bread, but they did not consult the LORD. ¹⁵Then Joshua went ahead and signed a peace treaty with them, and the leaders of Israel ratified their agreement with a binding oath.

¹⁶Three days later, the facts came out—these people of Gibeon lived nearby! ¹⁷The Israelites set out at once to investigate and reached their towns in three days. The names of these towns were Gibeon, Kephirah, Beeroth, and Kiriath-jearim. ¹⁸But the Israelites did not attack the towns, for their leaders had made a vow to the LORD, the God of Israel.

The people of Israel grumbled against their leaders because of the treaty. ¹⁹But the leaders replied, "We have sworn an oath in the presence of the LORD, the God of Israel. We cannot touch them. ²⁰We must let them live, for God would be angry with us if we broke our oath. ²¹Let them live. But we will make them chop the wood and carry the water for the entire community."

So the Israelites kept their promise to the Gibeonites. ²²But Joshua called together the Gibeonite leaders and said, "Why did you lie to us? Why did you say that you live in a distant land when you live right here among us? ²³May you be cursed! From now on you will chop wood and carry water for the house of my God."

²⁴They replied, "We did it because we were told that the LORD your God instructed his servant Moses to conquer this entire land and destroy all the people living in it. So we feared for our lives because of you. That is why we have done it. ²⁵Now we are at your mercy—do whatever you think is right."

²⁶Joshua did not allow the people of Israel to kill them. ²⁷But that day he made the Gibeonites the woodchoppers and water carriers for the people of Israel and for the altar

of the LORD—wherever the LORD would choose to build it. That arrangement continues to this day.

ISRAEL DEFEATS THE SOUTHERN KINGS

10 Now Adoni-zedek, king of Jerusalem, heard that Joshua had captured and completely destroyed* Ai and killed its king, just as he had destroyed the city of Jericho and killed its king. He also learned that the Gibeonites had made peace with Israel and were now their allies. ²He and his people became very afraid when they heard all this because Gibeon was a large city—as large as the royal cities and larger than Ai. And the Gibeonite men were mighty warriors. ³So King Adoni-zedek of Jerusalem sent messengers to several other kings: Hoham of Hebron, Piram of Jarmuth, Japhia of Lachish, and Debir of Eglon. ⁴"Come and help me destroy Gibeon," he urged them, "for they have made peace with Joshua and the people of Israel." ⁵So these five Amorite kings combined their armies for a united attack. They moved all their troops into place and attacked Gibeon.

⁶The men of Gibeon quickly sent messengers to Joshua at Gilgal, "Don't abandon your servants now!" they pleaded. "Come quickly and save us! For all the Amorite kings who live in the hill country have come out against us with their armies."

⁷So Joshua and the entire Israelite army left Gilgal and set out to rescue Gibeon. ⁸"Do not be afraid of them," the LORD said to Joshua, "for I will give you victory over them. Not a single one of them will be able to stand up to you."

⁹Joshua traveled all night from Gilgal and took the Amorite armies by surprise. ¹⁰The LORD threw them into a panic, and the Israelites slaughtered them in great numbers at Gibeon. Then the Israelites chased the enemy along the road to Beth-horon and attacked them at Azekah and Makkedah, killing them along the way. ¹¹As the Amorites retreated down the road from Beth-horon, the LORD destroyed them with a terrible hailstorm that continued until they reached Azekah. The hail killed more of the enemy than the Israelites killed with the sword.

¹²On the day the LORD gave the Israelites victory over the Amorites, Joshua prayed to the LORD in front of all the people of Israel. He said,

"Let the sun stand still over Gibeon,
    and the moon over the valley of Aijalon."

¹³So the sun and moon stood still until the Israelites had defeated their enemies.

Is this event not recorded in *The Book of Jashar**? The sun stopped in the middle of the sky, and it did not set as on a normal day. ¹⁴The LORD fought for Israel that day. Never before or since has there been a day like that one, when the LORD answered such a request from a human being.

¹⁵Then Joshua and the Israelite army returned to their camp at Gilgal.

JOSHUA KILLS THE FIVE SOUTHERN KINGS

¹⁶During the battle, the five kings escaped and hid in a cave at Makkedah. ¹⁷When Joshua heard that they had been found, ¹⁸he issued this command: "Cover the opening of the cave with large rocks and place guards at the entrance to keep the kings inside. ¹⁹The rest of you continue chasing the enemy and cut them down from the rear. Don't let them get back to their cities, for the LORD your God has given you victory over them."

²⁰So Joshua and the Israelite army continued the slaughter and wiped out the five armies except for a tiny remnant that managed to reach their fortified cities. ²¹Then the Israelites returned safely to their camp at Makkedah. After that, no one dared to speak a word against Israel.

10:1 The Hebrew term used here refers to the complete consecration of things or people to the LORD, either by destroying them or by giving them as an offering; also in 10:28, 35, 37, 39, 40. **10:13** Or *The Book of the Upright.*

²²Then Joshua said, "Remove the rocks covering the opening of the cave and bring the five kings to me." ²³So they brought the five kings out of the cave—the kings of Jerusalem, Hebron, Jarmuth, Lachish, and Eglon. ²⁴Joshua told the captains of his army, "Come and put your feet on the kings' necks." And they did as they were told.

²⁵"Don't ever be afraid or discouraged," Joshua told his men. "Be strong and courageous, for the LORD is going to do this to all of your enemies." ²⁶Then Joshua killed each of the five kings and hung them on five trees until evening.

²⁷As the sun was going down, Joshua gave instructions for the bodies of the kings to be taken down from the trees and thrown into the cave where they had been hiding. Then they covered the opening of the cave with a large pile of stones, which remains to this very day.

ISRAEL DESTROYS THE SOUTHERN CITIES

²⁸That same day Joshua completely destroyed the city of Makkedah, killing everyone in it, including the king. Not one person in the city was left alive. He killed the king of Makkedah as he had killed the king of Jericho. ²⁹Then Joshua and the Israelites went to Libnah and attacked it. ³⁰There, too, the LORD gave them the city and its king. They slaughtered everyone in the city and left no survivors. Then Joshua killed the king of Libnah just as he had killed the king of Jericho.

³¹From Libnah, Joshua and the Israelites went to Lachish and attacked it. ³²And the LORD gave it to them on the second day. Here, too, the entire population was slaughtered, just as at Libnah. ³³During the attack on Lachish, King Horam of Gezer had arrived with his army to help defend the city. But Joshua's men killed him and destroyed his entire army.

³⁴Then Joshua and the Israelite army went to Eglon and attacked it. ³⁵They captured it in one day, and as at Lachish, they completely destroyed everyone in the city. ³⁶After leaving Eglon, they attacked Hebron, ³⁷capturing it and all of its surrounding towns. And just as they had done at Eglon, they completely destroyed the entire population. Not one person was left alive. ³⁸Then they turned back and attacked Debir. ³⁹They captured the city, its king, and all of its surrounding villages. And they killed everyone in it, leaving no survivors. They completely destroyed Debir just as they had destroyed Libnah and Hebron.

⁴⁰So Joshua conquered the whole region— the kings and people of the hill country, the Negev, the western foothills,* and the mountain slopes. He completely destroyed everyone in the land, leaving no survivors, just as the LORD, the God of Israel, had commanded. ⁴¹Joshua slaughtered them from Kadesh-barnea to Gaza and from Goshen to Gibeon. ⁴²In a single campaign Joshua conquered all these kings and their land, for the LORD, the God of Israel, was fighting for his people. ⁴³Then Joshua and the Israelite army returned to their camp at Gilgal.

ISRAEL DEFEATS THE NORTHERN KINGS

11 When King Jabin of Hazor heard what had happened, he sent urgent messages to the following kings: King Jobab of Madon; the king of Shimron; the king of Acshaph; ²all the kings of the northern hill country; the kings in the Jordan Valley* south of Galilee*; the kings in the western foothills*; the kings of Naphoth-dor on the west; ³the kings of Canaan, both east and west; the kings of the Amorites; the kings of the Hittites; the kings of the Perizzites; the kings in the Jebusite hill country; and the Hivites in the towns on the slopes of Mount Hermon, in the land of Mizpah.

⁴All these kings responded by mobilizing their warriors and uniting to fight against

10:40 Hebrew *the Shephelah.* **11:2a** Hebrew *the Arabah;* also in 11:16. **11:2b** Hebrew *of Kinnereth.* **11:2c** Hebrew *the Shephelah;* also in 11:16.

Israel. Their combined armies, along with a vast array of horses and chariots, covered the landscape like the sand on the seashore. ⁵They established their camp around the water near Merom to fight against Israel.

⁶Then the LORD said to Joshua, "Do not be afraid of them. By this time tomorrow they will all be dead. Cripple their horses and burn their chariots."

⁷So Joshua and his warriors traveled to the water near Merom and attacked suddenly. ⁸And the LORD gave them victory over their enemies. The Israelites chased them as far as Great Sidon and Misrephoth-maim, and eastward into the valley of Mizpah, until not one enemy warrior was left alive. ⁹Then Joshua crippled the horses and burned all the chariots, as the LORD had instructed.

¹⁰Joshua then turned back and captured Hazor and killed its king. (Hazor had at one time been the capital of the federation of all these kingdoms.) ¹¹The Israelites completely destroyed* every living thing in the city. Not a single person was spared. And then Joshua burned the city.

¹²Joshua slaughtered all the other kings and their people, completely destroying them, just as Moses, the servant of the LORD, had commanded. ¹³However, Joshua did not burn any of the cities built on mounds except Hazor. ¹⁴And the Israelites took all the captured goods and cattle of the ravaged cities for themselves, but they killed all the people. ¹⁵As the LORD had commanded his servant Moses, so Moses commanded Joshua. And Joshua did as he was told, carefully obeying all of the LORD's instructions to Moses.

¹⁶So Joshua conquered the entire region— the hill country, the Negev, the land of Goshen, the western foothills, the Jordan Valley, and the mountains and lowlands of Israel. ¹⁷The Israelite territory now extended all the way from Mount Halak, which leads up to Seir, to Baal-gad at the foot of Mount Hermon in the valley of Lebanon. Joshua

> *We are often so caught up in our activities that we tend to worship our work, work at our play, and play at our worship.*
>
> CHARLES SWINDOLL

killed all the kings of those territories, ¹⁸waging war for a long time to accomplish this. ¹⁹No one in this region made peace with the Israelites except the Hivites of Gibeon. All the others were defeated. ²⁰For the LORD hardened their hearts and caused them to fight the Israelites instead of asking for peace. So they were completely and mercilessly destroyed, as the LORD had commanded Moses.

²¹During this period, Joshua destroyed all the descendants of Anak, who lived in the hill country of Hebron, Debir, Anab, and the entire hill country of Judah and Israel. He killed them all and completely destroyed their towns. ²²Not one was left in all the land of Israel, though some still remained in Gaza, Gath, and Ashdod.

²³So Joshua took control of the entire land, just as the LORD had instructed Moses. He gave it to the people of Israel as their special possession, dividing the land among the tribes. So the land finally had rest from war.

KINGS DEFEATED EAST OF THE JORDAN

12 These are the kings east of the Jordan River who had been killed and whose land was taken. Their territory extended from the Arnon Gorge to Mount Hermon and included all the land east of the Jordan Valley.*

²King Sihon of the Amorites, who lived in

11:11 The Hebrew term used here refers to the complete consecration of things or people to the LORD, either by destroying them or by giving them as an offering; also in 11:12, 20, 21. 12:1 Hebrew *the Arabah;* also in 12:3, 8.

Heshbon, was defeated. His kingdom included Aroer, on the edge of the Arnon Gorge, and extended from the middle of the Arnon Gorge to the Jabbok River, which serves as a boundary for the Ammonites. This territory included half of the present area of Gilead, which lies north of the Jabbok River. ³Sihon also controlled the Jordan Valley as far north as the western shores of the Sea of Galilee* and as far south as the Dead Sea,* from Beth-jeshimoth to the slopes of Pisgah.

⁴King Og of Bashan, the last of the Rephaites, lived at Ashtaroth and Edrei. ⁵He ruled a territory stretching from Mount Hermon to Salecah in the north and to all of Bashan in the east, and westward to the boundaries of the kingdoms of Geshur and Maacah. His kingdom included the northern half of Gilead, the other portion of which was in the territory of King Sihon of Heshbon. ⁶Moses, the servant of the LORD, and the Israelites had destroyed the people of King Sihon and King Og. And Moses gave their land to the tribes of Reuben, Gad, and the half-tribe of Manasseh.

KINGS DEFEATED WEST OF THE JORDAN

⁷The following is a list of the kings Joshua and the Israelite armies defeated on the west side of the Jordan, from Baal-gad in the valley of Lebanon to Mount Halak, which leads up to Seir. (Joshua allotted this land to the tribes of Israel as their inheritance, ⁸including the hill country, the western foothills,* the Jordan Valley, the mountain slopes, the Judean wilderness, and the Negev. The people who lived in this region were the Hittites, the Amorites, the Canaanites, the Perizzites, the Hivites, and the Jebusites.) These are the kings Israel defeated:

⁹ The king of Jericho
    The king of Ai, near Bethel
¹⁰ The king of Jerusalem

The king of Hebron
¹¹ The king of Jarmuth
    The king of Lachish
¹² The king of Eglon
    The king of Gezer
¹³ The king of Debir
    The king of Geder
¹⁴ The king of Hormah
    The king of Arad
¹⁵ The king of Libnah
    The king of Adullam
¹⁶ The king of Makkedah
    The king of Bethel
¹⁷ The king of Tappuah
    The king of Hepher
¹⁸ The king of Aphek
    The king of Lasharon
¹⁹ The king of Madon
    The king of Hazor
²⁰ The king of Shimron-meron
    The king of Acshaph
²¹ The king of Taanach
    The king of Megiddo
²² The king of Kedesh
    The king of Jokneam in Carmel
²³ The king of Dor in the city of
        Naphoth-dor*
    The king of Goyim in Gilgal*
²⁴ The king of Tirzah.

In all, thirty-one kings and their cities were destroyed.

THE LAND YET TO BE CONQUERED

13 When Joshua was an old man, the LORD said to him, "You are growing old, and much land remains to be conquered. ²The people still need to occupy the land of the Philistines and the Geshurites—³territory that belongs to the Canaanites. This land extends from the stream of Shihor, which is on the boundary of Egypt, northward to the boundary of Ekron, ⁴and includes the five Philistine cities of Gaza, Ashdod, Ashkelon,

12:3a Hebrew *sea of Kinnereth.* **12:3b** Hebrew *the sea of the Arabah, the Salt Sea.* **12:8** Hebrew *the Shephelah.* **12:23a** Hebrew *Naphath-dor,* a variant name for Naphoth-dor. **12:23b** Greek version reads *Goyim in Galilee.*

Gath, and Ekron. The land of the Avvites in the south also remains to be conquered. In the north, this area has not yet been conquered: all the land of the Canaanites, including Mearah (which belongs to the Sidonians), stretching northward to Aphek on the border of the Amorites; [5]the land of the Gebalites and all of the Lebanon mountain area to the east, from Baal-gad beneath Mount Hermon to Lebo-hamath; [6]and all the hill country from Lebanon to Misrephoth-maim, including all the land of the Sidonians.

"I will drive these people out of the land for the Israelites. So be sure to give this land to Israel as a special possession, just as I have commanded you. [7]Include all this territory as Israel's inheritance when you divide the land among the nine tribes and the half-tribe of Manasseh."

THE LAND DIVIDED EAST OF THE JORDAN

[8]Half the tribe of Manasseh and the tribes of Reuben and Gad had already received their inheritance on the east side of the Jordan, for Moses, the servant of the LORD, had previously assigned this land to them.

[9]Their territory extended from Aroer on the edge of the Arnon Gorge (including the town in the middle of the gorge) to the plain beyond Medeba, as far as Dibon. [10]It also included all the towns of King Sihon of the Amorites, who reigned in Heshbon, and extended as far as the borders of Ammon. [11]It included Gilead, the territory of the kingdoms of Geshur and Maacah, all of Mount Hermon, all of Bashan as far as Salecah, [12]and all the territory of King Og of Bashan, who had reigned in Ashtaroth and Edrei. King Og was the last of the Rephaites, for Moses had attacked them and driven them out. [13]But the Israelites failed to drive out the people of Geshur and Maacah, so they continue to live among the Israelites to this day.

AN INHERITANCE FOR THE TRIBE OF LEVI

[14]Moses did not assign any land to the tribe of Levi. Instead, as the LORD had promised them, their inheritance came from the offerings burned on the altar to the LORD, the God of Israel.

THE LAND GIVEN TO THE TRIBE OF REUBEN

[15]Moses had assigned the following area to the families of the tribe of Reuben.

[16]Their territory extended from Aroer on the edge of the Arnon Gorge (including the town in the middle of the gorge) to the plain beyond Medeba. [17]It included Heshbon and the other towns on the plain—Dibon, Bamoth-baal, Beth-baal-meon, [18]Jahaz, Kedemoth, Mephaath, [19]Kiriathaim, Sibmah, Zereth-shahar on the hill above the valley, [20]Beth-peor, the slopes of Pisgah, and Beth-jeshimoth.

[21]The land of Reuben also included all the towns of the plain and the entire kingdom of Sihon. Sihon was the Amorite king who had reigned in Heshbon and was killed by Moses along with the chiefs of Midian—Evi, Rekem, Zur, Hur, and Reba—princes living in the region who were allied with Sihon. [22]The Israelites also killed Balaam the magician, the son of Beor. [23]The Jordan River marked the western boundary for the tribe of Reuben. The towns and villages in this area were given as an inheritance to the families of the tribe of Reuben.

THE LAND GIVEN TO THE TRIBE OF GAD

[24]Moses had assigned the following area to the families of the tribe of Gad.

[25]Their territory included Jazer, all the towns of Gilead, and half of the land of Ammon, as far as the town of Aroer just west of Rabbah. [26]It extended from

My Daily Worship

CLAIMING REAL WEALTH NOW!

JOSHUA 12:1–19:51

But Moses gave no land to the tribe of Levi, for the LORD, the God of Israel,
had promised to be their inheritance (13:33).

[i reflect]

Moses and Joshua served as executors of Jacob's estate. The descendants of Jacob's twelve sons gathered to receive their inheritance, property in the Promised Land. When Levi's turn came, his tribe obtained no land. Instead, that tribe received something much better than property—a special relationship with the God of Israel. They would represent God's presence and receive from the other tribes tithes, gifts, and benefits dedicated to God.

God has filled his Word with wonderful promises. Not only has he declared that he will be present for those who trust him, he also offers an eternal inheritance that will never spoil, fade, or perish to those who trust in Jesus (Ephesians 3:6). That inheritance is not made up of possessions that eventually will rot, rust, or get stolen. The inheritance promised to the people of God is not financial, but something worth much more—eternal life (Titus 3:6–7).

We are often distracted from worship by a preoccupation with the things of this world. We have bills to pay and other obligations. We invest in the stock market hoping for a little security in our later years, only to discover that all we have put away can be wiped out literally overnight. The eyes of faith, however, see beyond the gains and losses of this life to an eternal inheritance waiting for us.

An old gospel chorus put it this way: "I've got a home in glory land that outshines the sun!" God himself is the inheritance of the one who worships him in spirit and in truth. Go on, get excited about spending your inheritance; you'll have eternity in which to do it.

As you go through the day, look at the people you encounter, your material possessions, and even your "to-do" list from an eternal perspective and focus on what God has in store for you.

[i pray]

Lord, when I think about the inheritance waiting for me in heaven, I can hardly contain my joy. Today I choose to focus not on what is lacking in this life but on what is coming to me in the next.

[i respond]

Imagine God has written you a will, leaving his inheritance to you. What specifically is included in the will? Write a list of the eternal inheritance promised you.

Heshbon to Ramath-mizpeh and Betonim, and from Mahanaim to Lo-debar.* ²⁷In the valley were Beth-haram, Beth-nimrah, Succoth, Zaphon, and the rest of the kingdom of King Sihon of Heshbon. The Jordan River was the western border, extending as far north as the Sea of Galilee.* ²⁸The towns and villages in this area were given as an inheritance to the families of the tribe of Gad.

THE LAND GIVEN TO THE HALF-TRIBE OF MANASSEH

²⁹Moses had assigned the following area to the families of the half-tribe of Manasseh.

³⁰Their territory extended from Mahanaim, including all of Bashan, all the former kingdom of King Og, and the sixty towns of Jair in Bashan. ³¹It also included half of Gilead and King Og's royal cities of Ashtaroth and Edrei. All this was given to the descendants of Makir, who was Manasseh's son.

³²These are the allotments Moses had made while he was on the plains of Moab, across the Jordan River, east of Jericho. ³³But Moses gave no land to the tribe of Levi, for the LORD, the God of Israel, had promised to be their inheritance.

THE LAND DIVIDED WEST OF THE JORDAN

14 The remaining tribes of Israel inherited land in Canaan as allotted by Eleazar the priest, Joshua son of Nun, and the tribal leaders. ²These nine and a half tribes received their inheritance by means of sacred lots, in accordance with the LORD's command through Moses. ³Moses had already given an inheritance of land to the two and a half tribes on the east side of the Jordan River. ⁴The tribe of Joseph had become two separate tribes—Manasseh and Ephraim. And the Levites were given no land at all, only towns to live in and the surrounding pasturelands for their flocks and herds. ⁵So the distribution of the land was in strict accordance with the LORD's instructions to Moses.

CALEB REQUESTS HIS LAND

⁶A delegation from the tribe of Judah, led by Caleb son of Jephunneh the Kenizzite, came to Joshua at Gilgal. Caleb said to Joshua, "Remember what the LORD said to Moses, the man of God, about you and me when we were at Kadesh-barnea. ⁷I was forty years old when Moses, the servant of the LORD, sent me from Kadesh-barnea to explore the land of Canaan. I returned and gave from my heart a good report, ⁸but my brothers who went with me frightened the people and discouraged them from entering the Promised Land. For my part, I followed the LORD my God completely. ⁹So that day Moses promised me, 'The land of Canaan on which you were just walking will be your special possession and that of your descendants forever, because you wholeheartedly followed the LORD my God.'

¹⁰"Now, as you can see, the LORD has kept me alive and well as he promised for all these forty-five years since Moses made this promise—even while Israel wandered in the wilderness. Today I am eighty-five years old. ¹¹I am as strong now as I was when Moses sent me on that journey, and I can still travel and fight as well as I could then. ¹²So I'm asking you to give me the hill country that the LORD promised me. You will remember that as scouts we found the Anakites living there in great, walled cities. But if the LORD is with me, I will drive them out of the land, just as the LORD said."

¹³So Joshua blessed Caleb son of Jephunneh and gave Hebron to him as an inheritance. ¹⁴Hebron still belongs to the descendants of Caleb son of Jephunneh the Kenizzite because he wholeheartedly followed the LORD, the God of Israel. ¹⁵(Previously Hebron had been called Kiriath-arba. It had been named after Arba, a great hero of the Anakites.)

And the land had rest from war.

13:26 Or *to the territory of Debir.* 13:27 Hebrew *sea of Kinnereth.*

THE LAND GIVEN TO THE TRIBE OF JUDAH

15 The land assigned to the families of the tribe of Judah reached southward to the border of Edom, with the wilderness of Zin being its southernmost point.

²The southern boundary began at the south bay of the Dead Sea,* ³ran south of Scorpion Pass* into the wilderness of Zin and went south of Kadesh-barnea to Hezron. Then it went up to Addar, where it turned toward Karka. ⁴From there it passed to Azmon, until it finally reached the brook of Egypt, which it followed to the Mediterranean Sea.* This was their* southern boundary.

⁵The eastern boundary extended along the Dead Sea to the mouth of the Jordan River.

The northern boundary began at the bay where the Jordan River empties into the Dead Sea, ⁶crossed to Beth-hoglah, then proceeded north of Beth-arabah to the stone of Bohan. (Bohan was Reuben's son.) ⁷From that point it went through the valley of Achor to Debir, turning north toward Gilgal, which is across from the slopes of Adummim on the south side of the valley. From there the border extended to the springs at En-shemesh and on to En-rogel. ⁸The boundary then passed through the valley of the son of Hinnom, along the southern slopes of the Jebusites, where the city of Jerusalem is located. Then it went west to the top of the mountain above the valley of Hinnom, and on up to the northern end of the valley of Rephaim. ⁹From there the border extended from the top of the mountain to the spring at the waters of Nephtoah,* and from there to the towns on Mount Ephron. Then it turned toward Baalah (that is, Kiriath-jearim). ¹⁰The border circled west of Baalah to Mount Seir, passed along to the town of Kesalon on the northern slope of Mount Jearim, and went down to Beth-shemesh and on to Timnah. ¹¹The boundary line then proceeded to the slope of the hill north of Ekron, where it turned toward Shikkeron and Mount Baalah. It passed Jabneel and ended at the Mediterranean Sea.

¹²The western boundary was the shoreline of the Mediterranean Sea.*

These are the boundaries for the families of the tribe of Judah.

THE LAND GIVEN TO CALEB

¹³The LORD instructed Joshua to assign some of Judah's territory to Caleb son of Jephunneh. So Caleb was given the city of Arba (that is, Hebron), which had been named after Anak's ancestor. ¹⁴Caleb drove out the three Anakites—Sheshai, Ahiman, and Talmai—descendants of Anak.

¹⁵Then he fought against the people living in the town of Debir (formerly called Kiriath-sepher). ¹⁶Caleb said, "I will give my daughter Acsah in marriage to the one who attacks and captures Kiriath-sepher." ¹⁷Othniel, the son of Caleb's brother Kenaz, was the one who conquered it, so Acsah became Othniel's wife.

¹⁸When Acsah married Othniel, she urged him* to ask her father for an additional field. As she got down off her donkey, Caleb asked her, "What is it? What can I do for you?"

¹⁹She said, "Give me a further blessing. You have been kind enough to give me land in the Negev; please give me springs as well." So Caleb gave her the upper and lower springs.

THE TOWNS JUDAH INHERITED

²⁰This was the inheritance given to the families of the tribe of Judah.

²¹The towns of Judah situated along the borders of Edom in the extreme south are Kabzeel, Eder, Jagur, ²²Kinah, Dimonah,

15:2 Hebrew *the Salt Sea;* also in 15:5. **15:3** Hebrew *Akrabbim.* **15:4a** Hebrew *the sea;* also in 15:11. **15:4b** Hebrew *your.* **15:9** Or *the spring at Me-nephtoah.* **15:12** Hebrew *the Great Sea;* also in 15:47. **15:18** Some Greek manuscripts read *Othniel urged her.*

IDOL, IDOLATRY

Idol, Idolatry—Hebrew *gil-lul* "idol, image"; *'a-tsav* "idol, image"; **bo**-*sheth* "shame"; **to'e-vah** "detestable thing"; Greek *ei-do-lon* "idol"; *ei-do-la-***trei**-*a* "idolatry." The Old Testament does not have a word for the abstract concept of idolatry, but expresses the idea concretely in terms of the possession or worship of images of false gods. The terms *bosheth* and *to'evah* are substitutions for a word meaning "idol" or for the name of a false god. Other expressions occur.

Idolatry is sneaky, taking many shapes. It can be the worship of false gods, or the false worship of the true God. The prophets of Israel attacked it in all forms, calling the people back to faithfulness. It is one thing to worship an idol, which is nothing but a worthless image of our own making (Isaiah 44:9–11). It is another to pretend to worship the Lord while forsaking his just ways. Such disguised idolatry the Lord equally despises (Amos 5:21–24).

The First Commandment for God's people is to worship him alone. Jesus reinforced this principle (Matthew 22:37–38), but the danger of idolatry remains. The Tenth Commandment forbids coveting what is not ours, and Paul calls such greed *idolatry* (Colossians 3:5). If we put our desires first, we make ourselves into gods in place of the One who is God. Approaching him in prayer and worship, we always listen for his voice: "For I am God; there is no other" (Isaiah 45:22).

Adadah, 23Kedesh, Hazor, Ithnan, 24Ziph, Telem, Bealoth, 25Hazor-hadattah, Kerioth-hezron (that is, Hazor), 26Amam, Shema, Moladah, 27Hazar-gaddah, Heshmon, Beth-pelet, 28Hazar-shual, Beersheba, Biziothiah, 29Baalah, Iim, Ezem, 30Eltolad, Kesil, Hormah, 31Ziklag, Madmannah, Sansannah, 32Lebaoth, Shilhim, Ain, and Rimmon. In all, there were twenty-nine of these towns with their surrounding villages.

33The following towns situated in the western foothills* were also given to Judah: Eshtaol, Zorah, Ashnah, 34Zanoah, En-gannim, Tappuah, Enam, 35Jarmuth, Adullam, Socoh, Azekah, 36Shaaraim, Adithaim, Gederah, and Gederothaim. In all, there were fourteen towns with their surrounding villages.

37Also included were Zenan, Hadashah, Migdal-gad, 38Dilean, Mizpeh, Joktheel, 39Lachish, Bozkath, Eglon, 40Cabbon, Lahmam, Kitlish, 41Gederoth, Beth-dagon, Naamah, and Makkedah—sixteen towns with their surrounding villages. 42Besides these, there were Libnah, Ether, Ashan, 43Iphtah, Ashnah, Nezib, 44Keilah, Aczib, and Mareshah—nine towns with their surrounding villages.

45The territory of the tribe of Judah also included all the towns and villages of Ekron. 46From Ekron the boundary extended west and included the towns near Ashdod with their surrounding villages. 47It also included Ashdod with its towns and villages and Gaza with its towns and villages, as far as the brook of Egypt and along the coast of the Mediterranean Sea.

48Judah also received the following towns in the hill country: Shamir, Jattir, Socoh, 49Dannah, Kiriath-sannah (that is, Debir), 50Anab, Eshtemoh, Anim, 51Goshen, Holon, and Giloh—eleven towns with their surrounding villages.

52Also included were the towns of Arab, Dumah, Eshan, 53Janim, Beth-tappuah, Aphekah, 54Humtah, Kiriath-arba (that is, Hebron), and Zior—nine towns with their surrounding villages.

15:33 Hebrew *the Shephelah*.

⁵⁵Besides these, there were Maon, Carmel, Ziph, Juttah, ⁵⁶Jezreel, Jokdeam, Zanoah, ⁵⁷Kain, Gibeah, and Timnah—ten towns with their surrounding villages.

⁵⁸In addition, there were Halhul, Beth-zur, Gedor, ⁵⁹Maarath, Beth-anoth, and Eltekon—six towns with their surrounding villages. ⁶⁰There were also Kiriath-baal (that is, Kiriath-jearim) and Rabbah—two towns with their surrounding villages.

⁶¹In the wilderness there were the towns of Beth-arabah, Middin, Secacah, ⁶²Nibshan, the City of Salt, and En-gedi—six towns with their surrounding villages.

⁶³But the tribe of Judah could not drive out the Jebusites, who lived in the city of Jerusalem, so the Jebusites live there among the people of Judah to this day.

THE INHERITANCE OF EPHRAIM AND WEST MANASSEH

16 The allotment to the descendants of Joseph extended from the Jordan River near Jericho, east of the waters of Jericho, through the wilderness and into the hill country of Bethel. ²From Bethel (that is, Luz)* it ran over to Ataroth in the territory of the Arkites. ³Then it descended westward to the territory of the Japhletites as far as Lower Beth-horon, then to Gezer and on over to the Mediterranean Sea.*

THE LAND GIVEN TO EPHRAIM

⁴The families of Joseph's sons, Manasseh and Ephraim, received their inheritance.

⁵The following territory was given to the families of the tribe of Ephraim as their inheritance.

The eastern boundary of their inheritance began at Ataroth-addar. From there it ran to Upper Beth-horon, ⁶then on to the Mediterranean Sea. The northern boundary began at the Mediterranean, ran east past Micmethath, then curved eastward past Taanath-shiloh to the east of Janoah. ⁷From Janoah it turned southward to Ataroth and Naarah, touched Jericho, and ended at the Jordan River. ⁸From Tappuah the border extended westward, following the Kanah Ravine to the Mediterranean Sea. This is the inheritance given to the families of the tribe of Ephraim.

⁹Ephraim was also given some towns with surrounding villages in the territory of the half-tribe of Manasseh. ¹⁰They did not drive the Canaanites out of Gezer, however, so the people of Gezer live as slaves among the people of Ephraim to this day.

THE LAND GIVEN TO WEST MANASSEH

17 The next allotment of land was given to the half-tribe of Manasseh, the descendants of Joseph's older son. Gilead and Bashan on the east side of the Jordan had already been given to the family of Makir because he was a great warrior. (Makir was Manasseh's oldest son and was the father of Gilead.) ²Land on the west side of the Jordan was allotted to the remaining families within the tribe of Manasseh: Abiezer, Helek, Asriel, Shechem, Hepher, and Shemida.

³However, Zelophehad son of Hepher, who was a descendant of Manasseh, Makir, and Gilead, had no sons. Instead, he had five daughters. Their names were Mahlah, Noah, Hoglah, Milcah, and Tirzah. ⁴These women came to Eleazar the priest, Joshua son of Nun, and the Israelite leaders and said, "The LORD commanded Moses to give us an inheritance along with the men of our tribe."

So Joshua gave them an inheritance along with their uncles, as the LORD had commanded. ⁵As a result, Manasseh's inheritance came to ten parcels of land, in addition to the

---

16:2 As in Greek version (also see 18:13); Hebrew reads *From Bethel to Luz.* 16:3 Hebrew *the sea;* also in 16:6, 8.

land of Gilead and Bashan across the Jordan River, [6]because the female descendants of Manasseh received an inheritance along with the male descendants. (The land of Gilead was given to the rest of the male descendants of Manasseh.)

[7]The boundary of the tribe of Manasseh extended from the border of Asher to Micmethath, which is east of Shechem. Then the boundary went south from Micmethath to the people living near the spring of Tappuah. [8](The land surrounding Tappuah belonged to Manasseh, but the town of Tappuah, on the border of Manasseh's territory, belonged to the tribe of Ephraim.) [9]From the spring of Tappuah, the border of Manasseh followed the northern side of the Kanah Ravine to the Mediterranean Sea.* (Several towns in Manasseh's territory belonged to the tribe of Ephraim.) [10]The land south of the ravine belonged to Ephraim, and the land north of the ravine belonged to Manasseh, with the Mediterranean Sea forming Manasseh's western border. North of Manasseh was the territory of Asher, and to the east was the territory of Issachar.

[11]The following towns within the territory of Issachar and Asher were given to Manasseh: Beth-shan,* Ibleam, Dor (that is, Naphoth-dor),* Endor, Taanach, and Megiddo, with their respective villages. [12]But the descendants of Manasseh were unable to occupy these towns. They could not drive out the Canaanites who continued to live there. [13]Later on, however, when the Israelites became strong enough, they forced the Canaanites to work as slaves. But they did not drive them out of the land.

[14]The descendants of Joseph came to Joshua and asked, "Why have you given us only one portion of land when the LORD has given us so many people?"

[15]Joshua replied, "If the hill country of Ephraim is not large enough for you, clear out land for yourselves in the forest where the Perizzites and Rephaites live."

[16]They said, "The hill country is not enough for us, and the Canaanites in the lowlands around Beth-shan and the valley of Jezreel have iron chariots—they are too strong for us."

[17]Then Joshua said to the tribes of Ephraim and Manasseh, the descendants of Joseph, "Since you are so large and strong, you will be given more than one portion. [18]The forests of the hill country will be yours as well. Clear as much of the land as you wish and live there. And I am sure you can drive out the Canaanites from the valleys, too, even though they are strong and have iron chariots."

THE ALLOTMENTS OF THE REMAINING LAND

18 Now that the land was under Israelite control, the entire Israelite assembly gathered at Shiloh and set up the Tabernacle.* [2]But there remained seven tribes who had not yet been allotted their inheritance.

[3]Then Joshua asked them, "How long are you going to wait before taking possession of the remaining land the LORD, the God of your ancestors, has given to you? [4]Select three men from each tribe, and I will send them out to survey the unconquered territory. They will

> *What greater calamity can befall a nation than the loss of worship?*
>
> RALPH WALDO EMERSON

17:9 Hebrew *the sea;* also in 17:10.   17:11a Hebrew *Beth-shean,* a variant name for Beth-shan; also in 17:16.   17:11b The meaning of the Hebrew here is uncertain.   18:1 Hebrew *Tent of Meeting.*

return to me with a written report of their proposed divisions of the inheritance. [5]The scouts will map the land into seven sections, excluding Judah's territory in the south and Joseph's territory in the north. [6]Then I will cast sacred lots in the presence of the LORD our God to decide which section will be assigned to each tribe. [7]However, the Levites will not receive any land. Their role as priests of the LORD is their inheritance. And the tribes of Gad, Reuben, and the half-tribe of Manasseh won't receive any more land, for they have already received their inheritance, which Moses, the servant of the LORD, gave them on the east side of the Jordan River."

[8]As the men who were mapping out the land started on their way, Joshua commanded them, "Go and survey the land. Then return to me with your written report, and I will assign the land to the tribes by casting sacred lots in the presence of the LORD here at Shiloh." [9]The men did as they were told and mapped the entire territory into seven sections, listing the towns in each section. Then they returned to Joshua in the camp at Shiloh. [10]There at Shiloh, Joshua cast sacred lots in the presence of the LORD to determine which tribe should have each section.

THE LAND GIVEN TO BENJAMIN

[11]The first allotment of land went to the families of the tribe of Benjamin. It lay between the territory previously assigned to the tribes of Judah and Joseph.

[12]The northern boundary began at the Jordan River, went north of the slope of Jericho, then west through the hill country and the wilderness of Beth-aven. [13]From there the boundary went south to Luz (that is, Bethel) and proceeded down to Ataroth-addar to the top of the hill south of Lower Beth-horon.

[14]The boundary then ran south along the western edge of the hill facing Beth-horon, ending at the village of Kiriath-baal (that is, Kiriath-jearim), one of the towns belonging to the tribe of Judah. This was the western boundary.

[15]The southern boundary began at the outskirts of Kiriath-jearim. From there it ran westward* to the spring at the waters of Nephtoah,* [16]and down to the base of the mountain beside the valley of the son of Hinnom, at the northern end of the valley of Rephaim. From there it went down the valley of Hinnom, crossing south of the slope where the Jebusites lived, and continued down to En-rogel. [17]From En-rogel the boundary proceeded northeast to En-shemesh and on to Geliloth (which is across from the slopes of Adummim). Then it went down to the stone of Bohan. (Bohan was Reuben's son.) [18]From there it passed along the north side of the slope overlooking the Jordan Valley.* The border then went down into the valley, [19]ran past the north slope of Beth-hoglah, and ended at the north bay of the Dead Sea,* which is the southern end of the Jordan River. [20]The eastern boundary was the Jordan River.

This was the inheritance for the families of the tribe of Benjamin.

THE TOWNS GIVEN TO BENJAMIN

[21]These were the towns given to the families of the tribe of Benjamin.

Jericho, Beth-hoglah, Emek-keziz, [22]Beth-arabah, Zemaraim, Bethel, [23]Avvim, Parah, Ophrah, [24]Kephar-ammoni, Ophni, and Geba—twelve towns with their villages. [25]Also Gibeon, Ramah, Beeroth, [26]Mizpeh, Kephirah, Mozah, [27]Rekem, Irpeel, Taralah, [28]Zela, Haeleph, Jebus (that is, Jerusalem), Gibeah, and

18:15a Or it went to Ephron, and. The meaning of the Hebrew is uncertain.　18:15b Or the spring at Me-nephtoah.　18:18 Hebrew the Arabah.　18:19 Hebrew Salt Sea.

Kiriath-jearim*—fourteen towns with their villages.

This was the inheritance given to the families of the tribe of Benjamin.

THE LAND GIVEN TO SIMEON

19 The second allotment of land went to the families of the tribe of Simeon. Their inheritance was surrounded by Judah's territory.

²Simeon's inheritance included Beersheba, Sheba, Moladah, ³Hazar-shual, Balah, Ezem, ⁴Eltolad, Bethul, Hormah, ⁵Ziklag, Beth-marcaboth, Hazar-susah, ⁶Beth-lebaoth, and Sharuhen— thirteen towns with their villages. ⁷It also included Ain, Rimmon, Ether, and Ashan—four towns with their villages, ⁸including all the villages as far south as Baalath-beer (also known as Ramah of the Negev).

This was the inheritance of the families of the tribe of Simeon. ⁹Their inheritance came from part of what had been given to Judah because Judah's territory was too large for them. So the tribe of Simeon received an inheritance within the territory of Judah.

THE LAND GIVEN TO ZEBULUN

¹⁰The third allotment of land went to the families of the tribe of Zebulun.

The boundary of Zebulun's inheritance started at Sarid. ¹¹From there it went west, going past Maralah, touching Dabbesheth, and proceeding to the brook east of Jokneam. ¹²In the other direction, the boundary line went east from Sarid to the border of Kisloth-tabor, and from there to Daberath and up to Japhia. ¹³Then it continued east to Gath-hepher, Eth-kazin, and Rimmon and turned toward Neah. ¹⁴The

northern boundary of Zebulun passed Hannathon and ended at the valley of Iphtah-el. ¹⁵The towns in these areas included Kattath, Nahalal, Shimron, Idalah, and Bethlehem—twelve towns with their surrounding villages.

¹⁶This was the inheritance of the families of the tribe of Zebulun.

THE LAND GIVEN TO ISSACHAR

¹⁷The fourth allotment of land went to the families of the tribe of Issachar.

¹⁸Its boundaries included the following towns: Jezreel, Kesulloth, Shunem, ¹⁹Hapharaim, Shion, Anaharath, ²⁰Rabbith, Kishion, Ebez, ²¹Remeth, En-gannim, En-haddah, and Beth-pazzez. ²²The boundary also touched Tabor, Shahazumah, and Beth-shemesh, ending at the Jordan River—sixteen towns with their surrounding villages.

²³This was the inheritance of the families of the tribe of Issachar.

THE LAND GIVEN TO ASHER

²⁴The fifth allotment of land went to the families of the tribe of Asher.

²⁵Its boundaries included these towns: Helkath, Hali, Beten, Acshaph, ²⁶Allammelech, Amad, and Mishal. The boundary on the west went from Carmel to Shihor-libnath, ²⁷turned east toward Beth-dagon, and ran as far as Zebulun in the valley of Iphtah-el, running north to Beth-emek and Neiel. It then continued north to Cabul, ²⁸Abdon,* Rehob, Hammon, Kanah, and as far as Greater Sidon. ²⁹Then the boundary turned toward Ramah and the fortified city of Tyre and came to the Mediterranean Sea* at Hosah. The territory also included Mehebel, Aczib, ³⁰Ummah,

18:28 As in Greek version; Hebrew reads *Kiriath.* 19:28 As in some Hebrew manuscripts (see also 21:30); most Hebrew manuscripts read *Ebron.* 19:29 Hebrew *the sea.*

Aphek, and Rehob—twenty-two towns with their surrounding villages.

³¹This was the inheritance of the families of the tribe of Asher.

THE LAND GIVEN TO NAPHTALI

³²The sixth allotment of land went to the families of the tribe of Naphtali.

³³Its boundary ran from Heleph, from the oak at Zaanannim, and extended across to Adami-nekeb, Jabneel, and as far as Lakkum, ending at the Jordan River. ³⁴The western boundary ran past Aznoth-tabor, then to Hukkok, and touched the boundary of Zebulun in the south, the boundary of Asher on the west, and the Jordan River* on the east. ³⁵The fortified cities included in this territory were Ziddim, Zer, Hammath, Rakkath, Kinnereth, ³⁶Adamah, Ramah, Hazor, ³⁷Kedesh, Edrei, En-hazor, ³⁸Yiron, Migdal-el, Horem, Beth-anath, and Beth-shemesh— nineteen cities with their surrounding villages.

³⁹This was the inheritance of the families of the tribe of Naphtali.

THE LAND GIVEN TO DAN

⁴⁰The seventh and last allotment of land went to the families of the tribe of Dan.

⁴¹The towns within Dan's inheritance included Zorah, Eshtaol, Ir-shemesh, ⁴²Shaalabbin, Aijalon, Ithlah, ⁴³Elon, Timnah, Ekron, ⁴⁴Eltekeh, Gibbethon, Baalath, ⁴⁵Jehud, Bene-berak, Gath-rimmon, ⁴⁶and Me-jarkon, also Rakkon along with the territory across from Joppa.

⁴⁷But the tribe of Dan had trouble taking possession of their land, so they fought against the town of Laish.* They captured it, slaughtered its people, and settled there.

They renamed the city Dan after their ancestor.

⁴⁸This was the inheritance of the families of the tribe of Dan—these towns with their villages.

THE LAND GIVEN TO JOSHUA

⁴⁹After all the land was divided among the tribes, the Israelites gave a special piece of land to Joshua as his inheritance. ⁵⁰For the LORD had said he could have any town he wanted. He chose Timnath-serah in the hill country of Ephraim. He rebuilt the town and lived there.

⁵¹These are the territories that Eleazar the priest, Joshua son of Nun, and the tribal leaders gave as an inheritance to the tribes of Israel by casting sacred lots in the presence of the LORD at the entrance of the Tabernacle* at Shiloh. So the division of the land was completed.

THE CITIES OF REFUGE

20 The LORD said to Joshua, ²"Now tell the Israelites to designate the cities of refuge, as I instructed Moses. ³Anyone who kills another person unintentionally can run to one of these cities and be protected from the relatives of the one who was killed, for the relatives may seek to avenge the killing.

⁴"Upon reaching one of these cities, the one who caused the accidental death will appear before the leaders at the city gate and explain what happened. They must allow the accused to enter the city and live there among them. ⁵If the relatives of the victim come to avenge the killing, the leaders must not release the accused to them, for the death was accidental. ⁶But the person who caused the death must stay in that city and be tried by the community and found innocent. Then the one declared innocent because the death was accidental must continue to live in that city until the death of the high priest who was in office at the time of the accident. After that, the one found innocent is free to return home."

19:34 Hebrew *and Judah at the Jordan River.* 19:47 Hebrew *Leshem,* another name for Laish. 19:51 Hebrew *Tent of Meeting.*

⁷The following cities were designated as cities of refuge: Kedesh of Galilee, in the hill country of Naphtali; Shechem, in the hill country of Ephraim; and Kiriath-arba (that is, Hebron), in the hill country of Judah. ⁸On the east side of the Jordan River, across from Jericho, the following cities were designated as cities of refuge: Bezer, in the wilderness plain of the tribe of Reuben; Ramoth in Gilead, in the territory of the tribe of Gad; and Golan in Bashan, in the land of the tribe of Manasseh. ⁹These cities were set apart for Israelites as well as the foreigners living among them. Anyone who accidentally killed another person could take refuge in one of these cities. In this way, they could escape being killed in revenge prior to standing trial before the community.

THE TOWNS GIVEN TO THE LEVITES

21 Then the leaders of the tribe of Levi came to consult with Eleazar the priest, Joshua son of Nun, and the leaders of the other tribes of Israel. ²They spoke to them at Shiloh in the land of Canaan, saying, "The LORD instructed Moses to give us towns to live in and pasturelands for our cattle." ³So by the command of the LORD the Levites were given as their inheritance the following towns with their pasturelands.

⁴The descendants of Aaron, who were members of the Kohathite clan within the tribe of Levi, were given thirteen towns that were originally assigned to the tribes of Judah, Simeon, and Benjamin. ⁵The other families of the Kohathite clan were allotted ten towns from the territories of Ephraim, Dan, and the half-tribe of Manasseh.

⁶The clan of Gershon received thirteen towns from the tribes of Issachar, Asher, Naphtali, and the half-tribe of Manasseh in Bashan.

⁷The clan of Merari received twelve cities from the tribes of Reuben, Gad, and Zebulun.

⁸So the Israelites obeyed the LORD's command to Moses and assigned these towns

and pasturelands to the Levites by casting sacred lots.

⁹The Israelites gave the following towns from the tribes of Judah and Simeon ¹⁰to the descendants of Aaron, who were members of the Kohathite clan within the tribe of Levi, since the sacred lot fell to them first: ¹¹Kiriath-arba (that is, Hebron), in the hill country of

---

Words of Worship

JEHOVAH JIREH

Jehovah Jireh (Yahweh Yir'eh)—While sometimes taken as a name for the Lord, this is really a name given to a place where the Lord's provision was revealed (Genesis 22:14).

"This is only a test." We might hear these words over the radio, in a check of the emergency broadcasting network. But Abraham didn't hear them when God told him to sacrifice Isaac. He assumed this was for real, and even raised the knife to slay his son. When the Lord, Jehovah Jireh, saw that Abraham was completely obedient—which is what it means to have faith—he intervened just in time and provided a ram as a substitute sacrifice.

Perhaps we can hardly understand what Abraham was asked to do. Before Jesus Christ had been raised from death and opened the way to eternal life, any hope Abraham had for his own future rested on Isaac. God had given him a son in his old age, fulfilling his promise to make him a great people (Genesis 12:2). Now, he was being asked to throw away his own future—as an act of worship! Yet he was willing. Can we approach the Lord with the same trust, knowing he will provide the means for both our worship and our ongoing life? For he has already provided the Lamb!

Judah, along with its surrounding pasture-lands. (Arba was an ancestor of Anak.) ¹²But the fields beyond the city and the surrounding villages were given to Caleb son of Jephunneh.

¹³The following towns with their pasture-lands were given to the descendants of Aaron the priest: Hebron (a city of refuge for those who accidentally killed someone), Libnah, ¹⁴Jattir, Eshtemoa, ¹⁵Holon, Debir, ¹⁶Ain, Juttah, and Beth-shemesh—nine towns from these two tribes.

¹⁷From the tribe of Benjamin the priests were given the following towns with their surrounding pasturelands: Gibeon, Geba, ¹⁸Anathoth, and Almon—four towns. ¹⁹So thirteen towns were given to the priests, the descendants of Aaron.

²⁰The rest of the Kohathite clan from the tribe of Levi was allotted these towns and pasturelands from the tribe of Ephraim: ²¹Shechem (a city of refuge for those who accidentally killed someone), Gezer, ²²Kibzaim, and Beth-horon—four towns.

²³The following towns and pasturelands were allotted to the priests from the tribe of Dan: Eltekeh, Gibbethon, ²⁴Aijalon, and Gath-rimmon—four towns.

²⁵The half-tribe of Manasseh allotted the following towns with their pasturelands to the priests: Taanach and Gath-rimmon—two towns. ²⁶So ten towns with their pasture-lands were given to the rest of the Kohathite clan.

²⁷The descendants of Gershon, another clan within the tribe of Levi, received two towns with their pasturelands from the half-tribe of Manasseh: Golan in Bashan (a city of refuge) and Be-eshterah.

²⁸From the tribe of Issachar they received Kishion, Daberath, ²⁹Jarmuth, and En-gan-nim—four towns with their pasturelands.

³⁰From the tribe of Asher they received Mishal, Abdon, ³¹Helkath, and Rehob—four towns and their pasturelands.

³²From the tribe of Naphtali they received Kedesh in Galilee (a city of refuge), Hammoth-dor, and Kartan—three towns with their pas-turelands.

³³So thirteen towns and their pasturelands were allotted to the clan of Gershon.

³⁴The rest of the Levites—the Merari clan—were given the following towns from the tribe of Zebulun: Jokneam, Kartah, ³⁵Dimnah, and Nahalal—four towns with their pasturelands.

³⁶From the tribe of Reuben they received Bezer, Jahaz,* ³⁷Kedemoth, and Mephaath—four towns with their pasturelands.

³⁸From the tribe of Gad they received Ramoth in Gilead (a city of refuge), Maha-naim, ³⁹Heshbon, and Jazer—four towns with their pasturelands. ⁴⁰So twelve towns were allotted to the clan of Merari.

⁴¹The total number of towns and pasture-lands within Israelite territory given to the Levites came to forty-eight. ⁴²Every one of these towns had pasturelands surrounding it.

⁴³So the LORD gave to Israel all the land he had sworn to give their ancestors, and they conquered it and settled there. ⁴⁴And the LORD gave them rest on every side, just as he had solemnly promised their ancestors. None of their enemies could stand against them, for the LORD helped them conquer all their ene-mies. ⁴⁵All of the good promises that the LORD had given Israel came true.

THE EASTERN TRIBES RETURN HOME

22 Then Joshua called together the tribes of Reuben, Gad, and the half-tribe of Manasseh. ²He told them, "You have done as Moses, the servant of the LORD, commanded you, and you have obeyed every order I have given you. ³You have not deserted the other tribes, even though the campaign has lasted for such a long time. You have been careful to obey the commands of the LORD your God up to the present day. ⁴And now the LORD your God has given the other tribes rest, as he promised them. So go home now to the land Moses, the servant of the LORD, gave you on the east side of the Jordan River. ⁵But be very

21:36 Hebrew *Jahzah,* a variant name for Jahaz.

careful to obey all the commands and the law that Moses gave to you. Love the LORD your God, walk in all his ways, obey his commands, be faithful to him, and serve him with all your heart and all your soul."

⁶So Joshua blessed them and sent them home. ⁷Now Moses had given the land of Bashan to the half-tribe of Manasseh east of the Jordan. The other half of the tribe was given land west of the Jordan. As Joshua sent them away, he blessed them ⁸and said, "Share with your relatives back home the great wealth you have taken from your enemies. Share with them your large herds of cattle, your silver and gold, your bronze and iron, and your clothing."

⁹So the men of Reuben, Gad, and the half-tribe of Manasseh left the rest of Israel at Shiloh in the land of Canaan. They started the journey back to their own land of Gilead, the territory that belonged to them according to the LORD's command through Moses.

THE EASTERN TRIBES BUILD A MEMORIAL

¹⁰But while they were still in Canaan, before they crossed the Jordan River, Reuben, Gad, and the half-tribe of Manasseh built a very large altar near the Jordan River at a place called Geliloth.

¹¹When the rest of Israel heard they had built the altar at Geliloth west of the Jordan River, in the land of Canaan, ¹²the whole assembly gathered at Shiloh and prepared to go to war against their brother tribes. ¹³First, however, they sent a delegation led by Phinehas son of Eleazar, the priest. They crossed the river to talk with the tribes of Reuben, Gad, and the half-tribe of Manasseh. ¹⁴In this delegation were ten high officials of Israel, one from each of the ten tribes, and each a leader within the family divisions of Israel.

¹⁵When they arrived in the land of Gilead, they said to the tribes of Reuben, Gad, and the half-tribe of Manasseh, ¹⁶"The whole commu-

nity of the LORD demands to know why you are betraying the God of Israel. How could you turn away from the LORD and build an altar in rebellion against him? ¹⁷Was our sin at Peor not enough? We are not yet fully cleansed of it, even after the plague that struck the entire assembly of the LORD. ¹⁸And yet today you are turning away from following the LORD. If you rebel against the LORD today, he will be angry with all of us tomorrow. ¹⁹If you need the altar because your land is defiled, then join us on our side of the river, where the LORD lives among us in his Tabernacle, and we will share our land with you. But do not rebel against the LORD or draw us into your rebellion by building another altar for yourselves. There is only one true altar of the LORD our God. ²⁰Didn't God punish all the people of Israel when Achan, a member of the clan of Zerah, sinned by stealing the things set apart for the LORD*? He was not the only one who died because of that sin."

²¹Then the people of Reuben, Gad, and the half-tribe of Manasseh answered these high officials: ²²"The LORD alone is God! The LORD alone is God! We have not built the altar in rebellion against the LORD. If we have done so, do not spare our lives this day. But the LORD knows, and let all Israel know, too, ²³that we have not built an altar for ourselves to turn away from the LORD. Nor will we use it for our burnt offerings or grain offerings or peace offerings. If we have built it for this purpose, may the LORD himself punish us.

²⁴"We have built this altar because we fear that in the future your descendants will say to ours, 'What right do you have to worship the LORD, the God of Israel? ²⁵The LORD has placed the Jordan River as a barrier between our people and your people. You have no claim to the LORD.' And your descendants may make our descendants stop worshiping the LORD. ²⁶So we decided to build the altar, not for burnt sacrifices, ²⁷but as a memorial. It will

---

22:20 The Hebrew term used here refers to the complete consecration of things or people to the LORD, either by destroying them or by giving them as an offering.

remind our descendants and your descendants that we, too, have the right to worship the LORD at his sanctuary with our burnt offerings, sacrifices, and peace offerings. Then your descendants will not be able to say to ours, 'You have no claim to the LORD.' [28]If they say this, our descendants can reply, 'Look at this copy of the LORD's altar that our ancestors made. It is not for burnt offerings or sacrifices; it is a reminder of the relationship both of us have with the LORD.' [29]Far be it from us to rebel against the LORD or turn away from him by building our own altar for burnt offerings, grain offerings, or sacrifices. Only the altar of the LORD our God that stands in front of the Tabernacle may be used for that purpose."

[30]When Phinehas the priest and the high officials heard this from the tribes of Reuben, Gad, and the half-tribe of Manasseh, they were satisfied. [31]Phinehas son of Eleazar, the priest, replied to them, "Today we know the LORD is among us because you have not sinned against the LORD as we thought. Instead, you have rescued Israel from being destroyed by the LORD."

[32]Then Phinehas son of Eleazar, the priest, and the ten high officials left the tribes of Reuben and Gad in Gilead and returned to the land of Canaan to tell the Israelites what had happened. [33]And all the Israelites were satisfied and praised God and spoke no more of war against Reuben and Gad. [34]The people of Reuben and Gad named the altar "Witness,"* for they said, "It is a witness between us and them that the LORD is our God, too."

JOSHUA'S FINAL WORDS TO ISRAEL

23 The years passed, and the LORD had given the people of Israel rest from all their enemies. Joshua, who was now very old, [2]called together all the elders, leaders, judges, and officers of Israel. He said to them, "I am an old man now. [3]You have seen everything the LORD your God has done for you during my lifetime. The LORD your God has fought for you against your enemies. [4]I have allotted to you as an inheritance all the land of the nations yet unconquered, as well as the land of those we have already conquered—from the Jordan River to the Mediterranean Sea* in the west. [5]This land will be yours, for the LORD your God will drive out all the people living there now. You will live there instead of them, just as the LORD your God promised you.

[6]"So be strong! Be very careful to follow all the instructions written in the Book of the Law of Moses. Do not deviate from them in any way. [7]Make sure you do not associate with the other people still remaining in the land. Do not even mention the names of their gods, much less swear by them or worship them. [8]But be faithful to the LORD your God as you have done until now.

[9]"For the LORD has driven out great and powerful nations for you, and no one has yet been able to defeat you. [10]Each one of you will put to flight a thousand of the enemy, for the LORD your God fights for you, just as he has promised. [11]So be very careful to love the LORD your God.

[12]"But if you turn away from him and intermarry with the survivors of these nations remaining among you, [13]then know for certain that the LORD your God will no longer drive them out from your land. Instead, they will be a snare and a trap to you, a pain in your side and a thorn in your eyes, and you will be wiped out from this good land the LORD your God has given you.

[14]"Soon I will die, going the way of all the earth. Deep in your hearts you know that every promise of the LORD your God has come true. Not a single one has failed! [15]But as surely as the LORD your God has given you the good things he promised, he will also bring disaster on you if you disobey him. He will completely wipe you out from this good land he has given you. [16]If you break the covenant of the LORD your God by worshiping and

22:34 Hebrew *edh*. Some manuscripts lack this word. 23:4 Hebrew *the Great Sea*.

serving other gods, his anger will burn against you, and you will quickly be wiped out from the good land he has given you."

THE LORD'S COVENANT RENEWED

24 Then Joshua summoned all the people of Israel to Shechem, along with their elders, leaders, judges, and officers. So they came and presented themselves to God.

²Joshua said to the people, "This is what the LORD, the God of Israel, says: Your ancestors, including Terah, the father of Abraham and Nahor, lived beyond the Euphrates River,* and they worshiped other gods. ³But I took your ancestor Abraham from the land beyond the Euphrates and led him into the land of Canaan. I gave him many descendants through his son Isaac. ⁴To Isaac I gave Jacob and Esau. To Esau I gave the hill country of Seir, while Jacob and his children went down into Egypt.

⁵"Then I sent Moses and Aaron, and I brought terrible plagues on Egypt; and afterward I brought you out as a free people. ⁶But when your ancestors arrived at the Red Sea,* the Egyptians chased after you with chariots and horses. ⁷When you cried out to the LORD, I put darkness between you and the Egyptians. I brought the sea crashing down on the Egyptians, drowning them. With your very own eyes you saw what I did. Then you lived in the wilderness for many years.

⁸"Finally, I brought you into the land of the Amorites on the east side of the Jordan. They fought against you, but I gave you victory over them, and you took possession of their land. ⁹Then Balak son of Zippor, king of Moab, started a war against Israel. He asked Balaam son of Beor to curse you, ¹⁰but I would not listen to him. Instead, I made Balaam bless you, and so I rescued you from Balak.

¹¹"When you crossed the Jordan River and came to Jericho, the men of Jericho fought against you. There were also many others who fought you, including the Amorites, the Perizzites, the Canaanites, the Hittites, the Girgashites, the Hivites, and the Jebusites. But

I gave you victory over them. ¹²And I sent hornets ahead of you to drive out the two kings of the Amorites. It was not your swords or bows that brought you victory. ¹³I gave you land you had not worked for, and I gave you cities you did not build—the cities in which you are now living. I gave you vineyards and olive groves for food, though you did not plant them.

¹⁴"So honor the LORD and serve him wholeheartedly. Put away forever the idols your ancestors worshiped when they lived beyond the Euphrates River and in Egypt. Serve the LORD alone. ¹⁵But if you are unwilling to serve the LORD, then choose today whom you will serve. Would you prefer the gods your ancestors served beyond the Euphrates? Or will it be the gods of the Amorites in whose land you now live? But as for me and my family, we will serve the LORD."

¹⁶The people replied, "We would never forsake the LORD and worship other gods. ¹⁷For the LORD our God is the one who rescued us and our ancestors from slavery in the land of Egypt. He performed mighty miracles before our very eyes. As we traveled through the wilderness among our enemies, he preserved us. ¹⁸It was the LORD who drove out the Amorites and the other nations living here in the land. So we, too, will serve the LORD, for he alone is our God."

¹⁹Then Joshua said to the people, "You are not able to serve the LORD, for he is a holy and jealous God. He will not forgive your rebellion and sins. ²⁰If you forsake the LORD and serve other gods, he will turn against you and destroy you, even though he has been so good to you."

²¹But the people answered Joshua, saying, "No, we are determined to serve the LORD!"

²²"You are accountable for this decision," Joshua said. "You have chosen to serve the LORD."

"Yes," they replied, "we are accountable."

²³"All right then," Joshua said, "destroy the idols among you, and turn your hearts to the LORD, the God of Israel."

24:2 Hebrew *the river*; also in 24:3, 14, 15. 24:6 Hebrew *sea of reeds*.

My Daily Worship

— *February 24* —

IT'S YOUR CHOICE

JOSHUA 20:1–24:33

But if you are unwilling to serve the LORD, then choose today whom you will serve.
Would you prefer the gods your ancestors served beyond the Euphrates?
Or will it be the gods of the Amorites in whose land you now live?
But as for me and my family, we will serve the LORD (24:15).

[i reflect]

When two roads diverge in the woods of life, you can't follow both. You can't even be sure that choosing the one less traveled by will make the right difference. What you can be sure of is that whichever route you choose will soon diverge again. From the moment you roll out of bed in the morning, you're making decisions—some big, some small. You decide how you'll cover your body with clothing or fuel it with food. You select people to speak to and topics of conversation. You choose between an endless variety of ways that you can spend your leisure time.

Choices. Joshua had them too. Some small and mundane, some large. God had put him in charge of a nation of people who had to decide whether to put their faith in local gods or in the living God. They had to choose whom they were going to worship: idols made by human hands or the One holding the entire world in his hands.

We face the same choices. Daily, we must choose where we will place our faith, and whom we will serve. The true worshiper chooses to serve the living God.

Today you may be tempted to call in sick to work, or make up an excuse as to why you can't attend the weekly prayer meeting. A friend may ask you to lie for them, or you may be tempted to cheat on your expense report. Ask what it means in each situation to worship and serve the living God. Then choose.

[i pray]

God, you know I find it easy to follow you when I'm surrounded by other believers
who are singing your praises. It's so much harder when I feel alone in
my faith. Give me the strength daily to make the right choices.

[i respond]

List the key decisions ahead of you this week regarding the use of your time, your resources, and your relationships with others. Prayerfully consider each decision, then write down how you can choose to put God first in each choice you need to make.

²⁴The people said to Joshua, "We will serve the LORD our God. We will obey him alone."

²⁵So Joshua made a covenant with the people that day at Shechem, committing them to a permanent and binding contract between themselves and the LORD. ²⁶Joshua recorded these things in the Book of the Law of God. As a reminder of their agreement, he took a huge stone and rolled it beneath the oak tree beside the Tabernacle of the LORD.

²⁷Joshua said to all the people, "This stone has heard everything the LORD said to us. It will be a witness to testify against you if you go back on your word to God."

²⁸Then Joshua sent the people away, each to his own inheritance.

LEADERS BURIED IN THE PROMISED LAND

²⁹Soon after this, Joshua son of Nun, the servant of the LORD, died at the age of 110. ³⁰They buried him in the land he had inherited, at Timnath-serah in the hill country of Ephraim, north of Mount Gaash.

³¹Israel served the LORD throughout the lifetime of Joshua and of the leaders who outlived him—those who had personally experienced all that the LORD had done for Israel.

³²The bones of Joseph, which the Israelites had brought along with them when they left Egypt, were buried at Shechem, in the parcel of ground Jacob had bought from the sons of Hamor for one hundred pieces of silver.* This land was located in the territory allotted to the tribes of Ephraim and Manasseh, the descendants of Joseph.

³³Eleazar son of Aaron also died. He was buried in the hill country of Ephraim, in the town of Gibeah, which had been given to his son Phinehas.

24:32 Hebrew *100 kesitahs;* the value or weight of the kesitah is no longer known.

Judges

When Israel's leaders take charge, and the people gladly follow—bless the LORD! (5:2).

Losing Sight of God

A room full of little children play under the watchful eye of a supervisor, who has their welfare at heart. On a table in their midst is an open box of chocolate chip cookies. Left to themselves, the chances are that the children will succumb to temptation and quickly devour the cookies, even if they've been told to wait for the delicious, nourishing lunch awaiting them.

In the days of the judges, the Israelites, just like little children, find themselves unable to resist the temptations that exist around them. The Promised Land has been conquered, but the Israelites haven't removed the original inhabitants or their gods as God told them to do (1:21–36). After Joshua dies (2:6–9), the new generation of Israelites, who do not acknowledge God or remember what he has done, turn their eyes from him to worship idols. This angers the Lord (2:20–3:5) and he brings punishment upon Israel.

Judges tells a sad story of the continual cycle of complacency, sin, punishment, repentance, blessing, and complacency again. Over the three centuries that span this book, a series of national leaders, called judges, come to the rescue of the Israelites, drawing them back to God. But as soon as a strong, faithful leader dies, the people lose sight of God and return to their idol-worshiping ways. Notable leaders during this period include Deborah, Gideon, and Samson.

The concluding phrase of the book of Judges states, "In those days Israel had no king, so the people did whatever seemed right in their own eyes" (21:25). This seems to imply that a king would have solved Israel's problems. But was having a king the answer? Perhaps the lesson of the book of Judges is the impossibility of humanity worshiping God and obeying his Law, and the need for the coming of the only judge, leader, or king who can make a difference—the Righteous Judge, Jesus.

Don't lose sight of the one true Judge. Worship and keep your eyes on him.

Worship Moments

- When God rebuked the Israelites, the people wept, pleaded, and offered sacrifices to demonstrate their change of heart (2:1–5; cf. 6:6–10; 10:10–16; 21:2–4).

- After Deborah and Barak's mighty victory over the Canaanites, they sang a song of praise to the Lord (5:1–31).

- In this book God is praised as the "Sovereign LORD" (6:22; 16:28); "The LORD Is Peace" (6:24); and "the LORD, who is judge" (11:27).

JUDAH AND SIMEON CONQUER THE LAND

1 After Joshua died, the Israelites asked the LORD, "Which tribe should attack the Canaanites first?"

²The LORD answered, "Judah, for I have given them victory over the land."

³The leaders of Judah said to their relatives from the tribe of Simeon, "Join with us to fight against the Canaanites living in the territory allotted to us. Then we will help you conquer your territory." So the men of Simeon went with Judah.

⁴When the men of Judah attacked, the LORD gave them victory over the Canaanites and Perizzites, and they killed ten thousand enemy warriors at the town of Bezek. ⁵While at Bezek they encountered King Adoni-bezek and fought against him, and the Canaanites and Perizzites were defeated. ⁶Adoni-bezek escaped, but the Israelites soon captured him and cut off his thumbs and big toes. ⁷Adoni-bezek said, "I once had seventy kings with thumbs and big toes cut off, eating scraps from under my table. Now God has paid me back for what I did to them." They took him to Jerusalem, and he died there.

⁸The men of Judah attacked Jerusalem and captured it, killing all its people and setting the city on fire. ⁹Then they turned south to fight the Canaanites living in the hill country, the Negev, and the western foothills.* ¹⁰Judah marched against the Canaanites in Hebron (formerly called Kiriath-arba), defeating the forces of Sheshai, Ahiman, and Talmai. ¹¹From there they marched against the people living in the town of Debir (formerly called Kiriath-sepher).

¹²Then Caleb said, "I will give my daughter Acsah in marriage to the one who attacks and captures Kiriath-sepher." ¹³Othniel, the son of Caleb's younger brother Kenaz, was the one who conquered it, so Acsah became Othniel's wife.

¹⁴When Acsah married Othniel, she urged him* to ask her father for an additional field. As she got down off her donkey, Caleb asked her, "What is it? What can I do for you?"

¹⁵She said, "Give me a further blessing. You have been kind enough to give me land in the Negev; please give me springs as well." So Caleb gave her the upper and lower springs.

¹⁶When the tribe of Judah left Jericho,* the Kenites, who were descendants of Moses' father-in-law, traveled with them into the wilderness of Judah. They settled among the people there, near the town of Arad in the Negev.

¹⁷Then Judah joined with Simeon to fight against the Canaanites living in Zephath, and they completely destroyed* the town. So the town was named Hormah.* ¹⁸In addition, Judah captured the cities of Gaza, Ashkelon, and Ekron, along with their surrounding territories.

ISRAEL FAILS TO CONQUER THE LAND

¹⁹The LORD was with the people of Judah, and they took possession of the hill country. But they failed to drive out the people living in the plains because the people there had iron chariots. ²⁰The city of Hebron was given to Caleb as Moses had promised. And Caleb drove out the people living there, who were descendants of the three sons of Anak. ²¹The tribe of Benjamin, however, failed to drive out the Jebusites, who were living in Jerusalem. So to this day the Jebusites live in Jerusalem among the people of Benjamin.

²²The descendants of Joseph attacked the town of Bethel, and the LORD was with them. ²³They sent spies to Bethel (formerly known as Luz), ²⁴who confronted a man coming out of the city. They said to him, "Show us a way into the city, and we will have mercy on you." ²⁵So he showed them a way in, and they killed everyone in the city except for this man and his family. ²⁶Later the man moved to the land of the Hittites, where he built a city. He named

---

1:9 Hebrew *the Shephelah*. 1:14 Greek version and Latin Vulgate read *he urged her*. 1:16 Hebrew *the city of palms*. 1:17a The Hebrew term used here refers to the complete consecration of things or people to the LORD, either by destroying them or by giving them as an offering. 1:17b *Hormah* means "destruction."

the city Luz, and it is known by that name to this day.

²⁷The tribe of Manasseh failed to drive out the people living in Beth-shan,* Taanach, Dor, Ibleam, Megiddo, and their surrounding villages, because the Canaanites were determined to stay in that region. ²⁸When the Israelites grew stronger, they forced the Canaanites to work as slaves, but they never did drive them out of the land.

²⁹The tribe of Ephraim also failed to drive out the Canaanites living in Gezer, and so the Canaanites continued to live there among them.

³⁰The tribe of Zebulun also failed to drive out the Canaanites living in Kitron and Nahalol, who continued to live among them. But they forced them to work as slaves.

³¹The tribe of Asher also failed to drive out the residents of Acco, Sidon, Ahlab, Aczib, Helbah, Aphik, and Rehob. ³²In fact, because they did not drive them out, the Canaanites dominated the land where the people of Asher lived.

³³The tribe of Naphtali also failed to drive out the residents of Beth-shemesh and Beth-anath. Instead, the Canaanites dominated the land where they lived. Nevertheless, the people of Beth-shemesh and Beth-anath were sometimes forced to work as slaves for the people of Naphtali.

³⁴As for the tribe of Dan, the Amorites forced them into the hill country and would not let them come down into the plains. ³⁵The Amorites were determined to stay in Mount Heres, Aijalon, and Shaalbim, but when the descendants of Joseph became stronger, they forced the Amorites to work as slaves. ³⁶The boundary of the Amorites ran from Scorpion Pass* to Sela and continued upward from there.

THE LORD'S MESSENGER COMES TO BOKIM

2 The angel of the LORD went up from Gilgal to Bokim with a message for the Israelites. He told them, "I brought you out of Egypt into this land that I swore to give your ancestors, and I said I would never break my covenant with you. ²For your part, you were not to make any covenants with the people living in this land; instead, you were to destroy their altars. Why, then, have you disobeyed my command? ³Since you have done this, I will no longer drive out the people living in your land. They will be thorns in your sides, and their gods will be a constant temptation to you." ⁴When the angel of the LORD finished speaking, the Israelites wept loudly. ⁵So they called the place "Weeping,"* and they offered sacrifices to the LORD.

THE DEATH OF JOSHUA

⁶After Joshua sent the people away, each of the tribes left to take possession of the land allotted to them. ⁷And the Israelites served the LORD throughout the lifetime of Joshua and the leaders who outlived him—those who had seen all the great things the LORD had done for Israel.

⁸Then Joshua son of Nun, the servant of the LORD, died at the age of 110. ⁹They buried him in the land he had inherited, at Timnath-serah* in the hill country of Ephraim, north of Mount Gaash.

ISRAEL DISOBEYS THE LORD

¹⁰After that generation died, another generation grew up who did not acknowledge the LORD or remember the mighty things he had done for Israel. ¹¹Then the Israelites did what was evil in the LORD's sight and worshiped the images of Baal. ¹²They abandoned the LORD, the God of their ancestors, who had brought them out of Egypt. They chased after other gods, worshiping the gods of the people around them. And they angered the LORD. ¹³They abandoned the LORD to serve Baal and the images of Ashtoreth. ¹⁴This made the LORD burn with anger against Israel, so he handed them over to marauders who stole their possessions. He sold them to their enemies all

---

1:27 Hebrew *Beth-shean*, a variant name for Beth-shan. 1:36 Hebrew *Akrabbim*. 2:5 Hebrew *Bokim*. 2:9 Hebrew *Timnath-heres*, a variant name for Timnath-serah.

around, and they were no longer able to resist them. [15]Every time Israel went out to battle, the LORD fought against them, bringing them defeat, just as he promised. And the people were very distressed.

THE LORD RESCUES HIS PEOPLE

[16]Then the LORD raised up judges to rescue the Israelites from their enemies. [17]Yet Israel did not listen to the judges but prostituted themselves to other gods, bowing down to them. How quickly they turned away from the path of their ancestors, who had walked in obedience to the LORD's commands. [18]Whenever the LORD placed a judge over Israel, he was with that judge and rescued the people from their enemies throughout the judge's lifetime. For the LORD took pity on his people, who were burdened by oppression and suffering. [19]But when the judge died, the people returned to their corrupt ways, behaving worse than those who had lived before them. They followed other gods, worshiping and bowing down to them. And they refused to give up their evil practices and stubborn ways.

[20]So the LORD burned with anger against Israel. He said, "Because these people have violated the covenant I made with their ancestors and have ignored my commands, [21]I will no longer drive out the nations that Joshua left unconquered when he died. [22]I did this to test Israel—to see whether or not they would obey the LORD as their ancestors did." [23]That is why the LORD did not quickly drive the nations out or allow Joshua to conquer them all.

THE NATIONS LEFT IN CANAAN

3 The LORD left certain nations in the land to test those Israelites who had not participated in the wars of Canaan. [2]He did this to teach warfare to generations of Israelites who had no experience in battle. [3]These were the nations: the Philistines (those living under the five Philistine rulers), all the Canaanites, the Sidonians, and the Hivites living in the hill country of Lebanon from Mount Baal-hermon to Lebo-hamath. [4]These people were left to test the Israelites—to see whether they would obey the commands the LORD had given to their ancestors through Moses.

[5]So Israel lived among the Canaanites, Hittites, Amorites, Perizzites, Hivites, and Jebusites, [6]and they intermarried with them. Israelite sons married their daughters, and Israelite daughters were given in marriage to their sons. And the Israelites worshiped their gods.

OTHNIEL BECOMES ISRAEL'S JUDGE

[7]The Israelites did what was evil in the LORD's sight. They forgot about the LORD their God, and they worshiped the images of Baal and the Asherah poles. [8]Then the LORD burned with anger against Israel, and he handed them over to King Cushan-rishathaim of Aram-naharaim.* And the Israelites were subject to Cushan-rishathaim for eight years.

[9]But when Israel cried out to the LORD for help, the LORD raised up a man to rescue them. His name was Othniel, the son of Caleb's younger brother, Kenaz. [10]The Spirit of the LORD came upon him, and he became Israel's judge. He went to war against King Cushan-rishathaim of Aram, and the LORD gave Othniel victory over him. [11]So there was peace in the land for forty years. Then Othniel son of Kenaz died.

EHUD BECOMES ISRAEL'S JUDGE

[12]Once again the Israelites did what was evil in the LORD's sight, so the LORD gave King Eglon of Moab control over Israel. [13]Together with the Ammonites and Amalekites, Eglon attacked Israel and took possession of Jericho.* [14]And the Israelites were subject to Eglon of Moab for eighteen years.

[15]But when Israel cried out to the LORD for help, the LORD raised up a man to rescue

---

3:8 *Aram-naharaim* means "Aram of the two rivers," thought to have been located between the Euphrates and Balih Rivers in northwestern Mesopotamia. 3:13 Hebrew *the city of palms.*

My Daily Worship

NO COMPROMISE POLICY

JUDGES 1:1—3:6

For your part, you were not to make any covenants with the people living in this land; instead,
you were to destroy their altars. Why, then, have you disobeyed my command? (2:2).

[i reflect]

God's explicit command to his people had two parts. In their new land they were to: 1) destroy existing altars; and 2) refuse to enter agreements (covenants) with the current residents. God wanted a no-tolerance and no-compromise policy. They were not to compromise their present situation by allowing the symbols of unbelief to stand. They were not to compromise their future by making commitments that would affect their ability to obey God. But, despite God's clarity, within a generation he had to confront his people with a question: Why have you disobeyed?

We also worship in foreign lands. We have become citizens of God's kingdom through faith in Christ, but we still dwell in territory controlled by the enemy. Spiritually speaking, we can't call any place on earth our Promised Land. Our King has instructed us that though we live *in* the world, we are not to be *of* the world.

Meanwhile, God's no-tolerance and no-compromise command still applies. God alone deserves our worship, so the ideas, symbols, and objects worshiped by the world must not serve that purpose in our lives. Our relationships with those in the world must not include commitments or promises that compete with our obedience to God.

What could be easier than lifting up praise and gratitude to the One who has promised never to break his covenant with us? And yet we face the same temptations that repeatedly defeated the people of Israel. But their story doesn't have to be ours. As we draw close to God, he promises to draw close to us (James 4:8). Sin separates, but repentance is a divine U-turn that brings us right back to him again. What a glorious place to be!

Check how tightly you hold on to worldly possessions. When making promises, ask yourself how they will affect your freedom to live for God. Guard against the daily compromises—small and large—that may jeopardize your worship and relationship with God.

[i pray]

Lord, I admit that I have broken your covenant of love through failure to drive sin from my life.
I confess my personal disobedience and ask you to fill me again with the joy of your presence.

[i respond]

If you are longing for the unfettered times of worship you once knew, take a spiritual inventory and ask the Holy Spirit to make areas of compromise clear to you. Write them down and pray about each one. Joy is just on the other side!

them. His name was Ehud son of Gera, of the tribe of Benjamin, who was left-handed. The Israelites sent Ehud to deliver their tax money to King Eglon of Moab. ¹⁶So Ehud made himself a double-edged dagger that was eighteen inches* long, and he strapped it to his right thigh, keeping it hidden under his clothing. ¹⁷He brought the tax money to Eglon, who was very fat. ¹⁸After delivering the payment, Ehud sent home those who had carried the tax money.

¹⁹But when Ehud reached the stone carvings near Gilgal, he turned back. He came to Eglon and said, "I have a secret message for you." So the king commanded his servants to be silent and sent them all out of the room. ²⁰Ehud walked over to Eglon as he was sitting alone in a cool upstairs room and said, "I have a message for you from God!" As King Eglon rose from his seat, ²¹Ehud reached with his left hand, pulled out the dagger strapped to his right thigh, and plunged it into the king's belly. ²²The dagger went so deep that the handle disappeared beneath the king's fat. So Ehud left the dagger in, and the king's bowels emptied. ²³Then Ehud closed and locked the doors and climbed down the latrine and escaped through the sewage access.

²⁴After Ehud was gone, the king's servants returned and found the doors to the upstairs room locked. They thought he might be using the latrine, ²⁵so they waited. But when the king didn't come out after a long delay, they became concerned and got a key. And when they opened the door, they found their master dead on the floor.

²⁶While the servants were waiting, Ehud escaped, passing the idols on his way to Seirah. ²⁷When he arrived in the hill country of Ephraim, Ehud sounded a call to arms. Then he led a band of Israelites down from the hills. ²⁸"Follow me," he said, "for the LORD has given you victory over Moab your enemy." So they followed him. And the Israelites took control of the shallows of the Jordan River across from Moab, preventing anyone from crossing. ²⁹They attacked the Moabites and killed about ten thousand of their strongest and bravest warriors. Not one of them escaped. ³⁰So Moab was conquered by Israel that day, and the land was at peace for eighty years.

SHAMGAR BECOMES ISRAEL'S JUDGE

³¹After Ehud, Shamgar son of Anath rescued Israel. He killed six hundred Philistines with an ox goad.

DEBORAH BECOMES ISRAEL'S JUDGE

4 After Ehud's death, the Israelites again did what was evil in the LORD's sight. ²So the LORD handed them over to King Jabin of Hazor, a Canaanite king. The commander of his army was Sisera, who lived in Harosheth-haggoyim. ³Sisera, who had nine hundred iron chariots, ruthlessly oppressed the Israelites for twenty years. Then the Israelites cried out to the LORD for help.

⁴Deborah, the wife of Lappidoth, was a prophet who had become a judge in Israel. ⁵She would hold court under the Palm of Deborah, which stood between Ramah and Bethel in the hill country of Ephraim, and the Israelites came to her to settle their disputes. ⁶One day she sent for Barak son of Abinoam, who lived in Kedesh in the land of Naphtali. She said to him, "This is what the LORD, the God of Israel, commands you: Assemble ten thousand warriors from the tribes of Naphtali and Zebulun at Mount Tabor. ⁷I will lure Sisera, commander of Jabin's army, along with his chariots and warriors, to the Kishon River. There I will give you victory over him."

⁸Barak told her, "I will go, but only if you go with me!"

⁹"Very well," she replied, "I will go with you. But since you have made this choice, you will receive no honor. For the LORD's victory over Sisera will be at the hands of a woman." So

3:16 Hebrew *1 cubit* [45 centimeters].

Deborah went with Barak to Kedesh. ¹⁰At Kedesh, Barak called together the tribes of Zebulun and Naphtali, and ten thousand warriors marched up with him. Deborah also marched with them.

¹¹Now Heber the Kenite, a descendant of Moses' brother-in-law* Hobab, had moved away from the other members of his tribe and pitched his tent by the Oak of Zaanannim, near Kedesh.

¹²When Sisera was told that Barak son of Abinoam had gone up to Mount Tabor, ¹³he called for all nine hundred of his iron chariots and all of his warriors, and they marched from Harosheth-haggoyim to the Kishon River.

¹⁴Then Deborah said to Barak, "Get ready! Today the LORD will give you victory over Sisera, for the LORD is marching ahead of you." So Barak led his ten thousand warriors down the slopes of Mount Tabor into battle. ¹⁵When Barak attacked, the LORD threw Sisera and all his charioteers and warriors into a panic. Then Sisera leaped down from his chariot and escaped on foot. ¹⁶Barak chased the enemy and their chariots all the way to Harosheth-haggoyim, killing all of Sisera's warriors. Not a single one was left alive.

¹⁷Meanwhile, Sisera ran to the tent of Jael, the wife of Heber the Kenite, because Heber's family was on friendly terms with King Jabin of Hazor. ¹⁸Jael went out to meet Sisera and said to him, "Come into my tent, sir. Come in. Don't be afraid." So he went into her tent, and she covered him with a blanket.

¹⁹"Please give me some water," he said. "I'm thirsty." So she gave him some milk to drink and covered him again.

²⁰"Stand at the door of the tent," he told her. "If anybody comes and asks you if there is anyone here, say no."

²¹But when Sisera fell asleep from exhaustion, Jael quietly crept up to him with a hammer and tent peg. Then she drove the tent peg through his temple and into the ground, and so he died.

²²When Barak came looking for Sisera, Jael went out to meet him. She said, "Come, and I will show you the man you are looking for." So he followed her into the tent and found Sisera lying there dead, with the tent peg through his temple.

²³So on that day Israel saw God subdue Jabin, the Canaanite king. ²⁴And from that time on Israel became stronger and stronger against King Jabin, until they finally destroyed him.

THE SONG OF DEBORAH

5 On that day Deborah and Barak son of Abinoam sang this song:

² "When Israel's leaders take charge,
    and the people gladly follow—
bless the LORD!

³ "Listen, you kings!
    Pay attention, you mighty rulers!
For I will sing to the LORD.
    I will lift up my song to the LORD, the
        God of Israel.

⁴ "LORD, when you set out from Seir
    and marched across the fields of Edom,
the earth trembled
    and the cloudy skies poured down rain.
⁵ The mountains quaked at the coming of
        the LORD.
    Even Mount Sinai shook in the presence
        of the LORD, the God of Israel.

⁶ "In the days of Shamgar son of Anath, and
        in the days of Jael,
    people avoided the main roads,
    and travelers stayed on crooked side paths.
⁷ There were few people left in the villages of
        Israel—
    until Deborah arose as a mother for Israel.
⁸ When Israel chose new gods,
    war erupted at the city gates.
Yet not a shield or spear could be seen
    among forty thousand warriors in Israel!

4:11 Or *father-in-law.*

9 My heart goes out to Israel's leaders,
    and to those who gladly followed.
      Bless the LORD!

10 "You who ride on fine donkeys
    and sit on fancy saddle blankets, listen!
    And you who must walk along the road,
      listen!
11 Listen to the village musicians* gathered at
      the watering holes.
    They recount the righteous victories of
      the LORD,
    and the victories of his villagers in Israel.
  Then the people of the LORD
    marched down to the city gates.

12 "Wake up, Deborah, wake up!
    Wake up, wake up, and sing a song!
  Arise, Barak!
    Lead your captives away, son of Abinoam!

13 "Down from Tabor marched the remnant
      against the mighty.
    The people of the LORD marched down
      against mighty warriors.
14 They came down from Ephraim—a land
      that once belonged to the Amalekites,
    and Benjamin also followed you.
  From Makir the commanders marched down;
      from Zebulun came those who carry the
      rod of authority.
15 The princes of Issachar were with Deborah
      and Barak.
    They followed Barak, rushing into the valley.
  But in the tribe of Reuben
      there was great indecision.
16 Why did you sit at home among the
      sheepfolds—
    to hear the shepherds whistle for their
      flocks?
  In the tribe of Reuben
      there was great indecision.
17 Gilead remained east of the Jordan.
    And Dan, why did he stay home?
  Asher sat unmoved at the seashore,
      remaining in his harbors.

5:11 The meaning of the Hebrew is uncertain.

18 But Zebulun risked his life,
    as did Naphtali, on the battlefield.

19 "The kings of Canaan fought at Taanach
      near Megiddo's springs,
    but they carried off no treasures of
      battle.
20 The stars fought from heaven.
    The stars in their orbits fought against
      Sisera.
21 The Kishon River swept them away—
    that ancient river, the Kishon.
  March on, my soul, with courage!
22 Then the horses' hooves hammered the
      ground,
    the galloping, galloping of Sisera's
      mighty steeds.
23 'Let the people of Meroz be cursed,' said
      the angel of the LORD.
  'Let them be utterly cursed
  because they did not come to help the LORD,
    to help the LORD against the mighty
      warriors.'

24 "Most blessed is Jael,
    the wife of Heber the Kenite.
    May she be blessed above all women
      who live in tents.
25 Sisera asked for water,
    and Jael gave him milk.
  In a bowl fit for kings,
    she brought him yogurt.
26 Then with her left hand she reached for a
      tent peg,
    and with her right hand she reached for
      the workman's hammer.
  She hit Sisera, crushing his head.
    She pounded the tent peg through his
      head, piercing his temples.
27 He sank, he fell,
    he lay dead at her feet.

28 "From the window Sisera's mother looked
      out.
    Through the window she watched for
      his return, saying,

My Daily Worship

PAY ATTENTION AND CELEBRATE!

JUDGES 3:7 – 5:31

Listen, you kings! Pay attention, you mighty rulers! For I will sing to the LORD.
I will lift up my song to the LORD, the God of Israel (5:3).

[i reflect]

Everyone has battles. The conflicts we face may not be on the scale of a full-fledged military contest, such as the one Deborah and the Israelites faced against the forces led by General Sisera of Hazor. But we struggle daily. A battle against cancer. A battle to save a marriage, hold on to a job, fight off depression. Everyone has battles.

Few people enjoy conflict. Deborah and Barak were no exception. Deborah was Israel's judge, and God gave her specific instructions to command Barak to mobilize the Israelites for war. When he refused to go alone, she agreed to accompany him, but warned that any honor due the conquering hero would now be denied him.

When victory was handed to Israel, Deborah responded with worship: "Listen, you kings! Pay attention, you mighty rulers! For I will sing to the LORD. I will lift up my song to the LORD, the God of Israel." In a beautiful praise song, Deborah focused on the source of their great victory and recounted for all to hear the wondrous work of God. Such worship not only honors God, but it also encourages us in facing our next battle.

When we see God do something amazing as Deborah did, when we see his hand clearly in our lives, the only appropriate response is worship. "Listen!" Deborah said. "Pay attention!" Look for the many ways that God gives us victories daily. Pay attention to how he is guiding us and carrying us through each struggle. Then we will lift up our song to God in thanksgiving and praise.

What victory has God given to you? Shout thanks to him! How has God provided for you? Offer a song of praise to him!

[i pray]

Lord, I confess that too often I fail to take time to adequately thank you for the victories you have given me in life's battles. Help me today to shout and sing my thanks to you.

[i respond]

Name the battle you are facing right now. Write out a battle plan that will give the victory God already has planned for you. Celebrate!

'Why is his chariot so long in coming?
Why don't we hear the sound of chariot
wheels?'
29 A reply comes from her wise women,
and she repeats these words to herself:
30 'They are dividing the captured goods they
found—
a woman or two for every man.
There are gorgeous robes for Sisera,
and colorful, beautifully embroidered
robes for me.'

31 "LORD, may all your enemies die as Sisera
did!
But may those who love you rise like the
sun at full strength!"

Then there was peace in the land for forty
years.

GIDEON BECOMES ISRAEL'S JUDGE

6 Again the Israelites did what was evil in
the LORD's sight. So the LORD handed
them over to the Midianites for seven years.
²The Midianites were so cruel that the
Israelites fled to the mountains, where they
made hiding places for themselves in caves
and dens. ³Whenever the Israelites planted
their crops, marauders from Midian, Amalek,
and the people of the east would attack Israel,
⁴camping in the land and destroying crops as
far away as Gaza. They left the Israelites with
nothing to eat, taking all the sheep, oxen, and
donkeys. ⁵These enemy hordes, coming with
their cattle and tents as thick as locusts,
arrived on droves of camels too numerous to
count. And they stayed until the land was
stripped bare. ⁶So Israel was reduced to starvation by the Midianites. Then the Israelites
cried out to the LORD for help.

⁷When they cried out to the LORD because
of Midian, ⁸the LORD sent a prophet to the
Israelites. He said, "This is what the LORD, the
God of Israel, says: I brought you up out of
slavery in Egypt ⁹and rescued you from the
Egyptians and from all who oppressed you. I
drove out your enemies and gave you their
land. ¹⁰I told you, 'I am the LORD your God.
You must not worship the gods of the
Amorites, in whose land you now live.' But
you have not listened to me."

¹¹Then the angel of the LORD came and sat
beneath the oak tree at Ophrah, which
belonged to Joash of the clan of Abiezer.
Gideon son of Joash had been threshing
wheat at the bottom of a winepress to hide the
grain from the Midianites. ¹²The angel of the
LORD appeared to him and said, "Mighty hero,
the LORD is with you!"

¹³"Sir," Gideon replied, "if the LORD is with
us, why has all this happened to us? And
where are all the miracles our ancestors told
us about? Didn't they say, 'The LORD brought
us up out of Egypt'? But now the LORD has
abandoned us and handed us over to the
Midianites."

¹⁴Then the LORD turned to him and said,
"Go with the strength you have and rescue
Israel from the Midianites. I am sending you!"

¹⁵"But Lord," Gideon replied, "how can I
rescue Israel? My clan is the weakest in the
whole tribe of Manasseh, and I am the least in
my entire family!"

¹⁶The LORD said to him, "I will be with you.
And you will destroy the Midianites as if you
were fighting against one man."

¹⁷Gideon replied, "If you are truly going to
help me, show me a sign to prove that it is
really the LORD speaking to me. ¹⁸Don't go
away until I come back and bring my offering
to you."

The LORD answered, "I will stay here until
you return."

¹⁹Gideon hurried home. He cooked a young
goat, and with half a bushel* of flour he baked
some bread without yeast. Then, carrying the
meat in a basket and the broth in a pot, he
brought them out and presented them to the
angel, who was under the oak tree.

²⁰The angel of God said to him, "Place the

6:19 Hebrew *1 ephah* [18 liters].

My Daily Worship

— *February 27* —

HOW CAN I POSSIBLY DO THAT?

JUDGES 6:1–8:35

"But Lord," Gideon replied, "how can I rescue Israel?
My clan is the weakest in the whole tribe of Manasseh,
and I am the least in my entire family!" (6:15).

[i reflect]

Gideon wasn't posing a rhetorical question here. If God sat down with you for a chat, wouldn't you seize the opportunity to ask a few urgent questions? Maybe your questions would be like Gideon's: *Why are you asking this of me? How can I possibly fulfill this assignment? Lord, don't you think you picked the wrong person?*

The wonderful news is that God welcomes our questions. They don't put him off. He doesn't get angry when we question our circumstances or his plan for our life. Look how he responded to Gideon. Far from being annoyed by Gideon's questions, God actually responded to him with patience, reassurance, and a commission for service, "Go with the strength you have and rescue Israel from the Midianites. I am sending you!" (6:14).

The God whom we worship is not distressed by our questions. He knows that, like Gideon, we often feel weak, inadequate, or overwhelmed by life. He desires our honesty in worship and wants us to bring to him those issues, questions, and doubts that are on our minds. As you enter into earnest dialogue with him through prayer, you can bring everything to him—your praise, your thanks, your doubts, and even your questions. The Lord's response to Gideon's questions is true for you today as well: "I will be with you" (6:16).

Be honest with God. Don't allow your questions to prevent you from coming to him in worship. Bring your questions as a sacrifice to him. God can handle them.

[i pray]

Lord, many times I feel just like Gideon—questioning what you want me to do,
or why you have brought these circumstances into my life. Help me draw
strength from your promise to be with me, no matter what.

[i respond]

What questions weigh on your mind? Ask them out loud to God. Spend some time in silence before God, listening for his answer.

meat and the unleavened bread on this rock, and pour the broth over it." And Gideon did as he was told. [21]Then the angel of the LORD touched the meat and bread with the staff in his hand, and fire flamed up from the rock and consumed all he had brought. And the angel of the LORD disappeared.

[22]When Gideon realized that it was the angel of the LORD, he cried out, "Sovereign LORD, I have seen the angel of the LORD face to face!"

[23]"It is all right," the LORD replied. "Do not be afraid. You will not die." [24]And Gideon built an altar to the LORD there and named it "The LORD Is Peace."* The altar remains in Ophrah in the land of the clan of Abiezer to this day.

[25]That night the LORD said to Gideon, "Take the second best bull from your father's herd, the one that is seven years old. Pull down your father's altar to Baal, and cut down the Asherah pole standing beside it. [26]Then build an altar to the LORD your God here on this hill, laying the stones carefully. Sacrifice the bull as a burnt offering on the altar, using as fuel the wood of the Asherah pole you cut down." [27]So Gideon took ten of his servants and did as the LORD had commanded. But he did it at night because he was afraid of the other members of his father's household and the people of the town. He knew what would happen if they found out who had done it.

[28]Early the next morning, as the people of the town began to stir, someone discovered that the altar of Baal had been knocked down and that the Asherah pole beside it was gone. In their place a new altar had been built, and it had the remains of a sacrifice on it. [29]The people said to each other, "Who did this?" And after asking around and making a careful search, they learned that it was Gideon, the son of Joash.

[30]"Bring out your son," they shouted to Joash. "He must die for destroying the altar of Baal and for cutting down the Asherah pole."

[31]But Joash shouted to the mob, "Why are you defending Baal? Will you argue his case?

Whoever pleads his case will be put to death by morning! If Baal truly is a god, let him defend himself and destroy the one who knocked down his altar!" [32]From then on Gideon was called Jerubbaal, which means "Let Baal defend himself," because he knocked down Baal's altar.

[33]Soon afterward the armies of Midian, Amalek, and the people of the east formed an alliance against Israel and crossed the Jordan, camping in the valley of Jezreel. [34]Then the Spirit of the LORD took possession of Gideon. He blew a ram's horn as a call to arms, and the men of the clan of Abiezer came to him. [35]He also sent messengers throughout Manasseh, Asher, Zebulun, and Naphtali, summoning their warriors, and all of them responded.

[36]Then Gideon said to God, "If you are truly going to use me to rescue Israel as you promised, [37]prove it to me in this way. I will put some wool on the threshing floor tonight. If the fleece is wet with dew in the morning but the ground is dry, then I will know that you are going to help me rescue Israel as you promised." [38]And it happened just that way. When Gideon got up the next morning, he squeezed the fleece and wrung out a whole bowlful of water.

[39]Then Gideon said to God, "Please don't be angry with me, but let me make one more request. This time let the fleece remain dry while the ground around it is wet with dew." [40]So that night God did as Gideon asked. The fleece was dry in the morning, but the ground was covered with dew.

GIDEON DEFEATS THE MIDIANITES

7 So Jerubbaal (that is, Gideon) and his army got up early and went as far as the spring of Harod. The armies of Midian were camped north of them in the valley near the hill of Moreh. [2]The LORD said to Gideon, "You have too many warriors with you. If I let all of you fight the Midianites, the Israelites will boast to me that they saved themselves by

6:24 Hebrew *Yahweh Shalom.*

their own strength. ³Therefore, tell the people, 'Whoever is timid or afraid may leave*' and go home.' " Twenty-two thousand of them went home, leaving only ten thousand who were willing to fight.

⁴But the LORD told Gideon, "There are still too many! Bring them down to the spring, and I will sort out who will go with you and who will not." ⁵When Gideon took his warriors down to the water, the LORD told him, "Divide the men into two groups. In one group put all those who cup water in their hands and lap it up with their tongues like dogs. In the other group put all those who kneel down and drink with their mouths in the stream." ⁶Only three hundred of the men drank from their hands. All the others got down on their knees and drank with their mouths in the stream. ⁷The LORD told Gideon, "With these three hundred men I will rescue you and give you victory over the Midianites. Send all the others home." ⁸So Gideon collected the provisions and rams' horns of the other warriors and sent them home. But he kept the three hundred men with him.

Now the Midianite camp was in the valley just below Gideon. ⁹During the night, the LORD said, "Get up! Go down into the Midianite camp, for I have given you victory over them! ¹⁰But if you are afraid to attack, go down to the camp with your servant Purah. ¹¹Listen to what the Midianites are saying, and you will be greatly encouraged. Then you will be eager to attack."

So Gideon took Purah and went down to the outposts of the enemy camp. ¹²The armies of Midian, Amalek, and the people of the east had settled in the valley like a swarm of locusts. Their camels were like grains of sand on the seashore—too many to count! ¹³Gideon crept up just as a man was telling his friend about a dream. The man said, "I had this dream, and in my dream a loaf of barley bread came tumbling down into the Midianite camp. It hit a tent, turned it over, and knocked it flat!"

¹⁴His friend said, "Your dream can mean only one thing—God has given Gideon son of Joash, the Israelite, victory over all the armies united with Midian!"

¹⁵When Gideon heard the dream and its interpretation, he thanked God. Then he returned to the Israelite camp and shouted, "Get up! For the LORD has given you victory over the Midianites!" ¹⁶He divided the three hundred men into three groups and gave each man a ram's horn and a clay jar with a torch in it. ¹⁷Then he said to them, "Keep your eyes on me. When I come to the edge of the camp, do just as I do. ¹⁸As soon as my group blows the rams' horns, those of you on the other sides of the camp blow your horns and shout, 'For the LORD and for Gideon!' "

¹⁹It was just after midnight, after the changing of the guard, when Gideon and the one hundred men with him reached the outer edge of the Midianite camp. Suddenly, they blew the horns and broke their clay jars. ²⁰Then all three groups blew their horns and broke their jars. They held the blazing torches in their left hands and the horns in their right hands and shouted, "A sword for the LORD and for Gideon!" ²¹Each man stood at his position around the camp and watched as all the Midianites rushed around in a panic, shouting as they ran. ²²When the three hundred Israelites blew their horns, the LORD caused the warriors in the camp to fight against each other with their swords. Those who were not killed fled to places as far away as Beth-shittah near Zererah and to the border of Abel-meholah near Tabbath.

²³Then Gideon sent for the warriors of Naphtali, Asher, and Manasseh, who joined in the chase after the fleeing army of Midian. ²⁴Gideon also sent messengers throughout the hill country of Ephraim, saying, "Come down to attack the Midianites. Cut them off at the shallows of the Jordan River at Beth-barah." And the men of Ephraim did as they were told. ²⁵They captured Oreb and Zeeb, the two

7:3 Hebrew *leave Mount Gilead*. The identity of Mount Gilead is uncertain in this context. It is perhaps used here as another name for Mount Gilboa.

Midianite generals, killing Oreb at the rock of Oreb, and Zeeb at the winepress of Zeeb. And they continued to chase the Midianites. Afterward the Israelites brought the heads of Oreb and Zeeb to Gideon, who was by the Jordan.

GIDEON KILLS ZEBAH AND ZALMUNNA

8 Then the people of Ephraim asked Gideon, "Why have you treated us this way? Why didn't you send for us when you first went out to fight the Midianites?" And they argued heatedly with Gideon.

²But Gideon replied, "What have I done compared to you? Aren't the last grapes of Ephraim's harvest better than the entire crop of my little clan of Abiezer? ³God gave you victory over Oreb and Zeeb, the generals of the Midianite army. What have I done compared to that?" When the men of Ephraim heard Gideon's answer, they were no longer angry.

⁴Gideon then crossed the Jordan River with his three hundred men, and though they were exhausted, they continued to chase the enemy. ⁵When they reached Succoth, Gideon asked the leaders of the town, "Will you please give my warriors some food? They are very tired. I am chasing Zebah and Zalmunna, the kings of Midian."

⁶But the leaders of Succoth replied, "You haven't caught Zebah and Zalmunna yet. Catch them first, and then we will feed your warriors."

⁷So Gideon said, "After the LORD gives me victory over Zebah and Zalmunna, I will return and tear your flesh with the thorns and briers of the wilderness."

⁸From there Gideon went up to Peniel* and asked for food, but he got the same answer. ⁹So he said to the people of Peniel, "After I return in victory, I will tear down this tower."

¹⁰By this time Zebah and Zalmunna were in Karkor with a remnant of 15,000 warriors—all that remained of the allied armies of the east—for 120,000 had already been killed.

¹¹Gideon circled around by the caravan route east of Nobah and Jogbehah, taking the Midianite army by surprise. ¹²Zebah and Zalmunna, the two Midianite kings, fled, but Gideon chased them down and captured all their warriors.

¹³After this, Gideon returned by way of Heres Pass. ¹⁴There he captured a young man from Succoth and demanded that he write down the names of all the seventy-seven rulers and leaders in the town. ¹⁵Gideon then returned to Succoth and said to the leaders, "Here are Zebah and Zalmunna. When we were here before, you taunted me, saying, 'You haven't caught Zebah and Zalmunna yet. Catch them first, and then we will feed your exhausted warriors.'" ¹⁶Then Gideon took the leaders of the town and taught them a lesson, punishing them with thorns and briers from the wilderness. ¹⁷He also knocked down the tower of Peniel and killed all the men in the town.

¹⁸Then Gideon asked Zebah and Zalmunna, "The men you killed at Tabor—what were they like?"

"Like you," they replied. "They all had the look of a king's son."

¹⁹"They were my brothers!" Gideon exclaimed. "As surely as the LORD lives, I wouldn't kill you if you hadn't killed them."

²⁰Turning to Jether, his oldest son, he said, "Kill them!" But Jether did not draw his sword, for he was only a boy and was afraid.

²¹Then Zebah and Zalmunna said to Gideon, "Don't ask a boy to do a man's job! Do it yourself!" So Gideon killed them both and took the royal ornaments from the necks of their camels.

GIDEON'S SACRED EPHOD

²²Then the Israelites said to Gideon, "Be our ruler! You and your son and your grandson will be our rulers, for you have rescued us from Midian."

²³But Gideon replied, "I will not rule over you, nor will my son. The LORD will rule over

8:8 Hebrew *Penuel,* a variant name for Peniel; also in 8:9, 17.

you! 24However, I have one request. Each of you can give me an earring out of the treasures you collected from your fallen enemies." (The enemies, being Ishmaelites, all wore gold earrings.)

25"Gladly!" they replied. They spread out a cloak, and each one threw in a gold earring he had gathered. 26The weight of the gold earrings was forty-three pounds,* not including the crescents and pendants, the royal clothing of the kings, or the chains around the necks of their camels. 27Gideon made a sacred ephod from the gold and put it in Ophrah, his hometown. But soon all the Israelites prostituted themselves by worshiping it, and it became a trap for Gideon and his family.

28That is the story of how Israel subdued Midian, which never recovered. Throughout the rest of Gideon's lifetime—about forty years—the land was at peace.

29Then Gideon* son of Joash returned home. 30He had seventy sons, for he had many wives. 31He also had a concubine in Shechem, who bore him a son named Abimelech. 32Gideon died when he was very old, and he was buried in the grave of his father, Joash, at Ophrah in the land of the clan of Abiezer.

33As soon as Gideon was dead, the Israelites prostituted themselves by worshiping the images of Baal, making Baal-berith their god. 34They forgot the LORD their God, who had rescued them from all their enemies surrounding them. 35Nor did they show any loyalty to the family of Jerubbaal (that is, Gideon), despite all the good he had done for Israel.

ABIMELECH RULES OVER SHECHEM

9 One day Gideon's* son Abimelech went to Shechem to visit his mother's brothers. He said to them and to the rest of his mother's family, 2"Ask the people of Shechem whether they want to be ruled by all seventy of Gideon's sons or by one man. And remember, I am your own flesh and blood!"

3So Abimelech's uncles spoke to all the people of Shechem on his behalf. And after listening to their proposal, they decided in favor of Abimelech because he was their relative. 4They gave him seventy silver coins from the temple of Baal-berith, which he used to hire some soldiers who agreed to follow him. 5He took the soldiers to his father's home at Ophrah, and there, on one stone, they killed all seventy of his half brothers. But the youngest brother, Jotham, escaped and hid. 6Then the people of Shechem and Beth-millo called a meeting under the oak beside the pillar* at Shechem and made Abimelech their king.

JOTHAM'S PARABLE

7When Jotham heard about this, he climbed to the top of Mount Gerizim and shouted, "Listen to me, people of Shechem! Listen to me if you want God to listen to you! 8Once upon a time the trees decided to elect a king. First they said to the olive tree, 'Be our king!' 9But it refused, saying, 'Should I quit producing the olive oil that blesses both God and people, just to wave back and forth over the trees?'

10"Then they said to the fig tree, 'You be our king!' 11But the fig tree also refused, saying, 'Should I quit producing my sweet fruit just to wave back and forth over the trees?'

12"Then they said to the grapevine, 'You be our king!' 13But the grapevine replied, 'Should I quit producing the wine that cheers both God and people, just to wave back and forth over the trees?'

14"Then all the trees finally turned to the thornbush and said, 'Come, you be our king!' 15And the thornbush replied, 'If you truly want to make me your king, come and take shelter in my shade. If not, let fire come out from me and devour the cedars of Lebanon.'

16"Now make sure you have acted honorably and in good faith by making Abimelech your king, and that you have done right by Gideon* and all of his descendants. Have you

---

8:26 Hebrew *1,700 shekels* [19.4 kilograms]. 8:29 Hebrew *Jerubbaal;* see 6:32. 9:1 Hebrew *Jerubbaal's* (see 6:32); also in 9:2, 24. 9:6 The meaning of the Hebrew is uncertain. 9:16 Hebrew *Jerubbaal* (see 6:32); also in 9:19, 28, 57.

treated my father with the honor he deserves? [17]For he fought for you and risked his life when he rescued you from the Midianites. [18]But now you have revolted against my father and his descendants, killing his seventy sons on one stone. And you have chosen his slave woman's son, Abimelech, to be your king just because he is your relative. [19]If you have acted honorably and in good faith toward Gideon and his descendants, then may you find joy in Abimelech, and may he find joy in you. [20]But if you have not acted in good faith, then may fire come out from Abimelech and devour the people of Shechem and Beth-millo; and may fire come out from the people of Shechem and Beth-millo and devour Abimelech!" [21]Then Jotham escaped and lived in Beer because he was afraid of his brother Abimelech.

Shechem's Revolt against Abimelech

[22]After Abimelech had ruled over Israel for three years, [23]God stirred up trouble* between Abimelech and the people of Shechem, and they revolted. [24]In the events that followed, God punished Abimelech and the men of Shechem for murdering Gideon's seventy sons. [25]The people of Shechem set an ambush for Abimelech on the hilltops and robbed everyone who passed that way. But someone warned Abimelech about their plot.

[26]At that time Gaal son of Ebed moved to Shechem with his brothers and gained the confidence of the people of Shechem. [27]During the annual harvest festival at Shechem, held in the temple of the local god, the wine flowed freely, and everyone began cursing Abimelech. [28]"Who is Abimelech?" Gaal shouted. "He's not a true descendant of Shechem!* Why should we be Abimelech's servants? He's merely the son of Gideon, and Zebul is his administrator. Serve the men of Hamor, who are Shechem's true descendants. Why should we serve Abimelech? [29]If I were in

charge, I would get rid of Abimelech. I would say* to him, 'Get some more soldiers, and come out and fight!'"

[30]But when Zebul, the leader of the city, heard what Gaal was saying, he was furious. [31]He sent messengers to Abimelech in Arumah,* telling him, "Gaal son of Ebed and his brothers have come to live in Shechem, and now they are inciting the city to rebel against you. [32]Come by night with an army and hide out in the fields. [33]In the morning, as soon as it is daylight, storm the city. When Gaal and those who are with him come out against you, you can do with them as you wish."

[34]So Abimelech and his men went by night and split into four groups, stationing themselves around Shechem. [35]Gaal was standing at the city gates when Abimelech and his army came out of hiding. [36]When Gaal saw them, he said to Zebul, "Look, there are people coming down from the hilltops!"

Zebul replied, "It's just the shadows of the hills that look like men."

[37]But again Gaal said, "No, people are coming down from the hills.* And another group is coming down the road past the Diviners' Oak.*"

[38]Then Zebul turned on him triumphantly. "Now where is that big mouth of yours?" he demanded. "Wasn't it you that said, 'Who is Abimelech, and why should we be his servants?' The men you mocked are right outside the city! Go out and fight them!"

[39]Gaal then led the men of Shechem into battle against Abimelech, [40]but he was defeated and ran away. Many of Shechem's warriors were killed, and the ground was covered with dead bodies all the way to the city gate. [41]Abimelech stayed in Arumah, and Zebul drove Gaal and his brothers out of Shechem.

[42]The next day the people of Shechem went out into the fields to battle. When Abimelech heard about it, [43]he divided his men into three groups and set an ambush in the fields. When

9:23 Hebrew *sent a disturbing spirit.*   9:28 Hebrew *Who is Shechem?*   9:29 As in Greek version; Hebrew reads *And he said.*
9:31 Hebrew *Tormah;* see 9:41.   9:37a Or *the center of the land.*   9:37b Hebrew *Elon-meonenim.*

Abimelech saw the people coming out of the city, he and his men jumped up from their hiding places and attacked them. [44]Abimelech and his group stormed the city gate to keep the men of Shechem from getting back in, while Abimelech's other two groups cut them down in the fields. [45]The battle went on all day before Abimelech finally captured the city. He killed the people, leveled the city, and scattered salt all over the ground.

[46]When the people who lived in the tower of Shechem heard what had happened, they took refuge within the walls of the temple of Baal-berith.* [47]Someone reported to Abimelech that the people were gathered together in the temple, [48]so he led his forces to Mount Zalmon. He took an ax and chopped some branches from a tree, and he put them on his shoulder. "Quick, do as I have done!" he told his men. [49]So each of them cut down some branches, following Abimelech's example. They piled the branches against the walls of the temple and set them on fire. So all the people who had lived in the tower of Shechem died, about a thousand men and women.

[50]Then Abimelech attacked the city of Thebez and captured it. [51]But there was a strong tower inside the city, and the entire population fled to it. They barricaded themselves in and climbed up to the roof of the tower. [52]Abimelech followed them to attack the tower. But as he prepared to set fire to the entrance, [53]a woman on the roof threw down a millstone that landed on Abimelech's head and crushed his skull. [54]He said to his young armor bearer, "Draw your sword and kill me! Don't let it be said that a woman killed Abimelech!" So the young man stabbed him with his sword, and he died. [55]When Abimelech's men saw that he was dead, they disbanded and returned to their homes.

[56]Thus, God punished Abimelech for the evil he had done against his father by murdering his seventy brothers. [57]God also punished the men of Shechem for all their evil. So the curse of Jotham son of Gideon came true.

TOLA BECOMES ISRAEL'S JUDGE

10 After Abimelech's death, Tola, the son of Puah and descendant of Dodo, came to rescue Israel. He was from the tribe of Issachar but lived in the town of Shamir in the hill country of Ephraim. [2]He was Israel's judge for twenty-three years. When he died, he was buried in Shamir.

JAIR BECOMES ISRAEL'S JUDGE

[3]After Tola died, a man from Gilead named Jair judged Israel for twenty-two years. [4]His thirty sons rode around on thirty donkeys, and they owned thirty towns in the land of Gilead, which are still called the Towns of Jair.* [5]When Jair died, he was buried in Kamon.

THE AMMONITES OPPRESS ISRAEL

[6]Again the Israelites did evil in the LORD's sight. They worshiped images of Baal and Ashtoreth, and the gods of Aram, Sidon, Moab, Ammon, and Philistia. Not only this, but they abandoned the LORD and no longer served him at all. [7]So the LORD burned with anger against Israel, and he handed them over to the Philistines and the Ammonites, [8]who began to oppress them that year. For eighteen years they oppressed all the Israelites east of the Jordan River in the land of the Amorites (that is, in Gilead). [9]The Ammonites also crossed to the west side of the Jordan and attacked Judah, Benjamin, and Ephraim. The Israelites were in great distress. [10]Finally, they cried out to the LORD, saying, "We have sinned against you because we have abandoned you as our God and have served the images of Baal."

[11]The LORD replied, "Did I not rescue you from the Egyptians, the Amorites, the Ammonites, the Philistines, [12]the Sidonians, the Amalekites, and the Maonites? When they oppressed you, you cried out to me, and I rescued you. [13]Yet you have abandoned me and served other gods. So I will not rescue you anymore. [14]Go and cry out to the gods you

---

9:46 Hebrew *El-berith*, another name for Baal-berith; compare 9:4. **10:4** Hebrew *Havvoth-jair*.

have chosen! Let them rescue you in your hour of distress!"

¹⁵But the Israelites pleaded with the LORD and said, "We have sinned. Punish us as you see fit, only rescue us today from our enemies." ¹⁶Then the Israelites put aside their foreign gods and served the LORD. And he was grieved by their misery.

¹⁷At that time the armies of Ammon had gathered for war and were camped in Gilead, preparing to attack Israel's army at Mizpah. ¹⁸The leaders of Gilead said to each other, "Whoever attacks the Ammonites first will become ruler over all the people of Gilead."

JEPHTHAH BECOMES ISRAEL'S JUDGE

11 Now Jephthah of Gilead was a great warrior. He was the son of Gilead, but his mother was a prostitute. ²Gilead's wife also had several sons, and when these half brothers grew up, they chased Jephthah off the land. "You will not get any of our father's inheritance," they said, "for you are the son of a prostitute." ³So Jephthah fled from his brothers and lived in the land of Tob. Soon he had a large band of rebels following him.

⁴At about this time, the Ammonites began their war against Israel. ⁵When the Ammonites attacked, the leaders of Gilead sent for Jephthah in the land of Tob. They said, ⁶"Come and be our commander! Help us fight the Ammonites!"

⁷But Jephthah said to them, "Aren't you the ones who hated me and drove me from my father's house? Why do you come to me now when you're in trouble?"

⁸"Because we need you," they replied. "If you will lead us in battle against the Ammonites, we will make you ruler over all the people of Gilead."

⁹Jephthah said, "If I come with you and if the LORD gives me victory over the Ammonites, will you really make me ruler over all the people?"

¹⁰"The LORD is our witness," the leaders replied. "We promise to do whatever you say."

¹¹So Jephthah went with the leaders of Gilead, and he became their ruler and commander of the army. At Mizpah, in the presence of the LORD, Jephthah repeated what he had said to the leaders.

¹²Then Jephthah sent messengers to the king of Ammon, demanding to know why Israel was being attacked. ¹³The king of Ammon answered Jephthah's messengers, "When the Israelites came out of Egypt, they stole my land from the Arnon River to the Jabbok River and all the way to the Jordan. Now then, give back the land peaceably."

¹⁴Jephthah sent this message back to the Ammonite king:

¹⁵"This is what Jephthah says: Israel did not steal any land from Moab or Ammon. ¹⁶When the people of Israel arrived at Kadesh on their journey from Egypt after crossing the Red Sea,* ¹⁷they sent messengers to the king of Edom asking for permission to pass through his land. But their request was denied. Then they asked the king of Moab for similar permission, but he wouldn't let them pass through either. So the people of Israel stayed in Kadesh.

¹⁸"Finally, they went around Edom and Moab through the wilderness. They traveled along Moab's eastern border and camped on the other side of the Arnon River. But they never once crossed the Arnon River into Moab. ¹⁹"Then Israel sent messengers to King Sihon of the Amorites, who ruled from Heshbon, asking for permission to cross through his land to get to their destination. ²⁰But King Sihon didn't trust Israel to pass through his land. Instead, he mobilized his army at Jahaz and attacked them. ²¹But the LORD, the God of Israel, gave his people victory over King Sihon. So Israel took control of all the land of

11:16 Hebrew *sea of reeds.*

My Daily Worship

RETURN TO YOUR FIRST LOVE

JUDGES 9:1–12:15

But the Israelites pleaded with the LORD and said, "We have sinned. Punish us as you see fit, only rescue us today from our enemies" (10:15).

[i reflect]

"I'll never leave you," the husband whispered tenderly to his new bride on their honeymoon. Five years later, she came home to a note that read, "I'm leaving you for another woman." Forgotten was the promise given that honeymoon night. Ignored and discarded were the marriage vows so solemnly exchanged.

Our faith often resembles that of a wayward spouse. "Lord, I worship you. Only you are worthy of praise," we shout when our faith is new. We sing praises. We study his Word. We tell others of the wondrous things he has done. We do good works. But, little by little, our enthusiasm wanes. Our attention wanders, and we coast along. We allow sin to creep in and separate us from God.

The tale is a familiar one. "We would never forsake the LORD and worship other gods. . . . We, too, will serve the LORD, for he alone is our God" (Joshua 24:16,18). So said the people of Israel in the last days of Joshua. But as years went by in the time of Judges, the people forgot the mighty acts of the Lord. They began to worship the gods Baal and Ashtoreth, and other gods of the nations around them. Eventually they did not worship the Lord at all.

We may forget all about the Lord, but he does not forget about us. Just as he allowed Israel to suffer at the hands of their enemies, he allows us to suffer in order to bring us back to himself. The worship God desires comes from a broken and repentant heart. In his mercy, he forgives and restores us. "Though he brings grief, he also shows compassion according to the greatness of his unfailing love" (Lamentations 3:32).

How far have you wandered from your first love? What will it take to restore and refresh your relationship with the One whose love is unfailing? Use this time to renew your vows with him as an act of worship.

[i pray]

Lord, you are my first love, but I have drifted away. I have allowed sin to creep into my life and separate me from your love. Please forgive me. Renew my spirit that I might worship you with my whole heart.

[i respond]

Consider the ways you have wandered from God in the past week. Write a vow of renewed love for God, telling him specifically how you plan to refresh and restore your relationship with him.

the Amorites, who lived in that region, [22]from the Arnon River to the Jabbok River, and from the wilderness to the Jordan.

[23]"So you see, it was the LORD, the God of Israel, who took away the land from the Amorites and gave it to Israel. Why, then, should we give it to you? [24]You keep whatever your god Chemosh gives you, and we will keep whatever the LORD our God gives us. [25]Are you any better than Balak son of Zippor, king of Moab? Did he try to make a case against Israel for disputed land? Did he go to war? No, of course not. [26]But now after three hundred years you make an issue of this! Israel has been living here all this time, spread across the land from Heshbon to Aroer and in all the towns along the Arnon River. Why have you made no effort to recover it before now? [27]I have not sinned against you. Rather, you have wronged me by attacking me. Let the LORD, who is judge, decide today which of us is right—Israel or Ammon."

[28]But the king of Ammon paid no attention to Jephthah's message.

JEPHTHAH'S VOW

[29]At that time the Spirit of the LORD came upon Jephthah, and he went throughout the land of Gilead and Manasseh, including Mizpah in Gilead, and led an army against the Ammonites. [30]And Jephthah made a vow to the LORD. He said, "If you give me victory over the Ammonites, [31]I will give to the LORD the first thing coming out of my house to greet me when I return in triumph. I will sacrifice it as a burnt offering."

[32]So Jephthah led his army against the Ammonites, and the LORD gave him victory. [33]He thoroughly defeated the Ammonites from Aroer to an area near Minnith—twenty towns—and as far away as Abel-keramim. Thus Israel subdued the Ammonites.

[34]When Jephthah returned home to Miz-pah, his daughter—his only child—ran out to meet him, playing on a tambourine and dancing for joy. [35]When he saw her, he tore his clothes in anguish. "My daughter!" he cried out. "My heart is breaking! What a tragedy that you came out to greet me. For I have made a vow to the LORD and cannot take it back."

[36]And she said, "Father, you have made a promise to the LORD. You must do to me what you have promised, for the LORD has given you a great victory over your enemies, the Ammonites. [37]But first let me go up and roam in the hills and weep with my friends for two months, because I will die a virgin."

[38]"You may go," Jephthah said. And he let her go away for two months. She and her friends went into the hills and wept because she would never have children. [39]When she returned home, her father kept his vow, and she died a virgin. So it has become a custom in Israel [40]for young Israelite women to go away for four days each year to lament the fate of Jephthah's daughter.

EPHRAIM FIGHTS WITH JEPHTHAH

12 Then the tribe of Ephraim mobilized its army and crossed over to Zaphon. They sent this message to Jephthah: "Why didn't you call for us to help you fight against Ammon? We are going to burn down your house with you in it!"

[2]"I summoned you at the beginning of the dispute, but you refused to come!" Jephthah said. "You failed to help us in our struggle against Ammon. [3]So I risked my life and went to battle without you, and the LORD gave me victory over the Ammonites. So why have you come to fight me?"

[4]The leaders of Ephraim responded, "The men of Gilead are nothing more than rejects from Ephraim and Manasseh." So Jephthah called out his army and attacked the men of Ephraim and defeated them.

[5]Jephthah captured the shallows of the Jordan, and whenever a fugitive from Ephraim

tried to go back across, the men of Gilead would challenge him. "Are you a member of the tribe of Ephraim?" they would ask. If the man said, "No, I'm not," ⁶they would tell him to say "Shibboleth." If he was from Ephraim, he would say "Sibboleth," because people from Ephraim cannot pronounce the word correctly. Then they would take him and kill him at the shallows of the Jordan River. So forty-two thousand Ephraimites were killed at that time.

⁷Jephthah was Israel's judge for six years. When he died, he was buried in one of the towns of Gilead.

IBZAN BECOMES ISRAEL'S JUDGE

⁸After Jephthah, Ibzan became Israel's judge. He lived in Bethlehem, ⁹and he had thirty sons and thirty daughters. He married his daughters to men outside his clan and brought in thirty young women from outside his clan to marry his sons. Ibzan judged Israel for seven years. ¹⁰When he died, he was buried at Bethlehem.

ELON BECOMES ISRAEL'S JUDGE

¹¹After him, Elon from Zebulun became Israel's judge. He judged Israel for ten years. ¹²When he died, he was buried at Aijalon in Zebulun.

ABDON BECOMES ISRAEL'S JUDGE

¹³After Elon died, Abdon son of Hillel, from Pirathon, became Israel's judge. ¹⁴He had forty sons and thirty grandsons, who rode on seventy donkeys. He was Israel's judge for eight years. ¹⁵Then he died and was buried at Pirathon in Ephraim, in the hill country of the Amalekites.

THE BIRTH OF SAMSON

13 Again the Israelites did what was evil in the LORD's sight, so the LORD handed them over to the Philistines, who kept them in subjection for forty years.

²In those days, a man named Manoah from the tribe of Dan lived in the town of Zorah. His wife was unable to become pregnant, and they had no children. ³The angel of the LORD appeared to Manoah's wife and said, "Even though you have been unable to have children, you will soon become pregnant and give birth to a son. ⁴You must not drink wine or any other alcoholic drink or eat any forbidden food. ⁵You will become pregnant and give birth to a son, and his hair must never be cut. For he will be dedicated to God as a Nazirite from birth. He will rescue Israel from the Philistines."

⁶The woman ran and told her husband, "A man of God appeared to me! He was like one of God's angels, terrifying to look at. I didn't ask where he was from, and he didn't tell me his name. ⁷But he told me, 'You will become pregnant and give birth to a son. You must not drink wine or any other alcoholic drink or eat

any forbidden food. For your son will be dedicated to God as a Nazirite from the moment of his birth until the day of his death.'"

⁸Then Manoah prayed to the LORD. He said, "Lord, please let the man of God come back to us again and give us more instructions about this son who is to be born."

⁹God answered his prayer, and the angel of God appeared once again to his wife as she was sitting in the field. But her husband, Manoah, was not with her. ¹⁰So she quickly ran and told her husband, "The man who appeared to me the other day is here again!"

¹¹Manoah ran back with his wife and asked, "Are you the man who talked to my wife the other day?"

"Yes," he replied, "I am."

¹²So Manoah asked him, "When your words come true, what kind of rules should govern the boy's life and work?"

¹³The angel of the LORD replied, "Be sure your wife follows the instructions I gave her. ¹⁴She must not eat grapes or raisins, drink wine or any other alcoholic drink, or eat any forbidden food."

¹⁵Then Manoah said to the angel of the LORD, "Please stay here until we can prepare a young goat for you to eat."

¹⁶"I will stay," the angel of the LORD replied, "but I will not eat anything. However, you may prepare a burnt offering as a sacrifice to the LORD." (Manoah didn't realize it was the angel of the LORD.)

¹⁷Then Manoah asked the angel of the LORD, "What is your name? For when all this comes true, we want to honor you."

¹⁸"Why do you ask my name?" the angel of the LORD replied. "You wouldn't understand if I told you."

¹⁹Then Manoah took a young goat and a grain offering and offered it on a rock as a sacrifice to the LORD. And as Manoah and his wife watched, the LORD did an amazing thing. ²⁰As the flames from the altar shot up toward the sky, the angel of the LORD ascended in the fire. When Manoah and his wife saw this, they fell with their faces to the ground.

²¹The angel did not appear again to Manoah and his wife. Manoah finally realized it was the angel of the LORD, ²²and he said to his wife, "We will die, for we have seen God!"

²³But his wife said, "If the LORD were going to kill us, he wouldn't have accepted our burnt offering and grain offering. He wouldn't have appeared to us and told us this wonderful thing and done these miracles."

²⁴When her son was born, they named him Samson. And the LORD blessed him as he grew up. ²⁵And in Mahaneh-dan, which is located between the towns of Zorah and Eshtaol, the Spirit of the LORD began to take hold of him.

SAMSON'S RIDDLE

14 One day when Samson was in Timnah, he noticed a certain Philistine woman. ²When he returned home, he told his father and mother, "I want to marry a young Philistine woman I saw in Timnah."

³His father and mother objected strenuously, "Isn't there one woman in our tribe or among all the Israelites you could marry? Why must you go to the pagan Philistines to find a wife?"

But Samson told his father, "Get her for me. She is the one I want." ⁴His father and mother didn't realize the LORD was at work in this, creating an opportunity to disrupt the Philistines, who ruled over Israel at that time.

⁵As Samson and his parents were going down to Timnah, a young lion attacked Samson near the vineyards of Timnah. ⁶At that moment

> *True worship is when the spirit,*
> *the immortal and invisible part*
> *of man, speaks to and meets*
> *with God, who is immortal*
> *and invisible.*
>
> WILLIAM BARCLAY

the Spirit of the LORD powerfully took control of him, and he ripped the lion's jaws apart with his bare hands. He did it as easily as if it were a young goat. But he didn't tell his father or mother about it. ⁷When Samson arrived in Timnah, he talked with the woman and was very pleased with her.

⁸Later, when he returned to Timnah for the wedding, he turned off the path to look at the carcass of the lion. And he found that a swarm of bees had made some honey in the carcass. ⁹He scooped some of the honey into his hands and ate it along the way. He also gave some to his father and mother, and they ate it. But he didn't tell them he had taken the honey from the carcass of the lion.

¹⁰As his father was making final arrangements for the marriage, Samson threw a party at Timnah, as was the custom of the day. ¹¹Thirty young men from the town were invited to be his companions. ¹²Samson said to them, "Let me tell you a riddle. If you solve my riddle during these seven days of the celebration, I will give you thirty plain linen robes and thirty fancy robes. ¹³But if you can't solve it, then you must give me thirty linen robes and thirty fancy robes."

"All right," they agreed, "let's hear your riddle."
¹⁴So he said:

"From the one who eats came something to eat;
    out of the strong came something sweet."

Three days later they were still trying to figure it out. ¹⁵On the fourth* day they said to Samson's wife, "Get the answer to the riddle from your husband, or we will burn down your father's house with you in it. Did you invite us to this party just to make us poor?"

¹⁶So Samson's wife came to him in tears and said, "You don't love me; you hate me! You have given my people a riddle, but you haven't told me the answer."

"I haven't even given the answer to my father or mother," he replied. "Why should I tell you?" ¹⁷So she cried whenever she was with him and kept it up for the rest of the celebration. At last, on the seventh day, he told her the answer because of her persistent nagging. Then she gave the answer to the young men.

¹⁸So before sunset of the seventh day, the men of the town came to Samson with their answer:

"What is sweeter than honey?
    What is stronger than a lion?"

Samson replied, "If you hadn't plowed with my heifer, you wouldn't have found the answer to my riddle!" ¹⁹Then the Spirit of the LORD powerfully took control of him. He went down to the town of Ashkelon, killed thirty men, took their belongings, and gave their clothing to the men who had answered his riddle. But Samson was furious about what had happened, and he went back home to live with his father and mother. ²⁰So his wife was given in marriage to the man who had been Samson's best man at the wedding.

SAMSON'S VENGEANCE ON THE PHILISTINES

15 Later on, during the wheat harvest, Samson took a young goat as a present to his wife. He intended to sleep with her, but her father wouldn't let him in. ²"I really thought you hated her," her father explained, "so I gave her in marriage to your best man. But look, her sister is more beautiful than she is. Marry her instead."

³Samson said, "This time I cannot be blamed for everything I am going to do to you Philistines." ⁴Then he went out and caught three hundred foxes. He tied their tails together in pairs, and he fastened a torch to each pair of tails. ⁵Then he lit the torches and let the foxes run through the fields of the Philistines. He burned all their grain to the ground, including the grain still in piles and

14:15 As in Greek version; Hebrew reads *seventh*.

all that had been bundled. He also destroyed their grapevines and olive trees.

⁶"Who did this?" the Philistines demanded.

"Samson," was the reply, "because his father-in-law from Timnah gave Samson's wife to be married to his best man." So the Philistines went and got the woman and her father and burned them to death.

⁷"Because you did this," Samson vowed, "I will take my revenge on you, and I won't stop until I'm satisfied!" ⁸So he attacked the Philistines with great fury and killed many of them. Then he went to live in a cave in the rock of Etam.

⁹The Philistines retaliated by setting up camp in Judah and raiding the town of Lehi. ¹⁰The men of Judah asked the Philistines, "Why have you attacked us?"

The Philistines replied, "We've come to capture Samson. We have come to pay him back for what he did to us."

¹¹So three thousand men of Judah went down to get Samson at the cave in the rock of Etam. They said to Samson, "Don't you realize the Philistines rule over us? What are you doing to us?"

But Samson replied, "I only paid them back for what they did to me."

¹²But the men of Judah told him, "We have come to tie you up and hand you over to the Philistines."

"All right," Samson said. "But promise that you won't kill me yourselves."

¹³"We will tie you up and hand you over to the Philistines," they replied. "We won't kill you." So they tied him up with two new ropes and led him away from the rock.

¹⁴As Samson arrived at Lehi, the Philistines came shouting in triumph. But the Spirit of the LORD powerfully took control of Samson, and he snapped the ropes on his arms as if they were burnt strands of flax, and they fell from his wrists. ¹⁵Then he picked up a donkey's jawbone that was lying on the ground and killed a thousand Philistines with it. ¹⁶And Samson said,

"With the jawbone of a donkey,
    I've made heaps on heaps!
With the jawbone of a donkey,
    I've killed a thousand men!"

¹⁷When he finished speaking, he threw away the jawbone; and the place was named Jawbone Hill.*

¹⁸Now Samson was very thirsty, and he cried out to the LORD, "You have accomplished this great victory by the strength of your servant. Must I now die of thirst and fall into the hands of these pagan people?" ¹⁹So God caused water to gush out of a hollow in the ground at Lehi, and Samson was revived as he drank. Then he named that place "The Spring of the One Who Cried Out,"* and it is still in Lehi to this day.

²⁰Samson was Israel's judge for twenty years, while the Philistines ruled the land.

SAMSON REMOVES GAZA'S GATES

16 One day Samson went to the Philistine city of Gaza and spent the night with a prostitute. ²Word soon spread that Samson was there, so the men of Gaza gathered together and waited all night at the city gates. They kept quiet during the night, saying to themselves, "When the light of morning comes, we will kill him."

³But Samson stayed in bed only until midnight. Then he got up, took hold of the city gates with its two posts, and lifted them, bar and all, right out of the ground. He put them on his shoulders and carried them all the way to the top of the hill across from Hebron.

SAMSON AND DELILAH

⁴Later Samson fell in love with a woman named Delilah, who lived in the valley of Sorek. ⁵The leaders of the Philistines went to her and said, "Find out from Samson what makes him so strong and how he can be overpowered and tied up securely. Then each of us will give you eleven hundred pieces* of silver."

15:17 Hebrew *Ramath-lehi.*   15:19 Hebrew *En-hakkore.*   16:5 Hebrew *1,100 shekels,* about 28 pounds or 12.5 kilograms in weight.

My Daily Worship

— March 1 —

BREAK DOWN YOUR WALLS!

JUDGES 13:1–16:31

"Let me die with the Philistines," he prayed. And the temple crashed down
on the Philistine leaders and all the people. So he killed more people
when he died than he had during his entire lifetime (16:30).

[i reflect]

In his last moments, Samson finally placed his life in God's hands. Alone and sightless, his amazing potential had been humbled and humiliated as a result of his own poor choices. God provided tools to build a life that could have helped many of his people, but instead Samson constructed a life that separated him from God. Samson's hands did not make the temple walls that surrounded him, but the invisible prison that actually held him resulted from his own efforts.

The walls of separation are built by sin. Only repentance can tear it down. Grinding grain in a Philistine prison, Samson had time to reflect on his sin and ask forgiveness. The wall that had separated him from God crumbled. Samson asked the Lord to allow him to defeat the Philistines one last time. The strength of the Lord returned to Samson and he brought down the Philistine temple in a spectacular crash.

You sing of his mercy and you lift your arms in praise, but in your heart you are far from God. A stone wall surrounds you and keeps you from the One who is worthy of all praise. Some of the stones are unconfessed sin. Others are needless worry. Many have a "to do" list engraved there. Every stone is a barrier between you and the one true God.

Take a look at the wall that separates you from God. Is the shame of unconfessed sin keeping you from wholehearted worship? Do you worry ceaselessly, or do you humbly trust God with your future? Do you entirely fill up your day with activity, or do you reserve time to worship God? When we cherish sin in our hearts we lose the desire to worship. "But if we confess our sins to him, he is faithful and just to forgive us and to cleanse us from every wrong" (1 John 1:9). Tear down that wall!

[i pray]

Father, you are so holy and I am so sinful. Only you can release me from the power of sin.
In your mercy, forgive me and allow me to worship you with all my heart.

[i respond]

What one sin contributes the most to the wall that inhibits your own growth? Find a friend today, in person or on the phone, and confess that sin. Ask for prayer.

⁶So Delilah said to Samson, "Please tell me what makes you so strong and what it would take to tie you up securely."

⁷Samson replied, "If I am tied up with seven new bowstrings that have not yet been dried, I will be as weak as anyone else."

⁸So the Philistine leaders brought Delilah seven new bowstrings, and she tied Samson up with them. ⁹She had hidden some men in one of the rooms of her house, and she cried out, "Samson! The Philistines have come to capture you!" But Samson snapped the bowstrings as if they were string that had been burned in a fire. So the secret of his strength was not discovered.

¹⁰Afterward Delilah said to him, "You made fun of me and told me a lie! Now please tell me how you can be tied up securely."

¹¹Samson replied, "If I am tied up with brand-new ropes that have never been used, I will be as weak as anyone else."

¹²So Delilah took new ropes and tied him up with them. The men were hiding in the room as before, and again Delilah cried out, "Samson! The Philistines have come to capture you!" But Samson snapped the ropes from his arms as if they were thread.

¹³Then Delilah said, "You have been making fun of me and telling me lies! Won't you please tell me how you can be tied up securely?"

Samson replied, "If you weave the seven braids of my hair into the fabric on your loom and tighten it with the loom shuttle,* I will be as weak as anyone else."

So while he slept, Delilah wove the seven braids of his hair into the fabric ¹⁴and tightened it with the loom shuttle. Again she cried out, "Samson! The Philistines have come to capture you!" But Samson woke up, pulled back the loom shuttle, and yanked his hair away from the loom and the fabric.

¹⁵Then Delilah pouted, "How can you say you love me when you don't confide in me? You've made fun of me three times now, and you still haven't told me what makes you so strong!"

¹⁶So day after day she nagged him until he couldn't stand it any longer.

¹⁷Finally, Samson told her his secret. "My hair has never been cut," he confessed, "for I was dedicated to God as a Nazirite from birth. If my head were shaved, my strength would leave me, and I would become as weak as anyone else."

¹⁸Delilah realized he had finally told her the truth, so she sent for the Philistine leaders. "Come back one more time," she said, "for he has told me everything." So the Philistine leaders returned and brought the money with them. ¹⁹Delilah lulled Samson to sleep with his head in her lap, and she called in a man to shave off his hair, making his capture certain. And his strength left him. ²⁰Then she cried out, "Samson! The Philistines have come to capture you!"

When he woke up, he thought, "I will do as before and shake myself free." But he didn't realize the LORD had left him.

²¹So the Philistines captured him and gouged out his eyes. They took him to Gaza, where he was bound with bronze chains and made to grind grain in the prison. ²²But before long his hair began to grow back.

SAMSON'S FINAL VICTORY

²³The Philistine leaders held a great festival, offering sacrifices and praising their god, Dagon. They said, "Our god has given us victory over our enemy Samson!"

²⁴When the people saw him, they praised their god, saying, "Our god has delivered our enemy to us! The one who killed so many of us is now in our power!"

²⁵Half drunk by now, the people demanded, "Bring out Samson so he can perform for us!" So he was brought from the prison and made to stand at the center of the temple, between the two pillars supporting the roof. ²⁶Samson said to the servant who was leading him by the hand, "Place my hands against the two pillars. I want to rest against them." ²⁷The temple was completely filled with people. All the Philistine leaders were there, and

16:13 As in Greek version; Hebrew lacks *on your loom and tighten it with the loom shuttle.*

there were about three thousand on the roof who were watching Samson and making fun of him.

²⁸Then Samson prayed to the LORD, "Sovereign LORD, remember me again. O God, please strengthen me one more time so that I may pay back the Philistines for the loss of my eyes." ²⁹Then Samson put his hands on the center pillars of the temple and pushed against them with all his might. ³⁰"Let me die with the Philistines," he prayed. And the temple crashed down on the Philistine leaders and all the people. So he killed more people when he died than he had during his entire lifetime.

³¹Later his brothers and other relatives went down to get his body. They took him back home and buried him between Zorah and Eshtaol, where his father, Manoah, was buried. Samson had been Israel's judge for twenty years.

MICAH'S IDOLS

17 A man named Micah lived in the hill country of Ephraim. ²One day he said to his mother, "I heard you curse the thief who stole eleven hundred pieces* of silver from you. Well, here they are. I was the one who took them."

"The LORD bless you for admitting it," his mother replied. ³He returned the money to her, and she said, "I now dedicate these silver coins to the LORD. In honor of my son, I will have an image carved and an idol cast." ⁴So his mother took two hundred of the silver coins to a silversmith, who made them into an image and an idol. And these were placed in Micah's house.

⁵Micah set up a shrine, and he made a sacred ephod and some household idols. Then he installed one of his sons as the priest. ⁶In those days Israel had no king, so the people did whatever seemed right in their own eyes.

⁷One day a young Levite from Bethlehem in Judah ⁸arrived in that area of Ephraim, looking for a good place to live. He happened to stop at Micah's house as he was traveling through. ⁹"Where are you from?" Micah asked him.

And he replied, "I am a Levite from Bethlehem in Judah, and I am looking for a place to live."

¹⁰"Stay here with me," Micah said, "and you can be a father and priest to me. I will give you ten pieces* of silver a year, plus a change of clothes and your food." ¹¹The Levite agreed to this and became like one of Micah's sons. ¹²So Micah ordained the Levite as his personal priest, and he lived in Micah's house. ¹³"I know the LORD will bless me now," Micah said, "because I have a Levite serving as my priest."

IDOLATRY IN THE TRIBE OF DAN

18 Now in those days Israel had no king. And the tribe of Dan was trying to find a place to settle, for they had not yet driven out the people who lived in the land assigned to them. ²So the men of Dan chose five warriors from among their clans, who lived in the towns of Zorah and Eshtaol, to scout out a land for them to settle in.

When these warriors arrived in the hill country of Ephraim, they came to Micah's home and spent the night there. ³Noticing the young Levite's accent, they took him aside and asked him, "Who brought you here, and what are you doing? Why are you here?" ⁴He told them about his agreement with Micah and that he was Micah's personal priest.

⁵Then they said, "Ask God whether or not our journey will be successful."

⁶"Go in peace," the priest replied. "For the LORD will go ahead of you on your journey."

⁷So the five men went on to the town of Laish, where they noticed the people living carefree lives, like the Sidonians; they were peaceful and secure. The people were also wealthy because their land was very fertile.

17:2 Hebrew *1,100 shekels*, about 28 pounds or 12.5 kilograms in weight. **17:10** Hebrew *10 shekels*, about 4 ounces or 114 grams in weight.

And they lived a great distance from Sidon and had no allies nearby.

⁸When the men returned to Zorah and Eshtaol, their relatives asked them, "What did you find?"

⁹The men replied, "Let's attack! We have seen the land, and it is very good. You should not hesitate to go and take possession of it. ¹⁰When you get there, you will find the people living carefree lives. God has given us a spacious and fertile land, lacking in nothing!"

¹¹So six hundred warriors from the tribe of Dan set out from Zorah and Eshtaol. ¹²They camped at a place west of Kiriath-jearim in Judah, which is called Mahaneh-dan* to this day. ¹³Then they went up into the hill country of Ephraim and came to the house of Micah.

¹⁴The five men who had scouted out the land around Laish said to the others, "There is a shrine here with a sacred ephod, some household idols, a carved image, and a cast idol. It's obvious what we ought to do." ¹⁵So the five men went over to Micah's house, where the young Levite lived, and greeted him kindly. ¹⁶As the six hundred warriors from the tribe of Dan stood just outside the gate, ¹⁷the five spies entered the shrine and took the carved image, the sacred ephod, the household idols, and the cast idol.

¹⁸When the priest saw the men carrying all the sacred objects out of Micah's shrine, he said, "What are you doing?"

¹⁹"Be quiet and come with us," they said. "Be a father and priest to all of us. Isn't it better to be a priest for an entire tribe of Israel than just for the household of one man?" ²⁰The young priest was quite happy to go with them, so he took along the sacred ephod, the household idols, and the carved image. ²¹They started on their way again, placing their children, livestock, and possessions in front of them.

²²When the people from the tribe of Dan were quite a distance from Micah's home, Micah and some of his neighbors came chasing after them. ²³They were shouting as they

caught up with them. The men of Dan turned around and said, "What do you want? Why have you called these men together and chased after us like this?"

²⁴"What do you mean, What do I want?" Micah replied. "You've taken away all my gods and my priest, and I have nothing left!"

²⁵The men of Dan said, "Watch what you say! Some of us are short-tempered, and they might get angry and kill you and your family." ²⁶So the men of Dan went on their way. When Micah saw that there were too many of them

---

Words of Worship

REPENT, REPENTANCE

Repent, Repentance—Hebrew *shuv* "turn, return"; Greek *me-ta-no-e-o* "change one's mind, repent"; *me-ta-noi-a* "change of mind, repentance."

Driving down the expressway, we read the sign and realize we've missed our exit. Continuing in the direction we're headed will only take us farther from our destination. We know we need to turn around, and at the first interchange we get off the road and head the other way. That's what repentance looks like. We see our error, change our mind, and turn from the mistaken course of action.

Repentance isn't the same as regret or remorse. We might be sorry about a mistake we've made or a course we've chosen, but until we've changed our behavior, we haven't repented. Paul said, "Sorrow without repentance is the kind that results in death" (2 Corinthians 7:10). We're still an accident waiting to happen. Bringing our guilt and frustration to the Lord in prayer is a good first move. But then we need to ask him for directions, and steer our lives along his way to life.

18:12 *Mahaneh-dan* means "the camp of Dan."

for him to attack, he turned around and went home.

²⁷Then, with Micah's idols and his priest, the men of Dan came to the town of Laish, whose people were peaceful and secure. They attacked and killed all the people and burned the town to the ground. ²⁸There was no one to rescue the residents of the town, for they lived a great distance from Sidon and had no allies nearby. This happened in the valley near Beth-rehob.

Then the people of the tribe of Dan rebuilt the town and lived there. ²⁹They renamed the town Dan after their ancestor, Israel's son, but it had originally been called Laish.

³⁰Then they set up the carved image, and they appointed Jonathan son of Gershom, a descendant of Moses,* as their priest. This family continued as priests for the tribe of Dan until the Exile. ³¹So Micah's carved image was worshiped by the tribe of Dan as long as the Tabernacle of God remained at Shiloh.

THE LEVITE AND HIS CONCUBINE

19 Now in those days Israel had no king. There was a man from the tribe of Levi living in a remote area of the hill country of Ephraim. One day he brought home a woman from Bethlehem in Judah to be his concubine. ²But she was unfaithful to him and returned to her father's home in Bethlehem. After about four months, ³her husband took a servant and an extra donkey to Bethlehem to persuade her to come back. When he arrived at her father's house, she took him inside, and her father welcomed him. ⁴Her father urged him to stay awhile, so he stayed three days, eating, drinking, and sleeping there.

⁵On the fourth day the man was up early, ready to leave, but the woman's father said, "Have something to eat before you go." ⁶So the two of them sat down together and had something to eat and drink. Then the woman's father said, "Please stay the night and enjoy yourself." ⁷The man got up to leave, but his father-in-law kept urging him to stay, so he finally gave in and stayed the night. ⁸On the morning of the fifth day he was up early again, ready to leave, and again the woman's father said, "Have something to eat; then you can leave some time this afternoon." So they had another day of feasting.

⁹That afternoon, as he and his concubine and servant were preparing to leave, his father-in-law said, "Look, it's getting late. Stay the night and enjoy yourself. Tomorrow you can get up early and be on your way."

¹⁰But this time the man was determined to leave. So he took his two saddled donkeys and his concubine and headed in the direction of Jebus (that is, Jerusalem). ¹¹It was late in the day when they reached Jebus, and the man's servant said to him, "It's getting too late to travel; let's stay in this Jebusite city tonight."

¹²"No," his master said, "we can't stay in this foreign city where there are no Israelites. We will go on to Gibeah. ¹³We will find a place to spend the night in either Gibeah or Ramah." ¹⁴So they went on. The sun was setting as they came to Gibeah, a town in the land of Benjamin, ¹⁵so they stopped there to spend the night. They rested in the town square, but no one took them in for the night.

¹⁶That evening an old man came home from his work in the fields. He was from the hill country of Ephraim, but he was living in Gibeah in the territory of Benjamin. ¹⁷When he saw the travelers sitting in the town square, he asked them where they were from and where they were going.

¹⁸"We have been in Bethlehem in Judah," the man replied. "We are on our way home to a remote area in the hill country of Ephraim, and we're going to the Tabernacle of the LORD. But no one has taken us in for the night, ¹⁹even though we have everything we need. We have straw and fodder for our donkeys and plenty of bread and wine for ourselves."

²⁰"You are welcome to stay with me," the old man said. "I will give you anything you might need. But whatever you do, don't spend the

18:30 As in an ancient Hebrew tradition, some Greek manuscripts, and Latin Vulgate; Masoretic Text reads *of Manasseh.*

night in the square." [21]So he took them home with him and fed their donkeys. After they washed their feet, they had supper together.

[22]While they were enjoying themselves, some of the wicked men in the town surrounded the house. They began beating at the door and shouting to the old man, "Bring out the man who is staying with you so we can have sex with him."

[23]The old man stepped outside to talk to them. "No, my brothers, don't do such an evil thing. For this man is my guest, and such a thing would be shameful. [24]Here, take my virgin daughter and this man's concubine. I will bring them out to you, and you can do whatever you like to them. But don't do such a shameful thing to this man."

[25]But they wouldn't listen to him. Then the Levite took his concubine and pushed her out the door. The men of the town abused her all night, taking turns raping her until morning. Finally, at dawn, they let her go. [26]At daybreak the woman returned to the house where her husband was staying. She collapsed at the door of the house and lay there until it was light.

[27]When her husband opened the door to leave, he found her there. She was lying face down, with her hands on the threshold. [28]He said, "Get up! Let's go!" But there was no answer.* So he put her body on his donkey and took her home.

[29]When he got home, he took a knife and cut his concubine's body into twelve pieces. Then he sent one piece to each tribe of Israel. [30]Everyone who saw it said, "Such a horrible crime has not been committed since Israel left Egypt. Shouldn't we speak up and do something about this?"

ISRAEL'S WAR WITH BENJAMIN

20 Then all the Israelites, from Dan to Beersheba and from the land of Gilead, came together in one large assembly and stood in the presence of the LORD at Mizpah. [2]The leaders of all the people and all the tribes of Israel—400,000 warriors armed with swords—took their positions in the assembly of the people of God. [3](Word soon reached the land of Benjamin that the other tribes had gone up to Mizpah.) The Israelites then asked how this terrible crime had happened.

[4]The Levite, the husband of the woman who had been murdered, said, "My concubine and I came to Gibeah, a town in the land of Benjamin, to spend the night. [5]That night some of the leaders of Gibeah surrounded the house, planning to kill me, and they raped my concubine until she was dead. [6]So I cut her body into twelve pieces and sent the pieces throughout the land of Israel, for these men have committed this terrible and shameful crime. [7]Now then, the entire community of Israel must decide what should be done about this!"

[8]And all the people stood up together and replied, "Not one of us will return home. [9]Instead, we will draw lots to decide who will attack Gibeah. [10]One tenth of the men from each tribe will be chosen to supply the warriors with food, and the rest of us will take revenge on Gibeah* for this shameful thing they have done in Israel." [11]So all the Israelites were united, and they gathered together to attack the town.

[12]The Israelites sent messengers to the tribe of Benjamin, saying, "What a terrible thing

> *Worship is the highest act of which man is capable.*
>
> SAMUEL H. MILLER

19:28 Greek version adds *for she was dead.* 20:10 Hebrew *Geba*, in this case, a variant for Gibeah; also in 20:33.

has been done among you! [13]Give up these evil men from Gibeah so we can execute them and purge Israel of this evil."

But the people of Benjamin would not listen. [14]Instead, they came from their towns and gathered at Gibeah to fight the Israelites. [15]Twenty-six thousand of their warriors armed with swords arrived in Gibeah to join the seven hundred warriors who lived there. [16]Seven hundred of Benjamin's warriors were left-handed, each of whom could sling a rock and hit a target within a hairsbreadth, without missing. [17]Israel had 400,000 warriors armed with swords, not counting Benjamin's warriors.

[18]Before the battle the Israelites went to Bethel and asked God, "Which tribe should lead the attack against the people of Benjamin?"

The LORD answered, "Judah is to go first."

[19]So the Israelites left early the next morning and camped near Gibeah. [20]Then they advanced toward Gibeah to attack the men of Benjamin. [21]But Benjamin's warriors, who were defending the town, came out and killed twenty-two thousand Israelites in the field that day.

[22]But the Israelites took courage and assembled at the same place they had fought the previous day. [23](For they had gone up to Bethel and wept in the presence of the LORD until evening. Then they asked the LORD, "Should we fight against our relatives from Benjamin again?" And the LORD said, "Go out and fight against them.")

[24]So they went out to fight against the warriors of Benjamin, [25]but the men of Benjamin killed another eighteen thousand Israelites, all of whom were experienced with a sword.

[26]Then all the Israelites went up to Bethel and wept in the presence of the LORD and fasted until evening. They also brought burnt offerings and peace offerings to the LORD. [27]And the Israelites went up seeking direction from the LORD. (In those days the Ark of the Covenant of God was in Bethel, [28]and Phinehas son of Eleazar and grandson of Aaron was the

priest.) The Israelites asked the LORD, "Should we fight against our relatives from Benjamin again or should we stop?"

The LORD said, "Go! Tomorrow I will give you victory over them."

[29]So the Israelites set an ambush all around Gibeah. [30]They went out on the third day and assembled at the same place as before. [31]When the warriors of Benjamin came out to attack, they were drawn away from the town. And as they had done before, they began to kill the Israelites. About thirty Israelites died in the open fields and along the roads leading to Bethel and Gibeah.

[32]Then the warriors of Benjamin shouted, "We're defeating them as we did in the first battle!" But the Israelites had agreed in advance to run away so that the men of Benjamin would chase them along the roads and be drawn away from the town.

[33]When the main group of Israelite warriors reached Baal-tamar, they turned and prepared to attack. Then the Israelites hiding in ambush west of Gibeah jumped up from where they were [34]and advanced against Benjamin from behind. The fighting was so heavy that Benjamin didn't realize the impending disaster. [35]So the LORD helped Israel defeat Benjamin, and that day the Israelites killed 25,100 of Benjamin's warriors, all of whom were experienced with a sword. [36]Then the men of Benjamin saw that they were beaten.

The Israelites had retreated from Benjamin's warriors in order to give those hiding in ambush more room to maneuver. [37]Then those who were in hiding rushed in from all sides and killed everyone in the town. [38]They sent up a large cloud of smoke from the town, [39]which was the signal for the Israelites to turn and attack Benjamin's warriors.

By that time Benjamin's warriors had killed about thirty Israelites, and they shouted, "We're defeating them as we did in the first battle!" [40]But when the warriors of Benjamin looked behind them and saw the smoke rising into the sky from every part of the town, [41]the

Israelites turned and attacked. At this point Benjamin's warriors realized disaster was near and became terrified. ⁴²So they ran toward the wilderness, but the Israelites chased after them and killed them. ⁴³The Israelites surrounded the men of Benjamin and were relentless in chasing them down, finally overtaking them east of Gibeah. ⁴⁴Eighteen thousand of Benjamin's greatest warriors died in that day's battle. ⁴⁵The survivors fled into the wilderness toward the rock of Rimmon, but Israel killed five thousand of them along the road. They continued the chase until they had killed another two thousand near Gidom.

⁴⁶So the tribe of Benjamin lost twenty-five thousand brave warriors that day, ⁴⁷leaving only six hundred men who escaped to the rock of Rimmon, where they lived for four months. ⁴⁸Then the Israelites returned and slaughtered every living thing in all the towns—the people, the cattle—everything. They also burned down every town they came to.

ISRAEL PROVIDES WIVES FOR BENJAMIN

21 The Israelites had vowed at Mizpah never to give their daughters in marriage to a man from the tribe of Benjamin. ²And the people went to Bethel and sat in the presence of God until evening, raising their voices and weeping bitterly. ³"O LORD, God of Israel," they cried out, "why has this happened? Now one of our tribes is missing!"

⁴Early the next morning the people built an altar and presented their burnt offerings and peace offerings on it. ⁵Then they said, "Was any tribe of Israel not represented when we held our council in the presence of the LORD at Mizpah?" At that time they had taken a solemn oath in the LORD's presence, vowing that anyone who refused to come must die.

⁶The Israelites felt deep sadness for Benjamin and said, "Today we have lost one of the tribes from our family; it is nearly wiped out. ⁷How can we find wives for the few who remain, since we have sworn by the LORD not to give them our daughters in marriage?"

⁸So they asked, "Was anyone absent when we presented ourselves to the LORD at Mizpah?" And they discovered that no one from Jabesh-gilead had attended. ⁹For after they counted all the people, no one from Jabesh-gilead was present. ¹⁰So they sent twelve thousand warriors to Jabesh-gilead with orders to kill everyone there, including women and children. ¹¹"This is what you are to do," they said. "Completely destroy* all the males and every woman who is not a virgin." ¹²Among the residents of Jabesh-gilead they found four hundred young virgins who had never slept with a man, and they brought them to the camp at Shiloh in the land of Canaan.

¹³The Israelite assembly sent a peace delegation to the little remnant of Benjamin who were living at the rock of Rimmon. ¹⁴Then the men of Benjamin returned to their homes, and the four hundred women of Jabesh-gilead who were spared were given to them as wives. But there were not enough women for all of them.

¹⁵The people felt sorry for Benjamin because the LORD had left this gap in the tribes of Israel. ¹⁶So the Israelite leaders asked, "How can we find wives for the few who remain, since all the women of the tribe of Benjamin are dead? ¹⁷There must be heirs for the survivors so that an entire tribe of Israel will not be lost forever. ¹⁸But we cannot give them our own daughters in marriage because we have sworn with a solemn oath that anyone who does this will fall under God's curse."

¹⁹Then they thought of the annual festival of the LORD held in Shiloh, between Lebonah and Bethel, along the east side of the road that goes from Bethel to Shechem. ²⁰They told the men of Benjamin who still needed wives, "Go and hide in the vineyards. ²¹When the women of Shiloh come out for their dances, rush out from the vineyards, and each of you can take

21:11 The Hebrew term used here refers to the complete consecration of things or people to the LORD, either by destroying them or by giving them as an offering.

My Daily Worship

RUNNING IN SIN CIRCLES

JUDGES 17:1–21:25

In those days Israel had no king,
so the people did whatever seemed right in their own eyes (21:25).

[i reflect]

History does not run in circles, but people do. Generation after generation, children repeat their parents' sins. We claim great progress, yet in the most significant ways remain unchanged. What phrase better describes our cycle of sin than "the people did whatever seemed right in their own eyes"?

The last verse of the book of Judges could serve as a description for every generation, including ours. Whether or not a king or some other authority structure is in place only affects external behavior. Inwardly, we want to decide for ourselves about right and wrong. Children and adults may use different words to express themselves, but all of us exhibit at our core a willfulness that says, "You can't tell me what to do! I decide that!"

But we are wrong. God *can* tell us what to do. God *has* told us what to do. Notice the irony in the opening phrase above, "Israel [God's people] had no king." They had no need for a king because they had God. Instead, they forgot God and made themselves kings over their own lives. Just like them, when we forget God or fail to obey him, what seems right in our eyes usually turns out to be wrong. As soon as we acknowledge God's direction in our lives we begin to break the sin cycle.

Our tendency to run our lives has such deep roots in us that worship must always include an awareness of our rebelliousness. We turn humbly to God as we realize we can't trust ourselves. The cycle of sin can only be broken by the power of the Holy Spirit. "So I advise you to live according to your new life in the Holy Spirit. Then you won't be doing what your sinful nature craves" (Galatians 5:16). Learning to do what God wants rather than what looks good to us keeps us from running in sin circles.

[i pray]

Dear Father, I want to break the cycle of sin in my life. Send your Holy Spirit to show
me the areas in which I am "doing whatever seems right" in my own eyes.
Help me to confess those areas and break that cycle.

[i respond]

At some point in worship, the need to confess sin will almost always come. In fact, facing and acknowledging our sin tendencies can clear the atmosphere for worship. The next time you prepare to worship, begin this way, "Lord, I recognize in this moment that you are God and I am not."

one of them home to be your wife! [22]And when their fathers and brothers come to us in protest, we will tell them, 'Please be understanding. Let them have your daughters, for we didn't find enough wives for them when we destroyed Jabesh-gilead. And you are not guilty of breaking the vow since you did not give your daughters in marriage to them.'"

[23]So the men of Benjamin did as they were told. They kidnapped the women who took part in the celebration and carried them off to the land of their own inheritance. Then they rebuilt their towns and lived in them. [24]So the assembly of Israel departed by tribes and families, and they returned to their own homes.

[25]In those days Israel had no king, so the people did whatever seemed right in their own eyes.

Ruth

Your God will be my God (1:16).

God to the Rescue

Riveted to the television, millions watched the unfolding drama as firemen and rescue teams labored around the clock to save a group of Pennsylvania miners stranded deep underground. People, united in their mutual concern, waited for each morsel of news. Finally, everyone rejoiced when all the miners were rescued and brought safely back to the surface. Dramatic rescue stories such as this capture and touch people's hearts, restoring their faith and filling them with hopefulness.

That's the book of Ruth, a powerful and dramatic story of rescue. It is also a gentle and beautiful story of love, loyalty, faithfulness, compassion, and salvation, in which two helpless women throw themselves on the mercy of God's people. When Naomi's husband and two sons died, she decided to go home, urging daughter-in-law Ruth to remain in Moab. But Ruth chose to go with Naomi, saying: "Don't ask me to leave you. . . . Your people will be my people, and your God will be my God" (1:16). The two widows traveled back to Bethlehem in Judah.

Ruth gathered leftover grain to support herself and Naomi. In the barley fields, she met the owner of the land, Boaz, who welcomed her (2:11), commending her for her loyalty and kindness. In Boaz, Naomi recognizes a close relative and, therefore, a "family redeemer" (2:20; 3:9, 12; 4:14). According to Israel's custom, the family redeemer was a person obligated to rescue impoverished relatives to keep their property within the clan.

Notice that Boaz's rescue of Ruth parallels God's love relationship with Israel and also his relationship with us. We come to Jesus totally impoverished, with empty hands like Ruth and Naomi. He graciously accepts us, rescues us from our destitution, and begins a love relationship with us, inspiring us to love him in return. Implicit in this book is an attitude of love, respect, and worship for the gracious God of Israel, who accepts and blesses all who earnestly seek him.

Worship Moments

- Ruth's declaration of steadfast trust in God is one of the most moving statements of faith in all of Scripture (1:16).

- The leaders of the people pronounce a blessing on Boaz and Ruth (4:11).

- In this book, God is the One who blesses (1:6); the One under whose wings Ruth takes refuge (2:12); the Almighty (1:20–21).

Elimelech Moves His Family to Moab

1 In the days when the judges ruled in Israel, a man from Bethlehem in Judah left the country because of a severe famine. He took his wife and two sons and went to live in the country of Moab. [2]The man's name was Elimelech, and his wife was Naomi. Their two sons were Mahlon and Kilion. They were Ephrathites from Bethlehem in the land of Judah. During their stay in Moab, [3]Elimelech died and Naomi was left with her two sons. [4]The two sons married Moabite women. One married a woman named Orpah, and the other a woman named Ruth. But about ten years later, [5]both Mahlon and Kilion died. This left Naomi alone, without her husband or sons.

Naomi and Ruth Return

[6]Then Naomi heard in Moab that the LORD had blessed his people in Judah by giving them good crops again. So Naomi and her daughters-in-law got ready to leave Moab to return to her homeland. [7]With her two daughters-in-law she set out from the place where she had been living, and they took the road that would lead them back to Judah.

[8]But on the way, Naomi said to her two daughters-in-law, "Go back to your mothers' homes instead of coming with me. And may the LORD reward you for your kindness to your husbands and to me. [9]May the LORD bless you with the security of another marriage." Then she kissed them good-bye, and they all broke down and wept.

[10]"No," they said. "We want to go with you to your people."

[11]But Naomi replied, "Why should you go on with me? Can I still give birth to other sons who could grow up to be your husbands? [12]No, my daughters, return to your parents' homes, for I am too old to marry again. And even if it were possible, and I were to get married tonight and bear sons, then what? [13]Would you wait for them to grow up and refuse to marry someone else? No, of course not, my daughters! Things are far more bitter for me than for you, because the LORD himself has caused me to suffer."

[14]And again they wept together, and Orpah kissed her mother-in-law good-bye. But Ruth insisted on staying with Naomi. [15]"See," Naomi said to her, "your sister-in-law has gone back to her people and to her gods. You should do the same."

[16]But Ruth replied, "Don't ask me to leave you and turn back. I will go wherever you go and live wherever you live. Your people will be my people, and your God will be my God. [17]I will die where you die and will be buried there. May the LORD punish me severely if I allow anything but death to separate us!" [18]So when Naomi saw that Ruth had made up her mind to go with her, she stopped urging her.

[19]So the two of them continued on their journey. When they came to Bethlehem, the entire town was stirred by their arrival. "Is it really Naomi?" the women asked.

[20]"Don't call me Naomi," she told them. "Instead, call me Mara,* for the Almighty has made life very bitter for me. [21]I went away full, but the LORD has brought me home empty. Why should you call me Naomi when the LORD has caused me to suffer* and the Almighty has sent such tragedy?"

[22]So Naomi returned from Moab, accompanied by her daughter-in-law Ruth, the young Moabite woman. They arrived in Bethlehem at the beginning of the barley harvest.

Ruth Works in Boaz's Field

2 Now there was a wealthy and influential man in Bethlehem named Boaz, who was a relative of Naomi's husband, Elimelech.

[2]One day Ruth said to Naomi, "Let me go out into the fields to gather leftover grain behind anyone who will let me do it."

And Naomi said, "All right, my daughter, go ahead." [3]So Ruth went out to gather grain behind the harvesters. And as it happened, she

---

1:20 *Naomi* means "pleasant"; *Mara* means "bitter." **1:21** Or *has testified against me.*

My Daily Worship

WHAT SHOULD YOU LEAVE BEHIND?

RUTH 1:1–2:23

But Ruth replied, "Don't ask me to leave you and turn back. I will go wherever you go and live wherever you live. Your people will be my people, and your God will be my God" (1:16).

[i reflect]

"We're moving." Two words sure to set up a flurry of activity. Decision after decision. What do we pack? What do we leave behind? Farewell to family and friends and all that is familiar. Moving is as difficult today as it was in the days of Ruth and Naomi.

Panting from exertion, the two women stopped to rest at the crest of the hill. The high plains of Moab lay behind; the road to Judah snaked through the hills ahead. "Go home," Naomi urged, and Ruth considered. Home to her family and friends, to her culture, to her gods. *But Naomi is my family,* Ruth thought, *and now my home is with her, wherever that might be.* With love Ruth replied, "I will go wherever you go."

Ruth's decision reached far beyond compassion for her mother-in-law, for she added, "Your people will be my people, and your God will be my God" (1:16). With these words, Ruth abandoned the gods of her ancestors and took refuge under the wings of the God of Israel (2:12). Now she would worship the one true God.

What must you abandon to worship the one true God? False beliefs and practices of the past? A relationship or an activity that does not honor God? Possessions that weigh heavy? A sin that blocks him from your sight? Or is God calling you to leave your home (or your comfort zone) to follow him to a new place?

Worshiping God involves sacrifice, but he "gives his riches to all who ask for them" (Romans 10:12). God honored Ruth's faith by blessing her new life in Israel and giving her a place in the lineage of Jesus (Matthew 1:5). How has God blessed you since you put your faith in him?

Consider what God is calling you to leave behind today. Like Ruth, follow your heart and obey God.

[i pray]

Creator of heaven and earth, I bow down to worship you alone. I cast out all that has come between us. Please release me from the sin that entangles and purify me so that I may stand in your presence.

[i respond]

You are moving to a new relationship with God. Examine your activities, your possessions, your attitudes. Make two lists: What will you pack? What will you leave behind? If you find anything that is not worthy to bring into the presence of God, throw it away.

found herself working in a field that belonged to Boaz, the relative of her father-in-law, Elimelech.

⁴While she was there, Boaz arrived from Bethlehem and greeted the harvesters. "The LORD be with you!" he said.

"The LORD bless you!" the harvesters replied.

⁵Then Boaz asked his foreman, "Who is that girl over there?"

⁶And the foreman replied, "She is the young woman from Moab who came back with Naomi. ⁷She asked me this morning if she could gather grain behind the harvesters. She has been hard at work ever since, except for a few minutes' rest over there in the shelter."

⁸Boaz went over and said to Ruth, "Listen, my daughter. Stay right here with us when you gather grain; don't go to any other fields. Stay right behind the women working in my field. ⁹See which part of the field they are harvesting, and then follow them. I have warned the young men not to bother you. And when you are thirsty, help yourself to the water they have drawn from the well."

¹⁰Ruth fell at his feet and thanked him warmly. "Why are you being so kind to me?" she asked. "I am only a foreigner."

¹¹"Yes, I know," Boaz replied. "But I also know about the love and kindness you have shown your mother-in-law since the death of your husband. I have heard how you left your father and mother and your own land to live here among complete strangers. ¹²May the LORD, the God of Israel, under whose wings you have come to take refuge, reward you fully."

¹³"I hope I continue to please you, sir," she replied. "You have comforted me by speaking so kindly to me, even though I am not as worthy as your workers."

¹⁴At lunchtime Boaz called to her, "Come over here and help yourself to some of our food. You can dip your bread in the wine if you like." So she sat with his harvesters, and Boaz gave her food—more than she could eat.

¹⁵When Ruth went back to work again, Boaz ordered his young men, "Let her gather grain right among the sheaves without stopping her. ¹⁶And pull out some heads of barley from the bundles and drop them on purpose for her. Let her pick them up, and don't give her a hard time!"

¹⁷So Ruth gathered barley there all day, and when she beat out the grain that evening, it came to about half a bushel.* ¹⁸She carried it back into town and showed it to her mother-in-law. Ruth also gave her the food that was left over from her lunch.

¹⁹"So much!" Naomi exclaimed. "Where did you gather all this grain today? Where did you work? May the LORD bless the one who helped you!"

So Ruth told her mother-in-law about the man in whose field she had worked. And she said, "The man I worked with today is named Boaz."

²⁰"May the LORD bless him!" Naomi told her daughter-in-law. "He is showing his kindness to us as well as to your dead husband.* That man is one of our closest relatives, one of our family redeemers."

²¹Then Ruth said, "What's more, Boaz even told me to come back and stay with his harvesters until the entire harvest is completed."

²²"This is wonderful!" Naomi exclaimed. "Do as he said. Stay with his workers right through the whole harvest. You will be safe there, unlike in other fields."

²³So Ruth worked alongside the women in Boaz's fields and gathered grain with them until the end of the barley harvest. Then she worked with them through the wheat harvest, too. But all the while she lived with her mother-in-law.

RUTH AT THE THRESHING FLOOR

3 One day Naomi said to Ruth, "My daughter, it's time that I found a permanent home for you, so that you will be provided for. ²Boaz is a close relative of ours, and he's been

---

2:17 Hebrew *about an ephah* [18 liters]. 2:20 Hebrew *to the living and to the dead.*

My Daily Worship

— M a r c h   4 —

WHEN THERE'S NO PLACE TO GO!

RUTH 3:1–4:22

"I am your servant Ruth," she replied. "Spread the corner of your covering over me, for you are my family redeemer" (3:9).

[i reflect]

Walking slowly behind the harvesters, Ruth gathered the grain that had been left behind. This was God's provision, that grain be left in the field for the poor and widowed. Hard and demeaning work it was. Was this to be her life? No husband, no children, no home? Was she to be allotted only the leftovers of life?

In desperation, she turned to Boaz. "Spread the corner of your covering over me," she pleaded. In other words: "Marry me (for this was a marriage proposal) and redeem my life. Cast the cover of redemption over me. Cover me as a bird covers its young with its wing. Take away my loneliness and despair, and give me hope. Protect me, cherish me, love me, for you are my family redeemer."

The family redeemer was a relative who volunteered to take responsibility for the extended family. In agreeing to care for Ruth and Naomi, Boaz showed great kindness by buying back land to guarantee Ruth and Naomi's inheritance. But Boaz is more than just a model of kindness to two poor widows—he is a picture of the kindness and grace that we find in our own family redeemer—Jesus.

For we also are in desperate need of a family redeemer. "For all have sinned; all fall short of God's glorious standard" (Romans 3:23). The Day of Judgment is coming. Our sins will be exposed and we will stand naked and alone, condemned before a holy God. Yet, Jesus, in his love and compassion, will spread the cover of his redemption over us. He will cover us completely, so that only his own glorious work will be seen. Then he will bring us into the very presence of God, and we will be found "holy and blameless as [we] stand before him without a single fault" (Colossian 1:22).

This is only the beginning of redemption, for Jesus seeks to redeem every aspect of our lives. Turn to him in your poverty and despair, and ask for his redemption. He will take your loss, your failure, your loneliness, and he will use it for God's glory. Give him your hopes and dreams, for his "purpose is to give life in all its fullness" (John 10:10).

[i pray]

Cast your cover of redemption over me, Jesus, my Lord and my Redeemer. Cover me completely with your love and protection. Redeem my life, so I may live only for our Father's glory.

[i respond]

Make a list of the ways that Jesus, your family redeemer, has covered you with his kindness and love in the past twenty-four hours. Take time to thank him for each act of grace, kindness, redemption, and love.

very kind by letting you gather grain with his workers. Tonight he will be winnowing barley at the threshing floor. ³Now do as I tell you— take a bath and put on perfume and dress in your nicest clothes. Then go to the threshing floor, but don't let Boaz see you until he has finished his meal. ⁴Be sure to notice where he lies down; then go and uncover his feet and lie down there. He will tell you what to do."

⁵"I will do everything you say," Ruth replied. ⁶So she went down to the threshing floor that night and followed the instructions of her mother-in-law.

⁷After Boaz had finished his meal and was in good spirits, he lay down beside the heap of grain and went to sleep. Then Ruth came quietly, uncovered his feet, and lay down. ⁸Around midnight, Boaz suddenly woke up and turned over. He was surprised to find a woman lying at his feet! ⁹"Who are you?" he demanded.

"I am your servant Ruth," she replied. "Spread the corner of your covering over me, for you are my family redeemer."

¹⁰"The LORD bless you, my daughter!" Boaz exclaimed. "You are showing more family loyalty now than ever by not running after a younger man, whether rich or poor. ¹¹Now don't worry about a thing, my daughter. I will do what is necessary, for everyone in town knows you are an honorable woman. ¹²But there is one problem. While it is true that I am one of your family redeemers, there is another man who is more closely related to you than I am. ¹³Stay here tonight, and in the morning I will talk to him. If he is willing to redeem you, then let him marry you. But if he is not willing, then as surely as the LORD lives, I will marry you! Now lie down here until morning."

¹⁴So Ruth lay at Boaz's feet until the morning, but she got up before it was light enough for people to recognize each other. For Boaz said, "No one must know that a woman was here at the threshing floor." ¹⁵Boaz also said to her, "Bring your cloak and spread it out." He measured out six scoops* of barley into the cloak and helped her put it on her back. Then Boaz* returned to the town.

¹⁶When Ruth went back to her mother-in-law, Naomi asked, "What happened, my daughter?"

Ruth told Naomi everything Boaz had done for her, ¹⁷and she added, "He gave me these six scoops of barley and said, 'Don't go back to your mother-in-law empty-handed.'"

¹⁸Then Naomi said to her, "Just be patient, my daughter, until we hear what happens. The man won't rest until he has followed through on this. He will settle it today."

BOAZ MARRIES RUTH

4 So Boaz went to the town gate and took a seat there. When the family redeemer he had mentioned came by, Boaz called out to him, "Come over here, friend. I want to talk to you." So they sat down together. ²Then Boaz called ten leaders from the town and asked them to sit as witnesses. ³And Boaz said to the family redeemer, "You know Naomi, who came back from Moab. She is selling the land that belonged to our relative Elimelech. ⁴I felt that I should speak to you about it so that you can redeem it if you wish. If you want the land, then buy it here in the presence of these witnesses. But if you don't want it, let me know right away, because I am next in line to redeem it after you."

The man replied, "All right, I'll redeem it."

⁵Then Boaz told him, "Of course, your purchase of the land from Naomi also requires that you marry Ruth, the Moabite widow. That way, she can have children who will carry on her husband's name and keep the land in the family."

⁶"Then I can't redeem it," the family redeemer replied, "because this might endanger my own estate. You redeem the land; I cannot do it."

⁷In those days it was the custom in Israel for anyone transferring a right of purchase to

---

3:15a Hebrew *six measures*, an unknown quantity. 3:15b Most Hebrew manuscripts read *he*; many Hebrew manuscripts, Syriac version, and Latin Vulgate read *she*.

remove his sandal and hand it to the other party. This publicly validated the transaction. [8]So the other family redeemer drew off his sandal as he said to Boaz, "You buy the land."

[9]Then Boaz said to the leaders and to the crowd standing around, "You are witnesses that today I have bought from Naomi all the property of Elimelech, Kilion, and Mahlon. [10]And with the land I have acquired Ruth, the Moabite widow of Mahlon, to be my wife. This way she can have a son to carry on the family name of her dead husband and to inherit the family property here in his home-town. You are all witnesses today."

[11]Then the leaders and all the people stand-ing there replied, "We are witnesses! May the LORD make the woman who is now coming into your home like Rachel and Leah, from whom all the nation of Israel descended! May you be great in Ephrathah and famous in Bethlehem. [12]And may the LORD give you descendants by this young woman who will be like those of our ancestor Perez, the son of Tamar and Judah."

THE DESCENDANTS OF BOAZ

[13]So Boaz married Ruth and took her home to live with him. When he slept with her, the LORD enabled her to become pregnant, and she gave birth to a son. [14]And the women of the town said to Naomi, "Praise the LORD who has given you a family redeemer today! May he be famous in Israel. [15]May this child restore your youth and care for you in your old age. For he is the son of your daughter-in-law who loves you so much and who has been better to you than seven sons!"

[16]Naomi took care of the baby and cared for him as if he were her own. [17]The neighbor women said, "Now at last Naomi has a son again!" And they named him Obed. He became the father of Jesse and the grandfather of David.

[18]This is their family line beginning with their ancestor Perez:

Perez was the father of Hezron.
[19] Hezron was the father of Ram.
Ram was the father of Amminadab.
[20] Amminadab was the father of Nahshon.
Nahshon was the father of Salmon.
[21] Salmon was the father of Boaz.
Boaz was the father of Obed.
[22] Obed was the father of Jesse.
Jesse was the father of David.

1 Samuel

*Worship the LORD with all your heart and . . . don't turn
your back on him in any way (12:20).*

A Heart for God

Which man is more likely to be successful? The first stands tall and strong, with striking good looks, a charismatic figure, and he owns an impeccable pedigree as the son of a wealthy and influential father. The second is just a boy, a farmer's kid, the youngest of seven sons, who has spent most of his life in the field (literally). Most would not hesitate even a moment to choose the first. Yet looks can be deceiving, and even the most talented individual can underachieve or squander those gifts.

That's the story we discover in 1 Samuel: two men, two life-directions, and two very different legacies.

Saul was called "the most handsome man in Israel—head and shoulders taller than anyone else" (9:2). An all-star. The most likely candidate for king. And for that role he was chosen by God and anointed by Samuel. But he took just a few years to squander his opportunities and lose his throne.

In contrast, David was no one special, a boy-shepherd, minding his own business and his father's flocks. Yet a few decades later he became a great, conquering king.

The difference was in the heart. Samuel made that point when informing Saul that his dynasty would end: "The LORD has sought out a man after his own heart" (13:14). A short time later, God underscored that truth when he told Samuel as he looked for a successor, "The LORD doesn't make decisions the way you do! People judge by outward appearance, but the LORD looks at a person's thoughts and intentions" (16:7).

Saul began strong, but his life spiraled downward and finally ended in suicide. A tragic figure, a symbol of self-centered futility. David, despite his humble beginnings, became Israel's greatest king and the ancient ancestor of the Messiah. Was David perfect? No. But his heart was right.

As you read through 1 Samuel, consider the "heart" choices made by both David and Saul. Ask God to bring your heart in line with his.

Worship Moments

- Samuel's mother, Hannah, composes a beautiful psalm of praise to God (2:1–10).

- Samuel offers a burnt offering to the Lord and pleads with him to help Israel (7:9).

- God is called "the LORD Almighty" (1:3); our "Rock" (2:2); "the LORD judges" (2:10); "holy God" (6:20); "your king" (12:12); "the Glory of Israel" (15:29); and "the living God" (17:26).

ELKANAH AND HIS FAMILY

1 There was a man named Elkanah who lived in Ramah* in the hill country of Ephraim. He was the son of Jeroham and grandson of Elihu, from the family of Tohu and the clan of Zuph. ²Elkanah had two wives, Hannah and Peninnah. Peninnah had children, while Hannah did not.

³Each year Elkanah and his family would travel to Shiloh to worship and sacrifice to the LORD Almighty at the Tabernacle. The priests of the LORD at that time were the two sons of Eli—Hophni and Phinehas. ⁴On the day Elkanah presented his sacrifice, he would give portions of the sacrifice to Peninnah and each of her children. ⁵But he gave Hannah a special portion* because he loved her very much, even though the LORD had given her no children. ⁶But Peninnah made fun of Hannah because the LORD had closed her womb. ⁷Year after year it was the same—Peninnah would taunt Hannah as they went to the Tabernacle.* Hannah would finally be reduced to tears and would not even eat.

⁸"What's the matter, Hannah?" Elkanah would ask. "Why aren't you eating? Why be so sad just because you have no children? You have me—isn't that better than having ten sons?"

HANNAH'S PRAYER FOR A SON

⁹Once when they were at Shiloh, Hannah went over to the Tabernacle* after supper to pray to the LORD. Eli the priest was sitting at his customary place beside the entrance. ¹⁰Hannah was in deep anguish, crying bitterly as she prayed to the LORD. ¹¹And she made this vow: "O LORD Almighty, if you will look down upon my sorrow and answer my prayer and give me a son, then I will give him back to you. He will be yours for his entire lifetime, and as a sign that he has been dedicated to the LORD, his hair will never be cut."*

¹²As she was praying to the LORD, Eli watched her. ¹³Seeing her lips moving but hearing no sound, he thought she had been drinking. ¹⁴"Must you come here drunk?" he demanded. "Throw away your wine!"

¹⁵"Oh no, sir!" she replied, "I'm not drunk! But I am very sad, and I was pouring out my heart to the LORD. ¹⁶Please don't think I am a wicked woman! For I have been praying out of great anguish and sorrow."

¹⁷"In that case," Eli said, "cheer up! May the God of Israel grant the request you have asked of him."

¹⁸"Oh, thank you, sir!" she exclaimed. Then she went back and began to eat again, and she was no longer sad.

SAMUEL'S BIRTH AND DEDICATION

¹⁹The entire family got up early the next morning and went to worship the LORD once more. Then they returned home to Ramah. When Elkanah slept with Hannah, the LORD remembered her request, ²⁰and in due time she gave birth to a son. She named him Samuel,* for she said, "I asked the LORD for him."

²¹The next year Elkanah, Peninnah, and their children went on their annual trip to offer a sacrifice to the LORD. ²²But Hannah did not go. She told her husband, "Wait until the baby is weaned. Then I will take him to the Tabernacle and leave him there with the LORD permanently."*

²³"Whatever you think is best," Elkanah agreed. "Stay here for now, and may the LORD help you keep your promise." So she stayed home and nursed the baby.

²⁴When the child was weaned, Hannah took him to the Tabernacle in Shiloh. They brought along a three-year-old bull* for the sacrifice and half a bushel* of flour and some wine. ²⁵After sacrificing the bull, they took the child to Eli. ²⁶"Sir, do you remember me?" Hannah

---

1:1 Hebrew *Ramathaim-zophim*; compare 1:19. 1:5 Or *a double portion*. The meaning of the Hebrew is uncertain. 1:7 Hebrew *the house of the LORD*; also in 1:24. 1:9 Hebrew *the Temple of the LORD*. 1:11 Some manuscripts add *He will drink neither wine nor intoxicants.* 1:20 *Samuel* sounds like the Hebrew term for "asked of God" or "heard by God." 1:22 Some manuscripts add *I will offer him as a Nazirite for all time.* 1:24a As in Dead Sea Scrolls, Greek and Syriac versions; Masoretic Text reads *3 bulls*. 1:24b Hebrew *and an ephah* [18 liters].

asked. "I am the woman who stood here several years ago praying to the LORD. [27] I asked the LORD to give me this child, and he has given me my request. [28] Now I am giving him to the LORD, and he will belong to the LORD his whole life." And they* worshiped the LORD there.

HANNAH'S PRAYER OF PRAISE

2 Then Hannah prayed:

"My heart rejoices in the LORD!
  Oh, how the LORD has blessed me!
Now I have an answer for my enemies,
  as I delight in your deliverance.
[2] No one is holy like the LORD!
  There is no one besides you;
  there is no Rock like our God.

[3] "Stop acting so proud and haughty!
  Don't speak with such arrogance!
The LORD is a God who knows your deeds;
  and he will judge you for what you have
    done.
[4] Those who were mighty are mighty no
    more;
  and those who were weak are now strong.
[5] Those who were well fed are now starving;
  and those who were starving are now
    full.
The barren woman now has seven
    children;
  but the woman with many children will
    have no more.
[6] The LORD brings both death and life;
  he brings some down to the grave but
    raises others up.
[7] The LORD makes one poor and another
    rich;
  he brings one down and lifts another up.
[8] He lifts the poor from the dust—
  yes, from a pile of ashes!
He treats them like princes,
  placing them in seats of honor.

"For all the earth is the LORD's,
  and he has set the world in order.
[9] He will protect his godly ones,
  but the wicked will perish in darkness.
No one will succeed by strength alone.
[10] Those who fight against the LORD will be
    broken.
He thunders against them from heaven;
  the LORD judges throughout the earth.
He gives mighty strength to his king;
  he increases the might of his anointed one."

[11] Then Elkanah and Hannah returned home to Ramah without Samuel. And the boy became the LORD's helper, for he assisted Eli the priest.

ELI'S WICKED SONS

[12] Now the sons of Eli were scoundrels who had no respect for the LORD [13] or for their duties as priests. Whenever anyone offered a sacrifice, Eli's sons would send over a servant with a three-pronged fork. While the meat of the sacrificed animal was still boiling, [14] the servant would stick the fork into the pot and demand that whatever it brought up be given to Eli's sons. All the Israelites who came to worship at Shiloh were treated this way. [15] Sometimes the servant would come even before the animal's fat had been burned on the altar. He would demand raw meat before it had been boiled so that it could be used for roasting.

[16] The man offering the sacrifice might reply, "Take as much as you want, but the fat must first be burned." Then the servant would demand, "No, give it to me now, or I'll take it by force." [17] So the sin of these young men was very serious in the LORD's sight, for they treated the LORD's offerings with contempt.

[18] Now Samuel, though only a boy, was the LORD's helper. He wore a linen tunic just like that of a priest.* [19] Each year his mother made a small coat for him and brought it to him when she came with her husband for the sacrifice. [20] Before they returned home, Eli would bless Elkanah and his wife and say, "May the

1:28 Or he. 2:18 Hebrew He wore a linen ephod.

My Daily Worship

— March 5 —

CLINGING TO THE ROCK

1 SAMUEL 1:1–3:21

*No one is holy like the LORD! There is no one besides you;
there is no Rock like our God (2:2).*

[i reflect]

Desperate. Tormented. Mocked and ridiculed. Perhaps you have felt these things when you have been desperate for a miracle as Hannah was.

Imagine Hannah's pain. Her husband's other wife, Peninnah, mocked and ridiculed her because she had no children. It was bad enough to be childless in her day, when childbearing gave women value. But then to be tormented by this woman who had borne sons to Hannah's own husband was too much. Her grief was great.

She poured her heart out to God, and he answered her prayer and gave her a son. Her pain was transformed to joy. Hannah had made a promise to God in her hour of anguish, as many people do, and she kept her promise when he granted her heart's desire. She dedicated her son to God and gave him up to be raised and trained for God's service in the Temple (Tabernacle) at Shiloh.

When have you experienced amazing answered prayer? Was your response praise and thanksgiving? Did you freely give back to God what he had so graciously given to you, or did you clutch it to yourself, now that you finally had what you longed for?

In Hannah's prayer of praise, she acknowledged the true source of her deliverance. She praised God's holiness, his steadfastness, his power, his protection, and his strength. And she lifted up her precious son and returned him to God.

God has given us so much. Too often, we forget what God has done for us or we simply take it for granted. This day look for his answers and, like Hannah, give him praise.

[i pray]

God, thank you for hearing and answering my prayers, whether the answer is "Yes," "No, it's not best for you," or "Wait on this one." Forgive me for sometimes forgetting it was you who delivered me in my hour of desperate need. Help me to worship and praise you today!

[i respond]

Read Hannah's praise prayer out loud (2:1–10). Consider your own situation. How has God provided for you, protected you, and answered your prayers? Write (or say) your own two- to three-sentence praise prayer.

LORD give you other children to take the place of this one she gave to the LORD.*" ²¹And the LORD gave Hannah three sons and two daughters. Meanwhile, Samuel grew up in the presence of the LORD.

²²Now Eli was very old, but he was aware of what his sons were doing to the people of Israel. He knew, for instance, that his sons were seducing the young women who assisted at the entrance of the Tabernacle.* ²³Eli said to them, "I have been hearing reports from the people about the wicked things you are doing. Why do you keep sinning? ²⁴You must stop, my sons! The reports I hear among the LORD's people are not good. ²⁵If someone sins against another person, God* can mediate for the guilty party. But if someone sins against the LORD, who can intercede?" But Eli's sons wouldn't listen to their father, for the LORD was already planning to put them to death.

²⁶Meanwhile, as young Samuel grew taller, he also continued to gain favor with the LORD and with the people.

A WARNING FOR ELI'S FAMILY

²⁷One day a prophet came to Eli and gave him this message from the LORD: "Didn't I reveal myself to your ancestors when the people of Israel were slaves in Egypt? ²⁸I chose your ancestor Aaron* from among all his relatives to be my priest, to offer sacrifices on my altar, to burn incense, and to wear the priestly garments* as he served me. And I assigned the sacrificial offerings to you priests. ²⁹So why do you scorn my sacrifices and offerings? Why do you honor your sons more than me—for you and they have become fat from the best offerings of my people!

³⁰"Therefore, the LORD, the God of Israel, says: The terrible things you are doing cannot continue! I had promised that your branch of the tribe of Levi* would always be my priests. But I will honor only those who honor me, and I will despise those who despise me. ³¹I

will put an end to your family, so it will no longer serve as my priests. All the members of your family will die before their time. None will live to a ripe old age. ³²You will watch with envy as I pour out prosperity on the people of Israel. But no members of your family will ever live out their days. ³³Those who are left alive will live in sadness and grief, and their children will die a violent death.* ³⁴And to prove that what I have said will come true, I will cause your two sons, Hophni and Phinehas, to die on the same day!

³⁵"Then I will raise up a faithful priest who will serve me and do what I tell him to do. I will bless his descendants, and his family will be priests to my anointed kings forever. ³⁶Then all of your descendants will bow before his descendants, begging for money and food. 'Please,' they will say, 'give us jobs among the priests so we will have enough to eat.'"

THE LORD SPEAKS TO SAMUEL

3 Meanwhile, the boy Samuel was serving the LORD by assisting Eli. Now in those days messages from the LORD were very rare, and visions were quite uncommon.

²One night Eli, who was almost blind by now, had just gone to bed. ³The lamp of God had not yet gone out, and Samuel was sleeping in the Tabernacle* near the Ark of God. ⁴Suddenly, the LORD called out, "Samuel! Samuel!"

"Yes?" Samuel replied. "What is it?" ⁵He jumped up and ran to Eli. "Here I am. What do you need?"

"I didn't call you," Eli replied. "Go on back to bed." So he did.

⁶Then the LORD called out again, "Samuel!"

Again Samuel jumped up and ran to Eli. "Here I am," he said. "What do you need?"

"I didn't call you, my son," Eli said. "Go on back to bed."

⁷Samuel did not yet know the LORD because

2:20 As in Greek version; Hebrew reads *this one she requested of the LORD in prayer.* 2:22 Hebrew *Tent of Meeting.* Some manuscripts lack this entire sentence. 2:25 Or *the judges.* 2:28a Hebrew *your father.* 2:28b Hebrew *an ephod.* 2:30 Hebrew *that your house and your father's house.* 2:33 As in Dead Sea Scrolls, which read *die by the sword;* Masoretic Text reads *die like mortals.* 3:3 Hebrew *the Temple of the LORD.*

Words of Worship

SERVANT

Servant—Hebrew *'e-ved*; Greek *dou-los*. Both words refer to servants in general, but the Greek word especially signifies service as a slave, one bound to a master.

In Scripture, a speaker often refers to himself as "your servant" when addressing someone of higher status. And when a worshiper is asking the Lord to rescue him from danger, we may hear something like, "Don't hide from your servant; answer me quickly, for I am in deep trouble!" (Psalm 69:17). Paul applies the title "Christ's servant" to himself and other believers (Galatians 1:10).

In our day, calling yourself a servant may seem like a putdown. In some ways, however, it's more like a badge of honor. A servant of the King of kings is on a mission for the King and enjoys his protection. To bring the Lord his due praise is an important and serious task, and he entrusts it to those made in his own image, "a kingdom of priests," or royal priesthood (1 Peter 2:9). His promise to his servants is that we will reign with Christ, for "the God of peace will soon crush Satan under your feet" (Romans 16:20). Serve the Lord with gladness!

he had never had a message from the LORD before. ⁸So now the LORD called a third time, and once more Samuel jumped up and ran to Eli. "Here I am," he said. "What do you need?"

Then Eli realized it was the LORD who was calling the boy. ⁹So he said to Samuel, "Go and lie down again, and if someone calls again, say, 'Yes, LORD, your servant is listening.' " So Samuel went back to bed.

¹⁰And the LORD came and called as before, "Samuel! Samuel!"

And Samuel replied, "Yes, your servant is listening."

¹¹Then the LORD said to Samuel, "I am about to do a shocking thing in Israel. ¹²I am going to carry out all my threats against Eli and his family. ¹³I have warned him continually that judgment is coming for his family, because his sons are blaspheming God* and he hasn't disciplined them. ¹⁴So I have vowed that the sins of Eli and his sons will never be forgiven by sacrifices or offerings."

SAMUEL SPEAKS FOR THE LORD

¹⁵Samuel stayed in bed until morning, then got up and opened the doors of the Tabernacle* as usual. He was afraid to tell Eli what the LORD had said to him. ¹⁶But Eli called out to him, "Samuel, my son."

"Here I am," Samuel replied.

¹⁷"What did the LORD say to you? Tell me everything. And may God punish you if you hide anything from me!" ¹⁸So Samuel told Eli everything; he didn't hold anything back. "It is the LORD's will," Eli replied. "Let him do what he thinks best."

¹⁹As Samuel grew up, the LORD was with him, and everything Samuel said was wise and helpful. ²⁰All the people of Israel from one end of the land to the other knew that Samuel was confirmed as a prophet of the LORD. ²¹The LORD continued to appear at Shiloh and gave messages to Samuel there at the Tabernacle. ¹And Samuel's words went out to all the people of Israel.

THE PHILISTINES CAPTURE THE ARK

4 At that time Israel was at war with the Philistines. The Israelite army was camped near Ebenezer, and the Philistines were at Aphek. ²The Philistines attacked and defeated the army of Israel, killing four thousand men. ³After the battle was over, the army of Israel retreated to their camp, and their leaders asked, "Why did the LORD allow us to

3:13 As in Greek version; Hebrew reads *his sons have made themselves contemptible.* 3:15 Hebrew *the house of the LORD.*

be defeated by the Philistines?" Then they said, "Let's bring the Ark of the Covenant of the LORD from Shiloh. If we carry it into battle with us, it* will save us from our enemies."

⁴So they sent men to Shiloh to bring back the Ark of the Covenant of the LORD Almighty, who is enthroned between the cherubim. Hophni and Phinehas, the sons of Eli, helped carry the Ark of God to where the battle was being fought. ⁵When the Israelites saw the Ark of the Covenant of the LORD coming into the camp, their shout of joy was so loud that it made the ground shake!

⁶"What's going on?" the Philistines asked. "What's all the shouting about in the Hebrew camp?" When they were told it was because the Ark of the LORD had arrived, ⁷they panicked. "The gods have* come into their camp!" they cried. "This is a disaster! We have never had to face anything like this before! ⁸Who can save us from these mighty gods of Israel? They are the same gods who destroyed the Egyptians with plagues when Israel was in the wilderness. ⁹Fight as you never have before, Philistines! If you don't, we will become the Hebrews' slaves just as they have been ours!"

¹⁰So the Philistines fought desperately, and Israel was defeated again. The slaughter was great; thirty thousand Israelite men died that day. The survivors turned and fled to their tents. ¹¹The Ark of God was captured, and Hophni and Phinehas, the two sons of Eli, were killed.

THE DEATH OF ELI

¹²A man from the tribe of Benjamin ran from the battlefront and arrived at Shiloh later that same day. He had torn his clothes and put dust on his head to show his grief. ¹³Eli was waiting beside the road to hear the news of the battle, for his heart trembled for the safety of the Ark of God. When the messenger arrived and told what had happened, an outcry resounded throughout the town. ¹⁴"What is all the noise about?" Eli asked.

4:3 Or *he.* 4:7 Or *A god has.*

The messenger rushed over to Eli, ¹⁵who was ninety-eight years old and blind. ¹⁶He said to Eli, "I have just come from the battlefront—I was there this very day."

"What happened?" Eli demanded.

¹⁷"Israel has been defeated," the messenger replied. "Thousands of Israelite troops are dead on the battlefield. Your two sons, Hophni and Phinehas, were killed, too. And the Ark of God has been captured."

¹⁸When the messenger mentioned what had happened to the Ark, Eli fell backward from his seat beside the gate. He broke his neck and died, for he was old and very fat. He had led Israel for forty years.

¹⁹Eli's daughter-in-law, the wife of Phinehas, was pregnant and near her time of delivery. When she heard that the Ark of God had been captured and that her husband and father-in-law were dead, her labor pains suddenly began. ²⁰She died in childbirth, but before she passed away the midwives tried to encourage her. "Don't be afraid," they said. "You have a baby boy!" But she did not answer or respond in any way.

²¹She named the child Ichabod—"Where is the glory?"—murmuring, "Israel's glory is gone." She named him this because the Ark of God had been captured and because her husband and her father-in-law were dead. ²²Then she said, "The glory has departed from Israel, for the Ark of God has been captured."

The responsible person seeks to make his or her whole life a response to the question and call of God.

DIETRICH BONHOEFFER

THE ARK IN PHILISTIA

5 After the Philistines captured the Ark of God, they took it from the battleground at Ebenezer to the city of Ashdod. ²They carried the Ark of God into the temple of Dagon and placed it beside the idol of Dagon. ³But when the citizens of Ashdod went to see it the next morning, Dagon had fallen with his face to the ground in front of the Ark of the LORD! So they set the idol up again. ⁴But the next morning the same thing happened—the idol had fallen face down before the Ark of the LORD again. This time his head and hands had broken off and were lying in the doorway. Only the trunk of his body was left intact. ⁵That is why to this day neither the priests of Dagon nor anyone who enters the temple of Dagon will step on its threshold.

⁶Then the LORD began to afflict the people of Ashdod and the nearby villages with a plague of tumors.* ⁷When the people realized what was happening, they cried out, "We can't keep the Ark of the God of Israel here any longer! He is against us! We will all be destroyed along with our god Dagon." ⁸So they called together the rulers of the five Philistine cities and asked, "What should we do with the Ark of the God of Israel?"

The rulers discussed it and replied, "Move it to the city of Gath." So they moved the Ark of the God of Israel to Gath. ⁹But when the Ark arrived at Gath, the LORD began afflicting its people, young and old, with a plague of tumors, and there was a great panic.

¹⁰So they sent the Ark of God to the city of Ekron, but when the people of Ekron saw it coming they cried out, "They are bringing the Ark of the God of Israel here to kill us, too!" ¹¹So the people summoned the rulers again and begged them, "Please send the Ark of the God of Israel back to its own country, or it* will kill us all." For the plague from God had already begun, and great fear was sweeping across the city. ¹²Those who didn't die were afflicted with tumors; and there was weeping everywhere.

THE PHILISTINES RETURN THE ARK

6 The Ark of the LORD remained in Philistine territory seven months in all. ²Then the Philistines called in their priests and diviners and asked them, "What should we do about the Ark of the LORD? Tell us how to return it to its own land."

³"Send the Ark of the God of Israel back, along with a gift," they were told. "Send a guilt offering so the plague will stop. Then, if the plague doesn't stop, you will know that God didn't send the plague after all."

⁴"What sort of guilt offering should we send?" they asked.

And they were told, "Since the plague has struck both you and your five rulers, make five gold tumors and five gold rats, just like those that have ravaged your land. ⁵Make these things to show honor to the God of Israel. Perhaps then he will stop afflicting you, your gods, and your land. ⁶Don't be stubborn and rebellious as Pharaoh and the Egyptians were. They wouldn't let Israel go until God had ravaged them with dreadful plagues. ⁷Now build a new cart, and find two cows that have just had calves. Make sure the cows have never been yoked to a cart. Hitch the cows to the cart, but shut their calves away from them in a pen. ⁸Put the Ark of the LORD on the cart, and beside it place a chest containing the gold rats and gold tumors. Then let the cows go wherever they want. ⁹If they cross the border of our land and go to Beth-shemesh, we will know it was the LORD who brought this great disaster upon us. If they don't, we will know that the plague was simply a coincidence and was not sent by the LORD at all."

¹⁰So these instructions were carried out. Two cows with newborn calves were hitched to the cart, and their calves were shut up in a pen. ¹¹Then the Ark of the LORD and the chest

---

5:6 Greek version and Latin Vulgate read *tumors. And rats appeared in their land, and death and destruction were throughout the city.*
5:11 Or *he.*

containing the gold rats and gold tumors were placed on the cart. ¹²And sure enough, the cows went straight along the road toward Beth-shemesh, lowing as they went. The Philistine rulers followed them as far as the border of Beth-shemesh.

¹³The people of Beth-shemesh were harvesting wheat in the valley, and when they saw the Ark, they were overjoyed! ¹⁴The cart came into the field of a man named Joshua and stopped beside a large rock. So the people broke up the wood of the cart for a fire and killed the cows and sacrificed them to the LORD as a burnt offering. ¹⁵Several men of the tribe of Levi lifted the Ark of the LORD and the chest containing the gold rats and gold tumors from the cart and placed them on the large rock. Many burnt offerings and sacrifices were offered to the LORD that day by the people of Beth-shemesh. ¹⁶The five Philistine rulers watched all this and then returned to Ekron that same day.

¹⁷The five gold tumors that were sent by the Philistines as a guilt offering to the LORD were gifts from the rulers of Ashdod, Gaza, Ashkelon, Gath, and Ekron. ¹⁸The five gold rats represented the five Philistine cities and their surrounding villages, which were controlled by the five rulers. The large rock at Beth-shemesh, where they set the Ark of the LORD, still stands in the field of Joshua as a reminder of what happened there.

THE ARK MOVED TO KIRIATH-JEARIM

¹⁹But the LORD killed seventy men* from Beth-shemesh because they looked into the Ark of the LORD. And the people mourned greatly because of what the LORD had done. ²⁰"Who is able to stand in the presence of the LORD, this holy God?" they cried out. "Where can we send the Ark from here?" ²¹So they sent messengers to the people at Kiriath-jearim and told them, "The Philistines have returned the Ark of the LORD. Please come here and get it!"

⁷So the men of Kiriath-jearim came to get the Ark of the LORD. They took it to the hillside home of Abinadab and ordained Eleazar, his son, to be in charge of it. ²The Ark remained in Kiriath-jearim for a long time—twenty years in all. During that time, all Israel mourned because it seemed that the LORD had abandoned them.

SAMUEL LEADS ISRAEL TO VICTORY

³Then Samuel said to all the people of Israel, "If you are really serious about wanting to return to the LORD, get rid of your foreign gods and your images of Ashtoreth. Determine to obey only the LORD; then he will rescue you from the Philistines." ⁴So the Israelites destroyed their images of Baal and Ashtoreth and worshiped only the LORD.

⁵Then Samuel told them, "Come to Mizpah, all of you. I will pray to the LORD for you." ⁶So they gathered there and, in a great ceremony, drew water from a well and poured it out before the LORD. They also went without food all day and confessed that they had sinned against the LORD. So it was at Mizpah that Samuel became Israel's judge.

⁷When the Philistine rulers heard that all Israel had gathered at Mizpah, they mobilized their army and advanced. The Israelites were badly frightened when they learned that the Philistines were approaching. ⁸"Plead with the LORD our God to save us from the Philistines!" they begged Samuel. ⁹So Samuel took a young lamb and offered it to the LORD as a whole burnt offering. He pleaded with the LORD to help Israel, and the LORD answered.

¹⁰Just as Samuel was sacrificing the burnt offering, the Philistines arrived for battle. But the LORD spoke with a mighty voice of thunder from heaven, and the Philistines were thrown into such confusion that the Israelites defeated them. ¹¹The men of Israel chased them from Mizpah to Beth-car, slaughtering them all along the way.

6:19 As in a few Hebrew manuscripts; most Hebrew manuscripts and Greek version read *50,070 men.* Perhaps the text should be understood to read *the LORD killed 70 men and 50 oxen.*

My Daily Worship

— March 6 —

ARE YOU SERIOUS?

1 SAMUEL 4:1–7:17

Then Samuel said to all the people of Israel, "If you are really serious about wanting to return
to the Lord, get rid of your foreign gods and your images of Ashtoreth. Determine
to obey only the Lord; then he will rescue you from the Philistines" (7:3).

[i reflect]

How often have you started out with the best of intentions—to lose weight, live within your budget, get involved in a ministry or Bible study—only to forget all about it within a week or two? All too frequently we talk about personal change but do nothing to make it happen. That type of behavior begs the question: Are we really serious about making those changes? The Israelites in this passage had to answer the same question, "If you are really serious . . . "

For twenty long years the people of Israel had grieved, feeling as though God had abandoned them. But Samuel recognized that it was the other way around—the people had abandoned God. Samuel gave them the solution to their misery, reminding them of God's faithfulness and mercy. He got right to the point, telling the people what they had to do. If they would get rid of their idols and return to God and obey him, he would rescue them.

Samuel didn't waste words. It was time for the people to stop feeling sorry for themselves and take some action. If you're really sorry, he told them, if you really mean it, then get serious. Do something about it. Get rid of whatever it is that is keeping you from worshiping God, and he will be there again for you. Samuel very well could have been speaking to us.

Imagine he is standing in front of you. Samuel begins by saying, "If you are really serious about wanting to return to the Lord . . . " How would you finish that sentence? What would it mean for you to get serious about your relationship with God? It might mean removing an "idol," or doing what you know God wants you to do. It might mean changing an attitude, or not feeling sorry for yourself.

In response to Samuel's message, the people of Israel destroyed their idols and worshiped God. And God rescued them. They got serious about returning to God and took the necessary steps to restore a healthy relationship with him. Their very act of obedience was an act of worship.

Today, think about what it might mean for you to get serious about a relationship with God. Then worship him with a clear conscience and with your whole heart.

[i pray]

Lord, show me what I need to do to "get serious" about my faith. Show me the
attitudes or habits that keep me from worshiping you with my whole heart.

[i respond]

For one day, take an inventory of your attitudes and actions. Look for ways you may have fallen into flippant or casual attitudes toward your relationship with God. Then list one or two ways you might get more serious about your faith.

[12]Samuel then took a large stone and placed it between the towns of Mizpah and Jeshanah.* He named it Ebenezer—"the stone of help"—for he said, "Up to this point the LORD has helped us!" [13]So the Philistines were subdued and didn't invade Israel again for a long time. And throughout Samuel's lifetime, the LORD's powerful hand was raised against the Philistines. [14]The Israelite towns near Ekron and Gath that the Philistines had captured were restored to Israel, along with the rest of the territory that the Philistines had taken. And there was also peace between Israel and the Amorites in those days.

[15]Samuel continued as Israel's judge for the rest of his life. [16]Each year he traveled around, setting up his court first at Bethel, then at Gilgal, and then at Mizpah. He judged the people of Israel at each of these places. [17]Then he would return to his home at Ramah, and he would hear cases there, too. And Samuel built an altar to the LORD at Ramah.

ISRAEL REQUESTS A KING

8 As Samuel grew old, he appointed his sons to be judges over Israel. [2]Joel and Abijah, his oldest sons, held court in Beersheba. [3]But they were not like their father, for they were greedy for money. They accepted bribes and perverted justice.

[4]Finally, the leaders of Israel met at Ramah to discuss the matter with Samuel. [5]"Look," they told him, "you are now old, and your sons are not like you. Give us a king like all the other nations have."

[6]Samuel was very upset with their request and went to the LORD for advice. [7]"Do as they say," the LORD replied, "for it is me they are rejecting, not you. They don't want me to be their king any longer. [8]Ever since I brought them from Egypt they have continually forsaken me and followed other gods. And now they are giving you the same treatment. [9]Do as they ask, but solemnly warn them about how a king will treat them."

SAMUEL WARNS AGAINST A KINGDOM

[10]So Samuel passed on the LORD's warning to the people. [11]"This is how a king will treat you," Samuel said. "The king will draft your sons into his army and make them run before his chariots. [12]Some will be commanders of his troops, while others will be slave laborers. Some will be forced to plow in his fields and harvest his crops, while others will make his weapons and chariot equipment. [13]The king will take your daughters from you and force them to cook and bake and make perfumes for him. [14]He will take away the best of your fields and vineyards and olive groves and give them to his own servants. [15]He will take a tenth of your harvest and distribute it among his officers and attendants. [16]He will want your male and female slaves and demand the finest of your cattle* and donkeys for his own use. [17]He will demand a tenth of your flocks, and you will be his slaves. [18]When that day comes, you will beg for relief from this king you are demanding, but the LORD will not help you."

[19]But the people refused to listen to Samuel's warning. "Even so, we still want a king," they said. [20]"We want to be like the nations around us. Our king will govern us and lead us into battle."

[21]So Samuel told the LORD what the people had said, [22]and the LORD replied, "Do as they say, and give them a king." Then Samuel agreed and sent the people home.

SAUL MEETS SAMUEL

9 Kish was a rich, influential man from the tribe of Benjamin. He was the son of Abiel and grandson of Zeror, from the family of Becorath and the clan of Aphiah. [2]His son Saul was the most handsome man in Israel— head and shoulders taller than anyone else in the land.

[3]One day Kish's donkeys strayed away, and he told Saul, "Take a servant with you, and go

7:12 As in Greek version; Hebrew reads *Shen.*   8:16 As in Greek version; Hebrew reads *young men.*

Words of Worship

DANCING

Dance, Dancing—Hebrew *ma-chol* "a round dance"; *ro-qed* "to dance"; Greek *a-gal-li-a-o* "leap for joy." Other words are used.

We might not be very good at dancing and may fall all over ourselves trying to match the beat and keep in step. Surely that couldn't be part of worship. Besides, isn't dancing something that could take our minds off the Lord and focus it on other things that might not honor him?

But wait! The psalmist is inviting us to praise the Lord with dancing (Psalm 150:4). So what if we won't win a prize in the ballroom? Maybe any kind of repeated movement, done for the glory of God, is a sort of dance to him—even if it's just the repetition of going to our place of prayer, kneeling, then standing again, and returning. That simple action could be part of what Paul means when he says, "Give yourselves completely to God since you have been given new life. And use your whole body as a tool to do what is right for the glory of God" (Romans 6:13). Or we could do more than that, when it's appropriate. Every part of us belongs to him, and sometimes we just have to *move*!

look for them." ⁴So Saul took one of his servants and traveled all through the hill country of Ephraim, the land of Shalishah, the Shaalim area, and the entire land of Benjamin, but they couldn't find the donkeys anywhere. ⁵Finally, they entered the region of Zuph, and Saul said to his servant, "Let's go home. By now my father will be more worried about us than about the donkeys!"

⁶But the servant said, "I've just thought of something! There is a man of God who lives here in this town. He is held in high honor by all the people because everything he says comes true. Let's go find him. Perhaps he can tell us which way to go."

⁷"But we don't have anything to offer him," Saul replied. "Even our food is gone, and we don't have a thing to give him."

⁸"Well," the servant said, "I have one small silver piece.* We can at least offer it to him and see what happens!" ⁹(In those days if people wanted a message from God, they would say, "Let's go and ask the seer," for prophets used to be called seers.)

¹⁰"All right," Saul agreed, "let's try it!" So they started into the town where the man of God was.

¹¹As they were climbing a hill toward the town, they met some young women coming out to draw water. So Saul and his servant asked, "Is the seer here today?"

¹²"Yes," they replied. "Stay right on this road. He is at the town gates. He has just arrived to take part in a public sacrifice up on the hill. ¹³Hurry and catch him before he goes up the hill to eat. The guests won't start until he arrives to bless the food."

¹⁴So they entered the town, and as they passed through the gates, Samuel was coming out toward them to climb the hill. ¹⁵Now the LORD had told Samuel the previous day, ¹⁶"About this time tomorrow I will send you a man from the land of Benjamin. Anoint him to be the leader of my people, Israel. He will rescue them from the Philistines, for I have looked down on my people in mercy and have heard their cry."

¹⁷When Samuel noticed Saul, the LORD said, "That's the man I told you about! He will rule my people."

¹⁸Just then Saul approached Samuel at the gateway and asked, "Can you please tell me where the seer's house is?"

¹⁹"I am the seer!" Samuel replied. "Go on up the hill ahead of me to the place of sacrifice,

---

9:8 Hebrew ¼ *shekel of silver*, about 0.1 ounces or 3 grams in weight.

and we'll eat there together. In the morning I will tell you what you want to know and send you on your way. ²⁰And don't worry about those donkeys that were lost three days ago, for they have been found. And I am here to tell you that you and your family are the focus of all Israel's hopes."

²¹Saul replied, "But I'm only from Benjamin, the smallest tribe in Israel, and my family is the least important of all the families of that tribe! Why are you talking like this to me?"

²²Then Samuel brought Saul and his servant into the great hall and placed them at the head of the table, honoring them above the thirty special guests. ²³Samuel then instructed the cook to bring Saul the finest cut of meat, the piece that had been set aside for the guest of honor. ²⁴So the cook brought it in and placed it before Saul. "Go ahead and eat it," Samuel said. "I was saving it for you even before I invited these others!" So Saul ate with Samuel.

²⁵After the feast, when they had returned to the town, Samuel took Saul up to the roof of the house and prepared a bed for him there.* ²⁶At daybreak the next morning, Samuel called up to Saul, "Get up! It's time you were on your way." So Saul got ready, and he and Samuel left the house together. ²⁷When they reached the edge of town, Samuel told Saul to send his servant on ahead. After the servant was gone, Samuel said, "Stay here, for I have received a special message for you from God."

SAMUEL ANOINTS SAUL AS KING

10 Then Samuel took a flask of olive oil and poured it over Saul's head. He kissed Saul on the cheek and said, "I am doing this because the LORD has appointed you to be the leader of his people Israel.* ²When you leave me today, you will see two men beside Rachel's tomb at Zelzah, on the border of Benjamin. They will tell you that the donkeys have been found and that your father is wor-

ried about you and is asking, 'Have you seen my son?'

³"When you get to the oak of Tabor, you will see three men coming toward you who are on their way to worship God at Bethel. One will be bringing three young goats, another will have three loaves of bread, and the third will be carrying a skin of wine. ⁴They will greet you and offer you two of the loaves, which you are to accept.

⁵"When you arrive at Gibeah of God,* where the garrison of the Philistines is located, you will meet a band of prophets coming down from the altar on the hill. They will be playing a harp, a tambourine, a flute, and a lyre, and they will be prophesying. ⁶At that time the Spirit of the LORD will come upon you with power, and you will prophesy with them. You will be changed into a different person. ⁷After these signs take place, do whatever you think is best, for God will be with you. ⁸Then go down to Gilgal ahead of me and wait for me there seven days. I will join you there to sacrifice burnt offerings and peace offerings. When I arrive, I will give you further instructions."

SAMUEL'S SIGNS ARE FULFILLED

⁹As Saul turned and started to leave, God changed his heart, and all Samuel's signs were fulfilled that day. ¹⁰When Saul and his servant arrived at Gibeah, they saw the prophets coming toward them. Then the Spirit of God came upon Saul, and he, too, began to prophesy. ¹¹When his friends heard about it, they exclaimed, "What? Is Saul a prophet? How did the son of Kish become a prophet?" ¹²But one of the neighbors responded, "It doesn't matter who his father is; anyone can become a prophet."* So that is the origin of the saying "Is Saul a prophet?"

¹³When Saul had finished prophesying, he climbed the hill to the altar. ¹⁴"Where in the world have you been?" Saul's uncle asked him.

9:25 As in Greek version; Hebrew reads *and talked with him there.*   **10:1** Greek version reads *Israel. And you will rule over the LORD's people and save them from their enemies around them. This will be the sign to you that the LORD has appointed you to be leader over his inheritance.*   **10:5** Hebrew *Gibeath-elohim.*   **10:12** Hebrew *responded, "Who is their father?"*

"We went to look for the donkeys," Saul replied, "but we couldn't find them. So we went to the prophet Samuel to ask him where they were."

[15]"Oh? And what did he say?" his uncle asked.

[16]"He said the donkeys had been found," Saul replied. But Saul didn't tell his uncle that Samuel had anointed him to be king.

SAUL IS ACCLAIMED KING

[17]Later Samuel called all the people of Israel to meet before the LORD at Mizpah. [18]And he gave them this message from the LORD, the God of Israel: "I brought you from Egypt and rescued you from the Egyptians and from all of the nations that were oppressing you. [19]But though I have done so much for you, you have rejected me and said, 'We want a king instead!' Now, therefore, present yourselves before the LORD by tribes and clans."

[20]So Samuel called the tribal leaders together before the LORD, and the tribe of Benjamin was chosen.* [21]Then he brought each family of the tribe of Benjamin before the LORD, and the family of the Matrites was chosen. And finally Saul son of Kish was chosen from among them. But when they looked for him, he had disappeared! [22]So they asked the LORD, "Where is he?"

And the LORD replied, "He is hiding among the baggage." [23]So they found him and brought him out, and he stood head and shoulders above anyone else.

[24]Then Samuel said to all the people, "This is the man the LORD has chosen as your king. No one in all Israel is his equal!"

And all the people shouted, "Long live the king!"

[25]Then Samuel told the people what the rights and duties of a king were. He wrote them down on a scroll and placed it before the LORD. Then Samuel sent the people home again.

[26]When Saul returned to his home at Gibeah, a band of men whose hearts God had touched became his constant companions. [27]But there were some wicked men who complained, "How can this man save us?" And they despised him and refused to bring him gifts. But Saul ignored them.*

SAUL DEFEATS THE AMMONITES

11 About a month later,* King Nahash of Ammon led his army against the Israelite city of Jabesh-gilead. But the citizens of Jabesh asked for peace. "Make a treaty with us, and we will be your servants," they pleaded.

[2]"All right," Nahash said, "but only on one condition. I will gouge out the right eye of every one of you as a disgrace to all Israel!"

[3]"Give us seven days to send messengers throughout Israel!" replied the leaders of Jabesh. "If none of our relatives will come to save us, we will agree to your terms."

[4]When the messengers came to Gibeah, Saul's hometown, and told the people about their plight, everyone broke into tears. [5]Saul was plowing in the field, and when he returned to town, he asked, "What's the matter? Why is everyone crying?" So they told him about the message from Jabesh.

[6]Then the Spirit of God came mightily upon Saul, and he became very angry. [7]He took two oxen and cut them into pieces and sent the messengers to carry them throughout Israel with this message: "This is what will happen to the oxen of anyone who refuses to follow Saul and Samuel into battle!" And the LORD made the people afraid of Saul's anger, and all of them came out together as one. [8]When Saul mobilized them at Bezek, he found that there were 300,000 men of Israel, in addition to 30,000* from Judah.

[9]So Saul sent the messengers back to Jabesh-gilead to say, "We will rescue you by noontime

---

10:20 Hebrew *chosen by lot*; also in 10:21. 10:27 Dead Sea Scroll 4QSamᵃ continues: *Nahash, king of the Ammonites, had been grievously oppressing the Gadites and Reubenites who lived east of the Jordan River. He gouged out the right eye of each of the Israelites living there, and he didn't allow anyone to come and rescue them. In fact, of all the Israelites east of the Jordan, there wasn't a single one whose right eye Nahash had not gouged out. But there were seven thousand men who had escaped from the Ammonites, and they had settled in Jabesh-gilead.* 11:1 As in Greek version; Hebrew lacks *About a month later.* 11:8 Dead Sea Scrolls and Greek version read *70,000.*

tomorrow!" What joy there was throughout the city when that message arrived!

¹⁰The men of Jabesh then told their enemies, "Tomorrow we will come out to you, and you can do to us as you wish." ¹¹But before dawn the next morning, Saul arrived, having divided his army into three detachments. He launched a surprise attack against the Ammonites and slaughtered them the whole morning. The remnant of their army was so badly scattered that no two of them were left together.

¹²Then the people exclaimed to Samuel, "Now where are those men who said Saul shouldn't rule over us? Bring them here, and we will kill them!"

¹³But Saul replied, "No one will be executed today, for today the LORD has rescued Israel!"

¹⁴Then Samuel said to the people, "Come, let us all go to Gilgal to reaffirm Saul's kingship." ¹⁵So they went to Gilgal, and in a solemn ceremony before the LORD they crowned him king. Then they offered peace offerings to the LORD, and Saul and all the Israelites were very happy.

SAMUEL'S FAREWELL ADDRESS

12 Then Samuel addressed the people again: "I have done as you asked and given you a king. ²I have selected him ahead of my own sons, and I stand here, an old, gray-haired man. I have served as your leader since I was a boy. ³Now tell me as I stand before the LORD and before his anointed one—whose ox or donkey have I stolen? Have I ever cheated any of you? Have I ever oppressed you? Have I ever taken a bribe? Tell me and I will make right whatever I have done wrong."

⁴"No," they replied, "you have never cheated or oppressed us in any way, and you have never taken even a single bribe."

⁵"The LORD and his anointed one are my witnesses," Samuel declared, "that you can never accuse me of robbing you."

"Yes, it is true," they replied.

⁶"It was the LORD who appointed Moses and Aaron," Samuel continued. "He brought your ancestors out of the land of Egypt. ⁷Now stand here quietly before the LORD as I remind you of all the great things the LORD has done for you and your ancestors.

⁸"When the Israelites were* in Egypt and cried out to the LORD, he sent Moses and Aaron to rescue them from Egypt and to bring them into this land. ⁹But the people soon forgot about the LORD their God, so he let them be conquered by Sisera, the general of Hazor's army, and by the Philistines and the king of Moab.

¹⁰"Then they cried to the LORD again and confessed, 'We have sinned by turning away from the LORD and worshiping the images of Baal and Ashtoreth. But we will worship you and you alone if you will rescue us from our enemies.' ¹¹Then the LORD sent Gideon,* Barak,* Jephthah, and Samuel* to save you, and you lived in safety.

¹²"But when you were afraid of Nahash, the king of Ammon, you came to me and said that you wanted a king to reign over you, even though the LORD your God was already your king. ¹³All right, here is the king you have chosen. Look him over. You asked for him, and the LORD has granted your request.

¹⁴"Now if you will fear and worship the LORD and listen to his voice, and if you do not rebel against the LORD's commands, and if you and your king follow the LORD your God, then all will be well. ¹⁵But if you rebel against the LORD's commands and refuse to listen to him, then his hand will be as heavy upon you as it was upon your ancestors.

¹⁶"Now stand here and see the great thing the LORD is about to do. ¹⁷You know that it does not rain at this time of the year during the wheat harvest. I will ask the LORD to send thunder and rain today. Then you will realize how wicked you have been in asking the LORD for a king!"

¹⁸So Samuel called to the LORD, and the

12:8 Hebrew *When Jacob was.*   12:11a Hebrew *Jerubbaal,* another name for Gideon; see Judg 7:1.   12:11b As in Greek and Syriac versions; Hebrew reads *Bedan.*   12:11c Greek and Syriac versions read *Samson.*

My Daily Worship
— March 7 —

NEVER, NEVER, NEVER GIVE UP!
1 SAMUEL 8:1–12:25

As for me, I will certainly not sin against the LORD by ending my prayers for you.
And I will continue to teach you what is good and right (12:23–24).

[i reflect]

Samuel was not happy with the people. They insisted upon having a king, when they already had the Creator of the universe as their leader. Apparently, they had forgotten all that God had given to them and had done for them. It would be understandable if Samuel were to just wash his hands of the whole affair and walk away from these ungrateful people. Perfectly understandable.

But note Samuel's response. Instead of giving up on these people, he declared that he would not stop praying for them. And rather than leave the people to their own devices, Samuel said he would continue to teach them. God had given Samuel a call, a duty, a mission, and he was determined to remain faithful to that—regardless of the outcome.

When have you felt like quitting? Maybe it was when the person you've been praying for still shows no interest in God. When have you felt like walking away? Perhaps a friend whom you have been counseling turned away and took other advice. The lesson of Samuel is clear: Never give up. Don't give up on your children who may be running with the wrong friends, on changing your own habits and attitudes, or on that person who has yet to turn to God.

Remember Samuel. Remember whom you are serving. God has called you, and God will take care of the results. He wants you to be faithful. Tell him how you feel and renew your commitment to worship him through your service and obedience.

[i pray]

Lord, there are times when I just feel like giving up and walking away.
Help me to remember that it's you I am serving.
Strengthen my faith. Help me renew my commitment to serve you.

[i respond]

What has God called you to do? Make a list of those commitments and responsibilities. Using the verses from 1 Samuel 12:23–24, fill in the sentences: "I will not sin against the Lord by ending my prayers for _____," and "I will continue to _____ ."

LORD sent thunder and rain. And all the people were terrified of the LORD and of Samuel. [19]"Pray to the LORD your God for us, or we will die!" they cried out to Samuel. "For now we have added to our sins by asking for a king."

[20]"Don't be afraid," Samuel reassured them. "You have certainly done wrong, but make sure now that you worship the LORD with all your heart and that you don't turn your back on him in any way. [21]Don't go back to worshiping worthless idols that cannot help or rescue you—they really are useless! [22]The LORD will not abandon his chosen people, for that would dishonor his great name. He made you a special nation for himself.

[23]"As for me, I will certainly not sin against the LORD by ending my prayers for you. And I will continue to teach you what is good and right. [24]But be sure to fear the LORD and sincerely worship him. Think of all the wonderful things he has done for you. [25]But if you continue to sin, you and your king will be destroyed."

CONTINUED WAR WITH PHILISTIA

13 Saul was thirty* years old when he became king, and he reigned for forty-two years.*

[2]Saul selected three thousand special troops from the army of Israel and sent the rest of the men home. He took two thousand of the chosen men with him to Micmash and the hill country of Bethel. The other thousand went with Saul's son Jonathan to Gibeah in the land of Benjamin.

[3]Soon after this, Jonathan attacked and defeated the garrison of Philistines at Geba. The news spread quickly among the Philistines that Israel was in revolt, so Saul sounded the call to arms throughout Israel. [4]He announced that the Philistine garrison at Geba had been destroyed, and he warned the people that the Philistines now hated the Israelites more than ever. So the entire Israelite army mobilized again and met Saul at Gilgal.

[5]The Philistines mustered a mighty army of three thousand* chariots, six thousand horsemen, and as many warriors as the grains of sand along the seashore! They camped at Micmash east of Beth-aven. [6]When the men of Israel saw the vast number of enemy troops, they lost their nerve entirely and tried to hide in caves, holes, rocks, tombs, and cisterns. [7]Some of them crossed the Jordan River and escaped into the land of Gad and Gilead.

SAUL'S DISOBEDIENCE AND SAMUEL'S REBUKE

Meanwhile, Saul stayed at Gilgal, and his men were trembling with fear. [8]Saul waited there seven days for Samuel, as Samuel had instructed him earlier, but Samuel still didn't come. Saul realized that his troops were rapidly slipping away. [9]So he demanded, "Bring me the burnt offering and the peace offerings!" And Saul sacrificed the burnt offering himself. [10]Just as Saul was finishing with the burnt offering, Samuel arrived. Saul went out to meet and welcome him, [11]but Samuel said, "What is this you have done?"

Saul replied, "I saw my men scattering from me, and you didn't arrive when you said you would, and the Philistines are at Micmash ready for battle. [12]So I said, 'The Philistines are ready to march against us, and I haven't even asked for the LORD's help!' So I felt obliged to offer the burnt offering myself before you came."

[13]"How foolish!" Samuel exclaimed. "You have disobeyed the command of the LORD your God. Had you obeyed, the LORD would have established your kingdom over Israel forever. [14]But now your dynasty must end, for the LORD has sought out a man after his own heart. The LORD has already chosen him to be king over his people, for you have not obeyed the LORD's command."

13:1a As in a few Greek manuscripts; the number is missing in the Hebrew.   13:1b Hebrew *reigned . . . and two;* the number is incomplete in the Hebrew. Compare Acts 13:21.   13:5 As in Greek and Syriac versions; Hebrew reads *30,000.*

Israel's Military Disadvantage

[15]Samuel then left Gilgal and went on his way, but the rest of the troops went with Saul to meet the army. They went up from Gilgal to Gibeah in the land of Benjamin.* When Saul counted the men who were still with him, he found only six hundred left! [16]Saul and Jonathan and the troops with them were staying at Geba, near Gibeah, in the land of Benjamin. The Philistines set up their camp at Micmash. [17]Three raiding parties soon left the camp of the Philistines. One went north toward Ophrah in the land of Shual, [18]another went west to Beth-horon, and the third moved toward the border above the valley of Zeboim near the wilderness.

[19]There were no blacksmiths in the land of Israel in those days. The Philistines wouldn't allow them for fear they would make swords and spears for the Hebrews. [20]So whenever the Israelites needed to sharpen their plowshares, picks, axes, or sickles,* they had to take them to a Philistine blacksmith. [21](The schedule of charges was as follows: a quarter of an ounce of silver* for sharpening a plowshare or a pick, and an eighth of an ounce* for sharpening an ax, a sickle, or an ox goad.) [22]So none of the people of Israel had a sword or spear, except for Saul and Jonathan.

[23]The pass at Micmash had meanwhile been secured by a contingent of the Philistine army.

Jonathan's Daring Plan

14 One day Jonathan said to the young man who carried his armor, "Come on, let's go over to where the Philistines have their outpost." But Jonathan did not tell his father what he was doing. [2]Meanwhile, Saul and his six hundred men were camped on the outskirts of Gibeah, around the pomegranate tree at Migron. [3](Among Saul's men was Ahijah the priest, who was wearing the linen ephod. Ahijah was the son of Ahitub, Ichabod's brother. Ahitub was the son of Phinehas and the grandson of Eli, the priest of the LORD who had served at Shiloh.)

No one realized that Jonathan had left the Israelite camp. [4]To reach the Philistine outpost, Jonathan had to go down between two rocky cliffs that were called Bozez and Seneh. [5]The cliff on the north was in front of Micmash, and the one on the south was in front of Geba. [6]"Let's go across to see those pagans," Jonathan said to his armor bearer. "Perhaps the LORD will help us, for nothing can hinder the LORD. He can win a battle whether he has many warriors or only a few!"

[7]"Do what you think is best," the youth replied. "I'm with you completely, whatever you decide."

[8]"All right then," Jonathan told him. "We will cross over and let them see us. [9]If they say to us, 'Stay where you are or we'll kill you,' then we will stop and not go up to them. [10]But if they say, 'Come on up and fight,' then we will go up. That will be the LORD's sign that he will help us defeat them."

[11]When the Philistines saw them coming, they shouted, "Look! The Hebrews are crawling out of their holes!" [12]Then they shouted to Jonathan, "Come on up here, and we'll teach you a lesson!"

"Come on, climb right behind me," Jonathan said to his armor bearer, "for the LORD will help us defeat them!" [13]So they climbed up using both hands and feet, and the Philistines fell back as Jonathan and his armor bearer killed them right and left. [14]They killed about twenty men in all, and their bodies were scattered over about half an acre.* [15]Suddenly, panic broke out in the Philistine army, both in the camp and in the field, including even the outposts and raiding parties. And just then an earthquake struck, and everyone was terrified.

Israel Defeats the Philistines

[16]Saul's lookouts in Gibeah saw a strange sight—the vast army of Philistines began to

---

13:15 As in Greek version; Hebrew reads *Samuel left Gilgal and went to Gibeah in the land of Benjamin.* 13:20 As in Greek version; Hebrew reads *or plowshares.* 13:21a Hebrew *1 pim* [8 grams]. 13:21b Hebrew *¹/₃ of a shekel* [4 grams]. 14:14 Hebrew *half a yoke;* a "yoke" was the amount of land plowed by a pair of yoked oxen in one day.

melt away in every direction. [17]"Find out who isn't here," Saul ordered. And when they checked, they found that Jonathan and his armor bearer were gone. [18]Then Saul shouted to Ahijah, "Bring the ephod here!" For at that time Ahijah was wearing the ephod in front of the Israelites.* [19]But while Saul was talking to the priest, the shouting and confusion in the Philistine camp grew louder and louder. So Saul said to Ahijah, "Never mind; let's get going!"*

[20]Then Saul and his six hundred men rushed out to the battle and found the Philistines killing each other. There was terrible confusion everywhere. [21]Even the Hebrews who had gone over to the Philistine army revolted and joined in with Saul, Jonathan, and the rest of the Israelites. [22]Likewise, the men who were hiding in the hills joined the chase when they saw the Philistines running away. [23]So the LORD saved Israel that day, and the battle continued to rage even out beyond Beth-aven.

Saul's Foolish Oath

[24]Now the men of Israel were worn out that day, because Saul had made them take an oath, saying, "Let a curse fall on anyone who eats before evening—before I have full revenge on my enemies." So no one ate a thing all day, [25]even though they found honeycomb on the ground in the forest. [26]They didn't even touch the honey because they all feared the oath they had taken.

[27]But Jonathan had not heard his father's command, and he dipped a stick into a piece of honeycomb and ate the honey. After he had eaten it, he felt much better. [28]But one of the men saw him and said, "Your father made the army take a strict oath that anyone who eats food today will be cursed. That is why everyone is weary and faint."

[29]"My father has made trouble for us all!" Jonathan exclaimed. "A command like that only hurts us. See how much better I feel now

that I have eaten this little bit of honey. [30]If the men had been allowed to eat freely from the food they found among our enemies, think how many more we could have killed!"

[31]But hungry as they were, they chased and killed the Philistines all day from Micmash to Aijalon, growing more and more faint. [32]That evening they flew upon the battle plunder and butchered the sheep, cattle, and calves, but they ate them without draining the blood. [33]Someone reported to Saul, "Look, the men are sinning against the LORD by eating meat that still has blood in it."

"That is very wrong," Saul said. "Find a large stone and roll it over here. [34]Then go out among the troops and tell them, 'Bring the cattle and sheep here to kill them and drain the blood. Do not sin against the LORD by eating meat with the blood still in it.'" So that night all the troops brought their animals and slaughtered them there. [35]And Saul built an altar to the LORD, the first one he had ever built.

[36]Then Saul said, "Let's chase the Philistines all night and destroy every last one of them."

His men replied, "We'll do whatever you think is best."

But the priest said, "Let's ask God first."

[37]So Saul asked God, "Should we go after the Philistines? Will you help us defeat them?" But God made no reply that day.

[38]Then Saul said to the leaders, "Something's wrong! I want all my army commanders to come here. We must find out what sin was committed today. [39]I vow by the name of the LORD who rescued Israel that the sinner will surely die, even if it is my own son Jonathan!" But no one would tell him what the trouble was. [40]Then Saul said, "Jonathan and I will stand over here, and all of you stand over there." And the people agreed.

[41]Then Saul prayed, "O LORD, God of Israel, please show us who is guilty and who is innocent. Are Jonathan and I guilty, or is the sin among the others?"* And Jonathan and Saul

---

14:18 As in some Greek manuscripts; Hebrew reads *"Bring the Ark of God."* For at that time the Ark of God was with the Israelites. 14:19 Hebrew *Withdraw your hand.* 14:41a Greek version adds *If the fault is with me or my son Jonathan, respond with Urim; but if the men of Israel are at fault, respond with Thummim.*

were chosen* as the guilty ones, and the people were declared innocent.

42Then Saul said, "Now choose* between me and Jonathan." And Jonathan was shown to be the guilty one.

43"Tell me what you have done," Saul demanded of Jonathan.

"I tasted a little honey," Jonathan admitted. "It was only a little bit on the end of a stick. Does that deserve death?"

44"Yes, Jonathan," Saul said, "you must die! May God strike me dead if you are not executed for this."

45But the people broke in and said to Saul, "Should Jonathan, who saved Israel today, die? Far from it! As surely as the LORD lives, not one hair on his head will be touched, for he has been used of God to do a mighty miracle today." So the people rescued Jonathan, and he was not put to death. 46Then Saul called back the army from chasing the Philistines, and the Philistines returned home.

SAUL'S MILITARY SUCCESSES

47Now when Saul had secured his grasp on Israel's throne, he fought against his enemies in every direction—against Moab, Ammon, Edom, the kings of Zobah, and the Philistines. And wherever he turned, he was victorious. 48He did great deeds and conquered the Amalekites, saving Israel from all those who had plundered them.

49Saul's sons included Jonathan, Ishbosheth,* and Malkishua. He also had two daughters: Merab, who was older, and Michal. 50Saul's wife was Ahinoam, the daughter of Ahimaaz. The commander of Saul's army was his cousin Abner, his uncle Ner's son. 51Abner's father, Ner, and Saul's father, Kish, were brothers; both were sons of Abiel.

52The Israelites fought constantly with the Philistines throughout Saul's lifetime. So whenever Saul saw a young man who was brave and strong, he drafted him into his army.

SAUL DESTROYS THE AMALEKITES

15 One day Samuel said to Saul, "I anointed you king of Israel because the LORD told me to. Now listen to this message from the LORD! 2This is what the LORD Almighty says: 'I have decided to settle accounts with the nation of Amalek for opposing Israel when they came from Egypt. 3Now go and completely destroy* the entire Amalekite nation—men, women, children, babies, cattle, sheep, camels, and donkeys.'"

4So Saul mobilized his army at Telaim. There were 200,000 troops in addition to 10,000 men from Judah. 5Then Saul went to the city of Amalek and lay in wait in the valley. 6Saul sent this message to the Kenites: "Move away from where the Amalekites live or else you will die with them. For you were kind to the people of Israel when they came up from Egypt." So the Kenites packed up and left.

7Then Saul slaughtered the Amalekites from Havilah all the way to Shur, east of Egypt. 8He captured Agag, the Amalekite king, but completely destroyed everyone else. 9Saul and his men spared Agag's life and kept the best of the sheep and cattle, the fat calves and lambs—everything, in fact, that appealed to them. They destroyed only what was worthless or of poor quality.

THE LORD REJECTS SAUL

10Then the LORD said to Samuel, 11"I am sorry that I ever made Saul king, for he has not been loyal to me and has again refused to obey me." Samuel was so deeply moved when he heard this that he cried out to the LORD all night.

12Early the next morning Samuel went to find Saul. Someone told him, "Saul went to Carmel to set up a monument to himself; then he went on to Gilgal."

13When Samuel finally found him, Saul greeted him cheerfully. "May the LORD bless you," he said. "I have carried out the LORD's command!"

14:41b Hebrew *chosen by lot.* 14:42 Hebrew *draw lots.* 14:49 Hebrew *Ishvi,* a variant name for Ishbosheth; also known as Eshbaal. 15:3 The Hebrew term used here refers to the complete consecration of things or people to the LORD, either by destroying them or by giving them as an offering; also in 15:8, 9, 15, 18, 20, 21.

[14]"Then what is all the bleating of sheep and lowing of cattle I hear?" Samuel demanded.

[15]"It's true that the army spared the best of the sheep and cattle," Saul admitted. "But they are going to sacrifice them to the LORD your God. We have destroyed everything else."

[16]Then Samuel said to Saul, "Stop! Listen to what the LORD told me last night!"

"What was it?" Saul asked.

[17]And Samuel told him, "Although you may think little of yourself, are you not the leader of the tribes of Israel? The LORD has anointed you king of Israel. [18]And the LORD sent you on a mission and told you, 'Go and completely destroy the sinners, the Amalekites, until they are all dead.' [19]Why haven't you obeyed the LORD? Why did you rush for the plunder and do exactly what the LORD said not to do?"

[20]"But I did obey the LORD," Saul insisted. "I carried out the mission he gave me. I brought back King Agag, but I destroyed everyone else. [21]Then my troops brought in the best of the sheep and cattle and plunder to sacrifice to the LORD your God in Gilgal."

[22]But Samuel replied, "What is more pleasing to the LORD: your burnt offerings and sacrifices or your obedience to his voice? Obedience is far better than sacrifice. Listening to him is much better than offering the fat of rams. [23]Rebellion is as bad as the sin of witchcraft, and stubbornness is as bad as worshiping idols. So because you have rejected the word of the LORD, he has rejected you from being king."

SAUL PLEADS FOR FORGIVENESS

[24]Then Saul finally admitted, "Yes, I have sinned. I have disobeyed your instructions and the LORD's command, for I was afraid of the people and did what they demanded. [25]Oh, please, forgive my sin now and go with me to worship the LORD."

[26]But Samuel replied, "I will not return with you! Since you have rejected the LORD's command, he has rejected you from being the king of Israel."

[27]As Samuel turned to go, Saul grabbed at him to try to hold him back and tore his robe. [28]And Samuel said to him, "See? The LORD has torn the kingdom of Israel from you today and has given it to someone else—one who is better than you. [29]And he who is the Glory of Israel will not lie, nor will he change his mind, for he is not human that he should change his mind!"

[30]Then Saul pleaded again, "I know I have sinned. But please, at least honor me before the leaders and before my people by going with me to worship the LORD your God." [31]So Samuel finally agreed and went with him, and Saul worshiped the LORD.

SAMUEL EXECUTES KING AGAG

[32]Then Samuel said, "Bring King Agag to me." Agag arrived full of smiles, for he thought, "Surely the worst is over, and I have been spared!"* [33]But Samuel said, "As your sword has killed the sons of many mothers, now your mother will be childless." And Samuel cut Agag to pieces before the LORD at Gilgal. [34]Then Samuel went home to Ramah, and Saul returned to his house at Gibeah. [35]Samuel never went to meet with Saul again, but he mourned constantly for him. And the LORD was sorry he had ever made Saul king of Israel.

SAMUEL ANOINTS DAVID AS KING

16 Finally, the LORD said to Samuel, "You have mourned long enough for Saul. I have rejected him as king of Israel. Now fill your horn with olive oil and go to Bethlehem. Find a man named Jesse who lives there, for I have selected one of his sons to be my new king."

[2]But Samuel asked, "How can I do that? If Saul hears about it, he will kill me."

"Take a heifer with you," the LORD replied, "and say that you have come to make a sacrifice to the LORD. [3]Invite Jesse to the sacrifice, and I will show you which of his sons to anoint for me."

15:32 Dead Sea Scrolls and Greek version read *Agag arrived hesitantly, for he thought, "Surely this is the bitterness of death."*

My Daily Worship

— M A R C H   8 —

H IT THE PAUSE BUTTON

1 S A M U E L   1 3 : 1 – 1 5 : 3 5

But Samuel replied, "What is more pleasing to the LORD: your burnt offerings and
sacrifices or your obedience to his voice? Obedience is far better than sacrifice.
Listening to him is much better than offering the fat of rams" (15:22).

[i reflect]

Sacrifices. We make them daily—getting up early to drive the children to school for an activity,
assisting a colleague with a difficult assignment, taking time to listen to a hurting friend. Then
think about church and all the sacrifices we've made there in terms of our time, our talents, and
our money. Everyone makes sacrifices. Yet, it's evident from Samuel's words to the Israelites that
making sacrifices is not enough.

The Israelites had been diligent in bringing the proper sacrifices to the Lord, but something was
missing. In following the letter of the law, the Israelites had missed out on what was most important—obeying God, listening to him, and spending time with him. Sacrifices are noble. In fact,
sacrifices were instituted by God as a symbol of his redemptive plan. But, as Samuel reminded
the people, developing a deeper relationship with God is more important and more pleasing to him.

No matter what we're sacrificing, God wants our heart. He wants our obedience as our worship.

What's your schedule like? Do you sacrifice your time, your energy, maybe even your family, for
other activities, including serving at church, leaving precious little time for other important matters? We can wear ourselves out serving God and miss out on what he desires most: our obedience,
our love, and our worship. We don't have time to love him, or anyone else, if we're running from
activity to activity without a moment to spare.

Slow down. Take time to truly listen to God. Look for opportunities throughout the day when you
can pause and worship. Instead of frantically changing lanes on the way to the office or doing
errands, get in the slow lane and whisper a prayer to God. Intentionally get in the longer lines at
the grocery store so you can offer him thanks for his provisions.

[i pray]

Lord, show me what you would have me do. I long to serve you, but I run so fast
that I don't have time to listen carefully to you, my spouse, or my children.
Help me stop this busyness so I can concentrate on what's truly important.

[i respond]

Make a list of your weekly commitments. Prayerfully consider each one in light of what you know
God desires from you.

⁴So Samuel did as the LORD instructed him. When he arrived at Bethlehem, the leaders of the town became afraid. "What's wrong?" they asked. "Do you come in peace?"

⁵"Yes," Samuel replied. "I have come to sacrifice to the LORD. Purify yourselves and come with me to the sacrifice." Then Samuel performed the purification rite for Jesse and his sons and invited them, too.

⁶When they arrived, Samuel took one look at Eliab and thought, "Surely this is the LORD's anointed!" ⁷But the LORD said to Samuel, "Don't judge by his appearance or height, for I have rejected him. The LORD doesn't make decisions the way you do! People judge by outward appearance, but the LORD looks at a person's thoughts and intentions."

⁸Then Jesse told his son Abinadab to step forward and walk in front of Samuel. But Samuel said, "This is not the one the LORD has chosen." ⁹Next Jesse summoned Shammah, but Samuel said, "Neither is this the one the LORD has chosen." ¹⁰In the same way all seven of Jesse's sons were presented to Samuel. But Samuel said to Jesse, "The LORD has not chosen any of these." ¹¹Then Samuel asked, "Are these all the sons you have?"

"There is still the youngest," Jesse replied. "But he's out in the fields watching the sheep."

"Send for him at once," Samuel said. "We will not sit down to eat until he arrives."

¹²So Jesse sent for him. He was ruddy and handsome, with pleasant eyes. And the LORD said, "This is the one; anoint him."

¹³So as David stood there among his brothers, Samuel took the olive oil he had brought and poured it on David's head. And the Spirit of the LORD came mightily upon him from that day on. Then Samuel returned to Ramah.

DAVID SERVES IN SAUL'S COURT

¹⁴Now the Spirit of the LORD had left Saul, and the LORD sent a tormenting spirit that filled him with depression and fear. ¹⁵Some of Saul's servants suggested a remedy. "It is clear that a spirit from God is tormenting you," they said. ¹⁶"Let us find a good musician to play the harp for you whenever the tormenting spirit is bothering you. The harp music will quiet you, and you will soon be well again."

¹⁷"All right," Saul said. "Find me someone who plays well and bring him here."

¹⁸One of the servants said to Saul, "The son of Jesse is a talented harp player. Not only that; he is brave and strong and has good judgment. He is also a fine-looking young man, and the LORD is with him."

¹⁹So Saul sent messengers to Jesse to say, "Send me your son David, the shepherd." ²⁰Jesse responded by sending David to Saul, along with a young goat and a donkey loaded down with food and wine. ²¹So David went to Saul and served him. Saul liked David very much, and David became one of Saul's armor bearers.

²²Then Saul sent word to Jesse asking, "Please let David join my staff, for I am very pleased with him." ²³And whenever the tormenting spirit from God troubled Saul, David would play the harp. Then Saul would feel better, and the tormenting spirit would go away.

GOLIATH CHALLENGES THE ISRAELITES

17 The Philistines now mustered their army for battle and camped between Socoh in Judah and Azekah at Ephes-dammim. ²Saul countered by gathering his troops near the valley of Elah. ³So the Philistines and Israelites faced each other on opposite hills, with the valley between them.

⁴Then Goliath, a Philistine champion from Gath, came out of the Philistine ranks to face the forces of Israel. He was a giant of a man, measuring over nine feet* tall! ⁵He wore a bronze helmet and a coat of mail that weighed 125 pounds.* ⁶He also wore bronze leggings, and he slung a bronze javelin over his back. ⁷The shaft of his spear was as heavy and thick

---

17:4 Hebrew 6 cubits and 1 span [which totals about 9.75 feet or 3 meters]; Greek version and Dead Sea Scrolls read 4 cubits and 1 span [which totals about 6.75 feet or 2 meters]. 17:5 Hebrew 5,000 shekels [57 kilograms].

My Daily Worship

— *March 9* —

BE LEAST BUT NOT LAST!

1 SAMUEL 16:1–17:58

But the LORD said to Samuel, "Don't judge by his appearance or height, for I have rejected him. The LORD doesn't make decisions the way you do! People judge by outward appearance, but the LORD looks at a person's thoughts and intentions" (16:7).

[i reflect]

When have you been overlooked or left out because you just didn't measure up in some way? Maybe you were passed over for a promotion because your colleague landed a bigger deal than you did. Or maybe you didn't get to sing that solo because you just couldn't reach the high notes like the other soprano.

Susan G. didn't measure up. She had limped all her life. Complications at birth had left her abnormally short, her leg twisted. She was always picked last for sports teams in school because the other kids knew she was a slow runner. She had never been invited to a school dance.

Despite her obvious physical limitations, Susan remained cheerful and optimistic. If she minded being left out of activities, she never showed it. She just concentrated on her studies and on being a good friend. So at the end of her senior year in high school, imagine Susan's surprise when she was voted the "Girl with the Biggest Heart." Although Susan had often been left out, her classmates recognized her as an invaluable member of their class.

It's great to know that God doesn't care if we limp or can't sing or tell a good joke. He's not impressed with our bank account, nice house, or important job. Instead, he's concerned about what's inside our hearts. That's what he told Samuel when he was looking for a future king, "The LORD looks at a person's thoughts and intentions." The exterior doesn't matter; it's what's inside that counts.

Being "right" on the inside begins with worship. Turn your attention to God and ask him to make you his person.

[i pray]

Lord, thank you for not looking at me like people do. I'm so glad that you care more about what I think and say than about how I look, and that you don't judge me by outward standards of beauty or brilliance or possessions.

[i respond]

Look into a mirror. Note all your characteristics—the good ones along with the ones you don't care for. Tell God right now that you know none of this matters to him. Hear his voice tell you how beautiful you are inside—and that's what counts.

as a weaver's beam, tipped with an iron spear-head that weighed fifteen pounds.* An armor bearer walked ahead of him carrying a huge shield.

[8]Goliath stood and shouted across to the Israelites, "Do you need a whole army to settle this? Choose someone to fight for you, and I will represent the Philistines. We will settle this dispute in single combat! [9]If your man is able to kill me, then we will be your slaves. But if I kill him, you will be our slaves! [10]I defy the armies of Israel! Send me a man who will fight with me!" [11]When Saul and the Israelites heard this, they were terrified and deeply shaken.

JESSE SENDS DAVID TO SAUL'S CAMP

[12]Now David was the son of a man named Jesse, an Ephrathite from Bethlehem in the land of Judah. Jesse was an old man at that time, and he had eight sons in all. [13]Jesse's three oldest sons—Eliab, Abinadab, and Shammah—had already joined Saul's army to fight the Philistines. [14]David was the youngest of Jesse's sons. Since David's three oldest brothers were in the army, they stayed with Saul's forces all the time. [15]But David went back and forth between working for Saul and helping his father with the sheep in Beth-lehem.

[16]For forty days, twice a day, morning and evening, the Philistine giant strutted in front of the Israelite army.

[17]One day Jesse said to David, "Take this half-bushel* of roasted grain and these ten loaves of bread to your brothers. [18]And give these ten cuts of cheese to their captain. See how your brothers are getting along, and bring me back a letter from them.*"

[19]David's brothers were with Saul and the Israelite army at the valley of Elah, fighting against the Philistines. [20]So David left the sheep with another shepherd and set out early the next morning with the gifts. He arrived at the outskirts of the camp just as the Israelite army was leaving for the battlefield with shouts and battle cries. [21]Soon the Israelite and Philistine forces stood facing each other, army against army. [22]David left his things with the keeper of supplies and hurried out to the ranks to greet his brothers. [23]As he was talking with them, he saw Goliath, the champion from Gath, come out from the Philistine ranks, shouting his challenge to the army of Israel.

[24]As soon as the Israelite army saw him, they began to run away in fright. [25]"Have you seen the giant?" the men were asking. "He comes out each day to challenge Israel. And have you heard about the huge reward the king has offered to anyone who kills him? The king will give him one of his daughters for a wife, and his whole family will be exempted from pay-ing taxes!"

[26]David talked to some others standing there to verify the report. "What will a man get for killing this Philistine and putting an end to his abuse of Israel?" he asked them. "Who is this pagan Philistine anyway, that he is allowed to defy the armies of the living God?" [27]And David received the same reply as before: "What you have been hearing is true. That is the reward for killing the giant."

[28]But when David's oldest brother, Eliab, heard David talking to the men, he was angry. "What are you doing around here anyway?" he demanded. "What about those few sheep you're supposed to be taking care of? I know about your pride and dishonesty. You just want to see the battle!"

[29]"What have I done now?" David replied. "I was only asking a question!" [30]He walked over to some others and asked them the same thing and received the same answer. [31]Then David's question was reported to King Saul, and the king sent for him.

DAVID KILLS GOLIATH

[32]"Don't worry about a thing," David told Saul. "I'll go fight this Philistine!"

[33]"Don't be ridiculous!" Saul replied. "There is no way you can go against this Philistine.

17:7 Hebrew *600 shekels* [6.8 kilograms].   17:17 Hebrew *ephah* [18 liters].   17:18 Hebrew *and take their pledge.*

You are only a boy, and he has been in the army since he was a boy!"

³⁴But David persisted. "I have been taking care of my father's sheep," he said. "When a lion or a bear comes to steal a lamb from the flock, ³⁵I go after it with a club and take the lamb from its mouth. If the animal turns on me, I catch it by the jaw and club it to death. ³⁶I have done this to both lions and bears, and I'll do it to this pagan Philistine, too, for he has defied the armies of the living God! ³⁷The LORD who saved me from the claws of the lion and the bear will save me from this Philistine!"

Saul finally consented. "All right, go ahead," he said. "And may the LORD be with you!"

³⁸Then Saul gave David his own armor—a bronze helmet and a coat of mail. ³⁹David put it on, strapped the sword over it, and took a step or two to see what it was like, for he had never worn such things before. "I can't go in these," he protested. "I'm not used to them." So he took them off again. ⁴⁰He picked up five smooth stones from a stream and put them in his shepherd's bag. Then, armed only with his shepherd's staff and sling, he started across to fight Goliath.

⁴¹Goliath walked out toward David with his shield bearer ahead of him, ⁴²sneering in contempt at this ruddy-faced boy. ⁴³"Am I a dog," he roared at David, "that you come at me with a stick?" And he cursed David by the names of his gods. ⁴⁴"Come over here, and I'll give your flesh to the birds and wild animals!" Goliath yelled.

⁴⁵David shouted in reply, "You come to me with sword, spear, and javelin, but I come to you in the name of the LORD Almighty—the God of the armies of Israel, whom you have defied. ⁴⁶Today the LORD will conquer you, and I will kill you and cut off your head. And then I will give the dead bodies of your men to the birds and wild animals, and the whole world will know that there is a God in Israel! ⁴⁷And everyone will know that the LORD does not need weapons to rescue his people. It is

his battle, not ours. The LORD will give you to us!"

⁴⁸As Goliath moved closer to attack, David quickly ran out to meet him. ⁴⁹Reaching into his shepherd's bag and taking out a stone, he hurled it from his sling and hit the Philistine in the forehead. The stone sank in, and Goliath stumbled and fell face downward to the ground. ⁵⁰So David triumphed over the Philistine giant with only a stone and sling. And since he had no sword, ⁵¹he ran over and pulled Goliath's sword from its sheath. David used it to kill the giant and cut off his head.

ISRAEL ROUTS THE PHILISTINES

When the Philistines saw that their champion was dead, they turned and ran. ⁵²Then the Israelites gave a great shout of triumph and rushed after the Philistines, chasing them as far as Gath* and the gates of Ekron. The bodies of the dead and wounded Philistines were strewn all along the road from Shaaraim, as far as Gath and Ekron. ⁵³Then the Israelite army returned and plundered the deserted Philistine camp. ⁵⁴(David took Goliath's head to Jerusalem, but he stored the Philistine's armor in his own tent.)

⁵⁵As Saul watched David go out to fight Goliath, he asked Abner, the general of his army, "Abner, whose son is he?"

"I really don't know," Abner said.

⁵⁶"Well, find out!" the king told him.

⁵⁷After David had killed Goliath, Abner brought him to Saul with the Philistine's head still in his hand. ⁵⁸"Tell me about your father, my boy," Saul said.

And David replied, "His name is Jesse, and we live in Bethlehem."

SAUL BECOMES JEALOUS OF DAVID

18 After David had finished talking with Saul, he met Jonathan, the king's son. There was an immediate bond of love between them, and they became the best of

17:52 As in some Greek manuscripts; Hebrew reads *a valley.*

friends. ²From that day on Saul kept David with him at the palace and wouldn't let him return home. ³And Jonathan made a special vow to be David's friend, ⁴and he sealed the pact by giving him his robe, tunic, sword, bow, and belt.

⁵Whatever Saul asked David to do, David did it successfully. So Saul made him a commander in his army, an appointment that was applauded by the fighting men and officers alike. ⁶But something happened when the victorious Israelite army was returning home after David had killed Goliath. Women came out from all the towns along the way to celebrate and to cheer for King Saul, and they sang and danced for joy with tambourines and cymbals.* ⁷This was their song:

"Saul has killed his thousands,
    and David his ten thousands!"

⁸This made Saul very angry. "What's this?" he said. "They credit David with ten thousands and me with only thousands. Next they'll be making him their king!" ⁹So from that time on Saul kept a jealous eye on David.

¹⁰The very next day, in fact, a tormenting spirit from God overwhelmed Saul, and he began to rave like a madman. David began to play the harp, as he did whenever this happened. But Saul, who had a spear in his hand, ¹¹suddenly hurled it at David, intending to pin him to the wall. But David jumped aside and escaped. This happened another time, too, ¹²for Saul was afraid of him, and he was jealous because the LORD had left him and was now with David. ¹³Finally, Saul banned him from his presence and appointed him commander over only a thousand men, but David faithfully led his troops into battle.

¹⁴David continued to succeed in everything he did, for the LORD was with him. ¹⁵When Saul recognized this, he became even more afraid of him. ¹⁶But all Israel and Judah loved David because he was so successful at leading his troops into battle.

DAVID MARRIES SAUL'S DAUGHTER

¹⁷One day Saul said to David, "I am ready to give you my older daughter, Merab, as your wife. But first you must prove yourself to be a real warrior by fighting the LORD's battles." For Saul thought to himself, "I'll send him out against the Philistines and let them kill him rather than doing it myself."

¹⁸"Who am I, and what is my family in Israel that I should be the king's son-in-law?" David exclaimed. "My father's family is nothing!" ¹⁹So* when the time came for the wedding, Saul gave Merab in marriage to Adriel, a man from Meholah.

²⁰In the meantime, Saul's daughter Michal had fallen in love with David, and Saul was delighted when he heard about it. ²¹"Here's another chance to see him killed by the Philistines!" Saul said to himself. But to David he said, "I have a way for you to become my son-in-law after all!"

²²Then Saul told his men to say confidentially to David, "The king really likes you, and so do we. Why don't you accept the king's offer and become his son-in-law?"

²³When Saul's men said these things to David, he replied, "How can a poor man from a humble family afford the bride price for the daughter of a king?"

²⁴When Saul's men reported this back to the king, ²⁵he told them, "Tell David that all I want for the bride price is one hundred Philistine foreskins! Vengeance on my enemies is all I really want." But what Saul had in mind was that David would be killed in the fight.

²⁶David was delighted to accept the offer. So before the time limit expired, ²⁷he and his men went out and killed two hundred Philistines and presented all their foreskins to the king. So Saul gave Michal to David to be his wife.

²⁸When the king realized how much the LORD was with David and how much Michal loved him, ²⁹he became even more afraid of him, and he remained David's enemy for the rest of his life. ³⁰Whenever the Philistine army

18:6 The type of instrument represented by the final word is uncertain.   18:19 Or But.

My Daily Worship

— March 10 —

THE GIFT OF FRIENDSHIP
1 SAMUEL 18:1–20:42

After David had finished talking with Saul, he met Jonathan, the king's son.
There was an immediate bond of love between them,
and they became the best of friends (18:1).

[i reflect]

What does it take to form a friendship? Sometimes it's a bond that develops over years of shared experiences. Sometimes, as in the case of David and Jonathan, the bond was formed almost immediately. Whatever the circumstances, friends are those special people with whom we can laugh and cry. They encourage us and stay close to us during the difficult times.

Just the word *friend* can bring a smile. Whether it's the person you call when you get good news or the person who accompanies you through your dark valleys, that friend is a rich gift from God. But the greatest friendship gift is with God himself. Think about it. God not only gives us the gift of friendship, but he also offers us *his* friendship. The Creator of the universe promises to be with us always, to encourage us when we are down, and to comfort us when we are grieving.

Just as Jonathan and David were loyal to each other through great difficulties, God is faithful to us as we stay close to him. His promise is true—he will never leave or abandon us. He encourages us to lay our deepest burdens and concerns upon him. He offers to guide us and walk with us through the storms. That is a friendship worth keeping and maintaining.

Celebrate the gift of God's friendship—and friendship itself—by worshiping him with a close friend. Share your concerns with that person. Ask that person to lift you up in prayer as you pray for them. God intends for us to live in community—with him and with each other—as we worship and as we go through the ups and downs of daily life.

[i pray]

God, thank you for my friends. I am so glad that I don't walk through life alone,
but that you have placed each of my "favored companions" alongside me, so
we can travel our paths together. Thank you for being my Friend of friends.

[i respond]

Ask a friend to be your prayer partner. Establish a set time when you can reach one another during the week and pray for each other's concerns.

attacked, David was more successful against them than all the rest of Saul's officers. So David's name became very famous throughout the land.

SAUL TRIES TO KILL DAVID

19 Saul now urged his servants and his son Jonathan to assassinate David. But Jonathan, because of his close friendship with David, [2]told him what his father was planning. "Tomorrow morning," he warned him, "you must find a hiding place out in the fields. [3]I'll ask my father to go out there with me, and I'll talk to him about you. Then I'll tell you everything I can find out."

[4]The next morning Jonathan spoke with his father about David, saying many good things about him. "Please don't sin against David," Jonathan pleaded. "He's never done anything to harm you. He has always helped you in any way he could. [5]Have you forgotten about the time he risked his life to kill the Philistine giant and how the LORD brought a great victory to Israel as a result? You were certainly happy about it then. Why should you murder an innocent man like David? There is no reason for it at all!"

[6]So Saul listened to Jonathan and vowed, "As surely as the LORD lives, David will not be killed." [7]Afterward Jonathan called David and told him what had happened. Then he took David to see Saul, and everything was as it had been before.

[8]War broke out shortly after that, and David led his troops against the Philistines. He attacked them with such fury that they all ran away.

[9]But one day as Saul was sitting at home, the tormenting spirit from the LORD suddenly came upon him again. As David played his harp for the king, [10]Saul hurled his spear at David in an attempt to kill him. But David dodged out of the way and escaped into the night, leaving the spear stuck in the wall.

MICHAL SAVES DAVID'S LIFE

[11]Then Saul sent troops to watch David's house. They were told to kill David when he came out the next morning. But Michal, David's wife, warned him, "If you don't get away tonight, you will be dead by morning." [12]So she helped him climb out through a window, and he escaped. [13]Then she took an idol* and put it in his bed, covered it with blankets, and put a cushion of goat's hair at its head. [14]When the troops came to arrest David, she told them he was sick and couldn't get out of bed.

[15]"Then bring him to me in his bed," Saul ordered, "so I can kill him as he lies there!" And he sent them back to David's house. [16]But when they came to carry David out, they discovered that it was only an idol in the bed with a cushion of goat's hair at its head.

[17]"Why have you tricked me and let my enemy escape?" Saul demanded of Michal.

"I had to," Michal replied. "He threatened to kill me if I didn't help him."

[18]So David got away and went to Ramah to see Samuel, and he told him all that Saul had done to him. Then Samuel took David with him to live at Naioth. [19]When the report reached Saul that David was at Naioth in Ramah, [20]he sent troops to capture him. But when they arrived and saw Samuel and the other prophets prophesying, the Spirit of God came upon Saul's men, and they also began to prophesy. [21]When Saul heard what had happened, he sent other troops, but they, too, prophesied! The same thing happened a third time! [22]Finally, Saul himself went to Ramah and arrived at the great well in Secu. "Where are Samuel and David?" he demanded.

"They are at Naioth in Ramah," someone told him. [23]But on the way to Naioth the Spirit of God came upon Saul, and he, too, began to prophesy! [24]He tore off his clothes and lay on the ground all day and all night, prophesying in the presence of Samuel. The people who were watching exclaimed, "What? Is Saul a prophet, too?"

19:13 Hebrew *teraphim;* also in 19:16.

JONATHAN HELPS DAVID

20 David now fled from Naioth in Ramah and found Jonathan. "What have I done?" he exclaimed. "What is my crime? How have I offended your father that he is so determined to kill me?"

²"That's not true!" Jonathan protested. "I'm sure he's not planning any such thing, for he always tells me everything he's going to do, even the little things. I know he wouldn't hide something like this from me. It just isn't so!"

³Then David took an oath before Jonathan and said, "Your father knows perfectly well about our friendship, so he has said to himself, 'I won't tell Jonathan—why should I hurt him?' But I swear to you that I am only a step away from death! I swear it by the LORD and by your own soul!"

⁴"Tell me what I can do!" Jonathan exclaimed.

⁵David replied, "Tomorrow we celebrate the new moon festival. I've always eaten with your father on this occasion, but tomorrow I'll hide in the field and stay there until the evening of the third day. ⁶If your father asks where I am, tell him I asked permission to go home to Bethlehem for an annual family sacrifice. ⁷If he says, 'Fine!' then you will know all is well. But if he is angry and loses his temper, then you will know he was planning to kill me. ⁸Show me this kindness as my sworn friend—for we made a covenant together before the LORD—or kill me yourself if I have sinned against your father. But please don't betray me to him!"

⁹"Never!" Jonathan exclaimed. "You know that if I had the slightest notion my father was planning to kill you, I would tell you at once."

¹⁰Then David asked, "How will I know whether or not your father is angry?"

¹¹"Come out to the field with me," Jonathan replied. And they went out there together. ¹²Then Jonathan told David, "I promise by the LORD, the God of Israel, that by this time tomorrow, or the next day at the latest, I will talk to my father and let you know at once how he feels about you. If he speaks favorably about you, I will let you know. ¹³But if he is angry and wants you killed, may the LORD kill me if I don't warn you so you can escape and live. May the LORD be with you as he used to be with my father. ¹⁴And may you treat me with the faithful love of the LORD as long as I live. But if I die, ¹⁵treat my family with this faithful love, even when the LORD destroys all your enemies."

¹⁶So Jonathan made a covenant with David,* saying, "May the LORD destroy all your enemies!" ¹⁷And Jonathan made David reaffirm his vow of friendship again, for Jonathan loved David as much as he loved himself.

¹⁸Then Jonathan said, "Tomorrow we celebrate the new moon festival. You will be missed when your place at the table is empty. ¹⁹The day after tomorrow, toward evening, go to the place where you hid before, and wait there by the stone pile.* ²⁰I will come out and shoot three arrows to the side of the stone pile as though I were shooting at a target. ²¹Then I will send a boy to bring the arrows back. If you hear me tell him, 'They're on this side,' then you will know, as surely as the LORD lives, that all is well, and there is no trouble. ²²But if I tell him, 'Go farther—the arrows are still ahead of you,' then it will mean that you must leave immediately, for the LORD is sending you away. ²³And may the LORD make us keep our promises to each other, for he has witnessed them."

> Strong affections for God
> rooted in truth
> are the bone and marrow
> of biblical worship.
>
> JOHN PIPER

20:16 Hebrew *with the house of David.* 20:19 Hebrew *the stone Ezel.* The meaning of the Hebrew is uncertain.

²⁴So David hid himself in the field, and when the new moon festival began, the king sat down to eat. ²⁵He sat at his usual place against the wall, with Jonathan sitting opposite him* and Abner beside him. But David's place was empty. ²⁶Saul didn't say anything about it that day, for he said to himself, "Something must have made David ceremonially unclean. Yes, that must be why he's not here." ²⁷But when David's place was empty again the next day, Saul asked Jonathan, "Why hasn't the son of Jesse been here for dinner either yesterday or today?"

²⁸Jonathan replied, "David earnestly asked me if he could go to Bethlehem. ²⁹He wanted to take part in a family sacrifice. His brother demanded that he be there, so I told him he could go. That's why he isn't here."

³⁰Saul boiled with rage at Jonathan. "You stupid son of a whore!"* he swore at him. "Do you think I don't know that you want David to be king in your place, shaming yourself and your mother? ³¹As long as that son of Jesse is alive, you'll never be king. Now go and get him so I can kill him!"

³²"But what has he done?" Jonathan demanded. "Why should he be put to death?" ³³Then Saul hurled his spear at Jonathan, intending to kill him. So at last Jonathan realized that his father was really determined to kill David. ³⁴Jonathan left the table in fierce anger and refused to eat all that day, for he was crushed by his father's shameful behavior toward David.

³⁵The next morning, as agreed, Jonathan went out into the field and took a young boy with him to gather his arrows. ³⁶"Start running," he told the boy, "so you can find the arrows as I shoot them." So the boy ran, and Jonathan shot an arrow beyond him. ³⁷When the boy had almost reached the arrow, Jonathan shouted, "The arrow is still ahead of you. ³⁸Hurry, hurry, don't wait." So the boy quickly gathered up the arrows and ran back to his master. ³⁹He, of course, didn't understand what Jonathan meant; only Jonathan and David knew. ⁴⁰Then Jonathan gave his bow and arrows to the boy and told him to take them back to the city.

⁴¹As soon as the boy was gone, David came out from where he had been hiding near the stone pile.* Then David bowed to Jonathan with his face to the ground. Both of them were in tears as they embraced each other and said good-bye, especially David. ⁴²At last Jonathan said to David, "Go in peace, for we have made a pact in the LORD's name. We have entrusted each other and each other's children into the LORD's hands forever." Then David left, and Jonathan returned to the city.

DAVID RUNS FROM SAUL

21 David went to the city of Nob to see Ahimelech the priest. Ahimelech trembled when he saw him. "Why are you alone?" he asked. "Why is no one with you?"

²"The king has sent me on a private matter," David said. "He told me not to tell anyone why I am here. I have told my men where to meet me later. ³Now, what is there to eat? Give me five loaves of bread or anything else you have."

⁴"We don't have any regular bread," the priest replied. "But there is the holy bread, which I guess you can have if your young men have not slept with any women recently."

⁵"Don't worry," David replied. "I never allow my men to be with women when they are on a campaign. And since they stay clean even on ordinary trips, how much more on this one!"

⁶So, since there was no other food available, the priest gave him the holy bread—the Bread of the Presence that was placed before the LORD in the Tabernacle. It had just been replaced that day with fresh bread.

⁷Now Doeg the Edomite, Saul's chief herdsman, was there that day for ceremonial purification.*

⁸David asked Ahimelech, "Do you have a

20:25 As in Greek version; Hebrew reads *with Jonathan standing.*   20:30 Hebrew *You son of a perverse and rebellious woman.*
20:41 As in Greek version; Hebrew reads *near the south edge.*   21:7 Hebrew *was detained before the LORD.*

spear or sword? The king's business was so urgent that I didn't even have time to grab a weapon!"

9"I only have the sword of Goliath the Philistine, whom you killed in the valley of Elah," the priest replied. "It is wrapped in a cloth behind the ephod. Take that if you want it, for there is nothing else here."

"There is nothing like it!" David replied. "Give it to me!"

10So David escaped from Saul and went to King Achish of Gath. 11But Achish's officers weren't happy about his being there. "Isn't this David, the king of the land?" they asked. "Isn't he the one the people honor with dances, singing, 'Saul has killed his thousands, and David his ten thousands'?"

12David heard these comments and was afraid of what King Achish might do to him. 13So he pretended to be insane, scratching on doors and drooling down his beard. 14Finally, King Achish said to his men, "Must you bring me a madman? 15We already have enough of them around here! Why should I let someone like this be my guest?"

DAVID AT THE CAVE OF ADULLAM

22 So David left Gath and escaped to the cave of Adullam. Soon his brothers and other relatives joined him there. 2Then others began coming—men who were in trouble or in debt or who were just discontented—until David was the leader of about four hundred men.

3Later David went to Mizpeh in Moab, where he asked the king, "Would you let my father and mother live here under royal protection until I know what God is going to do for me?" 4The king agreed, and David's parents stayed in Moab while David was living in his stronghold.

5One day the prophet Gad told David, "Leave the stronghold and return to the land of Judah." So David went to the forest of Hereth. 6The news of his arrival in Judah soon reached Saul. At the time, the king was sitting beneath a tamarisk tree on the hill at Gibeah, holding his spear and surrounded by his officers.

7"Listen here, you men of Benjamin!" Saul shouted when he heard the news. "Has David promised you fields and vineyards? Has he promised to make you commanders in his army? 8Is that why you have conspired against me? For not one of you has ever told me that my own son is on David's side. You're not even sorry for me. Think of it! My own son—encouraging David to try and kill me!"

9Then Doeg the Edomite, who was standing there with Saul's men, spoke up. "When I was at Nob," he said, "I saw David talking to Ahimelech the priest. 10Ahimelech consulted the LORD to find out what David should do. Then he gave David food and the sword of Goliath the Philistine."

THE SLAUGHTER OF THE PRIESTS

11King Saul immediately sent for Ahimelech and all his family, who served as priests at Nob. 12When they arrived, Saul shouted at him, "Listen to me, you son of Ahitub!"

"What is it, my king?" Ahimelech asked.

13"Why have you and David conspired against me?" Saul demanded. "Why did you give him food and a sword? Why have you inquired of God for him? Why did you encourage him to revolt against me and to come here and attack me?"

14"But sir," Ahimelech replied, "is there anyone among all your servants who is as faithful as David, your son-in-law? Why, he is the captain of your bodyguard and a highly honored member of your household! 15This was certainly not the first time I had consulted God for him! Please don't accuse me and my family in this matter, for I knew nothing of any plot against you."

16"You will surely die, Ahimelech, along with your entire family!" the king shouted. 17And he ordered his bodyguards, "Kill these priests of the LORD, for they are allies and conspirators with David! They knew he was running away from me, but they didn't tell me!" But Saul's men refused to kill the LORD's priests.

[18]Then the king said to Doeg, "You do it." So Doeg turned on them and killed them, eighty-five priests in all, all still wearing their priestly tunics. [19]Then he went to Nob, the city of the priests, and killed the priests' families—men and women, children and babies, and all the cattle, donkeys, and sheep.

[20]Only Abiathar, one of the sons of Ahimelech, escaped and fled to David. [21]When he told David that Saul had killed the priests of the LORD, [22]David exclaimed, "I knew it! When I saw Doeg there that day, I knew he would tell Saul. Now I have caused the death of all your father's family. [23]Stay here with me, and I will protect you with my own life, for the same person wants to kill us both."

DAVID PROTECTS THE TOWN OF KEILAH

23 One day news came to David that the Philistines were at Keilah stealing grain from the threshing floors. [2]David asked the LORD, "Should I go and attack them?"

"Yes, go and save Keilah," the LORD told him.

[3]But David's men said, "We're afraid even here in Judah. We certainly don't want to go to Keilah to fight the whole Philistine army!"

[4]So David asked the LORD again, and again the LORD replied, "Go down to Keilah, for I will help you conquer the Philistines."

[5]So David and his men went to Keilah. They slaughtered the Philistines and took all their livestock and rescued the people of Keilah. [6]Abiathar the priest went to Keilah with David, taking the ephod with him to get answers for David from the LORD.

[7]Saul soon learned that David was at Keilah. "Good!" he exclaimed. "We've got him now! God has handed him over to me, for he has trapped himself in a walled city!"

[8]So Saul mobilized his entire army to march to Keilah and attack David and his men. [9]But David learned of Saul's plan and told Abiathar the priest to bring the ephod and ask the LORD

> *Praise is where God lives.*
>
> UNKNOWN

what he should do. [10]And David prayed, "O LORD, God of Israel, I have heard that Saul is planning to come and destroy Keilah because I am here. [11]Will the men of Keilah surrender me to him?* And will Saul actually come as I have heard? O LORD, God of Israel, please tell me."

And the LORD said, "He will come."

[12]Again David asked, "Will these men of Keilah really betray me and my men to Saul?"

And the LORD replied, "Yes, they will betray you."

DAVID HIDES IN THE WILDERNESS

[13]So David and his men—about six hundred of them now—left Keilah and began roaming the countryside. Word soon reached Saul that David had escaped, so he didn't go to Keilah after all. [14]David now stayed in the strongholds of the wilderness and in the hill country of Ziph. Saul hunted him day after day, but God didn't let him be found.

[15]One day near Horesh, David received the news that Saul was on the way to Ziph to search for him and kill him. [16]Jonathan went to find David and encouraged him to stay strong in his faith in God. [17]"Don't be afraid," Jonathan reassured him. "My father will never find you! You are going to be the king of Israel, and I will be next to you, as my father is well aware." [18]So the two of them renewed their covenant of friendship before the LORD.

23:11 Some manuscripts lack the first sentence of 23:11.

Then Jonathan returned home, while David stayed at Horesh.

¹⁹But now the men of Ziph went to Saul in Gibeah and betrayed David to him. "We know where David is hiding," they said. "He is in the strongholds of Horesh on the hill of Hakilah, which is in the southern part of Jeshimon. ²⁰Come down whenever you're ready, O king, and we will catch him and hand him over to you!"

²¹"The LORD bless you," Saul said. "At last someone is concerned about me! ²²Go and check again to be sure of where he is staying and who has seen him there, for I know that he is very crafty. ²³Discover his hiding places, and come back with a more definite report. Then I'll go with you. And if he is in the area at all, I'll track him down, even if I have to search every hiding place in Judah!"

²⁴So the men of Ziph returned home ahead of Saul. Meanwhile, David and his men had moved into the wilderness of Maon in the Arabah Valley south of Jeshimon. ²⁵When David heard that Saul and his men were searching for him, he went even farther into the wilderness to the great rock, and he remained there in the wilderness of Maon. But Saul kept after him. ²⁶He and David were now on opposite sides of a mountain. Just as Saul and his men began to close in on David and his men, ²⁷an urgent message reached Saul that the Philistines were raiding Israel again. ²⁸So Saul quit the chase and returned to fight the Philistines. Ever since that time, the place where David was camped has been called the Rock of Escape.* ²⁹David then went to live in the strongholds of En-gedi.

DAVID SPARES SAUL'S LIFE

24 After Saul returned from fighting the Philistines, he was told that David had gone into the wilderness of En-gedi. ²So Saul chose three thousand special troops from throughout Israel and went to search for David and his men near the rocks of the wild goats. ³At the place where the road passes some sheepfolds, Saul went into a cave to relieve himself. But as it happened, David and his men were hiding in that very cave!

⁴"Now's your opportunity!" David's men whispered to him. "Today is the day the LORD was talking about when he said, 'I will certainly put Saul into your power, to do with as you wish.'" Then David crept forward and cut off a piece of Saul's robe.

⁵But then David's conscience began bothering him because he had cut Saul's robe. ⁶"The LORD knows I shouldn't have done it," he said to his men. "It is a serious thing to attack the LORD's anointed one, for the LORD himself has chosen him." ⁷So David sharply rebuked his men and did not let them kill Saul.

After Saul had left the cave and gone on his way, ⁸David came out and shouted after him, "My lord the king!" And when Saul looked around, David bowed low before him.

⁹Then he shouted to Saul, "Why do you listen to the people who say I am trying to harm you? ¹⁰This very day you can see with your own eyes it isn't true. For the LORD placed you at my mercy back there in the cave, and some of my men told me to kill you, but I spared you. For I said, 'I will never harm him—he is the LORD's anointed one.' ¹¹Look, my father, at what I have in my hand. It is a piece of your robe! I cut it off, but I didn't kill you. This proves that I am not trying to harm you and that I have not sinned against you, even though you have been hunting for me to kill me. ¹²The LORD will decide between us. Perhaps the LORD will punish you for what you are trying to do to me, but I will never harm you. ¹³As that old proverb says, 'From evil people come evil deeds.' So you can be sure I will never harm you. ¹⁴Who is the king of Israel trying to catch anyway? Should he spend his time chasing one who is as worthless as a dead dog or a flea? ¹⁵May the LORD judge which of us is right and punish the guilty one. He is my advocate, and he will rescue me from your power!"

23:28 Hebrew *Sela-hammahlekoth.*

[16]Saul called back, "Is that really you, my son David?" Then he began to cry. [17]And he said to David, "You are a better man than I am, for you have repaid me good for evil. [18]Yes, you have been wonderfully kind to me today, for when the LORD put me in a place where you could have killed me, you didn't do it. [19]Who else would let his enemy get away when he had him in his power? May the LORD reward you well for the kindness you have shown me today. [20]And now I realize that you are surely going to be king, and Israel will flourish under your rule. [21]Now, swear to me by the LORD that when that happens you will not kill my family and destroy my line of descendants!"

[22]So David promised, and Saul went home. But David and his men went back to their stronghold.

THE DEATH OF SAMUEL

25 Now Samuel died, and all Israel gathered for his funeral. They buried him near his home at Ramah.

NABAL ANGERS DAVID

Then David moved down to the wilderness of Maon.* [2]There was a wealthy man from Maon who owned property near the village of Carmel. He had three thousand sheep and a thousand goats, and it was sheep-shearing time. [3]This man's name was Nabal, and his wife, Abigail, was a sensible and beautiful woman. But Nabal, a descendant of Caleb, was mean and dishonest in all his dealings.

[4]When David heard that Nabal was shearing his sheep, [5]he sent ten of his young men to Carmel. He told them to deliver this message: [6]"Peace and prosperity to you, your family, and everything you own! [7]I am told that you are shearing your sheep and goats. While your shepherds stayed among us near Carmel, we never harmed them, and nothing was ever stolen from them. [8]Ask your own servants, and they will tell you this is true. So would you please be kind to us, since we have come

at a time of celebration? Please give us any provisions you might have on hand." [9]David's young men gave this message to Nabal and waited for his reply.

[10]"Who is this fellow David?" Nabal sneered. "Who does this son of Jesse think he is? There are lots of servants these days who run away from their masters. [11]Should I take my bread and water and the meat I've slaughtered for my shearers and give it to a band of outlaws who come from who knows where?" [12]So David's messengers returned and told him what Nabal had said.

[13]"Get your swords!" was David's reply as he strapped on his own. Four hundred men started off with David, and two hundred remained behind to guard their equipment.

[14]Meanwhile, one of Nabal's servants went to Abigail and told her, "David sent men from the wilderness to talk to our master, and he insulted them. [15]But David's men were very good to us, and we never suffered any harm from them. Nothing was stolen from us the whole time they were with us. [16]In fact, day and night they were like a wall of protection to us and the sheep. [17]You'd better think fast, for there is going to be trouble for our master and his whole family. He's so ill-tempered that no one can even talk to him!"

[18]Abigail lost no time. She quickly gathered two hundred loaves of bread, two skins of wine, five dressed sheep, nearly a bushel* of roasted grain, one hundred raisin cakes, and two hundred fig cakes. She packed them on donkeys and said to her servants, [19]"Go on ahead. I will follow you shortly." But she didn't tell her husband what she was doing.

[20]As she was riding her donkey into a mountain ravine, she saw David and his men coming toward her. [21]David had just been saying, "A lot of good it did to help this fellow. We protected his flocks in the wilderness, and nothing he owned was lost or stolen. But he has repaid me evil for good. [22]May God deal with me severely if even one man of his household is still alive tomorrow morning!"

25:1 As in Greek version; Hebrew reads *Paran*. 25:18 Hebrew *5 seahs* [30 liters].

My Daily Worship

— March 11 —

GETTING REVENGE OR RELEASE

1 SAMUEL 21:1–24:22

May the LORD judge which of us is right and punish the guilty one. He is
my advocate, and he will rescue me from your power! (24:15).

[i reflect]

David held up a piece of King Saul's robe as he shouted the words above. Moments before, Saul had been unguarded and vulnerable in a cave where David and his men had been hiding. Saul was at David's mercy, and David had mercy. Instead of killing the king, David sliced off a corner of the royal robe. He spared the king's life out of deliberate trust in God. He refused to take the throne by force. He didn't want to be king unless God placed him in that position.

Perhaps the hardest work we can do during worship is the work of forgiveness. Anytime we are faced with the opportunity for revenge we have also been given the opportunity to release. And there's nothing like the quietness and reflection of worship to bring to mind offenses, hurts, anger, and unsettled issues in our lives. Jesus described just such a situation in Matthew 5:23–25. Worship is on hold until we release those we need to forgive. David understood worship.

David transformed a tense moment of temptation into an act of worship by sparing Saul's life and publicly announcing his ongoing trust in God. He released Saul for God's judgment by not taking revenge into his own hands. His was costly worship. David demonstrated that he was a man after God's heart by his shameless persistence in trusting God, even when that trust put his own life at risk.

Forgiveness may not be risky for you, but it will be hard work. We don't forgive easily, especially if our cause is just. But, like David, we demonstrate our understanding of the depth of God's forgiveness of us by the way we go about forgiving others. Worship includes receiving and giving forgiveness. We certainly need God's help to do both.

[i pray]

Lord, I want to release those I am struggling to forgive because I want to be truly
free to worship you. Help me let you handle my case, giving up my plans to
repay evil with evil. I trust you to do what is right in every situation.

[i respond]

Isn't it time to give up that old hurt, the one that still nags at you almost every day? Remembering, reliving, and regretting only eat at you, not at the other person. Write a note to that person, expressing love and concern, asking for their prayers and forgiveness for harboring that offense.

Words of Worship

HUMILITY, BEING HUMBLE

Humility, Being Humble—Hebrew *nich-na'* "humble oneself"; *'a-nah* "poor, humble"; *'a-na-vah* "humility, lowliness"; Greek *ta-pei-no-o* "humble oneself"; *ta-pei-no-phro-su-ne* "humility."

It's hard to see the Lord working in our lives when we forget how much we need him. Sometimes we think we can handle it all ourselves—everything's under control, thank you! Then we start looking for God, and he seems to have stepped out for a moment.

One thing the Scriptures are clear about is that the Lord isn't fond of proud people (1 Peter 5:5). But his Word is full of wonderful promises to those who fear him and, in humility, admit their dependence on him. To the humble he offers "riches, honor, and long life" (Proverbs 22:4). He offers his salvation—a deliverance from those things that come against us (Psalm 149:4). But perhaps greatest of all is his promise that, when we come to him with humble worship, he will abide with us. "I live in that high and holy place with those whose spirits are contrite and humble" (Isaiah 57:15).

ABIGAIL INTERCEDES FOR NABAL

²³When Abigail saw David, she quickly got off her donkey and bowed low before him. ²⁴She fell at his feet and said, "I accept all blame in this matter, my lord. Please listen to what I have to say. ²⁵I know Nabal is a wicked and ill-tempered man; please don't pay any attention to him. He is a fool, just as his name suggests.* But I never even saw the messengers you sent.

²⁶"Now, my lord, as surely as the LORD lives and you yourself live, since the LORD has kept you from murdering and taking vengeance into your own hands, let all your enemies be as cursed as Nabal is. ²⁷And here is a present I have brought to you and your young men. ²⁸Please forgive me if I have offended in any way. The LORD will surely reward you with a lasting dynasty, for you are fighting the LORD's battles. And you have not done wrong throughout your entire life.

²⁹"Even when you are chased by those who seek your life, you are safe in the care of the LORD your God, secure in his treasure pouch! But the lives of your enemies will disappear like stones shot from a sling! ³⁰When the LORD has done all he promised and has made you leader of Israel, ³¹don't let this be a blemish on your record. Then you won't have to carry on your conscience the staggering burden of needless bloodshed and vengeance. And when the LORD has done these great things for you, please remember me!"

³²David replied to Abigail, "Praise the LORD, the God of Israel, who has sent you to meet me today! ³³Thank God for your good sense! Bless you for keeping me from murdering the man and carrying out vengeance with my own hands. ³⁴For I swear by the LORD, the God of Israel, who has kept me from hurting you, that if you had not hurried out to meet me, not one of Nabal's men would be alive tomorrow morning." ³⁵Then David accepted her gifts and told her, "Return home in peace. We will not kill your husband."

³⁶When Abigail arrived home, she found that Nabal had thrown a big party and was celebrating like a king. He was very drunk, so she didn't tell him anything about her meeting with David until the next morning. ³⁷The next morning when he was sober, she told him what had happened. As a result he had a stroke,* and he lay on his bed paralyzed. ³⁸About ten days later, the LORD struck him and he died.

25:25 The name *Nabal* means "fool." 25:37 Hebrew *his heart failed him.*

DAVID MARRIES ABIGAIL

³⁹When David heard that Nabal was dead, he said, "Praise the LORD, who has paid back Nabal and kept me from doing it myself. Nabal has received the punishment for his sin." Then David wasted no time in sending messengers to Abigail to ask her to become his wife.

⁴⁰When the messengers arrived at Carmel, they told Abigail, "David has sent us to ask if you will marry him."

⁴¹She bowed low to the ground and responded, "Yes, I am even willing to become a slave to David's servants!" ⁴²Quickly getting ready, she took along five of her servant girls as attendants, mounted her donkey, and went with David's messengers. And so she became his wife. ⁴³David also married Ahinoam from Jezreel, making both of them his wives. ⁴⁴Saul, meanwhile, had given his daughter Michal, David's wife, to a man from Gallim named Palti son of Laish.

DAVID SPARES SAUL AGAIN

26 Now some messengers from Ziph came back to Saul at Gibeah to tell him, "David is hiding on the hill of Hakilah, which overlooks Jeshimon." ²So Saul took three thousand of his best troops and went to hunt him down in the wilderness of Ziph. ³Saul camped along the road beside the hill of Hakilah, near Jeshimon, where David was hiding. But David knew of Saul's arrival, ⁴so he sent out spies to watch his movements.

⁵David slipped over to Saul's camp one night to look around. Saul and his general, Abner son of Ner, were sleeping inside a ring formed by the slumbering warriors. ⁶"Will anyone volunteer to go in there with me?" David asked Ahimelech the Hittite and Abishai son of Zeruiah, Joab's brother.

"I'll go with you," Abishai replied. ⁷So David and Abishai went right into Saul's camp and found him asleep, with his spear stuck in the ground beside his head. Abner and the warriors were lying asleep around him. ⁸"God has

surely handed your enemy over to you this time!" Abishai whispered to David. "Let me thrust that spear through him. I'll pin him to the ground, and I won't need to strike twice!"

⁹"No!" David said. "Don't kill him. For who can remain innocent after attacking the LORD's anointed one? ¹⁰Surely the LORD will strike Saul down someday, or he will die in battle or of old age. ¹¹But the LORD forbid that I should kill the one he has anointed! But I'll tell you what—we'll take his spear and his jug of water and then get out of here!"

¹²So David took the spear and jug of water that were near Saul's head. Then he and Abishai got away without anyone seeing them or even waking up, because the LORD had put Saul's men into a deep sleep. ¹³David climbed the hill opposite the camp until he was at a safe distance. ¹⁴Then he shouted down to Abner and Saul, "Wake up, Abner!"

"Who is it?" Abner demanded.

¹⁵"Well, Abner, you're a great man, aren't you?" David taunted. "Where in all Israel is there anyone as mighty? So why haven't you guarded your master the king when someone came to kill him? ¹⁶This isn't good at all! I swear by the LORD that you and your men deserve to die, because you failed to protect your master, the LORD's anointed! Look around! Where are the king's spear and the jug of water that were beside his head?"

¹⁷Saul recognized David's voice and called out, "Is that you, my son David?"

And David replied, "Yes, my lord the king. ¹⁸Why are you chasing me? What have I done? What is my crime? ¹⁹But now let my lord the king listen to his servant. If the LORD has stirred you up against me, then let him accept my offering. But if this is simply a human scheme, then may those involved be cursed by the LORD. For you have driven me from my home, so I can no longer live among the LORD's people and worship as I should. ²⁰Must I die on foreign soil, far from the presence of the LORD? Why has the king of Israel come out to search for a single flea? Why does he hunt me down like a partridge on the mountains?"

²¹Then Saul confessed, "I have sinned. Come back home, my son, and I will no longer try to harm you, for you valued my life today. I have been a fool and very, very wrong."

²²"Here is your spear, O king," David replied. "Let one of your young men come over and get it. ²³The LORD gives his own reward for doing good and for being loyal, and I refused to kill you even when the LORD placed you in my power, for you are the LORD's anointed one. ²⁴Now may the LORD value my life, even as I have valued yours today. May he rescue me from all my troubles."

²⁵And Saul said to David, "Blessings on you, my son David. You will do heroic deeds and be a great conqueror." Then David went away, and Saul returned home.

DAVID AMONG THE PHILISTINES

27 But David kept thinking to himself, "Someday Saul is going to get me. The best thing for me to do is escape to the Philistines. Then Saul will stop hunting for me, and I will finally be safe."

²So David took his six hundred men and their families and went to live at Gath under the protection of King Achish. ³David brought his two wives along with him—Ahinoam of Jezreel and Abigail of Carmel, Nabal's widow. ⁴Word soon reached Saul that David had fled to Gath, so he stopped hunting for him.

⁵One day David said to Achish, "If it is all right with you, we would rather live in one of the country towns instead of here in the royal city." ⁶So Achish gave him the town of Ziklag (which still belongs to the kings of Judah to this day), ⁷and they lived there among the Philistines for a year and four months.

⁸David and his men spent their time raiding the Geshurites, the Girzites, and the Amalekites—people who had lived near Shur, along the road to Egypt, since ancient times. ⁹David didn't leave one person alive in the villages he attacked. He took the sheep, cattle, donkeys, camels, and clothing before returning home to see King Achish.

¹⁰"Where did you make your raid today?" Achish would ask.

And David would reply, "Against the south of Judah, the Jerahmeelites, and the Kenites."

¹¹No one was left alive to come to Gath and tell where he had really been. This happened again and again while he was living among the Philistines. ¹²Achish believed David and thought to himself, "By now the people of Israel must hate him bitterly. Now he will have to stay here and serve me forever!"

SAUL CONSULTS A MEDIUM

28 About that time the Philistines mustered their armies for another war with Israel. King Achish told David, "You and your men will be expected to join me in battle."

²"Very well!" David agreed. "Now you will see for yourself what we can do."

Then Achish told David, "I will make you my personal bodyguard for life."

³Meanwhile, Samuel had died, and all Israel had mourned for him. He was buried in Ramah, his hometown. And Saul had banned all mediums and psychics from the land of Israel.

⁴The Philistines set up their camp at Shunem, and Saul and the armies of Israel camped at Gilboa. ⁵When Saul saw the vast Philistine army, he became frantic with fear. ⁶He asked the LORD what he should do, but the LORD refused to answer him, either by dreams or by sacred lots* or by the prophets. ⁷Saul then said to his advisers, "Find a woman who is a medium, so I can go and ask her what to do."

His advisers replied, "There is a medium at Endor."

⁸So Saul disguised himself by wearing ordinary clothing instead of his royal robes. Then he went to the woman's home at night, accompanied by two of his men.

28:6 Hebrew *by Urim.*

My Daily Worship

— March 12 —

HURRY UP AND WAIT

1 SAMUEL 25:1–28:25

He asked the LORD what he should do, but the LORD refused to answer him,
either by dreams or by sacred lots or by the prophets (28:6).

[i reflect]

No one likes to wait, whether it's in a long line at the grocery store or waiting for a family member to get ready for church. Waiting is tough, especially when it comes to the big issues:

- Waiting for a wayward child to come back to his faith roots
- Waiting for the results of a medical test
- Waiting for the outcome of a job interview
- Waiting to see the results of a company merger

Waiting can be tough. Often we ask God for patience while we're waiting for an answer to prayer, and then get impatient when the answer doesn't come! Consider Saul's response to waiting. This passage explains that he was waiting for an answer from God. But when he didn't get one, he took an impatient weird turn and went to a medium for advice.

God doesn't always answer when we think he should or how we think he should, but he always answers prayer. Our part is to trust him when the answers aren't forthcoming. He doesn't want us to run to another god for help; he wants us to wait patiently for him.

Have you been praying about an issue and found God silent? What has your response been? David exclaimed: "I waited patiently for the LORD to help me, and he turned to me and heard my cry. He lifted me out of the pit of despair, out of the mud and the mire. He set my feet on solid ground and steadied me as I walked along" (Psalm 40:1–2).

Come back to him now, today. He's going to answer. He promised, and he always keeps his promises. Spend some time in prayerful worship, thanking God for how he is going to answer your concerns.

[i pray]

God, I've waited so long for your answer. Please don't be silent any longer, Lord.
Help me to wait on you, to accept your timing and not demand my own.

[i respond]

Spend the next five to ten minutes being still before God. Present to him what is foremost on your mind, and then "Be silent, and know that I am God!" (Psalm 46:10).

"I have to talk to a man who has died," he said. "Will you call up his spirit for me?"

⁹"Are you trying to get me killed?" the woman demanded. "You know that Saul has expelled all the mediums and psychics from the land. Why are you setting a trap for me?"

¹⁰But Saul took an oath in the name of the LORD and promised, "As surely as the LORD lives, nothing bad will happen to you for doing this."

¹¹Finally, the woman said, "Well, whose spirit do you want me to call up?"

"Call up Samuel," Saul replied.

¹²When the woman saw Samuel, she screamed, "You've deceived me! You are Saul!"

¹³"Don't be afraid!" the king told her. "What do you see?"

"I see a god* coming up out of the earth," she said.

¹⁴"What does he look like?" Saul asked.

"He is an old man wrapped in a robe," she replied. Saul realized that it was Samuel, and he fell to the ground before him.

¹⁵"Why have you disturbed me by calling me back?" Samuel asked.

"Because I am in deep trouble," Saul replied. "The Philistines are at war with us, and God has left me and won't reply by prophets or dreams. So I have called for you to tell me what to do."

¹⁶But Samuel replied, "Why ask me if the LORD has left you and has become your enemy? ¹⁷The LORD has done just as he said he would. He has taken the kingdom from you and given it to your rival, David. ¹⁸The LORD has done this because you did not obey his instructions concerning the Amalekites. ¹⁹What's more, the LORD will hand you and the army of Israel over to the Philistines tomorrow, and you and your sons will be here with me. The LORD will bring the entire army of Israel down in defeat."

²⁰Saul fell full length on the ground, paralyzed with fright because of Samuel's words. He was also faint with hunger, for he had eaten nothing all day and all night. ²¹When the woman saw how distraught he was, she said, "Sir, I obeyed your command at the risk of my life. ²²Now do what I say, and let me give you something to eat so you can regain your strength for the trip back."

²³But Saul refused. The men who were with him also urged him to eat, so he finally yielded and got up from the ground and sat on the couch. ²⁴The woman had been fattening a calf, so she hurried out and killed it. She kneaded dough and baked unleavened bread. ²⁵She brought the meal to Saul and his men, and they ate it. Then they went out into the night.

THE PHILISTINES REJECT DAVID

29 The entire Philistine army now mobilized at Aphek, and the Israelites camped at the spring in Jezreel. ²As the Philistine rulers were leading out their troops in groups of one hundred and one thousand, David and his men marched at the rear with King Achish. ³But the Philistine commanders demanded, "What are these Hebrews doing here?"

And Achish told them, "This is David, the man who ran away from King Saul of Israel. He's been with me for years, and I've never found a single fault in him since he defected to me."

⁴But the Philistine commanders were angry. "Send him back!" they demanded. "He can't go into the battle with us. What if he turns against us? Is there any better way for him to reconcile himself with his master than by turning on us in battle? ⁵Isn't this the same David about whom the women of Israel sing in their dances, 'Saul has killed his thousands, and David his ten thousands'?"

⁶So Achish finally summoned David and his men. "I swear by the LORD," he told them, "you are some of the finest men I've ever met. I think you should go with us, but the other Philistine rulers won't hear of it. ⁷Please don't upset them, but go back quietly."

⁸"What have I done to deserve this treatment?"

28:13 Or *gods*.

My Daily Worship

— March 13 —

SHARING IS OUR THANKS-GIVING

1 SAMUEL 29:1–31:13

But David said, "No, my brothers! Don't be selfish with what the LORD has given us.
He has kept us safe and helped us defeat the enemy" (30:23).

[i reflect]

David's men grumbled. They didn't want to share the goods they had recovered from the Amalekites with men who hadn't been a part of David's rescue party. But David showed the generosity of his divine descendant, Jesus Christ, when he told the men to "share and share alike" (30:24). He also reminded his men that generosity toward others could express gratitude to God for his help.

People who visit Third-World countries are often amazed at the Christian community's generosity, despite their lack of material goods. They may share all the food they have for a week at a special meal for guests. Believers stretch what little they have to benefit many. Their generosity expresses worship to the God who provides all they have, and they gladly share it. They live out what David instructed his men, "Don't be selfish with what the LORD has given us."

What has God given you so that you can share it with others? Perhaps you have resources that could help your church provide for that ministry need? Or you could give a word of encouragement that would enable a struggling friend to keep going? Perhaps you could share the gift of your time so that your neighbor who cares for an elderly loved one can take a break?

Worship in the form of sharing with others doesn't have to wait until you can afford it. Paul says of the believers in Macedonia, "Though they have been going through much trouble and hard times, their wonderful joy and deep poverty have overflowed in rich generosity. For I can testify that they gave not only what they could afford but far more. And they did it of their own free will" (2 Corinthians 8:2–3).

Who could use your help? Why not call right now and offer to share what you have with that person?

[i pray]

God, thank you for all you have given me. You have provided abundantly.
I lift it all up to you now with open hands, asking that you would help me
share what I have as an act of worship and gratitude to you.

[i respond]

How difficult is it for you to share with others? Make a list of three specific items you own that could be of assistance to someone else (clothes, tools, food, money). Ask God to lead you to those who can receive your effort to express gratitude to God.

David demanded. "Why can't I fight the enemies of my lord, the king?"

⁹But Achish insisted, "As far as I'm concerned, you're as perfect as an angel of God. But my commanders are afraid to have you with them in the battle. ¹⁰Now get up early in the morning, and leave with your men as soon as it gets light." ¹¹So David headed back into the land of the Philistines, while the Philistine army went on to Jezreel.

DAVID DESTROYS THE AMALEKITES

30 Three days later, when David and his men arrived home at their town of Ziklag, they found that the Amalekites had made a raid into the Negev and had burned Ziklag to the ground. ²They had carried off the women and children and everyone else but without killing anyone. ³When David and his men saw the ruins and realized what had happened to their families, ⁴they wept until they could weep no more. ⁵David's two wives, Ahinoam of Jezreel and Abigail, the widow of Nabal of Carmel, were among those captured. ⁶David was now in serious trouble because his men were very bitter about losing their wives and children, and they began to talk of stoning him. But David found strength in the LORD his God.

⁷Then he said to Abiathar the priest, "Bring me the ephod!" So Abiathar brought it. ⁸Then David asked the LORD, "Should I chase them? Will I catch them?"

And the LORD told him, "Yes, go after them. You will surely recover everything that was taken from you!" ⁹So David and his six hundred men set out, and they soon came to Besor Brook. ¹⁰But two hundred of the men were too exhausted to cross the brook, so David continued the pursuit with his four hundred remaining troops.

¹¹Some of David's troops found an Egyptian man in a field and brought him to David. They gave him some bread to eat and some water to drink. ¹²They also gave him part of a fig cake and two clusters of raisins because he hadn't had anything to eat or drink for three days and nights. It wasn't long before his strength returned.

¹³"To whom do you belong, and where do you come from?" David asked him.

"I am an Egyptian—the slave of an Amalekite," he replied. "My master left me behind three days ago because I was sick. ¹⁴We were on our way back from raiding the Kerethites in the Negev, the territory of Judah, and the land of Caleb, and we had just burned Ziklag."

¹⁵"Will you lead me to them?" David asked.

The young man replied, "If you swear by God's name that you will not kill me or give me back to my master, then I will guide you to them."

¹⁶So the Egyptian led them to the Amalekite encampment. When David and his men arrived, the Amalekites were spread out across the fields, eating and drinking and dancing with joy because of the vast amount of plunder they had taken from the Philistines and the land of Judah. ¹⁷David and his men rushed in among them and slaughtered them throughout that night and the entire next day until evening. None of the Amalekites escaped except four hundred young men who fled on camels. ¹⁸David got back everything the Amalekites had taken, and he rescued his two wives. ¹⁹Nothing was missing: small or great, son or daughter, nor anything else that had been taken. David brought everything back. ²⁰His troops rounded up all the flocks and herds and drove them on ahead. "These all belong to David as his reward!" they said.

²¹When they reached Besor Brook and met the two hundred men who had been too tired to go with them, David greeted them joyfully. ²²But some troublemakers among David's men said, "They didn't go with us, so they can't have any of the plunder. Give them their wives and children, and tell them to be gone."

²³But David said, "No, my brothers! Don't be selfish with what the LORD has given us. He has kept us safe and helped us defeat the enemy. ²⁴Do you think anyone will listen to you when you talk like this? We share and

share alike—those who go to battle and those who guard the equipment." ²⁵From then on David made this a law for all of Israel, and it is still followed.

²⁶When he arrived at Ziklag, David sent part of the plunder to the leaders of Judah, who were his friends. "Here is a present for you, taken from the LORD's enemies," he said. ²⁷The gifts were sent to the leaders of the following towns where David and his men had been: Bethel, Ramoth-negev, Jattir, ²⁸Aroer, Siphmoth, Eshtemoa, ²⁹Racal,* the towns of the Jerahmeelites, the towns of the Kenites, ³⁰Hormah, Bor-ashan, Athach, ³¹Hebron, and all the other places they had visited.

THE DEATH OF SAUL

31 Now the Philistines attacked Israel, forcing the Israelites to flee. Many were slaughtered on the slopes of Mount Gilboa. ²The Philistines closed in on Saul and his sons, and they killed three of his sons—Jonathan, Abinadab, and Malkishua. ³The fighting grew very fierce around Saul, and the Philistine archers caught up with him and wounded him severely. ⁴Saul groaned to his armor bearer, "Take your sword and kill me before these pagan Philistines run me through and humiliate me." But his armor bearer was afraid and would not do it. So Saul took his own sword and fell on it. ⁵When his armor bearer realized that Saul was dead, he fell on his own sword and died beside the king. ⁶So Saul, three of his sons, his armor bearer, and his troops all died together that same day.

⁷When the Israelites on the other side of the Jezreel Valley and beyond the Jordan saw that their army had been routed and that Saul and his sons were dead, they abandoned their towns and fled. So the Philistines moved in and occupied their towns.

⁸The next day, when the Philistines went out to strip the dead, they found the bodies of Saul and his three sons on Mount Gilboa. ⁹So they cut off Saul's head and stripped off his armor. Then they proclaimed the news of Saul's death in their pagan temple and to the people throughout the land of Philistia. ¹⁰They placed his armor in the temple of the Ashtoreths, and they fastened his body to the wall of the city of Beth-shan.

¹¹But when the people of Jabesh-gilead heard what the Philistines had done to Saul, ¹²their warriors traveled all night to Beth-shan and took the bodies of Saul and his sons down from the wall. They brought them to Jabesh, where they burned the bodies. ¹³Then they took their remains and buried them beneath the tamarisk tree at Jabesh, and they fasted for seven days.

30:29 Greek version reads *Carmel.*

2 Samuel

O LORD, you are my light; . . . you light up my darkness (22:29).

God's Unfailing Love

I f only . . . if only . . . if only. Regrets—"should have's," "could have's," and "what if's"—can plague us for years. Although David was one of Israel's great kings, he had no doubt spent some sleepless nights recounting his regrets: *If only I hadn't looked, . . . if only if I hadn't invited, . . . if only I hadn't let my desires. . . .*

Second Samuel not only tells us the long sorry tale of what caused his regrets; it also is a story about David's experience of grace and God's unfailing love. But if we focus on David's mistakes, we will miss it. Certainly David's relationship with God was disrupted by sin, and David felt its sting after the prophet Nathan confronted him about his affair with Bathsheba. Distraught, David was quick to acknowledge his sin, and Nathan assured him of his forgiveness (12:13). The lesson is clear—God willingly and lovingly restores our relationship with him when we turn from our sin.

The book begins with everything going well for David. He won a civil war (1:1–4:12), was anointed king (5:1–5), and made Jerusalem his capital (5:6–15). He was a passionate man who celebrated the return of the Ark (6:14), wept bitterly at the death of his son Absalom (18:33), and deeply desired to build a temple for God (7:1–2). But David's passion was a two-edged sword. He lusted after Bathsheba and ignored God. David repented, but experienced the consequences of his sin. The child of their union died, a son raped a daughter, another son murdered the rapist, and yet another son incited a rebellion.

Nevertheless, we see glimpses of grace. Notice the contrast between David's susceptibility to sin and his assurance of God's mercy. David says, "I am blameless before God; . . . [he is] like the refreshing rains" (22:24; 23:4). Look for examples of God's grace toward sinners throughout this book and be encouraged that the God we worship is full of love, compassion, and forgiveness toward his fallen people.

Worship Moments

- David is filled with wonder that God plans to found a kingly dynasty through him (7:18–29).

- David's repentance for his grievous sin included fasting and lying all night on the ground (12:16).

- God is called: "LORD God Almighty" (5:10); "the Lord who bursts through" (5:20); "Sovereign LORD" (7:18); "my rock, my fortress, . . . my savior" (22:2); "my shield, . . . my stronghold, my high tower" (22:3–4); and "the Most High" (22:14).

David Learns of Saul's Death

1 After the death of Saul, David returned from his victory over the Amalekites and spent two days in Ziklag. [2] On the third day after David's return, a man arrived from the Israelite battlefront. He had torn his clothes and put dirt on his head to show that he was in mourning. He fell to the ground before David in deep respect.

[3] "Where have you come from?" David asked.

"I escaped from the Israelite camp," the man replied.

[4] "What happened?" David demanded. "Tell me how the battle went."

The man replied, "Our entire army fled. Many men are dead and wounded on the battlefield, and Saul and his son Jonathan have been killed."

[5] "How do you know that Saul and Jonathan are dead?" David demanded.

[6] The young man answered, "I happened to be on Mount Gilboa. I saw Saul there leaning on his spear with the enemy chariots closing in on him. [7] When he turned and saw me, he cried out for me to come to him. 'How can I help?' I asked him. [8] And he said to me, 'Who are you?' I replied, 'I am an Amalekite.' [9] Then he begged me, 'Come over here and put me out of my misery, for I am in terrible pain and want to die.'

[10] "So I killed him," the Amalekite told David, "for I knew he couldn't live. Then I took his crown and one of his bracelets so I could bring them to you, my lord."

[11] David and his men tore their clothes in sorrow when they heard the news. [12] They mourned and wept and fasted all day for Saul and his son Jonathan, and for the LORD's army and the nation of Israel, because so many had died that day. [13] Then David said to the young man who had brought the news, "Where are you from?"

And he replied, "I am a foreigner, an Amalekite, who lives in your land."

[14] "Were you not afraid to kill the LORD's anointed one?" David asked. [15] Then David said to one of his men, "Kill him!" So the man thrust his sword into the Amalekite and killed him. [16] "You die self-condemned," David said, "for you yourself confessed that you killed the LORD's anointed one."

David's Song for Saul and Jonathan

[17] Then David composed a funeral song for Saul and Jonathan. [18] Later he commanded that it be taught to all the people of Judah. It is known as the Song of the Bow, and it is recorded in *The Book of Jashar.* *

[19] Your pride and joy, O Israel, lies dead on
    the hills!
  How the mighty heroes have fallen!
[20] Don't announce the news in Gath,
    or the Philistines will rejoice.
  Don't proclaim it in the streets of Ashkelon,
    or the pagans will laugh in triumph.

[21] O mountains of Gilboa,
    let there be no dew or rain upon you or
    your slopes.
  For there the shield of the mighty was defiled;
    the shield of Saul will no longer be
    anointed with oil.
[22] Both Saul and Jonathan killed their
    strongest foes;
  they did not return from battle
    empty-handed.

[23] How beloved and gracious were Saul and
    Jonathan!
  They were together in life and in death.
  They were swifter than eagles;
    they were stronger than lions.

[24] O women of Israel, weep for Saul,
    for he dressed you in fine clothing and
    gold ornaments.

[25] How the mighty heroes have fallen in battle!
  Jonathan lies dead upon the hills.
[26] How I weep for you, my brother Jonathan!

1:18 Or *The Book of the Upright.*

Oh, how much I loved you!
And your love for me was deep,
  deeper than the love of women!

27 How the mighty heroes have fallen!
  Stripped of their weapons, they lie dead.

DAVID ANOINTED KING OF JUDAH

2 After this, David asked the LORD, "Should I move back to Judah?"

And the LORD replied, "Yes."

Then David asked, "Which town should I go to?"

And the LORD replied, "Hebron."

²David's wives were Ahinoam from Jezreel and Abigail, the widow of Nabal from Carmel. So David and his wives ³and his men and their families all moved to Judah, and they settled near the town of Hebron. ⁴Then Judah's leaders came to David and crowned him king over the tribe of Judah.

When David heard that the men of Jabesh-gilead had buried Saul, ⁵he sent them this message: "May the LORD bless you for being so loyal to your king and giving him a decent burial. ⁶May the LORD be loyal to you in return and reward you with his unfailing love! And I, too, will reward you for what you have done. ⁷And now that Saul is dead, I ask you to be my strong and loyal subjects like the people of Judah, who have anointed me as their new king."

ISHBOSHETH CROWNED KING OF ISRAEL

⁸But Abner son of Ner, the commander of Saul's army, had already gone to Mahanaim with Saul's son Ishbosheth.* ⁹There he proclaimed Ishbosheth king over Gilead, Jezreel, Ephraim, Benjamin, the land of the Ashurites, and all the rest of Israel. ¹⁰Ishbosheth was forty years old when he became king, and he ruled from Mahanaim for two years. Meanwhile, the tribe of Judah remained loyal to David. ¹¹David made Hebron his capital, and he ruled as king of Judah for seven and a half years.

WAR BETWEEN ISRAEL AND JUDAH

¹²One day Abner led some of Ishbosheth's troops from Mahanaim to Gibeon. ¹³About the same time, Joab son of Zeruiah led David's troops from Hebron, and they met Abner at the pool of Gibeon. The two groups sat down there, facing each other from opposite sides of the pool. ¹⁴Then Abner suggested to Joab, "Let's have a few of our warriors put on an exhibition of hand-to-hand combat."

"All right," Joab agreed. ¹⁵So twelve men were chosen from each side to fight against each other. ¹⁶Each one grabbed his opponent by the hair and thrust his sword into the other's side so that all of them died. The place has been known ever since as the Field of Swords.* ¹⁷The two armies then began to fight each other, and by the end of the day Abner and the men of Israel had been defeated by the forces of David.

THE DEATH OF ASAHEL

¹⁸Joab, Abishai, and Asahel, the three sons of Zeruiah, were among David's forces that day. Asahel could run like a deer, ¹⁹and he began chasing Abner. He was relentless and single-minded in his pursuit. ²⁰When Abner looked back and saw him coming, he called out, "Is that you, Asahel?"

"Yes, it is," he replied.

²¹"Go fight someone else!" Abner warned. "Take on one of the younger men and strip him of his weapons." But Asahel refused and kept right on chasing Abner.

²²Again Abner shouted to him, "Get away from here! I will never be able to face your brother Joab if I have to kill you!" ²³But Asahel would not give up, so Abner thrust the butt end of his spear through Asahel's stomach, and the spear came out through his back. He stumbled to the ground and died there. And everyone who came by that spot stopped and stood still when they saw Asahel lying there.

2:8 Also known as *Eshbaal*.   2:16 Hebrew *Helkath-hazzurim*.

My Daily Worship

— March 14 —

HOW TO LIVE WITH LOSS

2 SAMUEL 1:1–4:12

They mourned and wept and fasted all day for Saul and his son Jonathan, and for the
LORD's army and the nation of Israel, because so many had died that day (1:12).

[i reflect]

Loss. Grief. Anguish of soul. Tragedy and disaster take their toll on us. Death is so painful to those left behind. David had lost two people he loved very much, in addition to many men in his army. He openly expressed his grief; he tore his clothes in sorrow.

When loss hits home, it can feel as if you'll never stop aching; that your pain will never stop being a sharp torture.

What loss are you feeling today? Was it the death of a beloved friend, like David's Jonathan? Or the death of a parent, a brother, or even your child? Was it the death of your dream of a solid and lasting marriage that ended in divorce? Or the successful career that disintegrated when your business collapsed?

Even though you may not want to, expressing grief is healthy and necessary if you're ever to heal. It may be a long, slow process, but as David and his men did, admit your grief, feel your pain, mourn your losses.

This is the time to grieve and to cry (Ecclesiastes 3:4). God knows how you feel, and he hurts with you. After all, Jesus was "a man of sorrows, acquainted with bitterest grief" (Isaiah 53:3). Cyprian wrote: "[Jesus is] the Teacher of humility, endurance, and suffering. What He tells us to do, He did first. And what He urges us to suffer, He suffered first for us." Go to him; ask him to help you bear it, and he will.

[i pray]

God, when I think of my losses, I'm tempted to retreat to that black emotional place,
to isolate myself from others—even from you. It hurts too much to do anything else.
Hold me close, Lord, wipe my tears. Remind me of the day there will be no grief.

[i respond]

Learning to express your grief can be a healthy step toward healing. Tell God exactly how you feel and how much you are hurting. Write him a letter. Draw a picture. Shout aloud. God knows.

²⁴When Joab and Abishai found out what had happened, they set out after Abner. The sun was just going down as they arrived at the hill of Ammah near Giah, along the road to the wilderness of Gibeon. ²⁵Abner's troops from the tribe of Benjamin regrouped there at the top of the hill to take a stand. ²⁶Abner shouted down to Joab, "Must we always solve our differences with swords? Don't you realize the only thing we will gain is bitterness toward each other? When will you call off your men from chasing their Israelite brothers?"

²⁷Then Joab said, "God only knows what would have happened if you hadn't spoken, for we would have chased you all night if necessary." ²⁸So Joab blew his trumpet, and his men stopped chasing the troops of Israel.

²⁹All that night Abner and his men retreated through the Jordan Valley.* They crossed the Jordan River, traveling all through the morning,* and they did not stop until they arrived at Mahanaim.

³⁰Meanwhile, Joab and his men also returned home. When Joab counted his casualties, he discovered that only nineteen men were missing, in addition to Asahel. ³¹But three hundred and sixty of Abner's men, all from the tribe of Benjamin, had been killed. ³²Joab and his men took Asahel's body to Bethlehem and buried him there beside his father. Then they traveled all night and reached Hebron at daybreak.

3 That was the beginning of a long war between those who had been loyal to Saul and those who were loyal to David. As time passed David became stronger and stronger, while Saul's dynasty became weaker and weaker.

DAVID'S SONS BORN IN HEBRON

²These were the sons who were born to David in Hebron:

The oldest was Amnon, whose mother was Ahinoam of Jezreel.

³ The second was Kileab, whose mother was Abigail, the widow of Nabal from Carmel.

The third was Absalom, whose mother was Maacah, the daughter of Talmai, king of Geshur.

Words of Worship

GLORY

Glory, Glorify—Hebrew *ka-**vod*** "weight, glory, honor"; *kib-**bed*** "to glorify, honor"; Greek *dox-a-zo* "glorify"; ***dox**-a* "glory, honor."

"Seeing is believing." Maybe if we could see God, our doubts would vanish. Moses might have felt that way when he prayed, "Please let me see your glorious presence." God didn't reveal his face, for no human can see it and live. Moses saw only the aftermath of God's glory (Exodus 33:18–23). In the Bible, God's glory is like a brilliant envelope around him. The Hebrew word for *glory* refers to mass or heaviness. When we meet the Lord, we sense his weighty presence. We're confronted by something our ordinary experience can't comprehend. As Paul wrote, God "lives in light so brilliant that no human can approach him" (1 Timothy 6:16).

The more wonder, then, that Jesus revealed another side to God's glory—the compassionate, merciful side hidden behind his radiance. God's glory isn't just our idea of his greatness but the love we sense when we meet him. "For God, who said, 'Let there be light in the darkness,' has made us to understand that this light is the brightness of the glory of God that is seen in the face of Jesus Christ" (2 Corinthians 4:6). Scripture proclaims the hope that, through Jesus, we will share in that glory (Romans 5:2).

2:29a Hebrew *the Arabah.* **2:29b** Or *continued on through the Bithron.* The meaning of the Hebrew is uncertain.

⁴ The fourth was Adonijah, whose mother was Haggith.
The fifth was Shephatiah, whose mother was Abital.
⁵ The sixth was Ithream, whose mother was David's wife Eglah.

These sons were all born to David in Hebron.

ABNER JOINS FORCES WITH DAVID

⁶As the war went on, Abner became a powerful leader among those who were loyal to Saul's dynasty. ⁷One day Ishbosheth,* Saul's son, accused Abner of sleeping with one of his father's concubines, a woman named Rizpah. ⁸Abner became furious. "Am I a Judean dog to be kicked around like this?" he shouted. "After all I have done for you and your father by not betraying you to David, is this my reward—that you find fault with me about this woman? ⁹May God deal harshly with me if I don't help David get all that the LORD has promised him! ¹⁰I should just go ahead and give David the rest of Saul's kingdom. I should set him up as king over Israel as well as Judah, from Dan to Beersheba." ¹¹Ishbosheth didn't dare say another word because he was afraid of what Abner might do.

¹²Then Abner sent messengers to David, saying, "Let's make an agreement, and I will help turn the entire nation of Israel over to you."

¹³"All right," David replied, "but I will not negotiate with you unless you bring back my wife Michal, Saul's daughter, when you come."

¹⁴David then sent this message to Ishbosheth, Saul's son: "Give me back my wife Michal, for I bought her with the lives of one hundred Philistines." ¹⁵So Ishbosheth took Michal away from her husband Palti* son of Laish. ¹⁶Palti followed along behind her as far as Bahurim, weeping as he went. Then Abner told him, "Go back home!" So Palti returned.

¹⁷Meanwhile, Abner had consulted with the leaders of Israel. "For some time now," he told them, "you have wanted to make David your king. ¹⁸Now is the time! For the LORD has said, 'I have chosen David to save my people from the Philistines and from all their other enemies.'" ¹⁹Abner also spoke with the leaders of the tribe of Benjamin. Then he went to Hebron to tell David that all the people of Israel and Benjamin supported him.

²⁰When Abner came to Hebron with his twenty men, David entertained them with a great feast. ²¹Then Abner said to David, "Let me go and call all the people of Israel to your side. They will make a covenant with you to make you their king. Then you will be able to rule over everything your heart desires." So David sent Abner safely on his way.

JOAB MURDERS ABNER

²²But just after Abner left, Joab and some of David's troops returned from a raid, bringing much plunder with them. ²³When Joab was told that Abner had just been there visiting the king and had been sent away in safety, ²⁴he rushed to see the king. "What have you done?" he demanded. "What do you mean by letting Abner get away? ²⁵You know perfectly well that he came to spy on you and to discover everything you are doing!"

²⁶Joab then left David and sent messengers to catch up with Abner. They found him at the pool of Sirah and brought him back with them. But David knew nothing about it. ²⁷When Abner arrived at Hebron, Joab took him aside at the gateway as if to speak with him privately. But then he drew his dagger and killed Abner in revenge for killing his brother Asahel.

²⁸When David heard about it, he declared, "I vow by the LORD that I and my people are innocent of this crime against Abner. ²⁹Joab and his family are the guilty ones. May his family in every generation be cursed with a man who has open sores or leprosy* or who walks on crutches* or who dies by the sword or who begs for food!"

3:7 Also known as *Eshbaal*. 3:15 As in 1 Sam 25:44; Hebrew reads *Paltiel*, a variant name for Palti. 3:29a Or *or a contagious skin disease.* The Hebrew word used here can describe various skin diseases. 3:29b Or *who is effeminate*; Hebrew reads *who handles a spindle.*

³⁰So Joab and his brother Abishai killed Abner because Abner had killed their brother Asahel at the battle of Gibeon.

DAVID MOURNS ABNER'S DEATH

³¹Then David said to Joab and all those who were with him, "Tear your clothes and put on sackcloth. Go into deep mourning for Abner." And King David himself walked behind the procession to the grave. ³²They buried Abner in Hebron, and the king and all the people wept at his graveside. ³³Then the king sang this funeral song for Abner:

"Should Abner have died as fools die?
³⁴ Your hands were not bound;
    your feet were not chained.
No, you were murdered—
    the victim of a wicked plot."

All the people wept again for Abner. ³⁵David had refused to eat anything the day of the funeral, and now everyone begged him to eat. But David had made a vow, saying, "May God kill me if I eat anything before sundown." ³⁶This pleased the people very much. In fact, everything the king did pleased them! ³⁷So everyone in Judah and Israel knew that David was not responsible for Abner's death.

³⁸Then King David said to the people, "Do you not realize that a great leader and a great man has fallen today in Israel? ³⁹And even though I am the anointed king, these two sons of Zeruiah—Joab and Abishai—are too strong for me to control. So may the LORD repay these wicked men for their wicked deeds."

THE MURDER OF ISHBOSHETH

4 When Ishbosheth* heard about Abner's death at Hebron, he lost all courage, and his people were paralyzed with fear. ²Now there were two brothers, Baanah and Recab, who were captains of Ishbosheth's raiding parties. They were sons of Rimmon, a mem-ber of the tribe of Benjamin who lived in Beeroth. The town of Beeroth is now part of Benjamin's territory ³because the original people of Beeroth fled to Gittaim, where they still live as foreigners.

⁴(Saul's son Jonathan had a son named Mephibosheth,* who was crippled as a child. He was five years old when Saul and Jonathan were killed at the battle of Jezreel. When news of the battle reached the capital, the child's nurse grabbed him and fled. But she fell and dropped him as she was running, and he became crippled as a result.)

⁵One day Recab and Baanah, the sons of Rimmon from Beeroth, went to Ishbosheth's home around noon as he was taking a nap. ⁶The doorkeeper, who had been sifting wheat, became drowsy and fell asleep. So Recab and Baanah slipped past the doorkeeper, went into Ishbosheth's bedroom, and stabbed him in the stomach. Then they escaped. ⁷But before leaving, they cut off his head as he lay there on his bed. Taking his head with them, they fled across the Jordan Valley* through the night. ⁸They arrived at Hebron and presented Ishbosheth's head to David. "Look!" they exclaimed. "Here is the head of Ishbosheth, the son of your enemy Saul who tried to kill you. Today the LORD has given you revenge on Saul and his entire family!"

⁹But David said to Recab and Baanah, "As surely as the LORD lives, the one who saves me from my enemies, I will tell you the truth. ¹⁰Once before, someone told me, 'Saul is dead,' thinking he was bringing me good news. But I seized him and killed him at Ziklag. That's the reward I gave him for his news! ¹¹Now what reward should I give the wicked men who have killed an innocent man in his own house and on his own bed? Should I not also demand your very lives?" ¹²So David ordered his young men to kill them, and they did. They cut off their hands and feet and hung their bodies beside the pool in Hebron. Then they took Ishbosheth's head and buried it in Abner's tomb in Hebron.

4:1 Also known as *Eshbaal.* 4:4 Also known as *Meribbaal.* 4:7 Hebrew *the Arabah.*

DAVID BECOMES KING OF ALL ISRAEL

5 Then all the tribes of Israel went to David at Hebron and told him, "We are all members of your family. ²For a long time, even while Saul was our king, you were the one who really led Israel. And the LORD has told you, 'You will be the shepherd of my people Israel. You will be their leader.' " ³So there at Hebron, David made a covenant with the leaders of Israel before the LORD. And they anointed him king of Israel.

⁴David was thirty years old when he began to reign, and he reigned forty years in all. ⁵He had reigned over Judah from Hebron for seven years and six months, and from Jerusalem he reigned over all Israel and Judah for thirty-three years.

DAVID CAPTURES JERUSALEM

⁶David then led his troops to Jerusalem to fight against the Jebusites. "You'll never get in here," the Jebusites taunted. "Even the blind and lame could keep you out!" For the Jebusites thought they were safe. ⁷But David captured the fortress of Zion, now called the City of David.

⁸When the insulting message from the defenders of the city reached David, he told his own troops, "Go up through the water tunnel into the city and destroy those 'lame' and 'blind' Jebusites. How I hate them." That is the origin of the saying, "The blind and the lame may not enter the house."* ⁹So David made the fortress his home, and he called it the City of David. He built additional fortifications around the city, starting at the Millo* and working inward. ¹⁰And David became more and more powerful, because the LORD God Almighty was with him.

¹¹Then King Hiram of Tyre sent messengers to David, along with carpenters and stonemasons to build him a palace. Hiram also sent many cedar logs for lumber. ¹²And David realized that the LORD had made him king over Israel and had made his kingdom great for the sake of his people Israel.

¹³After moving from Hebron to Jerusalem, David married more wives and concubines, and he had many sons and daughters. ¹⁴These are the names of David's sons who were born in Jerusalem: Shimea,* Shobab, Nathan, Solomon, ¹⁵Ibhar, Elishua, Nepheg, Japhia, ¹⁶Elishama, Eliada, and Eliphelet.

DAVID CONQUERS THE PHILISTINES

¹⁷When the Philistines heard that David had been anointed king of Israel, they mobilized all their forces to capture him. But David was told they were coming and went into the stronghold. ¹⁸The Philistines arrived and spread out across the valley of Rephaim. ¹⁹So David asked the LORD, "Should I go out to fight the Philistines? Will you hand them over to me?"

The LORD replied, "Yes, go ahead. I will certainly give you the victory."

²⁰So David went to Baal-perazim and defeated the Philistines there. "The LORD has done it!" David exclaimed. "He burst through my enemies like a raging flood!" So David named that place Baal-perazim (which means "the Lord who bursts through"). ²¹The Philistines had abandoned their idols there, so David and his troops confiscated them.

²²But after a while the Philistines returned and again spread out across the valley of Rephaim. ²³And once again David asked the LORD what to do. "Do not attack them straight on," the LORD replied. "Instead, circle around behind them and attack them near the balsam trees. ²⁴When you hear a sound like marching feet in the tops of the balsam trees, attack! That will be the signal that the LORD is moving ahead of you to strike down the Philistines." ²⁵So David did what the LORD commanded, and he struck down the Philistines all the way from Gibeon* to Gezer.

5:8 The meaning of this saying is uncertain.   5:9 Or *the supporting terraces.* The meaning of the Hebrew is uncertain.   5:14 As in parallel text at 1 Chr 3:5; Hebrew reads *Shammua,* a variant name for Shimea.   5:25 As in Greek version (see also 1 Chr 14:16); Hebrew reads *Geba.*

The Ark Brought to Jerusalem

6 Then David mobilized thirty thousand special troops. ²He led them to Baalah of Judah* to bring home the Ark of God, which bears the name of the LORD Almighty, who is enthroned between the cherubim. ³They placed the Ark of God on a new cart and brought it from the hillside home of Abinadab. Uzzah and Ahio, Abinadab's sons, were guiding the cart ⁴with the Ark of God on it, with Ahio walking in front. ⁵David and all the people of Israel were celebrating before the LORD with all their might, singing songs* and playing all kinds of musical instruments—lyres, harps, tambourines, castanets, and cymbals.

⁶But when they arrived at the threshing floor of Nacon, the oxen stumbled, and Uzzah put out his hand to steady the Ark of God. ⁷Then the LORD's anger blazed out against Uzzah for doing this, and God struck him dead beside the Ark of God. ⁸David was angry because the LORD's anger had blazed out against Uzzah. He named that place Perezuzzah (which means "outbreak against Uzzah"). It is still called that today.

⁹David was now afraid of the LORD and asked, "How can I ever bring the Ark of the LORD back into my care?" ¹⁰So David decided not to move the Ark of the LORD into the City of David. He took it instead to the home of Obed-edom of Gath. ¹¹The Ark of the LORD remained there with the family of Obed-edom for three months, and the LORD blessed him and his entire household.

¹²Then King David was told, "The LORD has blessed Obed-edom's home and everything he has because of the Ark of God." So David went there and brought the Ark to the City of David with a great celebration. ¹³After the men who were carrying it had gone six steps, they stopped and waited so David could sacrifice an ox and a fattened calf. ¹⁴And David danced before the LORD with all his might, wearing a priestly tunic.* ¹⁵So David and all Israel brought up the Ark of the LORD with much shouting and blowing of trumpets.

Michal's Contempt for David

¹⁶But as the Ark of the LORD entered the City of David, Michal, the daughter of Saul, looked down from her window. When she saw King David leaping and dancing before the LORD, she was filled with contempt for him.

¹⁷The Ark of the LORD was placed inside the special tent that David had prepared for it. And David sacrificed burnt offerings and peace offerings to the LORD. ¹⁸When he had finished, David blessed the people in the name of the LORD Almighty. ¹⁹Then he gave a gift of food to every man and woman in Israel: a loaf of bread, a cake of dates,* and a cake of raisins. Then everyone went home.

²⁰When David returned home to bless his family, Michal came out to meet him and said in disgust, "How glorious the king of Israel looked today! He exposed himself to the servant girls like any indecent person might do!"

²¹David retorted to Michal, "I was dancing before the LORD, who chose me above your father and his family! He appointed me as the leader of Israel, the people of the LORD. So I am willing to act like a fool in order to show my joy in the LORD. ²²Yes, and I am willing to look even more foolish than this, but I will be held in honor by the girls of whom you have spoken!" ²³So Michal, the daughter of Saul, remained childless throughout her life.

The Lord's Covenant Promise to David

7 When the LORD had brought peace to the land and King David was settled in his palace, ²David summoned Nathan the prophet. "Look!" David said. "Here I am living in this beautiful cedar palace, but the Ark of God is out in a tent!"

³Nathan replied, "Go ahead and do what you have in mind, for the LORD is with you."

6:2 *Baalah of Judah* is another name for Kiriath-jearim; compare 1 Chr 13:6.   6:5 As in Greek version (see also 1 Chr 13:8); Hebrew reads *cypress trees.*   6:14 Hebrew *a linen ephod.*   6:19 Or *a portion of meat.* The meaning of the Hebrew is uncertain.

My Daily Worship

— *March 15* —

LIVING WITH WILD ABANDON

2 SAMUEL 5:1–7:29

And David danced before the LORD with all his might, wearing a priestly tunic.
So David and all Israel brought up the Ark of the LORD with
much shouting and blowing of trumpets (6:14–15).

[i reflect]

In some churches, celebrate really means *celebrate*. People clap, sing, laugh, and lift their hands to God in praise. They don't care who's looking, what they are thinking, or what anyone else is doing. They're going to praise him in their own way and do it with enthusiasm.

For other people, praise and worship are internal processes with little or no outward sign of celebration, although they're just as thankful and joyful as the more demonstrative believers.

David fell into the first group. He reveled in God's goodness, dancing for all he was worth. He was later criticized for his exuberance, but all that mattered to him was raising his voice and his heart to his wonderful God.

Which type of worshiper are you? Are you a quiet worshiper whose awe and love for God flow out in silent prayer? Or do you raise the roof with your vocal and active worship? Isn't it great to remember that God loves both kinds of worship? The loud kind and the quiet kind. The private worship and the public worship.

Your worship might be enriched by trying something new. If you're quiet, try clapping your hands. If you're a dancer, try standing still and focusing all that energy upward to God in silent prayer.

David didn't mind making a fool of himself for God, and whether we do that in bold witness or uncompromising standards or a particular style of worship—looking foolish is well worth it if it can bring glory to God.

Try worshiping in different ways throughout the day. Lift your voice in song as you drive to work. Spend a moment in silent prayer as you prepare dinner. Dance in the privacy of your bedroom. Worship him!

[i pray]

Lord, forgive me for being judgmental about the way others worship you. I haven't really
said it out loud, but the way some people worship in church makes me uncomfortable.
Help me, God, to be so focused on you that I don't even see what they're doing.

[i respond]

Try something "foolish" today for Jesus. Maybe answer the phone, "God bless you!" Or crank up the CD player and play your favorite praise song at maximum volume. Lift your hands to God as you pray, or actually get down on your knees and worship him.

4But that same night the LORD said to Nathan,

5"Go and tell my servant David, 'This is what the LORD says: Are you the one to build me a temple to live in? 6I have never lived in a temple, from the day I brought the Israelites out of Egypt until now. My home has always been a tent, moving from one place to another. 7And I have never once complained to Israel's leaders, the shepherds of my people Israel. I have never asked them, "Why haven't you built me a beautiful cedar temple?" '

8"Now go and say to my servant David, 'This is what the LORD Almighty says: I chose you to lead my people Israel when you were just a shepherd boy, tending your sheep out in the pasture. 9I have been with you wherever you have gone, and I have destroyed all your enemies. Now I will make your name famous throughout the earth! 10And I have provided a permanent homeland for my people Israel, a secure place where they will never be disturbed. It will be their own land where wicked nations won't oppress them as they did in the past, 11from the time I appointed judges to rule my people. And I will keep you safe from all your enemies.

" 'And now the LORD declares that he will build a house for you—a dynasty of kings! 12For when you die, I will raise up one of your descendants, and I will make his kingdom strong. 13He is the one who will build a house—a temple—for my name. And I will establish the throne of his kingdom forever. 14I will be his father, and he will be my son. If he sins, I will use other nations to punish him. 15But my unfailing love will not be taken from him as I took it from Saul, whom I removed before you. 16Your dynasty and your kingdom will continue for all time before me, and your throne will be secure forever.' "

17So Nathan went back to David and told him everything the LORD had said.

DAVID'S PRAYER OF THANKS

18Then King David went in and sat before the LORD and prayed, "Who am I, O Sovereign LORD, and what is my family, that you have brought me this far? 19And now, Sovereign LORD, in addition to everything else, you speak of giving me a lasting dynasty! Do you deal with everyone this way,* O Sovereign LORD? 20What more can I say? You know what I am really like, Sovereign LORD. 21For the sake of your promise and according to your will, you have done all these great things and have shown them to me.

22"How great you are, O Sovereign LORD! There is no one like you—there is no other God. We have never even heard of another god like you! 23What other nation on earth is like Israel? What other nation, O God, have you redeemed from slavery to be your own people? You made a great name for yourself when you rescued your people from Egypt. You performed awesome miracles and drove out the nations and gods that stood in their way. 24You made Israel your people forever, and you, O LORD, became their God.

25"And now, O LORD God, do as you have promised concerning me and my family. Confirm it as a promise that will last forever. 26And may your name be honored forever so that all the world will say, 'The LORD Almighty is God over Israel!' And may the dynasty of your servant David be established in your presence.

27"O LORD Almighty, God of Israel, I have been bold enough to pray this prayer because you have revealed that you will build a house for me—an eternal dynasty! 28For you are God, O Sovereign LORD. Your words are truth, and you have promised these good things to

7:19 The meaning of the Hebrew is uncertain.

me, your servant. ²⁹And now, may it please you to bless me and my family so that our dynasty may continue forever before you. For when you grant a blessing to your servant, O Sovereign LORD, it is an eternal blessing!"

DAVID'S MILITARY VICTORIES

8 After this, David subdued and humbled the Philistines by conquering Gath, their largest city.* ²David also conquered the land of Moab. He made the people lie down on the ground in a row, and he measured them off in groups with a length of rope. He measured off two groups to be executed for every one group to be spared. The Moabites who were spared became David's servants and brought him tribute money.

³David also destroyed the forces of Hadadezer son of Rehob, king of Zobah, when Hadadezer marched out to strengthen his control along the Euphrates River. ⁴David captured seventeen hundred charioteers* and twenty thousand foot soldiers. Then he crippled all but one hundred of the chariot horses.

⁵When Arameans from Damascus arrived to help Hadadezer, David killed twenty-two thousand of them. ⁶Then he placed several army garrisons in Damascus, the Aramean capital, and the Arameans became David's subjects and brought him tribute money. So the LORD gave David victory wherever he went. ⁷David brought the gold shields of Hadadezer's officers to Jerusalem, ⁸along with a large amount of bronze from Hadadezer's cities of Tebah* and Berothai.

⁹When King Toi of Hamath heard that David had destroyed the army of Hadadezer, ¹⁰he sent his son Joram to congratulate David on his success. Hadadezer and Toi had long been enemies, and there had been many wars between them. Joram presented David with many gifts of silver, gold, and bronze. ¹¹King David dedicated all these gifts to the LORD, along with the silver and gold he had set apart from the other nations he had subdued— ¹²Edom,* Moab, Ammon, Philistia, and Amalek—and from Hadadezer son of Rehob, king of Zobah.

¹³So David became very famous. After his return he destroyed eighteen thousand Edomites* in the Valley of Salt. ¹⁴He placed army garrisons throughout Edom, and all the Edomites became David's subjects. This was another example of how the LORD made David victorious wherever he went.

¹⁵David reigned over all Israel and was fair to everyone. ¹⁶Joab son of Zeruiah was commander of the army. Jehoshaphat son of Ahilud was the royal historian. ¹⁷Zadok son of Ahitub and Ahimelech son of Abiathar were the priests. Seraiah was the court secretary. ¹⁸Benaiah son of Jehoiada was captain of the king's bodyguard.* David's sons served as priestly leaders.*

DAVID'S KINDNESS TO MEPHIBOSHETH

9 One day David began wondering if anyone in Saul's family was still alive, for he had promised Jonathan that he would show kindness to them. ²He summoned a man named Ziba, who had been one of Saul's servants. "Are you Ziba?" the king asked.

"Yes sir, I am," Ziba replied.

³The king then asked him, "Is anyone still alive from Saul's family? If so, I want to show God's kindness to them in any way I can."

Ziba replied, "Yes, one of Jonathan's sons is still alive, but he is crippled."

⁴"Where is he?" the king asked.

"In Lo-debar," Ziba told him, "at the home of Makir son of Ammiel." ⁵So David sent for him and brought him from Makir's home.

8:1 Hebrew *by conquering Metheg-ammah,* a name which means "the bridle," possibly referring to the size of the city or the tribute money taken from it. Compare 1 Chr 18:1.   **8:4** Greek version reads *1,000 chariots and 7,000 charioteers;* compare 1 Chr 18:4.
8:8 As in some Greek manuscripts (see also 1 Chr 18:8); Hebrew reads *Betah.*   **8:12** As in a few Hebrew manuscripts and Greek and Syriac versions (see also 8:14; 1 Chr 18:11); most Hebrew manuscripts read *Aram.*   **8:13** As in a few Hebrew manuscripts and Greek and Syriac versions (see also 8:14; 1 Chr 18:12); most Hebrew manuscripts read *Arameans.*   **8:18a** Hebrew *of the Kerethites and Pelethites.*
8:18b Hebrew *David's sons were priests;* compare parallel text at 1 Chr 18:17.

⁶His name was Mephibosheth*; he was Jonathan's son and Saul's grandson. When he came to David, he bowed low in great fear and said, "I am your servant."

⁷But David said, "Don't be afraid! I've asked you to come so that I can be kind to you because of my vow to your father, Jonathan. I will give you all the land that once belonged to your grandfather Saul, and you may live here with me at the palace!"

⁸Mephibosheth fell to the ground before the king. "Should the king show such kindness to a dead dog like me?" he exclaimed.

⁹Then the king summoned Saul's servant Ziba and said, "I have given your master's grandson everything that belonged to Saul and his family. ¹⁰You and your sons and servants are to farm the land for him to produce food for his family. But Mephibosheth will live here at the palace with me."

Ziba, who had fifteen sons and twenty servants, replied, ¹¹"Yes, my lord; I will do all that you have commanded." And from that time on, Mephibosheth ate regularly with David, as though he were one of his own sons. ¹²Mephibosheth had a young son named Mica. And from then on, all the members of Ziba's household were Mephibosheth's servants. ¹³And Mephibosheth, who was crippled in both feet, moved to Jerusalem to live at the palace.

DAVID DEFEATS THE AMMONITES

10 Some time after this, King Nahash of the Ammonites died, and his son Hanun became king. ²David said, "I am going to show complete loyalty to Hanun because his father, Nahash, was always completely loyal to me." So David sent ambassadors to express sympathy to Hanun about his father's death.

But when David's ambassadors arrived in the land of Ammon, ³Hanun's advisers said to their master, "Do you really think these men are coming here to honor your father? No!

David has sent them to spy out the city so that they can come in and conquer it!" ⁴So Hanun seized David's ambassadors and shaved off half of each man's beard, cut off their robes at the buttocks, and sent them back to David in shame. ⁵When David heard what had happened, he sent messengers to tell the men to stay at Jericho until their beards grew out, for they were very embarrassed by their appearance.

⁶Now the people of Ammon realized how seriously they had angered David, so they hired twenty thousand Aramean mercenaries from the lands of Beth-rehob and Zobah, one thousand from the king of Maacah, and twelve thousand from the land of Tob. ⁷When David heard about this, he sent Joab and the entire Israelite army to fight them. ⁸The Ammonite troops drew up their battle lines at the entrance of the city gates, while the Arameans from Zobah and Rehob and the men from Tob and Maacah positioned themselves to fight in the open fields.

⁹When Joab saw that he would have to fight on two fronts, he chose the best troops in his army. He placed them under his personal command and led them out to fight the Arameans in the fields. ¹⁰He left the rest of the army under the command of his brother Abishai, who was to attack the Ammonites. ¹¹"If the Arameans are too strong for me, then come over and help me," Joab told his brother. "And if the Ammonites are too strong for you, I will come and help you. ¹²Be courageous! Let us fight bravely to save our people and the cities of our God. May the LORD's will be done."

¹³When Joab and his troops attacked, the Arameans began to run away. ¹⁴And when the Ammonites saw the Arameans running, they ran from Abishai and retreated into the city. After the battle was over, Joab returned to Jerusalem.

¹⁵The Arameans now realized that they were no match for Israel. So when they regrouped, ¹⁶they were joined by additional Aramean

9:6 Also known as *Meribbaal.*

My Daily Worship

— *March 16* —

A DEAD DOG LIKE ME

2 SAMUEL 8:1–10:19

*Mephibosheth fell to the ground before the king. "Should the king
show such kindness to a dead dog like me?" he exclaimed (9:8).*

[i reflect]

A wayward son, an adulterous wife, a rebellious nation. In the Bible, God's mercy extends to all three, and more. He is lavish—not stingy—with his mercy. He grants it generously to us who are so undeserving.

Yet it can be hard to show mercy to someone who has wronged you, to someone who has harmed your child or betrayed your trust. A more likely human response would be anger or a desire for revenge, or to simply tune-out and not deal with the offender.

Again and again, David provided a powerful example of God's mercy. He had no legal responsibility to Jonathan's son; he didn't even know the young man was alive. Nor had Mephibosheth come to David asking for help. In fact, when David invited him to his palace, Mephibosheth feared for his life, believing himself to be unworthy to come before the king.

But in a show of God-like extravagant compassion and grace, David sought him out, called him to himself, and gave Mephibosheth a place at his table. Imagine. God does the same for us. He seeks us out, draws us to himself with his love, and tenderly provides and cares for us, his children. It's only because of his grace that we are saved. It's only because of his love that we are invited to feast at his table.

Who might benefit from a lavish display of mercy from you today? Is there someone you haven't thought of in a long time who could use your help? Someone everyone else has forgotten? Someone who once wronged you in some way? It may be hard, and you may not want to. But why not search that person out and give him or her a healthy dose of God's mercy displayed through you?

As an act of worship, make a conscious effort to extend God's grace to others today. Instead of judgment, show mercy. Instead of revenge, give forgiveness. Instead of anger, show love.

[i pray]

*Lord, I need your help to be merciful. It doesn't always come naturally.
Awaken my compassion, God, and make my heart soft like yours.*

[i respond]

Think of your day's agenda. Name one person with whom you are likely to cross paths; then think of one specific way to show that person God's compassion.

troops summoned by Hadadezer from the other side of the Euphrates River.* These troops arrived at Helam under the command of Shobach, the commander of all Hadadezer's forces. [17]When David heard what was happening, he mobilized all Israel, crossed the Jordan River, and led the army to Helam. The Arameans positioned themselves there in battle formation and then attacked David. [18]But again the Arameans fled from the Israelites. This time David's forces killed seven hundred charioteers and forty thousand horsemen,* including Shobach, the commander of their army. [19]When Hadadezer and his Aramean allies realized they had been defeated by Israel, they surrendered to them and became their subjects. After that, the Arameans were afraid to help the Ammonites.

DAVID AND BATHSHEBA

11 The following spring, the time of year when kings go to war, David sent Joab and the Israelite army to destroy the Ammonites. In the process they laid siege to the city of Rabbah. But David stayed behind in Jerusalem.

[2]Late one afternoon David got out of bed after taking a nap and went for a stroll on the roof of the palace. As he looked out over the city, he noticed a woman of unusual beauty taking a bath. [3]He sent someone to find out who she was, and he was told, "She is Bathsheba, the daughter of Eliam and the wife of Uriah the Hittite." [4]Then David sent for her; and when she came to the palace, he slept with her. (She had just completed the purification rites after having her menstrual period.) Then she returned home. [5]Later, when Bathsheba discovered that she was pregnant, she sent a message to inform David.

[6]So David sent word to Joab: "Send me Uriah the Hittite." [7]When Uriah arrived, David asked him how Joab and the army were getting along and how the war was progressing. [8]Then he told Uriah, "Go on home and

relax." David even sent a gift to Uriah after he had left the palace. [9]But Uriah wouldn't go home. He stayed that night at the palace entrance with some of the king's other servants.

[10]When David heard what Uriah had done, he summoned him and asked, "What's the matter with you? Why didn't you go home last night after being away for so long?"

[11]Uriah replied, "The Ark and the armies of Israel and Judah are living in tents,* and Joab and his officers are camping in the open fields. How could I go home to wine and dine and sleep with my wife? I swear that I will never be guilty of acting like that."

[12]"Well, stay here tonight," David told him, "and tomorrow you may return to the army." So Uriah stayed in Jerusalem that day and the next. [13]Then David invited him to dinner and got him drunk. But even then he couldn't get Uriah to go home to his wife. Again he slept at the palace entrance.

DAVID ARRANGES FOR URIAH'S DEATH

[14]So the next morning David wrote a letter to Joab and gave it to Uriah to deliver. [15]The letter instructed Joab, "Station Uriah on the front lines where the battle is fiercest. Then pull back so that he will be killed." [16]So Joab assigned Uriah to a spot close to the city wall where he knew the enemy's strongest men were fighting. [17]And Uriah was killed along with several other Israelite soldiers.

[18]Then Joab sent a battle report to David. [19]He told his messenger, "Report all the news of the battle to the king. [20]But he might get angry and ask, 'Why did the troops go so close to the city? Didn't they know there would be shooting from the walls? [21]Wasn't Gideon's son Abimelech killed* at Thebez by a woman who threw a millstone down on him?' Then tell him, 'Uriah the Hittite was killed, too.'"

[22]So the messenger went to Jerusalem and gave a complete report to David. [23]"The

10:16 Hebrew *the river.* 10:18 Some Greek manuscripts read *foot soldiers;* compare parallel text at 1 Chr 19:18. 11:11 Or *at Succoth.*
11:21 Hebrew *Was not Abimelech son of Jerubbesheth killed.*

enemy came out against us," he said. "And as we chased them back to the city gates, "the archers on the wall shot arrows at us. Some of our men were killed, including Uriah the Hittite."

²⁵"Well, tell Joab not to be discouraged," David said. "The sword kills one as well as another! Fight harder next time, and conquer the city!"

²⁶When Bathsheba heard that her husband was dead, she mourned for him. ²⁷When the period of mourning was over, David sent for her and brought her to the palace, and she became one of his wives. Then she gave birth to a son. But the LORD was very displeased with what David had done.

NATHAN REBUKES DAVID

12 So the LORD sent Nathan the prophet to tell David this story: "There were two men in a certain town. One was rich, and one was poor. ²The rich man owned many sheep and cattle. ³The poor man owned nothing but a little lamb he had worked hard to buy. He raised that little lamb, and it grew up with his children. It ate from the man's own plate and drank from his cup. He cuddled it in his arms like a baby daughter. ⁴One day a guest arrived at the home of the rich man. But instead of killing a lamb from his own flocks for food, he took the poor man's lamb and killed it and served it to his guest."

⁵David was furious. "As surely as the LORD lives," he vowed, "any man who would do such a thing deserves to die! ⁶He must repay four lambs to the poor man for the one he stole and for having no pity."

⁷Then Nathan said to David, "You are that man! The LORD, the God of Israel, says, 'I anointed you king of Israel and saved you from the power of Saul. ⁸I gave you his house and his wives and the kingdoms of Israel and Judah. And if that had not been enough, I would have given you much, much more. ⁹Why, then, have you despised the word of the LORD and done this horrible deed? For you have murdered Uriah and stolen his wife.

¹⁰From this time on, the sword will be a constant threat to your family, because you have despised me by taking Uriah's wife to be your own.

¹¹" 'Because of what you have done, I, the LORD, will cause your own household to rebel against you. I will give your wives to another man, and he will go to bed with them in public view. ¹²You did it secretly, but I will do this to you openly in the sight of all Israel.' "

DAVID CONFESSES HIS GUILT

¹³Then David confessed to Nathan, "I have sinned against the LORD."

Nathan replied, "Yes, but the LORD has forgiven you, and you won't die for this sin. ¹⁴But you have given the enemies of the LORD great opportunity to despise and blaspheme him, so your child will die."

¹⁵After Nathan returned to his home, the LORD made Bathsheba's baby deathly ill. ¹⁶David begged God to spare the child. He went without food and lay all night on the bare ground. ¹⁷The leaders of the nation pleaded with him to get up and eat with them, but he refused. ¹⁸Then on the seventh day the baby died. David's advisers were afraid to tell him. "He was so broken up about the baby being sick," they said. "What will he do to himself when we tell him the child is dead?"

¹⁹But when David saw them whispering, he realized what had happened. "Is the baby dead?" he asked.

"Yes," they replied. ²⁰Then David got up from the ground, washed himself, put on lotions, and changed his clothes. Then he went to the Tabernacle and worshiped the LORD. After that, he returned to the palace and ate. ²¹His advisers were amazed. "We don't understand you," they told him. "While the baby was still living, you wept and refused to eat. But now that the baby is dead, you have stopped your mourning and are eating again."

²²David replied, "I fasted and wept while the child was alive, for I said, 'Perhaps the LORD will be gracious to me and let the child live.' ²³But why should I fast when he is dead? Can I

bring him back again? I will go to him one day, but he cannot return to me."

²⁴Then David comforted Bathsheba, his wife, and slept with her. She became pregnant and gave birth to a son, and they named him Solomon. The LORD loved the child ²⁵and sent word through Nathan the prophet that his name should be Jedidiah—"beloved of the LORD"—because the LORD loved him.

DAVID CAPTURES RABBAH

²⁶Meanwhile, Joab and the Israelite army were successfully ending their siege of Rabbah, the capital of Ammon. ²⁷Joab sent messengers to tell David, "I have fought against Rabbah and captured its water supply.* ²⁸Now bring the rest of the army and finish the job, so you will get credit for the victory instead of me."

²⁹So David led the rest of his army to Rabbah and captured it. ³⁰David removed the crown from the king's head,* and it was placed on David's own head. The crown was made of gold and set with gems, and it weighed about seventy-five pounds.* David took a vast amount of plunder from the city. ³¹He also made slaves of the people of Rabbah and forced them to labor with saws, picks, and axes, and to work in the brick kilns. That is how he dealt with the people of all the Ammonite cities. Then David and his army returned to Jerusalem.

THE RAPE OF TAMAR

13 David's son Absalom had a beautiful sister named Tamar. And Amnon, her half brother, fell desperately in love with her. ²Amnon became so obsessed with Tamar that he became ill. She was a virgin, and it seemed impossible that he could ever fulfill his love for her.

³Now Amnon had a very crafty friend—his cousin Jonadab. He was the son of David's brother Shimea.* ⁴One day Jonadab said to Amnon, "What's the trouble? Why should the son of a king look so dejected morning after morning?"

So Amnon told him, "I am in love with Tamar, Absalom's sister."

⁵"Well," Jonadab said, "I'll tell you what to do. Go back to bed and pretend you are sick. When your father comes to see you, ask him to let Tamar come and prepare some food for you. Tell him you'll feel better if she feeds you."

⁶So Amnon pretended to be sick. And when the king came to see him, Amnon asked him, "Please let Tamar come to take care of me and cook something for me to eat." ⁷So David agreed and sent Tamar to Amnon's house to prepare some food for him.

⁸When Tamar arrived at Amnon's house, she went to the room where he was lying down so he could watch her mix some dough. Then she baked some special bread for him. ⁹But when she set the serving tray before him, he refused to eat. "Everyone get out of here," Amnon told his servants. So they all left. ¹⁰Then he said to Tamar, "Now bring the food into my bedroom and feed it to me here." So Tamar took it to him. ¹¹But as she was feeding him, he grabbed her and demanded, "Come to bed with me, my darling sister."

¹²"No, my brother!" she cried. "Don't be foolish! Don't do this to me! You know what a serious crime it is to do such a thing in Israel. ¹³Where could I go in my shame? And you would be called one of the greatest fools in Israel. Please, just speak to the king about it, and he will let you marry me."

¹⁴But Amnon wouldn't listen to her, and since he was stronger than she was, he raped her. ¹⁵Then suddenly Amnon's love turned to hate, and he hated her even more than he had loved her. "Get out of here!" he snarled at her.

¹⁶"No, no!" Tamar cried. "To reject me now is a greater wrong than what you have already done to me."

But Amnon wouldn't listen to her. ¹⁷He

12:27 Or *captured the city of water.* **12:30a** Greek version reads *removed the crown of Milcom;* compare 1 Kgs 11:5. Milcom, also called Molech, was the god of the Ammonites. **12:30b** Hebrew *1 talent* [34 kilograms]. **13:3** Hebrew *Shimeah* (also in 13:32), a variant name for Shimea; compare 1 Chr 2:13.

My Daily Worship

— March 17 —

When the Truth Hurts

2 Samuel 11:1–14:39

Then Nathan said to David, "You are that man! The Lord, the God of Israel, says, 'I anointed
you king of Israel and saved you from the power of Saul. . . . Why then, have you
despised the word of the Lord and done this horrible deed?'" (12:7, 9).

[i reflect]

The game comes to an abrupt halt as the referee blows the whistle. "Foul!" he shouts, as he calls
out your number and points at you. All eyes are directed at you. Everyone in the gym knows what
you did wrong. You stand guilty—"you are that man!"

In this passage, David thought he had gotten away with his sins of adultery and murder. But God
saw them, and Nathan knew his secret crimes. Then, like the referee, Nathan blew the whistle on
his friend, called a foul, and confronted David with the truth. *You are that man, David.*

The truth hurts. We'd rather not hear it. We'd rather hide from it, or pretend that everything is OK
and that no one had noticed. But we need to be confronted with the truth—the truth of our own
sins—and confess them before God. Perhaps David's greatest strength was his willingness to confess his sins and repent. While David still suffered the consequences of his sins, God did forgive
him and restored their relationship, so that he called David "a man after my own heart" (Acts
13:22).

It's hard to admit we are wrong or that we did wrong. It's embarrassing to be truthful about what
we have done. But the alternative—denial—is much worse than having sin found out.
Unconfessed sin eats away at us. It separates us from God; it hinders our prayers; it separates us
from loved ones. The cure is so easy and so hard. Admit it; agree with God that it was wrong and
turn away from it. He will forgive you, welcome you back to his loving arms, and call you a person
"after his own heart."

Confession is at the heart of worship. Be honest with God and admit your sins. Remove anything
that comes between you and your relationship with God. He already knows, and he stands at the
end of your prayer, waiting to forgive.

[i pray]

Lord, I confess my sins to you. In my heart right now, I'm agreeing with you that I've
done wrong in the specific areas that I'm going to name right now. Forgive me,
Lord, so that I can worship you, freed from my sins.

[i respond]

Take with you a reminder to confess your sins. At the top of a piece of paper, write, "I agree with
God that I . . ." Throughout the day, write down what you need to confess as God brings those sins
to mind.

shouted for his servant and demanded, "Throw this woman out, and lock the door behind her!"

¹⁸So the servant put her out. She was wearing a long, beautiful robe,* as was the custom in those days for the king's virgin daughters. ¹⁹But now Tamar tore her robe and put ashes on her head. And then, with her face in her hands, she went away crying.

²⁰Her brother Absalom saw her and asked, "Is it true that Amnon has been with you? Well, don't be so upset. Since he's your brother anyway, don't worry about it." So Tamar lived as a desolate woman in Absalom's house. ²¹When King David heard what had happened, he was very angry. ²²And though Absalom never spoke to Amnon about it, he hated Amnon deeply because of what he had done to his sister.

ABSALOM'S REVENGE ON AMNON

²³Two years later, when Absalom's sheep were being sheared at Baal-hazor near Ephraim, Absalom invited all the king's sons to come to a feast. ²⁴He went to the king and said, "My sheep-shearers are now at work. Would the king and his servants please come to celebrate the occasion with me?"

²⁵The king replied, "No, my son. If we all came, we would be too much of a burden on you." Absalom pressed him, but the king wouldn't come, though he sent his thanks.

²⁶"Well, then," Absalom said, "if you can't come, how about sending my brother Amnon instead?"

"Why Amnon?" the king asked. ²⁷But Absalom kept on pressing the king until he finally agreed to let all his sons attend, including Amnon.

²⁸Absalom told his men, "Wait until Amnon gets drunk; then at my signal, kill him! Don't be afraid. I'm the one who has given the command. Take courage and do it!" ²⁹So at Absalom's signal they murdered Amnon. Then

> *Worship is God's enjoyment of us and our enjoyment of him. Worship is a response to the father/child relationship.*
>
> GRAHAM KENDRICK

the other sons of the king jumped on their mules and fled.

³⁰As they were on the way back to Jerusalem, this report reached David: "Absalom has killed all your sons; not one is left alive!" ³¹The king jumped up, tore his robe, and fell prostrate on the ground. His advisers also tore their clothes in horror and sorrow.

³²But just then Jonadab, the son of David's brother Shimea, arrived and said, "No, not all your sons have been killed! It was only Amnon! Absalom has been plotting this ever since Amnon raped his sister Tamar. ³³No, your sons aren't all dead! It was only Amnon." ³⁴Meanwhile Absalom escaped.

Then the watchman on the Jerusalem wall saw a great crowd coming toward the city from the west. He ran to tell the king, "I see a crowd of people coming from the Horonaim road* along the side of the hill."

³⁵"Look!" Jonadab told the king. "There they are now! Your sons are coming, just as I said." ³⁶They soon arrived, weeping and sobbing, and the king and his officials wept bitterly with them. ³⁷And David mourned many days for his son Amnon.

Absalom fled to his grandfather, Talmai son of Ammihud, the king of Geshur. ³⁸He stayed there in Geshur for three years. ³⁹And David, now reconciled to Amnon's death, longed to be reunited with his son Absalom.*

13:18 Or *a robe with sleeves,* or *an ornamented robe.* The meaning of the Hebrew is uncertain. **13:34** As in Greek version; Hebrew reads *from the road behind him.* **13:39** Or *no longer felt a need to go out after Absalom.*

JOAB ARRANGES FOR ABSALOM'S RETURN

14 Joab realized how much the king longed to see Absalom. ²So he sent for a woman from Tekoa who had a reputation for great wisdom. He said to her, "Pretend you are in mourning; wear mourning clothes and don't bathe or wear any perfume. Act like a woman who has been in deep sorrow for a long time. ³Then go to the king and tell him the story I am about to tell you." Then Joab told her what to say.

⁴When the woman approached the king, she fell with her face down to the floor in front of him and cried out, "O king! Help me!"

⁵"What's the trouble?" the king asked.

"I am a widow," she replied. ⁶"My two sons had a fight out in the field. And since no one was there to stop it, one of them was killed. ⁷Now the rest of the family is demanding, 'Let us have your son. We will execute him for murdering his brother. He doesn't deserve to inherit his family's property.' But if I do that, I will have no one left, and my husband's name and family will disappear from the face of the earth."

⁸"Leave it to me," the king told her. "Go home, and I'll see to it that no one touches him."

⁹"Oh, thank you, my lord," she replied. "And I'll take the responsibility if you are criticized for helping me like this."

¹⁰"Don't worry about that!" the king said. "If anyone objects, bring them to me. I can assure you they will never complain again!"

¹¹Then she said, "Please swear to me by the LORD your God that you won't let anyone take vengeance against my son. I want no more bloodshed."

"As surely as the LORD lives," he replied, "not a hair on your son's head will be disturbed!"

¹²"Please let me ask one more thing of you!" she said.

"Go ahead," he urged. "Speak!"

¹³She replied, "Why don't you do as much for all the people of God as you have promised to do for me? You have convicted yourself in making this decision, because you have refused to bring home your own banished son. ¹⁴All of us must die eventually. Our lives are like water spilled out on the ground, which cannot be gathered up again. That is why God tries to bring us back when we have been separated from him. He does not sweep away the lives of those he cares about—and neither should you!

¹⁵"But I have come to plead with you for my son because my life and my son's life have been threatened. I said to myself, 'Perhaps the king will listen to me ¹⁶and rescue us from those who would cut us off from God's people. ¹⁷Yes, the king will give us peace of mind again.' I know that you are like an angel of God and can discern good from evil. May the LORD your God be with you."

¹⁸"I want to know one thing," the king replied.

"Yes, my lord?" she asked.

¹⁹"Did Joab send you here?"

And the woman replied, "My lord the king, how can I deny it? Nobody can hide anything from you. Yes, Joab sent me and told me what to say. ²⁰He did it to place the matter before you in a different light. But you are as wise as an angel of God, and you understand everything that happens among us!"

²¹So the king sent for Joab and told him, "All right, go and bring back the young man Absalom."

²²Joab fell to the ground before the king and blessed him and said, "At last I know that I have gained your approval, for you have granted me this request!"

²³Then Joab went to Geshur and brought Absalom back to Jerusalem. ²⁴But the king gave this order: "Absalom may go to his own house, but he must never come into my presence." So Absalom did not see the king.

ABSALOM RECONCILED TO DAVID

²⁵Now no one in Israel was as handsome as Absalom. From head to foot, he was the perfect specimen of a man. ²⁶He cut his hair only once a year, and then only because it was too

heavy to carry around. When he weighed it out, it came to five pounds!* ²⁷He had three sons and one daughter. His daughter's name was Tamar, and she was very beautiful.

²⁸Absalom lived in Jerusalem for two years without getting to see the king. ²⁹Then Absalom sent for Joab to ask him to intercede for him, but Joab refused to come. Absalom sent for him a second time, but again Joab refused to come. ³⁰So Absalom said to his servants, "Go and set fire to Joab's barley field, the field next to mine." So they set his field on fire, as Absalom had commanded.

³¹Then Joab came to Absalom and demanded, "Why did your servants set my field on fire?"

³²And Absalom replied, "Because I wanted you to ask the king why he brought me back from Geshur if he didn't intend to see me. I might as well have stayed there. Let me see the king; if he finds me guilty of anything, then let him execute me."

³³So Joab told the king what Absalom had said. Then at last David summoned his estranged son, and Absalom came and bowed low before the king, and David kissed him.

ABSALOM'S REBELLION

15 After this, Absalom bought a chariot and horses, and he hired fifty footmen to run ahead of him. ²He got up early every morning and went out to the gate of the city. When people brought a case to the king for judgment, Absalom would ask where they were from, and they would tell him their tribe. ³Then Absalom would say, "You've really got a strong case here! It's too bad the king doesn't have anyone to hear it. ⁴I wish I were the judge. Then people could bring their problems to me, and I would give them justice!" ⁵And when people tried to bow before him, Absalom wouldn't let them. Instead, he took them by the hand and embraced them. ⁶So in this way, Absalom stole the hearts of all the people of Israel.

⁷After four years,* Absalom said to the king,

"Let me go to Hebron to offer a sacrifice to the LORD in fulfillment of a vow I made to him. ⁸For while I was at Geshur, I promised to sacrifice to him in Hebron if he would bring me back to Jerusalem."

⁹"All right," the king told him. "Go and fulfill your vow."

So Absalom went to Hebron. ¹⁰But while he was there, he sent secret messengers to every part of Israel to stir up a rebellion against the king. "As soon as you hear the trumpets," his message read, "you will know that Absalom has been crowned king in Hebron." ¹¹He took two hundred men from Jerusalem with him as guests, but they knew nothing of his intentions. ¹²While he was offering the sacrifices, he sent for Ahithophel, one of David's counselors who lived in Giloh. Soon many others also joined Absalom, and the conspiracy gained momentum.

DAVID ESCAPES FROM JERUSALEM

¹³A messenger soon arrived in Jerusalem to tell King David, "All Israel has joined Absalom in a conspiracy against you!"

¹⁴"Then we must flee at once, or it will be too late!" David urged his men. "Hurry! If we get out of the city before he arrives, both we and the city of Jerusalem will be spared from disaster."

¹⁵"We are with you," his advisers replied. "Do what you think is best." ¹⁶So the king and his household set out at once. He left no one behind except ten of his concubines to keep the palace in order. ¹⁷The king and his people set out on foot, and they paused at the edge of the city ¹⁸to let David's troops move past to lead the way. There were six hundred Gittites who had come with David from Gath, along with the king's bodyguard.* ¹⁹Then the king turned to Ittai, the captain of the Gittites, and asked, "Why are you coming with us? Go on back with your men to King Absalom, for you are a guest in Israel, a foreigner in exile. ²⁰You arrived only yesterday,

14:26 Hebrew *200 shekels* [2.3 kilograms] *by the royal standard.* 15:7 As in Greek and Syriac versions; Hebrew reads *40 years.* 15:18 Hebrew *the Kerethites and Pelethites.*

Words of Worship

THE LORD

The LORD, the Lord—Hebrew *Yah-veh* [shortened form *Yah*] "Yahweh, Jehovah"; *'a-don* "husband, master"; *'a-do-nai* "lord, lordship"; Greek *Ku-ri-os* "lord, master." The pronunciation *Yahveh*, or *Yahweh*, does not occur in the Hebrew Bible since *'Adonai* is traditionally read in its place. The Hebrew text lacks vowel letters, so the vowel signs for *'Adonai* are placed with the letters YHWH. Where this occurs, English translations usually print LORD (in capital letters). Where *'Adonai* occurs in Hebrew along with YHWH, English translations may print "Lord GOD" or another expression such as "Sovereign LORD." The traditional name "Jehovah" results from combining the letters YHWH with the vowel sounds for *'Adonai*. In the New Testament, *Kurios* is applied both to the Old Testament name, *Yahweh*, and to the Lord Jesus Christ.

You might be the president of your company, but "President" isn't your name. Your family, friends, and associates know you by a different "handle"—your proper name. In the same way, "God" is not the name of the One we worship. It's his office or title. But he does have a proper name, YHWH, known to his worshipers.

In the Bible, names often have meaning. The Lord explained his name to Moses when he said, "I AM THE ONE WHO ALWAYS IS" (Exodus 3:14). The name YHWH is related to the verb meaning "to be." It signifies his ongoing involvement in the history of his people, for he is "the God of Abraham, the God of Isaac, and the God of Jacob" (Exodus 3:15). We know him, in other words, because he has been involved with us in the course of our lives. It's not surprising, then, that Christians began to call Jesus "the Lord," using the same words used for Yahweh. For they saw clearly that "God was in Christ, reconciling the world to himself" (2 Corinthians 5:19).

and now should I force you to wander with us? I don't even know where we will go. Go on back and take your troops with you, and may the LORD show you his unfailing love and faithfulness.*"

[21]But Ittai said to the king, "I vow by the LORD and by your own life that I will go wherever you go, no matter what happens—whether it means life or death."

[22]David replied, "All right, come with us." So Ittai and his six hundred men and their families went along.

[23]There was deep sadness throughout the land as the king and his followers passed by. They crossed the Kidron Valley and then went out toward the wilderness.

[24]Abiathar and Zadok and the Levites took the Ark of the Covenant of God and set it down beside the road. Then they offered sacrifices there until everyone had passed by. [25]David instructed Zadok to take the Ark of God back into the city. "If the LORD sees fit," David said, "he will bring me back to see the Ark and the Tabernacle again. [26]But if he is through with me, then let him do what seems best to him."

[27]Then the king told Zadok the priest, "Look,* here is my plan. You and Abiathar* should return quietly to the city with your son Ahimaaz and Abiathar's son Jonathan. [28]I will stop at the shallows of the Jordan River* and wait there for a message from you. Let me know what happens in Jerusalem before I disappear into the wilderness." [29]So Zadok and Abiathar took the Ark of God back to the city and stayed there.

[30]David walked up the road that led to the Mount of Olives, weeping as he went. His head was covered and his feet were bare as a sign of mourning. And the people who were with him covered their heads and wept as they climbed the mountain. [31]When someone told David that his adviser Ahithophel was now backing Absalom, David prayed, "O LORD, let Ahithophel give Absalom foolish advice!"

15:20 As in Greek version; Hebrew reads *and may unfailing love and faithfulness go with you.* 15:27a As in Greek version; Hebrew reads *Are you a seer?* or *Do you see?* 15:27b Hebrew lacks *and Abiathar*; compare 15:29. 15:28 Hebrew *at the crossing points of the wilderness.*

³²As they reached the spot at the top of the Mount of Olives where people worshiped God, David found Hushai the Arkite waiting for him. Hushai had torn his clothing and put dirt on his head as a sign of mourning. ³³But David told him, "If you go with me, you will only be a burden. ³⁴Return to Jerusalem and tell Absalom, 'I will now be your adviser, just as I was your father's adviser in the past.' Then you can frustrate and counter Ahithophel's advice. ³⁵Zadok and Abiathar, the priests, are there. Tell them the plans that are being made to capture me, ³⁶and they will send their sons Ahimaaz and Jonathan to find me and tell me what is going on." ³⁷So David's friend Hushai returned to Jerusalem, getting there just as Absalom arrived.

DAVID AND ZIBA

16 David was just past the top of the hill when Ziba, the servant of Mephibosheth,* caught up with him. He was leading two donkeys loaded with two hundred loaves of bread, one hundred clusters of raisins, one hundred bunches of summer fruit, and a skin of wine. ²"What are these for?" the king asked Ziba.

And Ziba replied, "The donkeys are for your people to ride on, and the bread and summer fruit are for the young men to eat. The wine is to be taken with you into the wilderness for those who become faint."

³"And where is Mephibosheth?" the king asked him.

"He stayed in Jerusalem," Ziba replied. "He said, 'Today I will get back the kingdom of my grandfather Saul.'"

⁴"In that case," the king told Ziba, "I give you everything Mephibosheth owns."

"Thank you, sir," Ziba replied. "I will always do whatever you want me to do."

SHIMEI CURSES DAVID

⁵As David and his party passed Bahurim, a man came out of the village cursing them. It was Shimei son of Gera, a member of Saul's family. ⁶He threw stones at the king and the king's officers and all the mighty warriors who surrounded them. ⁷"Get out of here, you murderer, you scoundrel!" he shouted at David. ⁸"The LORD is paying you back for murdering Saul and his family. You stole his throne, and now the LORD has given it to your son Absalom. At last you will taste some of your own medicine, you murderer!"

⁹"Why should this dead dog curse my lord the king?" Abishai son of Zeruiah demanded. "Let me go over and cut off his head!"

¹⁰"No!" the king said. "What am I going to do with you sons of Zeruiah! If the LORD has told him to curse me, who am I to stop him?" ¹¹Then David said to Abishai and the other officers, "My own son is trying to kill me. Shouldn't this relative of Saul* have even more reason to do so? Leave him alone and let him curse, for the LORD has told him to do it. ¹²And perhaps the LORD will see that I am being wronged and will bless me because of these curses." ¹³So David and his men continued on, and Shimei kept pace with them on a nearby hillside, cursing as he went and throwing stones at David and tossing dust into the air.

¹⁴The king and all who were with him grew weary along the way, so they rested when they reached the Jordan River.*

AHITHOPHEL ADVISES ABSALOM

¹⁵Meanwhile, Absalom and his men arrived at Jerusalem, accompanied by Ahithophel. ¹⁶When David's friend Hushai the Arkite arrived, he went immediately to see Absalom. "Long live the king!" he exclaimed. "Long live the king!"

¹⁷"Is this the way you treat your friend David?" Absalom asked him. "Why aren't you with him?"

¹⁸"I'm here because I work for the man who is chosen by the LORD and by Israel," Hushai replied. ¹⁹"And anyway, why shouldn't I serve

---

16:1 Also known as *Meribbaal.* **16:11** Hebrew *this Benjaminite.* **16:14** As in Greek version (see also 17:16); Hebrew reads *when they reached their destination.*

you? I helped your father, and now I will help you!"

²⁰Then Absalom turned to Ahithophel and asked him, "What should I do next?"

²¹Ahithophel told him, "Go and sleep with your father's concubines, for he has left them here to keep the house. Then all Israel will know that you have insulted him beyond hope of reconciliation, and they will give you their support." ²²So they set up a tent on the palace roof where everyone could see it, and Absalom went into the tent to sleep with his father's concubines.

²³Absalom followed Ahithophel's advice, just as David had done. For every word Ahithophel spoke seemed as wise as though it had come directly from the mouth of God.

17 Now Ahithophel urged Absalom, "Let me choose twelve thousand men to start out after David tonight. ²I will catch up to him while he is weary and discouraged. He and his troops will panic, and everyone will run away. Then I will kill only the king, ³and I will bring all the people back to you as a bride returns to her husband. After all, it is only this man's life that you seek.* Then all the people will remain unharmed and peaceful." ⁴This plan seemed good to Absalom and to all the other leaders of Israel.

HUSHAI COUNTERS AHITHOPHEL'S ADVICE

⁵But then Absalom said, "Bring in Hushai the Arkite. Let's see what he thinks about this." ⁶When Hushai arrived, Absalom told him what Ahithophel had said. Then he asked, "What is your opinion? Should we follow Ahithophel's advice? If not, speak up."

⁷"Well," Hushai replied, "this time I think Ahithophel has made a mistake. ⁸You know your father and his men; they are mighty warriors. Right now they are probably as enraged as a mother bear who has been robbed of her cubs. And remember that your father is an experienced soldier. He won't be spending the night among the troops. ⁹He has probably already hidden in some pit or cave. And when he comes out and attacks and a few of your men fall, there will be panic among your troops, and everyone will start shouting that your men are being slaughtered. ¹⁰Then even the bravest of them, though they have the heart of a lion, will be paralyzed with fear. For all Israel knows what a mighty man your father is and how courageous his warriors are.

¹¹"I suggest that you mobilize the entire army of Israel, bringing them from as far away as Dan and Beersheba. That way you will have an army as numerous as the sand on the seashore. And I think that you should personally lead the troops. ¹²When we find David, we can descend on him like the dew that falls to the ground, so that not one of his men is left alive. ¹³And if David has escaped into some city, you will have the entire army of Israel there at your command. Then we can take ropes and drag the walls of the city into the nearest valley until every stone is torn down."

¹⁴Then Absalom and all the leaders of Israel said, "Hushai's advice is better than Ahithophel's." For the LORD had arranged to defeat the counsel of Ahithophel, which really was the better plan, so that he could bring disaster upon Absalom!

HUSHAI WARNS DAVID TO ESCAPE

¹⁵Then Hushai reported to Zadok and Abiathar, the priests, what Ahithophel had said and what he himself had suggested instead. ¹⁶"Quick!" he told them. "Find David and urge him not to stay at the shallows of the Jordan River* tonight. He must go across at once into the wilderness beyond. Otherwise he will die and his entire army with him."

¹⁷Jonathan and Ahimaaz had been staying at En-rogel so as not to be seen entering and leaving the city. Arrangements had been made for a servant girl to bring them the message

---

17:3 As in Greek version; Hebrew reads *like the return of all is the man whom you seek.* **17:16** Hebrew *at the crossing points of the wilderness.*

they were to take to King David. [18]But a boy saw them leaving En-rogel to go to David, and he told Absalom about it. Meanwhile, they escaped to Bahurim, where a man hid them inside a well in his courtyard. [19]The man's wife put a cloth over the top of the well with grain on it to dry in the sun; so no one suspected they were there.

[20]When Absalom's men arrived, they asked her, "Have you seen Ahimaaz and Jonathan?"

She replied, "They were here, but they crossed the brook." Absalom's men looked for them without success and returned to Jerusalem.

[21]Then the two men crawled out of the well and hurried on to King David. "Quick!" they told him, "cross the Jordan tonight!" And they told him how Ahithophel had advised that he be captured and killed. [22]So David and all the people with him went across the Jordan River during the night, and they were all on the other bank before dawn.

[23]Meanwhile, Ahithophel was publicly disgraced when Absalom refused his advice. So he saddled his donkey, went to his hometown, set his affairs in order, and hanged himself. He died there and was buried beside his father.

[24]David soon arrived at Mahanaim. By now, Absalom had mobilized the entire army of Israel and was leading his troops across the Jordan River. [25]Absalom had appointed Amasa as commander of his army, replacing Joab, who had been commander under David.

Man's chief end is
to glorify God
and to enjoy Him
forever.

THE WESTMINSTER CATECHISM

(Amasa was Joab's cousin. His father was Jether,* an Ishmaelite.* His mother, Abigail daughter of Nahash, was the sister of Joab's mother, Zeruiah.) [26]Absalom and the Israelite army set up camp in the land of Gilead.

[27]When David arrived at Mahanaim, he was warmly greeted by Shobi son of Nahash of Rabbah, an Ammonite, and by Makir son of Ammiel of Lo-debar, and by Barzillai of Gilead from Rogelim. [28]They brought sleeping mats, cooking pots, serving bowls, wheat and barley flour, roasted grain, beans, lentils, [29]honey, butter, sheep, and cheese for David and those who were with him. For they said, "You must all be very tired and hungry and thirsty after your long march through the wilderness."

ABSALOM'S DEFEAT AND DEATH

18 David now appointed generals and captains to lead his troops. [2]One-third were placed under Joab, one-third under Joab's brother Abishai son of Zeruiah, and one-third under Ittai the Gittite. The king told his troops, "I am going out with you."

[3]But his men objected strongly. "You must not go," they urged. "If we have to turn and run—and even if half of us die—it will make no difference to Absalom's troops; they will be looking only for you. You are worth ten thousand of us, and it is better that you stay here in the city and send us help if we need it."

[4]"If you think that's the best plan, I'll do it," the king finally agreed. So he stood at the gate of the city as all the divisions of troops passed by. [5]And the king gave this command to Joab, Abishai, and Ittai: "For my sake, deal gently with young Absalom." And all the troops heard the king give this order to his commanders.

[6]So the battle began in the forest of Ephraim, [7]and the Israelite troops were beaten back by David's men. There was a great slaughter, and twenty thousand men laid down their lives that day. [8]The battle raged all

---

17:25a Hebrew *Ithra*, a variant name for Jether.   17:25b As in some Greek manuscripts (see also 1 Chr 2:17); Hebrew reads *an Israelite*.

across the countryside, and more men died because of the forest than were killed by the sword.

⁹During the battle, Absalom came unexpectedly upon some of David's men. He tried to escape on his mule, but as he rode beneath the thick branches of a great oak, his head got caught. His mule kept going and left him dangling in the air. ¹⁰One of David's men saw what had happened and told Joab, "I saw Absalom dangling in a tree."

¹¹"What?" Joab demanded. "You saw him there and didn't kill him? I would have rewarded you with ten pieces of silver* and a hero's belt!"

¹²"I wouldn't do it for a thousand pieces of silver,*" the man replied. "We all heard the king say to you and Abishai and Ittai, 'For my sake, please don't harm young Absalom.' ¹³And if I had betrayed the king by killing his son—and the king would certainly find out who did it—you yourself would be the first to abandon me."

¹⁴"Enough of this nonsense," Joab said. Then he took three daggers and plunged them into Absalom's heart as he dangled from the oak still alive. ¹⁵Ten of Joab's young armor bearers then surrounded Absalom and killed him. ¹⁶Then Joab blew the trumpet, and his men returned from chasing the army of Israel. ¹⁷They threw Absalom's body into a deep pit in the forest and piled a great heap of stones over it. And the army of Israel fled to their homes.

¹⁸During his lifetime, Absalom had built a monument to himself in the King's Valley, for he had said, "I have no son to carry on my name." He named the monument after himself, and it is known as Absalom's Monument to this day.

DAVID MOURNS ABSALOM'S DEATH

¹⁹Then Zadok's son Ahimaaz said, "Let me run to the king with the good news that the LORD has saved him from his enemy Absalom."

²⁰"No," Joab told him, "it wouldn't be good news to the king that his son is dead. You can be my messenger some other time, but not today."

²¹Then Joab said to a man from Cush, "Go tell the king what you have seen." The man bowed and ran off.

²²But Ahimaaz continued to plead with Joab, "Whatever happens, please let me go, too."

"Why should you go, my son?" Joab replied. "There will be no reward for you."

²³"Yes, but let me go anyway," he begged.

Joab finally said, "All right, go ahead." Then Ahimaaz took a shortcut across the plain of the Jordan and got to Mahanaim ahead of the man from Cush.

²⁴While David was sitting at the city gate, the watchman climbed to the roof of the gateway by the wall. As he looked, he saw a lone man running toward them. ²⁵He shouted the news down to David, and the king replied, "If he is alone, he has news."

As the messenger came closer, ²⁶the watchman saw another man running toward them. He shouted down, "Here comes another one!"

The king replied, "He also will have news."

²⁷"The first man runs like Ahimaaz son of Zadok," the watchman said.

"He is a good man and comes with good news," the king replied.

²⁸Then Ahimaaz cried out to the king, "All is well!" He bowed low with his face to the ground and said, "Blessed be the LORD your God, who has handed over the rebels who dared to stand against you."

²⁹"What about young Absalom?" the king demanded. "Is he all right?"

Ahimaaz replied, "When Joab told me to come, there was a lot of commotion. But I didn't know what was happening."

³⁰"Wait here," the king told him. So Ahimaaz stepped aside.

³¹Then the man from Cush arrived and said, "I have good news for my lord the king. Today

18:11 Hebrew *10 shekels of silver*, about 4 ounces or 114 grams in weight. 18:12 Hebrew *1,000 shekels*, about 25 pounds or 11.4 kilograms in weight.

the Lord has rescued you from all those who rebelled against you."

[32]"What about young Absalom?" the king demanded. "Is he all right?"

And the Cushite replied, "May all of your enemies, both now and in the future, be as that young man is!"

[33]The king was overcome with emotion. He went up to his room over the gateway and burst into tears. And as he went, he cried, "O my son Absalom! My son, my son Absalom! If only I could have died instead of you! O Absalom, my son, my son."

JOAB REBUKES THE KING

19 Word soon reached Joab that the king was weeping and mourning for Absalom. [2]As the troops heard of the king's deep grief for his son, the joy of that day's victory was turned into deep sadness. [3]They crept back into the city as though they were ashamed and had been beaten in battle. [4]The king covered his face with his hands and kept on weeping, "O my son Absalom! O Absalom, my son, my son!"

[5]Then Joab went to the king's room and said to him, "We saved your life today and the lives of your sons, your daughters, and your wives and concubines. Yet you act like this, making us feel ashamed, as though we had done something wrong. [6]You seem to love those who hate you and hate those who love you. You made it clear today that we mean nothing to you. If Absalom had lived and all of us had died, you would be pleased. [7]Now go out there and congratulate the troops, for I swear by the Lord that if you don't, not a single one of them will remain here tonight. Then you will be worse off than you have ever been." [8]So the king went out and sat at the city gate, and as the news spread throughout the city that he was there, everyone went to him.

Meanwhile, the Israelites who supported Absalom had fled to their homes. [9]And throughout the tribes of Israel there was much discussion and argument going on. The people were saying, "The king saved us from our enemies, the Philistines, but Absalom chased him out of the country. [10]Now Absalom, whom we anointed to rule over us, is dead. Let's ask David to come back and be our king again."

[11]Then King David sent Zadok and Abiathar, the priests, to say to the leaders of Judah, "Why are you the last ones to reinstate the king? For I have heard that all Israel is ready, and only you are holding out. [12]Yet you are my relatives, my own tribe, my own flesh and blood! Why are you the last ones to welcome me back?" [13]And David told them to tell Amasa, "Since you are my nephew, may God strike me dead if I do not appoint you as commander of my army in place of Joab." [14]Then Amasa convinced all the leaders of Judah, and they responded unanimously. They sent word to the king, "Return to us, and bring back all those who are with you."

DAVID'S RETURN TO JERUSALEM

[15]So the king started back to Jerusalem. And when he arrived at the Jordan River, the people of Judah came to Gilgal to meet him and escort him across the river. [16]Then Shimei son of Gera, the man from Bahurim in Benjamin, hurried across with the men of Judah to welcome King David. [17]A thousand men from the tribe of Benjamin were with him, including Ziba, the servant of Saul, and Ziba's fifteen sons and twenty servants. They rushed down to the Jordan to arrive ahead of the king. [18]They all crossed the ford and worked hard ferrying the king's household across the river, helping them in every way they could.

DAVID'S MERCY TO SHIMEI

As the king was about to cross the river, Shimei fell down before him. [19]"My lord the king, please forgive me," he pleaded. "Forget the terrible thing I did when you left Jerusalem. [20]I know how much I sinned. That is why I have come here today, the very first person in all Israel* to greet you."

19:20 Hebrew *the house of Joseph.*

My Daily Worship

— *March 18* —

STAYING CLOSE IN YOUR GRIEF

2 SAMUEL 15:1–19:43

*So the king went out and sat at the city gate, and as the news spread throughout
the city that he was there, everyone went to him (19:8).*

[i reflect]

"Your child is dead." Those words crush the spirit, overwhelming a parent with grief. More than once did David hear those words. More than once was he devastated with sorrow. The loss of Bathsheba's baby, Amnon, and now his son, Absalom, made the shadowy valley of death an all-too-familiar place for David. He was overwhelmed with sorrow.

We don't know what David was thinking about God in those moments, but Joab confronted David with the need to set his grief alongside his duty to fulfill his God-given role as the king. Grief changes, but it doesn't stop life. Grief itself doesn't remain the same for long. After the initial blow that turns the world upside down, grief begins to transform into either a series of deep episodes of genuine sorrow over the loss or a series of bouts with self-pity.

Grief affects us in many ways. One clue that we are not responding to grief in a healthy way is when we try to stop the world so we can grieve. So David, with tear-stained face, walked to the city gate and sat in silent tribute to his men for their courageous defense of his throne. They came to him, not because he was grieving nor because of the great victory, but because they realized he didn't blame them for his grief.

In times of grief we discover just how close we are to God. Death creates a distance that only a vital relationship can bridge. Although David was sorrow-filled, his grief did not become a barrier between him and God. David continually experienced God as his Shepherd because he experienced God as Lord. The time we spend in communion with God when life seems normal actually prepares us for those times when life takes a sudden turn into the dark valley.

Keep close to God now through worship, prayer, and Bible study. Experience God as Lord so you will know him as your Shepherd when the time comes.

[i pray]

*God, thank you for being with me in both the good times and the times of anguish. Help
me to reach for you and cling to you when the pain is overwhelming. Help me to hear
your voice in my pain and rest in your arms when I feel like I'm falling apart.*

[i respond]

Experience God as your Shepherd. Write down all the qualities of a shepherd that come to mind. Underline those characteristics that you need from God right now.

[21]Then Abishai son of Zeruiah said, "Shimei should die, for he cursed the LORD's anointed king!"

[22]"What am I going to do with you sons of Zeruiah!" David exclaimed. "This is not a day for execution but for celebration! I am once again the king of Israel!" [23]Then, turning to Shimei, David vowed, "Your life will be spared."

DAVID'S KINDNESS TO MEPHIBOSHETH

[24]Now Mephibosheth,* Saul's grandson, arrived from Jerusalem to meet the king. He had not washed his feet or clothes nor trimmed his beard since the day the king left Jerusalem. [25]"Why didn't you come with me, Mephibosheth?" the king asked him.

[26]Mephibosheth replied, "My lord the king, my servant Ziba deceived me. I told him, 'Saddle my donkey so that I can go with the king.' For as you know I am crippled. [27]Ziba has slandered me by saying that I refused to come. But I know that you are like an angel of God, so do what you think is best. [28]All my relatives and I could expect only death from you, my lord, but instead you have honored me among those who eat at your own table! So how can I complain?"

[29]"All right," David replied. "My decision is that you and Ziba will divide your land equally between you."

[30]"Give him all of it," Mephibosheth said. "I am content just to have you back again, my lord!"

DAVID'S KINDNESS TO BARZILLAI

[31]Barzillai of Gilead now arrived from Rogelim to conduct the king across the Jordan. [32]He was very old, about eighty, and very wealthy. He was the one who had provided food for the king during his stay in Mahanaim. [33]"Come across with me and live in Jerusalem," the king said to Barzillai. "I will take care of you there."

[34]"No," he replied, "I am far too old for that. [35]I am eighty years old today, and I can no longer enjoy anything. Food and wine are no longer tasty, and I cannot hear the musicians as they play. I would only be a burden to my lord the king. [36]Just to go across the river with you is all the honor I need! [37]Then let me return again to die in my own town, where my father and mother are buried. But here is my son Kimham. Let him go with you and receive whatever good things you want to give him."

[38]"Good," the king agreed. "Kimham will go with me, and I will do for him whatever I would have done for you." [39]So all the people crossed the Jordan with the king. After David had blessed and embraced him, Barzillai returned to his own home. [40]The king then went on to Gilgal, taking Kimham with him. All the army of Judah and half the army of Israel escorted him across the river.

AN ARGUMENT OVER THE KING

[41]But the men of Israel complained to the king that the men of Judah had gotten to do most of the work in helping him cross the Jordan. [42]"Why not?" the men of Judah replied. "The king is one of our own tribe. Why should this make you angry? We have charged him nothing. And he hasn't fed us or even given us gifts!"

[43]"But there are ten tribes in Israel," the others replied. "So we have ten times as much right to the king as you do. Why did you treat us with such contempt? Remember, we were the first to speak of bringing him back to be our king again." The argument continued back and forth, and the men of Judah were very harsh in their replies.

THE REVOLT OF SHEBA

20 Then a troublemaker named Sheba son of Bicri, a man from the tribe of Benjamin, blew a trumpet and shouted, "We have nothing to do with David. We want no part of this son of Jesse. Come on, you men of Israel, let's all go home!" [2]So the men of Israel deserted David and followed Sheba. But the

19:24 Also known as *Meribbaal*.

men of Judah stayed with their king and escorted him from the Jordan River to Jerusalem.

³When the king arrived at his palace in Jerusalem, he instructed that the ten concubines he had left to keep house should be placed in seclusion. Their needs were to be cared for, he said, but he would no longer sleep with them. So each of them lived like a widow until she died.

⁴Then the king instructed Amasa to mobilize the army of Judah within three days and to report back at that time. ⁵So Amasa went out to notify the troops, but it took him longer than the three days he had been given. ⁶Then David said to Abishai, "That troublemaker Sheba is going to hurt us more than Absalom did. Quick, take my troops and chase after him before he gets into a fortified city where we can't reach him."

⁷So Abishai and Joab set out after Sheba with an elite guard from Joab's army and the king's own bodyguard.* ⁸As they arrived at the great stone in Gibeon, Amasa met them, coming from the opposite direction. Joab was wearing his uniform with a dagger strapped to his belt. As he stepped forward to greet Amasa, he secretly slipped the dagger from its sheath. ⁹"How are you, my cousin?" Joab said and took him by the beard with his right hand as though to kiss him. ¹⁰Amasa didn't notice the dagger in his left hand, and Joab stabbed him in the stomach with it so that his insides gushed out onto the ground. Joab did not need to strike again, and Amasa soon died. Joab and his brother Abishai left him lying there and continued after Sheba.

¹¹One of Joab's young officers shouted to Amasa's troops, "If you are for Joab and David, come and follow Joab." ¹²But Amasa lay in his blood in the middle of the road, and Joab's officer saw that a crowd was gathering around to stare at him. So he pulled him off the road into a field and threw a cloak over him. ¹³With Amasa's body out of the way, everyone went on with Joab to capture Sheba.

¹⁴Meanwhile, Sheba had traveled across Israel to mobilize his own clan of Bicri at the city of Abel-beth-maacah. ¹⁵When Joab's forces arrived, they attacked Abel-beth-maacah and built a ramp against the city wall and began battering it down. ¹⁶But a wise woman in the city called out to Joab, "Listen to me, Joab. Come over here so I can talk to you." ¹⁷As he approached, the woman asked, "Are you Joab?"

"I am," he replied.

So she said, "Listen carefully to your servant."

"I'm listening," he said.

¹⁸Then she continued, "There used to be a saying, 'If you want to settle an argument, ask advice at the city of Abel.' ¹⁹I am one who is peace loving and faithful in Israel. But you are destroying a loyal city. Why do you want to destroy what belongs to the LORD?"

²⁰And Joab replied, "Believe me, I don't want to destroy your city! ²¹All I want is a man named Sheba son of Bicri from the hill country of Ephraim, who has revolted against King David. If you hand him over to me, we will leave the city in peace."

"All right," the woman replied, "we will throw his head over the wall to you." ²²Then the woman went to the people with her wise advice, and they cut off Sheba's head and threw it out to Joab. So he blew the trumpet and called his troops back from the attack, and they all returned to their homes. Joab returned to the king at Jerusalem.

²³Joab once again became the commander of David's army. Benaiah son of Jehoiada was commander of the king's bodyguard. ²⁴Adoniram* was in charge of the labor force. Jehoshaphat son of Ahilud was the royal historian. ²⁵Sheva was the court secretary. Zadok and Abiathar were the priests. ²⁶Ira the Jairite was David's personal priest.

DAVID AVENGES THE GIBEONITES

21 There was a famine during David's reign that lasted for three years, so David asked the LORD about it. And the LORD

20:7 Hebrew *the Kerethites and Pelethites*; also in 20:23. 20:24 As in Greek version (see also 1 Kgs 4:6; 5:14); Hebrew reads *Adoram*.

said, "The famine has come because Saul and his family are guilty of murdering the Gibeonites."

²So King David summoned the Gibeonites. They were not part of Israel but were all that was left of the nation of the Amorites. Israel had sworn not to kill them, but Saul, in his zeal, had tried to wipe them out. ³David asked them, "What can I do for you to make amends? Tell me so that the LORD will bless his people again."

⁴"Well, money won't do it," the Gibeonites replied. "And we don't want to see the Israelites executed in revenge."

"What can I do then?" David asked. "Just tell me and I will do it for you."

⁵Then they replied, "It was Saul who planned to destroy us, to keep us from having any place at all in Israel. ⁶So let seven of Saul's sons or grandsons be handed over to us, and we will execute them before the LORD at Gibeon, on the mountain of the LORD.*"

"All right," the king said, "I will do it." ⁷David spared Jonathan's son Mephibosheth,* who was Saul's grandson, because of the oath David and Jonathan had sworn before the LORD. ⁸But he gave them Saul's two sons Armoni and Mephibosheth, whose mother was Rizpah daughter of Aiah. He also gave them the five sons of Saul's daughter Merab,* the wife of Adriel son of Barzillai from Meholah. ⁹The men of Gibeon executed them on the mountain before the LORD. So all seven of them died together at the beginning of the barley harvest.

¹⁰Then Rizpah, the mother of two of the men, spread sackcloth on a rock and stayed there the entire harvest season. She prevented vultures from tearing at their bodies during the day and stopped wild animals from eating them at night. ¹¹When David learned what Rizpah, Saul's concubine, had done, ¹²he went to the people of Jabesh-gilead and asked for the bones of Saul and his son Jonathan. (When Saul and Jonathan had died in a battle with the Philistines, it was the people of Jabesh-gilead who had retrieved their bodies from the public square of the Philistine city of Beth-shan.) ¹³So David brought the bones of Saul and Jonathan, as well as the bones of the men the Gibeonites had executed. ¹⁴He buried them all in the tomb of Kish, Saul's father, at the town of Zela in the land of Benjamin. After that, God ended the famine in the land of Israel.

BATTLES AGAINST PHILISTINE GIANTS

¹⁵Once again the Philistines were at war with Israel. And when David and his men were in the thick of battle, David became weak and exhausted. ¹⁶Ishbi-benob was a descendant of the giants* ; his bronze spearhead weighed more than seven pounds,* and he was armed with a new sword. He had cornered David and was about to kill him. ¹⁷But Abishai son of Zeruiah came to his rescue and killed the Philistine. After that, David's men declared, "You are not going out to battle again! Why should we risk snuffing out the light of Israel?"

¹⁸After this, there was another battle against the Philistines at Gob. As they fought, Sibbecai from Hushah killed Saph, another descendant of the giants. ¹⁹In still another battle at Gob, Elhanan son of Jair* from Bethlehem killed the brother of Goliath of Gath.* The handle of his spear was as thick as a weaver's beam! ²⁰In another battle with the Philistines at Gath, a huge man with six fingers on each hand and six toes on each foot—a descendant of the giants—²¹defied and taunted Israel. But he was killed by Jonathan, the son of David's brother Shimea.* ²²These four Philistines were descended from the giants of Gath, but they were killed by David and his warriors.

21:6 As in Greek version (see also 21:9); Hebrew reads *at Gibeah of Saul, the chosen of the LORD.* 21:7 Also known as *Meribbaal.* 21:8 As in a few Hebrew and Greek manuscripts and Syriac version (see also 1 Sam 18:19); most Hebrew manuscripts read *Michal.* 21:16a As in Greek version; Hebrew reads *a descendant of the Rephaites;* also in 21:18, 20, 22. 21:16b Hebrew *300 shekels* [3.4 kilograms]. 21:19a As in parallel text at 1 Chr 20:5; Hebrew reads *son of Jaare-oregim.* 21:19b As in parallel text at 1 Chr 20:5; Hebrew reads *killed Goliath of Gath.* 21:21 As in parallel text at 1 Chr 20:7; Hebrew reads *Shimei,* a variant name for Shimea.

DAVID'S SONG OF PRAISE

22 David sang this song to the LORD after the LORD had rescued him from all his enemies and from Saul. ²These are the words he sang:

"The LORD is my rock, my fortress, and my
      savior;
³   my God is my rock, in whom I find
      protection.
He is my shield, the strength of my
      salvation, and my stronghold,
   my high tower, my savior, the one who
      saves me from violence.
⁴ I will call on the LORD, who is worthy of
      praise,
   for he saves me from my enemies.

⁵ "The waves of death surrounded me;
      the floods of destruction swept over me.
⁶ The grave* wrapped its ropes around me;
      death itself stared me in the face.
⁷ But in my distress I cried out to the
      LORD;
   yes, I called to my God for help.
He heard me from his sanctuary;
   my cry reached his ears.

⁸ "Then the earth quaked and trembled;
   the foundations of the heavens shook;
   they quaked because of his anger.
⁹ Smoke poured from his nostrils;
   fierce flames leaped from his mouth;
   glowing coals flamed forth from him.
¹⁰ He opened the heavens and came down;
   dark storm clouds were beneath his feet.
¹¹ Mounted on a mighty angel,* he flew,
   soaring* on the wings of the wind.
¹² He shrouded himself in darkness,
   veiling his approach with dense rain
      clouds.
¹³ A great brightness shone before him,
   and bolts of lightning blazed forth.
¹⁴ The LORD thundered from heaven;
   the Most High gave a mighty shout.

¹⁵ He shot his arrows and scattered his
      enemies;
   his lightning flashed, and they were
      confused.
¹⁶ Then at the command of the LORD,
   at the blast of his breath,
the bottom of the sea could be seen,
   and the foundations of the earth were
      laid bare.

¹⁷ "He reached down from heaven and
      rescued me;
   he drew me out of deep waters.
¹⁸ He delivered me from my powerful
      enemies,
   from those who hated me and were too
      strong for me.
¹⁹ They attacked me at a moment when I was
      weakest,
   but the LORD upheld me.
²⁰ He led me to a place of safety;
   he rescued me because he delights in me.
²¹ The LORD rewarded me for doing right;
   he compensated me because of my
      innocence.
²² For I have kept the ways of the LORD;
   I have not turned from my God to
      follow evil.
²³ For all his laws are constantly before me;
   I have never abandoned his principles.
²⁴ I am blameless before God;
   I have kept myself from sin.
²⁵ The LORD rewarded me for doing right,
   because of my innocence in his sight.

²⁶ "To the faithful you show yourself faithful;
   to those with integrity you show integrity.
²⁷ To the pure you show yourself pure,
   but to the wicked you show yourself
      hostile.
²⁸ You rescue those who are humble,
   but your eyes are on the proud to
      humiliate them.
²⁹ O LORD, you are my light;
   yes, LORD, you light up my darkness.

22:6 Hebrew *Sheol.* **22:11a** Hebrew *cherub.* **22:11b** As in some Hebrew manuscripts (see also Ps 18:10); other Hebrew manuscripts read *appearing.*

³⁰ In your strength I can crush an army;
  with my God I can scale any wall.

³¹ "As for God, his way is perfect.
  All the LORD's promises prove true.
  He is a shield for all who look to him for
    protection.
³² For who is God except the LORD?
  Who but our God is a solid rock?
³³ God is my strong fortress;
  he has made my way safe.
³⁴ He makes me as surefooted as a deer,
  leading me safely along the mountain
    heights.
³⁵ He prepares me for battle;
  he strengthens me to draw a bow of
    bronze.
³⁶ You have given me the shield of your
    salvation;
  your help* has made me great.
³⁷ You have made a wide path for my feet
  to keep them from slipping.
³⁸ "I chased my enemies and destroyed them;
  I did not stop until they were conquered.
³⁹ I consumed them; I struck them down so
    they could not get up;
  they fell beneath my feet.
⁴⁰ You have armed me with strength for the
    battle;
  you have subdued my enemies under my
    feet.
⁴¹ You made them turn and run;
  I have destroyed all who hated me.
⁴² They called for help, but no one came to
    rescue them.
  They cried to the LORD, but he refused
    to answer them.
⁴³ I ground them as fine as the dust of the
    earth;
  I swept them into the gutter like dirt.

⁴⁴ "You gave me victory over my accusers.
  You preserved me as the ruler over
    nations;
  people I don't even know now serve me.

⁴⁵ Foreigners cringe before me;
  as soon as they hear of me, they submit.
⁴⁶ They all lose their courage
  and come trembling from their
    strongholds.

⁴⁷ "The LORD lives! Blessed be my rock!
  May God, the rock of my salvation, be
    exalted!
⁴⁸ He is the God who pays back those who
    harm me;
  he subdues the nations under me
⁴⁹ and rescues me from my enemies.
  You hold me safe beyond the reach of my
    enemies;
  you save me from violent opponents.
⁵⁰ For this, O LORD, I will praise you among
    the nations;
  I will sing joyfully to your name.
⁵¹ You give great victories to your king;
  you show unfailing love to your anointed,
  to David and all his descendants
    forever."

DAVID'S LAST WORDS

23

These are the last words of David:

"David, the son of Jesse, speaks—
  David, the man to whom God gave such
    wonderful success,
  David, the man anointed by the God of
    Jacob,
  David, the sweet psalmist of Israel.

² "The Spirit of the LORD speaks through me;
  his words are upon my tongue.
³ The God of Israel spoke.
  The Rock of Israel said to me:
'The person who rules righteously,
  who rules in the fear of God,
⁴ he is like the light of the morning,
  like the sunrise bursting forth in a
    cloudless sky,
  like the refreshing rains that bring
    tender grass from the earth.'

22:36 As in Dead Sea Scrolls; most Hebrew manuscripts read *your answering.*

My Daily Worship

— March 19 —

WHAT'S YOUR SECURITY BLANKET?

2 SAMUEL 20:1–24:25

He is my shield, the strength of my salvation, and my stronghold, my high tower,
my savior, the one who saves me from violence (22:3).

[i reflect]

Perhaps your toddler carried a blanket with him wherever he went. Or maybe your child clung to a favorite stuffed animal that she absolutely could not sleep without. We smile when we see these youngsters clutching their security symbols because it's cute—they are babies. But as adults, we too cling to "security blankets," and that's not so cute.

Our blankets may be a relationship that we absolutely need in order to feel secure. Or perhaps it's a job title, the right address, model of car, or type of house. Maybe we're clinging to the idea of fame or power or prestige based on our abilities and talents. Whatever our "security blanket" may be, the truth is that none of these things offer the least bit of security. They can be stolen, lost, or taken away, and each will fail at the critical moment.

That's why we need to realize, as David did in this heartfelt song, that our security rests solely on our God and our relationship with him. Consider the words David used to describe his security: "rock," "fortress," "stronghold," "high tower," "shield." The words paint a picture of an impenetrable, permanent place of refuge and safety. David knew from his personal experience that God alone could provide that type of security.

How about you? Have you experienced God as rock and fortress and stronghold? Have you sought safety and refuge within your relationship with him? Bring before him those issues and needs that threaten your security and offer them to him as worship. Then build your future on the *rock*—God almighty. Depend on him. He will not disappoint.

[i pray]

Lord, uncertainty swirls around me, and I don't know what tomorrow might bring. I become
frightened when I imagine all that could happen. Help me to leave my life and my
future with you, knowing that you will take care of me and mine.

[i respond]

Write down your top three concerns for tomorrow. Now talk to God about them, your uncertainties, your fears. Then put the paper in your Bible, and let God carry those future concerns today.

⁵ "It is my family God has chosen!
   Yes, he has made an everlasting covenant
      with me.
   His agreement is eternal, final, sealed.
   He will constantly look after my safety
      and success.
⁶ But the godless are like thorns to be
      thrown away,
   for they tear the hand that touches them.
⁷ One must be armed to chop them down;
   they will be utterly consumed with fire."

DAVID'S MIGHTIEST MEN

⁸These are the names of David's mightiest men. The first was Jashobeam the Hacmonite,* who was commander of the Three—the three greatest warriors among David's men. He once used his spear to kill eight hundred enemy warriors in a single battle.*

⁹Next in rank among the Three was Eleazar son of Dodai, a descendant of Ahoah. Once Eleazar and David stood together against the Philistines when the entire Israelite army had fled. ¹⁰He killed Philistines until his hand was too tired to lift his sword, and the LORD gave him a great victory that day. The rest of the army did not return until it was time to collect the plunder!

¹¹Next in rank was Shammah son of Agee from Harar. One time the Philistines gathered at Lehi and attacked the Israelites in a field full of lentils. The Israelite army fled, ¹²but Shammah held his ground in the middle of the field and beat back the Philistines. So the LORD brought about a great victory.

¹³Once during harvesttime, when David was at the cave of Adullam, the Philistine army was camped in the valley of Rephaim. The Three (who were among the Thirty—an elite group among David's fighting men) went down to meet him there. ¹⁴David was staying in the stronghold at the time, and a Philistine detachment had occupied the town of Bethlehem. ¹⁵David remarked longingly to his men, "Oh, how I would love some of that good water from the well in Bethlehem, the one by the gate." ¹⁶So the Three broke through the Philistine lines, drew some water from the well, and brought it back to David. But he refused to drink it. Instead, he poured it out before the LORD. ¹⁷"The LORD forbid that I should drink this!" he exclaimed. "This water is as precious as the blood of these men who risked their lives to bring it to me." So David did not drink it. This is an example of the exploits of the Three.

DAVID'S THIRTY MIGHTY MEN

¹⁸Abishai son of Zeruiah, the brother of Joab, was the leader of the Thirty.* He once used his spear to kill three hundred enemy warriors in a single battle. It was by such feats that he became as famous as the Three. ¹⁹Abishai was the most famous of the Thirty* and was their commander, though he was not one of the Three.

²⁰There was also Benaiah son of Jehoiada, a valiant warrior from Kabzeel. He did many heroic deeds, which included killing two of Moab's mightiest warriors. Another time he chased a lion down into a pit. Then, despite the snow and slippery ground, he caught the lion and killed it. ²¹Another time, armed only with a club, he killed a great Egyptian warrior who was armed with a spear. Benaiah wrenched the spear from the Egyptian's hand and killed him with it. ²²These are some of the deeds that made Benaiah almost as famous as the Three. ²³He was more honored than the other members of the Thirty, though he was not one of the Three. And David made him commander of his bodyguard.

²⁴Other members of the Thirty included:

   Asahel, Joab's brother;
   Elhanan son of Dodo from Bethlehem;
²⁵ Shammah from Harod;
   Elika from Harod;

23:8a As in parallel text at 1 Chr 11:11; Hebrew reads *Josheb-basshebeth the Tahkemonite.* 23:8b As in some Greek manuscripts (see also 1 Chr 11:11); the Hebrew is uncertain, though it might be rendered *the Three. It was Adino the Eznite who killed eight hundred men at one time.* 23:18 As in a few Hebrew manuscripts and Syriac version; most Hebrew manuscripts read *the Three.* 23:19 As in Syriac version; Hebrew reads *the Three.*

²⁶ Helez from Pelon*;
Ira son of Ikkesh from Tekoa;
²⁷ Abiezer from Anathoth;
Sibbecai* from Hushah;
²⁸ Zalmon from Ahoah;
Maharai from Netophah;
²⁹ Heled* son of Baanah from Netophah;
Ithai* son of Ribai from Gibeah (from the
tribe of Benjamin);
³⁰ Benaiah from Pirathon;
Hurai* from Nahale-gaash*;
³¹ Abi-albon the Arbathite;
Azmaveth from Bahurim;
³² Eliahba from Shaalbon;
the sons of Jashen;
³³ Jonathan son of Shagee* from Harar;
Ahiam son of Sharar from Harar;
³⁴ Eliphelet son of Ahasbai from Maacah;
Eliam son of Ahithophel from Giloh;
³⁵ Hezro from Carmel;
Paarai from Arba;
³⁶ Igal son of Nathan from Zobah;
Bani from Gad;
³⁷ Zelek from Ammon;
Naharai from Beeroth (Joab's armor bearer);
³⁸ Ira from Jattir;
Gareb from Jattir;
³⁹ Uriah the Hittite.

There were thirty-seven in all.

DAVID TAKES A CENSUS

24 Once again the anger of the LORD burned against Israel, and he caused David to harm them by taking a census. "Go and count the people of Israel and Judah," the LORD told him.

²So the king said to Joab, the commander of his army, "Take a census of all the people in the land—from Dan in the north to Beersheba in the south—so that I may know how many people there are."

³But Joab replied to the king, "May the LORD your God let you live until there are a hundred times as many people in your kingdom as there are now! But why do you want to do this?"

⁴But the king insisted that they take the census, so Joab and his officers went out to count the people of Israel. ⁵First they crossed the Jordan and camped at Aroer, south of the town in the valley, in the direction of Gad. Then they went on to Jazer, ⁶then to Gilead in the land of Tahtim-hodshi* and to Dan-jaan and around to Sidon. ⁷Then they came to the stronghold of Tyre, and all the cities of the Hivites and Canaanites. Finally, they went south to Judah as far as Beersheba. ⁸Having gone through the entire land, they completed their task in nine months and twenty days and then returned to Jerusalem. ⁹Joab reported the number of people to the king. There were 800,000 men of military age in Israel and 500,000 in Judah.

JUDGMENT FOR DAVID'S SIN

¹⁰But after he had taken the census, David's conscience began to bother him. And he said to the LORD, "I have sinned greatly and shouldn't have taken the census. Please forgive me, LORD, for doing this foolish thing."

¹¹The next morning the word of the LORD came to the prophet Gad, who was David's seer. This was the message: ¹²"Go and say to David, 'This is what the LORD says: I will give you three choices. Choose one of these punishments, and I will do it.'"

¹³So Gad came to David and asked him, "Will you choose three* years of famine throughout the land, three months of fleeing from your enemies, or three days of severe plague throughout your land? Think this over and let me know what answer to give the LORD."

23:26 As in parallel text at 1 Chr 11:27 (see also 1 Chr 27:10); Hebrew reads *from Palti.* 23:27 As in some Greek manuscripts (see also 1 Chr 11:29); Hebrew reads *Mebunnai.* 23:29a As in some Hebrew manuscripts (see also 1 Chr 11:30); most Hebrew manuscripts read *Heleb.* 23:29b As in parallel text at 1 Chr 11:31; Hebrew reads *Ittai.* 23:30a As in some Greek manuscripts (see also 1 Chr 11:32); Hebrew reads *Hiddai.* 23:30b Or *from the ravines of Gaash.* 23:33 As in parallel text at 1 Chr 11:34; Hebrew reads *Jonathan, Shammah;* some Greek manuscripts read *Jonathan son of Shammah.* 24:6 Greek version reads *to Gilead and to Kadesh in the land of the Hittites.* 24:13 As in Greek version (see also 1 Chr 21:12); Hebrew reads *seven.*

[14]"This is a desperate situation!" David replied to Gad. "But let us fall into the hands of the LORD, for his mercy is great. Do not let me fall into human hands."

[15]So the LORD sent a plague upon Israel that morning, and it lasted for three days. Seventy thousand people died throughout the nation. [16]But as the death angel was preparing to destroy Jerusalem, the LORD relented and said to the angel, "Stop! That is enough!" At that moment the angel of the LORD was by the threshing floor of Araunah the Jebusite.

[17]When David saw the angel, he said to the LORD, "I am the one who has sinned and done wrong! But these people are innocent—what have they done? Let your anger fall against me and my family."

David Builds an Altar

[18]That day Gad came to David and said to him, "Go and build an altar to the LORD on the threshing floor of Araunah the Jebusite."

[19]So David went to do what the LORD had commanded him. [20]When Araunah saw the king and his men coming toward him, he came forward and bowed before the king with his face to the ground. [21]"Why have you come, my lord?" Araunah asked.

And David replied, "I have come to buy your threshing floor and to build an altar to the LORD there, so that the LORD will stop the plague."

[22]"Take it, my lord, and use it as you wish," Araunah said to David. "Here are oxen for the burnt offering, and you can use the threshing tools and ox yokes for wood to build a fire on the altar. [23]I will give it all to you, and may the LORD your God accept your sacrifice."

[24]But the king replied to Araunah, "No, I insist on buying it, for I cannot present burnt offerings to the LORD my God that have cost me nothing." So David paid him fifty pieces of silver* for the threshing floor and the oxen. [25]David built an altar there to the LORD and offered burnt offerings and peace offerings. And the LORD answered his prayer, and the plague was stopped.

24:24 Hebrew *50 shekels of silver*, about 20 ounces or 570 grams in weight.

1 Kings

The LORD is God! The LORD is God! (18:39).

Wholehearted Devotion

Olympic athletes know it takes single-minded determination to win gold. In a sprint, a quick sideways glance at an opponent can mean the difference between first and fourth place. No wonder coaches and trainers insist: Keep your eye on the finish line!

Why is it, then, that in the race of life we so often try to divide our time between focusing on God's best and looking away?

The book of 1 Kings is all about the necessity of wholehearted devotion to the one true God, keeping focused on his finishing line. If we divide our loyalties between God and something else, that something else will almost always steal our heart away—and bring us to ruin.

We see this in the life of Israel's wisest, wealthiest, and most powerful king—Solomon, the one God anointed to build his Temple in Jerusalem. Twice God appeared to Solomon and blessed him more than any man alive at that time (chapters 3–10). Later in life, however, Solomon allowed his foreign wives to turn his heart's affection from God to other so-called gods (chapter 11).

Solomon's downfall soon became a snare for the whole nation (chapters 12–22). Even when the Israelites were called back to the one true God under the prophet Elijah (18:22–40), their repentance was short-lived.

As you read 1 Kings, renew your vow to always love the Lord your God with all your heart, soul, strength, and mind, and to keep your eyes on his goal.

Worship Moments

- After securing his position as king, Solomon went to the local altar at Gibeon and offered a thousand burnt offerings. God appeared to Solomon, asked him what he wanted, and then promised to give him far more! (3:1–15).

- After building the Temple in Jerusalem, the glorious presence of the Lord filled the place. Solomon lifted up a magnificent prayer of dedication and then offered tens of thousands of sacrifices to God. God appeared to Solomon a second time and warned him to abandon his worship for idols (8:1–9:9).

- After the kingdom split, Jeroboam, the king of the northern tribes, formed a new religion that turned the people's hearts further away from God. A prophet from the southern kingdom condemned this idolatry (12:25–13:10).

- In this book God is praised as the "Sovereign LORD" (2:26; 8:53); "the LORD Almighty" (18:15); and "the LORD God Almighty" (19:10, 14).

DAVID IN HIS OLD AGE

1 Now King David was very old, and no matter how many blankets covered him, he could not keep warm. ²So his advisers told him, "We will find a young virgin who will wait on you and be your nurse. She will lie in your arms and keep you warm." ³So they searched throughout the country for a beautiful girl, and they found Abishag from Shunem and brought her to the king. ⁴The girl was very beautiful, and she waited on the king and took care of him. But the king had no sexual relations with her.

ADONIJAH CLAIMS THE THRONE

⁵About that time David's son Adonijah, whose mother was Haggith, decided to make himself king in place of his aged father. So he provided himself with chariots and horses* and recruited fifty men to run in front of him. ⁶Now his father, King David, had never disciplined him at any time, even by asking, "What are you doing?" Adonijah was a very handsome man and had been born next after Absalom. ⁷Adonijah took Joab son of Zeruiah and Abiathar the priest into his confidence, and they agreed to help him become king. ⁸But among those who remained loyal to David and refused to support Adonijah were Zadok the priest, Benaiah son of Jehoiada, Nathan the prophet, Shimei, Rei, and David's personal bodyguard.

⁹Adonijah went to the stone of Zoheleth* near the spring of En-rogel, where he sacrificed sheep, oxen, and fattened calves. He invited all his brothers—the other sons of King David—and all the royal officials of Judah. ¹⁰But he did not invite Nathan the prophet, or Benaiah, or the king's bodyguard, or his brother Solomon.

¹¹Then Nathan the prophet went to Bathsheba, Solomon's mother, and asked her, "Did you realize that Haggith's son, Adonijah, has made himself king and that our lord David doesn't even know about it? ¹²If you want to save your own life and the life of your son Solomon, follow my counsel. ¹³Go at once to King David and say to him, 'My lord, didn't you promise me that my son Solomon would be the next king and would sit upon your throne? Then why has Adonijah become king?' ¹⁴And while you are still talking with him, I will come and confirm everything you have said."

¹⁵So Bathsheba went into the king's bedroom. He was very old now, and Abishag was taking care of him. ¹⁶Bathsheba bowed low before him.

"What can I do for you?" he asked her.

¹⁷She replied, "My lord, you vowed to me by the LORD your God that my son Solomon would be the next king and would sit on your throne. ¹⁸But instead, Adonijah has become the new king, and you do not even know about it. ¹⁹He has sacrificed many oxen, fattened calves, and sheep, and he has invited all your sons and Abiathar the priest and Joab, the commander of the army. But he did not invite your servant Solomon. ²⁰And now, my lord the king, all Israel is waiting for your decision as to who will become king after you. ²¹If you do not act, my son Solomon and I will be treated as criminals as soon as you are dead."

²²While she was still speaking with the king, Nathan the prophet arrived. ²³The king's advisers told him, "Nathan the prophet is here to see you."

Nathan went in and bowed low before the

> We only learn to behave ourselves
> in the presence of God.
>
> C. S. LEWIS

1:5 Or *and charioteers.*   1:9 Or *to the Serpent's Stone;* Greek version supports reading *Zoheleth* as a proper name.

king. ²⁴He asked, "My lord, have you decided that Adonijah will be the next king and that he will sit on your throne? ²⁵Today he has sacrificed many oxen, fattened calves, and sheep, and he has invited your sons to attend the celebration. He also invited Joab, the commander of the army,* and Abiathar the priest. They are feasting and drinking with him and shouting, 'Long live King Adonijah!' ²⁶But I myself, your servant, was not invited; neither were Zadok the priest, Benaiah son of Jehoiada, nor Solomon. ²⁷Has my lord really done this without letting any of his servants know who should be the next king?"

DAVID MAKES SOLOMON KING

²⁸"Call Bathsheba," David said. So she came back in and stood before the king. ²⁹And the king vowed, "As surely as the LORD lives, who has rescued me from every danger, ³⁰today I decree that your son Solomon will be the next king and will sit on my throne, just as I swore to you before the LORD, the God of Israel."

³¹Then Bathsheba bowed low before him again and exclaimed, "May my lord King David live forever!"

³²Then King David ordered, "Call Zadok the priest, Nathan the prophet, and Benaiah son of Jehoiada." When they came into the king's presence, ³³the king said to them, "Take Solomon and my officers down to Gihon Spring. Solomon is to ride on my personal mule. ³⁴There Zadok the priest and Nathan the prophet are to anoint him king over Israel. Then blow the trumpets and shout, 'Long live King Solomon!' ³⁵When you bring him back here, he will sit on my throne. He will succeed me as king, for I have appointed him to be ruler over Israel and Judah."

³⁶"Amen!" Benaiah son of Jehoiada replied. "May the LORD, the God of my lord the king, decree it to be so. ³⁷And may the LORD be with Solomon as he has been with you, and may he make Solomon's reign even greater than yours!"

³⁸So Zadok the priest, Nathan the prophet,

Benaiah son of Jehoiada, and the king's bodyguard* took Solomon down to Gihon Spring, and Solomon rode on King David's personal mule. ³⁹There Zadok the priest took a flask of olive oil from the sacred tent and poured it on Solomon's head. Then the trumpets were blown, and all the people shouted, "Long live King Solomon!" ⁴⁰And all the people returned with Solomon to Jerusalem, playing flutes and shouting for joy. The celebration was so joyous and noisy that the earth shook with the sound.

⁴¹Adonijah and his guests heard the celebrating and shouting just as they were finishing their banquet. When Joab heard the sound of trumpets, he asked, "What's going on? Why is the city in such an uproar?"

⁴²And while he was still speaking, Jonathan son of Abiathar the priest arrived. "Come in," Adonijah said to him, "for you are a good man. You must have good news."

⁴³"Not at all!" Jonathan replied. "Our lord King David has just declared Solomon king! ⁴⁴The king sent him down to Gihon Spring with Zadok the priest, Nathan the prophet, and Benaiah son of Jehoiada, protected by the king's bodyguard. They had him ride on the king's own mule, ⁴⁵and Zadok and Nathan have anointed him as the new king. They have just returned, and the whole city is celebrating and rejoicing. That's what all the noise is about. ⁴⁶Moreover, Solomon is now sitting on the royal throne as king. ⁴⁷All the royal officials went to King David and congratulated him, saying, 'May your God make Solomon's fame even greater than your own, and may Solomon's kingdom be even greater than yours!' Then the king bowed his head in worship as he lay in his bed, ⁴⁸and he spoke these words: 'Blessed be the LORD, the God of Israel, who today has chosen someone to sit on my throne while I am still alive to see it.'"

⁴⁹Then all of Adonijah's guests jumped up in panic from the banquet table and quickly went their separate ways. ⁵⁰Adonijah himself was afraid of Solomon, so he rushed to the

1:25 As in Greek version; Hebrew reads *invited the commanders of the army.* 1:38 Hebrew *the Kerethites and Pelethites;* also in 1:44.

sacred tent and caught hold of the horns of the altar. [51]Word soon reached Solomon that Adonijah had seized the horns of the altar and that he was pleading, "Let Solomon swear today that he will not kill me!"

[52]Solomon replied, "If he proves himself to be loyal, he will not be harmed.* But if he does not, he will die." [53]So King Solomon summoned Adonijah, and they brought him down from the altar. He came and bowed low before the king, and Solomon dismissed him, saying, "Go on home."

DAVID'S FINAL INSTRUCTIONS TO SOLOMON

2 As the time of King David's death approached, he gave this charge to his son Solomon: [2]"I am going where everyone on earth must someday go. Take courage and be a man. [3]Observe the requirements of the LORD your God and follow all his ways. Keep each of the laws, commands, regulations, and stipulations written in the law of Moses so that you will be successful in all you do and wherever you go. [4]If you do this, then the LORD will keep the promise he made to me: 'If your descendants live as they should and follow me faithfully with all their heart and soul, one of them will always sit on the throne of Israel.'

[5]"And there is something else. You know that Joab son of Zeruiah murdered my two army commanders, Abner son of Ner and Amasa son of Jether. He pretended that it was an act of war, but it was done in a time of peace,* staining his belt and sandals with the blood of war. [6]Do with him what you think best, but don't let him die in peace.

[7]"Be kind to the sons of Barzillai of Gilead. Make them permanent guests of the king, for they took care of me when I fled from your brother Absalom.

[8]"And remember Shimei son of Gera, the man from Bahurim in Benjamin. He cursed me with a terrible curse as I was fleeing to Mahanaim. When he came down to meet me

at the Jordan River, I swore by the LORD that I would not kill him. [9]But that oath does not make him innocent. You are a wise man, and you will know how to arrange a bloody death for him."

[10]Then David died and was buried in the City of David. [11]He had reigned over Israel for forty years, seven of them in Hebron and thirty-three in Jerusalem. [12]Solomon succeeded him as king, replacing his father, David, and he was firmly established on the throne.

SOLOMON ESTABLISHES HIS RULE

[13]One day Adonijah, whose mother was Haggith, came to see Bathsheba, Solomon's mother. "Have you come to make trouble?" she asked him.

"No," he said, "I come in peace. [14]In fact, I have a favor to ask of you."

"What is it?" she asked.

[15]He replied, "As you know, the kingdom was mine; everyone expected me to be the next king. But the tables were turned, and everything went to my brother instead; for that is the way the LORD wanted it. [16]So now I have just one favor to ask of you. Please don't turn me down."

"What is it?" she asked.

[17]He replied, "Speak to King Solomon on my behalf, for I know he will do anything you request. Ask him to give me Abishag, the girl from Shunem, as my wife."

[18]"All right," Bathsheba replied. "I will speak to the king for you."

[19]So Bathsheba went to King Solomon to speak on Adonijah's behalf. The king rose from his throne to meet her, and he bowed down before her. When he sat down on his throne again, he ordered that a throne be brought for his mother, and she sat at his right hand.

[20]"I have one small request to make of you," she said. "I hope you won't turn me down."

"What is it, my mother?" he asked. "You know I won't refuse you."

1:52 Hebrew *not a hair on his head will be touched.* 2:5 Or *He murdered them during a time of peace as revenge for deaths they had caused in time of war.*

²¹"Then let your brother Adonijah marry Abishag, the girl from Shunem," she replied.

²²"How can you possibly ask me to give Abishag to Adonijah?" Solomon demanded. "You might as well be asking me to give him the kingdom! You know that he is my older brother, and that he has Abiathar the priest and Joab son of Zeruiah on his side." ²³Then King Solomon swore solemnly by the LORD: "May God strike me dead if Adonijah has not sealed his fate with this request. ²⁴The LORD has confirmed me and placed me on the throne of my father, David; he has established my dynasty as he promised. So as surely as the LORD lives, Adonijah will die this very day!" ²⁵So King Solomon ordered Benaiah son of Jehoiada to execute him, and Adonijah was put to death.

²⁶Then the king said to Abiathar the priest, "Go back to your home in Anathoth. You deserve to die, but I will not kill you now, because you carried the Ark of the Sovereign LORD for my father, and you suffered right along with him through all his troubles." ²⁷So Solomon deposed Abiathar from his position as priest of the LORD, thereby fulfilling the decree the LORD had made at Shiloh concerning the descendants of Eli.

²⁸Although he had not followed Absalom earlier, Joab had also joined Adonijah's revolt. When Joab heard about Adonijah's death, he ran to the sacred tent of the LORD and caught hold of the horns of the altar. ²⁹When news of this reached King Solomon, he sent Benaiah son of Jehoiada to execute him.

³⁰Benaiah went into the sacred tent of the LORD and said to Joab, "The king orders you to come out!"

But Joab answered, "No, I will die here."

So Benaiah returned to the king and told him what Joab had said.

³¹"Do as he said," the king replied. "Kill him there beside the altar and bury him. This will remove the guilt of his senseless murders from me and from my father's family. ³²Then the LORD will repay him for the murders of two men who were more righteous and better

than he. For my father was no party to the deaths of Abner son of Ner, commander of the army of Israel, and Amasa son of Jether, commander of the army of Judah. ³³May Joab and his descendants be forever guilty of these murders, and may the LORD grant peace to David and his descendants and to his throne forever."

³⁴So Benaiah son of Jehoiada returned to the sacred tent and killed Joab, and Joab was buried at his home in the wilderness. ³⁵Then the king appointed Benaiah to command the army in place of Joab, and he installed Zadok the priest to take the place of Abiathar.

³⁶The king then sent for Shimei and told him, "Build a house here in Jerusalem and live there. But don't step outside the city to go anywhere else. ³⁷On the day you cross the Kidron Valley, you will surely die; your blood will be on your own head."

³⁸Shimei replied, "Your sentence is fair; I will do whatever my lord the king commands." So Shimei lived in Jerusalem for a long time.

³⁹But three years later, two of Shimei's slaves escaped to King Achish of Gath. When Shimei learned where they were, ⁴⁰he saddled his donkey and went to Gath to search for them. When he had found them, he took them back to Jerusalem.

⁴¹Solomon heard that Shimei had left Jerusalem and had gone to Gath and returned. ⁴²So he sent for Shimei and demanded, "Didn't I make you swear by the LORD and warn you not to go anywhere else, or you would surely die? And you replied, 'The sentence is fair; I will do as you say.' ⁴³Then why haven't you kept your oath to the LORD and obeyed my command?"

⁴⁴The king also said to Shimei, "You surely remember all the wicked things you did to my father, King David. May the LORD punish you for them. ⁴⁵But may I receive the LORD's rich blessings, and may one of David's descendants always sit on this throne." ⁴⁶Then, at the king's command, Benaiah son of Jehoiada took Shimei outside and killed him.

So the kingdom was now firmly in Solomon's grip.

SOLOMON ASKS FOR WISDOM

3 Solomon made an alliance with Pharaoh, the king of Egypt, and married one of his daughters. He brought her to live in the City of David until he could finish building his palace and the Temple of the LORD and the wall around the city. ²At that time the people of Israel sacrificed their offerings at local altars, for a temple honoring the name of the LORD had not yet been built.

³Solomon loved the LORD and followed all the instructions of his father, David, except that Solomon, too, offered sacrifices and burned incense at the local altars. ⁴The most important of these altars was at Gibeon, so the king went there and sacrificed one thousand burnt offerings. ⁵That night the LORD appeared to Solomon in a dream, and God said, "What do you want? Ask, and I will give it to you!"

⁶Solomon replied, "You were wonderfully kind to my father, David, because he was honest and true and faithful to you. And you have continued this great kindness to him today by giving him a son to succeed him. ⁷O LORD my God, now you have made me king instead of my father, David, but I am like a little child who doesn't know his way around. ⁸And here I am among your own chosen people, a nation so great they are too numerous to count! ⁹Give me an understanding mind so that I can govern your people well and know the difference between right and wrong. For who by himself is able to govern this great nation of yours?"

¹⁰The Lord was pleased with Solomon's reply and was glad that he had asked for wisdom. ¹¹So God replied, "Because you have asked for wisdom in governing my people and have not asked for a long life or riches for yourself or the death of your enemies—¹²I will give you what you asked for! I will give you a wise and understanding mind such as no one else has ever had or ever will have! ¹³And I will also give you what you did not ask for—rich-es and honor! No other king in all the world will be compared to you for the rest of your life! ¹⁴And if you follow me and obey my commands as your father, David, did, I will give you a long life."

¹⁵Then Solomon woke up and realized it had been a dream. He returned to Jerusalem and stood before the Ark of the Lord's covenant, where he sacrificed burnt offerings and peace offerings. Then he invited all his officials to a great banquet.

SOLOMON JUDGES WISELY

¹⁶Some time later, two prostitutes came to the king to have an argument settled. ¹⁷"Please, my lord," one of them began, "this woman and I live in the same house. I gave birth to a baby while she was with me in the house. ¹⁸Three days later, she also had a baby. We were alone; there were only two of us in the house. ¹⁹But her baby died during the night when she rolled over on it. ²⁰Then she got up in the night and took my son from beside me while I was asleep. She laid her dead child in my arms and took mine to sleep beside her. ²¹And in the morning when I tried to nurse my son, he was dead! But when I looked more closely in the morning light, I saw that it wasn't my son at all."

²²Then the other woman interrupted, "It certainly was your son, and the living child is mine."

"No," the first woman said, "the dead one is yours, and the living one is mine." And so they argued back and forth before the king.

²³Then the king said, "Let's get the facts straight. Both of you claim the living child is yours, and each says that the dead child belongs to the other. ²⁴All right, bring me a sword." So a sword was brought to the king. ²⁵Then he said, "Cut the living child in two and give half to each of these women!"

²⁶Then the woman who really was the mother of the living child, and who loved him very much, cried out, "Oh no, my lord! Give her the child—please do not kill him!"

But the other woman said, "All right, he will

My Daily Worship

— March 20 —

A DIVINE BLANK CHECK

1 KINGS 1:1–4:34

*Give me an understanding mind so that I can govern your people well and
know the difference between right and wrong. For who by himself
is able to govern this great nation of yours? (3:9).*

[i reflect]

Heaven and earth paused in silence. All creation listened. God had just spoken. "What do you want? Ask, and I will give it to you" (3:5b). How would the new king answer? Solomon had just been given the equivalent of a divine blank check. What amount would he write down? What would he ask God to give him?

Given the same opportunity, how would you respond? Solomon paused long enough to review the events that had brought him to this moment. He expressed humble gratitude over the legacy God had preserved through his father, David. He acknowledged God's mighty power in forming a great people. And he admitted his awareness of the difference between his abilities and the task before him. He confessed his ineptness.

Solomon made a God-centered request when he answered God's invitation. He identified God as the source of understanding and discernment. He recognized God's divine ownership over the people he was called to lead. He again acknowledged his inability to govern God's people on his own. He asked for God's provision and participation. God answered with that and much more.

If the wisest king who ever lived bowed in humble adoration to Almighty God, you would be wise to follow Solomon's example. Like Solomon, you undoubtedly have aspects of your life that point out your shortcomings and inabilities. You need wisdom you know you don't have. That's not a bad place to be. People who come to God in Solomon's footsteps find that God answers the same way. He says to us, "What do you want? Ask and I will give it to you." (See James 1:5–8.)

Wise worship always flows out of a deep and humble desire to see God more clearly. He wants to clarify our vision. Use those moments throughout the day when you feel stymied by the task facing you, to turn to him and ask for wisdom.

[i pray]

Lord, in you I trust. With wise King Solomon, I recognize my need of guidance. Forgive me for the many times I attempt to go it alone. Give me the wisdom today to trust you in all I do. Amen.

[i respond]

Draft a personal prayer to the Lord, acknowledging areas in your life in which you need to trust him. Post this on a bulletin board in your home and consult it regularly.

be neither yours nor mine; divide him between us!"

²⁷Then the king said, "Do not kill him, but give the baby to the woman who wants him to live, for she is his mother!"

²⁸Word of the king's decision spread quickly throughout all Israel, and the people were awed as they realized the great wisdom God had given him to render decisions with justice.

SOLOMON'S OFFICIALS AND GOVERNORS

4 So Solomon was king over all Israel, ²and these were his high officials:

Azariah son of Zadok was the priest.
³ Elihoreph and Ahijah, the sons of Shisha, were court secretaries.
Jehoshaphat son of Ahilud was the royal historian.
⁴ Benaiah son of Jehoiada was commander of the army.
Zadok and Abiathar were the priests.
⁵ Azariah son of Nathan presided over the district governors.
Zabud son of Nathan, a priest, was a trusted adviser to the king.
⁶ Ahishar was manager of palace affairs.
Adoniram son of Abda was in charge of the labor force.

⁷Solomon also had twelve district governors who were over all Israel. They were responsible for providing food from the people for the king's household. Each of them arranged provisions for one month of the year. ⁸These are the names of the twelve governors:

Ben-hur, in the hill country of Ephraim.
⁹ Ben-deker, in Makaz, Shaalbim, Beth-shemesh, and Elon-bethhanan.
¹⁰ Ben-hesed, in Arubboth, including Socoh and all the land of Hepher.

¹¹ Ben-abinadab, in Naphoth-dor.* (He was married to Taphath, one of Solomon's daughters.)
¹² Baana son of Ahilud, in Taanach and Megiddo, all of Beth-shan* near Zarethan below Jezreel, and all the territory from Beth-shan to Abel-meholah and over to Jokmeam.
¹³ Ben-geber, in Ramoth-gilead, including the Towns of Jair (named for Jair son of Manasseh) in Gilead, and in the Argob region of Bashan, including sixty great fortified cities with gates barred with bronze.
¹⁴ Ahinadab son of Iddo, in Mahanaim.
¹⁵ Ahimaaz, in Naphtali. (He was married to Basemath, another of Solomon's daughters.)
¹⁶ Baana son of Hushai, in Asher and in Aloth.
¹⁷ Jehoshaphat son of Paruah, in Issachar.
¹⁸ Shimei son of Ela, in Benjamin.
¹⁹ Geber son of Uri, in the land of Gilead,* including the territories of King Sihon of the Amorites and King Og of Bashan.

And there was one governor over the land of Judah.*

SOLOMON'S PROSPERITY AND WISDOM

²⁰The people of Judah and Israel were as numerous as the sand on the seashore. They were very contented, with plenty to eat and drink. ²¹King Solomon ruled all the kingdoms from the Euphrates River* to the land of the Philistines, as far south as the border of Egypt. The conquered peoples of those lands sent tribute money to Solomon and continued to serve him throughout his lifetime.

²²The daily food requirements for Solomon's palace were 150 bushels of choice flour and 300 bushels of meal,* ²³ten oxen from the fattening pens, twenty pasture-fed

---

4:11 Hebrew *Naphath-dor*, a variant name for Naphoth-dor. **4:12** Hebrew *Beth-shean*, a variant name for Beth-shan; also in 4:12b. **4:19a** Greek version reads *of Gad*; compare 4:13. **4:19b** As in some Greek manuscripts; Hebrew lacks *of Judah*. The meaning of the Hebrew is uncertain. **4:21** Hebrew *the river*; also in 4:24. **4:22** Hebrew *30 cors* [5.5 kiloliters] *of choice flour and 60 cors* [11 kiloliters] *of meal.*

cattle, one hundred sheep or goats, as well as deer, gazelles, roebucks, and choice fowl.

²⁴Solomon's dominion extended over all the kingdoms west of the Euphrates River, from Tiphsah to Gaza. And there was peace throughout the entire land. ²⁵Throughout the lifetime of Solomon, all of Judah and Israel lived in peace and safety. And from Dan to Beersheba, each family had its own home and garden.

²⁶Solomon had four thousand* stalls for his chariot horses and twelve thousand horses.* ²⁷The district governors faithfully provided food for King Solomon and his court, each during his assigned month. ²⁸They also brought the necessary barley and straw for the royal horses in the stables.

²⁹God gave Solomon great wisdom and understanding, and knowledge too vast to be measured. ³⁰In fact, his wisdom exceeded that of all the wise men of the East and the wise men of Egypt. ³¹He was wiser than anyone else, including Ethan the Ezrahite and Heman, Calcol, and Darda—the sons of Mahol. His fame spread throughout all the surrounding nations. ³²He composed some 3,000 proverbs and wrote 1,005 songs. ³³He could speak with authority about all kinds of plants, from the great cedar of Lebanon to the tiny hyssop that grows from cracks in a wall. He could also speak about animals, birds, reptiles, and fish. ³⁴And kings from every nation sent their ambassadors to listen to the wisdom of Solomon.

PREPARATIONS FOR BUILDING THE TEMPLE

5 King Hiram of Tyre had always been a loyal friend of David, so when he learned that David's son Solomon was the new king of Israel, Hiram sent ambassadors to congratulate him. ²Then Solomon sent this message back to Hiram:

³"You know that my father, David, was not able to build a Temple to honor the name

---

Words of Worship

WORK

Work, Doing—Hebrew *'a-sah* "to do, make"; *me-la'-chah* "work"; Greek *er-ga-zo-mai* "to work, accomplish"; *er-gon* "work"; *poi-e-o* "to do." Other words are used.

The alarm goes off, and we're jolted to some semblance of an awakened state. Another work day and we have to get up and trudge back to the "salt mines." Or we've been working on an absorbing project all day. The office has emptied out, but we're still hard at it, with just the cleaning woman for company. They're waiting for us at home, but our work is too important, too fascinating!

No matter which way we look at it—drudgery or obsession—we need an attitude adjustment. Work is good, but it can become a curse unless we put it in perspective. We can resent it, run from it, define ourselves by it, lose ourselves in it. Or we can offer it to the Lord as an act of worship. Paul says that whatever we do, we are to do it as an act of thanksgiving to God (Colossians 3:17). Work for his glory.

---

of the LORD his God because of the many wars he waged with surrounding nations. He could not build until the LORD gave him victory over all his enemies. ⁴But now the LORD my God has given me peace on every side, and I have no enemies and all is well. ⁵So I am planning to build a Temple to honor the name of the LORD my God, just as he instructed my father that I should do. For the LORD told him, 'Your son, whom I will place on your throne, will build the Temple to honor my name.' ⁶Now please command that cedars from

---

4:26a As in some Greek manuscripts (see also 2 Chr 9:25); Hebrew reads *40,000.* 4:26b Or *12,000 charioteers.*

Lebanon be cut for me. Let my men work alongside yours, and I will pay your men whatever wages you ask. As you know, there is no one among us who can cut timber like you Sidonians!"

[7]When Hiram received Solomon's message, he was very pleased and said, "Praise the LORD for giving David a wise son to be king of the great nation of Israel." [8]Then he sent this reply to Solomon:

"I have received your message, and I will do as you have asked concerning the timber. I can supply you with both cedar and cypress. [9]My servants will bring the logs from the Lebanon mountains to the Mediterranean Sea and build them into rafts. We will float them along the coast to whatever place you choose. Then we will break the rafts apart and deliver the timber to you. You can pay me with food for my household."

[10]So Hiram produced for Solomon as much cedar and cypress timber as he desired. [11]In return Solomon sent him an annual payment of 100,000 bushels* of wheat for his household and 110,000 gallons* of olive oil. [12]So the LORD gave great wisdom to Solomon just as he had promised. And Hiram and Solomon made a formal alliance of peace.

[13]Then King Solomon enlisted 30,000 laborers from all Israel. [14]He sent them to Lebanon in shifts, 10,000 every month, so that each man would be one month in Lebanon and two months at home. Adoniram was in charge of this labor force. [15]Solomon also enlisted 70,000 common laborers, 80,000 stonecutters in the hill country, [16]and 3,600* foremen to supervise the work. [17]At the king's command, the stonecutters quarried and shaped costly

blocks of stone for the foundation of the Temple. [18]Men from the city of Gebal helped Solomon's and Hiram's builders prepare the timber and stone for the Temple.

SOLOMON BUILDS THE TEMPLE

6 It was in midspring,* during the fourth year of Solomon's reign, that he began the construction of the Temple of the LORD. This was 480 years after the people of Israel were delivered from their slavery in the land of Egypt.

[2]The Temple that King Solomon built for the LORD was 90 feet long, 30 feet wide, and 45 feet high.* [3]The foyer at the front of the Temple was 30 feet wide, running across the entire width of the Temple. It projected outward 15 feet from the front of the Temple. [4]Solomon also made narrow, recessed windows throughout the Temple.

[5]A complex of rooms was built against the outer walls of the Temple, all the way around the sides and rear of the building. [6]The complex was three stories high, the bottom floor being 7½ feet wide, the second floor 9 feet wide, and the top floor 10½ feet wide. The rooms were connected to the walls of the Temple by beams resting on ledges built out from the wall. So the beams were not inserted into the walls themselves.

[7]The stones used in the construction of the Temple were prefinished at the quarry, so the entire structure was built without the sound of hammer, ax, or any other iron tool at the building site.

[8]The entrance to the bottom floor* was on the south side of the Temple. There were winding stairs going up to the second floor, and another flight of stairs between the second and third floors. [9]After completing the Temple structure, Solomon put in a ceiling made of beams and planks of cedar. [10]As

---

5:11a Hebrew *20,000 cors* [3,640 kiloliters].   **5:11b** As in Greek version, which reads *20,000 baths* [420 kiloliters] (see also 2 Chr 2:10); Hebrew reads *20 cors*, about 800 gallons or 3.6 kiloliters in volume.   **5:16** As in some Greek manuscripts (see also 2 Chr 2:2, 18); Hebrew reads *3,300*.   **6:1** Hebrew *in the month of Ziv, which is the second month.* This month of the Hebrew lunar calendar usually occurs in April and May.   **6:2** Hebrew *60 cubits* [27 meters] *long, 20 cubits* [9 meters] *wide, and 30 cubits* [13.5 meters] *high.* In this chapter, the distance measures are calculated from the Hebrew cubit at a ratio of 18 inches or 45 centimeters per cubit.   **6:8** As in Greek version; Hebrew reads *middle floor.*

already stated, there was a complex of rooms on three sides of the building, attached to the Temple walls by cedar timbers. Each story of the complex was 7½ feet high.

[11]Then the LORD gave this message to Solomon: [12]"Concerning this Temple you are building, if you keep all my laws and regulations and obey all my commands, I will fulfill through you the promise I made to your father, David. [13]I will live among the people of Israel and never forsake my people."

THE TEMPLE'S INTERIOR

[14]So Solomon finished building the Temple. [15]The entire inside, from floor to ceiling, was paneled with wood. He paneled the walls and ceilings with cedar, and he used cypress for the floors. [16]He partitioned off an inner sanctuary—the Most Holy Place—at the far end of the Temple. It was 30 feet deep and was paneled with cedar from floor to ceiling. [17]The main room of the Temple, outside the Most Holy Place, was 60 feet long. [18]Cedar paneling completely covered the stone walls throughout the Temple, and the paneling was decorated with carvings of gourds and open flowers.

[19]Solomon prepared the inner sanctuary in the rear of the Temple, where the Ark of the LORD's covenant would be placed. [20]This inner sanctuary was 30 feet long, 30 feet wide, and 30 feet high. Solomon overlaid its walls and ceiling with pure gold. He also overlaid the altar made of cedar.* [21]Then he overlaid the rest of the Temple's interior with pure gold, and he made gold chains to protect the entrance to the Most Holy Place. [22]So he finished overlaying the entire Temple with gold, including the altar that belonged to the Most Holy Place.

[23]Within the inner sanctuary Solomon placed two cherubim made of olive wood, each 15 feet tall. [24]The wingspan of each of the cherubim was 15 feet, each wing being 7½ feet long. [25]The two cherubim were identical in shape and size; [26]each was 15 feet tall. [27]Solomon placed them side by side in the inner sanctuary of the Temple. Their outspread wings reached from wall to wall, while their inner wings touched at the center of the room. [28]He overlaid the two cherubim with gold.

[29]All the walls of the inner sanctuary and the main room were decorated with carvings of cherubim, palm trees, and open flowers. [30]The floor in both rooms was overlaid with gold.

[31]For the entrance to the inner sanctuary, Solomon made double doors of olive wood with five-sided doorposts. [32]These doors were decorated with carvings of cherubim, palm trees, and open flowers, and the doors were overlaid with gold.

[33]Then he made four-sided doorposts of olive wood for the entrance to the Temple. [34]There were two folding doors of cypress wood, and each door was hinged to fold back upon itself. [35]These doors were decorated with carvings of cherubim, palm trees, and open flowers, and the doors were overlaid with gold.

[36]The walls of the inner courtyard were built so that there was one layer of cedar beams after every three layers of hewn stone.

[37]The foundation of the LORD's Temple was laid in midspring* of the fourth year of Solomon's reign. [38]The entire building was completed in every detail by midautumn* of the eleventh year of his reign. So it took seven years to build the Temple.

SOLOMON BUILDS HIS PALACE

7 Solomon also built a palace for himself, and it took him thirteen years to complete the construction.

[2]One of Solomon's buildings was called the Palace of the Forest of Lebanon. It was 150 feet long, 75 feet wide, and 45 feet high.* The

---

6:20 Or overlaid the altar with cedar. The meaning of the Hebrew is uncertain. 6:37 Hebrew in the month of Ziv. This month of the Hebrew lunar calendar usually occurs in April and May. 6:38 Hebrew in the month of Bul, which is the eighth month. This month of the Hebrew lunar calendar usually occurs in October and November. 7:2 Hebrew 100 cubits [45 meters] long, 50 cubits [22.5 meters] wide, and 30 cubits [13.5 meters] high. In this chapter, the distance measures are calculated from the Hebrew cubit at a ratio of 18 inches or 45 centimeters per cubit.

great cedar ceiling beams rested on four rows of cedar pillars. [3]It had a cedar roof supported by forty-five rafters that rested on three rows of pillars, fifteen in each row. [4]On each of the side walls there were three rows of windows facing each other. [5]All the doorways were rectangular in frame; they were in sets of three, facing each other.

[6]He also built the Hall of Pillars, which was 75 feet long and 45 feet wide. There was a porch at its front, covered by a canopy that was supported by pillars.

[7]There was also the Hall of the Throne, also known as the Hall of Judgment, where Solomon sat to hear legal matters. It was paneled with cedar from floor to ceiling.* [8]Solomon's living quarters surrounded a courtyard behind this hall; they were built the same way. He also built similar living quarters for Pharaoh's daughter, one of his wives. [9]All these buildings were built entirely from huge, costly blocks of stone, cut and trimmed to exact measure on all sides. [10]Some of the huge foundation stones were 15 feet long, and some were 12 feet long. [11]The costly blocks of stone used in the walls were also cut to measure, and cedar beams were also used. [12]The walls of the great courtyard were built so that there was one layer of cedar beams after every three layers of hewn stone, just like the walls of the inner courtyard of the LORD's Temple with its entrance foyer.

FURNISHINGS FOR THE TEMPLE

[13]King Solomon then asked for a man named Huram* to come from Tyre, [14]for he was a craftsman skilled in bronze work. He was half Israelite, since his mother was a widow from the tribe of Naphtali, and his father had been a foundry worker from Tyre. So he came to work for King Solomon.

[15]Huram cast two bronze pillars, each 27 feet tall and 18 feet in circumference. [16]For the tops of the pillars he made capitals of molded bronze, each 7½ feet tall. [17]Each capital was decorated with seven sets of latticework and interwoven chains. [18]He also made two rows of pomegranates that encircled the latticework to decorate the capitals over the pillars. [19]The capitals on the columns inside the foyer were shaped like lilies, and they were 6 feet tall. [20]Each capital on the two pillars had two hundred pomegranates in two rows around them, beside the rounded surface next to the latticework. [21]Huram set the pillars at the entrance of the Temple, one toward the south and one toward the north. He named the one on the south Jakin, and the one on the north Boaz.* [22]The capitals on the pillars were shaped like lilies. And so the work on the pillars was finished.

[23]Then Huram cast a large round tank, 15 feet across from rim to rim; it was called the Sea. It was 7½ feet deep and about 45 feet in circumference. [24]The Sea was encircled just below its rim by two rows of decorative gourds. There were about six gourds per foot* all the way around, and they had been cast as part of the tank.

[25]The Sea rested on a base of twelve bronze oxen, all facing outward. Three faced north, three faced west, three faced south, and three faced east. [26]The walls of the Sea were about three inches* thick, and its rim flared out like a cup and resembled a lily blossom. It could hold about 11,000 gallons* of water.

> *Make worship the guiding light of your very existence, the goal of your life mission, and you will know love as you've never known it.*
>
> DAVID JEREMIAH

²⁷Huram also made ten bronze water carts, each 6 feet long, 6 feet wide, and 4½ feet tall. ²⁸They were constructed with side panels braced with crossbars. ²⁹Both the panels and the crossbars were decorated with carved lions, oxen, and cherubim. Above and below the lions and oxen were wreath decorations. ³⁰Each of these carts had four bronze wheels and bronze axles. At each corner of the carts were supporting posts for the bronze basins; these supports were decorated with carvings of wreaths on each side. ³¹The top of each cart had a circular frame for the basin. It projected 1½ feet above the cart's top like a round pedestal, and its opening was 2¼ feet across; it was decorated on the outside with carvings of wreaths. The panels of the carts were square, not round. ³²Under the panels were four wheels that were connected to axles that had been cast as one unit with the cart. The wheels were 2¼ feet in diameter ³³and were similar to chariot wheels. The axles, spokes, rims, and hubs were all cast from molten bronze.

³⁴There were supports at each of the four corners of the carts, and these, too, were cast as one unit with the cart. ³⁵Around the top of each cart there was a rim 9 inches wide.* The supports and side panels were cast as one unit with the cart. ³⁶Carvings of cherubim, lions, and palm trees decorated the panels and supports wherever there was room, and there were wreaths all around. ³⁷All ten water carts were the same size and were made alike, for each was cast from the same mold.

³⁸Huram also made ten bronze basins, one for each cart. Each basin was 6 feet across and could hold 220 gallons* of water. ³⁹He arranged five water carts on the south side of the Temple and five on the north side. The Sea was placed at the southeast corner of the Temple. ⁴⁰He also made the necessary pots, shovels, and basins.

So at last Huram completed everything King Solomon had assigned him to make for the Temple of the LORD:

⁴¹ two pillars,
two bowl-shaped capitals on top of the pillars,
two networks of chains that decorated the capitals,
⁴² four hundred pomegranates that hung from the chains on the capitals (two rows of pomegranates for each of the chain networks that were hung around the capitals on top of the pillars),
⁴³ the ten water carts holding the ten basins,
⁴⁴ the Sea and the twelve oxen under it,
⁴⁵ the pots, the shovels, and the basins.

All these utensils for the Temple of the LORD that Huram made for Solomon were made of burnished bronze. ⁴⁶The king had them cast in clay molds in the Jordan Valley between Succoth and Zarethan. ⁴⁷Solomon did not weigh all the utensils because there were so many; the weight of the bronze could not be measured.

⁴⁸So Solomon made all the furnishings of the Temple of the LORD:

the gold altar,
the gold table for the Bread of the Presence,
⁴⁹ the gold lampstands, five on the south and five on the north, in front of the Most Holy Place,
the flower decorations, lamps, and tongs, all of gold,
⁵⁰ the cups, lamp snuffers, basins, dishes, and firepans, all of pure gold,
the doors for the entrances to the Most Holy Place and the main room of the Temple, with their fronts overlaid with gold.

⁵¹So King Solomon finished all his work on the Temple of the LORD. Then Solomon brought all the gifts his father, David, had dedicated—the silver, the gold, and the other utensils—and he stored them in the treasuries of the LORD's Temple.

7:35 Hebrew *half a cubit wide* [22.5 centimeters]. 7:38 Hebrew *40 baths* [840 liters].

THE ARK BROUGHT TO THE TEMPLE

8 Solomon then summoned the leaders of all the tribes and families of Israel to assemble in Jerusalem. They were to bring the Ark of the LORD's covenant from its location in the City of David, also known as Zion, to its new place in the Temple. [2]They all assembled before the king at the annual Festival of Shelters in early autumn.* [3]When all the leaders of Israel arrived, the priests picked up the Ark. [4]Then the priests and Levites took the Ark of the LORD, along with the Tabernacle* and all its sacred utensils, and carried them up to the Temple. [5]King Solomon and the entire community of Israel sacrificed sheep and oxen before the Ark in such numbers that no one could keep count!

[6]Then the priests carried the Ark of the LORD's covenant into the inner sanctuary of the Temple—the Most Holy Place—and placed it beneath the wings of the cherubim. [7]The cherubim spread their wings over the Ark, forming a canopy over the Ark and its carrying poles. [8]These poles were so long that their ends could be seen from the front entrance of the Temple's main room—the Holy Place—but not from outside it. They are still there to this day. [9]Nothing was in the Ark except the two stone tablets that Moses had placed there at Mount Sinai,* where the LORD made a covenant with the people of Israel as they were leaving the land of Egypt.

[10]As the priests came out of the inner sanctuary, a cloud filled the Temple of the LORD. [11]The priests could not continue their work because the glorious presence of the LORD filled the Temple.

SOLOMON BLESSES THE PEOPLE

[12]Then Solomon prayed, "O LORD, you have said that you would live in thick darkness. [13]But I have built a glorious Temple for you, where you can live forever!"

[14]Then the king turned around to the entire community of Israel standing before him and gave this blessing: [15]"Blessed be the LORD, the God of Israel, who has kept the promise he made to my father, David. [16]For he told my father, 'From the day I brought my people Israel out of Egypt, I have never chosen a city among the tribes of Israel as the place where a temple should be built to honor my name. But now I have chosen David to be king over my people.'"

[17]Then Solomon said, "My father, David, wanted to build this Temple to honor the name of the LORD, the God of Israel. [18]But the LORD told him, 'It is right for you to want to build the Temple to honor my name, [19]but you are not the one to do it. One of your sons will build it instead.'

[20]"And now the LORD has done what he promised, for I have become king in my father's place. I have built this Temple to honor the name of the LORD, the God of Israel. [21]And I have prepared a place there for the Ark, which contains the covenant that the LORD made with our ancestors when he brought them out of Egypt."

SOLOMON'S PRAYER OF DEDICATION

[22]Then Solomon stood with his hands lifted toward heaven before the altar of the LORD in front of the entire community of Israel. [23]He prayed, "O LORD, God of Israel, there is no God like you in all of heaven or earth. You keep your promises and show unfailing love to all who obey you and are eager to do your will. [24]You have kept your promise to your servant David, my father. You made that promise with your own mouth, and today you have fulfilled it with your own hands. [25]And now, O LORD, God of Israel, carry out your further promise to your servant David, my father. For you said to him, 'If your descendants guard their behavior as you have done, they will

8:2 Hebrew at the festival in the month Ethanim, which is the seventh month. The Festival of Shelters began on the fifteenth day of the seventh month on the Hebrew lunar calendar. This occurs on our calendar in late September or early October.   8:4 Hebrew Tent of Meeting.   8:9 Hebrew at Horeb, another name for Sinai.

My Daily Worship

— March 21 —

UP IN THE AIR

1 KINGS 5:1–8:66

*Then Solomon stood with his hands lifted toward heaven before the altar of the LORD
in front of the entire community of Israel. He prayed, "O LORD, God of Israel,
there is no God like you in all of heaven or earth" (8:22–23).*

[i reflect]

There's an old joke that goes like this: Did you hear about the church that couldn't agree whether or not to let worshipers raise their hands during worship? The members reached a compromise. Those who felt the need to lift their hands could only lift one. They signed an "arms limitation treaty."

Sadly, this kind of body language has been divisive in some congregations. But contrary to the opinion of many, praying with uplifted arms is not a practice that began with the charismatic renewal movement. Solomon "with his hands lifted toward heaven" when he prayed. It was a tangible way of lifting his heart to the Lord. By raising his arms, the king reached for the Lord. It was almost as if he were attempting to hand over his requests as he made contact through prayer.

His example provides us with a picture of animated surrender. Can't you feel the drama of this scene? It's a way of self-disclosure in personal worship that has nothing to do with our understanding of the Holy Spirit. It's simply a way of reaching out beyond ourselves when we talk to the Lord.

Instead of nervously clutching your fingers together as you sometimes do, relax them. Open your palms. Say, "Lord, I'm tired of carrying these concerns. I surrender them to you." Allow the Lord to take whatever it is you are holding on to. What could possibly keep you from handing those concerns over to him? Lifting your arms to the Lord, remind yourself (and him) that he's all you need today.

[i pray]

*Lord, I know in my head that you are all I need. My heart sometimes lags behind.
As I lift my hands in an expression of my childlike dependence on you,
cause my heart to catch up. Amen.*

[i respond]

Pray with outstretched hands for the next week. After incorporating this ancient body language into your daily prayer for several days, evaluate if this posture serves to increase your intimacy with the Lord.

always reign over Israel.' ²⁶Now, O God of Israel, fulfill this promise to your servant David, my father.

²⁷"But will God really live on earth? Why, even the highest heavens cannot contain you. How much less this Temple I have built! ²⁸Listen to my prayer and my request, O LORD my God. Hear the cry and the prayer that your servant is making to you today. ²⁹May you watch over this Temple both day and night, this place where you have said you would put your name. May you always hear the prayers I make toward this place. ³⁰May you hear the humble and earnest requests from me and your people Israel when we pray toward this place. Yes, hear us from heaven where you live, and when you hear, forgive.

³¹"If someone wrongs another person and is required to take an oath of innocence in front of the altar at this Temple, ³²then hear from heaven and judge between your servants—the accuser and the accused. Punish the guilty party and acquit the one who is innocent.

³³"If your people Israel are defeated by their enemies because they have sinned against you, and if they turn to you and call on your name and pray to you here in this Temple, ³⁴then hear from heaven and forgive their sins and return them to this land you gave their ancestors.

³⁵"If the skies are shut up and there is no rain because your people have sinned against you, and then they pray toward this Temple and confess your name and turn from their sins because you have punished them, ³⁶then hear from heaven and forgive the sins of your servants, your people Israel. Teach them to do what is right, and send rain on your land that you have given to your people as their special possession.

³⁷"If there is a famine in the land, or plagues, or crop disease, or attacks of locusts or caterpillars, or if your people's enemies are in the land besieging their towns—whatever the trouble is—³⁸and if your people offer a prayer concerning their troubles or sorrow, raising their hands toward this Temple, ³⁹then

hear from heaven where you live, and forgive. Give your people whatever they deserve, for you alone know the human heart. ⁴⁰Then they will fear you and walk in your ways as long as they live in the land you gave to our ancestors.

⁴¹"And when foreigners hear of you and come from distant lands to worship your great name—⁴²for they will hear of you and of your mighty miracles and your power—and when they pray toward this Temple, ⁴³then hear from heaven where you live, and grant what they ask of you. Then all the people of the earth will come to know and fear you, just as your own people Israel do. They, too, will know that this Temple I have built bears your name.

⁴⁴"If your people go out at your command to fight their enemies, and if they pray to the LORD toward this city that you have chosen and toward this Temple that I have built for your name, ⁴⁵then hear their prayers from heaven and uphold their cause.

⁴⁶"If they sin against you—and who has never sinned?—you may become angry with them and let their enemies conquer them and take them captive to a foreign land far or near. ⁴⁷But in that land of exile, they may turn to you again in repentance and pray, 'We have sinned, done evil, and acted wickedly.' ⁴⁸Then if they turn to you with their whole heart and soul and pray toward the land you gave to their ancestors, toward this city you have chosen, and toward this Temple I have built to honor your name, ⁴⁹then hear their prayers from heaven where you live. Uphold their cause ⁵⁰and forgive your people who have sinned against you. Make their captors merciful to them, ⁵¹for they are your people—your special possession—whom you brought out of the iron-smelting furnace of Egypt.

⁵²"May your eyes be open to my requests and to the requests of your people Israel. Hear and answer them whenever they cry out to you. ⁵³For when you brought our ancestors out of Egypt, O Sovereign LORD, you told your servant Moses that you had separated Israel

from among all the nations of the earth to be your own special possession."

THE DEDICATION OF THE TEMPLE

⁵⁴When Solomon finished making these prayers and requests to the LORD, he stood up in front of the altar of the LORD, where he had been kneeling with his hands raised toward heaven. ⁵⁵He stood there and shouted this blessing over the entire community of Israel: ⁵⁶"Praise the LORD who has given rest to his people Israel, just as he promised. Not one word has failed of all the wonderful promises he gave through his servant Moses. ⁵⁷May the LORD our God be with us as he was with our ancestors; may he never forsake us. ⁵⁸May he give us the desire to do his will in everything and to obey all the commands, laws, and regulations that he gave our ancestors. ⁵⁹And may these words that I have prayed in the presence of the LORD be before him constantly, day and night, so that the LORD our God may uphold my cause and the cause of his people Israel, fulfilling our daily needs. ⁶⁰May people all over the earth know that the LORD is God and that there is no other god. ⁶¹And may you, his people, always be faithful to the LORD our God. May you always obey his laws and commands, just as you are doing today."

⁶²Then the king and all Israel with him offered sacrifices to the LORD. ⁶³Solomon sacrificed peace offerings to the LORD numbering 22,000 oxen and 120,000 sheep. And so the king and all Israel dedicated the Temple of the LORD. ⁶⁴That same day the king dedicated the central area of the courtyard in front of the LORD's Temple. He offered burnt offerings, grain offerings, and the fat of peace offerings there, because the bronze altar in the LORD's presence was too small to handle so many offerings.

⁶⁵Then Solomon and all Israel celebrated the Festival of Shelters* in the presence of the LORD their God. A large crowd had gathered from as far away as Lebo-hamath in the north to the brook of Egypt in the south. The celebration went on for fourteen days in all— seven days for the dedication of the altar and seven days for the Festival of Shelters.* ⁶⁶After the festival was over,* Solomon sent the people home. They blessed the king as they went, and they were all joyful and happy because the LORD had been good to his servant David and to his people Israel.

THE LORD'S RESPONSE TO SOLOMON

9 So Solomon finished building the Temple of the LORD, as well as the royal palace. He completed everything he had planned to do. ²Then the LORD appeared to Solomon a second time, as he had done before at Gibeon. ³The LORD said to him, "I have heard your prayer and your request. I have set apart this Temple you have built so that my name will be honored there forever. I will always watch over it and care for it. ⁴As for you, if you will follow me with integrity and godliness, as David your father did, always obeying my commands and keeping my laws and regulations, ⁵then I will establish the throne of your dynasty over Israel forever. For I made this promise to your father, David: 'You will never fail to have a successor on the throne of Israel.'

⁶"But if you or your descendants abandon me and disobey my commands and laws, and if you go and worship other gods, ⁷then I will uproot the people of Israel from this land I have given them. I will reject this Temple that I have set apart to honor my name. I will make Israel an object of mockery and ridicule among the nations. ⁸And though this Temple is impressive now, it will become an appalling sight for all who pass by. They will scoff and ask, 'Why did the LORD do such terrible things to his land and to his Temple?' ⁹And the answer will be, 'Because his people forgot the

---

8:65a Hebrew *the festival;* see note on 8:2. **8:65b** Hebrew *seven days and seven days, fourteen days;* compare parallel text at 2 Chr 7:8-10. **8:66** Hebrew *On the eighth day,* probably referring to the day following the seven-day Festival of Shelters; compare parallel text at 2 Chr 7:9-10.

LORD their God, who brought their ancestors out of Egypt, and they worshiped other gods instead. That is why the LORD has brought all these disasters upon them.'"

SOLOMON'S AGREEMENT WITH HIRAM

¹⁰Now at the end of the twenty years during which Solomon built the Temple of the LORD and the royal palace, ¹¹Solomon gave twenty towns in the land of Galilee to King Hiram of Tyre as payment for all the cedar and cypress lumber and gold he had furnished for the construction of the buildings. ¹²Hiram came from Tyre to see the towns Solomon had given him, but he was not at all pleased with them. ¹³"What kind of towns are these, my brother?" he asked. "These towns are worthless!" So Hiram called that area Cabul—"worthless"—as it is still known today. ¹⁴Hiram had sent Solomon nine thousand pounds* of gold.

SOLOMON'S MANY ACHIEVEMENTS

¹⁵This is the account of the forced labor that Solomon conscripted to build the LORD's Temple, the royal palace, the Millo,* the wall of Jerusalem, and the cities of Hazor, Megiddo, and Gezer. ¹⁶(The king of Egypt had attacked and captured Gezer, killing the Canaanite population and burning it down. He gave the city to his daughter as a wedding gift when she married Solomon. ¹⁷So Solomon rebuilt the city of Gezer.) He also built up the towns of Lower Beth-horon, ¹⁸Baalath, and Tamar* in the desert, within his land. ¹⁹He built towns as supply centers and constructed cities where his chariots and horses* could be kept. He built to his heart's content in Jerusalem and Lebanon and throughout the entire realm.

²⁰There were still some people living in the land who were not Israelites, including Amorites, Hittites, Perizzites, Hivites, and Jebusites. ²¹These were descendants of the nations that Israel had not completely destroyed.* So Solomon conscripted them for his labor force, and they serve in the labor force to this day. ²²But Solomon did not conscript any of the Israelites for forced labor. Instead, he assigned them to serve as fighting men, government officials, officers in his army, commanders of his chariots, and charioteers. ²³He also appointed 550 of them to supervise the various projects.

²⁴After Solomon moved his wife, Pharaoh's daughter, from the City of David to the new palace he had built for her, he constructed the Millo.

²⁵Three times each year Solomon offered burnt offerings and peace offerings to the LORD on the altar he had built. He also burned incense to the LORD. And so he finished the work of building the Temple.

²⁶Later King Solomon built a fleet of ships at Ezion-geber, a port near Elath* in the land of Edom, along the shore of the Red Sea.* ²⁷Hiram sent experienced crews of sailors to sail the ships with Solomon's men. ²⁸They sailed to Ophir and brought back to Solomon some sixteen tons* of gold.

THE QUEEN OF SHEBA'S VISIT

10 When the queen of Sheba heard of Solomon's reputation, which brought honor to the name of the LORD, she came to test him with hard questions. ²She arrived in Jerusalem with a large group of attendants and a great caravan of camels loaded with spices, huge quantities of gold, and precious jewels. When she met with Solomon, they talked about everything she had on her mind. ³Solomon answered all her questions; nothing was too hard for the king to explain to her. ⁴When the queen of Sheba realized how wise Solomon was, and when she saw the palace he had built, ⁵she was breathless. She was also

9:14 Hebrew *120 talents* [4 metric tons]. 9:15 Or *the supporting terraces;* also in 9:24. 9:18 The marginal *Qere* reading of the Masoretic Text reads *Tadmor.* 9:19 Or *and charioteers.* 9:21 The Hebrew term used here refers to the complete consecration of things or people to the LORD, either by destroying them or by giving them as an offering. 9:26a As in Greek version (see also 2 Kgs 14:22; 16:6); Hebrew reads *Eloth.* 9:26b Hebrew *sea of reeds.* 9:28 Hebrew *420 talents* [14 metric tons].

amazed at the food on his tables, the organization of his officials and their splendid clothing, the cup-bearers and their robes, and the burnt offerings Solomon made at the Temple of the LORD.

⁶She exclaimed to the king, "Everything I heard in my country about your achievements and wisdom is true! ⁷I didn't believe it until I arrived here and saw it with my own eyes. Truly I had not heard the half of it! Your wisdom and prosperity are far greater than what I was told. ⁸How happy these people must be! What a privilege for your officials to stand here day after day, listening to your wisdom! ⁹The LORD your God is great indeed! He delights in you and has placed you on the throne of Israel. Because the LORD loves Israel with an eternal love, he has made you king so you can rule with justice and righteousness."

¹⁰Then she gave the king a gift of nine thousand pounds* of gold, and great quantities of spices and precious jewels. Never again were so many spices brought in as those the queen of Sheba gave to Solomon.

¹¹(When Hiram's ships brought gold from Ophir, they also brought rich cargoes of almug wood and precious jewels. ¹²The king used the almug wood to make railings for the Temple of the LORD and the royal palace, and to construct harps and lyres for the musicians. Never before or since has there been such a supply of beautiful almug wood.)

¹³King Solomon gave the queen of Sheba whatever she asked for, besides all the other customary gifts he had so generously given. Then she and all her attendants left and returned to their own land.

SOLOMON'S WEALTH AND SPLENDOR

¹⁴Each year Solomon received about twenty-five tons* of gold. ¹⁵This did not include the additional revenue he received from merchants and traders, all the kings of Arabia, and the governors of the land.

¹⁶King Solomon made two hundred large shields of hammered gold, each containing over fifteen pounds* of gold. ¹⁷He also made three hundred smaller shields of hammered gold, each containing nearly four pounds* of gold. The king placed these shields in the Palace of the Forest of Lebanon.

¹⁸Then the king made a huge ivory throne and overlaid it with pure gold. ¹⁹The throne had six steps and a rounded back. On both sides of the seat were armrests, with the figure of a lion standing on each side of the throne. ²⁰Solomon made twelve other lion figures, one standing on each end of each of the six steps. No other throne in all the world could be compared with it!

²¹All of King Solomon's drinking cups were solid gold, as were all the utensils in the Palace of the Forest of Lebanon. They were not made of silver because silver was considered of little value in Solomon's day!

²²The king had a fleet of trading ships* that sailed with Hiram's fleet. Once every three years the ships returned, loaded down with gold, silver, ivory, apes, and peacocks.*

²³So King Solomon became richer and wiser than any other king in all the earth. ²⁴People from every nation came to visit him and to hear the wisdom God had given him. ²⁵Year after year, everyone who came to visit brought him gifts of silver and gold, clothing, weapons, spices, horses, and mules.

²⁶Solomon built up a huge force of chariots and horses. He had fourteen hundred chariots and twelve thousand horses.* He stationed many of them in the chariot cities, and some near him in Jerusalem. ²⁷The king made silver as plentiful in Jerusalem as stones. And valuable cedarwood was as common as the sycamore wood that grows in the foothills of Judah.* ²⁸Solomon's horses were imported from Egypt* and from Cilicia*; the king's

---

10:10 Hebrew *120 talents* [4 metric tons]. 10:14 Hebrew *666 talents* [23 metric tons]. 10:16 Hebrew *600 shekels* [6.8 kilograms]. 10:17 Hebrew *3 minas* [1.8 kilograms]. 10:22a Hebrew *fleet of ships of Tarshish.* 10:22b Or *and baboons.* 10:26 Or *12,000 charioteers.* 10:27 Hebrew *the Shephelah.* 10:28a Possibly *Muzur,* a district near Cilicia; also in 10:29. 10:28b Hebrew *Kue,* probably another name for Cilicia.

traders acquired them from Cilicia at the standard price. ²⁹At that time, Egyptian chariots delivered to Jerusalem could be purchased for 600 pieces of silver,* and horses could be bought for 150 pieces of silver.* Many of these were then resold to the kings of the Hittites and the kings of Aram.

SOLOMON'S MANY WIVES

11 Now King Solomon loved many foreign women. Besides Pharaoh's daughter, he married women from Moab, Ammon, Edom, Sidon, and from among the Hittites. ²The LORD had clearly instructed his people not to intermarry with those nations, because the women they married would lead them to worship their gods. Yet Solomon insisted on loving them anyway. ³He had seven hundred wives and three hundred concubines. And sure enough, they led his heart away from the LORD. ⁴In Solomon's old age, they turned his heart to worship their gods instead of trusting only in the LORD his God, as his father, David, had done. ⁵Solomon worshiped Ashtoreth, the goddess of the Sidonians, and Molech,* the detestable god of the Ammonites. ⁶Thus, Solomon did what was evil in the LORD's sight; he refused to follow the LORD completely, as his father, David, had done. ⁷On the Mount of Olives, east of Jerusalem, he even built a shrine for Chemosh, the detestable god of Moab, and another for Molech, the detestable god of the Ammonites. ⁸Solomon built such shrines for all his foreign wives to use for burning incense and sacrificing to their gods.

⁹The LORD was very angry with Solomon, for his heart had turned away from the LORD, the God of Israel, who had appeared to him twice. ¹⁰He had warned Solomon specifically about worshiping other gods, but Solomon did not listen to the LORD's command. ¹¹So now the LORD said to him, "Since you have not kept my covenant and have disobeyed my laws, I will surely tear the kingdom away from

you and give it to one of your servants. ¹²But for the sake of your father, David, I will not do this while you are still alive. I will take the kingdom away from your son. ¹³And even so, I will let him be king of one tribe, for the sake of my servant David and for the sake of Jerusalem, my chosen city."

SOLOMON'S ENEMIES

¹⁴Then the LORD raised up Hadad the Edomite, a member of Edom's royal family, to be an enemy against Solomon. ¹⁵Years before, David had gone to Edom with Joab, his army commander, to bury some Israelites who had died in battle. While there, the Israelite army had killed nearly every male in Edom. ¹⁶Joab and the army had stayed there for six months, killing them. ¹⁷But Hadad and a few of his father's royal officials had fled. (Hadad was a very small child at the time.) ¹⁸They escaped from Midian and went to Paran, where others joined them. Then they traveled to Egypt and went to Pharaoh, who gave them a home, food, and some land. ¹⁹Pharaoh grew very fond of Hadad, and he gave him a wife—the sister of Queen Tahpenes. ²⁰She bore him a son, Genubath, who was brought up in Pharaoh's palace among Pharaoh's own sons.

²¹When the news reached Hadad in Egypt that David and his commander Joab were both dead, he said to Pharaoh, "Let me return to my own country."

²²"Why?" Pharaoh asked him. "What do you lack here? How have we disappointed you that you want to go home?"

"Nothing is wrong," he replied. "But even so, I must return home."

²³God also raised up Rezon son of Eliada to be an enemy against Solomon. Rezon had fled from his master, King Hadadezer of Zobah, ²⁴and had become the leader of a gang of rebels. After David conquered Hadadezer, Rezon and his men fled to Damascus, where he became king. ²⁵Rezon was Israel's bitter enemy for the rest of Solomon's reign, and he

10:29a Hebrew *600 shekels of silver*, about 15 pounds or 6.8 kilograms in weight. 10:29b Hebrew *150 [shekels]*, about 3.8 pounds or 1.7 kilograms in weight. 11:5 Hebrew *Milcom*, a variant name for Molech; also in 11:33.

My Daily Worship

— March 22 —

LESSONS FROM TURNING LEAVES

1 KINGS 9:1–11:43

In Solomon's old age, they turned his heart to worship their gods instead of trusting only in the LORD his God, as his father, David, had done (11:4).

[i reflect]

Autumn leaves don't turn red, yellow, orange, and brown because of "peer pressure." To the uninformed observer, it might appear that one solitary green leaf changes its appearance, and then soon after, those nearby follow suit. But what appears at first blush to be the case is not at all the cause. Rather, leaves are transformed in color because something has died inside. The sap that once nourished each leaf has ceased to run as it did during the spring and summer. The flow of chloroform has been cut off.

You might think that Solomon's willingness to start worshiping pagan gods was simply because of the pressure put on him by his Gentile wives. But that explanation would be far too simple. Most likely, as with the leaves of fall, something had begun to die within the king's soul. The God-ward flow within his heart had begun to dry up.

His fiery passion for the Lord gradually cooled through neglected spiritual disciplines. His tendency to turn away from the God of his father was not peer pressure as much as it was a spiritual vacuum that needed to be filled. Solomon's wives can't be blamed for his apostasy. The fact that the king was willing to marry non-Jewish women indicates that he had already begun to turn away from the Lord.

It's oh-so-subtle, but oh-so-dangerous. The negative influence of other people in your life only starts to take a toll when you have shut off the Holy Spirit's influence. The invitation of friends to join them for sporting events on Sunday seems more attractive when you haven't prioritized personal worship during the week. It's when you have slacked off on reading God's Word that you're more apt to read a racy novel or watch sexually explicit entertainment.

But that isn't what you want, is it? You long for intimacy with your Father, and yet you know how the daily grind so easily leaves you vulnerable to slacking off. The Lord longs for you to come into his presence. It breaks his heart when you hold him at arm's length. It's never too late; you can still run into his arms today.

[i pray]

Lord, I'm shocked by what Solomon did. But when I look in the mirror and recognize how easy it is to slowly distance myself from you an inch at a time, I can't be too quick to judge him. I know how prone I am to wander from you. Draw me to yourself today.

[i respond]

Find a dry brown leaf in your backyard or a nearby park. Tack it to a bulletin board near to where you work each day. Allow that symbol to remind you of the price of holding God at arm's length.

made trouble, just as Hadad did. Rezon hated Israel intensely and continued to reign in Aram.

JEROBOAM REBELS AGAINST SOLOMON

²⁶Another rebel leader was Jeroboam son of Nebat, one of Solomon's own officials. He came from the city of Zeredah in Ephraim, and his mother was Zeruah, a widow. ²⁷This is the story behind his rebellion. Solomon was rebuilding the Millo* and repairing the walls of the city of his father, David. ²⁸Jeroboam was a very capable young man, and when Solomon saw how industrious he was, he put him in charge of the labor force from the tribes of Ephraim and Manasseh.*

²⁹One day as Jeroboam was leaving Jerusalem, the prophet Ahijah from Shiloh met him on the road, wearing a new cloak. The two of them were alone in a field, ³⁰and Ahijah took the new cloak he was wearing and tore it into twelve pieces. ³¹Then he said to Jeroboam, "Take ten of these pieces, for this is what the LORD, the God of Israel, says: 'I am about to tear the kingdom from the hand of Solomon, and I will give ten of the tribes to you! ³²But I will leave him one tribe for the sake of my servant David and for the sake of Jerusalem, which I have chosen out of all the tribes of Israel. ³³For Solomon has abandoned me and worshiped Ashtoreth, the goddess of the Sidonians; Chemosh, the god of Moab; and Molech, the god of the Ammonites. He has not followed my ways and done what is pleasing in my sight. He has not obeyed my laws and regulations as his father, David, did.

³⁴" 'But I will not take the entire kingdom from Solomon at this time. For the sake of my servant David, the one whom I chose and who obeyed my commands and laws, I will let Solomon reign for the rest of his life. ³⁵But I will take the kingdom away from his son and give ten of the tribes to you. ³⁶His son will have one tribe so that the descendants of David my servant will continue to reign* in Jerusalem, the city I have chosen to be the place for my name. ³⁷And I will place you on the throne of Israel, and you will rule over all that your heart desires. ³⁸If you listen to what I tell you and follow my ways and do whatever I consider to be right, and if you obey my laws and commands, as my servant David did, then I will always be with you. I will establish an enduring dynasty for you as I did for David, and I will give Israel to you. ³⁹But I will punish the descendants of David because of Solomon's sin—though not forever.' "

⁴⁰Solomon tried to kill Jeroboam, but he fled to King Shishak of Egypt and stayed there until Solomon died.

⁴¹The rest of the events in Solomon's reign, including his wisdom, are recorded in *The Book of the Acts of Solomon.* ⁴²Solomon ruled in Jerusalem over all Israel for forty years. ⁴³When Solomon died, he was buried in the city of his father, David. Then his son Rehoboam became the next king.

THE NORTHERN TRIBES REVOLT

12 Rehoboam went to Shechem, where all Israel had gathered to make him king. ²When Jeroboam son of Nebat heard of Solomon's death, he returned from Egypt,* for he had fled to Egypt to escape from King Solomon. ³The leaders of Israel sent for Jeroboam, and the whole assembly of Israel went to speak with Rehoboam. ⁴"Your father was a hard master," they said. "Lighten the harsh labor demands and heavy taxes that your father imposed on us. Then we will be your loyal subjects."

⁵Rehoboam replied, "Give me three days to think this over. Then come back for my answer." So the people went away.

⁶Then King Rehoboam went to discuss the matter with the older men who had counseled his father, Solomon. "What is your advice?" he asked. "How should I answer these people?"

⁷The older counselors replied, "If you are

11:27 Or *the supporting terraces.* **11:28** Hebrew *from the house of Joseph.* **11:36** Hebrew *will continue to have a lamp.* **12:2** As in Greek version and Latin Vulgate (see also 2 Chr 10:2); Hebrew reads *he lived in Egypt.*

willing to serve the people today and give them a favorable answer, they will always be your loyal subjects."

⁸But Rehoboam rejected the advice of the elders and instead asked the opinion of the young men who had grown up with him and who were now his advisers. ⁹"What is your advice?" he asked them. "How should I answer these people who want me to lighten the burdens imposed by my father?"

¹⁰The young men replied, "This is what you should tell those complainers: 'My little finger is thicker than my father's waist—if you think he was hard on you, just wait and see what I'll be like! ¹¹Yes, my father was harsh on you, but I'll be even harsher! My father used whips on you, but I'll use scorpions!' "

¹²Three days later, Jeroboam and all the people returned to hear Rehoboam's decision, just as the king had requested. ¹³But Rehoboam spoke harshly to them, for he rejected the advice of the older counselors ¹⁴and followed the counsel of his younger advisers. He told the people, "My father was harsh on you, but I'll be even harsher! My father used whips on you, but I'll use scorpions!" ¹⁵So the king paid no attention to the people's demands. This turn of events was the will of the LORD, for it fulfilled the LORD's message to Jeroboam son of Nebat through the prophet Ahijah from Shiloh.

¹⁶When all Israel realized that the king had rejected their request, they shouted, "Down with David and his dynasty! We have no share in Jesse's son! Let's go home, Israel! Look out for your own house, O David!" So the people of Israel returned home. ¹⁷But Rehoboam continued to rule over the Israelites who lived in the towns of Judah.

¹⁸King Rehoboam sent Adoniram,* who was in charge of the labor force, to restore order, but all Israel stoned him to death. When this news reached King Rehoboam, he quickly jumped into his chariot and fled to Jerusalem. ¹⁹The northern tribes of Israel have refused to be ruled by a descendant of David to this day.

²⁰When the people of Israel learned of Jeroboam's return from Egypt, they called an assembly and made him king over all Israel. So only the tribe of Judah remained loyal to the family of David.

SHEMAIAH'S PROPHECY

²¹When Rehoboam arrived at Jerusalem, he mobilized the armies of Judah and Benjamin—180,000 select troops—to fight against the army of Israel and to restore the kingdom to himself. ²²But God said to Shemaiah, the man of God, ²³"Say to Rehoboam son of Solomon, king of Judah, and to all the people of Judah and Benjamin, ²⁴'This is what the LORD says: Do not fight against your relatives, the Israelites. Go back home, for what has happened is my doing!' " So they obeyed the message of the LORD and went home, as the LORD had commanded.

JEROBOAM MAKES GOLD CALVES

²⁵Jeroboam then built up the city of Shechem in the hill country of Ephraim, and it became his capital. Later he went and built up the town of Peniel.* ²⁶Jeroboam thought to himself, "Unless I am careful, the kingdom will return to the dynasty of David. ²⁷When they go to Jerusalem to offer sacrifices at the Temple of the LORD, they will again give their allegiance to King Rehoboam of Judah. They will kill me and make him their king instead."

²⁸So on the advice of his counselors, the king made two gold calves. He said to the people, "It is too much trouble for you to worship in Jerusalem. O Israel, these are the gods who brought you out of Egypt!"

²⁹He placed these calf idols at the southern and northern ends of Israel—in Bethel and in Dan. ³⁰This became a great sin, for the people worshiped them, traveling even as far as Dan. ³¹Jeroboam built shrines at the pagan high places and ordained priests from the rank and

---

12:18 As in some Greek manuscripts and Syriac version (see also 4:6; 5:14); Hebrew reads *Adoram.*   12:25 Hebrew *Penuel,* a variant name for Peniel.

file of the people—those who were not from the priestly tribe of Levi. ³²Jeroboam also instituted a religious festival in Bethel, held on a day in midautumn,* similar to the annual Festival of Shelters in Judah. There at Bethel he himself offered sacrifices to the calves he had made. And it was at Bethel that he appointed priests for the pagan shrines he had made. ³³So on the appointed day in midautumn, a day that he himself had designated, Jeroboam offered sacrifices on the altar at Bethel. He instituted a religious festival for Israel, and he went up to the altar to burn incense.

A PROPHET DENOUNCES JEROBOAM

13 At the LORD's command, a man of God from Judah went to Bethel, and he arrived there just as Jeroboam was approaching the altar to offer a sacrifice. ²Then at the LORD's command, he shouted, "O altar, altar! This is what the LORD says: A child named Josiah will be born into the dynasty of David. On you he will sacrifice the priests from the pagan shrines who come here to burn incense, and human bones will be burned on you." ³That same day the man of God gave a sign to prove his message, and he said, "The LORD has promised to give this sign: This altar will split apart, and its ashes will be poured out on the ground."

⁴King Jeroboam was very angry with the man of God for speaking against the altar. So he pointed at the man and shouted, "Seize that man!" But instantly the king's hand became paralyzed in that position, and he couldn't pull it back. ⁵At the same time a wide crack appeared in the altar, and the ashes poured out, just as the man of God had predicted in his message from the LORD.

⁶The king cried out to the man of God, "Please ask the LORD your God to restore my hand again!" So the man of God prayed to the LORD, and the king's hand became normal again.

Words of Worship

KNEEL

Kneel—Hebrew *be-rech* "kneel"; Greek *go-nu-pe-te-o* "kneel."

"Come, let us worship and bow down," the psalm writer invites us. "Let us kneel before the LORD our maker" (Psalm 95:5). Kneeling is a gesture of respect toward an authority. While few of us have knelt before a monarch or pontiff, we understand what it means to be on our knees before the Lord, the highest of authorities. We kneel to seek his mercy and forgiveness, as Solomon knelt at the dedication of the Temple (1 Kings 8:54). We kneel in fervent pleading for his intervention, as Jesus knelt before his Father in Gethsemane (Luke 22:41–42).

The Hebrew word for *kneel* is related to the word for *bless*. The Lord is blessed by our posture of respect. When we humble ourselves before him, he will lift us up and grant his benefits (James 4:10). As John Ellerton wrote in a well-known hymn, "We stand to bless thee, ere our worship cease; then, lowly kneeling, wait thy word of peace."

---

⁷Then the king said to the man of God, "Come to the palace with me and have something to eat, and I will give you a gift."

⁸But the man of God said to the king, "Even if you gave me half of everything you own, I would not go with you. I would not eat any food or drink any water in this place. ⁹For the LORD gave me this command: 'You must not eat any food or drink any water while you are there, and do not return to Judah by the same way you came.'" ¹⁰So he left Bethel and went home another way.

¹¹As it happened, there was an old prophet

12:32 Hebrew *on the fifteenth day of the eighth month* (also in 12:33). This day of the Hebrew lunar calendar occurs in late October or early November, exactly one month after the annual Festival of Shelters in Judah (see Lev 23:34).

living in Bethel, and his sons came home and told him what the man of God had done in Bethel that day. They also told him what he had said to the king. [12]The old prophet asked them, "Which way did he go?" So they told their father which road the man of God had taken. [13]"Quick, saddle the donkey," the old man said. And when they had saddled the donkey for him, [14]he rode after the man of God and found him sitting under an oak tree.

The old prophet asked him, "Are you the man of God who came from Judah?"

"Yes," he replied, "I am."

[15]Then he said to the man of God, "Come home with me and eat some food."

[16]"No, I cannot," he replied. "I am not allowed to eat any food or drink any water here in this place. [17]For the LORD gave me this command: 'You must not eat any food or drink any water while you are there, and do not return to Judah by the same way you came.'"

[18]But the old prophet answered, "I am a prophet, too, just as you are. And an angel gave me this message from the LORD: 'Bring him home with you, and give him food to eat and water to drink.'" But the old man was lying to him. [19]So they went back together, and the man of God ate some food and drank some water at the prophet's home.

[20]Then while they were sitting at the table, a message from the LORD came to the old prophet. [21]He cried out to the man of God from Judah, "This is what the LORD says: You have defied the LORD's message and have disobeyed the command the LORD your God gave you. [22]You came back to this place and ate food and drank water where he told you not to eat or drink. Because of this, your body will not be buried in the grave of your ancestors."

[23]Now after the man of God had finished eating and drinking, the prophet saddled his own donkey for him, [24]and the man of God started off again. But as he was traveling along, a lion came out and killed him. His body lay there on the road, with the donkey and the lion standing beside it. [25]People came

by and saw the body lying in the road and the lion standing beside it, and they went and reported it in Bethel, where the old prophet lived.

[26]When the old prophet heard the report, he said, "It is the man of God who disobeyed the LORD's command. The LORD has fulfilled his word by causing the lion to attack and kill him."

[27]Then the prophet said to his sons, "Saddle a donkey for me." So they saddled a donkey, [28]and he went out and found the body lying in the road. The donkey and lion were still standing there beside it, for the lion had not eaten the body nor attacked the donkey. [29]So the prophet laid the body of the man of God on the donkey and took it back to the city to mourn over him and bury him. [30]He laid the body in his own grave, crying out in grief, "Oh, my brother!"

[31]Afterward the prophet said to his sons, "When I die, bury me in the grave where the man of God is buried. Lay my bones beside his bones. [32]For the message the LORD told him to proclaim against the altar in Bethel and against the pagan shrines in the towns of Samaria will surely come true."

[33]But even after this, Jeroboam did not turn from his evil ways. He continued to choose priests from the rank and file of the people. Anyone who wanted to could become a priest for the pagan shrines. [34]This became a great sin and resulted in the destruction of Jeroboam's kingdom and the death of all his family.

AHIJAH'S PROPHECY AGAINST JEROBOAM

14 At that time Jeroboam's son Abijah became very sick. [2]So Jeroboam told his wife, "Disguise yourself so that no one will recognize you as the queen. Then go to the prophet Ahijah at Shiloh—the man who told me I would become king. [3]Take him a gift of ten loaves of bread, some cakes, and a jar of honey, and ask him what will happen to the boy."

⁴So Jeroboam's wife went to Ahijah's home at Shiloh. He was an old man now and could no longer see. ⁵But the LORD had told Ahijah, "Jeroboam's wife will come here, pretending to be someone else. She will ask you about her son, for he is very sick. You must give her the answer that I give you."

⁶So when Ahijah heard her footsteps at the door, he called out, "Come in, wife of Jeroboam! Why are you pretending to be someone else?" Then he told her, "I have bad news for you. ⁷Give your husband, Jeroboam, this message from the LORD, the God of Israel: 'I promoted you from the ranks of the common people and made you ruler over my people Israel. ⁸I ripped the kingdom away from the family of David and gave it to you. But you have not been like my servant David, who obeyed my commands and followed me with all his heart and always did whatever I wanted him to do. ⁹You have done more evil than all who lived before you. You have made other gods and have made me furious with your gold calves. And since you have turned your back on me, ¹⁰I will bring disaster on your dynasty and kill all your sons, slave or free alike. I will burn up your royal dynasty as one burns up trash until it is all gone. ¹¹I, the LORD, vow that the members of your family who die in the city will be eaten by dogs, and those who die in the field will be eaten by vultures.'"

¹²Then Ahijah said to Jeroboam's wife, "Go on home, and when you enter the city, the child will die. ¹³All Israel will mourn for him and bury him. He is the only member of your family who will have a proper burial, for this child is the only good thing that the LORD, the God of Israel, sees in the entire family of Jeroboam. ¹⁴And the LORD will raise up a king over Israel who will destroy the family of Jeroboam. This will happen today, even now! ¹⁵Then the LORD will shake Israel like a reed whipped about in a stream. He will uproot the people of Israel from this good land that he gave their ancestors and will scatter them beyond the Euphrates River,* for they have angered the LORD by worshiping Asherah poles. ¹⁶He will abandon Israel because Jeroboam sinned and made all of Israel sin along with him."

¹⁷So Jeroboam's wife returned to Tirzah, and the child died just as she walked through the door of her home. ¹⁸When the people of Israel buried him, they mourned for him, as the LORD had promised through the prophet Ahijah.

¹⁹The rest of the events of Jeroboam's reign, all his wars and how he ruled, are recorded in *The Book of the History of the Kings of Israel.* ²⁰Jeroboam reigned in Israel twenty-two years. When Jeroboam died, his son Nadab became the next king.

REHOBOAM RULES IN JUDAH

²¹Meanwhile, Rehoboam son of Solomon was king in Judah. He was forty-one years old when he became king, and he reigned seventeen years in Jerusalem, the city the LORD had chosen from among all the tribes of Israel as the place to honor his name. Rehoboam's mother was Naamah, an Ammonite woman. ²²During Rehoboam's reign, the people of Judah did what was evil in the LORD's sight, arousing his anger with their sin, for it was even worse than that of their ancestors. ²³They built pagan shrines and set up sacred pillars and Asherah poles on every high hill and under every green tree. ²⁴There were even shrine prostitutes throughout the land. The people imitated the detestable practices of the pagan nations the LORD had driven from the land ahead of the Israelites.

²⁵In the fifth year of King Rehoboam's reign, King Shishak of Egypt came up and attacked Jerusalem. ²⁶He ransacked the Temple of the LORD and the royal palace and stole everything, including all the gold shields Solomon had made. ²⁷Afterward Rehoboam made bronze shields as substitutes, and he entrusted them to the care of the palace guard officers. ²⁸Whenever the king went to the Temple of the LORD, the guards would carry them along and then return them to the guardroom.

14:15 Hebrew *the river.*

²⁹The rest of the events in Rehoboam's reign and all his deeds are recorded in *The Book of the History of the Kings of Judah.* ³⁰There was constant war between Rehoboam and Jeroboam. ³¹When Rehoboam died, he was buried among his ancestors in the City of David. His mother was Naamah, an Ammonite woman. Then his son Abijam* became the next king.

ABIJAM RULES IN JUDAH

15 Abijam* began to rule over Judah in the eighteenth year of Jeroboam's reign in Israel. ²He reigned in Jerusalem three years. His mother was Maacah, the daughter of Absalom.* ³He committed the same sins as his father before him, and his heart was not right with the LORD his God, as the heart of his ancestor David had been. ⁴But for David's sake, the LORD his God allowed his dynasty to continue,* and he gave Abijam a son to rule after him in Jerusalem. ⁵For David had done what was pleasing in the LORD's sight and had obeyed the LORD's commands throughout his life, except in the affair concerning Uriah the Hittite.

⁶There was war between Abijam and Jeroboam* throughout Abijam's reign. ⁷The rest of the events in Abijam's reign and all his deeds are recorded in *The Book of the History of the Kings of Judah.* There was constant war between Abijam and Jeroboam. ⁸When Abijam died, he was buried in the City of David. Then his son Asa became the next king.

ASA RULES IN JUDAH

⁹Asa began to rule over Judah in the twentieth year of Jeroboam's reign in Israel. ¹⁰He reigned in Jerusalem forty-one years. His grandmother* was Maacah, the daughter of Absalom. ¹¹Asa did what was pleasing in the LORD's sight, as his ancestor David had done. ¹²He banished the shrine prostitutes from the land and removed all the idols his ancestors had made.

¹³He even deposed his grandmother Maacah from her position as queen mother because she had made an obscene Asherah pole. He cut down the pole and burned it in the Kidron Valley. ¹⁴Although the pagan shrines were not completely removed, Asa remained faithful to the LORD throughout his life. ¹⁵He brought into the Temple of the LORD the silver and gold and the utensils that he and his father had dedicated.

¹⁶There was constant war between King Asa of Judah and King Baasha of Israel. ¹⁷King Baasha of Israel invaded Judah and fortified Ramah in order to prevent anyone from entering or leaving King Asa's territory in Judah. ¹⁸Asa responded by taking all the silver and gold that was left in the treasuries of the LORD's Temple and the royal palace. He sent it with some of his officials to Ben-hadad son of Tabrimmon and grandson of Hezion, the king of Aram, who was ruling in Damascus, along with this message:

¹⁹"Let us renew the treaty that existed between your father and my father. See, I am sending you a gift of silver and gold. Break your treaty with King Baasha of Israel so that he will leave me alone."

²⁰Ben-hadad agreed to King Asa's request and sent his armies to attack Israel. They conquered the towns of Ijon, Dan, Abel-beth-maacah, and all Kinnereth, with all the land of Naphtali. ²¹As soon as Baasha of Israel heard what was happening, he abandoned his project of fortifying Ramah and withdrew to Tirzah. ²²Then King Asa sent an order throughout Judah, requiring that everyone, without exception, help to carry away the building stones and timbers that Baasha had been using to fortify Ramah. Asa used these materials to fortify the town of Geba in Benjamin and the town of Mizpah.

²³The rest of the events in Asa's reign, the

14:31 Also known as *Abijah.* **15:1** Also known as *Abijah.* **15:2** Hebrew *Abishalom* (also in 15:10), a variant name for Absalom; compare 2 Chr 11:20. **15:4** Hebrew *gave him a lamp in Jerusalem.* **15:6** As in a few Hebrew manuscripts; most Hebrew manuscripts read *between Rehoboam and Jeroboam.* **15:10** Hebrew *his mother* (also in 15:13); compare 15:2.

extent of his power, and the names of the cities he built are recorded in *The Book of the History of the Kings of Judah*. In his old age his feet became diseased. ²⁴When Asa died, he was buried with his ancestors in the City of David. Then his son Jehoshaphat became the next king.

NADAB RULES IN ISRAEL

²⁵Nadab son of Jeroboam began to rule over Israel in the second year of King Asa's reign in Judah. He reigned in Israel two years. ²⁶But he did what was evil in the LORD's sight and followed the example of his father, continuing the sins of idolatry that Jeroboam had led Israel to commit.

²⁷Then Baasha son of Ahijah, from the tribe of Issachar, plotted against Nadab and assassinated him while he and the Israelite army were laying siege to the Philistine town of Gibbethon. ²⁸Baasha killed Nadab in the third year of King Asa's reign in Judah, and he became the next king of Israel. ²⁹He immediately killed all the descendants of King Jeroboam, so that not one of the royal family was left, just as the LORD had promised concerning Jeroboam by the prophet Ahijah from Shiloh. ³⁰This was done because Jeroboam had aroused the anger of the LORD, the God of Israel, by the sins he had committed and the sins he had led Israel to commit. ³¹The rest of the events in Nadab's reign and all his deeds are recorded in *The Book of the History of the Kings of Israel*.

BAASHA RULES IN ISRAEL

³²There was constant war between Asa and King Baasha of Israel. ³³Baasha began to rule over Israel in the third year of King Asa's reign in Judah. Baasha reigned in Tirzah twenty-four years. ³⁴But he did what was evil in the LORD's sight and followed the example of Jeroboam, continuing the sins of idolatry that Jeroboam had led Israel to commit.

16 This message from the LORD was delivered to King Baasha by the prophet Jehu son of Hanani: ²"I lifted you out of the dust to make you ruler of my people Israel, but you have followed the evil example of Jeroboam. You have aroused my anger by causing my people to sin. ³So now I will destroy you and your family, just as I destroyed the descendants of Jeroboam son of Nebat. ⁴Those of your family who die in the city will be eaten by dogs, and those who die in the field will be eaten by the vultures."

⁵The rest of the events in Baasha's reign and the extent of his power are recorded in *The Book of the History of the Kings of Israel*. ⁶When Baasha died, he was buried in Tirzah. Then his son Elah became the next king.

⁷This message from the LORD had been spoken against Baasha and his family through the prophet Jehu son of Hanani. It was delivered because Baasha had done what was evil in the LORD's sight, arousing him to anger by his sins, just like the family of Jeroboam, and also because Baasha had destroyed the family of Jeroboam.

ELAH RULES IN ISRAEL

⁸Elah son of Baasha began to rule over Israel from Tirzah in the twenty-sixth year of King Asa's reign in Judah. He reigned in Israel two years. ⁹Then Zimri, who commanded half of the royal chariots, made plans to kill him. One day in Tirzah, Elah was getting drunk at the home of Arza, the supervisor of the palace. ¹⁰Zimri walked in and struck him down and killed him. This happened in the twenty-seventh year of King Asa's reign in Judah. Then Zimri became the next king.

¹¹Zimri immediately killed the entire royal family of Baasha, and he did not leave a single male child. He even destroyed distant relatives and friends. ¹²So Zimri destroyed the dynasty of Baasha as the LORD had promised through the prophet Jehu. ¹³This happened because of the sins of Baasha and his son Elah and because of all the sins they led Israel to commit, arousing the anger of the LORD, the God of Israel, with their idols. ¹⁴The rest of the events in Elah's reign and all his deeds are

My Daily Worship

— *March 23* —

DAFFODILS IN THE DUNG HEAP

1 KINGS 12:1–16:34

Although the pagan shrines were not completely removed, Asa remained faithful to the LORD
throughout his life. He brought into the Temple of the LORD the silver and
gold and the utensils that he and his father had dedicated (15:14–15).

[i reflect]

The key to accomplishing anything in politics is compromise. Just ask Mark Hatfield. This retired United States Senator should know. As a Christian who let his light shine in national politics, Senator Hatfield attempted to lobby for legislation that cared for the poor and oppressed, respected the rights of the individual, and reflected Judeo-Christian values.

But this veteran politician would be the first to admit that given the backdrop of a fallen world, you can't expect perfection. You have to give in to what you don't fully endorse in order to hold on to what really matters. In politics, little happens without a willingness to compromise.

King Asa understood that. In contrast to the corruption that had characterized Jewish religious life prior to his reign, he was a saint. All the same, he wasn't successful in getting rid of all the garbage that had accumulated in the Temple. Certain pagan practices and shrines remained in spite of his influence.

Still, Asa remained faithful to the Lord. He continued to worship God with a pure and undivided heart even when there was proof of heresy around him. He didn't compromise his beliefs, but he recognized that he couldn't legislate others' choices. His life was not without evidences of short-comings, but he stayed on course.

Encouraging? You bet it is. That's the kind of world you live in. Not everything in your house is in order. Like Asa, you're in process. Your marriage isn't perfect. Your kids may have turned away from their spiritual foundation. Still, you can follow after God and make progress.

Confess to the Lord your desire to stay focused on him in spite of what remains a blur around you. That type of admission is an act of worship.

[i pray]

Lord, thanks for the reminder from your Word today. I'm encouraged that you recognized spiritual
progress in Asa's life even though there wasn't perfection in his world. Give me the
determination to do what I can, and not to be derailed by what I can't. Amen.

[i respond]

Be aware of evidences of imperfection in your world today. When you notice a ding on the car door, or a scratch on the coffee table, thank the Lord that spiritual growth doesn't depend on everything being in order.

recorded in *The Book of the History of the Kings of Israel.*

ZIMRI RULES IN ISRAEL

¹⁵Zimri began to rule over Israel from Tirzah in the twenty-seventh year of King Asa's reign in Judah, but he reigned only seven days. When the army of Israel, which was then engaged in attacking the Philistine town of Gibbethon, ¹⁶heard that Zimri had assassinated the king, they chose Omri, commander of the army, as their new king. ¹⁷So Omri led the army of Israel away from Gibbethon to attack Tirzah, Israel's capital. ¹⁸When Zimri saw that the city had been taken, he went into the citadel of the king's house and burned it down over himself and died in the flames. ¹⁹For he, too, had done what was evil in the LORD's sight and followed the example of Jeroboam, continuing the sins of idolatry that Jeroboam had led Israel to commit. ²⁰The rest of the events of Zimri's reign and his conspiracy are recorded in *The Book of the History of the Kings of Israel.*

OMRI RULES IN ISRAEL

²¹But now the people of Israel were divided into two groups. Half the people tried to make Tibni son of Ginath their king, while the other half supported Omri. ²²But Omri's supporters defeated the supporters of Tibni son of Ginath. So Tibni was killed, and Omri became the next king.

²³Omri began to rule over Israel in the thirty-first year of King Asa's reign in Judah. He reigned twelve years in all, six of them in Tirzah. ²⁴Then Omri bought the hill now known as Samaria from its owner, Shemer, for 150 pounds of silver.* He built a city on it and called the city Samaria in honor of Shemer. ²⁵But Omri did what was evil in the LORD's sight, even more than any of the kings before him. ²⁶He followed the example of Jeroboam, continuing the sins of idolatry that Jeroboam had led Israel to commit. Thus, he aroused the anger of the LORD, the God of Israel. ²⁷The rest of the events in Omri's reign, the extent of his

power, and all his deeds are recorded in *The Book of the History of the Kings of Israel.* ²⁸When Omri died, he was buried in Samaria. Then his son Ahab became the next king.

AHAB RULES IN ISRAEL

²⁹Ahab son of Omri began to rule over Israel in the thirty-eighth year of King Asa's reign in Judah. He reigned in Samaria twenty-two years. ³⁰But Ahab did what was evil in the Lord's sight, even more than any of the kings before him. ³¹And as though it were not enough to live like Jeroboam, he married Jezebel, the daughter of King Ethbaal of the Sidonians, and he began to worship Baal. ³²First he built a temple and an altar for Baal in Samaria. ³³Then he set up an Asherah pole. He did more to arouse the anger of the LORD, the God of Israel, than any of the other kings of Israel before him.

³⁴It was during his reign that Hiel, a man from Bethel, rebuilt Jericho. When he laid the foundations, his oldest son, Abiram, died. And when he finally completed it by setting up the gates, his youngest son, Segub, died. This all happened according to the message from the LORD concerning Jericho spoken by Joshua son of Nun.

ELIJAH FED BY RAVENS

17 Now Elijah, who was from Tishbe in Gilead, told King Ahab, "As surely as the LORD, the God of Israel, lives—the God

---

16:24 Hebrew *for 2 talents* [68 kilograms] *of silver.*

whom I worship and serve—there will be no dew or rain during the next few years unless I give the word!"

²Then the LORD said to Elijah, ³"Go to the east and hide by Kerith Brook at a place east of where it enters the Jordan River. ⁴Drink from the brook and eat what the ravens bring you, for I have commanded them to bring you food."

⁵So Elijah did as the LORD had told him and camped beside Kerith Brook. ⁶The ravens brought him bread and meat each morning and evening, and he drank from the brook. ⁷But after a while the brook dried up, for there was no rainfall anywhere in the land.

THE WIDOW AT ZAREPHATH

⁸Then the LORD said to Elijah, ⁹"Go and live in the village of Zarephath, near the city of Sidon. There is a widow there who will feed you. I have given her my instructions."

¹⁰So he went to Zarephath. As he arrived at the gates of the village, he saw a widow gathering sticks, and he asked her, "Would you please bring me a cup of water?" ¹¹As she was going to get it, he called to her, "Bring me a bite of bread, too."

¹²But she said, "I swear by the LORD your God that I don't have a single piece of bread in the house. And I have only a handful of flour left in the jar and a little cooking oil in the bottom of the jug. I was just gathering a few sticks to cook this last meal, and then my son and I will die."

¹³But Elijah said to her, "Don't be afraid! Go ahead and cook that 'last meal,' but bake me a little loaf of bread first. Afterward there will still be enough food for you and your son. ¹⁴For this is what the LORD, the God of Israel, says: There will always be plenty of flour and oil left in your containers until the time when the LORD sends rain and the crops grow again!"

¹⁵So she did as Elijah said, and she and Elijah and her son continued to eat from her supply of flour and oil for many days. ¹⁶For no matter how much they used, there was always enough left in the containers, just as the LORD had promised through Elijah.

¹⁷Some time later, the woman's son became sick. He grew worse and worse, and finally he died. ¹⁸She then said to Elijah, "O man of God, what have you done to me? Have you come here to punish my sins by killing my son?"

¹⁹But Elijah replied, "Give me your son." And he took the boy's body from her, carried him up to the upper room, where he lived, and laid the body on his bed. ²⁰Then Elijah cried out to the LORD, "O LORD my God, why have you brought tragedy on this widow who has opened her home to me, causing her son to die?"

²¹And he stretched himself out over the child three times and cried out to the LORD, "O LORD my God, please let this child's life return to him." ²²The LORD heard Elijah's prayer, and the life of the child returned, and he came back to life! ²³Then Elijah brought him down from the upper room and gave him to his mother. "Look, your son is alive!" he said.

²⁴Then the woman told Elijah, "Now I know for sure that you are a man of God, and that the LORD truly speaks through you."

THE CONTEST ON MOUNT CARMEL

18 After many months passed, in the third year of the drought, the LORD said to Elijah, "Go and present yourself to King Ahab. Tell him that I will soon send rain!" ²So Elijah went to appear before Ahab.

Meanwhile, the famine had become very severe in Samaria. ³So Ahab summoned Obadiah, who was in charge of the palace. (Now Obadiah was a devoted follower of the LORD. ⁴Once when Jezebel had tried to kill all the LORD's prophets, Obadiah had hidden one hundred of them in two caves. He had put fifty prophets in each cave and had supplied them with food and water.) ⁵Ahab said to Obadiah, "We must check every spring and valley to see if we can find enough grass to save at least some of my horses and mules."

⁶So they divided the land between them. Ahab went one way by himself, and Obadiah went another way by himself.

⁷As Obadiah was walking along, he saw Elijah coming toward him. Obadiah recognized him at once and fell to the ground before him. "Is it really you, my lord Elijah?" he asked.

⁸"Yes, it is," Elijah replied. "Now go and tell your master I am here."

⁹"Oh, sir," Obadiah protested, "what harm have I done to you that you are sending me to my death at the hands of Ahab? ¹⁰For I swear by the LORD your God that the king has searched every nation and kingdom on earth from end to end to find you. And each time when he was told, 'Elijah isn't here,' King Ahab forced the king of that nation to swear to the truth of his claim. ¹¹And now you say, 'Go and tell your master that Elijah is here'! ¹²But as soon as I leave you, the Spirit of the LORD will carry you away to who knows where. When Ahab comes and cannot find you, he will kill me. Yet I have been a true servant of the LORD all my life. ¹³Has no one told you, my lord, about the time when Jezebel was trying to kill the LORD's prophets? I hid a hundred of them in two caves and supplied them with food and water. ¹⁴And now you say, 'Go and tell your master that Elijah is here'! Sir, if I do that, I'm as good as dead!"

¹⁵But Elijah said, "I swear by the LORD Almighty, in whose presence I stand, that I will present myself to Ahab today."

¹⁶So Obadiah went to tell Ahab that Elijah had come, and Ahab went out to meet him. ¹⁷"So it's you, is it—Israel's troublemaker?" Ahab asked when he saw him.

¹⁸"I have made no trouble for Israel," Elijah replied. "You and your family are the troublemakers, for you have refused to obey the commands of the LORD and have worshiped the images of Baal instead. ¹⁹Now bring all the people of Israel to Mount Carmel, with all 450 prophets of Baal and the 400 prophets of Asherah, who are supported by Jezebel."

²⁰So Ahab summoned all the people and the prophets to Mount Carmel. ²¹Then Elijah stood in front of them and said, "How long are you going to waver between two opinions? If the LORD is God, follow him! But if Baal is God, then follow him!" But the people were completely silent.

²²Then Elijah said to them, "I am the only prophet of the LORD who is left, but Baal has 450 prophets. ²³Now bring two bulls. The prophets of Baal may choose whichever one they wish and cut it into pieces and lay it on the wood of their altar, but without setting fire to it. I will prepare the other bull and lay it on the wood on the altar, but not set fire to it. ²⁴Then call on the name of your god, and I will call on the name of the LORD. The god who answers by setting fire to the wood is the true God!" And all the people agreed.

²⁵Then Elijah said to the prophets of Baal, "You go first, for there are many of you. Choose one of the bulls and prepare it and call on the name of your god. But do not set fire to the wood."

²⁶So they prepared one of the bulls and placed it on the altar. Then they called on the name of Baal all morning, shouting, "O Baal, answer us!" But there was no reply of any kind. Then they danced wildly around the altar they had made.

²⁷About noontime Elijah began mocking them. "You'll have to shout louder," he scoffed, "for surely he is a god! Perhaps he is deep in thought, or he is relieving himself. Or maybe he is away on a trip, or he is asleep and needs to be wakened!"

²⁸So they shouted louder, and following their normal custom, they cut themselves with knives and swords until the blood gushed out. ²⁹They raved all afternoon until the time of the evening sacrifice, but still there was no reply, no voice, no answer.

³⁰Then Elijah called to the people, "Come over here!" They all crowded around him as he repaired the altar of the LORD that had been torn down. ³¹He took twelve stones, one

My Daily Worship

— *March 24* —

IT'S TIME TO CHOOSE

1 KINGS 17:1–19:21

Then Elijah stood in front of them and said, "How long are you going to waver
between two opinions? If the LORD is God, follow him! But if Baal is God,
then follow him!" But the people were completely silent (18:21).

[i reflect]

Living in a democracy, we have the privilege of expressing our opinions through the ballot box every year. Yet, in the most recent presidential election, only 51 percent of all registered voters cared enough to exercise this right. It's tempting to think that one vote doesn't really count, but history proves otherwise:

- In 1776, one vote gave America the English language instead of the German language.

- In 1868, one vote saved President Andrew Johnson from impeachment.

- In 1941, one vote preserved the draft just twelve weeks before the Japanese attack on Pearl Harbor.

- In 1960, Richard Nixon lost the presidential election and John F. Kennedy won it by less than one vote per precinct in the United States.

Although it wasn't an election, the people of Israel had to make a choice. Elijah had given them all the facts. They were capable of making the right choice but they remained silent. They couldn't bring themselves to choose. Yet, with their silence they voted. Only after Elijah called on the Lord to demonstrate his power in dramatic ways did his apathetic audience weigh in.

God will not accept the role of default deity. He will not share recognition or position with any other god. The role of God, by definition, fits only One. Those who do not decide *for* God are automatically voting *against* him, even if they haven't decided exactly for whom they are voting. The consequences for those who refuse to choose God are the same as for those who choose against him.

As was the case with the ancient Israelites, God has given you adequate proof that he has the right to rule in your life. Every day you're given a chance to affirm his leadership. It's not as difficult as you might think. Submit your agenda to him in prayer. Express your willingness for him to overrule your plans. With gratitude in your heart, be proactive in your praise today. There's no need to wait for someone to ask who you will follow.

[i pray]

Lord, I want to be quick in my confession of dependence on you. I also want to be immediately
responsive when you indicate to me something I should say or do. Unlike those who
waiver in their commitment, I want to be known as a loyal supporter.

[i respond]

Come up with a clever slogan that announces you are a follower of the Lord. Use it to create your own campaign button (i.e., "He's got my vote!" or "I'm a loyal follower!"). Wear it during your designated time of worship each day.

to represent each of the tribes of Israel,* ³²and he used the stones to rebuild the LORD's altar. Then he dug a trench around the altar large enough to hold about three gallons.* ³³He piled wood on the altar, cut the bull into pieces, and laid the pieces on the wood. Then he said, "Fill four large jars with water, and pour the water over the offering and the wood." After they had done this, ³⁴he said, "Do the same thing again!" And when they were finished, he said, "Now do it a third time!" So they did as he said, ³⁵and the water ran around the altar and even overflowed the trench.

³⁶At the customary time for offering the evening sacrifice, Elijah the prophet walked up to the altar and prayed, "O LORD, God of Abraham, Isaac, and Jacob,* prove today that you are God in Israel and that I am your servant. Prove that I have done all this at your command. ³⁷O LORD, answer me! Answer me so these people will know that you, O LORD, are God and that you have brought them back to yourself."

³⁸Immediately the fire of the LORD flashed down from heaven and burned up the young bull, the wood, the stones, and the dust. It even licked up all the water in the ditch! ³⁹And when the people saw it, they fell on their faces and cried out, "The LORD is God! The LORD is God!"

⁴⁰Then Elijah commanded, "Seize all the prophets of Baal. Don't let a single one escape!" So the people seized them all, and Elijah took them down to the Kishon Valley and killed them there.

ELIJAH PRAYS FOR RAIN

⁴¹Then Elijah said to Ahab, "Go and enjoy a good meal! For I hear a mighty rainstorm coming!"

⁴²So Ahab prepared a feast. But Elijah climbed to the top of Mount Carmel and fell to the ground and prayed. ⁴³Then he said to his servant, "Go and look out toward the sea."

The servant went and looked, but he returned to Elijah and said, "I didn't see anything." Seven times Elijah told him to go and look, and seven times he went. ⁴⁴Finally the seventh time, his servant told him, "I saw a little cloud about the size of a hand rising from the sea."

Then Elijah shouted, "Hurry to Ahab and tell him, 'Climb into your chariot and go back home. If you don't hurry, the rain will stop you!' "

⁴⁵And sure enough, the sky was soon black with clouds. A heavy wind brought a terrific rainstorm, and Ahab left quickly for Jezreel. ⁴⁶Now the LORD gave special strength to Elijah. He tucked his cloak into his belt and ran ahead of Ahab's chariot all the way to the entrance of Jezreel.

ELIJAH FLEES TO SINAI

19 When Ahab got home, he told Jezebel what Elijah had done and that he had slaughtered the prophets of Baal. ²So Jezebel sent this message to Elijah: "May the gods also kill me if by this time tomorrow I have failed to take your life like those whom you killed."

³Elijah was afraid and fled for his life. He went to Beersheba, a town in Judah, and he left his servant there. ⁴Then he went on alone into the desert, traveling all day. He sat down under a solitary broom tree and prayed that he might die. "I have had enough, LORD," he said. "Take my life, for I am no better than my ancestors."

⁵Then he lay down and slept under the broom tree. But as he was sleeping, an angel touched him and told him, "Get up and eat!" ⁶He looked around and saw some bread baked on hot stones and a jar of water! So he ate and drank and lay down again.

⁷Then the angel of the LORD came again and touched him and said, "Get up and eat some more, for there is a long journey ahead of you."

⁸So he got up and ate and drank, and the food gave him enough strength to travel forty

18:31 Hebrew *each of the tribes of the sons of Jacob to whom the LORD had said, "Your name will be Israel."* 18:32 Hebrew *2 seahs* [12 liters] *of seed.* 18:36 Hebrew *and Israel.*

Words of Worship

REJOICE

Rejoice, Joy—Hebrew *sa-me-ach* "be joyful"; *sim-chah* "joy"; *gil* "to dance" (in a circle); Greek *chai-ro* "rejoice"; *cha-ra* "joy." The same words are used for being glad.

The Scriptures say much about rejoicing and being happy in the Lord. Sometimes it's almost a command: "O worshipers of the LORD, rejoice!" (Psalm 105:3). It's our duty, as the Lord's worshipers, to rejoice just because he wants us to. Even if we don't feel like it, we can do it to obey him. This is not a matter of feelings but of *action;* one of the biblical words for rejoicing actually means "to dance around."

What does rejoicing do for us? It takes us out of ourselves, redirecting our attention to how wonderful God is and what he has done for his people. It puts Jesus' love into the center of our thoughts. It brings healing to our wounded souls. Sometimes rejoicing is difficult when life isn't going well. We get so preoccupied with our problems that we forget to be joyful. But Paul urged Christians to a life of rejoicing. "Always be full of joy in the Lord. I say it again—rejoice!" (Philippians 4:4). He knew he'd have to tell some of us twice.

days and forty nights to Mount Sinai,* the mountain of God. ⁹There he came to a cave, where he spent the night.

THE LORD SPEAKS TO ELIJAH

But the LORD said to him, "What are you doing here, Elijah?"

¹⁰Elijah replied, "I have zealously served the LORD God Almighty. But the people of Israel

19:8 Hebrew *Horeb*, another name for Sinai.

have broken their covenant with you, torn down your altars, and killed every one of your prophets. I alone am left, and now they are trying to kill me, too."

¹¹"Go out and stand before me on the mountain," the LORD told him. And as Elijah stood there, the LORD passed by, and a mighty windstorm hit the mountain. It was such a terrible blast that the rocks were torn loose, but the LORD was not in the wind. After the wind there was an earthquake, but the LORD was not in the earthquake. ¹²And after the earthquake there was a fire, but the LORD was not in the fire. And after the fire there was the sound of a gentle whisper. ¹³When Elijah heard it, he wrapped his face in his cloak and went out and stood at the entrance of the cave.

And a voice said, "What are you doing here, Elijah?"

¹⁴He replied again, "I have zealously served the LORD God Almighty. But the people of Israel have broken their covenant with you, torn down your altars, and killed every one of your prophets. I alone am left, and now they are trying to kill me, too."

¹⁵Then the LORD told him, "Go back the way you came, and travel to the wilderness of Damascus. When you arrive there, anoint Hazael to be king of Aram. ¹⁶Then anoint Jehu son of Nimshi to be king of Israel, and anoint Elisha son of Shaphat from Abel-meholah to replace you as my prophet. ¹⁷Anyone who escapes from Hazael will be killed by Jehu, and those who escape Jehu will be killed by Elisha! ¹⁸Yet I will preserve seven thousand others in Israel who have never bowed to Baal or kissed him!"

THE CALL OF ELISHA

¹⁹So Elijah went and found Elisha son of Shaphat plowing a field with a team of oxen. There were eleven teams of oxen ahead of him, and he was plowing with the twelfth team. Elijah went over to him and threw his cloak across his shoulders and walked away

again. ²⁰Elisha left the oxen standing there, ran after Elijah, and said to him, "First let me go and kiss my father and mother good-bye, and then I will go with you!"

Elijah replied, "Go on back! But consider what I have done to you."

²¹Elisha then returned to his oxen, killed them, and used the wood from the plow to build a fire to roast their flesh. He passed around the meat to the other plowmen, and they all ate. Then he went with Elijah as his assistant.

BEN-HADAD ATTACKS SAMARIA

20 Now King Ben-hadad of Aram mobilized his army, supported by the chariots and horses of thirty-two allied kings. They went to besiege Samaria, the Israelite capital, and launched attacks against it. ²Ben-hadad sent messengers into the city to relay this message to King Ahab of Israel: "This is what Ben-hadad says: ³'Your silver and gold are mine, and so are the best of your wives and children!'"

⁴"All right, my lord," Ahab replied. "All that I have is yours!"

⁵Soon Ben-hadad's messengers returned again and said, "This is what Ben-hadad says: 'I have already demanded that you give me your silver, gold, wives, and children. ⁶But about this time tomorrow I will send my officials to search your palace and the homes of your people. They will take away everything you consider valuable!'"

⁷Then Ahab summoned all the leaders of the land and said to them, "Look how this man is stirring up trouble! I already agreed when he sent the message demanding that I give him my wives and children and silver and gold."

⁸"Don't give in to any more demands," the leaders and people advised.

⁹So Ahab told the messengers from Ben-hadad, "Say this to my lord the king: 'I will give you everything you asked for the first time, but this last demand of yours I simply cannot meet.'" So the messengers returned to Ben-hadad with the response.

¹⁰Then Ben-hadad sent this message to Ahab: "May the gods bring tragedy on me, and even worse than that, if there remains enough dust from Samaria to provide more than a handful for each of my soldiers."

¹¹The king of Israel sent back this answer: "A warrior still dressing for battle should not boast like a warrior who has already won."

¹²This reply of Ahab's reached Ben-hadad and the other kings as they were drinking in their tents.* "Prepare to attack!" Ben-hadad commanded his officers. So they prepared to attack the city.

AHAB'S VICTORY OVER BEN-HADAD

¹³Then a prophet came to see King Ahab and told him, "This is what the LORD says: Do you see all these enemy forces? Today I will hand them all over to you. Then you will know that I am the LORD."

¹⁴Ahab asked, "How will he do it?"

And the prophet replied, "This is what the LORD says: The troops of the provincial commanders will do it."

"Should we attack first?" Ahab asked.

"Yes," the prophet answered.

¹⁵So Ahab mustered the troops of the 232 provincial commanders. Then he called out the rest of his army of seven thousand men. ¹⁶About noontime, as Ben-hadad and the thirty-two allied kings were still in their tents getting drunk, ¹⁷the troops of the provincial commanders marched out of the city. As they approached, Ben-hadad's scouts reported to him, "Some troops are coming from Samaria."

¹⁸"Take them alive," Ben-hadad commanded, "whether they have come for peace or for war."

¹⁹But by now Ahab's provincial commanders had led the army out to fight. ²⁰Each Israelite soldier killed his Aramean opponent, and suddenly the entire Aramean army panicked and fled. The Israelites chased them, but King

20:12 Or *in Succoth;* also in 20:16.

Ben-hadad and a few others escaped on horses. [21]However, the other horses and chariots were destroyed, and the Arameans were killed in a great slaughter.

[22]Afterward the prophet said to King Ahab, "Get ready for another attack by the king of Aram next spring."

BEN-HADAD'S SECOND ATTACK

[23]After their defeat, Ben-hadad's officers said to him, "The Israelite gods are gods of the hills; that is why they won. But we can beat them easily on the plains. [24]Only this time replace the kings with field commanders! [25]Recruit another army like the one you lost. Give us the same number of horses, chariots, and men, and we will fight against them in the plains. There's not a shadow of a doubt that we will beat them." So King Ben-hadad did as they suggested. [26]The following spring he called up the Aramean army and marched out against Israel, this time at Aphek. [27]Israel then mustered its army, set up supply lines, and moved into the battle. But the Israelite army looked like two little flocks of goats in comparison to the vast Aramean forces that filled the countryside!

[28]Then the man of God went to the king of Israel and said, "This is what the LORD says: The Arameans have said that the LORD is a god of the hills and not of the plains. So I will help you defeat this vast army. Then you will know that I am the LORD."

[29]The two armies camped opposite each other for seven days, and on the seventh day the battle began. The Israelites killed 100,000 Aramean foot soldiers in one day. [30]The rest fled behind the walls of Aphek, but the wall fell on them and killed another 27,000. Ben-hadad fled into the city and hid in a secret room. [31]Ben-hadad's officers said to him, "Sir, we have heard that the kings of Israel are very merciful. So let's humble ourselves by wearing sackcloth and putting ropes on our heads. Then perhaps King Ahab will let you live."

[32]So they put on sackcloth and ropes and went to the king of Israel and begged, "Your servant Ben-hadad says, 'Please let me live!'"

The king of Israel responded, "Is he still alive? He is my brother!"

[33]The men were quick to grasp at this straw of hope, and they replied, "Yes, your brother Ben-hadad!"

"Go and get him," the king of Israel told them. And when Ben-hadad arrived, Ahab invited him up into his chariot!

[34]Ben-hadad told him, "I will give back the towns my father took from your father, and you may establish places of trade in Damascus, as my father did in Samaria."

Then Ahab said, "I will let you go under these conditions." So they made a treaty, and Ben-hadad was set free.

A PROPHET CONDEMNS AHAB

[35]Meanwhile, the LORD instructed one of the group of prophets to say to another man, "Strike me!" But the man refused to strike the prophet. [36]Then the prophet told him, "Because you have not obeyed the voice of the LORD, a lion will kill you as soon as you leave me." And sure enough, when he had gone, a lion attacked and killed him.

[37]Then the prophet turned to another man and said, "Strike me!" So he struck the prophet and wounded him.

[38]The prophet waited for the king beside the road, having placed a bandage over his eyes to disguise himself. [39]As the king passed by, the prophet called out to him, "Sir, I was in the battle, and a man brought me a prisoner. He said, 'Guard this man; if for any reason he gets away, you will either die or pay a fine of seventy-five pounds* of silver!' [40]But while I was busy doing something else, the prisoner disappeared!"

"Well, it's your own fault," the king replied. "You have determined your own judgment."

[41]Then the prophet pulled the bandage from his eyes, and the king of Israel recognized him as one of the prophets. [42]And the prophet told him, "This is what the LORD says: Because you

20:39 Hebrew *1 talent* [34 kilograms].

have spared the man I said must be destroyed,* now you must die in his place, and your people will die instead of his people." ⁴³So the king of Israel went home to Samaria angry and sullen.

NABOTH'S VINEYARD

21 King Ahab had a palace in Jezreel, and near the palace was a vineyard owned by a man named Naboth. ²One day Ahab said to Naboth, "Since your vineyard is so convenient to the palace, I would like to buy it to use as a vegetable garden. I will give you a better vineyard in exchange, or if you prefer, I will pay you for it."

³But Naboth replied, "The LORD forbid that I should give you the inheritance that was passed down by my ancestors." ⁴So Ahab went home angry and sullen because of Naboth's answer. The king went to bed with his face to the wall and refused to eat!

⁵"What in the world is the matter?" his wife, Jezebel, asked him. "What has made you so upset that you are not eating?"

⁶"I asked Naboth to sell me his vineyard or to trade it, and he refused!" Ahab told her.

⁷"Are you the king of Israel or not?" Jezebel asked. "Get up and eat and don't worry about it. I'll get you Naboth's vineyard!"

⁸So she wrote letters in Ahab's name, sealed them with his seal, and sent them to the elders and other leaders of the city where Naboth lived. ⁹In her letters she commanded: "Call the citizens together for fasting and prayer and give Naboth a place of honor. ¹⁰Find two scoundrels* who will accuse him of cursing God and the king. Then take him out and stone him to death."

¹¹So the elders and other leaders followed the instructions Jezebel had written in the letters. ¹²They called for a fast and put Naboth at a prominent place before the people. ¹³Then two scoundrels accused him before all the people of cursing God and the king. So he was dragged outside the city and stoned to death. ¹⁴The city officials then sent word to

Jezebel, "Naboth has been stoned to death."

¹⁵When Jezebel heard the news, she said to Ahab, "You know the vineyard Naboth wouldn't sell you? Well, you can have it now! He's dead!" ¹⁶So Ahab immediately went down to the vineyard to claim it.

¹⁷But the LORD said to Elijah, who was from Tishbe, ¹⁸"Go down to meet King Ahab, who rules in Samaria. He will be at Naboth's vineyard in Jezreel, taking possession of it. ¹⁹Give him this message: 'This is what the LORD says: Isn't killing Naboth bad enough? Must you rob him, too? Because you have done this, dogs will lick your blood outside the city just as they licked the blood of Naboth!' "

²⁰"So my enemy has found me!" Ahab exclaimed to Elijah.

"Yes," Elijah answered, "I have come because you have sold yourself to what is evil in the LORD's sight. ²¹The LORD is going to bring disaster to you and sweep you away. He will not let a single one of your male descendants, slave or free alike, survive in Israel! ²²He is going to destroy your family as he did the family of Jeroboam son of Nebat and the family of Baasha son of Ahijah, for you have made him very angry and have led all of Israel into sin. ²³The LORD has also told me that the dogs of Jezreel will eat the body of your wife, Jezebel, at the city wall. ²⁴The members of your family who die in the city will be eaten by dogs, and those who die in the field will be eaten by vultures."

²⁵No one else so completely sold himself to what was evil in the LORD's sight as did Ahab, for his wife, Jezebel, influenced him. ²⁶He was especially guilty because he worshiped idols just as the Amorites had done—the people whom the LORD had driven from the land ahead of the Israelites.

²⁷When Ahab heard this message, he tore his clothing, dressed in sackcloth, and fasted. He even slept in sackcloth and went about in deep mourning.

²⁸Then another message from the LORD

20:42 The Hebrew term used here refers to the complete consecration of things or people to the LORD, either by destroying them or by giving them as an offering.   21:10 Hebrew *two sons of Belial;* also in 21:13.

My Daily Worship

— *March 25* —

WHEN GOD SPEAKS, LISTEN!

1 KINGS 20:1–22:53

When Ahab heard this message, he tore his clothing, dressed in sackcloth, and fasted.
He even slept in sackcloth and went about in deep mourning (21:27).

[i reflect]

Back in the seventies E. F. Hutton, a well-known investment firm, took to the airwaves with a successful marketing campaign. It called attention to how much stock Hutton investors put in their broker's advice. The popular tag line to the television ads was this: "When E. F. Hutton speaks, people listen!"

Who's to say how accurate those commercials were? One thing we do know for sure is that when our E (Everlasting) F (Father) God speaks, even those who are not accustomed to hearing his voice, listen up. Ahab is a case in point. When approached by Elijah with a word from the Lord, this wicked king from Samaria humbled himself. God's disapproval with Ahab's past behavior was obvious. The Lord had succeeded in getting Ahab's attention. Unfortunately for this Machiavellian monarch, his humility was short-lived.

We are so grateful that God still speaks. Unwilling to let us wander off into a spiritual wasteland, he holds a mirror to our faces. In lieu of Elijah, he sometimes uses the prophetic voice of a pastor or friend. But more often than not, you hear him speaking through the pages of the Bible.

Have you heard that familiar voice yet today? More than likely it will require silencing the din of daily activities. Easier said than done, right? Babies need changing. Kids need to be fed. Deadlines need to be met. But hearing from One who has your best interests at heart is worth finding the time. All it takes is five minutes to center down and listen up. Go ahead and cup your ear for your Father's voice.

[i pray]

Lord, I'm grateful that prayer is not one-way communication. It's comforting to know
that you hear me when I bring my requests to you. It's encouraging that you take
delight in directing my steps and confronting my sin. As I pause before
you in silence, I await the whisper of your presence. Amen.

[i respond]

Carve out five minutes today to spend in an undistracted place, with your Bible and a notebook. Jot down what you think the Lord is saying to you about applying the passage you've just read.

came to Elijah, who was from Tishbe: [29]"Do you see how Ahab has humbled himself before me? Because he has done this, I will not do what I promised during his lifetime. It will happen to his sons; I will destroy all his descendants."

Jehoshaphat and Ahab

22 For three years there was no war between Aram and Israel. [2]Then during the third year, King Jehoshaphat of Judah went to visit King Ahab of Israel. [3]During the visit, Ahab said to his officials, "Do you realize that the Arameans are still occupying our city of Ramoth-gilead? And we haven't done a thing about it!" [4]Then he turned to Jehoshaphat and asked, "Will you join me in fighting against Ramoth-gilead?"

And Jehoshaphat replied to King Ahab, "Why, of course! You and I are brothers, and my troops are yours to command. Even my horses are at your service." [5]Then Jehoshaphat added, "But first let's find out what the LORD says."

[6]So King Ahab summoned his prophets, about four hundred of them, and asked them, "Should I go to war against Ramoth-gilead or not?"

They all replied, "Go right ahead! The Lord will give you a glorious victory!"

[7]But Jehoshaphat asked, "Isn't there a prophet of the LORD around, too? I would like to ask him the same question."

[8]King Ahab replied, "There is still one prophet of the LORD, but I hate him. He never prophesies anything but bad news for me! His name is Micaiah son of Imlah."

"You shouldn't talk like that," Jehoshaphat said. "Let's hear what he has to say."

[9]So the king of Israel called one of his officials and said, "Quick! Go and get Micaiah son of Imlah."

Micaiah Prophesies against Ahab

[10]King Ahab of Israel and King Jehoshaphat of Judah, dressed in their royal robes, were sitting on thrones at the threshing floor near the gate of Samaria. All of Ahab's prophets were prophesying there in front of them. [11]One of them, Zedekiah son of Kenaanah, made some iron horns and proclaimed, "This is what the LORD says: With these horns you will gore the Arameans to death!"

[12]All the other prophets agreed. "Yes," they said, "go up to Ramoth-gilead and be victorious, for the LORD will give you victory!"

[13]Meanwhile, the messenger who went to get Micaiah said to him, "Look, all the prophets are promising victory for the king. Be sure that you agree with them and promise success."

[14]But Micaiah replied, "As surely as the LORD lives, I will say only what the LORD tells me to say."

[15]When Micaiah arrived before the king, Ahab asked him, "Micaiah, should we go to war against Ramoth-gilead or not?"

And Micaiah replied, "Go right ahead! The LORD will give the king a glorious victory!"

[16]But the king replied sharply, "How many times must I demand that you speak only the truth when you speak for the LORD?"

[17]So Micaiah told him, "In a vision I saw all Israel scattered on the mountains, like sheep without a shepherd. And the LORD said, 'Their master has been killed. Send them home in peace.'"

[18]"Didn't I tell you?" the king of Israel said to Jehoshaphat. "He does it every time. He never prophesies anything but bad news for me."

[19]Then Micaiah continued, "Listen to what the LORD says! I saw the LORD sitting on his throne with all the armies of heaven around him, on his right and on his left. [20]And the LORD said, 'Who can entice Ahab to go into battle against Ramoth-gilead so that he can be killed there?' There were many suggestions, [21]until finally a spirit approached the LORD and said, 'I can do it!'

[22]" 'How will you do this?' the LORD asked.

"And the spirit replied, 'I will go out and inspire all Ahab's prophets to speak lies.'

" 'You will succeed,' said the LORD. 'Go ahead and do it.'

²³"So you see, the LORD has put a lying spirit in the mouths of your prophets. For the LORD has determined disaster for you."

²⁴Then Zedekiah son of Kenaanah walked up to Micaiah and slapped him across the face. "When did the Spirit of the LORD leave me to speak to you?" he demanded.

²⁵And Micaiah replied, "You will find out soon enough when you find yourself hiding in some secret room!"

²⁶King Ahab of Israel then ordered, "Arrest Micaiah and take him back to Amon, the governor of the city, and to my son Joash. ²⁷Give them this order from the king: 'Put this man in prison, and feed him nothing but bread and water until I return safely from the battle!'"

²⁸But Micaiah replied, "If you return safely, the LORD has not spoken through me!" Then he added to those standing around, "Take note of what I have said."

THE DEATH OF AHAB

²⁹So the king of Israel and King Jehoshaphat of Judah led their armies against Ramoth-gilead. ³⁰Now King Ahab said to Jehoshaphat, "As we go into battle, I will disguise myself so no one will recognize me, but you wear your royal robes." So Ahab disguised himself, and they went into battle.

³¹Now the king of Aram had issued these orders to his thirty-two charioteers: "Attack only the king of Israel!" ³²So when the Aramean charioteers saw Jehoshaphat in his royal robes, they went after him. "There is the king of Israel!" they shouted. But when Jehoshaphat cried out, ³³the charioteers realized he was not the king of Israel, and they stopped chasing him.

³⁴An Aramean soldier, however, randomly shot an arrow at the Israelite troops, and the arrow hit the king of Israel between the joints of his armor. "Get me out of here!" Ahab groaned to the driver of his chariot. "I have been badly wounded!" ³⁵The battle raged all that day, and Ahab was propped up in his chariot facing the Arameans. The blood from his wound ran down to the floor of his chariot, and as evening arrived he died. ³⁶Just as the sun was setting, the cry ran through his troops: "It's all over—return home!" ³⁷So the king died, and his body was taken to Samaria and buried there. ³⁸Then his chariot was washed beside the pool of Samaria, where the prostitutes bathed, and dogs came and licked the king's blood, just as the LORD had promised.

³⁹The rest of the events in Ahab's reign and the story of the ivory palace and the cities he built are recorded in *The Book of the History of the Kings of Israel.* ⁴⁰When Ahab died, he was buried among his ancestors. Then his son Ahaziah became the next king.

JEHOSHAPHAT RULES IN JUDAH

⁴¹Jehoshaphat son of Asa began to rule over Judah in the fourth year of King Ahab's reign in Israel. ⁴²He was thirty-five years old when he became king, and he reigned in Jerusalem twenty-five years. His mother was Azubah, the daughter of Shilhi. ⁴³Jehoshaphat was a good king, following the example of his father, Asa. He did what was pleasing in the LORD's sight. During his reign, however, he failed to remove all the pagan shrines, and the people still offered sacrifices and burned incense there. ⁴⁴Jehoshaphat also made peace with the king of Israel.

⁴⁵The rest of the events in Jehoshaphat's reign, the extent of his power, and the wars he waged are recorded in *The Book of the History of the Kings of Judah.* ⁴⁶He banished from the land the rest of the shrine prostitutes, who still continued their practices from the days of his father, Asa. ⁴⁷There was no king in Edom at that time, only a deputy.

⁴⁸Jehoshaphat also built a fleet of trading ships* to sail to Ophir for gold. But the ships never set sail, for they were wrecked at Ezion-geber. ⁴⁹At that time Ahaziah son of Ahab proposed to Jehoshaphat, "Let my men sail an

22:48 Hebrew *fleet of ships of Tarshish.*

expedition with your men." But Jehoshaphat refused the offer.

⁵⁰When Jehoshaphat died, he was buried with his ancestors in the City of David. Then his son Jehoram became the next king.

AHAZIAH RULES IN ISRAEL

⁵¹Ahaziah son of Ahab began to rule over Israel in the seventeenth year of King Jehoshaphat's reign in Judah. He reigned in Samaria two years. ⁵²But he did what was evil in the LORD's sight, following the example of his father and mother and the example of Jeroboam son of Nebat, who had led Israel into the sin of idolatry. ⁵³He served Baal and worshiped him, arousing the anger of the LORD, the God of Israel, just as his father had done.

2 Kings

You alone are God of all the kingdoms of the earth (19:15).

Have You Made the Right Choice?

American presidential history is rich in detail. The story of George Washington chopping down a cherry tree is as vivid in many school children's minds as Lincoln's address at Gettysburg. We have preserved a host of personal trivia of our leaders' lives, as well as records of their stance on every political issue of import. In the same manner, the book of 2 Kings preserves a history of those who ruled from the thrones of the divided kingdoms of Judah and Israel. We don't find much detail about their personal or political life. Instead, the book remembers each king for a single personal choice regarding one pivotal issue—worship.

The stories of good kings, like the boy-king Joash who chose to worship God alone, are scarce. But the record of ruler after ruler who flagrantly chose to worship false gods is overwhelming. Even the prophet Elisha (who performed more recorded miracles than any other person in the Old Testament) could not dissuade the people from following along with their leaders' disastrous decisions during the crucial years before the Babylonians and Assyrians took God's people captive.

God could have forced singular devotion on his people. He could have demanded their allegiance. But God withholds his divine right to dominion when it comes to the domain of our hearts. Although he alone is worthy and deserving of our worship, this book reminds us that God permits us to come to that critical conclusion on our own.

Like the kings in this book, when future generations ponder our own personal history, they may look at much of our lives as insignificant. The daily decisions and details of our past will seem trivial. However, regarding what and whom we chose to worship—our life's devotion—that alone is noteworthy. Will they see we made the right choice? God has left the answer up to us.

Worship Moments

- Jehoiada, the priest, established young Joash as the rightful king of Judah, the southern kingdom. Years later, they worked together to restore worship of God in the Temple (11:4–12:16).

- The fall of Israel, the northern kingdom, was the direct result of Israel's worship of idols instead of the one true God (17:7–23).

- After the reign of evil king Manasseh, King Josiah once again restored the worship of God, which included the reading of God's Law and celebrating Passover (22:1–23:28).

- In this book God is praised as "the LORD Almighty" (3:14; 19:31); "the living God" (19:4, 16; cf. 2:2, 4, 6; 3:14; 4:30; 5:16, 20); and "God of all the kingdoms of the earth" (19:15).

ELIJAH CONFRONTS KING AHAZIAH

1 After King Ahab's death, the nation of Moab declared its independence from Israel.

²One day Israel's new king, Ahaziah, fell through the latticework of an upper room at his palace in Samaria, and he was seriously injured. So he sent messengers to the temple of Baal-zebub, the god of Ekron, to ask whether he would recover.

³But the angel of the LORD told Elijah, who was from Tishbe, "Go and meet the messengers of the king of Samaria and ask them, 'Why are you going to Baal-zebub, the god of Ekron, to ask whether the king will get well? Is there no God in Israel? ⁴Now, therefore, this is what the LORD says: You will never leave the bed on which you are lying, but you will surely die.'" So Elijah went to deliver the message.

⁵When the messengers returned to the king, he asked them, "Why have you returned so soon?"

⁶They replied, "A man came up to us and said, 'Go back to the king and give him this message from the LORD: Why are you sending men to Baal-zebub, the god of Ekron, to ask whether you will get well? Is there no God in Israel? Now, since you have done this, you will never leave the bed on which you are lying, but you will surely die.'"

⁷"Who was this man?" the king demanded. "What did he look like?"

⁸They replied, "He was a hairy man,* and he wore a leather belt around his waist."

"It was Elijah from Tishbe!" the king exclaimed. ⁹Then he sent an army captain with fifty soldiers to arrest him. They found him sitting on top of a hill. The captain said to him, "Man of God, the king has commanded you to come along with us."

¹⁰But Elijah replied to the captain, "If I am a man of God, let fire come down from heaven and destroy you and your fifty men!" Then fire fell from heaven and killed them all.

¹¹So the king sent another captain with fifty men. The captain said to him, "Man of God, the king says that you must come down right away."

¹²Elijah replied, "If I am a man of God, let fire come down from heaven and destroy you and your fifty men!" And again the fire of God fell from heaven and killed them all.

¹³Once more the king sent a captain with fifty men. But this time the captain fell to his knees before Elijah. He pleaded with him, "O man of God, please spare my life and the lives of these, your fifty servants. ¹⁴See how the fire from heaven has destroyed the first two groups. But now please spare my life!"

¹⁵Then the angel of the LORD said to Elijah, "Don't be afraid. Go with him." So Elijah got up and went to the king.

¹⁶And Elijah said to the king, "This is what the LORD says: Why did you send messengers to Baal-zebub, the god of Ekron, to ask whether you will get well? Is there no God in Israel? Now, since you have done this, you will never leave the bed on which you are lying, but you will surely die."

¹⁷So Ahaziah died, just as the LORD had promised through Elijah. Since Ahaziah did not have a son to succeed him, his brother Joram* became the next king. This took place in the second year of the reign of Jehoram son of Jehoshaphat, king of Judah. ¹⁸The rest of the events in Ahaziah's reign are recorded in *The Book of the History of the Kings of Israel.*

ELIJAH TAKEN INTO HEAVEN

2 When the LORD was about to take Elijah up to heaven in a whirlwind, Elijah and Elisha were traveling from Gilgal. ²And Elijah said to Elisha, "Stay here, for the LORD has told me to go to Bethel."

But Elisha replied, "As surely as the LORD lives and you yourself live, I will never leave you!" So they went on together to Bethel.

³The group of prophets from Bethel came to Elisha and asked him, "Did you know that

1:8 Or *He was wearing clothing made of hair.* 1:17 Hebrew *Jehoram,* a variant name for Joram.

FAST, FASTING

Fast, Fasting—Hebrew *tsum* "to fast"; *tsom* "a fast, fasting"; Greek *ne-**steu**-o* "to fast"; *ne-**stei**-a* "a fast, fasting."

Saints of all ages have practiced fasting, abstaining from food in varying degrees for a period of time while devoting themselves to prayer. Self-denial is a worthy contrast to the world's pressure to consume—to be full of food and full of ourselves. The tendency is to think that we are more righteous than others because we practice certain disciplines. But the record of the heroes and heroines of our faith shows that those who have consistently fasted have been most conscious of their own unworthiness before God and most aware of his purpose in their lives.

To fast is to tell the Lord what he already knows, but we tend to forget: Our bodies, along with our time, are not our own to do with as we please. They are his, for he gave them to us, and our urges do not rule over us as they do those whom Paul described, "Their god is their appetite . . . and all they think about is this life here on earth" (Philippians 3:19). Instead, by fasting we recognize that our body is the temple of the Spirit of God, a sanctuary devoted to exalting his name.

Scripture teaches that the earnest prayers of the righteous get results (James 5:16). Does our fasting give us greater leverage with God than simple prayer? Trying to coerce God into answering our prayers, by any means, is more like magic than faith! God is sovereign, and our prayers are best answered when we ask according to his purposes (1 John 5:14). But if fasting heightens our sensitivity to the voice of the Spirit, we will pray more effectively—and see the results God wants!

---

the LORD is going to take your master away from you today?"

"Quiet!" Elisha answered. "Of course I know it."

⁴Then Elijah said to Elisha, "Stay here, for the LORD has told me to go to Jericho."

But Elisha replied again, "As surely as the LORD lives and you yourself live, I will never leave you." So they went on together to Jericho.

⁵Then the group of prophets from Jericho came to Elisha and asked him, "Did you know that the LORD is going to take your master away from you today?"

"Quiet!" he answered again. "Of course I know it."

⁶Then Elijah said to Elisha, "Stay here, for the LORD has told me to go to the Jordan River."

But again Elisha replied, "As surely as the LORD lives and you yourself live, I will never leave you." So they went on together.

⁷Fifty men from the group of prophets also went and watched from a distance as Elijah and Elisha stopped beside the Jordan River. ⁸Then Elijah folded his cloak together and struck the water with it. The river divided, and the two of them went across on dry ground!

⁹When they came to the other side, Elijah said to Elisha, "What can I do for you before I am taken away?"

And Elisha replied, "Please let me become your rightful successor."*

¹⁰"You have asked a difficult thing," Elijah replied. "If you see me when I am taken from you, then you will get your request. But if not, then you won't."

¹¹As they were walking along and talking, suddenly a chariot of fire appeared, drawn by horses of fire. It drove between them, separating them, and Elijah was carried by a whirlwind into heaven. ¹²Elisha saw it and cried out, "My father! My father! The chariots and charioteers of Israel!" And as they disappeared from sight, Elisha tore his robe in two.

¹³Then Elisha picked up Elijah's cloak and

2:9 Hebrew *Let me inherit a double share of your spirit.*

returned to the bank of the Jordan River. ¹⁴He struck the water with the cloak and cried out, "Where is the LORD, the God of Elijah?" Then the river divided, and Elisha went across.

¹⁵When the group of prophets from Jericho saw what happened, they exclaimed, "Elisha has become Elijah's successor!"* And they went to meet him and bowed down before him. ¹⁶"Sir," they said, "just say the word and fifty of our strongest men will search the wilderness for your master. Perhaps the Spirit of the LORD has left him on some mountain or in some valley."

"No," Elisha said, "don't send them." ¹⁷But they kept urging him until he was embarrassed, and he finally said, "All right, send them." So fifty men searched for three days but did not find Elijah. ¹⁸Elisha was still at Jericho when they returned. "Didn't I tell you not to go?" he asked.

ELISHA'S FIRST MIRACLES

¹⁹Now the leaders of the town of Jericho visited Elisha. "We have a problem, my lord," they told him. "This town is located in beautiful natural surroundings, as you can see. But the water is bad, and the land is unproductive."

²⁰Elisha said, "Bring me a new bowl with salt in it." So they brought it to him. ²¹Then he went out to the spring that supplied the town with water and threw the salt into it. And he said, "This is what the LORD says: I have made this water wholesome. It will no longer cause death or infertility.*" ²²And sure enough! The water has remained wholesome ever since, just as Elisha said.

²³Elisha left Jericho and went up to Bethel. As he was walking along the road, a group of boys from the town began mocking and making fun of him. "Go away, you baldhead!" they chanted. "Go away, you baldhead!" ²⁴Elisha turned around and looked at them, and he cursed them in the name of the LORD. Then two bears came out of the woods and mauled forty-two of them. ²⁵From there

Elisha went to Mount Carmel and finally returned to Samaria.

WAR BETWEEN ISRAEL AND MOAB

3 Ahab's son Joram* began to rule over Israel in the eighteenth year of King Jehoshaphat's reign in Judah. He reigned in Samaria twelve years. ²He did what was evil in the LORD's sight, but he was not as wicked as his father and mother. He at least tore down the sacred pillar of Baal that his father had set up. ³Nevertheless he continued in the sins of idolatry that Jeroboam son of Nebat had led the people of Israel to commit.

⁴King Mesha of Moab and his people were sheep breeders. They used to pay the king of Israel an annual tribute of 100,000 lambs and the wool of 100,000 rams. ⁵But after Ahab's death, the king of Moab rebelled against the king of Israel. ⁶So King Joram mustered the army of Israel and marched from Samaria. ⁷On the way, he sent this message to King Jehoshaphat of Judah: "The king of Moab has rebelled against me. Will you help me fight him?"

And Jehoshaphat replied, "Why, of course! You and I are brothers, and my troops are yours to command. Even my horses are at your service." ⁸Then Jehoshaphat asked, "What route will we take?"

"We will attack from the wilderness of Edom," Joram replied. ⁹The king of Edom and his troops joined them, and all three armies traveled along a roundabout route through the wilderness for seven days. But there was no water for the men or their pack animals.

¹⁰"What should we do?" the king of Israel cried out. "The LORD has brought the three of us here to let the king of Moab defeat us."

¹¹But King Jehoshaphat of Judah asked, "Is there no prophet of the LORD with us? If there is, we can ask the LORD what to do."

One of King Joram's officers replied, "Elisha son of Shaphat is here. He used to be Elijah's personal assistant.*"

2:15 Hebrew *The spirit of Elijah rests upon Elisha.* 2:21 Or *or make the land unproductive.* 3:1 Hebrew *Jehoram,* a variant name for Joram; also in 3:6. 3:11 Hebrew *He used to pour water on the hands of Elijah.*

¹²Jehoshaphat said, "Then the LORD will speak through him." So the kings of Israel, Judah, and Edom went to consult with Elisha.

¹³"I want no part of you," Elisha said to the king of Israel. "Go to the pagan prophets of your father and mother!"

But King Joram said, "No! For it was the LORD who called us three kings here to be destroyed by the king of Moab!"

¹⁴Elisha replied, "As surely as the LORD Almighty lives, whom I serve, I would not bother with you except for my respect for King Jehoshaphat of Judah. ¹⁵Now bring me someone who can play the harp."

While the harp was being played, the power of the LORD came upon Elisha, ¹⁶and he said, "This is what the LORD says: This dry valley will be filled with pools of water! ¹⁷You will see neither wind nor rain, says the LORD, but this valley will be filled with water. You will have plenty for yourselves and for your cattle and your other animals. ¹⁸But this is only a simple thing for the LORD, for he will make you victorious over the army of Moab! ¹⁹You will conquer the best of their cities, even the fortified ones. You will cut down all their trees, stop up all their springs, and ruin all their good land with stones."

²⁰And sure enough, the next day at about the time when the morning sacrifice was offered, water suddenly appeared! It was flowing from the direction of Edom, and soon there was water everywhere.

²¹Meanwhile, when the people of Moab heard about the three armies marching against them, they mobilized every man who could fight, young and old, and stationed themselves along their border. ²²But when they got up the next morning, the sun was shining across the water, making it look as red as blood. ²³"It's blood!" the Moabites exclaimed. "The three armies have attacked and killed each other! Let's go and collect the plunder!"

²⁴When they arrived at the Israelite camp, the army of Israel rushed out and attacked the Moabites, who turned and ran. The army of Israel chased them into the land of Moab, destroying everything as they went. ²⁵They destroyed the cities, covered their good land with stones, stopped up the springs, and cut down the good trees. Finally, only Kir-hareseth was left, but even that came under attack.*

²⁶When the king of Moab saw that he was losing the battle, he led seven hundred of his warriors in a desperate attempt to break through the enemy lines near the king of Edom, but they failed to escape. ²⁷So he took his oldest son, who would have been the next king, and sacrificed him as a burnt offering on the wall. As a result, the anger against Israel was great, so they withdrew and returned to their own land.

ELISHA HELPS A POOR WIDOW

4 One day the widow of one of Elisha's fellow prophets came to Elisha and cried out to him, "My husband who served you is dead, and you know how he feared the LORD. But now a creditor has come, threatening to take my two sons as slaves."

²"What can I do to help you?" Elisha asked. "Tell me, what do you have in the house?"

"Nothing at all, except a flask of olive oil," she replied.

³And Elisha said, "Borrow as many empty jars as you can from your friends and neighbors. ⁴Then go into your house with your sons and shut the door behind you. Pour olive oil from your flask into the jars, setting the jars aside as they are filled."

⁵So she did as she was told. Her sons brought many jars to her, and she filled one after another. ⁶Soon every container was full to the brim!

"Bring me another jar," she said to one of her sons.

"There aren't any more!" he told her. And then the olive oil stopped flowing.

⁷When she told the man of God what had

3:25 Hebrew *until only Kir-hareseth was left, with its stones, but the slingers surrounded and attacked it.*

happened, he said to her, "Now sell the olive oil and pay your debts, and there will be enough money left over to support you and your sons."

ELISHA AND THE WOMAN FROM SHUNEM

[8] One day Elisha went to the town of Shunem. A wealthy woman lived there, and she invited him to eat some food. From then on, whenever he passed that way, he would stop there to eat.

[9] She said to her husband, "I am sure this man who stops in from time to time is a holy man of God. [10] Let's make a little room for him on the roof and furnish it with a bed, a table, a chair, and a lamp. Then he will have a place to stay whenever he comes by."

[11] One day Elisha returned to Shunem, and he went up to his room to rest. [12] He said to his servant Gehazi, "Tell the woman I want to speak to her." When she arrived, [13] Elisha said to Gehazi, "Tell her that we appreciate the kind concern she has shown us. Now ask her what we can do for her. Does she want me to put in a good word for her to the king or to the commander of the army?"

"No," she replied, "my family takes good care of me."

[14] Later Elisha asked Gehazi, "What do you think we can do for her?"

He suggested, "She doesn't have a son, and her husband is an old man."

[15] "Call her back again," Elisha told him. When the woman returned, Elisha said to her as she stood in the doorway, [16] "Next year at about this time you will be holding a son in your arms!"

"No, my lord!" she protested. "Please don't lie to me like that, O man of God." [17] But sure enough, the woman soon became pregnant. And at that time the following year she had a son, just as Elisha had said.

[18] One day when her child was older, he went out to visit his father, who was working with the harvesters. [19] Suddenly he complained, "My head hurts! My head hurts!"

His father said to one of the servants, "Carry him home to his mother."

[20] So the servant took him home, and his mother held him on her lap. But around noontime he died. [21] She carried him up to the bed of the man of God, then shut the door and left him there. [22] She sent a message to her husband: "Send one of the servants and a donkey so that I can hurry to the man of God and come right back."

[23] "Why today?" he asked. "It is neither a new moon festival nor a Sabbath."

But she said, "It's all right." [24] So she saddled the donkey and said to the servant, "Hurry! Don't slow down on my account unless I tell you to."

[25] As she approached the man of God at Mount Carmel, Elisha saw her in the distance. He said to Gehazi, "Look, the woman from Shunem is coming. [26] Run out to meet her and ask her, 'Is everything all right with you, with your husband, and with your child?'"

"Yes," the woman told Gehazi, "everything is fine."

[27] But when she came to the man of God at the mountain, she fell to the ground before him and caught hold of his feet. Gehazi began to push her away, but the man of God said, "Leave her alone. Something is troubling her deeply, and the LORD has not told me what it is."

[28] Then she said, "It was you, my lord, who said I would have a son. And didn't I tell you not to raise my hopes?"

[29] Then Elisha said to Gehazi, "Get ready to

The heart of God loves a persevering worshiper who, though overwhelmed by many troubles, is overwhelmed even more by the beauty of God.

MATT REDMAN

travel; take my staff and go! Don't talk to anyone along the way. Go quickly and lay the staff on the child's face."

³⁰But the boy's mother said, "As surely as the LORD lives and you yourself live, I won't go home unless you go with me." So Elisha returned with her.

³¹Gehazi hurried on ahead and laid the staff on the child's face, but nothing happened. There was no sign of life. He returned to meet Elisha and told him, "The child is still dead."

³²When Elisha arrived, the child was indeed dead, lying there on the prophet's bed. ³³He went in alone and shut the door behind him and prayed to the LORD. ³⁴Then he lay down on the child's body, placing his mouth on the child's mouth, his eyes on the child's eyes, and his hands on the child's hands. And the child's body began to grow warm again! ³⁵Elisha got up and walked back and forth in the room a few times. Then he stretched himself out again on the child. This time the boy sneezed seven times and opened his eyes!

³⁶Then Elisha summoned Gehazi. "Call the child's mother!" he said. And when she came in, Elisha said, "Here, take your son!" ³⁷She fell at his feet, overwhelmed with gratitude. Then she picked up her son and carried him downstairs.

MIRACLES DURING A FAMINE

³⁸Elisha now returned to Gilgal, but there was a famine in the land. One day as the group of prophets was seated before him, he said to his servant, "Put on a large kettle and make some stew for these men."

³⁹One of the young men went out into the field to gather vegetables and came back with a pocketful of wild gourds. He shredded them and put them into the kettle without realizing they were poisonous. ⁴⁰But after the men had eaten a bite or two they cried out, "Man of God, there's poison in this stew!" So they would not eat it.

⁴¹Elisha said, "Bring me some flour." Then he threw it into the kettle and said, "Now it's all right, go ahead and eat." And then it did not harm them!

⁴²One day a man from Baal-shalishah brought the man of God a sack of fresh grain and twenty loaves of barley bread made from the first grain of his harvest. Elisha said, "Give it to the group of prophets* so they can eat."

⁴³"What?" his servant exclaimed. "Feed one hundred people with only this?"

But Elisha repeated, "Give it to the group of prophets so they can eat, for the LORD says there will be plenty for all. There will even be some left over!" ⁴⁴And sure enough, there was plenty for all and some left over, just as the LORD had promised.

THE HEALING OF NAAMAN

5 The king of Aram had high admiration for Naaman, the commander of his army, because through him the LORD had given Aram great victories. But though Naaman was a mighty warrior, he suffered from leprosy.*

²Now groups of Aramean raiders had invaded the land of Israel, and among their captives was a young girl who had been given to Naaman's wife as a maid. ³One day the girl said to her mistress, "I wish my master would go to see the prophet in Samaria. He would heal him of his leprosy."

⁴So Naaman told the king what the young girl from Israel had said. ⁵"Go and visit the prophet," the king told him. "I will send a letter of introduction for you to carry to the king of Israel." So Naaman started out, taking as gifts 750 pounds of silver, 150 pounds of gold,* and ten sets of clothing. ⁶The letter to the king of Israel said: "With this letter I present my servant Naaman. I want you to heal him of his leprosy."

⁷When the king of Israel read it, he tore his clothes in dismay and said, "This man sends me a leper to heal! Am I God, that I can kill and give life? He is only trying to find an excuse to invade us again."

4:42 Hebrew *to the people*; also in 4:43. 5:1 Or *from a contagious skin disease*. The Hebrew word used here and throughout this passage can describe various skin diseases. 5:5 Hebrew *10 talents* [340 kilograms] *of silver, 6,000 shekels* [68 kilograms] *of gold*.

⁸But when Elisha, the man of God, heard about the king's reaction, he sent this message to him: "Why are you so upset? Send Naaman to me, and he will learn that there is a true prophet here in Israel."

⁹So Naaman went with his horses and chariots and waited at the door of Elisha's house. ¹⁰But Elisha sent a messenger out to him with this message: "Go and wash yourself seven times in the Jordan River. Then your skin will be restored, and you will be healed of leprosy."

¹¹But Naaman became angry and stalked away. "I thought he would surely come out to meet me!" he said. "I expected him to wave his hand over the leprosy and call on the name of the LORD his God and heal me! ¹²Aren't the Abana River and Pharpar River of Damascus better than all the rivers of Israel put together? Why shouldn't I wash in them and be healed?" So Naaman turned and went away in a rage.

¹³But his officers tried to reason with him and said, "Sir, if the prophet had told you to do some great thing, wouldn't you have done it? So you should certainly obey him when he says simply to go and wash and be cured!" ¹⁴So Naaman went down to the Jordan River and dipped himself seven times, as the man of God had instructed him. And his flesh became as healthy as a young child's, and he was healed!

¹⁵Then Naaman and his entire party went back to find the man of God. They stood before him, and Naaman said, "I know at last that there is no God in all the world except in Israel. Now please accept my gifts."

¹⁶But Elisha replied, "As surely as the LORD lives, whom I serve, I will not accept any gifts." And though Naaman urged him to take the gifts, Elisha refused.

¹⁷Then Naaman said, "All right, but please allow me to load two of my mules with earth from this place, and I will take it back home with me. From now on I will never again offer any burnt offerings or sacrifices to any other god except the LORD. ¹⁸However, may the LORD pardon me in this one thing. When my master the king goes into the temple of the god Rimmon to worship there and leans on my arm, may the LORD pardon me when I bow, too."

¹⁹"Go in peace," Elisha said. So Naaman started home again.

THE GREED OF GEHAZI

²⁰But Gehazi, Elisha's servant, said to himself, "My master should not have let this Aramean get away without accepting his gifts. As surely as the LORD lives, I will chase after him and get something from him." ²¹So Gehazi set off after him.

When Naaman saw him running after him, he climbed down from his chariot and went to meet him. "Is everything all right?" Naaman asked.

²²"Yes," Gehazi said, "but my master has sent me to tell you that two young prophets from the hill country of Ephraim have just arrived. He would like 75 pounds* of silver and two sets of clothing to give to them."

²³"By all means, take 150 pounds* of silver," Naaman insisted. He gave him two sets of clothing, tied up the money in two bags, and sent two of his servants to carry the gifts for Gehazi. ²⁴But when they arrived at the hill, Gehazi took the gifts from the servants and sent the men back. Then he hid the gifts inside the house.

²⁵When he went in to his master, Elisha asked him, "Where have you been, Gehazi?"

"I haven't been anywhere," he replied.

²⁶But Elisha asked him, "Don't you realize that I was there in spirit when Naaman stepped down from his chariot to meet you? Is this the time to receive money and clothing and olive groves and vineyards and sheep and oxen and servants? ²⁷Because you have done this, you and your children and your children's children will suffer from Naaman's leprosy forever." When Gehazi left the room, he was leprous; his skin was as white as snow.

5:22 Hebrew *1 talent* [34 kilograms]. 5:23 Hebrew *2 talents* [68 kilograms].

THE FLOATING AX HEAD

6 One day the group of prophets came to Elisha and told him, "As you can see, this place where we meet with you is too small. ²Let's go down to the Jordan River, where there are plenty of logs. There we can build a new place for us to meet."

"All right," he told them, "go ahead."

³"Please come with us," someone suggested.

"I will," he said.

⁴When they arrived at the Jordan, they began cutting down trees. ⁵But as one of them was chopping, his ax head fell into the river. "Ah, my lord!" he cried. "It was a borrowed ax!"

⁶"Where did it fall?" the man of God asked. When he showed him the place, Elisha cut a stick and threw it into the water. Then the ax head rose to the surface and floated. ⁷"Grab it," Elisha said to him. And the man reached out and grabbed it.

ELISHA TRAPS THE ARAMEANS

⁸When the king of Aram was at war with Israel, he would confer with his officers and say, "We will mobilize our forces at such and such a place."

⁹But immediately Elisha, the man of God, would warn the king of Israel, "Do not go near that place, for the Arameans are planning to mobilize their troops there." ¹⁰So the king of Israel would send word to the place indicated by the man of God, warning the people there to be on their guard. This happened several times.

¹¹The king of Aram became very upset over this. He called in his officers and demanded, "Which of you is the traitor? Who has been informing the king of Israel of my plans?"

¹²"It's not us, my lord," one of the officers replied. "Elisha, the prophet in Israel, tells the king of Israel even the words you speak in the privacy of your bedroom!"

¹³The king commanded, "Go and find out where Elisha is, and we will send troops to seize him."

And the report came back: "Elisha is at Dothan." ¹⁴So one night the king of Aram sent a great army with many chariots and horses to surround the city. ¹⁵When the servant of the man of God got up early the next morning and went outside, there were troops, horses, and chariots everywhere.

"Ah, my lord, what will we do now?" he cried out to Elisha.

¹⁶"Don't be afraid!" Elisha told him. "For there are more on our side than on theirs!" ¹⁷Then Elisha prayed, "O LORD, open his eyes and let him see!" The LORD opened his servant's eyes, and when he looked up, he saw that the hillside around Elisha was filled with horses and chariots of fire.

¹⁸As the Aramean army advanced toward them, Elisha prayed, "O LORD, please make them blind." And the LORD did as Elisha asked. ¹⁹Then Elisha went out and told them, "You have come the wrong way! This isn't the right city! Follow me, and I will take you to the man you are looking for." And he led them to Samaria. ²⁰As soon as they had entered Samaria, Elisha prayed, "O LORD, now open their eyes and let them see." And the LORD did, and they discovered that they were in Samaria.

²¹When the king of Israel saw them, he shouted to Elisha, "My father, should I kill them?"

²²"Of course not!" Elisha told him. "Do we kill prisoners of war? Give them food and drink and send them home again to their master."

²³So the king made a great feast for them and then sent them home to their king. After that, the Aramean raiders stayed away from the land of Israel.

BEN-HADAD BESIEGES SAMARIA

²⁴Some time later, however, King Ben-hadad of Aram mobilized his entire army and besieged Samaria. ²⁵As a result there was a great famine in the city. After a while even a donkey's head sold for two pounds of silver,

and a cup of dove's dung cost about two ounces* of silver.

²⁶One day as the king of Israel was walking along the wall of the city, a woman called to him, "Please help me, my lord the king!"

²⁷"If the LORD doesn't help you, what can I do?" he retorted. "I have neither food nor wine to give you." ²⁸But then the king asked, "What is the matter?"

She replied, "This woman proposed that we eat my son one day and her son the next. ²⁹So we cooked my son and ate him. Then the next day I said, 'Kill your son so we can eat him,' but she had hidden him."

³⁰When the king heard this, he tore his clothes in despair. And as the king walked along the wall, the people could see that he was wearing sackcloth underneath next to his skin. ³¹"May God kill me if I don't execute Elisha son of Shaphat this very day," the king vowed.

³²Elisha was sitting in his house at a meeting with the leaders of Israel when the king sent a messenger to summon him. But before the messenger arrived, Elisha said to the leaders, "A murderer has sent a man to kill me. When he arrives, shut the door and keep him out. His master will soon follow him."

³³While Elisha was still saying this, the messenger arrived. And the king* said, "It is the LORD who has brought this trouble on us! Why should I wait any longer for the LORD?"

7 Elisha replied, "Hear this message from the LORD! This is what the LORD says: By this time tomorrow in the markets of Samaria, five quarts of fine flour will cost only half an ounce of silver,* and ten quarts of barley grain will cost only half an ounce of silver.*"

²The officer assisting the king said to the man of God, "That couldn't happen even if the LORD opened the windows of heaven!"

But Elisha replied, "You will see it happen, but you won't be able to eat any of it!"

LEPERS VISIT THE ENEMY CAMP

³Now there were four men with leprosy* sitting at the entrance of the city gates. "Why should we sit here waiting to die?" they asked each other. ⁴"We will starve if we stay here, and we will starve if we go back into the city. So we might as well go out and surrender to the Aramean army. If they let us live, so much the better. But if they kill us, we would have died anyway."

⁵So that evening they went out to the camp of the Arameans, but no one was there! ⁶For the Lord had caused the whole army of Aram to hear the clatter of speeding chariots and the galloping of horses and the sounds of a great army approaching. "The king of Israel has hired the Hittites and Egyptians* to attack us!" they cried out. ⁷So they panicked and fled into the night, abandoning their tents, horses, donkeys, and everything else, and they fled for their lives.

⁸When the lepers arrived at the edge of the camp, they went into one tent after another, eating, drinking wine, and carrying out silver and gold and clothing and hiding it. ⁹Finally, they said to each other, "This is not right. This is wonderful news, and we aren't sharing it with anyone! If we wait until morning, some terrible calamity will certainly fall upon us. Come on, let's go back and tell the people at the palace."

¹⁰So they went back to the city and told the gatekeepers what had happened—that they had gone out to the Aramean camp and no one was there! The horses and donkeys were tethered and the tents were all in order, but there was not a single person around. ¹¹Then the gatekeepers shouted the news to the people in the palace.

6:25 Hebrew *sold for 80 shekels* [0.9 kilograms] *of silver, and* 1/4 *of a cab* [0.3 liters] *of dove's dung cost 5 shekels* [57 grams]. *Dove's dung may be a variety of wild vegetable.* 6:33 Hebrew *he.* 7:1a Hebrew *1 seah* [6 liters] *of fine flour will cost 1 shekel* [11 grams]; also in 7:16, 18. 7:1b Hebrew *2 seahs* [12 liters] *of barley grain will cost 1 shekel* [11 grams]; also in 7:16, 18. 7:3 Or *with a contagious skin disease.* The Hebrew word used here and throughout this passage can describe various skin diseases. 7:6 Possibly *and the people of Muzur,* a district near Cilicia.

My Daily Worship

US VERSUS THEM

2 KINGS 1:1–8:15

*"Don't be afraid!" Elisha told him. "For there are
more on our side than on theirs!" (6:16).*

[i reflect]

Daybreak. The first to rise, the servant goes outside to begin the morning preparations for his master—Elisha, the prophet of Israel. *What is this?* the servant thought. *How did an army with chariots and horses assemble during the night? The Arameans will surely kill us all!* He runs to tell Elisha.

The prophet is not surprised by the news. He seems to have expected it. Elisha reassures his servant, for he also expected something else . . . and sees it. The servant thinks, *More on our side? Is my lord blind? There are troops, horses, and chariot everywhere!*

Elisha is not blind. Indeed, he intercedes for his servant, "O LORD, open his eyes and let him see!" (6:17). Yes, let him see beyond what his eyes are telling him. Horses and chariots of fire—the very symbol of power that Elisha saw the LORD use to sweep Elijah to heaven (2:11)—have come to fill the hillsides. The enemy army had assembled during the night, but so had God's army.

Enemies, named or unnamed, human or inhuman, surround us at times. The word *outnumbered* scarcely begins to describe how we feel at times. Do we panic, as Elisha's servant did at first? Or do we ask for a new vision of what's there, for the eyes to "see" the other army that has assembled during the night?

Lawrence Scupoli, a sixteenth-century priest, wrote in *The Spiritual Combat*, "If your strength fails you, ask for some more from God. He will not refuse your request. Even if your enemies are great in number, the love of God which holds you is infinitely greater. His angels are more numerous."

As you lift your heart in the morning in prayer and praise, may you also lift your eyes to see what God has provided.

[i pray]

*O Lord, open my eyes that I may see the forces that you have assembled
on the hillsides of my life. I trust in your strength and your provision.*

[i respond]

Who or what are the enemies you face? Write them down, then turn the paper face down. Now walk to a window or an open door. Look to the horizon and imagine the forces that God has assembled on your behalf.

ISRAEL PLUNDERS THE CAMP

[12]The king got out of bed in the middle of the night and told his officers, "I know what has happened. The Arameans know we are starving, so they have left their camp and have hidden in the fields. They are expecting us to leave the city, and then they will take us alive and capture the city."

[13]One of his officers replied, "We had better send out scouts to check into this. Let them take five of the remaining horses. If something happens to them, it won't be a greater loss than if they stay here and die with the rest of us."

[14]So two chariots with horses were prepared, and the king sent scouts to see what had happened to the Aramean army. [15]They went all the way to the Jordan River, following a trail of clothing and equipment that the Arameans had thrown away in their mad rush to escape. The scouts returned and told the king about it. [16]Then the people of Samaria rushed out and plundered the Aramean camp. So it was true that five quarts of fine flour were sold that day for half an ounce of silver, and ten quarts of barley grain were sold for half an ounce of silver, just as the LORD had promised. [17]The king appointed his officer to control the traffic at the gate, but he was knocked down and trampled to death as the people rushed out.

So everything happened exactly as the man of God had predicted when the king came to his house. [18]The man of God had said to the king, "By this time tomorrow in the markets of Samaria, five quarts of fine flour will cost half an ounce of silver, and ten quarts of barley grain will cost half an ounce of silver." [19]The king's officer had replied, "That couldn't happen even if the LORD opened the windows of heaven!" And the man of God had said, "You will see it happen, but you won't be able to eat any of it!" [20]And so it was, for the people trampled him to death at the gate!

8:11 Hebrew *He stared at him.*

THE WOMAN FROM SHUNEM RETURNS HOME

8 Elisha had told the woman whose son he had brought back to life, "Take your family and move to some other place, for the LORD has called for a famine on Israel that will last for seven years." [2]So the woman did as the man of God instructed. She took her family and lived in the land of the Philistines for seven years.

[3]After the famine ended she returned to the land of Israel, and she went to see the king about getting back her house and land. [4]As she came in, the king was talking with Gehazi, the servant of the man of God. The king had just said, "Tell me some stories about the great things Elisha has done." [5]And Gehazi was telling the king about the time Elisha had brought a boy back to life. At that very moment, the mother of the boy walked in to make her appeal to the king.

"Look, my lord!" Gehazi exclaimed. "Here is the woman now, and this is her son—the very one Elisha brought back to life!"

[6]"Is this true?" the king asked her. And she told him that it was. So he directed one of his officials to see to it that everything she had lost was restored to her, including the value of any crops that had been harvested during her absence.

HAZAEL MURDERS BEN-HADAD

[7]Now Elisha went to Damascus, the capital of Aram, where King Ben-hadad lay sick. Someone told the king that the man of God had come. [8]When the king heard the news, he said to Hazael, "Take a gift to the man of God. Then tell him to ask the LORD if I will get well again."

[9]So Hazael loaded down forty camels with the finest products of Damascus as a gift for Elisha. He went in to him and said, "Your servant Ben-hadad, the king of Aram, has sent me to ask you if he will recover."

[10]And Elisha replied, "Go and tell him, 'You will recover.' But the LORD has shown me that he will actually die!" [11]Elisha stared at Hazael*

with a fixed gaze until Hazael became uneasy. Then the man of God started weeping.

¹²"What's the matter, my lord?" Hazael asked him.

Elisha replied, "I know the terrible things you will do to the people of Israel. You will burn their fortified cities, kill their young men, dash their children to the ground, and rip open their pregnant women!"

¹³Then Hazael replied, "How could a nobody like me* ever accomplish such a great feat?"

But Elisha answered, "The LORD has shown me that you are going to be the king of Aram."

¹⁴When Hazael went back, the king asked him, "What did Elisha tell you?"

And Hazael replied, "He told me that you will surely recover."

¹⁵But the next day Hazael took a blanket, soaked it in water, and held it over the king's face until he died. Then Hazael became the next king of Aram.

JEHORAM RULES IN JUDAH

¹⁶Jehoram son of King Jehoshaphat of Judah began to rule over Judah in the fifth year of King Joram's reign in Israel. Joram was the son of Ahab. ¹⁷Jehoram was thirty-two years old when he became king, and he reigned in Jerusalem eight years. ¹⁸But Jehoram followed the example of the kings of Israel and was as wicked as King Ahab, for he had married one of Ahab's daughters. So Jehoram did what was evil in the LORD's sight. ¹⁹But the LORD was not willing to destroy Judah, for he had made a covenant with David and promised that his descendants would continue to rule forever.*

²⁰During Jehoram's reign, the Edomites revolted against Judah and crowned their own king. ²¹So Jehoram* went with all his chariots to attack the town of Zair.* The Edomites surrounded him and his charioteers, but he escaped at night under cover of darkness. Jehoram's army, however, deserted him and fled. ²²Edom has been independent from Judah to this day. The town of Libnah revolted about that same time.

²³The rest of the events in Jehoram's reign and all his deeds are recorded in *The Book of the History of the Kings of Judah.* ²⁴When Jehoram died, he was buried with his ancestors in the City of David. Then his son Ahaziah became the next king.

AHAZIAH RULES IN JUDAH

²⁵Ahaziah son of Jehoram began to rule over Judah in the twelfth year of King Joram's reign in Israel. King Joram was the son of Ahab. ²⁶Ahaziah was twenty-two years old when he became king, and he reigned in Jerusalem one year. His mother was Athaliah, a granddaughter of King Omri of Israel. ²⁷Ahaziah followed the evil example of King Ahab's family, doing what was evil in the LORD's sight, because he was related by marriage to the family of Ahab.

²⁸Ahaziah joined King Joram of Israel in his war against King Hazael of Aram at Ramoth-gilead. When King Joram was wounded in the battle, ²⁹he returned to Jezreel to recover from his wounds. While Joram was there, King Ahaziah of Judah went to visit him.

JEHU ANOINTED KING OF ISRAEL

9 Meanwhile, Elisha the prophet had summoned a member of the group of prophets. "Get ready to go to Ramoth-gilead," he told him. "Take this vial of olive oil with you, ²and find Jehu son of Jehoshaphat and grandson of Nimshi. Call him into a back room away from his friends, ³and pour the oil over his head. Say to him, 'This is what the LORD says: I anoint you to be the king over Israel.' Then open the door and run for your life!"

⁴So the young prophet did as he was told and went to Ramoth-gilead. ⁵When he arrived there, he found Jehu sitting in a meeting with the other army officers. "I have a message for you, Commander," he said.

"For which one of us?" Jehu asked.

8:13 Hebrew *a dog.* 8:19 Hebrew *promised to give a lamp to David and his descendants forever.* 8:21a Hebrew *Joram,* a variant name for Jehoram; also in 8:23, 24. 8:21b Greek version reads *Seir.*

"For you, Commander," he replied.

⁶So Jehu left the others and went into the house. Then the young prophet poured the oil over Jehu's head and said, "This is what the LORD, the God of Israel, says: I anoint you king over the LORD's people, Israel. ⁷You are to destroy the family of Ahab, your master. In this way, I will avenge the murder of my prophets and all the LORD's servants who were killed by Jezebel. ⁸The entire family of Ahab must be wiped out—every male, slave and free alike, in Israel. ⁹I will destroy the family of Ahab as I destroyed the families of Jeroboam son of Nebat and of Baasha son of Ahijah. ¹⁰Dogs will eat Ahab's wife, Jezebel, at the plot of land in Jezreel, and no one will bury her." Then the young prophet opened the door and ran.

¹¹Jehu went back to his fellow officers, and one of them asked him, "What did that crazy fellow want? Is everything all right?"

"You know the way such a man babbles on," Jehu replied.

¹²"You're lying," they said. "Tell us." So Jehu told them what the man had said and that at the LORD's command he had been anointed king over Israel.

¹³They quickly spread out their cloaks on the bare steps and blew a trumpet, shouting, "Jehu is king!"

JEHU KILLS JORAM AND AHAZIAH

¹⁴So Jehu son of Jehoshaphat and grandson of Nimshi formed a conspiracy against King Joram. (Now Joram had been with the army at Ramoth-gilead, defending Israel against the forces of King Hazael of Aram. ¹⁵But Joram* had been wounded in the fighting and had returned to Jezreel to recover from his wounds.) So Jehu told the men with him, "Since you want me to be king, don't let anyone escape to Jezreel to report what we have done."

¹⁶Then Jehu got into a chariot and rode to Jezreel to find King Joram, who was lying there wounded. King Ahaziah of Judah was

there, too, for he had gone to visit him. ¹⁷The watchman on the tower of Jezreel saw Jehu and his company approaching, so he shouted to Joram, "I see a company of troops coming!"

"Send out a rider to find out if they are coming in peace," King Joram shouted back.

¹⁸So a rider went out to meet Jehu and said, "The king wants to know whether you are coming in peace."

Jehu replied, "What do you know about peace? Get behind me!"

The watchman called out to the king, "The rider has met them, but he is not returning."

¹⁹So the king sent out a second rider. He rode up to them and demanded, "The king wants to know whether you come in peace."

Again Jehu answered, "What do you know about peace? Get behind me!"

²⁰The watchman exclaimed, "The rider has met them, but he isn't returning either! It must be Jehu son of Nimshi, for he is driving so recklessly."

²¹"Quick! Get my chariot ready!" King Joram commanded.

Then King Joram of Israel and King Ahaziah of Judah rode out in their chariots to meet Jehu. They met him at the field that had belonged to Naboth of Jezreel. ²²King Joram demanded, "Do you come in peace, Jehu?"

Jehu replied, "How can there be peace as long as the idolatry and witchcraft of your mother, Jezebel, are all around us?"

²³Then King Joram reined the chariot horses around and fled, shouting to King Ahaziah, "Treason, Ahaziah!" ²⁴Then Jehu drew his bow and shot Joram between the shoulders. The arrow pierced his heart, and he sank down dead in his chariot.

²⁵Jehu said to Bidkar, his officer, "Throw him into the field of Naboth of Jezreel. Do you remember when you and I were riding along behind his father, Ahab? The LORD pronounced this message against him: ²⁶'I solemnly swear that I will repay him here on Naboth's property, says the LORD, for the murder of Naboth and his sons that I saw

9:15 Hebrew *Jehoram,* a variant name for Joram; also in 9:17, 21, 22, 23, 24.

I Choose You!

2 Kings 8:16–10:36

Then the young prophet poured the oil over Jehu's head and said, "This is what the LORD,
the God of Israel, says: I anoint you king over the LORD's people, Israel" (9:6).

[i reflect]

The young prophet lifts the vial over Jehu's head. Are his hands shaking? Who could blame him if they are? God has chosen a warrior to be the next king of Israel, one who—if he fulfills prophecy—will be known for his violence. Elisha had even warned this young prophet that, after the anointing, he should "open the door and run for [his] life!" (9:3). An unusual anointing, to say the least.

Stop for a moment. An unusual anointing? The passage is a double anointing; not one but two men were set apart by God for a special task. Jehu was called "into a back room away from his friends," ultimately away from the litany of kings who did what was evil in the Lord's sight. But the nameless "young prophet" was equally called for a special task. No olive oil was poured from a vial over his head, yet his anointing was as much from God as Jehu's. Anointed to anoint.

From the beginning, our God has been calling, anointing, setting apart. In Exodus 30:22–33, even the anointing oil is anointed, specially set apart to anoint Aaron and his sons to be priests. So the question is not "Will we be anointed," but, rather, "Are we attuned to his call?" Do we feel the invisible oil poured on the tops of our heads, dripping down? Do we take to heart the words of David, another who was anointed for a special task in God's service? "You can be sure of this: The LORD has set apart the godly for himself" (Psalm 4:3).

We can sit with the disciples in the Upper Room of our relationship with God. As you listen to Jesus' words—"You didn't choose me. I chose you. I appointed you to go and produce fruit that will last" (John 15:16)—take comfort and take action.

Today, think of the special tasks for which God has appointed—and anointed—you.

[i pray]

Call me, dear God, for I am listening. Anoint me, for I am waiting. Set me apart; send me
where you will. Just do not set me aside while you have a special task for me.

[i respond]

Sit in a quiet place and close your eyes. Imagine a vial of oil being lifted over your head, then poured over you. Feel the cool liquid as it drips down over your hair. Listen to the words, "I chose you." Respond to God in willingness and love, asking him to lead and direct you, whom he has anointed.

yesterday.' So throw him out on Naboth's field, just as the LORD said."

²⁷When King Ahaziah of Judah saw what was happening, he fled along the road to Beth-haggan. Jehu rode after him, shouting, "Shoot him, too!" So they shot Ahaziah in his chariot at the Ascent of Gur, near Ibleam. He was able to go on as far as Megiddo, but he died there. ²⁸His officials took him by chariot to Jerusalem, where they buried him with his ancestors in the City of David. ²⁹Ahaziah's reign over Judah had begun in the eleventh year of King Joram's reign in Israel.

THE DEATH OF JEZEBEL

³⁰When Jezebel, the queen mother, heard that Jehu had come to Jezreel, she painted her eyelids and fixed her hair and sat at a window. ³¹When Jehu entered the gate of the palace, she shouted at him, "Have you come in peace, you murderer? You are just like Zimri, who murdered his master!"

³²Jehu looked up and saw her at the window and shouted, "Who is on my side?" And two or three eunuchs looked out at him. ³³"Throw her down!" Jehu yelled. So they threw her out the window, and some of her blood spattered against the wall and on the horses. And Jehu trampled her body under his horses' hooves.

³⁴Then Jehu went into the palace and ate and drank. Afterward he said, "Someone go and bury this cursed woman, for she is the daughter of a king." ³⁵But when they went out to bury her, they found only her skull, her feet, and her hands.

³⁶When they returned and told Jehu, he stated, "This fulfills the message from the LORD, which he spoke through his servant Elijah from Tishbe: 'At the plot of land in Jezreel, dogs will eat Jezebel's flesh. ³⁷Her body will be scattered like dung on the field of Jezreel, so that no one will be able to recognize her.'"

JEHU KILLS AHAB'S FAMILY

10 Now Ahab had seventy sons living in the city of Samaria. So Jehu wrote a letter and sent copies to Samaria, to the officials of the city,* to the leaders of the people, and to the guardians of King Ahab's sons. The letter said, ²"The king's sons are with you, and you have at your disposal chariots, horses, a fortified city, and weapons. As soon as you receive this letter, ³select the best qualified of King Ahab's sons to be your king, and prepare to fight for Ahab's dynasty."

⁴But they were paralyzed with fear and said, "Two kings couldn't stand against this man! What can we do?" ⁵So the palace and city administrators, together with the other leaders and the guardians of the king's sons, sent this message to Jehu: "We are your servants and will do anything you tell us. We will not make anyone king; do whatever you think is best."

⁶Jehu responded with a second letter: "If you are on my side and are going to obey me, bring the heads of the king's sons to me at Jezreel at about this time tomorrow."

Now the seventy sons of the king were being cared for by the leaders of Samaria, where they had been raised since childhood. ⁷When the letter arrived, the leaders killed all seventy of the king's sons. They placed their heads in baskets and presented them to Jehu at Jezreel. ⁸A messenger went to Jehu and said, "They have brought the heads of the king's sons."

So Jehu ordered, "Pile them in two heaps at the entrance of the city gate, and leave them there until morning."

⁹In the morning he went out and spoke to the crowd that had gathered around them. "You aren't to blame," he told them. "I am the one who conspired against my master and killed him. But who killed all these? ¹⁰You can be sure that the message of the LORD that was spoken concerning Ahab's family will not fail. The LORD declared through his servant Elijah that this would happen." ¹¹Then Jehu killed all

---

10:1 As in some Greek manuscripts and Latin Vulgate (see also 10:6); Hebrew reads *of Jezreel.*

of Ahab's relatives living in Jezreel and all his important officials, personal friends, and priests. So Ahab was left without a single survivor.

¹²Then Jehu set out for Samaria. Along the way, while he was at Beth-eked of the Shepherds, ¹³he met some relatives of King Ahaziah of Judah. "Who are you?" he asked them.

And they replied, "We are relatives of King Ahaziah. We are going to visit the sons of King Ahab and the queen mother."

¹⁴"Take them alive!" Jehu shouted to his men. And they captured all forty-two of them and killed them at the well of Beth-eked. None of them escaped.

¹⁵When Jehu left there, he met Jehonadab son of Recab, who was coming to meet him. After they had greeted each other, Jehu said to him, "Are you as loyal to me as I am to you?"

"Yes, I am," Jehonadab replied.

"If you are," Jehu said, "then give me your hand." So Jehonadab put out his hand, and Jehu helped him into the chariot. ¹⁶Then Jehu said, "Now come with me, and see how devoted I am to the LORD." So Jehonadab rode along with him. ¹⁷When Jehu arrived in Samaria, he killed everyone who was left there from Ahab's family, just as the LORD had promised through Elijah.

JEHU KILLS THE PRIESTS OF BAAL

¹⁸Then Jehu called a meeting of all the people of the city and said to them, "Ahab hardly worshiped Baal at all compared to the way I will worship him! ¹⁹Summon all the prophets and worshipers of Baal, and call together all his priests. See to it that every one of them comes, for I am going to offer a great sacrifice to Baal. Any of Baal's worshipers who fail to come will be put to death." But Jehu's plan was to destroy all the worshipers of Baal.

²⁰Then Jehu ordered, "Prepare a solemn assembly to worship Baal!" So they did. ²¹He sent messengers throughout all Israel summoning those who worshiped Baal. They all came and filled the temple of Baal from one end to the other. ²²And Jehu instructed the keeper of the wardrobe, "Be sure that every worshiper of Baal wears one of these robes." So robes were given to them.

²³Then Jehu went into the temple of Baal with Jehonadab son of Recab. Jehu said to the worshipers of Baal, "Make sure that only those who worship Baal are here. Don't let anyone in who worships the LORD!" ²⁴So they were all inside the temple to offer sacrifices and burnt offerings. Now Jehu had surrounded the building with eighty of his men and had warned them, "If you let anyone escape, you will pay for it with your own life."

²⁵As soon as Jehu had finished sacrificing the burnt offering, he commanded his guards and officers, "Go in and kill all of them. Don't let a single one escape!" So they killed them all with their swords, and the guards and officers dragged their bodies outside. Then Jehu's men went into the fortress* of the temple of Baal. ²⁶They dragged out the sacred pillar used in the worship of Baal and destroyed it. ²⁷They broke down the sacred pillar of Baal and wrecked the temple of Baal, converting it into a public toilet. That is what it is used for to this day. ²⁸Thus, Jehu destroyed every trace of Baal worship from Israel. ²⁹He did not, however, destroy the gold calves at Bethel and Dan, the great sin that Jeroboam son of Nebat had led Israel to commit.

³⁰Nonetheless the LORD said to Jehu, "You have done well in following my instructions to destroy the family of Ahab. Because of this I will cause your descendants to be the kings of Israel down to the fourth generation." ³¹But Jehu did not obey the law of the LORD, the God of Israel, with all his heart. He refused to turn from the sins of idolatry that Jeroboam had led Israel to commit.

THE DEATH OF JEHU

³²At about this time the LORD began to reduce the size of Israel's territory. King Hazael conquered several sections of the country ³³east of

10:25 Hebrew *city.*

the Jordan River, including all of Gilead, Gad, Reuben, and Manasseh. He conquered the area from the town of Aroer by the Arnon Gorge to as far north as Gilead and Bashan.

34The rest of the events in Jehu's reign and all his deeds and achievements are recorded in *The Book of the History of the Kings of Israel.* 35When Jehu died, he was buried with his ancestors in Samaria. Then his son Jehoahaz became the next king. 36In all, Jehu reigned over Israel from Samaria for twenty-eight years.

ATHALIAH RULES IN JUDAH

11 When Athaliah, the mother of King Ahaziah of Judah, learned that her son was dead, she set out to destroy the rest of the royal family. 2But Ahaziah's sister Jehosheba, the daughter of King Jehoram,* took Ahaziah's infant son, Joash, and stole him away from among the rest of the king's children, who were about to be killed. Jehosheba put Joash and his nurse in a bedroom to hide him from Athaliah, so the child was not murdered. 3Joash and his nurse remained hidden in the Temple of the LORD for six years while Athaliah ruled over the land.

REVOLT AGAINST ATHALIAH

4In the seventh year of Athaliah's reign, Jehoiada the priest summoned the commanders, the Carite mercenaries, and the guards to come to the Temple of the LORD. He made a pact with them and made them swear an oath of loyalty there in the LORD's Temple; then he showed them the king's son.

5Jehoiada told them, "This is what you must do. A third of you who are on duty on the Sabbath are to guard the royal palace itself. 6Another third of you are to stand guard at the Sur Gate. And the final third must stand guard behind the palace guard. These three groups will all guard the palace. 7The other two units who are off duty on the Sabbath must stand guard for the king at the LORD's Temple. 8Form a bodyguard for the king and keep your weapons in hand. Any unauthorized person who approaches you must be killed. Stay right beside the king at all times."

9So the commanders did everything just as Jehoiada the priest ordered. The commanders took charge of the men reporting for duty that Sabbath, as well as those who were going off duty. They brought them all to Jehoiada the priest, 10and he supplied them with the spears and shields that had once belonged to King David and were stored in the Temple of the LORD. 11The guards stationed themselves around the king, with their weapons ready. They formed a line from the south side of the Temple around to the north side and all around the altar.

12Then Jehoiada brought out Joash, the king's son, and placed the crown on his head. He presented Joash with a copy of God's covenant and proclaimed him king. They anointed him, and all the people clapped their hands and shouted, "Long live the king!"

THE DEATH OF ATHALIAH

13When Athaliah heard all the noise made by the guards and the people, she hurried to the LORD's Temple to see what was happening. 14And she saw the newly crowned king standing in his place of authority by the pillar, as was the custom at times of coronation. The officers and trumpeters were surrounding him, and people from all over the land were rejoicing and blowing trumpets. When Athaliah saw all this, she tore her clothes in despair and shouted, "Treason! Treason!"

15Then Jehoiada the priest ordered the commanders who were in charge of the troops, "Take her out of the Temple, and kill anyone who tries to rescue her. Do not kill her here in the Temple of the LORD." 16So they seized her and led her out to the gate where horses enter the palace grounds, and she was killed there.

JEHOIADA'S RELIGIOUS REFORMS

17Then Jehoiada made a covenant between the LORD and the king and the people that they

11:2 Hebrew *Joram,* a variant name for Jehoram.

would be the LORD's people. He also made a covenant between the king and the people. [18]And all the people of the land went over to the temple of Baal and tore it down. They demolished the altars and smashed the idols to pieces, and they killed Mattan the priest of Baal in front of the altars.

Jehoiada the priest stationed guards at the Temple of the LORD. [19]Then the commanders, the Carite mercenaries, the guards, and all the people of the land escorted the king from the Temple of the LORD. They went through the gate of the guards and into the palace, and the king took his seat on the royal throne. [20]So all the people of the land rejoiced, and the city was peaceful because Athaliah had been killed at the king's palace.

[21]Joash* was seven years old when he became king.

JOASH REPAIRS THE TEMPLE

12 Joash* began to rule over Judah in the seventh year of King Jehu's reign in Israel. He reigned in Jerusalem forty years. His mother was Zibiah, from Beersheba. [2]All his life Joash did what was pleasing in the LORD's sight because Jehoiada the priest instructed him. [3]Yet even so, he did not destroy the pagan shrines, and the people still offered sacrifices and burned incense there.

[4]One day King Joash said to the priests, "Collect all the money brought as a sacred offering to the LORD's Temple, whether it is a regular assessment, a payment of vows, or a voluntary gift. [5]Let the priests take some of that money to pay for whatever repairs are needed at the Temple."

[6]But by the twenty-third year of Joash's reign, the priests still had not repaired the Temple. [7]So King Joash called for Jehoiada and the other priests and asked them, "Why haven't you repaired the Temple? Don't use any more gifts for your own needs. From now on, it must all be spent on getting the Temple into good condition." [8]So the priests agreed not to collect any more money from the people, and they also agreed not to undertake the repairs of the Temple themselves.

[9]Then Jehoiada the priest bored a hole in the lid of a large chest and set it on the right-hand side of the altar at the entrance of the Temple of the LORD. The priests guarding the entrance put all of the people's contributions into the chest. [10]Whenever the chest became full, the court secretary and the high priest counted the money that had been brought to the LORD's Temple and put it into bags. [11]Then they gave the money to the construction supervisors, who used it to pay the people working on the LORD's Temple—the carpenters, the builders, [12]the masons, and the stone-cutters. They also used the money to buy timber and cut stone for repairing the LORD's Temple, and they paid any other expenses related to the Temple's restoration.

[13]The money brought to the Temple was not used for making silver cups, lamp snuffers, basins, trumpets, or other articles of gold or silver for the Temple of the LORD. [14]It was paid out to the workmen, who used it for the Temple repairs. [15]No accounting was required from the construction supervisors, because they were honest and faithful workers. [16]However, the money that was contributed for guilt offerings and sin offerings was not brought into the LORD's Temple. It was given to the priests for their own use.

THE END OF JOASH'S REIGN

[17]About this time King Hazael of Aram went to war against Gath and captured it. Then he turned to attack Jerusalem. [18]King Joash collected all the sacred objects that Jehoshaphat, Jehoram, and Ahaziah, the previous kings of Judah, had dedicated, along with what he himself had dedicated. He sent them all to Hazael, along with all the gold in the treasuries of the LORD's Temple and the royal palace. So Hazael called off his attack on Jerusalem.

[19]The rest of the events in Joash's reign and all his deeds are recorded in *The Book of the*

11:21 Hebrew *Jehoash*, a variant name for Joash. 12:1 Hebrew *Jehoash*, a variant name for Joash; also in 12:2, 4, 6, 7, 18.

History of the Kings of Judah. ²⁰But his officers plotted against him and assassinated him at Beth-millo on the road to Silla. ²¹The assassins were Jozabad son of Shimeath and Jehozabad son of Shomer—both trusted advisers. Joash was buried with his ancestors in the City of David. Then his son Amaziah became the next king.

JEHOAHAZ RULES IN ISRAEL

13 Jehoahaz son of Jehu began to rule over Israel in the twenty-third year of King Joash's reign in Judah. He reigned in Samaria seventeen years. ²But he did what was evil in the LORD's sight. He followed the example of Jeroboam son of Nebat, continuing the sins of idolatry that Jeroboam son of Nebat had led Israel to commit. ³So the LORD was very angry with Israel, and he allowed King Hazael of Aram and his son Ben-hadad to defeat them time after time.

⁴Then Jehoahaz prayed for the LORD's help, and the LORD heard his prayer. The LORD could see how terribly the king of Aram was oppressing Israel. ⁵So the LORD raised up a deliverer to rescue the Israelites from the tyranny of the Arameans. Then Israel lived in safety again as they had in former days. ⁶But they continued to sin, following the evil example of Jeroboam. They even set up an Asherah pole in Samaria. ⁷Finally, Jehoahaz's army was reduced to fifty mounted troops, ten chariots, and ten thousand foot soldiers. The king of Aram had killed the others like they were dust under his feet.

⁸The rest of the events in Jehoahaz's reign and all his deeds, including the extent of his power, are recorded in *The Book of the History of the Kings of Israel.* ⁹When Jehoahaz died, he was buried in Samaria with his ancestors. Then his son Jehoash* became the next king.

JEHOASH RULES IN ISRAEL

¹⁰Jehoash son of Jehoahaz began to rule over Israel in the thirty-seventh year of King Joash's reign in Judah. He reigned in Samaria sixteen years. ¹¹But he did what was evil in the LORD's sight. He refused to turn from the sins of idolatry that Jeroboam son of Nebat had led Israel to commit. ¹²The rest of the events in Jehoash's reign and all his deeds, including the extent of his power and his war with King Amaziah of Judah, are recorded in *The Book of the History of the Kings of Israel.* ¹³When Jehoash died, he was buried with his ancestors in Samaria. Then his son Jeroboam II became the next king.

ELISHA'S FINAL PROPHECY

¹⁴When Elisha was in his last illness, King Jehoash of Israel visited him and wept over him. "My father! My father! The chariots and charioteers of Israel!" he cried.

¹⁵Elisha told him, "Get a bow and some arrows." And the king did as he was told. ¹⁶Then Elisha told the king of Israel to put his hand on the bow, and Elisha laid his own hands on the king's hands. ¹⁷Then he commanded, "Open that eastern window," and he opened it. Then he said, "Shoot!" So he did.

Then Elisha proclaimed, "This is the LORD's arrow, full of victory over Aram, for you will completely conquer the Arameans at Aphek. ¹⁸Now pick up the other arrows and strike them against the ground." So the king picked them up and struck the ground three times. ¹⁹But the man of God was angry with him. "You should have struck the ground five or six times!" he exclaimed. "Then you would have beaten Aram until they were entirely destroyed. Now you will be victorious only three times."

²⁰Then Elisha died and was buried.

Groups of Moabite raiders used to invade the land each spring. ²¹Once when some Israelites were burying a man, they spied a band of these raiders. So they hastily threw the body they were burying into the tomb of Elisha. But as soon as the body touched Elisha's bones, the dead man revived and jumped to his feet!

13:9 Hebrew *Joash,* a variant name for Jehoash; also in 13:10, 12, 13, 14, 25.

My Daily Worship
— *March 28* —

SPECIAL PLACES, DIVINE SPACES
2 KINGS 11:1–13:25

So King Joash called for Jehoiada and the other priests and asked them, "Why haven't you repaired the Temple? Don't use any more gifts for your own needs. From now on, it must all be spent on getting the Temple into good condition" (12:7).

[i reflect]

The place is quiet, though not oppressively silent. All is in order—aisles full of bookshelves, the reference section, the periodicals area, computers, kiosks providing space and privacy to study. The place is a library, of course, a space dedicated to reading, to learning, to study. The librarians keep it true to its purpose, complete and ready to serve those who frequent it.

The people of God had a space dedicated to the worship of God, the Temple at Jerusalem. They had priests who were to ensure that the magnificent edifice built by Solomon would stay ready and true to its purpose. But the Temple, constructed in every detail to express the worthiness and perfection of the Lord, was now in terrible shape. Its treasures had been plundered, the very building was in disrepair, and its walls were cluttered with the symbols of pagan deities. "Why haven't you fixed this yet?" Joash laments. Beyond the physical damage, however, was the spiritual disarray. The Temple's singular purpose had been compromised.

What we see, what we touch, what we hear—it all affects us. We must be aware and responsible lest we, like the Israelites, allow our inner house of worship to fall into disrepair or compromise. The result will be the same as in the days of the kings: People pulled away from worship. Do we glory in the new organ, the polished candlesticks, the reupholstered pews? Certainly not. We do not bow down to the altar, but rather, as David urged, "Worship the LORD in the splendor of his holiness" (Psalm 29:2). Honor God by honoring the singular purpose of his house. The Lord is holy and our worship of him must also be holy. The Lord is wholly divine, and so must our worship places be.

Set apart a portion of your devotional time specifically for praise and prayer. Perhaps you may want to "set apart" a new place also, just for time with him.

[i pray]

God, I honor you and praise you. You alone are worthy of worship.
Thank you for places set apart to worship you.

[i respond]

What physical things encouraged prayer and praise? What sounds, smells, or feelings do you remember as you were directed toward God in worship? Choose at least one of these things you can use or adapt for your personal worship.

²²King Hazael of Aram had oppressed Israel during the entire reign of King Jehoahaz. ²³But the LORD was gracious to the people of Israel, and they were not totally destroyed. He pitied them because of his covenant with Abraham, Isaac, and Jacob. And to this day he still has not completely destroyed them or banished them from his presence.

²⁴King Hazael of Aram died, and his son Ben-hadad became the next king. ²⁵Then Jehoash son of Jehoahaz recaptured from Ben-hadad son of Hazael the towns that Hazael had taken from Jehoash's father, Jehoahaz. Jehoash defeated Ben-hadad on three occasions, and so recovered the Israelite towns.

AMAZIAH RULES IN JUDAH

14 Amaziah son of Joash began to rule over Judah in the second year of the reign of King Jehoash* of Israel. ²Amaziah was twenty-five years old when he became king, and he reigned in Jerusalem twenty-nine years. His mother was Jehoaddin, from Jerusalem. ³Amaziah did what was pleasing in the LORD's sight, but not like his ancestor David. Instead, he followed the example of his father, Joash. ⁴Amaziah did not destroy the pagan shrines, where the people offered sacrifices and burned incense.

⁵When Amaziah was well established as king, he executed the men who had assassinated his father. ⁶However, he did not kill the children of the assassins, for he obeyed the command of the LORD written in the Book of the Law of Moses: "Parents must not be put to death for the sins of their children, nor the children for the sins of their parents. Those worthy of death must be executed for their own crimes."*

⁷It was Amaziah who killed ten thousand Edomites in the Valley of Salt. He also conquered Sela and changed its name to Joktheel, as it is called to this day.

⁸One day Amaziah sent this challenge to

Israel's king Jehoash, the son of Jehoahaz and grandson of Jehu: "Come and meet me in battle!"

⁹But King Jehoash of Israel replied to King Amaziah of Judah with this story: "Out in the Lebanon mountains a thistle sent a message to a mighty cedar tree: 'Give your daughter in marriage to my son.' But just then a wild animal came by and stepped on the thistle, crushing it! ¹⁰You have indeed destroyed Edom and are very proud about it. Be content with your victory and stay at home! Why stir up trouble that will bring disaster on you and the people of Judah?"

¹¹But Amaziah refused to listen, so King

14:1 Hebrew *Joash*, a variant name for Jehoash; also in 14:13, 23, 27. **14:6** Deut 24:16.

Jehoash of Israel mobilized his army against King Amaziah of Judah. The two armies drew up their battle lines at Beth-shemesh in Judah. [12]Judah was routed by the army of Israel, and its army scattered and fled for home. [13]King Jehoash of Israel captured King Amaziah of Judah at Beth-shemesh and marched on to Jerusalem. Then Jehoash ordered his army to demolish six hundred feet* of Jerusalem's wall, from the Ephraim Gate to the Corner Gate. [14]He carried off all the gold and silver and all the utensils from the Temple of the LORD, as well as from the palace treasury. He also took hostages and returned to Samaria.

[15]The rest of the events in Jehoash's reign, including the extent of his power and his war with King Amaziah of Judah, are recorded in *The Book of the History of the Kings of Israel.* [16]When Jehoash died, he was buried with his ancestors in Samaria. Then his son Jeroboam II became the next king.

[17]King Amaziah of Judah lived on for fifteen years after the death of King Jehoash of Israel. [18]The rest of the events in Amaziah's reign are recorded in *The Book of the History of the Kings of Judah.* [19]There was a conspiracy against Amaziah's life in Jerusalem, and he fled to Lachish. But his enemies sent assassins after him, and they killed him there. [20]They brought him back to Jerusalem on a horse, and he was buried with his ancestors in the City of David.

[21]The people of Judah then crowned Amaziah's sixteen-year-old son, Uzziah,* as their next king. [22]After his father's death, Uzziah rebuilt the town of Elath and restored it to Judah.

JEROBOAM II RULES IN ISRAEL

[23]Jeroboam II, the son of Jehoash, began to rule over Israel in the fifteenth year of King Amaziah's reign in Judah. Jeroboam reigned in Samaria forty-one years. [24]He did what was evil in the LORD's sight. He refused to turn from the sins of idolatry that Jeroboam son of Nebat had led Israel to commit. [25]Jeroboam II recovered the territories of Israel between Lebo-hamath and the Dead Sea,* just as the LORD, the God of Israel, had promised through Jonah son of Amittai, the prophet from Gath-hepher. [26]For the LORD saw the bitter suffering of everyone in Israel, and how they had absolutely no one to help them. [27]And because the LORD had not said he would blot out the name of Israel completely, he used Jeroboam II, the son of Jehoash, to save them.

[28]The rest of the events in the reign of Jeroboam II and all his deeds, including the extent of his power, his wars, and how he recovered for Israel both Damascus and Hamath, which had belonged to Judah,* are recorded in *The Book of the History of the Kings of Israel.* [29]When Jeroboam II died, he was buried with his ancestors, the kings of Israel. Then his son Zechariah became the next king.

UZZIAH RULES IN JUDAH

15 Uzziah* son of Amaziah began to rule over Judah in the twenty-seventh year of the reign of King Jeroboam II of Israel. [2]He was sixteen years old when he became king, and he reigned in Jerusalem fifty-two years. His mother was Jecoliah, from Jerusalem. [3]He did what was pleasing in the LORD's sight, just as his father, Amaziah, had done. [4]But he did not destroy the pagan shrines, where the people offered sacrifices and burned incense. [5]The LORD struck the king with leprosy,* which lasted until the day of his death; he lived in a house by himself. The king's son Jotham was put in charge of the royal palace, and he governed the people of the land.

[6]The rest of the events in Uzziah's reign and all his deeds are recorded in *The Book of the History of the Kings of Judah.* [7]When Uzziah died, he was buried near his ancestors in the

---

14:13 Hebrew *400 cubits* [180 meters]. 14:21 Hebrew *Azariah,* a variant name for Uzziah. 14:25 Hebrew *the sea of the Arabah.* 14:28 Or *to Yaudi.* 15:1 Hebrew *Azariah,* a variant name for Uzziah; also in 15:6, 7, 8, 17, 23, 27. 15:5 Or *with a contagious skin disease.* The Hebrew word used here and throughout this passage can describe various skin diseases.

City of David. Then his son Jotham became the next king.

ZECHARIAH RULES IN ISRAEL

[8]Zechariah son of Jeroboam II began to rule over Israel in the thirty-eighth year of King Uzziah's reign in Judah. He reigned in Samaria six months. [9]Zechariah did what was evil in the LORD's sight, as his ancestors had done. He refused to turn from the sins of idolatry that Jeroboam son of Nebat had led Israel to commit. [10]Then Shallum son of Jabesh conspired against Zechariah, assassinated him in public,* and became the next king. [11]The rest of the events in Zechariah's reign are recorded in *The Book of the History of the Kings of Israel.* [12]So the LORD's message to Jehu came true: "Your descendants will be kings of Israel down to the fourth generation."

SHALLUM RULES IN ISRAEL

[13]Shallum son of Jabesh began to rule over Israel in the thirty-ninth year of King Uzziah's reign in Judah. Shallum reigned in Samaria only one month. [14]Then Menahem son of Gadi went to Samaria from Tirzah and assassinated him, and he became the next king. [15]The rest of the events in Shallum's reign, including his conspiracy, are recorded in *The Book of the History of the Kings of Israel.*

MENAHEM RULES IN ISRAEL

[16]At that time Menahem destroyed the town of Tappuah* and all the surrounding countryside as far as Tirzah, because its citizens refused to surrender the town. He killed the entire population and ripped open the pregnant women.

[17]Menahem son of Gadi began to rule over Israel in the thirty-ninth year of King Uzziah's reign in Judah. He reigned in Samaria ten years. [18]But Menahem did what was evil in the LORD's sight. During his entire reign, he refused to turn from the sins of idolatry that Jeroboam son of Nebat had led Israel to commit. [19]Then King Tiglath-pileser* of Assyria invaded the land. But Menahem paid him thirty-seven tons* of silver to gain his support in tightening his grip on royal power. [20]Menahem extorted the money from the rich of Israel, demanding that each of them pay twenty ounces* of silver in the form of a special tax. So the king of Assyria turned from attacking Israel and did not stay in the land. [21]The rest of the events in Menahem's reign and all his deeds are recorded in *The Book of the History of the Kings of Israel.* [22]When Menahem died, his son Pekahiah became the next king.

PEKAHIAH RULES IN ISRAEL

[23]Pekahiah son of Menahem began to rule over Israel in the fiftieth year of King Uzziah's reign in Judah. He reigned in Samaria two years. [24]But Pekahiah did what was evil in the LORD's sight. He refused to turn from the sins of idolatry that Jeroboam son of Nebat had led Israel to commit.

[25]Then Pekah son of Remaliah, the commander of Pekahiah's army, conspired against him. With fifty men from Gilead, Pekah assassinated the king, along with Argob and Arieh, in the citadel of the palace at Samaria. Pekah then became the next king of Israel. [26]The rest of the events in Pekahiah's reign and all his deeds are recorded in *The Book of the History of the Kings of Israel.*

PEKAH RULES IN ISRAEL

[27]Pekah son of Remaliah began to rule over Israel in the fifty-second year of King Uzziah's reign in Judah. He reigned in Samaria twenty years. [28]But Pekah did what was evil in the LORD's sight. He refused to turn from the sins of idolatry that Jeroboam son of Nebat had led Israel to commit. [29]During his reign, King Tiglath-pileser of Assyria attacked Israel again, and he captured the towns of Ijon, Abel-beth-maacah, Janoah, Kedesh, and Hazor. He also conquered the regions of

15:10 Or *at Ibleam.* 15:16 As in some Greek manuscripts; Hebrew reads *Tiphsah.* 15:19a Hebrew *Pul,* another name for Tiglath-pileser. 15:19b Hebrew *1,000 talents* [34 metric tons]. 15:20 Hebrew *50 shekels* [570 grams].

Gilead, Galilee, and Naphtali, and he took the people to Assyria as captives. [30]Then Hoshea son of Elah conspired against Pekah and assassinated him. He began to rule over Israel in the twentieth year of Jotham son of Uzziah. [31]The rest of the events in Pekah's reign and all his deeds are recorded in *The Book of the History of the Kings of Israel.*

JOTHAM RULES IN JUDAH

[32]Jotham son of Uzziah began to rule over Judah in the second year of King Pekah's reign in Israel. [33]He was twenty-five years old when he became king, and he reigned in Jerusalem sixteen years. His mother was Jerusha, the daughter of Zadok.

[34]Jotham did what was pleasing in the LORD's sight, just as his father Uzziah had done. [35]But he did not destroy the pagan shrines, where the people offered sacrifices and burned incense. He was the one who rebuilt the upper gate of the Temple of the LORD.

[36]The rest of the events in Jotham's reign and all his deeds are recorded in *The Book of the History of the Kings of Judah.* [37]In those days the LORD began to send King Rezin of Aram and King Pekah of Israel to attack Judah. [38]When Jotham died, he was buried with his ancestors in the City of David. Then his son Ahaz became the next king.

AHAZ RULES IN JUDAH

16 Ahaz son of Jotham began to rule over Judah in the seventeenth year of King Pekah's reign in Israel. [2]Ahaz was twenty years old when he became king, and he reigned in Jerusalem sixteen years. He did not do what was pleasing in the sight of the LORD his God, as his ancestor David had done. [3]Instead, he followed the example of the kings of Israel, even sacrificing his own son in the fire.* He imitated the detestable practices of the pagan nations the LORD had driven from the land

> *Stand true to God and he will bring out his truth in a way that will make your life an expression of worship.*
>
> OSWALD CHAMBERS

ahead of the Israelites. [4]He offered sacrifices and burned incense at the pagan shrines and on the hills and under every green tree.

[5]Then King Rezin of Aram and King Pekah of Israel declared war on Ahaz. They besieged Jerusalem but did not conquer it. [6]At that time the king of Edom* recovered the town of Elath for Edom.* He drove out the people of Judah and sent Edomites* to live there, as they do to this day.

[7]King Ahaz sent messengers to King Tiglath-pileser of Assyria with this message: "I am your servant and your vassal.* Come up and rescue me from the attacking armies of Aram and Israel." [8]Then Ahaz took the silver and gold from the Temple of the LORD and the palace treasury and sent it as a gift to the Assyrian king. [9]So the Assyrians attacked the Aramean capital of Damascus and led its population away as captives, resettling them in Kir. They also killed King Rezin.

[10]King Ahaz then went to Damascus to meet with King Tiglath-pileser of Assyria. While he was there, he noticed an unusual altar. So he sent a model of the altar to Uriah the priest, along with its design in full detail. [11]Uriah built an altar just like it by following the king's instructions, and it was ready for the king when he returned from Damascus. [12]When the king returned, he inspected the altar and made offerings on it. [13]The king presented a burnt offering and a grain offering, poured a

16:3 Or *even making his son pass through the fire.* 16:6a As in Latin Vulgate; Hebrew reads *Rezin king of Aram.* 16:6b As in Latin Vulgate; Hebrew reads *Aram.* 16:6c As in marginal *Qere* reading of the Masoretic Text, Greek version, and Latin Vulgate; Hebrew reads *Arameans.* 16:7 Hebrew *your son.*

drink offering over it, and sprinkled the blood of peace offerings on it.

[14]Then King Ahaz removed the old bronze altar from the front of the LORD's Temple, which had stood between the entrance and the new altar, and placed it on the north side of the new altar. [15]He said to Uriah the priest, "Use the new altar for the morning sacrifices of burnt offering, the evening grain offering, the king's burnt offering and grain offering, and the offerings of the people, including their drink offerings. The blood from the burnt offerings and sacrifices should be sprinkled over the new altar. The old bronze altar will be only for my personal use." [16]Uriah the priest did just as King Ahaz instructed him.

[17]Then the king removed the side panels and basins from the portable water carts. He also removed the Sea from the backs of the bronze oxen and placed it on the stone pavement. [18]In deference to the king of Assyria, he also removed the canopy that had been constructed inside the palace for use on the Sabbath day,* as well as the king's outer entrance to the Temple of the LORD.

[19]The rest of the events in Ahaz's reign and his deeds are recorded in *The Book of the History of the Kings of Judah.* [20]When Ahaz died, he was buried with his ancestors in the City of David. Then his son Hezekiah became the next king.

HOSHEA RULES IN ISRAEL

17 Hoshea son of Elah began to rule over Israel in the twelfth year of King Ahaz's reign in Judah. He reigned in Samaria nine years. [2]He did what was evil in the LORD's sight, but not as much as the kings of Israel who ruled before him.

[3]King Shalmaneser of Assyria attacked and defeated King Hoshea, so Israel was forced to pay heavy annual tribute to Assyria. [4]Then Hoshea conspired against the king of Assyria by asking King So of Egypt* to help him shake free of Assyria's power and by refusing to pay the annual tribute to Assyria. When the king of Assyria discovered this treachery, he arrested him and put him in prison for his rebellion.

[5]Then the king of Assyria invaded the entire land, and for three years he besieged Samaria. [6]Finally, in the ninth year of King Hoshea's reign, Samaria fell, and the people of Israel were exiled to Assyria. They were settled in colonies in Halah, along the banks of the Habor River in Gozan, and among the cities of the Medes.

SAMARIA FALLS TO ASSYRIA

[7]This disaster came upon the nation of Israel because the people worshiped other gods, sinning against the LORD their God, who had brought them safely out of their slavery in Egypt. [8]They had imitated the practices of the pagan nations the LORD had driven from the land before them, as well as the practices the kings of Israel had introduced. [9]The people of Israel had also secretly done many things that were not pleasing to the LORD their God. They built pagan shrines for themselves in all their towns, from the smallest outpost to the largest walled city. [10]They set up sacred pillars and Asherah poles at the top of every hill and under every green tree. [11]They burned incense at the shrines, just like the nations the LORD had driven from the land ahead of them. So the people of Israel had done many evil things, arousing the LORD's anger. [12]Yes, they worshiped idols, despite the LORD's specific and repeated warnings. [13]Again and again the LORD had sent his prophets and seers to warn both Israel and Judah: "Turn from all your evil ways. Obey my commands and laws, which are contained in the whole law that I commanded your ancestors and which I gave you through my servants the prophets."

[14]But the Israelites would not listen. They were as stubborn as their ancestors and refused to believe in the LORD their God. [15]They rejected his laws and the covenant he had made with their ancestors, and they

16:18 The meaning of the Hebrew is uncertain.   17:4 Or *by asking the king of Egypt at Sais.*

My Daily Worship

— *March 29* —

ONLY ONE IS WORTHY

2 KINGS 14:1–17:41

Worship only the LORD, who brought you out of Egypt with such mighty miracles and power.
You must worship him and bow before him; offer sacrifices to him alone (17:36).

[i reflect]

"*God of our fathers, with his almighty hand accomplished great things . . . True, but that was then.*
This is now. Today."

"*We need a more modern god for modern times. In fact, things are so complicated we could prob-*
ably use several gods."

"*Look at the world. It's full of gods. Surely, ours isn't that special. When it comes to deities, you*
can never have too many, can you?"

Is this how the people of Israel thought about worship? It is certainly how they acted. The result?
"They . . . became worthless themselves" (17:15b), for worship shapes our character into a likeness of the object of our worship. Though created in the image of the one true God, when they
worshipped false gods, their souls became increasingly similar to their substitute deities. Caught
in the confusion, their worship became a bazaar of the bizarre. So in this passage we see that they
have to be continually reminded to worship God *alone*.

Were God's commandments given through Moses not clear enough? Did they wonder, like *we* wonder, what did God *really* mean? Surely God's word couldn't apply in all situations, for all times,
right? No, the words were clear, the meaning transparent: "I am the LORD your God, who rescued
you from slavery in Egypt. Do not worship any other gods besides me. Do not make idols of any
kind. . . . You must never worship or bow down to them" (Exodus 20:2–5). Do not. Do not. Never.
So many generations later, "the Israelites would not listen. They were as stubborn as their ancestors and refused to believe in the LORD their God" (17:14). God really meant what he said.

"Holy, Holy, Holy," a hymn written generations ago, calls us to worship: "Only Thou art holy; there
is none beside Thee, / Perfect in pow'r, in love, and purity." It is God alone whom we worship. To
him alone, each day, offer your sacrifice of praise.

[i pray]

God, you alone are holy, holy, holy. You alone are worthy to worship as God. There truly
is none beside Thee. I bow down before you. You alone are holy, holy, holy.

[i respond]

Look at a recent issue of a news magazine. What are the "gods" of today, that try to pull you away
from worshiping God alone? Think about your words, choices, and actions. In what ways do you
"bow down," "serve," or "offer sacrifice" to these gods?

despised all his warnings. They worshiped worthless idols and became worthless themselves. They followed the example of the nations around them, disobeying the LORD's command not to imitate them. ¹⁶They defied all the commands of the LORD their God and made two calves from metal. They set up an Asherah pole and worshiped Baal and all the forces of heaven. ¹⁷They even sacrificed their own sons and daughters in the fire.* They consulted fortune-tellers and used sorcery and sold themselves to evil, arousing the LORD's anger.

¹⁸And because the LORD was angry, he swept them from his presence. Only the tribe of Judah remained in the land. ¹⁹But even the people of Judah refused to obey the commands of the LORD their God. They walked down the same evil paths that Israel had established. ²⁰So the LORD rejected all the descendants of Israel. He punished them by handing them over to their attackers until they were destroyed. ²¹For when the LORD tore Israel away from the kingdom of David, they chose Jeroboam son of Nebat as their king. Then Jeroboam drew Israel away from following the LORD and made them commit a great sin. ²²And the people of Israel persisted in all the evil ways of Jeroboam. They did not turn from these sins of idolatry ²³until the LORD finally swept them away, just as all his prophets had warned would happen. So Israel was carried off to the land of Assyria, where they remain to this day.

FOREIGNERS SETTLE IN ISRAEL

²⁴And the king of Assyria transported groups of people from Babylon, Cuthah, Avva, Hamath, and Sepharvaim and resettled them in the towns of Samaria, replacing the people of Israel. So the Assyrians took over Samaria and the other towns of Israel. ²⁵But since these foreign settlers did not worship the LORD when they first arrived, the LORD sent lions among them to kill some of them.

²⁶So a message was sent to the king of Assyria: "The people whom you have resettled in the towns of Israel* do not know how to worship the God of the land. He has sent lions among them to destroy them because they have not worshiped him correctly."

²⁷The king of Assyria then commanded, "Send one of the exiled priests from Samaria back to Israel. Let him teach the new residents the religious customs of the God of the land." ²⁸So one of the priests who had been exiled from Samaria returned to Bethel and taught the new residents how to worship the LORD.

²⁹But these various groups of foreigners also continued to worship their own gods. In town after town where they lived, they placed their idols at the pagan shrines that the people of Israel had built. ³⁰Those from Babylon worshiped idols of their god Succoth-benoth. Those from Cuthah worshiped their god Nergal. And those from Hamath worshiped Ashima. ³¹The Avvites worshiped their gods Nibhaz and Tartak. And the people from Sepharvaim even burned their own children as sacrifices to Adrammelech and Anammelech.

³²These new residents worshiped the LORD, but they appointed from among themselves priests to offer sacrifices at the pagan shrines. ³³And though they worshiped the LORD, they continued to follow the religious customs of the nations from which they came. ³⁴And this is still going on among them today. They follow their former practices instead of truly worshiping the LORD and obeying the laws, regulations, instructions, and commands he gave the descendants of Jacob, whose name he changed to Israel. ³⁵For the LORD had made a covenant with the descendants of Jacob and commanded them: "Do not worship any other gods or bow before them or serve them or offer sacrifices to them. ³⁶Worship only the LORD, who brought you out of Egypt with such mighty miracles and power. You must worship him and bow before him; offer sacrifices to him alone. ³⁷Be careful to obey all the laws, regulations, instructions, and com-

17:17 Or *They even made their sons and daughters pass through the fire.*   17:26 Hebrew *of Samaria;* also in 17:29.

mands that he wrote for you. You must not worship any other gods. ³⁸Do not forget the covenant I made with you, and do not worship other gods. ³⁹You must worship only the LORD your God. He is the one who will rescue you from all your enemies."

⁴⁰But the people would not listen and continued to follow their old ways. ⁴¹So while these new residents worshiped the LORD, they also worshiped their idols. And to this day their descendants do the same.

HEZEKIAH RULES IN JUDAH

18 Hezekiah son of Ahaz began to rule over Judah in the third year of King Hoshea's reign in Israel. ²He was twenty-five years old when he became king, and he reigned in Jerusalem twenty-nine years. His mother was Abijah,* the daughter of Zechariah. ³He did what was pleasing in the LORD's sight, just as his ancestor David had done. ⁴He removed the pagan shrines, smashed the sacred pillars, and knocked down the Asherah poles. He broke up the bronze serpent that Moses had made, because the people of Israel had begun to worship it by burning incense to it. The bronze serpent was called Nehushtan.*

⁵Hezekiah trusted in the LORD, the God of Israel. There was never another king like him in the land of Judah, either before or after his time. ⁶He remained faithful to the LORD in everything, and he carefully obeyed all the commands the LORD had given Moses. ⁷So the LORD was with him, and Hezekiah was successful in everything he did. He revolted against the king of Assyria and refused to pay him tribute. ⁸He also conquered the Philistines as far distant as Gaza and its territory, from their smallest outpost to their largest walled city.

⁹During the fourth year of Hezekiah's reign, which was the seventh year of King Hoshea's reign in Israel, King Shalmaneser of Assyria attacked Israel and began a siege on the city of Samaria. ¹⁰Three years later, during the sixth year of King Hezekiah's reign and the ninth year of King Hoshea's reign in Israel, Samaria fell. ¹¹At that time the king of Assyria deported the Israelites to Assyria and put them in colonies in Halah, along the banks of the Habor River in Gozan, and among the cities of the Medes. ¹²For they had refused to listen to the LORD their God. Instead, they had violated his covenant—all the laws the LORD had given through his servant Moses.

ASSYRIA INVADES JUDAH

¹³In the fourteenth year of King Hezekiah's reign, King Sennacherib of Assyria came to attack the fortified cities of Judah and conquered them. ¹⁴King Hezekiah sent this message to the king of Assyria at Lachish: "I have done wrong. I will pay whatever tribute money you demand if you will only go away." The king of Assyria then demanded a settlement of more than eleven tons of silver and about one ton of gold.* ¹⁵To gather this amount, King Hezekiah used all the silver stored in the Temple of the LORD and in the palace treasury. ¹⁶Hezekiah even stripped the gold from the doors of the LORD's Temple and from the doorposts he had overlaid with gold, and he gave it all to the Assyrian king.

¹⁷Nevertheless the king of Assyria sent his commander in chief, his field commander, and his personal representative from Lachish with a huge army to confront King Hezekiah in Jerusalem. The Assyrians stopped beside the aqueduct that feeds water into the upper pool, near the road leading to the field where cloth is bleached. ¹⁸They summoned King Hezekiah, but the king sent these officials to meet with them: Eliakim son of Hilkiah, the palace administrator, Shebna the court secretary, and Joah son of Asaph, the royal historian.

SENNACHERIB THREATENS JERUSALEM

¹⁹Then the Assyrian king's personal representative sent this message to King Hezekiah:

18:2 As in parallel text at 2 Chr 29:1; Hebrew reads *Abi,* a variant name for Abijah. **18:4** *Nehushtan* sounds like the Hebrew terms that mean "snake," "bronze," and "unclean thing." **18:14** Hebrew *300 talents* [10 metric tons] *of silver and 30 talents* [1 metric ton] *of gold.*

"This is what the great king of Assyria says: What are you trusting in that makes you so confident? [20]Do you think that mere words can substitute for military skill and strength? Which of your allies will give you any military backing against Assyria? [21]Will Egypt? If you lean on Egypt, you will find it to be a stick that breaks beneath your weight and pierces your hand. The pharaoh of Egypt is completely unreliable!

[22]"But perhaps you will say, 'We are trusting in the LORD our God!' But isn't he the one who was insulted by King Hezekiah? Didn't Hezekiah tear down his shrines and altars and make everyone in Judah worship only at the altar here in Jerusalem?

[23]"I'll tell you what! My master, the king of Assyria, will strike a bargain with you. If you can find two thousand horsemen in your entire army, he will give you two thousand horses for them to ride on! [24]With your tiny army, how can you think of challenging even the weakest contingent of my master's troops, even with the help of Egypt's chariots and horsemen*? [25]What's more, do you think we have invaded your land without the LORD's direction? The LORD himself told us, 'Go and destroy it!'"

[26]Then Eliakim son of Hilkiah, Shebna, and Joah said to the king's representative, "Please speak to us in Aramaic, for we understand it well. Don't speak in Hebrew, for the people on the wall will hear."

[27]But Sennacherib's representative replied, "My master wants everyone in Jerusalem to hear this, not just you. He wants them to know that if you do not surrender, this city will be put under siege. The people will become so hungry and thirsty that they will eat their own dung and drink their own urine."

[28]Then he stood and shouted in Hebrew to the people on the wall, "Listen to this message from the great king of Assyria! [29]This is what the king says: Don't let King Hezekiah deceive you. He will never be able to rescue you from my power. [30]Don't let him fool you into trusting in the LORD by saying, 'The LORD will rescue us! This city will never be handed over to the Assyrian king.'

[31]"Don't listen to Hezekiah! These are the terms the king of Assyria is offering: Make peace with me—open the gates and come out. Then I will allow each of you to continue eating from your own garden and drinking from your own well. [32]Then I will arrange to take you to another land like this one—a country with bountiful harvests of grain and wine, bread and vineyards, olive trees and honey—a land of plenty. Choose life instead of death!

"Don't listen to Hezekiah when he tries to mislead you by saying, 'The LORD will rescue us!' [33]Have the gods of any other nations ever saved their people from the king of Assyria? [34]What happened to the gods of Hamath and Arpad? And what about the gods of Sepharvaim, Hena, and Ivvah? Did they rescue Samaria from my power? [35]What god of any nation has ever been able to save its people from my power? Name just one! So what makes you think that the LORD can rescue Jerusalem?"

[36]But the people were silent and did not answer because Hezekiah had told them not to speak. [37]Then Eliakim son of Hilkiah, the palace administrator, Shebna the court secretary, and Joah son of Asaph, the royal historian, went back to Hezekiah. They tore their clothes in despair, and they went in to see the king and told him what the Assyrian representative had said.

HEZEKIAH SEEKS THE LORD'S HELP

19 When King Hezekiah heard their report, he tore his clothes and put on sackcloth and went into the Temple of the

18:24 Or *and charioteers.*

LORD to pray. ²And he sent Eliakim the palace administrator, Shebna the court secretary, and the leading priests, all dressed in sackcloth, to the prophet Isaiah son of Amoz. ³They told him, "This is what King Hezekiah says: This is a day of trouble, insult, and disgrace. It is like when a child is ready to be born, but the mother has no strength to deliver it. ⁴But perhaps the LORD your God has heard the Assyrian representative defying the living God and will punish him for his words. Oh, pray for those of us who are left!"

⁵After King Hezekiah's officials delivered the king's message to Isaiah, ⁶the prophet replied, "Say to your master, 'This is what the LORD says: Do not be disturbed by this blasphemous speech against me from the Assyrian king's messengers. ⁷Listen! I myself will move against him, and the king will receive a report from Assyria telling him that he is needed at home. Then I will make him want to return to his land, where I will have him killed with a sword.'"

⁸Meanwhile, the Assyrian representative left Jerusalem and went to consult his king, who had left Lachish and was attacking Libnah. ⁹Soon afterward King Sennacherib received word that King Tirhakah of Ethiopia* was leading an army to fight against him. Before leaving to meet the attack, he sent this message back to Hezekiah in Jerusalem:

¹⁰"This message is for King Hezekiah of Judah. Don't let this God you trust deceive you with promises that Jerusalem will not be captured by the king of Assyria. ¹¹You know perfectly well what the kings of Assyria have done wherever they have gone. They have crushed everyone who stood in their way! Why should you be any different? ¹²Have the gods of other nations rescued them—such nations as Gozan, Haran, Rezeph, and the people of Eden who were in Tel-assar? The former kings of Assyria destroyed them all! ¹³What happened to the king of Hamath and the king of Arpad? What happened to the kings of Sepharvaim, Hena, and Ivvah?"

¹⁴After Hezekiah received the letter and read it, he went up to the LORD's Temple and spread it out before the LORD. ¹⁵And Hezekiah prayed this prayer before the LORD: "O LORD, God of Israel, you are enthroned between the mighty cherubim! You alone are God of all the kingdoms of the earth. You alone created the heavens and the earth. ¹⁶Listen to me, O LORD, and hear! Open your eyes, O LORD, and see! Listen to Sennacherib's words of defiance against the living God.

¹⁷"It is true, LORD, that the kings of Assyria have destroyed all these nations, just as the message says. ¹⁸And they have thrown the gods of these nations into the fire and burned them. But of course the Assyrians could destroy them! They were not gods at all—only idols of wood and stone shaped by human hands. ¹⁹Now, O LORD our God, rescue us from his power; then all the kingdoms of the earth will know that you alone, O LORD, are God."

ISAIAH PREDICTS JUDAH'S DELIVERANCE

²⁰Then Isaiah son of Amoz sent this message to Hezekiah: "This is what the LORD, the God of Israel, says: I have heard your prayer about King Sennacherib of Assyria. ²¹This is the message that the LORD has spoken against him:

'The virgin daughter of Zion
  despises you and laughs at you.
The daughter of Jerusalem
  scoffs and shakes her head as you flee.

²² 'Whom do you think you have been
  insulting and ridiculing?
Against whom did you raise your voice?
At whom did you look in such proud
  condescension?
It was the Holy One of Israel!

19:9 Hebrew *of Cush.*

²³ By your messengers you have mocked the
    Lord.
  You have said, "With my many chariots
    I have conquered the highest mountains—
    yes, the remotest peaks of Lebanon.
  I have cut down its tallest cedars
    and its choicest cypress trees.
  I have reached its farthest corners
    and explored its deepest forests.
²⁴ I have dug wells in many a foreign land
    and refreshed myself with their water.
  I even stopped up the rivers of Egypt
    so that my armies could go across!"

²⁵ 'But have you not heard?
    It was I, the LORD, who decided this long
    ago.
  Long ago I planned what I am now
    causing to happen,
    that you should crush fortified cities
    into heaps of rubble.
²⁶ That is why their people have so little
    power
    and are such easy prey for you.
  They are as helpless as the grass,
    as easily trampled as tender green shoots.
  They are like grass sprouting on a
    housetop,
    easily scorched by the sun.

²⁷ 'But I know you well—
    your comings and goings and all you do.
    I know the way you have raged against me.
²⁸ And because of your arrogance against me,
    which I have heard for myself,
  I will put my hook in your nose
    and my bridle in your mouth.
  I will make you return
    by the road on which you came.'"

²⁹Then Isaiah said to Hezekiah, "Here is the
proof that the LORD will protect this city from
Assyria's king. This year you will eat only what
grows up by itself, and next year you will eat
what springs up from that. But in the third
year you will plant crops and harvest them;

you will tend vineyards and eat their fruit.
³⁰And you who are left in Judah, who have
escaped the ravages of the siege, will take root
again in your own soil, and you will flourish
and multiply. ³¹For a remnant of my people
will spread out from Jerusalem, a group of
survivors from Mount Zion. The passion of
the LORD Almighty will make this happen!

³²"And this is what the LORD says about the
king of Assyria: His armies will not enter
Jerusalem to shoot their arrows. They will not
march outside its gates with their shields and
build banks of earth against its walls. ³³The king
will return to his own country by the road on
which he came. He will not enter this city, says
the LORD. ³⁴For my own honor and for the
sake of my servant David, I will defend it."

³⁵That night the angel of the LORD went out
to the Assyrian camp and killed 185,000
Assyrian troops. When the surviving Assyrians* woke up the next morning, they found
corpses everywhere. ³⁶Then King Sennacherib
of Assyria broke camp and returned to his
own land. He went home to his capital of
Nineveh and stayed there. ³⁷One day while he
was worshiping in the temple of his god
Nisroch, his sons Adrammelech and Sharezer
killed him with their swords. They then
escaped to the land of Ararat, and another son,
Esarhaddon, became the next king of Assyria.

HEZEKIAH'S SICKNESS
AND RECOVERY

20 About that time Hezekiah became
deathly ill, and the prophet Isaiah son
of Amoz went to visit him. He gave the king
this message: "This is what the LORD says: Set
your affairs in order, for you are going to die.
You will not recover from this illness."

²When Hezekiah heard this, he turned his
face to the wall and prayed to the LORD,
³"Remember, O LORD, how I have always tried
to be faithful to you and do what is pleasing in
your sight." Then he broke down and wept
bitterly.

19:35 Hebrew When they.

My Daily Worship

— *March 30* —

FIRST RESPONSE OR LAST RESORT?

2 KINGS 18:1–21:26

After Hezekiah received the letter and read it, he went up to the
LORD's Temple and spread it out before the LORD (19:14).

[i reflect]

At least it was a letter. At least the threats were not shouted on the roadside, as before, for all passersby to hear. Still, the threatening words Hezekiah read were as bold and as enormous as the literal threat posed by King Sennacherib and his mighty army. Whatever the form of communication, whatever the messenger, the situation for Judah seemed as desperate as it could get.

Was Hezekiah tempted to take the deal, to surrender with the promise of a good life for his people? The prophet Isaiah, after the shouted threats, *had* delivered God's own message: "Do not be disturbed by this blasphemous speech against me from the Assyrian king's messengers. Listen! I myself will move against him" (19:6–7). But this letter was different . . .

No, Hezekiah did not hesitate. He did not meet with his advisors to analyze the letter. He showed his faithfulness to the Lord in everything. Hezekiah hurried to the Temple with only one response. He "spread it out before the LORD," and then he spread himself out in prayer. "You alone are God. . . . You alone created. . . . O LORD our God, rescue us." The Assyrians were indeed defeated, as God alone could accomplish.

We all face threats of many kinds. Desperate situations, people offering deals and compromises, problems that redefine the word *hopeless*. What do we do first? Seek human counsel? Construct a chart of pros and cons? Read the latest self-help book? Instead, spread it out before the Lord. With complete honesty, a bow-before-the-Almighty, pleading prayer must be our first response.

As you encounter difficulties or trials during the day, remember Hezekiah, and "spread it out before the LORD."

[i pray]

God, you know the ways your name is dishonored. You know the threats I face. You alone
offer rescue from desperate situations. I come to you first, not as a last resort.

[i respond]

Who or what is threatening you today? Is it in a tangible form, such as a letter, an overdue bill, or something described in a newspaper article? Is it an intangible enemy? Write it on a piece of paper. Spread that threat on the floor, and bow before God in honest, pleading prayer.

⁴But before Isaiah had left the middle court-yard, this message came to him from the LORD: ⁵"Go back to Hezekiah, the leader of my people. Tell him, 'This is what the LORD, the God of your ancestor David, says: I have heard your prayer and seen your tears. I will heal you, and three days from now you will get out of bed and go to the Temple of the LORD. ⁶I will add fifteen years to your life, and I will rescue you and this city from the king of Assyria. I will do this to defend my honor and for the sake of my servant David.' "

⁷Then Isaiah said to Hezekiah's servants, "Make an ointment from figs and spread it over the boil." They did this, and Hezekiah recovered!

⁸Meanwhile, Hezekiah had said to Isaiah, "What sign will the LORD give to prove that he will heal me and that I will go to the Temple of the LORD three days from now?"

⁹Isaiah replied, "This is the sign that the LORD will give you to prove he will do as he promised. Would you like the shadow on the sundial to go forward ten steps or backward ten steps?"

¹⁰"The shadow always moves forward," Hezekiah replied. "Make it go backward instead." ¹¹So Isaiah asked the LORD to do this, and he caused the shadow to move ten steps backward on the sundial of Ahaz!

ENVOYS FROM BABYLON

¹²Soon after this, Merodach-baladan son of Baladan, king of Babylon, sent Hezekiah his best wishes and a gift, for he had heard that Hezekiah had been very sick. ¹³Hezekiah welcomed the Babylonian envoys and showed them everything in his treasure-houses—the silver, the gold, the spices, and the aromatic oils. He also took them to see his armory and showed them all his other treasures—everything! There was nothing in his palace or kingdom that Hezekiah did not show them.

¹⁴Then Isaiah the prophet went to King Hezekiah and asked him, "What did those men want? Where were they from?"

Hezekiah replied, "They came from the distant land of Babylon."

¹⁵"What did they see in your palace?" Isaiah asked.

"They saw everything," Hezekiah replied. "I showed them everything I own—all my treasures."

¹⁶Then Isaiah said to Hezekiah, "Listen to this message from the LORD: ¹⁷The time is coming when everything you have—all the treasures stored up by your ancestors—will be carried off to Babylon. Nothing will be left, says the LORD. ¹⁸Some of your own descendants will be taken away into exile. They will become eunuchs who will serve in the palace of Babylon's king."

¹⁹Then Hezekiah said to Isaiah, "This message you have given me from the LORD is good." But the king was thinking, "At least there will be peace and security during my lifetime."

²⁰The rest of the events in Hezekiah's reign, including the extent of his power and how he built a pool and dug a tunnel to bring water into the city, are recorded in *The Book of the History of the Kings of Judah.* ²¹When Hezekiah died, his son Manasseh became the next king.

MANASSEH RULES IN JUDAH

21 Manasseh was twelve years old when he became king, and he reigned in Jerusalem fifty-five years. His mother was Hephzibah. ²He did what was evil in the LORD's sight, imitating the detestable practices of the pagan nations whom the LORD had driven from the land ahead of the Israelites. ³He rebuilt the pagan shrines his father, Hezekiah, had destroyed. He constructed altars for Baal and set up an Asherah pole, just as King Ahab of Israel had done. He also bowed before all the forces of heaven and worshiped them. ⁴He even built pagan altars in the Temple of the LORD, the place where the LORD had said his name should be honored. ⁵He built these altars for all the forces of heaven in both courtyards of the LORD's Temple. ⁶Manasseh even sacrificed his own

---

Words of Worship

SERVE

Serve—Hebrew *'a-vad*; Greek *dou-lo-o*; *la-treu-o*. In the Old Testament, *'avad* is a general word for any kind of work or service. In the New Testament, *douloo* suggests service as a slave, whereas *latreuo* refers to service for hire, and religious service.

To serve others is to respond to their needs and wants, like the "server" in our favorite restaurant. That's what we as worshipers want to do for God. He has called us to serve him and to serve others, putting them ahead of ourselves. Jesus reminded his disciples he had not come to be served, but to serve (Mark 10:45). Washing their feet, he set an example of service (John 13:14–15).

In the Bible, the word *serve* describes the work of priests at God's altar as well as meeting the needs of others. To worship the Lord is to respond to what he wants; therefore, we speak of a "service of worship." All of life, lived sacrificially with the benefit of others in mind, can be our service (Romans 12:1). When we pray to or praise the Lord, or join other believers in doing these things, we are reminded who it is we truly serve.

---

son in the fire.* He practiced sorcery and divination, and he consulted with mediums and psychics. He did much that was evil in the LORD's sight, arousing his anger.

⁷Manasseh even took an Asherah pole he had made and set it up in the Temple, the very place where the LORD had told David and his son Solomon: "My name will be honored here forever in this Temple and in Jerusalem—the city I have chosen from among all the other tribes of Israel. ⁸If the Israelites will obey my commands—the whole law that was given through my servant Moses—I will not send them into exile from this land that I gave their ancestors." ⁹But the people refused to listen, and Manasseh led them to do even more evil than the pagan nations whom the LORD had destroyed when the Israelites entered the land.

¹⁰Then the LORD said through his servants the prophets: ¹¹"King Manasseh of Judah has done many detestable things. He is even more wicked than the Amorites, who lived in this land before Israel. He has led the people of Judah into idolatry. ¹²So this is what the LORD, the God of Israel, says: I will bring such disaster on Jerusalem and Judah that the ears of those who hear about it will tingle with horror. ¹³I will judge Jerusalem by the same standard I used for Samaria and by the same measure I used for the family of Ahab. I will wipe away the people of Jerusalem as one wipes a dish and turns it upside down. ¹⁴Then I will reject even those few of my people who are left, and I will hand them over as plunder for their enemies. ¹⁵For they have done great evil in my sight and have angered me ever since their ancestors came out of Egypt."

¹⁶Manasseh also murdered many innocent people until Jerusalem was filled from one end to the other with innocent blood. This was in addition to the sin that he caused the people of Judah to commit, leading them to do evil in the LORD's sight.

¹⁷The rest of the events in Manasseh's reign and all his deeds, including the sins he committed, are recorded in *The Book of the History of the Kings of Judah.* ¹⁸When Manasseh died, he was buried in the palace garden, the garden of Uzza. Then his son Amon became the next king.

AMON RULES IN JUDAH

¹⁹Amon was twenty-two years old when he became king, and he reigned in Jerusalem two years. His mother was Meshullemeth, the daughter of Haruz from Jotbah. ²⁰He did what was evil in the LORD's sight, just as his father,

---

21:6 Or *even made his son pass through the fire.*

Manasseh, had done. [21]He followed the example of his father, worshiping the same idols that his father had worshiped. [22]He abandoned the LORD, the God of his ancestors, and he refused to follow the LORD's ways.

[23]Then Amon's own servants plotted against him and assassinated him in his palace. [24]But the people of the land killed all those who had conspired against King Amon, and they made his son Josiah the next king.

[25]The rest of the events in Amon's reign and all his deeds are recorded in *The Book of the History of the Kings of Judah.* [26]He was buried in his tomb in the garden of Uzza. Then his son Josiah became the next king.

JOSIAH RULES IN JUDAH

22 Josiah was eight years old when he became king, and he reigned in Jerusalem thirty-one years. His mother was Jedidah, the daughter of Adaiah from Bozkath. [2]He did what was pleasing in the LORD's sight and followed the example of his ancestor David. He did not turn aside from doing what was right.

[3]In the eighteenth year of his reign, King Josiah sent Shaphan son of Azaliah and grandson of Meshullam, the court secretary, to the Temple of the LORD. He told him, [4]"Go up to Hilkiah the high priest and have him count the money the gatekeepers have collected from the people at the LORD's Temple. [5]Entrust this money to the men assigned to supervise the Temple's restoration. Then they can use it to pay workers to repair the Temple of the LORD. [6]They will need to hire carpenters, builders, and masons. Also have them buy the timber and the cut stone needed to repair the Temple. [7]But there will be no need for the construction supervisors to keep account of the money they receive, for they are honest people."

HILKIAH DISCOVERS GOD'S LAW

[8]Hilkiah the high priest said to Shaphan the court secretary, "I have found the Book of the Law in the LORD's Temple!" Then Hilkiah gave the scroll to Shaphan, and he read it.

[9]Shaphan returned to the king and reported, "Your officials have given the money collected at the Temple of the LORD to the workers and supervisors at the Temple." [10]Shaphan also said to the king, "Hilkiah the priest has given me a scroll." So Shaphan read it to the king.

[11]When the king heard what was written in the Book of the Law, he tore his clothes in despair. [12]Then he gave these orders to Hilkiah the priest, Ahikam son of Shaphan, Acbor son of Micaiah, Shaphan the court secretary, and Asaiah the king's personal adviser: [13]"Go to the Temple and speak to the LORD for me and for the people and for all Judah. Ask him about the words written in this scroll that has been found. The LORD's anger is burning against us because our ancestors have not obeyed the words in this scroll. We have not been doing what this scroll says we must do."

[14]So Hilkiah the priest, Ahikam, Acbor, Shaphan, and Asaiah went to the newer Mishneh section* of Jerusalem to consult with the prophet Huldah. She was the wife of Shallum son of Tikvah and grandson of Harhas, the keeper of the Temple wardrobe. [15]She said to them, "The LORD, the God of Israel, has spoken! Go and tell the man who sent you, [16]'This is what the LORD says: I will destroy this city and its people, just as I stated in the scroll you read. [17]For my people have abandoned me and worshiped pagan gods, and I am very angry with them for everything they have done. My anger is burning against this place, and it will not be quenched.'

[18]"But go to the king of Judah who sent you to seek the LORD and tell him: 'This is what the LORD, the God of Israel, says concerning the message you have just heard: [19]You were sorry and humbled yourself before the LORD when you heard what I said against this city and its people, that this land would be cursed and become desolate. You tore your clothing in despair and wept before me in repentance. So

22:14 Or *the Second Quarter*, a newer section of Jerusalem.

I have indeed heard you, says the LORD. [20]I will not send the promised disaster against this city until after you have died and been buried in peace. You will not see the disaster I am going to bring on this place.'" So they took her message back to the king.

JOSIAH'S RELIGIOUS REFORMS

23 Then the king summoned all the leaders of Judah and Jerusalem. [2]And the king went up to the Temple of the LORD with all the people of Judah and Jerusalem, and the priests, and the prophets—all the people from the least to the greatest. There the king read to them the entire Book of the Covenant that had been found in the LORD's Temple. [3]The king took his place of authority beside the pillar and renewed the covenant in the LORD's presence. He pledged to obey the LORD by keeping all his commands, regulations, and laws with all his heart and soul. In this way, he confirmed all the terms of the covenant that were written in the scroll, and all the people pledged themselves to the covenant.

[4]Then the king instructed Hilkiah the high priest and the leading priests and the Temple gatekeepers to remove from the LORD's Temple all the utensils that were used to worship Baal, Asherah, and all the forces of heaven. The king had all these things burned outside Jerusalem on the terraces of the Kidron Valley, and he carried the ashes away to Bethel. [5]He did away with the pagan priests, who had been appointed by the previous kings of Judah, for they had burned incense at the pagan shrines throughout Judah and even in the vicinity of Jerusalem. They had also offered incense to Baal, and to the sun, the moon, the constellations, and to all the forces of heaven. [6]The king removed the Asherah pole from the LORD's Temple and took it outside Jerusalem to the Kidron Valley, where he burned it. Then he ground the pole to dust and threw the dust in the public cemetery. [7]He also tore down the houses of the shrine prostitutes that were inside the Temple of the LORD, where the women wove coverings for the Asherah pole.

[8]Josiah brought back to Jerusalem all the priests of the LORD, who were living in other towns of Judah. He also defiled all the pagan shrines, where they had burned incense, from Geba to Beersheba. He destroyed the shrines at the entrance to the gate of Joshua, the governor of Jerusalem. This gate was located to the left of the city gate as one enters the city. [9]The priests who had served at the pagan shrines were not allowed to serve at the LORD's altar in Jerusalem, but they were allowed to eat unleavened bread with the other priests.

[10]Then the king defiled the altar of Topheth in the valley of Ben-hinnom, so no one could ever again use it to sacrifice a son or daughter in the fire* as an offering to Molech. [11]He removed from the entrance of the LORD's Temple the horse statues that the former kings of Judah had dedicated to the sun. They were near the quarters of Nathan-melech the eunuch, an officer of the court. The king also burned the chariots dedicated to the sun.

[12]Josiah tore down the altars that the kings of Judah had built on the palace roof above the upper room of Ahaz. The king destroyed the altars that Manasseh had built in the two courtyards of the LORD's Temple. He smashed them to bits and scattered the pieces in the Kidron Valley. [13]The king also desecrated the pagan shrines east of Jerusalem and south of the Mount of Corruption, where King Solomon of Israel had built shrines for Ashtoreth, the detestable goddess of the Sidonians; and for Chemosh, the detestable god of the Moabites; and for Molech,* the detestable god of the Ammonites. [14]He smashed the sacred pillars and cut down the Asherah poles. Then he desecrated these places by scattering human bones over them.

[15]The king also tore down the altar at Bethel, the pagan shrine that Jeroboam son of Nebat had made when he led Israel into sin. Josiah crushed the stones to dust and burned

23:10 Or *to make a son or daughter pass through the fire.*   **23:13** Hebrew *Milcom,* a variant name for Molech.

the Asherah pole. [16]Then as Josiah was looking around, he noticed several tombs in the side of the hill. He ordered that the bones be brought out, and he burned them on the altar at Bethel to desecrate it. This happened just as the LORD had promised through the man of God as Jeroboam stood beside the altar at the festival. Then Josiah turned and looked up at the tomb of the man of God* who had predicted these things. [17]"What is that monument over there?" Josiah asked.

And the people of the town told him, "It is the tomb of the man of God who came from Judah and predicted the very things that you have just done to the altar at Bethel!"

[18]Josiah replied, "Leave it alone. Don't disturb his bones." So they did not burn his bones or those of the old prophet from Samaria.

[19]Then Josiah demolished all the buildings at the pagan shrines in the towns of Samaria, just as he had done at Bethel. They had been built by the various kings of Israel and had made the LORD very angry. [20]He executed the priests of the pagan shrines on their own altars, and he burned human bones on the altars to desecrate them. Finally, he returned to Jerusalem.

JOSIAH CELEBRATES PASSOVER

[21]King Josiah then issued this order to all the people: "You must celebrate the Passover to the LORD your God, as it is written in the Book of the Covenant." [22]There had not been a Passover celebration like that since the time when the judges ruled in Israel, throughout all the years of the kings of Israel and Judah. [23]This Passover was celebrated to the LORD in Jerusalem during the eighteenth year of King Josiah's reign.

[24]Josiah also exterminated the mediums and psychics, the household gods, and every other kind of idol worship, both in Jerusalem and throughout the land of Judah. He did this in obedience to all the laws written in the scroll that Hilkiah the priest had found in the LORD's Temple. [25]Never before had there been a king like Josiah, who turned to the LORD with all his heart and soul and strength, obeying all the laws of Moses. And there has never been a king like him since.

[26]Even so, the LORD's anger burned against Judah because of all the great evils of King Manasseh, and he did not hold back his fierce anger from them. [27]For the LORD had said, "I will destroy Judah just as I have destroyed Israel. I will banish the people from my presence and reject my chosen city of Jerusalem and the Temple where my name was to be honored."

[28]The rest of the events in Josiah's reign and all his deeds are recorded in *The Book of the History of the Kings of Judah.*

[29]While Josiah was king, Pharaoh Neco, king of Egypt, went to the Euphrates River to help the king of Assyria. King Josiah marched out with his army to fight him, but King Neco killed him when they met at Megiddo. [30]Josiah's officers took his body back in a chariot from Megiddo to Jerusalem and buried him in his own tomb. Then the people anointed his son Jehoahaz and made him the next king.

JEHOAHAZ RULES IN JUDAH

[31]Jehoahaz was twenty-three years old when he became king, and he reigned in Jerusalem three months. His mother was Hamutal, the daughter of Jeremiah from Libnah. [32]He did what was evil in the LORD's sight, just as his ancestors had done.

[33]Pharaoh Neco put Jehoahaz in prison at Riblah in the land of Hamath to prevent him from ruling from Jerusalem. He also demanded that Judah pay 7,500 pounds of silver and 75 pounds of gold* as tribute. [34]Pharaoh Neco then installed Eliakim, another of Josiah's sons, to reign in place of his father, and he changed Eliakim's name to Jehoiakim. Jehoahaz was taken to Egypt as a prisoner, where he died.

23:16 As in Greek version; Hebrew lacks *as Jeroboam stood beside the altar at the festival. Then Josiah turned and looked up at the tomb of the man of God.* 23:33 Hebrew *100 talents* [3.4 metric tons] *of silver and 1 talent* [34 kilograms] *of gold.*

My Daily Worship

— *March 31* —

YOUR BURIED TREASURE

2 KINGS 22:1–25:30

Josiah also exterminated the mediums and psychics, the household gods, and every other kind of idol worship, both in Jerusalem and throughout the land of Judah. He did this in obedience to all the laws written in the scroll that Hilkiah the priest had found in the LORD's Temple (23:24).

[i reflect]

Imagine a buried treasure. But this treasure is not intentionally buried for safekeeping, like a chest hidden away by planning and cunning. Its worth is not even known by those who lose it, who push it aside, toss it to the back of the closet, heap other stuff on top of it.

Such was the fate of the Law of God, the very words given through Moses. The scroll containing God's covenant and law was buried and lost in the Temple, so forgotten by God's people that for centuries they had not even known how to celebrate Passover. Then came Hilkiah. "I have found the Book of the Law!" the priest yelled to the court secretary. After they read the incredible words, they knew what to do: "We must bring it to King Josiah; he will know what to do."

Crying out. Clothes torn in despair. But indeed the reformer does know what to do. Get back to the truth, the way we should live, the shape of holy worship. They had sunk so far—especially under Josiah's father, Amon, and grandfather, Manasseh, one of the most evil of all the kings of Judah— but Josiah aspired to climb to the higher ground of his great-grandfather, Hezekiah. Josiah even went beyond that, restoring of God's Word as a treasure in the people's hearts as it should have been treasured in the Temple: "Never before had there been a king like Josiah, who turned to the LORD with all his heart and soul and strength, obeying all the laws of Moses" (23:25).

Where is the treasure of God's Word today? Where in our churches? Where in your life? May our lives express the conviction of the hymn, "Book of books, our people's strength, statesman's, teacher's, hero's treasure." May this treasure be seen in the riches that are your prayers and praises throughout the day.

[i pray]

God, I am grateful beyond words for your Word. Help me to treasure it, to know it, to live it. Guide me in the truth of your Scripture; let it be a lamp for my path.

[i respond]

Is there a portion of the Scriptures that is "buried treasure" to you? Choose a passage—such as a psalm or a New Testament letter—that you do not know well. Read it through at least twice, then choose a verse or verses to memorize today. Then do just that.

JEHOIAKIM RULES IN JUDAH

[35]In order to get the silver and gold demanded as tribute by Pharaoh Neco, Jehoiakim collected a tax from the people of Judah, requiring them to pay in proportion to their wealth.

[36]Jehoiakim was twenty-five years old when he became king, and he reigned in Jerusalem eleven years. His mother was Zebidah, the daughter of Pedaiah from Rumah. [37]He did what was evil in the LORD's sight, just as his ancestors had done.

24 During Jehoiakim's reign, King Nebuchadnezzar of Babylon invaded the land of Judah. Jehoiakim surrendered and paid him tribute for three years but then rebelled. [2]Then the LORD sent bands of Babylonian,* Aramean, Moabite, and Ammonite raiders against Judah to destroy it, just as the LORD had promised through his prophets. [3]These disasters happened to Judah according to the LORD's command. He had decided to remove Judah from his presence because of the many sins of Manasseh. [4]He had filled Jerusalem with innocent blood, and the LORD would not forgive this.

[5]The rest of the events in Jehoiakim's reign and all his deeds are recorded in *The Book of the History of the Kings of Judah.* [6]When Jehoiakim died, his son Jehoiachin became the next king. [7]The king of Egypt never returned after that, for the king of Babylon occupied the entire area formerly claimed by Egypt—from the brook of Egypt to the Euphrates River.

JEHOIACHIN RULES IN JUDAH

[8]Jehoiachin was eighteen years old when he became king, and he reigned in Jerusalem three months. His mother was Nehushta, the daughter of Elnathan from Jerusalem. [9]Jehoiachin did what was evil in the LORD's sight, just as his father had done.

[10]During Jehoiachin's reign, the officers of King Nebuchadnezzar of Babylon came up against Jerusalem and besieged it. [11]Nebuchadnezzar himself arrived at the city during the siege. [12]Then King Jehoiachin, along with his advisers, nobles, and officials, and the queen mother, surrendered to the Babylonians.

In the eighth year of Nebuchadnezzar's reign, he took Jehoiachin prisoner. [13]As the LORD had said beforehand, Nebuchadnezzar carried away all the treasures from the LORD's Temple and the royal palace. They cut apart all the gold vessels that King Solomon of Israel had placed in the Temple. [14]King Nebuchadnezzar took ten thousand captives from Jerusalem, including all the princes and the best of the soldiers, craftsmen, and smiths. So only the poorest people were left in the land.

[15]Nebuchadnezzar led King Jehoiachin away as a captive to Babylon, along with his wives and officials, the queen mother, and all Jerusalem's elite. [16]He also took seven thousand of the best troops and one thousand craftsmen and smiths, all of whom were strong and fit for war. [17]Then the king of Babylon installed Mattaniah, Jehoiachin's uncle, as the next king, and he changed Mattaniah's name to Zedekiah.

ZEDEKIAH RULES IN JUDAH

[18]Zedekiah was twenty-one years old when he became king, and he reigned in Jerusalem eleven years. His mother was Hamutal, the daughter of Jeremiah from Libnah. [19]But Zedekiah did what was evil in the LORD's sight, just as Jehoiakim had done. [20]So the LORD, in his anger, finally banished the people of Jerusalem and Judah from his presence and sent them into exile.

THE FALL OF JERUSALEM

Then Zedekiah rebelled against the king of Babylon.

25 So on January 15,* during the ninth year of Zedekiah's reign, King Nebuchadnezzar of Babylon led his entire army

---

24:2 Or *Chaldean.* 25:1 Hebrew *on the tenth day of the tenth month,* of the Hebrew calendar. A number of events in 2 Kings can be cross-checked with dates in surviving Babylonian records and related accurately to our modern calendar. This event occurred on January 15, 588 B.C.

against Jerusalem. They surrounded the city and built siege ramps against its walls. ²Jerusalem was kept under siege until the eleventh year of King Zedekiah's reign.

³By July 18 of Zedekiah's eleventh year,* the famine in the city had become very severe, with the last of the food entirely gone. ⁴Then a section of the city wall was broken down, and all the soldiers made plans to escape from the city. But since the city was surrounded by the Babylonians,* they waited for nightfall and fled through the gate between the two walls behind the king's gardens. They made a dash across the fields, in the direction of the Jordan Valley.*

⁵But the Babylonians chased after them and caught the king on the plains of Jericho, for by then his men had all abandoned him. ⁶They brought him to the king of Babylon at Riblah, where sentence was passed against him. ⁷The king of Babylon made Zedekiah watch as all his sons were killed. Then they gouged out Zedekiah's eyes, bound him in bronze chains, and led him away to Babylon.

THE TEMPLE DESTROYED

⁸On August 14 of that year,* which was the nineteenth year of Nebuchadnezzar's reign, Nebuzaradan, captain of the guard, an official of the Babylonian king, arrived in Jerusalem. ⁹He burned down the Temple of the LORD, the royal palace, and all the houses of Jerusalem. He destroyed all the important buildings in the city. ¹⁰Then the captain of the guard supervised the entire Babylonian* army as they tore down the walls of Jerusalem. ¹¹Nebuzaradan, captain of the guard, then took as exiles those who remained in the city, along with the rest of the people and the troops who had declared their allegiance to the king of Babylon. ¹²But the captain of the guard allowed some of the poorest people to stay behind in Judah to care for the vineyards and fields.

¹³The Babylonians broke up the bronze pillars, the bronze water carts, and the bronze Sea that were at the LORD's Temple, and they carried all the bronze away to Babylon. ¹⁴They also took all the pots, shovels, lamp snuffers, dishes, and all the other bronze utensils used for making sacrifices at the Temple. ¹⁵Nebuzaradan, captain of the guard, also took the firepans and basins, and all the other utensils made of pure gold or silver.

¹⁶The bronze from the two pillars, the water carts, and the Sea was too great to be weighed. These things had been made for the LORD's Temple in the days of King Solomon. ¹⁷Each of the pillars was 27 feet* tall. The bronze capital on top of each pillar was 7½ feet* high and was decorated with a network of bronze pomegranates all the way around.

¹⁸The captain of the guard took with him as prisoners Seraiah the chief priest, his assistant Zephaniah, and the three chief gatekeepers. ¹⁹And of the people still hiding in the city, he took an officer of the Judean army, five of the king's personal advisers, the army commander's chief secretary, who was in charge of recruitment, and sixty other citizens. ²⁰Nebuzaradan the commander took them all to the king of Babylon at Riblah. ²¹And there at Riblah, in the land of Hamath, the king of Babylon had them all put to death. So the people of Judah were sent into exile from their land.

GEDALIAH GOVERNS IN JUDAH

²²Then King Nebuchadnezzar appointed Gedaliah son of Ahikam and grandson of Shaphan as governor over the people left in Judah. ²³When all the army commanders and their men learned that the king of Babylon had appointed Gedaliah as governor, they joined him at Mizpah. These included Ishmael son of Nethaniah, Johanan son of Kareah, Seraiah son of Tanhumeth the Netophathite, and

---

25:3 Hebrew *By the ninth day,* that is, "of the fourth month of Zedekiah's eleventh year" (compare Jer 52:6 and the note there). This event of the Hebrew lunar calendar occurred on July 18, 586 B.C.; also see note on 25:1.   **25:4a** Or *the Chaldeans;* also in 25:5, 13, 25, 26.   **25:4b** Hebrew *the Arabah.*   **25:8** Hebrew *On the seventh day of the fifth month,* of the Hebrew calendar. This day was August 14, 586 B.C.; also see note on 25:1.   **25:10** Or *Chaldean;* also in 25:24.   **25:17a** Hebrew *18 cubits* [8.1 meters].   **25:17b** As in parallel texts at 1 Kgs 7:16, 2 Chr 3:15, and Jer 52:22, all of which read *5 cubits* [2.3 meters]; Hebrew reads *3 cubits,* which is 4.5 feet or 1.4 meters.

> *If our knowledge of God is superficial,*
> *our worship will be superficial.*
>
> R. C. SPROUL

Jaazaniah son of the Maacathite, and all their men.

[24]Gedaliah vowed to them that the Babylonian officials meant them no harm. "Live in the land and serve the king of Babylon, and all will go well for you," he promised. [25]But in midautumn of that year,* Ishmael son of Nethaniah and grandson of Elishama, who was of the royal family, went to Mizpah with ten men and assassinated Gedaliah and everyone with him, both Judeans and Babylonians.

[26]Then all the people of Judah, from the least to the greatest, as well as the army commanders, fled in panic to Egypt, for they were afraid of what the Babylonians would do to them.

HOPE FOR ISRAEL'S ROYAL LINE

[27]In the thirty-seventh year of King Jehoiachin's exile in Babylon, Evil-merodach ascended to the Babylonian throne. He was kind to Jehoiachin and released him from prison on April 2 of that year.* [28]He spoke pleasantly to Jehoiachin and gave him preferential treatment over all the other exiled kings in Babylon. [29]He supplied Jehoiachin with new clothes to replace his prison garb and allowed him to dine at the king's table for the rest of his life. [30]The Babylonian king also gave him a regular allowance to cover his living expenses until the day of his death.

25:25 Hebrew *in the seventh month,* of the Hebrew calendar. This month occurred in October and November 586 B.C. 25:27 Hebrew *on the twenty-seventh day of the twelfth month,* of the Hebrew calendar. This day was April 2, 561 B.C.; also see note on 25:1.

1 Chronicles

Yours, O LORD, is the greatness, the power, the glory, the victory, and the majesty.

Everything in the heavens and on earth is yours, O LORD, and this is your kingdom (29:11).

Signs of the Times

Reading 1 Chronicles is like opening a time capsule—a treasure of names, history, and traditions preserved for future generations to experience. At first glance, a collection of yellowed newspaper clippings and photos in a time capsule may not seem like much. Upon closer inspection, however, a unified theme begins to emerge, and the remnants from another time, another place, and its people take on greater significance.

In the same way, we must examine what the writer of 1 Chronicles has left behind, piece by piece, chapter by chapter, to gain a sense of the story. It doesn't take long to discover that the book chronicles the journey of how God's people came to love and worship him. What begins as a genealogy in the opening chapters represents more than just a list of names. Tracing the line of David reveals a legacy of worshipers who committed themselves to be God's followers. It makes David's own story of devotion to God all the more meaningful. The focus on the preparations for building the Temple proves it was more than a historical building. Beyond its stone, timber, and mortar is a story of the God who met his worshipers there.

First Chronicles challenges us to reflect on our own stories as God's followers. Can you recall a place where you experienced meaningful worship with God? Can you think of a time when you connected with his majesty? Or when your mind preserved a snapshot of his grace and love? As you read this book, reflect on the moments that chronicle your worship relationship with God.

Worship Moments

- Jabez, a descendant of Judah, prayed in faith to the God of Israel (4:9–10).

- David brought the ark of God into Jerusalem with a great musical celebration of joy and dancing before the Lord (13:1–14; 15:1–29).

- David's worship involved prayers and psalms of humble praise and thanksgiving (16:7–36; 17:16–27; 29:10–20).

- God is praised as "the LORD Almighty" (11:9; 17:7, 24) and the "God of our salvation" (16:35). God's Spirit also is at work (12:18; cf. 28:19).

FROM ADAM TO NOAH'S SONS

1 The descendants of Adam were Seth, Enosh, [2]Kenan, Mahalalel, Jared, [3]Enoch, Methuselah, Lamech, [4]and Noah.

The sons of Noah were* Shem, Ham, and Japheth.

DESCENDANTS OF JAPHETH

[5]The descendants of Japheth were Gomer, Magog, Madai, Javan, Tubal, Meshech, and Tiras.

[6]The descendants of Gomer were Ashkenaz, Riphath,* and Togarmah.

[7]The descendants of Javan were Elishah, Tarshish, Kittim, and Rodanim.

DESCENDANTS OF HAM

[8]The descendants of Ham were Cush, Mizraim,* Put, and Canaan.

[9]The descendants of Cush were Seba, Havilah, Sabtah, Raamah, and Sabteca. The descendants of Raamah were Sheba and Dedan. [10]Cush was also the ancestor of Nimrod, who was known across the earth as a heroic warrior.

[11]Mizraim was the ancestor of the Ludites, Anamites, Lehabites, Naphtuhites, [12]Pathrusites, Casluhites, and the Caphtorites, from whom the Philistines came.*

[13]Canaan's oldest son was Sidon, the ancestor of the Sidonians. Canaan was also the ancestor of the Hittites, [14]Jebusites, Amorites, Girgashites, [15]Hivites, Arkites, Sinites, [16]Arvadites, Zemarites, and Hamathites.

DESCENDANTS OF SHEM

[17]The descendants of Shem were Elam, Asshur, Arphaxad, Lud, and Aram.

The descendants of Aram were* Uz, Hul, Gether, and Mash.*

[18]Arphaxad was the father of Shelah. Shelah was the father of Eber. [19]Eber had two sons. The first was named Peleg—"division"—for during his lifetime the people of the world were divided into different language groups and dispersed. His brother's name was Joktan.

[20]Joktan was the ancestor of Almodad, Sheleph, Hazarmaveth, Jerah, [21]Hadoram, Uzal, Diklah, [22]Obal,* Abimael, Sheba, [23]Ophir, Havilah, and Jobab. All these were descendants of Joktan.

[24]So this is the family line descended from Shem: Arphaxad, Shelah,* [25]Eber, Peleg, Reu, [26]Serug, Nahor, Terah, [27]and Abram, later known as Abraham.

DESCENDANTS OF ABRAHAM

[28]The sons of Abraham were Isaac and Ishmael.

[29]The sons of Ishmael were Nebaioth (the oldest), Kedar, Adbeel, Mibsam, [30]Mishma, Dumah, Massa, Hadad, Tema, [31]Jetur, Naphish, and Kedemah. These were the sons of Ishmael.

[32]The sons of Keturah, Abraham's concubine, were Zimran, Jokshan, Medan, Midian, Ishbak, and Shuah.

The sons of Jokshan were Sheba and Dedan.

[33]The sons of Midian were Ephah, Epher, Hanoch, Abida, and Eldaah.

All these were sons of Abraham by his concubine Keturah.

DESCENDANTS OF ISAAC

[34]Abraham was the father of Isaac. The sons of Isaac were Esau and Israel.*

DESCENDANTS OF ESAU

[35]The sons of Esau were Eliphaz, Reuel, Jeush, Jalam, and Korah.

1:4 As in Greek version (see also Gen 5:3-32); Hebrew lacks *The sons of Noah were*. 1:6 As in some Hebrew manuscripts and Greek version (see also Gen 10:3); most Hebrew manuscripts read *Diphath*. 1:8 Or *Egypt;* also in 1:11. 1:12 Hebrew *Casluhites, from whom the Philistines came, Caphtorites.* See Jer 47:4; Amos 9:7. 1:17a As in one Hebrew manuscript and some Greek manuscripts (see also Gen 10:23); most Hebrew manuscripts lack *The descendants of Aram were*. 1:17b As in parallel text at Gen 10:23; Hebrew reads *and Meshech*. 1:22 As in some Hebrew manuscripts and Syriac version (see also Gen 10:28); most Hebrew manuscripts read *Ebal*. 1:24 Some Greek manuscripts read *Arphaxad, Cainan, Shelah*. See notes on Gen 10:24; 11:12-13. 1:34 *Israel* is the name that God gave to Jacob.

³⁶The sons of Eliphaz were Teman, Omar, Zepho,* Gatam, Kenaz, and Amalek, who was born to Timna.*
³⁷The sons of Reuel were Nahath, Zerah, Shammah, and Mizzah.

ORIGINAL PEOPLES OF EDOM

³⁸The sons of Seir were Lotan, Shobal, Zibeon, Anah, Dishon, Ezer, and Dishan.
³⁹The sons of Lotan were Hori and Heman.* Lotan's sister was named Timna.
⁴⁰The sons of Shobal were Alvan,* Manahath, Ebal, Shepho,* and Onam.
The sons of Zibeon were Aiah and Anah.
⁴¹The son of Anah was Dishon.
The sons of Dishon were Hemdan,* Eshban, Ithran, and Keran.
⁴²The sons of Ezer were Bilhan, Zaavan, and Akan.*
The sons of Dishan* were Uz and Aran.

RULERS OF EDOM

⁴³These are the kings who ruled in Edom before there were kings in Israel*:

Bela son of Beor, who ruled from his city of Dinhabah.
⁴⁴When Bela died, Jobab son of Zerah from Bozrah became king.
⁴⁵When Jobab died, Husham from the land of the Temanites became king.
⁴⁶When Husham died, Hadad son of Bedad became king and ruled from the city of Avith. He was the one who destroyed the Midianite army in the land of Moab.
⁴⁷When Hadad died, Samlah from the city of Masrekah became king.
⁴⁸When Samlah died, Shaul from the city of Rehoboth on the Euphrates River* became king.
⁴⁹When Shaul died, Baal-hanan son of Acbor became king.
⁵⁰When Baal-hanan died, Hadad became king and ruled from the city of Pau.* His wife was Mehetabel, the daughter of Matred and granddaughter of Me-zahab. ⁵¹Then Hadad died.

The clan leaders of Edom were Timna, Alvah,* Jetheth, ⁵²Oholibamah, Elah, Pinon, ⁵³Kenaz, Teman, Mibzar, ⁵⁴Magdiel, and Iram. These were the clan leaders of Edom.

DESCENDANTS OF ISRAEL

2 The sons of Israel* were Reuben, Simeon, Levi, Judah, Issachar, Zebulun, ²Dan, Joseph, Benjamin, Naphtali, Gad, and Asher.

DESCENDANTS OF JUDAH

³Judah had three sons through Bathshua, a Canaanite woman. Their names were Er, Onan, and Shelah. But the oldest son, Er, was a wicked man, so the LORD killed him. ⁴Later Judah had twin sons through Tamar, his widowed daughter-in-law. Their names were Perez and Zerah. So Judah had five sons in all.
⁵The sons of Perez were Hezron and Hamul.
⁶The sons of Zerah were Zimri, Ethan, Heman, Calcol, and Darda*—five in all.
⁷Achan* son of Carmi, one of Zerah's descendants, brought disaster on Israel by taking plunder that had been set apart for the LORD.*
⁸The son of Ethan was Azariah.

1:36a As in many Hebrew manuscripts and a few Greek manuscripts (see also Gen 36:11); most Hebrew manuscripts read *Zephi.* **1:36b** As in some Greek manuscripts (see also Gen 36:12); Hebrew reads *Kenaz, Timna, and Amalek.* **1:39** As in parallel text at Gen 36:22; Hebrew reads *and Homam.* **1:40a** As in many Hebrew manuscripts and a few Greek manuscripts (see also Gen 36:23); most Hebrew manuscripts read *Alian.* **1:40b** As in some Hebrew manuscripts (see also Gen 36:23); most Hebrew manuscripts read *Shephi.* **1:41** As in many Hebrew manuscripts and some Greek manuscripts (see also Gen 36:26); most Hebrew manuscripts read *Hamran.* **1:42a** As in many Hebrew and Greek manuscripts (see also Gen 36:27); most Hebrew manuscripts read *Jaakan.* **1:42b** Hebrew *Dishon;* compare 1:38 and parallel text at Gen 36:28. **1:43** Or *before an Israelite king ruled over them.* **1:48** Hebrew *the river.* **1:50** As in many Hebrew manuscripts, some Greek manuscripts, Syriac version, and Latin Vulgate (see also Gen 36:39); most Hebrew manuscripts read *Pai.* **1:51** As in parallel text at Gen 36:40; Hebrew reads *Aliah.* **2:1** *Israel* is the name that God gave to Jacob. **2:6** As in many Hebrew manuscripts, some Greek manuscripts, and Syriac version (see also 1 Kgs 4:31); Hebrew reads *Dara.* **2:7a** Hebrew *Achar;* compare Josh 7:1. *Achar* means "disaster." **2:7b** The Hebrew term used here refers to the complete consecration of things or people to the LORD, either by destroying them or by giving them as an offering.

FROM JUDAH'S GRANDSON HEZRON TO DAVID

9The sons of Hezron were Jerahmeel, Ram, and Caleb.*

10 Ram was the father of Amminadab. Amminadab was the father of Nahshon, a leader of Judah.

11 Nahshon was the father of Salmon.* Salmon was the father of Boaz.

12 Boaz was the father of Obed. Obed was the father of Jesse.

13Jesse's first son was Eliab, his second was Abinadab, his third was Shimea, 14his fourth was Nethanel, his fifth was Raddai, 15his sixth was Ozem, and his seventh was David.

16Their sisters were named Zeruiah and Abigail. Zeruiah had three sons named Abishai, Joab, and Asahel.

17Abigail married a man named Jether, an Ishmaelite, and they had a son named Amasa.

DESCENDANTS OF HEZRON'S SON CALEB

18Hezron's son Caleb had two wives named Azubah and Jerioth. Azubah's sons were named Jesher, Shobab, and Ardon. 19After Azubah died, Caleb married Ephrathah,* and they had a son named Hur. 20Hur was the father of Uri. Uri was the father of Bezalel.

21When Hezron was sixty years old, he married Gilead's sister, the daughter of Makir. They had a son named Segub. 22Segub was the father of Jair, who ruled twenty-three towns in the land of Gilead. 23(Later Geshur and Aram captured the Towns of Jair* and also took Kenath and its sixty surrounding villages.) All these were descendants of Makir, the father of Gilead.

24Soon after Hezron died in the town of Caleb-ephrathah, his wife Abijah gave birth to a son named Ashhur (the father of* Tekoa).

DESCENDANTS OF HEZRON'S SON JERAHMEEL

25The sons of Jerahmeel, the oldest son of Hezron, were Ram (the oldest), Bunah, Oren, Ozem, and Ahijah. 26Jerahmeel had a second wife named Atarah. She was the mother of Onam.

27The sons of Ram, the oldest son of Jerahmeel, were Maaz, Jamin, and Eker.

28The sons of Onam were Shammai and Jada. The sons of Shammai were Nadab and Abishur.

29 The sons of Abishur and his wife Abihail were Ahban and Molid.

30 The sons of Nadab were Seled and Appaim. Seled died without children, 31but Appaim had a son named Ishi. The son of Ishi was Sheshan. Sheshan had a descendant named Ahlai.

32Shammai's brother, Jada, had two sons named Jether and Jonathan. Jether died without children, 33but Jonathan had two sons named Peleth and Zaza. These were all descendants of Jerahmeel.

34Sheshan had no sons, though he did have daughters. He also had an Egyptian servant named Jarha. 35Sheshan gave one of his daughters to be the wife of Jarha, and they had a son named Attai.

36 Attai was the father of Nathan. Nathan was the father of Zabad.

37 Zabad was the father of Ephlal. Ephlal was the father of Obed.

38 Obed was the father of Jehu. Jehu was the father of Azariah.

39 Azariah was the father of Helez. Helez was the father of Eleasah.

40 Eleasah was the father of Sismai. Sismai was the father of Shallum.

2:9 Hebrew *Kelubai,* a variant name for Caleb; compare 2:18. **2:11** As in Greek version (see also Ruth 4:21); Hebrew reads *Salma.* **2:19** Hebrew *Ephrath,* a variant name for Ephrathah; compare 2:50 and 4:4. **2:23** Or *captured Havvoth-jair.* **2:24** Or *the founder of;* also in 2:42, 45, 49-52 and perhaps other instances where the text reads *the father of.*

41 Shallum was the father of Jekamiah. Jekamiah was the father of Elishama.

DESCENDANTS OF HEZRON'S SON CALEB

42 The oldest son of Caleb, the brother of Jerahmeel, was Mesha, the father of Ziph. Caleb's second son was Mareshah, the father of Hebron.* 43 The sons of Hebron were Korah, Tappuah, Rekem, and Shema. 44 Shema was the father of Raham. Raham was the father of Jorkeam. Rekem was the father of Shammai. 45 The son of Shammai was Maon. Maon was the father of Beth-zur. 46 Caleb's concubine Ephah gave birth to Haran, Moza, and Gazez. Haran was the father of Gazez. 47 The sons of Jahdai were Regem, Jotham, Geshan, Pelet, Ephah, and Shaaph. 48 Another of Caleb's concubines, Maacah, gave birth to Sheber and Tirhanah. 49 She also gave birth to Shaaph (the father of Madmannah) and Sheva (the father of Macbenah and Gibea). Caleb also had a daughter named Acsah. 50 These were all descendants of Caleb.

DESCENDANTS OF CALEB'S SON HUR

The sons of Hur, the oldest son of Caleb's wife Ephrathah, were Shobal (the father of Kiriath-jearim), 51 Salma (the father of Bethlehem), and Hareph (the father of Beth-gader). 52 The descendants of Shobal (the father of Kiriath-jearim) were Haroeh, half the Manahathites, 53 and the families of Kiriath-jearim—the Ithrites, Puthites, Shumathites, and Mishraites, from whom came the people of Zorah and Eshtaol. 54 The descendants of Salma were Bethlehem, the Netophathites, Atroth-beth-joab, the other half of the Manahathites, the Zorites, 55 and the families of scribes living at Jabez—the Tirathites, Shimeathites, and Sucathites. All these were Kenites who descended from Hammath, the father of the family of Recab.*

DESCENDANTS OF DAVID

3 These were the sons who were born to David in Hebron:

The oldest was Amnon, whose mother was Ahinoam of Jezreel.
The second was Kileab,* whose mother was Abigail from Carmel.
2 The third was Absalom, whose mother was Maacah, the daughter of Talmai, king of Geshur.
The fourth was Adonijah, whose mother was Haggith.
3 The fifth was Shephatiah, whose mother was Abital.
The sixth was Ithream, whose mother was Eglah.

4 These six sons were born to David in Hebron, where he reigned seven and a half years.

Then David moved the capital to Jerusalem, where he reigned another thirty-three years. 5 The sons born to David in Jerusalem included Shimea, Shobab, Nathan, and Solomon. Bathsheba,* the daughter of Ammiel, was the mother of these sons. 6 David also had nine other sons: Ibhar, Elishua,* Elpelet,* 7 Nogah, Nepheg, Japhia, 8 Elishama, Eliada, and Eliphelet. 9 These were the sons of David, not including the sons of his concubines. David also had a daughter named Tamar.

DESCENDANTS OF SOLOMON

10 The descendants of Solomon were Rehoboam, Abijah, Asa, Jehoshaphat,

---

2:42 The meaning of the Hebrew is uncertain. 2:55 Or *the founder of Beth-recab*. 3:1 As in parallel text at 2 Sam 3:3; Hebrew reads *Daniel*. 3:5 Hebrew *Bathshua*, a variant name for Bathsheba. 3:6a As in some Hebrew and Greek manuscripts (see also 14:5-7 and 2 Sam 5:15); most Hebrew manuscripts read *Elishama*. 3:6b Hebrew *Eliphelet*; compare parallel text at 14:5-7.

[11]Jehoram,* Ahaziah, Joash, [12]Amaziah, Uzziah,* Jotham, [13]Ahaz, Hezekiah, Manasseh, [14]Amon, and Josiah.

[15]The sons of Josiah were Johanan (the oldest), Jehoiakim (the second), Zedekiah (the third), and Jehoahaz* (the fourth).

[16]Jehoiakim was succeeded by his son Jehoiachin; he, in turn, was succeeded by his uncle Zedekiah.*

DESCENDANTS OF JEHOIACHIN

[17]The sons of Jehoiachin,* who was taken prisoner by the Babylonians, were Shealtiel, [18]Malkiram, Pedaiah, Shenazzar, Jekamiah, Hoshama, and Nedabiah.

[19]The sons of Pedaiah were Zerubbabel and Shimei.

The sons of Zerubbabel were Meshullam and Hananiah. He also had a daughter named Shelomith. [20]His five other sons were Hashubah, Ohel, Berekiah, Hasadiah, and Jushab-hesed.

[21]The sons of Hananiah were Pelatiah and Jeshaiah. Jeshaiah's son was Rephaiah. Rephaiah's son was Arnan. Arnan's son was Obadiah. Obadiah's son was Shecaniah.

[22]Shecaniah's descendants were Shemaiah and his sons, Hattush, Igal, Bariah, Neariah, and Shaphat—six in all.

[23]The sons of Neariah were Elioenai, Hizkiah, and Azrikam—three in all.

[24]The sons of Elioenai were Hodaviah, Eliashib, Pelaiah, Akkub, Johanan, Delaiah, and Anani—seven in all.

OTHER DESCENDANTS OF JUDAH

4 Some of the descendants of Judah were Perez, Hezron, Carmi, Hur, and Shobal.

[2]Shobal's son Reaiah was the father of Jahath. Jahath was the father of Ahumai and Lahad. These were the families of the Zorathites.

Words of Worship

WORSHIP

Worship—Hebrew *hish-tach-e-vah* "bow down, prostrate oneself"; Greek *pros-ku-ne-o* "bow down, prostrate oneself." The words refer to the act of paying homage to a ruler, which in ancient times was expressed through bowing or falling down before the person.

One of the best known descriptions of worship is that of A. W. Tozer: "Worship is the normal employment of moral beings." It's normal for people to recognize that they are not God and that they need to seek the One who is. Failing to do so is abnormal and leads to painful distortions of human life. Paul mentioned the warped state of those who "wouldn't worship [God] as God or even give him thanks" (Romans 1:21). Paul's comments sound like a catalog of the cultural ills of our time.

The biblical words for *worship* mean to bow down before the Lord, and biblical expressions of worship focus on God's sovereignty and greatness. The heart of worship is the expression of humility and the recognition that God alone is our authority and Source. But far from demeaning us, worship lifts us to what we can be: servants and partners with God, patterned after his own image (Genesis 1:27) and sharing in his divine nature (2 Peter 1:4).

---

[3]The descendants of* Etam were Jezreel, Ishma, Idbash, Hazzelelponi (his daughter), [4]Penuel (the father of* Gedor), and Ezer (the father of Hushah). These were

---

3:11 Hebrew *Joram*, a variant name for Jehoram. **3:12** Hebrew *Azariah*, a variant name for Uzziah. **3:15** Hebrew *Shallum*, another name for Jehoahaz. **3:16** Hebrew *The descendants of Jehoiakim were his son Jeconiah* [a variant name for Jehoiachin] *and his son Zedekiah.* **3:17** Hebrew *Jeconiah*, a variant name for Jehoiachin. **4:3** As in Greek version; Hebrew reads *father of*. The meaning of the Hebrew is uncertain. **4:4** Or *the founder of*; also in 4:12, 14, 17-18, and perhaps other instances where the text reads *the father of*.

the descendants of Hur (the firstborn of Ephrathah), the ancestor of Bethlehem. [5]Ashhur (the father of Tekoa) had two wives, named Helah and Naarah. [6]Naarah gave birth to Ahuzzam, Hepher, Temeni, and Haahashtari. [7]Helah gave birth to Zereth, Izhar, Ethnan, [8]and Koz, who became the ancestor of Anub, Zobebah, and all the families of Aharhel son of Harum.

[9]There was a man named Jabez who was more distinguished than any of his brothers. His mother named him Jabez* because his birth had been so painful. [10]He was the one who prayed to the God of Israel, "Oh, that you would bless me and extend my lands! Please be with me in all that I do, and keep me from all trouble and pain!" And God granted him his request.

[11]Kelub (the brother of Shuhah) was the father of Mehir. Mehir was the father of Eshton. [12]Eshton was the father of Beth-rapha, Paseah, and Tehinnah. Tehinnah was the father of Ir-nahash. These were the descendants of Recah.

[13]The sons of Kenaz were Othniel and Seraiah. Othniel's sons were Hathath and Meonothai.* [14]Meonothai was the father of Ophrah. Seraiah was the father of Joab, the founder of the Valley of Craftsmen,* so called because many craftsmen lived there.

[15]The sons of Caleb son of Jephunneh were Iru, Elah, and Naam. The son of Elah was Kenaz.

[16]The sons of Jehallelel were Ziph, Ziphah, Tiria, and Asarel.

[17]The sons of Ezrah were Jether, Mered, Epher, and Jalon. Mered married an Egyptian woman, who became the mother of Miriam, Shammai, and Ishbah (the father of Eshtemoa). [18]Mered also married a woman of Judah, who became the mother of Jered (the father of Gedor),

Heber (the father of Soco), and Jekuthiel (the father of Zanoah). Mered's Egyptian wife was named Bithiah, and she was an Egyptian princess.

[19]Hodiah's wife was the sister of Naham. One of her sons was the father of Keilah the Garmite, and another was the father of Eshtemoa the Maacathite.

[20]The sons of Shimon were Amnon, Rinnah, Ben-hanan, and Tilon.

The descendants of Ishi were Zoheth and Ben-zoheth.

DESCENDANTS OF JUDAH'S SON SHELAH

[21]Shelah was one of Judah's sons. The descendants of Shelah were Er (the father of Lecah), Laadah (the father of Mareshah), the families of linen workers at Beth-ashbea, [22]Jokim, the people of Cozeba, Joash, and Saraph, who ruled over Moab and Jashubi-lehem. These names all come from ancient records. [23]They were the potters who lived in Netaim and Gederah. They all worked for the king.

DESCENDANTS OF SIMEON

[24]The sons of Simeon were Nemuel, Jamin, Jarib, Zerah, and Shaul.

[25]The descendants of Shaul were Shallum, Mibsam, and Mishma.

[26]The descendants of Mishma were Hammuel, Zaccur, and Shimei.

[27]Shimei had sixteen sons and six daughters, but none of his brothers had large families. So Simeon's tribe never became as large as the tribe of Judah.

[28]They lived in Beersheba, Moladah, Hazar-shual, [29]Bilhah, Ezem, Tolad, [30]Bethuel, Hormah, Ziklag, [31]Beth-marcaboth, Hazar-susim, Beth-biri, and Shaaraim. These towns were under their control until the time of King David.

4:9 Jabez sounds like a Hebrew term meaning "distress" or "pain." 4:13 As in some Greek manuscripts and Latin Vulgate; Hebrew lacks and Meonothai. 4:14 Or Joab, the father of Ge-harashim.

[32]Their descendants also lived in Etam, Ain, Rimmon, Token, and Ashan—five towns [33]and their surrounding villages as far away as Baalath.* This was their territory, and these names are recorded in their family genealogy.

[34]Other descendants of Simeon included Meshobab, Jamlech, Joshah son of Amaziah, [35]Joel, Jehu son of Joshibiah, son of Seraiah, son of Asiel, [36]Elioenai, Jaakobah, Jeshohaiah, Asaiah, Adiel, Jesimiel, Benaiah, [37]and Ziza son of Shiphi, son of Allon, son of Jedaiah, son of Shimri, son of Shemaiah.

[38]These were the names of some of the leaders of Simeon's wealthy clans, [39]who traveled to the region of Gedor, in the east part of the valley, seeking pastureland for their flocks. [40]They found lush pastures there, and the land was quiet and peaceful.

Some of Ham's descendants had been living in the region of Gedor. [41]But during the reign of King Hezekiah of Judah, the leaders of Simeon invaded it and completely destroyed* the homes of the descendants of Ham and of the Meunites. They killed everyone who lived there and took the land for themselves, because they wanted its good pastureland for their flocks. [42]Five hundred of these invaders from the tribe of Simeon went to Mount Seir, led by Pelatiah, Neariah, Rephaiah, and Uzziel—all sons of Ishi. [43]They destroyed the few Amalekites who had survived, and they have lived there ever since.

DESCENDANTS OF REUBEN

5 The oldest son of Israel* was Reuben. But since he dishonored his father by sleeping with one of his father's concubines, his birthright was given to the sons of his brother Joseph. For this reason, Reuben is not listed in the genealogy as the firstborn son. [2]It was the descendants of Judah that became the most powerful tribe and provided a ruler for the nation,* but the birthright belonged to Joseph.

[3]The sons of Reuben, the oldest son of Israel, were Hanoch, Pallu, Hezron, and Carmi.

[4]The descendants of Joel were Shemaiah, Gog, Shimei, [5]Micah, Reaiah, Baal, [6]and Beerah.

Beerah was the leader of the Reubenites when they were taken into captivity by King Tiglath-pileser* of Assyria.

[7]Beerah's relatives are listed in their genealogy by their clans: Jeiel (the leader), Zechariah, [8]and Bela son of Azaz, son of Shema, son of Joel.

These Reubenites lived in the area that stretches from Aroer to Nebo and Baal-meon. [9]And since they had so many cattle in the land of Gilead, they spread eastward toward the edge of the desert that stretches to the Euphrates River.

[10]During the reign of Saul, the Reubenites defeated the Hagrites in battle. Then they moved into the Hagrite settlements all along the eastern edge of Gilead.

DESCENDANTS OF GAD

[11]Across from the Reubenites in the land of Bashan lived the descendants of Gad, who were spread as far east as Salecah. [12]Joel was the leader in the land of Bashan, and Shapham was second-in-command, along with Janai and Shaphat.

[13]Their relatives, the leaders of seven other clans, were Michael, Meshullam, Sheba, Jorai, Jacan, Zia, and Eber. [14]These were all descendants of Abihail son of Huri, son of Jaroah, son of Gilead, son of Michael, son of Jeshishai, son of Jahdo, son

4:33 As in some Greek manuscripts (see also Josh 19:8); Hebrew reads *Baal*. 4:41 The Hebrew term used here refers to the complete consecration of things or people to the LORD, either by destroying them or by giving them as an offering. 5:1 *Israel* is the name that God gave to Jacob. 5:2 Or *and from Judah came a prince*. 5:6 Hebrew *Tilgath-pilneser*, a variant name for Tiglath-pileser; also in 5:26.

> *Man is never more truly man*
> *than when he worships God.*
>
> JAMES B. TORRANCE

of Buz. [15]Ahi son of Abdiel, son of Guni, was the leader of their clans.

[16]The Gadites lived in the land of Gilead, in Bashan and its villages, and throughout the Sharon Plain. [17]All of these were listed in the genealogical records during the days of King Jotham of Judah and King Jeroboam of Israel.

THE TRIBES EAST OF THE JORDAN

[18]There were 44,760 skilled warriors in the armies of Reuben, Gad, and the half-tribe of Manasseh. They were all skilled in combat and armed with shields, swords, and bows. [19]They waged war against the Hagrites, the Jeturites, the Naphishites, and the Nodabites. [20]They cried out to God during the battle, and he answered their prayer because they trusted in him. So the Hagrites and all their allies were defeated. [21]The plunder taken from the Hagrites included 50,000 camels, 250,000 sheep, 2,000 donkeys, and 100,000 captives. [22]Many of the Hagrites were killed in the battle because God was fighting against them. So they lived in their land until they were taken away into exile.

[23]The half-tribe of Manasseh spread through the land from Bashan to Baal-hermon, Senir, and Mount Hermon. They were very numerous. [24]These were the leaders of their clans: Epher, Ishi, Eliel, Azriel, Jeremiah, Hodaviah, and Jahdiel. Each of these men had a great reputation as a warrior and leader.

[25]But they were unfaithful and violated their covenant with the God of their ancestors. They worshiped the gods of the nations that God had destroyed. [26]So the God of Israel caused King Pul of Assyria (also known as Tiglath-pileser) to invade the land and lead away the people of Reuben, Gad, and the half-tribe of Manasseh as captives. The Assyrians exiled them to Halah, Habor, Hara, and the Gozan River, where they remain to this day.

THE PRIESTLY LINE

6 The sons of Levi were Gershon, Kohath, and Merari.
[2]The descendants of Kohath included Amram, Izhar, Hebron, and Uzziel.
[3]The children of Amram were Aaron, Moses, and Miriam.
The sons of Aaron were Nadab, Abihu, Eleazar, and Ithamar.

[4] Eleazar was the father of Phinehas. Phinehas was the father of Abishua.
[5] Abishua was the father of Bukki. Bukki was the father of Uzzi.
[6] Uzzi was the father of Zerahiah. Zerahiah was the father of Meraioth.
[7] Meraioth was the father of Amariah. Amariah was the father of Ahitub.
[8] Ahitub was the father of Zadok. Zadok was the father of Ahimaaz.
[9] Ahimaaz was the father of Azariah. Azariah was the father of Johanan.
[10] Johanan was the father of Azariah, the high priest at the Temple built by Solomon in Jerusalem.
[11] Azariah was the father of Amariah. Amariah was the father of Ahitub.
[12] Ahitub was the father of Zadok. Zadok was the father of Shallum.
[13] Shallum was the father of Hilkiah. Hilkiah was the father of Azariah.
[14] Azariah was the father of Seraiah. Seraiah was the father of Jehozadak, [15]who went into exile when the LORD sent the people of Judah and Jerusalem into captivity under Nebuchadnezzar.

THE LEVITE CLANS

[16]The sons of Levi were Gershon,* Kohath, and Merari.

[17]The descendants of Gershon included Libni and Shimei.

[18]The descendants of Kohath included Amram, Izhar, Hebron, and Uzziel.

[19]The descendants of Merari included Mahli and Mushi.

The following were the Levite clans, listed according to their ancestral descent:

[20]The descendants of Gershon included Libni, Jahath, Zimmah, [21]Joah, Iddo, Zerah, and Jeatherai.

[22]The descendants of Kohath included Amminadab, Korah, Assir, [23]Elkanah, Abiasaph,* Assir, [24]Tahath, Uriel, Uzziah, and Shaul.

[25]The descendants of Elkanah included Amasai, Ahimoth, [26]Elkanah, Zophai, Nahath, [27]Eliab, Jeroham, Elkanah, and Samuel.*

[28]The sons of Samuel were Joel* (the older) and Abijah (the second).

[29]The descendants of Merari included Mahli, Libni, Shimei, Uzzah, [30]Shimea, Haggiah, and Asaiah.

THE TEMPLE MUSICIANS

[31]David assigned the following men to lead the music at the house of the LORD after he put the Ark there. [32]They ministered with music there at the Tabernacle* until Solomon built the Temple of the LORD in Jerusalem. Then they carried on their work there, following all the regulations handed down to them. [33]These are the men who served, along with their sons:

Heman the musician was from the clan of Kohath. His genealogy was traced back through Joel, Samuel, [34]Elkanah, Jeroham, Eliel, Toah, [35]Zuph, Elkanah, Mahath, Amasai, [36]Elkanah, Joel, Azariah, Zephaniah, [37]Tahath, Assir, Abiasaph, Korah, [38]Izhar, Kohath, Levi, and Israel.*

[39]Heman's first assistant was Asaph from the clan of Gershon.* Asaph's genealogy was traced back through Berekiah, Shimea, [40]Michael, Baaseiah, Malkijah, [41]Ethni, Zerah, Adaiah, [42]Ethan, Zimmah, Shimei, [43]Jahath, Gershon, and Levi.

[44]Heman's second assistant was Ethan from the clan of Merari. Ethan's genealogy was traced back through Kishi, Abdi, Malluch, [45]Hashabiah, Amaziah, Hilkiah, [46]Amzi, Bani, Shemer, [47]Mahli, Mushi, Merari, and Levi.

[48]Their relatives, also Levites, were appointed to various other tasks in the Tabernacle, the house of God.

AARON'S DESCENDANTS

[49]Only Aaron and his descendants served as priests. They presented the offerings on the altar of burnt offering and the altar of incense, and they performed all the other duties related to the Most Holy Place. They made atonement for Israel by following all the commands that Moses, the servant of God, had given them.

[50]The descendants of Aaron were Eleazar, Phinehas, Abishua, [51]Bukki, Uzzi, Zerahiah, [52]Meraioth, Amariah, Ahitub, [53]Zadok, and Ahimaaz.

TERRITORY FOR THE LEVITES

[54]This is a record of the towns and territory assigned by means of sacred lots to the descendants of Aaron who were from the clan of Kohath. [55]This included Hebron and its surrounding pasturelands in Judah, [56]but the fields and outlying areas were given to Caleb

---

6:16 Hebrew *Gershom,* a variant name for Gershon (see 6:1); also in 6:17, 20, 43, 62, 71. 6:23 Hebrew *Ebiasaph,* a variant name for Abiasaph (also in 6:37); compare parallel text at Exod 6:24. 6:27 As in some Greek manuscripts (see also 6:33-34); Hebrew lacks *and Samuel.* 6:28 As in some Greek manuscripts and the Syriac version (see also 6:33 and 1 Sam 8:2); Hebrew lacks *Joel.* 6:32 Hebrew *the Tabernacle, the Tent of Meeting.* 6:38 *Israel* is the name that God gave to Jacob. 6:39 Hebrew lacks *from the clan of Gershon;* see 6:43.

son of Jephunneh. ⁵⁷So the descendants of Aaron were given the following towns, each with its surrounding pasturelands: Hebron (a city of refuge), Libnah, Jattir, Eshtemoa, ⁵⁸Holon,* Debir, ⁵⁹Ain,* Juttah,* and Beth-shemesh. ⁶⁰And from the territory of Benjamin they were given Gibeon,* Geba, Alemeth, and Anathoth, each with its pasturelands. So a total of thirteen towns was given to the descendants of Aaron. ⁶¹The remaining descendants of Kohath received ten towns from the territory of the half-tribe of Manasseh by means of sacred lots.

⁶²The descendants of Gershon received by sacred lots thirteen towns from the territories of Issachar, Asher, Naphtali, and from the Bashan area of Manasseh, east of the Jordan.

⁶³The descendants of Merari received by sacred lots twelve towns from the territories of Reuben, Gad, and Zebulun.

⁶⁴So the people of Israel assigned all these towns and pasturelands to the Levites. ⁶⁵The towns in the territories of Judah, Simeon, and Benjamin, mentioned above, were also assigned by means of sacred lots.

⁶⁶The descendants of Kohath received from the territory of Ephraim these towns, each with its surrounding pasturelands: ⁶⁷Shechem (a city of refuge in the hill country of Ephraim), Gezer, ⁶⁸Jokmeam, Beth-horon, ⁶⁹Aijalon, and Gath-rimmon. ⁷⁰The remaining descendants of Kohath were assigned these towns from the territory of the half-tribe of Manasseh: Aner and Bileam, each with its pasturelands.

⁷¹The descendants of Gershon received from the territory of the half-tribe of Manasseh the town of Golan in Bashan with its pasturelands and Ashtaroth with its pasturelands. ⁷²From the territory of Issachar, they were given Kedesh, Daberath, ⁷³Ramoth, and Anem, with their pasturelands. ⁷⁴From the territory of Asher, they received Mashal, Abdon, ⁷⁵Hukok, and Rehob, each with its

pasturelands. ⁷⁶From the territory of Naphtali, they were given Kedesh in Galilee, Hammon, and Kiriathaim, each with its pasturelands.

⁷⁷The remaining descendants of Merari received from the territory of Zebulun the towns of Jokneam, Kartah,* Rimmono, and Tabor, each with its pasturelands. ⁷⁸From the territory of Reuben, east of the Jordan River opposite Jericho, they received Bezer (a desert town), Jahaz,* ⁷⁹Kedemoth, and Mephaath, each with its pasturelands. ⁸⁰And from the territory of Gad, they received Ramoth in Gilead, Mahanaim, ⁸¹Heshbon, and Jazer, each with its pasturelands.

DESCENDANTS OF ISSACHAR

7 The four sons of Issachar were Tola, Puah, Jashub, and Shimron.
²The sons of Tola were Uzzi, Rephaiah, Jeriel, Jahmai, Ibsam, and Shemuel. Each of them was the leader of an ancestral clan. At the time of King David, the total number of men available for military service from these families was 22,600.
³The son of Uzzi was Izrahiah. The sons of Izrahiah were Michael, Obadiah, Joel, and Isshiah. These five became the leaders of clans. ⁴The total number of men available for military service among their descendants was 36,000, for all five of them had many wives and many sons.

⁵The total number of men available for military service from all the clans of the tribe of Issachar was 87,000. All of them were listed in their tribal genealogy.

DESCENDANTS OF BENJAMIN

⁶Three of Benjamin's sons were Bela, Beker, and Jediael.
⁷The sons of Bela were Ezbon, Uzzi, Uzziel, Jerimoth, and Iri. These five warriors were the leaders of clans. The total number of men available for military service among

6:58 As in parallel text at Josh 21:15; Hebrew reads *Hilen.* 6:59a As in parallel text at Josh 21:16; Hebrew reads *Ashan.* 6:59b As in Syriac version (see also Josh 21:16); Hebrew lacks *Juttah.* 6:60 As in parallel text at Josh 21:17; Hebrew lacks *Gibeon.* 6:77 As in Greek version (see also Josh 21:34); Hebrew lacks *Jokneam, Kartah.* 6:78 Hebrew *Jahzah,* a variant name for Jahaz.

their descendants was 22,034. All of them were listed in their family genealogy.

[8]The sons of Beker were Zemirah, Joash, Eliezer, Elioenai, Omri, Jeremoth, Abijah, Anathoth, and Alemeth. [9]According to their family genealogy, there were 20,200 men available for military service among their descendants, in addition to their clan leaders.

[10]The son of Jediael was Bilhan. The sons of Bilhan were Jeush, Benjamin, Ehud, Kenaanah, Zethan, Tarshish, and Ahishahar. [11]They were the leaders of the clans of Jediael, and their descendants included 17,200 men available for military service.

[12]The sons of Ir were Shuppim and Huppim. Hushim was the son of Aher.

DESCENDANTS OF NAPHTALI

[13]The sons of Naphtali were Jahzeel,* Guni, Jezer, and Shillem.* They were all descendants of Jacob's wife Bilhah.

DESCENDANTS OF MANASSEH

[14]The sons of Manasseh, born to his Aramean concubine, were Asriel and Makir. Makir was the father of Gilead.

[15]Makir found wives for Huppim and Shuppim. Makir's sister was named Maacah. One of his descendants was Zelophehad, who had only daughters.

[16]Makir's wife, Maacah, gave birth to a son whom she named Peresh. His brother's name was Sheresh. The sons of Peresh were Ulam and Rakem. [17]The son of Ulam was Bedan. All these were considered Gileadites, descendants of Makir son of Manasseh.

[18]Makir's sister Hammoleketh gave birth to Ishhod, Abiezer, and Mahlah.

[19]The sons of Shemida were Ahian, Shechem, Likhi, and Aniam.

Words of Worship

INSTRUMENTS

Instruments—Hebrew *ke-lei hash-shir* "implements of song." The Hebrew word *keli*, like the English word "instrument," is used for any kind of implement or apparatus, including cooking pots, tools, and weapons.

In Israel's worship, instruments were used in the praise of the Lord (Psalm 150). Musical instruments of several types were used— string, wind, percussion—and each had its special function. Trumpets, horns, and clashing cymbals summoned the people to festivals or lifted up high praise. Reed instruments expressed the worshiper's longing for the Lord. Lyres or other stringed instruments accompanied singers, and tambourines kept rhythm to the dance. The voice was also an instrument, offering praise through song.

Instruments don't play themselves. Their use for God's glory depends on the motivation of those who play them. As the Lord's worshipers, we are like instruments. The Holy Spirit moves upon our lives to make them a song—a song that exalts him and blesses others with the awareness of his presence and purpose. As Francis of Assisi prayed, "Lord, make me an instrument of your peace."

DESCENDANTS OF EPHRAIM

[20]The descendants of Ephraim were Shuthelah, Bered, Tahath, Eleadah, Tahath, [21]Zabad, and Shuthelah.

Ephraim's sons Ezer and Elead were killed trying to steal livestock from the local farmers near Gath. [22]Their father, Ephraim, mourned for them a long time, and his relatives came to comfort him.

7:13a As in parallel text at Gen 46:24; Hebrew reads *Jahziel*, a variant name for Jahzeel. **7:13b** As in some Hebrew and Greek manuscripts (see also Gen 46:24; Num 26:49); most Hebrew manuscripts read *Shallum*.

²³Afterward Ephraim slept with his wife, and she became pregnant and gave birth to a son. Ephraim named him Beriah* because of the tragedy his family had suffered.

²⁴Ephraim had a daughter named Sheerah. She built the towns of Lower and Upper Beth-horon and Uzzen-sheerah.

²⁵Ephraim's line of descent was Rephah, Resheph, Telah, Tahan, ²⁶Ladan, Ammihud, Elishama, ²⁷Nun, and Joshua.

²⁸The descendants of Ephraim lived in the territory that included Bethel and its surrounding towns to the south, Naaran to the east, Gezer and its villages to the west, and Shechem and its surrounding villages to the north as far as Ayyah and its towns. ²⁹Along the border of Manasseh were the towns of Beth-shan,* Taanach, Megiddo, Dor, and their surrounding villages. The descendants of Joseph son of Israel* lived in these towns.

DESCENDANTS OF ASHER

³⁰The sons of Asher were Imnah, Ishvah, Ishvi, and Beriah. They had a sister named Serah.

³¹The sons of Beriah were Heber and Malkiel (the father of Birzaith).

³²The sons of Heber were Japhlet, Shomer, and Hotham. They had a sister named Shua.

³³The sons of Japhlet were Pasach, Bimhal, and Ashvath.

³⁴The sons of Shomer were Ahi, Rohgah, Hubbah, and Aram.

³⁵The sons of his brother Helem* were Zophah, Imna, Shelesh, and Amal.

³⁶The sons of Zophah were Suah, Harnepher, Shual, Beri, Imrah, ³⁷Bezer, Hod, Shamma, Shilshah, Ithran,* and Beera.

³⁸The sons of Jether were Jephunneh, Pispah, and Ara.

³⁹The sons of Ulla were Arah, Hanniel, and Rizia.

⁴⁰Each of these descendants of Asher was the head of an ancestral clan. They were all skilled warriors and prominent leaders. There were 26,000 men available for military service among the descendants listed in their tribal genealogy.

DESCENDANTS OF BENJAMIN

8 The sons of Benjamin, in order of age, included Bela (the oldest), Ashbel, Aharah, ²Nohah, and Rapha.

³The sons of Bela were Addar, Gera, Abihud,* ⁴Abishua, Naaman, Ahoah, ⁵Gera, Shephuphan, and Huram.

⁶The sons of Ehud, leaders of the clans living at Geba, were driven out and moved to Manahath. ⁷Ehud's sons were Naaman, Ahijah, and Gera. Gera, the father of Uzza and Ahihud, led them when they moved.

⁸After Shaharaim divorced his wives Hushim and Baara, he had children in the land of Moab. ⁹Hodesh, his new wife, gave birth to Jobab, Zibia, Mesha, Malcam, ¹⁰Jeuz, Sakia, and Mirmah. These sons all became the leaders of clans.

¹¹Shaharaim's wife Hushim had already given birth to Abitub and Elpaal. ¹²The sons of Elpaal were Eber, Misham, Shemed (who built Ono and Lod and their villages), ¹³Beriah, and Shema. They were the leaders of the clans living in Aijalon, and they drove out the inhabitants of Gath.

¹⁴Ahio, Shashak, Jeremoth, ¹⁵Zebadiah, Arad, Eder, ¹⁶Michael, Ishpah, and Joha were the sons of Beriah.

¹⁷Zebadiah, Meshullam, Hizki, Heber, ¹⁸Ishmerai, Izliah, and Jobab were the sons of Elpaal.

¹⁹Jakim, Zicri, Zabdi, ²⁰Elienai, Zillethai, Eliel,

7:23 Beriah sounds like a Hebrew term meaning "tragedy" or "misfortune." 7:29a Hebrew Beth-shan, a variant name for Beth-shan. 7:29b Israel is the name that God gave to Jacob. 7:35 Possibly another name for Hotham; compare 7:32. 7:37 Possibly another name for Jether; compare 7:38. 8:3 Possibly Gera the father of Ehud; compare 8:6.

²¹Adaiah, Beraiah, and Shimrath were the sons of Shimei.

²²Ishpan, Eber, Eliel, ²³Abdon, Zicri, Hanan, ²⁴Hananiah, Elam, Anthothijah, ²⁵Iphdeiah, and Penuel were the sons of Shashak.

²⁶Shamsherai, Shehariah, Athaliah, ²⁷Jaareshiah, Elijah, and Zicri were the sons of Jeroham.

²⁸These were the leaders of the ancestral clans, and they were listed in their tribal genealogy. They all lived in Jerusalem.

THE FAMILY OF SAUL

²⁹Jeiel* (the father of* Gibeon) lived in Gibeon. His wife's name was Maacah, ³⁰and his oldest son was named Abdon. Jeiel's other sons were Zur, Kish, Baal, Ner,* Nadab, ³¹Gedor, Ahio, Zechariah,* ³²and Mikloth, who was the father of Shimeam.* All these families lived near each other in Jerusalem.

³³Ner was the father of Kish. Kish was the father of Saul. Saul was the father of Jonathan, Malkishua, Abinadab, and Eshbaal.

³⁴Jonathan was the father of Meribbaal. Meribbaal was the father of Micah. ³⁵Micah was the father of Pithon, Melech, Tahrea,* and Ahaz.

³⁶ Ahaz was the father of Jadah.* Jadah was the father of Alemeth, Azmaveth, and Zimri. Zimri was the father of Moza.

³⁷ Moza was the father of Binea. Binea was the father of Rephaiah.* Rephaiah was the father of Eleasah. Eleasah was the father of Azel.

³⁸Azel had six sons: Azrikam, Bokeru, Ishmael, Sheariah, Obadiah, and Hanan. These were the sons of Azel.

³⁹Azel's brother Eshek had three sons: Ulam (the oldest), Jeush (the second), and Eliphelet (the third). ⁴⁰The sons of Ulam were all skilled warriors and expert archers. They had many sons and grandsons—150 in all.

All these were descendants of Benjamin.

9 All Israel was listed in the genealogical record in *The Book of the Kings of Israel.*

THE RETURNING EXILES

The people of Judah were exiled to Babylon because they were unfaithful to the LORD. ²The first to return to their property in their former towns were common people. With them came some of the priests, Levites, and Temple assistants. ³People from the tribes of Judah, Benjamin, Ephraim, and Manasseh came and settled in Jerusalem.

⁴One family that returned was that of Uthai son of Ammihud, son of Omri, son of Imri, son of Bani, a descendant of Perez son of Judah.

⁵Others returned from the Shilonite clan, including Asaiah (the oldest) and his sons.

⁶From the Zerahite clan, Jeuel returned with his relatives. In all, 690 families from the tribe of Judah returned.

⁷From the tribe of Benjamin came Sallu son of Meshullam, son of Hodaviah, son of Hassenuah; ⁸Ibneiah son of Jeroham; Elah son of Uzzi, son of Micri; Meshullam son of Shephatiah, son of Reuel, son of Ibnijah.

⁹These men were all leaders of clans, and they were listed in their tribal genealogy. In all,

---

8:29a As in some Greek manuscripts (see also 9:35); Hebrew lacks *Jeiel.* 8:29b Or *the founder of.* 8:30 As in some Greek manuscripts (see also 9:36); Hebrew lacks *Ner.* 8:31 As in parallel text at 9:37; Hebrew reads *Zeker,* a variant name for Zechariah. 8:32 As in parallel text at 9:38; Hebrew reads *Shimeah,* a variant name for Shimeam. 8:35 As in parallel text at 9:41; Hebrew reads *Tarea,* a variant name for Tahrea. 8:36 As in parallel text at 9:42; Hebrew reads *Jehoaddah,* a variant name for Jadah. 8:37 As in parallel text at 9:43; Hebrew reads *Raphah,* a variant name for Rephaiah.

My Daily Worship

— April 1 —

No Small Part in God's House

1 Chronicles 1:1–9:44

Some of the gatekeepers were assigned to care for the various utensils used in worship. They checked them in and out to avoid any loss. Others were responsible for the furnishings, the items in the sanctuary, and the supplies such as choice flour, wine, olive oil, incense, and spices. But it was the priests who prepared the spices and incense (9:28–30).

[i reflect]

M. Craig Barnes, pastor of the National Presbyterian Church in Washington, D.C., conducted the funeral for a man who helped develop the famous Boeing 747 aircraft. Following the service, he spoke with his widow and commented on how marvelous it was that her late husband had helped build that remarkable aircraft. The wife replied, "The truth is, he worked on one little switchbox smaller than a loaf of bread. That's all he worked on for fifteen years. But when that 747 lifted off the ground for the first time, it was the happiest day of his life."

God's household is in many ways like the team of individuals who each contributed in some small, but significant way to the success of the 747. While Jesus suggested that those who followed him are like a family, the apostle Paul compared the mutual ministry of Christians in community to the human body. Every body part and organ is indispensable to the other. Each has a critical part to play.

That's the picture we have in this passage of Scripture. Although the priests in the Old Testament were responsible for worship, God did not expect them to carry it off all by themselves. Sure, they were called and set apart. But their holy calling was not disconnected from the Israelites. The priests choreographed a sacred liturgy, but the people of God were very much involved. Each person had a part to play. There was something for those without an "official" calling to contribute. That hasn't changed. When coming before the Lord with a heart of worship, you don't have to wait for Sunday. You don't need a pastor. God is an audience of one, and he welcomes your soliloquy of praise. In your own inimitable way, you can celebrate his greatness and glory with silence, singing, prayer, a prostrate act of surrender, or even a homespun ballet.

[i pray]

Lord, for too long I've thought of worship as something that only happens in the sanctuary on Sunday. I'm sorry for forfeiting so many opportunities throughout the week—or even the day—to bring my love and unique gifts and lay them at your feet. It's great to know you desire my worship every day. Amen.

[i respond]

Think of a way you can remind yourself that your home is as much a sanctuary as the church. You might light a candle near to where you pray each day or hang a cross on the wall.

956 families from the tribe of Benjamin returned.

THE RETURNING PRIESTS

[10]Among the priests who returned were Jedaiah, Jehoiarib, Jakin, [11]Azariah son of Hilkiah, son of Meshullam, son of Zadok, son of Meraioth, son of Ahitub. Azariah was the chief officer of the house of God.

[12]Other returning priests were Adaiah son of Jeroham, son of Pashhur, son of Malkijah, and Maasai son of Adiel, son of Jahzerah, son of Meshullam, son of Meshillemith, son of Immer.

[13]In all, 1,760 priests returned. They were heads of clans and very able men. They were responsible for ministering at the house of God.

THE RETURNING LEVITES

[14]The Levites who returned were Shemaiah son of Hasshub, son of Azrikam, son of Hashabiah, a descendant of Merari; [15]Bakbakkar; Heresh; Galal; Mattaniah son of Mica, son of Zicri, son of Asaph; [16]Obadiah son of Shemaiah, son of Galal, son of Jeduthun; and Berekiah son of Asa, son of Elkanah, who lived in the area of Netophah.

[17]The gatekeepers who returned were Shallum, Akkub, Talmon, Ahiman, and their relatives. Shallum was the chief gatekeeper. [18]Prior to this time, they were responsible for the King's Gate on the east side. These men served as gatekeepers for the camps of the Levites. [19]Shallum was the son of Kore, a descendant of Abiasaph,* from the clan of Korah. He and his relatives, the Korahites, were responsible for guarding the entrance to the sanctuary, just as their ancestors had guarded the Tabernacle in the camp of the LORD.

[20]Phinehas son of Eleazar had been in charge of the gatekeepers in earlier times, and the LORD had been with him. [21]And later Zechariah son of Meshelemiah had been responsible for guarding the entrance to the Tabernacle.*

[22]In all, there were 212 gatekeepers in those days, and they were listed by genealogies in their villages. David and Samuel the seer had appointed their ancestors because they were reliable men. [23]These gatekeepers and their descendants, by their divisions, were responsible for guarding the entrance to the house of the LORD, the house that was formerly a tent. [24]The gatekeepers were stationed on all four sides—east, west, north, and south. [25]From time to time, their relatives in the villages came to share their duties for seven-day periods.

[26]The four chief gatekeepers, all Levites, were in an office of great trust, for they were responsible for the rooms and treasuries at the house of God. [27]They would spend the night around the house of God, since it was their duty to guard it. It was also their job to open the gates every morning.

[28]Some of the gatekeepers were assigned to care for the various utensils used in worship. They checked them in and out to avoid any loss. [29]Others were responsible for the furnishings, the items in the sanctuary, and the supplies such as choice flour, wine, olive oil, incense, and spices. [30]But it was the priests who prepared the spices and incense. [31]Mattithiah, a Levite and the oldest son of Shallum the Korahite, was entrusted with baking the bread used in the offerings. [32]And some members of the clan of Kohath were in charge of preparing the bread to be set on the table each Sabbath day.

[33]The musicians, all prominent Levites, lived at the Temple. They were exempt from other responsibilities there since they were on duty at all hours. [34]All these men lived in Jerusalem. They were the heads of Levite families and were listed as prominent leaders in their tribal genealogy.

9:19 Hebrew *Ebiasaph,* a variant name for Abiasaph; compare Exod 6:24. **9:21** Hebrew *Tent of Meeting.*

KING SAUL'S FAMILY TREE

35Jeiel (the father of* Gibeon) lived in Gibeon. His wife's name was Maacah, 36and his oldest son was named Abdon. Jeiel's other sons were Zur, Kish, Baal, Ner, Nadab, 37Gedor, Ahio, Zechariah, and Mikloth. 38Mikloth was the father of Shimeam. All these families lived near each other in Jerusalem.

39Ner was the father of Kish. Kish was the father of Saul. Saul was the father of Jonathan, Malkishua, Abinadab, and Eshbaal.

40Jonathan was the father of Meribbaal. Meribbaal was the father of Micah. 41The sons of Micah were Pithon, Melech, Tahrea, and Ahaz.*

42 Ahaz was the father of Jadah.*
Jadah was the father of Alemeth,
    Azmaveth, and Zimri.
Zimri was the father of Moza.

43 Moza was the father of Binea.
Binea's son was Rephaiah.
Rephaiah's son was Eleasah.
Eleasah's son was Azel.

44Azel had six sons, and their names were Azrikam, Bokeru, Ishmael, Sheariah, Obadiah, and Hanan. These were the sons of Azel.

THE DEATH OF KING SAUL

10 Now the Philistines attacked Israel, forcing the Israelites to flee. Many were slaughtered on the slopes of Mount Gilboa. 2The Philistines closed in on Saul and his sons, and they killed three of his sons—Jonathan, Abinadab, and Malkishua. 3The fighting grew very fierce around Saul, and the Philistine archers caught up with him and wounded him severely. 4Saul groaned to his armor bearer, "Take your sword and run me through before these pagan Philistines come and humiliate me." But his armor bearer was afraid and would not do it. So Saul took his own sword and fell on it. 5When his armor bearer realized that Saul was dead, he fell on his own sword and died. 6So Saul and his three sons died there together, bringing his dynasty to an end.

7When the Israelites in the Jezreel Valley saw that their army had been routed and that Saul and his sons were dead, they abandoned their towns and fled. So the Philistines moved in and occupied their towns.

8The next day when the Philistines went out to strip the dead, they found the bodies of Saul and his sons on Mount Gilboa. 9So they stripped off Saul's armor and cut off his head. Then they proclaimed the news of Saul's death before their idols and to the people throughout the land of Philistia. 10They placed his armor in the temple of their gods, and they fastened his head to the wall in the temple of Dagon.

11But when the people of Jabesh-gilead heard what the Philistines had done to Saul, 12their warriors went out and brought the bodies of Saul and his three sons back to Jabesh. Then they buried their remains beneath the oak tree at Jabesh, and they fasted for seven days.

13So Saul died because he was unfaithful to the LORD. He failed to obey the LORD's command, and he even consulted a medium 14instead of asking the LORD for guidance. So the LORD killed him and turned his kingdom over to David son of Jesse.

DAVID BECOMES KING OF ALL ISRAEL

11 Then all Israel went to David at Hebron and told him, "We are all members of your family. 2For a long time, even while Saul was our king, you were the one who really led Israel. And the LORD your God has told you, 'You will be the shepherd of my people Israel. You will be their leader.'" 3So there at Hebron David made a covenant with the leaders of Israel before the LORD. They

9:35 Or the founder of. 9:41 As in Syriac version and Latin Vulgate (see also 8:35); Hebrew lacks and Ahaz. 9:42 As in some Hebrew manuscripts and Greek version (see also 8:36); Hebrew reads Jarah.

anointed him king of Israel, just as the LORD had promised through Samuel.

DAVID CAPTURES JERUSALEM

⁴Then David and all Israel went to Jerusalem (or Jebus, as it used to be called), where the Jebusites, original inhabitants of the land, lived. ⁵The people of Jebus said to David, "You will never get in here!" But David captured the fortress of Zion, now called the City of David.

⁶David had said to his troops, "Whoever leads the attack against the Jebusites will become the commander of my armies!" And Joab, the son of David's sister Zeruiah, led the attack, so he became the commander of David's armies.

⁷David made the fortress his home, and that is why it is called the City of David. ⁸He extended the city from the Millo* to the surrounding area, while Joab rebuilt the rest of Jerusalem. ⁹And David became more and more powerful, because the LORD Almighty was with him.

DAVID'S MIGHTIEST MEN

¹⁰These are the leaders of David's mighty men. Together with all Israel, they determined to make David their king, just as the LORD had promised concerning Israel. ¹¹Here is the record of David's mightiest men:

The first was Jashobeam the Hacmonite, who was commander of the Three—the three greatest warriors among David's men.* He once used his spear to kill three hundred enemy warriors in a single battle.

¹²Next in rank among the Three was Eleazar son of Dodai,* a descendant of Ahoah. ¹³He was with David in the battle against the Philistines at Pas-dammim. The battle took place in a field full of barley, and the Israelite army fled. ¹⁴But Eleazar and David held their ground in the middle of the field and beat back the Philistines. So the LORD saved them by giving them a great victory.

¹⁵Once when David was at the rock near the cave of Adullam, the Philistine army was camped in the valley of Rephaim. The Three (who were among the Thirty—an elite group among David's fighting men) went down to meet him there. ¹⁶David was staying in the stronghold at the time, and a Philistine detachment had occupied the town of Bethlehem. ¹⁷David remarked longingly to his men, "Oh, how I would love some of that good water from the well in Bethlehem, the one by the gate." ¹⁸So the Three broke through the Philistine lines, drew some water from the well, and brought it back to David. But David refused to drink it. Instead, he poured it out before the LORD. ¹⁹"God forbid that I should drink this!" he exclaimed. "This water is as precious as the blood of these men who risked their lives to bring it to me." So David did not drink it. This is an example of the exploits of the Three.

DAVID'S THIRTY MIGHTY MEN

²⁰Abishai, the brother of Joab, was the leader of the Thirty.* He once used his spear to kill three hundred enemy warriors in a single battle. It was by such feats that he became as famous as the Three. ²¹Abishai was the most famous of the Thirty and was their commander, though he was not one of the Three.

²²There was also Benaiah son of Jehoiada, a valiant warrior from Kabzeel. He did many heroic deeds, which included killing two of Moab's mightiest warriors. Another time he chased a lion down into a pit. Then, despite the snow and slippery ground, he caught the lion and killed it. ²³Another time, armed with only a club, he killed an Egyptian warrior who was seven and a half feet* tall and whose spear was as thick as a weaver's beam. Benaiah wrenched the spear from the Egyptian's hand and killed him with it. ²⁴These are some of the deeds that made Benaiah as famous as the Three. ²⁵He was more honored than the other

---

11:8 Or *the supporting terraces.* The meaning of the Hebrew is uncertain.   11:11 As in some Greek manuscripts (see also 2 Sam 23:8); Hebrew *commander of the Thirty,* or *commander of the captains.*   11:12 As in parallel text at 2 Sam 23:9 (see also 1 Chr 27:4); Hebrew reads *Dodo,* a variant name for Dodai.   11:20 As in Syriac version; Hebrew reads *the Three;* also in 11:21.   11:23 Hebrew *5 cubits* [2.3 meters].

My Daily Worship

— April 2 —

POUR YOU!

1 CHRONICLES 10:1–12:40

David remarked longingly to his men, "Oh, how I would love some of that good water from the well in Bethlehem, the one by the gate." So the Three broke through the Philistine lines, drew some water from the well, and brought it back to David. But David refused to drink it. Instead he poured it out before the LORD (11:17–18).

[i reflect]

Sacrifice. That's a synonym for worship. When you willingly give up doing what you would rather do to spend time in the presence of the Lord, you are worshiping. When you forgo what is valuable to you in order to take stock of the priceless worth of God, you are worshiping. This is what David, the crowned prince of God, did as he hid from Saul.

While a fugitive, David longed for the cool refreshing water in his hometown. That well-known well would provide him with a tangible connection with family and memories of home. It would connect David to the place where the prophet Samuel had anointed him as the king-elect. It would remind him that God had called him.

His men knew that. Because of their love for their leader, they risked their lives to bring back to David a leather pouch of water. And to their amazement, the future king emptied the contents on the ground in front of them. Oh, he was grateful all right. He was conscious of how costly such an act of love was. Recognizing the value of the water, David poured it out as an act of worship to the Lord. He could have drunk it. He could have enjoyed it. But he didn't. David remembered that the source of his call was not his hometown, but the Lord himself. He modeled for his men the costliness of worship.

Three thousand years later, King David still models for us why sacrifice and worship are synonyms. Do you catch the significance of it all? Perhaps you're exhausted from projects accomplished and dreading more deadlines to come. The fact that you are still willing to spend time with the Lord instead of doing what you long to do or feel you deserve to do, that's a part of worship. Isn't that what you want to do as a way of affirming to the Lord what he deserves? Then why not tell him now?

[i pray]

Lord, I'm not sure I could have done what David did. Even now, I can almost taste that cool pure water from the well in Bethlehem. The fact that I resist sacrifice points to how selfish I am. Forgive me, Lord, for my tendency to please myself instead of you.

[i respond]

Make an act of sacrifice today to show that God is more worthy of your worship than you are of having your needs met. Go without a meal to spend more time in prayer, make a sacrificial financial contribution to a relief ministry or missions organization, or donate your time to a ministry at your local church.

members of the Thirty, though he was not one of the Three. And David made him commander of his bodyguard.

²⁶These were also included among David's mighty men:

Asahel, Joab's brother;
Elhanan son of Dodo from Bethlehem;
²⁷ Shammah from Harod;*
Helez from Pelon;
²⁸ Ira son of Ikkesh from Tekoa;
Abiezer from Anathoth;
²⁹ Sibbecai from Hushah;
Zalmon* from Ahoah;
³⁰ Maharai from Netophah;
Heled son of Baanah from Netophah;
³¹ Ithai son of Ribai from Gibeah (from the tribe of Benjamin);
Benaiah from Pirathon;
³² Hurai from near Nahale-gaash*;
Abi-albon* the Arbathite;
³³ Azmaveth from Bahurim*;
Eliahba from Shaalbon;
³⁴ the sons of Jashen* from Gizon;
Jonathan son of Shagee from Harar;
³⁵ Ahiam son of Sharar* from Harar;
Eliphal son of Ur;
³⁶ Hepher from Mekerah;
Ahijah from Pelon;
³⁷ Hezro from Carmel;
Paarai* son of Ezbai;
³⁸ Joel, the brother of Nathan;
Mibhar son of Hagri;
³⁹ Zelek from Ammon;
Naharai from Beeroth (Joab's armor bearer);
⁴⁰ Ira from Jattir;
Gareb from Jattir;
⁴¹ Uriah the Hittite;
Zabad son of Ahlai;
⁴² Adina son of Shiza, the Reubenite leader who had thirty men with him;
⁴³ Hanan son of Maacah;
Joshaphat from Mithna;
⁴⁴ Uzzia from Ashtaroth;
Shama and Jeiel, the sons of Hotham, from Aroer;
⁴⁵ Jediael son of Shimri;
Joha, his brother, from Tiz;
⁴⁶ Eliel from Mahavah;
Jeribai and Joshaviah, the sons of Elnaam;
Ithmah from Moab;
⁴⁷ Eliel and Obed;
Jaasiel from Zobah.

WARRIORS JOIN DAVID'S ARMY

12 The following men joined David at Ziklag while he was hiding from Saul son of Kish. They were among the warriors who fought beside David in battle. ²All of them were expert archers, and they could shoot arrows or sling stones with their left hand as well as their right. They were all relatives of Saul from the tribe of Benjamin. ³Their leader was Ahiezer son of Shemaah from Gibeah; his brother Joash was second-in-command. These were the other warriors:

Jeziel and Pelet, sons of Azmaveth;
Beracah and Jehu from Anathoth;
⁴ Ishmaiah from Gibeon, a famous warrior and leader among the Thirty;
Jeremiah, Jahaziel, Johanan, and Jozabad from Gederah;
⁵ Eluzai, Jerimoth, Bealiah, Shemariah, and Shephatiah from Haruph;
⁶ Elkanah, Isshiah, Azarel, Joezer, and Jashobeam, who were Korahites;
⁷ Joelah and Zebadiah, sons of Jeroham from Gedor.

⁸Some brave and experienced warriors from the tribe of Gad also defected to David while he was at the stronghold in the wilderness. They were expert with both shield and spear, as fierce as lions and as swift as deer on the mountains.

11:27 As in parallel text at 2 Sam 23:25; Hebrew reads *Shammoth from Haror.* 11:29 As in parallel text at 2 Sam 23:28; Hebrew reads *Ilai.* 11:32a Or *from the ravines of Gaash.* 11:32b As in parallel text at 2 Sam 23:31; Hebrew reads *Abiel.* 11:33 As in parallel text at 2 Sam 23:31; Hebrew reads *Baharum.* 11:34 As in parallel text at 2 Sam 23:32; Hebrew reads *sons of Hashem.* 11:35 As in parallel text at 2 Sam 23:33; Hebrew reads *son of Sacar.* 11:37 As in parallel text at 2 Sam 23:35; Hebrew reads *Naarai.*

⁹ Ezer was their leader.
  Obadiah was second.
  Eliab was third.
¹⁰ Mishmannah was fourth.
  Jeremiah was fifth.
¹¹ Attai was sixth.
  Eliel was seventh.
¹² Johanan was eighth.
  Elzabad was ninth.
¹³ Jeremiah was tenth.
  Macbannai was eleventh.

¹⁴These warriors from Gad were army commanders. The weakest among them could take on a hundred regular troops, and the strongest could take on a thousand! ¹⁵They crossed the Jordan River during its seasonal flooding at the beginning of the year and drove out all the people living in the lowlands on both the east and west banks.

¹⁶Others from Benjamin and Judah came to David at the stronghold. ¹⁷David went out to meet them and said, "If you have come in peace to help me, we are friends. But if you have come to betray me to my enemies when I am innocent, then may the God of our ancestors see and judge you."

¹⁸Then the Spirit came upon Amasai, who later became a leader among the Thirty, and he said,

"We are yours, David!
  We are on your side, son of Jesse.
Peace and prosperity be with you,
  and success to all who help you,
    for your God is the one who helps you."

So David let them join him, and he made them officers over his troops.

¹⁹Some men from Manasseh defected from the Israelite army and joined David when he went with the Philistines to fight against Saul. But as it turned out, the Philistine leaders refused to let David and his men go with them. After much discussion, they sent them back, for they said, "It will cost us our lives if David switches loyalties to Saul and turns against us."

²⁰Here is a list of the men from Manasseh who defected to David as he was returning to Ziklag: Adnah, Jozabad, Jediael, Michael, Jozabad, Elihu, and Zillethai. Each commanded a thousand troops from the tribe of Manasseh. ²¹They helped David chase down bands of raiders, for they were all brave and able warriors who became commanders in his army. ²²Day after day more men joined David until he had a great army, like the army of God.

²³These are the numbers of armed warriors who joined David at Hebron. They were all eager to see David become king instead of Saul, just as the LORD had promised.

²⁴From the tribe of Judah, there were 6,800 warriors armed with shields and spears.
²⁵From the tribe of Simeon, there were 7,100 warriors.
²⁶From the tribe of Levi, there were 4,600 troops. ²⁷This included Jehoiada, leader of the family of Aaron, who had 3,700 under his command. ²⁸This also included Zadok, a young warrior, with twenty-two members of his family who were all officers.
²⁹From the tribe of Benjamin, Saul's relatives, there were 3,000 warriors. Most of the men from Benjamin had remained loyal to Saul until this time.
³⁰From the tribe of Ephraim, there were 20,800 warriors, each famous in his own clan.
³¹From the half-tribe of Manasseh west of the Jordan, 18,000 men were sent for the express purpose of helping David become king.
³²From the tribe of Issachar, there were 200 leaders of the tribe with their relatives. All these men understood the temper of the times and knew the best course for Israel to take.
³³From the tribe of Zebulun, there were 50,000 skilled warriors. They were fully armed and prepared for battle and completely loyal to David.

³⁴From the tribe of Naphtali, there were 1,000 officers and 37,000 warriors armed with shields and spears.

³⁵From the tribe of Dan, there were 28,600 warriors, all prepared for battle.

³⁶From the tribe of Asher, there were 40,000 trained warriors, all prepared for battle.

³⁷From the east side of the Jordan River— where the tribes of Reuben and Gad and the half-tribe of Manasseh lived—there were 120,000 troops armed with every kind of weapon.

³⁸All these men came in battle array to Hebron with the single purpose of making David the king of Israel. In fact, all Israel agreed that David should be their king. ³⁹They feasted and drank with David for three days, for preparations had been made by their relatives for their arrival. ⁴⁰And people from as far away as Issachar, Zebulun, and Naphtali brought food on donkeys, camels, mules, and oxen. Vast supplies of flour, fig cakes, raisins, wine, olive oil, cattle, and sheep were brought to the celebration. There was great joy throughout the land of Israel.

DAVID ATTEMPTS TO MOVE THE ARK

13 David consulted with all his officials, including the generals and captains of his army. ²Then he addressed the entire assembly of Israel as follows: "If you approve and if it is the will of the LORD our God, let us send messages to all the Israelites throughout the land, including the priests and Levites in their towns and pasturelands. Let us invite them to come and join us. ³It is time to bring back the Ark of our God, for we neglected it during the reign of Saul."

⁴The whole assembly agreed to this, for the people could see it was the right thing to do. ⁵So David summoned all the people of Israel, from one end of the country to the other,* to join in bringing the Ark of God from Kiriath-jearim. ⁶Then David and all Israel went to Baalah of Judah (also called Kiriath-jearim) to bring back the Ark of God, which bears the name of the LORD who is enthroned between the cherubim. ⁷They transported the Ark of God from the house of Abinadab on a new cart, with Uzzah and Ahio guiding it. ⁸David and all Israel were celebrating before God with all their might, singing and playing all kinds of musical instruments—lyres, harps, tambourines, cymbals, and trumpets.

⁹But when they arrived at the threshing floor of Nacon,* the oxen stumbled, and Uzzah put out his hand to steady the Ark. ¹⁰Then the LORD's anger blazed out against Uzzah, and he struck him dead because he had laid his hand on the Ark. So Uzzah died there in the presence of God. ¹¹David was angry because the LORD's anger had blazed out against Uzzah. He named that place Perez-uzzah (which means "outbreak against Uzzah"). It is still called that today.

¹²David was now afraid of God and asked, "How can I ever bring the Ark of God back into my care?" ¹³So David decided not to move the Ark into the City of David. He took it instead to the home of Obed-edom of Gath. ¹⁴The Ark of God remained there with the family of Obed-edom for three months, and the LORD blessed him and his entire household.

> *Praising God is one of the highest and purest acts in religion. In prayer we act like men; in praise we act like angels.*
>
> THOMAS WATSON

13:5 Hebrew *from the Shihor of Egypt to Lebo-hamath.* 13:9 As in parallel text at 2 Sam 6:6; Hebrew reads *Kidon.*

DAVID'S PALACE AND FAMILY

14 Now King Hiram of Tyre sent messengers to David, along with stonemasons and carpenters to build him a palace. Hiram also sent many cedar logs for lumber. ²And David realized that the LORD had made him king over Israel and had made his kingdom very great for the sake of his people Israel.

³Then David married more wives in Jerusalem, and they had many sons and daughters. ⁴These are the names of David's sons who were born in Jerusalem: Shimea,* Shobab, Nathan, Solomon, ⁵Ibhar, Elishua, Elpelet, ⁶Nogah, Nepheg, Japhia, ⁷Elishama, Eliada,* and Eliphelet.

DAVID CONQUERS THE PHILISTINES

⁸When the Philistines heard that David had been anointed king over all Israel, they mobilized all their forces to capture him. But David was told they were coming, so he and his men marched out to meet them. ⁹The Philistines had arrived in the valley of Rephaim and raided it. ¹⁰So David asked God, "Should I go out to fight the Philistines? Will you hand them over to me?"

The LORD replied, "Yes, go ahead. I will give you the victory."

¹¹So David and his troops went to Baal-perazim and defeated the Philistines there. "God has done it!" David exclaimed. "He used me to burst through my enemies like a raging flood!" So that place was named Baal-perazim (which means "the Lord who bursts through"). ¹²The Philistines had abandoned their idols* there, so David gave orders to burn them up.

¹³But after a while, the Philistines returned and raided the valley again. ¹⁴And once again David asked God what to do. "Do not attack them straight on," God replied. "Instead, circle around behind them and attack them near the balsam trees. ¹⁵When you hear a sound like marching feet in the tops of the balsam trees, attack! That will be the signal that God is moving ahead of you to strike down the Philistines." ¹⁶So David did what God commanded, and he struck down the Philistine army all the way from Gibeon to Gezer.

¹⁷So David's fame spread everywhere, and the LORD caused all the nations to fear David.

PREPARING TO MOVE THE ARK

15 David now built several buildings for himself in the City of David. He also prepared a place for the Ark of God and set up a special tent there to shelter it. ²Then he issued these instructions: "When we transport the Ark of God this time, no one except the Levites may carry it. The LORD has chosen them to carry the Ark of the LORD and to minister before him forever."

³Then David summoned all the Israelites to Jerusalem to bring the Ark of the LORD to the place he had prepared for it. ⁴These are the priests* and Levites who were called together:

⁵There were 120 from the clan of Kohath, with Uriel as their leader.
⁶There were 220 from the clan of Merari, with Asaiah as their leader.
⁷There were 130 from the clan of Gershon,* with Joel as their leader.
⁸There were 200 descendants of Elizaphan, with Shemaiah as their leader.
⁹There were 80 descendants of Hebron, with Eliel as their leader.
¹⁰There were 112 descendants of Uzziel, with Amminadab as their leader.

¹¹Then David summoned the priests, Zadok and Abiathar, and these Levite leaders: Uriel, Asaiah, Joel, Shemaiah, Eliel, and Amminadab. ¹²He said to them, "You are the leaders of the Levite families. You must purify yourselves and all your fellow Levites, so you can bring the Ark of the LORD, the God of Israel, to the

---

14:4 Hebrew *Shammua,* a variant name for Shimea; compare 3:5. 14:7 Hebrew *Beeliada,* a variant name for Eliada; compare 3:8 and parallel text at 2 Sam 5:16. 14:12 Hebrew *their gods;* compare parallel text at 2 Sam 5:21. 15:4 Hebrew *descendants of Aaron.* 15:7 Hebrew *Gershom,* a variant name for Gershon.

place I have prepared for it. [13]Because you Levites did not carry the Ark the first time, the anger of the LORD our God burst out against us. We failed to ask God how to move it in the proper way." [14]So the priests and the Levites purified themselves in order to bring the Ark of the LORD, the God of Israel, to Jerusalem. [15]Then the Levites carried the Ark of God on their shoulders with its carrying poles, just as the LORD had instructed Moses.

[16]David also ordered the Levite leaders to appoint a choir of Levites who were singers and musicians to sing joyful songs to the accompaniment of lyres, harps, and cymbals. [17]So the Levites appointed Heman son of Joel, Asaph son of Berekiah, and Ethan son of Kushaiah from the clan of Merari to direct the musicians. [18]The following men were chosen as their assistants: Zechariah, Jaaziel, Shemiramoth, Jehiel, Unni, Eliab, Benaiah, Maaseiah, Mattithiah, Eliphelehu, Mikneiah, and the gatekeepers, Obed-edom and Jeiel.

[19]Heman, Asaph, and Ethan were chosen to sound the bronze cymbals. [20]Zechariah, Aziel, Shemiramoth, Jehiel, Unni, Eliab, Maaseiah, and Benaiah were chosen to play the lyres.* [21]Mattithiah, Eliphelehu, Mikneiah, Obed-edom, Jeiel, and Azaziah were chosen to play the harps.* [22]Kenaniah, the head Levite, was chosen as the choir leader because of his skill.

[23]Berekiah and Elkanah were chosen to guard the Ark. [24]Shebaniah, Joshaphat, Nethanel, Amasai, Zechariah, Benaiah, and Eliezer—all of whom were priests—were chosen to blow the trumpets as they marched in front of the Ark of God. Obed-edom and Jehiah were chosen to guard the Ark.

MOVING THE ARK TO JERUSALEM

[25]Then David and the leaders of Israel and the generals of the army went to the home of Obed-edom to bring the Ark of the LORD's covenant up to Jerusalem with a great celebration. [26]And because God was clearly helping the Levites as they carried the Ark of the LORD's covenant, they sacrificed seven bulls and seven lambs. [27]David was dressed in a robe of fine linen, as were the Levites who carried the Ark, the singers, and Kenaniah the song leader. David was also wearing a priestly tunic.* [28]So all Israel brought up the Ark of the LORD's covenant to Jerusalem with shouts of joy, the blowing of horns and trumpets, the crashing of cymbals, and loud playing on harps and lyres.

[29]But as the Ark of the LORD's covenant entered the City of David, Michal, the daughter of Saul, looked down from her window. When she saw King David dancing and leaping for joy, she was filled with contempt for him.

16 So they brought the Ark of God into the special tent David had prepared for it, and they sacrificed burnt offerings and peace offerings before God. [2]When he had finished, David blessed the people in the name of the LORD. [3]Then he gave a gift of food to every man and woman in Israel: a loaf of bread, a cake of dates,* and a cake of raisins.

[4]David appointed the following Levites to lead the people in worship before the Ark of the LORD by asking for his blessings and giving thanks and praise to the LORD, the God of Israel. [5]Asaph, the leader of this group, sounded the cymbals. His assistants were Zechariah (the second), then Jeiel, Shemiramoth, Jehiel, Mattithiah, Eliab, Benaiah, Obed-edom, and Jeiel. They played the harps and lyres. [6]The priests, Benaiah and Jahaziel, played the trumpets regularly before the Ark of God's covenant.

DAVID'S SONG OF PRAISE

[7]That day David gave to Asaph and his fellow Levites this song of thanksgiving to the LORD:

[8] Give thanks to the LORD and proclaim his
  greatness.

15:20 Hebrew adds *according to Alamoth*, which is probably a musical term. The meaning of the Hebrew is uncertain. 15:21 Hebrew adds *according to the Sheminith*, which is probably a musical term. The meaning of the Hebrew is uncertain. 15:27 Hebrew *a linen ephod.* 16:3 Or *a portion of meat.* The meaning of the Hebrew is uncertain.

Let the whole world know what he has
done.
⁹ Sing to him; yes, sing his praises.
Tell everyone about his miracles.
¹⁰ Exult in his holy name;
O worshipers of the LORD, rejoice!
¹¹ Search for the LORD and for his strength,
and keep on searching.
¹² Think of the wonderful works he has
done,
the miracles, and the judgments he
handed down,
¹³ O children of Israel, God's servant,
O descendants of Jacob, God's chosen
one.

¹⁴ He is the LORD our God.
His rule is seen throughout the land.
¹⁵ He always stands by his covenant*—
the commitment he made to a thousand
generations.
¹⁶ This is the covenant he made with
Abraham
and the oath he swore to Isaac.
¹⁷ He confirmed it to Jacob as a decree,
to the people of Israel as a never-ending
treaty:
¹⁸ "I will give you the land of Canaan
as your special possession."

¹⁹ He said this when they were few in
number,
a tiny group of strangers in Canaan.
²⁰ They wandered back and forth between
nations,
from one kingdom to another.
²¹ Yet he did not let anyone oppress them.
He warned kings on their behalf:
²² "Do not touch these people I have chosen,
and do not hurt my prophets."

²³ Let the whole earth sing to the LORD!
Each day proclaim the good news that
he saves.
²⁴ Publish his glorious deeds among the
nations.

Tell everyone about the amazing things
he does.
²⁵ Great is the LORD! He is most worthy of
praise!
He is to be revered above all gods.
²⁶ The gods of other nations are merely idols,
but the LORD made the heavens!
²⁷ Honor and majesty surround him;
strength and beauty are in his dwelling.

²⁸ O nations of the world, recognize the
LORD,
recognize that the LORD is glorious and
strong.
²⁹ Give to the LORD the glory he deserves!
Bring your offering and come to
worship him.
Worship the LORD in all his holy splendor.
³⁰ Let all the earth tremble before him.
The world is firmly established and
cannot be shaken.

³¹ Let the heavens be glad, and let the earth
rejoice!
Tell all the nations that the LORD is king.
³² Let the sea and everything in it shout his
praise!
Let the fields and their crops burst forth
with joy!
³³ Let the trees of the forest rustle with praise
before the LORD!
For he is coming to judge the earth.

³⁴ Give thanks to the LORD, for he is good!
His faithful love endures forever.
³⁵ Cry out, "Save us, O God of our salvation!
Gather and rescue us from among the
nations,
so we can thank your holy name
and rejoice and praise you."

³⁶ Blessed be the LORD, the God of Israel,
from everlasting to everlasting!

And all the people shouted "Amen!" and
praised the LORD.

16:15 As in some Greek manuscripts (see also Ps 105:8); Hebrew reads *Remember his covenant forever.*

WORSHIP AT JERUSALEM AND GIBEON

37David arranged for Asaph and his fellow Levites to minister regularly before the Ark of the LORD's covenant, doing whatever needed to be done each day. 38This group included Obed-edom (son of Jeduthun), Hosah, and sixty-eight other Levites as gatekeepers.

39Meanwhile, David stationed Zadok the priest and his fellow priests at the Tabernacle of the LORD on the hill of Gibeon, where they continued to minister before the LORD. 40They sacrificed the regular burnt offerings to the LORD each morning and evening on the altar set aside for that purpose, obeying everything written in the law of the LORD, which he had given to Israel. 41David also appointed Heman, Jeduthun, and the others chosen by name to give thanks to the LORD, "for his faithful love endures forever." 42They used their trumpets, cymbals, and other instruments to accompany the songs of praise to God. And the sons of Jeduthun were appointed as gatekeepers.

43Then all the people returned to their homes, and David returned home to bless his family.

THE LORD'S COVENANT PROMISE TO DAVID

17 Now when David was settled in his palace, he said to Nathan the prophet, "Here I am living in this beautiful cedar palace, but the Ark of the LORD's covenant is out in a tent!"

2Nathan replied, "Go ahead with what you have in mind, for God is with you."

3But that same night God said to Nathan,

4"Go and tell my servant David, 'This is what the LORD says: You are not the one to build me a temple to live in. 5I have never lived in a temple, from the day I brought the Israelites out of Egypt until now. My home has always been a tent, moving from one place to another. 6And I never once complained to Israel's leaders,* the shepherds of my people. I have never asked them, "Why haven't you built me a beautiful cedar temple?"'

7"Now go and say to my servant David, 'This is what the LORD Almighty says: I chose you to lead my people Israel when you were just a shepherd boy, tending your sheep out in the pasture. 8I have been with you wherever you have gone, and I have destroyed all your enemies. Now I will make your name famous throughout the earth! 9And I have provided a permanent homeland for my people Israel, a secure place where they will never be disturbed. It will be their own land where wicked nations won't oppress them as they did in the past, 10from the time I appointed judges to rule my people. And I will subdue all your enemies.

" 'And now I declare that the LORD will build a house for you—a dynasty of kings! 11For when you die, I will raise up one of your sons, and I will make his kingdom strong. 12He is the one who will build a house—a temple—for me. And I will establish his throne forever. 13I will be his father, and he will be my son. I will not take my unfailing love from him as I took it from Saul, who ruled before you. 14I will establish him over my dynasty and my kingdom for all time, and his throne will be secure forever.'"

15So Nathan went back to David and told him everything the LORD had said.

DAVID'S PRAYER OF THANKS

16Then King David went in and sat before the LORD and prayed, "Who am I, O LORD God, and what is my family, that you have brought me this far? 17And now, O God, in addition to everything else, you speak of giving me a lasting dynasty! You speak as though I were someone very great,* O LORD God! 18What

---

17:6 As in Greek version (see also 2 Sam 7:7); Hebrew reads *judges*. 17:17 The meaning of the Hebrew is uncertain.

My Daily Worship
— *April 3* —

DANCING THE HOLY TWO-STEP
1 CHRONICLES 13:1–16:43

Give thanks to the LORD and proclaim his greatness. Let the whole world know what he has done. Sing to him; yes, sing his praises. Tell everyone about his miracles (16:8–9).

[i reflect]

The graceful movements of a dancer as she pirouettes to a praise song. The eloquent gestures and motions that underscore the words of a hymn. Dance can be a wonderful expression of worship. But have you ever thought of worship itself as a dance? In a manner of speaking, that's exactly what it is. Worship is a holy two-step.

In this passage, David is like a dance-caller. Listen carefully to his instructions and you'll begin to hear the two-directional movement he suggests. "Give thanks to the LORD!" That's the primary step of worship. It's with an open heart that we move toward the Lord. But it doesn't stop there. David calls us to turn and "proclaim his greatness!" That's another step in which, with our words, we move toward those around us who may not understand just how awesome our great God is.

And the dance continues. "Let the whole world know what he has done." Again we step toward people around us, proclaiming the incredible works that God has done in our lives. Then it's back to the first step in which we move toward God. "Sing to him, . . . sing his praises!" But we don't stop there. David, the dance-caller, reminds us to "tell everyone about his miracles."

Toward the Lord, then toward our neighbors. Gratefully singing to God, then confidently bragging about him to people around us. One step. Two step. Repeat. Step. Step. Feel the rhythm? Wherever you are, whatever you are doing, the cadence of worship is all-encompassing.

When all of your life is lived mindful of being in the presence of the Lord, then how you approach him as well as how you represent him is worship. Doesn't that just make you want to join the dance?

[i pray]

Lord, I'm putting on my dancing shoes today. It's such a freeing thought that my worship is not restricted to fifteen minutes of Bible reading and prayer. Please give me the ability to go about my routines today mindful of you. Amen.

[i respond]

As you drive around your community, allow the signal lights at intersections to remind you of the stop-and-go flow of worship. Red light means wait in the Lord's presence. Green light means go be a witness to the great wonders that he's done in your life.

more can I say about the way you have honored me? You know what I am really like. ¹⁹For my sake, O LORD, and according to your will, you have done all these great things and have made them known.

²⁰"O LORD, there is no one like you—there is no other God. We have never even heard of another god like you! ²¹What other nation on earth is like Israel? What other nation, O God, have you redeemed from slavery to be your own people? You made a great name for yourself when you rescued your people from Egypt. You performed awesome miracles and drove out the nations that stood in their way. ²²You chose Israel to be your people forever, and you, O LORD, have become their God.

²³"And now, O LORD, do as you have promised concerning me and my family. May it be a promise that will last forever. ²⁴And may your name be established and honored forever so that all the world will say, 'The LORD Almighty is God over Israel!' And may the dynasty of your servant David be established in your presence.

²⁵"O my God, I have been bold enough to pray this prayer because you have revealed that you will build a house for me—an eternal dynasty! ²⁶For you are God, O LORD. And you have promised these good things to me, your servant. ²⁷And now, it has pleased you to bless me and my family so that our dynasty will continue forever before you. For when you grant a blessing, O LORD, it is an eternal blessing!"

DAVID'S MILITARY VICTORIES

18 After this, David subdued and humbled the Philistines by conquering Gath and its surrounding towns. ²David also conquered the land of Moab, and the Moabites became David's subjects and brought him tribute money.

³Then David destroyed the forces of King Hadadezer of Zobah, as far as Hamath,* when Hadadezer marched out to strengthen his control along the Euphrates River. ⁴David captured one thousand chariots, seven thousand charioteers, and twenty thousand foot soldiers. Then he crippled all but one hundred of the chariot horses.

⁵When Arameans from Damascus arrived to help Hadadezer, David killed twenty-two thousand of them. ⁶Then he placed several army garrisons in Damascus, the Aramean capital, and the Arameans became David's subjects and brought him tribute money. So the LORD gave David victory wherever he went. ⁷David brought the gold shields of Hadadezer's officers to Jerusalem, ⁸along with a large amount of bronze from Hadadezer's cities of Tebah* and Cun. Later Solomon melted the bronze and used it for the Temple. He molded it into the bronze Sea, the pillars, and the various bronze utensils used at the Temple.

⁹When King Toi* of Hamath heard that David had destroyed the army of King Hadadezer of Zobah, ¹⁰he sent his son Joram* to congratulate David on his success. Hadadezer and Toi had long been enemies, and there had been many wars between them. Joram presented David with many gifts of gold, silver, and bronze. ¹¹King David dedicated all these gifts to the LORD, along with the silver and gold he had taken from the other nations he had subdued—Edom, Moab, Ammon, Philistia, and Amalek.

¹²Abishai son of Zeruiah destroyed eighteen thousand Edomites in the Valley of Salt. ¹³He placed army garrisons throughout Edom, and all the Edomites became David's subjects. This was another example of how the LORD made David victorious wherever he went.

¹⁴David reigned over all Israel and was fair to everyone. ¹⁵Joab son of Zeruiah was commander of the army. Jehoshaphat son of Ahilud was the royal historian. ¹⁶Zadok son of Ahitub and Ahimelech* son of Abiathar were the priests. Seraiah* was the court secretary.

18:3 The meaning of the Hebrew is uncertain. **18:8** Hebrew reads *Tibhath,* a variant name for Tebah; compare parallel text at 2 Sam 8:8. **18:9** As in parallel text at 2 Sam 8:9; Hebrew reads *Tou;* also in 18:10. **18:10** As in parallel text at 2 Sam 8:10; Hebrew reads *Hadoram,* a variant name for Joram. **18:16a** As in some Hebrew manuscripts, Syriac version, and Latin Vulgate (see also 2 Sam 8:17); most Hebrew manuscripts read *Abimelech.* **18:16b** As in parallel text at 2 Sam 8:17; Hebrew reads *Shavsha.*

My Daily Worship

— *April 4* —

CLAIMING GOD'S PROMISES

1 CHRONICLES 17:1—22:1

And now, O LORD, do as you have promised concerning me and my family. May it be a promise
that will last forever. And may your name be established and honored forever so that
all the world will say, "The LORD Almighty is God over Israel!" (17:23–24).

[i reflect]

Margaret had been raised in the Blue Ridge mountains of Virginia. When her mother died, she had to drop out of school to make a home for her grieving father and her two brothers. As a result, she never had the opportunity to go to college. With the Lord's help, she did the best she could to teach herself.

Although she loved to read, Margaret never outgrew an insecurity when carrying on conversations with highly educated folk. But when it came to carrying on conversations with the Lord, she knew what she was talking about . . . and to whom. When Margaret moved to Idaho to stay with cousins, she met and married a Greek immigrant who worked on the railroad. The love she shared with Harry resulted in six children. And the love she had for her Lord meant that she committed her children into his care each day.

In addition to reading from a dog-eared leather-bound Bible each morning after breakfast, Margaret would pull a Scripture card from a little wooden box on her kitchen table. She called it her "box of promises." It was filled with individual verses from the Bible documenting the myriad ways God had guaranteed to intervene on behalf of his people. Margaret would claim the promises of God and pray them back to the Lord on behalf of her family.

King David did the same. Taking God at his word and living each day with the assurance of his involvement was the way David coped with his stress as Israel's ruler.

You can deal with the challenges you face in the same way, too. When you identify one of God's promises and then request what he's offered, you are falling at his feet in joyful (and expectant) dependence. What is it you need today? Claim it. Then offer that promise back to God as a sacrifice of thanksgiving and trust.

[i pray]

"O Jesus, I have promised to serve you to the end." I know the words of this
hymn by heart, but my life seems to lag behind my lips. Help me today
to put more stock in your promises than in mine. Amen.

[i respond]

Begin your own "promise box." As you read through the Scriptures, copy on an index card those promises God makes to his people that you think also apply to you. Compile your growing stack of cards in a little box. Then pull out a card each day.

[17]Benaiah son of Jehoiada was captain of the king's bodyguard.* David's sons served as the king's chief assistants.

DAVID DEFEATS THE AMMONITES

19 Some time after this, King Nahash of the Ammonites died, and his son Hanun* became king. [2]David said, "I am going to show complete loyalty to Hanun because his father, Nahash, was always completely loyal to me." So David sent ambassadors to express sympathy to Hanun about his father's death.

But when David's ambassadors arrived in the land of Ammon, [3]Hanun's advisers said to him, "Do you really think these men are coming here to honor your father? No! David has sent them to spy out the land so that they can come in and conquer it!" [4]So Hanun seized David's ambassadors and shaved their beards, cut off their robes at the buttocks, and sent them back to David in shame. [5]When David heard what had happened, he sent messengers to tell the men to stay at Jericho until their beards grew out, for they were very embarrassed by their appearance.

[6]Now the people of Ammon realized how seriously they had angered David, so Hanun and the Ammonites sent thirty-eight tons* of silver to hire chariots and troops from Aram-naharaim, Aram-maacah, and Zobah. [7]They also hired thirty-two thousand chariots and secured the support of the king of Maacah and his army. These forces camped at Medeba, where they were joined by the Ammonite troops that Hanun had recruited from his own towns. [8]When David heard about this, he sent Joab and all his warriors to fight them. [9]The Ammonite troops drew up their battle lines at the gate of the city, while the other kings positioned themselves to fight in the open fields.

[10]When Joab saw that he would have to fight on two fronts, he chose the best troops in his army. He placed them under his personal command and led them out to fight the Arameans in the fields. [11]He left the rest of the army under the command of his brother Abishai, who was to attack the Ammonites. [12]"If the Arameans are too strong for me, then come over and help me," Joab told his brother. "And if the Ammonites are too strong for you, I will help you. [13]Be courageous! Let us fight bravely to save our people and the cities of our God. May the LORD's will be done."

[14]When Joab and his troops attacked, the Arameans began to run away. [15]And when the Ammonites saw the Arameans running, they ran from Abishai and retreated into the city. Then Joab returned to Jerusalem.

[16]The Arameans now realized that they were no match for Israel, so they summoned additional Aramean troops from the other side of the Euphrates River.* These troops arrived under the command of Shobach,* the commander of all Hadadezer's forces. [17]When David heard what was happening, he mobilized all Israel, crossed the Jordan River, and positioned his troops in battle formation. Then he engaged the enemy troops in battle, and they fought against him. [18]But again the Arameans fled from the Israelites. This time David's forces killed seven thousand charioteers and forty thousand foot soldiers, including Shobach, the commander of their army. [19]When the servants of Hadadezer realized they had been defeated by Israel, they surrendered to David and became his subjects. After that, the Arameans were no longer willing to help the Ammonites.

THE CAPTURE OF RABBAH

20 The following spring, the time of year when kings go to war, Joab led the Israelite army in successful attacks against the towns and villages of the Ammonites. In the process they laid siege to the city of Rabbah and destroyed it. But David had stayed behind in Jerusalem.

[2]When David arrived at Rabbah, he

18:17 Hebrew *of the Kerethites and Pelethites.* **19:1** Hebrew lacks *Hanun;* compare parallel text at 2 Sam 10:1. **19:6** Hebrew *1,000 talents* [34 metric tons]. **19:16a** Hebrew *the river.* **19:16b** As in parallel text at 2 Sam 10:16; Hebrew reads *Shophach;* also in 19:18.

Words of Worship

FAVOR

Favor—Hebrew *chen* "favor, graciousness"; *ra-tson* "favor"; Greek *cha-ris* "favor, grace."

In prayer we seek the Lord's favor, his approval, and blessing on our endeavors. If, through our own merit and efforts, we could make everything work out the way we want, we wouldn't need to ask for his favor. We wouldn't even have to pray! God's favor comes not because we've earned it but because he chooses to give it.

We don't need to be afraid to ask for God's favor, even if we don't think we deserve it. The Lord constantly searches our hearts and understands our motives (1 Chronicles 28:9). We can trust him not to favor us with something we will misuse or that will harm us. John reminds us, "We can be confident that he will listen to us whenever we ask him for anything in line with his will" (1 John 5:14).

removed the crown from the king's head,* and it was placed on David's own head. The crown was made of gold and set with gems, and it weighed about seventy-five pounds.* David took a vast amount of plunder from the city. ³He also made slaves of the people of Rabbah and forced them to labor with saws, picks, and axes.* That is how he dealt with the people of all the Ammonite cities. Then David and his army returned to Jerusalem.

BATTLES AGAINST THE PHILISTINES

⁴After this, war broke out with the Philistines at Gezer. As they fought, Sibbecai from Hushah killed Saph,* a descendant of the giants,* and so the Philistines were subdued. ⁵During another battle with the Philistines, Elhanan son of Jair killed Lahmi, the brother of Goliath of Gath. The handle of Lahmi's spear was as thick as a weaver's beam! ⁶In another battle with the Philistines at Gath, a huge man with six fingers on each hand and six toes on each foot—a descendant of the giants—⁷defied and taunted Israel. But he was killed by Jonathan, the son of David's brother Shimea. ⁸These Philistines were descendants of the giants of Gath, but they were killed by David and his warriors.

DAVID TAKES A CENSUS

21 Satan rose up against Israel and caused David to take a census of the Israelites. ²David gave these orders to Joab and his commanders: "Take a census of all the people in the land—from Beersheba in the south to Dan in the north—and bring me the totals so I may know how many there are."

³But Joab replied, "May the LORD increase the number of his people a hundred times over! But why, my lord, do you want to do this? Are they not all your servants? Why must you cause Israel to sin?"

⁴But the king insisted that Joab take the census, so Joab traveled throughout Israel to count the people. Then he returned to Jerusalem ⁵and reported the number of people to David. There were 1,100,000 men of military age in Israel, and 470,000 in Judah. ⁶But Joab did not include the tribes of Levi and Benjamin in the census because he was so distressed at what the king had made him do.

JUDGMENT FOR DAVID'S SIN

⁷God was very displeased with the census, and he punished Israel for it. ⁸Then David said to God, "I have sinned greatly and shouldn't have taken the census. Please forgive me for doing this foolish thing."

20:2a Greek version and Latin Vulgate read *removed the crown of Milcom;* compare 1 Kgs 11:5. Milcom, also called Molech, was the god of the Ammonites. **20:2b** Hebrew *1 talent* [34 kilograms]. **20:3** As in parallel text at 2 Sam 12:31; Hebrew reads *and saws.* **20:4a** As in parallel text at 2 Sam 21:18; Hebrew reads *Sippai.* **20:4b** Hebrew *descendant of the Rephaites;* also in 20:6, 8.

⁹Then the LORD spoke to Gad, David's seer. This was the message; ¹⁰"Go and say to David, 'This is what the LORD says: I will give you three choices. Choose one of these punishments, and I will do it.'"

¹¹So Gad came to David and said, "These are the choices the LORD has given you. ¹²You may choose three years of famine, three months of destruction by your enemies, or three days of severe plague as the angel of the LORD brings devastation throughout the land of Israel. Think this over and let me know what answer to give the LORD."

¹³"This is a desperate situation!" David replied to Gad. "But let me fall into the hands of the LORD, for his mercy is very great. Do not let me fall into human hands."

¹⁴So the LORD sent a plague upon Israel, and seventy thousand people died as a result. ¹⁵And God sent an angel to destroy Jerusalem. But just as the angel was preparing to destroy it, the LORD relented and said to the death angel, "Stop! That is enough!" At that moment the angel of the LORD was standing by the threshing floor of Araunah* the Jebusite.

¹⁶David looked up and saw the angel of the LORD standing between heaven and earth with his sword drawn, stretched out over Jerusalem. So David and the leaders of Israel put on sackcloth to show their distress and fell down with their faces to the ground. ¹⁷And David said to God, "I am the one who called for the census! I am the one who has sinned and done wrong! But these people are innocent—what have they done? O LORD my God, let your anger fall against me and my family, but do not destroy your people."

DAVID BUILDS AN ALTAR

¹⁸Then the angel of the LORD told Gad to instruct David to build an altar to the LORD at the threshing floor of Araunah the Jebusite. ¹⁹So David obeyed the instructions the LORD had given him through Gad. ²⁰Araunah, who was busy threshing wheat at the time, turned and saw the angel there. His four sons, who were with him, ran away and hid. ²¹When Araunah saw the king approaching, he left his threshing floor and bowed to the ground before David.

²²David said to Araunah, "Let me buy this threshing floor from you at its full price. Then I will build an altar to the LORD there, so that he will stop the plague."

²³"Take it, my lord, and use it as you wish," Araunah said to David. "Here are oxen for the burnt offerings, and you can use the threshing tools for wood to build a fire on the altar. And take the wheat for the grain offering. I will give it all to you."

²⁴But the king replied to Araunah, "No, I insist on paying what it is worth. I cannot take what is yours and give it to the LORD. I will not offer a burnt offering that has cost me nothing!" ²⁵So David gave Araunah six hundred pieces of gold* in payment for the threshing floor. ²⁶David built an altar there to the LORD and sacrificed burnt offerings and peace offerings. And when David prayed, the LORD answered him by sending fire from heaven to burn up the offering on the altar. ²⁷Then the LORD spoke to the angel, who put the sword back into its sheath.

²⁸When David saw that the LORD had answered his prayer, he offered sacrifices there at Araunah's threshing floor. ²⁹At that time, the Tabernacle of the LORD and the altar that Moses made in the wilderness were located at the hill of Gibeon. ³⁰But David was not able to go there to inquire of God, because he was terrified by the drawn sword of the angel of the LORD.

22 Then David said, "This will be the location for the Temple of the LORD God and the place of the altar for Israel's burnt offerings!"

PREPARATIONS FOR THE TEMPLE

²So David gave orders to call together the foreigners living in Israel, and he assigned them

---

21:15 As in parallel text at 2 Sam 24:16; Hebrew reads *Ornan,* another name for Araunah; also in 21:18-28. **21:25** Hebrew *600 shekels of gold,* about 15 pounds or 6.8 kilograms in weight.

> *To be with God wondering,*
> *that is adoration.*
>
> MICHAEL RAMSEY,
> ARCHBISHOP OF CANTERBURY

the task of preparing blocks of stone for building the Temple of God. ³David provided large amounts of iron for the nails that would be needed for the doors in the gates and for the clamps, and more bronze than they could ever weigh. ⁴He also provided innumerable cedar logs, for the men of Tyre and Sidon had brought vast amounts of cedar to David. ⁵David said, "My son Solomon is still young and inexperienced, and the Temple of the LORD must be a magnificent structure, famous and glorious throughout the world. So I will begin making preparations for it now." So David collected vast amounts of building materials before his death.

⁶Then David sent for his son Solomon and instructed him to build a Temple for the LORD, the God of Israel. ⁷"I wanted to build a Temple to honor the name of the LORD my God," David told him. ⁸"But the LORD said to me, 'You have killed many men in the great battles you have fought. And since you have shed so much blood before me, you will not be the one to build a Temple to honor my name. ⁹But you will have a son who will experience peace and rest. I will give him peace with his enemies in all the surrounding lands. His name will be Solomon,* and I will give peace and quiet to Israel during his reign. ¹⁰He is the one who will build a Temple to honor my name. He will be my son, and I will be his father. And I will establish the throne of his kingdom over Israel forever.'

¹¹"Now, my son, may the LORD be with you and give you success as you follow his instructions in building the Temple of the LORD your God. ¹²And may the LORD give you wisdom and understanding, that you may obey the law of the LORD your God as you rule over Israel. ¹³For if you carefully obey the laws and regulations that the LORD gave to Israel through Moses, you will be successful. Be strong and courageous; do not be afraid or lose heart!

¹⁴"I have worked hard to provide materials for building the Temple of the LORD—nearly four thousand tons of gold, nearly forty thousand tons of silver,* and so much iron and bronze that it cannot be weighed. I have also gathered lumber and stone for the walls, though you may need to add more. ¹⁵You have many skilled stonemasons and carpenters and craftsmen of every kind available to you. ¹⁶They are expert goldsmiths and silversmiths and workers of bronze and iron. Now begin the work, and may the LORD be with you!"

¹⁷Then David ordered all the leaders of Israel to assist Solomon in this project. ¹⁸"The LORD your God is with you," he declared. "He has given you peace with the surrounding nations. He has handed them over to me, and they are now subject to the LORD and his people. ¹⁹Now seek the LORD your God with all your heart. Build the sanctuary of the LORD God so that you can bring the Ark of the LORD's covenant and the holy vessels of God into the Temple built to honor the LORD's name."

DUTIES OF THE LEVITES

23 When David was an old man, he appointed his son Solomon to be king over Israel. ²David summoned all the political leaders of Israel, together with the priests and Levites, for the coronation ceremony. ³All the Levites who were thirty years old or older were counted, and the total came to thirty-eight thousand. ⁴Then David said, "Twenty-four thousand of them will supervise the

---

22:9 *Solomon* sounds like and is probably derived from the Hebrew word for "peace." 22:14 Hebrew *100,000 talents* [3,400 metric tons] *of gold, 1,000,000 talents* [34,000 metric tons] *of silver.*

work at the Temple of the LORD. Six thousand are to serve as officials and judges. ⁵Four thousand will work as gatekeepers, and another four thousand will praise the LORD with the musical instruments I have made." ⁶Then David divided the Levites into divisions named after the clans descended from the three sons of Levi—Gershon, Kohath, and Merari.

THE GERSHONITES

⁷The Gershonite family units were defined by their lines of descent from Libni* and Shimei, the sons of Gershon. ⁸Three of the descendants of Libni were Jehiel (the family leader), Zetham, and Joel. ⁹These were the leaders of the family of Libni.

Three of the descendants of Shimei were Shelomoth, Haziel, and Haran. ¹⁰Four other descendants of Shimei were Jahath, Ziza,* Jeush, and Beriah. ¹¹Jahath was the family leader, and Ziza was next. Jeush and Beriah were counted as a single family because neither had many sons.

THE KOHATHITES

¹²The descendants of Kohath included Amram, Izhar, Hebron, and Uzziel. ¹³The sons of Amram were Aaron and Moses. Aaron and his descendants were set apart to dedicate the most holy things, to offer sacrifices in the LORD's presence, to serve the LORD, and to pronounce blessings in his name forever.

¹⁴As for Moses, the man of God, his sons were included with the tribe of Levi. ¹⁵The sons of Moses were Gershom and Eliezer. ¹⁶The descendants of Gershom included Shebuel, the family leader. ¹⁷Eliezer had only one son, Rehabiah, the family leader. Rehabiah had numerous descendants. ¹⁸The descendants of Izhar included Shelomith, the family leader.

¹⁹The descendants of Hebron included Jeriah (the family leader), Amariah (the second), Jahaziel (the third), and Jekameam (the fourth). ²⁰The descendants of Uzziel included Micah (the family leader) and Isshiah (the second).

THE MERARITES

²¹The descendants of Merari included Mahli and Mushi.

The sons of Mahli were Eleazar and Kish. ²²Eleazar died with no sons, only daughters. His daughters married their cousins, the sons of Kish. ²³The three sons of Mushi were Mahli, Eder, and Jerimoth.

²⁴These were the descendants of Levi by clans, the leaders of their family groups, registered carefully by name. Each had to be twenty years old or older to qualify for service in the house of the LORD. ²⁵For David said, "The LORD, the God of Israel, has given us peace, and he will always live in Jerusalem. ²⁶Now the Levites will no longer need to carry the Tabernacle and its utensils from place to place." ²⁷It was according to David's final instructions that all the Levites twenty years old or older were registered for service.

²⁸The work of the Levites was to assist the priests, the descendants of Aaron, as they served at the house of the LORD. They also took care of the courtyards and side rooms, helped perform the ceremonies of purification, and served in many other ways in the house of God. ²⁹They were in charge of the sacred bread that was set out on the table, the choice flour for the grain offerings, the wafers made without yeast, the cakes cooked in olive oil, and the other mixed breads. They were also responsible to check all the weights and measures. ³⁰And each morning and evening they stood before the LORD to sing songs of thanks and praise to him. ³¹They

---

23:7 Hebrew *Ladan* (also in 23:8-9), another name for Libni; compare 6:17.   23:10 As in Greek version and Latin Vulgate (see also 23:11); Hebrew reads *Zina.*

assisted with the burnt offerings that were presented to the LORD on Sabbath days, at new moon celebrations, and at all the appointed festivals. The proper number of Levites served in the LORD's presence at all times, following all the procedures they had been given.

³²And so, under the supervision of the priests, the Levites watched over the Tabernacle and the Temple* and faithfully carried out their duties of service at the house of the LORD.

DUTIES OF THE PRIESTS

24 This is how Aaron's descendants, the priests, were divided into groups for service. The sons of Aaron were Nadab, Abihu, Eleazar, and Ithamar. ²But Nadab and Abihu died before their father did, and they had no sons. So only Eleazar and Ithamar were left to carry on as priests.

³With the help of Zadok, who was a descendant of Eleazar, and of Ahimelech, who was a descendant of Ithamar, David divided Aaron's descendants into groups according to their various duties. ⁴Eleazar's descendants were divided into sixteen groups and Ithamar's into eight, for there were more family leaders among the descendants of Eleazar.

⁵All tasks were assigned to the various groups by means of sacred lots so that no preference would be shown, for there were many qualified officials serving God in the sanctuary from among the descendants of both Eleazar and Ithamar. ⁶Shemaiah son of Nethanel, a Levite, acted as secretary and wrote down the names and assignments in the presence of the king, Zadok the priest, Ahimelech son of Abiathar, and the family leaders of the priests and Levites. The descendants of Eleazar and Ithamar took turns casting lots.

⁷ The first lot fell to Jehoiarib.
The second lot fell to Jedaiah.
⁸ The third lot fell to Harim.
The fourth lot fell to Seorim.

⁹ The fifth lot fell to Malkijah.
The sixth lot fell to Mijamin.
¹⁰ The seventh lot fell to Hakkoz.
The eighth lot fell to Abijah.
¹¹ The ninth lot fell to Jeshua.
The tenth lot fell to Shecaniah.
¹² The eleventh lot fell to Eliashib.
The twelfth lot fell to Jakim.
¹³ The thirteenth lot fell to Huppah.
The fourteenth lot fell to Jeshebeab.
¹⁴ The fifteenth lot fell to Bilgah.
The sixteenth lot fell to Immer.
¹⁵ The seventeenth lot fell to Hezir.
The eighteenth lot fell to Happizzez.
¹⁶ The nineteenth lot fell to Pethahiah.
The twentieth lot fell to Jehezkel.
¹⁷ The twenty-first lot fell to Jakin.
The twenty-second lot fell to Gamul.
¹⁸ The twenty-third lot fell to Delaiah.
The twenty-fourth lot fell to Maaziah.

¹⁹Each group carried out its duties in the house of the LORD according to the procedures established by their ancestor Aaron in obedience to the commands of the LORD, the God of Israel.

FAMILY LEADERS AMONG THE LEVITES

²⁰These were the other family leaders descended from Levi:

From the descendants of Amram, the leader was Shebuel.*
From the descendants of Shebuel, the leader was Jehdeiah.
²¹ From the descendants of Rehabiah, the leader was Isshiah.
²² From the descendants of Izhar, the leader was Shelomith.*
From the descendants of Shelomith, the leader was Jahath.
²³ From the descendants of Hebron, Jeriah was the leader,* Amariah was

23:32 Hebrew *the Tent of Meeting and the sanctuary.* 24:20 Hebrew *Shubael* (also in 24:20b), a variant name for Shebuel; compare 23:16 and 26:24. 24:22 Hebrew *Shelomoth* (also in 24:22b), a variant name for Shelomith; compare 23:18. 24:23 Hebrew *From the descendants of Jeriah;* compare 23:19.

second-in-command, Jahaziel was third, and Jekameam was fourth.

²⁴ From the descendants of Uzziel, the leader was Micah.

From the descendants of Micah, the leader was Shamir, ²⁵along with Isshiah, the brother of Micah.

From the descendants of Isshiah, the leader was Zechariah.

²⁶ From the descendants of Merari, the leaders were Mahli and Mushi.

From the descendants of Jaaziah, the leader was Beno.

²⁷ From the descendants of Merari through Jaaziah, the leaders were Beno, Shoham, Zaccur, and Ibri.

²⁸ From the descendants of Mahli, the leader was Eleazar, though he had no sons.

²⁹ From the descendants of Kish, the leader was Jerahmeel.

³⁰ From the descendants of Mushi, the leaders were Mahli, Eder, and Jerimoth.

These were the descendants of Levi in their various families. ³¹Like the descendants of Aaron, they were assigned to their duties by means of sacred lots, without regard to age or rank. It was done in the presence of King David, Zadok, Ahimelech, and the family leaders of the priests and the Levites.

DUTIES OF THE MUSICIANS

25 David and the army commanders then appointed men from the families of Asaph, Heman, and Jeduthun to proclaim God's messages to the accompaniment of harps, lyres, and cymbals. Here is a list of their names and their work:

²From the sons of Asaph, there were Zaccur, Joseph, Nethaniah, and Asarelah. They worked under the direction of their father, Asaph, who proclaimed God's messages by the king's orders.

³Jeduthun had six sons: Gedaliah, Zeri, Jeshaiah, Shimei,* Hashabiah, and Mattithiah. They worked under the direction of their father, Jeduthun, who proclaimed God's messages to the accompaniment of the harp, offering thanks and praise to the LORD.

⁴Heman's sons were Bukkiah, Mattaniah, Uzziel, Shubael,* Jerimoth, Hananiah, Hanani, Eliathah, Geddalti, Romamti-ezer, Joshbekashah, Mallothi, Hothir, and Mahazioth. ⁵All these were the sons of Heman, the king's seer, for God had honored him with fourteen sons and three daughters.

⁶All these men were under the direction of their fathers as they made music at the house of the LORD. Their responsibilities included the playing of cymbals, lyres, and harps at the house of God. Asaph, Jeduthun, and Heman reported directly to the king. ⁷They and their families were all trained in making music before the LORD, and each of them—288 in all—was an accomplished musician. ⁸The musicians were appointed to their particular term of service by means of sacred lots, without regard to whether they were young or old, teacher or student.

⁹ The first lot fell to Joseph of the Asaph clan and twelve of his sons and relatives.*

The second lot fell to Gedaliah and twelve of his sons and relatives.

¹⁰ The third lot fell to Zaccur and twelve of his sons and relatives.

¹¹ The fourth lot fell to Zeri* and twelve of his sons and relatives.

¹² The fifth lot fell to Nethaniah and twelve of his sons and relatives.

¹³ The sixth lot fell to Bukkiah and twelve of his sons and relatives.

25:3 As in one Hebrew manuscript and some Greek manuscripts (see also 25:17); most Hebrew manuscripts lack *Shimei*. 25:4 Hebrew *Shebuel*, a variant name for Shubael; compare 25:20. 25:9 As in Greek version; Hebrew lacks *and twelve of his sons and relatives*. 25:11 Hebrew *Izri*, a variant name for Zeri; compare 25:3.

My Daily Worship

— April 5 —

MAKING MUSICAL MEMORIES

1 CHRONICLES 22:2–27:34

David and the army commanders then appointed men from the families
of Asaph, Heman, and Jeduthun to proclaim God's messages
to the accompaniment of harps, lyres, and cymbals (25:1).

[i reflect]

Our memory likes to play tricks on us. It's time to leave for work and you can't remember where you left the car keys. You walk into a room to get something only to discover you have forgotten what it is you need. Forgetfulness—it plagues us all. We struggle to recall names and phone numbers and where we put our glasses. But more than that, we tend to forget things we value as significant while remembering events or thoughts we'd rather forget.

Perhaps that's why memorizing God's Word is so difficult. Try as you will, you can't seem to hide it in your heart. What causes you to keep trying, however, is the joy you've experienced in the past when you quoted a verse from memory to someone who wanted to know what God had to say on a certain topic. Being able to recite a passage of Scripture when the truth it celebrates describes a given life situation is wonderfully freeing. But lest you think it impossible, try adding music.

When David and the army commanders instructed certain families to put a musical accompaniment to the words of God, they were doing us a big favor. It's funny, but putting Scripture to music makes memorizing it easier. That's been tested and proven. In fact, you probably already have memorized Scripture without even knowing it because some praise songs you sing come straight out of the Bible.

By listening to worship music as you work around the house or drive back and forth to your place of employment, you will sing those lyrics over and over until they become part of you. And guess what? In the process of listening, singing, and memorizing the Word of God, you'll be worshiping him. Sing a different tune today, and hide God's Word in your heart.

[i pray]

Lord, thank you for the gift of music. Melody, harmony, rhythm, and lyrics create
space in my heart so that your words can live there. It's wonderful to be alive
today with access to such wonderful worship music. As I listen and sing
along, surround me with a sense of your holy presence. Amen.

[i respond]

Take some time to read the liner notes of a favorite worship CD or tape. Select a song that is based on Scripture, and then play that tune until you know the words by heart.

¹⁴ The seventh lot fell to Asarelah* and twelve of his sons and relatives.

¹⁵ The eighth lot fell to Jeshaiah and twelve of his sons and relatives.

¹⁶ The ninth lot fell to Mattaniah and twelve of his sons and relatives.

¹⁷ The tenth lot fell to Shimei and twelve of his sons and relatives.

¹⁸ The eleventh lot fell to Uzziel* and twelve of his sons and relatives.

¹⁹ The twelfth lot fell to Hashabiah and twelve of his sons and relatives.

²⁰ The thirteenth lot fell to Shubael and twelve of his sons and relatives.

²¹ The fourteenth lot fell to Mattithiah and twelve of his sons and relatives.

²² The fifteenth lot fell to Jerimoth* and twelve of his sons and relatives.

²³ The sixteenth lot fell to Hananiah and twelve of his sons and relatives.

²⁴ The seventeenth lot fell to Joshbekashah* and twelve of his sons and relatives.

²⁵ The eighteenth lot fell to Hanani and twelve of his sons and relatives.

²⁶ The nineteenth lot fell to Mallothi and twelve of his sons and relatives.

²⁷ The twentieth lot fell to Eliathah and twelve of his sons and relatives.

²⁸ The twenty-first lot fell to Hothir and twelve of his sons and relatives.

²⁹ The twenty-second lot fell to Geddalti* and twelve of his sons and relatives.

³⁰ The twenty-third lot fell to Mahazioth and twelve of his sons and relatives.

³¹ The twenty-fourth lot fell to Romamti-ezer and twelve of his sons and relatives.

DUTIES OF THE GATEKEEPERS

26 ¹ These are the divisions of the gatekeepers:

From the Korahites, there was Meshelemiah son of Kore, of the family of Asaph. ²The sons of Meshelemiah were Zechariah (the oldest), Jediael (the second), Zebadiah (the third), Jathniel (the fourth), ³Elam (the fifth), Jehohanan (the sixth), and Eliehoenai (the seventh).

⁴The sons of Obed-edom, also gatekeepers, were Shemaiah (the oldest), Jehozabad (the second), Joah (the third), Sacar (the fourth), Nethanel (the fifth), ⁵Ammiel (the sixth), Issachar (the seventh), and Peullethai (the eighth). God had richly blessed Obed-edom.

⁶Obed-edom's son Shemaiah had sons with great ability who earned positions of great authority in the clan. ⁷Their names were Othni, Rephael, Obed, and Elzabad. Their relatives, Elihu and Semakiah, were also very capable men.

⁸All of these descendants of Obed-edom, including their sons and grandsons—sixty-two of them in all—were very capable men, well qualified for their work.

⁹Meshelemiah's eighteen sons and relatives were also very capable men.

¹⁰Hosah, of the Merari clan, appointed Shimri as the leader among his sons, though he was not the oldest. ¹¹His other sons included Hilkiah (the second), Tebaliah (the third), and Zechariah (the fourth). Hosah's sons and relatives, who served as gatekeepers, numbered thirteen in all.

¹²These divisions of the gatekeepers were named for their family leaders, and like the other Levites, they served at the house of the LORD. ¹³They were assigned by families for guard duty at the various gates, without regard to age or training, for it was all decided by means of sacred lots.

¹⁴The responsibility for the east gate went to

25:14 Hebrew *Jesharelah*, a variant name for Asarelah; compare 25:2. 25:18 Hebrew *Azarel*, a variant name for Uzziel; compare 25:4.
25:22 Hebrew *Jeremoth*, a variant name for Jerimoth; compare 25:4. 25:24 Hebrew *Joshbekasha*, a variant name for Joshbekashah; compare 25:4. 25:29 Hebrew *Giddalti*, a variant name for Geddalti; compare 25:4.

Meshelemiah* and his group. The north gate was assigned to his son Zechariah, a man of unusual wisdom. [15]The south gate went to Obed-edom, and his sons were put in charge of the storehouses. [16]Shuppim and Hosah were assigned the west gate and the gateway leading up to the Temple.* Guard duties were divided evenly. [17]Six Levites were assigned each day to the east gate, four to the north gate, four to the south gate, and two to each of the storehouses. [18]Six were assigned each day to the west gate, four to the gateway leading up to the Temple, and two to the courtyard.*

[19]These were the divisions of the gatekeepers from the clans of Korah and Merari.

TREASURERS AND OTHER OFFICIALS

[20]Other Levites, led by Ahijah, were in charge of the treasuries of the house of God and the storerooms. [21]From the family of Libni* in the clan of Gershon, Jehiel* was the leader. [22]The sons of Jehiel, Zetham and his brother Joel, were in charge of the treasuries of the house of the LORD.

[23]These are the leaders that descended from Amram, Izhar, Hebron, and Uzziel:

[24]From the clan of Amram, Shebuel was a descendant of Gershom son of Moses. He was the chief officer of the treasuries. [25]His relatives through Eliezer were Rehabiah, Jeshaiah, Joram, Zicri, and Shelomoth.

[26]Shelomoth and his relatives were in charge of the treasuries that held all the things dedicated to the LORD by King David, the family leaders, and the generals and captains and other officers of the army. [27]These men had dedicated some of the plunder they had gained in battle to maintain the house of the LORD. [28]Shelomoth and his relatives also cared for the items dedicated to the LORD by Samuel the seer, Saul son of Kish, Abner son of Ner, and Joab son of Zeruiah. All the other dedicated items were in their care, too.

[29]From the clan of Izhar came Kenaniah. He and his sons were appointed to serve as public administrators and judges throughout Israel.

[30]From the clan of Hebron came Hashabiah. He and his relatives—seventeen hundred capable men—were put in charge of the Israelite lands west of the Jordan River. They were responsible for all matters related to the things of the LORD and the service of the king in that area.

[31]Also from the clan of Hebron came Jeriah,* who was the leader of the Hebronites according to the genealogical records. (In the fortieth year of David's reign, a search was made in the records, and capable men from the clan of Hebron were found at Jazer in the land of Gilead.) [32]There were twenty-seven hundred capable men among the relatives of Jeriah. King David sent them to the east side of the Jordan River and put them in charge of the tribes of Reuben and Gad and the half-tribe of Manasseh. They were responsible for all matters related to the things of God and the service of the king.

MILITARY COMMANDERS AND DIVISIONS

27 This is the list of Israelite generals and captains, and their officers, who served the king by supervising the army divisions that were on duty each month of the year. Each division served for one month and had twenty-four thousand troops.

[2]Jashobeam son of Zabdiel was commander of the first division, which was on duty

---

26:14 Hebrew *Shelemiah,* a variant name for Meshelemiah; compare 26:2. 26:16 Or *the gate of Shalleketh on the upper road* (also in 26:18). The meaning of the Hebrew is uncertain. 26:18 Or *the colonnade.* The meaning of the Hebrew is uncertain. 26:21a Hebrew *Ladan,* another name for Libni; compare 6:17. 26:21b Hebrew *Jehieli* (also in 26:22), a variant name for Jehiel; compare 23:8. 26:31 Hebrew *Jerijah,* a variant name for Jeriah; compare 23:19.

during the first month. There were twenty-four thousand troops in his division. ³He was a descendant of Perez and was in charge of all the army officers for the first month.

⁴Dodai, a descendant of Ahoah, was commander of the second division, which was on duty during the second month. There were twenty-four thousand troops in his division, and Mikloth was his chief officer.

⁵Benaiah son of Jehoiada the priest was commander of the third division, which was on duty during the third month. There were twenty-four thousand troops in his division. ⁶This was the Benaiah who commanded David's elite military group known as the Thirty. His son Ammizabad was his chief officer.

⁷Asahel, the brother of Joab, was commander of the fourth division, which was on duty during the fourth month. There were twenty-four thousand troops in his division. Asahel was succeeded by his son Zebadiah.

⁸Shammah* the Izrahite was commander of the fifth division, which was on duty during the fifth month. There were twenty-four thousand troops in his division.

⁹Ira son of Ikkesh from Tekoa was commander of the sixth division, which was on duty during the sixth month. There were twenty-four thousand troops in his division.

¹⁰Helez, a descendant of Ephraim from Pelon, was commander of the seventh division, which was on duty during the seventh month. There were twenty-four thousand troops in his division.

¹¹Sibbecai, a descendant of Zerah from Hushah, was commander of the eighth division, which was on duty during the eighth month. There were twenty-four thousand troops in his division.

¹²Abiezer from Anathoth in the territory of Benjamin was commander of the ninth division, which was on duty during the ninth month. There were twenty-four thousand troops in his division.

¹³Maharai, a descendant of Zerah from Netophah, was commander of the tenth division, which was on duty during the tenth month. There were twenty-four thousand troops in his division.

¹⁴Benaiah from Pirathon in Ephraim was commander of the eleventh division, which was on duty during the eleventh month. There were twenty-four thousand troops in his division.

¹⁵Heled,* a descendant of Othniel from Netophah, was commander of the twelfth division, which was on duty during the twelfth month. There were twenty-four thousand troops in his division.

LEADERS OF THE TRIBES

¹⁶The following were the tribes of Israel and their leaders:

Tribe	Leader
Reuben	Eliezer son of Zicri
Simeon	Shephatiah son of Maacah
¹⁷ Levi	Hashabiah son of Kemuel
Aaron (the priests)	Zadok
¹⁸ Judah	Elihu (a brother of David)
Issachar	Omri son of Michael
¹⁹ Zebulun	Ishmaiah son of Obadiah
Naphtali	Jeremoth son of Azriel
²⁰ Ephraim	Hoshea son of Azaziah
Manasseh (west)	Joel son of Pedaiah
²¹ Manasseh (east*)	Iddo son of Zechariah
Benjamin	Jaasiel son of Abner
²² Dan	Azarel son of Jeroham

These were the leaders of the tribes of Israel.

²³When David took his census, he did not count those who were younger than twenty years of age, because the LORD had promised to make the Israelites as numerous as the

---

27:8 Hebrew *Shamhuth,* another name for Shammah; compare 11:27 and 2 Sam 23:25.   27:15 Hebrew *Heldai,* a variant name for Heled; compare 11:30 and 2 Sam 23:29.   27:21 Hebrew *in Gilead.*

stars in heaven. [24]Joab began the census but never finished it because the anger of God broke out against Israel. The final total was never recorded in King David's official records.

OFFICIALS OF DAVID'S KINGDOM

[25]Azmaveth son of Adiel was in charge of the palace treasuries.

Jonathan son of Uzziah was in charge of the regional treasuries throughout the towns, villages, and fortresses of Israel.

[26]Ezri son of Kelub was in charge of the field workers who farmed the king's lands.

[27]Shimei from Ramah was in charge of the king's vineyards.

Zabdi from Shepham was responsible for the grapes and the supplies of wine.

[28]Baal-hanan from Geder was in charge of the king's olive groves and sycamore-fig trees in the foothills of Judah.*

Joash was responsible for the supplies of olive oil.

[29]Shitrai from Sharon was in charge of the cattle on the Sharon Plain.

Shaphat son of Adlai was responsible for the cattle in the valleys.

[30]Obil the Ishmaelite was in charge of the camels.

Jehdeiah from Meronoth was in charge of the donkeys.

[31]Jaziz the Hagrite was in charge of the king's sheep.

All these officials were overseers of King David's property.

[32]Jonathan, David's uncle, was a wise counselor to the king, a man of great insight, and a scribe. Jehiel the Hacmonite was responsible to teach the king's sons. [33]Ahithophel was the royal adviser. Hushai the Arkite was the king's friend. [34]Ahithophel was succeeded by Jehoiada son of Benaiah and by Abiathar. Joab was commander of the Israelite army.

27:28 Hebrew *the Shephelah.*

DAVID'S INSTRUCTIONS TO SOLOMON

28 David summoned all his officials to Jerusalem—the leaders of the tribes, the commanders of the twelve army divisions, the other generals and captains, the overseers of the royal property and livestock, the palace officials, the mighty men, and all the other warriors in the kingdom. [2]David rose and stood before them and addressed them as follows: "My brothers and my people! It was my desire to build a temple where the Ark of the LORD's covenant, God's footstool, could rest permanently. I made the necessary preparations for building it, [3]but God said to me, 'You must not build a temple to honor my name, for you are a warrior and have shed much blood.'

[4]"Yet the LORD, the God of Israel, has chosen me from among all my father's family to be king over Israel forever. For he has chosen the tribe of Judah to rule, and from among the families of Judah, he chose my father's family. And from among my father's sons, the LORD was pleased to make me king over all Israel. [5]And from among my sons—for the LORD has given me many children—he chose Solomon to succeed me on the throne of his kingdom of Israel. [6]He said to me, 'Your son Solomon will build my Temple and its courtyards, for I have chosen him as my son, and I will be his father. [7]And if he continues to obey my commands and regulations as he does now, I will make his kingdom last forever.' [8]So now, with God as our witness, I give you this charge for all Israel, the LORD's assembly: Be careful to obey all the commands of the LORD your God, so that you may possess this good land and leave it to your children as a permanent inheritance.

[9]"And Solomon, my son, get to know the God of your ancestors. Worship and serve him with your whole heart and with a willing mind. For the LORD sees every heart and understands and knows every plan and thought. If you seek him, you will find him.

But if you forsake him, he will reject you forever. [10]So take this seriously. The LORD has chosen you to build a Temple as his sanctuary. Be strong, and do the work."

[11]Then David gave Solomon the plans for the Temple and its surroundings, including the treasuries, the upstairs rooms, the inner rooms, and the inner sanctuary where the Ark's cover—the place of atonement—would be kept. [12]David also gave Solomon all the plans he had in mind* for the courtyards of the LORD's Temple, the outside rooms, the treasuries of God's Temple, and the rooms for the dedicated gifts. [13]The king also gave Solomon the instructions concerning the work of the various divisions of priests and Levites in the Temple of the LORD. And he gave specifications for the items in the LORD's Temple which were to be used for worship and sacrifice.

[14]David gave instructions regarding how much gold and silver should be used to make the necessary items. [15]He told Solomon the amount of gold needed for the gold lampstands and lamps, and the amount of silver for the silver lampstands and lamps, depending on how each would be used. [16]He designated the amount of gold for the table on which the Bread of the Presence would be placed and the amount of silver for other tables.

[17]David also designated the amount of gold for the solid gold meat hooks used to handle the sacrificial meat and for the basins, pitchers, and dishes, as well as the amount of silver for every dish. [18]Finally, he designated the amount of refined gold for the altar of incense and for the gold cherubim, whose wings were stretched out over the Ark of the LORD's covenant. [19]"Every part of this plan," David told Solomon, "was given to me in writing from the hand of the LORD.*"

[20]Then David continued, "Be strong and courageous, and do the work. Don't be afraid or discouraged by the size of the task, for the LORD God, my God, is with you. He will not fail you or forsake you. He will see to it that all the work related to the Temple of the LORD is finished correctly. [21]The various divisions of priests and Levites will serve in the Temple of God. Others with skills of every kind will volunteer, and the leaders and the entire nation are at your command."

GIFTS FOR BUILDING THE TEMPLE

29 Then King David turned to the entire assembly and said, "My son Solomon, whom God has chosen to be the next king of Israel, is still young and inexperienced. The work ahead of him is enormous, for the Temple he will build is not just another building—it is for the LORD God himself! [2]Using every resource at my command, I have gathered as much as I could for building the Temple of my God. Now there is enough gold, silver, bronze, iron, and wood, as well as great quantities of onyx, other precious stones, costly jewels, and all kinds of fine stone and marble. [3]And now because of my devotion to the Temple of my God, I am giving all of my own private treasures of gold and silver to help in the construction. This is in addition to the building materials I have already collected for his holy Temple. [4]I am donating more than 112 tons of gold* from Ophir and over 262 tons of refined silver* to be used for overlaying the walls of the buildings [5]and for the other gold and silver work to be done by the craftsmen. Now then, who will follow my example? Who is willing to give offerings to the LORD today?"

[6]Then the family leaders, the leaders of the tribes of Israel, the generals and captains of the army, and the king's administrative officers all gave willingly. [7]For the construction of the Temple of God, they gave almost 188 tons of gold,* 10,000 gold coins,* about 375 tons

---

28:12 Or *the plans of the spirit that was with him.* **28:19** Or *was written under the direction of the LORD.* **29:4a** Hebrew *3,000 talents* [102 metric tons] *of gold.* **29:4b** Hebrew *7,000 talents* [238 metric tons] *of silver.* **29:7a** Hebrew *5,000 talents* [170 metric tons] *of gold.* **29:7b** Hebrew *10,000 darics* [a Persian coin] *of gold,* about 185 pounds or 84 kilograms in weight.

My Daily Worship

— *April 6* —

PASSING THE BATON OF FAITH

1 CHRONICLES 28:1–29:30

And Solomon, my son, get to know the God of your ancestors. Worship and
serve him with your whole heart and with a willing mind (28:9).

[i reflect]

Harold Barnes didn't always have a knack for memorizing the Bible and for good reason. Hal was over forty when he became a Christian. Once he trusted Christ as his Savior, Hal developed an insatiable hunger for God's Word. He loved to read and meditate on Scripture. This traveling sales-man kept a pocket-sized version of the Bible wherever he went. As he drove several hundred miles between clients, Hal would read and audibly recite long passages.

When he turned eighty, Harold Barnes had memorized over 170 chapters of the Bible. The amount of truth he hid in his mind and heart was the by-product of spending time in personal worship. Just as David hoped his son Solomon would do, Hal worshiped and served the Lord with his whole heart and a willing mind. Because he did, Hal shared his joy and inner peace with his clients, his neighbors, and his family.

In fact, when his grandson Jacob turned thirteen, Grandpa Hal was invited to speak at the birth-day celebration. As he stood up in front of a roomful of invited guests, the elderly man challenged the boy to seek the Lord and spend time in his Word. More than anything Hal wanted the faith he had found in midlife to be passed on to family members who would come after him. Holding up a worn copy of the Scriptures, Hal said, "Jake, this book will keep you from sin or sin will keep you from this book!"

Essentially that's what David was saying to his son when he challenged him to "get to know the God of your ancestors." It's what the Lord would have someone say to you. He longs to have you curl up in a chair, focus on him, and pay attention to his words so that they become engraved on your heart.

[i pray]

Lord, I'm grateful for those who have passed the baton of faith to me. Because of the influence of
those who loved me enough to be honest with me, I am spending time in your book on a regular
basis. Help me be that kind of an influencer in the lives of those who look up to me. Amen.

[i respond]

Try memorizing a chapter of the Bible. Look for a relatively short psalm. Spend ten minutes each day reading it aloud (with expression), "as unto the Lord."

of silver,* about 675 tons of bronze,* and about 3,750 tons of iron.* ⁸They also contributed numerous precious stones, which were deposited in the treasury of the house of the LORD under the care of Jehiel, a descendant of Gershon. ⁹The people rejoiced over the offerings, for they had given freely and wholeheartedly to the LORD, and King David was filled with joy.

DAVID'S PRAYER OF PRAISE

¹⁰Then David praised the LORD in the presence of the whole assembly: "O LORD, the God of our ancestor Israel,* may you be praised forever and ever! ¹¹Yours, O LORD, is the greatness, the power, the glory, the victory, and the majesty. Everything in the heavens and on earth is yours, O LORD, and this is your kingdom. We adore you as the one who is over all things. ¹²Riches and honor come from you alone, for you rule over everything. Power and might are in your hand, and it is at your discretion that people are made great and given strength.

¹³"O our God, we thank you and praise your glorious name! ¹⁴But who am I, and who are my people, that we could give anything to you? Everything we have has come from you, and we give you only what you have already given us! ¹⁵We are here for only a moment, visitors and strangers in the land as our ancestors were before us. Our days on earth are like a shadow, gone so soon without a trace.

¹⁶"O LORD our God, even these materials that we have gathered to build a Temple to honor your holy name come from you! It all belongs to you! ¹⁷I know, my God, that you examine our hearts and rejoice when you find integrity there. You know I have done all this with good motives, and I have watched your people offer their gifts willingly and joyously.

¹⁸"O LORD, the God of our ancestors Abraham, Isaac, and Israel, make your people always want to obey you. See to it that their love for you never changes. ¹⁹Give my son Solomon the wholehearted desire to obey all your commands, decrees, and principles, and to build this Temple, for which I have made all these preparations."

²⁰Then David said to the whole assembly, "Give praise to the LORD your God!" And the entire assembly praised the LORD, the God of their ancestors, and they bowed low and knelt before the LORD and the king.

SOLOMON NAMED AS KING

²¹The next day they brought a thousand bulls, a thousand rams, and a thousand male lambs as burnt offerings to the LORD. They also brought drink offerings and many other sacrifices on behalf of Israel. ²²They feasted and drank in the LORD's presence with great joy that day.

And again they crowned David's son Solomon as their new king. They anointed him before the LORD as their leader, and they anointed Zadok as their priest. ²³So Solomon took the throne of the LORD in place of his father, David, and he prospered greatly, and all Israel obeyed him. ²⁴All the royal officials, the army commanders, and the sons of King David pledged their loyalty to King Solomon. ²⁵And the LORD exalted Solomon so the entire nation of Israel stood in awe of him, and he gave Solomon even greater wealth and honor than his father.

SUMMARY OF DAVID'S REIGN

²⁶So David son of Jesse reigned over all Israel. ²⁷He ruled Israel for forty years in all, seven years from Hebron and thirty-three years from Jerusalem. ²⁸He died at a ripe old age, having enjoyed long life, wealth, and honor. Then his son Solomon ruled in his place. ²⁹All the events of King David's reign, from beginning to end, are written in *The Record of Samuel the Seer, The Record of Nathan the Prophet,* and *The Record of Gad the Seer.* ³⁰These accounts include the mighty deeds of his reign and everything that happened to him and to Israel and to all the surrounding kingdoms.

29:7c Hebrew *10,000 talents* [340 metric tons] *of silver.* **29:7d** Hebrew *18,000 talents* [612 metric tons] *of bronze.* **29:7e** Hebrew *100,000 talents* [3,400 metric tons] *of iron.* **29:10** *Israel* is the name that God gave to Jacob.

2 Chronicles

The eyes of the LORD search the whole earth in order to strengthen
those whose hearts are fully committed to him (16:9).

What's Your Heart Condition?

Total release. It's the picture of marathon runners stretching and straining every ligament in their bodies just to touch the tape at the finish line. It's the commitment seen in athletes at the top of their game—abandoned to their art. It's the bungee jumper in freefall, and the cliff diver seconds before the splash. And total release is also a part of true worship, seen in the people of God who built the Temple and committed themselves to God.

Solomon led his people to hold nothing back when it came to worship. The people gladly invested their intense labor and sweat into building the Temple, as if to devote every ounce of their being in honor of God's glory. The pure gold overlays, the massive winged cherubim in the Most Holy Place, the bronze oxen—no expense was spared inside or outside the Temple to glorify God! The entire community of Israel sacrificed countless animals at the Temple's dedication and considered it a mere pittance of praise.

Second Chronicles, however, goes on to reveal the true standard for commitment through the stories of the kings who followed Solomon. Through their foibles and their faithfulness, we see that worship involves more than externals such as our wallets and our wealth. The picture of true worship is the total release of our hearts and wills to God. When God searches for and finds a heart that wholly belongs to him, his eyes brighten and he summons the whole of heaven in support.

As you read through 2 Chronicles, check your heart of worship against God's standards.

Worship Moments

- After Solomon completed all the work on the Temple, he offered a remarkable prayer of praise and commitment, dedicating the Temple to God (6:14–42).

- God's fire came down from heaven as the people offered sacrifices to the Lord in worship and praise (7:1–4).

- King Jehoshaphat committed himself to seek God. Before battle he bowed down in prayer before God and led the people in praising God with loud shouts (19:3–20:19).

- In this book God is praised as "an awesome God" (2:5); "the God who is in heaven" (20:6; 32:20); and "the LORD, the God of heaven" (36:23). We also see the Spirit of God at work (15:1; 20:14; 24:20).

SOLOMON ASKS FOR WISDOM

1 Solomon, the son of King David, now took firm control of the kingdom, for the LORD his God was with him and made him very powerful. [2]He called together all Israel—the generals and captains of the army, the judges, and all the political and clan leaders. [3]Then Solomon led the entire assembly to the hill at Gibeon where God's Tabernacle* was located. This was the Tabernacle that Moses, the LORD's servant, had constructed in the wilderness. [4]David had already moved the Ark of God from Kiriath-jearim to the special tent he had prepared for it in Jerusalem. [5]But the bronze altar made by Bezalel son of Uri and grandson of Hur was still at Gibeon in front of the Tabernacle of the LORD. So Solomon and the people gathered in front of it to consult the LORD. [6]There in front of the Tabernacle, Solomon went up to the bronze altar in the LORD's presence and sacrificed a thousand burnt offerings on it.

[7]That night God appeared to Solomon in a dream and said, "What do you want? Ask, and I will give it to you!"

[8]Solomon replied to God, "You have been so faithful and kind to my father, David, and now you have made me king in his place. [9]Now, LORD God, please keep your promise to David my father, for you have made me king over a people as numerous as the dust of the earth! [10]Give me wisdom and knowledge to rule them properly, for who is able to govern this great nation of yours?"

[11]God said to Solomon, "Because your greatest desire is to help your people, and you did not ask for personal wealth and honor or the death of your enemies or even a long life, but rather you asked for wisdom and knowledge to properly govern my people, [12]I will certainly give you the wisdom and knowledge you requested. And I will also give you riches, wealth, and honor such as no other king has ever had before you or will ever have again!"

[13]Then Solomon returned to Jerusalem from the Tabernacle at the hill of Gibeon, and he reigned over Israel.

[14]Solomon built up a huge military force, which included fourteen hundred chariots and twelve thousand horses.* He stationed many of them in the chariot cities, and some near him in Jerusalem. [15]During Solomon's reign, silver and gold were as plentiful in Jerusalem as stones. And valuable cedarwood was as common as the sycamore wood that grows in the foothills of Judah.* [16]Solomon's horses were imported from Egypt* and from Cilicia*; the king's traders acquired them from Cilicia at the standard price. [17]At that time, Egyptian chariots delivered to Jerusalem could be purchased for 600 pieces of silver,* and horses could be bought for 150 pieces of silver.* Many of these were then resold to the kings of the Hittites and the kings of Aram.

PREPARATIONS FOR BUILDING THE TEMPLE

2 Solomon now decided that the time had come to build a Temple for the LORD and a royal palace for himself. [2]He enlisted a force of 70,000 common laborers, 80,000 stonecutters in the hill country, and 3,600 foremen. [3]Solomon also sent this message to King Hiram* at Tyre:

"Send me cedar logs like the ones that were supplied to my father, David, when he was building his palace. [4]I am about to build a Temple to honor the name of the LORD my God. It will be a place set apart to burn incense and sweet spices before him, to display the special sacrificial bread, and to sacrifice burnt offerings each morning and evening, on the Sabbaths, at new moon celebrations, and at the other appointed festivals of the LORD our God.

1:3 Hebrew *Tent of Meeting*; also in 1:6, 13. 1:14 Or *12,000 charioteers*. 1:15 Hebrew *the Shephelah*. 1:16a Possibly *Muzur*, a district near Cilicia; also in 1:17. 1:16b Hebrew *Kue*, probably another name for Cilicia. 1:17a Hebrew *600 shekels of silver*, about 15 pounds or 6.8 kilograms in weight. 1:17b Hebrew *150 shekels*, about 3.8 pounds or 1.7 kilograms in weight. 2:3 Hebrew *Huram*, a variant name for Hiram; also in 2:11, 12.

My Daily Worship

— *April 7* —

AWESOME ARCHITECTURE

2 CHRONICLES 1:1–5:1

*This will be a magnificent Temple because our God is
an awesome God, greater than any other (2:5).*

[i reflect]

Finally. A Temple worthy of God was going to be built. Cedar from Lebanon, gold, bronze, purple cloth. The house for God that David had envisioned so long ago was finally under way.

Dearly had David wanted to construct a true Temple, saying to the prophet Nathan, "Here I am living in this beautiful cedar palace, but the Ark of God is out in a tent!" (2 Samuel 7:2). Although his heart was "after God's own heart" (Acts 13:22), David's hands were those of the battlefield. God said to him, "You must not build a temple to honor my name, for you are a warrior and have shed much blood" (1 Chronicles 28:3).

Solomon, granted extraordinary wisdom, was entrusted with the extraordinary task. Demonstrating his God-given wisdom, he acknowledged his limitations. What if this Temple was but a paltry reflection of our awesome God, who is greater than any other, whom the very heavens cannot contain? "Who am I," he wondered, "to consider building a Temple for him?" So, in addition to the exquisite supplies and the enormous work force, he sought and found a master craftsman who could work with the other craftsmen to turn all these fine materials into *the* Temple. Only the best of the best artisans, shaping the best of the best materials, could make it magnificent.

Centuries later, medieval builder and designer Michel di Giovanni, put it this way, "Church architecture ought to be an earthly and temporal fulfillment of the Savior's own prophecy that though the voices of men be still, the rocks and stones themselves will cry out with the laud and praise and honor due unto the King of kings and the Lord of lords."

Awesome architecture for an awesome God. Believer, whatever gifts, abilities, or talents you possess, give your best and give your all, so that your life of praise honors him to the fullest.

[i pray]

*O Lord, I kneel in awe of you, for you are an awesome God. May our places of worship
and our attitudes of worship cry out that you are greater than any other.*

[i respond]

Go to a place in nature where you feel as though the rocks and stones are crying out, reminding you of the God who is to be praised. Offer up your prayers, gifts, and abilities to the Lord.

He has commanded Israel to do these things forever.

⁵"This will be a magnificent Temple because our God is an awesome God, greater than any other. ⁶But who can really build him a worthy home? Not even the highest heavens can contain him! So who am I to consider building a Temple for him, except as a place to burn sacrifices to him?

⁷"So send me a master craftsman who can work with gold, silver, bronze, and iron; someone who is expert at dyeing purple, scarlet, and blue cloth; and a skilled engraver who can work with the craftsmen of Judah and Jerusalem who were selected by my father, David. ⁸Also send me cedar, cypress, and almug* logs from Lebanon, for I know that your men are without equal at cutting timber. I will send my men to help them. ⁹An immense amount of timber will be needed, for the Temple I am going to build will be very large and magnificent. ¹⁰I will pay your men 100,000 bushels of crushed wheat, 100,000 bushels of barley,* 110,000 gallons of wine, and 110,000 gallons of olive oil.*"

¹¹King Hiram sent this letter of reply to Solomon:

"It is because the LORD loves his people that he has made you their king! ¹²Blessed be the LORD, the God of Israel, who made the heavens and the earth! He has given David a wise son, gifted with skill and understanding, who will build a Temple for the LORD and a royal palace for himself.

¹³"I am sending you a master craftsman named Huram-abi. He is a brilliant man, ¹⁴the son of a woman from Dan in Israel; his father is from Tyre. He is skillful at making things from gold, silver, bronze, and iron. He also knows all about stonework, carpentry, and weaving. He is an expert in dyeing purple, blue, and scarlet cloth and in working with linen. He is also an engraver and can follow any design given to him. He will work with your craftsmen and those appointed by my lord David, your father.

¹⁵"Send along the wheat, barley, olive oil, and wine that you mentioned. ¹⁶We will cut whatever timber you need from the Lebanon mountains and will float the logs in rafts down the coast of the Mediterranean Sea to Joppa. From there you can transport the logs up to Jerusalem."

¹⁷Solomon took a census of all foreigners in the land of Israel, like the census his father had taken, and he counted 153,600. ¹⁸He enlisted 70,000 of them as common laborers, 80,000 as stonecutters in the hill country, and 3,600 as foremen.

SOLOMON BUILDS THE TEMPLE

3 So Solomon began to build the Temple of the LORD in Jerusalem on Mount Moriah, where the LORD had appeared to Solomon's father, King David. The Temple was built on the threshing floor of Araunah* the Jebusite, the site that David had selected. ²The construction began in midspring,* during the fourth year of Solomon's reign.

³The foundation for the Temple of God was ninety feet long and thirty feet wide.* ⁴The foyer at the front of the Temple was thirty feet wide, running across the entire width of the Temple. The inner walls of the foyer and the ceiling were overlaid with pure gold. The roof of the foyer was thirty feet* high.

2:8 Hebrew *algum*, a variant name for almug; compare 9:10-11 and parallel text at 1 Kgs 10:11-12. 2:10a Hebrew *20,000 cors* [3,640 kiloliters] *of crushed wheat, 20,000 cors of barley.* 2:10b Hebrew *20,000 baths* [420 kiloliters] *of wine, and 20,000 baths of olive oil.* 3:1 Hebrew reads *Ornan*, another name for Araunah; compare 2 Sam 24:16. 3:2 Hebrew *on the second day of the second month.* This day of the Hebrew lunar calendar occurs in April or early May. 3:3 Hebrew *60 cubits* [27 meters] *long and 20 cubits* [9 meters] *wide.* In this chapter, the distance measures are calculated from the Hebrew cubit at a ratio of 18 inches or 45 centimeters per cubit. 3:4 As in some Greek and Syriac manuscripts, which read *20 cubits* [9 meters]; Hebrew reads *120 cubits,* which is 180 feet or 54 meters.

⁵The main room of the Temple was paneled with cypress wood, overlaid with pure gold, and decorated with carvings of palm trees and chains. ⁶The walls of the Temple were decorated with beautiful jewels and with pure gold from the land of Parvaim. ⁷All the walls, beams, doors, and thresholds throughout the Temple were overlaid with gold, and figures of cherubim were carved on the walls.

⁸The Most Holy Place was thirty feet wide, corresponding to the width of the Temple, and it was also thirty feet deep. Its interior was overlaid with about twenty-three tons* of pure gold. ⁹They used gold nails that weighed about twenty ounces* each. The walls of the upper rooms were also overlaid with pure gold.

¹⁰Solomon made two figures shaped like cherubim and overlaid them with gold. These were placed in the Most Holy Place. ¹¹The total wingspan of the two cherubim standing side by side was 30 feet. One wing of the first figure was 7½ feet long, and it touched the Temple wall. The other wing, also 7½ feet long, touched one of the wings of the second figure. ¹²In the same way, the second figure had one wing 7½ feet long that touched the opposite wall. The other wing, also 7½ feet long, touched the wing of the first figure. ¹³So the wingspan of both cherubim together was 30 feet. They both stood and faced out toward the main room of the Temple. ¹⁴Across the entrance of the Most Holy Place, Solomon hung a curtain made of fine linen and blue, purple, and scarlet yarn, with figures of cherubim embroidered on it.

¹⁵For the front of the Temple, Solomon made two pillars that were 27 feet* tall, each topped by a capital extending upward another 7½ feet. ¹⁶He made a network of interwoven chains and used them to decorate the tops of the pillars. He also made one hundred decorative pomegranates and attached them to the chains. ¹⁷Then he set up the two pillars at the entrance of the Temple, one to the south of the entrance and the other to the north. He named the one on the south Jakin, and the one on the north Boaz.*

FURNISHINGS FOR THE TEMPLE

4 Solomon also made a bronze altar 30 feet long, 30 feet wide, and 15 feet high.* ²Then he cast a large round tank, 15 feet across from rim to rim; it was called the Sea. It was 7½ feet deep and about 45 feet in circumference. ³The Sea was encircled just below its rim by two rows of figures that resembled oxen. There were about six oxen per foot* all the way around, and they had been cast as part of the tank.

⁴The Sea rested on a base of twelve bronze oxen, all facing outward. Three faced north, three faced west, three faced south, and three faced east. ⁵The walls of the Sea were about three inches* thick, and its rim flared out like a cup and resembled a lily blossom. It could hold about 16,500 gallons* of water.

⁶He also made ten basins for water to wash the offerings, five to the south of the Sea and five to the north. The priests used the Sea itself, and not the basins, for their own washing.

⁷Solomon then cast ten gold lampstands according to the specifications that had been given and put them in the Temple. Five were placed against the south wall, and five were placed against the north wall. ⁸He also built ten tables and placed them in the Temple, five along the south wall and five along the north wall. Then he molded one hundred gold basins.

⁹Solomon also built a courtyard for the priests and the large outer courtyard. He made doors for the courtyard entrances and overlaid

---

3:8 Hebrew *600 talents* [20.4 metric tons].   3:9 Hebrew *50 shekels* [570 grams].   3:15 As in Syriac version (see also 1 Kgs 7:15; 2 Kgs 25:17; Jer 52:21), which reads *18 cubits* [8.1 meters]; Hebrew reads *35 cubits*, which is 52.5 feet or 15.8 meters. 3:17 Jakin probably means "he establishes"; Boaz probably means "in him is strength." 4:1 Hebrew *20 cubits* [9 meters] *long, 20 cubits wide, and 10 cubits* [4.5 meters] *high.* In this chapter, the distance measures are calculated from the Hebrew cubit at a ratio of 18 inches or 45 centimeters per cubit. 4:3 Or *20 oxen per meter*; Hebrew reads *10 per cubit.* 4:5a Hebrew *a handbreadth* [8 centimeters]. 4:5b Hebrew *3,000 baths* [63 kiloliters].

¹³ four hundred pomegranates that hung from the chains on the capitals (two rows of pomegranates for each of the chain networks that were hung around the capitals on top of the pillars),

¹⁴ the water carts holding the basins,

¹⁵ the Sea and the twelve oxen under it,

¹⁶ the pots, the shovels, the meat hooks, and all the related utensils.

Huram-abi made all these things out of burnished bronze for the Temple of the LORD, just as King Solomon had requested. ¹⁷The king had them cast in clay molds in the Jordan Valley between Succoth and Zarethan.* ¹⁸Such great quantities of bronze were used that its weight could not be determined.

¹⁹So Solomon made all the furnishings for the Temple of God:

the gold altar;

the tables for the Bread of the Presence;

²⁰ the lampstands and their lamps of pure gold to burn in front of the Most Holy Place as prescribed;

²¹ the flower decorations, lamps, and tongs, all of pure gold;

²² the lamp snuffers, basins, dishes, and firepans, all of pure gold;

the doors for the entrances to the Most Holy Place and the main room of the Temple, overlaid with gold.

THE ARK BROUGHT TO THE TEMPLE

5 When Solomon had finished all the work related to building the Temple of the LORD, he brought in the gifts dedicated by his father, King David, including all the silver and gold and all the utensils. These were stored in the treasuries of the Temple of God.

²Solomon then summoned the leaders of all the tribes and families of Israel to assemble in Jerusalem. They were to bring the Ark of the

---

Words of Worship

SING

Sing, Singing, Song—Hebrew *shir* "to sing"; *shir, shi-rah* "song"; *za-mar,* "to sing (with a stringed instrument or psaltery); *rin-nen* "to sing out"; Greek *ai-do* "to sing"; *psal-lo* "to sing psalms"; *o-de* "song." Other words are used.

Something about music reaches us at a deep level. Even words that seem ordinary when spoken can take on that extra punch when we sing them. Usually, we remember words we've sung more readily than those we've only said.

One way to let God's Word penetrate the heart is to sing it, and many parts of the Bible were composed to be sung. Singing our own praise to him gives it greater impact. This is how God made us, so it's no wonder the psalmist invites us to "come before him, singing with joy" (Psalm 100:2). Paul suggests that our life in Christ is a life of song, of "making music to the Lord" (Ephesians 5:19). Expressed in song, our praise of the Lord becomes both deeper and higher. Sing to the Lord!

---

them with bronze. ¹⁰The Sea was placed near the southeast corner of the Temple.

¹¹Huram-abi also made the necessary pots, shovels, and basins.

So at last Huram-abi completed everything King Solomon had assigned him to make for the Temple of God:

¹² two pillars,

two bowl-shaped capitals on top of the pillars,

two networks of chains that decorated the capitals,

4:17 As in parallel text at 1 Kgs 7:46; Hebrew reads *Zeredah.*

LORD's covenant from its location in the City of David, also known as Zion, to its new place in the Temple. ³They all assembled before the king at the annual Festival of Shelters in early autumn.* ⁴When all the leaders of Israel arrived, the Levites moved the Ark, ⁵along with the special tent* and all its sacred utensils. The Levitical priests carried them all up to the Temple. ⁶King Solomon and the entire community of Israel sacrificed sheep and oxen before the Ark in such numbers that no one could keep count!

⁷Then the priests carried the Ark of the LORD's covenant into the inner sanctuary of the Temple—the Most Holy Place—and placed it beneath the wings of the cherubim. ⁸The cherubim spread their wings out over the Ark, forming a canopy over the Ark and its carrying poles. ⁹These poles were so long that their ends could be seen from the front entrance of the Temple's main room—the Holy Place—but not from outside it. They are still there to this day. ¹⁰Nothing was in the Ark except the two stone tablets that Moses had placed there at Mount Sinai,* when the LORD made a covenant with the people of Israel after they left Egypt.

¹¹Then the priests left the Holy Place. All the priests who were present had purified themselves, whether or not they were on duty that day. ¹²And the Levites who were musicians—Asaph, Heman, Jeduthun, and all their sons and brothers—were dressed in fine linen robes and stood at the east side of the altar playing cymbals, harps, and lyres. They were joined by 120 priests who were playing trumpets. ¹³The trumpeters and singers performed together in unison to praise and give thanks to the LORD. Accompanied by trumpets, cymbals, and other instruments, they raised their voices and praised the LORD with these words:

"He is so good!
His faithful love endures forever!"

At that moment a cloud filled the Temple of the LORD. ¹⁴The priests could not continue their work because the glorious presence of the LORD filled the Temple of God.

SOLOMON BLESSES THE PEOPLE

6 Then Solomon prayed, "O LORD, you have said that you would live in thick darkness. ²But I have built a glorious Temple for you, where you can live forever!"

³Then the king turned around to the entire community of Israel standing before him and gave this blessing: ⁴"Blessed be the LORD, the God of Israel, who has kept the promise he made to my father, David. For he told my father, ⁵'From the day I brought my people out of Egypt, I have never chosen a city among the tribes of Israel as the place where a temple should be built to honor my name. Nor have I chosen a king to lead my people Israel. ⁶But now I have chosen Jerusalem as that city, and David as that king.'"

⁷Then Solomon said, "My father, David, wanted to build this Temple to honor the name of the LORD, the God of Israel. ⁸But the LORD told him, 'It is right for you to want to build the Temple to honor my name, ⁹but you will not be the one to do it. One of your sons will build it instead.'

¹⁰"And now the LORD has done what he promised, for I have become king in my father's place. I have built this Temple to honor the name of the LORD, the God of Israel. ¹¹There I have placed the Ark, and in the Ark is the covenant that the LORD made with the people of Israel."

SOLOMON'S PRAYER OF DEDICATION

¹²Then Solomon stood with his hands spread out before the altar of the LORD in front of the entire community of Israel. ¹³He had made a bronze platform 7½ feet long, 7½ feet wide, and 4½ feet high* and had placed it at the

---

5:3 Hebrew *at the festival that is in the seventh month.* The Festival of Shelters began on the fifteenth day of the seventh month of the Hebrew lunar calendar. This occurs on our calendar in late September or early October.   5:5 Hebrew *Tent of Meeting.*
5:10 Hebrew *Horeb,* another name for Sinai.   6:13 Hebrew *5 cubits* [2.3 meters] *long, 5 cubits wide, and 3 cubits* [1.4 meters] *high.*

center of the Temple's outer courtyard. He stood on the platform before the entire assembly, and then he knelt down and lifted his hands toward heaven. [14]He prayed, "O LORD, God of Israel, there is no God like you in all of heaven and earth. You keep your promises and show unfailing love to all who obey you and are eager to do your will. [15]You have kept your promise to your servant David, my father. You made that promise with your own mouth, and today you have fulfilled it with your own hands. [16]And now, O LORD, God of Israel, carry out your further promise to your servant David, my father. For you said to him, 'If your descendants guard their behavior and obey my law as you have done, they will always reign over Israel.' [17]Now, O LORD, God of Israel, fulfill this promise to your servant David.

[18]"But will God really live on earth among people? Why, even the highest heavens cannot contain you. How much less this Temple I have built! [19]Listen to my prayer and my request, O LORD my God. Hear the cry and the prayer that your servant is making to you. [20]May you watch over this Temple both day and night, this place where you have said you would put your name. May you always hear the prayers I make toward this place. [21]May you hear the humble and earnest requests from me and your people Israel when we pray toward this place. Yes, hear us from heaven where you live, and when you hear, forgive.

[22]"If someone wrongs another person and is required to take an oath of innocence in front of the altar at this Temple, [23]then hear from heaven and judge between your servants—the accuser and the accused. Punish the guilty party, and acquit the one who is innocent.

[24]"If your people Israel are defeated by their enemies because they have sinned against you, and if they turn to you and call on your name and pray to you here in this Temple, [25]then hear from heaven and forgive their sins and return them to this land you gave their ancestors.

[26]"If the skies are shut up and there is no rain because your people have sinned against you, and then they pray toward this Temple and confess your name and turn from their sins because you have punished them, [27]then hear from heaven and forgive the sins of your servants, your people Israel. Teach them to do what is right, and send rain on your land that you have given to your people as their special possession.

[28]"If there is a famine in the land, or plagues, or crop disease, or attacks of locusts or caterpillars, or if your people's enemies are in the land besieging their towns—whatever the trouble is—[29]and if your people offer a prayer concerning their troubles or sorrow, raising their hands toward this Temple, [30]then hear from heaven where you live, and forgive. Give your people whatever they deserve, for you alone know the human heart. [31]Then they will fear you and walk in your ways as long as they live in the land you gave to our ancestors.

[32]"And when foreigners hear of you and your mighty miracles, and they come from distant lands to worship your great name and to pray toward this Temple, [33]then hear from heaven where you live, and grant what they ask of you. Then all the people of the earth will come to know and fear you, just as your own people Israel do. They, too, will know that this Temple I have built bears your name.

[34]"If your people go out at your command to fight their enemies, and if they pray to you toward this city that you have chosen and toward this Temple that I have built for your name, [35]then hear their prayers from heaven and uphold their cause.

[36]"If they sin against you—and who has never sinned?—you may become angry with them and let their enemies conquer them and take them captive to a foreign land far or near. [37]But in that land of exile, they may turn to you again in repentance and pray, 'We have sinned, done evil, and acted wickedly.' [38]Then if they turn to you with their whole heart and soul and pray toward the land you gave to their ancestors, toward this city you have cho-sen, and toward this Temple I have built to

honor your name, [39]then hear their prayers from heaven where you live. Uphold their cause and forgive your people who have sinned against you.

[40]"O my God, be attentive to all the prayers made to you in this place. [41]And now, O LORD God, arise and enter this resting place of yours, where your magnificent Ark has been placed. May your priests, O LORD God, be clothed with salvation, and may your saints rejoice in your goodness. [42]O LORD God, do not reject your anointed one. Remember your unfailing love for your servant David.*"

THE DEDICATION OF THE TEMPLE

7 When Solomon finished praying, fire flashed down from heaven and burned up the burnt offerings and sacrifices, and the glorious presence of the LORD filled the Temple. [2]The priests could not even enter the Temple of the LORD because the glorious presence of the LORD filled it. [3]When all the people of Israel saw the fire coming down and the glorious presence of the LORD filling the Temple, they fell face down on the ground and worshiped and praised the LORD, saying,

"He is so good!
His faithful love endures forever!"

[4]Then the king and all the people offered sacrifices to the LORD. [5]King Solomon offered a sacrifice of 22,000 oxen and 120,000 sheep. And so the king and all the people dedicated the Temple of God. [6]The priests took their assigned positions, and so did the Levites who were singing, "His faithful love endures forever!" They accompanied the singing with music from the instruments King David had made for praising the LORD. On the other side of the Levites, the priests blew the trumpets, while all Israel stood.

[7]Solomon then dedicated the central area of the courtyard in front of the LORD's Temple so they could present burnt offerings and the fat from peace offerings there. He did this because the bronze altar he had built could not handle all the burnt offerings, grain offerings, and sacrificial fat.

[8]For the next seven days they celebrated the Festival of Shelters* with huge crowds gathered from all the tribes of Israel. They came from as far away as Lebo-hamath in the north, to the brook of Egypt in the south. [9]On the eighth day they had a closing ceremony, for they had celebrated the dedication of the altar for seven days and the Festival of Shelters for seven days. [10]Then at the end of the celebration,* Solomon sent the people home. They were all joyful and happy because the LORD had been so good to David and Solomon and to his people Israel.

THE LORD'S RESPONSE TO SOLOMON

[11]So Solomon finished building the Temple of the LORD, as well as the royal palace. He completed everything he had planned to do. [12]Then one night the LORD appeared to Solomon and said, "I have heard your prayer and have chosen this Temple as the place for making sacrifices. [13]At times I might shut up the heavens so that no rain falls, or I might command locusts to devour your crops, or I might send plagues among you. [14]Then if my people who are called by my name will humble themselves and pray and seek my face and turn from their wicked ways, I will hear from heaven and will forgive their sins and heal their land. [15]I will listen to every prayer made in this place, [16]for I have chosen this Temple and set it apart to be my home forever. My eyes and my heart will always be here.

[17]"As for you, if you follow me as your father, David, did and obey all my commands, laws, and regulations, [18]then I will not let anyone take away your throne. This is the same promise I gave your father, David, when I said, 'You will never fail to have a successor who rules over Israel.'

6:42 Or Remember the faithfulness of your servant David. 7:8 Hebrew the festival (also in 7:9); see note on 5:3. 7:10 Hebrew Then on the twenty-seventh day of the seventh month. This day of the Hebrew lunar calendar occurs in late September or early October.

¹⁹"But if you abandon me and disobey the laws and commands I have given you, and if you go and worship other gods, ²⁰then I will uproot the people of Israel from this land of mine that I have given them. I will reject this Temple that I have set apart to honor my name. I will make it a spectacle of contempt among the nations. ²¹And though this Temple is impressive now, it will become an appalling sight to all who pass by. They will ask, 'Why has the LORD done such terrible things to his land and to his Temple?' ²²And the answer will be, 'Because his people abandoned the LORD, the God of their ancestors, who brought them out of Egypt, and they worshiped other gods instead. That is why he brought all these disasters upon them.'"

SOLOMON'S MANY ACHIEVEMENTS

8 It was now twenty years since Solomon had become king, and the great building projects of the LORD's Temple and his own royal palace were completed. ²Solomon now turned his attention to rebuilding the towns that King Hiram* had given him, and he settled Israelites in them. ³It was at this time, too, that Solomon fought against the city of Hamath-zobah and conquered it. ⁴He rebuilt Tadmor in the desert and built towns in the region of Hamath as supply centers. ⁵He fortified the cities of Upper Beth-horon and Lower Beth-horon, rebuilding their walls and installing barred gates. ⁶He also rebuilt Baalath and other supply centers at this time and constructed cities where his chariots and horses* could be kept. He built to his heart's content in Jerusalem and Lebanon and throughout the entire realm.

⁷There were still some people living in the land who were not Israelites, including Hittites, Amorites, Perizzites, Hivites, and Jebusites. ⁸These were descendants of the nations that Israel had not completely destroyed. So Solomon conscripted them for his labor force, and they serve in the labor force to this day. ⁹But Solomon did not conscript any of the Israelites for forced labor. Instead, he assigned them to serve as fighting men, officers in his army, commanders of his chariots, and charioteers. ¹⁰King Solomon also appointed 250 of them to supervise the various projects.

¹¹Solomon moved his wife, Pharaoh's daughter, from the City of David to the new palace he had built for her. He said, "My wife must not live in King David's palace, for the Ark of the LORD has been there, and it is holy ground."

¹²Then Solomon sacrificed burnt offerings to the LORD on the altar he had built in front of the foyer of the Temple. ¹³The number of sacrifices varied from day to day according to the commands Moses had given. Extra sacrifices were offered on the Sabbaths, on new moon festivals, and at the three annual festivals—the Passover celebration, the Festival of Harvest,* and the Festival of Shelters. ¹⁴In assigning the priests to their duties, Solomon followed the regulations of his father, David. He also assigned the Levites to lead the people in praise and to assist the priests in their daily duties. And he assigned the gatekeepers to their gates by their divisions, following the commands of David, the man of God. ¹⁵Solomon did not deviate in any way from David's commands concerning the priests and Levites and the treasuries.

¹⁶So Solomon made sure that all the work related to building the Temple of the LORD was carried out, from the day its foundation was laid to the day of its completion.

¹⁷Later Solomon went to Ezion-geber and Elath,* ports in the land of Edom, along the shore of the Red Sea.* ¹⁸Hiram sent him ships commanded by his own officers and manned by experienced crews of sailors. These ships sailed to the land of Ophir with Solomon's men and brought back to Solomon almost seventeen tons* of gold.

8:2 Hebrew *Huram,* a variant name for Hiram; also in 8:18. **8:6** Or *and charioteers.* **8:13** Or *Festival of Weeks.* **8:17a** As in Greek version (see also 2 Kgs 14:22; 16:6); Hebrew reads *Eloth.* **8:17b** Hebrew *the sea.* **8:18** Hebrew *450 talents* [15.3 metric tons].

My Daily Worship

— *April 8* —

GOD HEARS AND HEALS

2 CHRONICLES 5:2-9:31

*Then if my people who are called by my name will humble themselves and pray
and seek my face and turn from their wicked ways, I will hear from
heaven and will forgive their sins and heal their land (7:14).*

[i reflect]

"Hear us from heaven. . . . Hear their prayers from heaven where you live. . . . Be attentive to all the prayers made to you."

He had stood on a platform before the entire assembly. Then he knelt, lifting his hands high toward heaven. King Solomon prayed with eloquence and passion, dedicating the Temple. Now—months later, maybe years later—the Lord appears to Solomon at night. "I *have* heard your prayer," he assures the king, "and have chosen this Temple as the place for making sacrifices" (7:12).

Does God think that, from this point on, his people will never stray? That they will continually offer sacrifices with clean hearts and hands? No, he knows them too well, these people called by his name. Their wicked ways will return, and with them droughts and locusts and plagues. Still, there will be mercy and healing, *if* the people humble themselves, pray, seek God's face, and repent. "I will listen to every prayer made in this place," he promises, "for I have chosen this Temple and set it apart" (7:15–16).

But what of us? The great Temple at Jerusalem is no more, the building but a part of history. Yet God still hears us from heaven, still calls us to the same humility, prayer, seeking of his face, and repentance. The early Christians could be certain of this, and so can we: "So humble yourselves before God. . . . Draw close to God, and God will draw close to you. . . . Let there be tears for the wrong things you have done. Let there be sorrow and deep grief. . . . When you bow down before the Lord and admit your dependence on him, he will lift you up and give you honor" (James 4:7–10).

Bow down before the Lord; humble yourself even to tears. As you rise and move through the day, still your heart before him, continually confessing.

[i pray]

*O Lord, hear me from heaven. I bow before you, I seek your face, I turn to you. Honor
your promise to Solomon, as you have for your people ever since. Forgive and heal.*

[i respond]

Before whom are you humble? Your family? Your superiors at work? Your pastor? In what ways are you humble before God? Describe how you respond to others and to God when you have done wrong.

The Queen of Sheba's Visit

9 When the queen of Sheba heard of Solomon's reputation, she came to Jerusalem to test him with hard questions. She arrived with a large group of attendants and a great caravan of camels loaded with spices, huge quantities of gold, and precious jewels. ²When she met with Solomon, they talked about everything she had on her mind. Solomon answered all her questions; nothing was too hard for him to explain to her. ³When the queen of Sheba realized how wise Solomon was, and when she saw the palace he had built, ⁴she was breathless. She was also amazed at the food on his tables, the organization of his officials and their splendid clothing, the cup-bearers and their robes, and the burnt offerings Solomon made at the Temple of the LORD.

⁵She exclaimed to the king, "Everything I heard in my country about your achievements and wisdom is true! ⁶I didn't believe it until I arrived here and saw it with my own eyes. Truly I had not heard the half of it! Your wisdom is far greater than what I was told. ⁷How happy these people must be! What a privilege for your officials to stand here day after day, listening to your wisdom! ⁸The LORD your God is great indeed! He delights in you and has placed you on the throne to rule for him. Because God loves Israel so much and desires this kingdom to last forever, he has made you king so you can rule with justice and righteousness."

⁹Then she gave the king a gift of nine thousand pounds* of gold, and great quantities of spices and precious jewels. Never before had there been spices as fine as those the queen of Sheba gave to Solomon.

¹⁰(When the crews of Hiram and Solomon brought gold from Ophir, they also brought rich cargoes of almug wood* and precious jewels. ¹¹The king used the almug wood to make steps* for the Temple of the LORD and the royal palace, and to construct harps and lyres for the musicians. Never before had there been such beautiful instruments in Judah.)

¹²King Solomon gave the queen of Sheba whatever she asked for—gifts of greater value than the gifts she had given him. Then she and all her attendants left and returned to their own land.

Solomon's Wealth and Splendor

¹³Each year Solomon received about 25 tons* of gold. ¹⁴This did not include the additional revenue he received from merchants and traders. All the kings of Arabia and the governors of the land also brought gold and silver to Solomon.

¹⁵King Solomon made two hundred large shields of hammered gold, each containing over 15 pounds* of gold. ¹⁶He also made three hundred smaller shields of hammered gold, each containing about 7½ pounds* of gold. The king placed these shields in the Palace of the Forest of Lebanon.

¹⁷Then the king made a huge ivory throne and overlaid it with pure gold. ¹⁸The throne had six steps, and there was a footstool of gold attached to it. On both sides of the seat were armrests, with the figure of a lion standing on each side of the throne. ¹⁹Solomon made

> *The essence of idolatry is the entertainment of thoughts about God that are not worthy of him.*
>
> A.W. TOZER

9:9 Hebrew *120 talents* [4 metric tons]. 9:10 Hebrew *algum wood* (also in 9:11); compare parallel text at 1 Kgs 10:11-12. 9:11 Or *gateways*. The meaning of the Hebrew is uncertain. 9:13 Hebrew *666 talents* [23 metric tons]. 9:15 Hebrew *600 shekels* [6.8 kilograms]. 9:16 Hebrew *300 shekels* [3.4 kilograms].

twelve other lion figures, one standing on each end of each of the six steps. No other throne in all the world could be compared with it!

²⁰All of King Solomon's drinking cups were solid gold, as were all the utensils in the Palace of the Forest of Lebanon. They were not made of silver because silver was considered of little value in Solomon's day!

²¹The king had a fleet of trading ships* manned by the sailors sent by Hiram.* Once every three years the ships returned, loaded down with gold, silver, ivory, apes, and peacocks.*

²²So King Solomon became richer and wiser than any other king in all the earth. ²³Kings from every nation came to visit him and to hear the wisdom God had given him. ²⁴Year after year, everyone who came to visit brought him gifts of silver and gold, clothing, weapons, spices, horses, and mules.

²⁵Solomon had four thousand stalls for his chariot horses and twelve thousand horses.* He stationed many of them in the chariot cities, and some near him in Jerusalem. ²⁶He ruled over all the kings from the Euphrates River* to the land of the Philistines and the border of Egypt. ²⁷The king made silver as plentiful in Jerusalem as stones. And valuable cedarwood was as common as the sycamore wood that grows in the foothills of Judah.* ²⁸Solomon's horses were imported from Egypt* and many other countries.

SUMMARY OF SOLOMON'S REIGN

²⁹The rest of the events of Solomon's reign, from beginning to end, are recorded in *The Record of Nathan the Prophet* and in *The Prophecy of Ahijah from Shiloh,* and also in *The Visions of Iddo the Seer,* concerning Jeroboam son of Nebat. ³⁰Solomon ruled in Jerusalem over all Israel for forty years. ³¹When he died, he was buried in the city of his father, David. Then his son Rehoboam became the next king.

THE NORTHERN TRIBES REVOLT

10 Rehoboam went to Shechem, where all Israel had gathered to make him king. ²When Jeroboam son of Nebat heard of Solomon's death, he returned from Egypt, for he had fled to Egypt to escape from King Solomon. ³The leaders of Israel sent for Jeroboam, and he and all Israel went together to speak with Rehoboam. ⁴"Your father was a hard master," they said. "Lighten the harsh labor demands and heavy taxes that your father imposed on us. Then we will be your loyal subjects."

⁵Rehoboam replied, "Come back in three days for my answer." So the people went away.

⁶Then King Rehoboam went to discuss the matter with the older men who had counseled his father, Solomon. "What is your advice?" he asked. "How should I answer these people?"

⁷The older counselors replied, "If you are good to the people and show them kindness and do your best to please them, they will always be your loyal subjects."

⁸But Rehoboam rejected the advice of the elders and instead asked the opinion of the young men who had grown up with him and who were now his advisers. ⁹"What is your advice?" he asked them. "How should I answer these people who want me to lighten the burdens imposed by my father?"

¹⁰The young men replied, "This is what you should tell those complainers: 'My little finger is thicker than my father's waist—if you think he was hard on you, just wait and see what I'll be like! ¹¹Yes, my father was harsh on you, but I'll be even harsher! My father used whips on you, but I'll use scorpions!'"

¹²Three days later, Jeroboam and all the people returned to hear Rehoboam's decision, just as the king had requested. ¹³But Rehoboam spoke harshly to them, for he rejected the advice of the older counselors ¹⁴and followed the counsel of his younger advisers. He told the people, "My father was harsh on you, but I'll be even harsher! My father used whips

9:21a Hebrew *fleet of ships that could sail to Tarshish.* 9:21b Hebrew *Huram,* a variant name for Hiram. 9:21c Or *and baboons.* 9:25 Or *12,000 charioteers.* 9:26 Hebrew *the river.* 9:27 Hebrew *the Shephelah.* 9:28 Possibly *Muzur,* a district near Cilicia.

on you, but I'll use scorpions!" ¹⁵So the king paid no attention to the people's demands. This turn of events was the will of God, for it fulfilled the prophecy of the LORD spoken to Jeroboam son of Nebat by the prophet Ahijah from Shiloh.

¹⁶When all Israel realized that the king had rejected their request, they shouted, "Down with David and his dynasty! We have no share in Jesse's son! Let's go home, Israel! Look out for your own house, O David!" So all Israel returned home. ¹⁷But Rehoboam continued to rule over the Israelites who lived in the towns of Judah.

¹⁸King Rehoboam sent Adoniram,* who was in charge of the labor force, to restore order, but the Israelites stoned him to death. When this news reached King Rehoboam, he quickly jumped into his chariot and fled to Jerusalem. ¹⁹The northern tribes of Israel have refused to be ruled by a descendant of David to this day.

SHEMAIAH'S PROPHECY

11 When Rehoboam arrived at Jerusalem, he mobilized the armies of Judah and Benjamin—180,000 select troops—to fight against the army of Israel and to restore the kingdom to himself. ²But the LORD said to Shemaiah, the man of God, ³"Say to Rehoboam son of Solomon, king of Judah, and to all the Israelites in Judah and Benjamin: ⁴'This is what the LORD says: Do not fight against your relatives. Go back home, for what has happened is my doing!'" So they obeyed the message of the LORD and did not fight against Jeroboam.

REHOBOAM FORTIFIES JUDAH

⁵Rehoboam remained in Jerusalem and fortified various cities for the defense of Judah. ⁶He built up Bethlehem, Etam, Tekoa, ⁷Bethzur, Soco, Adullam, ⁸Gath, Mareshah, Ziph, ⁹Adoraim, Lachish, Azekah, ¹⁰Zorah, Aijalon, and Hebron. These became the fortified cities of Judah and Benjamin. ¹¹Rehoboam strengthened their defenses and stationed commanders in them. In each of them, he stored supplies of food, olive oil, and wine. ¹²He also put shields and spears in these towns as a further safety measure. So only Judah and Benjamin remained under his control.

¹³But all the priests and Levites living among the northern tribes of Israel sided with Rehoboam. ¹⁴The Levites even abandoned their homes and property and moved to Judah and Jerusalem, because Jeroboam and his sons would not allow them to serve the LORD as priests. ¹⁵Jeroboam appointed his own priests to serve at the pagan shrines, where they worshiped the goat and calf idols he had made. ¹⁶From all over Israel, those who sincerely wanted to worship the LORD, the God of Israel, followed the Levites to Jerusalem, where they could offer sacrifices to the LORD, the God of their ancestors. ¹⁷This strengthened the kingdom of Judah, and for three years they supported Rehoboam son of Solomon and earnestly sought to obey the LORD as they had done during the reigns of David and Solomon.

REHOBOAM'S FAMILY

¹⁸Rehoboam married his cousin Mahalath, the daughter of David's son Jerimoth and of Abihail, the daughter of Eliab. (Eliab was one of David's brothers, a son of Jesse.) ¹⁹Mahalath had three sons—Jeush, Shemariah, and Zaham.

²⁰Later Rehoboam married another cousin, Maacah, the daughter of Absalom. Maacah gave birth to Abijah, Attai, Ziza, and Shelomith. ²¹Rehoboam loved Maacah more than any of his other wives and concubines. In all, he had eighteen wives and sixty concubines, and they gave birth to twenty-eight sons and sixty daughters. ²²Rehoboam made Maacah's son Abijah chief among the princes, making it clear that he would be the next king. ²³Rehoboam also wisely gave responsibilities to his other sons and stationed them in the

10:18 Hebrew *Hadoram*, a variant name for Adoniram; compare 1 Kgs 4:6; 5:14; 12:18.

fortified cities throughout the land of Judah and Benjamin. He provided them with generous provisions and arranged for each of them to have several wives.

EGYPT INVADES JUDAH

12 But when Rehoboam was firmly established and strong, he abandoned the law of the LORD, and all Israel followed him in this sin. ²Because they were unfaithful to the LORD, King Shishak of Egypt attacked Jerusalem in the fifth year of King Rehoboam's reign. ³He came with twelve hundred chariots, sixty thousand horsemen, and a countless army of foot soldiers, including Libyans, Sukkites, and Ethiopians.* ⁴Shishak conquered Judah's fortified cities and then advanced to attack Jerusalem.

⁵The prophet Shemaiah then met with Rehoboam and Judah's leaders, who had all fled to Jerusalem because of Shishak. Shemaiah told them, "This is what the LORD says: You have abandoned me, so I am abandoning you to Shishak."

⁶The king and the leaders of Israel humbled themselves and said, "The LORD is right in doing this to us!"

⁷When the LORD saw their change of heart, he gave this message to Shemaiah: "Since the people have humbled themselves, I will not completely destroy them and will soon give them some relief. I will not use Shishak to pour out my anger on Jerusalem. ⁸But they will become his subjects, so that they can learn how much better it is to serve me than to serve earthly rulers."

⁹So King Shishak of Egypt came to Jerusalem and took away all the treasures of the Temple of the LORD and of the royal palace, including all of Solomon's gold shields. ¹⁰King Rehoboam later replaced them with bronze shields and entrusted them to the care of the captain of his bodyguard. ¹¹Whenever the king went to the Temple of the LORD, the guards would carry them along and then return them to the guardroom. ¹²Because Rehoboam humbled himself, the LORD's anger was turned aside, and he did not destroy him completely. And there was still goodness in the land of Judah.

SUMMARY OF REHOBOAM'S REIGN

¹³King Rehoboam firmly established himself in Jerusalem and continued to rule. He was forty-one years old when he became king, and he reigned seventeen years in Jerusalem, the city the LORD had chosen from among all the tribes of Israel as the place to honor his name. Rehoboam's mother was Naamah, a woman from Ammon. ¹⁴But he was an evil king, for he did not seek the LORD with all his heart.

¹⁵The rest of the events of Rehoboam's reign, from beginning to end, are recorded in *The Record of Shemaiah the Prophet* and in *The Record of Iddo the Seer,* which are part of the genealogical record. Rehoboam and Jeroboam were continually at war with each other. ¹⁶When Rehoboam died, he was buried in the City of David. Then his son Abijah became the next king.

ABIJAH'S WAR WITH JEROBOAM

13 Abijah began to rule over Judah in the eighteenth year of Jeroboam's reign in Israel. ²He reigned in Jerusalem three years. His mother was Maacah,* a daughter of Uriel from Gibeah.

Then war broke out between Abijah and Jeroboam. ³Judah, led by King Abijah, fielded 400,000 seasoned warriors, while Jeroboam mustered 800,000 courageous men from Israel. ⁴When the army of Judah arrived in the hill country of Ephraim, Abijah stood on Mount Zemaraim and shouted to Jeroboam and the Israelite army: "Listen to me! ⁵Don't you realize that the LORD, the God of Israel, made an unbreakable covenant* with David, giving him and his descendants the throne of Israel forever? ⁶Yet Jeroboam son of Nebat, who was a mere servant of David's son

12:3 Hebrew *and Cushites.*   13:2 As in most Greek manuscripts and Syriac version (see also 2 Chr 11:20-21; 1 Kgs 15:2); Hebrew reads *Micaiah.*   13:5 Hebrew *a covenant of salt.*

Solomon, became a traitor to his master. [7]Then a whole gang of scoundrels joined him, defying Solomon's son Rehoboam when he was young and inexperienced and could not stand up to them. [8]Do you really think you can stand against the kingdom of the LORD that is led by the descendants of David? Your army is vast indeed, but with you are those gold calves that Jeroboam made as your gods! [9]And you have chased away the priests of the LORD and the Levites and have appointed your own priests, just like the pagan nations. You let anyone become a priest these days! Whoever comes to be dedicated with a young bull and seven rams can become a priest of these so-called gods of yours!

[10]"But as for us, the LORD is our God, and we have not abandoned him. Only the descendants of Aaron serve the LORD as priests, and the Levites alone may help them in their work. [11]They present burnt offerings and fragrant incense to the LORD every morning and evening. They place the Bread of the Presence on the holy table, and they light the gold lampstand every evening. We are following the instructions of the LORD our God, but you have abandoned him. [12]So you see, God is with us. He is our leader. His priests blow their trumpets and lead us into battle against you. O people of Israel, do not fight against the LORD, the God of your ancestors, for you will not succeed!"

[13]Meanwhile, Jeroboam had secretly sent part of his army around behind the men of Judah to ambush them. [14]When Judah realized that they were being attacked from the front and the rear, they cried out to the LORD for help. Then the priests blew the trumpets, [15]and the men of Judah began to shout. At the sound of their battle cry, God defeated Jeroboam and the Israelite army and routed them before Abijah and the army of Judah. [16]The Israelite army fled from Judah, and God handed them over to Judah in defeat. [17]Abijah and his army inflicted heavy losses on them; there were 500,000 casualties among Israel's finest troops that day. [18]So Judah defeated Israel because they trusted in the LORD, the God of their ancestors. [19]Abijah and his army pursued Jeroboam's troops and captured some of his towns, including Bethel, Jeshanah, and Ephron, along with their surrounding villages.

[20]So Jeroboam of Israel never regained his power during Abijah's lifetime, and finally the LORD struck him down and he died. [21]By contrast, Abijah of Judah grew more and more powerful. He married fourteen wives and had twenty-two sons and sixteen daughters. [22]The rest of the events of Abijah's reign, including his words and deeds, are recorded in *The Commentary of Iddo the Prophet.*

EARLY YEARS OF ASA'S REIGN

14 When Abijah died, he was buried in the City of David. Then his son Asa became the next king. There was peace in the land for ten years, [2]for Asa did what was pleasing and good in the sight of the LORD his God. [3]He removed the pagan altars and the shrines. He smashed the sacred pillars and cut down the Asherah poles. [4]He commanded the people of Judah to seek the LORD, the God of their ancestors, and to obey his law and his commands. [5]Asa also removed the pagan shrines, as well as the incense altars from every one of Judah's towns. So Asa's kingdom enjoyed a period of peace. [6]During those peaceful years, he was able to build up the fortified cities throughout Judah. No one tried to make war against him at this time, for the LORD was giving him rest from his enemies. [7]Asa told the people of Judah, "Let us build towns and fortify them with walls, towers, gates, and bars. The land is ours because we sought the LORD our God, and he has given us rest from our enemies." So they went ahead with these projects and brought them to completion.

[8]King Asa had an army of 300,000 warriors from the tribe of Judah, armed with large shields and spears. He also had an army of 280,000 warriors from the tribe of Benjamin, armed with small shields and bows. Both armies were composed of courageous fighting men.

My Daily Worship

— *April 9* —

THE PRICE WE PAY

2 CHRONICLES 10:1–13:22

I will not use Shishak to pour out my anger on Jerusalem. But they will
become his subjects, so that they can learn how much better it
is to serve me than to serve earthly rulers (12:7–8).

[i reflect]

The people had clamored for a king way back in the days of the judges. "Give us a king," they had told Samuel. "Give us a king like all the other nations have." Although they had grieved Samuel, the Lord knew their true motives: "It is me they are rejecting, not you. They don't want me to be their king any longer" (1 Samuel 8:5, 7).

Now it was happening again. King Rehoboam, Solomon's son, was firmly established, but he soon abandoned the law of the Lord. All God's people followed Rehoboam in sin. Consequently, God allowed the king of Egypt, Shishak, to terrorize Jerusalem into subjection. But because God did not let the Egyptians completely destroy Judah, some missed his point. Those unwilling to see God's correction may have even said, "Well, things could be worse." In reality, life could have been so much better. They could have been following wholeheartedly the one true God, through his chosen earthly king.

Becoming Shishak's subjects showed the people that a cruel master can be much worse than a holy One. But did the people of God learn to whom they should ultimately swear allegiance? Do we? The price we pay for wrongful allegiance may not be as obvious as Judah's subjection to a ruthless rule, but the bondage can be just as real. Enslavement to debt, or destructive philosophies, or twisted religious structures may result from an unwillingness to serve and obey the Lord.

God alone demonstrates his worthiness for our ultimate allegiance. Anyone or anything that replaces God in our lives will exact too high a price in return. When you see a flag today, let it remind you of your ultimate allegiance to the worthy One.

[i pray]

King of kings, you alone are worthy to reign in my heart. I pledge to you my honor
and my loyalty, even onto the spiritual battlefields of this life.

[i respond]

Meditate on this verse of a classic hymn or find it in a hymnal and sing it: "Lead on, O King eternal: we follow, not with fears; / for gladness breaks like morning where'er thy face appears. / Thy cross is lifted o'er us; we journey in its light; / the crown awaits the conquest; lead on, O God of might!"

⁹Once an Ethiopian* named Zerah attacked Judah with an army of a million men* and three hundred chariots. They advanced to the city of Mareshah, ¹⁰so Asa deployed his armies for battle in the valley north of Mareshah.* ¹¹Then Asa cried out to the LORD his God, "O LORD, no one but you can help the powerless against the mighty! Help us, O LORD our God, for we trust in you alone. It is in your name that we have come against this vast horde. O LORD, you are our God; do not let mere men prevail against you!"

¹²So the LORD defeated the Ethiopians* in the presence of Asa and the army of Judah, and the enemy fled. ¹³Asa and his army pursued them as far as Gerar, and so many Ethiopians fell that they were unable to rally. They were destroyed by the LORD and his army, and the army of Judah carried off vast quantities of plunder. ¹⁴While they were at Gerar, they attacked all the towns in that area, and terror from the LORD came upon the people there. As a result, vast quantities of plunder were taken from these towns, too. ¹⁵They also attacked the camps of herdsmen and captured many sheep and camels before finally returning to Jerusalem.

ASA'S RELIGIOUS REFORMS

15 Then the Spirit of God came upon Azariah son of Oded, ²and he went out to meet King Asa as he was returning from the battle. "Listen to me, Asa!" he shouted. "Listen, all you people of Judah and Benjamin! The LORD will stay with you as long as you stay with him! Whenever you seek him, you will find him. But if you abandon him, he will abandon you. ³For a long time, Israel was without the true God, without a priest to teach them, and without God's law. ⁴But whenever you were in distress and turned to the LORD, the God of Israel, and sought him out, you found him. ⁵During those dark times, it was not safe to travel. Problems troubled the nation on every hand. ⁶Nation fought against nation, and city against city, for God was troubling you with every kind of problem. ⁷And now, you men of Judah, be strong and courageous, for your work will be rewarded."

⁸When Asa heard this message from Azariah the prophet,* he took courage and removed all the idols in the land of Judah and Benjamin and in the towns he had captured in

---

Words of Worship

PRAY, PRAYER

Pray, Prayer—Hebrew *hit-pal-lel* "intercede, pray"; *te-fil-lah* "prayer"; *te-hin-nah* "supplication"; *qa-ra'* "call [to the Lord]"; Greek *pros-eu-cho-mai* "pray"; *pros-eu-che* "prayer." Other words are used.

"Keep on praying," Paul wrote (1 Thessalonians 5:17). The Bible's drama is a story of prayer, its cast of leading characters made up of men and women of prayer—Abraham, Moses, Elijah, David, Jeremiah, Daniel, Mary, Paul, the Lord Jesus himself. Through prayer, the cry of their hearts, they exalted God, received his guidance, knew his deliverance, were confirmed in their faith—and changed the course of history.

We may think we aren't very good at praying. Jesus' disciples must have felt the same way when they asked, "Lord, teach us to pray" (Luke 11:1). In response, he taught them a brief prayer acknowledging our heavenly Father's authority and asking his provision, forgiveness, and protection. Our prayers can be as simple as this, for prayer—whatever form it takes—is simply talking with God. If he's our Father, it's normal family conversation.

14:9a Hebrew *a Cushite.*   **14:9b** Or *an army of thousands and thousands;* Hebrew reads *an army of a thousand thousands.*
14:10 Or *in the Zephathah Valley near Mareshah.*   **14:12** Hebrew *Cushites;* also in 14:13.   **15:8** As in Syriac version and Latin Vulgate (see also 15:1); Hebrew reads *from Oded the prophet.*

the hill country of Ephraim. And he repaired the altar of the LORD, which stood in front of the foyer of the LORD's Temple.

⁹Then Asa called together all the people of Judah and Benjamin, along with the people of Ephraim, Manasseh, and Simeon who had settled among them. Many had moved to Judah during Asa's reign when they saw that the LORD his God was with him. ¹⁰The people gathered at Jerusalem in late spring,* during the fifteenth year of Asa's reign. ¹¹On that day they sacrificed to the LORD some of the animals they had taken as plunder in the battle— seven hundred oxen and seven thousand sheep and goats. ¹²Then they entered into a covenant to seek the LORD, the God of their ancestors, with all their heart and soul. ¹³They agreed that anyone who refused to seek the LORD, the God of Israel, would be put to death—whether young or old, man or woman. ¹⁴They shouted out their oath of loyalty to the LORD with trumpets blaring and horns sounding. ¹⁵All were happy about this covenant, for they had entered into it with all their hearts. Eagerly they sought after God, and they found him. And the LORD gave them rest from their enemies on every side.

¹⁶King Asa even deposed his grandmother Maacah from her position as queen mother because she had made an obscene Asherah pole. He cut down the pole, broke it up, and burned it in the Kidron Valley. ¹⁷Although the pagan shrines were not completely removed from Israel, Asa remained fully committed to the LORD throughout his life. ¹⁸He brought into the Temple of God the silver and gold and the utensils that he and his father had dedicated. ¹⁹So there was no more war until the thirty-fifth year of Asa's reign.

FINAL YEARS OF ASA'S REIGN

16 In the thirty-sixth year of Asa's reign, King Baasha of Israel invaded Judah and fortified Ramah in order to prevent anyone from entering or leaving King Asa's territory in Judah. ²Asa responded by taking the silver and gold from the treasuries of the LORD's Temple and from the royal palace. He sent it to King Ben-hadad of Aram, who was ruling in Damascus, along with this message:

³"Let us renew the treaty that existed between your father and my father. See, I am sending you a gift of silver and gold. Break your treaty with King Baasha of Israel so that he will leave me alone."

⁴Ben-hadad agreed to King Asa's request and sent his armies to attack Israel. They conquered the towns of Ijon, Dan, Abel-beth-maacah,* and all the store cities in Naphtali. ⁵As soon as Baasha of Israel heard what was happening, he abandoned his project of fortifying Ramah. ⁶Then King Asa called out all the men of Judah to carry away the building stones and timbers that Baasha had been using to fortify Ramah. Asa used these materials to fortify the towns of Geba and Mizpah.

⁷At that time Hanani the seer came to King Asa and told him, "Because you have put your trust in the king of Aram instead of in the LORD your God, you missed your chance to destroy the army of the king of Aram. ⁸Don't you remember what happened to the Ethiopians* and Libyans and their vast army, with all of their chariots and horsemen*? At that time you relied on the LORD, and he handed them all over to you. ⁹The eyes of the LORD search the whole earth in order to strengthen those whose hearts are fully committed to him. What a fool you have been! From now on, you will be at war." ¹⁰Asa became so angry with Hanani for saying this that he threw him into prison. At that time, Asa also began to oppress some of his people.

SUMMARY OF ASA'S REIGN

¹¹The rest of the events of Asa's reign, from beginning to end, are recorded in *The Book of*

15:10 Hebrew *in the third month.* This month of the Hebrew lunar calendar usually occurs in May and June.   **16:4** As in parallel text at 1 Kgs 15:20; Hebrew reads *Abel-maim,* another name for Abel-beth-maacah.   **16:8a** Hebrew *Cushites.*   **16:8b** Or *and charioteers.*

the Kings of Judah and Israel. ¹²In the thirty-ninth year of his reign, Asa developed a serious foot disease. Even when the disease became life threatening, he did not seek the LORD's help but sought help only from his physicians. ¹³So he died in the forty-first year of his reign. ¹⁴He was buried in the tomb he had carved out for himself in the City of David. He was laid on a bed perfumed with sweet spices and ointments, and at his funeral the people built a huge fire in his honor.

JEHOSHAPHAT RULES IN JUDAH

17 Then Jehoshaphat, Asa's son, became the next king. He strengthened Judah to stand against any attack from Israel. ²He stationed troops in all the fortified cities of Judah, and he assigned additional garrisons to the land of Judah and to the towns of Ephraim that his father, Asa, had conquered.

³The LORD was with Jehoshaphat because he followed the example of his father's early years* and did not worship the images of Baal. ⁴He sought his father's God and obeyed his commands instead of following the practices of the kingdom of Israel. ⁵So the LORD established Jehoshaphat's control over the kingdom of Judah. All the people of Judah brought gifts to Jehoshaphat, so he became very wealthy and highly esteemed. ⁶He was committed to the ways of the LORD. He knocked down the pagan shrines and destroyed the Asherah poles.

⁷In the third year of his reign, Jehoshaphat sent out his officials to teach in all the towns of Judah. These officials included Ben-hail, Obadiah, Zechariah, Nethanel, and Micaiah. ⁸He sent Levites along with them, including Shemaiah, Nethaniah, Zebadiah, Asahel, Shemiramoth, Jehonathan, Adonijah, Tobijah, and Tob-adonijah. He also sent out the priests, Elishama and Jehoram. ⁹They took copies of the Book of the Law of the LORD and traveled around through all the towns of Judah, teaching the people.

¹⁰Then the fear of the LORD fell over all the surrounding kingdoms so that none of them declared war on Jehoshaphat. ¹¹Some of the Philistines brought him gifts and silver as tribute, and the Arabs brought seventy-seven hundred rams and seventy-seven hundred male goats.

¹²So Jehoshaphat became more and more powerful and built fortresses and store cities throughout Judah. ¹³He stored numerous supplies in Judah's towns and stationed an army of seasoned troops at Jerusalem. ¹⁴His army was enrolled according to ancestral clans.

From Judah, there were 300,000 troops organized in units of one thousand, under the command of Adnah. ¹⁵Next in command was Jehohanan, who commanded 280,000 troops. ¹⁶Next was Amasiah son of Zicri, who volunteered for the LORD's service, with 200,000 troops under his command.

¹⁷From Benjamin, there were 200,000 troops equipped with bows and shields. They were under the command of Eliada, a veteran soldier. ¹⁸Next in command was Jehozabad, who commanded 180,000 armed men.

¹⁹These were the troops stationed in Jerusalem to serve the king, besides those Jehoshaphat stationed in the fortified cities throughout Judah.

JEHOSHAPHAT AND AHAB

18 Now Jehoshaphat enjoyed great riches and high esteem, and he arranged for his son to marry the daughter of King Ahab of Israel. ²A few years later, he went to Samaria to visit Ahab, who prepared a great banquet for him and his officials. They butchered great numbers of sheep and oxen for the feast. Then Ahab enticed Jehoshaphat to join forces with him to attack Ramoth-gilead. ³"Will you join me in fighting against Ramoth-gilead?" Ahab asked.

17:3 Some Hebrew manuscripts read *the example of his father, David.*

My Daily Worship

— *April 10* —

FULLY COMMITTED OR FOOLISHLY CLEVER?

2 CHRONICLES 14:1 – 16:14

The eyes of the LORD search the whole earth in order to strengthen
those whose hearts are fully committed to him (16:9).

[i reflect]

It had seemed like a prudent move. Strategic diplomacy, some might say. "Let us renew the treaty"—what could be better than such negotiations?

What could be better? A lot, said the Lord to King Asa, through Hanani the seer. "Because you have put your trust in the king of Aram instead of in the LORD your God, you missed your chance to destroy the army of the king of Aram" (16:7). And this was after years of successfully trusting God against the Ethiopians and the Libyans, the idols and the Asherah poles. "What a fool you have been!" accused Hanani, when he saw that Asa had so quickly forgotten how the Lord had helped them.

Having trusted in the Lord and relied on his power, Asa now was trusting in a foreign ruler to bring peace and, later, would be relying only on his physicians to heal his foot disease. Had he not experienced for himself the words of Azariah that "the LORD will stay with you as long as you stay with him! Whenever you seek him, you will find him" (15:2)? How else could Asa have found the courage to remove all the idols from Judah? Now he would experience the other half of the truth told by Azariah: "But if you abandon him, he will abandon you."

We shake our heads. How could Asa be so foolish? Having trusted in God and found him trustworthy, how could he place that trust in anything or anybody else? Then we remember. The temptation to give up, give it over, hang it up, hand it over. *Certainly,* we say, *God would have done something by now, if he were going to.* Or perhaps we cloak our misplaced trust in words such as, *Maybe I'll just try this too. The Lord helps those who help themselves, right?*

In what situations are you trusting something or someone other than the Lord? Turn those over to the Lord. He willingly helps all who come to him, fully committed, worshiping him.

[i pray]

O God, search me and know me. I want to be fully committed to you,
that I may experience your restorative and empowering love.

[i respond]

Close your eyes and imagine a searchlight moving over a large area, perhaps a field. The light stops on you. Is it a harsh glare? Or is it a glow, warming and transferring power? Has the Lord found your heart "fully committed to him"? Write down those aspects of your relationship with him that need his strengthening.

And Jehoshaphat replied, "Why, of course! You and I are brothers, and my troops are yours to command. We will certainly join you in battle." ⁴Then Jehoshaphat added, "But first let's find out what the LORD says."

⁵So King Ahab summoned his prophets, four hundred of them, and asked them, "Should we go to war against Ramoth-gilead or not?"

They all replied, "Go ahead, for God will give you a great victory!"

⁶But Jehoshaphat asked, "Isn't there a prophet of the LORD around, too? I would like to ask him the same question."

⁷King Ahab replied, "There is still one prophet of the LORD, but I hate him. He never prophesies anything but bad news for me! His name is Micaiah son of Imlah."

"You shouldn't talk like that," Jehoshaphat said. "Let's hear what he has to say."

⁸So the king of Israel called one of his officials and said, "Quick! Go and get Micaiah son of Imlah."

MICAIAH PROPHESIES AGAINST AHAB

⁹King Ahab of Israel and King Jehoshaphat of Judah, dressed in their royal robes, were sitting on thrones at the threshing floor near the gate of Samaria. All of Ahab's prophets were prophesying there in front of them. ¹⁰One of them, Zedekiah son of Kenaanah, made some iron horns and proclaimed, "This is what the LORD says: With these horns you will gore the Arameans to death!"

¹¹All the other prophets agreed. "Yes," they said, "go up to Ramoth-gilead and be victorious. The LORD will give you a glorious victory!"

¹²Meanwhile, the messenger who went to get Micaiah said to him, "Look, all the prophets are promising victory for the king. Be sure that you agree with them and promise success."

¹³But Micaiah replied, "As surely as the LORD lives, I will say only what my God tells me to say."

> *What we worship determines what we become.*
>
> HARVEY F. AMMERMAN

¹⁴When Micaiah arrived before the king, Ahab asked him, "Micaiah, should we go to war against Ramoth-gilead or not?"

And Micaiah replied, "Go right ahead! It will be a glorious victory!"

¹⁵But the king replied sharply, "How many times must I demand that you speak only the truth when you speak for the LORD?"

¹⁶So Micaiah told him, "In a vision I saw all Israel scattered on the mountains, like sheep without a shepherd. And the LORD said, 'Their master has been killed. Send them home in peace.'"

¹⁷"Didn't I tell you?" the king of Israel said to Jehoshaphat. "He does it every time. He never prophesies anything but bad news for me."

¹⁸Then Micaiah continued, "Listen to what the LORD says! I saw the LORD sitting on his throne with all the armies of heaven on his right and on his left. ¹⁹And the LORD said, 'Who can entice King Ahab of Israel to go into battle against Ramoth-gilead so that he can be killed there?' There were many suggestions, ²⁰until finally a spirit approached the LORD and said, 'I can do it!'

"'How will you do this?' the LORD asked.

²¹"And the spirit replied, 'I will go out and inspire all Ahab's prophets to speak lies.'

"'You will succeed,' said the LORD. 'Go ahead and do it.'

²²"So you see, the LORD has put a lying spirit in the mouths of your prophets. For the LORD has determined disaster for you."

²³Then Zedekiah son of Kenaanah walked up to Micaiah and slapped him across the face. "When did the Spirit of the LORD leave me to speak to you?" he demanded.

²⁴And Micaiah replied, "You will find out soon enough, when you find yourself hiding in some secret room!"

²⁵King Ahab of Israel then ordered, "Arrest Micaiah and take him back to Amon, the governor of the city, and to my son Joash. ²⁶Give them this order from the king: 'Put this man in prison, and feed him nothing but bread and water until I return safely from the battle!'"

²⁷But Micaiah replied, "If you return safely, the LORD has not spoken through me!" Then he added to those standing around, "Take note of what I have said."

THE DEATH OF AHAB

²⁸So the king of Israel and King Jehoshaphat of Judah led their armies against Ramoth-gilead. ²⁹Now King Ahab said to Jehoshaphat, "As we go into battle, I will disguise myself so no one will recognize me, but you wear your royal robes." So Ahab disguised himself, and they went into battle.

³⁰Now the king of Aram had issued these orders to his charioteers: "Attack only the king of Israel!" ³¹So when the Aramean charioteers saw Jehoshaphat in his royal robes, they went after him. "There is the king of Israel!" they shouted. But Jehoshaphat cried out to the LORD to save him, and God helped him by turning the attack away from him. ³²As soon as the charioteers realized he was not the king of Israel, they stopped chasing him.

³³An Aramean soldier, however, randomly shot an arrow at the Israelite troops, and the arrow hit the king of Israel between the joints of his armor. "Get me out of here!" Ahab groaned to the driver of his chariot. "I have been badly wounded!" ³⁴The battle raged all that day, and Ahab propped himself up in his chariot facing the Arameans until evening. Then, just as the sun was setting, he died.

JEHOSHAPHAT APPOINTS JUDGES

19 When King Jehoshaphat of Judah arrived safely home to Jerusalem, ²Jehu son of Hanani the seer went out to meet him. "Why should you help the wicked and love those who hate the LORD?" he asked the king. "What you have done has brought the LORD's anger against you. ³There is some good in you, however, for you have removed the Asherah poles throughout the land, and you have committed yourself to seeking God."

⁴So Jehoshaphat lived in Jerusalem, but he went out among the people, traveling from Beersheba to the hill country of Ephraim, encouraging the people to return to the LORD, the God of their ancestors. ⁵He appointed judges throughout the nation in all the fortified cities, ⁶and he gave them these instructions: "Always think carefully before pronouncing judgment. Remember that you do not judge to please people but to please the LORD. He will be with you when you render the verdict in each case that comes before you. ⁷Fear the LORD and judge with care, for the LORD our God does not tolerate perverted justice, partiality, or the taking of bribes."

⁸Jehoshaphat appointed some of the Levites and priests and clan leaders in Israel to serve as judges in Jerusalem for cases concerning both the law of the LORD and civil disputes. ⁹These were his instructions to them: "You must always act in the fear of the LORD, with integrity and with undivided hearts. ¹⁰Whenever a case comes to you from fellow citizens in an outlying town, whether a murder case or some other violation of God's instructions, commands, laws, or regulations, you must warn them not to sin against the LORD, so that his anger will not come against you and them. Do this and you will not be guilty.

¹¹"Amariah the high priest will have final say in all cases concerning the LORD. Zebadiah son of Ishmael, a leader from the tribe of Judah, will have final say in all civil cases. The Levites will assist you in making sure that justice is served. Take courage as you fulfill your

duties, and may the LORD be with those who do what is right."

WAR WITH MOAB, AMMON, AND EDOM

20 After this, the armies of the Moabites, Ammonites, and some of the Meunites* declared war on Jehoshaphat. ²Messengers came and told Jehoshaphat, "A vast army from Edom* is marching against you from beyond the Dead Sea.* They are already at Hazazon-tamar." (This was another name for En-gedi.) ³Jehoshaphat was alarmed by this news and sought the LORD for guidance. He also gave orders that everyone throughout Judah should observe a fast. ⁴So people from all the towns of Judah came to Jerusalem to seek the LORD.

⁵Jehoshaphat stood before the people of Judah and Jerusalem in front of the new courtyard at the Temple of the LORD. ⁶He prayed, "O LORD, God of our ancestors, you alone are the God who is in heaven. You are ruler of all the kingdoms of the earth. You are powerful and mighty; no one can stand against you! ⁷O our God, did you not drive out those who lived in this land when your people arrived? And did you not give this land forever to the descendants of your friend Abraham? ⁸Your people settled here and built this Temple for you. ⁹They said, 'Whenever we are faced with any calamity such as war, disease, or famine, we can come to stand in your presence before this Temple where your name is honored. We can cry out to you to save us, and you will hear us and rescue us.'

¹⁰"And now see what the armies of Ammon, Moab, and Mount Seir are doing. You would not let our ancestors invade those nations when Israel left Egypt, so they went around them and did not destroy them. ¹¹Now see how they reward us! For they have come to throw us out of your land, which you gave us as an inheritance. ¹²O our God, won't you stop them? We are powerless against this mighty army that is about to attack us. We do not know what to do, but we are looking to you for help."

¹³As all the men of Judah stood before the LORD with their little ones, wives, and children, ¹⁴the Spirit of the LORD came upon one of the men standing there. His name was Jahaziel son of Zechariah, son of Benaiah, son of Jeiel, son of Mattaniah, a Levite who was a descendant of Asaph. ¹⁵He said, "Listen, King Jehoshaphat! Listen, all you people of Judah and Jerusalem! This is what the LORD says: Do not be afraid! Don't be discouraged by this mighty army, for the battle is not yours, but God's. ¹⁶Tomorrow, march out against them. You will find them coming up through the ascent of Ziz at the end of the valley that opens into the wilderness of Jeruel. ¹⁷But you will not even need to fight. Take your positions; then stand still and watch the LORD's victory. He is with you, O people of Judah and Jerusalem. Do not be afraid or discouraged. Go out there tomorrow, for the LORD is with you!"

¹⁸Then King Jehoshaphat bowed down with his face to the ground. And all the people of Judah and Jerusalem did the same, worshiping the LORD. ¹⁹Then the Levites from the clans of Kohath and Korah stood to praise the LORD, the God of Israel, with a very loud shout.

²⁰Early the next morning the army of Judah went out into the wilderness of Tekoa. On the way Jehoshaphat stopped and said, "Listen to me, all you people of Judah and Jerusalem! Believe in the LORD your God, and you will be able to stand firm. Believe in his prophets, and you will succeed." ²¹After consulting the leaders of the people, the king appointed singers to walk ahead of the army, singing to the LORD and praising him for his holy splendor. This is what they sang:

"Give thanks to the LORD;
  his faithful love endures forever!"

20:1 As in some Greek manuscripts (see also 26:7); Hebrew reads *Ammonites.* 20:2a As in one Hebrew manuscript; most Hebrew manuscripts and ancient versions read *Aram.* 20:2b Hebrew *the sea.*

— *April 11* —

SING BEFORE YOUR BATTLES!

2 CHRONICLES 17:1–20:37

After consulting the leaders of the people, the king appointed singers to walk ahead of
the army, singing to the LORD and praising him for his holy splendor. This is what
they sang: "Give thanks to the LORD; his faithful love endures forever!" (20:21).

[i reflect]

What an unusual way to start a battle! The people of Judah were facing three armies determined to wipe their nation from the earth—and they put a choir in the front lines! In this wonderful story, God promised to deliver Judah from her enemies, and the people believed his word. The singers were not praying and beseeching God to protect them and give them victory. They were simply praising him for his faithful love to them. They were worshiping his holy splendor, without fear of the enemy spread before them.

But notice the significance of the sequence of events in this battle. The people sang their praise to God *before* the battle. They praised him based on their knowledge of his character—not the outcome. It's easy to thank God when we receive the promotion, or the test results come back negative, or our prayer is answered in the way we imagined. But thanking God *before* we know the outcome? That requires putting our faith and trust in the One who is in control.

What battle are you facing right now? Perhaps you are waiting to hear back from a recent job interview. Or maybe you are in a broken relationship that you are trying desperately to reconcile. Perhaps you are battling a life-threatening illness or an addiction, or a sinful habit that just seems to defeat your best efforts. Whatever it is, praise God right now. Offer your thanksgiving to him for his holy splendor and for his faithful love.

What kept the Israelites singing that day as they advanced into battle? God's assurance not to be discouraged by the size of the army, but to march forward, knowing that the battle is his. God promises the same to you. No matter what you're facing, the battle is the Lord's. Believe him, as the Israelites did. Then offer your praise to God. *Before.*

[i pray]

Lord, too often I wait to see what will happen before I thank you. Too often, I trust
in the results rather than in the One who promises to fight the battle for me.
Help me to praise right now—at this moment—before I face my day.

[i respond]

Name the battle that is facing you today. Thank God for how he is going before you into battle. Praise him now for the outcome.

²²At the moment they began to sing and give praise, the LORD caused the armies of Ammon, Moab, and Mount Seir to start fighting among themselves. ²³The armies of Moab and Ammon turned against their allies from Mount Seir and killed every one of them. After they had finished off the army of Seir, they turned on each other.

²⁴So when the army of Judah arrived at the lookout point in the wilderness, there were dead bodies lying on the ground for as far as they could see. Not a single one of the enemy had escaped. ²⁵King Jehoshaphat and his men went out to gather the plunder. They found vast amounts of equipment, clothing,* and other valuables—more than they could carry. There was so much plunder that it took them three days just to collect it all! ²⁶On the fourth day they gathered in the Valley of Blessing,* which got its name that day because the people praised and thanked the LORD there. It is still called the Valley of Blessing today.

²⁷Then they returned to Jerusalem, with Jehoshaphat leading them, full of joy that the LORD had given them victory over their enemies. ²⁸They marched into Jerusalem to the music of harps, lyres, and trumpets and proceeded to the Temple of the LORD. ²⁹When the surrounding kingdoms heard that the LORD himself had fought against the enemies of Israel, the fear of God came over them. ³⁰So Jehoshaphat's kingdom was at peace, for his God had given him rest on every side.

SUMMARY OF JEHOSHAPHAT'S REIGN

³¹So Jehoshaphat ruled over the land of Judah. He was thirty-five years old when he became king, and he reigned in Jerusalem twenty-five years. His mother was Azubah, the daughter of Shilhi. ³²Jehoshaphat was a good king, following the ways of his father, Asa. He did what was pleasing in the LORD's sight. ³³During his reign, however, he failed to remove all the pagan shrines, and the people never fully committed themselves to following the God of their ancestors. ³⁴The rest of the events of Jehoshaphat's reign, from beginning to end, are recorded in *The Record of Jehu Son of Hanani,* which is included in *The Book of the Kings of Israel.*

³⁵But near the end of his life, King Jehoshaphat of Judah made an alliance with King Ahaziah of Israel, who was a very wicked man.* ³⁶Together they built a fleet of trading ships* at the port of Ezion-geber. ³⁷Then Eliezer son of Dodavahu from Mareshah prophesied against Jehoshaphat. He said, "Because you have allied yourself with King Ahaziah, the LORD will destroy your work." So the ships met with disaster and never put out to sea.*

JEHORAM RULES IN JUDAH

21 When Jehoshaphat died, he was buried with his ancestors in the City of David. Then his son Jehoram became the next king. ²Jehoram's brothers—the other sons of Jehoshaphat—were Azariah, Jehiel, Zechariah, Azariahu, Michael, and Shephatiah. ³Their father had given each of them valuable gifts of silver, gold, and costly items, and also the ownership of some of Judah's fortified cities. However, Jehoram became king because he was the oldest. ⁴But when Jehoram had become solidly established as king, he killed all his brothers and some of the other leaders of Israel.

⁵Jehoram was thirty-two years old when he became king, and he reigned in Jerusalem eight years. ⁶But Jehoram followed the example of the kings of Israel and was as wicked as King Ahab, for he had married one of Ahab's daughters. So Jehoram did what was evil in the LORD's sight. ⁷But the LORD was not willing to destroy David's dynasty, for he had made a covenant with David and promised that his descendants would continue to rule forever.*

20:25 As in some Hebrew manuscripts and Latin Vulgate; most Hebrew manuscripts read *corpses.* 20:26 Hebrew *valley of Beracah.* 20:35 Or *who made him do what was wrong.* 20:36 Hebrew *fleet of ships that could go to Tarshish.* 20:37 Hebrew *never set sail for Tarshish.* 21:7 Hebrew *promised to give a lamp to David and his descendants forever.*

⁸During Jehoram's reign, the Edomites revolted against Judah and crowned their own king. ⁹So Jehoram went to attack Edom with his full army and all his chariots. The Edomites surrounded him and his charioteers, but he escaped at night under cover of darkness. ¹⁰Edom has been independent from Judah to this day. The town of Libnah revolted about that same time, because Jehoram had abandoned the LORD, the God of his ancestors. ¹¹He had built pagan shrines in the hill country of Judah and had led the people of Jerusalem and Judah to give themselves to pagan gods.

¹²Then Elijah the prophet wrote Jehoram this letter:

"This is what the LORD, the God of your ancestor David, says: You have not followed the good example of your father, Jehoshaphat, or your grandfather King Asa of Judah. ¹³Instead, you have been as evil as the kings of Israel. You have led the people of Jerusalem and Judah to worship idols, just as King Ahab did in Israel. And you have even killed your own brothers, men who were better than you. ¹⁴So now the LORD is about to strike you, your people, your children, your wives, and all that is yours with a heavy blow. ¹⁵You yourself will be stricken with a severe intestinal disease until it causes your bowels to come out."

¹⁶Then the LORD stirred up the Philistines and the Arabs, who lived near the Ethiopians,* to attack Jehoram. ¹⁷They marched against Judah, broke down its defenses, and carried away everything of value in the royal palace, including his sons and his wives. Only his youngest son, Ahaziah,* was spared.

¹⁸It was after this that the LORD struck Jehoram with the severe intestinal disease. ¹⁹In the course of time, at the end of two years, the disease caused his bowels to come out, and he died in agony. His people did not build a great fire to honor him at his funeral as they had done for his ancestors. ²⁰Jehoram was thirty-two years old when he became king, and he reigned in Jerusalem eight years. No one was sorry when he died. He was buried in the City of David, but not in the royal cemetery.

AHAZIAH RULES IN JUDAH

22 Then the people of Jerusalem made Ahaziah, Jehoram's youngest son, their next king. The marauding bands of Arabs had killed all the older sons. So Ahaziah son of Jehoram reigned as king of Judah. ²Ahaziah was twenty-two* years old when he became king, and he reigned in Jerusalem one year. His mother was Athaliah, a granddaughter of King Omri of Israel. ³Ahaziah also followed the evil example of King Ahab's family, for his mother encouraged him in doing wrong. ⁴He did what was evil in the LORD's sight, just as Ahab had done. After the death of his father, members of Ahab's family became his advisers, and they led him to ruin.

⁵Following their evil advice, Ahaziah made an alliance with King Joram,* the son of King Ahab of Israel. They went out to fight King Hazael of Aram at Ramoth-gilead, and the Arameans wounded Joram in the battle. ⁶Joram returned to Jezreel to recover from his wounds, and King Ahaziah* of Judah went to Jezreel to visit him. ⁷But this turned out to be a fatal mistake, for God had decided to punish Ahaziah. It was during this visit that Ahaziah went out with Joram to meet Jehu son of Nimshi, whom the LORD had appointed to end the dynasty of Ahab.

⁸While Jehu was executing judgment against the family of Ahab, he happened to meet some of Judah's officials and Ahaziah's relatives* who were attending Ahaziah. So Jehu killed them all. ⁹Then Jehu's men

21:16 Hebrew *the Cushites.* 21:17 Hebrew *Jehoahaz,* a variant name for Ahaziah; compare 22:1. 22:2 As in some Greek manuscripts and Syriac version (see also 2 Kgs 8:26); Hebrew reads *forty-two.* 22:5 Hebrew *Jehoram,* a variant name for Joram; also in 22:6, 7. 22:6 Some Hebrew manuscripts, Greek and Syriac versions, and Latin Vulgate (see also 2 Kgs 8:29); most Hebrew manuscripts read *Azariah.* 22:8 As in Greek version (see also 2 Kgs 10:13); Hebrew reads *and sons of the brothers of Ahaziah.*

searched for Ahaziah, and they found him hiding in the city of Samaria. They brought him to Jehu, who killed him. Ahaziah was given a decent burial because the people said, "He was the grandson of Jehoshaphat—a man who sought the LORD with all his heart." None of the surviving members of Ahaziah's family was capable of ruling the kingdom.

ATHALIAH RULES IN JUDAH

¹⁰When Athaliah, the mother of King Ahaziah of Judah, learned that her son was dead, she set out to destroy the rest of Judah's royal family. ¹¹But Ahaziah's sister Jehosheba,* the daughter of King Jehoram, took Ahaziah's infant son, Joash, and stole him away from among the rest of the king's children, who were about to be killed. She put Joash and his nurse in a bedroom. In this way, Jehosheba, the wife of Jehoiada the priest, hid the child so that Athaliah could not murder him. ¹²Joash remained hidden in the Temple of God for six years while Athaliah ruled over the land.

REVOLT AGAINST ATHALIAH

23 In the seventh year of Athaliah's reign, Jehoiada the priest decided to act. He got up his courage and made a pact with five army commanders: Azariah son of Jeroham, Ishmael son of Jehohanan, Azariah son of Obed, Maaseiah son of Adaiah, and Elishaphat son of Zicri. ²These men traveled secretly throughout Judah and summoned the Levites and clan leaders in Judah's towns to come to Jerusalem. ³They all gathered at the Temple of God, where they made a covenant with Joash, the young king.

Jehoiada said to them, "The time has come for the king's son to reign! The LORD has promised that a descendant of David will be our king. ⁴This is what you must do. When the priests and Levites come on duty on the Sabbath, a third of them will serve as gatekeepers. ⁵Another third will go over to the royal palace, and the final third will be at the Foundation Gate. Everyone else should stay in the courtyards of the LORD's Temple. ⁶Remember, only the priests and Levites on duty may enter the Temple of the LORD, for they are set apart as holy. The rest of the people must obey the LORD's instructions and stay outside. ⁷You Levites, form a bodyguard for the king and keep your weapons in hand. Any unauthorized person who enters the Temple must be killed. Stay right beside the king at all times."

⁸So the Levites and the people did everything just as Jehoiada the priest ordered. The commanders took charge of the men reporting for duty that Sabbath, as well as those who were going off duty. Jehoiada the priest did not let anyone go home after their shift ended. ⁹Then Jehoiada supplied the commanders with the spears and shields that had once belonged to King David and were stored in the Temple of God. ¹⁰He stationed the guards around the king, with their weapons ready. They formed a line from the south side of the Temple around to the north side and all around the altar.

¹¹Then Jehoiada and his sons brought out Joash, the king's son, and placed the crown on his head. They presented Joash with a copy of God's laws and proclaimed him king. Then they anointed him, and everyone shouted, "Long live the king!"

THE DEATH OF ATHALIAH

¹²When Athaliah heard the noise of the people running and the shouts of praise to the king, she hurried to the LORD's Temple to see what was happening. ¹³And she saw the newly crowned king standing in his place of authority by the pillar at the Temple entrance. The officers and trumpeters were surrounding him, and people from all over the land were rejoicing and blowing trumpets. Singers with musical instruments were leading the people in a great celebration. When Athaliah saw all this, she tore her clothes in despair and shouted, "Treason! Treason!"

22:11 As in parallel text at 2 Kgs 11:2; Hebrew reads *Jehoshabeath*, a variant name for Jehosheba.

My Daily Worship

— *April 12* —

COURAGEOUS WORSHIP

2 CHRONICLES 21:1–24:27

In the seventh year of Athaliah's reign, Jehoiada the priest decided to act. He got up his courage and made a pact with five army commanders. . . . Then Jehoiada made a covenant between himself and the king and the people that they would be the LORD's people (23:1, 16).

[i reflect]

Ask the typical churchgoer to describe what worship involves, and you most likely will receive answers such as: singing, confession, praying, thanksgiving, praising, celebrating, dancing. The list goes on. But would you include "courage to take a stand"as part of worship? Sometimes our worship requires just that.

Jehoiada the priest decided to act to restore the throne to a descendant of David, according to God's promise to his people. God used Jehoiada's courage and willingness to act to bring about his purposes. After Joash became king, Jehoida continued to demonstrate worship through action, making a covenant with the king and the people that they would be the Lord's people. Because of Jehoiada's actions, the Temple of God was restored during Joash's reign, and the people lived in peace.

In your relationship with God, when have you had to exercise courage? What actions in personal or public worship would require bravery on your part if God called on you to participate or lead? God treasures the private time you spend with him reading his Word, praying, and honoring his power and greatness. Yet, he also desires your honoring his presence out in public. If that thought immediately grips your soul with dread, then you are a candidate for God's gift of courage.

Ask him what he wants you to do to demonstrate your love for him, and then trust him for the courage to carry it out. Perhaps you need to take a stand against the type of jokes told around the office, or confront a friend who is walking away from God. Whatever, and wherever, God is calling you to take a stand today. Remember—he will supply the courage when you need it.

[i pray]

Help me to learn to worship you with my actions. Show me what I should do today that will bring honor and glory to you. Help me to respond to your love with acts of love toward others.

[i respond]

Right where you are, stand up and pray to God that throughout the day you will have the courage to speak freely and boldly about your faith with others.

[14]Then Jehoiada the priest ordered the commanders who were in charge of the troops, "Take her out of the Temple, and kill anyone who tries to rescue her. Do not kill her here in the Temple of the LORD." [15]So they seized her and led her out to the gate where horses enter the palace grounds, and they killed her there.

JEHOIADA'S RELIGIOUS REFORMS

[16]Then Jehoiada made a covenant between himself and the king and the people that they would be the LORD's people. [17]And all the people went over to the temple of Baal and tore it down. They demolished the altars and smashed the idols, and they killed Mattan the priest of Baal in front of the altars.

[18]Jehoiada now put the Levitical priests in charge of the Temple of the LORD, following all the instructions given by David. He also commanded them to present burnt offerings to the LORD, as prescribed by the law of Moses, and to sing and rejoice as David had instructed. [19]He stationed gatekeepers at the gates of the LORD's Temple to keep those who were ceremonially unclean from entering.

[20]Then the commanders, nobles, rulers, and all the people escorted the king from the Temple of the LORD. They went through the Upper Gate and into the palace, and they seated the king on the royal throne. [21]So all the people of the land rejoiced, and the city was peaceful because Athaliah had been killed.

JOASH REPAIRS THE TEMPLE

24 Joash was seven years old when he became king, and he reigned in Jerusalem forty years. His mother was Zibiah, from Beersheba. [2]Joash did what was pleasing in the LORD's sight throughout the lifetime of Jehoiada the priest. [3]Jehoiada chose two wives for Joash, and he had sons and daughters.

[4]Some time later, Joash decided to repair and restore the Temple of the LORD. [5]He summoned the priests and Levites and gave them these instructions: "Go at once to all the towns of Judah and collect the required annual offerings, so that we can repair the Temple of your God. Do not delay!" But the Levites did not act right away.

[6]So the king called for Jehoiada the high priest and asked him, "Why haven't you demanded that the Levites go out and collect the Temple taxes from the towns of Judah and from Jerusalem? Moses, the servant of the LORD, levied this tax on the community of Israel in order to maintain the Tabernacle of the Covenant.*"

[7]Over the years, the followers of wicked Athaliah had broken into the Temple of God, and they had used all the dedicated things from the Temple of the LORD to worship the images of Baal. [8]So now Joash gave instructions for a chest to be made and set outside the gate leading to the Temple of the LORD. [9]Then a proclamation was sent throughout Judah and Jerusalem, telling the people to bring to the LORD the tax that Moses, the servant of God, had required of the Israelites in the wilderness. [10]This pleased all the leaders and the people, and they gladly brought their money and filled the chest with it.

[11]Whenever the chest became full, the Levites carried it to the king's officials. Then the court secretary and an officer of the high priest counted the money and took the chest back to the Temple again. This went on day after day, and a large amount of money was collected. [12]The king and Jehoiada gave the money to the construction supervisors, who hired masons and carpenters to restore the Temple of the LORD. They also hired metalworkers, who made articles of iron and bronze for the LORD's Temple.

[13]So the men in charge of the renovation worked hard, and they made steady progress. They restored the Temple of God according to its original design and strengthened it. [14]When all the repairs were finished, they brought the remaining money to the king and Jehoiada. It was used to make utensils for the Temple of the LORD—utensils for worship services and

24:6 Hebrew *Tent of the Testimony.*

for burnt offerings, including ladles and other vessels made of gold and silver. And the burnt offerings were sacrificed continually in the Temple of the LORD during the lifetime of Jehoiada the priest.

¹⁵Jehoiada lived to a very old age, finally dying at 130. ¹⁶He was buried among the kings in the City of David, because he had done so much good in Israel for God and his Temple.

JEHOIADA'S REFORMS REVERSED

¹⁷But after Jehoiada's death, the leaders of Judah came and bowed before King Joash and persuaded the king to listen to their advice. ¹⁸They decided to abandon the Temple of the LORD, the God of their ancestors, and they worshiped Asherah poles and idols instead! Then the anger of God burned against Judah and Jerusalem because of their sin. ¹⁹The LORD sent prophets to bring them back to him, but the people would not listen.

²⁰Then the Spirit of God came upon Zechariah son of Jehoiada the priest. He stood before the people and said, "This is what God says: Why do you disobey the LORD's commands so that you cannot prosper? You have abandoned the LORD, and now he has abandoned you!"

²¹Then the leaders plotted to kill Zechariah, and by order of King Joash himself, they stoned him to death in the courtyard of the LORD's Temple. ²²That was how King Joash repaid Jehoiada for his love and loyalty—by killing his son. Zechariah's last words as he died were, "May the LORD see what they are doing and hold them accountable!"

THE END OF JOASH'S REIGN

²³At the beginning of the year, the Aramean army marched against Joash. They invaded Judah and Jerusalem and killed all the leaders of the nation. Then they sent all the plunder back to their king in Damascus. ²⁴Although the Arameans attacked with only a small army, the LORD helped them conquer the much larger army of Judah. The people of Judah had abandoned the LORD, the God of their ancestors, so judgment was executed against Joash.

²⁵The Arameans withdrew, leaving Joash severely wounded. But his own officials decided to kill him for murdering the son of Jehoiada the priest. They assassinated him as he lay in bed. Then he was buried in the City of David, but not in the royal cemetery. ²⁶The assassins were Jozabad,* the son of an Ammonite woman named Shimeath, and Jehozabad, the son of a Moabite woman named Shomer.*

²⁷The complete story about the sons of Joash, the prophecies about him, and the record of his restoration of the Temple of God are written in *The Commentary on the Book of the Kings.* When Joash died, his son Amaziah became the next king.

AMAZIAH RULES IN JUDAH

25 Amaziah was twenty-five years old when he became king, and he reigned in Jerusalem twenty-nine years. His mother was Jehoaddin,* from Jerusalem. ²Amaziah did what was pleasing in the LORD's sight, but not wholeheartedly.

³When Amaziah was well established as king, he executed the men who had assassinated his father. ⁴However, he did not kill the children of the assassins, for he obeyed the command of the LORD written in the Book of the Law of Moses: "Parents must not be put to death for the sins of their children, nor the children for the sins of their parents. Those worthy of death must be executed for their own crimes."*

⁵Another thing Amaziah did was to organize the army, assigning leaders to each clan from Judah and Benjamin. Then he took a census and found that he had an army of 300,000 men twenty years old and older, all trained in the use of spear and shield. ⁶He also

24:26a As in parallel text at 2 Kgs 12:21; Hebrew reads *Zabad.* 24:26b As in parallel text at 2 Kgs 12:21; Hebrew reads *Shimrith.* 25:1 As in parallel text at 2 Kgs 14:2; Hebrew reads *Jehoaddan,* a variant name for Jehoaddin. 25:4 Deut 24:16.

paid about 7,500 pounds* of silver to hire 100,000 experienced fighting men from Israel. 7But a man of God came to the king and said, "O king, do not hire troops from Israel, for the LORD is not with Israel. He will not help those people of Ephraim! 8If you let them go with your troops into battle, you will be defeated no matter how well you fight. God will overthrow you, for he has the power to help or to frustrate."

9Amaziah asked the man of God, "But what should I do about the silver I paid to hire the army of Israel?"

The man of God replied, "The LORD is able to give you much more than this!" 10So Amaziah discharged the hired troops and sent them back to Ephraim. This made them angry with Judah, and they returned home in a great rage.

11Then Amaziah summoned his courage and led his army to the Valley of Salt, where they killed ten thousand Edomite troops from Seir. 12They captured another ten thousand and took them to the top of a cliff and threw them off, dashing them to pieces on the rocks below.

13Meanwhile, the hired troops that Amaziah had sent home raided several of the towns of Judah between Samaria and Beth-horon, killing three thousand people and carrying off great quantities of plunder.

14When King Amaziah returned from defeating the Edomites, he brought with him idols taken from the people of Seir. He set them up as his own gods, bowed down in front of them, and presented sacrifices to them! 15This made the LORD very angry, and he sent a prophet to ask, "Why have you worshiped gods who could not even save their own people from you?"

16But the king interrupted him and said, "Since when have I asked your advice? Be quiet now before I have you killed!"

So the prophet left with this warning: "I know that God has determined to destroy you because you have done this and have not accepted my counsel."

17After consulting with his advisers, King Amaziah of Judah sent this challenge to Israel's king Jehoash,* the son of Jehoahaz and grandson of Jehu: "Come and meet me in battle!"

18But King Jehoash of Israel replied to King Amaziah of Judah with this story: "Out in the Lebanon mountains, a thistle sent a message to a mighty cedar tree: 'Give your daughter in marriage to my son.' But just then a wild animal came by and stepped on the thistle, crushing it! 19You may be very proud of your conquest of Edom, but my advice is to stay home. Why stir up trouble that will bring disaster on you and the people of Judah?"

20But Amaziah would not listen, for God was arranging to destroy him for worshiping the gods of Edom. 21So King Jehoash of Israel mobilized his army against King Amaziah of Judah. The two armies drew up their battle lines at Beth-shemesh in Judah. 22Judah was routed by the army of Israel, and its army scattered and fled for home. 23King Jehoash of Israel captured King Amaziah of Judah at Beth-shemesh and brought him back to Jerusalem. Then Jehoash ordered his army to demolish six hundred feet* of Jerusalem's wall, from the Ephraim Gate to the Corner Gate. 24He carried off all the gold and silver and all the utensils from the Temple of God that had been in the care of Obed-edom. He also seized the treasures of the royal palace, along with hostages, and then returned to Samaria.

25King Amaziah of Judah lived on for fifteen years after the death of King Jehoash of Israel. 26The rest of the events of Amaziah's reign, from beginning to end, are recorded in *The Book of the Kings of Judah and Israel.* 27After Amaziah turned away from the LORD, there was a conspiracy against his life in Jerusalem, and he fled to Lachish. But his enemies sent assassins after him, and they killed him there.

25:6 Hebrew *100 talents* [3.4 metric tons].   25:17 Hebrew *Joash,* a variant name for Jehoash; also in 25:18, 21, 23, 25.   25:23 Hebrew *400 cubits* [180 meters].

²⁸They brought him back to Jerusalem on a horse, and he was buried with his ancestors in the City of David.*

UZZIAH RULES IN JUDAH

26 The people of Judah then crowned Amaziah's sixteen-year-old son, Uzziah, as their next king. ²After his father's death, Uzziah rebuilt the town of Elath* and restored it to Judah. ³Uzziah was sixteen when he became king, and he reigned in Jerusalem fifty-two years. His mother was Jecoliah, from Jerusalem. ⁴He did what was pleasing in the LORD's sight, just as his father, Amaziah, had done. ⁵Uzziah sought God during the days of Zechariah, who instructed him in the fear of God. And as long as the king sought the LORD, God gave him success.

⁶He declared war on the Philistines and broke down the walls of Gath, Jabneh, and Ashdod. Then he built new towns in the Ashdod area and in other parts of Philistia. ⁷God helped him not only with his wars against the Philistines, but also in his battles with the Arabs of Gur* and in his wars with the Meunites. ⁸The Meunites* paid annual tribute to him, and his fame spread even to Egypt, for he had become very powerful.

⁹Uzziah built fortified towers in Jerusalem at the Corner Gate, at the Valley Gate, and at the angle in the wall. ¹⁰He also constructed forts in the wilderness and dug many water cisterns, because he kept great herds of livestock in the foothills of Judah* and on the plains. He was also a man who loved the soil. He had many workers who cared for his farms and vineyards, both on the hillsides and in the fertile valleys.

¹¹Uzziah had an army of well-trained warriors, ready to march into battle, unit by unit. This great army of fighting men had been mustered and organized by Jeiel, the secretary of the army, and his assistant, Maaseiah. They were under the direction of Hananiah, one of the king's officials. ¹²Twenty-six hundred clan leaders commanded these regiments of seasoned warriors. ¹³The army consisted of 307,500 men, all elite troops. They were prepared to assist the king against any enemy. ¹⁴Uzziah provided the entire army with shields, spears, helmets, coats of mail, bows, and sling stones. ¹⁵And he produced machines mounted on the walls of Jerusalem, designed by brilliant men to shoot arrows and hurl stones* from the towers and the corners of the wall. His fame spread far and wide, for the LORD helped him wonderfully until he became very powerful.

UZZIAH'S SIN AND PUNISHMENT

¹⁶But when he had become powerful, he also became proud, which led to his downfall. He sinned against the LORD his God by entering the sanctuary of the LORD's Temple and personally burning incense on the altar. ¹⁷Azariah the high priest went in after him with eighty other priests of the LORD, all brave men. ¹⁸They confronted King Uzziah and said, "It is not for you, Uzziah, to burn incense to the LORD. That is the work of the priests alone, the sons of Aaron who are set apart for this work. Get out of the sanctuary, for you have sinned. The LORD God will not honor you for this!"

¹⁹Uzziah was furious and refused to set down the incense burner he was holding. But as he was standing there with the priests before the incense altar in the LORD's Temple, leprosy* suddenly broke out on his forehead. ²⁰When Azariah and the other priests saw the leprosy, they rushed him out. And the king himself was eager to get out because the LORD had struck him. ²¹So King Uzziah had leprosy until the day he died. He lived in isolation, excluded from the Temple of the LORD. His son Jotham was put in charge of the royal palace, and he governed the people of the land.

25:28 As in some Hebrew manuscripts and other ancient versions (see also 2 Kgs 14:20); most Hebrew manuscripts read *the city of Judah.* **26:2** As in Greek version (see also 2 Kgs 14:22; 16:6); Hebrew reads *Eloth.* **26:7** As in Greek version; Hebrew reads *Gur-baal.* **26:8** As in Greek version; Hebrew reads *Ammonites.* Compare 26:7. **26:10** Hebrew *the Shephelah.* **26:15** Or *designed by brilliant men to protect those who shot arrows and stones.* **26:19** Or *a contagious skin disease.* The Hebrew word used here and throughout this passage can describe various skin diseases.

²²The rest of the events of Uzziah's reign, from beginning to end, are recorded by the prophet Isaiah son of Amoz. ²³So Uzziah died, and since he had leprosy, he was buried nearby in a burial field belonging to the kings. Then his son Jotham became the next king.

JOTHAM RULES IN JUDAH

27 Jotham was twenty-five years old when he became king, and he reigned in Jerusalem sixteen years. His mother was Jerusha, the daughter of Zadok. ²He did what was pleasing in the LORD's sight, just as his father, Uzziah, had done. But unlike him, Jotham did not enter the Temple of the LORD. Nevertheless, the people continued in their corrupt ways.

³Jotham rebuilt the Upper Gate to the LORD's Temple and also did extensive rebuilding on the wall at the hill of Ophel. ⁴He built towns in the hill country of Judah and constructed fortresses and towers in the wooded areas. ⁵Jotham waged war against the Ammonites and conquered them. For the next three years, he received from them an annual tribute of 7,500 pounds* of silver, 50,000 bushels of wheat, and 50,000 bushels of barley.*

⁶King Jotham became powerful because he was careful to live in obedience to the LORD his God.

⁷The rest of the events of Jotham's reign, including his wars and other activities, are recorded in *The Book of the Kings of Israel and Judah.* ⁸He was twenty-five years old when he became king, and he reigned in Jerusalem sixteen years. ⁹When he died, he was buried in the City of David, and his son Ahaz became the next king.

AHAZ RULES IN JUDAH

28 Ahaz was twenty years old when he became king, and he reigned in Jerusalem sixteen years. He did not do what was pleasing in the sight of the LORD, as his

ancestor David had done. ²Instead, he followed the example of the kings of Israel and cast images for the worship of Baal. ³He offered sacrifices in the valley of the son of Hinnom, even sacrificing his own sons in the fire.* He imitated the detestable practices of the pagan nations whom the LORD had driven from the land ahead of the Israelites. ⁴He offered sacrifices and burned incense at the pagan shrines and on the hills and under every green tree.

⁵That is why the LORD his God allowed the king of Aram to defeat Ahaz and to exile large numbers of his people to Damascus. The armies of Israel also defeated Ahaz and inflicted many casualties on his army. ⁶In a single day Pekah son of Remaliah, Israel's king, killed 120,000 of Judah's troops because they had abandoned the LORD, the God of their ancestors. ⁷Then Zicri, a warrior from Ephraim, killed Maaseiah, the king's son; Azrikam, the king's palace commander; and Elkanah, the king's second-in-command. ⁸The armies of Israel captured 200,000 women and children from Judah and took tremendous amounts of plunder, which they took back to Samaria.

⁹But a prophet of the LORD named Oded was there in Samaria when the army of Israel returned home. He went out to meet them and said, "The LORD, the God of your ancestors, was angry with Judah and let you defeat them. But you have gone too far, killing them without mercy, and all heaven is disturbed. ¹⁰And now you are planning to make slaves of these people from Judah and Jerusalem. What about your own sins against the LORD your God? ¹¹Listen to me and return these captives you have taken, for they are your own relatives. Watch out, because now the LORD's fierce anger has been turned against you!"

¹²Then some of the leaders of Israel*— Azariah son of Jehohanan, Berekiah son of Meshillemoth, Jehizkiah son of Shallum, and Amasa son of Hadlai—agreed with this and

---

27:5a Hebrew *100 talents* [3.4 metric tons]. **27:5b** Hebrew *10,000 cors* [1,820 kiloliters] *of wheat, and 10,000 cors of barley.* **28:3** Or *even making his sons pass through the fire.* **28:12** Hebrew *Ephraim,* referring to the northern kingdom of Israel.

My Daily Worship

— *April 13* —

PRIDE, POWER, AND PRAISE

2 CHRONICLES 25:1–28:27

But when [Uzziah] had become powerful, he also became proud, which led to his
downfall. He sinned against the LORD his God by entering the sanctuary of
the LORD's Temple and personally burning incense on the altar (26:16).

[i reflect]

"I'm so proud of you," we say when our daughter masters a difficult task. "I'm proud of you," we tell our son when he earns his college degree. "I'm proud of you," we encourage our successful spouse. So what's wrong with pride? When those we love are proud of us, it gives us a sense of dignity, value, and self-respect.

The danger in pride comes when we take our eyes off God and begin to think we are in charge of our lives. J. C. Ryle made the following observation: "[Pride] prevents repentance, keeps people back from Christ, checks brotherly love and nips spiritual concern in the bud. Let us watch against it and be on our guard." Pride causes us to become arrogant, haughty, and disdainful of others.

Uzziah's pride led him to believe he did not need a priest to offer sacrifices on his behalf. Is pride a problem for you? If you continually seek the Lord and allow yourself to be instructed in the fear of God, you will be successful spiritually, which is far more important than your bank balance, your professional accomplishments, the size of the house you live in, or the model of car you drive.

Those who have direct power over others, such as business executives, government officials, and judges have a special responsibility to keep pride in check and not abuse their power. But it's just as easy to be guilty of pride about our spirituality, to think we are better than others who may not feel as close to God as we do.

If we seek his face, God promises to be with us. With God's presence, we have power—his power—to praise him, to claim victory over sin and circumstances, to use the talents and gifts he has given us for his glory, to love others as he has loved us, to transform our pride into praise. Worship God today for *his* power, not yours.

[i pray]

God, forgive me for those times I take my eyes off you and start to think I'm responsible for my
success. What comfort it is to know that you are in charge, not me! I praise you for your power.

[i respond]

Think about a recent success you have had. Analyze how those successes have affected your relationship with God and with others. If pride has crept in, ask God to forgive you and to help you transform your pride into praise.

TREMBLE

Tremble—Hebrew *cha-rad* "tremble"; *chul* "twist, tremble"; *ra-gaz* "quiver"; *ra-'ash* "shake"; Greek *tro-mos* "a trembling." Other words are used in both Old Testament and New Testament. Though none of these words appears more than a few times, the variety of terms employed in Scripture suggests that trembling of some sort was a response to be expected upon encountering the Lord's powerful and mysterious presence.

We can't get our minds around God. Yes, we can know him and his love—supremely in Jesus Christ. But there's still that element of mystery, that sense of being in the presence of a power we can't control. He's the Creator of the universe, and we're only human. Like Jacob, we're filled with awe when God shows up (Genesis 28:17). We come to him not casually, but in fear and trembling, because "it is a terrible thing to fall into the hands of the living God" (Hebrews 10:31).

A God who doesn't fill us with awe would be a tame imitation, the product of our own wishful thinking. When God breaks through to us in his might, we fall before him as John did in the presence of the risen Christ (Revelation 1:17). Then, trembling before him, we feel his comforting touch and hear his voice: "Don't be afraid!"

handed over the plunder in the sight of all the leaders and people. [15]Then the four men mentioned by name came forward and distributed clothes from the plunder to the prisoners who were naked. They provided clothing and sandals to wear, gave them enough food and drink, and dressed their wounds with olive oil. They put those who were weak on donkeys and took all the prisoners back to their own land—to Jericho, the city of palms. Then they returned to Samaria.

AHAZ CLOSES THE TEMPLE

[16]About that time King Ahaz of Judah asked the king of Assyria for help against his enemies. [17]The armies of Edom had again invaded Judah and taken captives. [18]And the Philistines had raided towns located in the foothills of Judah* and in the Negev. They had already captured Beth-shemesh, Aijalon, Gederoth, Soco with its villages, Timnah with its villages, and Gimzo with its villages, and the Philistines had occupied these towns. [19]The LORD was humbling Judah because of King Ahaz of Judah,* for he had encouraged his people to sin and had been utterly unfaithful to the LORD. [20]So when King Tiglath-pileser* of Assyria arrived, he oppressed King Ahaz instead of helping him. [21]Ahaz took valuable items from the LORD's Temple, the royal palace, and from the homes of his officials and gave them to the king of Assyria as tribute. But even this did not help him.

[22]And when trouble came to King Ahaz, he became even more unfaithful to the LORD. [23]He offered sacrifices to the gods of Damascus who had defeated him, for he said, "These gods helped the kings of Aram, so they will help me, too, if I sacrifice to them." But instead, they led to his ruin and the ruin of all Israel. [24]The king took the utensils from the Temple of God and broke them into pieces. He shut the doors of the LORD's Temple so that no one could worship there and then set up altars to pagan gods in every corner of Jerusalem. [25]He made pagan shrines in all the

confronted the men returning from battle. [13]"You must not bring the prisoners here!" they declared. "We cannot afford to add to our sins and guilt. Our guilt is already great, and the LORD's fierce anger is already turned against Israel."

[14]So the warriors released the prisoners and

28:18 Hebrew *the Shephelah.* **28:19** Hebrew *of Israel.* **28:20** Hebrew *Tilgath-pilneser,* a variant name for Tiglath-pileser.

towns of Judah for offering sacrifices to other gods. In this way, he aroused the anger of the LORD, the God of his ancestors.

²⁶The rest of the events of Ahaz's reign and all his dealings, from beginning to end, are recorded in *The Book of the Kings of Judah and Israel.* ²⁷When King Ahaz died, he was buried in Jerusalem but not in the royal cemetery. Then his son Hezekiah became the next king.

HEZEKIAH RULES IN JUDAH

29 Hezekiah was twenty-five years old when he became the king of Judah, and he reigned in Jerusalem twenty-nine years. His mother was Abijah, the daughter of Zechariah. ²He did what was pleasing in the LORD's sight, just as his ancestor David had done.

HEZEKIAH REOPENS THE TEMPLE

³In the very first month of the first year of his reign, Hezekiah reopened the doors of the Temple of the LORD and repaired them. ⁴He summoned the priests and Levites to meet him at the courtyard east of the Temple. ⁵He said to them, "Listen to me, you Levites! Purify yourselves, and purify the Temple of the LORD, the God of your ancestors. Remove all the defiled things from the sanctuary. ⁶Our ancestors were unfaithful and did what was evil in the sight of the LORD our God. They abandoned the LORD and his Temple; they turned their backs on him. ⁷They also shut the doors to the Temple's foyer, and they snuffed out the lamps. They stopped burning incense and presenting burnt offerings at the sanctuary of the God of Israel. ⁸That is why the LORD's anger has fallen upon Judah and Jerusalem. He has made us an object of dread, horror, and ridicule, as you can so plainly see. ⁹Our fathers have been killed in battle, and our sons and daughters and wives are in captivity. ¹⁰But now I will make a covenant with the LORD, the God of Israel, so that his fierce anger will turn away from us. ¹¹My dear

Levites, do not neglect your duties any longer! The LORD has chosen you to stand in his presence, to minister to him, and to lead the people in worship and make offerings to him."

¹²Then these Levites got right to work:

From the clan of Kohath: Mahath son of Amasai and Joel son of Azariah.
From the clan of Merari: Kish son of Abdi and Azariah son of Jehallelel.
From the clan of Gershon: Joah son of Zimmah and Eden son of Joah.
¹³ From the family of Elizaphan: Shimri and Jeiel.
From the family of Asaph: Zechariah and Mattaniah.
¹⁴ From the family of Heman: Jehiel and Shimei.
From the family of Jeduthun: Shemaiah and Uzziel.

¹⁵These men called together their fellow Levites, and they purified themselves. Then they began to purify the Temple of the LORD, just as the king had commanded. They were careful to follow all the LORD's instructions in their work. ¹⁶The priests went into the sanctuary of the Temple of the LORD to cleanse it, and they took out to the Temple courtyard all the defiled things they found. From there the Levites carted it all out to the Kidron Valley.

¹⁷The work began on a day in early spring,* and in eight days they had reached the foyer of the LORD's Temple. Then they purified the Temple of the LORD itself, which took another eight days. So the entire task was completed in sixteen days.

THE TEMPLE REDEDICATION

¹⁸Then the Levites went to King Hezekiah and gave him this report: "We have purified the Temple of the LORD, the altar of burnt offering with all its utensils, and the table of the Bread of the Presence with all its utensils. ¹⁹We have also recovered all the utensils taken by King Ahaz when he was unfaithful and closed

---

29:17 Hebrew *on the first day of the first month.* This day of the Hebrew lunar calendar occurs in March or early April.

the Temple. They are now in front of the altar of the LORD, purified and ready for use."

²⁰Early the next morning King Hezekiah gathered the city officials and went to the Temple of the LORD. ²¹They brought seven bulls, seven rams, seven lambs, and seven male goats as a sin offering for the kingdom, for the Temple, and for Judah. The king commanded the priests, who were descendants of Aaron, to sacrifice the animals on the altar of the LORD. ²²So they killed the bulls, and the priests took the blood and sprinkled it on the altar. Next they killed the rams and sprinkled their blood on the altar. And finally, they did the same with the lambs. ²³The male goats for the sin offering were then brought before the king and the assembly of people, who laid their hands on them. ²⁴The priests then killed the goats as a sin offering and sprinkled their blood on the altar to make atonement for the sins of all Israel. The king had specifically commanded that this burnt offering and sin offering should be made for all Israel.

²⁵King Hezekiah then stationed the Levites at the Temple of the LORD with cymbals, harps, and lyres. He obeyed all the commands that the LORD had given to King David through Gad, the king's seer, and the prophet Nathan. ²⁶The Levites then took their positions around the Temple with the instruments of David, and the priests took their positions with the trumpets. ²⁷Then Hezekiah ordered that the burnt offering be placed on the altar. As the burnt offering was presented, songs of praise to the LORD were begun, accompanied by the trumpets and other instruments of David, king of Israel. ²⁸The entire assembly worshiped the LORD as the singers sang and the trumpets blew, until all the burnt offerings were finished. ²⁹Then the king and everyone with him bowed down in worship. ³⁰King Hezekiah and the officials ordered the Levites to praise the LORD with the psalms of David and Asaph the seer. So they offered joyous praise and bowed down in worship.

³¹Then Hezekiah declared, "The dedication ceremony has come to an end. Now bring your sacrifices and thanksgiving offerings to the Temple of the LORD." So the people brought their sacrifices and thanksgiving offerings, and those whose hearts were willing brought burnt offerings, too. ³²The people brought to the LORD seventy bulls, one hundred rams, and two hundred lambs for burnt offerings. ³³They also brought six hundred bulls and three thousand sheep as sacrifices. ³⁴But there were too few priests to prepare all the burnt offerings, so their relatives the Levites helped them until the work was finished and until more priests had been purified. For the Levites had been more conscientious about purifying themselves than the priests. ³⁵There was an abundance of burnt offerings, along with the usual drink offerings, and a great deal of fat from the many peace offerings. So the Temple of the LORD was restored to service. ³⁶And Hezekiah and all the people rejoiced greatly because of what God had done for the people, for everything had been accomplished so quickly.

PREPARATIONS FOR PASSOVER

30 King Hezekiah now sent word to all Israel and Judah, and he wrote letters of invitation to Ephraim and Manasseh. He asked everyone to come to the Temple of the LORD at Jerusalem to celebrate the Passover of the LORD, the God of Israel. ²The king, his officials, and all the community of Jerusalem decided to celebrate Passover a month later than usual.* ³They were unable to celebrate it at the regular time because not enough priests could be purified by then, and the people had not yet assembled at Jerusalem. ⁴This plan for keeping the Passover seemed right to the king and all the people. ⁵So they sent a proclamation throughout all Israel, from Beersheba in the south to Dan in the north, inviting everyone to come to Jerusalem to celebrate the Passover of the LORD, the God of Israel. The

30:2 Hebrew *in the second month.* This month of the Hebrew lunar calendar usually occurs in April and May.

people had not been celebrating it in great numbers as prescribed in the law.

[6]At the king's command, messengers were sent throughout Israel and Judah. They carried letters which said:

"O people of Israel, return to the LORD, the God of Abraham, Isaac, and Israel,* so that he will return to the few of us who have survived the conquest of the Assyrian kings. [7]Do not be like your ancestors and relatives who abandoned the LORD, the God of their ancestors, and became an object of derision, as you yourselves can see. [8]Do not be stubborn, as they were, but submit yourselves to the LORD. Come to his Temple which he has set apart as holy forever. Worship the LORD your God so that his fierce anger will turn away from you. [9]For if you return to the LORD, your relatives and your children will be treated mercifully by their captors, and they will be able to return to this land. For the LORD your God is gracious and merciful. If you return to him, he will not continue to turn his face from you."

CELEBRATION OF PASSOVER

[10]The messengers went from town to town throughout Ephraim and Manasseh and as far as the territory of Zebulun. But most of the people just laughed at the messengers and made fun of them. [11]However, some from Asher, Manasseh, and Zebulun humbled themselves and went to Jerusalem. [12]At the same time, God's hand was on the people in the land of Judah, giving them a strong desire to unite in obeying the orders of the king and his officials, who were following the word of the LORD. [13]And so a huge crowd assembled at Jerusalem in midspring* to celebrate Passover and the Festival of Unleavened Bread. [14]They set to work and removed the pagan altars from Jerusalem. They took away all the incense altars and threw them into the Kidron Valley.

[15]On the appointed day in midspring, one month later than usual,* the people slaughtered their Passover lambs. Then the priests and Levites became ashamed, so they purified themselves and brought burnt offerings to the Temple of the LORD. [16]They took their places at the Temple according to the regulations found in the law of Moses, the man of God. The Levites brought the sacrificial blood to the priests, who then sprinkled it on the altar.

[17]Since many of the people there had not purified themselves, the Levites had to slaughter their Passover lambs for them, to set them apart for the LORD. [18]Most of those who came from Ephraim, Manasseh, Issachar, and Zebulun had not purified themselves. But King Hezekiah prayed for them, and they were allowed to eat the Passover meal anyway, even though this was contrary to God's laws. For Hezekiah said, "May the LORD, who is good, pardon those [19]who decide to follow the LORD, the God of their ancestors, even though they are not properly cleansed for the ceremony." [20]And the LORD listened to Hezekiah's prayer and healed the people.

[21]So the people of Israel who were present in Jerusalem celebrated the Festival of Unleavened Bread for seven days with great joy. Each day the Levites and priests sang to the LORD, accompanied by loud instruments.* [22]Hezekiah encouraged the Levites for the skill they displayed as they served the LORD. So for seven days the celebration continued. Peace offerings were sacrificed, and the people confessed their sins to the LORD, the God of their ancestors.

[23]The entire assembly then decided to continue the festival another seven days, so they celebrated joyfully for another week. [24]King Hezekiah gave the people one thousand bulls and seven thousand sheep for offerings, and

---

30:6 *Israel* is the name that God gave to Jacob. 30:13 Hebrew *in the second month.* This month of the Hebrew lunar calendar usually occurs in April and May. 30:15 Hebrew *On the fourteenth day of the second month.* This day of the Hebrew lunar calendar occurs in late April or early May. 30:21 Or *sang to the LORD with all their strength.*

the officials donated one thousand bulls and ten thousand sheep. Meanwhile, many more priests purified themselves.

²⁵The entire assembly of Judah rejoiced, including the priests, the Levites, all who came from the land of Israel, the foreigners who came to the festival, and all those who lived in Judah. ²⁶There was great joy in the city, for Jerusalem had not seen a celebration like this one since the days of Solomon, King David's son. ²⁷Then the Levitical priests stood and blessed the people, and God heard them from his holy dwelling in heaven.

HEZEKIAH'S RELIGIOUS REFORMS

31 Now when the festival ended, the Israelites who attended went to all the towns of Judah, Benjamin, Ephraim, and Manasseh, and they smashed the sacred pillars, cut down the Asherah poles, and removed the pagan shrines and altars. After this, the Israelites returned to their own towns and homes.

²Hezekiah then organized the priests and Levites into divisions to offer the burnt offerings and peace offerings, and to worship and give thanks and praise to the LORD at the gates of the Temple. ³The king also made a personal contribution of animals for the daily morning and evening burnt offerings, as well as for the weekly Sabbath festivals and monthly new moon festivals, and for the other annual festivals as required in the law of the LORD. ⁴In addition, he required the people in Jerusalem to bring the prescribed portion of their income to the priests and Levites, so they could devote themselves fully to the law of the LORD.

⁵The people responded immediately and generously with the first of their crops and grain, new wine, olive oil, honey, and all the produce of their fields. They brought a tithe of all they owned. ⁶The people who had moved to Judah from Israel, and the people of Judah themselves, brought in the tithes of their cattle and sheep and a tithe of the things that had been dedicated to the LORD their God, and they piled them up in great heaps. ⁷The first of these tithes was brought in late spring,* and the heaps continued to grow until early autumn.* ⁸When Hezekiah and his officials came and saw these huge piles, they thanked the LORD and his people Israel!

⁹"Where did all this come from?" Hezekiah asked the priests and Levites.

¹⁰And Azariah the high priest, from the family of Zadok, replied, "Since the people began bringing their gifts to the LORD's Temple, we have had enough to eat and plenty to spare, for the LORD has blessed his people."

¹¹Hezekiah decided to have storerooms prepared in the Temple of the LORD, and this was done. ¹²Then all the gifts and tithes were faithfully brought to the Temple. Conaniah the Levite was put in charge, assisted by his brother Shimei. ¹³The supervisors under them were Jehiel, Azaziah, Nahath, Asahel, Jerimoth, Jozabad, Eliel, Ismakiah, Mahath, and Benaiah. These appointments were made by King Hezekiah and Azariah, the chief official in the Temple of God.

¹⁴Kore son of Imnah the Levite, who was the gatekeeper at the East Gate, was put in charge of distributing the freewill offerings of God, the gifts, and the things that had been dedicated to the LORD. ¹⁵His faithful assistants were Eden, Miniamin, Jeshua, Shemaiah, Amariah, and Shecaniah. They distributed the gifts among the families of priests in their towns, by their divisions, dividing the gifts fairly among young and old alike. ¹⁶They also distributed the gifts to all males three years old or older, regardless of their place in the genealogical records, who came daily to the LORD's Temple to perform their official duties, by their divisions. ¹⁷And they distributed gifts to the priests who were listed in the genealogical records by families, and to the Levites twenty years old or older who were listed according to their jobs and their divisions.

31:7a Hebrew *in the third month*. This month of the Hebrew lunar calendar usually occurs in May and June. 31:7b Hebrew *in the seventh month*. This month of the Hebrew lunar calendar usually occurs in September and October.

My Daily Worship

— *April 14* —

COME TO THE PARTY!

2 CHRONICLES 29:1 – 32:33

There was great joy in the city, for Jerusalem had not seen a celebration
like this one since the days of Solomon, King David's son (30:26).

[i reflect]

Have you ever wondered why we tend to observe the Lord's Supper at church in a somber mood? You'd almost think you were at a funeral. Curiously, the earliest Christians celebrated the Lord's Supper at the end of a fellowship meal called a "love feast." It was a most fitting setting for what was a New Testament equivalent of the Jewish Passover celebration that was filled with feasting, family, and joy. After all, both the Passover and the Lord's Supper recalled salvation and freedom. Both celebrations were occasions to do just that . . . celebrate!

No wonder the passage in 2 Chronicles 30 describes a party-like atmosphere of the Passover festival during the godly reign of King Hezekiah. Read 2 Chronicles 30:20–27 again and see how God is being honored while the reality of his presence provided an up-beat cadence.

William Willimon addresses the need to restore joy and celebration into the Lord's Supper, "We have celebrated the Lord's Supper as a funereal, doleful memorial to a departed hero rather than as the joyous Sunday Resurrection meal it is intended to be. . . . When we eat together, our focus is upon the whole saving work of God in Christ—birth, life, service, Passion, death, Resurrection, Ascension, and present reign."

Just as the Israelites celebrated the Passover with joy and feasting, communion should be cause for rejoicing. It reminds us that Jesus died, came back to life, and is returning to earth for us. So the next time you are served communion in church, make a point to sing in full voice and smile broadly as you contemplate the Lord's gift of himself. But you don't need to wait to factor joy into your worship. Your personal quiet time each day is another kind of communion worthy of joy and celebration. After all, based on what we read in this passage, the Lord hears those who come before him.

[i pray]

Lord, I'm determined to factor joy into my times with you (both at church and at home).
Forgive me, for acting as if Jesus were still dead. The reality of Easter means
I have sufficient reason to celebrate in your presence, especially when
I recall my "exodus" from personal slavery to sin. Amen.

[i respond]

Write down what brings you joy—whether it's being with a particular person, listening to a specific song, or being in a particular place. Choose one of those experiences to have today.

¹⁸Food allotments were also given to all the families listed in the genealogical records, including the little babies, the wives, and the sons and daughters. For they had all been faithful in purifying themselves. ¹⁹As for the priests, the descendants of Aaron, who were living in the open villages around the towns, men were appointed to distribute portions to every male among the priests and to all the Levites listed in the genealogical records.

²⁰In this way, King Hezekiah handled the distribution throughout all Judah, doing what was pleasing and good in the sight of the LORD his God. ²¹In all that he did in the service of the Temple of God and in his efforts to follow the law and the commands, Hezekiah sought his God wholeheartedly. As a result, he was very successful.

ASSYRIA INVADES JUDAH

32 After Hezekiah had faithfully carried out this work, King Sennacherib of Assyria invaded Judah. He laid siege to the fortified cities, giving orders for his army to break through their walls. ²When Hezekiah realized that Sennacherib also intended to attack Jerusalem, ³he consulted with his officials and military advisers, and they decided to stop the flow of the springs outside the city. ⁴They organized a huge work crew to stop the flow of the springs, cutting off the brook that ran through the fields. For they said, "Why should the kings of Assyria come here and find plenty of water?"

⁵Then Hezekiah further strengthened his defenses by repairing the wall wherever it was broken down and by adding to the fortifications and constructing a second wall outside the first. He also reinforced the Millo* in the City of David and manufactured large numbers of weapons and shields. ⁶He appointed military officers over the people and asked them to assemble before him in the square at the city gate. Then Hezekiah encouraged them with this address: ⁷"Be strong and courageous! Don't be afraid of the king of Assyria or his mighty army, for there is a power far greater on our side! ⁸He may have a great army, but they are just men. We have the LORD our God to help us and to fight our battles for us!" These words greatly encouraged the people.

SENNACHERIB THREATENS JERUSALEM

⁹Then King Sennacherib of Assyria, while still besieging the town of Lachish, sent officials to Jerusalem with this message for Hezekiah and all the people in the city:

¹⁰"This is what King Sennacherib of Assyria says: What are you trusting in that makes you think you can survive my siege of Jerusalem? ¹¹Hezekiah has said, 'The LORD our God will rescue us from the king of Assyria.' Surely Hezekiah is misleading you, sentencing you to death by famine and thirst! ¹²Surely you must realize that Hezekiah is the very person who destroyed all the LORD's shrines and altars. He commanded Judah and Jerusalem to worship at only the one altar at the Temple and to make sacrifices on it alone.

¹³"Surely you must realize what I and the other kings of Assyria before me have done to all the people of the earth! Were any of the gods of those nations able to rescue their people from my power? ¹⁴Name just one time when any god, anywhere, was able to rescue his people from me! What makes you think your God can do any better? ¹⁵Don't let Hezekiah fool you! Don't let him deceive you like this! I say it again—no god of any nation has ever yet been able to rescue his people from me or my ancestors. How much less will your God rescue you from my power!"

¹⁶And Sennacherib's officials further mocked the LORD God and his servant

32:5 Or *the supporting terraces.*

Hezekiah, heaping insult upon insult. ¹⁷The king also sent letters scorning the LORD, the God of Israel. He wrote, "Just as the gods of all the other nations failed to rescue their people from my power, so the God of Hezekiah will also fail." ¹⁸The Assyrian officials who brought the letters shouted this in the Hebrew language to the people gathered on the walls of the city, trying to terrify them so it would be easier to capture the city. ¹⁹These officials talked about the God of Jerusalem as though he were one of the pagan gods, made by human hands.

²⁰Then King Hezekiah and the prophet Isaiah son of Amoz cried out in prayer to God in heaven. ²¹And the LORD sent an angel who destroyed the Assyrian army with all its commanders and officers. So Sennacherib returned home in disgrace to his own land. And when he entered the temple of his god, some of his own sons killed him there with a sword. ²²That is how the LORD rescued Hezekiah and the people of Jerusalem from King Sennacherib of Assyria and from all the others who threatened them. So there was peace at last throughout the land. ²³From then on King Hezekiah became highly respected among the surrounding nations, and many gifts for the LORD arrived at Jerusalem, with valuable presents for King Hezekiah, too.

Hezekiah's Sickness and Recovery

²⁴About that time, Hezekiah became deathly ill. He prayed to the LORD, who healed him and gave him a miraculous sign. ²⁵But Hezekiah did not respond appropriately to the kindness shown him, and he became proud. So the LORD's anger came against him and against Judah and Jerusalem. ²⁶Then Hezekiah repented of his pride, and the people of Jerusalem humbled themselves. So the LORD's anger did not come against them during Hezekiah's lifetime.

²⁷Hezekiah was very wealthy and held in high esteem. He had to build special treasury buildings for his silver, gold, precious stones, and spices, and for his shields and other valuable items. ²⁸He also constructed many storehouses for his grain, new wine, and olive oil; and he made many stalls for his cattle and folds for his flocks of sheep and goats. ²⁹He built many towns and acquired vast flocks and herds, for God had given him great wealth. ³⁰He blocked up the upper spring of Gihon and brought the water down through a tunnel to the west side of the City of David. And so he succeeded in everything he did.

³¹However, when ambassadors arrived from Babylon to ask about the remarkable events that had taken place in the land, God withdrew from Hezekiah in order to test him and to see what was really in his heart.

Summary of Hezekiah's Reign

³²The rest of the events of Hezekiah's reign and his acts of devotion are recorded in *The Vision of the Prophet Isaiah Son of Amoz,* which is included in *The Book of the Kings of Judah and Israel.* ³³When Hezekiah died, he was buried in the upper area of the royal cemetery, and all Judah and Jerusalem honored him at his death. Then his son Manasseh became the next king.

Manasseh Rules in Judah

33 Manasseh was twelve years old when he became king, and he reigned in Jerusalem fifty-five years. ²He did what was evil in the LORD's sight, imitating the detestable practices of the pagan nations whom the LORD had driven from the land ahead of the Israelites. ³He rebuilt the pagan shrines his father Hezekiah had destroyed. He constructed altars for the images of Baal and set up Asherah poles. He also bowed before all the stars of heaven and worshiped them. ⁴He even built pagan altars in the Temple of the LORD, the place where the LORD had said his name should be honored forever. ⁵He put these altars for the stars of heaven in both courtyards of the LORD's Temple. ⁶Manasseh even sacrificed his own sons in the fire* in the valley of the son of Hinnom. He practiced sorcery, divination, and witchcraft, and he consulted with mediums and psychics. He did much that was evil in the LORD's sight, arousing his anger.

⁷Manasseh even took a carved idol he had made and set it up in God's Temple, the very place where God had told David and his son Solomon: "My name will be honored here forever in this Temple and in Jerusalem—the city I have chosen from among all the other tribes of Israel. ⁸If the Israelites will obey my commands—all the instructions, laws, and regulations given through Moses—I will not send them into exile from this land that I gave their ancestors." ⁹But Manasseh led the people of Judah and Jerusalem to do even more evil than the pagan nations whom the LORD had destroyed when the Israelites entered the land.

¹⁰The LORD spoke to Manasseh and his people, but they ignored all his warnings. ¹¹So the LORD sent the Assyrian armies, and they took Manasseh prisoner. They put a ring through his nose, bound him in bronze chains, and led him away to Babylon. ¹²But while in deep distress, Manasseh sought the LORD his God and cried out humbly to the God of his ancestors. ¹³And when he prayed, the LORD listened to him and was moved by his request for help. So the LORD let Manasseh return to Jerusalem and to his kingdom. Manasseh had finally realized that the LORD alone is God!

¹⁴It was after this that Manasseh rebuilt the outer wall of the City of David, from west of the Gihon Spring in the Kidron Valley to the Fish Gate, and continuing around the hill of Ophel, where it was built very high. And he stationed his military officers in all of the fortified cities of Judah. ¹⁵Manasseh also removed the foreign gods from the hills and the idol from the LORD's Temple. He tore down all the altars he had built on the hill where the Temple stood and all the altars that were in Jerusalem, and he dumped them outside the city. ¹⁶Then he restored the altar of the LORD

and sacrificed peace offerings and thanksgiving offerings on it. He also encouraged the people of Judah to worship the LORD, the God of Israel. ¹⁷However, the people still sacrificed at the pagan shrines, but only to the LORD their God.

¹⁸The rest of the events of Manasseh's reign, his prayer to God, and the words the seers spoke to him in the name of the LORD, the God of Israel, are recorded in *The Book of the Kings of Israel.* ¹⁹Manasseh's prayer, the account of the way God answered him, and an account of all his sins and unfaithfulness are recorded in *The Record of the Seers.** It includes a list of the locations where he built pagan shrines and set up Asherah poles and idols before he repented. ²⁰When Manasseh died, he was buried at his palace. Then his son Amon became the next king.

AMON RULES IN JUDAH

²¹Amon was twenty-two years old when he became king, and he reigned in Jerusalem two years. ²²He did what was evil in the LORD's sight, just as his father Manasseh had done. He worshiped and sacrificed to all the idols his father had made. ²³But unlike his father, he did not humble himself before the LORD. Instead, Amon sinned even more.

²⁴At last Amon's own officials plotted against him and assassinated him in his palace. ²⁵But the people of the land killed all those who had conspired against King Amon, and they made his son Josiah the next king.

JOSIAH RULES IN JUDAH

34 Josiah was eight years old when he became king, and he reigned in Jerusalem thirty-one years. ²He did what was pleasing in the LORD's sight and followed the example of his ancestor David. He did not turn aside from doing what was right.

³During the eighth year of his reign, while he was still young, Josiah began to seek the God of his ancestor David. Then in the twelfth

---

33:6 Or *even made his sons pass through the fire.*   33:19 Or *The Record of Hozai.*

My Daily Worship

— April 15 —

OUR EMOTIONAL GOD

2 CHRONICLES 33:1–36:23

But while in deep distress, Manasseh sought the LORD his God and cried out humbly to the
God of his ancestors. And when he prayed, the LORD listened to him and was moved by his
request for help. So the LORD let Manasseh return to Jerusalem and to his kingdom.
Manasseh had finally realized that the LORD alone is God! (33:12–13).

[i reflect]

King Manasseh paid a heavy price for his unfaithfulness to God. He lost his throne and was led away in chains to prison in a foreign land. Manasseh deserved his punishment—and worse. He did terrible things, even sacrificing his own sons to a heathen god. But Manasseh's story includes more than punishment. When he humbled himself before God, the Lord *was moved* by his request for help! God forgave Manasseh and restored his kingdom.

Imagine. God is moved by our prayers of confession. But that's not an easy concept for us to accept. Because we know that God is the all-powerful Creator, we may assume that he is aloof and disinterested. Even if we acknowledge that he loves us, we often have trouble believing that he really does care about us personally. Yet, God grieves when we disobey him, burns with anger at our sin, and is moved with compassion when we humbly bow before him in confession.

Jesus offers us another glimpse of the Father's delight with us through the parable of the lost coin (Luke 15:8–10). He relates the joyous celebration that the heavenly angels throw every time "even one sinner repents." *Even one.* Every individual is precious before God, and he is moved as we come to him in total dependence and repentance.

Today, remember that you are created in God's image, and that image includes emotions. Your actions affect him! As you worship, confess any disobedience and ask God to forgive you, and know that he will respond to your request for help. Worship involves your feelings as well, so freely express to God your emotions towards others and what steps you may need to take to restore relationships with them.

[i pray]

God, help me to realize that my attitudes and actions have an emotional impact
on you. Help me to bring you joy today, not sorrow. Help me to serve
you humbly, with love and gratitude for your great mercy.

[i respond]

Review your actions over the past twenty-four hours. How do you think your actions affected God emotionally? What steps do you need to take right now to restore the joy of fellowship with him?

year, he began to purify Judah and Jerusalem, destroying all the pagan shrines, the Asherah poles, and the carved idols and cast images. [4]He saw to it that the altars for the images of Baal and their incense altars were torn down. He also made sure that the Asherah poles, the carved idols, and the cast images were smashed and scattered over the graves of those who had sacrificed to them. [5]Then he burned the bones of the pagan priests on their own altars, and so he purified Judah and Jerusalem.

[6]He did the same thing in the towns of Manasseh, Ephraim, and Simeon, even as far as Naphtali. [7]He destroyed the pagan altars and the Asherah poles, and he crushed the idols into dust. He cut down the incense altars throughout the land of Israel and then returned to Jerusalem.

[8]In the eighteenth year of his reign, after he had purified the land and the Temple, Josiah appointed Shaphan son of Azaliah, Maaseiah the governor of Jerusalem, and Joah son of Joahaz, the royal historian, to repair the Temple of the LORD his God. [9]They gave Hilkiah the high priest the money that had been collected by the Levites who served as gatekeepers at the Temple of God. The gifts were brought by people from Manasseh, Ephraim, and from all the remnant of Israel, as well as from all Judah, Benjamin, and the people of Jerusalem. [10]He entrusted the money to the men assigned to supervise the restoration of the LORD's Temple. Then they paid the workers who did the repairs and renovation. [11]Thus, they hired carpenters and masons and purchased cut stone for the walls and timber for the rafters and beams. They restored what earlier kings of Judah had allowed to fall into ruin.

[12]The workers served faithfully under the leadership of Jahath and Obadiah, Levites of the Merarite clan, and Zechariah and Meshullam, Levites of the Kohathite clan. Other Levites, all of whom were skilled musicians, [13]were put in charge of the laborers of the various trades. Still others assisted as secretaries, officials, and gatekeepers.

HILKIAH DISCOVERS GOD'S LAW

[14]As Hilkiah the high priest was recording the money collected at the LORD's Temple, he found the Book of the Law of the LORD as it had been given through Moses. [15]Hilkiah said to Shaphan the court secretary, "I have found the Book of the Law in the LORD's Temple!" Then Hilkiah gave the scroll to Shaphan.

[16]Shaphan took the scroll to the king and reported, "Your officials are doing everything they were assigned to do. [17]The money that was collected at the Temple of the LORD has been given to the supervisors and workmen." [18]Shaphan also said to the king, "Hilkiah the priest has given me a scroll." So Shaphan read it to the king.

[19]When the king heard what was written in the law, he tore his clothes in despair. [20]Then he gave these orders to Hilkiah, Ahikam son of Shaphan, Acbor son of Micaiah,* Shaphan the court secretary, and Asaiah the king's personal adviser: [21]"Go to the Temple and speak to the LORD for me and for all the remnant of Israel and Judah. Ask him about the words written in this scroll that has been found. The LORD's anger has been poured out against us because our ancestors have not obeyed the word of the LORD. We have not been doing what this scroll says we must do."

[22]So Hilkiah and the other men went to the newer Mishneh section* of Jerusalem to consult with the prophet Huldah. She was the wife of Shallum son of Tikvah and grandson of Harhas,* the keeper of the Temple wardrobe. [23]She said to them, "The LORD, the God of Israel, has spoken! Go and tell the man who sent you, [24]This is what the LORD says: I will certainly destroy this city and its people. All the curses written in the scroll you have read will come true. [25]For the people of Judah have abandoned me and worshiped pagan gods,

34:20 As in parallel text at 2 Kgs 22:12; Hebrew reads *Abdon son of Micah.* 34:22a Or *the Second Quarter,* a newer section of Jerusalem. 34:22b As in parallel text at 2 Kgs 22:14; Hebrew reads *son of Tokhath, son of Hasrah.*

and I am very angry with them for everything they have done. My anger will be poured out against this place, and nothing will be able to stop it.'

²⁶"But go to the king of Judah who sent you to seek the LORD and tell him: 'This is what the LORD, the God of Israel, says concerning the message you have just heard: ²⁷You were sorry and humbled yourself before God when you heard what I said against this city and its people. You humbled yourself and tore your clothing in despair and wept before me in repentance. So I have indeed heard you, says the LORD. ²⁸I will not send the promised disaster against this city and its people until after you have died and been buried in peace. You will not see the disaster I am going to bring on this place.' " So they took her message back to the king.

JOSIAH'S RELIGIOUS REFORMS

²⁹Then the king summoned all the leaders of Judah and Jerusalem. ³⁰And the king went up to the Temple of the LORD with all the people of Judah and Jerusalem and the priests and the Levites—all the people from the greatest to the least. There the king read to them the entire Book of the Covenant that had been found in the LORD's Temple. ³¹The king took his place of authority beside the pillar and renewed the covenant in the LORD's presence. He pledged to obey the LORD by keeping all his commands, regulations, and laws with all his heart and soul. He promised to obey all the terms of the covenant that were written in the scroll. ³²And he required everyone in Jerusalem and the people of Benjamin to make a similar pledge. As the people of Jerusalem did this, they renewed their covenant with God, the God of their ancestors.

³³So Josiah removed all detestable idols from the entire land of Israel and required everyone to worship the LORD their God. And throughout the rest of his lifetime, they did not turn away from the LORD, the God of their ancestors.

JOSIAH CELEBRATES PASSOVER

35 Then Josiah announced that the Passover of the LORD would be celebrated in Jerusalem on the appointed day in early spring.* The Passover lambs were slaughtered at twilight of that day. ²Josiah also assigned the priests to their duties and encouraged them in their work at the Temple of the LORD. ³He issued this order to the Levites, who had been set apart to serve the LORD and were teachers in Israel: "Since the Ark is now in Solomon's Temple and you do not need to carry it back and forth on your shoulders, spend your time serving the LORD your God and his people Israel. ⁴Report for duty according to the family divisions of your ancestors, following the written instructions of King David of Israel and the instructions of his son Solomon. ⁵Then stand in your appointed holy places and help the families assigned to you as they bring their offerings to the Temple. ⁶Slaughter the Passover lambs, purify yourselves, and prepare to help those who come. Follow all the instructions that the LORD gave through Moses."

⁷Then Josiah contributed from his personal property thirty thousand lambs and young goats for the people's Passover offerings, and three thousand bulls. ⁸The king's officials also made willing contributions to the people, priests, and Levites. Hilkiah, Zechariah, and Jehiel, the administrators of God's Temple, gave the priests twenty-six hundred lambs and young goats and three hundred bulls as Passover offerings. ⁹The Levite leaders—Conaniah and his brothers Shemaiah and Nethanel, and Hashabiah, Jeiel, and Jozabad—gave five thousand lambs and young goats and five hundred bulls to the Levites for their Passover offerings.

¹⁰When everything was ready for the Passover celebration, the priests and the Levites took their places, organized by their divisions, according to the king's orders. ¹¹The Levites then slaughtered the Passover lambs and presented the blood to the priests, who

---

35:1 Hebrew *on the fourteenth day of the first month.* This day of the Hebrew lunar calendar occurs in late March or early April.

> *Worship is pure adoration,*
> *the lifting up of the redeemed spirit*
> *toward God in contemplation*
> *of His holy perfection.*
>
> JERRY SOLOMON

sprinkled the blood on the altar while the Levites prepared the animals. [12]They divided the burnt offerings among the people by their family groups, so they could offer them to the LORD according to the instructions recorded in the Book of Moses. They did the same with the bulls. [13]Then they roasted the Passover lambs as prescribed; and they boiled the holy offerings in pots, kettles, and pans, and brought them out quickly so the people could eat them.

[14]Afterward the Levites prepared a meal for themselves and for the priests, because the priests had been busy from morning till night offering the burnt offerings and the fat portions. The Levites took responsibility for all these preparations. [15]The musicians, descendants of Asaph, were in their assigned places, following the orders given by David, Asaph, Heman, and Jeduthun, the king's seer. The gatekeepers guarded the gates and did not need to leave their posts of duty, for their meals were brought to them by their fellow Levites.

[16]The entire ceremony for the LORD's Passover was completed that day. All the burnt offerings were sacrificed on the altar of the LORD, as King Josiah had ordered. [17]All the Israelites present in Jerusalem celebrated Passover and the Festival of Unleavened Bread for seven days. [18]Never since the time of the prophet Samuel had there been such a Passover. None of the kings of Israel had ever kept a Passover as Josiah did, involving all the priests and Levites, all the people of Jerusalem, and people from all over Judah and

Israel. [19]This Passover celebration took place in the eighteenth year of Josiah's reign.

JOSIAH DIES IN BATTLE

[20]After Josiah had finished restoring the Temple, King Neco of Egypt led his army up from Egypt to do battle at Carchemish on the Euphrates River, and Josiah and his army marched out to fight him. [21]But King Neco sent ambassadors to Josiah with this message:

"What do you want with me, king of Judah? I have no quarrel with you today! I only want to fight the nation with which I am at war. And God has told me to hurry! Do not interfere with God, who is with me, or he will destroy you."

[22]But Josiah refused to listen to Neco, to whom God had indeed spoken, and he would not turn back. Instead, he led his army into battle on the plain of Megiddo. He laid aside his royal robes so the enemy would not recognize him. [23]But the enemy archers hit King Josiah with their arrows and wounded him. He cried out to his men, "Take me from the battle, for I am badly wounded!"

[24]So they lifted Josiah out of his chariot and placed him in another chariot. Then they brought him back to Jerusalem, where he died. He was buried there in the royal cemetery. And all Judah and Jerusalem mourned for him. [25]The prophet Jeremiah composed funeral songs for Josiah, and to this day choirs still sing these sad songs about his death. These songs of sorrow have become a tradition and are recorded in *The Book of Laments.* [26]The rest of the events of Josiah's reign and his acts of devotion done according to the written law of the LORD, [27]from beginning to end, are recorded in *The Book of the Kings of Israel and Judah.*

JEHOAHAZ RULES IN JUDAH

36 Then the people of the land took Josiah's son Jehoahaz and made him

the next king in Jerusalem. ²Jehoahaz* was twenty-three years old when he became king, but he reigned only three months. ³Then he was deposed by Neco, the king of Egypt, who demanded a tribute from Judah of 7,500 pounds of silver and 75 pounds of gold.* ⁴The king of Egypt appointed Eliakim, the brother of Jehoahaz, as the next king of Judah and Jerusalem, and he changed Eliakim's name to Jehoiakim. Then Neco took Jehoahaz to Egypt as a prisoner.

JEHOIAKIM RULES IN JUDAH

⁵Jehoiakim was twenty-five years old when he became king, and he reigned in Jerusalem eleven years. But he did what was evil in the sight of the LORD his God. ⁶Then King Nebuchadnezzar of Babylon came to Jerusalem and captured it, and he bound Jehoiakim in chains and led him away to Babylon. ⁷Nebuchadnezzar also took some of the treasures from the Temple of the LORD, and he placed them in his palace* in Babylon. ⁸The rest of the events of Jehoiakim's reign, including all the evil things he did and everything found against him, are recorded in *The Book of the Kings of Israel and Judah.* Then his son Jehoiachin became the next king.

JEHOIACHIN RULES IN JUDAH

⁹Jehoiachin was eighteen* years old when he became king, but he reigned in Jerusalem only three months and ten days. Jehoiachin did what was evil in the LORD's sight. ¹⁰In the spring of the following year, Jehoiachin was summoned to Babylon by King Nebuchadnezzar. Many treasures from the Temple of the LORD were taken to Babylon at that time. And Nebuchadnezzar appointed Jehoiachin's uncle,* Zedekiah, to be the next king in Judah and Jerusalem.

ZEDEKIAH RULES IN JUDAH

¹¹Zedekiah was twenty-one years old when he became king, and he reigned in Jerusalem eleven years. ¹²He did what was evil in the sight of the LORD his God, and he refused to humble himself in the presence of the prophet Jeremiah, who spoke for the LORD. ¹³He also rebelled against King Nebuchadnezzar, even though he had taken an oath of loyalty in God's name. Zedekiah was a hard and stubborn man, refusing to turn to the LORD, the God of Israel.

¹⁴All the leaders of the priests and the people became more and more unfaithful. They followed the pagan practices of the surrounding nations, desecrating the Temple of the LORD in Jerusalem.

¹⁵The LORD, the God of their ancestors, repeatedly sent his prophets to warn them, for he had compassion on his people and his Temple. ¹⁶But the people mocked these messengers of God and despised their words. They scoffed at the prophets until the LORD's anger could no longer be restrained and there was no remedy.

THE FALL OF JERUSALEM

¹⁷So the LORD brought the king of Babylon against them. The Babylonians* killed Judah's young men, even chasing after them into the Temple. They had no pity on the people, killing both young and old, men and women, healthy and sick. God handed them all over to Nebuchadnezzar. ¹⁸The king also took home to Babylon all the utensils, large and small, used in the Temple of God, and the treasures from both the LORD's Temple and the royal palace. He also took with him all the royal princes. ¹⁹Then his army set fire to the Temple of God, broke down the walls of Jerusalem, burned all the palaces, and completely destroyed everything of value.* ²⁰The few who survived were taken away to Babylon, and they became servants to the king and his sons

---

36:2 Hebrew *Joahaz,* a variant name for Jehoahaz; also in 36:4. **36:3** Hebrew *100 talents* [3.4 metric tons] *of silver and 1 talent* [34 kilograms] *of gold.* **36:7** Or *temple.* **36:9** As in one Hebrew manuscript, some Greek manuscripts, and Syriac version (see also 2 Kgs 24:8); most Hebrew manuscripts read *eight.* **36:10** As in parallel text at 2 Kgs 24:17; Hebrew reads *brother,* or *relative.* **36:17** Or *Chaldeans.* **36:19** Or *destroyed all the valuable Temple utensils.*

until the kingdom of Persia came to power. [21]So the message of the LORD spoken through Jeremiah was fulfilled. The land finally enjoyed its Sabbath rest, lying desolate for seventy years, just as the prophet had said.

CYRUS ALLOWS THE EXILES TO RETURN

[22]In the first year of King Cyrus of Persia,* the LORD fulfilled Jeremiah's prophecy by stirring the heart of Cyrus to put this proclamation into writing and to send it throughout his kingdom:

[23]"This is what King Cyrus of Persia says: The LORD, the God of heaven, has given me all the kingdoms of the earth. He has appointed me to build him a Temple at Jerusalem in the land of Judah. All of you who are the LORD's people may return to Israel for this task. May the LORD your God be with you!"

36:22 The first year of Cyrus's reign was 538 B.C.

Ezra

With praise and thanks, they sang this song to the LORD: "He is so good! His faithful love for Israel endures forever!" Then all the people gave a great shout, praising the LORD because the foundation of the LORD's temple had been laid (3:11).

Rediscovering Our Roots

They say one can never "come home" again, as much as we may want to. Life changes. People move. The city or house may not feel, look, or even smell the same as it does in our memories! Yet, we yearn not so much to come back to a place as much as we long to return to our roots—the foundation of who we are, our hopes and dreams. This is the story told in the book of Ezra—the plight of God's people returning home after years of captivity in a foreign land, far from their roots.

They returned to a geographical place, Jerusalem. More significantly, however, they returned to the heart of God, back to making the worship of God the center point of their lives. They went to work rebuilding the destroyed Temple and scraping away the silt of a generation of disobedience from its foundation. While rebuilding the Temple they encountered resistance. Even so, they rediscovered much about the people they were called to be. Going home to their roots, they rediscovered the heart of worship.

Many people make a similar journey away from God. Perhaps, like Israel, we wander away due to disobedience, disinterest, or a season of discontent. Regardless of the reason for our wanderings, God woos us back to worship him again. At our homecoming, we rekindle intimacy with God and fellowship is restored. Like the Israelites returning to Jerusalem, we sense this is where we belong. And we hear God saying to us, "Welcome home."

Worship Moments

- The people came together, in community, to begin the long process of recovering true worship. They rebuilt the altar in order to worship God again with their sacrifices (3:1–2).

- Worship was done with great joy and extravagance, as the people dedicated the Temple to God (6:16–18).

- Fasting is one way to focus on worship. Ezra led the people in fasting and praying for God's protection (8:21).

- Worship must be done with clean hearts. Ezra mourned for and confessed the sins of the people, praying for God's mercy (9:1–15).

Cyrus Allows the Exiles to Return

1 In the first year of King Cyrus of Persia,* the LORD fulfilled Jeremiah's prophecy by stirring the heart of Cyrus to put this proclamation into writing and to send it throughout his kingdom:

²"This is what King Cyrus of Persia says: The LORD, the God of heaven, has given me all the kingdoms of the earth. He has appointed me to build him a Temple at Jerusalem in the land of Judah. ³All of you who are his people may return to Jerusalem in Judah to rebuild this Temple of the LORD, the God of Israel, who lives in Jerusalem. And may your God be with you! ⁴Those who live in any place where Jewish survivors are found should contribute toward their expenses by supplying them with silver and gold, supplies for the journey, and livestock, as well as a freewill offering for the Temple of God in Jerusalem."

⁵Then God stirred the hearts of the priests and Levites and the leaders of the tribes of Judah and Benjamin to return to Jerusalem to rebuild the Temple of the LORD. ⁶And all their neighbors assisted by giving them vessels of silver and gold, supplies for the journey, and livestock. They gave them many choice gifts in addition to all the freewill offerings.

⁷King Cyrus himself brought out the valuable items which King Nebuchadnezzar had taken from the LORD's Temple in Jerusalem and had placed in the temple of his own gods. ⁸Cyrus directed Mithredath, the treasurer of Persia, to count these items and present them to Sheshbazzar, the leader of the exiles returning to Judah.*

⁹These were the items Cyrus donated:

gold trays	30
silver trays	1,000
silver censers*	29
¹⁰ gold bowls	30
silver bowls	410
other items	1,000

¹¹In all, 5,400 gold and silver items were turned over to Sheshbazzar to take back to Jerusalem when the exiles returned there from Babylon.

Exiles Who Returned with Zerubbabel

2 Here is the list of the Jewish exiles of the provinces who returned from their captivity to Jerusalem and to the other towns of Judah. They had been deported to Babylon by King Nebuchadnezzar. ²Their leaders were Zerubbabel, Jeshua, Nehemiah, Seraiah, Reelaiah, Mordecai, Bilshan, Mispar, Bigvai, Rehum, and Baanah. This is the number of the men of Israel who returned from exile:

³ The family of Parosh	2,172
⁴ The family of Shephatiah	372
⁵ The family of Arah	775
⁶ The family of Pahath-moab (descendants of Jeshua and Joab)	2,812
⁷ The family of Elam	1,254
⁸ The family of Zattu	945
⁹ The family of Zaccai	760
¹⁰ The family of Bani	642
¹¹ The family of Bebai	623
¹² The family of Azgad	1,222
¹³ The family of Adonikam	666
¹⁴ The family of Bigvai	2,056
¹⁵ The family of Adin	454
¹⁶ The family of Ater (descendants of Hezekiah)	98
¹⁷ The family of Bezai	323
¹⁸ The family of Jorah	112
¹⁹ The family of Hashum	223
²⁰ The family of Gibbar	95
²¹ The people of Bethlehem	123
²² The people of Netophah	56
²³ The people of Anathoth	128
²⁴ The people of Beth-azmaveth*	42
²⁵ The peoples of Kiriath-jearim,* Kephirah, and Beeroth	743
²⁶ The peoples of Ramah and Geba	621

1:1 The first year of Cyrus's reign was 538 B.C. 1:8 Hebrew *Sheshbazzar, the prince of Judah.* 1:9 The meaning of this Hebrew word is uncertain. 2:24 As in parallel text at Neh 7:28; Hebrew reads *Azmaveth.* 2:25 As in some Hebrew manuscripts and Greek version (see also Neh 7:29); Hebrew reads *Kiriath-arim.*

My Daily Worship

— April 16 —

GOD WORKS OUTSIDE THE BOX

EZRA 1:1–3:13

In the first year of King Cyrus of Persia, the LORD fulfilled Jeremiah's
prophecy by stirring the heart of Cyrus to put this proclamation
into writing and to send it throughout his kingdom (1:1).

[i reflect]

It's not hard for us to comprehend that God would use other Christians to work in our lives and in our circumstances. We readily give him credit for the blessings that come our way through the church. What we don't expect, however, is for God to use our secular boss, our unbelieving friends, or even a pagan ruler to accomplish his plans.

The book of Ezra shows us that God's plans encompass it all—the secular and the sacred—and he will use whatever he chooses to move his story forward. God stirred the pagan heart of King Cyrus to issue a decree for the Jews to return home to Jerusalem to rebuild their Temple. Although Cyrus himself wasn't a worshiper, God used his desire to win the Jew's loyalty to bring good to his people. As Proverbs 21:1 reminds us, "The king's heart is like a stream of water directed by the LORD; he turns it wherever he pleases."

God is always taking the initiative to call his people to himself, and he will work through whatever means available to do so. Nothing is outside of God's power to control. He can stir the hearts of people who don't know him. He can use their misguided desires and work through their worldly roles. We can be glad that whenever we think we know how God works, he breaks out of our box. His boundless love uses anything to move his people one step closer to his plans for them.

Think about the people in your own life—believers and nonbelievers. How is God using them to work in your life? Take time to thank him that he is not bound by our preconceived ideas about who is "worthy" or not to do his bidding.

[i pray]

God, help me stop dividing my life into things you're "in" and things you're "not in." You are
God of everything. Open my eyes to your plans as they unfold in my workplace, in my
neighborhood, and in the world. Thank you for using it all to accomplish your will.

[i respond]

Choose a specific place where you spend much of your day—whether it's as a volunteer at school, at the workplace, or at home. Think about the various people you encounter there. Put them on your prayer list, and watch to see what God does.

27 The people of Micmash	122
28 The peoples of Bethel and Ai	223
29 The citizens of Nebo	52
30 The citizens of Magbish	156
31 The citizens of Elam	1,254
32 The citizens of Harim	320
33 The citizens of Lod, Hadid, and Ono	725
34 The citizens of Jericho	345
35 The citizens of Senaah	3,630

36These are the priests who returned from exile:

The family of Jedaiah (through the line of Jeshua)	973
37 The family of Immer	1,052
38 The family of Pashhur	1,247
39 The family of Harim	1,017

40These are the Levites who returned from exile:

The families of Jeshua and Kadmiel (descendants of Hodaviah)	74
41 The singers of the family of Asaph	128
42 The gatekeepers of the families of Shallum, Ater, Talmon, Akkub, Hatita, and Shobai	139

43The descendants of the following Temple servants returned from exile:
Ziha, Hasupha, Tabbaoth,
44 Keros, Siaha, Padon,
45 Lebanah, Hagabah, Akkub,
46 Hagab, Shalmai,* Hanan,
47 Giddel, Gahar, Reaiah,
48 Rezin, Nekoda, Gazzam,
49 Uzza, Paseah, Besai,
50 Asnah, Meunim, Nephusim,
51 Bakbuk, Hakupha, Harhur,
52 Bazluth, Mehida, Harsha,
53 Barkos, Sisera, Temah,
54 Neziah, and Hatipha.

55The descendants of these servants of King Solomon returned from exile:
Sotai, Sophereth,* Peruda,
56 Jaalah, Darkon, Giddel,

57 Shephatiah, Hattil, Pokereth-hazzebaim, and Ami.

58In all, the Temple servants and the descendants of Solomon's servants numbered 392.

59Another group returned to Jerusalem at this time from the towns of Tel-melah, Tel-harsha, Kerub, Addan, and Immer. However, they could not prove that they or their families were descendants of Israel. 60This group consisted of the families of Delaiah, Tobiah, and Nekoda—a total of 652 people.

61Three families of priests—Hobaiah, Hakkoz, and Barzillai—also returned to Jerusalem. (This Barzillai had married a woman who was a descendant of Barzillai of Gilead, and he had taken her family name.) 62But they had lost their genealogical records, so they were not allowed to serve as priests. 63The governor would not even let them eat the priests' share of food from the sacrifices until there was a priest who could consult the LORD about the matter by means of sacred lots.*

64So a total of 42,360 people returned to Judah, 65in addition to 7,337 servants and 200 singers, both men and women. 66They took with them 736 horses, 245 mules, 67435 camels, and 6,720 donkeys.

68When they arrived at the Temple of the LORD in Jerusalem, some of the family leaders gave generously toward the rebuilding of God's Temple on its original site, 69and each leader gave as much as he could. The total of their gifts came to 61,000 gold coins,* 6,250 pounds* of silver, and 100 robes for the priests.

70So the priests, the Levites, the singers, the gatekeepers, the Temple servants, and some of the common people settled in villages near Jerusalem. The rest of the people returned to the other towns of Judah from which they had come.

2:46 As in the marginal Qere reading of the Masoretic Text (see also Neh 7:48); Hebrew text reads Shamlai. 2:55 As in parallel text at Neh 7:57; Hebrew reads Hassophereth. 2:63 Hebrew consult the Urim and Thummim about the matter. 2:69a Hebrew 61,000 darics of gold, about 1,100 pounds or 500 kilograms in weight. 2:69b Hebrew 5,000 minas [3 metric tons].

THE ALTAR IS REBUILT

3 Now in early autumn,* when the Israelites had settled in their towns, all the people assembled together as one person in Jerusalem. ²Then Jeshua son of Jehozadak* with his fellow priests and Zerubbabel son of Shealtiel with his family began to rebuild the altar of the God of Israel so they could sacrifice burnt offerings on it, as instructed in the law of Moses, the man of God. ³Even though the people were afraid of the local residents, they rebuilt the altar at its old site. Then they immediately began to sacrifice burnt offerings on the altar to the LORD. They did this each morning and evening.

⁴They celebrated the Festival of Shelters as prescribed in the law of Moses, sacrificing the burnt offerings specified for each day of the festival. ⁵They also offered the regular burnt offerings and the offerings required for the new moon celebrations and the other annual festivals to the LORD. Freewill offerings were also sacrificed to the LORD by the people. ⁶Fifteen days before the Festival of Shelters began,* the priests had begun to sacrifice burnt offerings to the LORD. This was also before they had started to lay the foundation of the LORD's Temple.

THE PEOPLE REBUILD THE TEMPLE

⁷Then they hired masons and carpenters and bought cedar logs from the people of Tyre and Sidon, paying them with food, wine, and olive oil. The logs were brought down from the Lebanon mountains and floated along the coast of the Mediterranean Sea to Joppa, for King Cyrus had given permission for this.

⁸The construction of the Temple of God began in midspring,* during the second year after they arrived in Jerusalem. The work force was made up of everyone who had returned from exile, including Zerubbabel son of Shealtiel, Jeshua son of Jehozadak and his fellow priests, and all the Levites. The Levites who were twenty years old or older were put in charge of rebuilding the LORD's Temple. ⁹The workers at the Temple of God

---

Words of Worship

TEACHING

Teaching—Hebrew *mu-sar* "instruction"; *to-rah*, "instruction, law"; Greek *di-da-che* "teaching."

What's the purpose of teaching or instruction? In our culture, much teaching—especially in public education—is intended simply to impart information or skills. It's up to the learner to apply this learning in whatever way he or she sees fit. Teaching in the Bible has a different purpose: to help people "receive instruction in discipline, good conduct, and doing what is right, just, and fair" (Proverbs 1:3). Even the law or *torah* of Moses is not legislation as we understand it, but instruction, meant to equip the learner to live in a way that pleases God.

Christian teaching isn't just dispensing facts. Its purpose is "to equip God's people to do his work and build up the church, the body of Christ" (Ephesians 4:12). As we learn from the Word of God, whether in the worship assembly or in personal study and devotion, our question is, "How does this knowledge help me become a more committed, compassionate, and effective servant of the Lord Jesus Christ?" Often the best teaching comes through the godly example of others. Christian living, as is sometimes said, is "more caught than taught."

3:1 Hebrew *in the seventh month.* The year is not specific, so it may have been during Cyrus's first year (538 B.C.) or second year (537 B.C.). The seventh month of the Hebrew lunar calendar occurred in September/October 538 B.C. and October/November 537 B.C. **3:2** Hebrew *Jozadak,* a variant name for Jehozadak; also in 3:8. **3:6** Hebrew *On the first day of the seventh month.* This day of the Hebrew lunar calendar occurs in September or October. The Festival of Shelters began on the fifteenth day of the seventh month. **3:8** Hebrew *in the second month.* This month of the Hebrew lunar calendar occurred in April and May 536 B.C.

were supervised by Jeshua with his sons and relatives, and Kadmiel and his sons, all descendants of Hodaviah.* They were helped in this task by the Levites of the family of Henadad.

[10]When the builders completed the foundation of the LORD's Temple, the priests put on their robes and took their places to blow their trumpets. And the Levites, descendants of Asaph, clashed their cymbals to praise the LORD, just as King David had prescribed. [11]With praise and thanks, they sang this song to the LORD:

"He is so good!
His faithful love for Israel endures
forever!"

Then all the people gave a great shout, praising the LORD because the foundation of the LORD's Temple had been laid.

[12]Many of the older priests, Levites, and other leaders remembered the first Temple, and they wept aloud when they saw the new Temple's foundation. The others, however, were shouting for joy. [13]The joyful shouting and weeping mingled together in a loud commotion that could be heard far in the distance.

ENEMIES OPPOSE THE REBUILDING

4 The enemies of Judah and Benjamin heard that the exiles were rebuilding a Temple to the LORD, the God of Israel. [2]So they approached Zerubbabel and the other leaders and said, "Let us build with you, for we worship your God just as you do. We have sacrificed to him ever since King Esarhaddon of Assyria brought us here."

[3]But Zerubbabel, Jeshua, and the other leaders of Israel replied, "You may have no part in this work, for we have nothing in common. We alone will build the Temple for the LORD, the God of Israel, just as King Cyrus of Persia commanded us."

[4]Then the local residents tried to discourage and frighten the people of Judah to keep them from their work. [5]They bribed agents to work against them and to frustrate their aims. This went on during the entire reign of King Cyrus of Persia and lasted until King Darius of Persia took the throne.

LATER OPPOSITION UNDER KING ARTAXERXES

[6]Years later when Xerxes* began his reign, the enemies of Judah wrote him a letter of accusation against the people of Judah and Jerusalem. [7]And even later, during the reign of King Artaxerxes of Persia,* the enemies of Judah, led by Bishlam, Mithredath, and Tabeel, sent a letter to Artaxerxes in the Aramaic language, and it was translated for the king. [8]Rehum* the governor and Shimshai the court secretary wrote the letter, telling King Artaxerxes about the situation in Jerusalem. [9]They greeted the king for all their colleagues—the judges and local leaders, the people of Tarpel, the Persians, the Babylonians, and the people of Erech and Susa (that is, Elam). [10]They also sent greetings from the rest of the people whom the great and noble Ashurbanipal* had deported and relocated in Samaria and throughout the neighboring lands of the province west of the Euphrates River. [11]This is a copy of the letter they sent him:

"To Artaxerxes, from your loyal subjects
in the province west of the Euphrates
River.

[12]"Please be informed that the Jews who came here to Jerusalem from Babylon are rebuilding this rebellious and evil city. They have already laid the foundation for

---

3:9 Hebrew *sons of Judah* (i.e., *bene Yehudah*). *Bene* might also be read here as the proper name Binnui; *Yehudah* is probably another name for Hodaviah. Compare 2:40; Neh 7:43; 1 Esdras 5:58. **4:6** Hebrew *Ahasuerus*, another name for Xerxes. He reigned 486–465 B.C. **4:7** Artaxerxes reigned 465–424 B.C. **4:8** The original text of 4:8–6:18 is in Aramaic. **4:10** Aramaic *Osnappar*, another name for Ashurbanipal.

its walls and will soon complete them. [13]But we wish you to know that if this city is rebuilt and its walls are completed, it will be much to your disadvantage, for the Jews will then refuse to pay their tribute, customs, and tolls to you.

[14]"Since we are loyal to you as your subjects and we do not want to see you dishonored in this way, we have sent you this information. [15]We suggest that you search your ancestors' records, where you will discover what a rebellious city this has been in the past. In fact, it was destroyed because of its long history of sedition against the kings and countries who attempted to control it. [16]We declare that if this city is rebuilt and its walls are completed, the province west of the Euphrates River will be lost to you."

[17]Then Artaxerxes made this reply:

"To Rehum the governor, Shimshai the court secretary, and their colleagues living in Samaria and throughout the province west of the Euphrates River.

[18]"Greetings. The letter you sent has been translated and read to me. [19]I have ordered a search to be made of the records and have indeed found that Jerusalem has in times past been a hotbed of insurrection against many kings. In fact, rebellion and sedition are normal there! [20]Powerful kings have ruled over Jerusalem and the entire province west of the Euphrates River and have received vast tribute, customs, and tolls. [21]Therefore, issue orders to have these people stop their work. That city must not be rebuilt except at my express command. [22]Do not delay, for we must not permit the situation to get out of control."

[23]When this letter from King Artaxerxes was read to Rehum, Shimshai, and their colleagues, they hurried to Jerusalem and forced the Jews to stop building.

THE REBUILDING RESUMES

[24]The work on the Temple of God in Jerusalem had stopped, and it remained at a standstill until the second year of the reign of King Darius of Persia.*

5 At that time the prophets Haggai and Zechariah son of Iddo prophesied in the name of the God of Israel to the Jews in Judah and Jerusalem. [2]Zerubbabel son of Shealtiel and Jeshua son of Jehozadak* responded by beginning the task of rebuilding the Temple of God in Jerusalem. And the prophets of God were with them and helped them.

[3]But Tattenai, governor of the province west of the Euphrates, and Shethar-bozenai and their colleagues soon arrived in Jerusalem and asked, "Who gave you permission to rebuild this Temple and restore this structure?" [4]They also asked for a list of the names of all the people who were working on the Temple. [5]But because their God was watching over them, the leaders of the Jews were not prevented from building until a report was sent to Darius and he returned his decision.

TATTENAI'S LETTER TO KING DARIUS

[6]This is the letter that Tattenai the governor, Shethar-bozenai, and the other officials of the province west of the Euphrates River sent to King Darius:

[7]"Greetings to King Darius. [8]We wish to inform you that we went to the construction site of the Temple of the great God in the province of Judah. It is being rebuilt with specially prepared stones, and timber is being laid in its walls. The work is going forward with great energy and success. [9]We asked the leaders, 'Who gave you permission to rebuild this Temple and restore this structure?' [10]And we demanded their

---

4:24 The second year of Darius's reign was 520 B.C. 5:2 Aramaic *Jozadak*, a variant name for Jehozadak.

> The time has come for a revival
> of public worship as the finest of
> the fine arts . . . . While there is a call
> for strong preaching there is even a
> greater need for uplifting worship.
>
> ANDREW W. BLACKWOOD

names so that we could tell you who the leaders were.

[11]"This was their answer: 'We are the servants of the God of heaven and earth, and we are rebuilding the Temple that was built here many years ago by a great king of Israel. [12]But because our ancestors angered the God of heaven, he abandoned them to King Nebuchadnezzar of Babylon,* who destroyed this Temple and exiled the people to Babylonia. [13]However, King Cyrus of Babylon,* during the first year of his reign, issued a decree that the Temple of God should be rebuilt. [14]King Cyrus returned the gold and silver utensils that Nebuchadnezzar had taken from the Temple of God in Jerusalem and had placed in the temple of Babylon. These items were taken from that temple and delivered into the safekeeping of a man named Sheshbazzar, whom King Cyrus appointed as governor of Judah. [15]The king instructed him to return the utensils to their place in Jerusalem and to rebuild the Temple of God there as it had been before. [16]So this Sheshbazzar came and laid the foundations of the Temple of God in Jerusalem. The people have been working on it ever since, though it is not yet completed.'

[17]"So now, if it pleases the king, we request that you search in the royal archives of Babylon to discover whether King Cyrus ever issued a decree to rebuild God's Temple in Jerusalem. And then let the king send us his decision in this matter."

DARIUS APPROVES THE REBUILDING

6 So King Darius issued orders that a search be made in the Babylonian archives, where treasures were stored. [2]But it was at the fortress at Ecbatana in the province of Media that a scroll was found. This is what it said:

[3]"Memorandum:

"In the first year of King Cyrus's reign, a decree was sent out concerning the Temple of God at Jerusalem. It must be rebuilt on the site where Jews used to offer their sacrifices, retaining the original foundations. Its height will be ninety feet, and its width will be ninety feet.* [4]Every three layers of specially prepared stones will be topped by a layer of timber. All expenses will be paid by the royal treasury. [5]And the gold and silver utensils, which were taken to Babylon by Nebuchadnezzar from the Temple of God in Jerusalem, will be taken back to Jerusalem and put into God's Temple as they were before."

[6]So King Darius sent this message:

"To Tattenai, governor of the province west of the Euphrates River, to Shethar-bozenai, and to your colleagues and other officials west of the Euphrates:

"Stay away from there! [7]Do not disturb the construction of the Temple of God. Let it be rebuilt on its former site, and do not

---

5:12 Aramaic *Nebuchadnezzar the Chaldean.* 5:13 King Cyrus of Persia is here identified as the king of Babylon because Persia had conquered the Babylonian Empire. 6:3 Aramaic *Its height will be 60 cubits* [27 meters], *and its width will be 60 cubits.* It is commonly held that this verse should be emended to read: "Its height will be 45 feet, its length will be 90 feet, and its width will be 30 feet"; compare 1 Kgs 6:2. The emendation regarding the width is supported by the Syriac version.

My Daily Worship

— *April 17* —

How Much Do You Want It?

Ezra 4:1–6:22

There was great joy throughout the land because the LORD had changed
the attitude of the king of Assyria toward them, so that he helped
them to rebuild the Temple of God, the God of Israel (6:22).

[i reflect]

Real worship can be quite a challenge. The whole house may be quiet, until you pick up your Bible or sit down to pray. That's when the kids start arguing, the dog needs to go out, you remember the phone calls you haven't returned, and feel guilty for ignoring it all to worship God.

The scene Ezra describes is no different. The flesh, the devil, and the world all worked against God's people rebuilding the Temple. Their desire to put God first met with opposition from within and without.

First, enemies approached, deceitfully claiming their allegiance to God (4:2). What a picture of our lives. If we look closely inside, despite our soul's longing for God, parts of us still want to rebel. Our flesh values self-inflation, blessings, and ease above relationship with God.

Second, Satan tried to defeat God's people with bribes and frustration (4:5). Similarly, he bribes us with promises of more time if we'll just push worship aside. He tells us that taking care of other "needs," more than worship, will satisfy us.

Third, the world accused the Jews of disloyalty (4:13–14) in an effort to prohibit their progress. Still today when we spend time focusing on God, the world competes for our loyalty with its many worries and concerns.

Thankfully, God's people pushed through the obstacles and pursued God's plan to worship him. God rewarded their perseverance with great joy! As they did what they could, God did what only he could, and changed the king's attitude to grant them success. When nothing can stop our desire to put God first, he takes care of the rest.

[i pray]

Lord, forgive me for being so easily distracted from the one activity you want,
my worship. Help me see the obstacles to worship as enemies of my trust
and rest in you. Increase my desire to put you first and love you best.

[i respond]

In what areas of your life do you need to ensure that God is first? With your family? At your workplace? Within your ministry? Consider each area of your life and write down one or two ways that you can make God your top priority in that arena.

hinder the governor of Judah and the leaders of the Jews in their work. [8]Moreover I hereby decree that you are to help these leaders of the Jews as they rebuild this Temple of God. You must pay the full construction costs without delay from my taxes collected in your province so that the work will not be discontinued. [9]Give the priests in Jerusalem whatever is needed in the way of young bulls, rams, and lambs for the burnt offerings presented to the God of heaven. And without fail, provide them with the wheat, salt, wine, and olive oil that they need each day. [10]Then they will be able to offer acceptable sacrifices to the God of heaven and pray for me and my sons.

[11]"Those who violate this decree in any way will have a beam pulled from their house. Then they will be tied to it and flogged, and their house will be reduced to a pile of rubble.* [12]May the God who has chosen the city of Jerusalem as the place to honor his name destroy any king or nation that violates this command and destroys this Temple. I, Darius, have issued this decree. Let it be obeyed with all diligence."

THE TEMPLE'S DEDICATION

[13]Tattenai, governor of the province west of the Euphrates River, and Shethar-bozenai and their colleagues complied at once with the command of King Darius. [14]So the Jewish leaders continued their work, and they were greatly encouraged by the preaching of the prophets Haggai and Zechariah son of Iddo. The Temple was finally finished, as had been commanded by the God of Israel and decreed by Cyrus, Darius, and Artaxerxes, the kings of Persia. [15]The Temple was completed on March 12,* during the sixth year of King Darius's reign.

[16]The Temple of God was then dedicated with great joy by the people of Israel, the priests, the Levites, and the rest of the people who had returned from exile. [17]During the dedication ceremony for the Temple of God, one hundred young bulls, two hundred rams, and four hundred lambs were sacrificed. And twelve male goats were presented as a sin offering for the twelve tribes of Israel. [18]Then the priests and Levites were divided into their various divisions to serve at the Temple of God in Jerusalem, following all the instructions recorded in the Book of Moses.

CELEBRATION OF PASSOVER

[19]On April 21* the returned exiles celebrated Passover. [20]The priests and Levites had purified themselves and were ceremonially clean. So they slaughtered the Passover lamb for all the returned exiles, for the other priests, and for themselves. [21]The Passover meal was eaten by the people of Israel who had returned from exile and by the others in the land who had turned from their immoral customs to worship the LORD, the God of Israel. [22]They ate the Passover meal and celebrated the Festival of Unleavened Bread for seven days. There was great joy throughout the land because the LORD had changed the attitude of the king of Assyria* toward them, so that he helped them to rebuild the Temple of God, the God of Israel.

EZRA ARRIVES IN JERUSALEM

7 Many years later, during the reign of King Artaxerxes of Persia,* there was a man named Ezra. He was the son* of Seraiah, son of Azariah, son of Hilkiah, [2]son of Shallum, son of Zadok, son of Ahitub, [3]son of Amariah, son of Azariah, son* of Meraioth, [4]son of Zerahiah, son of Uzzi, son of Bukki, [5]son of Abishua, son of Phinehas, son of Eleazar, son of Aaron the high priest. [6]This Ezra was a scribe, well versed in the law of Moses, which

---

6:11 Aramaic *a dunghill.* 6:15 Aramaic *on the third day of the month Adar,* of the Hebrew calendar. This event occurred on March 12, 515 B.C.; also see note on 3:1. 6:19 Hebrew *On the fourteenth day of the first month,* of the Hebrew calendar. This event occurred on April 21, 515 B.C.; also see note on 3:1. 6:22 King Darius of Persia is here identified as the king of Assyria because Persia had conquered the Babylonian Empire, which included the earlier Assyrian Empire. 7:1a Artaxerxes reigned 465–424 B.C. 7:1b Or *descendant;* see 1 Chr 6:14. 7:3 Or *descendant;* see 1 Chr 6:6-10.

the LORD, the God of Israel, had given to the people of Israel. He came up to Jerusalem from Babylon, and the king gave him everything he asked for, because the gracious hand of the LORD his God was on him. [7]Some of the people of Israel, as well as some of the priests, Levites, singers, gatekeepers, and Temple servants, traveled up to Jerusalem with him in the seventh year of King Artaxerxes' reign.

[8]Ezra arrived in Jerusalem in August* of that year. [9]He had left Babylon on April 8* and came to Jerusalem on August 4,* for the gracious hand of his God was on him. [10]This was because Ezra had determined to study and obey the law of the LORD and to teach those laws and regulations to the people of Israel.

ARTAXERXES' LETTER TO EZRA

[11]King Artaxerxes had given a copy of the following letter to Ezra, the priest and scribe who studied and taught the commands and laws of the LORD to Israel:

[12]"Greetings* from Artaxerxes, the king of kings, to Ezra the priest, the teacher of the law of the God of heaven.

[13]"I decree that any of the people of Israel in my kingdom, including the priests and Levites, may volunteer to return to Jerusalem with you. [14]I and my Council of Seven hereby instruct you to conduct an inquiry into the situation in Judah and Jerusalem, based on your God's law, which is in your hand. [15]We also commission you to take with you some silver and gold, which we are freely presenting as an offering to the God of Israel who lives in Jerusalem.

[16]"Moreover you are to take any silver and gold which you may obtain from the province of Babylon, as well as the freewill offerings of the people and the priests that are presented for the Temple of their God in Jerusalem. [17]These donations are to be used specifically for the purchase of bulls, rams, lambs, and the appropriate grain offerings and drink offerings, all of which will be offered on the altar of the Temple of your God in Jerusalem. [18]Any money that is left over may be used in whatever way you and your colleagues feel is the will of your God. [19]But as for the utensils we are entrusting to you for the service of the Temple of your God, deliver them in full to the God of Jerusalem. [20]If you run short of money for anything necessary for your God's Temple or for any similar needs, you may requisition funds from the royal treasury.

[21]"I, Artaxerxes the king, hereby send this decree to all the treasurers in the province west of the Euphrates River: 'You are to give Ezra whatever he requests of you, for he is a priest and teacher of the law of the God of heaven. [22]You are to give him up to 7,500 pounds* of silver, 500 bushels* of wheat, 550 gallons of wine, 550 gallons of olive oil,* and an unlimited supply of salt. [23]Be careful to provide whatever the God of heaven demands for his Temple, for why should we risk bringing God's anger against the realm of the king and his sons? [24]I also decree that no priest, Levite, singer, gatekeeper, Temple servant, or other worker in this Temple of God will be required to pay taxes of any kind.'

[25]"And you, Ezra, are to use the wisdom God has given you to appoint magistrates and judges who know your God's laws to govern all the people in the province west of the Euphrates River. If the people are not familiar with those laws, you must teach them. [26]Anyone who refuses to obey the law of your God and the law of the king will be punished immediately by

---

7:8 Hebrew *in the fifth month.* This month of the Hebrew lunar calendar occurred in August and September 458 B.C. 7:9a Hebrew *on the first day of the first month,* of the Hebrew calendar. This event occurred on April 8, 458 B.C.; also see note on 3:1. 7:9b Hebrew *on the first day of the fifth month,* of the Hebrew calendar. This event occurred on August 4, 458 B.C.; also see note on 3:1. 7:12 The original text of 7:12-26 is in Aramaic. 7:22a Aramaic *100 talents* [3.4 metric tons]. 7:22b Aramaic *100 cors* [18.2 kiloliters]. 7:22c Aramaic *100 baths* [2.1 kiloliters] *of wine, 100 baths of olive oil.*

death, banishment, confiscation of goods, or imprisonment."

EZRA PRAISES THE LORD

[27] Praise the LORD, the God of our ancestors, who made the king want to beautify the Temple of the LORD in Jerusalem! [28] And praise him for demonstrating such unfailing love to me by honoring me before the king, his council, and all his mighty princes! I felt encouraged because the gracious hand of the LORD my God was on me. And I gathered some of the leaders of Israel to return with me to Jerusalem.

EXILES WHO RETURNED WITH EZRA

8 Here is a list of the family leaders and the genealogies of those who came with me from Babylon during the reign of King Artaxerxes:

[2] From the family of Phinehas: Gershom.
From the family of Ithamar: Daniel.
[3] From the family of David: Hattush son of Shecaniah.
From the family of Parosh: Zechariah and 150 other men.
[4] From the family of Pahath-moab: Eliehoenai son of Zerahiah and 200 other men.
[5] From the family of Zattu*: Shecaniah son of Jahaziel and 300 other men.
[6] From the family of Adin: Ebed son of Jonathan and 50 other men.
[7] From the family of Elam: Jeshaiah son of Athaliah and 70 other men.
[8] From the family of Shephatiah: Zebadiah son of Michael and 80 other men.
[9] From the family of Joab: Obadiah son of Jehiel and 218 other men.
[10] From the family of Bani*: Shelomith son of Josiphiah and 160 other men.
[11] From the family of Bebai: Zechariah son of Bebai and 28 other men.

[12] From the family of Azgad: Johanan son of Hakkatan and 110 other men.
[13] From the family of Adonikam, who came later*: Eliphelet, Jeuel, Shemaiah, and 60 other men.
[14] From the family of Bigvai: Uthai, Zaccur, and 70 other men.

EZRA'S JOURNEY TO JERUSALEM

[15] I assembled the exiles at the Ahava Canal, and we camped there for three days while I went over the lists of the people and the priests who had arrived. I found that not one Levite had volunteered to come along. [16] So I sent for Eliezer, Ariel, Shemaiah, Elnathan, Jarib, Elnathan, Nathan, Zechariah, and Meshullam, who were leaders of the people. I also sent for Joiarib and Elnathan, who were very wise men. [17] I sent them to Iddo, the leader of the Levites at Casiphia, to ask him and his relatives and the Temple servants to send us ministers for the Temple of God at Jerusalem. [18] Since the gracious hand of our God was on us, they sent us a man named Sherebiah, along with eighteen of his sons and brothers. He was a very astute man and a descendant of Mahli, who was a descendant of Levi son of Israel.* [19] They also sent Hashabiah, together with Jeshaiah from the descendants of Merari, and twenty of his sons and brothers, [20] and 220 Temple servants. The Temple servants were assistants to the Levites—a group of Temple workers first instituted by King David. They were all listed by name.

[21] And there by the Ahava Canal, I gave orders for all of us to fast and humble ourselves before our God. We prayed that he would give us a safe journey and protect us, our children, and our goods as we traveled. [22] For I was ashamed to ask the king for soldiers and horsemen to accompany us and protect us from enemies along the way. After all, we had told the king, "Our God protects all those who worship him, but his fierce anger

---

8:5 As in some Greek manuscripts (see also 1 Esdras 8:32); Hebrew lacks *Zattu*. 8:10 As in some Greek manuscripts (see also 1 Esdras 8:36); Hebrew lacks *Bani*. 8:13 The meaning of the Hebrew for this phrase is uncertain. 8:18 *Israel* is the name that God gave to Jacob.

rages against those who abandon him." ²³So we fasted and earnestly prayed that our God would take care of us, and he heard our prayer.

²⁴I appointed twelve leaders of the priests—Sherebiah, Hashabiah, and ten other priests—²⁵to be in charge of transporting the silver, the gold, the gold bowls, and the other items that the king, his council, his leaders, and the people of Israel had presented for the Temple of God. ²⁶I weighed the treasure as I gave it to them and found the totals to be as follows:

24 tons* of silver,
7,500 pounds* of silver utensils,
7,500 pounds* of gold,
²⁷ 20 gold bowls, equal in value to 1,000 gold coins,*
2 fine articles of polished bronze, as precious as gold.

²⁸And I said to these priests, "You and these treasures have been set apart as holy to the LORD. This silver and gold is a freewill offering to the LORD, the God of our ancestors. ²⁹Guard these treasures well until you present them, without an ounce lost, to the leading priests, the Levites, and the leaders of Israel at the storerooms of the LORD's Temple in Jerusalem." ³⁰So the priests and the Levites accepted the task of transporting these treasures to the Temple of our God in Jerusalem.

³¹We broke camp at the Ahava Canal on April 19* and started off to Jerusalem. And the gracious hand of our God protected us and saved us from enemies and bandits along the way. ³²So at last we arrived safely in Jerusalem, where we rested for three days.

³³On the fourth day after our arrival, the silver, gold, and other valuables were weighed at the Temple of our God and entrusted to Meremoth son of Uriah the priest and to Eleazar son of Phinehas, along with Jozabad son of Jeshua and Noadiah son of Binnui—both of whom were Levites. ³⁴Everything was accounted for by number and weight, and the total weight was officially recorded.

³⁵Then the exiles who had returned from captivity sacrificed burnt offerings to the God of Israel. They presented twelve oxen for the people of Israel, as well as ninety-six rams and seventy-seven lambs. They also offered twelve goats as a sin offering. All this was given as a burnt offering to the LORD. ³⁶The king's decrees were delivered to his lieutenants and the governors of the province west of the Euphrates River, who then cooperated by supporting the people and the Temple of God.

EZRA'S PRAYER CONCERNING INTERMARRIAGE

9 But then the Jewish leaders came to me and said, "Many of the people of Israel, and even some of the priests and Levites, have not kept themselves separate from the other peoples living in the land. They have taken up the detestable practices of the Canaanites, Hittites, Perizzites, Jebusites, Ammonites, Moabites, Egyptians, and Amorites. ²For the men of Israel have married women from these people and have taken them as wives for their sons. So the holy race has become polluted by these mixed marriages. To make matters worse, the officials and leaders are some of the worst offenders."

³When I heard this, I tore my clothing, pulled hair from my head and beard, and sat down utterly shocked. ⁴Then all who trembled at the words of the God of Israel came and sat with me because of this unfaithfulness of his people. And I sat there utterly appalled until the time of the evening sacrifice.

⁵At the time of the sacrifice, I stood up from where I had sat in mourning with my clothes torn. I fell to my knees, lifted my hands to the LORD my God. ⁶I prayed, "O my God, I am utterly ashamed; I blush to lift up my face to you. For our sins are piled higher than our

8:26a Hebrew *650 talents* [22 metric tons]. 8:26b Hebrew *100 talents* [3.4 metric tons]. 8:26c Hebrew *100 talents* [3.4 metric tons].
8:27 Hebrew *1,000 darics*, about 19 pounds or 8.6 kilograms in weight. 8:31 Hebrew *on the twelfth day of the first month*, of the Hebrew calendar. This event occurred on April 19, 458 B.C.; see note on 7:9a.

heads, and our guilt has reached to the heavens. [7]Our whole history has been one of great sin. That is why we and our kings and our priests have been at the mercy of the pagan kings of the land. We have been killed, captured, robbed, and disgraced, just as we are today.

[8]"But now we have been given a brief moment of grace, for the LORD our God has allowed a few of us to survive as a remnant. He has given us security in this holy place. Our God has brightened our eyes and granted us some relief from our slavery. [9]For we were slaves, but in his unfailing love our God did not abandon us in our slavery. Instead, he caused the kings of Persia to treat us favorably. He revived us so that we were able to rebuild the Temple of our God and repair its ruins. He has given us a protective wall in Judah and Jerusalem.

[10]"And now, O our God, what can we say after all of this? For once again we have ignored your commands! [11]Your servants the prophets warned us that the land we would possess was totally defiled by the detestable practices of the people living there. From one end to the other, the land is filled with corruption. [12]You told us not to let our daughters marry their sons, and not to let our sons marry their daughters, and not to help those nations in any way. You promised that if we avoided these things, we would become a prosperous nation. You promised that we would enjoy the good produce of the land and leave this prosperity to our children as an inheritance forever.

[13]"Now we are being punished because of our wickedness and our great guilt. But we have actually been punished far less than we deserve, for you, our God, have allowed some of us to survive as a remnant. [14]But now we are again breaking your commands and intermarrying with people who do these detestable things. Surely your anger will destroy us until even this little remnant no longer survives. [15]O LORD, God of Israel, you are just. We stand before you in our guilt as nothing but an escaped remnant, though in such a condition none of us can stand in your presence."

THE PEOPLE CONFESS THEIR SIN

10 While Ezra prayed and made this confession, weeping and throwing himself to the ground in front of the Temple of God, a large crowd of people from Israel—men, women, and children—gathered and wept bitterly with him. [2]Then Shecaniah son of Jehiel, a descendant of Elam, said to Ezra, "We confess that we have been unfaithful to our God, for we have married these pagan women of the land. But there is hope for Israel in spite of this. [3]Let us now make a covenant with our God to divorce our pagan wives and to send them away with their children. We will follow the advice given by you and by the others who respect the commands of our God. We will obey the law of God. [4]Take courage, for it is your duty to tell us how to proceed in setting things straight, and we will cooperate fully."

[5]So Ezra stood up and demanded that the leaders of the priests and the Levites and all the people of Israel swear that they would do as Shecaniah had said. And they all swore a solemn oath. [6]Then Ezra left the front of the Temple of God and went to the room of Jehohanan son of Eliashib. He spent the night* there, but he did not eat any food or drink. He was still in mourning because of the unfaithfulness of the returned exiles. [7]Then a proclamation was made throughout Judah and Jerusalem that all the returned exiles should come to Jerusalem. [8]Those who failed to come within three days would, if the leaders and elders so decided, forfeit all their property and be expelled from the assembly of the exiles.

[9]Within three days, all the people of Judah and Benjamin had gathered in Jerusalem. This took place on December 19,* and all the people were sitting in the square before the Temple of God. They were trembling both

---

10:6 As in parallel text at 1 Esdras 9:2; Hebrew reads *He went.*   10:9 Hebrew *on the twentieth day of the ninth month,* of the Hebrew calendar. This event occurred on December 19, 458 B.C.; also see note on 7:9a.

My Daily Worship

— April 18 —

MY STUPID SINS

EZRA 7:1–10:44

I prayed, "O my God, I am utterly ashamed; I blush to lift up my face to you. For our sins are piled higher than our heads, and our guilt has reached to the heavens" (9:6).

[i reflect]

Where do we get the strength to stand against sin? How can we live in a society that continually compromises without desiring to do the same? Why is sin so *not* worth it? Ezra knew the answer to all of these troubling questions was to worship God.

Ezra shines like a star among the darkened hearts of his people. They had disobeyed God by marrying unbelievers and accepting their pagan ways. Brokenhearted, Ezra mourned over such sin. He saw it so clearly and refused it so easily because he practiced three key elements of worship: He understood God's laws, experienced God's favor, and accepted his need for God.

First, in worship we affirm that everything God says and does is right. We see his laws, not as restrictive prohibitions against enjoyment, but as protective guidelines for abundant living. Then second, this leads us to abandon ourselves more and more into God's loving care for us. Through worship, we remember how much God cares for everything that matters to us, and we entrust him with our heart's desires. We're able to relax our sinful grasping and rest in his favor. Third, worship changes our demanding nature to one of humility that acknowledges, as Ezra did, "God of Israel, you are just. We stand before you . . . as nothing but an escaped remnant" (9:15).

Ezra was living proof that when we know God's Word (7:6), experience God's favor (7:28), and accept our dependency (9:15), nothing can entice us to return to life without him. In comparison, sin just seems plain stupid.

As you go through your daily activities, consider which of these three areas you need to grow in to remain in constant worship with God.

[i pray]

Dear God, I bring all that I know about myself into your presence.
Search me and show me the things that block my wholehearted
worship. Lead me to remove them so I might delight in you.

[i respond]

How resistant have you been to sins that surround you? If assessing yourself in this way is difficult, ask a friend to lovingly point out any sin that you may be harboring. Spend some time with God reading his Word, receiving his favor, and accepting your dependency on him.

because of the seriousness of the matter and because it was raining. [10]Then Ezra the priest stood and said to them: "You have sinned, for you have married pagan women. Now we are even more deeply under condemnation than we were before. [11]Confess your sin to the LORD, the God of your ancestors, and do what he demands. Separate yourselves from the people of the land and from these pagan women."

[12]Then the whole assembly raised their voices and answered, "Yes, you are right; we must do as you say!" [13]Then they added, "This isn't something that can be done in a day or two, for many of us are involved in this extremely sinful affair. This is the rainy season, so we cannot stay out here much longer. [14]Let our leaders act on behalf of us all. Everyone who has a pagan wife will come at the scheduled time with the leaders and judges of his city, so that the fierce anger of our God may be turned away from us concerning this affair." [15]Only Jonathan son of Asahel and Jahzeiah son of Tikvah opposed this course of action, and Meshullam and Shabbethai the Levite supported them.

[16]So this was the plan that they followed. Ezra selected leaders to represent their families, designating each of the representatives by name. On December 29,* the leaders sat down to investigate the matter. [17]By March 27 of the next year* they had finished dealing with all the men who had married pagan wives.

THOSE GUILTY OF INTERMARRIAGE

[18]These are the priests who had married pagan wives:

From the family of Jeshua son of Jehozadak* and his brothers: Maaseiah, Eliezer, Jarib, and Gedaliah. [19]They vowed to divorce their wives, and they each acknowledged their guilt by offering a ram as a guilt offering.

[20]From the family of Immer: Hanani and Zebadiah.

[21]From the family of Harim: Maaseiah, Elijah, Shemaiah, Jehiel, and Uzziah.

[22]From the family of Pashhur: Elioenai, Maaseiah, Ishmael, Nethanel, Jozabad, and Elasah.

[23]These are the Levites who were guilty: Jozabad, Shimei, Kelaiah (also called Kelita), Pethahiah, Judah, and Eliezer.

[24]This is the singer who was guilty: Eliashib.

These are the gatekeepers who were guilty: Shallum, Telem, and Uri.

[25]These are the other people of Israel who were guilty:

From the family of Parosh: Ramiah, Izziah, Malkijah, Mijamin, Eleazar, Hashabiah,* and Benaiah.

[26]From the family of Elam: Mattaniah, Zechariah, Jehiel, Abdi, Jeremoth, and Elijah.

[27]From the family of Zattu: Elioenai, Eliashib, Mattaniah, Jeremoth, Zabad, and Aziza.

[28]From the family of Bebai: Jehohanan, Hananiah, Zabbai, and Athlai.

[29]From the family of Bani: Meshullam, Malluch, Adaiah, Jashub, Sheal, and Jeremoth.

[30]From the family of Pahath-moab: Adna, Kelal, Benaiah, Maaseiah, Mattaniah, Bezalel, Binnui, and Manasseh.

[31]From the family of Harim: Eliezer, Ishijah, Malkijah, Shemaiah, Shimeon, [32]Benjamin, Malluch, and Shemariah.

[33]From the family of Hashum: Mattenai, Mattattah, Zabad, Eliphelet, Jeremai, Manasseh, and Shimei.

10:16 Hebrew *On the first day of the tenth month,* of the Hebrew calendar. This event occurred on December 29, 458 B.C.; also see note on 7:9a.   10:17 Hebrew *By the first day of the first month,* of the Hebrew calendar. This event occurred on March 27, 457 B.C.; also see note on 7:9a.   10:18 Hebrew *Jozadak,* a variant name for Jehozadak.   10:25 As in parallel text at 1 Esdras 9:26; Hebrew reads *Malkijah.*

³⁴From the family of Bani: Maadai, Amram, Uel, ³⁵Benaiah, Bedeiah, Keluhi, ³⁶Vaniah, Meremoth, Eliashib, ³⁷Mattaniah, Mattenai, and Jaasu.

³⁸From the family of Binnui*: Shimei, ³⁹Shelemiah, Nathan, Adaiah, ⁴⁰Macnadebai, Shashai, Sharai, ⁴¹Azarel, Shelemiah, Shemariah, ⁴²Shallum, Amariah, and Joseph.

⁴³From the family of Nebo: Jeiel, Mattithiah, Zabad, Zebina, Jaddai, Joel, and Benaiah.

⁴⁴Each of these men had a pagan wife, and some even had children by these wives.*

Nehemiah

During the dedication . . . . the Levites throughout the land were asked to come to Jerusalem to assist in the ceremonies. They were to take part in the joyous occasion with their songs of thanksgiving and with music of cymbals, lyres, and harps (12:27).

Roof-Raising Worship

Some trips are leisurely excursions for the purpose of pleasure, relaxation, and fun. Other trips we have to take because of a family emergency or for a job. Nehemiah's journey falls into the second category—a family emergency that became his God-given mission.

Thirteen years after Ezra had returned to Jerusalem, Nehemiah followed the same 900-mile route from Babylon to Jerusalem. He traveled with the urgency of someone racing to a rescue—every minute counted. The problem was strategic: Without defensive walls around the city, the Temple project would stall. All the construction lay vulnerable to regional thugs and marauders, of which there was no shortage. God led Nehemiah to take charge of building the walls around Jerusalem. Only then could the Temple be safely completed.

Most of the book of Nehemiah reads like a work roster: Baruch son of Sabbai built this, while Meremoth son of Uriah built that. But the plot takes a turn when Sanballat appeared with his side-kick Tobiah to harass and pester the workers. Nehemiah responded by organizing a militia. While half of the workers stood guard, the other half worked on the walls.

Nehemiah was a political person, close to power, and a capable administrator with a big heart for worship. Finally, when the wall was completed and Jerusalem was secure, he and Ezra responded with a real roof-raising worship experience. Work done, the people gathered to praise God.

As you read this book, look for how Nehemiah models prayer and worship as integral parts of his leadership.

Worship Moments

- The people gathered to hear God's law read as the day of worship began. They praised a God they could learn about. Their minds joined their hearts in praise (8:6).

- Repentance is often done in a mood of sorrow and guilt. But that mood must give way to the joy of forgiveness and reconciliation (8:9–10).

- Fasting is often part of worship, especially personal worship, but so is feasting (8:12).

- The people asked God for help, and made a solemn promise: "We will not neglect the Temple of our God" (10:39).

1

These are the memoirs of Nehemiah son of Hacaliah.

NEHEMIAH'S CONCERN FOR JERUSALEM

In late autumn of the twentieth year of King Artaxerxes' reign,* I was at the fortress of Susa. ²Hanani, one of my brothers, came to visit me with some other men who had just arrived from Judah. I asked them about the Jews who had survived the captivity and about how things were going in Jerusalem. ³They said to me, "Things are not going well for those who returned to the province of Judah. They are in great trouble and disgrace. The wall of Jerusalem has been torn down, and the gates have been burned."

⁴When I heard this, I sat down and wept. In fact, for days I mourned, fasted, and prayed to the God of heaven. ⁵Then I said, "O LORD, God of heaven, the great and awesome God who keeps his covenant of unfailing love with those who love him and obey his commands, ⁶listen to my prayer! Look down and see me praying night and day for your people Israel. I confess that we have sinned against you. Yes, even my own family and I have sinned! ⁷We have sinned terribly by not obeying the commands, laws, and regulations that you gave us through your servant Moses.

⁸"Please remember what you told your servant Moses: 'If you sin, I will scatter you among the nations. ⁹But if you return to me and obey my commands, even if you are exiled to the ends of the earth, I will bring you back to the place I have chosen for my name to be honored.'

¹⁰"We are your servants, the people you rescued by your great power and might. ¹¹O LORD, please hear my prayer! Listen to the prayers of those of us who delight in honoring you. Please grant me success now as I go to ask the king* for a great favor. Put it into his heart to be kind to me."

In those days I was the king's cup-bearer.

NEHEMIAH GOES TO JERUSALEM

2

Early the following spring,* during the twentieth year of King Artaxerxes' reign, I was serving the king his wine. I had never appeared sad in his presence before this time. ²So the king asked me, "Why are you so sad? You aren't sick, are you? You look like a man with deep troubles."

Then I was badly frightened, ³but I replied, "Long live the king! Why shouldn't I be sad? For the city where my ancestors are buried is in ruins, and the gates have been burned down."

⁴The king asked, "Well, how can I help you?"

With a prayer to the God of heaven, ⁵I replied, "If it please Your Majesty and if you are pleased with me, your servant, send me to Judah to rebuild the city where my ancestors are buried."

⁶The king, with the queen sitting beside him, asked, "How long will you be gone? When will you return?" So the king agreed, and I set a date for my departure.

⁷I also said to the king, "If it please Your Majesty, give me letters to the governors of the province west of the Euphrates River, instructing them to let me travel safely through their territories on my way to Judah. ⁸And please send a letter to Asaph, the manager of the king's forest, instructing him to give me timber. I will need it to make beams for the gates of the Temple fortress, for the city walls, and for a house for myself." And the king granted these requests, because the gracious hand of God was on me.

⁹When I came to the governors of the province west of the Euphrates River, I delivered the king's letters to them. The king, I should add, had sent along army officers and horsemen to protect me. ¹⁰But when Sanballat the Horonite and Tobiah the Ammonite official heard of my arrival, they were very angry that someone had come who was interested in helping Israel.

1:1 Hebrew *In the month of Kislev of the twentieth year.* A number of dates in the book of Nehemiah can be cross-checked with dates in surviving Persian records and related accurately to our modern calendar. This month of the Hebrew lunar calendar occurred in November and December 446 B.C. The *twentieth year* probably refers to the reign of King Artaxerxes I; compare 2:1; 5:14. 1:11 Hebrew *stand before this man.* 2:1 Hebrew *In the month of Nisan.* This month of the Hebrew lunar calendar occurred in April and May 445 B.C.

Nehemiah Inspects Jerusalem's Wall

[11]Three days after my arrival at Jerusalem, [12]I slipped out during the night, taking only a few others with me. I had not told anyone about the plans God had put in my heart for Jerusalem. We took no pack animals with us, except the donkey that I myself was riding. [13]I went out through the Valley Gate, past the Jackal's Well,* and over to the Dung Gate to inspect the broken walls and burned gates. [14]Then I went to the Fountain Gate and to the King's Pool, but my donkey couldn't get through the rubble. [15]So I went up the Kidron Valley* instead, inspecting the wall before I turned back and entered again at the Valley Gate.

[16]The city officials did not know I had been out there or what I was doing, for I had not yet said anything to anyone about my plans. I had not yet spoken to the religious and political leaders, the officials, or anyone else in the administration. [17]But now I said to them, "You know full well the tragedy of our city. It lies in ruins, and its gates are burned. Let us rebuild the wall of Jerusalem and rid ourselves of this disgrace!" [18]Then I told them about how the gracious hand of God had been on me, and about my conversation with the king.

They replied at once, "Good! Let's rebuild the wall!" So they began the good work.

[19]But when Sanballat, Tobiah, and Geshem the Arab heard of our plan, they scoffed contemptuously. "What are you doing, rebelling against the king like this?" they asked.

[20]But I replied, "The God of heaven will help us succeed. We his servants will start rebuilding this wall. But you have no stake or claim in Jerusalem."

Rebuilding the Wall of Jerusalem

3 Then Eliashib the high priest and the other priests started to rebuild at the Sheep Gate. They dedicated it and set up its doors, building the wall as far as the Tower of the Hundred, which they dedicated, and the Tower of Hananel. [2]People from the city of Jericho worked next to them, and beyond them was Zaccur son of Imri.

[3]The Fish Gate was built by the sons of Hassenaah. They did the whole thing—laid the beams, hung the doors, and put the bolts and bars in place. [4]Meremoth son of Uriah and grandson of Hakkoz repaired the next section of wall. Beside him were Meshullam son of Berekiah and grandson of Meshezabel, and then Zadok son of Baana. [5]Next were the people from Tekoa, though their leaders refused to help.

[6]The Old City Gate* was repaired by Joiada son of Paseah and Meshullam son of Besodeiah. They laid the beams, set up the doors, and installed the bolts and bars. [7]Next to them were Melatiah from Gibeon, Jadon from Meronoth, and people from Gibeon and Mizpah, the headquarters of the governor of the province west of the Euphrates River. [8]Next was Uzziel son of Harhaiah, a goldsmith by trade, who also worked on the wall. Beyond him was Hananiah, a manufacturer of perfumes. They left out* a section of Jerusalem as far as the Broad Wall.

[9]Rephaiah son of Hur, the leader of half the district of Jerusalem, was next to them on the wall. [10]Next Jedaiah son of Harumaph repaired the wall beside his own house, and next to him was Hattush son of Hashabneiah. [11]Then came Malkijah son of Harim and Hasshub son of Pahath-moab, who repaired the Tower of the Ovens, in addition to another section of the wall. [12]Shallum son of Hallohesh and his daughters repaired the next section. He was the leader of the other half of the district of Jerusalem.

[13]The people from Zanoah, led by Hanun, rebuilt the Valley Gate, hung its doors, and installed the bolts and bars. They also repaired the fifteen hundred feet* of wall to the Dung Gate.

2:13 Or *Serpent's Well.* **2:15** Hebrew *the valley.* **3:6** Or *The Mishneh Gate,* or *The Jeshanah Gate.* **3:8** Or *They restored.* **3:13** Hebrew *1,000 cubits* [450 meters].

My Daily Worship

— *April 19* —

LONGING FOR HOME

NEHEMIAH 1:1—4:23

They said to me, "Things are not going well for those who returned to the province of Judah.
They are in great trouble and disgrace. The wall of Jerusalem has been torn down,
and the gates have been burned." When I heard this, I sat down and wept. In fact,
for days I mourned, fasted, and prayed to the God of heaven (1:3–4).

[i reflect]

The opening verses of Nehemiah may strike us as just a factual account of the setting for the book and the reason for its being written. That is true; but something else about this passage is equally important, something that is easy to overlook.

Nehemiah was a Jew living in exile in Susa, the capital city of Persia near the Persian Gulf. He was in service to King Artaxerxes. *Nehemiah had never lived in Jerusalem.* For all we know, he had never even been there. Yet his heart turned to Jerusalem, the city of his ancestors, longing for it as his true home.

Is there a place like that in your memory? A place where life seemed happier, simpler, or at least less hectic? A place that you think of as *home?* Most of us would say yes, but even if earth holds no place like that for you, heaven does. There our heavenly Father waits to greet us as beloved children, and welcome us home with the words, "Well done."

Worship, whether corporate or individual, evokes in us a longing for a better world, a world where God himself will be with us, where he will remove all of our sorrows, and there will be no more death or sorrow or crying or pain, "for the old world and its evils are gone forever" (Revelation 21:4).

Nehemiah was homesick for a place he had never been before. He longed to go there. Worshiping God will have the same effect on us. As you come before him today, thank God for the place that he is preparing for you.

[i pray]

Father, awaken in me a desire for my rightful dwelling place, even as
I continue my sojourn through this far country. Help me not grow so
accustomed to my surroundings that I mistake them for home.

[i respond]

C. S. Lewis wrote that the "Christians who did most for the present world were those who thought most of the next." What do you think of when you hear the word heaven? Think of as many adjectives as you can to describe the home awaiting you there.

[14]The Dung Gate was repaired by Malkijah son of Recab, the leader of the Beth-hakkerem district. After rebuilding it, he hung the doors and installed the bolts and bars.

[15]Shallum son of Col-hozeh, the leader of the Mizpah district, repaired the Fountain Gate. He rebuilt it, roofed it, hung its doors, and installed its bolts and bars. Then he repaired the wall of the pool of Siloam* near the king's garden, and he rebuilt the wall as far as the stairs that descend from the City of David. [16]Next to him was Nehemiah son of Azbuk, the leader of half the district of Beth-zur. He rebuilt the wall to a place opposite the royal cemetery as far as the water reservoir and the House of the Warriors.

[17]Next was a group of Levites working under the supervision of Rehum son of Bani. Then came Hashabiah, the leader of half the district of Keilah, who supervised the building of the wall on behalf of his own district. [18]Next down the line were his countrymen led by Binnui* son of Henadad, the leader of the other half of the district of Keilah.

[19]Next to them, Ezer son of Jeshua, the leader of Mizpah, repaired another section of wall opposite the armory by the buttress. [20]Next to him was Baruch son of Zabbai, who repaired an additional section from the buttress to the door of the home of Eliashib the high priest. [21]Meremoth son of Uriah and grandson of Hakkoz rebuilt another section of the wall extending from a point opposite the door of Eliashib's house to the side of the house.

[22]Then came the priests from the surrounding region. [23]After them, Benjamin, Hasshub, and Azariah son of Maaseiah and grandson of Ananiah repaired the sections next to their own houses. [24]Next was Binnui son of Henadad, who rebuilt another section of the wall from Azariah's house to the buttress and the corner. [25]Palal son of Uzai carried on the work from a point opposite the buttress and the corner to the upper tower that projects from the king's house beside the court of the guard. Next to him were Pedaiah son of Parosh [26]and the Temple servants living on the hill of Ophel, who repaired the wall as far as the Water Gate toward the east and the projecting tower. [27]Then came the people of Tekoa, who repaired another section opposite the great projecting tower and over to the wall of Ophel.

[28]The priests repaired the wall up the hill

Words of Worship

ASSEMBLY, CONGREGATION

Assembly, Congregation—Hebrew *'e-dah* "congregation, assembly"; *qa-hal* "congregation, assembly"; Greek *ek-kle-si-a* "assembly, church."

In the intimacy and tender devotion of our personal time with the Lord, we should remember that, as the poet John Donne said, no one is an "island." As Christ's worshipers we are part of his body, pledged to bear the burdens of our brothers and sisters. For this reason, we don't neglect to meet with others for encouragement, as we look to Christ together (Hebrews 10:25).

The Bible often mentions the congregation, or assembly, of the people of God. The Greek word for the gathering of Christian believers, *ekklesia*, is related to the word for "call" and describes a community summoned for a special purpose. No other group of people in the world will do what the Christian assembly does. It lifts up the name of Jesus in prayer and celebration, and declares the goodness of God who "has called you out of the darkness into his wonderful light" (1 Peter 2:9). We are called to be a people of praise.

3:15 Hebrew *pool of Shelah,* another name for the pool of Siloam. **3:18** As in a few Hebrew manuscripts, some Greek manuscripts, and Syriac version (see also 3:24; 10:9); most Hebrew manuscripts read *Bavvai.*

from the Horse Gate, each one doing the section immediately opposite his own house. ²⁹Next Zadok son of Immer also rebuilt the wall next to his own house, and beyond him was Shemaiah son of Shecaniah, the gatekeeper of the East Gate. ³⁰Next Hananiah son of Shelemiah and Hanun, the sixth son of Zalaph, repaired another section, while Meshullam son of Berekiah rebuilt the wall next to his own house. ³¹Malkijah, one of the goldsmiths, repaired the wall as far as the housing for the Temple servants and merchants, opposite the Inspection Gate. Then he continued as far as the upper room at the corner. ³²The other goldsmiths and merchants repaired the wall from that corner to the Sheep Gate.

ENEMIES OPPOSE THE REBUILDING

4 Sanballat was very angry when he learned that we were rebuilding the wall. He flew into a rage and mocked the Jews, ²saying in front of his friends and the Samarian army officers, "What does this bunch of poor, feeble Jews think they are doing? Do they think they can build the wall in a day if they offer enough sacrifices? Look at those charred stones they are pulling out of the rubbish and using again!"

³Tobiah the Ammonite, who was standing beside him, remarked, "That stone wall would collapse if even a fox walked along the top of it!"

⁴Then I prayed, "Hear us, O our God, for we are being mocked. May their scoffing fall back on their own heads, and may they themselves become captives in a foreign land! ⁵Do not ignore their guilt. Do not blot out their sins, for they have provoked you to anger here in the presence of* the builders."

⁶At last the wall was completed to half its original height around the entire city, for the people had worked very hard. ⁷But when Sanballat and Tobiah and the Arabs, Ammonites, and Ashdodites heard that the work was going ahead and that the gaps in the wall were being repaired, they became furious. ⁸They all made plans to come and fight against Jerusalem and to bring about confusion there. ⁹But we prayed to our God and guarded the city day and night to protect ourselves.

¹⁰Then the people of Judah began to complain that the workers were becoming tired. There was so much rubble to be moved that we could never get it done by ourselves. ¹¹Meanwhile, our enemies were saying, "Before they know what's happening, we will swoop down on them and kill them and end their work."

¹²The Jews who lived near the enemy came and told us again and again, "They will come from all directions and attack us!"* ¹³So I placed armed guards behind the lowest parts of the wall in the exposed areas. I stationed the people to stand guard by families, armed with swords, spears, and bows.

¹⁴Then as I looked over the situation, I called together the leaders and the people and said to them, "Don't be afraid of the enemy! Remember the Lord, who is great and glorious, and fight for your friends, your families, and your homes!"

¹⁵When our enemies heard that we knew of their plans and that God had frustrated them, we all returned to our work on the wall. ¹⁶But from then on, only half my men worked while the other half stood guard with spears, shields, bows, and coats of mail. The officers stationed themselves behind the people of Judah ¹⁷who were building the wall. The common laborers carried on their work with one hand supporting their load and one hand holding a weapon. ¹⁸All the builders had a sword belted to their side. The trumpeter stayed with me to sound the alarm.

¹⁹Then I explained to the nobles and officials and all the people, "The work is very spread out, and we are widely separated from each other along the wall. ²⁰When you hear the

---

4:5 Or *for they have thrown insults in the face of.* 4:12 The meaning of the Hebrew is uncertain.

blast of the trumpet, rush to wherever it is sounding. Then our God will fight for us!"

²¹We worked early and late, from sunrise to sunset. And half the men were always on guard. ²²I also told everyone living outside the walls to move into Jerusalem. That way they and their servants could go on guard duty at night as well as work during the day. ²³During this time, none of us—not I, nor my relatives, nor my servants, nor the guards who were with me—ever took off our clothes. We carried our weapons with us at all times, even when we went for water.*

NEHEMIAH DEFENDS THE OPPRESSED

5 About this time some of the men and their wives raised a cry of protest against their fellow Jews. ²They were saying, "We have such large families. We need more money just so we can buy the food we need to survive." ³Others said, "We have mortgaged our fields, vineyards, and homes to get food during the famine." ⁴And others said, "We have already borrowed to the limit on our fields and vineyards to pay our taxes. ⁵We belong to the same family, and our children are just like theirs. Yet we must sell our children into slavery just to get enough money to live. We have already sold some of our daughters, and we are helpless to do anything about it, for our fields and vineyards are already mortgaged to others."

⁶When I heard their complaints, I was very angry. ⁷After thinking about the situation, I spoke out against these nobles and officials. I told them, "You are oppressing your own relatives by charging them interest when they borrow money!" Then I called a public meeting to deal with the problem.

⁸At the meeting I said to them, "The rest of us are doing all we can to redeem our Jewish relatives who have had to sell themselves to pagan foreigners, but you are selling them back into slavery again. How often must we

redeem them?" And they had nothing to say in their defense.

⁹Then I pressed further, "What you are doing is not right! Should you not walk in the fear of our God in order to avoid being mocked by enemy nations? ¹⁰I myself, as well as my brothers and my workers, have been lending the people money and grain, but now let us stop this business of loans. ¹¹You must restore their fields, vineyards, olive groves, and homes to them this very day. Repay the interest you charged on their money, grain, wine, and olive oil."

¹²Then they replied, "We will give back everything and demand nothing more from the people. We will do as you say." Then I called the priests and made the nobles and officials formally vow to do what they had promised.

¹³I shook out the fold of my robe and said, "If you fail to keep your promise, may God shake you from your homes and from your property!"

The whole assembly responded, "Amen," and they praised the LORD. And the people did as they had promised.

¹⁴I would like to mention that for the entire twelve years that I was governor of Judah—from the twentieth until the thirty-second year of the reign of King Artaxerxes*—neither I nor my officials drew on our official food allowance. ¹⁵This was quite a contrast to the former governors who had laid heavy burdens

> *If you truly meet God,*
> *you will worship;*
> *and if you truly worship,*
> *others will be drawn to God.*
>
> GERRIT GUSTAFSON

4:23 Hebrew *Each his weapon the water*. The meaning of the Hebrew is uncertain. 5:14 That is, from 445 to 433 B.C.

on the people, demanding a daily ration of food and wine, besides a pound* of silver. Even their assistants took advantage of the people. But because of my fear of God, I did not act that way. [16]I devoted myself to working on the wall and refused to acquire any land. And I required all my officials to spend time working on the wall. [17]I asked for nothing, even though I regularly fed 150 Jewish officials at my table, besides all the visitors from other lands! [18]The provisions required at my expense for each day were one ox, six fat sheep, and a large number of domestic fowl. And every ten days we needed a large supply of all kinds of wine. Yet I refused to claim the governor's food allowance because the people were already having a difficult time.

[19]Remember, O my God, all that I have done for these people, and bless me for it.

CONTINUED OPPOSITION TO REBUILDING

6 When Sanballat, Tobiah, Geshem the Arab, and the rest of our enemies found out that I had finished rebuilding the wall and that no gaps remained—though we had not yet hung the doors in the gates—[2]Sanballat and Geshem sent me a message asking me to meet them at one of the villages* in the plain of Ono. But I realized they were plotting to harm me, [3]so I replied by sending this message to them: "I am doing a great work! I cannot stop to come and meet with you."

[4]Four times they sent the same message, and each time I gave the same reply. [5]The fifth time, Sanballat's servant came with an open letter in his hand, [6]and this is what it said:

"Geshem* tells me that everywhere he goes he hears that you and the Jews are planning to rebel and that is why you are building the wall. According to his reports, you plan to be their king. [7]He also reports that you have appointed prophets to prophesy about you in Jerusalem, saying, 'Look! There is a king in Judah!'

"You can be very sure that this report will get back to the king, so I suggest that you come and talk it over with me."

[8]My reply was, "You know you are lying. There is no truth in any part of your story." [9]They were just trying to intimidate us, imagining that they could break our resolve and stop the work. So I prayed for strength to continue the work.

[10]Later I went to visit Shemaiah son of Delaiah and grandson of Mehetabel, who was confined to his home. He said, "Let us meet together inside the Temple of God and bolt the doors shut. Your enemies are coming to kill you tonight."

[11]But I replied, "Should someone in my position run away from danger? Should someone in my position enter the Temple to save his life? No, I won't do it!" [12]I realized that God had not spoken to him, but that he had uttered this prophecy against me because Tobiah and Sanballat had hired him. [13]They were hoping to intimidate me and make me sin by following his suggestion. Then they would be able to accuse and discredit me.

[14]Remember, O my God, all the evil things that Tobiah and Sanballat have done. And remember Noadiah the prophet and all the prophets like her who have tried to intimidate me.

THE BUILDERS COMPLETE THE WALL

[15]So on October 2* the wall was finally finished—just fifty-two days after we had begun. [16]When our enemies and the surrounding nations heard about it, they were frightened

5:15 Hebrew *40 shekels* [456 grams]. 6:2 As in Greek version; Hebrew reads *at Kephirim*. 6:6 Hebrew *Gashmu*, another name for Geshem. 6:15 Hebrew *on the twenty-fifth day of the month Elul*, of the Hebrew calendar. This event occurred on October 2, 445 B.C.; also see note on 1:1.

and humiliated. They realized that this work had been done with the help of our God.

[17]During those fifty-two days, many letters went back and forth between Tobiah and the officials of Judah. [18]For many in Judah had sworn allegiance to him because his father-in-law was Shecaniah son of Arah and because his son Jehohanan was married to the daughter of Meshullam son of Berekiah. [19]They kept telling me what a wonderful man Tobiah was, and then they told him everything I said. And Tobiah sent many threatening letters to intimidate me.

7 After the wall was finished and I had hung the doors in the gates, the gatekeepers, singers, and Levites were appointed. [2]I gave the responsibility of governing Jerusalem to my brother Hanani, along with Hananiah, the commander of the fortress, for he was a faithful man who feared God more than most. [3]I said to them, "Do not leave the gates open during the hottest part of the day.* And while the gatekeepers are still on duty, have them shut and bar the doors. Appoint the residents of Jerusalem to act as guards, everyone on a regular watch. Some will serve at their regular posts and some in front of their own homes."

NEHEMIAH REGISTERS THE PEOPLE

[4]At that time the city was large and spacious, but the population was small. And only a few houses were scattered throughout the city. [5]So my God gave me the idea to call together all the leaders of the city, along with the ordinary citizens, for registration. I had found the genealogical record of those who had first returned to Judah. This is what was written there:

[6]"Here is the list of the Jewish exiles of the provinces who returned from their captivity to Jerusalem and to the other towns of Judah.

They had been deported to Babylon by King Nebuchadnezzar. [7]Their leaders were Zerubbabel, Jeshua, Nehemiah, Seraiah,* Reelaiah,* Nahamani, Mordecai, Bilshan, Mispar,* Bigvai, Rehum,* and Baanah. This is the number of men of Israel who returned from exile:

[8]	The family of Parosh	2,172
[9]	The family of Shephatiah	372
[10]	The family of Arah	652
[11]	The family of Pahath-moab (descendants of Jeshua and Joab)	2,818
[12]	The family of Elam	1,254
[13]	The family of Zattu	845
[14]	The family of Zaccai	760
[15]	The family of Bani*	648
[16]	The family of Bebai	628
[17]	The family of Azgad	2,322
[18]	The family of Adonikam	667
[19]	The family of Bigvai	2,067
[20]	The family of Adin	655
[21]	The family of Ater (descendants of Hezekiah)	98
[22]	The family of Hashum	328
[23]	The family of Bezai	324
[24]	The family of Jorah*	112
[25]	The family of Gibbar*	95
[26]	The peoples of Bethlehem and Netophah	188
[27]	The people of Anathoth	128
[28]	The people of Beth-azmaveth	42
[29]	The peoples of Kiriath-jearim, Kephirah, and Beeroth	743
[30]	The peoples of Ramah and Geba	621
[31]	The people of Micmash	122
[32]	The peoples of Bethel and Ai	123
[33]	The people of Nebo	52
[34]	The citizens of Elam	1,254
[35]	The citizens of Harim	320
[36]	The citizens of Jericho	345
[37]	The citizens of Lod, Hadid, and Ono	721
[38]	The citizens of Senaah	3,930

[39]"These are the priests who returned from exile:

	The family of Jedaiah (through the line of Jeshua)	973
[40]	The family of Immer	1,052
[41]	The family of Pashhur	1,247
[42]	The family of Harim	1,017

7:3 Or *Keep the gates of Jerusalem closed until the sun is hot.* 7:7a As in parallel text at Ezra 2:2; Hebrew reads *Azariah.* 7:7b As in parallel text at Ezra 2:2; Hebrew reads *Raamiah.* 7:7c As in parallel text at Ezra 2:2; Hebrew reads *Mispereth.* 7:7d As in parallel text at Ezra 2:2; Hebrew reads *Nehum.* 7:15 As in parallel text at Ezra 2:10; Hebrew reads *Binnui.* 7:24 As in parallel text at Ezra 2:18; Hebrew reads *Hariph.* 7:25 As in parallel text at Ezra 2:20; Hebrew reads *Gibeon.*

My Daily Worship

— April 20 —

A JOB WELL DONE

NEHEMIAH 5:1–7:73

So on October 2 the wall was finally finished—just fifty-two days after we had begun. When our enemies and the surrounding nations heard about it, they were frightened and humiliated. They realized that this work had been done with the help of our God (6:15–16).

[i reflect]

The boy was so slow to learn to talk that his parents thought he was abnormal. His teachers called him a misfit. His classmates avoided him and seldom invited him to play with them. He failed his first college entrance exam at a college in Zurich, Switzerland. A year later he tried again. In time he became world-famous. His name? Albert Einstein.

Perhaps you have not achieved (yet) to the level of an Albert Einstein, but accomplishing something in spite of great difficulties or active opposition is cause for great satisfaction and pride. That's a normal reaction, and that sort of pride is not all wrong. As C. S. Lewis once observed, there are two kinds of pride. One is the opposite of humility, and that's bad; the other is the opposite of shame, and that's good. Taking pride in doing a job well is acceptable.

Nehemiah undoubtedly felt some of that when he and his fellow workers finished rebuilding the wall around Jerusalem in just fifty-two days. His opponents had mocked and scoffed, but Nehemiah's team had persevered and had overcome their opposition. Even so, he eschewed taking the credit himself, giving the accolades to God. This is an integral part of worship: giving God the honor and the tribute he deserves for the gifts he has given us—including our abilities, such as leadership and perseverance.

When we serve God faithfully, using our spiritual gifts, we have a sense of fulfillment and satisfaction, a sense of connectedness to him that we find nowhere else. This is true in our everyday lives and it is especially true in worship. When we offer praise and tribute to God for his goodness to us, we experience the completeness of knowing, "This is what I was born to do." Like Nehemiah surveying that improbable wall, take pride—the right kind of pride—in offering up to the Lord your accomplishments and abilities today.

[i pray]

Father, help me offer you the kind of worship you deserve. I can't do that in my own strength and ability, so I ask that you would by your grace make up for my lack. Help me give worship worthy of your holiness, majesty, mercy, and love.

[i respond]

What accomplishment has been a source of satisfaction and pride to you? Write a credit line to God for how he helped you accomplish this and thank him for what he is going to do.

⁴³"These are the Levites who returned from exile:

The families of Jeshua and Kadmiel
(descendants of Hodaviah*) 74
⁴⁴ The singers of the family of Asaph 148
⁴⁵ The gatekeepers of the families of
Shallum, Ater, Talmon, Akkub,
Hatita, and Shobai 138

⁴⁶"The descendants of the following Temple servants returned from exile:
Ziha, Hasupha, Tabbaoth,
⁴⁷ Keros, Siaha,* Padon,
⁴⁸ Lebanah, Hagabah, Shalmai,
⁴⁹ Hanan, Giddel, Gahar,
⁵⁰ Reaiah, Rezin, Nekoda,
⁵¹ Gazzam, Uzza, Paseah,
⁵² Besai, Meunim, Nephusim,*
⁵³ Bakbuk, Hakupha, Harhur,
⁵⁴ Bazluth,* Mehida, Harsha,
⁵⁵ Barkos, Sisera, Temah,
⁵⁶ Neziah, and Hatipha.

⁵⁷"The descendants of these servants of King Solomon returned from exile:
Sotai, Sophereth, Peruda,*
⁵⁸ Jaalah,* Darkon, Giddel,
⁵⁹ Shephatiah, Hattil, Pokereth-hazzebaim, and Ami.*

⁶⁰"In all, the Temple servants and the descendants of Solomon's servants numbered 392.

⁶¹"Another group returned to Jerusalem at this time from the towns of Tel-melah, Tel-harsha, Kerub, Addan,* and Immer. However, they could not prove that they or their families were descendants of Israel. ⁶²This group included the families of Delaiah, Tobiah, and Nekoda—a total of 642 people.

⁶³"Three families of priests—Hobaiah, Hakkoz, and Barzillai—also returned to Jerusalem. (This Barzillai had married a woman who was a descendant of Barzillai of Gilead, and he had taken her family name.) ⁶⁴But they had lost their genealogical records, so they were not allowed to serve as priests. ⁶⁵The governor would not even let them eat the priests' share of food from the sacrifices until there was a priest who could consult the LORD about the matter by means of sacred lots.*

⁶⁶"So a total of 42,360 people returned to Judah, ⁶⁷in addition to 7,337 servants and 245 singers, both men and women. ⁶⁸They took with them 736 horses, 245 mules,* ⁶⁹435 camels, and 6,720 donkeys.

⁷⁰"Some of the family leaders gave gifts for the work. The governor gave to the treasury 1,000 gold coins,* 50 gold basins, and 530 robes for the priests. ⁷¹The other leaders gave to the treasury a total of 20,000 gold coins* and some 2,750 pounds* of silver for the work. ⁷²The rest of the people gave 20,000 gold coins, about 2,500 pounds* of silver, and 67 robes for the priests.

⁷³"So the priests, the Levites, the gatekeepers, the singers, the Temple servants, along with some of the people—that is to say, all Israel—settled in their own towns."

EZRA READS THE LAW

Now in midautumn,* when the Israelites had settled in their towns, ¹all the people assembled together as one person at the square just inside the Water Gate. They asked Ezra the scribe to bring out the Book of the Law of Moses, which the LORD had given for Israel to obey.

8 ²So on October 8* Ezra the priest brought the scroll of the law before the assembly,

---

7:43 As in parallel text at Ezra 2:40; Hebrew reads *Hodevah.* **7:47** As in parallel text at Ezra 2:44; Hebrew reads *Sia.* **7:52** As in parallel text at Ezra 2:50; Hebrew reads *Nephushesim.* **7:54** As in parallel text at Ezra 2:52; Hebrew reads *Bazlith.* **7:57** As in parallel text at Ezra 2:55; Hebrew reads *Perida.* **7:58** As in parallel text at Ezra 2:56; Hebrew reads *Jaala.* **7:59** As in parallel text at Ezra 2:57; Hebrew reads *Amon.* **7:61** As in parallel text at Ezra 2:59; Hebrew reads *Addon.* **7:65** Hebrew *consult the Urim and Thummim about the matter.* **7:68** As in some Hebrew manuscripts (see also Ezra 2:66); most Hebrew manuscripts lack this verse. **7:70** Hebrew *1,000 darics of gold,* about 19 pounds or 8.6 kilograms in weight. **7:71a** Hebrew *20,000 darics of gold,* about 375 pounds or 170 kilograms in weight; also in 7:72. **7:71b** Hebrew *2,200 minas* [1.3 metric tons]. **7:72** Hebrew *2,000 minas* [1.2 metric tons]. **7:73** Hebrew *in the seventh month.* This month of the Hebrew lunar calendar occurred in October and November 445 B.C. **8:2** Hebrew *on the first day of the seventh month,* of the Hebrew calendar. This event occurred on October 8, 445 B.C.; also see note on 1:1.

which included the men and women and all the children old enough to understand. ³He faced the square just inside the Water Gate from early morning until noon and read aloud to everyone who could understand. All the people paid close attention to the Book of the Law. ⁴Ezra the scribe stood on a high wooden platform that had been made for the occasion. To his right stood Mattithiah, Shema, Anaiah, Uriah, Hilkiah, and Maaseiah. To his left stood Pedaiah, Mishael, Malkijah, Hashum, Hashbaddanah, Zechariah, and Meshullam. ⁵Ezra stood on the platform in full view of all the people. When they saw him open the book, they all rose to their feet.

⁶Then Ezra praised the LORD, the great God, and all the people chanted, "Amen! Amen!" as they lifted their hands toward heaven. Then they bowed down and worshiped the LORD with their faces to the ground.

⁷Now the Levites—Jeshua, Bani, Sherebiah, Jamin, Akkub, Shabbethai, Hodiah, Maaseiah, Kelita, Azariah, Jozabad, Hanan, and Pelaiah—instructed the people who were standing there. ⁸They read from the Book of the Law of God and clearly explained the meaning of what was being read, helping the people understand each passage. ⁹Then Nehemiah the governor, Ezra the priest and scribe, and the Levites who were interpreting for the people said to them, "Don't weep on such a day as this! For today is a sacred day before the LORD your God." All the people had been weeping as they listened to the words of the law.

¹⁰And Nehemiah* continued, "Go and celebrate with a feast of choice foods and sweet drinks, and share gifts of food with people who have nothing prepared. This is a sacred day before our Lord. Don't be dejected and sad, for the joy of the LORD is your strength!"

¹¹And the Levites, too, quieted the people, telling them, "Hush! Don't weep! For this is a sacred day." ¹²So the people went away to eat and drink at a festive meal, to share gifts of food, and to celebrate with great joy because they had heard God's words and understood them.

THE FESTIVAL OF SHELTERS

¹³On October 9* the family leaders and the priests and Levites met with Ezra to go over the law in greater detail. ¹⁴As they studied the law, they discovered that the LORD had commanded through Moses that the Israelites should live in shelters during the festival to be held that month.* ¹⁵He had said that a proclamation should be made throughout their towns and especially in Jerusalem, telling the people to go to the hills to get branches from olive, wild olive, myrtle, palm, and fig trees. They were to use these branches to make shelters in which they would live during the festival, as it was prescribed in the law.

¹⁶So the people went out and cut branches and used them to build shelters on the roofs of their houses, in their courtyards, in the courtyards of God's Temple, or in the squares just inside the Water Gate and the Ephraim Gate. ¹⁷So everyone who had returned from captivity lived in these shelters for the seven days of the festival, and everyone was filled with great joy! The Israelites had not celebrated this way since the days of Joshua son of Nun. ¹⁸Ezra read from the Book of the Law of God on each of the seven days of the festival. Then on October 15* they held a solemn assembly, as the law of Moses required.

THE PEOPLE CONFESS THEIR SINS

9 On October 31* the people returned for another observance. This time they fasted and dressed in sackcloth and sprinkled dust

8:10 Hebrew *he.* 8:13 Hebrew *On the second day,* of the seventh month of the Hebrew calendar. This event occurred on October 9, 445 B.C.; also see notes on 1:1 and 8:2. 8:14 Hebrew *in the seventh month.* This month of the Hebrew lunar calendar usually occurs in September and October. See Lev 23:39-43. 8:18 Hebrew *on the eighth day,* of the seventh month of the Hebrew calendar. This event occurred on October 15, 445 B.C.; also see notes on 1:1 and 8:2. 9:1 Hebrew *On the twenty-fourth day of that same month,* the seventh month of the Hebrew calendar. This event occurred on October 31, 445 B.C.; also see note on 1:1.

on their heads. [2]Those of Israelite descent separated themselves from all foreigners as they confessed their own sins and the sins of their ancestors. [3]The Book of the Law of the LORD their God was read aloud to them for about three hours.* Then for three more hours they took turns confessing their sins and worshiping the LORD their God. [4]Some of the Levites were standing on the stairs, crying out to the LORD their God. Their names were Jeshua, Bani, Kadmiel, Shebaniah, Bunni, Sherebiah, Bani, and Kenani.

[5]Then the leaders of the Levites—Jeshua, Kadmiel, Bani, Hashabneiah, Sherebiah, Hodiah, Shebaniah, and Pethahiah—called out to the people: "Stand up and praise the LORD your God, for he lives from everlasting to everlasting!"

Then they continued, "Praise his glorious name! It is far greater than we can think or say. [6]You alone are the LORD. You made the skies and the heavens and all the stars. You made the earth and the seas and everything in them. You preserve and give life to everything, and all the angels of heaven worship you.

[7]"You are the LORD God, who chose Abram and brought him from Ur of the Chaldeans and renamed him Abraham. [8]When he had proved himself faithful, you made a covenant with him to give him and his descendants the land of the Canaanites, Hittites, Amorites, Perizzites, Jebusites, and Girgashites. And you have done what you promised, for you are always true to your word.

[9]"You saw the sufferings and sorrows of our ancestors in Egypt, and you heard their cries from beside the Red Sea.* [10]You displayed miraculous signs and wonders against Pharaoh, his servants, and all his people, for you knew how arrogantly the Egyptians were treating them. You have a glorious reputation that has never been forgotten. [11]You divided the sea for your people so they could walk through on dry land! And then you hurled their enemies into the depths of the sea. They sank like stones beneath the mighty waters.

[12]You led our ancestors by a pillar of cloud during the day and a pillar of fire at night so that they could find their way.

[13]"You came down on Mount Sinai and spoke to them from heaven. You gave them regulations and instructions that were just, and laws and commands that were true. [14]You instructed them concerning the laws of your holy Sabbath. And you commanded them, through Moses your servant, to obey all your commands, laws, and instructions.

[15]"You gave them bread from heaven when they were hungry and water from the rock when they were thirsty. You commanded them to go and take possession of the land you had sworn to give them. [16]But our ancestors were a proud and stubborn lot, and they refused to obey your commands.

[17]"They refused to listen and did not remember the miracles you had done for them. Instead, they rebelled and appointed a leader to take them back to their slavery in Egypt! But you are a God of forgiveness, gracious and merciful, slow to become angry, and full of unfailing love and mercy. You did not abandon them, [18]even though they made an idol shaped like a calf and said, 'This is your god who brought you out of Egypt!' They sinned and committed terrible blasphemies. [19]But in your great mercy you did not abandon them to die in the wilderness. The pillar of cloud still led them forward by day, and the pillar of fire showed them the way through the night. [20]You sent your good Spirit to instruct them, and you did not stop giving them bread from heaven or water for their thirst. [21]For forty years you sustained them in the wilderness. They lacked nothing in all that time. Their clothes did not wear out, and their feet did not swell!

[22]"Then you helped our ancestors conquer great kingdoms and many nations, and you placed your people in every corner of the land. They completely took over the land of King Sihon of Heshbon and the land of King Og of Bashan. [23]You made their descendants

9:3 Hebrew *for a quarter of a day.* **9:9** Hebrew *sea of reeds.*

My Daily Worship

— April 21 —

LOOK UP!

NEHEMIAH 8:1–10:39

*You alone are the LORD. You made the skies and the heavens and all the stars. You made
the earth and the seas and everything in them. You preserve and give life
to everything, and all the angels of heaven worship you (9:6).*

[i reflect]

What natural phenomenon fills you most with awe and wonder? A beautiful sunrise or sunset . . .
waves crashing on a beach . . . a majestic, snowcapped mountain peak . . . whales breaching and
spraying water in a foaming frenzy . . . the night sky splashed with stars, glittering like diamonds
on black velvet . . . your newborn child . . . the development, growth, and intricate workings of the
human body?

As you stand awed and amazed, remember the One who ordained that the cosmos and our planet
should work in such a marvelous fashion, who formed us in his own image, and who holds it all
together by his will. (See Colossians 1:15–17.)

The One we worship is a God of beauty and order. Many early scientists were driven to discover
the great truths about nature and nature's laws by their logical convictions that the creation must
have a Creator and that natural laws must have been given by a Lawgiver. They were convinced,
as are a growing number of scientists today, that such a beautiful and well-ordered universe could
not be the result of accident and chance, but was engineered by an Intelligent Designer.

The Levites—Israel's worship leaders—expressed similar ideas as they exhorted the people that
day to worship the Lord, the Creator and Sustainer of the universe. That must have been some
worship service! But they didn't know what we know: how the first creation points toward the *new*
creation, when all things are made new in Christ.

The next time you have the opportunity to watch the sunrise in all its gold-orange-red-blue glory, or
hold a baby and marvel at the wonder of birth, be sure to give thanks to the One who created them.

[i pray]

*Lord, help me see you in all things, from the infinitesimal to the infinite. Remind me
that there is no corner of the universe where you are not present and sovereign.*

[i respond]

In his poem "The Tyger," William Blake penned the words, "What immortal hand or eye could
frame thy fearful symmetry?" From your vantage point, what can you see that inspires wonder at
the works of God? Pause right now and consider God's handiwork.

as numerous as the stars in the sky and brought them into the land you had promised to their ancestors. ²⁴They went in and took possession of the land. You subdued whole nations before them. Even the kings and the Canaanites, who inhabited the land, were powerless! Your people could deal with them as they pleased. ²⁵Our ancestors captured fortified cities and fertile land. They took over houses full of good things, with cisterns already dug and vineyards and olive groves and orchards in abundance. So they ate until they were full and grew fat and enjoyed themselves in all your blessings.

²⁶"But despite all this, they were disobedient and rebelled against you. They threw away your law, they killed the prophets who encouraged them to return to you, and they committed terrible blasphemies. ²⁷So you handed them over to their enemies. But in their time of trouble they cried to you, and you heard them from heaven. In great mercy, you sent them deliverers who rescued them from their enemies.

²⁸"But when all was going well, your people turned to sin again, and once more you let their enemies conquer them. Yet whenever your people cried to you again for help, you listened once more from heaven. In your wonderful mercy, you rescued them repeatedly! ²⁹You warned them to return to your law, but they became proud and obstinate and disobeyed your commands. They did not follow your regulations, by which people will find life if only they obey. They stubbornly turned their backs on you and refused to listen. ³⁰In your love, you were patient with them for many years. You sent your Spirit, who, through the prophets, warned them about their sins. But still they wouldn't listen! So once again you allowed the pagan inhabitants of the land to conquer them. ³¹But in your great mercy, you did not destroy them completely or abandon them forever. What a gracious and merciful God you are!

³²"And now, our God, the great and mighty and awesome God, who keeps his covenant of unfailing love, do not let all the hardships we have suffered be as nothing to you. Great trouble has come upon us and upon our kings and princes and priests and prophets and ancestors from the days when the kings of Assyria first triumphed over us until now. ³³Every time you punished us you were being just. We have sinned greatly, and you gave us only what we deserved. ³⁴Our kings, princes, priests, and ancestors did not obey your law or listen to your commands and solemn warnings. ³⁵Even while they had their own kingdom, they did not serve you even though you showered your goodness on them. You gave them a large, fertile land, but they refused to turn from their wickedness.

³⁶"So now today we are slaves here in the land of plenty that you gave to our ancestors! We are slaves among all this abundance! ³⁷The lush produce of this land piles up in the hands of the kings whom you have set over us because of our sins. They have power over us and our cattle. We serve them at their pleasure, and we are in great misery.

³⁸"Yet in spite of all this,* we are making a solemn promise and putting it in writing. On this sealed document are the names of our princes and Levites and priests."

THE PEOPLE AGREE TO OBEY

10 The document was ratified and sealed with the following names:

Nehemiah the governor, the son of Hacaliah. The priests who signed were Zedekiah, ²Seraiah, Azariah, Jeremiah, ³Pashhur, Amariah, Malkijah, ⁴Hattush, Shebaniah, Malluch, ⁵Harim, Meremoth, Obadiah, ⁶Daniel, Ginnethon, Baruch, ⁷Meshullam, Abijah, Mijamin, ⁸Maaziah, Bilgai, and Shemaiah. These were the priests.

⁹The Levites who signed were Jeshua son of Azaniah, Binnui from the family of

9:38 Or *Because of all this.*

Henadad, Kadmiel, [10]and their fellow Levites: Shebaniah, Hodiah, Kelita, Pelaiah, Hanan, [11]Mica, Rehob, Hashabiah, [12]Zaccur, Sherebiah, Shebaniah, [13]Hodiah, Bani, and Beninu.

[14]The leaders who signed were Parosh, Pahath-moab, Elam, Zattu, Bani, [15]Bunni, Azgad, Bebai, [16]Adonijah, Bigvai, Adin, [17]Ater, Hezekiah, Azzur, [18]Hodiah, Hashum, Bezai, [19]Hariph, Anathoth, Nebai, [20]Magpiash, Meshullam, Hezir, [21]Meshezabel, Zadok, Jaddua, [22]Pelatiah, Hanan, Anaiah, [23]Hoshea, Hananiah, Hasshub, [24]Hallohesh, Pilha, Shobek, [25]Rehum, Hashabnah, Maaseiah, [26]Ahiah, Hanan, Anan, [27]Malluch, Harim, and Baanah.

[28]The rest of the people—the priests, Levites, gatekeepers, singers, Temple servants, and all who had separated themselves from the pagan people of the land in order to serve God, and who were old enough to understand—[29]now all heartily bound themselves with an oath. They vowed to accept the curse of God if they failed to obey the law of God as issued by his servant Moses. They solemnly promised to carefully follow all the commands, laws, and regulations of the LORD their Lord.

THE VOW OF THE PEOPLE

[30]"We promise not to let our daughters marry the pagan people of the land, nor to let our sons marry their daughters. [31]We further promise that if the people of the land should bring any merchandise or grain to be sold on the Sabbath or on any other holy day, we will refuse to buy it. And we promise not to do any work every seventh year and to cancel the debts owed to us by other Jews.

[32]"In addition, we promise to obey the command to pay the annual Temple tax of an eighth of an ounce of silver,* so that there will be enough money to care for the Temple of our God. [33]This will provide for the Bread of the Presence; for the regular grain offerings and burnt offerings; for the offerings on the Sabbaths, the new moon celebrations, and the annual festivals; for the holy offerings; and for the sin offerings to make atonement for Israel. It will also provide for the other items necessary for the work of the Temple of our God.

[34]"We have cast sacred lots to determine when—at regular times each year—the families of the priests, Levites, and the common people should bring wood to God's Temple to be burned on the altar of the LORD our God, as required in the law.

[35]"We promise always to bring the first part of every harvest to the LORD's Temple—whether it be a crop from the soil or from our fruit trees. [36]We agree to give to God our oldest sons and the firstborn of all our herds and flocks, just as the law requires. We will present them to the priests who minister in the Temple of our God. [37]We will store the produce in the storerooms of the Temple of our God. We will bring the best of our flour and other grain offerings, the best of our fruit, and the best of our new wine and olive oil. And we promise to bring to the Levites a tenth of everything our land produces, for it is the Levites who collect the tithes in all our rural towns. [38]A priest—a descendant of Aaron—will be with the Levites as they receive these tithes. And a tenth of all that is collected as tithes will be delivered by the Levites to the Temple of our God and placed in the storerooms. [39]The people and the Levites must bring these offerings of grain, new wine, and olive oil to the Temple and place them in the sacred containers near the ministering priests, the gatekeepers, and the singers.

"So we promise together not to neglect the Temple of our God."

THE PEOPLE OCCUPY JERUSALEM

11 Now the leaders of the people were living in Jerusalem, the holy city, at this time. A tenth of the people from the other

---

10:32 Hebrew *tax of ⅓ of a shekel* [4 grams].

towns of Judah and Benjamin were chosen by sacred lots to live there, too, while the rest stayed where they were. [2]And the people commended everyone who volunteered to resettle in Jerusalem.

[3]Here is a list of the names of the provincial officials who came to Jerusalem. Most of the people, priests, Levites, Temple servants, and descendants of Solomon's servants continued to live in their own homes in the various towns of Judah, [4]but some of the people from Judah and Benjamin resettled in Jerusalem.

From the tribe of Judah: Athaiah son of Uzziah, son of Zechariah, son of Amariah, son of Shephatiah, son of Mahalalel, of the family of Perez; [5]and Maaseiah son of Baruch, son of Col-hozeh, son of Hazaiah, son of Adaiah, son of Joiarib, son of Zechariah, of the family of Shelah.*
[6]There were also 468 descendants of Perez who lived in Jerusalem—all outstanding men.
[7]From the tribe of Benjamin: Sallu son of Meshullam, son of Joed, son of Pedaiah, son of Kolaiah, son of Maaseiah, son of Ithiel, son of Jeshaiah; [8]and after him there were Gabbai and Sallai, and a total of 928 relatives. [9]Their chief officer was Joel son of Zicri, who was assisted by Judah son of Hassenuah, second-in-command over the city.
[10]From the priests: Jedaiah son of Joiarib; Jakin; [11]and Seraiah son of Hilkiah, son of Meshullam, son of Zadok, son of Meraioth, son of Ahitub, the supervisor of the Temple of God; [12]together with 822 of their associates, who worked at the Temple. Also, there was Adaiah son of Jeroham, son of Pelaliah, son of Amzi, son of Zechariah, son of Pashhur, son of Malkijah; [13]and 242 of his associates, who were heads of their families. There were also Amashsai son of Azarel, son of Ahzai, son of Meshillemoth, son of Immer; [14]and 128 of his outstanding associates. Their

chief officer was Zabdiel son of Haggedolim.
[15]From the Levites: Shemaiah son of Hasshub, son of Azrikam, son of Hashabiah, son of Bunni; [16]Shabbethai and Jozabad, who were in charge of the work outside the Temple of God; [17]Mattaniah son of Mica, son of Zabdi, a descendant of Asaph, who opened the thanksgiving services with prayer; Bakbukiah, who was Mattaniah's assistant; and Abda son of Shammua, son of Galal, son of Jeduthun. [18]In all, there were 284 Levites in the holy city.
[19]From the gatekeepers: Akkub, Talmon, and 172 of their associates, who guarded the gates.

[20]The other priests, Levites, and the rest of the Israelites lived wherever their family inheritance was located in any of the towns of Judah. [21]However, the Temple servants, whose leaders were Ziha and Gishpa, all lived on the hill of Ophel.
[22]The chief officer of the Levites in Jerusalem was Uzzi son of Bani, son of Hashabiah, son of Mattaniah, son of Mica, a descendant of Asaph, whose family served as singers at God's Temple. [23]They were under royal orders, which determined their daily activities.
[24]Pethahiah son of Meshezabel, a descendant of Zerah son of Judah, was the king's agent in all matters of public administration.
[25]Some of the people of Judah lived in Kiriath-arba with its villages, Dibon with its villages, and Jekabzeel with its villages. [26]They also lived in Jeshua, Moladah, Beth-pelet, [27]Hazar-shual, Beersheba with its villages, [28]Ziklag, and Meconah with its villages. [29]They were also in En-rimmon, Zorah, Jarmuth, [30]Zanoah, and Adullam with their villages. They were also in Lachish and its nearby fields and Azekah with its surrounding villages. So the people of Judah were living all the way from Beersheba to the valley of Hinnom. [31]Some of the people of Benjamin lived

11:5 Hebrew *son of the Shilonite.*

at Geba, Micmash, Aija, and Bethel with its surrounding villages. [32]They were also in Anathoth, Nob, Ananiah, [33]Hazor, Ramah, Gittaim, [34]Hadid, Zeboim, Neballat, [35]Lod, Ono, and the Valley of Craftsmen.* [36]Some of the Levites who lived in Judah were sent to live with the tribe of Benjamin.

A History of the Priests and Levites

12 Here is the list of the priests and Levites who had returned with Zerubbabel son of Shealtiel and Jeshua the high priest:

Seraiah, Jeremiah, Ezra,
[2] Amariah, Malluch, Hattush,
[3] Shecaniah, Harim,* Meremoth,
[4] Iddo, Ginnethon,* Abijah,
[5] Miniamin, Moadiah,* Bilgah,
[6] Shemaiah, Joiarib, Jedaiah,
[7] Sallu, Amok, Hilkiah, and Jedaiah.

These were the leaders of the priests and their associates in the days of Jeshua.

[8]The Levites who had returned with them were Jeshua, Binnui, Kadmiel, Sherebiah, Judah, and Mattaniah, who with his associates was in charge of the songs of thanksgiving. [9]Their associates, Bakbukiah and Unni, stood opposite them during the service.

[10] Jeshua the high priest was the father of Joiakim.
Joiakim was the father of Eliashib.
Eliashib was the father of Joiada.
[11] Joiada was the father of Johanan.*
Johanan was the father of Jaddua.

[12]Now when Joiakim was high priest, the family leaders of the priests were as follows:

Meraiah was leader of the family of Seraiah.
Hananiah was leader of the family of Jeremiah.
[13] Meshullam was leader of the family of Ezra.
Jehohanan was leader of the family of Amariah.
[14] Jonathan was leader of the family of Malluch.*
Joseph was leader of the family of Shecaniah.*
[15] Adna was leader of the family of Harim.
Helkai was leader of the family of Meremoth.*
[16] Zechariah was leader of the family of Iddo.
Meshullam was leader of the family of Ginnethon.
[17] Zicri was leader of the family of Abijah.
There was also a* leader of the family of Miniamin.
Piltai was leader of the family of Moadiah.
[18] Shammua was leader of the family of Bilgah.
Jehonathan was leader of the family of Shemaiah.
[19] Mattenai was leader of the family of Joiarib.
Uzzi was leader of the family of Jedaiah.
[20] Kallai was leader of the family of Sallu.*
Eber was leader of the family of Amok.
[21] Hashabiah was leader of the family of Hilkiah.
Nethanel was leader of the family of Jedaiah.

[22]During the reign of Darius II of Persia,* a list was compiled of the family leaders of the Levites and the priests in the days of the following high priests: Eliashib, Joiada, Johanan, and Jaddua. [23]The heads of the Levite families were recorded in *The Book of History* down to the days of Johanan, the grandson* of Eliashib.

11:35 Or *and Ge-harashim.* 12:3 Hebrew *Rehum;* compare 7:42; 12:15; Ezra 2:39. 12:4 As in some Hebrew manuscripts and Latin Vulgate (see also 12:16); most Hebrew manuscripts read *Ginnethoi.* 12:5 Hebrew *Mijamin, Maadiah;* compare 12:17. 12:11 Hebrew *Jonathan;* compare 12:22. 12:14a As in Greek version (see also 10:4; 12:2); Hebrew reads *Malluchi.* 12:14b As in many Hebrew manuscripts, some Greek manuscripts, and Syriac version (see also 12:3); most Hebrew manuscripts read *Shebaniah.* 12:15 As in some Greek manuscripts (see also 12:3); Hebrew reads *Meraioth.* 12:17 Hebrew lacks the name of this family leader. 12:20 Hebrew *Sallai;* compare 12:7. 12:22 Hebrew *Darius the Persian.* 12:23 Hebrew *son;* compare 12:10-11.

[24]These were the family leaders of the Levites: Hashabiah, Sherebiah, Jeshua, Binnui,* Kadmiel, and other associates, who stood opposite them during the ceremonies of praise and thanksgiving, one section responding to the other, just as commanded by David, the man of God. [25]This included Mattaniah, Bakbukiah, and Obadiah.

Meshullam, Talmon, and Akkub were the gatekeepers in charge of the storerooms at the gates. [26]These all served in the days of Joiakim son of Jeshua, son of Jehozadak,* and in the days of Nehemiah the governor and of Ezra the priest and scribe.

DEDICATION OF JERUSALEM'S WALL

[27]During the dedication of the new wall of Jerusalem, the Levites throughout the land were asked to come to Jerusalem to assist in the ceremonies. They were to take part in the joyous occasion with their songs of thanksgiving and with the music of cymbals, lyres, and harps. [28]The singers were brought together from Jerusalem and its surrounding villages and from the villages of the Netophathites. [29]They also came from Beth-gilgal and the area of Geba and Azmaveth, for the singers had built their own villages around Jerusalem. [30]The priests and Levites first dedicated themselves, then the people, the gates, and the wall.

[31]I led the leaders of Judah to the top of the wall and organized two large choirs to give thanks. One of the choirs proceeded southward* along the top of the wall to the Dung Gate. [32]Hoshaiah and half the leaders of Judah followed them, [33]along with Azariah, Ezra, Meshullam, [34]Judah, Benjamin, Shemaiah, Jeremiah, [35]and some priests who played trumpets. Then came Zechariah son of Jonathan, son of Shemaiah, son of Mattaniah, son of Micaiah, son of Zaccur, a descendant of Asaph. [36]And finally came Zechariah's colleagues Shemaiah, Azarel, Milalai, Gilalai, Maai, Nethanel, Judah, and Hanani. They used the musical instruments prescribed by David, the man of God. Ezra the scribe led this procession. [37]At the Fountain Gate they went straight up the steps on the ascent of the city wall toward the City of David. They passed the house of David and then proceeded to the Water Gate on the east.

[38]The second choir went northward* around the other way to meet them. I followed them, with the other half of the people, along the top of the wall past the Tower of the Ovens to the Broad Wall, [39]then past the Ephraim Gate to the Old City Gate,* past the Fish Gate and the Tower of Hananel, and went on to the Tower of the Hundred. Then we continued on to the Sheep Gate and stopped at the Guard Gate.

[40]The two choirs that were giving thanks then proceeded to the Temple of God, where they took their places. So did I, together with the group of leaders who were with me. [41]We went together with the trumpet-playing priests—Eliakim, Maaseiah, Miniamin, Micaiah, Elioenai, Zechariah, and Hananiah—[42]and the singers—Maaseiah, Shemaiah, Eleazar, Uzzi, Jehohanan, Malkijah, Elam, and Ezer. They played and sang loudly and clearly under the direction of Jezrahiah the choir director.

[43]Many sacrifices were offered on that joyous day, for God had given the people cause for great joy. The women and children also participated in the celebration, and the joy of the people of Jerusalem could be heard far away.

PROVISIONS FOR TEMPLE WORSHIP

[44]On that day men were appointed to be in charge of the storerooms for the gifts, the first part of the harvest, and the tithes. They were responsible to collect these from the fields as required by the law for the priests and Levites,

---

12:24 Hebrew *son of* (i.e., *ben*), which should probably be read here as the proper name Binnui; compare Ezra 3:9 and the note there. 12:26 Hebrew *Jozadak*, a variant name for Jehozadak. 12:31 Hebrew *to the right*. 12:38 Hebrew *to the left*. 12:39 Or *the Mishneh Gate*, or *the Jeshanah Gate*.

My Daily Worship

— April 22 —

NOT JUST A SPECTATOR SPORT

NEHEMIAH 11:1–13:31

Here is the list of the priests and Levites who had returned with Zerubbabel son
of Shealtiel and Jeshua the high priest: Seraiah, Jeremiah, Ezra, . . . (12:1).

[i reflect]

Most people tend to skip this kind of chapter in their devotional reading. What could be duller than a list of people who attended a religious ceremony in Jerusalem in 444 B.C.? These men, women, and young people are completely unknown (except for Nehemiah, Ezra, and maybe Asaph). Yet they have something important to teach us about worship.

For one thing, *biblical worship is not a spectator sport.* Judging from the names included in Nehemiah 12, it would have been easier to name the people who were *not* involved in this worship service. The list includes priests, Levites, singers, trumpet players, choirs, scribes, and the governor himself—and those are just the people *on the wall* surrounding the city. Worship is meant to involve *everyone*, not just the worship leaders and the "professionals."

For another, *biblical worship places great emphasis on holiness.* In Nehemiah 12:30, the word translated "dedicated" means to cleanse or purify. In other words, we don't come into the presence of a holy God in a slovenly, disrespectful way, but with our best and purest efforts.

And finally, *biblical worship places a premium on joy.* Nehemiah 12:43 alone uses the root word for "joy" four times. Worship must be reverent, of course, and never flippant or shallow, but it should be joyful. If God is in the house, there will be joy. Not cheap, superficial laughter—the kind you get watching most sitcoms—but real, genuine, heartfelt joy.

C. S. Lewis wrote, "We are half-hearted creatures, fooling about with drink and sex and ambition when infinite joy is offered us, like an ignorant child who wants to go on making mud pies in a slum because he cannot imagine what is meant by the offer of a holiday at the sea. We are far too easily pleased."

Participation, holiness, joy . . . are these present in your worship? Have you experienced the fullness and richness of true worship? If not, ask God to help you grow in these areas.

[i pray]

Father, help me worship you with all my heart, soul, mind, body, and will. Grant that
I will never again be satisfied with going through the motions. Give me a hunger
for your holiness and a sense of the true joy to be found only in you.

[i respond]

Write down these three headings: participation, holiness, joy. Consider how you have experienced each of these in your worship. Jot down how you can incorporate these elements into your worship.

for all the people of Judah valued the priests and Levites and their work. ⁴⁵They performed the service of their God and the service of purification, as required by the laws of David and his son Solomon, and so did the singers and the gatekeepers. ⁴⁶The custom of having choir directors to lead the choirs in hymns of praise and thanks to God began long ago in the days of David and Asaph. ⁴⁷So now, in the days of Zerubbabel and of Nehemiah, the people brought a daily supply of food for the singers, the gatekeepers, and the Levites. The Levites, in turn, gave a portion of what they received to the priests, the descendants of Aaron.

NEHEMIAH'S VARIOUS REFORMS

13 On that same day, as the Book of Moses was being read, the people found a statement which said that no Ammonite or Moabite should ever be permitted to enter the assembly of God. ²For they had not been friendly to the Israelites when they left Egypt. Instead, they hired Balaam to curse them, though our God turned the curse into a blessing. ³When this law was read, all those of mixed ancestry were immediately expelled from the assembly.

⁴Before this had happened, Eliashib the priest, who had been appointed as supervisor of the storerooms of the Temple of our God and who was also a relative of Tobiah, ⁵had converted a large storage room and placed it at Tobiah's disposal. The room had previously been used for storing the grain offerings, frankincense, Temple utensils, and tithes of grain, new wine, olive oil, and the special portion set aside for the priests. Moses had decreed that these offerings belonged to the Levites, the singers, and the gatekeepers.

⁶I was not in Jerusalem at that time, for I had returned to the king in the thirty-second year of the reign of King Artaxerxes of Babylon,* though I later received his permission to return. ⁷When I arrived back in Jerusalem and learned the extent of this evil deed of Eliashib—that he had provided Tobiah with a room in the courtyards of the Temple of God—⁸I became very upset and threw all of Tobiah's belongings from the room. ⁹Then I demanded that the rooms be purified, and I brought back the utensils for God's Temple, the grain offerings, and the frankincense.

¹⁰I also discovered that the Levites had not been given what was due them, so they and the singers who were to conduct the worship services had all returned to work their fields. ¹¹I immediately confronted the leaders and demanded, "Why has the Temple of God been neglected?" Then I called all the Levites back again and restored them to their proper duties. ¹²And once more all the people of Judah began bringing their tithes of grain, new wine, and olive oil to the Temple storerooms.

¹³I put Shelemiah the priest, Zadok the scribe, and Pedaiah, one of the Levites, in charge of the storerooms. And I appointed Hanan son of Zaccur and grandson of Mattaniah as their assistant. These men had an excellent reputation, and it was their job to make honest distributions to their fellow Levites.

¹⁴Remember this good deed, O my God, and do not forget all that I have faithfully done for the Temple of my God.

¹⁵One Sabbath day I saw some men of Judah treading their winepresses. They were also bringing in bundles of grain and loading them on their donkeys. And on that day they were bringing their wine, grapes, figs, and all sorts of produce to Jerusalem to sell. So I rebuked them for selling their produce on the Sabbath. ¹⁶There were also some men from Tyre bringing in fish and all kinds of merchandise. They were selling it on the Sabbath to the people of Judah—and in Jerusalem at that!

13:6 The thirty-second year of Artaxerxes was 433 B.C.

¹⁷So I confronted the leaders of Judah, "Why are you profaning the Sabbath in this evil way? ¹⁸Wasn't it enough that your ancestors did this sort of thing, so that our God brought the present troubles upon us and our city? Now you are bringing even more wrath upon the people of Israel by permitting the Sabbath to be desecrated in this way!" ¹⁹So I commanded that from then on the gates of the city should be shut as darkness fell every Friday evening,* not to be opened until the Sabbath ended. I also sent some of my own servants to guard the gates so that no merchandise could be brought in on the Sabbath day. ²⁰The merchants and tradesmen with a variety of wares camped outside Jerusalem once or twice. ²¹But I spoke sharply to them and said, "What are you doing out here, camping around the wall? If you do this again, I will arrest you!" And that was the last time they came on the Sabbath. ²²Then I commanded the Levites to purify themselves and to guard the gates in order to preserve the holiness of the Sabbath.

Remember this good deed also, O my God! Have compassion on me according to your great and unfailing love.

²³About the same time I realized that some of the men of Judah had married women from Ashdod, Ammon, and Moab. ²⁴Even worse, half their children spoke in the language of Ashdod or some other people and could not speak the language of Judah at all. ²⁵So I confronted them and called down curses on them. I beat some of them and pulled out their hair. I made them swear before God that they would not let their children intermarry with the pagan people of the land. ²⁶"Wasn't this exactly what led King Solomon of Israel into sin?" I demanded. "There was no king from any nation who could compare to him, and God loved him and made him king over all Israel. But even he was led into sin by his foreign wives. ²⁷How could you even think of committing this sinful deed and acting unfaithfully toward God by marrying foreign women?"

²⁸One of the sons of Joiada* son of Eliashib the high priest had married a daughter of Sanballat the Horonite, so I banished him from my presence.

²⁹Remember them, O my God, for they have defiled the priesthood and the promises and vows of the priests and Levites.

³⁰So I purged out everything foreign and assigned tasks to the priests and Levites, making certain that each knew his work. ³¹I also made sure that the supply of wood for the altar was brought at the proper times and that the first part of the harvest was collected for the priests.

Remember this in my favor, O my God.

13:19 Hebrew *on the day before the Sabbath.* 13:28 Hebrew *Jehoiada,* a variant name for Joiada.

Esther

Haman approached King Xerxes and said, "There is a certain race of people scattered through all the provinces of your empire. Their laws are different from those of any other nation, and they refuse to obey even the laws of the king" (3:8).

Faithful to God's Leading

This dramatic story of Israel's persecution and deliverance never mentions worship. Nor does it mention God, prayer, songs, or sacrifice—not once. A reader might think that the drama had been purged of religious reference to attract a secular audience, or worse, that faith did not count for these people. But that theory does not work.

Throughout this adventure of risk, choice, cunning, and vengeance, the sovereign hand of God is everywhere evident and surely at work. The absence of God from the narrative is not the absence of God in the story. At all the crucial turning points, God's control over the ways of kings, ambitious princes, and his faithful people provides the clear backdrop and key to understanding the meaning of this rescue.

Was Mordecai wise to refuse to honor the arrogant Haman? Was Esther deceptive to withhold her ethnic identity during the run-off for queen? In all these twists and turns, a people who remained faithful despite their oppression found their rescue, not through armed struggle but through the courage of a woman nourished on God's promises and faithful to God's leading.

Esther is not described here attending to worship, but no one could rise to her challenge apart from a life spent kneeling before the all-caring God whose work is true all the time. The book's author (unknown by name) gives much more attention to Esther's physical beauty than to her spiritual development, but everything depends on the latter as the story reaches its climax.

Read Esther and be encouraged. You may not be aware of God working on your behalf, but he is there—behind the scenes, in all circumstances—accomplishing his great purpose and plan.

Worship Moments

- Mordecai understood that God was in control (4:14). Praise and worship for God's care is the unspoken, underlying storyline here, the script behind the script.

- God moves the hearts of all people, at all levels. Xerxes, bothered by holy restlessness, seeks his peace in late night study of his own history and discovers God's care for him (6:1–2).

- The people celebrate Purim, marking the deliverance by God through Esther. Celebrations are important ways to remember God's specific acts (9:26–27).

THE KING'S BANQUET

1 This happened in the days of King Xerxes,* who reigned over 127 provinces stretching from India to Ethiopia.* ²At that time he ruled his empire from his throne at the fortress of Susa. ³In the third year of his reign, he gave a banquet for all his princes and officials. He invited all the military officers of Media and Persia, as well as the noblemen and provincial officials. ⁴The celebration lasted six months*—a tremendous display of the opulent wealth and glory of his empire.

⁵When it was all over, the king gave a special banquet for all the palace servants and officials—from the greatest to the least. It lasted for seven days and was held at Susa in the courtyard of the palace garden. ⁶The courtyard was decorated with beautifully woven white and blue linen hangings, fastened by purple ribbons to silver rings embedded in marble pillars. Gold and silver couches stood on a mosaic pavement of porphyry, marble, mother-of-pearl, and other costly stones. ⁷Drinks were served in gold goblets of many designs, and there was an abundance of royal wine, just as the king had commanded. ⁸The only restriction on the drinking was that no one should be compelled to take more than he wanted. But those who wished could have as much as they pleased, for the king had instructed his staff to let everyone decide this matter for himself.

⁹Queen Vashti gave a banquet for the women of the palace at the same time.

QUEEN VASHTI DEPOSED

¹⁰On the seventh day of the feast, when King Xerxes was half drunk with wine, he told Mehuman, Biztha, Harbona, Bigtha, Abagtha, Zethar, and Carcas, the seven eunuchs who attended him, ¹¹to bring Queen Vashti to him with the royal crown on her head. He wanted all the men to gaze on her beauty, for she was a very beautiful woman. ¹²But when they conveyed the king's order to Queen Vashti, she refused to come. This made the king furious, and he burned with anger.

¹³He immediately consulted with his advisers, who knew all the Persian laws and customs, for he always asked their advice. ¹⁴The names of these men were Carshena, Shethar, Admatha, Tarshish, Meres, Marsena, and Memucan—seven high officials of Persia and Media. They were his closest associates and held the highest positions in the empire. ¹⁵"What must be done to Queen Vashti?" the king demanded. "What penalty does the law provide for a queen who refuses to obey the king's orders, properly sent through his eunuchs?"

¹⁶Memucan answered the king and his princes, "Queen Vashti has wronged not only the king but also every official and citizen throughout your empire. ¹⁷Women everywhere will begin to despise their husbands when they learn that Queen Vashti has refused to appear before the king. ¹⁸Before this day is out, the wife of every one of us, your officials throughout the empire, will hear what the queen did and will start talking to their husbands the same way. There will be no end to the contempt and anger throughout your realm. ¹⁹So if it please the king, we suggest that you issue a written decree, a law of the Persians and Medes that cannot be revoked. It should order that Queen Vashti be forever banished from your presence and that you choose another queen more worthy than she. ²⁰When this decree is published throughout your vast empire, husbands everywhere, whatever their rank, will receive proper respect from their wives!"

²¹The king and his princes thought this made good sense, so he followed Memucan's counsel. ²²He sent letters to all parts of the empire, to each province in its own script and language, proclaiming that every man should be the ruler of his home.

1:1a Hebrew *Ahasuerus*, another name for Xerxes; also throughout the book of Esther.   1:1b Hebrew *to Cush*.   1:4 Hebrew *180 days*.

ESTHER BECOMES QUEEN

2 But after Xerxes' anger had cooled, he began thinking about Vashti and what she had done and the decree he had made. [2]So his attendants suggested, "Let us search the empire to find beautiful young virgins for the king. [3]Let the king appoint agents in each province to bring these beautiful young women into the royal harem at Susa. Hegai, the eunuch in charge, will see that they are all given beauty treatments. [4]After that, the young woman who pleases you most will be made queen instead of Vashti." This advice was very appealing to the king, so he put the plan into effect immediately.

[5]Now at the fortress of Susa there was a certain Jew named Mordecai son of Jair. He was from the tribe of Benjamin and was a descendant of Kish and Shimei. [6]His family* had been exiled from Jerusalem to Babylon by King Nebuchadnezzar, along with King Jehoiachin* of Judah and many others. [7]This man had a beautiful and lovely young cousin, Hadassah, who was also called Esther. When her father and mother had died, Mordecai adopted her into his family and raised her as his own daughter. [8]As a result of the king's decree, Esther, along with many other young women, was brought to the king's harem at the fortress of Susa and placed in Hegai's care. [9]Hegai was very impressed with Esther and treated her kindly. He quickly ordered a special menu for her and provided her with beauty treatments. He also assigned her seven maids specially chosen from the king's palace, and he moved her and her maids into the best place in the harem.

[10]Esther had not told anyone of her nationality and family background, for Mordecai had told her not to. [11]Every day Mordecai would take a walk near the courtyard of the harem to ask about Esther and to find out what was happening to her.

[12]Before each young woman was taken to the king's bed, she was given the prescribed twelve months of beauty treatments—six

months with oil of myrrh, followed by six months with special perfumes and ointments. [13]When the time came for her to go in to the king, she was given her choice of whatever clothing or jewelry she wanted to enhance her beauty. [14]That evening she was taken to the king's private rooms, and the next morning she was brought to the second harem,* where the king's wives lived. There she would be under the care of Shaashgaz, another of the king's eunuchs. She would live there for the rest of her life, never going to the king again unless he had especially enjoyed her and requested her by name.

[15]When it was Esther's turn* to go to the

2:6a Hebrew *He.* **2:6b** Hebrew *Jeconiah,* a variant name for Jehoiachin. **2:14** Or *to another part of the harem.* **2:15** Hebrew *the turn of Esther, the daughter of Abihail, who was Mordecai's uncle, who had adopted her.*

king, she accepted the advice of Hegai, the eunuch in charge of the harem. She asked for nothing except what he suggested, and she was admired by everyone who saw her. ¹⁶When Esther was taken to King Xerxes at the royal palace in early winter* of the seventh year of his reign, ¹⁷the king loved her more than any of the other young women. He was so delighted with her that he set the royal crown on her head and declared her queen instead of Vashti. ¹⁸To celebrate the occasion, he gave a banquet in Esther's honor for all his princes and servants, giving generous gifts to everyone and declaring a public festival for the provinces.

¹⁹Even after all the young women had been transferred to the second harem* and Mordecai had become a palace official, ²⁰Esther continued to keep her nationality and family background a secret. She was still following Mordecai's orders, just as she did when she was living in his home.

MORDECAI'S LOYALTY TO THE KING

²¹One day as Mordecai was on duty at the palace, two of the king's eunuchs, Bigthana* and Teresh—who were guards at the door of the king's private quarters—became angry at King Xerxes and plotted to assassinate him. ²²But Mordecai heard about the plot and passed the information on to Queen Esther. She then told the king about it and gave Mordecai credit for the report. ²³When an investigation was made and Mordecai's story was found to be true, the two men were hanged on a gallows.* This was all duly recorded in *The Book of the History of King Xerxes' Reign.*

HAMAN'S PLOT AGAINST THE JEWS

3 Some time later, King Xerxes promoted Haman son of Hammedatha the Agagite

to prime minister, making him the most powerful official in the empire next to the king himself. ²All the king's officials would bow down before Haman to show him respect whenever he passed by, for so the king had commanded. But Mordecai refused to bow down or show him respect.

³Then the palace officials at the king's gate asked Mordecai, "Why are you disobeying the king's command?" ⁴They spoke to him day after day, but still he refused to comply with the order. So they spoke to Haman about this to see if he would tolerate Mordecai's conduct, since Mordecai had told them he was a Jew.

⁵When Haman saw that Mordecai would not bow down or show him respect, he was filled with rage. ⁶So he decided it was not enough to lay hands on Mordecai alone. Since he had learned that Mordecai was a Jew, he decided to destroy all the Jews throughout the entire empire of Xerxes.

⁷So in the month of April,* during the twelfth year of King Xerxes' reign, lots were cast (the lots were called *purim*) to determine the best day and month to take action. And the day selected was March 7, nearly a year later.*

⁸Then Haman approached King Xerxes and said, "There is a certain race of people scattered through all the provinces of your empire. Their laws are different from those of any other nation, and they refuse to obey even the laws of the king. So it is not in the king's interest to let them live. ⁹If it please Your Majesty, issue a decree that they be destroyed, and I will give 375 tons* of silver to the government administrators so they can put it into the royal treasury."

¹⁰The king agreed, confirming his decision by removing his signet ring from his finger and giving it to Haman son of Hammedatha

---

2:16 Hebrew *in the tenth month, the month of Tebeth.* A number of dates in the book of Esther can be cross-checked with dates in surviving Persian records and related accurately to our modern calendar. This month of the Hebrew lunar calendar occurred in December 479 B.C. and January 478 B.C. 2:19 The meaning of the Hebrew is uncertain. 2:21 Hebrew *Bigthan;* compare 6:2. 2:23 Or *on a pole.* 3:7a Hebrew *in the first month, the month of Nisan.* This month of the Hebrew lunar calendar occurred in April and May 474 B.C.; also see note on 2:16. 3:7b As in Greek version, which reads *the thirteenth day of the twelfth month, the month of Adar* (see also 3:13). Hebrew reads *in the twelfth month,* of the Hebrew calendar. The date selected was March 7, 473 B.C.; also see note on 2:16. 3:9 Hebrew *10,000 talents* [340 metric tons].

the Agagite—the enemy of the Jews. [11]"Keep the money," the king told Haman, "but go ahead and do as you like with these people."

[12]On April 17* Haman called in the king's secretaries and dictated letters to the princes, the governors of the respective provinces, and the local officials of each province in their own scripts and languages. These letters were signed in the name of King Xerxes, sealed with his ring, [13]and sent by messengers into all the provinces of the empire. The letters decreed that all Jews—young and old, including women and children—must be killed, slaughtered, and annihilated on a single day. This was scheduled to happen nearly a year later on March 7.* The property of the Jews would be given to those who killed them. [14]A copy of this decree was to be issued in every province and made known to all the people, so that they would be ready to do their duty on the appointed day. [15]At the king's command, the decree went out by the swiftest messengers, and it was proclaimed in the fortress of Susa. Then the king and Haman sat down to drink, but the city of Susa fell into confusion.

MORDECAI REQUESTS ESTHER'S HELP

4 When Mordecai learned what had been done, he tore his clothes, put on sackcloth and ashes, and went out into the city, crying with a loud and bitter wail. [2]He stood outside the gate of the palace, for no one was allowed to enter while wearing clothes of mourning. [3]And as news of the king's decree reached all the provinces, there was great mourning among the Jews. They fasted, wept, and wailed, and many people lay in sackcloth and ashes.

[4]When Queen Esther's maids and eunuchs came and told her about Mordecai, she was deeply distressed. She sent clothing to him to replace the sackcloth, but he refused it. [5]Then Esther sent for Hathach, one of the king's

eunuchs who had been appointed as her attendant. She ordered him to go to Mordecai and find out what was troubling him and why he was in mourning. [6]So Hathach went out to Mordecai in the square in front of the palace gate.

[7]Mordecai told him the whole story and told him how much money Haman had promised to pay into the royal treasury for the destruction of the Jews. [8]Mordecai gave Hathach a copy of the decree issued in Susa that called for the death of all Jews, and he asked Hathach to show it to Esther. He also asked Hathach to explain it to her and to urge her to go to the king to beg for mercy and plead for her people. [9]So Hathach returned to Esther with Mordecai's message.

[10]Then Esther told Hathach to go back and relay this message to Mordecai: [11]"The whole world knows that anyone who appears before the king in his inner court without being invited is doomed to die unless the king holds out his gold scepter. And the king has not called for me to come to him in more than a month." [12]So Hathach gave Esther's message to Mordecai.

[13]Mordecai sent back this reply to Esther: "Don't think for a moment that you will escape there in the palace when all other Jews are killed. [14]If you keep quiet at a time like this, deliverance for the Jews will arise from some other place, but you and your relatives will die. What's more, who can say but that you have been elevated to the palace for just such a time as this?"

[15]Then Esther sent this reply to Mordecai: [16]"Go and gather together all the Jews of Susa and fast for me. Do not eat or drink for three days, night or day. My maids and I will do the same. And then, though it is against the law, I will go in to see the king. If I must die, I am willing to die." [17]So Mordecai went away and did as Esther told him.

3:12 Hebrew *On the thirteenth day of the first month,* of the Hebrew calendar. This event occurred on April 17, 474 B.C.; also see note on 2:16. **3:13** Hebrew *on the thirteenth day of the twelfth month, the month of Adar,* of the Hebrew calendar. The date selected was March 7, 473 B.C.; also see note on 2:16.

My Daily Worship

— *April 23* —

FOR SUCH A TIME AS THIS
ESTHER 1:1–4:17

If you keep quiet at a time, like this deliverance for the Jews will arise from some other place,
but you and your relatives will die. What's more, who can say but that you have
been elevated to the palace for just such a time as this? (4:14).

[i reflect]

His name was Clarke Bynum, not Clark Kent. But to the 398 passengers on British Air flight #2069, the 6' 7" insurance salesman from Sumter, South Carolina, was a real-life Superman. Clarke was on his way to Uganda for a two-week missions opportunity when something happened at 35,000 feet that would drastically alter his plans.

Clarke Bynum had been placed in a dramatic opportunity to play a role just as Queen Esther did thousands of years before. Mordacai could have been speaking to Bynum with the words he used to challenge his niece to speak up for her people: *Who can say but that you have been put on this plane for just such a time as this?*

In the midst of a seven-hour flight from London to Nairobi, Clarke had drifted off to sleep but was jarred awake by the biggest "air pocket" he'd ever experienced. Noises from the cockpit indicated something was wrong. A mentally deranged Kenyan bent on killing himself and all 398 on board had commandeered the control panel bringing the jumbo jet into a virtual nosedive. In ninety seconds the plane plummeted from 35,000 feet to 17,000 feet.

Concentrating on the fact that he had to do something, Clarke forced his way into the cockpit with confidence he didn't know he had. He tackled the 27-year-old Kenyan from behind while the pilot feverishly pushed buttons and grabbed the controls to pull the plane out of its death dive. Because of his quick-thinking actions, the people on that plane were saved.

You probably will never have as dramatic an opportunity as Clarke Bynum or Esther, but God still places you in circumstances and situations where you can make a difference. As part of your worship today, ask God to help you see your current situation from the eyes of One who can make a difference. Submit yourself to him for whatever he has in mind today.

[i pray]

Lord, help me believe that you put me in this time and place with my abilities and resources
because you had a purpose in mind. Show me how to overcome whatever may
hold me back so that I can become a proactive player in your kingdom.

[i respond]

Do you believe that you have everything you need to live the life God wants you to live? Make a list of your qualities, gifts, passions, drives, desires, and resources. Then consider how you can use them to move forward into God's purposes for you.

ESTHER'S REQUEST TO THE KING

5 Three days later, Esther put on her royal robes and entered the inner court of the palace, just across from the king's hall. The king was sitting on his royal throne, facing the entrance. ²When he saw Queen Esther standing there in the inner court, he welcomed her, holding out the gold scepter to her. So Esther approached and touched its tip.

³Then the king asked her, "What do you want, Queen Esther? What is your request? I will give it to you, even if it is half the kingdom!"

⁴And Esther replied, "If it please Your Majesty, let the king and Haman come today to a banquet I have prepared for the king."

⁵The king turned to his attendants and said, "Tell Haman to come quickly to a banquet, as Esther has requested." So the king and Haman went to Esther's banquet.

⁶And while they were drinking wine, the king said to Esther, "Now tell me what you really want. What is your request? I will give it to you, even if it is half the kingdom!"

⁷Esther replied, "This is my request and deepest wish. ⁸If Your Majesty is pleased with me and wants to grant my request, please come with Haman tomorrow to the banquet I will prepare for you. Then tomorrow I will explain what this is all about."

HAMAN'S PLAN TO KILL MORDECAI

⁹What a happy man Haman was as he left the banquet! But when he saw Mordecai sitting at the gate, not standing up or trembling nervously before him, he was furious. ¹⁰However, he restrained himself and went on home. Then he gathered together his friends and Zeresh, his wife, ¹¹and boasted to them about his great wealth and his many children. He bragged about the honors the king had given him and how he had been promoted over all the other officials and leaders.

¹²Then Haman added, "And that's not all! Queen Esther invited only me and the king himself to the banquet she prepared for us. And she has invited me to dine with her and the king again tomorrow!" ¹³Then he added, "But all this is meaningless as long as I see Mordecai the Jew just sitting there at the palace gate."

¹⁴So Haman's wife, Zeresh, and all his friends suggested, "Set up a gallows* that stands seventy-five feet* tall, and in the morning ask the king to hang Mordecai on it. When this is done, you can go on your merry way to the banquet with the king." This pleased Haman immensely, and he ordered the gallows set up.

THE KING HONORS MORDECAI

6 That night the king had trouble sleeping, so he ordered an attendant to bring the historical records of his kingdom so they could be read to him. ²In those records he discovered an account of how Mordecai had exposed the plot of Bigthana and Teresh, two of the eunuchs who guarded the door to the king's private quarters. They had plotted to assassinate the king. ³"What reward or recognition did we ever give Mordecai for this?" the king asked.

His attendants replied, "Nothing has been done."

⁴"Who is that in the outer court?" the king inquired. Now, as it happened, Haman had just arrived in the outer court of the palace to ask the king to hang Mordecai from the gallows* he had prepared.

⁵So the attendants replied to the king, "Haman is out there."

"Bring him in," the king ordered. ⁶So Haman came in, and the king said, "What should I do to honor a man who truly pleases me?"

Haman thought to himself, "Whom would the king wish to honor more than me?" ⁷So he replied, "If the king wishes to honor someone, ⁸he should bring out one of the king's own royal robes, as well as the king's own horse

---

5:14a Or *a pole.* 5:14b Hebrew *50 cubits* [22.5 meters]. 6:4 Or *from the pole.*

> *The whole person, with all his senses, with both mind and body, needs to be involved in genuine worship.*
>
> JERRY KERNS

with a royal emblem on its head. ⁹Instruct one of the king's most noble princes to dress the man in the king's robe and to lead him through the city square on the king's own horse. Have the prince shout as they go, 'This is what happens to those the king wishes to honor!'"

¹⁰"Excellent!" the king said to Haman. "Hurry and get the robe and my horse, and do just as you have said for Mordecai the Jew, who sits at the gate of the palace. Do not fail to carry out everything you have suggested."

¹¹So Haman took the robe and put it on Mordecai, placed him on the king's own horse, and led him through the city square, shouting, "This is what happens to those the king wishes to honor!" ¹²Afterward Mordecai returned to the palace gate, but Haman hurried home dejected and completely humiliated.

¹³When Haman told his wife, Zeresh, and all his friends what had happened, they said, "Since Mordecai—this man who has humiliated you—is a Jew, you will never succeed in your plans against him. It will be fatal to continue to oppose him." ¹⁴While they were still talking, the king's eunuchs arrived to take Haman to the banquet Esther had prepared.

THE KING EXECUTES HAMAN

7 So the king and Haman went to Queen Esther's banquet. ²And while they were drinking wine that day, the king again asked her, "Tell me what you want, Queen Esther. What is your request? I will give it to you, even if it is half the kingdom!"

³And so Queen Esther replied, "If Your Majesty is pleased with me and wants to grant my request, my petition is that my life and the lives of my people will be spared. ⁴For my people and I have been sold to those who would kill, slaughter, and annihilate us. If we had only been sold as slaves, I could remain quiet, for that would have been a matter too trivial to warrant disturbing the king."

⁵"Who would do such a thing?" King Xerxes demanded. "Who would dare touch you?"

⁶Esther replied, "This wicked Haman is our enemy." Haman grew pale with fright before the king and queen. ⁷Then the king jumped to his feet in a rage and went out into the palace garden.

But Haman stayed behind to plead for his life with Queen Esther, for he knew that he was doomed. ⁸In despair he fell on the couch where Queen Esther was reclining, just as the king returned from the palace garden. "Will he even assault the queen right here in the palace, before my very eyes?" the king roared. And as soon as the king spoke, his attendants covered Haman's face, signaling his doom.

⁹Then Harbona, one of the king's eunuchs, said, "Haman has set up a gallows* that stands seventy-five feet* tall in his own courtyard. He intended to use it to hang Mordecai, the man who saved the king from assassination."

"Then hang Haman on it!" the king ordered. ¹⁰So they hanged Haman on the gallows he had set up for Mordecai, and the king's anger was pacified.

A DECREE TO HELP THE JEWS

8 On that same day King Xerxes gave the estate of Haman, the enemy of the Jews, to Queen Esther. Then Mordecai was brought before the king, for Esther had told the king how they were related. ²The king took off his signet ring—which he had taken back from

7:9a Or *a pole;* also in 7:10. **7:9b** Hebrew *50 cubits* [22.5 meters].

Haman—and gave it to Mordecai. And Esther appointed Mordecai to be in charge of Haman's property.

[3]Now once more Esther came before the king, falling down at his feet and begging him with tears to stop Haman's evil plot against the Jews. [4]Again the king held out the gold scepter to Esther. So she rose and stood before him [5]and said, "If Your Majesty is pleased with me and if he thinks it is right, send out a decree reversing Haman's orders to destroy the Jews throughout all the provinces of the king. [6]For how can I endure to see my people and my family slaughtered and destroyed?"

[7]Then King Xerxes said to Queen Esther and Mordecai the Jew, "I have given Esther the estate of Haman, and he has been hanged on the gallows* because he tried to destroy the Jews. [8]Now go ahead and send a message to the Jews in the king's name, telling them whatever you want, and seal it with the king's signet ring. But remember that whatever is written in the king's name and sealed with his ring can never be revoked."

[9]So on June 25* the king's secretaries were summoned. As Mordecai dictated, they wrote a decree to the Jews and to the princes, governors, and local officials of all the 127 provinces stretching from India to Ethiopia.* The decree was written in the scripts and languages of all the peoples of the empire, including the Jews. [10]Mordecai wrote in the name of King Xerxes and sealed the message with the king's signet ring. He sent the letters by swift messengers, who rode horses especially bred for the king's service.

[11]The king's decree gave the Jews in every city authority to unite to defend their lives. They were allowed to kill, slaughter, and annihilate anyone of any nationality or province who might attack them or their children and wives, and to take the property of their enemies. [12]The day chosen for this event throughout all the provinces of King Xerxes was

March 7 of the next year.* [13]A copy of this decree was to be recognized as law in every province and proclaimed to all the people. That way the Jews would be ready on that day to take revenge on their enemies. [14]So urged on by the king's command, the messengers rode out swiftly on horses bred for the king's service. The same decree was also issued at the fortress of Susa.

[15]Then Mordecai put on the royal robe of blue and white and the great crown of gold, and he wore an outer cloak of fine linen and purple. And the people of Susa celebrated the new decree. [16]The Jews were filled with joy and gladness and were honored everywhere. [17]In every city and province, wherever the king's decree arrived, the Jews rejoiced and had a great celebration and declared a public festival and holiday. And many of the people of the land became Jews themselves, for they feared what the Jews might do to them.

The Victory of the Jews

9 So on March 7* the two decrees of the king were put into effect. On that day, the enemies of the Jews had hoped to destroy them, but quite the opposite happened. [2]The Jews gathered in their cities throughout all the king's provinces to defend themselves against anyone who might try to harm them. But no one could make a stand against them, for everyone was afraid of them. [3]And all the commanders of the provinces, the princes, the governors, and the royal officials helped the Jews for fear of Mordecai. [4]For Mordecai had been promoted in the king's palace, and his fame spread throughout all the provinces as he became more and more powerful.

[5]But the Jews went ahead on the appointed day and struck down their enemies with the sword. They killed and annihilated their enemies and did as they pleased with those who hated them. [6]They killed five hundred

---

8:7 Or *on the pole.* 8:9a Hebrew *on the twenty-third day of the third month, the month of Sivan,* of the Hebrew calendar. This event occurred on June 25, 474 B.C.; also see note on 2:16. 8:9b Hebrew *to Cush.* 8:12 Hebrew *the thirteenth day of the twelfth month, the month of Adar,* of the Hebrew calendar. The date selected was March 7, 473 B.C.; also see note on 2:16. 9:1 Hebrew *on the thirteenth day of the twelfth month, the month of Adar,* of the Hebrew calendar. This event occurred on March 7, 473 B.C.; also see note on 2:16.

My Daily Worship

— April 24 —

FINDING GOD BETWEEN THE LINES

ESTHER 5:1–10:3

He told them to celebrate these days with feasting and gladness and by giving gifts to each other and to the poor. This would commemorate a time when the Jews gained relief from their enemies, when their sorrow was turned into gladness and their mourning into joy (9:22).

[i reflect]

If you want to find God in the book of Esther, you'll have to read between the lines. The plot reveals a hotheaded king, a beautiful orphaned Jewish girl, a murderous small-minded official, and a wise old uncle. But God is never mentioned by name throughout this book. Yet, he is behind the scenes, actively working to turn a nation's mourning into joy.

What a powerful lesson! We may only see an overbearing boss, a crippling grief, or a spiteful enemy. To find God's prevailing goodness requires that we read between the lines of our lives. That happens when we worship. Worship shifts our focus off the action of our lives, on to the Director of it. Rather than giving in to the worries, anxieties, and fears clamoring for our attention, we focus on our center, our real life. In God's presence, we come to trust his goodness even when we can't see his hand.

In Esther we find God working effectively even without anyone's conscious knowledge of it. He is working between the lines of your story, too—between any plots against you, between any fears about your future, even between the glimpses of your understanding and your perceptions of his presence. Always active. Always loving. His ever-present, transcendent caring fills every space. Trusting that fact changes our sorrows into gladness and our mourning into joy.

Look between the lines of your life. God is there.

[i pray]

God, I confess that so often I get caught up in the action of my life and I forget to look for how you are working behind the scenes. I bring to you the events, activities, and schedule I've been keeping. Tune my heart to how you are working, so I can cooperate with your plans.

[i respond]

Imagine how the book of Esther would have unfolded without God. No Esther to intervene. No "accidental" overhearing of an assassination plot by Mordecai. No ousting of Haman. No victory for the Jews. Now think back over your last few days, and imagine them without God. What would have changed in your life?

people in the fortress of Susa. ⁷They also killed Parshandatha, Dalphon, Aspatha, ⁸Poratha, Adalia, Aridatha, ⁹Parmashta, Arisai, Aridai, and Vaizatha—¹⁰the ten sons of Haman son of Hammedatha, the enemy of the Jews. But they did not take any plunder.

¹¹That evening, when the king was informed of the number of people killed in the fortress of Susa, ¹²he called for Queen Esther and said, "The Jews have killed five hundred people in the fortress of Susa alone and also Haman's ten sons. If they have done that here, what has happened in the rest of the provinces? But now, what more do you want? It will be granted to you; tell me and I will do it."

¹³And Esther said, "If it please Your Majesty, give the Jews in Susa permission to do again tomorrow as they have done today, and have the bodies of Haman's ten sons hung from the gallows.*"

¹⁴So the king agreed, and the decree was announced in Susa. They also hung the bodies of Haman's ten sons from the gallows. ¹⁵Then the Jews at Susa gathered together on March 8* and killed three hundred more people, though again they took no plunder.

¹⁶Meanwhile, the other Jews throughout the king's provinces had gathered together to defend their lives. They gained relief from all their enemies, killing seventy-five thousand of those who hated them. But they did not take any plunder. ¹⁷Throughout the provinces this was done on March 7.* Then on the following day* they rested, celebrating their victory with a day of feasting and gladness. ¹⁸But the Jews at Susa continued killing their enemies on the second day also, and then rested on the third day,* making that their day of feasting and gladness. ¹⁹So to this day, rural Jews living in unwalled villages celebrate an annual festival and holiday in late winter,* when they rejoice and send gifts to each other.

THE FESTIVAL OF PURIM

²⁰Mordecai recorded these events and sent letters to the Jews near and far, throughout all the king's provinces, ²¹encouraging them to celebrate an annual festival on these two days. ²²He told them to celebrate these days with feasting and gladness and by giving gifts to each other and to the poor. This would commemorate a time when the Jews gained relief from their enemies, when their sorrow was turned into gladness and their mourning into joy.

²³So the Jews adopted Mordecai's suggestion and began this annual custom. ²⁴Haman son of Hammedatha the Agagite, the enemy of the Jews, had plotted to crush and destroy them on the day and month determined by casting lots (the lots were called *purim*). ²⁵But when Esther came before the king, he issued a decree causing Haman's evil plot to backfire, and Haman and his sons were hanged on the gallows. ²⁶(That is why this celebration is called Purim, because it is the ancient word for casting lots.) So because of Mordecai's letter and because of what they had experienced, ²⁷the Jews throughout the realm agreed to inaugurate this tradition and to pass it on to their descendants and to all who became Jews. They declared they would never fail to celebrate these two prescribed days at the appointed time each year. ²⁸These days would be remembered and kept from generation to generation and celebrated by every family throughout the provinces and cities of the empire. These days would never cease to be celebrated among the Jews, nor would the memory of what happened ever die out among their descendants.

²⁹Then Queen Esther, the daughter of Abihail, along with Mordecai the Jew, wrote another letter putting the queen's full author-

---

9:13 Or *the pole;* also in 9:14, 25. 9:15 Hebrew *the fourteenth day of the month of Adar,* of the Hebrew calendar. This event occurred on March 8, 473 B.C.; also see note on 2:16. 9:17a Hebrew *on the thirteenth day of the month of Adar,* of the Hebrew calendar. This event occurred on March 7, 473 B.C.; also see note on 2:16. 9:17b Hebrew *on the fourteenth day,* of the Hebrew month of Adar. 9:18 Hebrew *killing their enemies on the thirteenth day and the fourteenth day, and then rested on the fifteenth day,* of the Hebrew month of Adar. 9:19 Hebrew *on the fourteenth day of the month of Adar.* This day of the Hebrew lunar calendar usually occurs in March.

ity behind Mordecai's letter to establish the Festival of Purim. [30]In addition, letters wishing peace and security were sent to the Jews throughout the 127 provinces of the empire of Xerxes. [31]These letters established the Festival of Purim—an annual celebration of these days at the appointed time, decreed by both Mordecai the Jew and Queen Esther. (The people decided to observe this festival, just as they had decided for themselves and their descendants to establish the times of fasting and mourning.) [32]So the command of Esther confirmed the practices of Purim, and it was all written down in the records.

THE GREATNESS OF XERXES AND MORDECAI

10 King Xerxes imposed tribute throughout his empire, even to the distant coastlands. [2]His great achievements and the full account of the greatness of Mordecai, whom the king had promoted, are recorded in *The Book of the History of the Kings of Media and Persia*. [3]Mordecai the Jew became the prime minister, with authority next to that of King Xerxes himself. He was very great among the Jews, who held him in high esteem, because he worked for the good of his people and was a friend at the royal court for all of them.

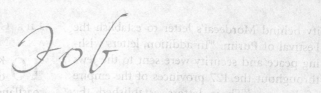

I had heard about you before, but now I have seen you with my own eyes. I take back everything I said, and I sit in dust and ashes to show my repentance (42:5–6).

When the Going Gets Tough

I f life followed a straight-line path from right living to reward, Job's story would have never been told. Because life is unfair—good people suffer, innocent people die, children go hungry—Job's dialogues, and even his silence before God, are a record of perhaps the most important conversations in history.

No one in this book, neither the straight-arrow, God-fearing types nor the once-happy-brought-low types can understand. Job, the one who lets his heart spill out, forgetting restraint and decorum, comes closest, but still he has no answers. Life has spun way outside the fairness orbit. Good people cannot explain it.

Finally God speaks, but not to apologize for the inequities and suffering, not to correct all this theological flutter. Rather, God reminds this weary group that he is God. Through a series of pointed questions, the Lord reminds them that their calling is not to weigh the reasonableness of his sovereign action but instead to worship. Everything else comes later.

Reflecting on these conversations between Job and God, G. K. Chesterton wrote, "Job flings at God one riddle, God flings back at Job a hundred riddles, and Job is at peace; he is comforted with conundrums." In the end, Job understands that God is God.

Too often, we worship as a way of collecting credit points so that when God cashes us out down the road, we will be happy. Wrong approach. Job's story reminds us that we worship God because God is God and we are not. No ledgers, no deals, no terms or conditions. God is God. That's enough.

Worship Moments

- Job is a worshiping man. He is wealthy and his family is large. He does not neglect to acknowledge the source of it all (1:5).

- Job rejects the advice that he renounce God, that he end his life of reverence (2:9–10). To do so would be to annul, cancel, rescind his life of worship. No amount of loss drives him to that fatal point.

- Whenever we approach God, the tone is to be worshipful, not argumentative. We don't call God to account. We don't present the ledger and demand cosmic fairness as something God owes us. All words to God must be worship words (40:1–5).

PROLOGUE

1 There was a man named Job who lived in the land of Uz. He was blameless, a man of complete integrity. He feared God and stayed away from evil. ²He had seven sons and three daughters. ³He owned seven thousand sheep, three thousand camels, five hundred teams of oxen, and five hundred female donkeys, and he employed many servants. He was, in fact, the richest person in that entire area.

⁴Every year when Job's sons had birthdays, they invited their brothers and sisters to join them for a celebration. On these occasions they would get together to eat and drink. ⁵When these celebrations ended—and sometimes they lasted several days—Job would purify his children. He would get up early in the morning and offer a burnt offering for each of them. For Job said to himself, "Perhaps my children have sinned and have cursed God in their hearts." This was Job's regular practice.

JOB'S FIRST TEST

⁶One day the angels* came to present themselves before the LORD, and Satan the Accuser came with them. ⁷"Where have you come from?" the LORD asked Satan.

And Satan answered the LORD, "I have been going back and forth across the earth, watching everything that's going on."

⁸Then the LORD asked Satan, "Have you noticed my servant Job? He is the finest man in all the earth—a man of complete integrity. He fears God and will have nothing to do with evil."

⁹Satan replied to the LORD, "Yes, Job fears God, but not without good reason! ¹⁰You have always protected him and his home and his property from harm. You have made him prosperous in everything he does. Look how rich he is! ¹¹But take away everything he has, and he will surely curse you to your face!"

¹²"All right, you may test him," the LORD said to Satan. "Do whatever you want with everything he possesses, but don't harm him physically." So Satan left the LORD's presence.

¹³One day when Job's sons and daughters were dining at the oldest brother's house, ¹⁴a messenger arrived at Job's home with this news: "Your oxen were plowing, with the donkeys feeding beside them, ¹⁵when the Sabeans raided us. They stole all the animals and killed all the farmhands. I am the only one who escaped to tell you."

¹⁶While he was still speaking, another messenger arrived with this news: "The fire of God has fallen from heaven and burned up your sheep and all the shepherds. I am the only one who escaped to tell you."

¹⁷While he was still speaking, a third messenger arrived with this news: "Three bands of Chaldean raiders have stolen your camels and killed your servants. I am the only one who escaped to tell you."

¹⁸While he was still speaking, another messenger arrived with this news: "Your sons and daughters were feasting in their oldest brother's home. ¹⁹Suddenly, a powerful wind swept in from the desert and hit the house on all sides. The house collapsed, and all your children are dead. I am the only one who escaped to tell you."

²⁰Job stood up and tore his robe in grief. Then he shaved his head and fell to the ground before God. ²¹He said,

"I came naked from my mother's womb,
 and I will be stripped of everything
  when I die.
The LORD gave me everything I had,
 and the LORD has taken it away.
Praise the name of the LORD!"

²²In all of this, Job did not sin by blaming God.

JOB'S SECOND TEST

2 One day the angels* came again to present themselves before the LORD, and Satan the Accuser came with them. ²"Where have you come from?" the LORD asked Satan.

1:6 Hebrew *the sons of God.* 2:1 Hebrew *the sons of God.*

And Satan answered the LORD, "I have been going back and forth across the earth, watching everything that's going on."

³Then the LORD asked Satan, "Have you noticed my servant Job? He is the finest man in all the earth—a man of complete integrity. He fears God and will have nothing to do with evil. And he has maintained his integrity, even though you persuaded me to harm him without cause."

⁴Satan replied to the LORD, "Skin for skin—he blesses you only because you bless him. A man will give up everything he has to save his life. ⁵But take away his health, and he will surely curse you to your face!"

⁶"All right, do with him as you please," the LORD said to Satan. "But spare his life." ⁷So Satan left the LORD's presence, and he struck Job with a terrible case of boils from head to foot.

⁸Then Job scraped his skin with a piece of broken pottery as he sat among the ashes. ⁹His wife said to him, "Are you still trying to maintain your integrity? Curse God and die."

¹⁰But Job replied, "You talk like a godless woman. Should we accept only good things from the hand of God and never anything bad?" So in all this, Job said nothing wrong.

JOB'S THREE FRIENDS SHARE HIS ANGUISH

¹¹Three of Job's friends were Eliphaz the Temanite, Bildad the Shuhite, and Zophar the Naamathite. When they heard of the tragedy he had suffered, they got together and traveled from their homes to comfort and console him. ¹²When they saw Job from a distance, they scarcely recognized him. Wailing loudly, they tore their robes and threw dust into the air over their heads to demonstrate their grief. ¹³Then they sat on the ground with him for seven days and nights. And no one said a word, for they saw that his suffering was too great for words.

3:8 Hebrew *rouse Leviathan.*

JOB'S FIRST SPEECH

3 At last Job spoke, and he cursed the day of his birth. ²He said:

³"Cursed be the day of my birth, and cursed be the night when I was conceived. ⁴Let that day be turned to darkness. Let it be lost even to God on high, and let it be shrouded in darkness. ⁵Yes, let the darkness and utter gloom claim it for its own. Let a black cloud overshadow it, and let the darkness terrify it. ⁶Let that night be blotted off the calendar, never again to be counted among the days of the year, never again to appear among the months. ⁷Let that night be barren. Let it have no joy. ⁸Let those who are experts at cursing—those who are ready to rouse the sea monster*—curse that day. ⁹Let its morning stars remain dark. Let it hope for light, but in vain; may it never see the morning light. ¹⁰Curse it for its failure to shut my mother's womb, for letting me be born to all this trouble.

¹¹"Why didn't I die at birth as I came from the womb? ¹²Why did my mother let me live? Why did she nurse me at her breasts? ¹³For if I had died at birth, I would be at peace now, asleep and at rest. ¹⁴I would rest with the world's kings and prime ministers, famous for their great construction projects. ¹⁵I would rest with wealthy princes whose palaces were filled with gold and silver. ¹⁶Why was I not buried like a stillborn child, like a baby who never lives to see the light? ¹⁷For in death the wicked cease from troubling, and the weary are at rest. ¹⁸Even prisoners are at ease in death, with no guards to curse them. ¹⁹Rich and poor are there alike, and the slave is free from his master.

²⁰"Oh, why should light be given to the weary, and life to those in misery? ²¹They long for death, and it won't come. They search for death more eagerly than for hidden treasure. ²²It is a blessed relief when they finally die, when they find the grave. ²³Why is life given to those with no future, those destined by God to live in distress? ²⁴I cannot eat for sighing; my groans pour out like water. ²⁵What I always

My Daily Worship

— April 25 —

Is It in the Cards?
JOB 1:1–5:27

He said, "I came naked from my mother's womb, and I will be stripped of everything when I die. The LORD gave me everything I had, and the LORD has taken it away. Praise the name of the LORD!" In all of this, Job did not sin by blaming God (1:21–22).

[i reflect]

Try this exercise: Take five index cards. Write down the five most important things and people in your life, one on each card. Now buckle in.

A hurricane (tornado, earthquake, fire, mudslide—whatever natural disasters you have where you live) hits your home. You lose all your possessions. If you had any material possessions written down—house, car, boat, baseball card collection, whatever—tear up those cards.

Your family is in a car accident. Only you and your spouse survive. If you have anyone else in your family written down, lose those cards, too.

"Wait a minute," you're thinking. "This is not an uplifting, worshipful exercise. I'm not doing this." Hold that thought and hang in for one more jolt, OK?

The doctor calls you in, looking very grim. "I have your test results . . . it's not good." If your health was one of your top five, toss that card, too.

How are you feeling? Besides angry at this morbid little exercise, that is. It has a purpose, and if you're familiar with Job's story, you know what it is. This depressing scenario is a thinly veiled retelling of what happened to that godly man long, long ago. How did Job respond to such overwhelming loss and sorrow? Unbelievably, he responded by worshiping God. Job refused to give in to the grief and pain he undoubtedly felt, instead choosing to let God be God and to remain faithful to his Lord.

If any of this were to happen to you, certainly you would feel angry, sad, hurt, confused, depressed, and other tough emotions. God understands; he gave you the capacity to have all those feelings. But when sorrow comes, remember to do what Job did: Take your grief and pain *to* him. Don't try to carry them all on your own.

Whatever your troubles or stressful circumstances today, turn to God. Let him carry your burdens.

[i pray]

Lord, I never want to face anything like the nightmare Job had to go through. I cannot imagine being able to deal with it as he did, and I don't ever want the opportunity to find out. But when my times of testing come, I ask you for the grace to bow before you in childlike submission, not to turn away in childish rage.

[i respond]

What sorrow, loss, or hardship are you experiencing right now? Express your emotions out loud to God. Tell him exactly how you are feeling. Give your pain and hurt to him.

COUNSEL, WARNING

Counsel, Warning—Hebrew *ya-'ats* "to advise, counsel"; *'e-tsah* "prudence, counsel"; Greek *nou-the-te-o* "warn, admonish"; *nou-the-si-a* "warning, admonition"; *bou-le* "counsel."

During worship, we may hear the Lord speaking to us with a word of counsel or warning. This will be true to the extent that reading and studying of the Scriptures are part of our worship. As we listen to the words of those upon whom the Holy Spirit moved through the ages, we hear also the voice of God: "Listen to me, O my people, while I give you stern warnings" (Psalm 81:8).

Maybe we think we know what is right for us without asking for anyone else's advice. But Jeremiah reminds us that feelings and desires can easily deceive (Jeremiah 17:9). We need the counsel of God to make right and wise decisions. We need his Word, and we need other worshipers to help us hear it. "Use his words to teach and counsel each other" (Colossians 3:16).

feared has happened to me. What I dreaded has come to be. ²⁶I have no peace, no quietness. I have no rest; instead, only trouble comes."

ELIPHAZ'S FIRST RESPONSE TO JOB

4 Then Eliphaz the Temanite replied to Job:

²"Will you be patient and let me say a word? For who could keep from speaking out?

³"In the past you have encouraged many a troubled soul to trust in God; you have supported those who were weak. ⁴Your words have strengthened the fallen; you steadied those who wavered. ⁵But now when trouble strikes, you faint and are broken. ⁶Does your reverence for God give you no confidence? Shouldn't you believe that God will care for those who are upright?

⁷"Stop and think! Does the innocent person perish? When has the upright person been destroyed? ⁸My experience shows that those who plant trouble and cultivate evil will harvest the same. ⁹They perish by a breath from God. They vanish in a blast of his anger. ¹⁰Though they are fierce young lions, they will all be broken and destroyed. ¹¹The fierce lion will starve, and the cubs of the lioness will be scattered.

¹²"This truth was given me in secret, as though whispered in my ear. ¹³It came in a vision at night as others slept. ¹⁴Fear gripped me; I trembled and shook with terror. ¹⁵A spirit* swept past my face. Its wind sent shivers up my spine. ¹⁶It stopped, but I couldn't see its shape. There was a form before my eyes, and a hushed voice said, ¹⁷'Can a mortal be just and upright before God? Can a person be pure before the Creator?'

¹⁸"If God cannot trust his own angels and has charged some of them with folly, ¹⁹how much less will he trust those made of clay! Their foundation is dust, and they are crushed as easily as moths. ²⁰They are alive in the morning, but by evening they are dead, gone forever without a trace. ²¹Their tent collapses; they die in ignorance.

ELIPHAZ'S RESPONSE CONTINUES

5 "You may cry for help, but no one listens. You may turn to the angels,* but they give you no help. ²Surely resentment destroys the fool, and jealousy kills the simple. ³From my experience, I know that fools who turn from God may be successful for the moment, but then comes sudden disaster. ⁴Their children

4:15 Or *wind.* **5:1** Hebrew *the holy ones.*

are abandoned far from help, with no one to defend them. ⁵Their harvests are stolen, and their wealth satisfies the thirst of many others, not themselves! ⁶But evil does not spring from the soil, and trouble does not sprout from the earth. ⁷People are born for trouble as predictably as sparks fly upward from a fire.

> *Praise is a soul in flower.*
>
> THOMAS WATSON

⁸"My advice to you is this: Go to God and present your case to him. ⁹For he does great works too marvelous to understand. He performs miracles without number. ¹⁰He gives rain for the earth. He sends water for the fields. ¹¹He gives prosperity to the poor and humble, and he takes sufferers to safety. ¹²He frustrates the plans of the crafty, so their efforts will not succeed. ¹³He catches those who think they are wise in their own cleverness, so that their cunning schemes are thwarted. ¹⁴They grope in the daylight as though they were blind; they see no better in the daytime than at night. ¹⁵He rescues the poor from the cutting words of the strong. He saves them from the clutches of the powerful. ¹⁶And so at last the poor have hope, and the fangs of the wicked are broken.

¹⁷"But consider the joy of those corrected by God! Do not despise the chastening of the Almighty when you sin. ¹⁸For though he wounds, he also bandages. He strikes, but his hands also heal. ¹⁹He will rescue you again and again so that no evil can touch you. ²⁰He will save you from death in time of famine, from the power of the sword in time of war. ²¹You will be safe from slander and will have no fear

of destruction when it comes. ²²You will laugh at destruction and famine; wild animals will not terrify you. ²³You will be at peace with the stones of the field, and its wild animals will be at peace with you. ²⁴You will know that your home is kept safe. When you visit your pastures, nothing will be missing. ²⁵Your children will be many; your descendants will be as plentiful as grass! ²⁶You will live to a good old age. You will not be harvested until the proper time!

²⁷"We have found from experience that all this is true. Listen to my counsel, and apply it to yourself."

JOB'S SECOND SPEECH: A RESPONSE TO ELIPHAZ

6 Then Job spoke again:

²"If my sadness could be weighed and my troubles be put on the scales, ³they would be heavier than all the sands of the sea. That is why I spoke so rashly. ⁴For the Almighty has struck me down with his arrows. He has sent his poisoned arrows deep within my spirit. All God's terrors are arrayed against me. ⁵Don't I have a right to complain? Wild donkeys bray when they find no green grass, and oxen low when they have no food. ⁶People complain when there is no salt in their food. And how tasteless is the uncooked white of an egg! ⁷My appetite disappears when I look at it; I gag at the thought of eating it!

⁸"Oh, that I might have my request, that God would grant my hope. ⁹I wish he would crush me. I wish he would reach out his hand and kill me. ¹⁰At least I can take comfort in this: Despite the pain, I have not denied the words of the Holy One. ¹¹But I do not have the strength to endure. I do not have a goal that encourages me to carry on. ¹²Do I have strength as hard as stone? Is my body made of bronze? ¹³No, I am utterly helpless, without any chance of success.

¹⁴"One should be kind to a fainting friend, but you have accused me without the slightest fear of the Almighty. ¹⁵My brother, you have proved as unreliable as a seasonal brook that

overflows its banks in the spring ¹⁶when it is swollen with ice and melting snow. ¹⁷But when the hot weather arrives, the water disappears. The brook vanishes in the heat. ¹⁸The caravans turn aside to be refreshed, but there is nothing there to drink, and so they perish in the desert. ¹⁹With high hopes, the caravans from Tema and from Sheba stop for water, ²⁰but finding none, their hopes are dashed. ²¹You, too, have proved to be of no help. You have seen my calamity, and you are afraid. ²²But why? Have I ever asked you for a gift? Have I begged you to use any of your wealth on my behalf? ²³Have I ever asked you to rescue me from my enemies? Have I asked you to save me from ruthless people?

²⁴"All I want is a reasonable answer—then I will keep quiet. Tell me, what have I done wrong? ²⁵Honest words are painful, but what do your criticisms amount to? ²⁶Do you think your words are convincing when you disregard my cry of desperation? ²⁷You would even send an orphan into slavery* or sell a friend. ²⁸Look at me! Would I lie to your face? ²⁹Stop assuming my guilt, for I am righteous. Don't be so unjust. ³⁰Do you think I am lying? Don't I know the difference between right and wrong?

7 "Is this not the struggle of all humanity? A person's life is long and hard, like that of a hired hand, ²like a worker who longs for the day to end, like a servant waiting to be paid. ³I, too, have been assigned months of futility, long and weary nights of misery. ⁴When I go to bed, I think, 'When will it be morning?' But the night drags on, and I toss till dawn. ⁵My skin is filled with worms and scabs. My flesh breaks open, full of pus.

JOB CRIES OUT TO GOD

⁶"My days are swifter than a weaver's shuttle flying back and forth. They end without hope. ⁷O God, remember that my life is but a breath, and I will never again experience pleasure. ⁸You see me now, but not for long. Your eyes

Words of Worship

LIFT THE EYES

Lift the Eyes—Hebrew *na-sa' 'ei-na-yim* "lift up the eyes." A typical Hebraic idiom for looking at, or regarding, an object of one's focus.

"I lift my eyes to you, O God, enthroned in heaven" (Psalm 123:1). How concrete is the language of Scripture, so full of vivid images and specific actions! There's a powerful insight here. Looking at something is not just passive observation. It's an active process that involves us, even changes us. When we focus on something, we're investing ourselves in it.

That's why we should avoid "lifting our eyes" toward objects, people, or possessions that can't really help us, or could even do us harm. Instead, we should look to Jesus in prayer, keeping our eyes on the One on whom our faith depends (Hebrews 12:2). And we have Scripture's promise, "When he comes we will be like him, for we will see him as he really is" (1 John 3:2).

will be on me, but I will be dead. ⁹Just as a cloud dissipates and vanishes, those who die will not come back. ¹⁰They are gone forever from their home—never to be seen again.

¹¹"I cannot keep from speaking. I must express my anguish. I must complain in my bitterness. ¹²Am I a sea monster that you place a guard on me? ¹³If I think, 'My bed will comfort me, and I will try to forget my misery with sleep,' ¹⁴you shatter me with dreams. You terrify me with visions. ¹⁵I would rather die of strangulation than go on and on like this. ¹⁶I hate my life. I do not want to go on living. Oh, leave me alone for these few remaining days.

¹⁷"What are mere mortals, that you should

make so much of us? ¹⁸For you examine us every morning and test us every moment. ¹⁹Why won't you leave me alone—even for a moment*? ²⁰Have I sinned? What have I done to you, O watcher of all humanity? Why have you made me your target? Am I a burden to you? ²¹Why not just pardon my sin and take away my guilt? For soon I will lie down in the dust and die. When you look for me, I will be gone."

BILDAD'S FIRST RESPONSE TO JOB

8 Then Bildad the Shuhite replied to Job:

²"How long will you go on like this? Your words are a blustering wind. ³Does God twist justice? Does the Almighty twist what is right? ⁴Your children obviously sinned against him, so their punishment was well deserved. ⁵But if you pray to God and seek the favor of the Almighty, ⁶if you are pure and live with complete integrity, he will rise up and restore your happy home. ⁷And though you started with little, you will end with much.

⁸"Just ask the former generation. Pay attention to the experience of our ancestors. ⁹For we were born but yesterday and know so little. Our days on earth are as transient as a shadow. ¹⁰But those who came before us will teach you. They will teach you from the wisdom of former generations.

¹¹"Can papyrus reeds grow where there is no marsh? Can bulrushes flourish where there is no water? ¹²While they are still flowering, not ready to be cut, they begin to wither. ¹³Such is the fate of all who forget God. The hope of the godless comes to nothing. ¹⁴Everything they count on will collapse. They are leaning on a spiderweb. ¹⁵They cling to their home for security, but it won't last. They try to hold it fast, but it will not endure. ¹⁶The godless seem so strong, like a lush plant growing in the sunshine, its branches spreading across the garden. ¹⁷Its roots grow down through a pile of rocks to hold it firm. ¹⁸But when it is uprooted, it isn't even missed!

¹⁹That is the end of its life, and others spring up from the earth to replace it.

²⁰"But look! God will not reject a person of integrity, nor will he make evildoers prosper. ²¹He will yet fill your mouth with laughter and your lips with shouts of joy. ²²Those who hate you will be clothed with shame, and the tent of the wicked will be destroyed."

JOB'S THIRD SPEECH: A RESPONSE TO BILDAD

9 Then Job spoke again:

²"Yes, I know this is all true in principle. But how can a person be declared innocent in the eyes of God? ³If someone wanted to take God to court,* would it be possible to answer him even once in a thousand times? ⁴For God is so wise and so mighty. Who has ever challenged him successfully?

⁵"Without warning, he moves the mountains, overturning them in his anger. ⁶He shakes the earth from its place, and its foundations tremble. ⁷If he commands it, the sun won't rise and the stars won't shine. ⁸He alone has spread out the heavens and marches on the waves of the sea. ⁹He made all the stars— the Bear, Orion, the Pleiades, and the constellations of the southern sky. ¹⁰His great works are too marvelous to understand. He performs miracles without number.

¹¹"Yet when he comes near, I cannot see him. When he moves on, I do not see him go. ¹²If he sends death to snatch someone away, who can stop him? Who dares to ask him, 'What are you doing?' ¹³And God does not restrain his anger. The mightiest forces against him* are crushed beneath his feet.

¹⁴"And who am I, that I should try to answer God or even reason with him? ¹⁵Even if I were innocent, I would have no defense. I could only plead for mercy. ¹⁶And even if I summoned him and he responded, he would never listen to me. ¹⁷For he attacks me without reason,* and he multiplies my wounds without cause. ¹⁸He will not let me catch my

---

7:19 Hebrew *long enough to swallow my spittle.*   9:3 Or *If God wanted to take a person to court.*   9:13 Hebrew *The helpers of Rahab,* the name of a mythical sea monster that represents chaos in ancient literature.   9:17 As in Syriac version; Hebrew reads *with a storm.*

breath, but fills me instead with bitter sorrows. ¹⁹As for strength, he has it. As for justice, who can challenge him? ²⁰Though I am innocent, my own mouth would pronounce me guilty. Though I am blameless, it* would prove me wicked.

²¹"I am innocent, but it makes no difference to me—I despise my life. ²²Innocent or wicked, it is all the same to him. That is why I say, 'He destroys both the blameless and the wicked.' ²³He laughs when a plague suddenly kills the innocent. ²⁴The whole earth is in the hands of the wicked, and God blinds the eyes of the judges and lets them be unfair. If not he, then who?

²⁵"My life passes more swiftly than a runner. It flees away, filled with tragedy. ²⁶It disappears like a swift boat, like an eagle that swoops down on its prey. ²⁷If I decided to forget my complaints, if I decided to end my sadness and be cheerful, ²⁸I would dread all the pain he would send. For I know you will not hold me innocent, O God. ²⁹Whatever happens, I will be found guilty. So what's the use of trying? ³⁰Even if I were to wash myself with soap and cleanse my hands with lye to make them absolutely clean, ³¹you would plunge me into a muddy ditch, and I would be so filthy my own clothing would hate me.

³²"God is not a mortal like me, so I cannot argue with him or take him to trial. ³³If only there were a mediator who could bring us together, but there is none. ³⁴The mediator could make God stop beating me, and I would no longer live in terror of his punishment. ³⁵Then I could speak to him without fear, but I cannot do that in my own strength.

JOB FRAMES HIS PLEA TO GOD

10 "I am disgusted with my life. Let me complain freely. I will speak in the bitterness of my soul. ²I will say to God, 'Don't simply condemn me—tell me the charge you are bringing against me. ³What do you gain by oppressing me? Why do you reject me, the work of your own hands, while sending joy and prosperity to the wicked? ⁴Are your eyes only those of a human? Do you see things as people see them? ⁵Is your lifetime merely human? Is your life so short ⁶that you are in a hurry to probe for my guilt, to search for my sin? ⁷Although you know I am not guilty, no one can rescue me from your power.

⁸" 'You formed me with your hands; you made me, and yet you completely destroy me. ⁹Remember that I am made of dust—will you turn me back to dust so soon? ¹⁰You guided my conception and formed me in the womb.* ¹¹You clothed me with skin and flesh, and you knit my bones and sinews together. ¹²You gave me life and showed me your unfailing love. My life was preserved by your care.

¹³" 'Yet your real motive—I know this was your intent—¹⁴was to watch me, and if I sinned, you would not forgive my iniquity. ¹⁵If I am guilty, too bad for me. And even if I'm innocent, I am filled with shame and misery so that I can't hold my head high. ¹⁶And if I hold my head high, you hunt me like a lion and display your awesome power against me. ¹⁷Again and again you witness against me. You pour out an ever-increasing volume of anger upon me and bring fresh armies against me.

¹⁸" 'Why, then, did you bring me out of my mother's womb? Why didn't you let me die at birth? ¹⁹Then I would have been spared this miserable existence. I would have gone directly from the womb to the grave. ²⁰I have only a little time left, so leave me alone—that I may have a little moment of comfort ²¹before I leave for the land of darkness and utter gloom, never to return. ²²It is a land as dark as midnight, a land of utter gloom where confusion reigns and the light is as dark as midnight.' "

ZOPHAR'S FIRST RESPONSE TO JOB

11 Then Zophar the Naamathite replied to Job:

9:20 Or *he.* **10:10** Hebrew *You poured me out like milk and curdled me like cheese.*

My Daily Worship

— April 26 —

It's the Honest Truth

JOB 6:1–14:22

I am disgusted with my life. Let me complain freely.
I will speak in the bitterness of my soul (10:1).

[i reflect]

Wait a minute—isn't this the same person who earlier refused to become bitter and turn away from God? He's changed his tune pretty radically, hasn't he? Well, yes and no.

When we read Job's words in 1:21–22, we were amazed at his faithfulness and his refusal to sin against God in spite of his unspeakable loss. Here he is freely and openly acknowledging his bitterness and disillusionment with his Maker. (When people tell you the Bible is a nice little book filled with nice little stories, open it up to Job and let them read a little bit of his life.) Yes, Job is expressing his hurt and frustration now—after all, it's been quite some time since his troubles began, and still no relief in sight—but don't miss the key aspect of his lament. He's still pouring his heart out *to* God, not turning his face *away from* him.

It's all right to be honest with God about your feelings, even the dark, negative ones you don't want anyone else to see. Do you think he'll be surprised or disappointed? He already knows how you feel, and he isn't the least bit threatened by it. What parent doesn't want his child to come to him when he or she is hurt?

You can be completely honest with God. If not with him, then who? He is the one we can count on to never leave us or abandon us, even when we're in our darkest times. Corrie ten Boom wrote, "When a train goes through a tunnel and it gets dark, you don't throw away the ticket and jump off. You sit still and trust the engineer."

Sit still before God right now. Tell him what you are experiencing; then worship the One who will never leave you.

[i pray]

Father, no more pious words and spiritual-sounding platitudes. I'm going to be
honest with you about my hurts, my doubts, and my frustrations, trusting
that you are big enough to handle it, and gracious enough to allow it.

[i respond]

Re-read Job's words from today's passage as if they are coming from your heart. Identify your own complaints, and tell God the specifics. Ask God to help you work through your circumstances.

²"Shouldn't someone answer this torrent of words? Is a person proved innocent just by talking a lot? ³Should I remain silent while you babble on? When you mock God, shouldn't someone make you ashamed? ⁴You claim, 'My teaching is pure,' and 'I am clean in the sight of God.' ⁵If only God would speak; if only he would tell you what he thinks! ⁶If only he would tell you the secrets of wisdom, for true wisdom is not a simple matter. Listen! God is doubtless punishing you far less than you deserve!

⁷"Can you solve the mysteries of God? Can you discover everything there is to know about the Almighty? ⁸Such knowledge is higher than the heavens—but who are you? It is deeper than the underworld*—what can you know in comparison to him? ⁹It is broader than the earth and wider than the sea. ¹⁰If God comes along and puts a person in prison, or if he calls the court to order, who is going to stop him? ¹¹For he knows those who are false, and he takes note of all their sins. ¹²An empty-headed person won't become wise any more than a wild donkey can bear human offspring*!

¹³"If only you would prepare your heart and lift up your hands to him in prayer! ¹⁴Get rid of your sins and leave all iniquity behind you. ¹⁵Then your face will brighten in innocence. You will be strong and free of fear. ¹⁶You will forget your misery. It will all be gone like water under the bridge. ¹⁷Your life will be brighter than the noonday. Any darkness will be as bright as morning. ¹⁸You will have courage because you will have hope. You will be protected and will rest in safety. ¹⁹You will lie down unafraid, and many will look to you for help. ²⁰But the wicked will lose hope. They have no escape. Their hope becomes despair."

Job's Fourth Speech: A Response to Zophar

12 Then Job spoke again:

²"You really know everything, don't you? And when you die, wisdom will die with you! ³Well, I know a few things myself—and you're no better than I am. Who doesn't know these things you've been saying? ⁴Yet my friends laugh at me. I am a man who calls on God and receives an answer. I am a just and blameless man, yet they laugh at me. ⁵People who are at ease mock those in trouble. They give a push to people who are stumbling. ⁶But even robbers are left in peace, and those who provoke God—and God has them in his power—live in safety!

⁷"Ask the animals, and they will teach you. Ask the birds of the sky, and they will tell you. ⁸Speak to the earth, and it will instruct you. Let the fish of the sea speak to you. ⁹They all know that the LORD has done this. ¹⁰For the life of every living thing is in his hand, and the breath of all humanity. ¹¹Just as the mouth tastes good food, so the ear tests the words it hears. ¹²Wisdom belongs to the aged, and understanding to those who have lived many years.

¹³"But true wisdom and power are with God; counsel and understanding are his. ¹⁴What he destroys cannot be rebuilt. When he closes in on someone, there is no escape. ¹⁵If he holds back the rain, the earth becomes a desert. If he releases the waters, they flood the earth.

¹⁶"Yes, strength and wisdom are with him; deceivers and deceived are both in his power. ¹⁷He leads counselors away stripped of good judgment; he drives judges to madness. ¹⁸He removes the royal robe of kings. With ropes around their waist, they are led away. ¹⁹He leads priests away stripped of status; he overthrows the mighty. ²⁰He silences the trusted adviser, and he removes the insight of the elders. ²¹He pours disgrace upon princes and confiscates weapons from the strong.

²²"He floods the darkness with light; he brings light to the deepest gloom. ²³He raises up nations, and he destroys them. He makes nations expand, and he abandons them. ²⁴He takes away the understanding of kings, and he

11:8 Hebrew *Sheol.*   11:12 Or *bear a tame colt.*

leaves them wandering in a wasteland without a path. ²⁵They grope in the darkness without a light. He makes them stagger like drunkards.

Job Wants to Argue His Case with God

13 "Look, I have seen many instances such as you describe. I understand what you are saying. ²I know as much as you do. You are no better than I am. ³Oh, how I long to speak directly to the Almighty. I want to argue my case with God himself. ⁴For you are smearing me with lies. As doctors, you are worthless quacks. ⁵Please be quiet! That's the smartest thing you could do. ⁶Listen to my charge; pay attention to my arguments.

⁷"Are you defending God by means of lies and dishonest arguments? ⁸You should be impartial witnesses, but will you slant your testimony in his favor? Will you argue God's case for him? ⁹Be careful that he doesn't find out what you are doing! Or do you think you can fool him as easily as you fool people? ¹⁰No, you will be in serious trouble with him if even in your hearts you slant your testimony in his favor. ¹¹Doesn't his majesty strike terror into your heart? Does not your fear of him seize you? ¹²Your statements have about as much value as ashes. Your defense is as fragile as a clay pot.

¹³"Be silent now and leave me alone. Let me speak—and I will face the consequences. ¹⁴Yes, I will take my life in my hands and say what I really think. ¹⁵God might kill me, but I cannot wait. I am going to argue my case with him. ¹⁶But this is what will save me: that I am not godless. If I were, I would be thrown from his presence.

¹⁷"Listen closely to what I am about to say. Hear me out. ¹⁸I have prepared my case; I will be proved innocent. ¹⁹Who can argue with me over this? If you could prove me wrong, I would remain silent until I die.

Job Asks How He Has Sinned

²⁰"O God, there are two things I beg of you, and I will be able to face you. ²¹Remove your

---

Words of Worship

PROCLAIM, PROCLAMATION

Proclaim, Proclamation—Hebrew *hig-gid* "bring out, reveal"; *sip-per* "recount"; *ho-di-a'* "make known"; *'a-mar* "say, speak"; Greek *ex-an-gel-lo* "declare, proclaim"; *kat-an-gel-lo* "announce." Other words are used.

"I will proclaim your greatness," the psalmist declared (Psalm 145:6). Our worship is a proclamation that God is in control of his universe and of our lives. When we call on him in prayer and praise, we are announcing that his kingdom has come—he has arrived, and he is taking over! As we worship the Lord, we herald his appearance in the midst of his people, to bless them and correct whatever is amiss.

Worship proclaims the good news of Jesus Christ. Paul summarized it: "Christ appeared in the flesh and was shown to be righteous by the Spirit. He was seen by angels and was announced to the nations. He was believed on in the world and was taken up into heaven" (1 Timothy 3:16). As we worship the Lord, we declare the message of Christ to earthly authorities, to spiritual powers, and to ourselves.

---

hand from me, and don't terrify me with your awesome presence. ²²Now summon me, and I will answer! Or let me speak to you, and you reply. ²³Tell me, what have I done wrong? Show me my rebellion and my sin. ²⁴Why do you turn away from me? Why do you consider me your enemy? ²⁵Would you terrify a leaf that is blown by the wind? Would you chase a dry stalk of grass?

²⁶"You write bitter accusations against me and bring up all the sins of my youth. ²⁷You

put my feet in stocks. You watch all my paths. You trace all my footprints. [28]I waste away like rotting wood, like a moth-eaten coat.

14 "How frail is humanity! How short is life, and how full of trouble! [2]Like a flower, we blossom for a moment and then wither. Like the shadow of a passing cloud, we quickly disappear. [3]Must you keep an eye on such a frail creature and demand an accounting from me? [4]Who can create purity in one born impure? No one! [5]You have decided the length of our lives. You know how many months we will live, and we are not given a minute longer. [6]So give us a little rest, won't you? Turn away your angry stare. We are like hired hands, so let us finish the task you have given us.

[7]"If a tree is cut down, there is hope that it will sprout again and grow new branches. [8]Though its roots have grown old in the earth and its stump decays, [9]at the scent of water it may bud and sprout again like a new seedling.

[10]"But when people die, they lose all strength. They breathe their last, and then where are they? [11]As water evaporates from a lake and as a river disappears in drought, [12]people lie down and do not rise again. Until the heavens are no more, they will not wake up nor be roused from their sleep.

[13]"I wish you would hide me with the dead and forget me there until your anger has passed. But mark your calendar to think of me again! [14]If mortals die, can they live again? This thought would give me hope, and through my struggle I would eagerly wait for release. [15]You would call and I would answer, and you would yearn for me, your handiwork. [16]For then you would count my steps, instead of watching for my sins. [17]My sins would be sealed in a pouch, and you would cover over my iniquity.

[18]"But as mountains fall and crumble and as rocks fall from a cliff, [19]as water wears away the stones and floods wash away the soil, so you destroy people's hope. [20]You always overpower them, and then they pass from the scene. You disfigure them in death and send them away. [21]They never know if their sons grow up in honor or sink to insignificance. [22]They are absorbed in their own pain and grief."

ELIPHAZ'S SECOND RESPONSE TO JOB

15 Then Eliphaz the Temanite replied: [2]"You are supposed to be a wise man, and yet you give us all this foolish talk. You are nothing but a windbag. [3]It isn't right to speak so foolishly. What good do such words do? [4]Have you no fear of God, no reverence for him? [5]Your sins are telling your mouth what to say. Your words are based on clever deception. [6]But why should I condemn you? Your own mouth does!

[7]"Were you the first person ever born? Were you born before the hills were made? [8]Were you listening at God's secret council? Do you have a monopoly on wisdom? [9]What do you know that we don't? What do you understand that we don't? [10]On our side are aged, gray-haired men much older than your father!

[11]"Is God's comfort too little for you? Is his gentle word not enough? [12]What has captured your reason? What has weakened your vision, [13]that you turn against God and say all these evil things? [14]Can a mortal be pure? Can a human be just? [15]Why, God doesn't even trust the angels*! Even the heavens cannot be absolutely pure in his sight. [16]How much less pure is a corrupt and sinful person with a thirst for wickedness!

[17]"If you will listen, I will answer you from my own experience. [18]And it is confirmed by the experience of wise men who have heard the same thing from their fathers, [19]those to whom the land was given long before any foreigners arrived.

[20]"Wicked people are in pain throughout

15:15 Hebrew *the holy ones.*

> *Worship is giving God the best that he has given you. Be careful what you do with the best you have.*
>
> OSWALD CHAMBERS

their lives. ²¹They are surrounded by terrors, and even on good days they fear the attack of the destroyer. ²²They dare not go out into the darkness for fear they will be murdered. ²³They wander abroad for bread, saying, 'Where is it?'* They know their ruin is certain. ²⁴That dark day terrifies them. They live in distress and anguish, like a king preparing for an attack. ²⁵For they have clenched their fists against God, defying the Almighty. ²⁶Holding their strong shields, they defiantly charge against him.

²⁷"These wicked people are fat and rich, ²⁸but their cities will be ruined. They will live in abandoned houses that are ready to tumble down. ²⁹They will not continue to be rich. Their wealth will not endure, and their possessions will no longer spread across the horizon.

³⁰"They will not escape the darkness. The flame will burn them up, and the breath of God will destroy everything they have. ³¹Let them no longer trust in empty riches. They are only fooling themselves, for emptiness will be their only reward. ³²They will be cut down in the prime of life, and all they counted on will disappear. ³³They will be like a vine whose grapes are harvested before they are ripe, like an olive tree that sheds its blossoms so the fruit cannot form. ³⁴For the godless are barren. Their homes, enriched through bribery, will be consumed by fire. ³⁵They conceive trouble and evil, and their hearts give birth only to deceit."

JOB'S FIFTH SPEECH: A RESPONSE TO ELIPHAZ

16 Then Job spoke again:

²"I have heard all this before. What miserable comforters you are! ³Won't you ever stop your flow of foolish words? What have I said that makes you speak so endlessly? ⁴I could say the same things if you were in my place. I could spout off my criticisms against you and shake my head at you. ⁵But that's not what I would do. I would speak in a way that helps you. I would try to take away your grief. ⁶But as it is, my grief remains no matter how I defend myself. And it does not help if I refuse to speak.

⁷"O God, you have ground me down and devastated my family. ⁸You have reduced me to skin and bones—as proof, they say, of my sins. ⁹God hates me and tears angrily at my flesh. He gnashes his teeth at me and pierces me with his eyes. ¹⁰People jeer and laugh at me. They slap my cheek in contempt. A mob gathers against me. ¹¹God has handed me over to sinners. He has tossed me into the hands of the wicked.

¹²"I was living quietly until he broke me apart. He took me by the neck and dashed me to pieces. Then he set me up as his target. ¹³His archers surrounded me, and his arrows pierced me without mercy. The ground is wet with my blood.* ¹⁴Again and again he smashed me, charging at me like a warrior. ¹⁵Here I sit in sackcloth. I have surrendered, and I sit in the dust. ¹⁶My eyes are red with weeping; darkness covers my eyes. ¹⁷Yet I am innocent, and my prayer is pure.

¹⁸"O earth, do not conceal my blood. Let it cry out on my behalf. ¹⁹Even now my witness is in heaven. My advocate is there on high. ²⁰My friends scorn me, but I pour out my tears to God. ²¹Oh, that someone would mediate between God and me, as a person mediates between friends. ²²For soon I must go down that road from which I will never return.

15:23 Greek version reads *He is appointed to be food for a vulture.*   **16:13** Hebrew *my gall.*

JOB CONTINUES TO DEFEND HIS INNOCENCE

17 "My spirit is crushed, and I am near death. The grave is ready to receive me. ²I am surrounded by mockers. I watch how bitterly they taunt me.

³"You must defend my innocence, O God, since no one else will stand up for me. ⁴You have closed their minds to understanding, but do not let them triumph. ⁵They denounce their companions for their own advantage, so let their children faint with hunger.

⁶"God has made a mockery of me among the people; they spit in my face. ⁷My eyes are dim with weeping, and I am but a shadow of my former self. ⁸The upright are astonished when they see me. The innocent are aroused against the ungodly. ⁹The righteous will move onward and forward, and those with pure hearts will become stronger and stronger.

¹⁰"As for all of you, come back and try again! But I will not find a wise man among you. ¹¹My days are over. My hopes have disappeared. My heart's desires are broken. ¹²They say that night is day and day is night; how they pervert the truth! ¹³I might go to the grave and make my bed in darkness. ¹⁴And I might call the grave my father, and the worm my mother and my sister. ¹⁵But where then is my hope? Can anyone find it? ¹⁶No, my hope will go down with me to the grave. We will rest together in the dust!"

BILDAD'S SECOND RESPONSE TO JOB

18 Then Bildad the Shuhite replied: ²"How long before you stop talking? Speak sense if you want us to answer! ³Do you think we are cattle? Do you think we have no intelligence? ⁴You may tear your hair out in anger, but will that cause the earth to be abandoned? Will it make rocks fall from a cliff?

⁵"The truth remains that the light of the wicked will be snuffed out. The sparks of their fire will not glow. ⁶The light in their tent will grow dark. The lamp hanging above them will be quenched. ⁷The confident stride of the wicked will be shortened. Their own schemes will be their downfall.

⁸"The wicked walk into a net. They fall into a pit that's been dug in the path. ⁹A trap grabs them by the heel. A noose tightens around them. ¹⁰A snare lies hidden in the ground. A rope lies coiled on their path.

¹¹"Terrors surround the wicked and trouble them at every step. ¹²Their vigor is depleted by hunger, and calamity waits for them to stumble. ¹³Disease eats their skin; death devours their limbs. ¹⁴They are torn from the security of their tent, and they are brought down to the king of terrors. ¹⁵The home of the wicked will disappear beneath a fiery barrage of burning sulfur. ¹⁶Their roots will dry up, and their branches will wither. ¹⁷All memory of their existence will perish from the earth. No one will remember them. ¹⁸They will be thrust from light into darkness, driven from the world. ¹⁹They will have neither children nor grandchildren, nor any survivor in their home country. ²⁰People in the west are appalled at their fate; people in the east are horrified. ²¹They will say, 'This was the home of a wicked person, the place of one who rejected God.'"

JOB'S SIXTH SPEECH: A RESPONSE TO BILDAD

19 Then Job spoke again: ²"How long will you torture me? How long will you try to break me with your words? ³Ten times now you have meant to insult me. You should be ashamed of dealing with me so harshly. ⁴And even if I have sinned, that is my concern, not yours. ⁵You are trying to overcome me, using my humiliation as evidence of my sin, ⁶but it is God who has wronged me. I cannot defend myself, for I am like a city under siege.

⁷"I cry out for help, but no one hears me. I protest, but there is no justice. ⁸God has blocked my way and plunged my path into darkness. ⁹He has stripped me of my honor and removed the crown from my head. ¹⁰He has demolished me on every side, and I am

My Daily Worship

— *April 27* —

What Do You Know?

JOB 15:1–21:34

But as for me, I know that my Redeemer lives, and that he will stand upon the earth at last.
And after my body has decayed, yet in my body I will see God! (19:25–26).

[i reflect]

"Eat health food—jog daily—die anyway."

You may remember that bumper sticker from some years back. The point it makes, rather darkly, is that our bodies are not designed to last forever in their current condition. No matter how well (or how poorly) we maintain them, they will wear out sooner or later. The question confronts everyone: *What then?*

The Bible makes it clear: "It is destined that each person dies only once and after that comes judgment" (Hebrews 9:27). We live, we die, we stand before God to give account for our lives. Does that thought fill you with anticipation or dread? For the man or woman who does not know the atoning power of Christ's death on the cross, the thought of appearing before a holy God should be a terrifying prospect.

But we who have accepted the payment Jesus made on our behalf, need have no fear or apprehension. We stand justified—*made right*—before him. Romans 8:1 proclaims: "So now there is no condemnation for those who belong to Christ Jesus." *No condemnation*—only love, forgiveness, mercy, and grace.

The Old Testament only specifically addresses life after death in a relative handful of places, and nowhere more compellingly than here in 19:25–27. In spite of his great suffering, or perhaps because of it, Job lifted his eyes and his thoughts to eternity and found great comfort there: *As for me, I know that my Redeemer lives . . . . [and] I will see him for myself*. As we grow older, and the prospect of our own mortality becomes more real with each birthday, let us set our gaze in that same place, find that same comfort and assurance. He's *our* Redeemer, too.

Set your eyes on your Redeemer today and worship him.

[i pray]

Lord Jesus, you are my sure and certain hope of eternal life. I do not trust in my own works
of righteousness, but in your work of sacrifice and atonement on my behalf. Who do I
have in heaven but you? And what more do I need? Help me to see death not as a
wall, but a door through which I will some day pass and see you face-to-face.

[i respond]

Create your own slogan that reflects your view of what awaits you beyond this world. Display it in a place that will be a reminder that "my Redeemer lives."

finished. He has destroyed my hope. ¹¹His fury burns against me; he counts me as an enemy. ¹²His troops advance. They build up roads to attack me. They camp all around my tent.

¹³"My relatives stay far away, and my friends have turned against me. ¹⁴My neighbors and my close friends are all gone. ¹⁵The members of my household have forgotten me. The servant girls consider me a stranger. I am like a foreigner to them. ¹⁶I call my servant, but he doesn't come; I even plead with him! ¹⁷My breath is repulsive to my wife. I am loathsome to my own family. ¹⁸Even young children despise me. When I stand to speak, they turn their backs on me. ¹⁹My close friends abhor me. Those I loved have turned against me. ²⁰I have been reduced to skin and bones and have escaped death by the skin of my teeth.

²¹"Have mercy on me, my friends, have mercy, for the hand of God has struck me. ²²Why must you persecute me as God does? Why aren't you satisfied with my anguish?

²³"Oh, that my words could be written. Oh, that they could be inscribed on a monument, ²⁴carved with an iron chisel and filled with lead, engraved forever in the rock.

²⁵"But as for me, I know that my Redeemer lives, and that he will stand upon the earth at last. ²⁶And after my body has decayed, yet in my body I will see God*! ²⁷I will see him for myself. Yes, I will see him with my own eyes. I am overwhelmed at the thought!

²⁸"How dare you go on persecuting me, saying, 'It's his own fault'? ²⁹I warn you, you yourselves are in danger of punishment for your attitude. Then you will know that there is judgment."

Zophar's Second Response to Job

20 Then Zophar the Naamathite replied:

²"I must reply because I am greatly disturbed. ³I have had to endure your insults, but now my spirit prompts me to reply.

⁴"Don't you realize that ever since people were first placed on the earth, ⁵the triumph of the wicked has been short-lived and the joy of the godless has been only temporary? ⁶Though the godless man's pride reaches to the heavens and though his head touches the clouds, ⁷yet he will perish forever, thrown away like his own dung. Those who knew him will ask, 'Where is he?' ⁸He will fade like a dream and not be found. He will vanish like a vision in the night. ⁹Neither his friends nor his family will ever see him again. ¹⁰His children will beg from the poor, for he must give back his ill-gotten wealth. ¹¹He was just a young man, but his bones will lie in the dust.

¹²"He enjoyed the taste of his wickedness, letting it melt under his tongue. ¹³He savored it, holding it long in his mouth. ¹⁴But suddenly, the food he has eaten turns sour within him, a poisonous venom in his stomach. ¹⁵He will vomit the wealth he swallowed. God won't let him keep it down. ¹⁶He will suck the poison of snakes. The viper will kill him. ¹⁷He will never again enjoy abundant streams of olive oil or rivers of milk and honey. ¹⁸His labors will not be rewarded. His wealth will bring him no joy. ¹⁹For he oppressed the poor and left them destitute. He foreclosed on their homes. ²⁰He was always greedy but never satisfied. Of all the things he dreamed about, nothing remains. ²¹Nothing is left after he finishes gorging himself; therefore, his prosperity will not endure.

²²"In the midst of plenty, he will run into trouble, and disasters will destroy him. ²³May God give him a bellyful of trouble. May God rain down his anger upon him. ²⁴He will try to escape, but God's arrow will pierce him. ²⁵The arrow is pulled from his body, and the arrowhead glistens with blood.* The terrors of death are upon him.

²⁶"His treasures will be lost in deepest darkness. A wildfire will devour his goods, consuming all he has left. ²⁷The heavens will reveal his guilt, and the earth will give testimony against him. ²⁸A flood will sweep away

---

19:26 Or *without my body I will see God.*   20:25 Hebrew *with gall.*

his house. God's anger will descend on him in torrents. ²⁹This is the fate that awaits the wicked. It is the inheritance decreed by God."

Job's Seventh Speech: A Response to Zophar

21 Then Job spoke again: ²"Listen closely to what I am saying. You can console me by listening to me. ³Bear with me, and let me speak. After I have spoken, you may mock me.

⁴"My complaint is with God, not with people. No wonder I'm so impatient. ⁵Look at me and be stunned. Put your hand over your mouth in shock. ⁶When I think about what I am saying, I shudder. My body trembles.

⁷"The truth is that the wicked live to a good old age. They grow old and wealthy. ⁸They live to see their children grow to maturity, and they enjoy their grandchildren. ⁹Their homes are safe from every fear, and God does not punish them. ¹⁰Their bulls never fail to breed. Their cows bear calves without miscarriage. ¹¹Their children skip about like lambs in a flock of sheep. ¹²They sing with tambourine and harp. They make merry to the sound of the flute. ¹³They spend their days in prosperity; then they go down to the grave in peace. ¹⁴All this, even though they say to God, 'Go away. We want no part of you and your ways.¹⁵Who is the Almighty, and why should we obey him? What good will it do us if we pray?' ¹⁶But their prosperity is not of their own doing, so I will have nothing to do with that kind of thinking.

¹⁷"Yet the wicked get away with it time and time again. They rarely have trouble, and God skips them when he distributes sorrows in his anger. ¹⁸Are they driven before the wind like straw? Are they carried away by the storm? Not at all!

¹⁹" 'Well,' you say, 'at least God will punish their children!' But I say that God should punish the ones who sin, not their children! Let them feel their own penalty. ²⁰Let their own eyes see their destruction. Let them drink

> *If we want to worship in spirit and in truth, we need to rediscover the capacity to wonder that God placed within each of us.*
>
> — David Jeremiah

deeply of the anger of the Almighty. ²¹For when they are dead, they will not care what happens to their family.

²²"But who can teach a lesson to God, the supreme Judge? ²³One person dies in prosperity and security, ²⁴the very picture of good health. ²⁵Another person dies in bitter poverty, never having tasted the good life. ²⁶Both alike are buried in the same dust, both eaten by the same worms.

²⁷"Look, I know your thoughts. I know the schemes you plot against me. ²⁸You will tell me of rich and wicked people who came to disaster because of their sins. ²⁹But I tell you to ask those who have been around, and they can tell you the truth. ³⁰Evil people are spared in times of calamity and are allowed to escape. ³¹No one rebukes them openly. No one repays them for what they have done. ³²When they are carried to the grave, an honor guard keeps watch at their tomb. ³³A great funeral procession goes to the cemetery. Many pay their respects as the body is laid to rest and the earth gives sweet repose.

³⁴"How can you comfort me? All your explanations are wrong!"

Eliphaz's Third Response to Job

22 Then Eliphaz the Temanite replied: ²"Can a person's actions be of benefit to God? Can even a wise person be helpful to him? ³Is it any pleasure to the Almighty if you are righteous? Would it be

any gain to him if you were perfect? ⁴Is it because of your reverence for him that he accuses and judges you? ⁵Not at all! It is because of your wickedness! Your guilt has no limit!

⁶"For example, you must have lent money to your friend and then kept the clothing he gave you as a pledge. Yes, you stripped him to the bone. ⁷You must have refused water for the thirsty and food for the hungry. ⁸After all, you think the land belongs to the powerful and that those who are privileged have a right to it! ⁹You must have sent widows away without helping them and crushed the strength of orphans. ¹⁰That is why you are surrounded by traps and sudden fears. ¹¹That is why you cannot see in the darkness, and waves of water cover you.

¹²"God is so great—higher than the heavens, higher than the farthest stars. ¹³But you reply, 'That's why God can't see what I am doing! How can he judge through the thick darkness? ¹⁴For thick clouds swirl about him, and he cannot see us. He is way up there, walking on the vault of heaven.'

¹⁵"Will you continue on the old paths where evil people have walked? ¹⁶They were snatched away in the prime of life, and the foundations of their lives were washed away forever. ¹⁷For they said to God, 'Leave us alone! What can the Almighty do for us?' ¹⁸But they forgot that he had filled their homes with good things, so I will have nothing to do with that kind of thinking.

¹⁹"Now the righteous will be happy to see the wicked destroyed, and the innocent will laugh them to scorn. ²⁰They will say, 'Surely our enemies have been destroyed. The last of them have been consumed in the fire.'

²¹"Stop quarreling with God! If you agree with him, you will have peace at last, and things will go well for you. ²²Listen to his instructions, and store them in your heart. ²³If you return to the Almighty and clean up your life, you will be restored. ²⁴Give up your lust for money, and throw your precious gold into the river. ²⁵Then the Almighty himself will be your treasure. He will be your precious silver!

²⁶"Then you will delight yourself in the Almighty and look up to God. ²⁷You will pray to him, and he will hear you, and you will fulfill your vows to him. ²⁸Whatever you decide to do will be accomplished, and light will shine on the road ahead of you. ²⁹If someone is brought low and you say, 'Help him up,' God will save the downcast. ³⁰Then even sinners will be rescued by your pure hands."

JOB'S EIGHTH SPEECH: A RESPONSE TO ELIPHAZ

23 Then Job spoke again:

²"My complaint today is still a bitter one, and I try hard not to groan aloud. ³If only I knew where to find God, I would go to his throne and talk with him there. ⁴I would lay out my case and present my arguments. ⁵Then I would listen to his reply and understand what he says to me. ⁶Would he merely argue with me in his greatness? No, he would give me a fair hearing. ⁷Fair and honest people can reason with him, so I would be acquitted by my Judge.

⁸"I go east, but he is not there. I go west, but I cannot find him. ⁹I do not see him in the north, for he is hidden. I turn to the south, but I cannot find him. ¹⁰But he knows where I am going. And when he has tested me like gold in a fire, he will pronounce me innocent.

¹¹"For I have stayed in God's paths; I have followed his ways and not turned aside. ¹²I have not departed from his commands but have treasured his word in my heart. ¹³Nevertheless, his mind concerning me remains unchanged, and who can turn him from his purposes? Whatever he wants to do, he does. ¹⁴So he will do for me all he has planned. He controls my destiny. ¹⁵No wonder I am so terrified in his presence. When I think of it, terror grips me. ¹⁶God has made my heart faint; the Almighty has terrified me. ¹⁷Darkness is all around me; thick, impenetrable darkness is everywhere.

JOB ASKS WHY THE WICKED ARE NOT PUNISHED

24 "Why doesn't the Almighty open the court and bring judgment? Why must the godly wait for him in vain? ²Evil people steal land by moving the boundary markers. They steal flocks of sheep, ³and they even take donkeys from the poor and fatherless. A poor widow must surrender her valuable ox as collateral for a loan. ⁴The poor are kicked aside; the needy must hide together for safety. ⁵Like the wild donkeys in the desert, the poor must spend all their time just getting enough to keep body and soul together. They go into the desert to search for food for their children.

⁶They harvest a field they do not own, and they glean in the vineyards of the wicked. ⁷All night they lie naked in the cold, without clothing or covering. ⁸They are soaked by mountain showers, and they huddle against the rocks for want of a home.

⁹"The wicked snatch a widow's child from her breast; they take the baby as a pledge for a loan. ¹⁰The poor must go about naked, without any clothing. They are forced to carry food while they themselves are starving. ¹¹They press out olive oil without being allowed to taste it, and they tread in the winepress as they suffer from thirst. ¹²The groans of the dying rise from the city, and the wounded cry for help, yet God does not respond to their moaning.

¹³"Wicked people rebel against the light. They refuse to acknowledge its ways. They will not stay in its paths. ¹⁴The murderer rises in the early dawn to kill the poor and needy; at night he is a thief. ¹⁵The adulterer waits for the twilight, for he says, 'No one will see me then.' He masks his face so no one will know him. ¹⁶They break into houses at night and sleep in the daytime. They are not acquainted with the light. ¹⁷The black night is their morning. They ally themselves with the terrors of the darkness.

¹⁸"But they disappear from the earth as quickly as foam is swept down a river. Everything they own is cursed, so that no one enters their vineyard. ¹⁹Death consumes sinners just as drought and heat consume snow. ²⁰Even the sinner's own mother will forget him. Worms will find him sweet to eat. No one will remember him. Wicked people are broken like a tree in the storm. ²¹For they have taken advantage of the childless who have no protecting sons. They refuse to help the needy widows.

²²"God, in his power, drags away the rich. They may rise high, but they have no assurance in life. ²³They may be allowed to live in security, but God is always watching them. ²⁴And though they are great now, in a moment they will be gone like all others, withered like heads of grain.

²⁵"Can anyone claim otherwise? Who can prove me wrong?"

BILDAD'S THIRD RESPONSE TO JOB

25 Then Bildad the Shuhite replied:
²"God is powerful and dreadful. He enforces peace in the heavens. ³Who is able to count his heavenly army? Does his light not shine on all the earth? ⁴How can a mere mortal stand before God and claim to be righteous? Who in all the earth is pure? ⁵God is so glorious that even the moon and stars scarcely shine compared to him. ⁶How much less are mere people, who are but worms in his sight?"

JOB'S NINTH SPEECH: A RESPONSE TO BILDAD

26 Then Job spoke again:
²"How you have helped the powerless! How you have saved a person who has no strength! ³How you have enlightened my stupidity! What wise things you have said! ⁴Where have you gotten all these wise sayings? Whose spirit speaks through you?

⁵"The dead tremble in their place beneath the waters. ⁶The underworld* is naked in God's presence. There is no cover for the place of destruction. ⁷God stretches the northern sky over empty space and hangs the earth on nothing. ⁸He wraps the rain in his thick clouds, and the clouds do not burst with the weight. ⁹He shrouds his throne with his clouds. ¹⁰He created the horizon when he separated the waters; he set the boundaries for day and night. ¹¹The foundations of heaven tremble at his rebuke. ¹²By his power the sea grew calm. By his skill he crushed the great sea monster.* ¹³His Spirit made the heavens beautiful, and his power pierced the gliding serpent.

¹⁴"These are some of the minor things he does, merely a whisper of his power. Who can understand the thunder of his power?"

JOB'S FINAL SPEECH

27 Job continued speaking:
²"I make this vow by the living God, who has taken away my rights, by the Almighty who has embittered my soul. ³As long as I live, while I have breath from God, ⁴my lips will speak no evil, and my tongue will speak no lies. ⁵I will never concede that you are right; until I die, I will defend my innocence. ⁶I will maintain my innocence without wavering. My conscience is clear for as long as I live.

⁷"May my enemy be punished like the wicked, my adversary like evil men. ⁸For what hope do the godless have when God cuts them off and takes away their life? ⁹Will God listen to their cry when trouble comes upon them? ¹⁰Can they take delight in the Almighty? Can they call to God at any time?

¹¹"I will teach you about God's power. I will not conceal anything that concerns the Almighty. ¹²But I don't need to, for you yourselves have seen all this; yet you are saying all these useless things to me.

¹³"This is what the wicked will receive from God; this is their inheritance from the Almighty. ¹⁴If they have a multitude of children, their children will die in war or starve to death. ¹⁵Those who survive will be brought down to the grave by a plague, with no one to mourn them, not even their wives.

¹⁶"Evil people may have all the money in the world, and they may store away mounds of

> *I know I have an immortal soul,*
> *because I have immortal longings.*
>
> ANNE FRANK

26:6 Hebrew *Sheol.*   26:12 Hebrew *Rahab,* the name of a mythical sea monster that represents chaos in ancient literature.

clothing. ¹⁷But the righteous will wear that clothing, and the innocent will divide all that money. ¹⁸The houses built by the wicked are as fragile as a spiderweb, as flimsy as a shelter made of branches.

¹⁹"The wicked go to bed rich but wake up to find that all their wealth is gone. ²⁰Terror overwhelms them, and they are blown away in the storms of the night. ²¹The east wind carries them away, and they are gone. It sweeps them away. ²²It whirls down on them without mercy. They struggle to flee from its power. ²³But everyone jeers at them and mocks them.

Job Speaks of Wisdom and Understanding

28 "People know how to mine silver and refine gold. ²They know how to dig iron from the earth and smelt copper from stone. ³They know how to put light into darkness and explore the farthest, darkest regions of the earth as they search for ore. ⁴They sink a mine shaft into the earth far from where anyone lives. They descend on ropes, swinging back and forth. ⁵Bread comes from the earth, but below the surface the earth is melted as by fire.

⁶"People know how to find sapphires and gold dust—⁷treasures that no bird of prey can see, no falcon's eye observe—⁸for they are deep within the mines. No wild animal has ever walked upon those treasures; no lion has set his paw there. ⁹People know how to tear apart flinty rocks and overturn the roots of mountains. ¹⁰They cut tunnels in the rocks and uncover precious stones. ¹¹They dam up the trickling streams and bring to light the hidden treasures.

¹²"But do people know where to find wisdom? Where can they find understanding? ¹³No one knows where to find it, for it is not found among the living. ¹⁴'It is not here,' says the ocean. 'Nor is it here,' says the sea.

¹⁵"It cannot be bought for gold or silver. ¹⁶Its value is greater than all the gold of Ophir, greater than precious onyx stone or sapphires. ¹⁷Wisdom is far more valuable than gold and crystal. It cannot be purchased with jewels mounted in fine gold. ¹⁸Coral and valuable rock crystal are worthless in trying to get it. The price of wisdom is far above pearls. ¹⁹Topaz from Ethiopia* cannot be exchanged for it. Its value is greater than the purest gold.

²⁰"But do people know where to find wisdom? Where can they find understanding? ²¹For it is hidden from the eyes of all humanity. Even the sharp-eyed birds in the sky cannot discover it. ²²But Destruction and Death say, 'We have heard a rumor of where wisdom can be found.'

²³"God surely knows where it can be found, ²⁴for he looks throughout the whole earth, under all the heavens. ²⁵He made the winds blow and determined how much rain should fall. ²⁶He made the laws of the rain and prepared a path for the lightning. ²⁷Then, when he had done all this, he saw wisdom and measured it. He established it and examined it thoroughly. ²⁸And this is what he says to all humanity: 'The fear of the Lord is true wisdom; to forsake evil is real understanding.'"

Job Speaks of His Former Blessings

29 Job continued speaking:
²"I long for the years gone by when God took care of me, ³when he lighted the way before me and I walked safely through the darkness. ⁴In my early years, the friendship of God was felt in my home. ⁵The Almighty was still with me, and my children were around me. ⁶In those days my cows produced milk in abundance, and my olive groves poured out streams of olive oil.

⁷"Those were the days when I went to the city gate and took my place among the honored leaders. ⁸The young stepped aside when they saw me, and even the aged rose in respect at my coming. ⁹The princes stood in silence and put their hands over their mouths. ¹⁰The

28:19 Hebrew *from Cush.*

highest officials of the city stood quietly, holding their tongues in respect.

¹¹"All who heard of me praised me. All who saw me spoke well of me. ¹²For I helped the poor in their need and the orphans who had no one to help them. ¹³I helped those who had lost hope, and they blessed me. And I caused the widows' hearts to sing for joy. ¹⁴All I did was just and honest. Righteousness covered me like a robe, and I wore justice like a turban. ¹⁵I served as eyes for the blind and feet for the lame. ¹⁶I was a father to the poor and made sure that even strangers received a fair trial. ¹⁷I broke the jaws of godless oppressors and made them release their victims.

¹⁸"I thought, 'Surely I will die surrounded by my family after a long, good life. ¹⁹For I am like a tree whose roots reach the water, whose branches are refreshed with the dew. ²⁰New honors are constantly bestowed on me, and my strength is continually renewed.'

²¹"Everyone listened to me and valued my advice. They were silent as they waited for me to speak. ²²And after I spoke, they had nothing to add, for my counsel satisfied them. ²³They longed for me to speak as they longed for rain. They waited eagerly, for my words were as refreshing as the spring rain. ²⁴When they were discouraged, I smiled at them. My look of approval was precious to them. ²⁵I told them what they should do and presided over them as their chief. I lived as a king among his troops and as one who comforts those who mourn.

JOB SPEAKS OF HIS ANGUISH

30 "But now I am mocked by those who are younger than I, by young men whose fathers are not worthy to run with my sheepdogs. ²A lot of good they are to me—those worn-out wretches! ³They are gaunt with hunger and flee to the deserts and the wastelands, desolate and gloomy. ⁴They eat coarse leaves, and they burn the roots of shrubs for heat. ⁵They are driven from civilization, and people shout after them as if they were thieves. ⁶So now they live in frightening ravines and in caves and among the rocks. ⁷They sound like animals as they howl among the bushes; they huddle together for shelter beneath the nettles. ⁸They are nameless fools, outcasts of civilization.

⁹"And now their sons mock me with their vulgar song! They taunt me! ¹⁰They despise me and won't come near me, except to spit in my face. ¹¹For God has cut the cords of my tent. He has humbled me, so they have thrown off all restraint. ¹²These outcasts oppose me to my face. They send me sprawling; they lay traps in my path. ¹³They block my road and do everything they can to hasten my calamity, knowing full well that I have no one to help me. ¹⁴They come at me from all directions. They rush upon me when I am down. ¹⁵I live in terror now. They hold me in contempt, and my prosperity has vanished as a cloud before a strong wind.

¹⁶"And now my heart is broken. Depression haunts my days. ¹⁷My weary nights are filled with pain as though something were relentlessly gnawing at my bones. ¹⁸With a strong hand, God grabs my garment. He grips me by the collar of my tunic. ¹⁹He has thrown me into the mud. I have become as dust and ashes.

²⁰"I cry to you, O God, but you don't answer me. I stand before you, and you don't bother to look. ²¹You have become cruel toward me. You persecute me with your great power. ²²You throw me into the whirlwind and destroy me in the storm. ²³And I know that you are sending me to my death—the destination of all who live.

²⁴"Surely no one would turn against the needy when they cry for help. ²⁵Did I not weep for those in trouble? Was I not deeply grieved for the needy? ²⁶So I looked for good, but evil came instead. I waited for the light, but darkness fell. ²⁷My heart is troubled and restless. Days of affliction have come upon me. ²⁸I walk in gloom, without sunlight. I stand in the public square and cry for help. ²⁹But instead, I am considered a brother to jackals and a companion to ostriches. ³⁰My skin has turned

My Daily Worship

— *April 28* —

IT'S A MYSTERY TO ME

JOB 22:1–31:40

God surely knows where it can be found, for he looks throughout the whole earth, under
all the heavens. . . . And this is what he says to all humanity: "The fear of the
Lord is true wisdom; to forsake evil is real understanding" (28:23, 28).

[i reflect]

When we suffer—and everyone does, at some level, from the princess in the palace to the Jobs of the world who suffer unbelievable pain and hardship—it is almost reflexive that our first reaction is to raise our voice and ask, *"Why me?* Did I do something to deserve this? Is God angry with me, punishing me for some sin I've committed? Is God involved in my pain at all?"

"Why?" is a question we are free to ask God (Job certainly did, over and over); yet God is not bound to answer. Sometimes he provides glimpses into his purposes in our pain, but not always. Often the reason for our suffering remains a mystery to us. In those times it is good to focus on what we *do* know—the character of our God.

Job acknowledged that, even though he could not penetrate the veil of mystery surrounding God's plan for his trials, he still accepted that wisdom begins with, resides in, and ends with God. We may not understand his ways, but *he* does, and he understands ours as well. Our lives, including the dark parts, the parts where all we see is darkness all around us and every sensation is pain, are part of the great tapestry of God's unfolding plan of redemption. We may not know what his purpose is, but knowing that he has a purpose is what keeps us from giving in to despair.

Viktor Frankl, a psychotherapist and Holocaust survivor (echoing the German philosopher Frederick Nietzsche), said: "Man can endure almost any *'what'* as long as he has a *'why.'"* Our "why" is knowing that our sovereign God is still in control of our lives and our circumstances even when we are not, and that we can still trust in his goodness, holiness, compassion, and grace. When you confront a "what" today, something beyond your understanding, take time to thank God that he has answered your "whys."

[i pray]

Father, help me to trust you even when I do not understand you. Remind me often
that you are working out your purposes in my life in ways that go far beyond my
understanding. Even though I will not always like it or comprehend it, help me
to accept that your plan for me is perfect and your grace for me is sufficient.

[i respond]

Oswald Chambers wrote, "God does not waste suffering, nor does he discipline out of caprice. If he plows, it is because he proposes a crop." What crop do you think God is plowing right now in your life? Write it down; then thank God for how he is specifically working in you.

Words of Worship

LORD ALMIGHTY

Lord Almighty—Hebrew *Yah-veh tse-va-'ot* "Yahweh of armies"; ***ku**-ri-os sa-ba-**oth*** "Lord of hosts." In the New Testament, *sabaoth* is a transliteration of the Hebrew *tseva'ot* and is mainly found in a few quotations from the Old Testament.

The Ark of the Covenant was a sacred container, topped by the golden figures of the cherubim that held the tablets of the commandments. It symbolized Yahweh's presence with his people, and he was said to be "enthroned between the mighty cherubim" (2 Kings 19:15). Because the ark went before the people of Israel as they wandered through the wilderness and also as they went into battle, Yahweh's name came to be linked with the massed forces of his worshipers. He was called "Yahweh of armies," or Lord Almighty, especially in the psalms and the prophetic writings.

It may seem strange that the "God of peace" (Hebrews 13:20) is also the God of armies. But worship is also warfare. When we praise the Lord, we do battle in the Spirit "against the evil rulers and authorities of the unseen world" (Ephesians 6:12). We have enlisted in the army of the Lord Almighty, and the taste of victory is ours.

---

dark, and my bones burn with fever. ³¹My harp plays sad music, and my flute accompanies those who weep.

JOB'S FINAL PROTEST OF INNOCENCE

31 "I made a covenant with my eyes not to look with lust upon a young woman. ²What has God above chosen for us? What is our inheritance from the Almighty on high? ³It is calamity for the wicked, misfortune for those who do evil. ⁴He sees everything I do and every step I take.

⁵"Have I lied to anyone or deceived anyone? ⁶Let God judge me on the scales of justice, for he knows my integrity. ⁷If I have strayed from his pathway, or if my heart has lusted for what my eyes have seen, or if I am guilty of any other sin, ⁸then let someone else harvest the crops I have planted, and let all that I have planted be uprooted.

⁹"If my heart has been seduced by a woman, or if I have lusted for my neighbor's wife, ¹⁰then may my wife belong to another man; may other men sleep with her. ¹¹For lust is a shameful sin, a crime that should be punished. ¹²It is a devastating fire that destroys to hell. It would wipe out everything I own.

¹³"If I have been unfair to my male or female servants, if I have refused to hear their complaints, ¹⁴how could I face God? What could I say when he questioned me about it? ¹⁵For God created both me and my servants. He created us both.

¹⁶"Have I refused to help the poor, or crushed the hopes of widows who looked to me for help? ¹⁷Have I been stingy with my food and refused to share it with hungry orphans? ¹⁸No, from childhood I have cared for orphans, and all my life I have cared for widows. ¹⁹Whenever I saw someone who was homeless and without clothes, ²⁰did they not praise me for providing wool clothing to keep them warm? ²¹If my arm has abused an orphan because I thought I could get away with it, ²²then let my shoulder be wrenched out of place! Let my arm be torn from its socket! ²³That would be better than facing the judgment sent by God. For if the majesty of God opposes me, what hope is there?

²⁴"Have I put my trust in money or felt secure because of my gold? ²⁵Does my happiness depend on my wealth and all that I own? ²⁶Have I looked at the sun shining in the skies, or the moon walking down its silver pathway, ²⁷and been secretly enticed in my heart to worship them? ²⁸If so, I should be punished by the

judges, for it would mean I had denied the God of heaven.

²⁹"Have I ever rejoiced when my enemies came to ruin or become excited when harm came their way? ³⁰No, I have never cursed anyone or asked for revenge. ³¹My servants have never let others go hungry. ³²I have never turned away a stranger but have opened my doors to everyone. ³³Have I tried to hide my sins as people normally do, hiding my guilt in a closet? ³⁴Have I feared the crowd and its contempt, so that I refused to acknowledge my sin and would not go outside?

³⁵"If only I had someone who would listen to me and try to see my side! Look, I will sign my name to my defense. Let the Almighty show me that I am wrong. Let my accuser write out the charges against me. ³⁶I would face the accusation proudly. I would treasure it like a crown. ³⁷For I would tell him exactly what I have done. I would come before him like a prince.

³⁸"If my land accuses me and all its furrows weep together, ³⁹or if I have stolen its crops or murdered its owners, ⁴⁰then let thistles grow on that land instead of wheat and weeds instead of barley."

Job's words are ended.

ELIHU RESPONDS TO JOB'S FRIENDS

32 Job's three friends refused to reply further to him because he kept insisting on his innocence.

²Then Elihu son of Barakel the Buzite, of the clan of Ram, became angry. He was angry because Job refused to admit that he had sinned and that God was right in punishing him. ³He was also angry with Job's three friends because they had condemned God* by their inability to answer Job's arguments. ⁴Elihu had waited for the others to speak because they were older than he. ⁵But when he saw that they had no further reply, he spoke out angrily.

⁶Elihu son of Barakel the Buzite said, "I am young and you are old, so I held back and did not dare to tell you what I think. ⁷I thought, 'Those who are older should speak, for wisdom comes with age.' ⁸Surely it is God's Spirit within people, the breath of the Almighty within them, that makes them intelligent. ⁹But sometimes the elders are not wise. Sometimes the aged do not understand justice. ¹⁰So listen to me and let me express my opinion.

> *Timid, tame domesticated adoration plays no part in heaven's chorus.*
>
> D. A. CARSON

¹¹"I have waited all this time, listening very carefully to your arguments, listening to you grope for words. ¹²I have listened, but not one of you has refuted Job or answered his arguments. ¹³And don't tell me, 'He is too wise for us. Only God can convince him.' ¹⁴If Job had been arguing with me, I would not answer with that kind of logic! ¹⁵You sit there baffled, with no further response. ¹⁶Should I continue to wait, now that you are silent? Must I also remain silent? ¹⁷No, I will say my piece. I will speak my mind. I surely will. ¹⁸For I am pent up and full of words, and the spirit within me urges me on. ¹⁹I am like a wine cask without a vent. My words are ready to burst out! ²⁰I must speak to find relief, so let me give my answers. ²¹I won't play favorites or try to flatter anyone. ²²And if I tried, my Creator would soon do away with me.

ELIHU PRESENTS HIS CASE AGAINST JOB

33 "Listen, Job, to what I have to say. ²Now that I have begun to speak, let

32:3 As in ancient Hebrew scribal tradition; the Masoretic Text makes no reference to God.

me continue. ³I speak with all sincerity; I speak the truth. ⁴For the Spirit of God has made me, and the breath of the Almighty gives me life. ⁵Answer me, if you can; make your case and take your stand.

⁶"Look, you and I are the same before God. I, too, was formed from clay. ⁷So you don't need to be afraid of me. I am not some great person to make you nervous and afraid.

⁸"You have said it in my hearing. I have heard your very words. ⁹You said, 'I am pure; I am innocent; I have not sinned. ¹⁰God is picking a quarrel with me, and he considers me to be his enemy. ¹¹He puts my feet in the stocks and watches every move I make.'

¹²"In this you are not right, and I will show you why. As you yourself have said, 'God is greater than any person.' ¹³So why are you bringing a charge against him? You say, 'He does not respond to people's complaints.' ¹⁴But God speaks again and again, though people do not recognize it. ¹⁵He speaks in dreams, in visions of the night when deep sleep falls on people as they lie in bed. ¹⁶He whispers in their ear and terrifies them with his warning. ¹⁷He causes them to change their minds; he keeps them from pride. ¹⁸He keeps them from the grave, from crossing over the river of death. ¹⁹Or God disciplines people with sickness and pain, with ceaseless aching in their bones. ²⁰They lose their appetite and do not care for even the most delicious food. ²¹They waste away to skin and bones. ²²They are at death's door; the angels of death wait for them.

²³"But if a special messenger from heaven is there to intercede for a person, to declare that he is upright, ²⁴God will be gracious and say, 'Set him free. Do not make him die, for I have found a ransom for his life.' ²⁵Then his body will become as healthy as a child's, firm and youthful again. ²⁶When he prays to God, he will be accepted. And God will receive him with joy and restore him to good standing. ²⁷He will declare to his friends, 'I sinned, but it was not worth it. ²⁸God rescued me from the grave, and now my life is filled with light.'

²⁹"Yes, God often does these things for people. ³⁰He rescues them from the grave so they may live in the light of the living. ³¹Mark this well, Job. Listen to me, and let me say more. ³²But if you have anything to say, go ahead. I want to hear it, for I am anxious to see you justified. ³³But if not, then listen to me. Keep silent and I will teach you wisdom!"

Elihu Accuses Job of Arrogance

34 Then Elihu said:

²"Listen to me, you wise men. Pay attention, you who have knowledge. ³Just as the mouth tastes good food, the ear tests the words it hears.' ⁴So let us discern for ourselves what is right; let us learn together what is good. ⁵For Job has said, 'I am innocent, but God has taken away my rights. ⁶I am innocent, but they call me a liar. My suffering is incurable, even though I have not sinned.'

⁷"Has there ever been a man as arrogant as Job, with his thirst for irreverent talk? ⁸He seeks the companionship of evil people. He spends his time with wicked men. ⁹He has even said, 'Why waste time trying to please God?'

¹⁰"Listen to me, you who have understanding. Everyone knows that God doesn't sin! The Almighty can do no wrong. ¹¹He repays people according to their deeds. He treats people according to their ways. ¹²There is no truer statement than this: God will not do wrong. The Almighty cannot twist justice. ¹³Who put the world in his care? Who has set the whole world in place? ¹⁴If God were to take back his spirit* and withdraw his breath, ¹⁵all life would cease, and humanity would turn again to dust.

¹⁶"Listen now and try to understand. ¹⁷Could God govern if he hated justice? Are you going to condemn the almighty Judge? ¹⁸For he says to kings and nobles, 'You are wicked and unjust.' ¹⁹He doesn't care how

34:14 Or *his Spirit*.

great a person may be, and he doesn't pay any more attention to the rich than to the poor. He made them all. ²⁰In a moment they die. At midnight they all pass away; the mighty are removed without human hand.

²¹"For God carefully watches the way people live; he sees everything they do. ²²No darkness is thick enough to hide the wicked from his eyes. ²³For it is not up to mortals to decide when to come before God in judgment. ²⁴He brings the mighty to ruin without asking anyone, and he sets up others in their places. ²⁵He watches what they do, and in the night he overturns them, destroying them. ²⁶He openly strikes them down for their wickedness. ²⁷For they turned aside from following him. They have no respect for any of his ways. ²⁸So they cause the poor to cry out, catching God's attention. Yes, he hears the cries of the needy. ²⁹When he is quiet, who can make trouble? But when he hides his face, who can find him? ³⁰He prevents the godless from ruling so they cannot be a snare to the people.

³¹"Why don't people say to God, 'I have sinned, but I will sin no more'? ³²Or 'I don't know what evil I have done; tell me, and I will stop at once'?

³³"Must God tailor his justice to your demands? But you have rejected him! The choice is yours, not mine. Go ahead, share your wisdom with us. ³⁴After all, bright people will tell me, and wise people will hear me say, ³⁵'Job speaks without knowledge; his words lack insight.' ³⁶Job, you deserve the maximum penalty for the wicked way you have talked. ³⁷For now you have added rebellion and blasphemy against God to your other sins."

ELIHU REMINDS JOB OF GOD'S JUSTICE

35 Then Elihu said:

²"Do you think it is right for you to claim, 'I am righteous before God'? ³Yet you also ask, 'What's the use of living a righteous life? How will it benefit me?'

⁴"I will answer you and all your friends, too. ⁵Look up into the sky and see the clouds high

---

Words of Worship

SEEK

Seek—Hebrew *biq-qesh* "seek, inquire"; *da-rash* "seek out, follow"; *shi-char* "seek eagerly"; Greek *ze-te-o* "seek, search out." The Bible's emphasis on seeking God is evident in the number of times it uses expressions such as "seek the LORD," "seek God" or "seek his face" (used more than 100 times). The importance of seeking God is also underscored by the use of several different words for this concept.

God isn't playing "hide and seek" with us. And he isn't lost. When the Bible refers to seeking the Lord, that simply means to call upon him in worship and prayer. Isaiah makes that clear when he uses two parallel expressions: "Seek the LORD while you can find him. Call on him now while he is near" (Isaiah 55:6). Jesus told Philip, "Anyone who has seen me has seen the Father!" (John 14:9). As Christians, we always know where to find God.

But God is seeking, too. As Jesus said, "True worshipers will worship the Father in spirit and in truth. The Father is looking for anyone who will worship him that way" (John 4:23). Let's not try to play "hide and seek" with *him!*

---

above you. ⁶If you sin, what do you accomplish against him? Even if you sin again and again, what effect will it have on him? ⁷If you are good, is this some great gift to him? What could you possibly give him? ⁸No, your sins affect only people like yourself, and your good deeds affect only other people.

⁹"The oppressed cry out beneath the wrongs that are done to them. They groan beneath the power of the mighty. ¹⁰Yet they don't ask, 'Where is God my Creator, the one

who gives songs in the night? ¹¹Where is the one who makes us wiser than the animals and birds?'

¹²"And if they do cry out and God does not answer, it is because of their pride. ¹³But it is wrong to say God doesn't listen, to say the Almighty isn't concerned. ¹⁴And it is even more false to say he doesn't see what is going on. He will bring about justice if you will only wait. ¹⁵But do you cry out against him because he does not respond in anger? ¹⁶Job, you have protested in vain. You have spoken like a fool."

36 Elihu continued speaking:
²"Let me go on, and I will show you the truth of what I am saying. For I have not finished defending God! ³I will give you many illustrations of the righteousness of my Creator. ⁴I am telling you the honest truth, for I am a man of well-rounded knowledge.

⁵"God is mighty, yet he does not despise anyone! He is mighty in both power and understanding. ⁶He does not let the wicked live but gives justice to the afflicted. ⁷His eyes never leave the innocent, but he establishes and exalts them with kings forever. ⁸If troubles come upon them and they are enslaved and afflicted, ⁹he takes the trouble to show them the reason. He shows them their sins, for they have behaved proudly. ¹⁰He gets their attention and says they must turn away from evil.

¹¹"If they listen and obey God, then they will be blessed with prosperity throughout their lives. All their years will be pleasant. ¹²But if they refuse to listen to him, they will perish in battle and die from lack of understanding. ¹³For the godless are full of resentment. Even when he punishes them, they refuse to cry out to him for help. ¹⁴They die young after wasting their lives in immoral living. ¹⁵But by means of their suffering, he rescues those who suffer. For he gets their attention through adversity.

¹⁶"God has led you away from danger, giving you freedom. You have prospered in a wide and pleasant valley. ¹⁷But you are too obsessed with judgment on the godless. Don't worry, justice will be upheld. ¹⁸But watch out, or you may be seduced with wealth. Don't let yourself be bribed into sin. ¹⁹Could all your wealth and mighty efforts keep you from distress? ²⁰Do not long for the cover of night, for that is when people will be destroyed. ²¹Be on guard! Turn back from evil, for it was to prevent you from getting into a life of evil that God sent this suffering.

Elihu Reminds Job of God's Power

²²"Look, God is all-powerful. Who is a teacher like him? ²³No one can tell him what to do. No one can say to him, 'You have done wrong.' ²⁴Instead, glorify his mighty works, singing songs of praise. ²⁵Everyone has seen these things, but only from a distance.

²⁶"Look, God is exalted beyond what we can understand. His years are without number. ²⁷He draws up the water vapor and then distills it into rain. ²⁸The rain pours down from the clouds, and everyone benefits from it. ²⁹Can anyone really understand the spreading of the clouds and the thunder that rolls forth from heaven? ³⁰See how he spreads the lightning around him and how it lights up the depths of the sea. ³¹By his mighty acts he governs the people, giving them food in abundance. ³²He fills his hands with lightning bolts. He hurls each at its target. ³³The thunder announces his presence; the storm announces his indignant anger.*

37 "My heart pounds as I think of this. It leaps within me. ²Listen carefully to the thunder of God's voice as it rolls from his mouth. ³It rolls across the heavens, and his lightning flashes out in every direction. ⁴Then comes the roaring of the thunder—the tremendous voice of his majesty. He does not restrain the thunder when he speaks. ⁵God's voice is glorious in the thunder. We cannot comprehend the greatness of his power.

36:33 Or *even the cattle know when a storm is coming.* The meaning of the Hebrew is uncertain.

My Daily Worship

— *April 29* —

RULING BY GRACE

JOB 32:1–37:24

We cannot imagine the power of the Almighty, yet he is so just and merciful
that he does not oppress us. No wonder people everywhere fear him.
People who are truly wise show him reverence (37:23–24).

[i reflect]

If you were a king or a dictator with absolute, unchallenged power over your domain, how would you deal with rebels, with those who chafed at living under your rule?

God rules his Creation by his unlimited, sovereign power. He can control this planet and its inhabitants in any way he sees fit, and the Bible makes it clear that the inhabitants are all guilty of revolting against him (Romans 3). How would we expect a just God to deal with such rebels?

He could deal with us harshly, pouring out the penalties our sins deserve. Who could blame him or say he was being unfair? Yet he chooses to be merciful, extending to us forgiveness, compassion, and grace. It is what makes Christianity unique. In his book *What's So Amazing About Grace?*, Philip Yancey recounts a debate among the attendees at a British conference on comparative religions about what belief is unique to the Christian faith. C. S. Lewis ended the debate with one word: grace.

Writes Yancey, "The notion of God's love coming to us free of charge, no strings attached seems to go against every instinct of humanity. The Buddhist eight-fold path, the Hindu doctrine of Karma, the Jewish covenant, and the Muslim code of law—each of these offers a way to earn approval. Only Christianity dares to make God's love unconditional."

Do you need a reason to praise God today? Thank him for his power, his majesty, and his sovereignty. Thank him that he poured out the wrath our sins deserve on his Son, Jesus. And thank him for his grace.

[i pray]

Father, forgive me for the times I have thought that I deserved your love and
forgiveness. I know you love me in spite of what I am, not because of it.
Thank you for granting me mercy instead of giving me justice.

[i respond]

In what ways have you rebelled against God recently, or just lived as if he didn't exist? Describe your rebellion in one or two sentences. Then thank God for his graciousness, mercy, and forgiveness.

⁶"He directs the snow to fall on the earth and tells the rain to pour down. ⁷Everyone stops working at such a time so they can recognize his power. ⁸The wild animals hide in the rocks or in their dens. ⁹The stormy wind comes from its chamber, and the driving winds bring the cold. ¹⁰God's breath sends the ice, freezing wide expanses of water. ¹¹He loads the clouds with moisture, and they flash with his lightning. ¹²The clouds turn around and around under his direction. They do whatever he commands throughout the earth. ¹³He causes things to happen on earth, either as a punishment or as a sign of his unfailing love.

¹⁴"Listen, Job; stop and consider the wonderful miracles of God! ¹⁵Do you know how God controls the storm and causes the lightning to flash forth from his clouds? ¹⁶Do you understand how he balances the clouds with wonderful perfection and skill? ¹⁷When you are sweltering in your clothes and the south wind dies down and everything is still, ¹⁸he makes the skies reflect the heat like a giant mirror. Can you do that?

¹⁹"You think you know so much, so teach the rest of us what to say to God. We are too ignorant to make our own arguments. ²⁰Should God be told that I want to speak? Can we speak when we are confused? ²¹We cannot look at the sun, for it shines brightly in the sky when the wind clears away the clouds. ²²Golden splendor comes from the mountain of God. He is clothed in dazzling splendor. ²³We cannot imagine the power of the Almighty, yet he is so just and merciful that he does not oppress us. ²⁴No wonder people everywhere fear him. People who are truly wise show him reverence."

The Lord Challenges Job

38 Then the LORD answered Job from the whirlwind:

²"Who is this that questions my wisdom with such ignorant words? ³Brace yourself, because I have some questions for you, and you must answer them.

⁴"Where were you when I laid the foundations of the earth? Tell me, if you know so much. ⁵Do you know how its dimensions were determined and who did the surveying? ⁶What supports its foundations, and who laid its cornerstone ⁷as the morning stars sang together and all the angels* shouted for joy?

⁸"Who defined the boundaries of the sea as it burst from the womb, ⁹and as I clothed it with clouds and thick darkness? ¹⁰For I locked it behind barred gates, limiting its shores. ¹¹I said, 'Thus far and no farther will you come. Here your proud waves must stop!'

¹²"Have you ever commanded the morning to appear and caused the dawn to rise in the east? ¹³Have you ever told the daylight to spread to the ends of the earth, to bring an end to the night's wickedness? ¹⁴For the features of the earth take shape as the light approaches, and the dawn is robed in red. ¹⁵The light disturbs the haunts of the wicked, and it stops the arm that is raised in violence.

¹⁶"Have you explored the springs from which the seas come? Have you walked about and explored their depths? ¹⁷Do you know where the gates of death are located? Have you seen the gates of utter gloom? ¹⁸Do you realize the extent of the earth? Tell me about it if you know!

¹⁹"Where does the light come from, and where does the darkness go? ²⁰Can you take it to its home? Do you know how to get there? ²¹But of course you know all this! For you were born before it was all created, and you are so very experienced!

²²"Have you visited the treasuries of the snow? Have you seen where the hail is made and stored? ²³I have reserved it for the time of trouble, for the day of battle and war. ²⁴Where is the path to the origin of light? Where is the home of the east wind?

²⁵"Who created a channel for the torrents of rain? Who laid out the path for the lightning? ²⁶Who makes the rain fall on barren land, in a

38:7 Hebrew *sons of God.*

desert where no one lives? ²⁷Who sends the rain that satisfies the parched ground and makes the tender grass spring up?

²⁸"Does the rain have a father? Where does dew come from? ²⁹Who is the mother of the ice? Who gives birth to the frost from the heavens? ³⁰For the water turns to ice as hard as rock, and the surface of the water freezes.

³¹"Can you hold back the movements of the stars? Are you able to restrain the Pleiades or Orion? ³²Can you ensure the proper sequence of the seasons or guide the constellation of the Bear with her cubs across the heavens? ³³Do you know the laws of the universe and how God rules the earth?

³⁴"Can you shout to the clouds and make it rain? ³⁵Can you make lightning appear and cause it to strike as you direct it? ³⁶Who gives intuition and instinct? ³⁷Who is wise enough to count all the clouds? Who can tilt the water jars of heaven, ³⁸turning the dry dust to clumps of mud?

³⁹"Can you stalk prey for a lioness and satisfy the young lions' appetites ⁴⁰as they lie in their dens or crouch in the thicket? ⁴¹Who provides food for the ravens when their young cry out to God as they wander about in hunger?

THE LORD'S CHALLENGE CONTINUES

39 "Do you know when the mountain goats give birth? Have you watched as the wild deer are born? ²Do you know how many months they carry their young? Are you aware of the time of their delivery? ³They crouch down to give birth to their young and deliver their offspring. ⁴Their young grow up in the open fields, then leave their parents and never return.

⁵"Who makes the wild donkey wild? ⁶I have placed it in the wilderness; its home is the wasteland. ⁷It hates the noise of the city, and it has no driver to shout at it. ⁸The mountains are its pastureland, where it searches for every blade of grass.

⁹"Will the wild ox consent to being tamed? Will it stay in your stall? ¹⁰Can you hitch a wild ox to a plow? Will it plow a field for you? ¹¹Since it is so strong, can you trust it? Can you go away and trust the ox to do your work? ¹²Can you rely on it to return, bringing your grain to the threshing floor?

¹³"The ostrich flaps her wings grandly, but they are no match for the feathers of the stork. ¹⁴She lays her eggs on top of the earth, letting them be warmed in the dust. ¹⁵She doesn't worry that a foot might crush them or that wild animals might destroy them. ¹⁶She is harsh toward her young, as if they were not her own. She is unconcerned though they die, ¹⁷for God has deprived her of wisdom. He has given her no understanding. ¹⁸But whenever she jumps up to run, she passes the swiftest horse with its rider.

¹⁹"Have you given the horse its strength or clothed its neck with a flowing mane? ²⁰Did you give it the ability to leap forward like a locust? Its majestic snorting is something to hear! ²¹It paws the earth and rejoices in its strength. When it charges to war, ²²it is unafraid. It does not run from the sword. ²³The arrows rattle against it, and the spear and javelin flash. ²⁴Fiercely it paws the ground and rushes forward into battle when the trumpet blows. ²⁵It snorts at the sound of the bugle. It senses the battle even at a distance. It quivers at the noise of battle and the shout of the captain's commands.

²⁶"Are you the one who makes the hawk soar and spread its wings to the south? ²⁷Is it at your command that the eagle rises to the heights to make its nest? ²⁸It lives on the cliffs, making its home on a distant, rocky crag. ²⁹From there it hunts its prey, keeping watch with piercing eyes. ³⁰Its nestlings gulp down blood, for it feeds on the carcass of the slaughtered."

40 Then the LORD said to Job, ²"Do you still want to argue with the Almighty? You are God's critic, but do you have the answers?"

JOB RESPONDS TO THE LORD

[3] Then Job replied to the LORD, [4] "I am nothing—how could I ever find the answers? I will put my hand over my mouth in silence. [5] I have said too much already. I have nothing more to say."

THE LORD CHALLENGES JOB AGAIN

[6] Then the LORD answered Job from the whirlwind:

[7] "Brace yourself, because I have some questions for you, and you must answer them. [8] Are you going to discredit my justice and condemn me so you can say you are right? [9] Are you as strong as God, and can you thunder with a voice like his? [10] All right then, put on your robes of state, your majesty and splendor. [11] Give vent to your anger. Let it overflow against the proud. [12] Humiliate the proud with a glance; walk on the wicked where they stand. [13] Bury them in the dust. Imprison them in the world of the dead. [14] Then even I would praise you, for your own strength would save you.

[15] "Take a look at the mighty hippopotamus.* I made it, just as I made you. It eats grass like an ox. [16] See its powerful loins and the muscles of its belly. [17] Its tail is as straight as a cedar. The sinews of its thighs are tightly knit together. [18] Its bones are tubes of bronze. Its limbs are bars of iron. [19] It is a prime example of God's amazing handiwork. Only its Creator can threaten it. [20] The mountains offer it their best food, where all the wild animals play. [21] It lies down under the lotus plants, hidden by the reeds. [22] The lotus plants give it shade among the willows beside the stream. [23] It is not disturbed by raging rivers, not even when the swelling Jordan rushes down upon it. [24] No one can catch it off guard or put a ring in its nose and lead it away.

THE LORD'S CHALLENGE CONTINUES

41 "Can you catch a crocodile* with a hook or put a noose around its jaw? [2] Can you tie it with a rope through the nose or pierce its jaw with a spike? [3] Will it beg you for mercy or implore you for pity? [4] Will it agree to work for you? Can you make it be your slave for life? [5] Can you make it a pet like a bird, or give it to your little girls to play with? [6] Will merchants try to buy it? Will they sell it in their shops? [7] Will its hide be hurt by darts, or its head by a harpoon? [8] If you lay a hand on it, you will never forget the battle that follows, and you will never try it again!

[9] "No, it is useless to try to capture it. The hunter who attempts it will be thrown down. [10] And since no one dares to disturb the crocodile, who would dare to stand up to me? [11] Who will confront me and remain safe*? Everything under heaven is mine.

[12] "I want to emphasize the tremendous strength in the crocodile's limbs and throughout its enormous frame. [13] Who can strip off its hide, and who can penetrate its double layer of armor*? [14] Who could pry open its jaws? For its teeth are terrible! [15] The overlapping scales on its back make a shield. [16] They are close together so no air can get between them. [17] They lock together so nothing can penetrate them.

[18] "When it sneezes, it flashes light! Its eyes are like the red of dawn. [19] Fire and sparks leap from its mouth. [20] Smoke streams from its nostrils like steam from a boiling pot on a fire of dry rushes. [21] Yes, its breath would kindle coals, for flames shoot from its mouth.

[22] "The tremendous strength in its neck strikes terror wherever it goes. [23] Its flesh is hard and firm, not soft and fat. [24] Its heart is as hard as rock, as hard as a millstone. [25] When it rises, the mighty are afraid, gripped by terror. [26] No sword can stop it, nor spear nor dart nor pointed shaft. [27] To the crocodile, iron is nothing but straw, and bronze is rotten wood. [28] Arrows cannot make it flee. Stones shot from a sling are as ineffective as straw. [29] Clubs do no good, and it laughs at the swish of the javelins. [30] Its belly is covered with scales as sharp as

---

40:15 Hebrew at behemoth. 41:1 Hebrew Leviathan; also throughout the following passage. 41:11 As in Greek version; Hebrew reads confront me that I must pay. 41:13 As in Greek version; Hebrew reads its bridle.

My Daily Worship

— *April 30* —

HIS LOVE LEAVES ME SPEECHLESS

JOB 38:1 – 42:17

Then Job replied to the LORD, "I am nothing—how could I ever find the answers? I will put my hand over my mouth in silence. I have said too much already. I have nothing more to say" (40:3–5).

[i reflect]

The chorus of the title track on Steven Curtis Chapman's *Speechless* CD captures the songwriter's response to encountering the Creator's love, majesty, and provision: "And I am speechless, I'm astonished and amazed; I am silenced by your wondrous grace." Silence. Dumbfounded. Without words. Indeed, speechless.

Some 4,000 years before Mr. Chapman *sang* those words, the Old Testament saint Job *lived* them.

Job, as most everyone knows, was the man who found himself at the center of a cosmic wager. Satan charged that Job's "faith" was a thin veneer, built solely on the blessings of God. "Take away your favor," the evil one snarls at God, "and watch him curse you!"

God takes the bet. He lets Satan assault his servant with a malevolence rarely seen on earth. Job is devastated in every conceivable way. He pours out his shattered soul to God, even as he doggedly tries to hang on to his flagging faith.

For most of the book, God says nothing as Job cries out in his confusion. And heaven remains silent, even when Job's advisers offer their multiple theories on suffering.

At last, God speaks. He thunders forth with an avalanche of questions that leave Job dumbfounded. God's point? "I AM in control. I AM also wise and good." Humbled, Job realizes that sometimes the most appropriate form of worship is simply to shut one's mouth before the Almighty.

Today, as you go about your routine, make it your goal to talk less and listen more. Focus on the fact that the God of the universe has a personal interest in you and wants a relationship with *you*. Allow his love to leave you speechless.

[i pray]

Lord God, do whatever it takes to leave me speechless.

[i respond]

Practicing silence and solitude is a rare spiritual discipline in the modern, Western church. Carve out thirty minutes in your day to get alone with God. Don't "do" anything. Just sit quietly in his presence. Listen to what he wants to say to you. Be speechless this entire time.

glass. They tear up the ground as it drags through the mud.

³¹"The crocodile makes the water boil with its commotion. It churns the depths. ³²The water glistens in its wake. One would think the sea had turned white. ³³There is nothing else so fearless anywhere on earth. ³⁴Of all the creatures, it is the proudest. It is the king of beasts."

JOB RESPONDS TO THE LORD

42 Then Job replied to the LORD: ²"I know that you can do anything, and no one can stop you. ³You ask, 'Who is this that questions my wisdom with such ignorance?' It is I. And I was talking about things I did not understand, things far too wonderful for me.

⁴"You said, 'Listen and I will speak! I have some questions for you, and you must answer them.'

⁵"I had heard about you before, but now I have seen you with my own eyes. ⁶I take back everything I said, and I sit in dust and ashes to show my repentance."

CONCLUSION: THE LORD BLESSES JOB

⁷After the LORD had finished speaking to Job, he said to Eliphaz the Temanite: "I am angry with you and with your two friends, for you have not been right in what you said about me, as my servant Job was. ⁸Now take seven young bulls and seven rams and go to my servant Job and offer a burnt offering for yourselves. My servant Job will pray for you, and I will accept his prayer on your behalf. I will not treat you as you deserve, for you have not been right in what you said about me, as my servant Job was."

⁹So Eliphaz the Temanite, Bildad the

Shuhite, and Zophar the Naamathite did as the LORD commanded them, and the LORD accepted Job's prayer.

¹⁰When Job prayed for his friends, the LORD restored his fortunes. In fact, the LORD gave him twice as much as before! ¹¹Then all his brothers, sisters, and former friends came and feasted with him in his home. And they consoled him and comforted him because of all the trials the LORD had brought against him. And each of them brought him a gift of money* and a gold ring.

¹²So the LORD blessed Job in the second half of his life even more than in the beginning. For now he had fourteen thousand sheep, six thousand camels, one thousand teams of oxen, and one thousand female donkeys. ¹³He also gave Job seven more sons and three more daughters. ¹⁴He named his first daughter Jemimah, the second Keziah, and the third Keren-happuch. ¹⁵In all the land there were no other women as lovely as the daughters of Job. And their father put them into his will along with their brothers.

¹⁶Job lived 140 years after that, living to see four generations of his children and grandchildren. ¹⁷Then he died, an old man who had lived a long, good life.

> *Praise and worship is a choice, not just a feeling!*
>
> KENT HENRY

42:11 Hebrew *a kesitah;* the value or weight of the kesitah is no longer known.

Psalms

And I will live in the house of the LORD forever (23:6).

Songs of the Heart

The book of Psalms is the songbook for all who worship God. Here the heart soars in praise, the voice lifts in prayer, and the anguish of sin and the joy of salvation come together to say, "Thank you, Lord. You are all I need."

David, the shepherd-king, wrote many of these songs. He captured such a range of emotions—sometimes despair and anger, sometimes sweet peace—and always focused on God's loving-kindness. That's why worship is the right place to use these songs. In worship we celebrate God's radical, amazing, ever-flowing love. In such a setting, the heart sings. To remain silent and stoic would require the rocks to sing out, something rocks cannot do. But we must.

Psalms is divided into five books, or collections, based on style and date. Each book ends with a doxology, an "Amen" to God for everything said and sung before. Some of these psalms are sung on a pilgrim's journey, some pray that God will destroy enemies, some flow out of struggle and sadness, all point to God as Savior, Redeemer, and the answer to the cry of every heart.

People who are wounded in spirit often turn to the psalms to lead them into worship. These songs reassure them that God knows and cares. When our world goes insane, we need a song to center our hearts or to vent our rage or to ask for the help we cannot find anywhere else. Most of all, we need to know our place in the world.

In worship, we find that place created by the One who fills our cup, leads us through valleys, and takes our fear away. This Great Shepherd will be there at the end of the day. Our home is to be with him—that's where the heart wants to rest. And sing.

Worship Moments

- David worshiped in gladness and joy, with shouting and singing (100:1–2).

- David confessed his sin before God, as preparation for worship (51:2–4).

- Honest words of lament and grief were part of David's prayers and worship (22:1–31; 42:1–11).

- God is worshiped as Creator (8:3–9); as a "rock" and "fortress" (18:2); the "Most High" (91:1); as "king" and "judge of all the earth" (98:9).

BOOK ONE (PSALMS 1–41)

PSALM 1

1 Oh, the joys of those
   who do not follow the advice of the
      wicked,
   or stand around with sinners,
   or join in with scoffers.
2 But they delight in doing everything the
      LORD wants;
   day and night they think about his law.
3 They are like trees planted along the
      riverbank,
   bearing fruit each season without fail.
   Their leaves never wither,
   and in all they do, they prosper.

4 But this is not true of the wicked.
   They are like worthless chaff, scattered
      by the wind.
5 They will be condemned at the time of
      judgment.
   Sinners will have no place among the
      godly.

6 For the LORD watches over the path of the
      godly,
   but the path of the wicked leads to
      destruction.

PSALM 2

1 Why do the nations rage?
   Why do the people waste their time with
      futile plans?
2 The kings of the earth prepare for battle;
   the rulers plot together
against the LORD
   and against his anointed one.
3 "Let us break their chains," they cry,
   "and free ourselves from this slavery."

4 But the one who rules in heaven laughs.
   The Lord scoffs at them.
5 Then in anger he rebukes them,
   terrifying them with his fierce fury.

> *A Christian should be
> an alleluia
> from head to foot.*
>
> AUGUSTINE

6 For the LORD declares, "I have placed my
      chosen king on the throne
   in Jerusalem, my holy city.*"

7 The king proclaims the LORD's decree:
"The LORD said to me, 'You are my son.*
   Today I have become your Father.*
8 Only ask, and I will give you the nations as
      your inheritance,
   the ends of the earth as your
      possession.
9 You will break them with an iron rod
   and smash them like clay pots.' "

10 Now then, you kings, act wisely!
   Be warned, you rulers of the earth!
11 Serve the LORD with reverent fear,
   and rejoice with trembling.
12 Submit to God's royal son, or he will
      become angry,
   and you will be destroyed in the midst of
      your pursuits—
   for his anger can flare up in an instant.

But what joy for all who find protection
   in him!

PSALM 3

*A psalm of David, regarding the time David
fled from his son Absalom.*

1 O LORD, I have so many enemies;
   so many are against me.

2:6 Hebrew *on Zion, my holy mountain.*   **2:7a** Or *Son; also in 2:12.*   **2:7b** Or *Today I reveal you as my son.*

² So many are saying,
   "God will never rescue him!" *Interlude**

³ But you, O Lord, are a shield around me,
   my glory, and the one who lifts my head
      high.

⁴ I cried out to the Lord,
   and he answered me from his holy
      mountain. *Interlude*

⁵ I lay down and slept.
   I woke up in safety,
   for the Lord was watching over me.

⁶ I am not afraid of ten thousand enemies
   who surround me on every side.

⁷ Arise, O Lord!
   Rescue me, my God!
   Slap all my enemies in the face!
   Shatter the teeth of the wicked!

⁸ Victory comes from you, O Lord.
   May your blessings rest on your people.
      Interlude

PSALM 4

*For the choir director: A psalm of David, to be
accompanied by stringed instruments.*

¹ Answer me when I call,
   O God who declares me innocent.
   Take away my distress.
   Have mercy on me and hear my prayer.

² How long will you people ruin my
      reputation?
   How long will you make these
      groundless accusations?
   How long will you pursue lies? *Interlude*

³ You can be sure of this:
   The Lord has set apart the godly for
      himself.
   The Lord will answer when I call
      to him.

⁴ Don't sin by letting anger gain control over
      you.
   Think about it overnight and remain
      silent. *Interlude*

⁵ Offer proper sacrifices,
   and trust in the Lord.

⁶ Many people say, "Who will show us better
      times?"
   Let the smile of your face shine on us,
      Lord.

⁷ You have given me greater joy
   than those who have abundant harvests
      of grain and wine.

⁸ I will lie down in peace and sleep,
   for you alone, O Lord, will keep me safe.

PSALM 5

*For the choir director: A psalm of David, to be
accompanied by the flute.*

¹ O Lord, hear me as I pray;
   pay attention to my groaning.

² Listen to my cry for help, my King and
      my God,
   for I will never pray to anyone but you.

³ Listen to my voice in the morning, Lord.
   Each morning I bring my requests to
      you and wait expectantly.

⁴ O God, you take no pleasure in
      wickedness;
   you cannot tolerate the slightest sin.

⁵ Therefore, the proud will not be allowed to
      stand in your presence,
   for you hate all who do evil.

⁶ You will destroy those who tell lies.
   The Lord detests murderers and
      deceivers.

⁷ Because of your unfailing love, I can enter
      your house;
   with deepest awe I will worship at your
      Temple.

3:2 Hebrew *Selah*. The meaning of this word is uncertain, though it is probably a musical or literary term. It is rendered *Interlude*
throughout the Psalms.

8 Lead me in the right path, O LORD,
   or my enemies will conquer me.
Tell me clearly what to do,
   and show me which way to turn.

9 My enemies cannot speak one truthful
      word.
   Their deepest desire is to destroy others.
Their talk is foul, like the stench from an
      open grave.
   Their speech is filled with flattery.
10 O God, declare them guilty.
   Let them be caught in their own traps.
Drive them away because of their many
      sins,
   for they rebel against you.

11 But let all who take refuge in you
      rejoice;
   let them sing joyful praises forever.
Protect them,
   so all who love your name may be filled
      with joy.
12 For you bless the godly, O LORD,
   surrounding them with your shield of
      love.

PSALM 6

*For the choir director: A psalm of David, to
be accompanied by an eight-stringed
instrument.**

1 O LORD, do not rebuke me in your anger
   or discipline me in your rage.
2 Have compassion on me, LORD, for I am
      weak.
   Heal me, LORD, for my body is in agony.
3 I am sick at heart.
   How long, O LORD, until you
      restore me?

4 Return, O LORD, and rescue me.
   Save me because of your unfailing love.
5 For in death, who remembers you?
   Who can praise you from the grave?

6 I am worn out from sobbing.
   Every night tears drench my bed;
      my pillow is wet from weeping.
7 My vision is blurred by grief;
   my eyes are worn out because of all my
      enemies.

8 Go away, all you who do evil,
   for the LORD has heard my crying.
9 The LORD has heard my plea;
   the LORD will answer my prayer.
10 May all my enemies be disgraced and
      terrified.
   May they suddenly turn back in shame.

PSALM 7

*A psalm of David, which he sang to the LORD
concerning Cush of the tribe of Benjamin.*

1 I come to you for protection, O LORD
      my God.
   Save me from my persecutors—
      rescue me!
2 If you don't, they will maul me like a lion,
   tearing me to pieces with no one to
      rescue me.

3 O LORD my God, if I have done wrong
   or am guilty of injustice,
4 if I have betrayed a friend
   or plundered my enemy without cause,
5 then let my enemies capture me.
   Let them trample me into the ground.
   Let my honor be left in the dust.
                                    Interlude

6 Arise, O LORD, in anger!
   Stand up against the fury of my
      enemies!
   Wake up, my God, and bring justice!
7 Gather the nations before you.
   Sit on your throne high above them.
8 The LORD passes judgment on the nations.
   Declare me righteous, O LORD,
   for I am innocent, O Most High!

6:TITLE Hebrew *with stringed instruments; according to the sheminith.*

My Daily Worship

— *May 1* —

WIDE AWAKE AND WIDE ALIVE!

PSALMS 1:1–4:8

I will lie down in peace and sleep,
for you alone, O LORD, will keep me safe (4:8).

[i reflect]

Doesn't that sound wonderful—to lie down in peace and sleep restfully, completely? For many of us, though, a peaceful night's sleep is more a dream than a reality. In fact, one of the most widely prescribed classes of pharmaceuticals is sleep aids. Insomnia is at epidemic levels as people pack their days with busyness and then stay up half the night worrying about what they didn't get done, what they didn't do well, and what they have to accomplish tomorrow.

Sweet sleep can come, however, when we sense, bone deep, that God is in control. That means spending our days not in a heightened state of activity, but in a heightened state of attunement toward God. Sleeping well at night, we might say, is a by-product of being more than wide awake—rather, being *wide alive*—during the day.

What does it mean to be "wide alive"?

You may be familiar with the quote by Irenaeus that says, "The glory of God is a man fully alive." But do you know how the whole quote runs? "The glory of God is a man fully alive, *and the life of man consists in beholding God."* Wide-aliveness, then, is living with a God-focus.

Living with a God-focus does not imply inactivity. We may, in fact, have a rather full schedule. But at the same time, we're always testing the wind to see where the Spirit is blowing. We're living in purest freedom because we know his eagle eye is searching the skies to guard us from the circling raptors.

Everything is going to be all right. Keep your focus and worship on the One who will keep you safe, and rest assured.

[i pray]

In the day, Lord, and in the night, let me sense your presence so that I
may rest assured that you are near. Help me to live with a God-focus,
wide-alive, so that I may be attuned to you throughout my day.

[i respond]

Before you go to sleep, mentally—or physically—list the concerns, issues, or situations that are weighing on your mind. Check off each one as you hand it over to God. Thank him that he watches over you and keeps you safe.

9 End the wickedness of the ungodly,
    but help all those who obey you.
  For you look deep within the mind and
      heart,
    O righteous God.

10 God is my shield,
    saving those whose hearts are true and
      right.
11 God is a judge who is perfectly fair.
    He is angry with the wicked every day.

12 If a person does not repent,
    God* will sharpen his sword;
  he will bend and string his bow.
13 He will prepare his deadly weapons
    and ignite his flaming arrows.

14 The wicked conceive evil;
    they are pregnant with trouble
  and give birth to lies.
15 They dig a pit to trap others
    and then fall into it themselves.
16 They make trouble,
    but it backfires on them.
  They plan violence for others,
    but it falls on their own heads.

17 I will thank the Lord because he is just;
    I will sing praise to the name of the
      Lord Most High.

PSALM 8

*For the choir director: A psalm of David, to be
accompanied by a stringed instrument.**

1 O Lord, our Lord, the majesty of your
      name fills the earth!
    Your glory is higher than the heavens.

2 You have taught children and nursing
      infants
    to give you praise.*
  They silence your enemies
    who were seeking revenge.

3 When I look at the night sky and see the
      work of your fingers—
    the moon and the stars you have set in
      place—
4 what are mortals that you should think
      of us,
    mere humans that you should care
      for us?*
5 For you made us only a little lower than
      God,*
    and you crowned us with glory and
      honor.
6 You put us in charge of everything you
      made,
    giving us authority over all things—
7 the sheep and the cattle
    and all the wild animals,
8 the birds in the sky, the fish in the sea,
    and everything that swims the ocean
      currents.

9 O Lord, our Lord, the majesty of your
      name fills the earth!

PSALM 9

*For the choir director: A psalm of David, to be
sung to the tune "Death of the Son."*

1 I will thank you, Lord, with all my heart;
    I will tell of all the marvelous things you
      have done.
2 I will be filled with joy because of you.
    I will sing praises to your name,
      O Most High.

3 My enemies turn away in retreat;
    they are overthrown and destroyed
      before you.
4 For you have judged in my favor;
    from your throne, you have judged with
      fairness.
5 You have rebuked the nations and
      destroyed the wicked;
    you have wiped out their names forever.

7:12 Hebrew *he.* 8:TITLE Hebrew *according to the gittith.* 8:2 As in Greek version; Hebrew reads *to show strength.* 8:4 Hebrew *what is
man that you should think of him, the son of man that you should care for him?* 8:5 Or *a little lower than the angels;* Hebrew reads *Elohim.*

My Daily Worship

— *May 2* —

STARRY, STARRY NIGHT

PSALMS 5:1–8:9

When I look at the night sky and see the work of your fingers—
. . . what are mortals that you should think of us? (8:3–4).

[i reflect]

David gazed into the night sky and was overwhelmed by the greatness of God displayed before him. He was not the first to be confronted and confounded by the vast expanse of God's creation.

When Abraham stepped outside his tent one night, awed to learn that his descendants would be vast in number like the stars (Genesis 15:5–6), how many stars did he actually see? About two thousand, if he had average eyesight. Yet astronomers tell us that our galaxy alone contains hundreds of billions of stars—and the Milky Way is just one of hundreds of millions of galaxies.

Another stargazer, Job, identified God as the One responsible for placing the constellation Orion in the sky (Job 9:9). Little did he dream, however, that Betelgeuse (the star forming the right shoulder of Orion) is so big that if you were to put it where our sun is, it would engulf the planets Mercury, Venus, Earth, and Mars.

And Solomon, in his guise as the Teacher, assured us that there is nothing new under the sun (Ecclesiastes 1:9). But he could not know that if we were to drive a car sixty miles per hour for twenty-four hours a day, it would take us more than three years to reach the sun. Nor could he have known that if the sun were the size of the dot over a letter "i," the nearest star would be a dot ten miles away.

Astronomy keeps expanding our vision of what the universe is. This and other scientific disciplines, whether they use telescopes or microscopes, should expand even more our vision of how great the Creator of the universe is. And when we add in the comprehension that this great God stoops to love us and wants a relationship with us . . . well, worship alone is the proper response.

As you observe a sunrise, a sunset, or gaze into the starry night, join David, Abraham, and Job in worshiping the awesome splendor of our God.

[i pray]

Around the bend of our pockmarked Moon, through the glittering rings of Saturn, past the glowing Crab nebula, you, O Lord, are most marvelous to behold! Thank you that you consider us more highly valued than your incredible handiwork.

[i respond]

Worship God by starlight tonight. As you look at the wonder and beauty of the night sky, take time to thank him that he has crowned you with glory and honor.

⁶ My enemies have met their doom;
  their cities are perpetual ruins.
  Even the memory of their uprooted
    cities is lost.

⁷ But the LORD reigns forever,
  executing judgment from his throne.
⁸ He will judge the world with justice
  and rule the nations with fairness.

⁹ The LORD is a shelter for the oppressed,
  a refuge in times of trouble.
¹⁰ Those who know your name trust in you,
  for you, O LORD, have never abandoned
    anyone who searches for you.

¹¹ Sing praises to the LORD who reigns in
    Jerusalem.*
  Tell the world about his unforgettable
    deeds.
¹² For he who avenges murder cares for the
    helpless.
  He does not ignore those who cry to
    him for help.

¹³ LORD, have mercy on me.
  See how I suffer at the hands of those
    who hate me.
  Snatch me back from the jaws of
    death.
¹⁴ Save me, so I can praise you publicly at
    Jerusalem's gates,
  so I can rejoice that you have rescued me.

¹⁵ The nations have fallen into the pit they
    dug for others.
  They have been caught in their own
    trap.
¹⁶ The LORD is known for his justice.
  The wicked have trapped themselves in
    their own snares.   *Quiet Interlude**

¹⁷ The wicked will go down to the grave.*
  This is the fate of all the nations who
    ignore God.
¹⁸ For the needy will not be forgotten forever;

the hopes of the poor will not always be
    crushed.

¹⁹ Arise, O LORD!
  Do not let mere mortals defy you!
  Let the nations be judged in your
    presence!
²⁰ Make them tremble in fear, O LORD.
  Let them know they are merely human.

                                    Interlude

PSALM 10

¹ O LORD, why do you stand so far away?
  Why do you hide when I need you the
    most?
² Proud and wicked people viciously oppress
    the poor.
  Let them be caught in the evil they plan
    for others.
³ For they brag about their evil desires;
  they praise the greedy and curse the
    LORD.
⁴ These wicked people are too proud to
    seek God.
  They seem to think that God is dead.
⁵ Yet they succeed in everything they do.
  They do not see your punishment
    awaiting them.
  They pour scorn on all their enemies.
⁶ They say to themselves, "Nothing bad will
    ever happen to us!
  We will be free of trouble forever!"

⁷ Their mouths are full of cursing, lies, and
    threats.
  Trouble and evil are on the tips of their
    tongues.
⁸ They lurk in dark alleys,
  murdering the innocent who pass by.

They are always searching
  for some helpless victim.
⁹ Like lions they crouch silently,
  waiting to pounce on the helpless.
  Like hunters they capture their victims

9:11 Hebrew *Zion;* also in 9:14. 9:16 Hebrew *Higgaion Selah.* The meaning of this phrase is uncertain. 9:17 Hebrew *to Sheol.*

My Daily Worship

— May 3 —

FURTHER UP AND FURTHER IN
PSALMS 9:1–12:8

Those who know your name trust in you, for you,
O LORD, have never abandoned anyone who searches for you (9:10).

[i reflect]

In *The Last Battle,* the concluding volume of the Chronicles of Narnia, author C. S. Lewis describes his characters' first encounter with the "new Narnia" (a picture of heaven). The call that goes out to them again and again is, "Further up and further in!" The children find themselves in a land that is not only more wonderful, and somehow more *right,* than any other they have ever known, but also infinite in its variety and scope. Racing effortlessly across the landscape, they find they can explore deeper into the new Narnia without ever exhausting its possibilities, each more wonderful than the last.

As is heaven, so is her Master. In eternity, we will discover more and ever more of the excellencies of our Lord. But why wait until then? In this life—in the "old Narnia," so to speak—we can be busy about a discovery process that has God as its objective. In fact, what else is a devotional life for? So-called Christians who think they have arrived at a destination and can stop moving, who have lost their sense of wonder and adventure, who think they know all there is to know of God— these are the ones who know least of all.

Unbelievers are not the only spiritual seekers. As today's passage informs us, we who know God's name and trust in him search for him too. We seek to understand better his nature and his will for us. We search for better ways of living in his presence. And our search for God will not be fruitless, for we *will* find him—or rather, he will find us (Galatians 4:9).

Renew your resolve, like David, to know and worship the name of the One you trust and to continue searching for him "further up and further in."

[i pray]

Inexhaustible God, show me a new vista of your holiness. Open up a fresh path into the
interior of your love. Draw me over a mountain pass toward your vale of mercy.

[i respond]

Write down three questions you have about God, his character, or your relationship with him. Commit to finding the answers to these questions through Bible study, prayer, conversations with other believers, or through reading Christian authors.

and drag them away in nets.
10 The helpless are overwhelmed and
collapse;
they fall beneath the strength of the
wicked.
11 The wicked say to themselves, "God isn't
watching!
He will never notice!"

12 Arise, O LORD!
Punish the wicked, O God!
Do not forget the helpless!
13 Why do the wicked get away with cursing
God?
How can they think, "God will never call
us to account"?

14 But you do see the trouble and grief they
cause.
You take note of it and punish them.
The helpless put their trust in you.
You are the defender of orphans.

15 Break the arms of these wicked, evil
people!
Go after them until the last one is
destroyed!
16 The LORD is king forever and ever!
Let those who worship other gods be
swept from the land.

17 LORD, you know the hopes of the helpless.
Surely you will listen to their cries and
comfort them.
18 You will bring justice to the orphans and
the oppressed,
so people can no longer terrify them.

PSALM 11

For the choir director: A psalm of David.

1 I trust in the LORD for protection.
So why do you say to me,
"Fly to the mountains for safety!
2 The wicked are stringing their bows
and setting their arrows in the
bowstrings.
They shoot from the shadows at those
who do right.
3 The foundations of law and order have
collapsed.
What can the righteous do?"

4 But the LORD is in his holy Temple;
the LORD still rules from heaven.
He watches everything closely,
examining everyone on earth.
5 The LORD examines both the righteous and
the wicked.
He hates everyone who loves violence.
6 He rains down blazing coals on the
wicked,
punishing them with burning sulfur and
scorching winds.
7 For the LORD is righteous, and he loves
justice.
Those who do what is right will see his
face.

PSALM 12

*For the choir director: A psalm of David,
to be accompanied by an eight-stringed
instrument.**

1 Help, O LORD, for the godly are fast
disappearing!
The faithful have vanished from the
earth!
2 Neighbors lie to each other,
speaking with flattering lips and
insincere hearts.
3 May the LORD bring their flattery to an end
and silence their proud tongues.
4 They say, "We will lie to our hearts'
content.
Our lips are our own—who can
stop us?"

5 The LORD replies, "I have seen violence
done to the helpless,

12:TITLE Hebrew *according to the sheminith.*

and I have heard the groans of the poor.
Now I will rise up to rescue them,
as they have longed for me to do."
6 The LORD's promises are pure,
like silver refined in a furnace,
purified seven times over.

7 Therefore, LORD, we know you will protect
the oppressed,
preserving them forever from this lying
generation,
8 even though the wicked strut about,
and evil is praised throughout the land.

PSALM 13

For the choir director: A psalm of David.

1 O LORD, how long will you forget me?
Forever?
How long will you look the other way?
2 How long must I struggle with anguish in
my soul,
with sorrow in my heart every day?
How long will my enemy have the upper
hand?

3 Turn and answer me, O LORD my God!
Restore the light to my eyes, or I will die.
4 Don't let my enemies gloat, saying, "We
have defeated him!"
Don't let them rejoice at my downfall.

5 But I trust in your unfailing love.
I will rejoice because you have rescued
me.
6 I will sing to the LORD
because he has been so good to me.

PSALM 14

For the choir director: A psalm of David.

1 Only fools say in their hearts,
"There is no God."
They are corrupt, and their actions are
evil;
no one does good!

2 The LORD looks down from heaven
on the entire human race;
he looks to see if there is even one with
real understanding,
one who seeks for God.
3 But no, all have turned away from God;
all have become corrupt.
No one does good,
not even one!

4 Will those who do evil never learn?
They eat up my people like bread;
they wouldn't think of praying to the
LORD.
5 Terror will grip them,
for God is with those who obey him.
6 The wicked frustrate the plans of the
oppressed,
but the LORD will protect his people.

7 Oh, that salvation would come from
Mount Zion to rescue Israel!
For when the LORD restores his people,
Jacob will shout with joy, and Israel will
rejoice.

PSALM 15

A psalm of David.

1 Who may worship in your sanctuary,
LORD?
Who may enter your presence on your
holy hill?

2 Those who lead blameless lives
and do what is right,
speaking the truth from sincere hearts.
3 Those who refuse to slander others
or harm their neighbors
or speak evil of their friends.
4 Those who despise persistent sinners,
and honor the faithful followers of the
LORD
and keep their promises even when it
hurts.
5 Those who do not charge interest on the
money they lend,

and who refuse to accept bribes to testify
against the innocent.

Such people will stand firm forever.

PSALM 16

A psalm of David.

1 Keep me safe, O God,
for I have come to you for refuge.

2 I said to the LORD, "You are my Master!
All the good things I have are from you."
3 The godly people in the land
are my true heroes!
I take pleasure in them!
4 Those who chase after other gods will be
filled with sorrow.
I will not take part in their sacrifices
or even speak the names of their gods.

5 LORD, you alone are my inheritance, my
cup of blessing.
You guard all that is mine.
6 The land you have given me is a pleasant
land.
What a wonderful inheritance!

7 I will bless the LORD who guides me;
even at night my heart instructs me.
8 I know the LORD is always with me.
I will not be shaken, for he is right
beside me.

9 No wonder my heart is filled with joy,
and my mouth* shouts his praises!
My body rests in safety.
10 For you will not leave my soul among the
dead*
or allow your godly one* to rot in the
grave.
11 You will show me the way of life,
granting me the joy of your presence
and the pleasures of living with you
forever.

PSALM 17

A prayer of David.

1 O LORD, hear my plea for justice.
Listen to my cry for help.
Pay attention to my prayer,
for it comes from an honest heart.
2 Declare me innocent,
for you know those who do right.

3 You have tested my thoughts and
examined my heart in the night.
You have scrutinized me and found
nothing amiss,
for I am determined not to sin in what
I say.
4 I have followed your commands,
which have kept me from going along
with cruel and evil people.
5 My steps have stayed on your path;
I have not wavered from following you.

6 I am praying to you because I know you
will answer, O God.
Bend down and listen as I pray.
7 Show me your unfailing love in wonderful
ways.
You save with your strength
those who seek refuge from their
enemies.
8 Guard me as the apple of your eye.
Hide me in the shadow of your wings.
9 Protect me from wicked people who
attack me,
from murderous enemies who
surround me.
10 They are without pity.
Listen to their boasting.
11 They track me down, surround me,
and throw me to the ground.
12 They are like hungry lions, eager to tear
me apart—
like young lions in hiding, waiting for
their chance.

16:9 As in Greek version; Hebrew reads *glory.*   **16:10a** Hebrew *in Sheol.*   **16:10b** Or *your Holy One.*

My Daily Worship

— May 4 —

THE SINGING AND DANCING KING

PSALMS 13:1–16:11

I will sing to the LORD because he has been so good to me (13:6).

[i reflect]

If an award were given for being the most human person in history (with all the good and bad that entails), David, son of Jesse, might well deserve the honor. Shepherd boy, great king. Champion, rebel leader, collaborator, commander-in-chief, civil warrior. Son, brother, friend, husband, father. Devout believer, great sinner. Capable of astonishing variations of emotion. Bold in acting; nimble in reacting. Enduring long.

Yet among all this variety, one lasting quality of David was his love of music. David first came to royal notice as "a talented harp player" called in to soothe King Saul (1 Samuel 16:18). Ironically, a ditty sung by women ("Saul has killed his thousands, and David his ten thousands!" 1 Samuel 18:7) almost doomed David by arousing the jealousy of Saul. Yet David later sang a funeral song for Saul and Jonathan—and another for the general Abner (2 Samuel 1:17–27; 3:33–34). Even in this short psalm, while David cried out to God from the depths of his despair, he still found reason to sing to the Lord, "because he has been so good to me."

David refused to squelch his musical inclinations when he became king. As the ark was brought to Jerusalem, "David and all the people of Israel were celebrating before the LORD with all their might, singing songs and playing all kinds of musical instruments—lyres, harps, tambourines, castanets, and cymbals" (2 Samuel 6:5). And later David gave orders for the establishment of a Levite choir and appointed men "to proclaim God's messages to the accompaniment of harps, lyres, and cymbals" (1 Chronicles 15:16; 25:1). David himself was responsible for a large portion of Israel's hymnbook, the Psalms.

As the book of Psalms models, music has a power to inspire emotion and to express it. Music is among the fittest vehicles for communicating to and about God.

What song can you sing today to God? Like David, sing to the Lord because he has been so good to you.

[i pray]

I trust in your unfailing love, O God. I rejoice because you have rescued me.
I will sing to you because you have been so good to me.

[i respond]

C. S. Lewis said, "The most valuable thing the Psalms do for me is to express the same delight in God which made David dance." As part of your personal worship, flip through the book of Psalms and find lines of praise that move you; then pray them—or better yet, sing them—to God.

¹³ Arise, O LORD!
Stand against them and bring them to
their knees!
Rescue me from the wicked with your
sword!
¹⁴ Save me by your mighty hand, O LORD,
from those whose only concern is
earthly gain.
May they have their punishment in full.
May their children inherit more of the
same,
and may the judgment continue to their
children's children.

¹⁵ But because I have done what is right, I
will see you.
When I awake, I will be fully satisfied,
for I will see you face to face.

PSALM 18

*For the choir director: A psalm of David, the
servant of the LORD. He sang this song to the
LORD on the day the LORD rescued him from
all his enemies and from Saul.*

¹ I love you, LORD; you are my strength.
² The LORD is my rock, my fortress, and my
savior;
my God is my rock, in whom I find
protection.
He is my shield, the strength of my
salvation, and my stronghold.
³ I will call on the LORD, who is worthy of
praise,
for he saves me from my enemies.

⁴ The ropes of death surrounded me;
the floods of destruction swept over me.
⁵ The grave* wrapped its ropes around me;
death itself stared me in the face.
⁶ But in my distress I cried out to the LORD;
yes, I prayed to my God for help.
He heard me from his sanctuary;
my cry reached his ears.

⁷ Then the earth quaked and trembled;
the foundations of the mountains
shook;
they quaked because of his anger.
⁸ Smoke poured from his nostrils;
fierce flames leaped from his mouth;
glowing coals flamed forth from him.
⁹ He opened the heavens and came down;
dark storm clouds were beneath his feet.
¹⁰ Mounted on a mighty angel,* he flew,
soaring on the wings of the wind.
¹¹ He shrouded himself in darkness,
veiling his approach with dense rain
clouds.
¹² The brilliance of his presence broke
through the clouds,
raining down hail and burning coals.
¹³ The LORD thundered from heaven;
the Most High gave a mighty shout.*
¹⁴ He shot his arrows and scattered his
enemies;
his lightning flashed, and they were
greatly confused.
¹⁵ Then at your command, O LORD,
at the blast of your breath,
the bottom of the sea could be seen,
and the foundations of the earth were
laid bare.

¹⁶ He reached down from heaven and
rescued me;
he drew me out of deep waters.
¹⁷ He delivered me from my powerful
enemies,
from those who hated me and were too
strong for me.
¹⁸ They attacked me at a moment when I was
weakest,
but the LORD upheld me.
¹⁹ He led me to a place of safety;
he rescued me because he delights in me.
²⁰ The LORD rewarded me for doing right;
he compensated me because of my
innocence.
²¹ For I have kept the ways of the LORD;

18:5 Hebrew *Sheol.* **18:10** Hebrew *a cherub.* **18:13** As in Greek version (see also 2 Sam 22:14); Hebrew adds *raining down hail and burning coals.*

My Daily Worship

— *May 5* —

HIDING IN THE SHADOWS

PSALMS 17:1–20:9

Hide me in the shadow of your wings. Protect me from wicked people who attack me,
from murderous enemies who surround me (17:8–9).

[i reflect]

While being persecuted by King Saul, David wrote this psalm as a plea for justice in the face of false accusations. David offered up this entreaty with the confidence of someone who knows that his prayer will be answered and that he is praying to the One who could protect him and hide him.

Christians throughout the centuries, particularly early believers, have encountered harsh opposition. Yet, they too prevailed because of their confidence in the One who had overcome the world and who had promised them a secure future. We see this unassailable faith in a portion of the second-century *Letter to Diognetius:*

> [The Christians] pass their days on earth, but they are citizens of heaven. They obey the prescribed laws and at the same time surpass the laws by their lives. They love all men and are persecuted by all. They are poor yet make many rich. They are dishonored and yet in their very dishonor are glorified. They are evilly spoken of and yet are justified. They are insulted and repay the insult with honor. They do good yet are punished as evildoers. When punished, they rejoice as if quickened into life. They are assailed by the Jews as foreigners and are persecuted by the Greeks, yet those who hate them are unable to assign any reason for their hatred.

To sum up, what the soul is in the body, that is what Christians are in the world.

Christ said, "Here on earth you will have many trials and sorrows. But take heart, because I have overcome the world" (John 16:33). Are we ready to accept opposition from the world? Are we ready to trust that God will be with us, covering us in the shadow of his wings?

Tell Jesus what trials you are facing, what enemies are surrounding you today. Use these times of opposition as opportunities to worship the One who hides you in the shadows of his wings.

[i pray]

Sometimes I bring attacks on myself, God, I know it. Other times, though, I am victim to the evil that rages against all people, most intensely against yours. Spread your strong wings over me.

[i respond]

What does it mean to you to live in the shadow of God's wings? Think of the past several days. How has God protected you, your family during that time? Write a brief note of thanks for how God has covered you with his wings.

I have not turned from my God to
   follow evil.
²² For all his laws are constantly before me;
   I have never abandoned his principles.
²³ I am blameless before God;
   I have kept myself from sin.
²⁴ The LORD rewarded me for doing right,
   because of the innocence of my hands in
   his sight.

²⁵ To the faithful you show yourself faithful;
   to those with integrity you show
   integrity.
²⁶ To the pure you show yourself pure,
   but to the wicked you show yourself
   hostile.
²⁷ You rescue those who are humble,
   but you humiliate the proud.
²⁸ LORD, you have brought light to my life;
   my God, you light up my darkness.
²⁹ In your strength I can crush an army;
   with my God I can scale any wall.

³⁰ As for God, his way is perfect.
   All the LORD's promises prove true.
   He is a shield for all who look to him for
   protection.
³¹ For who is God except the LORD?
   Who but our God is a solid rock?
³² God arms me with strength;
   he has made my way safe.
³³ He makes me as surefooted as a deer,
   leading me safely along the mountain
   heights.
³⁴ He prepares me for battle;
   he strengthens me to draw a bow of bronze.
³⁵ You have given me the shield of your
   salvation.
   Your right hand supports me;
   your gentleness has made me great.
³⁶ You have made a wide path for my feet
   to keep them from slipping.

³⁷ I chased my enemies and caught them;
   I did not stop until they were conquered.
³⁸ I struck them down so they could not get up;
   they fell beneath my feet.

³⁹ You have armed me with strength for the
   battle;
   you have subdued my enemies under my
   feet.
⁴⁰ You made them turn and run;
   I have destroyed all who hated me.
⁴¹ They called for help, but no one came to
   rescue them.
   They cried to the LORD, but he refused
   to answer them.
⁴² I ground them as fine as dust carried by
   the wind.
   I swept them into the gutter like dirt.

⁴³ You gave me victory over my accusers.
   You appointed me as the ruler over
   nations;
   people I don't even know now serve me.
⁴⁴ As soon as they hear of me, they submit;
   foreigners cringe before me.
⁴⁵ They all lose their courage
   and come trembling from their
   strongholds.

⁴⁶ The LORD lives! Blessed be my rock!
   May the God of my salvation be exalted!
⁴⁷ He is the God who pays back those who
   harm me;
   he subdues the nations under me
⁴⁸ and rescues me from my enemies.
   You hold me safe beyond the reach of my
   enemies;
   you save me from violent opponents.
⁴⁹ For this, O LORD, I will praise you among
   the nations;
   I will sing joyfully to your name.
⁵⁰ You give great victories to your king;
   you show unfailing love to your
   anointed,
   to David and all his descendants forever.

PSALM 19

For the choir director: A psalm of David.

¹ The heavens tell of the glory of God.
   The skies display his marvelous
   craftsmanship.

2 Day after day they continue to speak;
   night after night they make him known.
3 They speak without a sound or a word;
   their voice is silent in the skies;*
4 yet their message has gone out to all the
      earth,
   and their words to all the world.

The sun lives in the heavens
   where God placed it.
5 It bursts forth like a radiant bridegroom
   after his wedding.
It rejoices like a great athlete
   eager to run the race.
6 The sun rises at one end of the heavens
   and follows its course to the other end.
   Nothing can hide from its heat.

7 The law of the LORD is perfect,
   reviving the soul.
The decrees of the LORD are trustworthy,
   making wise the simple.
8 The commandments of the LORD are right,
   bringing joy to the heart.
The commands of the LORD are clear,
   giving insight to life.
9 Reverence for the LORD is pure,
   lasting forever.
The laws of the LORD are true;
   each one is fair.
10 They are more desirable than gold,
   even the finest gold.
They are sweeter than honey,
   even honey dripping from the comb.
11 They are a warning to those who hear them;
   there is great reward for those who obey
      them.

12 How can I know all the sins lurking in my
      heart?
   Cleanse me from these hidden faults.
13 Keep me from deliberate sins!
   Don't let them control me.
Then I will be free of guilt
   and innocent of great sin.

14 May the words of my mouth and the
      thoughts of my heart
   be pleasing to you,
   O LORD, my rock and my redeemer.

PSALM 20

For the choir director: A psalm of David.

1 In times of trouble, may the LORD respond
   to your cry.
May the God of Israel* keep you safe
   from all harm.
2 May he send you help from his sanctuary
   and strengthen you from Jerusalem.*
3 May he remember all your gifts
   and look favorably on your burnt
      offerings.   *Interlude*

4 May he grant your heart's desire
   and fulfill all your plans.
5 May we shout for joy when we hear of
      your victory,
   flying banners to honor our God.
May the LORD answer all your prayers.

6 Now I know that the LORD saves his
      anointed king.
He will answer him from his holy heaven
   and rescue him by his great power.
7 Some nations boast of their armies and
      weapons,*
   but we boast in the LORD our God.
8 Those nations will fall down and collapse,
   but we will rise up and stand firm.

9 Give victory to our king, O LORD!
   Respond to our cry for help.

PSALM 21

For the choir director: A psalm of David.

1 How the king rejoices in your strength,
      O LORD!
   He shouts with joy because of your
      victory.

19:3 Or *There is no speech or language where their voice is not heard.* 20:1 Hebrew *of Jacob.* 20:2 Hebrew *Zion.* 20:7 Hebrew *chariots and horses.*

² For you have given him his heart's
desire;
you have held back nothing that he
requested.   *Interlude*

³ You welcomed him back with success and
prosperity.
You placed a crown of finest gold on his
head.
⁴ He asked you to preserve his life,
and you have granted his request.
The days of his life stretch on
forever.
⁵ Your victory brings him great honor,
and you have clothed him with splendor
and majesty.
⁶ You have endowed him with eternal
blessings.
You have given him the joy of being in
your presence.
⁷ For the king trusts in the LORD.
The unfailing love of the Most High will
keep him from stumbling.

⁸ You will capture all your enemies.
Your strong right hand will seize all
those who hate you.
⁹ You will destroy them as in a flaming
furnace
when you appear.
The LORD will consume them in his
anger;
fire will devour them.
¹⁰ You will wipe their children from the face
of the earth;
they will never have descendants.
¹¹ Although they plot against you,
their evil schemes will never succeed.
¹² For they will turn and run
when they see your arrows aimed at
them.

¹³ We praise you, LORD, for all your glorious
power.
With music and singing we celebrate
your mighty acts.

PSALM 22

*For the choir director: A psalm of David, to be
sung to the tune "Doe of the Dawn."*

¹ My God, my God! Why have you
forsaken me?
Why do you remain so distant?
Why do you ignore my cries for help?
² Every day I call to you, my God, but you
do not answer.
Every night you hear my voice, but I find
no relief.

³ Yet you are holy.
The praises of Israel surround your
throne.
⁴ Our ancestors trusted in you,
and you rescued them.
⁵ You heard their cries for help and saved
them.
They put their trust in you and were
never disappointed.

⁶ But I am a worm and not a man.
I am scorned and despised by all!
⁷ Everyone who sees me mocks me.
They sneer and shake their heads, saying,
⁸ "Is this the one who relies on the LORD?
Then let the LORD save him!
If the LORD loves him so much,
let the LORD rescue him!"

⁹ Yet you brought me safely from my
mother's womb
and led me to trust you when I was a
nursing infant.
¹⁰ I was thrust upon you at my birth.
You have been my God from the
moment I was born.

¹¹ Do not stay so far from me,
for trouble is near,
and no one else can help me.
¹² My enemies surround me like a herd of
bulls;
fierce bulls of Bashan have hemmed
me in!

¹³ Like roaring lions attacking their prey,
    they come at me with open mouths.
¹⁴ My life is poured out like water,
    and all my bones are out of joint.
  My heart is like wax,
    melting within me.
¹⁵ My strength has dried up like sunbaked
    clay.
  My tongue sticks to the roof of my
    mouth.
  You have laid me in the dust and left me
    for dead.

¹⁶ My enemies surround me like a pack of
    dogs;
  an evil gang closes in on me.
  They have pierced my hands and feet.
¹⁷ I can count every bone in my body.
  My enemies stare at me and gloat.
¹⁸ They divide my clothes among themselves
    and throw dice* for my garments.

¹⁹ O LORD, do not stay away!
  You are my strength; come quickly to
    my aid!
²⁰ Rescue me from a violent death;
    spare my precious life from these dogs.
²¹ Snatch me from the lions' jaws,
    and from the horns of these wild oxen.

²² Then I will declare the wonder of your
    name to my brothers and sisters.
  I will praise you among all your people.
²³ Praise the LORD, all you who fear him!
  Honor him, all you descendants of Jacob!
  Show him reverence, all you descendants
    of Israel!
²⁴ For he has not ignored the suffering of the
    needy.
  He has not turned and walked away.
  He has listened to their cries for help.

²⁵ I will praise you among all the people;
  I will fulfill my vows in the presence of
    those who worship you.
²⁶ The poor will eat and be satisfied.

All who seek the LORD will praise him.
  Their hearts will rejoice with everlasting
    joy.
²⁷ The whole earth will acknowledge the
    LORD and return to him.
  People from every nation will bow down
    before him.
²⁸ For the LORD is king!
  He rules all the nations.

²⁹ Let the rich of the earth feast and worship.
  Let all mortals—those born to die—bow
    down in his presence.
³⁰ Future generations will also serve him.
  Our children will hear about the
    wonders of the Lord.
³¹ His righteous acts will be told to those yet
    unborn.
  They will hear about everything he has
    done.

PSALM 23
A psalm of David.

¹ The LORD is my shepherd;
    I have everything I need.
² He lets me rest in green meadows;
    he leads me beside peaceful streams.
³   He renews my strength.
  He guides me along right paths,
    bringing honor to his name.

⁴ Even when I walk
    through the dark valley of death,*
  I will not be afraid,
    for you are close beside me.
  Your rod and your staff
    protect and comfort me.

⁵ You prepare a feast for me
    in the presence of my enemies.
  You welcome me as a guest,
    anointing my head with oil.
  My cup overflows with blessings.
⁶ Surely your goodness and unfailing love
    will pursue me

22:18 Hebrew *cast lots.* 23:4 Or *the darkest valley.*

all the days of my life,
and I will live in the house of the LORD
forever.

PSALM 24
A psalm of David.

¹ The earth is the LORD's, and everything in it.
The world and all its people belong to him.
² For he laid the earth's foundation on the
seas
and built it on the ocean depths.

³ Who may climb the mountain of the
LORD?
Who may stand in his holy place?
⁴ Only those whose hands and hearts are
pure,
who do not worship idols
and never tell lies.
⁵ They will receive the LORD's blessing
and have right standing with God their
savior.
⁶ They alone may enter God's presence
and worship the God of Israel.*

Interlude

⁷ Open up, ancient gates!
Open up, ancient doors,
and let the King of glory enter.
⁸ Who is the King of glory?
The LORD, strong and mighty,
the LORD, invincible in battle.
⁹ Open up, ancient gates!
Open up, ancient doors,
and let the King of glory enter.
¹⁰ Who is the King of glory?
The LORD Almighty—
he is the King of glory.   *Interlude*

PSALM 25
A psalm of David.

¹ To you, O LORD, I lift up my soul.
² I trust in you, my God!

24:6 Hebrew *of Jacob.*

Do not let me be disgraced,
or let my enemies rejoice in my defeat.
³ No one who trusts in you will ever be
disgraced,
but disgrace comes to those who try to
deceive others.

⁴ Show me the path where I should walk,
O LORD;
point out the right road for me to
follow.
⁵ Lead me by your truth and teach me,
for you are the God who saves me.
All day long I put my hope in you.

⁶ Remember, O LORD, your unfailing love
and compassion,
which you have shown from long ages
past.
⁷ Forgive the rebellious sins of my youth;
look instead through the eyes of your
unfailing love,
for you are merciful, O LORD.

⁸ The LORD is good and does what is right;
he shows the proper path to those who
go astray.
⁹ He leads the humble in what is right,
teaching them his way.
¹⁰ The LORD leads with unfailing love and
faithfulness
all those who keep his covenant and
obey his decrees.

¹¹ For the honor of your name, O LORD,
forgive my many, many sins.
¹² Who are those who fear the LORD?
He will show them the path they should
choose.
¹³ They will live in prosperity,
and their children will inherit the
Promised Land.
¹⁴ Friendship with the LORD is reserved for
those who fear him.
With them he shares the secrets of his
covenant.

My Daily Worship
— May 6 —

TAKE A BREAK
PSALMS 21:1–24:10

He lets me rest in green meadows; he leads me beside peaceful streams (23:2).

[i reflect]

Nighttime and daytime, sleep and wakefulness, workday and weekend, motion and stillness, labor and rest—life has a rhythm, impressed into earthly existence when the mold was still wet. God himself rested after laboring six days to make the world, and he declared a Sabbath for his people.

Still, sometimes we denigrate the restful side of the equation. "If I can just skip lunch, just go to bed later, just work through the weekend, I can get so much more done." It doesn't work, or at least not for long. The always-on lifestyle is likely to be switched off prematurely.

Nothing is wrong with hard work, of course. After all, Jesus pushed himself pretty hard to meet the needs of the people who came to him. But he also made time to get away for prayer and to escape the press of the crowds. We, similarly, ought to be grateful when our Shepherd leads us to grassy meadows where we can lie down and rest.

Rest times can then become special times of worship. In our leisure we can turn our focus upon God with a concentration not possible amid the distractions of our busy days. Worship, in fact, can become an aid in our resting. As Richard Clarke Cabot said, "Worship renews the spirit as sleep renews the body."

The times are coming when we will have to walk through the valley of the shadow of death. Let us settle gratefully in the meadows while we have them.

As you go through your daily routines, find ways to schedule mini-Sabbath times with the Lord. Take a break to sit and reflect upon God. Let this time renew you and refresh you.

[i pray]

Shepherd of my soul, let me not become lazy out of a selfish desire for comfort. Nor let me work frantically, as if ignorant of your promise to provide for me. But let me live by the rhythm you set every day, every week, all my life—and meet you there.

[i respond]

Be creative in incorporating "break times" with God today. Instead of having coffee with a friend or coworker, spend that time with God. Before embarking on a new activity or errand, spend a moment thanking God for how your day is going.

¹⁵ My eyes are always looking to the LORD for
help,
for he alone can rescue me from the
traps of my enemies.

¹⁶ Turn to me and have mercy on me,
for I am alone and in deep distress.
¹⁷ My problems go from bad to worse.
Oh, save me from them all!
¹⁸ Feel my pain and see my trouble.
Forgive all my sins.
¹⁹ See how many enemies I have,
and how viciously they hate me!
²⁰ Protect me! Rescue my life from them!
Do not let me be disgraced, for I trust
in you.
²¹ May integrity and honesty protect me,
for I put my hope in you.

²² O God, ransom Israel
from all its troubles.

PSALM 26

A psalm of David.

¹ Declare me innocent, O LORD,
for I have acted with integrity;
I have trusted in the LORD without
wavering.
² Put me on trial, LORD, and
cross-examine me.
Test my motives and affections.
³ For I am constantly aware of your
unfailing love,
and I have lived according to your truth.

⁴ I do not spend time with liars
or go along with hypocrites.
⁵ I hate the gatherings of those who do
evil,
and I refuse to join in with the wicked.

⁶ I wash my hands to declare my
innocence.
I come to your altar, O LORD,
⁷ singing a song of thanksgiving
and telling of all your miracles.

Words of Worship

PSALMS

Psalms—Hebrew *miz-**mor*** "psalm"; *te-hil-**lim***
"praises"; Greek ***psal**-mos* "psalm." A psalm,
strictly speaking, is a lyric sung to the
accompaniment of a stringed instrument.
While some of the psalms of the Bible are
called "psalms" in this musical sense, the
Hebrew title for the book of Psalms is the
word for "praises."

The book of Psalms is a treasury of faith and
devotion. Though we sometimes think of a
psalm as a song of exultation, psalms cover
every mood, every expression of our approach
to God—from despair to delight, from confession to confidence, from petitioning God
for help to praising him for his answer. They
speak of the Lord's Anointed, the Christ. In
the psalms, God speaks words of comfort and
reassurance back to his worshipers. In a similar way, our cries to God in prayer and personal worship may range across the same
emotional spectrum. Seeking his face in
prayer, we can do no better than to come
before him with psalms—the psalms of
Scripture, or psalms of our own!

---

⁸ I love your sanctuary, LORD,
the place where your glory shines.

⁹ Don't let me suffer the fate of sinners.
Don't condemn me along with
murderers.
¹⁰ Their hands are dirty with wicked
schemes,
and they constantly take bribes.

¹¹ But I am not like that; I do what is right.
So in your mercy, save me.
¹² I have taken a stand,
and I will publicly praise the LORD.

PSALM 27

A psalm of David.

1 The LORD is my light and my salvation—
    so why should I be afraid?
    The LORD protects me from danger—
    so why should I tremble?

2 When evil people come to destroy me,
    when my enemies and foes attack me,
    they will stumble and fall.
3 Though a mighty army surrounds me,
    my heart will know no fear.
    Even if they attack me,
    I remain confident.

4 The one thing I ask of the LORD—
    the thing I seek most—
    is to live in the house of the LORD all the
        days of my life,
    delighting in the LORD's perfections
    and meditating in his Temple.
5 For he will conceal me there when troubles
        come;
    he will hide me in his sanctuary.
    He will place me out of reach on a high
        rock.
6 Then I will hold my head high,
    above my enemies who surround me.
    At his Tabernacle I will offer sacrifices with
        shouts of joy,
    singing and praising the LORD with
        music.

7 Listen to my pleading, O LORD.
    Be merciful and answer me!
8 My heart has heard you say, "Come and
        talk with me."
    And my heart responds, "LORD, I am
        coming."
9 Do not hide yourself from me.
    Do not reject your servant in anger.
    You have always been my helper.
    Don't leave me now; don't abandon me,
    O God of my salvation!
10 Even if my father and mother abandon me,
    the LORD will hold me close.

11 Teach me how to live, O LORD.
    Lead me along the path of honesty,
    for my enemies are waiting for me to
        fall.
12 Do not let me fall into their hands.
    For they accuse me of things I've never
        done
    and breathe out violence against me.
13 Yet I am confident that I will see the
        LORD's goodness
    while I am here in the land of the living.

14 Wait patiently for the LORD.
    Be brave and courageous.
    Yes, wait patiently for the LORD.

PSALM 28

A psalm of David.

1 O LORD, you are my rock of safety.
    Please help me; don't refuse to answer
        me.
    For if you are silent,
    I might as well give up and die.
2 Listen to my prayer for mercy
    as I cry out to you for help,
    as I lift my hands toward your holy
        sanctuary.

3 Don't drag me away with the wicked—
    with those who do evil—
    those who speak friendly words to their
        neighbors
    while planning evil in their hearts.
4 Give them the punishment they so richly
        deserve!
    Measure it out in proportion to their
        wickedness.
    Pay them back for all their evil deeds!
    Give them a taste of what they have
        done to others.
5 They care nothing for what the LORD has
        done
    or for what his hands have made.
    So he will tear them down like old
        buildings,
    and they will never be rebuilt!

⁶ Praise the LORD!
  For he has heard my cry for mercy.
⁷ The LORD is my strength, my shield from
    every danger.
  I trust in him with all my heart.
  He helps me, and my heart is filled
    with joy.
  I burst out in songs of thanksgiving.

⁸ The LORD protects his people
  and gives victory to his anointed king.
⁹ Save your people!
  Bless Israel, your special possession!
  Lead them like a shepherd,
    and carry them forever in your arms.

PSALM 29

A psalm of David.

¹ Give honor to the LORD, you angels;
  give honor to the LORD for his glory and
    strength.
² Give honor to the LORD for the glory of his
    name.
  Worship the LORD in the splendor of his
    holiness.

³ The voice of the LORD echoes above the
    sea.
  The God of glory thunders.
  The LORD thunders over the mighty sea.
⁴ The voice of the LORD is powerful;
  the voice of the LORD is full of majesty.
⁵ The voice of the LORD splits the mighty
    cedars;
  the LORD shatters the cedars of Lebanon.
⁶ He makes Lebanon's mountains skip like a
    calf
  and Mount Hermon* to leap like a
    young bull.
⁷ The voice of the LORD strikes with
    lightning bolts.
⁸ The voice of the LORD makes the desert
    quake;
  the LORD shakes the desert of Kadesh.

⁹ The voice of the LORD twists mighty oaks*
  and strips the forests bare.
  In his Temple everyone shouts, "Glory!"

¹⁰ The LORD rules over the floodwaters.
  The LORD reigns as king forever.
¹¹ The LORD gives his people strength.
  The LORD blesses them with peace.

PSALM 30

*A psalm of David, sung at the dedication of
the Temple.*

¹ I will praise you, LORD, for you have
    rescued me.
  You refused to let my enemies triumph
    over me.
² O LORD my God, I cried out to you for
    help,
  and you restored my health.
³ You brought me up from the grave,
    O LORD.
  You kept me from falling into the pit of
    death.

⁴ Sing to the LORD, all you godly ones!
  Praise his holy name.
⁵ His anger lasts for a moment,
  but his favor lasts a lifetime!
  Weeping may go on all night,
  but joy comes with the morning.

⁶ When I was prosperous I said,
  "Nothing can stop me now!"
⁷ Your favor, O LORD, made me as secure as
    a mountain.
  Then you turned away from me, and I
    was shattered.

⁸ I cried out to you, O LORD.
  I begged the Lord for mercy, saying,
⁹ "What will you gain if I die,
  if I sink down into the grave?
  Can my dust praise you from the grave?
  Can it tell the world of your faithfulness?

29:6 Hebrew *Sirion,* another name for Mount Hermon.   **29:9** Or *causes the deer to writhe in labor.*

My Daily Worship

— May 7 —

In God's Waiting Room

Psalms 25:1–28:9

Wait patiently for the LORD. Be brave and courageous.
Yes, wait patiently for the LORD (27:14).

[i reflect]

In a world that honors assertive action, it comes as something of a shock to realize how many of the great heroes of faith spent some of the best years of their lives in what must have seemed unendurable waiting. Sarah's hope ran out as she waited decades to conceive her promised son. Jacob could trade nothing more than smiles with the woman he fancied, while he worked the seven years required to receive her. Moses loitered in the wilderness for forty years before he could move his crowd toward the Promised Land. Elijah was prepared to become vulture bait in a ravine after giving it all he had on Mount Carmel to no avail. The Jewish exiles had to let the prophesied seventy years elapse before they could return to Jerusalem.

David was no stranger to God's waiting room. He had been anointed as king at age sixteen, but didn't take the throne until he was thirty. In the intervening twenty-four years, David was chased through the wilderness by the jealous Saul. Waiting on God's timing was not easy.

What is God thinking when he lets his servants smolder in inactivity? And what are we supposed to do in our stymied times?

Let's be honest: waiting is never easy. It is not only the soldiers on the brink of war who need a reminder to be brave; those who wait need courage like iron forged in their souls. They also need to know that waiting is a something and not a nothing, for it is a time when God is working on *who we are* more so than on *what we do*. And it is a time when we can learn to worship God for who he is rather than for the immediate benefits we receive.

For what are you waiting today? While you are in God's waiting room, thank him now for the molding and refining he is doing in you.

[i pray]

For you, a thousand years are as a day, Lord, but for me, a day is a day.
Have mercy on me in my waiting. Yet as long as my waiting lasts, and
longer still, so long will I trust in you. Most of all, be near me.

[i respond]

Are you in a waiting period? Briefly describe your situation now and assess your spiritual maturity. Place the paper in your Bible at a point where you can later read and see how God has worked in you through the coming days.

> *The most valuable thing the Psalms
> do for me is to express the
> same delight in God
> which made David dance.*
>
> C. S. L E W I S

¹⁰ Hear me, LORD, and have mercy on me.
  Help me, O LORD."

¹¹ You have turned my mourning into joyful
   dancing.
   You have taken away my clothes of
   mourning and clothed me with joy,
¹² that I might sing praises to you and not be
   silent.
   O LORD my God, I will give you thanks
   forever!

PSALM 31

For the choir director: A psalm of David.

¹ O LORD, I have come to you for
  protection;
  don't let me be put to shame.
  Rescue me, for you always do what is
  right.
² Bend down and listen to me;
  rescue me quickly.
  Be for me a great rock of safety,
  a fortress where my enemies cannot
  reach me.

³ You are my rock and my fortress.
  For the honor of your name, lead me
  out of this peril.
⁴ Pull me from the trap my enemies set
  for me,
  for I find protection in you alone.
⁵ I entrust my spirit into your hand.

Rescue me, LORD, for you are a faithful
  God.

⁶ I hate those who worship worthless idols.
  I trust in the LORD.
⁷ I am overcome with joy because of your
  unfailing love,
  for you have seen my troubles,
  and you care about the anguish of my
  soul.
⁸ You have not handed me over to my
  enemy
  but have set me in a safe place.

⁹ Have mercy on me, LORD, for I am in
  distress.
  My sight is blurred because of my tears.
  My body and soul are withering away.
¹⁰ I am dying from grief;
   my years are shortened by sadness.
  Misery* has drained my strength;
  I am wasting away from within.
¹¹ I am scorned by all my enemies
   and despised by my neighbors—
   even my friends are afraid to come near
   me.
  When they see me on the street,
  they turn the other way.
¹² I have been ignored as if I were dead,
   as if I were a broken pot.
¹³ I have heard the many rumors about me,
   and I am surrounded by terror.
  My enemies conspire against me,
  plotting to take my life.

¹⁴ But I am trusting you, O LORD,
   saying, "You are my God!"
¹⁵ My future is in your hands.
  Rescue me from those who hunt me
  down relentlessly.
¹⁶ Let your favor shine on your servant.
  In your unfailing love, save me.
¹⁷ Don't let me be disgraced, O LORD,
   for I call out to you for help.
  Let the wicked be disgraced;
  let them lie silent in the grave.

31:10 Or *Sin.*

18 May their lying lips be silenced—
those proud and arrogant lips that
accuse the godly.

19 Your goodness is so great!
You have stored up great blessings for
those who honor you.
You have done so much for those who
come to you for protection,
blessing them before the watching world.
20 You hide them in the shelter of your
presence,
safe from those who conspire against
them.
You shelter them in your presence,
far from accusing tongues.

21 Praise the LORD,
for he has shown me his unfailing love.
He kept me safe when my city was under
attack.
22 In sudden fear I had cried out,
"I have been cut off from the LORD!"
But you heard my cry for mercy
and answered my call for help.

23 Love the LORD, all you faithful ones!
For the LORD protects those who are
loyal to him,
but he harshly punishes all who are
arrogant.
24 So be strong and take courage,
all you who put your hope in the LORD!

PSALM 32

A psalm of David.

1 Oh, what joy for those
whose rebellion is forgiven,
whose sin is put out of sight!
2 Yes, what joy for those
whose record the LORD has cleared of sin,
whose lives are lived in complete honesty!

3 When I refused to confess my sin,
I was weak and miserable,
and I groaned all day long.

4 Day and night your hand of discipline was
heavy on me.
My strength evaporated like water in the
summer heat. *Interlude*

5 Finally, I confessed all my sins to you
and stopped trying to hide them.
I said to myself, "I will confess my
rebellion to the LORD."
And you forgave me! All my guilt is
gone. *Interlude*

6 Therefore, let all the godly confess their
rebellion to you while there is time,
that they may not drown in the
floodwaters of judgment.
7 For you are my hiding place;
you protect me from trouble.
You surround me with songs of victory.
Interlude

8 The LORD says, "I will guide you along the
best pathway for your life.
I will advise you and watch over you.
9 Do not be like a senseless horse or
mule
that needs a bit and bridle to keep it
under control."

10 Many sorrows come to the wicked,
but unfailing love surrounds those who
trust the LORD.
11 So rejoice in the LORD and be glad, all you
who obey him!
Shout for joy, all you whose hearts are
pure!

PSALM 33

1 Let the godly sing with joy to the LORD,
for it is fitting to praise him.
2 Praise the LORD with melodies on the
lyre;
make music for him on the ten-stringed
harp.
3 Sing new songs of praise to him;
play skillfully on the harp and sing with
joy.

⁴ For the word of the LORD holds true,
  and everything he does is worthy of our
    trust.
⁵ He loves whatever is just and good,
  and his unfailing love fills the earth.

⁶ The LORD merely spoke,
  and the heavens were created.
He breathed the word,
  and all the stars were born.
⁷ He gave the sea its boundaries
  and locked the oceans in vast reservoirs.

⁸ Let everyone in the world fear the LORD,
  and let everyone stand in awe of him.
⁹ For when he spoke, the world began!
  It appeared at his command.

¹⁰ The LORD shatters the plans of the nations
  and thwarts all their schemes.
¹¹ But the LORD's plans stand firm forever;
  his intentions can never be shaken.

¹² What joy for the nation whose God is the
    LORD,
  whose people he has chosen for his own.

¹³ The LORD looks down from heaven
  and sees the whole human race.
¹⁴ From his throne he observes
  all who live on the earth.
¹⁵ He made their hearts,
  so he understands everything they do.

¹⁶ The best-equipped army cannot save a
    king,
  nor is great strength enough to save a
    warrior.
¹⁷ Don't count on your warhorse to give you
    victory—
  for all its strength, it cannot save you.

¹⁸ But the LORD watches over those who fear
    him,
  those who rely on his unfailing love.
¹⁹ He rescues them from death
  and keeps them alive in times of famine.

²⁰ We depend on the LORD alone to save us.
  Only he can help us, protecting us like a
    shield.
²¹ In him our hearts rejoice,
  for we are trusting in his holy name.
²² Let your unfailing love surround us, LORD,
  for our hope is in you alone.

PSALM 34

*A psalm of David, regarding the time he
pretended to be insane in front of Abimelech,
who sent him away.*

¹ I will praise the LORD at all times.
  I will constantly speak his praises.
² I will boast only in the LORD;
  let all who are discouraged take heart.
³ Come, let us tell of the LORD's greatness;
  let us exalt his name together.

⁴ I prayed to the LORD, and he answered me,
  freeing me from all my fears.
⁵ Those who look to him for help will be
    radiant with joy;
  no shadow of shame will darken their
    faces.
⁶ I cried out to the LORD in my suffering,
  and he heard me.
He set me free from all my fears.
⁷ For the angel of the LORD guards all who
    fear him,
  and he rescues them.

⁸ Taste and see that the LORD is good.
  Oh, the joys of those who trust in him!
⁹ Let the LORD's people show him reverence,
  for those who honor him will have all
    they need.
¹⁰ Even strong young lions sometimes go
    hungry,
  but those who trust in the LORD will
    never lack any good thing.

¹¹ Come, my children, and listen to me,
  and I will teach you to fear the LORD.
¹² Do any of you want to live
  a life that is long and good?

My Daily Worship

— May 8 —

HEAVEN ON EARTH

PSALMS 29:1–32:11

Oh, what joy for those whose rebellion is forgiven,
whose sin is put out of sight! (32:1).

[i reflect]

In the summer of A.D. 430, knowing that his illness must surely prove mortal, what did the great churchman and theologian Augustine request as a singular favor? He asked that the words of Psalm 32 might be painted on the walls of his bedroom where he could view them as long as his eyes held sight.

Somehow it seems appropriate that the writer who gave us an autobiography entitled *Confessions* (still a must-read for the thinking Christian) wanted to meditate until the end upon a psalm about confession of sin.

Augustine was seventy-five at the time of his death. Unless something goes seriously askew in our spirits, we never outgrow our awe of the kindness of Christ. We experience, like David did in this passage, the indescribable joy that comes when God has put our sin out of sight, when our "rebellion is forgiven." Divine grace for sinners is a perennial theme of worship.

Refusing to confess sin produces a kind of pent-up internal pressure that builds and builds, resulting in every manner of misery for body and spirit. Psalm 32 speaks of this effect as well. But, oh, the relief of confession, as the pressure flows out with the penitent's tears! Praise then becomes as natural and as necessary as breathing. Confession renews worship.

Eternal life begins at salvation. Surely the joy of the forgiven sinner, then, is the natural reaction of what is dead coming to life. And it's a joy we can know in a fresh filling every time we repent.

What do you need to confess before God? Tell him what's burdening your heart, then rejoice in a life lived in complete honesty and forgiveness.

[i pray]

I can't thank you enough, Father, for clearing my record of sin when I first believed
in your Son. Help me not to sin, but when I do sin, help me to turn
immediately and discover the joy of renewed forgiveness.

[i respond]

Memorize Psalm 32:1–2. Paint this passage on the walls of your mind so that you can cast your attention toward it whenever you are tempted to hoard your sin like a measly minded miser or whenever you need a sure motive to praise God.

¹³ Then watch your tongue!
    Keep your lips from telling lies!
¹⁴ Turn away from evil and do good.
    Work hard at living in peace with others.

¹⁵ The eyes of the LORD watch over those
        who do right;
    his ears are open to their cries for help.
¹⁶ But the LORD turns his face against those
        who do evil;
    he will erase their memory from the
        earth.

¹⁷ The LORD hears his people when they call
        to him for help.
    He rescues them from all their troubles.
¹⁸ The LORD is close to the brokenhearted;
    he rescues those who are crushed in
        spirit.

¹⁹ The righteous face many troubles,
    but the LORD rescues them from each
        and every one.
²⁰ For the LORD protects them from harm—
    not one of their bones* will be broken!

²¹ Calamity will surely overtake the wicked,
    and those who hate the righteous will be
        punished.
²² But the LORD will redeem those who serve
        him.
    Everyone who trusts in him will be
        freely pardoned.

PSALM 35

A psalm of David.

¹ O LORD, oppose those who oppose me.
    Declare war on those who are attacking
        me.
² Put on your armor, and take up your
        shield.
    Prepare for battle, and come to my aid.
³ Lift up your spear and javelin
    and block the way of my enemies.
    Let me hear you say,
        "I am your salvation!"

⁴ Humiliate and disgrace those trying to kill
        me;
    turn them back in confusion.
⁵ Blow them away like chaff in the wind—
    a wind sent by the angel of the LORD.
⁶ Make their path dark and slippery,
    with the angel of the LORD pursuing
        them.
⁷ Although I did them no wrong,
    they laid a trap for me.
    Although I did them no wrong,
    they dug a pit for me.
⁸ So let sudden ruin overtake them!
    Let them be caught in the snare they set
        for me!
    Let them fall to destruction in the pit
        they dug for me.

⁹ Then I will rejoice in the LORD.
    I will be glad because he rescues me.
¹⁰ I will praise him from the bottom of my
        heart:
    "LORD, who can compare with you?
    Who else rescues the weak and helpless
        from the strong?
    Who else protects the poor and needy
        from those who want to rob them?"

¹¹ Malicious witnesses testify against me.
    They accuse me of things I don't even
        know about.
¹² They repay me with evil for the good I do.
    I am sick with despair.
¹³ Yet when they were ill,
    I grieved for them.
    I even fasted and prayed for them,
    but my prayers returned unanswered.
¹⁴ I was sad, as though they were my friends
        or family,
    as if I were grieving for my own mother.

¹⁵ But they are glad now that I am in trouble;
    they gleefully join together against me.

34:20 Hebrew *protects him from harm—not one of his bones.*

I am attacked by people I don't even know;
   they hurl slander at me continually.
¹⁶ They mock me with the worst kind of
     profanity,
   and they snarl at me.

¹⁷ How long, O Lord, will you look on and
     do nothing?
   Rescue me from their fierce attacks.
   Protect my life from these lions!
¹⁸ Then I will thank you in front of the entire
     congregation.
   I will praise you before all the people.

¹⁹ Don't let my treacherous enemies
   rejoice over my defeat.
   Don't let those who hate me without
     cause
   gloat over my sorrow.
²⁰ They don't talk of peace;
   they plot against innocent people
   who are minding their own business.
²¹ They shout that they have seen me doing
     wrong.
   "Aha," they say. "Aha!
   With our own eyes we saw him do it!"

²² O Lord, you know all about this.
   Do not stay silent.
   Don't abandon me now, O Lord.
²³ Wake up! Rise to my defense!
   Take up my case, my God and my Lord.
²⁴ Declare me "not guilty," O Lord my God,
   for you give justice.
   Don't let my enemies laugh about me in
     my troubles.
²⁵ Don't let them say, "Look! We have what
     we wanted!
   Now we will eat him alive!"

²⁶ May those who rejoice at my troubles
   be humiliated and disgraced.
   May those who triumph over me
   be covered with shame and dishonor.
²⁷ But give great joy to those
   who have stood with me in my defense.

Let them continually say, "Great is the
   Lord,
   who enjoys helping his servant."
²⁸ Then I will tell everyone of your justice
     and goodness,
   and I will praise you all day long.

Psalm 36

*For the choir director: A psalm of David, the
servant of the Lord.*

¹ Sin whispers to the wicked, deep within
     their hearts.
   They have no fear of God to restrain
     them.
² In their blind conceit,
   they cannot see how wicked they really
     are.
³ Everything they say is crooked and
     deceitful.
   They refuse to act wisely or do what is
     good.
⁴ They lie awake at night, hatching sinful
     plots.
   Their course of action is never good.
   They make no attempt to turn from evil.

⁵ Your unfailing love, O Lord, is as vast as
     the heavens;
   your faithfulness reaches beyond the
     clouds.
⁶ Your righteousness is like the mighty
     mountains,
   your justice like the ocean depths.
   You care for people and animals alike,
     O Lord.
⁷   How precious is your unfailing love,
     O God!
   All humanity finds shelter
   in the shadow of your wings.
⁸ You feed them from the abundance of
     your own house,
   letting them drink from your rivers of
     delight.
⁹ For you are the fountain of life,
   the light by which we see.

¹⁰ Pour out your unfailing love on those who
love you;
give justice to those with honest hearts.
¹¹ Don't let the proud trample me;
don't let the wicked push me around.
¹² Look! They have fallen!
They have been thrown down, never to
rise again.

PSALM 37

A psalm of David.

¹ Don't worry about the wicked.
Don't envy those who do wrong.
² For like grass, they soon fade away.
Like springtime flowers, they soon
wither.

³ Trust in the LORD and do good.
Then you will live safely in the land and
prosper.
⁴ Take delight in the LORD,
and he will give you your heart's desires.

⁵ Commit everything you do to the LORD.
Trust him, and he will help you.
⁶ He will make your innocence as clear as
the dawn,
and the justice of your cause will shine
like the noonday sun.

⁷ Be still in the presence of the LORD,
and wait patiently for him to act.
Don't worry about evil people who prosper
or fret about their wicked schemes.

⁸ Stop your anger!
Turn from your rage!
Do not envy others—
it only leads to harm.
⁹ For the wicked will be destroyed,
but those who trust in the LORD will
possess the land.

¹⁰ In a little while, the wicked will disappear.
Though you look for them, they will be
gone.

¹¹ Those who are gentle and lowly will
possess the land;
they will live in prosperous security.

¹² The wicked plot against the godly;
they snarl at them in defiance.
¹³ But the Lord just laughs,
for he sees their day of judgment coming.

¹⁴ The wicked draw their swords
and string their bows
to kill the poor and the oppressed,
to slaughter those who do right.
¹⁵ But they will be stabbed through the heart
with their own swords,
and their bows will be broken.

¹⁶ It is better to be godly and have little
than to be evil and possess much.
¹⁷ For the strength of the wicked will be
shattered,
but the LORD takes care of the godly.

¹⁸ Day by day the LORD takes care of the
innocent,
and they will receive a reward that lasts
forever.
¹⁹ They will survive through hard times;
even in famine they will have more than
enough.

²⁰ But the wicked will perish.
The LORD's enemies are like flowers in a
field—
they will disappear like smoke.

²¹ The wicked borrow and never repay,
but the godly are generous givers.
²² Those blessed by the LORD will inherit the
land,
but those cursed by him will die.

²³ The steps of the godly are directed by the
LORD.
He delights in every detail of their lives.
²⁴ Though they stumble, they will not fall,
for the LORD holds them by the hand.

My Daily Worship

— *May 9* —

RECOVERING MY "OH!"

PSALMS 33:1–36:12

You feed them from the abundance of your own house,
letting them drink from your rivers of delight (36:8).

[i reflect]

What a contrast David paints in this passage between those who are blinded to their sin and those who truly see the knee-bending, heart-stopping "oh!" of God's unfailing love and righteousness. The truth is that we can lose our "oh" when we allow our relationship with God to become routine, dry, and predictable. We no longer experience the "rivers of delight" because we are slogging through the mud of daily existence.

As A. W. Tozer posed the question, "Are we losing our 'Oh!'? When the heart on its knees moves into the awesome presence, and hears with fear and wonder things not lawful to utter, the mind falls flat, and words, previously its faithful servants, become weak and totally incapable of telling what the heart hears and sees. In that awful moment, the worshiper can only cry 'Oh!' "

Not only God himself but also his gifts are greater than we can express. Seen aright, so-called "ordinary," everyday events and scenes are, in fact, rivers of delight gushing from heaven.

Annie Dillard, in *Pilgrim at Tinker Creek,* writes of trying to see the world like someone who has been blind all her life but can suddenly see: "I saw the backyard cedar where the mourning doves roost charged and transfigured, each cell buzzing with flame. I stood on the grass with the lights in it, grass that was wholly fire, utterly focused and utterly dreamed."

Dillard continues, "I have since only very rarely seen the tree with the lights in it. The vision comes and goes, mostly goes, but I live for it, for the moment when the mountains open and a new light roars in, spate through the crack, and the mountains slam."

The good news is that you can always regain your "oh!" if you find yourself bogged down in a spiritual rut. Look for the "oh" in your familiar routine—as you drive to work, as you run errands, as you walk through your day.

[i pray]

Words are not enough, God above, to thank you for the rivers of delight you send.
I want to drink from them—and to realize what I'm drinking.

[i respond]

Today, walk through your day while looking at "ordinary" places and people with new eyes. What makes you say "Oh!"? How will you worship, wordlessly or word-fully, the awesome Presence?

25 Once I was young, and now I am old.
  Yet I have never seen the godly forsaken,
  nor seen their children begging for bread.
26 The godly always give generous loans to
    others,
  and their children are a blessing.

27 Turn from evil and do good,
  and you will live in the land forever.
28 For the LORD loves justice,
  and he will never abandon the godly.

He will keep them safe forever,
  but the children of the wicked will
    perish.
29 The godly will inherit the land
  and will live there forever.

30 The godly offer good counsel;
  they know what is right from wrong.
31 They fill their hearts with God's law,
  so they will never slip from his path.

32 Those who are evil spy on the godly,
  waiting for an excuse to kill them.
33 But the LORD will not let the wicked
    succeed
  or let the godly be condemned when
    they are brought before the judge.

34 Don't be impatient for the LORD to act!
  Travel steadily along his path.
He will honor you, giving you the land.
  You will see the wicked destroyed.

35 I myself have seen it happen—
  proud and evil people thriving like
    mighty trees.
36 But when I looked again, they were gone!
  Though I searched for them, I could not
    find them!

37 Look at those who are honest and good,
  for a wonderful future lies before those
    who love peace.
38 But the wicked will be destroyed;
  they have no future.

39 The LORD saves the godly;
  he is their fortress in times of trouble.
40 The LORD helps them,
  rescuing them from the wicked.
He saves them,
  and they find shelter in him.

PSALM 38

*A psalm of David, to bring us to the LORD's
remembrance.*

1 O LORD, don't rebuke me in your anger!
  Don't discipline me in your rage!
2 Your arrows have struck deep,
  and your blows are crushing me.

3 Because of your anger, my whole body is
    sick;
  my health is broken because of my sins.
4 My guilt overwhelms me—
  it is a burden too heavy to bear.
5 My wounds fester and stink
  because of my foolish sins.
6 I am bent over and racked with pain.
  My days are filled with grief.
7 A raging fever burns within me,
  and my health is broken.
8 I am exhausted and completely crushed.
  My groans come from an anguished
    heart.

9 You know what I long for, Lord;
  you hear my every sigh.
10 My heart beats wildly, my strength fails,
  and I am going blind.
11 My loved ones and friends stay away,
  fearing my disease.
  Even my own family stands at a distance.
12 Meanwhile, my enemies lay traps for me;
  they make plans to ruin me.
  They think up treacherous deeds all day
    long.
13 But I am deaf to all their threats.
  I am silent before them as one who
    cannot speak.
14 I choose to hear nothing,
  and I make no reply.

My Daily Worship

— *May 10* —

UNCONDITIONAL SURRENDER

PSALMS 37:1–41:13

Commit everything you do to the LORD. Trust him,
and he will help you (37:5).

[i reflect]

Like many artists, Judson Van de Venter was good, but not good enough to survive solely on what he earned from selling his paintings. So in order to pay his bills, Judson taught school. His income as a schoolteacher allowed him to pursue a passion that filled his heart with great joy. *Would he ever be able to fully devote himself to what he loved,* Judson wondered.

When a series of evangelistic services were held in the church he attended, the artistically inclined teacher volunteered to help. As individuals came forward to acknowledge their need of Christ, Judson would counsel them at the front of the church. His gifts in working with people were obvious to his friends. It was clear to them he had the gift of an evangelist.

For five years Judson vacillated between his abilities as an artist and an increasingly apparent giftedness for ministry. Finally, he understood the truth of the psalm writer who committed everything he did to the Lord. When he finally surrendered to God's call on his life, Judson wrote lyrics to a hymn of consecration we continue to sing more than a century after it was first published.

It begins, "All to Jesus I surrender, all to him I freely give." But those aren't just his words. They can be your words as well. Even though you may have abilities that bring you indescribable joy when you express them, don't allow those God-given gifts to come between you and what God wants for you. Examine your gifts and abilities in light of Judson Van de Venter's song. What do you need to surrender to God, to freely give him today?

Kneel down right now and tell the Lord he has access to all you have and are and ever will be. Now that's a portrait of surrender he will prize as a masterpiece.

[i pray]

Lord, I identify with Judson's struggle. I, too, have passions and abilities that bring me joy. But I surrender those to you today. Please use them for your glory and not mine alone. Amen.

[i respond]

Why not start an I Surrender chart? At the top of a sheet of paper, write "I Surrender . . ." Post it where you will see it each morning. Every day write something on it that conceivably could come between you and your relationship with the Lord. Commit that to him today.

¹⁵ For I am waiting for you, O LORD.
  You must answer for me, O Lord my
    God.
¹⁶ I prayed, "Don't let my enemies gloat over
    me
  or rejoice at my downfall."
¹⁷ I am on the verge of collapse,
  facing constant pain.
¹⁸ But I confess my sins;
  I am deeply sorry for what I have done.
¹⁹ My enemies are many;
  they hate me though I have done
    nothing against them.
²⁰ They repay me evil for good
  and oppose me because I stand for the
    right.

²¹ Do not abandon me, LORD.
  Do not stand at a distance, my God.
²² Come quickly to help me, O Lord my
    savior.

PSALM 39

*For Jeduthun, the choir director: A psalm
of David.*

¹ I said to myself, "I will watch what I do
  and not sin in what I say.
  I will curb my tongue
    when the ungodly are around me."
² But as I stood there in silence—
  not even speaking of good things—
  the turmoil within me grew to the
    bursting point.
³ My thoughts grew hot within me
  and began to burn,
  igniting a fire of words:
⁴ "LORD, remind me how brief my time on
    earth will be.
  Remind me that my days are numbered,
  and that my life is fleeing away.
⁵ My life is no longer than the width of my
    hand.
  An entire lifetime is just a moment to
    you;
  human existence is but a breath."
                                    Interlude

⁶ We are merely moving shadows,
  and all our busy rushing ends in nothing.
  We heap up wealth for someone else to
    spend.

⁷ And so, Lord, where do I put my hope?
  My only hope is in you.
⁸ Rescue me from my rebellion,
  for even fools mock me when I rebel.
⁹ I am silent before you; I won't say a word.
  For my punishment is from you.
¹⁰ Please, don't punish me anymore!
  I am exhausted by the blows from your
    hand.
¹¹ When you discipline people for their sins,
  their lives can be crushed like the life of
    a moth.
  Human existence is as frail as breath.
                                    Interlude

¹² Hear my prayer, O LORD!
  Listen to my cries for help!
  Don't ignore my tears.
  For I am your guest—
    a traveler passing through,
  as my ancestors were before me.
¹³ Spare me so I can smile again
  before I am gone and exist no more.

PSALM 40

For the choir director: A psalm of David.

¹ I waited patiently for the LORD to help me,
  and he turned to me and heard my cry.
² He lifted me out of the pit of despair,
  out of the mud and the mire.
  He set my feet on solid ground
  and steadied me as I walked along.
³ He has given me a new song to sing,
  a hymn of praise to our God.
  Many will see what he has done and be
    astounded.
  They will put their trust in the LORD.

⁴ Oh, the joys of those who trust the LORD,
  who have no confidence in the proud,
  or in those who worship idols.

⁵ O LORD my God, you have done many
        miracles for us.
    Your plans for us are too numerous to
        list.
    If I tried to recite all your wonderful deeds,
        I would never come to the end of them.

⁶ You take no delight in sacrifices or
        offerings.
    Now that you have made me listen, I
        finally understand—
    you don't require burnt offerings or sin
        offerings.
⁷ Then I said, "Look, I have come.
    And this has been written about me in
        your scroll:
⁸ I take joy in doing your will, my God,
    for your law is written on my heart."

⁹ I have told all your people about your
        justice.
    I have not been afraid to speak out,
        as you, O LORD, well know.
¹⁰ I have not kept this good news hidden in
        my heart;
    I have talked about your faithfulness and
        saving power.
    I have told everyone in the great assembly
        of your unfailing love and faithfulness.

¹¹ LORD, don't hold back your tender mercies
        from me.
    My only hope is in your unfailing love
        and faithfulness.
¹² For troubles surround me—
        too many to count!
    They pile up so high
        I can't see my way out.
    They are more numerous than the hairs on
        my head.
    I have lost all my courage.

¹³ Please, LORD, rescue me!
    Come quickly, LORD, and help me.
¹⁴ May those who try to destroy me
        be humiliated and put to shame.
    May those who take delight in my trouble

    be turned back in disgrace.
¹⁵ Let them be horrified by their shame,
    for they said, "Aha! We've got him now!"

¹⁶ But may all who search for you
        be filled with joy and gladness.
    May those who love your salvation
        repeatedly shout, "The LORD is great!"

¹⁷ As for me, I am poor and needy,
    but the Lord is thinking about me right
        now.
    You are my helper and my savior.
    Do not delay, O my God.

PSALM 41

For the choir director: A psalm of David.

¹ Oh, the joys of those who are kind to the
        poor.
    The LORD rescues them in times of
        trouble.
² The LORD protects them
        and keeps them alive.
    He gives them prosperity
        and rescues them from their enemies.
³ The LORD nurses them when they are sick
        and eases their pain and discomfort.

⁴ "O LORD," I prayed, "have mercy on me.
    Heal me, for I have sinned against you."
⁵ But my enemies say nothing but evil about
        me.
    "How soon will he die and be
        forgotten?" they ask.
⁶ They visit me as if they are my friends,
    but all the while they gather gossip,
    and when they leave, they spread it
        everywhere.
⁷ All who hate me whisper about me,
        imagining the worst for me.
⁸ "Whatever he has, it is fatal," they say.
    "He will never get out of that bed!"
⁹ Even my best friend, the one I trusted
        completely,
    the one who shared my food,
        has turned against me.

¹⁰ LORD, have mercy on me.
    Make me well again, so I can pay them
        back!
¹¹ I know that you are pleased with me,
    for you have not let my enemy triumph
        over me.
¹² You have preserved my life because I am
        innocent;
    you have brought me into your presence
        forever.

¹³ Bless the LORD, the God of Israel,
    who lives forever from eternal ages past.
    Amen and amen!

BOOK TWO (PSALMS 42–72)

PSALM 42

*For the choir director: A psalm of the
descendants of Korah.*

¹ As the deer pants for streams of water,
    so I long for you, O God.
² I thirst for God, the living God.
    When can I come and stand before him?
³ Day and night, I have only tears for food,
    while my enemies continually taunt me,
        saying,
    "Where is this God of yours?"

⁴ My heart is breaking
    as I remember how it used to be:
I walked among the crowds of worshipers,
    leading a great procession to the house
        of God,
singing for joy and giving thanks—
    it was the sound of a great celebration!

⁵ Why am I discouraged?
    Why so sad?
I will put my hope in God!
    I will praise him again—
    my Savior and ⁶my God!

Now I am deeply discouraged,
    but I will remember your kindness—

from Mount Hermon, the source of the
        Jordan,
    from the land of Mount Mizar.
⁷ I hear the tumult of the raging seas
    as your waves and surging tides sweep
        over me.

⁸ Through each day the LORD pours his
        unfailing love upon me,
    and through each night I sing his songs,
        praying to God who gives me life.

⁹ "O God my rock," I cry,
    "Why have you forsaken me?
Why must I wander in darkness,
    oppressed by my enemies?"
¹⁰ Their taunts pierce me like a fatal wound.
    They scoff, "Where is this God of yours?"

¹¹ Why am I discouraged?
    Why so sad?
I will put my hope in God!
    I will praise him again—
    my Savior and my God!

PSALM 43

¹ O God, take up my cause!
    Defend me against these ungodly
        people.
    Rescue me from these unjust liars.
² For you are God, my only safe haven.
    Why have you tossed me aside?
Why must I wander around in darkness,
    oppressed by my enemies?

³ Send out your light and your truth;
    let them guide me.
Let them lead me to your holy mountain,
    to the place where you live.
⁴ There I will go to the altar of God,
    to God—the source of all my joy.
I will praise you with my harp,
    O God, my God!

⁵ Why am I discouraged?
    Why so sad?
I will put my hope in God!

My Daily Worship

— May 11 —

MOONLIT MELODIES

PSALMS 42:1–45:17

Through each day the LORD pours his unfailing love upon me, and through each night I sing his songs, praying to God who gives me life (42:8).

[i reflect]

In 1943 a young Wheaton College graduate by the name of Billy Graham became pastor of Western Springs Baptist Church near Chicago. Billy and his new wife had barely settled into life in the pastorate when a well-known radio evangelist by the name of Torrey Johnson challenged the young pastor with an opportunity.

In addition to being a local church pastor, Torrey wondered if Billy would like to broaden the influence of his new ministry by becoming the regular speaker on a Sunday evening radio broadcast called *Songs in the Night*. Graham nervously accepted and proceeded to seek out a popular staff announcer at WMBI radio at Moody Bible Institute in Chicago to work with him. So began the ministry partnership of George Beverly Shea and Billy Graham.

Each week Billy would relate biblical promises to current events while Shea would sing hymns that celebrated God's faithfulness. *Songs in the Night* provided a vocabulary of praise with which listeners could close out the Lord's Day in preparation for the challenges of a new week. Although Billy only hosted the program for a brief time, its popularity continued. More than sixty years later, the program continues to guide late night reflections to those who drift off to sleep mindful of the Lord's goodness.

Millennia before radio, the psalm writer recognized the importance of reflection and singing at the end of the day. For him it was a natural expression of faith and the means to focus on the "the God who gives me life" as we lay our heads down to sleep. Can you relate to that? If ever there was a time to commit your concerns to the Lord and think about his love, it's as you relax beneath your covers in the stillness of the night. Go ahead. Hum a few bars of a favorite worship song or reflect on lyrics you know by heart. It's a way of giving the Lord a goodnight hug.

[i pray]

Lord Jesus, I know you are always in tune with my life. But there's just something about nighttime that causes me to feel close to you. In the quiet of the dark, hear the lyrics of love that cannot be contained in my grateful heart.

[i respond]

Why not try something new? Instead of just using your clock radio to wake you in the morning, use the timer on it to listen to a Christian station or a praise tape as you're drifting off to sleep.

I will praise him again—
my Savior and my God!

PSALM 44

For the choir director: A psalm of the descendants of Korah.

1 O God, we have heard it with our own
ears—
our ancestors have told us
of all you did in other days,
in days long ago:
2 You drove out the pagan nations
and gave all the land to our ancestors;
you crushed their enemies,
setting our ancestors free.
3 They did not conquer the land with their
swords;
it was not their own strength that gave
them victory.
It was by your mighty power that they
succeeded;
it was because you favored them and
smiled on them.

4 You are my King and my God.
You command victories for your people.*
5 Only by your power can we push back our
enemies;
only in your name can we trample our
foes.
6 I do not trust my bow;
I do not count on my sword to save me.
7 It is you who gives us victory over our
enemies;
it is you who humbles those who hate us.
8 O God, we give glory to you all day long
and constantly praise your name.

Interlude

9 But now you have tossed us aside in
dishonor.
You no longer lead our armies to battle.
10 You make us retreat from our enemies
and allow them to plunder our land.

11 You have treated us like sheep waiting to
be slaughtered;
you have scattered us among the
nations.
12 You sold us—your precious people—for a
pittance.
You valued us at nothing at all.

13 You have caused all our neighbors to mock
us.
We are an object of scorn and derision
to the nations around us.
14 You have made us the butt of their jokes;
we are scorned by the whole world.
15 We can't escape the constant humiliation;
shame is written across our faces.
16 All we hear are the taunts of our mockers.
All we see are our vengeful enemies.

17 All this has happened despite our loyalty
to you.
We have not violated your covenant.
18 Our hearts have not deserted you.
We have not strayed from your path.
19 Yet you have crushed us in the desert.
You have covered us with darkness and
death.

20 If we had turned away from worshiping
our God
or spread our hands in prayer to foreign
gods,
21 God would surely have known it,
for he knows the secrets of every heart.
22 For your sake we are killed every day;
we are being slaughtered like sheep.

23 Wake up, O Lord! Why do you sleep?
Get up! Do not reject us forever.
24 Why do you look the other way?
Why do you ignore our suffering and
oppression?
25 We collapse in the dust,
lying face down in the dirt.
26 Rise up! Come and help us!
Save us because of your unfailing love.

44:4 Hebrew *for Jacob.*

PSALM 45

For the choir director: A psalm of the descendants of Korah, to be sung to the tune "Lilies." A love song.

1 My heart overflows with a beautiful
        thought!
    I will recite a lovely poem to the king,
    for my tongue is like the pen of a skillful
        poet.

2 You are the most handsome of all.
    Gracious words stream from your lips.
    God himself has blessed you forever.
3 Put on your sword, O mighty warrior!
    You are so glorious, so majestic!
4 In your majesty, ride out to victory,
        defending truth, humility, and justice.
    Go forth to perform awe-inspiring deeds!
5 Your arrows are sharp,
        piercing your enemies' hearts.
    The nations fall before you,
        lying down beneath your feet.

6 Your throne, O God,* endures forever and
        ever.
    Your royal power is expressed in justice.
7 You love what is right and hate what is
        wrong.
    Therefore God, your God, has anointed
        you,
        pouring out the oil of joy on you more
        than on anyone else.
8 Your robes are perfumed with myrrh,
        aloes, and cassia.
    In palaces decorated with ivory,
        you are entertained by the music of
        harps.
9 Kings' daughters are among your
        concubines.
    At your right side stands the queen,
        wearing jewelry of finest gold from
        Ophir!

10 Listen to me, O royal daughter; take to
        heart what I say.

Forget your people and your homeland
        far away.
11 For your royal husband delights in your
        beauty;
    honor him, for he is your lord.
12 The princes of Tyre* will shower you with
        gifts.
    People of great wealth will entreat your
        favor.

13 The bride, a princess, waits within her
        chamber,
    dressed in a gown woven with gold.
14 In her beautiful robes, she is led to the
        king,
    accompanied by her bridesmaids.
15 What a joyful, enthusiastic procession
    as they enter the king's palace!

16 Your sons will become kings like their
        father.
    You will make them rulers over many
        lands.

17 I will bring honor to your name in every
        generation.
    Therefore, the nations will praise you
        forever and ever.

PSALM 46

For the choir director: A psalm of the descendants of Korah, to be sung by soprano voices. A song.*

1 God is our refuge and strength,
    always ready to help in times of trouble.
2 So we will not fear, even if earthquakes
        come
    and the mountains crumble into the sea.
3 Let the oceans roar and foam.
    Let the mountains tremble as the waters
        surge!   *Interlude*

4 A river brings joy to the city of our God,
    the sacred home of the Most High.

45:6 Or *Your divine throne.* **45:12** Hebrew *The daughter of Tyre.* **46:**TITLE Hebrew *according to alamoth.*

⁵ God himself lives in that city; it cannot be
    destroyed.
  God will protect it at the break of day.
⁶ The nations are in an uproar,
    and kingdoms crumble!
  God thunders,
    and the earth melts!

⁷ The LORD Almighty is here among us;
    the God of Israel* is our fortress.

Interlude

⁸ Come, see the glorious works of the LORD:
    See how he brings destruction upon the
    world
⁹ and causes wars to end throughout the
    earth.
  He breaks the bow and snaps the spear
    in two;
  he burns the shields with fire.

¹⁰ "Be silent, and know that I am God!
    I will be honored by every nation.
    I will be honored throughout the world."

¹¹ The LORD Almighty is here among us;
    the God of Israel is our fortress.

Interlude

PSALM 47

*For the choir director: A psalm of the
descendants of Korah.*

¹ Come, everyone, and clap your hands for
    joy!
  Shout to God with joyful praise!
² For the LORD Most High is awesome.
    He is the great King of all the earth.
³ He subdues the nations before us,
    putting our enemies beneath our feet.
⁴ He chose the Promised Land as our
    inheritance,
  the proud possession of Jacob's
    descendants, whom he loves.

Interlude

⁵ God has ascended with a mighty shout.
    The LORD has ascended with trumpets
    blaring.
⁶ Sing praise to God, sing praises;
    sing praise to our King, sing praises!

⁷ For God is the King over all the earth.
    Praise him with a psalm!
⁸ God reigns above the nations,
    sitting on his holy throne.
⁹ The rulers of the world have gathered
    together.
  They join us in praising the God of
    Abraham.
  For all the kings of the earth belong to
    God.
  He is highly honored everywhere.

PSALM 48

A psalm of the descendants of Korah. A song.

¹ How great is the LORD,
    and how much we should praise him
  in the city of our God,
    which is on his holy mountain!
² It is magnificent in elevation—
    the whole earth rejoices to see it!
  Mount Zion, the holy mountain,*
    is the city of the great King!
³ God himself is in Jerusalem's towers.
    He reveals himself as her defender.

⁴ The kings of the earth joined forces
    and advanced against the city.
⁵ But when they saw it, they were stunned;
    they were terrified and ran away.
⁶ They were gripped with terror,
    like a woman writhing in the pain of
    childbirth
⁷ or like the mighty ships of Tarshish
    being shattered by a powerful east wind.

⁸ We had heard of the city's glory,
    but now we have seen it ourselves—
  the city of the LORD Almighty.

46:7 Hebrew *of Jacob;* also in 46:11. 48:2 Or *Mount Zion, in the far north;* Hebrew reads *Mount Zion, the heights of Zaphon.*

My Daily Worship

— *May 12* —

THE SOUNDS OF SILENCE

PSALMS 46:1–49:20

Be silent, and know that I am God! I will be honored by every nation.
I will be honored throughout the world (46:10).

[*i reflect*]

It is possible to hear truth in silence. In a classic folk ballad of the sixties, singing duo Simon and Garfunkel challenged a superficial generation in the haunting words of "Sounds of Silence." With prophetic voices they invoked a nation to listen to what life had to say in the empty sounds of a shallow world.

At first glance, the words to that song appear to go along with what we read in Psalm 46—that knowledge is found by intentionally concentrating on what is beneath the surface of daily routines. Getting beyond the obvious allows one to understand the underlying truth. But if you took time to study the lyrics to "Sounds of Silence," you'd discover that the "silence" Simon and Garfunkel sang about is quite different from what God commands in Psalm 46.

When the sovereign Lord insists that we "be silent," he wants us to actually press the mute button on life. He knows (and we can discover) that only in a quiet place can we truly hear his inaudible whispers. In God's book, the sounds of silence have nothing to do with analyzing meaningless cultural chatter. Rather they have to do with the space we alone can create. A carved-out space distanced from the hue and cry of a too-fast and too-noisy world where we can contemplate the awesomeness of God without distraction.

Sound inviting? You bet it does. But where will you most likely create such a cocoon of quiet? In a hot bath? On a long walk in the woods? In an easy chair by the fire after everyone is in bed (and the TV is finally off)? Wherever it is for you, it's a space worth finding. The reason is this. God is the One who longs to meet us there in the silence. That's why he told us to be still and quiet in the first place.

[*i pray*]

Lord, forgive me for the tendency I have to turn prayer into a monologue. I'm inclined
to talk instead of listen. I know you are concerned about what's on my mind,
but I need to know what's on your heart even more. Amen.

[*i respond*]

As uncomfortable as it might be initially, don't speak a word as you pray today. Aim to listen in the most quiet place you can find at home or at work. It might require going out into the garage to sit in an empty parked car.

It is the city of our God;
he will make it safe forever.   *Interlude*

⁹ O God, we meditate on your unfailing love
as we worship in your Temple.
¹⁰ As your name deserves, O God,
you will be praised to the ends of the
earth.
Your strong right hand is filled with
victory.
¹¹ Let the people on Mount Zion rejoice.
Let the towns of Judah be glad,
for your judgments are just.

¹² Go, inspect the city of Jerusalem.*
Walk around and count the many
towers.
¹³ Take note of the fortified walls,
and tour all the citadels,
that you may describe them
to future generations.
¹⁴ For that is what God is like.
He is our God forever and ever,
and he will be our guide until we die.

PSALM 49

*For the choir director: A psalm of the
descendants of Korah.*

¹ Listen to this, all you people!
Pay attention, everyone in the world!
² High and low,
rich and poor—listen!
³ For my words are wise,
and my thoughts are filled with insight.
⁴ I listen carefully to many proverbs
and solve riddles with inspiration from a
harp.

⁵ There is no need to fear when times of
trouble come,
when enemies are surrounding me.
⁶ They trust in their wealth
and boast of great riches.
⁷ Yet they cannot redeem themselves from
death*

by paying a ransom to God.
⁸ Redemption does not come so easily,
for no one can ever pay enough
⁹ to live forever
and never see the grave.

¹⁰ Those who are wise must finally die,
just like the foolish and senseless,
leaving all their wealth behind.
¹¹ The grave is their eternal home,
where they will stay forever.
They may name their estates after
themselves,
but they leave their wealth to others.
¹² They will not last long despite their
riches—
they will die like the animals.
¹³ This is the fate of fools,
though they will be remembered as
being so wise.   *Interlude*
¹⁴ Like sheep, they are led to the grave,
where death will be their shepherd.
In the morning the godly will rule over
them.
Their bodies will rot in the grave,
far from their grand estates.
¹⁵ But as for me, God will redeem my life.
He will snatch me from the power of
death.   *Interlude*

¹⁶ So don't be dismayed when the wicked
grow rich,
and their homes become ever more
splendid.
¹⁷ For when they die, they carry nothing with
them.
Their wealth will not follow them into
the grave.
¹⁸ In this life they consider themselves
fortunate,
and the world loudly applauds their
success.
¹⁹ But they will die like all others before
them
and never again see the light of day.

48:12 Hebrew *Zion.* 49:7 Or *no one can redeem the life of another.*

²⁰ People who boast of their wealth don't
understand
that they will die like the animals.

PSALM 50

A psalm of Asaph.

¹ The mighty God, the LORD, has spoken;
he has summoned all humanity from
east to west!
² From Mount Zion, the perfection of
beauty,
God shines in glorious radiance.
³ Our God approaches with the noise of
thunder.
Fire devours everything in his way,
and a great storm rages around him.
⁴ Heaven and earth will be his witnesses
as he judges his people:
⁵ "Bring my faithful people to me—
those who made a covenant with me by
giving sacrifices."
⁶ Then let the heavens proclaim his justice,
for God himself will be the judge.

Interlude

⁷ "O my people, listen as I speak.
Here are my charges against you,
O Israel:
I am God, your God!
⁸ I have no complaint about your sacrifices
or the burnt offerings you constantly
bring to my altar.
⁹ But I want no more bulls from your
barns;
I want no more goats from your pens.
¹⁰ For all the animals of the forest are mine,
and I own the cattle on a thousand hills.
¹¹ Every bird of the mountains
and all the animals of the field belong to
me.
¹² If I were hungry, I would not mention it to
you,
for all the world is mine and everything
in it.
¹³ I don't need the bulls you sacrifice;
I don't need the blood of goats.

¹⁴ What I want instead is your true thanks
to God;
I want you to fulfill your vows to the
Most High.
¹⁵ Trust me in your times of trouble,
and I will rescue you,
and you will give me glory."

¹⁶ But God says to the wicked:
"Recite my laws no longer,
and don't pretend that you obey me.
¹⁷ For you refuse my discipline
and treat my laws like trash.
¹⁸ When you see a thief, you help him,
and you spend your time with adulterers.
¹⁹ Your mouths are filled with wickedness,
and your tongues are full of lies.
²⁰ You sit around and slander a brother—
your own mother's son.
²¹ While you did all this, I remained silent,
and you thought I didn't care.
But now I will rebuke you,
listing all my charges against you.
²² Repent, all of you who ignore me,
or I will tear you apart,
and no one will help you.
²³ But giving thanks is a sacrifice that truly
honors me.
If you keep to my path,
I will reveal to you the salvation of God."

PSALM 51

*For the choir director: A psalm of David,
regarding the time Nathan the prophet came to
him after David had committed adultery with
Bathsheba.*

¹ Have mercy on me, O God,
because of your unfailing love.
Because of your great compassion,
blot out the stain of my sins.
² Wash me clean from my guilt.
Purify me from my sin.

³ For I recognize my shameful deeds—
they haunt me day and night.
⁴ Against you, and you alone, have I sinned;

I have done what is evil in your sight.
You will be proved right in what you say,
and your judgment against me is just.

5 For I was born a sinner—
yes, from the moment my mother
conceived me.
6 But you desire honesty from the heart,
so you can teach me to be wise in my
inmost being.

7 Purify me from my sins,* and I will be
clean;
wash me, and I will be whiter than snow.
8 Oh, give me back my joy again;
you have broken me—
now let me rejoice.
9 Don't keep looking at my sins.
Remove the stain of my guilt.
10 Create in me a clean heart, O God.
Renew a right spirit within me.
11 Do not banish me from your presence,
and don't take your Holy Spirit from
me.
12 Restore to me again the joy of your
salvation,
and make me willing to obey you.
13 Then I will teach your ways to sinners,
and they will return to you.
14 Forgive me for shedding blood, O God
who saves;
then I will joyfully sing of your
forgiveness.
15 Unseal my lips, O Lord,
that I may praise you.

16 You would not be pleased with sacrifices,
or I would bring them.
If I brought you a burnt offering,
you would not accept it.
17 The sacrifice you want is a broken spirit.
A broken and repentant heart, O God,
you will not despise.

18 Look with favor on Zion and help her;
rebuild the walls of Jerusalem.

19 Then you will be pleased with worthy
sacrifices
and with our whole burnt offerings;
and bulls will again be sacrificed on your
altar.

PSALM 52

For the choir director: A psalm of David,
regarding the time Doeg the Edomite told Saul
that Ahimelech had given refuge to David.

1 You call yourself a hero, do you?
Why boast about this crime of yours,
you who have disgraced God's people?
2 All day long you plot destruction.
Your tongue cuts like a sharp razor;
you're an expert at telling lies.
3 You love evil more than good
and lies more than truth.   *Interlude*

4 You love to say things that harm others,
you liar!
5 But God will strike you down once and for
all.
He will pull you from your home
and drag you from the land of the living.
Interlude

6 The righteous will see it and be
amazed.
They will laugh and say,
7 "Look what happens to mighty warriors
who do not trust in God.
They trust their wealth instead
and grow more and more bold in their
wickedness."

8 But I am like an olive tree,
thriving in the house of God.
I trust in God's unfailing love
forever and ever.
9 I will praise you forever, O God,
for what you have done.
I will wait for your mercies
in the presence of your people.

51:7 Hebrew *Purify me with the hyssop branch.*

My Daily Worship

— *May 13* —

A CHILDLIKE HEART

PSALMS 50:1–53:6

The sacrifice you want is a broken spirit.
A broken and repentant heart,
O God, you will not despise (51:17).

[i reflect]

Jesus is the one who taught us that we have a lot to learn from children. In their wide-eyed curiosity, innocent trust, and unpolished honesty, we are given a picture of what God hopes we will be like when we grow up. Children also mirror the tenderness of heart our heavenly Father desires when we have been justly disciplined.

Broken and repentant hearts beat within the breasts of pint-sized humans. If you have ever been in the presence of a child who has been caught in an act of disobedience, you probably have witnessed the psalm writer's "broken and repentant heart." Caught with the proverbial hand in the cookie jar, or clasping the bat that just sent the ball careening through the neighbor's window, the child stands before the parent. The sounds of uncontrollable sobbing (interrupted only by a whispered admission of sorrow), tears rolling down a crestfallen face, and arms extended in search of a forgiving embrace soon follow.

These evidences of remorse are good indicators that the perpetrator is genuinely sorry. No reasonable parent would withhold love, acceptance, and forgiveness from one so broken. And neither does a loving God distance himself from his children who own up to their sin and humbly cast themselves on his mercy.

Doesn't a child's acknowledgement of wrong bring fresh light to this passage? You can feel the emotion. You can sense the humility. You are that child. So don't delay. The authentic worship you desire to offer a holy (yet approachable) God is fueled by childlike repentance. Tell him what is breaking your heart right now.

[i pray]

Loving God, I mislead myself when I think that rationalizing my self-centered actions
and attitudes is a sign of maturity. But I know I don't fool you. Help me become
more like a child who is quick to admit wrongs and willing to show emotions.

[i respond]

Next time you are in a waiting room at a doctor's office or between services at church, make note of the ways children act. Observe their honesty and disregard for faking what they feel. As you see what you lack, ask the Lord to instill that quality within you.

PSALM 53

For the choir director: A meditation of David.

1 Only fools say in their hearts,
   "There is no God."
They are corrupt, and their actions are
      evil;
   no one does good!

2 God looks down from heaven
   on the entire human race;
he looks to see if there is even one with
      real understanding,
   one who seeks for God.
3 But no, all have turned away from God;
   all have become corrupt.
No one does good,
   not even one!

4 Will those who do evil never learn?
   They eat up my people like bread;
   they wouldn't think of praying to God.
5 But then terror will grip them,
   terror like they have never known
      before.
God will scatter the bones of your
      enemies.
   You will put them to shame, for God has
      rejected them.

6 Oh, that salvation would come from
      Mount Zion to rescue Israel!
   For when God restores his people,
   Jacob will shout with joy, and Israel will
      rejoice.

PSALM 54

*For the choir director: A meditation of David,
regarding the time the Ziphites came and said
to Saul, "We know where David is hiding." To
be accompanied by stringed instruments.*

1 Come with great power, O God, and rescue
      me!
   Defend me with your might.
2 O God, listen to my prayer.
   Pay attention to my plea.

3 For strangers are attacking me;
   violent men are trying to kill me.
   They care nothing for God.   *Interlude*

4 But God is my helper.
   The Lord is the one who keeps me
      alive!
5 May my enemies' plans for evil be turned
      against them.
   Do as you promised and put an end to
      them.

6 I will sacrifice a voluntary offering to you;
   I will praise your name, O LORD,
      for it is good.
7 For you will rescue me from my troubles
   and help me to triumph over my
      enemies.

PSALM 55

*For the choir director: A psalm of David, to be
accompanied by stringed instruments.*

1 Listen to my prayer, O God.
   Do not ignore my cry for help!
2 Please listen and answer me,
   for I am overwhelmed by my troubles.
3 My enemies shout at me,
   making loud and wicked threats.
   They bring trouble on me,
   hunting me down in their anger.

4 My heart is in anguish.
   The terror of death overpowers me.
5 Fear and trembling overwhelm me.
   I can't stop shaking.
6 Oh, how I wish I had wings like a dove;
   then I would fly away and rest!
7 I would fly far away
   to the quiet of the wilderness.   *Interlude*

8 How quickly I would escape—
   far away from this wild storm of hatred.
9 Destroy them, Lord, and confuse their
      speech,
   for I see violence and strife in the city.

¹⁰ Its walls are patrolled day and night
against invaders,
but the real danger is wickedness within
the city.
¹¹ Murder and robbery are everywhere there;
threats and cheating are rampant in the
streets.

¹² It is not an enemy who taunts me—
I could bear that.
It is not my foes who so arrogantly insult
me—
I could have hidden from them.
¹³ Instead, it is you—my equal,
my companion and close friend.
¹⁴ What good fellowship we enjoyed
as we walked together to the house
of God.

¹⁵ Let death seize my enemies by surprise;
let the grave* swallow them alive,
for evil makes its home within them.

¹⁶ But I will call on God,
and the LORD will rescue me.
¹⁷ Morning, noon, and night
I plead aloud in my distress,
and the LORD hears my voice.
¹⁸ He rescues me and keeps me safe
from the battle waged against me,
even though many still oppose me.
¹⁹ God, who is king forever,
will hear me and will humble them.

Interlude

For my enemies refuse to change their ways;
they do not fear God.

²⁰ As for this friend of mine, he betrayed me;
he broke his promises.
²¹ His words are as smooth as cream,
but in his heart is war.
His words are as soothing as lotion,
but underneath are daggers!

²² Give your burdens to the LORD,
and he will take care of you.

He will not permit the godly to slip and
fall.
²³ But you, O God, will send the wicked
down to the pit of destruction.
Murderers and liars will die young,
but I am trusting you to save me.

PSALM 56

For the choir director: A psalm of David,
regarding the time the Philistines seized him in
Gath. To be sung to the tune "Dove on Distant
Oaks."

¹ O God, have mercy on me.
The enemy troops press in on me.
My foes attack me all day long.
² My slanderers hound me constantly,
and many are boldly attacking me.
³ But when I am afraid,
I put my trust in you.
⁴ O God, I praise your word.
I trust in God, so why should I be afraid?
What can mere mortals do to me?

⁵ They are always twisting what I say;
they spend their days plotting ways to
harm me.
⁶ They come together to spy on me—
watching my every step, eager to kill me.
⁷ Don't let them get away with their
wickedness;
in your anger, O God, throw them to the
ground.

⁸ You keep track of all my sorrows.
You have collected all my tears in your
bottle.
You have recorded each one in your
book.
⁹ On the very day I call to you for help,
my enemies will retreat.
This I know: God is on my side.*
¹⁰ O God, I praise your word.

55:15 Hebrew *let Sheol.* 56:9 Or *By this I will know that God is on my side.*

Yes, LORD, I praise your word.
¹¹ I trust in God, so why should I be afraid?
    What can mere mortals do to me?

¹² I will fulfill my vows to you, O God,
    and offer a sacrifice of thanks for your
      help.
¹³ For you have rescued me from death;
    you have kept my feet from slipping.
    So now I can walk in your presence, O God,
    in your life-giving light.

PSALM 57

*For the choir director: A psalm of David,
regarding the time he fled from Saul and went
into the cave. To be sung to the tune "Do Not
Destroy!"*

¹ Have mercy on me, O God, have mercy!
    I look to you for protection.
    I will hide beneath the shadow of your
      wings
    until this violent storm is past.

² I cry out to God Most High,
    to God who will fulfill his purpose for
      me.
³ He will send help from heaven to save me,
    rescuing me from those who are out to
      get me.   *Interlude*
    My God will send forth his unfailing love
    and faithfulness.

⁴ I am surrounded by fierce lions
    who greedily devour human prey—
    whose teeth pierce like spears and arrows,
    and whose tongues cut like swords.

⁵ Be exalted, O God, above the highest
    heavens!
    May your glory shine over all the
      earth.

⁶ My enemies have set a trap for me.
    I am weary from distress.

They have dug a deep pit in my path,
    but they themselves have fallen into it.
                Interlude

⁷ My heart is confident in you, O God;
    no wonder I can sing your praises!
⁸ Wake up, my soul!
    Wake up, O harp and lyre!
    I will waken the dawn with my song.
⁹ I will thank you, Lord, in front of all the
      people.
    I will sing your praises among the
      nations.
¹⁰ For your unfailing love is as high as the
    heavens.
    Your faithfulness reaches to the clouds.

¹¹ Be exalted, O God, above the highest
    heavens.
    May your glory shine over all the earth.

PSALM 58

*For the choir director: A psalm of David, to be
sung to the tune "Do Not Destroy!"*

¹ Justice—do you rulers know the meaning
    of the word?
    Do you judge the people fairly?
² No, all your dealings are crooked;
    you hand out violence instead of
      justice.
³ These wicked people are born sinners;
    even from birth they have lied and gone
      their own way.
⁴ They spit poison like deadly snakes;
    they are like cobras that refuse to listen,
⁵ ignoring the tunes of the snake charmers,
    no matter how skillfully they play.

⁶ Break off their fangs, O God!
    Smash the jaws of these lions, O LORD!
⁷ May they disappear like water into thirsty
    ground.
    Make their weapons useless in their
      hands.*

58:7 Or *Let them be trodden down and wither like grass.* The meaning of the Hebrew is uncertain.

My Daily Worship
— *May 14* —

FIGHTING OUR FEARS
PSALMS 54:1–56:13

But when I am afraid, I put my trust in you. O God, I praise your word. I trust in God,
so why should I be afraid? What can mere mortals do to me? (56:3–4).

[i reflect]

David's fears were very real—enemy troops pressing in on him; foes attacking him throughout the day; slanderers hounding him constantly; others who boldly were attacking him. Today, our fears often are not as imminent or life-threatening.

In fact, there's a phobia named for nearly every part of life. Have you noticed the number of things people are deathly afraid of? It's almost scary. Some are afraid of snakes, while others are afraid of spiders. Some fear rats, and some fear heights. There's a phobia of flying, of public speaking, of getting germs, and of being in a crowd. Some people are simply afraid of being afraid.

Evidently young Timothy, Paul's young disciple, was prone to getting sweaty palms. Overwhelmed by life. Intimidated by ministry. Afraid of failure perhaps? No wonder Paul encouraged his protégé with these words in 2 Timothy 1:7, "For God has not given us a spirit of fear and timidity, but of power, love, and self-discipline."

But being told that the fear factor doesn't have divine origin doesn't mean that anxiety evaporates. Having a relationship with God doesn't vaccinate a person from being afraid. David certainly was in tune with God, and yet fear tracked him down on occasions. He admits to the fact he was afraid at times. But when confronted with fear, David knew where to turn. When tempted to have a panic attack, he didn't turn his back and run. David dropped to his knees and called on the name of the Lord. Acknowledging his need of God in a time of anxiety was an expression of worship. And it can be for you too.

What grips your heart or leaves you feeling faint? Don't pretend you're unflappable. Admit your fear in the presence of God. Then admit your need of him. Such an admission is a type of praise the Lord loves to hear. He longs to wrap his arms around you and comfort you.

Kneel before him now. Tell him the fears that loom ahead of you this day. Allow him to hold and protect you.

[i pray]

Father, you know what I fear. Trying to hide my anxieties from you
is silly. Nonetheless, I continually struggle to admit my need. Remind me
that you are capable of calming my nervous and fearful heart.

[i respond]

Commit today's verse to memory. When you find yourself buckling to your personal phobia, recite this verse aloud and take comfort, as David did, knowing that God will be with you.

8 May they be like snails that dissolve into
slime,
like a stillborn child who will never see
the sun.
9 God will sweep them away, both young
and old,
faster than a pot heats on an open flame.

10 The godly will rejoice when they see
injustice avenged.
They will wash their feet in the blood of
the wicked.
11 Then at last everyone will say,
"There truly is a reward for those who
live for God;
surely there is a God who judges justly
here on earth."

PSALM 59

*For the choir director: A psalm of David,
regarding the time Saul sent soldiers to watch
David's house in order to kill him. To be sung
to the tune "Do Not Destroy!"*

1 Rescue me from my enemies, O God.
Protect me from those who have come
to destroy me.
2 Rescue me from these criminals;
save me from these murderers.

3 They have set an ambush for me.
Fierce enemies are out there waiting,
though I have done them no wrong,
O LORD.
4 Despite my innocence, they prepare to
kill me.
Rise up and help me! Look on my plight!
5 O LORD God Almighty, the God of Israel,
rise up to punish hostile nations.
Show no mercy to wicked traitors.
Interlude

6 They come at night,
snarling like vicious dogs
as they prowl the streets.

7 Listen to the filth that comes from their
mouths,
the piercing swords that fly from their
lips.
"Who can hurt us?" they sneer.
8 But LORD, you laugh at them.
You scoff at all the hostile nations.
9 You are my strength; I wait for you to
rescue me,
for you, O God, are my place of safety.
10 In his unfailing love, my God will come
and help me.
He will let me look down in triumph on
all my enemies.

11 Don't kill them, for my people soon forget
such lessons;
stagger them with your power, and bring
them to their knees,
O Lord our shield.
12 Because of the sinful things they say,
because of the evil that is on their lips,
let them be captured by their pride,
their curses, and their lies.
13 Destroy them in your anger!
Wipe them out completely!
Then the whole world will know
that God reigns in Israel.*   *Interlude*

14 My enemies come out at night,
snarling like vicious dogs
as they prowl the streets.
15 They scavenge for food
but go to sleep unsatisfied.*

16 But as for me, I will sing about your
power.
I will shout with joy each morning
because of your unfailing love.
For you have been my refuge,
a place of safety in the day of distress.

17 O my Strength, to you I sing praises,
for you, O God, are my refuge,
the God who shows me unfailing love.

59:13 Hebrew *in Jacob.* **59:15** Or *and growl if they don't get enough.*

My Daily Worship

— *May 15* —

A Song for All Nations

PSALMS 57:1–59:17

I will thank you, LORD, in front of all the people.
I will sing your praises among the nations (57:9).

[i reflect]

In 1984 an ordained minister by the name of Ray Barnett heard a BBC news report from Africa that disturbed him greatly. It described the plight of thousands of children in Uganda who were victims of the oppressive reign of dictator Idi Amin. Barnett, himself an orphan, was moved to help the suffering children robbed of parents and hope.

While traveling through Africa, he picked up a young boy who was hitchhiking between two cities. The entire length of the journey the boy sang simple melodies that inspired Barnett. He began to picture an entire choir of dark-skinned children, filled with the love of Jesus, touring the world. Not only would the choir provide a practical means of raising money to feed, clothe, and educate countless orphans, but the children also would bear witness to God's faithfulness through song.

Within a short period of time the African Children's Choir was formed. Since then, more than six thousand children from Uganda, Kenya, Rwanda, Nigeria, and Ghana have brought the words of David's psalm to life: "I will thank you, LORD, in front of all the people. I will sing your praises among the nations" (57:9). Grateful children have traveled the world giving public praise to God as they sing from the depths of grateful hearts.

The response of the nations has been humbling. Needy children not only are being cared for, but amazingly, the praise of children provides a practical means of enriching their lives. But you would expect that, right? Haven't you discovered the same?

When you grieve a loved one's death or you struggle with health issues, you have to choose between sulking or singing. When you find the means to call on the Lord, you're always glad you did. But what is more, when you allow neighbors or colleagues to look into your trusting heart, the praise of God multiplies. A life of praise pays big dividends. Sing his praises throughout the day!

[i pray]

Lord, thanks for Ray Barnett and his listening heart. Thanks for the African Children's Choir.
Thanks for what I've learned from them about availability and the power of praise to touch others.
As I continue to praise you, use me in the world in which I live.

[i respond]

When's the last time you wrote down praises to God? Scrawl your praises down on a 3 x 5 index card and keep it in your Bible for easy reference. Determine to brag about God the next time you have a chance.

PSALM 60

For the choir director: A psalm of David useful for teaching, regarding the time David fought Aram-naharaim and Aram-zobah, and Joab returned and killed twelve thousand Edomites in the Valley of Salt. To be sung to the tune "Lily of the Testimony."

¹ You have rejected us, O God, and broken
        our defenses.
    You have been angry with us; now
        restore us to your favor.
² You have shaken our land and split it
        open.
    Seal the cracks before it completely
        collapses.
³ You have been very hard on us,
    making us drink wine that sent us
        reeling.
⁴ But you have raised a banner for those
        who honor you—
    a rallying point in the face of attack.
                                        Interlude

⁵ Use your strong right arm to save us,
    and rescue your beloved people.
⁶ God has promised this by his holiness*:
    "I will divide up Shechem with joy.
    I will measure out the valley of Succoth.
⁷ Gilead is mine,
    and Manasseh is mine.
    Ephraim will produce my warriors,
    and Judah will produce my kings.
⁸ Moab will become my lowly servant,
    and Edom will be my slave.
    I will shout in triumph over the
        Philistines."

⁹ But who will bring me into the fortified
        city?
    Who will bring me victory over Edom?
¹⁰ Have you rejected us, O God?
    Will you no longer march with our
        armies?
¹¹ Oh, please help us against our enemies,
    for all human help is useless.

¹² With God's help we will do mighty things,
    for he will trample down our foes.

PSALM 61

For the choir director: A psalm of David, to be accompanied by stringed instruments.

¹ O God, listen to my cry!
    Hear my prayer!
² From the ends of the earth,
    I will cry to you for help,
    for my heart is overwhelmed.
    Lead me to the towering rock of safety,
³   for you are my safe refuge,
    a fortress where my enemies cannot
        reach me.
⁴ Let me live forever in your sanctuary,
    safe beneath the shelter of your wings!
                                        Interlude
⁵ For you have heard my vows, O God.
    You have given me an inheritance
        reserved for those who fear your name.

⁶ Add many years to the life of the king!
    May his years span the generations!
⁷ May he reign under God's protection
        forever.
    Appoint your unfailing love and
        faithfulness to watch over him.

⁸ Then I will always sing praises to your
        name
    as I fulfill my vows day after day.

PSALM 62

For Jeduthun, the choir director: A psalm of David.

¹ I wait quietly before God,
    for my salvation comes from him.
² He alone is my rock and my salvation,
    my fortress where I will never be shaken.

³ So many enemies against one man—
    all of them trying to kill me.

60:6 Or *in his sanctuary.*

My Daily Worship

— May 16 —

AN OPEN DOOR

PSALMS 60:1–63:11

O God, listen to my cry! Hear my prayer! From the ends of the earth,
I will cry to you for help, for my heart is overwhelmed (61:1–2).

[i reflect]

It's a scenario many a young mom can relate to. At the end of a long day, while dragging herself to bed, she passes her preschool-age boy's bedroom. The sound she hears pulls at her heartstrings. Opening the door and flipping on the light, she sees her son clutching his favorite blanket sitting upright on his bed. With knees pulled up to his quivering chin, his thumb is inserted into his mouth and his eyes are puddled with fresh tears.

Sitting down on the edge of the bed, the mother pulls her little guy close and embraces him. "Don't be frightened, sweetheart," she says calmly. "Daddy and I are just down the hall. Everything is okay. There is no reason to be scared." Then there's the classic closure to this familiar scene. As the comforted child lays back down on his bed watching his mother walk toward the hallway, he calls out, "Leave my door open and the light on in the hallway, okay, Mommy? It helps me know you're not far away."

It's called fear of being alone. David experienced it. In this psalm, most likely written after he had narrowly escaped Saul's effort to kill him, David was crying out for God's security and assurance of his presence. Listen again to his cry, "My heart is overwhelmed. Lead me to the towering rock of safety, for you are my safe refuge" (61:2–3).

Most likely you can relate to being overwhelmed by the thought of isolation. And, yet, just as that mother eased the panic in her child's heart by providing a reality check of her presence in the house, so God wants to do the same in your anxious heart. He hears our frantic cries for help. Just ask David. Revealing his love and promises in the Bible is God's way of leaving the door open.

So go ahead. In personal worship open his book and discover that the lights are on. Even in the dark night when you have fears for your safety or concerns about your children's choices, you may feel you are all alone. But you aren't. Feel his arms of safety around you.

[i pray]

Lord God, it's been years since I was three, but I relate to that little boy alone and afraid
in his bed. My monsters aren't invisible; they have names. Finances. Cancer. Stress.
Divorce. Prodigal kids. I'm grateful you hear when I call out to you.

[i respond]

Write down one or more of the verses you found in the Bible that are promises of God's security to you. Place them by your bed so you can read them before going to sleep. Let those select verses call to mind the continual nearness of your heavenly Father.

To them I'm just a broken-down wall
   or a tottering fence.
4 They plan to topple me from my high
     position.
   They delight in telling lies about me.
They are friendly to my face,
   but they curse me in their hearts.

                  Interlude

5 I wait quietly before God,
   for my hope is in him.
6 He alone is my rock and my salvation,
   my fortress where I will not be
     shaken.
7 My salvation and my honor come from
     God alone.
   He is my refuge, a rock where no enemy
     can reach me.

8 O my people, trust in him at all times.
   Pour out your heart to him,
   for God is our refuge.   *Interlude*

9 From the greatest to the lowliest—
   all are nothing in his sight.
If you weigh them on the scales,
   they are lighter than a puff of air.
10 Don't try to get rich
   by extortion or robbery.
And if your wealth increases,
   don't make it the center of your life.

11 God has spoken plainly,
   and I have heard it many times:
Power, O God, belongs to you;
12   unfailing love, O Lord, is yours.
Surely you judge all people
   according to what they have done.

PSALM 63

A psalm of David, regarding a time when
David was in the wilderness of Judah.

1 O God, you are my God;
   I earnestly search for you.
My soul thirsts for you;
   my whole body longs for you

in this parched and weary land
   where there is no water.
2 I have seen you in your sanctuary
   and gazed upon your power and glory.
3 Your unfailing love is better to me than life
     itself;
   how I praise you!
4 I will honor you as long as I live,
   lifting up my hands to you in prayer.
5 You satisfy me more than the richest of
     foods.
   I will praise you with songs of joy.

6 I lie awake thinking of you,
   meditating on you through the night.
7 I think how much you have helped me;
   I sing for joy in the shadow of your
     protecting wings.
8 I follow close behind you;
   your strong right hand holds me
     securely.

9 But those plotting to destroy me will come
     to ruin.
   They will go down into the depths of the
     earth.
10 They will die by the sword
   and become the food of jackals.
11 But the king will rejoice in God.
   All who trust in him will praise him,
   while liars will be silenced.

PSALM 64

For the choir director: A psalm of David.

1 O God, listen to my complaint.
   Do not let my enemies' threats
     overwhelm me.
2 Protect me from the plots of the wicked,
   from the scheming of those who do evil.
3 Sharp tongues are the swords they wield;
   bitter words are the arrows they aim.
4 They shoot from ambush at the innocent,
   attacking suddenly and fearlessly.
5 They encourage each other to do evil

and plan how to set their traps.
  "Who will ever notice?" they ask.
6 As they plot their crimes, they say,
  "We have devised the perfect plan!"
  Yes, the human heart and mind are
     cunning.

7 But God himself will shoot them down.
  Suddenly, his arrows will pierce them.
8 Their own words will be turned against
     them, destroying them.
  All who see it happening will shake their
     heads in scorn.
9 Then everyone will stand in awe,
  proclaiming the mighty acts of God,
  realizing all the amazing things he does.

10 The godly will rejoice in the LORD
  and find shelter in him.
  And those who do what is right
     will praise him.

PSALM 65

For the choir director: A psalm of David.
A song.

1 What mighty praise, O God,
  belongs to you in Zion.
  We will fulfill our vows to you,
2   for you answer our prayers,
  and to you all people will come.
3 Though our hearts are filled with sins,
  you forgive them all.
4 What joy for those you choose to bring
     near,
  those who live in your holy courts.
  What joys await us
  inside your holy Temple.

5 You faithfully answer our prayers with
     awesome deeds,
  O God our savior.
  You are the hope of everyone on earth,
  even those who sail on distant seas.
6 You formed the mountains by your power
  and armed yourself with mighty
     strength.

Words of Worship

MUSIC

Music—Hebrew *shir* "song." Scripture does not have a word for music in general but refers to specific kinds of music or instruments. The English word "music" derives from the Greek idea of the *muse*, the spirit thought to inspire poets and musicians. The biblical equivalent would be the phenomenon of prophecy. The Hebrew prophets heard from the Lord and then spoke his word.

It's not surprising that the Lord gave his people music as a way of approaching his mystery and expressing the joy of his presence. Some truths ordinary speech cannot fully convey. Words touch us through our conscious thought. But music touches us at a deeper, intuitive level. We can't explain its effect on us, but we know it's real and grips our emotions.

In the worship of Israel, vocal and instrumental music served as a "sacrifice of praise," an offering of song to accompany the offering of sacrifice. The early Christians also worshiped through music, singing "psalms, hymns and spiritual songs" (Ephesians 5:19). Revelation records a future time of highest praise, where a pageant of song begun by four living beings widens to include the praise of every creature (Revelation 5:8–14). We join that widening circle of praise today, singing with adoration words alone can't contain.

7 You quieted the raging oceans
  with their pounding waves
  and silenced the shouting of the nations.
8 Those who live at the ends of the earth
  stand in awe of your wonders.
  From where the sun rises to where it sets,
  you inspire shouts of joy.

9 You take care of the earth and water it,
    making it rich and fertile.
  The rivers of God will not run dry;
    they provide a bountiful harvest of
      grain,
    for you have ordered it so.
10 You drench the plowed ground with rain,
    melting the clods and leveling the
      ridges.
  You soften the earth with showers
    and bless its abundant crops.
11 You crown the year with a bountiful
    harvest;
    even the hard pathways overflow with
      abundance.
12 The wilderness becomes a lush pasture,
    and the hillsides blossom with joy.
13 The meadows are clothed with flocks of
    sheep,
    and the valleys are carpeted with
      grain.
    They all shout and sing for joy!

PSALM 66

For the choir director: A psalm. A song.

1 Shout joyful praises to God, all the earth!
2   Sing about the glory of his name!
    Tell the world how glorious he is.
3 Say to God, "How awesome are your
    deeds!
    Your enemies cringe before your mighty
      power.
4 Everything on earth will worship you;
    they will sing your praises,
    shouting your name in glorious songs."
                                    Interlude

5 Come and see what our God has done,
    what awesome miracles he does for his
      people!
6 He made a dry path through the Red Sea,*
    and his people went across on foot.
    Come, let us rejoice in who he is.
7 For by his great power he rules forever.

66:6 Hebrew *the sea.*

He watches every movement of the
    nations;
    let no rebel rise in defiance.   *Interlude*

8 Let the whole world bless our God
    and sing aloud his praises.
9 Our lives are in his hands,
    and he keeps our feet from stumbling.
10 You have tested us, O God;
    you have purified us like silver melted in
      a crucible.
11 You captured us in your net
    and laid the burden of slavery on our
      backs.
12 You sent troops to ride across our broken
    bodies.
  We went through fire and flood.
    But you brought us to a place of great
      abundance.

13 Now I come to your Temple with burnt
    offerings
    to fulfill the vows I made to you—
14 yes, the sacred vows you heard me make
    when I was in deep trouble.
15 That is why I am sacrificing burnt
    offerings to you—
    the best of my rams as a pleasing aroma.
    And I will sacrifice bulls and goats.
                                    Interlude

16 Come and listen, all you who fear God,
    and I will tell you what he did for me.
17 For I cried out to him for help,
    praising him as I spoke.
18 If I had not confessed the sin in my heart,
    my Lord would not have listened.
19 But God did listen!
    He paid attention to my prayer.

20 Praise God, who did not ignore my
    prayer
    and did not withdraw his unfailing love
      from me.

PSALM 67

For the choir director: A psalm, to be
accompanied by stringed instruments. A song.

¹ May God be merciful and bless us.
  May his face shine with favor upon us.
    Interlude
² May your ways be known throughout the
    earth,
  your saving power among people
    everywhere.
³ May the nations praise you, O God.
  Yes, may all the nations praise you.

⁴ How glad the nations will be, singing for
    joy,
  because you govern them with justice
  and direct the actions of the whole
    world.   *Interlude*
⁵ May the nations praise you, O God.
  Yes, may all the nations praise you.

⁶ Then the earth will yield its harvests,
  and God, our God, will richly bless us.
⁷ Yes, God will bless us,
  and people all over the world will fear
    him.

PSALM 68

For the choir director: A psalm of David.
A song.

¹ Arise, O God, and scatter your enemies.
  Let those who hate God run for their
    lives.
² Drive them off like smoke blown by the
    wind.
  Melt them like wax in fire.
  Let the wicked perish in the presence of
    God.
³ But let the godly rejoice.
  Let them be glad in God's presence.
  Let them be filled with joy.

⁴ Sing praises to God and to his name!
  Sing loud praises to him who rides the
    clouds.

His name is the LORD—
  rejoice in his presence!
⁵ Father to the fatherless, defender of
    widows—
  this is God, whose dwelling is holy.
⁶ God places the lonely in families;
  he sets the prisoners free and gives them
    joy.
  But for rebels, there is only famine and
    distress.

⁷ O God, when you led your people from
    Egypt,
  when you marched through the
    wilderness,   *Interlude*
⁸ the earth trembled, and the heavens
    poured rain
  before you, the God of Sinai,
  before God, the God of Israel.
⁹ You sent abundant rain, O God,
  to refresh the weary Promised Land.
¹⁰ There your people finally settled,
  and with a bountiful harvest, O God,
  you provided for your needy people.

¹¹ The Lord announces victory,
  and throngs of women shout the happy
    news.
¹² Enemy kings and their armies flee,
  while the women of Israel divide the
    plunder.
¹³ Though they lived among the sheepfolds,
  now they are covered with silver and
    gold,
  as a dove is covered by its wings.
¹⁴ The Almighty scattered the enemy kings
  like a blowing snowstorm on Mount
    Zalmon.

¹⁵ The majestic mountains of Bashan
  stretch high into the sky.
¹⁶ Why do you look with envy, O rugged
    mountains,
  at Mount Zion, where God has chosen
    to live,
  where the LORD himself will live forever?

¹⁷ Surrounded by unnumbered thousands of
  chariots,
    the Lord came from Mount Sinai into
    his sanctuary.
¹⁸ When you ascended to the heights,
    you led a crowd of captives.
  You received gifts from the people,
    even from those who rebelled against
    you.
  Now the LORD God will live among us
    here.

¹⁹ Praise the Lord; praise God our savior!
    For each day he carries us in his arms.
                                    Interlude
²⁰ Our God is a God who saves!
    The Sovereign LORD rescues us from
    death.

²¹ But God will smash the heads of his
  enemies,
    crushing the skulls of those who love
    their guilty ways.
²² The Lord says, "I will bring my enemies
    down from Bashan;
  I will bring them up from the depths of
    the sea.
²³ You, my people, will wash your feet in
    their blood,
  and even your dogs will get their share!"

²⁴ Your procession has come into view,
    O God—
  the procession of my God and King
    as he goes into the sanctuary.
²⁵ Singers are in front, musicians are
  behind;
    with them are young women playing
    tambourines.
²⁶ Praise God, all you people of Israel;
    praise the LORD, the source of Israel's
    life.
²⁷ Look, the little tribe of Benjamin leads the
    way.
  Then comes a great throng of rulers
    from Judah

and all the rulers of Zebulun and
    Naphtali.

²⁸ Summon your might, O God.
    Display your power, O God, as you have
    in the past.
²⁹ The kings of the earth are bringing tribute
    to your Temple in Jerusalem.
³⁰ Rebuke these enemy nations—
    these wild animals lurking in the reeds,
    this herd of bulls among the weaker
    calves.
  Humble those who demand tribute from
    us.*
    Scatter the nations that delight in war.
³¹ Let Egypt come with gifts of precious
    metals;
    let Ethiopia* bow in submission to God.
³² Sing to God, you kingdoms of the earth.
    Sing praises to the Lord.   *Interlude*

³³ Sing to the one who rides across the
    ancient heavens,
    his mighty voice thundering from the
    sky.
³⁴ Tell everyone about God's power.
    His majesty shines down on Israel;
    his strength is mighty in the heavens.
³⁵ God is awesome in his sanctuary.
    The God of Israel gives power and
    strength to his people.

  Praise be to God!

PSALM 69

*For the choir director: A psalm of David, to be
sung to the tune "Lilies."*

¹ Save me, O God,
    for the floodwaters are up to my neck.
² Deeper and deeper I sink into the mire;
    I can't find a foothold to stand on.
  I am in deep water,
    and the floods overwhelm me.
³ I am exhausted from crying for help;

68:30 Or *Humble them until they submit, bringing pieces of silver as tribute.* 68:31 Hebrew *Cush.*

My Daily Worship

— *May 17* —

IN THE ARMS OF GOD

PSALMS 64:1–68:35

Praise the LORD; praise God our savior!
For each day he carries us in his arms (68:19).

[i reflect]

On a hot July day in 1967, Joni Eareckson Tada's life changed forever. This athletic teenager dove into a shallow lake, breaking her neck and fracturing her spinal cord. Instantly she became a quadriplegic. Dreams of riding horses through a meadow remained just that. So, too, the hopes of walking along a beach at sunrise hand in hand with a boyfriend.

The next two years of hospitalization and therapy were excruciating, but Joni persevered. Eventually, she learned to paint with a brush between her teeth. Through a friend's witness, she also discovered a personal relationship with Jesus Christ and a faith that enabled her to rely on God's everlasting arms. Remarkably, Joni has not just experienced what it's like to be carried by the Lord through the predictable dark days; she has experienced it everyday.

But there's more. Although she will never walk hand in hand with a boyfriend on a beach this side of heaven, Joni knows the delight of holding hands with her husband, Ken. And it's through Ken's hands that Joni is able to grasp God's unconditional love in a tangible way. Each day Ken must lift and carry her from bed to wheelchair, from wheelchair to toilet seat, from house to car, and so on.

Every day Joni relies on another person to care for needs she cannot meet for herself. Another's strength compensates for her weakness. What a quadriplegic experiences literally, the psalm writer pictured metaphorically when he wrote of being carried daily by the arms of God.

Isn't that good news? What has happened today that has left you feeling weak? You don't have to be confined to a wheelchair to attest to the reality of God's care. When life cuts you off at the knees, he is there reaching out to help you stand up. Use those moments of weakness to celebrate and rejoice in God's strong arms!

[i pray]

O God, the story of Joni inspires me. You have carried her in so many ways. But when
I stop and think about it, you have carried me too. I need to rest on your never-failing
arms, Lord. Life continues to leave me weak. Give me the faith to lean on you.

[i respond]

During your quiet time, contemplate your open palms. Picture yourself in God's hands. If it helps, write your name in the middle of your hand as a reminder of how safe you are no matter what comes up the rest of the day.

my throat is parched and dry.
My eyes are swollen with weeping,
  waiting for my God to help me.

⁴ Those who hate me without cause
  are more numerous than the hairs on
    my head.
These enemies who seek to destroy me
  are doing so without cause.
They attack me with lies,
  demanding that I give back what I didn't
    steal.

⁵ O God, you know how foolish I am;
  my sins cannot be hidden from you.
⁶ Don't let those who trust in you stumble
    because of me,
  O Sovereign LORD Almighty.
Don't let me cause them to be humiliated,
  O God of Israel.
⁷ For I am mocked and shamed for your
    sake;
  humiliation is written all over my
    face.
⁸ Even my own brothers pretend they don't
    know me;
  they treat me like a stranger.

⁹ Passion for your house burns within me,
  so those who insult you are also
    insulting me.
¹⁰ When I weep and fast before the LORD,
  they scoff at me.
¹¹ When I dress in sackcloth to show sorrow,
  they make fun of me.
¹² I am the favorite topic of town gossip,
  and all the drunkards sing about me.

¹³ But I keep right on praying to you, LORD,
  hoping this is the time you will show me
    favor.
In your unfailing love, O God,
  answer my prayer with your sure
    salvation.
¹⁴ Pull me out of the mud;
  don't let me sink any deeper!
Rescue me from those who hate me,

and pull me from these deep waters.
¹⁵ Don't let the floods overwhelm me,
  or the deep waters swallow me,
  or the pit of death devour me.

¹⁶ Answer my prayers, O LORD,
  for your unfailing love is wonderful.
Turn and take care of me,
  for your mercy is so plentiful.
¹⁷ Don't hide from your servant;
  answer me quickly, for I am in deep
    trouble!
¹⁸ Come and rescue me;
  free me from all my enemies.

¹⁹ You know the insults I endure—
  the humiliation and disgrace.
You have seen all my enemies
  and know what they have said.
²⁰ Their insults have broken my heart,
  and I am in despair.
If only one person would show some pity;
  if only one would turn and comfort me.
²¹ But instead, they give me poison for food;
  they offer me sour wine to satisfy my
    thirst.

²² Let the bountiful table set before them
    become a snare,
  and let their security become a trap.
²³ Let their eyes go blind so they cannot see,
  and let their bodies grow weaker and
    weaker.
²⁴ Pour out your fury on them;
  consume them with your burning anger.
²⁵ May their homes become desolate
  and their tents be deserted.
²⁶ To those you have punished, they add
    insult to injury;
  they scoff at the pain of those you have
    hurt.
²⁷ Pile their sins up high,
  and don't let them go free.
²⁸ Erase their names from the Book of Life;
  don't let them be counted among the
    righteous.

29 I am suffering and in pain.
  Rescue me, O God, by your saving power.

30 Then I will praise God's name with
    singing,
  and I will honor him with thanksgiving.

31 For this will please the LORD more than
    sacrificing an ox
  or presenting a bull with its horns and
    hooves.

32 The humble will see their God at work and
    be glad.
  Let all who seek God's help live in joy.

33 For the LORD hears the cries of his needy
    ones;
  he does not despise his people who are
    oppressed.

34 Praise him, O heaven and earth,
  the seas and all that move in them.

35 For God will save Jerusalem*
  and rebuild the towns of Judah.
  His people will live there
    and take possession of the land.

36 The descendants of those who obey him
    will inherit the land,
  and those who love him will live there in
    safety.

PSALM 70

*For the choir director: A psalm of David, to
bring us to the LORD's remembrance.*

1 Please, God, rescue me!
  Come quickly, LORD, and help me.

2 May those who try to destroy me
  be humiliated and put to shame.
  May those who take delight in my trouble
  be turned back in disgrace.

3 Let them be horrified by their shame,
  for they said, "Aha! We've got him now!"

4 But may all who search for you
  be filled with joy and gladness.
  May those who love your salvation
  repeatedly shout, "God is great!"

5 But I am poor and needy;
  please hurry to my aid, O God.
  You are my helper and my savior;
  O LORD, do not delay!

PSALM 71

1 O LORD, you are my refuge;
  never let me be disgraced.

2 Rescue me! Save me from my enemies, for
    you are just.
  Turn your ear to listen and set me free.

3 Be to me a protecting rock of safety,
  where I am always welcome.
  Give the order to save me,
  for you are my rock and my fortress.

4 My God, rescue me from the power of the
    wicked,
  from the clutches of cruel oppressors.

5 O Lord, you alone are my hope.
  I've trusted you, O LORD, from
    childhood.

6 Yes, you have been with me from birth;
  from my mother's womb you have cared
    for me.
  No wonder I am always praising you!

7 My life is an example to many,
  because you have been my strength and
    protection.

8 That is why I can never stop praising you;
  I declare your glory all day long.

9 And now, in my old age, don't set me
    aside.
  Don't abandon me when my strength is
    failing.

10 For my enemies are whispering against me.
  They are plotting together to kill me.

11 They say, "God has abandoned him.
  Let's go and get him,
  for there is no one to help him now."

12 O God, don't stay away.
  My God, please hurry to help me.

69:35 Hebrew *Zion.*

13 Bring disgrace and destruction on those
    who accuse me.
  May humiliation and shame cover
    those who want to harm me.

14 But I will keep on hoping for you to help
    me;
  I will praise you more and more.
15 I will tell everyone about your
    righteousness.
  All day long I will proclaim your saving
    power,
  for I am overwhelmed by how much you
    have done for me.
16 I will praise your mighty deeds,
    O Sovereign LORD.
  I will tell everyone that you alone are
    just and good.

17 O God, you have taught me from my
    earliest childhood,
  and I have constantly told others about
    the wonderful things you do.
18 Now that I am old and gray,
    do not abandon me, O God.
  Let me proclaim your power to this new
    generation,
  your mighty miracles to all who come
    after me.

19 Your righteousness, O God, reaches to the
    highest heavens.
  You have done such wonderful things.
  Who can compare with you, O God?
20 You have allowed me to suffer much
    hardship,
  but you will restore me to life again
    and lift me up from the depths of the
    earth.
21 You will restore me to even greater honor
    and comfort me once again.

22 Then I will praise you with music on the
    harp,
  because you are faithful to your
    promises, O God.

I will sing for you with a lyre,
  O Holy One of Israel.
23 I will shout for joy and sing your praises,
    for you have redeemed me.
24 I will tell about your righteous deeds
    all day long,
  for everyone who tried to hurt me
    has been shamed and humiliated.

PSALM 72

A psalm of Solomon.

1 Give justice to the king, O God,
    and righteousness to the king's son.
2 Help him judge your people in the right
    way;
  let the poor always be treated fairly.
3 May the mountains yield prosperity for all,
    and may the hills be fruitful,
  because the king does what is right.
4 Help him to defend the poor,
    to rescue the children of the needy,
    and to crush their oppressors.
5 May he live* as long as the sun shines,
    as long as the moon continues in the
    skies.
  Yes, forever!
6 May his reign be as refreshing as the
    springtime rains—
  like the showers that water the earth.
7 May all the godly flourish during his reign.
  May there be abundant prosperity until
    the end of time.

8 May he reign from sea to sea,
    and from the Euphrates River* to the
    ends of the earth.
9 Desert nomads will bow before him;
    his enemies will fall before him in the
    dust.
10 The western kings of Tarshish and the
    islands
  will bring him tribute.
  The eastern kings of Sheba and Seba
    will bring him gifts.

72:5 As in Greek version; Hebrew reads *May they fear you.* **72:8** Hebrew *the river.*

My Daily Worship

— May 18 —

RUN FOR YOUR LIFE!

PSALMS 69:1–72:20

*O God, you have taught me from my earliest childhood, and I have constantly told others
about the wonderful things you do. Now that I am old and gray, do not abandon me,
O God. Let me proclaim your power to this new generation (71:17–18).*

[i reflect]

On January 21, 1925, the lives of countless children in Nome, Alaska, were at stake. An epidemic of diphtheria had broken out in the gold rush city, and they didn't have enough antitoxin to treat the sick. Dr. Curtis Welch telegraphed Fairbanks, Anchorage, Seward, and Juneau asking for help. The only serum in the entire Alaska Territory was found in Anchorage. The problem was how to get the needed medicine to Nome in the shortest time possible.

With the Bering Sea frozen and no railroad or roads extending to Nome's remote location, dog teams were the only solution. A doctor in Anchorage placed the serum on an overnight train to Nenana. From there, twenty sled dog mushers took turns transporting the precious medicine over 674 miles. The relay ended in Nome on February 2. In only 127 ½ hours the lifesaving serum arrived in time to save the next generation of Nome's future leaders.

According to the psalm writer, passing the faith from one generation to the next is like passing the baton in a relay race or a serum run. What God had taught him was precious truth. He felt an obligation to pass it on to those who came after him.

What a challenge for every believer. What we have received we can't just keep to ourselves. Our children need to know; so do our neighbor's children. Think about it. That's the way it is with worship. We catch a glimpse of God and then we help others focus on what we've seen.

Consider the people, as well as the children, whom you will encounter during your daily routine. How many of them know God? With whom can you pass on the baton of faith today?

[i pray]

*Lord, it's humbling to realize you desire to use imperfect people like me to keep
Christianity alive and thriving in our world. Knowing this boggles my mind. But it
also prompts me to want to spend more time in your presence so that I have
something significant to say to those you bring across my path.*

[i respond]

Think about those who have influenced your life spiritually. Thank the Lord for what they contributed to your life. Now ask the Lord to open your eyes to those who look up to *you* as a faith hero. Determine to be proactive in your friendship with them.

¹¹ All kings will bow before him,
and all nations will serve him.

¹² He will rescue the poor when they cry to
him;
he will help the oppressed, who have no
one to defend them.
¹³ He feels pity for the weak and the needy,
and he will rescue them.
¹⁴ He will save them from oppression and
from violence,
for their lives are precious to him.

¹⁵ Long live the king!
May the gold of Sheba be given to him.
May the people always pray for him
and bless him all day long.
¹⁶ May there be abundant crops throughout
the land,
flourishing even on the mountaintops.
May the fruit trees flourish as they do in
Lebanon,
sprouting up like grass in a field.
¹⁷ May the king's name endure forever;
may it continue as long as the sun shines.
May all nations be blessed through him
and bring him praise.

¹⁸ Bless the LORD God, the God of Israel,
who alone does such wonderful things.
¹⁹ Bless his glorious name forever!
Let the whole earth be filled with his
glory.
Amen and amen!

²⁰ (This ends the prayers of David son of
Jesse.)

BOOK THREE (PSALMS 73–89)

PSALM 73

A psalm of Asaph.

¹ Truly God is good to Israel,
to those whose hearts are pure.

² But as for me, I came so close to the edge
of the cliff!
My feet were slipping, and I was almost
gone.
³ For I envied the proud
when I saw them prosper despite their
wickedness.
⁴ They seem to live such a painless life;
their bodies are so healthy and strong.
⁵ They aren't troubled like other people
or plagued with problems like everyone
else.
⁶ They wear pride like a jeweled necklace,
and their clothing is woven of cruelty.
⁷ These fat cats have everything
their hearts could ever wish for!
⁸ They scoff and speak only evil;
in their pride they seek to crush
others.
⁹ They boast against the very heavens,
and their words strut throughout the
earth.
¹⁰ And so the people are dismayed and
confused,
drinking in all their words.
¹¹ "Does God realize what is going on?"
they ask.
"Is the Most High even aware of what is
happening?"
¹² Look at these arrogant people—
enjoying a life of ease while their riches
multiply.

¹³ Was it for nothing that I kept my heart
pure
and kept myself from doing wrong?
¹⁴ All I get is trouble all day long;
every morning brings me pain.

¹⁵ If I had really spoken this way,
I would have been a traitor to your
people.
¹⁶ So I tried to understand why the wicked
prosper.
But what a difficult task it is!
¹⁷ Then one day I went into your sanctuary,
O God,

My Daily Worship

— May 19 —

THE SINGLE-MINDED LIFE

PSALMS 73:1–75:10

Whom have I in heaven but you? I desire you more than anything on earth.
My health may fail, and my spirit may grow weak, but God remains
the strength of my heart; he is mine forever (73:25–26).

[i reflect]

In the movie *The Emperor's Club*, Kevin Klein plays William Hundert, a history teacher at St. Benedict's Academy for boys. He sees his role as a teacher to be far more than a job. It is a calling. Early on in the film, Mr. Hundert makes the statement that a person's character determines his future. If every person's life is a book, the end of the story is known long before the last chapter has been written. In other words, what a man or a woman values will filter their choices and brand their reputation.

That certainly is true of the psalm writer. Worshiping God was his sole focus. As a result it was his *soul* focus too. His desire was to grow a relationship with the living God, and that single-minded goal remained throughout his long life. To use Mr. Hundert's analogy, those who knew the writer as a young man would not have been surprised to see him die with praises on his lips. His passion defined his life, so at the end of his life, that single overriding passion sustained him.

What a beautiful picture. Doesn't that motivate you to spend more time with the Lord? As you read your Bible and listen to praise music, why not let the complicated issues that divide your loyalties fall by the wayside? Look to the Lord as the one worthy object of your affection (and attention).

It's a worthwhile effort, even though it may be difficult at first. But the truth Jesus taught remains: When we seek God's kingdom first, all our other legitimate needs will be supplied (Matthew 6:33). Praise God!

[i pray]

Jesus, what you taught your disciples wasn't all that new, was it? Those who wrote
the psalms were wise to the truth that a life governed by a singular purpose
yielded great dividends. I want to invest in that kind of long-term account.
Will you help me? I want to start today by lingering in your presence.

[i respond]

Review your "to do" list for the day. Make it a five-word list today: "Get to know God better!" Then make sure you do something during the day—whether it's reading selections by a Christian author, listening to Christian radio, or praying with a friend—to get to know God better.

and I thought about the destiny of the
wicked.
¹⁸ Truly, you put them on a slippery path
and send them sliding over the cliff to
destruction.
¹⁹ In an instant they are destroyed,
swept away by terrors.
²⁰ Their present life is only a dream
that is gone when they awake.
When you arise, O Lord,
you will make them vanish from this life.

²¹ Then I realized how bitter I had become,
how pained I had been by all I had seen.
²² I was so foolish and ignorant—
I must have seemed like a senseless
animal to you.
²³ Yet I still belong to you;
you are holding my right hand.
²⁴ You will keep on guiding me with your
counsel,
leading me to a glorious destiny.
²⁵ Whom have I in heaven but you?
I desire you more than anything on
earth.
²⁶ My health may fail, and my spirit may
grow weak,
but God remains the strength of my
heart;
he is mine forever.

²⁷ But those who desert him will perish,
for you destroy those who abandon you.
²⁸ But as for me, how good it is to be near
God!
I have made the Sovereign LORD my
shelter,
and I will tell everyone about the
wonderful things you do.

PSALM 74

A psalm of Asaph.

¹ O God, why have you rejected us
forever?

74:2 Hebrew *Mount Zion.*

Why is your anger so intense against the
sheep of your own pasture?
² Remember that we are the people you
chose in ancient times,
the tribe you redeemed as your own
special possession!
And remember Jerusalem,* your home
here on earth.
³ Walk through the awful ruins of the city;
see how the enemy has destroyed your
sanctuary.
⁴ There your enemies shouted their
victorious battle cries;
there they set up their battle standards.
⁵ They chopped down the entrance
like woodcutters in a forest.
⁶ With axes and picks,
they smashed the carved paneling.
⁷ They set the sanctuary on fire, burning it
to the ground.
They utterly defiled the place that bears
your holy name.
⁸ Then they thought, "Let's destroy
everything!"
So they burned down all the places
where God was worshiped.

⁹ We see no miraculous signs
as evidence that you will save us.
All the prophets are gone;
no one can tell us when it will end.
¹⁰ How long, O God, will you allow our
enemies to mock you?
Will you let them dishonor your name
forever?
¹¹ Why do you hold back your strong right
hand?
Unleash your powerful fist and deliver a
deathblow.

¹² You, O God, are my king from ages past,
bringing salvation to the earth.
¹³ You split the sea by your strength
and smashed the sea monster's heads.
¹⁴ You crushed the heads of Leviathan
and let the desert animals eat him.

¹⁵ You caused the springs and streams to
gush forth,
and you dried up rivers that never run
dry.
¹⁶ Both day and night belong to you;
you made the starlight* and the sun.
¹⁷ You set the boundaries of the earth,
and you make both summer and winter.

¹⁸ See how these enemies scoff at you, LORD.
A foolish nation has dishonored your
name.
¹⁹ Don't let these wild beasts destroy your
doves.
Don't forget your afflicted people
forever.

²⁰ Remember your covenant promises,
for the land is full of darkness and
violence!
²¹ Don't let the downtrodden be constantly
disgraced!
Instead, let these poor and needy ones
give praise to your name.

²² Arise, O God, and defend your cause.
Remember how these fools insult you all
day long.
²³ Don't overlook these things your enemies
have said.
Their uproar of rebellion grows ever
louder.

PSALM 75

*For the choir director: A psalm of Asaph,
to be sung to the tune "Do Not Destroy!"
A song.*

¹ We thank you, O God!
We give thanks because you are near.
People everywhere tell of your mighty
miracles.

² God says, "At the time I have planned,
I will bring justice against the wicked.

³ When the earth quakes and its people live
in turmoil,
I am the one who keeps its foundations
firm. *Interlude*

⁴ "I warned the proud, 'Stop your boasting!'
I told the wicked, 'Don't raise your fists!
⁵ Don't lift your fists in defiance at the
heavens
or speak with rebellious arrogance.' "

⁶ For no one on earth—from east or west,
or even from the wilderness—
can raise another person up.
⁷ It is God alone who judges;
he decides who will rise and who will fall.
⁸ For the LORD holds a cup in his hand;
it is full of foaming wine mixed with
spices.
He pours the wine out in judgment,
and all the wicked must drink it,
draining it to the dregs.

⁹ But as for me, I will always proclaim what
God has done;
I will sing praises to the God of Israel.*

¹⁰ For God says, "I will cut off the strength of
the wicked,
but I will increase the power of the
godly."

PSALM 76

*For the choir director: A psalm of Asaph,
to be accompanied by stringed instruments.
A song.*

¹ God is well known in Judah;
his name is great in Israel.
² Jerusalem* is where he lives;
Mount Zion is his home.
³ There he breaks the arrows of the enemy,
the shields and swords and weapons of
his foes. *Interlude*

74:16 Or *moon;* Hebrew reads *light.* 75:9 Hebrew *of Jacob.* 76:2 Hebrew *Salem,* another name for Jerusalem.

⁴ You are glorious and more majestic
 than the everlasting mountains.*
⁵ The mightiest of our enemies have been
 plundered.
 They lie before us in the sleep of death.
 No warrior could lift a hand against us.
⁶ When you rebuked them, O God of Jacob,
 their horses and chariots stood still.

⁷ No wonder you are greatly feared!
 Who can stand before you when your
 anger explodes?
⁸ From heaven you sentenced your enemies;
 the earth trembled and stood silent
 before you.
⁹ You stand up to judge those who do evil,
 O God,
 and to rescue the oppressed of the earth.
 Interlude

¹⁰ Human opposition only enhances your
 glory,
 for you use it as a sword of judgment.*

¹¹ Make vows to the LORD your God, and
 fulfill them.
 Let everyone bring tribute to the
 Awesome One.
¹² For he breaks the spirit of princes
 and is feared by the kings of the earth.

PSALM 77

*For Jeduthun, the choir director: A psalm
of Asaph.*

¹ I cry out to God without holding back.
 Oh, that God would listen to me!
² When I was in deep trouble,
 I searched for the Lord.
 All night long I pray, with hands lifted
 toward heaven, pleading.
 There can be no joy for me until he acts.
³ I think of God, and I moan,
 overwhelmed with longing for his help.
 Interlude

⁴ You don't let me sleep.
 I am too distressed even to pray!
⁵ I think of the good old days, long since
 ended,
⁶ when my nights were filled with joyful
 songs.
 I search my soul and think about the
 difference now.
⁷ Has the Lord rejected me forever?
 Will he never again show me favor?
⁸ Is his unfailing love gone forever?
 Have his promises permanently failed?
⁹ Has God forgotten to be kind?
 Has he slammed the door on his
 compassion? *Interlude*

¹⁰ And I said, "This is my fate,
 that the blessings of the Most High have
 changed to hatred."
¹¹ I recall all you have done, O LORD;
 I remember your wonderful deeds of
 long ago.
¹² They are constantly in my thoughts.
 I cannot stop thinking about them.

¹³ O God, your ways are holy.
 Is there any god as mighty as you?
¹⁴ You are the God of miracles and wonders!
 You demonstrate your awesome power
 among the nations.
¹⁵ You have redeemed your people by your
 strength,
 the descendants of Jacob and of Joseph
 by your might. *Interlude*

¹⁶ When the Red Sea* saw you, O God,
 its waters looked and trembled!
 The sea quaked to its very depths.
¹⁷ The clouds poured down their rain;
 the thunder rolled and crackled in the
 sky.
 Your arrows of lightning flashed.
¹⁸ Your thunder roared from the whirlwind;
 the lightning lit up the world!
 The earth trembled and shook.

76:4 As in Greek version; Hebrew reads *than mountains filled with beasts of prey.* 76:10 The meaning of the Hebrew is uncertain.
77:16 Hebrew *the waters.*

My Daily Worship

— *May 20* —

REMEMBER THE GOOD OLD DAYS?

PSALMS 76:1–78:72

O God, your ways are holy. Is there any god as mighty as you? You are the God of miracles and wonders! You demonstrate your awesome power among the nations. You have redeemed your people by your strength, the descendants of Jacob and of Joseph by your might (77:13–15).

[i reflect]

The night seems endless. The trouble is overwhelming. You have never been so sad. You toss and turn, but sleep eludes you. You cry out to God in anguish, but hear no answer. Is God even listening?

The author of Psalm 77 experienced such a night. With hands lifted up to heaven, he pled for mercy. The psalm writer yearned for God's help but heard no answer. Had the Lord slammed the door on compassion? Had the Lord rejected him forever?

Then he remembered the "good old days, long since ended, when my nights were filled with joyful songs" (77:5–6). He recalled the wonderful deeds of long ago, when the Lord parted the Red Sea and led his people out of Egypt. Soon his thoughts were filled with the miracles of the Lord.

At times, you may think your situation is hopeless, that the problems you face have no solutions or end in sight. At those times, remember that your God is "the God of miracles and wonders!" (77:14). Trapped between the Egyptians and the Red Sea, the nation of Israel faced certain destruction. But in one creative and unexpected act, the God of miracles parted the waters and redeemed his people. Surely he can be trusted to redeem your life as well.

Do you remember the good old days of your life? Starting with the miracle of your birth, think of the many wonders God has performed. Reflect on the blessings of health, family, and home. Recall his faithfulness in your darkest hours. List the ways he has rescued you from evil. Consider the countless answered prayers. Praise him for his love and compassion. Those were the good old days! Trust in the goodness of those days to see you through your current situation.

[i pray]

Mighty God, I praise you, for you are the God of miracles and wonders! I praise you for the wonders of your creation. I praise you for the miracle of life. I praise you for your mighty power.

[i respond]

Take time to record "the good old days" as they happen. Inscribe your prayers in a notebook and leave space to write the answers. When trouble comes, use these recordings to remember God's hand upon your life and have hope for the future.

¹⁹ Your road led through the sea,
　　your pathway through the mighty
　　　waters—
　　a pathway no one knew was there!
²⁰ You led your people along that road like a
　　flock of sheep,
　　with Moses and Aaron as their
　　　shepherds.

PSALM 78

A psalm of Asaph.

¹ O my people, listen to my teaching.
　　Open your ears to what I am saying,
² for I will speak to you in a parable.
　　I will teach you hidden lessons from our
　　　past—
³ stories we have heard and know,
　　stories our ancestors handed down to us.
⁴ We will not hide these truths from our
　　children
　　but will tell the next generation about
　　the glorious deeds of the LORD.
　　We will tell of his power and the mighty
　　miracles he did.
⁵ For he issued his decree to Jacob;
　　he gave his law to Israel.
　　He commanded our ancestors
　　to teach them to their children,
⁶ so the next generation might know
　　them—
　　even the children not yet born—
　　that they in turn might teach their
　　children.
⁷ So each generation can set its hope anew
　　on God,
　　remembering his glorious miracles
　　and obeying his commands.
⁸ Then they will not be like their
　　ancestors—
　　stubborn, rebellious, and unfaithful,
　　refusing to give their hearts to God.

⁹ The warriors of Ephraim, though fully
　　armed,
　　turned their backs and fled when the day
　　of battle came.

¹⁰ They did not keep God's covenant,
　　and they refused to live by his law.
¹¹ They forgot what he had done—
　　the wonderful miracles he had shown
　　them,
¹² the miracles he did for their ancestors in
　　Egypt, on the plain of Zoan.
¹³ For he divided the sea before them and led
　　them through!
　　The water stood up like walls beside
　　them!
¹⁴ In the daytime he led them by a cloud,
　　and at night by a pillar of fire.
¹⁵ He split open the rocks in the wilderness
　　to give them plenty of water, as from a
　　gushing spring.
¹⁶ He made streams pour from the rock,
　　making the waters flow down like a
　　river!

¹⁷ Yet they kept on with their sin,
　　rebelling against the Most High in the
　　desert.
¹⁸ They willfully tested God in their hearts,
　　demanding the foods they craved.
¹⁹ They even spoke against God himself,
　　saying,
　　"God can't give us food in the desert.
²⁰ Yes, he can strike a rock so water gushes
　　out,
　　but he can't give his people bread and
　　meat."
²¹ When the LORD heard them, he was angry.
　　The fire of his wrath burned against
　　Jacob.
　　Yes, his anger rose against Israel,
²² for they did not believe God
　　or trust him to care for them.
²³ But he commanded the skies to open—
　　he opened the doors of heaven—
²⁴ and rained down manna for them to eat.
　　He gave them bread from heaven.
²⁵ They ate the food of angels!
　　God gave them all they could hold.
²⁶ He released the east wind in the heavens
　　and guided the south wind by his
　　mighty power.

27 He rained down meat as thick as dust—
   birds as plentiful as the sands along the
      seashore!
28 He caused the birds to fall within their
      camp
   and all around their tents.
29 The people ate their fill.
   He gave them what they wanted.
30 But before they finished eating this food
      they had craved,
   while the meat was yet in their mouths,
31 the anger of God rose against them,
   and he killed their strongest men;
   he struck down the finest of Israel's
      young men.
32 But in spite of this, the people kept on
      sinning.
   They refused to believe in his miracles.
33 So he ended their lives in failure
   and gave them years of terror.
34 When God killed some of them, the rest
      finally sought him.
   They repented and turned to God.
35 Then they remembered that God was their
      rock,
   that their redeemer was the Most High.
36 But they followed him only with their
      words;
   they lied to him with their tongues.
37 Their hearts were not loyal to him.
   They did not keep his covenant.
38 Yet he was merciful and forgave their sins
   and didn't destroy them all.
   Many a time he held back his anger
   and did not unleash his fury!
39 For he remembered that they were merely
      mortal,
   gone in a moment like a breath of wind,
      never to return.

40 Oh, how often they rebelled against him in
      the desert
   and grieved his heart in the wilderness.
41 Again and again they tested God's patience
   and frustrated the Holy One of Israel.

42 They forgot about his power
   and how he rescued them from their
      enemies.
43 They forgot his miraculous signs in Egypt,
   his wonders on the plain of Zoan.
44 For he turned their rivers into blood,
   so no one could drink from the streams.
45 He sent vast swarms of flies to consume
      them
   and hordes of frogs to ruin them.
46 He gave their crops to caterpillars;
   their harvest was consumed by locusts.
47 He destroyed their grapevines with hail
   and shattered their sycamores with sleet.
48 He abandoned their cattle to the hail,
   their livestock to bolts of lightning.
49 He loosed on them his fierce anger—
   all his fury, rage, and hostility.
   He dispatched against them
   a band of destroying angels.
50 He turned his anger against them;
   he did not spare the Egyptians' lives
   but handed them over to the plague.
51 He killed the oldest son in each Egyptian
      family,
   the flower of youth throughout the land
      of Egypt.*
52 But he led his own people like a flock of
      sheep,
   guiding them safely through the
      wilderness.
53 He kept them safe so they were not afraid;
   but the sea closed in upon their enemies.
54 He brought them to the border of his holy
      land,
   to this land of hills he had won for
      them.
55 He drove out the nations before them;
   he gave them their inheritance by lot.
   He settled the tribes of Israel into their
      homes.

56 Yet though he did all this for them,
   they continued to test his patience.
   They rebelled against the Most High
   and refused to follow his decrees.

78:51 Hebrew *in the tents of Ham.*

57 They turned back and were as faithless as
  their parents had been.
  They were as useless as a crooked bow.
58 They made God angry by building altars to
  other gods;
  they made him jealous with their idols.
59 When God heard them, he was very angry,
  and he rejected Israel completely.
60 Then he abandoned his dwelling at Shiloh,
  the Tabernacle where he had lived
  among the people.
61 He allowed the Ark of his might to be
  captured;
  he surrendered his glory into enemy
  hands.
62 He gave his people over to be butchered by
  the sword,
  because he was so angry with his own
  people—his special possession.
63 Their young men were killed by fire;
  their young women died before singing
  their wedding songs.
64 Their priests were slaughtered,
  and their widows could not mourn their
  deaths.
65 Then the Lord rose up as though waking
  from sleep,
  like a mighty man aroused from a
  drunken stupor.
66 He routed his enemies
  and sent them to eternal shame.
67 But he rejected Joseph's descendants;
  he did not choose the tribe of Ephraim.
68 He chose instead the tribe of Judah,
  Mount Zion, which he loved.
69 There he built his towering sanctuary,
  as solid and enduring as the earth itself.
70 He chose his servant David,
  calling him from the sheep pens.
71 He took David from tending the ewes and
  lambs
  and made him the shepherd of Jacob's
  descendants—
  God's own people, Israel.
72 He cared for them with a true heart
  and led them with skillful hands.

PSALM 79
A psalm of Asaph.

1 O God, pagan nations have conquered
  your land, your special possession.
  They have defiled your holy Temple
  and made Jerusalem a heap of ruins.
2 They have left the bodies of your servants
  as food for the birds of heaven.
  The flesh of your godly ones
  has become food for the wild animals.
3 Blood has flowed like water all around
  Jerusalem;
  no one is left to bury the dead.
4 We are mocked by our neighbors,
  an object of scorn and derision to those
  around us.

5 O LORD, how long will you be angry with
  us? Forever?
  How long will your jealousy burn like
  fire?
6 Pour out your wrath on the nations that
  refuse to recognize you—
  on kingdoms that do not call upon your
  name.
7 For they have devoured your people
  Israel,*
  making the land a desolate wilderness.
8 Oh, do not hold us guilty for our former
  sins!
  Let your tenderhearted mercies quickly
  meet our needs,
  for we are brought low to the dust.
9 Help us, O God of our salvation!
  Help us for the honor of your name.
  Oh, save us and forgive our sins
  for the sake of your name.
10 Why should pagan nations be allowed to
  scoff,
  asking, "Where is their God?"
  Show us your vengeance against the
  nations,
  for they have spilled the blood of your
  servants.
11 Listen to the moaning of the prisoners.

79:7 Hebrew *Jacob.*

Demonstrate your great power by saving
    those condemned to die.

¹² O Lord, take sevenfold vengeance on our
    neighbors
    for the scorn they have hurled at you.
¹³ Then we your people, the sheep of your
    pasture,
    will thank you forever and ever,
    praising your greatness from generation
    to generation.

PSALM 80

*For the choir director: A psalm of Asaph,
to be sung to the tune "Lilies of the
Covenant."*

¹ Please listen, O Shepherd of Israel,
    you who lead Israel* like a flock.
    O God, enthroned above the cherubim,
    display your radiant glory
²   to Ephraim, Benjamin, and Manasseh.
    Show us your mighty power.
    Come to rescue us!

³ Turn us again to yourself, O God.
    Make your face shine down upon us.
    Only then will we be saved.

⁴ O LORD God Almighty,
    how long will you be angry and reject
    our prayers?
⁵ You have fed us with sorrow
    and made us drink tears by the
    bucketful.
⁶ You have made us the scorn of
    neighboring nations.
    Our enemies treat us as a joke.

⁷ Turn us again to yourself, O God
    Almighty.
    Make your face shine down upon us.
    Only then will we be saved.
⁸ You brought us from Egypt as though we
    were a tender vine;

you drove away the pagan nations and
    transplanted us into your land.
⁹ You cleared the ground for us,
    and we took root and filled the land.
¹⁰ The mountains were covered with our
    shade;
    the mighty cedars were covered with our
    branches.
¹¹ We spread our branches west to the
    Mediterranean Sea,
    our limbs east to the Euphrates River.*
¹² But now, why have you broken down our
    walls
    so that all who pass may steal our fruit?
¹³ The boar from the forest devours us,
    and the wild animals feed on us.

¹⁴ Come back, we beg you, O God Almighty.
    Look down from heaven and see our
    plight.
    Watch over and care for this vine
¹⁵   that you yourself have planted,
    this son you have raised for yourself.
¹⁶ For we are chopped up and burned by our
    enemies.
    May they perish at the sight of your
    frown.
¹⁷ Strengthen the man you love,
    the son of your choice.
¹⁸ Then we will never forsake you again.
    Revive us so we can call on your name
    once more.

¹⁹ Turn us again to yourself, O LORD God
    Almighty.
    Make your face shine down upon us.
    Only then will we be saved.

PSALM 81

*For the choir director: A psalm of Asaph, to be
accompanied by a stringed instrument.**

¹ Sing praises to God, our strength.
    Sing to the God of Israel.*
² Sing! Beat the tambourine.

80:1 Hebrew *Joseph.*   80:11 Hebrew *west to the sea, . . . east to the river.*   81:TITLE Hebrew *according to the gittith.*   81:1 Hebrew *of Jacob.*

Play the sweet lyre and the harp.
3 Sound the trumpet for a sacred feast
  when the moon is new,
  when the moon is full.
4 For this is required by the laws of Israel;
  it is a law of the God of Jacob.
5 He made it a decree for Israel*
  when he attacked Egypt to set us free.

I heard an unknown voice that said,
6 "Now I will relieve your shoulder of its
  burden;
  I will free your hands from their heavy
  tasks.
7 You cried to me in trouble, and I saved
  you;
  I answered out of the thundercloud.
  I tested your faith at Meribah,
  when you complained that there was no
  water.   *Interlude*

8 "Listen to me, O my people, while I give
  you stern warnings.
  O Israel, if you would only listen!
9 You must never have a foreign god;
  you must not bow down before a false
  god.
10 For it was I, the LORD your God,
  who rescued you from the land of Egypt.
  Open your mouth wide, and I will fill it
  with good things.

11 "But no, my people wouldn't listen.
  Israel did not want me around.
12 So I let them follow their blind and
  stubborn way,
  living according to their own desires.
13 But oh, that my people would listen to me!
  Oh, that Israel would follow me, walking
  in my paths!
14 How quickly I would then subdue their
  enemies!
  How soon my hands would be upon
  their foes!
15 Those who hate the LORD would cringe
  before him;

their desolation would last forever.
16 But I would feed you with the best of
  foods.
  I would satisfy you with wild honey
  from the rock."

PSALM 82
A psalm of Asaph.

1 God presides over heaven's court;
  he pronounces judgment on the judges:
2 "How long will you judges hand down
  unjust decisions?
  How long will you shower special favors
  on the wicked?   *Interlude*

3 "Give fair judgment to the poor and the
  orphan;
  uphold the rights of the oppressed and
  the destitute.
4 Rescue the poor and helpless;
  deliver them from the grasp of evil
  people.
5 But these oppressors know nothing;
  they are so ignorant!
  And because they are in darkness,
  the whole world is shaken to the core.
6 I say, 'You are gods
  and children of the Most High.
7 But in death you are mere men.
  You will fall as any prince,
  for all must die.'"

> *Your heart's desire,*
> *even if you haven't realized it,*
> *is to live every moment*
> *in the wonder of worship.*
>
> DAVID JEREMIAH

81:5 Hebrew *for Joseph.*

⁸ Rise up, O God, and judge the earth,
　for all the nations belong to you.

PSALM 83

A psalm of Asaph. A song.

¹ O God, don't sit idly by,
　silent and inactive!
² Don't you hear the tumult of your
　　enemies?
　Don't you see what your arrogant
　　enemies are doing?
³ They devise crafty schemes against your
　　people,
　laying plans against your precious ones.
⁴ "Come," they say, "let us wipe out Israel as
　　a nation.
　We will destroy the very memory of its
　　existence."
⁵ This was their unanimous decision.
　They signed a treaty as allies against you—
⁶ these Edomites and Ishmaelites,
　　Moabites and Hagrites,
⁷ Gebalites, Ammonites, and Amalekites,
　and people from Philistia and Tyre.
⁸ Assyria has joined them, too,
　and is allied with the descendants of Lot.
　　　　　　　　　　　　　　　Interlude

⁹ Do to them as you did to the Midianites
　　or as you did to Sisera and Jabin at the
　　Kishon River.
¹⁰ They were destroyed at Endor,
　and their decaying corpses fertilized the
　　soil.
¹¹ Let their mighty nobles die as Oreb and
　　Zeeb did.
　Let all their princes die like Zebah and
　　Zalmunna,
¹² for they said, "Let us seize for our own use
　these pasturelands of God!"
¹³ O my God, blow them away like whirling
　　dust,
　like chaff before the wind!

¹⁴ As a fire roars through a forest
　and as a flame sets mountains ablaze,
¹⁵ chase them with your fierce storms;
　terrify them with your tempests.
¹⁶ Utterly disgrace them
　until they submit to your name, O LORD.
¹⁷ Let them be ashamed and terrified forever.
　Make them failures in everything they
　　do,
¹⁸ until they learn that you alone are called
　　the LORD,
　that you alone are the Most High,
　　supreme over all the earth.

PSALM 84

*For the choir director: A psalm of the
descendants of Korah, to be accompanied by a
stringed instrument.*

¹ How lovely is your dwelling place,
　O LORD Almighty.
² I long, yes, I faint with longing
　to enter the courts of the LORD.
　With my whole being, body and soul,
　I will shout joyfully to the living God.
³ Even the sparrow finds a home there,
　　and the swallow builds her nest
　　and raises her young—
　at a place near your altar,
　　O LORD Almighty, my King and my God!
⁴ How happy are those who can live in your
　　house,
　always singing your praises.　　*Interlude*

⁵ Happy are those who are strong in the
　　LORD,
　who set their minds on a pilgrimage to
　　Jerusalem.
⁶ When they walk through the Valley of
　　Weeping,*
　it will become a place of refreshing
　　springs,
　where pools of blessing collect after the
　　rains!
⁷ They will continue to grow stronger,

84:TITLE Hebrew *according to the gittith.*　84:6 Hebrew *valley of Baca.*

and each of them will appear before
    God in Jerusalem.*

8 O LORD God Almighty, hear my prayer.
    Listen, O God of Israel.*   *Interlude*

9 O God, look with favor upon the king, our
    protector!
    Have mercy on the one you have
       anointed.

10 A single day in your courts
    is better than a thousand anywhere else!
    I would rather be a gatekeeper in the
       house of my God
    than live the good life in the homes of
       the wicked.
11 For the LORD God is our light and
       protector.
    He gives us grace and glory.
    No good thing will the LORD withhold
    from those who do what is right.
12 O LORD Almighty,
    happy are those who trust in you.

PSALM 85

*For the choir director: A psalm of the
descendants of Korah.*

1 LORD, you have poured out amazing
    blessings on your land!
    You have restored the fortunes of Israel.*
2 You have forgiven the guilt of your
       people—
    yes, you have covered all their sins.
                    Interlude

3 You have withdrawn your fury.
    You have ended your blazing anger.
4 Now turn to us again, O God of our
       salvation.
    Put aside your anger against us.
5 Will you be angry with us always?
    Will you prolong your wrath to distant
       generations?

6 Won't you revive us again,
    so your people can rejoice in you?
7 Show us your unfailing love, O LORD,
    and grant us your salvation.

8 I listen carefully to what God the LORD is
       saying,
    for he speaks peace to his people, his
       faithful ones.
    But let them not return to their foolish
       ways.
9 Surely his salvation is near to those who
       honor him;
    our land will be filled with his glory.

10 Unfailing love and truth have met together.
    Righteousness and peace have kissed!
11 Truth springs up from the earth,
    and righteousness smiles down from
       heaven.
12 Yes, the LORD pours down his blessings.
    Our land will yield its bountiful crops.
13 Righteousness goes as a herald before him,
    preparing the way for his steps.

PSALM 86

A prayer of David.

1 Bend down, O LORD, and hear my prayer;
    answer me, for I need your help.
2 Protect me, for I am devoted to you.
    Save me, for I serve you and trust you.
    You are my God.
3 Be merciful, O Lord,
    for I am calling on you constantly.
4 Give me happiness, O Lord,
    for my life depends on you.
5 O Lord, you are so good, so ready to
       forgive,
    so full of unfailing love for all who ask
       your aid.
6 Listen closely to my prayer, O LORD;
    hear my urgent cry.
7 I will call to you whenever trouble strikes,
    and you will answer me.

84:7 Hebrew *Zion*.   84:8 Hebrew *of Jacob*.   85:1 Hebrew *of Jacob*.

My Daily Worship

— May 21 —

A PLACE CALLED HOME

PSALM 79:1–84:12

How lovely is your dwelling place, O LORD Almighty.
I long, yes, I faint with longing to enter the courts of the LORD.
With my whole being, body and soul, I will shout joyfully to the living God (84:1–2).

[i reflect]

A soldier sits in a camp chair in a country far away and dreams of home. Home, where family and friends gather. Home, with comfortable chairs and familiar food. Home, where he is safe and secure. Home, the place where he belongs.

In much the same way, the psalm writer longed for home—to get away from the bustle and cares of this world and to be in the presence of his Lord. For the writer, being home with God meant physically being in God's dwelling place, his holy Temple. Just as the solider yearned for the physical presence of his home, the psalmist wrote with urgency "to enter the courts of the LORD" (84:2).

The truth is, God's dwelling place can be felt anywhere. He is at home in the quiet sanctuary of a stained-glass cathedral, as we sit in our cozy chair in the corner of a room, or walking outdoors under the leafy canopy of the woods. Wherever we go, God's presence is with us.

It is equally true that entering a church building provides a special place where we can escape, if only for a few hours, the busyness of our lives and find solitude to meditate and pray. There we can refresh and refocus through the music, the prayers, and the lessons taught. We find joy and strength from being with fellow worshipers. God is at home there as well.

No wonder the psalm writer faints with longing to enter God's home; it is the very place where he feels most at home. With his whole being he shouts praises to the living God. "How happy are those who can live in your house, always singing your praises" (84:4).

How about you? Are you happy to be in God's presence, in his home, singing his praises? Imagine that God is sitting with you right now. Celebrate his dwelling place with you and welcome him home!

[i pray]

O Lord Almighty, I long to be in your dwelling place. With my whole being, body
and soul, I long to be in your presence. My one true home is with you.

[i respond]

Meditate on Psalm 84. Where do you most feel "at home" with God? Go to that place today and create your own psalm of longing and praise.

8 Nowhere among the pagan gods is there a
  god like you, O Lord.
    There are no other miracles like yours.
9 All the nations—and you made each
  one—
    will come and bow before you, Lord;
    they will praise your great and holy
    name.
10 For you are great and perform great
  miracles.
    You alone are God.

11 Teach me your ways, O LORD,
    that I may live according to your truth!
  Grant me purity of heart,
    that I may honor you.
12 With all my heart I will praise you, O Lord
  my God.
    I will give glory to your name forever,
13 for your love for me is very great.
    You have rescued me from the depths of
    death*!

14 O God, insolent people rise up against me;
    violent people are trying to kill me.
    And you mean nothing to them.
15 But you, O Lord, are a merciful and
  gracious God,
    slow to get angry,
    full of unfailing love and truth.
16 Look down and have mercy on me.
    Give strength to your servant;

yes, save me, for I am your servant.
17 Send me a sign of your favor.
    Then those who hate me will be put to
    shame,
    for you, O LORD, help and comfort me.

PSALM 87

A psalm of the descendants of Korah. A song.

1 On the holy mountain stands the city
    founded by the LORD.
2 He loves the city of Jerusalem
    more than any other city in Israel.*
3 O city of God,
    what glorious things are said of you!
                                    Interlude

4 I will record Egypt* and Babylon among
    those who know me—
    also Philistia and Tyre, and even distant
    Ethiopia.*
    They have all become citizens of
    Jerusalem!
5 And it will be said of Jerusalem,*
    "Everyone has become a citizen here."
    And the Most High will personally bless
    this city.
6 When the LORD registers the nations,
    he will say, "This one has become a
    citizen of Jerusalem."   *Interlude*

7 At all the festivals, the people will sing,
    "The source of my life is in Jerusalem!"

PSALM 88

*For the choir director: A psalm of the
descendants of Korah, to be sung to the tune
"The Suffering of Affliction." A psalm of
Heman the Ezrahite. A song.*

1 O LORD, God of my salvation,
    I have cried out to you day and night.
2 Now hear my prayer;
    listen to my cry.

> Have an eye to God
> in every word you sing.
>
> JOHN WESLEY

86:13 Hebrew *of Sheol.* 87:2 Hebrew *He loves the gates of Zion more than all the dwellings of Jacob.* 87:4a Hebrew *Rahab,* the name of a mythical sea monster that represents chaos in ancient literature. The name is used here as a poetic name for Egypt. 87:4b Hebrew *Cush.* 87:5 Hebrew *Zion.*

³ For my life is full of troubles,
   and death draws near.
⁴ I have been dismissed as one who is dead,
   like a strong man with no strength left.
⁵ They have abandoned me to death,
   and I am as good as dead.
   I am forgotten,
   cut off from your care.
⁶ You have thrust me down to the lowest pit,
   into the darkest depths.
⁷ Your anger lies heavy on me;
   wave after wave engulfs me.   *Interlude*

⁸ You have caused my friends to loathe me;
   you have sent them all away.
   I am in a trap with no way of escape.
⁹ My eyes are blinded by my tears.
   Each day I beg for your help, O LORD;
   I lift my pleading hands to you for
   mercy.
¹⁰ Of what use to the dead are your miracles?
   Do the dead get up and praise you?
                                   Interlude

¹¹ Can those in the grave declare your
   unfailing love?
   In the place of destruction, can they
   proclaim your faithfulness?
¹² Can the darkness speak of your miracles?
   Can anyone in the land of forgetfulness
   talk about your righteousness?

¹³ O LORD, I cry out to you.
   I will keep on pleading day by day.
¹⁴ O LORD, why do you reject me?
   Why do you turn your face away from
   me?
¹⁵ I have been sickly and close to death since
   my youth.
   I stand helpless and desperate before
   your terrors.
¹⁶ Your fierce anger has overwhelmed me.
   Your terrors have cut me off.
¹⁷ They swirl around me like floodwaters all
   day long.
   They have encircled me completely.

¹⁸ You have taken away my companions and
   loved ones;
   only darkness remains.

PSALM 89

A psalm of Ethan the Ezrahite.

¹ I will sing of the tender mercies of the
   LORD forever!
   Young and old will hear of your
   faithfulness.
² Your unfailing love will last forever.
   Your faithfulness is as enduring as the
   heavens.

³ The LORD said, "I have made a solemn
   agreement with David, my chosen
   servant.
   I have sworn this oath to him:
⁴ 'I will establish your descendants as kings
   forever;
   they will sit on your throne from now
   until eternity.' "   *Interlude*

⁵ All heaven will praise your miracles, LORD;
   myriads of angels will praise you for
   your faithfulness.
⁶ For who in all of heaven can compare with
   the LORD?
   What mightiest angel is anything like the
   LORD?
⁷ The highest angelic powers stand in awe of
   God.
   He is far more awesome than those who
   surround his throne.
⁸ O LORD God Almighty!
   Where is there anyone as mighty as you,
   LORD?
   Faithfulness is your very character.

⁹ You are the one who rules the oceans.
   When their waves rise in fearful storms,
   you subdue them.
¹⁰ You are the one who crushed the great sea
   monster.*

89:10 Hebrew *Rahab*, the name of a mythical sea monster that represents chaos in ancient literature.

You scattered your enemies with your
mighty arm.
¹¹ The heavens are yours, and the earth is
yours;
everything in the world is yours—you
created it all.
¹² You created north and south.
Mount Tabor and Mount Hermon
praise your name.
¹³ Powerful is your arm!
Strong is your hand!
Your right hand is lifted high in glorious
strength.
¹⁴ Your throne is founded on two strong
pillars—righteousness and justice.
Unfailing love and truth walk before you
as attendants.
¹⁵ Happy are those who hear the joyful call to
worship,
for they will walk in the light of your
presence, LORD.
¹⁶ They rejoice all day long in your wonderful
reputation.
They exult in your righteousness.
¹⁷ You are their glorious strength.
Our power is based on your favor.
¹⁸ Yes, our protection comes from the LORD,
and he, the Holy One of Israel, has given
us our king.

¹⁹ You once spoke in a vision to your prophet
and said,
"I have given help to a warrior.
I have selected him from the common
people to be king.
²⁰ I have found my servant David.
I have anointed him with my holy oil.
²¹ I will steady him,
and I will make him strong.
²² His enemies will not get the best of him,
nor will the wicked overpower him.
²³ I will beat down his adversaries before him
and destroy those who hate him.
²⁴ My faithfulness and unfailing love will be
with him,
and he will rise to power because of me.

²⁵ I will extend his rule from the
Mediterranean Sea in the west
to the Tigris and Euphrates rivers in the
east.*
²⁶ And he will say to me, 'You are my
Father,
my God, and the Rock of my salvation.'
²⁷ I will make him my firstborn son,
the mightiest king on earth.
²⁸ I will love him and be kind to him
forever;
my covenant with him will never end.
²⁹ I will preserve an heir for him;
his throne will be as endless as the days
of heaven.
³⁰ But if his sons forsake my law
and fail to walk in my ways,
³¹ if they do not obey my decrees
and fail to keep my commands,
³² then I will punish their sin with the rod,
and their disobedience with beating.
³³ But I will never stop loving him,
nor let my promise to him fail.
³⁴ No, I will not break my covenant;
I will not take back a single word I said.
³⁵ I have sworn an oath to David,
and in my holiness I cannot lie:
³⁶ His dynasty will go on forever;
his throne is as secure as the sun,
³⁷ as eternal as the moon,
my faithful witness in the sky!" *Interlude*

³⁸ But now you have rejected him.
Why are you so angry with the one you
chose as king?
³⁹ You have renounced your covenant with
him,
for you have thrown his crown in the
dust.
⁴⁰ You have broken down the walls protecting
him
and laid in ruins every fort defending
him.
⁴¹ Everyone who comes along has robbed
him
while his neighbors mock.

89:25 Hebrew *I will set his hand on the sea, his right hand on the rivers.*

My Daily Worship
— May 22 —

LOVE ME FOREVER
PSALM 85:1-89:52

I will sing of the tender mercies of the LORD forever! Young and old will
hear of your faithfulness. Your unfailing love will last forever.
Your faithfulness is as enduring as the heavens (89:1–2).

[i reflect]

The young mother gazes on the face of her newborn son and her heart fills with love. She delights in his first word, his first step, his first day of school. She celebrates his victories and comforts him in defeat. As her son grows in stature, so also does the love in her heart. "I will love you forever," she sings.

Then one day a policeman knocks at her door. Her son is in trouble with the law. The problems are devastating; her sorrow overwhelming. Though family and friends abandon, the mother stands by her son. Her love never fails.

As the mother loves her son, how much more does our heavenly Father love his children? David, the man after God's own heart, sinned grievously. Yet God forgave him and promised, "I will love him and be kind to him forever; my covenant with him will never end" (89:28). God's love for David reached beyond the grave, for he also promised to love and bless David's heirs. "His dynasty will go on forever; his throne is as secure as the sun" (89:36).

No matter how great our trouble, God's love is greater still. The Scriptures are filled with testimonies to his unfathomable love for us. No ocean is deeper, no mountain higher, than the love our Father has for us. Human relationships may falter, but God's love never fails. Heaven and earth will pass away, but God's love will remain. His love endures forever.

Join David in song, praising God for his unfailing love. "With all my heart I will praise you, O LORD my God. I will give glory to your name forever, for your love for me is very great" (86:12–13).

[i pray]

With my lips I will glorify you, Lord, for your love never fails.
With my heart, I will honor you, for you are so good.
With my voice I will sing of your mercy forever.

[i respond]

Write down today's key verse on an index card. Carry this card with you in your wallet or purse throughout the day as a reminder that God's unfailing love will last forever.

⁴² You have strengthened his enemies against
  him
  and made them all rejoice.
⁴³ You have made his sword useless
  and have refused to help him in battle.
⁴⁴ You have ended his splendor
  and overturned his throne.
⁴⁵ You have made him old before his time
  and publicly disgraced him.   *Interlude*

⁴⁶ O LORD, how long will this go on?
  Will you hide yourself forever?
  How long will your anger burn like fire?
⁴⁷ Remember how short my life is,
  how empty and futile this human
  existence!
⁴⁸ No one can live forever; all will die.
  No one can escape the power of the
  grave.   *Interlude*

⁴⁹ Lord, where is your unfailing love?
  You promised it to David with a faithful
  pledge.
⁵⁰ Consider, Lord, how your servants are
  disgraced!
  I carry in my heart the insults of so
  many people.
⁵¹ Your enemies have mocked me, O LORD;
  they mock the one you anointed as
  king.

⁵² Blessed be the LORD forever!
  Amen and amen!

BOOK FOUR (PSALMS 90–106)

PSALM 90

A prayer of Moses, the man of God.

¹ Lord, through all the generations
  you have been our home!
² Before the mountains were created,
  before you made the earth and the
  world,
  you are God, without beginning or end.

³ You turn people back to dust, saying,
  "Return to dust!"
⁴ For you, a thousand years are as yesterday!
  They are like a few hours!
⁵ You sweep people away like dreams that
  disappear
  or like grass that springs up in the
  morning.
⁶ In the morning it blooms and flourishes,
  but by evening it is dry and withered.
⁷ We wither beneath your anger;
  we are overwhelmed by your fury.
⁸ You spread out our sins before you—
  our secret sins—and you see them all.
⁹ We live our lives beneath your wrath.
  We end our lives with a groan.

¹⁰ Seventy years are given to us!
  Some may even reach eighty.
  But even the best of these years are filled
  with pain and trouble;
  soon they disappear, and we are gone.
¹¹ Who can comprehend the power of your
  anger?
  Your wrath is as awesome as the fear you
  deserve.
¹² Teach us to make the most of our time,
  so that we may grow in wisdom.

¹³ O LORD, come back to us!
  How long will you delay?
  Take pity on your servants!
¹⁴ Satisfy us in the morning with your
  unfailing love,
  so we may sing for joy to the end of our
  lives.
¹⁵ Give us gladness in proportion to our
  former misery!
  Replace the evil years with good.
¹⁶ Let us see your miracles again;
  let our children see your glory at
  work.
¹⁷ And may the Lord our God show us his
  approval
  and make our efforts successful.
  Yes, make our efforts successful!

PSALM 91

1 Those who live in the shelter of the Most
High
will find rest in the shadow of the
Almighty.
2 This I declare of the LORD:
He alone is my refuge, my place of
safety;
he is my God, and I am trusting him.
3 For he will rescue you from every trap
and protect you from the fatal plague.
4 He will shield you with his wings.
He will shelter you with his feathers.
His faithful promises are your armor
and protection.
5 Do not be afraid of the terrors of the
night,
nor fear the dangers of the day,
6 nor dread the plague that stalks in
darkness,
nor the disaster that strikes at midday.
7 Though a thousand fall at your side,
though ten thousand are dying around
you,
these evils will not touch you.
8 But you will see it with your eyes;
you will see how the wicked are
punished.

9 If you make the LORD your refuge,
if you make the Most High your shelter,
10 no evil will conquer you;
no plague will come near your dwelling.
11 For he orders his angels
to protect you wherever you go.
12 They will hold you with their hands
to keep you from striking your foot on a
stone.
13 You will trample down lions and
poisonous snakes;
you will crush fierce lions and serpents
under your feet!

14 The LORD says, "I will rescue those who
love me.
I will protect those who trust in my
name.

15 When they call on me, I will answer;
I will be with them in trouble.
I will rescue them and honor them.
16 I will satisfy them with a long life
and give them my salvation."

PSALM 92

A psalm to be sung on the LORD's Day. A song.

1 It is good to give thanks to the LORD,
to sing praises to the Most High.
2 It is good to proclaim your unfailing love
in the morning,
your faithfulness in the evening,
3 accompanied by the harp and lute
and the harmony of the lyre.
4 You thrill me, LORD, with all you have
done for me!
I sing for joy because of what you have
done.

5 O LORD, what great miracles you do!
And how deep are your thoughts.
6 Only an ignorant person would not know
this!
Only a fool would not understand it.
7 Although the wicked flourish like weeds,
and evildoers blossom with success,
there is only eternal destruction ahead of
them.
8 But you are exalted in the heavens.
You, O LORD, continue forever.
9 Your enemies, LORD, will surely perish;
all evildoers will be scattered.

10 But you have made me as strong as a wild
bull.
How refreshed I am by your power!
11 With my own eyes I have seen the downfall
of my enemies;
with my own ears I have heard the
defeat of my wicked opponents.
12 But the godly will flourish like palm trees
and grow strong like the cedars of
Lebanon.
13 For they are transplanted into the LORD's
own house.

They flourish in the courts of our God.
¹⁴ Even in old age they will still produce fruit;
they will remain vital and green.
¹⁵ They will declare, "The LORD is just!
He is my rock!
There is nothing but goodness in him!"

PSALM 93

¹ The LORD is king! He is robed in majesty.
Indeed, the LORD is robed in majesty
and armed with strength.
The world is firmly established;
it cannot be shaken.

² Your throne, O LORD, has been established
from time immemorial.
You yourself are from the everlasting
past.
³ The mighty oceans have roared, O LORD.
The mighty oceans roar like thunder;
the mighty oceans roar as they pound
the shore.
⁴ But mightier than the violent raging of the
seas,
mightier than the breakers on the
shore—
the LORD above is mightier than these!
⁵ Your royal decrees cannot be changed.
The nature of your reign, O LORD, is
holiness forever.

PSALM 94

¹ O LORD, the God to whom vengeance
belongs,
O God of vengeance, let your glorious
justice be seen!
² Arise, O judge of the earth.
Sentence the proud to the penalties they
deserve.
³ How long, O LORD?
How long will the wicked be allowed to
gloat?
⁴ Hear their arrogance!
How these evildoers boast!
⁵ They oppress your people, LORD,

hurting those you love.
⁶ They kill widows and foreigners
and murder orphans.
⁷ "The LORD isn't looking," they say,
"and besides, the God of Israel* doesn't
care."

⁸ Think again, you fools!
When will you finally catch on?
⁹ Is the one who made your ears deaf?
Is the one who formed your eyes blind?
¹⁰ He punishes the nations—won't he also
punish you?
He knows everything—doesn't he also
know what you are doing?
¹¹ The LORD knows people's thoughts,
that they are worthless!

¹² Happy are those whom you discipline,
LORD,
and those whom you teach from your
law.
¹³ You give them relief from troubled times
until a pit is dug for the wicked.
¹⁴ The LORD will not reject his people;
he will not abandon his own special
possession.
¹⁵ Judgment will come again for the
righteous,
and those who are upright will have a
reward.

¹⁶ Who will protect me from the wicked?
Who will stand up for me against
evildoers?
¹⁷ Unless the LORD had helped me,
I would soon have died.
¹⁸ I cried out, "I'm slipping!"
and your unfailing love, O LORD,
supported me.
¹⁹ When doubts filled my mind,
your comfort gave me renewed hope
and cheer.

²⁰ Can unjust leaders claim that God is on
their side—

94:7 Hebrew *of Jacob.*

My Daily Worship

— *May 23* —

UNDER HIS WINGS

PSALMS 90:1–95:11

He will shield you with his wings. He will shelter you with his feathers.
His faithful promises are your armor and protection (91:4).

[i reflect]

The bird huddles over its young as the storm rages on. The tree sways crazily in the wind, but the nest holds fast. Sheets of rain pour over the bird, but the nestlings stay warm and dry. Lightning flashes, thunder booms, but the little birds are safe and secure under the wings of their protector.

Likewise, the psalm writer recognized that when life's storms hit, there is only one place to turn: "He alone is my refuge, my place of safety; he is my God, and I am trusting him" (91:2). In the midst of turmoil and danger, the psalm writer was confident that God would shelter him "with his feathers" and protect him with "his faithful promises."

Do the storms of life threaten to overpower you? Is your life swaying crazily out of control? Is trouble pouring down on your head? Find shelter and rest in the shadow of the Lord Almighty. Take refuge under the wings of the Most High. Draw close to him and he will shield you from the storm.

In medieval times a soldier wore heavy metal to deflect the arrows of the enemy, but we wear the promises of God. The Lord promises, "I will rescue those who love me. I will protect those who trust in my name. When they call on me, I will answer; . . . I will satisfy them with a long life and give them my salvation" (91:14–16). Put on the armor of God's promises and stand against the enemy.

What protection do you need today? Look to God's promises and claim them as your own. In each battle, worship the One who helps you overcome.

[i pray]

Lord Almighty, gather me under the wings of your protection.
Shelter me with your feathers and hold me close to your heart.
Shield me from the storms that rage and grant me your salvation.

[i respond]

Name the battle that you are facing today. What do you need from God to fight that battle? Love, patience, endurance, forgiveness, grace? Whatever it may be, look through God's Word for a promise related to that specific need. Write it down and carry it with you as your "protection."

leaders who permit injustice by their
laws?
21 They attack the righteous
and condemn the innocent to death.
22 But the LORD is my fortress;
my God is a mighty rock where I can
hide.
23 God will make the sins of evil people fall
back upon them.
He will destroy them for their sins.
The LORD our God will destroy them.

PSALM 95

1 Come, let us sing to the LORD!
Let us give a joyous shout to the rock of
our salvation!
2 Let us come before him with thanksgiving.
Let us sing him psalms of praise.
3 For the LORD is a great God,
the great King above all gods.
4 He owns the depths of the earth,
and even the mightiest mountains are
his.
5 The sea belongs to him, for he made it.
His hands formed the dry land, too.

6 Come, let us worship and bow down.
Let us kneel before the LORD our maker,
7 for he is our God.
We are the people he watches over,
the sheep under his care.

Oh, that you would listen to his voice
today!
8 The LORD says, "Don't harden your hearts
as Israel did at Meribah,
as they did at Massah in the wilderness.
9 For there your ancestors tried my patience;
they courted my wrath though they had
seen my many miracles.
10 For forty years I was angry with them, and
I said,
'They are a people whose hearts turn
away from me.
They refuse to do what I tell them.'
11 So in my anger I made a vow:
'They will never enter my place of rest.' "

PSALM 96

1 Sing a new song to the LORD!
Let the whole earth sing to the LORD!
2 Sing to the LORD; bless his name.
Each day proclaim the good news that
he saves.
3 Publish his glorious deeds among the
nations.
Tell everyone about the amazing things
he does.
4 Great is the LORD! He is most worthy of
praise!
He is to be revered above all the gods.
5 The gods of other nations are merely idols,
but the LORD made the heavens!
6 Honor and majesty surround him;
strength and beauty are in his sanctuary.
7 O nations of the world, recognize the
LORD;
recognize that the LORD is glorious and
strong.
8 Give to the LORD the glory he deserves!
Bring your offering and come to
worship him.
9 Worship the LORD in all his holy
splendor.
Let all the earth tremble before him.
10 Tell all the nations that the LORD is king.
The world is firmly established and
cannot be shaken.
He will judge all peoples fairly.

11 Let the heavens be glad, and let the earth
rejoice!
Let the sea and everything in it shout his
praise!
12 Let the fields and their crops burst forth
with joy!
Let the trees of the forest rustle with
praise 13before the LORD!
For the LORD is coming!
He is coming to judge the earth.
He will judge the world with
righteousness
and all the nations with his truth.

PSALM 97

1 The LORD is king! Let the earth rejoice!
Let the farthest islands be glad.
2 Clouds and darkness surround him.
Righteousness and justice are the
foundation of his throne.
3 Fire goes forth before him
and burns up all his foes.
4 His lightning flashes out across the
world.
The earth sees and trembles.
5 The mountains melt like wax before the
LORD,
before the Lord of all the earth.
6 The heavens declare his righteousness;
every nation sees his glory.
7 Those who worship idols are disgraced—
all who brag about their worthless
gods—
for every god must bow to him.
8 Jerusalem* has heard and rejoiced,
and all the cities of Judah are glad
because of your justice, LORD!
9 For you, O LORD, are most high over all
the earth;
you are exalted far above all gods.

10 You who love the LORD, hate evil!
He protects the lives of his godly
people
and rescues them from the power of the
wicked.
11 Light shines on the godly,
and joy on those who do right.
12 May all who are godly be happy in the
LORD
and praise his holy name!

PSALM 98

A psalm.

1 Sing a new song to the LORD,
for he has done wonderful deeds.
He has won a mighty victory
by his power and holiness.
2 The LORD has announced his victory

and has revealed his righteousness to
every nation!
3 He has remembered his promise to love
and be faithful to Israel.
The whole earth has seen the salvation
of our God.

4 Shout to the LORD, all the earth;
break out in praise and sing for joy!
5 Sing your praise to the LORD with the
harp,
with the harp and melodious song,

Words of Worship

ENTER

Enter—Hebrew *bo'* "go, enter"; Greek *eis-er-cho-mai* "go, enter."

The simple words *enter* and *go* don't seem very exalted or descriptive of how we worship the Lord. Yet both are critical actions in our personal devotion. If we never *go* to the Lord or *enter into* his presence, then nothing else is likely to happen. Worship begins when we respond to his call and move toward him.

The Scriptures invite us to come into the place of worship: "Enter his gates with thanksgiving, go into his courts with praise" (Psalm 100:4). Those "courts" may be a building, where we meet with others who love the Lord. Or they may be the hidden sanctuary of our heart, for we are his temple (1 Corinthians 3:17). We enter God's presence to worship him, but also to receive what he wants to give us in return—the wonderful repose of his peace. Focusing on ourselves, we're often torn by anxiety, wondering if we've done enough to earn the right to exist! In the Lord's presence, we're released from our striving, for "God's rest is there for people to enter" (Hebrews 4:6).

97:8 Hebrew *Zion.*

6 with trumpets and the sound of the
      ram's horn.
   Make a joyful symphony before the LORD,
      the King!

7 Let the sea and everything in it shout his
      praise!
   Let the earth and all living things join in.
8 Let the rivers clap their hands in glee!
   Let the hills sing out their songs of joy
9   before the LORD.
   For the LORD is coming to judge the earth.
   He will judge the world with justice,
   and the nations with fairness.

PSALM 99

1 The LORD is king!
      Let the nations tremble!
   He sits on his throne between the
      cherubim.
      Let the whole earth quake!
2 The LORD sits in majesty in Jerusalem,*
      supreme above all the nations.
3 Let them praise your great and awesome
      name.
      Your name is holy!
4 Mighty king, lover of justice,
      you have established fairness.
   You have acted with justice
      and righteousness throughout Israel.*
5 Exalt the LORD our God!
      Bow low before his feet, for he is holy!

6 Moses and Aaron were among his priests;
      Samuel also called on his name.
   They cried to the LORD for help,
      and he answered them.
7 He spoke to them from the pillar of cloud,
      and they followed the decrees and
         principles he gave them.
8 O LORD our God, you answered them.
      You were a forgiving God,
      but you punished them when they went
         wrong.

99:2 Hebrew *Zion.* 99:4 Hebrew *Jacob.*

9 Exalt the LORD our God
      and worship at his holy mountain in
         Jerusalem,
      for the LORD our God is holy!

PSALM 100

A psalm of thanksgiving.

1 Shout with joy to the LORD, O earth!
2   Worship the LORD with gladness.
   Come before him, singing with joy.
3 Acknowledge that the LORD is God!
      He made us, and we are his.
   We are his people, the sheep of his
      pasture.

4 Enter his gates with thanksgiving;
      go into his courts with praise.
   Give thanks to him and bless his name.
5 For the LORD is good.
      His unfailing love continues forever,
      and his faithfulness continues to each
         generation.

PSALM 101

A psalm of David.

1 I will sing of your love and justice.
      I will praise you, LORD, with songs.
2 I will be careful to live a blameless life—
      when will you come to my aid?
   I will lead a life of integrity
      in my own home.
3 I will refuse to look at
      anything vile and vulgar.
   I hate all crooked dealings;
      I will have nothing to do with them.
4 I will reject perverse ideas
      and stay away from every evil.
5 I will not tolerate people who slander their
      neighbors.
   I will not endure conceit and pride.

6 I will keep a protective eye on the godly,
      so they may dwell with me in safety.

My Daily Worship

— *May 24* —

S H O U T   I T   O U T!

P S A L M S   9 6 : 1 – 1 0 4 : 8

Shout with joy to the LORD, O earth! Worship the LORD with gladness.
Come before him, singing with joy (100:1–2).

[i reflect]

It's called March Madness. Every year the top sixty-four teams in college basketball battle it out for the right to be called national champions. As the field is whittled down from sixty-four to sixteen to eight to the "final four," those who watch see runaway victories, last-second thrillers, overtime nail-biters, and incredible come-from-behind victories. At last the final two teams compete—and only one emerges the victor. As those last seconds tick off, the fans stream onto the court with shouts and cheers, celebrating the victory.

Do the mighty deeds of the Lord generate that kind of enthusiasm in you? Do you shout with joy when you recall the wondrous things he has done? Or do you calmly go about your business, barely giving him a thought? Do you sing out in a strong, clear voice or do you mumble along, your mind on another planet? Do you tell others about Jesus or do you keep the good news to yourself?

Maybe you think you don't have much to shout about. What about the Lord's return? For he is coming soon. Tell everyone you meet about his amazing wonders. Proclaim the good news of his salvation every day. Make his name known to the nations, so they can bow down and worship him. "For the LORD is coming! He is coming to judge the earth. He will judge the world with righteousness and all the nations with his truth" (96:13).

Now is the time to sing a new song to the Lord. Leave behind the songs of bitterness and complaint. Bring out songs of glory and praise. Worship him in all his splendor. Praise him for the wonders of his creation. Exalt his holy name to all the earth. Laugh and shout and sing, for he is coming soon. Rejoice!

[i pray]

Lord, you are my king. I bow down low before you, for you are holy. You are glorious and strong.
You judge the earth with righteousness and truth. I exalt your name forever.

[i respond]

Take a moment to truly and honestly shout to the Lord! If you are inside, step outside your door and shout! Or find a closet, basement, or garage in which to raise your voice and shout that the Lord is good! Cheer for God! Yell!

Only those who are above reproach
will be allowed to serve me.
⁷ I will not allow deceivers to serve me,
and liars will not be allowed to enter my
presence.
⁸ My daily task will be to ferret out criminals
and free the city of the LORD from their
grip.

PSALM 102

A prayer of one overwhelmed with trouble,
pouring out problems before the LORD.

¹ LORD, hear my prayer!
Listen to my plea!
² Don't turn away from me
in my time of distress.
Bend down your ear
and answer me quickly when I call to
you,
³ for my days disappear like smoke,
and my bones burn like red-hot coals.
⁴ My heart is sick, withered like grass,
and I have lost my appetite.
⁵ Because of my groaning,
I am reduced to skin and bones.
⁶ I am like an owl in the desert,
like a lonely owl in a far-off wilderness.
⁷ I lie awake,
lonely as a solitary bird on the roof.
⁸ My enemies taunt me day after day.
They mock and curse me.
⁹ I eat ashes instead of my food.
My tears run down into my drink
¹⁰ because of your anger and wrath.
For you have picked me up and thrown
me out.
¹¹ My life passes as swiftly as the evening
shadows.
I am withering like grass.

¹² But you, O LORD, will rule forever.
Your fame will endure to every
generation.
¹³ You will arise and have mercy on
Jerusalem*—

and now is the time to pity her,
now is the time you promised to help.
¹⁴ For your people love every stone in her
walls
and show favor even to the dust in her
streets.
¹⁵ And the nations will tremble before the
LORD.
The kings of the earth will tremble
before his glory.
¹⁶ For the LORD will rebuild Jerusalem.
He will appear in his glory.
¹⁷ He will listen to the prayers of the
destitute.
He will not reject their pleas.

¹⁸ Let this be recorded for future generations,
so that a nation yet to be created will
praise the LORD.
¹⁹ Tell them the LORD looked down
from his heavenly sanctuary.
He looked to the earth from heaven
²⁰ to hear the groans of the prisoners,
to release those condemned to die.
²¹ And so the LORD's fame will be celebrated
in Zion,
his praises in Jerusalem,
²² when multitudes gather together
and kingdoms come to worship the
LORD.

²³ He has cut me down in midlife,
shortening my days.
²⁴ But I cried to him, "My God, who lives
forever,
don't take my life while I am still so
young!
²⁵ In ages past you laid the foundation of the
earth,
and the heavens are the work of your
hands.
²⁶ Even they will perish, but you remain
forever;
they will wear out like old clothing.
You will change them like a garment,
and they will fade away.

102:13 Hebrew *Zion;* also in 102:16.

My Daily Worship

— *May 25* —

THE PERFECT DAD

PSALMS 102:1–104:35

*The LORD is like a father to his children, tender and
compassionate to those who fear him (103:13).*

[i reflect]

David knew. He had felt the pain, experienced the shame of going so far astray that he thought he
would never get home again. He knew what it was like to admit all this to God the Father.

But he also knew what manner of Father his God was. The bellowing kind, determined to make an
example of David for his other children? The sullen kind, who is so hurt, so wounded in pride that
one of his sons could do wrong that he withdraws his love into sullen silence? The preoccupied,
"boys will be boys" kind, that barely acknowledges, much less punishes, a wayward child?

The great Lord of heaven—the One who had the power to bellow, the reason to withdraw, and a
universe of things occupying his attention—was none of those. He was like a *perfect* father, tender and compassionate. Why? "For he understands how weak we are; he knows we are only dust"
(103:14). David ran like the shepherd boy he was to such a Father.

David ran to worship as well, calling himself to praise: "Praise the LORD, I tell myself. . . . Praise
the LORD, I tell myself. . . . Praise the LORD, I tell myself" (103:1, 2; 104:1). Do we, children of
God just as dear to the Father as the great King David, respond in praise?

In the early 1800s Henry Lyte drew from these same psalms as he wrote the hymn, "Praise, My
Soul, the King of Heaven." The third verse echoes David's words: "Fatherlike, he tends and spares
us, well our feeble frame he knows. In his hands he gently bears us, rescues us from all our foes.
Alleluia! Alleluia! Widely as his mercy flows!"

As you go through the day, remember your tender, compassionate Father who stands ready to tend
and spare you, bear up and rescue you. Tell yourself to praise him!

[i pray]

*Father, I will praise you and bless you. With my whole heart, I will praise your holy name.
With my whole heart, I thank you for being such a tender and compassionate Father.*

[i respond]

Worshipfully read or sing the first verse of the hymn above: "Praise, my soul, the King of heaven,
to his feet your tribute bring. Ransomed, healed, restored, forgiven; who, like me, his praise should
sing? Alleluia! Alleluia! Praise the everlasting King!"

²⁷ But you are always the same;
    your years never end.
²⁸ The children of your people
    will live in security.
    Their children's children
    will thrive in your presence."

PSALM 103

A psalm of David.

¹ Praise the LORD, I tell myself;
    with my whole heart, I will praise his
    holy name.
² Praise the LORD, I tell myself,
    and never forget the good things he does
    for me.
³ He forgives all my sins
    and heals all my diseases.
⁴ He ransoms me from death
    and surrounds me with love and tender
    mercies.
⁵ He fills my life with good things.
    My youth is renewed like the eagle's!
⁶ The LORD gives righteousness
    and justice to all who are treated
    unfairly.
⁷ He revealed his character to Moses
    and his deeds to the people of Israel.
⁸ The LORD is merciful and gracious;
    he is slow to get angry and full of
    unfailing love.
⁹ He will not constantly accuse us,
    nor remain angry forever.
¹⁰ He has not punished us for all our sins,
    nor does he deal with us as we deserve.
¹¹ For his unfailing love toward those who
    fear him
    is as great as the height of the heavens
    above the earth.
¹² He has removed our rebellious acts
    as far away from us as the east is from
    the west.
¹³ The LORD is like a father to his children,
    tender and compassionate to those who
    fear him.
¹⁴ For he understands how weak we are;
    he knows we are only dust.

¹⁵ Our days on earth are like grass;
    like wildflowers, we bloom and die.
¹⁶ The wind blows, and we are gone—
    as though we had never been here.
¹⁷ But the love of the LORD remains forever
    with those who fear him.
    His salvation extends to the children's
    children
¹⁸   of those who are faithful to his covenant,
    of those who obey his commandments!

¹⁹ The LORD has made the heavens his
    throne;
    from there he rules over everything.
²⁰ Praise the LORD, you angels of his,
    you mighty creatures who carry out his
    plans,
    listening for each of his commands.
²¹ Yes, praise the LORD, you armies of angels
    who serve him and do his will!
²² Praise the LORD, everything he has created,
    everywhere in his kingdom.
    As for me—I, too, will praise the LORD.

PSALM 104

¹ Praise the LORD, I tell myself;
    O LORD my God, how great you are!
    You are robed with honor and with
    majesty;
²   you are dressed in a robe of light.
    You stretch out the starry curtain of the
    heavens;
³   you lay out the rafters of your home in
    the rain clouds.
    You make the clouds your chariots;
    you ride upon the wings of the wind.
⁴ The winds are your messengers;
    flames of fire are your servants.

⁵ You placed the world on its foundation
    so it would never be moved.
⁶ You clothed the earth with floods of water,
    water that covered even the mountains.
⁷ At the sound of your rebuke, the water
    fled;
    at the sound of your thunder, it fled
    away.

8 Mountains rose and valleys sank
   to the levels you decreed.
9 Then you set a firm boundary for the seas,
   so they would never again cover the
   earth.

10 You make the springs pour water into
   ravines,
   so streams gush down from the
   mountains.
11 They provide water for all the animals,
   and the wild donkeys quench their
   thirst.
12 The birds nest beside the streams
   and sing among the branches of the
   trees.
13 You send rain on the mountains from your
   heavenly home,
   and you fill the earth with the fruit of
   your labor.
14 You cause grass to grow for the cattle.
   You cause plants to grow for people to
   use.
   You allow them to produce food from the
   earth—
15 wine to make them glad,
   olive oil as lotion for their skin,
   and bread to give them strength.
16 The trees of the LORD are well cared for—
   the cedars of Lebanon that he planted.
17 There the birds make their nests,
   and the storks make their homes in the
   firs.
18 High in the mountains are pastures for the
   wild goats,
   and the rocks form a refuge for rock
   badgers.*
19 You made the moon to mark the seasons
   and the sun that knows when to set.
20 You send the darkness, and it becomes
   night,
   when all the forest animals prowl about.
21 Then the young lions roar for their food,
   but they are dependent on God.
22 At dawn they slink back
   into their dens to rest.

23 Then people go off to their work;
   they labor until the evening shadows fall
   again.

24 O LORD, what a variety of things you have
   made!
   In wisdom you have made them all.
   The earth is full of your creatures.
25 Here is the ocean, vast and wide,
   teeming with life of every kind,
   both great and small.
26 See the ships sailing along,
   and Leviathan, which you made to play
   in the sea.
27 Every one of these depends on you
   to give them their food as they need it.
28 When you supply it, they gather it.
   You open your hand to feed them, and
   they are satisfied.
29 But if you turn away from them, they
   panic.
   When you take away their breath, they
   die
   and turn again to dust.
30 When you send your Spirit, new life is
   born
   to replenish all the living of the earth.

31 May the glory of the LORD last forever!
   The LORD rejoices in all he has made!
32 The earth trembles at his glance;
   the mountains burst into flame at his
   touch.
33 I will sing to the LORD as long as I live.
   I will praise my God to my last
   breath!
34 May he be pleased by all these thoughts
   about him,
   for I rejoice in the LORD.
35 Let all sinners vanish from the face of the
   earth;
   let the wicked disappear forever.
   As for me—I will praise the LORD!

   Praise the LORD!

104:18 Or coneys, or hyraxes.

PSALM 105
1 Give thanks to the LORD and proclaim his
    greatness.
  Let the whole world know what he has
    done.
2 Sing to him; yes, sing his praises.
  Tell everyone about his miracles.
3 Exult in his holy name;
  O worshipers of the LORD, rejoice!
4 Search for the LORD and for his strength,
  and keep on searching.
5 Think of the wonderful works he has
    done,
  the miracles and the judgments he
    handed down,
6 O children of Abraham, God's servant,
  O descendants of Jacob, God's chosen
    one.
7 He is the LORD our God.
  His rule is seen throughout the land.
8 He always stands by his covenant—
  the commitment he made to a thousand
    generations.
9 This is the covenant he made with
    Abraham
  and the oath he swore to Isaac.
10 He confirmed it to Jacob as a decree,
  to the people of Israel as a never-ending
    treaty:
11 "I will give you the land of Canaan
  as your special possession."

12 He said this when they were few in
    number,
  a tiny group of strangers in Canaan.
13 They wandered back and forth between
    nations,
  from one kingdom to another.
14 Yet he did not let anyone oppress them.
  He warned kings on their behalf:
15 "Do not touch these people I have chosen,
  and do not hurt my prophets."
16 He called for a famine on the land of
    Canaan,
  cutting off its food supply.
17 Then he sent someone to Egypt ahead of
    them—

Joseph, who was sold as a slave.
18 There in prison, they bruised his feet with
    fetters
  and placed his neck in an iron collar.
19 Until the time came to fulfill his word,
  the LORD tested Joseph's character.
20 Then Pharaoh sent for him and set him
    free;
  the ruler of the nation opened his prison
    door.
21 Joseph was put in charge of all the king's
    household;
  he became ruler over all the king's
    possessions.
22 He could instruct the king's aides as he
    pleased
  and teach the king's advisers.

23 Then Israel arrived in Egypt;
  Jacob lived as a foreigner in the land of
    Ham.
24 And the LORD multiplied the people of
    Israel
  until they became too mighty for their
    enemies.
25 Then he turned the Egyptians against the
    Israelites,
  and they plotted against the LORD's
    servants.

26 But the LORD sent Moses his servant,
  along with Aaron, whom he had
    chosen.
27 They performed miraculous signs among
    the Egyptians,
  and miracles in the land of Ham.
28 The LORD blanketed Egypt in darkness,
  for they had defied his commands to let
    his people go.
29 He turned the nation's water into blood,
  poisoning all the fish.
30 Then frogs overran the land;
  they were found even in the king's
    private rooms.
31 When he spoke, flies descended on the
    Egyptians,
  and gnats swarmed across Egypt.

³² Instead of rain, he sent murderous hail,
    and flashes of lightning overwhelmed
      the land.
³³ He ruined their grapevines and fig trees
    and shattered all the trees.
³⁴ He spoke, and hordes of locusts came—
    locusts beyond number.
³⁵ They ate up everything green in the land,
    destroying all the crops.
³⁶ Then he killed the oldest child in each
      Egyptian home,
    the pride and joy of each family.

³⁷ But he brought his people safely out of
      Egypt, loaded with silver and gold;
    there were no sick or feeble people
      among them.
³⁸ Egypt was glad when they were gone,
    for the dread of them was great.
³⁹ The LORD spread out a cloud above them
      as a covering
    and gave them a great fire to light the
      darkness.
⁴⁰ They asked for meat, and he sent them
      quail;
    he gave them manna—bread from
      heaven.
⁴¹ He opened up a rock, and water gushed
      out
    to form a river through the dry and
      barren land.
⁴² For he remembered his sacred promise
    to Abraham his servant.
⁴³ So he brought his people out of Egypt
      with joy,
    his chosen ones with rejoicing.
⁴⁴ He gave his people the lands of pagan
      nations,
    and they harvested crops that others had
      planted.
⁴⁵ All this happened so they would follow his
      principles
    and obey his laws.

Praise the LORD!

PSALM 106

¹ Praise the LORD!

Give thanks to the LORD, for he is good!
    His faithful love endures forever.
² Who can list the glorious miracles of the
      LORD?
    Who can ever praise him half enough?
³ Happy are those who deal justly with
      others
    and always do what is right.

⁴ Remember me, too, LORD, when you show
      favor to your people;
    come to me with your salvation.
⁵ Let me share in the prosperity of your
      chosen ones.
    Let me rejoice in the joy of your people;
    let me praise you with those who are
      your heritage.

⁶ Both we and our ancestors have sinned.
    We have done wrong! We have acted
      wickedly!
⁷ Our ancestors in Egypt
    were not impressed by the LORD's
      miracles.
    They soon forgot his many acts of
      kindness to them.
    Instead, they rebelled against him at the
      Red Sea.*
⁸ Even so, he saved them—
    to defend the honor of his name
    and to demonstrate his mighty power.
⁹ He commanded the Red Sea* to divide,
    and a dry path appeared.
    He led Israel across the sea bottom that
      was as dry as a desert.
¹⁰ So he rescued them from their enemies
    and redeemed them from their foes.
¹¹ Then the water returned and covered their
      enemies;
    not one of them survived.
¹² Then at last his people believed his
      promises.
    Then they finally sang his praise.

106:7 Hebrew *at the sea, the sea of reeds.* 106:9 Hebrew *sea of reeds;* also in 106:22.

¹³ Yet how quickly they forgot what he had
   done!
   They wouldn't wait for his counsel!
¹⁴ In the wilderness, their desires ran wild,
   testing God's patience in that dry land.
¹⁵ So he gave them what they asked for,
   but he sent a plague along with it.
¹⁶ The people in the camp were jealous of
   Moses
   and envious of Aaron, the LORD's holy
   priest.
¹⁷ Because of this, the earth opened up;
   it swallowed Dathan
   and buried Abiram and the other
   rebels.
¹⁸ Fire fell upon their followers;
   a flame consumed the wicked.

¹⁹ The people made a calf at Mount Sinai*;
   they bowed before an image made of
   gold.
²⁰ They traded their glorious God
   for a statue of a grass-eating ox!
²¹ They forgot God, their savior,
   who had done such great things in
   Egypt—
²² such wonderful things in that land,
   such awesome deeds at the Red Sea.
²³ So he declared he would destroy them.
   But Moses, his chosen one, stepped
   between the LORD and the people.
   He begged him to turn from his anger
   and not destroy them.

²⁴ The people refused to enter the pleasant
   land,
   for they wouldn't believe his promise to
   care for them.
²⁵ Instead, they grumbled in their tents
   and refused to obey the LORD.
²⁶ Therefore, he swore
   that he would kill them in the
   wilderness,
²⁷ that he would scatter their descendants
   among the nations,
   exiling them to distant lands.

²⁸ Then our ancestors joined in the worship
   of Baal at Peor;
   they even ate sacrifices offered to the
   dead!
²⁹ They angered the LORD with all these
   things,
   so a plague broke out among them.
³⁰ But Phinehas had the courage to step in,
   and the plague was stopped.
³¹ So he has been regarded as a righteous
   man
   ever since that time.

³² At Meribah, too, they angered the LORD,
   causing Moses serious trouble.
³³ They made Moses angry,*
   and he spoke foolishly.

³⁴ Israel failed to destroy the nations in the
   land,
   as the LORD had told them to.
³⁵ Instead, they mingled among the pagans
   and adopted their evil customs.
³⁶ They worshiped their idols,
   and this led to their downfall.
³⁷ They even sacrificed their sons
   and their daughters to the demons.
³⁸ They shed innocent blood,
   the blood of their sons and daughters.
   By sacrificing them to the idols of Canaan,
   they polluted the land with murder.
³⁹ They defiled themselves by their evil deeds,
   and their love of idols was adultery in
   the LORD's sight.

⁴⁰ That is why the LORD's anger burned
   against his people,
   and he abhorred his own special
   possession.
⁴¹ He handed them over to pagan nations,
   and those who hated them ruled over
   them.
⁴² Their enemies crushed them
   and brought them under their cruel
   power.
⁴³ Again and again he delivered them,

106:19 Hebrew *at Horeb,* another name for Sinai.   106:33 Hebrew *They embittered his spirit.*

My Daily Worship

— M a y 2 6 —

TELL ME A STORY

PSALMS 105:1–107:43

Give thanks to the LORD, for he is good! His faithful love endures forever. . . .
Those who are wise will take all this to heart;
they will see in our history the faithful love of the LORD (107:1, 43).

[i reflect]

Telling and retelling stories is one of the most basic ways for people to communicate. From the birth of language, humans have remembered and shared stories.

For the people of God, it is more than a mere account; the telling of stories is the telling of *the* story, that of God's relationship with his people. From the song recounting God's deliverance of his people out of Egypt (Exodus 15:1–18), through Peter's and Paul's testimonies of the reality of Jesus' life and purpose, we see "in our history the faithful love of the LORD."

The anonymous psalm writers of today's readings richly recount God's deeds through the centuries. What moves them to move others, to remember together? It is the pull of worship. "Give thanks to the LORD and proclaim his greatness" (105:1). "Give thanks to the LORD, for he is good! His faithful love endures forever" (106:1; 107:1).

But keep listening. Centuries later, then coming down through the years to us, is a quiet recounting. A young woman speaks of the Lord's faithful love—how he has blessed her, how he has blessed his people, and how he has revealed his goodness. Yet the quiet recounting found in Luke 1:46–55 is known by a grand name, the Magnificat. "Oh, how I praise the Lord," Mary begins. "How I rejoice in God my Savior! . . . For he, the Mighty One, is holy, and he has done great things for me. . . . And how he has helped his servant Israel! He has not forgotten his promise to be merciful."

Are you wise, taking all this to heart? Are you seeing in your history the faithful love of the Lord? Use this time to reflect on your history with God. Like Mary, rejoice with a song of praise in your heart.

[i pray]

O Lord, how I praise your name. Your faithful love to your people is remarkable.
Your faithful love to me is my salvation. I give thanks to you,
for you are good beyond measure.

[i respond]

Consider the ways that God has revealed his goodness in your story. Compose your own psalm of gratitude, beginning "Give thanks to the LORD, for he is good! His faithful love endures forever."

but they continued to rebel against him,
and they were finally destroyed by their
sin.

44 Even so, he pitied them in their distress
and listened to their cries.

45 He remembered his covenant with them
and relented because of his unfailing
love.

46 He even caused their captors
to treat them with kindness.

47 O LORD our God, save us!
Gather us back from among the nations,
so we can thank your holy name
and rejoice and praise you.

48 Blessed be the LORD, the God of Israel,
from everlasting to everlasting!
Let all the people say, "Amen!"

Praise the LORD!

BOOK FIVE (PSALMS 107–150)

PSALM 107

1 Give thanks to the LORD, for he is good!
His faithful love endures forever.

2 Has the LORD redeemed you? Then speak
out!
Tell others he has saved you from your
enemies.

3 For he has gathered the exiles from many
lands,
from east and west, from north and
south.

4 Some wandered in the desert,
lost and homeless.

5 Hungry and thirsty,
they nearly died.

6 "LORD, help!" they cried in their trouble,
and he rescued them from their distress.

7 He led them straight to safety,
to a city where they could live.

8 Let them praise the LORD for his great love
and for all his wonderful deeds to them.

9 For he satisfies the thirsty
and fills the hungry with good things.

10 Some sat in darkness and deepest gloom,
miserable prisoners in chains.

11 They rebelled against the words of God,
scorning the counsel of the Most High.

12 That is why he broke them with hard
labor;
they fell, and no one helped them rise
again.

13 "LORD, help!" they cried in their trouble,
and he saved them from their distress.

14 He led them from the darkness and
deepest gloom;
he snapped their chains.

15 Let them praise the LORD for his great love
and for all his wonderful deeds to them.

16 For he broke down their prison gates of
bronze;
he cut apart their bars of iron.

17 Some were fools in their rebellion;
they suffered for their sins.

18 Their appetites were gone,
and death was near.

19 "LORD, help!" they cried in their trouble,
and he saved them from their distress.

20 He spoke, and they were healed—
snatched from the door of death.

21 Let them praise the LORD for his great love
and for all his wonderful deeds to them.

22 Let them offer sacrifices of thanksgiving
and sing joyfully about his glorious acts.

23 Some went off in ships,
plying the trade routes of the world.

24 They, too, observed the LORD's power in
action,
his impressive works on the deepest seas.

25 He spoke, and the winds rose,
stirring up the waves.

26 Their ships were tossed to the heavens
and sank again to the depths;
the sailors cringed in terror.

27 They reeled and staggered like drunkards
and were at their wits' end.

28 "LORD, help!" they cried in their trouble,
  and he saved them from their distress.
29 He calmed the storm to a whisper
  and stilled the waves.
30 What a blessing was that stillness
  as he brought them safely into harbor!
31 Let them praise the LORD for his great love
  and for all his wonderful deeds to them.
32 Let them exalt him publicly before the
    congregation
  and before the leaders of the nation.

33 He changes rivers into deserts,
  and springs of water into dry land.
34 He turns the fruitful land into salty
    wastelands,
  because of the wickedness of those who
    live there.
35 But he also turns deserts into pools of
    water,
  the dry land into flowing springs.
36 He brings the hungry to settle there
  and build their cities.
37 They sow their fields, plant their vineyards,
  and harvest their bumper crops.
38 How he blesses them!
  They raise large families there,
  and their herds of cattle increase.

39 When they decrease in number and
    become impoverished
  through oppression, trouble, and
    sorrow,
40 the LORD pours contempt on their princes,
  causing them to wander in trackless
    wastelands.
41 But he rescues the poor from their
    distress
  and increases their families like vast
    flocks of sheep.
42 The godly will see these things and be glad,
  while the wicked are stricken silent.
43 Those who are wise will take all this to
    heart;
  they will see in our history the faithful
    love of the LORD.

108:7 Or *in his sanctuary.*

PSALM 108

A psalm of David. A song.

1 My heart is confident in you, O God;
  no wonder I can sing your praises!
  Wake up, my soul!
2   Wake up, O harp and lyre!
  I will waken the dawn with my song.
3 I will thank you, LORD, in front of all the
    people.
  I will sing your praises among the
    nations.
4 For your unfailing love is higher than the
    heavens.
  Your faithfulness reaches to the clouds.
5 Be exalted, O God, above the highest
    heavens.
  May your glory shine over all the earth.

6 Use your strong right arm to save me,
  and rescue your beloved people.
7 God has promised this by his holiness*:
  "I will divide up Shechem with joy.
  I will measure out the valley of
    Succoth.
8 Gilead is mine,
  and Manasseh is mine.
  Ephraim will produce my warriors,
  and Judah will produce my kings.
9 Moab will become my lowly servant,
  and Edom will be my slave.
  I will shout in triumph over the
    Philistines."

10 But who will bring me into the fortified
    city?
  Who will bring me victory over Edom?
11 Have you rejected us, O God?
  Will you no longer march with our
    armies?
12 Oh, please help us against our enemies,
  for all human help is useless.
13 With God's help we will do mighty
    things,
  for he will trample down our foes.

PSALM 109

For the choir director: A psalm of David.

1 O God, whom I praise,
   don't stand silent and aloof
2 while the wicked slander me
   and tell lies about me.
3 They are all around me with their hateful
   words,
   and they fight against me for no reason.
4 I love them, but they try to destroy me—
   even as I am praying for them!
5 They return evil for good,
   and hatred for my love.

6 Arrange for an evil person to turn on him.
   Send an accuser to bring him to trial.
7 When his case is called for judgment,
   let him be pronounced guilty.
   Count his prayers as sins.
8 Let his years be few;
   let his position be given to someone else.
9 May his children become fatherless,
   and may his wife become a widow.
10 May his children wander as beggars;
   may they be evicted from their ruined
   homes.
11 May creditors seize his entire estate,
   and strangers take all he has earned.
12 Let no one be kind to him;
   let no one pity his fatherless children.
13 May all his offspring die.
   May his family name be blotted out in a
   single generation.
14 May the LORD never forget the sins of his
   ancestors;
   may his mother's sins never be erased
   from the record.
15 May these sins always remain before the
   LORD,
   but may his name be cut off from
   human memory.
16 For he refused all kindness to others;
   he persecuted the poor and needy,
   and he hounded the brokenhearted to
   death.
17 He loved to curse others;
   now you curse him.
   He never blessed others;
   now don't you bless him.
18 Cursing is as much a part of him as his
   clothing,
   or as the water he drinks,
   or the rich food he eats.
19 Now may his curses return and cling to
   him like clothing;
   may they be tied around him like a belt.

20 May those curses become the LORD's
   punishment for my accusers
   who are plotting against my life.
21 But deal well with me, O Sovereign LORD,
   for the sake of your own reputation!
   Rescue me because you are so faithful and
   good.
22 For I am poor and needy,
   and my heart is full of pain.
23 I am fading like a shadow at dusk;
   I am falling like a grasshopper that is
   brushed aside.
24 My knees are weak from fasting,
   and I am skin and bones.
25 I am an object of mockery to people
   everywhere;
   when they see me, they shake their
   heads.

26 Help me, O LORD my God!
   Save me because of your unfailing love.
27 Let them see that this is your doing,
   that you yourself have done it, LORD.
28 Then let them curse me if they like,
   but you will bless me!
   When they attack me, they will be
   disgraced!
   But I, your servant, will go right on
   rejoicing!
29 Make their humiliation obvious to all;
   clothe my accusers with disgrace.
30 But I will give repeated thanks to the LORD,
   praising him to everyone.
31 For he stands beside the needy,
   ready to save them from those who
   condemn them.

My Daily Worship

— May 27 —

IT'S NO WONDER!

PSALMS 108:1–112:10

My heart is confident in you, O God;
no wonder I can sing your praises! (108:1).

[i reflect]

The hooded figures begin to chant, "*Te Deum laudamus: te Dominum confitemur. Te aeternum Patrem omnis terra veneratur. . . . Sanctus, Sanctus, Sanctus, Dominus Deus Sabaoth. Pleni sunt coeli et terra maiestatis gloriae tuae. . . .*"

This composition, known as the *Te Deum laudamus,* was composed by Nicetas, bishop of Remesiana, in the early fifth century. It was heard in monasteries and convents every Sunday at the end of Matins, except during penitential seasons. Dark, depressing, devoid of life. Hardly in the same league as the psalm writer's confidence and claim to sing God's praises—"Wake up, my soul! Wake up, O harp and lyre! I will waken the dawn with my song. . . . I will sing your praises among the nations" (108:1–3).

But don't let the Latin fool you. "We praise thee, O God," begins the traditional English transla-tion of the *Te Deum laudamus.* "We acknowledge thee to be the Lord. All the earth doth worship thee, the Father everlasting. . . . Holy, holy, holy, Lord God of Sabaoth. Heaven and earth are full of the majesty of thy glory. . . ." The words continue: *laudabilis, laudat, laudamus,* "praise, praise, praise."

Still today, in convents, monasteries, churches, gatherings in homes, and in private meditations, God is praised, from the original Latin to a contemporary translation of the *Te Deum laudamus:* "You are God: we praise you; You are the Lord: we acclaim you; You are the eternal Father: all cre-ation worships you. . . . Holy, holy, holy Lord, God of power and might, heaven and earth are full of your glory."

Join the chorus. Reach back to David's psalms, through the *Te Deum laudamus,* to your own morn-ing worship. "My heart is confident in you, O God; no wonder I can sing your praises!"

[i pray]

God, it is no wonder I can sing your praises. You alone are full of power and might;
in you alone is my heart confident. You alone are God; I praise you. You
alone are Lord; I acclaim you. You alone are Father; I worship you.

[i respond]

Read and meditate on the entire text of the *Te Deum laudamus,* found in books of liturgy or reli-gious poetry (even on the Internet). Or listen to one of the musical settings by Purcell, Handel, Berlioz, Bruckner, Dvorák, and others to inspire your worship today.

PSALM 110

A psalm of David.

1 The LORD said to my Lord,
    "Sit in honor at my right hand
until I humble your enemies,
    making them a footstool under your
        feet."

2 The LORD will extend your powerful
        dominion from Jerusalem*;
    you will rule over your enemies.
3 In that day of battle,
    your people will serve you willingly.
Arrayed in holy garments,
    your vigor will be renewed each day like
        the morning dew.
4 The LORD has taken an oath and will not
        break his vow:
    "You are a priest forever in the line of
        Melchizedek."
5 The Lord stands at your right hand to
        protect you.
    He will strike down many kings in the
        day of his anger.
6 He will punish the nations
    and fill them with their dead;
he will shatter heads
    over the whole earth.
7 But he himself will be refreshed from
        brooks along the way.
    He will be victorious.

PSALM 111

1 Praise the LORD!

I will thank the LORD with all my heart
    as I meet with his godly people.
2 How amazing are the deeds of the LORD!
    All who delight in him should ponder
        them.
3 Everything he does reveals his glory and
        majesty.
    His righteousness never fails.
4 Who can forget the wonders he performs?
    How gracious and merciful is our LORD!

5 He gives food to those who trust him;
    he always remembers his covenant.
6 He has shown his great power to his
        people
    by giving them the lands of other
        nations.
7 All he does is just and good,
    and all his commandments are
        trustworthy.
8 They are forever true,
    to be obeyed faithfully and with
        integrity.

Words of Worship

SELAH

Selah—Hebrew *se-lah*. This term occurs seventy-one times in the Psalms and three times in Habakkuk. In the New Living Translation, the word *Selah* appears as *Interlude.*

The word *Selah* occurs at the end of some verses in various psalms or prayers meant to be sung. Nobody knows for sure what the word means. Some authorities relate it to the verb *salal*, meaning "lift up." It could refer to a momentary pause in the singing, perhaps for reflection. More likely, it refers to a musical interlude, a spontaneous "lifting up" of praise by instruments and perhaps voices too.

Whatever *Selah* means, it has something to teach us about worship. It's like a breath mark, indicating a break in the normal course of worship to allow something else to occur—a meditation, a spontaneous outburst of adoration, the chance for a voice to be heard other than our own. There is an ebb and flow of prayer and praise in our lives, as we not only put out, but also pause to take in what the Spirit wants to give us. *Selah.*

110:2 Hebrew *Zion.*

9 He has paid a full ransom for his people.
   He has guaranteed his covenant with
      them forever.
   What a holy, awe-inspiring name he has!
10 Reverence for the LORD is the foundation
      of true wisdom.
   The rewards of wisdom come to all who
      obey him.

Praise his name forever!

PSALM 112

1 Praise the LORD!

Happy are those who fear the LORD.
   Yes, happy are those who delight in
      doing what he commands.
2 Their children will be successful
      everywhere;
   an entire generation of godly people will
      be blessed.
3 They themselves will be wealthy,
   and their good deeds will never be
      forgotten.
4 When darkness overtakes the godly, light
      will come bursting in.
   They are* generous, compassionate, and
      righteous.
5 All goes well for those who are generous,
   who lend freely and conduct their
      business fairly.
6 Such people will not be overcome by evil
      circumstances.
   Those who are righteous will be long
      remembered.
7 They do not fear bad news;
   they confidently trust the LORD to care
      for them.
8 They are confident and fearless
   and can face their foes triumphantly.
9 They give generously to those in need.
   Their good deeds will never be
      forgotten.
   They will have influence and honor.
10 The wicked will be infuriated when they
      see this.

They will grind their teeth in anger;
   they will slink away, their hopes
      thwarted.

PSALM 113

1 Praise the LORD!

Yes, give praise, O servants of the LORD.
   Praise the name of the LORD!
2 Blessed be the name of the LORD
      forever and ever.
3 Everywhere—from east to west—
   praise the name of the LORD.
4 For the LORD is high above the nations;
   his glory is far greater than the heavens.

5 Who can be compared with the LORD our
      God,
   who is enthroned on high?
6 Far below him are the heavens and the
      earth.
   He stoops to look,
7 and he lifts the poor from the dirt
   and the needy from the garbage dump.
8 He sets them among princes,
   even the princes of his own people!
9 He gives the barren woman a home,
   so that she becomes a happy mother.

Praise the LORD!

PSALM 114

1 When the Israelites escaped from Egypt—
   when the family of Jacob left that
      foreign land—
2 the land of Judah became God's
      sanctuary,
   and Israel became his kingdom.

3 The Red Sea* saw them coming and
      hurried out of their way!
   The water of the Jordan River turned
      away.
4 The mountains skipped like rams,
   the little hills like lambs!

112:4 Greek version reads *The LORD is.*   114:3 Hebrew *the sea;* also in 114:5.

5 What's wrong, Red Sea, that made you
    hurry out of their way?
  What happened, Jordan River, that you
    turned away?
6 Why, mountains, did you skip like rams?
  Why, little hills, like lambs?

7 Tremble, O earth, at the presence of the
    Lord,
  at the presence of the God of Israel.*
8 He turned the rock into pools of water;
  yes, springs of water came from solid
    rock.

PSALM 115

1 Not to us, O LORD, but to you goes all the
    glory
  for your unfailing love and faithfulness.
2 Why let the nations say,
  "Where is their God?"
3 For our God is in the heavens,
  and he does as he wishes.
4 Their idols are merely things of silver and
    gold,
  shaped by human hands.
5 They cannot talk, though they have
    mouths,
  or see, though they have eyes!
6 They cannot hear with their ears,
  or smell with their noses,
7 or feel with their hands,
  or walk with their feet,
  or utter sounds with their throats!
8 And those who make them are just like
    them,
  as are all who trust in them.

9 O Israel, trust the LORD!
  He is your helper; he is your shield.
10 O priests of Aaron, trust the LORD!
  He is your helper; he is your shield.
11 All you who fear the LORD, trust the LORD!
  He is your helper; he is your shield.

12 The LORD remembers us,
  and he will surely bless us.

He will bless the people of Israel
  and the family of Aaron, the priests.
13 He will bless those who fear the LORD,
  both great and small.

14 May the LORD richly bless
  both you and your children.
15 May you be blessed by the LORD,
  who made heaven and earth.
16 The heavens belong to the LORD,
  but he has given the earth to all
    humanity.

17 The dead cannot sing praises to the LORD,
  for they have gone into the silence of the
    grave.
18 But we can praise the LORD
  both now and forever!

Praise the LORD!

PSALM 116

1 I love the LORD because he hears
  and answers my prayers.
2 Because he bends down and listens,
  I will pray as long as I have breath!
3 Death had its hands around my throat;
  the terrors of the grave* overtook me.
  I saw only trouble and sorrow.
4 Then I called on the name of the LORD:
  "Please, LORD, save me!"
5 How kind the LORD is! How good he is!
  So merciful, this God of ours!
6 The LORD protects those of childlike faith;
  I was facing death, and then he saved
    me.
7 Now I can rest again,
  for the LORD has been so good to me.
8 He has saved me from death,
  my eyes from tears,
  my feet from stumbling.
9 And so I walk in the LORD's presence
  as I live here on earth!
10 I believed in you, so I prayed,
  "I am deeply troubled, LORD."
11 In my anxiety I cried out to you,

114:7 Hebrew *of Jacob.* 116:3 Hebrew *of Sheol.*

My Daily Worship

— May 28 —

HE BENDS DOWN AND LISTENS

PSALMS 113:1–118:29

*I love the LORD because he hears and answers my prayers. Because he bends
down and listens, I will pray as long as I have breath! (116:1–2).*

[i reflect]

"She has been growing, but she is still just a little girl," the adults say, giving new meaning to the phrase "talking down to children." The girl is sad. Will they listen? They can barely hear her soft voice. "Besides," they say, "she's only a child."

Then God bends down and listens.

A young man has been running, stumbling, falling for years. Raised in a tough neighborhood, his so-called friends will not listen and enemies are deaf to his cries for mercy. Down in the dumps, down on his luck, down for the count.

Then God bends down and listens.

She is old now, and sick. The medical staff bustles in and out, dispensing pleasantries with the pills. Stopping neither to wait for the answer to their near-rhetorical questions nor to hear the questions she has. Besides, not a good idea to get "too close" to the dying.

Then God bends down and listens.

Any of the three could have written Psalm 116, because God bends down and listens. To the small, the beaten down, the weak, he hears and answers their prayers. Saving from death (verses 3,6), honoring childlike faith (verse 6), lifting those who stumble (verse 8), comforting the dying (verse 15). Bending down to you, giving you reason to pray as long as you have breath.

In *The Screwtape Letters* by C. S. Lewis, a senior devil laments God's view of prayer: "Whenever there is prayer, there is danger of His own immediate action. He is cynically indifferent to the dignity of His position, and ours, as pure spirits, and to human animals on their knees. He pours out self-knowledge in a quite shameless fashion."

Pray now, pray always to the One who is "indifferent to the dignity of his position," who bends down and listens and answers. Then, in thankfulness to answered prayer, worship him.

[i pray]

O God, I thank you for hearing and answering my prayers. You have saved me a thousand times over, for you first bend down and listen. Help me to pray now and always.

[i respond]

Think over the events of the past week. Write down the times you have stumbled or been low and God has bent down and listened to your prayers. Praise him for his answers.

"These people are all liars!"

12 What can I offer the LORD
    for all he has done for me?
13 I will lift up a cup symbolizing his
        salvation;
    I will praise the LORD's name for
        saving me.
14 I will keep my promises to the LORD
    in the presence of all his people.

15 The LORD's loved ones are precious
        to him;
    it grieves him when they die.
16 O LORD, I am your servant;
    yes, I am your servant, the son of your
        handmaid,
    and you have freed me from my
        bonds!
17 I will offer you a sacrifice of thanksgiving
    and call on the name of the LORD.
18 I will keep my promises to the LORD
    in the presence of all his people,
19 in the house of the LORD,
    in the heart of Jerusalem.

Praise the LORD!

PSALM 117
1 Praise the LORD, all you nations.
    Praise him, all you people of the earth.
2 For he loves us with unfailing love;
    the faithfulness of the LORD endures
        forever.

Praise the LORD!

PSALM 118
1 Give thanks to the LORD, for he is good!
    His faithful love endures forever.

2 Let the congregation of Israel repeat:
    "His faithful love endures forever."
3 Let Aaron's descendants, the priests,
        repeat:
    "His faithful love endures forever."
4 Let all who fear the LORD repeat:
    "His faithful love endures forever."

5 In my distress I prayed to the LORD,
    and the LORD answered me and
        rescued me.
6 The LORD is for me, so I will not be afraid.
    What can mere mortals do to me?
7 Yes, the LORD is for me; he will help me.
    I will look in triumph at those who
        hate me.
8 It is better to trust the LORD
    than to put confidence in people.
9 It is better to trust the LORD
    than to put confidence in princes.
10 Though hostile nations surrounded me,
    I destroyed them all in the name of the
        LORD.
11 Yes, they surrounded and attacked me,
    but I destroyed them all in the name of
        the LORD.
12 They swarmed around me like bees;
    they blazed against me like a roaring
        flame.
    But I destroyed them all in the name of
        the LORD.
13 You did your best to kill me, O my enemy,
    but the LORD helped me.
14 The LORD is my strength and my song;
    he has become my victory.
15 Songs of joy and victory are sung in the
        camp of the godly.
    The strong right arm of the LORD has
        done glorious things!
16 The strong right arm of the LORD is raised
        in triumph.
    The strong right arm of the LORD has
        done glorious things!
17 I will not die, but I will live
    to tell what the LORD has done.
18 The LORD has punished me severely,
    but he has not handed me over to death.

19 Open for me the gates where the righteous
        enter,
    and I will go in and thank the LORD.
20 Those gates lead to the presence of the
        LORD,
    and the godly enter there.

²¹ I thank you for answering my prayer
   and saving me!

²² The stone rejected by the builders
   has now become the cornerstone.
²³ This is the LORD's doing,
   and it is marvelous to see.
²⁴ This is the day the LORD has made.
   We will rejoice and be glad in it.
²⁵ Please, LORD, please save us.
   Please, LORD, please give us success.
²⁶ Bless the one who comes in the name of
   the LORD.
   We bless you from the house of the LORD.
²⁷ The LORD is God, shining upon us.
   Bring forward the sacrifice and put it on
   the altar.
²⁸ You are my God, and I will praise you!
   You are my God, and I will exalt you!

²⁹ Give thanks to the LORD, for he is good!
   His faithful love endures forever.

PSALM 119

¹ Happy are people of integrity,
   who follow the law of the LORD.
² Happy are those who obey his decrees
   and search for him with all their hearts.
³ They do not compromise with evil,
   and they walk only in his paths.
⁴ You have charged us
   to keep your commandments carefully.
⁵ Oh, that my actions would consistently
   reflect your principles!
⁶ Then I will not be disgraced
   when I compare my life with your
   commands.
⁷ When I learn your righteous laws,
   I will thank you by living as I should!
⁸ I will obey your principles.
   Please don't give up on me!

⁹ How can a young person stay pure?
   By obeying your word and following its
   rules.

¹⁰ I have tried my best to find you—
   don't let me wander from your
   commands.
¹¹ I have hidden your word in my heart,
   that I might not sin against you.
¹² Blessed are you, O LORD;
   teach me your principles.
¹³ I have recited aloud
   all the laws you have given us.
¹⁴ I have rejoiced in your decrees
   as much as in riches.
¹⁵ I will study your commandments
   and reflect on your ways.
¹⁶ I will delight in your principles
   and not forget your word.

¹⁷ Be good to your servant,
   that I may live and obey your word.
¹⁸ Open my eyes to see
   the wonderful truths in your law.
¹⁹ I am but a foreigner here on earth;
   I need the guidance of your commands.
   Don't hide them from me!
²⁰ I am overwhelmed continually
   with a desire for your laws.
²¹ You rebuke those cursed proud ones
   who wander from your commands.
²² Don't let them scorn and insult me,
   for I have obeyed your decrees.
²³ Even princes sit and speak against me,
   but I will meditate on your principles.
²⁴ Your decrees please me;
   they give me wise advice.

²⁵ I lie in the dust, completely discouraged;
   revive me by your word.
²⁶ I told you my plans, and you answered.
   Now teach me your principles.
²⁷ Help me understand the meaning of your
   commandments,
   and I will meditate on your wonderful
   miracles.
²⁸ I weep with grief;
   encourage me by your word.
²⁹ Keep me from lying to myself;

119 This psalm is a Hebrew acrostic poem; there are 22 stanzas, one for each letter of the Hebrew alphabet. The 8 verses within each stanza begin with the Hebrew letter of its section.

give me the privilege of knowing
your law.
³⁰ I have chosen to be faithful;
I have determined to live by your laws.
³¹ I cling to your decrees.
LORD, don't let me be put to shame!
³² If you will help me,
I will run to follow your commands.

³³ Teach me, O LORD,
to follow every one of your principles.
³⁴ Give me understanding and I will obey
your law;
I will put it into practice with all my
heart.
³⁵ Make me walk along the path of your
commands,
for that is where my happiness is found.
³⁶ Give me an eagerness for your decrees;
do not inflict me with love for money!
³⁷ Turn my eyes from worthless things,
and give me life through your word.*
³⁸ Reassure me of your promise,
which is for those who honor you.
³⁹ Help me abandon my shameful ways;
your laws are all I want in life.
⁴⁰ I long to obey your commandments!
Renew my life with your goodness.

⁴¹ LORD, give to me your unfailing love,
the salvation that you promised me.
⁴² Then I will have an answer for those who
taunt me,
for I trust in your word.
⁴³ Do not snatch your word of truth from
me,
for my only hope is in your laws.
⁴⁴ I will keep on obeying your law
forever and forever.
⁴⁵ I will walk in freedom,
for I have devoted myself to your
commandments.
⁴⁶ I will speak to kings about your decrees,
and I will not be ashamed.
⁴⁷ How I delight in your commands!
How I love them!

⁴⁸ I honor and love your commands.
I meditate on your principles.

⁴⁹ Remember your promise to me,
for it is my only hope.
⁵⁰ Your promise revives me;
it comforts me in all my troubles.
⁵¹ The proud hold me in utter contempt,
but I do not turn away from your law.
⁵² I meditate on your age-old laws;
O LORD, they comfort me.
⁵³ I am furious with the wicked,
those who reject your law.
⁵⁴ Your principles have been the music of my
life
throughout the years of my pilgrimage.
⁵⁵ I reflect at night on who you are, O LORD,
and I obey your law because of this.
⁵⁶ This is my happy way of life:
obeying your commandments.

⁵⁷ LORD, you are mine!
I promise to obey your words!
⁵⁸ With all my heart I want your blessings.
Be merciful just as you promised.
⁵⁹ I pondered the direction of my life,
and I turned to follow your statutes.
⁶⁰ I will hurry, without lingering,
to obey your commands.
⁶¹ Evil people try to drag me into sin,
but I am firmly anchored to your law.
⁶² At midnight I rise to thank you
for your just laws.
⁶³ Anyone who fears you is my friend—
anyone who obeys your
commandments.
⁶⁴ O LORD, the earth is full of your unfailing
love;
teach me your principles.

⁶⁵ You have done many good things for me,
LORD,
just as you promised.
⁶⁶ I believe in your commands;
now teach me good judgment and
knowledge.

119:37 Some manuscripts read *in your ways.*

My Daily Worship
— *May 29* —

THE WORD ON THE WORD
PSALM 119:1–88

I have tried my best to find you—don't let me wander from your commands.
I have hidden your word in my heart, that I might not sin against you (119:10–11).

[i reflect]

The facts to stack up about Psalm 119 are fascinating, the stuff to win party games—or at least impress the other guests.

- Longest psalm (176 verses)
- Longest chapter of the entire Bible
- An acrostic poem of twenty-two stanzas (one for each letter of the Hebrew alphabet), with the eight verses of each stanza starting with the Hebrew letter of that section
- Near the exact midpoint of many Bibles
- A remarkable array of terms for the Scriptures—laws, decrees, commandments, principles, word, statutes, commands

These facts may be fascinating, but following the Word of God is not a trivial pursuit. The psalmist was inspired to write Scripture about the Scriptures—the word on the Word—not to add to his credentials as an author. He was making a commitment to God himself and urging others to do the same. Wandering from these commands? You are wandering from God. Hiding this Word in your heart? You are hiding God himself there.

The contemporary Christian singer Sara Groves has written a song entitled "The Word," to express the vital connection we can have with God through the Scriptures. As the psalm writer realizes that the only way not to sin is to hide the Word in his heart, Groves recognizes that she has tried to help herself while her Bible sits upon the shelf. She delights that the Word was, and the Word is, and the Word will be.

We can bless and praise our God by learning his principles. We can live a life that sings God's Word. Recommit today to hide God's Word in your heart. Then celebrate the Word!

[i pray]

Thank you, O Lord, for your Word and for the life you have breathed into it.
I praise you for giving me the means to live a holy life.

[i respond]

Memorize Psalm 119:1–2, hiding it in your heart: "Happy are people of integrity, who follow the law of the LORD. Happy are those who obey his decrees and search for him with all their hearts."

67 I used to wander off until you disciplined
      me;
   but now I closely follow your word.
68 You are good and do only good;
   teach me your principles.
69 Arrogant people have made up lies about
      me,
   but in truth I obey your commandments
      with all my heart.
70 Their hearts are dull and stupid,
   but I delight in your law.
71 The suffering you sent was good for me,
   for it taught me to pay attention to your
      principles.
72 Your law is more valuable to me
   than millions in gold and silver!

73 You made me; you created me.
   Now give me the sense to follow your
      commands.
74 May all who fear you find in me a cause
      for joy,
   for I have put my hope in your word.
75 I know, O LORD, that your decisions are
      fair;
   you disciplined me because I needed it.
76 Now let your unfailing love comfort me,
   just as you promised me, your servant.
77 Surround me with your tender mercies so
      I may live,
   for your law is my delight.
78 Bring disgrace upon the arrogant people
      who lied about me;
   meanwhile, I will concentrate on your
      commandments.
79 Let me be reconciled
   with all who fear you and know your
      decrees.
80 May I be blameless in keeping your
      principles;
   then I will never have to be ashamed.

81 I faint with longing for your salvation;
   but I have put my hope in your word.
82 My eyes are straining to see your promises
      come true.
   When will you comfort me?

83 I am shriveled like a wineskin in the
      smoke, exhausted with waiting.
   But I cling to your principles and obey
      them.
84 How long must I wait?
   When will you punish those who
      persecute me?
85 These arrogant people who hate your law
   have dug deep pits for me to fall into.
86 All your commands are trustworthy.
   Protect me from those who hunt me
      down without cause.
87 They almost finished me off,
   but I refused to abandon your
      commandments.
88 In your unfailing love, spare my life;
   then I can continue to obey your
      decrees.

89 Forever, O LORD,
   your word stands firm in heaven.
90 Your faithfulness extends to every
      generation,
   as enduring as the earth you created.
91 Your laws remain true today,
   for everything serves your plans.
92 If your law hadn't sustained me with joy,
   I would have died in my misery.
93 I will never forget your commandments,
   for you have used them to restore my joy
      and health.
94 I am yours; save me!
   For I have applied myself to obey your
      commandments.
95 Though the wicked hide along the way to
      kill me,
   I will quietly keep my mind on your
      decrees.
96 Even perfection has its limits,
   but your commands have no limit.

97 Oh, how I love your law!
   I think about it all day long.
98 Your commands make me wiser than my
      enemies,
   for your commands are my constant
      guide.

My Daily Worship

— *May 30* —

SHINING IN THE DARKNESS

PSALMS 119:89–176

Your word is a lamp for my feet and a light for my path (119:105).

[i reflect]

Food. Clothing. Shelter. Warmth. The basics of life, the minimum to survive. But without another key resource, we are immobilized, too frightened to move. Light is what we need. Light, the first "Let there be" command that God spoke.

The psalm writer yearned for the light that is God's Word. Not a cozy fixture in the corner, God as interior designer. No, he needed a lamp for the feet, a light for the path. He had suffered, he had had sorrows, and his experience told him that only God's illumination would help (verses 107, 153).

The path, God's path, was dangerous. The wicked had set traps (verse 110), evils waited to take advantage of any misstep (verse 133). Even without these foes, darkness meant stumbling (verse 165) or even stubbornly wandering off the path (verse 176). "Please, God, give me the light of your lamp—your Word," the psalmist pleads, "that I may walk the straight and narrow."

The strength of the light intensifies through time, as Peter testifies to the early church. "We have even greater confidence in the message proclaimed by the prophets. Pay close attention to what they wrote, for their words are like a light shining in a dark place—until the day Christ appears and his brilliant light shines in your hearts" (2 Peter 1:19).

The psalm writer had the law. The early New Testament Christians had the law, the histories, the prophecies, and the Psalms. We have all this, plus the illumination of the New Testament books. But we also have the greatest light, the Word that became human, the Light who "gives light to everyone. The light shines through the darkness, and the darkness can never extinguish it" (John 1:4–5).

Walk the path of prayer and praise, guided by the light of God's Word. Ask God to illumine your way throughout the day. Thank him for his guidance.

[i pray]

O God, thank you for the lamp of your Word. Give me the will to use the light to see the dangers and to keep a sure footing, that I may walk your path in obedience.

[i respond]

Imagine yourself walking on a path called "The Next Few Days," or even, "The Next Few Hours." What are the dangers, possible missteps, and wrong turns looming ahead? Review the passage above and underline the verses that may help guide your steps today.

⁹⁹ Yes, I have more insight than my teachers,
  for I am always thinking of your decrees.
¹⁰⁰ I am even wiser than my elders,
  for I have kept your commandments.
¹⁰¹ I have refused to walk on any path of evil,
  that I may remain obedient to your
    word.
¹⁰² I haven't turned away from your laws,
  for you have taught me well.
¹⁰³ How sweet are your words to my taste;
  they are sweeter than honey.
¹⁰⁴ Your commandments give me
    understanding;
  no wonder I hate every false way of life.

¹⁰⁵ Your word is a lamp for my feet
  and a light for my path.
¹⁰⁶ I've promised it once, and I'll promise
    again:
  I will obey your wonderful laws.
¹⁰⁷ I have suffered much, O LORD;
  restore my life again, just as you
    promised.
¹⁰⁸ LORD, accept my grateful thanks
  and teach me your laws.
¹⁰⁹ My life constantly hangs in the balance,
  but I will not stop obeying your law.
¹¹⁰ The wicked have set their traps for me
    along your path,
  but I will not turn from your
    commandments.
¹¹¹ Your decrees are my treasure;
  they are truly my heart's delight.
¹¹² I am determined to keep your principles,
  even forever, to the very end.

¹¹³ I hate those who are undecided about you,
  but my choice is clear—I love your law.
¹¹⁴ You are my refuge and my shield;
  your word is my only source of hope.
¹¹⁵ Get out of my life, you evil-minded
    people,
  for I intend to obey the commands of
    my God.
¹¹⁶ LORD, sustain me as you promised, that I
    may live!
  Do not let my hope be crushed.

¹¹⁷ Sustain me, and I will be saved;
  then I will meditate on your principles
    continually.
¹¹⁸ But you have rejected all who stray from
    your principles.
  They are only fooling themselves.
¹¹⁹ All the wicked of the earth are the scum
    you skim off;
  no wonder I love to obey your decrees!
¹²⁰ I tremble in fear of you;
  I fear your judgments.

¹²¹ Don't leave me to the mercy of my
    enemies,
  for I have done what is just and right.
¹²² Please guarantee a blessing for me.
  Don't let those who are arrogant oppress
    me!
¹²³ My eyes strain to see your deliverance,
  to see the truth of your promise fulfilled.
¹²⁴ I am your servant;
  deal with me in unfailing love,
  and teach me your principles.
¹²⁵ Give discernment to me, your servant;
  then I will understand your decrees.
¹²⁶ LORD, it is time for you to act,
  for these evil people have broken your
    law.
¹²⁷ Truly, I love your commands
  more than gold, even the finest gold.
¹²⁸ Truly, each of your commandments is
    right.
  That is why I hate every false way.

¹²⁹ Your decrees are wonderful.
  No wonder I obey them!
¹³⁰ As your words are taught, they give light;
  even the simple can understand them.
¹³¹ I open my mouth, panting expectantly,
  longing for your commands.
¹³² Come and show me your mercy,
  as you do for all who love your name.
¹³³ Guide my steps by your word,
  so I will not be overcome by any evil.
¹³⁴ Rescue me from the oppression of evil
    people;
  then I can obey your commandments.

[135] Look down on me with love;
    teach me all your principles.
[136] Rivers of tears gush from my eyes
    because people disobey your law.

[137] O LORD, you are righteous,
    and your decisions are fair.
[138] Your decrees are perfect;
    they are entirely worthy of our trust.
[139] I am overwhelmed with rage,
    for my enemies have disregarded your
        words.
[140] Your promises have been thoroughly
        tested;
    that is why I love them so much.
[141] I am insignificant and despised,
    but I don't forget your commandments.
[142] Your justice is eternal,
    and your law is perfectly true.
[143] As pressure and stress bear down on me,
    I find joy in your commands.
[144] Your decrees are always fair;
    help me to understand them, that I may
        live.

[145] I pray with all my heart; answer me, LORD!
    I will obey your principles.
[146] I cry out to you; save me,
    that I may obey your decrees.
[147] I rise early, before the sun is up;
    I cry out for help and put my hope in
        your words.
[148] I stay awake through the night,
    thinking about your promise.
[149] In your faithful love, O LORD, hear my cry;
    in your justice, save my life.
[150] Those lawless people are coming near to
        attack me;
    they live far from your law.
[151] But you are near, O LORD,
    and all your commands are true.
[152] I have known from my earliest days
    that your decrees never change.

[153] Look down upon my sorrows and rescue
        me,
    for I have not forgotten your law.

[154] Argue my case; take my side!
    Protect my life as you promised.
[155] The wicked are far from salvation,
    for they do not bother with your
        principles.
[156] LORD, how great is your mercy;
    in your justice, give me back my life.
[157] Many persecute and trouble me,
    yet I have not swerved from your
        decrees.
[158] I hate these traitors
    because they care nothing for your
        word.
[159] See how I love your commandments,
        LORD.
    Give back my life because of your
        unfailing love.
[160] All your words are true;
    all your just laws will stand forever.

[161] Powerful people harass me without cause,
    but my heart trembles only at your
        word.
[162] I rejoice in your word
    like one who finds a great treasure.
[163] I hate and abhor all falsehood,
    but I love your law.
[164] I will praise you seven times a day
    because all your laws are just.
[165] Those who love your law have great
        peace
    and do not stumble.
[166] I long for your salvation, LORD,
    so I have obeyed your commands.
[167] I have obeyed your decrees,
    and I love them very much.
[168] Yes, I obey your commandments and
        decrees,
    because you know everything I do.

[169] O LORD, listen to my cry;
    give me the discerning mind you
        promised.
[170] Listen to my prayer;
    rescue me as you promised.
[171] Let my lips burst forth with praise,
    for you have taught me your principles.

172 Let my tongue sing about your word,
    for all your commands are right.
173 Stand ready to help me,
    for I have chosen to follow your
      commandments.
174 O Lord, I have longed for your salvation,
    and your law is my delight.
175 Let me live so I can praise you,
    and may your laws sustain me.
176 I have wandered away like a lost sheep;
    come and find me,
    for I have not forgotten your commands.

PSALM 120

A song for the ascent to Jerusalem.

1 I took my troubles to the Lord;
    I cried out to him, and he answered my
      prayer.
2 Rescue me, O Lord, from liars
    and from all deceitful people.
3 O deceptive tongue, what will God do to
    you?
    How will he increase your punishment?
4 You will be pierced with sharp arrows
    and burned with glowing coals.

5 How I suffer among these scoundrels of
    Meshech!
    It pains me to live with these people
      from Kedar!
6 I am tired of living here
    among people who hate peace.
7 As for me, I am for peace;
    but when I speak, they are for war!

PSALM 121

A song for the ascent to Jerusalem.

1 I look up to the mountains—
    does my help come from there?
2 My help comes from the Lord,
    who made the heavens and the earth!

3 He will not let you stumble and fall;
    the one who watches over you will not
      sleep.

4 Indeed, he who watches over Israel
    never tires and never sleeps.

5 The Lord himself watches over you!
    The Lord stands beside you as your
      protective shade.
6 The sun will not hurt you by day,
    nor the moon at night.
7 The Lord keeps you from all evil
    and preserves your life.
8 The Lord keeps watch over you as you
    come and go,
    both now and forever.

PSALM 122

*A song for the ascent to Jerusalem. A psalm
of David.*

1 I was glad when they said to me,
    "Let us go to the house of the Lord."
2 And now we are standing here
    inside your gates, O Jerusalem.
3 Jerusalem is a well-built city,
    knit together as a single unit.
4 All the people of Israel—the Lord's
      people—
    make their pilgrimage here.
    They come to give thanks to the name of
      the Lord
    as the law requires.
5 Here stand the thrones where judgment is
      given,
    the thrones of the dynasty of David.

6 Pray for the peace of Jerusalem.
    May all who love this city prosper.
7 O Jerusalem, may there be peace within
      your walls
    and prosperity in your palaces.
8 For the sake of my family and friends, I
      will say,
    "Peace be with you."
9 For the sake of the house of the Lord our
      God,
    I will seek what is best for you,
      O Jerusalem.

My Daily Worship
— May 31 —

MY HELP-LINE
PSALMS 120:1—126:6

I look up to the mountains—does my help come from there? (121:1).

[i reflect]

Flying into Portland or Seattle can be exhilarating. The ocean and mountain views in the Pacific Northwest are tremendous (when it's not raining!). Most beautiful are the conical volcanic mountains, with names like Adams, Hood, Rainier, and Baker, as they raise their massive, snowcapped peaks to the sky, sentinels of the coastlands.

One other mountain also stood sentinel in these high peaks. But in May 1980, in a spectacular and deadly display, Mount St. Helens blew its top. Thirteen hundred feet shorter than it used to be, Mount St. Helens today looks like a cone of sand that a child heaped up on the beach and then petulantly swatted with his hand. In this world of flux, even our grandest mountains are subject to change.

That's a lesson worth recalling when we're inclined to trust too much in any sort of worldly security. Great fortunes have been lost. Faithful allies have betrayed. Carefully guarded health has faltered. Knowledge, credentials, position—all have proved inadequate in the test. Even the earth itself, we're prewarned, will one day be swallowed up in fire (2 Peter 3:7).

Where, then, can we find real security during our times of need? It's a mark of wisdom to be able to say from the heart, "My help comes from the LORD, who made the heavens and the earth!" (121:2). This is a mark, too, of knowing what to value, whom to adore. That worship is righteous which has as its object the only One who is worthy. Let us cling in all ways to this caring Father and be safe.

As you go through the day, use the times when you find yourself needing help as a reason to turn to God.

[i pray]

You alone, my God, are my help-line. You alone never change and are worthy of trust.

[i respond]

Abraham Heschel said, "To worship is to rise to a higher level of existence, to see the world from the point of view of God." Write down three challenges, tasks, or situations you are facing today. Next, write down beside each situation the way that God might view them.

PSALM 123

A song for the ascent to Jerusalem.

1 I lift my eyes to you,
    O God, enthroned in heaven.
2 We look to the LORD our God for his mercy,
    just as servants keep their eyes on their
        master,
    as a slave girl watches her mistress for
        the slightest signal.

3 Have mercy on us, LORD, have mercy,
    for we have had our fill of contempt.
4 We have had our fill of the scoffing of the
        proud
    and the contempt of the arrogant.

PSALM 124

*A song for the ascent to Jerusalem. A psalm
of David.*

1 If the LORD had not been on our side—
    let Israel now say—
2 if the LORD had not been on our side
    when people rose up against us,
3 they would have swallowed us alive
    because of their burning anger against us.
4 The waters would have engulfed us;
    a torrent would have overwhelmed us.
5 Yes, the raging waters of their fury
    would have overwhelmed our very lives.

6 Blessed be the LORD,
    who did not let their teeth tear us apart!
7 We escaped like a bird from a hunter's
        trap.
    The trap is broken, and we are free!
8 Our help is from the LORD,
    who made the heavens and the earth.

PSALM 125

A song for the ascent to Jerusalem.

1 Those who trust in the LORD are as secure
    as Mount Zion;

they will not be defeated but will endure
    forever.
2 Just as the mountains surround and
        protect Jerusalem,
    so the LORD surrounds and protects his
        people, both now and forever.
3 The wicked will not rule the godly,
    for then the godly might be forced to do
        wrong.
4 O LORD, do good to those who are good,
    whose hearts are in tune with you.
5 But banish those who turn to crooked
        ways, O LORD.
    Take them away with those who do evil.
    And let Israel have quietness and peace.

PSALM 126

A song for the ascent to Jerusalem.

1 When the LORD restored his exiles to
        Jerusalem,*
    it was like a dream!
2 We were filled with laughter,
    and we sang for joy.
    And the other nations said,
    "What amazing things the LORD has
        done for them."
3 Yes, the LORD has done amazing things for
        us!
    What joy!

4 Restore our fortunes, LORD,
    as streams renew the desert.
5 Those who plant in tears
    will harvest with shouts of joy.
6 They weep as they go to plant their seed,
    but they sing as they return with the
        harvest.

PSALM 127

*A song for the ascent to Jerusalem. A psalm of
Solomon.*

1 Unless the LORD builds a house,
    the work of the builders is useless.

126:1 Hebrew *Zion.*

THE CONTRACTOR AND THE CREW

PSALMS 127:1–130:8

Unless the LORD builds a house, the work of the builders is useless (127:1).

[i reflect]

Solomon, the author of this psalm, knew a little something about building houses. After all, he had built one for the Lord.

No doubt Solomon had heard many times how his father, King David, desired to build a spectacular house for the Lord. God sent the prophet Nathan to the king with a message, essentially saying, "No, you will not build a house (Temple) for me, but I will build a house (dynasty) for you" (2 Samuel 7:11–16). David had to be content with knowing his son would fulfill David's construction dreams.

We can labor all we want at projects that seem desirable or meritorious to us, but if they are not in accordance with God's will, our efforts are in vain. Want to be a leader of the masses? It's no good if God gave you an artist's soul. Dream of a ministry that would be dangerous and all-consuming? Not while you're raising those little children God gave you.

We may get huffy sometimes at what seems God's stubborn insistence on his own way. But we're better off in every sense if we'll fall in with the will of God instead of trying to get him to fall in with ours. We'll be more productive and more satisfied if we'll accept God as the general contractor and take our place—and an honored place it is—as a carpenter on his crew.

"I want what God wants," declared Francis of Assisi. "That's why I am so merry."

What are your plans for today? What about the next year, or even five years? Ask God to be the builder of your plans both for today and the future. Thank him today for making you part of his crew.

[i pray]

In my little time on this planet, Lord, I want my work to matter.
Show me the right nail to strike.

[i respond]

Get a hammer (or another tool) from a toolbox. While you're holding it, think about any effort you have been putting out lately without seeming to make much headway. Does God want you to persevere at it (definitely a possibility), or does he want you to drop it and work on something else? In a time of private worship, rededicate yourself to seeking and doing God's will.

Unless the LORD protects a city,
  guarding it with sentries will do no
    good.
2 It is useless for you to work so hard
  from early morning until late at night,
anxiously working for food to eat;
  for God gives rest to his loved ones.

3 Children are a gift from the LORD;
  they are a reward from him.
4 Children born to a young man
  are like sharp arrows in a warrior's
    hands.
5 How happy is the man whose quiver is full
    of them!
  He will not be put to shame when he
    confronts his accusers at the city
    gates.

PSALM 128

A song for the ascent to Jerusalem.

1 How happy are those who fear the
    LORD—
  all who follow his ways!
2 You will enjoy the fruit of your labor.
  How happy you will be! How rich your
    life!
3 Your wife will be like a fruitful vine,
  flourishing within your home.
And look at all those children!
  There they sit around your table
  as vigorous and healthy as young olive
    trees.
4 That is the LORD's reward
  for those who fear him.

5 May the LORD continually bless you from
    Zion.
  May you see Jerusalem prosper as long
    as you live.
6 May you live to enjoy your
    grandchildren.
  And may Israel have quietness and
    peace.

129:5 Hebrew *Zion.*

PSALM 129

A song for the ascent to Jerusalem.

1 From my earliest youth my enemies have
    persecuted me—
  let Israel now say—
2 from my earliest youth my enemies have
    persecuted me,
  but they have never been able to finish
    me off.
3 My back is covered with cuts,
  as if a farmer had plowed long
    furrows.
4 But the LORD is good;
  he has cut the cords used by the ungodly
    to bind me.
5 May all who hate Jerusalem*
  be turned back in shameful defeat.
6 May they be as useless as grass on a
    rooftop,
  turning yellow when only half grown,
7 ignored by the harvester,
  despised by the binder.
8 And may those who pass by refuse to give
    them this blessing:
  "The LORD's blessings be upon you;
  we bless you in the LORD's name."

PSALM 130

A song for the ascent to Jerusalem.

1 From the depths of despair, O LORD,
  I call for your help.
2 Hear my cry, O Lord.
  Pay attention to my prayer.

3 LORD, if you kept a record of our sins,
  who, O Lord, could ever survive?
4 But you offer forgiveness,
  that we might learn to fear you.

5 I am counting on the LORD;
  yes, I am counting on him.
  I have put my hope in his word.

⁶ I long for the Lord
　　more than sentries long for the dawn,
　　yes, more than sentries long for the dawn.

⁷ O Israel, hope in the LORD;
　　for with the LORD there is unfailing love
　　and an overflowing supply of salvation.
⁸ He himself will free Israel
　　from every kind of sin.

PSALM 131

A song for the ascent to Jerusalem. A psalm of David.

¹ LORD, my heart is not proud;
　　my eyes are not haughty.
　I don't concern myself with matters too
　　　great
　　or awesome for me.
² But I have stilled and quieted myself,
　　just as a small child is quiet with its
　　　mother.
　　Yes, like a small child is my soul
　　　within me.

³ O Israel, put your hope in the LORD—
　　now and always.

PSALM 132

A song for the ascent to Jerusalem.

¹ LORD, remember David
　　and all that he suffered.
² He took an oath before the LORD.
　　He vowed to the Mighty One of Israel,*
³ "I will not go home;
　　I will not let myself rest.
⁴ I will not let my eyes sleep
　　nor close my eyelids in slumber
⁵ 　until I find a place to build a house for
　　　the LORD,
　　a sanctuary for the Mighty One of
　　　Israel."
⁶ We heard that the Ark was in Ephrathah;
　　then we found it in the distant
　　　countryside of Jaar.

⁷ Let us go to the dwelling place of the
　　LORD;
　　let us bow low before him.
⁸ Arise, O LORD, and enter your sanctuary,
　　along with the Ark, the symbol of your
　　　power.
⁹ Your priests will be agents of salvation;
　　may your loyal servants sing for joy.

¹⁰ For the sake of your servant David,
　　do not reject the king you chose for your
　　　people.
¹¹ The LORD swore to David
　　a promise he will never take back:
　"I will place one of your descendants on
　　your throne.
¹² If your descendants obey the terms of my
　　covenant
　　and follow the decrees that I teach
　　　them,
　then your royal line will never end."

¹³ For the LORD has chosen Jerusalem*;
　　he has desired it as his home.
¹⁴ "This is my home where I will live forever,"
　　he said.
　　"I will live here, for this is the place I
　　　desired.
¹⁵ I will make this city prosperous
　　and satisfy its poor with food.
¹⁶ I will make its priests the agents of
　　　salvation;
　　its godly people will sing for joy.
¹⁷ Here I will increase the power of David;
　　my anointed one will be a light for my
　　　people.
¹⁸ I will clothe his enemies with shame,
　　but he will be a glorious king."

PSALM 133

A song for the ascent to Jerusalem. A psalm of David.

¹ How wonderful it is, how pleasant,
　　when brothers live together in harmony!

132:2 Hebrew *of Jacob; also in 132:5.* 132:13 Hebrew *Zion.*

2 For harmony is as precious as the fragrant
anointing oil
that was poured over Aaron's head,
that ran down his beard
and onto the border of his robe.
3 Harmony is as refreshing as the dew from
Mount Hermon
that falls on the mountains of Zion.
And the LORD has pronounced his
blessing,
even life forevermore.

PSALM 134

A song for the ascent to Jerusalem.

1 Oh, bless the LORD, all you servants of the
LORD,
you who serve as night watchmen in the
house of the LORD.
2 Lift your hands in holiness,
and bless the LORD.

3 May the LORD, who made heaven and
earth,
bless you from Jerusalem.*

PSALM 135

1 Praise the LORD!

Praise the name of the LORD!
Praise him, you who serve the LORD,
2 you who serve in the house of the LORD,
in the courts of the house of our God.
3 Praise the LORD, for the LORD is good;
celebrate his wonderful name with
music.
4 For the LORD has chosen Jacob for himself,
Israel for his own special treasure.

5 I know the greatness of the LORD—
that our Lord is greater than any other
god.
6 The LORD does whatever pleases him
throughout all heaven and earth,
and on the seas and in their depths.

7 He causes the clouds to rise over the
earth.
He sends the lightning with the rain
and releases the wind from his
storehouses.
8 He destroyed the firstborn in each
Egyptian home,
both people and animals.
9 He performed miraculous signs and
wonders in Egypt;
Pharaoh and all his people watched.
10 He struck down great nations
and slaughtered mighty kings—
11 Sihon king of the Amorites,
Og king of Bashan,
and all the kings of Canaan.
12 He gave their land as an inheritance,
a special possession to his people
Israel.
13 Your name, O LORD, endures forever;
your fame, O LORD, is known to every
generation.
14 For the LORD will vindicate his people
and have compassion on his servants.

15 Their idols are merely things of silver and
gold,
shaped by human hands.
16 They cannot talk, though they have
mouths,
or see, though they have eyes!
17 They cannot hear with their ears
or smell with their noses.
18 And those who make them are just like
them,
as are all who trust in them.

19 O Israel, praise the LORD!
O priests of Aaron, praise the LORD!
20 O Levites, praise the LORD!
All you who fear the LORD, praise the
LORD!
21 The LORD be praised from Zion,
for he lives here in Jerusalem.

Praise the LORD!

134:3 Hebrew *Zion.*

My Daily Worship

— *June 2* —

LIVING IN HARMONY

PSALMS 131:1–136:26

How wonderful it is, how pleasant, when brothers live together in harmony! (133:1).

[i reflect]

In this brief psalm, David writes of the joy of harmonious relationships and how precious a commodity unity is. It *is* wonderful when brothers (or sisters) live together in harmony, but unfortunately, it is also very rare.

Consider the disciples Jesus chose—the very ones you would suppose would live and work together. There was a tax collector (known as collaborators with the Roman overlords) and there was a Zealot (committed to overthrowing the Romans). There was a pair of brothers who maneuvered for the top spots of influence, angering all the others, who wanted those spots for themselves. There was a hothead who sometimes had a bold faith but often slipped up, and who, after calling Jesus the Christ, betrayed him. There was even a traitor who cared more about gold than God. And this was the nucleus of the early church!

It seems that not much has changed. The church we know today is an inspiring, infuriating, faithful, hypocritical, cooperative, divisive, generous, selfish, foolish, wise conglomeration of half-reformed sinners. The bride of Christ—can't live with her, can't live without her. That's us, folks!

Yet Christ loves his bride, and so we must learn to do the same. We have to work at getting along, facing squarely our own flaws and bearing with the flaws of others. Unity is worth the effort, however much it may not seem to be. A cord of three strands is not easily broken. Fellow rejoicers double the joy of the rejoicer; fellow weepers halve the sorrow of the weeper. As the psalmist wrote, how wonderful when brothers and sisters live in harmony!

One more thing: Unity makes worship powerful. "May God . . . help you live in complete harmony with each other—each with the attitude of Christ Jesus toward the other. Then all of you can join together with one voice, giving praise and glory to God" (Romans 15:5–6).

Is there someone at work, at church, in your neighborhood, or even within your household, with whom you are out of tune? Look today for ways to live "in complete harmony with each other."

[i pray]

I acknowledge, Lord, that not only others but I, too, am responsible for
the problems in the church. Let progress toward unity begin with me.

[i respond]

Think of that one person with whom you have been struggling. Write down that person's name and then pray specifically about the next encounter you will have with that person. Ask that God will give you the attitude of Christ toward him or her.

PSALM 136

1 Give thanks to the LORD, for he is good!
His faithful love endures forever.
2 Give thanks to the God of gods.
His faithful love endures forever.
3 Give thanks to the Lord of lords.
His faithful love endures forever.

4 Give thanks to him who alone does mighty
miracles.
His faithful love endures forever.
5 Give thanks to him who made the heavens
so skillfully.
His faithful love endures forever.
6 Give thanks to him who placed the earth
on the water.
His faithful love endures forever.
7 Give thanks to him who made the
heavenly lights—
His faithful love endures forever.
8 the sun to rule the day,
His faithful love endures forever.
9 and the moon and stars to rule the
night.
His faithful love endures forever.

10 Give thanks to him who killed the
firstborn of Egypt.
His faithful love endures forever.
11 He brought Israel out of Egypt.
His faithful love endures forever.
12 He acted with a strong hand and powerful
arm.
His faithful love endures forever.
13 Give thanks to him who parted the
Red Sea.*
His faithful love endures forever.
14 He led Israel safely through,
His faithful love endures forever.
15 but he hurled Pharaoh and his army
into the sea.
His faithful love endures forever.
16 Give thanks to him who led his people
through the wilderness.
His faithful love endures forever.

17 Give thanks to him who struck down
mighty kings.
His faithful love endures forever.
18 He killed powerful kings—
His faithful love endures forever.
19 Sihon king of the Amorites,
His faithful love endures forever.
20 and Og king of Bashan.
His faithful love endures forever.
21 God gave the land of these kings as an
inheritance—
His faithful love endures forever.
22 a special possession to his servant Israel.
His faithful love endures forever.

23 He remembered our utter weakness.
His faithful love endures forever.
24 He saved us from our enemies.
His faithful love endures forever.
25 He gives food to every living thing.
His faithful love endures forever.

26 Give thanks to the God of heaven.
His faithful love endures forever.

PSALM 137

1 Beside the rivers of Babylon, we sat and
wept
as we thought of Jerusalem.*
2 We put away our lyres,
hanging them on the branches of the
willow trees.
3 For there our captors demanded a song
of us.
Our tormentors requested a joyful
hymn:
"Sing us one of those songs of
Jerusalem!"
4 But how can we sing the songs of the
LORD
while in a foreign land?

5 If I forget you, O Jerusalem,
let my right hand forget its skill upon
the harp.

136:13 Hebrew *sea of reeds;* also in 136:15.   137:1 Hebrew *Zion;* also in 137:3.

⁶ May my tongue stick to the roof of my
mouth
if I fail to remember you,
if I don't make Jerusalem my highest joy.

⁷ O LORD, remember what the Edomites did
on the day the armies of Babylon
captured Jerusalem.
"Destroy it!" they yelled.
"Level it to the ground!"
⁸ O Babylon, you will be destroyed.
Happy is the one who pays you back
for what you have done to us.
⁹ Happy is the one who takes your babies
and smashes them against the rocks!

PSALM 138

A psalm of David.

¹ I give you thanks, O LORD, with all my
heart;
I will sing your praises before the gods.
² I bow before your holy Temple as I worship.
I will give thanks to your name
for your unfailing love and faithfulness,
because your promises are backed
by all the honor of your name.
³ When I pray, you answer me;
you encourage me by giving me the
strength I need.

⁴ Every king in all the earth will give you
thanks, O LORD,
for all of them will hear your words.
⁵ Yes, they will sing about the LORD's ways,
for the glory of the LORD is very great.
⁶ Though the LORD is great, he cares for the
humble,
but he keeps his distance from the
proud.

⁷ Though I am surrounded by troubles,
you will preserve me against the anger of
my enemies.
You will clench your fist against my angry
enemies!

139:8 Hebrew *to Sheol.*

Your power will save me.
⁸ The LORD will work out his plans for my
life—
for your faithful love, O LORD, endures
forever.
Don't abandon me, for you made me.

PSALM 139

For the choir director: A psalm of David.

¹ O LORD, you have examined my heart
and know everything about me.
² You know when I sit down or stand up.
You know my every thought when far
away.
³ You chart the path ahead of me
and tell me where to stop and rest.
Every moment you know where I am.
⁴ You know what I am going to say
even before I say it, LORD.
⁵ You both precede and follow me.
You place your hand of blessing on my
head.
⁶ Such knowledge is too wonderful for me,
too great for me to know!

⁷ I can never escape from your spirit!
I can never get away from your
presence!
⁸ If I go up to heaven, you are there;
if I go down to the place of the dead,*
you are there.
⁹ If I ride the wings of the morning,
if I dwell by the farthest oceans,
¹⁰ even there your hand will guide me,
and your strength will support me.
¹¹ I could ask the darkness to hide me
and the light around me to become
night—
¹² but even in darkness I cannot hide
from you.
To you the night shines as bright as day.
Darkness and light are both alike to you.

¹³ You made all the delicate, inner parts of
my body

and knit me together in my mother's
womb.
14 Thank you for making me so wonderfully
complex!
Your workmanship is marvelous—and
how well I know it.
15 You watched me as I was being formed in
utter seclusion,
as I was woven together in the dark of
the womb.
16 You saw me before I was born.
Every day of my life was recorded in
your book.
Every moment was laid out
before a single day had passed.

17 How precious are your thoughts about
me,* O God!
They are innumerable!
18 I can't even count them;
they outnumber the grains of sand!
And when I wake up in the morning,
you are still with me!

19 O God, if only you would destroy the
wicked!
Get out of my life, you murderers!
20 They blaspheme you;
your enemies take your name in vain.
21 O Lord, shouldn't I hate those who
hate you?
Shouldn't I despise those who resist you?
22 Yes, I hate them with complete hatred,
for your enemies are my enemies.

23 Search me, O God, and know my heart;
test me and know my thoughts.
24 Point out anything in me that offends you,
and lead me along the path of
everlasting life.

PSALM 140

For the choir director: A psalm of David.

1 O Lord, rescue me from evil people.
Preserve me from those who are violent,

2 those who plot evil in their hearts
and stir up trouble all day long.
3 Their tongues sting like a snake;
the poison of a viper drips from their
lips. *Interlude*

4 O Lord, keep me out of the hands of the
wicked.
Preserve me from those who are violent,
for they are plotting against me.
5 The proud have set a trap to catch me;
they have stretched out a net;
they have placed traps all along the way.
Interlude

6 I said to the Lord, "You are my God!"
Listen, O Lord, to my cries for mercy!
7 O Sovereign Lord, my strong savior,
you protected me on the day of battle.
8 Lord, do not give in to their evil desires.
Do not let their evil schemes succeed,
O God. *Interlude*

9 Let my enemies be destroyed
by the very evil they have planned for me.
10 Let burning coals fall down on their heads,
or throw them into the fire,
or into deep pits from which they can't
escape.
11 Don't let liars prosper here in our land.
Cause disaster to fall with great force on
the violent.

12 But I know the Lord will surely help those
they persecute;
he will maintain the rights of the poor.
13 Surely the godly are praising your name,
for they will live in your presence.

PSALM 141

A psalm of David.

1 O Lord, I am calling to you. Please hurry!
Listen when I cry to you for help!
2 Accept my prayer as incense offered to you,

139:17 Or *How precious to me are your thoughts.*

My Daily Worship

— June 3 —

FULL EXPOSURE

PSALMS 137:1–140:13

*O LORD, you have examined my heart and know everything about me. You know when
I sit down or stand up. You know my every thought when far away (139:1–2).*

[i reflect]

Virtually every culture on the planet prefers the use of clothing in public, even if it is only a string or some paint. Clothing, of course, has functional and symbolic values. But beyond that, we put on clothes before meeting others because of something deep in the human psyche—something related to the shame of exposure.

It was not so for our first Mom and Pop. They wandered around Eden Botanical Preserve gloriously unconcerned about the lack of mediation between their bodies and the world. Only when they became guilty of wrongdoing did God sew them some clothes. A connection was forged then between sin (a matter of the spirit) and shame over nakedness (a matter of the body), because human beings are unitary spiritual-physical creatures: soulbodies.

The psalm writer realized this truth when he wrote, "Every moment you know where I am. You know what I am going to say even before I say it, LORD. You both precede and follow me" (139:3–5). Nowhere, the psalmist acknowledged, could he go where God was not present. No thought could he think or say that God did not already know.

Likewise, we may pile on all the clothes we like, but we're still exposed 100 percent before God. This is not a pleasing thought when we're feeling guilty. We may even want to run away from God like the prophet Jonah did, but we'll find he's still stirring things up for us no matter how far away we sail. The omnipresence, omniscience, and omnipotence of God are not such welcome qualities when we know we're at fault.

But when we come to believe—really believe—that God has forgiven us through Christ, we can begin to grow comfortable with our heart exposure before him. The relationship becomes the spiritual counterpart of a marriage, which by design is the safe place within which to overcome one's scruples about nudity. We can stop messing around with fig leaves, and when God calls, "Where are you?" we can answer immediately, "Here I am, Lord!"

[i pray]

*Father, with some trepidation I welcome your intimate attention to my life, for I realize
you are a true Friend. When it comes to my naked moral state, you see me not
as the sinner I am, but clothed in the righteousness of your Son, Jesus.*

[i respond]

First Corinthians 13:12 says one day we will know fully, just as we are fully known. What is the effect of guilt feelings upon your worship—the chief part in the process of knowing and being known by God? Write a brief answer.

and my upraised hands as an evening
offering.

3 Take control of what I say, O LORD,
and keep my lips sealed.
4 Don't let me lust for evil things;
don't let me participate in acts of
wickedness.
Don't let me share in the delicacies
of those who do evil.

5 Let the godly strike me!
It will be a kindness!
If they reprove me, it is soothing medicine.
Don't let me refuse it.

But I am in constant prayer
against the wicked and their deeds.
6 When their leaders are thrown down from
a cliff,
they will listen to my words and find
them pleasing.
7 Even as a farmer breaks up the soil and
brings up rocks,
so the bones of the wicked will be
scattered without a decent burial.

8 I look to you for help, O Sovereign LORD.
You are my refuge; don't let them
kill me.
9 Keep me out of the traps they have set
for me,
out of the snares of those who do evil.
10 Let the wicked fall into their own snares,
but let me escape.

PSALM 142

*A psalm of David, regarding his experience in
the cave. A prayer.*

1 I cry out to the LORD;
I plead for the LORD's mercy.
2 I pour out my complaints before him
and tell him all my troubles.
3 For I am overwhelmed,
and you alone know the way I should
turn.

Wherever I go,
my enemies have set traps for me.
4 I look for someone to come and help me,
but no one gives me a passing thought!
No one will help me;
no one cares a bit what happens to me.
5 Then I pray to you, O LORD.
I say, "You are my place of refuge.
You are all I really want in life.
6 Hear my cry,
for I am very low.
Rescue me from my persecutors,
for they are too strong for me.
7 Bring me out of prison
so I can thank you.
The godly will crowd around me,
for you treat me kindly."

PSALM 143

A psalm of David.

1 Hear my prayer, O LORD;
listen to my plea!
Answer me because you are faithful and
righteous.
2 Don't bring your servant to trial!
Compared to you, no one is perfect.
3 My enemy has chased me.
He has knocked me to the ground.
He forces me to live in darkness like
those in the grave.
4 I am losing all hope;
I am paralyzed with fear.
5 I remember the days of old.
I ponder all your great works.
I think about what you have done.
6 I reach out for you.
I thirst for you as parched land thirsts
for rain.   *Interlude*

7 Come quickly, LORD, and answer me,
for my depression deepens.
Don't turn away from me,
or I will die.
8 Let me hear of your unfailing love to me in
the morning,
for I am trusting you.

My Daily Worship

— *June 4* —

CRUEL WORLD, KIND LORD

PSALMS 141:1–144:15

Come quickly, LORD, and answer me, for my depression deepens.
Don't turn away from me, or I will die (143:7).

[i reflect]

Even from a cursory reading of this psalm, David's state of mind is clear. David was losing hope, caught in a downward spiral of fear and depression. We can almost hear the anguish in his voice: "I am losing all hope; I am paralyzed with fear. . . . Come quickly, LORD, and answer me, for my depression deepens."

David was not alone. According to the National Institute of Mental Health, 9 to 10 percent of Americans suffer from clinical depression in a given year. Women suffer from depression at twice the rate of men. And none of this even takes into account lighter and more fleeting cases of sadness, or "the blues," which surely affects all but the most Pollyanna-ish among us.

The causes of depression are diverse. Thankfully, psychotherapy or medical treatments are able to blow away the dark clouds for most depression-sufferers in time. Yet undoubtedly many cases of depression have a spiritual component. It is entirely appropriate for depression-sufferers to seek the Lord for relief of their mental state and its causes, as David did when he was penned in by his enemies.

Everyone would like a life that goes from victory to victory, attended by peace, comfort, and laughter. But God sees fit to take us through times when we must do what we thought we were incapable of, when we lose what we thought we could never live without, or when we are forced to give up dreams we thought constituted our reason for being. All of this naturally registers on our emotions.

We must recognize that suffering is due directly or indirectly to human sin and not to any cruelty on the part of God. Even more important, we must recognize that God works with us in our struggles, deepening and maturing our faith and making us richer human beings. And what of the worship from those who are in the midst of, or have come through, a testing period? It reaches depths of meaning and authenticity that a Pollyanna could never know.

When depression hits, do as David did. Turn toward the Lord, not away from him. Reach out to him in prayer and worship, trusting that he will come quickly.

[i pray]

Whether or not I can see you through the dark clouds that surround me,
it is in you I place my hope, most kind Lord.

[i respond]

Choose one: (1) If you are currently in a period of depression, renew your commitment to seek the Lord for help. (2) If you know someone who is depressed, ask how you can support that person.

Show me where to walk,
for I have come to you in prayer.
⁹ Save me from my enemies, LORD;
I run to you to hide me.
¹⁰ Teach me to do your will,
for you are my God.
May your gracious Spirit lead me forward
on a firm footing.
¹¹ For the glory of your name, O LORD, save
me.
In your righteousness, bring me out of
this distress.
¹² In your unfailing love, cut off all my
enemies
and destroy all my foes,
for I am your servant.

PSALM 144

A psalm of David.

¹ Bless the LORD, who is my rock.
He gives me strength for war
and skill for battle.
² He is my loving ally and my fortress,
my tower of safety, my deliverer.
He stands before me as a shield, and I take
refuge in him.
He subdues the nations* under me.

³ O LORD, what are mortals that you should
notice us,
mere humans that you should care for us?
⁴ For we are like a breath of air;
our days are like a passing shadow.

⁵ Bend down the heavens, LORD, and come
down.
Touch the mountains so they billow
smoke.
⁶ Release your lightning bolts and scatter
your enemies!
Release your arrows and confuse them!
⁷ Reach down from heaven and
rescue me;
deliver me from deep waters,
from the power of my enemies.

⁸ Their mouths are full of lies;
they swear to tell the truth, but they lie.

⁹ I will sing a new song to you, O God!
I will sing your praises with a
ten-stringed harp.
¹⁰ For you grant victory to kings!
You are the one who rescued your
servant David.
¹¹ Save me from the fatal sword!
Rescue me from the power of my
enemies.
Their mouths are full of lies;
they swear to tell the truth, but they lie.

¹² May our sons flourish in their youth
like well-nurtured plants.
May our daughters be like graceful pillars,
carved to beautify a palace.
¹³ May our farms be filled
with crops of every kind.
May the flocks in our fields multiply by the
thousands,
even tens of thousands,
¹⁴ and may our oxen be loaded down with
produce.
May there be no breached walls, no forced
exile,
no cries of distress in our squares.
¹⁵ Yes, happy are those who have it like this!
Happy indeed are those whose God is
the LORD.

PSALM 145

A psalm of praise of David.

¹ I will praise you, my God and King,
and bless your name forever and ever.
² I will bless you every day,
and I will praise you forever.
³ Great is the LORD! He is most worthy of
praise!
His greatness is beyond discovery!

⁴ Let each generation tell its children
of your mighty acts.

144:2 Some manuscripts read *my people.*

My Daily Worship

— June 5 —

THE GREAT BURDEN-BEARER

PSALMS 145:1–150:6

The LORD helps the fallen and lifts up those bent beneath their loads (145:14).

[i reflect]

Everyone has burdens—whether it's financial, health-related, or circumstantial. Sometimes though, as David expressed in this psalm, our burdens seem to be more than we can bear. We struggle and stumble under the weight of worries and concerns, wondering how we can go on.

In his book *Dark Symbols, Obscure Signs,* Riggins R. Earl Jr. recounts the story of a former slave, Charlie, who by chance encountered his old master thirty years after escaping. Here is how their conversation went:

The former master asked, "Charlie, do you remember me lacerating your back?"

Charlie said, "Yes, mars."

"Have you forgiven me?"

"Yes, I have forgiven you."

The white man next asked, "How can you forgive me, Charlie?"

Charlie replied, "I love you as though you never hit me a lick, for the God I serve is a God of love, and I can't go to his kingdom with hate in my heart."

The old master held out his hand and said, "I am sorry for what I did."

Shaking hands, Charlie answered, "That's all right, mars. I done left the past behind me."

God had lifted from Charlie the heavy burden of unjust servitude. Perhaps more importantly, God had lifted from Charlie a burden of bitterness that, while justifiable, could have become debilitating. It brings to mind Jesus' words: "Come to me, all of you who are weary and carry heavy burdens, and I will give you rest" (Matthew 11:28).

Such a burden-bearing God we willingly worship. Such a Lord—who knows firsthand what it is to go through this human existence—can be trusted to care when life has got us down. Such a Lord will pick us up and set us back on the road when we think we cannot go on. With his hand lifting our burden, the load becomes light enough to bear.

Consider what load or burden you can leave behind today. Mentally put that burden into the Lord's hands and trust him for the outcome.

[i pray]

I'm bending, Lord; I'm falling. Take from me the weight I bear,
and gladly I will wear your yoke of lightest wood.

[i respond]

Meditate for a few minutes on the grace—the unmerited goodness—with which God has rescued you so many times in the past. Meditate on your attitude about the burden you want lifted now.

5 I will meditate* on your majestic, glorious
   splendor
   and your wonderful miracles.
6 Your awe-inspiring deeds will be on every
   tongue;
   I will proclaim your greatness.
7 Everyone will share the story of your
   wonderful goodness;
   they will sing with joy of your
   righteousness.

8 The LORD is kind and merciful,
   slow to get angry, full of unfailing love.
9 The LORD is good to everyone.
   He showers compassion on all his
   creation.
10 All of your works will thank you, LORD,
   and your faithful followers will bless
   you.
11 They will talk together about the glory of
   your kingdom;
   they will celebrate examples of your
   power.
12 They will tell about your mighty deeds
   and about the majesty and glory of your
   reign.
13 For your kingdom is an everlasting
   kingdom.
   You rule generation after generation.

The LORD is faithful in all he says;
   he is gracious in all he does.*
14 The LORD helps the fallen
   and lifts up those bent beneath their
   loads.
15 All eyes look to you for help;
   you give them their food as they need it.
16 When you open your hand,
   you satisfy the hunger and thirst of every
   living thing.

17 The LORD is righteous in everything he
   does;
   he is filled with kindness.
18 The LORD is close to all who call on him,

yes, to all who call on him sincerely.
19 He fulfills the desires of those who fear
   him;
   he hears their cries for help and rescues
   them.
20 The LORD protects all those who love him,
   but he destroys the wicked.

21 I will praise the LORD,
   and everyone on earth will bless his holy
   name
   forever and forever.

PSALM 146
1 Praise the LORD!

Praise the LORD, I tell myself.
2 I will praise the LORD as long as I live.
   I will sing praises to my God even with
   my dying breath.

3 Don't put your confidence in powerful
   people;
   there is no help for you there.
4 When their breathing stops, they return to
   the earth,
   and in a moment all their plans come to
   an end.
5 But happy are those who have the God of
   Israel* as their helper,
   whose hope is in the LORD their God.
6 He is the one who made heaven and earth,
   the sea, and everything in them.
   He is the one who keeps every promise
   forever,
7 who gives justice to the oppressed
   and food to the hungry.
   The LORD frees the prisoners.
8 The LORD opens the eyes of the blind.
   The LORD lifts the burdens of those bent
   beneath their loads.
   The LORD loves the righteous.
9 The LORD protects the foreigners among us.
   He cares for the orphans and widows,
   but he frustrates the plans of the wicked.

145:5 Some manuscripts read *They will speak.* 145:13 The last two lines of 145:13 are not found in many of the ancient manuscripts.
146:5 Hebrew *of Jacob.*

10 The LORD will reign forever,
   O Jerusalem,* your God is King in every
    generation!

Praise the LORD!

PSALM 147

1 Praise the LORD!

How good it is to sing praises to our God!
   How delightful and how right!
2 The LORD is rebuilding Jerusalem
   and bringing the exiles back to Israel.
3 He heals the brokenhearted,
   binding up their wounds.
4 He counts the stars
   and calls them all by name.
5 How great is our Lord! His power is
    absolute!
   His understanding is beyond
    comprehension!
6 The LORD supports the humble,
   but he brings the wicked down into the
    dust.

7 Sing out your thanks to the LORD;
   sing praises to our God, accompanied by
    harps.
8 He covers the heavens with clouds,
   provides rain for the earth,
   and makes the green grass grow in
    mountain pastures.
9 He feeds the wild animals,
   and the young ravens cry to him for
    food.
10 The strength of a horse does not impress
    him;
   how puny in his sight is the strength of a
    man.
11 Rather, the LORD's delight is in those who
    honor him,
   those who put their hope in his
    unfailing love.

12 Praise the LORD, O Jerusalem!
   Praise your God, O Zion!

146:10 Hebrew *Zion.*

Words of Worship

PRAISE

Praise—Hebrew *hil-**lel*** "to praise, boast, commend"; *te-hil-**lah*** "praise, commendation"; Greek *e-pai-**ne**-o* "to praise, commend"; *e-pai-nos* "praise, commendation."

When we're proud of someone in our family, we want to boast about that person. As members of God's family, we want to boast about him—his great deeds that have set us free, the way of life he has outlined for us, his care for our needs, his forgiving love despite our weakness. Praise is boasting about God, for that's what the usual Hebrew words for praise mean.

For those who know the Lord, praise is a way of life, a daily walk. With the psalm writer we say, "I will praise you seven times a day because all your laws are just" (Psalm 119:164). Through Jesus, God's beloved Son, we have been brought into his family. In response, we become people of praise (Ephesians 1:5–6). We're not alone, for all of God's creation is invited to praise him. "Let everything that lives sing praises to the LORD!" (Psalm 150:6).

---

13 For he has fortified the bars of your gates
   and blessed your children within you.
14 He sends peace across your nation
   and satisfies you with plenty of the finest
    wheat.
15 He sends his orders to the world—
   how swiftly his word flies!
16 He sends the snow like white wool;
   he scatters frost upon the ground like
    ashes.
17 He hurls the hail like stones.
   Who can stand against his freezing cold?

18 Then, at his command, it all melts.
　 He sends his winds, and the ice thaws.

19 He has revealed his words to Jacob,
　 his principles and laws to Israel.
20 He has not done this with any other
　 nation;
　 they do not know his laws.

Praise the LORD!

PSALM 148

1 Praise the LORD!

Praise the LORD from the heavens!
　 Praise him from the skies!
2 Praise him, all his angels!
　 Praise him, all the armies of heaven!
3 Praise him, sun and moon!
　 Praise him, all you twinkling stars!
4 Praise him, skies above!
　 Praise him, vapors high above the
　 clouds!
5 Let every created thing give praise to the
　 LORD,
　 for he issued his command, and they
　 came into being.
6 He established them forever and forever.
　 His orders will never be revoked.

7 Praise the LORD from the earth,
　 you creatures of the ocean depths,
8 fire and hail, snow and storm,
　 wind and weather that obey him,
9 mountains and all hills,
　 fruit trees and all cedars,
10 wild animals and all livestock,
　 reptiles and birds,
11 kings of the earth and all people,
　 rulers and judges of the earth,
12 young men and maidens,
　 old men and children.
13 Let them all praise the name of the LORD.
　 For his name is very great;
　 his glory towers over the earth and
　 heaven!

149:2 Hebrew Zion.

14 He has made his people strong,
　 honoring his godly ones—
　 the people of Israel who are close to
　 him.

Praise the LORD!

PSALM 149

1 Praise the LORD!

Sing to the LORD a new song.
　 Sing his praises in the assembly of the
　 faithful.
2 O Israel, rejoice in your Maker.
　 O people of Jerusalem,* exult in your
　 King.
3 Praise his name with dancing,
　 accompanied by tambourine and
　 harp.
4 For the LORD delights in his people;
　 he crowns the humble with salvation.
5 Let the faithful rejoice in this honor.
　 Let them sing for joy as they lie on their
　 beds.
6 Let the praises of God be in their
　 mouths,
　 and a sharp sword in their hands—
7 to execute vengeance on the nations
　 and punishment on the peoples,
8 to bind their kings with shackles
　 and their leaders with iron chains,
9 to execute the judgment written against
　 them.
　 This is the glory of his faithful ones.

Praise the LORD!

PSALM 150

1 Praise the LORD!

Praise God in his heavenly dwelling;
　 praise him in his mighty heaven!
2 Praise him for his mighty works;
　 praise his unequaled greatness!
3 Praise him with a blast of the trumpet;
　 praise him with the lyre and harp!

> *God's training ground, where*
> *the missionary weapons are found,*
> *is the hidden, personal,*
> *worshiping life of the saint.*
> OSWALD CHAMBERS

[4] Praise him with the tambourine and
     dancing;
   praise him with stringed instruments
     and flutes!
[5] Praise him with a clash of cymbals;
   praise him with loud clanging
     cymbals.
[6] Let everything that lives sing praises to
     the LORD!

   Praise the LORD!

Psalm Song Chart

As songs of the Temple, the Psalms provide a glimpse into the way the Israelites worshiped God. They capture some of the nation's highs and lows, as well as the personal struggles and victories of individual believers. They're honest, heartfelt, and true—the very heart of worship. And they have inspired countless Christian songwriters throughout history to the present day. Use the chart below to compare the following hymns and praise songs to the psalms that prompted them. Take time to consider the glory of our God who has been worshiped throughout human history—and who will be worshiped forever in heaven.

Title	Songwriter	Where to Find
A Shield about Me	Donn Thomas and Charles Williams	Psalm 3:3
Give Ear to My Words	Bill Sprouse Jr.	Psalm 5:1–3
I Will Call Upon the Lord	Michael O'Shields	Psalm 18:46
The Lord My God My Shepherd Is	F. Bland Tucker	Psalm 23
The King of Love My Shepherd Is	Henry William Baker	Psalm 23
My Shepherd Will Supply My Need	Isaac Watts	Psalm 23
Show Me Your Ways	Russell Fragar	Psalm 25:4–5
You Are My Hiding Place	Michael Ledner	Psalm 32:7
Jesus, Lover of My Soul	John Ezzy, Daniel Grul, and Stephen McPherson	Psalm 40:2
As the Deer	Martin Nystrom	Psalm 42:1
Why So Downcast?	Frank Berrios, Tom Brooks, and Jeff Hamlin	Psalm 42:5–6
Create in Me	Mary Rice Hopkins	Psalm 51:10
Cares Chorus	Kelly Willard	Psalm 55:22
Be Exalted, O God	Brent Chambers	Psalm 57:5
Thy Loving Kindness	Hugh Mitchell	Psalm 63:3–4
Hail to the Lord's Anointed	James Montgomery	Psalm 72
How Lovely Is Thy Dwelling Place	Psalms of David in Meter (1650)	Psalm 84:1
Better Is One Day	Matt Redman	Psalm 84:10
Glorious Things of Thee Are Spoken	John Newton	Psalm 87:3
O God, Our Help in Ages Past	Isaac Watts	Psalm 90:1–5
Mighty Is Our God	Eugene Greco, Gerrit Gustafson, and Don Moen	Psalm 93:4
A Mighty Fortress Is Our God	Martin Luther	Psalm 94:22
Come Let Us Worship and Bow Down	Dave Doherty	Psalm 95:6
The Lord Reigns	Dan Stradwick	Psalm 97:1
Sing to the Lord	Paul and Rita Baloche	Psalm 98:1
He Has Made Me Glad	Leona Von Brethorst	Psalm 100:4–5
Bless the Lord, O My Soul	Pete Sanchez Jr.	Psalm 103:1–2
Let the Redeemed	Ward Ellis	Psalm 107:2
This Is the Day	Rick Shelton and Les Garrett	Psalm 118:24
Thy Word Is a Lamp Unto My Feet	Amy Grant and Michael W. Smith	Psalm 119:105
All Creatures of Our God and King	Francis of Assisi	Psalm 145
Great Is the Lord	Michael W. Smith and Deborah Smith	Psalm 145:3–4
O Praise Ye the Lord	Henry Williams Baker	Psalm 148
Let Everything That Has Breath	Rich Gomez	Psalm 150:6

Proverbs

Fear of the LORD is the beginning of knowledge (1:7).

Wisdom Is at the Heart of knowledge

If you were looking for advice on how to maintain a relationship or what to do about an annoying neighbor, you probably would skip over *Hints from Heloise* or Martha Stewart's column in the Sunday newspaper and turn right to *Dear Abby*. Similarly, if you wanted to learn how to worship God, you probably would not start with a study of Proverbs—a book known for its collection of wise sayings on practical living and moral truths. A careful reading of Proverbs, however, may prove more helpful than at first imagined for providing insights on worship.

At the very heart of wisdom is knowing God—and worship is all about knowing God. The author explains, "Fear of the LORD is the beginning of wisdom. Knowledge of the Holy One results in understanding" (9:10). True wisdom is not just about common sense or book knowledge. Rather, it is based on our knowing God and his ways and upon our reverence, or "fear" of God. A life filled with worship studying God's Word, spending time with him, praying, and meditating on his character—will prepare us for a life of wisdom. As we learn more about God, we can respond in obedience, living according to his standards.

Faithfulness is an important element of worship, and it's a recurring theme in this book as well— including faithfulness to one's spouse, to honesty, integrity, truthfulness, kindness, true worship, and to God. The final chapter of Proverbs (31) paints a picture of a wise and faithful wife, whose life stands in direct contrast to the foolish, unfaithful woman whose enticements and seductions destroy lives.

As you read through Proverbs, look for the many practical truths and lessons that you can apply to your life and gain wisdom. Then worship the Holy One who gives you understanding.

Worship Moments

- God recognizes sincere worship (20:27; 21:3, 27).

- Godliness is having God's attitude towards the helpless (19:17; 22:22–23; 29:7).

- God is revealed as protector and avenger of the poor (14:31; 23:10); as a fortress (18:10); and as unfailing love and faithfulness (20:28).

The Purpose of Proverbs

1 These are the proverbs of Solomon, David's son, king of Israel.

[2]The purpose of these proverbs is to teach people wisdom and discipline, and to help them understand wise sayings. [3]Through these proverbs, people will receive instruction in discipline, good conduct, and doing what is right, just, and fair. [4]These proverbs will make the simpleminded clever. They will give knowledge and purpose to young people.

[5]Let those who are wise listen to these proverbs and become even wiser. And let those who understand receive guidance [6]by exploring the depth of meaning in these proverbs, parables, wise sayings, and riddles.

[7]Fear of the LORD is the beginning of knowledge. Only fools despise wisdom and discipline.

A Father's Exhortation: Acquire Wisdom

[8]Listen, my child,* to what your father teaches you. Don't neglect your mother's teaching. [9]What you learn from them will crown you with grace and clothe you with honor.

[10]My child, if sinners entice you, turn your back on them! [11]They may say, "Come and join us. Let's hide and kill someone! Let's ambush the innocent! [12]Let's swallow them alive as the grave swallows its victims. Though they are in the prime of life, they will go down into the pit of death. [13]And the loot we'll get! We'll fill our houses with all kinds of things! [14]Come on, throw in your lot with us; we'll split our loot with you."

[15]Don't go along with them, my child! Stay far away from their paths. [16]They rush to commit crimes. They hurry to commit murder. [17]When a bird sees a trap being set, it stays away. [18]But not these people! They set an ambush for themselves; they booby-trap their own lives! [19]Such is the fate of all who are greedy for gain. It ends up robbing them of life.

Wisdom Shouts in the Streets

[20]Wisdom shouts in the streets. She cries out in the public square. [21]She calls out to the crowds along the main street, and to those in front of city hall. [22]"You simpletons!" she cries. "How long will you go on being simpleminded? How long will you mockers relish your mocking? How long will you fools fight the facts? [23]Come here and listen to me! I'll pour out the spirit of wisdom upon you and make you wise.

[24]"I called you so often, but you didn't come. I reached out to you, but you paid no attention. [25]You ignored my advice and rejected the correction I offered. [26]So I will laugh when you are in trouble! I will mock you when disaster overtakes you—[27]when calamity overcomes you like a storm, when you are engulfed by trouble, and when anguish and distress overwhelm you.

[28]"I will not answer when they cry for help. Even though they anxiously search for me, they will not find me. [29]For they hated knowledge and chose not to fear the LORD. [30]They rejected my advice and paid no attention when I corrected them. [31]That is why they must eat the bitter fruit of living their own way. They must experience the full terror of the path they have chosen. [32]For they are simpletons who turn away from me—to death. They are fools, and their own complacency will destroy them. [33]But all who listen to me will live in peace and safety, unafraid of harm."

The Benefits of Wisdom

2 My child,* listen to me and treasure my instructions. [2]Tune your ears to wisdom, and concentrate on understanding. [3]Cry out for insight and understanding. [4]Search for them as you would for lost money or hidden treasure. [5]Then you will understand what it means to fear the LORD, and you will gain knowledge of God. [6]For the LORD grants wisdom! From his mouth come knowledge and

---

1:8 Hebrew *my son;* also in 1:10, 15. 2:1 Hebrew *My son.*

My Daily Worship

— *June 6* —

A Treasure of Good Sense

Proverbs 1:1–2:22

For the LORD grants wisdom! From his mouth come knowledge and understanding.
He grants a treasure of good sense to the godly. He is their shield,
protecting those who walk with integrity (2:6–7).

[i reflect]

Decisions. Choices. Alternatives. Judgments. We face them every day. How we long for wisdom to make good decisions when the way ahead is not clear! How we wish we could know what is the right action to take in a difficult situation. How we yearn for fair judgment among choices that appear gray, rather than the black and white choices we would prefer. How badly we need *a treasure of good sense* to deal with the complexities of life.

"The LORD grants wisdom!" That's a promise we can claim. Nothing we will face is beyond the understanding of the One who created us. God's wisdom is available to us—but we need to ask for it. We need to pour out our lack of understanding, our confusion, our fears, and our doubts before him. We need to set aside our own opinions and prejudices. We need to admit we don't know what to do and that we need his knowledge and understanding. Then we need to be patient and wait for his sure response.

A short song, which appeared in the *Sarum Primer of 1514*, illustrates beautifully the need to commit daily to seeking and trusting God's wisdom and guidance in all aspects of life. The songwriter penned these words: "God be in my head, and in my understanding;/ God be in mine eyes, and in my looking;/ God be in my mouth, and in my speaking;/ God be in my heart, and in my thinking;/ God be at mine end, and at my departing."

Spend a few moments now committing your head, eyes, mouth, heart, and life to God as an act of worship. Ask him to guide you throughout the day, and turn to his "treasure of good sense" as you tackle the day's problems.

[i pray]

I praise you today, Lord, for your promise of wisdom. Oh, how much I need
your knowledge and understanding! Fill my treasure chest with good
sense today, so that I may be protected by your shield of wisdom.

[i respond]

Picture God's "treasure of good sense." What would you find in it? Write down at least five aspects of that treasure that you most need today. Then thank God that he already has granted that to you.

understanding. 7He grants a treasure of good sense to the godly. He is their shield, protecting those who walk with integrity. 8He guards the paths of justice and protects those who are faithful to him.

9Then you will understand what is right, just, and fair, and you will know how to find the right course of action every time. 10For wisdom will enter your heart, and knowledge will fill you with joy. 11Wise planning will watch over you. Understanding will keep you safe.

12Wisdom will save you from evil people, from those whose speech is corrupt. 13These people turn from right ways to walk down dark and evil paths. 14They rejoice in doing wrong, and they enjoy evil as it turns things upside down. 15What they do is crooked, and their ways are wrong.

16Wisdom will save you from the immoral woman, from the flattery of the adulterous woman. 17She has abandoned her husband and ignores the covenant she made before God. 18Entering her house leads to death; it is the road to hell.* 19The man who visits her is doomed. He will never reach the paths of life.

20Follow the steps of good men instead, and stay on the paths of the righteous. 21For only the upright will live in the land, and those who have integrity will remain in it. 22But the wicked will be removed from the land, and the treacherous will be destroyed.

TRUSTING IN THE LORD

3 My child,* never forget the things I have taught you. Store my commands in your heart, 2for they will give you a long and satisfying life. 3Never let loyalty and kindness get away from you! Wear them like a necklace; write them deep within your heart. 4Then you will find favor with both God and people, and you will gain a good reputation.

5Trust in the LORD with all your heart; do not depend on your own understanding. 6Seek his will in all you do, and he will direct your paths.

7Don't be impressed with your own wisdom. Instead, fear the LORD and turn your back on evil. 8Then you will gain renewed health and vitality.

9Honor the LORD with your wealth and with the best part of everything your land produces. 10Then he will fill your barns with grain, and your vats will overflow with the finest wine.

11My child, don't ignore it when the LORD disciplines you, and don't be discouraged when he corrects you. 12For the LORD corrects those he loves, just as a father corrects a child* in whom he delights.

13Happy is the person who finds wisdom and gains understanding. 14For the profit of wisdom is better than silver, and her wages are better than gold. 15Wisdom is more precious than rubies; nothing you desire can compare with her. 16She offers you life in her right hand, and riches and honor in her left. 17She will guide you down delightful paths; all her ways are satisfying. 18Wisdom is a tree of life to those who embrace her; happy are those who hold her tightly.

19By wisdom the LORD founded the earth; by understanding he established the heavens. 20By his knowledge the deep fountains of the earth burst forth, and the clouds poured down rain.

21My child, don't lose sight of good planning and insight. Hang on to them, 22for they fill you with life and bring you honor and respect. 23They keep you safe on your way and keep your feet from stumbling. 24You can lie down without fear and enjoy pleasant dreams. 25You need not be afraid of disaster or the destruction that comes upon the wicked, 26for the LORD is your security. He will keep your foot from being caught in a trap.

27Do not withhold good from those who deserve it when it's in your power to help them. 28If you can help your neighbor now, don't say, "Come back tomorrow, and then I'll help you."

2:18 Hebrew *to the spirits of the dead.* 3:1 Hebrew *My son;* also in 3:11, 21. 3:12 Hebrew *a son.*

My Daily Worship

— *June 7* —

WHAT ARE YOU WITHHOLDING?

PROVERBS 3:1–35

Honor the LORD with your wealth and with the best part of everything
your land produces. Then he will fill your barns with grain, and
your vats will overflow with the finest wine (3:9–10).

[i reflect]

As the opening stanza to the familiar hymn, "Take My Life, and Let It Be" floated through the congregation, the pastor instructed his congregation, "The words are so simple. And here it's set to Mozart's very singable Nottingham tune. Easy to go on musical autopilot. But don't you dare. Don't sing anything you don't mean. Especially verse four."

The first verse started strong: "Take my life, and let it be consecrated, Lord, to Thee." *And while you're at it, take my moments and my days.* Verses two and three continued the glad offerings: hands, feet, voice—*Hey, God, I'm singing my heart out for you!*—and lips. *What's so hard about this?* Then came the verse.

"Take my silver and my gold: Not a mite would I withhold." Suddenly the singing was more tentative. *Not a mite? What's a mite, anyway? God doesn't really mean . . .* But they knew he did mean it. They gained strength through the rest of the six verses, urging God, "Take my intellect, my will, my heart, my love."

In 1878, four years after writing the hymn, Havergal wrote to a friend, "'Take my silver and my gold' now means shipping off all my ornaments to the Church Missionary House, including a jewel cabinet that is really fit for a countess. . . . Nearly fifty articles are being packed up. I don't think I ever packed a box with such pleasure."

"Honor the LORD with your wealth," the proverb instructs. Don't withhold a mite. Consider today how you can honor God with your possessions—whether it's donating to a favorite ministry or mission group, taking a bag of groceries to the local food pantry, or helping out a family who is struggling financially.

[i pray]

God, I do want you to have every area of my life. Help me to reach deeply into my resources
to give you what is already yours, what you have entrusted to me for a time.

[i respond]

In many worship services, the following is said after the offering is brought forward: "All things come of thee, O Lord, and of thine own have we given thee." Say these words the next time you begin paying your monthly bills and tithe.

²⁹Do not plot against your neighbors, for they trust you. ³⁰Don't make accusations against someone who hasn't wronged you.

³¹Do not envy violent people; don't copy their ways. ³²Such wicked people are an abomination to the LORD, but he offers his friendship to the godly.

³³The curse of the LORD is on the house of the wicked, but his blessing is on the home of the upright.

³⁴The LORD mocks at mockers, but he shows favor to the humble.

³⁵The wise inherit honor, but fools are put to shame!

A FATHER'S WISE ADVICE

4 My children,* listen to me. Listen to your father's instruction. Pay attention and grow wise, ²for I am giving you good guidance. Don't turn away from my teaching. ³For I, too, was once my father's son, tenderly loved by my mother as an only child.

⁴My father told me, "Take my words to heart. Follow my instructions and you will live. ⁵Learn to be wise, and develop good judgment. Don't forget or turn away from my words. ⁶Don't turn your back on wisdom, for she will protect you. Love her, and she will guard you. ⁷Getting wisdom is the most important thing you can do! And whatever else you do, get good judgment. ⁸If you prize wisdom, she will exalt you. Embrace her and she will honor you. ⁹She will place a lovely wreath on your head; she will present you with a beautiful crown."

¹⁰My child,* listen to me and do as I say, and you will have a long, good life. ¹¹I will teach you wisdom's ways and lead you in straight paths. ¹²If you live a life guided by wisdom, you won't limp or stumble as you run. ¹³Carry out my instructions; don't forsake them. Guard them, for they will lead you to a fulfilled life.

¹⁴Do not do as the wicked do or follow the path of evildoers. ¹⁵Avoid their haunts. Turn away and go somewhere else, ¹⁶for evil people cannot sleep until they have done their evil deed for the day. They cannot rest unless they have caused someone to stumble. ¹⁷They eat wickedness and drink violence!

¹⁸The way of the righteous is like the first gleam of dawn, which shines ever brighter until the full light of day. ¹⁹But the way of the wicked is like complete darkness. Those who follow it have no idea what they are stumbling over.

²⁰Pay attention, my child, to what I say. Listen carefully. ²¹Don't lose sight of my words. Let them penetrate deep within your heart, ²²for they bring life and radiant health to anyone who discovers their meaning.

²³Above all else, guard your heart, for it affects everything you do.*

²⁴Avoid all perverse talk; stay far from corrupt speech.

²⁵Look straight ahead, and fix your eyes on what lies before you. ²⁶Mark out a straight path for your feet; then stick to the path and stay safe. ²⁷Don't get sidetracked; keep your feet from following evil.

AVOID IMMORAL WOMEN

5 My son, pay attention to my wisdom; listen carefully to my wise counsel. ²Then you will learn to be discreet and will store up knowledge.

³The lips of an immoral woman are as sweet as honey, and her mouth is smoother than oil. ⁴But the result is as bitter as poison, sharp as a double-edged sword. ⁵Her feet go down to death; her steps lead straight to the grave.* ⁶For she does not care about the path to life. She staggers down a crooked trail and doesn't even realize where it leads.

⁷So now, my sons, listen to me. Never stray from what I am about to say: ⁸Run from her! Don't go near the door of her house! ⁹If you do, you will lose your honor and hand over to merciless people everything you have achieved in life. ¹⁰Strangers will obtain your

---

4:1 Hebrew *My sons.* 4:10 Hebrew *My son;* also in 4:20. 4:23 Hebrew *for from it flow the springs of life.* 5:5 Hebrew *to Sheol.*

My Daily Worship

— *June 8* —

THE FIRST GLEAM OF DAWN

PROVERBS 4:1–5:23

The way of the righteous is like the first gleam of dawn, which
shines ever brighter until the full light of day (4:18).

[i reflect]

A thin line of deep rose appears in the charcoal sky. Slowly the light increases, and the color changes from rose to orange to gold. Stars fade and disappear. The sky lightens to palest blue, then deepens to the azure of a robin's egg. The first rays of sun streak across the landscape, heralding a new day. Darkness has fled.

The writer of Proverbs pictures the way of the righteous as being like that first gleam of dawn. God's wisdom gradually brings light to our journey and enables us to walk in straight paths (4:11). His understanding illuminates the dark places in our lives, bringing healing and new life, and transforming our confusion into his wisdom. *God is light and there is no darkness in him at all* (1 John 1:5). As we listen to his Word and obey his instructions, his light transforms us. We reflect back this light to the world like the gleam of dawn.

We can offer up the prayer first spoken in the sixth century, *"Hear us, O never-failing light, Lord our God, the fountain of light, the light of your angels, principalities, powers, and of all intelligent beings, who created the light of your saints. May our souls be lamps of yours, kindled and illumi-nated by you. May they shine and burn with the truth and never go out in darkness and ashes. May the gloom of sins be cleared away and the light of perpetual faith abide within us."*

In what areas of your life do you need God's light today? Perhaps it is an attitude that needs chang-ing, a relationship that requires forgiveness, or a neglected sin that should be brought to light and confessed. Ask God to shine his truth on you throughout the day.

[i pray]

Lord, warm me with the full light of your love. Melt my hardness. Banish my doubts.
Illuminate my darkness with your wisdom. Help me to reflect your light to others
who are hungry for the sunrise of your knowledge and understanding.

[i respond]

Write your own prayer of illumination, mentioning specific areas where you need God's light to shine. Read it aloud as you watch the sunrise.

wealth, and someone else will enjoy the fruit of your labor. [11]Afterward you will groan in anguish when disease consumes your body, [12]and you will say, "How I hated discipline! If only I had not demanded my own way! [13]Oh, why didn't I listen to my teachers? Why didn't I pay attention to those who gave me instruction? [14]I have come to the brink of utter ruin, and now I must face public disgrace."

[15]Drink water from your own well—share your love only with your wife.* [16]Why spill the water of your springs in public, having sex with just anyone?* [17]You should reserve it for yourselves. Don't share it with strangers.

[18]Let your wife be a fountain of blessing for you. Rejoice in the wife of your youth. [19]She is a loving doe, a graceful deer. Let her breasts satisfy you always. May you always be captivated by her love. [20]Why be captivated, my son, with an immoral woman, or embrace the breasts of an adulterous woman?

[21]For the LORD sees clearly what a man does, examining every path he takes. [22]An evil man is held captive by his own sins; they are ropes that catch and hold him. [23]He will die for lack of self-control; he will be lost because of his incredible folly.

LESSONS FOR DAILY LIFE

6 My child,* if you co-sign a loan for a friend or guarantee the debt of someone you hardly know—[2]if you have trapped yourself by your agreement and are caught by what you said—[3]quick, get out of it if you possibly can! You have placed yourself at your friend's mercy. Now swallow your pride; go and beg to have your name erased. [4]Don't put it off. Do it now! Don't rest until you do. [5]Save yourself like a deer escaping from a hunter, like a bird fleeing from a net.

[6]Take a lesson from the ants, you lazybones. Learn from their ways and be wise! [7]Even though they have no prince, governor, or ruler to make them work, [8]they labor hard all summer, gathering food for the winter. [9]But you,

lazybones, how long will you sleep? When will you wake up? I want you to learn this lesson: [10]A little extra sleep, a little more slumber, a little folding of the hands to rest—[11]and poverty will pounce on you like a bandit; scarcity will attack you like an armed robber.

[12]Here is a description of worthless and wicked people: They are constant liars, [13]signaling their true intentions to their friends by making signs with their eyes and feet and fingers. [14]Their perverted hearts plot evil. They stir up trouble constantly. [15]But they will be destroyed suddenly, broken beyond all hope of healing.

[16]There are six things the LORD hates—no, seven things he detests:
[17] haughty eyes,
  a lying tongue,
  hands that kill the innocent,
[18] a heart that plots evil,
  feet that race to do wrong,
[19] a false witness who pours out lies,
  a person who sows discord among
    brothers.

[20]My son, obey your father's commands, and don't neglect your mother's teaching. [21]Keep their words always in your heart. Tie them around your neck. [22]Wherever you walk, their counsel can lead you. When you sleep, they will protect you. When you wake up in the morning, they will advise you. [23]For these commands and this teaching are a lamp to light the way ahead of you. The correction of discipline is the way to life.

[24]These commands and this teaching will keep you from the immoral woman, from the smooth tongue of an adulterous woman. [25]Don't lust for her beauty. Don't let her coyness seduce you. [26]For a prostitute will bring you to poverty, and sleeping with another man's wife may cost you your very life. [27]Can a man scoop fire into his lap and not be burned? [28]Can he walk on hot coals and not

5:15 Hebrew *Drink water from your own cistern, flowing water from your own well.*   5:16 Hebrew *Why spill your springs in public, your streams in the streets?*   6:1 Hebrew *My son.*

My Daily Worship

— *June 9* —

THE MOST BELOVED FAMILY MEMBER

PROVERBS 6:1–7:27

*Love wisdom like a sister; make insight a
beloved member of your family (7:4).*

[i reflect]

"What *exactly* do you think you're doing?"

He tried to bluff his way through, muttering, "Don't worry. I know what I'm doing." It never worked. Not with her.

"Oh, you know, do you? Like you knew all the times before? Sit down. And listen this time. I *am* your sister, you know." Then firmly—but with a sister's concern in her voice and touch of her hand on his—she told him that the friendships he was pursuing were getting him further and further into trouble.

Wisdom is just such a relative. Often personified as a woman in the Bible, wisdom is deserving of love just as a caring sister deserves to be loved. Wisdom is the one to lead your head and your heart back to God. She cares enough to look at your life and your bad choices, and then point them out, lay it out, chew you out.

If a Christian's life is to be a holy act of worship every day, wisdom must have her say. And she must be heeded. The stakes are too high, the consequences too deep, the ramifications too wide. Solomon knew well from his own experience the importance of listening and heeding wise warnings.

How do you welcome God's insight? Is it like a sister's or brother's care to you, or a nagging voice that you tune out? God longs for his people—if they are truly to be called his people—to have minds and hearts shaped by and conformed to his ways.

Today, listen to the wisdom of the family members God sends to you, whether they are siblings, extended family, or the family of God. Let wisdom lead you back to the altar, with a holy heart and mind to praise him.

[i pray]

*Father God, help me to listen to your wisdom as to a caring sibling. Let me embrace it
as a sister. I thank you for the messengers of wisdom you have sent to me.*

[i respond]

Who have been messengers of wisdom in your life? How has the wisdom given through them helped make you holier, quicker to worship? Today, write one of them a letter thanking him or her for sharing that wisdom with you.

blister his feet? [29]So it is with the man who sleeps with another man's wife. He who embraces her will not go unpunished.

[30]Excuses might be found for a thief who steals because he is starving. [31]But if he is caught, he will be fined seven times as much as he stole, even if it means selling everything in his house to pay it back.

[32]But the man who commits adultery is an utter fool, for he destroys his own soul. [33]Wounds and constant disgrace are his lot. His shame will never be erased. [34]For the woman's husband will be furious in his jealousy, and he will have no mercy in his day of vengeance. [35]There is no compensation or bribe that will satisfy him.

ANOTHER WARNING ABOUT IMMORAL WOMEN

7 Follow my advice, my son; always treasure my commands. [2]Obey them and live! Guard my teachings as your most precious possession.* [3]Tie them on your fingers as a reminder. Write them deep within your heart.

[4]Love wisdom like a sister; make insight a beloved member of your family. [5]Let them hold you back from an affair with an immoral woman, from listening to the flattery of an adulterous woman.

[6]I was looking out the window of my house one day [7]and saw a simpleminded young man who lacked common sense. [8]He was crossing the street near the house of an immoral woman. He was strolling down the path by her house [9]at twilight, as the day was fading, as the dark of night set in. [10]The woman approached him, dressed seductively and sly of heart. [11]She was the brash, rebellious type who never stays at home. [12]She is often seen in the streets and markets, soliciting at every corner.

[13]She threw her arms around him and kissed him, and with a brazen look she said, [14]"I've offered my sacrifices and just finished my vows. [15]It's you I was looking for! I came

out to find you, and here you are! [16]My bed is spread with colored sheets of finest linen imported from Egypt. [17]I've perfumed my bed with myrrh, aloes, and cinnamon. [18]Come, let's drink our fill of love until morning. Let's enjoy each other's caresses, [19]for my husband is not home. He's away on a long trip. [20]He has taken a wallet full of money with him, and he won't return until later in the month."

[21]So she seduced him with her pretty speech. With her flattery she enticed him. [22]He followed her at once, like an ox going to the slaughter or like a trapped stag, [23]awaiting the arrow that would pierce its heart. He was like a bird flying into a snare, little knowing it would cost him his life.

[24]Listen to me, my sons, and pay attention to my words. [25]Don't let your hearts stray away toward her. Don't wander down her wayward path. [26]For she has been the ruin of many; numerous men have been her victims. [27]Her house is the road to the grave.* Her bedroom is the den of death.

WISDOM CALLS FOR A HEARING

8 Listen as wisdom calls out! Hear as understanding raises her voice! [2]She stands on the hilltop and at the crossroads. [3]At the entrance to the city, at the city gates, she cries aloud, [4]"I call to you, to all of you! I am raising my voice to all people. [5]How naive you are! Let me give you common sense. O foolish ones, let me give you understanding. [6]Listen to me! For I have excellent things to tell you. Everything I say is right, [7]for I speak the truth and hate every kind of deception. [8]My advice is wholesome and good. There is nothing crooked or twisted in it. [9]My words are plain to anyone with understanding, clear to those who want to learn.

[10]"Choose my instruction rather than silver, and knowledge over pure gold. [11]For wisdom is far more valuable than rubies. Nothing you desire can be compared with it.

[12]"I, Wisdom, live together with good judgment.

7:2 Hebrew *as the apple of your eye.* 7:27 Hebrew *to Sheol.*

My Daily Worship

— *June 10* —

BUILDING A WORSHIP FOUNDATION

PROVERBS 8:1–9:18

*Fear of the LORD is the beginning of wisdom. Knowledge of
the Holy One results in understanding (9:10).*

[i reflect]

At the height of her popularity, Ann Landers, the newspaper advice columnist, received an average of 10,000 letters each month, and nearly all of them from people burdened with problems. When asked if there was any one issue that predominated throughout the letters she received, her reply was the one problem above all others seemed to be fear. People were afraid of losing their health, their wealth, their loved ones. People were afraid of life itself.

None of us likes to be afraid. We associate fear with strong, negative emotions: dread, terror, anxiety, cowardice, panic, timidity, abhorrence, revulsion, and despair. Fear generates a fight-or-flight response deep within us. We avoid whatever makes us afraid whenever we can and fight against it when we can't escape it. So what, then, does it mean to fear the Lord? For those who do not know God, dread and terror of punishment are appropriate responses. But for those who truly seek knowledge of the Holy One, fear is transformed by love into reverence and awe.

Fear of the Lord is the very basis of our worship. It inspires within us reverence for God's majesty and power and illuminates the great gulf between our humanness and God's divinity. Fear induces us to obedience and service; it emboldens us to avoid sin and live a holy life. Fear galvanizes us to hate evil and treasure good. It quickens our hearts with worshipful respect for God and infuses us with the love of God.

The wonderful paradox of fear of the Lord is that *this* fear ultimately frees you from all other fears. Fear of God gives you wisdom to know he is in charge, not you. It brings knowledge of his holiness—and nothing can challenge that power. Fear of God brings understanding to all other fears and gladdens your heart. *Do not fear anything except the LORD Almighty. He alone is the Holy One. If you fear him, you need fear nothing else* (Isaiah 8:13).

Today, claim that freedom from your own personal fears as you worship the Holy One. Fear him. Nothing else.

[i pray]

*I bow before you in reverential awe, Lord. I praise you for your majesty and greatness.
I praise you for your holiness. I fear you because you are Creator and
I am merely your creature. Yet you love me! Amazing!*

[i respond]

Maybe you have never written to someone like Ann Landers, but you most likely have your own set of fears. What tops your list? Write them down. Tear up each one as you read aloud today's key verse.

I know where to discover knowledge and discernment. [13]All who fear the LORD will hate evil. That is why I hate pride, arrogance, corruption, and perverted speech. [14]Good advice and success belong to me. Insight and strength are mine. [15]Because of me, kings reign, and rulers make just laws. [16]Rulers lead with my help, and nobles make righteous judgments.

[17]"I love all who love me. Those who search for me will surely find me. [18]Unending riches, honor, wealth, and justice are mine to distribute. [19]My gifts are better than the purest gold, my wages better than sterling silver! [20]I walk in righteousness, in paths of justice. [21]Those who love me inherit wealth, for I fill their treasuries.

[22]"The LORD formed me from the beginning, before he created anything else. [23]I was appointed in ages past, at the very first, before the earth began. [24]I was born before the oceans were created, before the springs bubbled forth their waters. [25]Before the mountains and the hills were formed, I was born—[26]before he had made the earth and fields and the first handfuls of soil.

[27]"I was there when he established the heavens, when he drew the horizon on the oceans. [28]I was there when he set the clouds above, when he established the deep fountains of the earth. [29]I was there when he set the limits of the seas, so they would not spread beyond their boundaries. And when he marked off the earth's foundations, [30]I was the architect at his side. I was his constant delight, rejoicing always in his presence. [31]And how happy I was with what he created—his wide world and all the human family!

[32]"And so, my children,* listen to me, for happy are all who follow my ways. [33]Listen to my counsel and be wise. Don't ignore it.

[34]"Happy are those who listen to me, watching for me daily at my gates, waiting for me outside my home! [35]For whoever finds me finds life and wins approval from the LORD. [36]But those who miss me have injured themselves. All who hate me love death."

9 Wisdom has built her spacious house with seven pillars. [2]She has prepared a great banquet, mixed the wines, and set the table. [3]She has sent her servants to invite everyone to come. She calls out from the heights overlooking the city. [4]"Come home with me," she urges the simple. To those without good judgment, she says, [5]"Come, eat my food, and drink the wine I have mixed. [6]Leave your foolish ways behind, and begin to live; learn how to be wise."

[7]Anyone who rebukes a mocker will get a smart retort. Anyone who rebukes the wicked will get hurt. [8]So don't bother rebuking mockers; they will only hate you. But the wise, when rebuked, will love you all the more. [9]Teach the wise, and they will be wiser. Teach the righteous, and they will learn more.

[10]Fear of the LORD is the beginning of wisdom. Knowledge of the Holy One results in understanding. [11]Wisdom will multiply your days and add years to your life. [12]If you become wise, you will be the one to benefit. If you scorn wisdom, you will be the one to suffer.

FOLLY CALLS FOR A HEARING

[13]The woman named Folly is loud and brash. She is ignorant and doesn't even know it. [14]She sits in her doorway on the heights overlooking the city. [15]She calls out to men going by who are minding their own business. [16]"Come home with me," she urges the simple. To those without good judgment, she says, [17]"Stolen water is refreshing; food eaten in secret tastes the best!" [18]But the men don't realize that her former guests are now in the grave.*

THE PROVERBS OF SOLOMON

10 The proverbs of Solomon:
A wise child* brings joy to a father; a foolish child brings grief to a mother.

[2]Ill-gotten gain has no lasting value, but right living can save your life.

[3]The LORD will not let the godly starve to

8:32 Hebrew *my sons.* **9:18** Hebrew *in Sheol.* **10:1** Hebrew *son;* also in 10:1b.

My Daily Worship

— June 11 —

No Strain, No Gain

PROVERBS 10:1–11:31

Godly people find life; evil people find death (11:19).

[i reflect]

"Let us strain toward righteousness." So wrote Lactantius, a teacher of rhetoric and later, a defender of the Christian faith.

Some hear the cloister call. A few live a hermit's life. Perhaps for them, the pursuit of righteousness and godliness, which today's proverb urges, is easy. (Then again, perhaps not.) But for most of us, being godly people and living consistent, godly lives is a strain, to say the least.

Lactantius knew the challenge, the effort needed, the straining that leads to life. He also saw what evil leads to. In the early fourth century, at the request of the Emperor Diocletian, Lactantius moved from his native Africa to the city of Nicomedia, in what today is Turkey, to be a professor of rhetoric.

He became a Christian in Nicomedia. Ironically, the edicts and persecutions of this same Diocletian made it impossible for him to continue as a public teacher. He had some private students, but he was often in poverty. He wrote and wrote—an impassioned Christian apologist. We have many of his writings, which, set against the challenges of his life, urge others to be those "godly people" who "find life."

Lactantius wrote, "Let those who are hungry come and be fed with heavenly food that will satisfy continual hunger. . . . The supreme and honest Judge will raise to life and to eternal light whoever has trampled on the corruptions of the earth by their righteousness. . . . Let us strain toward righteousness. It alone, as an inseparable companion, will lead us to God."

Strain toward righteousness, toward godly living. Today, let it lead you as a companion to God's presence and the privilege of worshiping him.

[i pray]

O Lord, I want to travel the path that leads to you. Help me be counted among those godly people who find life. Help me strain toward righteousness and then cling to it as it leads me to you.

[i respond]

Proverbs 11:19–20 works together to call you to godliness. Read the verses, meditate on them, memorize them: "Godly people find life; evil people find death. The LORD hates people with twisted hearts, but he delights in those who have integrity."

death, but he refuses to satisfy the craving of the wicked.

⁴Lazy people are soon poor; hard workers get rich.

⁵A wise youth works hard all summer; a youth who sleeps away the hour of opportunity brings shame.

⁶The godly are showered with blessings; evil people cover up their harmful intentions.

⁷We all have happy memories of the godly, but the name of a wicked person rots away.

⁸The wise are glad to be instructed, but babbling fools fall flat on their faces.

⁹People with integrity have firm footing, but those who follow crooked paths will slip and fall.

¹⁰People who wink at wrong cause trouble, but a bold reproof promotes peace.*

¹¹The words of the godly lead to life; evil people cover up their harmful intentions.

¹²Hatred stirs up quarrels, but love covers all offenses.

¹³Wise words come from the lips of people with understanding, but fools will be punished with a rod.

¹⁴Wise people treasure knowledge, but the babbling of a fool invites trouble.

¹⁵The wealth of the rich is their fortress; the poverty of the poor is their calamity.

¹⁶The earnings of the godly enhance their lives, but evil people squander their money on sin.

¹⁷People who accept correction are on the pathway to life, but those who ignore it will lead others astray.

¹⁸To hide hatred is to be a liar; to slander is to be a fool.

¹⁹Don't talk too much, for it fosters sin. Be sensible and turn off the flow!

²⁰The words of the godly are like sterling silver; the heart of a fool is worthless.

²¹The godly give good advice, but fools are destroyed by their lack of common sense.

²²The blessing of the LORD makes a person rich, and he adds no sorrow with it.

²³Doing wrong is fun for a fool, while wise conduct is a pleasure to the wise.

²⁴The fears of the wicked will all come true; so will the hopes of the godly.

²⁵Disaster strikes like a cyclone, whirling the wicked away, but the godly have a lasting foundation.

²⁶Lazy people are a pain to their employer. They are like smoke in the eyes or vinegar that sets the teeth on edge.

²⁷Fear of the LORD lengthens one's life, but the years of the wicked are cut short.

²⁸The hopes of the godly result in happiness, but the expectations of the wicked are all in vain.

²⁹The LORD protects the upright but destroys the wicked.

³⁰The godly will never be disturbed, but the wicked will be removed from the land.

³¹The godly person gives wise advice, but the tongue that deceives will be cut off.

³²The godly speak words that are helpful, but the wicked speak only what is corrupt.

11 The LORD hates cheating, but he delights in honesty.

²Pride leads to disgrace, but with humility comes wisdom.

³Good people are guided by their honesty; treacherous people are destroyed by their dishonesty.

⁴Riches won't help on the day of judgment, but right living is a safeguard against death.

⁵The godly are directed by their honesty; the wicked fall beneath their load of sin.

⁶The godliness of good people rescues them; the ambition of treacherous people traps them.

⁷When the wicked die, their hopes all perish, for they rely on their own feeble strength.

⁸God rescues the godly from danger, but he lets the wicked fall into trouble.

⁹Evil words destroy one's friends; wise discernment rescues the godly.

¹⁰The whole city celebrates when the godly succeed; they shout for joy when the godless die.

10:10 As in Greek version; Hebrew reads *but babbling fools fall flat on their faces.*

¹¹Upright citizens bless a city and make it prosper, but the talk of the wicked tears it apart.

¹²It is foolish to belittle a neighbor; a person with good sense remains silent.

¹³A gossip goes around revealing secrets, but those who are trustworthy can keep a confidence.

¹⁴Without wise leadership, a nation falls; with many counselors, there is safety.

¹⁵Guaranteeing a loan for a stranger is dangerous; it is better to refuse than to suffer later.

¹⁶Beautiful women obtain wealth, and violent men get rich.

¹⁷Your own soul is nourished when you are kind, but you destroy yourself when you are cruel.

¹⁸Evil people get rich for the moment, but the reward of the godly will last.

¹⁹Godly people find life; evil people find death.

²⁰The LORD hates people with twisted hearts, but he delights in those who have integrity.

²¹You can be sure that evil people will be punished, but the children of the godly will go free.

²²A woman who is beautiful but lacks discretion is like a gold ring in a pig's snout.

²³The godly can look forward to happiness, while the wicked can expect only wrath.

²⁴It is possible to give freely and become more wealthy, but those who are stingy will lose everything.

²⁵The generous prosper and are satisfied; those who refresh others will themselves be refreshed.

²⁶People curse those who hold their grain for higher prices, but they bless the one who sells to them in their time of need.

²⁷If you search for good, you will find favor; but if you search for evil, it will find you!

²⁸Trust in your money and down you go! But the godly flourish like leaves in spring.

²⁹Those who bring trouble on their families inherit only the wind. The fool will be a servant to the wise.

³⁰The godly are like trees that bear life-giving fruit, and those who save lives are wise.

³¹If the righteous are rewarded here on earth, how much more true that the wicked and the sinner will get what they deserve!

12 To learn, you must love discipline; it is stupid to hate correction.

²The LORD approves of those who are good, but he condemns those who plan wickedness.

³Wickedness never brings stability; only the godly have deep roots.

⁴A worthy wife is her husband's joy and crown; a shameful wife saps his strength.

⁵The plans of the godly are just; the advice of the wicked is treacherous.

⁶The words of the wicked are like a murderous ambush, but the words of the godly save lives.

⁷The wicked perish and are gone, but the children of the godly stand firm.

⁸Everyone admires a person with good sense, but a warped mind is despised.

⁹It is better to be a nobody with a servant than to be self-important but have no food.

¹⁰The godly are concerned for the welfare of their animals, but even the kindness of the wicked is cruel.

¹¹Hard work means prosperity; only fools idle away their time.

¹²Thieves are jealous of each other's loot, while the godly bear their own fruit.

¹³The wicked are trapped by their own words, but the godly escape such trouble.

¹⁴People can get many good things by the words they say; the work of their hands also gives them many benefits.

¹⁵Fools think they need no advice, but the wise listen to others.

¹⁶A fool is quick-tempered, but a wise person stays calm when insulted.

¹⁷An honest witness tells the truth; a false witness tells lies.

¹⁸Some people make cutting remarks, but the words of the wise bring healing.

¹⁹Truth stands the test of time; lies are soon exposed.

²⁰Deceit fills hearts that are plotting evil; joy fills hearts that are planning peace!

²¹No real harm befalls the godly, but the wicked have their fill of trouble.

²²The LORD hates those who don't keep their word, but he delights in those who do.

²³Wise people don't make a show of their knowledge, but fools broadcast their folly.

²⁴Work hard and become a leader; be lazy and become a slave.

²⁵Worry weighs a person down; an encouraging word cheers a person up.

²⁶The godly give good advice to their friends;* the wicked lead them astray.

²⁷Lazy people don't even cook the game they catch, but the diligent make use of everything they find.

²⁸The way of the godly leads to life; their path does not lead to death.

13 A wise child* accepts a parent's discipline; a young mocker refuses to listen.

²Good people enjoy the positive results of their words, but those who are treacherous crave violence.

³Those who control their tongue will have a long life; a quick retort can ruin everything.

⁴Lazy people want much but get little, but those who work hard will prosper and be satisfied.

⁵Those who are godly hate lies; the wicked come to shame and disgrace.

⁶Godliness helps people all through life, while the evil are destroyed by their wickedness.

⁷Some who are poor pretend to be rich; others who are rich pretend to be poor.

⁸The rich can pay a ransom, but the poor won't even get threatened.

⁹The life of the godly is full of light and joy, but the sinner's light is snuffed out.

¹⁰Pride leads to arguments; those who take advice are wise.

¹¹Wealth from get-rich-quick schemes quickly disappears; wealth from hard work grows.

¹²Hope deferred makes the heart sick, but when dreams come true, there is life and joy.

¹³People who despise advice will find themselves in trouble; those who respect it will succeed.

¹⁴The advice of the wise is like a life-giving fountain; those who accept it avoid the snares of death.

¹⁵A person with good sense is respected; a treacherous person walks a rocky road.

¹⁶Wise people think before they act; fools don't and even brag about it!

¹⁷An unreliable messenger stumbles into trouble, but a reliable messenger brings healing.

¹⁸If you ignore criticism, you will end in poverty and disgrace; if you accept criticism, you will be honored.

¹⁹It is pleasant to see dreams come true, but fools will not turn from evil to attain them.

²⁰Whoever walks with the wise will become wise; whoever walks with fools will suffer harm.

²¹Trouble chases sinners, while blessings chase the righteous!

²²Good people leave an inheritance to their grandchildren, but the sinner's wealth passes to the godly.

²³A poor person's farm may produce much food, but injustice sweeps it all away.

²⁴If you refuse to discipline your children, it proves you don't love them; if you love your children, you will be prompt to discipline them.

²⁵The godly eat to their hearts' content, but the belly of the wicked goes hungry.

14 A wise woman builds her house; a foolish woman tears hers down with her own hands.

²Those who follow the right path fear the LORD; those who take the wrong path despise him.

³The talk of fools is a rod for their backs,* but the words of the wise keep them out of trouble.

12:26 Or *The godly are cautious in friendship,* or *the godly are freed from evil.* The meaning of the Hebrew is uncertain. **13:1** Hebrew *son.* **14:3** Hebrew *a rod of pride.*

My Daily Worship

— June 12 —

THE PLEASURE OF DISCIPLINE

PROVERBS 12:1–13:25

To learn, you must love discipline; it is stupid to hate correction (12:1).

[i reflect]

Discipline is one of those unfortunate words that is largely misunderstood and usually said with a frown and a sigh. It is continually cast in a negative light—doing hard, unpleasant things, or worse, having some measure of pain inflicted on you by another.

But what is it really? Discipline is training—training that frees you to be the best you can be. Good parents discipline their children not to hurt but to help, to protect them from ultimate harm, and to point them in a better way.

Champion athletes discipline themselves. Endlessly running and stretching and lifting weights. They spend hours perfecting subtle techniques—twisting this body part or that, dipping or spinning just so.

Why? Why do they put themselves through such a rigorous and exacting regimen? Are they masochists? No. They subject themselves to all this because they know discipline brings freedom and reward. To be prepared, to know you are ready for whatever comes, is a wonderful thing. To be able to respond successfully—is there a joy better than this? That is why the proverb writer exhorts us to "love discipline."

Worshiping God is no different. It takes discipline to get our selfish souls to acknowledge God, and it takes further discipline to learn to honor him rightly. That means reading, studying, observing. It means diligence. It means discomfort. It means a reordering of priorities. It means loving the process and accepting correction.

The Academy Award-winning movie *Chariots of Fire* tells the story of Eric Liddell, a Scottish Christian, a champion runner, and eventual missionary to China. When chastised by his sister for spending so much time training for the Olympics, Liddell replied, "When I run, I feel [God's] pleasure." What a great picture of the freedom and joy discipline brings! And what a great reminder of the pleasure we can know when we discipline our hearts to worship him today.

[i pray]

Lord, grant me the wisdom and endurance to keep pushing and prodding my lazy soul,
so that I become a disciplined worshiper, honoring you as you so richly deserve.
I want to feel your pleasure as I live for you in every way, every day of my life.

[i respond]

Set an alarm to go off at six o'clock, and when it beeps, spend six minutes worshiping God. Focus. Sing. Pray. Listen. But whatever you do, let God have your full attention and full affection. Allow this exercise to become a continual habit.

⁴An empty stable stays clean, but no income comes from an empty stable.

⁵A truthful witness does not lie; a false witness breathes lies.

⁶A mocker seeks wisdom and never finds it, but knowledge comes easily to those with understanding.

⁷Stay away from fools, for you won't find knowledge there.

⁸The wise look ahead to see what is coming, but fools deceive themselves.

⁹Fools make fun of guilt, but the godly acknowledge it and seek reconciliation.

¹⁰Each heart knows its own bitterness, and no one else can fully share its joy.

¹¹The house of the wicked will perish, but the tent of the godly will flourish.

¹²There is a path before each person that seems right, but it ends in death.

¹³Laughter can conceal a heavy heart; when the laughter ends, the grief remains.

¹⁴Backsliders get what they deserve; good people receive their reward.

¹⁵Only simpletons believe everything they are told! The prudent carefully consider their steps.

¹⁶The wise are cautious* and avoid danger; fools plunge ahead with great confidence.

¹⁷Those who are short-tempered do foolish things, and schemers are hated.

¹⁸The simpleton is clothed with folly, but the wise person is crowned with knowledge.

¹⁹Evil people will bow before good people; the wicked will bow at the gates of the godly.

²⁰The poor are despised even by their neighbors, while the rich have many "friends."

²¹It is sin to despise one's neighbors; blessed are those who help the poor.

²²If you plot evil, you will be lost; but if you plan good, you will be granted unfailing love and faithfulness.

²³Work brings profit, but mere talk leads to poverty!

²⁴Wealth is a crown for the wise; the effort of fools yields only folly.

²⁵A truthful witness saves lives, but a false witness is a traitor.

²⁶Those who fear the LORD are secure; he will be a place of refuge for their children.

²⁷Fear of the LORD is a life-giving fountain; it offers escape from the snares of death.

²⁸A growing population is a king's glory; a dwindling nation is his doom.

²⁹Those who control their anger have great understanding; those with a hasty temper will make mistakes.

³⁰A relaxed attitude lengthens life; jealousy rots it away.

³¹Those who oppress the poor insult their Maker, but those who help the poor honor him.

³²The wicked are crushed by their sins, but the godly have a refuge when they die.

³³Wisdom is enshrined in an understanding heart; wisdom is not* found among fools.

³⁴Godliness exalts a nation, but sin is a disgrace to any people.

³⁵A king rejoices in servants who know what they are doing; he is angry with those who cause trouble.

15 A gentle answer turns away wrath, but harsh words stir up anger.

²The wise person makes learning a joy; fools spout only foolishness.

³The LORD is watching everywhere, keeping his eye on both the evil and the good.

⁴Gentle words bring life and health; a deceitful tongue crushes the spirit.

⁵Only a fool despises a parent's discipline; whoever learns from correction is wise.

⁶There is treasure in the house of the godly, but the earnings of the wicked bring trouble.

⁷Only the wise can give good advice; fools cannot do so.

⁸The LORD hates the sacrifice of the wicked, but he delights in the prayers of the upright.

⁹The LORD despises the way of the wicked, but he loves those who pursue godliness.

¹⁰Whoever abandons the right path will be severely punished; whoever hates correction will die.

¹¹Even the depths of Death and Destruction*

14:16 Hebrew *The wise fear.* **14:33** As in Greek version; Hebrew lacks *not.* **15:11** Hebrew *Sheol and Abaddon.*

My Daily Worship

— *June 13* —

SECURITY THROUGH FEAR

PROVERBS 14:1–35

Those who fear the LORD are secure; he will be
a place of refuge for their children (14:26).

[i reflect]

Death. Disease. Disaster. People fear so many things in this troubled world. Even when we're not wrestling with big worries like financial ruin or terrorism, we're haunted by lesser, but still potent, demons—fears of aging, being alone, or fitting in. Author and psychologist Dr. Les Parrott writes, "We are living in the Age of Anxiety. Many see stress and anxiety as the most pervasive psychological phenomenon of our time."

The result of all these anxious thoughts is a pervading sense of insecurity. And so what do we typically do? We scramble about trying to guard against this contingency or ward off that possibility. And just about the time we think we've taken care of one worry, another problem appears on the horizon, setting off a whole new round of uncertainty. Is this any way to live?

Solomon's wise observation, "those who fear the LORD are secure," reminds us of a great truth. Real security is found in the Lord. He is the ultimate safe place. He is a cosmic version of those castles and round towers of Ireland that contain tiny doorways, leading to small staircases that twist upward to fortified "safe rooms" high within. In times of trouble, women and children found refuge and security in these hideaways that were inaccessible to the biggest, most fierce invaders. No wonder the psalms refer to God as our rock and fortress, our shield and stronghold (Psalm 31:2–3; 18:2).

But notice what else Solomon says. The ones who actually *experience* this security in the deepest and richest ways are those who "fear the LORD." In other words they revere him. They think of him, hold him in highest regard, and seek to know and please him. God-fearing folk have their minds and hearts set on him. To fear God is simply to worship him.

As you encounter stressful situations today, as anxious thoughts creep into your mind, or as fears begin to mount, use those moments to turn to God and worship him.

[i pray]

O, my Rock, my Shield, my Fortress, teach me to fear you, to worship you,
to love you, to seek you. And as I do, let me know true security and rest.

[i respond]

Memorize the verse above (Proverbs 14:26). Repeat it to yourself all through your day. Share it with at least three people.

are known by the LORD. How much more does he know the human heart!

¹²Mockers don't love those who rebuke them, so they stay away from the wise.

¹³A glad heart makes a happy face; a broken heart crushes the spirit.

¹⁴A wise person is hungry for truth, while the fool feeds on trash.

¹⁵For the poor, every day brings trouble; for the happy heart, life is a continual feast.

¹⁶It is better to have little with fear for the LORD than to have great treasure with turmoil.

¹⁷A bowl of soup with someone you love is better than steak with someone you hate.

¹⁸A hothead starts fights; a cool-tempered person tries to stop them.

¹⁹A lazy person has trouble all through life; the path of the upright is easy!

²⁰Sensible children bring joy to their father; foolish children despise their mother.

²¹Foolishness brings joy to those who have no sense; a sensible person stays on the right path.

²²Plans go wrong for lack of advice; many counselors bring success.

²³Everyone enjoys a fitting reply; it is wonderful to say the right thing at the right time!

²⁴The path of the wise leads to life above; they leave the grave* behind.

²⁵The LORD destroys the house of the proud, but he protects the property of widows.

²⁶The LORD despises the thoughts of the wicked, but he delights in pure words.

²⁷Dishonest money brings grief to the whole family, but those who hate bribes will live.

²⁸The godly think before speaking; the wicked spout evil words.

²⁹The LORD is far from the wicked, but he hears the prayers of the righteous.

³⁰A cheerful look brings joy to the heart; good news makes for good health.

³¹If you listen to constructive criticism, you will be at home among the wise.

³²If you reject criticism, you only harm yourself; but if you listen to correction, you grow in understanding.

³³Fear of the LORD teaches a person to be wise; humility precedes honor.

16 We can gather our thoughts, but the LORD gives the right answer.

²People may be pure in their own eyes, but the LORD examines their motives.

³Commit your work to the LORD, and then your plans will succeed.

⁴The LORD has made everything for his own purposes, even the wicked for punishment.

⁵The LORD despises pride; be assured that the proud will be punished.

⁶Unfailing love and faithfulness cover sin; evil is avoided by fear of the LORD.

⁷When the ways of people please the LORD, he makes even their enemies live at peace with them.

⁸It is better to be poor and godly than rich and dishonest.

⁹We can make our plans, but the LORD determines our steps.

¹⁰The king speaks with divine wisdom; he must never judge unfairly.

¹¹The LORD demands fairness in every business deal; he sets the standard.

¹²A king despises wrongdoing, for his rule depends on his justice.

¹³The king is pleased with righteous lips; he loves those who speak honestly.

¹⁴The anger of the king is a deadly threat; the wise do what they can to appease it.

¹⁵When the king smiles, there is life; his favor refreshes like a gentle rain.

¹⁶How much better to get wisdom than gold, and understanding than silver!

¹⁷The path of the upright leads away from evil; whoever follows that path is safe.

¹⁸Pride goes before destruction, and haughtiness before a fall.

¹⁹It is better to live humbly with the poor than to share plunder with the proud.

²⁰Those who listen to instruction will prosper; those who trust the LORD will be happy.

²¹The wise are known for their understanding,

15:24 Hebrew *Sheol.*

My Daily Worship

— *June 14* —

THE HEART OF THE MATTER

PROVERBS 15:1–33

The LORD hates the sacrifice of the wicked, but he delights
in the prayers of the upright (15:8).

[i reflect]

William Temple, Archbishop of Canterbury (1942–44), wrote: "Worship is the submission of all our nature to God. It is the quickening of conscience by his holiness; the nourishment of mind with his truth; the purifying of imagination by his beauty; the opening of the heart to his love; the surrender of will to his purpose—and all of this gathered up in adoration."

Contrast this breathtaking understanding of true worship with the prevailing popular view that worship is the attempt to please God by engaging in certain prescribed religious rituals. Sadly, for some people worship is the handful of "holy acts" one does at certain times and in certain places (churches, Christian camps, etc.). Bottom line, if you sing a few praise songs . . . if you put money in the offering plate . . . if you kneel and pray at the altar . . . if you stand and speak in tongues . . . if you have some kind of other emotional experience, you can say you have worshiped. God is satisfied, and now you can go back to your normal, everyday life.

The problem with this kind of thinking is that it turns God into a kind of religious "hall monitor," roaming up and down the aisles of churches, to see who is participating. He becomes the worship cop who wants to make sure we toe the line. At issue is our compliance—our bodies in the right places going through (literally) the right worship motions, our lips saying all the right things.

But God wants our hearts. All the religious gyrations in the world don't mean a thing if our hearts aren't right.

If you want to delight God, start with your heart. Allow your worship to flow from a heart that is centered on who God is and who you are in him.

[i pray]

Lord, remind me again and again, that your focus is more on who I am than
on what I do. Purify my heart. Cleanse my heart so that everything
about me, all day every day, is worship that honors you.

[i respond]

Go to a quiet place and meditate on Psalm 139:23–24. Ask God to show you any wrong attitudes and actions that need to be confessed and renounced. Listen for the whisper of the Spirit.

and instruction is appreciated if it's well presented.

²²Discretion is a life-giving fountain to those who possess it, but discipline is wasted on fools.

²³From a wise mind comes wise speech; the words of the wise are persuasive.

²⁴Kind words are like honey—sweet to the soul and healthy for the body.

²⁵There is a path before each person that seems right, but it ends in death.

²⁶It is good for workers to have an appetite; an empty stomach drives them on.

²⁷Scoundrels hunt for scandal; their words are a destructive blaze.

²⁸A troublemaker plants seeds of strife; gossip separates the best of friends.

²⁹Violent people deceive their companions, leading them down a harmful path.

³⁰With narrowed eyes, they plot evil; without a word, they plan their mischief.

³¹Gray hair is a crown of glory; it is gained by living a godly life.

³²It is better to be patient than powerful; it is better to have self-control than to conquer a city.

³³We may throw the dice, but the LORD determines how they fall.

17 A dry crust eaten in peace is better than a great feast with strife.

²A wise slave will rule over the master's shameful sons and will share their inheritance.

³Fire tests the purity of silver and gold, but the LORD tests the heart.

⁴Wrongdoers listen to wicked talk; liars pay attention to destructive words.

⁵Those who mock the poor insult their Maker; those who rejoice at the misfortune of others will be punished.

⁶Grandchildren are the crowning glory of the aged; parents are the pride of their children.

⁷Eloquent speech is not fitting for a fool; even less are lies fitting for a ruler.

⁸A bribe seems to work like magic for those who give it; they succeed in all they do.

⁹Disregarding another person's faults preserves love; telling about them separates close friends.

¹⁰A single rebuke does more for a person of understanding than a hundred lashes on the back of a fool.

¹¹Evil people seek rebellion, but they will be severely punished.

¹²It is safer to meet a bear robbed of her cubs than to confront a fool caught in folly.

¹³If you repay evil for good, evil will never leave your house.

¹⁴Beginning a quarrel is like opening a floodgate, so drop the matter before a dispute breaks out.

¹⁵The LORD despises those who acquit the guilty and condemn the innocent.

¹⁶It is senseless to pay tuition to educate a fool who has no heart for wisdom.

¹⁷A friend is always loyal, and a brother is born to help in time of need.

¹⁸It is poor judgment to co-sign a friend's note, to become responsible for a neighbor's debts.

¹⁹Anyone who loves to quarrel loves sin; anyone who speaks boastfully* invites disaster.

²⁰The crooked heart will not prosper; the twisted tongue tumbles into trouble.

²¹It is painful to be the parent of a fool; there is no joy for the father of a rebel.

²²A cheerful heart is good medicine, but a broken spirit saps a person's strength.

²³The wicked accept secret bribes to pervert justice.

²⁴Sensible people keep their eyes glued on wisdom, but a fool's eyes wander to the ends of the earth.

²⁵A foolish child* brings grief to a father and bitterness to a mother.

²⁶It is wrong to fine the godly for being good or to punish nobles for being honest!

²⁷A truly wise person uses few words; a person with understanding is even-tempered.

17:19 Or *who builds up defenses;* Hebrew reads *who makes a high gate.* **17:25** Hebrew *son.*

My Daily Worship

— June 15 —

Whose Agenda Is It Anyway?

PROVERBS 16:1–33

Commit your work to the LORD,
and then your plans will succeed (16:3).

[i reflect]

William Barclay said that work done for love always has a glory. But how many people work for love, or as Paul urged, for the glory of God (1 Corinthians 10:31)? Listen to conversations. You'll hear phrases like "my job," "my goals," and "my happiness." The fact is most people view their lives as their own. Even more astonishing, human nature subconsciously thinks, "What matters most in the world is me and how things affect me."

Then Christ enters the picture, messing up everything. To hear the Bible tell it, he is The Point. Life revolves around him, not us. Even more startling to self-absorbed, self-willed souls is the truth that he owns us, meaning he has the perfect right to command our lives. He did not come to be our copilot. Nor is his eternal job description to give us divine assistance in accomplishing all our self-centered plans and dreams. No, he came to invite us to have a meaningful part in fulfilling *his* agenda.

That's the idea behind today's often misunderstood verse. Read it again. Think of it against the backdrop of Proverbs 3:5–6: "Trust in the LORD with all your heart; do not depend on your own understanding. Seek his will in all you do, and he will direct your paths."

Do you see? Real life is found in trusting God, not ordering him around like a divine waiter. Satisfaction comes when we seek his will, rather than devising our own plans. When we make him central, when we give him our hearts and sign off on his plans, then—at last!—we find direction, success, and the significance our souls hunger for.

Your work as a worshiper today is to pursue God's agenda for the world at your workplace and in your neighborhood. When you commit to do that, you can never, ever fail.

[i pray]

Lord, speak to me. Show me the truth about my heart. Let me see if I am truly committed
to your work or to my own. Remind me that success in any venture that
excludes you or pushes you to the sidelines is actually failure.

[i respond]

Write out the goals and dreams you are currently pursuing. Have you committed those plans to God? Write either a "yes" or "no" next to each one as you answer that question. For every no, take time now to offer up those plans to him.

²⁸Even fools are thought to be wise when they keep silent; when they keep their mouths shut, they seem intelligent.

18 A recluse is self-indulgent, snarling at every sound principle of conduct.

²Fools have no interest in understanding; they only want to air their own opinions.

³When the wicked arrive, contempt, shame, and disgrace are sure to follow.

⁴A person's words can be life-giving water; words of true wisdom are as refreshing as a bubbling brook.

⁵It is wrong for a judge to favor the guilty or condemn the innocent.

⁶Fools get into constant quarrels; they are asking for a beating.

⁷The mouths of fools are their ruin; their lips get them into trouble.

⁸What dainty morsels rumors are—but they sink deep into one's heart.

⁹A lazy person is as bad as someone who destroys things.

¹⁰The name of the LORD is a strong fortress; the godly run to him and are safe.

¹¹The rich think of their wealth as an impregnable defense; they imagine it is a high wall of safety.

¹²Haughtiness goes before destruction; humility precedes honor.

¹³What a shame, what folly, to give advice before listening to the facts!

¹⁴The human spirit can endure a sick body, but who can bear it if the spirit is crushed?

¹⁵Intelligent people are always open to new ideas. In fact, they look for them.

¹⁶Giving a gift works wonders; it may bring you before important people!

¹⁷Any story sounds true until someone sets the record straight.

¹⁸Casting lots can end arguments and settle disputes between powerful opponents.

¹⁹It's harder to make amends with an offended friend than to capture a fortified city. Arguments separate friends like a gate locked with iron bars.

²⁰Words satisfy the soul as food satisfies the stomach; the right words on a person's lips bring satisfaction.

²¹Those who love to talk will experience the consequences, for the tongue can kill or nourish life.

²²The man who finds a wife finds a treasure and receives favor from the LORD.

²³The poor plead for mercy; the rich answer with insults.

²⁴There are "friends" who destroy each other, but a real friend sticks closer than a brother.

19 It is better to be poor and honest than to be a fool and dishonest.

²Zeal without knowledge is not good; a person who moves too quickly may go the wrong way.

³People ruin their lives by their own foolishness and then are angry at the LORD.

⁴Wealth makes many "friends"; poverty drives them away.

⁵A false witness will not go unpunished, nor will a liar escape.

⁶Many beg favors from a prince; everyone is the friend of a person who gives gifts!

⁷If the relatives of the poor despise them, how much more will their friends avoid them. The poor call after them, but they are gone.

⁸To acquire wisdom is to love oneself; people who cherish understanding will prosper.

⁹A false witness will not go unpunished, and a liar will be destroyed.

¹⁰It isn't right for a fool to live in luxury or for a slave to rule over princes!

¹¹People with good sense restrain their anger; they earn esteem by overlooking wrongs.

¹²The king's anger is like a lion's roar, but his favor is like dew on the grass.

¹³A foolish child* is a calamity to a father; a nagging wife annoys like a constant dripping.

¹⁴Parents can provide their sons with an inheritance of houses and wealth, but only the LORD can give an understanding wife.

19:13 Hebrew *son;* also in 19:27.

My Daily Worship

— *June 16* —

THE GREAT COVER-UP

PROVERBS 17:1–18:24

Disregarding another person's faults preserves love;
telling about them separates close friends (17:9).

[i reflect]

Close your eyes for a moment and remember the first secret you shared that someone didn't keep. Was it a whisper in third grade of hatred for a love unrequited? An embarrassing revelation made to a parent that was broadcast to the family? Perhaps as an adult you bared your soul to your best friend, only to have your kindred spirit involve others in your most intimate struggle.

Chances are you remember a moment of betrayal from your past; and even now, there's a tender spot in your heart that's strangely sore from the memory. Knowing this, it's even harder to admit that we ourselves have inflicted such pain on others. And looking at our hearts, we know that announcing another's faults has at some time made us look better.

That is why Solomon took time to remind us that "disregarding another person's faults preserves love." We should be willing to overlook the faults of another because, after all, isn't that what our God does for us? "He will not constantly accuse us, . . . For he understands how weak we are; he knows we are only dust" (Psalm 103:9, 14). How thankful we are that this all-powerful Savior, full of tenderness and compassion, doesn't do to us as we deserve! This "unfailing love toward those who fear him" (Psalm 103:11) blankets us with mercy, inspires our devotion, and reminds us to humbly overlook the faults of others.

Because we are made in his image, we are called to offer the ultimate form of worship: to be and act like him. "Dear friends, since God loved us that much, we surely ought to love each other" (1 John 4:11).

As an act of worship today, look for opportunities where you can disregard another person's faults and preserve love.

[i pray]

Sometimes I'm overwhelmed by your understanding. Please forgive me, once again,
for pointing out the faults of others. Help me to revel in your mercy and love,
and to offer the same to others as my act of worship to you.

[i respond]

What is in your heart that prompts you to reveal the faults of others? Make a list of the ways the Lord has forgiven you; then write down all the reasons you love him. Find one way to show forgiveness and love by disregarding the faults of someone else.

¹⁵A lazy person sleeps soundly—and goes hungry.

¹⁶Keep the commandments and keep your life; despising them leads to death.

¹⁷If you help the poor, you are lending to the LORD—and he will repay you!

¹⁸Discipline your children while there is hope. If you don't, you will ruin their lives.

¹⁹Short-tempered people must pay their own penalty. If you rescue them once, you will have to do it again.

²⁰Get all the advice and instruction you can, and be wise the rest of your life.

²¹You can make many plans, but the LORD's purpose will prevail.

²²Loyalty makes a person attractive. And it is better to be poor than dishonest.

²³Fear of the LORD gives life, security, and protection from harm.

²⁴Some people are so lazy that they won't even lift a finger to feed themselves.

²⁵If you punish a mocker, the simpleminded will learn a lesson; if you reprove the wise, they will be all the wiser.

²⁶Children who mistreat their father or chase away their mother are a public disgrace and an embarrassment.

²⁷If you stop listening to instruction, my child, you have turned your back on knowledge.

²⁸A corrupt witness makes a mockery of justice; the mouth of the wicked gulps down evil.

²⁹Mockers will be punished, and the backs of fools will be beaten.

20 Wine produces mockers; liquor leads to brawls. Whoever is led astray by drink cannot be wise.

²The king's fury is like a lion's roar; to rouse his anger is to risk your life.

³Avoiding a fight is a mark of honor; only fools insist on quarreling.

⁴If you are too lazy to plow in the right season, you will have no food at the harvest.

⁵Though good advice lies deep within a person's heart, the wise will draw it out.

⁶Many will say they are loyal friends, but who can find one who is really faithful?

⁷The godly walk with integrity; blessed are their children after them.

⁸When a king judges, he carefully weighs all the evidence, distinguishing the bad from the good.

⁹Who can say, "I have cleansed my heart; I am pure and free from sin"?

¹⁰The LORD despises double standards of every kind.

¹¹Even children are known by the way they act, whether their conduct is pure and right.

¹²Ears to hear and eyes to see—both are gifts from the LORD.

¹³If you love sleep, you will end in poverty. Keep your eyes open, and there will be plenty to eat!

¹⁴The buyer haggles over the price, saying, "It's worthless," then brags about getting a bargain!

¹⁵Wise speech is rarer and more valuable than gold and rubies.

¹⁶Be sure to get collateral from anyone who guarantees the debt of a stranger. Get a deposit if someone guarantees the debt of a foreigner.*

¹⁷Stolen bread tastes sweet, but it turns to gravel in the mouth.

¹⁸Plans succeed through good counsel; don't go to war without the advice of others.

¹⁹A gossip tells secrets, so don't hang around with someone who talks too much.

²⁰If you curse your father or mother, the lamp of your life will be snuffed out.

²¹An inheritance obtained early in life is not a blessing in the end.

²²Don't say, "I will get even for this wrong." Wait for the LORD to handle the matter.

²³The LORD despises double standards; he is not pleased by dishonest scales.

²⁴How can we understand the road we travel? It is the LORD who directs our steps.

²⁵It is dangerous to make a rash promise to God before counting the cost.

²⁶A wise king finds the wicked, lays them

20:16 An alternate reading in the Hebrew text is *the debt of an adulterous woman;* compare 27:13.

My Daily Worship

— June 17 —

WAIT BEFORE IT'S TOO LATE

PROVERBS 19:1–20:30

*Zeal without knowledge is not good; a person who moves
too quickly may go the wrong way (19:2).*

[i reflect]

Kings, nobles, and peasants. History shows people from all walks of life have made errors in judgment that cost them something. In the Shakespearean tragedy Romeo and Juliet, the love-smitten Romeo plots his own suicide upon the announcement that his Juliet is dead. In his haste, he ingests poison before he receives the message that she is not gone, but merely drugged. We cringe at the couple's misfortune and scoff at Romeo's hastiness.

It's true, as the proverb writer points out, that acting without the right information will often lead us down a wrong path. Consider another example of fear and misjudgment in the Old Testament when King Saul, in the heat of battle, refused to wait for the priest Samuel. Instead, Saul hastily offered up a burnt offering to the Lord. Samuel arrived, rebuked him, and named the price for Saul's lack of patience: "Had you obeyed, the LORD would have established your kingdom over Israel forever. But now your dynasty must end, for the LORD has sought out a man after his own heart" (1 Samuel 13:13–14a).

The stories of impetuous mistakes seem endless. And if we mentally review our past, we find our own errors in judgment. Unwritten, perhaps—yet not unseen by an all-knowing God. We excuse ourselves by saying that action must be better than inaction: At least we were doing *something*.

How strange that the very action we avoid is the one God requests of us: *wait*. Oh, the heartache, financial ruin, vocational distress, and relationships that might be spared if we rested in God's promise, "The LORD is wonderfully good to those who wait for him and seek him. So it is good to wait quietly for salvation from the LORD" (Lamentations 3:25–26).

Wait. Seek God today before each decision you need to make. Take time to mentally worship him, ask him for guidance and wisdom, and then wait.

[i pray]

*Forgive me, Father, for often running ahead of you. Give me a heart of wisdom and show me
how to wait on you—offering my gifts, energy, and time to you as a sacrifice of praise.*

[i respond]

On a note card, write down five things you can do while waiting on God (specific ways to pray, keeping track of circumstances in a journal, spending extra time in praise, etc). Have the list ready for your next season of waiting.

out like wheat, then runs the crushing wheel over them.

²⁷The LORD's searchlight penetrates the human spirit,* exposing every hidden motive.

²⁸Unfailing love and faithfulness protect the king; his throne is made secure through love.

²⁹The glory of the young is their strength; the gray hair of experience is the splendor of the old.

³⁰Physical punishment cleanses away evil;* such discipline purifies the heart.

21 The king's heart is like a stream of water directed by the LORD; he turns it wherever he pleases.

²People may think they are doing what is right, but the LORD examines the heart.

³The LORD is more pleased when we do what is just and right than when we give him sacrifices.

⁴Haughty eyes, a proud heart, and evil actions are all sin.

⁵Good planning and hard work lead to prosperity, but hasty shortcuts lead to poverty.

⁶Wealth created by lying is a vanishing mist and a deadly trap.*

⁷Because the wicked refuse to do what is just, their violence boomerangs and destroys them.

⁸The guilty walk a crooked path; the innocent travel a straight road.

⁹It is better to live alone in the corner of an attic than with a contentious wife in a lovely home.

¹⁰Evil people love to harm others; their neighbors get no mercy from them.

¹¹A simpleton can learn only by seeing mockers punished; a wise person learns from instruction.

¹²The Righteous One* knows what is going on in the homes of the wicked; he will bring the wicked to disaster.

¹³Those who shut their ears to the cries of the poor will be ignored in their own time of need.

¹⁴A secret gift calms anger; a secret bribe pacifies fury.

¹⁵Justice is a joy to the godly, but it causes dismay among evildoers.

¹⁶The person who strays from common sense will end up in the company of the dead.

¹⁷Those who love pleasure become poor; wine and luxury are not the way to riches.

¹⁸Sometimes the wicked are punished to save the godly, and the treacherous for the upright.

¹⁹It is better to live alone in the desert than with a crabby, complaining wife.

²⁰The wise have wealth and luxury, but fools spend whatever they get.

²¹Whoever pursues godliness and unfailing love will find life, godliness, and honor.

²²The wise conquer the city of the strong and level the fortress in which they trust.

²³If you keep your mouth shut, you will stay out of trouble.

²⁴Mockers are proud and haughty; they act with boundless arrogance.

²⁵The desires of lazy people will be their ruin, for their hands refuse to work. ²⁶They are always greedy for more, while the godly love to give!

²⁷God loathes the sacrifice of an evil person, especially when it is brought with ulterior motives.

²⁸A false witness will be cut off, but an attentive witness will be allowed to speak.

²⁹The wicked put up a bold front, but the upright proceed with care.

³⁰Human plans, no matter how wise or well advised, cannot stand against the LORD.

³¹The horses are prepared for battle, but the victory belongs to the LORD.

22 Choose a good reputation over great riches, for being held in high esteem is better than having silver or gold.

²The rich and the poor have this in common: The LORD made them both.

³A prudent person foresees the danger

20:27 Or *The human spirit is the LORD's searchlight.* 20:30 The meaning of the Hebrew is uncertain. 21:6 As in Greek version; Hebrew reads *mist for those who seek death.* 21:12 Or *The righteous man.*

My Daily Worship

— *June 18* —

PURSUING THE RIGHT STUFF

PROVERBS 21:1–22:29

*Whoever pursues godliness and unfailing love will
find life, godliness, and honor (21:21).*

[i reflect]

The old adage says "cleanliness is next to godliness." No one would argue that maintaining good hygiene is a positive pursuit, but *next to godliness?* What exactly does that mean? According to the proverb writer, the pursuit of godliness should be every believer's goal. But what does it take to be a godly man or woman?

The life of the apostle Paul is one illustration. A Pharisee with high credentials who persecuted Christians, his conversion was nothing short of a miracle. Paul's desire for godliness consumed him, as he counted all of his education, background, and position as nothing. "God forbid that I should boast about anything except the cross of our Lord Jesus Christ" (Galatians 6:14). Paul died a martyr for his faith, but he would be honored as the foremost writer of the New Testament, an apostle to the Gentiles, and a godly example to every believer.

The renowned preacher Jonathan Edwards offers another example. Consider his prayer of daily consecration, "I have given myself clear away and not retained anything of my own. I have been to God this morning and told him I have given myself wholly to him. . . . I take him as my whole portion and felicity, looking upon nothing else as any part of my happiness. His law is the constant rule of my obedience."

In today's world, our first priority is often making our life more comfortable. But God asks us to put first things first. His priorities are that we love him with all our being, walk in ways that glorify him, and share his love with others in everything we do and say. As Augustine wrote, "Let the desire for glory be surpassed by the love of righteousness." That's what it means to pursue godliness.

For a moment, forget about what others think of you or about your to-do list. Ask yourself if your worship includes pursuing God's priorities. When you put first things first, God promises "godliness, life, and honor" will follow.

[i pray]

*Please forgive me, Father, for the times I forget about your priorities. Thank you for accepting me
as I am, and help me to live out a life that overflows with godliness and love.*

[i respond]

Reserve three blank lines at the top of today's to-do list. Write: "love God with all my being," "walk in ways that glorify him," and "share his love with others," giving these things priority.

ahead and takes precautions; the simpleton goes blindly on and suffers the consequences.

⁴True humility and fear of the LORD lead to riches, honor, and long life.

⁵The deceitful walk a thorny, treacherous road; whoever values life will stay away.

⁶Teach your children to choose the right path, and when they are older, they will remain upon it.

⁷Just as the rich rule the poor, so the borrower is servant to the lender.

⁸Those who plant seeds of injustice will harvest disaster, and their reign of terror will end.

⁹Blessed are those who are generous, because they feed the poor.

¹⁰Throw out the mocker, and fighting, quarrels, and insults will disappear.

¹¹Anyone who loves a pure heart and gracious speech is the king's friend.

¹²The LORD preserves knowledge, but he ruins the plans of the deceitful.

¹³The lazy person is full of excuses, saying, "If I go outside, I might meet a lion in the street and be killed!"

¹⁴The mouth of an immoral woman is a deep pit; those living under the LORD's displeasure will fall into it.

¹⁵A youngster's heart is filled with foolishness, but discipline will drive it away.

¹⁶A person who gets ahead by oppressing the poor or by showering gifts on the rich will end in poverty.

THIRTY SAYINGS OF THE WISE

¹⁷Listen to the words of the wise; apply your heart to my instruction. ¹⁸For it is good to keep these sayings deep within yourself, always ready on your lips. ¹⁹I am teaching you today—yes, you—so you will trust in the LORD. ²⁰I have written thirty sayings for you, filled with advice and knowledge. ²¹In this way, you may know the truth and bring an accurate report to those who sent you.

²²Do not rob the poor because they are poor or exploit the needy in court. ²³For the LORD is their defender. He will injure anyone who injures them.

²⁴Keep away from angry, short-tempered people, ²⁵or you will learn to be like them and endanger your soul.

²⁶Do not co-sign another person's note or put up a guarantee for someone else's loan. ²⁷If you can't pay it, even your bed will be snatched from under you.

²⁸Do not steal your neighbor's property by moving the ancient boundary markers set up by your ancestors.

²⁹Do you see any truly competent workers? They will serve kings rather than ordinary people.

23 When dining with a ruler, pay attention to what is put before you. ²If you are a big eater, put a knife to your throat, ³and don't desire all the delicacies—deception may be involved.

⁴Don't weary yourself trying to get rich. Why waste your time? ⁵For riches can disappear as though they had the wings of a bird!

⁶Don't eat with people who are stingy; don't desire their delicacies. ⁷"Eat and drink," they say, but they don't mean it. They are always thinking about how much it costs. ⁸You will vomit up the delicious food they serve, and you will have to take back your words of appreciation for their "kindness."

⁹Don't waste your breath on fools, for they will despise the wisest advice.

¹⁰Don't steal the land of defenseless orphans by moving the ancient boundary markers, ¹¹for their Redeemer is strong. He himself will bring their charges against you.

¹²Commit yourself to instruction; attune your ears to hear words of knowledge.

¹³Don't fail to correct your children. They won't die if you spank them. ¹⁴Physical discipline may well save them from death.*

¹⁵My child,* how I will rejoice if you become wise. ¹⁶Yes, my heart will thrill when you speak what is right and just.

¹⁷Don't envy sinners, but always continue to

23:14 Hebrew *from Sheol.* 23:15 Hebrew *My son;* also in 23:19.

My Daily Worship

LOOKING UP, NOT SIDEWAYS

PROVERBS 23:1–35

Don't envy sinners, but always continue to fear the LORD. For surely you have
a future ahead of you; your hope will not be disappointed (23:17).

[i reflect]

Few of us like to admit to feelings of envy, yet few of us are immune from them either. Your neighbor pulls into his driveway behind the wheel of a new car and you feel a twinge of discontent with your older vehicle. A coworker is given the job promotion you hoped for, or perhaps a former classmate achieves the sort of success you've dreamed of. Envy can cause us to look sideways at what others have and down upon our own circumstances rather than up to God.

Neighbors, coworkers, and classmates may not be the type of "sinners" the proverb writer is referring to, but the command not to envy others applies to us all. Envy inhibits our ability to worship. When we focus on what others have, we take our attention away from all that God has done for us. It's been said that a discontented person has the attitude that everything he does for God is too much, and everything God does for him is too little.

The antidote to discontentment is found in today's key verse. Rather than experiencing envy of others, we are encouraged to develop a healthy reverence for the Lord. God alone has the power to satisfy us and he has promised to supply everything that we truly need. Author G. K. Chesterton once defined true contentment as "a real, even an active virtue—not only affirmative but creative. It is the power of getting out of any situation all there is in it."

Worship draws us closer to God so that we can begin to see our lives from his perspective. Whatever your present circumstances, look for ways today that you can draw every ounce of good from them. Remember that God has promised you both a future and a hope. Keep looking up!

[i pray]

Lord, I admit that at times I'm envious when I look at the lives of others
in my world. Please rid me of this insidious tendency to compare.
I know that true contentment is found in you alone.

[i respond]

As Chesterton said, true contentment is "an active virtue." Walk around your house, apartment, or office and look for all the possessions, people, and blessings that you have been given. Thank God for all you have.

fear the LORD. [18]For surely you have a future ahead of you; your hope will not be disappointed.

[19]My child, listen and be wise. Keep your heart on the right course. [20]Do not carouse with drunkards and gluttons, [21]for they are on their way to poverty. Too much sleep clothes a person with rags.

[22]Listen to your father, who gave you life, and don't despise your mother's experience when she is old. [23]Get the truth and don't ever sell it; also get wisdom, discipline, and discernment. [24]The father of godly children has cause for joy. What a pleasure it is to have wise children.* [25]So give your parents joy! May she who gave you birth be happy.

[26]O my son, give me your heart. May your eyes delight in my ways of wisdom. [27]A prostitute is a deep pit; an adulterous woman is treacherous.* [28]She hides and waits like a robber, looking for another victim who will be unfaithful to his wife.

[29]Who has anguish? Who has sorrow? Who is always fighting? Who is always complaining? Who has unnecessary bruises? Who has bloodshot eyes? [30]It is the one who spends long hours in the taverns, trying out new drinks. [31]Don't let the sparkle and smooth taste of wine deceive you. [32]For in the end it bites like a poisonous serpent; it stings like a viper. [33]You will see hallucinations, and you will say crazy things. [34]You will stagger like a sailor tossed at sea, clinging to a swaying mast. [35]And you will say, "They hit me, but I didn't feel it. I didn't even know it when they beat me up. When will I wake up so I can have another drink?"

24 Don't envy evil people; don't desire their company. [2]For they spend their days plotting violence, and their words are always stirring up trouble.

[3]A house is built by wisdom and becomes strong through good sense. [4]Through knowledge its rooms are filled with all sorts of precious riches and valuables.

[5]A wise man is mightier than a strong man,* and a man of knowledge is more powerful than a strong man. [6]So don't go to war without wise guidance; victory depends on having many counselors.

[7]Wisdom is too much for a fool. When the leaders gather, the fool has nothing to say.

[8]A person who plans evil will get a reputation as a troublemaker. [9]The schemes of a fool are sinful; everyone despises a mocker.

[10]If you fail under pressure, your strength is not very great.

[11]Rescue those who are unjustly sentenced to death; don't stand back and let them die. [12]Don't try to avoid responsibility by saying you didn't know about it. For God knows all hearts, and he sees you. He keeps watch over your soul, and he knows you knew! And he will judge all people according to what they have done.

[13]My child,* eat honey, for it is good, and the honeycomb is sweet to the taste. [14]In the same way, wisdom is sweet to your soul. If you find it, you will have a bright future, and your hopes will not be cut short.

[15]Do not lie in wait like an outlaw at the home of the godly. And don't raid the house where the godly live. [16]They may trip seven times, but each time they will rise again. But one calamity is enough to lay the wicked low.

[17]Do not rejoice when your enemies fall into trouble. Don't be happy when they stumble. [18]For the LORD will be displeased with you and will turn his anger away from them.

[19]Do not fret because of evildoers; don't envy the wicked. [20]For the evil have no future; their light will be snuffed out.

[21]My child, fear the LORD and the king, and don't associate with rebels. [22]For you will go down with them to sudden disaster. Who knows where the punishment from the LORD and the king will end?

MORE SAYINGS OF THE WISE

[23]Here are some further sayings of the wise:

23:24 Hebrew *a wise son.* 23:27 Hebrew *is a narrow well.* 24:5 As in Greek version; Hebrew reads *A wise man is strength.* 24:13 Hebrew *My son;* also in 24:21.

My Daily Worship

— *June 20* —

PAY BACK WITH LOVE

PROVERBS 24:1–34

Do not rejoice when your enemies fall into trouble.
Don't be happy when they stumble (24:17).

[i reflect]

A story is told about Abraham Lincoln in the closing days of the Civil War. A prominent senator took the floor of the Senate to demand that, as the enemy to the Union, the South should be destroyed. Lincoln listened quietly. When the politician finally ceased his diatribe, Lincoln was said to have calmly replied, "Do I not destroy my enemy when I make him my friend?"

We live in a world in which vengeance is common. Conventional wisdom demands that if you are struck, you strike back. If someone hurts you, you hurt him. Payback time. Tit for tat.

Proverbs speaks of the wisdom that comes from heaven, however—unconventional wisdom that is peace-loving and full of mercy. This is the type of wisdom that restrains us from gloating over the misfortunes of our enemies but shares their sorrows instead.

Paul's first letter to the Corinthians speaks of a love that does not delight in evil but rejoices with the truth (13:6.) It is only natural to feel a sense of satisfaction when those who have hurt us receive their "comeuppance." Yet today's key verse cautions us against such a response. How and where do we learn to love in such an unnatural fashion?

When we attempt to avenge the wrongs predicated upon us we assume the rightful role of God, who alone will judge the earth. Worship reminds us of our proper relationship: God is the one who judges justly; we do not. Scripture does not state that we always will be treated fairly on this side of heaven, but we are promised that one day God himself will avenge all wrongs.

When you are tempted to shout "unfair" today, remember the One you worship. Allow him to correct the wrongs while he strengthens you to show love and mercy.

[i pray]

I struggle with this, Lord. I may not try to get even with those who have hurt me,
but I confess that I'd feel a certain satisfaction if they fell into trouble.
I need your unconventional love for my adversaries.

[i respond]

Think of a person who has recently wronged you. Pay that person back with love by calling them on the phone, jotting them a note, or leaving them a small gift on their desk.

It is wrong to show favoritism when passing judgment. ²⁴A judge who says to the wicked, "You are innocent," will be cursed by many people and denounced by the nations. ²⁵But blessings are showered on those who convict the guilty.

²⁶It is an honor to receive an honest reply.

²⁷Develop your business first before building your house.

²⁸Do not testify spitefully against innocent neighbors; don't lie about them. ²⁹And don't say, "Now I can pay them back for all their meanness to me! I'll get even!"

³⁰I walked by the field of a lazy person, the vineyard of one lacking sense. ³¹I saw that it was overgrown with thorns. It was covered with weeds, and its walls were broken down. ³²Then, as I looked and thought about it, I learned this lesson: ³³A little extra sleep, a little more slumber, a little folding of the hands to rest—³⁴and poverty will pounce on you like a bandit; scarcity will attack you like an armed robber.

MORE PROVERBS OF SOLOMON

25 These are more proverbs of Solomon, collected by the advisers of King Hezekiah of Judah.

²It is God's privilege to conceal things and the king's privilege to discover them.

³No one can discover the height of heaven, the depth of the earth, or all that goes on in the king's mind!

⁴Remove the dross from silver, and the sterling will be ready for the silversmith. ⁵Remove the wicked from the king's court, and his reign will be made secure by justice.

⁶Don't demand an audience with the king or push for a place among the great. ⁷It is better to wait for an invitation than to be sent to the end of the line, publicly disgraced!

Just because you see something, ⁸don't be in a hurry to go to court. You might go down before your neighbors in shameful defeat. ⁹So discuss the matter with them privately. Don't tell anyone else, ¹⁰or others may accuse you of gossip. Then you will never regain your good reputation.

¹¹Timely advice is as lovely as golden apples in a silver basket.

¹²Valid criticism is as treasured by the one who heeds it as jewelry made from finest gold.

¹³Faithful messengers are as refreshing as snow in the heat of summer. They revive the spirit of their employer.

¹⁴A person who doesn't give a promised gift is like clouds and wind that don't bring rain.

¹⁵Patience can persuade a prince, and soft speech can crush strong opposition.

¹⁶Do you like honey? Don't eat too much of it, or it will make you sick!

¹⁷Don't visit your neighbors too often, or you will wear out your welcome.

¹⁸Telling lies about others is as harmful as hitting them with an ax, wounding them with a sword, or shooting them with a sharp arrow.

¹⁹Putting confidence in an unreliable person is like chewing with a toothache or walking on a broken foot.

²⁰Singing cheerful songs to a person whose heart is heavy is as bad as stealing someone's jacket in cold weather or rubbing salt in a wound.

²¹If your enemies are hungry, give them food to eat. If they are thirsty, give them water to drink. ²²You will heap burning coals on their heads, and the LORD will reward you.

²³As surely as a wind from the north brings rain, so a gossiping tongue causes anger!

²⁴It is better to live alone in the corner of an attic than with a contentious wife in a lovely home.

²⁵Good news from far away is like cold water to the thirsty.

²⁶If the godly compromise with the wicked, it is like polluting a fountain or muddying a spring.

²⁷Just as it is not good to eat too much honey, it is not good for people to think about all the honors they deserve.

²⁸A person without self-control is as defenseless as a city with broken-down walls.

My Daily Worship

— *June 21* —

HANDLING THE HEAT
PROVERBS 25:1–26:28

Timely advice is as lovely as golden apples in a silver basket. Valid criticism is as treasured by the one who heeds it as jewelry made from finest gold (25:11–12).

[i reflect]

"Let me offer you a small piece of advice . . . "

"You could have done a much better job on that project if only . . . "

What is it about words like these that can cause us to bristle? Both unsolicited advice and unexpected criticism can create an almost instantaneous negative reaction if we're not careful. We might feel we are being personally attacked or that our work has been judged to be inadequate.

When we become defensive, however, we are creating barriers to communication that can greatly inhibit our spiritual growth. Granted, not every recommendation or critique we receive is well-intended. The key passage describes certain types of advice and criticism in lyrical terms—comparing them to choice fruit and precious metal. The instruction is clear: We are to regard timely advice and valid criticism to be of high value.

The great preacher Charles Spurgeon, who was no stranger to criticism, once said: "Get a friend to tell you your faults, or better still, welcome an enemy who will watch you keenly and sting you savagely. What a blessing such an irritating critic will be to a wise man. What an intolerable nuisance to a fool!"

Responding in a godly fashion to others' suggestions, opinions, or critiques can be one of the most challenging disciplines to which we are called as followers of Christ. Thankfully, we have examples in Scripture—leaders such as Moses and David—whose response to complaints or godly rebuke is a model for us yet today.

We can't worship God if our own self-estimation is too high, and God in his wisdom sometimes sends critics not to hurt but to humble us. Today, as you may feel burned by the heat of criticism, remember to take your pain to your heavenly Father for comfort and counsel.

[i pray]

When I am criticized, my immediate reaction is to want to defend myself. Lord, help me instead to search for any grains of truth in the counsel I've been given, and then to apply it.

[i respond]

What jewels of valid criticism have you received recently? Take time today to thank that person for his or her advice.

26 Honor doesn't go with fools any more than snow with summer or rain with harvest.

²Like a fluttering sparrow or a darting swallow, an unfair curse will not land on its intended victim.

³Guide a horse with a whip, a donkey with a bridle, and a fool with a rod to his back!

⁴When arguing with fools, don't answer their foolish arguments, or you will become as foolish as they are.

⁵When arguing with fools, be sure to answer their foolish arguments, or they will become wise in their own estimation.

⁶Trusting a fool to convey a message is as foolish as cutting off one's feet or drinking poison!

⁷In the mouth of a fool, a proverb becomes as limp as a paralyzed leg.

⁸Honoring a fool is as foolish as tying a stone to a slingshot.

⁹A proverb in a fool's mouth is as dangerous as a thornbush brandished by a drunkard.

¹⁰An employer who hires a fool or a bystander is like an archer who shoots recklessly.

¹¹As a dog returns to its vomit, so a fool repeats his folly.

¹²There is more hope for fools than for people who think they are wise.

¹³The lazy person is full of excuses, saying, "I can't go outside because there might be a lion on the road! Yes, I'm sure there's a lion out there!"

¹⁴As a door turns back and forth on its hinges, so the lazy person turns over in bed.

¹⁵Some people are so lazy that they won't lift a finger to feed themselves.

¹⁶Lazy people consider themselves smarter than seven wise counselors.

¹⁷Yanking a dog's ears is as foolish as interfering in someone else's argument.

¹⁸Just as damaging as a mad man shooting a lethal weapon ¹⁹is someone who lies to a friend and then says, "I was only joking."

²⁰Fire goes out for lack of fuel, and quarrels disappear when gossip stops.

²¹A quarrelsome person starts fights as easily as hot embers light charcoal or fire lights wood.

²²What dainty morsels rumors are—but they sink deep into one's heart.

²³Smooth* words may hide a wicked heart, just as a pretty glaze covers a common clay pot.

²⁴People with hate in their hearts may sound pleasant enough, but don't believe them. ²⁵Though they pretend to be kind, their hearts are full of all kinds of evil. ²⁶While their hatred may be concealed by trickery, it will finally come to light for all to see.

²⁷If you set a trap for others, you will get caught in it yourself. If you roll a boulder down on others, it will roll back and crush you.

²⁸A lying tongue hates its victims, and flattery causes ruin.

27 Don't brag about tomorrow, since you don't know what the day will bring.

²Don't praise yourself; let others do it!

³A stone is heavy and sand is weighty, but the resentment caused by a fool is heavier than both.

⁴Anger is cruel, and wrath is like a flood, but who can survive the destructiveness of jealousy?

⁵An open rebuke is better than hidden love!

⁶Wounds from a friend are better than many kisses from an enemy.

⁷Honey seems tasteless to a person who is full, but even bitter food tastes sweet to the hungry.

⁸A person who strays from home is like a bird that strays from its nest.

⁹The heartfelt counsel of a friend is as sweet as perfume and incense.

¹⁰Never abandon a friend—either yours or your father's. Then in your time of need, you won't have to ask your relatives for assistance. It is better to go to a neighbor than to a relative who lives far away.

¹¹My child,* how happy I will be if you turn

26:23 As in Greek version; Hebrew reads *Burning.*   **27:11** Hebrew *My son.*

out to be wise! Then I will be able to answer my critics.

¹²A prudent person foresees the danger ahead and takes precautions. The simpleton goes blindly on and suffers the consequences.

¹³Be sure to get collateral from anyone who guarantees the debt of a stranger. Get a deposit if someone guarantees the debt of an adulterous woman.

¹⁴If you shout a pleasant greeting to your neighbor too early in the morning, it will be counted as a curse!

¹⁵A nagging wife is as annoying as the constant dripping on a rainy day. ¹⁶Trying to stop her complaints is like trying to stop the wind or hold something with greased hands.

¹⁷As iron sharpens iron, a friend sharpens a friend.

¹⁸Workers who tend a fig tree are allowed to eat its fruit. In the same way, workers who protect their employer's interests will be rewarded.

¹⁹As a face is reflected in water, so the heart reflects the person.

²⁰Just as Death and Destruction* are never satisfied, so human desire is never satisfied.

²¹Fire tests the purity of silver and gold, but a person is tested by being praised.

²²You cannot separate fools from their foolishness, even though you grind them like grain with mortar and pestle.

²³Know the state of your flocks, and put your heart into caring for your herds, ²⁴for riches don't last forever, and the crown might not be secure for the next generation. ²⁵After the hay is harvested, the new crop appears, and the mountain grasses are gathered in, ²⁶your sheep will provide wool for clothing, and your goats will be sold for the price of a field. ²⁷And you will have enough goats' milk for you, your family, and your servants.

28 The wicked run away when no one is chasing them, but the godly are as bold as lions.

²When there is moral rot within a nation, its government topples easily. But with wise and knowledgeable leaders, there is stability.

³A poor person who oppresses the poor is like a pounding rain that destroys the crops.

⁴To reject the law is to praise the wicked; to obey the law is to fight them.

⁵Evil people don't understand justice, but those who follow the LORD understand completely.

⁶It is better to be poor and honest than rich and crooked.

⁷Young people who obey the law are wise; those who seek out worthless companions bring shame to their parents.

⁸A person who makes money by charging interest will lose it. It will end up in the hands of someone who is kind to the poor.

⁹The prayers of a person who ignores the law are despised.

¹⁰Those who lead the upright into sin will fall into their own trap, but the honest will inherit good things.

¹¹Rich people picture themselves as wise, but their real poverty is evident to the poor.

¹²When the godly succeed, everyone is glad. When the wicked take charge, people go into hiding.

¹³People who cover over their sins will not prosper. But if they confess and forsake them, they will receive mercy.

¹⁴Blessed are those who have a tender conscience,* but the stubborn are headed for serious trouble.

¹⁵A wicked ruler is as dangerous to the poor as a lion or bear attacking them.

¹⁶Only a stupid prince will oppress his people, but a king will have a long reign if he hates dishonesty and bribes.

¹⁷A murderer's tormented conscience will drive him into the grave. Don't protect him!

¹⁸The honest will be rescued from harm, but those who are crooked will be destroyed.

¹⁹Hard workers have plenty of food; playing around brings poverty.

²⁰The trustworthy will get a rich reward. But

27:20 Hebrew *Sheol and Abaddon*. 28:14 Hebrew *those who fear*.

the person who wants to get rich quick will only get into trouble.

²¹Showing partiality is never good, yet some will do wrong for something as small as a piece of bread.

²²A greedy person tries to get rich quick, but it only leads to poverty.

²³In the end, people appreciate frankness more than flattery.

²⁴Robbing your parents and then saying, "What's wrong with that?" is as serious as committing murder.

²⁵Greed causes fighting; trusting the LORD leads to prosperity.

²⁶Trusting oneself is foolish, but those who walk in wisdom are safe.

²⁷Whoever gives to the poor will lack nothing. But a curse will come upon those who close their eyes to poverty.

²⁸When the wicked take charge, people hide. When the wicked meet disaster, the godly multiply.

29 Whoever stubbornly refuses to accept criticism will suddenly be broken beyond repair.

²When the godly are in authority, the people rejoice. But when the wicked are in power, they groan.

³The man who loves wisdom brings joy to his father, but if he hangs around with prostitutes, his wealth is wasted.

⁴A just king gives stability to his nation, but one who demands bribes destroys it.

⁵To flatter people is to lay a trap for their feet.

⁶Evil people are trapped by sin, but the righteous escape, shouting for joy.

⁷The godly know the rights of the poor; the wicked don't care to know.

⁸Mockers can get a whole town agitated, but those who are wise will calm anger.

⁹If a wise person takes a fool to court, there will be ranting and ridicule but no satisfaction.

¹⁰The bloodthirsty hate the honest, but the upright seek out the honest.

¹¹A fool gives full vent to anger, but a wise person quietly holds it back.

¹²If a ruler honors liars, all his advisers will be wicked.

¹³The poor and the oppressor have this in common—the LORD gives light to the eyes of both.

¹⁴A king who is fair to the poor will have a long reign.

¹⁵To discipline and reprimand a child produces wisdom, but a mother is disgraced by an undisciplined child.

¹⁶When the wicked are in authority, sin increases. But the godly will live to see the tyrant's downfall.

¹⁷Discipline your children, and they will give you happiness and peace of mind.

¹⁸When people do not accept divine guidance, they run wild. But whoever obeys the law is happy.

¹⁹For a servant, mere words are not enough—discipline is needed. For the words may be understood, but they are not heeded.

²⁰There is more hope for a fool than for someone who speaks without thinking.

²¹A servant who is pampered from childhood will later become a rebel.

²²A hot-tempered person starts fights and gets into all kinds of sin.

²³Pride ends in humiliation, while humility brings honor.

²⁴If you assist a thief, you are only hurting yourself. You will be punished if you report the crime, but you will be cursed if you don't.

²⁵Fearing people is a dangerous trap, but to trust the LORD means safety.

²⁶Many seek the ruler's favor, but justice comes from the LORD.

²⁷The godly despise the wicked; the wicked despise the godly.

THE SAYINGS OF AGUR

30 The message of Agur son of Jakeh. An oracle.*

I am weary, O God; I am weary and worn

30:1a Or *son of Jakeh from Massa.*

My Daily Worship

— June 22 —

FORGETTING FINANCIAL FANTASIES
PROVERBS 27:1, 29:27

Know the state of your flocks, and put your heart into caring for your herds, for riches don't last forever, and the crown might not be secure for the next generation (27:23–24).

[i reflect]

The legendary multimillionaire John D. Rockefeller, the wealthiest man of his generation, was once asked how much money it would take to satisfy him. His reported reply? "Just a little bit more."

At worst, his response reveals the innate greed of the human heart. At best, it highlights human-kind's universal feeling of restlessness, or perhaps insecurity about not having enough.

Clearly the great majority of us will never know firsthand what it's like to be "as rich as Rockefeller." But we can grasp the crucial truth that, contrary to our frequent financial daydreams, riches and social standing do not provide true security. Fortunes can and do disappear. Power and influence are quick to evaporate.

In today's passage, readers are encouraged to forget financial fantasies and to focus instead on down-to-earth realities like discipline and hard work. The common shepherds in Bible times who lived off the land found a simple but good life. In an agrarian society, they had no choice but to depend on God for his provision. And he proved faithful again and again.

The lessons for us? Be diligent. Do your work well. Exercise simple faith. No matter what your job or financial condition, being a true worshiper demands that as you work, you look to God and rely on him. The issue isn't the amount of money in your bank account, but the amount of trust and gratitude in your heart.

God wants us to pay careful attention not only to our hearts (Proverbs 4:23) but also to our herds (that is, work), because all of life is sacred. In other words, worship and work are not separate or opposing entities. On the contrary, your work today can and should be an act of worship. Whatever task or job you have to do today, offer it first to God and put your heart into it.

[i pray]

Lord, continually open my heart to the truth that worldly wealth does not equal true security, and that many of the things the world sees as mundane are highly significant in your eyes. Teach me to live out my calling and do my daily work in your strength, and to trust you to provide for all my needs.

[i respond]

Pick out one unglamorous task at work or home that really needs to be done and that you've been dreading. Carve out the necessary time and do the job right, with a good attitude, as an act of worship.

out, O God.* ²I am too ignorant to be human, and I lack common sense. ³I have not mastered human wisdom, nor do I know the Holy One.

⁴Who but God goes up to heaven and comes back down? Who holds the wind in his fists? Who wraps up the oceans in his cloak? Who has created the whole wide world? What is his name—and his son's name? Tell me if you know!

⁵Every word of God proves true. He defends all who come to him for protection. ⁶Do not add to his words, or he may rebuke you, and you will be found a liar. ⁷O God, I beg two favors from you before I die. ⁸First, help me never to tell a lie. Second, give me neither poverty nor riches! Give me just enough to satisfy my needs. ⁹For if I grow rich, I may deny you and say, "Who is the LORD?" And if I am too poor, I may steal and thus insult God's holy name.

¹⁰Never slander a person to his employer. If you do, the person will curse you, and you will pay for it.

¹¹Some people curse their father and do not thank their mother. ¹²They feel pure, but they are filthy and unwashed. ¹³They are proud beyond description and disdainful. ¹⁴They devour the poor with teeth as sharp as swords or knives. They destroy the needy from the face of the earth.

¹⁵The leech has two suckers that cry out, "More, more!"* There are three other things—no, four!—that are never satisfied:
¹⁶ the grave,
    the barren womb,
    the thirsty desert,
    the blazing fire.

¹⁷The eye that mocks a father and despises a mother will be plucked out by ravens of the valley and eaten by vultures.

¹⁸There are three things that amaze me—no, four things I do not understand:
¹⁹ how an eagle glides through the sky,
    how a snake slithers on a rock,
    how a ship navigates the ocean,
    how a man loves a woman.
²⁰Equally amazing is how an adulterous woman can satisfy her sexual appetite, shrug her shoulders, and then say, "What's wrong with that?"

²¹There are three things that make the earth tremble—no, four it cannot endure:
²² a slave who becomes a king,
    an overbearing fool who prospers,
²³ a bitter woman who finally gets a husband,
    a servant girl who supplants her mistress.

²⁴There are four things on earth that are small but unusually wise:
²⁵ Ants—they aren't strong,
    but they store up food for the winter.
²⁶ Rock badgers*—they aren't powerful,
    but they make their homes among the
      rocky cliffs.
²⁷ Locusts—they have no king,
    but they march like an army in ranks.
²⁸ Lizards—they are easy to catch,
    but they are found even in kings' palaces.

²⁹There are three stately monarchs on the earth—no, four:
³⁰ the lion, king of animals, who won't turn
      aside for anything,
³¹ the strutting rooster,
    the male goat,
    a king as he leads his army.

³²If you have been a fool by being proud or plotting evil, don't brag about it—cover your mouth with your hand in shame. ³³As the beating of cream yields butter, and a blow to the nose causes bleeding, so anger causes quarrels.

THE SAYINGS OF KING LEMUEL

31 These are the sayings of King Lemuel, an oracle* that his mother taught him.

30:1b The Hebrew can also be translated *The man declares this to Ithiel, to Ithiel and to Ucal.* 30:15 Hebrew *two daughters who cry out, "Give, give!"* 30:26 Or *coneys,* or *hyraxes.* 31:1 Or *of Lemuel, king of Massa.*

My Daily Worship

— *June 23* —

AN UNSOLVED MYSTERY

PROVERBS 30:1–33

Who but God goes up to heaven and comes back down? Who holds the wind in his fists?
Who wraps up the oceans in his cloak? Who has created the whole wide world?
What is his name—and his son's name? Tell me if you know! Every word of
God proves true. He defends all who come to him for protection (30:4–5).

[i reflect]

Author A. W. Tozer insisted that the single most important thing about any individual is what he or she believes about God.

Spiritually sensitive people know this is true. This probably explains why, through sermons, theology books, weekend seminars, and worship music we strive so hard to understand God for ourselves and struggle so much to explain him to others. But do we do all this in the humble effort to love and serve him better? Or is our deeper motive to figure God out and make him less mysterious?

One thing is for sure—if we could answer every nagging question about God's character and accurately predict his every action, then in a real sense, there would be no need for trust. We'd have God in a box. And we creatures, rather than the Creator, would have the upper hand.

It won't work. Trying to remove all mystery about the Almighty is futile. You may as well try to catch a hurricane in a Mason jar. The Lord surely cannot be contained in a definition or poked and prodded the way researchers examine lab rats. The great God of the Bible is inexplicable and unpredictable. The whole universe can't contain him. In fact, the only reason we know anything about him at all is because he has graciously revealed himself in creation, in Jesus, the living Word, and in the written Word.

It's not wrong to want to learn about God—in fact, that's what worship is all about. Christians should spend time reading and studying and trying to get to know him better. But keep in mind that finite creatures can never fully grasp an infinite Creator. It is this sense of mystery that keeps our hearts filled with wonder.

As you go through your daily routine, look for the mysteries about God that you encounter. Let those mysteries move you to awe-filled worship.

[i pray]

O Great Triune God, I praise you because your greatness is unsearchable and
your ways are mysterious and wonderful. Give me a heart that hungers
to know you and a humility that realizes you can't be "figured out."

[i respond]

Make a list of things you don't understand about God. Discuss the list with an older, wiser Christian friend or mentor. Which items have answers? Which require submission and trust?

²O my son, O son of my womb, O son of my promises, ³do not spend your strength on women, on those who ruin kings.

⁴And it is not for kings, O Lemuel, to guzzle wine. Rulers should not crave liquor. ⁵For if they drink, they may forget their duties and be unable to give justice to those who are oppressed. ⁶Liquor is for the dying, and wine for those in deep depression. ⁷Let them drink to forget their poverty and remember their troubles no more.

⁸Speak up for those who cannot speak for themselves; ensure justice for those who are perishing. ⁹Yes, speak up for the poor and helpless, and see that they get justice.

A Wife of Noble Character

¹⁰Who can find a virtuous and capable wife? She is worth more than precious rubies. ¹¹Her husband can trust her, and she will greatly enrich his life. ¹²She will not hinder him but help him all her life.

¹³She finds wool and flax and busily spins it. ¹⁴She is like a merchant's ship; she brings her food from afar. ¹⁵She gets up before dawn to prepare breakfast for her household and plan the day's work for her servant girls. ¹⁶She goes out to inspect a field and buys it; with her earnings she plants a vineyard.

¹⁷She is energetic and strong, a hard worker.

¹⁸She watches for bargains; her lights burn late into the night. ¹⁹Her hands are busy spinning thread, her fingers twisting fiber.

²⁰She extends a helping hand to the poor and opens her arms to the needy.

²¹She has no fear of winter for her household because all of them have warm* clothes. ²²She quilts her own bedspreads. She dresses like royalty in gowns of finest cloth.

²³Her husband is well known, for he sits in the council meeting with the other civic leaders.

²⁴She makes belted linen garments and sashes to sell to the merchants.

²⁵She is clothed with strength and dignity, and she laughs with no fear of the future. ²⁶When she speaks, her words are wise, and kindness is the rule when she gives instructions. ²⁷She carefully watches all that goes on in her household and does not have to bear the consequences of laziness.

²⁸Her children stand and bless her. Her husband praises her: ²⁹"There are many virtuous and capable women in the world, but you surpass them all!"

³⁰Charm is deceptive, and beauty does not last; but a woman who fears the LORD will be greatly praised. ³¹Reward her for all she has done. Let her deeds publicly declare her praise.

31:21 As in Greek version; Hebrew *scarlet*.

My Daily Worship
— June 24 —

THE WORK OF WORSHIP
PROVERBS 31:1–31

Speak up for those who cannot speak for themselves; ensure justice for those who are perishing.
Yes, speak up for the poor and helpless, and see that they get justice (31:8–9).

[i reflect]

When some people are asked what is their favorite verse in the Bible, they reply, "God helps those who help themselves." The only problem is that this so-called verse cannot be found in the Bible. Its source? Ben Franklin's *Poor Richard's Almanac, 1757.*

In fact, the Bible says almost the opposite—instructing God's people to help those who *can't* help themselves.

Take the passage above, for example. In the strictest, most literal sense, the first nine verses of Proverbs 31 are advice from a queen mother to her son, the king. She's urging him to rule his people with mercy and compassion, reminding him to use his exalted position and immense power to help the helpless. But the principles in the passage apply to all followers of Christ (see Psalm 82:3–4; 2 Corinthians 9:9). We're called to be imitators of God (Ephesians 5:1) and, let's face it, who cares for the poor more than he does (Proverbs 14:31)?

When was the last time you got your hands dirty helping out in a low-income neighborhood? Visited inmates in a nearby jail? Paid a visit to an orphanage or nursing home? Tutored kids from the inner city? Helped a mentally challenged person? Did something to advance the pro-life movement? Challenged unfair treatment of minorities or immigrants?

"What? Why suggest those kinds of activities in a Bible devoted to worship?" Because worship is not just about singing or praying at a certain time and in a certain place. It is a mindset. It is a way of life. It is a heart that beats for God and looks constantly for ways to spread his righteous reputation in the world. When we live as worshipers, every place is holy, every moment is significant, and every action is eternal.

Find opportunities to do the work of worship today.

[i pray]

Father, impress ever deeper on my heart the truth that I am blessed to be a blessing,
and that life is not about me but about you—about serving you by serving others.
Stir up a holy compassion in my heart today.

[i respond]

Pick one of the suggestions above, grab a friend or some family members, and spend a few hours making a difference in your world to the glory of God.

Ecclesiastes

Here is my final conclusion: Fear God and obey his commandments,
for this is the duty of every person (12:13).

Like Chasing the Wind

Consider what Leonard Woolf, literary editor of *The Nation,* had to say about his lifetime achievements: "I see clearly that I have achieved practically nothing. The world today and the history of the human anthill during the past five to seven years would be exactly the same if I had played Ping-Pong instead of sitting on committees and writing books and memoranda."

Woolf would have found a sympathetic ear from the Teacher in Ecclesiastes. His assessment after a lifetime of trying, testing, and tasting everything life had to offer? "Everything under the sun is meaningless, like chasing the wind" (1:14). Through his experiences, the Teacher had learned that true satisfaction and meaning in life could not be found in the paths the world typically pursues—knowledge, popularity, money, pleasure, or work. Rather, at the end of the book, the Teacher concludes that real satisfaction comes only from knowing God and obeying his commandments. Without God at the center of our lives, we will end up like the Teacher—empty and cynical.

While the tone of the book is largely negative and pessimistic, Ecclesiastes also offers us some important insights and wisdom. True enjoyment in life comes as we follow God's guidelines and stay connected to him (2:24–25); God's timing is perfect (3:1–8); satisfaction in life is a gift from God (3:13); and all our days are in God's hands (9:1). With insights like these, it's no wonder that the Teacher came to his ultimate conclusion, "Fear God and obey his commandments, for this is the duty of every person." In the end, the Teacher observed that God alone is worthy of worship simply because of who he is.

The lesson for us is clear: The pursuits of this world are empty without a vital and living relationship with God.

Worship Moments

- Accept the pleasures of food, drink, and hard work as gifts from God (2:24; 3:13; 9:7).

- Be quiet and listen carefully in the house of God (5:1).

- The cynical author has a strong belief in God. He reveals God's character as gift-giver (1:24–25; 3:13; 9:9); as righteous judge (3:17); as controller of our destiny (6:10); as a God to fear (8:12); and as the Creator whom we must not forget (12:1).

1

These are the words of the Teacher,* King David's son, who ruled in Jerusalem.

EVERYTHING IS MEANINGLESS

2"Everything is meaningless," says the Teacher, "utterly meaningless!"

3What do people get for all their hard work? 4Generations come and go, but nothing really changes. 5The sun rises and sets and hurries around to rise again. 6The wind blows south and north, here and there, twisting back and forth, getting nowhere. 7The rivers run into the sea, but the sea is never full. Then the water returns again to the rivers and flows again to the sea. 8Everything is so weary and tiresome! No matter how much we see, we are never satisfied. No matter how much we hear, we are not content.

9History merely repeats itself. It has all been done before. Nothing under the sun is truly new. 10What can you point to that is new? How do you know it didn't already exist long ago? 11We don't remember what happened in those former times. And in future generations, no one will remember what we are doing now.

THE FUTILITY OF WISDOM

12I, the Teacher, was king of Israel, and I lived in Jerusalem. 13I devoted myself to search for understanding and to explore by wisdom everything being done in the world. I soon discovered that God has dealt a tragic existence to the human race. 14Everything under the sun is meaningless, like chasing the wind. 15What is wrong cannot be righted. What is missing cannot be recovered.

16I said to myself, "Look, I am wiser than any of the kings who ruled in Jerusalem before me. I have greater wisdom and knowledge than any of them." 17So I worked hard to distinguish wisdom from foolishness. But now I realize that even this was like chasing the wind. 18For the greater my wisdom, the greater my grief. To increase knowledge only increases sorrow.

THE FUTILITY OF PLEASURE

2

I said to myself, "Come now, let's give pleasure a try. Let's look for the 'good things' in life." But I found that this, too, was meaningless. 2"It is silly to be laughing all the time," I said. "What good does it do to seek only pleasure?" 3After much thought, I decided to cheer myself with wine. While still seeking wisdom, I clutched at foolishness. In this way, I hoped to experience the only happiness most people find during their brief life in this world.

4I also tried to find meaning by building huge homes for myself and by planting beautiful vineyards. 5I made gardens and parks, filling them with all kinds of fruit trees. 6I built reservoirs to collect the water to irrigate my many flourishing groves. 7I bought slaves, both men and women, and others were born into my household. I also owned great herds and flocks, more than any of the kings who lived in Jerusalem before me. 8I collected great sums of silver and gold, the treasure of many kings and provinces. I hired wonderful singers, both men and women, and had many beautiful concubines. I had everything a man could desire!

9So I became greater than any of the kings who ruled in Jerusalem before me. And with it all, I remained clear-eyed so that I could evaluate all these things. 10Anything I wanted, I took. I did not restrain myself from any joy. I even found great pleasure in hard work, an additional reward for all my labors. 11But as I looked at everything I had worked so hard to accomplish, it was all so meaningless. It was like chasing the wind. There was nothing really worthwhile anywhere.

THE WISE AND THE FOOLISH

12So I decided to compare wisdom and folly, and anyone else would come to the same conclusions I did. 13Wisdom is of more value than foolishness, just as light is better than darkness. 14For the wise person sees, while the fool is blind. Yet I saw that wise and foolish people

---

1:1 Hebrew *Koheleth*; this term is rendered "the Teacher" throughout this book.

share the same fate. ¹⁵Both of them die. Just as the fool will die, so will I. So of what value is all my wisdom? Then I said to myself, "This is all so meaningless!" ¹⁶For the wise person and the fool both die, and in the days to come, both will be forgotten.

THE FUTILITY OF WORK

¹⁷So now I hate life because everything done here under the sun is so irrational. Everything is meaningless, like chasing the wind. ¹⁸I am disgusted that I must leave the fruits of my hard work to others. ¹⁹And who can tell whether my successors will be wise or foolish? And yet they will control everything I have gained by my skill and hard work. How meaningless!

²⁰So I turned in despair from hard work. It was not the answer to my search for satisfaction in this life. ²¹For though I do my work with wisdom, knowledge, and skill, I must leave everything I gain to people who haven't worked to earn it. This is not only foolish but highly unfair. ²²So what do people get for all their hard work? ²³Their days of labor are filled with pain and grief; even at night they cannot rest. It is all utterly meaningless.

²⁴So I decided there is nothing better than to enjoy food and drink and to find satisfaction in work. Then I realized that this pleasure is from the hand of God. ²⁵For who can eat or enjoy anything apart from him? ²⁶God gives wisdom, knowledge, and joy to those who please him. But if a sinner becomes wealthy, God takes the wealth away and gives it to those who please him. Even this, however, is meaningless, like chasing the wind.

A TIME FOR EVERYTHING

3 ¹There is a time for everything,
   a season for every activity under
      heaven.
² A time to be born and a time to die.
   A time to plant and a time to harvest.
³ A time to kill and a time to heal.

A time to tear down and a time to
   rebuild.
⁴ A time to cry and a time to laugh.
   A time to grieve and a time to dance.
⁵ A time to scatter stones and a time to
   gather stones.
   A time to embrace and a time to turn
      away.
⁶ A time to search and a time to lose.
   A time to keep and a time to throw
      away.
⁷ A time to tear and a time to mend.
   A time to be quiet and a time to speak up.
⁸ A time to love and a time to hate.
   A time for war and a time for peace.

⁹What do people really get for all their hard work? ¹⁰I have thought about this in connection with the various kinds of work God has given people to do. ¹¹God has made everything beautiful for its own time. He has planted eternity in the human heart, but even so, people cannot see the whole scope of God's work from beginning to end. ¹²So I concluded that there is nothing better for people than to be happy and to enjoy themselves as long as they can. ¹³And people should eat and drink and enjoy the fruits of their labor, for these are gifts from God.

¹⁴And I know that whatever God does is final. Nothing can be added to it or taken from it. God's purpose in this is that people should fear him. ¹⁵Whatever exists today and whatever will exist in the future has already existed in the past. For God calls each event back in its turn.*

THE INJUSTICES OF LIFE

¹⁶I also noticed that throughout the world there is evil in the courtroom. Yes, even the courts of law are corrupt! ¹⁷I said to myself, "In due season God will judge everyone, both good and bad, for all their deeds."

¹⁸Then I realized that God allows people to continue in their sinful ways so he can test them. That way, they can see for themselves

3:15 Hebrew *For God calls the past to account.*

My Daily Worship

FINDING MEANING IN LIFE

ECCLESIASTES 1:1–2:26

For who can eat or enjoy anything apart from him? God gives wisdom,
knowledge, and joy to those who please him (2:25).

[i reflect]

Mark Twain wistfully observed, "You don't know quite what it is you're looking for, but it just fairly makes your heart ache, you want it so."

Perhaps no one in history has illustrated this human longing for meaning more than Solomon. The product of a scandalous affair between David and Bathsheba, the boy grew up to become Israel's second king. Blessed with unearthly wisdom (1 Kings 4:29–34), Solomon enjoyed a reign of remarkable prosperity and unprecedented peace. He oversaw the building of Jerusalem's greatest and most glorious Temple. He dabbled in engineering and botany, and became famous worldwide. But over time, proving that even wise people can do stupid things, he accumulated a household of seven hundred wives and three hundred mistresses—many of them foreign and worshipers of other gods.

Not surprisingly, Solomon's heart for the one true God cooled. His restlessness multiplied. Eventually he found himself in the ultimate mid-life crisis—a time of frantic searching, boredom, and despair.

His diary from this period, the ancient book of Ecclesiastes, reads like the bitter ramblings of a depressed old skeptic: "Everything is meaningless, . . . utterly meaningless!" (1:2). Yet at the end, after experimenting with every pleasure and pursuit this world has to offer, he concluded, "Here is my final conclusion: Fear God and obey his commandments, for this is the duty of every person" (12:13).

What was Solomon's great discovery? That a life divorced from God is no life at all. That meaning and joy in life can only be found by relating rightly to the source of life. To fear God is to worship him. To worship him is to make him the top priority in your thoughts and actions.

Name the area in which you are experiencing the most discontent today—finances, health, work, family, church. Make sure that God is at the center of that area. Give it to him now.

[i pray]

Lord, teach me what it means to fear you. Give me the heart and the will to obey your commands.
Cause a desire for you and your glory to become the ruling passion in my life.

[i respond]

List the things (hobbies, possessions, relationships, pursuits, etc.) that have the tendency to capture your heart and turn your attention from God. Confess your need for the Lord and your desire to keep him central in your life. Then burn the list in your fireplace or grill.

that they are no better than animals. ¹⁹For humans and animals both breathe the same air,* and both die. So people have no real advantage over the animals. How meaningless! ²⁰Both go to the same place—the dust from which they came and to which they must return. ²¹For who can prove that the human spirit goes upward and the spirit of animals goes downward into the earth? ²²So I saw that there is nothing better for people than to be happy in their work. That is why they are here! No one will bring them back from death to enjoy life in the future.

4 Again I observed all the oppression that takes place in our world. I saw the tears of the oppressed, with no one to comfort them. The oppressors have great power, and the victims are helpless. ²So I concluded that the dead are better off than the living. ³And most fortunate of all are those who were never born. For they have never seen all the evil that is done in our world.

⁴Then I observed that most people are motivated to success by their envy of their neighbors. But this, too, is meaningless, like chasing the wind.

⁵Foolish people refuse to work and almost starve. ⁶They feel it is better to be lazy and barely survive than to work hard, especially when in the long run everything is so futile.

THE ADVANTAGES OF COMPANIONSHIP

⁷I observed yet another example of meaninglessness in our world. ⁸This is the case of a man who is all alone, without a child or a brother, yet who works hard to gain as much wealth as he can. But then he asks himself, "Who am I working for? Why am I giving up so much pleasure now?" It is all so meaningless and depressing.

⁹Two people can accomplish more than twice as much as one; they get a better return for their labor. ¹⁰If one person falls, the other can reach out and help. But people who are alone when they fall are in real trouble. ¹¹And on a cold night, two under the same blanket can gain warmth from each other. But how can one be warm alone? ¹²A person standing alone can be attacked and defeated, but two can stand back-to-back and conquer. Three are even better, for a triple-braided cord is not easily broken.

Words of Worship

EXALT

Exalt—Hebrew *ro-mem* "make high." Other terms for "lifting" or "raising up" can be found in both the Old Testament and the New Testament, but they do not mean "exalt" in the context of praise and worship.

"Be exalted, O God, above the highest heavens. May your glory shine over all the earth" (Psalm 108:5). The Bible uses concrete images to describe how we worship. When the psalm writer speaks of exalting the Lord, he uses a word that means to raise him up or make him high.

Think of some objects raised up in our world: our nation's flag flying in the breeze; historic monuments; statues of both the famous and infamous; proud civic towers; skyscrapers bearing the names of powerful companies; domes of the halls of government and justice; spires of cathedrals. All these, being raised up, call attention to themselves and the values they represent. In the same way, our worship is intended to call attention to our glorious God and the Lord Jesus Christ. Our exaltation makes them visible in our sight and in the eyes of those around us. "Come, let us tell of the LORD's greatness; let us exalt his name together" (Psalm 34:3).

3:19 Or *both have the same spirit.*

My Daily Worship

— *June 26* —

ETERNAL LONGINGS

ECCLESIASTES 3:1 – 5:20

*God has made everything beautiful for its own time. He has planted eternity
in the human heart, but even so, people cannot see the whole
scope of God's work from beginning to end (3:11).*

[i reflect]

The French author Simone Weil once remarked that beauty and affliction are the only two things that can pierce the human heart. King Solomon observed the same truth some ten centuries earlier in the book of Ecclesiastes.

Their point was that this world—and that includes *your* life—is full of mystery and transcendence. Haven't you experienced fleeting moments of such wonder and sweetness that you felt like laughing and weeping all at once? Haven't you faced head-scratching, heart-hurting hard times that rumbled like a hurricane through your soul? Of course you have. This is the universal human experience.

Tragically, most people plod through their days unaware of the deep drama unfolding all around them. They miss the world's haunting beauty (or quickly dismiss it) even as they try frantically to remove every shred of discomfort and pain from their lives. Their hearts are then numb to all the things in creation meant to point us to a better world still to come. Roses, sunsets, tax audits, even cancer—if we look with deeper eyes—can each direct our attention to the One who is writing, directing, and playing the lead role in the divine drama we call life.

Don't ignore, deny, or—worst of all—deaden the eternal longings deep in your heart. Savor the rich beauty all around you throughout the day. Search in and behind the affliction in your life. God is speaking. He is wooing you. The whole world is his sanctuary. Your entire life is meant to be a response to him. Let those who have ears to hear, let them hear.

[i pray]

*Father, thank you for the beauty in my life—even the strange beauty of affliction.
You are at work. I trust you, and believe that meaning and significance
and deep joy are found only in you. Open my eyes today.*

[i respond]

Take a leisure walk in your neighborhood and stop to carefully observe ten beautiful things you don't usually even notice. How do these works of God stir your heart? Thank and praise God for his amazing creation.

THE FUTILITY OF POLITICAL POWER

[13]It is better to be a poor but wise youth than to be an old and foolish king who refuses all advice. [14]Such a youth could come from prison and succeed. He might even become king, though he was born in poverty. [15]Everyone is eager to help such a youth, even to help him take the throne. [16]He might become the leader of millions and be very popular. But then the next generation grows up and rejects him! So again, it is all meaningless, like chasing the wind.

THE IMPORTANCE OF FEARING GOD

5 As you enter the house of God, keep your ears open and your mouth shut! Don't be a fool who doesn't realize that mindless offerings to God are evil. [2]And don't make rash promises to God, for he is in heaven, and you are only here on earth. So let your words be few.

[3]Just as being too busy gives you nightmares, being a fool makes you a blabbermouth.

[4]So when you make a promise to God, don't delay in following through, for God takes no pleasure in fools. Keep all the promises you make to him. [5]It is better to say nothing than to promise something that you don't follow through on. [6]In such cases, your mouth is making you sin. And don't defend yourself by telling the Temple messenger that the promise you made was a mistake. That would make God angry, and he might wipe out everything you have achieved.

[7]Dreaming all the time instead of working is foolishness. And there is ruin in a flood of empty words. Fear God instead.

THE FUTILITY OF WEALTH

[8]If you see a poor person being oppressed by the powerful and justice being miscarried throughout the land, don't be surprised! For every official is under orders from higher up, and matters of justice only get lost in red tape and bureaucracy. [9]Even the king milks the land for his own profit!*

[10]Those who love money will never have enough. How absurd to think that wealth brings true happiness! [11]The more you have, the more people come to help you spend it. So what is the advantage of wealth—except perhaps to watch it run through your fingers!

[12]People who work hard sleep well, whether they eat little or much. But the rich are always worrying and seldom get a good night's sleep.

[13]There is another serious problem I have seen in the world. Riches are sometimes hoarded to the harm of the saver, [14]or they are put into risky investments that turn sour, and everything is lost. In the end, there is nothing left to pass on to one's children. [15]People who live only for wealth come to the end of their lives as naked and empty-handed as on the day they were born.

[16]And this, too, is a very serious problem. As people come into this world, so they depart. All their hard work is for nothing. They have been working for the wind, and everything will be swept away. [17]Throughout their lives, they live under a cloud—frustrated, discouraged, and angry.

[18]Even so, I have noticed one thing, at least, that is good. It is good for people to eat well, drink a good glass of wine, and enjoy their work—whatever they do under the sun—for however long God lets them live. [19]And it is a good thing to receive wealth from God and the good health to enjoy it. To enjoy your work and accept your lot in life—that is indeed a gift from God. [20]People who do this rarely look with sorrow on the past, for God has given them reasons for joy.

6 There is another serious tragedy I have seen in our world. [2]God gives great wealth and honor to some people and gives them everything they could ever want, but then he doesn't give them the health to enjoy it. They

5:9 The meaning of the Hebrew is uncertain.

> *Worship is the strategy by which we interrupt our preoccupation with ourselves and attend to the presence of God.*
>
> EUGENE PETERSON

die, and others get it all! This is meaningless— a sickening tragedy.

³A man might have a hundred children and live to be very old. But if he finds no satisfaction in life and in the end does not even get a decent burial, I say he would have been better off born dead. ⁴I realize that his birth would have been meaningless and ended in darkness. He wouldn't even have had a name, ⁵and he would never have seen the sun or known of its existence. Yet he would have had more peace than he has in growing up to be an unhappy man. ⁶He might live a thousand years twice over but not find contentment. And since he must die like everyone else— well, what's the use?

⁷All people spend their lives scratching for food, but they never seem to have enough. ⁸Considering this, do wise people really have any advantage over fools? Do poor people gain anything by being wise and knowing how to act in front of others?

⁹Enjoy what you have rather than desiring what you don't have. Just dreaming about nice things is meaningless; it is like chasing the wind.

THE FUTURE—DETERMINED AND UNKNOWN

¹⁰Everything has already been decided. It was known long ago what each person would be. So there's no use arguing with God about your destiny.

¹¹The more words you speak, the less they mean. So why overdo it?

¹²In the few days of our empty lives, who knows how our days can best be spent? And who can tell what will happen in the future after we are gone?

WISDOM FOR LIFE

7 A good reputation is more valuable than the most expensive perfume. In the same way, the day you die is better than the day you are born.

²It is better to spend your time at funerals than at festivals. For you are going to die, and you should think about it while there is still time.

³Sorrow is better than laughter, for sadness has a refining influence on us.

⁴A wise person thinks much about death, while the fool thinks only about having a good time now.

⁵It is better to be criticized by a wise person than to be praised by a fool! ⁶Indeed, a fool's laughter is quickly gone, like thorns crackling in a fire. This also is meaningless.

⁷Extortion turns wise people into fools, and bribes corrupt the heart.

⁸Finishing is better than starting. Patience is better than pride.

⁹Don't be quick-tempered, for anger is the friend of fools.

¹⁰Don't long for "the good old days," for you don't know whether they were any better than today.

¹¹Being wise is as good as being rich; in fact, it is better. ¹²Wisdom or money can get you almost anything, but it's important to know that only wisdom can save your life.

¹³Notice the way God does things; then fall into line. Don't fight the ways of God, for who can straighten out what he has made crooked?

¹⁴Enjoy prosperity while you can. But when hard times strike, realize that both come from God. That way you will realize that nothing is certain in this life.

THE LIMITS OF HUMAN WISDOM

¹⁵In this meaningless life, I have seen everything, including the fact that some good

people die young and some wicked people live on and on. ¹⁶So don't be too good or too wise! Why destroy yourself? ¹⁷On the other hand, don't be too wicked either—don't be a fool! Why should you die before your time? ¹⁸So try to walk a middle course—but those who fear God will succeed either way.

¹⁹A wise person is stronger than the ten leading citizens of a town!

²⁰There is not a single person in all the earth who is always good and never sins.

²¹Don't eavesdrop on others—you may hear your servant laughing at you. ²²For you know how often you yourself have laughed at others.

²³All along I have tried my best to let wisdom guide my thoughts and actions. I said to myself, "I am determined to be wise." But it didn't really work. ²⁴Wisdom is always distant and very difficult to find. ²⁵I searched everywhere, determined to find wisdom and to understand the reason for things. I was determined to prove to myself that wickedness is stupid and that foolishness is madness.

²⁶I discovered that a seductive woman is more bitter than death. Her passion is a trap, and her soft hands will bind you. Those who please God will escape from her, but sinners will be caught in her snare.

²⁷"This is my conclusion," says the Teacher. "I came to this result after looking into the matter from every possible angle. ²⁸Just one out of every thousand men I interviewed can be said to be upright, but not one woman! ²⁹I discovered that God created people to be upright, but they have each turned to follow their own downward path."

8 How wonderful to be wise, to be able to analyze and interpret things. Wisdom lights up a person's face, softening its hardness.

OBEDIENCE TO THE KING

²Obey the king because you have vowed before God to do this. ³Don't try to avoid doing your duty, and don't take a stand with those who plot evil. For the king will punish those who disobey him. ⁴The king's command is backed by great power. No one can resist or question it. ⁵Those who obey him will not be punished. Those who are wise will find a time and a way to do what is right. ⁶Yes, there is a time and a way for everything, even as people's troubles lie heavily upon them.

⁷Indeed, how can people avoid what they don't know is going to happen? ⁸None of us can hold back our spirit from departing. None of us has the power to prevent the day of our death. There is no escaping that obligation, that dark battle. And in the face of death, wickedness will certainly not rescue those who practice it.

THE WICKED AND THE RIGHTEOUS

⁹I have thought deeply about all that goes on here in the world, where people have the power to hurt each other. ¹⁰I have seen wicked people buried with honor. How strange that they were the very ones who frequented the Temple and are praised* in the very city where they committed their crimes! ¹¹When a crime is not punished, people feel it is safe to do wrong. ¹²But even though a person sins a hundred times and still lives a long time, I know that those who fear God will be better off. ¹³The wicked will never live long, good lives, for they do not fear God. Their days will never grow long like the evening shadows.

¹⁴And this is not all that is meaningless in our world. In this life, good people are often treated as though they were wicked, and wicked people are often treated as though they were good. This is so meaningless!

¹⁵So I recommend having fun, because there is nothing better for people to do in this world than to eat, drink, and enjoy life. That way they will experience some happiness along with all the hard work God gives them.

¹⁶In my search for wisdom, I tried to observe everything that goes on all across the

---

8:10 As in some Hebrew manuscripts and Greek version; many Hebrew manuscripts read *and are forgotten.*

My Daily Worship
— June 27 —

GOD'S WARNING SIGNALS
ECCLESIASTES 6:1–8:17

Don't be quick-tempered, for anger is the friend of fools (7:9).

[i reflect]

Strong emotions—if we handle them wisely—can function like warning lights on the dashboards of our lives. Do you find yourself extremely discouraged, even depressed? Feeling insignificant, even worthless? How about anxious, or even panicky? If so, perhaps you need to pull over and "look under the hood." Or better yet, pull into "God's garage" for a quick check-up or tune-up.

Strong emotions are a flashing signal that something isn't quite right. If we ignore them and continue barreling on down the highway of life, pedal to the metal, we risk causing real damage to ourselves and others. What these powerful feelings are indicating is that it is time to stop driving. Find a rest area. Put your life up on blocks (even if only for a few minutes). Call time-out. Retreat and regroup. With God's help, examine your heart.

Nowhere is this more important than in dealing with the common emotion of anger. By developing this holy habit of regular heart monitoring and maintenance, we avoid the common tendency for minor irritations to escalate into full-scale rage. As we learn this important discipline, we also learn to avoid saying or doing things in anger that we later regret.

This kind of reflective living makes us proactive instead of reactive people. It turns potentially negative emotional moments into occasions for prayer and insight. It's just one more way to become a true-blue worshiper—a person who clings to God and leans on him in every situation of life, even the really volatile ones.

When you feel yourself starting to boil over today, stop. Pull over. Talk to God, and ask him to redirect your emotions.

[i pray]

Father, when I am filled with anger, prompt me to seek you out, so that together we can look at my heart and find out not only why I feel the way I do, but how I can proceed in a way that honors you.

[i respond]

Identify those areas, situations, or even times of day, where you tend to have a short fuse. Take time to pray about each situation beforehand.

earth. I discovered that there is ceaseless activity, day and night. [17]This reminded me that no one can discover everything God has created in our world, no matter how hard they work at it. Not even the wisest people know everything, even if they say they do.

DEATH COMES TO ALL

9 This, too, I carefully explored: Even though the actions of godly and wise people are in God's hands, no one knows whether or not God will show them favor in this life. [2]The same destiny ultimately awaits everyone, whether they are righteous or wicked, good or bad,* ceremonially clean or unclean, religious or irreligious. Good people receive the same treatment as sinners, and people who take oaths are treated like people who don't.

[3]It seems so tragic that one fate comes to all. That is why people are not more careful to be good. Instead, they choose their own mad course, for they have no hope. There is nothing ahead but death anyway. [4]There is hope only for the living. For as they say, "It is better to be a live dog than a dead lion!"

[5]The living at least know they will die, but the dead know nothing. They have no further reward, nor are they remembered. [6]Whatever they did in their lifetime—loving, hating, envying—is all long gone. They no longer have a part in anything here on earth. [7]So go ahead. Eat your food and drink your wine with a happy heart, for God approves of this! [8]Wear fine clothes, with a dash of cologne!

[9]Live happily with the woman you love through all the meaningless days of life that God has given you in this world. The wife God gives you is your reward for all your earthly toil. [10]Whatever you do, do well. For when you go to the grave, there will be no work or planning or knowledge or wisdom.

[11]I have observed something else in this world of ours. The fastest runner doesn't always win the race, and the strongest warrior doesn't always win the battle. The wise are

Words of Worship

HEART

Heart—Hebrew *le-vav* or *lev*; Greek *kar-di-a*. The Hebrew word is usually translated "heart," in the sense of the inner being—mind, will, memory. The Greek word in the New Testament follows the Hebrew usage.

We know that the heart pumps blood through the body, and if it stops beating, we stop living. But, as our innermost organ, the heart also represents something deep in our personality. In literature and entertainment the heart has come to stand for feeling, compassion, romance. In the Bible, by contrast, the heart refers to the intention or purpose to which a person devotes his or her life.

We can deceive ourselves about what we really want, but God sees our hearts—our true intentions. His living Word "exposes us for what we really are" (Hebrews 4:12), and the state of our heart determines what becomes of our life (Proverbs 4:23). Jesus said, "God blesses those whose hearts are pure, for they will see God" (Matthew 5:8). To have a pure heart means to have one intention, to worship God and behold him. When that is true for us, we can say with the psalmist, "With all my heart I will praise you, O LORD my God" (Psalm 86:12).

often poor, and the skillful are not necessarily wealthy. And those who are educated don't always lead successful lives. It is all decided by chance, by being at the right place at the right time.

[12]People can never predict when hard times might come. Like fish in a net or birds in a snare, people are often caught by sudden tragedy.

9:2 As in Greek and Syriac versions, and Latin Vulgate; Hebrew lacks *or bad.*

THOUGHTS ON WISDOM AND FOLLY

¹³Here is another bit of wisdom that has impressed me as I have watched the way our world works. ¹⁴There was a small town with only a few people living in it, and a great king came with his army and besieged it. ¹⁵There was a poor, wise man living there who knew how to save the town, and so it was rescued. But afterward no one thought any more about him. ¹⁶Then I realized that though wisdom is better than strength, those who are wise will be despised if they are poor. What they say will not be appreciated for long. ¹⁷But even so, the quiet words of a wise person are better than the shouts of a foolish king. ¹⁸A wise person can overcome weapons of war, but one sinner can destroy much that is good.

10 Dead flies will cause even a bottle of perfume to stink! Yes, an ounce of foolishness can outweigh a pound of wisdom and honor.

²The hearts of the wise lead them to do right, and the hearts of the foolish lead them to do evil. ³You can identify fools just by the way they walk down the street!

⁴If your boss is angry with you, don't quit! A quiet spirit can overcome even great mistakes.

⁵There is another evil I have seen as I have watched the world go by. Kings and rulers make a grave mistake ⁶if they give foolish people great authority, and if they fail to give people of proven worth their rightful place of dignity. ⁷I have even seen servants riding like princes—and princes walking like servants.

⁸When you dig a well, you may fall in. When you demolish an old wall, you could be bitten by a snake. ⁹When you work in a quarry, stones might fall and crush you! When you chop wood, there is danger with each stroke of your ax! Such are the risks of life.

¹⁰Since a dull ax requires great strength, sharpen the blade. That's the value of wisdom; it helps you succeed.

¹¹It does no good to charm a snake after it has bitten you.

¹²It is pleasant to listen to wise words, but the speech of fools brings them to ruin.

¹³Since fools base their thoughts on foolish premises, their conclusions will be wicked madness.

¹⁴Foolish people claim to know all about the future and tell everyone the details! But who can really know what is going to happen?

¹⁵Fools are so exhausted by a little work that they have no strength for even the simplest tasks.

¹⁶Destruction is certain for the land whose king is a child* and whose leaders feast in the morning. ¹⁷Happy is the land whose king is a nobleman and whose leaders feast only to gain strength for their work, not to get drunk.

¹⁸Laziness lets the roof leak, and soon the rafters begin to rot.

¹⁹A party gives laughter, and wine gives happiness, and money gives everything!

²⁰Never make light of the king, even in your thoughts. And don't make fun of a rich man, either. A little bird may tell them what you have said.

GENEROSITY AND DILIGENCE

11 Give generously, for your gifts will return to you later.* ²Divide your gifts among many, for you do not know what risks might lie ahead.

³When the clouds are heavy, the rains come down.

When a tree falls, whether south or north, there it lies.

⁴If you wait for perfect conditions, you will never get anything done.

⁵God's ways are as hard to discern as the pathways of the wind, and as mysterious as a tiny baby being formed in a mother's womb.

⁶Be sure to stay busy and plant a variety of crops, for you never know which will grow—perhaps they all will.

10:16 Or *whose king is a servant.*   11:1 Hebrew *Throw your bread on the waters, for after many days you will find it again.*

ADVICE FOR OLD AND YOUNG

⁷Light is sweet; it's wonderful to see the sun! ⁸When people live to be very old, let them rejoice in every day of life. But let them also remember that the dark days will be many. Everything still to come is meaningless.

⁹Young man, it's wonderful to be young! Enjoy every minute of it. Do everything you want to do; take it all in. But remember that you must give an account to God for everything you do. ¹⁰So banish grief and pain, but remember that youth, with a whole life before it, still faces the threat of meaninglessness.

12 Don't let the excitement of youth cause you to forget your Creator. Honor him in your youth before you grow old and no longer enjoy living. ²It will be too late then to remember him, when the light of the sun and moon and stars is dim to your old eyes, and there is no silver lining left among the clouds. ³Your limbs will tremble with age, and your strong legs will grow weak. Your teeth will be too few to do their work, and you will be blind, too. ⁴And when your teeth are gone, keep your lips tightly closed when you eat! Even the chirping of birds will wake you up. But you yourself will be deaf and tuneless, with a quavering voice. ⁵You will be afraid of heights and of falling, white-haired and withered, dragging along without any sexual desire. You will be standing at death's door. And as you near your everlasting home, the mourners will walk along the streets.

⁶Yes, remember your Creator now while you are young, before the silver cord of life snaps and the golden bowl is broken. Don't wait until the water jar is smashed at the spring and the pulley is broken at the well. ⁷For then the dust will return to the earth, and the spirit will return to God who gave it.

⁸"All is meaningless," says the Teacher, "utterly meaningless."

CONCLUDING THOUGHTS

⁹Because the Teacher was wise, he taught the people everything he knew. He collected proverbs and classified them. ¹⁰Indeed, the Teacher taught the plain truth, and he did so in an interesting way.

¹¹A wise teacher's words spur students to action and emphasize important truths. The collected sayings of the wise are like guidance from a shepherd.

¹²But, my child,* be warned: There is no end of opinions ready to be expressed. Studying them can go on forever and become very exhausting!

¹³Here is my final conclusion: Fear God and obey his commands, for this is the duty of every person. ¹⁴God will judge us for everything we do, including every secret thing, whether good or bad.

> *A glimpse of God will save you.*
> *To gaze at him will sanctify you.*
>
> MANLEY BEASLEY

12:12 Hebrew *my son.*

My Daily Worship

— *June 28* —

DILIGENT GENEROSITY
ECCLESIASTES 9:1–12:14

Give generously, for your gifts will return to you later (11:1).

[i reflect]

R. G. LeTourneau, owner of some two hundred patents, made a fortune designing and selling massive earth-moving equipment. He was perhaps most famous for his lavish charity. Later in life, he made it his goal to give away, not 10 percent of his income (the standard Christian tithe), but 90 percent! His reasoning, "God has a bigger shovel than I have."

Such generosity is hard for us to fathom because, well, it's an uncertain world. The stock market can always sink, and unemployment rates can always rise. No surprise, then, that human nature likes to hunker down, play it safe, hoard possessions, and look out for number one.

But then we come to a passage like this, which basically says: "Throw caution to the wind. Take financial risks. More specifically, be ready and willing to help others in trouble." Why? Why would anyone live like that? First, because of the way relationships tend to work. Generous people typically find help in trouble. Oftentimes the people they have helped are the ones to return the favor. On other occasions, the help comes from unexpected sources. Like the sayings in the book of Proverbs, this pithy maxim in the book of Ecclesiastes is not a surefire guarantee, but it is a pretty safe bet.

But even if we never "get it back" in this life, there is a second reason to be generous. Living by giving is a prime way we can worship God. Every time we write a check to charity or take a meal to someone in trouble, we have a prime opportunity to act out this prayer: "God, you have blessed me, so that I might bless others. You have been faithful to me in the past; I know you will be faithful in the future. I trust you to continue to provide. May this small gesture bring great honor to your Name."

When you lend a helping hand to people, turn a trusting heart heavenward. Give thanks. Acknowledge God as the provider of every good thing in your life. Worship.

[i pray]

Father, you have so richly blessed me! Give me a generous heart to go with all the good gifts you have showered on me. Prompt me to be unselfish with my time, talents, and treasures today. I want to be a diligent giver . . . and worshiper!

[i respond]

Go to your pantry and pick out three or four items. Grab some good things that you really enjoy—peanut butter, your favorite unopened box of cereal (not nasty stuff like canned beets!). Put it all in a sack and take it to a nearby food bank. Sing your favorite praise songs while you do this.

Song of Songs

Kiss me again and again, for your love is sweeter than wine (1:2).

A Lover's Exchange

Most modern weddings begin with a formal ceremony—either religious or secular—in which the bride and groom exchange vows and enter into a lifelong contract to be faithful to each other. This solemn ceremony is usually followed by a more lighthearted party of celebration, often with music and dancing, as well as complimentary speeches about each other by the bride, the groom, and others in the wedding party.

In the Song of Songs, we see a completely different wedding party. Here the bride and groom sing love songs to each other, with a wedding chorus joining in periodically, sometimes as narrator and sometimes to simply repeat what has already been said. The content of the songs is intimate—so much so that, because this is not our custom, if we attended such a wedding celebration and could understand the language, we would probably find it strange, if not embarrassing.

Song of Songs was written around the third century B.C., but its lyrical love poetry probably comes from much earlier. Some biblical historians say that this intimate exchange of love language is an allegory of Christ's love relationship with the church, or more specifically, his relationship with each individual Christian. It is, therefore, one of the Bible's richest examples of worship, even though the language is not what we would ordinarily use.

Poets, songwriters—many of them Christians from other eras—have produced works similar to this in their worship of the Lord. Perhaps a different approach to prayer would be to put yourself into some of the exchanges, accepting the love language as being addressed directly to you from the Lord himself. As you ponder this, ask the Holy Spirit to show you how the lover of your soul wants you to use this unfamiliar book of Scripture in your worship of him.

Worship Moments

- "How beautiful you are, my beloved, how beautiful! Your eyes are soft like doves" (1:15).

- "You have ravished my heart, my treasure, my bride" (4:9).

- "Place me like a seal over your heart, or like a seal on your arm" (8:6).

- Names that may refer to God: "my king" (1:4); "my love" (1:7); "my lover" (2:3); "beloved" (5:1); "my friend" (5:16).

1 This is Solomon's song of songs, more wonderful than any other.

*Young Woman:** ²"Kiss me again and again, for your love is sweeter than wine. ³How fragrant your cologne, and how pleasing your name! No wonder all the young women love you! ⁴Take me with you. Come, let's run! Bring me into your bedroom, O my king.*"

Young Women of Jerusalem: "How happy we are for him! We praise his love even more than wine."

Young Woman: "How right that the young women love you!

⁵"I am dark and beautiful, O women of Jerusalem, tanned as the dark tents of Kedar. Yes, even as the tents of Solomon!

⁶"Don't look down on me, you fair city girls, just because my complexion is so dark. The sun has burned my skin. My brothers were angry with me and sent me out to tend the vineyards in the hot sun. Now see what it has done to me!*

⁷"Tell me, O my love, where are you leading your flock today? Where will you rest your sheep at noon? For why should I wander like a prostitute* among the flocks of your companions?"

Young Man: ⁸"If you don't know, O most beautiful woman, follow the trail of my flock to the shepherds' tents, and there feed your young goats. ⁹What a lovely filly you are, my beloved one!* ¹⁰How lovely are your cheeks, with your earrings setting them afire! How stately is your neck, accented with a long string of jewels. ¹¹We will make earrings of gold for you and beads of silver."

Young Woman: ¹²"The king is lying on his couch, enchanted by the fragrance of my perfume. ¹³My lover is like a sachet of myrrh lying between my breasts. ¹⁴He is like a bouquet of flowers in the gardens of En-gedi."

Young Man: ¹⁵"How beautiful you are, my beloved, how beautiful! Your eyes are soft like doves."

Young Woman: ¹⁶"What a lovely, pleasant sight you are, my love, as we lie here on the grass, ¹⁷shaded by cedar trees and spreading firs."

2 *Young Woman:* "I am the rose of Sharon, the lily of the valley."

Young Man: ²"Yes, compared to other women, my beloved is like a lily among thorns."

Young Woman: ³"And compared to other youths, my lover is like the finest apple tree in the orchard. I am seated in his delightful shade, and his fruit is delicious to eat. ⁴He brings me to the banquet hall, so everyone can see how much he loves me. ⁵Oh, feed me with your love—your 'raisins' and your 'apples'—for I am utterly lovesick! ⁶His left hand is under my head, and his right hand embraces me.

⁷"Promise me, O women of Jerusalem, by the swift gazelles and the deer of the wild, not to awaken love until the time is right.*

⁸"Ah, I hear him—my lover! Here he comes, leaping on the mountains and bounding over the hills. ⁹My lover is like a

---

> *In worship, silence is far more that the absence of sound.*
>
> WELTON GADDY

1:1 The headings identifying the speakers are not in the original text, though the Hebrew usually gives clues by means of the gender of the person speaking.   1:4 Or *The king has brought me into his bedroom.*   1:6 Hebrew *My own vineyard I have neglected.*   1:7 Hebrew *like a veiled woman.*   1:9 Hebrew *I compare you, my beloved, to a mare among Pharaoh's chariots.*   2:7 Or *not to awaken love until it is ready.*

are budding, and the grapevines are in blossom. How delicious they smell! Yes, spring is here! Arise, my beloved, my fair one, and come away.'"

Young Man: [14]"My dove is hiding behind some rocks, behind an outcrop on the cliff. Let me see you; let me hear your voice. For your voice is pleasant, and you are lovely."

Young Women of Jerusalem: [15]"Quick! Catch all the little foxes before they ruin the vineyard of your love, for the grapevines are all in blossom."

Young Woman: [16]"My lover is mine, and I am his. He feeds among the lilies! [17]Before the dawn comes and the shadows flee away, come back to me, my love. Run like a gazelle or a young stag on the rugged mountains.*"

3 *Young Woman:* "One night as I lay in bed, I yearned deeply for my lover, but he did not come. [2]So I said to myself, 'I will get up now and roam the city, searching for him in all its streets and squares.' But my search was in vain. [3]The watchmen stopped me as they made their rounds, and I said to them, 'Have you seen him anywhere, this one I love so much?' [4]A little while later I found him and held him. I didn't let him go until I had brought him to my childhood home, into my mother's bedroom, where I had been conceived.

[5]"Promise me, O women of Jerusalem, by the swift gazelles and the deer of the wild, not to awaken love until the time is right.*"

Young Women of Jerusalem: [6]"Who is this sweeping in from the deserts like a cloud of smoke along the ground? Who is it that smells of myrrh and frankincense and every other spice? [7]Look, it is Solomon's carriage, with sixty of Israel's mightiest men surrounding it. [8]They are all skilled swordsmen and experienced warriors. Each one wears a sword on his thigh, ready

---

Words of Worship

HALLELUJAH, ALLELUIA

Hallelujah, Alleluia—Hebrew *hal-le-lu-jah* "praise Yah"; Greek *hal-le-lou-i-a*. The Hebrew phrase combines the verb *hillel* "to praise" with a shortened form of *Yahweh*, the personal name of God. The Greek word is simply a transcription of the Hebrew.

Every Christian can speak at least one phrase in Hebrew, for the exclamation "Hallelujah!" comes straight out of the Bible. We hear it more than twenty times in the book of Psalms (it appears as "Praise the Lord!" in newer English translations), and again near the end of the New Testament in the book of Revelation.

To exclaim or sing "Hallelujah!" is to recognize who is in charge of our universe and who is responsible for all the good that happens to us. Even when life isn't going as well as we might like, our "Hallelujah!" can take our anger, resentment, sorrow, or despair and put everything into proper perspective. We're not the center of our world, God is. When "Hallelujah!" reminds us of this, we can experience healing and deliverance. "Hallelujah! For the Lord our God, the Almighty, reigns" (Revelation 19:6).

---

swift gazelle or a young deer. Look, there he is behind the wall! Now he is looking in through the window, gazing into the room.

[10]"My lover said to me, 'Rise up, my beloved, my fair one, and come away. [11]For the winter is past, and the rain is over and gone. [12]The flowers are springing up, and the time of singing birds has come, even the cooing of turtledoves. [13]The fig trees

---

2:17 Or *on the hills of Bether.*   **3:5** Or *not to awaken love until it is ready.*

My Daily Worship

— *June 29* —

A REFLECTION OF GOD'S ROMANTIC HEART

SONG OF SONGS 1:1–4:16

You are like a private garden, my treasure, my bride! You are like a spring
that no one else can drink from, a fountain of my own (4:12).

[i reflect]

In his autobiography, *Just As I Am,* Billy Graham writes of his initial impressions of the woman he would one day marry, "If I had not been smitten with love at the first sight of Ruth Bell, I would certainly have been the exception. Many men at Wheaton thought she was stunning. Petite, vivacious, smart, talented, witty, stylish, amiable, and unattached. What more could a fellow ask for?"

Billy forgot one adjective in describing his future wife: determined. She felt God was calling her to be a missionary in Tibet, while Graham felt the call to preach the Gospel. Many months, discussions, and what might be termed arguments later over the future of their relationship, Billy finally put the question to Ruth, "Do you believe that God brought us together? When she answered "yes," he replied, "In that case, God will lead me, and you'll do the following."

Perhaps not the classic proposal, but when the answer "yes" came several months later, their union resulted in a relationship that turned into a lifetime commitment.

After more than a half a century of marriage and successfully raising five children, this starry-eyed husband and wife still celebrate the Creator's gift of intimacy. They look into the portrait of romantic love that King Solomon painted in Song of Songs as if it were a mirror. Not only do they see their love for each other in these verses, they also see a reflection of God's love.

Can't you see it too? Feel the arms of God embracing you with the gift of a new day. Listen as he calls you his beloved. Respond with a heart filled with love for the faithfulness and grace that he has lavished on you this day.

[i pray]

Lord, why should it surprise me that the gift of marital intimacy should be celebrated
in the Bible? Forgive me for making the false assumption that romance and sex are
of human origin. Thanks for the reminder that the most intimate love possible
is what you desire for man and woman and between yourself and me.

[i respond]

Contemplate two or three couples you know who have exceptional marriages. What do they do to keep their relationship fresh and growing? What correlation might you draw between that kind of love and the way you approach the Lord in personal worship?

to defend the king against an attack during the night.

⁹"King Solomon has built a carriage for himself from wood imported from Lebanon's forests. ¹⁰Its posts are of silver, its canopy is gold, and its seat is upholstered in purple cloth. Its interior was a gift of love from the young women of Jerusalem."

Young Woman: ¹¹"Go out to look upon King Solomon, O young women of Jerusalem.* See the crown with which his mother crowned him on his wedding day, the day of his gladness."

4 *Young Man:* "How beautiful you are, my beloved, how beautiful! Your eyes behind your veil are like doves. Your hair falls in waves, like a flock of goats frisking down the slopes of Gilead. ²Your teeth are as white as sheep, newly shorn and washed. They are perfectly matched; not one is missing. ³Your lips are like a ribbon of scarlet. Oh, how beautiful your mouth! Your cheeks behind your veil are like pomegranate halves—lovely and delicious. ⁴Your neck is as stately as the tower of David, jeweled with the shields of a thousand heroes. ⁵Your breasts are like twin fawns of a gazelle, feeding among the lilies. ⁶Before the dawn comes and the shadows flee away, I will go to the mountain of myrrh and to the hill of frankincense. ⁷You are so beautiful, my beloved, so perfect in every part.

⁸"Come with me from Lebanon, my bride. Come down* from the top of Mount Amana, from Mount Senir and Mount Hermon, where lions have their dens and panthers prowl. ⁹You have ravished my heart, my treasure, my bride. I am overcome by one glance of your eyes, by a single bead of your necklace. ¹⁰How sweet is your love, my treasure, my bride! How much better it is than wine! Your perfume is more fragrant than the richest of spices. ¹¹Your lips, my bride, are as sweet as honey. Yes, honey and cream are under your tongue. The scent of your clothing is like that of the mountains and the cedars of Lebanon.

¹²"You are like a private garden, my treasure, my bride! You are like a spring that no one else can drink from, a fountain of my own. ¹³You are like a lovely orchard bearing precious fruit, with the rarest of perfumes: ¹⁴nard and saffron, calamus and cinnamon, myrrh and aloes, perfume from every incense tree, and every other lovely spice. ¹⁵You are a garden fountain, a well of living water, as refreshing as the streams from the Lebanon mountains."

Young Woman: ¹⁶"Awake, north wind! Come, south wind! Blow on my garden and waft its lovely perfume to my lover. Let him come into his garden and eat its choicest fruits."

5 *Young Man:* "I am here in my garden, my treasure, my bride! I gather my myrrh with my spices and eat my honeycomb with my honey. I drink my wine with my milk."

Young Women of Jerusalem: "Oh, lover and beloved, eat and drink! Yes, drink deeply of this love!"

Young Woman: ²"One night as I was sleeping, my heart awakened in a dream. I heard the voice of my lover. He was knocking at my bedroom door. 'Open to me, my darling, my treasure, my lovely dove,' he said, 'for I have been out in the night. My head is soaked with dew, my hair with the wetness of the night.'

³"But I said, 'I have taken off my robe. Should I get dressed again? I have washed my feet. Should I get them soiled?'

⁴"My lover tried to unlatch the door, and my heart thrilled within me. ⁵I jumped up to open it. My hands dripped with perfume, my fingers with lovely myrrh,

3:11 Hebrew *Zion.*   **4:8** Or *Look down.*

> One should use praise to
> recognize what one is not.
>
> ELIAS CANETTI

as I pulled back the bolt. ⁶I opened to my lover, but he was gone. I yearned for even his voice! I searched for him, but I couldn't find him anywhere. I called to him, but there was no reply. ⁷The watchmen found me as they were making their rounds; they struck and wounded me. The watchman on the wall tore off my veil.

⁸"Make this promise to me, O women of Jerusalem! If you find my beloved one, tell him that I am sick with love."

Young Women of Jerusalem: ⁹"O woman of rare beauty, what is it about your loved one that brings you to tell us this?"

Young Woman: ¹⁰"My lover is dark and dazzling, better than ten thousand others! ¹¹His head is the finest gold, and his hair is wavy and black. ¹²His eyes are like doves beside brooks of water; they are set like jewels. ¹³His cheeks are like sweetly scented beds of spices. His lips are like perfumed lilies. His breath is like myrrh. ¹⁴His arms are like round bars of gold, set with chrysolite. His body is like bright ivory, aglow with sapphires. ¹⁵His legs are like pillars of marble set in sockets of the finest gold, strong as the cedars of Lebanon. None can rival him. ¹⁶His mouth is altogether sweet; he is lovely in every way. Such, O women of Jerusalem, is my lover, my friend."

6 *Young Women of Jerusalem:* "O rarest of beautiful women, where has your lover gone? We will help you find him."

Young Woman: ²"He has gone down to his garden, to his spice beds, to graze and to gather the lilies. ³I am my lover's, and my lover is mine. He grazes among the lilies!"

Young Man: ⁴"O my beloved, you are as beautiful as the lovely town of Tirzah. Yes, as beautiful as Jerusalem! You are as majestic as an army with banners! ⁵Look away, for your eyes overcome me! Your hair falls in waves, like a flock of goats frisking down the slopes of Gilead. ⁶Your teeth are as white as newly washed sheep. They are perfectly matched; not one is missing. ⁷Your cheeks behind your veil are like pomegranate halves—lovely and delicious. ⁸There may be sixty wives, all queens, and eighty concubines and unnumbered virgins available to me. ⁹But I would still choose my dove, my perfect one, the only beloved daughter of her mother! The young women are delighted when they see her; even queens and concubines sing her praises! ¹⁰Who is this,' they ask, 'arising like the dawn, as fair as the moon, as bright as the sun, as majestic as an army with banners?'

¹¹"I went down into the grove of nut trees and out to the valley to see the new growth brought on by spring. I wanted to see whether the grapevines were budding yet, or whether the pomegranates were blossoming. ¹²Before I realized it, I found myself in my princely bed with my beloved one.*"

Young Women of Jerusalem: ¹³"Return, return to us, O maid of Shulam. Come back, come back, that we may see you once again."

Young Man: "Why do you gaze so intently at this young woman of Shulam, as she moves so gracefully between two lines of dancers?*"

6:12 Or *among the royal chariots of my people,* or *among the chariots of Amminadab.* The meaning of the Hebrew is uncertain.   6:13 Or *as you would at the movements of two armies?* or *as you would at the dance of Mahanaim?* The meaning of the Hebrew is uncertain.

7 *Young Man:* "How beautiful are your sandaled feet, O queenly maiden. Your rounded thighs are like jewels, the work of a skilled craftsman. ²Your navel is as delicious as a goblet filled with wine. Your belly is lovely, like a heap of wheat set about with lilies. ³Your breasts are like twin fawns of a gazelle. ⁴Your neck is as stately as an ivory tower. Your eyes are like the sparkling pools in Heshbon by the gate of Bath-rabbim. Your nose is as fine as the tower of Lebanon overlooking Damascus. ⁵Your head is as majestic as Mount Carmel, and the sheen of your hair radiates royalty. A king is held captive in your queenly tresses.

⁶"Oh, how delightful you are, my beloved; how pleasant for utter delight! ⁷You are tall and slim like a palm tree, and your breasts are like its clusters of dates. ⁸I said, 'I will climb up into the palm tree and take hold of its branches.' Now may your breasts be like grape clusters, and the scent of your breath like apples. ⁹May your kisses be as exciting as the best wine, smooth and sweet, flowing gently over lips and teeth.*"

Young Woman: ¹⁰"I am my lover's, the one he desires. ¹¹Come, my love, let us go out into the fields and spend the night among the wildflowers.* ¹²Let us get up early and go out to the vineyards. Let us see whether the vines have budded, whether the blossoms have opened, and whether the pomegranates are in flower. And there I will give you my love. ¹³There the mandrakes give forth their fragrance, and the rarest fruits are at our doors, the new as well as old, for I have stored them up for you, my lover."

8 *Young Woman:* "Oh, if only you were my brother, who nursed at my mother's breast. Then I could kiss you no matter who was watching, and no one would criticize me. ²I would bring you to my childhood home, and there you would teach me. I would give you spiced wine to drink, my sweet pomegranate wine. ³Your left hand would be under my head and your right hand would embrace me.

⁴"I want you to promise, O women of Jerusalem, not to awaken love until the time is right.*"

Young Women of Jerusalem: ⁵"Who is this coming up from the desert, leaning on her lover?"

7:9 As in Greek and Syriac versions and Latin Vulgate; Hebrew reads *over lips of sleepers.* 7:11 Or *in the villages.* 8:4 Or *not to awaken love until it is ready.*

My Daily Worship

— June 30 —

GOD'S ETERNAL FLAME

SONG OF SONGS 5:1–8:14

Place me like a seal over your heart, or like a seal on your arm. For love is as strong as death, and its jealousy is as enduring as the grave. Love flashes like fire, the brightest kind of flame. Many waters cannot quench love; neither can rivers drown it (8:6–7).

[i reflect]

Every year 4.5 million people visit Arlington National Cemetery. Most of those pay their respects at the grave of President John F. Kennedy. It is marked by an eternal flame that was incorporated into the grave marker at the request of JFK's widow. Even though the flame apparatus had been tested to withstand rain and wind, a month after the assassinated president was buried a group of students from a Catholic school accidentally doused the flame by sprinkling holy water on it. An alert uniformed guard relit it with a portable lighter.

When the Kennedy grave was expanded in the late sixties, a more elaborate fuel line was constructed underground with a specially designed apparatus created by the Institute of Gas Technology of Chicago. As part of the plan, a constantly flashing electric spark near the tip of the nozzle relights the gas should the flame be extinguished accidentally. Curiously, the fuel is natural gas and is mixed with a controlled quantity of air to achieve the color and shape of the flame. All the same, for purposes of maintenance around the gravesite, the flame is occasionally turned off manually. It's not eternal, after all.

In contrast, the picture of love found in the these verses from Song of Solomon presents a real eternal flame. The love pictured here can't be quenched. Although the description is of human love, it also points to the giver of love. The intense flame of his affection can't ever be doused or turned off. That's why the apostle Paul wrote: "Nothing can ever separate us from his love" (Romans 8:38).

Human love can be strong. But the love of a heavenly Father is stronger still. It's a seal that is seen in two nail-pierced hands. Stretch your hands toward him now and say, "I love you!"

[i pray]

*Jesus, I can't thank you enough for bearing my sin. In your death on the cross
I see the seal of your love. As I ponder the nail prints in your hands and feet,
I am moved with humility and gratitude. I love you, Lord.*

[i respond]

Even though you may be familiar with 1 Corinthians 13, take time now to read this chapter aloud. As you do, substitute "God" for the word "love." Let this powerful reminder of the Father's love prompt you to respond in worship.

Young Woman: "I aroused you under the apple tree, where your mother gave you birth, where in great pain she delivered you. ⁶Place me like a seal over your heart, or like a seal on your arm. For love is as strong as death, and its jealousy is as enduring as the grave. Love flashes like fire, the brightest kind of flame. ⁷Many waters cannot quench love; neither can rivers drown it. If a man tried to buy love with everything he owned, his offer would be utterly despised."

The Young Woman's Brothers: ⁸"We have a little sister too young for breasts. What will we do if someone asks to marry her? ⁹If she is chaste, we will strengthen and encourage her. But if she is promiscuous, we will shut her off from men.*"

Young Woman: ¹⁰"I am chaste, and I am now full breasted. And my lover is content with me.

¹¹"Solomon has a vineyard at Baal-hamon, which he rents to some farmers there. Each of them pays one thousand pieces of silver* for its use. ¹²But as for my own vineyard, O Solomon, you can take my thousand pieces of silver. And I will give two hundred pieces of silver* to those who care for its vines."

Young Man: ¹³"O my beloved, lingering in the gardens, how wonderful that your companions can listen to your voice. Let me hear it, too!"

Young Woman: ¹⁴"Come quickly, my love! Move like a swift gazelle or a young deer on the mountains of spices."

8:9 Hebrew *If she is a wall, we will build battlements of silver on her; but if she is a door, we will surround her with panels of cedar.*
8:11 Hebrew *1,000 shekels of silver,* about 25 pounds or 11.4 kilograms in weight; also in 8:12. 8:12 Hebrew *200 [shekels],* about 5 pounds or 2.3 kilograms in weight.

Isaiah

Look, your Savior is coming. See, he brings his reward with him as he comes (62:11).

A Light Shining in the Darkness

Anyone reading the book of Isaiah certainly would be struck by the recurring themes of a wayward people and a longsuffering God. However, reading the book as one who is familiar with Jesus' life story, however, serves as a powerful reminder of how Jesus fulfilled Scripture in his lifetime.

The life of Jesus is clearly foretold, beginning with: "The virgin will conceive a child! She will give birth to a son and will call him Immanuel" (7:14); to "There will be a time in the future when Galilee of the Gentiles, . . . will be filled with glory" (9:1); to "Many were amazed when they saw him—beaten and bloodied, so disfigured one would scarcely know he was a person" (52:14). These are only a few of the many verses that foreshadow the coming Savior's ministry in which he makes the lame walk, the blind see, the deaf hear, and sets the captives free (35:6; 42:7).

Over and over the prophet speaks of the coming of light: "The people who walk in darkness will see a great light—a light that will shine on all who live in the land where death casts its shadow" (9:2); and "Arise, Jerusalem! Let your light shine for all the nations to see! For the glory of the LORD is shining upon you" (60:1). Isaiah truly focuses on the glory of the Lord—the Light of the world—the One who was appointed to bring good news to the poor (61:1).

As you read through this epic book, notice the frustrating inconsistencies of the people of Israel as contrasted with God's constant and faithful wooing of them. Notice, also, the verses that have a familiar ring to them because you have read them in the New Testament Gospels. This book is a great resource for worship. It reminds us of the wonder of the coming of the Messiah—and the fact that he has made himself accessible to each one of us.

Worship Moments

- The hosts of heaven worship God (6:2–3).

- "Listen in silence before me" is God's command (41:1).

- "I will also bless the Gentiles who . . . serve him and love his name" (56:6).

- "Enjoy the Sabbath, . . . don't follow your own desires" (58:13).

- The Lord is worshiped as "a refuge" (25:4); "the eternal Rock" (26:4); "the Potter" (29:16); and "the First and the Last" (44:6; 48:12).

1 These visions concerning Judah and Jerusalem came to Isaiah son of Amoz during the reigns of Uzziah, Jotham, Ahaz, and Hezekiah—all kings of Judah.

A Message for Rebellious Judah

[2]Hear, O heavens! Listen, O earth! This is what the LORD says: "The children I raised and cared for have turned against me. [3]Even the animals—the donkey and the ox—know their owner and appreciate his care, but not my people Israel. No matter what I do for them, they still do not understand."

[4]Oh, what a sinful nation they are! They are loaded down with a burden of guilt. They are evil and corrupt children who have turned away from the LORD. They have despised the Holy One of Israel, cutting themselves off from his help.

[5]Why do you continue to invite punishment? Must you rebel forever? Your head is injured, and your heart is sick. [6]You are sick from head to foot—covered with bruises, welts, and infected wounds—without any ointments or bandages. [7]Your country lies in ruins, and your cities are burned. As you watch, foreigners plunder your fields and destroy everything they see. [8]Jerusalem* stands abandoned like a watchman's shelter in a vineyard or field after the harvest is over. It is as helpless as a city under siege. [9]If the LORD Almighty had not spared a few of us, we would have been wiped out as completely as Sodom and Gomorrah.

[10]Listen to the LORD, you leaders of Israel! Listen to the law of our God, people of Israel. You act just like the rulers and people of Sodom and Gomorrah. [11]"I am sick of your sacrifices," says the LORD. "Don't bring me any more burnt offerings! I don't want the fat from your rams or other animals. I don't want to see the blood from your offerings of bulls and rams and goats. [12]Why do you keep parading through my courts with your worthless sacrifices? [13]The incense you bring me is a stench in my nostrils! Your celebrations of the new moon and the Sabbath day, and your special days for fasting—even your most pious meetings—are all sinful and false. I want nothing more to do with them. [14]I hate all your festivals and sacrifices. I cannot stand the sight of them! [15]From now on, when you lift up your hands in prayer, I will refuse to look. Even though you offer many prayers, I will not listen. For your hands are covered with the blood of your innocent victims. [16]Wash yourselves and be clean! Let me no longer see your evil deeds. Give up your wicked ways. [17]Learn to do good. Seek justice. Help the oppressed. Defend the orphan. Fight for the rights of widows.

[18]"Come now, let us argue this out," says the LORD. "No matter how deep the stain of your sins, I can remove it. I can make you as clean as freshly fallen snow. Even if you are stained as red as crimson, I can make you as white as wool. [19]If you will only obey me and let me help you, then you will have plenty to eat. [20]But if you keep turning away and refusing to listen, you will be destroyed by your enemies. I, the LORD, have spoken!"

Unfaithful Jerusalem

[21]See how Jerusalem, once so faithful, has become a prostitute. Once the home of justice and righteousness, she is now filled with murderers. [22]Once like pure silver, you have become like worthless slag. Once so pure, you are now like watered-down wine. [23]Your leaders are rebels, the companions of thieves. All of them take bribes and refuse to defend the orphans and the widows.

[24]Therefore, the Lord, the LORD Almighty, the Mighty One of Israel, says, "I will pour out my fury on you, my enemies! [25]I will turn against you. I will melt you down and skim off your slag. I will remove all your impurities. [26]Afterward I will give you good judges and wise counselors like the ones you used to have. Then Jerusalem will again be called the Home of Justice and the Faithful City."

1:8 Hebrew *The daughter of Zion.*

My Daily Worship

— July 1 —

FROM THE PRAYER CLOSET
TO THE STREET
ISAIAH 1:1–4:6

Learn to do good. Seek justice. Help the oppressed. Defend the orphan.
Fight for the rights of widows (1:17).

[i reflect]

She was born August 26, 1910, in Skopje, Macedonia. Her wealthy parents named her Agnes Gonxha Bojaxhiu. They had no idea that their daughter would some day change her name or change the course of history. In 1928 she joined a religious order and took the name Teresa. In 1950, this diminutive lady in her familiar white habit founded a religious order in Calcutta.

Under her "servant leadership," the Missionaries of Charity order operated hospitals, orphanages, and shelters for lepers and the dying poor. The ministry that Mother Teresa started grew to include branches in fifty Indian cities and thirty countries. She dedicated every day of her adult life caring for the dying, the cripple, the mentally ill, the unwanted, the unloved. As far as she was concerned, she was loving, cleaning, and feeding "Jesus in disguise."

In her eighty-seven years of life, this giant of the faith proved that worship is more than having personal devotions. It is personally serving the needy around us. That's what Isaiah is driving at in this passage. Genuine praise extends beyond the prayer closet to the people we encounter throughout the day.

Lactantius, an early church father, was on the same page with Mother Teresa as well as Isaiah. He wrote: "If it is piety to know God and, as a result, to worship him, then those who don't know God plainly don't know justice. For how can we know justice if we are unaware of its source?"

Even though lingering in the Lord's sweet presence is definitely easier than helping a homeless person to a shelter, it is incomplete. Worshiping with our hands and feet is harder than with our lips. Today, instead of folding your hands in your favorite chair, walk downtown and give someone a hand.

[i pray]

Help me, Father, to see the needs around me that break your heart. Don't allow me
to be so comfortable in my quiet time with you that I fail to hear
the blaring chaos of a world longing for justice and mercy.

[i respond]

For a week, use your normal devotional time to "do good": write a letter to the editor of your local paper lobbying for a just cause, help serve at a homeless shelter or soup kitchen, befriend an elderly widow at a nursing home, or other act of service.

²⁷Because the LORD is just and righteous, the repentant people of Jerusalem* will be redeemed. ²⁸But all sinners will be completely destroyed, for they refuse to come to the LORD.

²⁹Shame will cover you when you think of the times you offered sacrifices to idols in your groves of sacred oaks. You will blush when you think of all the sins you committed in your sacred gardens. ³⁰You will wither away like an oak or garden without water. ³¹The strongest among you will disappear like burning straw. Your evil deeds are the spark that will set the straw on fire, and no one will be able to put it out.

THE LORD'S FUTURE REIGN

2 This is another vision that Isaiah son of Amoz saw concerning Judah and Jerusalem:

²In the last days, the Temple of the LORD in Jerusalem will become the most important place on earth. People from all over the world will go there to worship. ³Many nations will come and say, "Come, let us go up to the mountain of the LORD, to the Temple of the God of Israel.* There he will teach us his ways, so that we may obey him." For in those days the LORD's teaching and his word will go out from Jerusalem.

⁴The LORD will settle international disputes. All the nations will beat their swords into plowshares and their spears into pruning hooks. All wars will stop, and military training will come to an end. ⁵Come, people of Israel, let us walk in the light of the LORD!

A WARNING OF JUDGMENT

⁶The LORD has rejected the people of Israel because they have made alliances with foreigners from the East who practice magic and divination, just like the Philistines. ⁷Israel has vast treasures of silver and gold and many horses and chariots. ⁸The land is filled with idols. The people bow down and worship these things they have made. ⁹So now everyone will be humbled and brought low. The LORD cannot simply ignore their sins!

¹⁰Crawl into caves in the rocks. Hide from the terror of the LORD and the glory of his majesty. ¹¹The day is coming when your pride will be brought low and the LORD alone will be exalted. ¹²In that day the LORD Almighty will punish the proud, bringing them down to the dust. ¹³He will cut down the tall cedars of Lebanon and the mighty oaks of Bashan. ¹⁴He will level the high mountains and hills. ¹⁵He will break down every high tower and wall. ¹⁶He will destroy the great trading ships* and all the small boats in the harbor. ¹⁷The arrogance of all people will be brought low. Their pride will lie in the dust. The LORD alone will be exalted! ¹⁸Idols will be utterly abolished and destroyed.

¹⁹When the LORD rises to shake the earth, his enemies will crawl with fear into holes in the ground. They will hide in caves in the rocks from the terror of the LORD and the glory of his majesty. ²⁰They will abandon their gold and silver idols to the moles and bats. ²¹They will crawl into caverns and hide among the jagged rocks at the tops of cliffs. In this way, they will try to escape the terror of the LORD and the glory of his majesty as he rises to shake the earth.

²²Stop putting your trust in mere humans. They are as frail as breath. How can they be of help to anyone?

JUDGMENT AGAINST JUDAH

3 The Lord, the LORD Almighty, will cut off the supplies of food and water from Jerusalem and Judah. ²He will destroy all the nation's leaders—the heroes, soldiers, judges, prophets, diviners, elders, ³army officers, honorable citizens, advisers, skilled magicians, and expert enchanters. ⁴Then he will appoint children to rule over them, and anarchy will prevail. ⁵People will take advantage of each other—man against man, neighbor fighting

1:27 Hebrew *Zion*. 2:3 Hebrew *of Jacob*; also in 2:5, 6. 2:16 Hebrew *every ship of Tarshish*.

Words of Worship

ALTAR

Altar—Hebrew *miz-be-ach*; Greek *thu-si-a-ste-ri-on*. Both the Hebrew and Greek terms are derived from words that mean "sacrifice, offering."

An altar is a structure on which sacrifices are offered. The altars of the tabernacle of Moses and the Temple of Jerusalem were made by craftsmen, but earlier altars were piles of uncut stones. When an offering was consumed by fire, it was understood that the Lord received it and showed favor to the worshiper. The sanctuary altar was a place of refuge, where one accused of manslaughter might be protected from an avenger.

When Jesus died on the cross, his followers understood that the traditional sacrifices no longer had value. God had accepted the sacrifice of the Lamb of God for the sins of his people. Nevertheless, the altar remains a powerful symbol. Many early Christians gave their lives in witness, and their blood cried out from under the altar of heaven (Revelation 6:9). The altar represents the place where we offer ourselves to the Lord in prayer (Romans 12:1), bring the sacrifice of praise (Hebrews 13:15), and seek refuge in Jesus (Hebrews 6:18). Our altar may not be an elegant piece of furniture. We may build it simply from the "uncut stones" (Exodus 20:25) of our lives.

---

[7]"No!" he will reply. "I can't help. I don't have any extra food or clothes. Don't ask me to get involved!"

[8]Judah and Jerusalem will lie in ruins because they speak out against the LORD and refuse to obey him. They have offended his glorious presence among them. [9]The very look on their faces gives them away and displays their guilt. They sin openly like the people of Sodom. They are not one bit ashamed. How terrible it will be for them! They have brought about their own destruction.

[10]But all will be well for those who are godly. Tell them, "You will receive a wonderful reward!" [11]But say to the wicked, "Your destruction is sure. You, too, will get what you deserve. Your well-earned punishment is on the way."

[12]Children oppress my people, and women rule over them. O my people, can't you see what fools your rulers are? They are leading you down a pretty garden path to destruction.

[13]The LORD takes his place in court. He is the great prosecuting attorney, presenting his case against his people! [14]The leaders and the princes will be the first to feel the LORD's judgment. "You have ruined Israel, which is my vineyard. You have taken advantage of the poor, filling your barns with grain extorted from helpless people. [15]How dare you grind my people into the dust like that!" demands the Lord, the LORD Almighty.

A WARNING FOR JERUSALEM'S WOMEN

[16]Next the LORD will judge the women of Jerusalem,* who walk around with their noses in the air, with tinkling ornaments on their ankles. Their eyes rove among the crowds, flirting with the men. [17]The Lord will send a plague of scabs to ornament their heads. Yes, the LORD will make them bald for all to see!

[18]The Lord will strip away their artful beauty—their ornaments, headbands, and crescent necklaces; [19]their earrings, bracelets, and veils of shimmering gauze. [20]Gone will be

---

neighbor. Young people will revolt against authority, and nobodies will sneer at honorable people.

[6]In those days a man will say to his brother, "Since you have a cloak, you be our leader! Take charge of this heap of ruins!"

3:16 Hebrew *the daughters of Zion.*

their scarves, ankle chains, sashes, perfumes, and charms; ²¹their rings, jewels, ²²party clothes, gowns, capes, and purses; ²³their mirrors, linen garments, head ornaments, and shawls. ²⁴Instead of smelling of sweet perfume, they will stink. They will wear ropes for sashes, and their well-set hair will fall out. They will wear rough sackcloth instead of rich robes. Their beauty will be gone. Only shame will be left to them.

²⁵The men of the city will die in battle. ²⁶The gates of Jerusalem* will weep and mourn. The city will be like a ravaged woman, huddled on the ground.

4 In that day few men will be left alive. Seven women will fight over each of them and say, "Let us all marry you! We will provide our own food and clothing. Only let us be called by your name so we won't be mocked as old maids."

A PROMISE OF RESTORATION

²But in the future, Israel—the branch of the LORD—will be lush and beautiful, and the fruit of the land will be the pride of its people. ³All those whose names are written down, who have survived the destruction of Jerusalem, will be a holy people. ⁴The Lord will wash the moral filth from the women of Jerusalem.* He will cleanse Jerusalem of its bloodstains by a spirit of judgment that burns like fire. ⁵Then the LORD will provide shade for Jerusalem* and all who assemble there. There will be a canopy of smoke and cloud throughout the day and clouds of fire at night, covering the glorious land. ⁶It will be a shelter from daytime heat and a hiding place from storms and rain.

A SONG ABOUT THE LORD'S VINEYARD

5 Now I will sing a song for the one I love about his vineyard:

My beloved has a vineyard
 on a rich and fertile hill.
² He plowed the land, cleared its stones,
 and planted it with choice vines.
In the middle he built a watchtower
 and carved a winepress in the nearby
 rocks.
Then he waited for a harvest of sweet
 grapes,
 but the grapes that grew were wild and
 sour.
³ "Now, you people of Jerusalem and Judah,
 you have heard the case; you be the
 judges.
⁴ What more could I have done
 to cultivate a rich harvest?
Why did my vineyard give me wild grapes
 when I expected sweet ones?
⁵ Now this is what I am going to do to my
 vineyard:
I will tear down its fences
 and let it be destroyed.
I will break down its walls
 and let the animals trample it.
⁶ I will make it a wild place.
 I will not prune the vines or hoe the
 ground.
 I will let it be overgrown with briers and
 thorns.
 I will command the clouds
 to drop no more rain on it."

⁷ This is the story of the LORD's people.
 They are the vineyard of the LORD
 Almighty.
 Israel and Judah are his pleasant garden.
 He expected them to yield a crop of
 justice,
 but instead he found bloodshed.
 He expected to find righteousness,
 but instead he heard cries of oppression.

JUDAH'S GUILT AND JUDGMENT

⁸Destruction is certain for you who buy up property so others have no place to live. Your homes are built on great estates so you can be

3:26 Hebrew *Zion.*   4:4 Hebrew *from the daughters of Zion.*   4:5 Hebrew *Mount Zion.*

alone in the land. ⁹But the LORD Almighty has sealed your awful fate. With my own ears I heard him say, "Many beautiful homes will stand deserted, the owners dead or gone. ¹⁰Ten acres* of vineyard will not produce even six gallons* of wine. Ten measures of seed will yield only one measure* of grain."

¹¹Destruction is certain for you who get up early to begin long drinking bouts that last late into the night. ¹²You furnish lovely music and wine at your grand parties; the harps, lyres, tambourines, and flutes are superb! But you never think about the LORD or notice what he is doing. ¹³So I will send my people into exile far away because they do not know me. The great and honored among them will starve, and the common people will die of thirst.

¹⁴The grave* is licking its chops in anticipation of Jerusalem, this delicious morsel. Her great and lowly will be swallowed up, with all her drunken crowds. ¹⁵In that day the arrogant will be brought down to the dust; the proud will be humbled. ¹⁶But the LORD Almighty is exalted by his justice. The holiness of God is displayed by his righteousness. ¹⁷In those days flocks will feed among the ruins; lambs and kids* will pasture there.

¹⁸Destruction is certain for those who drag their sins behind them, tied with cords of falsehood. ¹⁹They even mock the Holy One of Israel and say, "Hurry up and do something! Quick, show us what you can do. We want to see what you have planned."

²⁰Destruction is certain for those who say that evil is good and good is evil; that dark is light and light is dark; that bitter is sweet and sweet is bitter.

²¹Destruction is certain for those who think they are wise and consider themselves to be clever.

²²Destruction is certain for those who are heroes when it comes to drinking, who boast about all the liquor they can hold. ²³They take bribes to pervert justice. They let the wicked go free while punishing the innocent.

²⁴Therefore, they will all disappear like burning straw. Their roots will rot and their flowers wither, for they have rejected the law of the LORD Almighty. They have despised the word of the Holy One of Israel. ²⁵That is why the anger of the LORD burns against his people. That is why he has raised his fist to crush them. The hills tremble, and the rotting bodies of his people are thrown as garbage into the streets. But even then the LORD's anger will not be satisfied. His fist is still poised to strike!

²⁶He will send a signal to the nations far away. He will whistle to those at the ends of the earth, and they will come racing toward Jerusalem. ²⁷They will not get tired or stumble. They will run without stopping for rest or sleep. Not a belt will be loose, not a sandal thong broken. ²⁸Their arrows will be sharp and their bows ready for battle. Sparks will fly from their horses' hooves as the wheels of their chariots spin like the wind. ²⁹Roaring like lions, they will pounce on their prey. They will seize my people and carry them off into captivity, and no one will be there to rescue them. ³⁰The enemy nations will growl over their victims like the roaring of the sea. A cloud of darkness and sorrow will hover over Israel. The clouds will blot out the light.

ISAIAH'S CLEANSING AND CALL

6 In the year King Uzziah died, I saw the Lord. He was sitting on a lofty throne, and the train of his robe filled the Temple. ²Hovering around him were mighty seraphim, each with six wings. With two wings they covered their faces, with two they covered their feet, and with the remaining two they flew. ³In a great chorus they sang, "Holy, holy, holy is the LORD Almighty! The whole earth is filled with his glory!" ⁴The glorious singing shook the Temple to its foundations, and the entire sanctuary was filled with smoke.

5:10a Hebrew *A ten yoke,* that is, the area of land plowed by ten teams of oxen in one day. 5:10b Hebrew *a bath* [21 liters]. 5:10c Hebrew *A homer* [5 bushels or 182 liters] *of seed will yield only an ephah* [0.5 bushels or 18.2 liters]. 5:14 Hebrew *Sheol.* 5:17 As in Greek version; Hebrew reads *strangers.*

⁵Then I said, "My destruction is sealed, for I am a sinful man and a member of a sinful race. Yet I have seen the King, the LORD Almighty!"

⁶Then one of the seraphim flew over to the altar, and he picked up a burning coal with a pair of tongs. ⁷He touched my lips with it and said, "See, this coal has touched your lips. Now your guilt is removed, and your sins are forgiven."

⁸Then I heard the Lord asking, "Whom should I send as a messenger to my people? Who will go for us?"

And I said, "Lord, I'll go! Send me."

⁹And he said, "Yes, go. But tell my people this: 'You will hear my words, but you will not understand. You will see what I do, but you will not perceive its meaning.' ¹⁰Harden the hearts of these people. Close their ears, and shut their eyes. That way, they will not see with their eyes, hear with their ears, understand with their hearts, and turn to me for healing."

¹¹Then I said, "Lord, how long must I do this?"

And he replied, "Until their cities are destroyed, with no one left in them. Until their houses are deserted and the whole country is an utter wasteland. ¹²Do not stop until the LORD has sent everyone away to distant lands and the entire land of Israel lies deserted. ¹³Even if only a tenth—a remnant—survive, it will be invaded again and burned. Israel will remain a stump, like a tree that is cut down, but the stump will be a holy seed that will grow again."

A MESSAGE FOR AHAZ

7 During the reign of Ahaz son of Jotham and grandson of Uzziah, Jerusalem was attacked by King Rezin of Aram and King Pekah of Israel, the son of Remaliah. The city withstood the attack, however, and was not taken.

²The news had come to the royal court: "Aram is allied with Israel* against us!" So the hearts of the king and his people trembled with fear, just as trees shake in a storm.

³Then the LORD said to Isaiah, "Go out to meet King Ahaz, you and your son Shear-jashub.* You will find the king at the end of the aqueduct that feeds water into the upper pool, near the road leading to the field where cloth is bleached. ⁴Tell him to stop worrying. Tell him he doesn't need to fear the fierce anger of those two burned-out embers, King Rezin of Aram and Pekah son of Remaliah.

⁵"Yes, the kings of Aram and Israel are coming against you. They are saying, ⁶'We will invade Judah and throw its people into panic. Then we will fight our way into Jerusalem and install the son of Tabeel as Judah's king.'

⁷"But this is what the Sovereign LORD says: This invasion will never happen, ⁸because Aram is no stronger than its capital, Damascus. And Damascus is no stronger than its king, Rezin. As for Israel, within sixty-five years it will be crushed and completely destroyed. ⁹Israel is no stronger than its capital, Samaria. And Samaria is no stronger than its king, Pekah son of Remaliah. You do not believe me? If you want me to protect you, learn to believe what I say."

THE SIGN OF IMMANUEL

¹⁰Not long after this, the LORD sent this message to King Ahaz: ¹¹"Ask me for a sign, Ahaz, to prove that I will crush your enemies as I have promised. Ask for anything you like, and make it as difficult as you want."

¹²But the king refused. "No," he said, "I wouldn't test the LORD like that."

¹³Then Isaiah said, "Listen well, you royal family of David! You aren't satisfied to exhaust my patience. You exhaust the patience of God as well! ¹⁴All right then, the Lord himself will choose the sign. Look! The virgin* will conceive a child! She will give birth to a son and will call him Immanuel—'God is with us.' ¹⁵By the time this child is old enough

7:2 Hebrew *Ephraim,* referring to the northern kingdom of Israel; also in 7:5, 8, 9, 17. 7:3 *Shear-jashub* means "A remnant will return."
7:14 Or *young woman.*

My Daily Worship

— July 2 —

A TRUE VISION OF HOLINESS

ISAIAH 5:1–7:25

Then I said, "My destruction is sealed, for I am a sinful man and a member of a sinful race.
Yet I have seen the King, the LORD Almighty!" (6:5).

[i reflect]

In writing about Isaiah's encounter with the holiness of God in his classic *The Holiness of God,*
R. C. Sproul observes, "In that single moment all of [Isaiah's] self-esteem was shattered. In a brief
second he was exposed, made naked beneath the gaze of the absolute standard of holiness. . . .
The instant he measured himself by the ultimate standard, he was destroyed—morally and spiritually annihilated." Isaiah's own words reflect this, "My destruction is sealed, for I am a sinful
man and a member of a sinful race."

The Bible is filled with references to the way people respond to the holiness of God. Shortly after
creation, the guilty couple distanced themselves in the garden from a holy God. Camouflaging
themselves among the foliage, they played the first recorded game of hide and seek (Genesis 3:8).
When David recognized the gravity of his sin with Bathsheba, he cast himself on God's mercy, all
the while feeling estranged from the One he had ultimately violated (Psalm 51).

Through all these encounters runs a common thread of dread. The brilliance of God's pure presence reveals the imperfection of our sinful lives. We either want to run away and hide or we want
him to leave us alone. The disparity is normative. This awareness of his holiness and our unholi-
ness is redemptive knowledge. It motivates us to act on the feelings of guilt and shame now uncovered. It brings us to a point of seeking forgiveness and finding God's love anew. It reminds us that
the One we worship is truly worthy of our praise and adoration even though we aren't.

So what is it that you've failed to confess? It may be something you said to your spouse or
the way you reacted to your children. Allow the Lord to bring it to light today that he might deal
with it.

[i pray]

Lord, I apologize for the many times I've failed to hallow your presence and recognize
your glory. I love you so much that sometimes I respond to you with the rude informality
I use with my best friends. But in the process, Lord, I fail to fall on my face in silent
reverence and hear the rebuke you would offer me in love. Forgive me, holy God.

[i respond]

Remind yourself of the holy nature of our awesome God. As you prepare to meet with him today,
keep a pad of paper nearby to record the shortcomings the Lord brings to mind. Write them down
in order to deal with them one at a time as he prompts you.

to eat curds and honey, he will know enough to choose what is right and reject what is wrong. ¹⁶But before he knows right from wrong, the two kings you fear so much—the kings of Israel and Aram—will both be dead.

¹⁷"The LORD will bring a terrible curse on you, your nation, and your family. You will soon experience greater terror than has been known in all the years since Solomon's empire was divided into Israel and Judah. The mighty king of Assyria will come with his great army!"

> *Worship comes not as the fruit of our impulse, felt need, or creativity; it is the specific command of God.*
>
> DAVID JEREMIAH

¹⁸In that day the LORD will whistle for the army of Upper Egypt and for the army of Assyria. They will swarm around you like flies. Like bees, they will sting and kill. ¹⁹They will come in vast hordes, spreading across the whole land. They will settle in the fertile areas and also in the desolate valleys, caves, and thorny places. ²⁰In that day the Lord will take this "razor"—these Assyrians you have hired to protect you—and use it to shave off everything: your land, your crops, and your people.*

²¹When they finally stop plundering, a farmer will be fortunate to have a cow and two sheep left. ²²The few people still left in the land will live on curds and wild honey because that is all the land will produce. ²³In that day the lush vineyards, now worth as much as a thousand pieces of silver,* will become patches of briers and thorns. ²⁴The entire land will

be one vast brier patch, a hunting ground overrun by wildlife. ²⁵No one will go to the fertile hillsides where the gardens once grew, for briers and thorns will cover them. Cattle, sheep, and goats will graze there.

THE COMING ASSYRIAN INVASION

8 Again the LORD said to me, "Make a large signboard and clearly write this name on it: Maher-shalal-hash-baz.*" ²I asked Uriah the priest and Zechariah son of Jeberekiah, both known as honest men, to testify that I had written it before the child was conceived.

³Then I slept with my wife, and she became pregnant and had a son. And the LORD said, "Call him Maher-shalal-hash-baz. ⁴This name prophesies that within a couple of years, before this child is old enough to say 'Papa' or 'Mama,' the king of Assyria will invade both Damascus and Samaria and carry away their riches."

⁵Then the LORD spoke to me again and said, ⁶"The people of Judah have rejected my gentle care* and are rejoicing over what will happen to King Rezin and King Pekah. ⁷Therefore, the Lord will overwhelm them with a mighty flood from the Euphrates River*—the king of Assyria and all his mighty armies. ⁸This flood will overflow all its channels and sweep into Judah. It will submerge Immanuel's land from one end to the other.

⁹"The Assyrians will cry, 'Do your best to defend yourselves, but you will be shattered! Listen all you nations. Prepare for battle—and die! Yes, die! ¹⁰Call your councils of war, develop your strategies, prepare your plans of attack—and then die! For God is with us!*'"

A CALL TO TRUST THE LORD

¹¹The LORD has said to me in the strongest terms: "Do not think like everyone else does. ¹²Do not be afraid that some plan conceived behind closed doors will be the end of you. ¹³Do not fear anything except the LORD

7:20 Hebrew *shave off the head, the hair of the legs, and the beard.* 7:23 Hebrew *1,000 shekels of silver,* about 25 pounds or 11.4 kilograms in weight. 8:1 *Maher-shalal-hash-baz* means "Swift to plunder and quick to spoil." 8:6 Hebrew *rejected the gently flowing waters of Shiloah.* 8:7 Hebrew *the river.* 8:10 Hebrew *Immanuel!*

Almighty, He alone is the Holy One. If you fear him, you need fear nothing else. [14]He will keep you safe. But to Israel and Judah he will be a stone that causes people to stumble and a rock that makes them fall. And for the people of Jerusalem he will be a trap that entangles them. [15]Many of them will stumble and fall, never to rise again. Many will be captured."

[16]I will write down all these things as a testimony of what the LORD will do. I will entrust it to my disciples, who will pass it down to future generations. [17]I will wait for the LORD to help us, though he has turned away from the people of Israel.* My only hope is in him. [18]I and the children the LORD has given me have names* that reveal the plans the LORD Almighty has for his people. [19]So why are you trying to find out the future by consulting mediums and psychics? Do not listen to their whisperings and mutterings. Can the living find out the future from the dead? Why not ask your God?

[20]"Check their predictions against my testimony," says the LORD. "If their predictions are different from mine, it is because there is no light or truth in them. [21]My people will be led away as captives, weary and hungry. And because they are hungry, they will rage and shake their fists at heaven and curse their king and their God. [22]Wherever they look, there will be trouble and anguish and dark despair. They will be thrown out into the darkness."

HOPE IN THE MESSIAH

9 Nevertheless, that time of darkness and despair will not go on forever. The land of Zebulun and Naphtali will soon be humbled, but there will be a time in the future when Galilee of the Gentiles, which lies along the road that runs between the Jordan and the sea, will be filled with glory. [2]The people who walk in darkness will see a great light—a light that will shine on all who live in the land where death casts its shadow. [3]Israel will again

be great, and its people will rejoice as people rejoice at harvesttime. They will shout with joy like warriors dividing the plunder. [4]For God will break the chains that bind his people and the whip that scourges them, just as he did when he destroyed the army of Midian with Gideon's little band. [5]In that day of peace, battle gear will no longer be issued. Never again will uniforms be bloodstained by war. All such equipment will be burned.

[6]For a child is born to us, a son is given to us. And the government will rest on his shoulders. These will be his royal titles: Wonderful Counselor,* Mighty God, Everlasting Father, Prince of Peace. [7]His ever expanding, peaceful government will never end. He will rule forever with fairness and justice from the throne of his ancestor David. The passionate commitment of the LORD Almighty will guarantee this!

THE LORD'S ANGER AGAINST ISRAEL

[8]The Lord has spoken out against that braggart Israel, [9]and the people of Israel* and Samaria will soon discover it. In their pride and arrogance they say, [10]"Our land lies in ruins now, but we will rebuild it better than before. We will replace the broken bricks with cut stone, the fallen sycamore trees with cedars." [11]The LORD will reply to their bragging by bringing Rezin's enemies, the Assyrians, against them—[12]along with Arameans from the east and Philistines from the west. With bared fangs, they will devour Israel. But even then the LORD's anger will not be satisfied. His fist is still poised to strike. [13]For after all this punishment, the people will still not repent and turn to the LORD Almighty.

[14]Therefore, in a single day, the LORD will destroy both the head and the tail, the palm branch and the reed. [15]The leaders of Israel are the head, and the lying prophets are the tail.

8:17 Hebrew *the house of Jacob.* 8:18 *Isaiah* means "The LORD will save"; *Shear-jashub* means "A remnant will return"; and *Maher-shalal-hash-baz* means "Swift to plunder and quick to spoil." 9:6 Or *Wonderful, Counselor.* 9:9 Hebrew *of Ephraim,* referring to the northern kingdom of Israel.

[16]For the leaders of the people have led them down the path of destruction. [17]That is why the Lord has no joy in the young men and no mercy on even the widows and orphans. For they are all hypocrites, speaking wickedness with lies. But even then the LORD's anger will not be satisfied. His fist is still poised to strike.

[18]This wickedness is like a brushfire. It burns not only briers and thorns but the forests, too. Its burning sends up vast clouds of smoke. [19]The land is blackened by the fury of the LORD Almighty. The people are fuel for the fire, and no one spares anyone else. [20]They fight against their own neighbors to steal food, but they will still be hungry. In the end they will even eat their own children.* [21]Manasseh will feed on Ephraim, Ephraim will feed on Manasseh, and both will devour Judah. But even then the LORD's anger will not be satisfied. His fist is still poised to strike.

10 Destruction is certain for the unjust judges, for those who issue unfair laws. [2]They deprive the poor, the widows, and the orphans of justice. Yes, they rob widows and fatherless children! [3]What will you do when I send desolation upon you from a distant land? To whom will you turn for help? Where will your treasures be safe? [4]I will not help you. You will stumble along as prisoners or lie among the dead. But even then the LORD's anger will not be satisfied. His fist is still poised to strike.

JUDGMENT AGAINST ASSYRIA

[5]"Destruction is certain for Assyria, the whip of my anger. Its military power is a club in my hand. [6]Assyria will enslave my people, who are a godless nation. It will plunder them, trampling them like dirt beneath its feet. [7]But the king of Assyria will not know that it is I who sent him. He will merely think he is attacking my people as part of his plan to conquer the world. [8]He will say, 'Each of my princes will soon be a king, ruling a conquered land. [9]We will destroy Calno just as we did Carchemish. Hamath will fall before us as Arpad did. And we will destroy Samaria just as we did Damascus. [10]Yes, we have finished off many a kingdom whose gods were far greater than those in Jerusalem and Samaria. [11]So when we have defeated Samaria and her gods, we will destroy Jerusalem with hers.'"

[12]After the Lord has used the king of Assyria to accomplish his purposes in Jerusalem, he will turn against the king of Assyria and punish him—for he is proud and arrogant. [13]He boasts, "By my own power and wisdom I have won these wars. By my own strength I have captured many lands, destroyed their kings, and carried off their treasures. [14]By my greatness I have robbed their nests of riches and gathered up kingdoms as a farmer gathers eggs. No one can even flap a wing against me or utter a peep of protest."

[15]Can the ax boast greater power than the person who uses it? Is the saw greater than the person who saws? Can a whip strike unless a hand is moving it? Can a cane walk by itself?

[16]Listen now, king of Assyria! Because of all your evil boasting, the Lord, the LORD Almighty, will send a plague among your proud troops, and a flaming fire will ignite your glory. [17]The LORD, the Light of Israel and the Holy One, will be a flaming fire that will destroy them. In a single night he will burn those thorns and briers, the Assyrians. [18]Assyria's vast army is like a glorious forest, yet it will be destroyed. The LORD will completely destroy Assyria's warriors, and they will waste away like sick people in a plague. [19]Only a few from all that mighty army will survive—so few that a child could count them!

HOPE FOR THE LORD'S PEOPLE

[20]Then at last those left in Israel and Judah* will trust the LORD, the Holy One of Israel. They will no longer depend on the Assyrians, who would destroy them. [21]A remnant of them will return* to the Mighty God. [22]But

9:20 Or *eat their own arms.* **10:20** Hebrew *and the house of Jacob.* **10:21** Hebrew *Shear-jashub;* see 7:3; 8:18.

My Daily Worship

— *July 3* —

WHAT'S IN A NAME?
ISAIAH 8:1–11:16

For a child is born to us, a son is given to us. And the government will rest on his shoulders.
These will be his royal titles: Wonderful Counselor, Mighty God,
Everlasting Father, Prince of Peace (9:6).

[i reflect]

"For a child is born to us . . ." So begins the familiar passage read every year at Christmas—the assurance of a Child, a Son, who would enter our world to save it. Immediately we think of the manger and the baby born in a lowly stable. We know that this cute, cuddly infant is the Savior, the son promised for many. Yet Isaiah reminds us that he was so much more:

- Wonderful Counselor—The One we worship holds the counsels of God from eternity; he defends God's people with perfect integrity and grace.

- Mighty God—He is nothing less than the Almighty Creator in human flesh, the One who is capable of achieving the seemingly impossible.

- Everlasting Father—As the image of the invisible God, the Eternal One we worship is like a father. No distant diety here.

- Prince of Peace—He is the One who reconciles us to God; he is the giver of peace in our hearts and ultimately, when his kingdom is established, of peace among the nations.

Writes Matthew Henry, "To what earthly king or kingdom can these words apply? Give then, O Lord, to thy people to know thee by every endearing name, and in every glorious character. Give increase of grace in every heart of thy redeemed upon earth."

When we ponder and consider Christ's true identity, in all its facets and with all its promises, it makes us want to praise God for his unbelievable provision and love. Whisper these timeless names under your breath. Better yet, why not write all four titles on an empty sheet of paper and hang it on the refrigerator or near your place of work? During the day, as you glance at that sheet of paper, imagine the Lord invisibly serving you in the ways those names suggest.

[i pray]

Lord Jesus, I love the names Isaiah attributes to you. Each one is powerful yet precious.
As I speak your names, remind me that you delight in manifesting yourself
in my life in each of these needed ways.

[i respond]

Just for fun, try filling a blank sheet of paper with as many adjectives as you can think of that describe your experience of the Triune God. Begin with words like faithful, gracious, forgiving. Keep the sheet at hand as you spend quiet moments in the Lord's presence each day this week.

though the people of Israel are as numerous as the sand on the seashore, only a few of them will return at that time. The LORD has rightly decided to destroy his people. 23Yes, the Lord, the LORD Almighty, has already decided to consume them.

24So this is what the Lord, the LORD Almighty, says: "My people in Jerusalem,* do not be afraid of the Assyrians when they oppress you just as the Egyptians did long ago. 25It will not last very long. In a little while my anger against you will end, and then my anger will rise up to destroy them."

26The LORD Almighty will beat them with his whip, as he did when Gideon triumphed over the Midianites at the rock of Oreb, or when the LORD's staff was raised to drown the Egyptian army in the sea. 27In that day the LORD will end the bondage of his people. He will break the yoke of slavery and lift it from their shoulders.*

28Look, the mighty armies of Assyria are coming! They are now at Aiath, now at Migron. They are storing some of their equipment at Micmash. 29They are crossing the pass and are staying overnight at Geba. Fear strikes the city of Ramah. All the people of Gibeah—the city of Saul—are running for their lives. 30Well may you scream in terror, you people of Gallim! Shout out a warning to Laishah, for the mighty army comes. Poor Anathoth, what a fate is yours! 31There go the people of Madmenah, all fleeing. And the citizens of Gebim are preparing to run. 32But the enemy stops at Nob for the rest of that day. He shakes his fist at Mount Zion in Jerusalem.

33But look! The Lord, the LORD Almighty, will chop down the mighty tree! He will destroy all that vast army of Assyria—officers and high officials alike. 34The Mighty One will cut down the enemy as an ax cuts down the forest trees in Lebanon.

A BRANCH FROM DAVID'S LINE

11 Out of the stump of David's family* will grow a shoot—yes, a new Branch bearing fruit from the old root. 2And the Spirit of the LORD will rest on him—the Spirit of wisdom and understanding, the Spirit of counsel and might, the Spirit of knowledge and the fear of the LORD. 3He will delight in obeying the LORD. He will never judge by appearance, false evidence, or hearsay. 4He will defend the poor and the exploited. He will rule against the wicked and destroy them with the breath of his mouth. 5He will be clothed with fairness and truth.

6In that day the wolf and the lamb will live together; the leopard and the goat will be at peace. Calves and yearlings will be safe among lions, and a little child will lead them all. 7The cattle will graze among bears. Cubs and calves will lie down together. And lions will eat grass as the livestock do. 8Babies will crawl safely among poisonous snakes. Yes, a little child will put its hand in a nest of deadly snakes and pull it out unharmed. 9Nothing will hurt or destroy in all my holy mountain. And as the waters fill the sea, so the earth will be filled with people who know the LORD.

10In that day the heir to David's throne* will be a banner of salvation to all the world. The nations will rally to him, for the land where he lives will be a glorious place. 11In that day the Lord will bring back a remnant of his people for the second time, returning them to the land of Israel from Assyria, Lower Egypt, Upper Egypt, Ethiopia,* Elam, Babylonia,* Hamath, and all the distant coastlands.

12He will raise a flag among the nations for Israel to rally around. He will gather the scattered people of Judah from the ends of the earth. 13Then at last the jealousy between Israel* and Judah will end. They will not fight against each other anymore. 14They will join forces to swoop down on Philistia to the west. Together they will attack and plunder the

---

10:24 Hebrew *Zion.*   10:27 As in Greek version; Hebrew reads *The yoke will be broken, for you have grown so fat.*   11:1 Hebrew *the line of Jesse.* Jesse was King David's father.   11:10 Hebrew *the root of Jesse.*   11:11a Hebrew *Pathros, Cush.*   11:11b Hebrew *Shinar.*
11:13 Hebrew *Ephraim,* referring to the northern kingdom of Israel.

nations to the east. They will occupy all the lands of Edom, Moab, and Ammon.

¹⁵The LORD will make a dry path through the Red Sea.* He will wave his hand over the Euphrates River,* sending a mighty wind to divide it into seven streams that can easily be crossed. ¹⁶He will make a highway from Assyria for the remnant there, just as he did for Israel long ago when they returned from Egypt.

SONGS OF PRAISE FOR SALVATION

12 In that day you will sing:

"Praise the LORD!
He was angry with me,
  but now he comforts me.
² See, God has come to save me.
  I will trust in him and not be afraid.
The LORD GOD is my strength and my
    song;
  he has become my salvation."

³With joy you will drink deeply from the fountain of salvation! ⁴In that wonderful day you will sing:

"Thank the LORD!
  Praise his name!
Tell the world what he has done.
  Oh, how mighty he is!
⁵ Sing to the LORD,
  for he has done wonderful things.
  Make known his praise around the
    world.
⁶ Let all the people of Jerusalem* shout his
    praise with joy!
  For great is the Holy One of Israel who
    lives among you."

A MESSAGE ABOUT BABYLON

13 Isaiah son of Amoz received this message concerning the destruction of Babylon:

²"See the flags waving as the enemy attacks. Cheer them on, O Israel! Wave to them as they march against Babylon to destroy the palaces of the high and mighty. ³I, the LORD, have assigned this task to these armies, and they will rejoice when I am exalted. I have called them to satisfy my anger."

⁴Hear the noise on the mountains! Listen, as the armies march! It is the noise and the shout of many nations. The LORD Almighty has brought them here to form an army. ⁵They came from countries far away. They are the LORD's weapons; they carry his anger with them and will destroy the whole land. ⁶Scream in terror, for the LORD's time has arrived—the time for the Almighty to destroy. ⁷Every arm is paralyzed with fear. Even the strongest hearts melt ⁸and are afraid. Fear grips them with terrible pangs, like those of a woman about to give birth. They look helplessly at one another as the flames of the burning city reflect on their faces. ⁹For see, the day of the LORD is coming—the terrible day of his fury and fierce anger. The land will be destroyed and all the sinners with it. ¹⁰The heavens will be black above them. No light will shine from stars or sun or moon.

¹¹"I, the LORD, will punish the world for its evil and the wicked for their sin. I will crush the arrogance of the proud and the haughtiness of the mighty. ¹²Few will be left alive when I have finished my work. People will be as scarce as gold—more rare than the gold of Ophir. ¹³For I will shake the heavens, and the earth will move from its place. I, the LORD Almighty, will show my fury and fierce anger."

¹⁴Everyone will run until exhausted, rushing back to their own lands like hunted deer, wandering like sheep without a shepherd. ¹⁵Anyone who is captured will be run through with a sword. ¹⁶Their little children will be dashed to death right before their eyes. Their homes will be sacked and their wives raped by the attacking hordes. ¹⁷For I will stir up the Medes against Babylon, and no amount of silver or gold will buy them off. ¹⁸The attacking armies will shoot down the young people with

11:15a Hebrew *sea of Egypt.*   **11:15b** Hebrew *the river.*   **12:6** Hebrew *Zion.*

arrows. They will have no mercy on helpless babies and will show no compassion for the children.

[19]Babylon, the most glorious of kingdoms, the flower of Chaldean culture, will be devastated like Sodom and Gomorrah when God destroyed them. [20]Babylon will never rise again. Generation after generation will come and go, but the land will never again be lived in. Nomads will refuse to camp there, and shepherds will not allow their sheep to stay overnight. [21]Wild animals of the desert will move into the ruined city. The houses will be haunted by howling creatures. Ostriches will live among the ruins, and wild goats will come there to dance. [22]Hyenas will howl in its fortresses, and jackals will make their dens in its palaces. Babylon's days are numbered; its time of destruction will soon arrive.

A Taunt for Babylon's King

14 But the LORD will have mercy on the descendants of Jacob. Israel will be his special people once again. He will bring them back to settle once again in their own land. And people from many different nations will come and join them there and become a part of the people of Israel.* [2]The nations of the world will help the LORD's people to return, and those who come to live in their land will serve them. Those who captured Israel will be captured, and Israel will rule over its enemies.

[3]In that wonderful day when the LORD gives his people rest from sorrow and fear, from slavery and chains, [4]you will taunt the king of Babylon. You will say, "The mighty man has been destroyed. Yes, your insolence is ended. [5]For the LORD has crushed your wicked power and broken your evil rule. [6]You persecuted the people with unceasing blows of rage and held the nations in your angry grip. Your tyranny was unrestrained. [7]But at last the land is at rest and is quiet. Finally it can sing again! [8]Even the trees of the forest—the cypress trees and the cedars of Lebanon—sing out this joyous song: 'Your power is broken! No one will come to cut us down now!'

[9]"In the place of the dead* there is excitement over your arrival. World leaders and mighty kings long dead are there to see you. [10]With one voice they all cry out, 'Now you are as weak as we are! [11]Your might and power are gone; they were buried with you. All the pleasant music in your palace has ceased. Now maggots are your sheet and worms your blanket.'

[12]"How you are fallen from heaven, O shining star, son of the morning! You have been thrown down to the earth, you who destroyed the nations of the world. [13]For you said to yourself, 'I will ascend to heaven and set my throne above God's stars. I will preside on the mountain of the gods far away in the north. [14]I will climb to the highest heavens and be like the Most High.' [15]But instead, you will be brought down to the place of the dead, down to its lowest depths. [16]Everyone there will stare at you and ask, 'Can this be the one who shook the earth and the kingdoms of the world? [17]Is this the one who destroyed the world and made it into a wilderness? Is this the king who demolished the world's greatest cities and had no mercy on his prisoners?'

[18]"The kings of the nations lie in stately glory in their tombs, [19]but you will be thrown out of your grave like a worthless branch. Like a corpse trampled underfoot, you will be dumped into a mass grave with those killed in battle. You will descend to the pit. [20]You will not be given a proper burial, for you have destroyed your nation and slaughtered your people. Your son will not succeed you as king. [21]Kill the children of this sinner! Do not let them rise and conquer the land or rebuild the cities of the world."

[22]This is what the LORD Almighty says: "I, myself, have risen against him! I will destroy his children and his children's children, so they will never sit on his throne. [23]I will make Babylon into a desolate land, a place of porcupines, filled with swamps and marshes. I

14:1 Hebrew *the house of Jacob.* 14:9 Hebrew *Sheol;* also in 14:15.

My Daily Worship

— *July 4* —

GREETING DEATH WITH A SONG

ISAIAH 12:1–16:14

See, God has come to save me. I will trust in him and not be afraid.
The LORD GOD is my strength and my song;
he has become my salvation (12:2).

[i reflect]

Art Bernier was a devout Christian whose optimism was contagious. Those who encountered him at Seattle Pacific University where he worked as a custodian knew Art as spark plug. He made sure other peoples' days were filled with joy and life. His last days of life, however, were spent in a hospital filled with pain. Inoperable cancer was the cause.

As one nurse nervously attempted to find a vein in which to administer morphine, she hit a nerve. The discomfort was so intense, Art swore at his white uniformed helper. In addition to the intolerable pain, Art felt remorse. He pressed the call button summoning the nurse and begged her forgiveness. But that was only one of the indicators that Art Bernier was a believer.

As death drew nearer, this seventy-year-old man didn't recoil in fear. The words of Isaiah above described him. He found the ability in his heart to trust God and not be overwhelmed with anxiety. Although his strength was ebbing away on a daily basis, this man, who had sung in church most of his adult life, still attempted to sing from his hospital bed. He sang about Jesus and the strength his Savior gave. Whatever fear he might have had about journeying through the valley of death, he met with songs of praise.

The early church father Augustine could have been describing Art Bernier when he wrote, "Those who overcome the fear of death by their faith, will receive great glory and fair compensation for their faith." So don't minimize the place and power of praise in your life. Don't you see how critical it is? When personal worship becomes a pattern of life, it serves us well when death comes knocking. In the meantime, don't you feel like wrapping your lips around lyrics that celebrate the Savior's love? Do it now wherever you are.

[i pray]

Holy Father, the example of others who have proved your faithfulness in trying times inspires me.
Like Art Bernier, I want to be quick to apologize and have a ready song on my lips. Holy Spirit,
will you sensitize me and motivate me to praise you more than I do? Thanks, Lord.

[i respond]

Find an old hymnal. Use it as a companion to your Bible as you meet the Lord in worship each day. If you can follow the notes in the hymnal, sing the words. If you can't read music, just meditate on the lyrics. Treat them as devotional poetry.

Words of Worship

HOLY

Holy—Hebrew *qa-dosh*; Greek *ha-gi-os*.

Christian piety has often associated holiness with goodness—high moral standards, a life unstained by the degraded values of world cultures. In the Bible, being good is a secondary meaning of what it means to be holy. The primary sense of the Hebrew word has to do with being *separated* from what is common or ordinary. The Lord is holy because he is *extraordinary*, mysterious, not easily packaged into our neat categories. And people, and even sacred things, are "holy" not because of what they are in themselves, but because God has appropriated them for his own purposes.

That's a reassuring thought because in the New Testament we sometimes hear Christians referred to as "God's holy people" (Ephesians 1:1) or, to use the traditional term, "the saints." If our being holy depended on measuring up to some standard of goodness, then we might as well forget about it. As Jesus reminds us, "Only God is truly good" (Mark 10:18). But when our desire to worship the Lord leads us to set ourselves apart for him, then we share in his holiness. We, too, become extraordinary. "You must be holy because I, the LORD your God, am holy" (Leviticus 19:2).

will sweep the land with the broom of destruction. I, the LORD Almighty, have spoken!"

A MESSAGE ABOUT ASSYRIA

²⁴The LORD Almighty has sworn this oath: "It will all happen as I have planned. It will come about according to my purposes. ²⁵I will break the Assyrians when they are in Israel; I will trample them on my mountains. My people will no longer be their slaves. ²⁶I have a plan for the whole earth, for my mighty power reaches throughout the world. ²⁷The LORD Almighty has spoken—who can change his plans? When his hand moves, who can stop him?"

A MESSAGE ABOUT PHILISTIA

²⁸This message came to me the year King Ahaz died:

²⁹Do not rejoice, you Philistines, that the king who attacked you is dead. For even though that whip is broken, his son will be worse than his father ever was. From that snake a poisonous snake will be born, a fiery serpent to destroy you! ³⁰I will feed the poor in my pasture; the needy will lie down in peace. But as for you, I will wipe you out with famine. I will destroy the few who remain.

³¹Weep, you Philistine cities, for you are doomed! Melt in fear, for everyone will be destroyed. A powerful army is coming out of the north. Each soldier rushes forward ready to fight. ³²What should we tell the enemy messengers? Tell them that the LORD has built Jerusalem,* and that the poor of his people will find refuge in its walls.

A MESSAGE ABOUT MOAB

15 This message came to me concerning Moab:

In one night your cities of Ar and Kir will be destroyed. ²Your people in Dibon will mourn at their temples and shrines, weeping for the fate of Nebo and Medeba. They will shave their heads in sorrow and cut off their beards. ³They will wear sackcloth as they wander the streets. From every home will come the sound of weeping. ⁴The cries from the cities of Heshbon and Elealeh will be heard far away, even in Jahaz! The bravest warriors of Moab will cry out in utter terror.

14:32 Hebrew *Zion.*

⁵My heart weeps for Moab. Its people flee to Zoar and Eglath-shelishiyah. Weeping, they climb the road to Luhith. Their crying can be heard all along the road to Horonaim. ⁶Even the waters of Nimrim are dried up! The grassy banks are scorched, and the tender plants are gone. ⁷The desperate refugees take only the possessions they can carry and flee across the Ravine of Willows. ⁸The whole land of Moab is a land of weeping from one end to the other—from Eglaim to Beer-elim. ⁹The stream near Dibon* runs red with blood, but I am still not finished with Dibon! Lions will hunt down the survivors, both those who try to run and those who remain behind.

16 Moab's refugees at Sela send lambs to Jerusalem* as a token of alliance with the king of Judah. ²The women of Moab are left like homeless birds at the shallow crossings of the Arnon River. ³"Help us," they cry. "Defend us against our enemies. Protect us from their relentless attack. Do not betray us. ⁴Let our outcasts stay among you. Hide them from our enemies until the terror is past."

When oppression and destruction have ceased and enemy raiders have disappeared, ⁵then David's throne will be established by love. From that throne a faithful king will reign, one who always does what is just and right.

⁶Is this Moab, the proud land we have heard so much about? Its pride and insolence are all gone now! ⁷The entire land of Moab weeps. Yes, you people of Moab, mourn for the delicacies of Kir-hareseth. ⁸Weep for the abandoned farms of Heshbon and the vineyards at Sibmah. The wine from those vineyards used to make the rulers of the nations drunk. Moab was once like a spreading grapevine. Her tendrils spread out as far as Jazer and trailed out into the desert. Her shoots once reached as far as the Dead Sea.* ⁹But now the enemy has completely destroyed that vine. So I wail and lament for Jazer and the vineyards of Sibmah. My tears will flow for Heshbon and Elealeh, for their summer fruits and harvests have all been destroyed.

¹⁰Gone now is the gladness; gone is the joy of harvest. The happy singing in the vineyards will be heard no more. The treading out of grapes in the winepresses has ceased forever. I have ended all their harvest joys. ¹¹I will weep for Moab. My sorrow for Kir-hareseth* will be very great. ¹²On the hilltops the people of Moab will pray in anguish to their idols, but it will do them no good. They will cry to the gods in their temples, but no one will come to save them.

¹³The LORD has already said this about Moab in the past. ¹⁴But now the LORD says, "Within three years, without fail, the glory of Moab will be ended, and few of its people will be left alive."

A MESSAGE ABOUT DAMASCUS AND ISRAEL

17 This message came to me concerning Damascus:

"Look, Damascus will disappear! It will become a heap of ruins. ²The cities of Aroer will be deserted. Sheep will graze in the streets and lie down unafraid. There will be no one to chase them away. ³The fortified cities of Israel* will also be destroyed, and the power of Damascus will end. The few left in Aram will share the fate of Israel's departed glory," says the LORD Almighty.

⁴"In that day the glory of Israel* will be very dim, for poverty will stalk the land. ⁵Israel will be abandoned like the grainfields in the valley of Rephaim after the harvest. ⁶Only a few of its people will be left, like the stray olives left on the tree after the harvest. Only two or three remain in the highest branches, four or five out on the tips of the limbs. Yes, Israel will be stripped bare of people," says the LORD, the God of Israel.

15:9 As in Dead Sea Scrolls, some Greek manuscripts, and Latin Vulgate; Masoretic Text reads *Dimon;* also in 15:9b.   16:1 Hebrew *to the daughter of Zion.*   16:8 Hebrew *the sea.*   16:11 Hebrew *Kir-heres,* a variant name for Kir-hareseth.   17:3 Hebrew *of Ephraim,* referring to the northern kingdom of Israel.   17:4 Hebrew *of Jacob.*

> *The language of worship is found in prayer.*
>
> JACK HAYFORD

[7]Then at last the people will think of their Creator and have respect for the Holy One of Israel. [8]They will no longer ask their idols for help or worship what their own hands have made. They will never again bow down to their Asherah poles or burn incense on the altars they built.

[9]Their largest cities will be as deserted as overgrown thickets. They will become like the cities the Amorites abandoned when the Israelites came here so long ago. [10]Why? Because you have turned from the God who can save you—the Rock who can hide you. You may plant the finest imported grapevines, [11]and they may grow so well that they blossom on the very morning you plant them, but you will never pick any grapes from them. Your only harvest will be a load of grief and incurable pain.

[12]Look! The armies rush forward like waves thundering toward the shore. [13]But though they roar like breakers on a beach, God will silence them. They will flee like chaff scattered by the wind or like dust whirling before a storm. [14]In the evening Israel waits in terror, but by dawn its enemies are dead. This is the just reward of those who plunder and destroy the people of God.

A MESSAGE ABOUT ETHIOPIA

18 Destruction is certain for the land of Ethiopia,* which lies at the headwaters of the Nile. Its winged sailboats glide along the river, [2]and ambassadors are sent in fast boats down the Nile. Go home, swift messengers! Take a message to your land divided by rivers, to your tall, smooth-skinned people, who are feared far and wide for their conquests and destruction.

[3]When I raise my battle flag on the mountain, let all the world take notice. When I blow the trumpet, listen! [4]For the LORD has told me this: "I will watch quietly from my dwelling place—as quietly as the heat rises on a summer day, or as the dew forms on an autumn morning during the harvest."

[5]Even before you begin your attack, while your plans are ripening like grapes, the LORD will cut you off as though with pruning shears. He will snip your spreading branches. [6]Your mighty army will be left dead in the fields for the mountain birds and wild animals to eat. The vultures will tear at corpses all summer. The wild animals will gnaw at bones all winter.

[7]But the time will come when the LORD Almighty will receive gifts from this land divided by rivers, from this tall, smooth-skinned people, who are feared far and wide for their conquests and destruction. They will bring the gifts to the LORD Almighty in Jerusalem,* the place where his name dwells.

A MESSAGE ABOUT EGYPT

19 This message came to me concerning Egypt:

Look! The LORD is advancing against Egypt, riding on a swift cloud. The idols of Egypt tremble. The hearts of the Egyptians melt with fear.

[2]"I will make the Egyptians fight against each other—brother against brother, neighbor against neighbor, city against city, province against province. [3]The Egyptians will lose heart, and I will confuse their plans. They will plead with their idols for wisdom. They will call on spirits, mediums, and psychics to show them which way to turn. [4]I will hand

18:1 Hebrew *Cush*. 18:7 Hebrew *on Mount Zion*.

Egypt over to a hard, cruel master, to a fierce king," says the Lord, the LORD Almighty.

⁵The waters of the Nile will fail to rise and flood the fields. The riverbed will be parched and dry. ⁶The canals of the Nile will dry up, and the streams of Egypt will become foul with rotting reeds and rushes. ⁷All the greenery along the riverbank will wither and blow away. All the crops will dry up, and everything will die. ⁸The fishermen will weep for lack of work. Those who fish with hooks and those who use nets will all be unemployed. ⁹The weavers will have no flax or cotton, for the crops will fail. ¹⁰The weavers and all the workers will be sick at heart.

¹¹What fools are the counselors of Zoan! Their best counsel to the king of Egypt is stupid and wrong. Will they still boast of their wisdom? Will they dare tell Pharaoh about their long line of wise ancestors? ¹²What has happened to your wise counselors, Pharaoh? If they are so wise, let them tell you what the LORD Almighty is going to do to Egypt. ¹³The wise men from Zoan are fools, and those from Memphis* are deluded. The leaders of Egypt have ruined the land with their foolish counsel. ¹⁴The LORD has sent a spirit of foolishness on them, so all their suggestions are wrong. They cause the land of Egypt to stagger like a sick drunkard. ¹⁵Nobody in Egypt, whether rich or poor, important or unknown, can offer any help.

¹⁶In that day the Egyptians will be as weak as women. They will cower in fear beneath the upraised fist of the LORD Almighty. ¹⁷Just to speak the name of Israel will strike deep terror in their hearts, for the LORD Almighty has laid out his plans against them.

¹⁸In that day five of Egypt's cities will follow the LORD Almighty. They will even begin to speak the Hebrew language.* One of these will be Heliopolis, the City of the Sun. ¹⁹In that day there will be an altar to the LORD in the heart of Egypt, and there will be a monument to the LORD at its border. ²⁰It will be a sign and a witness to the LORD Almighty in the land of

---

Words of Worship

WORD

Word—Hebrew *da-var* "word, saying, matter"; Greek *lo-gos* "word, speaking, topic"; *rhe-ma* "word, expression." The Hebrew *davar* occurs some five hundred times in the Old Testament, with meanings ranging from the utterances of the Lord or his prophets all the way to a catchall expression, such as "something." The two Greek words differ in that *logos* (occurring about three hundred times in the New Testament) carries the nuance of a word as a concept or principle, whereas *rhema* (occurring about seventy times) tends to refer to a word actually spoken.

The expression "mere words" is not one we would hear from the people of the Bible. The Israelites and early Christians took words seriously, for life and reality were made up of them. While we use words to *describe* our world, people in biblical cultures used them to *build* their world. The more powerful the speaker, the more effective the word! God brought the universe into being by speaking: "Let there be light" (Genesis 1:3). He said of his Word, "It will accomplish all I want it to" (Isaiah 55:11).

No wonder, then, that Jesus Christ is called the Word, who "became human and lived here on earth among us" (John 1:14). Not only does he reveal God's glory and truth, but through him, we also are built into a new creation. As we worship our Lord, we remember how powerful words can be. When we use them in conformity with God's Word, we build up a universe to his praise.

Egypt. When the people cry to the LORD for help against those who oppress them, he will send them a savior who will rescue them.

19:13 Hebrew *Noph.* **19:18** Hebrew *the language of Canaan.*

²¹In that day the LORD will make himself known to the Egyptians. Yes, they will know the LORD and will give their sacrifices and offerings to him. They will make promises to the LORD and keep them. ²²The LORD will strike Egypt in a way that will bring healing. For the Egyptians will turn to the LORD, and he will listen to their pleas and heal them.

²³In that day Egypt and Assyria will be connected by a highway. The Egyptians and Assyrians will move freely between their lands, and they will worship the same God. ²⁴And Israel will be their ally. The three will be together, and Israel will be a blessing to them. ²⁵For the LORD Almighty will say, "Blessed be Egypt, my people. Blessed be Assyria, the land I have made. Blessed be Israel, my special possession!"

A MESSAGE ABOUT EGYPT AND ETHIOPIA

20 In the year when King Sargon of Assyria captured the Philistine city of Ashdod, ²the LORD told Isaiah son of Amoz, "Take off all your clothes, including your sandals." Isaiah did as he was told and walked around naked and barefoot.

³Then the LORD said, "My servant Isaiah has been walking around naked and barefoot for the last three years. This is a sign—a symbol of the terrible troubles I will bring upon Egypt and Ethiopia.* ⁴For the king of Assyria will take away the Egyptians and Ethiopians* as prisoners. He will make them walk naked and barefoot, both young and old, their buttocks uncovered, to the shame of Egypt. ⁵How dismayed will be the Philistines, who counted on the power of Ethiopia and boasted of their allies in Egypt! ⁶They will say, 'If this can happen to Egypt, what chance do we have? For we counted on Egypt to protect us from the king of Assyria.'"

A MESSAGE ABOUT BABYLON

21 This message came to me concerning the land of Babylonia*:

Disaster is roaring down on you from the desert, like a whirlwind sweeping in from the Negev. ²I see an awesome vision: I see you plundered and destroyed. Go ahead, you Elamites and Medes, take part in the siege. Babylon will fall, and the groaning of all the nations she enslaved will end. ³My stomach aches and burns with pain. Sharp pangs of horror are upon me, like the pangs of a woman giving birth. I grow faint when I hear what God is planning; I am blinded with dismay. ⁴My mind reels; my heart races. The sleep I once enjoyed at night is now a faint memory. I lie awake, trembling.

⁵Look! They are preparing a great feast. They are spreading rugs for people to sit on. Everyone is eating and drinking. Quick! Grab your shields and prepare for battle! You are being attacked!

⁶Meanwhile, the Lord said to me, "Put a watchman on the city wall to shout out what he sees. ⁷Tell him to sound the alert when he sees chariots drawn by horses and warriors mounted on donkeys and camels."

⁸Then the watchman* called out, "Day after day I have stood on the watchtower, my lord. Night after night I have remained at my post. ⁹Now at last—look! Here come the chariots and warriors!" Then the watchman said, "Babylon is fallen! All the idols of Babylon lie broken on the ground!"

¹⁰O my people, threshed and winnowed, I have told you everything the LORD Almighty, the God of Israel, has said.

A MESSAGE ABOUT EDOM

¹¹This message came to me concerning Edom*:

Someone from Edom* keeps calling to me, "Watchman, how much longer until morning? When will the night be over?"

¹²The watchman replies, "Morning is coming, but night will soon follow. If you wish to ask again, then come back and ask."

20:3 Hebrew *Cush;* also in 20:5. **20:4** Hebrew *Cushites.* **21:1** Hebrew *the desert of the sea.* **21:8** As in Dead Sea Scrolls and Syriac version; Masoretic Text reads *a lion.* **21:11a** Hebrew *Dumah,* which means "silence" or "stillness." It is a wordplay on the word *Edom.* **21:11b** Hebrew *Seir,* another name for Edom.

My Daily Worship

— July 5 —

OF KERNELS AND CROSSES
ISAIAH 17:1–23:18

O my people, threshed and winnowed, I have told you everything the LORD
Almighty, the God of Israel, has said (21:10).

[i reflect]

In biblical times, farmers would use their oxen to drag a heavy sledge back and forth across a pile of harvested grain to separate the kernels from the chaff. Afterward, they would toss the whole mess into the air with a pitchfork and let the wind blow the chaff away. Then they would gather up the grain and set fire to the chaff.

It's easy to see why threshing and winnowing became prominent biblical symbols, isn't it? For instance, trials in life can crush us, forcing us to give up our cherished sins (the chaff) and leaving only what is God-pleasing (the kernels). That's what happened to the Israelites in Isaiah's time, who suffered repeated enemy invasions and finally were taken away in exile before they gave up idolatry. It can happen to us, too. We can be "threshed and winnowed."

God is not the author of evil, but he permits evil to enter our lives when it suits his larger purposes for the world or his smaller purposes for our lives individually. As we are living for Christ, these trials become woven into the pattern of our discipleship. They are not just random troubles but "crosses" we have to bear.

Charles de Foucauld wrote, "We should accept, as we would a favor, every moment of our lives and whatever they may bring, whether it is good or bad, but the crosses with even greater gratitude than the rest. Crosses release us from this world and by doing so bind us to God."

Learning to accept God's winnowing and threshing work in our lives is graduate-level Christianity. We're justified in trembling before the prospect. But if we're committed to a path of devotion that will take us into the heart of God, we will choose to worship God even when the sledge is on our backs.

Today, thank God for the threshing and winnowing you are experiencing. Be specific.

[i pray]

It hurts to be threshed, God. Winnowing takes away from me what I like.
But go ahead—reduce me to a bare kernel of myself that is all for you.

[i respond]

In your personal worship time, seek God for insight into what affections or actions you should let go of. Praise him for doing whatever it takes to reveal more plainly what is godly in you.

A Message about Arabia

[13]This message came to me concerning Arabia:

O caravans from Dedan, hide in the deserts of Arabia. [14]O people of Tema, bring food and water to these weary refugees. [15]They have fled from drawn swords and sharp arrows and the terrors of war. [16]"But within a year,"* says the Lord, "all the glory of Kedar will come to an end. [17]Only a few of its courageous archers will survive. I, the LORD, the God of Israel, have spoken!"

A Message about Jerusalem

22 This message came to me concerning Jerusalem*:

What is happening? Why is everyone running to the rooftops? [2]The whole city is in a terrible uproar. What do I see in this reveling city? Bodies are lying everywhere, killed by famine and disease.* [3]All your leaders flee. They surrender without resistance. The people try to slip away, but they are captured, too. [4]Leave me alone to weep; do not try to comfort me. Let me cry for my people as I watch them being destroyed.

[5]Oh, what a day of crushing trouble! What a day of confusion and terror the Lord, the LORD Almighty, has brought upon the Valley of Vision! The walls of Jerusalem have been broken, and cries of death echo from the mountainsides. [6]Elamites are the archers; Arameans drive the chariots. The men of Kir hold up the shields. [7]They fill your beautiful valleys and crowd against your gates. [8]Judah's defenses have been stripped away. You run to the armory for your weapons. [9]You inspect the walls of Jerusalem* to see what needs to be repaired. You store up water in the lower pool. [10]You check the houses and tear some down to get stone to fix the walls. [11]Between the city walls, you build a reservoir for water from the old pool. But all your feverish plans are to no avail because you never ask God for help. He is the one who planned this long ago.

[12]The Lord, the LORD Almighty, called you to weep and mourn. He told you to shave your heads in sorrow for your sins and to wear clothes of sackcloth to show your remorse. [13]But instead, you dance and play; you slaughter sacrificial animals, feast on meat, and drink wine. "Let's eat, drink, and be merry," you say. "What's the difference, for tomorrow we die." [14]The LORD Almighty has revealed to me that this sin will never be forgiven you until the day you die. That is the judgment of the Lord, the LORD Almighty.

A Message for Shebna

[15]Furthermore, the Lord, the LORD Almighty, told me to confront Shebna, the palace administrator, and to give him this message: [16]"Who do you think you are, building a beautiful tomb for yourself in the rock? [17]For the LORD is about to seize you and hurl you away. He is going to send you into captivity, you strong man! [18]He will crumple you up into a ball and toss you away into a distant, barren land. There you will die, and there your glorious chariots will remain, broken and useless. You are a disgrace to your master.

[19]"Yes, I will drive you out of office," says the LORD. "I will pull you down from your high position. [20]And then I will call my servant Eliakim son of Hilkiah to replace you. [21]He will have your royal robes, your title, and your authority. And he will be a father to the people of Jerusalem and Judah. [22]I will give him the key to the house of David—the highest position in the royal court. He will open doors, and no one will be able to shut them; he will close doors, and no one will be able to open them. [23]He will bring honor to his family name, for I will drive him firmly in place like a tent stake. [24]He will be loaded down with responsibility, and he will bring honor to even the lowliest members of his family."

[25]The LORD Almighty says: "When that time comes, I will pull out the stake that seemed so firm. It will come out and fall to the ground.

21:16 Hebrew *Within a year, like the years of a hired hand.* Some ancient manuscripts read *Within three years*, as in 16:14. **22:1** Hebrew *concerning the Valley of Vision.* **22:2** Hebrew *killed, but not by sword and not in battle.* **22:9** Hebrew *the city of David.*

Everything it supports will fall with it. I, the LORD, have spoken!"

A MESSAGE ABOUT TYRE

23 This message came to me concerning Tyre:

Weep, O ships of Tarshish, returning home from distant lands! Weep for your harbor at Tyre because it is gone! The rumors you heard in Cyprus* are all true. ²Mourn in silence, you people of the coast and you merchants of Sidon. Your traders crossed the sea, ³sailing over deep waters. They brought you grain from Egypt* and harvests from along the Nile. You were the merchandise mart of the world.

Whenever the method of worship becomes more important than the Person of worship, we have already prostituted our worship.

JUDSON CORNWALL

⁴But now you are put to shame, city of Sidon, fortress on the sea. For the sea says, "Now I am childless; I have no sons or daughters." ⁵When Egypt hears the news about Tyre, there will be great sorrow. ⁶Flee now to Tarshish! Wail, you people who live by the sea! ⁷How can this silent ruin be all that is left of your once joyous city? What a history was yours! Think of all the colonists you sent to distant lands.

⁸Who has brought this disaster on Tyre, empire builder and chief trader of the world? ⁹The LORD Almighty has done it to destroy your pride and show his contempt for all human greatness. ¹⁰Come, Tarshish, sweep over your mother Tyre like the flooding Nile, for the city is defenseless. ¹¹The LORD holds out his hand over the seas. He shakes the king-doms of the earth. He has spoken out against Phoenicia* and depleted its strength. ¹²He says, "Never again will you rejoice, O daughter of Sidon. Once you were a lovely city, but you will never again be strong. Even if you flee to Cyprus, you will find no rest."

¹³Look at the land of Babylonia*—the people of that land are gone! The Assyrians have handed Babylon over to the wild beasts. They have built siege ramps against its walls, torn down its palaces, and turned it into a heap of rubble.

¹⁴Wail, O ships of Tarshish, for your home port is destroyed! ¹⁵For seventy years, the length of a king's life, Tyre will be forgotten. But then the city will come back to life and sing sweet songs like a prostitute. ¹⁶Long absent from her lovers, she will take a harp, walk the streets, and sing her songs, so that she will again be remembered. ¹⁷Yes, after seventy years the LORD will revive Tyre. But she will be no different than she was before. She will return again to all her evil ways around the world. ¹⁸But in the end her businesses will give their profits to the LORD. Her wealth will not be hoarded but will be used to provide good food and fine clothing for the LORD's priests.

DESTRUCTION OF THE EARTH

24 Look! The LORD is about to destroy the earth and make it a vast wasteland. See how he is scattering the people over the face of the earth. ²Priests and laypeople, servants and masters, maids and mistresses, buyers and sellers, lenders and borrowers, bankers and debtors—none will be spared. ³The earth will be completely emptied and looted. The LORD has spoken!

⁴The earth dries up, the crops wither, the skies refuse to rain. ⁵The earth suffers for the sins of its people, for they have twisted the instructions of God, violated his laws, and broken his everlasting covenant. ⁶Therefore, a curse consumes the earth and its people. They

---

23:1 Hebrew *Kittim;* also in 23:12. 23:3 Hebrew *from Shihor,* a branch of the Nile River. 23:11 Hebrew *Canaan.* 23:13 Or *Chaldea.*

are left desolate, destroyed by fire. Few will be left alive.

⁷All the joys of life will be gone. The grape harvest will fail, and there will be no wine. The merrymakers will sigh and mourn. ⁸The clash of tambourines will be stilled; the happy cries of celebration will be heard no more. The melodious chords of the harp will be silent. ⁹Gone are the joys of wine and song; strong drink now turns bitter in the mouth.

¹⁰The city writhes in chaos; every home is locked to keep out looters. ¹¹Mobs gather in the streets, crying out for wine. Joy has reached its lowest ebb. Gladness has been banished from the land. ¹²The city is left in ruins, with its gates battered down. ¹³Throughout the earth the story is the same—like the stray olives left on the tree or the few grapes left on the vine after harvest, only a remnant is left.

¹⁴But all who are left will shout and sing for joy. Those in the west will praise the LORD's majesty. ¹⁵In eastern lands, give glory to the LORD. In the coastlands of the sea, praise the name of the LORD, the God of Israel. ¹⁶Listen to them as they sing to the LORD from the ends of the earth. Hear them singing praises to the Righteous One!

But my heart is heavy with grief. I am discouraged, for evil still prevails, and treachery is everywhere. ¹⁷Terror and traps and snares will be your lot, you people of the earth. ¹⁸Those who flee in terror will fall into a trap, and those who escape the trap will step into a snare.

Destruction falls on you from the heavens. The world is shaken beneath you. ¹⁹The earth has broken down and has utterly collapsed. Everything is lost, abandoned, and confused. ²⁰The earth staggers like a drunkard. It trembles like a tent in a storm. It falls and will not rise again, for its sins are very great.

²¹In that day the LORD will punish the fallen angels in the heavens and the proud rulers of the nations on earth. ²²They will be rounded up and put in prison until they are tried and condemned. ²³Then the LORD Almighty will

mount his throne on Mount Zion. He will rule gloriously in Jerusalem, in the sight of all the leaders of his people. There will be such glory that the brightness of the sun and moon will seem to fade away.

PRAISE FOR JUDGMENT AND SALVATION

25 O LORD, I will honor and praise your name, for you are my God. You do such wonderful things! You planned them long ago, and now you have accomplished them. ²You turn mighty cities into heaps of ruins. Cities with strong walls are turned to rubble. Beautiful palaces in distant lands disappear and will never be rebuilt. ³Therefore, strong nations will declare your glory; ruthless nations will revere you.

⁴But to the poor, O LORD, you are a refuge from the storm. To the needy in distress, you are a shelter from the rain and the heat. For the oppressive acts of ruthless people are like a storm beating against a wall, ⁵or like the relentless heat of the desert. But you silence the roar of foreign nations. You cool the land with the shade of a cloud. So the boastful songs of ruthless people are stilled.

⁶In Jerusalem,* the LORD Almighty will spread a wonderful feast for everyone around the world. It will be a delicious feast of good food, with clear, well-aged wine and choice beef. ⁷In that day he will remove the cloud of gloom, the shadow of death that hangs over the earth. ⁸He will swallow up death forever! The Sovereign LORD will wipe away all tears. He will remove forever all insults and mockery against his land and people. The LORD has spoken!

⁹In that day the people will proclaim, "This is our God. We trusted in him, and he saved us. This is the LORD, in whom we trusted. Let us rejoice in the salvation he brings!" ¹⁰For the LORD's good hand will rest on Jerusalem.

Moab will be crushed like trampled straw and left to rot. ¹¹God will push down Moab's

25:6 Hebrew *On this mountain;* also in 25:10.

My Daily Worship

— *July 6* —

THE COST (AND GAIN) OF DISCIPLESHIP

ISAIAH 24:1–27:13

Trust in the LORD always, for the Lord God is the eternal Rock (26:4).

[i reflect]

"In Peru, Christians don't expect to get something for serving Jesus," said Pastor Zapata. "They expect to give something." To illustrate, Pastor Zapata showed his foreign guests a row of white crosses, each representing a local Christian killed by Communist insurgents. As if that wasn't proof enough, inside Pastor Zapata's village home was the body of another pastor who had been killed by guerrillas the night before. Expressing their grief, members of the dead man's family ringed his body where it lay covered with a blanket.

Outside, though, the scene was joyous. Despite a steady rain, the congregation of the murdered pastor were singing praise choruses. Guerrillas had killed their pastor, destroyed their church building, and burned many of their homes, yet they sang praise to God. They were still at risk from the guerrillas, but they magnified the Father anyway.

These believers, and countless others whose stories are shared through the Voice of the Martyrs, had learned the lesson that Isaiah taught: Trusting in God is never the wrong choice. He is the eternal Rock to whom we can cling in life and in death—we trust in him *always*.

For many believers, suffering won't reach levels anywhere nearing the pain known by the martyred church. For others, it may. Regardless of our circumstances, we need God's strength—a strength that endures.

The context of Isaiah's comment is one of victory. Similarly, the Bible tells us that the martyrs have their robes washed clean and stand before the throne of God. If we hold to the eternal Rock and do not let go, we will one day find ourselves in that place where a praise-inspiring vision of God fills our whole being.

Allow the testimony of Pastor Zapata to stir you today to pray for the persecuted church—that they will continue to trust in the Lord, the eternal Rock.

[i pray]

I will cling to you, eternal Rock, when the desperation of evil clutches at me.
May I wake up after the trials of this life are over still clinging to you.

[i respond]

Find a rock outside. With a permanent marker, write on it whatever trial or difficulty you are facing. Keep it at your workspace as a reminder to trust in your eternal Rock.

people as a swimmer pushes down water with his hands. He will end their pride and all their evil works. ¹²The high walls of Moab will be demolished and ground to dust.

A Song of Praise to the Lord

26 In that day, everyone in the land of Judah will sing this song:

Our city is now strong!
  We are surrounded by the walls of God's
    salvation.
² Open the gates to all who are righteous;
    allow the faithful to enter.
³ You will keep in perfect peace all who trust
    in you,
    whose thoughts are fixed on you!
⁴ Trust in the LORD always,
    for the LORD God is the eternal Rock.
⁵ He humbles the proud
    and brings the arrogant city to the dust.
  Its walls come crashing down!
⁶   The poor and oppressed trample it
      underfoot.

⁷ But for those who are righteous,
    the path is not steep and rough.
  You are a God of justice,
    and you smooth out the road ahead of
      them.
⁸ LORD, we love to obey your laws;
    our heart's desire is to glorify your name.
⁹ All night long I search for you;
    earnestly I seek for God.
  For only when you come to judge the earth
    will people turn from wickedness and do
      what is right.
¹⁰ Your kindness to the wicked does not
      make them do good.
    They keep doing wrong and take no
      notice of the LORD's majesty.
¹¹ O LORD, they do not listen when you threaten.
    They do not see your upraised fist.
  Show them your eagerness to defend your
      people.
    Perhaps then they will be ashamed.
    Let your fire consume your enemies.

¹² LORD, you will grant us peace,
    for all we have accomplished is really
      from you.
¹³ O LORD our God, others have ruled us,
    but we worship you alone.
¹⁴ Those we served before are dead and gone.
    Never again will they return!
  You attacked them and destroyed them,
    and they are long forgotten.
¹⁵ We praise you, LORD!
    You have made our nation great;
    you have extended our borders!

¹⁶ LORD, in distress we searched for you.
    We were bowed beneath the burden of
      your discipline.
¹⁷ We were like a woman about to give birth,
    writhing and crying out in pain.
  When we are in your presence, LORD,
¹⁸   we, too, writhe in agony,
    but nothing comes of our suffering.
  We have done nothing to rescue the
      world;
    no one has been born to populate the
      earth.
¹⁹ Yet we have this assurance:
    Those who belong to God will live;
    their bodies will rise again!
  Those who sleep in the earth
    will rise up and sing for joy!
  For God's light of life will fall like dew
    on his people in the place of the dead!

Restoration for Israel

²⁰Go home, my people, and lock your doors! Hide until the LORD's anger against your enemies has passed. ²¹Look! The LORD is coming from heaven to punish the people of the earth for their sins. The earth will no longer hide those who have been murdered. They will be brought out for all to see.

27 In that day the LORD will take his terrible, swift sword and punish Leviathan, the swiftly moving serpent, the coiling, writhing serpent, the dragon of the sea.
²"In that day we will sing of the pleasant

vineyard. ³I, the LORD, will watch over it and tend its fruitful vines. Each day I will water them; day and night I will watch to keep enemies away. ⁴My anger against Israel will be gone. If I find briers and thorns bothering her, I will burn them up. ⁵These enemies will be spared only if they surrender and beg for peace and protection."

⁶The time is coming when my people will take root. Israel will bud and blossom and fill the whole earth with her fruit! ⁷Has the LORD punished Israel in the same way he has punished her enemies? No, for he devastated her enemies, ⁸but he has punished Israel only a little. He has exiled her from her land as though blown away in a storm from the east. ⁹The LORD did this to purge away Israel's* sin. When he has finished, all the pagan altars will be crushed to dust. There won't be an Asherah pole or incense altar left standing. ¹⁰Israel's fortified cities will be silent and empty, the houses abandoned, the streets covered with grass. Cattle will graze there, chewing on twigs and branches.

¹¹The people are like the dead branches of a tree, broken off and used for kindling beneath the cooking pots. Israel is a foolish and stupid nation, for its people have turned away from God. Therefore, the one who made them will show them no pity or mercy. ¹²Yet the time will come when the LORD will gather them together one by one like handpicked grain. He will bring them to his great threshing floor— from the Euphrates River* in the east to the brook of Egypt in the west. ¹³In that day the great trumpet will sound. Many who were dying in exile in Assyria and Egypt will return to Jerusalem to worship the LORD on his holy mountain.

A Message about Samaria

28 Destruction is certain for the city of Samaria—the pride and joy of the drunkards of Israel*! It sits in a rich valley, but its glorious beauty will suddenly disappear. Destruction is certain for that city—the pride of a people brought low by wine. ²For the Lord will send the mighty Assyrian army against it. Like a mighty hailstorm and a torrential rain, they will burst upon it and dash it to the ground. ³The proud city of Samaria— the pride and joy of the drunkards of Israel— will be trampled beneath its enemies' feet. ⁴It sits in a fertile valley, but its glorious beauty will suddenly disappear. It will be greedily snatched up, as an early fig is hungrily picked and eaten.

⁵Then at last the LORD Almighty will himself be Israel's crowning glory. He will be the pride and joy of the remnant of his people. ⁶He will give a longing for justice to their judges. He will give great courage to their warriors who stand at the gates.

⁷Now, however, Israel is being led by drunks! The priests and prophets reel and stagger from beer and wine. They make stupid mistakes as they carry out their responsibilities. ⁸Their tables are covered with vomit; filth is everywhere. ⁹They say, "Who does the LORD think we are? Why does he speak to us like this? Are we little children, barely old enough to talk? ¹⁰He tells us everything over and over again, a line at a time, in very simple words!*"

¹¹Since they refuse to listen, God will speak to them through foreign oppressors who speak an unknown language! ¹²God's people could have rest in their own land if they would only obey him, but they will not listen. ¹³So the LORD will spell out his message for them again, repeating it over and over, a line at a time, in very simple words. Yet they will stumble over this simple, straightforward message. They will be injured, trapped, and captured.

¹⁴Therefore, listen to this message from the LORD, you scoffing rulers in Jerusalem. ¹⁵You boast that you have struck a bargain to avoid death and have made a deal to dodge the

27:9 Hebrew *Jacob's.* 27:12 Hebrew *the river.* 28:1 Hebrew *of Ephraim,* referring to the northern kingdom of Israel; also in 28:3.
28:10 The Hebrew text for this verse may simply be childish sounds that have no meaning, or perhaps a childish mimicking of the prophet's words. Also in 28:13.

grave.* You say, "The Assyrians can never touch us, for we have built a strong refuge made of lies and deception." [16]Therefore, this is what the Sovereign LORD says: "Look! I am placing a foundation stone in Jerusalem.* It is firm, a tested and precious cornerstone that is safe to build on. Whoever believes need never run away again.*

[17]"I will take the measuring line of justice and the plumb line of righteousness to check the foundation wall you have built. Your refuge looks strong, but since it is made of lies, a hailstorm will knock it down. Since it is made of deception, the enemy will come like a flood to sweep it away. [18]I will cancel the bargain you made to avoid death, and I will overturn your deal to dodge the grave. When the terrible enemy floods in, you will be trampled into the ground. [19]Again and again that flood will come, morning after morning, day and night, until you are carried away."

This message will bring terror to your people. [20]For you have no place of refuge—the bed you have made is too short to lie on. The blankets are too narrow to cover you. [21]The LORD will come suddenly and in anger, as he did against the Philistines at Mount Perazim and against the Amorites at Gibeon. He will come to do a strange, unusual thing: He will destroy his own people! [22]So scoff no more, or your punishment will be even greater. For the Lord, the LORD Almighty, has plainly told me that he is determined to crush you.

[23]Listen to me; listen as I plead! [24]Does a farmer always plow and never sow? Is he forever cultivating the soil and never planting it? [25]Does he not finally plant his seeds for dill, cumin, wheat, barley, and spelt, each in its own section of his land? [26]The farmer knows just what to do, for God has given him understanding. [27]He doesn't thresh all his crops the same way. A heavy sledge is never used on dill; rather, it is beaten with a light stick. A threshing wheel is never rolled on cumin; instead, it is beaten softly with a flail. [28]Bread grain is easily crushed, so he doesn't keep on pounding it. He threshes it under the wheels of a cart, but he doesn't pulverize it. [29]The LORD Almighty is a wonderful teacher, and he gives the farmer great wisdom.

A MESSAGE ABOUT JERUSALEM

29 "Destruction is certain for Ariel,* the City of David. Year after year you offer your many sacrifices. [2]Yet I will bring disaster upon you, and there will be much weeping and sorrow. For Jerusalem will become as her name Ariel means—an altar covered with blood. [3]I will be your enemy, surrounding Jerusalem and attacking its walls. I will build siege towers around it and will destroy it. [4]Your voice will whisper like a ghost from the earth where you will lie buried.

[5]"But suddenly, your ruthless enemies will be driven away like chaff before the wind. [6]In an instant, I, the LORD Almighty, will come against them with thunder and earthquake and great noise, with whirlwind and storm and consuming fire. [7]All the nations fighting against Jerusalem* will vanish like a dream! Those who are attacking her walls will vanish like a vision in the night. [8]A hungry person dreams of eating but is still hungry. A thirsty person dreams of drinking but is still faint from thirst when morning comes. In the same way, your enemies will dream of a victorious conquest over Jerusalem,* but all to no avail."

[9]Are you amazed and incredulous? Do you not believe it? Then go ahead and be blind if you must. You are stupid, but not from wine! You stagger, but not from beer! [10]For the LORD has poured out on you a spirit of deep sleep. He has closed the eyes of your prophets and visionaries. [11]All these future events are a sealed book to them. When you give it to those who can read, they will say, "We can't read it because it is sealed." [12]When you give it to those who cannot read, they will say, "Sorry, we don't know how to read."

[13]And so the Lord says, "These people say

28:15 Hebrew *Sheol;* also in 28:18. **28:16a** Hebrew *in Zion.* **28:16b** Greek version reads *Anyone who believes in him will not be disappointed.* **29:1** *Ariel* sounds like a Hebrew term that means "hearth" or "altar." **29:7** Hebrew *Ariel.* **29:8** Hebrew *Mount Zion.*

My Daily Worship

— *July 7* —

THE POTTER AND HIS WORKS

ISAIAH 28:1–31:9

Should the thing that was created say to the one who made it, "He didn't make us"?
Does a jar ever say, "The potter who made me is stupid"? (29:16).

[i reflect]

Did biomolecules build up on Earth's surface over eons, as naturalistic dogma predicts? It seems not. According to Hugh Ross and Fazale Rana in their book *Origins of Life,* Earth has been bombarded by massively destructive meteorites many times, narrowing the window of life sustainability to a period far too short for evolution.

Did life originate on early Earth in the form of extremophiles—tiny creatures that are able to withstand very high or very low temperatures? Apparently not, since biologists now admit that even the simplest extremophiles are too complex to have arisen on their own.

Did microscopic life arrive on Earth aboard a meteorite from some other place in the universe, perhaps Jupiter's watery moon, Europa? No. Europa's ice layer has now been proved much too thick (miles deep) to permit life to exist farther down. Meanwhile, numerous lines of evidence are making it look more and more like Earth is the only place in the universe capable of hosting life.

These are just a few of the theories that origin-of-life scientists have considered—and dropped. While evolution has worn an air of invincibility since the Scopes trial, the truth is that it's getting tougher and tougher to believe that life originated from nonlife. The proof just isn't there.

Meanwhile, we who believe in creation have no room for smugness. How many of us proclaim that God had a purpose for creating life in general, while at the same time we question whether God had a purpose in creating *us,* individually? How many of us, by hating our bodies or our brains or our circumstances, echo the thought of the jar, "The potter who made me is stupid"?

The Potter (to use Isaiah's imagery) knew just what he was doing when he made each of us "pots." Thank him for creating you exactly as you are and for each "pot and jar" that you encounter throughout the day.

[i pray]

For the life that greens this globe, especially for this body that is my
vehicle of movement and expression, I honor you, Lord. Help me
to make of the gift that is my life all you meant it to be.

[i respond]

Browse through a book about the human body, perhaps one on the development of babies in the womb. Truly, we are fearfully and wonderfully made! Worship our Maker, more wonderful still!

they are mine. They honor me with their lips, but their hearts are far away. And their worship of me amounts to nothing more than human laws learned by rote.* [14]Because of this, I will do wonders among these hypocrites. I will show that human wisdom is foolish and even the most brilliant people lack understanding."

[15]Destruction is certain for those who try to hide their plans from the LORD, who try to keep him in the dark concerning what they do! "The LORD can't see us," you say to yourselves. "He doesn't know what is going on!" [16]How stupid can you be? He is the Potter, and he is certainly greater than you. You are only the jars he makes! Should the thing that was created say to the one who made it, "He didn't make us"? Does a jar ever say, "The potter who made me is stupid"?

[17]Soon—and it will not be very long—the wilderness of Lebanon will be a fertile field once again. And the fertile fields will become a lush and fertile forest. [18]In that day deaf people will hear words read from a book, and blind people will see through the gloom and darkness. [19]The humble will be filled with fresh joy from the LORD. Those who are poor will rejoice in the Holy One of Israel. [20]Those who intimidate and harass will be gone, and all those who plot evil will be killed. [21]Those who make the innocent guilty by their false testimony will disappear. And those who use trickery to pervert justice and tell lies to tear down the innocent will be no more.

[22]That is why the LORD, who redeemed Abraham, says to the people of Israel,* "My people will no longer pale with fear or be ashamed. [23]For when they see their many children and material blessings, they will recognize the holiness of the Holy One of Israel. They will stand in awe of the God of Israel. [24]Those in error will then believe the truth, and those who constantly complain will accept instruction.

JUDAH'S WORTHLESS TREATY WITH EGYPT

30 "Destruction is certain for my rebellious children," says the LORD. "You make plans that are contrary to my will. You weave a web of plans that are not from my Spirit, thus piling up your sins. [2]For without consulting me, you have gone down to Egypt to find help. You have put your trust in Pharaoh for his protection. [3]But in trusting Pharaoh, you will be humiliated and disgraced. [4]For though his power extends to Zoan and Hanes, [5]it will all turn out to your shame. He will not help you even one little bit."

[6]Look at the animals moving slowly across the terrible desert to Egypt—donkeys and camels loaded with treasure to pay for Egypt's aid. On through the wilderness they go, where lions and poisonous snakes live. All this, and Egypt will give you nothing in return. [7]Egypt's promises are worthless! I call her the Harmless Dragon.*

A WARNING FOR REBELLIOUS JUDAH

[8]Now go and write down these words concerning Egypt. They will then stand until the end of time as a witness to Israel's unbelief. [9]For these people are stubborn rebels who refuse to pay any attention to the LORD's instructions.

[10]They tell the prophets, "Shut up! We don't want any more of your reports." They say, "Don't tell us the truth. Tell us nice things. Tell us lies. [11]Forget all this gloom. We have heard more than enough about your 'Holy One of Israel.' We are tired of listening to what he has to say."

[12]This is the reply of the Holy One of Israel: "Because you despise what I tell you and trust instead in oppression and lies, [13]calamity will come upon you suddenly. It will be like a bulging wall that bursts and falls. In an instant

---

29:13 Greek version reads *Their worship is a farce, for they merely teach human commands and teachings.* **29:22** Hebrew *of Jacob;* also in 29:23. **30:7** Hebrew *Rahab who sits still.* Rahab is the name of a mythical sea monster that represents chaos in ancient literature. The name is used here as a poetic name for Egypt.

it will collapse and come crashing down. [14]You will be smashed like a piece of pottery—shattered so completely that there won't be a piece left that is big enough to carry coals from a fireplace or a little water from the well."

[15]The Sovereign LORD, the Holy One of Israel, says, "Only in returning to me and waiting for me will you be saved. In quietness and confidence is your strength. But you would have none of it. [16]You said, 'No, we will get our help from Egypt. They will give us swift horses for riding into battle.' But the only swiftness you are going to see is the swiftness of your enemies chasing you! [17]One of them will chase a thousand of you. Five of them will make all of you flee. You will be left like a lonely flagpole on a distant mountaintop."

BLESSINGS FOR THE LORD'S PEOPLE

[18]But the LORD still waits for you to come to him so he can show you his love and compassion. For the LORD is a faithful God. Blessed are those who wait for him to help them.

[19]O people of Zion, who live in Jerusalem, you will weep no more. He will be gracious if you ask for help. He will respond instantly to the sound of your cries. [20]Though the Lord gave you adversity for food and affliction for drink, he will still be with you to teach you. You will see your teacher with your own eyes, [21]and you will hear a voice say, "This is the way; turn around and walk here." [22]Then you will destroy all your silver idols and gold images. You will throw them out like filthy rags. "Ugh!" you will say to them. "Begone!"

[23]Then the LORD will bless you with rain at planting time. There will be wonderful harvests and plenty of pastureland for your cattle. [24]The oxen and donkeys that till the ground will eat good grain, its chaff having been blown away by the wind. [25]In that day, when your enemies are slaughtered, there will be streams of water flowing down every mountain and hill. [26]The moon will be as bright as the sun, and the sun will be seven times brighter—like the light of seven days! So it will be when the LORD begins to heal his people and cure the wounds he gave them.

[27]Look! The LORD is coming from far away, burning with anger, surrounded by a thick, rising smoke. His lips are filled with fury; his words consume like fire. [28]His anger pours out like a flood on his enemies, sweeping them all away. He will sift out the proud nations. He will bridle them and lead them off to their destruction.

[29]But the people of God will sing a song of joy, like the songs at the holy festivals. You will be filled with joy, as when a flutist leads a group of pilgrims to Jerusalem—the mountain of the LORD—to the Rock of Israel. [30]And the LORD will make his majestic voice heard. With angry indignation he will bring down his mighty arm on his enemies. It will descend with devouring flames, with cloudbursts, thunderstorms, and huge hailstones, bringing their destruction. [31]At the LORD's command, the Assyrians will be shattered. He will strike them down with his rod. [32]And as the LORD strikes them, his people will keep time with the music of tambourines and harps. [33]Topheth—the place of burning—has long been ready for the Assyrian king; it has been piled high with wood. The breath of the LORD, like fire from a volcano, will set it ablaze.

THE FUTILITY OF RELYING ON EGYPT

31 Destruction is certain for those who look to Egypt for help, trusting their cavalry and chariots instead of looking to the LORD, the Holy One of Israel. [2]In his wisdom, the LORD will send great disaster; he will not change his mind. He will rise against those who are wicked, and he will crush their allies, too. [3]For these Egyptians are mere humans, not God! Their horses are puny flesh, not mighty spirits! When the LORD clenches his fist against them, they will stumble and fall among those they are trying to help. They will all fall down and die together.

[4]But the LORD has told me this: "When a

lion, even a young one, kills a sheep, it pays no attention to the shepherd's shouts and noise. It just goes right on eating. In the same way, the LORD Almighty will come and fight on Mount Zion. He will not be frightened away! [5]The LORD Almighty will hover over Jerusalem as a bird hovers around its nest. He will defend and save the city; he will pass over it and rescue it."

[6]Therefore, my people, though you are such wicked rebels, come and return to the LORD. [7]I know the glorious day will come when every one of you will throw away the gold idols and silver images that your sinful hands have made.

[8]"The Assyrians will be destroyed, but not by the swords of men. The sword of God will strike them, and they will panic and flee. The strong young Assyrians will be taken away as captives. [9]Even their generals will quake with terror and flee when they see the battle flags," says the LORD, whose flame burns brightly in Jerusalem.

ISRAEL'S ULTIMATE DELIVERANCE

32 Look, a righteous king is coming! And honest princes will rule under him. [2]He will shelter Israel from the storm and the wind. He will refresh her as a river in the desert and as the cool shadow of a large rock in a hot and weary land. [3]Then everyone who can see will be looking for God, and those who can hear will listen to his voice. [4]Even the hotheads among them will be full of sense and understanding. Those who stammer in uncertainty will speak out plainly.

[5]In that day ungodly fools will not be heroes. Wealthy cheaters will not be respected as outstanding citizens. [6]Everyone will recognize ungodly fools for what they are. They spread lies about the LORD; they deprive the hungry of food and give no water to the thirsty. [7]The smooth tricks of evil people will be exposed, including all the lies they use to oppress the poor in the courts. [8]But good people will be generous to others and will be blessed for all they do.

[9]Listen, you women who lie around in lazy ease. Listen to me, and I will tell you of your reward. [10]In a short time—in just a little more than a year—you careless ones will suddenly begin to care. For your fruit crop will fail, and the harvest will never take place. [11]Tremble, you women of ease; throw off your unconcern. Strip off your pretty clothes, and wear sackcloth in your grief. [12]Beat your breasts in sorrow for your bountiful farms that will soon be gone, and for those fruitful vines of other years. [13]For your land will be overgrown with thorns and briers. Your joyful homes and happy cities will be gone. [14]The palace and the city will be deserted, and busy towns will be empty. Herds of donkeys and goats will graze on the hills where the watchtowers are, [15]until at last the Spirit is poured down upon us from heaven. Then the wilderness will become a fertile field, and the fertile field will become a lush and fertile forest. [16]Justice will rule in the wilderness and righteousness in the fertile field. [17]And this righteousness will bring peace. Quietness and confidence will fill the land forever.

[18]My people will live in safety, quietly at home. They will be at rest. [19]Even though the forest will be destroyed and the city torn down, [20]God will greatly bless his people. Wherever they plant seed, bountiful crops will spring up. Their flocks and herds will graze in green pastures.

A MESSAGE ABOUT ASSYRIA

33 Destruction is certain for you Assyrians,* who have destroyed everything around you but have never felt destruction yourselves. You expect others to respect their promises to you, while you betray your promises to them. Now you, too, will be betrayed and destroyed!

[2]But LORD, be merciful to us, for we have

33:1 Hebrew *for you, O destroyer . . . O betrayer.* The Hebrew text does not specifically name Assyria as the object of this prophecy.

My Daily Worship

— *July 8* —

SHATTER YOUR COMPLACENCY

ISAIAH 32:1–35:10

Listen, you women who lie around in lazy ease. . . .
In a short time—in just a little more than a year—
you careless ones will suddenly begin to care (32:9–10).

[i reflect]

The nation's capital was still a country village when in 1814, the British invaded Washington. Until that moment, the War of 1812 had been "Mr. Madison's War," and the nation was unconcerned about any pending threat to them. Most citizens were, in a word, complacent.

Following the Battle of Bladensburg, near Washington, the attitude changed drastically. The capital's critics and residents alike fled before the invasion. As the White House was engulfed with flames and torches were tossed into the War Department building, complacency vanished. The enemy had touched the very heart of the nation. Overnight the citizenry had been awakened to the reality that this was *their* war.

That pattern of complacency is not limited to nations and wars. When we're healthy, the career is going well, and all aspects of life seemingly fall into place, we can grow complacent in our relationship with God. Then, suddenly, the enemy invades—a job is lost, the test is positive, a relationship is broken. Our complacent lives are shaken.

At the time Isaiah delivered this prophecy, the people of Israel's countryside were taking it easy after harvesting their crops. That would have been fine, except apparently they were feeling self-sufficient and complacent about God. They had no idea—until Isaiah warned them—that they were mere months away from seeing their pleasant fields and vineyards utterly devastated (perhaps by an invasion of the Assyrians). Their complacency was about to be shattered.

Where has complacency crept into your attitudes, habits, or relationships? Use this time as your personal wake-up call and confess those areas to God.

[i pray]

Father, I ask that you would reveal to me this day where I have grown complacent in my relationship with you. Place in me a renewed fervor and urgency in my relationship with you.

[i respond]

Jump-start your faith today by doing something totally different—pray with a friend on the telephone; use Christian music to inspire your devotional time; find a different location to spend time with God. Break the pattern of your time with God. Shatter your complacency.

waited for you. Be our strength each day and our salvation in times of trouble. [3]The enemy runs at the sound of your voice. When you stand up, the nations flee! [4]Just as locusts strip the fields and vines, so Jerusalem will strip the fallen army of Assyria!

[5]Though the LORD is very great and lives in heaven, he will make Jerusalem* his home of justice and righteousness. [6]In that day he will be your sure foundation, providing a rich store of salvation, wisdom, and knowledge. The fear of the LORD is the key to this treasure.

[7]But now your ambassadors weep in bitter disappointment, for Assyria has refused their petition for peace. [8]Your roads are deserted; no one travels them anymore. The Assyrians have broken their peace pact and care nothing for the promises they made before witnesses.* They have no respect for anyone. [9]All the land of Israel is in trouble. Lebanon has been destroyed. The plain of Sharon is now a wilderness. Bashan and Carmel have been plundered.

[10]But the LORD says: "I will stand up and show my power and might. [11]You Assyrians will gain nothing by all your efforts. Your own breath will turn to fire and kill you. [12]Your people will be burned up completely, like thorns cut down and tossed in a fire. [13]Listen to what I have done, you nations far away! And you that are near, acknowledge my might!"

[14]The sinners in Jerusalem* shake with fear. "Which one of us," they cry, "can live here in the presence of this all-consuming fire?" [15]The ones who can live here are those who are honest and fair, who reject making a profit by fraud, who stay far away from bribes, who refuse to listen to those who plot murder, who shut their eyes to all enticement to do wrong. [16]These are the ones who will dwell on high. The rocks of the mountains will be their fortress of safety. Food will be supplied to them, and they will have water in abundance.

[17]Your eyes will see the king in all his splendor, and you will see a land that stretches into the distance. [18]You will think back to this time of terror when the Assyrian officers outside your walls counted your towers and estimated how much plunder they would get from your fallen city. [19]But soon they will all be gone. These fierce, violent people with a strange, unknown language will disappear.

[20]Instead, you will see Zion as a place of worship and celebration. You will see Jerusalem, a city quiet and secure. [21]The LORD will be our Mighty One. He will be like a wide river of protection that no enemy can cross. [22]For the LORD is our judge, our lawgiver, and our king. He will care for us and save us. [23]The enemies' sails hang loose on broken masts with useless tackle. Their treasure will be divided by the people of God. Even the lame will win their share! [24]The people of Israel will no longer say, "We are sick and helpless," for the LORD will forgive their sins.

A MESSAGE FOR THE NATIONS

34 Come here and listen, O nations of the earth. Let the world and everything in it hear my words. [2]For the LORD is enraged against the nations. His fury is against all their armies. He will completely destroy* them, bringing about their slaughter. [3]Their dead will be left unburied, and the stench of rotting bodies will fill the land. The mountains will flow with their blood. [4]The heavens above will melt away and disappear like a rolled-up scroll. The stars will fall from the sky, just as withered leaves and fruit fall from a tree.

[5]And when my sword has finished its work in the heavens, then watch. It will fall upon Edom, the nation I have completely destroyed. [6]The sword of the LORD is drenched with blood. It is covered with fat as though it had been used for killing lambs and goats and rams for a sacrifice. Yes, the LORD will offer a great sacrifice in the rich city of Bozrah. He

---

33:5 Hebrew *Zion.* 33:8 As in Dead Sea Scrolls; Masoretic Text reads *care nothing for the cities.* 33:14 Hebrew *in Zion.* 34:2 The Hebrew term used here refers to the complete consecration of things or people to the LORD, either by destroying them or by giving them as an offering; also in 34:5.

MEDITATE

Meditate—Hebrew *biq-qer* "inquire, meditate"; *ha-gah* "mutter, groan"; *si-ach* "ponder, meditate"; *si-chah* "meditation."

We tend to think of meditation, thinking and reflecting on something, as an internal process. Not so for the biblical worshiper, whose meditation is a visible activity. For example, when the psalm writer describes righteous worshipers who "think about his law" (Psalm 1:2) day and night, he uses the word *hagah,* mutter. The worshiper is not just thinking about the Word of God, but is perhaps reciting it under his breath. And when the writer says that he longs to live in the house of the Lord, "meditating in his Temple" (Psalm 27:4), he uses the word *biqqer,* which means to inquire or penetrate, especially through prayer. In biblical cultures, even reading was not done silently but aloud.

Many Christians seek a daily quiet time with the Lord. But Scripture shows us that even our personal worship is never just a "head trip." Following biblical models, we might discover that our "quiet time" is not so quiet after all.

land will lie deserted from generation to generation. No one will live there anymore. [11]It will be haunted by the horned owl, the hawk, the screech owl, and the raven.* For God will bring chaos and destruction to that land. [12]It will be called the Land of Nothing, and its princes soon will all be gone. [13]Thorns will overrun its palaces; nettles will grow in its forts. The ruins will become a haunt for jackals and a home for ostriches. [14]Wild animals of the desert will mingle there with hyenas, their howls filling the night. Wild goats will bleat at one another among the ruins, and night creatures will come there to rest. [15]There the owl will make her nest and lay her eggs. She will hatch her young and cover them with her wings. And the vultures will come, each one with its mate.

[16]Search the book of the LORD, and see what he will do. He will not miss a single detail. Not one of these birds and animals will be missing, and none will lack a mate, for the LORD has promised this. His Spirit will make it all come true. [17]He has surveyed and divided the land and deeded it over to those creatures. They will possess it forever, from generation to generation.

HOPE FOR RESTORATION

35 Even the wilderness will rejoice in those days. The desert will blossom with flowers. [2]Yes, there will be an abundance of flowers and singing and joy! The deserts will become as green as the mountains of Lebanon, as lovely as Mount Carmel's pastures and the plain of Sharon. There the LORD will display his glory, the splendor of our God.

[3]With this news, strengthen those who have tired hands, and encourage those who have weak knees. [4]Say to those who are afraid, "Be strong, and do not fear, for your God is coming to destroy your enemies. He is coming to save you." [5]And when he comes, he will open the eyes of the blind and unstop the ears of the deaf. [6]The lame will leap like a deer, and

will make a mighty slaughter in Edom. [7]The strongest will die—veterans and young men, too. The land will be soaked with blood and the soil enriched with fat. [8]For it is the day of the LORD's vengeance, the year when Edom will be paid back for all it did to Israel.* [9]The streams of Edom will be filled with burning pitch, and the ground will be covered with fire. [10]This judgment on Edom will never end; the smoke of its burning will rise forever. The

34:8 Hebrew *to Zion.* **34:11** The identification of some of these birds is uncertain.

those who cannot speak will shout and sing! Springs will gush forth in the wilderness, and streams will water the desert. ⁷The parched ground will become a pool, and springs of water will satisfy the thirsty land. Marsh grass and reeds and rushes will flourish where desert jackals once lived.

⁸And a main road will go through that once deserted land. It will be named the Highway of Holiness. Evil-hearted people will never travel on it. It will be only for those who walk in God's ways; fools will never walk there. ⁹Lions will not lurk along its course, and there will be no other dangers. Only the redeemed will follow it. ¹⁰Those who have been ransomed by the LORD will return to Jerusalem,* singing songs of everlasting joy. Sorrow and mourning will disappear, and they will be overcome with joy and gladness.

ASSYRIA INVADES JUDAH

36 In the fourteenth year of King Hezekiah's reign, King Sennacherib of Assyria came to attack the fortified cities of Judah and conquered them. ²Then the king of Assyria sent his personal representative with a huge army from Lachish to confront King Hezekiah in Jerusalem. The Assyrians stopped beside the aqueduct that feeds water into the upper pool, near the road leading to the field where cloth is bleached.

³These are the officials who went out to meet with them: Eliakim son of Hilkiah, the palace administrator, Shebna the court secretary, and Joah son of Asaph, the royal historian. ⁴Then the Assyrian king's personal representative sent this message to King Hezekiah:

"This is what the great king of Assyria says: What are you trusting in that makes you so confident? ⁵Do you think that mere words can substitute for military skill and strength? Which of your allies will give you any military backing against Assyria? ⁶Will

Egypt? If you lean on Egypt, you will find it to be a stick that breaks beneath your weight and pierces your hand. The Pharaoh of Egypt is completely unreliable!

⁷"But perhaps you will say, 'We are trusting in the LORD our God!' But isn't he the one who was insulted by King Hezekiah? Didn't Hezekiah tear down his shrines and altars and make everyone in Judah worship only at the altar here in Jerusalem?

⁸"I'll tell you what! My master, the king of Assyria, will strike a bargain with you. If you can find two thousand horsemen in your entire army, he will give you two thousand horses for them to ride on! ⁹With your tiny army, how can you think of challenging even the weakest contingent of my master's troops, even with the help of Egypt's chariots and horsemen*? ¹⁰What's more, do you think we have invaded your land without the LORD's direction? The LORD himself told us, 'Go and destroy it!'"

¹¹Then Eliakim, Shebna, and Joah said to the king's representative, "Please speak to us in Aramaic, for we understand it well. Don't speak in Hebrew, for the people on the wall will hear."

¹²But Sennacherib's representative replied, "My master wants everyone in Jerusalem to hear this, not just you. He wants them to know that if you do not surrender, this city will be put under siege. The people will become so hungry and thirsty that they will eat their own dung and drink their own urine."

¹³Then he stood and shouted in Hebrew to the people on the wall, "Listen to this message from the great king of Assyria! ¹⁴This is what the king says: Don't let King Hezekiah deceive you. He will never be able to rescue you. ¹⁵Don't let him fool you into trusting in the LORD by saying, 'The LORD will rescue us! This

35:10 Hebrew *Zion.*   36:9 Or *and charioteers.*

city will never be handed over to the Assyrian king.'

16"Don't listen to Hezekiah! These are the terms the king of Assyria is offering: Make peace with me—open the gates and come out. Then I will allow each of you to continue eating from your own garden and drinking from your own well. 17Then I will arrange to take you to another land like this one—a country with bountiful harvests of grain and wine, bread and vineyards—a land of plenty.

18"Don't let Hezekiah mislead you by saying, 'The LORD will rescue us!' Have the gods of any other nations ever saved their people from the king of Assyria? 19What happened to the gods of Hamath and Arpad? And what about the gods of Sepharvaim? Did they rescue Samaria from my power? 20What god of any nation has ever been able to save its people from my power? Name just one! So what makes you think that the LORD can rescue Jerusalem?"

21But the people were silent and did not answer because Hezekiah had told them not to speak. 22Then Eliakim son of Hilkiah, the palace administrator, Shebna the court secretary, and Joah son of Asaph, the royal historian, went back to Hezekiah. They tore their clothes in despair, and they went in to see the king and told him what the Assyrian representative had said.

HEZEKIAH SEEKS THE LORD'S HELP

37 When King Hezekiah heard their report, he tore his clothes and put on sackcloth and went into the Temple of the LORD to pray. 2And he sent Eliakim the palace administrator, Shebna the court secretary, and the leading priests, all dressed in sackcloth, to the prophet Isaiah son of Amoz. 3They told him, "This is what King Hezekiah says: This is a day of trouble, insult, and disgrace. It is like when a child is ready to be born, but the mother has no strength to deliver it. 4But perhaps the LORD your God has heard the Assyrian representative defying the living God and will punish him for his words. Oh, pray for those of us who are left!"

5After King Hezekiah's officials delivered the king's message to Isaiah, 6the prophet replied, "Say to your master, 'This is what the LORD says: Do not be disturbed by this blasphemous speech against me from the Assyrian king's messengers. 7Listen! I myself will make sure that the king will receive a report from Assyria telling him that he is needed at home. Then I will make him want to return to his land, where I will have him killed with a sword.'"

8Meanwhile, the Assyrian representative left Jerusalem and went to consult his king, who had left Lachish and was attacking Libnah.

9Soon afterward King Sennacherib received word that King Tirhakah of Ethiopia* was leading an army to fight against him. Before leaving to meet the attack, he sent this message back to Hezekiah in Jerusalem:

10"This message is for King Hezekiah of Judah. Don't let this God you trust deceive you with promises that Jerusalem will not be captured by the king of Assyria. 11You know perfectly well what the kings of Assyria have done wherever they have gone. They have crushed everyone who stood in their way! Why should you be any different? 12Have the gods of other nations rescued them—such nations as Gozan, Haran, Rezeph, and the people of Eden who were in Tel-assar? The former kings of Assyria destroyed them all! 13What happened to the king of Hamath and the king of Arpad? What happened to the kings of Sepharvaim, Hena, and Ivvah?"

14After Hezekiah received the letter and read it, he went up to the LORD's Temple and spread it out before the LORD. 15And Hezekiah prayed this prayer before the LORD: 16"O LORD

37:9 Hebrew *of Cush.*

Almighty, God of Israel, you are enthroned between the mighty cherubim! You alone are God of all the kingdoms of the earth. You alone created the heavens and the earth. ¹⁷Listen to me, O LORD, and hear! Open your eyes, O LORD, and see! Listen to Sennacherib's words of defiance against the living God.

¹⁸"It is true, LORD, that the kings of Assyria have destroyed all these nations, just as the message says. ¹⁹And they have thrown the gods of these nations into the fire and burned them. But of course the Assyrians could destroy them! They were not gods at all—only idols of wood and stone shaped by human hands. ²⁰Now, O LORD our God, rescue us from his power; then all the kingdoms of the earth will know that you alone, O LORD, are God."

ISAIAH PREDICTS JUDAH'S DELIVERANCE

²¹Then Isaiah son of Amoz sent this message to Hezekiah: "This is what the LORD, the God of Israel, says: This is my answer to your prayer concerning King Sennacherib of Assyria. ²²This is the message that the LORD has spoken against him:

'The virgin daughter of Zion
  despises you and laughs at you.
The daughter of Jerusalem
  scoffs and shakes her head as you flee.

²³ 'Whom do you think you have been insulting and ridiculing?
  Against whom did you raise your voice?
At whom did you look in such proud
    condescension?
  It was the Holy One of Israel!
²⁴ By your messengers you have mocked the
    Lord.
  You have said, "With my many chariots
I have conquered the highest mountains—
    yes, the remotest peaks of Lebanon.
I have cut down its tallest cedars
  and its choicest cypress trees.
I have reached its farthest corners

and explored its deepest forests.
²⁵ I have dug wells in many a foreign land
  and refreshed myself with their water.
I even stopped up the rivers of Egypt
  so that my armies could go across!"

²⁶ 'But have you not heard?
  It was I, the LORD, who decided this long
    ago.
Long ago I planned what I am now
    causing to happen,
  that you should crush fortified cities
    into heaps of rubble.
²⁷ That is why their people have so little
    power
  and are such easy prey for you.
They are as helpless as the grass,
  as easily trampled as tender green
    shoots.
They are like grass sprouting on a
    housetop,
  easily scorched by the sun.

²⁸ 'But I know you well—
  your comings and goings and all
    you do.
I know the way you have raged against
    me.
²⁹ And because of your arrogance against me,
  which I have heard for myself,
I will put my hook in your nose
  and my bridle in your mouth.
I will make you return
  by the road on which you came.' "

³⁰Then Isaiah said to Hezekiah, "Here is the proof that the LORD will protect this city from Assyria's king. This year you will eat only what grows up by itself, and next year you will eat what springs up from that. But in the third year you will plant crops and harvest them; you will tend vineyards and eat their fruit. ³¹And you who are left in Judah, who have escaped the ravages of the siege, will take root again in your own soil, and you will flourish and multiply. ³²For a remnant of my people will spread out from Jerusalem, a group of

My Daily Worship

— July 9 —

THE SILENCE OF LISTENING PRAYER

ISAIAH 36:1–39:8

After Hezekiah received the letter and read it, he went up to
the LORD's Temple and spread it out before the LORD.
And Hezekiah prayed (37:14–15).

[i reflect]

"In worship," declared C. Welton Gaddy, "silence is far more than the absence of sound. Silence constitutes a vital part of the divine-human dialogue. In silence, worshipers can experience interchanges with God that will not be known where silence does not prevail."

Being silent before God may seem a strain for those of us who are not used to it; it can make us restless or uncomfortable. But prayer can never truly be two-way communication until we learn to listen as well as speak. In fact, if prayer ever feels like an unreal exercise to us, it may be because we are doing all the talking!

It is not that we should necessarily expect to hear God give us specific instruction on a matter (how nice when he does, as in the case of Hezekiah), or that we should even expect to feel the Spirit's "nudge" that some Christians talk about. It's more about stretching open a space in our spirits for God to begin to fill with himself. Listening prayer, in that way, changes us over time.

Brigid Herman said, "As we approach prayer by the spacious antechamber of silence, we come to realize that the first mover is not we but God." Through listening prayer, then, we learn more about this One to whom we are praying. We cannot "know that he is God" until we are willing to "be still" (see Psalm 46:10). Listening prayer has the power to bring our wills more nearly in line with God's will—that place where we can be assured of his best for us.

Facing a crisis or decision? As an act of worship today, spread it out before the Lord as Hezekiah did. Speak. Wait. And listen.

[i pray]

Thank you, Lord, for letting me babble on about matters you understand much
more than I do. It makes me feel better to tell you what I wonder about.
Yet speak now, Lord, for your servant is listening.

[i respond]

Go to the quietest place you know, some place where you can hear the dust settle. Then—to make up for the times you have failed to let God get a word in edgewise—spend ten minutes listening for every one minute you spend talking to God.

survivors from Mount Zion. The passion of the LORD Almighty will make this happen!

³³"And this is what the LORD says about the king of Assyria: His armies will not enter Jerusalem to shoot their arrows. They will not march outside its gates with their shields and build banks of earth against its walls. ³⁴The king will return to his own country by the road on which he came. He will not enter this city, says the LORD. ³⁵For my own honor and for the sake of my servant David, I will defend it."

³⁶That night the angel of the LORD went out to the Assyrian camp and killed 185,000 Assyrian troops. When the surviving Assyrians* woke up the next morning, they found corpses everywhere. ³⁷Then King Sennacherib of Assyria broke camp and returned to his own land. He went home to his capital of Nineveh and stayed there. ³⁸One day while he was worshiping in the temple of his god Nisroch, his sons Adrammelech and Sharezer killed him with their swords. They then escaped to the land of Ararat, and another son, Esarhaddon, became the next king of Assyria.

HEZEKIAH'S SICKNESS AND RECOVERY

38 About that time Hezekiah became deathly ill, and the prophet Isaiah son of Amoz went to visit him. He gave the king this message: "This is what the LORD says: Set your affairs in order, for you are going to die. You will not recover from this illness."

²When Hezekiah heard this, he turned his face to the wall and prayed to the LORD, ³"Remember, O LORD, how I have always tried to be faithful to you and do what is pleasing in your sight." Then he broke down and wept bitterly.

⁴Then this message came to Isaiah from the LORD: ⁵"Go back to Hezekiah and tell him, 'This is what the LORD, the God of your ancestor David, says: I have heard your prayer and

seen your tears. I will add fifteen years to your life, ⁶and I will rescue you and this city from the king of Assyria. Yes, I will defend this city.

⁷" 'And this is the sign that the LORD will give you to prove he will do as he promised: ⁸I will cause the sun's shadow to move ten steps backward on the sundial of Ahaz!' " So the shadow on the sundial moved backward ten steps.

HEZEKIAH'S POEM OF PRAISE

⁹When King Hezekiah was well again, he wrote this poem about his experience:

¹⁰ I said, "In the prime of my life,
    must I now enter the place of the dead?
    Am I to be robbed of my normal years?"
¹¹ I said, "Never again will I see the LORD
    GOD
    while still in the land of the living.
  Never again will I see my friends
    or laugh with those who live in this
    world.
¹² My life has been blown away
    like a shepherd's tent in a storm.
  It has been cut short,
    as when a weaver cuts cloth from a loom.
  Suddenly, my life was over.
¹³ I waited patiently all night,
    but I was torn apart as though by lions.
  Suddenly, my life was over.
¹⁴ Delirious, I chattered like a swallow or a
    crane,
    and then I moaned like a mourning
    dove.
  My eyes grew tired of looking to heaven
    for help.
  I am in trouble, Lord. Help me!"

¹⁵ But what could I say?
    For he himself had sent this sickness.
  Now I will walk humbly throughout my
    years
    because of this anguish I have felt.
¹⁶ Lord, your discipline is good,
    for it leads to life and health.

37:36 Hebrew *When they.*

You have restored my health
and have allowed me to live!
[17] Yes, it was good for me to suffer this
anguish,
for you have rescued me from death
and have forgiven all my sins.
[18] For the dead cannot praise you;
they cannot raise their voices in praise.
Those who go down to destruction
can no longer hope in your faithfulness.
[19] Only the living can praise you as I do
today.
Each generation can make known your
faithfulness to the next.
[20] Think of it—the LORD has healed me!
I will sing his praises with instruments
every day of my life
in the Temple of the LORD.

[21]Isaiah had said to Hezekiah's servants, "Make an ointment from figs and spread it over the boil, and Hezekiah will recover."

[22]And Hezekiah had asked, "What sign will prove that I will go to the Temple of the LORD three days from now?"

ENVOYS FROM BABYLON

39 Soon after this, Merodach-baladan son of Baladan, king of Babylon, sent Hezekiah his best wishes and a gift. He had heard that Hezekiah had been very sick and that he had recovered. [2]Hezekiah welcomed the Babylonian envoys and showed them everything in his treasure-houses—the silver, the gold, the spices, and the aromatic oils. He also took them to see his armory and showed them all his other treasures—everything! There was nothing in his palace or kingdom that Hezekiah did not show them.

[3]Then Isaiah the prophet went to King Hezekiah and asked him, "What did those men want? Where were they from?"

Hezekiah replied, "They came from the distant land of Babylon."

[4]"What did they see in your palace?" asked Isaiah.

"They saw everything," Hezekiah replied. "I

---

*I must take time to worship
the One whose name I bear.*

OSWALD CHAMBERS

---

showed them everything I own—all my treasures."

[5]Then Isaiah said to Hezekiah, "Listen to this message from the LORD Almighty: [6]The time is coming when everything you have— all the treasures stored up by your ancestors— will be carried off to Babylon. Nothing will be left, says the LORD. [7]Some of your own descendants will be taken away into exile. They will become eunuchs who will serve in the palace of Babylon's king."

[8]Then Hezekiah said to Isaiah, "This message you have given me from the LORD is good." But the king was thinking, "At least there will be peace and security during my lifetime."

COMFORT FOR GOD'S PEOPLE

40 "Comfort, comfort my people," says your God. [2]"Speak tenderly to Jerusalem. Tell her that her sad days are gone and that her sins are pardoned. Yes, the LORD has punished her in full for all her sins."

[3]Listen! I hear the voice of someone shouting, "Make a highway for the LORD through the wilderness. Make a straight, smooth road through the desert for our God. [4]Fill the valleys and level the hills. Straighten out the curves and smooth off the rough spots. [5]Then the glory of the LORD will be revealed, and all people will see it together. The LORD has spoken!"

[6]A voice said, "Shout!"

I asked, "What should I shout?"

"Shout that people are like the grass that

dies away. Their beauty fades as quickly as the beauty of flowers in a field. [7]The grass withers, and the flowers fade beneath the breath of the LORD. And so it is with people. [8]The grass withers, and the flowers fade, but the word of our God stands forever."

[9]Messenger of good news, shout to Zion from the mountaintops! Shout louder to Jerusalem—do not be afraid. Tell the towns of Judah, "Your God is coming!" [10]Yes, the Sovereign LORD is coming in all his glorious power. He will rule with awesome strength. See, he brings his reward with him as he comes. [11]He will feed his flock like a shepherd. He will carry the lambs in his arms, holding them close to his heart. He will gently lead the mother sheep with their young.

[12]Who else has held the oceans in his hand? Who has measured off the heavens with his fingers? Who else knows the weight of the earth or has weighed out the mountains and the hills? [13]Who is able to advise the Spirit of the LORD? Who knows enough to be his teacher or counselor? [14]Has the LORD ever needed anyone's advice? Does he need instruction about what is good or what is best? [15]No, for all the nations of the world are nothing in comparison with him. They are but a drop in the bucket, dust on the scales. He picks up the islands as though they had no weight at all. [16]All Lebanon's forests do not contain sufficient fuel to consume a sacrifice large enough to honor him. All Lebanon's sacrificial animals would not make an offering worthy of our God. [17]The nations of the world are as nothing to him. In his eyes they are less than nothing—mere emptiness and froth.

[18]To whom, then, can we compare God? What image might we find to resemble him? [19]Can he be compared to an idol formed in a mold, overlaid with gold, and decorated with silver chains? [20]Or is a poor person's wooden idol better? Can God be compared to an idol that must be placed on a stand so it won't fall down?

[21]Have you never heard or understood? Are you deaf to the words of God—the words he gave before the world began? Are you so ignorant? [22]It is God who sits above the circle of the earth. The people below must seem to him like grasshoppers! He is the one who spreads out the heavens like a curtain and makes his tent from them. [23]He judges the great people of the world and brings them all to nothing. [24]They hardly get started, barely taking root, when he blows on them and their work withers. The wind carries them off like straw.

[25]"To whom will you compare me? Who is my equal?" asks the Holy One.

[26]Look up into the heavens. Who created all the stars? He brings them out one after another, calling each by its name. And he counts them to see that none are lost or have strayed away.

[27]O Israel, how can you say the LORD does not see your troubles? How can you say God refuses to hear your case? [28]Have you never heard or understood? Don't you know that the LORD is the everlasting God, the Creator of all the earth? He never grows faint or weary. No one can measure the depths of his understanding. [29]He gives power to those who are tired and worn out; he offers strength to the weak. [30]Even youths will become exhausted, and young men will give up. [31]But those who wait on the LORD will find new strength. They will fly high on wings like eagles. They will run and not grow weary. They will walk and not faint.

GOD'S HELP FOR ISRAEL

41 "Listen in silence before me, you lands beyond the sea. Bring your strongest arguments. Come now and speak. The court is ready for your case.

[2]"Who has stirred up this king from the east, who meets victory at every step? Who, indeed, but the LORD? He gives him victory over many nations and permits him to trample their kings underfoot. He puts entire armies to the sword. He scatters them in the wind with his bow. [3]He chases them away and goes on safely, though he is walking over unfamiliar ground. [4]Who has done such mighty

deeds, directing the affairs of the human race as each new generation marches by? It is I, the LORD, the First and the Last. I alone am he."

⁵The lands beyond the sea watch in fear. Remote lands tremble and mobilize for war. ⁶They encourage one another with the words, "Be strong!" ⁷The craftsmen rush to make new idols. The carver hurries the goldsmith, and the molder helps at the anvil. "Good," they say. "It's coming along fine." Carefully they join the parts together, then fasten the thing in place so it won't fall over.

⁸"But as for you, Israel my servant, Jacob my chosen one, descended from my friend Abraham, ⁹I have called you back from the ends of the earth so you can serve me. For I have chosen you and will not throw you away. ¹⁰Don't be afraid, for I am with you. Do not be dismayed, for I am your God. I will strengthen you. I will help you. I will uphold you with my victorious right hand.

¹¹"See, all your angry enemies lie there, confused and ashamed. Anyone who opposes you will die. ¹²You will look for them in vain. They will all be gone! ¹³I am holding you by your right hand—I, the LORD your God. And I say to you, 'Do not be afraid. I am here to help you. ¹⁴Despised though you are, O Israel, don't be afraid, for I will help you. I am the LORD, your Redeemer. I am the Holy One of Israel.' ¹⁵You will be a new threshing instrument with many sharp teeth. You will tear all your enemies apart, making chaff of mountains. ¹⁶You will toss them in the air, and the wind will blow them all away; a whirlwind will scatter them. And the joy of the LORD will fill you to overflowing. You will glory in the Holy One of Israel.

¹⁷"When the poor and needy search for water and there is none, and their tongues are parched from thirst, then I, the LORD, will answer them. I, the God of Israel, will never forsake them. ¹⁸I will open up rivers for them on high plateaus. I will give them fountains of water in the valleys. In the deserts they will find pools of water. Rivers fed by springs

will flow across the dry, parched ground. ¹⁹I will plant trees—cedar, acacia, myrtle, olive, cypress, fir, and pine—on barren land. ²⁰Everyone will see this miracle and understand that it is the LORD, the Holy One of Israel, who did it.

²¹"Can your idols make such claims as these? Let them come and show what they can do!" says the LORD, the King of Israel.* ²²"Let them try to tell us what happened long ago or what the future holds. ²³Yes, that's it! If you are gods, tell what will occur in the days ahead. Or perform a mighty miracle that will fill us with amazement and fear. Do something, whether good or bad! ²⁴But no! You are less than nothing and can do nothing at all. Anyone who chooses you becomes filthy, just like you!

²⁵"But I have stirred up a leader from the north and east. He will come against the nations and call on my name, and I will give him victory over kings and princes. He will trample them as a potter treads on clay.

²⁶"Who but I have told you this would happen? Who else predicted this, making you admit that he was right? No one else said a word! ²⁷I was the first to tell Jerusalem, 'Look! Help is on the way!' ²⁸Not one of your idols told you this. Not one gave any answer when I asked. ²⁹See, they are all foolish, worthless things. Your idols are all as empty as the wind.

THE LORD'S CHOSEN SERVANT

42 "Look at my servant, whom I strengthen. He is my chosen one, and I am pleased with him. I have put my Spirit upon him. He will reveal justice to the nations. ²He will be gentle—he will not shout or raise his voice in public. ³He will not crush those who are weak or quench the smallest hope. He will bring full justice to all who have been wronged. ⁴He will not stop until truth and righteousness prevail throughout the earth. Even distant lands beyond the sea will wait for his instruction."

⁵God, the LORD, created the heavens and

41:21 Hebrew *the King of Jacob.*

stretched them out. He created the earth and everything in it. He gives breath and life to everyone in all the world. And it is he who says, [6]"I, the LORD, have called you to demonstrate my righteousness. I will guard and support you, for I have given you to my people as the personal confirmation of my covenant with them. And you will be a light to guide all nations to me. [7]You will open the eyes of the blind and free the captives from prison. You will release those who sit in dark dungeons.

[8]"I am the LORD; that is my name! I will not give my glory to anyone else. I will not share my praise with carved idols. [9]Everything I prophesied has come true, and now I will prophesy again. I will tell you the future before it happens."

A SONG OF PRAISE TO THE LORD

[10] Sing a new song to the LORD!
    Sing his praises from the ends of the
        earth!
    Sing, all you who sail the seas,
        all you who live in distant coastlands.
[11] Join in the chorus, you desert towns;
        let the villages of Kedar rejoice!
    Let the people of Sela sing for joy;
        shout praises from the mountaintops!
[12] Let the coastlands glorify the LORD;
        let them sing his praise.
[13] The LORD will march forth like a mighty
        man;
    he will come out like a warrior, full of
        fury.
    He will shout his thundering battle cry,
        and he will crush all his enemies.
[14] He will say, "I have long been silent;
        yes, I have restrained myself.
    But now I will give full vent to my fury;
        I will gasp and pant like a woman giving
            birth.
[15] I will level the mountains and hills
        and bring a blight on all their greenery.
    I will turn the rivers into dry land
        and will dry up all the pools.
[16] I will lead blind Israel down a new path,
        guiding them along an unfamiliar way.

    I will make the darkness bright before
        them
        and smooth out the road ahead of them.
    Yes, I will indeed do these things;
        I will not forsake them.
[17] But those who trust in idols,
        calling them their gods—
        they will be turned away in shame.

ISRAEL'S FAILURE TO SEE AND LISTEN

[18]"Oh, how deaf and blind you are toward me! Why won't you listen? Why do you refuse to see? [19]Who in all the world is as blind as my own people, my servant? Who is as deaf as my messengers? Who is as blind as my chosen people, the servant of the LORD? [20]You see and understand what is right but refuse to act on it. You hear, but you don't really listen."

[21]The LORD has magnified his law and made it truly glorious. Through it he had planned to show the world that he is righteous. [22]But what a sight his people are, for they have been robbed, enslaved, imprisoned, and trapped. They are fair game for all and have no one to protect them. [23]Will not even one of you apply these lessons from the past and see the ruin that awaits you? [24]Who allowed Israel to be robbed and hurt? Was it not the LORD? It was the LORD whom we sinned against, for the people would not go where he sent them, nor would they obey his law. [25]That is why he poured out such fury on them and destroyed them in battle. They were set on fire and burned, but they still refused to understand.

THE SAVIOR OF ISRAEL

43 But now, O Israel, the LORD who created you says: "Do not be afraid, for I have ransomed you. I have called you by name; you are mine. [2]When you go through deep waters and great trouble, I will be with you. When you go through rivers of difficulty, you will not drown! When you walk through the fire of oppression, you will not be burned up; the flames will not consume you. [3]For I am the LORD, your God, the Holy One of

My Daily Worship

— *July 10* —

A NEW SONG FOR ALL NATIONS
ISAIAH 40:1–44:28

Sing a new song to the LORD! Sing his praises from the ends of the earth!
Sing, all you who sail the seas, all you who live in distant coastlands (42:10).

[i reflect]

"Missions is not the ultimate goal of the church. Worship is," declared John Piper in his book *Let the Nations Be Glad!* "Missions exists because worship doesn't."

Indeed, you could say that the goal of missions is to enculturate the worship of God in the widest possible way. Only when "new songs" are sung to God in the Yaminahuas language (Amazon), the Buhi language (Philippines), the Occitan language (Provence)—as well as in every other language and via every culture on earth—only then will the praise of God swell to its fullest extent, every harmonic layer adding to the richness of the chords. God deserves and desires no less.

Piper continued, "When this age is over, and the countless millions of the redeemed fall on their faces before the throne of God, missions will be no more. It is a temporary necessity. But worship abides forever."

In fact, we know that's just what will happen. After peeking into heaven, the apostle John reported, "I saw a vast crowd, too great to count, from every nation and tribe and people and language, standing in front of the throne and before the Lamb. They were clothed in white and held palm branches in their hands. And they were shouting with a mighty shout, 'Salvation comes from our God on the throne and from the Lamb!' " (Revelation 7:9–10). In John's vision, the angels added their Amen to the praise coming from the diverse crowd of human beings (verses 11–12). Let us do the same.

Today, look for ways to incorporate an aspect or style of another culture into your worship routine. Celebrate the diversity that God has given to us.

[i pray]

Amen! Blessing and glory and wisdom and thanksgiving and honor and
power and strength belong to our God forever and forever. Amen!

[i respond]

The next time you get a chance, ask a Christian of a different ethnicity to teach you a "new song" of praise from his or her culture. Also, in a personal worship time, ask God how he would have you help to spread his song of salvation around the globe.

Israel, your Savior. I gave Egypt, Ethiopia,* and Seba as a ransom for your freedom. ⁴Others died that you might live. I traded their lives for yours because you are precious to me. You are honored, and I love you.

⁵"Do not be afraid, for I am with you. I will gather you and your children from east and west ⁶and from north and south. I will bring my sons and daughters back to Israel from the distant corners of the earth. ⁷All who claim me as their God will come, for I have made them for my glory. It was I who created them."

⁸Bring out the people who have eyes but are blind, who have ears but are deaf. ⁹Gather the nations together! Which of their idols has ever foretold such things? Can any of them predict something even a single day in advance? Where are the witnesses of such predictions? Who can verify that they spoke the truth?

¹⁰"But you are my witnesses, O Israel!" says the LORD. "And you are my servant. You have been chosen to know me, believe in me, and understand that I alone am God. There is no other God; there never has been and never will be. ¹¹I am the LORD, and there is no other Savior. ¹²First I predicted your deliverance; I declared what I would do, and then I did it— I saved you. No foreign god has ever done this before. You are witnesses that I am the only God," says the LORD. ¹³"From eternity to eternity I am God. No one can oppose what I do. No one can reverse my actions."

THE LORD'S PROMISE OF VICTORY

¹⁴The LORD your Redeemer, the Holy One of Israel, says: "For your sakes I will send an invading army against Babylon. And the Babylonians* will be forced to flee in those ships they are so proud of. ¹⁵I am the LORD, your Holy One, Israel's Creator and King. ¹⁶I am the LORD, who opened a way through the waters, making a dry path through the sea. ¹⁷I called forth the mighty army of Egypt with all its chariots and horses. I drew them beneath the waves, and they drowned, their lives snuffed out like a smoldering candlewick.

¹⁸"But forget all that—it is nothing compared to what I am going to do. ¹⁹For I am about to do a brand-new thing. See, I have already begun! Do you not see it? I will make a pathway through the wilderness for my people to come home. I will create rivers for them in the desert! ²⁰The wild animals in the fields will thank me, the jackals and ostriches, too, for giving them water in the wilderness. Yes, I will make springs in the desert, so that my chosen people can be refreshed. ²¹I have made Israel for myself, and they will someday honor me before the whole world.

²²"But, my dear people, you refuse to ask for my help. You have grown tired of me! ²³You have not brought me lambs for burnt offerings. You have not honored me with sacrifices, though I have not burdened and wearied you with my requests for grain offerings and incense. ²⁴You have not brought me fragrant incense or pleased me with the fat from sacrifices. Instead, you have burdened me with your sins and wearied me with your faults.

²⁵"I—yes, I alone—am the one who blots out your sins for my own sake and will never think of them again. ²⁶Let us review the situation together, and you can present your case if you have one. ²⁷From the very beginning, your ancestors sinned against me—all your leaders broke my laws. ²⁸That is why I have disgraced your priests and assigned Israel a future of complete destruction* and shame.

44 "But now, listen to me, Jacob my servant, Israel my chosen one. ²The LORD who made you and helps you says: O Jacob, my servant, do not be afraid. O Israel,* my chosen one, do not fear. ³For I will give you abundant water to quench your thirst and to moisten your parched fields. And I will pour out my Spirit and my blessings on your children. ⁴They will thrive like watered grass, like willows on a riverbank. ⁵Some will proudly

---

43:3 Hebrew *Cush.* **43:14** Or *Chaldeans.* **43:28** The Hebrew term used here refers to the complete consecration of things or people to the LORD, either by destroying them or by giving them as an offering. **44:2** Hebrew *Jeshurun,* a term of endearment for Israel.

claim, 'I belong to the LORD.' Others will say, 'I am a descendant of Jacob.' Some will write the LORD's name on their hands and will take the honored name of Israel as their own.

THE FOOLISHNESS OF IDOLS

⁶"This is what the LORD, Israel's King and Redeemer, the LORD Almighty, says: I am the First and the Last; there is no other God. ⁷Who else can tell you what is going to happen in the days ahead? Let them tell you if they can and thus prove their power. Let them do as I have done since ancient times. ⁸Do not tremble; do not be afraid. Have I not proclaimed from ages past what my purposes are for you? You are my witnesses—is there any other God? No! There is no other Rock—not one!"

⁹How foolish are those who manufacture idols to be their gods. These highly valued objects are really worthless. They themselves are witnesses that this is so, for their idols neither see nor know. No wonder those who worship them are put to shame. ¹⁰Who but a fool would make his own god—an idol that cannot help him one bit! ¹¹All who worship idols will stand before the LORD in shame, along with all these craftsmen—mere humans—who claim they can make a god. Together they will stand in terror and shame.

¹²The blacksmith stands at his forge to make a sharp tool, pounding and shaping it with all his might. His work makes him hungry and thirsty, weak and faint. ¹³Then the wood-carver measures and marks out a block of wood, takes the tool, and carves the figure of a man. Now he has a wonderful idol that cannot even move from where it is placed! ¹⁴He cuts down cedars; he selects the cypress and the oak; he plants the cedar in the forest to be nourished by the rain. ¹⁵And after his care, he uses part of the wood to make a fire to warm himself and bake his bread. Then—yes, it's true—he takes the rest of it and makes himself a god for people to worship! He makes an idol and bows down and praises it! ¹⁶He burns part of the tree to roast his meat and to keep himself warm. ¹⁷Then he takes what's left and

---

Words of Worship

DOXOLOGY

Doxology—Greek *doxa* "glory," combined with *logos* "word, saying." The combination, meaning "an ascription of glory," does not occur in the New Testament, though both words occur frequently.

"Praise God, from whom all blessings flow!" Many Christian worshipers know these familiar words as "the Doxology." But Scripture includes other doxologies. Any outburst of praise and glory to God is considered a doxology. One of the fullest is David's: "Yours, O LORD, is the greatness, the power, the glory, the victory, and the majesty" (1 Chronicles 29:11). It finds an echo in the praise of every creature in John's vision of universal worship: "Blessing and honor and glory and power belong to the one sitting on the throne and to the Lamb forever and ever" (Revelation 5:13).

As we enter a time of personal worship, we're anxious to bring before God our needs and the needs of others. We want to offer expressions of love for our Savior and thanksgiving for what he's done for us. We expect to hear the Lord's word of wisdom and guidance. But let's frame all we bring to him in doxologies, and "give to the Lord the glory he deserves" (Psalm 96:8).

---

makes his god: a carved idol! He falls down in front of it, worshiping and praying to it. "Rescue me!" he says. "You are my god!"

¹⁸Such stupidity and ignorance! Their eyes are closed, and they cannot see. Their minds are shut, and they cannot think. ¹⁹The person who made the idol never stops to reflect, "Why, it's just a block of wood! I burned half of it for heat and used it to bake my bread and roast my meat. How can the rest of it be a god?

Should I bow down to worship a chunk of wood?" [20]The poor, deluded fool feeds on ashes. He is trusting something that can give him no help at all. Yet he cannot bring himself to ask, "Is this thing, this idol that I'm holding in my hand, a lie?"

RESTORATION FOR JERUSALEM

[21]"Pay attention, O Israel, for you are my servant. I, the LORD, made you, and I will not forget to help you. [22]I have swept away your sins like the morning mists. I have scattered your offenses like the clouds. Oh, return to me, for I have paid the price to set you free."

[23]Sing, O heavens, for the LORD has done this wondrous thing. Shout, O earth! Break forth into song, O mountains and forests and every tree! For the LORD has redeemed Jacob and is glorified in Israel.

[24]The LORD, your Redeemer and Creator, says: "I am the LORD, who made all things. I alone stretched out the heavens. By myself I made the earth and everything in it. [25]I am the one who exposes the false prophets as liars by causing events to happen that are contrary to their predictions. I cause wise people to give bad advice, thus proving them to be fools. [26]But I carry out the predictions of my prophets! When they say Jerusalem will be saved and the towns of Judah will be lived in once again, it will be done! [27]When I speak to the rivers and say, 'Be dry!' they will be dry. [28]When I say of Cyrus, 'He is my shepherd,' he will certainly do as I say. He will command that Jerusalem be rebuilt and that the Temple be restored."

CYRUS, THE LORD'S CHOSEN ONE

45 This is what the LORD says to Cyrus, his anointed one, whose right hand he will empower. Before him, mighty kings will be paralyzed with fear. Their fortress gates will be opened, never again to shut against him. [2]This is what the LORD says: "I will go before you, Cyrus, and level the mountains.* I will smash down gates of bronze and cut through

bars of iron. [3]And I will give you treasures hidden in the darkness—secret riches. I will do this so you may know that I am the LORD, the God of Israel, the one who calls you by name.

[4]"And why have I called you for this work? It is for the sake of Jacob my servant, Israel my chosen one. I called you by name when you did not know me. [5]I am the LORD; there is no other God. I have prepared you, even though you do not know me, [6]so all the world from east to west will know there is no other God. I am the LORD, and there is no other. [7]I am the one who creates the light and makes the darkness. I am the one who sends good times and bad times. I, the LORD, am the one who does these things. [8]Open up, O heavens, and pour out your righteousness. Let the earth open wide so salvation and righteousness can sprout up together. I, the LORD, created them.

[9]"Destruction is certain for those who argue with their Creator. Does a clay pot ever argue with its maker? Does the clay dispute with the one who shapes it, saying, 'Stop, you are doing it wrong!' Does the pot exclaim, 'How clumsy can you be!' [10]How terrible it would be if a newborn baby said to its father and mother, 'Why was I born? Why did you make me this way?'"

[11]This is what the LORD, the Creator and Holy One of Israel, says: "Do you question what I do? Do you give me orders about the work of my hands? [12]I am the one who made the earth and created people to live on it. With my hands I stretched out the heavens. All the millions of stars are at my command. [13]I will raise up Cyrus to fulfill my righteous purpose, and I will guide all his actions. He will restore my city and free my captive people—and not for a reward! I, the LORD Almighty, have spoken!"

FUTURE CONVERSION OF GENTILES

[14]This is what the LORD says: "The Egyptians, Ethiopians,* and Sabeans will be subject to you. They will come to you with all their merchandise, and it will all be yours. They will

---

45:2 As in Dead Sea Scrolls and Greek version; Masoretic Text reads *the swellings.*   45:14 Hebrew *Cushites.*

My Daily Worship

— *July 11* —

A LONG OBEDIENCE IN
THE SAME DIRECTION

ISAIAH 45:1–48:22

I will be your God throughout your lifetime—until your hair is white with age.
I made you, and I will care for you (46:4).

[i reflect]

There's something charming about a young believer who is full of enthusiasm for the Lord. But there's something truly inspiring about a man or woman who has walked with God through all the stages of life, and in old age radiates a mature Christian confidence based on experience.

Time magazine profiled Billy Graham in an article titled "A Christian in Winter." The evangelist, over decades, fulfilled his calling and upheld moral standards, and so he has become an example of consistent obedience to Christ for a lifetime. What sort of Christians will we be in the winter of life? There's no question that God will remain faithful to us, as Isaiah 46:4 assures us; but will we be faithful to him all the way to the end?

Ecclesiastes 12:1–7 teaches us to start remembering our Creator in our youth, laying the foundation for a lifelong relationship with God. Then we will receive the blessings of old age, as so beautifully expressed by the late Dean of Westminster Abbey and Master of Balliol, Rev. Jowett, in a letter to a friend:

> Though I am growing old, I maintain that the best part is yet to come—the time when one may see things more dispassionately and know oneself and others more truly, and perhaps be able to do more, and in religion rest centered in a very few simple truths.

> I do not want to ignore the other side, that one will not be able to see so well, or walk so far, or read so much. But there may be more peace within, more communion with God, more real light instead of distraction about many things, better relations with others, fewer mistakes.

The truth is our bodies may fail us, but God never will. The habit of daily worship can help bind us to Christ with bonds time can never weaken.

[i pray]

I want to build a relationship with you, Lord, that will weather every storm in my forecast. Work in me so that, should I reach old age, my wrinkly face will glow with the reflection of your presence and my dentured smile will make others wonder what secret I know.

[i respond]

Write, or visit if you can, the godliest elderly Christian you know. Ask this senior citizen of the kingdom, "What do you now know about having a relationship with Christ that you wish you had known when you were my age?"

follow you as prisoners in chains. They will fall to their knees in front of you and say, 'God is with you, and he is the only God.' "

[15]Truly, O God of Israel, our Savior, you work in strange and mysterious ways. [16]All who make idols will be humiliated and disgraced. [17]But the LORD will save the people of Israel with eternal salvation. They will never again be humiliated and disgraced throughout everlasting ages. [18]For the LORD is God, and he created the heavens and earth and put everything in place. He made the world to be lived in, not to be a place of empty chaos.

"I am the LORD," he says, "and there is no other. [19]I publicly proclaim bold promises. I do not whisper obscurities in some dark corner so no one can understand what I mean. And I did not tell the people of Israel* to ask me for something I did not plan to give. I, the LORD, speak only what is true and right.

[20]"Gather together and come, you fugitives from surrounding nations. What fools they are who carry around their wooden idols and pray to gods that cannot save! [21]Consult together, argue your case, and state your proofs that idol worship pays. Who made these things known long ago? What idol ever told you they would happen? Was it not I, the LORD? For there is no other God but me—a just God and a Savior—no, not one! [22]Let all the world look to me for salvation! For I am God; there is no other. [23]I have sworn by my own name, and I will never go back on my word: Every knee will bow to me, and every tongue will confess allegiance to my name."

[24]The people will declare, "The LORD is the source of all my righteousness and strength." And all who were angry with him will come to him and be ashamed. [25]In the LORD all the generations of Israel will be justified, and in him they will boast.

BABYLON'S FALSE GODS

46 The idols of Babylon, Bel and Nebo, are being hauled away on ox carts. But look! The beasts are staggering under the weight! [2]Both the idols and the ones carrying them are bowed down. The gods cannot protect the people, and the people cannot protect the gods. They go off into captivity together.

[3]"Listen to me, all you who are left in Israel. I created you and have cared for you since before you were born. [4]I will be your God throughout your lifetime—until your hair is white with age. I made you, and I will care for you. I will carry you along and save you.

[5]"To whom will you compare me? Who is my equal? [6]Some people pour out their silver and gold and hire a craftsman to make a god from it. Then they bow down and worship it! [7]They carry it around on their shoulders, and when they set it down, it stays there. It cannot even move! And when someone prays to it, there is no answer. It has no power to get anyone out of trouble.

[8]"Do not forget this, you guilty ones. [9]And do not forget the things I have done throughout history. For I am God—I alone! I am God, and there is no one else like me. [10]Only I can tell you what is going to happen even before it happens. Everything I plan will come to pass, for I do whatever I wish. [11]I will call a swift bird of prey from the east—a leader from a distant land who will come and do my bidding. I have said I would do it, and I will. [12]Listen to me, you stubborn, evil people! [13]For I am ready to set things right, not in the distant future, but right now! I am ready to save Jerusalem* and give my glory to Israel.

PREDICTION OF BABYLON'S FALL

47 "Come, Babylon, unconquered one, sit in the dust. For your days of glory, pomp, and honor have ended. O daughter of Babylonia,* never again will you be the lovely princess, tender and delicate. [2]Take heavy millstones and grind the corn. Remove your veil and strip off your robe. Expose yourself to public view. [3]You will be naked and burdened

---

45:19 Hebrew *of Jacob.*   46:13 Hebrew *Zion.*   47:1 Or *Chaldea;* also in 47:5.

with shame. I will take vengeance against you and will not negotiate."

⁴Our Redeemer, whose name is the LORD Almighty, is the Holy One of Israel.

⁵"O daughter of Babylonia, sit now in darkness and silence. Never again will you be known as the queen of kingdoms. ⁶For I was angry with my chosen people and began their punishment by letting them fall into your hands. But you, Babylon, showed them no mercy. You have forced even the elderly to carry heavy burdens. ⁷You thought, 'I will reign forever as queen of the world!' You did not care at all about my people or think about the consequences of your actions.

⁸"You are a pleasure-crazy kingdom, living at ease and feeling secure, bragging as if you were the greatest in the world! You say, 'I'm self-sufficient and not accountable to anyone! I will never be a widow or lose my children.' ⁹Well, those two things will come upon you in a moment: widowhood and the loss of your children. Yes, these calamities will come upon you, despite all your witchcraft and magic.

¹⁰"You felt secure in all your wickedness. 'No one sees me,' you said. Your 'wisdom' and 'knowledge' have caused you to turn away from me and claim, 'I am self-sufficient and not accountable to anyone!' ¹¹So disaster will overtake you suddenly, and you won't be able to charm it away. Calamity will fall upon you, and you won't be able to buy your way out. A catastrophe will arise so fast that you won't know what hit you.

¹²"Call out the demon hordes you have worshiped all these years. Ask them to help you strike terror into the hearts of people once again. ¹³You have more than enough advisers, astrologers, and stargazers. Let them stand up and save you from what the future holds. ¹⁴But they are as useless as dried grass burning in a fire. They cannot even save themselves! You will get no help from them at all. Their hearth is not a place to sit for warmth. ¹⁵And all your friends, those with whom you have done business since childhood, will slip away and disappear, unable to help.

GOD'S STUBBORN PEOPLE

48 "Listen to me, O family of Jacob, who are called by the name of Israel and born into the family of Judah. Listen, you who take oaths in the name of the LORD and call on the God of Israel. You don't follow through on any of your promises, ²even though you call yourself the holy city and talk about depending on the God of Israel, whose name is the LORD Almighty. ³Time and again I warned you about what was going to happen in the future. Then suddenly I took action, and all my predictions came true.

⁴"I know how stubborn and obstinate you are. Your necks are as unbending as iron. You are as hardheaded as bronze. ⁵That is why I told you ahead of time what I was going to do. That way, you could never say, 'My idols did it. My wooden image and metal god commanded it to happen!' ⁶You have heard my predictions and seen them fulfilled, but you refuse to admit it. Now I will tell you new things I have not mentioned before, secrets you have not yet heard. ⁷They are brand new, not things from the past. So you cannot say, 'We knew that all the time!'

⁸"Yes, I will tell you of things that are entirely new, for I know so well what traitors you are. You have been rebels from your earliest childhood, rotten through and through. ⁹Yet for my own sake and for the honor of my name, I will hold back my anger and not wipe you out. ¹⁰I have refined you but not in the way silver is refined. Rather, I have refined you in the furnace of suffering. ¹¹I will rescue you for my sake—yes, for my own sake! That way, the pagan nations will not be able to claim that their gods have conquered me. I will not let them have my glory!

FREEDOM FROM BABYLON

¹²"Listen to me, O family of Jacob, Israel my chosen one! I alone am God, the First and the Last. ¹³It was my hand that laid the foundations of the earth. The palm of my right hand spread out the heavens above. I spoke, and they came into being.

¹⁴"Have any of your idols ever told you this? Come, all of you, and listen: 'The LORD has chosen Cyrus as his ally. He will use him to put an end to the empire of Babylon, destroying the Babylonian* armies.' ¹⁵I have said it: I am calling Cyrus! I will send him on this errand and will help him succeed. ¹⁶Come closer and listen. I have always told you plainly what would happen so you would have no trouble understanding."

And now the Sovereign LORD and his Spirit have sent me with this message: ¹⁷"The LORD, your Redeemer, the Holy One of Israel, says: I am the LORD your God, who teaches you what is good and leads you along the paths you should follow. ¹⁸Oh, that you had listened to my commands! Then you would have had peace flowing like a gentle river and righteousness rolling like waves. ¹⁹Then you would have become as numerous as the sands along the seashore—too many to count! There would have been no need for your destruction."

²⁰Yet even now, be free from your captivity! Leave Babylon and the Babylonians,* singing as you go! Shout to the ends of the earth that the LORD has redeemed his servants, the people of Israel.* ²¹They were not thirsty when he led them through the desert. He divided the rock, and water gushed out for them to drink.

²²"But there is no peace for the wicked," says the LORD.

THE LORD'S SERVANT COMMISSIONED

49 Listen to me, all of you in far-off lands! The LORD called me before my birth; from within the womb he called me by name. ²He made my words of judgment as sharp as a sword. He has hidden me in the shadow of his hand. I am like a sharp arrow in his quiver. ³He said to me, "You are my servant, Israel, and you will bring me glory."

⁴I replied, "But my work all seems so useless! I have spent my strength for nothing and to no purpose at all. Yet I leave it all in the LORD's hand; I will trust God for my reward."

⁵And now the LORD speaks—he who formed me in my mother's womb to be his servant, who commissioned me to bring his people of Israel back to him. The LORD has honored me, and my God has given me strength. ⁶He says, "You will do more than restore the people of Israel to me. I will make you a light to the Gentiles, and you will bring my salvation to the ends of the earth."

⁷The LORD, the Redeemer and Holy One of Israel, says to the one who is despised and rejected by a nation, to the one who is the servant of rulers: "Kings will stand at attention when you pass by. Princes will bow low because the LORD has chosen you. He, the faithful LORD, the Holy One of Israel, chooses you."

PROMISES OF ISRAEL'S RESTORATION

⁸This is what the LORD says: "At just the right time, I will respond to you. On the day of salvation, I will help you. I will give you as a token and pledge to Israel. This will prove that I will reestablish the land of Israel and reassign it to its own people again. ⁹Through you I am saying to the prisoners of darkness, 'Come out! I am giving you your freedom!' They will be my sheep, grazing in green pastures and on hills that were previously bare. ¹⁰They will neither hunger nor thirst. The searing sun and scorching desert winds will not reach them anymore. For the LORD in his mercy will lead them beside cool waters. ¹¹And I will make my mountains into level paths for them. The highways will be raised above the valleys. ¹²See, my people will return from far away, from lands to the north and west, and from as far south as Egypt.*"

¹³Sing for joy, O heavens! Rejoice, O earth! Burst into song, O mountains! For the LORD has comforted his people and will have compassion on them in their sorrow.

48:14 Or *Chaldean*.   48:20a Or *the Chaldeans*.   48:20b Hebrew *his servant, Jacob*.   49:12 As in Dead Sea Scrolls, which read *from the region of Aswan*, which is in southern Egypt. Masoretic Text reads *from the region of Sinim*.

My Daily Worship

— *July 12* —

HIS LOVE IS HAND-WRITTEN

ISAIAH 49:1–52:12

See, I have written your name on my hand (49:16).

[i reflect]

"No doubt about it," they lamented. "God has deserted us. Probably even forgotten us."

The poster children for short-term memory disorder, the people of Israel thought for the umpteenth time that they, the Chosen People, had become the Rejected People. Or perhaps they had felt like Tevye in the musical *Fiddler on the Roof:* "It is said we are the chosen people. Could you please choose somebody else?"

Isaiah encourages them, "For the LORD has comforted his people and will have compassion on them in their sorrow" (49:13). God *has* comforted and *will* comfort. Then a small word in the next verse reveals much: *Yet.* Despite the history, despite the promises, "Yet Jerusalem says, 'The LORD has deserted us; the Lord has forgotten us.'" Does *Yet* describe your response to God's faithfulness and promises to comfort? How strongly do you claim he has forgotten you?

His response to the charge of forgetting his people is the same as it always was: "Never! . . . I have written your name on my hand" (49:15–16). What do we know of this hand? It is a hand of power, of fighting and smiting, but also of such comfort and protection. Along with the people of Israel and Isaiah, we can say: "He has hidden me in the shadow of his hand" (49:2); "I leave it all in the LORD's hand" (49:4); and we are "hidden safely within" his hand (51:16).

God does not simply know us "like the back of his hand." He turns over his hands and shows us the palms—the same palms that later bore the nail prints of crucifixion, the ultimate proof that he has not forgotten us.

May we lift up *our* hands today in gratitude and praise.

[i pray]

O God, I thank you for your hands. Hands of comfort, hands of protection, hands that bear the marks that prove that you have never deserted me and will never forget me.

[i respond]

Isaiah describes the coming Messiah who is both Sovereign Lord and Suffering Servant. Write down what actions or characteristics of hands help describe the two different roles. Meditate on those images.

[14]Yet Jerusalem* says, "The LORD has deserted us; the Lord has forgotten us."

[15]"Never! Can a mother forget her nursing child? Can she feel no love for a child she has borne? But even if that were possible, I would not forget you! [16]See, I have written your name on my hand. Ever before me is a picture of Jerusalem's walls in ruins. [17]Soon your descendants will come back, and all who are trying to destroy you will go away. [18]Look and see, for all your children will come back to you. As surely as I live," says the LORD, "they will be like jewels or bridal ornaments for you to display.

[19]"Even the most desolate parts of your abandoned land will soon be crowded with your people. Your enemies who enslaved you will be far away. [20]The generations born in exile will return and say, 'We need more room! It's crowded here!' [21]Then you will think to yourself, 'Who has given me all these descendants? For most of my children were killed, and the rest were carried away into exile. I was left here all alone. Who bore these children? Who raised them for me?'"

[22]This is what the Sovereign LORD says: "See, I will give a signal to the godless nations. They will carry your little sons back to you in their arms; they will bring your daughters on their shoulders. [23]Kings and queens will serve you. They will care for all your needs. They will bow to the earth before you and lick the dust from your feet. Then you will know that I am the LORD. Those who wait for me will never be put to shame."

[24]Who can snatch the plunder of war from the hands of a warrior? Who can demand that a tyrant* let his captives go? [25]But the LORD says, "The captives of warriors will be released, and the plunder of tyrants will be retrieved. For I will fight those who fight you, and I will save your children. [26]I will feed your enemies with their own flesh. They will be drunk with rivers of their own blood. All the world will know that I, the LORD, am your Savior and Redeemer, the Mighty One of Israel.*"

50 The LORD asks, "Did I sell you as slaves to my creditors? Is that why you are not here? Is your mother gone because I divorced her and sent her away? No, you went away as captives because of your sins. And your mother, too, was taken because of your sins. [2]Was I too weak to save you? Is that why the house is silent and empty when I come home? Is it because I have no power to rescue? No, that is not the reason! For I can speak to the sea and make it dry! I can turn rivers into deserts covered with dying fish. [3]I am the one who sends darkness out across the skies, bringing it to a state of mourning."

> *Worship is the intentional attitudes and actions of focusing on God.*
>
> BYRON SPRADLIN

THE LORD'S OBEDIENT SERVANT

[4]The Sovereign LORD has given me his words of wisdom, so that I know what to say to all these weary ones. Morning by morning he wakens me and opens my understanding to his will. [5]The Sovereign LORD has spoken to me, and I have listened. I do not rebel or turn away. [6]I give my back to those who beat me and my cheeks to those who pull out my beard. I do not hide from shame, for they mock me and spit in my face.

[7]Because the Sovereign LORD helps me, I will not be dismayed. Therefore, I have set my face like a stone, determined to do his will. And I know that I will triumph. [8]He who gives

49:14 Hebrew *Zion*. 49:24 As in Dead Sea Scrolls, Syriac version, and Latin Vulgate (also see 49:25); Masoretic Text reads *a righteous person*. 49:26 Hebrew *of Jacob*.

me justice is near. Who will dare to oppose me now? Where are my enemies? Let them appear! [9]See, the Sovereign LORD is on my side! Who will declare me guilty? All my enemies will be destroyed like old clothes that have been eaten by moths!

[10]Who among you fears the LORD and obeys his servant? If you are walking in darkness, without a ray of light, trust in the LORD and rely on your God. [11]But watch out, you who live in your own light and warm yourselves by your own fires. This is the reward you will receive from me: You will soon lie down in great torment.

A CALL TO TRUST THE LORD

51 "Listen to me, all who hope for deliverance—all who seek the LORD! Consider the quarry from which you were mined, the rock from which you were cut! [2]Yes, think about your ancestors Abraham and Sarah, from whom you came. Abraham was alone when I called him. But when I blessed him, he became a great nation."

[3]The LORD will comfort Israel* again and make her deserts blossom. Her barren wilderness will become as beautiful as Eden—the garden of the LORD. Joy and gladness will be found there. Lovely songs of thanksgiving will fill the air.

[4]"Listen to me, my people. Hear me, Israel, for my law will be proclaimed, and my justice will become a light to the nations. [5]My mercy and justice are coming soon. Your salvation is on the way. I will rule the nations. They will wait for me and long for my power. [6]Look up to the skies above, and gaze down on the earth beneath. For the skies will disappear like smoke, and the earth will wear out like a piece of clothing. The people of the earth will die like flies, but my salvation lasts forever. My righteous rule will never end!

[7]"Listen to me, you who know right from wrong and cherish my law in your hearts. Do not be afraid of people's scorn or their slan-derous talk. [8]For the moth will destroy them as it destroys clothing. The worm will eat away at them as it eats wool. But my righteousness will last forever. My salvation will continue from generation to generation."

[9]Wake up, LORD! Robe yourself with strength! Rouse yourself as in the days of old when you slew Egypt, the dragon of the Nile.* [10]Are you not the same today, the one who dried up the sea, making a path of escape when you saved your people? [11]Those who have been ransomed by the LORD will return to Jerusalem,* singing songs of everlasting joy. Sorrow and mourning will disappear, and they will be overcome with joy and gladness.

[12]"I, even I, am the one who comforts you. So why are you afraid of mere humans, who wither like the grass and disappear? [13]Yet you have forgotten the LORD, your Creator, the one who put the stars in the sky and established the earth. Will you remain in constant dread of human oppression? Will you continue to fear the anger of your enemies from morning till night? [14]Soon all you captives will be released! Imprisonment, starvation, and death will not be your fate! [15]For I am the LORD your God, who stirs up the sea, causing its waves to roar. My name is the LORD Almighty. [16]And I have put my words in your mouth and hidden you safely within my hand. I set all the stars in space and established the earth. I am the one who says to Israel, 'You are mine!'"

[17]Wake up, wake up, O Jerusalem! You have drunk enough from the cup of the LORD's fury. You have drunk the cup of terror, tipping out its last drops. [18]Not one of your children is left alive to help you or tell you what to do. [19]These two things have been your lot: desolation and destruction, famine and war. And who is left to sympathize? Who is left to comfort you? [20]For your children have fainted and lie in the streets, helpless as antelopes caught in a net. The LORD has poured out his fury; God has rebuked them.

51:3 Hebrew *Zion;* also in 51:16. **51:9** Hebrew *slew Rahab the dragon.* Rahab is the name of a mythical sea monster that represents chaos in ancient literature. The name is used here as a poetic name for Egypt. **51:11** Hebrew *Zion.*

²¹But now listen to this, you afflicted ones, who sit in a drunken stupor, though not from drinking wine. ²²This is what the Sovereign LORD, your God and Defender, says: "See, I am taking the terrible cup from your hands. You will drink no more of my fury. It is gone at last! ²³But I will put that cup into the hands of those who tormented you. I will give it to those who trampled you into the dust and walked on your backs."

DELIVERANCE FOR JERUSALEM

52 Wake up, wake up, O Zion! Clothe yourselves with strength. Put on your beautiful clothes, O holy city of Jerusalem, for unclean and godless people will no longer enter your gates. ²Rise from the dust, O Jerusalem. Remove the slave bands from your neck, O captive daughter of Zion. ³For this is what the LORD says: "When I sold you into exile, I received no payment. Now I can redeem you without paying for you."

⁴This is what the Sovereign LORD says: "Long ago my people went to live as resident foreigners in Egypt. Now they have been oppressed without cause by Assyria. ⁵And now, what is this?" asks the LORD. "Why are my people enslaved again? Those who rule them shout in exultation. My name is being blasphemed all day long. ⁶But I will reveal my name to my people, and they will come to know its power. Then at last they will recognize that it is I who speaks to them."

⁷How beautiful on the mountains are the feet of those who bring good news of peace and salvation, the news that the God of Israel* reigns! ⁸The watchmen shout and sing with joy, for before their very eyes they see the LORD bringing his people home to Jerusalem.* ⁹Let the ruins of Jerusalem break into joyful song, for the LORD has comforted his people. He has redeemed Jerusalem. ¹⁰The LORD will demonstrate his holy power before the eyes of all the nations. The ends of the earth will see the salvation of our God.

52:7 Hebrew *of Zion.* 52:8 Hebrew *to Zion.*

Words of Worship

FATHER

Father—Hebrew *'av;* Aramaic *'ab-ba';* Greek *pa-ter.* The Aramaic *'abba'* is an intense form of *'av,* and one of several Aramaic words preserved in the New Testament.

Some have claimed that when Jesus called God "Father," and taught his followers to do so, he revealed a tender side of God that the Israelite worshiper never knew. True, God isn't often called Father in the Old Testament. But the awareness that he is Father to his people undergirds the relationship of the covenant, so basic to biblical faith. Jesus built on what his people already knew about God, calling them back to an intimacy long clouded over by tradition. When the gospel message was translated into Greek, Christian worshipers still joined the Aramaic word to the Greek one, crying out "Abba Father" or "dear Father" (Galatians 4:6).

We shouldn't confuse God's fatherhood with the spineless situation-comedy fathers of today's media. In biblical times and cultures, a father was a figure of great authority. The burden of his family's welfare and reputation fell squarely on his shoulders, and his word counted in the lives of his children. Even the prodigal son realized the need for his father's protection. The wonder, as Jesus tells the story, is that this dignified father *ran* to greet his returning son—just as God yearns for his children to come home! In worship, we come home to him always when we pray, "Our Father in heaven . . ."

---

¹¹Go now, leave your bonds and slavery. Put Babylon behind you, with everything it represents, for it is unclean to you. You are the

LORD's holy people. Purify yourselves, you who carry home the vessels of the LORD. [12]You will not leave in a hurry, running for your lives. For the LORD will go ahead of you, and the God of Israel will protect you from behind.

THE LORD'S SUFFERING SERVANT

[13]See, my servant will prosper; he will be highly exalted. [14]Many were amazed when they saw him*—beaten and bloodied, so disfigured one would scarcely know he was a person. [15]And he will again startle* many nations. Kings will stand speechless in his presence. For they will see what they had not previously been told about; they will understand what they had not heard about.

53 Who has believed our message? To whom will the LORD reveal his saving power? [2]My servant grew up in the LORD's presence like a tender green shoot, sprouting from a root in dry and sterile ground. There was nothing beautiful or majestic about his appearance, nothing to attract us to him. [3]He was despised and rejected—a man of sorrows, acquainted with bitterest grief. We turned our backs on him and looked the other way when he went by. He was despised, and we did not care.

[4]Yet it was our weaknesses he carried; it was our sorrows* that weighed him down. And we thought his troubles were a punishment from God for his own sins! [5]But he was wounded and crushed for our sins. He was beaten that we might have peace. He was whipped, and we were healed! [6]All of us have strayed away like sheep. We have left God's paths to follow our own. Yet the LORD laid on him the guilt and sins of us all.

[7]He was oppressed and treated harshly, yet he never said a word. He was led as a lamb to the slaughter. And as a sheep is silent before the shearers, he did not open his mouth. [8]From prison and trial they led him away to his death. But who among the people realized that he was dying for their sins—that he was suffering their punishment? [9]He had done no wrong, and he never deceived anyone. But he was buried like a criminal; he was put in a rich man's grave.

[10]But it was the LORD's good plan to crush him and fill him with grief. Yet when his life is made an offering for sin, he will have a multitude of children, many heirs. He will enjoy a long life, and the LORD's plan will prosper in his hands. [11]When he sees all that is accomplished by his anguish, he will be satisfied. And because of what he has experienced, my righteous servant will make it possible for many to be counted righteous, for he will bear all their sins. [12]I will give him the honors of one who is mighty and great, because he exposed himself to death. He was counted among those who were sinners. He bore the sins of many and interceded for sinners.

FUTURE GLORY FOR JERUSALEM

54 "Sing, O childless woman! Break forth into loud and joyful song, O Jerusalem, even though you never gave birth to a child. For the woman who could bear no children now has more than all the other women," says the LORD. [2]"Enlarge your house; build an addition; spread out your home! [3]For you will soon be bursting at the seams. Your descendants will take over other nations and live in their cities.

[4]"Fear not; you will no longer live in shame. The shame of your youth and the sorrows of widowhood will be remembered no more, [5]for your Creator will be your husband. The LORD Almighty is his name! He is your Redeemer, the Holy One of Israel, the God of all the earth. [6]For the LORD has called you back from your grief—as though you were a young wife abandoned by her husband," says your God. [7]"For a brief moment I abandoned you, but with great compassion I will take you back. [8]In a moment of anger I turned my face away for a little while. But with everlasting love I will have compassion on you," says the LORD, your Redeemer.

52:14 As in Syriac version; Hebrew reads *you.* 52:15 Or *cleanse.* 53:4 Or *Yet it was our sicknesses he carried; it was our diseases.*

⁹"Just as I swore in the time of Noah that I would never again let a flood cover the earth and destroy its life, so now I swear that I will never again pour out my anger on you. ¹⁰For the mountains may depart and the hills disappear, but even then I will remain loyal to you. My covenant of blessing will never be broken," says the LORD, who has mercy on you.

¹¹"O storm-battered city, troubled and desolate! I will rebuild you on a foundation of sapphires and make the walls of your houses from precious jewels. ¹²I will make your towers of sparkling rubies and your gates and walls of shining gems. ¹³I will teach all your citizens, and their prosperity will be great. ¹⁴You will live under a government that is just and fair. Your enemies will stay far away; you will live in peace. Terror will not come near. ¹⁵If any nation comes to fight you, it will not be because I sent them to punish you. Your enemies will always be defeated because I am on your side. ¹⁶I have created the blacksmith who fans the coals beneath the forge and makes the weapons of destruction. And I have created the armies that destroy. ¹⁷But in that coming day, no weapon turned against you will succeed. And everyone who tells lies in court will be brought to justice. These benefits are enjoyed by the servants of the LORD; their vindication will come from me. I, the LORD, have spoken!

INVITATION TO THE LORD'S SALVATION

55 "Is anyone thirsty? Come and drink—even if you have no money! Come, take your choice of wine or milk—it's all free! ²Why spend your money on food that does not give you strength? Why pay for food that does you no good? Listen, and I will tell you where to get food that is good for the soul!

³"Come to me with your ears wide open. Listen, for the life of your soul is at stake. I am ready to make an everlasting covenant with you. I will give you all the mercies and unfailing love that I promised to David. ⁴He displayed my power by being my witness and a leader among the nations. ⁵You also will command the nations, and they will come running to obey, because I, the LORD your God, the Holy One of Israel, have made you glorious."

⁶Seek the LORD while you can find him. Call on him now while he is near. ⁷Let the people turn from their wicked deeds. Let them banish from their minds the very thought of doing wrong! Let them turn to the LORD that he may have mercy on them. Yes, turn to our God, for he will abundantly pardon.

⁸"My thoughts are completely different from yours," says the LORD. "And my ways are far beyond anything you could imagine. ⁹For just as the heavens are higher than the earth, so are my ways higher than your ways and my thoughts higher than your thoughts.

¹⁰"The rain and snow come down from the heavens and stay on the ground to water the earth. They cause the grain to grow, producing seed for the farmer and bread for the hungry. ¹¹It is the same with my word. I send it out, and it always produces fruit. It will accomplish all I want it to, and it will prosper everywhere I send it. ¹²You will live in joy and peace. The mountains and hills will burst into song, and the trees of the field will clap their hands! ¹³Where once there were thorns, cypress trees will grow. Where briers grew, myrtles will sprout up. This miracle will bring great honor to the LORD's name; it will be an everlasting sign of his power and love.

BLESSINGS FOR ALL NATIONS

56 "Be just and fair to all," says the LORD. "Do what is right and good, for I am coming soon to rescue you. ²Blessed are those who are careful to do this. Blessed are those who honor my Sabbath days of rest by refusing to work. And blessed are those who keep themselves from doing wrong.

³"And my blessings are for Gentiles, too, when they commit themselves to the LORD. Do not let them think that I consider them second-class citizens. And my blessings are also for the eunuchs. They are as much mine

My Daily Worship

— July 13 —

BEYOND OUR IMAGININGS

ISAIAH 52:13–55:13

"My thoughts are completely different from yours," says the LORD. "And my ways are far beyond anything you could imagine. For just as the heavens are higher than the earth, so are my ways higher than your ways and my thoughts higher than your thoughts" (55:8–9).

[i reflect]

In his article "God's Sovereignty: The Ultimate Question," John Strumbo wrote, "At human birth the brain weighs, on average, 14 ounces. It usually reaches its maximum size at age 15 (proving the size of the brain has nothing to do with intelligence). At its maximum size, the brain weighs an average of 46 ounces, slightly less than three pounds. In liquid measurement, that's about a Big Gulp from the soda machine at the local gas station."

And with this brain, Strumbo continues, "We're going to comprehend the infinite, decipher the mysteries of the millenniums, we're going to answer all the questions? Right!"

Put in those terms, it's absurd to think that we can comprehend the greatness and vastness of God. Yet we try. Much of the time we tend to think of God as simply a large human. He's big; we're little. He thinks huge thoughts and does great things; we think little thoughts and do little things. Wrong. No matter how large we make God, or how small we make ourselves, we get a distorted picture.

Honest, humble, and heartfelt worship often begins at the moment we recognize and acknowledge the differences between God and us. We have the amazing honor of being made in God's image, which means we are a reflection of God, not miniature gods. We, though creatures, can get to know and worship our Creator. We reflect God; but there's no one else like him.

"My thoughts are completely different from yours." "My ways are far beyond anything that you could imagine." That is the God that we worship. That is the God who *is* in control. Today, allow that image of an all-knowing and all-powerful, yet all-loving God, to fill and guide you.

[i pray]

Your ways, O God, are so much higher than mine. Your thoughts, O God, dwarf anything that I or anyone could think. Thank you for the way your Word rains down on my life. I thank you most of all for the seed of salvation that you imagined, planted, and brought to harvest in me.

[i respond]

Read through Isaiah 55 again, jotting down particular phrases that strike you as God's unique thoughts. Ask God to show you at least one moment in your life today where you can use or apply his thoughts to that situation.

as anyone else. ⁴For I say this to the eunuchs who keep my Sabbath days holy, who choose to do what pleases me and commit their lives to me: ⁵I will give them—in my house, within my walls—a memorial and a name far greater than the honor they would have received by having sons and daughters. For the name I give them is an everlasting one. It will never disappear!

> *Surely that which occupies the total time and energies of heaven must be a fitting pattern for earth.*
>
> PAUL E. BILLHEIMER

⁶"I will also bless the Gentiles who commit themselves to the LORD and serve him and love his name, who worship him and do not desecrate the Sabbath day of rest, and who have accepted his covenant. ⁷I will bring them also to my holy mountain of Jerusalem and will fill them with joy in my house of prayer. I will accept their burnt offerings and sacrifices, because my Temple will be called a house of prayer for all nations. ⁸For the Sovereign LORD, who brings back the outcasts of Israel, says: I will bring others, too, besides my people Israel."

SINFUL LEADERS CONDEMNED

⁹Come, wild animals of the field! Come, wild animals of the forest! Come and devour my people! ¹⁰For the leaders of my people—the LORD's watchmen, his shepherds—are blind to every danger. They are like silent watchdogs that give no warning when danger comes. They love to lie around, sleeping and dreaming. ¹¹And they are as greedy as dogs, never satisfied. They are stupid shepherds, all fol-

lowing their own path, all of them intent on personal gain.

¹²"Come," they say. "We will get some wine and have a party. Let's all get drunk. Let this go on and on, and tomorrow will be even better."

57 The righteous pass away; the godly often die before their time. And no one seems to care or wonder why. No one seems to understand that God is protecting them from the evil to come. ²For the godly who die will rest in peace.

IDOLATROUS WORSHIP CONDEMNED

³"But you—come here, you witches' children, you offspring of adulterers and prostitutes! ⁴Whom do you mock, making faces and sticking out your tongues? You children of sinners and liars! ⁵You worship your idols with great passion beneath every green tree. You slaughter your children as human sacrifices down in the valleys, under overhanging rocks. ⁶Your gods are the smooth stones in the valleys. You worship them with drink offerings and grain offerings. They, not I, are your inheritance. Does all this make me happy? ⁷You have committed adultery on the mountaintops by worshiping idols there, and so you have been unfaithful to me. ⁸Behind closed doors, you have set up your idols and worship them instead of me. This is adultery, for you are loving these idols instead of loving me. You have climbed right into bed with these detestable gods. ⁹You have given olive oil and perfume to Molech* as your gift. You have traveled far, even into the world of the dead,* to find new gods to love. ¹⁰You grew weary in your search, but you never gave up. You strengthened yourself and went on. ¹¹Why were you more afraid of them than of me? How is it that you don't even remember me or think about me? Is it because I have not corrected you that you have no fear of me?

¹²"Now I will expose your so-called good

57:9a Or *to the king.* 57:9b Hebrew *into Sheol.*

deeds that you consider so righteous. None of them will benefit or save you. ¹³Let's see if your idols can do anything for you when you cry to them for help. They are so helpless that a breath of wind can knock them down! But whoever trusts in me will possess the land and inherit my holy mountain. ¹⁴I will say, 'Rebuild the road! Clear away the rocks and stones so my people can return from captivity.'"

GOD FORGIVES THE REPENTANT

¹⁵The high and lofty one who inhabits eternity, the Holy One, says this: "I live in that high and holy place with those whose spirits are contrite and humble. I refresh the humble and give new courage to those with repentant hearts. ¹⁶For I will not fight against you forever; I will not always show my anger. If I did, all people would pass away—all the souls I have made. ¹⁷I was angry and punished these greedy people. I withdrew myself from them, but they went right on sinning. ¹⁸I have seen what they do, but I will heal them anyway! I will lead them and comfort those who mourn. ¹⁹Then words of praise will be on their lips. May they have peace, both near and far, for I will heal them all," says the LORD. ²⁰"But those who still reject me are like the restless sea. It is never still but continually churns up mire and dirt. ²¹There is no peace for the wicked," says my God.

TRUE AND FALSE WORSHIP

58 "Shout with the voice of a trumpet blast. Tell my people Israel* of their sins! ²Yet they act so pious! They come to the Temple every day and seem delighted to hear my laws. You would almost think this was a righteous nation that would never abandon its God. They love to make a show of coming to me and asking me to take action on their behalf. ³'We have fasted before you!' they say. 'Why aren't you impressed? We have done much penance, and you don't even notice it!'

"I will tell you why! It's because you are living for yourselves even while you are fasting. You keep right on oppressing your workers. ⁴What good is fasting when you keep on fighting and quarreling? This kind of fasting will never get you anywhere with me. ⁵You humble yourselves by going through the motions of penance, bowing your heads like a blade of grass in the wind. You dress in sackcloth and cover yourselves with ashes. Is this what you call fasting? Do you really think this will please the LORD?

⁶"No, the kind of fasting I want calls you to free those who are wrongly imprisoned and to stop oppressing those who work for you. Treat them fairly and give them what they earn. ⁷I want you to share your food with the hungry and to welcome poor wanderers into your homes. Give clothes to those who need them, and do not hide from relatives who need your help.

⁸"If you do these things, your salvation will come like the dawn. Yes, your healing will come quickly. Your godliness will lead you forward, and the glory of the LORD will protect you from behind. ⁹Then when you call, the LORD will answer. 'Yes, I am here,' he will quickly reply.

"Stop oppressing the helpless and stop making false accusations and spreading vicious rumors! ¹⁰Feed the hungry and help those in trouble. Then your light will shine out from the darkness, and the darkness around you will be as bright as day. ¹¹The LORD will guide you continually, watering your life when you are dry and keeping you healthy, too. You will be like a well-watered garden, like an ever-flowing spring. ¹²Your children will rebuild the deserted ruins of your cities. Then you will be known as the people who rebuild their walls and cities.

¹³"Keep the Sabbath day holy. Don't pursue your own interests on that day, but enjoy the Sabbath and speak of it with delight as the LORD's holy day. Honor the LORD in everything you do, and don't follow your own

58:1 Hebrew *Jacob*.

desires or talk idly. If you do this, [14]the LORD will be your delight. I will give you great honor and give you your full share of the inheritance I promised to Jacob, your ancestor. I, the LORD, have spoken!"

WARNINGS AGAINST SIN

59 Listen! The LORD is not too weak to save you, and he is not becoming deaf. He can hear you when you call. [2]But there is a problem—your sins have cut you off from God. Because of your sin, he has turned away and will not listen anymore. [3]Your hands are the hands of murderers, and your fingers are filthy with sin. Your mouth is full of lies, and your lips are tainted with corruption.

[4]No one cares about being fair and honest. Their lawsuits are based on lies. They spend their time plotting evil deeds and then doing them. [5]They spend their time and energy spinning evil plans that end up in deadly actions. [6]They cheat and shortchange everyone. Nothing they do is productive; all their activity is filled with sin. Violence is their trademark. [7]Their feet run to do evil, and they rush to commit murder. They think only about sinning. Wherever they go, misery and destruction follow them. [8]They do not know what true peace is or what it means to be just and good. They continually do wrong, and those who follow them cannot experience a moment's peace.

[9]It is because of all this evil that deliverance is far from us. That is why God doesn't punish those who injure us. No wonder we are in darkness when we expected light. No wonder we are walking in the gloom. [10]No wonder we grope like blind people and stumble along. Even at brightest noontime, we fall down as though it were dark. No wonder we are like corpses when compared to vigorous young men! [11]We growl like hungry bears; we moan like mournful doves. We look for justice, but it is nowhere to be found. We look to be rescued, but it is far away from us. [12]For our sins

are piled up before God and testify against us. Yes, we know what sinners we are. [13]We know that we have rebelled against the LORD. We have turned our backs on God. We know how unfair and oppressive we have been, carefully planning our deceitful lies. [14]Our courts oppose people who are righteous, and justice is nowhere to be found. Truth falls dead in the streets, and fairness has been outlawed. [15]Yes, truth is gone, and anyone who tries to live a godly life is soon attacked.

The LORD looked and was displeased to find that there was no justice. [16]He was amazed to see that no one intervened to help the oppressed. So he himself stepped in to save them with his mighty power and justice. [17]He put on righteousness as his body armor and placed the helmet of salvation on his head. He clothed himself with the robes of vengeance and godly fury. [18]He will repay his enemies for their evil deeds. His fury will fall on his foes in distant lands. [19]Then at last they will respect and glorify the name of the LORD throughout the world. For he will come like a flood tide driven by the breath of the LORD.

[20]"The Redeemer will come to Jerusalem,*" says the LORD, "to buy back those in Israel* who have turned from their sins. [21]And this is my covenant with them," says the LORD. "My Spirit will not leave them, and neither will these words I have given you. They will be on your lips and on the lips of your children and your children's children forever. I, the LORD, have spoken!

FUTURE GLORY FOR JERUSALEM

60 "Arise, Jerusalem! Let your light shine for all the nations to see! For the glory of the LORD is shining upon you. [2]Darkness as black as night will cover all the nations of the earth, but the glory of the LORD will shine over you. [3]All nations will come to your light. Mighty kings will come to see your radiance.

[4]"Look and see, for everyone is coming home! Your sons are coming from distant

59:20a Hebrew *to Zion.* **59:20b** Hebrew *in Jacob.*

My Daily Worship

— July 14 —

THAT OLD SIN PROBLEM

ISAIAH 56:1-59:21

But there is a problem—your sins have cut you off from God. Because of your sin,
he has turned away and will not listen anymore (59:2).

[i reflect]

He seems to have finally lost patience with his wayward children. About time, some said. He is ready to cut them out of the will. They say they want to visit, but he will likely turn them away.

Such was the relationship between God and a young man of high intelligence but low morals, who was born in A.D. 354 in what is now known as Algeria. He struggled with God intellectually, as a student and teacher of rhetoric and philosophy. He struggled with God spiritually, as the son of a devout Christian and protégé of Saint Ambrose, the great bishop of Milan.

His name was Augustine. His writings are legendary, as was his leadership of the early church following his baptism, ordination as a priest, and eventual consecration as the bishop of Hippo. Augustine understood as few others have the enormity of the "problem" Isaiah described in the key verse above—"your sins have cut you off from God." When Augustine sinned, he knew God had turned away from him; indeed, his most famous book is the autobiographical *Confessions.*

We can join Augustine in his yearnings to God: "My soul is constricted. Expand it, so that you can enter in. It is in ruins, restore it. It will offend your eyes. I confess and know this, but who will cleanse it? Whom can I cry out to but to you? Cleanse me from my secret sins, O Lord."

What reason is there for hope that God will save us? Isaiah's words ring eternally true: "Listen! The LORD is not too weak to save you, and he is not becoming deaf. He can hear you when you call" (59:1).

Call to him now. He will turn back. He will listen.

[i pray]

Father God, I know that my sins have cut me off from you. I turn to you; please turn
back to me. I pray that you will listen and help me back into your presence.

[i respond]

Read about the life of Saint Augustine in his *Confessions* or the many biographical accounts in books, encyclopedias, and on the Internet. Thank God that he offers you the same listening ear and restorative grace as he did to Augustine.

lands; your little daughters will be carried home. ⁵Your eyes will shine, and your hearts will thrill with joy, for merchants from around the world will come to you. They will bring you the wealth of many lands. ⁶Vast caravans of camels will converge on you, the camels of Midian and Ephah. From Sheba they will bring gold and incense for the worship of the LORD. ⁷The flocks of Kedar will be given to you, and the rams of Nebaioth will be brought for my altars. In that day I will make my Temple glorious.

⁸"And what do I see flying like clouds to Israel, like doves to their nests? ⁹They are the ships of Tarshish, reserved to bring the people of Israel home. They will bring their wealth with them, and it will bring great honor to the LORD your God, the Holy One of Israel, for he will fill you with splendor.

¹⁰"Foreigners will come to rebuild your cities. Kings and rulers will send you aid. For though I have destroyed you in my anger, I will have mercy on you through my grace. ¹¹Your gates will stay open around the clock to receive the wealth of many lands. The kings of the world will be led as captives in a victory procession. ¹²For the nations that refuse to be your allies will be destroyed. ¹³The glory of Lebanon will be yours—the forests of cypress, fir, and pine—to beautify my sanctuary. My Temple will be glorious!

¹⁴"The children of your tormentors will come and bow before you. Those who despised you will kiss your feet. They will call you the City of the LORD, and Zion of the Holy One of Israel.

¹⁵"Though you were once despised and hated and rebuffed by all, you will be beautiful forever. You will be a joy to all generations, for I will make you so. ¹⁶Powerful kings and mighty nations will bring the best of their goods to satisfy your every need. You will know at last that I, the LORD, am your Savior and Redeemer, the Mighty One of Israel.* ¹⁷I will exchange your bronze for gold, your iron for silver, your wood for bronze, and your stones for iron. Peace and righteousness will be your leaders! ¹⁸Violence will disappear from your land; the desolation and destruction of war will end. Salvation will surround you like city walls, and praise will be on the lips of all who enter there.

¹⁹"No longer will you need the sun or moon to give you light, for the LORD your God will be your everlasting light, and he will be your glory. ²⁰The sun will never set; the moon will not go down. For the LORD will be your everlasting light. Your days of mourning will come to an end. ²¹All your people will be righteous. They will possess their land forever, for I will plant them there with my own hands in order to bring myself glory. ²²The smallest family will multiply into a large clan. The tiniest group will become a mighty nation. I, the LORD, will bring it all to pass at the right time."

GOOD NEWS FOR THE OPPRESSED

61 The Spirit of the Sovereign LORD is upon me, because the LORD has appointed me to bring good news to the poor. He has sent me to comfort the brokenhearted and to announce that captives will be released and prisoners will be freed.* ²He has sent me to tell those who mourn that the time of the LORD's favor has come,* and with it, the day of God's anger against their enemies. ³To all who mourn in Israel,* he will give beauty for ashes, joy instead of mourning, praise instead of despair. For the LORD has planted them like strong and graceful oaks for his own glory.

⁴They will rebuild the ancient ruins, repairing cities long ago destroyed. They will revive them, though they have been empty for many generations. ⁵Foreigners will be your servants. They will feed your flocks and plow your fields and tend your vineyards. ⁶You will be called priests of the LORD, ministers of our God. You will be fed with the treasures of the

60:16 Hebrew *of Jacob.* 61:1 Greek version reads *and the blind will see.* 61:2 Or *to proclaim the acceptable year of the LORD.* 61:3 Hebrew *in Zion.*

Words of Worship

PROPHECY

Prophecy—Hebrew *hit-nab-be'* "to prophesy"; *na-vi'* "prophet"; Greek *pro-phe-teu-o* "to prophesy"; *pro-phe-tes* "prophet"; *pro-phe-tei-a* "prophecy."

The idea of prophecy is often associated with predicting future events, but in Scripture, it has a broader meaning. A prophet is not a "foreteller" but a "forthteller"—one who hears from God and speaks forth his word of judgment or consolation. What the Lord speaks through his prophets is not just for tomorrow, but for today.

Paul says, "One who prophesies is helping others grow in the Lord, encouraging and comforting them" (1 Corinthians 14:3). Prophecy is a sign that God is present (1 Corinthians 14:25). As we let God's Word flow into us and through us, even the unbeliever will be moved to acknowledge and worship him. Every believer is to seek all the gifts of the Holy Spirit, Paul reminds us, but "especially the gift of prophecy" (1 Corinthians 14:1).

clothing of salvation and draped me in a robe of righteousness. I am like a bridegroom in his wedding suit or a bride with her jewels. ¹¹The Sovereign LORD will show his justice to the nations of the world. Everyone will praise him! His righteousness will be like a garden in early spring, filled with young plants springing up everywhere.

ISAIAH'S PRAYER FOR JERUSALEM

62 Because I love Zion, because my heart yearns for Jerusalem, I cannot remain silent. I will not stop praying for her until her righteousness shines like the dawn, and her salvation blazes like a burning torch.

²The nations will see your righteousness. Kings will be blinded by your glory. And the LORD will give you a new name. ³The LORD will hold you in his hands for all to see—a splendid crown in the hands of God. ⁴Never again will you be called the Godforsaken City* or the Desolate Land.* Your new name will be the City of God's Delight* and the Bride of God,* for the LORD delights in you and will claim you as his own. ⁵Your children will care for you with joy, O Jerusalem, just as a young man cares for his bride. Then God will rejoice over you as a bridegroom rejoices over his bride.

⁶O Jerusalem, I have posted watchmen on your walls; they will pray to the LORD day and night for the fulfillment of his promises. Take no rest, all you who pray. ⁷Give the LORD no rest until he makes Jerusalem the object of praise throughout the earth. ⁸The LORD has sworn to Jerusalem by his own strength: "I will never again hand you over to your enemies. Never again will foreign warriors come and take away your grain and wine. ⁹You raised it, and you will keep it, praising the LORD. Within the courtyards of the Temple, you yourselves will drink the wine that you have pressed."

¹⁰Go out! Prepare the highway for my people to return! Smooth out the road; pull out

nations and will boast in their riches. ⁷Instead of shame and dishonor, you will inherit a double portion of prosperity and everlasting joy.

⁸"For I, the LORD, love justice. I hate robbery and wrongdoing. I will faithfully reward my people for their suffering and make an everlasting covenant with them. ⁹Their descendants will be known and honored among the nations. Everyone will realize that they are a people the LORD has blessed."

¹⁰I am overwhelmed with joy in the LORD my God! For he has dressed me with the

---

62:4a Hebrew *Azubah,* which means "forsaken." 62:4b Hebrew *Shemamah,* which means "desolate." 62:4c Hebrew *Hephzibah,* which means "my delight is in her." 62:4d Hebrew *Beulah,* which means "married."

the boulders; raise a flag for all the nations to see. ¹¹The LORD has sent this message to every land: "Tell the people of Israel,* 'Look, your Savior is coming. See, he brings his reward with him as he comes.' " ¹²They will be called the Holy People and the People Redeemed by the LORD. And Jerusalem will be known as the Desirable Place and the City No Longer Forsaken.

JUDGMENT AGAINST THE LORD'S ENEMIES

63 Who is this who comes from Edom, from the city of Bozrah, with his clothing stained red? Who is this in royal robes, marching in the greatness of his strength?

"It is I, the LORD, announcing your salvation! It is I, the LORD, who is mighty to save!"

²Why are your clothes so red, as if you have been treading out grapes?

³"I have trodden the winepress alone; no one was there to help me. In my anger I have trampled my enemies as if they were grapes. In my fury I have trampled my foes. It is their blood that has stained my clothes. ⁴For the time has come for me to avenge my people, to ransom them from their oppressors. ⁵I looked, but no one came to help my people. I was amazed and appalled at what I saw. So I executed vengeance alone; unaided, I passed down judgment. ⁶I crushed the nations in my anger and made them stagger and fall to the ground."

PRAISE FOR DELIVERANCE

⁷I will tell of the LORD's unfailing love. I will praise the LORD for all he has done. I will rejoice in his great goodness to Israel, which he has granted according to his mercy and love. ⁸He said, "They are my very own people. Surely they will not be false again." And he became their Savior. ⁹In all their suffering he also suffered, and he personally rescued them. In his love and mercy he redeemed them. He lifted them up and carried them through all the years.

¹⁰But they rebelled against him and grieved his Holy Spirit. That is why he became their enemy and fought against them. ¹¹Then they remembered those days of old when Moses led his people out of Egypt. They cried out, "Where is the one who brought Israel through the sea, with Moses as their shepherd? Where is the one who sent his Holy Spirit to be among his people? ¹²Where is the one whose power divided the sea before them, when Moses lifted up his hand, establishing his reputation forever? ¹³Where is the one who led them through the bottom of the sea? They were like fine stallions racing through the desert, never stumbling. ¹⁴As with cattle going down into a peaceful valley, the Spirit of the LORD gave them rest. You led your people, LORD, and gained a magnificent reputation."

PRAYER FOR MERCY AND PARDON

¹⁵LORD, look down from heaven and see us from your holy, glorious home. Where is the passion and the might you used to show on our behalf? Where are your mercy and compassion now? ¹⁶Surely you are still our Father! Even if Abraham and Jacob* would disown us, LORD, you would still be our Father. You are our Redeemer from ages past. ¹⁷LORD, why have you allowed us to turn from your path? Why have you given us stubborn hearts so we no longer fear you? Return and help us, for we are your servants and your special possession. ¹⁸How briefly your holy people possessed the holy place, and now our enemies have destroyed it. ¹⁹LORD, why do you treat us as though we never belonged to you? Why do you act as though we had never been known as your people?

64 Oh, that you would burst from the heavens and come down! How the mountains would quake in your presence! ²As fire causes wood to burn and water to boil, your coming would make the nations trem-

62:11 Hebrew *Tell the daughter of Zion.* 63:16 Hebrew *Israel.*

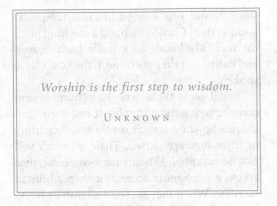

Worship is the first step to wisdom.

UNKNOWN

ble. Then your enemies would learn the reason for your fame! ³When you came down long ago, you did awesome things beyond our highest expectations. And oh, how the mountains quaked! ⁴For since the world began, no ear has heard, and no eye has seen a God like you, who works for those who wait for him! ⁵You welcome those who cheerfully do good, who follow godly ways.

But we are not godly. We are constant sinners, so your anger is heavy on us. How can people like us be saved? ⁶We are all infected and impure with sin. When we proudly display our righteous deeds, we find they are but filthy rags. Like autumn leaves, we wither and fall. And our sins, like the wind, sweep us away. ⁷Yet no one calls on your name or pleads with you for mercy. Therefore, you have turned away from us and turned us over to our sins.

⁸And yet, LORD, you are our Father. We are the clay, and you are the potter. We are all formed by your hand. ⁹Oh, don't be so angry with us, LORD. Please don't remember our sins forever. Look at us, we pray, and see that we are all your people.

¹⁰Your holy cities are destroyed; even Jerusalem is a desolate wilderness. ¹¹The holy, beautiful Temple where our ancestors praised you has been burned down, and all the things of beauty are destroyed. ¹²After all this, LORD, must you still refuse to help us? Will you continue to be silent and punish us?

65:9 Hebrew *remnant of Jacob.*

JUDGMENT AND FINAL SALVATION

65 The LORD says, "People who never before inquired about me are now asking about me. I am being found by people who were not looking for me. To them I have said, 'I am here!'

²"I opened my arms to my own people all day long, but they have rebelled. They follow their own evil paths and thoughts. ³All day long they insult me to my face by worshiping idols in their sacred gardens. They burn incense on the rooftops of their homes. ⁴At night they go out among the graves and secret places to worship evil spirits. They also eat pork and other forbidden foods. ⁵Yet they say to each other, 'Don't come too close or you will defile me! I am holier than you!' They are a stench in my nostrils, an acrid smell that never goes away.

⁶"Look, my decree is written out in front of me: I will not stand silent; I will repay them in full! Yes, I will repay them—⁷both for their own sins and for those of their ancestors," says the LORD. "For they also burned incense on the mountains and insulted me on the hills. I will pay them back in full!

⁸"But I will not destroy them all," says the LORD. "For just as good grapes are found among a cluster of bad ones (and someone will say, 'Don't throw them all away—there are some good grapes there!'), so I will not destroy all Israel. For I still have true servants there. ⁹I will preserve a remnant of the people of Israel* and of Judah to possess my land. Those I choose will inherit it and serve me there. ¹⁰For my people who have searched for me, the plain of Sharon will again be filled with flocks, and the valley of Achor will be a place to pasture herds.

¹¹"But because the rest of you have forsaken the LORD and his Temple and worship the gods of Fate and Destiny, ¹²I will 'destine' you to the sword. All of you will bow before the executioner, for when I called, you did not answer. When I spoke, you did not listen. You deliberately sinned—before my very eyes—and chose to do what you know I despise."

¹³Therefore, this is what the Sovereign LORD says: "You will starve, but my servants will eat. You will be thirsty, but they will drink. You will be sad and ashamed, but they will rejoice. ¹⁴You will cry in sorrow and despair, while my servants sing for joy. ¹⁵Your name will be a curse word among my people, for the Sovereign LORD will destroy you and call his true servants by another name. ¹⁶All who invoke a blessing or take an oath will do so by the God of truth. For I will put aside my anger and forget the evil of earlier days.

¹⁷"Look! I am creating new heavens and a new earth—so wonderful that no one will even think about the old ones anymore. ¹⁸Be glad; rejoice forever in my creation! And look! I will create Jerusalem as a place of happiness. Her people will be a source of joy. ¹⁹I will rejoice in Jerusalem and delight in my people. And the sound of weeping and crying will be heard no more.

²⁰"No longer will babies die when only a few days old. No longer will adults die before they have lived a full life. No longer will people be considered old at one hundred! Only sinners will die that young! ²¹In those days, people will live in the houses they build and eat the fruit of their own vineyards. ²²It will not be like the past, when invaders took the houses and confiscated the vineyards. For my people will live as long as trees and will have time to enjoy their hard-won gains. ²³They will not work in vain, and their children will not be doomed to misfortune. For they are people blessed by the LORD, and their children, too, will be blessed. ²⁴I will answer them before they even call to me. While they are still talking to me about their needs, I will go ahead and answer their prayers! ²⁵The wolf and lamb will feed together. The lion will eat straw like the ox. Poisonous snakes will strike no more. In those days, no one will be hurt or destroyed on my holy mountain. I, the LORD, have spoken!"

66 This is what the LORD says: "Heaven is my throne, and the earth is my footstool. Could you ever build me a temple as good as that? Could you build a dwelling place for me? ²My hands have made both heaven and earth, and they are mine. I, the LORD, have spoken!

"I will bless those who have humble and contrite hearts, who tremble at my word. ³But those who choose their own ways, delighting in their sins, are cursed. Their offerings will not be accepted. When such people sacrifice an ox, it is no more acceptable than a human sacrifice. When they sacrifice a lamb or bring an offering of grain, it is as bad as putting a dog or the blood of a pig on the altar! When they burn incense, it is as if they had blessed an idol. ⁴I will send great troubles against them—all the things they feared. For when I called, they did not answer. When I spoke, they did not listen. They deliberately sinned—before my very eyes—and chose to do what they know I despise."

⁵Hear this message from the LORD, and tremble at his words: "Your close relatives hate you and throw you out for being loyal to my name. 'Let the LORD be honored!' they scoff. 'Be joyful in him!' But they will be put to shame. ⁶What is all the commotion in the city? What is that terrible noise from the Temple? It is the voice of the LORD taking vengeance against his enemies.

⁷"Before the birth pains even begin, Jerusalem gives birth to a son. ⁸Who has ever seen or heard of anything as strange as this? Has a nation ever been born in a single day? Has a country ever come forth in a mere moment? But by the time Jerusalem's* birth pains begin, the baby will be born; the nation will come forth. ⁹Would I ever bring this nation to the point of birth and then not deliver it?" asks the LORD. "No! I would never keep this nation from being born," says your God.

¹⁰"Rejoice with Jerusalem! Be glad with her, all you who love her and mourn for her. ¹¹Delight in Jerusalem! Drink deeply of her glory even as an infant drinks at its mother's generous breasts. ¹²Peace and prosperity will

66:8 Hebrew *Zion's.*

My Daily Worship

— July 15 —

A Name of Fame

Isaiah 60:1–66:24

"As surely as my new heavens and earth will remain, so will you always be my people, with a name that will never disappear," says the LORD. (66:22).

[i reflect]

After a battle in which his namesake had fled from a skirmish, Alexander the Great approached the young soldier and rebuked him, "Either change your name or live up to it."

Names, particularly family names, carry great import. Passing on the family name—be it in a business or simply an enduring lineage—has been important since history began. For some, it can even become an obsession: "It's the end of an era. If he doesn't produce a son, he's the last of the line. The family name dies with him."

Names are important to God, too. Consider the emphasis given in Scripture to *the* name: "At the name of Jesus . . . the name that is above all names" (Ephesians 2:9–10). To conclude the prophecy given through Isaiah, however, God chose to emphasize not his own name but that of his people. They will have "a name that will never disappear."

By reaffirming that they will "always be my people," God is assuring them that through the Messiah that would be born, they will always be his family. The family name will never die out, never disappear.

"Look ahead!" the Father beckons. "God's Son is far greater than the angels, just as the name God gave him is far greater than their names" (Hebrews 1:4). "Look ahead further still," the Father seems to say, "to that new heaven and earth. Believers will have the Son's and the Father's name written on their foreheads!" (Revelation 14:1).

Always part of God's people. Always one of his children. Always with his name—written not as earthly names on birth certificates and tombstones, but on your forehead . . . and on your heart, that you may praise him wholeheartedly.

How will you honor God's name today?

[i pray]

Father God, I praise you and thank you for calling me by your name, for giving me a future and a hope and a family here on earth and in heaven.

[i respond]

Write down a few of the characteristics, personality traits, or events that are associated with your family's name. Which cause you pride and a sense of well-being? Which cause you shame? How do these compare with associations of having God's name as your heritage?

overflow Jerusalem like a river," says the LORD. "The wealth of the nations will flow to her. Her children will be nursed at her breasts, carried in her arms, and treated with love. [13]I will comfort you there as a child is comforted by its mother."

[14]When you see these things, your heart will rejoice. Vigorous health will be yours! Everyone will see the good hand of the LORD on his people—and his anger against his enemies. [15]See, the LORD is coming with fire, and his swift chariots of destruction roar like a whirlwind. He will bring punishment with the fury of his anger and the flaming fire of his hot rebuke. [16]The LORD will punish the world by fire and by his sword, and many will be killed by the LORD.

[17]"Those who 'purify' themselves in a sacred garden, feasting on pork and rats and other forbidden meats, will come to a terrible end," says the LORD. [18]"I can see what they are doing, and I know what they are thinking. So I will gather all nations and peoples together, and they will see my glory. [19]I will perform a sign among them. And I will send those who sur-vive to be messengers to the nations—to Tarshish, to the Libyans* and Lydians* (who are famous as archers), to Tubal and Greece,* and to all the lands beyond the sea that have not heard of my fame or seen my glory. There they will declare my glory to the nations. [20]They will bring the remnant of your people back from every nation. They will bring them to my holy mountain in Jerusalem as an offering to the LORD. They will ride on horses, in chariots and wagons, and on mules and camels," says the LORD. [21]"And I will appoint some of those who return to be my priests and Levites. I, the LORD, have spoken!

[22]"As surely as my new heavens and earth will remain, so will you always be my people, with a name that will never disappear," says the LORD. [23]"All humanity will come to worship me from week to week and from month to month. [24]And as they go out, they will see the dead bodies of those who have rebelled against me. For the worms that devour them will never die, and the fire that burns them will never go out. All who pass by will view them with utter horror."

66:19a As in some Greek manuscripts, which read *Put* [Libya]; Hebrew reads *Pul*.   66:19b Hebrew *Lud*.   66:19c Hebrew *Javan*.

Jeremiah

Come back to me, and I will heal your wayward hearts (3:22).

Taking Drastic Measures

"Do that one more time, and I'll . . . !" A mother's angry words can be heard above the din of a small child's howling and whining. It's a scene that more often than not repeats itself in a crowded grocery store, or while waiting in the doctor's office, or in any place not conducive to children. Usually, we don't know how the situation gets resolved—whether the mother finally appeases the child, the child acquiesces, or if discipline is administered. Sometimes drastic measures are required for misbehavior.

That's the subject of the book of Jeremiah—drastic measures for a nation's misbehavior. Throughout Jeremiah's lifetime, the prophet had the unenviable task of telling the people of God that God was going to punish them for their sinful lifestyles. Jeremiah warned that Israel's evil ways—especially their cruelty to the poor, the needy, and the helpless (5:28–29)—would not go unpunished. God was preparing a powerful army to come and destroy Jerusalem (6:1–2), and to carry its people off as captives if they did not change their sinful behaviors.

When our hearts have become "hard ground" (4:3), and we have lost all sense of what is right and wrong, the unpleasant truth is that God may use drastic measures to cause us to repent. That's the bad news. The good news, however, is when we do repent and turn from our sins, God assures us that he will heal our wayward hearts and write his laws on them (31:33).

Jeremiah had a difficult message for the people of his day, but he also looked ahead to the time when the Righteous One (23:5) would come. "His name is the LORD Almighty. He will defend [his people] and give them rest" (50:34). Jeremiah speaks for all of us when he asks God to "correct me, LORD, but please be gentle" (10:24). If we are wise, we will accept correction, and return to love and worship the Lord.

Worship Moments

- "Plow up the hard ground of your hearts!" True worship begins with repentance (4:3).

- Jeremiah sings a hymn of praise to God (51:15–19).

- God is: "merciful" (3:12); "just and righteous" (9:24); the "Hope of Israel" (14:8); "your lawyer to plead your case" (51:36). Jeremiah calls God: "my strength and fortress, my refuge" (16:19); and "my hope" (17:17).

1 These are the words of Jeremiah son of Hilkiah, one of the priests from Anathoth, a town in the land of Benjamin. ²The LORD first gave messages to Jeremiah during the thirteenth year of King Josiah's reign in Judah.* ³He continued to give messages throughout the reign of Josiah's son, King Jehoiakim, until the eleventh year of King Zedekiah's reign in Judah. In August of that year,* the people of Jerusalem were taken away as captives.

JEREMIAH'S CALL AND FIRST VISIONS

⁴The LORD gave me a message. He said, ⁵"I knew you before I formed you in your mother's womb. Before you were born I set you apart and appointed you as my spokesman to the world."

⁶"O Sovereign LORD," I said, "I can't speak for you! I'm too young!"

⁷"Don't say that," the LORD replied, "for you must go wherever I send you and say whatever I tell you. ⁸And don't be afraid of the people, for I will be with you and take care of you. I, the LORD, have spoken!"

⁹Then the LORD touched my mouth and said, "See, I have put my words in your mouth! ¹⁰Today I appoint you to stand up against nations and kingdoms. You are to uproot some and tear them down, to destroy and overthrow them. You are to build others up and plant them."

¹¹Then the LORD said to me, "Look, Jeremiah! What do you see?"

And I replied, "I see a branch from an almond tree."

¹²And the LORD said, "That's right, and it means that I am watching,* and I will surely carry out my threats of punishment."

¹³Then the LORD spoke to me again and asked, "What do you see now?"

And I replied, "I see a pot of boiling water, tipping from the north."

¹⁴"Yes," the LORD said, "for terror from the north will boil out on the people of this land. ¹⁵Listen! I am calling the armies of the kingdoms of the north to come to Jerusalem. They will set their thrones at the gates of the city. They will attack its walls and all the other towns of Judah. ¹⁶I will pronounce judgment on my people for all their evil—for deserting me and worshiping other gods. Yes, they worship idols that they themselves have made!

¹⁷"Get up and get dressed. Go out, and tell them whatever I tell you to say. Do not be afraid of them, or I will make you look foolish in front of them. ¹⁸For see, today I have made you immune to their attacks. You are strong like a fortified city that cannot be captured, like an iron pillar or a bronze wall. None of the kings, officials, priests, or people of Judah will be able to stand against you. ¹⁹They will try, but they will fail. For I am with you, and I will take care of you. I, the LORD, have spoken!"

THE LORD'S CASE AGAINST HIS PEOPLE

2 The LORD gave me another message. He said, ²"Go and shout in Jerusalem's streets: 'This is what the LORD says: I remember how eager you were to please me as a young bride long ago, how you loved me and followed me even through the barren wilderness. ³In those days Israel was holy to the LORD, the first of my children.* All who harmed my people were considered guilty, and disaster fell upon them. I, the LORD, have spoken!'"

⁴Listen to the word of the LORD, people of Jacob—all you families of Israel! ⁵This is what the LORD says: "What sin did your ancestors find in me that led them to stray so far? They worshiped foolish idols, only to become foolish themselves. ⁶They did not ask, 'Where is the LORD who brought us safely out of Egypt

---

1:2 The thirteenth year of Josiah's reign was 627 B.C. 1:3 Hebrew *In the fifth month,* of the Hebrew calendar. A number of events in Jeremiah can be cross-checked with dates in surviving Babylonian records and related accurately to our modern calendar. This month in the eleventh year of Zedekiah's reign occurred in August and September 586 B.C. Also see 52:12 and the note there. 1:12 The Hebrew word for "watching" sounds like the word for "almond tree." 2:3 Hebrew *the firstfruits of his harvest.*

My Daily Worship

— July 16 —

FROM THE START

JEREMIAH 1:1 – 4:31

I knew you before I formed you in your mother's womb. Before
you were born I set you apart and appointed you
as my spokesman to the world (1:5).

[i reflect]

Dr. Lloyd Ogilvie, longtime chaplain of the United States Senate, once preached a sermon called "When God First Thought of You." In this memorable message, Dr. Ogilvie contended that each of us existed in the mind of our Creator before we were conceived in our mother's womb. His point was this: When God first decided that we would be given life on earth, there was a purpose in his plan. It wasn't random. It was by design.

That's the same principle presented by Jeremiah in the opening chapter of his book. God has a personal knowledge of those he has created. His love is specific and personal. He knows intimately those he loves and his knowledge is complete. From the very point of conception, a loving God is aware of what makes each person special.

In light of that keen awareness, God weaves together a meaningful plan that is based on the needs and gifts of each person. Jeremiah's assignment was to speak prophetically to the unresponsive nation of Israel. For you, his call to love your neighbor might seem equally as challenging. But it is just as meaningful because God knows what you can uniquely accomplish for his sake.

Realizing that God knows all about us—the bad as well as the good—can be troubling. Nothing about your thoughts, attitudes, and actions escapes his all-seeing eyes. This may call for personal confession of sin. But understanding that God knows all might just as easily prompt you to praise him. Imagine—the Creator of the Universe understands you like none other—and still loves you. Amazing! So whether you need to confess or praise him, do it now. Personal worship includes both.

[i pray]

Lord, your knowledge of me is both troubling and comforting. Forgive me for attempting
to rationalize my sins as if I could fool you. Help me to be aware of you as I make
choices each day. And thanks, Lord, for guiding my path in life
according to the unique way you wired me. Amen.

[i respond]

On an index card, jot down some of your abilities and interests. Once you have made your list, reflect on the fact that God gave you the particular bents and gifts you have because he wants to use them. Thank him for the fact that he knows and understands you like no one else.

and led us through the barren wilderness—a land of deserts and pits, of drought and death, where no one lives or even travels?'

[7]"And when I brought you into a fruitful land to enjoy its bounty and goodness, you defiled my land and corrupted the inheritance I had promised you. [8]The priests did not ask, 'Where is the LORD?' The judges ignored me, the rulers turned against me, and the prophets spoke in the name of Baal, wasting their time on nonsense. [9]Therefore, I will bring my case against you and will keep on accusing you, even against your children's children in the years to come. I, the LORD, have spoken!

[10]"Go west to the land of Cyprus*; go east to the land of Kedar. Think about what you see there. See if anyone has ever heard of anything as strange as this. [11]Has any nation ever exchanged its gods for another god, even though its gods are nothing? Yet my people have exchanged their glorious God* for worthless idols! [12]The heavens are shocked at such a thing and shrink back in horror and dismay, says the LORD. [13]For my people have done two evil things: They have forsaken me—the fountain of living water. And they have dug for themselves cracked cisterns that can hold no water at all!

THE RESULTS OF ISRAEL'S SIN

[14]"Why has Israel become a nation of slaves? Why has she been carried away as plunder? [15]Lions have roared against her. The land has been destroyed, and the cities are now in ruins. No one lives in them anymore. [16]Egyptians, marching from their cities of Memphis* and Tahpanhes, have utterly destroyed Israel's glory and power. [17]And you have brought this on yourselves by rebelling against the LORD your God when he wanted to lead you and show you the way!

[18]"What have you gained by your alliances with Egypt and Assyria? What good to you are the waters of the Nile* and the Euphrates*? [19]Your own wickedness will punish you. You will see what an evil, bitter thing it is to forsake the LORD your God, having no fear of him. I, the Lord, the LORD Almighty, have spoken! [20]Long ago I broke your yoke and tore away the chains of your slavery, but still you would not obey me. On every hill and under every green tree, you have prostituted yourselves by bowing down to idols.

[21]"How could this happen? When I planted you, I chose a vine of the purest stock—the very best. How did you grow into this corrupt wild vine? [22]No amount of soap or lye can make you clean. You are stained with guilt that cannot be washed away. I, the Sovereign LORD, have spoken!

ISRAEL, AN UNFAITHFUL WIFE

[23]"You say, 'That's not true! We haven't worshiped the images of Baal!' But how can you say that? Go and look in any valley in the land! Face the awful sins you have done. You are like a restless female camel, desperate for a male! [24]You are like a wild donkey, sniffing the wind at mating time. Who can restrain your lust? Those who desire you do not even need to search, for you come running to them! [25]Why do you refuse to turn from all this running after other gods? But you say, 'Don't waste your breath. I have fallen in love with these foreign gods, and I can't stop loving them now!'

[26]"Like a thief, Israel feels shame only when she gets caught. Kings, officials, priests, and prophets—all are alike in this. [27]To an image carved from a piece of wood they say, 'You are my father.' To an idol chiseled out of stone they say, 'You are my mother.' They turn their backs on me, but in times of trouble they cry out for me to save them! [28]Why don't you call on these gods you have made? When danger comes, let them save you if they can! For you have as many gods as there are cities and towns in Judah. [29]Why do you accuse me of doing wrong? You are the ones who have rebelled, says the LORD. [30]I have punished your children, but it did them no good. They still

2:10 Hebrew *Kittim.* 2:11 Hebrew *their Glory.* 2:16 Hebrew *Noph.* 2:18a Hebrew *of Shihor,* a branch of the Nile River. 2:18b Hebrew *the river.*

refuse to obey. You yourselves have killed your prophets as a lion kills its prey.

[31]"O my people, listen to the words of the LORD! Have I been like a desert to Israel? Have I been to them a land of darkness? Why then do my people say, 'At last we are free from God! We won't have anything to do with him anymore!' [32]Does a young woman forget her jewelry? Does a bride hide her wedding dress? No! Yet for years on end my people have forgotten me.

[33]"How you plot and scheme to win your lovers. The most experienced prostitute could learn from you! [34]Your clothing is stained with the blood of the innocent and the poor. You killed them even though they didn't break into your houses! [35]And yet you say, 'I haven't done anything wrong. Surely he isn't angry with me!' Now I will punish you severely because you claim you have not sinned.

[36]"First here, then there—you flit from one ally to another asking for help. But your new friends in Egypt will let you down, just as Assyria did before. [37]In despair, you will be led into exile with your hands on your heads, for the LORD has rejected the nations you trust. You will not succeed despite their help.

3 "If a man divorces a woman and she marries someone else, he is not to take her back again, for that would surely corrupt the land. But you have prostituted yourself with many lovers, says the LORD. Yet I am still calling you to come back to me.

[2]"Look all around you. Is there anywhere in the entire land where you have not been defiled by your adulteries? You sit like a prostitute beside the road waiting for a client. You sit alone like a nomad in the desert. You have polluted the land with your prostitution and wickedness. [3]That is why even the spring rains have failed. For you are a prostitute and are completely unashamed. [4]Yet you say to me, 'Father, you have been my guide since the days of my youth. [5]Surely you won't be angry about such a little thing! Surely you can forget it!' So you talk, and keep right on doing all the evil you can."

Words of Worship

FELLOWSHIP, SHARING

Fellowship, Sharing —Hebrew *re-gesh* "throng"; Greek *koi-no-ni-a* "communion, sharing, participation, fellowship." The Hebrew word describes a crowd, such as a group gathering for a festival.

The Christian life is one of fellowship with brothers and sisters in the faith, through which we build up one another. But sometimes our *fellowship* becomes "fallowship," where nothing grows; or "shallowship," a superficial getting together that doesn't create lasting loyalties. The psalm writer discovered this difference, to his sorrow. "What good fellowship we enjoyed," he said of his friend, "as we walked together to the house of God" (Psalm 55:14)—but his friend had turned against him.

In the New Testament, the word *koinonia* describes fellowship among Christians, but it's hard to translate. It means something deeper than just getting together with friends, or even sharing with others. It describes a family relationship of intimacy and bonding. We can't enjoy this kind of fellowship at the human level alone, for first of all "our fellowship is with the Father and with his Son, Jesus Christ" (1 John 1:3), a communion in the Holy Spirit (Philippians 2:1). We have been brought into this deep sharing only through the cross of Christ, the covenant made by his blood (1 Corinthians 10:16).

JUDAH FOLLOWS ISRAEL'S EXAMPLE

[6]During the reign of King Josiah, the LORD said to me, "Have you seen what fickle Israel

does? Like a wife who commits adultery, Israel has worshiped other gods on every hill and under every green tree. ⁷I thought that after she had done all this she would return to me. But she did not come back. And though her faithless sister Judah saw this, ⁸she paid no attention. She saw that I had divorced faithless Israel and sent her away. But now Judah, too, has left me and given herself to prostitution. ⁹Israel treated it all so lightly—she thought nothing of committing adultery by worshiping idols made of wood and stone. So now the land has been greatly defiled. ¹⁰But in spite of all this, her faithless sister Judah has never sincerely returned to me. She has only pretended to be sorry," says the LORD.

HOPE FOR WAYWARD ISRAEL

¹¹Then the LORD said to me, "Even faithless Israel is less guilty than treacherous Judah! ¹²Therefore, go and say these words to Israel,* 'This is what the LORD says: O Israel, my faithless people, come home to me again, for I am merciful. I will not be angry with you forever. ¹³Only acknowledge your guilt. Admit that you rebelled against the LORD your God and committed adultery against him by worshiping idols under every green tree. Confess that you refused to follow me. I, the LORD, have spoken!'"

¹⁴"Return home, you wayward children," says the LORD, "for I am your husband. I will bring you again to the land of Israel*—one from here and two from there, from wherever you are scattered. ¹⁵And I will give you leaders after my own heart, who will guide you with knowledge and understanding.

¹⁶"And when your land is once more filled with people," says the LORD, "you will no longer wish for 'the good old days' when you possessed the Ark of the LORD's covenant. Those days will not be missed or even thought about, and there will be no need to rebuild the Ark. ¹⁷In that day Jerusalem will be known as The Throne of the LORD. All nations will come there to honor the LORD. They will no

longer stubbornly follow their own evil desires. ¹⁸In those days the people of Judah and Israel will return together from exile in the north. They will return to the land I gave their ancestors as an inheritance forever.

¹⁹"I thought to myself, 'I would love to treat you as my own children!' I wanted nothing more than to give you this beautiful land— the finest inheritance in the world. I looked forward to your calling me 'Father,' and I thought you would never turn away from me again. ²⁰But you have betrayed me, you people of Israel! You have been like a faithless wife who leaves her husband," says the LORD.

²¹Voices are heard high on the windswept mountains, the weeping and pleading of Israel's people. For they have forgotten the LORD their God and wandered far from his ways.

²²"My wayward children," says the LORD, "come back to me, and I will heal your wayward hearts."

"Yes, we will come," the people reply, "for you are the LORD our God. ²³Our worship of idols and our religious orgies on the hills and mountains are completely false. Only in the LORD our God will Israel ever find salvation. ²⁴From childhood we have watched as everything our ancestors worked for—their flocks and herds, their sons and daughters—was squandered on a delusion. ²⁵Let us now lie down in shame and dishonor, for we and our ancestors have always sinned against the LORD our God. We have never obeyed him."

4 "O Israel, come back to me," says the LORD. "If you will throw away your detestable idols and go astray no more, ²and if you will swear by my name alone, and begin to live good, honest lives and uphold justice, then you will be a blessing to the nations of the world, and all people will come and praise my name."

COMING JUDGMENT AGAINST JUDAH

³This is what the LORD says to the people of Judah and Jerusalem: "Plow up the hard

3:12 Hebrew *toward the north.*   3:14 Hebrew *to Zion.*

ground of your hearts! Do not waste your good seed among thorns. ⁴Cleanse your minds and hearts before the LORD, or my anger will burn like an unquenchable fire because of all your sins.

⁵"Shout to Jerusalem and to all Judah! Tell them to sound the alarm throughout the land: 'Run for your lives! Flee to the fortified cities!' ⁶Send a signal toward Jerusalem*: 'Flee now! Do not delay!' For I am bringing terrible destruction upon you from the north."

⁷A lion stalks from its den, a destroyer of nations. And it is headed for your land! Your

> *Not only must our relationship to God be right, but the outward expression of that relationship must also be right.*
>
> OSWALD CHAMBERS

towns will lie in ruins, empty of people. ⁸So put on clothes of mourning and weep with broken hearts, for the fierce anger of the LORD is still upon us.

⁹"In that day," says the LORD, "the king and the officials will tremble in fear. The priests and the prophets will be struck with horror."

¹⁰Then I said, "O Sovereign LORD, the people have been deceived by what you said, for you promised peace for Jerusalem. Yet the sword is even now poised to strike them dead!"

¹¹The time is coming when the LORD will say to the people of Jerusalem, "A burning wind is blowing in from the desert. It is not a gentle breeze useful for winnowing grain. ¹²It is a roaring blast sent by me! Now I will pronounce your destruction!"

¹³Our enemy rushes down on us like a storm wind! His chariots are like whirlwinds; his horses are swifter than eagles. How terrible it will be! Our destruction is sure! ¹⁴O Jerusalem, cleanse your hearts that you may be saved. How long will you harbor your evil thoughts? ¹⁵From Dan and the hill country of Ephraim, your destruction has been announced.

¹⁶"Warn the surrounding nations and announce to Jerusalem: 'The enemy is coming from a distant land, raising a battle cry against the towns of Judah. ¹⁷They surround Jerusalem like watchmen surrounding a field, for my people have rebelled against me,'" says the LORD. ¹⁸"Your own actions have brought this upon you. This punishment is a bitter dose of your own medicine. It has pierced you to the heart!"

JEREMIAH WEEPS FOR HIS PEOPLE

¹⁹My heart, my heart—I writhe in pain! My heart pounds within me! I cannot be still. For I have heard the blast of enemy trumpets and the roar of their battle cries. ²⁰Waves of destruction roll over the land, until it lies in complete desolation. Suddenly, every tent is destroyed; in a moment, every shelter is crushed. ²¹How long must this go on? How long must I be surrounded by war and death?

²²"My people are foolish and do not know me," says the LORD. "They are senseless children who have no understanding. They are clever enough at doing wrong, but they have no talent at all for doing right!"

JEREMIAH'S VISION OF COMING DISASTER

²³I looked at the earth, and it was empty and formless. I looked at the heavens, and there was no light. ²⁴I looked at the mountains and hills, and they trembled and shook. ²⁵I looked, and all the people were gone. All the birds of the sky had flown away. ²⁶I looked, and the fertile fields had become a wilderness. The cities lay in ruins, crushed by the LORD's fierce anger.

4:6 Hebrew *Zion.*

[27]This is what the LORD says: "The whole land will be ruined, but I will not destroy it completely. [28]The earth will mourn, the heavens will be draped in black, because of my decree against my people. I have made up my mind and will not change it."

[29]At the noise of marching armies, the people flee in terror from the cities. They hide in the bushes and run for the mountains. All the cities have been abandoned—not a person remains! [30]What are you doing, you who have been plundered? Why do you dress up in your most beautiful clothing and jewelry? Why do you brighten your eyes with mascara? It will do you no good! Your allies despise you and will kill you.

[31]I hear a great cry, like that of a woman giving birth to her first child. It is the cry of Jerusalem's people* gasping for breath, pleading for help, prostrate before their murderers.

THE SINS OF JUDAH

5 "Run up and down every street in Jerusalem," says the LORD. "Look high and low; search throughout the city! If you can find even one person who is just and honest, I will not destroy the city. [2]Even when they are under oath, saying, 'As surely as the LORD lives,' they all tell lies!"

[3]LORD, you are searching for honesty. You struck your people, but they paid no attention. You crushed them, but they refused to turn from sin. They are determined, with faces set like stone; they have refused to repent.

[4]Then I said, "But what can we expect from the poor and ignorant? They don't know the ways of the LORD. They don't understand what God expects of them. [5]I will go and speak to their leaders. Surely they will know the LORD's ways and what God requires of them." But the leaders, too, had utterly rejected their God. [6]So now a lion from the forest will attack them; a wolf from the desert will pounce on them. A leopard will lurk near

their towns, tearing apart any who dare to venture out. For their rebellion is great, and their sins are many.

[7]"How can I pardon you? For even your children have turned from me. They have sworn by gods that are not gods at all! I fed my people until they were fully satisfied. But they thanked me by committing adultery and lining up at the city's brothels. [8]They are well-fed, lusty stallions, each neighing for his neighbor's wife. [9]Should I not punish them for this?" asks the LORD. "Should I not avenge myself against a nation such as this?

[10]"Go down the rows of the vineyards and destroy them, but leave a scattered few alive. Strip the branches from the vine, for they do not belong to the LORD. [11]The people of Israel and Judah are full of treachery against me," says the LORD. [12]"They have lied about the LORD and have said, 'He won't bother us! No disasters will come upon us! There will be no war or famine! [13]God's prophets are windbags full of words with no divine authority. Their predictions of disaster will fall on themselves!'"

[14]Therefore, this is what the LORD God Almighty says: "Because the people are talking like this, I will give you messages that will burn them up as if they were kindling wood. [15]O Israel, I will bring a distant nation against you," says the LORD. "It is a mighty nation, an ancient nation, a people whose language you do not know, whose speech you cannot understand. [16]Their weapons are deadly; their warriors are mighty. [17]They will eat your harvests and your children's bread, your flocks of sheep and your herds of cattle. Yes, they will eat your grapes and figs. And they will destroy your fortified cities, which you think are so safe.

[18]"Yet even in those days I will not blot you out completely," says the LORD. [19]"And when your people ask, 'Why is the LORD our God doing this to us?' you must reply, 'You rejected him and gave yourselves to foreign gods in your own land. Now you will serve foreigners in a land that is not your own.'

4:31 Hebrew *the daughter of Zion.*

A Warning for God's People

20"Make this announcement to Israel* and to Judah: 21Listen, you foolish and senseless people—who have eyes but do not see, who have ears but do not hear. 22Do you have no respect for me? Why do you not tremble in my presence? I, the LORD, am the one who defines the ocean's sandy shoreline, an everlasting boundary that the waters cannot cross. The waves may toss and roar, but they can never pass the bounds I set.

23"But my people have stubborn and rebellious hearts. They have turned against me and have chosen to practice idolatry. 24They do not say from the heart, 'Let us live in awe of the LORD our God, for he gives us rain each spring and fall, assuring us of plentiful harvests.' 25Your wickedness has deprived you of these wonderful blessings. Your sin has robbed you of all these good things.

26"Among my people are wicked men who lie in wait for victims like a hunter hiding in a blind. They are continually setting traps for other people. 27Like a cage filled with birds, their homes are filled with evil plots. And the result? Now they are great and rich. 28They are well fed and well groomed, and there is no limit to their wicked deeds. They refuse justice to orphans and deny the rights of the poor. 29Should I not punish them for this?" asks the LORD. "Should I not avenge myself against a nation such as this?

30"A horrible and shocking thing has happened in this land—31the prophets give false prophecies, and the priests rule with an iron hand. And worse yet, my people like it that way! But what will you do when the end comes?

Jerusalem's Last Warning

6 "Run for your lives, you people of Benjamin! Flee from Jerusalem! Sound the alarm in Tekoa! Send up a signal at Beth-hakkerem! Warn everyone that a powerful army is coming from the north to destroy this nation. 2O Jerusalem,* you are my beautiful and delicate daughter—but I will destroy you! 3Enemy shepherds will surround you. They will set up camp around the city and divide your pastures for their flocks. 4They shout, 'Prepare for battle and attack at noon! But now the day is fading, and the evening shadows are falling. 5So let us attack by night and destroy her palaces!'"

6This is what the LORD Almighty says: "Cut down the trees for battering rams. Build ramps against the walls of Jerusalem. This is the city to be punished, for she is wicked through and through. 7She spouts evil like a fountain! Her streets echo with the sounds of violence and destruction. Her sickness and sores are ever before me. 8This is your last warning, Jerusalem! If you do not listen, I will empty the land."

9This is what the LORD Almighty says: "Disaster will fall upon you. Even the few who remain in Israel will be gleaned again, as when a harvester checks each vine a second time to pick the grapes that were missed."

Israel's Constant Rebellion

10To whom can I give warning? Who will listen when I speak? Their ears are closed, and they cannot hear. They scorn the word of the LORD. They don't want to listen at all. 11So now I am filled with the LORD's fury. Yes, I am weary of holding it in!

"I will pour out my fury over Jerusalem, even on children playing in the streets, on gatherings of young men, and on husbands and wives and grandparents. 12Their homes will be turned over to their enemies, and so will their fields and their wives. For I will punish the people of this land," says the LORD. 13"From the least to the greatest, they trick others to get what does not belong to them. Yes, even my prophets and priests are like that! 14They offer superficial treatments for my people's mortal wound. They give assurances of peace when all is war. 15Are they ashamed when they do these disgusting things? No, not

5:20 Hebrew *to the house of Jacob.* 6:2 Hebrew *Zion.*

at all—they don't even blush! Therefore, they will lie among the slaughtered. They will be humbled beneath my punishing anger," says the LORD.

ISRAEL REJECTS THE LORD'S WAY

[16]So now the LORD says, "Stop right where you are! Look for the old, godly way, and walk in it. Travel its path, and you will find rest for your souls. But you reply, 'No, that's not the road we want!' [17]I set watchmen over you who said, 'Listen for the sound of the trumpet!' But you replied, 'No! We won't pay attention!'

[18]"Therefore, listen to this, all you nations. Take note of my people's condition. [19]Listen, all the earth! I will bring disaster upon my people. It is the fruit of their own sin because they refuse to listen to me. They have rejected all my instructions. [20]There is no use now in offering me sweet incense from Sheba. Keep your expensive perfumes! I cannot accept your burnt offerings. Your sacrifices have no sweet fragrance for me."

[21]Therefore, this is what the LORD says: "I will put obstacles in my people's path. Fathers and sons will both fall over them. Neighbors and friends will collapse together."

AN INVASION FROM THE NORTH

[22]This is what the LORD says: "See a great army marching from the north! A great nation is rising against you from far-off lands. [23]They are fully armed for slaughter. They are cruel and show no mercy. As they ride forward, the noise of their army is like a roaring sea. They are marching in battle formation to destroy you, Jerusalem.*"

[24]We have heard reports about the enemy, and we are weak with fright. Fear and pain have gripped us, like that of a woman about to give birth. [25]Don't go out to the fields! Don't travel the roads! The enemy is everywhere, and they are ready to kill. We are terrorized at every turn! [26]Now my people, dress yourselves in sackcloth, and sit among the ashes. Mourn and weep bitterly, as for the loss of an only

son. For suddenly, the destroying armies will be upon you!

[27]"Jeremiah, I have made you a tester of metals, that you may determine the quality of my people. [28]Are they not the worst of rebels, full of slander? They are as insolent as bronze, as hard and cruel as iron. All of them lead others into corruption. [29]The bellows blow fiercely. The refining fire grows hotter. But it will never purify and cleanse them because there is no purity in them to refine. [30]I will label them 'Rejected Silver' because I, the LORD, am discarding them."

JEREMIAH SPEAKS AT THE TEMPLE

7 The LORD gave another message to Jeremiah. He said, [2]"Go to the entrance of the LORD's Temple, and give this message to the people: 'O Judah, listen to this message from the LORD! Listen to it, all of you who worship here! [3]The LORD Almighty, the God of Israel, says: Even now, if you quit your evil ways, I will let you stay in your own land. [4]But do not be fooled by those who repeatedly promise your safety because the Temple of the LORD is here. [5]I will be merciful only if you stop your wicked thoughts and deeds and are fair to others; [6]and if you stop exploiting foreigners, orphans, and widows; and if you stop your murdering; and if you stop worshiping idols as you now do to your own harm. [7]Then I will let you stay in this land that I gave to your ancestors to keep forever.

[8]" 'Do you think that because the Temple is here you will never suffer? Don't fool yourselves! [9]Do you really think you can steal, murder, commit adultery, lie, and worship Baal and all those other new gods of yours, [10]and then come here and stand before me in my Temple and chant, "We are safe!"—only to go right back to all those evils again? [11]Do you think this Temple, which honors my name, is a den of thieves? I see all the evil going on there, says the LORD.

6:23 Hebrew *daughter of Zion.*

My Daily Worship
— July 17 —

BE HONEST TO GOD!
JEREMIAH 5:1–8:17

But do not be fooled by those who repeatedly promise your safety because
the Temple of the LORD is here. I will be merciful only if you stop your
wicked thoughts and deeds and are fair to others (7:4–5).

[i reflect]

A pastor in a liturgical church attempted to welcome his congregation from the pulpit with the ritualistic greeting, "The Lord be with you!" But the microphone wasn't working properly. After several failed attempts at being heard, he cleared his throat and loudly said, "Something appears to
be wrong with the sound system." Without thinking, the congregation replied with the usual liturgical response, "And also with you!"

This story may coax a smile, but it hints at a timeless tendency. It is possible to codify our worship so that it becomes routine and not sincere. Symbols and memorized sayings can replace a
sincere encounter with the living God. In Jeremiah's day, the Temple in Jerusalem was such a symbol. As long as God's people could look up and see the sun glistening off the gold-gilded roof of
Solomon's Temple, they felt that they were safe from God's judgment. Their walk with the Lord
had been reduced to superstitious reliance on external relics and repeated practices.

Perhaps you recognize that tendency in yourself at times. You catch yourself saying "Praise God!"
out of force of habit. The prayer you say before dinner is repetitious and offered without much
thought. Reprogramming your pattern of praise may not be as easy as you think. If you're willing,
however, it can be done.

As you think about the kind of vital relationship you desire with the Lord, speak your mind.
Wouldn't you like to be entirely honest? Well, you can. Avoid God-talk. Don't resort to religious
clichés. Speak to God in prayer as you would to your best friend in the world. Tell him how much
you love him and thank him for all he has done for you.

[i pray]

Lord, you must weary of the clichés and traditions we Christians rely on to satisfy
our need for security. Our superstitious approach to prayer and worship must
make you sad. Forgive me, Lord, for not speaking my mind and
allowing my actions of mercy to speak louder than my words.

[i respond]

Catch the number of times you talk "Christian-ese"—words you only use in church or in prayer.
Make a list of these words and try to write definitions for them. Find some new words that are part
of your daily vocabulary to replace them.

¹²" 'Go to the place at Shiloh where I once put the Tabernacle to honor my name. See what I did there because of all the wickedness of my people, the Israelites. ¹³While you were doing these wicked things, says the LORD, I spoke to you about it repeatedly, but you would not listen. I called out to you, but you refused to answer. ¹⁴So just as I destroyed Shiloh, I will now destroy this Temple that was built to honor my name, this Temple that you trust for help, this place that I gave to you and your ancestors. ¹⁵And I will send you into exile, just as I did your relatives, the people of Israel.*'

JUDAH'S PERSISTENT IDOLATRY

¹⁶"Pray no more for these people, Jeremiah. Do not weep or pray for them, and don't beg me to help them, for I will not listen to you. ¹⁷Do you not see what they are doing throughout the towns of Judah and in the streets of Jerusalem? ¹⁸No wonder I am so angry! Watch how the children gather wood and the fathers build sacrificial fires. See how the women knead dough and make cakes to offer to the Queen of Heaven. And they give drink offerings to their other idol gods! ¹⁹Am I the one they are hurting?" asks the LORD. "Most of all, they hurt themselves, to their own shame."

²⁰So the Sovereign LORD says: "I will pour out my terrible fury on this place. Its people, animals, trees, and crops will be consumed by the unquenchable fire of my anger."

²¹This is what the LORD Almighty, the God of Israel, says: "Away with your burnt offerings and sacrifices! Eat them yourselves! ²²When I led your ancestors out of Egypt, it was not burnt offerings and sacrifices I wanted from them. ²³This is what I told them: 'Obey me, and I will be your God, and you will be my people. Only do as I say, and all will be well!'

²⁴"But my people would not listen to me. They kept on doing whatever they wanted, following the stubborn desires of their evil hearts. They went backward instead of forward. ²⁵From the day your ancestors left Egypt

until now, I have continued to send my prophets—day in and day out. ²⁶But my people have not listened to me or even tried to hear. They have been stubborn and sinful—even worse than their ancestors.

²⁷"Tell them all this, but do not expect them to listen. Shout out your warnings, but do not expect them to respond. ²⁸Say to them, 'This is the nation whose people will not obey the LORD their God and who refuse to be taught. Truth has vanished from among them; it is no longer heard on their lips. ²⁹O Jerusalem, shave your head in mourning, and weep alone on the mountains. For the LORD has rejected and forsaken this generation that has provoked his fury.'

THE VALLEY OF SLAUGHTER

³⁰"The people of Judah have sinned before my very eyes," says the LORD. "They have set up their abominable idols right in my own Temple, defiling it. ³¹They have built the pagan shrines of Topheth in the valley of the son of Hinnom, where they sacrifice their little sons and daughters in the fire. I have never commanded such a horrible deed; it never even crossed my mind to command such a thing! ³²So beware, for the time is coming," says the LORD, "when that place will no longer be called Topheth or the valley of the son of Hinnom, but the Valley of Slaughter. They will bury so many bodies in Topheth that there won't be room for all the graves. ³³The corpses of my people will be food for the vultures and wild animals, and no one will be left to scare them away. ³⁴I will put an end to the happy singing and laughter in the streets of Jerusalem. The joyful voices of bridegrooms and brides will no longer be heard in the towns of Judah. The land will lie in complete desolation.

8 "In that day," says the LORD, "the enemy will break open the graves of the kings and officials of Judah, and the graves of the priests, prophets, and common people. ²They

---

7:15 Hebrew *of Ephraim,* referring to the northern kingdom of Israel.

will dig out their bones and spread them out on the ground before the sun, moon, and stars—the gods my people have loved, served, and worshiped. Their bones will not be gathered up again or buried but will be scattered on the ground like dung. ³And the people of this evil nation who survive will wish to die rather than live where I will send them. I, the LORD Almighty, have spoken!

DECEPTION BY FALSE PROPHETS

⁴"Jeremiah, say to the people, 'This is what the LORD says: When people fall down, don't they get up again? When they start down the wrong road and discover their mistake, don't they turn back? ⁵Then why do these people keep going along their self-destructive path, refusing to turn back, even though I have warned them? ⁶I listen to their conversations, and what do I hear? Is anyone sorry for sin? Does anyone say, "What a terrible thing I have done"? No! All are running down the path of sin as swiftly as a horse rushing into battle! ⁷The stork knows the time of her migration, as do the turtledove, the swallow, and the crane.* They all return at the proper time each year. But not my people! They do not know what the LORD requires of them.

⁸" 'How can you say, "We are wise because we have the law of the LORD," when your teachers have twisted it so badly? ⁹These wise teachers will be shamed by exile for their sin, for they have rejected the word of the LORD. Are they so wise after all? ¹⁰I will give their wives and their farms to others. From the least to the greatest, they trick others to get what does not belong to them. Yes, even my prophets and priests are like that. ¹¹They offer superficial treatments for my people's mortal wound. They give assurances of peace when all is war. ¹²Are they ashamed when they do these disgusting things? No, not at all—they don't even blush! Therefore, they will lie among the slaughtered. They will be humbled when they are punished, says the LORD. ¹³I will take away their rich harvests of figs and grapes. Their fruit trees will all die. All the good things I prepared for them will soon be gone. I, the LORD, have spoken!'

¹⁴"Then the people will say, 'Why should we wait here to die? Come, let's go to the fortified cities to die there. For the LORD our God has decreed our destruction and has given us a cup of poison to drink because we sinned against the LORD. ¹⁵We hoped for peace, but no peace came. We hoped for a time of healing, but found only terror. ¹⁶The snorting of the enemies' warhorses can be heard all the way from the land of Dan in the north! The whole land trembles at the approach of the terrible army, for it is coming to devour the land and everything in it—cities and people alike.'

¹⁷"I will send these enemy troops among you like poisonous snakes you cannot charm," says the LORD. "No matter what you do, they will bite you, and you will die."

JEREMIAH WEEPS FOR SINFUL JUDAH

¹⁸My grief is beyond healing; my heart is broken. ¹⁹Listen to the weeping of my people; it can be heard all across the land.

"Has the LORD abandoned Jerusalem*?" the people ask. "Is her King no longer there?"

"Oh, why have they angered me with their carved idols and worthless gods?" asks the LORD.

²⁰"The harvest is finished, and the summer is gone," the people cry, "yet we are not saved!"

²¹I weep for the hurt of my people. I am stunned and silent, mute with grief. ²²Is there no medicine in Gilead? Is there no physician there? Why is there no healing for the wounds of my people?

9 Oh, that my eyes were a fountain of tears; I would weep forever! I would sob day and night for all my people who have been slaughtered. ²Oh, that I could go away and forget them and live in a shack in the desert, for they are all adulterous and treacherous.

8:7 The identification of some of these birds is uncertain. 8:19 Hebrew *Zion*.

JUDGMENT FOR DISOBEDIENCE

³"My people bend their tongues like bows to shoot lies. They refuse to stand up for the truth. And they only go from bad to worse! They care nothing for me," says the LORD.

⁴"Beware of your neighbor! Beware of your brother! They all take advantage of one another and spread their slanderous lies. ⁵They all fool and defraud each other; no one tells the truth. With practiced tongues they tell lies; they wear themselves out with all their sinning. ⁶They pile lie upon lie and utterly refuse to come to me," says the LORD.

⁷Therefore, the LORD Almighty says, "See, I will melt them in a crucible and test them like metal. What else can I do with them? ⁸For their tongues aim lies like poisoned arrows. They promise peace to their neighbors while planning to kill them. ⁹Should I not punish them for this?" asks the LORD. "Should I not avenge myself against a nation such as this?"

¹⁰I will weep for the mountains and wail for the desert pastures. For they are desolate and empty of life; the lowing of cattle is heard no more; the birds and wild animals all have fled.

¹¹"I will make Jerusalem into a heap of ruins," says the LORD. "It will be a place haunted by jackals. The towns of Judah will be ghost towns, with no one living in them."

¹²Who is wise enough to understand all this? Who has been instructed by the LORD and can explain it to others? Why has the land been ruined so completely that no one even dares to travel through it?

¹³The LORD replies, "This has happened because my people have abandoned the instructions I gave them; they have refused to obey my law. ¹⁴Instead, they have stubbornly followed their own desires and worshiped the images of Baal, as their ancestors taught them. ¹⁵So now, listen to what the LORD Almighty, the God of Israel, says: Look! I will feed them with bitterness and give them poison to drink. ¹⁶I will scatter them around the world, and they will be strangers in distant lands. Their enemies will chase them with the sword until I have destroyed them completely."

WEEPING IN JERUSALEM

¹⁷This is what the LORD Almighty says: "Think about what is going on! Call for the mourners to come. ¹⁸Quick! Begin your weeping! Let the tears flow from your eyes. ¹⁹Hear the people of Jerusalem* crying in despair, 'We are ruined! Disaster has come upon us! We must leave our land, because our homes have been torn down.'"

²⁰Listen, you women, to the words of the LORD; open your ears to what he has to say. Teach your daughters to wail; teach one another how to lament. ²¹For death has crept in through our windows and has entered our mansions. It has killed off the flower of our youth: Children no longer play in the streets, and young men no longer gather in the squares. ²²And the LORD says, "Bodies will be scattered across the fields like dung, or like bundles of grain after the harvest. No one will be left to bury them."

²³This is what the LORD says: "Let not the wise man gloat in his wisdom, or the mighty man in his might, or the rich man in his riches. ²⁴Let them boast in this alone: that they truly know me and understand that I am the LORD who is just and righteous, whose love is unfailing, and that I delight in these things. I, the LORD, have spoken!

²⁵"A time is coming," says the LORD, "when I will punish all those who are circumcised in body but not in spirit—²⁶the Egyptians, Edomites, Ammonites, Moabites, the people who live in distant places,* and yes, even the people of Judah. Like all these pagan nations, the people of Israel also have uncircumcised hearts."

IDOLATRY BRINGS DESTRUCTION

10 Hear the word of the LORD, O Israel! ²This is what the LORD says: "Do not act like other nations who try to read their

---

9:19 Hebrew *Zion.*   9:26 Or *the people who clip the corners of their hair.*

My Daily Worship

GETTING TO KNOW HIM

JEREMIAH 8:18–12:17

Let them boast in this alone: that they truly know me and understand that
I am the LORD who is just and righteous, whose love is unfailing and
that I delight in these things. I, the LORD, have spoken! (9:24).

[i reflect]

Obtaining knowledge is a core value of the human experience. But not every person embraces that value with equal affection. An Arab proverb goes, "He who knows and knows that he knows is wise. Follow him. He who knows and knows not that he knows is asleep. Wake him. He who knows not and knows not that he knows not is uneducated. Teach him. He who knows not and knows that he knows not is a fool. Shun him."

As far as God is concerned, our knowledge of him is the most important possession we have. That comes through loud and clear in this passage from Jeremiah. For Hugh Steven, veteran missionary with Wycliffe Bible Translators, that was the credo of his life. When asked what our purpose in this life is all about, he would say: "To develop a capacity for knowing God so we will have the means by which to worship and enjoy him in the world to come."

Basil, one of the early church fathers, would agree. He wrote, "The primary function of our mind is to know God, as much as the very small can know the infinitely great. When our eyes first perceive visible objects, all visible objects aren't brought into sight at once. The hemisphere of heaven isn't seen with one glance. However, we are surrounded by the appearance of something, in reality, that is many things."

In other words, our ability to truly know God is rooted in our willingness to listen and observe. But that sure is difficult when spouses, children, and work deadlines demand attention. Yet, God says our knowledge of him is unequalled by any task on earth (no matter how noble). That should trigger within us the desire to sit in his presence and learn.

What is it you want—or need—to know about God today? Write down one question; then find time to pursue finding the answer. Make this a habit to "truly know and understand" God.

[i pray]

Lord, I am thrilled with the thought that I can know you. You are not some distant deity.
You are a caring Creator that desires a relationship with me. I want to
know that I know you by persistently seeking your face.

[i respond]

Jeremiah 9:24 is a great verse to memorize. As you do, hear God speaking these words to you.

future in the stars. Do not be afraid of their predictions, even though other nations are terrified by them. ³Their ways are futile and foolish. They cut down a tree and carve an idol. ⁴They decorate it with gold and silver and then fasten it securely with hammer and nails so it won't fall over. ⁵There stands their god like a helpless scarecrow in a garden! It cannot speak, and it needs to be carried because it cannot walk. Do not be afraid of such gods, for they can neither harm you nor do you any good."

⁶LORD, there is no one like you! For you are great, and your name is full of power. ⁷Who would not fear you, O King of nations? That title belongs to you alone! Among all the wise people of the earth and in all the kingdoms of the world, there is no one like you.

⁸The wisest of people who worship idols are stupid and foolish. The things they worship are made of wood! ⁹They bring beaten sheets of silver from Tarshish and gold from Uphaz, and they give these materials to skillful craftsmen who make their idols. Then they dress these gods in royal purple robes made by expert tailors. ¹⁰But the LORD is the only true God, the living God. He is the everlasting King! The whole earth trembles at his anger. The nations hide before his wrath.

¹¹Say this to those who worship other gods: "Your so-called gods, who did not make the heavens and earth, will vanish from the earth."*

¹² But God made the earth by his power,
  and he preserves it by his wisdom.
 He has stretched out the heavens
  by his understanding.
¹³ When he speaks, there is thunder in the
  heavens.
 He causes the clouds to rise over the earth.
 He sends the lightning with the rain
  and releases the wind from his
  storehouses.
¹⁴ Compared to him, all people are foolish
  and have no knowledge at all!
 They make idols, but the idols will disgrace
  their makers,

 for they are frauds.
 They have no life or power in them.
¹⁵ Idols are worthless; they are lies!
  The time is coming when they will all be
  destroyed.
¹⁶ But the God of Israel* is no idol!
 He is the Creator of everything that exists,
  including Israel, his own special
  possession.
 The LORD Almighty is his name!

THE COMING DESTRUCTION

¹⁷"Pack your bag and prepare to leave; the siege is about to begin," ¹⁸says the LORD. "For suddenly, I will fling you from this land and pour great troubles upon you. At last you will feel my anger."

¹⁹My wound is desperate, and my grief is great. My sickness is incurable, but I must bear it. ²⁰My home is gone, and no one is left to help me rebuild it. My children have been taken away, and I will never see them again. ²¹The shepherds of my people have lost their senses. They no longer follow the LORD or ask what he wants of them. Therefore, they fail completely, and their flocks are scattered. ²²Listen! Hear the terrifying roar of great armies as they roll down from the north. The towns of Judah will be destroyed and will become a haunt for jackals.

JEREMIAH'S PRAYER

²³I know, LORD, that a person's life is not his own. No one is able to plan his own course. ²⁴So correct me, LORD, but please be gentle. Do not correct me in anger, for I would die. ²⁵Pour out your wrath on the nations that refuse to recognize you—on nations that do not call upon your name. For they have utterly devoured your people Israel,* making the land a desolate wilderness.

JUDAH'S BROKEN COVENANT

11 The LORD gave another message to Jeremiah. He said, ²"Remind the peo-

---

10:11 The original text of this verse is in Aramaic. **10:16** Hebrew *the Portion of Jacob.* **10:25** Hebrew *Jacob.*

ple of Judah and Jerusalem about the terms of their covenant with me. ³Say to them, 'This is what the LORD, the God of Israel, says: Cursed is anyone who does not obey the terms of my covenant! ⁴For I said to your ancestors when I brought them out of slavery in Egypt, "If you obey me and do whatever I command you, then you will be my people, and I will be your God." ⁵I said this so I could keep my promise to your ancestors to give you a land flowing with milk and honey—the land you live in today.'"

Then I replied, "So be it,* LORD!"

⁶Then the LORD said, "Broadcast this message in the streets of Jerusalem. Go from town to town throughout the land and say, 'Remember the covenant your ancestors made, and do everything they promised. ⁷For I solemnly warned your ancestors when I brought them out of Egypt, repeating over and over again to this day: "Obey me!" ⁸But your ancestors did not pay any attention; they would not even listen. Instead, they stubbornly followed their own evil desires. And because they refused to obey, I brought upon them all the curses described in our covenant.'"

⁹Again the LORD spoke to me and said, "I have discovered a conspiracy against me among the people of Judah and Jerusalem. ¹⁰They have returned to the sins of their forefathers. They have refused to listen to me and are worshiping idols. Israel and Judah have both broken the covenant I made with their ancestors. ¹¹Therefore, says the LORD, I am going to bring calamity upon them, and they will not escape. Though they beg for mercy, I will not listen to their cries. ¹²Then the people of Judah and Jerusalem will pray to their idols and offer incense before them. But the idols will not save them when disaster strikes! ¹³Look now, people of Judah, you have as many gods as there are cities and towns. Your altars of shame—altars for burning incense to your god Baal—are along every street in Jerusalem.

11:5 Hebrew *Amen.*

Words of Worship

TEMPLE

Temple—Hebrew *beyt Yah-veh* "house of Yahweh"; *hey-chal* "palace, temple"; *miq-dash* "sanctuary"; Greek *na-os* "shrine, temple, sanctuary." In the Old Testament, "house of Yahweh" occurs more than 250 times. The New Testament uses *naos* for the Old Testament terms.

When ancient people wanted to symbolize the presence of their gods, they erected palaces for them, like a king's palace. Usually they would put a statue of the deity in its holiest place, or sanctuary. In the Bible, the same expressions—palace, sanctuary—are used for the Temple of the Lord, even though no image of him was permitted. In the Old Testament, however, the usual expression is "house of the LORD."

A palace is where royalty is enthroned, but a *house* is the dwelling of a family. Israel understood that no building could really hold God—not even the heavens could contain him (1 Kings 8:27). But God says, "I will live among the people of Israel and be their God" (Exodus 29:45). The Temple in Jerusalem was an earthly symbol of the presence of the God of heaven, a focal point for the faithful. Jesus and his apostles knew this Temple would soon pass away. But the real dwelling of God would remain—the consecrated family of the New Covenant. "For God's temple is holy, and you Christians are that temple" (1 Corinthians 3:17).

---

¹⁴"Pray no more for these people, Jeremiah. Do not weep or pray for them, for I will not listen to them when they cry out to me in distress. ¹⁵What right do my beloved people have

to come to my Temple, where they have done so many immoral things? Can their sacrifices avert their destruction? They actually rejoice in doing evil!

16"I, the LORD, once called them a thriving olive tree, beautiful to see and full of good fruit. But now I have sent the fury of their enemies to burn them with fire, leaving them charred and broken. 17I, the LORD Almighty, who planted this olive tree, have ordered it destroyed. For the people of Israel and Judah have done evil, provoking my anger by offering incense to Baal."

A PLOT AGAINST JEREMIAH

18Then the LORD told me about the plots my enemies were making against me. 19I had been as unaware as a lamb on the way to its slaughter. I had no idea that they were planning to kill me! "Let's destroy this man and all his words," they said. "Let's kill him, so his name will be forgotten forever."

20O LORD Almighty, you are just, and you examine the deepest thoughts of hearts and minds. Let me see your vengeance against them, for I have committed my cause to you.

21The men of Anathoth wanted me dead. They said they would kill me if I did not stop speaking in the LORD's name. 22So this is what the LORD Almighty says about them: "I will punish them! Their young men will die in battle, and their little boys and girls will starve. 23Not one of these plotters from Anathoth will survive, for I will bring disaster upon them when their time of punishment comes."

JEREMIAH QUESTIONS THE LORD'S JUSTICE

12 LORD, you always give me justice when I bring a case before you. Now let me bring you this complaint: Why are the wicked so prosperous? Why are evil people so happy? 2You have planted them, and they have taken root and prospered. Your name is on their lips, but in their hearts they give you no credit at all. 3But as for me, LORD, you know my

heart. You see me and test my thoughts. Drag these people away like helpless sheep to be butchered! Set them aside to be slaughtered!

4How long must this land weep? Even the grass in the fields has withered. The wild animals and birds have disappeared because of the evil in the land. Yet the people say, "The LORD won't do anything!"

THE LORD'S REPLY TO JEREMIAH

5Then the LORD replied to me, "If racing against mere men makes you tired, how will you race against horses? If you stumble and fall on open ground, what will you do in the thickets near the Jordan? 6Even your own brothers, members of your own family, have turned on you. They have plotted, raising a cry against you. Do not trust them, no matter how pleasantly they speak.

7"I have abandoned my people, my special possession. I have surrendered my dearest ones to their enemies. 8My chosen people have roared at me like a lion of the forest, so I have treated them as though I hated them. 9My chosen people have become as disgusting to me as a vulture. And indeed, they are surrounded by vultures. Bring on the wild beasts to pick their corpses clean!

10"Many rulers have ravaged my vineyard, trampling down the vines and turning all its beauty into a barren wilderness. 11They have made it an empty wasteland; I hear its mournful cry. The whole land is desolate, and no one even cares. 12Destroying armies plunder the land. The sword of the LORD kills people from one end of the nation to the other. No one will escape! 13My people have planted wheat but are harvesting thorns. They have worked hard, but it has done them no good. They will harvest a crop of shame, for the fierce anger of the LORD is upon them."

A MESSAGE FOR ISRAEL'S NEIGHBORS

14Now this is what the LORD says: "As for all the evil nations reaching out for the inheritance I gave my people Israel, I will uproot them from their lands just as Judah will be uprooted from hers. [15]But afterward I will return and have compassion on all of them. I will bring them home to their own lands again, each nation to its own inheritance. [16]And if these nations quickly learn the ways of my people, and if they learn to swear by my name, saying, 'As surely as the LORD lives' (just as they taught my people to swear by the name of Baal), then they will be given a place among my people. [17]But any nation who refuses to obey me will be uprooted and destroyed. I, the LORD, have spoken!"

JEREMIAH'S LINEN BELT

13 This is what the LORD said to me: "Go and buy a linen belt and put it around your waist, but do not wash it." [2]So I bought the belt as the LORD directed me and put it around my waist. [3]Then the LORD gave me another message: [4]"Take the linen belt you are wearing, and go to the Euphrates River.* Hide it there in a hole in the rocks." [5]So I went and hid it at the Euphrates as the LORD had instructed me.

[6]A long time afterward, the LORD said to me, "Go back to the Euphrates and get the linen belt that I told you to hide there." [7]So I went to the Euphrates and dug it out of the hole where I had hidden it. But now it was mildewed and falling apart. The belt was useless.

[8]Then I received this message from the LORD: [9]"The LORD says: This illustrates how I will rot away the pride of Judah and Jerusalem. [10]These wicked people refuse to listen to me. They stubbornly follow their own desires and worship idols. Therefore, they will become like this linen belt—good for nothing! [11]As a belt clings to a person's waist, so I created Judah and Israel to cling to me," says the LORD. "They were to be my people, my pride, my glory—an honor to my name. But they would not listen to me.

[12]"So tell them, 'The LORD, the God of Israel, says: All your wineskins will be full of wine.' And they will reply, 'Of course, you don't need to tell us how prosperous we will be!' [13]Then tell them, 'No, this is what the LORD means: I will make everyone in this land so confused that they will seem drunk—from the king sitting on David's throne and from the priests and the prophets, right on down to the common people. [14]I will smash them one against the other, even parents against children, says the LORD. I will not let my pity or mercy or compassion keep me from destroying them.'"

A WARNING AGAINST PRIDE

[15]Listen! Do not be proud, for the LORD has spoken. [16]Give glory to the LORD your God before it is too late. Acknowledge him before he brings darkness upon you, causing you to stumble and fall on the dark mountains. For then, when you look for light, you will find only terrible darkness. [17]And if you still refuse to listen, I will weep alone because of your pride. My eyes will overflow with tears because the LORD's flock will be led away into exile.

[18]Say to the king and his mother, "Come down from your thrones and sit in the dust, for your glorious crowns will soon be snatched from your heads." [19]The towns of the Negev will close their gates, and no one will be able to open them. The people of Judah will be taken away as captives. They will all be carried into exile.

[20]See the armies marching down from the north! Where is your flock—your beautiful flock—that he gave you to care for? [21]How will you feel when the LORD sets your foreign allies over you as rulers? You will writhe in pain like a woman giving birth! [22]You may ask yourself, "Why is all this happening to me?" It is because of your many sins! That is why you have been raped and destroyed by invading armies. [23]Can an Ethiopian* change the color of his skin? Can a leopard take away its spots? Neither can you start doing good, for you always do evil.

13:4 Hebrew *Perath;* also in 13:5, 6, 7. 13:23 Hebrew *a Cushite.*

²⁴"I will scatter you, just as chaff is scattered by the winds blowing in from the desert. ²⁵This is your allotment, that which is due you," says the LORD. "I have measured it out especially for you, because you have forgotten me and put your trust in false gods. ²⁶I myself will expose you to shame. ²⁷I am keenly aware of your adultery and lust, and your abominable idol worship out in the fields and on the hills. Your destruction is sure, Jerusalem! How long will it be before you are pure?"

JUDAH'S TERRIBLE DROUGHT

14 This message came to Jeremiah from the LORD, explaining why he was holding back the rain: ²"Judah wilts; her businesses have ground to a halt. All the people sit on the ground in mourning, and a great cry rises from Jerusalem. ³The nobles send servants to get water, but all the wells are dry. The servants return with empty pitchers, confused and desperate, covering their heads in grief. ⁴The ground is parched and cracked for lack of rain. The farmers are afraid; they, too, cover their heads. ⁵The deer abandons her newborn fawn because there is no grass. ⁶The wild donkeys stand on the bare hills panting like thirsty jackals. They strain their eyes looking for grass to eat, but there is none to be found."

⁷The people say, "LORD, our wickedness has caught up with us. We have sinned against you. So please, help us for the sake of your own reputation. ⁸O Hope of Israel, our Savior in times of trouble! Why are you like a stranger to us? Why are you like someone passing through the land, stopping only for the night? ⁹Are you also confused? Are you helpless to save us? You are right here among us, LORD. We are known as your people. Please don't abandon us now!"

¹⁰So the LORD replies to his people, "You love to wander far from me and do not follow in my paths. Now I will no longer accept you as my people. I will remember all your wickedness and will punish you for your sins."

THE LORD FORBIDS JEREMIAH TO INTERCEDE

¹¹Then the LORD said to me, "Do not pray for these people anymore. ¹²When they fast in my presence, I will pay no attention. When they present their burnt offerings and grain offerings to me, I will not accept them. In return, I will give them only war, famine, and disease."

¹³Then I said, "O Sovereign LORD, their prophets are telling them, 'All is well—no war or famine will come. The LORD will surely send you peace.'"

¹⁴Then the LORD said, "These prophets are telling lies in my name. I did not send them or tell them to speak. I did not give them any messages. They prophesy of visions and revelations they have never seen or heard. They speak foolishness made up in their own lying hearts. ¹⁵Therefore, says the LORD, I will punish these lying prophets, for they have spoken in my name even though I never sent them. They say that no war or famine will come, but they themselves will die by war and famine! ¹⁶As for the people to whom they prophesy—their bodies will be thrown out into the streets of Jerusalem, victims of famine and war. There will be no one left to bury them. Husbands, wives, sons, and daughters—all will be gone. For I will pour out their own wickedness on them.

¹⁷"Now, Jeremiah, say this to them: 'Night and day my eyes overflow with tears. I cannot stop weeping, for my virgin daughter—my precious people—has been run through with a sword and lies mortally wounded on the ground. ¹⁸If I go out into the fields, I see the bodies of people slaughtered by the enemy. If I walk the city streets, there I see people who have died of starvation. The prophets and priests continue with their work, but they do not know what they are doing.'"

A PRAYER FOR HEALING

¹⁹LORD, have you completely rejected Judah? Do you really hate Jerusalem*? Why have you wounded us past all hope of healing? We

14:19 Hebrew *Zion.*

My Daily Worship

— *July 19* —

A Near Impossibility

JEREMIAH 13:1–16:21

Can an Ethiopian change the color of his skin? Can a leopard take away its spots?
Neither can you start doing good, for you always do evil (13:23).

[i reflect]

In the fall of 1959, author John Howard Griffin set out on a personal odyssey. He exchanged the privileged life he'd known as a Southern white man for the disenfranchised world of a jobless black man by undergoing a medical procedure to change his skin color. His best-selling book *Black Like Me* chronicles his eye-opening lessons. But his skin didn't stay black, and he returned to life as a Caucasian.

Tired of hypocrisy and sin, we often try to change and remake ourselves too. But apart from God we're unsuccessful. As Origen once wrote, "A man will abandon other habits (although it may be hard to tear himself from them) more easily than he will surrender his opinions." The attitudes and values with which we are raised are more powerful than we realize. When coupled with our human nature that seeks pleasure over morality and self-interest over justice, choosing to do what is right is more easily agreed to than accomplished.

These words Jeremiah recorded leave little wiggle room and they make us uncomfortable. In fact these words invade the very center of our will. We may want desperately to change an attitude, behavior, or thought pattern, but we simply aren't strong enough. There is no way we can do it. We can't stop displeasing the Lord and being hurtful to others on our own. That is a fact of human nature.

Only the Lord, through his Spirit, can bring about the means for us to take on a new identity. It's called being born again. That's the only way our "spots of sin" are removed. Every day of our lives, God is about the process of changing us and making us more like Christ. What "spots" do you want taken away today? Ask God for his help and trust him to remove them.

[i pray]

Heavenly Father, change is really hard. I can't believe how difficult it is for me to reprogram
my self-centered heart. I'm reminded today how "spotted" my heart is with sin. Wash me,
Lord. Cleanse me of wrong attitudes toward people you love. Amen.

[i respond]

Examine what values you have inherited from your family of origin. Which ones are worth passing on to your children? Reflect on how the negative values you've inherited may impact your ability to worship the Lord.

hoped for peace, but no peace came. We hoped for a time of healing but found only terror.

20LORD, we confess our wickedness and that of our ancestors, too. We all have sinned against you. 21For the sake of your own name, LORD, do not abandon us. Do not disgrace yourself and the throne of your glory. Do not break your covenant with us. Please don't forget us!

22Can any of the foreign gods send us rain? Does it fall from the sky by itself? No, it comes from you, the LORD our God! Only you can do such things. So we will wait for you to help us.

JUDAH'S INEVITABLE DOOM

15 Then the LORD said to me, "Even if Moses and Samuel stood before me pleading for these people, I wouldn't help them. Away with them! Get them out of my sight! 2And if they say to you, 'But where can we go?' tell them, 'This is what the LORD says: Those who are destined for death, to death; those who are destined for war, to war; those who are destined for famine, to famine; those who are destined for captivity, to captivity.'

3"I will send four kinds of destroyers against them," says the LORD. "I will send the sword to kill, the dogs to drag away, the vultures to devour, and the wild animals to finish up what is left. 4Because of the wicked things Manasseh son of Hezekiah, king of Judah, did in Jerusalem, I will make my people an object of horror to all the kingdoms of the earth.

5"Who will feel sorry for you, Jerusalem? Who will weep for you? Who will even bother to ask how you are? 6You have forsaken me and turned your back on me," says the LORD. "Therefore, I will raise my clenched fists to destroy you. I am tired of always giving you another chance. 7I will winnow you like grain at the gates of your cities and take away everything you hold dear. I will destroy my own people, because they refuse to turn back to me from all their evil ways.

8"There will be more widows than the grains of sand along the seashore. At noon-time I will bring a destroyer against the mothers of young men. I will cause anguish and terror to come upon them suddenly. 9The mother of seven grows faint and gasps for breath; her sun has gone down while it is yet day. She sits childless now, disgraced and humiliated. And those who are left, I will hand over to the enemy to be killed," says the LORD.

God saves men to make them worshipers.

A. W. TOZER

JEREMIAH'S COMPLAINT

10Then I said, "What sadness is mine, my mother. Oh, that I had died at birth! I am hated everywhere I go. I am neither a lender who has threatened to foreclose nor a borrower who refuses to pay—yet they all curse me."

11The LORD replied, "All will be well with you, Jeremiah. Your enemies will ask you to plead on their behalf in times of trouble and distress. 12Can a man break a bar of iron from the north, or a bar of bronze? 13Because of all my people's sins against me, I will hand over their wealth and treasures as plunder to the enemy. 14I will tell their enemies to take them as captives to a foreign land. For my anger blazes forth like fire, and it will consume them."

15Then I said, "LORD, you know I am suffering for your sake. Punish my persecutors! Don't let them kill me! Be merciful to me and give them what they deserve! 16Your words are what sustain me. They bring me great joy and are my heart's delight, for I bear your name, O LORD God Almighty. 17I never joined the people in their merry feasts. I sat alone because your hand was on me. I burst with indignation at their sins. [18]Why then does my suffering continue? Why is my wound so incurable? Your help seems as uncertain as a seasonal brook. It is like a spring that has gone dry."

[19]The LORD replied, "If you return to me, I will restore you so you can continue to serve me. If you speak words that are worthy, you will be my spokesman. You are to influence them; do not let them influence you! [20]They will fight against you like an attacking army, but I will make you as secure as a fortified wall. They will not conquer you, for I will protect and deliver you. I, the LORD, have spoken! [21]Yes, I will certainly keep you safe from these wicked men. I will rescue you from their cruel hands."

JEREMIAH FORBIDDEN TO MARRY

16 The LORD gave me another message. He said, [2]"Do not marry or have children in this place. [3]For this is what the LORD says about the children born here in this city and about their mothers and fathers: [4]They will die from terrible diseases. No one will mourn for them or bury them, and they will lie scattered on the ground like dung. They will die from war and famine, and their bodies will be food for the vultures and wild animals.

JUDAH'S COMING PUNISHMENT

[5]"Do not go to their funerals to mourn and show sympathy for them," says the LORD, "for I have removed my protection and peace from them. I have taken away my unfailing love and my mercy. [6]Both the great and the lowly will die in this land. No one will bury them or mourn for them. Their friends will not cut themselves or shave their heads in sadness. [7]No one will offer a meal to comfort those who mourn for the dead—not even for the death of a mother or a father. No one will send a cup of wine to console them.

[8]"And do not go to their feasts and parties. Do not eat and drink with them at all. [9]For the LORD Almighty, the God of Israel, says: In your own lifetime, before your very eyes, I will put an end to the happy singing and laughter in this land. The joyful voices of bridegrooms and brides will no longer be heard.

[10]"When you tell the people all these things, they will ask, 'Why has the LORD decreed such terrible things against us? What have we done to deserve such treatment? What is our sin against the LORD our God?' [11]Tell them that this is the LORD's reply: It is because your ancestors were unfaithful to me. They worshiped other gods and served them. They abandoned me. They did not keep my law. [12]And you are even worse than your ancestors! You stubbornly follow your own evil desires and refuse to listen to me. [13]So I will throw you out of this land and send you into a foreign land where you and your ancestors have never been. There you can worship idols all you like—and I will grant you no favors!

HOPE DESPITE THE DISASTER

[14]"But the time is coming," says the LORD, "when people who are taking an oath will no longer say, 'As surely as the LORD lives, who rescued the people of Israel from the land of Egypt.' [15]Instead, they will say, 'As surely as the LORD lives, who brought the people of Israel back to their own land from the land of the north and from all the countries to which he had exiled them.' For I will bring them back to this land that I gave their ancestors.

[16]"But now I am sending for many fishermen who will catch them," says the LORD. "I am sending for hunters who will search for them in the forests and caves. [17]I am watching them closely, and I see every sin. They cannot hope to hide from me. [18]I will punish them doubly for all their sins, because they have defiled my land with lifeless images of their detestable gods and filled my inheritance with their evil deeds."

JEREMIAH'S PRAYER OF CONFIDENCE

[19]LORD, you are my strength and fortress, my refuge in the day of trouble! Nations from

around the world will come to you and say, "Our ancestors were foolish, for they worshiped worthless idols. 20Can people make their own god? The gods they make are not real gods at all!"

21"So now I will show them my power and might," says the LORD. "At last they will know that I am the LORD."

JUDAH'S SIN AND PUNISHMENT

17 The LORD says, "My people act as though their evil ways are laws to be obeyed, inscribed with a diamond point on their stony hearts, or with an iron chisel on the corners of their altars. 2Even their children go to worship at their sacred altars and Asherah poles, beneath every green tree and on every high hill. 3So I will give all your wealth and treasures—together with your pagan shrines—as plunder to your enemies, for sin runs rampant in your land. 4The wonderful inheritance I have reserved for you will slip out of your hands, and I will send you away as captives to a foreign land. For you have kindled my anger into a roaring fire that will burn forever."

WISDOM FROM THE LORD

5This is what the LORD says: "Cursed are those who put their trust in mere humans and turn their hearts away from the LORD. 6They are like stunted shrubs in the desert, with no hope for the future. They will live in the barren wilderness, on the salty flats where no one lives.

7"But blessed are those who trust in the LORD and have made the LORD their hope and confidence. 8They are like trees planted along a riverbank, with roots that reach deep into the water. Such trees are not bothered by the heat or worried by long months of drought. Their leaves stay green, and they go right on producing delicious fruit.

9"The human heart is most deceitful and desperately wicked. Who really knows how bad it is? 10But I know! I, the LORD, search all hearts and examine secret motives. I give all people their due rewards, according to what their actions deserve."

JEREMIAH'S TRUST IN THE LORD

11Like a bird that hatches eggs she has not laid, so are those who get their wealth by unjust means. Sooner or later they will lose their riches and, at the end of their lives, will become poor old fools.

12But we worship at your throne—eternal, high, and glorious! 13O LORD, the hope of Israel, all who turn away from you will be disgraced and shamed. They will be buried in a dry and dusty grave, for they have forsaken the LORD, the fountain of living water.

14O LORD, you alone can heal me; you alone can save. My praises are for you alone! 15People scoff at me and say, "What is this 'message from the LORD' you keep talking about? Why don't your predictions come true?"

16LORD, I have not abandoned my job as a shepherd for your people. I have not urged you to send disaster. It is your message I have given them, not my own. 17LORD, do not desert me now! You alone are my hope in the day of disaster. 18Bring shame and terror on all who persecute me, but give me peace. Yes, bring double destruction upon them!

OBSERVING THE SABBATH

19Then the LORD said to me, "Go and stand in the gates of Jerusalem, first at the gate where the king goes out, and then at each of the other gates. 20Say to all the people, 'Listen to this message from the LORD, you kings of Judah and all you people of Judah and everyone living in Jerusalem. 21This is what the LORD says: Listen to my warning and live! Stop carrying on your trade at Jerusalem's gates on the Sabbath day. 22Do not do your work on the Sabbath, but make it a holy day. I gave this command to your ancestors, 23but they did not listen or obey. They stubbornly refused to pay attention and would not respond to discipline.

My Daily Worship

— July 20 —

IN SEARCH OF GREENER PASTURES

JEREMIAH 17:1–20:18

But blessed are those who trust in the LORD and have made the LORD their hope and confidence.
They are like trees planted along a riverbank, with roots that reach deep into the water.
Such trees are not bothered by the heat or worried by long months of drought. Their
leaves stay green and they go right on producing delicious fruit (17:7–8).

[i reflect]

Washington is called "the Evergreen State," which is somewhat misleading. It is only the western side of the Cascade Mountains that is lush and green. Eastern Washington state is flat and arid, actually resembling the wheat fields of Kansas. The portion of the state that is dotted with inlets and lakes and benefits from the runoff of melting snow from Mount Rainier boasts a year-round vibrancy.

All the precipitation ordinarily associated with the Pacific Northwest allows the residential lawns and grassy parks in the "Emerald City" of Seattle to remain green twelve months of the year. It's a state of contrasts. Where there is moisture and proximity to bodies of water, there is life and color. Where there is the absence of those natural resources, there is brown wilderness.

In this passage, Jeremiah isn't giving us an agricultural lesson on growing healthy plants and fruit-bearing trees. He's calling us to observe that what's true in nature is also true for our spiritual lives. People who trust in the Lord and who make him their hope and confidence will be like the trees the prophet describes—lush and fruitful. Jeremiah's still life is intended to be a metaphor for the life of the believer.

No doubt you can imagine that scene in your mind. It can be descriptive of your life if you are being irrigated by remaining in the presence of the Lord. Haven't you found that the water of God's Word stimulates spiritual growth? Make sure you prioritize your regular exposure to it. Let the roots of your life go deep to find the refreshing springs that await you in God's continual presence.

When you find dry times during your day, when you feel under stress or far from God, allow this image of lush greenery to stir your thoughts to God, the One who can refresh you.

[i pray]

Lord, in all honesty my life is desert-like too much of the time. When I'm feeling spiritually dry,
I don't want to spend time with you. What makes those times worse are the memories I
have of special times when I'm thriving and growing. Refresh my arid heart today.

[i respond]

Next time there's a weather forecast that calls for rain, determine to put on your rain gear and go for a nice long walk. As you do, let the drenching shower refresh and "green up" your sense of God's presence and what he uses in your life to grow you.

²⁴" 'But if you obey me, says the LORD, and do not carry on your trade or work on the Sabbath day, and if you keep it holy, ²⁵then this nation will continue forever. There will always be a descendant of David sitting on the throne here in Jerusalem. Kings and their officials will always ride among the people of Judah in chariots and on horses, and this city will remain forever. ²⁶And from all around Jerusalem, from the towns of Judah and Benjamin, from the western foothills* and the hill country and the Negev, the people will come with their burnt offerings and sacrifices. They will bring their grain offerings, incense, and thanksgiving offerings to the LORD's Temple.

²⁷" 'But if you do not listen to me and refuse to keep the Sabbath holy, and if on the Sabbath day you bring loads of merchandise through the gates of Jerusalem just as on other days, then I will set fire to these gates. The fire will spread to the palaces, and no one will be able to put out the roaring flames.' "

THE POTTER AND THE CLAY

18 The LORD gave another message to Jeremiah. He said, ²"Go down to the shop where clay pots and jars are made. I will speak to you while you are there." ³So I did as he told me and found the potter working at his wheel. ⁴But the jar he was making did not turn out as he had hoped, so the potter squashed the jar into a lump of clay and started again.

⁵Then the LORD gave me this message: ⁶"O Israel, can I not do to you as this potter has done to his clay? As the clay is in the potter's hand, so are you in my hand. ⁷If I announce that a certain nation or kingdom is to be uprooted, torn down, and destroyed, ⁸but then that nation renounces its evil ways, I will not destroy it as I had planned. ⁹And if I announce that I will build up and plant a certain nation or kingdom, making it strong and great, ¹⁰but then that nation turns to evil and

refuses to obey me, I will not bless that nation as I had said I would.

¹¹"Therefore, Jeremiah, go and warn all Judah and Jerusalem. Say to them, 'This is what the LORD says: I am planning disaster against you instead of good. So turn from your evil ways, each of you, and do what is right.' "

¹²But they replied, "Don't waste your breath. We will continue to live as we want to, following our own evil desires."

¹³Then the LORD said, "Has anyone ever heard of such a thing, even among the pagan nations? My virgin Israel has done something too terrible to understand! ¹⁴Does the snow ever melt high up in the mountains of Lebanon? Do the cold, flowing streams from the crags of Mount Hermon ever run dry? ¹⁵These can be counted on, but not my people! For they have deserted me and turned to worthless idols. They have stumbled off the ancient highways of good, and they walk the muddy paths of sin. ¹⁶Therefore, their land will become desolate, a monument to their stupidity. All who pass by will be astonished and shake their heads in amazement at its utter desolation. ¹⁷I will scatter my people before their enemies as the east wind scatters dust. And in all their trouble I will turn my back on them and refuse to notice their distress."

A PLOT AGAINST JEREMIAH

¹⁸Then the people said, "Come on, let's find a way to stop Jeremiah. We have our own priests and wise men and prophets. We don't need him to teach the law and give us advice and prophecies. Let's spread rumors about him and ignore what he says."

¹⁹LORD, help me! Listen to what they are planning to do to me! ²⁰Should they repay evil for good? They have set a trap to kill me, though I pleaded for them and tried to protect them from your anger. ²¹So let their children starve! Let the sword pour out their blood! Let their wives become widows with-

17:26 Hebrew *the Shephelah.*

out any children! Let their old men die in a plague, and let their young men be killed in battle! ²²Let screaming be heard from their homes as warriors come suddenly upon them. For they have dug a pit for me, and they have hidden traps along my path.

²³LORD, you know all about their murderous plots against me. Don't forgive their crimes and blot out their sins. Let them die before you. Deal with them in your anger.

JEREMIAH'S SHATTERED JAR

19 The LORD said to me, "Go and buy a clay jar. Then ask some of the leaders of the people and of the priests to follow you. ²Go out into the valley of the son of Hinnom by the entrance to the Potsherd Gate, and repeat to them the words that I give you. ³Say to them, 'Listen to this message from the LORD, you kings of Judah and citizens of Jerusalem! This is what the LORD Almighty, the God of Israel, says: I will bring such a terrible disaster on this place that the ears of those who hear about it will ring!

⁴" 'For Israel has forsaken me and turned this valley into a place of wickedness. The people burn incense to foreign gods—idols never before worshiped by this generation, by their ancestors, or by the kings of Judah. And they have filled this place with the blood of innocent children. ⁵They have built pagan shrines to Baal, and there they burn their sons as sacrifices to Baal. I have never commanded such a horrible deed; it never even crossed my mind to command such a thing! ⁶So beware, for the time is coming, says the LORD, when this place will no longer be called Topheth or the valley of the son of Hinnom, but the Valley of Slaughter. ⁷For I will upset the battle plans of Judah and Jerusalem and let invading armies slaughter them. The enemy will leave the dead bodies as food for the vultures and wild animals. ⁸I will wipe Jerusalem from the face of the earth, making it a monument to their stupidity. All who pass by will be appalled and will gasp at the destruction they see there. ⁹I will see to it that your enemies lay

> *A vital ingredient of worship is expectancy: believing that something good is going to happen.*
>
> R.T. KENDALL

siege to the city until all the food is gone. Then those trapped inside will have to eat their own sons and daughters and friends. They will be driven to utter despair.'

¹⁰"As these men watch, Jeremiah, smash the jar you brought with you. ¹¹Then say to them, 'This is what the LORD Almighty says: As this jar lies shattered, so I will shatter the people of Judah and Jerusalem beyond all hope of repair. They will bury the bodies in Topheth until there is no more room. ¹²This is what I will do to this place and its people, says the LORD. I will cause this city to become defiled like Topheth. ¹³Yes, all the houses in Jerusalem, including the palace of Judah's kings, will become like Topheth—all the houses where you burned incense on the rooftops to your star gods, and where drink offerings were poured out to your idols.' "

¹⁴Then Jeremiah returned from Topheth where he had delivered this message, and he stopped in front of the Temple of the LORD. He said to the people there, ¹⁵"This is what the LORD Almighty, the God of Israel, says: I will bring disaster upon this city and its surrounding towns just as I promised, because you have stubbornly refused to listen to me."

JEREMIAH AND PASHHUR

20 Now Pashhur son of Immer, the priest in charge of the Temple of the LORD, heard what Jeremiah was saying. ²So he arrested Jeremiah the prophet and had him whipped and put in stocks at the Benjamin Gate of the LORD's Temple.

³The next day, when Pashhur finally released him, Jeremiah said, "Pashhur, the LORD has changed your name. From now on you are to be called 'The Man Who Lives in Terror.'* ⁴For this is what the LORD says: I will send terror upon you and all your friends, and you will watch as they are slaughtered by the swords of the enemy. I will hand the people of Judah over to the king of Babylon. He will take them captive to Babylon or run them through with the sword. ⁵And I will let your enemies plunder Jerusalem. All the famed treasures of the city—the precious jewels and gold and silver of your kings—will be carried off to Babylon. ⁶As for you, Pashhur, you and all your household will go as captives to Babylon. There you will die and be buried, you and all your friends to whom you promised that everything would be all right."

JEREMIAH'S COMPLAINT

⁷O LORD, you persuaded me, and I allowed myself to be persuaded. You are stronger than I am, and you overpowered me. Now I am mocked by everyone in the city. ⁸Whenever I speak, the words come out in a violent outburst. "Violence and destruction!" I shout. So these messages from the LORD have made me a household joke. ⁹And I can't stop! If I say I'll never mention the LORD or speak in his name, his word burns in my heart like a fire. It's like a fire in my bones! I am weary of holding it in!

¹⁰I have heard the many rumors about me. They call me "The Man Who Lives in Terror." And they say, "If you say anything, we will report it." Even my old friends are watching me, waiting for a fatal slip. "He will trap himself," they say, "and then we will get our revenge on him."

¹¹But the LORD stands beside me like a great warrior. Before him they will stumble. They cannot defeat me. They will be shamed and thoroughly humiliated. Their dishonor will never be forgotten. ¹²O LORD Almighty! You know those who are righteous, and you examine the deepest thoughts of hearts and minds. Let me see your vengeance against them, for I have committed my cause to you. ¹³Now I will sing out my thanks to the LORD! Praise the LORD! For though I was poor and needy, he delivered me from my oppressors.

¹⁴Yet I curse the day I was born! May the day of my birth not be blessed. ¹⁵I curse the messenger who told my father, "Good news—you have a son!" ¹⁶Let him be destroyed like the cities of old that the LORD overthrew without mercy. Terrify him all day long with battle shouts, ¹⁷for he did not kill me at birth. Oh, that I had died in my mother's womb, that her body had been my grave! ¹⁸Why was I ever born? My entire life has been filled with trouble, sorrow, and shame.

NO DELIVERANCE FROM BABYLON

21 The LORD spoke through Jeremiah when King Zedekiah sent Pashhur son of Malkijah and Zephaniah son of Maaseiah, the priest, to speak with him. They begged Jeremiah, ²"Please ask the LORD to help us. King Nebuchadnezzar* of Babylon has begun his attack on Judah. Perhaps the LORD will be gracious and do a mighty miracle as he has done in the past. Perhaps he will force Nebuchadnezzar to withdraw his armies."

³Jeremiah replied, "Go back to King Zedekiah and tell him, ⁴'This is what the LORD, the God of Israel, says: I will make your weapons useless against the king of Babylon and the Babylonians* who are attacking you. Yes, I will bring your enemies right into the heart of this city. ⁵I myself will fight against you with great power, for I am very angry. You have made me furious! ⁶I will send a terrible plague upon this city, and both people and animals will die. ⁷And then, says the LORD, even after King Zedekiah, his officials, and everyone else in the city have survived war, famine, and disease, I will hand them over to King Nebuchadnezzar of Babylon. He will

20:3 Hebrew *Magor-missabib,* which means "surrounded by terror"; also in 20:10. 21:2 Hebrew *Nebuchadrezzar,* a variant name for Nebuchadnezzar; also in 21:7. 21:4 Or *Chaldeans;* also in 21:9.

Words of Worship

NEW SONG

New Song—Hebrew *shir cha-dash*; Greek *o-de kai-ne*.

Sometimes the Psalmist invites us to "sing a new song to the LORD" (Psalm 96:1). We hear of it again in the Bible's final chapters when a choir sings "a wonderful new song in front of the throne of God" (Revelation 14:3). Scripture often refers to singing, but something is different about a *new song*. Perhaps what is meant is a song with a new exultation in God's love and mercy, a break from traditional pleading for help. Or perhaps the "new song" is a spontaneous outburst, free-flowing praise by instruments or voices (see also **Selah**). Authorities have no pat answers for us here.

One thing to bear in mind is that the Bible makes no real difference between what is *new* and what is *renewed*. When the old receives fresh life, it becomes new. So it is with our worship. We may come before the Lord with the same praises, prayers, and petitions—but with a fresh touch from the Spirit of the risen Christ they become new! God, the builder of our lives, is also in the renovation business: "I am making all things new" (Revelation 21:5).

slaughter them all without mercy, pity, or compassion.'

8"Tell all the people, 'This is what the LORD says: Take your choice of life or death! 9Everyone who stays in Jerusalem will die from war, famine, or disease, but those who go out and surrender to the Babylonians will live. 10For I have decided to bring disaster and not good upon this city, says the LORD. It will be captured by the king of Babylon, and he will reduce it to ashes.'

JUDGMENT ON JUDAH'S KINGS

11"Say to the royal family of Judah, 'Listen to this message from the LORD! 12This is what the LORD says to the dynasty of David: Give justice to the people you judge! Help those who have been robbed; rescue them from their oppressors. Do what is right, or my anger will burn like an unquenchable fire because of all your sins. 13I will fight against this city of Jerusalem that boasts, "We are safe on our mountain! No one can touch us here." 14And I myself will punish you for your sinfulness, says the LORD. I will light a fire in your forests that will burn up everything around you.'"

A MESSAGE FOR JUDAH'S KINGS

22 Then the LORD said to me, "Go over and speak directly to the king of Judah. Say to him, 2'Listen to this message from the LORD, you king of Judah, sitting on David's throne. Let your officials and your people listen, too. 3This is what the LORD says: Be fair-minded and just. Do what is right! Help those who have been robbed; rescue them from their oppressors. Quit your evil deeds! Do not mistreat foreigners, orphans, and widows. Stop murdering the innocent! 4If you obey me, there will always be a descendant of David sitting on the throne here in Jerusalem. The king will ride through the palace gates in chariots and on horses, with his parade of officials and subjects. 5But if you refuse to pay attention to this warning, I swear by my own name, says the LORD, that this palace will become a pile of rubble.'"

A MESSAGE ABOUT THE PALACE

6Now this is what the LORD says concerning the royal palace: "You are as beloved to me as fruitful Gilead and the green forests of Lebanon. But I will destroy you and leave you deserted, with no one living within your walls. 7I will call for wreckers, who will bring out their tools to dismantle you. They will tear out all your fine cedar beams and throw them on the fire. 8People from many nations will pass by the ruins of this city and say to one another, 'Why did the LORD destroy such a great city?' ⁹And the answer will be, 'Because they violated their covenant with the LORD their God by worshiping other gods.' "

A MESSAGE ABOUT JEHOAHAZ

¹⁰Do not weep for the dead king or mourn his loss. Instead, weep for the captive king being led away! For he will never return to see his native land again. ¹¹For this is what the LORD says about Jehoahaz,* who succeeded his father, King Josiah, and was taken away as a captive: "He will never return. ¹²He will die in a distant land and never again see his own country."

A MESSAGE ABOUT JEHOIAKIM

¹³And the LORD says, "Destruction is certain for Jehoiakim,* who builds his palace with forced labor.* By not paying wages, he builds injustice into its walls and oppression into its doorframes and ceilings. ¹⁴He says, 'I will build a magnificent palace with huge rooms and many windows, paneled throughout with fragrant cedar and painted a lovely red.'

¹⁵"But a beautiful palace does not make a great king! Why did your father, Josiah, reign so long? Because he was just and right in all his dealings. That is why God blessed him. ¹⁶He made sure that justice and help were given to the poor and needy, and everything went well for him. Isn't that what it means to know me?" asks the LORD. ¹⁷"But you! You are full of selfish greed and dishonesty! You murder the innocent, oppress the poor, and reign ruthlessly."

¹⁸Therefore, this is the LORD's decree of punishment against King Jehoiakim, who succeeded his father, Josiah, on the throne: "His family will not weep for him when he dies. His subjects will not even care that he is dead. ¹⁹He will be buried like a dead donkey—dragged out of Jerusalem and dumped outside the gate! ²⁰Weep, for your allies are all gone. Search for them in Lebanon. Shout for them at Bashan. Search for them in the regions east of the river.* See, they are all destroyed. Not one is left to help you.

²¹"When you were prosperous, I warned you, but you replied, 'Don't bother me.' Since childhood you have been that way—you simply will not listen! ²²And now your allies have all disappeared with a puff of wind. All your friends have been taken away as captives. Surely at last you will see your wickedness and be ashamed. ²³It may be nice to live in a beautiful palace lined with lumber from the cedars of Lebanon, but soon you will cry and groan in anguish—anguish like that of a woman about to give birth.

A MESSAGE FOR JEHOIACHIN

²⁴"And as surely as I live," says the LORD, "I will abandon you, Jehoiachin* son of Jehoiakim, king of Judah. Even if you were the signet ring on my right hand, I would pull you off. ²⁵I will hand you over to those who seek to kill you, of whom you are so desperately afraid—to King Nebuchadnezzar* of Babylon and the mighty Babylonian* army. ²⁶I will expel you and your mother from this land, and you will die in a foreign country. ²⁷You will never again return to the land of your desire.

²⁸"Why is this man Jehoiachin like a discarded, broken dish? Why are he and his children to be exiled to distant lands? ²⁹O earth, earth, earth! Listen to this message from the LORD! ³⁰This is what the LORD says: Let the record show that this man Jehoiachin was childless, for none of his children will ever sit on the throne of David to rule in Judah. His life will amount to nothing."

THE RIGHTEOUS BRANCH

23 "I will send disaster upon the leaders of my people—the shepherds of my sheep—for they have destroyed and scattered the very ones they were expected to care for," says the LORD.

22:11 Hebrew *Shallum,* another name for Jehoahaz. 22:13a The brother and successor of the exiled Jehoahaz. 22:13b Hebrew *by unrighteousness.* 22:20 Hebrew *in Abarim.* 22:24 Hebrew *Coniah,* a variant name for Jehoiachin; also in 22:28, 30. 22:25a Hebrew *Nebuchadrezzar,* a variant name for Nebuchadnezzar. 22:25b Or *Chaldean.*

My Daily Worship

— July 21 —

IN THE NAME OF GOD

JEREMIAH 21:1–24:10

But stop using this phrase, "prophecy from the LORD." For people are using it
to give authority to their own ideas, turning upside down the words
of our God, the living God, the LORD Almighty (23:36).

[i reflect]

Jim Jones was a popular pastor in Northern California. This effective communicator had a charismatic personality and was successful in bridging the chasms that often divided whites and blacks. His interracial church was known as the People's Temple. But something in Pastor Jones snapped. He became consumed with his own ideas.

To get support from the congregation, he would attribute his inspiration to divine revelations. It was one of those "revelations" that resulted in the majority of the People's Temple relocating to the small country of Guyana in South America. The communal cult was known as Jonestown. Relatives of church members who followed Pastor Jones were troubled. They had reason to believe that Jim Jones was a demagogue, but they had no idea what the tragic consequences of his leadership would be. On November 18, 1978, 914 members of the People's Temple committed mass suicide because a man, who equated himself to God, told them to drink Kool-Aid laced with poison.

That kind of cult phenomenon is not without precedent. Israel's history was stained with evidence of such scandal. Jeremiah had harsh words for those false prophets who claimed their words were from God. Even today it's tempting at times to attribute our gut instincts as being from God, when they are often selfish desires wanting to be fulfilled. Be honest when you evaluate why you want to change churches, why you're tempted at times to leave your mate, why you reinterpret Scripture in order to be politically correct.

As you quiet yourself before the Lord with the newspaper in one hand and your Bible in the other, remember which carries more weight. God alone is our authority.

[i pray]

Lord, the events of Jonestown are chilling to think about. But I wonder if you are sometimes
equally disturbed by my tendency to bring you down to my level. Forgive me, Lord,
for taking Bible verses out of context to rationalize my inappropriate behavior.

[i respond]

Who are the authorities that you trust? Make a list of names. Pray for each one, asking that God would reveal who or what sometimes carries more weight in your life than him.

[2]This is what the LORD, the God of Israel, says to these shepherds: "Instead of leading my flock to safety, you have deserted them and driven them to destruction. Now I will pour out judgment on you for the evil you have done to them. [3]But I will gather together the remnant of my flock from wherever I have driven them. I will bring them back into their own fold, and they will be fruitful and increase in number. [4]Then I will appoint responsible shepherds to care for them, and they will never be afraid again. Not a single one of them will be lost or missing," says the LORD.

[5]"For the time is coming," says the LORD, "when I will place a righteous Branch on King David's throne. He will be a King who rules with wisdom. He will do what is just and right throughout the land. [6]And this is his name: 'The LORD Is Our Righteousness.'* In that day Judah will be saved, and Israel will live in safety.

[7]"In that day," says the LORD, "when people are taking an oath, they will no longer say, 'As surely as the LORD lives, who rescued the people of Israel from the land of Egypt.' [8]Instead, they will say, 'As surely as the LORD lives, who brought the people of Israel back to their own land from the land of the north and from all the countries to which he had exiled them.' Then they will live in their own land."

JUDGMENT ON FALSE PROPHETS

[9]My heart is broken because of the false prophets, and I tremble uncontrollably. I stagger like a drunkard, like someone overcome by wine, because of the holy words the LORD has spoken against them. [10]For the land is full of adultery, and it lies under a curse. The land itself is in mourning—its pastures are dried up. For the prophets do evil and abuse their power.

[11]"The priests are like the prophets, all ungodly, wicked men. I have seen their despicable acts right here in my own Temple," says the LORD. [12]"Therefore, their paths will be dark and slippery. They will be chased down dark and treacherous trails, where they will fall. For I will bring disaster upon them when their time of punishment comes. I, the LORD, have spoken!

[13]"I saw that the prophets of Samaria were terribly evil, for they prophesied by Baal and led my people of Israel into sin. [14]But now I see that the prophets of Jerusalem are even worse! They commit adultery, and they love dishonesty. They encourage those who are doing evil instead of turning them away from their sins. These prophets are as wicked as the people of Sodom and Gomorrah once were."

[15]Therefore, this is what the LORD Almighty says concerning the prophets: "I will feed them with bitterness and give them poison to drink. For it is because of Jerusalem's prophets that wickedness fills this land. [16]This is my warning to my people," says the LORD Almighty. "Do not listen to these prophets when they prophesy to you, filling you with futile hopes. They are making up everything they say. They do not speak for the LORD! [17]They keep saying to these rebels who despise my word, 'Don't worry! The LORD says you will have peace!' And to those who stubbornly follow their own evil desires, they say, 'No harm will come your way!'

[18]"But can you name even one of these prophets who knows the LORD well enough to hear what he is saying? Has even one of them cared enough to listen? [19]Look! The LORD's anger bursts out like a storm, a whirlwind that swirls down on the heads of the wicked. [20]The anger of the LORD will not diminish until it has finished all his plans. In the days to come, you will understand all this very clearly.

[21]"I have not sent these prophets, yet they claim to speak for me. I have given them no message, yet they prophesy. [22]If they had listened to me, they would have spoken my words and turned my people from their evil ways. [23]Am I a God who is only in one place?" asks the LORD. "Do they think I cannot see what they are doing? [24]Can anyone hide from

23:6 Hebrew *Yahweh Tsidqenu.*

me? Am I not everywhere in all the heavens and earth?" asks the LORD.

²⁵"I have heard these prophets say, 'Listen to the dream I had from God last night.' And then they proceed to tell lies in my name. ²⁶How long will this go on? If they are prophets, they are prophets of deceit, inventing everything they say. ²⁷By telling these false dreams, they are trying to get my people to forget me, just as their ancestors did by worshiping the idols of Baal. ²⁸Let these false prophets tell their dreams, but let my true messengers faithfully proclaim my every word. There is a difference between chaff and wheat! ²⁹Does not my word burn like fire?" asks the LORD. "Is it not like a mighty hammer that smashes rock to pieces?

³⁰"Therefore," says the LORD, "I stand against these prophets who get their messages from each other—³¹these smooth-tongued prophets who say, 'This prophecy is from the LORD!' ³²Their imaginary dreams are flagrant lies that lead my people into sin. I did not send or appoint them, and they have no message at all for my people," says the LORD.

FALSE PROPHECIES AND FALSE PROPHETS

³³"Suppose one of the people or one of the prophets or priests asks you, 'What prophecy has the LORD burdened you with now?' You must reply, 'You are the burden!* The LORD says he will abandon you!' ³⁴If any prophet, priest, or anyone else says, 'I have a prophecy from the LORD,' I will punish that person along with his entire family. ³⁵You should keep asking each other, 'What is the LORD's answer?' or 'What is the LORD saying?' ³⁶But stop using this phrase, 'prophecy from the LORD.' For people are using it to give authority to their own ideas, turning upside down the words of our God, the living God, the LORD Almighty.

³⁷"This is what you should say to the prophets: 'What is the LORD's answer?' or 'What is the LORD saying?' ³⁸But suppose they respond, 'This is a prophecy from the LORD!' Then you should say, 'This is what the LORD says: Because you have used this phrase, "prophecy from the LORD," even though I warned you not to use it, ³⁹I will forget you completely. I will expel you from my presence, along with this city that I gave to you and your ancestors. ⁴⁰And I will make you an object of ridicule, and your name will be infamous throughout the ages.'"

GOOD AND BAD FIGS

24 After King Nebuchadnezzar* of Babylon exiled Jehoiachin* son of Jehoiakim, king of Judah, to Babylon along with the princes of Judah and all the skilled craftsmen, the LORD gave me this vision. I saw two baskets of figs placed in front of the LORD's Temple in Jerusalem. ²One basket was filled with fresh, ripe figs, while the other was filled with figs that were spoiled and could not be eaten.

³Then the LORD said to me, "What do you see, Jeremiah?"

I replied, "Figs, some very good and some very bad."

⁴Then the LORD gave me this message: ⁵"This is what the LORD, the God of Israel, says: The good figs represent the exiles I sent from Judah to the land of the Babylonians.* ⁶I have sent them into captivity for their own good. I will see that they are well treated, and I will bring them back here again. I will build them up and not tear them down. I will plant them and not uproot them. ⁷I will give them hearts that will recognize me as the LORD. They will be my people, and I will be their God, for they will return to me wholeheartedly.

⁸"But the rotten figs," the LORD said, "represent King Zedekiah of Judah, his officials, all the people left in Jerusalem, and those who live in Egypt. I will treat them like spoiled figs, too rotten to eat. ⁹I will make them an object of horror and evil to every nation on earth.

23:33 As in Greek version and Latin Vulgate; Hebrew reads *What burden?* 24:1a Hebrew *Nebuchadrezzar,* a variant name for Nebuchadnezzar. 24:1b Hebrew *Jeconiah,* a variant name for Jehoiachin. 24:5 Or *Chaldeans.*

They will be disgraced and mocked, taunted and cursed, wherever I send them. [10]I will send war, famine, and disease until they have vanished from the land of Israel, which I gave to them and their ancestors."

> *Worship in spirit and truth involves the total human being—spirit, mind, emotions, and body.*
>
> JACK HAYFORD

SEVENTY YEARS OF CAPTIVITY

25 This message for all the people of Judah came to Jeremiah from the LORD during the fourth year of Jehoiakim's reign* over Judah. This was the year when King Nebuchadnezzar* of Babylon began his reign.

[2]Jeremiah the prophet said to the people in Judah and Jerusalem, [3]"For the past twenty-three years—from the thirteenth year of Josiah son of Amon,* king of Judah, until now—the LORD has been giving me his messages. I have faithfully passed them on to you, but you have not listened.

[4]"Again and again, the LORD has sent you his prophets, but you have not listened or even tried to hear. [5]Each time the message was this: 'Turn from the evil road you are traveling and from the evil things you are doing. Only then will I let you live in this land that the LORD gave to you and your ancestors forever. [6]Do not make me angry by worshiping the idols you have made. Then I will not harm you.'

[7]"But you would not listen to me," says the LORD. "You made me furious by worshiping your idols, bringing on yourselves all the disasters you now suffer. [8]And now the LORD Almighty says: Because you have not listened to me, [9]I will gather together all the armies of the north under King Nebuchadnezzar of Babylon, whom I have appointed as my deputy. I will bring them all against this land and its people and against the other nations near you. I will completely destroy* you and make you an object of horror and contempt and a ruin forever. [10]I will take away your happy singing and laughter. The joyful voices of bridegrooms and brides will no longer be heard. Your businesses will fail, and all your homes will stand silent and dark. [11]This entire land will become a desolate wasteland. Israel and her neighboring lands will serve the king of Babylon for seventy years.

[12]"Then, after the seventy years of captivity are over, I will punish the king of Babylon and his people for their sins, says the LORD. I will make the country of the Babylonians* an everlasting wasteland. [13]I will bring upon them all the terrors I have promised in this book—all the penalties announced by Jeremiah against the nations. [14]Many nations and great kings will enslave the Babylonians, just as they enslaved my people. I will punish them in proportion to the suffering they cause my people."

THE CUP OF THE LORD'S ANGER

[15]Then the LORD, the God of Israel, said to me, "Take from my hand this cup filled to the brim with my anger, and make all the nations to whom I send you drink from it. [16]When they drink from it, they will stagger, crazed by the warfare I will send against them."

[17]So I took the cup of anger from the LORD and made all the nations drink from it—every nation the LORD sent me to. [18]I went to Jerusalem and the other towns of Judah, and their kings and officials drank from the cup. From that day until this, they have been a desolate ruin, an object of horror, contempt, and

---

25:1a The fourth year of Jehoiakim's reign and the accession year of Nebuchadnezzar's reign was 605 B.C. 25:1b Hebrew *Nebuchadrezzar*, a variant name for Nebuchadnezzar; also in 25:9. 25:3 The thirteenth year of Josiah's reign was 627 B.C. 25:9 The Hebrew term used here refers to the complete consecration of things or people to the LORD, either by destroying them or by giving them as an offering. 25:12 Or *Chaldeans.*

cursing. [19]I went to Egypt and spoke to Pharaoh, his officials, his princes, and his people. They, too, drank from that terrible cup, [20]along with all the foreigners living in that land. So did all the kings of the land of Uz and the kings of the Philistine cities of Ashkelon, Gaza, Ekron, and what remains of Ashdod. [21]Then I went to the nations of Edom, Moab, and Ammon, [22]and the kings of Tyre and Sidon, and the kings of the regions across the sea. [23]I went to Dedan, Tema, and Buz, and to the people who live in distant places.* [24]I went to the kings of Arabia, the kings of the nomadic tribes of the desert, [25]and to the kings of Zimri, Elam, and Media. [26]And I went to the kings of the northern countries, far and near, one after the other—all the kingdoms of the world. And finally, the king of Babylon* himself drank from the cup of the LORD's anger.

[27]Then the LORD said to me, "Now tell them, 'The LORD Almighty, the God of Israel, says: Drink from this cup of my anger. Get drunk and vomit, and you will fall to rise no more, for I am sending terrible wars against you.' [28]And if they refuse to accept the cup, tell them, 'The LORD Almighty says: You must drink from it. You cannot escape! [29]I have begun to punish Jerusalem, the city where my own name is honored. Now should I let you go unpunished? No, you will not escape disaster. I will call for war against all the nations of the earth. I, the LORD Almighty, have spoken!'

[30]"Now prophesy all these things, and say to them, 'The LORD will roar loudly against his own land from his holy dwelling in heaven. He will shout against everyone on the earth, like the harvesters do as they crush juice from the grapes. [31]His cry of judgment will reach the ends of the earth, for the LORD will bring his case against all the nations. He will judge all the people of the earth, slaughtering the wicked with his sword. The LORD has spoken!'"

[32]This is what the LORD Almighty says:

"Look! Disaster will fall upon nation after nation! A great whirlwind of fury is rising from the most distant corners of the earth!"

[33]In that day those the LORD has slaughtered will fill the earth from one end to the other. No one will mourn for them or gather up their bodies to bury them. They will be scattered like dung on the ground.

[34]Weep and moan, you evil shepherds! Roll in the dust, you leaders of the flock! The time of your slaughter has arrived; you will fall and shatter like fragile pottery. [35]You will find no place to hide; there will be no way to escape.

[36]Listen to the frantic cries of the shepherds, to the leaders of the flock shouting in despair, for the LORD is spoiling their pastures. [37]Peaceful meadows will be turned into a wasteland by the LORD's fierce anger. [38]He has left his den like a lion seeking its prey, and their land will be made desolate by the sword of the enemy and the LORD's fierce anger.

JEREMIAH'S ESCAPE FROM DEATH

26 This message came to Jeremiah from the LORD early in the reign of Jehoiakim son of Josiah,* king of Judah. [2]The LORD said, "Stand out in front of the Temple of the LORD, and make an announcement to the people who have come there to worship from all over Judah. Give them my entire message; include every word. [3]Perhaps they will listen and turn from their evil ways. Then I will be able to withhold the disaster I am ready to pour out on them because of their sins.

[4]"Say to them, 'This is what the LORD says: If you will not listen to me and obey the law I have given you, [5]and if you will not listen to my servants, the prophets—for I sent them again and again to warn you, but you would not listen to them—[6]then I will destroy this Temple as I destroyed Shiloh, the place where the Tabernacle was located. And I will make Jerusalem an object of cursing in every nation on earth.'"

25:23 Or who clip the corners of their hair.   25:26 Hebrew of Sheshach, a code name for Babylon.   26:1 The first year of Jehoiakim's reign was 608 B.C.

[7]The priests, the prophets, and all the people listened to Jeremiah as he spoke in front of the LORD's Temple. [8]But when Jeremiah had finished his message, saying everything the LORD had told him to say, the priests and prophets and all the people at the Temple mobbed him. "Kill him!" they shouted. [9]"What right do you have to prophesy in the LORD's name that this Temple will be destroyed like Shiloh? What do you mean, saying that Jerusalem will be destroyed?" And all the people threatened him as he stood in front of the Temple.

[10]When the officials of Judah heard what was happening, they rushed over from the palace and sat down at the New Gate of the Temple to hold court. [11]The priests and prophets presented their accusations to the officials and the people. "This man should die!" they said. "You have heard with your own ears what a traitor he is, for he has prophesied against this city."

[12]Then Jeremiah spoke in his own defense. "The LORD sent me to prophesy against this Temple and this city," he said. "The LORD gave me every word that I have spoken. [13]But if you stop your sinning and begin to obey the LORD your God, he will cancel this disaster that he has announced against you. [14]As for me, I am helpless and in your power—do with me as you think best. [15]But if you kill me, rest assured that you will be killing an innocent man! The responsibility for such a deed will lie on you, on this city, and on every person living in it. For it is absolutely true that the LORD sent me to speak every word you have heard."

[16]Then the officials and the people said to the priests and prophets, "This man does not deserve the death sentence, for he has spoken to us in the name of the LORD our God."

[17]Then some of the wise old men stood and spoke to the people there. [18]They said, "Think back to the days when Micah of Moresheth prophesied during the reign of King Hezekiah of Judah. He told the people of Judah, 'This is what the LORD Almighty says: Mount Zion will be plowed like an open field; Jerusalem will be reduced to rubble! A great forest will grow on the hilltop, where the Temple now stands.'* [19]But did King Hezekiah and the people kill him for saying this? No, they turned from their sins and worshiped the LORD. They begged him to have mercy on them. Then the LORD held back the terrible disaster he had pronounced against them. If we kill Jeremiah, who knows what will happen to us?"

[20](At this time, Uriah son of Shemaiah from Kiriath-jearim was also prophesying for the LORD. And he predicted the same terrible disaster against the city and nation as Jeremiah did. [21]When King Jehoiakim and the army officers and officials heard what he was saying, the king sent someone to kill him. But Uriah heard about the plot and escaped to Egypt. [22]Then King Jehoiakim sent Elnathan son of Acbor to Egypt along with several other men to capture Uriah. [23]They took him prisoner and brought him back to King Jehoiakim. The king then killed Uriah with a sword and had him buried in an unmarked grave.)

[24]Ahikam son of Shaphan also stood with Jeremiah and persuaded the court not to turn him over to the mob to be killed.

JEREMIAH WEARS AN OX YOKE

27 This message came to Jeremiah from the LORD early in the reign of Zedekiah* son of Josiah, king of Judah.

[2]The LORD said to me, "Make a yoke, and fasten it on your neck with leather thongs. [3]Then send messages to the kings of Edom, Moab, Ammon, Tyre, and Sidon through their ambassadors to King Zedekiah in Jerusalem. [4]Give them this message for their masters: 'This is what the LORD Almighty, the God of Israel, says: [5]By my great power I have made the earth and all its people and every animal. I can give these things of mine to anyone I choose. [6]Now I will give your countries to

26:18 Mic 3:12.   27:1 As in some Hebrew manuscripts and Syriac version (see also 27:3, 12); most Hebrew manuscripts read *Jehoiakim*.

send war, famine, and disease upon that nation until Babylon has conquered it.

[9] "'Do not listen to your false prophets, fortune-tellers, interpreters of dreams, mediums, and sorcerers who say, "The king of Babylon will not conquer you." [10]They are all liars, and I will drive you from your land and send you far away to die. [11]But the people of any nation that submits to the king of Babylon will be allowed to stay in their own country to farm the land as usual. I, the LORD, have spoken!'"

[12]Then I repeated this same message to King Zedekiah of Judah. "If you want to live, submit to the king of Babylon and his people," I said. [13]"Why do you insist on dying—you and your people? Why should you choose war, famine, and disease, which the LORD will bring against every nation that refuses to submit to Babylon's king? [14]Do not listen to the false prophets who keep telling you, 'The king of Babylon will not conquer you.' They are liars. [15]This is what the LORD says: I have not sent these prophets! They are telling you lies in my name, so I will drive you from this land. You will all die—you and all these prophets, too."

[16]Then I spoke to the priests and the people and said, "This is what the LORD says: Do not listen to your prophets who claim that soon the gold utensils taken from my Temple will be returned from Babylon. It is all a lie! [17]Do not listen to them. Surrender to the king of Babylon, and you will live. Why should this whole city be destroyed? [18]If they really are the LORD's prophets, let them pray to the LORD Almighty about the gold utensils that are still left in the LORD's Temple and in the king's palace and in the palaces of Jerusalem. Let them pray that these remaining articles will not be carried away with you to Babylon!

[19]"For this is what the LORD Almighty says about the bronze pillars in front of the Temple, the bronze Sea in the Temple courtyard, the bronze water carts, and all the other ceremonial articles. [20]King Nebuchadnezzar of Babylon left them here when he exiled Jehoiachin* son of Jehoiakim, king of Judah,

---

Words of Worship

FAITH, FAITHFULNESS

Faith, Faithfulness—Hebrew *'e-mu-nah* "faithfulness, firmness"; Greek *pistis* "faith, conviction."

Faith, in Scripture, has several meanings. It is first of all *faithfulness*, our firm commitment to the Lord and his ways. It is *reliance* in God, our trust in his help and direction for our lives. It is the *assurance* that God's promises are reliable, even when we don't always see them working out in our present circumstances. It is the core of our *beliefs* about God and his salvation, our understanding of what is true.

Worship involves all these facets of faith. We come to God as his committed people, loyal to his covenant. We rely on him to provide for us. We are convinced he has the answer to our questions and needs. What he tells us governs the way we look at life and all reality. Jesus' disciples said to him, "We need more faith; tell us how to get it" (Luke 17:5). That's our request, and it is answered in worship when we hear the word of Christ through prayer, song, or study, for "faith comes from listening to this message of good news" (Romans 10:17).

King Nebuchadnezzar of Babylon, who is my servant. I have put everything, even the wild animals, under his control. [7]All the nations will serve him and his son and his grandson until his time is up. But then many nations and great kings will conquer and rule over Babylon. [8]So you must submit to Babylon's king and serve him; put your neck under Babylon's yoke! I will punish any nation that refuses to be his slave, says the LORD. I will

27:20 Hebrew *Jeconiah*, a variant name for Jehoiachin.

to Babylon, along with all the other important people of Judah and Jerusalem. ²¹Yes, this is what the LORD Almighty, the God of Israel, says about the precious things kept in the Temple and in the palace of Judah's king: ²²They will all be carried away to Babylon and will stay there until I send for them, says the LORD. But someday I will bring them back to Jerusalem again."

JEREMIAH CONDEMNS HANANIAH

28 One day in late summer* of that same year—the fourth year of the reign of Zedekiah, king of Judah—Hananiah son of Azzur, a prophet from Gibeon, addressed me publicly in the Temple while all the priests and people listened. He said, ²"The LORD Almighty, the God of Israel, says: I will remove the yoke of the king of Babylon from your necks. ³Within two years, I will bring back all the Temple treasures that King Nebuchadnezzar carried off to Babylon. ⁴And I will bring back Jehoiachin* son of Jehoiakim, king of Judah, and all the other captives that were taken to Babylon. I will surely break the yoke that the king of Babylon has put on your necks. I, the LORD, have spoken!"

⁵Jeremiah responded to Hananiah as they stood in front of all the priests and people at the Temple. ⁶He said, "Amen! May your prophecies come true! I hope the LORD does everything you say. I hope he does bring back from Babylon the treasures of this Temple and all our loved ones. ⁷But listen now to the solemn words I speak to you in the presence of all these people. ⁸The ancient prophets who preceded you and me spoke against many nations, always warning of war, famine, and disease. ⁹So a prophet who predicts peace must carry the burden of proof. Only when his predictions come true can it be known that he is really from the LORD."

¹⁰Then Hananiah the prophet took the yoke off Jeremiah's neck and broke it. ¹¹And Hananiah said again to the crowd that had gathered, "The LORD has promised that within two years he will break the yoke of oppression from all the nations now subject to King Nebuchadnezzar of Babylon." At that, Jeremiah left the Temple area.

¹²Soon afterward the LORD gave this message to Jeremiah: ¹³"Go and tell Hananiah, 'This is what the LORD says: You have broken a wooden yoke, but you have replaced it with a yoke of iron. ¹⁴The LORD Almighty, the God of Israel, says: I have put a yoke of iron on the necks of all these nations, forcing them into slavery under King Nebuchadnezzar of Babylon. I have put everything, even the wild animals, under his control.'"

¹⁵Then Jeremiah the prophet said to Hananiah, "Listen, Hananiah! The LORD has not sent you, but the people believe your lies. ¹⁶Therefore, the LORD says you must die. Your life will end this very year because you have rebelled against the LORD."

¹⁷Two months later,* Hananiah died.

A LETTER TO THE EXILES

29 Jeremiah wrote a letter from Jerusalem to the elders, priests, prophets, and all the people who had been exiled to Babylon by King Nebuchadnezzar. ²This was after King Jehoiachin,* the queen mother, the court officials, the leaders of Judah, and all the craftsmen had been deported from Jerusalem. ³He sent the letter with Elasah son of Shaphan and Gemariah son of Hilkiah, when they went to Babylon as King Zedekiah's ambassadors to Nebuchadnezzar. This is what Jeremiah's letter said:

⁴The LORD Almighty, the God of Israel,
sends this message to all the captives he
has exiled to Babylon from Jerusalem:
⁵"Build homes, and plan to stay. Plant
gardens, and eat the food you produce.

28:1 Hebrew *In the fifth month,* of the Hebrew calendar. This month in the fourth year of Zedekiah's reign occurred in August and September 593 B.C. Also see note on 1:3.   28:4 Hebrew *Jeconiah,* a variant name for Jehoiachin.   28:17 Hebrew *In the seventh month of that same year.* See 28:1 and the note there.   29:2 Hebrew *Jeconiah,* a variant name for Jehoiachin.

My Daily Worship

— July 22 —

AN ANTIDOTE TO MOTION SICKNESS

JEREMIAH 25:1–29:32

*"For I know the plans I have for you," says the LORD. "They are plans for good
and not for disaster, to give you a future and a hope" (29:11).*

[i reflect]

Perspective is everything. When you have a view of what's up ahead, your current circumstances aren't as troubling as they might otherwise be. For example, have you ever noticed that the person driving the car never gets carsick? That's because the driver sees the upcoming curves and makes the necessary mental adjustment in advance of what his body (and the car) will later experience.

Curiously, a person's equilibrium is somehow impacted by a knowledge of what's ahead. Perhaps it also has to do with the fact that the person behind the steering wheel is in control of the speed at which the bends in the road are encountered. In other words, the one who is in control of the situation is not caught off-guard and is therefore able to steer his passengers with confidence (even though they may lack a similar sense of security).

In these familiar words recorded in Jeremiah, God reminds us that he is in complete control. Even though we can't see around the bend, he can. Our lives are following an itinerary of his choosing. And despite the fact that we sometimes get upset or lose our balance on the journey, he reminds us that his route is a good one. Our destination is a future filled with hope, and our safe arrival is guaranteed.

Isn't that enough to cause a smile to creep across your face? Thinking about the recent disappointments or disasters you've had to endure, isn't it good to know that God is in control? As you enter into his presence through prayer and praise today, be thankful that God knows your life story from beginning to end. Let the fact that nothing catches him by surprise penetrate your heart. Surrender your "motion sickness" to him as you deal with the curves up ahead.

[i pray]

*Father God, you know that when I don't have answers to questions about tomorrow, I tend
to stress out. Help me break the cycle of this self-destructive pattern. Remind me,
Lord, that as long as you can see what's coming, I don't need to worry.*

[i respond]

If you have never memorized Jeremiah 29:11, do it today. Write a paraphrase of this verse in your own words. For example, "God knows exactly where he's taking me, and he doesn't want me to worry about the path he'll lead me on to get there."

⁶Marry, and have children. Then find spouses for them, and have many grandchildren. Multiply! Do not dwindle away! ⁷And work for the peace and prosperity of Babylon. Pray to the LORD for that city where you are held captive, for if Babylon has peace, so will you."

⁸The LORD Almighty, the God of Israel, says, "Do not let the prophets and mediums who are there in Babylon trick you. Do not listen to their dreams ⁹because they prophesy lies in my name. I have not sent them," says the LORD. ¹⁰"The truth is that you will be in Babylon for seventy years. But then I will come and do for you all the good things I have promised, and I will bring you home again. ¹¹For I know the plans I have for you," says the LORD. "They are plans for good and not for disaster, to give you a future and a hope. ¹²In those days when you pray, I will listen. ¹³If you look for me in earnest, you will find me when you seek me. ¹⁴I will be found by you," says the LORD. "I will end your captivity and restore your fortunes. I will gather you out of the nations where I sent you and bring you home again to your own land."

¹⁵You may claim that the LORD has raised up prophets for you in Babylon. ¹⁶But this is what the LORD says about the king who sits on David's throne and all those still living here in Jerusalem—your relatives who were not exiled to Babylon. ¹⁷This is what the LORD Almighty says: "I will send war, famine, and disease upon them and make them like rotting figs—too bad to eat. ¹⁸Yes, I will pursue them with war, famine, and disease, and I will scatter them around the world. In every nation where I send them, I will make them an object of damnation, horror, contempt, and mockery. ¹⁹For they refuse to listen to me, though I have spoken to them repeatedly through my prophets.

And you who are in exile have not listened either," says the LORD.

²⁰Therefore, listen to this message from the LORD, all you captives there in Babylon. ²¹This is what the LORD Almighty, the God of Israel, says about your prophets—Ahab son of Kolaiah and Zedekiah son of Maaseiah—who are telling you lies in my name: "I will turn them over to Nebuchadnezzar* for a public execution. ²²Their terrible fate will become proverbial, so that whenever the Judean exiles want to curse someone they will say, 'May the LORD make you like Zedekiah and Ahab, whom the king of Babylon burned alive!' ²³For these men have done terrible things among my people. They have committed adultery with their neighbors' wives and have lied in my name. I am a witness to this," says the LORD.

A Message for Shemaiah

²⁴The LORD sent this message to Shemaiah the Nehelamite in Babylon: ²⁵"This is what the LORD Almighty, the God of Israel, says: You wrote a letter on your own authority to Zephaniah son of Maaseiah, the priest, and you sent copies to the other priests and people in Jerusalem. You said to Zephaniah, ²⁶"The LORD has appointed you to replace Jehoiada as the priest in charge of the house of the LORD. You are responsible to put anyone who claims to be a prophet in the stocks and neck irons. ²⁷So why have you done nothing to stop Jeremiah from Anathoth, who pretends to be a prophet among you? ²⁸Jeremiah sent a letter here to Babylon, predicting that our captivity will be a long one. He said we should build homes and plan to stay for many years. He said we should plant fruit trees, because we will be here to eat the fruit for many years to come.' "

²⁹But when Zephaniah the priest received Shemaiah's letter, he took it to Jeremiah and read it to him. ³⁰Then the LORD gave this mes-

29:21 Hebrew *Nebuchadrezzar*, a variant name for Nebuchadnezzar.

sage to Jeremiah: [31]"Send an open letter to all the exiles in Babylon. Tell them, 'This is what the LORD says concerning Shemaiah the Nehelamite: Since he has prophesied to you when I did not send him and has tricked you into believing his lies, [32]I will punish him and his family. None of his descendants will see the good things I will do for my people, for he has taught you to rebel against me. I, the LORD, have spoken!'"

PROMISES OF DELIVERANCE

30 The LORD gave another message to Jeremiah. He said, [2]"This is what the LORD, the God of Israel, says: Write down for the record everything I have said to you, Jeremiah. [3]For the time is coming when I will restore the fortunes of my people of Israel and Judah. I will bring them home to this land that I gave to their ancestors, and they will possess it and live here again. I, the LORD, have spoken!"

[4]This is the message the LORD gave concerning Israel and Judah: [5]"This is what the LORD says: I have heard the people crying; there is only fear and trembling. [6]Now let me ask you a question: Do men give birth to babies? Then why do they stand there, ashen-faced, hands pressed against their sides like women about to give birth? [7]In all history there has never been such a time of terror. It will be a time of trouble for my people Israel.* Yet in the end, they will be saved!

[8]"For in that day, says the LORD Almighty, I will break the yoke from their necks and snap their chains. Foreigners will no longer be their masters. [9]For my people will serve the LORD their God and David their king, whom I will raise up for them.

[10]"So do not be afraid, Jacob, my servant; do not be dismayed, Israel, says the LORD. For I will bring you home again from distant lands, and your children will return from their exile. Israel will return and will have peace and quiet in their own land, and no one will make

them afraid. [11]For I am with you and will save you, says the LORD. I will completely destroy the nations where I have scattered you, but I will not destroy you. But I must discipline you; I cannot let you go unpunished.

[12]"This is what the LORD says: Yours is an incurable bruise, a terrible wound. [13]There is no one to help you or bind up your injury. You are beyond the help of any medicine. [14]All your allies have left you and do not care about you anymore. I have wounded you cruelly, as though I were your enemy. For your sins are many, and your guilt is great. [15]Why do you protest your punishment—this wound that has no cure? I have had to punish you because your sins are many and your guilt is great.

[16]"But in that coming day, all who destroy you will be destroyed, and all your enemies will be sent into exile. Those who plunder you will be plundered, and those who attack you will be attacked. [17]I will give you back your health and heal your wounds, says the LORD.

"Now you are called an outcast—'Jerusalem* for whom nobody cares.' [18]But the LORD says this: When I bring you home again from your captivity and restore your fortunes, Jerusalem will be rebuilt on her ruins. The palace will be reconstructed as it was before. [19]There will be joy and songs of thanksgiving, and I will multiply my people and make of them a great and honored nation. [20]Their children will prosper as they did long ago. I will establish them as a nation before me, and I will punish anyone who hurts them. [21]They will have their own ruler again, and he will not be a foreigner. I will invite him to approach me, says the LORD, for who would dare to come unless invited? [22]You will be my people, and I will be your God."

[23]Look! The LORD's anger bursts out like a storm, a driving wind that swirls down on the heads of the wicked. [24]The fierce anger of the LORD will not diminish until it has finished all his plans. In the days to come, you will understand all this.

30:7 Hebrew *Jacob;* also in 30:10b.   30:17 Hebrew *Zion.*

HOPE FOR RESTORATION

31 "In that day," says the LORD, "I will be the God of all the families of Israel, and they will be my people. ²I will care for the survivors as they travel through the wilderness. I will again come to give rest to the people of Israel."

³Long ago the LORD said to Israel: "I have loved you, my people, with an everlasting love. With unfailing love I have drawn you to myself. ⁴I will rebuild you, my virgin Israel. You will again be happy and dance merrily with tambourines. ⁵Again you will plant your vineyards on the mountains of Samaria and eat from your own gardens there. ⁶The day will come when watchmen will shout from the hill country of Ephraim, 'Come, let us go up to Jerusalem* to worship the LORD our God.'"

⁷Now this is what the LORD says: "Sing with joy for Israel*! Shout for the greatest of nations! Shout out with praise and joy: 'Save your people, O LORD, the remnant of Israel!' ⁸For I will bring them from the north and from the distant corners of the earth. I will not forget the blind and lame, the expectant mothers and women about to give birth. A great company will return! ⁹Tears of joy will stream down their faces, and I will lead them home with great care. They will walk beside quiet streams and not stumble. For I am Israel's father, and Ephraim is my oldest child.

¹⁰"Listen to this message from the LORD, you nations of the world; proclaim it in distant coastlands: The LORD, who scattered his people, will gather them together and watch over them as a shepherd does his flock. ¹¹For the LORD has redeemed Israel from those too strong for them. ¹²They will come home and sing songs of joy on the heights of Jerusalem. They will be radiant because of the many gifts the LORD has given them—the good crops of wheat, wine, and oil, and the healthy flocks and herds. Their life will be like a watered garden, and all their sorrows will be gone. ¹³The

young women will dance for joy, and the men—old and young—will join in the celebration. I will turn their mourning into joy. I will comfort them and exchange their sorrow for rejoicing. ¹⁴I will supply the priests with an abundance of offerings. I will satisfy my people with my bounty. I, the LORD, have spoken!"

RACHEL'S SADNESS TURNS TO JOY

¹⁵This is what the LORD says: "A cry of anguish is heard in Ramah—mourning and weeping unrestrained. Rachel weeps for her children, refusing to be comforted—for her children are dead."

¹⁶But now the LORD says, "Do not weep any longer, for I will reward you. Your children will come back to you from the distant land of the enemy. ¹⁷There is hope for your future," says the LORD. "Your children will come again to their own land. ¹⁸I have heard Israel* saying, 'You disciplined me severely, but I deserved it. I was like a calf that needed to be trained for the yoke and plow. Turn me again to you and restore me, for you alone are the LORD my God. ¹⁹I turned away from God, but then I was sorry. I kicked myself for my stupidity! I was thoroughly ashamed of all I did in my younger days.'

²⁰"Is not Israel still my son, my darling child?" asks the LORD. "I had to punish him, but I still love him. I long for him and surely will have mercy on him.

²¹"Set up road signs; put up guideposts. Mark well the path by which you came. Come back again, my virgin Israel; return to your cities here. ²²How long will you wander, my wayward daughter? For the LORD will cause something new and different to happen—Israel will embrace her God.*"

²³This is what the LORD Almighty, the God of Israel, says: "When I bring them back again, the people of Judah and its cities will again say, 'The LORD bless you—O righteous home, O holy mountain!' ²⁴And city dwellers and

31:6 Hebrew Zion; also in 31:12.   31:7 Hebrew Jacob; also in 31:11.   31:18 Hebrew Ephraim, referring to the northern kingdom of Israel; also in 31:20.   31:22 Hebrew a woman will court a suitor.

My Daily Worship

— July 23 —

PUT ON YOUR DANCING SHOES

JEREMIAH 30:1–33:26

*The young women will dance for joy, and the men—old and young—will join
in the celebration. I will turn their mourning into joy. I will comfort
them and exchange their sorrow for rejoicing (31:13).*

[i reflect]

When residents of Palestine, West Virginia, think back on the war with Iraq, one soldier's name and face comes to mind more than any other—19-year-old PFC Jessica Lynch. This homegrown hero was among the soldiers of the 507th Ordinance Maintenance Company who were ambushed, captured, and feared dead. More than a week after the ambush, U.S. Special Forces raided the hospital near Baghdad where the wounded POW was being held as a hostage. The mourning of a small town tucked away in the Appalachian Mountains gave way to incredible joy.

Amazingly that scene is very similar to the one Jeremiah describes. Anticipating the return of the exiled Jews to Jerusalem, he pictures God's people dancing before the Lord in worshipful joy. No ballroom dancing here. This dancing is a spiritual celebration, a tangible act of praise by which God's faithfulness is celebrated against the backdrop of peril and injustice.

Based on what the prophet says, we have every reason to believe that turning mourning into danc-ing and sadness into joy is normative with God. That's his plan. Because we know him, our ulti-mate destiny is heaven, and we have the solid assurance that one day all sickness, death, and sorrow will be banished—we will be perfect and complete. Actually, all of this earth, including our pain and sorrow, is temporary. Only our joy and dancing will last forever!

Whatever your sorrow is today, keep your eyes on Christ and gain God's eternal perspective. Then, join in the celebration and get ready to dance!

[i pray]

*Lord, thanks to you I have cause for kicking up my heels. Time and time again you
have rescued me from what I was convinced was a dead end. Thanks for the gift
of laughter and joy that allow me to respond to you with gratitude when you
come through for me. Receive my celebration as a gift of worship now.*

[i respond]

Think about when God has reversed your sorrow and given you cause for joy. Write these moments down in the back of your Bible for easy reference, especially to review when you are going through tough times.

farmers and shepherds alike will live together in peace and happiness. ²⁵For I have given rest to the weary and joy to the sorrowing."

²⁶At this, I woke up and looked around. My sleep had been very sweet.

²⁷"The time will come," says the LORD, "when I will greatly increase the population and multiply the number of cattle here in Israel and Judah. ²⁸In the past I uprooted and tore down this nation. I overthrew it, destroyed it, and brought disaster upon it. But in the future I will plant it and build it up," says the LORD.

²⁹"The people will no longer quote this proverb: 'The parents eat sour grapes, but their children's mouths pucker at the taste.' ³⁰All people will die for their own sins—those who eat the sour grapes will be the ones whose mouths will pucker.

³¹"The day will come," says the LORD, "when I will make a new covenant with the people of Israel and Judah. ³²This covenant will not be like the one I made with their ancestors when I took them by the hand and brought them out of the land of Egypt. They broke that covenant, though I loved them as a husband loves his wife," says the LORD.

³³"But this is the new covenant I will make with the people of Israel on that day," says the LORD. "I will put my laws in their minds, and I will write them on their hearts. I will be their God, and they will be my people. ³⁴And they will not need to teach their neighbors, nor will they need to teach their family, saying, 'You should know the LORD.' For everyone, from the least to the greatest, will already know me," says the LORD. "And I will forgive their wickedness and will never again remember their sins."

³⁵It is the LORD who provides the sun to light the day and the moon and stars to light the night. It is he who stirs the sea into roaring waves. His name is the LORD Almighty, and this is what he says: ³⁶"I am as likely to reject my people Israel as I am to do away with the laws of nature! ³⁷Just as the heavens cannot be measured and the foundation of the earth cannot be explored, so I will not consider casting them away forever for their sins. I, the LORD, have spoken!

³⁸"The time is coming," says the LORD, "when all Jerusalem will be rebuilt for me, from the Tower of Hananel to the Corner Gate. ³⁹A measuring line will be stretched out over the hill of Gareb and across to Goah. ⁴⁰And the entire area—including the graveyard and ash dump in the valley, and all the fields out to the Kidron Valley on the east as far as the Horse Gate—will be holy to the LORD. The city will never again be captured or destroyed."

JEREMIAH'S LAND PURCHASE

32 The following message came to Jeremiah from the LORD in the tenth year of the reign of Zedekiah,* king of Judah. This was also the eighteenth year of the reign of King Nebuchadnezzar.* ²Jerusalem was under siege from the Babylonian army, and Jeremiah was imprisoned in the courtyard of the guard in the royal palace. ³King Zedekiah had put him there because he continued to give this prophecy: "This is what the LORD says: I am about to hand this city over to the king of Babylon. ⁴King Zedekiah will be captured by the Babylonians* and taken to the king of Babylon to be judged and sentenced. ⁵I will take Zedekiah to Babylon and will deal with him there. If you fight against the Babylonians, you will never succeed."

⁶At that time the LORD sent me a message. He said, ⁷"Your cousin Hanamel son of Shallum will come and say to you, 'Buy my field at Anathoth. By law you have the right to buy it before it is offered to anyone else.'"

⁸Then, just as the LORD had said he would, Hanamel came and visited me in the prison. He said, "Buy my field at Anathoth in the land of Benjamin. By law you have the right to buy it before it is offered to anyone else, so buy it

---

32:1a The tenth year of Zedekiah's reign and the eighteenth year of Nebuchadnezzar's reign was 587 B.C.   32:1b Hebrew *Nebuchadrezzar*, a variant name for Nebuchadnezzar; also in 32:28.   32:4 Or *Chaldeans*; also in 32:5, 24, 25, 28, 29, 43.

for yourself." Then I knew for sure that the message I had heard was from the LORD.

⁹So I bought the field at Anathoth, paying Hanamel seventeen pieces* of silver for it. ¹⁰I signed and sealed the deed of purchase before witnesses, weighed out the silver, and paid him. ¹¹Then I took the sealed deed and an unsealed copy of the deed, which contained the terms and conditions of the purchase, ¹²and I handed them to Baruch son of Neriah and grandson of Mahseiah. I did all this in the presence of my cousin Hanamel, the witnesses who had signed the deed, and all the men of Judah who were there.

¹³Then I said to Baruch as they all listened, ¹⁴"The LORD Almighty, the God of Israel, says: Take both this sealed deed and the unsealed copy, and put them into a pottery jar to preserve them for a long time. ¹⁵For the LORD Almighty, the God of Israel, says: Someday people will again own property here in this land and will buy and sell houses and vineyards and fields."

JEREMIAH'S PRAYER

¹⁶Then after I had given the papers to Baruch, I prayed to the LORD: ¹⁷"O Sovereign LORD! You have made the heavens and earth by your great power. Nothing is too hard for you! ¹⁸You are loving and kind to thousands, though children suffer for their parents' sins. You are the great and powerful God, the LORD Almighty. ¹⁹You have all wisdom and do great and mighty miracles. You are very aware of the conduct of all people, and you reward them according to their deeds. ²⁰You performed miraculous signs and wonders in the land of Egypt—things still remembered to this day! And you have continued to do great miracles in Israel and all around the world. You have made your name very great, as it is today.

²¹"You brought Israel out of Egypt with mighty signs and wonders, with great power and overwhelming terror. ²²You gave the people of Israel this land that you had promised their ancestors long before—a land flowing with milk and honey. ²³Our ancestors came and conquered it and lived in it, but they refused to obey you or follow your law. They have hardly done one thing you told them to! That is why you have sent this terrible disaster upon them.

²⁴"See how the siege ramps have been built against the city walls! Because of war, famine, and disease, the city has been handed over to the Babylonians, who will conquer it. Everything has happened just as you said it would. ²⁵And yet, O Sovereign LORD, you have told me to buy the field—paying good money for it before these witnesses—even though the city will soon belong to the Babylonians."

A PREDICTION OF JERUSALEM'S FALL

²⁶Then this message came to Jeremiah from the LORD: ²⁷"I am the LORD, the God of all the peoples of the world. Is anything too hard for me? ²⁸I will hand this city over to the Babylonians and to Nebuchadnezzar, king of Babylon, and he will capture it. ²⁹The Babylonians outside the walls will come in and set fire to the city. They will burn down all these houses, where the people caused my fury to rise by offering incense to Baal on the rooftops and by pouring out drink offerings to other gods. ³⁰Israel and Judah have done nothing but wrong since their earliest days. They have infuriated me with all their evil deeds," says the LORD. ³¹"From the time this city was built until now, it has done nothing but anger me, so I am determined to get rid of it.

³²"The sins of Israel and Judah—the sins of the people of Jerusalem, the kings, the officials, the priests, and the prophets—stir up my anger. ³³My people have turned their backs on me and have refused to return. Day after day, year after year, I taught them right from wrong, but they would not listen or obey. ³⁴They have set up their abominable idols right in my own Temple, defiling it. ³⁵They have built pagan shrines to Baal in the valley

---

32:9 Hebrew *17 shekels,* about 7 ounces or 194 grams in weight.

of the son of Hinnom, and there they sacrifice their sons and daughters to Molech. I have never commanded such a horrible deed; it never even crossed my mind to command such a thing. What an incredible evil, causing Judah to sin so greatly!

A Promise of Restoration

36"Now I want to say something more about this city. You have been saying, 'It will fall to the king of Babylon through war, famine, and disease.' But this is what the LORD, the God of Israel, says: 37I will surely bring my people back again from all the countries where I will scatter them in my fury. I will bring them back to this very city and let them live in peace and safety. 38They will be my people, and I will be their God. 39And I will give them one heart and mind to worship me forever, for their own good and for the good of all their descendants.

40"And I will make an everlasting covenant with them, promising not to stop doing good for them. I will put a desire in their hearts to worship me, and they will never leave me. 41I will rejoice in doing good to them and will faithfully and wholeheartedly replant them in this land. 42Just as I have sent all these calamities upon them, so I will do all the good I have promised them. I, the LORD, have spoken!

43"Fields will again be bought and sold in this land about which you now say, 'It has been ravaged by the Babylonians, a land where people and animals have all disappeared.' 44Yes, fields will once again be bought and sold—deeds signed and sealed and witnessed—in the land of Benjamin and here in Jerusalem, in the towns of Judah and in the hill country, in the foothills of Judah* and in the Negev, too. For someday I will restore prosperity to them. I, the LORD, have spoken!"

Promises of Peace and Prosperity

33 While Jeremiah was still confined in the courtyard of the guard, the LORD gave him this second message: 2"The LORD, the Maker of the heavens and earth—the LORD is his name—says this: 3Ask me and I will tell you some remarkable secrets about what is going to happen here. 4For this is what the LORD, the God of Israel, says: Though you have torn down the houses of this city and even the king's palace to get materials to strengthen the walls against the siege weapons of the enemy, 5the Babylonians* will still enter. The men of this city are already as good as dead, for I have determined to destroy them in my terrible anger. I have abandoned them because of all their wickedness.

6"Nevertheless, the time will come when I will heal Jerusalem's damage and give her prosperity and peace. 7I will restore the fortunes of Judah and Israel and rebuild their cities. 8I will cleanse away their sins against me, and I will forgive all their sins of rebellion. 9Then this city will bring me joy, glory, and honor before all the nations of the earth! The people of the world will see the good I do for my people and will tremble with awe!

10"This is what the LORD says: You say, 'This land has been ravaged, and the people and animals have all disappeared.' Yet in the empty streets of Jerusalem and Judah's other towns, there will be heard once more 11the sounds of joy and laughter. The joyful voices of bridegrooms and brides will be heard again, along with the joyous songs of people bringing thanksgiving offerings to the LORD. They will sing,

'Give thanks to the LORD Almighty, for the
    LORD is good.
His faithful love endures forever!'

For I will restore the prosperity of this land to what it was in the past, says the LORD.

12"This is what the LORD Almighty says: This land—though it is now desolate and the people and animals have all disappeared—will once more see shepherds leading sheep and lambs. 13Once again their flocks will prosper

32:44 Hebrew *the Shephelah.* 33:5 Or *Chaldeans.*

IMMANUEL

Immanuel—Hebrew *'Im-ma-nu 'El*; Greek *Em-ma-nu-el*.

It was a time of national distress. Judah was under invasion from both the Arameans and their own brothers in the kingdom of Israel, astray from the Lord. But God's prophet had a sign of encouragement for the beleaguered King of Judah. Pointing out a young woman, Isaiah told the king that by the time she could have a baby and wean him, the foreign threat would be gone! The baby's name would be *Immanuel*—"God is with us" (Isaiah 7:14).

When Jesus was to be born, the same prophecy came in a dream to Mary's husband Joseph (Matthew 1:23). Her son would bear this message of hope to God's people centuries after Isaiah's time: "God is with us!" In Jesus, Christians behold the Word of God in human form (John 1:14), and receive his promise: "I will never forsake you" (Hebrews 13:5). At worship, we know that the Lord God Almighty and the Lamb dwell with us in the city of our praise and adoration (Revelation 21–22). Let trials and difficulties come our way, if they must. "Our present troubles are quite small and won't last very long" (2 Corinthians 4:17), for God is with us!

in the towns of the hill country, the foothills of Judah,* the Negev, the land of Benjamin, the vicinity of Jerusalem, and all the towns of Judah. I, the LORD, have spoken!

[14]"The day will come, says the LORD, when I will do for Israel and Judah all the good I have promised them. [15]At that time I will bring to

the throne of David a righteous descendant,* and he will do what is just and right throughout the land. [16]In that day Judah will be saved, and Jerusalem will live in safety. And their motto will be 'The LORD is our righteousness!' [17]For this is what the LORD says: David will forever have a descendant sitting on the throne of Israel. [18]And there will always be Levitical priests to offer burnt offerings and grain offerings and sacrifices to me."

[19]Then this message came to Jeremiah from the LORD: [20]"If you can break my covenant with the day and the night so that they do not come on their usual schedule, [21]only then will my covenant with David, my servant, be broken. Only then will he no longer have a descendant to reign on his throne. The same is true for my covenant with the Levitical priests who minister before me. [22]And as the stars cannot be counted and the sand on the seashores cannot be measured, so I will multiply the descendants of David, my servant, and the Levites who minister before me."

[23]The LORD gave another message to Jeremiah. He said, [24]"Have you heard what people are saying?—'The LORD chose Judah and Israel and then abandoned them!' They are sneering and saying that Israel is not worthy to be counted as a nation. [25]But this is the LORD's reply: I would no more reject my people than I would change my laws of night and day, of earth and sky. [26]I will never abandon the descendants of Jacob or David, my servant, or change the plan that David's descendants will rule the descendants of Abraham, Isaac, and Jacob. Instead, I will restore them to their land and have mercy on them."

A WARNING FOR ZEDEKIAH

34 King Nebuchadnezzar of Babylon came with all the armies from the kingdoms he ruled, and he fought against Jerusalem and the towns of Judah. At that time this message came to Jeremiah from the LORD: [2]"Go to King Zedekiah of Judah, and

33:13 Hebrew *the Shephelah.* **33:15** Hebrew *a righteous Branch.*

tell him, 'This is what the LORD, the God of Israel, says: I am about to hand this city over to the king of Babylon, and he will burn it. ³You will not escape his grasp but will be taken into captivity. You will stand before the king of Babylon to be judged and sentenced. Then you will be exiled to Babylon.'

⁴"But listen to this promise from the LORD, O Zedekiah, king of Judah. This is what the LORD says: 'You will not be killed in war ⁵but will die peacefully among your people. They will burn incense in your memory, just as they did for your ancestors. They will weep for you and say, "Alas, our king is dead!" This I have decreed, says the LORD.'"

⁶So Jeremiah the prophet delivered the message to King Zedekiah of Judah. ⁷At this time the Babylonian army was besieging Jerusalem, Lachish, and Azekah—the only cities of Judah with their walls still standing.

FREEDOM FOR HEBREW SLAVES

⁸This message came to Jeremiah from the LORD after King Zedekiah made a covenant with the people, proclaiming freedom for the slaves. ⁹He had ordered all the people to free their Hebrew slaves—both men and women. No one was to keep a fellow Judean in bondage. ¹⁰The officials and all the people had obeyed the king's command, ¹¹but later they changed their minds. They took back the people they had freed, making them slaves again.

¹²So the LORD gave them this message through Jeremiah: ¹³"This is what the LORD, the God of Israel, says: I made a covenant with your ancestors long ago when I rescued them from their slavery in Egypt. ¹⁴I told them that every Hebrew slave must be freed after serving six years. But this was never done. ¹⁵Recently you repented and did what was right, following my command. You freed your slaves and made a solemn covenant with me in my Temple. ¹⁶But now you have shrugged off your oath and defiled my name by taking back the men and women you had freed, making them slaves once again.

¹⁷"Therefore, this is what the LORD says: Since you have not obeyed me by setting your countrymen free, I will set you free to be destroyed by war, famine, and disease. You will be considered a disgrace by all the nations of the earth. ¹⁸Because you have refused the terms of our covenant, I will cut you apart just as you cut apart the calf when you walked between its halves to solemnize your vows. ¹⁹Yes, I will cut you apart, whether you are officials of Judah or Jerusalem, court officials, priests, or common people—for you have broken your oath. ²⁰I will give you to your enemies, and they will kill you. Your bodies will be food for the vultures and wild animals. ²¹I will hand over King Zedekiah of Judah and his officials to the army of the king of Babylon. And though Babylon's king has left this city for a while, ²²I will call the Babylonian armies back again. They will fight against this city and will capture and burn it. I will see to it that all the towns of Judah are destroyed and left completely empty."

THE FAITHFUL RECABITES

35 This is the message the LORD gave Jeremiah when Jehoiakim son of Josiah was king of Judah: ²"Go to the settlement where the families of the Recabites live, and invite them to the LORD's Temple. Take them into one of the inner rooms, and offer them some wine."

³So I went to see Jaazaniah son of Jeremiah and grandson of Habazziniah and all his brothers and sons—representing all the Recabite families. ⁴I took them to the Temple, and we went into the room assigned to the sons of Hanan son of Igdaliah, a man of God. This room was located next to the one used by the palace officials, directly above the room of Maaseiah son of Shallum, the Temple gatekeeper.

⁵I set cups and jugs of wine before them and invited them to have a drink, ⁶but they refused. "No," they said. "We don't drink wine, because Jehonadab* son of Recab, our ances-

---

35:6 Hebrew *Jonadab,* a variant name for Jehonadab; also in 35:10, 14, 18, 19. See 2 Kgs 10:15.

tom, gave us this command: 'You and your descendants must never drink wine. [7]And do not build houses or plant crops or vineyards, but always live in tents. If you follow these commands, you will live long, good lives in the land.' [8]So we have obeyed him in all these things. We have never had a drink of wine since then, nor have our wives, our sons, or our daughters. [9]We haven't built houses or owned vineyards or farms or planted crops. [10]We have lived in tents and have fully obeyed all the commands of Jehonadab, our ancestor. [11]But when King Nebuchadnezzar* of Babylon arrived in this country, we were afraid of the Babylonian* and Aramean armies. So we decided to move to Jerusalem. That is why we are here."

[12]Then the LORD gave this message to Jeremiah: [13]"The LORD Almighty, the God of Israel, says: Go and say to the people in Judah and Jerusalem, 'Come and learn a lesson about how to obey me. [14]The Recabites do not drink wine because their ancestor Jehonadab told them not to. But I have spoken to you again and again, and you refuse to listen or obey. [15]I have sent you prophet after prophet to tell you to turn from your wicked ways and to stop worshiping other gods, so that you might live in peace here in the land I gave to you and your ancestors. But you would not listen to me or obey. [16]The families of Recab have obeyed their ancestor completely, but you have refused to listen to me.'

[17]"Therefore, the LORD God Almighty, the God of Israel, says: Because you refuse to listen or answer when I call, I will send upon Judah and Jerusalem all the disasters I have threatened."

[18]Then Jeremiah turned to the Recabites and said, "This is what the LORD Almighty, the God of Israel, says: You have obeyed your ancestor Jehonadab in every respect, following all his instructions. [19]Because of this, Jehonadab son of Recab will always

have descendants who serve me. I, the LORD Almighty, the God of Israel, have spoken!"

BARUCH READS THE LORD'S MESSAGES

36 During the fourth year that Jehoiakim son of Josiah was king in Judah,* the LORD gave this message to Jeremiah: [2]"Get a scroll, and write down all my messages against Israel, Judah, and the other nations. Begin with the first message back in the days of Josiah, and write down every message you have given, right up to the present time. [3]Perhaps the people of Judah will repent if they see in writing all the terrible things I have planned for them. Then I will be able to forgive their sins and wrongdoings."

[4]So Jeremiah sent for Baruch son of Neriah, and as Jeremiah dictated, Baruch wrote down all the prophecies that the LORD had given him. [5]Then Jeremiah said to Baruch, "I am a prisoner here and unable to go to the Temple. [6]So you go to the Temple on the next day of fasting, and read the messages from the LORD that are on this scroll. On that day people will be there from all over Judah. [7]Perhaps even yet they will turn from their evil ways and ask the LORD's forgiveness before it is too late. For the LORD's terrible anger has been pronounced against them."

[8]Baruch did as Jeremiah told him and read these messages from the LORD to the people at the Temple. [9]This happened on the day of sacred fasting held in late autumn,* during the fifth year of the reign of Jehoiakim son of Josiah. People from all over Judah came to attend the services at the Temple on that day. [10]Baruch read Jeremiah's words to all the people from the Temple room of Gemariah son of Shaphan. This room was just off the upper courtyard of the Temple, near the New Gate entrance.

[11]When Micaiah son of Gemariah and

35:11a Hebrew *Nebuchadrezzar*, a variant name for Nebuchadnezzar. **35:11b** Or *Chaldean.* **36:1** The fourth year of Jehoiakim's reign was 605 B.C. **36:9** Hebrew *in the ninth month*, of the Hebrew calendar (also in 36:22). This month in the fifth year of Jehoiakim's reign occurred in November and December 604 B.C. Also see note on 1:3.

grandson of Shaphan heard the messages from the LORD, [12]he went down to the secretary's room in the palace where the administrative officials were meeting. Elishama the secretary was there, along with Delaiah son of Shemaiah, Elnathan son of Acbor, Gemariah son of Shaphan, Zedekiah son of Hananiah, and all the others with official responsibilities. [13]When Micaiah told them about the messages Baruch was reading to the people, [14]the officials sent Jehudi son of Nethaniah, grandson of Shelemiah, and great-grandson of Cushi, to ask Baruch to come and read the messages to them, too. So Baruch took the scroll and went to them. [15]"Sit down and read the scroll to us," the officials said, and Baruch did as they requested.

[16]By the time Baruch had finished reading, they were badly frightened. "We must tell the king what we have heard," they said. [17]"But first, tell us how you got these messages. Did they come directly from Jeremiah?"

[18]So Baruch explained, "Jeremiah dictated them to me word by word, and I wrote down his words with ink on this scroll."

[19]"You and Jeremiah should both hide," the officials told Baruch. "Don't tell anyone where you are!" [20]Then the officials left the scroll for safekeeping in the room of Elishama the secretary and went to tell the king.

KING JEHOIAKIM BURNS THE SCROLL

[21]The king sent Jehudi to get the scroll. Jehudi brought it from Elishama's room and read it to the king as all his officials stood by. [22]It was late autumn, and the king was in a winterized part of the palace, sitting in front of a fire to keep warm. [23]Whenever Jehudi finished reading three or four columns, the king took his knife and cut off that section of the scroll. He then threw it into the fire, section by section, until the whole scroll was burned up. [24]Neither the king nor his officials showed any signs of fear or repentance at what they heard. [25]Even when Elnathan, Delaiah, and Gemariah begged the king not to burn the scroll, he wouldn't listen.

[26]Then the king commanded his son Jerahmeel, Seraiah son of Azriel, and Shelemiah son of Abdeel to arrest Baruch and Jeremiah. But the LORD had hidden them.

JEREMIAH REWRITES THE SCROLL

[27]After the king had burned Jeremiah's scroll, the LORD gave Jeremiah another message. He said, [28]"Get another scroll, and write everything again just as you did on the scroll King Jehoiakim burned. [29]Then say to the king, 'This is what the LORD says: You burned the scroll because it said the king of Babylon would destroy this land and everything in it. [30]Now this is what the LORD says about King Jehoiakim of Judah: He will have no heirs to sit on the throne of David. His dead body will be thrown out to lie unburied—exposed to hot days and frosty nights. [31]I will punish him and his family and his officials because of their sins. I will pour out on them and on all the people of Judah and Jerusalem all the disasters I have promised, for they would not listen to my warnings.'"

[32]Then Jeremiah took another scroll and dictated again to his secretary Baruch. He wrote everything that had been on the scroll King Jehoiakim had burned in the fire. Only this time, he added much more!

ZEDEKIAH CALLS FOR JEREMIAH

37 Zedekiah son of Josiah succeeded Jehoiachin* son of Jehoiakim as the king of Judah. He was appointed by King Nebuchadnezzar* of Babylon. [2]But neither King Zedekiah nor his officials nor the people who were left in the land listened to what the LORD said through Jeremiah. [3]Nevertheless, King Zedekiah sent Jehucal son of Shelemiah and Zephaniah the priest, son of Maaseiah, to ask Jeremiah, "Please pray to the LORD our God for us." [4]Jeremiah had not yet been imprisoned, so he could come and go as he pleased.

37:1a Hebrew *Coniah*, a variant name for Jehoiachin.   **37:1b** Hebrew *Nebuchadrezzar*, a variant name for Nebuchadnezzar.

My Daily Worship

— July 24 —

THE WRITE STUFF

JEREMIAH 34:1–38:28

Then Jeremiah took another scroll and dictated again to his secretary Baruch.
He wrote everything that had been on the scroll King Jehoiakim had
burned in the fire. Only this time, he added much more! (36:32).

[i reflect]

Kenneth Taylor was concerned that his ten children weren't understanding the family's devotional reading of the King James Version of the Bible. After all, it was in seventeenth-century English. So, beginning in 1954, as he rode the commuter train to his job in Chicago, Taylor started paraphrasing the New Testament into modern English.

After seven years of writing and rewriting, he submitted the manuscript to several publishing houses. Much to his chagrin, he was rejected by every one of them. Still, Taylor was convinced there was value in the work for more than just his own children. He refused to give up. At last, he and his wife, Margaret, decided to use their limited savings to self-publish. The result was a best-selling translation called *The Living Bible*, and the beginnings of an even more successful publishing company known as Tyndale House.

That same determination characterized Jeremiah. When King Jehoiakim destroyed the prophet's one and only copy of his prophecy, he could have despaired. But he didn't. It was too early to mourn. Jeremiah picked his devastated ego up off the ground and started all over again. This time, according to Scripture, he "added much more!"

We long to have the bravado to start over when detractors or circumstances destroy our "treasures." It's nearly impossible to sing praises to God when a reputation we have spent a lifetime building has been stained by false rumors. It's asking too much to put on a smile when the enemy is a diagnosis of cancer. But it's not entirely impossible.

Jeremiah went far and away beyond what any of his peers would have expected. And you know the reason: God planted in his heart the ability to persevere. He also will give you whatever courage is necessary to face your detractors or overcome your circumstances. Expect him to help you today.

[i pray]

Lord, it's so easy to quit when the rug is pulled out from under us. But I
don't want to bail out. I want to persevere and hold out to the end.
Give me the strength to regroup and pick up where I left off.

[i respond]

Though it may not be New Year's Day, make a "new" resolution today to trust God in your difficult circumstance. Write it in your Bible, and then ask God to help you persevere like Jeremiah did.

⁵At this time the army of Pharaoh Hophra* of Egypt appeared at the southern border of Judah. When the Babylonian* army heard about it, they withdrew from their siege of Jerusalem. ⁶Then the LORD gave this message to Jeremiah: ⁷"This is what the LORD, the God of Israel, says: Tell the king of Judah, who sent you to ask me what is going to happen, that Pharaoh's army is about to return to Egypt, though he came here to help you. ⁸Then the Babylonians* will come back and capture this city and burn it to the ground. ⁹The LORD says: Do not fool yourselves that the Babylonians are gone for good. They aren't! ¹⁰Even if you were to destroy the entire Babylonian army, leaving only a handful of wounded survivors, they would still stagger from their tents and burn this city to the ground!"

JEREMIAH IS IMPRISONED

¹¹When the Babylonian army left Jerusalem because of Pharaoh's approaching army, ¹²Jeremiah started to leave the city on his way to the land of Benjamin, to see the property he had bought. ¹³But as he was walking through the Benjamin Gate, a sentry arrested him and said, "You are defecting to the Babylonians!" The sentry making the arrest was Irijah son of Shelemiah and grandson of Hananiah.

¹⁴"That's not true!" Jeremiah protested. "I had no intention of doing any such thing." But Irijah wouldn't listen, and he took Jeremiah before the officials. ¹⁵They were furious with Jeremiah and had him flogged and imprisoned in the house of Jonathan the secretary. Jonathan's house had been converted into a prison. ¹⁶Jeremiah was put into a dungeon cell, where he remained for many days.

¹⁷Later King Zedekiah secretly requested that Jeremiah come to the palace, where the king asked him, "Do you have any messages from the LORD?"

"Yes, I do!" said Jeremiah. "You will be defeated by the king of Babylon."

¹⁸Then Jeremiah asked the king, "What crime have I committed? What have I done against you, your officials, or the people that I should be imprisoned like this? ¹⁹Where are your prophets now who told you the king of Babylon would not attack you? ²⁰Listen, my lord the king, I beg you. Don't send me back to the dungeon in the house of Jonathan the secretary, for I will die there."

²¹So King Zedekiah commanded that Jeremiah not be returned to the dungeon. Instead, he was imprisoned in the courtyard of the guard in the royal palace. The king also commanded that Jeremiah be given a loaf of fresh bread every day as long as there was any left in the city. So Jeremiah was put in the palace prison.

JEREMIAH IN A CISTERN

38 Now Shephatiah son of Mattan, Gedaliah son of Pashhur, Jehucal* son of Shelemiah, and Pashhur son of Malkijah heard what Jeremiah had been telling the people. He was saying, ²"This is what the LORD says: Everyone who stays in Jerusalem will die from war, famine, or disease, but those who surrender to the Babylonians* will live. ³The LORD also says: The city of Jerusalem will surely be handed over to the army of the king of Babylon, who will capture it."

⁴So these officials went to the king and said, "Sir, this man must die! That kind of talk will undermine the morale of the few fighting men we have left, as well as that of all the people, too. This man is a traitor!"

⁵So King Zedekiah agreed. "All right," he said. "Do as you like. I will do nothing to stop you."

⁶So the officials took Jeremiah from his cell and lowered him by ropes into an empty cistern in the prison yard. It belonged to Malkijah, a member of the royal family. There was no water in the cistern, but there was a thick layer of mud at the bottom, and Jeremiah sank down into it.

37:5a Hebrew *army of Pharaoh;* see 44:30. 37:5b Or *Chaldean;* also in 37:10, 11. 37:8 Or *Chaldeans;* also in 37:9, 13. 38:1 Hebrew *Jucal,* a variant name for Jehucal; see 37:3. 38:2 Or *Chaldeans;* also in 38:18, 19, 23.

> *We are changed, after all,*
> *by a smile from a stranger;*
> *how can we not be changed*
> *when we look at the face*
> *of Love himself.*
>
> N. T. WRIGHT

[7]But Ebed-melech the Ethiopian,* an important palace official, heard that Jeremiah was in the cistern. At that time the king was holding court at the Benjamin Gate, [8]so Ebed-melech rushed from the palace to speak with him. [9]"My lord the king," he said, "these men have done a very evil thing in putting Jeremiah the prophet into the cistern. He will soon die of hunger, for almost all the bread in the city is gone."

[10]So the king told Ebed-melech, "Take along thirty of my men, and pull Jeremiah out of the cistern before he dies."

[11]So Ebed-melech took the men with him and went to a room in the palace beneath the treasury, where he found some old rags and discarded clothing. He carried these to the cistern and lowered them to Jeremiah on a rope. [12]Ebed-melech called down to Jeremiah, "Put these rags under your armpits to protect you from the ropes." Then when Jeremiah was ready, [13]they pulled him out. So Jeremiah was returned to the courtyard of the guard—the palace prison—where he remained.

ZEDEKIAH QUESTIONS JEREMIAH

[14]One day King Zedekiah sent for Jeremiah to meet him at the third entrance of the LORD's Temple. "I want to ask you something," the king said. "And don't try to hide the truth."

[15]Jeremiah said, "If I tell you the truth, you will kill me. And if I give you advice, you won't listen to me anyway."

[16]So King Zedekiah secretly promised him, "As surely as the LORD our Creator lives, I will not kill you or hand you over to the men who want you dead."

[17]Then Jeremiah said to Zedekiah, "The LORD God Almighty, the God of Israel, says: If you surrender to Babylon, you and your family will live, and the city will not be burned. [18]But if you refuse to surrender, you will not escape! This city will be handed over to the Babylonians, and they will burn it to the ground."

[19]"But I am afraid to surrender," the king said, "for the Babylonians will hand me over to the Judeans who have defected to them. And who knows what they will do to me?"

[20]Jeremiah replied, "You won't be handed over to them if you choose to obey the LORD. Your life will be spared, and all will go well for you. [21]But if you refuse to surrender, this is what the LORD has revealed to me: [22]All the women left in your palace will be brought out and given to the officers of the Babylonian army. Then the women will taunt you, saying, 'What fine friends you have! They have betrayed and misled you. When your feet sank in the mud, they left you to your fate!' [23]All your wives and children will be led out to the Babylonians, and you will not escape. You will be seized by the king of Babylon, and this city will be burned."

[24]Then Zedekiah said to Jeremiah, "Don't tell anyone you told me this, or you will die! [25]My officials may hear that I spoke to you. Then they may say to you, 'Tell us what you and the king were talking about. If you don't tell us, we will kill you.' [26]If this happens, just tell them you begged me not to send you back to Jonathan's dungeon, for fear you would die there."

[27]Sure enough, it wasn't long before the king's officials came to Jeremiah and asked him why the king had called for him. But Jeremiah followed the king's instructions, and they left without finding out the truth. No one had overheard the conversation between

38:7 Hebrew *the Cushite.*

Jeremiah and the king. ²⁸And Jeremiah remained a prisoner in the courtyard of the guard until the day Jerusalem was captured.

THE FALL OF JERUSALEM

39 It was in January* during the ninth year of King Zedekiah's reign that King Nebuchadnezzar* and his army returned to besiege Jerusalem. ²Two and a half years later, on July 18,* the Babylonians broke through the wall, and the city fell. ³All the officers of the Babylonian army came in and sat in triumph at the Middle Gate: Nergal-sharezer of Samgar, and Nebo-sarsekim,* a chief officer, and Nergal-sharezer, the king's adviser, and many others.

⁴King Zedekiah and his royal guard saw the Babylonians in the city gate, so they fled when the darkness of night arrived. They went out through a gate between the two walls behind the king's garden and headed toward the Jordan Valley.* ⁵But the Babylonians* chased the king and caught him on the plains of Jericho. They took him to King Nebuchadnezzar of Babylon, who was at Riblah in the land of Hamath. There the king of Babylon pronounced judgment upon Zedekiah. ⁶He made Zedekiah watch as they killed his sons and all the nobles of Judah. ⁷Then he gouged out Zedekiah's eyes, bound him in chains, and sent him away to exile in Babylon.

⁸Meanwhile, the Babylonians burned Jerusalem, including the palace, and tore down the walls of the city. ⁹Then Nebuzaradan, the captain of the guard, sent to Babylon the remnant of the population as well as those who had defected to him. ¹⁰But Nebuzaradan left a few of the poorest people in Judah, and he assigned them fields and vineyards to care for.

JEREMIAH REMAINS IN JUDAH

¹¹King Nebuchadnezzar had told Nebuzaradan to find Jeremiah. ¹²"See that he isn't hurt," he had said. "Look after him well, and give him anything he wants." ¹³So Nebuzaradan, the captain of the guard, and Nebushazban, a chief officer, and Nergal-sharezer, the king's adviser, and the other officers of Babylon's king ¹⁴sent messengers to bring Jeremiah out of the prison. They put him under the care of Gedaliah son of Ahikam and grandson of Shaphan, who was to take him back to his home. So Jeremiah stayed in Judah among his own people.

¹⁵The LORD had given the following message to Jeremiah while he was still in prison: ¹⁶"Say to Ebed-melech the Ethiopian,* 'The LORD Almighty, the God of Israel, says: I will do to this city everything I have threatened. I will send disaster, not prosperity. You will see its destruction, ¹⁷but I will rescue you from those you fear so much. ¹⁸Because you trusted me, I will preserve your life and keep you safe. I, the LORD, have spoken!' "

40 The LORD gave a message to Jeremiah after Nebuzaradan, captain of the guard, had released him at Ramah. He had found Jeremiah bound in chains among the captives of Jerusalem and Judah who were being sent to exile in Babylon.

²The captain of the guard called for Jeremiah and said, "The LORD your God has brought this disaster on this land, ³just as he said he would. For these people have sinned against the LORD and disobeyed him. That is why it happened. ⁴Now I am going to take off your chains and let you go. If you want to come with me to Babylon, you are welcome. I will see that you are well cared for. But if you don't want to come, you may stay here. The whole land is before you—go wherever you like. ⁵If you decide to stay, then return to Gedaliah son of Ahikam and grandson of Shaphan. He has been appointed governor of Judah by the king of Babylon. Stay there with

---

39:1a Hebrew *in the tenth month,* of the Hebrew calendar. A number of events in Jeremiah can be cross-checked with dates in surviving Babylonian records and related accurately to our modern calendar. This event occurred on January 15, 588 B.C.; see 52:4 and the note there. 39:1b Hebrew *Nebuchadrezzar,* a variant name for Nebuchadnezzar; also in 39:11. 39:2 Hebrew *On the ninth day of the fourth month of the eleventh year of Zedekiah.* This event occurred on July 18, 586 B.C.; also see note on 39:1. 39:3 Or *Nergal-sharezer, Samgar-nebo, Sarsekim.* 39:4 Hebrew *the Arabah.* 39:5 Or *Chaldeans;* also in 39:8. 39:16 Hebrew *the Cushite.*

the people he rules. But it's up to you; go wherever you like."

Then Nebuzaradan gave Jeremiah some food and money and let him go. [6]So Jeremiah returned to Gedaliah son of Ahikam at Mizpah and lived in Judah with the few who were still left in the land.

GEDALIAH GOVERNS IN JUDAH

[7]The leaders of the Judean guerrilla bands in the countryside heard that the king of Babylon had appointed Gedaliah son of Ahikam as governor over the poor people who were left behind in Judah, and that he hadn't exiled everyone to Babylon. [8]So they came to see Gedaliah at Mizpah. These are the names of the leaders who came: Ishmael son of Nethaniah, Johanan and Jonathan, sons of Kareah, Seraiah son of Tanhumeth, the sons of Ephai the Netophathite, Jaazaniah* son of the Maacathite, and all their men.

[9]Gedaliah assured them that it would be safe for them to surrender to the Babylonians.* "Stay here, and serve the king of Babylon," he said, "and all will go well for you. [10]As for me, I will stay at Mizpah to represent you before the Babylonians who come to meet with us. Settle in any town you wish, and live off the land. Harvest the grapes and summer fruits and olives, and store them away."

[11]When the Judeans in Moab, Ammon, Edom, and the other nearby countries heard that the king of Babylon had left a few people in Judah and that Gedaliah was the governor, [12]they began to return to Judah from the places to which they had fled. They stopped at Mizpah to discuss their plans with Gedaliah and then went out into the Judean countryside to gather a great harvest of grapes and other crops.

A PLOT AGAINST GEDALIAH

[13]Soon after this, Johanan son of Kareah and the other guerrilla leaders came to Gedaliah at Mizpah. [14]They said to him, "Did you know that Baalis, king of Ammon, has sent Ishmael son of Nethaniah to assassinate you?" But Gedaliah refused to believe them.

[15]Later Johanan had a private conference with Gedaliah and volunteered to kill Ishmael secretly. "Why should we let him come and murder you?" Johanan asked. "What will happen then to the Judeans who have returned? Why should the few of us who are still left be scattered and lost?"

[16]But Gedaliah said to Johanan, "I forbid you to do any such thing, for you are lying about Ishmael."

THE MURDER OF GEDALIAH

41 But in midautumn,* Ishmael son of Nethaniah and grandson of Elishama, who was a member of the royal family, arrived in Mizpah accompanied by ten men. Gedaliah invited them to dinner. While they were eating, [2]Ishmael and his ten men suddenly drew their swords and killed Gedaliah, whom the king of Babylon had appointed governor. [3]Then they went out and slaughtered all the Judean officials and Babylonian* soldiers who were with Gedaliah at Mizpah.

[4]The next day, before anyone had heard about Gedaliah's murder, [5]eighty men arrived from Shechem, Shiloh, and Samaria. They had come to worship at the Temple of the LORD. They had shaved off their beards, torn their clothes, and cut themselves, and had brought along grain offerings and incense. [6]Ishmael left Mizpah to meet them, weeping as he went. When he reached them, he said, "Oh, come and see what has happened to Gedaliah!"

[7]But as soon as they were all inside the town, Ishmael and his men killed all but ten of them and threw their bodies into a cistern. [8]The other ten had talked Ishmael into letting them go by promising to bring him their stores of wheat, barley, oil, and honey that

---

40:8 As in parallel text at 2 Kgs 25:23; Hebrew reads *Jezaniah,* a variant name for Jaazaniah. **40:9** Or *Chaldeans;* also in 40:10. **41:1** Hebrew *in the seventh month,* of the Hebrew calendar. This month occurred in October and November 586 B.C. Also see note on 39:1. **41:3** Or *Chaldean.*

him at the pool near Gibeon. [13]The people Ishmael had captured shouted for joy when they saw Johanan and his men. [14]And all the captives from Mizpah escaped and began to help Johanan. [15]Meanwhile, Ishmael and eight of his men escaped from Johanan into the land of Ammon.

[16]Then Johanan son of Kareah and his officers led away all the people they had rescued—warriors, women, children, and palace officials.* [17]They took them all to the village of Geruth-kimham near Bethlehem, where they prepared to leave for Egypt. [18]They were afraid of what the Babylonians* would do when they heard that Ishmael had killed Gedaliah, the governor appointed by the Babylonian king.

WARNING TO STAY IN JUDAH

42 Then all the army officers, including Johanan son of Kareah and Jezaniah* son of Hoshaiah, and all the people, from the least to the greatest, approached [2]Jeremiah the prophet. They said, "Please pray to the LORD your God for us. As you know, we are only a tiny remnant compared to what we were before. [3]Beg the LORD your God to show us what to do and where to go."

[4]"All right," Jeremiah replied. "I will pray to the LORD your God, and I will tell you everything he says. I will hide nothing from you."

[5]Then they said to Jeremiah, "May the LORD your God be a faithful witness against us if we refuse to obey whatever he tells us to do! [6]Whether we like it or not, we will obey the LORD our God to whom we send you with our plea. For if we obey him, everything will turn out well for us."

[7]Ten days later, the LORD gave his reply to Jeremiah. [8]So he called for Johanan son of Kareah and the army officers, and for all the people, from the least to the greatest. [9]He said to them, "You sent me to the LORD, the God of Israel, with your request, and this is his reply: [10]Stay here in this land. If you do, I will build

they had hidden away. [9]The cistern where Ishmael dumped the bodies of the men he murdered was the large one made by King Asa when he fortified Mizpah to protect himself against King Baasha of Israel. Ishmael son of Nethaniah filled it with corpses.

[10]Ishmael made captives of the king's daughters and the other people who had been left under Gedaliah's care in Mizpah by Nebuzaradan, captain of the guard. Taking them with him, he started back toward the land of Ammon.

[11]But when Johanan son of Kareah and the rest of the guerrilla leaders heard what Ishmael had done, [12]they took all their men and set out to stop him. They caught up with

41:16 Or *eunuchs.* 41:18 Or *Chaldeans.* 42:1 Greek version reads *Azariah;* compare 43:2.

you up and not tear you down; I will plant you and not uproot you. For I am sorry for all the punishment I have had to bring upon you. [11]Do not fear the king of Babylon anymore, says the LORD. For I am with you and will save you and rescue you from his power. [12]I will be merciful to you by making him kind, so he will let you stay here in your land.'

[13]"But if you refuse to obey the LORD your God and say, 'We will not stay here,' [14]and if you insist on going to live in Egypt where you think you will be free from war, famine, and alarms, [15]then this is what the LORD says to the remnant of Judah. The LORD Almighty, the God of Israel, says: 'If you insist on going to Egypt, [16]the war and famine you fear will follow close behind you, and you will die there. [17]That is the fate awaiting every one of you who insists on going to live in Egypt. Yes, you will die from war, famine, and disease. None of you will escape from the disaster I will bring upon you there.'

[18]"For the LORD Almighty, the God of Israel, says: 'Just as my anger and fury were poured out on the people of Jerusalem, so they will be poured out on you when you enter Egypt. You will become an object of damnation, horror, cursing, and mockery. And you will never see your homeland again.'

[19]"Listen, you remnant of Judah. The LORD has told you: 'Do not go to Egypt!' Don't forget this warning I have given you today. [20]For you were deceitful when you sent me to pray to the LORD your God for you, saying, 'Just tell us what the LORD our God says, and we will do it!' [21]And today I have told you exactly what he said, but you will not obey the LORD your God any better now than you have in the past. [22]So you can be sure that you will die from war, famine, and disease in Egypt, where you insist on going."

JEREMIAH TAKEN TO EGYPT

43 When Jeremiah had finished giving this message from the LORD their God to all the people, [2]Azariah son of Hoshaiah and Johanan son of Kareah and all the other proud men said to Jeremiah, "You lie! The LORD our God hasn't forbidden us to go to Egypt! [3]Baruch son of Neriah has convinced you to say this, so we will stay here and be killed by the Babylonians* or be carried off into exile."

[4]So Johanan and all the army officers and all the people refused to obey the LORD's command to stay in Judah. [5]Johanan and his officers took with them all the people who had returned from the nearby countries to which they had fled. [6]In the crowd were men, women, and children, the king's daughters, and all those whom Nebuzaradan, the captain of the guard, had left with Gedaliah. Also included were the prophet Jeremiah and Baruch. [7]The people refused to obey the LORD and went to Egypt, going as far as the city of Tahpanhes.

[8]Then at Tahpanhes, the LORD gave another message to Jeremiah. He said, [9]"While the people of Judah are watching, bury large rocks between the pavement stones at the entrance of Pharaoh's palace here in Tahpanhes. [10]Then say to the people of Judah, 'The LORD Almighty, the God of Israel, says: I will surely bring my servant Nebuchadnezzar,* king of Babylon, here to Egypt. I will set his throne on these stones that I have hidden. He will spread his royal canopy over them. [11]And when he comes, he will destroy the land of Egypt. He will bring death to those destined for death; he will bring captivity to those destined for captivity; he will bring the sword against those destined for the sword. [12]He will set fire to the temples of Egypt's gods, burning all their idols and carrying away the people as captives. He will pick clean the land of Egypt as a shepherd picks fleas from his cloak. And he himself will leave unharmed. [13]He will break down the sacred pillars standing in the temple of the sun* in Egypt, and he will burn down the temples of Egypt's gods.'"

43:3 Or *Chaldeans.* **43:10** Hebrew *Nebuchadrezzar,* a variant name for Nebuchadnezzar. **43:13** Or *in Heliopolis.*

JUDGMENT FOR IDOLATRY

44 This is the message Jeremiah received concerning the Judeans living in northern Egypt in the cities of Migdol, Tahpanhes, and Memphis,* and throughout southern Egypt as well: ²"This is what the LORD Almighty, the God of Israel, says: You saw what I did to Jerusalem and to all the towns of Judah. They now lie in ruins, and no one lives in them. ³Because of all their wickedness, my anger rose high against them. They burned incense and worshiped other gods—gods that neither they nor you nor any of your ancestors have ever known.

⁴"Again and again I sent my servants, the prophets, to plead with them, 'Don't do these horrible things that I hate so much.' ⁵But my people would not listen or turn back from their wicked ways. They kept right on burning incense to these gods. ⁶And so my fury boiled over and fell like fire on the towns of Judah and into the streets of Jerusalem, and now they are a desolate ruin.

⁷"And now the LORD God Almighty, the God of Israel, asks you: Why are you destroying yourselves? For not one of you will survive—not a man, woman, or child among you who has come here from Judah, not even the babies in your arms. ⁸Why arouse my anger by burning incense to the idols you have made here in Egypt? You will only destroy yourselves and make yourselves an object of cursing and mockery for all the nations of the earth. ⁹Have you forgotten the sins of your ancestors, the sins of the kings and queens of Judah, and the sins you and your wives committed in Judah and Jerusalem? ¹⁰To this very hour you have shown no remorse or reverence. No one has chosen to follow my law and the decrees I gave to you and your ancestors before you.

¹¹"Therefore, the LORD Almighty, the God of Israel, says: I have made up my mind to destroy every one of you! ¹²I will take this remnant of Judah that insisted on coming here to Egypt, and I will consume them. They will fall here in Egypt, killed by war and famine. All will die, from the least to the greatest. They will be an object of damnation, horror, cursing, and mockery. ¹³I will punish them in Egypt just as I punished them in Jerusalem, by war, famine, and disease. ¹⁴Of those who fled to Egypt with dreams of returning home to Judah, only a handful will escape."

¹⁵Then all the women present and all the men who knew that their wives had burned incense to idols—a great crowd of all the Judeans living in Pathros, the southern region of Egypt—answered Jeremiah, ¹⁶"We will not listen to your messages from the LORD! ¹⁷We will do whatever we want. We will burn incense to the Queen of Heaven and sacrifice to her just as much as we like—just as we and our ancestors did before us, and as our kings and princes have always done in the towns of Judah and in the streets of Jerusalem. For in those days we had plenty to eat, and we were well off and had no troubles! ¹⁸But ever since we quit burning incense to the Queen of Heaven and stopped worshiping her, we have been in great trouble and have suffered the effects of war and famine."

¹⁹"And," the women added, "do you suppose that we were worshiping the Queen of Heaven, pouring out drink offerings to her, and making cakes marked with her image, without our husbands knowing it and helping us? Of course not!"

²⁰Then Jeremiah said to all of them, men and women alike, who had given him that answer, ²¹"Do you think the LORD did not know that you and your ancestors, your kings and officials, and all the people were burning incense to idols in the towns of Judah and in the streets of Jerusalem? ²²It was because the LORD could no longer bear all the evil things you were doing that he made your land an object of cursing—a desolate ruin without a single inhabitant—as it is today. ²³The very reason all these terrible things have happened to you is because you have burned incense to

44:1 Hebrew *Noph.*

My Daily Worship

— July 25 —

TOPPLING YOUR TOWER OF STRENGTH

JEREMIAH 39:1–45:5

Are you seeking great things for yourself? Don't do it! But don't be discouraged.
I will bring great disaster upon all these people, but I will protect
you wherever you go. I, the LORD, have spoken! (45:5).

[i reflect]

As American troops moved from the Persian Gulf into the major cities of Iraq during the recent war, they encountered towering statues bearing the likeness of Saddam Hussein. Within days of Iraq's liberation these images were toppled and destroyed. The destruction of these statues was a symbol of the regime's demise.

The larger-than-life likenesses that dominated towns and cities throughout this dictator's land show that the tendency to seek great things for one's self is true today as it was in Jeremiah's day. The desire to exercise godlike control over others and to seek glory for ourselves is not bound by culture or time, and it is not limited to despots. It is an ongoing temptation in a fallen world.

Still, for God's people we have a choice of whether to cave in to those impulses or resist them. For most people the temptation is not to become a Saddam-like dictator. Rather, it is to make a name for ourselves or try and take control of a situation that overwhelms. Ever been there? Sure you have. We all have. Ever since the couple in the Garden opted to hedge their bets and ended up hiding from God, we are naturally oriented to seek great things for ourselves.

When you feel this urge to glorify yourself, pause and turn to God. Ask him to reveal your hidden motives. Confess your tendencies to him; then seek his help. Such a time with the Lord in quiet reflection can lead to a special time of worship and praise.

[i pray]

Lord, I need you. I admit it. I've grown weary of attempting to be God in my life and with
those around me. Forgive me when I seek the glory that belongs to you alone.

[i respond]

Spend some moments recalling those dramatic scenes in Iraq, or in the former Soviet Union when statues of Lenin were bulldozed to the ground. As you visualize those symbols of regime change, ask the Lord to topple your ego a notch or two.

idols and sinned against the LORD, refusing to obey him and follow his instructions, laws, and stipulations."

²⁴Then Jeremiah said to them all, including the women, "Listen to this message from the LORD, all you citizens of Judah who live in Egypt. ²⁵The LORD Almighty, the God of Israel, says: You and your wives have said that you will never give up your devotion and sacrifices to the Queen of Heaven, and you have proved it by your actions. Then go ahead and carry out your promises and vows to her!

²⁶"But listen to this message from the LORD, all you Judeans now living in Egypt: I have sworn by my great name, says the LORD, that my name will no longer be spoken by any of the Judeans in the land of Egypt. None of you may invoke my name or use this oath: 'As surely as the Sovereign LORD lives!' ²⁷For I will watch over you to bring you disaster and not good. You will suffer war and famine until all of you are dead.

²⁸"Only a small number will escape death and return to Judah from Egypt. Then all those who came to Egypt will find out whose words are true, mine or theirs! ²⁹And this is the proof I give you, says the LORD, that all I have threatened will happen to you and that I will punish you here: ³⁰I will turn Pharaoh Hophra, king of Egypt, over to his enemies who want to kill him, just as I turned King Zedekiah of Judah over to King Nebuchadnezzar* of Babylon. I, the LORD, have spoken!"

A MESSAGE FOR BARUCH

45 The prophet Jeremiah gave a message to Baruch son of Neriah in the fourth year of the reign of Jehoiakim son of Josiah,* after Baruch had written down everything Jeremiah had dictated to him. He said, ²"This is what the LORD, the God of Israel, says to you, Baruch: ³You have said, 'I am overwhelmed with trouble! Haven't I had enough pain already? And now the LORD has added

more! I am weary of my own sighing and can find no rest.'

⁴"Baruch, this is what the LORD says: I will destroy this nation that I built. I will uproot what I planted. ⁵Are you seeking great things for yourself? Don't do it! But don't be discouraged. I will bring great disaster upon all these people, but I will protect you wherever you go. I, the LORD, have spoken!"

MESSAGES FOR THE NATIONS

46 The following messages were given to Jeremiah the prophet from the LORD concerning foreign nations.

MESSAGES ABOUT EGYPT

²This message concerning Egypt was given in the fourth year of the reign of Jehoiakim son of Josiah,* the king of Judah, on the occasion of the battle of Carchemish when Pharaoh Neco, king of Egypt, and his army were defeated beside the Euphrates River by King Nebuchadnezzar* of Babylon.

³"Buckle on your armor and advance into battle! ⁴Harness the horses, and prepare to mount them. Put on your helmets, sharpen your spears, and prepare your armor. ⁵But look! The Egyptian army flees in terror. The bravest of its fighting men run without a backward glance. They are terrorized at every turn, says the LORD. ⁶The swiftest cannot flee; the mightiest warriors cannot escape. By the Euphrates River to the north they stumble and fall.

⁷"Who is this, rising like the Nile River at floodtime, overflowing all the land? ⁸It is the Egyptian army, boasting that it will cover the earth like a flood, destroying every foe. ⁹Then come, you horses and chariots and mighty warriors of Egypt! Come, all you allies from Ethiopia, Libya, and Lydia* who are skilled with the shield and bow! ¹⁰For this is the day of the Lord, the LORD Almighty, a day of vengeance on his enemies. The sword will

---

44:30 Hebrew *Nebuchadrezzar,* a variant name for Nebuchadnezzar.   **45:1** The fourth year of Jehoiakim's reign was 605 B.C.   **46:2a** The fourth year of Jehoiakim's reign was 605 B.C.   **46:2b** Hebrew *Nebuchadrezzar,* a variant name for Nebuchadnezzar; also in 46:13, 26. **46:9** Hebrew *Cush, Put, and Lud.*

devour until it is satisfied, yes, drunk with your blood! The Lord, the LORD Almighty, will receive a sacrifice today in the north country beside the Euphrates River. ¹¹Go up to Gilead to get ointment, O virgin daughter of Egypt! But your many medicines will bring you no healing. ¹²The nations have heard of your shame. The earth is filled with your cries of despair. Your mightiest warriors will stumble across each other and fall together."

¹³Then the LORD gave the prophet Jeremiah this message about King Nebuchadnezzar's plans to attack Egypt.

¹⁴"Shout it out in Egypt! Publish it in the cities of Migdol, Memphis,* and Tahpanhes! Mobilize for battle, for the sword of destruction will devour everyone around you. ¹⁵Why have your warriors fled in terror? They cannot stand because the LORD has driven them away. ¹⁶They stumble and fall over each other and say among themselves, 'Come, let's go back to our homeland where we were born. Let's get away from the sword of the enemy!' ¹⁷There they will say, 'Pharaoh, the king of Egypt, is a loudmouth who missed his opportunity!'

¹⁸"As surely as I live," says the King, whose name is the LORD Almighty, "one is coming against Egypt who is as tall as Mount Tabor or Mount Carmel by the sea! ¹⁹Pack up! Get ready to leave for exile, you citizens of Egypt! The city of Memphis will be destroyed, without a single person living there. ²⁰Egypt is as sleek as a young cow, but a gadfly from the north is on its way! ²¹Egypt's famed mercenaries have become like fattened calves. They turn and run, for it is a day of great disaster for Egypt, a time of great punishment. ²²Silent as a serpent gliding away, Egypt flees. The invading army marches in; they come against her with axes like woodsmen. ²³They will cut down her people like trees," says the LORD, "for they are more numerous than grasshoppers. ²⁴Egypt will be humiliated; she will be handed over to men from the north."

²⁵The LORD Almighty, the God of Israel, says: "I will punish Amon, the god of Thebes,*

and all the other gods of Egypt. I will punish its rulers and Pharaoh, too, and all who trust in him. ²⁶I will hand them over to those who want them killed—to King Nebuchadnezzar of Babylon and his army. But afterward the land will recover from the ravages of war. I, the LORD, have spoken!

²⁷"But do not be afraid, Jacob, my servant; do not be dismayed, Israel. For I will bring you home again from distant lands, and your children will return from their exile. Israel* will return and will have peace and quiet, and nothing will make them afraid. ²⁸Fear not, Jacob, my servant," says the LORD, "for I am with you. I will destroy the nations to which I have exiled you, but I will not destroy you. But I must discipline you; I cannot let you go unpunished."

A MESSAGE ABOUT PHILISTIA

47 This is the LORD's message to the prophet Jeremiah concerning the Philistines of Gaza, before it was captured by the Egyptian army.

²This is what the LORD says: "A flood is coming from the north to overflow the land. It will destroy the land and everything in it—cities and people alike. People will scream in terror, and everyone in the land will weep. ³Hear the clatter of hooves and the rumble of wheels as the chariots rush by. Terrified fathers run madly, without a backward glance at their helpless children.

⁴"The time has come for the Philistines to be destroyed, along with their allies from Tyre and Sidon. Yes, the LORD is destroying the Philistines, those colonists from Crete.* ⁵The city of Gaza will be demolished; Ashkelon will lie in ruins. You remnant of the Mediterranean plain,* how long will you lament and mourn?

⁶"Now, O sword of the LORD, when will you be at rest again? Go back into your sheath; rest and be still! ⁷But how can it be still when the LORD has sent it on an errand? For the city of

---

46:14 Hebrew *Noph*; also in 46:19. 46:25 Hebrew *No*. 46:27 Hebrew *Jacob*. 47:4 Hebrew *from Caphtor*. 47:5 Hebrew *the plain*.

> *Praise is deeper than the lips.*
>
> ROBERT BROWNING

Ashkelon and the people living along the sea must be destroyed."

A MESSAGE ABOUT MOAB

48 This message was given concerning Moab.

This is what the LORD Almighty, the God of Israel, says: "Destruction is certain for the city of Nebo; it will soon lie in ruins. The city of Kiriathaim will be humiliated and captured; the fortress will be humiliated and broken down. ²No one will ever brag about Moab again, for there is a plot against her life. In Heshbon plans have been completed to destroy her. 'Come,' they say, 'we will cut her off from being a nation.' The city of Madmen,* too, will be silenced; the sword will follow you there. ³And then the roar of battle will surge against Horonaim, ⁴for all Moab is being destroyed. Her little ones will cry out.* ⁵Her refugees will climb the hills of Luhith, weeping bitterly, while cries of terror rise from Horonaim below. ⁶Flee for your lives! Hide in the wilderness!* ⁷Because you have trusted in your wealth and skill, you will be taken captive. Your god Chemosh, with his priests and princes, will be exiled to distant lands!

⁸"All the towns will be destroyed, both on the plateaus and in the valleys, for the LORD has spoken. ⁹Oh, that Moab had wings so she could fly away, for her cities will be left empty, with no one living in them. ¹⁰Cursed be those who refuse to do the work the LORD has given them, who hold back their swords from shedding blood!

¹¹"From her earliest history, Moab has lived in peace. She is like wine that has been allowed to settle. She has not been poured from flask to flask, and she is now fragrant and smooth. ¹²But the time is coming soon," says the LORD, "when I will send troublemakers to pour her from her jar. They will pour her out, then shatter the jar! ¹³At last Moab will be ashamed of her idol Chemosh, as Israel was ashamed of her gold calf at Bethel.*

¹⁴"You used to boast, 'We are heroes, mighty men of war.' ¹⁵But now Moab and her towns will be destroyed. Her most promising youth are doomed to slaughter," says the King, whose name is the LORD Almighty. ¹⁶"Calamity is coming fast to Moab; it threatens ominously.

¹⁷"You friends of Moab, weep for her and cry! See how the strong scepter is broken, how the beautiful staff is shattered! ¹⁸Come down from your glory and sit in the dust, you people of Dibon, for those who destroy Moab will shatter Dibon, too. They will tear down all your towers. ¹⁹The people of Aroer stand anxiously beside the road to watch. They shout to those who flee from Moab, 'What has happened there?'

²⁰"And the reply comes back, 'Moab lies in ruins; weep and wail! Tell it by the banks of the Arnon River: Moab has been destroyed!' ²¹All the cities of the plateau lie in ruins, too. Judgment has been poured out on them all—on Holon and Jahaz* and Mephaath, ²²and on Dibon and Nebo and Beth-diblathaim, ²³and on Kiriathaim and Beth-gamul and Beth-meon, ²⁴and on Kerioth and Bozrah—all the cities of Moab, far and near.

²⁵"The strength of Moab has ended. Her horns have been cut off, and her arms have been broken," says the LORD. ²⁶"Let her stagger

---

48:2 *Madmen* sounds like the Hebrew word for "silence"; it should not be confused with the English word *madmen.* 48:4 Greek version reads *Her cries are heard as far away as Zoar.* 48:6 Or *Be like* [the town of] *Aroer in the wilderness.* 48:13 Hebrew *ashamed when they trusted in Bethel.* 48:21 Hebrew *Jahzah,* a variant name for Jahaz.

and fall like a drunkard, for she has rebelled against the LORD. Moab will wallow in her own vomit, ridiculed by all. ²⁷Did you not make Israel the object of your ridicule? Was she caught in the company of thieves that you should despise her as you do?

²⁸"You people of Moab, flee from your cities and towns! Live in the caves like doves that nest in the clefts of the rocks. ²⁹We have heard of the pride of Moab, for it is very great. We know of her loftiness, her arrogance, and her haughty heart. ³⁰I know about her insolence," says the LORD, "but her boasts are false; they accomplish nothing. ³¹Yes, I wail for Moab; my heart is broken for the men of Kir-hareseth.*

³²"You people of Sibmah, rich in vineyards, I will weep for you even more than I did for Jazer. Your spreading vines once reached as far as the Dead Sea,* but the destroyer has stripped you bare! He has harvested your grapes and summer fruits. ³³Joy and gladness are gone from fruitful Moab. The presses yield no wine. No one treads the grapes with shouts of joy. There is shouting, yes, but not of joy. ³⁴Instead, their awful cries of terror can be heard from Heshbon clear across to Elealeh and Jahaz; from Zoar all the way to Horonaim and Eglath-shelishiyah. Even the waters of Nimrim are dried up now.

³⁵"I will put an end to Moab," says the LORD, "for they offer sacrifices at the pagan shrines and burn incense to their false gods. ³⁶My heart moans like a flute for Moab and Kir-hareseth, for all their wealth has disappeared. ³⁷They shave their heads and beards in mourning. They slash their hands and put on clothes made of sackcloth. ³⁸Crying and sorrow will be in every Moabite home and on every street. For I have smashed Moab like an old, unwanted bottle. ³⁹How it is broken! Hear the wailing! See the shame of Moab! She has become an object of ridicule, an example of ruin to all her neighbors.

⁴⁰"An eagle swoops down on the land of Moab," says the LORD. ⁴¹"Her cities will fall; her strongholds will be seized. Even the mightiest warriors will be as frightened as a woman about to give birth. ⁴²Moab will no longer be a nation, for she has boasted against the LORD.

⁴³"Terror and traps and snares will be your lot, O Moab," says the LORD. ⁴⁴"Those who flee in terror will fall into a trap, and those who escape the trap will step into a snare. I will see to it that you do not get away, for the time of your judgment has come," says the LORD. ⁴⁵"The people flee as far as Heshbon but are unable to go on. For a fire comes from Heshbon, King Sihon's ancestral home, to devour the entire land with all its rebellious people.

⁴⁶"O Moab, your destruction is sure! The people of the god Chemosh are destroyed! Your sons and daughters have been taken away as captives. ⁴⁷But in the latter days I will restore the fortunes of Moab," says the LORD.

This is the end of Jeremiah's prophecy concerning Moab.

A MESSAGE ABOUT AMMON

49 This message was given concerning the Ammonites.

This is what the LORD says: "What are you doing? Are there no descendants of Israel to inherit the land of Gad? Why are you, who worship Molech,* living in its towns? ²I will punish you for this," says the LORD, "by destroying your city of Rabbah. It will become a desolate heap, and the neighboring towns will be burned. Then Israel will come and take back the land you took from her," says the LORD.

³"Cry out, O Heshbon, for the town of Ai is destroyed. Weep, O people of Rabbah! Put on your clothes of mourning. Weep and wail, hiding in the hedges, for your god Molech will be exiled along with his princes and priests. ⁴You are proud of your fertile valleys, but they will soon be ruined. You rebellious daughter, you trusted in your wealth and thought no one

48:31 Hebrew *Kir-heres*, a variant name for Kir-hareseth; also in 48:36.   48:32 Hebrew *the sea of Jazer*.   49:1 Hebrew *Milcom*, a variant name for Molech; also in 49:3.

could ever harm you. ⁵But look! I will bring terror upon you," says the Lord, the LORD Almighty. "Your neighbors will chase you from your land, and no one will help your exiles as they flee. ⁶But afterward I will restore the fortunes of the Ammonites," says the LORD.

MESSAGES ABOUT EDOM

⁷This message was given concerning Edom.

This is what the LORD Almighty says: "Where are all the wise men of Teman? Is there no one left to give wise counsel? ⁸Turn and flee! Hide in deep caves, you people of Dedan! For when I bring disaster on Edom,* I will punish you, too! ⁹Those who harvest grapes always leave a few for the poor. If thieves came at night, even they would not take everything. ¹⁰But I will strip bare the land of Edom, and there will be no place left to hide. Its children, its brothers, and its neighbors—all will be destroyed—and Edom itself will be no more. ¹¹But I will preserve the orphans who remain among you. Your widows, too, will be able to depend on me for help."

¹²And this is what the LORD says: "If the innocent must suffer, how much more must you! You will not go unpunished! You must drink this cup of judgment! ¹³For I have sworn by my own name," says the LORD, "that Bozrah will become an object of horror and a heap of rubble; it will be mocked and cursed. All its towns and villages will be desolate forever."

¹⁴I have heard a message from the LORD that an ambassador was sent to the nations to say, "Form a coalition against Edom, and prepare for battle!"

¹⁵This is what the LORD says: "I will cut you down to size among the nations, Edom. You will be despised by all. ¹⁶You are proud that you inspire fear in others. And you are proud because you live in a rock fortress and hide high in the mountains. But don't fool yourselves! Though you live among the peaks with the eagles, I will bring you crashing down," says the LORD.

¹⁷"Edom will be an object of horror. All who pass by will be appalled and will gasp at the destruction they see there. ¹⁸It will be like the destruction of Sodom and Gomorrah and their neighboring towns," says the LORD. "No one will live there anymore. ¹⁹I will come like a lion from the thickets of the Jordan, leaping on the sheep in the pasture. I will chase Edom from its land, and I will appoint the leader of my choice. For who is like me, and who can challenge me? What ruler can oppose my will?"

²⁰Listen to the LORD's plans for Edom and the people of Teman. Even the little children will be dragged off, and their homes will be empty. ²¹The earth will shake with the noise of Edom's fall, and its cry of despair will be heard all the way to the Red Sea.* ²²The enemy will come as swiftly as an eagle, and he will spread his wings against Bozrah. Even the mightiest warriors will be as frightened as a woman about to give birth.

A MESSAGE ABOUT DAMASCUS

²³This message was given concerning Damascus.

This is what the LORD says: "The towns of Hamath and Arpad are struck with fear, for they have heard the news of their destruction. Their hearts are troubled like a wild sea in a raging storm. ²⁴Damascus has become feeble, and all her people turn to flee. Fear, anguish, and pain have gripped her as they do a woman giving birth. ²⁵That famous city, a city of joy, will be forsaken! ²⁶Her young men will fall in the streets and die. Her warriors will all be killed," says the LORD Almighty. ²⁷"And I will start a fire at the edge of Damascus that will burn up the palaces of Ben-hadad."

A MESSAGE ABOUT KEDAR AND HAZOR

²⁸This message was given concerning Kedar and the kingdoms of Hazor, which were attacked by King Nebuchadnezzar* of Babylon.

49:8 Hebrew *Esau;* also in 49:10. 49:21 Hebrew *sea of reeds.* 49:28 Hebrew *Nebuchadrezzar,* a variant name for Nebuchadnezzar; also in 49:30.

My Daily Worship

— *July 26* —

A FALSE SENSE OF SECURITY

JEREMIAH 46:1–49:39

"You are proud that you inspire fear in others. And you are proud because you live in a rock fortress and hide high in the mountains. But don't fool yourselves! Though you live among the peaks with the eagles, I will bring you crashing down," says the LORD (49:16).

[i reflect]

The city of Petra flourished in the sixth century B.C. It lay about three hours south of Amman in modern day Jordan. Taking advantage of the soft stone, the residents of this ancient town carved cliff dwellings and caves in which to live. The ornate architecture has survived amazingly well in the arid climate of the Middle East, the most famous of which was the Treasury building.

Surrounded by towering hills of rust-colored sandstone, Petra enjoyed natural protection against invaders. A narrow canyon leading into the valley of Petra no more than ten feet across (and less than four feet at some points) also provided increased security. The Lord's warning against pride and a false sense of security recorded by Jeremiah applies very well to this forgotten empire. Although the ancient Edomites claimed the safe vantage point of eagles and the enviable fortress-like surroundings, they were destroyed. When they failed to honor and worship Israel's God, their glory was reduced to a ghost town.

If you climb the hills of Petra today, you can easily see how futile it is to build a life on anything but the firm foundation of a growing faith in God. But it doesn't take a trip to the Middle East to grasp that truth. Go ahead and re-read these verses from Jeremiah. Feel the passion with which the Lord speaks. Hear the cry of the eagle in flight. See the weeping refugees of a civilization being led away into captivity. Ask the Lord what false securities exist in your life. Ask him to chip away at the beautiful veneer that prevents you from daily acknowledging your need of him.

[i pray]

Lord, I don't want the sad saga of the city of Petra to be true of me. Although I feel impervious to danger and spiritual attack, I know in my heart I am very vulnerable. Father, I turn to you today and admit my need of you.

[i respond]

Look up pictures of Petra on the Internet or in an encyclopedia. As you admire the ornate beauty carved in sandstone, think of what Jesus said about the Pharisees' "outer" spiritual piety—beneath the surface, there wasn't anything real there. Write down two ways that this is true in your life.

This is what the LORD says: "Advance against Kedar! Blot out the warriors from the East! ²⁹Their flocks and tents will be captured, and their household goods and camels will be taken away. Everywhere shouts of panic will be heard: 'We are terrorized at every turn!' ³⁰Flee for your lives," says the LORD. "Hide yourselves in deep caves, you people of Hazor, for King Nebuchadnezzar of Babylon has plotted against you and is preparing to destroy you.

³¹"Go up and attack those self-sufficient nomadic tribes," says the LORD. "They live alone in the desert without walls or gates. ³²Their camels and cattle will all be yours. I will scatter to the winds these people who live in distant places.* I will bring calamity upon them from every direction," says the LORD. ³³"Hazor will be inhabited by jackals, and it will be desolate forever. No one will live there anymore."

A MESSAGE ABOUT ELAM

³⁴This message concerning Elam came to the prophet Jeremiah from the LORD at the beginning of the reign of King Zedekiah of Judah.

³⁵This is what the LORD Almighty says: "I will destroy the archers of Elam—the best of their marksmen. ³⁶I will bring enemies from all directions, and I will scatter the people of Elam to the four winds. They will be exiled to countries around the world. ³⁷I myself will go with Elam's enemies to shatter it. My fierce anger will bring great disaster upon the people of Elam," says the LORD. "Their enemies will chase them with the sword until I have destroyed them completely. ³⁸I will set my throne in Elam," says the LORD, "and I will destroy its king and princes. ³⁹But in the latter days I will restore the fortunes of Elam," says the LORD.

A MESSAGE ABOUT BABYLON

50 The LORD gave Jeremiah the prophet this message concerning Babylon and the land of the Babylonians.*

²This is what the LORD says: "Tell the whole world, and keep nothing back! Raise a signal flag so everyone will know that Babylon will fall! Her images and idols will be shattered. Her gods Bel and Marduk will be utterly disgraced. ³For a nation will attack her from the north and bring such destruction that no one will live in her again. Everything will be gone; both people and animals will flee.

HOPE FOR ISRAEL AND JUDAH

⁴"Then the people of Israel and Judah will join together," says the LORD, "weeping and seeking the LORD their God. ⁵They will ask the way to Jerusalem* and will start back home again. They will bind themselves to the LORD with an eternal covenant that will never again be broken.

⁶"My people have been lost sheep. Their shepherds have led them astray and turned them loose in the mountains. They have lost their way and cannot remember how to get back to the fold. ⁷All who found them devoured them. Their enemies said, 'We are allowed to attack them freely, for they have sinned against the LORD, their place of rest, the hope of their ancestors.'

⁸"But now, flee from Babylon! Leave the land of the Babylonians. Lead my people home again. ⁹For look, I am raising up an army of great nations from the north. I will bring them against Babylon to attack her, and she will be captured. The enemies' arrows will go straight to the mark; they will not miss! ¹⁰Babylonia* will be plundered until the attackers are glutted with plunder," says the LORD.

BABYLON'S SURE FALL

¹¹"You rejoice and are glad, you plunderers of my chosen people. You frisk about like a calf in a meadow and neigh like a stallion. ¹²But your homeland* will be overwhelmed with shame and disgrace. You will become the least of nations—a wilderness, a dry and desolate

49:32 Or *who clip the corners of their hair.* 50:1 Or *Chaldeans;* also in 50:8, 25, 35, 45. 50:5 Hebrew *Zion;* also in 50:28. 50:10 Or *Chaldea.* 50:12 Hebrew *your mother.*

My Daily Worship

— July 27 —

IN PRAISE OF GODLY SHEPHERDS

JEREMIAH 50:1–52:34

My people have been lost sheep. Their shepherds have led them astray and
turned them loose in the mountains. They have lost their way
and cannot remember how to get back to the fold (50:6).

[i reflect]

Robert G. Tuttle Jr. is a respected theologian and author. Although he had gleaned much about biblical culture from his graduate work, he made a firsthand discovery about shepherds while escorting a tour group in Israel. One morning, the group climbed aboard a bus for a ride through the Judean countryside. The Israeli tour guide explained to Dr. Tuttle and his companions that shepherds in the Middle East never drive their flocks from behind. Instead, he said, they always lead them by going ahead of them.

Within a few minutes, Tuttle called to the front of the bus asking the guide to look out to the hillside. "I thought you said that shepherds in this part of the world never drive their sheep," he said. "Look over there!" As the guide looked through the bus windows, he saw a man charging after a flock of sheep attempting to get away. "Oh, sir," the tour guide said with a chuckle in his voice. "That's not a shepherd. That's a butcher."

Dr. Tuttle had not seen a wayward shepherd after all, but there were many wayward shepherds in Jeremiah's day. The spiritual shepherds of God's flock did not live up to what was expected of them. Their lives lacked integrity and their concern for the people of God left much to be desired.

Hopefully, you attend a church where your pastor/shepherd considers the call to care for your soul a privilege. If so, thank the Lord as you quietly intercede for significant others in your life. Ask God to fill your pastor with insight and inspiration as he feeds you each week in worship.

Of course, God is ultimately our Great Shepherd. He knows our needs and is committed to care for us. Before you start your day, or before you lay down for the night, read the Psalm 23. Personalize David's words as your own. Hold on to the phrase that you need most today.

[i pray]

Lord, I want to praise you for the gift of pastors. Unlike the apostate priests in Old Testament
times, they honor you by the way they care for the church. Give them a sense
of your presence, Lord, as they prepare to lead your flock even now.

[i respond]

Believe it or not, when it comes to the church, sheep can impact their shepherds for good. As a member of your shepherd's flock, write your pastor a note this week expressing gratitude for the way his or her ministry has impacted your life. Cite a specific instance.

land. ¹³Because of the LORD's anger, Babylon will become a deserted wasteland. All who pass by will be horrified and will gasp at the destruction they see there.

¹⁴"Yes, prepare to attack Babylon, all you nations round about. Let your archers shoot at her. Spare no arrows, for she has sinned against the LORD. ¹⁵Shout against her from every side. Look! She surrenders! Her walls have fallen. The LORD has taken vengeance, so do not spare her. Do to her as she has done to others! ¹⁶Lead from Babylon all those who plant crops; send all the harvesters away. Let the captives escape the sword of the enemy and rush back to their own lands.

HOPE FOR GOD'S PEOPLE

¹⁷"The Israelites are like sheep that have been scattered by lions. First the king of Assyria ate them up. Then King Nebuchadnezzar* of Babylon cracked their bones." ¹⁸Therefore, the LORD Almighty, the God of Israel, says: "Now I will punish the king of Babylon and his land, just as I punished the king of Assyria. ¹⁹And I will bring Israel home again to her own land, to feed in the fields of Carmel and Bashan, and to be satisfied once more on the hill country of Ephraim and Gilead. ²⁰In those days," says the LORD, "no sin will be found in Israel or in Judah, for I will forgive the remnant I preserve.

THE LORD'S JUDGMENT ON BABYLON

²¹"Go up, my warriors, against the land of Merathaim and against the people of Pekod. Yes, march against Babylon, the land of rebels, a land that I will judge! Pursue, kill, and completely destroy* them, as I have commanded you," says the LORD. ²²"Let the battle cry be heard in the land, a shout of great destruction. ²³Babylon, the mightiest hammer in all the earth, lies broken and shattered. Babylon is desolate among the nations! ²⁴Listen, Babylon, for I have set a trap for you. You are caught, for you have fought against the LORD.

²⁵"The LORD has opened his armory and brought out weapons to vent his fury against his enemies. The terror that falls upon the Babylonians will be the work of the Sovereign LORD Almighty. ²⁶Yes, come against her from distant lands. Break open her granaries. Crush her walls and houses into heaps of rubble. Destroy her completely, and leave nothing! ²⁷Even destroy her cattle—it will be terrible for them, too! Slaughter them all! For the time has come for Babylon to be devastated. ²⁸Listen to the people who have escaped from Babylon, as they declare in Jerusalem how the LORD our God has taken vengeance against those who destroyed his Temple.

²⁹"Send out a call for archers to come to Babylon. Surround the city so none can escape. Do to her as she has done to others, for she has defied the LORD, the Holy One of Israel. ³⁰Her young men will fall in the streets and die. Her warriors will all be killed," says the LORD.

³¹"See, I am your enemy, O proud people," says the Lord, the LORD Almighty. "Your day of reckoning has arrived. ³²O land of pride, you will stumble and fall, and no one will raise you up. For I will light a fire in the cities of Babylon that will burn everything around them."

³³And now the LORD Almighty says this: "The people of Israel and Judah have been wronged. Their captors hold them and refuse to let them go. ³⁴But the one who redeems them is strong. His name is the LORD Almighty. He will defend them and give them rest again in Israel. But the people of Babylon—there will be no rest for them!

³⁵"The sword of destruction will strike the Babylonians," says the LORD. "It will strike the people of Babylon—her princes and wise men, too. ³⁶And when it strikes her wise counselors, they will become fools! When it strikes her mightiest warriors, panic will seize them!

50:17 Hebrew *Nebuchadrezzar*, a variant name for Nebuchadnezzar. 50:21 The Hebrew term used here refers to the complete consecration of things or people to the LORD, either by destroying them or by giving them as an offering.

³⁷When it strikes her horses and chariots, her allies from other lands will become as weak as women. When it strikes her treasures, they all will be plundered. ³⁸It will even strike her water supply, causing it to dry up. And why? Because the whole land is filled with idols, and the people are madly in love with them.

³⁹"Soon this city of Babylon will be inhabited by ostriches and jackals. It will be a home for the wild animals of the desert. Never again will people live there; it will lie desolate forever. ⁴⁰I will destroy it just as I* destroyed Sodom and Gomorrah and their neighboring towns," says the LORD. "No one will live there anymore.

⁴¹"Look! A great army is marching from the north! A great nation and many kings are rising against you from far-off lands. ⁴²They are fully armed for slaughter. They are cruel and show no mercy. As they ride forward, the noise of their army is like a roaring sea. They are marching in battle formation to destroy you, Babylon. ⁴³The king of Babylon has received reports about the enemy, and he is weak with fright. Fear and pain have gripped him, like that of a woman about to give birth.

⁴⁴"I will come like a lion from the thickets of the Jordan, leaping on the sheep in the pasture. I will chase Babylon from its land, and I will appoint the leader of my choice. For who is like me, and who can challenge me? What ruler can oppose my will?"

⁴⁵Listen to the LORD's plans against Babylon and the land of the Babylonians. Even little children will be dragged off, and their homes will be empty. ⁴⁶The earth will shake with the noise of Babylon's fall, and her cry of despair will be heard around the world.

51 This is what the LORD says: "I will stir up a destroyer against Babylon and the people of Babylonia.* ²Foreigners will come and winnow her, blowing her away as chaff. They will come from every side to rise against her in her day of trouble. ³Don't let the archers put on their armor or draw their bows. No one will be spared! Young and old alike will be completely destroyed.* ⁴They will fall dead in the land of the Babylonians,* slashed to death in her streets. ⁵For the LORD Almighty has not forsaken Israel and Judah. He is still their God, even though their land was filled with sin against the Holy One of Israel."

⁶Flee from Babylon! Save yourselves! Don't get trapped in her punishment! It is the LORD's time for vengeance; he will fully repay her. ⁷Babylon has been like a golden cup in the LORD's hands, a cup from which he made the whole earth drink and go mad. ⁸But now suddenly, Babylon, too, has fallen. Weep for her, and give her medicine. Perhaps she can yet be healed. ⁹We would have helped her if we could, but nothing can save her now. Let her go; abandon her. Return now to your own land, for her judgment will be so great it cannot be measured. ¹⁰The LORD has vindicated us. Come, let us announce in Jerusalem* everything the LORD our God has done.

¹¹Sharpen the arrows! Lift up the shields! For the LORD has stirred up the spirit of the kings of the Medes to march against Babylon and destroy her. This is his vengeance against those who desecrated his Temple. ¹²Raise the battle flag against Babylon! Reinforce the guard and station the watchmen. Prepare an ambush, for the LORD will fulfill all his plans against Babylon.

¹³You are a city rich with water, a great center of commerce, but your end has come. The thread of your life is cut. ¹⁴The LORD Almighty has taken this vow and has sworn to it by his own name: "Your cities will be filled with enemies, like fields filled with locusts, and they will lift their shouts of triumph over you."

A HYMN OF PRAISE TO THE LORD

¹⁵ He made the earth by his power,
   and he preserves it by his wisdom.

50:40 Hebrew *just as God.* 51:1 Hebrew *of Leb-kamai,* a code name for Babylonia. 51:3 The Hebrew term used here refers to the complete consecration of things or people to the LORD, either by destroying them or by giving them as an offering. 51:4 Or *Chaldeans;* also in 51:54. 51:10 Hebrew *Zion;* also in 51:24, 35a.

He has stretched out the heavens
    by his understanding.
[16] When he speaks, there is thunder in the
    heavens.
He causes the clouds to rise over the
    earth.
He sends the lightning with the rain
    and releases the wind from his
    storehouses.
[17] Compared to him, all people are foolish
    and have no knowledge at all!
They make idols, but the idols will disgrace
    their makers,
    for they are frauds.
They have no life or power in them.
[18] Idols are worthless; they are lies!
The time is coming when they will all be
    destroyed.
[19] But the God of Israel* is no idol!
He is the Creator of everything that
    exists,
    including his people, his own special
    possession.
The LORD Almighty is his name!

BABYLON'S GREAT PUNISHMENT

[20]"You* are my battle-ax and sword," says the
LORD. "With you I will shatter nations and
destroy many kingdoms. [21]With you I will
shatter armies, destroying the horse and rider,
the chariot and charioteer. [22]With you I will
shatter men and women, old people and children, young men and maidens. [23]With you I
will shatter shepherds and flocks, farmers and
oxen, captains and rulers.

[24]"As you watch, I will repay Babylon and
the people of Babylonia* for all the wrong
they have done to my people in Jerusalem,"
says the LORD.

[25]"Look, O mighty mountain, destroyer of
the earth! I am your enemy," says the LORD. "I
will raise my fist against you, to roll you down
from the heights. When I am finished, you
will be nothing but a heap of rubble. [26]You will
be desolate forever. Even your stones will
never again be used for building. You will be
completely wiped out," says the LORD.

[27]Signal many nations to mobilize for war
against Babylon. Sound the battle cry! Bring
out the armies of Ararat, Minni, and
Ashkenaz. Appoint a leader, and bring a multitude of horses! [28]Bring against her the armies
of the kings of the Medes and their generals,
and the armies of all the countries they rule.

[29]Babylon trembles and writhes in pain, for
everything the LORD has planned against her
stands unchanged. Babylon will be left desolate without a single inhabitant. [30]Her mightiest warriors no longer fight. They stay in their
barracks. Their courage is gone. They have
become as fearful as women. The invaders
have burned the houses and broken down the
city gates. [31]Messengers from every side come
running to the king to tell him all is lost! [32]All
the escape routes are blocked. The fortifications are burning, and the army is in panic.

[33]For the LORD Almighty, the God of Israel,
says: "Babylon is like wheat on a threshing
floor, about to be trampled. In just a little
while her harvest will begin."

[34]"King Nebuchadnezzar* of Babylon has
eaten and crushed us and emptied out our
strength. He has swallowed us like a great
monster and filled his belly with our riches.
He has thrown us out of our own country.
[35]May Babylon be repaid for all the violence
she did to us," say the people of Jerusalem.
"May the people of Babylonia be paid in full
for all the blood they spilled," says Jerusalem.

THE LORD'S VENGEANCE ON BABYLON

[36]The LORD says to Jerusalem, "I will be your
lawyer to plead your case, and I will avenge
you. I will dry up her river, her water supply,
[37]and Babylon will become a heap of rubble,
haunted by jackals. It will be an object of horror and contempt, without a single person living there.

[38]"In their drunken feasts, the people of

51:19 Hebrew *the Portion of Jacob.* **51:20** Possibly Cyrus, who was used of God to conquer Babylon. Compare Isa 44:28; 45:1.
51:24 Or *Chaldea;* also in 51:35. **51:34** Hebrew *Nebuchadrezzar,* a variant name for Nebuchadnezzar.

Babylon roar like lions. ³⁹And while they lie inflamed with all their wine, I will prepare a different kind of feast for them. I will make them drink until they fall asleep, never again to waken," says the LORD. ⁴⁰"I will bring them like lambs to the slaughter, like rams and goats to be sacrificed.

⁴¹"How Babylon* is fallen—great Babylon, praised throughout the earth! The world can scarcely believe its eyes at her fall! ⁴²The sea has risen over Babylon; she is covered by its waves. ⁴³Her cities now lie in ruins; she is a dry wilderness where no one lives or even passes by. ⁴⁴And I will punish Bel, the god of Babylon, and pull from his mouth what he has taken. The nations will no longer come and worship him. The wall of Babylon has fallen.

A Message for the Exiles

⁴⁵"Listen, my people, flee from Babylon. Save yourselves! Run from the LORD's fierce anger. ⁴⁶But do not panic when you hear the first rumor of approaching forces. For rumors will keep coming year by year. Then there will be a time of violence as the leaders fight against each other. ⁴⁷For the time is surely coming when I will punish this great city and all her idols. Her whole land will be disgraced, and her dead will lie in the streets. ⁴⁸The heavens and earth will rejoice, for out of the north will come destroying armies against Babylon," says the LORD. ⁴⁹"Just as Babylon killed the people of Israel and others throughout the world, so must her people be killed. ⁵⁰Go, you who escaped the sword! Do not stand and watch—flee while you can! Remember the LORD, even though you are in a far-off land, and think about your home in Jerusalem."

⁵¹"We are ashamed," the people say. "We are insulted and disgraced because the LORD's Temple has been defiled by foreigners."

⁵²"Yes," says the LORD, "but the time is coming when Babylon's idols will be destroyed. The groans of her wounded people will be heard throughout the land. ⁵³Though Babylon reaches as high as the heavens, and though she increases her strength immeasurably, I will send enemies to plunder her," says the LORD.

Babylon's Complete Destruction

⁵⁴Listen! Hear the cry of Babylon, the sound of great destruction from the land of the Babylonians. ⁵⁵For the LORD is destroying Babylon. He will silence her. Waves of enemies pound against her; the noise of battle rings through the city. ⁵⁶Destroying armies come against Babylon. Her mighty men are captured, and their weapons break in their hands. For the LORD is a God who gives just punishment, and he is giving Babylon all she deserves.

⁵⁷"I will make drunk her officials, wise men, rulers, captains, and warriors," says the King, whose name is the LORD Almighty. "They will fall asleep and never wake up again!"

⁵⁸This is what the LORD Almighty says: "The wide walls of Babylon will be leveled to the ground, and her high gates will be burned. The builders from many lands have worked in vain, for their work will be destroyed by fire!"

Jeremiah's Message Sent to Babylon

⁵⁹The prophet Jeremiah gave this message to Zedekiah's staff officer, Seraiah son of Neriah and grandson of Mahseiah, when he went to Babylon with King Zedekiah of Judah. This was during the fourth year of Zedekiah's reign.* ⁶⁰Jeremiah had recorded on a scroll all the terrible disasters that would soon come upon Babylon. ⁶¹He said to Seraiah, "When you get to Babylon, read aloud everything on this scroll. ⁶²Then say, 'LORD, you have said that you will destroy Babylon so that neither people nor animals will remain here. She will lie empty and abandoned forever.' ⁶³Then, when you have finished reading the scroll, tie it to a stone, and throw it into the Euphrates River. ⁶⁴Then say, 'In this same way Babylon and her people will sink, never again to rise,

51:41 Hebrew *Sheshach*, a code name for Babylon. 51:59 The fourth year of Zedekiah's reign was 593 B.C.

because of the disasters I will bring upon her.'"

This is the end of Jeremiah's messages.

The Fall of Jerusalem

52 Zedekiah was twenty-one years old when he became king, and he reigned in Jerusalem eleven years. His mother's name was Hamutal, the daughter of Jeremiah from Libnah. ²But Zedekiah did what was evil in the LORD's sight, just as Jehoiakim had done. ³So the LORD, in his anger, finally banished the people of Jerusalem and Judah from his presence and sent them into exile.

Then Zedekiah rebelled against the king of Babylon. ⁴So on January 15,* during the ninth year of Zedekiah's reign, King Nebuchadnezzar* of Babylon led his entire army against Jerusalem. They surrounded the city and built siege ramps against its walls. ⁵Jerusalem was kept under siege until the eleventh year of King Zedekiah's reign.

⁶By July 18 of Zedekiah's eleventh year,* the famine in the city had become very severe, with the last of the food entirely gone. ⁷Then a section of the city wall was broken down, and all the soldiers made plans to escape from the city. But since the city was surrounded by the Babylonians,* they waited for nightfall and fled through the gate between the two walls behind the king's gardens. They made a dash across the fields, in the direction of the Jordan Valley.*

⁸But the Babylonians chased after them and caught King Zedekiah on the plains of Jericho, for by then his men had all abandoned him. ⁹They brought him to the king of Babylon at Riblah, in the land of Hamath, where sentence was passed against him. ¹⁰There at Riblah, the king of Babylon made Zedekiah watch as all his sons were killed; they also killed all the other leaders of Judah.

¹¹Then they gouged out Zedekiah's eyes, bound him in bronze chains, and led him away to Babylon. Zedekiah remained there in prison for the rest of his life.

The Temple Destroyed

¹²On August 17 of that year,* which was the nineteenth year of Nebuchadnezzar's reign, Nebuzaradan, captain of the guard, an official of the Babylonian king, arrived in Jerusalem. ¹³He burned down the Temple of the LORD, the royal palace, and all the houses of Jerusalem. He destroyed all the important buildings in the city. ¹⁴Then the captain of the guard supervised the entire Babylonian* army as they tore down the walls of Jerusalem. ¹⁵Nebuzaradan, captain of the guard, then took as exiles some of the poorest of the people and those who remained in the city, along with the rest of the craftsmen and the troops who had declared their allegiance to the king of Babylon. ¹⁶But Nebuzaradan allowed some of the poorest people to stay behind in Judah to care for the vineyards and fields.

¹⁷The Babylonians broke up the bronze pillars, the bronze water carts, and the bronze Sea that were at the LORD's Temple, and they carried all the bronze away to Babylon. ¹⁸They also took all the pots, shovels, lamp snuffers, basins, dishes, and all the other bronze utensils used for making sacrifices at the Temple. ¹⁹Nebuzaradan, captain of the guard, also took the small bowls, firepans, basins, pots, lampstands, dishes, bowls used for drink offerings, and all the other utensils made of pure gold or silver.

²⁰The bronze from the two pillars, the water carts, and the Sea with the twelve bulls beneath it was too great to be measured. These things had been made for the LORD's Temple in the days of King Solomon. ²¹Each of the pillars was 27 feet tall and 18 feet in cir-

---

52:4a Hebrew *on the tenth day of the tenth month,* of the Hebrew calendar. A number of events in Jeremiah can be cross-checked with dates in surviving Babylonian records and related accurately to our modern calendar. This event occurred on January 15, 588 B.C. 52:4b Hebrew *Nebuchadrezzar,* a variant name for Nebuchadnezzar; also in 52:12, 28, 29, 30. 52:6 Hebrew *By the ninth day of the fourth month* [of Zedekiah's eleventh year]. This event of the Hebrew lunar calendar occurred on July 18, 586 B.C.; also see note on 52:4a. 52:7a Or *Chaldeans;* also in 52:8, 17. 52:7b Hebrew *the Arabah.* 52:12 Hebrew *On the tenth day of the fifth month,* of the Hebrew calendar. This day was August 17, 586 B.C.; also see note on 52:4a. 52:14 Or *Chaldean.*

cumference.* They were hollow, with walls 3 inches thick.* ²²The bronze capital on top of each pillar was 7½ feet* high and was decorated with a network of bronze pomegranates all the way around. ²³There were ninety-six pomegranates on the sides, and a total of one hundred on the network around the top.

²⁴The captain of the guard took with him as prisoners Seraiah the chief priest, his assistant Zephaniah, and the three chief gatekeepers. ²⁵And of the people still hiding in the city, he took an officer of the Judean army, seven of the king's personal advisers, the army commander's chief secretary, who was in charge of recruitment, and sixty other citizens. ²⁶Nebuzaradan the commander took them all to the king of Babylon at Riblah. ²⁷And there at Riblah in the land of Hamath, the king of Babylon had them all put to death. So the people of Judah were sent into exile from their land.

²⁸The number of captives taken to Babylon in the seventh year of Nebuchadnezzar's reign* was 3,023. ²⁹Then in Nebuchadnezzar's eighteenth year* he took 832 more. ³⁰In his twenty-third year* he sent Nebuzaradan, his captain of the guard, who took 745 more—a total of 4,600 captives in all.

HOPE FOR ISRAEL'S ROYAL LINE

³¹In the thirty-seventh year of King Jehoiachin's exile in Babylon, Evil-merodach ascended to the Babylonian throne. He was kind to Jehoiachin and released him from prison on March 31 of that year.* ³²He spoke pleasantly to Jehoiachin and gave him preferential treatment over all the other exiled kings in Babylon. ³³He supplied Jehoiachin with new clothes to replace his prison garb and allowed him to dine at the king's table for the rest of his life. ³⁴The Babylonian king also gave him a regular allowance to cover his living expenses until the day of his death.

52:21a Hebrew *18 cubits* [8.1 meters] *tall and 12 cubits* [5.4 meters] *in circumference.*   52:21b Hebrew *4 fingers thick* [8 centimeters].
52:22 Hebrew *5 cubits* [2.3 meters].   52:28 This exile in the seventh year of Nebuchadnezzar's reign occurred in 597 B.C.   52:29 This exile in the eighteenth year of Nebuchadnezzar's reign occurred in 586 B.C.   52:30 This exile in the twenty-third year of Nebuchadnezzar's reign occurred in 581 B.C.   52:31 Hebrew *on the twenty-fifth day of the twelfth month,* of the Hebrew calendar. This day was March 31, 561 B.C.; also see note on 52:4a.

Lamentations

It is good to wait quietly for salvation from the LORD (3:26).

A Time for Mourning

There is one kind of sadness in our world that comes from being swept up in tragic circumstances beyond our control. In such dark moments, we worship by clinging to God and trusting that, despite appearances to the contrary, he really is in control.

A second (and perhaps more common) kind of sorrow is the bitter grief of a self-made mess. On these occasions we experience needless pain and trouble because we have failed to obey God.

Lamentations is a stark picture of this second type of anguish. God had sent an army of prophets to his rebellious nation of Judah urging them to change their ways. When they turned a deaf ear to these warnings, God sent an army of another kind. Jeremiah and his countrymen could only watch helplessly and weep as the invading Babylonians obliterated their beloved Jerusalem. Reading Jeremiah's diary of this regrettable episode takes us inside the soul of a vanquished people and into the heart of a holy and faithful God.

Apparently written to be recited in public on days of national mourning, Jeremiah's words spoke of a city and a people who sat alone and mourned, who were forsaken by friends, and who finally were forced to admit that their own sins had brought them to this sorry state. There was a point when it seemed that even God had forsaken them, when God wasn't hearing their prayers anymore: "He has walled me in, . . . and though I cry and shout, he shuts out my prayers" (3:7–8).

But Jeremiah wrote, "I still dare to hope when I remember this: The unfailing love of the LORD never ends. . . . Great is his faithfulness" (3:21–23). And in the end, God did hear his cries (3:55–57).

Lamentations tells us that there is a time for mourning, for sorrow, and for repentance. And after that, there is a time for rejoicing, knowing that God's faithfulness and unfailing love sets us free to turn to him once again in wholehearted worship.

Worship Moments

- Repentance is an appropriate act of worship. "LORD, see my anguish! My heart is broken" (1:20).

- In worship, discipline is involved: "It is good for the young to submit to the yoke of his discipline" (3:27).

- The author of Lamentations sees God as his "inheritance" (3:24); as his "lawyer," the One who pleads his case (3:58); and as "judge" (3:59). The Lord remains "the same forever" (5:19).

SORROW IN JERUSALEM

1 Jerusalem's streets,* once bustling with people, are now silent. Like a widow broken with grief, she sits alone in her mourning. Once the queen of nations, she is now a slave.

2She sobs through the night; tears stream down her cheeks. Among all her lovers, there is no one left to help her. All her friends have betrayed her; they are now her enemies.

3Judah has been led away into captivity, afflicted and enslaved. She lives among foreign nations and has no place of rest. Her enemies have chased her down, and she has nowhere to turn.

4The roads to Jerusalem* are in mourning, no longer filled with crowds on their way to celebrate the Temple festivals. The city gates are silent, her priests groan, her young women are crying—how bitterly Jerusalem weeps!

5Her oppressors have become her masters, and her enemies prosper, for the LORD has punished Jerusalem for her many sins. Her children have been captured and taken away to distant lands.

6All the beauty and majesty of Jerusalem* are gone. Her princes are like starving deer searching for pasture, too weak to run from the pursuing enemy.

7And now in the midst of her sadness and wandering, Jerusalem remembers her ancient splendor. But then she fell to her enemy, and there was no one to help her. Her enemy struck her down and laughed as she fell.

8Jerusalem has sinned greatly, so she has been tossed away like a filthy rag. All who once honored her now despise her, for they have seen her stripped naked and humiliated. All she can do is groan and hide her face.

9She defiled herself with immorality with no thought of the punishment that would follow. Now she lies in the gutter with no one to lift her out. "LORD, see my deep misery," she cries. "The enemy has triumphed."

10The enemy has plundered her completely, taking everything precious that she owns. She has seen foreigners violate her sacred Temple, the place the LORD had forbidden them to enter.

11Her people groan as they search for bread. They have sold their treasures for food to stay alive. "O LORD, look," she mourns, "and see how I am despised.

12"Is it nothing to you, all you who pass by? Look around and see if there is any suffering like mine, which the LORD brought on me in the day of his fierce anger.

13"He has sent fire from heaven that burns in my bones. He has placed a trap in my path and turned me back. He has made me desolate, racked with sickness all day long.

14"He wove my sins into ropes to hitch me to a yoke of captivity. The Lord sapped my strength and gave me to my enemies; I am helpless in their hands.

15"The Lord has treated my mighty men with contempt. At his command a great army has come to crush my young warriors. The Lord has trampled his beloved city* as grapes are trampled in a winepress.

16"For all these things I weep; tears flow down my cheeks. No one is here to comfort me; any who might encourage me are far away. My children have no future, for the enemy has conquered us."

17Jerusalem pleads for help, but no one comforts her. Regarding his people,* the LORD has said, "Let their neighbors be their enemies! Let them be thrown away like a filthy rag!"

18"And the LORD is right," she groans, "for I rebelled against him. Listen, people everywhere; look upon my anguish and despair, for my sons and daughters have been taken captive to distant lands.

19"I begged my allies for help, but they betrayed me. My priests and leaders starved to death in the city, even as they searched for food to save their lives.

1:1 Each of the first four chapters of this book is an acrostic, laid out in the order of the Hebrew alphabet. The first word of each verse begins with a successive Hebrew letter. Chapters 1, 2, and 4 have one verse for each of the 22 Hebrew letters. Chapter 3 contains 22 stanzas of three verses each. Though chapter 5 is not an acrostic, it also has 22 verses. 1:4 Hebrew *Zion;* also in 1:17. 1:6 Hebrew *the daughter of Zion.* 1:15 Hebrew *the virgin daughter of Judah.* 1:17 Hebrew *Jacob.*

²⁰"LORD, see my anguish! My heart is broken and my soul despairs, for I have rebelled against you. In the streets the sword kills, and at home there is only death.

²¹"Others heard my groans, but no one turned to comfort me. When my enemies heard of my troubles, they were happy to see what you had done. Oh, bring the day you promised, when you will destroy them as you have destroyed me.

²²"Look at all their evil deeds, LORD. Punish them, as you have punished me for all my sins. My groans are many, and my heart is faint."

GOD'S ANGER AT SIN

2 The Lord in his anger has cast a dark shadow over Jerusalem.* The fairest of Israel's cities lies in the dust, thrown down from the heights of heaven. In his day of awesome fury, the Lord has shown no mercy even to his Temple.*

²Without mercy the Lord has destroyed every home in Israel.* In his anger he has broken down the fortress walls of Jerusalem.* He has brought to dust the kingdom and all its rulers.

³All the strength of Israel vanishes beneath his fury. The Lord has withdrawn his protection as the enemy attacks. He consumes the whole land of Israel like a raging fire.

⁴He bends his bow against his people as though he were their enemy. His strength is used against them to kill their finest youth. His fury is poured out like fire on beautiful Jerusalem.*

⁵Yes, the Lord has vanquished Israel like an enemy. He has destroyed her forts and palaces. He has brought unending sorrow and tears to Jerusalem.

⁶He has broken down his Temple as though it were merely a garden shelter. The LORD has blotted out all memory of the holy festivals and Sabbath days. Kings and priests fall together before his anger.

⁷The Lord has rejected his own altar; he despises his own sanctuary. He has given Jerusalem's palaces to her enemies. They shout in the LORD's Temple as though it were a day of celebration.

⁸The LORD was determined to destroy the walls of Jerusalem. He made careful plans for their destruction, then he went ahead and did it. Therefore, the ramparts and walls have fallen down before him.

⁹Jerusalem's gates have sunk into the ground. All their locks and bars are destroyed, for he has smashed them. Her kings and princes have been exiled to distant lands; the law is no more. Her prophets receive no more visions from the LORD.

¹⁰The leaders of Jerusalem sit on the ground in silence, clothed in sackcloth. They throw dust on their heads in sorrow and despair. The young women of Jerusalem hang their heads in shame.

¹¹I have cried until the tears no longer come. My heart is broken, my spirit poured out, as I see what has happened to my people. Little children and tiny babies are fainting and dying in the streets.

¹²"Mama, we want food," they cry, and then collapse in their mothers' arms. Their lives ebb away like the life of a warrior wounded in battle.

¹³In all the world has there ever been such sorrow? O daughter of Jerusalem, to what can I compare your anguish? O virgin daughter of Zion, how can I comfort you? For your wound is as deep as the sea. Who can heal you?

¹⁴Your "prophets" have said so many foolish things, false to the core. They did not try to hold you back from exile by pointing out your sins. Instead, they painted false pictures, filling you with false hope.

¹⁵All who pass by jeer at you. They scoff and insult Jerusalem,* saying, "Is this the city called 'Most Beautiful in All the World' and 'Joy of All the Earth'?"

¹⁶All your enemies deride you. They scoff and grind their teeth and say, "We have

2:1a Hebrew *the daughter of Zion*; also in 2:8, 10, 18. 2:1b Hebrew *footstool.* 2:2a Hebrew *Jacob*; also in 2:3. 2:2b Hebrew *the daughter of Judah*; also in 2:5. 2:4 Hebrew *on the tent of the daughter of Zion.* 2:15 Hebrew *the daughter of Jerusalem.*

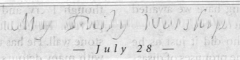

OUR ONLY REAL HELP

LAMENTATIONS 1:1–2:22

Rise during the night and cry out. Pour out your hearts like water
to the Lord. Lift up your hands to him in prayer. Plead for your
children as they faint with hunger in the streets (2:19).

[i reflect]

Horatius Bonar said, "In the day of prosperity we have many refuges to resort to; in the day of adversity, only one." The prophet Jeremiah experienced this truth firsthand as he served God, and the people of God, six centuries before the coming of Christ.

The era was not good for prophets. The nation was a spiritual and moral mess. The people had turned their backs on the one true God. Worse, they had begun worshiping pagan gods and participating in the vile rituals of their neighbors. Despite countless warnings from numerous prophets, the populace refused to turn from their self-willed ways.

At last God sent judgment on his beloved people in the form of the invading Babylonians. Lamentations describes this tragic event—a disaster that easily could have been avoided—the divine judgment of Jerusalem in 586 B.C.

Lamentations is a grim and gritty book. What does it have to do with worship? On one level it is a stark warning against worshiping anything or anyone other than God. On another level, it is a reminder that even when we have been unfaithful to God and are wallowing in the consequences of our rebellion, he is still the One we need. And he stands ready to forgive and restore us.

Feeling far away from God? Realizing some wrong choices? Wanting to come back to God? Then do as the prophet urges: Pour out your heart to God. Reach up to him in prayer. In the words of Catherine Marshall, "Crises bring us face to face with our inadequacy, and our inadequacy in turn leads us to the inexhaustible sufficiency of God."

[i pray]

Lord, not only in times of trouble, but on every occasion, teach me to pour out my soul to you.
Be my closest confidant. I want to walk with you, honor you . . . and cling to you.

[i respond]

As part of their worship, the ancient Hebrews would pour wine as an offering around the base of the altar (Numbers 15:1–10; see also 2 Timothy 4:6). Make this symbolism a part of your next devotional time. Pour out a glass of water to illustrate your desire to pour out your life for God, and to pour out your heart to him.

destroyed her at last! Long have we awaited this day, and it is finally here!"

¹⁷But it is the LORD who did it just as he warned. He has fulfilled the promises of disaster he made long ago. He has destroyed Jerusalem without mercy and caused her enemies to rejoice over her and boast of their power.

¹⁸Cry aloud* before the Lord, O walls of Jerusalem! Let your tears flow like a river. Give yourselves no rest from weeping day or night.

¹⁹Rise during the night and cry out. Pour out your hearts like water to the Lord. Lift up your hands to him in prayer. Plead for your children as they faint with hunger in the streets.

²⁰"O LORD, think about this!" Jerusalem cries. "You are doing this to your own people! Should mothers eat their little children, those they once bounced on their knees? Should priests and prophets die within the Lord's Temple?

²¹"See them lying in the streets—young and old, boys and girls, killed by the swords of the enemy. You have killed them in your anger, slaughtering them without mercy.

²²"You have invited terrors from all around as though you were calling them to a day of feasting. In the day of the LORD's anger, no one has escaped or survived. The enemy has killed all the children I bore and raised."

HOPE IN THE LORD'S FAITHFULNESS

3 I am the one who has seen the afflictions that come from the rod of the LORD's anger. ²He has brought me into deep darkness, shutting out all light. ³He has turned against me. Day and night his hand is heavy upon me.

⁴He has made my skin and flesh grow old. He has broken my bones. ⁵He has attacked me and surrounded me with anguish and distress. ⁶He has buried me in a dark place, like a person long dead.

⁷He has walled me in, and I cannot escape. He has bound me in heavy chains. ⁸And

though I cry and shout, he shuts out my prayers. ⁹He has blocked my path with a high stone wall. He has twisted the road before me with many detours.

¹⁰He hid like a bear or a lion, waiting to attack me. ¹¹He dragged me off the path and tore me with his claws, leaving me helpless and desolate. ¹²He bent his bow and aimed it squarely at me.

¹³He shot his arrows deep into my heart. ¹⁴My own people laugh at me. All day long they sing their mocking songs. ¹⁵He has filled me with bitterness. He has given me a cup of deep sorrow to drink.

¹⁶He has made me grind my teeth on gravel. He has rolled me in the dust. ¹⁷Peace has been stripped away, and I have forgotten what prosperity is. ¹⁸I cry out, "My splendor is gone! Everything I had hoped for from the LORD is lost!"

¹⁹The thought of my suffering and homelessness is bitter beyond words.* ²⁰I will never forget this awful time, as I grieve over my loss. ²¹Yet I still dare to hope when I remember this:

²²The unfailing love of the LORD never ends! By his mercies we have been kept from complete destruction. ²³Great is his faithfulness; his mercies begin afresh each day. ²⁴I say to myself, "The LORD is my inheritance; therefore, I will hope in him!"

²⁵The LORD is wonderfully good to those who wait for him and seek him. ²⁶So it is good to wait quietly for salvation from the LORD. ²⁷And it is good for the young to submit to the yoke of his discipline.

²⁸Let them sit alone in silence beneath the LORD's demands. ²⁹Let them lie face down in the dust; then at last there is hope for them. ³⁰Let them turn the other cheek to those who strike them. Let them accept the insults of their enemies.

³¹For the Lord does not abandon anyone forever. ³²Though he brings grief, he also shows compassion according to the greatness of his unfailing love. ³³For he does not enjoy hurting people or causing them sorrow.

2:18 Hebrew *Their heart cried.*   **3:19** Hebrew *is wormwood and gall.*

LAMENTATIONS 3

My Daily Worship

— *July 29* —

LOST IN WONDERING LOVE

LAMENTATIONS 3:1–5:22

The unfailing love of the LORD never ends! By his mercies we have been kept from complete destruction. Great is his faithfulness; his mercies begin afresh each day (3:22–23).

[i reflect]

Renowned Bible commentator William Barclay wrote: "When men worship Jesus Christ, they do not fall at his feet in broken submission, but in wondering love. A man does not say, 'I cannot resist a might like that.' He says, 'Love so amazing, so divine, demands my life, my soul, my all.' A man does not say, 'I am battered into surrender.' He says, 'I am lost in wonder, love, and praise.' "

That thought perfectly describes the prophet Jeremiah's career. The rebellious southern kingdom of Judah had resisted God's repeated appeals to turn away from their sinful ways. They had not been swayed by the fall of the northern kingdom of Israel. They had ignored every warning of impending judgment. Yet when, on divine cue, the brutal Babylonians arrived to destroy Jerusalem, the prophet was not so much shocked and amazed by God's power and justice as lost in wonder at God's faithful compassion. In the midst of all the violence and suffering, Jeremiah saw fresh, daily reminders of God's tender mercy.

What an amazing promise! No wonder so many Christians memorize this passage or display it in a frame on the living room wall. God's love is unfailing and endless. Judgment cannot obliterate his great mercy. It comes to us daily, like a gorgeous sunrise. And—don't miss this—he is *faithful!* He will do what he says. We can lean fully on him.

Perhaps the most stunning aspect about Jeremiah's great testimony of trust is the fact that he utters it in the bleakest of times. His unexpected actions call to mind the observation of William Law, "It is certain that whatever seeming calamity happens to you, if you thank and praise God for it, you will turn it into a blessing."

God's faithful mercy surrounds you today. Wonder at it; then respond with praise.

[i pray]

Give me eyes to see your unfailing love, Lord. I want to be lost in wonder at your great faithfulness. Move me to worship as I experience the fresh mercies of each new day.

[i respond]

Carry an umbrella with you today (regardless of the weather forecast). Let it remind you of the truth that God, in his love and mercy, is faithful to shower blessings on his children.

³⁴But the leaders of his people trampled prisoners underfoot. ³⁵They deprived people of their God-given rights in defiance of the Most High. ³⁶They perverted justice in the courts. Do they think the Lord didn't see it?

³⁷Can anything happen without the Lord's permission? ³⁸Is it not the Most High who helps one and harms another? ³⁹Then why should we, mere humans, complain when we are punished for our sins?

⁴⁰Instead, let us test and examine our ways. Let us turn again in repentance to the LORD. ⁴¹Let us lift our hearts and hands to God in heaven and say, ⁴²"We have sinned and rebelled, and you have not forgiven us.

⁴³"You have engulfed us with your anger, chased us down, and slaughtered us without mercy. ⁴⁴You have hidden yourself in a cloud so our prayers cannot reach you. ⁴⁵You have discarded us as refuse and garbage among the nations.

⁴⁶"All our enemies have spoken out against us. ⁴⁷We are filled with fear, for we are trapped, desolate, and ruined." ⁴⁸Streams of tears flow from my eyes because of the destruction of my people!

⁴⁹My tears flow down endlessly. They will not stop ⁵⁰until the LORD looks down from heaven and sees. ⁵¹My heart is breaking over the fate of all the women of Jerusalem.

⁵²My enemies, whom I have never harmed, chased me like a bird. ⁵³They threw me into a pit and dropped stones on me. ⁵⁴The water flowed above my head, and I cried out, "This is the end!"

⁵⁵But I called on your name, LORD, from deep within the well, ⁵⁶and you heard me! You listened to my pleading; you heard my weeping! ⁵⁷Yes, you came at my despairing cry and told me, "Do not fear."

⁵⁸Lord, you are my lawyer! Plead my case! For you have redeemed my life. ⁵⁹You have seen the wrong they have done to me, LORD. Be my judge, and prove me right. ⁶⁰You have seen the plots my enemies have laid against me.

⁶¹LORD, you have heard the vile names they call me. You know all about the plans they have made—⁶²the plots my enemies whisper and mutter against me all day long. ⁶³Look at them! In all their activities, they constantly mock me with their songs.

⁶⁴Pay them back, LORD, for all the evil they have done. ⁶⁵Give them hard and stubborn hearts, and then let your curse fall upon them! ⁶⁶Chase them down in your anger, destroying them from beneath the LORD's heavens.

GOD'S ANGER SATISFIED

4 How the gold has lost its luster! Even the finest gold has become dull. The sacred gemstones lie scattered in the streets!

²See how the precious children of Jerusalem,* worth their weight in gold, are now treated like pots of clay.

³Even the jackals feed their young, but not my people Israel. They ignore their children's cries, like the ostriches of the desert.

⁴The parched tongues of their little ones stick with thirst to the roofs of their mouths. The children cry for bread, but no one has any to give them.

⁵The people who once ate only the richest foods now beg in the streets for anything they can get. Those who once lived in palaces now search the garbage pits for food.

⁶The guilt* of my people is greater than that of Sodom, where utter disaster struck in a moment with no one to help them.

⁷Our princes were once glowing with health; they were as clean as snow and as elegant as jewels.

⁸But now their faces are blacker than soot. No one even recognizes them. Their skin sticks to their bones; it is as dry and hard as wood.

⁹Those killed by the sword are far better off than those who die of hunger, wasting away for want of food.

¹⁰Tenderhearted women have cooked their own children and eaten them in order to survive the siege.

4:2 Hebrew *sons of Zion.*   4:6 Or *punishment.*

¹¹But now the anger of the LORD is satisfied. His fiercest anger has now been poured out. He started a fire in Jerusalem* that burned the city to its foundations.

¹²Not a king in all the earth—no one in all the world—would have believed an enemy could march through the gates of Jerusalem.

¹³Yet it happened because of the sins of her prophets and priests, who defiled the city by shedding innocent blood.

¹⁴They wandered blindly through the streets, so defiled by blood that no one dared to touch them.

¹⁵"Get away!" the people shouted at them. "You are defiled! Don't touch us!" So they fled to distant lands and wandered there among foreign nations, but none would let them stay.

¹⁶The LORD himself has scattered them, and he no longer helps them. The priests and leaders are no longer honored and respected.

¹⁷We looked in vain for our allies to come and save us, but we were looking to nations that could offer no help at all.

¹⁸We couldn't go into the streets without danger to our lives. Our end was near; our days were numbered. We were doomed!

¹⁹Our enemies were swifter than the eagles. If we fled to the mountains, they found us. If we hid in the wilderness, they were waiting for us there.

²⁰Our king, the LORD's anointed, the very life of our nation, was caught in their snares. We had foolishly boasted that under his protection we could hold our own against any nation on earth!

²¹Are you rejoicing in the land of Uz, O people of Edom? But you, too, must drink from the cup of the LORD's anger. You, too, will be stripped naked in your drunkenness.

²²O Jerusalem,* your punishment will end; you will soon return from exile. But Edom, your punishment is just beginning; soon your many sins will be revealed.

PRAYER FOR RESTORATION

5 LORD, remember everything that has happened to us. See all the sorrows we bear! ²Our inheritance has been turned over to strangers, our homes to foreigners. ³We are orphaned and fatherless. Our mothers are widowed. ⁴We have to pay for water to drink, and even firewood is expensive. ⁵Those who pursue us are at our heels; we are exhausted but are given no rest. ⁶We submitted to Egypt and Assyria to get enough food to survive. ⁷It was our ancestors who sinned, but they died before the hand of judgment fell. We have suffered the punishment they deserved!

⁸Slaves have now become our masters; there is no one left to rescue us. ⁹We must hunt for food in the wilderness at the risk of our lives. ¹⁰Because of the famine, our skin has been blackened as though baked in an oven. ¹¹Our enemies rape the women and young girls in Jerusalem* and throughout the towns of Judah. ¹²Our princes are being hanged by their thumbs, and the old men are treated with contempt. ¹³The young men are led away to work at millstones, and the children stagger under heavy loads of wood. ¹⁴The old men no longer sit in the city gates; the young men no longer dance and sing.

¹⁵The joy of our hearts has ended; our dancing has turned to mourning. ¹⁶The garlands have* fallen from our heads. Disaster has fallen upon us because we have sinned. ¹⁷Our hearts are sick and weary, and our eyes grow dim with tears. ¹⁸For Jerusalem* is empty and desolate, a place haunted by jackals.

¹⁹But LORD, you remain the same forever! Your throne continues from generation to generation. ²⁰Why do you continue to forget us? Why have you forsaken us for so long? ²¹Restore us, O LORD, and bring us back to you again! Give us back the joys we once had! ²²Or have you utterly rejected us? Are you angry with us still?

4:11 Hebrew *in Zion.* 4:22 Hebrew *daughter of Zion.* 5:11 Hebrew *Zion.* 5:16 Or *The crown has.* 5:18 Hebrew *Mount Zion.*

Ezekiel

I will take away their hearts of stone, and give them tender hearts (11:19).

Giving Us New Hearts

Looking at a family member's vacation photos of the Grand Canyon, an old man growled, "Well, if you ask me, it just looks like a big hole in the ground." "Oh, no!" came the reply. "You have to see it in person to appreciate all its beauty and grandeur!" "I believe I'll pass," the old man sniffed. "I mean, when you've seen one hole, you've seen them all."

Sadly, this is the mind-set of many Bible readers when they come to the Old Testament prophets. If you took a poll, you might just discover that Ezekiel is the least read of the seventeen prophetic books.

Granted, it is long and filled with dire warnings and weird visions. But to dismiss Ezekiel out of hand is to miss a story of breathtaking wonder. It's a morality tale—a sobering reminder of what happens when human creatures declare their independence from their Creator. It's a love story—chronicling God's stubborn affection for his unfaithful people. Best of all, it's a true-life fairy tale, a drama of ultimate redemption—the Hero rescuing his beauty just in the nick of time and making plans to live with her happily ever after.

While Jeremiah was preaching in Jerusalem that the city would soon fall, Ezekiel was giving the same message to the Israelites already taken captive in Babylon. Like Jeremiah, Ezekiel desperately wanted the people to understand the seriousness of their rebellion. But as in Jeremiah, the people stubbornly refused to listen. Even as captives, the people could not accept the fact that Jerusalem would fall.

One of the overriding themes in Ezekiel is God's mercy and grace to his people. God would give them a new heart, replacing their hearts of stone with tender hearts (11:19). The prophet told the people that God would cleanse them by sprinkling clean water upon them (36:25). Ezekiel described God as a shepherd who watches over his sheep and leads them to new pastures (34:11–16).

As you read Ezekiel, look for these and other images that speak of God's amazing mercy. Use these images to help you focus on God's character as you come before him in worship.

Worship Moments

- Repentance is important. God says, "Remember your sins and cover your mouth in silence and shame when I forgive you" (16:63).

- The Spirit of God's ability to restore his people is illustrated through the startling image of dry bones that are brought back to life (37:1–14).

- God says, "I will be a sanctuary" (11:16); "they will truly be my people, and I will be their God" (11:20); and "I will show how holy my great name is" (36:23).

A Vision of Living Beings

1 On July 31* of my thirtieth year,* while I was with the Judean exiles beside the Kebar River in Babylon, the heavens were opened to me, and I saw visions of God. ²This happened during the fifth year of King Jehoiachin's captivity. ³The LORD gave a message to me, Ezekiel son of Buzi, a priest, there beside the Kebar River in the land of the Babylonians,* and I felt the hand of the LORD take hold of me.

⁴As I looked, I saw a great storm coming toward me from the north, driving before it a huge cloud that flashed with lightning and shone with brilliant light. The fire inside the cloud glowed like gleaming amber. ⁵From the center of the cloud came four living beings that looked human, ⁶except that each had four faces and two pairs of wings. ⁷Their legs were straight like human legs, but their feet were split like calves' feet and shone like burnished bronze. ⁸Beneath each of their wings I could see human hands. ⁹The wings of each living being touched the wings of the two beings beside it. The living beings were able to fly in any direction without turning around. ¹⁰Each had a human face in the front, the face of a lion on the right side, the face of an ox on the left side, and the face of an eagle at the back. ¹¹Each had two pairs of outstretched wings— one pair stretched out to touch the wings of the living beings on either side of it, and the other pair covered its body. ¹²They went in whatever direction the spirit chose, and they moved straight forward in all directions without having to turn around.

¹³The living beings looked like bright coals of fire or brilliant torches, and it looked as though lightning was flashing back and forth among them. ¹⁴And the living beings darted to and fro like flashes of lightning.

¹⁵As I looked at these beings, I saw four wheels on the ground beneath them, one wheel belonging to each. ¹⁶The wheels sparkled as if made of chrysolite. All four wheels looked the same; each wheel had a second wheel turning crosswise within it. ¹⁷The beings could move forward in any of the four directions they faced, without turning as they moved. ¹⁸The rims of the four wheels were awesomely tall, and they were covered with eyes all around the edges. ¹⁹When the four living beings moved, the wheels moved with them. When they flew upward, the wheels went up, too. ²⁰The spirit of the four living beings was in the wheels. So wherever the spirit went, the wheels and the living beings went, too. ²¹When the living beings moved, the wheels moved. When the living beings stopped, the wheels stopped. When the living beings flew into the air, the wheels rose up. For the spirit of the living beings was in the wheels.

²²There was a surface spread out above them like the sky. It sparkled like crystal. ²³Beneath this surface the wings of each living being stretched out to touch the others' wings, and each had two wings covering its body. ²⁴As they flew their wings roared like waves crashing against the shore, or like the voice of the Almighty,* or like the shouting of a mighty army. When they stopped, they let down their wings. ²⁵As they stood with their wings lowered, a voice spoke from beyond the crystal surface above them.

²⁶Above the surface over their heads was what looked like a throne made of blue sapphire. And high above this throne was a figure whose appearance was like that of a man. ²⁷From his waist up, he looked like gleaming amber, flickering like a fire. And from his waist down, he looked like a burning flame, shining with splendor. ²⁸All around him was a glowing halo, like a rainbow shining through the clouds. This was the way the glory of the LORD appeared to me. When I saw it, I fell face down in the dust, and I heard someone's voice speaking to me.

1:1a Hebrew *On the fifth day of the fourth month,* of the Hebrew calendar. A number of dates in Ezekiel can be cross-checked with dates in surviving Babylonian records and related accurately to our modern calendar. This event occurred on July 31, 593 B.C. **1:1b** Or *in the thirtieth year.* **1:3** Or *Chaldeans.* **1:24** Hebrew *Shaddai.*

EZEKIEL'S CALL AND COMMISSION

2 "Stand up, son of man," said the voice. "I want to speak with you." [2]The Spirit came into me as he spoke and set me on my feet. I listened carefully to his words. [3]"Son of man," he said, "I am sending you to the nation of Israel, a nation that is rebelling against me. Their ancestors have rebelled against me from the beginning, and they are still in revolt to this very day. [4]They are a hard-hearted and stubborn people. But I am sending you to say to them, 'This is what the Sovereign LORD says!' [5]And whether they listen or not—for remember, they are rebels—at least they will know they have had a prophet among them.

[6]"Son of man, do not fear them. Don't be afraid even though their threats are sharp as thorns and barbed like briers, and they sting like scorpions. Do not be dismayed by their dark scowls. For remember, they are rebels! [7]You must give them my messages whether they listen or not. But they won't listen, for they are completely rebellious! [8]Son of man, listen to what I say to you. Do not join them in being a rebel. Open your mouth, and eat what I give you."

[9]Then I looked and saw a hand reaching out to me, and it held a scroll. [10]He unrolled it, and I saw that both sides were covered with funeral songs, other words of sorrow, and pronouncements of doom.

3 The voice said to me, "Son of man, eat what I am giving you—eat this scroll! Then go and give its message to the people of Israel." [2]So I opened my mouth, and he fed me the scroll. [3]"Eat it all," he said. And when I ate it, it tasted as sweet as honey.

[4]Then he said, "Son of man, go to the people of Israel with my messages. [5]I am not sending you to some foreign people whose language you cannot understand. [6]No, I am not sending you to people with strange and difficult speech. If I did, they would listen! [7]I

am sending you to the people of Israel, but they won't listen to you any more than they listen to me! For the whole lot of them are hard-hearted and stubborn. [8]But look, I have made you as hard and stubborn as they are. [9]I have made you as hard as rock! So don't be afraid of them or fear their angry looks, even though they are such rebels."

[10]Then he added, "Son of man, let all my words sink deep into your own heart first. Listen to them carefully for yourself. [11]Then go to your people in exile and say to them, 'This is what the Sovereign LORD says!' Do this whether they listen to you or not."

[12]Then the Spirit lifted me up, and I heard a loud rumbling sound behind me. (May the glory of the LORD be praised in his place!)* [13]It was the sound of the wings of the living beings as they brushed against each other and the rumbling of their wheels beneath them.

[14]The Spirit lifted me up and took me away. I went in bitterness and turmoil, but the LORD's hold on me was strong. [15]Then I came to the colony of Judean exiles in Tel-abib, beside the Kebar River. I sat there among them for seven days, overwhelmed.

A WATCHMAN FOR ISRAEL

[16]At the end of the seven days, the LORD gave me a message. He said, [17]"Son of man, I have appointed you as a watchman for Israel. Whenever you receive a message from me, pass it on to the people immediately. [18]If I warn the wicked, saying, 'You are under the penalty of death,' but you fail to deliver the warning, they will die in their sins. And I will hold you responsible, demanding your blood for theirs. [19]If you warn them and they keep on sinning and refuse to repent, they will die in their sins. But you will have saved your life because you did what you were told to do. [20]If good people turn bad and don't listen to my warning, they will die. If you did not warn them of the consequences, then they will die in their sins. Their previous good deeds won't

---

3:12 A likely reading for this verse is *Then the Spirit lifted me up, and as the glory of the LORD rose from its place, I heard behind me a loud rumbling sound.*

My Daily Worship

— *July 30* —

IN HIS PRESENCE

EZEKIEL 1:1–5:17

All around him was a glowing halo, like a rainbow shining through the clouds. This was
the way the glory of the LORD appeared to me. When I saw it, I fell face down
in the dust, and I heard someone's voice speaking to me (1:28).

[*i reflect*]

John of the Cross, a sixteenth-century monk and mystic, is remembered for his passionate devotion to Christ. "I no longer want just to hear about you, beloved Lord, through messengers," he once wrote. "I no longer want to hear doctrines about you, nor to have my emotions stirred by people speaking of you. I yearn for your presence."

This is the hunger of every redeemed heart—to be with God. To see him face-to-face. To bask in his presence. To revel in his grace and love.

It only makes sense. Scripture says we were made by him and for him (Colossians 1:16). He is our true home. No wonder we never quite fit anywhere else. As Augustine put it, "You have made us for yourself, O God. And our hearts are restless until they find their rest in you."

Of course, those who encounter God as Ezekiel did in this passage are bowled over and forever changed. Moses glowed. Jacob built altars. Job shut his mouth and, as far as we know, never questioned God again. David wrote songs and danced with all his might. Isaiah came unglued. Zechariah was struck dumb. Mary sat in adoring wonder.

One truth is that we are always in the presence of God. We can go no place where he is not (see Psalm 139). Every moment of every day offers opportunities for worship.

Another truth is that life contains rare and precious occasions when God chooses to reveal himself in unmistakable and remarkable ways. We cannot program or predict these moments. But when they come, they mark us forever and give us unique opportunities to respond to God.

Today, take advantage of every moment—mundane or miraculous—to respond to God's precious presence.

[*i pray*]

Lord, I long to see you, to be with you, to love you. Open the eyes of my heart.
Become so real to me, that I cannot help being consumed with you.

[*i respond*]

Write in your journal, or on a piece of paper, about an occasion in which God seemed so real that you found yourself swallowed up in praise and adoration. Tell a friend about this experience.

Words of Worship

SOVEREIGN LORD

Sovereign Lord—Hebrew *'A-do-nai Yah-veh* " or *Yah-veh 'A-do-nai* "Lord Yahweh"; Greek *des-po-tes* "master, lord." The Hebrew expression occurs more than 280 times in the Old Testament, with 217 uses in Ezekiel alone. Older translations may use the expression "Lord God," the capital letters indicating the presence of the divine name Yahweh rather than the word for God (*'Elohim*), when used in parallel with *'Adonai*.

The Bible describes our relationship with the Lord in terms drawn from everyday human interaction. But people living in a democracy might find the term "Lord"—someone who controls our lives—hard to understand. We all resent a despot, to use the Greek equivalent. As adults we aren't used to having another person control our lives, and when that situation exists, we consider it dysfunctional. Perhaps the best equivalent to *'Adonai* is the word "boss"; but even our boss doesn't dictate what we do outside the work environment. In modern Israeli Hebrew, the related word *adon* is just a polite form of address, equivalent to "sir" or "Mister."

The biblical worshiper lived in a different culture and understood all too well what it meant to be accountable to God as his or her Sovereign Lord. Left to our own devices, we may find our lives going nowhere or even falling apart. When that happens, it's high time to acknowledge our Sovereign Lord and start taking direction from him.

²²Then the LORD took hold of me, and he said to me, "Go out into the valley, and I will talk to you there." ²³So I got up and went, and there I saw the glory of the LORD, just as I had seen it in my first vision by the Kebar River. And I fell face down in the dust.

²⁴Then the Spirit came into me and set me on my feet. He talked to me and said, "Go, shut yourself up in your house. ²⁵There you will be bound with ropes so you cannot go out among the people. ²⁶And I will make your tongue stick to the roof of your mouth so you won't be able to pray for them, for they are rebellious. ²⁷But whenever I give you a message, I will loosen your tongue and let you speak. Then you will say to them, 'This is what the Sovereign LORD says!' Some of them will listen, but some will ignore you, for they are rebels.

A SIGN OF THE COMING SIEGE

4 "And now, son of man, take a large brick and set it down in front of you. Then draw a map of the city of Jerusalem on it. ²Build siege ramps against the city walls. Surround it with enemy camps and battering rams. ³Then take an iron griddle and place it between you and the city. Turn toward it and demonstrate how the enemy will attack Jerusalem. This will be a warning to the people of Israel.

⁴"Now lie on your left side and place the sins of Israel on yourself. You are to bear their sins for the number of days you lie there on your side. ⁵You will bear Israel's sins for 390 days—one day for each year of their sin. ⁶After that, turn over and lie on your right side for 40 days—one day for each year of Judah's sin.

⁷"Meanwhile, continue your demonstration of the siege of Jerusalem. Lie there with your arm bared and prophesy her destruction. ⁸I will tie you up with ropes so you won't be able to turn from side to side until the days of your siege have been completed.

⁹"Now go and get some wheat, barley, beans, lentils, millet, and spelt, and mix them together in a storage jar. Use this food to make

help them, and I will hold you responsible, demanding your blood for theirs. ²¹But if you warn them and they repent, they will live, and you will have saved your own life, too."

bread for yourself during the 390 days you will be lying on your side. ¹⁰Ration this out to yourself, eight ounces* of food for each day, and eat it at set times. ¹¹Then measure out a jar* of water for each day, and drink it at set times. ¹²Each day prepare your bread as you would barley cakes. While all the people are watching, bake it over a fire using dried human dung as fuel and then eat the bread. ¹³For this is what the LORD says: Israel will eat defiled bread in the Gentile lands, where I will banish them!"

¹⁴Then I said, "O Sovereign LORD, must I be defiled by using human dung? For I have never been defiled before. From the time I was a child until now I have never eaten any animal that died of sickness or that I found dead. And I have never eaten any of the animals that our laws forbid."

¹⁵"All right," the LORD said. "You may bake your bread with cow dung instead of human dung." ¹⁶Then he told me, "Son of man, I will cause food to be very scarce in Jerusalem. It will be weighed out with great care and eaten fearfully. The water will be portioned out drop by drop, and the people will drink it with dismay. ¹⁷Food and water will be so scarce that the people will look at one another in terror, and they will waste away under their punishment.

A SIGN OF THE COMING JUDGMENT

5 "Son of man, take a sharp sword and use it as a razor to shave your head and beard. Use a scale to weigh the hair into three equal parts. ²Place a third of it at the center of your map of Jerusalem. After acting out the siege, burn it there. Scatter another third across your map and slash at it with a sword. Scatter the last third to the wind, for I will scatter my people with the sword. ³Keep just a bit of the hair and tie it up in your robe. ⁴Then take a few of these hairs out and throw them into the fire, burning them up. A fire will then spread from this remnant and destroy all of Israel.

⁵"This is what the Sovereign LORD says: This is an illustration of what will happen to Jerusalem. I placed her at the center of the nations, ⁶but she has rebelled against my regulations and has been even more wicked than the surrounding nations. She has refused to obey the laws I gave her to follow. ⁷So this is what the Sovereign LORD says: Since you have refused to obey my laws and regulations and have behaved even worse than your neighbors, ⁸I myself, the Sovereign LORD, am now your enemy. I will punish you publicly while all the nations watch. ⁹Because of your detestable idols, I will punish you more severely than I have punished anyone before or ever will again. ¹⁰Parents will eat their own children, and children will eat their parents. And I will punish you by scattering the few who survive to the far reaches of the earth.

> As worship begins in holy expectancy,
> it ends in holy obedience. Holy obedience
> saves worship from becoming an opiate,
> an escape from the pressing
> needs of modern life.
>
> RICHARD FOSTER

¹¹"As surely as I live, says the Sovereign LORD, I will cut you off completely. I will show you no pity at all because you have defiled my Temple with idols and vile practices. ¹²A third of your people will die in the city from famine and disease. A third of them will be slaughtered by the enemy outside the city walls. And I will scatter a third to the winds and chase them with my sword. ¹³Then at last my anger will be spent, and I will be satisfied. And when my fury against them has subsided, all Israel will know that I, the LORD, have spoken to them in my jealous anger.

4:10 Hebrew *20 shekels* [228 grams]. 4:11 Hebrew ⅙ *of a hin,* about 1.3 pints or 0.6 liters.

[14]"So I will turn you into a ruin, a mockery in the eyes of the surrounding nations and to everyone who travels by. [15]You will become an object of mockery and taunting and horror. You will be a warning to all the nations around you. They will see what happens when the LORD turns against a nation in furious rebuke. I, the LORD, have spoken!

[16]"I will shower you with the deadly arrows of famine to destroy you. The famine will become more and more severe until every crumb of food is gone. [17]And along with the famine, wild animals will attack you, robbing you of your children. Disease and war will stalk your land, and I will bring the sword of the enemy against you. I, the LORD, have spoken!"

JUDGMENT AGAINST ISRAEL'S MOUNTAINS

6 Again a message came to me from the LORD: [2]"Son of man, look over toward the mountains of Israel and prophesy against them. [3]Give the mountains of Israel this message from the Sovereign LORD. This is what the Sovereign LORD says to the mountains and hills and to the ravines and valleys: I am about to bring war upon you, and I will destroy your pagan shrines. [4]All your altars will be demolished, and your incense altars will be smashed. I will kill your people in front of your idols. [5]I will lay your corpses in front of your idols and scatter your bones around your altars. [6]Wherever you live there will be desolation. I will destroy your pagan shrines, your altars, your idols, your incense altars, and all the other religious objects you have made. [7]Then when the place is littered with corpses, you will know that I am the LORD.

[8]"But I will let a few of my people escape destruction, and they will be scattered among the nations of the world. [9]Then when they are exiled among the nations, they will remember me. They will recognize how grieved I am by their unfaithful hearts and lustful eyes that long for other gods. Then at last they will hate themselves for all their wickedness. [10]They will know that I alone am the LORD and that I was serious when I predicted that all this would happen to them.

[11]"This is what the Sovereign LORD says: Clap your hands in horror, and stamp your feet. Cry out, 'Alas!' because of all the evil that the people of Israel have done. Now they are going to die from war and famine and disease. [12]Disease will strike down those who are far away in exile. War will destroy those who are nearby. And anyone who survives will be killed by famine. So at last I will spend my fury on them. [13]When their dead lie scattered among their idols and altars, on every hill and mountain and under every green tree and great oak where they offered incense to their gods, then they will know that I alone am the LORD. [14]I will crush them and make their cities desolate from the wilderness in the south to Riblah* in the north. Then they will know that I am the LORD."

THE COMING OF THE END

7 Then this message came to me from the LORD: [2]"Son of man, this is what the Sovereign LORD says to Israel: The end is here! Wherever you look—east, west, north, or south—your land is finished. [3]No hope remains, for I will unleash my anger against you. I will call you to account for all your disgusting behavior. [4]I will turn my eyes away and show no pity, repaying you in full for all your evil. Then you will know that I am the LORD!

[5]"This is what the Sovereign LORD says: With one blow after another I will bring total disaster! [6]The end has come! It has finally arrived! Your final doom is waiting! [7]O people of Israel, the day of your destruction is dawning. The time has come; the day of trouble is near. It will ring with shouts of anguish, not shouts of joy. [8]Soon I will pour out my fury to complete your punishment for all your dis-

6:14 As in some Hebrew manuscripts; most Hebrew manuscripts read *Diblah*.

gusting behavior. ⁹I will neither spare nor pity you. I will repay you for all your detestable practices. Then you will know that it is I, the LORD, who is striking the blow.

¹⁰"The day of judgment is here; your destruction awaits! The people's wickedness and pride have reached a climax. ¹¹Their violence will fall back on them as punishment for their wickedness. None of these proud and wicked people will survive. All their wealth will be swept away. ¹²Yes, the time has come; the day is here! There is no reason for buyers to rejoice over the bargains they find or for sellers to grieve over their losses, for all of them will fall under my terrible anger. ¹³And if any merchants should survive, they will never return to their business. For what God has said applies to everyone—it will not be changed! Not one person whose life is twisted by sin will recover.

THE DESOLATION OF ISRAEL

¹⁴"The trumpets call Israel's army to mobilize, but no one listens, for my fury is against them all. ¹⁵Any who leave the city walls will be killed by enemy swords. Those who stay inside will die of famine and disease. ¹⁶The few who survive and escape to the mountains will moan like doves, weeping for their sins. ¹⁷Everyone's hands will be feeble; their knees will be as weak as water. ¹⁸They will dress themselves in sackcloth; horror and shame will cover them. They will shave their heads in sorrow and remorse.

¹⁹"They will throw away their money, tossing it out like worthless trash. It won't buy their deliverance in that day of the LORD's anger. It will neither satisfy nor feed them, for their love of money made them stumble into sin. ²⁰They were proud of their gold jewelry and used it to make vile and detestable idols. That is why I will make all their wealth disgusting to them. ²¹I will give it as plunder to foreigners from the most wicked of nations, and they will defile it. ²²I will hide my eyes as

these robbers invade my treasured land and corrupt it.

²³"Prepare chains for my people, for the land is bloodied by terrible crimes. Jerusalem is filled with violence. ²⁴I will bring the most ruthless of nations to occupy their homes. I will break down their proud fortresses and defile their sanctuaries. ²⁵Terror and trembling will overcome my people. They will look for peace but will not find it. ²⁶Calamity will follow calamity; rumor will follow rumor. They will look in vain for a vision from the prophets. They will receive no teaching from the priests and no counsel from the leaders. ²⁷The king and the prince will stand helpless, weeping in despair, and the people's hands will tremble with fear. I will bring against them the evil they have done to others, and they will receive the punishment they so richly deserve. Then they will know that I am the LORD!"

IDOLATRY IN THE TEMPLE

8 Then on September 17,* during the sixth year of King Jehoiachin's captivity, while the leaders of Judah were in my home, the Sovereign LORD took hold of me. ²I saw a figure that appeared to be a man. From the waist down he looked like a burning flame. From the waist up he looked like gleaming amber. ³He put out what seemed to be a hand and took me by the hair. Then the Spirit lifted me up into the sky and transported me in a vision of God to Jerusalem. I was taken to the north gate of the inner courtyard of the Temple, where there is a large idol that has made the LORD very angry. ⁴Suddenly, the glory of the God of Israel was there, just as I had seen it before in the valley.

⁵Then the LORD said to me, "Son of man, look toward the north." So I looked, and there to the north, beside the entrance to the gate of the altar, stood the idol that had made the LORD so angry.

⁶"Son of man," he said, "do you see what

8:1 Hebrew *on the fifth day of the sixth month*, of the Hebrew calendar. This event occurred on September 17, 592 B.C.; also see note on 1:1.

Words of Worship

HEALING

Healing—Hebrew *mar-pe'* "healing"; *te-ru-fah* "healing"; *rif-'ot* "health"; Greek *the-ra-pei-a* "healing, therapy."

In a glorious vision of Israel's renewed worship, Ezekiel saw a river flowing from the threshold of the Temple, bringing life to all the surrounding area. Thriving trees lined the river's banks, "for they are watered by the river flowing from the Temple. The fruit will be for food and the leaves for healing" (Ezekiel 47:12). This image of the healing that comes from worshiping the Lord returns on the Bible's closing page, in John's vision of living waters flowing from the throne of God and the Lamb (Revelation 22:1–2).

Physical ills, emotional distress, and moral distortion can affect our personal wholeness. But worship heals—or, more accurately, God works his therapy when we worship him. One reason is that many of our ills result from a preoccupation with *self*. When the Lord God and the Lamb come into the center of our focus, *self* falls into its proper perspective. Pride loses its power to block God's purpose. Then the Lord can do his restoring, healing work, as his river of life begins to flow within us.

they are doing? Do you see the great sins the people of Israel are doing to drive me from my Temple? But come, and you will see even greater sins than these!" ⁷Then he brought me to the door of the Temple courtyard, where I could see an opening in the wall. ⁸He said to me, "Now, son of man, dig into the wall." So I dug into the wall and uncovered a door to a hidden room.

⁹"Go in," he said, "and see the unspeakable wickedness going on in there!" ¹⁰So I went in and saw the walls engraved with all kinds of snakes, lizards, and hideous creatures. I also saw the various idols worshiped by the people of Israel. ¹¹Seventy leaders of Israel were standing there with Jaazaniah son of Shaphan in the middle. Each of them held an incense burner, so there was a thick cloud of incense above their heads.

¹²Then the LORD said to me, "Son of man, have you seen what the leaders of Israel are doing with their idols in dark rooms? They are saying, 'The LORD doesn't see us; he has deserted our land!' " ¹³Then he added, "Come, and I will show you greater sins than these!"

¹⁴He brought me to the north gate of the LORD's Temple, and some women were sitting there, weeping for the god Tammuz. ¹⁵"Have you seen this?" he asked. "But I will show you even greater sins than these!"

¹⁶Then he brought me into the inner courtyard of the LORD's Temple. At the entrance, between the foyer and the bronze altar, about twenty-five men were standing with their backs to the LORD's Temple. They were facing eastward, worshiping the sun!

¹⁷"Have you seen this, son of man?" he asked. "Is it nothing to the people of Judah that they commit these terrible sins, leading the whole nation into violence, thumbing their noses at me, and rousing my fury against them? ¹⁸Therefore, I will deal with them in fury. I will neither pity nor spare them. And though they scream for mercy, I will not listen."

THE SLAUGHTER OF IDOLATERS

9 Then the LORD thundered, "Bring on the men appointed to punish the city! Tell them to bring their weapons with them!" ²Six men soon appeared from the upper gate that faces north, each carrying a battle club in his hand. One of them was dressed in linen and carried a writer's case strapped to his side. They all went into the Temple courtyard and stood beside the bronze altar.

³Then the glory of the God of Israel rose up from between the cherubim, where it had rested, and moved to the entrance of the

Temple. And the LORD called to the man dressed in linen who was carrying the writer's case. ⁴He said to him, "Walk through the streets of Jerusalem and put a mark on the foreheads of all those who weep and sigh because of the sins they see around them."

⁵Then I heard the LORD say to the other men, "Follow him through the city and kill everyone whose forehead is not marked. Show no mercy; have no pity! ⁶Kill them all—old and young, girls and women and little children. But do not touch anyone with the mark. Begin your task right here at the Temple." So they began by killing the seventy leaders. ⁷"Defile the Temple!" the LORD commanded. "Fill its courtyards with the bodies of those you kill! Go!" So they went throughout the city and did as they were told.

⁸While they were carrying out their orders, I was all alone. I fell face down in the dust and cried out, "O Sovereign LORD! Will your fury against Jerusalem wipe out everyone left in Israel?"

⁹Then he said to me, "The sins of the people of Israel and Judah are very great. The entire land is full of murder; the city is filled with injustice. They are saying, 'The LORD doesn't see it! The LORD has forsaken the land!' ¹⁰So I will not spare them or have any pity on them. I will fully repay them for all they have done."

¹¹Then the man in linen clothing, who carried the writer's case, reported back and said, "I have finished the work you gave me to do."

THE LORD'S GLORY LEAVES THE TEMPLE

10 As I looked, I saw what appeared to be a throne of blue sapphire above the crystal surface over the heads of the cherubim. ²Then the LORD spoke to the man in linen clothing and said, "Go in between the whirling wheels beneath the cherubim, and take a handful of glowing coals and scatter them over the city." He did this as I watched. ³The cherubim were standing at the south end

of the Temple when the man went in, and the cloud of glory filled the inner courtyard. ⁴Then the glory of the LORD rose up from above the cherubim and went over to the door of the Temple. The Temple was filled with this cloud of glory, and the Temple courtyard glowed brightly with the glory of the LORD. ⁵The moving wings of the cherubim sounded like the voice of God Almighty and could be heard clearly in the outer courtyard.

⁶The LORD said to the man in linen clothing, "Go between the cherubim and take some burning coals from between the wheels." So the man went in and stood beside one of the wheels. ⁷Then one of the cherubim reached out his hand and took some live coals from the fire burning among them. He put the coals into the hands of the man in linen clothing, and the man took them and went out. ⁸(All the cherubim had what looked like human hands hidden beneath their wings.)

⁹Each of the four cherubim had a wheel beside him, and the wheels sparkled like chrysolite. ¹⁰All four wheels looked the same; each wheel had a second wheel turning crosswise within it. ¹¹The cherubim could move forward in any of the four directions they faced, without turning as they moved. They went straight in the direction in which their heads were turned, never turning aside. ¹²Both the cherubim and the wheels were covered with eyes. The cherubim had eyes all over their bodies, including their hands, their backs, and their wings. ¹³I heard someone refer to the wheels as "the whirling wheels." ¹⁴Each of the four cherubim had four faces— the first was the face of an ox,* the second was a human face, the third was the face of a lion, and the fourth was the face of an eagle.

¹⁵Then the cherubim rose upward. These were the same living beings I had seen beside the Kebar River. ¹⁶When the cherubim moved, the wheels moved with them. When they rose into the air, the wheels stayed beside them, going with them as they flew. ¹⁷When the cherubim stood still, the wheels also stopped,

10:14 Hebrew *the face of a cherub;* compare 1:10.

for the spirit of the living beings was in the wheels.

[18]Then the glory of the LORD moved from the door of the Temple and hovered above the cherubim. [19]And as I watched, the cherubim flew with their wheels to the east gate of the LORD's Temple. And the glory of the God of Israel hovered above them.

[20]These were the same living beings I had seen beneath the God of Israel when I was by the Kebar River. I knew they were cherubim, [21]for each had four faces and four wings and what looked like human hands under their wings. [22]Their faces, too, were just like the faces of the beings I had seen at the Kebar, and they traveled straight ahead, just as the others had.

JUDGMENT ON ISRAEL'S LEADERS

11 Then the Spirit lifted me and brought me over to the east gateway of the LORD's Temple, where I saw twenty-five prominent men of the city. Among them were Jaazaniah son of Azzur and Pelatiah son of Benaiah, who were leaders among the people.

[2]Then the Spirit said to me, "Son of man, these are the men who are responsible for the wicked counsel being given in this city. [3]They say to the people, 'Is it not a good time to build houses? Our city is like an iron pot. Inside it we will be like meat—safe from all harm.'* [4]Therefore, son of man, prophesy against them loudly and clearly."

[5]Then the Spirit of the LORD came upon me, and he told me to say, "This is what the LORD says to the people of Israel: Is that what you are saying? Yes, I know it is, for I know every thought that comes into your minds. [6]You have murdered endlessly and filled your streets with the dead.

[7]"Therefore, this is what the Sovereign LORD says: This city is an iron pot, but the victims of your injustice are the pieces of meat. And you are not safe, for I will soon drag you from the city. [8]I will expose you to the war you so greatly fear, says the Sovereign LORD. [9]I will drive you out of Jerusalem and hand you over to foreigners who will carry out my judgments against you. [10]You will be slaughtered all the way to the borders of Israel, and then you will know that I am the LORD. [11]No, this city will not be an iron pot for you, and you will not be the meat, safe inside. I will judge you even to the borders of Israel, [12]and you will know that I am the LORD. For you have refused to obey me; instead, you have copied the sins of the nations around you."

[13]While I was still speaking, Pelatiah son of Benaiah suddenly died. Then I fell face down in the dust and cried out, "O Sovereign LORD, are you going to kill everyone in Israel?"

HOPE FOR EXILED ISRAEL

[14]Then this message came to me from the LORD: [15]"Son of man, the people still left in Jerusalem are talking about their relatives in exile, saying, 'They are far away from the LORD, so now he has given their land to us!' [16]Therefore, give the exiles this message from the Sovereign LORD: Although I have scattered you in the countries of the world, I will be a sanctuary to you during your time in exile. [17]I, the Sovereign LORD, will gather you back from the nations where you are scattered, and I will give you the land of Israel once again.

[18]"When the people return to their homeland, they will remove every trace of their detestable idol worship. [19]And I will give them singleness of heart and put a new spirit within them. I will take away their hearts of stone and give them tender hearts* instead, [20]so they will obey my laws and regulations. Then they will truly be my people, and I will be their God. [21]But as for those who long for idols, I will repay them fully for their sins, says the Sovereign LORD."

THE LORD'S GLORY LEAVES JERUSALEM

[22]Then the cherubim lifted their wings and rose into the air with their wheels beside

11:3 Hebrew *This city is the pot, and we are the meat.* 11:19 Hebrew *hearts of flesh.*

My Daily Worship

— July 31 —

OUR NEW AND IMPROVED HEARTS!

EZEKIEL 6:1–11:25

And I will give them singleness of heart and put a new spirit within them. I will take away their hearts of stone and give them tender hearts instead, so they will obey my laws and regulations. Then they will truly be my people, and I will be their God (11:19–20).

[i reflect]

"Change my heart, O God. Make it ever true," the old praise chorus goes. "Change my heart, O God. Let me be like you."

It's a beloved song and a wonderful sentiment. But if you want to get picky theologically, it's an unnecessary request for Christians to make—sort of like praying for God to be with us.

The fact is, every believer in Jesus already has a changed heart. It's a done deal. That's the promise and the essence of the gospel, the new covenant. When we put our trust in Christ, an invisible but very real spiritual heart transplant occurs—your old, hard, sin-prone heart gets replaced with a new heart. That's what this passage in Ezekiel was alluding to—a new heart that can respond to God and connect with him. It's a heart that longs to know and serve and please God. It is a God-filled heart. And it is, despite what many believe and even teach, essentially good.

This explains why the apostle Paul speaks about believers having a brand-new nature (2 Corinthians 5:17). We really *are* brand-new people. And now we have new desires and new capacities to honor God.

So, if all this is true (and it *is*, according to the Bible), the Christian life is a matter of learning to say no to the impulses of our unredeemed human nature and letting our new, true nature surface in our daily lives. The God who lives in us wants to direct us, fill us, use us, and satisfy us. Becoming a fully devoted worshiper starts in the heart.

Today, consider singing that chorus this way, "Change my mind, O God. Let me see what's true. Change my mind, O God. You have made me new!"

[i pray]

Thank you, God, for changing me from the inside out. Show me
how to live for you out of my new, true nature.

[i respond]

Skim through a magazine or newspaper and search for the ads that claim "new and improved" products. Write down several ways that you are "new and improved" through your identity in Christ.

them, and the glory of the God of Israel hovered above them. [23]Then the glory of the LORD went up from the city and stopped above the mountain to the east.

[24]Afterward the Spirit of God carried me back again to Babylonia,* to the Judeans in exile there. And so ended the vision of my visit to Jerusalem. [25]And I told the exiles everything the LORD had shown me.

SIGNS OF THE COMING EXILE

12 Again a message came to me from the LORD: [2]"Son of man, you live among rebels who could see the truth if they wanted to, but they don't want to. They could hear me if they would listen, but they won't listen because they are rebellious. [3]So now put on a demonstration to show them what it will be like to go off into exile. Pack whatever you can carry on your back and leave your home to go on a journey. Make your preparations in broad daylight so the people can see you, for perhaps they will even yet consider what this means, even though they are such rebels. [4]Bring your baggage outside during the day so they can watch you. Then as they are watching, leave your house in the evening, just as captives do when they begin a long march to distant lands. [5]Dig a hole through the wall while they are watching and carry your possessions out through it. [6]As they watch, lift your pack to your shoulders and walk away into the night. Cover your face and don't look around. All of these actions will be a sign for the people of Israel."

[7]So I did as I was told. In broad daylight I brought my pack outside, filled with the things I might carry into exile. Then in the evening while the people looked on, I dug through the wall with my hands and went out into the darkness with my pack on my shoulder.

[8]The next morning this message came to me from the LORD: [9]"Son of man, these rebels, the people of Israel, have asked you what all this means. [10]Say to them, 'This is what the Sovereign LORD says: These actions contain a message for Zedekiah in Jerusalem* and for all the people of Israel.' [11]Then explain that your actions are a demonstration of what will soon happen to them, for they will be driven from their homes and sent away into exile.

[12]"Even Zedekiah will leave Jerusalem at night through a hole in the wall, taking only what he can carry with him. He will cover his face, and his eyes will never see his homeland again. [13]Then I will spread out my net and capture him in my snare. I will bring him to Babylon, the land of the Babylonians,* though he will never see it, and he will die there. [14]I will scatter his servants and guards to the four winds and send the sword after them. [15]And when I scatter them among the nations, they will know that I am the LORD. [16]But I will spare a few of them from death by war, famine, or disease, so they can confess to their captors about how wicked they have been. Then they will know that I am the LORD!"

[17]Then this message came to me from the LORD: [18]"Son of man, tremble as you eat your food. Drink your water with fear, as if it were your last. [19]Give the people this message from the Sovereign LORD concerning those living in Israel and Jerusalem: They will eat their food with trembling and sip their tiny portions of water in utter despair, because their land will be stripped bare on account of their violence. [20]The cities will be destroyed and the farmland deserted. Then you will know that I am the LORD."

A NEW PROVERB FOR ISRAEL

[21]Again a message came to me from the LORD: [22]"Son of man, what is that proverb they quote in Israel: 'Time passes, making a liar of every prophet'? [23]Give the people this message from the Sovereign LORD: I will put an end to this proverb, and you will soon stop quoting it. Now give them this new proverb to replace the old one: 'The time has come for every prophecy to be fulfilled!'

11:24 Or *Chaldea.* 12:10 Hebrew *the prince in Jerusalem;* also in 12:12. 12:13 Or *Chaldeans.*

²⁴"Then you will see what becomes of all the false visions and misleading predictions about peace in Israel. ²⁵For I am the LORD! What I threaten always happens. There will be no more delays, you rebels of Israel! I will fulfill my threat of destruction in your own lifetime, says the Sovereign LORD."

²⁶Then this message came to me from the LORD: ²⁷"Son of man, the people of Israel are saying, 'His visions won't come true for a long, long time.' ²⁸Therefore, give them this message from the Sovereign LORD: No more delay! I will now do everything I have threatened! I, the Sovereign LORD, have spoken!"

JUDGMENT AGAINST FALSE PROPHETS

13 Then this message came to me from the LORD: ²"Son of man, speak against the false prophets of Israel who are inventing their own prophecies. Tell them to listen to the word of the LORD. ³This is what the Sovereign LORD says: Destruction is certain for the false prophets who are following their own imaginations and have seen nothing at all!

⁴"O people of Israel, these prophets of yours are like jackals digging around in the ruins. ⁵They have done nothing to strengthen the breaks in the walls around the nation. They have not helped it to stand firm in battle on the day of the LORD. ⁶Instead, they have lied and said, 'My message is from the LORD,' even though the LORD never sent them. And yet they expect him to fulfill their prophecies! ⁷Can your visions be anything but false if you claim, 'This message is from the LORD,' when I have not even spoken to you?

⁸"Therefore, this is what the Sovereign LORD says: Because what you say is false and your visions are a lie, I will stand against you, says the Sovereign LORD. ⁹I will raise my fist against all the lying prophets, and they will be banished from the community of Israel. I will blot their names from Israel's record books, and they will never again see their own land. Then you will know that I am the Sovereign LORD!

¹⁰"These evil prophets deceive my people by saying, 'All is peaceful!' when there is no peace at all! It's as if the people have built a flimsy wall, and these prophets are trying to hold it together by covering it with whitewash! ¹¹Tell these whitewashers that their wall will soon fall down. A heavy rainstorm will undermine it; great hailstones and mighty winds will knock it down. ¹²And when the wall falls, the people will cry out, 'Where is the whitewash you applied?'

> *The man who cannot wonder,*
> *who does not habitually wonder and*
> *worship, is but a pair of spectacles*
> *behind which there is no eye.*
> THOMAS CARLYLE

¹³"Therefore, this is what the Sovereign LORD says: I will sweep away your whitewashed wall with a storm of indignation, with a great flood of anger, and with hailstones of fury. ¹⁴I will break down your wall right to the foundation, and when it falls, it will crush you. Then you will know that I am the LORD! ¹⁵At last my anger against the wall and those who covered it with whitewash will be satisfied. Then I will say to you: 'The wall and those who whitewashed it are both gone. ¹⁶They were lying prophets who claimed peace would come to Jerusalem when there was no peace. I, the Sovereign LORD, have spoken!'

JUDGMENT AGAINST FALSE WOMEN PROPHETS

¹⁷"Now, son of man, also speak out against the women who prophesy from their own imaginations. ¹⁸This is what the Sovereign LORD says: Destruction is certain for you women who are ensnaring the souls of my people, both young and old alike. You tie magic

charms on their wrists and furnish them with magic veils. Do you think you can trap others without bringing destruction on yourselves? [19]You turn my people away from me for a few handfuls of barley or a piece of bread. By lying to my people who love to listen to lies, you kill those who should not die, and you promise life to those who should not live.

[20]"And so the Sovereign LORD says: I am against all your magic charms, which you use to ensnare my people like birds. I will tear them from your arms, setting my people free like birds set free from a cage. [21]I will tear off the magic veils and save my people from your grasp. They will no longer be your victims. Then you will know that I am the LORD. [22]You have discouraged the righteous with your lies, when I didn't want them to suffer grief. And you have encouraged the wicked by promising them life, even though they continue in their sins. [23]But you will no longer talk of seeing visions that you never saw, nor will you practice your magic. For I will rescue my people from your grasp. Then you will know that I am the LORD."

THE IDOLATRY OF ISRAEL'S LEADERS

14 Then some of the leaders of Israel visited me, and while they were there, [2]this message came to me from the LORD: [3]"Son of man, these leaders have set up idols in their hearts. They have embraced things that lead them into sin. Why should I let them ask me anything? [4]Give them this message from the Sovereign LORD: I, the LORD, will punish the people of Israel who set up idols in their hearts so they fall into sin and then come to a prophet asking for help. [5]I will do this to capture the minds and hearts of all my people who have turned from me to worship their detestable idols.

[6]"Therefore, give the people of Israel this message from the Sovereign LORD: Repent and turn away from your idols, and stop all your loathsome practices. [7]I, the LORD, will punish all those, both Israelites and foreigners, who

reject me and set up idols in their hearts so they fall into sin, and who then come to a prophet asking for my advice. [8]I will turn against such people and make a terrible example of them, destroying them. Then you will know that I am the LORD. [9]And if a prophet is deceived and gives a message anyway, it is because I, the LORD, have deceived that prophet. I will stand against such prophets and cut them off from the community of Israel. [10]False prophets and hypocrites—evil people who claim to want my advice—will all be punished for their sins. [11]In this way, the people of Israel will learn not to stray from me, polluting themselves with sin. They will be my people, and I will be their God, says the Sovereign LORD."

THE CERTAINTY OF THE LORD'S JUDGMENT

[12]Then this message came to me from the LORD: [13]"Son of man, suppose the people of a country were to sin against me, and I lifted my fist to crush them, cutting off their food supply and sending a famine to destroy both people and animals alike. [14]Even if Noah, Daniel, and Job were there, their righteousness would save no one but themselves, declares the Sovereign LORD.

[15]"Or suppose I were to send an invasion of dangerous wild animals to devastate the land and kill the people. [16]Even if these three men were there, the Sovereign LORD swears that it would do no good—it wouldn't save the people from destruction. Those three alone would be saved, but the land would be devastated.

[17]"Or suppose I were to bring war against the land, and I told enemy armies to come and destroy everything. [18]Even if these three men were in the land, the Sovereign LORD swears that they could not save the people. They alone would be saved.

[19]"Or suppose I were to pour out my fury by sending an epidemic of disease into the land, and the plague killed people and animals alike. [20]Even if Noah, Daniel, and Job were

living there, the Sovereign LORD swears that they could not save the people. They alone would be saved by their righteousness.

²¹"Now this is what the Sovereign LORD says: How terrible it will be when all four of these fearsome punishments fall upon Jerusalem—war, famine, beasts, and plague—destroying all her people and animals. ²²Yet there will be survivors, and they will come here to join you as exiles in Babylon. You will see with your own eyes how wicked they are, and then you will feel better about what I have done to Jerusalem. ²³When you meet them and see their behavior, you will agree that these things are not being done to Israel without cause, says the Sovereign LORD."

JERUSALEM—A USELESS VINE

15 Then this message came to me from the LORD: ²"Son of man, how does a grapevine compare to a tree? Is a vine's wood as useful as the wood of a tree? ³Can its wood be used for making things, like pegs to hang up pots and pans? ⁴No, it can only be used for fuel, and even as fuel, it burns too quickly. ⁵Vine branches are useless both before and after being put into the fire!

⁶"And this is what the Sovereign LORD says: The people of Jerusalem are like grapevines growing among the trees of the forest. Since they are useless, I have set them aside to be burned! ⁷And I will see to it that if they escape from one fire, they will fall into another. When this happens, you will know that I am the LORD. ⁸And I will make the land desolate because my people have been unfaithful to me, says the Sovereign LORD."

JERUSALEM—AN UNFAITHFUL WIFE

16 Then another message came to me from the LORD: ²"Son of man, confront Jerusalem with her loathsome sins. ³Give her this message from the Sovereign LORD: You are nothing but a Canaanite! Your father was an Amorite and your mother a Hittite! ⁴When you were born, no one cared about you. Your umbilical cord was left uncut, and you were never washed, rubbed with salt, and dressed in warm clothing. ⁵No one had the slightest interest in you; no one pitied you or cared for you. On the day you were born, you were dumped in a field and left to die, unwanted.

⁶"But I came by and saw you there, helplessly kicking about in your own blood. As you lay there, I said, 'Live!' ⁷And I helped you to thrive like a plant in the field. You grew up and became a beautiful jewel. Your breasts became full, and your hair grew, though you were still naked. ⁸And when I passed by and saw you again, you were old enough to be married. So I wrapped my cloak around you to cover your nakedness and declared my marriage vows. I made a covenant with you, says the Sovereign LORD, and you became mine.

⁹"Then I bathed you and washed off your blood, and I rubbed fragrant oils into your skin. ¹⁰I gave you expensive clothing of linen and silk, beautifully embroidered, and sandals made of fine leather. ¹¹I gave you lovely jewelry, bracelets, and beautiful necklaces, ¹²a ring for your nose and earrings for your ears, and a lovely crown for your head. ¹³And so you were made beautiful with gold and silver. Your clothes were made of fine linen and were beautifully embroidered. You ate the finest foods—fine flour, honey, and olive oil—and became more beautiful than ever. You looked like a queen, and so you were! ¹⁴Your fame soon spread throughout the world on account of your beauty, because the splendor I bestowed on you perfected your beauty, says the Sovereign LORD.

¹⁵"But you thought you could get along without me, so you trusted instead in your fame and beauty. You gave yourself as a prostitute to every man who came along. Your beauty was theirs for the asking! ¹⁶You used the lovely things I gave you to make shrines for idols, where you carried out your acts of prostitution. Unbelievable! How could such a thing ever happen? ¹⁷You took the very jewels and gold and silver ornaments I had given you and made statues of men and worshiped

them, which is adultery against me. [18]You used the beautifully embroidered clothes I gave you to cover your idols. Then you used my oil and incense to worship them. [19]Imagine it! You set before them as a lovely sacrifice the fine flour and oil and honey I had given you, says the Sovereign LORD.

[20]"Then you took your sons and daughters—the children you had borne to me—and sacrificed them to your gods. Was it not enough that you should be a prostitute? [21]Must you also slaughter my children by sacrificing them to idols? [22]In all your years of adultery and loathsome sin, you have not once thought of the days long ago when you lay naked in a field, kicking about in your own blood.

[23]"Your destruction is certain, says the Sovereign LORD. In addition to all your other wickedness, [24]you built a pagan shrine and put altars to idols in every town square. [25]On every street corner you defiled your beauty, offering your body to every passerby in an endless stream of prostitution. [26]Then you added lustful Egypt to your lovers, fanning the flames of my anger with your increasing promiscuity. [27]That is why I struck you with my fist and reduced your boundaries. I handed you over to your enemies, the Philistines, and even they were shocked by your lewd conduct! [28]You have prostituted yourselves with the Assyrians, too. It seems you can never find enough new lovers! And after your prostitution there, you still were not satisfied. [29]You added to your lovers by embracing that great merchant land of Babylonia*—but you still weren't satisfied!

[30]"What a sick heart you have, says the Sovereign LORD, to do such things as these, acting like a shameless prostitute. [31]You build your pagan shrines on every street corner and your altars to idols in every square. You have been worse than a prostitute, so eager for sin that you have not even demanded payment for your love! [32]Yes, you are an adulterous wife who takes in strangers instead of her own husband. [33]Prostitutes charge for their services—but not you! You give gifts to your lovers, bribing them to come to you. [34]So you are the opposite of other prostitutes. No one pays you; instead, you pay them!

JUDGMENT ON JERUSALEM'S PROSTITUTION

[35]"Therefore, you prostitute, listen to this message from the LORD! [36]This is what the Sovereign LORD says: Because you have exposed yourself in prostitution to all your lovers, and because you have worshiped detestable idols, and because you have slaughtered your children as sacrifices to your gods, [37]this is what I am going to do. I will gather together all your allies—these lovers of yours with whom you have sinned, both those you loved and those you hated—and I will strip you naked in front of them so they can stare at you. [38]I will punish you for your murder and adultery. I will cover you with blood in my jealous fury. [39]Then I will give you to your lovers—these many nations—and they will destroy you. They will knock down your pagan shrines and the altars to your idols. They will strip you and take your beautiful jewels, leaving you completely naked and ashamed. [40]They will band together in a mob to stone you and run you through with swords. [41]They will burn your homes and punish you in front of many women. I will see to it that you stop your prostitution and end your payments to your many lovers.

[42]"Then at last my fury against you will be spent, and my jealous anger will subside. I will be calm and will not be angry with you anymore. [43]But first, because you have not remembered your youth but have angered me by doing all these evil things, I will fully repay you for all of your sins, says the Sovereign LORD. For to all your disgusting sins, you have added these lewd acts. [44]Everyone who makes up proverbs will say of you, 'Like mother, like daughter.' [45]For your mother loathed her husband and her children, and so do you. And

16:29 Or *Chaldea.*

My Daily Worship

— *August 1* —

FOR BETTER, FOR WORSE

EZEKIEL 12:1–16:63

And when I passed by and saw you again, you were old enough to be married. So I wrapped
my cloak around you to cover your nakedness and declared my marriage vows. I made
a covenant with you, says the Sovereign LORD, and you became mine (16:8).

[i reflect]

Writing about God's wondrous love in his book *God in the Dock*, British author C. S. Lewis observed: "He loves people in spite of their faults. He goes on loving. He does not let go. Don't say, 'It's all very well for him; he hasn't got to live with them.' He has. He is inside them as well as outside them. Every vile thought within their minds (and ours), every moment of spite, envy, arrogance, greed and self-conceit comes right up against his patient and longing love, and grieves his spirit more than it grieves ours."

This is precisely the point of Ezekiel 16. Here is a breathtakingly tragic chapter that recites God's long-term love and faithfulness for the southern kingdom of Judah and her callous tendency to play with God's affections. Anyone who has ever felt the bitter sting of unrequited love—or worse, the piercing pain of betrayal—will identify with God's wounded heart.

The sobering truth is that the ancient Jews weren't the only ones who treated God in this manner. We all have a tendency towards spiritual adultery. We are forever tempted to chase after other gods. The amazing thing is that, in spite of our hurtful habits, God doesn't cut his losses and move on. He keeps pursuing and wooing and loving. He loves us, for better or for worse.

How can we wrestle with these facts and not be moved? How can we not be changed? God wants you desperately, despite all your fickleness and failure. He wants *you* for his glory and for your deep, eternal happiness. Do you dare believe it?

Find a ring that you typically don't wear and put it on your right ring finger as a reminder today of God's never-failing covenant to you.

[i pray]

Pondering your stubborn love, I'm tempted to ask, "Why, Lord? Why me? Why such love?"
I pray that I might comprehend this love in a new way. And I pray, as a result, that I
might become a more faithful worshiper and a more devoted lover.

[i respond]

Find a quiet place and sing your favorite hymn or praise song to God. Let it come from a heart filled with appreciation and love.

you are exactly like your sisters, for they despised their husbands and their children. Truly your mother must have been a Hittite and your father an Amorite.

⁴⁶"Your older sister was Samaria, who lived with her daughters in the north. Your younger sister was Sodom, who lived with her daughters in the south. ⁴⁷But you have not merely sinned as they did—no, that was nothing to you. In a very short time you far surpassed them! ⁴⁸As surely as I live, says the Sovereign LORD, Sodom and her daughters were never as wicked as you and your daughters. ⁴⁹Sodom's sins were pride, laziness, and gluttony, while the poor and needy suffered outside her door. ⁵⁰She was proud and did loathsome things, so I wiped her out, as you have seen.

⁵¹"Even Samaria did not commit half your sins. You have done far more loathsome things than your sisters ever did. They seem righteous compared to you! ⁵²You should be deeply ashamed because your sins are so terrible. In comparison, you make your sisters seem innocent!

⁵³"But someday I will restore the fortunes of Sodom and Samaria, and I will restore you, too. ⁵⁴Then you will be truly ashamed of everything you have done, for your sins make them feel good in comparison. ⁵⁵Yes, your sisters, Sodom and Samaria, and all their people will be restored, and at that time you also will be restored. ⁵⁶In your proud days you held Sodom in contempt. ⁵⁷But now your greater wickedness has been exposed to all the world, and you are the one who is scorned—by Edom* and all her neighbors and by Philistia. ⁵⁸This is your punishment for all your disgusting sins, says the LORD.

⁵⁹"Now this is what the Sovereign LORD says: I will give you what you deserve, for you have taken your solemn vows lightly by breaking your covenant. ⁶⁰Yet I will keep the covenant I made with you when you were young, and I will establish an everlasting covenant with you. ⁶¹Then you will remember with shame all the evil you have done. I will make your sis-

ters, Samaria and Sodom, to be your daughters, even though they are not part of our covenant. ⁶²And I will reaffirm my covenant with you, and you will know that I am the LORD. ⁶³You will remember your sins and cover your mouth in silence and shame when I forgive you of all that you have done, says the Sovereign LORD."

A STORY OF TWO EAGLES

17 Then this message came to me from the LORD: ²"Son of man, tell this story to the people of Israel. ³Give them this message from the Sovereign LORD: A great eagle with broad wings full of many-colored feathers came to Lebanon. He took hold of the highest branch of a cedar tree ⁴and plucked off its topmost shoot. Then he carried it away to a city filled with merchants, where he planted it.

⁵"Then he planted one of its seedlings in fertile ground beside a broad river, where it would grow as quickly as a willow tree. ⁶It took root there and grew into a low, spreading vine. Its branches turned up toward the eagle, and its roots grew down beneath it. It soon produced strong branches and luxuriant leaves. ⁷But then another great eagle with broad wings and full plumage came along. So the vine sent its roots and branches out toward him for water. ⁸The vine did this even though it was already planted in good soil and had plenty of water so it could grow into a splendid vine and produce rich leaves and luscious fruit.

⁹"So now the Sovereign LORD asks: Should I let this vine grow and prosper? No! I will pull it out, roots and all! I will cut off its fruit and let its leaves wither and die. I will pull it out easily enough—it won't take a strong arm or a large army to do it. ¹⁰Then when the vine is transplanted, will it thrive? No, it will wither away completely when the east wind blows against it. It will die in the same good soil where it had grown so well."

16:57 Many ancient manuscripts read *Aram.*

THE RIDDLE EXPLAINED

[11]Then this message came to me from the LORD: [12]"Say to these rebels of Israel: Don't you understand the meaning of this riddle of the eagles? I will tell you, says the Sovereign LORD. The king of Babylon came to Jerusalem, took away her king and princes, and brought them to Babylon. [13]He made a treaty with a member of the royal family and made him take an oath of loyalty. He also exiled Israel's most influential leaders, [14]so Israel would not become strong again and revolt. Only by keeping her treaty with Babylon could Israel maintain her national identity.

[15]"Nevertheless, this man of Israel's royal family rebelled against Babylon, sending ambassadors to Egypt to request a great army and many horses. Can Israel break her sworn treaties like that and get away with it? [16]No! For as surely as I live, says the Sovereign LORD, the king of Israel will die in Babylon, the land of the king who put him in power and whose treaty he despised and broke. [17]Pharaoh and all his mighty army will fail to help Israel when the king of Babylon lays siege to Jerusalem again and destroys the lives of many. [18]For the king of Israel broke his treaty after swearing to obey; therefore, he will not escape.

[19]"So this is what the Sovereign LORD says: As surely as I live, I will punish him for breaking my covenant and despising the solemn oath he made in my name. [20]I will throw my net over him and capture him in my snare. I will bring him to Babylon and deal with him there for this treason against me. [21]And all the best warriors of Israel will be killed in battle, and those remaining in the city will be scattered to the four winds. Then you will know that I, the LORD, have spoken these words.

[22]"And the Sovereign LORD says: I will take a tender shoot from the top of a tall cedar, and I will plant it on the top of Israel's highest mountain. [23]It will become a noble cedar, sending forth its branches and producing seed. Birds of every sort will nest in it, finding shelter beneath its branches. [24]And all the trees will know that it is I, the LORD, who cuts down the tall tree and helps the short tree to grow tall. It is I who makes the green tree wither and gives new life to the dead tree. I, the LORD, have spoken! I will do what I have said."

THE JUSTICE OF A RIGHTEOUS GOD

18 Then another message came to me from the LORD: [2]"Why do you quote this proverb in the land of Israel: 'The parents have eaten sour grapes, but their children's mouths pucker at the taste'? [3]As surely as I live, says the Sovereign LORD, you will not say this proverb anymore in Israel. [4]For all people are mine to judge—both parents and children alike. And this is my rule: The person who sins will be the one who dies.

[5]"Suppose a certain man is just and does what is lawful and right, [6]and he has not feasted in the mountains before Israel's idols or worshiped them. And suppose he does not commit adultery or have intercourse with a woman during her menstrual period. [7]Suppose he is a merciful creditor, not keeping the items given in pledge by poor debtors, and does not rob the poor but instead gives food to the hungry and provides clothes for people in need. [8]And suppose he grants loans without interest, stays away from injustice, is honest and fair when judging others, [9]and faithfully obeys my laws and regulations. Anyone who does these things is just and will surely live, says the Sovereign LORD.

[10]"But suppose that man has a son who grows up to be a robber or murderer and refuses to do what is right. [11]And suppose that son does all the evil things his father would never do—worships idols on the mountains, commits adultery, [12]oppresses the poor and helpless, steals from debtors by refusing to let them redeem what they have given in pledge, worships idols and takes part in loathsome practices, [13]and lends money at interest. Should such a sinful person live? No! He must die and must take full blame.

[14]"But suppose that sinful son, in turn, has a

son who sees his father's wickedness but decides against that kind of life. ¹⁵Suppose this son refuses to worship idols on the mountains, does not commit adultery, ¹⁶and does not exploit the poor, but instead is fair to debtors and does not rob them. And suppose this son feeds the hungry, provides clothes for the needy, ¹⁷helps the poor, does not lend money at interest, and obeys all my regulations and laws. Such a person will not die because of his father's sins; he will surely live. ¹⁸But the father will die for the many sins he committed—for being cruel and robbing close relatives, doing what was clearly wrong among his people.

¹⁹" 'What?' you ask. 'Doesn't the child pay for the parent's sins?' No! For if the child does what is right and keeps my laws, that child will surely live. ²⁰The one who sins is the one who dies. The child will not be punished for the parent's sins, and the parent will not be punished for the child's sins. Righteous people will be rewarded for their own goodness, and wicked people will be punished for their own wickedness. ²¹But if wicked people turn away from all their sins and begin to obey my laws and do what is just and right, they will surely live and not die. ²²All their past sins will be forgotten, and they will live because of the righteous things they have done.

²³"Do you think, asks the Sovereign LORD, that I like to see wicked people die? Of course not! I only want them to turn from their wicked ways and live. ²⁴However, if righteous people turn to sinful ways and start acting like other sinners, should they be allowed to live? No, of course not! All their previous goodness will be forgotten, and they will die for their sins.

²⁵"Yet you say, 'The Lord isn't being just!' Listen to me, O people of Israel. Am I the one who is unjust, or is it you? ²⁶When righteous people turn from being good and start doing sinful things, they will die for it. Yes, they will die because of their sinful deeds. ²⁷And if wicked people turn away from their wicked-

ness, obey the law, and do what is just and right, they will save their lives. ²⁸They will live, because after thinking it over, they decided to turn from their sins. Such people will not die. ²⁹And yet the people of Israel keep saying, 'The Lord is unjust!' O people of Israel, it is you who are unjust, not I.

³⁰"Therefore, I will judge each of you, O people of Israel, according to your actions, says the Sovereign LORD. Turn from your sins! Don't let them destroy you! ³¹Put all your rebellion behind you, and get for yourselves a new heart and a new spirit. For why should you die, O people of Israel? ³²I don't want you to die, says the Sovereign LORD. Turn back and live!

A FUNERAL SONG FOR ISRAEL'S KINGS

19 "Sing this funeral song for the princes of Israel:

² 'What is your mother?
  A lioness among lions!
She lay down among the young lions
  and reared her cubs.
³ She raised one of her cubs
  to become a strong young lion.
He learned to catch and devour prey,
  and he became a man-eater.
⁴ Then the nations heard about him,
  and he was trapped in their pit.
They led him away in chains
  to the land of Egypt.

⁵ 'When the mother lion saw
  that all her hopes for him were gone,
she took another of her cubs
  and taught him to be a strong lion.
⁶ He prowled among the other lions
  and became a leader among them.
He learned to catch and devour prey,
  and he, too, became a man-eater.
⁷ He demolished fortresses in nearby nations*
  and destroyed their towns and cities.

19:7 As in Greek version; Hebrew reads *He consorted with widows.*

My Daily Worship

MAKING A SPIRITUAL U-TURN

EZEKIEL 17:1–21:32

Put all your rebellion behind you, and get for yourselves a new heart and a new spirit.
For why should you die, O people of Israel? I don't want you to die,
says the Sovereign LORD. Turn back and live! (18:31–32).

[i reflect]

What is repentance, and why is it important? Simply defined, the word means to "change one's mind," and it implies a turning away from sin to God. Writer Oswald Chambers called repentance the "bedrock of Christianity" and said it is "a gift from God." Preacher Charles Spurgeon further described it as "the grace of a lifetime."

In referring to repentance in these terms ("gift" and "grace"), these two giants of the faith are echoing the above words of the prophet Ezekiel. Look at them again.

Repentance is God's deepest wish for his creatures. He yearns for people to have life, spiritual life, eternal life. The clear message of Jesus is that our Creator longs for us to enjoy the richest existence imaginable (John 10:10). He desperately wants us to experience his vast mercy and grace and to be spared his perfect yet severe justice. We cannot experience God's amazing favor, however, until, like the prodigal son of the New Testament, we acknowledge our foolish actions and make a U-turn for home.

Even after we've become the children of God through faith in Christ (John 1:12), we need a kind of ongoing repentance. Daily we wander off course. Daily we need to stop, turn, and come back to God. And every time we do this—every single time—we find God to be like the father in the prodigal son story (Luke 15:11-32). Arms open wide, eyes filled with joy and relief, ready to throw a party in your honor! As the old country preachers used to say, "If that doesn't ring your bell, your clapper's broke."

As you go about your errands and routine today, allow each U-turn sign you see on the road to prompt you to thank God for his grace and mercy that awaits you as you turn back to him.

[i pray]

God, your patient love and desire to bless stuns me into silence. What a merciful Creator you are!
Thank you for calling me home and welcoming me even when I have been rebellious.

[i respond]

Throw a "Prodigal Party." Invite some friends over to celebrate God's lavish love and forgiveness. Or just give out party hats to members of your family and turn your evening meal into a special occasion for praise.

Their farms were desolated,
and their crops were destroyed.
Everyone in the land trembled in fear
when they heard him roar.
8 Then the armies of the nations attacked him,
surrounding him from every direction.
They spread out their nets for him
and captured him in their pit.
9 With hooks, they dragged him into a cage
and brought him before the king of
Babylon.
They held him in captivity,
so his voice could never again be heard
on the mountains of Israel.

10 'Your mother was like a vine
planted by the water's edge.
It had lush, green foliage
because of the abundant water.
11 Its branches became very strong,
strong enough to be a ruler's scepter.
It soon became very tall,
towering above all the others.
It stood out because of its height
and because of its many lush branches.
12 But the vine was uprooted in fury
and thrown down to the ground.
The desert wind dried up its fruit
and tore off its branches.
Its stem was destroyed by fire.
13 Now the vine is growing in the wilderness,
where the ground is hard and dry.
14 A fire has come from its branches
and devoured its fruit.
None of the remaining limbs
is strong enough to be a ruler's scepter.'

This is a funeral song, and it is now time for
the funeral."

THE REBELLION OF ISRAEL

20 On August 14,* during the seventh
year of King Jehoiachin's captivity,
some of the leaders of Israel came to request a
message from the LORD. They sat down in
front of me to wait for his reply. 2Then this
message came to me from the LORD: 3"Son of
man, give the leaders of Israel this message
from the Sovereign LORD: How dare you come
to ask for my help? As surely as I live, I will tell
you nothing. This is the word of the Sovereign
LORD!

4"Son of man, bring judgment against them
and condemn them. Make them realize how
loathsome the actions of their ancestors really
were. 5Give them this message from the
Sovereign LORD: When I chose Israel and
revealed myself to her in Egypt, I swore that I,
the LORD, would be her God. 6I promised that
I would bring her and her descendants out of
Egypt to a land I had discovered and
explored for them—a good land, a land flowing with milk and honey, the best of all lands
anywhere. 7Then I said to them, 'Each of you,
get rid of your idols. Do not defile yourselves
with the Egyptian gods, for I am the LORD
your God.'

8"But they rebelled against me and would
not listen. They did not get rid of their idols
or forsake the gods of Egypt. Then I threatened to pour out my fury on them to satisfy
my anger while they were still in Egypt. 9But I
didn't do it, for I acted to protect the honor of
my name. That way the surrounding nations
wouldn't be able to laugh at Israel's God, who
had promised to deliver his people. 10So I
brought my people out of Egypt and led them
into the wilderness. 11There I gave them my
laws so they could live by keeping them. Yes,
all those who keep them will live! 12And I gave
them my Sabbath days of rest as a sign
between them and me. It was to remind them
that I, the LORD, had set them apart to be holy,
making them my special people.

13"But the people of Israel rebelled against
me, and they refused to obey my laws there in
the wilderness. They wouldn't obey my
instructions even though obedience would
have given them life. And they also violated
my Sabbath days. So I threatened to pour out
my fury on them, and I made plans to utterly

20:1 Hebrew *In the fifth month, on the tenth day,* of the Hebrew calendar. This event occurred on August 14, 591 B.C.; also see note on 1:1.

consume them in the desert. ¹⁴But again I held back in order to protect the honor of my name. That way the nations who saw me lead my people out of Egypt wouldn't be able to claim I destroyed them because I couldn't take care of them. ¹⁵But I swore to them in the wilderness that I would not bring them into the land I had given them, a land flowing with milk and honey, the most beautiful place on earth. ¹⁶I told them this because they had rejected my laws, ignored my will for them, and violated my Sabbath days. Their hearts were given to their idols. ¹⁷Nevertheless, I pitied them and held back from destroying them in the wilderness.

¹⁸"Then I warned their children and told them not to follow in their parents' footsteps, defiling themselves with their idols. ¹⁹'I am the LORD your God,' I told them. 'Follow my laws, pay attention to my instructions, ²⁰and keep my Sabbath days holy, for they are a sign to remind you that I am the LORD your God.'

²¹"But their children, too, rebelled against me. They refused to keep my laws and follow my instructions, even though obeying them would have given them life. And they also violated my Sabbath days. So again I threatened to pour out my fury on them in the wilderness. ²²Nevertheless, I withdrew my judgment against them to protect the honor of my name among the nations who had seen my power in bringing them out of Egypt. ²³But I took a solemn oath against them while they were in the wilderness. I vowed I would scatter them among all the nations ²⁴because they did not obey my laws. They scorned my instructions by violating my Sabbath days and longing for the idols of their ancestors. ²⁵I gave them over to worthless customs and laws that would not lead to life. ²⁶I let them pollute themselves with the very gifts I had given them, and I allowed them to give their firstborn children as offerings to their gods—so I might devastate them and show them that I alone am the LORD.

JUDGMENT AND RESTORATION

²⁷"Therefore, son of man, give the people of Israel this message from the Sovereign LORD: Your ancestors continued to blaspheme and betray me, ²⁸for when I brought them into the land I had promised them, they offered sacrifices and incense on every high hill and under every green tree they saw! They roused my fury as they offered up sacrifices to their gods. They brought their perfumes and incense and poured out their drink offerings to them! ²⁹I said to them, 'What is this high place where you are going?' (This idol shrine has been called Bamah—'high place'—ever since.)

³⁰"Therefore, give the people of Israel this message from the Sovereign LORD: Do you plan to pollute yourselves just as your ancestors did? Do you intend to keep prostituting yourselves by worshiping detestable idols? ³¹For when you offer gifts to them and give your little children to be burned as sacrifices,* you continue to pollute yourselves to this day. Should I listen to you or help you, O people of Israel? As surely as I live, says the Sovereign LORD, I will not give you a message even though you have come to me requesting one.

³²"You say, 'We want to be like the nations all around us, who serve idols of wood and stone.' But what you have in mind will never happen. ³³As surely as I live, says the Sovereign LORD, I will rule you with an iron fist in great anger and with awesome power. ³⁴With might and fury I will bring you out from the lands where you are scattered. ³⁵I will bring you into the wilderness of the nations, and there I will judge you face to face. ³⁶I will judge you there just as I did your ancestors in the wilderness after bringing them out of Egypt, says the Sovereign LORD. ³⁷I will count you carefully and hold you to the terms of the covenant. ³⁸I will purge you of all those who rebel and sin against me. I will bring them out of the countries where they are in exile, but they will never enter the land of Israel. And when that happens, you will know that I am the LORD.

³⁹"As for you, O people of Israel, this is what

20:31 Or *and make your little children pass through the fire.*

the Sovereign LORD says: If you insist, go right ahead and worship your idols, but then don't turn around and bring gifts to me. Such desecration of my holy name must stop! ⁴⁰For on my holy mountain, says the Sovereign LORD, the people of Israel will someday worship me, and I will accept them. There I will require that you bring me all your offerings and choice gifts and sacrifices. ⁴¹When I bring you home from exile, you will be as pleasing to me as an offering of perfumed incense. And I will display my holiness in you as all the nations watch. ⁴²Then when I have brought you home to the land I promised your ancestors, you will know that I am the LORD. ⁴³You will look back at all your sins and hate yourselves because of the evil you have done. ⁴⁴You will know that I am the LORD, O people of Israel, when I have honored my name by treating you mercifully in spite of your wickedness, says the Sovereign LORD."

JUDGMENT AGAINST THE NEGEV

⁴⁵Then this message came to me from the LORD: ⁴⁶"Son of man, look toward the south* and speak out against it; prophesy against the fields of the Negev. ⁴⁷Give the southern wilderness this message from the Sovereign LORD: Hear the word of the LORD! I will set you on fire, O forest, and every tree will be burned—green and dry trees alike. The terrible flames will not be quenched; they will scorch everything from south to north. ⁴⁸And all the world will see that I, the LORD, have set this fire. It will not be put out."

⁴⁹Then I said, "O Sovereign LORD, they are saying of me, 'He only talks in riddles!' "

THE LORD'S SWORD OF JUDGMENT

21 Then this message came to me from the LORD: ²"Son of man, look toward Jerusalem and prophesy against Israel and her sanctuaries. ³Give her this message from the LORD: I am your enemy, O Israel, and I am about to unsheath my sword to destroy your

20:46 Hebrew *Teman.*

Words of Worship

MOST HOLY PLACE, HOLY PLACE

Most Holy Place, Holy Place—Hebrew *qe-dosh haq-qe-do-shim* "holy of holies, most holy [place]"; *de-vir* "inner sanctuary, oracle"; *ma-qom qa-dosh* "holy place"; Greek *ta ha-gi-a* "the holy place, sanctuary." The third Hebrew expression may refer to the entire Temple, while the first two refer specifically to the inmost sanctuary.

The sanctuary of Israel had three sections: The altar of sacrifice stood in the outer court, the inner court contained the altar of incense; the "most holy place" held the ark of the covenant, the symbol of God's presence with his people. Only the priests could approach the Lord's altars, and only the high priest could enter the inmost sanctuary.

In Christian worship the Temple of Jerusalem lost its central role, but remained a powerful word symbol of God's communion with his people. Every Christian is a temple of God's indwelling Spirit (1 Corinthians 3:16). In the city of praise "the Lord God Almighty and the Lamb are its temple" (Revelation 21:22). And the three-part structure of the Israelite sanctuary pictures our progression through worship. First we offer ourselves to God. Then we bring our "prayer as incense offered" (Psalm 141:2). Finally we enjoy God's abiding presence in the "most holy place" of heartfelt adoration.

---

people—the righteous and the wicked alike. ⁴Yes, I will not spare even the righteous! I will make a clean sweep throughout the land from south to north. ⁵All the world will know that I am the LORD. My sword is in my hand, and it will not return to its sheath until its work is finished.

[6]"Son of man, groan before the people! Groan before them with bitter anguish and a broken heart. [7]When they ask you why, tell them, 'I groan because of the terrifying news I have heard. When it comes true, the boldest heart will melt with fear; all strength will disappear. Every spirit will faint; strong knees will tremble and become as weak as water. And the Sovereign LORD says: It is coming! It's on its way!'"

[8]Then the LORD said to me, [9]"Son of man, give the people this message from the LORD: A sword is being sharpened and polished. [10]It is being prepared for terrible slaughter; it will flash like lightning! Now will you laugh? Those far stronger than you have fallen beneath its power!* [11]Yes, the sword is now being sharpened and polished; it is being prepared for the executioner!

[12]"Son of man, cry out and wail; pound your thighs in anguish, for that sword will slaughter my people and their leaders—everyone will die! [13]It will put them all to the test! So now the Sovereign LORD asks: What chance do they have?*

[14]"Son of man, prophesy to them and clap your hands vigorously. Then take the sword and brandish it twice, even three times, to symbolize the great massacre they will face! [15]Let their hearts melt with terror, for the sword glitters at every gate. It flashes like lightning; it is polished for slaughter! [16]O sword, slash to the right, and slash to the left, wherever you will, wherever you want. [17]I, too, will clap my hands, and I will satisfy my fury. I, the LORD, have spoken!"

A SIGNPOST FOR BABYLON'S KING

[18]Then this message came to me from the LORD: [19]"Son of man, make a map and trace two routes on it for the sword of Babylon's king to follow. Put a signpost on the road that comes out of Babylon where the road forks into two—[20]one road going to Ammon and its capital, Rabbah, and the other to Judah and fortified Jerusalem. [21]The king of Babylon now stands at the fork, uncertain whether to attack Jerusalem or Rabbah. He will call his magicians to use divination. They will cast lots by shaking arrows from the quiver. They will inspect the livers of their animal sacrifices. [22]Then they will decide to turn toward Jerusalem! With battering rams they will go against the gates, shouting for the kill. They will put up siege towers and build ramps against the walls to reach the top. [23]The people of Jerusalem will think it is a mistake, because of their treaty with the Babylonians. But the king of Babylon will remind the people of their rebellion. Then he will attack and capture them.

[24]"Therefore, this is what the Sovereign LORD says: Again and again your guilt cries out against you, for you are not ashamed of your sin. You don't even try to hide it! Wherever you go, whatever you do, all your actions are filled with sin. So now the time of your punishment has come!

[25]"O you corrupt and wicked prince of Israel, your final day of reckoning is here! [26]Take off your jeweled crown, says the Sovereign LORD. The old order changes—now the lowly are exalted, and the mighty are brought low. [27]Destruction! Destruction! I will surely destroy the kingdom. And it will not be restored until the one appears who has the right to judge it. Then I will hand it over to him.

A MESSAGE FOR THE AMMONITES

[28]"And now, son of man, prophesy concerning the Ammonites and their mockery. Give them this message from the Sovereign LORD: My sword is drawn for your slaughter; it is sharpened to destroy, flashing like lightning! [29]Your magicians and false prophets have given false visions and told lies about the sword. And now it will fall with even greater force on the wicked for whom the day of final reckoning

21:10 The meaning of the Hebrew is uncertain.   21:13 The meaning of the Hebrew is uncertain.

has come. ³⁰Should I return my sword to its sheath before I deal with you? No, I will destroy you in your own country, the land of your birth. ³¹I will pour out my fury on you and blow on you with the fire of my anger. I will hand you over to cruel men who are skilled in destruction. ³²You are fuel for the fire, and your blood will be spilled in your own land. You will be utterly wiped out, your memory lost to history. I, the LORD, have spoken!"

THE SINS OF JERUSALEM

22 Now this message came to me from the LORD: ²"Son of man, are you ready to judge Jerusalem? Are you ready to judge this city of murderers? Denounce her terrible deeds in public, ³and give her this message from the Sovereign LORD: O city of murderers, doomed and damned—city of idols, filthy and foul—⁴you are guilty of both murder and idolatry. Your day of destruction has come! You have reached the end of your years. I will make you an object of mockery throughout the world. ⁵O infamous city, filled with confusion, you will be mocked by people both far and near.

⁶"Every leader in Israel who lives within your walls is bent on murder. ⁷Fathers and mothers are contemptuously ignored. Resident foreigners are forced to pay for protection. Orphans and widows are wronged and oppressed. ⁸Inside your walls you despise my holy things and violate my Sabbath days of rest. ⁹People accuse others falsely and send them to their death. You are filled with idol worshipers and people who take part in lewd activities. ¹⁰Men sleep with their fathers' wives and have intercourse with women who are menstruating. ¹¹Within your walls live men who commit adultery with their neighbors' wives, who defile their daughters-in-law or who rape their own sisters. ¹²There are hired murderers, loan racketeers, and extortioners everywhere! They never even think of me and

my commands, says the Sovereign LORD. ¹³"But now I clap my hands in indignation over your dishonest gain and bloodshed. ¹⁴How strong and courageous will you be in my day of reckoning? I, the LORD, have spoken! I will do what I have said. ¹⁵I will scatter you among the nations and purge you of your wickedness. ¹⁶And when you have been dishonored among the nations, you will know that I am the LORD."

THE LORD'S REFINING FURNACE

¹⁷Then this message came to me from the LORD: ¹⁸"Son of man, the people of Israel are the worthless slag that remains after silver is smelted. They are the dross that is left over—a useless mixture of copper, tin, iron, and lead. ¹⁹So give them this message from the Sovereign LORD: Because you are all worthless slag, I will bring you to my crucible in Jerusalem. ²⁰I will melt you down in the heat of my fury, just as copper, tin, iron, and lead are melted down in a furnace. ²¹I will gather you together and blow the fire of my anger upon you, ²²and you will melt like silver in fierce heat. Then you will know that I, the LORD, have poured out my fury on you."

THE SINS OF ISRAEL'S LEADERS

²³Again a message came to me from the LORD: ²⁴"Son of man, give the people of Israel this message: In the day of my indignation, you will become like an uncleared wilderness or a desert without rain. ²⁵Your princes* plot conspiracies just as lions stalk their prey. They devour innocent people, seizing treasures and extorting wealth. They increase the number of widows in the land. ²⁶Your priests have violated my laws and defiled my holy things. To them there is no difference between what is holy and what is not. And they do not teach my people the difference between what is ceremonially clean and unclean. They disregard my Sabbath days so that my holy name is greatly dishonored among them. ²⁷Your leaders are like wolves, who tear apart their vic-

22:25 As in Greek version; Hebrew reads *prophets.*

tims. They actually destroy people's lives for profit! ²⁸And your prophets announce false visions and speak false messages. They say, 'My message is from the Sovereign LORD,' when the LORD hasn't spoken a single word to them. They repair cracked walls with whitewash! ²⁹Even common people oppress the poor, rob the needy, and deprive foreigners of justice.

³⁰"I looked for someone who might rebuild the wall of righteousness that guards the land. I searched for someone to stand in the gap in the wall so I wouldn't have to destroy the land, but I found no one. ³¹So now I will pour out my fury on them, consuming them in the fire of my anger. I will heap on them the full penalty for all their sins, says the Sovereign LORD."

THE ADULTERY OF TWO SISTERS

23 This message came to me from the LORD: ²"Son of man, once there were two sisters who were daughters of the same mother. ³They became prostitutes in Egypt. Even as young girls, they allowed themselves to be fondled and caressed. ⁴The older girl was named Oholah, and her sister was Oholibah. I married them, and they bore me sons and daughters. I am speaking of Samaria and Jerusalem, for Oholah is Samaria and Oholibah is Jerusalem.

⁵"Then Oholah lusted after other lovers instead of me, and she gave her love to the Assyrians, her neighbors. ⁶They were all attractive young men, captains and commanders dressed in handsome blue, dashing about on their horses. ⁷And so she prostituted herself with the most desirable men of Assyria, worshiping their idols and defiling herself. ⁸For when she left Egypt, she did not leave her spirit of prostitution behind. She was still as lewd as in her youth, when the Egyptians satisfied their lusts with her and robbed her of her virginity. ⁹And so I handed her over to her Assyrian lovers, whom she

desired so much. ¹⁰They stripped her and killed her and took away her children as their slaves. Her name was known to every woman in the land as a sinner who had received what she deserved.

¹¹"Yet even though Oholibah saw what had happened to Oholah, her sister, she followed right in her footsteps. And she was even more depraved, abandoning herself to her lust and prostitution. ¹²She fawned over her Assyrian neighbors, those handsome young men on fine horses, those captains and commanders in handsome uniforms—all of them desirable. ¹³I saw the way she was going, defiling herself just like her older sister.

¹⁴"Then she carried her prostitution even further. She fell in love with pictures that were painted on a wall—pictures of Babylonian* military officers, outfitted in striking red uniforms. ¹⁵Handsome belts encircled their waists, and flowing turbans crowned their heads. They were dressed like chariot officers from the land of Babylonia.* ¹⁶When she saw these paintings, she longed to give herself to them, so she sent messengers to Babylonia to invite them to come to her. ¹⁷So they came and committed adultery with her, defiling her in the bed of love. But later, she became disgusted with them and broke off their relationship.

¹⁸"So I became disgusted with Oholibah, just as I was with her sister, because she flaunted herself before them and gave herself to satisfy their lusts. ¹⁹But that didn't bother her. She turned to even greater prostitution, remembering her youth when she was a prostitute in Egypt. ²⁰She lusted after lovers whose attentions were gross and bestial. ²¹And so, Oholibah, you celebrated your former days as a young girl in Egypt, when you first allowed yourself to be fondled and caressed.

THE LORD'S JUDGMENT OF OHOLIBAH

²²"Therefore, Oholibah, this is what the Sovereign LORD says: I will send your lovers against you—those very nations from which

23:14 Or *Chaldean.* 23:15 Or *Chaldea;* also in 23:16.

you turned away in disgust. ²³For the Babylonians will come with all the Chaldeans from Pekod and Shoa and Koa. And all the Assyrians will come with them—handsome young captains, commanders, chariot officers, and other high-ranking officers, riding their horses. ²⁴They will all come against you from the north with chariots, wagons, and a great army fully prepared for attack. They will take up positions on every side, surrounding you with men armed for battle. And I will hand you over to them so they can do with you as they please. ²⁵I will turn my jealous anger against you, and they will deal furiously with you. They will cut off your nose and ears, and any survivors will then be slaughtered by the sword. Your children will be taken away as captives, and everything that is left will be burned. ²⁶They will strip you of your beautiful clothes and jewels. ²⁷In this way, I will put a stop to the lewdness and prostitution you brought from Egypt. You will never again cast longing eyes on those things or fondly remember your time in Egypt.

²⁸"For this is what the Sovereign LORD says: I will surely hand you over to your enemies, to those you loathe. ²⁹They will deal with you in hatred and rob you of all you own, leaving you naked and bare. The shame of your prostitution will be exposed to all the world. ³⁰You brought all this on yourself by prostituting yourself to other nations, defiling yourself with all their idols. ³¹Because you have followed in your sister's footsteps, I will punish you with the same terrors that destroyed her.

³²"Yes, this is what the Sovereign LORD says: You will drink from the same cup of terror as your sister—a cup that is large and deep. And all the world will mock and scorn you in your desolation. ³³You will reel like a drunkard beneath the awful blows of sorrow and distress, just as your sister Samaria did. ³⁴In deep anguish you will drain that cup of terror to the very bottom. Then you will smash it to pieces and beat your breast in anguish. For I, the Sovereign LORD, have spoken! ³⁵And because you have forgotten me and turned your back on me, says the Sovereign LORD, you must bear the consequences of all your lewdness and prostitution."

THE LORD'S JUDGMENT ON BOTH SISTERS

³⁶The LORD said to me, "Son of man, you must accuse Oholah and Oholibah of all their awful deeds. ³⁷They have committed both adultery and murder—adultery by worshiping idols and murder by burning their children as sacrifices on their altars. ³⁸Then after doing these terrible things, they defiled my Temple and violated my Sabbath day! ³⁹On the very day that they murdered their children in front of their idols, they boldly came into my Temple to worship! They came in and defiled my house!

⁴⁰"You sisters sent messengers to distant lands to get men. Then when they arrived, you bathed yourselves, painted your eyelids, and put on your finest jewels for them. ⁴¹You sat with them on a beautifully embroidered couch and put my incense and my oil on a table that was spread before you. ⁴²From your room came the sound of many men carousing. They were lustful men and drunkards from the wilderness, who put bracelets on your wrists and beautiful crowns on your heads. ⁴³Then I said, 'If they really want to sleep with worn-out, old prostitutes like these, let them!' ⁴⁴And that is what they did. They slept with Oholah and Oholibah, these shameless prostitutes, with all the zest of lustful young men. ⁴⁵But righteous people will judge these sister cities for what they really are—adulteresses and murderers. They will sentence them to all the punishment they deserve.

⁴⁶"Now this is what the Sovereign LORD says: Bring an army against them and hand them over to be terrorized and plundered. ⁴⁷For their enemies will stone them and kill them with swords. They will butcher their sons and daughters and burn their homes. ⁴⁸In this way, I will put an end to lewdness and idolatry in the land, and my judgment will be a warning

My Daily Worship

— *August 3* —

EXHIBIT A FOR GOD'S TRUTH

EZEKIEL 22:1–26:21

Son of man, I am going to take away your dearest treasure. Suddenly she will die.
Yet you must not show any sorrow. Do not weep; let there be no tears (24:16).

[i reflect]

The life of Gladys Aylward, a missionary to China during and after World War II, reveals a stirring story of faithful obedience to God. Incredibly, she rescued a hundred orphans from the Japanese, crossing the mountains of China to safety in Siam.

Upon delivering her precious cargo, Gladys was gravely ill and almost delirious. She had suffered beatings from the Japanese; she was ill from relapsing fever, typhus, pneumonia, malnutrition, shock, and fatigue. Yet, through her ordeal, Gladys had learned to choose Christ over anything else life had to offer—so much so that she turned down a marriage proposal from the man she loved. Gladys knew she could not continue God's work with the children if she were married.

It is a lesson many obedient servants of God have had to learn. Take Ezekiel, and the passage above. There was Ezekiel the faithful prophet, tending to God's business, doing right, when, as an object lesson to the nation, God took his beloved wife. She had been the light of Ezekiel's life. What a terrible loss! Then came the odd (unique to this one situation) command: Ezekiel is forbidden to mourn.

Ezekiel's experience is a strange but powerful reminder that we are part of a story that is much bigger than our own private lives. We have important roles to play, and huge, cosmic realities are at stake—like God's reputation and his glory, as well as the need for a lost and rebellious world to be pierced by the power and trustworthiness of God.

Here's the truth we need to grasp: When we suffer in this life and continue to cling to and trust God, we become "exhibit A"—a walking advertisement for the truth and the power of the gospel. Today, use your problems and struggles as opportunities to present your faith and trust in God.

[i pray]

Father, when I struggle and hurt, give me the grace to refuse self-pity. I want
to turn my difficulties and pain into opportunities to point others to you.

[i respond]

Make a list of three trials in your life that you have a tendency to complain or grumble about. Make these struggles the focus of your own mini-praise service. Thank God for how he can teach you and shape you and use you in the midst of these messes.

to others not to follow their wicked example. [49]You will be fully repaid for all your prostitution—your worship of idols. Yes, you will suffer the full penalty! Then you will know that I am the Sovereign LORD."

THE SIGN OF THE COOKING POT

24 On January 15,* during the ninth year of King Jehoiachin's captivity, this message came to me from the LORD: [2]"Son of man, write down today's date, because on this very day the king of Babylon is beginning his attack against Jerusalem. [3]Then show these rebels an illustration; give them a message from the Sovereign LORD. Put a pot of water on the fire to boil. [4]Fill it with choice meat—the rump and the shoulder and all the most tender cuts. [5]Use only the best sheep from the flock and heap fuel on the fire beneath the pot. Bring the pot to a boil, and cook the bones along with the meat.

[6]"Now this is what the Sovereign LORD says: Destruction is certain for Jerusalem, the city of murderers! She is a pot filled with corruption. So take the meat out chunk by chunk in whatever order it comes, [7]for her wickedness is evident to all. She murders boldly, leaving blood on the rocks for all to see. She doesn't even try to cover it! [8]So I will splash her blood on a rock as an open expression of my anger and vengeance against her.

[9]"This is what the Sovereign LORD says: Destruction is certain for Jerusalem, the city of murderers! I myself will pile up the fuel beneath her. [10]Yes, heap on the wood! Let the fire roar to make the pot boil. Cook the meat well with many spices. Then empty the pot and burn the bones. [11]Now set the empty pot on the coals to scorch away the filth and corruption. [12]But it's hopeless; the corruption remains. So throw it into the fire! [13]It is the filth and corruption of your lewdness and idolatry. And now, because I tried to cleanse you but you refused, you will remain filthy until my fury against you has been satisfied.

[14]I, the LORD, have spoken! The time has come and I won't hold back; I will not change my mind. You will be judged on the basis of all your wicked actions, says the Sovereign LORD."

THE DEATH OF EZEKIEL'S WIFE

[15]Then this message came to me from the LORD: [16]"Son of man, I am going to take away your dearest treasure. Suddenly she will die. Yet you must not show any sorrow. Do not weep; let there be no tears. [17]You may sigh but only quietly. Let there be no wailing at her grave. Do not uncover your head or take off your sandals. Do not perform the rituals of mourning or accept any food brought to you by consoling friends."

[18]So I proclaimed this to the people the next morning, and in the evening my wife died. The next morning I did everything I had been told to do. [19]Then the people asked, "What does all this mean? What are you trying to tell us?"

[20]So I said to them, "A message came to me from the LORD, [21]and I was told to give this message to the people of Israel. This is what the Sovereign LORD says: I will desecrate my Temple, the source of your security and pride. Your sons and daughters in Judea will be slaughtered by the sword. [22]Then you will do as Ezekiel has done. You will not mourn in public or console yourselves by eating the food brought to you by sympathetic friends. [23]Your heads must remain covered, and your sandals must not be taken off. You will not mourn or weep, but you will waste away because of your sins. You will mourn privately for all the evil you have done. [24]Ezekiel is an example for you to follow; you will do as he has done. And when that time comes, you will know that I am the LORD."

[25]Then the LORD said to me, "Son of man, on the day I take away their stronghold—their joy and glory, their heart's desire, their dearest treasure—I will also take away their sons and

---

24:1 Hebrew *On the tenth day of the tenth month,* of the Hebrew calendar. This event occurred on January 15, 588 B.C.; also see note on 1:1.

daughters. ²⁶And on that day a refugee from Jerusalem will come to you in Babylon and tell you what has happened. ²⁷And when he arrives, your voice will suddenly return so you can talk to him, and you will be a symbol for these people. Then they will know that I am the LORD."

A MESSAGE FOR AMMON

25 Then this message came to me from the LORD: ²"Son of man, look toward the land of Ammon and prophesy against its people. ³Give the Ammonites this message from the Sovereign LORD: Hear the word of the Sovereign LORD! Because you scoffed when my Temple was desecrated, mocked Israel in her desolation, and laughed at Judah as she went away into exile, ⁴I will allow nomads from the eastern deserts to overrun your country. They will set up their camps among you and pitch their tents on your land. They will harvest all your fruit and steal your livestock. ⁵And I will turn the city of Rabbah into a pasture for camels, and all the land of the Ammonites into an enclosure for sheep. Then you will know that I am the LORD.

⁶"And the Sovereign LORD says: Because you clapped and stamped and cheered with glee at the destruction of my people, ⁷I will lift up my fist against you. I will give you as plunder to many nations. I will cut you off from being a nation and destroy you completely. Then you will know that I am the LORD.

A MESSAGE FOR MOAB

⁸"And the Sovereign LORD says: Because the people of Moab have said that Judah is just like all the other nations, ⁹I will open up their eastern flank and wipe out their glorious frontier cities—Beth-jeshimoth, Baal-meon, and Kiriathaim. ¹⁰And I will hand Moab over to nomads from the eastern deserts, just as I handed over Ammon. Yes, the Ammonites will no longer be counted among the nations.

¹¹And in the same way, I will bring my judgment down on the Moabites. Then they will know that I am the LORD.

A MESSAGE FOR EDOM

¹²"And the Sovereign LORD says: The people of Edom have sinned greatly by avenging themselves against the people of Judah. ¹³Therefore, says the Sovereign LORD, I will raise my fist of judgment against Edom. I will wipe out their people, cattle, and flocks with the sword. I will make a wasteland of everything from Teman to Dedan. ¹⁴By the hand of my people of Israel, I will accomplish this. They will carry out my furious vengeance, and Edom will know it is from me. I, the Sovereign LORD, have spoken!

A MESSAGE FOR PHILISTIA

¹⁵"And the Sovereign LORD says: The people of Philistia have acted against Judah out of revenge and long-standing contempt. ¹⁶Therefore, says the Sovereign LORD, I will raise my fist of judgment against the land of the Philistines. I will wipe out the Kerethites and utterly destroy the people who live by the sea. ¹⁷I will execute terrible vengeance against them to rebuke them for what they have done. And when I have inflicted my revenge, then they will know that I am the LORD."

A MESSAGE FOR TYRE

26 On February 3, during the twelfth year of King Jehoiachin's captivity,* this message came to me from the LORD: ²"Son of man, Tyre has rejoiced over the fall of Jerusalem, saying, 'Ha! She who controlled the rich trade routes to the east has been broken, and I am the heir! Because she has been destroyed, I will become wealthy!'

³"Therefore, this is what the Sovereign LORD says: I am your enemy, O Tyre, and I will bring many nations against you, like the waves of the sea crashing against your shoreline. ⁴They

---

26:1 Hebrew *In the eleventh year, on the first day of the month,* of the Hebrew calendar year. Since an element is missing in the date formula here, scholars have reconstructed this probable reading: *In the eleventh [month of the twelfth] year, on the first day of the month.* This reading would put this message on February 3, 585 B.C.; also see note on 1:1.

will destroy the walls of Tyre and tear down its towers. I will scrape away its soil and make it a bare rock! [5]The island of Tyre will become uninhabited. It will be a place for fishermen to spread their nets, for I have spoken, says the Sovereign LORD. Tyre will become the prey of many nations, [6]and its mainland villages will be destroyed by the sword. Then they will know that I am the LORD.

> *Worship is the highest elevation of the spirit, and yet the lowliest prostration of the soul.*
>
> CHARLES H. SPURGEON

[7]"For the Sovereign LORD says: I will bring King Nebuchadnezzar* of Babylon—the king of kings from the north—against Tyre with his cavalry, chariots, and great army. [8]First he will destroy your mainland villages. Then he will attack you by building a siege wall, constructing a ramp, and raising a roof of shields against you. [9]He will pound your walls with battering rams and demolish your towers with sledgehammers. [10]The hooves of his cavalry will choke the city with dust, and your walls will shake as the horses gallop through your broken gates, pulling chariots behind them. [11]His horsemen will trample every street in the city. They will butcher your people, and your famous pillars will topple.

[12]"They will plunder all your riches and merchandise and break down your walls. They will destroy your lovely homes and dump your stones and timbers and even your dust into the sea. [13]I will stop the music of your songs. No more will the sound of harps be heard among your people. [14]I will make your island a bare rock, a place for fishermen to spread their nets. You will never be rebuilt, for I, the LORD, have spoken! This is the word of the Sovereign LORD.

THE EFFECT OF TYRE'S DESTRUCTION

[15]"This is what the Sovereign LORD says to Tyre: The whole coastline will tremble at the sound of your fall, as the screams of the wounded echo in the continuing slaughter. [16]All the seaport rulers will step down from their thrones and take off their royal robes and beautiful clothing. They will sit on the ground trembling with horror at what they have seen. [17]Then they will wail for you, singing this funeral song:

'O famous island city,
   once ruler of the sea,
   how you have been destroyed!
Your people, with their naval power,
   once spread fear around the world.
[18] Now the coastlands tremble at your fall.
   The islands are dismayed as you pass
    away.'

[19]"For the Sovereign LORD says: I will make Tyre an uninhabited ruin. You will sink beneath the terrible waves of enemy attack. Great seas will swallow you. [20]I will send you to the pit to lie there with those who descended there long ago. Your city will lie in ruins, buried beneath the earth, like those in the pit who have entered the world of the dead. Never again will you be given a position of respect here in the land of the living. [21]I will bring you to a terrible end, and you will be no more. You will be looked for, but you will never be found. I, the Sovereign LORD, have spoken!"

THE END OF TYRE'S GLORY

27 Then this message came to me from the LORD: [2]"Son of man, sing a funeral song for Tyre, [3]that mighty gateway to the sea,

26:7 Hebrew *Nebuchadrezzar,* a variant name for Nebuchadnezzar.

the trading center of the world. Give Tyre this message from the Sovereign LORD: You claimed, O Tyre, to be perfect in beauty. 4You extended your boundaries into the sea. Your builders made you glorious! 5You were like a great ship built of the finest cypress from Senir.* They took a cedar from Lebanon to make a mast for you. 6They carved oars for you from the oaks of Bashan. They made your deck of pine wood, brought from the southern coasts of Cyprus.* Then they inlaid it with ivory. 7Your sails were made of Egypt's finest linen, and they flew as a banner above you. You stood beneath blue and purple awnings made bright with dyes from the coasts of Elishah.

8"Your oarsmen came from Sidon and Arvad; your helmsmen were skilled men from Tyre itself. 9Wise old craftsmen from Gebal did all the caulking. Ships came with goods from every land to barter for your trade. 10Men from distant Persia, Lydia, and Libya* served in your great army. They hung their shields and helmets on your walls, giving you great honor. 11Men from Arvad and from Helech stood on your walls as sentinels. Your towers were manned by men from Gammad. Their shields hung on your walls, perfecting your splendor.

12"Tarshish was your agent, trading your wares in exchange for silver, iron, tin, and lead. 13Merchants from Greece,* Tubal, and Meshech brought slaves and bronze dishes. 14From Togarmah came riding horses, chariot horses, and mules. All these things were exchanged for your manufactured goods. 15Merchants came to you from Dedan.* Numerous coastlands were your captive markets; they brought payment in ivory tusks and ebony wood.

16"Aram* sent merchants to buy your wares. They traded turquoise, purple dyes, embroidery, fine linen, and jewelry of coral and rubies. 17Judah and Israel traded for your wares, offer-

ing wheat from Minnith, early figs,* honey, oil, and balm. 18Damascus traded for your rich variety of goods, bringing wine from Helbon and white wool from Zahar. 19Greeks from Uzal* came to trade for your merchandise. Wrought iron, cassia, and calamus were bartered for your wares. 20Dedan traded their expensive saddle blankets with you.

21"The Arabians and the princes of Kedar brought lambs and rams and goats in trade for your goods. 22The merchants of Sheba and Raamah came with all kinds of spices, jewels, and gold in exchange for your wares. 23Haran, Canneh, Eden, Sheba, Asshur, and Kilmad came with their merchandise, too. 24They brought choice fabrics to trade—blue cloth, embroidery, and many-colored carpets bound with cords and made secure. 25The ships of Tarshish were your ocean caravans. Your island warehouse was filled to the brim!

THE DESTRUCTION OF TYRE

26"But look! Your oarsmen are rowing your ship of state into a hurricane! Your mighty vessel flounders in the heavy eastern gale. You are shipwrecked in the heart of the sea! 27Everything is lost—your riches and wares, your sailors and helmsmen, your ship builders, merchants, and warriors. On that day of vast ruin, everyone on board sinks into the depths of the sea.

28"Your cities by the sea tremble as your helmsmen cry out in terror. 29All the oarsmen abandon their ships; the sailors and helmsmen come to stand on the shore. 30They weep bitterly as they throw dust on their heads and roll in ashes. 31They shave their heads in grief because of you and dress themselves in sackcloth. They weep for you with bitter anguish and deep mourning. 32As they wail and mourn, they sing this sad funeral song:

'Was there ever such a city as Tyre,
now silent at the bottom of the sea?

27:5 Or *Hermon.* 27:6 Hebrew *Kittim.* 27:10 Hebrew *Paras, Lud, and Put.* 27:13 Hebrew *Javan.* 27:15 Greek version reads *Rhodes.* 27:16 Some manuscripts read *Edom.* 27:17 The meaning of the Hebrew is uncertain. 27:19 Hebrew *Vedan and Javan from Uzal.* The meaning of the Hebrew is uncertain.

³³ The merchandise you traded
　　satisfied the needs of many nations.
　Kings at the ends of the earth
　　were enriched by your trade.
³⁴ Now you are a wrecked ship,
　　broken at the bottom of the sea.
　All your merchandise and your crew
　　have passed away with you.
³⁵ All who live along the coastlands
　　are appalled at your terrible fate.
　Their kings are filled with horror
　　and look on with twisted faces.
³⁶ The merchants of the nations
　　shake their heads at the sight of you,*
　for you have come to a horrible end
　　and will be no more.'"

A Message for Tyre's King

28 Then this message came to me from the LORD: ²"Son of man, give the prince of Tyre this message from the Sovereign LORD: In your great pride you claim, 'I am a god! I sit on a divine throne in the heart of the sea.' But you are only a man and not a god, though you boast that you are like a god. ³You regard yourself as wiser than Daniel and think no secret is hidden from you. ⁴With your wisdom and understanding you have amassed great wealth—gold and silver for your treasuries. ⁵Yes, your wisdom has made you very rich, and your riches have made you very proud.

⁶"Therefore, this is what the Sovereign LORD says: Because you think you are as wise as a god, ⁷I will bring against you an enemy army, the terror of the nations. They will suddenly draw their swords against your marvelous wisdom and defile your splendor! ⁸They will bring you down to the pit, and you will die there on your island home in the heart of the sea, pierced with many wounds. ⁹Will you then boast, 'I am a god!' to those who kill you? To them you will be no god but merely a man! ¹⁰You will die like an outcast at the hands of foreigners. I, the Sovereign LORD, have spoken!"

¹¹Then this further message came to me from the LORD: ¹²"Son of man, weep for the king of Tyre. Give him this message from the Sovereign LORD: You were the perfection of wisdom and beauty. ¹³You were in Eden, the garden of God. Your clothing was adorned with every precious stone*—red carnelian, chrysolite, white moonstone, beryl, onyx, jasper, sapphire, turquoise, and emerald—all beautifully crafted for you and set in the finest gold. They were given to you on the day you were created. ¹⁴I ordained and anointed you as the mighty angelic guardian.* You had access to the holy mountain of God and walked among the stones of fire.

¹⁵"You were blameless in all you did from the day you were created until the day evil was found in you. ¹⁶Your great wealth filled you with violence, and you sinned. So I banished you from the mountain of God. I expelled you, O mighty guardian, from your place among the stones of fire. ¹⁷Your heart was filled with pride because of all your beauty. You corrupted your wisdom for the sake of your splendor. So I threw you to the earth and exposed you to the curious gaze of kings. ¹⁸You defiled your sanctuaries with your many sins and your dishonest trade. So I brought fire from within you, and it consumed you. I let it burn you to ashes on the ground in the sight of all who were watching. ¹⁹All who knew you are appalled at your fate. You have come to a terrible end, and you are no more."

A Message for Sidon

²⁰Then another message came to me from the LORD: ²¹"Son of man, look toward the city of Sidon and prophesy against it. ²²Give the people of Sidon this message from the Sovereign LORD: I am your enemy, O Sidon, and I will reveal my glory by what happens to you. When I bring judgment against you and reveal my holiness among you, everyone watching will know that I am the LORD. ²³I will send a plague against you, and blood will be

---

27:36 Hebrew *hiss at you.*　**28:13** The identification of some of these gemstones is uncertain.　**28:14** Hebrew *guardian cherub;* also in 28:16.

spilled in your streets. The attack will come from every direction, and your people will lie slaughtered within your walls. Then everyone will know that I am the LORD. [24]No longer will Israel's scornful neighbors prick and tear at her like thorns and briers. For then they will know that I am the Sovereign LORD.

RESTORATION FOR ISRAEL

[25]"This is what the Sovereign LORD says: The people of Israel will again live in their own land, the land I gave my servant Jacob. For I will gather them from the distant lands where I have scattered them. I will reveal to the nations of the world my holiness among my people. [26]They will live safely in Israel and build their homes and plant their vineyards. And when I punish the neighboring nations that treated them with contempt, they will know that I am the LORD their God."

A MESSAGE FOR EGYPT

29 On January 7,* during the tenth year of King Jehoiachin's captivity, this message came to me from the LORD: [2]"Son of man, turn toward Egypt and prophesy against Pharaoh the king and all the people of Egypt. [3]Give them this message from the Sovereign LORD: I am your enemy, O Pharaoh, king of Egypt—you great monster, lurking in the streams of the Nile. For you have said, 'The Nile River is mine; I made it for myself!' [4]I will put hooks in your jaws and drag you out on the land with fish sticking to your scales. [5]I will leave you and all your fish stranded in the desert to die. You will lie unburied on the open ground, for I have given you as food to the wild animals and birds.

[6]"All the people of Egypt will discover that I am the LORD, for you collapsed like a reed when Israel looked to you for help. [7]Israel leaned on you, but like a cracked staff, you splintered and stabbed her in the armpit.

When she put her weight on you, you gave way, and her back was thrown out of joint. [8]So now the Sovereign LORD says: I will bring an army against you, O Egypt, and destroy both people and animals. [9]The land of Egypt will become a desolate wasteland, and the Egyptians will know that I am the LORD.

"Because you said, 'The Nile River is mine; I made it,' [10]I am now the enemy of both you and your river. I will utterly destroy the land of Egypt, from Migdol to Aswan, as far south as the border of Ethiopia.* [11]For forty years not a soul will pass that way, neither people nor animals. It will be completely uninhabited. [12]I will make Egypt desolate, and it will be surrounded by other desolate nations. Its cities will be empty and desolate for forty years, surrounded by other desolate cities. I will scatter the Egyptians to distant lands.

[13]"But the Sovereign LORD also says: At the end of the forty years I will bring the Egyptians home again from the nations to which they have been scattered. [14]I will restore the prosperity of Egypt and bring its people back to the land of Pathros in southern Egypt from which they came. But Egypt will remain an unimportant, minor kingdom. [15]It will be the lowliest of all the nations, never again great enough to rise above its neighbors.

[16]"Then Israel will no longer be tempted to trust in Egypt for help. Egypt's shattered condition will remind Israel of how sinful she was to trust Egypt in earlier days. Then Israel will know that I alone am the Sovereign LORD."

NEBUCHADNEZZAR TO CONQUER EGYPT

[17]On April 26,* during the twenty-seventh year of King Jehoiachin's captivity, this message came to me from the LORD: [18]"Son of man, the army of King Nebuchadnezzar* of Babylon fought so hard against Tyre that the warriors' heads were rubbed bare and their shoulders were raw and blistered. Yet

---

29:1 Hebrew *On the twelfth day of the tenth month,* of the Hebrew calendar. A number of dates in Ezekiel can be cross-checked with dates in surviving Babylonian records and related accurately to our modern calendar. This event occurred on January 7, 587 B.C.
29:10 Hebrew *Cush.* 29:17 Hebrew *On the first day of the first month,* of the Hebrew calendar. This event occurred on April 26, 571 B.C.; also see note on 29:1. 29:18 Hebrew *Nebuchadrezzar,* a variant name for Nebuchadnezzar; also in 29:19.

Nebuchadnezzar and his army won no plunder to compensate them for all their work. [19]Therefore, this is what the Sovereign LORD says: I will give the land of Egypt to Nebuchadnezzar, king of Babylon. He will carry off their wealth, plundering everything they have to pay his army. [20]Yes, I have given him the land of Egypt as a reward for his work, says the Sovereign LORD, because he was working for me when he destroyed Tyre.

[21]"And the day will come when I will cause the ancient glory of Israel to revive, and then at last your words will be respected. Then they will know that I am the LORD."

A Sad Day for Egypt

30 This is another message that came to me from the LORD: [2]"Son of man, prophesy and give this message from the Sovereign LORD: Weep, [3]for the terrible day is almost here—the day of the LORD! It is a day of clouds and gloom, a day of despair for the nations! [4]A sword will come against Egypt, and those who are slaughtered will cover the ground. Their wealth will be carried away and their foundations destroyed. The land of Ethiopia* will be ravished. [5]Ethiopia, Libya,* Lydia,* and Arabia, with all their other allies, will be destroyed in that war.

[6]"For this is what the LORD says: All of Egypt's allies will fall, and the pride of their power will end. From Migdol to Aswan they will be slaughtered by the sword, says the Sovereign LORD. [7]Egypt will be desolate, surrounded by desolate nations, and its cities will be in ruins, surrounded by other ruined cities. [8]And the people of Egypt will know that I am the LORD when I have set Egypt on fire and destroyed all their allies. [9]At that time I will send swift messengers in ships to terrify the complacent Ethiopians. Great panic will come upon them on that day of Egypt's certain destruction.

[10]"For this is what the Sovereign LORD says: Through King Nebuchadnezzar* of Babylon, I will destroy the hordes of Egypt. [11]He and his armies—ruthless among the nations—have been sent to demolish the land. They will make war against Egypt until slaughtered Egyptians cover the ground. [12]I will dry up the Nile River and hand the land over to wicked men. I will destroy the land of Egypt and everything in it, using foreigners to do it. I, the LORD, have spoken!

[13]"This is what the Sovereign LORD says: I will smash the idols of Egypt and the images at Memphis.* There will be no rulers left in Egypt; anarchy will prevail throughout the land! [14]I will destroy Pathros, Zoan, and Thebes,* and they will lie in ruins, burned up by my anger. [15]I will pour out my fury on Pelusium,* the strongest fortress of Egypt, and I will stamp out the people of Thebes. [16]Yes, I will set fire to all Egypt! Pelusium will be racked with pain; Thebes will be torn apart; Memphis will live in constant terror. [17]The young men of Heliopolis and Bubastis* will die in battle, and the women* will be taken away as slaves. [18]When I come to break the proud strength of Egypt, it will be a dark day for Tahpanhes, too. A dark cloud will cover Tahpanhes, and its daughters will be led away as captives. [19]And so I will greatly punish Egypt, and they will know that I am the LORD."

The Broken Arms of Pharaoh

[20]On April 29,* during the eleventh year of King Jehoiachin's captivity, this message came to me from the LORD: [21]"Son of man, I have broken the arm of Pharaoh, the king of Egypt. His arm has not been put in a cast so that it may heal. Neither has it been bound up with a splint to make it strong enough to hold a sword. [22]Therefore, this is what the Sovereign LORD says: I am the enemy of Pharaoh, the

---

30:4 Hebrew *Cush;* also in 30:5, 9. **30:5a** Hebrew *Put . . . Kub.* Both *Put* and *Kub* are associated with Libya. **30:5b** Hebrew *Lud.* **30:10** Hebrew *Nebuchadrezzar,* a variant name for Nebuchadnezzar. **30:13** Hebrew *Noph;* also in 30:16. **30:14** Hebrew *No;* also in 30:15, 16. **30:15** Hebrew *Sin;* also in 30:16. **30:17a** Hebrew *of Awen and Pi-beseth.* **30:17b** Or *her cities.* **30:20** Hebrew *On the seventh day of the first month,* of the Hebrew calendar. This event occurred on April 29, 587 B.C.; also see note on 29:1.

My Daily Worship

— *August 4* —

THE GOD OF EARTH AND TIME

EZEKIEL 27:1–32:32

I will restore the prosperity of Egypt and bring its people back to the land of Pathros in southern Egypt from which they came. But Egypt will remain an unimportant, minor kingdom. . . . And the day will come when I will cause the ancient glory of Israel to revive, and then at last your words will be respected. Then they will know that I am the LORD (29:14, 21).

[i reflect]

Near the end of a long and interesting life, Benjamin Franklin stated, "I have lived a long time, sir, and the longer I live the more convincing proofs I see of this truth—that God governs in the affairs of men."

Franklin's observation echoes the testimony of the Bible. Scholars note that at least one-fourth of the Bible was prophecy at the time it was written. In other words, one out of every four verses announced in advance what God was planning to do on earth! And many of these prophecies, like the one above about Egypt, has already been fulfilled.

So what difference does this make to one who wants to be a worshiper of God? Fulfilled prophecies show us God's faithfulness and trustworthiness. What he says he will do! We can count on him.

Prophecy also demonstrates the sovereignty of God. The world—despite appearances to the contrary—is *not* spinning wildly out of control, but moving toward its appointed end. God truly *does* have the whole world—and all of human history—in his good, big hands.

Finally, the inclusion of so much prophecy in the Bible accentuates God's love and concern for his people. He wants us to understand what lies ahead. He wants us to be prepared for all that is to come.

Today as you look at the news headlines (probably including at least one story about the tension in the Middle East), pause and worship the God of Egypt, and Israel, and the entire world. He is worthy to be praised!

[i pray]

Father in heaven, I thank you for being the Alpha and Omega, the eternal God, who stands outside of time and space and who governs in the affairs of men. Thank you for controlling my life.

[i respond]

Get a globe or a world map. Study part of it closely for a few minutes. Spend some time praising God for what he has done in history and what he will do in the future in that place.

king of Egypt! I will break both of his arms—the good arm along with the broken one—and I will make his sword clatter to the ground. ²³I will scatter the Egyptians to many lands throughout the world. ²⁴I will strengthen the arms of Babylon's king and put my sword in his hand. But I will break the arms of Pharaoh, king of Egypt, and he will lie there mortally wounded, groaning in pain. ²⁵I will strengthen the arms of the king of Babylon, while the arms of Pharaoh fall useless to his sides. And when I put my sword in the hand of Babylon's king and he brings it against the land of Egypt, Egypt will know that I am the LORD. ²⁶I will scatter the Egyptians among the nations. Then they will know that I am the LORD."

EGYPT COMPARED TO FALLEN ASSYRIA

31 On June 21,* during the eleventh year of King Jehoiachin's captivity, this message came to me from the LORD: ²"Son of man, give this message to Pharaoh, king of Egypt, and all his people: To whom would you compare your greatness? ³You are as Assyria was—a great and mighty nation. Assyria, too, was once like a cedar of Lebanon, full of thick branches that cast deep forest shade with its top high among the clouds. ⁴Deep springs watered it and helped it to grow tall and luxuriant. The water was so abundant that there was enough for all the trees nearby. ⁵This great tree towered above all the other trees around it. It prospered and grew long thick branches because of all the water at its roots. ⁶The birds nested in its branches, and in its shade all the wild animals gave birth to their young. All the great nations of the world lived in its shadow. ⁷It was strong and beautiful, for its roots went deep into abundant water. ⁸This tree became taller than any of the other cedars in the garden of God. No cypress had branches equal to it; no plane tree had boughs to compare. No tree in the garden of God came close to it in beauty. ⁹Because of the magnificence I gave this tree, it was the envy of all the other trees of Eden, the garden of God.

¹⁰"Therefore, this is what the Sovereign LORD says: Because it became proud and arrogant, and because it set itself so high above the others, reaching to the clouds, ¹¹I handed it over to a mighty nation that destroyed it as its wickedness deserved. I myself discarded it. ¹²A foreign army—the terror of the nations—cut it down and left it fallen on the ground. Its branches were scattered across the mountains and valleys and ravines of the land. All those who lived beneath its shadow went away and left it lying there. ¹³The birds roosted on its fallen trunk, and the wild animals lay among its branches. ¹⁴Let no other nation proudly exult in its own prosperity, though it be higher than the clouds, for all are doomed. They will land in the pit along with all the proud people of the world.

¹⁵"This is what the Sovereign LORD says: When Assyria went down into the grave,* I made the deep places mourn, and I restrained the mighty waters. I clothed Lebanon in black and caused the trees of the field to wilt. ¹⁶I made the nations shake with fear at the sound of its fall, for I sent it down to the grave with all the others like it. And all the other proud trees of Eden, the most beautiful and the best of Lebanon, the ones whose roots went deep into the water, were relieved to find it there with them in the pit. ¹⁷Its allies, too, were all destroyed and had passed away. They had gone down to the grave—all those nations that had lived in its shade.

¹⁸"O Egypt, to which of the trees of Eden will you compare your strength and glory? You, too, will be brought down to the pit with all these other nations. You will lie there among the outcasts who have died by the sword. This will be the fate of Pharaoh and all his teeming hordes. I, the Sovereign LORD, have spoken!"

31:1 Hebrew *On the first day of the third month,* of the Hebrew calendar. This event occurred on June 21, 587 B.C.; also see note on 29:1. 31:15 Hebrew *to Sheol;* also in 31:16, 17.

A WARNING FOR PHARAOH

32 On March 3,* during the twelfth year of King Jehoiachin's captivity, this message came to me from the LORD: ²"Son of man, mourn for Pharaoh, king of Egypt, and give him this message: You think of yourself as a strong young lion among the nations, but you are really just a sea monster, heaving around in your own rivers, stirring up mud with your feet.

³"Therefore, this is what the Sovereign LORD says: I will send many people to catch you in my net and haul you out of the water. ⁴I will leave you stranded on the land to die. All the birds of the heavens will land on you, and the wild animals of the whole earth will gorge themselves on you. ⁵I will cover the hills with your flesh and fill the valleys with your bones. ⁶I will drench the earth with your gushing blood all the way to the mountains, filling the ravines to the brim. ⁷When I blot you out, I will veil the heavens and darken the stars. I will cover the sun with a cloud, and the moon will not give you its light. ⁸Yes, I will bring darkness everywhere across your land. Even the brightest stars will become dark above you. I, the Sovereign LORD, have spoken!

⁹"And when I bring your shattered remains to distant nations that you have never seen, I will disturb many hearts. ¹⁰Yes, I will bring terror to many lands, and their kings will be terrified because of all I do to you. They will shudder in fear for their lives as I brandish my sword before them on the day of your fall.

¹¹"For this is what the Sovereign LORD says: The sword of the king of Babylon will come against you. ¹²I will destroy you with the swords of mighty warriors—the terror of the nations. They will shatter the pride of Egypt, and all its hordes will be destroyed. ¹³I will destroy all your flocks and herds that graze beside the streams. Never again will people or animals disturb those waters with their feet. ¹⁴Then I will let the waters of Egypt become

calm again, and they will flow as smoothly as olive oil, says the Sovereign LORD. ¹⁵And when I destroy Egypt and wipe out everything you have and strike down all your people, then you will know that I am the LORD. ¹⁶Yes, this is the funeral song they will sing for Egypt. Let all the nations mourn for Egypt and its hordes. I, the Sovereign LORD, have spoken!"

EGYPT FALLS INTO THE PIT

¹⁷On March 17,* during the twelfth year, another message came to me from the LORD:

Words of Worship

GO, GO UP

Go, Go Up—Hebrew *ha-lach* "go, walk"; *'a-lah* "go up."

Some Internet browser screens have a button that says, "Go." We can enter all the right address information in the box, but if we never click "Go," we might stare at the same screen for a long time. It can be like that with our worship. All our thoughts about how we need to pray or what kind of praise we should offer or how we could be thanking the Lord, may come to nothing if we never hit the "Go" button.

Biblical worshipers understood that sometimes we need prompting to enter the Lord's presence. "I was glad when they said to me, 'Let us go to the house of the LORD'" (Psalm 122:1). Unlike the Israelite worshiper, we may not have to "go up to the mountain of the LORD" (Isaiah 2:3), but we still have to press into his presence. It's great to think about how wonderful worship might be, but it's even better for us—and for the Lord—when we follow the prompt and click "Go."

32:1 Hebrew *On the first day of the twelfth month*, of the Hebrew calendar. This event occurred on March 3, 585 B.C.; also see note on 29:1. **32:17** Hebrew *On the fifteenth day of the month*, presumably in the twelfth month of the Hebrew calendar (see 32:1). This would put this message at the end of King Jehoiachin's twelfth year of captivity, on March 17, 585 B.C.; also see note on 29:1. Greek version reads *On the fifteenth day of the first month*, which would put this message on April 27, 586 B.C., at the beginning of Jehoiachin's twelfth year.

¹⁸"Son of man, weep for the hordes of Egypt and for the other mighty nations. For I will send them down to the world below in company with those who descend to the pit. ¹⁹Say to them, 'O Egypt, are you lovelier than the other nations? No! So go down to the pit and lie there among the outcasts.' ²⁰The Egyptians will fall with the many who have died by the sword, for the sword is drawn against them. Egypt will be dragged away to its judgment. ²¹Down in the grave* mighty leaders will mockingly welcome Egypt and its allies, saying, 'They have come down; they lie among the outcasts, all victims of the sword.'

²²"Assyria lies there surrounded by the graves of all its people, those who were slaughtered by the sword. ²³Their graves are in the depths of the pit, and they are surrounded by their allies. These mighty men who once struck terror in the hearts of people everywhere are now dead at the hands of their enemies.

²⁴"Elam lies there buried with its hordes who descended as outcasts to the world below. They terrorized the nations while they lived, but now they lie in the pit and share the humiliation of those who have gone to the world of the dead. ²⁵They have a resting place among the slaughtered, surrounded by the graves of all their people. Yes, they terrorized the nations while they lived, but now they lie in shame in the pit, all of them outcasts, slaughtered by the sword.

²⁶"Meshech and Tubal are there, surrounded by the graves of all their hordes. They once struck terror into the hearts of all people. But now they are outcasts, all victims of the sword. ²⁷They are not buried in honor like the fallen heroes of the outcasts, who went down to the grave* with their weapons—their shields covering their bodies,* and their swords beneath their heads. They brought terror to everyone while they were still alive.

²⁸"You too, Egypt, will lie crushed and broken among the outcasts, all victims of the sword.

²⁹"Edom is there with its kings and princes. Mighty as they were, they also lie among those killed by the sword, with the outcasts who have gone down to the pit. ³⁰All the princes of the north and the Sidonians are there, all victims of the sword. Once a terror, they now lie there in shame. They lie there as outcasts with all the other dead who have descended to the pit.

³¹"When Pharaoh arrives, he will be relieved to find that he is not alone in having his entire army killed, says the Sovereign LORD. ³²For I have caused my terror to fall upon all the living. And Pharaoh and his hordes will lie there among the outcasts who have died by the sword. I, the Sovereign LORD, have spoken!"

EZEKIEL AS ISRAEL'S WATCHMAN

33 Once again a message came to me from the LORD: ²"Son of man, give your people this message: When I bring an army against a country, the people of that land choose a watchman. ³When the watchman sees the enemy coming, he blows the alarm to warn the people. ⁴Then if those who hear the alarm refuse to take action—well, it is their own fault if they die. ⁵They heard the warning but wouldn't listen, so the responsibility is theirs. If they had listened to the warning, they could have saved their lives. ⁶But if the watchman sees the enemy coming and doesn't sound the alarm to warn the people, he is responsible for their deaths. They will die in their sins, but I will hold the watchman accountable.

⁷"Now, son of man, I am making you a watchman for the people of Israel. Therefore, listen to what I say and warn them for me. ⁸If I announce that some wicked people are sure to die and you fail to warn them about changing their ways, then they will die in their sins, but I will hold you responsible for their deaths. ⁹But if you warn them to repent and they don't repent, they will die in their sins, but you will not be held responsible.

THE WATCHMAN'S MESSAGE

¹⁰"Son of man, give the people of Israel this message: You are saying, 'Our sins are heavy

32:21 Hebrew *in Sheol.* 32:27a Hebrew *to Sheol.* 32:27b The meaning of the Hebrew phrase here is uncertain.

upon us; we are wasting away! How can we survive?' ¹¹As surely as I live, says the Sovereign LORD, I take no pleasure in the death of wicked people. I only want them to turn from their wicked ways so they can live. Turn! Turn from your wickedness, O people of Israel! Why should you die?

¹²"Son of man, give your people this message: The good works of righteous people will not save them if they turn to sin, nor will the sins of evil people destroy them if they repent and turn from their sins. ¹³When I tell righteous people that they will live, but then they sin, expecting their past righteousness to save them, then none of their good deeds will be remembered. I will destroy them for their sins. ¹⁴And suppose I tell some wicked people that they will surely die, but then they turn from their sins and do what is just and right. ¹⁵For instance, they might give back a borrower's pledge, return what they have stolen, and obey my life-giving laws, no longer doing what is evil. If they do this, then they will surely live and not die. ¹⁶None of their past sins will be brought up again, for they have done what is just and right, and they will surely live.

¹⁷"Your people are saying, 'The Lord is not just,' but it is they who are not just. ¹⁸For again I say, when righteous people turn to evil, they will die. ¹⁹But if wicked people turn from their wickedness and do what is just and right, they will live. ²⁰O people of Israel, you are saying, 'The Lord is not just.' But I will judge each of you according to your deeds."

EXPLANATION OF JERUSALEM'S FALL

²¹On January 8,* during the twelfth year of our captivity, a man who had escaped from Jerusalem came to me and said, "The city has fallen!" ²²The previous evening the LORD had taken hold of me and opened my mouth, so I would be able to speak when this man arrived the next morning.

²³Then this message came to me from the LORD: ²⁴"Son of man, the scattered remnants of Judah living among the ruined cities keep saying, 'Abraham was only one man, and yet he gained possession of the entire land! We are many; surely the land should be given to us as a possession.' ²⁵Now give these people this message from the Sovereign LORD: You eat meat with blood in it, you worship idols, and you murder the innocent. Do you really think the land should be yours? ²⁶Murderers! Idolaters! Adulterers! Should the land belong to you?

²⁷"Give them this message from the Sovereign LORD: As surely as I live, those living in the ruins will die by the sword. Those living in the open fields will be eaten by wild animals. Those hiding in the forts and caves will die of disease. ²⁸I will destroy the land and demolish her pride. Her arrogant power will come to an end. The mountains of Israel will be so ruined that no one will even travel through them. ²⁹When I have ruined the land because of their disgusting sins, then they will know that I am the LORD.

³⁰"Son of man, your people are whispering behind your back. They talk about you in their houses and whisper about you at the doors, saying, 'Come on, let's have some fun! Let's go hear the prophet tell us what the LORD is saying!' ³¹So they come pretending to be sincere and sit before you listening. But they have no intention of doing what I tell them. They express love with their mouths, but their hearts seek only after money. ³²You are very entertaining to them, like someone who sings love songs with a beautiful voice or plays fine music on an instrument. They hear what you say, but they don't do it! ³³But when all these terrible things happen to them—as they certainly will—then they will know a prophet has been among them."

THE SHEPHERDS OF ISRAEL

34 Then this message came to me from the LORD: ²"Son of man, prophesy against the shepherds, the leaders of Israel.

33:21 Hebrew *On the fifth day of the tenth month,* of the Hebrew calendar. This event occurred on January 8, 585 B.C.; also see note on 29:1.

Give them this message from the Sovereign LORD: Destruction is certain for you shepherds who feed yourselves instead of your flocks. Shouldn't shepherds feed their sheep? [3]You drink the milk, wear the wool, and butcher the best animals, but you let your flocks starve. [4]You have not taken care of the weak. You have not tended the sick or bound up the broken bones. You have not gone looking for those who have wandered away and are lost. Instead, you have ruled them with force and cruelty. [5]So my sheep have been scattered without a shepherd. They are easy prey for any wild animal. [6]They have wandered through the mountains and hills, across the face of the earth, yet no one has gone to search for them.

[7]"Therefore, you shepherds, hear the word of the LORD: [8]As surely as I live, says the Sovereign LORD, you abandoned my flock and left them to be attacked by every wild animal. Though you were my shepherds, you didn't search for my sheep when they were lost. You took care of yourselves and left the sheep to starve. [9]Therefore, you shepherds, hear the word of the LORD. [10]This is what the Sovereign LORD says: I now consider these shepherds my enemies, and I will hold them responsible for what has happened to my flock. I will take away their right to feed the flock, along with their right to feed themselves. I will rescue my flock from their mouths; the sheep will no longer be their prey.

THE GOOD SHEPHERD

[11]"For this is what the Sovereign LORD says: I myself will search and find my sheep. [12]I will be like a shepherd looking for his scattered flock. I will find my sheep and rescue them from all the places to which they were scattered on that dark and cloudy day. [13]I will bring them back home to their own land of Israel from among the peoples and nations. I will feed them on the mountains of Israel and by the rivers in all the places where people live. [14]Yes, I will give them good pastureland on the high hills of Israel. There they will lie down in pleasant places and feed in lush mountain pastures. [15]I myself will tend my sheep and cause them to lie down in peace, says the Sovereign LORD. [16]I will search for my lost ones who strayed away, and I will bring them safely home again. I will bind up the injured and strengthen the weak. But I will destroy those who are fat and powerful. I will feed them, yes—feed them justice!

> *Worship can never be the sole work of the rational mind.*
>
> DAVID JEREMIAH

[17]"And as for you, my flock, my people, this is what the Sovereign LORD says: I will judge between one sheep and another, separating the sheep from the goats. [18]Is it not enough for you to keep the best of the pastures for yourselves? Must you also trample down the rest? Is it not enough for you to take the best water for yourselves? Must you also muddy the rest with your feet? [19]All that is left for my flock to eat is what you have trampled down. All they have to drink is water that you have fouled.

[20]"Therefore, this is what the Sovereign LORD says: I will surely judge between the fat sheep and the scrawny sheep. [21]For you fat sheep push and butt and crowd my sick and hungry flock until they are scattered to distant lands. [22]So I will rescue my flock, and they will no longer be abused and destroyed. And I will judge between one sheep and another. [23]And I will set one shepherd over them, even my servant David. He will feed them and be a shepherd to them. [24]And I, the LORD, will be their God, and my servant David will be a prince among my people. I, the LORD, have spoken!

The Lord's Covenant of Peace

25"I will make a covenant of peace with them and drive away the dangerous animals from the land. Then my people will be able to camp safely in the wildest places and sleep in the woods without fear. 26I will cause my people and their homes around my holy hill to be a blessing. And I will send showers, showers of blessings, which will come just when they are needed. 27The orchards and fields of my people will yield bumper crops, and everyone will live in safety. When I have broken their chains of slavery and rescued them from those who enslaved them, then they will know that I am the LORD. 28They will no longer be prey for other nations, and wild animals will no longer attack them. They will live in safety, and no one will make them afraid.

29"And I will give them a land famous for its crops, so my people will never again go hungry or be shamed by the scorn of foreign nations. 30In this way, they will know that I, the LORD their God, am with them. And they will know that they, the people of Israel, are my people, says the Sovereign LORD. 31You are my flock, the sheep of my pasture. You are my people, and I am your God, says the Sovereign LORD."

A Message for Edom

35 Again a message came to me from the LORD: 2"Son of man, turn toward Mount Seir, and prophesy against its people. 3Give them this message from the Sovereign LORD: I am your enemy, O Mount Seir, and I will raise my fist against you to destroy you completely. 4I will demolish your cities and make you desolate, and then you will know that I am the LORD. 5Your continual hatred for the people of Israel led you to butcher them when they were helpless, when I had already punished them for all their sins. 6As surely as I live, says the Sovereign LORD, since you show no distaste for blood, I will give you a bloodbath of your own. Your turn has come! 7I will make Mount Seir utterly desolate, killing off all who try to escape and any who return. 8I will fill your mountains with the dead. Your hills, your valleys, and your streams will be filled with people slaughtered by the sword. 9I will make you desolate forever. Your cities will never be rebuilt. Then you will know that I am the LORD.

10"For you said, 'The lands of Israel and Judah will be ours. We will take possession of them. What do we care that the LORD is there!' 11Therefore, as surely as I live, says the Sovereign LORD, I will pay back your angry deeds with mine. I will punish you for all your acts of anger, envy, and hatred. And I will bring honor to my name by what I do to you. 12Then you will know that I, the LORD, have heard every contemptuous word you spoke against the mountains of Israel. For you said, 'They have been destroyed; they have been given to us as food to eat!' 13In saying that, you boasted proudly against me, and I have heard it all!

14"This is what the Sovereign LORD says: The whole world will rejoice when I make you desolate. 15You rejoiced at the desolation of Israel's inheritance. Now I will rejoice at yours! You will be wiped out, you people of Mount Seir and all who live in Edom! Then you will know that I am the LORD!

Restoration for Israel

36 "Son of man, prophesy to Israel's mountains. Give them this message: O mountains of Israel, hear the word of the LORD! 2This is what the Sovereign LORD says: Your enemies have taunted you, saying, 'Aha! Now the ancient heights belong to us!' 3Therefore, son of man, give the mountains of Israel this message from the Sovereign LORD: Your enemies have attacked you from all directions, and now you are possessed by many nations. You are the object of much mocking and slander. 4Therefore, O mountains of Israel, hear the word of the Sovereign LORD. He speaks to the hills and mountains, ravines and valleys, and to ruined wastes and long-deserted cities that have been destroyed and mocked by foreign nations everywhere.

⁵This is what the Sovereign LORD says: My jealous anger is on fire against these nations, especially Edom, because they have shown utter contempt for me by gleefully taking my land for themselves as plunder.

⁶"Therefore, prophesy to the hills and mountains, the ravines and valleys of Israel. Give them this message from the Sovereign LORD: I am full of fury because you have suffered shame before the surrounding nations. ⁷Therefore, says the Sovereign LORD, I have raised my hand and sworn an oath that those nations will soon have their turn at suffering shame. ⁸But the mountains of Israel will produce heavy crops of fruit to prepare for my people's return—and they will be coming home again soon! ⁹See, I am concerned for you, and I will come to help you. Your ground will be tilled and your crops planted. ¹⁰I will greatly increase the population of Israel, and the ruined cities will be rebuilt and filled with people. ¹¹Not only the people, but your flocks and herds will also greatly multiply. O mountains of Israel, I will bring people to live on you once again. I will make you even more prosperous than you were before. Then you will know that I am the LORD. ¹²I will cause my people to walk on you once again, and you will be their inheritance. You will never again devour their children.

¹³"This is what the Sovereign LORD says: Now the other nations taunt you, saying, 'Israel is a land that devours her own people!' ¹⁴But you will never again devour your people or bereave your nation, says the Sovereign LORD. ¹⁵I will not allow those foreign nations to sneer at you, and you will no longer be shamed by them or cause your nation to fall, says the Sovereign LORD."

¹⁶Then this further message came to me from the LORD: ¹⁷"Son of man, when the people of Israel were living in their own land, they defiled it by their evil deeds. To me their conduct was as filthy as a bloody rag. ¹⁸They polluted the land with murder and by worshiping idols, so I poured out my fury on them. ¹⁹I

scattered them to many lands to punish them for the evil way they had lived. ²⁰But when they were scattered among the nations, they brought dishonor to my holy name. For the nations said, 'These are the people of the LORD, and he couldn't keep them safe in his own land!' ²¹Then I was concerned for my holy name, which had been dishonored by my people throughout the world.

²²"Therefore, give the people of Israel this message from the Sovereign LORD: I am bringing you back again but not because you deserve it. I am doing it to protect my holy name, which you dishonored while you were scattered among the nations. ²³I will show how holy my great name is—the name you dishonored among the nations. And when I reveal my holiness through you before their very eyes, says the Sovereign LORD, then the nations will know that I am the LORD. ²⁴For I will gather you up from all the nations and bring you home again to your land.

²⁵"Then I will sprinkle clean water on you, and you will be clean. Your filth will be washed away, and you will no longer worship idols. ²⁶And I will give you a new heart with new and right desires, and I will put a new spirit in you. I will take out your stony heart of sin and give you a new, obedient heart.* ²⁷And I will put my Spirit in you so you will obey my laws and do whatever I command.

²⁸"And you will live in Israel, the land I gave your ancestors long ago. You will be my people, and I will be your God. ²⁹I will cleanse you of your filthy behavior. I will give you good crops, and I will abolish famine in the land. ³⁰I will give you great harvests from your fruit trees and fields, and never again will the surrounding nations be able to scoff at your land for its famines. ³¹Then you will remember your past sins and hate yourselves for all the evil things you did. ³²But remember, says the Sovereign LORD, I am not doing this because you deserve it. O my people of Israel, you should be utterly ashamed of all you have done!

36:26 Hebrew *a heart of flesh.*

My Daily Worship

— *August 5* —

MAKING REAL CHANGE

EZEKIEL 33:1–37:28

And I will give you a new heart with new and right desires, and I will put a new spirit in you.
I will take out your stony heart of sin and give you a new, obedient heart (36:26).

[i reflect]

Two high school seniors concocted a plan to cure themselves of using foul language. Each time one heard the other curse, he would deliver a swift, hard punch to the offender's arm. At the end of this week-long experiment, both boys sported bruised, aching biceps. And their speech was just as crude as ever.

Regarding the subject of how people change, Henry Drummond, author of *The Greatest Thing in the World,* observed: "Souls are not made sweet by taking [ill tempers] out, but by putting something in—a great Love, a new Spirit, the Spirit of Christ. Christ, the Spirit of Christ, interpenetrating ours, sweetens, purifies, transforms all. This only can eradicate what is wrong, renovate and regenerate, and rehabilitate the inner man. Will-power does not change men. Time does not change men. Christ does."

This is the message God proclaimed to the world through the prophet Ezekiel. Call it "new covenant" theology. Under the old covenant, God gave his people laws on tablets of stone. Under the new arrangement, God gives his children totally new hearts. The old system pressured people from without; the new system empowers Christians from within.

Formerly, people were motivated by a sense of duty and obligation (for example, "I ought to obey God.") Now, because of the indwelling Christ, Christians are motivated by joy and holy passion (for example, "I get to live for Christ!"). We live differently because we are different. In the words of the apostle Paul: "You must display a new nature because you are a new person" (Ephesians 4:24).

Stop trying to change yourself by your own power. It doesn't work. Instead, let Christ bring the deep, fundamental changes of the new birth to the surface of your life. Lean on him and yield your will to his. This is the essence of a life of true worship.

Today, offer to Christ as a sacrifice of worship an attitude or habit you want him to change.

[i pray]

A new heart, with new desires, . . . a heart that longs to know you and serve you.
This is my real identity. Oh God, let me live today out of my new, true heart.

[i respond]

Make a list of five, often-ignored, God-honoring desires that you sense deep in your soul. Share this list with an older wiser Christian. Pick one of these desires and ask God to help you make it a reality in your life.

³³"This is what the Sovereign LORD says: When I cleanse you from your sins, I will bring people to live in your cities, and the ruins will be rebuilt. ³⁴The fields that used to lie empty and desolate—a shock to all who passed by—will again be farmed. ³⁵And when I bring you back, people will say, 'This godforsaken land is now like Eden's garden! The ruined cities now have strong walls, and they are filled with people!' ³⁶Then the nations all around—all those still left—will know that I, the LORD, rebuilt the ruins and planted lush crops in the wilderness. For I, the LORD, have promised this, and I will do it.

³⁷"This is what the Sovereign LORD says: I am ready to hear Israel's prayers for these blessings, and I am ready to grant them their requests. ³⁸I will multiply them like the sacred flocks that fill Jerusalem's streets at the time of her festivals. The ruined cities will be crowded with people once more, and everyone will know that I am the LORD."

A VALLEY OF DRY BONES

37 The LORD took hold of me, and I was carried away by the Spirit of the LORD to a valley filled with bones. ²He led me around among the old, dry bones that covered the valley floor. They were scattered everywhere across the ground. ³Then he asked me, "Son of man, can these bones become living people again?"

"O Sovereign LORD," I replied, "you alone know the answer to that."

⁴Then he said to me, "Speak to these bones and say, 'Dry bones, listen to the word of the LORD! ⁵This is what the Sovereign LORD says: Look! I am going to breathe into you and make you live again! ⁶I will put flesh and muscles on you and cover you with skin. I will put breath into you, and you will come to life. Then you will know that I am the LORD.'"

⁷So I spoke these words, just as he told me. Suddenly as I spoke, there was a rattling noise all across the valley. The bones of each body

came together and attached themselves as they had been before. ⁸Then as I watched, muscles and flesh formed over the bones. Then skin formed to cover their bodies, but they still had no breath in them.

⁹Then he said to me, "Speak to the winds and say: 'This is what the Sovereign LORD says: Come, O breath, from the four winds! Breathe into these dead bodies so that they may live again.'"

¹⁰So I spoke as he commanded me, and the wind entered the bodies, and they began to breathe. They all came to life and stood up on their feet—a great army of them.

¹¹Then he said to me, "Son of man, these bones represent the people of Israel. They are saying, 'We have become old, dry bones—all hope is gone.' ¹²Now give them this message from the Sovereign LORD: O my people, I will open your graves of exile and cause you to rise again. Then I will bring you back to the land of Israel. ¹³When this happens, O my people, you will know that I am the LORD. ¹⁴I will put my Spirit in you, and you will live and return home to your own land. Then you will know that I am the LORD. You will see that I have done everything just as I promised. I, the LORD, have spoken!"

REUNION OF ISRAEL AND JUDAH

¹⁵Again a message came to me from the LORD: ¹⁶"Son of man, take a stick and carve on it these words: 'This stick represents Judah and its allied tribes.' Then take another stick and carve these words on it: 'This stick represents the northern tribes of Israel.'* ¹⁷Now hold them together in your hand as one stick. ¹⁸When your people ask you what your actions mean, ¹⁹say to them, 'This is what the Sovereign LORD says: I will take the northern tribes and join them to Judah. I will make them one stick in my hand.' ²⁰Then hold out the sticks you have inscribed, so the people can see them. ²¹And give them this message from the Sovereign LORD: I will gather the people of Israel from among the nations. I will

37:16 Hebrew *Ephraim's stick, representing Joseph and all the house of Israel.*

bring them home to their own land from the places where they have been scattered. ²²I will unify them into one nation in the land. One king will rule them all; no longer will they be divided into two nations. ²³They will stop polluting themselves with their detestable idols and other sins, for I will save them from their sinful backsliding. I will cleanse them. Then they will truly be my people, and I will be their God.

²⁴"My servant David will be their king, and they will have only one shepherd. They will obey my regulations and keep my laws. ²⁵They will live in the land of Israel where their ancestors lived, the land I gave my servant Jacob. They and their children and their grandchildren after them will live there forever, generation after generation. And my servant David will be their prince forever. ²⁶And I will make a covenant of peace with them, an everlasting covenant. I will give them their land and multiply them, and I will put my Temple among them forever. ²⁷I will make my home among them. I will be their God, and they will be my people. ²⁸And since my Temple will remain among them forever, the nations will know that I, the LORD, have set Israel apart for myself to be holy."

A MESSAGE FOR GOG

38 This is another message that came to me from the LORD: ²"Son of man, prophesy against Gog of the land of Magog, the prince who rules over the nations of Meshech and Tubal. ³Give him this message from the Sovereign LORD: Gog, I am your enemy! ⁴I will turn you around and put hooks into your jaws to lead you out to your destruction. I will mobilize your troops and cavalry and make you a vast and mighty horde, all fully armed. ⁵Persia, Ethiopia, and Libya* will join you, too, with all their weapons. ⁶Gomer and all its hordes will also join you, along with the armies of Beth-togarmah from the distant north and many others.

⁷"Get ready; be prepared! Keep all the armies around you mobilized, and take command of them. ⁸A long time from now you will be called into action. In the distant future you will swoop down on the land of Israel, which will be lying in peace after her recovery from war and after the return of her people from many lands. ⁹You and all your allies—a vast and awesome horde—will roll down on them like a storm and cover the land like a cloud.

¹⁰"This is what the Sovereign LORD says: At that time evil thoughts will come to your mind, and you will devise a wicked scheme. ¹¹You will say, 'Israel is an unprotected land filled with unwalled villages! I will march against her and destroy these people who live in such confidence! ¹²I will go to those once-desolate cities that are again filled with people who have returned from exile in many nations. I will capture vast amounts of plunder and take many slaves, for the people are rich with cattle now, and they think the whole world revolves around them!' ¹³But Sheba and Dedan and the merchants of Tarshish will ask, 'Who are you to rob them of silver and gold? Who are you to drive away their cattle and seize their goods and make them poor?'

¹⁴"Therefore, son of man, prophesy against Gog. Give him this message from the Sovereign LORD: When my people are living in peace in their land, then you will rouse yourself.* ¹⁵You will come from your homeland in the distant north with your vast cavalry and your mighty army, ¹⁶and you will cover the land like a cloud. This will happen in the distant future. I will bring you against my land as everyone watches, and my holiness will be displayed by what happens to you. Then all the nations will know that I am the LORD.

¹⁷"This is what the Sovereign LORD says: You are the one I was talking about long ago, when I announced through Israel's prophets that in future days I would bring you against my people. ¹⁸But when Gog invades the land of Israel, says the Sovereign LORD, my fury will rise!

38:5 Hebrew *Paras, Cush, and Put.* **38:14** As in Greek version; Hebrew reads *then you will know.*

¹⁹For in my jealousy and blazing anger, I promise a mighty shaking in the land of Israel on that day. ²⁰All living things—all the fish, birds, animals, and people—will quake in terror at my presence. Mountains will be thrown down; cliffs will crumble; walls will fall to the earth. ²¹I will summon the sword against you throughout Israel, says the Sovereign LORD. Your men will turn against each other in mortal combat. ²²I will punish you and your hordes with disease and bloodshed; I will send torrential rain, hailstones, fire, and burning sulfur! ²³Thus will I show my greatness and holiness, and I will make myself known to all the nations of the world. Then they will know that I am the LORD!

THE SLAUGHTER OF GOG'S ARMIES

39 "Son of man, prophesy against Gog. Give him this message from the Sovereign LORD: I am your enemy, O Gog, ruler of the nations of Meshech and Tubal. ²I will turn you and drive you toward the mountains of Israel, bringing you from the distant north. ³I will knock your weapons from your hands and leave you helpless. ⁴You and all your vast hordes will die on the mountains. I will give you as food to the vultures and wild animals. ⁵You will fall in the open fields, for I have spoken, says the Sovereign LORD. ⁶And I will rain down fire on Magog and on all your allies who live safely on the coasts. Then they will know that I am the LORD.

⁷"Thus, I will make known my holy name among my people of Israel. I will not let it be desecrated anymore. And the nations, too, will know that I am the LORD, the Holy One of Israel. ⁸That day of judgment will come, says the Sovereign LORD. Everything will happen just as I have declared it.

⁹"Then the people in the towns of Israel will go out and pick up your small and large shields, bows and arrows, javelins and spears, and they will use them for fuel. There will be enough to last them seven years! ¹⁰They will need nothing else for their fires. They won't need to cut wood from the fields or forests, for these weapons will give them all they need. They will take plunder from those who planned to plunder them, says the Sovereign LORD.

¹¹"And I will make a vast graveyard for Gog and his hordes in the Valley of the Travelers, east of the Dead Sea.* The path of those who travel there will be blocked by this burial ground, and they will change the name of the place to the Valley of Gog's Hordes. ¹²It will take seven months for the people of Israel to cleanse the land by burying the bodies. ¹³Everyone in Israel will help, for it will be a glorious victory for Israel when I demonstrate my glory on that day, says the Sovereign LORD. ¹⁴At the end of the seven months, special crews will be appointed to search the land for any skeletons and to bury them, so the land will be made clean again. ¹⁵Whenever some bones are found, a marker will be set up beside them so the burial crews will see them and take them to be buried in the Valley of Gog's Hordes. ¹⁶(There will be a town there named Hamonah—which means 'horde.') And so the land will finally be cleansed.

¹⁷"And now, son of man, call all the birds and wild animals, says the Sovereign LORD. Say to them: Gather together for my great sacrificial feast. Come from far and near to the mountains of Israel, and there eat the flesh and drink the blood! ¹⁸Eat the flesh of mighty men and drink the blood of princes as though they were rams, lambs, goats, and fat young bulls of Bashan! ¹⁹Gorge yourselves with flesh until you are glutted; drink blood until you are drunk. This is the sacrificial feast I have prepared for you. ²⁰Feast at my banquet table—feast on horses, riders, and valiant warriors, says the Sovereign LORD.

²¹"Thus, I will demonstrate my glory among the nations. Everyone will see the punishment I have inflicted on them and the power I have demonstrated. ²²And from that time on the

39:11 Hebrew *the sea.*

My Daily Worship

— *August 6* —

JEALOUS FOR HIS REPUTATION

EZEKIEL 38:1–42:20

So now the Sovereign LORD says: "I will end the captivity of my people; I will have mercy on Israel, for I am jealous for my holy reputation!" (39:25).

[i reflect]

In the modern classic, *Desiring God*, John Piper writes: "God's overwhelming passion is to exalt the value of his own glory. To that end he seeks to display it, to oppose those who belittle it, and to vindicate it from all contempt. It is clearly the uppermost reality in his affections. He loves his glory infinitely. A moment's reflection reveals the inexorable justice of this fact. God would be unrighteous (just as *we* would) if he valued anything more than what is supremely valuable. But he himself is supremely valuable."

This helps us understand why God announced through Ezekiel that he is "jealous for [his] holy reputation." God jealous? Worried about his reputation?

Understand that God is not needy or insecure. He is not like the corrupt third-world dictators of our time who demand allegiance using fear and intimidation and who plaster their pictures and monuments all over the countryside in the pathetic attempt to hang on to power. On the contrary, God says, "Worship me, make me the focus of your life because, quite simply, I deserve nothing less. I am the great treasure of the universe. To give your life to anything or anyone else would be illogical—and wrong."

All that God did in the time of Ezekiel, and all that he does now, is designed to show the world his greatness. And—here's the mind-boggling part—he calls us to embrace that same job description. *We* are to be jealous for God's glory. *We* are to pray continually that his name might be honored (Matthew 6:9). *We* are to conduct our lives in such a way that everything we do—every single thing—enhances God's holy reputation (1 Corinthians 10:31).

In other words, live today so that people shake their heads in wonder, lift their eyes to heaven, and say, "Wow. What an amazing God!"

[i pray]

Lord, be the great passion of my life. Make me jealous for your glory, and cause my life to spread your righteous reputation.

[i respond]

If you're really gutsy, ask two non-Christian friends or neighbors that you know well to tell you what they think about God just from watching your life.

people of Israel will know that I am the LORD their God. [23]The nations will then know why Israel was sent away to exile—it was punishment for sin, for they acted in treachery against their God. Therefore, I turned my back on them and let their enemies destroy them. [24]I turned my face away and punished them in proportion to the vileness of their sins.

RESTORATION FOR GOD'S PEOPLE

[25]"So now the Sovereign LORD says: I will end the captivity of my people*; I will have mercy on Israel, for I am jealous for my holy reputation! [26]They will accept responsibility for their past shame and treachery against me after they come home to live in peace and safety in their own land. And then no one will bother them or make them afraid. [27]When I bring them home from the lands of their enemies, my holiness will be displayed to the nations. [28]Then my people will know that I am the LORD their God—responsible for sending them away to exile and responsible for bringing them home. I will leave none of my people behind. [29]And I will never again turn my back on them, for I will pour out my Spirit upon them, says the Sovereign LORD."

THE NEW TEMPLE AREA

40 On April 28,* during the twenty-fifth year of our captivity—fourteen years after the fall of Jerusalem—the LORD took hold of me. [2]In a vision of God he took me to the land of Israel and set me down on a very high mountain. From there I could see what appeared to be a city across from me toward the south. [3]As he brought me nearer, I saw a man whose face shone like bronze standing beside a gateway entrance. He was holding in his hand a measuring tape and a measuring rod.

[4]He said to me, "Son of man, watch and listen. Pay close attention to everything I show you. You have been brought here so I can show you many things. Then you will return to the people of Israel and tell them everything you have seen."

THE EAST GATEWAY

[5]I could see a wall completely surrounding the Temple area. The man took a measuring rod that was 10½ feet* long and measured the wall, and the wall was 10½ feet thick and 10½ feet high.

[6]Then he went over to the gateway that goes through the eastern wall. He climbed the steps and measured the threshold of the gateway; it was 10½ feet deep.* [7]There were guard alcoves on each side built into the gateway passage. Each of these alcoves was 10½ feet square, with a distance between them of 8¾ feet along the passage wall. The gateway's inner threshold, which led to the foyer at the inner end of the gateway passage, was 10½ feet deep. [8]He also measured the foyer of the gateway* [9]and found it to be 14 feet deep, with supporting columns 3½ feet thick. This foyer was at the inner end of the gateway structure, facing toward the Temple.

[10]There were three guard alcoves on each side of the gateway passage. Each had the same measurements, and the dividing walls separating them were also identical. [11]The man measured the gateway entrance, which was 17½ feet wide at the opening and 22¾ feet wide in the gateway passage. [12]In front of each of the guard alcoves was a 21-inch curb. The alcoves themselves were 10½ feet square. [13]Then he measured the entire width of the gateway, measuring the distance between the back walls of facing guard alcoves; this distance was 43¾ feet. [14]He measured the dividing walls all along the inside of the gateway up

---

39:25 Hebrew of Jacob. 40:1 Hebrew At the beginning of the year, on the tenth day of the month, of the Hebrew calendar. A number of dates in Ezekiel can be cross-checked with dates in surviving Babylonian records and related accurately to our modern calendar. This event occurred on April 28, 573 B.C. 40:5 Hebrew 6 long cubits [3.2 meters], each being a cubit [18 inches or 45 centimeters] and a handbreadth [3 inches or 8 centimeters] in length. In this chapter, the distance measures are calculated using the Hebrew long cubit, which equals 21 inches or 53 centimeters. 40:6 Greek version; Hebrew reads one rod [10.5 feet or 3.2 meters] deep, and one threshold, one rod deep. 40:8 Many Hebrew manuscripts add which faced inward toward the Temple; it was one rod [10.5 feet or 3.2 meters] deep.
[9]Then he measured the foyer of the gateway, . . .

to the gateway's foyer; this distance was 105 feet.* [15]The full length of the gateway passage was 87½ feet from one end to the other. [16]There were recessed windows that narrowed inward through the walls of the guard alcoves and their dividing walls. There were also windows in the foyer structure. The surfaces of the dividing walls were decorated with carved palm trees.

THE OUTER COURTYARD

[17]Then the man brought me through the gateway into the outer courtyard of the Temple. A stone pavement ran along the walls of the courtyard, and thirty rooms were built against the walls, opening onto the pavement. [18]This pavement flanked the gates and extended out from the walls into the courtyard the same distance as the gateway entrance. This was the lower pavement. [19]Then the man measured across the Temple's outer courtyard between the outer and inner gateways; the distance was 175 feet.

THE NORTH GATEWAY

[20]There was a gateway on the north just like the one on the east, and the man measured it. [21]Here, too, there were three guard alcoves on each side, with dividing walls and a foyer. All the measurements matched those of the east gateway. The gateway passage was 87½ feet long and 43¾ feet wide between the back walls of facing guard alcoves. [22]The windows, the foyer, and the palm tree decorations were identical to those in the east gateway. There were seven steps leading up to the gateway entrance, and the foyer was at the inner end of the gateway passage. [23]Here on the north side, just as on the east, there was another gateway leading to the Temple's inner courtyard directly opposite this outer gateway. The distance between the two gateways was 175 feet.

THE SOUTH GATEWAY

[24]Then the man took me around to the south gateway and measured its various parts, and

he found they were exactly the same as in the others. [25]It had windows along the walls as the others did, and there was a foyer where the gateway passage opened into the outer courtyard. And like the others, the gateway passage was 87½ feet long and 43¾ feet wide between the back walls of facing guard alcoves. [26]This gateway also had a stairway of seven steps leading up to it, and there were palm tree decorations along the dividing walls. [27]And here again, directly opposite the outer gateway, was another gateway that led into the inner courtyard. The distance between the two gateways was 175 feet.

GATEWAYS TO THE INNER COURTYARD

[28]Then the man took me to the south gateway leading into the inner courtyard. He measured it and found that it had the same measurements as the other gateways. [29]Its guard alcoves, dividing walls, and foyer were the same size as those in the others. It also had windows along its walls and in the foyer structure. And like the others, the gateway passage was 87½ feet long and 43¾ feet wide. [30](The foyers of the gateways leading into the inner courtyard were 8¾ feet deep and 43¾ feet wide.) [31]The foyer of the south gateway faced into the outer courtyard. It had palm tree decorations on its columns, and there were eight steps leading to its entrance.

[32]Then he took me to the east gateway leading to the inner courtyard. He measured it and found that it had the same measurements as the other gateways. [33]Its guard alcoves, dividing walls, and foyer were the same size as those of the others, and there were windows along the walls and in the foyer structure. The gateway passage measured 87½ feet long and 43¾ feet wide. [34]Its foyer faced into the outer courtyard. It had palm tree decorations on its columns, and there were eight steps leading to its entrance.

[35]Then he took me around to the north gateway leading to the inner courtyard. He

measured it and found that it had the same measurements as the other gateways. ³⁶The guard alcoves, dividing walls, and foyer of this gateway had the same measurements as in the others and the same window arrangements. The gateway passage measured 87½ feet long and 43¾ feet wide. ³⁷Its foyer faced into the outer courtyard, and it had palm tree decorations on the columns. There were eight steps leading to its entrance.

ROOMS FOR PREPARING SACRIFICES

³⁸A door led from the foyer of the inner gateway on the north side into a side room where the meat for sacrifices was washed before being taken to the altar. ³⁹On each side of this foyer were two tables, where the sacrificial animals were slaughtered for the burnt offerings, sin offerings, and guilt offerings. ⁴⁰Outside the foyer, on each side of the stairs going up to the north entrance, there were two more tables. ⁴¹So there were eight tables in all, four inside and four outside, where the sacrifices were cut up and prepared. ⁴²There were also four tables of hewn stone for preparation of the burnt offerings, each 31½ inches square and 21 inches high. On these tables were placed the butchering knives and other implements and the sacrificial animals. ⁴³There were hooks, each three inches* long, fastened to the foyer walls and set on the tables where the sacrificial meat was to be laid.

ROOMS FOR THE PRIESTS

⁴⁴Inside the inner courtyard there were two one-room buildings for the singers, one beside the north gateway, facing south, and the other beside the south* gateway, facing north. ⁴⁵And the man said to me, "The building beside the north inner gate is for the priests who supervise the Temple maintenance. ⁴⁶The building beside the south inner gate is for the priests in charge of the altar—the descendants of Zadok—for they alone of all the Levites may approach the LORD to minister to him."

THE INNER COURTYARD AND TEMPLE

⁴⁷Then the man measured the inner courtyard and found it to be 175 feet square. The altar stood there in the courtyard in front of the Temple. ⁴⁸Then he brought me to the foyer of the Temple. He measured its supporting columns and found them to be 8¾ feet square. The entrance was 24½ feet wide with walls 5¼ feet thick. ⁴⁹The depth of the foyer was 35 feet and the width was 19¼ feet. There were ten steps leading up to it, with a column on each side.

41 After that, the man brought me into the Holy Place, the large main room of the Temple, and he measured the columns that framed its doorway. They were 10½ feet* square. ²The entrance was 17½ feet wide, and the walls on each side were 8¾ feet wide. The Holy Place itself was 70 feet long and 35 feet wide.

³Then he went into the inner room at the end of the Holy Place. He measured the columns at the entrance and found them to be 3½ feet thick. The entrance was 10½ feet wide, and the walls on each side of the entrance extended 12¼ feet to the corners of the inner room. ⁴The inner room was 35 feet square. "This," he told me, "is the Most Holy Place."

⁵Then he measured the wall of the Temple and found that it was 10½ feet thick. There was a row of rooms along the outside wall; each room was 7 feet wide. ⁶These rooms were built in three levels, one above the other, with thirty rooms on each level. The supports for these rooms rested on ledges in the Temple wall, but the supports did not extend into the wall. ⁷Each level was wider than the one below it, corresponding to the narrowing of the Temple wall as it rose higher. A stairway led up

40:43 Hebrew a handbreadth [8 centimeters]. 40:44 As in Greek version; Hebrew reads east. 41:1 Hebrew 6 cubits [3.2 meters]. In this chapter, the distance measures are calculated using the Hebrew long cubit, which equals 21 inches or 53 centimeters.

bim, each with two faces, and there was a palm tree carving between each of the cherubim. ¹⁹One face—that of a man—looked toward the palm tree on one side. The other face—that of a young lion—looked toward the palm tree on the other side. The figures were carved all along the inside of the Temple, ²⁰from the floor to the top of the walls, including the outer wall of the Holy Place.

²¹There were square columns at the entrance to the Holy Place, and the ones at the entrance of the Most Holy Place were similar. ²²There was an altar made of wood, 3½ feet square and 5¼ feet high. Its corners, base, and sides were all made of wood. "This," the man told me, "is the table that stands in the LORD's presence."

²³Both the Holy Place and the Most Holy Place had double doorways, ²⁴each with two swinging doors. ²⁵The doors leading into the Holy Place were decorated with carved cherubim and palm trees just as on the walls. And there was a wooden canopy over the front of the Temple's foyer. ²⁶On both sides of the foyer there were recessed windows decorated with carved palm trees.

ROOMS FOR THE PRIESTS

42 Then the man led me out of the Temple courtyard by way of the north gateway. We entered the outer courtyard and came to a group of rooms against the north wall of the inner courtyard. ²This group of structures, whose entrance opened toward the north, was 175 feet long and 87½ feet wide.* ³One block of rooms overlooked the 35-foot width of the inner courtyard. Another block of rooms looked out onto the pavement of the outer courtyard. The two blocks were built three levels high and stood across from each other. ⁴Between the two blocks of rooms ran a walkway 17½ feet wide. It extended the entire 175 feet of the complex, and all the doors faced toward the north. ⁵Each of the two upper levels of rooms was narrower than the

from the bottom level through the middle level to the top level.

⁸I noticed that the Temple was built on a terrace, which provided a foundation for the side rooms. This terrace was 10½ feet high. ⁹The outer wall of the Temple's side rooms was 8¾ feet thick. This left an open area between these side rooms ¹⁰and the row of rooms along the outer wall of the inner courtyard. This open area measured 35 feet in width, and it went all the way around the Temple. ¹¹Two doors opened from the side rooms into the terrace yard, which was 8¾ feet wide. One door faced north and the other south.

¹²A large building stood on the west, facing the Temple courtyard. It was 122½ feet wide and 157½ feet long, and its walls were 8¾ feet thick. ¹³Then the man measured the Temple, and he found it to be 175 feet long. The courtyard around the building, including its walls, was an additional 175 feet in length. ¹⁴The inner courtyard to the east of the Temple was also 175 feet wide. ¹⁵The building to the west, including its two walls, was also 175 feet wide.

The Holy Place, the Most Holy Place, and the foyer of the Temple were all paneled with wood, ¹⁶as were the frames of the recessed windows. The inner walls of the Temple were paneled with wood above and below the windows. ¹⁷The space above the door leading into the Most Holy Place was also paneled. ¹⁸All the walls were decorated with carvings of cheru-

We are never nearer Christ than when we find ourselves lost in a holy amazement at His unspeakable love.

JOHN OWEN

42:2 Hebrew *100 cubits* [53 meters] *long and 50 cubits* [26.5 meters] *wide.* In this chapter, the distance measures are calculated using the Hebrew long cubit, which equals 21 inches or 53 centimeters.

one beneath it because the upper levels had to allow space for walkways in front of them. ⁶Since there were three levels and they did not have supporting columns as in the courtyards, each of the upper levels was set back from the level beneath it. ⁷There was an outer wall that separated the rooms from the outer courtyard; it was 87½ feet long. ⁸This wall added length to the outer block of rooms, which extended for only 87½ feet, while the inner block—the rooms toward the Temple—extended for 175 feet. ⁹There was an entrance from the outer courtyard to these rooms from the east.

¹⁰On the south* side of the Temple there were two blocks of rooms just south of the inner courtyard between the Temple and the outer courtyard. These rooms were arranged just like the rooms on the north. ¹¹There was a walkway between the two blocks of rooms just like the complex on the north side of the Temple. This complex of rooms was the same length and width as the other one, and it had the same entrances and doors. The dimensions of each were identical. ¹²So there was an entrance in the wall facing the doors of the inner block of rooms, and another on the east at the end of the interior walkway.

¹³Then the man told me, "These rooms that overlook the Temple from the north and south are holy. It is there that the priests who offer sacrifices to the LORD will eat the most holy offerings. And they will use these rooms to store the grain offerings, sin offerings, and guilt offerings because these rooms are holy. ¹⁴When the priests leave the Holy Place, they must not go directly to the outer courtyard. They must first take off the clothes they wore while ministering because these clothes are holy. They must put on other clothes before entering the parts of the building complex open to the public."

¹⁵When the man had finished taking these measurements, he led me out through the east gateway to measure the entire Temple area. ¹⁶He measured the east side; it was 875 feet long. ¹⁷He also measured the north side and got the same measurement. ¹⁸The south side was the same length, ¹⁹and so was the west side. ²⁰So the area was 875 feet on each side with a wall all around it to separate the holy places from the common.

THE LORD'S GLORY RETURNS

43 After this, the man brought me back around to the east gateway. ²Suddenly, the glory of the God of Israel appeared from the east. The sound of his coming was like the roar of rushing waters, and the whole landscape shone with his glory. ³This vision was just like the others I had seen, first by the Kebar River and then when he came to destroy Jerusalem. And I fell down before him with my face in the dust. ⁴And the glory of the LORD came into the Temple through the east gateway.

⁵Then the Spirit took me up and brought me into the inner courtyard, and the glory of the LORD filled the Temple. ⁶And I heard someone speaking to me from within the Temple. (The man who had been measuring was still standing beside me.) ⁷And the LORD said to me, "Son of man, this is the place of my throne and the place where I will rest my feet. I will remain here forever, living among the people of Israel. They and their kings will not defile my holy name any longer by their adulterous worship of other gods or by raising monuments in honor of their dead kings.* ⁸They put their idol altars right next to mine with only a wall between them and me. They defiled my holy name by such wickedness, so I consumed them in my anger. ⁹Now let them put away their idols and the sacred pillars erected to honor their kings, and I will live among them forever.

¹⁰"Son of man, describe to the people of Israel the Temple I have shown you. Tell them its appearance and its plan so they will be ashamed of all their sins. ¹¹And if they are ashamed of what they have done, describe to

42:10 As in Greek version; Hebrew reads *east*.   43:7 Or *by raising pillars on their high places.*

My Daily Worship

— *August 7* —

HEAVINESS AND LIGHT

E Z E K I E L   43:1–48:35

Then the Spirit took me up and brought me into the inner courtyard,
and the glory of the LORD filled the Temple (43:5).

[i reflect]

The great hymn "Immortal, Invisible" concludes with this verse:

"Great Father of glory, pure Father of light,
Thine angels adore Thee, all veiling their sight;
All praise we would render; O help us to see
'Tis only the splendor of light hideth Thee!"

Purity. Light. Brightness. Splendor—all to an infinite degree. This was Ezekiel's experience as, in a wild vision, he watched the glory of God fill the Temple.

The Hebrew word translated *glory* refers literally to the heaviness or worth of something. The idea is brilliance and greatness, beauty and perfection. In the days of Moses, the glory of God took the form of an immense cloud or a bright pillar of fire. In John's visions in Revelation, the glory of God is accompanied by smoke, and it causes a sparkling effect. It is brighter than the sun itself. Because it is always such an awesome thing, people hide their eyes in holy fear when confronted with the unveiled glory of God. They typically hug the ground, flattened by the breath-taking weight of his majesty.

There is a great scene in the Gospel of John, an often overlooked moment near the end of Christ's life, where we witness this phenomenon of awe in God's presence. It happened when the mob arrives to arrest Jesus.

Stepping forward to meet them, he asked, "Whom are you looking for?" "Jesus of
Nazareth," they replied. "I am he," Jesus said. Judas was standing there with
them when Jesus identified himself. And as he said, "I am he," they all fell back-
ward to the ground! (John 18:4–6)

Each day you are surrounded by the glory of God. And even harder to comprehend, you are indwelled by this same God of glory. Yes, you are his modern-day temple! The only question is, Will you have eyes to see? Will you make yourself a fit habitation for him? And will you respond in reverence and worship? Let each church building you pass today serve as a reminder of God's glory indwelling you.

[i pray]

Fill me, O God with your glory. Open my eyes. Awe me with your beauty and majesty.
I want to go about my day caught up in wonder and worship.

[i respond]

If you do not usually bow down when you pray and worship, do so today. Spend some time on your face before God in reverence and holy fear.

them all the specifications of its construction—including its entrances and doors—and everything else about it. Write down all these specifications and directions as they watch so they will be sure to remember them. ¹²And this is the basic law of the Temple: absolute holiness! The entire top of the hill where the Temple is built is holy. Yes, this is the primary law of the Temple.

THE ALTAR

¹³"These are the measurements of the altar*: There is a gutter all around the altar 21 inches wide and 21 inches deep, with a curb 9 inches* wide around its edge. And this is the height of the altar: ¹⁴From the gutter the altar rises 3½ feet to a ledge that surrounds the altar; this lower ledge is 21 inches wide. From the lower ledge the altar rises 7 feet to the upper ledge; this upper ledge is also 21 inches wide. ¹⁵The top of the altar, the hearth, rises still 7 feet higher, with a horn rising up from each of the four corners. ¹⁶The top of the altar is square, measuring 21 feet by 21 feet. ¹⁷The upper ledge also forms a square, measuring 24½ feet on each side, with a 21-inch gutter and a 10½-inch curb all around the edge. There are steps going up the east side of the altar."

¹⁸Then he said to me, "Son of man, this is what the Sovereign LORD says: These will be the regulations for the burning of offerings and the sprinkling of blood when the altar is built. ¹⁹At that time, the Levitical priests of the family of Zadok, who minister before me, are to be given a young bull for a sin offering, says the Sovereign LORD. ²⁰You will take some of its blood and smear it on the four horns of the altar, the four corners of the upper ledge, and the curb that runs around that ledge. This will cleanse and make atonement for the altar. ²¹Then take the young bull for the sin offering and burn it at the appointed place outside the Temple area.

²²"On the second day, sacrifice as a sin offering a young male goat that has no physical defects. Then cleanse and make atonement for the altar again, just as you did with the young bull. ²³When you have finished the cleansing ceremony, offer another young bull that has no defects and a perfect ram from the flock. ²⁴You are to present them to the LORD, and the priests are to sprinkle salt on them and offer them as a burnt offering to the LORD.

²⁵"Every day for seven days a male goat, a young bull, and a ram from the flock will be sacrificed as a sin offering. None of these animals may have physical defects of any kind. ²⁶Do this each day for seven days to cleanse and make atonement for the altar, thus setting it apart for holy use. ²⁷On the eighth day, and on each day afterward, the priests will sacrifice on the altar the burnt offerings and peace offerings of the people. Then I will accept you, says the Sovereign LORD."

THE PRINCE, LEVITES, AND PRIESTS

44 Then the man brought me back to the east gateway in the outer wall, but it was closed. ²And the LORD said to me, "This gate must remain closed; it will never again be opened. No man will ever pass through it, for the LORD, the God of Israel, entered here. Thus, it must always remain shut. ³Only the prince himself may sit inside this gateway to feast in the LORD's presence. But he may come and go only through the gateway's foyer."

⁴Then the man brought me through the north gateway to the front of the Temple. I looked and saw that the glory of the LORD filled the Temple of the LORD, and I fell to the ground with my face in the dust.

⁵And the LORD said to me, "Son of man, take careful notice; use eyes and ears. Listen to everything I tell you about the regulations concerning the LORD's Temple. Take careful note of who may be admitted to the Temple

43:13a Hebrew *measurements of the altar in long cubits, each being a cubit* [18 inches or 45 centimeters] *and a handbreadth* [3 inches or 8 centimeters] *in length.* In this chapter, the distance measures are calculated using the Hebrew long cubit, which equals 21 inches or 53 centimeters. 43:13b Hebrew *1 span* [23 centimeters].

and who is to be excluded from it. ⁶And give these rebels, the people of Israel, this message from the Sovereign LORD: O people of Israel, enough of your disgusting sins! ⁷You have brought uncircumcised foreigners into my sanctuary—people who have no heart for God. In this way, you profaned my Temple even as you offered me my food, the fat and blood of sacrifices. Thus, in addition to all your other disgusting sins, you have broken my covenant. ⁸You have not kept the laws I gave you concerning these sacred rituals, for you have hired foreigners to take charge of my sanctuary.

⁹"So this is what the Sovereign LORD says: No foreigners, including those who live among the people of Israel, will enter my sanctuary if they have not been circumcised and do not love the LORD. ¹⁰And the men of the tribe of Levi who abandoned me when Israel strayed away from me to worship idols must bear the consequences of their unfaithfulness. ¹¹They may still be Temple guards and gatemen, and they may still slaughter the animals brought for burnt offerings and be present to help the people. ¹²But they encouraged my people to worship other gods, causing Israel to fall into deep sin. So I have raised my hand and taken an oath that they must bear the consequences for their sins, says the Sovereign LORD. ¹³They may not approach me to minister as priests. They may not touch any of my holy things or the holy offerings, for they must bear the shame of all the sins they have committed. ¹⁴They are to serve as the Temple caretakers and are relegated to doing maintenance work and helping the people in a general way.

¹⁵"However, the Levitical priests of the family of Zadok continued to minister faithfully in the Temple when Israel abandoned me for idols. These men will serve as my ministers. They will stand in my presence and offer the fat and blood of the sacrifices, says the Sovereign LORD. ¹⁶They are the ones who will enter my sanctuary and approach my table to serve me. They are the ones who will fulfill all my requirements. ¹⁷When they enter the gateway to the inner courtyard, they must wear only linen clothing. They must wear no wool while on duty in the inner courtyard or in the Temple itself. ¹⁸They must wear linen turbans and linen undergarments. They must not wear anything that would cause them to perspire. ¹⁹When they return to the outer courtyard where the people are, they must take off the clothes they wear while ministering to me. They must leave them in the sacred rooms and put on other clothes so they do not harm the people by transmitting holiness to them through this clothing.

²⁰"They must neither let their hair grow too long nor shave it off completely. Instead, they must trim it regularly. ²¹The priests must never drink wine before entering the inner courtyard. ²²They may choose their wives only from among the virgins of Israel or the widows of the priests. They may not marry other widows or divorced women. ²³They will teach my people the difference between what is holy and what is common, what is ceremonially clean and unclean.

²⁴"They will serve as judges to resolve any disagreements among my people. Their decisions must be based on my regulations. And the priests themselves must obey my instructions and laws at all the sacred festivals, and they will see to it that the Sabbath is set apart as a holy day. ²⁵A priest must never defile himself by being in the presence of a dead person unless it is his father, mother, child, brother, or unmarried sister. In such cases it is permitted. ²⁶But such a priest can only return to his Temple duties after being ritually cleansed and then waiting for seven days. ²⁷The first day he returns to work and enters the inner courtyard and the sanctuary, he must offer a sin offering for himself, says the Sovereign LORD.

²⁸"As to property, the priests will not have any, for I alone am their inheritance. ²⁹Their food will come from the gifts and sacrifices brought to the Temple by the people—the grain offerings, the sin offerings, and the guilt

offerings. Whatever anyone sets apart* for the LORD will belong to the priests. ³⁰The first of the ripe fruits and all the gifts brought to the LORD will go to the priests. The first samples of each grain harvest and the first of your flour must also be given to the priests so the LORD will bless your homes. ³¹The priests may never eat meat from any bird or animal that dies a natural death or that dies after being attacked by another animal.

DIVISION OF THE LAND

45 "When you divide the land among the tribes of Israel, you must set aside a section of it for the LORD as his holy portion. This piece of land will be 8⅓ miles long and 6⅔ miles wide.* The entire area will be holy ground. ²A section of this land, measuring 875 feet by 875 feet, will be set aside for the Temple. An additional strip of land 87½ feet wide is to be left empty all around it. ³Within the larger sacred area, measure out a portion of land 8⅓ miles long and 3⅓ miles wide. Within it the sanctuary of the Most Holy Place will be located. ⁴This area will be a holy land, set aside for the priests who minister to the LORD in the sanctuary. They will use it for their homes, and my Temple will be located within it. ⁵The strip of sacred land next to it, also 8⅓ miles long and 3⅓ miles wide, will be a living area for the Levites who work at the Temple. It will be their possession and a place for their towns.*

⁶"Adjacent to the larger sacred area will be a section of land 8⅓ miles long and 1⅔ miles wide. This will be set aside to be a city where anyone in Israel can come and live.

⁷"Two special sections of land will be set apart for the prince. One section will share a border with the east side of the sacred lands and city, and the second section will share a border on the west side. Then the far eastern and western borders of the prince's lands will line up with the eastern and western boundaries of the tribal areas. ⁸These sections of land will be the prince's allotment.

RULES FOR THE PRINCE

"My princes will no longer oppress and rob my people; they will assign the rest of the land to the people, giving an allotment to each tribe. ⁹For this is what the Sovereign LORD says: Enough, you princes of Israel! Stop all your violence and oppression and do what is just and right. Quit robbing and cheating my people out of their land! Stop expelling them from their homes! ¹⁰You must use only honest weights and scales, honest dry volume measures, and honest liquid volume measures.* ¹¹The homer* will be your standard unit for measuring volume. The ephah and the bath* will each measure one-tenth of a homer. ¹²The standard unit for weight will be the silver shekel.* One shekel consists of twenty gerahs, and sixty shekels are equal to one mina.*

SPECIAL OFFERINGS AND CELEBRATIONS

¹³"This is the tax you must give to the prince: one bushel of wheat or barley for every sixty* you harvest, ¹⁴one percent of your olive oil,* ¹⁵and one sheep for every two hundred in your flocks in Israel. These will be the grain offerings, burnt offerings, and peace offerings that will make atonement for the people who bring them, says the Sovereign LORD. ¹⁶All the people of Israel must join the prince in bringing their offerings. ¹⁷The prince will be required to provide offerings that are given at the religious festivals, the new moon celebra-

---

44:29 The Hebrew term used here refers to the complete consecration of things or people to the LORD, either by destroying them or by giving them as an offering. 45:1 Reflecting the Greek reading *25,000 cubits* [13.3 kilometers] *long and 20,000 cubits* [10.6 kilometers] *wide;* Hebrew reads *25,000 cubits long and 10,000 cubits wide.* Compare 45:3, 5; 48:9. In this chapter, the distance measures are calculated using the Hebrew long cubit, which equals 21 inches or 53 centimeters. 45:5 As in Greek version; Hebrew reads *They will have as their possession 20 rooms.* 45:10 Hebrew *use honest scales, an honest ephah, and an honest bath.* 45:11a The *homer* measures about 40 gallons or 182 liters. 45:11b The *ephah* is a dry measure; the *bath* is a liquid measure. 45:12a The shekel weighs about 0.4 ounces or 11 grams. 45:12b Elsewhere the mina is equated to 50 shekels. 45:13 Hebrew *⅙ of an ephah from each homer of wheat . . . and of barley.* 45:14 Hebrew *the portion of oil, measured by the bath, is ¹⁄₁₀ of a bath from each cor, which consists of 10 baths or 1 homer, for 10 baths are equivalent to a homer.*

tions, the Sabbath days, and all other similar occasions. He will provide the sin offerings, burnt offerings, grain offerings, drink offerings, and peace offerings to make reconciliation for the people of Israel.

¹⁸"This is what the Sovereign LORD says: In early spring, on the first day of each new year,* sacrifice a young bull with no physical defects to purify the Temple. ¹⁹The priest will take some of the blood of this sin offering and put it on the doorposts of the Temple, the four corners of the upper ledge on the altar, and the gateposts at the entrance to the inner courtyard. ²⁰Do this also on the seventh day of the new year for anyone who has sinned through error or ignorance. In that way, you will make atonement for the Temple.

²¹"On the fourteenth day of the new year, you must celebrate the Passover. This festival will last for seven days. Only bread without yeast may be eaten during that time. ²²On the day of Passover the prince will provide a young bull as a sin offering for himself and the people of Israel. ²³On each of the seven days of the feast he will prepare a burnt offering to the LORD. This daily offering will consist of seven young bulls and seven rams without any defects. A male goat will also be given each day for a sin offering. ²⁴The prince will provide a half bushel of flour as a grain offering and a gallon of olive oil* with each young bull and ram.

²⁵"During the seven days of the Festival of Shelters, which occurs every year in early autumn,* the prince will provide these same sacrifices for the sin offering, the burnt offering, and the grain offering, along with the required olive oil.

46 "This is what the Sovereign LORD says: The east gateway of the inner wall will be closed during the six workdays each week, but it will be open on Sabbath days and the days of new moon celebrations. ²The prince will enter the foyer of the gateway from the outside. Then he will stand by the gatepost while the priest offers his burnt offering and peace offering. He will worship inside the gateway passage and then go back out the way he came. The gateway will not be closed until evening. ³The common people will worship the LORD in front of this gateway on Sabbath days and the days of new moon celebrations.

⁴"Each Sabbath day the prince will present to the LORD a burnt offering of six lambs and one ram, all with no physical defects. ⁵He will present a grain offering of a half bushel of

45:18 Hebrew *On the first day of the first month,* of the Hebrew calendar. This day of the Hebrew lunar calendar occurs in late March or early April. 45:24 Hebrew *an ephah* [18 liters] *of flour . . . a hin* [3.8 liters] *of olive oil.* 45:25 Hebrew *the festival which begins on the fifteenth day of the seventh month* (see Lev 23:33). This day of the Hebrew lunar calendar occurs in late September or October.

flour to go with the ram and whatever amount of flour he chooses to go with each lamb. He is to offer one gallon of olive oil* for each half bushel of flour. ⁶At the new moon celebrations, he will bring one young bull, six lambs, and one ram, all with no physical defects. ⁷With the young bull he must bring a half bushel of flour for a grain offering. With the ram he must bring another half bushel of flour. And with each lamb he is to bring whatever amount of flour that he decides to give. With each half bushel of flour he must offer one gallon of olive oil.

⁸"The prince must enter the gateway through the foyer, and he must leave the same way he came. ⁹But when the people come in through the north gateway to worship the LORD during the religious festivals, they must leave by the south gateway. And those who entered through the south gateway must leave by the north gateway. They must never leave by the same gateway they came in; they must always use the opposite gateway. ¹⁰The prince will enter and leave with the people on these occasions.

¹¹"So at the special feasts and sacred festivals, the grain offering will be a half bushel of flour with each young bull, another half bushel of flour with each ram, and as much flour as the prince chooses to give with each lamb. One gallon of oil is to be given with each half bushel of flour. ¹²Whenever the prince offers a voluntary burnt offering or peace offering to the LORD, the east gateway to the inner courtyard will be opened for him to enter, and he will offer his sacrifices just as he does on Sabbath days. Then he will turn and leave the way he entered, and the gateway will be shut behind him.

¹³"Each morning a year-old lamb with no physical defects must be sacrificed as a burnt offering to the LORD. ¹⁴With the lamb, a grain offering must also be given to the LORD— about two and a half quarts of flour with a third of a gallon of olive oil* to moisten the flour. This will be a permanent law for you. ¹⁵The lamb, the grain offering, and the olive oil must be given as a daily sacrifice every morning without fail.

¹⁶"This is what the Sovereign LORD says: If the prince gives a gift of land to one of his sons, it will belong to him and his descendants forever. ¹⁷But if he gives a gift of land to one of his servants, the servant may keep it only until the Year of Jubilee, which comes every fiftieth year.* At that time the servant will be set free, and the land will return to the prince. Only the gifts given to the prince's sons will be permanent. ¹⁸And the prince may never take anyone's property by force. If he gives property to his sons, it must be from his own land, for I do not want any of my people unjustly evicted from their property."

THE TEMPLE KITCHENS

¹⁹Then the man brought me through the entrance beside the gateway and led me to the sacred rooms assigned to the priests, which faced toward the north. He showed me a place at the extreme west end of these rooms. ²⁰He explained, "This is where the priests will cook the meat from the guilt offerings and sin offerings and bake the flour from the grain offerings into bread. They will do it here to avoid carrying the sacrifices through the outer courtyard and harming the people by transmitting holiness to them."

²¹Then he brought me back to the outer courtyard and led me to each of its four corners. In each corner I saw an enclosure. ²²Each of these enclosures was 70 feet long and 52½ feet wide,* surrounded by walls. ²³Along the inside of these walls was a ledge of stone with fireplaces under the ledge all the way around. ²⁴The man said to me, "These are the kitchens to be used by the Temple assistants to boil the sacrifices offered by the people."

46:5 Hebrew *an ephah* [18 liters] *of flour . . . a hin* [3.8 liters] *of olive oil;* also in 46:7, 11.   46:14 Hebrew *⅙ of an ephah* [2.9 liters] *of flour with ⅓ of a hin* [1.3 liters] *of olive oil.*   46:17 Hebrew *until the Year of Release;* see Lev 25:8-17.   46:22 Hebrew *40 cubits* [21.2 meters] *long and 30 cubits* [15.9 meters] *wide.* The distances are calculated using the Hebrew long cubit, which equals 21 inches or 53 centimeters.

THE RIVER OF HEALING

47 Then the man brought me back to the entrance of the Temple. There I saw a stream flowing eastward from beneath the Temple threshold. This stream then passed to the right of the altar on its south side. ²The man brought me outside the wall through the north gateway and led me around to the eastern entrance. There I could see the stream flowing out through the south side of the east gateway. ³Measuring as he went, he led me along the stream for 1,750 feet* and told me to go across. At that point the water was up to my ankles. ⁴He measured off another 1,750 feet and told me to go across again. This time the water was up to my knees. After another 1,750 feet, it was up to my waist. ⁵Then he measured another 1,750 feet, and the river was too deep to cross without swimming.

⁶He told me to keep in mind what I had seen; then he led me back along the riverbank. ⁷Suddenly, to my surprise, many trees were now growing on both sides of the river! ⁸Then he said to me, "This river flows east through the desert into the Jordan Valley,* where it enters the Dead Sea.* The waters of this stream will heal the salty waters of the Dead Sea and make them fresh and pure. ⁹Everything that touches the water of this river will live. Fish will abound in the Dead Sea, for its waters will be healed. Wherever this water flows, everything will live. ¹⁰Fishermen will stand along the shores of the Dead Sea, fishing all the way from En-gedi to En-eglaim. The shores will be covered with nets drying in the sun. Fish of every kind will fill the Dead Sea, just as they fill the Mediterranean*! ¹¹But the marshes and swamps will not be purified; they will be sources of salt. ¹²All kinds of fruit trees will grow along both sides of the river. The leaves of these trees will never turn brown and fall, and there will always be fruit on their branches. There will be a new crop every month, without fail! For they are watered by the river flowing from the Temple. The fruit will be for food and the leaves for healing."

BOUNDARIES FOR THE LAND

¹³This is what the Sovereign LORD says: "Follow these instructions for dividing the land for the twelve tribes of Israel: The tribe of Joseph will be given two shares of land.* ¹⁴Otherwise each tribe will receive an equal share. I swore that I would give this land to your ancestors, and it will now come to you as your inheritance.

¹⁵"The northern border will run from the Mediterranean toward Hethlon, then on through Lebo-hamath to Zedad; ¹⁶then it will run to Berothah and Sibraim, which are on the border between Damascus and Hamath, and finally to Hazer-hatticon, on the border of Hauran. ¹⁷So the northern border will run from the Mediterranean to Hazar-enan, on the border between Hamath to the north and Damascus to the south.

¹⁸"The eastern border starts at a point between Hauran and Damascus and runs southward along the Jordan River between Israel and Gilead, past the Dead Sea* and as far south as Tamar.* This will be the eastern border.

¹⁹"The southern border will go west from Tamar to the waters of Meribah at Kadesh* and then follow the course of the brook of Egypt to the Mediterranean. This will be the southern border.

²⁰"On the west side the Mediterranean itself will be your border from the southern border to the point where the northern border begins, opposite Lebo-hamath.

²¹"Divide the land within these boundaries among the tribes of Israel. ²²Distribute the land as an inheritance for yourselves and for

---

47:3 Hebrew *1,000 cubits* [530 meters]; also in 47:4, 5. The distances are calculated using the Hebrew long cubit, which equals 21 inches or 53 centimeters.   47:8a Hebrew *the Arabah.*   47:8b Hebrew *the sea;* also in 47:10.   47:10 Hebrew *the great sea;* also in 47:15, 17, 19, 20.   47:13 A share of land for each of Joseph's two oldest sons, Ephraim and Manasseh.   47:18a Hebrew *the eastern sea.*   47:18b As in Greek version; Hebrew reads *you will measure.*   47:19 Hebrew *waters of Meribath-kadesh.*

the foreigners who have joined you and are raising their families among you. They will be just like native-born Israelites to you, and they will receive an inheritance among the tribes. [23]All these immigrants are to be given land within the territory of the tribe with whom they now live. I, the Sovereign LORD, have spoken!

DIVISION OF THE LAND

48 "Here is the list of the tribes of Israel and the territory each is to receive. The territory of Dan is in the extreme north. Its boundary line follows the Hethlon road to Lebo-hamath and then runs on to Hazar-enan on the border of Damascus, with Hamath to the north. Dan's territory extends all the way across the land of Israel from east to west. [2]Asher's territory lies south of Dan's and also extends from east to west. [3]Naphtali's land lies south of Asher's, also extending from east to west. [4]Then comes Manasseh south of Naphtali, and its territory also extends from east to west. [5]South of Manasseh is Ephraim, [6]and then Reuben, [7]and then Judah, all of whose boundaries extend from east to west.

[8]"South of Judah is the land set aside for a special purpose. It will be 8⅓ miles wide and will extend as far east and west as the tribal territories, with the Temple at the center.

[9]"The area set aside for the LORD's Temple will be 8⅓ miles long and 6⅔ miles wide.* [10]For the priests there will be a strip of land measuring 8⅓ miles long by 3⅓ miles wide, with the LORD's Temple at the center. [11]This area is set aside for the ordained priests, the descendants of Zadok who obeyed me and did not go astray when the people of Israel and the rest of the Levites did. [12]It will be their special portion when the land is distributed, the most sacred land of all. Next to the priests' territory will lie the land where the other Levites will live. [13]The land allotted to the

> *From a heart so amazed by God and his wonders burns a love that will not be extinguished.*
>
> MATT REDMAN

Levites will be the same size and shape as that belonging to the priests—8⅓ miles long and 3⅓ miles wide. Together these portions of land will measure 8⅓ miles long by 6⅔ miles wide.* [14]None of this special land will ever be sold or traded or used by others, for it belongs to the LORD; it is set apart as holy.

[15]"An additional strip of land 8⅓ miles long by 1⅔ miles wide, south of the sacred Temple area, will be allotted for public use—homes, pasturelands, and common lands, with a city at the center. [16]The city will measure 1½ miles* on each side. [17]Open lands will surround the city for 150 yards* in every direction. [18]Outside the city there will be a farming area that stretches 3⅓ miles to the east and 3⅓ miles to the west along the border of the sacred area. This farmland will produce food for the people working in the city. [19]Those who come from the various tribes to work in the city may farm it. [20]This entire area—including the sacred lands and the city—is a square that measures 8⅓ miles on each side.

[21]"The areas that remain, to the east and to the west of the sacred lands and the city, will belong to the prince. Each of these areas will be 8⅓ miles wide, extending in opposite directions to the eastern and western borders of Israel. [22]So the prince's land will include everything between the territories allotted to

---

48:9 Reflecting the Greek reading in 45:1: *25,000 cubits* [13.3 kilometers] *long and 20,000 cubits* [10.6 kilometers] *wide*; Hebrew reads *25,000 cubits long and 10,000 cubits wide.* Compare 45:1-5; 48:10-13. In this chapter, the distance measures are calculated using the Hebrew long cubit, which equals 21 inches or 53 centimeters. **48:13** See note on 48:9. **48:16** Hebrew *4,500 cubits* [2.4 kilometers]; also in 48:30, 32, 33, 34. **48:17** Hebrew *250 cubits* [133 meters].

Judah and Benjamin, except for the are
aside for the sacred lands and the city.

²³"These are the territories allotted to
rest of the tribes. Benjamin's territory lies ju
south of the prince's lands, and it extend
across the entire land of Israel from east to
west. ²⁴South of Benjamin's territory lies that
of Simeon, also extending across the land
from east to west. ²⁵Next is the territory of
Issachar with the same eastern and western
boundaries. ²⁶Then comes the territory of
Zebulun, which also extends across the land
from east to west. ²⁷The territory of Gad is just
south of Zebulun with the same borders to
the east and west. ²⁸The southern border of
Gad runs from Tamar to the waters of
Meribah at Kadesh* and then follows the
brook of Egypt to the Mediterranean.*
²⁹These are the allotments that will be set aside

for each tribe's inheritance, says the
LORD.

THE GATES OF THE CITY

³⁰"These will be the exits to the city: On
north wall, which is 1½ miles long, ³¹there wi
be three gates, each one named after a tribe of
Israel. The first will be named for Reuben, the
ond for Judah, and the third for Levi. ³²On
east wall, also 1½ miles long, the gates will
b amed for Joseph, Benjamin, and Dan.
³³The outh wall, also 1½ miles long, will have
gates amed for Simeon, Issachar, and
Zebulun ³⁴And on the west wall, also 1½ miles
long, the ates will be named for Gad, Asher,
and Naphali.

³⁵"The distance around the entire city will
be six miles.* And from that day the name of
the city will be 'The LORD Is There.'*"

48:28a Hebrew *waters of Meribath-kadesh.* **48:28b** Hebrew *the great sea.* **48:35a** Hebrew *18,000 cubits* [9.6 kilometers]. **48:35b** Hebrew
Yahweh Shammah.

Daniel

The people who know ... God will be strong (11:32).

The Power of the Promise

"Will things *ever* change?" Here is the question that, at one time or another, haunts every human heart. Encounter a dark trial—a child's rebelliousness, a joyless marriage, illness, loneliness, jobessness, restlessness—and you will find yourself asking it.

What gets us through such ordeals? In a word, *hope*. Hope that God will intervene. Hope that our situations will eventually improve.

The people of Judah living 2500 years ago were no strangers to feelings of hopelessness. They had been conquered by the nation of Babylon and taken into captivity. They wondered if things would ever change, if they would ever see their homeland again. The prophet Daniel lived during that captivity, and his story encouraged his countrymen—and encourages us—to continue to hope in God despite discouraging circumstances.

Most people are familiar with the stories in Daniel: the rescue of the three faithful young men thrown into the fiery furnace; Daniel's night in a den of hungry lions; the writing on the wall warning the king of Babylon that his kingdom was about to fall because of his sin. Through these circumstances, Daniel's faith and prayerful relationship with God was what sustained him and offered hope to others. The last section of Daniel continues the message of encouragement by chronicling prophecies of Israel's future victories over her enemies.

Daniel had a uniquely intimate relationship with the Lord. Here is what God said of him through a vision, while Daniel stood there, "trembling with fear": "O Daniel, greatly loved of God. . . . Since the first day you began to pray for understanding and to humble yourself before your God, your request has been heard in heaven" (10:11,12). Then the one speaking used the same words to Daniel as Jesus used when he met with his disciples after his resurrection: "Don't be afraid. . . . Be at peace" (10:19).

Daniel's story is a message of ultimate hope. It reminds us of our great God—sovereign, merciful, faithful. Daniel challenges us to worship God even under the most difficult circumstances.

Worship Moments

- Daniel doesn't forget to praise God and acknowledge where wisdom comes from (2:23–24).
- Daniel continues his habit of prayer, despite threats to his life (6:10).
- Daniel prayed and confessed his sin and the sins of the people (9:20).
- God is called: "a great and awesome God . . . of unfailing love" (9:4); "merciful and forgiving" (9:9).

DANIEL IN NEBUCHADNEZZAR'S COURT

1 During the third year of King Jehoiakim's reign in Judah,* King Nebuchadnezzar of Babylon came to Jerusalem and besieged it with his armies. ²The Lord gave him victory over King Jehoiakim of Judah. When Nebuchadnezzar returned to Babylon, he took with him some of the sacred objects from the Temple of God and placed them in the treasure-house of his god in the land of Babylonia.*

³Then the king ordered Ashpenaz, who was in charge of the palace officials, to bring to the palace some of the young men of Judah's royal family and other noble families, who had been brought to Babylon as captives. ⁴"Select only strong, healthy, and good-looking young men," he said. "Make sure they are well versed in every branch of learning, are gifted with knowledge and good sense, and have the poise needed to serve in the royal palace. Teach these young men the language and literature of the Babylonians.*" ⁵The king assigned them a daily ration of the best food and wine from his own kitchens. They were to be trained for a three-year period, and then some of them would be made his advisers in the royal court.

⁶Daniel, Hananiah, Mishael, and Azariah were four of the young men chosen, all from the tribe of Judah. ⁷The chief official renamed them with these Babylonian names:

Daniel was called Belteshazzar.
Hananiah was called Shadrach.
Mishael was called Meshach.
Azariah was called Abednego.

⁸But Daniel made up his mind not to defile himself by eating the food and wine given to them by the king. He asked the chief official for permission to eat other things instead. ⁹Now God had given the chief official great respect for Daniel. ¹⁰But he was alarmed by Daniel's suggestion. "My lord the king has ordered that you eat this food and wine," he said. "If you become pale and thin compared to the other youths your age, I am afraid the king will have me beheaded for neglecting my duties."

¹¹Daniel talked it over with the attendant who had been appointed by the chief official to look after Daniel, Hananiah, Mishael, and Azariah. ¹²"Test us for ten days on a diet of vegetables and water," Daniel said. ¹³"At the end of the ten days, see how we look compared to the other young men who are eating the king's rich food. Then you can decide whether or not to let us continue eating our diet." ¹⁴So the attendant agreed to Daniel's suggestion and tested them for ten days.

¹⁵At the end of the ten days, Daniel and his three friends looked healthier and better nourished than the young men who had been eating the food assigned by the king. ¹⁶So after that, the attendant fed them only vegetables instead of the rich foods and wines. ¹⁷God gave these four young men an unusual aptitude for learning the literature and science of the time. And God gave Daniel special ability in understanding the meanings of visions and dreams.

¹⁸When the three-year training period ordered by the king was completed, the chief official brought all the young men to King Nebuchadnezzar. ¹⁹The king talked with each of them, and none of them impressed him as much as Daniel, Hananiah, Mishael, and Azariah. So they were appointed to his regular staff of advisers. ²⁰In all matters requiring wisdom and balanced judgment, the king found the advice of these young men to be ten times better than that of all the magicians and enchanters in his entire kingdom. ²¹Daniel remained there until the first year of King Cyrus's reign.*

NEBUCHADNEZZAR'S DREAM

2 One night during the second year of his reign,* Nebuchadnezzar had a dream that

---

1:1 The third year of Jehoiakim's reign, according to the Hebrew system of reckoning, was 605 B.C.   1:2 Hebrew *the land of Shinar.*
1:4 Or *of the Chaldeans.*   1:21 The first year of Cyrus's reign was 538 B.C.   2:1 The second year of Nebuchadnezzar's reign was 603 B.C.

disturbed him so much that he couldn't sleep. [2]He called in his magicians, enchanters, sorcerers, and astrologers,* and he demanded that they tell him what he had dreamed. As they stood before the king, [3]he said, "I have had a dream that troubles me. Tell me what I dreamed, for I must know what it means."

[4]Then the astrologers answered the king in Aramaic,* "Long live the king! Tell us the dream, and we will tell you what it means."

[5]But the king said to the astrologers, "I am serious about this. If you don't tell me what my dream was and what it means, you will be torn limb from limb, and your houses will be demolished into heaps of rubble! [6]But if you tell me what I dreamed and what the dream means, I will give you many wonderful gifts and honors. Just tell me the dream and what it means!"

[7]They said again, "Please, Your Majesty. Tell us the dream, and we will tell you what it means."

[8]The king replied, "I can see through your trick! You are trying to stall for time because you know I am serious about what I said. [9]If you don't tell me the dream, you will be condemned. You have conspired to tell me lies in hopes that something will change. But tell me the dream, and then I will know that you can tell me what it means."

[10]The astrologers replied to the king, "There isn't a man alive who can tell Your Majesty his dream! And no king, however great and powerful, has ever asked such a thing of any magician, enchanter, or astrologer! [11]This is an impossible thing the king requires. No one except the gods can tell you your dream, and they do not live among people."

[12]The king was furious when he heard this, and he sent out orders to execute all the wise men of Babylon. [13]And because of the king's decree, men were sent to find and kill Daniel and his friends. [14]When Arioch, the commander of the king's guard, came to kill them, Daniel handled the situation with wisdom and discretion. [15]He asked Arioch, "Why has the king issued such a harsh decree?" So Arioch told him all that had happened. [16]Daniel went at once to see the king and requested more time so he could tell the king what the dream meant.

[17]Then Daniel went home and told his friends Hananiah, Mishael, and Azariah what had happened. [18]He urged them to ask the God of heaven to show them his mercy by telling them the secret, so they would not be executed along with the other wise men of Babylon. [19]That night the secret was revealed to Daniel in a vision. Then Daniel praised the God of heaven, [20]saying,

"Praise the name of God forever and ever,
 for he alone has all wisdom and power.
[21] He determines the course of world events;
 he removes kings and sets others on the
 throne.
 He gives wisdom to the wise
 and knowledge to the scholars.
[22] He reveals deep and mysterious things
 and knows what lies hidden in
 darkness,
 though he himself is surrounded by
 light.
[23] I thank and praise you, God of my
 ancestors,
 for you have given me wisdom and
 strength.
 You have told me what we asked of you
 and revealed to us what the king
 demanded."

DANIEL INTERPRETS THE DREAM

[24]Then Daniel went in to see Arioch, who had been ordered to execute the wise men of Babylon. Daniel said to him, "Don't kill the wise men. Take me to the king, and I will tell him the meaning of his dream."

[25]Then Arioch quickly took Daniel to the king and said, "I have found one of the captives from Judah who will tell Your Majesty the meaning of your dream!"

[26]The king said to Daniel (also known as

2:2 Or *Chaldeans;* also in 2:4, 5, 10.   2:4 The original text from this point through chapter 7 is in Aramaic.

My Daily Worship

— August 8 —

LARGE AND IN CHARGE

DANIEL 1:1–3:30

He determines the course of world events; he removes kings and sets others on the throne.
He gives wisdom to the wise and knowledge to the scholars (2:21).

[i reflect]

Years ago, an American missionary couple serving on the African continent were given a telegram containing the worst news any parent can receive: their son had been killed in an automobile accident back in the United States. They wired back a two-word answer: *No accident*.

No accident? How could they respond this way in the face of such tragic news? Only because they knew that God is sovereign and that he oversees the affairs of men, women, cultures, and entire nations. "He determines the course of world events; he removes kings and sets others on the throne. He gives wisdom to the wise and knowledge to the scholars," said Daniel.

When tough times come for you and your family—death, illness, divorce, financial reversals—how do you respond? With hand-wringing, sleepless nights, desperation, and fear? Such reactions are certainly typical, even understandable. Yet the men and women who place their trust in our sovereign God can know that this is not a random, senseless universe. It is under the control of its Creator; there are *no accidents*. He is in charge.

That's good to know in a world where the words "Columbine," "terrorism," "9/11" and "weapons of mass destruction" have become part of our cultural lexicon and our collective consciousness. We have no guarantees of safety, security, health, wealth, and unending blessedness, but we do have the assurance that the God who "determines the course of world events" is pleased to allow us to call him "Father."

Look at the events in your circumstances today through the perspective of Daniel's praise song to God. Every delay, every encounter, every detail has been allowed by the One who is in charge.

[i pray]

Father, I confess how often I am driven by my fears and anxieties instead of
trusting your sovereignty and your compassion. Help me remember that
"Love has no fear because perfect love expels all fear" (1 John 4:18).
I ask that by your mercy, you will replace my fear with your love.

[i respond]

No accidents. Print those words on several index cards and place them where you can see them throughout the day—at the kitchen sink, in the bathroom, at your office. Use these cards as reminders that God is in control of all things.

Belteshazzar), "Is this true? Can you tell me what my dream was and what it means?"

[27]Daniel replied, "There are no wise men, enchanters, magicians, or fortune-tellers who can tell the king such things. [28]But there is a God in heaven who reveals secrets, and he has shown King Nebuchadnezzar what will happen in the future. Now I will tell you your dream and the visions you saw as you lay on your bed.

[29]"While Your Majesty was sleeping, you dreamed about coming events. The revealer of mysteries has shown you what is going to happen. [30]And it is not because I am wiser than any living person that I know the secret of your dream, but because God wanted you to understand what you were thinking about.

[31]"Your Majesty, in your vision you saw in front of you a huge and powerful statue of a man, shining brilliantly, frightening and awesome. [32]The head of the statue was made of fine gold, its chest and arms were of silver, its belly and thighs were of bronze, [33]its legs were of iron, and its feet were a combination of iron and clay. [34]But as you watched, a rock was cut from a mountain by supernatural means.* It struck the feet of iron and clay, smashing them to bits. [35]The whole statue collapsed into a heap of iron, clay, bronze, silver, and gold. The pieces were crushed as small as chaff on a threshing floor, and the wind blew them all away without a trace. But the rock that knocked the statue down became a great mountain that covered the whole earth.

[36]"That was the dream; now I will tell Your Majesty what it means. [37]Your Majesty, you are a king over many kings. The God of heaven has given you sovereignty, power, strength, and honor. [38]He has made you the ruler over all the inhabited world and has put even the animals and birds under your control. You are the head of gold.

[39]"But after your kingdom comes to an end, another great kingdom, inferior to yours, will rise to take your place. After that kingdom has fallen, yet a third great kingdom, represented by the bronze belly and thighs, will rise to rule the world. [40]Following that kingdom, there will be a fourth great kingdom, as strong as iron. That kingdom will smash and crush all previous empires, just as iron smashes and crushes everything it strikes. [41]The feet and toes you saw that were a combination of iron and clay show that this kingdom will be divided. [42]Some parts of it will be as strong as iron, and others as weak as clay. [43]This mixture of iron and clay also shows that these kingdoms will try to strengthen themselves by forming alliances with each other through intermarriage. But this will not succeed, just as iron and clay do not mix.

[44]"During the reigns of those kings, the God of heaven will set up a kingdom that will never be destroyed; no one will ever conquer it. It will shatter all these kingdoms into nothingness, but it will stand forever. [45]That is the meaning of the rock cut from the mountain by supernatural means, crushing to dust the statue of iron, bronze, clay, silver, and gold.

"The great God has shown Your Majesty what will happen in the future. The dream is true, and its meaning is certain."

NEBUCHADNEZZAR REWARDS DANIEL

[46]Then King Nebuchadnezzar bowed to the ground before Daniel and worshiped him, and he commanded his people to offer sacrifices and burn sweet incense before him. [47]The king said to Daniel, "Truly, your God is the God of gods, the Lord over kings, a revealer of mysteries, for you have been able to reveal this secret."

[48]Then the king appointed Daniel to a high position and gave him many valuable gifts. He made Daniel ruler over the whole province of Babylon, as well as chief over all his wise men. [49]At Daniel's request, the king appointed Shadrach, Meshach, and Abednego to be in charge of all the affairs of the province of Babylon, while Daniel remained in the king's court.

2:34 Aramaic *not by human hands;* also in 2:45.

NEBUCHADNEZZAR'S GOLD STATUE

3 King Nebuchadnezzar made a gold statue ninety feet tall and nine feet wide* and set it up on the plain of Dura in the province of Babylon. ²Then he sent messages to the princes, prefects, governors, advisers, counselors, judges, magistrates, and all the provincial officials to come to the dedication of the statue he had set up. ³When all these officials* had arrived and were standing before the image King Nebuchadnezzar had set up, ⁴a herald shouted out, "People of all races and nations and languages, listen to the king's command! ⁵When you hear the sound of the horn, flute, zither, lyre, harp, pipes, and other instruments,* bow to the ground to worship King Nebuchadnezzar's gold statue. ⁶Anyone who refuses to obey will immediately be thrown into a blazing furnace."

⁷So at the sound of the musical instruments,* all the people, whatever their race or nation or language, bowed to the ground and worshiped the statue that King Nebuchadnezzar had set up.

⁸But some of the astrologers* went to the king and informed on the Jews. ⁹They said to King Nebuchadnezzar, "Long live the king! ¹⁰You issued a decree requiring all the people to bow down and worship the gold statue when they hear the sound of the musical instruments.* ¹¹That decree also states that those who refuse to obey must be thrown into a blazing furnace. ¹²But there are some Jews—Shadrach, Meshach, and Abednego—whom you have put in charge of the province of Babylon. They have defied Your Majesty by refusing to serve your gods or to worship the gold statue you have set up."

¹³Then Nebuchadnezzar flew into a rage and ordered Shadrach, Meshach, and Abednego to be brought before him. When they were brought in, ¹⁴Nebuchadnezzar said to them, "Is it true, Shadrach, Meshach, and Abednego, that you refuse to serve my gods or to worship the gold statue I have set up? ¹⁵I will give you one more chance. If you bow down and worship the statue I have made when you hear the sound of the musical instruments, all will be well. But if you refuse, you will be thrown immediately into the blazing furnace. What god will be able to rescue you from my power then?"

¹⁶Shadrach, Meshach, and Abednego replied, "O Nebuchadnezzar, we do not need to defend ourselves before you. ¹⁷If we are thrown into the blazing furnace, the God whom we serve is able to save us. He will rescue us from your power, Your Majesty. ¹⁸But even if he doesn't, Your Majesty can be sure that we will never serve your gods or worship the gold statue you have set up."

THE BLAZING FURNACE

¹⁹Nebuchadnezzar was so furious with Shadrach, Meshach, and Abednego that his face became distorted with rage. He commanded that the furnace be heated seven times hotter than usual. ²⁰Then he ordered some of the strongest men of his army to bind Shadrach, Meshach, and Abednego and throw them into the blazing furnace. ²¹So they tied them up and threw them into the furnace, fully clothed. ²²And because the king, in his anger, had demanded such a hot fire in the furnace, the flames leaped out and killed the soldiers as they threw the three men in! ²³So Shadrach, Meshach, and Abednego, securely tied, fell down into the roaring flames.

²⁴But suddenly, as he was watching, Nebuchadnezzar jumped up in amazement and exclaimed to his advisers, "Didn't we tie up three men and throw them into the furnace?"

"Yes," they said, "we did indeed, Your Majesty."

²⁵"Look!" Nebuchadnezzar shouted. "I see four men, unbound, walking around in the

---

3:1 Aramaic *60 cubits* [27 meters] *tall and 6 cubits* [2.7 meters] *wide.* **3:3** Aramaic *the princes, prefects, governors, advisers, counselors, judges, magistrates, and all the provincial officials.* **3:5** The identification of some of these musical instruments is uncertain. **3:7** Aramaic *the horn, flute, zither, lyre, harp, and other instruments of the musical ensemble.* **3:8** Aramaic *Chaldeans.* **3:10** Aramaic *the horn, flute, zither, lyre, harp, pipes, and other instruments of the musical ensemble;* also in 3:15.

fire. They aren't even hurt by the flames! And the fourth looks like a divine being*!"

²⁶Then Nebuchadnezzar came as close as he could to the door of the flaming furnace and shouted: "Shadrach, Meshach, and Abednego, servants of the Most High God, come out! Come here!" So Shadrach, Meshach, and Abednego stepped out of the fire. ²⁷Then the princes, prefects, governors, and advisers crowded around them and saw that the fire had not touched them. Not a hair on their heads was singed, and their clothing was not scorched. They didn't even smell of smoke!

²⁸Then Nebuchadnezzar said, "Praise to the God of Shadrach, Meshach, and Abednego! He sent his angel to rescue his servants who trusted in him. They defied the king's command and were willing to die rather than serve or worship any god except their own God. ²⁹Therefore, I make this decree: If any people, whatever their race or nation or language, speak a word against the God of Shadrach, Meshach, and Abednego, they will be torn limb from limb, and their houses will be crushed into heaps of rubble. There is no other god who can rescue like this!" ³⁰Then the king promoted Shadrach, Meshach, and Abednego to even higher positions in the province of Babylon.

NEBUCHADNEZZAR'S DREAM ABOUT A TREE

4 King Nebuchadnezzar sent this message to the people of every race and nation and language throughout the world:

"Peace and prosperity to you!

²"I want you all to know about the miraculous signs and wonders the Most High God has performed for me.

³ How great are his signs,
   how powerful his wonders!

His kingdom will last forever,
   his rule through all generations.

⁴"I, Nebuchadnezzar, was living in my palace in comfort and prosperity. ⁵But one night I had a dream that greatly frightened me; I saw visions that terrified me as I lay in my bed. ⁶So I issued an order

---

Words of Worship

TABERNACLE, TENT

Tabernacle, Tent—Hebrew *'o-hel* "tent, dwelling"; *mish-kan* "tent, dwelling"; Greek *ske-ne* "tent, hut"; *ske-no-ma* "encampment."

Israel's first worship center was the Tabernacle, or tent. The Jerusalem Temple was a continuation of the Tabernacle and followed its plan. But the Tabernacle embodied a truth that the Temple could not convey. As the Lord told David, through Nathan the prophet, "My home has always been a tent, moving from one place to another." God never complained about the temporary tent (2 Samuel 7:6–7). On the plane of human history, he prefers to be on the move.

So as we seek the Lord in worship, we need to be aware that he can be a moving target. If our devotional practices go on autopilot, ignoring fresh input from God's Word, we can lose sight of him. By his Word we know that his true Tabernacle is in heaven (Revelation 15:5), and we set our sights on him there. But we can also ask him to encamp with us as we follow him in this life. We can pray, with Charles Wesley, "O thou who didst on earth appear, by faith conceived, thyself impart; pitch thy tabernacle here in my believing heart."

3:25 Aramaic *like a son of the gods.*

calling in all the wise men of Babylon, so they could tell me what my dream meant. [7]When all the magicians, enchanters, astrologers,* and fortune-tellers came in, I told them the dream, but they could not tell me what it meant. [8]At last Daniel came in before me, and I told him the dream. (He was named Belteshazzar after my god, and the spirit of the holy gods is in him.)

[9]"I said to him, 'O Belteshazzar, master magician, I know that the spirit of the holy gods is in you and that no mystery is too great for you to solve. Now tell me what my dream means.

[10]"While I was lying in my bed, this is what I dreamed. I saw a large tree in the middle of the earth. [11]The tree grew very tall and strong, reaching high into the heavens for all the world to see. [12]It had fresh green leaves, and it was loaded with fruit for all to eat. Wild animals lived in its shade, and birds nested in its branches. All the world was fed from this tree.

[13]"Then as I lay there dreaming, I saw a messenger,* a holy one, coming down from heaven. [14]The messenger shouted, "Cut down the tree; lop off its branches! Shake off its leaves, and scatter its fruit! Chase the animals from its shade and the birds from its branches. [15]But leave the stump and the roots in the ground, bound with a band of iron and bronze and surrounded by tender grass. Now let him be drenched with the dew of heaven, and let him live like an animal among the plants of the fields. [16]For seven periods of time, let him have the mind of an animal instead of a human. [17]For this has been decreed by the messengers*; it is commanded by the holy ones. The purpose of this decree is that the whole world may understand that the Most High rules over the kingdoms of the world and gives them to anyone he chooses—even to the lowliest of humans."

[18]" 'O Belteshazzar, that was the dream that I, King Nebuchadnezzar, had. Now tell me what it means, for no one else can help me. All the wisest men of my kingdom have failed me. But you can tell me because the spirit of the holy gods is in you.'

DANIEL EXPLAINS THE DREAM

[19]"Upon hearing this, Daniel (also known as Belteshazzar) was overcome for a time, aghast at the meaning of the dream. Finally, the king said to him, 'Belteshazzar, don't be alarmed by the dream and what it means.'

"Belteshazzar replied, 'Oh, how I wish the events foreshadowed in this dream would happen to your enemies, my lord, and not to you! [20]You saw a tree growing very tall and strong, reaching high into the heavens for all the world to see. [21]It had fresh green leaves, and it was loaded with fruit for all to eat. Wild animals lived in its shade, and birds nested in its branches. [22]That tree, Your Majesty, is you. For you have grown strong and great; your greatness reaches up to heaven, and your rule to the ends of the earth.

[23]" 'Then you saw a messenger, a holy one, coming down from heaven and saying, "Cut down the tree and destroy it. But leave the stump and the roots in the ground, bound with a band of iron and bronze and surrounded by tender grass. Let him be drenched with the dew of heaven. Let him eat grass with the animals of the field for seven periods of time."

[24]" 'This is what the dream means, Your Majesty, and what the Most High has declared will happen to you. [25]You will be driven from human society, and you will live in the fields with the wild animals. You will eat grass like a cow, and you will be

---

4:7 Or *Chaldeans.*   4:13 Aramaic *a watcher;* also in 4:23.   4:17 Aramaic *the watchers.*

drenched with the dew of heaven. Seven periods of time will pass while you live this way, until you learn that the Most High rules over the kingdoms of the world and gives them to anyone he chooses. ²⁶But the stump and the roots were left in the ground. This means that you will receive your kingdom back again when you have learned that heaven rules.

²⁷" 'O King Nebuchadnezzar, please listen to me. Stop sinning and do what is right. Break from your wicked past by being merciful to the poor. Perhaps then you will continue to prosper.'

The Dream's Fulfillment

²⁸"But all these things did happen to King Nebuchadnezzar. ²⁹Twelve months later, he was taking a walk on the flat roof of the royal palace in Babylon. ³⁰As he looked out across the city, he said, 'Just look at this great city of Babylon! I, by my own mighty power, have built this beautiful city as my royal residence and as an expression of my royal splendor.'

³¹"While he was still speaking these words, a voice called down from heaven, 'O King Nebuchadnezzar, this message is for you! You are no longer ruler of this kingdom. ³²You will be driven from human society. You will live in the fields with the wild animals, and you will eat grass like a cow. Seven periods of time will pass while you live this way, until you learn that the Most High rules over the kingdoms of the world and gives them to anyone he chooses.'

³³"That very same hour the prophecy was fulfilled, and Nebuchadnezzar was driven from human society. He ate grass like a cow, and he was drenched with the dew of heaven. He lived this way until his hair was as long as eagles' feathers and his nails were like birds' claws.

Nebuchadnezzar Praises God

³⁴"After this time had passed, I, Nebuchadnezzar, looked up to heaven. My sanity returned, and I praised and worshiped the Most High and honored the one who lives forever.

His rule is everlasting,
  and his kingdom is eternal.
³⁵ All the people of the earth
  are nothing compared to him.
He has the power to do as he pleases
  among the angels of heaven
  and with those who live on earth.
No one can stop him or challenge
  him,
  saying, 'What do you mean by doing
    these things?'

³⁶"When my sanity returned to me, so did my honor and glory and kingdom. My advisers and officers sought me out, and I was reestablished as head of my kingdom, with even greater honor than before.

³⁷"Now I, Nebuchadnezzar, praise and glorify and honor the King of heaven. All his acts are just and true, and he is able to humble those who are proud."

The Writing on the Wall

5 A number of years later, King Belshazzar gave a great feast for a thousand of his nobles and drank wine with them. ²While Belshazzar was drinking, he gave orders to bring in the gold and silver cups that his predecessor,* Nebuchadnezzar, had taken from the Temple in Jerusalem, so that he and his nobles, his wives, and his concubines might drink from them. ³So they brought these gold cups taken from the Temple of God in Jerusalem, and the king and his nobles, his wives, and his concubines drank from them. ⁴They drank toasts from them to honor their idols made of gold, silver, bronze, iron, wood, and stone.

5:2 Aramaic *father;* also in 5:11, 13, 18.

[5]At that very moment they saw the fingers of a human hand writing on the plaster wall of the king's palace, near the lampstand. The king himself saw the hand as it wrote, [6]and his face turned pale with fear. Such terror gripped him that his knees knocked together and his legs gave way beneath him.

[7]The king shouted for the enchanters, astrologers,* and fortune-tellers to be brought before him. He said to these wise men of Babylon, "Whoever can read this writing and tell me what it means will be dressed in purple robes of royal honor and will wear a gold chain around his neck. He will become the third highest ruler in the kingdom!" [8]But when all the king's wise men came in, none of them could read the writing or tell him what it meant. [9]So the king grew even more alarmed, and his face turned ashen white. His nobles, too, were shaken.

[10]But when the queen mother heard what was happening, she hurried to the banquet hall. She said to Belshazzar, "Long live the king! Don't be so pale and afraid about this. [11]There is a man in your kingdom who has within him the spirit of the holy gods. During Nebuchadnezzar's reign, this man was found to have insight, understanding, and wisdom as though he himself were a god. Your predecessor, King Nebuchadnezzar, made him chief over all the magicians, enchanters, astrologers, and fortune-tellers of Babylon. [12]This man Daniel, whom the king named Belteshazzar, has a sharp mind and is filled with divine knowledge and understanding. He can interpret dreams, explain riddles, and solve difficult problems. Call for Daniel, and he will tell you what the writing means."

DANIEL EXPLAINS THE WRITING

[13]So Daniel was brought in before the king. The king asked him, "Are you Daniel, who was exiled from Judah by my predecessor, King Nebuchadnezzar? [14]I have heard that you have the spirit of the gods within you and that you are filled with insight, understanding, and wisdom. [15]My wise men and enchanters have tried to read this writing on the wall, but they cannot. [16]I am told that you can give interpretations and solve difficult problems. If you can read these words and tell me their meaning, you will be clothed in purple robes of royal honor, and you will wear a gold chain around your neck. You will become the third highest ruler in the kingdom."

[17]Daniel answered the king, "Keep your gifts or give them to someone else, but I will tell you what the writing means. [18]Your Majesty, the Most High God gave sovereignty, majesty, glory, and honor to your predecessor, Nebuchadnezzar. [19]He made him so great that people of all races and nations and languages trembled before him in fear. He killed those he wanted to kill and spared those he wanted to spare. He honored those he wanted to honor and disgraced those he wanted to disgrace. [20]But when his heart and mind were hardened with pride, he was brought down from his royal throne and stripped of his glory. [21]He was driven from human society. He was given the mind of an animal, and he lived among the wild donkeys. He ate grass like a cow, and he was drenched with the dew of heaven, until he learned that the Most High God rules the kingdoms of the world and appoints anyone he desires to rule over them.

[22]"You are his successor,* O Belshazzar, and you knew all this, yet you have not humbled yourself. [23]For you have defied the Lord of heaven and have had these cups from his Temple brought before you. You and your nobles and your wives and concubines have been drinking wine from them while praising gods of silver, gold, bronze, iron, wood, and stone—gods that neither see nor hear nor know anything at all. But you have not honored the God who gives you the breath of life and controls your destiny! [24]So God has sent this hand to write a message.

[25]"This is the message that was written: MENE, MENE, TEKEL, PARSIN. [26]This is what these words mean:

5:7 Or *Chaldeans*; also in 5:11. 5:22 Aramaic *son*.

Mene means 'numbered'—God has numbered the days of your reign and has brought it to an end.

²⁷ *Tekel* means 'weighed'—you have been weighed on the balances and have failed the test.

²⁸ *Parsin** means 'divided'—your kingdom has been divided and given to the Medes and Persians."

²⁹Then at Belshazzar's command, Daniel was dressed in purple robes, a gold chain was hung around his neck, and he was proclaimed the third highest ruler in the kingdom.

³⁰That very night Belshazzar, the Babylonian* king, was killed.* ³¹And Darius the Mede took over the kingdom at the age of sixty-two.

DANIEL IN THE LIONS' DEN

6 Darius the Mede decided to divide the kingdom into 120 provinces, and he appointed a prince to rule over each province. ²The king also chose Daniel and two others as administrators to supervise the princes and to watch out for the king's interests. ³Daniel soon proved himself more capable than all the other administrators and princes. Because of his great ability, the king made plans to place him over the entire empire. ⁴Then the other administrators and princes began searching for some fault in the way Daniel was handling his affairs, but they couldn't find anything to criticize. He was faithful and honest and always responsible. ⁵So they concluded, "Our only chance of finding grounds for accusing Daniel will be in connection with the requirements of his religion."

⁶So the administrators and princes went to the king and said, "Long live King Darius! ⁷We administrators, prefects, princes, advisers, and other officials have unanimously agreed that Your Majesty should make a law that will be strictly enforced. Give orders that for the next thirty days anyone who prays to anyone,

divine or human—except to Your Majesty—will be thrown to the lions. ⁸And let Your Majesty issue and sign this law so it cannot be changed, a law of the Medes and Persians, which cannot be revoked." ⁹So King Darius signed the law.

¹⁰But when Daniel learned that the law had been signed, he went home and knelt down as usual in his upstairs room, with its windows open toward Jerusalem. He prayed three times a day, just as he had always done, giving thanks to his God. ¹¹The officials went together to Daniel's house and found him praying and asking for God's help. ¹²So they went back to the king and reminded him about his law. "Did you not sign a law that for the next thirty days anyone who prays to anyone, divine or human—except to Your Majesty—will be thrown to the lions?"

"Yes," the king replied, "that decision stands; it is a law of the Medes and Persians, which cannot be revoked."

¹³Then they told the king, "That man Daniel, one of the captives from Judah, is paying no attention to you or your law. He still prays to his God three times a day."

¹⁴Hearing this, the king was very angry with himself for signing the law, and he tried to find a way to save Daniel. He spent the rest of the day looking for a way to get Daniel out of this predicament. ¹⁵In the evening the men went together to the king and said, "Your Majesty knows that according to the law of the Medes and the Persians, no law that the king signs can be changed."

¹⁶So at last the king gave orders for Daniel to be arrested and thrown into the den of lions. The king said to him, "May your God, whom you worship continually, rescue you." ¹⁷A stone was brought and placed over the mouth of the den. The king sealed the stone with his own royal seal and the seals of his nobles, so that no one could rescue Daniel from the lions. ¹⁸Then the king returned to his palace and spent the night fasting. He refused his

5:28 Aramaic *Peres*, the singular of *Parsin*. **5:30a** Or *Chaldean*. **5:30b** The Persians and Medes conquered Babylon in October 539 B.C.

My Daily Worship

— *August 9* —

NONNEGOTIABLE

DANIEL 4:1–6:28

But when Daniel learned that the law had been signed, he went home and knelt down
as usual in his upstairs room, with its windows open toward Jerusalem. He prayed
three times a day, just as he had always done, giving thanks to his God (6:10).

[*i reflect*]

Rosalind Rinker, in her book *Prayer: Conversing with God,* wrote, "Prayer is the expression of the human heart in conversation with God. The more natural the prayer, the more real he becomes. It has all been simplified for me to this extent: prayer is a dialogue between two persons who love each other."

Daniel certainly built his relationship with God on a foundation of love and trust. Prayer was as natural to Daniel as breathing and eating. It was the expression of his heart in conversation with his God. Throughout his life, from the time he was brought as a young foreign captive into the Babylonian king's court to each succeeding administration in which he served, Daniel indulged in prayer. It was his lifelong habit.

So when the edict was handed down that anyone praying to any god would be put to death, Daniel didn't flinch. Daniel refused to let anything keep him from spending time in prayer. It was, for him, a nonnegotiable. Nothing mattered more than his communion with his God—not food, drink, the opinions of others, or even a death threat. If we could have just a fraction of that dedication!

Contrast our often tepid prayer lives with that of Daniel—who refused to let a little thing like a death threat keep him from going before the Lord openly and regularly. If we're honest, most of us struggle with regularly meeting and communicating with God. We're pressed for time, concerned about how others see us, not as consistent in our prayer life as we know we should be. For many Christians, prayer is the first thing to go when life gets hectic and out of control.

Fortunately, God meets us where we are, not where we ought to be. Confess your lack of prayer and even your lack of desire to pray, and ask God to fan the flame. Then take this advice from Max Lucado, "Pray. Don't prepare to pray. Just pray. Don't read about prayer. Just pray."

[*i pray*]

Father, you know how weak my will is, and how easily I get distracted when it comes to spending
time with you. Be patient with me as you would with any young child. Give me the desire—and
the will—to talk with you daily as my forebear Daniel did, knowing that my relationship
with you is more important than anything else I have in my life today.

[*i respond*]

Look at your calendar or appointment book for the next several days. Pencil in "prayer time with God" as part of your daily routine. Commit to meeting with God during those times. Like Daniel, make prayer a habit!

usual entertainment and couldn't sleep at all that night.

¹⁹Very early the next morning, the king hurried out to the lions' den. ²⁰When he got there, he called out in anguish, "Daniel, servant of the living God! Was your God, whom you worship continually, able to rescue you from the lions?"

²¹Daniel answered, "Long live the king! ²²My God sent his angel to shut the lions' mouths so that they would not hurt me, for I have been found innocent in his sight. And I have not wronged you, Your Majesty."

²³The king was overjoyed and ordered that Daniel be lifted from the den. Not a scratch was found on him because he had trusted in his God. ²⁴Then the king gave orders to arrest the men who had maliciously accused Daniel. He had them thrown into the lions' den, along with their wives and children. The lions leaped on them and tore them apart before they even hit the floor of the den.

²⁵Then King Darius sent this message to the people of every race and nation and language throughout the world:

"Peace and prosperity to you!

²⁶"I decree that everyone throughout my kingdom should tremble with fear before the God of Daniel.

For he is the living God,
    and he will endure forever.
His kingdom will never be
    destroyed,
    and his rule will never end.
²⁷ He rescues and saves his people;
    he performs miraculous signs and
        wonders
    in the heavens and on earth.
He has rescued Daniel
    from the power of the lions."

²⁸So Daniel prospered during the reign of Darius and the reign of Cyrus the Persian.*

DANIEL'S VISION OF FOUR BEASTS

7 Earlier, during the first year of King Belshazzar's reign in Babylon, Daniel had a dream and saw visions as he lay in his bed. He wrote the dream down, and this is what he saw.

²In my vision that night, I, Daniel, saw a great storm churning the surface of a great sea, with strong winds blowing from every direction. ³Then four huge beasts came up out of the water, each different from the others.

⁴The first beast was like a lion with eagles' wings. As I watched, its wings were pulled off, and it was left standing with its two hind feet on the ground, like a human being. And a human mind was given to it.

⁵Then I saw a second beast, and it looked like a bear. It was rearing up on one side, and it had three ribs in its mouth between its teeth. And I heard a voice saying to it, "Get up! Devour many people!"

⁶Then the third of these strange beasts appeared, and it looked like a leopard. It had four wings like birds' wings on its back, and it had four heads. Great authority was given to this beast.

⁷Then in my vision that night, I saw a fourth beast, terrifying, dreadful, and very strong. It devoured and crushed its victims with huge iron teeth and trampled what was left beneath its feet. It was different from any of the other beasts, and it had ten horns. ⁸As I was looking at the horns, suddenly another small horn appeared among them. Three of the first horns were wrenched out, roots and all, to make room for it. This little horn had eyes like human eyes and a mouth that was boasting arrogantly.

⁹I watched as thrones were put in place and the Ancient One* sat down to judge. His clothing was as white as snow, his hair like whitest wool. He sat on a fiery throne with wheels of blazing fire, ¹⁰and a river of fire flowed from his presence. Millions of angels ministered to him, and a hundred million

6:28 Or of Darius, that is, the reign of Cyrus the Persian.   7:9 Aramaic an Ancient of Days; also in 7:13, 22.

stood to attend him. Then the court began its session, and the books were opened.

[11]I continued to watch because I could hear the little horn's boastful speech. I kept watching until the fourth beast was killed and its body was destroyed by fire. [12]As for the other three beasts, their authority was taken from them, but they were allowed to live for a while longer.*

[13]As my vision continued that night, I saw someone who looked like a man* coming with the clouds of heaven. He approached the Ancient One and was led into his presence. [14]He was given authority, honor, and royal power over all the nations of the world, so that people of every race and nation and language would obey him. His rule is eternal—it will never end. His kingdom will never be destroyed.

The Vision Is Explained

[15]I, Daniel, was troubled by all I had seen, and my visions terrified me. [16]So I approached one of those standing beside the throne and asked him what it all meant. He explained it to me like this: [17]"These four huge beasts represent four kingdoms that will arise from the earth. [18]But in the end, the holy people of the Most High will be given the kingdom, and they will rule forever and ever."

[19]Then I wanted to know the true meaning of the fourth beast, the one so different from the others and so terrifying. It devoured and crushed its victims with iron teeth and bronze claws, and it trampled what was left beneath its feet. [20]I also asked about the ten horns on the fourth beast's head and the little horn that came up afterward and destroyed three of the other horns. This was the horn that seemed greater than the others and had human eyes and a mouth that was boasting arrogantly. [21]As I watched, this horn was waging war against the holy people and was defeating them, [22]until the Ancient One came and judged in favor of the holy people of the Most

High. Then the time arrived for the holy people to take over the kingdom.

[23]Then he said to me, "This fourth beast is the fourth world power that will rule the earth. It will be different from all the others. It will devour the whole world, trampling everything in its path. [24]Its ten horns are ten kings that will rule that empire. Then another king will arise, different from the other ten, who will subdue three of them. [25]He will defy the Most High and wear down the holy people of the Most High. He will try to change their sacred festivals and laws, and they will be placed under his control for a time, times, and half a time.

[26]"But then the court will pass judgment, and all his power will be taken away and completely destroyed. [27]Then the sovereignty, power, and greatness of all the kingdoms under heaven will be given to the holy people of the Most High. They will rule forever, and all rulers will serve and obey them."

[28]That was the end of the vision. I, Daniel, was terrified by my thoughts and my face was pale with fear, but I kept these things to myself.

Daniel's Vision of a Ram and Goat

8 During the third year of King Belshazzar's reign, I, Daniel, saw another vision, following the one that had already appeared to me. [2]This time I was at the fortress of Susa, in the province of Elam, standing beside the Ulai River.*

[3]As I looked up, I saw in front of me a ram with two long horns standing beside the river.* One of the horns was longer than the other, even though it had begun to grow later than the shorter one. [4]The ram butted everything out of its way to the west, to the north, and to the south, and no one could stand against it or help its victims. It did as it pleased and became very great.

[5]While I was watching, suddenly a male goat appeared from the west, crossing the land

---

7:12 Aramaic *for a season and a time.* 7:13 Or *like a Son of Man;* Aramaic reads *like a son of man.* 8:2 Or *the Ulai Gate;* also in 8:16.
8:3 Or *the gate;* also in 8:6.

so swiftly that it didn't even touch the ground. This goat, which had one very large horn between its eyes, [6]headed toward the two-horned ram that I had seen standing beside the river. [7]The goat charged furiously at the ram and struck it, breaking off both its horns. Now the ram was helpless, and the goat knocked it down and trampled it. There was no one who could rescue the ram from the goat's power.

[8]The goat became very powerful. But at the height of its power, its large horn was broken off. In the large horn's place grew four prominent horns pointing in the four directions of the earth. [9]From one of the prominent horns came a small horn whose power grew very great. It extended toward the south and the east and toward the glorious land of Israel. [10]His power reached to the heavens where it attacked the heavenly armies, throwing some of the heavenly beings and stars to the ground and trampling them. [11]He even challenged the Commander of heaven's armies by canceling the daily sacrifices offered to him and by destroying his Temple. [12]But the army of heaven was restrained from destroying him for this sin. As a result, sacrilege was committed against the Temple ceremonies, and truth was overthrown. The horn succeeded in everything it did.*

[13]Then I heard two of the holy ones talking to each other. One of them said, "How long will the events of this vision last? How long will the rebellion that causes desecration stop the daily sacrifices? How long will the Temple and heaven's armies be trampled on?"

[14]The other replied, "It will take twenty-three hundred evenings and mornings; then the Temple will be restored."

GABRIEL EXPLAINS THE VISION

[15]As I, Daniel, was trying to understand the meaning of this vision, someone who looked like a man suddenly stood in front of me. [16]And I heard a human voice calling out from the Ulai River, "Gabriel, tell this man the meaning of his vision."

[17]As Gabriel approached the place where I was standing, I became so terrified that I fell to the ground. "Son of man," he said, "you must understand that the events you have seen in your vision relate to the time of the end."

> God is not greater
> if you reverence him,
> but you are greater
> if you serve him.
>
> AUGUSTINE

[18]While he was speaking, I fainted and lay there with my face to the ground. But Gabriel roused me with a touch and helped me to my feet. [19]Then he said, "I am here to tell you what will happen later in the time of wrath. What you have seen pertains to the very end of time. [20]The two-horned ram represents the kings of Media and Persia. [21]The shaggy male goat represents the king of Greece,* and the large horn between its eyes represents the first king of the Greek Empire. [22]The four prominent horns that replaced the one large horn show that the Greek Empire will break into four sections with four kings, none of them as great as the first.

[23]"At the end of their rule, when their sin is at its height, a fierce king, a master of intrigue, will rise to power. [24]He will become very strong, but not by his own power. He will cause a shocking amount of destruction and succeed in everything he does. He will destroy powerful leaders and devastate the holy people. [25]He will be a master of deception, defeating many by catching them off guard. Without warning he will destroy them. He will even take on the Prince of princes in

8:11-12 The meaning of the Hebrew for these verses is uncertain. 8:21 Hebrew of Javan.

battle, but he will be broken, though not by human power.

26"This vision about the twenty-three hundred evenings and mornings* is true. But none of these things will happen for a long time, so do not tell anyone about them yet."

27Then I, Daniel, was overcome and lay sick for several days. Afterward I got up and performed my duties for the king, but I was greatly troubled by the vision and could not understand it.

DANIEL'S PRAYER FOR HIS PEOPLE

9 It was the first year of the reign of Darius the Mede, the son of Ahasuerus, who became king of the Babylonians.* 2During the first year of his reign, I, Daniel, was studying the writings of the prophets. I learned from the word of the LORD, as recorded by Jeremiah the prophet, that Jerusalem must lie desolate for seventy years.* 3So I turned to the Lord God and pleaded with him in prayer and fasting. I wore rough sackcloth and sprinkled myself with ashes.

4I prayed to the LORD my God and confessed: "O Lord, you are a great and awesome God! You always fulfill your promises of unfailing love to those who love you and keep your commands. 5But we have sinned and done wrong. We have rebelled against you and scorned your commands and regulations. 6We have refused to listen to your servants the prophets, who spoke your messages to our kings and princes and ancestors and to all the people of the land.

7"Lord, you are in the right; but our faces are covered with shame, just as you see us now. This is true of us all, including the people of Judah and Jerusalem and all Israel, scattered near and far, wherever you have driven us because of our disloyalty to you. 8O LORD, we and our kings, princes, and ancestors are covered with shame because we have sinned against you. 9But the Lord our God is merciful and forgiving, even though we have rebelled against him. 10We have not obeyed the LORD our God, for we have not followed the laws he gave us through his servants the prophets. 11All Israel has disobeyed your law and turned away, refusing to listen to your voice.

"So now the solemn curses and judgments written in the law of Moses, the servant of God, have been poured out against us because of our sin. 12You have done exactly what you warned you would do against us and our rulers. Never in all history has there been a disaster like the one that happened in Jerusalem. 13Every curse written against us in the law of Moses has come true. All the troubles he predicted have taken place. But we have refused to seek mercy from the LORD our God by turning from our sins and recognizing his truth. 14The LORD has brought against us the disaster he prepared, for we did not obey him, and the LORD our God is just in everything he does.

15"O Lord our God, you brought lasting honor to your name by rescuing your people from Egypt in a great display of power. But we have sinned and are full of wickedness. 16In view of all your faithful mercies, Lord, please turn your furious anger away from your city of Jerusalem, your holy mountain. All the neighboring nations mock Jerusalem and your people because of our sins and the sins of our ancestors.

17"O our God, hear your servant's prayer! Listen as I plead. For your own sake, Lord, smile again on your desolate sanctuary.

18"O my God, listen to me and hear my request. Open your eyes and see our wretchedness. See how your city lies in ruins—for everyone knows that it is yours. We do not ask because we deserve help, but because you are so merciful.

19"O Lord, hear. O Lord, forgive. O Lord, listen and act! For your own sake, O my God, do not delay, for your people and your city bear your name."

8:26 Hebrew *about the evenings and mornings;* compare 8:14. **9:1** Or *the Chaldeans.* **9:2** See Jer 25:11-12; 29:10.

GABRIEL'S MESSAGE ABOUT THE EXILE

²⁰I went on praying and confessing my sin and the sins of my people, pleading with the LORD my God for Jerusalem, his holy mountain. ²¹As I was praying, Gabriel, whom I had seen in the earlier vision, came swiftly to me at the time of the evening sacrifice. ²²He explained to me, "Daniel, I have come here to give you insight and understanding. ²³The moment you began praying, a command was given. I am here to tell you what it was, for God loves you very much. Now listen, so you can understand the meaning of your vision.

²⁴"A period of seventy sets of seven* has been decreed for your people and your holy city to put down rebellion, to bring an end to sin, to atone for guilt, to bring in everlasting righteousness, to confirm the prophetic vision, and to anoint the Most Holy Place.* ²⁵Now listen and understand! Seven sets of seven plus sixty-two sets of seven* will pass from the time the command is given to rebuild Jerusalem until the Anointed One* comes. Jerusalem will be rebuilt with streets and strong defenses,* despite the perilous times.

²⁶"After this period of sixty-two sets of seven,* the Anointed One will be killed, appearing to have accomplished nothing, and a ruler will arise whose armies will destroy the city and the Temple. The end will come with a flood, and war and its miseries are decreed from that time to the very end. ²⁷He will make a treaty with the people for a period of one set of seven,* but after half this time, he will put an end to the sacrifices and offerings. Then as a climax to all his terrible deeds,* he will set up a sacrilegious object that causes desecration,* until the end that has been decreed is poured out on this defiler."

DANIEL'S VISION OF A MESSENGER

10 In the third year of the reign of King Cyrus of Persia, Daniel (also known as Belteshazzar) had another vision. It concerned events certain to happen in the future—times of war and great hardship—and Daniel understood what the vision meant.

²When this vision came to me, I, Daniel, had been in mourning for three weeks. ³All that time I had eaten no rich food or meat, had drunk no wine, and had used no fragrant oils. ⁴On April 23,* as I was standing beside the great Tigris River, ⁵I looked up and saw a man dressed in linen clothing, with a belt of pure gold around his waist. ⁶His body looked like a dazzling gem. From his face came flashes like lightning, and his eyes were like flaming torches. His arms and feet shone like polished bronze, and his voice was like the roaring of a vast multitude of people.

⁷I, Daniel, am the only one who saw this vision. The men with me saw nothing, but they were suddenly terrified and ran away to hide. ⁸So I was left there all alone to watch this amazing vision. My strength left me, my face grew deathly pale, and I felt very weak. ⁹When I heard him speak, I fainted and lay there with my face to the ground.

¹⁰Just then a hand touched me and lifted me, still trembling, to my hands and knees. ¹¹And the man said to me, "O Daniel, greatly loved of God, listen carefully to what I have to say to you. Stand up, for I have been sent to you." When he said this to me, I stood up, still trembling with fear.

¹²Then he said, "Don't be afraid, Daniel. Since the first day you began to pray for understanding and to humble yourself before your God, your request has been heard in heaven. I have come in answer to your prayer. ¹³But for

9:24a Hebrew *70 sevens.* 9:24b Or *the Most Holy One.* 9:25a Hebrew *Seven sevens plus 62 sevens.* 9:25b Or *an anointed one.* 9:25c Or *and a moat,* or *and trenches.* 9:26 Hebrew *After 62 sevens.* 9:27a Hebrew *for one seven.* 9:27b Hebrew *on the wing of abominations;* the meaning of the Hebrew is uncertain. 9:27c Hebrew *an abomination of desolation.* 10:4 Hebrew *On the twenty-fourth day of the first month.* This date in the book of Daniel can be cross-checked with dates in surviving Persian records and can be related accurately to our modern calendar. This day of the Hebrew lunar calendar occurred on April 23, 536 B.C.

My Daily Worship

— *August 10* —

THIS MEANS WAR
DANIEL 7:1–12:13

*Then he said, "Don't be afraid, Daniel. Since the first day you began to pray for understanding
and to humble yourself before your God, your request has been heard in heaven. I have come
in answer to your prayer. But for twenty-one days the spirit prince of the kingdom of
Persia blocked my way. Then Michael, one of the archangels, came to help me, and
I left him there with the spirit prince of the kingdom of Persia"(10:12–13).*

[i reflect]

Have you noticed how many distractions, obstacles, and detours you encounter on your way to
church or even in your own devotions? Weird, out of the ordinary kinds of happenings that conspire to keep you from spending time with God and other Christians?

Daniel 10:12–13 makes it clear that there is conflict in the spiritual realm when God's people pray
(see also Ephesians 6:10–18). Prayer is one of our mightiest weapons in this battle—the supernatural equivalent of air support in a military campaign—and our enemies will try to neutralize this
advantage and keep us from praying if they can.

C. S. Lewis once wrote, "There are two equal and opposite errors people fall into regarding the
devil and demons. One is to have an unhealthy and excessive interest in them; the other is to dis-
believe in their existence altogether. The devil is equally pleased with either one."

We must recognize the reality of Satan, demons, and spiritual warfare in our walk with the Lord.
(Jesus certainly did! See his confrontation with Satan in Matthew 4:1–11.) If we don't, we're sitting ducks. The battle is difficult enough fighting our own sin and spiritual inertia. Don't make it
harder by underestimating or discounting the truth about our opposition and the intensity of the
conflict. That's a sure-fire way to become a casualty in the spiritual war.

Make an assessment today of the defenses you already have in place to conduct spiritual warfare.
How would you assess your prayer life? Do you have prayer warriors you can call upon when tough
struggles come? Based on your evaluation, devise a strategy so that you will be battle-ready when
Satan and his cohorts attempt to derail you and undermine your faith.

[i pray]

*Lord, open my eyes to the reality of the battle going on in the spiritual realm. Teach me
to use the spiritual weapons and armor available to your people. Above all,
help me persevere and not lose heart as I come to you in prayer.*

[i respond]

Find a copy of C.S. Lewis' *The Screwtape Letters*. Read it with fresh eyes as to how Satan tries to
deceive and trip up God's children.

twenty-one days the spirit prince* of the kingdom of Persia blocked my way. Then Michael, one of the archangels,* came to help me, and I left him there with the spirit prince of the kingdom of Persia.* ¹⁴Now I am here to explain what will happen to your people in the future, for this vision concerns a time yet to come."

¹⁵While he was speaking to me, I looked down at the ground, unable to say a word. ¹⁶Then the one who looked like a man* touched my lips, and I opened my mouth and began to speak. I said to the one standing in front of me, "I am terrified by the vision I have seen, my lord, and I am very weak. ¹⁷How can someone like me, your servant, talk to you, my lord? My strength is gone, and I can hardly breathe."

¹⁸Then the one who looked like a man touched me again, and I felt my strength returning. ¹⁹"Don't be afraid," he said, "for you are deeply loved by God. Be at peace; take heart and be strong!"

As he spoke these words, I suddenly felt stronger and said to him, "Now you may speak, my lord, for you have strengthened me."

²⁰He replied, "Do you know why I have come? Soon I must return to fight against the spirit prince of the kingdom of Persia, and then against the spirit prince of the kingdom of Greece.* ²¹But before I do that, I will tell you what is written in the Book of Truth. (There is no one to help me against these spirit princes except Michael, your spirit prince.* ¹I have been standing beside Michael* as his support and defense since the first year of the reign of Darius the Mede.)

KINGS OF THE SOUTH AND NORTH

11 ²"Now then, I will reveal the truth to you. Three more Persian kings will reign, to be succeeded by a fourth, far richer than the others. Using his wealth for political

advantage, he will stir up everyone to war against the kingdom of Greece.*

³"Then a mighty king will rise to power who will rule a vast kingdom and accomplish everything he sets out to do. ⁴But at the height of his power, his kingdom will be broken apart and divided into four parts. It will not be ruled by the king's descendants, nor will the kingdom hold the authority it once had. For his empire will be uprooted and given to others.

⁵"The king of the south will increase in power, but one of this king's own officials will become more powerful than he and will rule his kingdom with great strength.

⁶"Some years later, an alliance will be formed between the king of the north and the king of the south. The daughter of the king of the south will be given in marriage to the king of the north to secure the alliance, but she will lose her influence over him, and so will her father. She will be given up along with her supporters. ⁷But when one of her relatives* becomes king of the south, he will raise an army and enter the fortress of the king of the north and defeat him. ⁸When he returns again to Egypt, he will carry back their idols with him, along with priceless gold and silver dishes. For some years afterward he will leave the king of the north alone.

⁹"Later the king of the north will invade the realm of the king of the south but will soon return to his own land. ¹⁰However, the sons of the king of the north will assemble a mighty army that will advance like a flood and carry the battle as far as the enemy's fortress. ¹¹Then the king of the south, in great anger, will rally against the vast forces assembled by the king of the north and will defeat them. ¹²After the enemy army is swept away, the king of the south will be filled with pride and will have many thousands of his enemies killed. But his success will be short lived.

¹³"A few years later, the king of the north will return with a fully equipped army far

---

10:13a Hebrew *the prince;* also in 10:13c, 20. **10:13b** Hebrew *the chief princes.* **10:13c** As in one Greek version; Hebrew reads *and I was left there with the kings of Persia.* The meaning of the Hebrew is uncertain. **10:16** As in most manuscripts of the Masoretic Text; one manuscript of the Masoretic Text and one Greek version read *Then something that looked like a human hand.* **10:20** Hebrew *of Javan.* **10:21** Hebrew *against these except Michael, your prince.* **11:1** Hebrew *him.* **11:2** Hebrew *of Javan.* **11:7** Hebrew *a branch from her roots.*

greater than the one he lost. ¹⁴At that time there will be a general uprising against the king of the south. Lawless ones among your own people will join them in order to fulfill the vision, but they will not succeed. ¹⁵Then the king of the north will come and lay siege to a fortified city and capture it. The best troops of the south will not be able to stand in the face of the onslaught.

¹⁶"The king of the north will march onward unopposed; none will be able to stop him. He will pause in the glorious land of Israel, intent on destroying it. ¹⁷He will make plans to come with the might of his entire kingdom and will form an alliance with the king of the south. He will give him a daughter in marriage in order to overthrow the kingdom from within, but his plan will fail.

¹⁸"After this, he will turn his attention to the coastal cities and conquer many. But a commander from another land will put an end to his insolence and will cause him to retreat in shame. ¹⁹He will take refuge in his own fortresses but will stumble and fall, and he will be seen no more.

²⁰"His successor will be remembered as the king who sent a tax collector to maintain the royal splendor, but after a very brief reign, he will die, though neither in battle nor open conflict.

²¹"The next to come to power will be a despicable man who is not directly in line for royal succession. But he will slip in when least expected and take over the kingdom by flattery and intrigue. ²²Before him great armies will be swept away, including a covenant prince. ²³By making deceitful promises, he will make various alliances. With a mere handful of followers, he will become strong. ²⁴Without warning he will enter the richest areas of the land and do something that none of his predecessors ever did—distribute among his followers the plunder and wealth of the rich. He will plot the overthrow of strongholds, but this will last for only a short while.

²⁵"Then he will stir up his courage and raise a great army against the king of the south. The king of the south will go to battle with a mighty army, but to no avail, for plots against him will succeed. ²⁶Those of his own household will bring his downfall. His army will be swept away, and many will be killed. ²⁷Seeking nothing but each other's harm, these kings will plot against each other at the conference table, attempting to deceive each other. But it will make no difference, for an end will still come at the appointed time.

²⁸"The king of the north will then return home with great riches. On the way he will set himself against the people of the holy covenant, doing much damage before continuing his journey.

²⁹"Then at the appointed time he will once again invade the south, but this time the result will be different. ³⁰For warships from western coastlands* will scare him off, and he will withdraw and return home. But he will vent his anger against the people of the holy covenant and reward those who forsake the covenant. ³¹His army will take over the Temple fortress, polluting the sanctuary, putting a stop to the daily sacrifices, and setting up the sacrilegious object that causes desecration.* ³²He will flatter those who have violated the covenant and win them over to his side. But the people who know their God will be strong and will resist him.

³³"Those who are wise will give instruction to many. But for a time many of these teachers will die by fire and sword, or they will be jailed and robbed. ³⁴While all these persecutions are going on, a little help will arrive, though many who join them will not be sincere. ³⁵And some who are wise will fall victim to persecution. In this way, they will be refined and cleansed and made pure until the time of the end, for the appointed time is still to come.

³⁶"The king will do as he pleases, exalting himself and claiming to be greater than every god there is, even blaspheming the God of

---

11:30 Hebrew *from Kittim.* 11:31 Hebrew *the abomination of desolation.*

gods. He will succeed—until the time of wrath is completed. For what has been determined will surely take place. [37]He will have no regard for the gods of his ancestors, or for the god beloved of women, or for any other god, for he will boast that he is greater than them all. [38]Instead of these, he will worship the god of fortresses—a god his ancestors never knew—and lavish on him gold, silver, precious stones, and costly gifts. [39]Claiming this foreign god's help, he will attack the strongest fortresses. He will honor those who submit to him, appointing them to positions of authority and dividing the land among them as their reward.*

[40]"Then at the time of the end, the king of the south will attack him, and the king of the north will storm out against him with chariots, cavalry, and a vast navy. He will invade various lands and sweep through them like a flood. [41]He will enter the glorious land of Israel, and many nations will fall, but Moab, Edom, and the best part of Ammon will escape. [42]He will conquer many countries, and Egypt will not escape. [43]He will gain control over the gold, silver, and treasures of Egypt, and the Libyans and Ethiopians* will be his servants.

[44]"But then news from the east and the north will alarm him, and he will set out in great anger to destroy many as he goes. [45]He will halt between the glorious holy mountain and the sea and will pitch his royal tents there, but while he is there, his time will suddenly run out, and there will be no one to help him.

THE TIME OF THE END

12 "At that time Michael, the archangel* who stands guard over your nation, will arise. Then there will be a time of anguish greater than any since nations first came into existence. But at that time every one of your people whose name is written in the book will be rescued. [2]Many of those whose bodies lie dead and buried will rise up, some to everlasting life and some to shame and everlasting contempt. [3]Those who are wise will shine as bright as the sky, and those who turn many to righteousness will shine like stars forever. [4]But you, Daniel, keep this prophecy a secret; seal up the book until the time of the end. Many will rush here and there, and knowledge will increase."

[5]Then I, Daniel, looked and saw two others standing on opposite banks of the river. [6]One of them asked the man dressed in linen, who was now standing above the river, "How long will it be until these shocking events happen?"

[7]The man dressed in linen, who was standing above the river, raised both his hands toward heaven and took this solemn oath by the one who lives forever: "It will go on for a time, times, and half a time. When the shattering of the holy people has finally come to an end, all these things will have happened."

[8]I heard what he said, but I did not understand what he meant. So I asked, "How will all this finally end, my lord?"

[9]But he said, "Go now, Daniel, for what I have said is for the time of the end. [10]Many will be purified, cleansed, and refined by these trials. But the wicked will continue in their wickedness, and none of them will understand. Only those who are wise will know what it means.

[11]"From the time the daily sacrifice is taken away and the sacrilegious object that causes desecration* is set up to be worshiped, there will be 1,290 days. [12]And blessed are those who wait and remain until the end of the 1,335 days!

[13]"As for you, go your way until the end. You will rest, and then at the end of the days, you will rise again to receive the inheritance set aside for you."

11:39 Or *at a price.* **11:43** Hebrew *Cushites.* **12:1** Hebrew *the great prince.* **12:11** Hebrew *the abomination of desolation.*

Hosea

I will heal you of your idolatry and faithlessness, and my love will know no bounds (14:4).

His Boundless Love

If you've ever had to listen to a knock-down, drag-out marital fight through thin apartment walls, then you've got the sense of the Old Testament book of Hosea. It's painful to read. And it is truly shocking. What is *this* doing in the Bible? God commanding one of his prophets to set up house with a whore?

Yet in this moving story that is precisely what God told Hosea to do: marry the town prostitute. And why? "This will illustrate the way my people have been untrue to me" (1:2). Devotion (or the lack of it) is the dominant theme throughout this book: faithfulness on God's part, faithlessness on the part of his people.

With Israel already under Assyrian occupation for chasing after other gods, God pleaded with Judah to avoid a similar fate. He declared Israel "is no longer my wife, and I no longer her husband" (2:1). Yet, almost in the same breath, he said mournfully: "I will win her back once again. I will lead her out into the desert and speak tenderly to her there" (2:14). It is a wonderful window into God's heart—a breathtaking glimpse of his incredible, never-ending love for his unfaithful people.

In the time of Hosea, Judah's idolatry was sapping her strength and causing her to behave like "silly, witless doves" (7:11). The people were continuing to come to the Temple to worship, but it was all a sham (8:12). Filled with anger, God knew he must punish his beloved, but wounded to the core of his being, he cried, "How can I destroy you . . . ? My heart is torn within me" (11:8).

In a stunning picture of redemption, Hosea bought back his wife, exhorting the nation to see the larger truth behind his own odd, sad story: "Return, O Israel, to the LORD your God. . . . Say to him, 'Forgive all our sins and graciously receive us, so that we may offer you the sacrifice of praise'" (14:1–2).

As you read this book, reflect on the wonder of God's gracious love for you. Check your heart. Examine your own faithfulness. Use this opportunity to offer him your own "sacrifice of praise."

Worship Moments

- "Help us, for you are our God!" is the people's cry of repentance (8:2).
- God's call to worship: "Plow up the hard ground of your hearts, for now is the time to seek the LORD" (10:12).
- Names God uses to describe himself: master and husband (2:16); Maker (8:14); LORD God Almighty (12:5); savior (13:4); a refreshing dew (14:5); a tree that is always green (14:8).

1 The LORD gave these messages to Hosea son of Beeri during the years when Uzziah, Jotham, Ahaz, and Hezekiah were kings of Judah, and Jeroboam son of Jehoash* was king of Israel.

HOSEA'S WIFE AND CHILDREN

2When the LORD first began speaking to Israel through Hosea, he said to him, "Go and marry a prostitute,* so some of her children will be born to you from other men. This will illustrate the way my people have been untrue to me, openly committing adultery against the LORD by worshiping other gods."

3So Hosea married Gomer, the daughter of Diblaim, and she became pregnant and gave Hosea a son. 4And the LORD said, "Name the child Jezreel, for I am about to punish King Jehu's dynasty to avenge the murders he committed at Jezreel. 5In fact, I will put an end to Israel's independence by breaking its military power in the Jezreel Valley."

6Soon Gomer became pregnant again and gave birth to a daughter. And the LORD said to Hosea, "Name your daughter Lo-ruhamah— 'Not loved'—for I will no longer show love to the people of Israel or forgive them. 7But I, the LORD their God, will show love to the people of Judah. I will personally free them from their enemies without any help from weapons or armies."

8After Gomer had weaned Lo-ruhamah, she again became pregnant and gave birth to a second son. 9And the LORD said, "Name him Lo-ammi—'Not my people'—for Israel is not my people, and I am not their God. 10Yet the time will come when Israel will prosper and become a great nation. In that day its people will be like the sands of the seashore—too many to count! Then, at the place where they were told, 'You are not my people,' it will be said, 'You are children of the living God.' 11Then the people of Judah and Israel will unite under one leader, and they will return from exile together. What a day that will be—

the day of Jezreel*—when God will again plant his people in his land. 1In that day you will call your brothers Ammi—'My people.' And you will call your sisters Ruhamah—'The ones I love.'

CHARGES AGAINST AN UNFAITHFUL WIFE

2 2"But now, call Israel* to account, for she is no longer my wife, and I am no longer her husband. Tell her to take off her garish makeup and suggestive clothing and to stop playing the prostitute. 3If she doesn't, I will strip her as naked as she was on the day she was born. I will leave her to die of thirst, as in a desert or a dry and barren wilderness. 4And I will not love her children as I would my own because they are not my children! They were conceived in adultery. 5For their mother is a shameless prostitute and became pregnant in a shameful way. She said, 'I'll run after other lovers and sell myself to them for food and drink, for clothing of wool and linen, and for olive oil.'

6"But I will fence her in with thornbushes. I will block the road to make her lose her way. 7When she runs after her lovers, she won't be able to catch up with them. She will search for them but not find them. Then she will think, 'I might as well return to my husband because I was better off with him than I am now.' 8She doesn't realize that it was I who gave her everything she has—the grain, the wine, the olive oil. Even the gold and silver she used in worshiping the god Baal were gifts from me!

9"But now I will take back the wine and ripened grain I generously provided each harvest season. I will take away the linen and wool clothing I gave her to cover her nakedness. 10I will strip her naked in public, while all her lovers look on. No one will be able to rescue her from my hands. 11I will put an end to her annual festivals, her new moon celebrations, and her Sabbath days—all her appointed festivals. 12I will destroy her vineyards and

---

1:1 Hebrew *Joash,* a variant name for Jehoash. 1:2 Or *a promiscuous woman.* 1:11 *Jezreel* means "God plants." 2:2 Hebrew *call your mother.*

orchards, things she claims her lovers gave her. I will let them grow into tangled thickets, where only wild animals will eat the fruit. [13]I will punish her for all the times she deserted me, when she burned incense to her images of Baal, put on her earrings and jewels, and went out looking for her lovers," says the LORD.

THE LORD'S LOVE FOR UNFAITHFUL ISRAEL

[14]"But then I will win her back once again. I will lead her out into the desert and speak tenderly to her there. [15]I will return her vineyards to her and transform the Valley of Trouble* into a gateway of hope. She will give herself to me there, as she did long ago when she was young, when I freed her from her captivity in Egypt.

[16]"In that coming day," says the LORD, "you will call me 'my husband' instead of 'my master.'* [17]O Israel, I will cause you to forget your images of Baal; even their names will no longer be spoken. [18]At that time I will make a covenant with all the wild animals and the birds and the animals that scurry along the ground so that they will not harm you. I will remove all weapons of war from the land, all swords and bows, so you can live unafraid in peace and safety. [19]I will make you my wife forever, showing you righteousness and justice, unfailing love and compassion. [20]I will be faithful to you and make you mine, and you will finally know me as LORD.

[21]"In that day," says the LORD, "I will answer the pleading of the sky for clouds, which will pour down water on the earth in answer to its cries for rain. [22]Then the earth will answer the thirsty cries of the grain, the grapes, and the olive trees for moisture. And the whole grand chorus will sing together, 'Jezreel'—'God plants!'

[23]"At that time I will plant a crop of Israelites and raise them for myself! I will show love to those I called 'Not loved.'* And to those I called 'Not my people,'* I will say, 'Now you are my people.' Then they will reply, 'You are our God!'"

HOSEA'S WIFE IS REDEEMED

3 Then the LORD said to me, "Go and get your wife again. Bring her back to you and love her, even though she loves adultery. For the LORD still loves Israel even though the people have turned to other gods, offering them choice gifts.*"

[2]So I bought her back for fifteen pieces of silver* and about five bushels of barley and a measure of wine.* [3]Then I said to her, "You must live in my house for many days and stop your prostitution. During this time, you will not have sexual intercourse with anyone, not even with me.*"

[4]This illustrates that Israel will be a long time without a king or prince, and without sacrifices, temple, priests, or even idols! [5]But afterward the people will return to the LORD their God and to David's descendant, their king.* They will come trembling in awe to the LORD, and they will receive his good gifts in the last days.

THE LORD'S CASE AGAINST ISRAEL

4 Hear the word of the LORD, O people of Israel! The LORD has filed a lawsuit against you, saying: "There is no faithfulness, no kindness, no knowledge of God in your land. [2]You curse and lie and kill and steal and commit adultery. There is violence everywhere, with one murder after another. [3]That is why your land is not producing. It is filled with sadness, and all living things are becoming sick and dying. Even the animals, birds, and fish have begun to disappear.

[4]"Don't point your finger at someone else and try to pass the blame! Look, you priests, my complaint is with you!* [5]As a sentence for

---

2:15 Hebrew *valley of Achor.* 2:16 Hebrew *'my baal.'* 2:23a Hebrew *Lo-ruhamah;* see 1:6. 2:23b Hebrew *Lo-ammi;* see 1:9. 3:1 Hebrew *raisin cakes.* 3:2a Hebrew *15 shekels of silver,* about 6 ounces or 171 grams in weight. 3:2b As in Greek version, which reads *a homer* [182 liters] *of barley and a measure of wine;* Hebrew reads *a homer of barley and a lethech* [2.5 bushels or 91 liters] *of barley.* 3:3 Or *and I will live with you.* 3:5 Hebrew *to David their king.* 4:4 Hebrew *Your people are like those with a complaint against the priests.*

your crimes, you will stumble in broad daylight, just as you might at night, and so will your false prophets. And I will destroy your mother, Israel. [6]My people are being destroyed because they don't know me. It is all your fault, you priests, for you yourselves refuse to know me. Now I refuse to recognize you as my priests. Since you have forgotten the laws of your God, I will forget to bless your children. [7]The more priests there are, the more they sin against me. They have exchanged* the glory of God for the disgrace of idols.

[8]"The priests get fed when the people sin and bring their sin offerings to them. So the priests are glad when the people sin! [9]Like priests, like people'—since the priests are wicked, the people are wicked, too. So now I will punish both priests and people for all their wicked deeds. [10]They will eat and still be hungry. Though they do a big business as prostitutes, they will have no children, for they have deserted the LORD to worship other gods.

[11]"Alcohol and prostitution have robbed my people of their brains. [12]They are asking a piece of wood to tell them what to do! They think a stick can tell them the future! Longing after idols has made them foolish. They have played the prostitute, serving other gods and deserting their God. [13]They offer sacrifices to idols on the tops of mountains. They go up into the hills to burn incense in the pleasant shade of oaks, poplars, and other trees.

"That is why your daughters turn to prostitution, and your daughters-in-law commit adultery. [14]Why should I punish them? For you men are doing the same thing, sinning with whores and shrine prostitutes. O foolish people! You will be destroyed, for you refuse to understand.

[15]"Though Israel is a prostitute, may Judah avoid such guilt. O Judah, do not join with those who worship me insincerely at Gilgal and at Beth-aven.* Their worship is mere pre-

tense as they take oaths in the LORD's name. [16]Israel is as stubborn as a heifer, so the LORD will put her out to pasture. She will stand alone and unprotected, like a helpless lamb in an open field. [17]Leave her alone because she is married to idolatry. [18]The men of Israel finish up their drinking bouts and off they go to find some prostitutes. Their love for shame is greater than their love for honor.* [19]So a mighty wind will sweep them away. They will die in shame because they offer sacrifices to idols.

THE FAILURE OF ISRAEL'S LEADERS

5 "Hear this, you priests and all of Israel's leaders! Listen, all you men of the royal family! These words of judgment are for you: You are doomed! For you have led the people into a snare by worshiping the idols at Mizpah and Tabor. [2]You have dug a deep pit to trap them at Acacia.* But never forget—I will settle with all of you for what you have done. [3]I know what you are like, O Israel! You have left me as a prostitute leaves her husband; you are utterly defiled. [4]Your deeds won't let you return to your God. You are a prostitute through and through, and you cannot know the LORD.

[5]"The arrogance of Israel* testifies against her; she will stumble under her load of guilt. Judah, too, will fall with her. [6]Then at last, they will come with their flocks and herds to offer sacrifices to the LORD. But it will be too late! They will not find him, because he has withdrawn from them, and they are now alone. [7]For they have betrayed the honor of the LORD, bearing children that aren't his. Now their false religion will devour them, along with their wealth.

[8]"Blow the ram's horn in Gibeah! Sound the alarm in Ramah! Raise the battle cry in Beth-aven*! Lead on into battle, O warriors of

---

4:7 As in Syriac version and an ancient Hebrew tradition; Masoretic Text reads *I will exchange.* 4:15 Beth-aven means "house of wickedness"; it is being used as another name for Bethel, which means "house of God." 4:18 As in Greek version; the meaning of the Hebrew is uncertain. 5:2 Hebrew *at Shittim.* The meaning of the Hebrew for this sentence is uncertain. 5:5 Hebrew *Israel and Ephraim.* 5:8 Beth-aven means "house of wickedness"; it is being used as another name for Bethel, which means "house of God."

My Daily Worship

— *August 11* —

KEEPING WORSHIP REAL

HOSEA 1:1 – 5:15

O Judah, do not join with those who worship me insincerely at Gilgal and at Beth-aven.
Their worship is mere pretense as they take oaths in the LORD's name (4:15).

[i reflect]

Home for the summer after her freshman year in college, Beth was eager to share what God had been doing in her life. Her pastor invited her to be a "guest preacher."

She hesitated, confident in her spirit but not in her speech. "Would you like me to ask Mr. Kelly to give you some tips?" the pastor asked. Yes, that would be great. Although known primarily as director of their incredible choir, Mr. Kelly was quite a public speaker.

His instruction helped immensely. As her last lesson ended, Beth handed Mr. Kelly a small gift. He read the note on which she had written of how God had blessed her and how grateful she was that Mr. Kelly had helped her praise God through her speaking.

"There's something you should know about me," he said as he pulled out his wallet and showed her his membership card in the Thomas Huxley Society. He was an actual card-carrying agnostic.

Beth was shocked. "But the choir? your solos? the hymns? the amazing anthems glorifying God?"

"I simply love good music and pulling off a good performance. Plus, you can't beat the acoustics in this sanctuary."

If the word *hypocrisy* was in an illustrated dictionary, a picture of Mr. Kelly might well be in the margin, alongside the people at Gilgal and Beth-aven. Now look at the word's origin in the Greek, *hupokrisis,* "playing a part on a stage." God beseeches his people today, even as he did centuries ago through the prophet Hosea, to worship him sincerely. In truth. Without pretense. The antithesis of hypocrisy.

Pause right now to consider your own worship habits. What part, if any, of your worship is merely playing a part? Act like you mean to worship him, . . . yet don't be an actor.

[i pray]

O God, I honor you and praise your name. May my worship be sincere. If I am in any way
a hypocrite playing the part of a worshiper, reprimand me. Redeem me. Restore me.

[i respond]

During your devotional time the next few days, watch the sincerity of your worship. Are you masking your true feelings? Are your responses akin to lifeless reading from a script? Write down two ways that you can "keep it real."

Benjamin! ⁹One thing is certain, Israel*: When your day of punishment comes, you will become a heap of rubble.

¹⁰"The leaders of Judah have become as bad as thieves.* So I will pour my anger down on them like a waterfall. ¹¹The people of Israel will be crushed and broken by my judgment because they are determined to worship idols. ¹²I will destroy Israel as a moth consumes wool. I will sap Judah's strength as dry rot weakens wood.

¹³"When Israel and Judah saw how sick they were, Israel turned to Assyria, to the great king there, but he could neither help nor cure them. ¹⁴I will tear at Israel and Judah as a lion rips apart its prey. I will carry them off, and there will be no one left to rescue them. ¹⁵Then I will return to my place until they admit their guilt and look to me for help. For as soon as trouble comes, they will search for me."

A Call to Repentance

6 "Come, let us return to the LORD! He has torn us in pieces; now he will heal us. He has injured us; now he will bandage our wounds. ²In just a short time, he will restore us so we can live in his presence. ³Oh, that we might know the LORD! Let us press on to know him! Then he will respond to us as surely as the arrival of dawn or the coming of rains in early spring."

⁴"O Israel* and Judah, what should I do with you?" asks the LORD. "For your love vanishes like the morning mist and disappears like dew in the sunlight. ⁵I sent my prophets to cut you to pieces. I have slaughtered you with my words, threatening you with death. My judgment will strike you as surely as day follows night. ⁶I want you to be merciful; I don't want your sacrifices. I want you to know God; that's more important than burnt offerings.

⁷"But like Adam, you broke my covenant and rebelled against me. ⁸Gilead is a city of

---

Words of Worship

WAIT

Wait—Hebrew *qa-vah* "wait, expect"; *du-miy-yah* "[wait] in silence"; *chik-kah* "wait."

In an activity-oriented culture, we don't usually associate *waiting* with worship. The biblical worshiper, on the other hand, sometimes speaks of waiting quietly for the Lord in the context of worshiping him (Psalm 62:1). It is a waiting of hope and expectation, as God's answer to prayer begins to appear over time.

Waiting for the Lord says a lot about our faith in him. Sometimes, when we face difficulties, we're tempted to take control and try to solve our own problems. But the adage that "God helps those who help themselves" is not in the Bible. (As a matter of fact, Benjamin Franklin gets credit for saying it.) Getting an accurate grasp of our needs and exploring prudent ways to resolve them is not wrong. But if waiting on God is left out of the picture, unintended consequences can result in a mess. As we seek him in worship, God's promise is renewed: "Those who wait on the LORD will find new strength" (Isaiah 40:31).

---

sinners, tracked with footprints of blood. ⁹Its citizens are bands of robbers, lying in ambush for their victims. Gangs of priests murder travelers along the road to Shechem and practice every kind of sin. ¹⁰Yes, I have seen a horrible thing in Israel: My people have defiled themselves by chasing after other gods!

¹¹"O Judah, a harvest of punishment is also waiting for you, though I wanted so much to restore the fortunes of my people!

5:9 Hebrew *Ephraim,* referring to the northern kingdom of Israel; also in 5:11, 12, 13, 14. **5:10** Hebrew *have become as those who move a boundary marker.* **6:4** Hebrew *Ephraim,* referring to the northern kingdom of Israel.

Israel's Love for Wickedness

7 "I wanted to heal Israel, but its sins were far too great. Samaria is filled with liars, thieves, and bandits! [2]Its people don't realize I am watching them. Their sinful deeds are all around them; I see them all! [3]The people make the king glad with their wickedness. The princes laugh about the people's many lies. [4]They are all adulterers, always aflame with lust. They are like an oven that is kept hot even while the baker is still kneading the dough.

[5]"On royal holidays, the princes get drunk. The king makes a fool of himself and drinks with those who are making fun of him. [6]Their hearts blaze like a furnace with intrigue. Their plot smolders through the night, and in the morning it flames forth like a raging fire. [7]They kill their kings one after another, and no one cries out to me for help.

[8]"My people of Israel* mingle with godless foreigners, picking up their evil ways. Now they have become as worthless as a half-baked cake! [9]Worshiping foreign gods has sapped their strength, but they don't even know it. Israel is like an old man with graying hair, unaware of how weak and old he has become. [10]His arrogance testifies against him, yet he doesn't return to the Lord his God or even try to find him.

[11]"The people of Israel have become like silly, witless doves, first calling to Egypt, then flying to Assyria. [12]But as they fly about, I will throw my net over them and bring them down like a bird from the sky. I will punish them for all their evil ways.*

[13]"How terrible it will be for my people who have deserted me! Let them die, for they have rebelled against me. I wanted to redeem them, but they have only spoken lies about me. [14]They do not cry out to me with sincere hearts. Instead, they sit on their couches and wail. They cut themselves, begging foreign gods for crops and prosperity.

[15]"I trained them and made them strong, yet now they plot evil against me. [16]They look everywhere except to heaven, to the Most High. They are like a crooked bow that always misses its target. Their leaders will be killed by their enemies because of their insolence toward me. Then the people of Egypt will laugh at them.

Israel Harvests the Whirlwind

8 "Sound the alarm! The enemy descends like an eagle on the people of the Lord, for they have broken my covenant and revolted against my law. [2]Now Israel pleads with me, 'Help us, for you are our God!' [3]But it is too late! The people of Israel have rejected what is good, and now their enemies will chase after them. [4]The people have appointed kings and princes, but not with my consent. By making idols for themselves from their silver and gold, they have brought about their own destruction.

[5]"O Samaria, I reject this calf—this idol you have made. My fury burns against you. How long will you be incapable of innocence? [6]This calf you worship was crafted by your own hands! It is not God! Therefore, it must be smashed to bits.

[7]"They have planted the wind and will harvest the whirlwind. The stalks of wheat wither, producing no grain. And if there is any grain, foreigners will eat it. [8]The people of Israel have been swallowed up; they lie among the nations like an old pot that no one wants. [9]Like a wild donkey looking for a mate, they have gone up to Assyria. The people of Israel* have sold themselves to many lovers. [10]But though they have sold themselves to many lands, I will now gather them together. Then they will writhe under the burden of the great king!

[11]"Israel has built many altars to take away sin, but these very altars became places for sinning! [12]Even though I gave them all my laws, they act as if those laws don't apply to

7:8 Hebrew *Ephraim*, referring to the northern kingdom of Israel; also in 7:11.   7:12 Hebrew *I will punish them because of what was reported against them in the assembly.*   8:9 Hebrew *Ephraim*, referring to the northern kingdom of Israel; also in 8:11.

them. [13]The people of Israel love their rituals of sacrifice, but to me their sacrifices are all meaningless! I will call my people to account for their sins, and I will punish them. They will go back down to Egypt.

[14]"Israel has built great palaces, and Judah has fortified its cities. But they have both forgotten their Maker. Therefore, I will send down fire on their palaces and burn their fortresses."

HOSEA ANNOUNCES ISRAEL'S PUNISHMENT

9 O people of Israel, do not rejoice as others do. For you have been unfaithful to your God, hiring yourselves out like prostitutes, offering sacrifices to other gods on every threshing floor. [2]So now your harvests will be too small to feed you. The grapes you gather will not quench your thirst. [3]You may no longer stay here in this land of the LORD. You will be carried off to Egypt and Assyria, where you will live on food that is ceremonially unclean.

[4]There, far from home, you will not be allowed to pour out wine as a sacrifice to the LORD. None of the sacrifices you offer there will please him. Such sacrifices will be unclean, just as food touched by a person in mourning is unclean. All who present such sacrifices will be defiled. They may eat this food to feed themselves, but they may not offer it to the LORD.

[5]What then will you do on festival days? What will you do on days of feasting in the LORD's presence? [6]Even if you escape destruction from Assyria, you will be conquered by Egypt. Memphis* will bury you. Briers will take over your treasures of silver; brambles will fill your homes.

[7]The time of Israel's punishment has come; the day of payment is almost here. Soon Israel will know this all too well. "The prophets are crazy!" the people shout. "The inspired men are mad!" So they taunt, for the nation is burdened with sin and shows only hatred for those who love God.

[8]The prophet is a watchman for my God over Israel,* yet traps are laid in front of him wherever he goes. He faces hostility even in the house of God. [9]The things my people do are as depraved as what they did in Gibeah long ago. God will not forget. He will surely punish them for their sins.

[10]The LORD says, "O Israel, when I first found you, it was like finding fresh grapes in the desert! When I saw your ancestors, it was like seeing the first ripe figs of the season! But then they deserted me for Baal-peor, giving themselves to that shameful idol. Soon they became as vile as the god they worshiped. [11]The glory of Israel will fly away like a bird, for your children will die at birth or perish in the womb or never even be conceived. [12]Even if your children do survive to grow up, I will take them from you. It will be a terrible day when I turn away and leave you alone. [13]I have watched Israel become as beautiful and pleasant as Tyre. But now Israel will bring out her children to be slaughtered."

[14]O LORD, what should I request for your people? I will ask for wombs that don't give birth and breasts that give no milk.

[15]The LORD says, "All their wickedness began at Gilgal; there I began to hate them. I will drive them from my land because of their evil actions. I will love them no more because all their leaders are rebels. [16]The people of Israel are stricken. Their roots are dried up; they will bear no more fruit. And if they give birth, I will slaughter their beloved children."

[17]My God will reject the people of Israel because they will not listen or obey. They will be wanderers, homeless among the nations.

THE LORD'S JUDGMENT AGAINST ISRAEL

10 How prosperous Israel is—a luxuriant vine loaded with fruit! But the more wealth the people got, the more they poured it

9:6 Memphis was the capital of northern Egypt. 9:8 Hebrew *Ephraim*, referring to the northern kingdom of Israel; also in 9:11, 13, 16.

My Daily Worship

— *August 12* —

THE SEEDS OF RIGHTEOUSNESS
HOSEA 6:1–10:15

I said, "Plant the good seeds of righteousness, and you will harvest a crop of my love.
Plow up the hard ground of your hearts, for now is the time to seek the LORD,
that he may come and shower righteousness upon you (10:12).

[i reflect]

An impossible task. How could this ground ever yield a harvest?

"Let us trust Mother Nature," they say. "Her sun and rain, the nutrients in her soil—these are the true means of growth."

"What?" the others counter. "Stop your poetic ramblings. They don't begin to disguise your laziness. We have days of work ahead of us to have any hope of producing crops. Especially with this drought."

What produces crops? Faith or good works? Tears or sweat? In farming, the answer is both. And in the soil of our own hearts, the answer is also both faith and work. God will shine his light on us, shower us with righteousness, and feed us from his Word. But we must get our hearts ready, we must break up any hard ground, we must clear out the rocks and stones, we must allow seeds of only high quality to be planted.

Saint Augustine pondered this dichotomy and wrote, "So then, what about those who acknowledge they don't have righteousness, but believe they can find it within themselves instead of seeking their Creator, the source of all righteousness? Yet it isn't a question of prayers alone, as if we don't need to include our willful efforts. For although God is 'our Helper,' nobody can be helped if they don't make some effort of their own. God doesn't work out our salvation in us as if we are dull stones or creatures without reason nor will."

What hard ground do you need to break up today so that God may find the soil of your heart ready for planting and receptive to the best seed? Confess those areas to God and ask that he will warm, water, and feed a righteous heart, willing and able to praise him.

[i pray]

God, I know the soil of my heart is often hard and rocky. Strengthen me and push me to get it ready for the seeds of righteousness you have, that my life may yield a crop worthy of you.

[i respond]

Read and memorize James 1:21: "So get rid of all the filth and evil in your lives, and humbly accept the message God has planted in your hearts, for it is strong enough to save your souls."

on the altars of their foreign gods. The richer the harvests they brought in, the more beautiful the statues and idols they built. ²The hearts of the people are fickle; they are guilty and must be punished. The LORD will break down their foreign altars and smash their many idols.

³Then they will say, "We have no king because we didn't fear the LORD. But what's the difference? What could a king do for us anyway?" ⁴They spout empty words and make promises they don't intend to keep. So perverted justice springs up among them like poisonous weeds in a farmer's field.

⁵The people of Samaria tremble for their calf idol at Beth-aven.* The people mourn over it, and the priests wail for it, because its glory will be stripped away. ⁶This idol they love so much will be carted away with them when they go as captives to Assyria, a gift to the great king there. Israel will be laughed at and shamed because its people have trusted in this idol. ⁷Samaria will be cut off, and its king will disappear like a chip of wood on an ocean wave. ⁸And the pagan shrines of Aven,* the place of Israel's sin, will crumble. Thorns and thistles will grow up around them. They will beg the mountains to bury them and the hills to fall on them.

⁹The LORD says, "O Israel, ever since that awful night in Gibeah, there has been only sin and more sin! You have made no progress whatsoever. Was it not right that the wicked men of Gibeah were attacked? ¹⁰Now I will attack you, too, for your rebellion and disobedience. I will call out the armies of the nations to punish you for your multiplied sins.

¹¹"Israel* is like a trained heifer accustomed to treading out the grain—an easy job that she loves. Now I will put a heavy yoke on her tender neck. I will drive her in front of the plow. Israel* and Judah must now break up the hard ground; their days of ease are gone. ¹²I said, 'Plant the good seeds of righteousness, and you will harvest a crop of my love. Plow up the hard ground of your hearts, for now is the time to seek the LORD, that he may come and shower righteousness upon you.'

¹³"But you have cultivated wickedness and raised a thriving crop of sins. You have eaten the fruit of lies—trusting in your military might, believing that great armies could make your nation safe! ¹⁴Now the terrors of war will rise among your people. All your fortifications will fall, just as they did when Shalman destroyed Beth-arbel. Even mothers and children were dashed to death there. ¹⁵You will share that fate, Bethel, because of your great wickedness. When the day of judgment dawns, the king of Israel will be completely destroyed.

THE LORD'S LOVE FOR ISRAEL

11 "When Israel was a child, I loved him as a son, and I called my son out of Egypt. ²But the more I* called to him, the more he rebelled, offering sacrifices to the images of Baal and burning incense to idols. ³It was I who taught Israel* how to walk, leading him along by the hand. But he doesn't know or even care that it was I who took care of him. ⁴I led Israel along with my ropes of kindness and love. I lifted the yoke from his neck, and I myself stooped to feed him.

⁵"But since my people refuse to return to me, they will go back to Egypt and will be forced to serve Assyria. ⁶War will swirl through their cities; their enemies will crash through their gates and destroy them, trapping them in their own evil plans. ⁷For my people are determined to desert me. They call me the Most High, but they don't truly honor me.

⁸"Oh, how can I give you up, Israel? How can I let you go? How can I destroy you like Admah and Zeboiim? My heart is torn within me, and my compassion overflows. ⁹No, I will

---

10:5 Beth-aven means "house of wickedness"; it is being used as another name for Bethel, which means "house of God." **10:8** Aven is a reference to Beth-aven; see 10:5 and the note there. **10:11a** Hebrew Ephraim, referring to the northern kingdom of Israel. **10:11b** Hebrew Jacob. **11:2** As in Greek version; Hebrew reads they. **11:3** Hebrew Ephraim, referring to the northern kingdom of Israel; also in 11:8, 9, 12.

not punish you as much as my burning anger tells me to. I will not completely destroy Israel, for I am God and not a mere mortal. I am the Holy One living among you, and I will not come to destroy.

¹⁰"For someday the people will follow the LORD. I will roar like a lion, and my people will return trembling from the west. ¹¹Like a flock of birds, they will come from Egypt. Flying like doves, they will return from Assyria. And I will bring them home again," says the LORD.

CHARGES AGAINST ISRAEL AND JUDAH

¹²Israel surrounds me with lies and deceit, but Judah still walks with God and is faithful to the Holy One.*

12 The people of Israel* feed on the wind; they chase after the east wind all day long. They multiply lies and violence; they make alliances with Assyria and cut deals with the Egyptians.

²Now the LORD is bringing a lawsuit against Judah. He is about to punish Jacob* for all his deceitful ways. ³Before Jacob was born, he struggled with his brother; when he became a man, he even fought with God. ⁴Yes, he wrestled with the angel and won. He wept and pleaded for a blessing from him. There at Bethel he met God face to face, and God spoke to him*—⁵the LORD God Almighty, the LORD is his name! ⁶So now, come back to your God! Act on the principles of love and justice, and always live in confident dependence on your God.

⁷But no, the people are like crafty merchants selling from dishonest scales—they love to cheat. ⁸Israel boasts, "I am rich, and I've gotten it all by myself! No one can say I got it by cheating! My record is spotless!"

⁹"I am the LORD your God, who rescued you from your slavery in Egypt. And I will make

---

If I find in myself a desire which no experience in this world can satisfy, the most probable explanation is that I was made for another world.

C. S. LEWIS

---

you live in tents again, as you do each year when you celebrate the Festival of Shelters.* ¹⁰I sent my prophets to warn you with many visions and parables."

¹¹But Gilead is filled with sinners who worship idols. And in Gilgal, too, they sacrifice bulls; their altars are lined up like the heaps of stone along the edges of a plowed field. ¹²Jacob fled to the land of Aram and earned a wife by tending sheep. ¹³Then the LORD led Jacob's descendants, the Israelites, out of Egypt by a prophet, who guided and protected them. ¹⁴But the people of Israel have bitterly provoked the LORD, so their Lord will now sentence them to death in payment for their sins.

THE LORD'S ANGER AGAINST ISRAEL

13 In the past when the tribe of Ephraim spoke, the people shook with fear because the other Israelite tribes looked up to them. But the people of Ephraim sinned by worshiping Baal and thus sealed their destruction. ²Now they keep on sinning by making silver idols to worship—images shaped skillfully with human hands. "Sacrifice to these," they cry, "and kiss the calf idols!" ³Therefore, they will disappear like the morning mist, like dew in the morning sun, like chaff blown by the wind, like smoke from a chimney.

⁴"I am the LORD your God, who rescued you from your slavery in Egypt. You have no God

---

11:12 Or *and Judah is unruly against God, the faithful Holy One.*   12:1 Hebrew *Ephraim,* referring to the northern kingdom of Israel; also in 12:8, 14.   12:2 *Jacob* means "he grasps at the heel"; this can also figuratively mean "he deceives."   12:4 As in Greek and Syriac versions; Hebrew reads *to us.*   12:9 Hebrew *as in the days of your appointed feast.*

but me, for there is no other savior. [5]I took care of you in the wilderness, in that dry and thirsty land. [6]But when you had eaten and were satisfied, then you became proud and forgot me. [7]So now I will attack you like a lion, or like a leopard that lurks along the road. [8]I will rip you to pieces like a bear whose cubs have been taken away. I will tear you apart and devour you like a hungry lion.

[9]"You are about to be destroyed, O Israel, though I am your helper. [10]Where now is* your king? Why don't you call on him for help? Where are all the leaders of the land? You asked for them, now let them save you! [11]In my anger I gave you kings, and in my fury I took them away.

[12]"The sins of Ephraim have been collected and stored away for punishment. [13]The people have been offered new birth, but they are like a child who resists being born. How stubborn they are! How foolish! [14]Should I ransom them from the grave? Should I redeem them from death? O death, bring forth your terrors! O grave, bring forth your plagues! For I will not relent! [15]Ephraim was the most fruitful of all his brothers, but the east wind—a blast from the LORD—will arise in the desert. It will blow hard against the people of Ephraim, drying up their land. All their flowing springs and wells will disappear. Every precious thing they have will be plundered and carried away. [16]The people of Samaria must bear the consequences of their guilt because they rebelled against their God. They will be killed by an invading army, their little ones dashed to death against the ground, their pregnant women ripped open by swords."

HEALING FOR THE REPENTANT

14 Return, O Israel, to the LORD your God, for your sins have brought you down. [2]Bring your petitions, and return to the LORD. Say to him, "Forgive all our sins and graciously receive us, so that we may offer you the sacrifice of praise. [3]Assyria cannot save us, nor can our strength in battle. Never again will we call the idols we have made 'our gods.' No, in you alone do the orphans find mercy."

[4]The LORD says, "Then I will heal you of your idolatry and faithlessness, and my love will know no bounds, for my anger will be gone forever! [5]I will be to Israel like a refreshing dew from heaven. It will blossom like the lily; it will send roots deep into the soil like the cedars in Lebanon. [6]Its branches will spread out like those of beautiful olive trees, as fragrant as the cedar forests of Lebanon. [7]My people will return again to the safety of their land. They will flourish like grain and blossom like grapevines. They will be as fragrant as the wines of Lebanon.

[8]"O Israel,* stay away from idols! I am the one who looks after you and cares for you. I am like a tree that is always green, giving my fruit to you all through the year."

[9]Let those who are wise understand these things. Let those who are discerning listen carefully. The paths of the LORD are true and right, and righteous people live by walking in them. But sinners stumble and fall along the way.

13:10 As in Greek and Syriac versions and Latin Vulgate; Hebrew reads *I will be.*   14:8 Hebrew *Ephraim,* referring to the northern kingdom of Israel.

My Daily Worship

— *August 13* —

OFFER YOUR SACRIFICE OF PRAISE
HOSEA 11:1–14:9

Bring your petitions, and return to the LORD. Say to him, "Forgive all our sins and graciously receive us, so that we may offer you the sacrifice of praise" (14:2).

[i reflect]

Giving thanks before serving Holy Communion, the Celebrant says: "We celebrate the memorial of our redemption, O Father, in this sacrifice of praise and thanksgiving. Recalling his death, resurrection, and ascension, we offer you these gifts."

These words are from the *Book of Common Prayer,* the worship "manual" of the Episcopal Church. But the call to a sacrifice of praise and thanksgiving is for individuals as well. And it has gone out for millennia. "Put it all before the LORD," said the prophets and priests. "Offer your petitions. Offer yourself. But then, forgiven one, do not stop offering. Offer the sacrifice of praise."

Why a *sacrifice* of praise? A sacrifice of praise refers to thank offerings to God—real, heartfelt repentance, not just going through the motions. It is a continual reminder that we are to offer something of value. And sometimes it costs. "It's a real sacrifice of time," complains the person who really would rather not part with those precious minutes. "I'd be sacrificing my career advancement," says the employee who debates cutting back on hours to care for a family member. "I'd be sacrificing feeling hurt and deprived," thinks the one not used to giving thanks during the hard times.

The author of the letter to the Hebrews echoed the phrase from Hosea, "With Jesus' help, let us continually offer our sacrifice of praise to God by proclaiming the glory of his name" (13:15).

Offer your petitions today. Offer yourself. Offer the sacrifice of praise.

[i pray]

LORD God, I am in awe of all that you are. I am grateful for all you have given to me.
Accept my prayer, a sacrifice of praise and thanksgiving to you.

[i respond]

Devote some time to offering a sacrifice of praise and thanksgiving. Write a litany of at least seven lines, with each line beginning, "I offer a sacrifice of praise for . . ." Pray it each day this week in your devotional time.

Joel

Turn to me now, . . . Give me your hearts (2:12).

A Time of Judgment

The thick dark cloud looms over the horizon. As the day wears on, the cloud moves closer, larger, more ominous, until it completely blocks the sun. Not one raindrop does the cloud contain. Instead, it is a moving, thunderous cacophony of thousands upon thousands of locusts. Then the cloud lowers near the ground, and the armies of grasshoppers invade, devouring every piece of vegetation in their path, leaving in their wake a denuded, desolate wasteland.

That sounds like a scene from a science fiction movie, but it's real. Many centuries ago, Joel warned of such an invasion: "Ahead of them the land lies fair as the Garden of Eden. . . . Behind them is nothing but desolation; . . . They swarm over the city and run along its walls. . . . The sun and moon grow dark" (2:3, 9, 10).

As terrible and horrifying as the prophecy of a locust plague, it would only be a foretaste of the future day of judgment. Behind the locust was Joel's message to the people of Judah, calling them to repent of their idolatry. He pleaded with the people, "The LORD says, 'Turn to me now, while there is time! Give me your hearts. . . . Don't tear your clothing in your grief; instead, tear your hearts.' Return to the LORD your God, for he is gracious and merciful" (2:12–13).

If Judah didn't repent, Joel warned, then God was going to bring a great invading army—not just a plague of locusts—to destroy the land and carry the people away. Yet, into this disturbing news he also weaves a message of hope, of God's kindness and blessings. God promised that, ultimately, "anyone who calls on the name of the LORD will be saved" (2:32).

It's easy to gloss over Joel's message as one meant for a specific people at a specific time. But, we, too, need to grasp Joel's vision of God's power and might and of his ultimate judgment of sin. The message is clear—as part of our personal worship, we need to repent and "tear our hearts" for God.

Worship Moments

- Prayers of intercession and repentance are part of worship. "The priests . . . will stand between the people and the altar, weeping. Let them pray, 'Spare your people, LORD!'" (2:17).

- Rejoicing is an essential part of worship. "Rejoice in the LORD your God!" (2:23).

- Salvation is accessible: "Anyone who calls on the name of the LORD will be saved" (2:32).

- God's dwelling place is with his people. "I, the LORD your God, live in Zion, my holy mountain" (3:17).

1

The LORD gave this message to Joel son of Pethuel.

MOURNING OVER THE LOCUST PLAGUE

²Hear this, you leaders of the people! Everyone listen! In all your history, has anything like this ever happened before? ³Tell your children about it in the years to come. Pass the awful story down from generation to generation. ⁴After the cutting locusts finished eating the crops, the swarming locusts took what was left! After them came the hopping locusts, and then the stripping locusts,* too!

⁵Wake up, you drunkards, and weep! All the grapes are ruined, and all your new wine is gone! ⁶A vast army of locusts* has invaded my land. It is a terrible army, too numerous to count! Its teeth are as sharp as the teeth of lions! ⁷They have destroyed my grapevines and fig trees, stripping their bark and leaving the branches white and bare.

⁸Weep with sorrow, as a virgin weeps when her fiancé has died. ⁹There is no grain or wine to offer at the Temple of the LORD. The priests are mourning because there are no offerings. Listen to the weeping of these ministers of the LORD! ¹⁰The fields are ruined and empty of crops. The grain, the wine, and the olive oil are gone.

¹¹Despair, all you farmers! Wail, all you vine growers! Weep, because the wheat and barley—yes, all the field crops—are ruined. ¹²The grapevines and the fig trees have all withered. The pomegranate trees, palm trees, and apple trees—yes, all the fruit trees—have dried up. All joy has dried up with them.

¹³Dress yourselves in sackcloth, you priests! Wail, you who serve before the altar! Come, spend the night in sackcloth, you ministers of my God! There is no grain or wine to offer at the Temple of your God. ¹⁴Announce a time of fasting; call the people together for a solemn meeting. Bring the leaders and all the people into the Temple of the LORD your God, and cry out to him there. ¹⁵The day of the LORD is on the way, the day when destruction comes from the Almighty. How terrible that day will be!

¹⁶We watch as our food disappears before our very eyes. There are no joyful celebrations in the house of our God. ¹⁷The seeds die in the parched ground, and the grain crops fail. The barns and granaries stand empty and abandoned. ¹⁸How the animals moan with hunger! The cattle wander about confused because there is no pasture for them. The sheep bleat in misery.

¹⁹LORD, help us! The fire has consumed the pastures and burned up all the trees. ²⁰Even the wild animals cry out to you because they have no water to drink. The streams have dried up, and fire has consumed the pastures.

LOCUSTS INVADE LIKE AN ARMY

2

Blow the trumpet in Jerusalem*! Sound the alarm on my holy mountain! Let everyone tremble in fear because the day of the LORD is upon us. ²It is a day of darkness and gloom, a day of thick clouds and deep blackness. Suddenly, like dawn spreading across the mountains, a mighty army appears! How great and powerful they are! The likes of them have not been seen before and never will be seen again.

³Fire burns in front of them and follows them in every direction! Ahead of them the land lies as fair as the Garden of Eden in all its beauty. Behind them is nothing but desolation; not one thing escapes. ⁴They look like tiny horses, and they run as fast. ⁵Look at them as they leap along the mountaintops! Listen to the noise they make—like the rumbling of chariots, like the roar of a fire sweeping across a field, or like a mighty army moving into battle.

⁶Fear grips all the people; every face grows pale with fright. ⁷The attackers march like warriors and scale city walls like trained soldiers. Straight forward they march, never

---

1:4 The precise identification of the four kinds of locusts mentioned here is uncertain. 1:6 Hebrew *A nation*. 2:1 Hebrew *Zion*; also in 2:15, 23.

breaking rank. [8]They never jostle each other; each moves in exactly the right place. They lunge through the gaps, and no weapon can stop them. [9]They swarm over the city and run along its walls. They enter all the houses, climbing like thieves through the windows.

[10]The earth quakes as they advance, and the heavens tremble. The sun and moon grow dark, and the stars no longer shine. [11]The LORD leads them with a shout! This is his mighty army, and they follow his orders. The day of the LORD is an awesome, terrible thing. Who can endure it?

A Call to Repentance

[12]That is why the LORD says, "Turn to me now, while there is time! Give me your hearts. Come with fasting, weeping, and mourning. [13]Don't tear your clothing in your grief; instead, tear your hearts." Return to the LORD your God, for he is gracious and merciful. He is not easily angered. He is filled with kindness and is eager not to punish you. [14]Who knows? Perhaps even yet he will give you a reprieve, sending you a blessing instead of this terrible curse. Perhaps he will give you so much that you will be able to offer grain and wine to the LORD your God as before!

[15]Blow the trumpet in Jerusalem! Announce a time of fasting; call the people together for a solemn meeting. [16]Bring everyone—the elders, the children, and even the babies. Call the bridegroom from his quarters and the bride from her private room. [17]The priests, who minister in the LORD's presence, will stand between the people and the altar, weeping. Let them pray, "Spare your people, LORD! They belong to you, so don't let them become an object of mockery. Don't let their name become a proverb of unbelieving foreigners who say, 'Where is the God of Israel? He must be helpless!'"

The Lord's Promise of Restoration

[18]Then the LORD will pity his people and be indignant for the honor of his land! [19]He will reply, "Look! I am sending you grain and wine and olive oil, enough to satisfy your needs. You will no longer be an object of mockery among the surrounding nations. [20]I will remove these armies from the north and send them far away. I will drive them back into the parched wastelands, where they will die. Those in the rear will go into the Dead Sea; those at the front will go into the Mediterranean.* The stench of their rotting bodies will rise over the land."

Surely the LORD has done great things! [21]Don't be afraid, my people! Be glad now and rejoice because the LORD has done great things. [22]Don't be afraid, you animals of the field! The pastures will soon be green. The trees will again be filled with luscious fruit; fig trees and grapevines will flourish once more. [23]Rejoice, you people of Jerusalem! Rejoice in the LORD your God! For the rains he sends are an expression of his grace. Once more the autumn rains will come, as well as the rains of spring. [24]The threshing floors will again be piled high with grain, and the presses will overflow with wine and olive oil.

[25]The LORD says, "I will give you back what you lost to the stripping locusts, the cutting locusts, the swarming locusts, and the hopping locusts.* It was I who sent this great destroying army against you. [26]Once again you will have all the food you want, and you will praise the LORD your God, who does these miracles for you. Never again will my people be disgraced like this. [27]Then you will know that I am here among my people of Israel and that I alone am the LORD your God. My people will never again be disgraced like this.

The Lord's Promise of His Spirit

[28]"Then after I have poured out my rains again, I will pour out my Spirit upon all people. Your sons and daughters will prophesy. Your old men will dream dreams. Your young men will see visions. [29]In those days, I will

---

2:20 Hebrew *the eastern sea; . . . the western sea.*   **2:25** The precise identification of the four kinds of locusts mentioned here is uncertain.

My Daily Worship

— August 14 —

A CHANGE OF HEART

JOEL 1:1–3:21

That is why the LORD says, "Turn to me now, while there is time!
Give me your hearts. Come with fasting, weeping, and mourning" (2:12).

[i reflect]

"But, God, they are *still* turned the wrong way! I wonder if they are even *able* to change. When are you going to say 'Enough is enough'?"

Repent, turn, change, the prophet Joel had been telling the people of Judah. Faithful communicator of God's message to his people, did he wonder if it were a limited-time offer? Was there a freshness date, or small print saying, "Must be redeemed by ____"?

"Yes, Joel, my people can change," God seems to say. "And I continue to be gracious and merciful. Slow to anger. Tell the people again, 'Return to the LORD your God.' My offer still stands."

We, too, can marvel at God's patience and God's offer. The same invitation, the same call to repentance hits our ears. "Turn to me now. . . . Give me your hearts." How will you respond?

In the mid-1990s, the devotional classic *My Utmost for His Highest* was updated using today's language. A group of Christian artists turned some of the devotions into music. Bryan Duncan expressed his gratitude that our gracious God could accept and redeem us in the song "A Heart Like Mine." That God could want him and seek him, with such a sinful heart, how could he be worthy? It is only God's redemption that made it so, the song continues. With abandon, every beat of our redeemed hearts can beat to a new purpose.

Repent, turn, change. Come to him today with "fasting, weeping, and mourning" for those areas in your life that need a change of heart.

[i pray]

I am grateful that you could love a heart like mine. I am thankful for your offer to redeem me
when I turn from sin. O gracious and merciful God, my heart beats for you.

[i respond]

What turns your heart away from God? Take a symbol of that (for example, an advertisement, a photograph, a dollar bill) and place it on a table. While seated, deliberately turn *away* from it and picture yourself turning *toward* God.

pour out my Spirit even on servants, men and women alike.

[30]"I will cause wonders in the heavens and on the earth—blood and fire and pillars of smoke. [31]The sun will be turned into darkness, and the moon will turn bloodred before that great and terrible day of the LORD arrives. [32]And anyone who calls on the name of the LORD will be saved. There will be people on Mount Zion in Jerusalem who escape, just as the LORD has said. These will be among the survivors whom the LORD has called.

JUDGMENT AGAINST ENEMY NATIONS

3 "At that time, when I restore the prosperity of Judah and Jerusalem," says the LORD, [2]"I will gather the armies of the world into the valley of Jehoshaphat.* There I will judge them for harming my people, for scattering my inheritance among the nations, and for dividing up my land. [3]They cast lots to decide which of my people would be their slaves. They traded young boys for prostitutes and little girls for enough wine to get drunk.

[4]"What do you have against me, Tyre and Sidon and you cities of Philistia? Are you trying to take revenge on me? If you are, then watch out! I will strike swiftly and pay you back for everything you have done. [5]You have taken my silver and gold and all my precious treasures, and you have carried them off to your pagan temples. [6]You have sold the people of Judah and Jerusalem to the Greeks,* who took them far from their homeland. [7]But I will bring them back again from all these places to which you sold them, and I will pay you back for all you have done. [8]I will sell your sons and daughters to the people of Judah, and they will sell them to the peoples of Arabia,* a nation far away. I, the LORD, have spoken!"

[9]Say to the nations far and wide: "Get ready for war! Call out your best warriors! Let all your fighting men advance for the attack! [10]Beat your plowshares into swords and your pruning hooks into spears. Train even your weaklings to be warriors. [11]Come quickly, all you nations everywhere! Gather together in the valley."

And now, O LORD, call out your warriors!

[12]"Let the nations be called to arms. Let them march to the valley of Jehoshaphat. There I, the LORD, will sit to pronounce judgment on them all. [13]Now let the sickle do its work, for the harvest is ripe. Come, tread the winepress because it is full. The storage vats are overflowing with the wickedness of these people."

[14]Thousands upon thousands are waiting in the valley of decision. It is there that the day of the LORD will soon arrive. [15]The sun and moon will grow dark, and the stars will no longer shine. [16]The LORD's voice will roar from Zion and thunder from Jerusalem, and the earth and heavens will begin to shake. But to his people of Israel, the LORD will be a welcoming refuge and a strong fortress.

BLESSINGS FOR GOD'S PEOPLE

[17]"Then you will know that I, the LORD your God, live in Zion, my holy mountain. Jerusalem will be holy forever, and foreign armies will never conquer her again. [18]In that day the mountains will drip with sweet wine, and the hills will flow with milk. Water will fill the dry streambeds of Judah, and a fountain will burst forth from the LORD's Temple, watering the arid valley of acacias.* [19]Egypt will become a wasteland and Edom a wilderness, because they attacked Judah and killed her innocent people.

[20]"But Judah will remain forever, and Jerusalem will endure through all future generations. [21]I will pardon my people's crimes, which I have not yet pardoned; and I, the LORD, will make my home in Jerusalem* with my people."

3:2 Jehoshaphat means "the LORD judges." **3:6** Hebrew to the peoples of Javan. **3:8** Hebrew to the Sabeans. **3:18** Hebrew valley of Shittim. **3:21** Hebrew Zion.

Amos

Do what is good and run from evil—that you may live! (5:14).

Stop Cheating on God!

When we walk through the front doors of church on Sunday, our all-is-well-with-the-world smile gets plastered on. We greet others with cheerful hellos, asking "How are you?" but never really stopping to hear the answer or to give an honest one in return. We look good and cleaned up on the outside, but inside is a different story. Behind the façade of well-being, we are hurting, depressed, angry, fearful, and anxious people. But no one would ever know it by looking at our appearance.

The same was true in Amos's day. The people looked good religiously. They brought sacrifices, went to the Temple, fasted, went through all the right motions, but their faith was empty. They worshiped idols, oppressed the poor, and had grown so complacent in their relationship with God that they had forgotten God's standards.

God tells Amos that, even though his people appear religious, they were cheating on him by cheating others: "You who rob the poor and trample the needy! . . . You measure out your grain in false measures" (8:4–5). Worse, they had neglected God's word. "My people have forgotten what it means to do right, . . . Therefore, . . . an enemy is coming!" (3:10–11).

God scolded the people of Amos's time—just as he scolds us when we put on a religious show and pretend to be good, but "can't wait for the Sabbath to be over . . . so you can get back to cheating the helpless" (8:5).

This book is about a hypocritical people who put on a happy, religious face for God. The Lord is not impressed by what we do to appear good. Never has been. Never will be. As you read Amos, ask yourself, Where does truth and justice fit into my life? How real is my own worship of the Lord? Like the people of Amos's day, we are being called to hate evil and do what is good. We are being called to return to the Lord—and live!

Worship Moments

- Worship the Lord with holy living. "Away with your hymns of praise! . . . I want to see a mighty flood of justice, a river of righteous living" (5:23–24).

- "O Sovereign Lord, please forgive your people!" Amos intercedes on their behalf (7:2).

- God is called: "the Lord who created the stars, . . . who turns darkness into morning, . . . who draws up water from the oceans" (5:8).

1 This message was given to Amos, a shepherd from the town of Tekoa in Judah. He received this message in visions two years before the earthquake, when Uzziah was king of Judah and Jeroboam II, the son of Jehoash,* was king of Israel.

²This is his report of what he saw and heard: "The LORD's voice roars from his Temple on Mount Zion; he thunders from Jerusalem! Suddenly, the lush pastures of the shepherds dry up. All the grass on Mount Carmel withers and dies."

GOD'S JUDGMENT ON ISRAEL'S NEIGHBORS

³This is what the LORD says: "The people of Damascus have sinned again and again, and I will not forget it. I will not let them go unpunished any longer! They beat down my people in Gilead as grain is threshed with threshing sledges of iron. ⁴So I will send down fire on King Hazael's palace, and the fortresses of King Ben-hadad will be destroyed. ⁵I will break down the gates of Damascus and slaughter its people all the way to the valley of Aven.* I will destroy the ruler in Beth-eden, and the people of Aram will return to Kir as slaves. I, the LORD, have spoken!"

⁶This is what the LORD says: "The people of Gaza have sinned again and again, and I will not forget it. I will not let them go unpunished any longer! They sent my people into exile, selling them as slaves in Edom. ⁷So I will send down fire on the walls of Gaza, and all its fortresses will be destroyed. ⁸I will slaughter the people of Ashdod and destroy the king of Ashkelon. Then I will turn to attack Ekron, and the few Philistines still left will be killed. I, the Sovereign LORD, have spoken!"

⁹This is what the LORD says: "The people of Tyre have sinned again and again, and I will not forget it. I will not let them go unpunished any longer! They broke their treaty of brotherhood with Israel, selling whole villages as slaves to Edom. ¹⁰So I will send down fire

on the walls of Tyre, and all its fortresses will be destroyed."

¹¹This is what the LORD says: "The people of Edom have sinned again and again, and I will not forget it. I will not let them go unpunished any longer! They chased down their relatives, the Israelites, with swords. They showed them no mercy and were unrelenting in their anger. ¹²So I will send down fire on Teman, and the fortresses of Bozrah will be destroyed."

> *Most of the verses written about praise in God's Word were voiced by people faced with crushing heartaches, injustice, treachery, slander, and scores of other difficult situations.*
>
> JONI EARECKSON TADA

¹³This is what the LORD says: "The people of Ammon have sinned again and again, and I will not forget it. I will not let them go unpunished any longer! When they attacked Gilead to extend their borders, they committed cruel crimes, ripping open pregnant women with their swords. ¹⁴So I will send down fire on the walls of Rabbah, and all its fortresses will be destroyed. There will be wild shouts during the battle, swirling like a whirlwind in a mighty storm. ¹⁵And their king* and his princes will go into exile together. I, the LORD, have spoken!"

2 This is what the LORD says: "The people of Moab have sinned again and again, and I will not forget it. I will not let them go unpunished any longer! They desecrated the tomb of Edom's king and burned his bones to ashes. ²So I will send down fire on the land of Moab, and all the fortresses in Kerioth will be destroyed. The people will fall in the noise of

1:1 Hebrew *Joash*, a variant name for Jehoash. 1:5 *Aven* means "wickedness." 1:15 Hebrew *malcam*, possibly referring to their god Molech.

battle, as the warriors shout and the trumpets blare. ³And I will destroy their king and slaughter all their princes. I, the LORD, have spoken!"

GOD'S JUDGMENT ON JUDAH AND ISRAEL

⁴This is what the LORD says: "The people of Judah have sinned again and again, and I will not forget it. I will not let them go unpunished any longer! They have rejected the laws of the LORD, refusing to obey him. They have been led astray by the same lies that deceived their ancestors. ⁵So I will send down fire on Judah, and all the fortresses of Jerusalem will be destroyed."

⁶This is what the LORD says: "The people of Israel have sinned again and again, and I will not forget it. I will not let them go unpunished any longer! They have perverted justice by selling honest people for silver and poor people for a pair of sandals. ⁷They trample helpless people in the dust and deny justice to those who are oppressed. Both father and son sleep with the same woman, corrupting my holy name. ⁸At their religious festivals, they lounge around in clothing stolen from their debtors. In the house of their god, they present offerings of wine purchased with stolen money.

⁹"Yet think of all I did for my people! I destroyed the Amorites before my people arrived in the land. The Amorites were as tall as cedar trees and strong as oaks, but I destroyed their fruit and dug out their roots. ¹⁰It was I who rescued you from Egypt and led you through the desert for forty years so you could possess the land of the Amorites. ¹¹I chose some of your sons to be prophets and others to be Nazirites. Can you deny this, my people of Israel?" asks the LORD. ¹²"But you caused the Nazirites to sin by making them drink your wine, and you said to my prophets, 'Shut up!'

¹³"So I will make you groan as a wagon groans when it is loaded down with grain.

¹⁴Your fastest runners will not get away. The strongest among you will become weak. Even the mightiest warriors will be unable to save themselves. ¹⁵The archers will fail to stand their ground. The swiftest soldiers won't be fast enough to escape. Even warriors on horses won't be able to outrun the danger. ¹⁶On that day, the most courageous of your fighting men will drop their weapons and run for their lives. I, the LORD, have spoken!"

3 Listen to this message that the LORD has spoken against you, O people of Israel and Judah—the entire family I rescued from Egypt: ²"From among all the families on the earth, I chose you alone. That is why I must punish you for all your sins."

WITNESSES AGAINST GUILTY ISRAEL

³Can two people walk together without agreeing on the direction? ⁴Does a lion ever roar in a thicket without first finding a victim? Does a young lion growl in its den without first catching its prey? ⁵Does a bird ever get caught in a trap that has no bait? Does a trap ever spring shut when there's nothing there to catch? ⁶When the war trumpet blares, shouldn't the people be alarmed? When disaster comes to a city, isn't it because the LORD planned it?

⁷"But always, first of all, I warn you through my servants the prophets. I, the Sovereign LORD, have now done this."

⁸The lion has roared—tremble in fear! The Sovereign LORD has spoken—I dare not refuse to proclaim his message!

⁹Announce this to the leaders of Philistia* and Egypt: "Take your seats now on the hills around Samaria, and witness the scandalous spectacle of all Israel's crimes."

¹⁰"My people have forgotten what it means to do right," says the LORD. "Their fortresses are filled with wealth taken by theft and violence. ¹¹Therefore," says the Sovereign LORD, "an enemy is coming! He will surround them

3:9 Hebrew *Ashdod.*

and shatter their defenses. Then he will plunder all their fortresses."

¹²This is what the LORD says: "A shepherd who tries to rescue a sheep from a lion's mouth will recover only two legs and a piece of ear. So it will be when the Israelites in Samaria are rescued with only a broken chair and a tattered pillow. ¹³Now listen to this, and announce it throughout all Israel,*" says the Lord, the LORD God Almighty. ¹⁴"On the very day I punish Israel for its sins, I will destroy the pagan altars at Bethel. The horns of the altar will be cut off and fall to the ground. ¹⁵And I will destroy the beautiful homes of the wealthy—their winter mansions and their summer houses, too—all their palaces filled with ivory. I, the LORD, have spoken!"

ISRAEL'S FAILURE TO LEARN

4 Listen to me, you "fat cows" of Samaria, you women who oppress the poor and crush the needy and who are always asking your husbands for another drink! ²The Sovereign LORD has sworn this by his holiness: "The time will come when you will be led away with hooks in your noses. Every last one of you will be dragged away like a fish on a hook! ³You will leave by going straight through the breaks in the wall; you will be thrown from your fortresses.* I, the LORD, have spoken!

⁴"Go ahead and offer your sacrifices to the idols at Bethel and Gilgal. Keep on disobeying—your sins are mounting up! Offer sacrifices each morning and bring your tithes every three days! ⁵Present your bread made with yeast as an offering of thanksgiving. Then give your extra voluntary offerings so you can brag about it everywhere! This is the kind of thing you Israelites love to do," says the Sovereign LORD.

⁶"I brought hunger to every city and famine to every town. But still you wouldn't return to me," says the LORD.

⁷"I kept the rain from falling when you needed it the most, ruining all your crops. I sent rain on one town but withheld it from another. Rain fell on one field, while another field withered away. ⁸People staggered from one town to another for a drink of water, but there was never enough. But still you wouldn't return to me," says the LORD.

⁹"I struck your farms and vineyards with blight and mildew. Locusts devoured all your fig and olive trees. But still you wouldn't return to me," says the LORD.

¹⁰"I sent plagues against you like the plagues I sent against Egypt long ago. I killed your young men in war and slaughtered all your horses. The stench of death filled the air! But still you wouldn't return to me," says the LORD.

¹¹"I destroyed some of your cities, as I destroyed* Sodom and Gomorrah. Those of you who survived were like half-burned sticks snatched from a fire. But still you wouldn't return to me," says the LORD.

¹²"Therefore, I will bring upon you all these further disasters I have announced. Prepare to meet your God as he comes in judgment, you people of Israel!"

¹³For the LORD is the one who shaped the mountains, stirs up the winds, and reveals his every thought. He turns the light of dawn into darkness and treads the mountains under his feet. The LORD God Almighty is his name!

A CALL TO REPENTANCE

5 Listen, you people of Israel! Listen to this funeral song I am singing:

² "The virgin Israel has fallen,
    never to rise again!
She lies forsaken on the ground,
    with none to raise her up."

³The Sovereign LORD says: "When one of your cities sends a thousand men to battle, only a hundred will return. When a town sends a hundred, only ten will come back alive."

3:13 Hebrew *the house of Jacob.* **4:3** Hebrew *thrown out toward Harmon,* possibly a reference to Mount Hermon. **4:11** Hebrew *as when God destroyed.*

My Daily Worship

— *August 15* —

DISCIPLINED IN LOVE

AMOS 1:1—4:13

From among all the families on the earth, I chose you alone.
That is why I must punish you for all your sins (3:2).

[i reflect]

"You don't love me anymore. That's why you're doing this."

A father is about to punish a child who is "getting too big for his britches." The child's words are not completely unexpected—after all, didn't he throw the same accusation at his own father? Nevertheless, it catches him up short.

"Don't love you anymore? Are you *kidding?* It's just because I love you that I'm doing this." The child waits for the next sentence that tests his young powers to comprehend parental logic: "This is going to hurt me more than it hurts you."

The children of God had been riding along on a caravan of prosperity. "Times are great. And with a king like Jeroboam, we can't lose. Who needs God when you're sittin' pretty like us?"

Israel's britches are about to split. They are sitting, but it's not pretty.

"Listen to this message," warned the prophet Amos. "God the Father chose you. You alone! Out of his great love he did this. He can't let you go on, as unpunished children."

After rescuing his chosen people from slavery in Egypt, he reminded them of his care, after the forty years in the wilderness. They were wanderers, yet still watched over. "So you should realize that just as a parent disciplines a child, the LORD your God disciplines you to help you" (Deuteronomy 8:5).

Centuries later, Solomon brings the message of love that cannot look the other way when we sin: "My child, don't ignore it when the LORD disciplines you, and don't be discouraged when he corrects you. For the LORD corrects those he loves, just as a father corrects a child in whom he delights" (Proverbs 3:11–12).

This is the way of God with his people, his beloved children. How has God brought his loving discipline into your life? Today, thank him for correcting your course because he loves you.

[i pray]

Father God, I know that I stray from your ways like a wayward child. Yet you chose me
and you still love me. Call me back. Convict me. Correct me.

[i respond]

What characteristics of discipline are effective with children you know? Write down three of these things that are parallel to how God the Father has dealt with you in recent years. Thank him for his loving ways.

⁴Now this is what the LORD says to the family of Israel: "Come back to me and live! ⁵Don't go to worship the idols of Bethel, Gilgal, or Beersheba. For the people of Gilgal will be dragged off into exile, and the people of Bethel will come to nothing."

⁶Come back to the LORD and live! If you don't, he will roar through Israel* like a fire, devouring you completely. Your gods in Bethel certainly won't be able to quench the flames! ⁷You wicked people! You twist justice, making it a bitter pill for the poor and oppressed. Righteousness and fair play are meaningless fictions to you.

⁸It is the LORD who created the stars, the Pleiades and Orion. It is he who turns darkness into morning and day into night. It is he who draws up water from the oceans and pours it down as rain on the land. The LORD is his name! ⁹With blinding speed and power he destroys the strong, crushing all their defenses.

¹⁰How you hate honest judges! How you despise people who tell the truth! ¹¹You trample the poor and steal what little they have through taxes and unfair rent. Therefore, you will never live in the beautiful stone houses you are building. You will never drink wine from the lush vineyards you are planting. ¹²For I know the vast number of your sins and rebellions. You oppress good people by taking bribes and deprive the poor of justice in the courts. ¹³So those who are wise will keep quiet, for it is an evil time.

¹⁴Do what is good and run from evil—that you may live! Then the LORD God Almighty will truly be your helper, just as you have claimed he is. ¹⁵Hate evil and love what is good; remodel your courts into true halls of justice. Perhaps even yet the LORD God Almighty will have mercy on his people who remain.*

¹⁶Therefore, this is what the Lord, the LORD God Almighty, says: "There will be crying in all the public squares and in every street. Call for the farmers to weep with you, and summon professional mourners to wail and lament. ¹⁷There will be wailing in every vineyard, for I will pass through and destroy them all. I, the LORD, have spoken!"

WARNING OF COMING JUDGMENT

¹⁸How terrible it will be for you who say, "If only the day of the LORD were here! For then the LORD would rescue us from all our enemies." But you have no idea what you are wishing for. That day will not bring light and prosperity, but darkness and disaster. ¹⁹In that day you will be like a man who runs from a lion—only to meet a bear. After escaping the bear, he leans his hand against a wall in his house—and is bitten by a snake. ²⁰Yes, the day of the LORD will be a dark and hopeless day, without a ray of joy or hope.

²¹"I hate all your show and pretense—the hypocrisy of your religious festivals and solemn assemblies. ²²I will not accept your burnt offerings and grain offerings. I won't even notice all your choice peace offerings. ²³Away with your hymns of praise! They are only noise to my ears. I will not listen to your music, no matter how lovely it is. ²⁴Instead, I want to see a mighty flood of justice, a river of righteous living that will never run dry.

²⁵"Was it to me you were bringing sacrifices and offerings during the forty years in the wilderness, Israel? ²⁶No, your real interest was in your pagan gods—Sakkuth your king god and Kaiwan your star god—the images you yourselves made.* ²⁷So I will send you into exile, to a land east of Damascus," says the LORD, whose name is God Almighty.

6 How terrible it will be for you who lounge in luxury and think you are secure in Jerusalem* and Samaria! You are famous and popular in Israel, you to whom the people go for help. ²Go over to Calneh and see what happened there. Then go to the great city of Hamath and on down to the Philistine city of

---

5:6 Hebrew *the house of Joseph.* **5:15** Hebrew *on the remnant of Joseph.* **5:26** Greek version reads *You took up the shrine of Molech, and the star of your god Rephan, and the images you made for yourselves.* **6:1** Hebrew *Zion.*

My Daily Worship

— August 16 —

WATERED-DOWN WORSHIP?

AMOS 5:1–9:15

*Away with your hymns of praise! They are only noise to my ears. I will not listen
to your music, no matter how lovely it is. Instead, I want to see a mighty flood
of justice, a river of righteous living that will never run dry (5:23–24).*

[i reflect]

"There are those who are asking the devotees of civil rights, 'When will you be satisfied?' We can never be satisfied as long as our bodies, heavy with the fatigue of travel, cannot gain lodging in the motels of the highways and the hotels of the cities. We cannot be satisfied as long as the Negro's basic mobility is from a smaller ghetto to a larger one. We can never be satisfied as long as a Negro in Mississippi cannot vote and a Negro in New York believes he has nothing for which to vote. No, no, we are not satisfied, and we will not be satisfied until justice rolls down like waters and righteousness like a mighty stream."

The speaker was Dr. Martin Luther King Jr., from the steps of the Lincoln Memorial on August 28, 1963. It was what came to be known as his "I Have a Dream" speech. His dream was for justice; his words were from Amos. He had used the same words in December 1955 to encourage the African-Americans of Montgomery, Alabama, at the start of the successful, 381-day bus boycott—a boycott begun through the quiet bravery of Rosa Parks.

Had the boy Martin heard the prophet's call for justice from his daddy's pulpit of Atlanta's Ebenezer Baptist Church? In the days before the boycott, had he preached from this passage as a young pastor there in Montgomery? For the call for justice is linked forever with the call to worship. The heart of God is grieved when our worship is hollow—our adoration becomes an abomination when we ignore injustice and the oppression of others.

Search out the small injustices that you come across today—where you can make a difference by standing up for the neglected, the overlooked, and the weak. Reach out to those you meet as an act of worship.

[i pray]

O God, you hear the cries of those to whom justice has been denied. Let the rivers of your justice move me, that I may work for justice. May I be a servant whose worship is pleasing to your ears.

[i respond]

Water dominates Maya Lin's Civil Rights Memorial in Montgomery, Alabama. Look at photos of it in reference books or on the Internet, remembering God's call for justice rolling down like waters and righteousness like a mighty stream.

Gath. You are no better than they were, and look at how they were destroyed. ³You push away every thought of coming disaster, but your actions only bring the day of judgment closer.

⁴How terrible it will be for you who sprawl on ivory beds surrounded with luxury, eating the meat of tender lambs and choice calves. ⁵You sing idle songs to the sound of the harp, and you fancy yourselves to be great musicians, as King David was. ⁶You drink wine by the bowlful, and you perfume yourselves with exotic fragrances, caring nothing at all that your nation* is going to ruin. ⁷Therefore, you will be the first to be led away as captives. Suddenly, all your revelry will end.

⁸The Sovereign LORD has sworn by his own name, and this is what he, the LORD God Almighty, says: "I despise the pride and false glory of Israel,* and I hate their beautiful homes. I will give this city and everything in it to their enemies."

⁹If there are ten men left in one house, they will all die. ¹⁰And when a close relative—one who is responsible for burning the dead—goes into the house to carry away a dead body, he will ask the last survivor, "Is there anyone else with you?" And the person will answer, "No!" Then he will say, "Hush! Don't even whisper the name of the LORD. He might hear you!"

¹¹When the LORD gives the command, homes both great and small will be smashed to pieces. ¹²Can horses gallop over rocks? Can oxen be used to plow rocks? Stupid even to ask—but that's how stupid you are when you turn justice into poison and make bitter the sweet fruit of righteousness. ¹³And just as stupid is this bragging about your conquest of Lo-debar.* You boast, "Didn't we take Karnaim* by our own strength and power?"

¹⁴"O people of Israel, I am about to bring an enemy nation against you," says the LORD God Almighty. "It will oppress you bitterly throughout your land—from Lebo-hamath in the north to the Arabah Valley in the south."

A VISION OF LOCUSTS

7 The Sovereign LORD showed me a vision. I saw him preparing to send a vast swarm of locusts over the land. This was after the king's share had been harvested from the fields and as the main crop was coming up. ²In my vision the locusts ate everything in sight that was green. Then I said, "O Sovereign LORD, please forgive your people! Unless you relent, Israel* will not survive, for we are only a small nation."

³So the LORD relented and did not fulfill the vision. "I won't do it," he said.

A VISION OF FIRE

⁴Then the Sovereign LORD showed me another vision. I saw him preparing to punish his people with a great fire. The fire had burned up the depths of the sea and was devouring the entire land. ⁵Then I said, "O Sovereign LORD, please don't do it. Unless you relent, Israel will not survive, for we are only a small nation."

⁶Then the LORD turned from this plan, too. "I won't do that either," said the Sovereign LORD.

A VISION OF A PLUMB LINE

⁷Then he showed me another vision. I saw the Lord standing beside a wall that had been built using a plumb line. He was checking it with a plumb line to see if it was straight. ⁸And the LORD said to me, "Amos, what do you see?"

I answered, "A plumb line."

And the Lord replied, "I will test my people with this plumb line. I will no longer ignore all their sins. ⁹The pagan shrines of your ancestors* and the temples of Israel will be destroyed, and I will bring the dynasty of King Jeroboam to a sudden end."

AMOS AND AMAZIAH

¹⁰But when Amaziah, the priest of Bethel, heard what Amos was saying, he rushed a message to King Jeroboam: "Amos is hatching

---

6:6 Hebrew *Joseph.* 6:8 Hebrew *Jacob.* 6:13a *Lo-debar* means "nothing." 6:13b *Karnaim* means "horns," a term that symbolizes strength. 7:2 Hebrew *Jacob;* also in 7:5. 7:9 Hebrew *of Isaac.*

---

a plot against you right here on your very doorstep! What he is saying is intolerable. It will lead to rebellion all across the land. ¹¹He is saying, 'Jeroboam will soon be killed and the people of Israel will be sent away into exile.' "

¹²Then Amaziah sent orders to Amos: "Get out of here, you seer! Go on back to the land of Judah and do your preaching there! ¹³Don't bother us here in Bethel with your prophecies, especially not here where the royal sanctuary is!"

¹⁴But Amos replied, "I'm not one of your professional prophets. I certainly never trained to be one. I'm just a shepherd, and I take care of fig trees. ¹⁵But the LORD called me away from my flock and told me, 'Go and prophesy to my people in Israel.'

¹⁶"Now then, listen to this message from the LORD! You say, 'Don't prophesy against Israel. Stop preaching against my people.'* ¹⁷But this is what the LORD says: Because you have refused to listen, your wife will become a prostitute in this city, and your sons and daughters will be killed. Your land will be divided up, and you yourself will die in a foreign land. And the people of Israel will certainly become captives in exile, far from their homeland."

A VISION OF RIPE FRUIT

8 Then the Sovereign LORD showed me another vision. In it I saw a basket filled with ripe fruit. ²"What do you see, Amos?" he asked.

I replied, "A basket full of ripe fruit."

Then the LORD said, "This fruit represents my people of Israel—ripe for punishment! I will not delay their punishment again. ³In that day the riotous sounds of singing in the Temple will turn to wailing. Dead bodies will be scattered everywhere. They will be carried out of the city in silence. I, the Sovereign LORD, have spoken!"

⁴Listen to this, you who rob the poor and trample the needy! ⁵You can't wait for the Sabbath day to be over and the religious festivals to end so you can get back to cheating the helpless. You measure out your grain in false measures and weigh it out on dishonest scales. ⁶And you mix the wheat you sell with chaff swept from the floor! Then you enslave poor people for a debt of one piece of silver or a pair of sandals.

⁷Now the LORD has sworn this oath by his own name, the Pride of Israel*: "I will never forget the wicked things you have done! ⁸The earth will tremble for your deeds, and

---

7:16 Hebrew *against the house of Isaac.* 8:7 Hebrew *the pride of Jacob.*

everyone will mourn. The land will rise up like the Nile River at floodtime, toss about, and sink again. ⁹At that time," says the Sovereign LORD, "I will make the sun go down at noon and darken the earth while it is still day. ¹⁰I will turn your celebrations into times of mourning, and your songs of joy will be turned to weeping. You will wear funeral clothes and shave your heads as signs of sorrow, as if your only son had died. How very bitter that day will be!

¹¹"The time is surely coming," says the Sovereign LORD, "when I will send a famine on the land—not a famine of bread or water but of hearing the words of the LORD. ¹²People will stagger everywhere from sea to sea, searching for the word of the LORD, running here and going there, but they will not find it. ¹³Beautiful girls and fine young men will grow faint and weary, thirsting for the LORD's word. ¹⁴And those who worship and swear by the idols of Samaria, Dan, and Beersheba will fall down, never to rise again."

A VISION OF GOD AT THE ALTAR

9 Then I saw a vision of the Lord standing beside the altar. He said, "Strike the tops of the Temple columns so hard that the foundation will shake. Smash the columns so the roof will crash down on the people below. Then those who survive will be slaughtered in battle. No one will escape!

²"Even if they dig down to the place of the dead,* I will reach down and pull them up. Even if they climb up into the heavens, I will bring them down. ³Even if they hide at the very top of Mount Carmel, I will search them out and capture them. Even if they hide at the bottom of the ocean, I will send the great sea serpent after them to bite and destroy them. ⁴Even if they are driven into exile, I will command the sword to kill them there. I am determined to bring disaster upon them and not to help them."

⁵The Lord, the LORD Almighty, touches the land and it melts, and all its people mourn. The ground rises like the Nile River at floodtime, and then it sinks again. ⁶The upper stories of the LORD's home are in the heavens, while its foundation is on the earth. He draws up water from the oceans and pours it down as rain on the land. The LORD is his name!

⁷"Do you Israelites think you are more important to me than the Ethiopians*?" asks the LORD. "I brought you out of Egypt, but have I not done as much for other nations, too? I brought the Philistines from Crete* and led the Arameans out of Kir.

⁸"I, the Sovereign LORD, am watching this sinful nation of Israel, and I will uproot it and scatter its people across the earth. Yet I have promised that I will never completely destroy the family of Israel,* " says the LORD. ⁹"For I have commanded that Israel be persecuted by the other nations as grain is sifted in a sieve, yet not one true kernel will be lost. ¹⁰But all the sinners will die by the sword—all those who say, 'Nothing bad will happen to us.'

A PROMISE OF RESTORATION

¹¹"In that day I will restore the fallen kingdom of David. It is now like a house in ruins, but I will rebuild its walls and restore its former glory. ¹²And Israel will possess what is left of Edom and all the nations I have called to be mine. I, the LORD, have spoken, and I will do these things.

¹³"The time will come," says the LORD, "when the grain and grapes will grow faster than they can be harvested. Then the terraced vineyards on the hills of Israel will drip with sweet wine! ¹⁴I will bring my exiled people of Israel back from distant lands, and they will rebuild their ruined cities and live in them again. They will plant vineyards and gardens; they will eat their crops and drink their wine. ¹⁵I will firmly plant them there in the land I have given them," says the LORD your God. "Then they will never be uprooted again."

9:2 Hebrew to Sheol.   9:7a Hebrew the Cushites.   9:7b Hebrew Caphtor.   9:8 Hebrew the house of Jacob.

Obadiah

The exiles of Israel will return to their land. . . . And the LORD himself will be king! (vv. 20, 21).

Don't Touch My Kids!

Squabbling between brothers—sibling rivalry—is common in most families. If allowed to carry on, it can often lead to disaster. Jacob and Esau were twins born to Rebekah and Isaac. And, like many brothers, their relationship was stormy. Esau was the elder, but Jacob was wily. It didn't help their relationship at all when Jacob deceived Esau into giving up his inheritance as the firstborn (Genesis 25–27). From then on the animosity between them and their descendants was very real. Jacob, whose name was changed to Israel, entered into a covenant with God and received many blessings. Esau, however, whose descendants became the nation of Edom, remained on the fringes, always looking for an opportunity to take advantage of Israel.

Obadiah's vision of prophecy warned that Edom—who should have known better than to defy God in this way—would be punished for gloating over Israel's misfortune when they went into captivity (v. 12). God warned Edom that judgment would come on them for their attitude and for encouraging the enemies of Israel to attack.

God's message to Edom was clear: Hurt my children and you will pay for it. Listen to God's indictment: "You deserted your relatives in Israel during their time of greatest need. You stood aloof, refusing to lift a finger to help when foreigners carried off their wealth. . . . You acted as though you were one of Israel's enemies" (v. 11). God would not tolerate rivalries, sibling or otherwise, or carrying grudges.

As you read this book, notice how a righteous and loving God cares for and protects his children. Those who mistreat them will pay for it. When we choose the Lord himself as our king, we can rejoice and worship him for his protective care of us.

Worship Moments

- God speaks, and it behooves the people to listen (vv. 4, 18).
- Jerusalem will be a holy place (v. 17).
- God is called: "Sovereign LORD" (v.1); "the LORD" (vv. 4, 15, 18); the "judge" (v. 15); and "king" (v. 21).

This is the vision that the Sovereign LORD revealed to Obadiah concerning the land of Edom.

EDOM'S JUDGMENT ANNOUNCED

We have heard a message from the LORD that an ambassador was sent to the nations to say, "Get ready, everyone! Let's assemble our armies and attack Edom!"

²The LORD says, "I will cut you down to size among the nations, Edom; you will be small and despised. ³You are proud because you live in a rock fortress and make your home high in the mountains. 'Who can ever reach us way up here?' you ask boastfully. Don't fool yourselves! ⁴Though you soar as high as eagles and build your nest among the stars, I will bring you crashing down. I, the LORD, have spoken!

⁵"If thieves came at night and robbed you, they would not take everything. Those who harvest grapes always leave a few for the poor. But your enemies will wipe you out completely! ⁶Every nook and cranny of Edom* will be searched and looted. Every treasure will be found and taken.

⁷"All your allies will turn against you. They will help to chase you from your land. They will promise you peace, while plotting your destruction. Your trusted friends will set traps for you, and you won't even know about it. ⁸At that time not a single wise person will be left in the whole land of Edom!" says the LORD. "For on the mountains of Edom I will destroy everyone who has wisdom and understanding. ⁹The mightiest warriors of Teman will be terrified, and everyone on the mountains of Edom will be cut down in the slaughter.

REASONS FOR EDOM'S PUNISHMENT

¹⁰"And why? Because of the violence you did to your close relatives in Israel.* Now you will be destroyed completely and filled with shame forever. ¹¹For you deserted your relatives in Israel during their time of greatest need. You stood aloof, refusing to lift a finger to help when foreign invaders carried off their wealth and cast lots to divide up Jerusalem. You acted as though you were one of Israel's enemies.

¹²"You shouldn't have done this! You shouldn't have gloated when they exiled your relatives to distant lands. You shouldn't have rejoiced because they were suffering such misfortune. You shouldn't have crowed over them as they suffered these disasters. ¹³You shouldn't have plundered the land of Israel when they were suffering such calamity. You shouldn't have gloated over the destruction of your relatives, looting their homes and making yourselves rich at their expense. ¹⁴You shouldn't have stood at the crossroads, killing those who tried to escape. You shouldn't have captured the survivors, handing them over to their enemies in that terrible time of trouble.

EDOM DESTROYED, ISRAEL RESTORED

¹⁵"The day is near when I, the LORD, will judge the godless nations! As you have done to Israel, so it will be done to you. All your evil deeds will fall back on your own heads. ¹⁶Just as you swallowed up my people on my holy mountain, so you and the surrounding nations will swallow the punishment I pour out on you. Yes, you nations will drink and stagger and disappear from history, as though you had never even existed.

¹⁷"But Jerusalem* will become a refuge for those who escape; it will be a holy place. And the people of Israel* will come back to reclaim their inheritance. ¹⁸At that time Israel will be a raging fire, and Edom, a field of dry stubble. The fire will roar across the field, devouring everything and leaving no survivors in Edom. I, the LORD, have spoken!

¹⁹"Then my people living in the Negev will occupy the mountains of Edom. Those living in the foothills of Judah* will possess the Philistine plains and take over the fields of

---

6 Hebrew *Esau;* also in 8b, 9, 18, 19, 21. **10** Hebrew *your brother Jacob.* **17a** Hebrew *Mount Zion.* **17b** Hebrew *house of Jacob;* also in 18. **19** Hebrew *the Shephelah.*

My Daily Worship

— *August 17* —

THE LORD WILL BE KING!

OBADIAH 1–21

Deliverers will go up to Mount Zion in Jerusalem to rule over the mountains of Edom.
And the LORD himself will be king! (21).

[i reflect]

"Are we there yet?" the voice implores from the back seat. The driver sighs. It's going to be a long trip. Like the child on a car trip barely begun, we implore from the back seat, "Father God, are we there yet? When will this agony be over?"

"How long . . . how long . . . how long, O Lord?" God's people have implored from the back seat since their trip out of Egypt. But the Father's hands are firmly on the wheel—the destination *will* be met, the goal *will* be achieved, his kingdom *will* come. As the prophet Obadiah encouraged, "The LORD himself will be king!"

Julian of Norwich, a Benedictine nun, was born in 1342. She became deathly ill in her early thirties, but God miraculously restored her and gave her a unique, long-term perspective. In *Revelations of Divine Love* she wrote:

> I saw full surely that he changeth never his purpose in no manner of thing, nor never shall, without end. For there was no thing unknown to him in his rightful ordinance from without beginning. And therefore all thing was [sic] set in order ere anything was made, as it should stand without end; and no manner of thing shall fail of that point. . . .

> And all this shewed he full blissfully, signifying thus: See! I am God: see! I am in all thing: see! I do all thing: see! I lift never mine hands off my works, nor ever shall, without end: see! I lead all thing to the end I ordained it to from without beginning, by the same Might, Wisdom and Love whereby I made it. How should any thing be amiss?

At times, life seems amiss. The job search has stalled. Health concerns arise. A spouse walks out the door. At such times, it is easy to think that victory has been delayed, the final destination of God's kingdom far off. Yet, we need to remember, like Julian, that God leads all things to the end he ordains.

Worship the King. He is already there, awaiting you.

[i pray]

Father God, I am such an impatient child. I place my trust in your care and in your
ultimate victory. Your will will be done. Your kingdom will come. I praise you.

[i respond]

Consider some your prayer requests from a year ago, five years ago, ten years ago. How has God triumphed in ways you hardly dared expect? Write down his answers, and praise God that he is already king over today's concerns.

Ephraim and Samaria. And the people of Benjamin will occupy the land of Gilead. [20]The exiles of Israel will return to their land and occupy the Phoenician coast as far north as Zarephath. The captives from Jerusalem exiled in the north* will return to their homeland and resettle the villages of the Negev. [21]Deliverers will go up to* Mount Zion in Jerusalem to rule over the mountains of Edom. And the LORD himself will be king!"

20 Hebrew *in Sepharad.* 21 Or *from.*

Jonah

I cried out to the LORD in my great trouble, and he answered me (2:2).

Hitting Rock Bottom

Rock bottom. It's that place in life at the end of personal failure and dashed hopes where it's impossible to sink any lower. When we've sunk as low as we can in an emotional and spiritual sense, our choices are slim. We can go sideways and stay stuck, we can wallow along the bottom in sorrow, or we can realize, as the prophet Jonah did, that the only way to go is up.

Jonah learned firsthand what it meant to bottom out spiritually and emotionally. Instead of going north to Nineveh to fulfill God's call to preach repentance, Jonah ran away in the opposite direction. He reneged, resisted, and just plain rebelled. He despised the Assyrian city of Nineveh—a stronghold of wickedness, pride, and power. Why should he bring these pagans the good news of God's mercy?

Jonah's downward spiral continued—down to the seacoast city of Joppa to board a ship, down in the dark hold of the craft to sleep away his responsibility, and then down beneath the crashing waves and into the belly of a great fish. That's where it happened. Worship brought him from his descent into darkness into the light of God's presence once more. He cried out. He prayed. He sang desperate songs of praise. God's grace buoyed his heart and raised his spirits. Jonah surfaced from his depression and rebellion as a changed man—ready to do what God called him to do. Even if that meant going to Nineveh to preach repentance and mercy.

If we find ourselves at rock bottom today, we need to remember that the only way to go is up. Let Jonah's story remind us that in times of dismal failure we may actually be closer to a moment of mercy than we realize. We can't help but praise a God who loves us enough to lift us out of the depths of despair through his amazing grace.

Worship Moments

- Unbelievers are awestruck by God's power and offer a sacrifice (1:16).

- Jonah earnestly prayed to God in his holy temple, and offered songs of praise (2:7, 9).

- The Ninevites humbled themselves and prayed for mercy (3:6–10).

- Jonah praises God as: "the LORD, the God of heaven, who made the sea and the land" (1:9); "a gracious and compassionate God" (4:2).

JONAH RUNS FROM THE LORD

1 The LORD gave this message to Jonah son of Amittai: [2]"Get up and go to the great city of Nineveh! Announce my judgment against it because I have seen how wicked its people are."

[3]But Jonah got up and went in the opposite direction in order to get away from the LORD. He went down to the seacoast, to the port of Joppa, where he found a ship leaving for Tarshish. He bought a ticket and went on board, hoping that by going away to the west he could escape from the LORD.

[4]But as the ship was sailing along, suddenly the LORD flung a powerful wind over the sea, causing a violent storm that threatened to send them to the bottom. [5]Fearing for their lives, the desperate sailors shouted to their gods for help and threw the cargo overboard to lighten the ship. And all this time Jonah was sound asleep down in the hold. [6]So the captain went down after him. "How can you sleep at a time like this?" he shouted. "Get up and pray to your god! Maybe he will have mercy on us and spare our lives."

[7]Then the crew cast lots to see which of them had offended the gods and caused the terrible storm. When they did this, Jonah lost the toss. [8]"What have you done to bring this awful storm down on us?" they demanded. "Who are you? What is your line of work? What country are you from? What is your nationality?"

[9]And Jonah answered, "I am a Hebrew, and I worship the LORD, the God of heaven, who made the sea and the land." [10]Then he told them that he was running away from the LORD.

The sailors were terrified when they heard this. "Oh, why did you do it?" they groaned. [11]And since the storm was getting worse all the time, they asked him, "What should we do to you to stop this storm?"

[12]"Throw me into the sea," Jonah said, "and it will become calm again. For I know that this terrible storm is all my fault."

[13]Instead, the sailors tried even harder to row the boat ashore. But the stormy sea was too violent for them, and they couldn't make it. [14]Then they cried out to the LORD, Jonah's God. "O LORD," they pleaded, "don't make us die for this man's sin. And don't hold us responsible for his death, because it isn't our fault. O LORD, you have sent this storm upon him for your own good reasons."

[15]Then the sailors picked Jonah up and threw him into the raging sea, and the storm stopped at once! [16]The sailors were awestruck by the LORD's great power, and they offered him a sacrifice and vowed to serve him.

[17]Now the LORD had arranged for a great fish to swallow Jonah. And Jonah was inside the fish for three days and three nights.

JONAH'S PRAYER

2 Then Jonah prayed to the LORD his God from inside the fish. [2]He said, "I cried out to the LORD in my great trouble, and he answered me. I called to you from the world of the dead,* and LORD, you heard me! [3]You threw me into the ocean depths, and I sank down to the heart of the sea. I was buried beneath your wild and stormy waves. [4]Then I said, 'O LORD, you have driven me from your presence. How will I ever again see your holy Temple?'

[5]"I sank beneath the waves, and death was very near. The waters closed in around me, and seaweed wrapped itself around my head. [6]I sank down to the very roots of the mountains. I was locked out of life and imprisoned in the land of the dead. But you, O LORD my God, have snatched me from the yawning jaws of death!

[7]"When I had lost all hope, I turned my thoughts once more to the LORD. And my earnest prayer went out to you in your holy Temple. [8]Those who worship false gods turn their backs on all God's mercies. [9]But I will offer sacrifices to you with songs of praise, and I will fulfill all my vows. For my salvation comes from the LORD alone."

2:2 Hebrew *from Sheol.*

My Daily Worship

— *August 18* —

WHEN ALL HOPE IS LOST

JONAH 1:1–2:10

When I had lost all hope, I turned my thoughts once more to the LORD.
And my earnest prayer went out to you in your holy Temple (2:7).

[i reflect]

Helen Keller is a famous example of a "hopeless case" who proved to be not so hopeless after all. But lesser known is the fact that the woman who drew Helen Keller out of her dark and silent world, Anne Sullivan, was once considered a hopeless case too.

Anne was born in April 1866 to poor Irish immigrants in Massachusetts. Her father worked little and drank much, and her mother suffered from tuberculosis. Anne herself contracted trachoma, which went untreated and resulted in near-blindness. When her mother died, Anne and her brother, Jimmy, wound up in the state poorhouse in Tewksbury, where they boarded with prostitutes, mental patients, and other troubled persons. Before long, Jimmy died, and Anne was left with no caring relative, little eyesight, and no prospects.

The turning point came when a team from the Board of Charities arrived at the poorhouse. Anne literally threw herself at the head of the team and begged to be given an education at a school for the blind. Her plea was heard, and at age fourteen she was enrolled in the Perkins Institute for the Blind, where in six years she went from elementary school classes to graduation as valedictorian. During that time, a brilliant operation restored her sight, and Anne thereafter devoted herself to the care of the blind.

"Hope means hoping when things are hopeless, or it is no virtue at all," said G. K. Chesterton. This is a truth Helen Keller and Anne Sullivan knew. It is a truth Jonah knew, too, when he was sinking into the waters of the sea, little dreaming that rescue was swimming nearby in the form of a great fish.

When we're out of hope, that's when it's time to turn our thoughts to God and hope again. Today, when you feel overwhelmed or without hope, remember Jonah. Turn your thoughts once again to God.

[i pray]

Bring on the big fish, Lord. Do whatever it takes to snatch me up from the hopeless circumstances into which I am sinking. Surprise me with your mastery of events. I believe.

[i respond]

Max Lucado, in his book *A Love Worth Giving*, talks about an "olive leaf of hope," referring to the olive leaf the dove brought back to Noah, bringing with it a message of hope. Extend an "olive leaf of hope" to someone you know is hurting today.

¹⁰Then the LORD ordered the fish to spit up Jonah on the beach, and it did.

JONAH GOES TO NINEVEH

3 Then the LORD spoke to Jonah a second time: ²"Get up and go to the great city of Nineveh, and deliver the message of judgment I have given you."

³This time Jonah obeyed the LORD's command and went to Nineveh, a city so large that it took three days to see it all. ⁴On the day Jonah entered the city, he shouted to the crowds: "Forty days from now Nineveh will be destroyed!" ⁵The people of Nineveh believed God's message, and from the greatest to the least, they decided to go without food and wear sackcloth to show their sorrow.

⁶When the king of Nineveh heard what Jonah was saying, he stepped down from his throne and took off his royal robes. He dressed himself in sackcloth and sat on a heap of ashes. ⁷Then the king and his nobles sent this decree throughout the city: "No one, not even the animals, may eat or drink anything at all. ⁸Everyone is required to wear sackcloth and pray earnestly to God. Everyone must turn from their evil ways and stop all their violence. ⁹Who can tell? Perhaps even yet God will have pity on us and hold back his fierce anger from destroying us."

¹⁰When God saw that they had put a stop to their evil ways, he had mercy on them and didn't carry out the destruction he had threatened.

JONAH'S ANGER AT THE LORD'S MERCY

4 This change of plans upset Jonah, and he became very angry. ²So he complained to the LORD about it: "Didn't I say before I left home that you would do this, LORD? That is why I ran away to Tarshish! I knew that you were a gracious and compassionate God, slow to get angry and filled with unfailing love. I knew how easily you could cancel your plans for destroying these people. ³Just kill me now, LORD! I'd rather be dead than alive because nothing I predicted is going to happen."

⁴The LORD replied, "Is it right for you to be angry about this?"

⁵Then Jonah went out to the east side of the city and made a shelter to sit under as he waited to see if anything would happen to the city. ⁶And the LORD God arranged for a leafy plant to grow there, and soon it spread its broad leaves over Jonah's head, shading him from the sun. This eased some of his discomfort, and Jonah was very grateful for the plant.

⁷But God also prepared a worm! The next morning at dawn the worm ate through the stem of the plant, so that it soon died and withered away. ⁸And as the sun grew hot, God sent a scorching east wind to blow on Jonah. The sun beat down on his head until he grew faint and wished to die. "Death is certainly better than this!" he exclaimed.

⁹Then God said to Jonah, "Is it right for you to be angry because the plant died?"

"Yes," Jonah retorted, "even angry enough to die!"

¹⁰Then the LORD said, "You feel sorry about the plant, though you did nothing to put it there. And a plant is only, at best, short lived. ¹¹But Nineveh has more than 120,000 people living in spiritual darkness,* not to mention all the animals. Shouldn't I feel sorry for such a great city?"

4:11 Hebrew *people who don't know their right hands from their left.*

My Daily Worship

— *August 19* —

AMEN TO MERCY

JONAH 3:1–4:11

I knew that you were a gracious and compassionate God, slow to get angry
and filled with unfailing love. I knew how easily you could cancel
your plans for destroying these people (4:2).

[i reflect]

A man was all in favor when his church decided to start running evangelistic small groups in members' homes. He even volunteered to host one of the groups. Imagine his surprise when he opened his door on the first small-group night and saw standing there his neighbor—the one about whom he had called the police several times for playing music too loud and letting dogs bark. Oh sure, the host liked the idea of anonymous strangers responding to the invitations that had been posted around the neighborhood, but when a known and hated neighbor was the seeker, he slammed the door shut.

It's a reaction as old as Jonah.

The recital of God's graciousness and compassion, his slowness to anger and unfailing love, constitutes a virtual refrain in the Old Testament (see Exodus 34:6; Psalm 86:15; 103:8; Joel 2:13), recited to the praise of God. In the mouth of Jonah, however, God's great qualities of kindness are recast as liabilities. The reluctant prophet wanted to see the Ninevites, his nation's archenemies, served out with punishment, not mercy.

God knew that we, too, would probably be tempted to give this bad slant to his grace. So Jesus told a story about a young man who went sullen over the merciful treatment shown his prodigal brother (Luke 15:25–30), and another story about workers hired early in the day who complained about the equal payment given to people hired later (Matthew 20:1–16).

God has grace in store even for people we do not like. Commit to praying today for a person whom you really don't like—maybe even hate—as an act of celebrating God's grace.

[i pray]

You are gracious. Yes, Lord! And compassionate. Amen! You are slow to get angry.
Hallelujah! You are filled with unfailing love. Yes! Yes! Yes!

[i respond]

Reach out to someone with whom you have struggled to get along or do not feel compassion toward. Invite that person for coffee, or spend some time getting to know that person beyond the work, neighborhood, or church environment.

Micah

O people, the LORD has already told you what is good, and this is what he requires:
to do what is right, to love mercy, and to walk humbly with your God (6:8).

Worship from the Heart

"Give me the bottom line." "Get to the point." "Cut to the chase." When it comes to determining what God wants from us, we don't want to play a guessing game. When we scratch our heads and try to think what would please him most, many possibilities may come to mind. In Micah's day, the people thought of offering calves, rams, or enough olive oil to float a boat downstream. We might translate that same sentiment into offering God our perfect church attendance or a significant donation to the church building fund. Surely that would please him.

In response, God admits we are right about one thing—worship is definitely all about what pleases him. But what pleases God? Micah sums it up this way: obedience from the heart.

Doing what's right becomes an act of worship when we honor him with how we live day to day. Not because we want to impress him, but because we love him. As Micah noted, it's the difference between working to impress God and walking humbly with him. Whenever we neglect obedience, the very heart of worship, we miss the point altogether. This is why Micah described Israel, Judah, and the entire earth as being under God's judgment.

Perfect church attendance on Sunday becomes a joke if we then disobey God Monday through Saturday! Micah's formula is simple. No obedience? No worship. If we really want to worship God the way he deserves to be worshiped, we must first wholeheartedly do what he says. Want to please God and worship him as he deserves? Heed Micah's warning—obey him.

Worship Moments

- Micah describes the astonishing power and might of God (1:3–4)—worthy of our sincere worship and praise (6:6–8).

- The majestic "leader-king" foreshadowed here is Jesus—the Messiah—exalted before all the people (2:13; 5:2, 4).

- God is the only one worthy of worship. Many nations will come to the Temple of the God of Israel (4:2).

- God is described as: "Sovereign LORD" (1:2); "my light" (7:8); a God who pardons sin and shows mercy (7:18); and shows "faithfulness and unfailing love" (7:20).

1

The LORD gave these messages to Micah of Moresheth during the years when Jotham, Ahaz, and Hezekiah were kings of Judah. The messages concerned both Samaria and Jerusalem, and they came to Micah in the form of visions.

GRIEF OVER SAMARIA AND JERUSALEM

²Attention! Let all the people of the world listen! The Sovereign LORD has made accusations against you; the Lord speaks from his holy Temple.

³Look! The LORD is coming! He leaves his throne in heaven and comes to earth, walking on the high places. ⁴They melt beneath his feet and flow into the valleys like wax in a fire, like water pouring down a hill.

⁵And why is this happening? Because of the sins and rebellion of Israel and Judah.* Who is to blame for Israel's rebellion? Samaria, its capital city! Where is the center of idolatry in Judah? In Jerusalem, its capital!

⁶"So I, the LORD, will make the city of Samaria a heap of rubble. Her streets will be plowed up for planting vineyards. I will roll the stones of her walls down into the valley below, exposing all her foundations. ⁷All her carved images will be smashed to pieces. All her sacred treasures will be burned up. These things were bought with the money earned by her prostitution, and they will now be carried away to pay prostitutes elsewhere."

⁸Because of all this, I will mourn and lament. I will walk around naked and barefoot in sorrow and shame. I will howl like a jackal and wail like an ostrich. ⁹For my people's wound is far too deep to heal. It has reached into Judah, even to the gates of Jerusalem.

¹⁰Don't tell our enemies in the city of Gath*; don't weep at all.* You people in Beth-leaphrah,* roll in the dust to show your anguish and despair. ¹¹You people of Shaphir,* go as captives into exile—naked and ashamed. The people of Zaanan* dare not come outside their walls. The people of Beth-ezel* mourn because the very foundations of their city have been swept away. ¹²The people of Maroth* anxiously wait for relief, but only bitterness awaits them as the LORD's judgment reaches even to the gates of Jerusalem.

¹³Quick! Use your swiftest chariots and flee, you people of Lachish.* You were the first city in Judah to follow Israel in the sin of idol worship, and so you led Jerusalem* into sin. ¹⁴Send a farewell gift to Moresheth-gath; there is no hope of saving it. The town of Aczib* has deceived the kings of Israel, for it promised help it could not give. ¹⁵You people of Mareshah,* I will bring a conqueror to capture your town. And the leaders* of Israel will go to Adullam.

¹⁶Weep, you people of Judah! Shave your heads in sorrow, for the children you love will be snatched away, and you will never see them again. Make yourselves as bald as an eagle, for your little ones will be exiled to distant lands.

JUDGMENT AGAINST WEALTHY OPPRESSORS

2

How terrible it will be for you who lie awake at night, thinking up evil plans. You rise at dawn and hurry to carry out any of the wicked schemes you have power to accomplish. ²When you want a certain piece of land, you find a way to seize it. When you want someone's house, you take it by fraud and violence. No one's family or inheritance is safe with you around!

³But this is what the LORD says: "I will reward your evil with evil; you won't be able to escape! After I am through with you, none of you will ever again walk proudly in the streets."

⁴In that day your enemies will make fun of

1:5 Hebrew *and Jacob.* 1:10a *Gath* sounds like the Hebrew term for "tell." 1:10b Greek version reads *weep not in Acco.* 1:10c *Beth-leaphrah* means "house of dust." 1:11a *Shaphir* means "pleasant." 1:11b *Zaanan* sounds like the Hebrew term for "come out." 1:11c *Beth-ezel* means "adjoining house." 1:12 *Maroth* sounds like the Hebrew term for "bitter." 1:13a *Lachish* sounds like the Hebrew term for "team of horses." 1:13b Hebrew *the daughter of Zion.* 1:14 *Aczib* means "deception." 1:15a *Mareshah* sounds like the Hebrew term for "conqueror." 1:15b Hebrew *the glory.*

you by singing this song of despair about your experience:

"We are finished,
    completely ruined!
God has confiscated our land,
    taking it from us.
He has given our fields
    to those who betrayed us.*"

⁵Others will set your boundaries then, and the LORD's people will have no say in how the land is divided.

TRUE AND FALSE PROPHETS

⁶"Don't say such things," the people say. "Don't prophesy like that. Such disasters will never come our way!"

⁷Should you talk that way, O family of Israel*? Will the LORD have patience with such behavior? If you would do what is right, you would find my words to be good. ⁸Yet to this very hour my people rise against me! You steal the shirts right off the backs of those who trusted you, making them as ragged as men who have just come home from battle. ⁹You have evicted women from their homes and stripped their children of all their God-given rights. ¹⁰Up! Begone! This is no longer your land and home, for you have filled it with sin and ruined it completely.

¹¹Suppose a prophet full of lies were to say to you, "I'll preach to you the joys of wine and drink!" That's just the kind of prophet you would like!

HOPE FOR RESTORATION

¹²"Someday, O Israel, I will gather the few of you who are left. I will bring you together again like sheep in a fold, like a flock in its pasture. Yes, your land will again be filled with noisy crowds! ¹³Your leader will break out and lead you out of exile. He will bring you through the gates of your cities of captivity, back to your own land. Your king will lead you; the LORD himself will guide you."

2:4 Or *to those who took us captive.*   2:7 Hebrew *house of Jacob.*

Words of Worship

TITHE, TITHING

Tithe, Tithing—Hebrew *ma-a-sar* "tenth"; Greek *de-ka-to-o* "pay a tithe."

A tithe is a tenth of whatever we gain through our work and the investment of our resources. Its purpose is to provide for the worship of the Lord. The tithe was given to the priests, who had no territory of their own, allowing them to carry out their responsibilities in the sanctuary. Christians, too, provide for the conduct of worship through tithes and offerings. People of the Bible lived close to the soil, and their tithe was usually offered from the grain harvest. When distance from the sanctuary required it, the tithe could be converted into money (Deuteronomy 14:24–26).

In whatever form, tithing symbolizes that prosperity comes from the Lord's favor, not our efforts. To busy ourselves, as the Lord says, with "building your own fine houses" while neglecting the needs of his house affects our ability to prosper (Haggai 1:9). David prayed, "Everything we have has come from you, and we give you only what you have already given us!" (1 Chronicles 29:14) Remembering this makes us better stewards of God's riches.

JUDGMENT AGAINST ISRAEL'S LEADERS

3 Listen, you leaders of Israel! You are supposed to know right from wrong, ²but you are the very ones who hate good and love evil. You skin my people alive and tear the flesh off their bones. ³You eat my people's flesh, cut away their skin, and break their bones. You chop them up like meat for the cooking pot.

⁴Then you beg the LORD for help in times of trouble! Do you really expect him to listen? After all the evil you have done, he won't even look at you!

⁵This is what the LORD says to you false prophets: "You are leading my people astray! You promise peace for those who give you food, but you declare war on anyone who refuses to pay you. ⁶Now the night will close around you, cutting off all your visions. Darkness will cover you, making it impossible for you to predict the future. The sun will set for you prophets, and your day will come to an end. ⁷Then you seers will cover your faces in shame, and you diviners will be disgraced. And you will admit that your messages were not from God."

⁸But as for me, I am filled with power and the Spirit of the LORD. I am filled with justice and might, fearlessly pointing out Israel's sin and rebellion. ⁹Listen to me, you leaders of Israel! You hate justice and twist all that is right. ¹⁰You are building Jerusalem on a foundation of murder and corruption. ¹¹You rulers govern for the bribes you can get; you priests teach God's laws only for a price; you prophets won't prophesy unless you are paid. Yet all of you claim you are depending on the LORD. "No harm can come to us," you say, "for the LORD is here among us."

¹²So because of you, Mount Zion will be plowed like an open field; Jerusalem will be reduced to rubble! A great forest will grow on the hilltop, where the Temple now stands.

THE LORD'S FUTURE REIGN

4 In the last days, the Temple of the LORD in Jerusalem will become the most important place on earth. People from all over the world will go there to worship. ²Many nations will come and say, "Come, let us go up to the mountain of the LORD, to the Temple of the God of Israel.* There he will teach us his ways, so that we may obey him." For in those days the LORD's teaching and his word will go out from Jerusalem.

³The LORD will settle international disputes. All the nations will beat their swords into plowshares and their spears into pruning hooks. All wars will stop, and military training will come to an end. ⁴Everyone will live quietly in their own homes in peace and prosperity, for there will be nothing to fear. The LORD Almighty has promised this! ⁵Even though the nations around us worship idols, we will follow the LORD our God forever and ever.

ISRAEL'S RETURN FROM EXILE

⁶"In that coming day," says the LORD, "I will gather together my people who are lame, who have been exiles, filled with grief. ⁷They are weak and far from home, but I will make them strong again, a mighty nation. Then I, the LORD, will rule from Jerusalem* as their king forever."

⁸As for you, O Jerusalem, the citadel of God's people, your royal might and power will come back to you again. The kingship will be restored to my precious Jerusalem. ⁹But why are you now screaming in terror? Have you no king to lead you? He is dead! Have you no wise people to counsel you? All are gone! Pain has gripped you like it does a woman in labor. ¹⁰Writhe and groan in terrible pain, you people of Jerusalem,* for you must leave this city to live in the open fields. You will soon be sent into exile in distant Babylon. But the LORD will rescue you there; he will redeem you from the grip of your enemies.

¹¹True, many nations have gathered together against you, calling for your blood, eager to gloat over your destruction. ¹²But they do not know the LORD's thoughts or understand his plan. These nations don't know that he is gathering them together to be beaten and trampled like bundles of grain on a threshing floor.

¹³"Rise up and destroy the nations, O Jerusalem!"* says the LORD. "For I will give you iron horns and bronze hooves, so you can trample many nations to pieces. Then you will give all the wealth they acquired as offerings to me, the Lord of all the earth."

4:2 Hebrew *of Jacob.*   4:7 Hebrew *Mount Zion.*   4:10 Hebrew *O daughter of Zion.*   4:13 Hebrew *"Rise up and thresh, O daughter of Zion."*

A Ruler from Bethlehem

5 Mobilize! Marshal your troops! The enemy is laying siege to Jerusalem. With a rod they will strike the leader of Israel in the face.

²But you, O Bethlehem Ephrathah, are only a small village in Judah. Yet a ruler of Israel will come from you, one whose origins are from the distant past. ³The people of Israel will be abandoned to their enemies until the time when the woman in labor gives birth to her son. Then at last his fellow countrymen will return from exile to their own land. ⁴And he will stand to lead his flock with the LORD's strength, in the majesty of the name of the LORD his God. Then his people will live there undisturbed, for he will be highly honored all around the world. ⁵And he will be the source of our peace.

When the Assyrians invade our land and break through our defenses, we will appoint seven rulers to watch over us, eight princes to lead us. ⁶They will rule Assyria with drawn swords and enter the gates of the land of Nimrod. They* will rescue us from the Assyrians when they pour over the borders to invade our land.

The Remnant Purified

⁷Then the few left in Israel* will go out among the nations. They will be like dew sent by the LORD or like rain falling on the grass, which no one can hold back. ⁸The remnant of Israel will go out among the nations and be as strong as a lion. And the other nations will be like helpless sheep, with no one to rescue them. ⁹The people of Israel will stand up to their foes, and all their enemies will be wiped out.

¹⁰"At that same time," says the LORD, "I will destroy all your weapons—your horses and chariots. ¹¹I will tear down your walls and demolish the defenses of your cities. ¹²I will put an end to all witchcraft; there will be no more fortune-tellers to consult. ¹³I will destroy all your idols and sacred pillars, so you will never again worship the work of your own hands. ¹⁴I will abolish your pagan shrines with their Asherah poles and destroy the cities where your idol temples stand. ¹⁵I will pour out my vengeance on all the nations that refuse to obey me."

The Lord's Case against Israel

6 Listen to what the LORD is saying: "Stand up and state your case against me. Let the mountains and hills be called to witness your complaints.

²"And now, O mountains, listen to the LORD's complaint! He has a case against his people Israel! He will prosecute them to the full extent of the law. ³O my people, what have I done to make you turn from me? Tell me why your patience is exhausted! Answer me! ⁴For I brought you out of Egypt and redeemed you from your slavery. I sent Moses, Aaron, and Miriam to help you.

⁵"Don't you remember, my people, how King Balak of Moab tried to have you cursed and how Balaam son of Beor blessed you instead? And remember your journey from Acacia* to Gilgal, when I, the LORD, did everything I could to teach you about my faithfulness."

⁶What can we bring to the LORD to make up for what we've done? Should we bow before God with offerings of yearling calves? ⁷Should we offer him thousands of rams and tens of thousands of rivers of olive oil? Would that please the LORD? Should we sacrifice our first-born children to pay for the sins of our souls? Would that make him glad?

⁸No, O people, the LORD has already told you what is good, and this is what he requires: to do what is right, to love mercy, and to walk humbly with your God.

Israel's Guilt and Punishment

⁹Listen! Fear the LORD if you are wise! His voice is calling out to everyone in Jerusalem:

5:6 Hebrew *He.* 5:7 Hebrew *Jacob;* also in 5:8. 6:5 Hebrew *Shittim.*

My Daily Worship

— August 20 —

WHEN YOU FACE PERSECUTION

MICAH 1:1–4:13

True, many nations have gathered together against you, calling for your blood, eager to gloat over your destruction. But they do not know the LORD's thoughts or understand his plan (4:11–12).

[i reflect]

In part, Micah may have been looking ahead to the near future when God would give the Israelites victory over their foes. But in another way, Micah probably was also looking toward the distant future, the end times, when God will decisively destroy the enemies ranged against his people. With either perspective, the principle is the same: *God protects his own.*

That's good to remember in a world where claiming the name of Christ can put your life at risk. Did you know that more Christians were martyred in the twentieth century (about 26 million) than in all the preceding centuries of the Christian era combined (an estimated 17 million up to the year 1900)? Did you know that today around 200 million Christians in sixty nations face persecution in some form, whether it's the enslavement of Christians in Sudan or the imprisonment of pastors in Vietnam or massacres in churches in India?

We might reasonably ask, Where is God? He is suffering with them, and preparing a glory for them weightier by far than what they endured (Romans 8:18).

We might also ask what this means for those of us who face little persecution. Some believe that as our society embraces generalized spirituality and relativized morality, persons who defend the exclusive claims of Christ will become an embattled minority, resembling the early church. But even if this scenario does not play out, "the world"—understood as the system that opposes God— is always going to reject us as it rejected our Lord (John 15:18). But remember, they do not know the Lord's thoughts or understand his plans.

Pray for the persecuted church today. Also, if any persons are persecuting you, ask Christ to reveal himself to them, as he did to the persecutor Saul of Tarsus, so that they might escape the judgment awaiting those who set themselves against God's people.

[i pray]

Sometimes, God, your opponents in the world seem numerous and fearsome. Protect me, I pray. Yet whatever happens to me in this life, I thank you that I am on the winning side.

[i respond]

Become more aware of the persecuted church in the world today. Visit a website such as Voice of the Martyrs to learn more about what is happening to believers around the globe.

"The armies of destruction are coming; the LORD is sending them.* [10]Will there be no end of your getting rich by cheating? The homes of the wicked are filled with treasures gained by dishonestly measuring out grain in short measures.* [11]And how can I tolerate all your merchants who use dishonest scales and weights? [12]The rich among you have become wealthy through extortion and violence. Your citizens are so used to lying that their tongues can no longer tell the truth.

[13]"Therefore, I will wound you! I will bring you to ruin for all your sins. [14]You will eat but never have enough. Your hunger pangs and emptiness will still remain. And though you try to save your money, it will come to nothing in the end. You will save a little, but I will give it to those who conquer you. [15]You will plant crops but not harvest them. You will press your olives but not get enough oil to anoint yourselves. You will trample the grapes but get no juice to make your wine.

[16]"The only laws you keep are those of evil King Omri; the only example you follow is that of wicked King Ahab! Therefore, I will make an example of you, bringing you to complete ruin. You will be treated with contempt, mocked by all who see you."

MISERY TURNED TO HOPE

7 What misery is mine! I feel like the fruit picker after the harvest who can find nothing to eat. Not a cluster of grapes or a single fig can be found to satisfy my hunger. [2]The godly people have all disappeared; not one fair-minded person is left on the earth. They are all murderers, even setting traps for their own brothers. [3]They go about their evil deeds with both hands. How skilled they are at using them! Officials and judges alike demand bribes. The people with money and influence pay them off, and together they scheme to twist justice. [4]Even the best of them is like a brier; the straightest is more crooked than a hedge of thorns. But your judgment day is coming swiftly now. Your time of punishment is here.

[5]Don't trust anyone—not your best friend or even your wife! [6]For the son despises his father. The daughter defies her mother. The daughter-in-law defies her mother-in-law. Your enemies will be right in your own household.

[7]As for me, I look to the LORD for his help. I wait confidently for God to save me, and my God will certainly hear me. [8]Do not gloat over me, my enemies! For though I fall, I will rise again. Though I sit in darkness, the LORD himself will be my light. [9]I will be patient as the LORD punishes me, for I have sinned against him. But after that, he will take up my case and punish my enemies for all the evil they have done to me. The LORD will bring me out of my darkness into the light, and I will see his righteousness. [10]Then my enemies will see that the LORD is on my side. They will be ashamed that they taunted me, saying, "Where is the LORD—that God of yours?" With my own eyes I will see them trampled down like mud in the streets.

[11]In that day, Israel, your cities will be rebuilt, and your borders will be extended. [12]People from many lands will come and honor you—from Assyria all the way to the towns of Egypt, and from Egypt all the way to the Euphrates River,* and from many distant seas and mountains. [13]But the land* will become empty and desolate because of the wickedness of those who live there.

THE LORD'S COMPASSION ON ISRAEL

[14]O LORD, come and rule your people; lead your flock in green pastures. Help them to live in peace and prosperity. Let them enjoy the fertile pastures of Bashan and Gilead as they did long ago.

[15]"Yes," says the LORD, "I will do mighty miracles for you, like those I did when I rescued you from slavery in Egypt."

6:9 Hebrew "Listen to the rod. Who appointed it?" **6:10** Hebrew by using the short ephah; the ephah was a unit for measuring grain. **7:12** Hebrew the river. **7:13** Or earth.

My Daily Worship
— August 21 —

SIMPLE GOODNESS
MICAH 5:1–7:20

O people, the LORD has already told you what is good, and this is what he requires:
to do what is right, to love mercy, and to walk humbly with your God (6:8).

[i reflect]

Prior to this key verse, the prophet Micah posed some rhetorical questions on behalf of his fellow Israelites. God had indicted the nation of Israel for plunging into all manner of immorality and idolatry. So Micah asked, "Should we offer him thousands of rams and tens of thousands of rivers of olive oil? Would that please the LORD? Should we sacrifice our firstborn children to pay for the sins of our souls? Would that make him glad?" (6:7). Answer: *no!* The people needed no new act of contrition. What they needed to do was to start obeying and living out the simple commands of justice and righteousness that God had already given them.

How could those Israelites have been so foolish to think they could buy off God? we think. But wait! Do we ever try to "make up" for our sins by going to more church services? Volunteering for more ministry projects? Adding a zero to the check we drop in the offering plate? Praying until our knees bear a permanent impression of the carpet? Fasting till we look like famine victims? Sometimes we may. In this, we're no more wise than the guilty Israelites.

In fact, we who know about grace coming through faith in Christ have even less justification for trying to buy off God with worship than did our Old Testament predecessors. We can make no "sacrifice" that will strike a single one of our sins off God's ledger, nor should we try. We have only to believe in God's Son and then do what we know is right.

"Just as worship begins in holy expectancy," said Richard Foster, "it ends in holy obedience. If worship does not propel us into greater obedience, it has not been worship."

Do what is right. Love mercy. Walk humbly with your God.

Spend time in silence before God right now. Ask him during that time to reveal to you where you need to be more obedient, more merciful, and more humble.

[i pray]

The light you have already given is enough for me to see my way by, Lord. Help me to do
what I know is right out of humble gratitude for your mercy to this sinner,
not proudly in a vain attempt to earn your good favor.

[i respond]

Rather than some extravagant act of devotion calculated to catch God's eye, today perform an act of kindness to another person in secret.

[16]All the nations of the world will stand amazed at what the LORD will do for you. They will be embarrassed that their power is so insignificant. They will stand in silent awe, deaf to everything around them. [17]They will come to realize what lowly creatures they really are. Like snakes crawling from their holes, they will come out to meet the LORD our God. They will fear him greatly, trembling in terror at his presence.

[18]Where is another God like you, who pardons the sins of the survivors among his people? You cannot stay angry with your people forever, because you delight in showing mercy. [19]Once again you will have compassion on us. You will trample our sins under your feet and throw them into the depths of the ocean! [20]You will show us your faithfulness and unfailing love as you promised with an oath to our ancestors Abraham and Jacob long ago.

Nahum

The LORD is slow to get angry, but his power is great,

and he never lets the guilty go unpunished (1:3).

Lessons Learned

How quickly we forget. It seems the lessons we learn the hard way and promise to remember are often the first to fade to black. Nahum reminds us of this fact through the tragic story of mighty Nineveh. About a generation after donning sackcloth and ashes to plead with Jonah for God's mercy, the people returned to their former sinful practices. Worshiping idols. Delving in wickedness. God-worship once again came to a screeching halt.

When the prophet Nahum entered the scene, however, his message was hardly a reminder to shape up. It was too late for that. Judgment was already on its way. He described Assyria's terrifying destruction in terrible detail—an event that would come to pass a mere fifty years later.

What's more surprising? The fact that one of the most influential cities in the world and the capital of the Assyrian Empire, repented at all, or that a hundred years later they took a 180-degree turn back to wickedness? The truth is this tendency shouldn't surprise us at all. It's part of human nature. The people of Nineveh were no exception; and neither are we. We forget to read God's Word. We slack off in prayer. We let other things crowd out our personal worship time with God. And according to Nahum, it's a slippery slope to all-out rebellion. Just look at Nineveh. Who would have guessed these God-worshipers in Jonah's time would be back to their same old wicked habits so soon?

As you read through this brief book, let Nahum's prophetic words sink into your heart. Refuse to let your worship slide or else reap the consequences.

Worship Moments

- We worship a God of awesome power seen through nature—a fierce whirlwind, quaking mountains, melting hills, and blazing fire (1:3–6).

- Nahum warns against worshiping false gods (3:4).

- God is described as: "a jealous God" (1:2); "good" and a "strong refuge (1:7); "the LORD Almighty" (3:5).

1

This message concerning Nineveh came as a vision to Nahum, who lived in Elkosh.

THE LORD'S ANGER AGAINST NINEVEH

²The LORD is a jealous God, filled with vengeance and wrath. He takes revenge on all who oppose him and furiously destroys his enemies! ³The LORD is slow to get angry, but his power is great, and he never lets the guilty go unpunished. He displays his power in the whirlwind and the storm. The billowing clouds are the dust beneath his feet. ⁴At his command the oceans and rivers dry up, the lush pastures of Bashan and Carmel fade, and the green forests of Lebanon wilt. ⁵In his presence the mountains quake, and the hills melt away; the earth trembles, and its people are destroyed. ⁶Who can stand before his fierce anger? Who can survive his burning fury? His rage blazes forth like fire, and the mountains crumble to dust in his presence.

⁷The LORD is good. When trouble comes, he is a strong refuge. And he knows everyone who trusts in him. ⁸But he sweeps away his enemies in an overwhelming flood. He pursues his foes into the darkness of night.

⁹Why are you scheming against the LORD? He will destroy you with one blow; he won't need to strike twice! ¹⁰His enemies, tangled up like thorns, staggering like drunks, will be burned like dry straw in a field. ¹¹Who is this king of yours who dares to plot evil against the LORD?

¹²This is what the LORD says: "Even though the Assyrians have many allies, they will be destroyed and disappear. O my people, I have already punished you once, and I will not do it again. ¹³Now I will break your chains and release you from Assyrian oppression."

¹⁴And this is what the LORD says concerning the Assyrians in Nineveh: "You will have no more children to carry on your name. I will destroy all the idols in the temples of your gods. I am preparing a grave for you because you are despicable and don't deserve to live!"

¹⁵Look! A messenger is coming over the mountains with good news! He is bringing a message of peace. Celebrate your festivals, O people of Judah, and fulfill all your vows, for your enemies from Nineveh will never invade your land again. They have been completely destroyed!

THE FALL OF NINEVEH

2

Nineveh, you are already surrounded by enemy armies! Sound the alarm! Man the ramparts! Muster your defenses, and keep a sharp watch for the enemy attack to begin! ²For the land of Israel lies empty and broken after your attacks, but the LORD will restore its honor and power again.

³Shields flash red in the sunlight! The attack begins! See their scarlet uniforms! Watch as their glittering chariots move into position, with a forest of spears waving above them. ⁴The chariots race recklessly along the streets and through the squares, swift as lightning, flickering like torches. ⁵The king shouts to his officers; they stumble in their haste, rushing to the walls to set up their defenses. ⁶But too late! The river gates are open! The enemy has entered! The palace is about to collapse!

⁷Nineveh's exile has been decreed, and all the servant girls mourn its capture. Listen to them moan like doves; watch them beat their breasts in sorrow. ⁸Nineveh is like a leaking water reservoir! The people are slipping away. "Stop, stop!" someone shouts, but the people just keep on running.

⁹Loot the silver! Plunder the gold! There seems no end to Nineveh's many treasures—its vast, uncounted wealth. ¹⁰Soon the city is an empty shambles, stripped of its wealth. Hearts melt in horror, and knees shake. The people stand aghast, their faces pale and trembling.

¹¹Where now is that great Nineveh, lion of the nations, full of fight and boldness, where the old and feeble and the young and tender lived with nothing to fear? ¹²O Nineveh, you were once a mighty lion! You crushed your enemies to feed your cubs and your mate. You

My Daily Worship

— August 22 —

FINDING SAFETY IN THE BATTLE

NAHUM 1:1–3:19

The LORD is good. When trouble comes, he is a strong refuge.
And he knows everyone who trusts in him (1:7).

[i reflect]

Herbert, an aging World War II veteran, set his granddaughter Alyssa on his knee one day and told her that he had a special gift for her. He brought out a small leather-covered Bible. "I carried this Bible with me all through the war," he explained. "As I tramped across Europe, fighting battles or just wondering what was going to happen next, this book was my comfort. It helped me trust that God would take care of me and my wife and baby back home."

Next, Herbert opened the Bible to a well-thumbed page and read Nahum 1:7 aloud. "This verse was my special promise," he told Alyssa. "In the war, I clung to the truth that God was with me, even in times of trouble. Somehow, knowing that God was aware of my fear helped me enter the refuge of his peace. And after all these years, what I know is that the Lord is good." As he handed over the worn leather Bible, he knew that the truth he had shared was the gift Alyssa would come to value greater in years to come.

Reading Nahum on the march in Europe, Herbert may or may not have realized that this little prophetic book was written in a context of war similar to what he was experiencing. The "Nazis" of Nahum's day were the Assyrians, who had already conquered the northern kingdom of Israel. Would they conquer the southern kingdom of Judah, too? No, the Lord would be a refuge to protect the remnant of his followers in the land.

The Lord is still good. He knows each of us by name and knows what we face in the "battles" of our lives. We can trust that, when trouble comes, he will be our strong refuge.

Sing a hymn of protection, such as Luther's great anthem, "A Mighty Fortress Is Our God." Pray for safety from the attacks you are enduring.

[i pray]

Be my safe place, O God, my God. Draw me into your shelter,
where I need have no fear. Whisper words of peace to me.

[i respond]

Memorize today's key verse. Recite it several times a day so that when you are in the midst of battle, you can turn to those words.

filled your city and your homes with captives and plunder.

¹³"I am your enemy!" says the LORD Almighty. "Your chariots will soon go up in smoke. The finest of your youth will be killed in battle. Never again will you bring back plunder from conquered nations. Never again will the voices of your proud messengers be heard."

THE LORD'S JUDGMENT AGAINST NINEVEH

3 How terrible it will be for Nineveh, the city of murder and lies! She is crammed with wealth to be plundered. ²Listen! Hear the crack of the whips as the chariots rush forward against her. Wheels rumble, horses' hooves pound, and chariots clatter as they bump wildly through the streets. ³See the flashing swords and glittering spears in the upraised arms of the cavalry! The dead are lying in the streets—dead bodies, heaps of bodies, everywhere. People stumble over them, scramble to their feet, and fall again. ⁴All this because Nineveh, the beautiful and faithless city, mistress of deadly charms, enticed the nations with her beauty. She taught them all to worship her false gods, enchanting people everywhere.

⁵"No wonder I am your enemy!" declares the LORD Almighty. "And now I will lift your skirts so all the earth will see your nakedness and shame. ⁶I will cover you with filth and show the world how vile you really are. ⁷All who see you will shrink back in horror and say, 'Nineveh lies in utter ruin.' Yet no one anywhere will regret your destruction."

⁸Are you any better than Thebes,* surrounded by rivers, protected by water on all sides? ⁹Ethiopia* and the land of Egypt were the source of her strength, which seemed without limit. The nations of Put and Libya also helped and supported her. ¹⁰Yet Thebes fell, and her people were led away as captives. Her babies were dashed to death against the stones of the streets. Soldiers cast lots to see who would get the Egyptian officers as servants. All their leaders were bound in chains.

¹¹And you, Nineveh, will also stagger like a drunkard. You will hide for fear of the attacking enemy. ¹²All your fortresses will fall. They will be devoured like the ripe figs that fall into the mouths of those who shake the trees. ¹³Your troops will be as weak and helpless as women. The gates of your land will be opened wide to the enemy and set on fire and burned.

¹⁴Get ready for the siege! Store up water! Strengthen the defenses! Make bricks to repair the walls! Go into the pits to trample clay, and pack it into molds! ¹⁵But in the middle of your preparations, the fire will devour you; the sword will cut you down. The enemy will consume you like locusts, devouring everything they see. There will be no escape, even if you multiply like grasshoppers. ¹⁶Merchants, as numerous as the stars, have filled your city with vast wealth. But like a swarm of locusts, they strip the land and then fly away. ¹⁷Your princes and officials are also like locusts, crowding together in the hedges to survive the cold. But like locusts that fly away when the sun comes up to warm the earth, all of them will fly away and disappear.

¹⁸O Assyrian king, your princes lie dead in the dust. Your people are scattered across the mountains. There is no longer a shepherd to gather them together. ¹⁹There is no healing for your wound; your injury is fatal. All who hear of your destruction will clap their hands for joy. Where can anyone be found who has not suffered from your cruelty?

3:8 Hebrew *No-amon;* also in 3:10. **3:9** Hebrew *Cush.*

Habakkuk

I will wait quietly for the coming day (3:16).

Worship While You Wait

Waiting. Everyone must do it, but no one really enjoys it. It tries our patience. The more important our need, the more waiting it seems to involve. Receiving a much-anticipated letter from a college admissions office takes forever. Finding out if we're going to receive that promotion is an eternity. Why must we often wait for what we really want?

Habakkuk wondered much the same thing as he pondered God's apparent delay. Judah, his homeland, was a mess. Idolatry was rampant. Wickedness was abundant. *And just where was God during this?* Habakkuk wanted to know. When could he count on God to show up and take charge? Habakkuk could hardly hold his anticipation in check as he launched into the lengthy conversation with God recorded here.

God responded to Habakkuk's tough questions with equal passion. He acknowledged that Habakkuk was waiting on him to act. Yet he instructed Habakkuk to worship while he waited. "Consider my attributes." "Ponder my power." "Muse on my might." Worshiping God instead of worrying about unanswered questions enabled Habakkuk to end his book with a message of hope.

Whenever we find ourselves waiting for God to act or answer us, worshiping him becomes all the more vital. When we see the rampant evil in our world today, we can ease our worries by bringing images of God's inexhaustible might, his fervent power, and his unquestionable authority to mind. This God is well worth the wait. Worshiping him while we wait for him to move in our world today makes us trust him for the answers—even if it takes until we get to heaven to receive them. Wait and worship.

Worship Moments

- Habakkuk worships with honest prayer (1:2–4).

- God's glory will fill the earth (2:14); his brilliant splendor fills the heavens (3:3).

- God is described as: "My God, my Holy One" (1:12; 3:3), "our Rock" (1:12), "wonderful God" (3:3); powerful and awesome (3:4, 6); and the "Sovereign LORD" (3:19).

1 This is the message that the prophet Habakkuk received from the LORD in a vision.

HABAKKUK'S COMPLAINT

²How long, O LORD, must I call for help? But you do not listen! "Violence!" I cry, but you do not come to save. ³Must I forever see this sin and misery all around me? Wherever I look, I see destruction and violence. I am surrounded by people who love to argue and fight. ⁴The law has become paralyzed and useless, and there is no justice given in the courts. The wicked far outnumber the righteous, and justice is perverted with bribes and trickery.

THE LORD'S REPLY

⁵The LORD replied, "Look at the nations and be amazed! Watch and be astounded at what I will do! For I am doing something in your own day, something you wouldn't believe even if someone told you about it. ⁶I am raising up the Babylonians* to be a new power on the world scene. They are a cruel and violent nation who will march across the world and conquer it. ⁷They are notorious for their cruelty. They do as they like, and no one can stop them. ⁸Their horses are swifter than leopards. They are a fierce people, more fierce than wolves at dusk. Their horsemen race forward from distant places. Like eagles they swoop down to pounce on their prey.

⁹"On they come, all of them bent on violence. Their hordes advance like a wind from the desert, sweeping captives ahead of them like sand. ¹⁰They scoff at kings and princes and scorn all their defenses. They simply pile ramps of earth against their walls and capture them! ¹¹They sweep past like the wind and are gone. But they are deeply guilty, for their own strength is their god."

HABAKKUK'S SECOND COMPLAINT

¹²O LORD my God, my Holy One, you who are eternal—is your plan in all of this to wipe us out? Surely not! O LORD our Rock, you have decreed the rise of these Babylonians to punish and correct us for our terrible sins. ¹³You are perfectly just in this. But will you, who cannot allow sin in any form, stand idly by while they swallow us up? Should you be silent while the wicked destroy people who are more righteous than they?

¹⁴Are we but fish to be caught and killed? Are we but creeping things that have no leader to defend them from their enemies? ¹⁵Must we be strung up on their hooks and dragged out in their nets while they rejoice? ¹⁶Then they will worship their nets and burn incense in front of them. "These nets are the gods who have made us rich!" they will claim.

¹⁷Will you let them get away with this forever? Will they succeed forever in their heartless conquests?

2 I will climb up into my watchtower now and wait to see what the LORD will say to me and how he will answer my complaint.

THE LORD'S SECOND REPLY

²Then the LORD said to me, "Write my answer in large, clear letters on a tablet, so that a runner can read it and tell everyone else. ³But these things I plan won't happen right away. Slowly, steadily, surely, the time approaches when the vision will be fulfilled. If it seems slow, wait patiently, for it will surely take place. It will not be delayed.

⁴"Look at the proud! They trust in themselves, and their lives are crooked;* but the righteous will live by their faith.* ⁵Wealth* is treacherous, and the arrogant are never at rest. They range far and wide, with their mouths opened as wide as death,* but they are never satisfied. In their greed they have gathered up many nations and peoples. ⁶But the time is coming when all their captives will taunt them, saying, 'You thieves! At last justice has caught up with you! Now you will get what you deserve for your oppression and

---

1:6 Or *Chaldeans.*   2:4a Greek version reads *I will have no pleasure in anyone who turns away.*   2:4b Or *the just will live by their faithfulness.*   2:5a As in Dead Sea Scroll 1QpHab; other Hebrew manuscripts read *Wine.*   2:5b Hebrew *as Sheol.*

My Daily Worship

— *August 23* —

MADE RIGHT BY FAITH ALONE

HABAKKUK 1:1–3:19

Look at the proud! They trust in themselves, and their lives are crooked;
but the righteous will live by their faith (2:4).

[i reflect]

That's one small step for a man, one giant leap for mankind.

Ask not what your country can do for you, but what you can do for your country.

Give me liberty, or give me death.

Most Americans (hopefully!) can identify those quotes as being spoken by Neil Armstrong, John F. Kennedy, and Patrick Henry, respectively. In the different times these words were spoken, they galvanized a nation and changed the course of history.

Less well-known to us are these words from the prophet Habakkuk, written around 600 B.C., "The righteous will live by their faith." This message (just three words in the original Hebrew text), echoed by the apostle Paul in Romans 1:17, set forth the uniquely biblical message that we are made right with God not by any works of righteousness, but strictly by faith. This doctrine of justification by faith sets Christianity apart. It also makes it difficult for many people to come to terms with God's wonderful salvation. We don't do anything to earn it; we don't add anything to it; we just receive it by his grace, through faith, period.

The truth that we are made right with God by faith, not works, changed the lives of great men and women through the centuries and helped launch the Protestant Reformation. Martin Luther wrote, "When the article of justification has fallen, everything has fallen. This is the chief article from which all other doctrines have flowed. It alone begets, nourishes, builds, preserves and defends the church of God; and without it the church of God cannot exist for one hour. [The doctrine of justification is] the master and prince, the lord, the ruler, and the judge over all kinds of doctrines."

Salvation is the gift of God from first to last. Let the beauty and the wonder of that cause you to bow before our gracious God in adoration, gratitude, and praise.

[i pray]

Lord, you know—and I confess—that my natural inclination is to try to work my way into your
favor. Forgive my lack of appreciation that it is only through the cross of Christ that
I am saved, not through any righteousness of my own. Thank you that I am
made right with you by faith; help me now also live by that same faith.

[i respond]

John Calvin called the doctrine of justification by faith "the main hinge on which religion turns." Write this in the front of your Bible as a constant reminder of the bedrock of your faith: *I am saved by God's grace through faith in Christ alone—period.*

extortion!' ⁷Suddenly, your debtors will rise up in anger. They will turn on you and take all you have, while you stand trembling and helpless. ⁸You have plundered many nations; now they will plunder you. You murderers! You have filled the countryside with violence and all the cities, too.

⁹"How terrible it will be for you who get rich by unjust means! You believe your wealth will buy security, putting your families beyond the reach of danger. ¹⁰But by the murders you committed, you have shamed your name and forfeited your lives. ¹¹The very stones in the walls of your houses cry out against you, and the beams in the ceilings echo the complaint.

¹²"How terrible it will be for you who build cities with money gained by murder and corruption! ¹³Has not the LORD Almighty promised that the wealth of nations will turn to ashes? They work so hard, but all in vain! ¹⁴For the time will come when all the earth will be filled, as the waters fill the sea, with an awareness of the glory of the LORD.

¹⁵"How terrible it will be for you who make your neighbors drunk! You force your cup on them so that you can gloat over their nakedness and shame. ¹⁶But soon it will be your turn! Come, drink and be exposed! Drink from the cup of the LORD's judgment, and all your glory will be turned to shame. ¹⁷You cut down the forests of Lebanon. Now you will be cut down! You terrified the wild animals you caught in your traps. Now terror will strike you because of your murder and violence in cities everywhere!

¹⁸"What have you gained by worshiping all your man-made idols? How foolish to trust in something made by your own hands! What fools you are to believe such lies! ¹⁹How terrible it will be for you who beg lifeless wooden idols to save you. You ask speechless stone images to tell you what to do. Can an idol speak for God? They may be overlaid with gold and silver, but they are lifeless inside. ²⁰But the LORD is in his holy Temple. Let all the earth be silent before him.'"

HABAKKUK'S PRAYER

3 This prayer was sung by the prophet Habakkuk:*

²I have heard all about you, LORD, and I am filled with awe by the amazing things you have done. In this time of our deep need, begin again to help us, as you did in years gone by. Show us your power to save us. And in your anger, remember your mercy.

³I see God, the Holy One, moving across the deserts from Edom* and Mount Paran.* His brilliant splendor fills the heavens, and the earth is filled with his praise! What a wonderful God he is! ⁴Rays of brilliant light flash from his hands. He rejoices in his awesome power.* ⁵Pestilence marches before him; plague follows close behind. ⁶When he stops, the earth shakes. When he looks, the nations tremble. He shatters the everlasting mountains and levels the eternal hills. But his power is not diminished in the least! ⁷I see the peoples of Cushan and Midian trembling in terror.

⁸Was it in anger, LORD, that you struck the rivers and parted the sea? Were you displeased with them? No, you were sending your chariots of salvation! ⁹You were commanding your weapons of power! You split open the earth with flowing rivers! ¹⁰The mountains watched and trembled. Onward swept the raging waters. The mighty deep cried out, lifting its hands to the LORD. ¹¹The lofty sun and moon began to fade, obscured by brilliance from your arrows and the flashing of your glittering spear.

¹²You marched across the land in awesome anger and trampled the nations in your fury. ¹³You went out to rescue your chosen people, to save your anointed ones. You crushed the heads of the wicked and laid bare their bones

---

3:1 Hebrew adds *according to shigionoth,* probably indicating the musical setting for the prayer. **3:3a** Hebrew *Teman.* **3:3b** Hebrew adds *selah;* also in 3:9, 13. The meaning of this Hebrew term is uncertain; it is probably a musical or literary term. **3:4** Or *He veils his awesome power.*

from head to toe. ¹⁴With their own weapons, you destroyed those who rushed out like a whirlwind, thinking Israel would be easy prey. ¹⁵You trampled the sea with your horses, and the mighty waters piled high.

¹⁶I trembled inside when I heard all this; my lips quivered with fear. My legs gave way beneath me,* and I shook in terror. I will wait quietly for the coming day when disaster will strike the people who invade us. ¹⁷Even though the fig trees have no blossoms, and there are no grapes on the vine; even though the olive crop fails, and the fields lie empty and barren; even though the flocks die in the fields, and the cattle barns are empty, ¹⁸yet I will rejoice in the LORD! I will be joyful in the God of my salvation. ¹⁹The Sovereign LORD is my strength! He will make me as surefooted as a deer* and bring me safely over the mountains.

(For the choir director: This prayer is to be accompanied by stringed instruments.)

3:16 Hebrew *Decay entered my bones.*   **3:19** Or *will give me the speed of a deer.*

Zephaniah

At last your troubles will be over, and you will fear disaster no more (3:15).

At Last

Everyone likes a story with a good ending. As children, we loved the fairy-tale idea of living "happily ever after." By the time we've experienced real life with its ups and downs, however, cynicism sets in, and we decide that "happily ever after" is only reserved for fairy tales and nursery rhymes. Zephaniah would disagree. He wrote his book to describe the "day of the LORD"—the ultimate "happily ever after" story for God's people.

The "day of the LORD" will be a day of everlasting and terrible judgment for the wicked. God is flawless, Zephaniah explained, and he will judge sin. The priests of Zephaniah's day who mixed pagan practices with worship and the influx of idolatry among the people revealed the rampant ungodliness in Judah. In Judah's time, judgment came in the form of a Babylonian conquest. Yet his words had a future meaning, too. In the last days, no one will be able to defend themselves against Zephaniah's terrible descriptions of impending judgment.

Yet for the righteous, this future day of the Lord will be the first day of eternal happiness. God will do away with evil forever and he will live among us (3:15). At last, our idea of a fairy-tale ending will come true. Until that time, however, life can be hard. Relationships suffer. Jobs change. Children rebel against their parents. Money is tight. Even when we can't find anything in our earthly lives to bring us hope (and let's admit it, some days that seems so true), we do have a storehouse of hope awaiting us in heaven. The day will come when there will be no tears. No sorrow. No pain. No death. We will worship Jesus forever at last.

Worship Moments

- Zephaniah speaks out against idolatrous practices instead of seeking guidance and blessing from God (1:4–5).

- Zephaniah envisions the day when all nations will worship God (2:11; 3:9).

- God is called: "the LORD their God" (2:7); "the LORD Almighty, the God of Israel" (2:9); and the "King of Israel" (3:15).

1

The LORD gave these messages to Zephaniah when Josiah son of Amon was king of Judah. Zephaniah was the son of Cushi, son of Gedaliah, son of Amariah, son of Hezekiah.

COMING JUDGMENT AGAINST JUDAH

[2]"I will sweep away everything in all your land," says the LORD. [3]"I will sweep away both people and animals alike. Even the birds of the air and the fish in the sea will die. I will reduce the wicked to heaps of rubble,* along with the rest of humanity," says the LORD. [4]"I will crush Judah and Jerusalem with my fist and destroy every last trace of their Baal worship. I will put an end to all the idolatrous priests, so that even the memory of them will disappear. [5]For they go up to their roofs and bow to the sun, moon, and stars. They claim to follow the LORD, but then they worship Molech,* too. So now I will destroy them! [6]And I will destroy those who used to worship me but now no longer do. They no longer ask for the LORD's guidance or seek my blessings."

[7]Stand in silence in the presence of the Sovereign LORD, for the awesome day of the LORD's judgment has come. The LORD has prepared his people for a great slaughter and has chosen their executioners.* [8]"On that day of judgment," says the LORD, "I will punish the leaders and princes of Judah and all those following pagan customs. [9]Yes, I will punish those who participate in pagan worship ceremonies, and those who steal and kill to fill their masters' homes with loot.

[10]"On that day," says the LORD, "a cry of alarm will come from the Fish Gate and echo throughout the newer Mishneh section* of the city. And a great crashing sound will come from the surrounding hills. [11]Wail in sorrow, all you who live in the market area, for all who buy and sell there will die.

[12]"I will search with lanterns in Jerusalem's darkest corners to find and punish those who sit contented in their sins, indifferent to the LORD, thinking he will do nothing at all to them. [13]They are the very ones whose property will be plundered by the enemy, whose homes will be ransacked. They will never have a chance to live in the new homes they have built. They will never drink wine from the vineyards they have planted.

[14]"That terrible day of the LORD is near. Swiftly it comes—a day when strong men will cry bitterly. [15]It is a day when the LORD's anger will be poured out. It is a day of terrible distress and anguish, a day of ruin and desolation, a day of darkness and gloom, of clouds, blackness, [16]trumpet calls, and battle cries. Down go the walled cities and strongest battlements!

[17]"Because you have sinned against the LORD, I will make you as helpless as a blind man searching for a path. Your blood will be poured out into the dust, and your bodies will lie there rotting on the ground."

[18]Your silver and gold will be of no use to you on that day of the LORD's anger. For the whole land will be devoured by the fire of his jealousy. He will make a terrifying end of all the people on earth.*

A CALL TO REPENTANCE

2

Gather together and pray, you shameless nation. [2]Gather while there is still time, before judgment begins and your opportunity is blown away like chaff. Act now, before the fierce fury of the LORD falls and the terrible day of the LORD's anger begins. [3]Beg the LORD to save you—all you who are humble, all you who uphold justice. Walk humbly and do what is right. Perhaps even yet the LORD will protect you from his anger on that day of destruction.

JUDGMENT AGAINST PHILISTIA

[4]Gaza, Ashkelon, Ashdod, Ekron—these Philistine cities, too, will be rooted out and left in

---

1:3 The meaning of the Hebrew is uncertain. 1:5 Hebrew *Malcam*, another name for Molech; or it could possibly mean *their king*. 1:7 Hebrew *has prepared a sacrifice and sanctified his guests*. 1:10 Or *the Second Quarter*, a newer section of Jerusalem. 1:18 Or *the people living in the land*.

desolation. ⁵And how terrible it will be for you Philistines* who live along the coast and in the land of Canaan, for this judgment is against you, too! The LORD will destroy you until not one of you is left. ⁶The coastal area will become a pasture, a place of shepherd camps and enclosures for sheep.

⁷The few survivors of the tribe of Judah will pasture there. They will lie down to rest in the abandoned houses in Ashkelon. For the LORD their God will visit his people in kindness and restore their prosperity again.

JUDGMENT AGAINST MOAB AND AMMON

⁸"I have heard the taunts of the people of Moab and Ammon, mocking my people and invading their borders. ⁹Now, as surely as I live," says the LORD Almighty, the God of Israel, "Moab and Ammon will be destroyed as completely as Sodom and Gomorrah. Their land will become a place of stinging nettles, salt pits, and eternal desolation. Those of my people who are left will plunder them and take their land."

¹⁰They will receive the wages of their pride, for they have scoffed at the people of the LORD Almighty. ¹¹The LORD will terrify them as he destroys all the gods in the land. Then people from nations around the world will worship the LORD, each in their own land.

JUDGMENT AGAINST ETHIOPIA AND ASSYRIA

¹²"You Ethiopians* will also be slaughtered by my sword," says the LORD.

¹³And the LORD will strike the lands of the north with his fist. He will destroy Assyria and make its great capital, Nineveh, a desolate wasteland, parched like a desert. ¹⁴The city that once was so proud will become a pasture for sheep and cattle. All sorts of wild animals will settle there. Owls of many kinds will live among the ruins of its palaces, hooting from the gaping windows. Rubble will block all the doorways, and the cedar paneling will lie open to the wind and weather.

¹⁵This is the fate of that boisterous city, once so secure. "In all the world there is no city as great as I," it boasted. But now, look how it has become an utter ruin, a place where animals live! Everyone passing that way will laugh in derision or shake a defiant fist.

JERUSALEM'S REBELLION AND REDEMPTION

3 How terrible it will be for rebellious, polluted Jerusalem, the city of violence and crime. ²It proudly refuses to listen even to the voice of the LORD. No one can tell it anything; it refuses all correction. It does not trust in the LORD or draw near to its God.

³Its leaders are like roaring lions hunting for their victims—out for everything they can get. Its judges are like ravenous wolves at evening time, who by dawn have left no trace of their prey. ⁴Its prophets are arrogant liars seeking their own gain. Its priests defile the Temple by disobeying God's laws. ⁵But the LORD is still there in the city, and he does no wrong. Day by day his justice is more evident, but no one takes notice—the wicked know no shame.

⁶"I have wiped out many nations, devastating their fortress walls and towers. Their cities are now deserted; their streets are in silent ruin. There are no survivors to even tell what happened. ⁷I thought, 'Surely they will have reverence for me now! Surely they will listen to my warnings, so I won't need to strike again.' But no; however much I punish them, they continue their evil practices from dawn till dusk and dusk till dawn." ⁸So now the LORD says: "Be patient; the time is coming soon when I will stand up and accuse these evil nations. For it is my decision to gather together the kingdoms of the earth and pour out my fiercest anger and fury on them. All the earth will be devoured by the fire of my jealousy.

⁹"On that day I will purify the lips of all people, so that everyone will be able to

2:5 Hebrew *Kerethites.*   2:12 Hebrew *Cushites.*

My Daily Worship

— August 24 —

A FATHER'S JOYFUL SONG

ZEPHANIAH 1:1–3:20

For the LORD your God has arrived to live among you. He is a mighty savior. He will
rejoice over you with great gladness. With his love, he will calm all your fears.
He will exult over you by singing a happy song (3:17).

[i reflect]

Ask any new parent (if you are one, you won't have to ask) if there is any more difficult, demanding, or time-consuming job than raising a child. You lose sleep, patience, money, time, hair, and, occasionally, your sanity. You make unbelievable sacrifices for a little person you only met recently, who has no marketable skills, adds nothing to the family finances, makes incredible demands on you at all hours of the day and night (especially the night), and doesn't even say "Thank you." Yet . . .

When it's time for bed or even a nap, there is nothing more satisfying than holding that little person close to your heart, singing a lullaby. For many parents, those are their most cherished memories.

It seems unbelievable, but that is how God feels about you. Zephaniah 3:17 says, "He will rejoice over you with great gladness. With his love, he will calm all your fears. He will exult over you by singing a happy song." Does that not sound like a picture of a proud father or mother, cuddling his or her child close, totally content just to be with him or her?

Jan Karon writes in her book *A New Song*, "God wants to be with us. That, in fact, is his name: Immanuel, God with us. And why is that so hard to imagine, when indeed, he made us for himself? Please hear that, . . . the One who made us, . . . made us for himself. We're reminded in the book of Revelation that he created all things—for his pleasure. Many of us believe that he created all things, but we forget the very best part—that he created us . . . for his pleasure."

As amazing as it seems, God thoroughly enjoys spending time with you. Remember this truth, especially on those days when it would be easier just to roll over and reset the alarm, or turn a deaf ear to his call.

[i pray]

Father, in those times when my own enthusiasm wanes, remind me that my relationship
with you is not just for me and my benefit, but that for some mysterious reason,
you actually enjoy my company. Let that knowledge motivate me to seek you more faithfully.

[i respond]

Plan a "date" with God, spending time doing nothing more than enjoying the absolute pleasure of his company. Choose a place that you enjoy—whether it's outdoors, a coffee shop, or a quiet retreat in your home. Don't plan any Bible study or serious meditation. Just revel in God's presence and his absolute joy in spending time with you.

worship the LORD together. [10]My scattered people who live beyond the rivers of Ethiopia* will come to present their offerings. [11]And then you will no longer need to be ashamed of yourselves, for you will no longer be rebels against me. I will remove all the proud and arrogant people from among you. There will be no pride on my holy mountain. [12]Those who are left will be the lowly and the humble, for it is they who trust in the name of the LORD. [13]The people of Israel who survive will do no wrong to each other, never telling lies or deceiving one another. They will live peaceful lives, lying down to sleep in safety; there will be no one to make them afraid."

[14]Sing, O daughter of Zion; shout aloud, O Israel! Be glad and rejoice with all your heart, O daughter of Jerusalem! [15]For the LORD will remove his hand of judgment and will disperse the armies of your enemy. And the LORD himself, the King of Israel, will live among you! At last your troubles will be over, and you will fear disaster no more.

[16]On that day the announcement to Jerusalem will be, "Cheer up, Zion! Don't be afraid! [17]For the LORD your God has arrived to live among you. He is a mighty savior. He will rejoice over you with great gladness. With his love, he will calm all your fears. He will exult over you by singing a happy song."

[18]"I will gather you who mourn for the appointed festivals; you will be disgraced no more.* [19]And I will deal severely with all who have oppressed you. I will save the weak and helpless ones; I will bring together those who were chased away. I will give glory and renown to my former exiles, who have been mocked and shamed. [20]On that day I will gather you together and bring you home again. I will give you a good name, a name of distinction among all the nations of the earth. They will praise you as I restore your fortunes before their very eyes. I, the LORD, have spoken!"

3:10 Hebrew *Cush.*   3:18 The meaning of the Hebrew for this verse is uncertain.

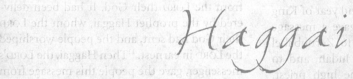

And the people worshiped the LORD in earnest (1:12).

First Things First

Everyone has the same time allotment each day. Twenty-four hours. However, the difference is in how we spend those hours. Sleeping. Eating. Driving. Thinking. Haggai is a crash course in time management regarding the Jews who returned to Jerusalem's ruins to rebuild the Temple and restore worship. While the people started well and set about rebuilding the Temple, they soon slipped back into wrong behavior. Sure, they had houses to build, fields to plant, and commerce to create. But fifteen years had passed since work on the Temple had stopped, and worship had ground to a halt.

Haggai stepped in and told the people to get their priorities straight. The time for excuses was over. "Why are you living in luxurious houses while my house is in ruins?" God said through the prophet (1:4). Haggai reminded them of what was most important: "Get back to work. The time to begin worship is now." Thanks to his exhortation, the people responded in earnest and experienced God's blessings as a result. They made building God's kingdom their top priority rather than building their own, and they began rebuilding the Temple structure stone upon stone. Everything else would just have to wait.

Likewise, if we paused for the precise moment when worship was convenient, we'd be waiting a long time. We will always face distractions that impede our worship experience. We run late. Sleep in. Get lazy, cranky, and busy. We are often tempted, like the Israelites, to put God on hold and bring our own worship to a standstill in deference to our personal schedule. However, Haggai's message remains the same. The time to worship God is now. Make it your priority.

Worship Moments

- Life devoid of worship was not good. There are consequences for ignoring worship (1:9–11).

- The people obeyed and offered heartfelt worship (1:12).

- God's presence and blessing is promised following worship (1:13; 2:4–5, 19).

- God is referred as: "the LORD Almighty" (1:5, 7, 9, 14; 2:6, 7, 8, 9, 11, 23); and the "LORD their God" (1:12).

A Call to Rebuild the Temple

1 On August 29* of the second year of King Darius's reign, the LORD gave a message through the prophet Haggai to Zerubbabel son of Shealtiel, governor of Judah, and to Jeshua* son of Jehozadak, the high priest. ²"This is what the LORD Almighty says: The people are saying, 'The time has not yet come to rebuild the LORD's house—the Temple.'"

³So the LORD sent this message through the prophet Haggai: ⁴"Why are you living in luxurious houses while my house lies in ruins? ⁵This is what the LORD Almighty says: Consider how things are going for you! ⁶You have planted much but harvested little. You have food to eat, but not enough to fill you up. You have wine to drink, but not enough to satisfy your thirst. You have clothing to wear, but not enough to keep you warm. Your wages disappear as though you were putting them in pockets filled with holes!

⁷"This is what the LORD Almighty says: Consider how things are going for you! ⁸Now go up into the hills, bring down timber, and rebuild my house. Then I will take pleasure in it and be honored, says the LORD. ⁹You hoped for rich harvests, but they were poor. And when you brought your harvest home, I blew it away. Why? Because my house lies in ruins, says the LORD Almighty, while you are all busy building your own fine houses. ¹⁰That is why the heavens have withheld the dew and the earth has withheld its crops. ¹¹I have called for a drought on your fields and hills—a drought to wither the grain and grapes and olives and all your other crops, a drought to starve both you and your cattle and to ruin everything you have worked so hard to get."

Obedience to God's Call

¹²Then Zerubbabel son of Shealtiel, Jeshua son of Jehozadak, the high priest, and the whole remnant of God's people obeyed the message from the LORD their God. It had been delivered by the prophet Haggai, whom the LORD their God had sent, and the people worshiped the LORD in earnest. ¹³Then Haggai, the LORD's messenger, gave the people this message from the LORD: "I am with you, says the LORD!" ¹⁴So the LORD sparked the enthusiasm of Zerubbabel son of Shealtiel, governor of Judah, Jeshua son of Jehozadak, the high priest, and the whole remnant of God's people. They came and began their work on the house of the LORD Almighty, their God. ¹⁵This was on September 21* of the second year of King Darius's reign.

The New Temple's Splendor

2 Then on October 17* of that same year, the LORD sent another message through the prophet Haggai. ²"Say this to Zerubbabel son of Shealtiel, governor of Judah, and to Jeshua* son of Jehozadak, the high priest, and to the remnant of God's people there in the land: ³Is there anyone who can remember this house—the Temple—as it was before? In comparison, how does it look to you now? It must seem like nothing at all! ⁴But now take courage, Zerubbabel, says the LORD. Take courage, Jeshua son of Jehozadak, the high priest. Take courage, all you people still left in the land, says the LORD. Take courage and work, for I am with you, says the LORD Almighty. ⁵My Spirit remains among you, just as I promised when you came out of Egypt. So do not be afraid.

⁶"For this is what the LORD Almighty says: In just a little while I will again shake the heavens and the earth. I will shake the oceans and the dry land, too. ⁷I will shake all the nations, and the treasures of all the nations will come to this Temple. I will fill this place with glory, says the LORD Almighty. ⁸The silver

---

1:1a Hebrew *On the first day of the sixth month,* of the Hebrew calendar. A number of dates in Haggai can be cross-checked with dates in surviving Persian records and related accurately to our modern calendar. This event occurred on August 29, 520 B.C. **1:1b** Hebrew *Joshua,* a variant name for Jeshua; also in 1:12, 14. **1:15** Hebrew *on the twenty-fourth day of the sixth month,* of the Hebrew calendar. This event occurred on September 21, 520 B.C.; also see note on 1:1a. **2:1** Hebrew *on the twenty-first day of the seventh month,* of the Hebrew calendar. This event occurred on October 17, 520 B.C.; also see note on 1:1a. **2:2** Hebrew *Joshua,* a variant name for Jeshua; also in 2:4.

My Daily Worship

— *August 25* —

FOR THE GLORY THAT WILL BE
HAGGAI 1:1–2:23

Take courage, all you people still left in the land, says the LORD.
Take courage and work, for I am with you, says the LORD Almighty (2:4).

[i reflect]

At age sixteen, in 1895, Edward bought his first camera and took fifty pictures. When he developed the film, however, he was distressed to see that only one had turned out—a picture of his sister by the piano. Edward's father criticized the effort, causing Edward to contemplate giving up photography. But then his mother praised the one successful photo, saying that it was beautiful and that it more than compensated for the forty-nine others. And so, with this encouragement, Edward Steichen went on to become one of the world's greatest photographers.

Timely encouragement can make the difference between premature surrender and glorious victory.

In 520 B.C., the Jewish exiles who had returned to Jerusalem began rebuilding the Temple. Yet as the days passed, instead of being proud that their work represented a turning point in the nation's religious life, they became disappointed in the structure they saw taking shape in front of them. Stone by stone, they were putting up the best worship house they could, but they knew it fell far short of the original temple in grandeur. They just did not have the resources King Solomon had had.

That's when God stepped in to encourage the builders. For the near term, he assured them of his presence. "Take courage, all you people still left in the land," he told them. "Take courage and work, for I am with you." For the long term, he painted a picture of the glory that would in time come to the temple. His encouragement gave them the extra push they needed to finish construction.

When we are attempting something for the glory of God, he has the same encouragement for us. He tells us, "I know your work seems lonely and futile now, my child, but I am working with you in it. And one day all will see a structure of marvelous strength and beauty. Don't quit!"

What is on your desk or on your to-do list that is overwhelming you right now? Remember God's words of encouragement and renew your commitment to "take courage and work" as an act of worship.

[i pray]

Let me know your nearness, God, and then I can go on. With you, all things are possible.

[i respond]

Pass on these words of encouragement to someone you know who is struggling to complete a task, ministry, or meet a deadline at work. Let them know that you are praying for them as well.

is mine, and the gold is mine, says the LORD Almighty. [9]The future glory of this Temple will be greater than its past glory, says the LORD Almighty. And in this place I will bring peace. I, the LORD Almighty, have spoken!"

BLESSINGS PROMISED
FOR OBEDIENCE

[10]On December 18* of the second year of King Darius's reign, the LORD sent this message to the prophet Haggai: [11]"This is what the LORD Almighty says! Ask the priests this question about the law: [12]If one of you is carrying a holy sacrifice in his robes and happens to brush against some bread or stew, wine or oil, or any other kind of food, will it also become holy?"

The priests replied, "No."

[13]Then Haggai asked, "But if someone becomes ceremonially unclean by touching a dead person and then brushes against any of the things mentioned, will it be defiled?"

And the priests answered, "Yes."

[14]Then Haggai said, "That is how it is with this people and this nation, says the LORD. Everything they do and everything they offer is defiled. [15]So think about this from now on—consider how things were going for you before you began to lay the foundation of the LORD's Temple. [16]When you hoped for a twenty-bushel crop, you harvested only ten. When you expected to draw fifty gallons from the winepress, you found only twenty. [17]I sent blight and mildew and hail to destroy all the produce of your labor. Yet, even so, you refused to return to me, says the LORD.

[18]"On this eighteenth day of December— the day when the foundation of the LORD's Temple was laid—carefully consider this: [19]I am giving you a promise now while the seed is still in the barn, before you have harvested your grain and before the grapevine, the fig tree, the pomegranate, and the olive tree have produced their crops. From this day onward I will bless you."

PROMISES FOR ZERUBBABEL

[20]The LORD sent this second message to Haggai on December 18*: [21]"Tell Zerubbabel, the governor of Judah, that I am about to shake the heavens and the earth. [22]I will overthrow royal thrones, destroying the power of foreign kingdoms. I will overturn their chariots and charioteers. The horses will fall, and their riders will kill each other. [23]But when this happens, says the LORD Almighty, I will honor you, Zerubbabel son of Shealtiel, my servant. I will treat you like a signet ring on my finger, says the LORD, for I have specially chosen you. I, the LORD Almighty, have spoken!"

2:10 Hebrew *On the twenty-fourth day of the ninth month,* of the Hebrew calendar (also in 2:18). This event occurred on December 18, 520 B.C.; also see note on 1:1a. **2:20** Hebrew *on the twenty-fourth day of the month;* see note on 2:10.

Zechariah

Rejoice greatly, O people of Zion! Shout in triumph,
O people of Jerusalem! Look, your king is coming to you (9:9).

A Reason to Worship

Electricity is in the air. Waves of excitement shoot across like lightning. The King is coming! And this is no ordinary king—it is King Jesus. Zechariah tells his contemporary Jewish audience about a dramatic future day when the Temple would one day be complete and the Messiah would come—not only once, but twice. The first time as a carpenter; the second time as King.

Zechariah's message uses precise imagery to predict details about the Messiah's first visit to planet Earth nearly five hundred years prior to his coming. He included his triumphal entry (9:9), his betrayal (11:13), and his manner of death (12:10), predicting these events with amazing accuracy. The artistry he uses to describe Jesus' Second Coming at the end of the age is just as awe inspiring. This "Day of the LORD," as Zechariah called it, will be the most cataclysmic event in history. It's a royal inauguration that no one in the world will miss.

Although Zechariah is primarily an apocalyptic book describing future events, we can feel the implications of those events here and now. That Jesus is returning some day as the King of the universe is reason enough to worship him today as the King of our hearts. "Why wait until the day his kingdom arrives to give him the praise he deserves?" Zechariah seems to ask with timeless urgency. Every day we spend in devotion to him now is only practice for what we'll do each day of eternity. Get ready! The King is coming!

Worship Moments

- Zechariah celebrates God's presence within the future restored city of Jerusalem (2:10).

- God desires worship from the heart that expresses itself in outward action (7:5–6, 8–10).

- Worship will be joyful and celebrative (8:19).

- Zechariah describes the largest worship service to date—a future day when the whole earth will worship God alone (14:9, 16).

- God is worshiped as: the "LORD Almighty" (1:3; 6:15; 8:1); the "Sovereign LORD" (9:14)"LORD their God" (9:16); the good shepherd (10:2-3); and the "King" (14:16).

A Call to Return to the Lord

1 In midautumn* of the second year of King Darius's reign, the LORD gave this message to the prophet Zechariah son of Berekiah and grandson of Iddo.

²"I, the LORD, was very angry with your ancestors. ³Therefore, say to the people, 'This is what the LORD Almighty says: Return to me, and I will return to you, says the LORD Almighty.' ⁴Do not be like your ancestors who would not listen when the earlier prophets said to them, 'This is what the LORD Almighty says: Turn from your evil ways and stop all your evil practices.'

⁵"Your ancestors and their prophets are now long dead. ⁶But all the things I said through my servants the prophets happened to your ancestors, just as I said they would. As a result, they repented and said, 'We have received what we deserved from the LORD Almighty. He has done what he said he would do.'"

A Man among the Myrtle Trees

⁷Then on February 15* of the second year of King Darius's reign, the LORD sent another message to the prophet Zechariah son of Berekiah and grandson of Iddo. Zechariah said:

⁸In a vision during the night, I saw a man sitting on a red horse that was standing among some myrtle trees in a small valley. Behind him were red, brown, and white horses, each with its own rider. ⁹I asked the angel who was talking with me, "My lord, what are all those horses for?"

"I will show you," the angel replied.

¹⁰So the man standing among the myrtle trees explained, "They are the ones the LORD has sent out to patrol the earth."

¹¹Then the other riders reported to the angel of the LORD, who was standing among the myrtle trees, "We have patrolled the earth, and the whole earth is at peace."

¹²Upon hearing this, the angel of the LORD prayed this prayer: "O LORD Almighty, for sev-enty years now you have been angry with Jerusalem and the towns of Judah. How long will it be until you again show mercy to them?" ¹³And the LORD spoke kind and comforting words to the angel who talked with me.

¹⁴Then the angel said to me, "Shout this message for all to hear: 'This is what the LORD Almighty says: My love for Jerusalem and Mount Zion is passionate and strong. ¹⁵But I am very angry with the other nations that enjoy peace and security. I was only a little angry with my people, but the nations punished them far beyond my intentions.

¹⁶"'Therefore, this is what the LORD says: I have returned to show mercy to Jerusalem. My Temple will be rebuilt, says the LORD Almighty, and plans will be made for the reconstruction of Jerusalem.'* ¹⁷Say this also: 'This is what the LORD Almighty says: The towns of Israel will again overflow with prosperity, and the LORD will again comfort Zion and choose Jerusalem as his own.'"

Four Horns and Four Blacksmiths

¹⁸Then I looked up and saw four animal horns. ¹⁹"What are these?" I asked the angel who was talking with me.

He replied, "These horns represent the world powers that scattered Judah, Israel, and Jerusalem."

²⁰Then the LORD showed me four blacksmiths. ²¹"What are these men coming to do?" I asked.

The angel replied, "The blacksmiths have come to terrify the four horns that scattered and humbled Judah. They will throw them down and destroy them."

Future Prosperity of Jerusalem

2 When I looked around me again, I saw a man with a measuring line in his hand. ²"Where are you going?" I asked.

1:1 Hebrew *In the eighth month.* A number of dates in Zechariah can be cross-checked with dates in surviving Persian records and related accurately to our modern calendar. This month of the Hebrew lunar calendar occurred in October and November 520 B.C. 1:7 Hebrew *on the twenty-fourth day of the eleventh month, the month of Shebat,* of the Hebrew calendar. This event occurred on February 15, 519 B.C.; also see note on 1:1. 1:16 Hebrew *and the measuring line will be stretched out over Jerusalem.*

He replied, "I am going to measure Jerusalem, to see how wide and how long it is."

³Then the angel who was with me went to meet a second angel who was coming toward him. ⁴The other angel said, "Hurry, and say to that young man, 'Jerusalem will someday be so full of people that it won't have room enough for everyone! Many will live outside the city walls, with all their livestock—and yet they will be safe. ⁵For I, myself, will be a wall of fire around Jerusalem, says the LORD. And I will be the glory inside the city!'"

THE EXILES ARE CALLED HOME

⁶The LORD says, "Come away! Flee from the north, for I have scattered you to the four winds. ⁷Come away! Escape to Jerusalem,* you who are exiled in Babylon!"

⁸"After a period of glory, the LORD Almighty sent me against the nations who oppressed you. For he said, 'Anyone who harms you harms my most precious possession.* ⁹I will raise my fist to crush them, and their own slaves will plunder them.' Then you will know that the LORD Almighty has sent me."

¹⁰The LORD says, "Shout and rejoice, O Jerusalem,* for I am coming to live among you. ¹¹Many nations will join themselves to the LORD on that day, and they, too, will be my people. I will live among you, and you will know that the LORD Almighty sent me to you. ¹²The land of Judah will be the LORD's inheritance in the holy land, and he will once again choose Jerusalem to be his own city. ¹³Be silent before the LORD, all humanity, for he is springing into action from his holy dwelling."

CLEANSING FOR THE HIGH PRIEST

3 Then the angel showed me Jeshua* the high priest standing before the angel of the LORD. Satan* was there at the angel's right hand, accusing Jeshua of many things. ²And the LORD said to Satan, "I, the LORD, reject your accusations, Satan. Yes, the LORD, who has chosen Jerusalem, rebukes you. This man is like a burning stick that has been snatched from a fire."

³Jeshua's clothing was filthy as he stood there before the angel. ⁴So the angel said to the others standing there, "Take off his filthy clothes." And turning to Jeshua he said, "See, I have taken away your sins, and now I am giving you these fine new clothes."

⁵Then I said, "Please, could he also have a clean turban on his head?" So they put a clean priestly turban on his head and dressed him in new clothes while the angel of the LORD stood by.

⁶Then the angel of the LORD spoke very solemnly to Jeshua and said, ⁷"This is what the LORD Almighty says: If you follow my ways and obey my requirements, then you will be given authority over my Temple and its courtyards. I will let you walk in and out of my presence along with these others standing here. ⁸Listen to me, O Jeshua the high priest, and all you other priests. You are symbols of the good things to come. Soon I am going to bring my servant, the Branch. ⁹Now look at the jewel I have set before Jeshua, a single stone with seven facets.* I will engrave an inscription on it, says the LORD Almighty, and I will remove the sins of this land in a single day. ¹⁰And on that day, says the LORD Almighty, each of you will invite your neighbor into your home to share your peace and prosperity."

A LAMPSTAND AND TWO OLIVE TREES

4 Then the angel who had been talking with me returned and woke me, as though I had been asleep. ²"What do you see now?" he asked.

I answered, "I see a solid gold lampstand with a bowl of oil on top of it. Around the bowl are seven lamps, each one having seven spouts with wicks. ³And I see two olive trees, one on each side of the bowl."

2:7 Hebrew *to Zion.* **2:8** Hebrew *harms the apple of my eye.* **2:10** Hebrew *O daughter of Zion.* **3:1a** Hebrew *Joshua,* a variant name for Jeshua; also in 3:3, 4, 6, 8, 9. **3:1b** Or *The Accuser;* Hebrew reads *The Adversary;* also in 3:2. **3:9** Hebrew *7 eyes.*

⁴Then I asked the angel, "What are these, my lord? What do they mean?"

⁵"Don't you know?" the angel asked.

"No, my lord," I replied.

⁶Then he said to me, "This is what the LORD says to Zerubbabel: It is not by force nor by strength, but by my Spirit, says the LORD Almighty. ⁷Nothing, not even a mighty mountain, will stand in Zerubbabel's way; it will flatten out before him! Then Zerubbabel will set the final stone of the Temple in place, and the people will shout: 'May God bless it! May God bless it!' "

⁸Then another message came to me from the LORD: ⁹"Zerubbabel is the one who laid the foundation of this Temple, and he will complete it. Then you will know that the LORD Almighty has sent me. ¹⁰Do not despise these small beginnings, for the LORD rejoices to see the work begin, to see the plumb line in Zerubbabel's hand. For these seven lamps represent the eyes of the LORD that search all around the world."

¹¹Then I asked the angel, "What are these two olive trees on each side of the lampstand, ¹²and what are the two olive branches that pour out golden oil through two gold tubes?"

¹³"Don't you know?" he asked.

"No, my lord," I replied.

¹⁴Then he said to me, "They represent the two anointed ones who assist the Lord of all the earth."

A FLYING SCROLL

5 I looked up again and saw a scroll flying through the air.

²"What do you see?" the angel asked.

"I see a flying scroll," I replied. "It appears to be about thirty feet long and fifteen feet wide.*"

³Then he said to me, "This scroll contains the curse that is going out over the entire land. One side says that those who steal will be banished from the land; the other side says that those who swear falsely will be banished from the land. ⁴And this is what the LORD Almighty says: I am sending this curse into the house of every thief and into the house of everyone who swears falsely by my name. And my curse will remain in that house until it is completely destroyed—even its timbers and stones."

A WOMAN IN A BASKET

⁵Then the angel who was talking with me came forward and said, "Look up! Something is appearing in the sky."

5:2 Hebrew *20 cubits* [9 meters] *long and 10 cubits* [4.5 meters] *wide.*

My Daily Worship

— *August 26* —

CHRIST, OUR PRECIOUS JEWEL
ZECHARIAH 1:1–4:14

Look at the jewel I have set before Jeshua, a single stone with seven facets.
I will engrave an inscription on it, says the LORD Almighty,
and I will remove the sins of this land in a single day (3:9).

[i reflect]

It was February 10, 1908, and Amsterdam diamond-cutter Joseph Asscher was feeling extremely nervous. This was the day set for Asscher to cut the largest diamond ever found—the Cullinan diamond, weighing 3,106 carats (1.37 lbs.). In attendance were representatives of the stone's owner, Britain's King Edward VII, as well as notary publics, a doctor, and two nurses.

Asscher had spent two months studying the rough diamond and making special tools for cutting and polishing this gem of unheard-of size. A slight miscalculation in his attack, and the stone could shatter into a thousand pieces. Slowly and carefully, Asscher lifted his mallet. Then, with finesse, he struck the blade. Nothing happened. Screwing up his courage again, Asscher struck a second time. This time the stone split perfectly. Asscher promptly fainted, then spent the next two weeks in a hospital recovering from nervous exhaustion.

The jewel that Zechariah saw in his vision may not have looked much like the Cullinan diamond, but it was much more valuable. In the possession of Jeshua (first high priest after the Jewish Exile), the stone in the vision had seven "eyes," or facets, indicating total awareness. Theologians concur: This jewel represents the Messiah, our Lord Jesus. His is the name engraved on the stone. He is the One who wipes out sins.

The remarkable thing is to think that we, in a sense, "possess" this matchless jewel, too. If Asscher would tremble before a hunk of compressed carbon, we should be in dumb awe that the Spirit of Christ has condescended to dwell with us. In the words of 2 Corinthians 4:7, we have "precious treasure" inside us!

Wear a piece of jewelry today that will help remind you to give thanks for the matchless jewel that you have in your possession.

[i pray]

What scares me, God, is that I don't even really know how blessed I am to have
Jesus living inside me. Help me to cherish this priceless gift.

[i respond]

List the pricetag for some of the possessions you have—such as your car, house, education, electronics, etc. Then list the priceless items you have—your family, health, relationships, etc., ending with the most priceless gift of all—Christ our jewel.

6"What is it?" I asked.

He replied, "It is a basket for measuring grain,* and it is filled with the sins* of everyone throughout the land."

7When the heavy lead cover was lifted off the basket, there was a woman sitting inside it. 8The angel said, "The woman's name is Wickedness," and he pushed her back into the basket and closed the heavy lid again.

9Then I looked up and saw two women flying toward us, with wings gliding on the wind. Their wings were like those of a stork, and they picked up the basket and flew with it into the sky.

10"Where are they taking the basket?" I asked the angel.

11He replied, "To the land of Babylonia,* where they will build a temple for the basket. And when the temple is ready, they will set the basket there on its pedestal."

Four Chariots

6 Then I looked up again and saw four chariots coming from between two bronze mountains. 2The first chariot was pulled by red horses, the second by black horses, 3the third by white horses, and the fourth by dappled-gray horses. 4"And what are these, my lord?" I asked the angel who was talking with me.

5He replied, "These are the four spirits* of heaven who stand before the Lord of all the earth. They are going out to do his work. 6The chariot with black horses is going north, the chariot with white horses is going west,* and the chariot with dappled-gray horses is going south."

7The powerful horses were eager to be off, to patrol back and forth across the earth. And the LORD said, "Go and patrol the earth!" So they left at once on their patrol.

8Then the LORD summoned me and said,

"Those who went north have vented the anger of my Spirit* there."

The Crowning of Jeshua

9Then I received another message from the LORD: 10"Heldai, Tobijah, and Jedaiah will bring gifts of silver and gold from the Jews exiled in Babylon. As soon as they arrive, meet them at the home of Josiah son of Zephaniah. 11Accept their gifts and make a crown* from the silver and gold. Then put the crown on the head of Jeshua* son of Jehozadak, the high priest. 12Tell him that the LORD Almighty says: Here is the man called the Branch. He will branch out where he is and build the Temple of the LORD. 13He will build the LORD's Temple, and he will receive royal honor and will rule as king from his throne. He will also serve as priest from his throne,* and there will be perfect harmony between the two.

14"The crown will be a memorial in the Temple of the LORD to honor those who gave it—Heldai,* Tobijah, Jedaiah, and Josiah* son of Zephaniah."

15Many will come from distant lands to rebuild the Temple of the LORD. And when this happens, you will know my messages have been from the LORD Almighty. All this will happen if you carefully obey the commands of the LORD your God.

A Call to Justice and Mercy

7 On December 7* of the fourth year of King Darius's reign, another message came to Zechariah from the LORD. 2The people of Bethel had sent Sharezer and Regemmelech,* along with their men, to seek the LORD's favor. 3They were to ask this question of the prophets and of the priests at the Temple of the LORD Almighty: "Should we continue to mourn and fast each summer on the anniversary of the Temple's destruction,* as we have done for so many years?"

5:6a Hebrew *an ephah*, about half a bushel or 18 liters; also in 5:7, 8, 9, 10, 11. **5:6b** As in Greek version; Hebrew reads *the appearance*. **5:11** Hebrew *the land of Shinar*. **6:5** Or *the four winds*. **6:6** Hebrew *is going after them*. **6:8** Hebrew *have given my Spirit rest*. **6:11a** As in Greek and Syriac versions; Hebrew reads *crowns*. **6:11b** Hebrew *Joshua*, a variant name for Jeshua. **6:13** Or *There will be a priest by his throne*. **6:14a** As in Syriac version (compare 6:10); Hebrew reads *Helem*. **6:14b** As in Syriac version (compare 6:10); Hebrew reads *Hen*. **7:1** Hebrew *On the fourth day of the ninth month, the month of Kislev*, of the Hebrew calendar. This event occurred on December 7, 518 B.C.; also see note on 1:1. **7:2** Or *Bethel-sharezer had sent Regemmelech*. **7:3** Hebrew *mourn and fast in the fifth month*. This month of the Hebrew lunar calendar usually occurs in July and August.

My Daily Worship

— August 27 —

NO POSERS ALLOWED

ZECHARIAH 5:1–9:17

During those seventy years of exile, when you fasted and mourned in the summer and at the festival in early autumn, was it really for me that you were fasting? And even now in your holy festivals, you don't think about me but only of pleasing yourselves (7:5–6).

[i reflect]

According to polling data, in a typical week in the United States:

- 43 percent of adults attend a religious service
- 25 percent of all adults attend Sunday school
- 42 percent of adults read the Bible
- Nearly 80 percent of adults pray

In view of all this religious activity, the question that begs to be asked is, So why isn't our nation more righteous? The answer is simple: It's perilously easy to *act* religious without really caring much about God.

Of course, hypocrisy is nothing new. In the period after the Jewish exiles returned to Judah from Babylon, they sent to inquire of God about whether they should continue to fast in the fifth and seventh months, as they had done during the Exile to mourn the destruction of Jerusalem. God essentially replied, "What difference does it make? You weren't really fasting for me while you were in exile, and to this day you're still thinking of yourself when it comes to worship."

Harsh words. It makes one wonder, what would God say about *our* worship?

What portion of the 43 percent of adults who attend a religious service do so for the selfish purpose of enjoying a "spiritual high" instead of to honor God? What portion of the 80 percent who pray do it to give themselves a sense of calm rather than to bring themselves into line with God's will? We may not be among those who have self-serving motives for our worship activity, but given God's attitude toward hypocrisy, it behooves us to check from time to time to make sure.

Worship is about making a real connection with him. Do a little worship quality control today. Assess your own motives in meeting with God—ask him to reveal any hidden agendas.

[i pray]

Show me my own motives for the "Christian" things I do, Lord, and help me to purify those motives where they are selfish. The real me wants the real you.

[i respond]

Make a list of all the activities you are involved with that you consider "religious." Put a question mark by the ones where you doubt your motives for participating in that activity. If necessary, take a "fast" from that particular activity until your motives are clearer to you.

[4]The LORD Almighty sent me this message: [5]"Say to all your people and your priests, 'During those seventy years of exile, when you fasted and mourned in the summer and at the festival in early autumn,* was it really for me that you were fasting? [6]And even now in your holy festivals, you don't think about me but only of pleasing yourselves. [7]Isn't this the same message the LORD proclaimed through the prophets years ago when Jerusalem and the towns of Judah were bustling with people, and the Negev and the foothills of Judah* were populated areas?' "

[8]Then this message came to Zechariah from the LORD: [9]"This is what the LORD Almighty says: Judge fairly and honestly, and show mercy and kindness to one another. [10]Do not oppress widows, orphans, foreigners, and poor people. And do not make evil plans to harm each other.

[11]"Your ancestors would not listen to this message. They turned stubbornly away and put their fingers in their ears to keep from hearing. [12]They made their hearts as hard as stone, so they could not hear the law or the messages that the LORD Almighty had sent them by his Spirit through the earlier prophets. That is why the LORD Almighty was so angry with them.

[13]"Since they refused to listen when I called to them, I would not listen when they called to me, says the LORD Almighty. [14]I scattered them as with a whirlwind among the distant nations, where they lived as strangers. Their land became so desolate that no one even traveled through it. The land that had been so pleasant became a desert."

PROMISED BLESSINGS FOR JERUSALEM

8 Then another message came to me from the LORD Almighty: [2]"This is what the LORD Almighty says: My love for Mount Zion is passionate and strong; I am consumed with passion for Jerusalem! [3]And now the LORD says: I am returning to Mount Zion, and I will live in Jerusalem. Then Jerusalem will be called the Faithful City; the mountain of the LORD Almighty will be called the Holy Mountain. [4]This is what the LORD Almighty says: Once again old men and women will walk Jerusalem's streets with a cane and sit together in the city squares. [5]And the streets of the city will be filled with boys and girls at play.

[6]"This is what the LORD Almighty says: All this may seem impossible to you now, a small and discouraged remnant of God's people. But do you think this is impossible for me, the LORD Almighty? [7]This is what the LORD Almighty says: You can be sure that I will rescue my people from the east and from the west. [8]I will bring them home again to live safely in Jerusalem. They will be my people, and I will be faithful and just toward them as their God.

[9]"This is what the LORD Almighty says: Take heart and finish the task! You have heard what the prophets have been saying about building the Temple of the LORD Almighty ever since the foundation was laid. [10]Before the work on the Temple began, there were no jobs and no wages for either people or animals. No traveler was safe from the enemy, for there were enemies on all sides. I had turned everyone against each other. [11]But now I will not treat the remnant of my people as I treated them before, says the LORD Almighty. [12]For I am planting seeds of peace and prosperity among you. The grapevines will be heavy with fruit. The earth will produce its crops, and the sky will release the dew. Once more I will make the remnant in Judah and Israel the heirs of these blessings. [13]Among the nations, Judah and Israel had become symbols of what it means to be cursed. But no longer! Now I will rescue you and make you both a symbol and a source of blessing! So don't be afraid or

---

7:5 Hebrew *fasted and mourned in the fifth and seventh months.* The fifth month of the Hebrew lunar calendar usually occurs in July and August. The seventh month usually occurs in September and October; both the Day of Atonement and the Festival of Shelters were celebrated in the seventh month.   7:7 Hebrew *the Shephelah.*

discouraged, but instead get on with rebuilding the Temple!

[14]"For this is what the LORD Almighty says: I did not change my mind when your ancestors angered me and I promised to punish them, says the LORD Almighty. [15]Neither will I change my decision to bless Jerusalem and the people of Judah. So don't be afraid. [16]But this is what you must do: Tell the truth to each other. Render verdicts in your courts that are just and that lead to peace. [17]Do not make evil plots to harm each other. And stop this habit of swearing to things that are false. I hate all these things, says the LORD."

[18]Here is another message that came to me from the LORD Almighty. [19]"This is what the LORD Almighty says: The traditional fasts and times of mourning you have kept in early summer, midsummer, autumn, and winter* are now ended. They will become festivals of joy and celebration for the people of Judah. So love truth and peace.

[20]"This is what the LORD Almighty says: People from nations and cities around the world will travel to Jerusalem. [21]The people of one city will say to the people in another, 'Let us go to Jerusalem to ask the LORD to bless us and to seek the LORD Almighty. We are planning to go ourselves.' [22]People from many nations, even powerful nations, will come to Jerusalem to seek the LORD Almighty and to ask the LORD to bless them.

[23]"This is what the LORD Almighty says: In those days ten people from nations and languages around the world will clutch at the hem of one Jew's robe. And they will say, 'Please let us walk with you, for we have heard that God is with you.'"

JUDGMENT AGAINST ISRAEL'S ENEMIES

9 This is the message* from the LORD against the land of Aram* and the city of Damascus, for the eyes of all humanity, including the people of Israel, are on the LORD. [2]Doom is certain for Hamath, near Damascus, and for the cities of Tyre and Sidon, too, though they are so clever. [3]Tyre has built a strong fortress and has piled up so much silver and gold that it is as common as dust in the streets! [4]But now the Lord will strip away Tyre's possessions and hurl its fortifications into the Mediterranean Sea.* Tyre will be set on fire and burned to the ground.

[5]The city of Ashkelon will see Tyre fall and will be filled with fear. Gaza will shake with terror, and so will Ekron, for their hopes will be dashed. Gaza will be conquered and its king killed, and Ashkelon will be completely deserted. [6]Foreigners will occupy the city of Ashdod. Thus, I will destroy the pride of the Philistines. [7]They will no longer eat meat with blood in it or feed on other forbidden foods. All the surviving Philistines will worship our God and be adopted as a new clan in Judah.* And the Philistines of Ekron will join my people, just as the Jebusites once did. [8]I will guard my Temple and protect it from invading armies. I am closely watching their movements. No foreign oppressor will ever again overrun my people's land.

ZION'S COMING KING

[9]Rejoice greatly, O people* of Zion! Shout in triumph, O people of Jerusalem! Look, your king is coming to you. He is righteous and victorious, yet he is humble, riding on a donkey—even on a donkey's colt. [10]I will remove the battle chariots from Israel* and the warhorses from Jerusalem, and I will destroy all the weapons used in battle. Your king will bring peace to the nations. His realm will stretch from sea to sea and from the Euphrates River* to the ends of the earth.*

[11]Because of the covenant I made with you, sealed with blood, I will free your prisoners

---

8:19 Hebrew *in the fourth, fifth, seventh, and tenth months.* The fourth month of the Hebrew lunar calendar usually occurs in June and July. The fifth month usually occurs in July and August. The seventh month usually occurs in September and October. The tenth month usually occurs in December and January. 9:1a Hebrew *An Oracle: The message.* 9:1b Hebrew *land of Hadrach.* 9:4 Hebrew *the sea.* 9:7 Hebrew *and will become a leader in Judah.* 9:9 Hebrew *daughter.* 9:10a Hebrew *from Ephraim;* also in 9:13. 9:10b Hebrew *the river.* 9:10c Or *the end of the land.*

from death in a waterless dungeon. [12]Come back to the place of safety, all you prisoners, for there is yet hope! I promise this very day that I will repay you two mercies for each of your woes! [13]Judah is my bow, and Israel is my arrow! Jerusalem* is my sword, and like a warrior, I will brandish it against the Greeks.*

[14]The LORD will appear above his people; his arrows will fly like lightning! The Sovereign LORD will sound the trumpet; he will go out against his enemies like a whirlwind from the southern desert. [15]The LORD Almighty will protect his people, and they will subdue their enemies with sling stones. They will shout in battle as though drunk with wine, shedding the blood of their enemies. They will be filled with blood like a bowl, drenched with blood like the corners of the altar.

[16]When that day arrives, the LORD their God will rescue his people, just as a shepherd rescues his sheep. They will sparkle in his land like jewels in a crown. [17]How wonderful and beautiful they will be! The young men and women will thrive on the abundance of grain and new wine.

THE LORD WILL RESTORE HIS PEOPLE

10 Ask the LORD for rain in the spring, and he will give it. It is the LORD who makes storm clouds that drop showers of rain so that every field becomes a lush pasture.

[2]Household gods give false advice, fortune-tellers predict only lies, and interpreters of dreams pronounce comfortless falsehoods. So my people are wandering like lost sheep, without a shepherd to protect and guide them.

[3]"My anger burns against your shepherds, and I will punish these leaders.* For the LORD Almighty has arrived to look after his flock of Judah; he will make them strong and glorious, like a proud warhorse in battle. [4]From Judah will come the cornerstone, the tent peg, the battle bow, and all the rulers. [5]They will be like mighty warriors in battle, trampling their

> *Worship is recognizing God for who he is; it is ascribing worth to him; it is God's people telling him about the worth they see in him.*
>
> DON WEAVER

enemies in the mud under their feet. Since the LORD is with them as they fight, they will overthrow even the horsemen of the enemy.

[6]"I will strengthen Judah and save Israel*; I will reestablish them because I love them. It will be as though I had never rejected them, for I am the LORD their God, who will hear their cries. [7]The people of Israel* will become like mighty warriors, and their hearts will be happy as if by wine. Their children, too, will see it all and be glad; their hearts will rejoice in the LORD. [8]When I whistle to them, they will come running, for I have redeemed them. From the few that are left, their population will grow again to its former size. [9]Though I have scattered them like seeds among the nations, still they will remember me in distant lands. With their children, they will survive and come home again to Israel. [10]I will bring them back from Egypt and Assyria and resettle them in Gilead and Lebanon. There won't be enough room for them all! [11]They will pass safely through the sea of distress,* for the waves of the sea will be held back. And the waters of the Nile will become dry. The pride of Assyria will be crushed, and the rule of Egypt will end. [12]I will make my people strong in my power, and they will go wherever they wish by my authority. I, the LORD, have spoken!"

11 Open your doors, Lebanon, so that fire may sweep through your cedar forests.

9:13a Hebrew *Zion.* 9:13b Hebrew *the sons of Javan.* 10:3 Or *these male goats.* 10:6 Hebrew *save the house of Joseph.* 10:7 Hebrew *of Ephraim.* 10:11 Or *the sea of Egypt,* referring to the Red Sea.

²Weep, you cypress trees, for all the ruined cedars; the tallest and most beautiful of them are fallen. Weep, you oaks of Bashan, as you watch the thickest forests being felled. ³Listen to the wailing of the shepherds, for their wealth is gone. Hear the young lions roaring, for their thickets in the Jordan Valley have been destroyed.

THE GOOD AND EVIL SHEPHERDS

⁴This is what the LORD my God says: "Go and care for a flock that is intended for slaughter. ⁵The buyers will slaughter their sheep without remorse. The sellers will say, 'Praise the LORD, I am now rich!' Even the shepherds have no compassion for them. ⁶And likewise, I will no longer have pity on the inhabitants of the land," says the LORD. "I will let them fall into each other's clutches, as well as into the clutches of their king. They will turn the land into a wilderness, and I will not protect them."

⁷So I cared for the flock intended for slaughter—the flock that was oppressed. Then I took two shepherd's staffs and named one Favor and the other Union. ⁸I got rid of their three evil shepherds in a single month. But I became impatient with these sheep—this nation—and they hated me, too. ⁹So I told them, "I won't be your shepherd any longer. If you die, you die. If you are killed, you are killed. And those who remain will devour each other!"

¹⁰Then I took my staff called Favor and snapped it in two, showing that I had revoked the covenant I had made with all the nations. ¹¹That was the end of my covenant with them. Those who bought and sold sheep were watching me, and they knew that the LORD was speaking to them through my actions. ¹²And I said to them, "If you like, give me my wages, whatever I am worth; but only if you want to." So they counted out for my wages thirty pieces* of silver.

¹³And the LORD said to me, "Throw it to the potters*"—this magnificent sum at which they valued me! So I took the thirty coins and threw them to the potters in the Temple of the LORD. ¹⁴Then I broke my other staff, Union, to show that the bond of unity between Judah and Israel was broken.

¹⁵Then the LORD said to me, "Go again and play the part of a worthless shepherd. ¹⁶This will illustrate how I will give this nation a shepherd who will not care for the sheep that are threatened by death, nor look after the young, nor heal the injured, nor feed the healthy. Instead, this shepherd will eat the meat of the fattest sheep and tear off their hooves. ¹⁷Doom is certain for this worthless shepherd who abandons the flock! The sword will cut his arm and pierce his right eye! His arm will become useless, and his right eye completely blind!"

FUTURE DELIVERANCE FOR JERUSALEM

12 This* message concerning the fate of Israel came from the LORD: "This message is from the LORD, who stretched out the heavens, laid the foundations of the earth, and formed the spirit within humans. ²I will make Jerusalem and Judah like an intoxicating drink to all the nearby nations that send their armies to besiege Jerusalem. ³On that day I will make Jerusalem a heavy stone, a burden for the world. None of the nations who try to lift it will escape unscathed.

⁴"On that day, says the LORD, I will cause every horse to panic and every rider to lose his nerve. I will watch over the people of Judah, but I will blind the horses of her enemies. ⁵And the clans of Judah will say to themselves, 'The people of Jerusalem have found strength in the LORD Almighty, their God.'

⁶"On that day I will make the clans of Judah like a brazier that sets a woodpile ablaze or like a burning torch among sheaves of grain. They will burn up all the neighboring nations right and left, while the people living in Jerusalem remain secure. ⁷The LORD will give

---

11:12 Hebrew *30 shekels,* about 12 ounces or 342 grams in weight. 11:13 Syriac version reads *into the treasury;* also in 11:13b.
12:1 Hebrew *An Oracle: This.*

victory to the rest of Judah first, before Jerusalem, so that the people of Jerusalem and the royal line of David will not have greater honor than the rest of Judah. [8]On that day the LORD will defend the people of Jerusalem; the weakest among them will be as mighty as King David! And the royal descendants will be like God, like the angel of the LORD who goes before them! [9]For my plan is to destroy all the nations that come against Jerusalem.

[10]"Then I will pour out a spirit of grace and prayer on the family of David and on all the people of Jerusalem. They will look on me whom they have pierced and mourn for him as for an only son. They will grieve bitterly for him as for a firstborn son who has died. [11]The sorrow and mourning in Jerusalem on that day will be like the grievous mourning of Hadad-rimmon in the valley of Megiddo.

[12]"All Israel will weep in profound sorrow, each family by itself, with the husbands and wives in separate groups. The family of David will mourn, along with the family of Nathan, [13]the family of Levi, and the family of Shimei. [14]Each of the surviving families from Judah will mourn separately, husbands and wives apart.

A FOUNTAIN OF CLEANSING

13 "On that day a fountain will be opened for the dynasty of David and for the people of Jerusalem, a fountain to cleanse them from all their sins and defilement.

[2]"And on that day, says the LORD Almighty, I will get rid of every trace of idol worship throughout the land, so that even the names of the idols will be forgotten. I will remove from the land all false prophets and the unclean spirits that inspire them. [3]If anyone begins prophesying again, his own father and mother will tell him, 'You must die, for you have prophesied lies in the name of the LORD.' Then his own father and mother will stab him.

[4]"No one will be boasting then of a prophetic gift! No one will wear prophet's clothes to try to fool the people. [5]'No,' he will say. 'I'm not a prophet; I'm a farmer. The soil has been my means of livelihood from my earliest youth.' [6]And if someone asks, 'Then what are those scars on your chest*?' he will say, 'I was wounded at the home of friends!'

THE SCATTERING OF THE SHEEP

[7]"Awake, O sword, against my shepherd, the man who is my partner, says the LORD Almighty. Strike down the shepherd, and the sheep will be scattered, and I will turn against the lambs. [8]Two-thirds of the people in the land will be cut off and die, says the LORD. But a third will be left in the land. [9]I will bring that group through the fire and make them pure, just as gold and silver are refined and purified by fire. They will call on my name, and I will answer them. I will say, 'These are my people,' and they will say, 'The LORD is our God.'"

THE LORD WILL RULE THE EARTH

14 Watch, for the day of the LORD is coming when your possessions will be plundered right in front of you! [2]On that day I will gather all the nations to fight against Jerusalem. The city will be taken, the houses plundered, and the women raped. Half the population will be taken away into captivity, and half will be left among the ruins of the city.

[3]Then the LORD will go out to fight against those nations, as he has fought in times past. [4]On that day his feet will stand on the Mount of Olives, which faces Jerusalem on the east. And the Mount of Olives will split apart, making a wide valley running from east to west, for half the mountain will move toward the north and half toward the south. [5]You will flee through this valley, for it will reach across to Azal.* Yes, you will flee as you did from the earthquake in the days of King Uzziah of Judah. Then the LORD my God will come, and all his holy ones with him.*

13:6 Or *scars between your hands.*   **14:5a** The meaning of the Hebrew is uncertain.   **14:5b** As in Greek version; Hebrew reads *with you.*

My Daily Worship

— *August 28* —

THE FACE IN THE CRUCIBLE

ZECHARIAH 10:1–14:21

I will bring that group through the fire and make them pure, just as gold and silver are refined and purified by fire. They will call on my name, and I will answer them. I will say, "These are my people," and they will say, "The LORD is our God" (13:9).

[i reflect]

Kay Arthur begins her book *As Silver Refined* by describing the patient labor of a craftsman as he builds a fire, crushes silver ore, fills his crucible with the mineral, watches the metal melt and impurities rise to the top, and repeatedly reheats the silver and skims off the dross. Then, "Once more he bends over the crucible, and this time he catches his breath. There it is! In the silver he sees what he has waited for so patiently: a clear image of himself, distinct and sharp."

It's easy to see why biblical writers turned to the practice of metal refinement for symbols of spiritual realities (Psalm 12:6; 66:10; Proverbs 17:3; 27:21). In Zechariah's case, a remnant of people left in the land were to be purified by their experience, so they would renew their covenant with God. But the message is of more than historical interest; we, too, may be refined like silver. God uses the flames of tribulation to burn away sinful impurities from our heart so that his image in us shows through distinct and sharp.

But let's not be overly pious. Oswald Chambers delivered a cold splash of reality when he said, "It is nonsense to say that suffering makes saints; it makes some people devils." Still, there is a suffering that *forms* rather than *deforms*. Chambers noted, "Suffering 'according to the will of God' raises us to a freedom and felicity that baffles all language to express." Let us, then, put off our asbestos overcoat when God sends his refining fire.

"Suffering," declared Henri Frédéric Amiel, "becomes a purification of the soul, a sacred trial sent by eternal love, a divine dispensation meant to sanctify and ennoble us, an acceptable aid to faith, a strange initiation into happiness."

Thank God today for the refining process you are undergoing right now.

[i pray]

Lord, suffering is indeed a strange initiation into happiness. Yet, show me how my pain is making me more like you. I will accept it, for I trust in you.

[i respond]

If you sense that your current hardship may be God's way of purifying you and bringing out his image in your life, then in prayer, dedicate yourself to cooperate with him. Afterward, light a match, quickly blow it out, and carry the charred match with you as a reminder of God's refining work.

⁶On that day the sources of light will no longer shine,* ⁷yet there will be continuous day! Only the LORD knows how this could happen! There will be no normal day and night, for at evening time it will still be light. ⁸On that day life-giving waters will flow out from Jerusalem, half toward the Dead Sea and half toward the Mediterranean,* flowing continuously both in summer and in winter.

⁹And the LORD will be king over all the earth. On that day there will be one LORD— his name alone will be worshiped. ¹⁰All the land from Geba, north of Judah, to Rimmon, south of Jerusalem, will become one vast plain. But Jerusalem will be raised up in its original place and will be inhabited all the way from the Benjamin Gate over to the site of the old gate, then to the Corner Gate, and from the Tower of Hananel to the king's winepresses. ¹¹And Jerusalem will be filled, safe at last, never again to be cursed and destroyed.

¹²And the LORD will send a plague on all the nations that fought against Jerusalem. Their people will become like walking corpses, their flesh rotting away. Their eyes will shrivel in their sockets, and their tongues will decay in their mouths. ¹³On that day they will be terrified, stricken by the LORD with great panic. They will fight against each other in hand-to-hand combat; ¹⁴Judah, too, will be fighting at Jerusalem. The wealth of all the neighboring nations will be captured—great quantities of gold and silver and fine clothing. ¹⁵This same plague will strike the horses, mules, camels, donkeys, and all the other animals in the enemy camps.

¹⁶In the end, the enemies of Jerusalem who survive the plague will go up to Jerusalem each year to worship the King, the LORD Almighty, and to celebrate the Festival of Shelters. ¹⁷And any nation anywhere in the world that refuses to come to Jerusalem to worship the King, the LORD Almighty, will have no rain. ¹⁸And if the people of Egypt refuse to attend the festival, the LORD will punish them with the same plague that he sends on the other nations who refuse to go. ¹⁹Egypt and the other nations will all be punished if they don't go to celebrate the festival.

²⁰On that day even the harness bells of the horses will be inscribed with these words: SET APART AS HOLY TO THE LORD. And the cooking pots in the Temple of the LORD will be as sacred as the basins used beside the altar. ²¹In fact, every cooking pot in Jerusalem and Judah will be set apart as holy to the LORD Almighty. All who come to worship will be free to use any of these pots to boil their sacrifices. And on that day there will no longer be traders* in the Temple of the LORD Almighty.

14:6 Hebrew *there will be no light, no cold or frost.* The meaning of the Hebrew is uncertain. 14:8 Hebrew *half toward the eastern sea and half toward the western sea.* 14:21 Hebrew *Canaanites.*

Malachi

"Cursed is the cheat who promises to give a fine ram from his flock
but then sacrifices a defective one to the Lord. For I am a great king,"
says the LORD Almighty, "and my name is feared among the nations!" (1:14).

Way Too Casual

"Casual day" in corporate offices has undergone a dramatic makeover in recent years. A time when slacks and a sports coat used to be considered dressing down is gone, replaced with baggy jeans and polo shirts. It's an "anything goes" society where sleeveless and backless are considered as appropriate as tailored clothes.

Malachi addressed the "casual day" in his time. He was talking about worship and the casual attitude the Jews had developed toward it. Although they completed the Temple after their return from Babylon, they still struggled to maintain focus. Their worship services had become sloppy, and the priests had neglected God's commands. As a result, the people were careless and lackadaisical about the idea of devoting their lives to the God who had saved them. Their "take it or leave it" mentality toward worship led them into trouble.

Through an interesting dialogue between the people and God, Malachi upheld the standard expected of priests and leaders and encouraged them to assume their responsibilities once again. He reminded the people that the Messiah is already on his way to punish the unjust and rescue the faithful few.

Does Malachi have a few words for worshipers today? Definitely. The same laziness plagues many people today whose best intentions to attend worship service go by the wayside when the alarm clock rings. The same carelessness haunts even the ones who make it to church physically but neglect to engage spiritually when it comes to worship. Casual attitudes lead to casual worship. Malachi's message to the church, though ancient, is still timely today. Casual day is for work, not for worship.

Worship Moments

- God does not want inferior offerings in our worship (1:7–10, 12–14). In contrast, Malachi highlights wholehearted worship worthy of an awesome God (1:11).

- Malachi describes the Messiah, worthy of pure worship offerings, as a blazing fire that sits in judgment (3:2–3).

- Malachi praises God as: the "LORD Almighty" (1:4); the unchanging God (3:6); the "Sun of Righteousness" (4:2).

1

This is the message* that the LORD gave to Israel through the prophet Malachi.*

THE LORD'S LOVE FOR ISRAEL

²"I have loved you deeply," says the LORD.

But you retort, "Really? How have you loved us?"

And the LORD replies, "I showed my love for you by loving your ancestor Jacob. Yet Esau was Jacob's brother, ³and I rejected Esau and devastated his hill country. I turned Esau's inheritance into a desert for jackals."

⁴And Esau's descendants in Edom may say, "We have been shattered, but we will rebuild the ruins."

But this is what the LORD Almighty says: "They may try to rebuild, but I will demolish them again! Their country will be known as 'The Land of Wickedness,' and their people will be called 'The People with Whom the LORD Is Forever Angry.' ⁵When you see the destruction for yourselves, you will say, 'Truly, the LORD's great power reaches far beyond our borders!'"

UNWORTHY SACRIFICES

⁶The LORD Almighty says to the priests: "A son honors his father, and a servant respects his master. I am your father and master, but where are the honor and respect I deserve? You have despised my name!

"But you ask, 'How have we ever despised your name?'

⁷"You have despised my name by offering defiled sacrifices on my altar.

"Then you ask, 'How have we defiled the sacrifices*?'

"You defile them by saying the altar of the LORD deserves no respect. ⁸When you give blind animals as sacrifices, isn't that wrong? And isn't it wrong to offer animals that are crippled and diseased? Try giving gifts like that to your governor, and see how pleased he is!" says the LORD Almighty.

⁹"Go ahead, beg God to be merciful to you!

But when you bring that kind of offering, why should he show you any favor at all?" asks the LORD Almighty.

¹⁰"I wish that someone among you would shut the Temple doors so that these worthless sacrifices could not be offered! I am not at all pleased with you," says the LORD Almighty, "and I will not accept your offerings. ¹¹But my name is honored by people of other nations from morning till night. All around the world they offer sweet incense and pure offerings in honor of my name. For my name is great among the nations," says the LORD Almighty. ¹²"But you dishonor my name with your actions. By bringing contemptible food, you are saying it's all right to defile the Lord's table. ¹³You say, 'It's too hard to serve the LORD,' and you turn up your noses at his commands," says the LORD Almighty. "Think of it! Animals that are stolen and mutilated, crippled and sick—presented as offerings! Should I accept from you such offerings as these?" asks the LORD. ¹⁴"Cursed is the cheat who promises to give a fine ram from his flock but then sacrifices a defective one to the Lord. For I am a great king," says the LORD Almighty, "and my name is feared among the nations!

A WARNING FOR THE PRIESTS

2

"Listen, you priests; this command is for you! ²Listen to me and take it to heart. Honor my name," says the LORD Almighty, "or I will bring a terrible curse against you. I will curse even the blessings you receive. Indeed, I have already cursed them, because you have not taken my warning seriously. ³I will rebuke your descendants and splatter your faces with the dung of your festival sacrifices, and I will add you to the dung heap. ⁴Then at last you will know it was I who sent you this warning so that my covenant with the Levites may continue," says the LORD Almighty.

⁵"The purpose of my covenant with the Levites was to bring life and peace, and this is what I gave them. This called for reverence

---

1:1a Hebrew *An Oracle: The message.*   1:1b *Malachi* means "my messenger."   1:7 As in Greek version; Hebrew reads *defiled you.*

My Daily Worship

— *August 29* —

ONLY OUR BEST WILL DO

MALACHI 1:1–2:17

"When you give blind animals as sacrifices, isn't that wrong? And isn't it wrong to offer animals that are crippled and diseased? Try giving gifts like that to your governor, and see how pleased he is!" says the LORD Almighty (1:8).

[i reflect]

In the movie version of the *Lord of the Rings,* there were battle scenes with scores of soldiers wearing chain mail. The designers decided that interconnected plastic rings would look most realistic on screen. So a pair of young men spent three and a half *years* linking 12.5 million plastic rings *by hand* for all the soldier costumes. In an interview, one of the young men gushed, "I would not have traded this experience for the world. It's been the most amazing time of my life."

Many people found the *Lord of the Rings* movies to be good entertainment, but would you want to spend three and a half years of your life attaching one plastic ring to another? Yet every day, people pour their whole souls into endeavors like lowering their time on the racecourse by a fraction of a second, recording and re-recording tracks for a demo CD that a music producer might possibly hear, or putting together a marketing plan that will knock the argyles off a client. The point is not that anything is wrong with these pursuits, but rather, do we give to God our very best, as others give to their vocations and avocations?

God criticized the priests of Israel for offering flawed animals on the altar even though the law clearly stated that God was to get only unblemished beasts. You can almost hear the hurt in God's voice because the flawed offerings showed how little the people cared about him. He must be hurt the same way when we approach our ministries in a slipshod, good-enough-for-church-work way. How thrilled he would be if we offered our lives as unblemished "living sacrifices" every day (Romans 12:1)!

Review your agenda for today. Commit to giving your best in each and every endeavor as an act of worship.

[i pray]

Lord, you gave me the perfect gift of your Son. You deserve nothing less than the very best of who I am. Watch and see how I'll give it!

[i respond]

Take inspiration from those who have used their gifts to the utmost for God's glory. For example, listen to a gospel recording by Mahalia Jackson, look at a print of a scriptural scene painted by Rembrandt, or read one of the sacred poems by John Donne.

from them, and they greatly revered me and stood in awe of my name. ⁶They passed on to the people all the truth they received from me. They did not lie or cheat; they walked with me, living good and righteous lives, and they turned many from lives of sin. ⁷The priests' lips should guard knowledge, and people should go to them for instruction, for the priests are the messengers of the LORD Almighty. ⁸But not you! You have left God's paths. Your 'guidance' has caused many to stumble into sin. You have corrupted the covenant I made with the Levites," says the LORD Almighty. ⁹"So I have made you despised and humiliated in the eyes of all the people. For you have not obeyed me but have shown partiality in your interpretation of the law."

A CALL TO FAITHFULNESS

¹⁰Are we not all children of the same Father? Are we not all created by the same God? Then why are we faithless to each other, violating the covenant of our ancestors? ¹¹In Judah, in Israel, and in Jerusalem there is treachery, for the men of Judah have defiled the LORD's beloved sanctuary by marrying women who worship idols. ¹²May the LORD cut off from the nation of Israel* every last man who has done this and yet brings an offering to the LORD Almighty.

¹³Here is another thing you do. You cover the LORD's altar with tears, weeping and groaning because he pays no attention to your offerings, and he doesn't accept them with pleasure. ¹⁴You cry out, "Why has the LORD abandoned us?" I'll tell you why! Because the LORD witnessed the vows you and your wife made to each other on your wedding day when you were young. But you have been disloyal to her, though she remained your faithful companion, the wife of your marriage vows. ¹⁵Didn't the LORD make you one with your wife? In body and spirit you are his.* And what does he want? Godly children from your union. So guard yourself; remain loyal to the wife of your youth. ¹⁶"For I hate divorce!" says the LORD, the God of Israel. "It is as cruel as putting on a victim's bloodstained coat," says the LORD Almighty. "So guard yourself; always remain loyal to your wife."

¹⁷You have wearied the LORD with your words.

"Wearied him?" you ask. "How have we wearied him?"

You have wearied him by suggesting that the LORD favors evildoers since he does not punish them. You have wearied him by asking, "Where is the God of justice?"

THE COMING DAY OF JUDGMENT

3 "Look! I am sending my messenger, and he will prepare the way before me. Then the Lord you are seeking will suddenly come to his Temple. The messenger of the covenant, whom you look for so eagerly, is surely coming," says the LORD Almighty. ²"But who will be able to endure it when he comes? Who will be able to stand and face him when he appears? For he will be like a blazing fire that refines metal or like a strong soap that whitens clothes. ³He will sit and judge like a refiner of silver, watching closely as the dross is burned away. He will purify the Levites, refining them like gold or silver, so that they may once again offer acceptable sacrifices to the LORD. ⁴Then once more the LORD will accept the offerings brought to him by the people of Judah and Jerusalem, as he did in former times. ⁵At that time I will put you on trial. I will be a ready witness against all sorcerers and adulterers and liars. I will speak against those who cheat employees of their wages, who oppress widows and orphans, or who deprive the foreigners living among you of justice, for these people do not fear me," says the LORD Almighty.

A CALL TO REPENTANCE

⁶"I am the LORD, and I do not change. That is why you descendants of Jacob are not already

---

2:12 Hebrew *from the tents of Jacob.* **2:15** Or *Did not one God make us and preserve our life and breath?* or *Did not one God make her, both flesh and spirit?* The meaning of the Hebrew is uncertain.

My Daily Worship

— *August 30* —

I-DOLATRY
MALACHI 3:1-4:6

The LORD Almighty says, "The day of judgment is coming, burning like a furnace.
The arrogant and the wicked will be burned up like straw on that day.
They will be consumed like a tree—roots and all" (4:1).

[i reflect]

Oscar-winning actress Meryl Streep in an interview once commented on the rampant pride in Hollywood: "It's sort of exhausting, this self-congratulatory atmosphere in which the movie community lives. It's unbearable. We're not that important in the world, but we certainly think we are. . . . It's so grand and the outfits are so incredible and the critique of how everybody looks and the desperation of people to make an impact—it really gets to me."

While pride is one of the classical seven deadly sins, it has long been recognized as somehow being the most fundamental sin. Pride is what caused Lucifer to be cast out of heaven; he preferred to be devil-in-chief rather than an angel commander saluting God. Pride in who we are or what we own or what we have accomplished likewise causes us to put ourselves in the place only God should occupy.

The Jews in Malachi's time had seen arrogant people temporarily getting away with doing what they wanted instead of obeying God. And so the people had concluded, "What's the use of serving God?" (3:14). But God assured everyone that the arrogant would in time certainly go through the fire of destruction—and a most thorough destruction at that (4:1).

Catherine of Siena reported that God said to her, "You are she who is not, and I am Who Is." Of course, each of us has value that has been given to us by God, and there is such a thing as justifiable pride in oneself. But in comparison to who God is, we are nothing. Let us put no other god—certainly not ourselves—before him.

Let your pride in your work—whether at home, school, or the office—take a backseat to God today. Whenever you are tempted to feel puffed up, turn your thoughts to the One who enables you to accomplish what you do.

[i pray]

To the I AM: I confess that you are God and I never will be. May I never envy the arrogant nor doubt that their pride will be judged. May I be the "last" whom you will make "first."

[i respond]

Chrysostom wrote, "Run from pride, for it is a passion more treacherous than any other." Inventory your latest accomplishments and achievements. Of which are you most proud? Call someone you know well and give the credit to God for that accomplishment or success.

completely destroyed. [7]Ever since the days of your ancestors, you have scorned my laws and failed to obey them. Now return to me, and I will return to you," says the LORD Almighty.

"But you ask, 'How can we return when we have never gone away?'

[8]"Should people cheat God? Yet you have cheated me!

"But you ask, 'What do you mean? When did we ever cheat you?'

"You have cheated me of the tithes and offerings due to me. [9]You are under a curse, for your whole nation has been cheating me. [10]Bring all the tithes into the storehouse so there will be enough food in my Temple. If you do," says the LORD Almighty, "I will open the windows of heaven for you. I will pour out a blessing so great you won't have enough room to take it in! Try it! Let me prove it to you! [11]Your crops will be abundant, for I will guard them from insects and disease.* Your grapes will not shrivel before they are ripe," says the LORD Almighty. [12]"Then all nations will call you blessed, for your land will be such a delight," says the LORD Almighty.

[13]"You have said terrible things about me," says the LORD.

"But you say, 'What do you mean? How have we spoken against you?'

[14]"You have said, 'What's the use of serving God? What have we gained by obeying his commands or by trying to show the LORD Almighty that we are sorry for our sins? [15]From now on we will say, "Blessed are the arrogant." For those who do evil get rich, and those who dare God to punish them go free of harm.'"

THE LORD'S PROMISE OF MERCY

[16]Then those who feared the LORD spoke with each other, and the LORD listened to what they said. In his presence, a scroll of remembrance was written to record the names of those who feared him and loved to think about him. [17]"They will be my people," says the LORD Almighty. "On the day when I act, they will be my own special treasure. I will spare them as a father spares an obedient and dutiful child. [18]Then you will again see the difference between the righteous and the wicked, between those who serve God and those who do not."

THE COMING DAY OF JUDGMENT

4 The LORD Almighty says, "The day of judgment is coming, burning like a furnace. The arrogant and the wicked will be burned up like straw on that day. They will be consumed like a tree—roots and all.

[2]"But for you who fear my name, the Sun of Righteousness will rise with healing in his wings.* And you will go free, leaping with joy like calves let out to pasture. [3]On the day when I act, you will tread upon the wicked as if they were dust under your feet," says the LORD Almighty.

[4]"Remember to obey the instructions of my servant Moses, all the laws and regulations that I gave him on Mount Sinai* for all Israel.

[5]"Look, I am sending you the prophet Elijah before the great and dreadful day of the LORD arrives. [6]His preaching will turn the hearts of parents* to their children, and the hearts of children to their parents. Otherwise I will come and strike the land with a curse."

3:11 Hebrew *from the devourer.* 4:2 Or *the sun of righteousness will rise with healing in its wings.* 4:4 Hebrew *Horeb,* another name for Sinai. 4:6 Hebrew *fathers;* also in 4:6b.

The New Testament

Matthew

Look! The virgin will conceive a child! She will give birth to a son, and
he will be called Immanuel (meaning, God is with us) (1:23).

The Promised One

For centuries, the Jews clung to the promises of the Old Testament. Desperate, downtrodden, beaten, overwhelmed, they looked to the words spoken through the prophets that God would send a deliverer, a rescuer. *Help is on the way.* Those words drove them to their knees in prayer during persecution. Those words lifted their eyes to heaven when doubts threatened to overwhelm them. Those words gave them hope when God seemed a million miles away. When? Where? How would this help come to them? As a Jew, Matthew knew that the Scriptures promised that God would send someone to deliver his people from all their suffering. He knew this deliverer as the Messiah.

This former tax collector, who later became one of Jesus' original twelve disciples, told his primarily Jewish audience that help was no longer *on the way.* The waiting was over; help had arrived. Jesus was indeed the promised Messiah. Matthew references the Old Testament more than any of the other three Gospels to show his audience how Jesus bridged the Old and New Testaments and fulfilled the prophecies. He demonstrated Jesus' authority as he preached a radical message in the Sermon on the Mount and challenged the Pharisees at every turn. He recorded Jesus as the Deliverer who healed the sick servant of a desperate Roman officer, cured the oozing sores of a leper, and released the twisted muscles of a paralyzed man.

Those whom Jesus rescued recognized him almost immediately. These individuals looked into their hero's eyes and knew that only one person on earth could do what he did—the Messiah.

Like them, we are in need of a deliverer, one who can come and rescue us from our sin. Like them, we need to know not only that help is on the way, but also that it is *here,* available to us at the cross. Jesus' death rescued us from certain death and secured our salvation. Help has arrived. You can gaze gratefully at his face and call your Deliverer by name. His name is Jesus.

Worship Moments

- Matthew shows that Jesus is worthy of worship from the very beginning at his birth (2:9–11).

- In the beginning and continuing throughout Jesus' ministry, some claim to worship him but have insincere motives (2:8; 15:7–9).

- Satan tempts Jesus to worship him instead of God the Father (4:1–11). However, Jesus declares that we must worship God alone (4:10).

- In this book, Jesus is emphasized as the descendant of David, the "Son of David"—a title reserved only for One worthy of worship (1:1; 9:27; 12:23; 15:22; 20:30–31; 21:9, 15; 22:41–45).

THE RECORD OF JESUS' ANCESTORS

1 This is a record of the ancestors of Jesus the Messiah, a descendant of King David and of Abraham:

2 Abraham was the father of Isaac.
Isaac was the father of Jacob.
Jacob was the father of Judah and his brothers.
3 Judah was the father of Perez and Zerah (their mother was Tamar).
Perez was the father of Hezron.
Hezron was the father of Ram.*
4 Ram was the father of Amminadab.
Amminadab was the father of Nahshon.
Nahshon was the father of Salmon.
5 Salmon was the father of Boaz (his mother was Rahab).
Boaz was the father of Obed (his mother was Ruth).
Obed was the father of Jesse.
6 Jesse was the father of King David.
David was the father of Solomon (his mother was Bathsheba, the widow of Uriah).
7 Solomon was the father of Rehoboam.
Rehoboam was the father of Abijah.
Abijah was the father of Asaph.*
8 Asaph was the father of Jehoshaphat.
Jehoshaphat was the father of Jehoram.*
Jehoram was the father* of Uzziah.
9 Uzziah was the father of Jotham.
Jotham was the father of Ahaz.
Ahaz was the father of Hezekiah.
10 Hezekiah was the father of Manasseh.
Manasseh was the father of Amos.*
Amos was the father of Josiah.
11 Josiah was the father of Jehoiachin* and his brothers (born at the time of the exile to Babylon).
12 After the Babylonian exile:
Jehoiachin was the father of Shealtiel.
Shealtiel was the father of Zerubbabel.

13 Zerubbabel was the father of Abiud.
Abiud was the father of Eliakim.
Eliakim was the father of Azor.
14 Azor was the father of Zadok.
Zadok was the father of Akim.
Akim was the father of Eliud.
15 Eliud was the father of Eleazar.
Eleazar was the father of Matthan.
Matthan was the father of Jacob.
16 Jacob was the father of Joseph, the husband of Mary.
Mary was the mother of Jesus, who is called the Messiah.

17 All those listed above include fourteen generations from Abraham to King David, and fourteen from David's time to the Babylonian exile, and fourteen from the Babylonian exile to the Messiah.

THE BIRTH OF JESUS THE MESSIAH

18 Now this is how Jesus the Messiah was born. His mother, Mary, was engaged to be married to Joseph. But while she was still a virgin, she became pregnant by the Holy Spirit. 19 Joseph, her fiancé, being a just man, decided to break the engagement quietly, so as not to disgrace her publicly.

20 As he considered this, he fell asleep, and an angel of the Lord appeared to him in a dream. "Joseph, son of David," the angel said, "do not be afraid to go ahead with your marriage to Mary. For the child within her has been conceived by the Holy Spirit. 21 And she will have a son, and you are to name him Jesus,* for he will save his people from their sins." 22 All of this happened to fulfill the Lord's message through his prophet:

23 "Look! The virgin will conceive a child!
She will give birth to a son,
and he will be called Immanuel*
(meaning, God is with us)."

1:3 Greek *Aram;* also in 1:4. See 1 Chr 2:9-10. **1:7** *Asaph* is the same person as Asa; also in 1:8. See 1 Chr 3:10. **1:8a** Greek *Joram.* See 1 Kgs 22:50 and note at 1 Chr 3:11. **1:8b** Or *ancestor;* also in 1:11. **1:10** *Amos* is the same person as Amon. See 1 Chr 3:14. **1:11** Greek *Jeconiah;* also in 1:12. See 2 Kgs 24:6 and note at 1 Chr 3:16. **1:21** *Jesus* means "The LORD saves." **1:23** Isa 7:14; 8:8, 10.

My Daily Worship

— *August 31* —

THE POWER OF ONE NAME

MATTHEW 1:1–2:23

And she will have a son, and you are to name him Jesus,
for he will save his people from their sins (1:21).

[i reflect]

As the new millennium was about to begin, Bryan Brand and his wife were hosting a Bible study on the book of Acts in their home. They observed how in the Scriptures people always responded very strongly to the name of Jesus. Sometimes it was favorably. Other times negatively. From those observations, Bryan got the idea to create billboards around St. Louis on which would appear simply the name of Jesus.

The first sign was put up in November 1999. Like those that appeared subsequently, it featured white letters on a green background to mimic interstate signs. The billboards carried no additional words, phone numbers, or attribution. Since the Jesus Name Project (as it was called) began, testimonies have been shared of marriages saved, a woman receiving forgiveness for abortion, a discouraged pastor gaining a renewed passion for ministry, plus many others—all through the power of one name.

For two millennia prior to Bryan Brand's brainstorm, the power of Jesus' name has resulted in freeing people from their sinful, self-destructive lifestyles. Since an angel instructed a carpenter to name his wife's child Jesus, the world has witnessed unimagined wonders that are rooted in the power of that name.

No doubt, you can attest to how simply whispering Jesus' name has calmed your fears. When you couldn't find a missing child, you called out "Jesus!" When the phone rang in the middle of the night with terrifying news, you spoke that wonderful name. No day is complete for the believer without saying or singing his name. Whether it be an ancient hymn like "At the Name of Jesus," that favorite Gaither tune "There's Just Something About That Name," or a brand new worship chorus that celebrates the Savior, sing it out today as a reminder that he takes delight in saving us from desperate situations through the power of his name.

[i pray]

Jesus, I love to say your name. Something about it calms my knotted nerves and renews my
confidence that you are in control. Lord Jesus, you are my only Savior. I need you today.

[i respond]

Find a hymnbook and look in the index for hymns that contain the name of Jesus in their titles. Spend the next few days reading those hymn verses and meditating on their meaning.

²⁴When Joseph woke up, he did what the angel of the Lord commanded. He brought Mary home to be his wife, ²⁵but she remained a virgin until her son was born. And Joseph named him Jesus.

THE VISIT OF THE WISE MEN

2 Jesus was born in the town of Bethlehem in Judea, during the reign of King Herod. About that time some wise men* from eastern lands arrived in Jerusalem, asking, ²"Where is the newborn king of the Jews? We have seen his star as it arose,* and we have come to worship him."

³Herod was deeply disturbed by their question, as was all of Jerusalem. ⁴He called a meeting of the leading priests and teachers of religious law. "Where did the prophets say the Messiah would be born?" he asked them.

⁵"In Bethlehem," they said, "for this is what the prophet wrote:

⁶ 'O Bethlehem of Judah,
 you are not just a lowly village in Judah,
 for a ruler will come from you
 who will be the shepherd for my people
  Israel.'*"

⁷Then Herod sent a private message to the wise men, asking them to come see him. At this meeting he learned the exact time when they first saw the star. ⁸Then he told them, "Go to Bethlehem and search carefully for the child. And when you find him, come back and tell me so that I can go and worship him, too!"

⁹After this interview the wise men went their way. Once again the star appeared to them, guiding them to Bethlehem. It went ahead of them and stopped over the place where the child was. ¹⁰When they saw the star, they were filled with joy! ¹¹They entered the house where the child and his mother, Mary, were, and they fell down before him and worshiped him. Then they opened their treasure chests and gave him gifts of gold, frankincense, and myrrh. ¹²But when it was time to leave, they went home another way, because God had warned them in a dream not to return to Herod.

THE ESCAPE TO EGYPT

¹³After the wise men were gone, an angel of the Lord appeared to Joseph in a dream. "Get up and flee to Egypt with the child and his mother," the angel said. "Stay there until I tell you to return, because Herod is going to try to

---

Words of Worship

JESUS

Jesus—Greek *Ie-sous.* The Greek name is a form of the Hebrew *Yeshua'* or *Yehoshua',* "Joshua."

"You are to name him Jesus," the angel said, "for he will save his people from their sins" (Matthew 1:21). So Joseph was told in a dream what the name of Mary's child would be, and its meaning. "Joshua" was a common enough Hebrew name, but given to the Son of God it had special force, for it declares, "His deliverance is the Lord."

In worship we call often upon Jesus, for "there is no other name in all of heaven for people to call on to save them" (Acts 4:12). Nothing is nebulous or vague about the *salvation* Jesus brings, for the biblical word simply means *deliverance.* Are we held back from what God wants us to be by a faulty self-image, destructive behavior patterns, a warped perspective on life, or some other enemy? By his death and resurrection, Jesus frees us from all these—and above all, from that sin of self-worship that would limit our fellowship with God, whether now or in eternity.

2:1 Or *royal astrologers;* Greek reads *magi;* also in 2:7, 16. 2:2 Or *in the east.* 2:6 Mic 5:2; 2 Sam 5:2.

kill the child." [14]That night Joseph left for Egypt with the child and Mary, his mother, [15]and they stayed there until Herod's death. This fulfilled what the Lord had spoken through the prophet: "I called my Son out of Egypt."*

[16]Herod was furious when he learned that the wise men had outwitted him. He sent soldiers to kill all the boys in and around Bethlehem who were two years old and under, because the wise men had told him the star first appeared to them about two years earlier.* [17]Herod's brutal action fulfilled the prophecy of Jeremiah:

[18] "A cry of anguish is heard in Ramah—
    weeping and mourning unrestrained.
  Rachel weeps for her children,
    refusing to be comforted—for they are
        dead."*

THE RETURN TO NAZARETH

[19]When Herod died, an angel of the Lord appeared in a dream to Joseph in Egypt and told him, [20]"Get up and take the child and his mother back to the land of Israel, because those who were trying to kill the child are dead." [21]So Joseph returned immediately to Israel with Jesus and his mother. [22]But when he learned that the new ruler was Herod's son Archelaus, he was afraid. Then, in another dream, he was warned to go to Galilee. [23]So they went and lived in a town called Nazareth. This fulfilled what was spoken by the prophets concerning the Messiah: "He will be called a Nazarene."

JOHN THE BAPTIST PREPARES THE WAY

3 In those days John the Baptist began preaching in the Judean wilderness. His message was, [2]"Turn from your sins and turn to God, because the Kingdom of Heaven is near.*" [3]Isaiah had spoken of John when he said,

"He is a voice shouting in the wilderness:
  'Prepare a pathway for the Lord's
      coming!
  Make a straight road for him!'*

[4]John's clothes were woven from camel hair, and he wore a leather belt; his food was locusts and wild honey. [5]People from Jerusalem and from every section of Judea and from all over the Jordan Valley went out to the wilderness to hear him preach. [6]And when they confessed their sins, he baptized them in the Jordan River.

[7]But when he saw many Pharisees and Sadducees coming to be baptized, he denounced them. "You brood of snakes!" he exclaimed. "Who warned you to flee God's coming judgment? [8]Prove by the way you live that you have really turned from your sins and turned to God. [9]Don't just say, 'We're safe—we're the descendants of Abraham.' That proves nothing. God can change these stones here into children of Abraham. [10]Even now the ax of God's judgment is poised, ready to sever your roots. Yes, every tree that does not produce good fruit will be chopped down and thrown into the fire.

[11]"I baptize with* water those who turn from their sins and turn to God. But someone is coming soon who is far greater than I am—so much greater that I am not even worthy to be his slave.* He will baptize you with the Holy Spirit and with fire.* [12]He is ready to separate the chaff from the grain with his winnowing fork. Then he will clean up the threshing area, storing the grain in his barn but burning the chaff with never-ending fire."

THE BAPTISM OF JESUS

[13]Then Jesus went from Galilee to the Jordan River to be baptized by John. [14]But John didn't want to baptize him. "I am the one who needs to be baptized by you," he said, "so why are you coming to me?"

[15]But Jesus said, "It must be done, because

2:15 Hos 11:1. 2:16 Or *according to the time he calculated from the wise men.* 2:18 Jer 31:15. 3:2 Or *has come,* or *is coming soon.*
3:3 Isa 40:3. 3:11a Or *in.* 3:11b Greek *to carry his sandals.* 3:11c Or *in the Holy Spirit and in fire.*

we must do everything that is right.*" So then John baptized him.

[16]After his baptism, as Jesus came up out of the water, the heavens were opened and he saw the Spirit of God descending like a dove and settling on him. [17]And a voice from heaven said, "This is my beloved Son, and I am fully pleased with him."

THE TEMPTATION OF JESUS

4 Then Jesus was led out into the wilderness by the Holy Spirit to be tempted there by the Devil. [2]For forty days and forty nights he ate nothing and became very hungry. [3]Then the Devil* came and said to him, "If you are the Son of God, change these stones into loaves of bread."

[4]But Jesus told him, "No! The Scriptures say,

'People need more than bread for their life;
   they must feed on every word of
      God.'*"

[5]Then the Devil took him to Jerusalem, to the highest point of the Temple, [6]and said, "If you are the Son of God, jump off! For the Scriptures say,

'He orders his angels to protect you.
And they will hold you with their hands
   to keep you from striking your foot on a
      stone.'*"

[7]Jesus responded, "The Scriptures also say, 'Do not test the Lord your God.'*"

[8]Next the Devil took him to the peak of a very high mountain and showed him the nations of the world and all their glory. [9]"I will give it all to you," he said, "if you will only kneel down and worship me."

[10]"Get out of here, Satan," Jesus told him. "For the Scriptures say,

'You must worship the Lord your God;
   serve only him.'*"

[11]Then the Devil went away, and angels came and cared for Jesus.

THE MINISTRY OF JESUS BEGINS

[12]When Jesus heard that John had been arrested, he left Judea and returned to Galilee. [13]But instead of going to Nazareth, he went to Capernaum, beside the Sea of Galilee, in the region of Zebulun and Naphtali. [14]This fulfilled Isaiah's prophecy:

[15] "In the land of Zebulun and of Naphtali,
   beside the sea, beyond the Jordan
      River—
   in Galilee where so many Gentiles live—
[16] the people who sat in darkness
   have seen a great light.
And for those who lived in the land where
   death casts its shadow,
   a light has shined."*

[17]From then on, Jesus began to preach, "Turn from your sins and turn to God, because the Kingdom of Heaven is near.*"

THE FIRST DISCIPLES

[18]One day as Jesus was walking along the shore beside the Sea of Galilee, he saw two brothers—Simon, also called Peter, and Andrew—fishing with a net, for they were commercial fishermen. [19]Jesus called out to them, "Come, be my disciples, and I will show you how to fish for people!" [20]And they left their nets at once and went with him.

[21]A little farther up the shore he saw two other brothers, James and John, sitting in a boat with their father, Zebedee, mending their nets. And he called them to come, too. [22]They immediately followed him, leaving the boat and their father behind.

THE MINISTRY OF JESUS IN GALILEE

[23]Jesus traveled throughout Galilee teaching in the synagogues, preaching everywhere the

---

3:15 Or *we must fulfill all righteousness.*   4:3 Greek *the tempter.*   4:4 Deut 8:3.   4:6 Ps 91:11-12.   4:7 Deut 6:16.   4:10 Deut 6:13.
4:15-16 Isa 9:1-2.   4:17 Or *has come,* or *is coming soon.*

My Daily Worship

— *September 1* —

Turn, Turn, Turn

MATTHEW 3:1–4:25

From then on, Jesus began to preach, "Turn from your sins and turn to God,
because the Kingdom of Heaven is near" (4:17).

[i reflect]

In the 60s, The Byrds released a song called "Turn, Turn, Turn." Although they were a secular rock group, this particular single that hit the Top 40 charts was straight out of Scripture. With alacrity and a singable tune, they taught a generation of flower children the words Solomon recorded in Ecclesiastes 3. The essence of the lyrics is quite straightforward. Every season of life with its distinct (and varied) occasions demands a unique response. Wise is the person who turns and faces the music (whether it be a jig or a dirge).

Jesus invites us to the kind of turning that is not seasonal. It is a turning that we must make throughout our lives. Because the broad stroke of sin paints us into a corner when we feel like rejoicing as well as when we feel like crying, we would do well to seek the Lord on a daily basis. It is always appropriate to turn from our self-centered ways and turn toward him.

Clement, an early church father, put it this way: "We must repent of our fleshly, evil deeds while we have the chance to repent with our whole heart, so that the Lord can save us." That's straightforward advice. Our experience probably would prove the wisdom of his words. When we fail to keep short accounts with the Lord, it takes its toll. Seasons of joy and content become fewer and farther between. Worship becomes more difficult and less meaningful.

As Clement wrote, as long as we are on this earth, we need to practice repentance. Daily. Hourly. By the minute if necessary. Keeping a short account with God today while we have the opportunity ensures that we will continue to experience peace, joy, contentment, and meaningful worship.

Today is your chance to turn, confess your sins, and accept the Lord's forgiveness.

[i pray]

I'm sorry, Father, for stringing you along. I've needed to turn away from
my sins long before now. I want to keep short accounts with you, Lord,
and taste the sweetness of your forgiveness on a daily basis.

[i respond]

Keep an account of your sins for a day or two as a way to practice repentance. As you turn from each one you list by confessing it and accepting God's forgiveness, cross it off your list. Keep short accounts with God!

Good News about the Kingdom. And he healed people who had every kind of sickness and disease. ²⁴News about him spread far beyond the borders of Galilee so that the sick were soon coming to be healed from as far away as Syria. And whatever their illness and pain, or if they were possessed by demons, or were epileptics, or were paralyzed—he healed them all. ²⁵Large crowds followed him wherever he went—people from Galilee, the Ten Towns,* Jerusalem, from all over Judea, and from east of the Jordan River.

THE SERMON ON THE MOUNT

5 One day as the crowds were gathering, Jesus went up the mountainside with his disciples and sat down to teach them.

THE BEATITUDES

²This is what he taught them:

³ "God blesses those who realize their need
    for him,*
    for the Kingdom of Heaven is given to
    them.
⁴ God blesses those who mourn,
    for they will be comforted.
⁵ God blesses those who are gentle and
    lowly,
    for the whole earth will belong to them.
⁶ God blesses those who are hungry and
    thirsty for justice,
    for they will receive it in full.
⁷ God blesses those who are merciful,
    for they will be shown mercy.
⁸ God blesses those whose hearts are pure,
    for they will see God.
⁹ God blesses those who work for peace,
    for they will be called the children of God.
¹⁰ God blesses those who are persecuted
    because they live for God,
    for the Kingdom of Heaven is theirs.

¹¹"God blesses you when you are mocked and persecuted and lied about because you are my followers. ¹²Be happy about it! Be very glad! For a great reward awaits you in heaven. And remember, the ancient prophets were persecuted, too.

TEACHING ABOUT SALT AND LIGHT

¹³"You are the salt of the earth. But what good is salt if it has lost its flavor? Can you make it useful again? It will be thrown out and trampled underfoot as worthless. ¹⁴You are the light of the world—like a city on a mountain, glowing in the night for all to see. ¹⁵Don't hide your light under a basket! Instead, put it on a stand and let it shine for all. ¹⁶In the same way, let your good deeds shine out for all to see, so that everyone will praise your heavenly Father.

TEACHING ABOUT THE LAW

¹⁷"Don't misunderstand why I have come. I did not come to abolish the law of Moses or the writings of the prophets. No, I came to fulfill them. ¹⁸I assure you, until heaven and earth disappear, even the smallest detail of God's law will remain until its purpose is achieved. ¹⁹So if you break the smallest commandment and teach others to do the same, you will be the least in the Kingdom of Heaven. But anyone who obeys God's laws and teaches them will be great in the Kingdom of Heaven.

²⁰"But I warn you—unless you obey God better than the teachers of religious law and the Pharisees do, you can't enter the Kingdom of Heaven at all!

TEACHING ABOUT ANGER

²¹"You have heard that the law of Moses says, 'Do not murder. If you commit murder, you are subject to judgment.'* ²²But I say, if you are angry with someone,* you are subject to judgment! If you call someone an idiot,* you are in danger of being brought before the high council. And if you curse someone,* you are in danger of the fires of hell.

4:25 Greek *Decapolis*. 5:3 Greek *the poor in spirit*. 5:21 Exod 20:13; Deut 5:17. 5:22a Greek *your brother*; also in 5:23. Some manuscripts add *without cause*. 5:22b Greek uses an Aramaic term of contempt: *If you say to your brother, 'Raca.'* 5:22c Greek *if you say, 'You fool.'*

My Daily Worship

— *September 2* —

THIS LITTLE LIGHT OF YOURS

MATTHEW 5:1–48

In the same way, let your good deeds shine out for all to see,
so that everyone will praise your heavenly Father (5:16).

[i reflect]

Before the summer Olympic Games or the winter Olympic Games, the routine is the same. A torch is lit from an eternal flame atop Mount Olympus in Greece. It is then transported to the country where the Games will be hosted. As excitement for the Olympics builds during the months prior to the opening ceremonies, ordinary citizens are given the privilege of carrying the torch for several hundred yards. Little by little, mile by mile, the Olympic flame makes its way toward the stadium in the city where the Games will be held. Local newspapers may herald the identity of individuals who run in the torch relay, but the significance is in the flame, calling attention to the events that it symbolizes.

Similarly, Christlike behavior and actions "shine out for all to see." They are not intended to draw attention to us, but to point to the goodness of God. Just as the Olympic torch reminds those who see it of the events soon to follow, so our good works remind others of the source of all goodness. Yet how easy it is for our passion for service to be doused. Worries over finances, stressing out over teenage kids, spending too much time with our personal hobbies—all can dim our flame. Fortunately, hearing the words of Jesus kindles a renewed desire to let our lights shine.

Do something today that will allow your good deeds to shine on your heavenly Father. Pick up the trash along a local roadway. Sweep a neighbor's sidewalk without telling him or her. If anyone asks, say you are doing it because you love Jesus!

[i pray]

Lord, I can be so self-centered sometimes. I love the limelight and the praise
of others. Forgive me for seeking affirmation when I do your work.
Help me instead to allow my service to draw attention to you.

[i respond]

Take ten minutes of quiet. Get a pad of paper and a pen. Allow God to bring to mind someone or something in your sphere of influence who could benefit from your help. Commit to helping "so that everyone will praise your heavenly Father."

²³"So if you are standing before the altar in the Temple, offering a sacrifice to God, and you suddenly remember that someone has something against you, ²⁴leave your sacrifice there beside the altar. Go and be reconciled to that person. Then come and offer your sacrifice to God. ²⁵Come to terms quickly with your enemy before it is too late and you are dragged into court, handed over to an officer, and thrown in jail. ²⁶I assure you that you won't be free again until you have paid the last penny.

Teaching about Adultery

²⁷"You have heard that the law of Moses says, 'Do not commit adultery.'* ²⁸But I say, anyone who even looks at a woman with lust in his eye has already committed adultery with her in his heart. ²⁹So if your eye—even if it is your good eye*—causes you to lust, gouge it out and throw it away. It is better for you to lose one part of your body than for your whole body to be thrown into hell. ³⁰And if your hand—even if it is your stronger hand*—causes you to sin, cut it off and throw it away. It is better for you to lose one part of your body than for your whole body to be thrown into hell.

Teaching about Divorce

³¹"You have heard that the law of Moses says, 'A man can divorce his wife by merely giving her a letter of divorce.'* ³²But I say that a man who divorces his wife, unless she has been unfaithful, causes her to commit adultery. And anyone who marries a divorced woman commits adultery.

Teaching about Vows

³³"Again, you have heard that the law of Moses says, 'Do not break your vows; you must carry out the vows you have made to the Lord.'* ³⁴But I say, don't make any vows! If you say, 'By heaven!' it is a sacred vow because heaven is God's throne. ³⁵And if you say, 'By the earth!'

it is a sacred vow because the earth is his footstool. And don't swear, 'By Jerusalem!' for Jerusalem is the city of the great King. ³⁶Don't even swear, 'By my head!' for you can't turn one hair white or black. ³⁷Just say a simple, 'Yes, I will,' or 'No, I won't.' Your word is enough. To strengthen your promise with a vow shows that something is wrong.*

Teaching about Revenge

³⁸"You have heard that the law of Moses says, 'If an eye is injured, injure the eye of the person who did it. If a tooth gets knocked out, knock out the tooth of the person who did it.'* ³⁹But I say, don't resist an evil person! If you are slapped on the right cheek, turn the other, too. ⁴⁰If you are ordered to court and your shirt is taken from you, give your coat, too. ⁴¹If a soldier demands that you carry his gear for a mile,* carry it two miles. ⁴²Give to those who ask, and don't turn away from those who want to borrow.

Teaching about Love for Enemies

⁴³"You have heard that the law of Moses says, 'Love your neighbor'* and hate your enemy. ⁴⁴But I say, love your enemies!* Pray for those who persecute you! ⁴⁵In that way, you will be acting as true children of your Father in heaven. For he gives his sunlight to both the evil and the good, and he sends rain on the just and on the unjust, too. ⁴⁶If you love only those who love you, what good is that? Even corrupt tax collectors do that much. ⁴⁷If you are kind only to your friends,* how are you different from anyone else? Even pagans do that. ⁴⁸But you are to be perfect, even as your Father in heaven is perfect.

Teaching about Giving to the Needy

6 "Take care! Don't do your good deeds publicly, to be admired, because then you

---

5:27 Exod 20:14; Deut 5:18. 5:29 Greek *your right eye.* 5:30 Greek *your right hand.* 5:31 Deut 24:1. 5:33 Num 30:2. 5:37 Or *Anything beyond this is from the evil one.* 5:38 Greek *'An eye for an eye and a tooth for a tooth.'* Exod 21:24; Lev 24:20; Deut 19:21. 5:41 Greek *milion* [4,854 feet or 1,478 meters]. 5:43 Lev 19:18. 5:44 Some manuscripts add *Bless those who curse you, do good to those who hate you.* 5:47 Greek *your brothers.*

My Daily Worship

— *September 3* —

TRY A CANDID CONVERSATION

MATTHEW 6:1–34

When you pray, don't babble on and on as people of other religions do.
They think their prayers are answered only by repeating
their words again and again (6:7).

[i reflect]

The hit Broadway musical *Fiddler on the Roof* offers its audience not only some first-class enter-tainment, but also a wonderful refresher course on intimate, candid prayer. The main character in the play is Tevye, a poor dairy farmer, who models candor and honesty in talking to God. He brings up small things—such as his poor son-in-law's need for a sewing machine. He talks to God about big things—like world peace.

Can't you hear Tevye as he gestures with animated passion and looks up to the sky as he speaks? Although many prayers punctuate the musical, one in particular illustrates Tevye's approach. He says, "Motel and Tzeitel have been married for some time now. They work very hard and they are as poor as squirrels in winter. But they are so happy they don't know how miserable they are. Motel keeps talking about a sewing machine. I know. You are very busy now. Wars. Revolutions. Floods and plagues. All these little things that bring people back to you. But couldn't you take a second and get him a sewing machine?" Then, before Tevye is finished, he lets the Lord know that he really needs a new horse.

As we hear this conversational approach to prayer, we can't help but think that this is what Jesus had in mind. In this passage, he makes a case for communication with the Father that is honest and spontaneous, not rote and ritualistic.

How would Jesus evaluate your prayers? Do they tend to follow a formula? Because of the fast pace at which life is lived, that's an easy pattern to fall into. Today, refresh your prayer life! Like Tevye, tell God even all the small matters that are weighing on your heart. Talk to God as if he is sitting right there beside you.

[i pray]

Dear God, I have to admit that the reason I don't talk to you as much as I should
is because prayer has become impersonal to me. I let words get in the way.
Please help me. I want to share with you what's on my heart.

[i respond]

When is the last time you wrote a letter to God? Try it. Be totally honest. Maybe you'd feel more comfortable writing him an e-mail on the computer. Tell God everything that is on your heart. He has promised to listen and to help.

will lose the reward from your Father in heaven. [2]When you give a gift to someone in need, don't shout about it as the hypocrites do—blowing trumpets in the synagogues and streets to call attention to their acts of charity! I assure you, they have received all the reward they will ever get. [3]But when you give to someone, don't tell your left hand what your right hand is doing. [4]Give your gifts in secret, and your Father, who knows all secrets, will reward you.

TEACHING ABOUT PRAYER AND FASTING

[5]"And now about prayer. When you pray, don't be like the hypocrites who love to pray publicly on street corners and in the synagogues where everyone can see them. I assure you, that is all the reward they will ever get. [6]But when you pray, go away by yourself, shut the door behind you, and pray to your Father secretly. Then your Father, who knows all secrets, will reward you.

[7]"When you pray, don't babble on and on as people of other religions do. They think their prayers are answered only by repeating their words again and again. [8]Don't be like them, because your Father knows exactly what you need even before you ask him! [9]Pray like this:

Our Father in heaven,
　may your name be honored.
[10] May your Kingdom come soon.
May your will be done here on earth,
　just as it is in heaven.
[11] Give us our food for today,*
[12] and forgive us our sins,
　just as we have forgiven those who have
　　sinned against us.
[13] And don't let us yield to temptation,
　but deliver us from the evil one.*

[14]"If you forgive those who sin against you, your heavenly Father will forgive you. [15]But if you refuse to forgive others, your Father will not forgive your sins.

[16]"And when you fast, don't make it obvious, as the hypocrites do, who try to look pale and disheveled so people will admire them for their fasting. I assure you, that is the only reward they will ever get. [17]But when you fast, comb your hair and wash your face. [18]Then no one will suspect you are fasting, except your Father, who knows what you do in secret. And your Father, who knows all secrets, will reward you.

TEACHING ABOUT MONEY AND POSSESSIONS

[19]"Don't store up treasures here on earth, where they can be eaten by moths and get rusty, and where thieves break in and steal. [20]Store your treasures in heaven, where they will never become moth-eaten or rusty and where they will be safe from thieves. [21]Wherever your treasure is, there your heart and thoughts will also be.

[22]"Your eye is a lamp for your body. A pure eye lets sunshine into your soul. [23]But an evil eye shuts out the light and plunges you into darkness. If the light you think you have is really darkness, how deep that darkness will be!

[24]"No one can serve two masters. For you will hate one and love the other, or be devoted to one and despise the other. You cannot serve both God and money.

[25]"So I tell you, don't worry about everyday life—whether you have enough food, drink, and clothes. Doesn't life consist of more than food and clothing? [26]Look at the birds. They don't need to plant or harvest or put food in barns because your heavenly Father feeds them. And you are far more valuable to him than they are. [27]Can all your worries add a single moment to your life? Of course not.

[28]"And why worry about your clothes? Look at the lilies and how they grow. They don't work or make their clothing, [29]yet Solomon in all his glory was not dressed as beautifully as they are. [30]And if God cares so wonderfully for flowers that are here today and gone tomor-

---

6:11 Or for tomorrow.   6:13 Or from evil. Some manuscripts add For yours is the kingdom and the power and the glory forever. Amen.

row, won't he more surely care for you? You have so little faith!

[31] "So don't worry about having enough food or drink or clothing. [32] Why be like the pagans who are so deeply concerned about these things? Your heavenly Father already knows all your needs, [33] and he will give you all you need from day to day if you live for him and make the Kingdom of God your primary concern.

[34] "So don't worry about tomorrow, for tomorrow will bring its own worries. Today's trouble is enough for today.

Don't Condemn Others

7 "Stop judging others, and you will not be judged. [2] For others will treat you as you treat them.* Whatever measure you use in judging others, it will be used to measure how you are judged. [3] And why worry about a speck in your friend's eye* when you have a log in your own? [4] How can you think of saying, 'Let me help you get rid of that speck in your eye,' when you can't see past the log in your own eye? [5] Hypocrite! First get rid of the log from your own eye; then perhaps you will see well enough to deal with the speck in your friend's eye.

[6] "Don't give what is holy to unholy people.* Don't give pearls to swine! They will trample the pearls, then turn and attack you.

Effective Prayer

[7] "Keep on asking, and you will be given what you ask for. Keep on looking, and you will find. Keep on knocking, and the door will be opened. [8] For everyone who asks, receives. Everyone who seeks, finds. And the door is opened to everyone who knocks. [9] You parents—if your children ask for a loaf of bread, do you give them a stone instead? [10] Or if they ask for a fish, do you give them a snake? Of course not! [11] If you sinful people know how to give good gifts to your children, how much more will your heavenly Father give good gifts to those who ask him.

The Golden Rule

[12] "Do for others what you would like them to do for you. This is a summary of all that is taught in the law and the prophets.

The Narrow Gate

[13] "You can enter God's Kingdom only through the narrow gate. The highway to hell* is broad, and its gate is wide for the many who choose the easy way. [14] But the gateway to life is small, and the road is narrow, and only a few ever find it.

The Tree and Its Fruit

[15] "Beware of false prophets who come disguised as harmless sheep, but are really wolves that will tear you apart. [16] You can detect them by the way they act, just as you can identify a tree by its fruit. You don't pick grapes from thornbushes, or figs from thistles. [17] A healthy tree produces good fruit, and an unhealthy tree produces bad fruit. [18] A good tree can't produce bad fruit, and a bad tree can't produce good fruit. [19] So every tree that does not produce good fruit is chopped down and thrown into the fire. [20] Yes, the way to identify a tree or a person is by the kind of fruit that is produced.

True Disciples

[21] "Not all people who sound religious are really godly. They may refer to me as 'Lord,' but they still won't enter the Kingdom of Heaven. The decisive issue is whether they obey my Father in heaven. [22] On judgment day many will tell me, 'Lord, Lord, we prophesied in your name and cast out demons in your name and performed many miracles in your name.' [23] But I will reply, 'I never knew you. Go away; the things you did were unauthorized.*'

Building on a Solid Foundation

[24] "Anyone who listens to my teaching and obeys me is wise, like a person who builds a

---

7:2 Or For God will treat you as you treat others; Greek reads For with the judgment you judge you will be judged. 7:3 Greek your brother's eye; also in 7:5. 7:6 Greek Don't give the sacred to dogs. 7:13 Greek The way that leads to destruction. 7:23 Or unlawful.

house on solid rock. ²⁵Though the rain comes in torrents and the floodwaters rise and the winds beat against that house, it won't collapse, because it is built on rock. ²⁶But anyone who hears my teaching and ignores it is foolish, like a person who builds a house on sand. ²⁷When the rains and floods come and the winds beat against that house, it will fall with a mighty crash."

²⁸After Jesus finished speaking, the crowds were amazed at his teaching, ²⁹for he taught as one who had real authority—quite unlike the teachers of religious law.

JESUS HEALS A MAN WITH LEPROSY

8 Large crowds followed Jesus as he came down the mountainside. ²Suddenly, a man with leprosy approached Jesus. He knelt before him, worshiping. "Lord," the man said, "if you want to, you can make me well again."

³Jesus touched him. "I want to," he said. "Be healed!" And instantly the leprosy disappeared. ⁴Then Jesus said to him, "Go right over to the priest and let him examine you. Don't talk to anyone along the way. Take along the offering required in the law of Moses for those who have been healed of leprosy, so everyone will have proof of your healing."

FAITH OF THE ROMAN OFFICER

⁵When Jesus arrived in Capernaum, a Roman officer came and pleaded with him, ⁶"Lord, my young servant lies in bed, paralyzed and racked with pain."

⁷Jesus said, "I will come and heal him."

⁸Then the officer said, "Lord, I am not worthy to have you come into my home. Just say the word from where you are, and my servant will be healed! ⁹I know, because I am under the authority of my superior officers and I have authority over my soldiers. I only need to say, 'Go,' and they go, or 'Come,' and they come. And if I say to my slaves, 'Do this or that,' they do it."

¹⁰When Jesus heard this, he was amazed. Turning to the crowd, he said, "I tell you the truth, I haven't seen faith like this in all the land of Israel! ¹¹And I tell you this, that many Gentiles will come from all over the world and sit down with Abraham, Isaac, and Jacob at the feast in the Kingdom of Heaven. ¹²But many Israelites—those for whom the Kingdom was prepared—will be cast into outer darkness, where there will be weeping and gnashing of teeth."

¹³Then Jesus said to the Roman officer, "Go on home. What you have believed has happened." And the young servant was healed that same hour.

JESUS HEALS MANY PEOPLE

¹⁴When Jesus arrived at Peter's house, Peter's mother-in-law was in bed with a high fever. ¹⁵But when Jesus touched her hand, the fever left her. Then she got up and prepared a meal for him.

¹⁶That evening many demon-possessed people were brought to Jesus. All the spirits fled when he commanded them to leave; and he healed all the sick. ¹⁷This fulfilled the word of the Lord through Isaiah, who said, "He took our sicknesses and removed our diseases."*

THE COST OF FOLLOWING JESUS

¹⁸When Jesus noticed how large the crowd was growing, he instructed his disciples to cross to the other side of the lake.

¹⁹Then one of the teachers of religious law said to him, "Teacher, I will follow you no matter where you go!"

²⁰But Jesus said, "Foxes have dens to live in, and birds have nests, but I, the Son of Man, have no home of my own, not even a place to lay my head."

²¹Another of his disciples said, "Lord, first let me return home and bury my father."

²²But Jesus told him, "Follow me now! Let those who are spiritually dead care for their own dead."*

8:17 Isa 53:4. **8:22** Greek *Let the dead bury their own dead.*

My Daily Worship

IT'S A BEAUTIFUL LIFE

MATTHEW 7:1–8:34

If you sinful people know how to give good gifts to your children,
how much more will your heavenly Father give
good gifts to those who ask him (7:11).

[i reflect]

While lecturing at Colorado College in 1893, Katherine Lee Bates hiked Pike's Peak where she was overwhelmed by the beauty of God's creation. From her viewpoint at the 14,110-foot summit, the thirty-four-year-old Wellesley professor gazed at the breathtaking panorama. Picking up her pen, she scratched out the lyrics to a song that celebrates the beauty of our country's natural resources.

"America the Beautiful" continues to be treasured as a portrait of God's blessings to those who claim the United States as their homeland. Although not specifically referring to this passage in Matthew, Katherine Bates' lyrics affirm it. As the song goes, God sheds his grace—his good gifts— on us, wherever we may call home. The wonder of creation displayed on every continent is unmistakable. So, too, are the gifts we often take for granted—health, food, shelter, clothing, employment, family, friends.

The gifts the heavenly Father wraps up and delivers are chosen with us in mind. They represent a personal knowledge of those who receive them. It is the kind of gift giving characterized by mothers and fathers who know exactly what their children need—and desire. It is the kind of gift giving that celebrates the uniqueness of the recipient.

Such beautiful gifts from a good God call for a response. Find a pen and a sheet of paper and begin to list what you're grateful for. Identify the gifts that God has given to you which celebrate the uniqueness of who you are.

Read it aloud to the Lord. Maybe, like Katherine Bates, you will feel inspired to write a poem about the beauty of God's blessings to you. Go for it!

[i pray]

Wonderful Father, thank you for how you have lavished me with good gifts—my family,
my friends, my livelihood. All have been tailor-made for me, specifically
chosen so that I would know the Giver and turn in worship to you.

[i respond]

Walk from room to room in your home. Go for a walk through your neighborhood. Take a visual inventory of your workplace. Look for the many gifts that God has given to you that are represented in these places. Pause to give him thanks for each one.

JESUS CALMS THE STORM

[23]Then Jesus got into the boat and started across the lake with his disciples. [24]Suddenly, a terrible storm came up, with waves breaking into the boat. But Jesus was sleeping. [25]The disciples went to him and woke him up, shouting, "Lord, save us! We're going to drown!"

[26]And Jesus answered, "Why are you afraid? You have so little faith!" Then he stood up and rebuked the wind and waves, and suddenly all was calm. [27]The disciples just sat there in awe. "Who is this?" they asked themselves. "Even the wind and waves obey him!"

> *This is true mature love—*
> *when all other affections have*
> *been completely abandoned for the*
> *love of the Son of God and the*
> *delight of doing His will.*
>
> BOB SORGE

JESUS HEALS TWO DEMON-POSSESSED MEN

[28]When Jesus arrived on the other side of the lake in the land of the Gadarenes,* two men who were possessed by demons met him. They lived in a cemetery and were so dangerous that no one could go through that area. [29]They began screaming at him, "Why are you bothering us, Son of God? You have no right to torture us before God's appointed time!" [30]A large herd of pigs was feeding in the distance, [31]so the demons begged, "If you cast us out, send us into that herd of pigs."

[32]"All right, go!" Jesus commanded them. So the demons came out of the men and entered the pigs, and the whole herd plunged down the steep hillside into the lake and drowned in the water. [33]The herdsmen fled to the nearby city, telling everyone what happened to the demon-possessed men. [34]The entire town came out to meet Jesus, but they begged him to go away and leave them alone.

JESUS HEALS A PARALYZED MAN

9 Jesus climbed into a boat and went back across the lake to his own town. [2]Some people brought to him a paralyzed man on a mat. Seeing their faith, Jesus said to the paralyzed man, "Take heart, son! Your sins are forgiven."

[3]"Blasphemy! This man talks like he is God!" some of the teachers of religious law said among themselves.

[4]Jesus knew what they were thinking, so he asked them, "Why are you thinking such evil thoughts? [5]Is it easier to say, 'Your sins are forgiven' or 'Get up and walk'? [6]I will prove that I, the Son of Man, have the authority on earth to forgive sins." Then Jesus turned to the paralyzed man and said, "Stand up, take your mat, and go on home, because you are healed!"

[7]And the man jumped up and went home! [8]Fear swept through the crowd as they saw this happen right before their eyes. They praised God for sending a man with such great authority.

JESUS CALLS MATTHEW

[9]As Jesus was going down the road, he saw Matthew sitting at his tax-collection booth. "Come, be my disciple," Jesus said to him. So Matthew got up and followed him.

[10]That night Matthew invited Jesus and his disciples to be his dinner guests, along with his fellow tax collectors and many other notorious sinners. [11]The Pharisees were indignant. "Why does your teacher eat with such scum*?" they asked his disciples.

[12]When he heard this, Jesus replied, "Healthy people don't need a doctor—sick people do." [13]Then he added, "Now go and learn the meaning of this Scripture: 'I want

---

8:28 Some manuscripts read *Gerasenes;* other manuscripts read *Gergesenes.* See Mark 5:1; Luke 8:26. 9:11 Greek *with tax collectors and sinners.*

you to be merciful; I don't want your sacrifices."* For I have come to call sinners, not those who think they are already good enough."

A DISCUSSION ABOUT FASTING

¹⁴One day the disciples of John the Baptist came to Jesus and asked him, "Why do we and the Pharisees fast, but your disciples don't fast?"

¹⁵Jesus responded, "Should the wedding guests mourn while celebrating with the groom? Someday he will be taken from them, and then they will fast. ¹⁶And who would patch an old garment with unshrunk cloth? For the patch shrinks and pulls away from the old cloth, leaving an even bigger hole than before. ¹⁷And no one puts new wine into old wineskins. The old skins would burst from the pressure, spilling the wine and ruining the skins. New wine must be stored in new wineskins. That way both the wine and the wineskins are preserved."

JESUS HEALS IN RESPONSE TO FAITH

¹⁸As Jesus was saying this, the leader of a synagogue came and knelt down before him. "My daughter has just died," he said, "but you can bring her back to life again if you just come and lay your hand upon her."

¹⁹As Jesus and the disciples were going to the official's home, ²⁰a woman who had had a hemorrhage for twelve years came up behind him. She touched the fringe of his robe, ²¹for she thought, "If I can just touch his robe, I will be healed."

²²Jesus turned around and said to her, "Daughter, be encouraged! Your faith has made you well." And the woman was healed at that moment.

²³When Jesus arrived at the official's home, he noticed the noisy crowds and heard the funeral music. ²⁴He said, "Go away, for the girl isn't dead; she's only asleep." But the crowd laughed at him. ²⁵When the crowd was finally outside, Jesus went in and took the girl by the hand, and she stood up! ²⁶The report of this miracle swept through the entire countryside.

JESUS HEALS THE BLIND AND MUTE

²⁷After Jesus left the girl's home, two blind men followed along behind him, shouting, "Son of David, have mercy on us!"

²⁸They went right into the house where he was staying, and Jesus asked them, "Do you believe I can make you see?"

"Yes, Lord," they told him, "we do."

²⁹Then he touched their eyes and said, "Because of your faith, it will happen." ³⁰And suddenly they could see! Jesus sternly warned them, "Don't tell anyone about this." ³¹But instead, they spread his fame all over the region.

³²When they left, some people brought to him a man who couldn't speak because he was possessed by a demon. ³³So Jesus cast out the demon, and instantly the man could talk. The crowds marveled. "Nothing like this has ever happened in Israel!" they exclaimed.

³⁴But the Pharisees said, "He can cast out demons because he is empowered by the prince of demons."

THE NEED FOR WORKERS

³⁵Jesus traveled through all the cities and villages of that area, teaching in the synagogues and announcing the Good News about the Kingdom. And wherever he went, he healed people of every sort of disease and illness. ³⁶He felt great pity for the crowds that came, because their problems were so great and they didn't know where to go for help. They were like sheep without a shepherd. ³⁷He said to his disciples, "The harvest is so great, but the workers are so few. ³⁸So pray to the Lord who is in charge of the harvest; ask him to send out more workers for his fields."

9:13 Hos 6:6.

JESUS SENDS OUT THE TWELVE APOSTLES

10 Jesus called his twelve disciples to him and gave them authority to cast out evil spirits and to heal every kind of disease and illness. ²Here are the names of the twelve apostles:

first Simon (also called Peter),
then Andrew (Peter's brother),
James (son of Zebedee),
John (James's brother),
³ Philip,
Bartholomew,
Thomas,
Matthew (the tax collector),
James (son of Alphaeus),
Thaddaeus,
⁴ Simon (the Zealot*),
Judas Iscariot (who later betrayed him).

⁵Jesus sent the twelve disciples out with these instructions: "Don't go to the Gentiles or the Samaritans, ⁶but only to the people of Israel—God's lost sheep. ⁷Go and announce to them that the Kingdom of Heaven is near.* ⁸Heal the sick, raise the dead, cure those with leprosy, and cast out demons. Give as freely as you have received!

⁹"Don't take any money with you. ¹⁰Don't carry a traveler's bag with an extra coat and sandals or even a walking stick. Don't hesitate to accept hospitality, because those who work deserve to be fed.* ¹¹Whenever you enter a city or village, search for a worthy man and stay in his home until you leave for the next town. ¹²When you are invited into someone's home, give it your blessing. ¹³If it turns out to be a worthy home, let your blessing stand; if it is not, take back the blessing. ¹⁴If a village doesn't welcome you or listen to you, shake off the dust of that place from your feet as you leave. ¹⁵I assure you, the wicked cities of Sodom and Gomorrah will be better off on the judgment day than that place will be.

¹⁶"Look, I am sending you out as sheep among wolves. Be as wary as snakes and harmless as doves. ¹⁷But beware! For you will be handed over to the courts and beaten in the synagogues. ¹⁸And you must stand trial before governors and kings because you are my followers. This will be your opportunity to tell them about me—yes, to witness to the world. ¹⁹When you are arrested, don't worry about what to say in your defense, because you will be given the right words at the right time. ²⁰For it won't be you doing the talking—it will be the Spirit of your Father speaking through you.

²¹"Brother will betray brother to death, fathers will betray their own children, and children will rise against their parents and cause them to be killed. ²²And everyone will hate you because of your allegiance to me. But those who endure to the end will be saved. ²³When you are persecuted in one town, flee to the next. I assure you that I, the Son of Man, will return before you have reached all the towns of Israel.

²⁴"A student is not greater than the teacher. A servant is not greater than the master. ²⁵The student shares the teacher's fate. The servant shares the master's fate. And since I, the master of the household, have been called the prince of demons,* how much more will it happen to you, the members of the household! ²⁶But don't be afraid of those who threaten you. For the time is coming when everything will be revealed; all that is secret will be made public. ²⁷What I tell you now in the darkness, shout abroad when daybreak comes. What I whisper in your ears, shout from the housetops for all to hear!

²⁸"Don't be afraid of those who want to kill you. They can only kill your body; they cannot touch your soul. Fear only God, who can destroy both soul and body in hell. ²⁹Not even a sparrow, worth only half a penny, can fall to the ground without your Father knowing it. ³⁰And the very hairs on your head are all numbered. ³¹So don't be afraid; you are more valuable to him than a whole flock of sparrows.

10:4 Greek *the Cananean.*   **10:7** Or *has come,* or *is coming soon.*   **10:10** Or *the worker is worthy of support.*   **10:25** Greek *Beelzeboul.*

My Daily Worship

— *September 5* —

A BIRD'S EYE VIEW

MATTHEW 9:1–10:42

Not even a sparrow, worth only half a penny, can fall to the ground without your Father knowing it. And the very hairs on your head are all numbered. So don't be afraid; you are more valuable to him than a whole flock of sparrows (10:29–31).

[i reflect]

Photos of earth taken from the space shuttle are incredible. These images photographed from hundreds of miles away have amazing clarity. Even more remarkable is how these images can be magnified and yet hold their crisp quality. The rooftops of high rises in a city's financial district are distinctly evident with this high-technology imaging. Zoom in more and you can even see the sidewalk in front of any given building.

In a sense, this technology helps us understand how it is possible for God to have the kind of omniscient knowledge Jesus attributes to him. If a camera mounted to an orbiting capsule can magnify activity on our planet with computer-governed precision, surely the Creator of the universe can focus on the most minute details of his creation. Nothing escapes his glance.

As a result, we have no reason to question our circumstances. As Ethel Waters, the great African-American singer, used to belt out, "Why should I be discouraged? His eye is on the sparrow and I know he watches me." God sees all and knows all.

As you struggle with issues at work or in your marriage that no one has a clue about, isn't it good to know that your Father in heaven is fully aware? Jesus is not exaggerating when he says that every hair on our heads is counted and known by the Father. Our lives are never out of view. Now that should give us great comfort. It is also a reality that motivates our praise. In fact, it frees us to praise God no matter where we are. Today as you are stuck in commuter traffic, struggling with a difficult situation, or merely mowing your lawn or shoveling snow, praise the One who is always watching!

[i pray]

Heavenly Father, so much of the worry and anxiety in my life would disappear if I'd simply cling to the fact that I am never off your radar screen. Forgive me for forgetting that truth. May your constant concern also motivate my obedience. I don't want to disappoint you, Lord.

[i respond]

Take time to look out the window. When you spot a small bird in a tree or on a telephone wire, remind yourself of the truth of these verses. In fact, every time you see a bird, try speaking to the Lord aloud, "Thanks for keeping your eye on me."

³²"If anyone acknowledges me publicly here on earth, I will openly acknowledge that person before my Father in heaven. ³³But if anyone denies me here on earth, I will deny that person before my Father in heaven.

³⁴"Don't imagine that I came to bring peace to the earth! No, I came to bring a sword. ³⁵I have come to set a man against his father, and a daughter against her mother, and a daughter-in-law against her mother-in-law. ³⁶Your enemies will be right in your own household! ³⁷If you love your father or mother more than you love me, you are not worthy of being mine; or if you love your son or daughter more than me, you are not worthy of being mine. ³⁸If you refuse to take up your cross and follow me, you are not worthy of being mine. ³⁹If you cling to your life, you will lose it; but if you give it up for me, you will find it.

⁴⁰"Anyone who welcomes you is welcoming me, and anyone who welcomes me is welcoming the Father who sent me. ⁴¹If you welcome a prophet as one who speaks for God,* you will receive the same reward a prophet gets. And if you welcome good and godly people because of their godliness, you will be given a reward like theirs. ⁴²And if you give even a cup of cold water to one of the least of my followers, you will surely be rewarded."

JESUS AND JOHN THE BAPTIST

11 When Jesus had finished giving these instructions to his twelve disciples, he went off teaching and preaching in towns throughout the country.

²John the Baptist, who was now in prison, heard about all the things the Messiah was doing. So he sent his disciples to ask Jesus, ³"Are you really the Messiah we've been waiting for, or should we keep looking for someone else?"

⁴Jesus told them, "Go back to John and tell him about what you have heard and seen— ⁵the blind see, the lame walk, the lepers are cured, the deaf hear, the dead are raised to life, and the Good News is being preached to the poor. ⁶And tell him: 'God blesses those who are not offended by me.*'"

⁷When John's disciples had gone, Jesus began talking about him to the crowds. "Who is this man in the wilderness that you went out to see? Did you find him weak as a reed, moved by every breath of wind? ⁸Or were you expecting to see a man dressed in expensive clothes? Those who dress like that live in palaces, not out in the wilderness. ⁹Were you looking for a prophet? Yes, and he is more than a prophet. ¹⁰John is the man to whom the Scriptures refer when they say,

'Look, I am sending my messenger before you,
and he will prepare your way before you.'*

¹¹"I assure you, of all who have ever lived, none is greater than John the Baptist. Yet even the most insignificant person in the Kingdom of Heaven is greater than he is! ¹²And from the time John the Baptist began preaching and baptizing until now, the Kingdom of Heaven has been forcefully advancing, and violent people attack it.* ¹³For before John came, all the teachings of the Scriptures looked forward to this present time. ¹⁴And if you are willing to accept what I say, he is Elijah, the one the prophets said would come.* ¹⁵Anyone who is willing to hear should listen and understand!

¹⁶"How shall I describe this generation? These people are like a group of children playing a game in the public square. They complain to their friends, ¹⁷'We played wedding songs, and you weren't happy, so we played funeral songs, but you weren't sad.' ¹⁸For John the Baptist didn't drink wine and he often fasted, and you say, 'He's demon possessed.' ¹⁹And I, the Son of Man, feast and drink, and you say, 'He's a glutton and a drunkard, and a friend of the worst sort of sinners!' But wisdom is shown to be right by what results from it."

10:41 Greek *welcome a prophet in the name of a prophet.* **11:6** Or *who don't fall away because of me.* **11:10** Mal 3:1. **11:12** Or *until now, eager multitudes have been pressing into the Kingdom of Heaven.* **11:14** See Mal 4:5.

My Daily Worship

— *September 6* —

LIBERTY'S ORIGINAL INVITATION

MATTHEW 11:1–12:50

*Then Jesus said, "Come to me, all of you who are weary and
carry heavy burdens, and I will give you rest" (11:28).*

[i reflect]

The Statue of Liberty is more than one of the most photographed landmarks in America. It symbolizes the legacy the United States has earned as a nation. Historically, we have welcomed the oppressed and homeless of many lands who have sought sanctuary within our borders. The colossal woman who stands in New York harbor symbolizes freedom. She beckons to all who pass with the inscription on her base: "Give me your tired, your poor, your huddled masses yearning to breathe free."

Nineteen centuries before the French artisan Frederic Auguste Bartholdi sculpted Lady Liberty, Jesus of Nazareth stood tall among a growing multitude of sin-weary followers and issued an even more attractive invitation to freedom. The Son of God did far more than offer would-be citizens a new form of government and the wide-open spaces of limitless opportunity. He invited them to immigrate to a spiritual realm, free from the unending exhaustion of carrying guilt. He offered them to give up the onerous pressure of running their own lives and allow him to take the wheel. Jesus held forth the torch of truth that would illuminate the path of following him.

Sound inviting? You bet it does. The stern copper lady serves as a beacon and promise of freedom, but really has no ability to deliver. Jesus, however, has made a promise and will get himself right down into your life to make sure it comes true. Can't you picture his smiling countenance? It's a loving glance that calls you to quit striving to please others or to prove yourself worthy. It calls you to complete freedom in him.

"Come to me," Jesus encourages, "and I will give you rest." Rest from the tyranny of your schedule. Rest from the anxieties and worries that burden you right now. Rest from the guilt of a sin-filled life. Enjoy this rest that comes from deep within the soul. Pause right now and in silent worship meditate on these words. Say them again to yourself. Give to Jesus whatever burdens you are bearing today. Find rest and freedom in him.

[i pray]

Lord Jesus, I've never looked at the Statue of Liberty as anything more than a patriotic symbol. But from now on it will trigger thoughts of how you stand at the threshold of my life inviting me to experience the freedom from sin that permits me to rest in your love. May your Word continue to teach me about the freedom and rest you have given me as I read it each day.

[i respond]

Find a picture of the Statue of Liberty on the Internet. Print it out and laminate it into a bookmark that you can keep in your Bible. Write at the bottom, "So if the Son sets you free, you will indeed be free" (quoted from John 8:36).

JUDGMENT FOR THE UNBELIEVERS

[20]Then Jesus began to denounce the cities where he had done most of his miracles, because they hadn't turned from their sins and turned to God. [21]"What horrors await you, Korazin and Bethsaida! For if the miracles I did in you had been done in wicked Tyre and Sidon, their people would have sat in deep repentance long ago, clothed in sackcloth and throwing ashes on their heads to show their remorse. [22]I assure you, Tyre and Sidon will be better off on the judgment day than you! [23]And you people of Capernaum, will you be exalted to heaven? No, you will be brought down to the place of the dead.* For if the miracles I did for you had been done in Sodom, it would still be here today. [24]I assure you, Sodom will be better off on the judgment day than you."

JESUS' PRAYER OF THANKSGIVING

[25]Then Jesus prayed this prayer: "O Father, Lord of heaven and earth, thank you for hiding the truth from those who think themselves so wise and clever, and for revealing it to the childlike. [26]Yes, Father, it pleased you to do it this way!

[27]"My Father has given me authority over everything. No one really knows the Son except the Father, and no one really knows the Father except the Son and those to whom the Son chooses to reveal him."

[28]Then Jesus said, "Come to me, all of you who are weary and carry heavy burdens, and I will give you rest. [29]Take my yoke upon you. Let me teach you, because I am humble and gentle, and you will find rest for your souls. [30]For my yoke fits perfectly, and the burden I give you is light."

CONTROVERSY ABOUT THE SABBATH

12 At about that time Jesus was walking through some grainfields on the Sabbath. His disciples were hungry, so they began breaking off heads of wheat and eating the grain. [2]Some Pharisees saw them do it and protested, "Your disciples shouldn't be doing that! It's against the law to work by harvesting grain on the Sabbath."

[3]But Jesus said to them, "Haven't you ever read in the Scriptures what King David did when he and his companions were hungry? [4]He went into the house of God, and they ate the special bread reserved for the priests alone. That was breaking the law, too. [5]And haven't you ever read in the law of Moses that the priests on duty in the Temple may work on the Sabbath? [6]I tell you, there is one here who is even greater than the Temple! [7]But you would not have condemned those who aren't guilty if you knew the meaning of this Scripture: 'I want you to be merciful; I don't want your sacrifices.'* [8]For I, the Son of Man, am master even of the Sabbath."

[9]Then he went over to the synagogue, [10]where he noticed a man with a deformed hand. The Pharisees asked Jesus, "Is it legal to work by healing on the Sabbath day?" (They were, of course, hoping he would say yes, so they could bring charges against him.)

[11]And he answered, "If you had one sheep, and it fell into a well on the Sabbath, wouldn't you get to work and pull it out? Of course you would. [12]And how much more valuable is a person than a sheep! Yes, it is right to do good on the Sabbath." [13]Then he said to the man, "Reach out your hand." The man reached out his hand, and it became normal, just like the other one. [14]Then the Pharisees called a meeting and discussed plans for killing Jesus.

JESUS, GOD'S CHOSEN SERVANT

[15]But Jesus knew what they were planning. He left that area, and many people followed him. He healed all the sick among them, [16]but he warned them not to say who he was. [17]This fulfilled the prophecy of Isaiah concerning him:

11:23 Greek *to Hades.* **12:7** Hos 6:6.

18 "Look at my Servant,
whom I have chosen.
He is my Beloved,
and I am very pleased with him.
I will put my Spirit upon him,
and he will proclaim justice to the
nations.
19 He will not fight or shout;
he will not raise his voice in public.
20 He will not crush those who are weak,
or quench the smallest hope,
until he brings full justice with his final
victory.
21 And his name will be the hope
of all the world."*

JESUS AND THE PRINCE OF DEMONS

22Then a demon-possessed man, who was both blind and unable to talk, was brought to Jesus. He healed the man so that he could both speak and see. 23The crowd was amazed. "Could it be that Jesus is the Son of David, the Messiah?" they wondered out loud.

24But when the Pharisees heard about the miracle, they said, "No wonder he can cast out demons. He gets his power from Satan,* the prince of demons."

25Jesus knew their thoughts and replied, "Any kingdom at war with itself is doomed. A city or home divided against itself is doomed. 26And if Satan is casting out Satan, he is fighting against himself. His own kingdom will not survive. 27And if I am empowered by the prince of demons,* what about your own followers? They cast out demons, too, so they will judge you for what you have said. 28But if I am casting out demons by the Spirit of God, then the Kingdom of God has arrived among you. 29Let me illustrate this. You can't enter a strong man's house and rob him without first tying him up. Only then can his house be robbed!* 30Anyone who isn't helping me opposes me, and anyone who isn't working with me is actually working against me.

31"Every sin or blasphemy can be forgiven—except blasphemy against the Holy Spirit, which can never be forgiven. 32Anyone who blasphemes against me, the Son of Man, can be forgiven, but blasphemy against the Holy Spirit will never be forgiven, either in this world or in the world to come.

33"A tree is identified by its fruit. Make a tree good, and its fruit will be good. Make a tree bad, and its fruit will be bad. 34You brood of snakes! How could evil men like you speak what is good and right? For whatever is in your heart determines what you say. 35A good person produces good words from a good heart, and an evil person produces evil words from an evil heart. 36And I tell you this, that you must give an account on judgment day of every idle word you speak. 37The words you say now reflect your fate then; either you will be justified by them or you will be condemned."

THE SIGN OF JONAH

38One day some teachers of religious law and Pharisees came to Jesus and said, "Teacher, we want you to show us a miraculous sign to prove that you are from God."

39But Jesus replied, "Only an evil, faithless generation would ask for a miraculous sign; but the only sign I will give them is the sign of the prophet Jonah. 40For as Jonah was in the belly of the great fish for three days and three nights, so I, the Son of Man, will be in the heart of the earth for three days and three nights. 41The people of Nineveh will rise up against this generation on judgment day and condemn it, because they repented at the preaching of Jonah. And now someone greater than Jonah is here—and you refuse to repent. 42The queen of Sheba* will also rise up against this generation on judgment day and condemn it, because she came from a distant land to hear the wisdom of Solomon. And now someone greater than Solomon is here—and you refuse to listen to him.

12:18-21 Isa 42:1-4. 12:24 Greek *Beelzeboul.* 12:27 Greek *by Beelzeboul.* 12:29 Or *One cannot rob Satan's kingdom without first tying him up. Only then can his demons be cast out.* 12:42 Greek *The queen of the south.*

43"When an evil spirit leaves a person, it goes into the desert, seeking rest but finding none. 44Then it says, 'I will return to the person I came from.' So it returns and finds its former home empty, swept, and clean. 45Then the spirit finds seven other spirits more evil than itself, and they all enter the person and live there. And so that person is worse off than before. That will be the experience of this evil generation."

THE TRUE FAMILY OF JESUS

46As Jesus was speaking to the crowd, his mother and brothers were outside, wanting to talk with him. 47Someone told Jesus, "Your mother and your brothers are outside, and they want to speak to you."

48Jesus asked, "Who is my mother? Who are my brothers?" 49Then he pointed to his disciples and said, "These are my mother and brothers. 50Anyone who does the will of my Father in heaven is my brother and sister and mother!"

STORY OF THE FARMER SCATTERING SEED

13 Later that same day, Jesus left the house and went down to the shore, 2where an immense crowd soon gathered. He got into a boat, where he sat and taught as the people listened on the shore. 3He told many stories such as this one:

"A farmer went out to plant some seed. 4As he scattered it across his field, some seeds fell on a footpath, and the birds came and ate them. 5Other seeds fell on shallow soil with underlying rock. The plants sprang up quickly, 6but they soon wilted beneath the hot sun and died because the roots had no nourishment in the shallow soil. 7Other seeds fell among thorns that shot up and choked out the tender blades. 8But some seeds fell on fertile soil and produced a crop that was thirty, sixty, and even a hundred times as much as had been planted. 9Anyone who is willing to hear should listen and understand!"

13:14-15 Isa 6:9-10.

10His disciples came and asked him, "Why do you always tell stories when you talk to the people?"

11Then he explained to them, "You have been permitted to understand the secrets of the Kingdom of Heaven, but others have not. 12To those who are open to my teaching, more understanding will be given, and they will have an abundance of knowledge. But to those who are not listening, even what they have will be taken away from them. 13That is why I tell these stories, because people see what I do, but they don't really see. They hear what I say, but they don't really hear, and they don't understand. 14This fulfills the prophecy of Isaiah, which says:

'You will hear my words,
  but you will not understand;
you will see what I do,
  but you will not perceive its meaning.
15 For the hearts of these people are
    hardened,
    and their ears cannot hear,
    and they have closed their eyes—
so their eyes cannot see,
    and their ears cannot hear,
    and their hearts cannot understand,
and they cannot turn to me
    and let me heal them.'*

16"But blessed are your eyes, because they see; and your ears, because they hear. 17I assure you, many prophets and godly people have longed to see and hear what you have seen and heard, but they could not.

18"Now here is the explanation of the story I told about the farmer sowing grain: 19The seed that fell on the hard path represents those who hear the Good News about the Kingdom and don't understand it. Then the evil one comes and snatches the seed away from their hearts. 20The rocky soil represents those who hear the message and receive it with joy. 21But like young plants in such soil, their roots don't go very deep. At first they get along fine, but

My Daily Worship

MORE THAN YOU BARGAINED FOR

MATTHEW 13:1–58

Again, the Kingdom of Heaven is like a pearl merchant on the lookout for choice pearls. When he discovered a pearl of great value, he sold everything he owned and bought it! (13:45–46).

[i reflect]

Originally it was called Seward's Icebox and Seward's Folly. Secretary of State William Seward convinced President Andrew Johnson to buy the Alaska Territory from the Russian government for $7.2 million. That reduces down to two cents per acre! Seward was aware that, in addition to the political presence the territory on the Bering Sea would represent, the wealth hidden within the vast wilderness of "the great land" was well worth the price the Czar demanded. Unfortunately, Seward didn't live long enough to fully realize the fortune in gold and oil beneath the soil of his purchase, let alone the awesome beauty of its natural resources. If he had known beforehand, he probably would have been willing to offer the Russians whatever it took to secure a land of such unprecedented abundance.

In this parable, Jesus compares the assurance of salvation to a priceless pearl. The merchant was so convinced of the pearl's value that he liquidated all of his other holdings in order to secure this one-of-a-kind discovery. Have you ever thought of what you have "in Christ" as worth giving up everything else to fully enjoy? When you put it like that, sacrificing "for the sake of Christ" becomes a plus and not a minus. Like the hidden resources of Alaska, personal salvation offers an abundance that can only be discovered after the fact, as you walk day by day with Christ.

No doubt you have experienced that for yourself. Nonetheless, at times it is easy to forget just how valuable this life is—a life of forgiveness and fulfillment that Jesus died to make possible for you.

What activities, pursuits, or priorities are preventing you from fully realizing the abundance of life in Christ? Like the pearl merchant, do whatever you need to in order to gain that which is priceless. As an act of worship, turn those over to Jesus today.

[i pray]

Jesus, forgive me when I take for granted the value of the investment I made when I exchanged my former life for a life "in you." Help me to explore the great expanse of my life that has yet to be developed by you. Let's explore the possibilities together.

[i respond]

What is the most priceless object or piece of jewelry that you own? Take some time to observe it and consider what makes it valuable. Compare and contrast your relationship with Jesus and this object.

they wilt as soon as they have problems or are persecuted because they believe the word. ²²The thorny ground represents those who hear and accept the Good News, but all too quickly the message is crowded out by the cares of this life and the lure of wealth, so no crop is produced. ²³The good soil represents the hearts of those who truly accept God's message and produce a huge harvest—thirty, sixty, or even a hundred times as much as had been planted."

STORY OF THE WHEAT AND WEEDS

²⁴Here is another story Jesus told: "The Kingdom of Heaven is like a farmer who planted good seed in his field. ²⁵But that night as everyone slept, his enemy came and planted weeds among the wheat. ²⁶When the crop began to grow and produce grain, the weeds also grew. ²⁷The farmer's servants came and told him, 'Sir, the field where you planted that good seed is full of weeds!'

²⁸"'An enemy has done it!' the farmer exclaimed.

"'Shall we pull out the weeds?' they asked.

²⁹"He replied, 'No, you'll hurt the wheat if you do. ³⁰Let both grow together until the harvest. Then I will tell the harvesters to sort out the weeds and burn them and to put the wheat in the barn.'"

ILLUSTRATION OF THE MUSTARD SEED

³¹Here is another illustration Jesus used: "The Kingdom of Heaven is like a mustard seed planted in a field. ³²It is the smallest of all seeds, but it becomes the largest of garden plants and grows into a tree where birds can come and find shelter in its branches."

ILLUSTRATION OF THE YEAST

³³Jesus also used this illustration: "The Kingdom of Heaven is like yeast used by a woman making bread. Even though she used a large amount* of flour, the yeast permeated every part of the dough."

³⁴Jesus always used stories and illustrations like these when speaking to the crowds. In fact, he never spoke to them without using such parables. ³⁵This fulfilled the prophecy that said,

"I will speak to you in parables.
 I will explain mysteries hidden since the creation of the world."*

THE WHEAT AND WEEDS EXPLAINED

³⁶Then, leaving the crowds outside, Jesus went into the house. His disciples said, "Please explain the story of the weeds in the field."

³⁷"All right," he said. "I, the Son of Man, am the farmer who plants the good seed. ³⁸The field is the world, and the good seed represents the people of the Kingdom. The weeds are the people who belong to the evil one. ³⁹The enemy who planted the weeds among the wheat is the Devil. The harvest is the end of the world, and the harvesters are the angels.

⁴⁰"Just as the weeds are separated out and burned, so it will be at the end of the world. ⁴¹I, the Son of Man, will send my angels, and they will remove from my Kingdom everything that causes sin and all who do evil, ⁴²and they will throw them into the furnace and burn them. There will be weeping and gnashing of teeth. ⁴³Then the godly will shine like the sun in their Father's Kingdom. Anyone who is willing to hear should listen and understand!

ILLUSTRATION OF THE HIDDEN TREASURE

⁴⁴"The Kingdom of Heaven is like a treasure that a man discovered hidden in a field. In his excitement, he hid it again and sold everything he owned to get enough money to buy the field—and to get the treasure, too!

13:33 Greek *3 measures.* 13:35 Ps 78:2.

ILLUSTRATION OF THE PEARL MERCHANT

45"Again, the Kingdom of Heaven is like a pearl merchant on the lookout for choice pearls. 46When he discovered a pearl of great value, he sold everything he owned and bought it!

ILLUSTRATION OF THE FISHING NET

47"Again, the Kingdom of Heaven is like a fishing net that is thrown into the water and gathers fish of every kind. 48When the net is full, they drag it up onto the shore, sit down, sort the good fish into crates, and throw the bad ones away. 49That is the way it will be at the end of the world. The angels will come and separate the wicked people from the godly, 50throwing the wicked into the fire. There will be weeping and gnashing of teeth. 51Do you understand?"

"Yes," they said, "we do."

52Then he added, "Every teacher of religious law who has become a disciple in the Kingdom of Heaven is like a person who brings out of the storehouse the new teachings as well as the old."

JESUS REJECTED AT NAZARETH

53When Jesus had finished telling these stories, he left that part of the country. 54He returned to Nazareth, his hometown. When he taught there in the synagogue, everyone was astonished and said, "Where does he get his wisdom and his miracles? 55He's just a carpenter's son, and we know Mary, his mother, and his brothers—James, Joseph, Simon, and Judas. 56All his sisters live right here among us. What makes him so great?" 57And they were deeply offended and refused to believe in him.

Then Jesus told them, "A prophet is honored everywhere except in his own hometown and among his own family." 58And so he did only a few miracles there because of their unbelief.

THE DEATH OF JOHN THE BAPTIST

14 When Herod Antipas* heard about Jesus, 2he said to his advisers, "This must be John the Baptist come back to life again! That is why he can do such miracles." 3For Herod had arrested and imprisoned John as a favor to his wife Herodias (the former wife of Herod's brother Philip). 4John kept telling Herod, "It is illegal for you to marry her." 5Herod would have executed John, but he was afraid of a riot, because all the people believed John was a prophet.

6But at a birthday party for Herod, Herodias's daughter performed a dance that greatly pleased him, 7so he promised with an oath to give her anything she wanted. 8At her mother's urging, the girl asked, "I want the head of John the Baptist on a tray!" 9The king was sorry, but because of his oath and because he didn't want to back down in front of his guests, he issued the necessary orders. 10So John was beheaded in the prison, 11and his head was brought on a tray and given to the girl, who took it to her mother. 12John's disciples came for his body and buried it. Then they told Jesus what had happened.

JESUS FEEDS FIVE THOUSAND

13As soon as Jesus heard the news, he went off by himself in a boat to a remote area to be alone. But the crowds heard where he was headed and followed by land from many villages. 14A vast crowd was there as he stepped from the boat, and he had compassion on them and healed their sick.

15That evening the disciples came to him and said, "This is a desolate place, and it is getting late. Send the crowds away so they can go to the villages and buy food for themselves."

16But Jesus replied, "That isn't necessary—you feed them."

17"Impossible!" they exclaimed. "We have only five loaves of bread and two fish!"

18"Bring them here," he said. 19Then he told the people to sit down on the grass. And he

14:1 Greek *Herod the tetrarch*. He was a son of King Herod and was ruler over one of the four districts in Palestine.

took the five loaves and two fish, looked up toward heaven, and asked God's blessing on the food. Breaking the loaves into pieces, he gave some of the bread and fish to each disciple, and the disciples gave them to the people. [20]They all ate as much as they wanted, and they picked up twelve baskets of leftovers. [21]About five thousand men had eaten from those five loaves, in addition to all the women and children!

JESUS WALKS ON WATER

[22]Immediately after this, Jesus made his disciples get back into the boat and cross to the other side of the lake while he sent the people home. [23]Afterward he went up into the hills by himself to pray. Night fell while he was there alone. [24]Meanwhile, the disciples were in trouble far away from land, for a strong wind had risen, and they were fighting heavy waves.

[25]About three o'clock in the morning* Jesus came to them, walking on the water. [26]When the disciples saw him, they screamed in terror, thinking he was a ghost. [27]But Jesus spoke to them at once. "It's all right," he said. "I am here! Don't be afraid."

[28]Then Peter called to him, "Lord, if it's really you, tell me to come to you by walking on water."

[29]"All right, come," Jesus said.

So Peter went over the side of the boat and walked on the water toward Jesus. [30]But when he looked around at the high waves, he was terrified and began to sink. "Save me, Lord!" he shouted.

[31]Instantly Jesus reached out his hand and grabbed him. "You don't have much faith," Jesus said. "Why did you doubt me?" [32]And when they climbed back into the boat, the wind stopped.

[33]Then the disciples worshiped him. "You really are the Son of God!" they exclaimed.

[34]After they had crossed the lake, they landed at Gennesaret. [35]The news of their arrival spread quickly throughout the whole sur-rounding area, and soon people were bringing all their sick to be healed. [36]The sick begged him to let them touch even the fringe of his robe, and all who touched it were healed.

JESUS TEACHES ABOUT INNER PURITY

15 Some Pharisees and teachers of religious law now arrived from Jerusalem to interview Jesus. [2]"Why do your disciples disobey our age-old traditions?" they demanded. "They ignore our tradition of ceremonial hand washing before they eat."

[3]Jesus replied, "And why do you, by your traditions, violate the direct commandments of God? [4]For instance, God says, 'Honor your father and mother,' and 'Anyone who speaks evil of father or mother must be put to death.'* [5]But you say, 'You don't need to honor your parents by caring for their needs if you give the money to God instead.' [6]And so, by your own tradition, you nullify the direct commandment of God. [7]You hypocrites! Isaiah was prophesying about you when he said,

[8] 'These people honor me with their lips,
    but their hearts are far away.
[9] Their worship is a farce,
    for they replace God's commands with
        their own man-made teachings.'*"

[10]Then Jesus called to the crowds and said, "Listen to what I say and try to understand. [11]You are not defiled by what you eat; you are defiled by what you say and do.*"

[12]Then the disciples came to him and asked, "Do you realize you offended the Pharisees by what you just said?"

[13]Jesus replied, "Every plant not planted by my heavenly Father will be rooted up, [14]so ignore them. They are blind guides leading the blind, and if one blind person guides another, they will both fall into a ditch."

[15]Then Peter asked Jesus, "Explain what you

14:25 Greek *In the fourth watch of the night.* 15:4 Exod 20:12; 21:17; Lev 20:9; Deut 5:16. 15:8-9 Isa 29:13. 15:11 Or *what comes out of the mouth defiles a person.*

My Daily Worship

— September 8 —

WORSHIP THAT IS GENUINE

MATTHEW 14:1–15:39

You hypocrites! Isaiah was prophesying about you when he said, "These people honor me with their lips, but their hearts are far away. Their worship is a farce, for they replace God's commands with their own man-made teachings" (15:7–9).

[i reflect]

The questions came fast. Intense. Double-edged. Fraught with traps.

A press conference? More like an inquisition. The Pharisees and religious teachers shot their arrows of interrogation at Jesus. He shot them right back. He who had walked on the water now deftly walked around their verbal traps. "Jesus, what are your motives? Where are your priorities?" these religious teachers asked.

Jesus didn't mince words with these leaders who had proven to be less than spiritual. "What are *yours?* Where are *yours?* You're just the sort of hypocrites the great prophet described." Then Jesus pointed back through the centuries, back to the messengers of old whose message was still current. As Ezekiel had written, "So they come pretending to be sincere and sit before you listening. But they have no intention of doing what I tell them. They express love with their mouths, but their hearts seek only after money" (Ezekiel 33:31).

Jesus may also have been pointing ahead to the apostle Paul's warnings against the worship of traditions instead of worshiping the only true God. "Such rules are mere human teaching about things that are gone as soon as we use them" (Colossians 2:22). "But some teachers have missed this whole point. They have turned away from these things and spend their time arguing and talking foolishness" (1 Timothy 1:6).

Do your lips honor God with prayers, with songs? Well and good. How far away is your heart? This is the test Jesus put before his "interviewers" from Jerusalem (15:1). At issue is nothing less than the genuineness of your worship. Are you responding to God's commands and not man-made teachings?

In your worship—both personal and corporate—what rules have you observed that have more to do with following human tradition than following God? Identify the one to which you are most prone and ask God's help in conquering it.

[i pray]

God in heaven, I want to honor you with my lips. I want to honor you with my heart as well. Draw me close, that I may respond to your commands and worship you with sincerity.

[i respond]

Read a book on worship that gives you fresh insight into God's heart and his commands. Ask your pastor or worship leader for suggestions, or try Matt Redman's *The Unquenchable Worshipper* as a beginning point.

meant when you said people aren't defiled by what they eat."

¹⁶"Don't you understand?" Jesus asked him. ¹⁷"Anything you eat passes through the stomach and then goes out of the body. ¹⁸But evil words come from an evil heart and defile the person who says them. ¹⁹For from the heart come evil thoughts, murder, adultery, all other sexual immorality, theft, lying, and slander. ²⁰These are what defile you. Eating with unwashed hands could never defile you and make you unacceptable to God!"

THE FAITH OF A GENTILE WOMAN

²¹Jesus then left Galilee and went north to the region of Tyre and Sidon. ²²A Gentile* woman who lived there came to him, pleading, "Have mercy on me, O Lord, Son of David! For my daughter has a demon in her, and it is severely tormenting her."

²³But Jesus gave her no reply—not even a word. Then his disciples urged him to send her away. "Tell her to leave," they said. "She is bothering us with all her begging."

²⁴Then he said to the woman, "I was sent only to help the people of Israel—God's lost sheep—not the Gentiles."

²⁵But she came and worshiped him and pleaded again, "Lord, help me!"

²⁶"It isn't right to take food from the children and throw it to the dogs," he said.

²⁷"Yes, Lord," she replied, "but even dogs are permitted to eat crumbs that fall beneath their master's table."

²⁸"Woman," Jesus said to her, "your faith is great. Your request is granted." And her daughter was instantly healed.

JESUS HEALS MANY PEOPLE

²⁹Jesus returned to the Sea of Galilee and climbed a hill and sat down. ³⁰A vast crowd brought him the lame, blind, crippled, mute, and many others with physical difficulties, and they laid them before Jesus. And he healed them all. ³¹The crowd was amazed!

Those who hadn't been able to speak were talking, the crippled were made well, the lame were walking around, and those who had been blind could see again! And they praised the God of Israel.

JESUS FEEDS FOUR THOUSAND

³²Then Jesus called his disciples to him and said, "I feel sorry for these people. They have been here with me for three days, and they have nothing left to eat. I don't want to send them away hungry, or they will faint along the road."

³³The disciples replied, "And where would we get enough food out here in the wilderness for all of them to eat?"

³⁴Jesus asked, "How many loaves of bread do you have?"

They replied, "Seven, and a few small fish."

³⁵So Jesus told all the people to sit down on the ground. ³⁶Then he took the seven loaves and the fish, thanked God for them, broke them into pieces, and gave them to the disciples, who distributed the food to the crowd.

³⁷They all ate until they were full, and when the scraps were picked up, there were seven large baskets of food left over! ³⁸There were four thousand men who were fed that day, in addition to all the women and children. ³⁹Then Jesus sent the people home, and he got into a boat and crossed over to the region of Magadan.

LEADERS DEMAND A MIRACULOUS SIGN

16 One day the Pharisees and Sadducees came to test Jesus' claims by asking him to show them a miraculous sign from heaven.

²He replied, "You know the saying, 'Red sky at night means fair weather tomorrow, ³red sky in the morning means foul weather all day.' You are good at reading the weather signs in the sky, but you can't read the obvious signs of the times!* ⁴Only an evil, faithless genera-

---

15:22 Greek *Canaanite.* 16:2-3 Several manuscripts do not include any of the words in 16:2-3 after *He replied.*

tion would ask for a miraculous sign, but the only sign I will give them is the sign of the prophet Jonah." Then Jesus left them and went away.

YEAST OF THE PHARISEES AND SADDUCEES

⁵Later, after they crossed to the other side of the lake, the disciples discovered they had forgotten to bring any food. ⁶"Watch out!" Jesus warned them. "Beware of the yeast of the Pharisees and Sadducees."

⁷They decided he was saying this because they hadn't brought any bread. ⁸Jesus knew what they were thinking, so he said, "You have so little faith! Why are you worried about having no food? ⁹Won't you ever understand? Don't you remember the five thousand I fed with five loaves, and the baskets of food that were left over? ¹⁰Don't you remember the four thousand I fed with seven loaves, with baskets of food left over? ¹¹How could you even think I was talking about food? So again I say, 'Beware of the yeast of the Pharisees and Sadducees.'"

¹²Then at last they understood that he wasn't speaking about yeast or bread but about the false teaching of the Pharisees and Sadducees.

PETER'S DECLARATION ABOUT JESUS

¹³When Jesus came to the region of Caesarea Philippi, he asked his disciples, "Who do people say that the Son of Man is?"

¹⁴"Well," they replied, "some say John the Baptist, some say Elijah, and others say Jeremiah or one of the other prophets."

¹⁵Then he asked them, "Who do you say I am?"

¹⁶Simon Peter answered, "You are the Messiah, the Son of the living God."

¹⁷Jesus replied, "You are blessed, Simon son of John,* because my Father in heaven has revealed this to you. You did not learn this from any human being. ¹⁸Now I say to you

---

Words of Worship

HYMNS

Hymns—Greek **hum**-*nos* "hymn." The Old Testament contains no direct equivalent. Although several words are used to describe the psalms, such as *mizmor* "psalm" and *shir* "song," only Psalm 145 is known by a title that could be translated "hymn of praise" (*tehillah*). Psalms 113–118, known as the "Egyptian Hallel," are associated with Passover and might have been the "hymn" sung by Jesus and his disciples after the Last Supper (Mark 14:26).

Anything sung in worship is usually called a hymn, especially if it's printed in a hymnal. Music scholars have a more precise definition. A hymn is a song addressed to the Lord or describing his glory, majesty, and great deeds. This God-centered focus is what makes a piece of music a hymn, whether it's in a book, on a screen, or flowing spontaneously from our lips. Many of the psalms of the Bible are hymns in this sense.

When we stop to think about it, some of our worship music isn't focused on the Lord. Instead, it focuses on *us*—our faith, our devotion, our needs. Songs like these are known as *devotional lyrics*, and they have their place in prayer and testimony. But when we want to bring our worship as an offering to God and center our devotion on his greatness, we turn to hymns.

---

that you are Peter,* and upon this rock I will build my church, and all the powers of hell* will not conquer it. ¹⁹And I will give you the keys of the Kingdom of Heaven. Whatever you lock on earth will be locked in heaven, and whatever you open on earth will be

---

16:17 Greek *Simon son of Jonah;* see John 1:42; 21:15-17.   **16:18a** *Peter* means "stone" or "rock."   **16:18b** Greek *and the gates of Hades.*

opened in heaven." [20]Then he sternly warned them not to tell anyone that he was the Messiah.

Jesus Predicts His Death

[21]From then on Jesus began to tell his disciples plainly that he had to go to Jerusalem, and he told them what would happen to him there. He would suffer at the hands of the leaders and the leading priests and the teachers of religious law. He would be killed, and he would be raised on the third day.

[22]But Peter took him aside and corrected him. "Heaven forbid, Lord," he said. "This will never happen to you!"

[23]Jesus turned to Peter and said, "Get away from me, Satan! You are a dangerous trap to me. You are seeing things merely from a human point of view, and not from God's."

[24]Then Jesus said to the disciples, "If any of you wants to be my follower, you must put aside your selfish ambition, shoulder your cross, and follow me. [25]If you try to keep your life for yourself, you will lose it. But if you give up your life for me, you will find true life. [26]And how do you benefit if you gain the whole world but lose your own soul* in the process? Is anything worth more than your soul? [27]For I, the Son of Man, will come in the glory of my Father with his angels and will judge all people according to their deeds. [28]And I assure you that some of you standing here right now will not die before you see me, the Son of Man, coming in my Kingdom."

The Transfiguration

17 Six days later Jesus took Peter and the two brothers, James and John, and led them up a high mountain. [2]As the men watched, Jesus' appearance changed so that his face shone like the sun, and his clothing became dazzling white. [3]Suddenly, Moses and Elijah appeared and began talking with Jesus. [4]Peter blurted out, "Lord, this is wonderful! If you want me to, I'll make three shrines,* one for you, one for Moses, and one for Elijah."

[5]But even as he said it, a bright cloud came over them, and a voice from the cloud said, "This is my beloved Son, and I am fully pleased with him. Listen to him." [6]The disciples were terrified and fell face down on the ground.

[7]Jesus came over and touched them. "Get up," he said, "don't be afraid." [8]And when they looked, they saw only Jesus with them. [9]As they descended the mountain, Jesus commanded them, "Don't tell anyone what you have seen until I, the Son of Man, have been raised from the dead."

[10]His disciples asked, "Why do the teachers of religious law insist that Elijah must return before the Messiah comes*?"

[11]Jesus replied, "Elijah is indeed coming first to set everything in order. [12]But I tell you, he has already come, but he wasn't recognized, and he was badly mistreated. And soon the Son of Man will also suffer at their hands." [13]Then the disciples realized he had been speaking of John the Baptist.

Jesus Heals a Demon-Possessed Boy

[14]When they arrived at the foot of the mountain, a huge crowd was waiting for them. A man came and knelt before Jesus and said, [15]"Lord, have mercy on my son, because he has seizures and suffers terribly. He often falls into the fire or into the water. [16]So I brought him to your disciples, but they couldn't heal him."

[17]Jesus replied, "You stubborn, faithless people! How long must I be with you until you believe? How long must I put up with you? Bring the boy to me." [18]Then Jesus rebuked the demon in the boy, and it left him. From that moment the boy was well.

[19]Afterward the disciples asked Jesus privately, "Why couldn't we cast out that demon?"

[20]"You didn't have enough faith," Jesus told them. "I assure you, even if you had faith as

---

16:26 Or *your life*; also in 16:26b.   **17:4** Or *shelters*; Greek reads *tabernacles*.   **17:10** Greek *that Elijah must come first.*

small as a mustard seed you could say to this mountain, 'Move from here to there,' and it would move. Nothing would be impossible."*

JESUS AGAIN PREDICTS HIS DEATH

²²One day after they had returned to Galilee, Jesus told them, "The Son of Man is going to be betrayed. ²³He will be killed, but three days later he will be raised from the dead." And the disciples' hearts were filled with grief.

PAYMENT OF THE TEMPLE TAX

²⁴On their arrival in Capernaum, the tax collectors for the Temple tax came to Peter and asked him, "Doesn't your teacher pay the Temple tax?"

²⁵"Of course he does," Peter replied. Then he went into the house to talk to Jesus about it.

But before he had a chance to speak, Jesus asked him, "What do you think, Peter*? Do kings tax their own people or the foreigners they have conquered?"

²⁶"They tax the foreigners," Peter replied.

"Well, then," Jesus said, "the citizens are free! ²⁷However, we don't want to offend them, so go down to the lake and throw in a line. Open the mouth of the first fish you catch, and you will find a coin. Take the coin and pay the tax for both of us."

THE GREATEST IN THE KINGDOM

18 About that time the disciples came to Jesus and asked, "Which of us is greatest in the Kingdom of Heaven?"

²Jesus called a small child over to him and put the child among them. ³Then he said, "I assure you, unless you turn from your sins and become as little children, you will never get into the Kingdom of Heaven. ⁴Therefore, anyone who becomes as humble as this little child is the greatest in the Kingdom of Heaven. ⁵And anyone who welcomes a little child like this on my behalf is welcoming me.

⁶But if anyone causes one of these little ones who trusts in me to lose faith, it would be better for that person to be thrown into the sea with a large millstone tied around the neck.

⁷"How terrible it will be for anyone who causes others to sin. Temptation to do wrong is inevitable, but how terrible it will be for the person who does the tempting. ⁸So if your hand or foot causes you to sin, cut it off and throw it away. It is better to enter heaven* crippled or lame than to be thrown into the unquenchable fire with both of your hands and feet. ⁹And if your eye causes you to sin, gouge it out and throw it away. It is better to enter heaven half blind than to have two eyes and be thrown into hell.

¹⁰"Beware that you don't despise a single one of these little ones. For I tell you that in heaven their angels are always in the presence of my heavenly Father.*

STORY OF THE LOST SHEEP

¹²"If a shepherd has one hundred sheep, and one wanders away and is lost, what will he do? Won't he leave the ninety-nine others and go out into the hills to search for the lost one? ¹³And if he finds it, he will surely rejoice over it more than over the ninety-nine that didn't wander away! ¹⁴In the same way, it is not my heavenly Father's will that even one of these little ones should perish.

CORRECTING A FELLOW BELIEVER

¹⁵"If another believer* sins against you, go privately and point out the fault. If the other person listens and confesses it, you have won that person back. ¹⁶But if you are unsuccessful, take one or two others with you and go back again, so that everything you say may be confirmed by two or three witnesses. ¹⁷If that person still refuses to listen, take your case to the church. If the church decides you are right, but the other person won't accept it, treat that person as a pagan or a corrupt tax collector. ¹⁸I tell

---

17:20 Some manuscripts add verse 21, *But this kind of demon won't leave unless you have prayed and fasted.* **17:25** Greek *Simon.*
18:8 Greek *enter life;* also in 18:9. **18:10** Some manuscripts add verse 11, *And I, the Son of Man, have come to save the lost.* **18:15** Greek *your brother.*

you this: Whatever you prohibit on earth is prohibited in heaven, and whatever you allow on earth is allowed in heaven.

19"I also tell you this: If two of you agree down here on earth concerning anything you ask, my Father in heaven will do it for you. 20For where two or three gather together because they are mine,* I am there among them."

STORY OF THE UNFORGIVING DEBTOR

21Then Peter came to him and asked, "Lord, how often should I forgive someone* who sins against me? Seven times?"

22"No!" Jesus replied, "seventy times seven!*

23"For this reason, the Kingdom of Heaven can be compared to a king who decided to bring his accounts up to date with servants who had borrowed money from him. 24In the process, one of his debtors was brought in who owed him millions of dollars.* 25He couldn't pay, so the king ordered that he, his wife, his children, and everything he had be sold to pay the debt. 26But the man fell down before the king and begged him, 'Oh, sir, be patient with me, and I will pay it all.' 27Then the king was filled with pity for him, and he released him and forgave his debt.

28"But when the man left the king, he went to a fellow servant who owed him a few thousand dollars.* He grabbed him by the throat and demanded instant payment. 29His fellow servant fell down before him and begged for a little more time. 'Be patient and I will pay it,' he pleaded. 30But his creditor wouldn't wait. He had the man arrested and jailed until the debt could be paid in full.

31"When some of the other servants saw this, they were very upset. They went to the king and told him what had happened. 32Then the king called in the man he had forgiven and said, 'You evil servant! I forgave you that tremendous debt because you pleaded with me. 33Shouldn't you have mercy on your fel-

low servant, just as I had mercy on you?' 34Then the angry king sent the man to prison until he had paid every penny.

35"That's what my heavenly Father will do to you if you refuse to forgive your brothers and sisters* in your heart."

DISCUSSION ABOUT DIVORCE AND MARRIAGE

19 After Jesus had finished saying these things, he left Galilee and went southward to the region of Judea and into the area east of the Jordan River. 2Vast crowds followed him there, and he healed their sick.

3Some Pharisees came and tried to trap him with this question: "Should a man be allowed to divorce his wife for any reason?"

4"Haven't you read the Scriptures?" Jesus replied. "They record that from the beginning 'God made them male and female.'* 5And he said, 'This explains why a man leaves his father and mother and is joined to his wife, and the two are united into one.'* 6Since they are no longer two but one, let no one separate them, for God has joined them together."

7"Then why did Moses say a man could merely write an official letter of divorce and send her away?"* they asked.

8Jesus replied, "Moses permitted divorce as a concession to your hard-hearted wickedness, but it was not what God had originally intended. 9And I tell you this, a man who divorces his wife and marries another commits adultery—unless his wife has been unfaithful.*"

10Jesus' disciples then said to him, "Then it is better not to marry!"

11"Not everyone can accept this statement," Jesus said. "Only those whom God helps. 12Some are born as eunuchs, some have been made that way by others, and some choose not to marry for the sake of the Kingdom of Heaven. Let anyone who can, accept this statement."

18:20 Greek gather together in my name.   18:21 Greek my brother.   18:22 Or 77 times.   8:24 Greek 10,000 talents.   18:28 Greek 100 denarii. A denarius was the equivalent of a full day's wage.   18:35 Greek your brother.   19:4 Gen 1:27; 5:2.   19:5 Gen 2:24. 19:7 Deut 24:1.   19:9 Some manuscripts add And the man who marries a divorced woman commits adultery.

My Daily Worship

— *September 9* —

A PEACE OF HIS MIND

MATTHEW 16:1–18:35

Then the king called in the man he had forgiven and said, "You evil servant! I forgave you that tremendous debt because you pleaded with me. Shouldn't you have mercy on your fellow servant, just as I had mercy on you?" (18:32–33).

[i reflect]

The parable of the unforgiving debtor is blunt and to the point.

Even more blunt are comments on it by Saint Athanasius, fourth-century bishop of Alexandria: "The Lord doesn't allow unthankful people to have peace. 'For there is no peace to the wicked, saith the Lord.' They work in pain and grief. The Lord didn't even forgive the one owing ten thousand talents. For this man, who had been forgiven of great things, forgot to be kind in little things. Therefore, he paid the penalty even for his previous debt."

Unthankful people are not *allowed* to have peace? Unforgiving equals wicked?

Yes, replies Jesus. He concludes the parable, "That's what my heavenly Father will do to you if you refuse to forgive your brothers and sisters in your heart" (18:35). Receiving forgiveness down from God, reaching up in thankfulness to God, releasing forgiveness out to others, rewarded back with the peace of God.

In God's great economy, the beneficiaries must soon be the benefactors. The debtor in the parable owed millions of dollars, yet the king forgave all of it. Our sin is the spiritual equivalent of such a debt, yet the King of kings paid the debt for us. The newly forgiven debtor in the parable was owed a comparatively small sum, perhaps a few thousand dollars, by another servant. Yet he would not extend any forgiveness. We are owed the spiritual equivalent of a pittance by our fellow servants of Christ. When we consider how much we have been forgiven, is it too much to ask that we forgive others?

Do we reach up in thankfulness, then reach out in forgiveness to others as an expression of that gratitude? Or do we make no connection at all between the two debts?

To whom do you need to extend forgiveness today? As an act of worship, reach up in thankfulness to God. Reach out with forgiveness to that person. Be rewarded back with peace.

[i pray]

King of kings, I am your servant. You have forgiven me a debt that I could never have repaid. I am grateful. Help me to reach out in forgiveness to others. I long for your peace.

[i respond]

Do you need to forgive someone—alive and well or long since dead? Write a letter of forgiveness to that person, and truly forgive. If he or she is alive, ask God's direction on whether to mail it.

JESUS BLESSES THE CHILDREN

¹³Some children were brought to Jesus so he could lay his hands on them and pray for them. The disciples told them not to bother him. ¹⁴But Jesus said, "Let the children come to me. Don't stop them! For the Kingdom of Heaven belongs to such as these." ¹⁵And he put his hands on their heads and blessed them before he left.

THE RICH YOUNG MAN

¹⁶Someone came to Jesus with this question: "Teacher,* what good things must I do to have eternal life?"

¹⁷"Why ask me about what is good?" Jesus replied. "Only God is good. But to answer your question, you can receive eternal life if you keep the commandments."

¹⁸"Which ones?" the man asked.

And Jesus replied: " 'Do not murder. Do not commit adultery. Do not steal. Do not testify falsely. ¹⁹Honor your father and mother. Love your neighbor as yourself.'*"

²⁰"I've obeyed all these commandments," the young man replied. "What else must I do?"

²¹Jesus told him, "If you want to be perfect, go and sell all you have and give the money to the poor, and you will have treasure in heaven. Then come, follow me." ²²But when the young man heard this, he went sadly away because he had many possessions.

²³Then Jesus said to his disciples, "I tell you the truth, it is very hard for a rich person to get into the Kingdom of Heaven. ²⁴I say it again—it is easier for a camel to go through the eye of a needle than for a rich person to enter the Kingdom of God!"

²⁵The disciples were astounded. "Then who in the world can be saved?" they asked.

²⁶Jesus looked at them intently and said, "Humanly speaking, it is impossible. But with God everything is possible."

²⁷Then Peter said to him, "We've given up everything to follow you. What will we get out of it?"

²⁸And Jesus replied, "I assure you that when I, the Son of Man, sit upon my glorious throne in the Kingdom,* you who have been my followers will also sit on twelve thrones, judging the twelve tribes of Israel. ²⁹And everyone who has given up houses or brothers or sisters or father or mother or children or property, for my sake, will receive a hundred times as much in return and will have eternal life. ³⁰But many who seem to be important now will be the least important then, and those who are considered least here will be the greatest then.*

STORY OF THE VINEYARD WORKERS

20 "For the Kingdom of Heaven is like the owner of an estate who went out early one morning to hire workers for his vineyard. ²He agreed to pay the normal daily wage* and sent them out to work.

³"At nine o'clock in the morning he was passing through the marketplace and saw some people standing around doing nothing. ⁴So he hired them, telling them he would pay them whatever was right at the end of the day. ⁵At noon and again around three o'clock he did the same thing. ⁶At five o'clock that evening he was in town again and saw some more people standing around. He asked them, 'Why haven't you been working today?'

⁷"They replied, 'Because no one hired us.'

"The owner of the estate told them, 'Then go on out and join the others in my vineyard.'

⁸"That evening he told the foreman to call the workers in and pay them, beginning with the last workers first. ⁹When those hired at five o'clock were paid, each received a full day's wage. ¹⁰When those hired earlier came to get their pay, they assumed they would receive more. But they, too, were paid a day's wage. ¹¹When they received their pay, they protested,

---

19:16 Some manuscripts read *Good Teacher.*   19:18-19 Exod 20:12-16; Lev 19:18; Deut 5:16-20.   19:28 Greek *in the regeneration.*
19:30 Greek *But many who are first will be last; and the last, first.*   20:2 Greek *a denarius,* the payment for a full day's labor; also in 20:9, 10, 13.

My Daily Worship

— *September 10* —

"BUT WITH GOD . . ."

MATTHEW 19:1–20:34

Jesus looked at them intently and said, "Humanly speaking, it is impossible.
But with God everything is possible" (19:26).

[i reflect]

Too bad he had already walked away. The rich young man never heard the words of possibility.

"Teacher, what good things must I do to have eternal life?" he had asked eagerly. He smiled at the reply; he had indeed obeyed all the commandments. *Could it really be this easy?*

"What else must I do?" he inquired further. But he soon stopped smiling, wondering if he could possibly have heard Jesus correctly. *Sell all I have? Give the money to the poor? The poor, of all people? Then follow Jesus?* The Gospel account tells us, "But when the young man heard this, he went sadly away because he had many possessions" (19:22).

Jesus watched him walk away, and then warned that it would indeed be hard for the rich to enter the kingdom of heaven. Even his disciples seemed to despair. Then the words, "But with God. . . ."

God's grace and power apply to far more than the salvation of a rich young man. *Everything* is possible. When we cannot do it, when others cannot do it or will not do it—God can and God will.

The contemporary singer Nicole C. Mullen expressed this conviction in her song "Call on Jesus." We can think we are beyond saving, we can be hiding, we can be in despair. But when we call on Jesus, "all things are possible"—mounting on wings like eagles, watching mountains fall, being assured that he will move heaven and earth to rescue us when we call.

The refrain continues—"But when you call on Jesus, all things are possible"—for his promise continues. His powerful grace. His gracious power.

Rejoice that all *is* possible with God. Drink in the hope that is poured into the words "But with God. . . ." In the presence of God, speak what is overwhelming you, what seems impossible to you. Then end your prayer with the words "But with God everything is possible."

[i pray]

God of the possible, I thank you for your grace. I am in awe of your power. I rejoice
that your grace and your power make you the God of all possibility.

[i respond]

Read through the whole account of "The Rich Young Man" and the discussion Jesus and the disciples had after the man left (19:16–30). Memorize verse 26 and let its hope be poured into you: "Humanly speaking, it is impossible. But with God everything is possible."

¹²"Those people worked only one hour, and yet you've paid them just as much as you paid us who worked all day in the scorching heat.'

¹³"He answered one of them, 'Friend, I haven't been unfair! Didn't you agree to work all day for the usual wage? ¹⁴Take it and go. I wanted to pay this last worker the same as you. ¹⁵Is it against the law for me to do what I want with my money? Should you be angry because I am kind?'

¹⁶"And so it is, that many who are first now will be last then; and those who are last now will be first then."

JESUS AGAIN PREDICTS HIS DEATH

¹⁷As Jesus was on the way to Jerusalem, he took the twelve disciples aside privately and told them what was going to happen to him. ¹⁸"When we get to Jerusalem," he said, "the Son of Man will be betrayed to the leading priests and the teachers of religious law. They will sentence him to die. ¹⁹Then they will hand him over to the Romans to be mocked, whipped, and crucified. But on the third day he will be raised from the dead."

JESUS TEACHES ABOUT SERVING OTHERS

²⁰Then the mother of James and John, the sons of Zebedee, came to Jesus with her sons. She knelt respectfully to ask a favor. ²¹"What is your request?" he asked.

She replied, "In your Kingdom, will you let my two sons sit in places of honor next to you, one at your right and the other at your left?"

²²But Jesus told them, "You don't know what you are asking! Are you able to drink from the bitter cup of sorrow I am about to drink?"

"Oh yes," they replied, "we are able!"

²³"You will indeed drink from it," he told them. "But I have no right to say who will sit on the thrones next to mine. My Father has prepared those places for the ones he has chosen."

²⁴When the ten other disciples heard what James and John had asked, they were indig-

> *The word worship is almost like the word love in our society; it has been tossed around until is has been stripped of all meaning.*
>
> DAVID JEREMIAH

nant. ²⁵But Jesus called them together and said, "You know that in this world kings are tyrants, and officials lord it over the people beneath them. ²⁶But among you it should be quite different. Whoever wants to be a leader among you must be your servant, ²⁷and whoever wants to be first must become your slave. ²⁸For even I, the Son of Man, came here not to be served but to serve others, and to give my life as a ransom for many."

JESUS HEALS TWO BLIND MEN

²⁹As Jesus and the disciples left the city of Jericho, a huge crowd followed behind. ³⁰Two blind men were sitting beside the road. When they heard that Jesus was coming that way, they began shouting, "Lord, Son of David, have mercy on us!" ³¹The crowd told them to be quiet, but they only shouted louder, "Lord, Son of David, have mercy on us!"

³²Jesus stopped in the road and called, "What do you want me to do for you?"

³³"Lord," they said, "we want to see!" ³⁴Jesus felt sorry for them and touched their eyes. Instantly they could see! Then they followed him.

THE TRIUMPHAL ENTRY

21 As Jesus and the disciples approached Jerusalem, they came to the town of Bethphage on the Mount of Olives. Jesus sent two of them on ahead. ²"Go into the village over there," he said, "and you will see a donkey tied there, with its colt beside it. Untie them and bring them here. ³If anyone asks what you are doing, just say, 'The Lord needs them,' and

My Daily Worship

— *September 11* —

THE PRAYER THAT CANNOT FAIL
MATTHEW 21:1–46

If you believe, you will receive whatever you ask for in prayer (21:22).

[i reflect]

"We must pray The Prayer That Cannot Fail. That's always the best way."

That advice is often heard from Father Tim Kavanaugh, an Episcopal priest who is the central character of a series of novels by Jan Karon, beginning with *At Home in Mitford*. The town might seem like a sleepy little place in North Carolina where nothing as serious-sounding as The Prayer That Cannot Fail would be needed. But it is. Always. Everywhere. By everyone.

Prayer in fervent belief—the kind that Jesus desired from his disciples—does get answered. In Mitford, Montana, Mexico City, Madagascar. But to come with such a guarantee of 100-percent effectiveness? Surely such a prayer must be long and deeply theological, probing the ontological nature of the Godhead.

Actually, The Prayer That Cannot Fail contains only four words. Four short words: "Your will be done."

Are you disappointed? Were you thinking that prayer paraprofessionals had discovered a new, more logical, empirically tested approach? A new posture? Perhaps a particular language that "got through" to God better and faster? Father Tim occasionally gets into this kind of thinking, as do his wife, parishioners, friends, and visitors to Mitford.

Go to God in prayer, confident prayer that is slapped with a label saying it will never fail. "Your will be done. . . ." Whatever comes after—a seemingly hopeless relationship, unemployment, a child who seems to be on the wrong path, illness, a difficult decision—comes under the never-fail umbrella.

"Your will be done," when said in utter honesty and genuine faith, is the perfect test of the saying, "Prayer changes things or it changes us." Open your hands and offer the something or the someone into God's care. Keep your hands open to receive back the answer—*his* answer.

[i pray]

Heavenly Father, hear The Prayer That Cannot Fail. Your will be done, this day and tomorrow and all my tomorrows. I am grateful that prayer does not fail because you never fail.

[i respond]

In your journal or on a sheet of paper, write your own extended Prayer That Cannot Fail. Write each concern you have today. Then under each write "Your will be done." Pray through the page.

he will immediately send them." ⁴This was done to fulfill the prophecy,

⁵ "Tell the people of Israel,*
'Look, your King is coming to you.
He is humble, riding on a donkey—
even on a donkey's colt.'"*

⁶The two disciples did as Jesus said. ⁷They brought the animals to him and threw their garments over the colt, and he sat on it.*

⁸Most of the crowd spread their coats on the road ahead of Jesus, and others cut branches from the trees and spread them on the road. ⁹He was in the center of the procession, and the crowds all around him were shouting,

"Praise God* for the Son of David!
Bless the one who comes in the name of
the Lord!
Praise God in highest heaven!"*

¹⁰The entire city of Jerusalem was stirred as he entered. "Who is this?" they asked.

¹¹And the crowds replied, "It's Jesus, the prophet from Nazareth in Galilee."

JESUS CLEARS THE TEMPLE

¹²Jesus entered the Temple and began to drive out the merchants and their customers. He knocked over the tables of the money changers and the stalls of those selling doves. ¹³He said, "The Scriptures declare, 'My Temple will be called a place of prayer,' but you have turned it into a den of thieves!"*

¹⁴The blind and the lame came to him, and he healed them there in the Temple. ¹⁵The leading priests and the teachers of religious law saw these wonderful miracles and heard even the little children in the Temple shouting, "Praise God for the Son of David." But they were indignant ¹⁶and asked Jesus, "Do you hear what these children are saying?"

"Yes," Jesus replied. "Haven't you ever read

the Scriptures? For they say, 'You have taught children and infants to give you praise.'*"

¹⁷Then he returned to Bethany, where he stayed overnight.

JESUS CURSES THE FIG TREE

¹⁸In the morning, as Jesus was returning to Jerusalem, he was hungry, ¹⁹and he noticed a fig tree beside the road. He went over to see if there were any figs on it, but there were only leaves. Then he said to it, "May you never bear fruit again!" And immediately the fig tree withered up.

²⁰The disciples were amazed when they saw this and asked, "How did the fig tree wither so quickly?"

²¹Then Jesus told them, "I assure you, if you have faith and don't doubt, you can do things like this and much more. You can even say to this mountain, 'May God lift you up and throw you into the sea,' and it will happen. ²²If you believe, you will receive whatever you ask for in prayer."

THE AUTHORITY OF JESUS CHALLENGED

²³When Jesus returned to the Temple and began teaching, the leading priests and other leaders came up to him. They demanded, "By whose authority did you drive out the merchants from the Temple?* Who gave you such authority?"

²⁴"I'll tell you who gave me the authority to do these things if you answer one question," Jesus replied. ²⁵"Did John's baptism come from heaven or was it merely human?"

They talked it over among themselves. "If we say it was from heaven, he will ask why we didn't believe him. ²⁶But if we say it was merely human, we'll be mobbed, because the people think he was a prophet." ²⁷So they finally replied, "We don't know."

And Jesus responded, "Then I won't answer your question either.

21:5a Greek *Tell the daughter of Zion.* Isa 62:11. 21:5b Zech 9:9. 21:7 Greek *over them, and he sat on them.* 21:9a Greek *Hosanna,* an exclamation of praise that literally means "save now"; also in 21:9b, 15. 21:9b Pss 118:25-26; 148:1. 21:13 Isa 56:7; Jer 7:11. 21:16 Ps 8:2. 21:23 Or *By whose authority do you do these things?*

STORY OF THE TWO SONS

28"But what do you think about this? A man with two sons told the older boy, 'Son, go out and work in the vineyard today.' 29The son answered, 'No, I won't go,' but later he changed his mind and went anyway. 30Then the father told the other son, 'You go,' and he said, 'Yes, sir, I will.' But he didn't go. 31Which of the two was obeying his father?"

They replied, "The first, of course."

Then Jesus explained his meaning: "I assure you, corrupt tax collectors and prostitutes will get into the Kingdom of God before you do. 32For John the Baptist came and showed you the way to life, and you didn't believe him, while tax collectors and prostitutes did. And even when you saw this happening, you refused to turn from your sins and believe him.

STORY OF THE EVIL FARMERS

33"Now listen to this story. A certain landowner planted a vineyard, built a wall around it, dug a pit for pressing out the grape juice, and built a lookout tower. Then he leased the vineyard to tenant farmers and moved to another country. 34At the time of the grape harvest he sent his servants to collect his share of the crop. 35But the farmers grabbed his servants, beat one, killed one, and stoned another. 36So the landowner sent a larger group of his servants to collect for him, but the results were the same.

37"Finally, the owner sent his son, thinking, 'Surely they will respect my son.'

38"But when the farmers saw his son coming, they said to one another, 'Here comes the heir to this estate. Come on, let's kill him and get the estate for ourselves!' 39So they grabbed him, took him out of the vineyard, and murdered him.

40"When the owner of the vineyard returns," Jesus asked, "what do you think he will do to those farmers?"

41The religious leaders replied, "He will put the wicked men to a horrible death and lease the vineyard to others who will give him his share of the crop after each harvest."

42Then Jesus asked them, "Didn't you ever read this in the Scriptures?

'The stone rejected by the builders
    has now become the cornerstone.
This is the Lord's doing,
    and it is marvelous to see.'*

43What I mean is that the Kingdom of God will be taken away from you and given to a nation that will produce the proper fruit. 44Anyone who stumbles over that stone will be broken to pieces, and it will crush anyone on whom it falls.*"

45When the leading priests and Pharisees heard Jesus, they realized he was pointing at them—that they were the farmers in his story. 46They wanted to arrest him, but they were afraid to try because the crowds considered Jesus to be a prophet.

STORY OF THE GREAT FEAST

22 Jesus told them several other stories to illustrate the Kingdom. He said, 2"The Kingdom of Heaven can be illustrated by the story of a king who prepared a great wedding feast for his son. 3Many guests were invited, and when the banquet was ready, he sent his servants to notify everyone that it was time to come. But they all refused! 4So he sent other servants to tell them, 'The feast has been prepared, and choice meats have been cooked. Everything is ready. Hurry!' 5But the guests he had invited ignored them and went about their business, one to his farm, another to his store. 6Others seized his messengers and treated them shamefully, even killing some of them.

7"Then the king became furious. He sent out his army to destroy the murderers and burn their city. 8And he said to his servants, 'The wedding feast is ready, and the guests I invited aren't worthy of the honor. 9Now go out to the street corners and invite everyone you see.'

21:42 Ps 118:22-23. 21:44 This verse is omitted in some early manuscripts.

10"So the servants brought in everyone they could find, good and bad alike, and the banquet hall was filled with guests. 11But when the king came in to meet the guests, he noticed a man who wasn't wearing the proper clothes for a wedding. 12'Friend,' he asked, 'how is it that you are here without wedding clothes?' And the man had no reply. 13Then the king said to his aides, 'Bind him hand and foot and throw him out into the outer darkness, where there is weeping and gnashing of teeth.' 14For many are called, but few are chosen."

TAXES FOR CAESAR

15Then the Pharisees met together to think of a way to trap Jesus into saying something for which they could accuse him. 16They decided to send some of their disciples, along with the supporters of Herod, to ask him this question: "Teacher, we know how honest you are. You teach about the way of God regardless of the consequences. You are impartial and don't play favorites. 17Now tell us what you think about this: Is it right to pay taxes to the Roman government or not?"

18But Jesus knew their evil motives. "You hypocrites!" he said. "Whom are you trying to fool with your trick questions? 19Here, show me the Roman coin used for the tax." When they handed him the coin,* 20he asked, "Whose picture and title are stamped on it?"

21"Caesar's," they replied.

"Well, then," he said, "give to Caesar what belongs to him. But everything that belongs to God must be given to God." 22His reply amazed them, and they went away.

DISCUSSION ABOUT RESURRECTION

23That same day some Sadducees stepped forward—a group of Jews who say there is no resurrection after death. They posed this question: 24"Teacher, Moses said, 'If a man dies without children, his brother should marry the widow and have a child who will be the brother's heir.'* 25Well, there were seven brothers. The oldest married and then died without children, so the second brother married the widow. 26This brother also died without children, and the wife was married to the next brother, and so on until she had been the wife of each of them. 27And then she also died. 28So tell us, whose wife will she be in the resurrection? For she was the wife of all seven of them!"

29Jesus replied, "Your problem is that you don't know the Scriptures, and you don't know the power of God. 30For when the dead rise, they won't be married. They will be like the angels in heaven. 31But now, as to whether there will be a resurrection of the dead— haven't you ever read about this in the Scriptures? Long after Abraham, Isaac, and Jacob had died, God said,* 32'I am the God of Abraham, the God of Isaac, and the God of Jacob.'* So he is the God of the living, not the dead."

33When the crowds heard him, they were impressed with his teaching.

THE MOST IMPORTANT COMMANDMENT

34But when the Pharisees heard that he had silenced the Sadducees with his reply, they thought up a fresh question of their own to ask him. 35One of them, an expert in religious law, tried to trap him with this question: 36"Teacher, which is the most important commandment in the law of Moses?"

37Jesus replied, "'You must love the Lord your God with all your heart, all your soul, and all your mind.'* 38This is the first and greatest commandment. 39A second is equally important: 'Love your neighbor as yourself.'* 40All the other commandments and all the demands of the prophets are based on these two commandments."

WHOSE SON IS THE MESSIAH?

41Then, surrounded by the Pharisees, Jesus asked them a question: 42"What do you think about the Messiah? Whose son is he?"

22:19 Greek *a denarius.* **22:24** Deut 25:5-6. **22:31** Greek *in the Scriptures? God said.* **22:32** Exod 3:6. **22:37** Deut 6:5. **22:39** Lev 19:18.

My Daily Worship

— September 12 —

ALL, ALL, ALL
MATTHEW 22:1–23:39

Jesus replied, "'You must love the Lord your God with all your heart, all your soul, and all your mind.' This is the first and greatest commandment" (22:37–38).

[i reflect]

The answer came so quickly. *How had he had time to sort through all 600 laws?* wondered the expert in religious law. *And that* commandment? *Why, even children know this. . . .*

Oh.

Are we sometimes like the Pharisees who questioned Jesus that day—asking him what we ought to already know? These "experts in religious law" more than likely had memorized these verses from Deuteronomy as young children: "Hear, O Israel! The LORD is our God, the Lord alone. And you must love the LORD your God with all your heart, all your soul, and all your strength. And you must commit yourselves wholeheartedly to these commands I am giving you today" (Deuteronomy 6:4–6). With his answer, Jesus reminded the religious leaders that nothing had changed—God's requirements were the same then and today.

"With all your heart." Is your affection for the Lord genuine, wholehearted? Halfhearted? An even smaller fraction?

"With all your soul." Is your soul sold out to God? Do you truly trust him for eternal life?

"With all your mind." Are your thoughts subject to the omniscient One? Do you thirst for truth and for him who is the source of knowledge?

The 17th-century poet George Herbert expressed this all-encompassing love of God in "Praise (II)," found in the collection *The Temple:*

"*King of Glorie, King of Peace, I will love thee: And that love may never cease, I will move thee. Wherefore with my utmost art I will sing thee, and the cream of all my heart I will bring thee.*"

You don't need to wonder about it; you already know what God expects. You know what he deserves. You must love the Lord your God with all . . . with all . . . with all. . . .

Give to God your all in love. Ask him to govern your mind. Tell him you love him wholeheartedly. Trust him with your very soul.

[i pray]

Lord God, I thank you that I do not have to guess and research and ponder what might be the most important commandment. I want to love you with all my heart, soul, and mind.

[i respond]

Write your own poem of all-out love for God. Bring in all three elements of this first and greatest commandment, expressing what it means to love him with all your heart, soul, and mind.

They replied, "He is the son of David."

43Jesus responded, "Then why does David, speaking under the inspiration of the Holy Spirit, call him Lord? For David said,

44 'The LORD said to my Lord,
  Sit in honor at my right hand
    until I humble your enemies beneath
      your feet.'*

45Since David called him Lord, how can he be his son at the same time?"

46No one could answer him. And after that, no one dared to ask him any more questions.

JESUS WARNS THE RELIGIOUS LEADERS

23 Then Jesus said to the crowds and to his disciples, 2"The teachers of religious law and the Pharisees are the official interpreters of the Scriptures. 3So practice and obey whatever they say to you, but don't follow their example. For they don't practice what they teach. 4They crush you with impossible religious demands and never lift a finger to help ease the burden.

5"Everything they do is for show. On their arms they wear extra wide prayer boxes with Scripture verses inside,* and they wear extra long tassels on their robes. 6And how they love to sit at the head table at banquets and in the most prominent seats in the synagogue! 7They enjoy the attention they get on the streets, and they enjoy being called 'Rabbi.'* 8Don't ever let anyone call you 'Rabbi,' for you have only one teacher, and all of you are on the same level as brothers and sisters.* 9And don't address anyone here on earth as 'Father,' for only God in heaven is your spiritual Father. 10And don't let anyone call you 'Master,' for there is only one master, the Messiah. 11The greatest among you must be a servant. 12But those who exalt themselves will be humbled, and those who humble themselves will be exalted.

Words of Worship

TRINITY

Trinity—This is a name for a Christian doctrine; the term does not occur in Scripture.

Throughout Christian history, the Trinity has occasioned great debate. Though this word isn't in the Bible, the teaching clearly is. So belief in "God in three Persons" has become a hallmark of orthodoxy. Nevertheless, theologians still struggle to define what the doctrine of the Trinity really says about God.

What's clear is that the men and women of the Scriptures sensed God impacting their lives as Father and Creator, as Jesus Christ his Son, and as the Holy Spirit bringing life to God's people. Paul put it this way: "We are all one body, we have the same Spirit, and we have all been called to the same glorious future. There is only one Lord, one faith, one baptism, and there is only one God and Father, who is over us all and in us all and living through us all" (Ephesians 4:4–6). At worship services, we often hear the familiar words: "in the name of the Father and the Son and the Holy Spirit" (Matthew 28:19). When we hear these words, we know we're in the presence of the Holy.

13"How terrible it will be for you teachers of religious law and you Pharisees. Hypocrites! For you won't let others enter the Kingdom of Heaven, and you won't go in yourselves.* 15Yes, how terrible it will be for you teachers of religious law and you Pharisees. For you cross land and sea to make one convert, and then you turn him into twice the son of hell as you yourselves are.

16"Blind guides! How terrible it will be for

22:44 Ps 110:1. 23:5 Greek *They enlarge their phylacteries.* 23:7 *Rabbi, from Aramaic, means "master" or "teacher."* 23:8 Greek *brothers.* 23:13 Some manuscripts add verse 14, *How terrible it will be for you teachers of religious law and you Pharisees. Hypocrites! You shamelessly cheat widows out of their property, and then, to cover up the kind of people you really are, you make long prayers in public. Because of this, your punishment will be the greater.*

you! For you say that it means nothing to swear 'by God's Temple'—you can break that oath. But then you say that it is binding to swear 'by the gold in the Temple.' [17]Blind fools! Which is greater, the gold, or the Temple that makes the gold sacred? [18]And you say that to take an oath 'by the altar' can be broken, but to swear 'by the gifts on the altar' is binding! [19]How blind! For which is greater, the gift on the altar, or the altar that makes the gift sacred? [20]When you swear 'by the altar,' you are swearing by it and by everything on it. [21]And when you swear 'by the Temple,' you are swearing by it and by God, who lives in it. [22]And when you swear 'by heaven,' you are swearing by the throne of God and by God, who sits on the throne.

[23]"How terrible it will be for you teachers of religious law and you Pharisees. Hypocrites! For you are careful to tithe even the tiniest part of your income,* but you ignore the important things of the law—justice, mercy, and faith. You should tithe, yes, but you should not leave undone the more important things. [24]Blind guides! You strain your water so you won't accidentally swallow a gnat; then you swallow a camel!

[25]"How terrible it will be for you teachers of religious law and you Pharisees. Hypocrites! You are so careful to clean the outside of the cup and the dish, but inside you are filthy—full of greed and self-indulgence! [26]Blind Pharisees! First wash the inside of the cup, and then the outside will become clean, too.

[27]"How terrible it will be for you teachers of religious law and you Pharisees. Hypocrites! You are like whitewashed tombs—beautiful on the outside but filled on the inside with dead people's bones and all sorts of impurity. [28]You try to look like upright people outwardly, but inside your hearts are filled with hypocrisy and lawlessness.

[29]"How terrible it will be for you teachers of religious law and you Pharisees. Hypocrites! For you build tombs for the prophets your ancestors killed and decorate the graves of the godly people your ancestors destroyed. [30]Then you say, 'We never would have joined them in killing the prophets.'

[31]"In saying that, you are accusing yourselves of being the descendants of those who murdered the prophets. [32]Go ahead. Finish what they started. [33]Snakes! Sons of vipers! How will you escape the judgment of hell? [34]I will send you prophets and wise men and teachers of religious law. You will kill some by crucifixion and whip others in your synagogues, chasing them from city to city. [35]As a result, you will become guilty of murdering all the godly people from righteous Abel to Zechariah son of Barachiah, whom you murdered in the Temple between the altar and the sanctuary. [36]I assure you, all the accumulated judgment of the centuries will break upon the heads of this very generation.

JESUS GRIEVES OVER JERUSALEM

[37]"O Jerusalem, Jerusalem, the city that kills the prophets and stones God's messengers! How often I have wanted to gather your children together as a hen protects her chicks beneath her wings, but you wouldn't let me. [38]And now look, your house is left to you, empty and desolate. [39]For I tell you this, you will never see me again until you say, 'Bless the one who comes in the name of the Lord!'*"

JESUS FORETELLS THE FUTURE

24 As Jesus was leaving the Temple grounds, his disciples pointed out to him the various Temple buildings. [2]But he told them, "Do you see all these buildings? I assure you, they will be so completely demolished that not one stone will be left on top of another!"

[3]Later, Jesus sat on the slopes of the Mount of Olives. His disciples came to him privately and asked, "When will all this take place? And will there be any sign ahead of time to signal your return and the end of the world*?"

[4]Jesus told them, "Don't let anyone mislead

23:23 Greek *to tithe the mint, the dill, and the cumin.* 23:39 Ps 118:26. 24:3 Or *the age.*

you. ⁵For many will come in my name, saying, 'I am the Messiah.' They will lead many astray. ⁶And wars will break out near and far, but don't panic. Yes, these things must come, but the end won't follow immediately. ⁷The nations and kingdoms will proclaim war against each other, and there will be famines and earthquakes in many parts of the world. ⁸But all this will be only the beginning of the horrors to come.

⁹"Then you will be arrested, persecuted, and killed. You will be hated all over the world because of your allegiance to me. ¹⁰And many will turn away from me and betray and hate each other. ¹¹And many false prophets will appear and will lead many people astray. ¹²Sin will be rampant everywhere, and the love of many will grow cold. ¹³But those who endure to the end will be saved. ¹⁴And the Good News about the Kingdom will be preached throughout the whole world, so that all nations will hear it; and then, finally, the end will come.

¹⁵"The time will come when you will see what Daniel the prophet spoke about: the sacrilegious object that causes desecration* standing in the Holy Place"—reader, pay attention! ¹⁶"Then those in Judea must flee to the hills. ¹⁷A person outside the house* must not go inside to pack. ¹⁸A person in the field must not return even to get a coat. ¹⁹How terrible it will be for pregnant women and for mothers nursing their babies in those days. ²⁰And pray that your flight will not be in winter or on the Sabbath. ²¹For that will be a time of greater horror than anything the world has ever seen or will ever see again. ²²In fact, unless that time of calamity is shortened, the entire human race will be destroyed. But it will be shortened for the sake of God's chosen ones.

²³"Then if anyone tells you, 'Look, here is the Messiah,' or 'There he is,' don't pay any attention. ²⁴For false messiahs and false prophets will rise up and perform great miraculous signs and wonders so as to deceive, if possible, even God's chosen ones. ²⁵See, I have warned you.

²⁶"So if someone tells you, 'Look, the Messiah is out in the desert,' don't bother to go and look. Or, 'Look, he is hiding here,' don't believe it! ²⁷For as the lightning lights up the entire sky, so it will be when the Son of Man comes. ²⁸Just as the gathering of vultures shows there is a carcass nearby, so these signs indicate that the end is near.*

²⁹"Immediately after those horrible days end,

the sun will be darkened,
   the moon will not give light,
the stars will fall from the sky,
   and the powers of heaven will be
      shaken.*

³⁰And then at last, the sign of the coming of the Son of Man will appear in the heavens, and there will be deep mourning among all the nations of the earth. And they will see the Son of Man arrive on the clouds of heaven with power and great glory.* ³¹And he will send forth his angels with the sound of a mighty trumpet blast, and they will gather together his chosen ones from the farthest ends of the earth and heaven.

³²"Now learn a lesson from the fig tree. When its buds become tender and its leaves begin to sprout, you know without being told that summer is near. ³³Just so, when you see the events I've described beginning to happen, you can know his return is very near, right at the door. ³⁴I assure you, this generation* will not pass from the scene before all these things take place. ³⁵Heaven and earth will disappear, but my words will remain forever.

³⁶"However, no one knows the day or the hour when these things will happen, not even the angels in heaven or the Son himself.* Only the Father knows.

24:15 Greek *the abomination of desolation*. See Dan 9:27; 11:31; 12:11.   24:17 Greek *on the roof*.   24:28 Greek *Wherever the carcass is, the vultures gather*.   24:29 See Isa 13:10; 34:4; Joel 2:10.   24:30 See Dan 7:13.   24:34 Or *this age*, or *this nation*.   24:36 Some manuscripts omit the phrase *or the Son himself*.

³⁷"When the Son of Man returns, it will be like it was in Noah's day. ³⁸In those days before the Flood, the people were enjoying banquets and parties and weddings right up to the time Noah entered his boat. ³⁹People didn't realize what was going to happen until the Flood came and swept them all away. That is the way it will be when the Son of Man comes.

⁴⁰"Two men will be working together in the field; one will be taken, the other left. ⁴¹Two women will be grinding flour at the mill; one will be taken, the other left. ⁴²So be prepared, because you don't know what day your Lord is coming.

⁴³"Know this: A homeowner who knew exactly when a burglar was coming would stay alert and not permit the house to be broken into. ⁴⁴You also must be ready all the time. For the Son of Man will come when least expected.

⁴⁵"Who is a faithful, sensible servant, to whom the master can give the responsibility of managing his household and feeding his family? ⁴⁶If the master returns and finds that the servant has done a good job, there will be a reward. ⁴⁷I assure you, the master will put that servant in charge of all he owns. ⁴⁸But if the servant is evil and thinks, 'My master won't be back for a while,' ⁴⁹and begins oppressing the other servants, partying, and getting drunk—⁵⁰well, the master will return unannounced and unexpected. ⁵¹He will tear the servant apart and banish him with the hypocrites. In that place there will be weeping and gnashing of teeth.

STORY OF THE TEN BRIDESMAIDS

25 "The Kingdom of Heaven can be illustrated by the story of ten bridesmaids* who took their lamps and went to meet the bridegroom. ²Five of them were foolish, and five were wise. ³The five who were foolish took no oil for their lamps, ⁴but the other five were wise enough to take along extra oil. ⁵When the bridegroom was delayed, they all lay down and slept. ⁶At midnight they were roused by the shout, 'Look, the bridegroom is coming! Come out and welcome him!'

⁷"All the bridesmaids got up and prepared their lamps. ⁸Then the five foolish ones asked the others, 'Please give us some of your oil because our lamps are going out.' ⁹But the others replied, 'We don't have enough for all of us. Go to a shop and buy some for yourselves.'

¹⁰"But while they were gone to buy oil, the bridegroom came, and those who were ready went in with him to the marriage feast, and the door was locked. ¹¹Later, when the other five bridesmaids returned, they stood outside, calling, 'Sir, open the door for us!' ¹²But he called back, 'I don't know you!'

¹³"So stay awake and be prepared, because you do not know the day or hour of my return.

STORY OF THE THREE SERVANTS

¹⁴"Again, the Kingdom of Heaven can be illustrated by the story of a man going on a trip. He called together his servants and gave them money to invest for him while he was gone. ¹⁵He gave five bags of gold* to one, two bags of gold to another, and one bag of gold to the last—dividing it in proportion to their abilities—and then left on his trip. ¹⁶The servant who received the five bags of gold began immediately to invest the money and soon doubled it. ¹⁷The servant with two bags of gold also went right to work and doubled the money. ¹⁸But the servant who received the one bag of gold dug a hole in the ground and hid the master's money for safekeeping.

¹⁹"After a long time their master returned from his trip and called them to give an account of how they had used his money. ²⁰The servant to whom he had entrusted the five bags of gold said, 'Sir, you gave me five bags of gold to invest, and I have doubled the amount.' ²¹The master was full of praise. 'Well done, my good and faithful servant. You have been faithful in handling this small amount, so now I will give you many more responsibilities. Let's celebrate together!'

25:1 Or *virgins*; also in 25:7, 11.   25:15 Greek *talents*; also throughout the story. A talent is equal to 75 pounds or 34 kilograms.

²²"Next came the servant who had received the two bags of gold, with the report, 'Sir, you gave me two bags of gold to invest, and I have doubled the amount.' ²³The master said, 'Well done, my good and faithful servant. You have been faithful in handling this small amount, so now I will give you many more responsibilities. Let's celebrate together!'

²⁴"Then the servant with the one bag of gold came and said, 'Sir, I know you are a hard man, harvesting crops you didn't plant and gathering crops you didn't cultivate. ²⁵I was afraid I would lose your money, so I hid it in the earth and here it is.'

²⁶"But the master replied, 'You wicked and lazy servant! You think I'm a hard man, do you, harvesting crops I didn't plant and gathering crops I didn't cultivate? ²⁷Well, you should at least have put my money into the bank so I could have some interest. ²⁸Take the money from this servant and give it to the one with the ten bags of gold. ²⁹To those who use well what they are given, even more will be given, and they will have an abundance. But from those who are unfaithful,* even what little they have will be taken away. ³⁰Now throw this useless servant into outer darkness, where there will be weeping and gnashing of teeth.'

THE FINAL JUDGMENT

³¹"But when the Son of Man comes in his glory, and all the angels with him, then he will sit upon his glorious throne. ³²All the nations will be gathered in his presence, and he will separate them as a shepherd separates the sheep from the goats. ³³He will place the sheep at his right hand and the goats at his left. ³⁴Then the King will say to those on the right, 'Come, you who are blessed by my Father, inherit the Kingdom prepared for you from the foundation of the world. ³⁵For I was hungry, and you fed me. I was thirsty, and you gave me a drink. I was a stranger, and you invited me into your home. ³⁶I was naked, and you gave me clothing. I was sick, and you cared for me. I was in prison, and you visited me.'

³⁷"Then these righteous ones will reply, 'Lord, when did we ever see you hungry and feed you? Or thirsty and give you something to drink? ³⁸Or a stranger and show you hospitality? Or naked and give you clothing? ³⁹When did we ever see you sick or in prison, and visit you?' ⁴⁰And the King will tell them, 'I assure you, when you did it to one of the least of these my brothers and sisters,* you were doing it to me!'

⁴¹"Then the King will turn to those on the left and say, 'Away with you, you cursed ones, into the eternal fire prepared for the Devil and his demons! ⁴²For I was hungry, and you didn't feed me. I was thirsty, and you didn't give me anything to drink. ⁴³I was a stranger, and you didn't invite me into your home. I was naked, and you gave me no clothing. I was sick and in prison, and you didn't visit me.'

⁴⁴"Then they will reply, 'Lord, when did we ever see you hungry or thirsty or a stranger or naked or sick or in prison, and not help you?' ⁴⁵And he will answer, 'I assure you, when you refused to help the least of these my brothers and sisters, you were refusing to help me.' ⁴⁶And they will go away into eternal punishment, but the righteous will go into eternal life."

THE PLOT TO KILL JESUS

26 When Jesus had finished saying these things, he said to his disciples, ²"As you know, the Passover celebration begins in two days, and I, the Son of Man, will be betrayed and crucified."

³At that same time the leading priests and other leaders were meeting at the residence of Caiaphas, the high priest, ⁴to discuss how to capture Jesus secretly and put him to death. ⁵"But not during the Passover," they agreed, "or there will be a riot."

JESUS ANOINTED AT BETHANY

⁶Meanwhile, Jesus was in Bethany at the home of Simon, a man who had leprosy. ⁷During

25:29 Or *who have nothing.* 25:40 Greek *my brothers.*

May Daily Worship

— *September 13* —

"WHEN DID WE EVER _____?"

MATTHEW 24:1–25:46

And he will answer, "I assure you, when you refused to help the least of these
my brothers and sisters, you were refusing to help me" (25:45).

[i reflect]

"But, Lord, when did we ever see you hungry or thirsty or in any kind of need and neglect you? We simply would not do that!"

Ah, but they had. And so have we.

Certainly Saint Francis of Assisi never neglected "the least" of Jesus' brothers and sisters, did he? Not the humble, kind, bless-the-beasts-and-the-children monk we see in paintings and in our imagination. In fact, a rule of his Franciscan order said, "They should be glad to live among social outcasts, among the poor and helpless, the sick and the lepers, and those who beg by the wayside."

Saint Francis was not always so concerned about the "least," however. Raised in luxury and privilege, he had done his best to avoid dealings with the disgusting outcasts of his day. Especially the lepers. When he got near them, he would hold his nose against the smell.

But he encountered God and was transformed into a remarkable servant who taught us how to serve Christ in all people. In *The Lessons of St. Francis*, John Michael Talbot describes one incident: "One day when Francis was riding down a road near Assisi he saw a leper approaching from a distance. He felt all the familiar feelings—the discomfort, the fear, the nausea, the desire to flee—as the lonely leper came closer and closer. But Francis, ennobled and enabled by God's grace, got down off his mule, walked up to the leper, and kissed him."

Later, Francis wrote, "Everything people leave after them in this world is lost, but for their charity and almsgiving they will receive a reward from God." Indeed, today's larger passage in Matthew links our compassion, or its lack, to Judgment Day (25:31–46).

Watch for "the least" today. Stop to talk with an elderly person. Assist a young mother, struggling with her groceries and young children. Send a note to a hurting friend. Give them your best. And by so doing, worship and serve the Most High.

[i pray]

Lord, have I seen you in any kind of need and not responded? Show me how
to love and serve you by loving and serving your people here around me.

[i respond]

Does your church help at a homeless shelter or related service? If you are not involved in this ministry, prayerfully consider this. If you are, are there ways to have more direct contact with those in need?

supper, a woman came in with a beautiful jar* of expensive perfume and poured it over his head. ⁸The disciples were indignant when they saw this. "What a waste of money," they said. ⁹"She could have sold it for a fortune and given the money to the poor."

¹⁰But Jesus replied, "Why berate her for doing such a good thing to me? ¹¹You will always have the poor among you, but I will not be here with you much longer. ¹²She has poured this perfume on me to prepare my body for burial. ¹³I assure you, wherever the Good News is preached throughout the world, this woman's deed will be talked about in her memory."

JUDAS AGREES TO BETRAY JESUS

¹⁴Then Judas Iscariot, one of the twelve disciples, went to the leading priests ¹⁵and asked, "How much will you pay me to betray Jesus to you?" And they gave him thirty pieces of silver. ¹⁶From that time on, Judas began looking for the right time and place to betray Jesus.

THE LAST SUPPER

¹⁷On the first day of the Festival of Unleavened Bread, the disciples came to Jesus and asked, "Where do you want us to prepare the Passover supper?"

¹⁸"As you go into the city," he told them, "you will see a certain man. Tell him, 'The Teacher says, My time has come, and I will eat the Passover meal with my disciples at your house.'" ¹⁹So the disciples did as Jesus told them and prepared the Passover supper there.

²⁰When it was evening, Jesus sat down at the table with the twelve disciples. ²¹While they were eating, he said, "The truth is, one of you will betray me."

²²Greatly distressed, one by one they began to ask him, "I'm not the one, am I, Lord?"

²³He replied, "One of you who is eating with me now* will betray me. ²⁴For I, the Son of Man, must die, as the Scriptures declared long ago. But how terrible it will be for my betrayer. Far better for him if he had never been born!"

²⁵Judas, the one who would betray him, also asked, "Teacher, I'm not the one, am I?"

And Jesus told him, "You have said it yourself."

²⁶As they were eating, Jesus took a loaf of bread and asked God's blessing on it. Then he broke it in pieces and gave it to the disciples, saying, "Take it and eat it, for this is my body." ²⁷And he took a cup of wine and gave thanks to God for it. He gave it to them and said, "Each of you drink from it, ²⁸for this is my blood, which seals the covenant* between God and his people. It is poured out to forgive the sins of many. ²⁹Mark my words—I will not drink wine again until the day I drink it new with you in my Father's Kingdom." ³⁰Then they sang a hymn and went out to the Mount of Olives.

JESUS PREDICTS PETER'S DENIAL

³¹"Tonight all of you will desert me," Jesus told them. "For the Scriptures say,

'God* will strike the Shepherd,
  and the sheep of the flock will be
    scattered.'*

³²But after I have been raised from the dead, I will go ahead of you to Galilee and meet you there."

³³Peter declared, "Even if everyone else deserts you, I never will."

³⁴"Peter," Jesus replied, "the truth is, this very night, before the rooster crows, you will deny me three times."

³⁵"No!" Peter insisted. "Not even if I have to die with you! I will never deny you!" And all the other disciples vowed the same.

JESUS PRAYS IN GETHSEMANE

³⁶Then Jesus brought them to an olive grove called Gethsemane, and he said, "Sit here while I go on ahead to pray." ³⁷He took Peter

26:7 Greek an alabaster jar. 26:23 Or The one who has dipped his hand in the bowl with me. 26:28 Some manuscripts read the new covenant. 26:31a Greek I. 26:31b Zech 13:7.

My Daily Worship

— September 14 —

EAT, DRINK, AND BE . . . THANKFUL

MATTHEW 26:1–74

"Take it and eat it, for this is my body." And he took a cup of wine and gave thanks to God for it. He gave it to them and said, "Each of you drink from it, for this is my blood, which seals the covenant between God and his people. It is poured out to forgive the sins of many" (26:26–28).

[i reflect]

Passover meal. The Last Supper. The Lord's Supper. Agape meal. The Blessed Sacrament. Mass. Communion. Known by many names, this meal began as the last, sad seder among friends one evening in Jerusalem. Today, we eat the bread and drink the wine in light of what happened the next few days.

Jesus broke the bread for them; his body was broken for you. He poured the wine for them; his blood was poured out for you. In the words of the apostle Paul, "For every time you eat this bread and drink this cup, you are announcing the Lord's death until he comes again" (1 Corinthians 11:26).

One of the most traditional names for the remembrance is the Eucharist. The word gets to the heart of why we celebrate, why we remember, for it derives from the Greek *eukharistia,* meaning "gratitude."

Henri J. M. Nouwen writes in *With Burning Hearts: A Meditation on the Eucharistic Life:* "The word 'Eucharist' means literally 'thanksgiving.' A Eucharistic life is one lived in gratitude. . . . Jesus gave us the Eucharist to enable us to choose gratitude. It is a choice we, ourselves, have to make. Nobody can make it for us. But the Eucharist prompts us to cry out to God for mercy, to listen to the words of Jesus, to invite him into our home, to enter into communion with him and proclaim good news to the world."

Nouwen reminds us that the Lord's Supper communicates, "Jesus is God giving himself completely, pouring himself out for us without reserve. . . . 'Eat, drink, this is my body, this is my blood . . . this is me for you!'"

Today as you eat bread or drink juice, allow these simple elements to remind you of Christ's body broken for you, of his blood shed for you. Then eat, drink, and be thankful.

[i pray]

Lord Jesus, I kneel before you in gratitude. I thank you that your body was broken for me, that your blood was shed for me. Help me live a eucharistic life of gratitude.

[i respond]

What prominence does thanksgiving have when you take Communion? The next time you receive Communion, note the words, perhaps even later writing them down, that communicate thankfulness and gratitude (for example, thanks, thankful, grateful).

and Zebedee's two sons, James and John, and he began to be filled with anguish and deep distress. [38]He told them, "My soul is crushed with grief to the point of death. Stay here and watch with me."

[39]He went on a little farther and fell face down on the ground, praying, "My Father! If it is possible, let this cup of suffering be taken away from me. Yet I want your will, not mine." [40]Then he returned to the disciples and found them asleep. He said to Peter, "Couldn't you stay awake and watch with me even one hour? [41]Keep alert and pray. Otherwise temptation will overpower you. For though the spirit is willing enough, the body is weak!"

[42]Again he left them and prayed, "My Father! If this cup cannot be taken away until I drink it, your will be done." [43]He returned to them again and found them sleeping, for they just couldn't keep their eyes open.

[44]So he went back to pray a third time, saying the same things again. [45]Then he came to the disciples and said, "Still sleeping? Still resting?* Look, the time has come. I, the Son of Man, am betrayed into the hands of sinners. [46]Up, let's be going. See, my betrayer is here!"

JESUS IS ARRESTED

[47]And even as he said this, Judas, one of the twelve disciples, arrived with a mob that was armed with swords and clubs. They had been sent out by the leading priests and other leaders of the people. [48]Judas had given them a prearranged signal: "You will know which one to arrest when I go over and give him the kiss of greeting." [49]So Judas came straight to Jesus. "Greetings, Teacher!" he exclaimed and gave him the kiss.

[50]Jesus said, "My friend, go ahead and do what you have come for." Then the others grabbed Jesus and arrested him. [51]One of the men with Jesus pulled out a sword and slashed off an ear of the high priest's servant.

[52]"Put away your sword," Jesus told him. "Those who use the sword will be killed by the sword. [53]Don't you realize that I could ask my Father for thousands* of angels to protect us, and he would send them instantly? [54]But if I did, how would the Scriptures be fulfilled that describe what must happen now?"

[55]Then Jesus said to the crowd, "Am I some dangerous criminal, that you have come armed with swords and clubs to arrest me? Why didn't you arrest me in the Temple? I was there teaching every day. [56]But this is all happening to fulfill the words of the prophets as recorded in the Scriptures." At that point, all the disciples deserted him and fled.

JESUS BEFORE THE COUNCIL

[57]Then the people who had arrested Jesus led him to the home of Caiaphas, the high priest, where the teachers of religious law and other leaders had gathered. [58]Meanwhile, Peter was following far behind and eventually came to the courtyard of the high priest's house. He went in, sat with the guards, and waited to see what was going to happen to Jesus.

[59]Inside, the leading priests and the entire high council* were trying to find witnesses who would lie about Jesus, so they could put him to death. [60]But even though they found many who agreed to give false witness, there was no testimony they could use. Finally, two men were found [61]who declared, "This man said, 'I am able to destroy the Temple of God and rebuild it in three days.'"

[62]Then the high priest stood up and said to Jesus, "Well, aren't you going to answer these charges? What do you have to say for yourself?" [63]But Jesus remained silent. Then the high priest said to him, "I demand in the name of the living God that you tell us whether you are the Messiah, the Son of God."

[64]Jesus replied, "Yes, it is as you say. And in the future you will see me, the Son of Man, sitting at God's right hand in the place of power and coming back on the clouds of heaven."*

[65]Then the high priest tore his clothing to show his horror, shouting, "Blasphemy! Why do we need other witnesses? You have all

26:45 Or *Sleep on, take your rest.* 26:53 Greek *12 legions.* 26:59 Greek *the Sanhedrin.* 26:64 See Ps 110:1; Dan 7:13.

heard his blasphemy. ⁶⁶"What is your verdict?"

"Guilty!" they shouted. "He must die!"

⁶⁷Then they spit in Jesus' face and hit him with their fists. And some slapped him, ⁶⁸saying, "Prophesy to us, you Messiah! Who hit you that time?"

PETER DENIES JESUS

⁶⁹Meanwhile, as Peter was sitting outside in the courtyard, a servant girl came over and said to him, "You were one of those with Jesus the Galilean."

⁷⁰But Peter denied it in front of everyone. "I don't know what you are talking about," he said.

⁷¹Later, out by the gate, another servant girl noticed him and said to those standing around, "This man was with Jesus of Nazareth."

⁷²Again Peter denied it, this time with an oath. "I don't even know the man," he said.

⁷³A little later some other bystanders came over to him and said, "You must be one of them; we can tell by your Galilean accent."

⁷⁴Peter said, "I swear by God, I don't know the man." And immediately the rooster crowed. ⁷⁵Suddenly, Jesus' words flashed through Peter's mind: "Before the rooster crows, you will deny me three times." And he went away, crying bitterly.

JUDAS HANGS HIMSELF

27 Very early in the morning, the leading priests and other leaders met again to discuss how to persuade the Roman government to sentence Jesus to death. ²Then they bound him and took him to Pilate, the Roman governor.

³When Judas, who had betrayed him, realized that Jesus had been condemned to die, he was filled with remorse. So he took the thirty pieces of silver back to the leading priests and other leaders. ⁴"I have sinned," he declared, "for I have betrayed an innocent man."

"What do we care?" they retorted. "That's your problem." ⁵Then Judas threw the money onto the floor of the Temple and went out and hanged himself. ⁶The leading priests picked up the money. "We can't put it in the Temple treasury," they said, "since it's against the law to accept money paid for murder." ⁷After some discussion they finally decided to buy the potter's field, and they made it into a cemetery for foreigners. ⁸That is why the field is still called the Field of Blood. ⁹This fulfilled the prophecy of Jeremiah that says,

"They took* the thirty pieces of silver—
    the price at which he was valued by the
      people of Israel—
¹⁰ and purchased the potter's field,
    as the Lord directed.*"

> *Worship and intercession must go together; one is impossible without the other.*
>
> OSWALD CHAMBERS

JESUS' TRIAL BEFORE PILATE

¹¹Now Jesus was standing before Pilate, the Roman governor. "Are you the King of the Jews?" the governor asked him.

Jesus replied, "Yes, it is as you say."

¹²But when the leading priests and other leaders made their accusations against him, Jesus remained silent. ¹³"Don't you hear their many charges against you?" Pilate demanded. ¹⁴But Jesus said nothing, much to the governor's great surprise.

¹⁵Now it was the governor's custom to release one prisoner to the crowd each year during the Passover celebration—anyone they wanted. ¹⁶This year there was a notorious criminal in prison, a man named Barabbas.*

27:9 Or *I took.* **27:9-10** Greek *as the Lord directed me.* Zech 11:12-13; Jer 32:6-9. **27:16** Some manuscripts read *Jesus Barabbas;* also in 27:17.

¹⁷As the crowds gathered before Pilate's house that morning, he asked them, "Which one do you want me to release to you—Barabbas, or Jesus who is called the Messiah?" ¹⁸(He knew very well that the Jewish leaders had arrested Jesus out of envy.)

¹⁹Just then, as Pilate was sitting on the judgment seat, his wife sent him this message: "Leave that innocent man alone, because I had a terrible nightmare about him last night."

²⁰Meanwhile, the leading priests and other leaders persuaded the crowds to ask for Barabbas to be released and for Jesus to be put to death. ²¹So when the governor asked again, "Which of these two do you want me to release to you?" the crowd shouted back their reply: "Barabbas!"

²²"But if I release Barabbas," Pilate asked them, "what should I do with Jesus who is called the Messiah?"

And they all shouted, "Crucify him!"

²³"Why?" Pilate demanded. "What crime has he committed?"

But the crowd only roared the louder, "Crucify him!"

²⁴Pilate saw that he wasn't getting anywhere and that a riot was developing. So he sent for a bowl of water and washed his hands before the crowd, saying, "I am innocent of the blood of this man. The responsibility is yours!"

²⁵And all the people yelled back, "We will take responsibility for his death—we and our children!"*

²⁶So Pilate released Barabbas to them. He ordered Jesus flogged with a lead-tipped whip, then turned him over to the Roman soldiers to crucify him.

THE SOLDIERS MOCK JESUS

²⁷Some of the governor's soldiers took Jesus into their headquarters and called out the entire battalion. ²⁸They stripped him and put a scarlet robe on him. ²⁹They made a crown of long, sharp thorns and put it on his head, and they placed a stick in his right hand as a scepter. Then they knelt before him in mockery, yelling, "Hail! King of the Jews!" ³⁰And they spit on him and grabbed the stick and beat him on the head with it. ³¹When they were finally tired of mocking him, they took off the robe and put his own clothes on him again. Then they led him away to be crucified.

THE CRUCIFIXION

³²As they were on the way, they came across a man named Simon, who was from Cyrene,* and they forced him to carry Jesus' cross. ³³Then they went out to a place called Golgotha (which means Skull Hill). ³⁴The soldiers gave him wine mixed with bitter gall, but when he had tasted it, he refused to drink it.

³⁵After they had nailed him to the cross, the soldiers gambled for his clothes by throwing dice.* ³⁶Then they sat around and kept guard as he hung there. ³⁷A signboard was fastened to the cross above Jesus' head, announcing the charge against him. It read: "This is Jesus, the King of the Jews."

³⁸Two criminals were crucified with him, their crosses on either side of his. ³⁹And the people passing by shouted abuse, shaking their heads in mockery. ⁴⁰"So! You can destroy the Temple and build it again in three days, can you? Well then, if you are the Son of God, save yourself and come down from the cross!"

⁴¹The leading priests, the teachers of religious law, and the other leaders also mocked Jesus. ⁴²"He saved others," they scoffed, "but he can't save himself! So he is the king of Israel, is he? Let him come down from the cross, and we will believe in him! ⁴³He trusted God—let God show his approval by delivering him! For he said, 'I am the Son of God.' ⁴⁴And the criminals who were crucified with him also shouted the same insults at him.

THE DEATH OF JESUS

⁴⁵At noon, darkness fell across the whole land until three o'clock. ⁴⁶At about three o'clock,

---

27:25 Greek "His blood be on us and on our children." 27:32 Cyrene was a city in northern Africa. 27:35 Greek by casting lots. A few late manuscripts add This fulfilled the word of the prophet: "They divided my clothes among themselves and cast lots for my robe." See Ps 22:18.

My Daily Worship

HIS COMMANDING PRESENCE

MATTHEW 27:1–28:20

Teach these new disciples to obey all the commands I have given you. And be sure of this:
I am with you always, even to the end of the age" (28:20).

[i reflect]

Jesus assured them, "I have been given complete authority in heaven and on earth."

That day up there on the mountain, Jesus assured his disciples of his remarkable power. Then he commissioned them with the greatest of commissions: "Go . . . make disciples . . . baptize . . . teach."

Assured, commissioned, and now reassured: "You now know *what* to do and *why* and *where*. Here is *how:* I will be with you. Always."

The God of complete authority. The God of complete assurance.

Jesus gives you, today's disciple, the same immense commission. Destinations and details will vary, but the greatness of the commission is constant. And something else also remains constant. "Be sure of this," Jesus says. "Be absolutely sure of this: I am with you always."

Mundane or magnificent, the assignments from God—the living of a life that is an act of worship to him—can overwhelm us. The promise of his presence remains.

Fernando Ortega's music often takes the lyrics and imagery of yesterday—including Scripture, liturgy that is centuries old, and traditional hymns—and gives them a fresh setting and instrumentation. In "Hear Me Calling, Great Redeemer," you can see yourself, like the disciples, coming down from the mountain, assured that God will "go before me through the valley." He goes *with* you through the valley as well, as you ask, "Hold my hand, hold my trembling hand."

Hold on to his hand, hold on to the truth that the commission he gives you comes with the same reassurance he gave the disciples. He will be with you. Always. Throughout today. To the end of the age.

[i pray]

God, I am humbled that you ask me to go, make disciples, baptize, and teach. I am
grateful that you do not abandon me with this commission. Be with me always.

[i respond]

To what people and places has Jesus sent you in the past five years? Identify three key missions (or mini-missions) and the ways he has kept his promise to be "with you always."

Jesus called out with a loud voice, "*Eli, Eli, lema sabachthani?*" which means, "My God, my God, why have you forsaken me?"*

47Some of the bystanders misunderstood and thought he was calling for the prophet Elijah. 48One of them ran and filled a sponge with sour wine, holding it up to him on a stick so he could drink. 49But the rest said, "Leave him alone. Let's see whether Elijah will come and save him."*

50Then Jesus shouted out again, and he gave up his spirit. 51At that moment the curtain in the Temple was torn in two, from top to bottom. The earth shook, rocks split apart, 52and tombs opened. The bodies of many godly men and women who had died were raised from the dead 53after Jesus' resurrection. They left the cemetery, went into the holy city of Jerusalem, and appeared to many people.*

54The Roman officer and the other soldiers at the crucifixion were terrified by the earthquake and all that had happened. They said, "Truly, this was the Son of God!"

55And many women who had come from Galilee with Jesus to care for him were watching from a distance. 56Among them were Mary Magdalene, Mary (the mother of James and Joseph), and Zebedee's wife, the mother of James and John.

The Burial of Jesus

57As evening approached, Joseph, a rich man from Arimathea who was one of Jesus' followers, 58went to Pilate and asked for Jesus' body. And Pilate issued an order to release it to him. 59Joseph took the body and wrapped it in a long linen cloth. 60He placed it in his own new tomb, which had been carved out of the rock. Then he rolled a great stone across the entrance as he left. 61Both Mary Magdalene and the other Mary were sitting nearby watching.

The Guard at the Tomb

62The next day—on the first day of the Passover ceremonies*—the leading priests and Pharisees went to see Pilate. 63They told him, "Sir, we remember what that deceiver once said while he was still alive: 'After three days I will be raised from the dead.' 64So we request that you seal the tomb until the third day. This will prevent his disciples from coming and stealing his body and then telling everyone he came back to life! If that happens, we'll be worse off than we were at first."

65Pilate replied, "Take guards and secure it the best you can." 66So they sealed the tomb and posted guards to protect it.

The Resurrection

28 Early on Sunday morning,* as the new day was dawning, Mary Magdalene and the other Mary went out to see the tomb. 2Suddenly there was a great earthquake, because an angel of the Lord came down from heaven and rolled aside the stone and sat on it. 3His face shone like lightning, and his clothing was as white as snow. 4The guards shook with fear when they saw him, and they fell into a dead faint.

5Then the angel spoke to the women. "Don't be afraid!" he said. "I know you are looking for Jesus, who was crucified. 6He isn't here! He has been raised from the dead, just as he said would happen. Come, see where his body was lying. 7And now, go quickly and tell his disciples he has been raised from the dead, and he is going ahead of you to Galilee. You will see him there. Remember, I have told you."

8The women ran quickly from the tomb. They were very frightened but also filled with great joy, and they rushed to find the disciples to give them the angel's message. 9And as they went, Jesus met them. "Greetings!" he said. And they ran to him, held his feet, and worshiped him. 10Then Jesus said to them, "Don't

---

27:46 Ps 22:1. 27:49 Some manuscripts add *And another took a spear and pierced his side, and out came water and blood.* 27:51-53 Or *The earth shook, rocks split apart, tombs opened, and the bodies of many godly men and women who had died were raised from the dead. After Jesus' resurrection, they left the cemetery, went into the holy city of Jerusalem, and appeared to many people.* 27:62 Or *On the next day, which is after the Preparation.* 28:1 Greek *After the Sabbath, on the first day of the week.*

be afraid! Go tell my brothers to leave for Galilee, and they will see me there."

THE REPORT OF THE GUARD

[11]As the women were on their way into the city, some of the men who had been guarding the tomb went to the leading priests and told them what had happened. [12]A meeting of all the religious leaders was called, and they decided to bribe the soldiers. [13]They told the soldiers, "You must say, 'Jesus' disciples came during the night while we were sleeping, and they stole his body.' [14]If the governor hears about it, we'll stand up for you and everything will be all right." [15]So the guards accepted the bribe and said what they were told to say.

Their story spread widely among the Jews, and they still tell it today.

THE GREAT COMMISSION

[16]Then the eleven disciples left for Galilee, going to the mountain where Jesus had told them to go. [17]When they saw him, they worshiped him—but some of them still doubted!

[18]Jesus came and told his disciples, "I have been given complete authority in heaven and on earth. [19]Therefore, go and make disciples of all the nations, baptizing them in the name of the Father and the Son and the Holy Spirit. [20]Teach these new disciples to obey all the commands I have given you. And be sure of this: I am with you always, even to the end of the age."

Mark

For even I, the Son of Man, came here not to be served but to serve others,
and to give my life as a ransom for many (10:45).

The Servant Model

I t's a kingdom turned upside down, where the first is last and the last is first. A place where the King's royal officials lovingly wait on the needy, the hurting, the forgotten, the sinners. No wonder Jesus' disciples took so long to understand the irony. They had never heard of a kingdom like this, much less a King who ruled by serving others.

Mark portrays Jesus as the surprising Servant who leads by loving the unlovable and doing the unthinkable. The shortest Gospel, Mark zeroes in on Jesus' ministering nature and records in rapid-fire succession his miracles, teachings, and work. This King of glory shed his royal robes and donned a tunic, eating at the table with those whom Mark said others considered to be scum. Mark also records more of Jesus' miracles than any of the four Gospels, demonstrating this Servant's position of strength. He described Jesus encasing a man's deformed hand in his powerful grip, calming a storm with a mere rebuke, and delivering the deranged from demons.

Mark's Gospel leaves little doubt as to why people longed to worship Jesus—the same reasons we long to worship him today. As Servant-Leader, he steps into our lives and does what no one else is willing to do. When life gets messy, others may pity our plight but keep their distance. Not Jesus. Stooping. Bending. Spreading the elbow-grease. Getting involved. It's all familiar territory to him. In his kingdom-turned-upside-down, Jesus set aside his glory to slip on a servant's skin, going to the cross to meet our greatest need. His initiative to serve us is the greatest irony in the Gospel. Remember, the One who was willing to become your Servant is the same One who became your Savior. Worship him as both.

Worship Moments

- Jesus assumes his glory during the Transfiguration at the top of a mountain—shining in dazzling white clothes and revealing himself as worthy of worship (9:1–8).

- The crowd cries out, "Praise God in highest heaven!" during Jesus' Triumphal Entry (11:9–10).

- A woman pours out her personal wealth on Jesus to worship and adore him (14:3–9).

- Mark emphasizes Jesus' divinity by referencing him as the Son of God (1:1, 11; 3:11; 5:7; 9:7; 12:1–11; 13:32; 15:39).

JOHN THE BAPTIST PREPARES THE WAY

1 Here begins the Good News about Jesus the Messiah, the Son of God.*

²In the book of the prophet Isaiah, God said,

"Look, I am sending my messenger before you,
   and he will prepare your way.*
³ He is a voice shouting in the wilderness:
   'Prepare a pathway for the Lord's coming!
   Make a straight road for him!'*"

⁴This messenger was John the Baptist. He lived in the wilderness and was preaching that people should be baptized to show that they had turned from their sins and turned to God to be forgiven.* ⁵People from Jerusalem and from all over Judea traveled out into the wilderness to see and hear John. And when they confessed their sins, he baptized them in the Jordan River. ⁶His clothes were woven from camel hair, and he wore a leather belt; his food was locusts and wild honey. ⁷He announced: "Someone is coming soon who is far greater than I am—so much greater that I am not even worthy to be his slave.* ⁸I baptize you with* water, but he will baptize you with the Holy Spirit!"

THE BAPTISM OF JESUS

⁹One day Jesus came from Nazareth in Galilee, and he was baptized by John in the Jordan River. ¹⁰And when Jesus came up out of the water, he saw the heavens split open and the Holy Spirit descending like a dove on him. ¹¹And a voice came from heaven saying, "You are my beloved Son, and I am fully pleased with you."

THE TEMPTATION OF JESUS

¹²Immediately the Holy Spirit compelled Jesus to go into the wilderness. ¹³He was there for forty days, being tempted by Satan. He was out among the wild animals, and angels took care of him.

THE FIRST DISCIPLES

¹⁴Later on, after John was arrested by Herod Antipas, Jesus went to Galilee to preach God's Good News. ¹⁵"At last the time has come!" he announced. "The Kingdom of God is near! Turn from your sins and believe this Good News!"

¹⁶One day as Jesus was walking along the shores of the Sea of Galilee, he saw Simon* and his brother, Andrew, fishing with a net, for they were commercial fishermen. ¹⁷Jesus called out to them, "Come, be my disciples, and I will show you how to fish for people!" ¹⁸And they left their nets at once and went with him.

¹⁹A little farther up the shore Jesus saw Zebedee's sons, James and John, in a boat mending their nets. ²⁰He called them, too, and immediately they left their father, Zebedee, in the boat with the hired men and went with him.

JESUS CASTS OUT AN EVIL SPIRIT

²¹Jesus and his companions went to the town of Capernaum, and every Sabbath day he went into the synagogue and taught the people. ²²They were amazed at his teaching, for he taught as one who had real authority—quite unlike the teachers of religious law.

²³A man possessed by an evil spirit was in the synagogue, ²⁴and he began shouting, "Why are you bothering us, Jesus of Nazareth? Have you come to destroy us? I know who you are—the Holy One sent from God!"

²⁵Jesus cut him short. "Be silent! Come out of the man." ²⁶At that, the evil spirit screamed and threw the man into a convulsion, but then he left him.

²⁷Amazement gripped the audience, and

1:1 Some manuscripts do not include *the Son of God*. 1:2 Mal 3:1. 1:3 Isa 40:3. 1:4 Greek *preaching a baptism of repentance for the forgiveness of sins*. 1:7 Greek *to stoop down and untie his sandals*. 1:8 Or *in*; also in 1:8b. 1:16 *Simon* is called *Peter* in 3:16 and thereafter.

they began to discuss what had happened. "What sort of new teaching is this?" they asked excitedly. "It has such authority! Even evil spirits obey his orders!" [28]The news of what he had done spread quickly through that entire area of Galilee.

Jesus Heals Many People

[29]After Jesus and his disciples left the synagogue, they went over to Simon and Andrew's home, and James and John were with them. [30]Simon's mother-in-law was sick in bed with a high fever. They told Jesus about her right away. [31]He went to her bedside, and as he took her by the hand and helped her to sit up, the fever suddenly left, and she got up and prepared a meal for them.

[32]That evening at sunset, many sick and demon-possessed people were brought to Jesus. [33]And a huge crowd of people from all over Capernaum gathered outside the door to watch. [34]So Jesus healed great numbers of sick people who had many different kinds of diseases, and he ordered many demons to come out of their victims. But because they knew who he was, he refused to allow the demons to speak.

Jesus Preaches in Galilee

[35]The next morning Jesus awoke long before daybreak and went out alone into the wilderness to pray. [36]Later Simon and the others went out to find him. [37]They said, "Everyone is asking for you."

[38]But he replied, "We must go on to other towns as well, and I will preach to them, too, because that is why I came." [39]So he traveled throughout the region of Galilee, preaching in the synagogues and expelling demons from many people.

Jesus Heals a Man with Leprosy

[40]A man with leprosy came and knelt in front of Jesus, begging to be healed. "If you want to, you can make me well again," he said.

[41]Moved with pity,* Jesus touched him. "I want to," he said. "Be healed!" [42]Instantly the leprosy disappeared—the man was healed. [43]Then Jesus sent him on his way and told him sternly, [44]"Go right over to the priest and let him examine you. Don't talk to anyone along the way. Take along the offering required in the law of Moses for those who have been healed of leprosy, so everyone will have proof of your healing."

[45]But as the man went on his way, he spread the news, telling everyone what had happened to him. As a result, such crowds soon surrounded Jesus that he couldn't enter a town anywhere publicly. He had to stay out in the secluded places, and people from everywhere came to him there.

Jesus Heals a Paralyzed Man

2 Several days later Jesus returned to Capernaum, and the news of his arrival spread quickly through the town. [2]Soon the house where he was staying was so packed with visitors that there wasn't room for one more person, not even outside the door. And he preached the word to them. [3]Four men arrived carrying a paralyzed man on a mat. [4]They couldn't get to Jesus through the crowd, so they dug through the clay roof above his head. Then they lowered the sick man on his mat, right down in front of Jesus. [5]Seeing their faith, Jesus said to the paralyzed man, "My son, your sins are forgiven."

[6]But some of the teachers of religious law who were sitting there said to themselves, [7]"What? This is blasphemy! Who but God can forgive sins!"

[8]Jesus knew what they were discussing among themselves, so he said to them, "Why do you think this is blasphemy? [9]Is it easier to say to the paralyzed man, 'Your sins are forgiven' or 'Get up, pick up your mat, and walk'? [10]I will prove that I, the Son of Man, have the authority on earth to forgive sins." Then Jesus turned to the paralyzed man and said,

---

1:41 Some manuscripts read *Moved with anger.*

My Daily Worship

— *September 16* —

CHANCE OF A LIFETIME

MARK 1:1–3:35

Jesus called out to them, "Come, be my disciples,
and I will show you how to fish for people!" (1:17).

[i reflect]

There's Abram, a businessman in Ur, hearing a voice and uprooting his family to go south to God only knows where. And because he's just crazy enough to follow this weird, wild call, he not only finds eternal treasure, he also changes the course of human history.

There's Moses, on the backside of nowhere, trying to keep up with a flock of smelly sheep, just killing time, when, out of the corner of his eye, he sees a flaming bush. He pauses to check it out. And his life—and the world—are never the same.

History is filled with men and women who heard God summon them and who dared to give up their small ambitions and pursue eternal realities. Countless saints, willing to hitch their wagons (and lives) to God's star and attempt outlandish, impossible things.

Such was the case with the disciples. Jesus gave the simple summons, "Come, be my disciples." Come and leave their families, their livelihoods, their *lives*? Follow a Nazarene carpenter-turned-preacher? But what about . . . what if . . . what if?

Here's the deal: Christ is still looking for disciples. He is still calling men, women, boys, and girls to himself. And, more amazingly, he continues to invite average—dare we say "flawed"—folks to join him in his cosmic cause. When we pursue Jesus, our lives take on a new and different urgency and go in new directions. Our gifts and abilities are suddenly focused on kingdom needs and opportunities.

Hey, since Jesus Christ *is* the focal point of the universe, the supreme value, the only truly worthy One, doesn't it make sense to follow him, to learn from him, and to encourage others to do the same?

Today, live with the abandon that comes from following Christ. Go where he leads. Use your talents in his service. Then watch what he does through you!

[i pray]

Lord Jesus, give me a wild heart full of reckless abandon for you and your purposes. Whole-life
worship means following you wherever you go, whatever it costs. That's what I want.

[i respond]

Find in Scripture the stories of three other biblical saints whose lives were turned upside down when they made God the great passion of their lives.

[11]"Stand up, take your mat, and go on home, because you are healed!"

[12]The man jumped up, took the mat, and pushed his way through the stunned onlookers. Then they all praised God. "We've never seen anything like this before!" they exclaimed.

JESUS CALLS LEVI (MATTHEW)

[13]Then Jesus went out to the lakeshore again and taught the crowds that gathered around him. [14]As he walked along, he saw Levi son of Alphaeus sitting at his tax-collection booth. "Come, be my disciple," Jesus said to him. So Levi got up and followed him.

[15]That night Levi invited Jesus and his disciples to be his dinner guests, along with his fellow tax collectors and many other notorious sinners. (There were many people of this kind among the crowds that followed Jesus.) [16]But when some of the teachers of religious law who were Pharisees* saw him eating with people like that, they said to his disciples, "Why does he eat with such scum*?"

[17]When Jesus heard this, he told them, "Healthy people don't need a doctor—sick people do. I have come to call sinners, not those who think they are already good enough."

A DISCUSSION ABOUT FASTING

[18]John's disciples and the Pharisees sometimes fasted. One day some people came to Jesus and asked, "Why do John's disciples and the Pharisees fast, but your disciples don't fast?"

[19]Jesus replied, "Do wedding guests fast while celebrating with the groom? Of course not. They can't fast while they are with the groom. [20]But someday he will be taken away from them, and then they will fast. [21]And who would patch an old garment with unshrunk cloth? For the new patch shrinks and pulls away from the old cloth, leaving an even bigger hole than before. [22]And no one puts new wine into old wineskins. The wine would burst the wineskins, spilling the wine and ruining the skins. New wine needs new wineskins."

A DISCUSSION ABOUT THE SABBATH

[23]One Sabbath day as Jesus was walking through some grainfields, his disciples began breaking off heads of wheat. [24]But the Pharisees said to Jesus, "They shouldn't be doing that! It's against the law to work by harvesting grain on the Sabbath."

2:16a Greek *the scribes of the Pharisees.*   **2:16b** Greek *with tax collectors and sinners.*

25But Jesus replied, "Haven't you ever read in the Scriptures what King David did when he and his companions were hungry? 26He went into the house of God (during the days when Abiathar was high priest), ate the special bread reserved for the priests alone, and then gave some to his companions. That was breaking the law, too." 27Then he said to them, "The Sabbath was made to benefit people, and not people to benefit the Sabbath. 28And I, the Son of Man, am master even of the Sabbath!"

JESUS HEALS ON THE SABBATH

3 Jesus went into the synagogue again and noticed a man with a deformed hand. 2Since it was the Sabbath, Jesus' enemies watched him closely. Would he heal the man's hand on the Sabbath? If he did, they planned to condemn him. 3Jesus said to the man, "Come and stand in front of everyone." 4Then he turned to his critics and asked, "Is it legal to do good deeds on the Sabbath, or is it a day for doing harm? Is this a day to save life or to destroy it?" But they wouldn't answer him. 5He looked around at them angrily, because he was deeply disturbed by their hard hearts. Then he said to the man, "Reach out your hand." The man reached out his hand, and it became normal again! 6At once the Pharisees went away and met with the supporters of Herod to discuss plans for killing Jesus.

CROWDS FOLLOW JESUS

7Jesus and his disciples went out to the lake, followed by a huge crowd from all over Galilee, Judea, 8Jerusalem, Idumea, from east of the Jordan River, and even from as far away as Tyre and Sidon. The news about his miracles had spread far and wide, and vast numbers of people came to see him for themselves. 9Jesus instructed his disciples to bring around a boat and to have it ready in case he was crowded off the beach. 10There had been many healings that day. As a result, many sick people were crowding around him, trying to touch him. 11And whenever those possessed by evil spirits caught sight of him, they would fall down in front of him shrieking, "You are the Son of God!" 12But Jesus strictly warned them not to say who he was.

JESUS CHOOSES THE TWELVE APOSTLES

13Afterward Jesus went up on a mountain and called the ones he wanted to go with him. And they came to him. 14Then he selected twelve of them to be his regular companions, calling them apostles.* He sent them out to preach, 15and he gave them authority to cast out demons. 16These are the names of the twelve he chose:

Simon (he renamed him Peter),
17 James and John (the sons of Zebedee, but Jesus nicknamed them "Sons of Thunder"*),
18 Andrew,
Philip,
Bartholomew,
Matthew,
Thomas,
James (son of Alphaeus),
Thaddaeus,
Simon (the Zealot*),
19 Judas Iscariot (who later betrayed him).

JESUS AND THE PRINCE OF DEMONS

20When Jesus returned to the house where he was staying, the crowds began to gather again, and soon he and his disciples couldn't even find time to eat. 21When his family heard what was happening, they tried to take him home with them. "He's out of his mind," they said.

22But the teachers of religious law who had arrived from Jerusalem said, "He's possessed by Satan,* the prince of demons. That's where he gets the power to cast out demons."

23Jesus called them over and said to them by way of illustration, "How can Satan cast out

3:14 Some manuscripts do not include *calling them apostles.* 3:17 Greek *whom he named Boanerges, which means Sons of Thunder.* 3:18 Greek *the Cananean.* 3:22 Greek *Beelzeboul.*

Satan? [24]A kingdom at war with itself will collapse. [25]A home divided against itself is doomed. [26]And if Satan is fighting against himself, how can he stand? He would never survive. [27]Let me illustrate this. You can't enter a strong man's house and rob him without first tying him up. Only then can his house be robbed!*

[28]"I assure you that any sin can be forgiven, including blasphemy; [29]but anyone who blasphemes against the Holy Spirit will never be forgiven. It is an eternal sin." [30]He told them this because they were saying he had an evil spirit.

THE TRUE FAMILY OF JESUS

[31]Jesus' mother and brothers arrived at the house where he was teaching. They stood outside and sent word for him to come out and talk with them. [32]There was a crowd around Jesus, and someone said, "Your mother and your brothers and sisters* are outside, asking for you."

[33]Jesus replied, "Who is my mother? Who are my brothers?" [34]Then he looked at those around him and said, "These are my mother and brothers. [35]Anyone who does God's will is my brother and sister and mother."

STORY OF THE FARMER SCATTERING SEED

4 Once again Jesus began teaching by the lakeshore. There was such a large crowd along the shore that he got into a boat and sat down and spoke from there. [2]He began to teach the people by telling many stories such as this one:

[3]"Listen! A farmer went out to plant some seed. [4]As he scattered it across his field, some seed fell on a footpath, and the birds came and ate it. [5]Other seed fell on shallow soil with underlying rock. The plant sprang up quickly, [6]but it soon wilted beneath the hot sun and died because the roots had no nourishment in the shallow soil. [7]Other seed fell among thorns that shot up and choked out the tender blades so that it produced no grain. [8]Still other seed fell on fertile soil and produced a crop that was thirty, sixty, and even a hundred times as much as had been planted." Then he said, [9]"Anyone who is willing to hear should listen and understand!"

[10]Later, when Jesus was alone with the twelve disciples and with the others who were gathered around, they asked him, "What do your stories mean?"

[11]He replied, "You are permitted to understand the secret about the Kingdom of God. But I am using these stories to conceal everything about it from outsiders, [12]so that the Scriptures might be fulfilled:

'They see what I do,
    but they don't perceive its meaning.
They hear my words,
    but they don't understand.
So they will not turn from their sins
    and be forgiven.'*

[13]"But if you can't understand this story, how will you understand all the others I am going to tell? [14]The farmer I talked about is the one who brings God's message to others. [15]The seed that fell on the hard path represents those who hear the message, but then Satan comes at once and takes it away from them. [16]The rocky soil represents those who hear the message and receive it with joy. [17]But like young plants in such soil, their roots don't go very deep. At first they get along fine, but they wilt as soon as they have problems or are persecuted because they believe the word. [18]The thorny ground represents those who hear and accept the Good News, [19]but all too quickly the message is crowded out by the cares of this life, the lure of wealth, and the desire for nice things, so no crop is produced. [20]But the good soil represents those who hear and accept God's message and produce a huge harvest—thirty, sixty, or even a hundred times as much as had been planted."

3:27 Or *One cannot rob Satan's kingdom without first tying him up. Only then can his demons be cast out.* 3:32 Some manuscripts do not include *and sisters.* 4:12 Isa 6:9-10.

⁹Then Jesus asked, "What is your name?"

And the spirit replied, "Legion, because there are many of us here inside this man." ¹⁰Then the spirits begged him again and again not to send them to some distant place. ¹¹There happened to be a large herd of pigs feeding on the hillside nearby. ¹²"Send us into those pigs," the evil spirits begged. ¹³Jesus gave them permission. So the evil spirits came out of the man and entered the pigs, and the entire herd of two thousand pigs plunged down the steep hillside into the lake, where they drowned.

> *Worship is rooted in an event—*
> *the living, dying, and rising again*
> *of Jesus Christ in history.*
> ROBERT WEBBER

¹⁴The herdsmen fled to the nearby city and the surrounding countryside, spreading the news as they ran. Everyone rushed out to see for themselves. ¹⁵A crowd soon gathered around Jesus, but they were frightened when they saw the man who had been demon possessed, for he was sitting there fully clothed and perfectly sane. ¹⁶Those who had seen what happened to the man and to the pigs told everyone about it, ¹⁷and the crowd began pleading with Jesus to go away and leave them alone.

¹⁸When Jesus got back into the boat, the man who had been demon possessed begged to go, too. ¹⁹But Jesus said, "No, go home to your friends, and tell them what wonderful things the Lord has done for you and how merciful he has been." ²⁰So the man started off to visit the Ten Towns* of that region and began to tell everyone about the great things

Jesus had done for him; and everyone was amazed at what he told them.

JESUS HEALS IN RESPONSE TO FAITH

²¹When Jesus went back across to the other side of the lake, a large crowd gathered around him on the shore. ²²A leader of the local synagogue, whose name was Jairus, came and fell down before him, ²³pleading with him to heal his little daughter. "She is about to die," he said in desperation. "Please come and place your hands on her; heal her so she can live."

²⁴Jesus went with him, and the crowd thronged behind. ²⁵And there was a woman in the crowd who had had a hemorrhage for twelve years. ²⁶She had suffered a great deal from many doctors through the years and had spent everything she had to pay them, but she had gotten no better. In fact, she was worse. ²⁷She had heard about Jesus, so she came up behind him through the crowd and touched the fringe of his robe. ²⁸For she thought to herself, "If I can just touch his clothing, I will be healed." ²⁹Immediately the bleeding stopped, and she could feel that she had been healed!

³⁰Jesus realized at once that healing power had gone out from him, so he turned around in the crowd and asked, "Who touched my clothes?"

³¹His disciples said to him, "All this crowd is pressing around you. How can you ask, 'Who touched me?'"

³²But he kept on looking around to see who had done it. ³³Then the frightened woman, trembling at the realization of what had happened to her, came and fell at his feet and told him what she had done. ³⁴And he said to her, "Daughter, your faith has made you well. Go in peace. You have been healed."

³⁵While he was still speaking to her, messengers arrived from Jairus's home with the message, "Your daughter is dead. There's no use troubling the Teacher now."

³⁶But Jesus ignored their comments and

5:20 Greek *Decapolis.*

said to Jairus, "Don't be afraid. Just trust me." ³⁷Then Jesus stopped the crowd and wouldn't let anyone go with him except Peter and James and John. ³⁸When they came to the home of the synagogue leader, Jesus saw the commotion and the weeping and wailing. ³⁹He went inside and spoke to the people. "Why all this weeping and commotion?" he asked. "The child isn't dead; she is only asleep."

⁴⁰The crowd laughed at him, but he told them all to go outside. Then he took the girl's father and mother and his three disciples into the room where the girl was lying. ⁴¹Holding her hand, he said to her, "Get up, little girl!"* ⁴²And the girl, who was twelve years old, immediately stood up and walked around! Her parents were absolutely overwhelmed. ⁴³Jesus commanded them not to tell anyone what had happened, and he told them to give her something to eat.

JESUS REJECTED AT NAZARETH

6 Jesus left that part of the country and returned with his disciples to Nazareth, his hometown. ²The next Sabbath he began teaching in the synagogue, and many who heard him were astonished. They asked, "Where did he get all his wisdom and the power to perform such miracles? ³He's just the carpenter, the son of Mary and brother of James, Joseph,* Judas, and Simon. And his sisters live right here among us." They were deeply offended and refused to believe in him.

⁴Then Jesus told them, "A prophet is honored everywhere except in his own hometown and among his relatives and his own family." ⁵And because of their unbelief, he couldn't do any mighty miracles among them except to place his hands on a few sick people and heal them. ⁶And he was amazed at their unbelief.

JESUS SENDS OUT THE TWELVE APOSTLES

Then Jesus went out from village to village, teaching. ⁷And he called his twelve disciples together and sent them out two by two, with authority to cast out evil spirits. ⁸He told them to take nothing with them except a walking stick—no food, no traveler's bag, no money. ⁹He told them to wear sandals but not to take even an extra coat. ¹⁰"When you enter each village, be a guest in only one home," he said. ¹¹"And if a village won't welcome you or listen to you, shake off its dust from your feet as you leave. It is a sign that you have abandoned that village to its fate."

¹²So the disciples went out, telling all they met to turn from their sins. ¹³And they cast out many demons and healed many sick people, anointing them with olive oil.

THE DEATH OF JOHN THE BAPTIST

¹⁴Herod Antipas, the king, soon heard about Jesus, because people everywhere were talking about him. Some were saying,* "This must be John the Baptist come back to life again. That is why he can do such miracles." ¹⁵Others thought Jesus was the ancient prophet Elijah. Still others thought he was a prophet like the other great prophets of the past. ¹⁶When Herod heard about Jesus, he said, "John, the man I beheaded, has come back from the dead." ¹⁷For Herod had sent soldiers to arrest and imprison John as a favor to Herodias. She had been his brother Philip's wife, but Herod had married her. ¹⁸John kept telling Herod, "It is illegal for you to marry your brother's wife." ¹⁹Herodias was enraged and wanted John killed in revenge, but without Herod's approval she was powerless. ²⁰And Herod respected John, knowing that he was a good and holy man, so he kept him under his protection. Herod was disturbed whenever he talked with John, but even so, he liked to listen to him.

²¹Herodias's chance finally came. It was Herod's birthday, and he gave a party for his palace aides, army officers, and the leading citizens of Galilee. ²²Then his daughter, also

---

5:41 Greek text uses Aramaic "*Talitha cumi*" and then translates it as "Get up, little girl." **6:3** Greek *Joses;* see Matt 13:55.
6:14 Some manuscripts read *He was saying.*

My Daily Worship

— *September 18* —

TIME TO RETREAT AND RECHARGE

MARK 6:1–56

The apostles returned to Jesus from their ministry tour and told him all
they had done and what they had taught. Then Jesus said,
"Let's get away from the crowds for a while and rest" (6:30–31).

[i reflect]

In *The Unquenchable Worshipper, Coming Back to the Heart of Worship*, Matt Redman observes: "So often when my worship has dried up, it's because I haven't been fueling the fire. I haven't set aside any time to soak myself under the showers of God's revelation. Often, time is the key factor. But if we can find space to soak ourselves in God's Word, his presence, his creation and spend time with other believers, then we'll find that the revelation floods back into our lives; and our hearts will respond with a blaze of worship once more."

The fact is we were designed by God to need a regular amount of down time. Jesus knew this. After sending his disciples out on a ministry tour, what did Jesus do? He told them it was time to get away and get some rest. And actually there is a work-rest rhythm built into the fabric of the universe. How else do we explain the seasons, hibernating animals, and dormant fruit trees? Sometimes the most fitting and God-honoring act is to simply *be* (with God) rather than to *do* (for him).

Ah, but we are a hyper-efficient, get it done, type-A generation with places to go, people to see, and things to do. Armed with our Palm Pilots and assorted "to do" lists, we launch into our days with a vengeance. Is it any wonder that our souls are weary and burned out? "Expend *extra* energy focusing on God? Give my time and my attention to him? Ha, I'm lucky to make it to church once a week!"

When our hearts are exhausted and drained, chances are we're thinking about anything but God. Today look at your schedule and ask God if you need a break from activity to focus on intimacy with him.

[i pray]

Lord, when my schedule is full and overflowing, it often means my heart is empty and dry. Teach
me the invaluable discipline of regularly excusing myself from the hustle and bustle of life.
I want to recharge in your presence so that my heart blazes again with worship.

[i respond]

Sit down with your calendar and plan out a day away with God—just you and him. If that's not possible, plan at least a half-day personal retreat. Tell a friend your plan and ask for some healthy accountability.

named Herodias,* came in and performed a dance that greatly pleased them all. "Ask me for anything you like," the king said to the girl, "and I will give it to you." ²³Then he promised, "I will give you whatever you ask, up to half of my kingdom!"

²⁴She went out and asked her mother, "What should I ask for?"

Her mother told her, "Ask for John the Baptist's head!"

²⁵So the girl hurried back to the king and told him, "I want the head of John the Baptist, right now, on a tray!"

²⁶Then the king was very sorry, but he was embarrassed to break his oath in front of his guests. ²⁷So he sent an executioner to the prison to cut off John's head and bring it to him. The soldier beheaded John in the prison, ²⁸brought his head on a tray, and gave it to the girl, who took it to her mother. ²⁹When John's disciples heard what had happened, they came for his body and buried it in a tomb.

JESUS FEEDS FIVE THOUSAND

³⁰The apostles returned to Jesus from their ministry tour and told him all they had done and what they had taught. ³¹Then Jesus said, "Let's get away from the crowds for a while and rest." There were so many people coming and going that Jesus and his apostles didn't even have time to eat. ³²They left by boat for a quieter spot. ³³But many people saw them leaving, and people from many towns ran ahead along the shore and met them as they landed. ³⁴A vast crowd was there as he stepped from the boat, and he had compassion on them because they were like sheep without a shepherd. So he taught them many things.

³⁵Late in the afternoon his disciples came to him and said, "This is a desolate place, and it is getting late. ³⁶Send the crowds away so they can go to the nearby farms and villages and buy themselves some food."

³⁷But Jesus said, "You feed them."

"With what?" they asked. "It would take a small fortune* to buy food for all this crowd!"

³⁸"How much food do you have?" he asked. "Go and find out."

They came back and reported, "We have five loaves of bread and two fish." ³⁹Then Jesus told the crowd to sit down in groups on the green grass. ⁴⁰So they sat in groups of fifty or a hundred.

⁴¹Jesus took the five loaves and two fish, looked up toward heaven, and asked God's blessing on the food. Breaking the loaves into pieces, he kept giving the bread and fish to the disciples to give to the people. ⁴²They all ate as much as they wanted, ⁴³and they picked up twelve baskets of leftover bread and fish. ⁴⁴Five thousand men had eaten from those five loaves!

JESUS WALKS ON WATER

⁴⁵Immediately after this, Jesus made his disciples get back into the boat and head out across the lake to Bethsaida, while he sent the people home. ⁴⁶Afterward he went up into the hills by himself to pray.

⁴⁷During the night, the disciples were in their boat out in the middle of the lake, and Jesus was alone on land. ⁴⁸He saw that they were in serious trouble, rowing hard and struggling against the wind and waves. About three o'clock in the morning* he came to them, walking on the water. He started to go past them, ⁴⁹but when they saw him walking on the water, they screamed in terror, thinking he was a ghost. ⁵⁰They were all terrified when they saw him. But Jesus spoke to them at once. "It's all right," he said. "I am here! Don't be afraid." ⁵¹Then he climbed into the boat, and the wind stopped. They were astonished at what they saw. ⁵²They still didn't understand the significance of the miracle of the multiplied loaves, for their hearts were hard and they did not believe.

⁵³When they arrived at Gennesaret on the other side of the lake, they anchored the boat ⁵⁴and climbed out. The people standing there

---

6:22 Some manuscripts read *the daughter of Herodias herself.* 6:37 Greek *200 denarii.* A denarius was the equivalent of a full day's wage. 6:48 Greek *About the fourth watch of the night.*

recognized him at once, [55]and they ran throughout the whole area and began carrying sick people to him on mats. [56]Wherever he went—in villages and cities and out on the farms—they laid the sick in the market plazas and streets. The sick begged him to let them at least touch the fringe of his robe, and all who touched it were healed.

JESUS TEACHES ABOUT INNER PURITY

7 One day some Pharisees and teachers of religious law arrived from Jerusalem to confront Jesus. [2]They noticed that some of Jesus' disciples failed to follow the usual Jewish ritual of hand washing before eating. [3](The Jews, especially the Pharisees, do not eat until they have poured water over their cupped hands,* as required by their ancient traditions. [4]Similarly, they eat nothing bought from the market unless they have immersed their hands in water. This is but one of many traditions they have clung to—such as their ceremony of washing cups, pitchers, and kettles.*) [5]So the Pharisees and teachers of religious law asked him, "Why don't your disciples follow our age-old customs? For they eat without first performing the hand-washing ceremony."

[6]Jesus replied, "You hypocrites! Isaiah was prophesying about you when he said,

[7] 'These people honor me with their lips,
　　but their hearts are far away.
　Their worship is a farce,
　　for they replace God's commands with
　　　their own man-made teachings.'*

[8]For you ignore God's specific laws and substitute your own traditions."

[9]Then he said, "You reject God's laws in order to hold on to your own traditions. [10]For instance, Moses gave you this law from God: 'Honor your father and mother,' and 'Anyone who speaks evil of father or mother must be put to death.'* [11]But you say it is all right for people to say to their parents, 'Sorry, I can't help you. For I have vowed to give to God what I could have given to you.'* [12]You let them disregard their needy parents. [13]As such, you break the law of God in order to protect your own tradition. And this is only one example. There are many, many others."

[14]Then Jesus called to the crowd to come and hear. "All of you listen," he said, "and try to understand. [15]You are not defiled by what you eat; you are defiled by what you say and do!*"

[17]Then Jesus went into a house to get away from the crowds, and his disciples asked him what he meant by the statement he had made. [18]"Don't you understand either?" he asked. "Can't you see that what you eat won't defile you? [19]Food doesn't come in contact with your heart, but only passes through the stomach and then comes out again." (By saying this, he showed that every kind of food is acceptable.)

[20]And then he added, "It is the thought-life that defiles you. [21]For from within, out of a person's heart, come evil thoughts, sexual immorality, theft, murder, [22]adultery, greed, wickedness, deceit, eagerness for lustful pleasure, envy, slander, pride, and foolishness. [23]All these vile things come from within; they are what defile you and make you unacceptable to God."

THE FAITH OF A GENTILE WOMAN

[24]Then Jesus left Galilee and went north to the region of Tyre.* He tried to keep it secret that he was there, but he couldn't. As usual, the news of his arrival spread fast. [25]Right away a woman came to him whose little girl was possessed by an evil spirit. She had heard about Jesus, and now she came and fell at his feet. [26]She begged him to release her child from the demon's control.

7:3 Greek *washed with the fist.*　7:4 Some Greek manuscripts add *and dining couches.*　7:7 Isa 29:13.　7:10 Exod 20:12; 21:17; Lev 20:9; Deut 5:16.　7:11 Greek *'What I could have given to you is Corban' (that is, a gift).*　7:15 Some manuscripts add verse 16, *Anyone who is willing to hear should listen and understand.*　7:24 Some Greek manuscripts add *and Sidon.*

Since she was a Gentile, born in Syrian Phoenicia, [27]Jesus told her, "First I should help my own family, the Jews.* It isn't right to take food from the children and throw it to the dogs."

[28]She replied, "That's true, Lord, but even the dogs under the table are given some crumbs from the children's plates."

[29]"Good answer!" he said. "And because you have answered so well, I have healed your daughter." [30]And when she arrived home, her little girl was lying quietly in bed, and the demon was gone.

JESUS HEALS A DEAF AND MUTE MAN

[31]Jesus left Tyre and went to Sidon, then back to the Sea of Galilee and the region of the Ten Towns.* [32]A deaf man with a speech impediment was brought to him, and the people begged Jesus to lay his hands on the man to heal him. [33]Jesus led him to a private place away from the crowd. He put his fingers into the man's ears. Then, spitting onto his own fingers, he touched the man's tongue with the spittle. [34]And looking up to heaven, he sighed and commanded, "Be opened!"* [35]Instantly the man could hear perfectly and speak plainly!

[36]Jesus told the crowd not to tell anyone, but the more he told them not to, the more they spread the news, [37]for they were completely amazed. Again and again they said, "Everything he does is wonderful. He even heals those who are deaf and mute."

JESUS FEEDS FOUR THOUSAND

8 About this time another great crowd had gathered, and the people ran out of food again. Jesus called his disciples and told them, [2]"I feel sorry for these people. They have been here with me for three days, and they have nothing left to eat. [3]And if I send them home without feeding them, they will faint along the road. For some of them have come a long distance."

[4]"How are we supposed to find enough food for them here in the wilderness?" his disciples asked.

[5]"How many loaves of bread do you have?" he asked.

"Seven," they replied. [6]So Jesus told all the people to sit down on the ground. Then he took the seven loaves, thanked God for them, broke them into pieces, and gave them to his disciples, who distributed the bread to the crowd. [7]A few small fish were found, too, so Jesus also blessed these and told the disciples to pass them out.

[8]They ate until they were full, and when the scraps were picked up, there were seven large baskets of food left over! [9]There were about four thousand people in the crowd that day, and he sent them home after they had eaten. [10]Immediately after this, he got into a boat with his disciples and crossed over to the region of Dalmanutha.

PHARISEES DEMAND A MIRACULOUS SIGN

[11]When the Pharisees heard that Jesus had arrived, they came to argue with him. Testing him to see if he was from God, they demanded, "Give us a miraculous sign from heaven to prove yourself."

[12]When he heard this, he sighed deeply and said, "Why do you people keep demanding a miraculous sign? I assure you, I will not give this generation any such sign." [13]So he got back into the boat and left them, and he crossed to the other side of the lake.

YEAST OF THE PHARISEES AND HEROD

[14]But the disciples discovered they had forgotten to bring any food, so there was only one loaf of bread with them in the boat. [15]As they were crossing the lake, Jesus warned them, "Beware of the yeast of the Pharisees and of Herod."

[16]They decided he was saying this because

7:27 Greek *Let the children eat first.* 7:31 Greek *Decapolis.* 7:34 Greek text uses Aramaic *"Ephphatha"* and then translates it as "Be opened."

My Daily Worship
— September 19 —

WHO IS HE REALLY?
MARK 7:1–8:38

Then Jesus asked, "Who do you say I am?"
Peter replied, "You are the Messiah" (8:29).

[i reflect]

No matter how much it tries, the world can't get over Jesus. Every couple of years or so, at least one of the major news magazines does a cover story on some aspect of his life or one of the networks airs a special about him. We are haunted by Christ, and rightly so.

Speaking of the uniqueness of Jesus in his book *Miracles,* C. S. Lewis writes: "Among these Jews there suddenly turns up a man who goes about talking as if he was God. He claims to forgive sins. He says he has always existed. He says he is coming to judge the world at the end of time . . . . And when you have grasped that, you will see that what this man said was, quite simply, the most shocking thing that has ever been uttered by human lips."

"*Who* do you say I am?" "Who do *you* say I am?" "Who do you say *I* am? No matter how it is posed, this is the question above all questions. It is the query Christ continues to ask each person and every generation. And whether or not we answer it with our lips, we will be answering it with our lives every day.

Peter got it right. He recognized that Jesus was much more than an intriguing political revolutionary, more than a good teacher, even more than a great prophet. He saw him rightly—as the long-promised Messiah—the Son of God sent to rescue people from sin, sent to reign over the world.

Later, writing to other worshipers of Jesus, Peter noted: "You love him even though you have never seen him. Though you do not see him, you trust him; and even now you are happy with a glorious, inexpressible joy. Your reward for trusting him will be the salvation of your souls" (1 Peter 1:8–9).

Today ask yourself the question: What does my life say to the world about who Jesus is? Let the "glorious, inexpressible joy" of knowing Jesus be evident in what you do and say throughout the day.

[i pray]

I believe in you, Jesus. You are my Savior and Lord. You are my King and Friend.
I love you. I trust you. Fill me with inexpressible joy as I center my life around you.

[i respond]

Pick one of these: (1) Tell ten unchurched neighbors or work associates that you're doing a religious project and your assignment is to ask: "Who, in your opinion, is Jesus?" Record the results (and pray for opportunities to talk further). (2) Write a letter to a friend describing who Jesus is. (3) Write a love song to Christ about who he is to you and what he's done for you.

they hadn't brought any bread. [17]Jesus knew what they were thinking, so he said, "Why are you so worried about having no food? Won't you ever learn or understand? Are your hearts too hard to take it in? [18]You have eyes—can't you see? You have ears—can't you hear?'* Don't you remember anything at all? [19]What about the five thousand men I fed with five loaves of bread? How many baskets of leftovers did you pick up afterward?"

"Twelve," they said.

[20]"And when I fed the four thousand with seven loaves, how many large baskets of leftovers did you pick up?"

"Seven," they said.

[21]"Don't you understand even yet?" he asked them.

JESUS HEALS A BLIND MAN

[22]When they arrived at Bethsaida, some people brought a blind man to Jesus, and they begged him to touch and heal the man. [23]Jesus took the blind man by the hand and led him out of the village. Then, spitting on the man's eyes, he laid his hands on him and asked, "Can you see anything now?"

[24]The man looked around. "Yes," he said, "I see people, but I can't see them very clearly. They look like trees walking around."

[25]Then Jesus placed his hands over the man's eyes again. As the man stared intently, his sight was completely restored, and he could see everything clearly. [26]Jesus sent him home, saying, "Don't go back into the village on your way home."

PETER'S DECLARATION ABOUT JESUS

[27]Jesus and his disciples left Galilee and went up to the villages of Caesarea Philippi. As they were walking along, he asked them, "Who do people say I am?"

[28]"Well," they replied, "some say John the Baptist, some say Elijah, and others say you are one of the other prophets."

[29]Then Jesus asked, "Who do you say I am?"

Peter replied, "You are the Messiah." [30]But Jesus warned them not to tell anyone about him.

JESUS PREDICTS HIS DEATH

[31]Then Jesus began to tell them that he, the Son of Man, would suffer many terrible things and be rejected by the leaders, the leading priests, and the teachers of religious law. He would be killed, and three days later he would rise again. [32]As he talked about this openly with his disciples, Peter took him aside and told him he shouldn't say things like that.*

[33]Jesus turned and looked at his disciples and then said to Peter very sternly, "Get away from me, Satan! You are seeing things merely from a human point of view, not from God's."

[34]Then he called his disciples and the crowds to come over and listen. "If any of you wants to be my follower," he told them, "you must put aside your selfish ambition, shoulder your cross, and follow me. [35]If you try to keep your life for yourself, you will lose it. But if you give up your life for my sake and for the sake of the Good News, you will find true life. [36]And how do you benefit if you gain the whole world but lose your own soul* in the process? [37]Is anything worth more than your soul? [38]If a person is ashamed of me and my message in these adulterous and sinful days, I, the Son of Man, will be ashamed of that person when I return in the glory of my Father with the holy angels."

9 Jesus went on to say, "I assure you that some of you standing here right now will not die before you see the Kingdom of God arrive in great power!"

THE TRANSFIGURATION

[2]Six days later Jesus took Peter, James, and John to the top of a mountain. No one else was there. As the men watched, Jesus' appearance changed, [3]and his clothing became dazzling white, far whiter than any earthly process could ever make it. [4]Then Elijah and

---

8:18 Jer 5:21. **8:32** Or *and began to correct him.* **8:36** Or *your life;* also in 8:37.

Moses appeared and began talking with Jesus.

⁵"Teacher, this is wonderful!" Peter exclaimed. "We will make three shrines*—one for you, one for Moses, and one for Elijah." ⁶He didn't really know what to say, for they were all terribly afraid.

⁷Then a cloud came over them, and a voice from the cloud said, "This is my beloved Son. Listen to him." ⁸Suddenly they looked around, and Moses and Elijah were gone, and only Jesus was with them. ⁹As they descended the mountainside, he told them not to tell anyone what they had seen until he, the Son of Man, had risen from the dead. ¹⁰So they kept it to themselves, but they often asked each other what he meant by "rising from the dead."

¹¹Now they began asking him, "Why do the teachers of religious law insist that Elijah must return before the Messiah comes?"

¹²Jesus responded, "Elijah is indeed coming first to set everything in order. Why then is it written in the Scriptures that the Son of Man must suffer and be treated with utter contempt? ¹³But I tell you, Elijah has already come, and he was badly mistreated, just as the Scriptures predicted."

JESUS HEALS A BOY POSSESSED BY AN EVIL SPIRIT

¹⁴At the foot of the mountain they found a great crowd surrounding the other disciples, as some teachers of religious law were arguing with them. ¹⁵The crowd watched Jesus in awe as he came toward them, and then they ran to greet him. ¹⁶"What is all this arguing about?" he asked.

¹⁷One of the men in the crowd spoke up and said, "Teacher, I brought my son for you to heal him. He can't speak because he is possessed by an evil spirit that won't let him talk. ¹⁸And whenever this evil spirit seizes him, it throws him violently to the ground and makes him foam at the mouth and grind his teeth and become rigid.* So I asked your disciples to cast out the evil spirit, but they couldn't do it."

¹⁹Jesus said to them, "You faithless people! How long must I be with you until you believe? How long must I put up with you? Bring the boy to me." ²⁰So they brought the boy. But when the evil spirit saw Jesus, it threw the child into a violent convulsion, and he fell to the ground, writhing and foaming at the mouth. ²¹"How long has this been happening?" Jesus asked the boy's father.

He replied, "Since he was very small. ²²The evil spirit often makes him fall into the fire or into water, trying to kill him. Have mercy on us and help us. Do something if you can."

²³"What do you mean, 'If I can'?" Jesus asked. "Anything is possible if a person believes."

²⁴The father instantly replied, "I do believe, but help me not to doubt!"

²⁵When Jesus saw that the crowd of onlookers was growing, he rebuked the evil spirit. "Spirit of deafness and muteness," he said, "I command you to come out of this child and never enter him again!" ²⁶Then the spirit screamed and threw the boy into another violent convulsion and left him. The boy lay there motionless, and he appeared to be dead. A murmur ran through the crowd, "He's dead." ²⁷But Jesus took him by the hand and helped him to his feet, and he stood up.

²⁸Afterward, when Jesus was alone in the house with his disciples, they asked him, "Why couldn't we cast out that evil spirit?"

²⁹Jesus replied, "This kind can be cast out only by prayer.*"

JESUS AGAIN PREDICTS HIS DEATH

³⁰Leaving that region, they traveled through Galilee. Jesus tried to avoid all publicity ³¹in order to spend more time with his disciples and teach them. He said to them, "The Son of Man is going to be betrayed. He will be killed, but three days later he will rise from the dead." ³²But they didn't understand what he was saying, and they were afraid to ask him what he meant.

9:5 Or *shelters;* Greek reads *tabernacles.* 9:18 Or *become weak.* 9:29 Some manuscripts add *and fasting.*

The Greatest in the Kingdom

[33]After they arrived at Capernaum, Jesus and his disciples settled in the house where they would be staying. Jesus asked them, "What were you discussing out on the road?" [34]But they didn't answer, because they had been arguing about which of them was the greatest. [35]He sat down and called the twelve disciples over to him. Then he said, "Anyone who wants to be the first must take last place and be the servant of everyone else."

[36]Then he put a little child among them. Taking the child in his arms, he said to them, [37]"Anyone who welcomes a little child like this on my behalf welcomes me, and anyone who welcomes me welcomes my Father who sent me."

Using the Name of Jesus

[38]John said to Jesus, "Teacher, we saw a man using your name to cast out demons, but we told him to stop because he isn't one of our group."

[39]"Don't stop him!" Jesus said. "No one who performs miracles in my name will soon be able to speak evil of me. [40]Anyone who is not against us is for us. [41]If anyone gives you even a cup of water because you belong to the Messiah, I assure you, that person will be rewarded.

[42]"But if anyone causes one of these little ones who trusts in me to lose faith, it would be better for that person to be thrown into the sea with a large millstone tied around the neck. [43]If your hand causes you to sin, cut it off. It is better to enter heaven* with only one hand than to go into the unquenchable fires of hell with two hands.* [45]If your foot causes you to sin, cut it off. It is better to enter heaven with only one foot than to be thrown into hell with two feet.* [47]And if your eye causes you to sin, gouge it out. It is better to enter the Kingdom of God half blind than to have two eyes and be thrown into hell, [48]where the worm never dies and the fire never goes out.'*

[49]"For everyone will be purified with fire.* [50]Salt is good for seasoning. But if it loses its flavor, how do you make it salty again? You must have the qualities of salt among yourselves and live in peace with each other."

Discussion about Divorce and Marriage

10 Then Jesus left Capernaum and went southward to the region of Judea and into the area east of the Jordan River. As always there were the crowds, and as usual he taught them.

[2]Some Pharisees came and tried to trap him with this question: "Should a man be allowed to divorce his wife?"

[3]"What did Moses say about divorce?" Jesus asked them.

[4]"Well, he permitted it," they replied. "He said a man merely has to write his wife an official letter of divorce and send her away."*

[5]But Jesus responded, "He wrote those instructions only as a concession to your hard-hearted wickedness. [6]But God's plan was seen from the beginning of creation, for 'He made them male and female.'* [7]This explains why a man leaves his father and mother and is joined to his wife,* [8]and the two are united into one.'* Since they are no longer two but one, [9]let no one separate them, for God has joined them together."

[10]Later, when he was alone with his disciples in the house, they brought up the subject again. [11]He told them, "Whoever divorces his wife and marries someone else commits adultery against her. [12]And if a woman divorces her husband and remarries, she commits adultery."

Jesus Blesses the Children

[13]One day some parents brought their children to Jesus so he could touch them and bless them, but the disciples told them not to

---

9:43a Greek *enter life;* also in 9:45. 9:43b Some manuscripts add verse 44 (which is identical with 9:48). 9:45 Some manuscripts add verse 46 (which is identical with 9:48). 9:48 Isa 66:24. 9:49 Greek *salted with fire.* Some manuscripts add *and every sacrifice will be salted with salt.* 10:4 Deut 24:1. 10:6 Gen 1:27; 5:2. 10:7 Some manuscripts do not include *and is joined to his wife.* 10:7-8 Gen 2:24.

My Daily Worship

— *September 20* —

FOR WHAT PURPOSE?

MARK 9:1–10:45

For even I, the Son of Man, came here not to be served but to serve others,
and to give my life as a ransom for many" (10:45).

[i reflect]

Why did Christ come into the world? To teach? Do miracles? Start a new religion?

In John 6:38 Jesus states his purpose this way, "I have come down from heaven to do the will of God who sent me, not to do what I want." And what exactly *was* the will of God for Jesus? Well, according to today's verse, it was to serve and to die. Or we might say, to serve *by* dying.

Pastor/author Rick Warren begins his best-selling book *The Purpose-Driven Life* with these penetrating words: "The purpose of your life is far greater than your own personal fulfillment, your peace of mind, or even your happiness. It's far greater than your family, your career, or even your wildest dreams and ambitions. If you want to know why you were placed on this planet, you must begin with God. You were born *by* his purpose and *for* his purpose."

Could it be that our purpose is similar to Christ's? Not to do what we want, but to die to our own agendas and live boldly for God's? To do the Father's will? To serve God by serving others?

And what if we take the risk? What if we give ourselves away—our whole lives as one giant sacrifice of worship to God? This is what Jesus did. It is how he lived. No wonder he was able to say, "I always do those things that are pleasing to him" (John 8:29). And no wonder the Father in heaven echoed this assessment, stating of Christ, "You are my beloved Son, and I am fully pleased with you" (Mark 1:11).

What would it mean for you to offer your life as a giant sacrifice of worship to God? Spend some time reflecting on what you need to change—attitudes, habits, daily schedule—so that your life focuses on serving others.

[i pray]

Father in heaven, I have learned that I can serve without worshiping, but I cannot
worship without service. My desire is to live fully for you. I want to give
my life to you in service to others. Teach me how to do that.

[i respond]

Think of a sacrificial act of service you could perform for someone this week—mowing a lawn, running an errand, scrubbing a toilet. Do it as a conscious act of worship to God.

bother him. [14]But when Jesus saw what was happening, he was very displeased with his disciples. He said to them, "Let the children come to me. Don't stop them! For the Kingdom of God belongs to such as these. [15]I assure you, anyone who doesn't have their kind of faith will never get into the Kingdom of God." [16]Then he took the children into his arms and placed his hands on their heads and blessed them.

THE RICH MAN

[17]As he was starting out on a trip, a man came running up to Jesus, knelt down, and asked, "Good Teacher, what should I do to get eternal life?"

[18]"Why do you call me good?" Jesus asked. "Only God is truly good. [19]But as for your question, you know the commandments: 'Do not murder. Do not commit adultery. Do not steal. Do not testify falsely. Do not cheat. Honor your father and mother.'*"

[20]"Teacher," the man replied, "I've obeyed all these commandments since I was a child."

[21]Jesus felt genuine love for this man as he looked at him. "You lack only one thing," he told him. "Go and sell all you have and give the money to the poor, and you will have treasure in heaven. Then come, follow me." [22]At this, the man's face fell, and he went sadly away because he had many possessions.

[23]Jesus looked around and said to his disciples, "How hard it is for rich people to get into the Kingdom of God!" [24]This amazed them. But Jesus said again, "Dear children, it is very hard* to get into the Kingdom of God. [25]It is easier for a camel to go through the eye of a needle than for a rich person to enter the Kingdom of God!"

[26]The disciples were astounded. "Then who in the world can be saved?" they asked.

[27]Jesus looked at them intently and said, "Humanly speaking, it is impossible. But not with God. Everything is possible with God."

[28]Then Peter began to mention all that he and the other disciples had left behind. "We've given up everything to follow you," he said.

[29]And Jesus replied, "I assure you that everyone who has given up house or brothers or sisters or mother or father or children or property, for my sake and for the Good News, [30]will receive now in return, a hundred times over, houses, brothers, sisters, mothers, children, and property—with persecutions. And in the world to come they will have eternal life. [31]But many who seem to be important now will be the least important then, and those who are considered least here will be the greatest then.*"

JESUS AGAIN PREDICTS HIS DEATH

[32]They were now on the way to Jerusalem, and Jesus was walking ahead of them. The disciples were filled with dread and the people following behind were overwhelmed with fear. Taking the twelve disciples aside, Jesus once more began to describe everything that was about to happen to him in Jerusalem. [33]"When we get to Jerusalem," he told them, "the Son of Man will be betrayed to the leading priests and the teachers of religious law. They will sentence him to die and hand him over to the Romans. [34]They will mock him, spit on him, beat him with their whips, and kill him, but after three days he will rise again."

JESUS TEACHES ABOUT SERVING OTHERS

[35]Then James and John, the sons of Zebedee, came over and spoke to him. "Teacher," they said, "we want you to do us a favor."

[36]"What is it?" he asked.

[37]"In your glorious Kingdom, we want to sit in places of honor next to you," they said, "one at your right and the other at your left."

[38]But Jesus answered, "You don't know what you are asking! Are you able to drink from the bitter cup of sorrow I am about to drink? Are

---

10:19 Exod 20:12-16; Deut 5:16-20. **10:24** Some manuscripts add *for those who trust in riches.* **10:31** Greek *But many who are first will be last; and the last, first.*

you able to be baptized with the baptism of suffering I must be baptized with?"

³⁹"Oh yes," they said, "we are able!"

And Jesus said, "You will indeed drink from my cup and be baptized with my baptism, ⁴⁰but I have no right to say who will sit on the thrones next to mine. God has prepared those places for the ones he has chosen."

⁴¹When the ten other disciples discovered what James and John had asked, they were indignant. ⁴²So Jesus called them together and said, "You know that in this world kings are tyrants, and officials lord it over the people beneath them. ⁴³But among you it should be quite different. Whoever wants to be a leader among you must be your servant, ⁴⁴and whoever wants to be first must be the slave of all. ⁴⁵For even I, the Son of Man, came here not to be served but to serve others, and to give my life as a ransom for many."

JESUS HEALS BLIND BARTIMAEUS

⁴⁶And so they reached Jericho. Later, as Jesus and his disciples left town, a great crowd was following. A blind beggar named Bartimaeus (son of Timaeus) was sitting beside the road as Jesus was going by. ⁴⁷When Bartimaeus heard that Jesus from Nazareth was nearby, he began to shout out, "Jesus, Son of David, have mercy on me!"

⁴⁸"Be quiet!" some of the people yelled at him.

But he only shouted louder, "Son of David, have mercy on me!"

⁴⁹When Jesus heard him, he stopped and said, "Tell him to come here."

So they called the blind man. "Cheer up," they said. "Come on, he's calling you!" ⁵⁰Bartimaeus threw aside his coat, jumped up, and came to Jesus.

⁵¹"What do you want me to do for you?" Jesus asked.

"Teacher," the blind man said, "I want to see!"

⁵²And Jesus said to him, "Go your way. Your faith has healed you." And instantly the blind man could see! Then he followed Jesus down the road.*

THE TRIUMPHAL ENTRY

11 As Jesus and his disciples approached Jerusalem, they came to the towns of Bethphage and Bethany, on the Mount of Olives. Jesus sent two of them on ahead. ²"Go into that village over there," he told them, "and as soon as you enter it, you will see a colt tied there that has never been ridden. Untie it and bring it here. ³If anyone asks what you are doing, just say, 'The Lord needs it and will return it soon.'"

⁴The two disciples left and found the colt standing in the street, tied outside a house. ⁵As they were untying it, some bystanders demanded, "What are you doing, untying that colt?" ⁶They said what Jesus had told them to say, and they were permitted to take it. ⁷Then they brought the colt to Jesus and threw their garments over it, and he sat on it.

⁸Many in the crowd spread their coats on the road ahead of Jesus, and others cut leafy branches in the fields and spread them along the way. ⁹He was in the center of the procession, and the crowds all around him were shouting,

"Praise God!*
Bless the one who comes in the name of the Lord!
¹⁰ Bless the coming kingdom of our ancestor David!
Praise God in highest heaven!"*

¹¹So Jesus came to Jerusalem and went into the Temple. He looked around carefully at everything, and then he left because it was late in the afternoon. Then he went out to Bethany with the twelve disciples.

JESUS CURSES THE FIG TREE

¹²The next morning as they were leaving Bethany, Jesus felt hungry. ¹³He noticed a fig

10:52 Or on the way.　11:9 Greek Hosanna, an exclamation of praise that literally means "save now"; also in 11:10.　11:9-10 Pss 118:25-26; 148:1.

BUILDING UP

Building Up—Greek *oi-ko-do-me* "edification, building up."

Giving directions for the church's worship, Paul wrote, "Everything that is done must be useful to all and build them up in the Lord" (1 Corinthians 14:26). Our individual worship should also be a building-up experience, helping us to mature in our faith and grow stronger in the Christian life.

In speaking of our being built up, Paul uses a word derived from the Greek word for *house*. A house has many parts. It's not all walls, or floors, or a roof, or windows and doors. All these must fit together to make it a livable, workable dwelling. Not only do we have our special role to play in the greater house of God's worshipers, but within our personal worship, all the right structures need to be present—prayer, praise, petition, study, and meditation. Christ himself, as Peter reminds us, is the cornerstone of the house into which God is building us up (1 Peter 2:4–5).

tree a little way off that was in full leaf, so he went over to see if he could find any figs on it. But there were only leaves because it was too early in the season for fruit. ¹⁴Then Jesus said to the tree, "May no one ever eat your fruit again!" And the disciples heard him say it.

JESUS CLEARS THE TEMPLE

¹⁵When they arrived back in Jerusalem, Jesus entered the Temple and began to drive out the merchants and their customers. He knocked over the tables of the money changers and the stalls of those selling doves, ¹⁶and he stopped everyone from bringing in merchandise. ¹⁷He taught them, "The Scriptures declare, 'My Temple will be called a place of prayer for all nations,' but you have turned it into a den of thieves."*

¹⁸When the leading priests and teachers of religious law heard what Jesus had done, they began planning how to kill him. But they were afraid of him because the people were so enthusiastic about Jesus' teaching. ¹⁹That evening Jesus and the disciples* left the city.

²⁰The next morning as they passed by the fig tree he had cursed, the disciples noticed it was withered from the roots. ²¹Peter remembered what Jesus had said to the tree on the previous day and exclaimed, "Look, Teacher! The fig tree you cursed has withered!"

²²Then Jesus said to the disciples, "Have faith in God. ²³I assure you that you can say to this mountain, 'May God lift you up and throw you into the sea,' and your command will be obeyed. All that's required is that you really believe and do not doubt in your heart. ²⁴Listen to me! You can pray for anything, and if you believe, you will have it. ²⁵But when you are praying, first forgive anyone you are holding a grudge against, so that your Father in heaven will forgive your sins, too.*"

THE AUTHORITY OF JESUS CHALLENGED

²⁷By this time they had arrived in Jerusalem again. As Jesus was walking through the Temple area, the leading priests, the teachers of religious law, and the other leaders came up to him. They demanded, ²⁸"By whose authority did you drive out the merchants from the Temple?* Who gave you such authority?"

²⁹"I'll tell who gave me authority to do these things if you answer one question," Jesus replied. ³⁰"Did John's baptism come from heaven or was it merely human? Answer me!"

³¹They talked it over among themselves. "If we say it was from heaven, he will ask why we didn't believe him. ³²But do we dare say it was

---

11:17 Isa 56:7; Jer 7:11. **11:19** Greek *they;* some manuscripts read *he.* **11:25** Some manuscripts add verse 26, *But if you do not forgive, neither will your Father who is in heaven forgive your sins.* **11:28** Or *By whose authority do you do these things?*

merely human?" For they were afraid that the people would start a riot, since everyone thought that John was a prophet. ³³So they finally replied, "We don't know."

And Jesus responded, "Then I won't answer your question either."

STORY OF THE EVIL FARMERS

12 Then Jesus began telling them stories: "A man planted a vineyard, built a wall around it, dug a pit for pressing out the grape juice, and built a lookout tower. Then he leased the vineyard to tenant farmers and moved to another country. ²At grape-picking time he sent one of his servants to collect his share of the crop. ³But the farmers grabbed the servant, beat him up, and sent him back empty-handed.

⁴"The owner then sent another servant, but they beat him over the head and treated him shamefully. ⁵The next servant he sent was killed. Others who were sent were either beaten or killed, ⁶until there was only one left—his son whom he loved dearly. The owner finally sent him, thinking, 'Surely they will respect my son.'

⁷"But the farmers said to one another, 'Here comes the heir to this estate. Let's kill him and get the estate for ourselves!' ⁸So they grabbed him and murdered him and threw his body out of the vineyard.

⁹"What do you suppose the owner of the vineyard will do?" Jesus asked. "I'll tell you— he will come and kill them all and lease the vineyard to others. ¹⁰Didn't you ever read this in the Scriptures?

'The stone rejected by the builders
    has now become the cornerstone.
¹¹ This is the Lord's doing,
    and it is marvelous to see.'*"

¹²The Jewish leaders wanted to arrest him for using this illustration because they realized he was pointing at them—they were the wicked farmers in his story. But they were afraid to touch him because of the crowds. So they left him and went away.

TAXES FOR CAESAR

¹³The leaders sent some Pharisees and supporters of Herod to try to trap Jesus into saying something for which he could be arrested. ¹⁴"Teacher," these men said, "we know how honest you are. You are impartial and don't play favorites. You sincerely teach the ways of God. Now tell us—is it right to pay taxes to the Roman government or not? ¹⁵Should we pay them, or should we not?"

Jesus saw through their hypocrisy and said, "Whom are you trying to fool with your trick questions? Show me a Roman coin,* and I'll tell you." ¹⁶When they handed it to him, he asked, "Whose picture and title are stamped on it?"

"Caesar's," they replied.

¹⁷"Well, then," Jesus said, "give to Caesar what belongs to him. But everything that belongs to God must be given to God." This reply completely amazed them.

DISCUSSION ABOUT RESURRECTION

¹⁸Then the Sadducees stepped forward—a group of Jews who say there is no resurrection after death. They posed this question: ¹⁹"Teacher, Moses gave us a law that if a man dies, leaving a wife without children, his brother should marry the widow and have a child who will be the brother's heir.* ²⁰Well, there were seven brothers. The oldest of them married and then died without children. ²¹So the second brother married the widow, but soon he too died and left no children. Then the next brother married her and died without children. ²²This continued until all the brothers had married her and died, and still there were no children. Last of all, the woman died, too. ²³So tell us, whose wife will she be in the resurrection? For all seven were married to her."

²⁴Jesus replied, "Your problem is that you

12:10-11 Ps 118:22-23. 12:15 Greek *a denarius.* 12:19 Deut 25:5-6.

don't know the Scriptures, and you don't know the power of God. [25]For when the dead rise, they won't be married. They will be like the angels in heaven. [26]But now, as to whether the dead will be raised—haven't you ever read about this in the writings of Moses, in the story of the burning bush? Long after Abraham, Isaac, and Jacob had died, God said to Moses,* 'I am the God of Abraham, the God of Isaac, and the God of Jacob.'* [27]So he is the God of the living, not the dead. You have made a serious error."

THE MOST IMPORTANT COMMANDMENT

[28]One of the teachers of religious law was standing there listening to the discussion. He realized that Jesus had answered well, so he asked, "Of all the commandments, which is the most important?"

[29]Jesus replied, "The most important commandment is this: 'Hear, O Israel! The Lord our God is the one and only Lord. [30]And you must love the Lord your God with all your heart, all your soul, all your mind, and all your strength.'* [31]The second is equally important: 'Love your neighbor as yourself.'* No other commandment is greater than these."

[32]The teacher of religious law replied, "Well said, Teacher. You have spoken the truth by saying that there is only one God and no other. [33]And I know it is important to love him with all my heart and all my understanding and all my strength, and to love my neighbors as myself. This is more important than to offer all of the burnt offerings and sacrifices required in the law."

[34]Realizing this man's understanding, Jesus said to him, "You are not far from the Kingdom of God." And after that, no one dared to ask him any more questions.

WHOSE SON IS THE MESSIAH?

[35]Later, as Jesus was teaching the people in the Temple, he asked, "Why do the teachers of religious law claim that the Messiah will be the son of David? [36]For David himself, speaking under the inspiration of the Holy Spirit, said,

'The LORD said to my Lord,
  Sit in honor at my right hand
    until I humble your enemies beneath
      your feet.'*

[37]Since David himself called him Lord, how can he be his son at the same time?" And the crowd listened to him with great interest.

[38]Here are some of the other things he taught them at this time: "Beware of these teachers of religious law! For they love to parade in flowing robes and to have everyone bow to them as they walk in the marketplaces. [39]And how they love the seats of honor in the synagogues and at banquets. [40]But they shamelessly cheat widows out of their property, and then, to cover up the kind of people they really are, they make long prayers in public. Because of this, their punishment will be the greater."

THE WIDOW'S OFFERING

[41]Jesus went over to the collection box in the Temple and sat and watched as the crowds dropped in their money. Many rich people put in large amounts. [42]Then a poor widow came and dropped in two pennies.* [43]He called his disciples to him and said, "I assure you, this poor widow has given more than all the others have given. [44]For they gave a tiny part of their surplus, but she, poor as she is, has given everything she has."

JESUS FORETELLS THE FUTURE

13 As Jesus was leaving the Temple that day, one of his disciples said, "Teacher, look at these tremendous buildings! Look at the massive stones in the walls!"

[2]Jesus replied, "These magnificent buildings will be so completely demolished that not one stone will be left on top of another."

12:26a Greek *in the story of the bush? God said to him.* 12:26b Exod 3:6. 12:29-30 Deut 6:4-5. 12:31 Lev 19:18. 12:36 Ps 110:1.
12:42 Greek *2 lepta, which is a kodrantes.*

My Daily Worship

— *September 21* —

GOD-WORTHY LOVE

MARK 10:46–12:34

And I know it is important to love him with all my heart and all my understanding and all my strength, and to love my neighbors as myself. This is more important than to offer all of the burnt offerings and sacrifices required in the law" (12:33).

[i reflect]

"Talk is cheap," the old saying goes, and nowhere is that more true than in the spiritual realm. It is one thing to know the right answers, to be able to quote chapter and verse, to discuss the finer points of theology. It is another matter altogether to put words into practice, to be doers of God's Word.

The discussion in today's passage—between Jesus and a devoutly religious young man—gets to the heart of worship, the essence of life. What's the bottom line? Why have we been created in the first place? How should we spend our lives? Of all the *good* things we could focus our attention on, what is the *best,* the most important?

The young man knew the truth in his head: Loving God with all that we are and have. Thinking of him. Pursuing him. Ordering our lives around him. Serving him. Seeking to honor him. And out of that consuming love, loving others compassionately. The man understood all this and could articulate it. He just wasn't able to live out the truth.

In his book, *The Pleasures of Loving God*, Mike Bickle observes: "It takes God to love God. We love him with the supernatural power of his own imparted love. God will reveal his love and impart it to us, and we will become fiery lovers with his love. For God burns with desire for the human heart—He is the ultimate lover. He is not passive. That same burning desire is imparted to us and seals our hearts with fire. The icy waters of sin, bondage, and persecution cannot extinguish this supernatural fire of God's love when we yield to its all-consuming power."

If you are struggling today to love God as he so richly deserves, call on him to fill you with heavenly passion. Ask him for God-worthy affection, and direct that love back toward heaven.

[i pray]

Lord, give me the insight and the power to take the knowledge I have and turn it into actions that I do. Fill me with your love so that I might love you with a deeper, purer, and more intense love.

[i respond]

List three things you could start doing and three things you should stop doing to better reflect your love for God. Make this exercise a sacrifice of praise. Commit by his grace to be different.

³Later, Jesus sat on the slopes of the Mount of Olives across the valley from the Temple. Peter, James, John, and Andrew came to him privately and asked him, ⁴"When will all this take place? And will there be any sign ahead of time to show us when all this will be fulfilled?"

⁵Jesus replied, "Don't let anyone mislead you, ⁶because many will come in my name, claiming to be the Messiah.* They will lead many astray. ⁷And wars will break out near and far, but don't panic. Yes, these things must come, but the end won't follow immediately. ⁸Nations and kingdoms will proclaim war against each other, and there will be earthquakes in many parts of the world, and famines. But all this will be only the beginning of the horrors to come. ⁹But when these things begin to happen, watch out! You will be handed over to the courts and beaten in the synagogues. You will be accused before governors and kings of being my followers. This will be your opportunity to tell them about me.* ¹⁰And the Good News must first be preached to every nation. ¹¹But when you are arrested and stand trial, don't worry about what to say in your defense. Just say what God tells you to. Then it is not you who will be speaking, but the Holy Spirit.

¹²"Brother will betray brother to death, fathers will betray their own children, and children will rise against their parents and cause them to be killed. ¹³And everyone will hate you because of your allegiance to me. But those who endure to the end will be saved.

¹⁴"The time will come when you will see the sacrilegious object that causes desecration* standing where it should not be"—reader, pay attention! "Then those in Judea must flee to the hills. ¹⁵A person outside the house* must not go back into the house to pack. ¹⁶A person in the field must not return even to get a coat. ¹⁷How terrible it will be for pregnant women and for mothers nursing their babies in those days. ¹⁸And pray that your flight will not be in winter. ¹⁹For those will be days of greater horror than at any time since God created the world. And it will never happen again. ²⁰In fact, unless the Lord shortens that time of calamity, the entire human race will be destroyed. But for the sake of his chosen ones he has shortened those days.

²¹"And then if anyone tells you, 'Look, here is the Messiah,' or, 'There he is,' don't pay any attention. ²²For false messiahs and false prophets will rise up and perform miraculous signs and wonders so as to deceive, if possible, even God's chosen ones. ²³Watch out! I have warned you!

²⁴"At that time, after those horrible days end,

the sun will be darkened,
   the moon will not give light,
²⁵ the stars will fall from the sky,
   and the powers of heaven will be shaken.*

²⁶Then everyone will see the Son of Man arrive on the clouds with great power and glory.* ²⁷And he will send forth his angels to gather together his chosen ones from all over the world—from the farthest ends of the earth and heaven.

²⁸"Now, learn a lesson from the fig tree. When its buds become tender and its leaves begin to sprout, you know without being told that summer is near. ²⁹Just so, when you see the events I've described beginning to happen, you can be sure that his return is very near, right at the door. ³⁰I assure you, this generation* will not pass from the scene until all these events have taken place. ³¹Heaven and earth will disappear, but my words will remain forever.

³²"However, no one knows the day or hour when these things will happen, not even the angels in heaven or the Son himself. Only the Father knows. ³³And since you don't know when they will happen, stay alert and keep watch.*

13:6 Greek name, saying, 'I am.' 13:9 Or This will be your testimony against them. 13:14 Greek the abomination of desolation. See Dan 9:27; 11:31; 12:11. 13:15 Greek on the roof. 13:24-25 See Isa 13:10; 34:4; Joel 2:10. 13:26 See Dan 7:13. 13:30 Or this age, or this nation. 13:33 Some manuscripts add and pray.

My Daily Worship

— *September 22* —

WORSHIP AND YOUR WEALTH

MARK 12:35–13:37

*He called his disciples to him and said, "I assure you, this poor widow has given more
than all the others have given. For they gave a tiny part of their surplus,
but she, poor as she is, has given everything she has" (12:43–44).*

[i reflect]

You don't need a Ph.D. in economics to know that it takes a chunk of money to live these days. We have basic needs: food, clothing, shelter. Paying taxes isn't optional. What about transportation, insurance, education costs, and saving for retirement? Pay for all the necessities (and maybe a small luxury every now and then) and watch your checking account balance drop precariously toward the red numbers.

So the million-dollar question is: Why would anyone in his or her right mind put money in a church offering plate? Or write out a check for world missions? We know the answer: How we handle money is perhaps the single best indicator of what we really believe. As the German theologian Helmut Thielicke once wisely observed, "Our pocketbooks have more to do with heaven and also with hell than our hymnbooks."

Jesus watched worshiper after worshiper come into the Temple and give God a few financial leftovers. It didn't cost these people anything. Then he noticed a destitute widow give her last two coins. There's no indication that she gave in order to get. Rather, it was a quiet act of love, a bold step of faith. If this life is all there is, she was nuts. If it really is possible to store up treasure in heaven (Matthew 6:19–21), she was a spiritual and financial genius.

What does handling of your material wealth today say about your spiritual health? Does it reflect a thankful heart absorbed with God and the business of God? Ponder the words of Amy Carmichael, "One can give without loving, but one cannot love without giving." Consider the wisdom of John Wesley, "When I have money, I get rid of it quickly lest it find a way into my heart."

Worship God today with your wealth—make an anonymous donation to your church or local charity.

[i pray]

*Search my heart, Lord, and examine my attitudes about wealth. Show me new ways I can worship
you by being generous. Remind me that you've blessed me so I can be a blessing.*

[i respond]

Look carefully at your checkbook register. Notice where your money is going. What do your spending habits say about you? About the worthiness of God and his work?

[34]"The coming of the Son of Man can be compared with that of a man who left home to go on a trip. He gave each of his employees instructions about the work they were to do, and he told the gatekeeper to watch for his return. [35]So keep a sharp lookout! For you do not know when the homeowner will return— at evening, midnight, early dawn, or late daybreak. [36]Don't let him find you sleeping when he arrives without warning. [37]What I say to you I say to everyone: Watch for his return!"

Jesus Anointed at Bethany

14 It was now two days before the Passover celebration and the Festival of Unleavened Bread. The leading priests and the teachers of religious law were still looking for an opportunity to capture Jesus secretly and put him to death. [2]"But not during the Passover," they agreed, "or there will be a riot."

[3]Meanwhile, Jesus was in Bethany at the home of Simon, a man who had leprosy. During supper, a woman came in with a beautiful jar of expensive perfume.* She broke the seal and poured the perfume over his head. [4]Some of those at the table were indignant. "Why was this expensive perfume wasted?" they asked. [5]"She could have sold it for a small fortune* and given the money to the poor!" And they scolded her harshly.

[6]But Jesus replied, "Leave her alone. Why berate her for doing such a good thing to me? [7]You will always have the poor among you, and you can help them whenever you want to. But I will not be here with you much longer. [8]She has done what she could and has anointed my body for burial ahead of time. [9]I assure you, wherever the Good News is preached throughout the world, this woman's deed will be talked about in her memory."

Judas Agrees to Betray Jesus

[10]Then Judas Iscariot, one of the twelve disciples, went to the leading priests to arrange to betray Jesus to them. [11]The leading priests were delighted when they heard why he had come, and they promised him a reward. So he began looking for the right time and place to betray Jesus.

The Last Supper

[12]On the first day of the Festival of Unleavened Bread (the day the Passover lambs were sacrificed), Jesus' disciples asked him, "Where do you want us to go to prepare the Passover supper?"

[13]So Jesus sent two of them into Jerusalem to make the arrangements. "As you go into the city," he told them, "a man carrying a pitcher of water will meet you. Follow him. [14]At the house he enters, say to the owner, 'The Teacher asks, Where is the guest room where I can eat the Passover meal with my disciples?' [15]He will take you upstairs to a large room that is already set up. That is the place; go ahead and prepare our supper there." [16]So the two disciples went on ahead into the city and found everything just as Jesus had said, and they prepared the Passover supper there.

[17]In the evening Jesus arrived with the twelve disciples. [18]As they were sitting around the table eating, Jesus said, "The truth is, one of you will betray me, one of you who is here eating with me."

[19]Greatly distressed, one by one they began to ask him, "I'm not the one, am I?"

[20]He replied, "It is one of you twelve, one who is eating with me now.* [21]For I, the Son of Man, must die, as the Scriptures declared long ago. But how terrible it will be for my betrayer. Far better for him if he had never been born!"

[22]As they were eating, Jesus took a loaf of bread and asked God's blessing on it. Then he broke it in pieces and gave it to the disciples, saying, "Take it, for this is my body."

[23]And he took a cup of wine and gave thanks to God for it. He gave it to them, and they all drank from it. [24]And he said to them, "This is my blood, poured out for many, sealing the covenant* between God and his

---

14:3 Greek *an alabaster jar of expensive ointment, pure nard.* 14:5 Greek *300 denarii.* A denarius was the equivalent of a full day's wage. 14:20 Or *one who is dipping bread into the bowl with me.* 14:24 Some manuscripts read *the new covenant.*

people. [25]I solemnly declare that I will not drink wine again until that day when I drink it new in the Kingdom of God." [26]Then they sang a hymn and went out to the Mount of Olives.

JESUS PREDICTS PETER'S DENIAL

[27]"All of you will desert me," Jesus told them. "For the Scriptures say,

'God* will strike the Shepherd,
and the sheep will be scattered.'*

[28]But after I am raised from the dead, I will go ahead of you to Galilee and meet you there."

[29]Peter said to him, "Even if everyone else deserts you, I never will."

[30]"Peter," Jesus replied, "the truth is, this very night, before the rooster crows twice, you will deny me three times."

[31]"No!" Peter insisted. "Not even if I have to die with you! I will never deny you!" And all the others vowed the same.

JESUS PRAYS IN GETHSEMANE

[32]And they came to an olive grove called Gethsemane, and Jesus said, "Sit here while I go and pray." [33]He took Peter, James, and John with him, and he began to be filled with horror and deep distress. [34]He told them, "My soul is crushed with grief to the point of death. Stay here and watch with me."

[35]He went on a little farther and fell face down on the ground. He prayed that, if it were possible, the awful hour awaiting him might pass him by. [36]"Abba,* Father," he said, "everything is possible for you. Please take this cup of suffering away from me. Yet I want your will, not mine."

[37]Then he returned and found the disciples asleep. "Simon!" he said to Peter. "Are you asleep? Couldn't you stay awake and watch with me even one hour? [38]Keep alert and pray. Otherwise temptation will overpower you. For though the spirit is willing enough, the body is weak."

[39]Then Jesus left them again and prayed, repeating his pleadings. [40]Again he returned to them and found them sleeping, for they just couldn't keep their eyes open. And they didn't know what to say.

[41]When he returned to them the third time, he said, "Still sleeping? Still resting?* Enough! The time has come. I, the Son of Man, am betrayed into the hands of sinners. [42]Up, let's be going. See, my betrayer is here!"

JESUS IS BETRAYED AND ARRESTED

[43]And immediately, as he said this, Judas, one of the twelve disciples, arrived with a mob that was armed with swords and clubs. They had been sent out by the leading priests, the teachers of religious law, and the other leaders. [44]Judas had given them a prearranged signal: "You will know which one to arrest when I go over and give him the kiss of greeting. Then you can take him away under guard."

[45]As soon as they arrived, Judas walked up to Jesus. "Teacher!" he exclaimed, and gave him the kiss. [46]Then the others grabbed Jesus and arrested him. [47]But someone pulled out a sword and slashed off an ear of the high priest's servant.

[48]Jesus asked them, "Am I some dangerous criminal, that you come armed with swords and clubs to arrest me? [49]Why didn't you arrest me in the Temple? I was there teaching every day. But these things are happening to fulfill what the Scriptures say about me."

[50]Meanwhile, all his disciples deserted him and ran away. [51]There was a young man following along behind, clothed only in a linen nightshirt. When the mob tried to grab him, [52]they tore off his clothes, but he escaped and ran away naked.

JESUS BEFORE THE COUNCIL

[53]Jesus was led to the high priest's home where the leading priests, other leaders, and teachers of religious law had gathered. [54]Meanwhile,

14:27a Greek I.   14:27b Zech 13:7.   14:36 *Abba* is an Aramaic term for "father."   14:41 Or *Sleep on, take your rest.*

Peter followed far behind and then slipped inside the gates of the high priest's courtyard. For a while he sat with the guards, warming himself by the fire.

55Inside, the leading priests and the entire high council* were trying to find witnesses who would testify against Jesus, so they could put him to death. But their efforts were in vain. 56Many false witnesses spoke against him, but they contradicted each other. 57Finally, some men stood up to testify against him with this lie: 58"We heard him say, 'I will destroy this Temple made with human hands, and in three days I will build another, made without human hands.'" 59But even then they didn't get their stories straight!

60Then the high priest stood up before the others and asked Jesus, "Well, aren't you going to answer these charges? What do you have to say for yourself?" 61Jesus made no reply. Then the high priest asked him, "Are you the Messiah, the Son of the blessed God?"

62Jesus said, "I am, and you will see me, the Son of Man, sitting at God's right hand in the place of power and coming back on the clouds of heaven."*

63Then the high priest tore his clothing to show his horror and said, "Why do we need other witnesses? 64You have all heard his blasphemy. What is your verdict?" And they all condemned him to death.

65Then some of them began to spit at him, and they blindfolded him and hit his face with their fists. "Who hit you that time, you prophet?" they jeered. And even the guards were hitting him as they led him away.

PETER DENIES JESUS

66Meanwhile, Peter was below in the courtyard. One of the servant girls who worked for the high priest 67noticed Peter warming himself at the fire. She looked at him closely and then said, "You were one of those with Jesus, the Nazarene."

68Peter denied it. "I don't know what you're talking about," he said, and he went out into the entryway. Just then, a rooster crowed.*

69The servant girl saw him standing there and began telling the others, "That man is definitely one of them!" 70Peter denied it again.

A little later some other bystanders began saying to Peter, "You must be one of them because you are from Galilee."

71Peter said, "I swear by God, I don't know this man you're talking about." 72And immediately the rooster crowed the second time. Suddenly, Jesus' words flashed through Peter's mind: "Before the rooster crows twice, you will deny me three times." And he broke down and cried.

JESUS' TRIAL BEFORE PILATE

15 Very early in the morning the leading priests, other leaders, and teachers of religious law—the entire high council*—met to discuss their next step. They bound Jesus and took him to Pilate, the Roman governor.

2Pilate asked Jesus, "Are you the King of the Jews?"

Jesus replied, "Yes, it is as you say."

3Then the leading priests accused him of many crimes, 4and Pilate asked him, "Aren't you going to say something? What about all these charges against you?" 5But Jesus said nothing, much to Pilate's surprise.

6Now it was the governor's custom to release one prisoner each year at Passover time—anyone the people requested. 7One of the prisoners at that time was Barabbas, convicted along with others for murder during an insurrection. 8The mob began to crowd in toward Pilate, asking him to release a prisoner as usual. 9"Should I give you the King of the Jews?" Pilate asked. 10(For he realized by now that the leading priests had arrested Jesus out of envy.) 11But at this point the leading priests stirred up the mob to demand the release of Barabbas instead of Jesus. 12"But if I release Barabbas," Pilate asked them, "what should I do with this man you call the King of the Jews?"

14:55 Greek *the Sanhedrin*. 14:62 See Ps 110:1; Dan 7:13. 14:68 Some manuscripts do not include *Just then, a rooster crowed*. 15:1 Greek *the Sanhedrin*; also in 15:43.

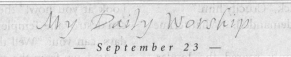

OUR HEROIC VICTIM

MARK 14:1–72

*"Abba, Father," he said, "everything is possible for you. Please take this cup
of suffering away from me. Yet I want your will, not mine" (14:36).*

[i reflect]

We look upon this agonizing scene in Gethsemane like we might gawk at a train wreck. It is stomach-turning and riveting, all at the same time. On the one hand, disasters—whatever form they take—*always* devastate lives. On the other hand, they almost always produce heroes. In this life-and-death moment, Christ is both.

He is about to become the ultimate "innocent victim," beaten senseless by a band of bored, brutal soldiers, then executed in cold blood. And why? For what crime? For speaking words of grace and truth.

But this kneeling figure, covered in blood, sweat, and tears, is also a hero of epic—no, make that *eternal*—proportions. His unselfish courage will make salvation possible for all. He will not only bear the sins of the world, but, as he hangs on that Roman cross, he will "be the offering for our sin" (2 Corinthians 5:21).

Jesus has willingly volunteered for this grimmest of duties. But who can fault him for the dread and horror that descends on his soul when the moment arrives?

Author Ken Gire in his book *Moments with the Savior* describes the scene well: "His hands are no longer clutching the grass in despair. They are no longer clasping each other in prayer. They are raised toward heaven, reaching for the cup from his Father's hand. And though it is a terrible cup, brimming with the wrath of God for the ferment of sin from centuries past and centuries yet to come, and though it is a cup he fears, he takes it. Because more than he fears the cup, he loves the hand from which it comes."

Today, worship Christ in two ways: first, by thanking him for his sacrifice, and second, by also living sacrificially yourself.

[i pray]

*Jesus, give me an ever-deepening appreciation for what you have done for me. I want
my whole life to be a worshipful response to who you are and how you have loved.*

[i respond]

Look for crosses today. Count them. But more than that, let each one prompt a pause in which you thank the Lord for his selfless sacrifice for you.

¹³They shouted back, "Crucify him!"

¹⁴"Why?" Pilate demanded. "What crime has he committed?"

But the crowd only roared the louder, "Crucify him!"

¹⁵So Pilate, anxious to please the crowd, released Barabbas to them. He ordered Jesus flogged with a lead-tipped whip, then turned him over to the Roman soldiers to crucify him.

THE SOLDIERS MOCK JESUS

¹⁶The soldiers took him into their headquarters* and called out the entire battalion. ¹⁷They dressed him in a purple robe and made a crown of long, sharp thorns and put it on his head. ¹⁸Then they saluted, yelling, "Hail! King of the Jews!" ¹⁹And they beat him on the head with a stick, spit on him, and dropped to their knees in mock worship. ²⁰When they were finally tired of mocking him, they took off the purple robe and put his own clothes on him again. Then they led him away to be crucified.

THE CRUCIFIXION

²¹A man named Simon, who was from Cyrene,* was coming in from the country just then, and they forced him to carry Jesus' cross. (Simon is the father of Alexander and Rufus.) ²²And they brought Jesus to a place called Golgotha (which means Skull Hill). ²³They offered him wine drugged with myrrh, but he refused it. ²⁴Then they nailed him to the cross. They gambled for his clothes, throwing dice* to decide who would get them.

²⁵It was nine o'clock in the morning when the crucifixion took place. ²⁶A signboard was fastened to the cross above Jesus' head, announcing the charge against him. It read: "The King of the Jews." ²⁷Two criminals were crucified with him, their crosses on either side of his.* ²⁹And the people passing by shouted abuse, shaking their heads in mockery. "Ha! Look at you now!" they yelled at him. "You can destroy the Temple and rebuild it in three days, can you? ³⁰Well then, save yourself and come down from the cross!"

³¹The leading priests and teachers of religious law also mocked Jesus. "He saved others," they scoffed, "but he can't save himself! ³²Let this Messiah, this king of Israel, come down from the cross so we can see it and believe him!" Even the two criminals who were being crucified with Jesus ridiculed him.

THE DEATH OF JESUS

³³At noon, darkness fell across the whole land until three o'clock. ³⁴Then, at that time Jesus called out with a loud voice, "*Eloi, Eloi, lema sabachthani?*" which means, "My God, my God, why have you forsaken me?"*

³⁵Some of the bystanders misunderstood and thought he was calling for the prophet Elijah. ³⁶One of them ran and filled a sponge with sour wine, holding it up to him on a stick so he could drink. "Leave him alone. Let's see whether Elijah will come and take him down!" he said.

³⁷Then Jesus uttered another loud cry and breathed his last. ³⁸And the curtain in the Temple was torn in two, from top to bottom. ³⁹When the Roman officer who stood facing him saw how he had died, he exclaimed, "Truly, this was the Son of God!"

⁴⁰Some women were there, watching from a distance, including Mary Magdalene, Mary (the mother of James the younger and of Joseph*), and Salome. ⁴¹They had been followers of Jesus and had cared for him while he was in Galilee. Then they and many other women had come with him to Jerusalem.

THE BURIAL OF JESUS

⁴²This all happened on Friday, the day of preparation,* the day before the Sabbath. As evening approached, ⁴³an honored member of the high council, Joseph from Arimathea

---

15:16 Greek *the courtyard, which is the praetorium.* **15:21** *Cyrene* was a city in northern Africa. **15:24** Greek *casting lots.* See Ps 22:18. **15:27** Some manuscripts add verse 28, *And the Scripture was fulfilled that said, "He was counted among those who were rebels."* See Isa 53:12. **15:34** Ps 22:1. **15:40** Greek *Joses;* also in 15:47. See Matt 27:56. **15:42** Greek *on the day of preparation.*

My Daily Worship

— *September 24* —

THE TORN CURTAIN

MARK 15:1–16:20

Then Jesus uttered another loud cry and breathed his last. And the curtain
in the Temple was torn in two, from top to bottom (15:37–38).

[i reflect]

Call it what it was. Obscene. Sickening. An ancient R-rated scene. A brutalized rabbi skewered to wood, bleeding, suffocating, crying out. Mockers laughed while mourners wept.

Writing about the crucifixion of Christ (and its eternal implications), C. S. Lewis noted in his book *The Four Loves*: "[God] creates the universe, already foreseeing . . . the buzzing cloud of flies about the cross, the flayed back pressed against the uneven stake, the nails driven through the mesial nerves, the repeated torture of back and arms as it is time after time, for breath's sake, hitched up. If I may dare the biological image, God is a 'host' who deliberately creates his own parasites; causes us to be that we may exploit and 'take advantage of' him. Herein is love."

Wrestle with that thought: God creates the human race knowing we will rebel, knowing we will put him (literally) through hell, knowing we will cost him the priceless life of his innocent Son.

But he implements the plan anyway. And the result? At the worst of moments, a mysterious phenomenon occurs. Scripture records that the veil inside the Jewish Temple is torn from top to bottom. This curtain is, for all practical purposes, the "wall," that signifies humanity's separation from God. The thick tapestry that keeps humans out of the "most holy place" is inexplicably ripped down the middle. Suddenly it is no more.

Herein is love. And here is the reason we worship. The torn curtain is why today we can worship our great God, talk to him, sing to him, praise him. It is why we dance with joy. It is why we lie face down before our Creator. He took the most horrifying incident in the universe and turned it into humanity's most hopeful hour. What an amazing God!

Thank God that because of the Cross, because of the torn curtain, you are in his presence right now. Spend a few moments there in grateful praise.

[i pray]

Father in heaven, let my thoughts be captured and let my life be propelled by
the love you showed at the cross. Thank you for opening a way of access
to you. You demand and you deserve my soul, my life, my all.

[i respond]

Sing with all your heart Isaac Watt's classic hymn, "When I Survey the Wondrous Cross," or sing the contemporary adaptation/arrangement "The Wonderful Cross" by J. D. Walt, Isaac Watts, Jesse Reeves, and Chris Tomlin.

(who was waiting for the Kingdom of God to come), gathered his courage and went to Pilate to ask for Jesus' body. [44]Pilate couldn't believe that Jesus was already dead, so he called for the Roman military officer in charge and asked him. [45]The officer confirmed the fact, and Pilate told Joseph he could have the body. [46]Joseph bought a long sheet of linen cloth, and taking Jesus' body down from the cross, he wrapped it in the cloth and laid it in a tomb that had been carved out of the rock. Then he rolled a stone in front of the entrance. [47]Mary Magdalene and Mary the mother of Joseph saw where Jesus' body was laid.

THE RESURRECTION

16 The next evening, when the Sabbath ended, Mary Magdalene and Salome and Mary the mother of James went out and purchased burial spices to put on Jesus' body. [2]Very early on Sunday morning,* just at sunrise, they came to the tomb. [3]On the way they were discussing who would roll the stone away from the entrance to the tomb. [4]But when they arrived, they looked up and saw that the stone—a very large one—had already been rolled aside. [5]So they entered the tomb, and there on the right sat a young man clothed in a white robe. The women were startled, [6]but the angel said, "Do not be so surprised. You are looking for Jesus, the Nazarene, who was crucified. He isn't here! He has been raised from the dead! Look, this is where they laid his body. [7]Now go and give this message to his disciples, including Peter: Jesus is going ahead of you to Galilee. You will see him there, just as he told you before he died!" [8]The women fled from the tomb, trembling and bewildered, saying nothing to anyone because they were too frightened to talk.*

[Shorter Ending of Mark]

Then they reported all these instructions briefly to Peter and his companions. Afterward Jesus himself sent them out from east to west with the sacred and unfailing message of salvation that gives eternal life. Amen.

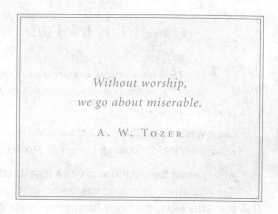

*Without worship,
we go about miserable.*

A. W. TOZER

[Longer Ending of Mark]

[9]It was early on Sunday morning when Jesus rose from the dead, and the first person who saw him was Mary Magdalene, the woman from whom he had cast out seven demons. [10]She went and found the disciples, who were grieving and weeping. [11]But when she told them that Jesus was alive and she had seen him, they didn't believe her.

[12]Afterward he appeared to two who were walking from Jerusalem into the country, but they didn't recognize him at first because he had changed his appearance. [13]When they realized who he was, they rushed back to tell the others, but no one believed them.

[14]Still later he appeared to the eleven disciples as they were eating together. He rebuked them for their unbelief—their stubborn refusal to believe those who had seen him after he had risen.

[15]And then he told them, "Go into all the world and preach the Good News to everyone, everywhere. [16]Anyone who believes and is baptized will be saved. But anyone who refuses to believe will be condemned. [17]These signs will accompany those who believe: They will cast out demons in my name, and they

---

16:2 Greek *on the first day of the week;* also in 16:9. **16:8** The most reliable early manuscripts conclude the Gospel of Mark at verse 8. Other manuscripts include various endings to the Gospel. Two of the more noteworthy endings are printed here.

will speak new languages.* [18]They will be able to handle snakes with safety, and if they drink anything poisonous, it won't hurt them. They will be able to place their hands on the sick and heal them."

[19]When the Lord Jesus had finished talking with them, he was taken up into heaven and sat down in the place of honor at God's right hand. [20]And the disciples went everywhere and preached, and the Lord worked with them, confirming what they said by many miraculous signs.

16:17 Or *new tongues; some manuscripts omit new.*

Luke

And I, the Son of Man, have come to seek and save those like him who are lost (19:10).

Just Like One of Us

It was extraordinary, yet ordinary. Amazing, yet mundane. Incredible, yet normal. The day God became a baby was unlike any other. Luke began his Gospel with Jesus' birth to demonstrate that it was the first of many ways that Jesus shared our common human existence. With precise details, the Gospel of Luke presents Jesus as the Son of Man who willingly abandoned his lofty throne in heaven to walk among us, experiencing the full range of human emotion.

Jesus tasted temptation early on and smelled the bitterness of Satan's whispered enticements to reject God. He sensed human sadness as he watched a grief-stricken widow during a funeral procession for her young son. His eyes observed the religious leaders' cruelty. His ears heard desperate cries for help. What joy he felt upon hearing the news of his disciples' successful ministry journey! And how he enjoyed welcoming the little children into his strong arms!

As God-man, he felt the sting of rejection and the pain of loneliness as his friends slept while he prayed on the night of his betrayal. On the cross, Jesus carried the shame of a world of sin on his shoulders. Every slanderous word that ever had been or ever would be spoken. Every murder. Every lie. Every prideful thought. He bore its crushing weight in his human frame for the purpose of purchasing our forgiveness with his blood.

Above all, Luke's letter reminds us why God had to become like us. Not to empathize with us. Not to pity us. But so that he might save us.

Worship Moments

- Jesus heals ten lepers and remarks about the human tendency to forget to give God praise when he works a miracle in our lives (17:11–19).

- The crowd erupts into praise when they witness Jesus healing a blind man (18:35–43).

- Jesus refers to himself as the "Son of Man" (5:24; 6:5, 22; 7:34; 9:22, 26, 44, 58; 11:30; 12:10, 40; 17:22, 24–26, 30; 18:8; 19:10; 21:27, 36; 22:22, 48, 69; 24:7).

- Luke details Jesus as the "Son of the Most High" (1:32), "Son of God" (1:35; 4:41; 22:70), and "Son of David" (18:38).

Introduction

1 Most honorable Theophilus:
Many people have written accounts about the events that took place* among us. ²They used as their source material the reports circulating among us from the early disciples and other eyewitnesses of what God has done in fulfillment of his promises. ³Having carefully investigated all of these accounts from the beginning, I have decided to write a careful summary for you, ⁴to reassure you of the truth of all you were taught.

The Birth of John the Baptist Foretold

⁵It all begins with a Jewish priest, Zechariah, who lived when Herod was king of Judea. Zechariah was a member of the priestly order of Abijah. His wife, Elizabeth, was also from the priestly line of Aaron. ⁶Zechariah and Elizabeth were righteous in God's eyes, careful to obey all of the Lord's commandments and regulations. ⁷They had no children because Elizabeth was barren, and now they were both very old.

⁸One day Zechariah was serving God in the Temple, for his order was on duty that week. ⁹As was the custom of the priests, he was chosen by lot to enter the sanctuary and burn incense in the Lord's presence. ¹⁰While the incense was being burned, a great crowd stood outside, praying.

¹¹Zechariah was in the sanctuary when an angel of the Lord appeared, standing to the right of the incense altar. ¹²Zechariah was overwhelmed with fear. ¹³But the angel said, "Don't be afraid, Zechariah! For God has heard your prayer, and your wife, Elizabeth, will bear you a son! And you are to name him John. ¹⁴You will have great joy and gladness, and many will rejoice with you at his birth, ¹⁵for he will be great in the eyes of the Lord. He must never touch wine or hard liquor, and he will be filled with the Holy Spirit, even before his birth.* ¹⁶And he will persuade many Israelites to turn to the Lord their God. ¹⁷He

will be a man with the spirit and power of Elijah, the prophet of old. He will precede the coming of the Lord, preparing the people for his arrival. He will turn the hearts of the fathers to their children, and he will change disobedient minds to accept godly wisdom."*

¹⁸Zechariah said to the angel, "How can I know this will happen? I'm an old man now, and my wife is also well along in years."

¹⁹Then the angel said, "I am Gabriel! I stand in the very presence of God. It was he who sent me to bring you this good news! ²⁰And now, since you didn't believe what I said, you won't be able to speak until the child is born. For my words will certainly come true at the proper time."

²¹Meanwhile, the people were waiting for Zechariah to come out, wondering why he was taking so long. ²²When he finally did come out, he couldn't speak to them. Then they realized from his gestures that he must have seen a vision in the Temple sanctuary.

²³He stayed at the Temple until his term of service was over, and then he returned home. ²⁴Soon afterward his wife, Elizabeth, became pregnant and went into seclusion for five months. ²⁵"How kind the Lord is!" she exclaimed. "He has taken away my disgrace of having no children!"

The Birth of Jesus Foretold

²⁶In the sixth month of Elizabeth's pregnancy, God sent the angel Gabriel to Nazareth, a village in Galilee, ²⁷to a virgin named Mary. She was engaged to be married to a man named Joseph, a descendant of King David. ²⁸Gabriel appeared to her and said, "Greetings, favored woman! The Lord is with you!*"

²⁹Confused and disturbed, Mary tried to think what the angel could mean. ³⁰"Don't be frightened, Mary," the angel told her, "for God has decided to bless you! ³¹You will become pregnant and have a son, and you are to name him Jesus. ³²He will be very great and will be called the Son of the Most High. And the Lord God will give him the throne of his ancestor

1:1 Or *have been fulfilled.* 1:15 Or *even from birth.* 1:17 See Mal 4:5-6. 1:28 Some manuscripts add *Blessed are you among women.*

David. ³³And he will reign over Israel* forever; his Kingdom will never end!"

³⁴Mary asked the angel, "But how can I have a baby? I am a virgin."

³⁵The angel replied, "The Holy Spirit will come upon you, and the power of the Most High will overshadow you. So the baby born to you will be holy, and he will be called the Son of God. ³⁶What's more, your relative Elizabeth has become pregnant in her old age! People used to say she was barren, but she's already in her sixth month. ³⁷For nothing is impossible with God."

³⁸Mary responded, "I am the Lord's servant, and I am willing to accept whatever he wants. May everything you have said come true." And then the angel left.

MARY VISITS ELIZABETH

³⁹A few days later Mary hurried to the hill country of Judea, to the town ⁴⁰where Zechariah lived. She entered the house and greeted Elizabeth. ⁴¹At the sound of Mary's greeting, Elizabeth's child leaped within her, and Elizabeth was filled with the Holy Spirit.

⁴²Elizabeth gave a glad cry and exclaimed to Mary, "You are blessed by God above all other women, and your child is blessed. ⁴³What an honor this is, that the mother of my Lord should visit me! ⁴⁴When you came in and greeted me, my baby jumped for joy the instant I heard your voice! ⁴⁵You are blessed, because you believed that the Lord would do what he said."

THE MAGNIFICAT: MARY'S SONG OF PRAISE

⁴⁶Mary responded,

"Oh, how I praise the Lord.
⁴⁷   How I rejoice in God my Savior!
⁴⁸ For he took notice of his lowly servant
         girl,
      and now generation after generation
         will call me blessed.
⁴⁹ For he, the Mighty One, is holy,

and he has done great things for me.
⁵⁰ His mercy goes on from generation to
         generation,
      to all who fear him.
⁵¹ His mighty arm does tremendous things!
      How he scatters the proud and haughty
         ones!
⁵² He has taken princes from their thrones
      and exalted the lowly.
⁵³ He has satisfied the hungry with good
         things
      and sent the rich away with empty
         hands.
⁵⁴ And how he has helped his servant Israel!
      He has not forgotten his promise to be
         merciful.
⁵⁵ For he promised our ancestors—Abraham
      and his children—
      to be merciful to them forever."

⁵⁶Mary stayed with Elizabeth about three months and then went back to her own home.

THE BIRTH OF JOHN THE BAPTIST

⁵⁷Now it was time for Elizabeth's baby to be born, and it was a boy. ⁵⁸The word spread quickly to her neighbors and relatives that the Lord had been very kind to her, and everyone rejoiced with her.

⁵⁹When the baby was eight days old, all the relatives and friends came for the circumcision ceremony. They wanted to name him Zechariah, after his father. ⁶⁰But Elizabeth said, "No! His name is John!"

⁶¹"What?" they exclaimed. "There is no one in all your family by that name." ⁶²So they asked the baby's father, communicating to him by making gestures. ⁶³He motioned for a writing tablet, and to everyone's surprise he wrote, "His name is John!" ⁶⁴Instantly Zechariah could speak again, and he began praising God.

⁶⁵Wonder fell upon the whole neighborhood, and the news of what had happened spread throughout the Judean hills. ⁶⁶Every-

1:33 Greek *over the house of Jacob.*

My Daily Worship

— September 25 —

GOD AND WE, INC.

LUKE 1:1–80

How I rejoice in God my Savior! For he took notice of his lowly servant girl,
and now generation after generation will call me blessed (1:47–48).

[i reflect]

Mary was right. Two thousand years after she lived, we still remember this humble village girl and wonder at how blessed she was to be chosen by God to become the mother of his Son.

All along, God has had a way of using ordinary people in extraordinary ways to further his plans. Paul commented about one early congregation, "Few of you were wise in the world's eyes, or powerful, or wealthy when God called you" (1 Corinthians 1:26). And ever since, the church has advanced largely through the work of humble folk.

In the fifth century, for example, the son of a minor church official in Britain was captured by pirates and sold as a slave in Ireland. He escaped several years later, but eventually returned to Ireland to preach the gospel. By the time of this ex-slave's death, practically the entire island had chosen Christianity. Today he is called Saint Patrick.

In the seventeenth century, a former soldier and office clerk named Nicholas Herman joined a religious order in France and spent decades working in the kitchen. His status was low, but that didn't stop him from writing the still-influential *Practice of the Presence of God* under his adopted name of Brother Lawrence.

At one time there was a fad for Christian businesspersons to name their companies "Lord & So-and-so" (the businessperson being "So-and-so") to indicate that God was their "senior partner." Perhaps we should not picture God as the senior partner in our enterprise; instead, we should see ourselves as the junior partners in *his*. While we may consider ourselves as less wealthy, less intelligent, or less highly placed than others, such conditions in no way prevent God from choosing us to partner with him in doing wonderful works. It's a blessed opportunity indeed.

Join God in carrying out his bidding throughout your regular routine today. Contemplate the fact that you are no longer ordinary; you are *extraordinary* because you worship an extraordinary God!

[i pray]

Sometimes I feel so unimportant, God, like I'm invisible. Help me not to focus on me,
but on you. Help me not to care who knows about me, but instead to desire the joy
of working alongside you as you move your glorious plan toward completion.

[i respond]

The book *Experiencing God,* by Henry Blackaby, became popular a few years ago with its challenging thesis that people ought to find out where God is acting and join in. If you haven't already, pick up a copy of this book and use it to change your thinking about "partnering" with God.

one who heard about it reflected on these events and asked, "I wonder what this child will turn out to be? For the hand of the Lord is surely upon him in a special way."

ZECHARIAH'S PROPHECY

[67] Then his father, Zechariah, was filled with the Holy Spirit and gave this prophecy:

[68] "Praise the Lord, the God of Israel,
because he has visited his people and
redeemed them.
[69] He has sent us a mighty Savior
from the royal line of his servant David,
[70] just as he promised
through his holy prophets long ago.
[71] Now we will be saved from our enemies
and from all who hate us.
[72] He has been merciful to our ancestors
by remembering his sacred covenant
with them,
[73] the covenant he gave to our ancestor
Abraham.
[74] We have been rescued from our enemies,
so we can serve God without fear,
[75] in holiness and righteousness forever.

[76] "And you, my little son,
will be called the prophet of the Most
High,
because you will prepare the way for the
Lord.
[77] You will tell his people how to find
salvation
through forgiveness of their sins.
[78] Because of God's tender mercy,
the light from heaven is about to break
upon us,
[79] to give light to those who sit in darkness
and in the shadow of death,
and to guide us to the path of peace."

[80] John grew up and became strong in spirit. Then he lived out in the wilderness until he began his public ministry to Israel.

THE BIRTH OF JESUS

2 At that time the Roman emperor, Augustus, decreed that a census should be taken throughout the Roman Empire. [2](This was the first census taken when Quirinius was governor of Syria.) [3]All returned to their own towns to register for this census. [4]And because Joseph was a descendant of King David, he had to go to Bethlehem in Judea, David's ancient home. He traveled there from the village of Nazareth in Galilee. [5]He took with him Mary, his fiancée, who was obviously pregnant by this time.

[6]And while they were there, the time came for her baby to be born. [7]She gave birth to her first child, a son. She wrapped him snugly in strips of cloth and laid him in a manger, because there was no room for them in the village inn.

THE SHEPHERDS AND ANGELS

[8]That night some shepherds were in the fields outside the village, guarding their flocks of sheep. [9]Suddenly, an angel of the Lord appeared among them, and the radiance of the Lord's glory surrounded them. They were terribly frightened, [10]but the angel reassured them. "Don't be afraid!" he said. "I bring you good news of great joy for everyone! [11]The Savior—yes, the Messiah, the Lord—has been born tonight in Bethlehem, the city of David! [12]And this is how you will recognize him: You will find a baby lying in a manger, wrapped snugly in strips of cloth!"

[13]Suddenly, the angel was joined by a vast host of others—the armies of heaven—praising God:

[14] "Glory to God in the highest heaven,
and peace on earth to all whom God
favors.*"

[15]When the angels had returned to heaven, the shepherds said to each other, "Come on, let's go to Bethlehem! Let's see this wonderful

2:14 Or *and peace on earth for all those pleasing God.* Some manuscripts read *and peace on earth, goodwill among people.*

My Daily Worship

— *September 26* —

HOMESICK FOR A PLACE
WE'VE NEVER BEEN

LUKE 2:1–51

She gave birth to her first child, a son. She wrapped him snugly in strips of cloth and laid him in a manger, because there was no room for them in the village inn (2:7).

[i reflect]

"If I find in myself a desire which no experience in this world can satisfy," said C. S. Lewis, "the most probable explanation is that I was made for another world." Many of us can attest to this same longing for heaven. We have moments (and they may occur at the oddest times, even when things are going well for us) when somehow, down deep, we think: *I don't belong here. This world is not my home.*

We can take comfort that it was the same way for Jesus. He was in the world, the world was made by him, but the world didn't recognize him for who he was (John 1:10). His displacement started when his mother gave birth to him in a stable because there was no room for them at the inn. Later he would say that he had no place to lay his head (Luke 9:58). Finally, in a parallel to his displaced birth, he would be crucified outside the walls of Jerusalem. Our Lord was an unwelcome stranger on this earth.

Now Jesus is at home in his Father's mansion, and he is preparing rooms for us there. Sojourners through this life, we are justified in every bit of longing we feel for heaven. Of course, God has a purpose for us on earth, just as he had for Jesus, and we must carry our cross to the end. And along the way, as it is possible and appropriate, we may enjoy the limited good this world has to offer. But the time will come—soon—when the door will open and we will hear the Father say, "Welcome home, my dear, dear child."

Allow the words of this familiar account of the Lord's birth to cause you to worship the One who does not belong to this world. Let it remind you that this is not your home, either.

[i pray]

I'm not at home in this world, Lord, and I don't want to be. May I make of my pilgrimage in these lower regions all that I ought, but never let me consider myself a permanent resident here. Where you are is where I belong.

[i respond]

Journal about what it means to you that Jesus left heaven and pitched a tent among us. Write also about when you have felt yourself to be an alien set loose on the face of the earth and have suffered the sharpest pangs of homesickness.

thing that has happened, which the Lord has told us about."

¹⁶They ran to the village and found Mary and Joseph. And there was the baby, lying in the manger. ¹⁷Then the shepherds told everyone what had happened and what the angel had said to them about this child. ¹⁸All who heard the shepherds' story were astonished, ¹⁹but Mary quietly treasured these things in her heart and thought about them often. ²⁰The shepherds went back to their fields and flocks, glorifying and praising God for what the angels had told them, and because they had seen the child, just as the angel had said.

JESUS IS PRESENTED IN THE TEMPLE

²¹Eight days later, when the baby was circumcised, he was named Jesus, the name given him by the angel even before he was conceived.

²²Then it was time for the purification offering, as required by the law of Moses after the birth of a child; so his parents took him to Jerusalem to present him to the Lord. ²³The law of the Lord says, "If a woman's first child is a boy, he must be dedicated to the Lord."* ²⁴So they offered a sacrifice according to what was required in the law of the Lord—"either a pair of turtledoves or two young pigeons."*

THE PROPHECY OF SIMEON

²⁵Now there was a man named Simeon who lived in Jerusalem. He was a righteous man and very devout. He was filled with the Holy Spirit, and he eagerly expected the Messiah to come and rescue Israel. ²⁶The Holy Spirit had revealed to him that he would not die until he had seen the Lord's Messiah. ²⁷That day the Spirit led him to the Temple. So when Mary and Joseph came to present the baby Jesus to the Lord as the law required, ²⁸Simeon was there. He took the child in his arms and praised God, saying,

²⁹ "Lord, now I can die in peace!
    As you promised me,

³⁰ I have seen the Savior
³¹   you have given to all people.
³² He is a light to reveal God to the nations,
    and he is the glory of your people Israel!"

³³Joseph and Mary were amazed at what was being said about Jesus. ³⁴Then Simeon blessed them, and he said to Mary, "This child will be rejected by many in Israel, and it will be their undoing. But he will be the greatest joy to many others. ³⁵Thus, the deepest thoughts of many hearts will be revealed. And a sword will pierce your very soul."

THE PROPHECY OF ANNA

³⁶Anna, a prophet, was also there in the Temple. She was the daughter of Phanuel, of the tribe of Asher, and was very old. She was a widow, for her husband had died when they had been married only seven years. ³⁷She was now eighty-four years old. She never left the Temple but stayed there day and night, worshiping God with fasting and prayer. ³⁸She came along just as Simeon was talking with Mary and Joseph, and she began praising God. She talked about Jesus to everyone who had been waiting for the promised King to come and deliver Jerusalem.

³⁹When Jesus' parents had fulfilled all the requirements of the law of the Lord, they returned home to Nazareth in Galilee. ⁴⁰There the child grew up healthy and strong. He was filled with wisdom beyond his years, and God placed his special favor upon him.

JESUS SPEAKS WITH THE TEACHERS

⁴¹Every year Jesus' parents went to Jerusalem for the Passover festival. ⁴²When Jesus was twelve years old, they attended the festival as usual. ⁴³After the celebration was over, they started home to Nazareth, but Jesus stayed behind in Jerusalem. His parents didn't miss him at first, ⁴⁴because they assumed he was with friends among the other travelers. But

2:23 Exod 13:2. 2:24 Lev 12:8.

when he didn't show up that evening, they started to look for him among their relatives and friends. ⁴⁵When they couldn't find him, they went back to Jerusalem to search for him there. ⁴⁶Three days later they finally discovered him. He was in the Temple, sitting among the religious teachers, discussing deep questions with them. ⁴⁷And all who heard him were amazed at his understanding and his answers.

⁴⁸His parents didn't know what to think. "Son!" his mother said to him. "Why have you done this to us? Your father and I have been frantic, searching for you everywhere."

⁴⁹"But why did you need to search?" he asked. "You should have known that I would be in my Father's house."* ⁵⁰But they didn't understand what he meant.

⁵¹Then he returned to Nazareth with them and was obedient to them; and his mother stored all these things in her heart. ⁵²So Jesus grew both in height and in wisdom, and he was loved by God and by all who knew him.

John the Baptist Prepares the Way

3 It was now the fifteenth year of the reign of Tiberius, the Roman emperor. Pilate was governor over Judea; Herod Antipas was ruler* over Galilee; his brother Philip was ruler* over Iturea and Traconitis; Lysanias was ruler over Abilene. ²Annas and Caiaphas were the high priests. At this time a message from God came to John son of Zechariah, who was living out in the wilderness. ³Then John went from place to place on both sides of the Jordan River, preaching that people should be baptized to show that they had turned from their sins and turned to God to be forgiven.* ⁴Isaiah had spoken of John when he said,

"He is a voice shouting in the wilderness:
'Prepare a pathway for the Lord's coming!
Make a straight road for him!
⁵ Fill in the valleys,

and level the mountains and hills!
Straighten the curves,
and smooth out the rough places!
⁶ And then all people will see
the salvation sent from God.'"*

⁷Here is a sample of John's preaching to the crowds that came for baptism: "You brood of snakes! Who warned you to flee God's coming judgment? ⁸Prove by the way you live that you have really turned from your sins and turned to God. Don't just say, 'We're safe—we're the descendants of Abraham.' That proves nothing. God can change these stones here into children of Abraham. ⁹Even now the ax of God's judgment is poised, ready to sever your roots. Yes, every tree that does not produce good fruit will be chopped down and thrown into the fire."

¹⁰The crowd asked, "What should we do?"

¹¹John replied, "If you have two coats, give one to the poor. If you have food, share it with those who are hungry."

¹²Even corrupt tax collectors came to be baptized and asked, "Teacher, what should we do?"

¹³"Show your honesty," he replied. "Make sure you collect no more taxes than the Roman government requires you to."

¹⁴"What should we do?" asked some soldiers.

John replied, "Don't extort money, and don't accuse people of things you know they didn't do. And be content with your pay."

¹⁵Everyone was expecting the Messiah to come soon, and they were eager to know whether John might be the Messiah. ¹⁶John answered their questions by saying, "I baptize with* water; but someone is coming soon who is greater than I am—so much greater that I am not even worthy to be his slave.* He will baptize you with the Holy Spirit and with fire.* ¹⁷He is ready to separate the chaff from the grain with his winnowing fork. Then he

2:49 Or *"Didn't you realize that I should be involved with my Father's affairs?"* **3:1a** Greek *Herod was tetrarch.* Herod Antipas was a son of King Herod. **3:1b** Greek *tetrarch;* also in 3:1c, 19. **3:3** Greek *preaching a baptism of repentance for the forgiveness of sins.* **3:4-6** Isa 40:3-5. **3:16a** Or *in.* **3:16b** Greek *to untie his sandals.* **3:16c** Or *in the Holy Spirit and in fire.*

will clean up the threshing area, storing the grain in his barn but burning the chaff with never-ending fire." [18]John used many such warnings as he announced the Good News to the people.

[19]John also publicly criticized Herod Antipas, ruler of Galilee, for marrying Herodias, his brother's wife, and for many other wrongs he had done. [20]So Herod put John in prison, adding this sin to his many others.

THE BAPTISM OF JESUS

[21]One day when the crowds were being baptized, Jesus himself was baptized. As he was praying, the heavens opened, [22]and the Holy Spirit descended on him in the form of a dove. And a voice from heaven said, "You are my beloved Son, and I am fully pleased with you.*"

THE RECORD OF JESUS' ANCESTORS

[23]Jesus was about thirty years old when he began his public ministry.

Jesus was known as the son of Joseph.
Joseph was the son of Heli.
[24]Heli was the son of Matthat.
Matthat was the son of Levi.
Levi was the son of Melki.
Melki was the son of Jannai.
Jannai was the son of Joseph.
[25]Joseph was the son of Mattathias.
Mattathias was the son of Amos.
Amos was the son of Nahum.
Nahum was the son of Esli.
Esli was the son of Naggai.
[26]Naggai was the son of Maath.
Maath was the son of Mattathias.
Mattathias was the son of Semein.
Semein was the son of Josech.
Josech was the son of Joda.
[27]Joda was the son of Joanan.
Joanan was the son of Rhesa.
Rhesa was the son of Zerubbabel.

Zerubbabel was the son of Shealtiel.
Shealtiel was the son of Neri.
[28]Neri was the son of Melki.
Melki was the son of Addi.
Addi was the son of Cosam.
Cosam was the son of Elmadam.
Elmadam was the son of Er.
[29]Er was the son of Joshua.
Joshua was the son of Eliezer.
Eliezer was the son of Jorim.
Jorim was the son of Matthat.
Matthat was the son of Levi.
[30]Levi was the son of Simeon.
Simeon was the son of Judah.
Judah was the son of Joseph.
Joseph was the son of Jonam.
Jonam was the son of Eliakim.
[31]Eliakim was the son of Melea.
Melea was the son of Menna.
Menna was the son of Mattatha.
Mattatha was the son of Nathan.
Nathan was the son of David.
[32]David was the son of Jesse.
Jesse was the son of Obed.
Obed was the son of Boaz.
Boaz was the son of Salmon.*
Salmon was the son of Nahshon.
[33]Nahshon was the son of Amminadab.
Amminadab was the son of Admin.
Admin was the son of Arni.*
Arni was the son of Hezron.
Hezron was the son of Perez.
Perez was the son of Judah.
[34]Judah was the son of Jacob.
Jacob was the son of Isaac.
Isaac was the son of Abraham.
Abraham was the son of Terah.
Terah was the son of Nahor.
[35]Nahor was the son of Serug.
Serug was the son of Reu.
Reu was the son of Peleg.
Peleg was the son of Eber.
Eber was the son of Shelah.
[36]Shelah was the son of Cainan.
Cainan was the son of Arphaxad.

3:22 Some manuscripts read *and today I have become your Father.* **3:32** Greek *Sala;* see Ruth 4:22. **3:33** *Arni* is the same person as Ram; see 1 Chr 2:9-10.

My Daily Worship

ALL CREATURES HERE BELOW

LUKE 3:1–4:13

One day when the crowds were being baptized, Jesus himself was baptized.
As he was praying, the heavens opened, and the Holy Spirit
descended on him in the form of a dove (3:21–22).

[i reflect]

J. Oswald Sanders, in *Enjoying Intimacy with God,* wrote, "We are now, and we will be in the future, only as intimate with God as we really choose to be."

Do you feel close to God right now? Do you desire to be closer to him? One way to grow closer to God is to know more about who he is. He reveals himself preeminently through Jesus.

One of the most striking characteristics of Jesus when he lived on earth was his humility. Jesus was not proud or conceited because he was the Son of the King; instead, he displayed humility from the start of his earthly ministry by submitting to baptism by John the Baptist, as we see in today's passage. Did he need to repent like other people, as baptism signified? No, the One who was fully God and fully man was completely sinless. He was baptized with all the other people because he wanted to identify with those he came to save.

Because of his humility and obedience, Jesus was accepted by the Father. As Jesus prayed, heaven was opened "and the Holy Spirit descended on him in the form of a dove." In company with this supernatural act, God announced in the overhearing of those present, "You are my beloved Son, and I am fully pleased with you" (3:22).

Though humble, Jesus is fully worthy of our worship. John, the man who baptized him, declared of Jesus, "He must become greater and greater, and I must become less and less" (John 3:30). In the same spirit, we should raise up Jesus and lower ourselves. As we do so, God will say of us, "You are my beloved son (or daughter), and I am pleased with you." This is the way to intimacy with God.

When pride and self-sufficiency bubble to the surface of your thoughts today, pause and focus on Jesus instead of yourself.

[i pray]

Jesus, I worship you because in your greatness you humbly came down from heaven, stepped down into the baptismal water, and were laid down lifeless in the tomb. And you did it all for me. Oh Lord, let my attitude always be "less of me, Lord, and more of you."

[i respond]

Imagine that your life has a "pride-o-meter," like a tachometer in a car measuring engine speed. What tends to rev up your pride-o-meter? Where is the needle pointing right now? How can you idle it back down?

Arphaxad was the son of Shem.
Shem was the son of Noah.
Noah was the son of Lamech.
[37] Lamech was the son of Methuselah.
Methuselah was the son of Enoch.
Enoch was the son of Jared.
Jared was the son of Mahalalel.
Mahalalel was the son of Kenan.
[38] Kenan was the son of Enosh.*
Enosh was the son of Seth.
Seth was the son of Adam.
Adam was the son of God.

THE TEMPTATION OF JESUS

4 Then Jesus, full of the Holy Spirit, left the Jordan River. He was led by the Spirit to go out into the wilderness, [2]where the Devil tempted him for forty days. He ate nothing all that time and was very hungry.

[3]Then the Devil said to him, "If you are the Son of God, change this stone into a loaf of bread."

[4]But Jesus told him, "No! The Scriptures say, 'People need more than bread for their life.'*"

[5]Then the Devil took him up and revealed to him all the kingdoms of the world in a moment of time. [6]The Devil told him, "I will give you the glory of these kingdoms and authority over them—because they are mine to give to anyone I please. [7]I will give it all to you if you will bow down and worship me."

[8]Jesus replied, "The Scriptures say,

'You must worship the Lord your God;
    serve only him.'*"

[9]Then the Devil took him to Jerusalem, to the highest point of the Temple, and said, "If you are the Son of God, jump off! [10]For the Scriptures say,

'He orders his angels to protect and guard
    you.
[11] And they will hold you with their hands

to keep you from striking your foot on a
    stone.'*"

[12]Jesus responded, "The Scriptures also say, 'Do not test the Lord your God.'*"

[13]When the Devil had finished tempting Jesus, he left him until the next opportunity came.

JESUS REJECTED AT NAZARETH

[14]Then Jesus returned to Galilee, filled with the Holy Spirit's power. Soon he became well known throughout the surrounding country. [15]He taught in their synagogues and was praised by everyone.

[16]When he came to the village of Nazareth, his boyhood home, he went as usual to the synagogue on the Sabbath and stood up to read the Scriptures. [17]The scroll containing the messages of Isaiah the prophet was handed to him, and he unrolled the scroll to the place where it says:

[18] "The Spirit of the Lord is upon me,
    for he has appointed me to preach Good
        News to the poor.
He has sent me to proclaim
    that captives will be released,
    that the blind will see,
    that the downtrodden will be freed from
        their oppressors,
[19]   and that the time of the Lord's favor has
        come.*"

[20]He rolled up the scroll, handed it back to the attendant, and sat down. Everyone in the synagogue stared at him intently. [21]Then he said, "This Scripture has come true today before your very eyes!"

[22]All who were there spoke well of him and were amazed by the gracious words that fell from his lips. "How can this be?" they asked. "Isn't this Joseph's son?"

[23]Then he said, "Probably you will quote me that proverb, 'Physician, heal yourself'—

3:38 Greek *Enos;* see Gen 5:6. **4:4** Deut 8:3. **4:8** Deut 6:13. **4:10-11** Ps 91:11-12. **4:12** Deut 6:16. **4:18-19** Or *and to proclaim the acceptable year of the Lord.* Isa 61:1-2.

My Daily Worship

— September 28 —

THE SERVANT-WORSHIPER

LUKE 4:14–5:39

The Spirit of the Lord is upon me, for he has appointed me
to preach Good News to the poor (4:18).

[i reflect]

John Teter, an evangelist with InterVarsity Christian Fellowship, tells about meeting a six-foot-tall, 280-pound wrestler who was a student at Compton College. The young man called himself Colossus.

Teter invited Colossus to attend a Bible study for spiritual seekers, and Colossus agreed. At the end of the first Bible study session, Teter asked Colossus to pray. The wrestler began, "O great Odin! This is your servant-warrior Colossus."

Startled, Teter interrupted and asked Colossus who he was praying to. "Odin," explained Colossus. "He is the Norse god of war. Me and my friends are into witchcraft. We're really into Odin right now."

Teter persuaded Colossus to try praying to Jesus instead. And by the end of the semester, Colossus had accepted Jesus as the sole Lord worthy of his worship. Now this new believer prays, "O great Yahweh, this is Colossus, your servant-warrior."

In a special sense, Jesus was appointed to preach good news. He acknowledged as much when he gave his inaugural sermon at a synagogue in Nazareth that we read about in today's passage. As the Messiah, he was fulfilling the prophecy from Isaiah 61:1–2 that he was reading in the synagogue that day.

In a more general sense, all of us are appointed to preach that same good news. Of course, in this day when people are worshiping gods and goddesses in a profusion unknown even in Old Testament times, sharing the gospel may get us into some interesting situations, as it did with Teter and Colossus. Yet as we allow others to see that our lives are oriented around worshiping Jesus, we may have the joy of seeing others take our Lord as theirs.

Prayerfully consider the people you will encounter today. Ask God to help you point to Jesus through your actions, your words, and your attitudes. Be a servant-worshiper!

[i pray]

O great Yahweh, you are the only true Lord. Let me never be so hypocritical as to hide
my faith in you from others. Let me make my worship and my witness one.

[i respond]

Memorize Luke 4:18–19, then meditate on the people in your life. Who among them constitute the "poor," the "captives," the "blind," the "downtrodden"? How can you show them Jesus?

meaning, 'Why don't you do miracles here in your hometown like those you did in Capernaum?' [24]But the truth is, no prophet is accepted in his own hometown.

[25]"Certainly there were many widows in Israel who needed help in Elijah's time, when there was no rain for three and a half years and hunger stalked the land. [26]Yet Elijah was not sent to any of them. He was sent instead to a widow of Zarephath—a foreigner in the land of Sidon. [27]Or think of the prophet Elisha, who healed Naaman, a Syrian, rather than the many lepers in Israel who needed help."

[28]When they heard this, the people in the synagogue were furious. [29]Jumping up, they mobbed him and took him to the edge of the hill on which the city was built. They intended to push him over the cliff, [30]but he slipped away through the crowd and left them.

JESUS CASTS OUT A DEMON

[31]Then Jesus went to Capernaum, a town in Galilee, and taught there in the synagogue every Sabbath day. [32]There, too, the people were amazed at the things he said, because he spoke with authority.

[33]Once when he was in the synagogue, a man possessed by a demon began shouting at Jesus, [34]"Go away! Why are you bothering us, Jesus of Nazareth? Have you come to destroy us? I know who you are—the Holy One sent from God."

[35]Jesus cut him short. "Be silent!" he told the demon. "Come out of the man!" The demon threw the man to the floor as the crowd watched; then it left him without hurting him further.

[36]Amazed, the people exclaimed, "What authority and power this man's words possess! Even evil spirits obey him and flee at his command!" [37]The story of what he had done spread like wildfire throughout the whole region.

JESUS HEALS MANY PEOPLE

[38]After leaving the synagogue that day, Jesus went to Simon's home, where he found Simon's mother-in-law very sick with a high fever. "Please heal her," everyone begged. [39]Standing at her bedside, he spoke to the fever, rebuking it, and immediately her temperature returned to normal. She got up at once and prepared a meal for them.

[40]As the sun went down that evening, people throughout the village brought sick family members to Jesus. No matter what their diseases were, the touch of his hand healed every one. [41]Some were possessed by demons; and the demons came out at his command, shouting, "You are the Son of God." But because they knew he was the Messiah, he stopped them and told them to be silent.

JESUS CONTINUES TO PREACH

[42]Early the next morning Jesus went out into the wilderness. The crowds searched everywhere for him, and when they finally found him, they begged him not to leave them. [43]But he replied, "I must preach the Good News of the Kingdom of God in other places, too, because that is why I was sent." [44]So he continued to travel around, preaching in synagogues throughout Judea.*

THE FIRST DISCIPLES

5 One day as Jesus was preaching on the shore of the Sea of Galilee,* great crowds pressed in on him to listen to the word of God. [2]He noticed two empty boats at the water's edge, for the fishermen had left them and were washing their nets. [3]Stepping into one of the boats, Jesus asked Simon,* its owner, to push it out into the water. So he sat in the boat and taught the crowds from there.

[4]When he had finished speaking, he said to Simon, "Now go out where it is deeper and let down your nets, and you will catch many fish."

[5]"Master," Simon replied, "we worked hard

4:44 Some manuscripts read *Galilee.* 5:1 Greek *Lake Gennesaret,* another name for the Sea of Galilee. 5:3 *Simon* is called *Peter* in 6:14 and thereafter.

all last night and didn't catch a thing. But if you say so, we'll try again." ⁶And this time their nets were so full they began to tear! ⁷A shout for help brought their partners in the other boat, and soon both boats were filled with fish and on the verge of sinking.

⁸When Simon Peter realized what had happened, he fell to his knees before Jesus and said, "Oh, Lord, please leave me—I'm too much of a sinner to be around you." ⁹For he was awestruck by the size of their catch, as were the others with him. ¹⁰His partners, James and John, the sons of Zebedee, were also amazed.

Jesus replied to Simon, "Don't be afraid! From now on you'll be fishing for people!" ¹¹And as soon as they landed, they left everything and followed Jesus.

JESUS HEALS A MAN WITH LEPROSY

¹²In one of the villages, Jesus met a man with an advanced case of leprosy. When the man saw Jesus, he fell to the ground, face down in the dust, begging to be healed. "Lord," he said, "if you want to, you can make me well again." ¹³Jesus reached out and touched the man. "I want to," he said. "Be healed!" And instantly the leprosy disappeared. ¹⁴Then Jesus instructed him not to tell anyone what had happened. He said, "Go right to the priest and let him examine you. Take along the offering required in the law of Moses for those who have been healed of leprosy, so everyone will have proof of your healing." ¹⁵Yet despite Jesus' instructions, the report of his power spread even faster, and vast crowds came to hear him preach and to be healed of their diseases. ¹⁶But Jesus often withdrew to the wilderness for prayer.

JESUS HEALS A PARALYZED MAN

¹⁷One day while Jesus was teaching, some Pharisees and teachers of religious law were sitting nearby. (It seemed that these men showed up from every village in all Galilee and Judea, as well as from Jerusalem.) And the

Words of Worship

MARANATHA

Maranatha—Greek *ma-ran a-tha*, from Aramaic *maran 'ata'* "Our Lord has come!" or *marana' ta'* "Our Lord, come!"

The everyday language of the earliest Christians was Aramaic, a sister language of Hebrew more widely spoken by the common people. Among several Aramaic expressions preserved in the Greek New Testament is *maranatha*. Paul uses it (1 Corinthians 16:22), "Our Lord, come!" as an expression of confidence in the return of the Lord Jesus. The phrase can be divided differently (in ancient manuscripts the words were often run together) however, with the meaning "Our Lord has come," indicating Jesus' presence with his people of the New Covenant.

Outside the New Testament, the earliest record of Christian worship is a late first-century document known as the *Didache*, or *Teaching*, which describes the gathering at the Lord's Table. Here *maranatha* is used at the end of the ceremony of the bread and cup. Did these early worshipers understand the Lord's Table as the anticipation of Christ's coming (1 Corinthians 11:26) or as a celebration of his presence (John 6:56)—or both? In any case, *maranatha!* is the cry of every worshiper longing for communion with the Lord, and for his help.

Lord's healing power was strongly with Jesus. ¹⁸Some men came carrying a paralyzed man on a sleeping mat. They tried to push through the crowd to Jesus, ¹⁹but they couldn't reach him. So they went up to the roof, took off some tiles, and lowered the sick man down into the crowd, still on his mat, right in front of Jesus. ²⁰Seeing their faith, Jesus said to the man, "Son, your sins are forgiven."

²¹"Who does this man think he is?" the Pharisees and teachers of religious law said to each other. "This is blasphemy! Who but God can forgive sins?"

²²Jesus knew what they were thinking, so he asked them, "Why do you think this is blasphemy? ²³Is it easier to say, 'Your sins are forgiven' or 'Get up and walk'? ²⁴I will prove that I, the Son of Man, have the authority on earth to forgive sins." Then Jesus turned to the paralyzed man and said, "Stand up, take your mat, and go on home, because you are healed!"

²⁵And immediately, as everyone watched, the man jumped to his feet, picked up his mat, and went home praising God. ²⁶Everyone was gripped with great wonder and awe. And they praised God, saying over and over again, "We have seen amazing things today."

Jesus Calls Levi (Matthew)

²⁷Later, as Jesus left the town, he saw a tax collector named Levi sitting at his tax-collection booth. "Come, be my disciple!" Jesus said to him. ²⁸So Levi got up, left everything, and followed him.

²⁹Soon Levi held a banquet in his home with Jesus as the guest of honor. Many of Levi's fellow tax collectors and other guests were there. ³⁰But the Pharisees and their teachers of religious law complained bitterly to Jesus' disciples, "Why do you eat and drink with such scum*?"

³¹Jesus answered them, "Healthy people don't need a doctor—sick people do. ³²I have come to call sinners to turn from their sins, not to spend my time with those who think they are already good enough."

A Discussion about Fasting

³³The religious leaders complained that Jesus' disciples were feasting instead of fasting. "John the Baptist's disciples always fast and pray," they declared, "and so do the disciples of the Pharisees. Why are yours always feasting?"

³⁴Jesus asked, "Do wedding guests fast while celebrating with the groom? ³⁵Someday he will be taken away from them, and then they will fast."

³⁶Then Jesus gave them this illustration: "No one tears a piece of cloth from a new garment and uses it to patch an old garment. For then the new garment would be torn, and the patch wouldn't even match the old garment. ³⁷And no one puts new wine into old wineskins. The new wine would burst the old skins, spilling the wine and ruining the skins. ³⁸New wine must be put into new wineskins. ³⁹But no one who drinks the old wine seems to want the fresh and the new. 'The old is better,' they say."

A Discussion about the Sabbath

6 One Sabbath day as Jesus was walking through some grainfields, his disciples broke off heads of wheat, rubbed off the husks in their hands, and ate the grains. ²But some Pharisees said, "You shouldn't be doing that! It's against the law to work by harvesting grain on the Sabbath."

³Jesus replied, "Haven't you ever read in the Scriptures what King David did when he and his companions were hungry? ⁴He went into the house of God, ate the special bread reserved for the priests alone, and then gave some to his friends. That was breaking the law, too." ⁵And Jesus added, "I, the Son of Man, am master even of the Sabbath."

Jesus Heals on the Sabbath

⁶On another Sabbath day, a man with a deformed right hand was in the synagogue while Jesus was teaching. ⁷The teachers of religious law and the Pharisees watched closely to see whether Jesus would heal the man on the Sabbath, because they were eager to find some legal charge to bring against him. ⁸But Jesus knew their thoughts. He said to the man with the deformed hand, "Come and stand here where everyone can see." So the man came forward. ⁹Then Jesus said to his critics, "I have

---

5:30 Greek *with tax collectors and sinners.*

a question for you. Is it legal to do good deeds on the Sabbath, or is it a day for doing harm? Is this a day to save life or to destroy it?" [10]He looked around at them one by one and then said to the man, "Reach out your hand." The man reached out his hand, and it became normal again! [11]At this, the enemies of Jesus were wild with rage and began to discuss what to do with him.

JESUS CHOOSES THE TWELVE APOSTLES

[12]One day soon afterward Jesus went to a mountain to pray, and he prayed to God all night. [13]At daybreak he called together all of his disciples and chose twelve of them to be apostles. Here are their names:

[14] Simon (he also called him Peter),
Andrew (Peter's brother),
James,
John,
Philip,
Bartholomew,
[15] Matthew,
Thomas,
James (son of Alphaeus),
Simon (the Zealot),
[16] Judas (son of James),
Judas Iscariot (who later betrayed him).

CROWDS FOLLOW JESUS

[17]When they came down the slopes of the mountain, the disciples stood with Jesus on a large, level area, surrounded by many of his followers and by the crowds. There were people from all over Judea and from Jerusalem and from as far north as the seacoasts of Tyre and Sidon. [18]They had come to hear him and to be healed, and Jesus cast out many evil spirits. [19]Everyone was trying to touch him, because healing power went out from him, and they were all cured.

THE BEATITUDES

[20]Then Jesus turned to his disciples and said,

"God blesses you who are poor,
for the Kingdom of God is given to you.
[21] God blesses you who are hungry now,
for you will be satisfied.
God blesses you who weep now,
for the time will come when you will laugh with joy.
[22] God blesses you who are hated and excluded and mocked and cursed because you are identified with me, the Son of Man.

[23]"When that happens, rejoice! Yes, leap for joy! For a great reward awaits you in heaven. And remember, the ancient prophets were also treated that way by your ancestors.

SORROWS FORETOLD

[24] "What sorrows await you who are rich,
for you have your only happiness now.
[25] What sorrows await you who are satisfied and prosperous now,
for a time of awful hunger is before you.
What sorrows await you who laugh carelessly,
for your laughing will turn to mourning and sorrow.
[26] What sorrows await you who are praised by the crowds,
for their ancestors also praised false prophets.

LOVE FOR ENEMIES

[27]"But if you are willing to listen, I say, love your enemies. Do good to those who hate you. [28]Pray for the happiness of those who curse you. Pray for those who hurt you. [29]If someone slaps you on one cheek, turn the other cheek. If someone demands your coat, offer your shirt also. [30]Give what you have to anyone who asks you for it; and when things are taken away from you, don't try to get them back. [31]Do for others as you would like them to do for you.

[32]"Do you think you deserve credit merely for loving those who love you? Even the sinners do that! [33]And if you do good only to

those who do good to you, is that so wonderful? Even sinners do that much! ³⁴And if you lend money only to those who can repay you, what good is that? Even sinners will lend to their own kind for a full return.

³⁵"Love your enemies! Do good to them! Lend to them! And don't be concerned that they might not repay. Then your reward from heaven will be very great, and you will truly be acting as children of the Most High, for he is kind to the unthankful and to those who are wicked. ³⁶You must be compassionate, just as your Father is compassionate.

Don't Condemn Others

³⁷"Stop judging others, and you will not be judged. Stop criticizing others, or it will all come back on you. If you forgive others, you will be forgiven. ³⁸If you give, you will receive. Your gift will return to you in full measure, pressed down, shaken together to make room for more, and running over. Whatever measure you use in giving—large or small—it will be used to measure what is given back to you."

³⁹Then Jesus gave the following illustration: "What good is it for one blind person to lead another? The first one will fall into a ditch and pull the other down also. ⁴⁰A student is not greater than the teacher. But the student who works hard will become like the teacher.

⁴¹"And why worry about a speck in your friend's eye* when you have a log in your own? ⁴²How can you think of saying, 'Friend,* let me help you get rid of that speck in your eye,' when you can't see past the log in your own eye? Hypocrite! First get rid of the log from your own eye; then perhaps you will see well enough to deal with the speck in your friend's eye.

The Tree and Its Fruit

⁴³"A good tree can't produce bad fruit, and a bad tree can't produce good fruit. ⁴⁴A tree is identified by the kind of fruit it produces. Figs never grow on thornbushes or grapes on bramble bushes. ⁴⁵A good person produces good

deeds from a good heart, and an evil person produces evil deeds from an evil heart. Whatever is in your heart determines what you say.

Building on a Solid Foundation

⁴⁶"So why do you call me 'Lord,' when you won't obey me? ⁴⁷I will show you what it's like when someone comes to me, listens to my teaching, and then obeys me. ⁴⁸It is like a person who builds a house on a strong foundation laid upon the underlying rock. When the floodwaters rise and break against the house, it stands firm because it is well built. ⁴⁹But anyone who listens and doesn't obey is like a person who builds a house without a foundation. When the floods sweep down against that house, it will crumble into a heap of ruins."

Faith of the Roman Officer

7 When Jesus had finished saying all this, he went back to Capernaum. ²Now the highly valued slave of a Roman officer was sick and near death. ³When the officer heard about Jesus, he sent some respected Jewish leaders to ask him to come and heal his slave. ⁴So they earnestly begged Jesus to come with them and help the man. "If anyone deserves your help, it is he," they said, ⁵"for he loves the Jews and even built a synagogue for us."

⁶So Jesus went with them. But just before they arrived at the house, the officer sent some friends to say, "Lord, don't trouble yourself by coming to my home, for I am not worthy of such an honor. ⁷I am not even worthy to come and meet you. Just say the word from where you are, and my servant will be healed. ⁸I know because I am under the authority of my superior officers, and I have authority over my soldiers. I only need to say, 'Go,' and they go, or 'Come,' and they come. And if I say to my slaves, 'Do this or that,' they do it."

⁹When Jesus heard this, he was amazed.

6:41 Greek *your brother's eye*; also in 6:42. 6:42 Greek *Brother*.

My Daily Worship

— *September 29* —

THE CROOKED KISS

LUKE 6:1–49

You must be compassionate, just as your Father is compassionate (6:36).

[i reflect]

Dr. Richard Selzer, in his book *Mortal Lessons: Notes on the Art of Surgery*, takes his readers into the hospital room where a young woman has just awakened after Selzer operated on her. In the process of removing the tumor from her cheek, Selzer unavoidably severed a nerve, causing her mouth to twist into a clownish shape. Now that she has awakened, Selzer has to inform her that the new shape of her mouth is permanent. The woman nods silently at the news. Then her husband, standing by the bed, says, "I like it. It's kind of cute." Selzer describes what the young husband does next: "Unmindful, he bends to kiss her crooked mouth, and I'm so close I can see how he twists his own lips to accommodate hers, to show her that their kiss still works."

We are like the woman with the twisted mouth. Our lives have been distorted by the effects of sin—our own sin and others' sin. But God loves us and accepts us as we are. Over time he'll straighten out our crookedness. That's the kind of compassion God has for us, Jesus taught his followers during his sermon on kingdom living from today's passage. And that's the kind of compassion we should have for others—a compassion that meets the needs of those made repulsive by the conditions of this wicked world.

If this sort of compassion seems too hard or too costly to you, remember that God promises to crown compassion with goodness. A preacher from the early church, John Chrysostom, said, "For those who have a treasure-house of blessings, a loving and merciful soul will make it overflow to meet all of their neighbors' needs. Such people will enjoy all the rewards God has prepared."

Seek God for direction on how you can show compassion to someone today.

[i pray]

*Lord, help me to see people as you see them so that I can look past
the ugly bents of their nature to a need you would have me meet.*

[i respond]

Check out the mercy ministries that your local church is involved with in your community. Investigate how you might get involved on a regular basis.

Turning to the crowd, he said, "I tell you, I haven't seen faith like this in all the land of Israel!" [10]And when the officer's friends returned to his house, they found the slave completely healed.

JESUS RAISES A WIDOW'S SON

[11]Soon afterward Jesus went with his disciples to the village of Nain, with a great crowd following him. [12]A funeral procession was coming out as he approached the village gate. The boy who had died was the only son of a widow, and many mourners from the village were with her. [13]When the Lord saw her, his heart overflowed with compassion. "Don't cry!" he said. [14]Then he walked over to the coffin and touched it, and the bearers stopped. "Young man," he said, "get up." [15]Then the dead boy sat up and began to talk to those around him! And Jesus gave him back to his mother.

[16]Great fear swept the crowd, and they praised God, saying, "A mighty prophet has risen among us," and "We have seen the hand of God at work today." [17]The report of what Jesus had done that day spread all over Judea and even out across its borders.

JESUS AND JOHN THE BAPTIST

[18]The disciples of John the Baptist told John about everything Jesus was doing. So John called for two of his disciples, [19]and he sent them to the Lord to ask him, "Are you the Messiah we've been expecting, or should we keep looking for someone else?"

[20]John's two disciples found Jesus and said to him, "John the Baptist sent us to ask, 'Are you the Messiah we've been expecting, or should we keep looking for someone else?'"

[21]At that very time, he cured many people of their various diseases, and he cast out evil spirits and restored sight to the blind. [22]Then he told John's disciples, "Go back to John and tell him what you have seen and heard—the blind see, the lame walk, the lepers are cured, the deaf hear, the dead are raised to life, and the Good News is being preached to the poor.

[23]And tell him, 'God blesses those who are not offended by me.*'"

[24]After they left, Jesus talked to the crowd about John. "Who is this man in the wilderness that you went out to see? Did you find him weak as a reed, moved by every breath of wind? [25]Or were you expecting to see a man dressed in expensive clothes? No, people who wear beautiful clothes and live in luxury are found in palaces, not in the wilderness. [26]Were you looking for a prophet? Yes, and he is more than a prophet. [27]John is the man to whom the Scriptures refer when they say,

'Look, I am sending my messenger before
   you,
   and he will prepare your way before you.'*

[28]I tell you, of all who have ever lived, none is greater than John. Yet even the most insignificant person in the Kingdom of God is greater than he is!"

[29]When they heard this, all the people, including the unjust tax collectors, agreed that God's plan was right,* for they had been baptized by John. [30]But the Pharisees and experts in religious law had rejected God's plan for them, for they had refused John's baptism.

[31]"How shall I describe this generation?" Jesus asked. "With what will I compare them? [32]They are like a group of children playing a game in the public square. They complain to their friends, 'We played wedding songs, and you weren't happy, so we played funeral songs, but you weren't sad.' [33]For John the Baptist didn't drink wine and he often fasted, and you say, 'He's demon possessed.' [34]And I, the Son of Man, feast and drink, and you say, 'He's a glutton and a drunkard, and a friend of the worst sort of sinners!' [35]But wisdom is shown to be right by the lives of those who follow it.*"

JESUS ANOINTED BY A SINFUL WOMAN

[36]One of the Pharisees asked Jesus to come to his home for a meal, so Jesus accepted the

---

7:23 Or *who don't fall away because of me.* 7:27 Mal 3:1. 7:29 Or *praised God.* 7:35 Or *But wisdom is justified by all her children.*

My Daily Worship

THE SMELL OF WORSHIP
LUKE 7:1–8:39

I tell you, her sins—and they are many—have been forgiven, so she has shown me much love.
But a person who is forgiven little shows only little love (7:47).

[i reflect]

Sigmund Freud said, "The quickest way to trigger an emotional response is with scent." And, in fact, scents have been shown to affect the limbic portion of the brain, the center of emotion and memory. With all of the personal and social implications attached to scent, it's little wonder that perfume has become a multibillion-dollar business today. Perfumes were popular even in biblical times.

In today's passage, the perfume that a woman poured over Jesus' feet was probably made from nard, an herb grown in India. It was kept in a small alabaster vase. Perfume was commonly offered to guests in Palestine, but as this honor had been withheld from Jesus by his host, the woman supplied the lack by cleaning, kissing, and anointing Jesus' feet with the expensive perfume. As the pleasing scent wafted to Christ's nostrils, he may have been reminded of the sweet odors of scented oil and incense used in Jewish worship (Exodus 30:22–38).

We don't know the backdrop to this event. Presumably, Jesus had recently met this woman, had showed her the need to repent, and had touched her heart with a pure love the likes of which she had never known before. The woman, in response, wanted to do something extravagant to show her gratitude. Thus, oblivious to what others might think, she barged into the dinner party Jesus was attending and performed the foot washing. Her act of worship was beautiful. Pity the religious folk at the table who were less sinful (or *thought* they were) and so could not know such joy in loving Jesus.

Myrna Reid Grant declared, "Transfixed with thanks, folded in love, I cannot adore enough." May the same attitude fill your heart. Let every scent you smell today cause you to give thanks and adoration to the Lord.

[i pray]

My sins have been many, Lord, but you have cleansed me of them all.
I fall to your feet, weeping in gratitude. I cannot adore you enough!

[i respond]

Put on a little of your best perfume or cologne. In your personal worship time, think of all the reasons you have to love Jesus. Send your prayer of gratitude heavenward as a sweet-smelling sacrifice of praise.

invitation and sat down to eat. [37]A certain immoral woman heard he was there and brought a beautiful jar* filled with expensive perfume. [38]Then she knelt behind him at his feet, weeping. Her tears fell on his feet, and she wiped them off with her hair. Then she kept kissing his feet and putting perfume on them.

[39]When the Pharisee who was the host saw what was happening and who the woman was, he said to himself, "This proves that Jesus is no prophet. If God had really sent him, he would know what kind of woman is touching him. She's a sinner!"

[40]Then Jesus spoke up and answered his thoughts. "Simon," he said to the Pharisee, "I have something to say to you."

"All right, Teacher," Simon replied, "go ahead."

[41]Then Jesus told him this story: "A man loaned money to two people—five hundred pieces of silver* to one and fifty pieces to the other. [42]But neither of them could repay him, so he kindly forgave them both, canceling their debts. Who do you suppose loved him more after that?"

[43]Simon answered, "I suppose the one for whom he canceled the larger debt."

"That's right," Jesus said. [44]Then he turned to the woman and said to Simon, "Look at this woman kneeling here. When I entered your home, you didn't offer me water to wash the dust from my feet, but she has washed them with her tears and wiped them with her hair. [45]You didn't give me a kiss of greeting, but she has kissed my feet again and again from the time I first came in. [46]You neglected the courtesy of olive oil to anoint my head, but she has anointed my feet with rare perfume. [47]I tell you, her sins—and they are many—have been forgiven, so she has shown me much love. But a person who is forgiven little shows only little love." [48]Then Jesus said to the woman, "Your sins are forgiven."

[49]The men at the table said among themselves, "Who does this man think he is, going around forgiving sins?"

[50]And Jesus said to the woman, "Your faith has saved you; go in peace."

WOMEN WHO FOLLOWED JESUS

8 Not long afterward Jesus began a tour of the nearby cities and villages to announce the Good News concerning the Kingdom of God. He took his twelve disciples with him, [2]along with some women he had healed and from whom he had cast out evil spirits. Among them were Mary Magdalene, from whom he had cast out seven demons; [3]Joanna, the wife of Chuza, Herod's business manager; Susanna; and many others who were contributing from their own resources to support Jesus and his disciples.

STORY OF THE FARMER SCATTERING SEED

[4]One day Jesus told this story to a large crowd that had gathered from many towns to hear him: [5]"A farmer went out to plant some seed. As he scattered it across his field, some seed fell on a footpath, where it was stepped on, and the birds came and ate it. [6]Other seed fell on shallow soil with underlying rock. This seed began to grow, but soon it withered and died for lack of moisture. [7]Other seed fell among thorns that shot up and choked out the tender blades. [8]Still other seed fell on fertile soil. This seed grew and produced a crop one hundred times as much as had been planted." When he had said this, he called out, "Anyone who is willing to hear should listen and understand!"

[9]His disciples asked him what the story meant. [10]He replied, "You have been permitted to understand the secrets of the Kingdom of God. But I am using these stories to conceal everything about it from outsiders, so that the Scriptures might be fulfilled:

'They see what I do,
  but they don't really see;

7:37 Greek *an alabaster jar*. 7:41 Greek *500 denarii*. A denarius was the equivalent of a full day's wage.

> *Worship changes the worshiper into the image of the One worshiped.*
>
> JACK HAYFORD

they hear what I say,
but they don't understand.'*

[11]"This is the meaning of the story: The seed is God's message. [12]The seed that fell on the hard path represents those who hear the message, but then the Devil comes and steals it away and prevents them from believing and being saved. [13]The rocky soil represents those who hear the message with joy. But like young plants in such soil, their roots don't go very deep. They believe for a while, but they wilt when the hot winds of testing blow. [14]The thorny ground represents those who hear and accept the message, but all too quickly the message is crowded out by the cares and riches and pleasures of this life. And so they never grow into maturity. [15]But the good soil represents honest, good-hearted people who hear God's message, cling to it, and steadily produce a huge harvest.

ILLUSTRATION OF THE LAMP

[16]"No one would light a lamp and then cover it up or put it under a bed. No, lamps are mounted in the open, where they can be seen by those entering the house. [17]For everything that is hidden or secret will eventually be brought to light and made plain to all. [18]So be sure to pay attention to what you hear. To those who are open to my teaching, more understanding will be given. But to those who are not listening, even what they think they have will be taken away from them."

THE TRUE FAMILY OF JESUS

[19]Once when Jesus' mother and brothers came to see him, they couldn't get to him because of the crowds. [20]Someone told Jesus, "Your mother and your brothers are outside, and they want to see you."

[21]Jesus replied, "My mother and my brothers are all those who hear the message of God and obey it."

JESUS CALMS THE STORM

[22]One day Jesus said to his disciples, "Let's cross over to the other side of the lake." So they got into a boat and started out. [23]On the way across, Jesus lay down for a nap, and while he was sleeping the wind began to rise. A fierce storm developed that threatened to swamp them, and they were in real danger.

[24]The disciples woke him up, shouting, "Master, Master, we're going to drown!"

So Jesus rebuked the wind and the raging waves. The storm stopped and all was calm! [25]Then he asked them, "Where is your faith?"

And they were filled with awe and amazement. They said to one another, "Who is this man, that even the winds and waves obey him?"

JESUS HEALS A DEMON-POSSESSED MAN

[26]So they arrived in the land of the Gerasenes,* across the lake from Galilee. [27]As Jesus was climbing out of the boat, a man who was possessed by demons came out to meet him. Homeless and naked, he had lived in a cemetery for a long time. [28]As soon as he saw Jesus, he shrieked and fell to the ground before him, screaming, "Why are you bothering me, Jesus, Son of the Most High God? Please, I beg you, don't torture me!" [29]For Jesus had already commanded the evil spirit to come out of him. This spirit had often taken control of the man. Even when he was shackled with chains, he simply broke them and rushed out into the wilderness, completely under the demon's power.

8:10 Isa 6:9. **8:26** Some manuscripts read *Gadarenes;* other manuscripts read *Gergesenes.* See Matt 8:28; Mark 5:1.

[30]"What is your name?" Jesus asked.

"Legion," he replied—for the man was filled with many demons. [31]The demons kept begging Jesus not to send them into the Bottomless Pit. [32]A large herd of pigs was feeding on the hillside nearby, and the demons pleaded with him to let them enter into the pigs. Jesus gave them permission. [33]So the demons came out of the man and entered the pigs, and the whole herd plunged down the steep hillside into the lake, where they drowned.

[34]When the herdsmen saw it, they fled to the nearby city and the surrounding countryside, spreading the news as they ran. [35]A crowd soon gathered around Jesus, for they wanted to see for themselves what had happened. And they saw the man who had been possessed by demons sitting quietly at Jesus' feet, clothed and sane. And the whole crowd was afraid. [36]Then those who had seen what happened told the others how the demon-possessed man had been healed. [37]And all the people in that region begged Jesus to go away and leave them alone, for a great wave of fear swept over them.

So Jesus returned to the boat and left, crossing back to the other side of the lake. [38]The man who had been demon possessed begged to go, too, but Jesus said, [39]"No, go back to your family and tell them all the wonderful things God has done for you." So he went all through the city telling about the great thing Jesus had done for him.

Jesus Heals in Response to Faith

[40]On the other side of the lake the crowds received Jesus with open arms because they had been waiting for him. [41]And now a man named Jairus, a leader of the local synagogue, came and fell down at Jesus' feet, begging him to come home with him. [42]His only child was dying, a little girl twelve years old.

As Jesus went with him, he was surrounded by the crowds. [43]And there was a woman in the crowd who had had a hemorrhage for twelve years. She had spent everything she had on doctors* and still could find no cure. [44]She came up behind Jesus and touched the fringe of his robe. Immediately, the bleeding stopped.

[45]"Who touched me?" Jesus asked.

Everyone denied it, and Peter said, "Master, this whole crowd is pressing up against you."

[46]But Jesus told him, "No, someone deliberately touched me, for I felt healing power go out from me." [47]When the woman realized that Jesus knew, she began to tremble and fell to her knees before him. The whole crowd heard her explain why she had touched him and that she had been immediately healed. [48]"Daughter," he said to her, "your faith has made you well. Go in peace."

[49]While he was still speaking to her, a messenger arrived from Jairus's home with the message, "Your little girl is dead. There's no use troubling the Teacher now."

[50]But when Jesus heard what had happened, he said to Jairus, "Don't be afraid. Just trust me, and she will be all right."

[51]When they arrived at the house, Jesus wouldn't let anyone go in with him except Peter, James, John, and the little girl's father and mother. [52]The house was filled with people weeping and wailing, but he said, "Stop the weeping! She isn't dead; she is only asleep."

[53]But the crowd laughed at him because they all knew she had died. [54]Then Jesus took her by the hand and said in a loud voice, "Get up, my child!" [55]And at that moment her life returned, and she immediately stood up! Then Jesus told them to give her something to eat. [56]Her parents were overwhelmed, but Jesus insisted that they not tell anyone what had happened.

Jesus Sends Out the Twelve Apostles

9 One day Jesus called together his twelve apostles and gave them power and

8:43 Some manuscripts omit *She had spent everything she had on doctors.*

authority to cast out demons and to heal all diseases. [2]Then he sent them out to tell everyone about the coming of the Kingdom of God and to heal the sick. [3]"Don't even take along a walking stick," he instructed them, "nor a traveler's bag, nor food, nor money. Not even an extra coat. [4]When you enter each village, be a guest in only one home. [5]If the people of the village won't receive your message when you enter it, shake off its dust from your feet as you leave. It is a sign that you have abandoned that village to its fate."

[6]So they began their circuit of the villages, preaching the Good News and healing the sick.

HEROD'S CONFUSION

[7]When reports of Jesus' miracles reached Herod Antipas,* he was worried and puzzled because some were saying, "This is John the Baptist come back to life again." [8]Others were saying, "It is Elijah or some other ancient prophet risen from the dead."

[9]"I beheaded John," Herod said, "so who is this man about whom I hear such strange stories?" And he tried to see him.

JESUS FEEDS FIVE THOUSAND

[10]When the apostles returned, they told Jesus everything they had done. Then he slipped quietly away with them toward the town of Bethsaida. [11]But the crowds found out where he was going, and they followed him. And he welcomed them, teaching them about the Kingdom of God and curing those who were ill. [12]Late in the afternoon the twelve disciples came to him and said, "Send the crowds away to the nearby villages and farms, so they can find food and lodging for the night. There is nothing to eat here in this deserted place."

[13]But Jesus said, "You feed them."

"Impossible!" they protested. "We have only five loaves of bread and two fish. Or are you expecting us to go and buy enough food for this whole crowd?" [14]For there were about five thousand men there.

"Just tell them to sit down on the ground in groups of about fifty each," Jesus replied. [15]So the people all sat down. [16]Jesus took the five loaves and two fish, looked up toward heaven, and asked God's blessing on the food. Breaking the loaves into pieces, he kept giving the bread and fish to the disciples to give to the people. [17]They all ate as much as they wanted, and they picked up twelve baskets of leftovers!

PETER'S DECLARATION ABOUT JESUS

[18]One day as Jesus was alone, praying, he came over to his disciples and asked them, "Who do people say I am?"

[19]"Well," they replied, "some say John the Baptist, some say Elijah, and others say you are one of the other ancient prophets risen from the dead."

[20]Then he asked them, "Who do you say I am?"

Peter replied, "You are the Messiah sent from God!"

JESUS PREDICTS HIS DEATH

[21]Jesus warned them not to tell anyone about this. [22]"For I, the Son of Man, must suffer many terrible things," he said. "I will be rejected by the leaders, the leading priests, and the teachers of religious law. I will be killed, but three days later I will be raised from the dead."

[23]Then he said to the crowd, "If any of you wants to be my follower, you must put aside your selfish ambition, shoulder your cross daily, and follow me. [24]If you try to keep your life for yourself, you will lose it. But if you give up your life for me, you will find true life. [25]And how do you benefit if you gain the whole world but lose or forfeit your own soul in the process? [26]If a person is ashamed of me and my message, I, the Son of Man, will be ashamed of that person when I return in my glory and in the glory of the Father and the holy angels. [27]And I assure you that some of you standing here right now will not die before you see the Kingdom of God."

9:7 Greek *Herod the tetrarch*. He was a son of King Herod and was ruler over one of the four districts in Palestine.

THE TRANSFIGURATION

[28]About eight days later Jesus took Peter, James, and John to a mountain to pray. [29]And as he was praying, the appearance of his face changed, and his clothing became dazzling white. [30]Then two men, Moses and Elijah, appeared and began talking with Jesus. [31]They were glorious to see. And they were speaking of how he was about to fulfill God's plan by dying in Jerusalem.

[32]Peter and the others were very drowsy and had fallen asleep. Now they woke up and saw Jesus' glory and the two men standing with him. [33]As Moses and Elijah were starting to leave, Peter, not even knowing what he was saying, blurted out, "Master, this is wonderful! We will make three shrines*—one for you, one for Moses, and one for Elijah." [34]But even as he was saying this, a cloud came over them; and terror gripped them as it covered them.

[35]Then a voice from the cloud said, "This is my Son, my Chosen One.* Listen to him." [36]When the voice died away, Jesus was there alone. They didn't tell anyone what they had seen until long after this happened.

JESUS HEALS A DEMON-POSSESSED BOY

[37]The next day, after they had come down the mountain, a huge crowd met Jesus. [38]A man in the crowd called out to him, "Teacher, look at my boy, who is my only son. [39]An evil spirit keeps seizing him, making him scream. It throws him into convulsions so that he foams at the mouth. It is always hitting and injuring him. It hardly ever leaves him alone. [40]I begged your disciples to cast the spirit out, but they couldn't do it."

[41]"You stubborn, faithless people," Jesus said, "how long must I be with you and put up with you? Bring him here." [42]As the boy came forward, the demon knocked him to the ground and threw him into a violent convulsion. But Jesus rebuked the evil spirit and healed the boy. Then he gave him back to his father. [43]Awe gripped the people as they saw this display of God's power.

JESUS AGAIN PREDICTS HIS DEATH

While everyone was marveling over all the wonderful things he was doing, Jesus said to his disciples, [44]"Listen to me and remember what I say. The Son of Man is going to be betrayed." [45]But they didn't know what he meant. Its significance was hidden from them, so they could not understand it, and they were afraid to ask him about it.

THE GREATEST IN THE KINGDOM

[46]Then there was an argument among them as to which of them would be the greatest. [47]But Jesus knew their thoughts, so he brought a little child to his side. [48]Then he said to them, "Anyone who welcomes a little child like this on my behalf welcomes me, and anyone who welcomes me welcomes my Father who sent me. Whoever is the least among you is the greatest."

USING THE NAME OF JESUS

[49]John said to Jesus, "Master, we saw someone using your name to cast out demons. We tried to stop him because he isn't in our group."

[50]But Jesus said, "Don't stop him! Anyone who is not against you is for you."

OPPOSITION FROM SAMARITANS

[51]As the time drew near for his return to heaven, Jesus resolutely set out for Jerusalem. [52]He sent messengers ahead to a Samaritan village to prepare for his arrival. [53]But they were turned away. The people of the village refused to have anything to do with Jesus because he had resolved to go to Jerusalem. [54]When James and John heard about it, they said to Jesus, "Lord, should we order down fire from heaven to burn them up*?" [55]But Jesus turned

9:33 Or *shelters;* Greek reads *tabernacles.*   **9:35** Some manuscripts read *This is my beloved Son.*   **9:54** Some manuscripts add *as Elijah did.*

My Daily Worship

— October 1 —

MADMAN, DEVIL, OR SON OF GOD?

LUKE 8:40–9:62

One day as Jesus was alone, praying, he came over to his disciples
and asked them, "Who do people say I am?" (9:18).

[i reflect]

Pope John Paul II was roundly criticized when he singled out certain entertainers for wearing a cross as jewelry when engaged in activities far removed from Christian morality. But John Paul was correctly picking up on modern culture's tendency to accept Jesus as an icon so long as it can interpret him in any manner it wants. Jesus is good, but then so are the Dalai Lama, Muhammad, and any number of other "spiritual" persons and symbols.

C. S. Lewis dealt with this issue decades ago when he addressed the seemingly benign practice of calling Jesus just a "great moral teacher."

"A man who was merely a man and said the sort of things Jesus said wouldn't be a great moral teacher," declared Lewis. "He'd be either a lunatic—on a level with a man who says he's a poached egg—or else he'd be the devil of hell. You must make your choice. Either this man was, and is, the Son of God, or else a madman or something worse."

In Jesus' own day, people were willing to accord him some limited prestige as a prophet. It took special insight from the Father for Peter to come up with the right answer. He told Jesus, "You are the Messiah sent from God!" (9:20).

Some people in our day might be excused for giving Jesus limited praise if they really don't know any better. But how many are subconsciously hoping to escape the full claims of Jesus on them by giving him partial approval? They're only passing judgment on themselves with their faint praise.

Reflect on your own answer to Jesus' question: *Who do you say I am?* Then worship him in the fullness of his claim as Messiah, God in human flesh.

[i pray]

Jesus, you are more than a good man, more than a prophet, more than a great
moral teacher. You are the Messiah sent from God. I bow before you.

[i respond]

Mentally, step outside yourself and try to see yourself as others do. What in your words or behavior faithfully reflects your belief that Jesus is the Son of God? What does not?

and rebuked them.* ⁵⁶So they went on to another village.

THE COST OF FOLLOWING JESUS

⁵⁷As they were walking along someone said to Jesus, "I will follow you no matter where you go."

⁵⁸But Jesus replied, "Foxes have dens to live in, and birds have nests, but I, the Son of Man, have no home of my own, not even a place to lay my head."

⁵⁹He said to another person, "Come, be my disciple."

The man agreed, but he said, "Lord, first let me return home and bury my father."

⁶⁰Jesus replied, "Let those who are spiritually dead care for their own dead.* Your duty is to go and preach the coming of the Kingdom of God."

⁶¹Another said, "Yes, Lord, I will follow you, but first let me say good-bye to my family."

⁶²But Jesus told him, "Anyone who puts a hand to the plow and then looks back is not fit for the Kingdom of God."

JESUS SENDS OUT HIS DISCIPLES

10 The Lord now chose seventy-two* other disciples and sent them on ahead in pairs to all the towns and villages he planned to visit. ²These were his instructions to them: "The harvest is so great, but the workers are so few. Pray to the Lord who is in charge of the harvest, and ask him to send out more workers for his fields. ³Go now, and remember that I am sending you out as lambs among wolves. ⁴Don't take along any money, or a traveler's bag, or even an extra pair of sandals. And don't stop to greet anyone on the road.

⁵"Whenever you enter a home, give it your blessing. ⁶If those who live there are worthy, the blessing will stand; if they are not, the blessing will return to you. ⁷When you enter a town, don't move around from home to home. Stay in one place, eating and drinking what they provide you. Don't hesitate to accept hospitality, because those who work deserve their pay.

⁸"If a town welcomes you, eat whatever is set before you ⁹and heal the sick. As you heal them, say, 'The Kingdom of God is near you now.' ¹⁰But if a town refuses to welcome you, go out into its streets and say, ¹¹"We wipe the dust of your town from our feet as a public announcement of your doom. And don't forget the Kingdom of God is near!' ¹²The truth is, even wicked Sodom will be better off than such a town on the judgment day.

¹³"What horrors await you, Korazin and Bethsaida! For if the miracles I did in you had been done in wicked Tyre and Sidon, their people would have sat in deep repentance long ago, clothed in sackcloth and throwing ashes on their heads to show their remorse. ¹⁴Yes, Tyre and Sidon will be better off on the judgment day than you. ¹⁵And you people of Capernaum, will you be exalted to heaven? No, you will be brought down to the place of the dead.*"

¹⁶Then he said to the disciples, "Anyone who accepts your message is also accepting me. And anyone who rejects you is rejecting me. And anyone who rejects me is rejecting God who sent me."

¹⁷When the seventy-two disciples returned, they joyfully reported to him, "Lord, even the demons obey us when we use your name!"

¹⁸"Yes," he told them, "I saw Satan falling from heaven as a flash of lightning! ¹⁹And I have given you authority over all the power of the enemy, and you can walk among snakes and scorpions and crush them. Nothing will injure you. ²⁰But don't rejoice just because evil spirits obey you; rejoice because your names are registered as citizens of heaven."

JESUS' PRAYER OF THANKSGIVING

²¹Then Jesus was filled with the joy of the Holy Spirit and said, "O Father, Lord of heaven and earth, thank you for hiding the truth from those who think themselves so wise and

---

9:55 Some manuscripts add *And he said, "You don't realize what your hearts are like.* ⁵⁶*For the Son of Man has not come to destroy men's lives, but to save them."* **9:60** Greek *Let the dead bury their own dead.* **10:1** Some manuscripts read *70;* also in 10:17. **10:15** Greek *to Hades.*

My Daily Worship

— O c t o b e r   2 —

ONLY ONE THING NEEDFUL

LUKE 10:1–11:36

But the Lord said to her, "My dear Martha, you are so upset over all these details!
There is really only one thing worth being concerned about. Mary has
discovered it—and I won't take it away from her" (10:41–42).

[i reflect]

Want to watch a movie on your DVD player? Great. But first you have to decide whether to watch the show in standard or wide-screen format, with or without subtitles, and with or without director's commentary. And then there's a whole menu of other "special features" to explore.

Want to save money by doing your own taxes? Good for you. Just remember that the instructions for Form 1040 alone now run to more than sixty pages of small print. As recently as 1992, the instructions were only twenty-seven pages long.

Need to buy a new computer? Sounds like fun. But do you want a desktop, a notebook, or a handheld? Which type of processor? How many gigs of memory? CRT monitor or flat panel? Do you want your printer to also make copies and receive faxes? Hurry up and decide; we haven't even started talking about software.

Life has become mighty complex, hasn't it? It's easy to get caught up in the practical details of living, just as Martha did when preparing dinner in this passage. But while the complexity of modern life makes our preoccupation with details understandable, it does not constitute an excuse for neglecting what's most important. We are still called to be like Mary, making a priority of sitting at the feet of Jesus to take in everything he teaches and give him our adoration in return.

What is the "one thing worth being concerned about"? It's spending time with Jesus. In the words of A. W. Tozer, "We are called to an everlasting preoccupation with God."

Even now, as you are spending time with God, what niggling details are crowding your mind? Write them down on a scrap of paper and set it aside for later. Then return your focus to God.

[i pray]

If my "kitchen work" never gets done, so be it. Lord, I want you first, you above all!
May nothing distract my gaze from your precious face.

[i respond]

Has time with Jesus been crowded out of your schedule by lesser callings? Get ruthless with your daily schedule. Sacrifice the good for the best. Establish a time now for uninterrupted communion with the Savior.

clever, and for revealing it to the childlike. Yes, Father, it pleased you to do it this way.

²²"My Father has given me authority over everything. No one really knows the Son except the Father, and no one really knows the Father except the Son and those to whom the Son chooses to reveal him."

²³Then when they were alone, he turned to the disciples and said, "How privileged you are to see what you have seen. ²⁴I tell you, many prophets and kings have longed to see and hear what you have seen and heard, but they could not."

THE MOST IMPORTANT COMMANDMENT

²⁵One day an expert in religious law stood up to test Jesus by asking him this question: "Teacher, what must I do to receive eternal life?"

²⁶Jesus replied, "What does the law of Moses say? How do you read it?"

²⁷The man answered, " 'You must love the Lord your God with all your heart, all your soul, all your strength, and all your mind.' And, 'Love your neighbor as yourself.' "*

²⁸"Right!" Jesus told him. "Do this and you will live!"

²⁹The man wanted to justify his actions, so he asked Jesus, "And who is my neighbor?"

STORY OF THE GOOD SAMARITAN

³⁰Jesus replied with an illustration: "A Jewish man was traveling on a trip from Jerusalem to Jericho, and he was attacked by bandits. They stripped him of his clothes and money, beat him up, and left him half dead beside the road.

³¹"By chance a Jewish priest came along; but when he saw the man lying there, he crossed to the other side of the road and passed him by. ³²A Temple assistant* walked over and looked at him lying there, but he also passed by on the other side.

³³"Then a despised Samaritan came along, and when he saw the man, he felt deep pity.

³⁴Kneeling beside him, the Samaritan soothed his wounds with medicine and bandaged them. Then he put the man on his own donkey and took him to an inn, where he took care of him. ³⁵The next day he handed the innkeeper two pieces of silver* and told him to take care of the man. 'If his bill runs higher than that,' he said, 'I'll pay the difference the next time I am here.'

³⁶"Now which of these three would you say was a neighbor to the man who was attacked by bandits?" Jesus asked.

³⁷The man replied, "The one who showed him mercy."

Then Jesus said, "Yes, now go and do the same."

JESUS VISITS MARTHA AND MARY

³⁸As Jesus and the disciples continued on their way to Jerusalem, they came to a village where a woman named Martha welcomed them into her home. ³⁹Her sister, Mary, sat at the Lord's feet, listening to what he taught. ⁴⁰But Martha was worrying over the big dinner she was preparing. She came to Jesus and said, "Lord, doesn't it seem unfair to you that my sister just sits here while I do all the work? Tell her to come and help me."

⁴¹But the Lord said to her, "My dear Martha, you are so upset over all these details! ⁴²There is really only one thing worth being concerned about. Mary has discovered it—and I won't take it away from her."

TEACHING ABOUT PRAYER

11 Once when Jesus had been out praying, one of his disciples came to him as he finished and said, "Lord, teach us to pray, just as John taught his disciples."

²He said, "This is how you should pray:

"Father, may your name be honored.
    May your Kingdom come soon.
³   Give us our food day by day.
⁴   And forgive us our sins—

10:27 Deut 6:5; Lev 19:18.   10:32 Greek *A Levite.*   10:35 Greek *2 denarii.* A denarius was the equivalent of a full day's wage.

just as we forgive those who have sinned against us.
And don't let us yield to temptation.*"

⁵Then, teaching them more about prayer, he used this illustration: "Suppose you went to a friend's house at midnight, wanting to borrow three loaves of bread. You would say to him, ⁶'A friend of mine has just arrived for a visit, and I have nothing for him to eat.' ⁷He would call out from his bedroom, 'Don't bother me. The door is locked for the night, and we are all in bed. I can't help you this time.' ⁸But I tell you this—though he won't do it as a friend, if you keep knocking long enough, he will get up and give you what you want so his reputation won't be damaged.*

⁹"And so I tell you, keep on asking, and you will be given what you ask for. Keep on looking, and you will find. Keep on knocking, and the door will be opened. ¹⁰For everyone who asks, receives. Everyone who seeks, finds. And the door is opened to everyone who knocks.

¹¹"You fathers—if your children ask* for a fish, do you give them a snake instead? ¹²Or if they ask for an egg, do you give them a scorpion? Of course not! ¹³If you sinful people know how to give good gifts to your children, how much more will your heavenly Father give the Holy Spirit to those who ask him."

JESUS AND THE PRINCE OF DEMONS

¹⁴One day Jesus cast a demon out of a man who couldn't speak, and the man's voice returned to him. The crowd was amazed, ¹⁵but some said, "No wonder he can cast out demons. He gets his power from Satan,* the prince of demons!" ¹⁶Trying to test Jesus, others asked for a miraculous sign from heaven to see if he was from God.

¹⁷He knew their thoughts, so he said, "Any kingdom at war with itself is doomed. A divided home is also doomed. ¹⁸You say I am empowered by the prince of demons.* But if Satan is fighting against himself by empowering me to cast out his demons, how can his kingdom survive? ¹⁹And if I am empowered by the prince of demons, what about your own followers? They cast out demons, too, so they will judge you for what you have said. ²⁰But if I am casting out demons by the power of God, then the Kingdom of God has arrived among you. ²¹For when Satan,* who is completely armed, guards his palace, it is safe—²²until someone who is stronger attacks and overpowers him, strips him of his weapons, and carries off his belongings.

²³"Anyone who isn't helping me opposes me, and anyone who isn't working with me is actually working against me.

²⁴"When an evil spirit leaves a person, it goes into the desert, searching for rest. But when it finds none, it says, 'I will return to the person I came from.' ²⁵So it returns and finds that its former home is all swept and clean. ²⁶Then the spirit finds seven other spirits more evil than itself, and they all enter the person and live there. And so that person is worse off than before."

²⁷As he was speaking, a woman in the crowd called out, "God bless your mother—the womb from which you came, and the breasts that nursed you!"

²⁸He replied, "But even more blessed are all who hear the word of God and put it into practice."

THE SIGN OF JONAH

²⁹As the crowd pressed in on Jesus, he said, "These are evil times, and this evil generation keeps asking me to show them a miraculous sign. But the only sign I will give them is the sign of the prophet Jonah. ³⁰What happened to him was a sign to the people of Nineveh that God had sent him. What happens to me will be a sign that God has sent me, the Son of Man, to these people.

11:2-4 Some manuscripts add additional portions of the Lord's Prayer as it reads in Matt 6:9-13.   11:8 Greek *in order to avoid shame*, or *because of [your] persistence.*   11:11 Some manuscripts add *for bread, do you give them a stone? Or if they ask.*   11:15 Greek *Beelzeboul.*
11:18 Greek *by Beelzeboul*; also in 11:19.   11:21 Greek *the strong one.*

31"The queen of Sheba* will rise up against this generation on judgment day and condemn it, because she came from a distant land to hear the wisdom of Solomon. And now someone greater than Solomon is here—and you refuse to listen to him. 32The people of Nineveh, too, will rise up against this generation on judgment day and condemn it, because they repented at the preaching of Jonah. And now someone greater than Jonah is here—and you refuse to repent.

RECEIVING THE LIGHT

33"No one lights a lamp and then hides it or puts it under a basket. Instead, it is put on a lampstand to give light to all who enter the room. 34Your eye is a lamp for your body. A pure eye lets sunshine into your soul. But an evil eye shuts out the light and plunges you into darkness. 35Make sure that the light you think you have is not really darkness. 36If you are filled with light, with no dark corners, then your whole life will be radiant, as though a floodlight is shining on you."

JESUS CRITICIZES THE RELIGIOUS LEADERS

37As Jesus was speaking, one of the Pharisees invited him home for a meal. So he went in and took his place at the table. 38His host was amazed to see that he sat down to eat without first performing the ceremonial washing required by Jewish custom. 39Then the Lord said to him, "You Pharisees are so careful to clean the outside of the cup and the dish, but inside you are still filthy—full of greed and wickedness! 40Fools! Didn't God make the inside as well as the outside? 41So give to the needy what you greedily possess, and you will be clean all over.

42"But how terrible it will be for you Pharisees! For you are careful to tithe even the tiniest part of your income,* but you completely forget about justice and the love of God. You should tithe, yes, but you should not leave undone the more important things.

43"How terrible it will be for you Pharisees! For how you love the seats of honor in the synagogues and the respectful greetings from everyone as you walk through the markets! 44Yes, how terrible it will be for you. For you are like hidden graves in a field. People walk over them without knowing the corruption they are stepping on."

45"Teacher," said an expert in religious law, "you have insulted us, too, in what you just said."

46"Yes," said Jesus, "how terrible it will be for you experts in religious law! For you crush people beneath impossible religious demands, and you never lift a finger to help ease the burden. 47How terrible it will be for you! For you build tombs for the very prophets your ancestors killed long ago. 48Murderers! You agree with your ancestors that what they did was right. You would have done the same yourselves. 49This is what God in his wisdom said about you:* 'I will send prophets and apostles to them, and they will kill some and persecute the others.'

50"And you of this generation will be held responsible for the murder of all God's prophets from the creation of the world— 51from the murder of Abel to the murder of Zechariah, who was killed between the altar and the sanctuary. Yes, it will surely be charged against you.

52"How terrible it will be for you experts in religious law! For you hide the key to knowledge from the people. You don't enter the Kingdom yourselves, and you prevent others from entering."

53As Jesus finished speaking, the Pharisees and teachers of religious law were furious. From that time on they grilled him with many hostile questions, 54trying to trap him into saying something they could use against him.

A WARNING AGAINST HYPOCRISY

12 Meanwhile, the crowds grew until thousands were milling about and

---

11:31 Greek *the queen of the south.*   **11:42** Greek *to tithe the mint and the rue and every herb.*   **11:49** Greek *Therefore, the wisdom of God said.*

My Daily Worship

— *October 3* —

HOW NOT TO BE A FOOL

LUKE 11:37–12:59

And I'll sit back and say to myself, My friend, you have enough stored away
for years to come. Now take it easy! Eat, drink, and be merry! (12:19).

[i reflect]

Just hours before dying of a pulmonary embolism during the 2003 Iraqi war, NBC anchor David Bloom wrote the following in an e-mail message to his wife:

> You can't begin to fathom, cannot begin to even glimpse the enormity of the changes I have and am continuing to undergo. God takes you to the depths of your being, until you're at rock bottom, and then, if you turn to him with utter and blind faith and resolve in your heart and mind to walk only with him and towards him, he picks you up with your bootstraps and leads you home. [I am] deeply saddened by the glimpses of death and destruction that I have seen, but at peace with my God and with you.

Bloom did not know that he was about to die, but clearly he was ready for it. In that sense, he presents the opposite example to the man described in Luke 12:16–21.

The wealthy farmer of Jesus' story had been blessed with a bountiful harvest and stored it all away. So far, so good. But his idea of what to do next reveals the problem: He did not take into account that he, like everyone else, lives day by day on the grace of God. While he envisioned a vast vista of hedonism stretching out before him, God had other plans. The following day was marked down on God's calendar as the farmer's exit day. The moral? "A person is a fool to store up earthly wealth but not have a rich relationship with God" (12:21).

Is your life focused on accumulating worldly wealth, like the farmer? Or is it focused on developing a rich relationship with God, like David Bloom?

Let every sign of worldly wealth you see throughout the day—banks, ATMs, stores—remind you of where true wealth is found. Thank God that he desires a relationship with you!

[i pray]

My treasure is in heaven, Lord. You are my treasure! Help me never to confuse
the relative values of my earthly possessions with my relationship with you.

[i respond]

If you were to write an e-mail message to a friend telling about the condition of your relationship with God, what would you honestly say? What would you identify as the changes you need to make? Write that message, and send it to a friend who could hold you accountable.

crushing each other. Jesus turned first to his disciples and warned them, "Beware of the yeast of the Pharisees—beware of their hypocrisy. ²The time is coming when everything will be revealed; all that is secret will be made public. ³Whatever you have said in the dark will be heard in the light, and what you have whispered behind closed doors will be shouted from the housetops for all to hear!

⁴"Dear friends, don't be afraid of those who want to kill you. They can only kill the body; they cannot do any more to you. ⁵But I'll tell you whom to fear. Fear God, who has the power to kill people and then throw them into hell.

⁶"What is the price of five sparrows? A couple of pennies? Yet God does not forget a single one of them. ⁷And the very hairs on your head are all numbered. So don't be afraid; you are more valuable to him than a whole flock of sparrows.

⁸"And I assure you of this: If anyone acknowledges me publicly here on earth, I, the Son of Man, will openly acknowledge that person in the presence of God's angels. ⁹But if anyone denies me here on earth, I will deny that person before God's angels. ¹⁰Yet those who speak against the Son of Man may be forgiven, but anyone who speaks blasphemies against the Holy Spirit will never be forgiven.

¹¹"And when you are brought to trial in the synagogues and before rulers and authorities, don't worry about what to say in your defense, ¹²for the Holy Spirit will teach you what needs to be said even as you are standing there."

STORY OF THE RICH FOOL

¹³Then someone called from the crowd, "Teacher, please tell my brother to divide our father's estate with me."

¹⁴Jesus replied, "Friend, who made me a judge over you to decide such things as that?" ¹⁵Then he said, "Beware! Don't be greedy for what you don't have. Real life is not measured by how much we own."

¹⁶And he gave an illustration: "A rich man had a fertile farm that produced fine crops. ¹⁷In fact, his barns were full to overflowing. ¹⁸So he said, 'I know! I'll tear down my barns and build bigger ones. Then I'll have room enough to store everything. ¹⁹And I'll sit back and say to myself, My friend, you have enough stored away for years to come. Now take it easy! Eat, drink, and be merry!'

²⁰"But God said to him, 'You fool! You will die this very night. Then who will get it all?'

²¹"Yes, a person is a fool to store up earthly wealth but not have a rich relationship with God."

TEACHING ABOUT MONEY AND POSSESSIONS

²²Then turning to his disciples, Jesus said, "So I tell you, don't worry about everyday life—whether you have enough food to eat or clothes to wear. ²³For life consists of far more than food and clothing. ²⁴Look at the ravens. They don't need to plant or harvest or put food in barns because God feeds them. And you are far more valuable to him than any birds! ²⁵Can all your worries add a single moment to your life? Of course not! ²⁶And if worry can't do little things like that, what's the use of worrying over bigger things?

²⁷"Look at the lilies and how they grow. They don't work or make their clothing, yet Solomon in all his glory was not dressed as beautifully as they are. ²⁸And if God cares so wonderfully for flowers that are here today and gone tomorrow, won't he more surely care for you? You have so little faith! ²⁹And don't worry about food—what to eat and drink. Don't worry whether God will provide it for you. ³⁰These things dominate the thoughts of most people, but your Father already knows your needs. ³¹He will give you all you need from day to day if you make the Kingdom of God your primary concern.

³²"So don't be afraid, little flock. For it gives your Father great happiness to give you the Kingdom.

³³"Sell what you have and give to those in need. This will store up treasure for you in

heaven! And the purses of heaven have no holes in them. Your treasure will be safe—no thief can steal it and no moth can destroy it. [34]Wherever your treasure is, there your heart and thoughts will also be.

BE READY FOR THE LORD'S COMING

[35]"Be dressed for service and well prepared, [36]as though you were waiting for your master to return from the wedding feast. Then you will be ready to open the door and let him in the moment he arrives and knocks. [37]There will be special favor for those who are ready and waiting for his return. I tell you, he himself will seat them, put on an apron, and serve them as they sit and eat! [38]He may come in the middle of the night or just before dawn.* But whenever he comes, there will be special favor for his servants who are ready!

[39]"Know this: A homeowner who knew exactly when a burglar was coming would not permit the house to be broken into. [40]You must be ready all the time, for the Son of Man will come when least expected."

[41]Peter asked, "Lord, is this illustration just for us or for everyone?"

[42]And the Lord replied, "I'm talking to any faithful, sensible servant to whom the master gives the responsibility of managing his household and feeding his family. [43]If the master returns and finds that the servant has done a good job, there will be a reward. [44]I assure you, the master will put that servant in charge of all he owns. [45]But if the servant thinks, 'My master won't be back for a while,' and begins oppressing the other servants, partying, and getting drunk—[46]well, the master will return unannounced and unexpected. He will tear the servant apart and banish him with the unfaithful. [47]The servant will be severely punished, for though he knew his duty, he refused to do it.

[48]"But people who are not aware that they are doing wrong will be punished only lightly. Much is required from those to whom much is given, and much more is required from those to whom much more is given.

JESUS CAUSES DIVISION

[49]"I have come to bring fire to the earth, and I wish that my task were already completed! [50]There is a terrible baptism ahead of me, and I am under a heavy burden until it is accomplished. [51]Do you think I have come to bring peace to the earth? No, I have come to bring strife and division! [52]From now on families will be split apart, three in favor of me, and two against—or the other way around. [53]There will be a division between father and son, mother and daughter, mother-in-law and daughter-in-law."

[54]Then Jesus turned to the crowd and said, "When you see clouds beginning to form in the west, you say, 'Here comes a shower.' And you are right. [55]When the south wind blows, you say, 'Today will be a scorcher.' And it is. [56]You hypocrites! You know how to interpret the appearance of the earth and the sky, but you can't interpret these present times.

[57]"Why can't you decide for yourselves what is right? [58]If you are on the way to court and you meet your accuser, try to settle the matter before it reaches the judge, or you may be sentenced and handed over to an officer and thrown in jail. [59]And if that happens, you won't be free again until you have paid the last penny."

A CALL TO REPENTANCE

13 About this time Jesus was informed that Pilate had murdered some people from Galilee as they were sacrificing at the Temple in Jerusalem. [2]"Do you think those Galileans were worse sinners than other people from Galilee?" he asked. "Is that why they suffered? [3]Not at all! And you will also perish unless you turn from your evil ways and turn to God. [4]And what about the eighteen men who died when the Tower of Siloam fell on them? Were they the worst sinners in

12:38 Greek *in the second or third watch.*

Jerusalem? ⁵No, and I tell you again that unless you repent, you will also perish."

ILLUSTRATION OF THE BARREN FIG TREE

⁶Then Jesus used this illustration: "A man planted a fig tree in his garden and came again and again to see if there was any fruit on it, but he was always disappointed. ⁷Finally, he said to his gardener, 'I've waited three years, and there hasn't been a single fig! Cut it down. It's taking up space we can use for something else.'

⁸"The gardener answered, 'Give it one more chance. Leave it another year, and I'll give it special attention and plenty of fertilizer. ⁹If we get figs next year, fine. If not, you can cut it down.'"

JESUS HEALS ON THE SABBATH

¹⁰One Sabbath day as Jesus was teaching in a synagogue, ¹¹he saw a woman who had been crippled by an evil spirit. She had been bent double for eighteen years and was unable to stand up straight. ¹²When Jesus saw her, he called her over and said, "Woman, you are healed of your sickness!" ¹³Then he touched her, and instantly she could stand straight. How she praised and thanked God!

¹⁴But the leader in charge of the synagogue was indignant that Jesus had healed her on the Sabbath day. "There are six days of the week for working," he said to the crowd. "Come on those days to be healed, not on the Sabbath."

¹⁵But the Lord replied, "You hypocrite! You work on the Sabbath day! Don't you untie your ox or your donkey from their stalls on the Sabbath and lead them out for water? ¹⁶Wasn't it necessary for me, even on the Sabbath day, to free this dear woman* from the bondage in which Satan has held her for eighteen years?" ¹⁷This shamed his enemies. And all the people rejoiced at the wonderful things he did.

ILLUSTRATION OF THE MUSTARD SEED

¹⁸Then Jesus said, "What is the Kingdom of God like? How can I illustrate it? ¹⁹It is like a tiny mustard seed planted in a garden; it grows and becomes a tree, and the birds come and find shelter among its branches."

ILLUSTRATION OF THE YEAST

²⁰He also asked, "What else is the Kingdom of God like? ²¹It is like yeast used by a woman making bread. Even though she used a large amount* of flour, the yeast permeated every part of the dough."

THE NARROW DOOR

²²Jesus went through the towns and villages, teaching as he went, always pressing on toward Jerusalem. ²³Someone asked him, "Lord, will only a few be saved?"

He replied, ²⁴"The door to heaven is narrow. Work hard to get in, because many will try to enter, ²⁵but when the head of the house has locked the door, it will be too late. Then you will stand outside knocking and pleading, 'Lord, open the door for us!' But he will reply, 'I do not know you.' ²⁶You will say, 'But we ate and drank with you, and you taught in our streets.' ²⁷And he will reply, 'I tell you, I don't know you. Go away, all you who do evil.'

²⁸"And there will be great weeping and gnashing of teeth, for you will see Abraham, Isaac, Jacob, and all the prophets within the Kingdom of God, but you will be thrown out. ²⁹Then people will come from all over the world to take their places in the Kingdom of God. ³⁰And note this: Some who are despised now will be greatly honored then; and some who are greatly honored now will be despised then.*"

JESUS GRIEVES OVER JERUSALEM

³¹A few minutes later some Pharisees said to him, "Get out of here if you want to live, because Herod Antipas wants to kill you!"

13:16 Greek *this woman, a daughter of Abraham.*   **13:21** Greek *3 measures.*   **13:30** Greek *Some are last who will be first, and some are first who will be last.*

My Daily Worship

— October 4 —

GATHER ME IN

LUKE 13:1–14:35

O Jerusalem, Jerusalem, the city that kills the prophets and stones God's messengers!
How often I have wanted to gather your children together as a hen protects
her chicks beneath her wings, but you wouldn't let me (13:34).

[i reflect]

The city bustled with life. Merchants bought and sold and haggled over prices. Old men sat by the gates and debated the fine points of the law. Women gathered at the wells and shared the latest news. Children laughed and shouted and chased one another down the street. And over all this, the Temple loomed, dominating the city with its splendor. Jerusalem, the city of David, soon to be destroyed.

O Jerusalem, Jesus mourned, how I long to gather you in, but you will not be gathered. Jerusalem, you who have rejected the prophets, have now rejected the Son of God. You long for the Messiah, but do not recognize the Anointed One standing in your midst. You call for justice, but you murder the King of kings. Your priests sacrifice animal after animal, but I am the perfect sacrifice for your sins. Come to me, come to me now, O Jerusalem, or face certain destruction.

It's easy to dismiss this passage as relevant only to the people of that day. But we face the same dilemma: Will we allow Jesus to gather us in or not? The Son of God has been revealed. He has died, he has risen, and he is now glorified. Accept him now, believe in him now, worship him now. Or reject him at your peril, just as Jerusalem did. Church membership will not shield you. Good deeds will not buy you favor. Judgment Day is coming and only those under the protection of Jesus will survive.

Consider your relationship with Jesus at this moment. He longs to gather you in, but will you be gathered? His welcoming arms await you. Run to Jesus your Savior. Draw close to him for he is your protector. Worship him for he is the Son of God. Bow down and give homage for he is your king.

[i pray]

Gather me in, Lord Jesus. I am willing. Gather me under your sheltering wings and hold me
close to you. Surround me with your love and do not let me stray from your protection.

[i respond]

Look for images of protection over the next few days—a parent holding the hand of a child; an elderly person clinging to the arm of a friend; a paramedic assisting someone in an accident; a mother bird feeding her young. Let these images cause you to remember how Jesus longs to gather and protect you.

[32]Jesus replied, "Go tell that fox that I will keep on casting out demons and doing miracles of healing today and tomorrow; and the third day I will accomplish my purpose. [33]Yes, today, tomorrow, and the next day I must proceed on my way. For it wouldn't do for a prophet of God to be killed except in Jerusalem!

[34]"O Jerusalem, Jerusalem, the city that kills the prophets and stones God's messengers! How often I have wanted to gather your children together as a hen protects her chicks beneath her wings, but you wouldn't let me. [35]And now look, your house is left to you empty. And you will never see me again until you say, 'Bless the one who comes in the name of the Lord!'*"

JESUS HEALS ON THE SABBATH

14 One Sabbath day Jesus was in the home of a leader of the Pharisees. The people were watching him closely, [2]because there was a man there whose arms and legs were swollen.* [3]Jesus asked the Pharisees and experts in religious law, "Well, is it permitted in the law to heal people on the Sabbath day, or not?" [4]When they refused to answer, Jesus touched the sick man and healed him and sent him away. [5]Then he turned to them and asked, "Which of you doesn't work on the Sabbath? If your son* or your cow falls into a pit, don't you proceed at once to get him out?" [6]Again they had no answer.

JESUS TEACHES ABOUT HUMILITY

[7]When Jesus noticed that all who had come to the dinner were trying to sit near the head of the table, he gave them this advice: [8]"If you are invited to a wedding feast, don't always head for the best seat. What if someone more respected than you has also been invited? [9]The host will say, 'Let this person sit here instead.' Then you will be embarrassed and will have to take whatever seat is left at the foot of the table! [10]"Do this instead—sit at the foot of the table. Then when your host sees you, he will come and say, 'Friend, we have a better place than this for you!' Then you will be honored in front of all the other guests. [11]For the proud will be humbled, but the humble will be honored."

[12]Then he turned to his host. "When you put on a luncheon or a dinner," he said, "don't invite your friends, brothers, relatives, and rich neighbors. For they will repay you by inviting you back. [13]Instead, invite the poor, the crippled, the lame, and the blind. [14]Then at the resurrection of the godly, God will reward you for inviting those who could not repay you."

STORY OF THE GREAT FEAST

[15]Hearing this, a man sitting at the table with Jesus exclaimed, "What a privilege it would be to have a share in the Kingdom of God!"

[16]Jesus replied with this illustration: "A man prepared a great feast and sent out many invitations. [17]When all was ready, he sent his servant around to notify the guests that it was time for them to come. [18]But they all began making excuses. One said he had just bought a field and wanted to inspect it, so he asked to be excused. [19]Another said he had just bought five pair of oxen and wanted to try them out. [20]Another had just been married, so he said he couldn't come.

[21]"The servant returned and told his master what they had said. His master was angry and said, 'Go quickly into the streets and alleys of the city and invite the poor, the crippled, the lame, and the blind.' [22]After the servant had done this, he reported, 'There is still room for more.' [23]So his master said, 'Go out into the country lanes and behind the hedges and urge anyone you find to come, so that the house will be full. [24]For none of those I invited first will get even the smallest taste of what I had prepared for them.'"

THE COST OF BEING A DISCIPLE

[25]Great crowds were following Jesus. He turned around and said to them, [26]"If you

---

13:35 Ps 118:26.   14:2 Traditionally translated *who had dropsy.*   14:5 Some manuscripts read *donkey.*

want to be my follower you must love me more than* your own father and mother, wife and children, brothers and sisters—yes, more than your own life. Otherwise, you cannot be my disciple. ²⁷And you cannot be my disciple if you do not carry your own cross and follow me.

²⁸"But don't begin until you count the cost. For who would begin construction of a building without first getting estimates and then checking to see if there is enough money to pay the bills? ²⁹Otherwise, you might complete only the foundation before running out of funds. And then how everyone would laugh at you! ³⁰They would say, 'There's the person who started that building and ran out of money before it was finished!'

³¹"Or what king would ever dream of going to war without first sitting down with his counselors and discussing whether his army of ten thousand is strong enough to defeat the twenty thousand soldiers who are marching against him? ³²If he is not able, then while the enemy is still far away, he will send a delegation to discuss terms of peace. ³³So no one can become my disciple without giving up everything for me.

³⁴"Salt is good for seasoning. But if it loses its flavor, how do you make it salty again? ³⁵Flavorless salt is good neither for the soil nor for fertilizer. It is thrown away. Anyone who is willing to hear should listen and understand!"

STORY OF THE LOST SHEEP

15 Tax collectors and other notorious sinners often came to listen to Jesus teach. ²This made the Pharisees and teachers of religious law complain that he was associating with such despicable people—even eating with them!

³So Jesus used this illustration: ⁴"If you had one hundred sheep, and one of them strayed away and was lost in the wilderness, wouldn't you leave the ninety-nine others to go and search for the lost one until you found it?

⁵And then you would joyfully carry it home on your shoulders. ⁶When you arrived, you would call together your friends and neighbors to rejoice with you because your lost sheep was found. ⁷In the same way, heaven will be happier over one lost sinner who returns to God than over ninety-nine others who are righteous and haven't strayed away!

STORY OF THE LOST COIN

⁸"Or suppose a woman has ten valuable silver coins* and loses one. Won't she light a lamp and look in every corner of the house and sweep every nook and cranny until she finds it? ⁹And when she finds it, she will call in her friends and neighbors to rejoice with her because she has found her lost coin. ¹⁰In the same way, there is joy in the presence of God's angels when even one sinner repents."

STORY OF THE LOST SON

¹¹To illustrate the point further, Jesus told them this story: "A man had two sons. ¹²The younger son told his father, 'I want my share of your estate now, instead of waiting until you die.' So his father agreed to divide his wealth between his sons.

¹³"A few days later this younger son packed all his belongings and took a trip to a distant land, and there he wasted all his money on wild living. ¹⁴About the time his money ran out, a great famine swept over the land, and he began to starve. ¹⁵He persuaded a local farmer to hire him to feed his pigs. ¹⁶The boy became so hungry that even the pods he was feeding the pigs looked good to him. But no one gave him anything.

¹⁷"When he finally came to his senses, he said to himself, 'At home even the hired men have food enough to spare, and here I am, dying of hunger! ¹⁸I will go home to my father and say, "Father, I have sinned against both heaven and you, ¹⁹and I am no longer worthy of being called your son. Please take me on as a hired man." '

²⁰"So he returned home to his father. And

14:26 Greek *you must hate.*   15:8 Greek *10 drachmas.* A drachma was the equivalent of a full day's wage.

while he was still a long distance away, his father saw him coming. Filled with love and compassion, he ran to his son, embraced him, and kissed him. ²¹His son said to him, 'Father, I have sinned against both heaven and you, and I am no longer worthy of being called your son.*'

²²"But his father said to the servants, 'Quick! Bring the finest robe in the house and put it on him. Get a ring for his finger, and sandals for his feet. ²³And kill the calf we have been fattening in the pen. We must celebrate with a feast, ²⁴for this son of mine was dead and has now returned to life. He was lost, but now he is found.' So the party began.

²⁵"Meanwhile, the older son was in the fields working. When he returned home, he heard music and dancing in the house, ²⁶and he asked one of the servants what was going on. ²⁷'Your brother is back,' he was told, 'and your father has killed the calf we were fattening and has prepared a great feast. We are celebrating because of his safe return.'

²⁸"The older brother was angry and wouldn't go in. His father came out and begged him, ²⁹but he replied, 'All these years I've worked hard for you and never once refused to do a single thing you told me to. And in all that time you never gave me even one young goat for a feast with my friends. ³⁰Yet when this son of yours comes back after squandering your money on prostitutes, you celebrate by killing the finest calf we have.'

³¹"His father said to him, 'Look, dear son, you and I are very close, and everything I have is yours. ³²We had to celebrate this happy day. For your brother was dead and has come back to life! He was lost, but now he is found!' "

STORY OF THE SHREWD MANAGER

16 Jesus told this story to his disciples: "A rich man hired a manager to handle his affairs, but soon a rumor went around that the manager was thoroughly dishonest. ²So his employer called him in and said, 'What's this I hear about your stealing from me? Get your report in order, because you are going to be dismissed.'

³"The manager thought to himself, 'Now what? I'm through here, and I don't have the strength to go out and dig ditches, and I'm too proud to beg. ⁴I know just the thing! And then I'll have plenty of friends to take care of me when I leave!'

⁵"So he invited each person who owed money to his employer to come and discuss the situation. He asked the first one, 'How much do you owe him?' ⁶The man replied, 'I owe him eight hundred gallons of olive oil.' So the manager told him, 'Tear up that bill and write another one for four hundred gallons.*'

⁷"'And how much do you owe my employer?' he asked the next man. 'A thousand bushels of wheat,' was the reply. 'Here,' the manager said, 'take your bill and replace it with one for only eight hundred bushels.*'

⁸"The rich man had to admire the dishonest rascal for being so shrewd. And it is true that the citizens of this world are more shrewd than the godly are. ⁹I tell you, use your worldly resources to benefit others and make friends. In this way, your generosity stores up a reward for you in heaven.*

¹⁰"Unless you are faithful in small matters, you won't be faithful in large ones. If you cheat even a little, you won't be honest with greater responsibilities. ¹¹And if you are untrustworthy about worldly wealth, who will trust you with the true riches of heaven? ¹²And if you are not faithful with other people's money, why should you be trusted with money of your own?

¹³"No one can serve two masters. For you will hate one and love the other, or be devoted to one and despise the other. You cannot serve both God and money."

¹⁴The Pharisees, who dearly loved their money, naturally scoffed at all this. ¹⁵Then he said to them, "You like to look good in public, but God knows your evil hearts. What this

---

15:21 Some manuscripts add *Please take me on as a hired man.* 16:6 Greek *100 baths . . . 50 [baths].* 16:7 Greek *100 korous . . . 80 [korous].* 16:9 Or *Then when you run out at the end of this life, your friends will welcome you into eternal homes.*

My Daily Worship

— October 5 —

WHAT WILL YOU ENDURE?

LUKE 15:1–16:31

In the same way, heaven will be happier over one lost sinner who returns to God than over ninety-nine others who are righteous and haven't strayed away! (15:7).

[i reflect]

A shepherd searching in the wilderness for the one lost sheep that has strayed from the flock. A woman turning her household upside down to find a lost coin. A father eagerly welcoming a wayward son who, after squandering his inheritance, returns home. In each instance, Jesus tells us the end result—a celebration when the lost has been found.

In this passage, Jesus reveals the heart of a Father who tenderly searches for sinners and then joyously forgives them. His love sent his Son to not only search for the lost, but to also endure the cross for their sake. God has the same extraordinary love for us today. He is still in the business of seeking and saving—and he calls us to join him.

Every person we meet is precious to God our Father. Every person needs to turn to him and be saved. And when that person does, oh the rejoicing! All of heaven, we are told, will be involved in an angelic celebration. So what are we willing to endure, how far are we willing to search, how much will we allow our "households" to be turned upside down in order to bring the lost to God?

Chrysostom wrote, "If God rejoices over the little one that is found, how do you despise those God earnestly cares for? We should give up even our lives for one of these little ones. But is the lost one weak and shabby? Then, it is even more important that we do everything we can to preserve them . . . For our neighbors' sake don't refuse to do any of the tasks that seem lowly and troublesome . . . although the work is hard and we must pass over mountains and valleys, endure everything for your neighbor's salvation."

As an act of worship to the One who came and saved you, consider your neighbors and take time to pray for their salvation. See them today with the eyes of your Father in heaven.

[i pray]

Jesus, thank you for redeeming my soul and giving me salvation. Help me to see others as those needing the same saving grace given to me.

[i respond]

Think of one person in your neighborhood who needs salvation. What lowly task can you perform to point him or her to Jesus? What sacrifice can you make to show the way to the Father? What will you endure for the sake of the lost?

world honors is an abomination in the sight of God.

16"Until John the Baptist began to preach, the laws of Moses and the messages of the prophets were your guides. But now the Good News of the Kingdom of God is preached, and eager multitudes are forcing their way in. 17But that doesn't mean that the law has lost its force in even the smallest point. It is stronger and more permanent than heaven and earth.

18"Anyone who divorces his wife and marries someone else commits adultery, and anyone who marries a divorced woman commits adultery."

THE RICH MAN AND LAZARUS

19Jesus said, "There was a certain rich man who was splendidly clothed and who lived each day in luxury. 20At his door lay a diseased beggar named Lazarus. 21As Lazarus lay there longing for scraps from the rich man's table, the dogs would come and lick his open sores. 22Finally, the beggar died and was carried by the angels to be with Abraham.* The rich man also died and was buried, 23and his soul went to the place of the dead.* There, in torment, he saw Lazarus in the far distance with Abraham.

24"The rich man shouted, 'Father Abraham, have some pity! Send Lazarus over here to dip the tip of his finger in water and cool my tongue, because I am in anguish in these flames.'

25"But Abraham said to him, 'Son, remember that during your lifetime you had everything you wanted, and Lazarus had nothing. So now he is here being comforted, and you are in anguish. 26And besides, there is a great chasm separating us. Anyone who wanted to cross over to you from here is stopped at its edge, and no one there can cross over to us.'

27"Then the rich man said, 'Please, Father Abraham, send him to my father's home. 28For I have five brothers, and I want him to warn them about this place of torment so they won't have to come here when they die.'

Words of Worship

SPIRITUAL SONGS

Spiritual Songs—Greek *o-dai* pneu-ma-ti-*kai* "spiritual songs."

"Sing psalms and hymns and spiritual songs to God with thankful hearts" (Colossians 3:16). When Paul wrote these words, he left us with a puzzle. Although scholars have wrestled with the question, no one can really be sure what he meant by *spiritual songs*. Was he referring to spontaneous singing, songs given as a word from the Holy Spirit, songs uttered in an unknown language—or all of the above, or something else?

We don't have to settle the issue to appreciate this truth: The Spirit of Christ motivates every genuine act of our worship. As Paul stated, "No one is able to say, 'Jesus is Lord,' except by the Holy Spirit" (1 Corinthians 12:3). When our worship in song celebrates Christ and lifts him up as Lord of our lives, we know we are offering spiritual songs.

29"But Abraham said, 'Moses and the prophets have warned them. Your brothers can read their writings anytime they want to.'

30"The rich man replied, 'No, Father Abraham! But if someone is sent to them from the dead, then they will turn from their sins.'

31"But Abraham said, 'If they won't listen to Moses and the prophets, they won't listen even if someone rises from the dead.'"

TEACHINGS ABOUT FORGIVENESS AND FAITH

17 One day Jesus said to his disciples, "There will always be temptations to

16:22 Greek *into Abraham's bosom.* 16:23 Greek *to Hades.*

My Daily Worship

— October 6 —

CLING TO THE CROSS

LUKE 17:1–18:43

One day the apostles said to the Lord,
"We need more faith; tell us how to get it" (17:5).

[i reflect]

In the beginning it was easy for the apostles to believe. They watched Jesus heal the sick and give sight to the blind. They saw him raise the widow's son from the dead and call Lazarus from the grave. They witnessed his power when he rebuked the wind and calmed the sea. But then Jesus began to confront the religious leaders with their sin and the trouble started. Soon the leaders plotted to have him arrested, and Jesus predicted his own death. The apostles were confused, so they pleaded with Jesus, "We need more faith; tell us how to get it" (17:5).

It's easy to trust God when times are good, but life is often difficult. Accidents, illness, job loss, broken relationships—all can leave us wondering if God's promises are true. Yet only in these situations can we really learn to trust God and humbly depend on him.

Jerome wrote, "It is hard to find undoubted faith in God. Suppose I stood to pray. I couldn't pray if I didn't believe. But if I really believed, I would cleanse my heart and beat my chest. The tears would stream down my cheeks, my body would shudder, my face grow pale. I would lie at my Lord's feet, weep over them, and wipe them with my hair. I would cling to the cross and not let go until I received mercy."

When we stumble in our faith, when we falter because of difficult circumstances, that's when we need to follow Jerome's lead and cling to the cross. Like the disciples, we need to turn to Jesus and ask him for more faith.

Today, as you spend time with God, tell him the doubts and trials that threaten to erode your faith. Ask him to point you to his promises and ask him to strengthen your faith.

[i pray]

Lord Jesus, I cling to the cross, for it has saved me. I come to you begging for mercy.
My sin is so great and my faith is so small. Increase my faith,
dear Jesus, so that I can bring glory to your name.

[i respond]

Look at your church library or local Christian bookstore for a promise book, if you don't have one already. Flip through the book for one of God's promises that you most need in your current situation. Write it on a separate piece of paper or in your journal, and then use it as a prayer tool in asking God for more faith to trust in his Word.

sin, but how terrible it will be for the person who does the tempting. ²It would be better to be thrown into the sea with a large millstone tied around the neck than to face the punishment in store for harming one of these little ones. ³I am warning you! If another believer* sins, rebuke him; then if he repents, forgive him. ⁴Even if he wrongs you seven times a day and each time turns again and asks forgiveness, forgive him."

⁵One day the apostles said to the Lord, "We need more faith; tell us how to get it."

⁶"Even if you had faith as small as a mustard seed," the Lord answered, "you could say to this mulberry tree, 'May God uproot you and throw you into the sea,' and it would obey you!

⁷"When a servant comes in from plowing or taking care of sheep, he doesn't just sit down and eat. ⁸He must first prepare his master's meal and serve him his supper before eating his own. ⁹And the servant is not even thanked, because he is merely doing what he is supposed to do. ¹⁰In the same way, when you obey me you should say, 'We are not worthy of praise. We are servants who have simply done our duty.'"

TEN HEALED OF LEPROSY

¹¹As Jesus continued on toward Jerusalem, he reached the border between Galilee and Samaria. ¹²As he entered a village there, ten lepers stood at a distance, ¹³crying out, "Jesus, Master, have mercy on us!"

¹⁴He looked at them and said, "Go show yourselves to the priests." And as they went, their leprosy disappeared.

¹⁵One of them, when he saw that he was healed, came back to Jesus, shouting, "Praise God, I'm healed!" ¹⁶He fell face down on the ground at Jesus' feet, thanking him for what he had done. This man was a Samaritan.

¹⁷Jesus asked, "Didn't I heal ten men? Where are the other nine? ¹⁸Does only this foreigner return to give glory to God?" ¹⁹And Jesus said to the man, "Stand up and go. Your faith has made you well."

THE COMING OF THE KINGDOM

²⁰One day the Pharisees asked Jesus, "When will the Kingdom of God come?"

Jesus replied, "The Kingdom of God isn't ushered in with visible signs.* ²¹You won't be able to say, 'Here it is!' or 'It's over there!' For the Kingdom of God is among you.*"

²²Later he talked again about this with his disciples. "The time is coming when you will long to share in the days of the Son of Man, but you won't be able to," he said. ²³"Reports will reach you that the Son of Man has returned and that he is in this place or that. Don't believe such reports or go out to look for him. ²⁴For when the Son of Man returns, you will know it beyond all doubt. It will be as evident as the lightning that flashes across the sky. ²⁵But first the Son of Man must suffer terribly* and be rejected by this generation.

²⁶"When the Son of Man returns, the world will be like the people were in Noah's day. ²⁷In those days before the Flood, the people enjoyed banquets and parties and weddings right up to the time Noah entered his boat and the Flood came to destroy them all.

²⁸"And the world will be as it was in the days of Lot. People went about their daily business—eating and drinking, buying and selling, farming and building—²⁹until the morning Lot left Sodom. Then fire and burning sulfur rained down from heaven and destroyed them all. ³⁰Yes, it will be 'business as usual' right up to the hour when the Son of Man returns.* ³¹On that day a person outside the house* must not go into the house to pack. A person in the field must not return to town. ³²Remember what happened to Lot's wife! ³³Whoever clings to this life will lose it, and whoever loses this life will save it. ³⁴That night two people will be asleep in one bed; one will be taken away, and the other will be left. ³⁵Two women will be grinding flour

---

17:3 Greek *your brother.* 17:20 Or *by your speculations.* 17:21 Or *within you.* 17:25 Or *suffer many things.* 17:30 Or *on the day the Son of Man is revealed.* 17:31 Greek *on the roof.*

together at the mill; one will be taken, the other left.*"

[37]"Lord, where will this happen?" the disciples asked.

Jesus replied, "Just as the gathering of vultures shows there is a carcass nearby, so these signs indicate that the end is near."*

STORY OF THE PERSISTENT WIDOW

18 One day Jesus told his disciples a story to illustrate their need for constant prayer and to show them that they must never give up. [2]"There was a judge in a certain city," he said, "who was a godless man with great contempt for everyone. [3]A widow of that city came to him repeatedly, appealing for justice against someone who had harmed her. [4]The judge ignored her for a while, but eventually she wore him out. 'I fear neither God nor man,' he said to himself, [5]'but this woman is driving me crazy. I'm going to see that she gets justice, because she is wearing me out with her constant requests!' "

[6]Then the Lord said, "Learn a lesson from this evil judge. [7]Even he rendered a just decision in the end, so don't you think God will surely give justice to his chosen people who plead with him day and night? Will he keep putting them off? [8]I tell you, he will grant justice to them quickly! But when I, the Son of Man, return, how many will I find who have faith?"

STORY OF THE PHARISEE AND TAX COLLECTOR

[9]Then Jesus told this story to some who had great self-confidence and scorned everyone else: [10]"Two men went to the Temple to pray. One was a Pharisee, and the other was a dishonest tax collector. [11]The proud Pharisee stood by himself and prayed this prayer: 'I thank you, God, that I am not a sinner like everyone else, especially like that tax collector over there! For I never cheat, I don't sin, I don't commit adultery, [12]I fast twice a week, and I give you a tenth of my income.'

[13]"But the tax collector stood at a distance and dared not even lift his eyes to heaven as he prayed. Instead, he beat his chest in sorrow, saying, 'O God, be merciful to me, for I am a sinner.' [14]I tell you, this sinner, not the Pharisee, returned home justified before God. For the proud will be humbled, but the humble will be honored."

JESUS BLESSES THE CHILDREN

[15]One day some parents brought their little children to Jesus so he could touch them and bless them, but the disciples told them not to bother him. [16]Then Jesus called for the children and said to the disciples, "Let the children come to me. Don't stop them! For the Kingdom of God belongs to such as these. [17]I assure you, anyone who doesn't have their kind of faith will never get into the Kingdom of God."

THE RICH MAN

[18]Once a religious leader asked Jesus this question: "Good teacher, what should I do to get eternal life?"

[19]"Why do you call me good?" Jesus asked him. "Only God is truly good. [20]But as for your question, you know the commandments: 'Do not commit adultery. Do not murder. Do not steal. Do not testify falsely. Honor your father and mother.'*"

[21]The man replied, "I've obeyed all these commandments since I was a child."

[22]"There is still one thing you lack," Jesus said. "Sell all you have and give the money to the poor, and you will have treasure in heaven. Then come, follow me." [23]But when the man heard this, he became sad because he was very rich.

[24]Jesus watched him go and then said to his disciples, "How hard it is for rich people to get into the Kingdom of God! [25]It is easier for a camel to go through the eye of a needle than

---

17:35 Some manuscripts add verse 36, *Two men will be working in the field; one will be taken, the other left.*   17:37 Greek *Wherever the carcass is, the vultures gather.*   18:20 Exod 20:12-16; Deut 5:16-20.

for a rich person to enter the Kingdom of God!"

²⁶Those who heard this said, "Then who in the world can be saved?"

²⁷He replied, "What is impossible from a human perspective is possible with God."

²⁸Peter said, "We have left our homes and followed you."

²⁹"Yes," Jesus replied, "and I assure you, everyone who has given up house or wife or brothers or parents or children, for the sake of the Kingdom of God, ³⁰will be repaid many times over in this life, as well as receiving eternal life in the world to come."

JESUS AGAIN PREDICTS HIS DEATH

³¹Gathering the twelve disciples around him, Jesus told them, "As you know, we are going to Jerusalem. And when we get there, all the predictions of the ancient prophets concerning the Son of Man will come true. ³²He will be handed over to the Romans to be mocked, treated shamefully, and spit upon. ³³They will whip him and kill him, but on the third day he will rise again."

³⁴But they didn't understand a thing he said. Its significance was hidden from them, and they failed to grasp what he was talking about.

JESUS HEALS A BLIND BEGGAR

³⁵As they approached Jericho, a blind beggar was sitting beside the road. ³⁶When he heard the noise of a crowd going past, he asked what was happening. ³⁷They told him that Jesus of Nazareth was going by. ³⁸So he began shouting, "Jesus, Son of David, have mercy on me!" ³⁹The crowds ahead of Jesus tried to hush the man, but he only shouted louder, "Son of David, have mercy on me!"

⁴⁰When Jesus heard him, he stopped and ordered that the man be brought to him. ⁴¹Then Jesus asked the man, "What do you want me to do for you?"

"Lord," he pleaded, "I want to see!"

⁴²And Jesus said, "All right, you can see!

Your faith has healed you." ⁴³Instantly the man could see, and he followed Jesus, praising God. And all who saw it praised God, too.

JESUS AND ZACCHAEUS

19 Jesus entered Jericho and made his way through the town. ²There was a man there named Zacchaeus. He was one of the most influential Jews in the Roman tax-collecting business, and he had become very rich. ³He tried to get a look at Jesus, but he was too short to see over the crowds. ⁴So he ran ahead and climbed a sycamore tree beside the road, so he could watch from there.

⁵When Jesus came by, he looked up at Zacchaeus and called him by name. "Zacchaeus!" he said. "Quick, come down! For I must be a guest in your home today."

⁶Zacchaeus quickly climbed down and took Jesus to his house in great excitement and joy. ⁷But the crowds were displeased. "He has gone to be the guest of a notorious sinner," they grumbled.

⁸Meanwhile, Zacchaeus stood there and said to the Lord, "I will give half my wealth to the poor, Lord, and if I have overcharged people on their taxes, I will give them back four times as much!"

⁹Jesus responded, "Salvation has come to this home today, for this man has shown himself to be a son of Abraham. ¹⁰And I, the Son of Man, have come to seek and save those like him who are lost."

STORY OF THE TEN SERVANTS

¹¹The crowd was listening to everything Jesus said. And because he was nearing Jerusalem, he told a story to correct the impression that the Kingdom of God would begin right away. ¹²He said, "A nobleman was called away to a distant empire to be crowned king and then return. ¹³Before he left, he called together ten servants and gave them ten pounds of silver* to invest for him while he was gone. ¹⁴But his people hated him and sent a delegation after

19:13 Greek *10 minas; 1 mina* was worth about 3 months' wages.

My Daily Worship

EVEN THE ROCKS WILL CHEER
LUKE 19:1–47

*He replied, "If they kept quiet, the stones along
the road would burst into cheers!" (19:40).*

[i reflect]

See the King in his triumphal entry. Mighty he is, yet humble. He rides the colt of a donkey. He comes in peace, our King. And our King is powerful. Did he not heal the blind, cure the leper, cause the lame to walk again? Did he not calm the sea? Throw down your garments in homage. Wave palm branches before him. Shout and sing as you follow him to Jerusalem. Praise God for all the miracles he has performed. Bless him, for he comes in the name of the Lord.

Now the King is glorified. He reigns in majesty at the right hand of his Father. He offers eternal life to those who call on his name. Throw down your time, your talents, and your possessions in service to your King. Lift your arms in worship. Praise him for all the wondrous things he has done. Sing and shout as you follow him all of your life.

The Pharisees protested that people should not give to Jesus the glory due to God. Even today, some refuse to believe that Jesus is the Son of the living God. But Jesus does not need our praise. Were we to remain silent "the stones along the road would burst into cheers!" (19:40). All creation declares his glory. It is our privilege to glorify our King and to serve him faithfully all our days.

On his deathbed, missionary David Brainerd said to his biographer, Jonathan Edwards, "I do not go to heaven to be advanced, but to give honor to God. It is no matter where I shall be stationed in heaven, whether I have a high or low seat there, but to live and please and glorify God. My heaven is to please God and glorify him, and give all to him, and to be wholly devoted to his glory."

It is our privilege to glorify God—in life and for all eternity. Go outside today and glorify God in his creation and with his creation. Remember, even the rocks one day will celebrate his glory!

[i pray]

*Jesus, you are my King and worthy of all my praise. I lift up my arms and glorify you.
It is my privilege to serve you. Take my life and use it to your glory.*

[i respond]

Find a rock and place it on your desk, by the kitchen sink, or on the dashboard of your car—wherever you spend the most time. Let it serve as a reminder of the great privilege you have to glorify and praise God.

him to say they did not want him to be their king.

¹⁵"When he returned, the king called in the servants to whom he had given the money. He wanted to find out what they had done with the money and what their profits were. ¹⁶The first servant reported a tremendous gain—ten times as much as the original amount! ¹⁷'Well done!' the king exclaimed. 'You are a trustworthy servant. You have been faithful with the little I entrusted to you, so you will be governor of ten cities as your reward.'

¹⁸"The next servant also reported a good gain—five times the original amount. ¹⁹'Well done!' the king said. 'You can be governor over five cities.'

²⁰"But the third servant brought back only the original amount of money and said, 'I hid it and kept it safe. ²¹I was afraid because you are a hard man to deal with, taking what isn't yours and harvesting crops you didn't plant.'

²²" 'You wicked servant!' the king roared. 'Hard, am I? If you knew so much about me and how tough I am, ²³why didn't you deposit the money in the bank so I could at least get some interest on it?' ²⁴Then turning to the others standing nearby, the king ordered, 'Take the money from this servant, and give it to the one who earned the most.'

²⁵" 'But, master,' they said, 'that servant has enough already!'

²⁶" 'Yes,' the king replied, 'but to those who use well what they are given, even more will be given. But from those who are unfaithful,* even what little they have will be taken away. ²⁷And now about these enemies of mine who didn't want me to be their king—bring them in and execute them right here in my presence.' "

THE TRIUMPHAL ENTRY

²⁸After telling this story, Jesus went on toward Jerusalem, walking ahead of his disciples. ²⁹As they came to the towns of Bethphage and Bethany, on the Mount of Olives, he sent two disciples ahead. ³⁰"Go into that village over there," he told them, "and as you enter it, you will see a colt tied there that has never been ridden. Untie it and bring it here. ³¹If anyone asks what you are doing, just say, 'The Lord needs it.' "

³²So they went and found the colt, just as Jesus had said. ³³And sure enough, as they were untying it, the owners asked them, "Why are you untying our colt?"

³⁴And the disciples simply replied, "The Lord needs it." ³⁵So they brought the colt to Jesus and threw their garments over it for him to ride on.

³⁶Then the crowds spread out their coats on the road ahead of Jesus. ³⁷As they reached the place where the road started down from the Mount of Olives, all of his followers began to shout and sing as they walked along, praising God for all the wonderful miracles they had seen.

³⁸ "Bless the King who comes in the name of
the Lord!
Peace in heaven
and glory in highest heaven!"*

³⁹But some of the Pharisees among the crowd said, "Teacher, rebuke your followers for saying things like that!"

⁴⁰He replied, "If they kept quiet, the stones along the road would burst into cheers!"

JESUS WEEPS OVER JERUSALEM

⁴¹But as they came closer to Jerusalem and Jesus saw the city ahead, he began to cry. ⁴²"I wish that even today you would find the way of peace. But now it is too late, and peace is hidden from you. ⁴³Before long your enemies will build ramparts against your walls and encircle you and close in on you. ⁴⁴They will crush you to the ground, and your children with you. Your enemies will not leave a single stone in place, because you have rejected the opportunity God offered you."

19:26 Or *who have nothing.* **19:38** Pss 118:26; 148:1.

Jesus Clears the Temple

⁴⁵Then Jesus entered the Temple and began to drive out the merchants from their stalls. ⁴⁶He told them, "The Scriptures declare, 'My Temple will be a place of prayer,' but you have turned it into a den of thieves."*

⁴⁷After that, he taught daily in the Temple, but the leading priests, the teachers of religious law, and the other leaders of the people began planning how to kill him. ⁴⁸But they could think of nothing, because all the people hung on every word he said.

The Authority of Jesus Challenged

20 One day as Jesus was teaching and preaching the Good News in the Temple, the leading priests and teachers of religious law and other leaders came up to him. ²They demanded, "By whose authority did you drive out the merchants from the Temple?* Who gave you such authority?"

³"Let me ask you a question first," he replied. ⁴"Did John's baptism come from heaven, or was it merely human?"

⁵They talked it over among themselves. "If we say it was from heaven, he will ask why we didn't believe him. ⁶But if we say it was merely human, the people will stone us, because they are convinced he was a prophet." ⁷Finally they replied, "We don't know."

⁸And Jesus responded, "Then I won't answer your question either."

Story of the Evil Farmers

⁹Now Jesus turned to the people again and told them this story: "A man planted a vineyard, leased it out to tenant farmers, and moved to another country to live for several years. ¹⁰At grape-picking time, he sent one of his servants to collect his share of the crop. But the farmers attacked the servant, beat him up, and sent him back empty-handed. ¹¹So the owner sent another servant, but the same thing happened; he was beaten up and treated

shamefully, and he went away empty-handed. ¹²A third man was sent and the same thing happened. He, too, was wounded and chased away.

¹³"'What will I do?' the owner asked himself. 'I know! I'll send my cherished son. Surely they will respect him.'

¹⁴"But when the farmers saw his son, they said to each other, 'Here comes the heir to this estate. Let's kill him and get the estate for ourselves!' ¹⁵So they dragged him out of the vineyard and murdered him.

"What do you suppose the owner of the vineyard will do to those farmers?" Jesus asked. ¹⁶"I'll tell you—he will come and kill them all and lease the vineyard to others."

"But God forbid that such a thing should ever happen," his listeners protested.

¹⁷Jesus looked at them and said, "Then what do the Scriptures mean?

'The stone rejected by the builders
    has now become the cornerstone.'*

¹⁸All who stumble over that stone will be broken to pieces, and it will crush anyone on whom it falls."

¹⁹When the teachers of religious law and the leading priests heard this story, they wanted to arrest Jesus immediately because they realized he was pointing at them—that they were the farmers in the story. But they were afraid there would be a riot if they arrested him.

Taxes for Caesar

²⁰Watching for their opportunity, the leaders sent secret agents pretending to be honest men. They tried to get Jesus to say something that could be reported to the Roman governor so he would arrest Jesus. ²¹They said, "Teacher, we know that you speak and teach what is right and are not influenced by what others think. You sincerely teach the ways of God. ²²Now tell us—is it right to pay taxes to the Roman government or not?"

²³He saw through their trickery and said,

19:46 Isa 56:7; Jer 7:11. **20:2** Or *By whose authority do you do these things?* **20:17** Ps 118:22.

²⁴"Show me a Roman coin.* Whose picture and title are stamped on it?"

"Caesar's," they replied.

²⁵"Well then," he said, "give to Caesar what belongs to him. But everything that belongs to God must be given to God." ²⁶So they failed to trap him in the presence of the people. Instead, they were amazed by his answer, and they were silenced.

DISCUSSION ABOUT RESURRECTION

²⁷Then some Sadducees stepped forward—a group of Jews who say there is no resurrection after death. ²⁸They posed this question: "Teacher, Moses gave us a law that if a man dies, leaving a wife but no children, his brother should marry the widow and have a child who will be the brother's heir.* ²⁹Well, there were seven brothers. The oldest married and then died without children. ³⁰His brother married the widow, but he also died. Still no children. ³¹And so it went, one after the other, until each of the seven had married her and died, leaving no children. ³²Finally, the woman died, too. ³³So tell us, whose wife will she be in the resurrection? For all seven were married to her!"

³⁴Jesus replied, "Marriage is for people here on earth. ³⁵But that is not the way it will be in the age to come. For those worthy of being raised from the dead won't be married then. ³⁶And they will never die again. In these respects they are like angels. They are children of God raised up to new life. ³⁷But now, as to whether the dead will be raised—even Moses proved this when he wrote about the burning bush. Long after Abraham, Isaac, and Jacob had died, he referred to the Lord* as 'the God of Abraham, the God of Isaac, and the God of Jacob.'* ³⁸So he is the God of the living, not the dead. They are all alive to him."

³⁹"Well said, Teacher!" remarked some of the teachers of religious law who were standing there. ⁴⁰And that ended their questions; no one dared to ask any more.

WHOSE SON IS THE MESSIAH?

⁴¹Then Jesus presented them with a question. "Why is it," he asked, "that the Messiah is said to be the son of David? ⁴²For David himself wrote in the book of Psalms:

'The LORD said to my Lord,
  Sit in honor at my right hand
⁴³ until I humble your enemies,
    making them a footstool under your
      feet.'*

⁴⁴Since David called him Lord, how can he be his son at the same time?"

⁴⁵Then, with the crowds listening, he turned to his disciples and said, ⁴⁶"Beware of these teachers of religious law! For they love to parade in flowing robes and to have everyone bow to them as they walk in the marketplaces. And how they love the seats of honor in the synagogues and at banquets. ⁴⁷But they shamelessly cheat widows out of their property, and then, to cover up the kind of people they really are, they make long prayers in public. Because of this, their punishment will be the greater."

THE WIDOW'S OFFERING

21 While Jesus was in the Temple, he watched the rich people putting their gifts into the collection box. ²Then a poor widow came by and dropped in two pennies.* ³"I assure you," he said, "this poor widow has given more than all the rest of them. ⁴For they have given a tiny part of their surplus, but she, poor as she is, has given everything she has."

JESUS FORETELLS THE FUTURE

⁵Some of his disciples began talking about the beautiful stonework of the Temple and the memorial decorations on the walls. But Jesus said, ⁶"The time is coming when all these things will be so completely demolished that not one stone will be left on top of another."

⁷"Teacher," they asked, "when will all this

20:24 Greek *a denarius.* 20:28 Deut 25:5-6. 20:37a Greek *when he wrote about the bush. He referred to the Lord.* 20:37b Exod 3:6.
20:42-43 Ps 110:1. 21:2 Greek *2 lepta.*

My Daily Worship

— October 8 —

WHAT BELONGS TO GOD

LUKE 20:1–21:37

He saw through their trickery and said, "Show me a Roman coin. Whose picture and title are stamped on it?" "Caesar's," they replied. "Well then," he said, "give to Caesar what belongs to him. But everything that belongs to God must be given to God" (20:23–25).

[i reflect]

The dining room is awash in paper. Stacks of cancelled checks line one side of the table. A mound of reports fills the center and piles of receipts spill over the edge. Pay stubs mingle with bank statements and a layer of tax forms covers the floor. Hours drag on as you calculate and re-calculate, but at last you are finished. You sign the form and attach a check. Sighing with relief, you drop it in the mailbox. Your taxes are paid for another year.

Taxes were no more popular in Jesus' day than in our own. The leaders tried to trick Jesus into saying it was wrong to pay taxes to Rome, but Jesus said, "Give to Caesar what belongs to him." It is our duty to submit to the authorities God has placed over us. But as difficult as it is to pay taxes, the second half of the verse presents a greater challenge. "But everything that belongs to God must be given to God." What belongs to God? Everything!

"The earth is the LORD's, and everything in it. The world and all its people belong to him" (Psalm 24:1). You are a child of the Lord. Do you submit to his authority or do you try to go your own way? Are you generous with the gifts God has given you or do you hold them tightly to yourself for your own pleasure? Remember, "Whatever is good and perfect comes to us from God above" (James 1:17).

The taxes we pay fund roads and schools and hospitals, but a life fully yielded to the Lord reaps benefits beyond measure. "For God has reserved a priceless inheritance for his children. It is kept in heaven for you, pure and undefiled, beyond the reach of change and decay" (1 Peter 1:4).

As an act of worship today, mentally surrender your time, your appointments, your errands, your encounters to God's authority and will.

[i pray]

Lord Almighty, I belong to you. I submit every thought and every action to your perfect will. Help me use the gifts you have given me for your glory.

[i respond]

Declare your "tax" to God. Make a list of the gifts God has given to you—talents, relationships, possessions, ministries. Thank him for each gift. Then write down one way you might use one of your gifts to glorify him.

take place? And will there be any sign ahead of time?"

[8]He replied, "Don't let anyone mislead you. For many will come in my name, claiming to be the Messiah* and saying, 'The time has come!' But don't believe them. [9]And when you hear of wars and insurrections, don't panic. Yes, these things must come, but the end won't follow immediately." [10]Then he added, "Nations and kingdoms will proclaim war against each other. [11]There will be great earthquakes, and there will be famines and epidemics in many lands, and there will be terrifying things and great miraculous signs in the heavens.

> *There is no more important activity of the human heart than to praise and worship God. This is the reason we exist. This is our purpose.*
>
> MICHAEL COLEMAN

[12]"But before all this occurs, there will be a time of great persecution. You will be dragged into synagogues and prisons, and you will be accused before kings and governors of being my followers. [13]This will be your opportunity to tell them about me. [14]So don't worry about how to answer the charges against you, [15]for I will give you the right words and such wisdom that none of your opponents will be able to reply! [16]Even those closest to you—your parents, brothers, relatives, and friends—will betray you. And some of you will be killed. [17]And everyone will hate you because of your allegiance to me. [18]But not a hair of your head will perish! [19]By standing firm, you will win your souls.

[20]"And when you see Jerusalem surrounded by armies, then you will know that the time of its destruction has arrived. [21]Then those in Judea must flee to the hills. Let those in Jerusalem escape, and those outside the city should not enter it for shelter. [22]For those will be days of God's vengeance, and the prophetic words of the Scriptures will be fulfilled. [23]How terrible it will be for pregnant women and for mothers nursing their babies. For there will be great distress in the land and wrath upon this people. [24]They will be brutally killed by the sword or sent away as captives to all the nations of the world. And Jerusalem will be conquered and trampled down by the Gentiles until the age of the Gentiles comes to an end.

[25]"And there will be strange events in the skies—signs in the sun, moon, and stars. And down here on earth the nations will be in turmoil, perplexed by the roaring seas and strange tides. [26]The courage of many people will falter because of the fearful fate they see coming upon the earth, because the stability of the very heavens will be broken up. [27]Then everyone will see the Son of Man arrive on the clouds with power and great glory.* [28]So when all these things begin to happen, stand straight and look up, for your salvation is near!"

[29]Then he gave them this illustration: "Notice the fig tree, or any other tree. [30]When the leaves come out, you know without being told that summer is near. [31]Just so, when you see the events I've described taking place, you can be sure that the Kingdom of God is near. [32]I assure you, this generation* will not pass from the scene until all these events have taken place. [33]Heaven and earth will disappear, but my words will remain forever.

[34]"Watch out! Don't let me find you living in careless ease and drunkenness, and filled with the worries of this life. Don't let that day catch you unaware, [35]as in a trap. For that day will come upon everyone living on the earth. [36]Keep a constant watch. And pray that, if possible, you may escape these horrors and stand before the Son of Man."

21:8 Greek *name, saying, 'I am.'* 21:27 See Dan 7:13. 21:32 Or *this age,* or *this nation.*

³⁷Every day Jesus went to the Temple to teach, and each evening he returned to spend the night on the Mount of Olives. ³⁸The crowds gathered early each morning to hear him.

JUDAS AGREES TO BETRAY JESUS

22 The Festival of Unleavened Bread, which begins with the Passover celebration, was drawing near. ²The leading priests and teachers of religious law were actively plotting Jesus' murder. But they wanted to kill him without starting a riot, a possibility they greatly feared.

³Then Satan entered into Judas Iscariot, who was one of the twelve disciples, ⁴and he went over to the leading priests and captains of the Temple guard to discuss the best way to betray Jesus to them. ⁵They were delighted that he was ready to help them, and they promised him a reward. ⁶So he began looking for an opportunity to betray Jesus so they could arrest him quietly when the crowds weren't around.

THE LAST SUPPER

⁷Now the Festival of Unleavened Bread arrived, when the Passover lambs were sacrificed. ⁸Jesus sent Peter and John ahead and said, "Go and prepare the Passover meal, so we can eat it together."

⁹"Where do you want us to go?" they asked him.

¹⁰He replied, "As soon as you enter Jerusalem, a man carrying a pitcher of water will meet you. Follow him. At the house he enters, ¹¹say to the owner, 'The Teacher asks, Where is the guest room where I can eat the Passover meal with my disciples?' ¹²He will take you upstairs to a large room that is already set up. That is the place. Go ahead and prepare our supper there." ¹³They went off to the city and found everything just as Jesus had said, and they prepared the Passover supper there.

¹⁴Then at the proper time Jesus and the twelve apostles sat down together at the table. ¹⁵Jesus said, "I have looked forward to this hour with deep longing, anxious to eat this Passover meal with you before my suffering begins. ¹⁶For I tell you now that I won't eat it again until it comes to fulfillment in the Kingdom of God."

¹⁷Then he took a cup of wine, and when he had given thanks for it, he said, "Take this and share it among yourselves. ¹⁸For I will not drink wine again until the Kingdom of God has come."

¹⁹Then he took a loaf of bread; and when he had thanked God for it, he broke it in pieces and gave it to the disciples, saying, "This is my body, given for you. Do this in remembrance of me." ²⁰After supper he took another cup of wine and said, "This wine is the token of God's new covenant to save you—an agreement sealed with the blood I will pour out for you.*

²¹"But here at this table, sitting among us as a friend, is the man who will betray me. ²²For I, the Son of Man, must die since it is part of God's plan. But how terrible it will be for my betrayer!" ²³Then the disciples began to ask each other which of them would ever do such a thing.

²⁴And they began to argue among themselves as to who would be the greatest in the coming Kingdom. ²⁵Jesus told them, "In this world the kings and great men order their people around, and yet they are called 'friends of the people.' ²⁶But among you, those who are the greatest should take the lowest rank, and the leader should be like a servant. ²⁷Normally the master sits at the table and is served by his servants. But not here! For I am your servant. ²⁸You have remained true to me in my time of trial. ²⁹And just as my Father has granted me a Kingdom, I now grant you the right ³⁰to eat and drink at my table in that Kingdom. And you will sit on thrones, judging the twelve tribes of Israel.

22:19-20 Some manuscripts omit 22:19b-20, *given for you . . . I will pour out for you.*

JESUS PREDICTS PETER'S DENIAL

[31]"Simon, Simon, Satan has asked to have all of you, to sift you like wheat. [32]But I have pleaded in prayer for you, Simon, that your faith should not fail. So when you have repented and turned to me again, strengthen and build up your brothers."

[33]Peter said, "Lord, I am ready to go to prison with you, and even to die with you."

[34]But Jesus said, "Peter, let me tell you something. The rooster will not crow tomorrow morning until you have denied three times that you even know me."

[35]Then Jesus asked them, "When I sent you out to preach the Good News and you did not have money, a traveler's bag, or extra clothing, did you lack anything?"

"No," they replied.

[36]"But now," he said, "take your money and a traveler's bag. And if you don't have a sword, sell your clothes and buy one! [37]For the time has come for this prophecy about me to be fulfilled: 'He was counted among those who were rebels.'* Yes, everything written about me by the prophets will come true."

[38]"Lord," they replied, "we have two swords among us."

"That's enough," he said.

JESUS PRAYS ON THE MOUNT OF OLIVES

[39]Then, accompanied by the disciples, Jesus left the upstairs room and went as usual to the Mount of Olives. [40]There he told them, "Pray that you will not be overcome by temptation."

[41]He walked away, about a stone's throw, and knelt down and prayed, [42]"Father, if you are willing, please take this cup of suffering away from me. Yet I want your will, not mine." [43]Then an angel from heaven appeared and strengthened him. [44]He prayed more fervently, and he was in such agony of spirit that his sweat fell to the ground like great drops of blood.* [45]At last he stood up again and returned to the disciples, only to find them asleep, exhausted from grief. [46]"Why are you sleeping?" he asked. "Get up and pray. Otherwise temptation will overpower you."

JESUS IS BETRAYED AND ARRESTED

[47]But even as he said this, a mob approached, led by Judas, one of his twelve disciples. Judas walked over to Jesus and greeted him with a kiss. [48]But Jesus said, "Judas, how can you betray me, the Son of Man, with a kiss?"

[49]When the other disciples saw what was about to happen, they exclaimed, "Lord, should we fight? We brought the swords!" [50]And one of them slashed at the high priest's servant and cut off his right ear.

[51]But Jesus said, "Don't resist anymore." And he touched the place where the man's ear had been and healed him. [52]Then Jesus spoke to the leading priests and captains of the Temple guard and the other leaders who headed the mob. "Am I some dangerous criminal," he asked, "that you have come armed with swords and clubs to arrest me? [53]Why didn't you arrest me in the Temple? I was there every day. But this is your moment, the time when the power of darkness reigns."

PETER DENIES JESUS

[54]So they arrested him and led him to the high priest's residence, and Peter was following far behind. [55]The guards lit a fire in the courtyard and sat around it, and Peter joined them there. [56]A servant girl noticed him in the firelight and began staring at him. Finally she said, "This man was one of Jesus' followers!"

[57]Peter denied it. "Woman," he said, "I don't even know the man!"

[58]After a while someone else looked at him and said, "You must be one of them!"

"No, man, I'm not!" Peter replied.

[59]About an hour later someone else insisted, "This must be one of Jesus' disciples because he is a Galilean, too."

[60]But Peter said, "Man, I don't know what you are talking about." And as soon as he said these words, the rooster crowed. [61]At that

---

22:37 Isa 53:12. 22:43-44 These verses are not included in many ancient manuscripts.

My Daily Worship

— October 9 —

THE TEARS OF OUR SAVIOR
LUKE 22:1–71

*He prayed more fervently, and he was in such agony of spirit that his sweat
fell to the ground like great drops of blood (22:44).*

[i reflect]

"The dungeon became to me as if it were a palace." So said Perpetua, a 22-year-old Christian from Carthage, North Africa, martyred around A.D. 200. Ripped away from the baby she was weaning, this woman of wealth and education was tortured and killed in an amphitheater. Onlookers claimed she went joyfully to her death, anticipating heaven.

We remember Perpetua for her bravery and unswerving devotion. Yet another martyr—the most famous in all of Christendom—cried out in anguish against his impending doom. As Jesus agonized, his sorrow expressed itself in what many believe were real drops of blood. Our Savior, the King of kings, was overwhelmed. Everything in him wanted to call off the pain that was about to sear his body and soul. And though sobs wracked the body that would soon be broken, the temptation finally subsided: "Yet I want your will [Father], not mine" (22:42).

Perhaps you shed tears of your own as you recount the precious story. You may wonder: "Did he have to be the victim of torture, harassment, malicious lies, surrounded by two-faced followers, taking the death penalty for another, separated from his Father, accompanied by friends who slept through his deepest pain . . . ?"

Yes. As Michael Card reminds us in *A Violent Grace*, "He was willing to lose all that we might win all." No crucifixion, no way to the Father. If there were no heart-wrenching agony, you would never know that Jesus stands with you through any suffering and temptation you face (Hebrews 2:18).

This truth transforms every sorrow into an opportunity for true intimacy and worship. It is in our pain that we "learn what it means to suffer with him, sharing in his death" (Philippians 3:10). As you worship him today, remember that he feels your hurts and provides everything you need for victory over temptation and death.

[i pray]

*I'm sorry, Lord, for often forgetting your agony. Teach me how to use my pain as an opportunity
to draw closer to you—and to claim the victory your costly sacrifice provides.*

[i respond]

Take a few quiet moments to remember the most painful event or circumstance of your life. Compare your suffering to the agony Christ experienced for you. Ask him how he wants to bring healing and victory through a trial you are facing right now.

moment the Lord turned and looked at Peter. Then Peter remembered that the Lord had said, "Before the rooster crows tomorrow morning, you will deny me three times." [62]And Peter left the courtyard, crying bitterly.

[63]Now the guards in charge of Jesus began mocking and beating him. [64]They blindfolded him; then they hit him and asked, "Who hit you that time, you prophet?" [65]And they threw all sorts of terrible insults at him.

JESUS BEFORE THE COUNCIL

[66]At daybreak all the leaders of the people assembled, including the leading priests and the teachers of religious law. Jesus was led before this high council,* [67]and they said, "Tell us if you are the Messiah."

But he replied, "If I tell you, you won't believe me. [68]And if I ask you a question, you won't answer. [69]But the time is soon coming when I, the Son of Man, will be sitting at God's right hand in the place of power."*

[70]They all shouted, "Then you claim you are the Son of God?"

And he replied, "You are right in saying that I am."

[71]"What need do we have for other witnesses?" they shouted. "We ourselves heard him say it."

JESUS' TRIAL BEFORE PILATE

23 Then the entire council took Jesus over to Pilate, the Roman governor. [2]They began at once to state their case: "This man has been leading our people to ruin by telling them not to pay their taxes to the Roman government and by claiming he is the Messiah, a king."

[3]So Pilate asked him, "Are you the King of the Jews?"

Jesus replied, "Yes, it is as you say."

[4]Pilate turned to the leading priests and to the crowd and said, "I find nothing wrong with this man!"

[5]Then they became desperate. "But he is causing riots everywhere he goes, all over Judea, from Galilee to Jerusalem!"

[6]"Oh, is he a Galilean?" Pilate asked. [7]When they answered that he was, Pilate sent him to Herod Antipas, because Galilee was under Herod's jurisdiction, and Herod happened to be in Jerusalem at the time.

[8]Herod was delighted at the opportunity to see Jesus, because he had heard about him and had been hoping for a long time to see him perform a miracle. [9]He asked Jesus question after question, but Jesus refused to answer. [10]Meanwhile, the leading priests and the teachers of religious law stood there shouting their accusations. [11]Now Herod and his soldiers began mocking and ridiculing Jesus. Then they put a royal robe on him and sent him back to Pilate. [12]Herod and Pilate, who had been enemies before, became friends that day.

[13]Then Pilate called together the leading priests and other religious leaders, along with the people, [14]and he announced his verdict. "You brought this man to me, accusing him of leading a revolt. I have examined him thoroughly on this point in your presence and find him innocent. [15]Herod came to the same conclusion and sent him back to us. Nothing this man has done calls for the death penalty. [16]So I will have him flogged, but then I will release him."*

[18]Then a mighty roar rose from the crowd, and with one voice they shouted, "Kill him, and release Barabbas to us!" [19](Barabbas was in prison for murder and for taking part in an insurrection in Jerusalem against the government.) [20]Pilate argued with them, because he wanted to release Jesus. [21]But they shouted, "Crucify him! Crucify him!"

[22]For the third time he demanded, "Why? What crime has he committed? I have found no reason to sentence him to death. I will therefore flog him and let him go."

[23]But the crowd shouted louder and louder for Jesus' death, and their voices prevailed.

22:66 Greek *before their Sanhedrin.* **22:69** See Ps 110:1. **23:16** Some manuscripts add verse 17, *For it was necessary for him to release one [prisoner] for them during the feast.*

My Daily Worship

— October 10 —

FORGOTTEN FORGIVENESS

LUKE 23:1–56

Jesus said, "Father, forgive these people, because they
don't know what they are doing" (23:34).

[i reflect]

"I'm forgiven because you were forsaken . . . ." asserts a popular worship song. When we first come to Christ, the words seem rich with meaning. We realize our brokenness and separation from a holy God and our hearts overflow with thanksgiving: "Thank you, Lord, for paying the price my forgiveness requires. Thank you that your forgiveness never ends!"

The funny thing about forgiveness, however, is that we often fail to remember how much we continue to need it. With our eternal destiny secured, we can become a bit less thankful for the mercy of God. In our honest moments, we may even admit that it doesn't move us like it used to. And it shows.

Traces of our ungratefulness poke through as we avoid Christian brothers and sisters who have offended us or spurn the coworker who betrayed our confidence. Our forgiveness has limits. In our hearts, we cry out like Peter did: "Lord, how often should I forgive someone who sins against me? Seven times?" (Matthew 18:21). It is all too easy for us to keep a record of wrongs.

In contrast, Jesus said, "Father, forgive these people, because they don't know what they are doing" (Luke 23:34a). A cry of mercy for the people who had mocked, tortured, and condemned him to a cruel death. Latin church father Ambrose said, "Who wouldn't learn to forgive their enemies when they see that, on the Cross, Christ prayed for those who persecuted him?" When he was seen at his weakest, Ambrose affirms, he was giving us the strength to bear insults with uncommon patience.

Today, allow your thinking to shift from those who have wronged you to the One who pardons all the wrongs you will ever commit. "The greater the insult [from others]," Ambrose offers, "the greater gratitude is due [to him]." Come to him in gratitude now for your forgiveness—then pass it on to others.

[i pray]

Sometimes I am less than grateful, Father—and I ask for your forgiveness. Show me how
to offer uncommon patience and forgiveness to others as my gift of gratitude to you.

[i respond]

Write down an offense someone has committed against you. Next, write down five ways you've wronged God and write the word "forgiven" across your list. Ask God to help you offer his forgiveness to the person who hurt you.

²⁴So Pilate sentenced Jesus to die as they demanded. ²⁵As they had requested, he released Barabbas, the man in prison for insurrection and murder. But he delivered Jesus over to them to do as they wished.

The Crucifixion

²⁶As they led Jesus away, Simon of Cyrene,* who was coming in from the country just then, was forced to follow Jesus and carry his cross. ²⁷Great crowds trailed along behind, including many grief-stricken women. ²⁸But Jesus turned and said to them, "Daughters of Jerusalem, don't weep for me, but weep for yourselves and for your children. ²⁹For the days are coming when they will say, 'Fortunate indeed are the women who are childless, the wombs that have not borne a child and the breasts that have never nursed.' ³⁰People will beg the mountains to fall on them and the hills to bury them. ³¹For if these things are done when the tree is green, what will happen when it is dry?*"

³²Two others, both criminals, were led out to be executed with him. ³³Finally, they came to a place called The Skull.* All three were crucified there—Jesus on the center cross, and the two criminals on either side.

³⁴Jesus said, "Father, forgive these people, because they don't know what they are doing."* And the soldiers gambled for his clothes by throwing dice.*

³⁵The crowd watched, and the leaders laughed and scoffed. "He saved others," they said, "let him save himself if he is really God's Chosen One, the Messiah." ³⁶The soldiers mocked him, too, by offering him a drink of sour wine. ³⁷They called out to him, "If you are the King of the Jews, save yourself!" ³⁸A signboard was nailed to the cross above him with these words: "This is the King of the Jews."

³⁹One of the criminals hanging beside him scoffed, "So you're the Messiah, are you? Prove it by saving yourself—and us, too, while you're at it!"

⁴⁰But the other criminal protested, "Don't you fear God even when you are dying? ⁴¹We deserve to die for our evil deeds, but this man hasn't done anything wrong." ⁴²Then he said, "Jesus, remember me when you come into your Kingdom."

⁴³And Jesus replied, "I assure you, today you will be with me in paradise."

The Death of Jesus

⁴⁴By this time it was noon, and darkness fell across the whole land until three o'clock. ⁴⁵The light from the sun was gone. And suddenly, the thick veil hanging in the Temple was torn apart. ⁴⁶Then Jesus shouted, "Father, I entrust my spirit into your hands!"* And with those words he breathed his last.

⁴⁷When the captain of the Roman soldiers handling the executions saw what had happened, he praised God and said, "Surely this man was innocent.*" ⁴⁸And when the crowd that came to see the crucifixion saw all that had happened, they went home in deep sorrow.* ⁴⁹But Jesus' friends, including the women who had followed him from Galilee, stood at a distance watching.

The Burial of Jesus

⁵⁰Now there was a good and righteous man named Joseph. He was a member of the Jewish high council, ⁵¹but he had not agreed with the decision and actions of the other religious leaders. He was from the town of Arimathea in Judea, and he had been waiting for the Kingdom of God to come. ⁵²He went to Pilate and asked for Jesus' body. ⁵³Then he took the body down from the cross and wrapped it in a long linen cloth and laid it in a new tomb that had been carved out of rock. ⁵⁴This was done late on Friday afternoon, the day of preparation* for the Sabbath. ⁵⁵As his body was taken away, the women

---

23:26 Cyrene was a city in northern Africa. 23:31 Or If these things are done to me, the living tree, what will happen to you, the dry tree? 23:33 Sometimes rendered Calvary, which comes from the Latin word for "skull." 23:34a This sentence is not included in many ancient manuscripts. 23:34b Greek by casting lots. See Ps 22:18. 23:46 Ps 31:5. 23:47 Or righteous. 23:48 Greek beating their breasts. 23:54 Greek on the day of preparation.

from Galilee followed and saw the tomb where they placed his body. [56]Then they went home and prepared spices and ointments to embalm him. But by the time they were finished it was the Sabbath, so they rested all that day as required by the law.

THE RESURRECTION

24 But very early on Sunday morning* the women came to the tomb, taking the spices they had prepared. [2]They found that the stone covering the entrance had been rolled aside. [3]So they went in, but they couldn't find the body of the Lord Jesus. [4]They were puzzled, trying to think what could have happened to it. Suddenly, two men appeared to them, clothed in dazzling robes. [5]The women were terrified and bowed low before them. Then the men asked, "Why are you looking in a tomb for someone who is alive? [6]He isn't here! He has risen from the dead! Don't you remember what he told you back in Galilee, [7]that the Son of Man must be betrayed into the hands of sinful men and be crucified, and that he would rise again the third day?"

[8]Then they remembered that he had said this. [9]So they rushed back to tell his eleven disciples—and everyone else—what had happened. [10]The women who went to the tomb were Mary Magdalene, Joanna, Mary the mother of James, and several others. They told the apostles what had happened, [11]but the story sounded like nonsense, so they didn't believe it. [12]However, Peter ran to the tomb to look. Stooping, he peered in and saw the empty linen wrappings; then he went home again, wondering what had happened.*

THE WALK TO EMMAUS

[13]That same day two of Jesus' followers were walking to the village of Emmaus, seven miles* out of Jerusalem. [14]As they walked along they were talking about everything that had happened. [15]Suddenly, Jesus himself came along and joined them and began walking beside them. [16]But they didn't know who he was, because God kept them from recognizing him.

[17]"You seem to be in a deep discussion about something," he said. "What are you so concerned about?"

They stopped short, sadness written across their faces. [18]Then one of them, Cleopas, replied, "You must be the only person in Jerusalem who hasn't heard about all the things that have happened there the last few days."

[19]"What things?" Jesus asked.

"The things that happened to Jesus, the man from Nazareth," they said. "He was a prophet who did wonderful miracles. He was a mighty teacher, highly regarded by both God and all the people. [20]But our leading priests and other religious leaders arrested him and handed him over to be condemned to death, and they crucified him. [21]We had thought he was the Messiah who had come to rescue Israel. That all happened three days ago. [22]Then some women from our group of his followers were at his tomb early this morning, and they came back with an amazing report. [23]They said his body was missing, and they had seen angels who told them Jesus is alive! [24]Some of our men ran out to see, and sure enough, Jesus' body was gone, just as the women had said."

[25]Then Jesus said to them, "You are such foolish people! You find it so hard to believe all that the prophets wrote in the Scriptures. [26]Wasn't it clearly predicted by the prophets that the Messiah would have to suffer all these things before entering his time of glory?" [27]Then Jesus quoted passages from the writings of Moses and all the prophets, explaining what all the Scriptures said about himself.

[28]By this time they were nearing Emmaus and the end of their journey. Jesus would have gone on, [29]but they begged him to stay the night with them, since it was getting late. So he went home with them. [30]As they sat down

24:1 Greek *But on the first day of the week, very early in the morning.* 24:12 Some manuscripts do not include this verse. 24:13 Greek *60 stadia* [11.1 kilometers].

to eat, he took a small loaf of bread, asked God's blessing on it, broke it, then gave it to them. [31]Suddenly, their eyes were opened, and they recognized him. And at that moment he disappeared!

[32]They said to each other, "Didn't our hearts feel strangely warm as he talked with us on the road and explained the Scriptures to us?" [33]And within the hour they were on their way back to Jerusalem, where the eleven disciples and the other followers of Jesus were gathered. When they arrived, they were greeted with the report, [34]"The Lord has really risen! He appeared to Peter[*]!"

JESUS APPEARS TO THE DISCIPLES

[35]Then the two from Emmaus told their story of how Jesus had appeared to them as they were walking along the road and how they had recognized him as he was breaking the bread. [36]And just as they were telling about it, Jesus himself was suddenly standing there among them. He said, "Peace be with you."[*] [37]But the whole group was terribly frightened, thinking they were seeing a ghost! [38]"Why are you frightened?" he asked. "Why do you doubt who I am? [39]Look at my hands. Look at my feet. You can see that it's really me. Touch me and make sure that I am not a ghost, because ghosts don't have bodies, as you see that I do!" [40]As he spoke, he held out his hands for them to see, and he showed them his feet.[*]

[41]Still they stood there doubting, filled with joy and wonder. Then he asked them, "Do you have anything here to eat?" [42]They gave him a piece of broiled fish, [43]and he ate it as they watched.

[44]Then he said, "When I was with you before, I told you that everything written about me by Moses and the prophets and in the Psalms must all come true." [45]Then he opened their minds to understand these many Scriptures. [46]And he said, "Yes, it was written long ago that the Messiah must suffer and die and rise again from the dead on the third day. [47]With my authority, take this message of repentance to all the nations, beginning in Jerusalem: 'There is forgiveness of sins for all who turn to me.' [48]You are witnesses of all these things.

[49]"And now I will send the Holy Spirit, just as my Father promised. But stay here in the city until the Holy Spirit comes and fills you with power from heaven."

THE ASCENSION

[50]Then Jesus led them to Bethany, and lifting his hands to heaven, he blessed them. [51]While he was blessing them, he left them and was taken up to heaven.[*] [52]They worshiped him and[*] then returned to Jerusalem filled with great joy. [53]And they spent all of their time in the Temple, praising God.

24:34 Greek Simon. 24:36 Some manuscripts do not include He said, "Peace be with you." 24:40 Some manuscripts do not include this verse. 24:51 Some manuscripts do not include and was taken up to heaven. 24:52 Some manuscripts do not include worshiped him and.

My Daily Worship

— *October 11* —

AN APPROPRIATE RESPONSE
LUKE 24:1–53

While he was blessing them, he left them and was taken up to heaven. They worshiped him and then returned to Jerusalem filled with great joy (24:51–52).

[i reflect]

On October 3, 1863, Abraham Lincoln issued a proclamation. It called all Americans to acknowledge their gratitude for God's many blessings. Even though America was still in the midst of the Civil War, the sixteenth president had recently experienced a personal dimension to his faith in Christ. In spite of continued conflict, he felt compelled to invite recipients of God's faithfulness to appropriately respond. The proclamation led to the establishment of our Thanksgiving holiday.

Lincoln was not the first to call for a national expression of gratitude to God for his goodness. Governor William Bradford formally called the Pilgrims to esteem the Almighty with worshipful hearts in what we now acknowledge to be the very first Thanksgiving in 1623. George Washington took his cue from Bradford and in 1789 proclaimed a national day of gratitude.

It's no wonder there have been multiple Thanksgiving proclamations. The principle is timeless. Recognition of God's gracious activity in our lives demands an appropriate response. Blessings require bowing before the One from whom they originate. But unlike our forefathers, the disciples had no need for someone to issue a proclamation that they express thanksgiving and worship. It was automatic. Having blessed his followers with the assurance of his presence and power, Jesus ascended into heaven while his followers returned to Jerusalem, filled with unstoppable thanks and joy.

If it has been a while since you've felt that joy, spend some time today contemplating how you have been showered with God's blessings. Start adding up your blessings. The most natural motivator for genuine worship is simple addition. But don't stop there. No matter how hectic the demands of this day may be, picture the risen Christ promising that he'll never leave you or forsake you.

[i pray]

O Lord Jesus, I truly am blessed. My life is filled with more than I deserve. Thank you for showering me with family, friends, food, and shelter, not to mention meaningful work. But I also know I'm wealthy because you have called me to represent you in my world.

[i respond]

Don't settle for "mental math." Go ahead and write out the material and spiritual possessions the Lord has allowed you to enjoy. Once you've filled a page, go back and circle the blessings that remind you on a daily basis that he is alive and at work in your life.

John

In the beginning the Word already existed. He was with God, and he was God (1:1).

Eyewitness to His Glory

Eyewitnesses speak from a privileged position. Their testimony is powerful because they are the authorities on what they have experienced. John, an eyewitness to the glory of Jesus Christ, didn't expect his readers to take his word for it, however. Thus, through his Gospel, John provides a detailed account of Jesus' divinity.

From the beginning, after watching Jesus turn water into wine at the wedding party, John knew that Jesus was extraordinary. Yet even John was skeptical at first. He needed convincing about who this Jesus really was. So he observed and learned. He witnessed the way Jesus talked with the religious leaders about his personal relationship with his heavenly Father. This carpenter spoke as if he knew God intimately. In fact, he spoke as if he were divine. Soon the evidence for that assumption began to mount at a rapid pace.

Jesus healed the sick, fed multitudes from a few loaves, and raised Lazarus from the dead. He taught with authority and expressed wisdom beyond human comprehension. When John penned his Gospel, he described Jesus' existence before time began. He called him the Creator of all things who had existed from all time. He wrote about Jesus as the bread of life who satisfies our spiritual hunger and as the living water who satisfies our thirst. John referred to him as the light of the world and the good shepherd. How did he know all this was true? He had seen the evidence firsthand. Jesus was—*is*—God.

So what difference does it make that Jesus *is* God? It makes all the difference when we consider our sin. God became flesh so that he could take care of sin. He was the only one who could. As fully man, he died on the cross, taking our punishment. As fully divine, he conquered death and offered the world forgiveness and the promise of eternal life. Only God could do that. Only God did.

So what difference does it make that Jesus *is* God? All the difference in the world!

Worship Moments

- Jesus teaches a Samaritan woman what it means to worship God "in spirit and in truth" (4:19–24).
- Jesus underscores his title, "the Messiah," and reveals his identity (4:26).
- Jesus explains that his greatest glory will come from something the disciples didn't yet understand—his death and resurrection (12:23–24). It would bring glory to God's name (12:28).
- John records many people who acknowledge Jesus by the name "Son of God" (1:34, 49; 11:27). John himself testifies that Jesus is the "Son of the Father" (1:14) and "the Messiah, the Son of God" (20:31).

CHRIST, THE ETERNAL WORD

1 In the beginning the Word already existed. He was with God, and he was God. [2]He was in the beginning with God. [3]He created everything there is. Nothing exists that he didn't make. [4]Life itself was in him, and this life gives light to everyone. [5]The light shines through the darkness, and the darkness can never extinguish it.

[6]God sent John the Baptist [7]to tell everyone about the light so that everyone might believe because of his testimony. [8]John himself was not the light; he was only a witness to the light. [9]The one who is the true light, who gives light to everyone, was going to come into the world.

[10]But although the world was made through him, the world didn't recognize him when he came. [11]Even in his own land and among his own people, he was not accepted. [12]But to all who believed him and accepted him, he gave the right to become children of God. [13]They are reborn! This is not a physical birth resulting from human passion or plan—this rebirth comes from God.

[14]So the Word became human and lived here on earth among us. He was full of unfailing love and faithfulness.* And we have seen his glory, the glory of the only Son of the Father.

[15]John pointed him out to the people. He shouted to the crowds, "This is the one I was talking about when I said, 'Someone is coming who is far greater than I am, for he existed long before I did.'"

[16]We have all benefited from the rich blessings he brought to us—one gracious blessing after another.* [17]For the law was given through Moses; God's unfailing love and faithfulness came through Jesus Christ. [18]No one has ever seen God. But his only Son, who is himself God,* is near to the Father's heart; he has told us about him.

THE TESTIMONY OF JOHN THE BAPTIST

[19]This was the testimony of John when the Jewish leaders sent priests and Temple assistants* from Jerusalem to ask John whether he claimed to be the Messiah. [20]He flatly denied it. "I am not the Messiah," he said.

[21]"Well then, who are you?" they asked. "Are you Elijah?"

"No," he replied.

"Are you the Prophet?"*

"No."

[22]"Then who are you? Tell us, so we can give an answer to those who sent us. What do you have to say about yourself?"

[23]John replied in the words of Isaiah:

"I am a voice shouting in the wilderness,
'Prepare a straight pathway for the
Lord's coming!'"*

[24]Then those who were sent by the Pharisees [25]asked him, "If you aren't the Messiah or Elijah or the Prophet, what right do you have to baptize?"

[26]John told them, "I baptize with* water, but right here in the crowd is someone you do not know, [27]who will soon begin his ministry. I am not even worthy to be his slave.*" [28]This incident took place at Bethany, a village east of the Jordan River, where John was baptizing.

JESUS, THE LAMB OF GOD

[29]The next day John saw Jesus coming toward him and said, "Look! There is the Lamb of God who takes away the sin of the world! [30]He is the one I was talking about when I said, 'Soon a man is coming who is far greater than I am, for he existed long before I did.' [31]I didn't know he was the one, but I have been baptizing with water in order to point him out to Israel."

[32]Then John said, "I saw the Holy Spirit descending like a dove from heaven and

1:14 Greek *grace and truth;* also in 1:17. **1:16** Greek *grace upon grace.* **1:18** Some manuscripts read *his one and only Son.* **1:19** Greek *and Levites.* **1:21** See Deut 18:15, 18; Mal 4:5-6. **1:23** Isa 40:3. **1:26** Or *in;* also in 1:31, 33. **1:27** Greek *to untie his sandals.*

resting upon him. ³³I didn't know he was the one, but when God sent me to baptize with water, he told me, 'When you see the Holy Spirit descending and resting upon someone, he is the one you are looking for. He is the one who baptizes with the Holy Spirit.' ³⁴I saw this happen to Jesus, so I testify that he is the Son of God.*"

THE FIRST DISCIPLES

³⁵The following day, John was again standing with two of his disciples. ³⁶As Jesus walked by, John looked at him and then declared, "Look! There is the Lamb of God!" ³⁷Then John's two disciples turned and followed Jesus.

³⁸Jesus looked around and saw them following. "What do you want?" he asked them.

They replied, "Rabbi" (which means Teacher), "where are you staying?"

³⁹"Come and see," he said. It was about four o'clock in the afternoon when they went with him to the place, and they stayed there the rest of the day.

⁴⁰Andrew, Simon Peter's brother, was one of these men who had heard what John said and then followed Jesus. ⁴¹The first thing Andrew did was to find his brother, Simon, and tell him, "We have found the Messiah" (which means the Christ).

⁴²Then Andrew brought Simon to meet Jesus. Looking intently at Simon, Jesus said, "You are Simon, the son of John—but you will be called Cephas" (which means Peter*).

⁴³The next day Jesus decided to go to Galilee. He found Philip and said to him, "Come, be my disciple." ⁴⁴Philip was from Bethsaida, Andrew and Peter's hometown.

⁴⁵Philip went off to look for Nathanael and told him, "We have found the very person Moses and the prophets wrote about! His name is Jesus, the son of Joseph from Nazareth."

⁴⁶"Nazareth!" exclaimed Nathanael. "Can anything good come from there?"

"Just come and see for yourself," Philip said.

⁴⁷As they approached, Jesus said, "Here comes an honest man—a true son of Israel."

⁴⁸"How do you know about me?" Nathanael asked.

And Jesus replied, "I could see you under the fig tree before Philip found you."

⁴⁹Nathanael replied, "Teacher, you are the Son of God—the King of Israel!"

⁵⁰Jesus asked him, "Do you believe all this just because I told you I had seen you under the fig tree? You will see greater things than this." ⁵¹Then he said, "The truth is, you will all see heaven open and the angels of God going up and down upon the Son of Man."*

THE WEDDING AT CANA

2 The next day* Jesus' mother was a guest at a wedding celebration in the village of Cana in Galilee. ²Jesus and his disciples were also invited to the celebration. ³The wine supply ran out during the festivities, so Jesus' mother spoke to him about the problem. "They have no more wine," she told him.

⁴"How does that concern you and me?" Jesus asked. "My time has not yet come."

⁵But his mother told the servants, "Do whatever he tells you."

⁶Six stone waterpots were standing there; they were used for Jewish ceremonial purposes and held twenty to thirty gallons* each. ⁷Jesus told the servants, "Fill the jars with water." When the jars had been filled to the brim, ⁸he said, "Dip some out and take it to the master of ceremonies." So they followed his instructions.

⁹When the master of ceremonies tasted the water that was now wine, not knowing where it had come from (though, of course, the servants knew), he called the bridegroom over. ¹⁰"Usually a host serves the best wine first," he said. "Then, when everyone is full and doesn't care, he brings out the less expensive wines. But you have kept the best until now!"

¹¹This miraculous sign at Cana in Galilee

1:34 Some manuscripts read *the chosen One of God.* **1:42** The names *Cephas* and *Peter* both mean "rock." **1:51** See Gen 28:10-17, the account of Jacob's ladder. **2:1** Greek *On the third day;* see 1:35, 43. **2:6** Greek *2 or 3 measures* [75 to 113 liters].

My Daily Worship

— *October 12* —

THE TRANSCENDENT, PERSONAL GOD

JOHN 1:1 – 2:12

In the beginning the Word already existed. He was with God, and he was God.
He was in the beginning with God. He created everything there is.
Nothing exists that he didn't make (1:1–3).

[i reflect]

In the beginning the Word already existed . . . What an odd way to begin an account of the life of the most important man who ever lived! What was in John's mind when he wrote those enigmatic words?

We cannot know for sure all he was thinking, but a couple of predominant thoughts seem clearly present. John was a Jew, and when a Jew heard the words, "In the beginning . . . ," he would of course think of the first words (actually, in Hebrew, the first *word*) of Genesis: *In the beginning* God created the heavens and the earth. *Creation* and *existence* itself—the great mystery of how the universe came into being.

John was a Jew, but he wrote in Greek. When a Greek heard the phrase, "In the beginning the Word already existed," he heard the word *logos*—from which we get our words "logic," "logical," "logistics," etc. He thought of that which gave *order* and *intelligence* to the cosmos.

Creation and existence, order and intelligence . . . they came together, wrapped in flesh, and entered the world through a stable in Bethlehem. Gene Edwards, in his book *The Birth,* put it this way, "At last, the Door opened, and like any other child ever born he was pushed forth in harsh agony, deep red blood, and from an envelope of protective water. He who had formed the world now made an entrance into that world . . ."

What a mind-boggling idea! So incredible, so outrageous—so *scandalous*—that it set off shock waves throughout Palestine and the rest of the ancient world. The ripples from that shock wave continue to this day, changing the lives of men, women, young people, entire cultures and nations, and the course of history itself.

When you worship, remember you praise the God who draws so near he became one of us.

[i pray]

Lord, you breathed creation into existence by the power of your creative Word, yet
you also draw close to me. I praise you for your transcendence, magnificence,
and splendor, and also for your mercy and compassion. Thank you for
being the God who rules over creation and also reigns in my heart.

[i respond]

List some of God's transcendent characteristics (he's the Creator, he's all-knowing, all-powerful, all-present, eternal, etc.) and his personal ones (he has a will, emotion, intellect, etc.). Underneath those lists, write a few sentences of praise for these characteristics of God.

was Jesus' first display of his glory. And his disciples believed in him.

¹²After the wedding he went to Capernaum for a few days with his mother, his brothers, and his disciples.

JESUS CLEARS THE TEMPLE

¹³It was time for the annual Passover celebration, and Jesus went to Jerusalem. ¹⁴In the Temple area he saw merchants selling cattle, sheep, and doves for sacrifices; and he saw money changers behind their counters. ¹⁵Jesus made a whip from some ropes and chased them all out of the Temple. He drove out the sheep and oxen, scattered the money changers' coins over the floor, and turned over their tables. ¹⁶Then, going over to the people who sold doves, he told them, "Get these things out of here. Don't turn my Father's house into a marketplace!"

¹⁷Then his disciples remembered this prophecy from the Scriptures: "Passion for God's house burns within me."*

¹⁸"What right do you have to do these things?" the Jewish leaders demanded. "If you have this authority from God, show us a miraculous sign to prove it."

¹⁹"All right," Jesus replied. "Destroy this temple, and in three days I will raise it up."

²⁰"What!" they exclaimed. "It took forty-six years to build this Temple, and you can do it in three days?" ²¹But by "this temple," Jesus meant his body. ²²After he was raised from the dead, the disciples remembered that he had said this. And they believed both Jesus and the Scriptures.

²³Because of the miraculous signs he did in Jerusalem at the Passover celebration, many people were convinced that he was indeed the Messiah. ²⁴But Jesus didn't trust them, because he knew what people were really like. ²⁵No one needed to tell him about human nature.

JESUS AND NICODEMUS

3 After dark one evening, a Jewish religious leader named Nicodemus, a Pharisee, ²came to speak with Jesus. "Teacher," he said, "we all know that God has sent you to teach us. Your miraculous signs are proof enough that God is with you."

³Jesus replied, "I assure you, unless you are born again,* you can never see the Kingdom of God."

⁴"What do you mean?" exclaimed Nicodemus. "How can an old man go back into his mother's womb and be born again?"

⁵Jesus replied, "The truth is, no one can enter the Kingdom of God without being born of water and the Spirit.* ⁶Humans can reproduce only human life, but the Holy Spirit gives new life from heaven. ⁷So don't be surprised at my statement that you* must be born again. ⁸Just as you can hear the wind but can't tell where it comes from or where it is going, so you can't explain how people are born of the Spirit."

⁹"What do you mean?" Nicodemus asked.

¹⁰Jesus replied, "You are a respected Jewish teacher, and yet you don't understand these things? ¹¹I assure you, I am telling you what we know and have seen, and yet you won't believe us. ¹²But if you don't even believe me when I tell you about things that happen here on earth, how can you possibly believe if I tell you what is going on in heaven? ¹³For only I, the Son of Man,* have come to earth and will return to heaven again. ¹⁴And as Moses lifted up the bronze snake on a pole in the wilderness, so I, the Son of Man, must be lifted up on a pole,* ¹⁵so that everyone who believes in me will have eternal life.

¹⁶"For God so loved the world that he gave his only Son, so that everyone who believes in him will not perish but have eternal life. ¹⁷God did not send his Son into the world to condemn it, but to save it.

¹⁸"There is no judgment awaiting those who

2:17 Or *"Concern for God's house will be my undoing."* Ps 69:9. 3:3 Or *born from above;* also in 3:7. 3:5 Or *spirit.* The Greek word for *Spirit* can also be translated *wind;* see 3:8. 3:7 The Greek word for *you* is plural; also in 3:12. 3:13 Some manuscripts add *who lives in heaven.* 3:14 Greek *must be lifted up.*

My Daily Worship

— *October 13* —

ONLY ONE WAY TO HEAVEN

JOHN 2:13–3:36

Jesus replied, "The truth is, no one can enter the Kingdom of God without being born of water and the Spirit" (3:5).

[i reflect]

How does a person get to heaven? A recent survey by the Barna Research Group showed that:

- 56 percent say good people can earn their way into heaven
- 44 percent say if people do not consciously accept Christ as Savior, they will be condemned to hell
- 44 percent say all people experience the same outcome after they die, regardless of their religious beliefs
- 39 percent say it doesn't matter what faith people embrace because all faiths teach the same lessons

But what does Jesus say? "I assure you, unless you are born again, you can never see the Kingdom of God" (3:3). Can you imagine how Nicodemus must have felt when he heard Jesus say that? Talk about a paradigm shift!

Nicodemus was a faithful Jew, a Pharisee, and an older man (a man didn't get into the Pharisees' club without a few gray hairs). Notice that he hadn't even asked Jesus anything up to this point in the passage. Yet Jesus dived right in, telling him that all his goodness and credentials didn't impress God. In order to be saved, Nicodemus needed to be *born again.*

Ephesians 2:8–9 says, "God saved you by his special favor when you believed. And you can't take credit for this; it is a gift from God. Salvation is not a reward for the good things we have done, so none of us can boast about it."

The gospel of grace runs counter to our every impulse. It is the natural condition of human beings to think we will get to heaven by being good. When people understand clearly the doctrine of grace—that we are powerless to save ourselves, that God must do it all for us—it is *shocking*, even *insulting*. But when we get really honest about who and what we are—sinners in the presence of a holy God—it is simply overwhelming. We must, by God's grace and against all human effort and reason, be *born again.*

Thank God today that he has made a way to be born again. It would be impossible without him.

[i pray]

Father, forgive my arrogance, presumptuousness, and simple forgetfulness when I think that my salvation had something to do with me. Remind me that I am saved by your grace, born again by your Spirit, and made acceptable in your sight by the death of your Son.

[i respond]

Who would truly shock you by becoming a Christian? Take a moment right now to think of that person. Write his or her name in your Bible. Commit to pray that God would do a supernatural work of grace in his or her heart.

trust him. But those who do not trust him have already been judged for not believing in the only Son of God. [19]Their judgment is based on this fact: The light from heaven came into the world, but they loved the darkness more than the light, for their actions were evil. [20]They hate the light because they want to sin in the darkness. They stay away from the light for fear their sins will be exposed and they will be punished. [21]But those who do what is right come to the light gladly, so everyone can see that they are doing what God wants."

JOHN THE BAPTIST EXALTS JESUS

[22]Afterward Jesus and his disciples left Jerusalem, but they stayed in Judea for a while and baptized there.

[23]At this time John the Baptist was baptizing at Aenon, near Salim, because there was plenty of water there and people kept coming to him for baptism. [24]This was before John was put into prison. [25]At that time a certain Jew began an argument with John's disciples over ceremonial cleansing. [26]John's disciples came to him and said, "Teacher, the man you met on the other side of the Jordan River, the one you said was the Messiah, is also baptizing people. And everybody is going over there instead of coming here to us."

[27]John replied, "God in heaven appoints each person's work. [28]You yourselves know how plainly I told you that I am not the Messiah. I am here to prepare the way for him—that is all. [29]The bride will go where the bridegroom is. A bridegroom's friend rejoices with him. I am the bridegroom's friend, and I am filled with joy at his success. [30]He must become greater and greater, and I must become less and less.

[31]"He has come from above and is greater than anyone else. I am of the earth, and my understanding is limited to the things of earth, but he has come from heaven.* [32]He tells what he has seen and heard, but how few believe what he tells them! [33]Those who

believe him discover that God is true. [34]For he is sent by God. He speaks God's words, for God's Spirit is upon him without measure or limit. [35]The Father loves his Son, and he has given him authority over everything. [36]And all who believe in God's Son have eternal life. Those who don't obey the Son will never experience eternal life, but the wrath of God remains upon them."

JESUS AND THE SAMARITAN WOMAN

4 Jesus* learned that the Pharisees had heard, "Jesus is baptizing and making more disciples than John" [2](though Jesus himself didn't baptize them—his disciples did). [3]So he left Judea to return to Galilee.

[4]He had to go through Samaria on the way. [5]Eventually he came to the Samaritan village of Sychar, near the parcel of ground that Jacob gave to his son Joseph. [6]Jacob's well was there; and Jesus, tired from the long walk, sat wearily beside the well about noontime. [7]Soon a Samaritan woman came to draw water, and Jesus said to her, "Please give me a drink." [8]He was alone at the time because his disciples had gone into the village to buy some food.

[9]The woman was surprised, for Jews refuse to have anything to do with Samaritans. She said to Jesus, "You are a Jew, and I am a Samaritan woman. Why are you asking me for a drink?"

[10]Jesus replied, "If you only knew the gift God has for you and who I am, you would ask me, and I would give you living water."

[11]"But sir, you don't have a rope or a bucket," she said, "and this is a very deep well. Where would you get this living water? [12]And besides, are you greater than our ancestor Jacob who gave us this well? How can you offer better water than he and his sons and his cattle enjoyed?"

[13]Jesus replied, "People soon become thirsty again after drinking this water. [14]But the water I give them takes away thirst altogether. It

---

3:31 Some manuscripts omit *but he has come from heaven.*   4:1 Some manuscripts read *The Lord.*

becomes a perpetual spring within them, giving them eternal life."

[15]"Please, sir," the woman said, "give me some of that water! Then I'll never be thirsty again, and I won't have to come here to haul water."

[16]"Go and get your husband," Jesus told her.

[17]"I don't have a husband," the woman replied.

Jesus said, "You're right! You don't have a husband—[18]for you have had five husbands, and you aren't even married to the man you're living with now."

[19]"Sir," the woman said, "you must be a prophet. [20]So tell me, why is it that you Jews insist that Jerusalem is the only place of worship, while we Samaritans claim it is here at Mount Gerizim,* where our ancestors worshiped?"

[21]Jesus replied, "Believe me, the time is coming when it will no longer matter whether you worship the Father here or in Jerusalem. [22]You Samaritans know so little about the one you worship, while we Jews know all about him, for salvation comes through the Jews. [23]But the time is coming and is already here when true worshipers will worship the Father in spirit and in truth. The Father is looking for anyone who will worship him that way. [24]For God is Spirit, so those who worship him must worship in spirit and in truth."

[25]The woman said, "I know the Messiah will come—the one who is called Christ. When he comes, he will explain everything to us."

[26]Then Jesus told her, "I am the Messiah!"*

[27]Just then his disciples arrived. They were astonished to find him talking to a woman, but none of them asked him why he was doing it or what they had been discussing. [28]The woman left her water jar beside the well and went back to the village and told everyone, [29]"Come and meet a man who told me everything I ever did! Can this be the Messiah?" [30]So the people came streaming from the village to see him.

[31]Meanwhile, the disciples were urging Jesus

to eat. [32]"No," he said, "I have food you don't know about."

[33]"Who brought it to him?" the disciples asked each other.

[34]Then Jesus explained: "My nourishment comes from doing the will of God, who sent me, and from finishing his work. [35]Do you think the work of harvesting will not begin until the summer ends four months from now? Look around you! Vast fields are ripening all around us and are ready now for the harvest. [36]The harvesters are paid good wages, and the fruit they harvest is people brought to eternal life. What joy awaits both the planter and the harvester alike! [37]You know the saying, 'One person plants and someone else harvests.' And it's true. [38]I sent you to harvest where you didn't plant; others had already done the work, and you will gather the harvest."

MANY SAMARITANS BELIEVE

[39]Many Samaritans from the village believed in Jesus because the woman had said, "He told me everything I ever did!" [40]When they came out to see him, they begged him to stay at their village. So he stayed for two days, [41]long enough for many of them to hear his message and believe. [42]Then they said to the woman, "Now we believe because we have heard him ourselves, not just because of what you told us. He is indeed the Savior of the world."

JESUS HEALS AN OFFICIAL'S SON

[43]At the end of the two days' stay, Jesus went on into Galilee. [44]He had previously said, "A prophet is honored everywhere except in his own country." [45]The Galileans welcomed him, for they had been in Jerusalem at the Passover celebration and had seen all his miraculous signs.

[46]In the course of his journey through Galilee, he arrived at the town of Cana, where he had turned the water into wine. There was a government official in the city of Capernaum whose son was very sick. [47]When he

---

4:20 Greek *on this mountain.* **4:26** Greek *"I am, the one speaking to you."*

heard that Jesus had come from Judea and was traveling in Galilee, he went over to Cana. He found Jesus and begged him to come to Capernaum with him to heal his son, who was about to die.

⁴⁸Jesus asked, "Must I do miraculous signs and wonders before you people will believe in me?"

⁴⁹The official pleaded, "Lord, please come now before my little boy dies."

⁵⁰Then Jesus told him, "Go back home. Your son will live!" And the man believed Jesus' word and started home.

⁵¹While he was on his way, some of his servants met him with the news that his son was alive and well. ⁵²He asked them when the boy had begun to feel better, and they replied, "Yesterday afternoon at one o'clock his fever suddenly disappeared!" ⁵³Then the father realized it was the same time that Jesus had told him, "Your son will live." And the officer and his entire household believed in Jesus. ⁵⁴This was Jesus' second miraculous sign in Galilee after coming from Judea.

JESUS HEALS A LAME MAN

5 Afterward Jesus returned to Jerusalem for one of the Jewish holy days. ²Inside the city, near the Sheep Gate, was the pool of Bethesda,* with five covered porches. ³Crowds of sick people—blind, lame, or paralyzed—lay on the porches.* ⁵One of the men lying there had been sick for thirty-eight years. ⁶When Jesus saw him and knew how long he had been ill, he asked him, "Would you like to get well?"

⁷"I can't, sir," the sick man said, "for I have no one to help me into the pool when the water is stirred up. While I am trying to get there, someone else always gets in ahead of me."

⁸Jesus told him, "Stand up, pick up your sleeping mat, and walk!"

⁹Instantly, the man was healed! He rolled up the mat and began walking! But this miracle happened on the Sabbath day. ¹⁰So the Jewish leaders objected. They said to the man who was cured, "You can't work on the Sabbath! It's illegal to carry that sleeping mat!"

¹¹He replied, "The man who healed me said to me, 'Pick up your sleeping mat and walk.' "

¹²"Who said such a thing as that?" they demanded.

¹³The man didn't know, for Jesus had disappeared into the crowd. ¹⁴But afterward Jesus found him in the Temple and told him, "Now you are well; so stop sinning, or something even worse may happen to you." ¹⁵Then the man went to find the Jewish leaders and told them it was Jesus who had healed him.

JESUS CLAIMS TO BE THE SON OF GOD

¹⁶So the Jewish leaders began harassing Jesus for breaking the Sabbath rules. ¹⁷But Jesus replied, "My Father never stops working, so why should I?" ¹⁸So the Jewish leaders tried all the more to kill him. In addition to disobeying the Sabbath rules, he had spoken of God as his Father, thereby making himself equal with God.

¹⁹Jesus replied, "I assure you, the Son can do nothing by himself. He does only what he sees the Father doing. Whatever the Father does, the Son also does. ²⁰For the Father loves the Son and tells him everything he is doing, and the Son will do far greater things than healing this man. You will be astonished at what he does. ²¹He will even raise from the dead anyone he wants to, just as the Father does. ²²And the Father leaves all judgment to his Son, ²³so that everyone will honor the Son, just as they honor the Father. But if you refuse to honor the Son, then you are certainly not honoring the Father who sent him.

²⁴"I assure you, those who listen to my message and believe in God who sent me have eternal life. They will never be condemned for

---

5:2 Some manuscripts read *Beth-zatha*; other manuscripts read *Bethsaida*. 5:3 Some manuscripts add *waiting for a certain movement of the water, 'for an angel of the Lord came from time to time and stirred up the water. And the first person to step down into it afterward was healed.*

My Daily Worship

In Spirit and Truth

JOHN 4:1–54

But the time is coming and is already here when true worshipers will worship the Father in spirit and in truth. The Father is looking for anyone who will worship him that way (4:23).

[i reflect]

What is worship? What do we mean when we talk about it?

Worship comes from the old English word *worthship*. Worship is ascribing worth to God—giving God his due. That's the heart of worship. Notice that the focus of attention in worship is not a preacher, a choir, a group of musicians, the kids . . . and it's not *us*, either. We're all important, but we are not the most important part of worship. In worship, God is the audience and we are the participants. So, what does it mean for us to "worship in spirit and in truth"?

In spirit. The Holy Spirit is not indicated here because the Greek text has no definite article; therefore, this refers to the human spirit. Worship engages the mind, but it should engage the whole person as well. Intellect, emotions, will, attitudes, bodies—our entire person should be involved in worship.

In truth. We must worship God *truthfully*. For Bible-believing Christians, that means we approach him in accordance with what the Bible tells us about him. Jesus says in John 17:17: "Make them pure and holy by teaching them your words of truth." We must worship God in truth, and that means according to the Scriptures.

It also means that we must approach God on the basis of what Jesus has done for us in his life, death, resurrection, and ascension. He *is* the truth. Jesus said, "I am the way, the truth, and the life. No one can come to the Father except through me" (John 14:6). Just as the Bible is the *written* Word, Jesus is the *living* Word.

Worship is not a spectator sport; it's full-contact spirituality. Engage yourself fully today in your time of worship—read, sing, meditate, dance, kneel—do whatever it takes to worship God fully.

[i pray]

Father, I confess there are times when I try to worship you and just go through the motions. I sit passively instead of truly being engaged in offering you my best, highest, and noblest efforts as an active participant. Forgive me, Father, and give me grace to worship you in spirit and in truth.

[i respond]

God wants you to worship him with all your heart, mind, emotions, body, and will. Evaluate your own personal worship, writing down each of these elements above. Next to each write one or two ways you can involve that aspect more in your worship.

their sins, but they have already passed from death into life.

²⁵"And I assure you that the time is coming, in fact it is here, when the dead will hear my voice—the voice of the Son of God. And those who listen will live. ²⁶The Father has life in himself, and he has granted his Son to have life in himself. ²⁷And he has given him authority to judge all mankind because he is the Son of Man. ²⁸Don't be so surprised! Indeed, the time is coming when all the dead in their graves will hear the voice of God's Son, ²⁹and they will rise again. Those who have done good will rise to eternal life, and those who have continued in evil will rise to judgment. ³⁰But I do nothing without consulting the Father. I judge as I am told. And my judgment is absolutely just, because it is according to the will of God who sent me; it is not merely my own.

WITNESSES TO JESUS

³¹"If I were to testify on my own behalf, my testimony would not be valid. ³²But someone else is also testifying about me, and I can assure you that everything he says about me is true. ³³In fact, you sent messengers to listen to John the Baptist, and he preached the truth. ³⁴But the best testimony about me is not from a man, though I have reminded you about John's testimony so you might be saved. ³⁵John shone brightly for a while, and you benefited and rejoiced. ³⁶But I have a greater witness than John—my teachings and my miracles. They have been assigned to me by the Father, and they testify that the Father has sent me. ³⁷And the Father himself has also testified about me. You have never heard his voice or seen him face to face, ³⁸and you do not have his message in your hearts, because you do not believe me—the one he sent to you.

³⁹"You search the Scriptures because you believe they give you eternal life. But the Scriptures point to me! ⁴⁰Yet you refuse to come to me so that I can give you this eternal life.

⁴¹"Your approval or disapproval means nothing to me, ⁴²because I know you don't have God's love within you. ⁴³For I have come to you representing my Father, and you refuse to welcome me, even though you readily accept others who represent only themselves. ⁴⁴No wonder you can't believe! For you gladly honor each other, but you don't care about the honor that comes from God alone.

⁴⁵"Yet it is not I who will accuse you of this before the Father. Moses will accuse you! Yes, Moses, on whom you set your hopes. ⁴⁶But if you had believed Moses, you would have believed me because he wrote about me. ⁴⁷And since you don't believe what he wrote, how will you believe what I say?"

JESUS FEEDS FIVE THOUSAND

6 After this, Jesus crossed over the Sea of Galilee, also known as the Sea of Tiberias. ²And a huge crowd kept following him wherever he went, because they saw his miracles as he healed the sick. ³Then Jesus went up into the hills and sat down with his disciples around him. ⁴(It was nearly time for the annual Passover celebration.) ⁵Jesus soon saw a great crowd of people climbing the hill, looking for him. Turning to Philip, he asked, "Philip, where can we buy bread to feed all these people?" ⁶He was testing Philip, for he already knew what he was going to do.

⁷Philip replied, "It would take a small fortune* to feed them!"

⁸Then Andrew, Simon Peter's brother, spoke up. ⁹"There's a young boy here with five barley loaves and two fish. But what good is that with this huge crowd?"

¹⁰"Tell everyone to sit down," Jesus ordered. So all of them—the men alone numbered five thousand—sat down on the grassy slopes. ¹¹Then Jesus took the loaves, gave thanks to God, and passed them out to the people. Afterward he did the same with the fish. And they all ate until they were full. ¹²"Now gather the leftovers," Jesus told his disciples, "so that

---

6:7 Greek *200 denarii*. A denarius was the equivalent of a full day's wage.

My Daily Worship

— October 15 —

A TALE OF TWO VOICES

JOHN 5:1–6:21

Soon a gale swept down upon them as they rowed, and the sea grew very rough. They were three or four miles out when suddenly they saw Jesus walking on the water toward the boat. They were terrified, but he called out to them, "I am here! Don't be afraid" (6:18–20).

[i reflect]

Everyone has to deal with some fear in his or her life. It comes in many different forms: fear of dying, of going to the dentist, of heights, of spiders, of small spaces, of speaking in public.

But fear also comes in other, more personally addressed packages:

- When its 2 A.M., and your daughter was supposed to be home at midnight
- When the doctor tells you that your test results are in, and you need to come in for a face-to-face consultation
- When the bills are piled up on the desk and there's not another paycheck in sight
- When your spouse says, "I don't love you anymore . . . I want out of this marriage"

Fear comes in different packages, but we've all received one or two . . . or 20 . . . .

It is interesting that in the Bible, whenever God makes an appearance to a human being—directly or in the form of the angel of the Lord—usually the first thing he says to the person is, "Fear not." Something about the presence of God causes us to fear; but something in his nature also will not allow fear to stay.

First John 4:18 says, "Such love has no fear because perfect love expels all fear." In his book *Lifesigns*, the late Henri Nouwen wrote: "Why is there no reason to fear any longer? Jesus himself answers this question succinctly when he approaches his frightened disciples walking on the lake: 'I am here. Do not be afraid.'"

We can face our fears with confidence, knowing that God is with us even in the storms. Take your fears to the One who alone can deal with and overcome them.

As you spend time with God right now, tell him your biggest fears. Then repeat Jesus' words, "I am here. Don't be afraid."

[i pray]

Father, you know how often I listen to the voice of fear instead of your voice. You know how often I allow my fears to drive my decisions, instead of love for you and for others. Help me learn to hear you above the clamor of my worries and anxieties, and to live accordingly.

[i respond]

Next time there is a storm, spend some time alone with God observing it. Use this act of nature to remind you that the Creator of the storm is with you always. Spend time in prayer and praise.

nothing is wasted." [13]There were only five barley loaves to start with, but twelve baskets were filled with the pieces of bread the people did not eat!

[14]When the people saw this miraculous sign, they exclaimed, "Surely, he is the Prophet* we have been expecting!" [15]Jesus saw that they were ready to take him by force and make him king, so he went higher into the hills alone.

JESUS WALKS ON WATER

[16]That evening his disciples went down to the shore to wait for him. [17]But as darkness fell and Jesus still hadn't come back, they got into the boat and headed out across the lake toward Capernaum. [18]Soon a gale swept down upon them as they rowed, and the sea grew very rough. [19]They were three or four miles* out when suddenly they saw Jesus walking on the water toward the boat. They were terrified, [20]but he called out to them, "I am here! Don't be afraid." [21]Then they were eager to let him in, and immediately the boat arrived at their destination!

JESUS, THE BREAD OF LIFE

[22]The next morning, back across the lake, crowds began gathering on the shore, waiting to see Jesus. For they knew that he and his disciples had come over together and that the disciples had gone off in their boat, leaving him behind. [23]Several boats from Tiberias landed near the place where the Lord had blessed the bread and the people had eaten. [24]When the crowd saw that Jesus wasn't there, nor his disciples, they got into the boats and went across to Capernaum to look for him. [25]When they arrived and found him, they asked, "Teacher, how did you get here?"

[26]Jesus replied, "The truth is, you want to be with me because I fed you, not because you saw the miraculous sign. [27]But you shouldn't be so concerned about perishable things like food. Spend your energy seeking the eternal life that I, the Son of Man, can give you. For

God the Father has sent me for that very purpose."

[28]They replied, "What does God want us to do?"

[29]Jesus told them, "This is what God wants you to do: Believe in the one he has sent."

[30]They replied, "You must show us a miraculous sign if you want us to believe in you. What will you do for us? [31]After all, our ancestors ate manna while they journeyed through the wilderness! As the Scriptures say, 'Moses gave them bread from heaven to eat.'* "

[32]Jesus said, "I assure you, Moses didn't give them bread from heaven. My Father did. And now he offers you the true bread from heaven. [33]The true bread of God is the one who comes down from heaven and gives life to the world."

[34]"Sir," they said, "give us that bread every day of our lives."

[35]Jesus replied, "I am the bread of life. No one who comes to me will ever be hungry again. Those who believe in me will never thirst. [36]But you haven't believed in me even though you have seen me. [37]However, those the Father has given me will come to me, and I will never reject them. [38]For I have come down from heaven to do the will of God who sent me, not to do what I want. [39]And this is the will of God, that I should not lose even one of all those he has given me, but that I should raise them to eternal life at the last day. [40]For it is my Father's will that all who see his Son and believe in him should have eternal life—that I should raise them at the last day."

[41]Then the people* began to murmur in disagreement because he had said, "I am the bread from heaven." [42]They said, "This is Jesus, the son of Joseph. We know his father and mother. How can he say, 'I came down from heaven'?"

[43]But Jesus replied, "Don't complain about what I said. [44]For people can't come to me unless the Father who sent me draws them to me, and at the last day I will raise them from the dead. [45]As it is written in the Scriptures,

6:14 See Deut 18:15, 18. 6:19 Greek *25 or 30 stadia* [4.6 or 5.5 kilometers]. 6:31 Exod 16:4; Ps 78:24. 6:41 Greek *Jewish people;* also in 6:52.

My Daily Worship

— *October 16* —

No More Hunger and Thirst

JOHN 6:22–7:9

"Sir," they said, "give us that bread every day of our lives." Jesus replied,
"I am the bread of life. No one who comes to me will ever be hungry again.
Those who believe in me will never thirst" (6:34–35).

[i reflect]

Going to parties, spending time with our families, heading to the mall, watching and playing sports, climbing the corporate ladder, watching TV, listening to music, even using alcohol and other drugs—what in the world do all these activities, the legal and illegal as well, have to do with each other?

Just this: Everyone is hungry and thirsty for life. All of these pursuits, most of which are perfectly legitimate, are often the means we use to satisfy those desires. With a couple of obvious exceptions, nothing is wrong with them in and of themselves, but they can never truly satisfy our "hunger and thirst" for the fullness of life. For that, we need something much more substantial.

Jesus told the people that he himself was the bread of life and the living water that would satisfy their hunger and thirst. They could—and we can—search anywhere and everywhere for something else to meet those needs, but that search is doomed to failure. Only God can meet our hunger and thirst—our desire for life in all its fullness.

The great French physicist and philosopher Blaise Paschal wrote that each person has a vacuum inside that only God can fill—it's God-shaped. Try as we may with all these other activities, objects, and even people, none of them can satisfy for long. Only the bread of life and the living water can do that. Feed regularly and drink deeply from him, both individually and corporately.

Today, whenever you feel hunger pangs or need something to drink, use these moments to prompt you to worship God as the only One able to satisfy your hunger and your thirst.

[i pray]

Lord, you know how often I go looking in other places and to other sources to meet
my wants, needs, and desires. Remind me that you alone have words of life—
that you are the bread of life and the living water. Help me to be content
with you and you alone and to never settle for anything less.

[i respond]

Go "spiritual food" shopping. Make a grocery list of the spiritual foods you need in order to feed regularly and drink deeply of God.

'They will all be taught by God.'* Everyone who hears and learns from the Father comes to me. [46](Not that anyone has ever seen the Father; only I, who was sent from God, have seen him.)

[47]"I assure you, anyone who believes in me already has eternal life. [48]Yes, I am the bread of life! [49]Your ancestors ate manna in the wilderness, but they all died. [50]However, the bread from heaven gives eternal life to everyone who eats it. [51]I am the living bread that came down out of heaven. Anyone who eats this bread will live forever; this bread is my flesh, offered so the world may live."

[52]Then the people began arguing with each other about what he meant. "How can this man give us his flesh to eat?" they asked.

[53]So Jesus said again, "I assure you, unless you eat the flesh of the Son of Man and drink his blood, you cannot have eternal life within you. [54]But those who eat my flesh and drink my blood have eternal life, and I will raise them at the last day. [55]For my flesh is the true food, and my blood is the true drink. [56]All who eat my flesh and drink my blood remain in me, and I in them. [57]I live by the power of the living Father who sent me; in the same way, those who partake of me will live because of me. [58]I am the true bread from heaven. Anyone who eats this bread will live forever and not die as your ancestors did, even though they ate the manna."

[59]He said these things while he was teaching in the synagogue in Capernaum.

MANY DISCIPLES DESERT JESUS

[60]Even his disciples said, "This is very hard to understand. How can anyone accept it?"

[61]Jesus knew within himself that his disciples were complaining, so he said to them, "Does this offend you? [62]Then what will you think if you see me, the Son of Man, return to heaven again? [63]It is the Spirit who gives eternal life. Human effort accomplishes nothing. And the very words I have spoken to you are spirit and life. [64]But some of you don't believe

me." (For Jesus knew from the beginning who didn't believe, and he knew who would betray him.) [65]Then he said, "That is what I meant when I said that people can't come to me unless the Father brings them to me."

[66]At this point many of his disciples turned away and deserted him. [67]Then Jesus turned to the Twelve and asked, "Are you going to leave, too?"

[68]Simon Peter replied, "Lord, to whom would we go? You alone have the words that give eternal life. [69]We believe them, and we know you are the Holy One of God."

[70]Then Jesus said, "I chose the twelve of you, but one is a devil." [71]He was speaking of Judas, son of Simon Iscariot, one of the Twelve, who would betray him.

JESUS AND HIS BROTHERS

7 After this, Jesus stayed in Galilee, going from village to village. He wanted to stay out of Judea where the Jewish leaders were plotting his death. [2]But soon it was time for the Festival of Shelters, [3]and Jesus' brothers urged him to go to Judea for the celebration. "Go where your followers can see your miracles!" they scoffed. [4]"You can't become a public figure if you hide like this! If you can do such wonderful things, prove it to the world!" [5]For even his brothers didn't believe in him.

[6]Jesus replied, "Now is not the right time for me to go. But you can go anytime, and it will make no difference. [7]The world can't hate you, but it does hate me because I accuse it of sin and evil. [8]You go on. I am not yet* ready to go to this festival, because my time has not yet come." [9]So Jesus remained in Galilee.

JESUS TEACHES OPENLY AT THE TEMPLE

[10]But after his brothers had left for the festival, Jesus also went, though secretly, staying out of public view. [11]The Jewish leaders tried to find him at the festival and kept asking if anyone had seen him. [12]There was a lot of discussion

6:45 Isa 54:13. 7:8 Some manuscripts omit *yet*.

about him among the crowds. Some said, "He's a wonderful man," while others said, "He's nothing but a fraud, deceiving the people." ¹³But no one had the courage to speak favorably about him in public, for they were afraid of getting in trouble with the Jewish leaders.

¹⁴Then, midway through the festival, Jesus went up to the Temple and began to teach. ¹⁵The Jewish leaders were surprised when they heard him. "How does he know so much when he hasn't studied everything we've studied?" they asked.

¹⁶So Jesus told them, "I'm not teaching my own ideas, but those of God who sent me. ¹⁷Anyone who wants to do the will of God will know whether my teaching is from God or is merely my own. ¹⁸Those who present their own ideas are looking for praise for themselves, but those who seek to honor the one who sent them are good and genuine. ¹⁹None of you obeys the law of Moses! In fact, you are trying to kill me."

²⁰The crowd replied, "You're demon possessed! Who's trying to kill you?"

²¹Jesus replied, "I worked on the Sabbath by healing a man, and you were offended. ²²But you work on the Sabbath, too, when you obey Moses' law of circumcision. (Actually, this tradition of circumcision is older than the law of Moses; it goes back to Abraham.) ²³For if the correct time for circumcising your son falls on the Sabbath, you go ahead and do it, so as not to break the law of Moses. So why should I be condemned for making a man completely well on the Sabbath? ²⁴Think this through and you will see that I am right."

Is Jesus the Messiah?

²⁵Some of the people who lived there in Jerusalem said among themselves, "Isn't this the man they are trying to kill? ²⁶But here he is, speaking in public, and they say nothing to him. Can it be that our leaders know that he really is the Messiah? ²⁷But how could he be?

For we know where this man comes from. When the Messiah comes, he will simply appear; no one will know where he comes from."

²⁸While Jesus was teaching in the Temple, he called out, "Yes, you know me, and you know where I come from. But I represent one you don't know, and he is true. ²⁹I know him because I have come from him, and he sent me to you." ³⁰Then the leaders tried to arrest him; but no one laid a hand on him, because his time had not yet come.

³¹Many among the crowds at the Temple believed in him. "After all," they said, "would you expect the Messiah to do more miraculous signs than this man has done?"

³²When the Pharisees heard that the crowds were murmuring such things, they and the leading priests sent Temple guards to arrest Jesus. ³³But Jesus told them, "I will be here a little longer. Then I will return to the one who sent me. ³⁴You will search for me but not find me. And you won't be able to come where I am."

³⁵The Jewish leaders were puzzled by this statement. "Where is he planning to go?" they asked. "Maybe he is thinking of leaving the country and going to the Jews in other lands, or maybe even to the Gentiles! ³⁶What does he mean when he says, 'You will search for me but not find me,' and 'You won't be able to come where I am'?"

Jesus Promises Living Water

³⁷On the last day, the climax of the festival, Jesus stood and shouted to the crowds, "If you are thirsty, come to me! ³⁸If you believe in me, come and drink! For the Scriptures declare that rivers of living water will flow out from within."* ³⁹(When he said "living water," he was speaking of the Spirit, who would be given to everyone believing in him. But the Spirit had not yet been given, because Jesus had not yet entered into his glory.)

7:37-38 Or "Let anyone who is thirsty come to me and drink. ³⁸For the Scriptures declare that rivers of living water will flow from the heart of those who believe in me."

DIVISION AND UNBELIEF

[40]When the crowds heard him say this, some of them declared, "This man surely is the Prophet."* [41]Others said, "He is the Messiah." Still others said, "But he can't be! Will the Messiah come from Galilee? [42]For the Scriptures clearly state that the Messiah will be born of the royal line of David, in Bethlehem, the village where King David was born."* [43]So the crowd was divided in their opinion about him. [44]And some wanted him arrested, but no one touched him.

[45]The Temple guards who had been sent to arrest him returned to the leading priests and Pharisees. "Why didn't you bring him in?" they demanded.

[46]"We have never heard anyone talk like this!" the guards responded.

[47]"Have you been led astray, too?" the Pharisees mocked. [48]"Is there a single one of us rulers or Pharisees who believes in him? [49]These ignorant crowds do, but what do they know about it? A curse on them anyway!"

[50]Nicodemus, the leader who had met with Jesus earlier, then spoke up. [51]"Is it legal to convict a man before he is given a hearing?" he asked.

[52]They replied, "Are you from Galilee, too? Search the Scriptures and see for yourself—no prophet ever comes from Galilee!"

[The most ancient Greek manuscripts do not include John 7:53–8:11.]

[53]Then the meeting broke up and everybody went home.

A WOMAN CAUGHT IN ADULTERY

8 Jesus returned to the Mount of Olives, [2]but early the next morning he was back again at the Temple. A crowd soon gathered, and he sat down and taught them. [3]As he was speaking, the teachers of religious law and Pharisees brought a woman they had caught in the act of adultery. They put her in front of the crowd.

[4]"Teacher," they said to Jesus, "this woman was caught in the very act of adultery. [5]The law of Moses says to stone her. What do you say?"

[6]They were trying to trap him into saying something they could use against him, but Jesus stooped down and wrote in the dust with his finger. [7]They kept demanding an answer, so he stood up again and said, "All right, stone her. But let those who have never sinned throw the first stones!" [8]Then he stooped down again and wrote in the dust.

[9]When the accusers heard this, they slipped away one by one, beginning with the oldest, until only Jesus was left in the middle of the crowd with the woman. [10]Then Jesus stood up again and said to her, "Where are your accusers? Didn't even one of them condemn you?"

[11]"No, Lord," she said.

And Jesus said, "Neither do I. Go and sin no more."

JESUS, THE LIGHT OF THE WORLD

[12]Jesus said to the people, "I am the light of the world. If you follow me, you won't be stumbling through the darkness, because you will have the light that leads to life."

[13]The Pharisees replied, "You are making false claims about yourself!"

[14]Jesus told them, "These claims are valid even though I make them about myself. For I know where I came from and where I am going, but you don't know this about me. [15]You judge me with all your human limitations,* but I am not judging anyone. [16]And if I did, my judgment would be correct in every respect because I am not alone—I have with me the Father who sent me. [17]Your own law says that if two people agree about something, their witness is accepted as fact.* [18]I am one witness, and my Father who sent me is the other."

[19]"Where is your father?" they asked.

Jesus answered, "Since you don't know who I am, you don't know who my Father is. If you

7:40 See Deut 18:15, 18. 7:42 See Mic 5:2. 8:15 Or *judge me by human standards.* 8:17 See Deut 19:15.

My Daily Worship

— *October 17* —

SEEING IN GOD'S LIGHT

JOHN 7:10–8:58

"I am the light of the world. If you follow me, you won't be stumbling through the darkness, because you will have the light that leads to life"(8:12).

[i reflect]

Musician and producer T-Bone Burnett once said, "I learned a long time ago that if you believe that Jesus is the light of the world, there are two kinds of songs you can write: You can write songs about that light, or about what you see by that light."

Think of all the places in the Bible that God reveals himself as light in some form, or when light accompanies God's revelation of himself:

- Exodus 3: the burning bush
- Luke 2: the birth of Jesus and the radiance of God's glory in the sky
- Matthew 17: the Transfiguration, when Jesus became radiant to the point where his face shone like the sun and his garments became white as light itself
- Revelation 21: the eternal city of God has no need for lamps or the sun or the moon because God himself is its light

Now, what does the light show us? The light shows us as we really are—and it's not a pretty picture. The Bible says, "No one is good—not even one. No one has real understanding; no one is seeking God. All have turned away from God; all have gone wrong" (Romans 3:10–12). Yet the light also shows us that we are God's image-bearers. From the beginning, God created us in his own image (Genesis 1:26–27).

In the light we see ourselves as we really are: radically and pervasively sinful, yet made in the very image of God. We also see that forgiveness comes from the grace of God manifested most fully in the cross of Christ. At the cross, the holiness of God and the sinfulness of humanity came together, and our salvation was accomplished.

Look in the mirror and thank God that you can see yourself clearly in his light—as a sinner saved by grace, made in his image and constantly being conformed more and more to the likeness of his Son.

[i pray]

Lord God Almighty, you are light itself, too pure and holy for human eyes to see. Still, I would see you as clearly as you enable me to so that I might praise you as I ought. Help me see myself and others in the light of your truth. Teach me to walk in the light of your truth.

[i respond]

What do you see by the light of the gospel and your relationship with Jesus that has changed the way you live? What other things do you see that need to change in light of God's truth? Ask God to shine the light of his truth into your heart and mind to give you grace to become more like Jesus.

knew me, then you would know my Father, too." [20]Jesus made these statements while he was teaching in the section of the Temple known as the Treasury. But he was not arrested, because his time had not yet come.

THE UNBELIEVING PEOPLE WARNED

[21]Later Jesus said to them again, "I am going away. You will search for me and die in your sin. You cannot come where I am going."

[22]The Jewish leaders asked, "Is he planning to commit suicide? What does he mean, 'You cannot come where I am going'?"

[23]Then he said to them, "You are from below; I am from above. You are of this world; I am not. [24]That is why I said that you will die in your sins; for unless you believe that I am who I say I am, you will die in your sins."

[25]"Tell us who you are," they demanded.

Jesus replied, "I am the one I have always claimed to be.* [26]I have much to say about you and much to condemn, but I won't. For I say only what I have heard from the one who sent me, and he is true." [27]But they still didn't understand that he was talking to them about his Father.

[28]So Jesus said, "When you have lifted up the Son of Man on the cross, then you will realize that I am he and that I do nothing on my own, but I speak what the Father taught me. [29]And the one who sent me is with me—he has not deserted me. For I always do those things that are pleasing to him." [30]Then many who heard him say these things believed in him.

JESUS AND ABRAHAM

[31]Jesus said to the people* who believed in him, "You are truly my disciples if you keep obeying my teachings. [32]And you will know the truth, and the truth will set you free."

[33]"But we are descendants of Abraham," they said. "We have never been slaves to anyone on earth. What do you mean, 'set free'?"

[34]Jesus replied, "I assure you that everyone who sins is a slave of sin. [35]A slave is not a permanent member of the family, but a son is part of the family forever. [36]So if the Son sets you free, you will indeed be free. [37]Yes, I realize that you are descendants of Abraham. And yet some of you are trying to kill me because my message does not find a place in your hearts. [38]I am telling you what I saw when I was with my Father. But you are following the advice of your father."

[39]"Our father is Abraham," they declared.

"No," Jesus replied, "for if you were children of Abraham, you would follow his good example.* [40]I told you the truth I heard from God, but you are trying to kill me. Abraham wouldn't do a thing like that. [41]No, you are obeying your real father when you act that way."

They replied, "We were not born out of wedlock! Our true Father is God himself."

[42]Jesus told them, "If God were your Father, you would love me, because I have come to you from God. I am not here on my own, but he sent me. [43]Why can't you understand what I am saying? It is because you are unable to do so! [44]For you are the children of your father the Devil, and you love to do the evil things he does. He was a murderer from the beginning and has always hated the truth. There is no truth in him. When he lies, it is consistent with his character; for he is a liar and the father of lies. [45]So when I tell the truth, you just naturally don't believe me! [46]Which of you can truthfully accuse me of sin? And since I am telling you the truth, why don't you believe me? [47]Anyone whose Father is God listens gladly to the words of God. Since you don't, it proves you aren't God's children."

[48]The people retorted, "You Samaritan devil! Didn't we say all along that you were possessed by a demon?"

[49]"No," Jesus said, "I have no demon in me. For I honor my Father—and you dishonor me. [50]And though I have no wish to glorify myself, God wants to glorify me. Let him be

---

8:25 Or "Why do I speak to you at all?" **8:31** Greek *Jewish people*; also in 8:48, 52, 57. **8:39** Some manuscripts read *if you are children of Abraham, follow his example.*

the judge. [51]I assure you, anyone who obeys my teaching will never die!"

[52]The people said, "Now we know you are possessed by a demon. Even Abraham and the prophets died, but you say that those who obey your teaching will never die! [53]Are you greater than our father Abraham, who died? Are you greater than the prophets, who died? Who do you think you are?"

[54]Jesus answered, "If I am merely boasting about myself, it doesn't count. But it is my Father who says these glorious things about me. You say, 'He is our God,' [55]but you do not even know him. I know him. If I said otherwise, I would be as great a liar as you! But it is true—I know him and obey him. [56]Your ancestor Abraham rejoiced as he looked forward to my coming. He saw it and was glad."

[57]The people said, "You aren't even fifty years old. How can you say you have seen Abraham?*"

[58]Jesus answered, "The truth is, I existed before Abraham was even born!"* [59]At that point they picked up stones to kill him. But Jesus hid himself from them and left the Temple.

JESUS HEALS A MAN BORN BLIND

9 As Jesus was walking along, he saw a man who had been blind from birth. [2]"Teacher," his disciples asked him, "why was this man born blind? Was it a result of his own sins or those of his parents?"

[3]"It was not because of his sins or his parents' sins," Jesus answered. "He was born blind so the power of God could be seen in him. [4]All of us must quickly carry out the tasks assigned us by the one who sent me, because there is little time left before the night falls and all work comes to an end. [5]But while I am still here in the world, I am the light of the world."

[6]Then he spit on the ground, made mud with the saliva, and smoothed the mud over the blind man's eyes. [7]He told him, "Go and wash in the pool of Siloam" (Siloam means

Sent). So the man went and washed, and came back seeing!

[8]His neighbors and others who knew him as a blind beggar asked each other, "Is this the same man—that beggar?" [9]Some said he was, and others said, "No, but he surely looks like him!"

And the beggar kept saying, "I am the same man!"

[10]They asked, "Who healed you? What happened?"

[11]He told them, "The man they call Jesus made mud and smoothed it over my eyes and told me, 'Go to the pool of Siloam and wash off the mud.' I went and washed, and now I can see!"

[12]"Where is he now?" they asked.

"I don't know," he replied.

[13]Then they took the man to the Pharisees. [14]Now as it happened, Jesus had healed the man on a Sabbath. [15]The Pharisees asked the man all about it. So he told them, "He smoothed the mud over my eyes, and when it was washed away, I could see!"

[16]Some of the Pharisees said, "This man Jesus is not from God, for he is working on the Sabbath." Others said, "But how could an ordinary sinner do such miraculous signs?" So there was a deep division of opinion among them.

[17]Then the Pharisees once again questioned the man who had been blind and demanded, "This man who opened your eyes—who do you say he is?"

The man replied, "I think he must be a prophet."

[18]The Jewish leaders wouldn't believe he had been blind, so they called in his parents. [19]They asked them, "Is this your son? Was he born blind? If so, how can he see?"

[20]His parents replied, "We know this is our son and that he was born blind, [21]but we don't know how he can see or who healed him. He is old enough to speak for himself. Ask him." [22]They said this because they were afraid of the Jewish leaders, who had announced that

---

8:57 Some manuscripts read *How can you say Abraham has seen you?* 8:58 Or *"Truly, truly, before Abraham was, I am."*

anyone saying Jesus was the Messiah would be expelled from the synagogue. [23]That's why they said, "He is old enough to speak for himself. Ask him."

[24]So for the second time they called in the man who had been blind and told him, "Give glory to God by telling the truth,* because we know Jesus is a sinner."

[25]"I don't know whether he is a sinner," the man replied. "But I know this: I was blind, and now I can see!"

[26]"But what did he do?" they asked. "How did he heal you?"

[27]"Look!" the man exclaimed. "I told you once. Didn't you listen? Why do you want to hear it again? Do you want to become his disciples, too?"

[28]Then they cursed him and said, "You are his disciple, but we are disciples of Moses. [29]We know God spoke to Moses, but as for this man, we don't know anything about him."

[30]"Why, that's very strange!" the man replied. "He healed my eyes, and yet you don't know anything about him! [31]Well, God doesn't listen to sinners, but he is ready to hear those who worship him and do his will. [32]Never since the world began has anyone been able to open the eyes of someone born blind. [33]If this man were not from God, he couldn't do it."

[34]"You were born in sin!" they answered. "Are you trying to teach us?" And they threw him out of the synagogue.

SPIRITUAL BLINDNESS

[35]When Jesus heard what had happened, he found the man and said, "Do you believe in the Son of Man*?"

[36]The man answered, "Who is he, sir, because I would like to."

[37]"You have seen him," Jesus said, "and he is speaking to you!"

[38]"Yes, Lord," the man said, "I believe!" And he worshiped Jesus.

[39]Then Jesus told him, "I have come to judge the world. I have come to give sight to the blind and to show those who think they see that they are blind."

[40]The Pharisees who were standing there heard him and asked, "Are you saying we are blind?"

[41]"If you were blind, you wouldn't be guilty," Jesus replied. "But you remain guilty because you claim you can see.

THE GOOD SHEPHERD AND HIS SHEEP

10 "I assure you, anyone who sneaks over the wall of a sheepfold, rather than going through the gate, must surely be a thief and a robber! [2]For a shepherd enters through the gate. [3]The gatekeeper opens the gate for him, and the sheep hear his voice and come to him. He calls his own sheep by name and leads them out. [4]After he has gathered his own flock, he walks ahead of them, and they follow him because they recognize his voice. [5]They won't follow a stranger; they will run from him because they don't recognize his voice."

[6]Those who heard Jesus use this illustration didn't understand what he meant, [7]so he explained it to them. "I assure you, I am the gate for the sheep," he said. [8]"All others who came before me were thieves and robbers. But the true sheep did not listen to them. [9]Yes, I am the gate. Those who come in through me will be saved. Wherever they go, they will find green pastures. [10]The thief's purpose is to steal and kill and destroy. My purpose is to give life in all its fullness.

[11]"I am the good shepherd. The good shepherd lays down his life for the sheep. [12]A hired hand will run when he sees a wolf coming. He will leave the sheep because they aren't his and he isn't their shepherd. And so the wolf attacks them and scatters the flock. [13]The hired hand runs away because he is merely hired and has no real concern for the sheep.

[14]"I am the good shepherd; I know my own sheep, and they know me, [15]just as my Father knows me and I know the Father. And I lay

9:24 Or *Give glory to God, not to Jesus*; Greek reads *Give glory to God.* 9:35 Some manuscripts read *the Son of God.*

My Daily Worship

— *October 18* —

THE POWER OF A CHANGED LIFE

JOHN 9:1–10:42

"Yes, Lord," the man said, "I believe!" And he worshiped Jesus (9:38).

[i reflect]

C. S. Lewis once said in an interview, "There are many different ways of bringing people into his Kingdom, even some ways that I specially dislike."

How did you become a Christian? Did someone answer all your questions, give you a crash course in apologetics, or show you the overwhelming evidence for the veracity of the Bible? Some people do come to faith in Christ that way, but most don't. Most come to believe that Jesus is Lord because someone they trust shares with them that Jesus can meet their deepest needs: for purpose, forgiveness, meaning, direction, truth, companionship, peace.

This man Jesus encountered in John 9 had an obvious need—he was born blind. He wanted to see, and Jesus gave him his sight. Is it any wonder he called Jesus "Lord" and proclaimed belief in him? Further, his belief in Jesus was unshakeable even in the face of intense, entrenched opposition. Someone who is knowledgeable or powerful might be able to intimidate you into renouncing your allegiance to a merely intellectual proposition. But you wouldn't renounce someone who changed your life!

How has knowing Jesus changed your life? Do you have different values, different principles, different lifestyle, different recreations, different ways of handling your money, time, and relationships? Knowing Jesus will, or *should*, change your life in every way. Knowing theology and apologetics is valuable, and you should "let God transform you into a new person by changing the way you think" (Romans 12:2). However, there is no more persuasive argument for the validity of your faith than your changed life.

Take time to reflect on the past year, the past five years, or even ten years. Thank God for the changes he has brought to your life during that time.

[i pray]

Father, I thank you for moving into my life and meeting my deepest needs. Thank you for loving me enough to accept me the way I am, and for loving me too much to leave me the way I was. May my changed life be a clear testimony to your power, grace, and love.

[i respond]

What in your life can only be explained in terms of the supernatural, that is to say, "God did it"? Make a list of the most significant changes God has made in your life. In prayer, thank him for what he has done for you; then look for an opportunity to share what you've learned with others.

BAPTISM

Baptism—Greek *bap-to* "baptize"; *bap-tis-ma* "baptism."

Baptism is the sign of our entrance into the family of God. Depending on the practice of our particular faith community, it may symbolize a commitment we make as adults, or one made on our behalf, usually our parents. However it is practiced, the waters of baptism symbolize our participation in Christ's death, that we might be united with him in his resurrection life.

Baptism is an encouragement to us in every aspect of our Christian walk, especially our worship. Doubts may arise in our minds about our standing in the Lord. We may wonder if we're serving him as we ought to, or whether he's inclined to hear our praise and our petitions. While it's always good to examine ourselves and monitor our own faithfulness to the Lord, our baptism is a reminder that we come to God not through our own worth but through our membership in Christ. When we doubt our relationship to God and hesitate to approach him, we can always tell ourselves, "I've been baptized!"

down my life for the sheep. ¹⁶I have other sheep, too, that are not in this sheepfold. I must bring them also, and they will listen to my voice; and there will be one flock with one shepherd.

¹⁷"The Father loves me because I lay down my life that I may have it back again. ¹⁸No one can take my life from me. I lay down my life voluntarily. For I have the right to lay it down when I want to and also the power to take it again. For my Father has given me this command."

¹⁹When he said these things, the people* were again divided in their opinions about him. ²⁰Some of them said, "He has a demon, or he's crazy. Why listen to a man like that?" ²¹Others said, "This doesn't sound like a man possessed by a demon! Can a demon open the eyes of the blind?"

JESUS CLAIMS TO BE THE SON OF GOD

²²It was now winter, and Jesus was in Jerusalem at the time of Hanukkah.* ²³He was at the Temple, walking through the section known as Solomon's Colonnade. ²⁴The Jewish leaders surrounded him and asked, "How long are you going to keep us in suspense? If you are the Messiah, tell us plainly."

²⁵Jesus replied, "I have already told you, and you don't believe me. The proof is what I do in the name of my Father. ²⁶But you don't believe me because you are not part of my flock. ²⁷My sheep recognize my voice; I know them, and they follow me. ²⁸I give them eternal life, and they will never perish. No one will snatch them away from me, ²⁹for my Father has given them to me, and he is more powerful than anyone else. So no one can take them from me. ³⁰The Father and I are one."

³¹Once again the Jewish leaders picked up stones to kill him. ³²Jesus said, "At my Father's direction I have done many things to help the people. For which one of these good deeds are you killing me?"

³³They replied, "Not for any good work, but for blasphemy, because you, a mere man, have made yourself God."

³⁴Jesus replied, "It is written in your own law that God said to certain leaders of the people, 'I say, you are gods!'* ³⁵And you know that the Scriptures cannot be altered. So if those people, who received God's message, were called 'gods,' ³⁶why do you call it blasphemy when the Holy One who was sent into the world by the Father says, 'I am the Son of God'? ³⁷Don't believe me unless I carry out my Father's

10:19 Greek *Jewish people.*   **10:22** Or *the Festival of Dedication.*   **10:34** Ps 82:6.

work. [38]But if I do his work, believe in what I have done, even if you don't believe me. Then you will realize that the Father is in me, and I am in the Father."

[39]Once again they tried to arrest him, but he got away and left them. [40]He went beyond the Jordan River to stay near the place where John was first baptizing. [41]And many followed him. "John didn't do miracles," they remarked to one another, "but all his predictions about this man have come true." [42]And many believed in him there.

THE DEATH OF LAZARUS

11 A man named Lazarus was sick. He lived in Bethany with his sisters, Mary and Martha. [2]This is the Mary who poured the expensive perfume on the Lord's feet and wiped them with her hair.* Her brother, Lazarus, was sick. [3]So the two sisters sent a message to Jesus telling him, "Lord, the one you love is very sick."

[4]But when Jesus heard about it he said, "Lazarus's sickness will not end in death. No, it is for the glory of God. I, the Son of God, will receive glory from this." [5]Although Jesus loved Martha, Mary, and Lazarus, [6]he stayed where he was for the next two days and did not go to them. [7]Finally after two days, he said to his disciples, "Let's go to Judea again."

[8]But his disciples objected. "Teacher," they said, "only a few days ago the Jewish leaders in Judea were trying to kill you. Are you going there again?"

[9]Jesus replied, "There are twelve hours of daylight every day. As long as it is light, people can walk safely. They can see because they have the light of this world. [10]Only at night is there danger of stumbling because there is no light." [11]Then he said, "Our friend Lazarus has fallen asleep, but now I will go and wake him up."

[12]The disciples said, "Lord, if he is sleeping, that means he is getting better!" [13]They thought Jesus meant Lazarus was having a good night's rest, but Jesus meant Lazarus had died.

[14]Then he told them plainly, "Lazarus is dead. [15]And for your sake, I am glad I wasn't there, because this will give you another opportunity to believe in me. Come, let's go see him."

[16]Thomas, nicknamed the Twin,* said to his fellow disciples, "Let's go, too—and die with Jesus."

[17]When Jesus arrived at Bethany, he was told that Lazarus had already been in his grave for four days. [18]Bethany was only a few miles* down the road from Jerusalem, [19]and many of the people* had come to pay their respects and console Martha and Mary on their loss. [20]When Martha got word that Jesus was coming, she went to meet him. But Mary stayed at home. [21]Martha said to Jesus, "Lord, if you had been here, my brother would not have died. [22]But even now I know that God will give you whatever you ask."

[23]Jesus told her, "Your brother will rise again."

[24]"Yes," Martha said, "when everyone else rises, on resurrection day."

[25]Jesus told her, "I am the resurrection and the life.* Those who believe in me, even though they die like everyone else, will live again. [26]They are given eternal life for believing in me and will never perish. Do you believe this, Martha?"

[27]"Yes, Lord," she told him. "I have always believed you are the Messiah, the Son of God, the one who has come into the world from God." [28]Then she left him and returned to Mary. She called Mary aside from the mourners and told her, "The Teacher is here and wants to see you." [29]So Mary immediately went to him.

[30]Now Jesus had stayed outside the village, at the place where Martha met him. [31]When the people who were at the house trying to console Mary saw her leave so hastily, they assumed she was going to Lazarus's grave to

11:2 This incident is recorded in chapter 12. 11:16 Greek *the one who was called Didymus.* 11:18 Greek *was about 15 stadia* [about 2.8 kilometers]. 11:19 Greek *Jewish people;* also 11:31, 33, 36, 45, 54. 11:25 Some manuscripts do not include *and the life.*

weep. So they followed her there. ³²When Mary arrived and saw Jesus, she fell down at his feet and said, "Lord, if you had been here, my brother would not have died."

³³When Jesus saw her weeping and saw the other people wailing with her, he was moved with indignation and was deeply troubled. ³⁴"Where have you put him?" he asked them.

They told him, "Lord, come and see." ³⁵Then Jesus wept. ³⁶The people who were standing nearby said, "See how much he loved him." ³⁷But some said, "This man healed a blind man. Why couldn't he keep Lazarus from dying?"

JESUS RAISES LAZARUS FROM THE DEAD

³⁸And again Jesus was deeply troubled. Then they came to the grave. It was a cave with a stone rolled across its entrance. ³⁹"Roll the stone aside," Jesus told them.

But Martha, the dead man's sister, said, "Lord, by now the smell will be terrible because he has been dead for four days."

⁴⁰Jesus responded, "Didn't I tell you that you will see God's glory if you believe?" ⁴¹So they rolled the stone aside. Then Jesus looked up to heaven and said, "Father, thank you for hearing me. ⁴²You always hear me, but I said it out loud for the sake of all these people standing here, so they will believe you sent me." ⁴³Then Jesus shouted, "Lazarus, come out!" ⁴⁴And Lazarus came out, bound in graveclothes, his face wrapped in a headcloth. Jesus told them, "Unwrap him and let him go!"

THE PLOT TO KILL JESUS

⁴⁵Many of the people who were with Mary believed in Jesus when they saw this happen. ⁴⁶But some went to the Pharisees and told them what Jesus had done. ⁴⁷Then the leading priests and Pharisees called the high council* together to discuss the situation. "What are we going to do?" they asked each other. "This man certainly performs many miraculous signs. ⁴⁸If we leave him alone, the whole nation will follow him, and then the Roman army will come and destroy both our Temple and our nation."

⁴⁹And one of them, Caiaphas, who was high priest that year, said, "How can you be so stupid? ⁵⁰Why should the whole nation be destroyed? Let this one man die for the people."

⁵¹This prophecy that Jesus should die for the entire nation came from Caiaphas in his position as high priest. He didn't think of it himself; he was inspired to say it. ⁵²It was a prediction that Jesus' death would be not for Israel only, but for the gathering together of all the children of God scattered around the world.

⁵³So from that time on the Jewish leaders began to plot Jesus' death. ⁵⁴As a result, Jesus stopped his public ministry among the people and left Jerusalem. He went to a place near the wilderness, to the village of Ephraim, and stayed there with his disciples.

⁵⁵It was now almost time for the celebration of Passover, and many people from the country arrived in Jerusalem several days early so they could go through the cleansing ceremony before the Passover began. ⁵⁶They wanted to see Jesus, and as they talked in the Temple, they asked each other, "What do you think? Will he come for the Passover?" ⁵⁷Meanwhile, the leading priests and Pharisees had publicly announced that anyone seeing Jesus must report him immediately so they could arrest him.

JESUS ANOINTED AT BETHANY

12 Six days before the Passover ceremonies began, Jesus arrived in Bethany, the home of Lazarus—the man he had raised from the dead. ²A dinner was prepared in Jesus' honor. Martha served, and Lazarus sat at the table with him. ³Then Mary took a twelve-ounce jar* of expensive perfume made from essence of nard, and she anointed Jesus' feet with it and wiped his feet with her hair. And the house was filled with fragrance.

11:47 Greek *the Sanhedrin.* **12:3** Greek *took 1 litra* [327 grams].

My Daily Worship

— October 19 —

PALM SUNDAYS
AND PROBLEM MONDAYS
JOHN 11:1–12:50

A huge crowd of Passover visitors took palm branches and went down the road
to meet him. They shouted, "Praise God! Bless the one who comes
in the name of the Lord! Hail to the King of Israel!" (12:12–13).

[i reflect]

The events surrounding Jesus' Triumphal Entry into Jerusalem are familiar to anyone who has ever attended a worship service on Palm Sunday. We sing hymns and praise choruses as our own hosannas, rejoicing over the royal reception our Lord received as he entered the city. We resonate with the roar of the approving crowd, the waving palm branches, and the shouted praise. *At last*, we think, *the King of Israel is receiving the honor due him. It's about time!*

Behavior that publicly demonstrates our love for Christ is an important part of worship. It provides an outlet for expressing the love we carry for the One who died for us on the cross. "Hail King Jesus!" we cry with the crowd on Sundays. "Blessed is the one who comes in the name of the Lord!"

We live in a world, however, where Palm Pilots are more prevalent than palm branches—where the realities of Monday's problems quickly eclipse the passion of Sunday's praise. The challenge for the contemporary Christian is to continue to honor Jesus after the hosannas have faded and the crowd has dispersed. Worship must be more than outward passion; it must also be inward devotion.

Brother Lawrence once reflected on what it means to worship God in spirit and truth. "[It] means to worship God as we ought to worship him. God is Spirit, so we must worship him in spirit and truth, that is, by a humble and true adoration of spirit in the depth and center of our souls. God alone can see this worship; we can repeat it so often that in the end it becomes as if it were natural to us, and as if God were one with our souls, and our souls one with him."

What comes most easily for you—public worship or private devotion? Take a few moments to think about your next Monday morning. How will you take your outward passion for Christ and inward devotion to him into the coming week?

[i pray]

Lord, I admit that worship comes easily on the Palm Sundays of my life, but when Problem Mondays arrive I don't feel much like praising you. Today I choose to exclaim "Hosanna!"

[i respond]

Take something from worship on Sunday—whether it's a hymn, words to a praise chorus, a Scripture reading, or a thought from the sermon—and incorporate it into your daily worship. Conversely, take a thought or reflection from your daily worship and use it to help you prepare for Sunday worship.

⁴But Judas Iscariot, one of his disciples—the one who would betray him—said, ⁵"That perfume was worth a small fortune.* It should have been sold and the money given to the poor." ⁶Not that he cared for the poor—he was a thief who was in charge of the disciples' funds, and he often took some for his own use.

⁷Jesus replied, "Leave her alone. She did it in preparation for my burial. ⁸You will always have the poor among you, but I will not be here with you much longer."

⁹When all the people* heard of Jesus' arrival, they flocked to see him and also to see Lazarus, the man Jesus had raised from the dead. ¹⁰Then the leading priests decided to kill Lazarus, too, ¹¹for it was because of him that many of the people had deserted them and believed in Jesus.

THE TRIUMPHAL ENTRY

¹²The next day, the news that Jesus was on the way to Jerusalem swept through the city. A huge crowd of Passover visitors ¹³took palm branches and went down the road to meet him. They shouted,

> "Praise God!*
> Bless the one who comes in the name of
>   the Lord!
> Hail to the King of Israel!"*

¹⁴Jesus found a young donkey and sat on it, fulfilling the prophecy that said:

> ¹⁵ "Don't be afraid, people of Israel.*
> Look, your King is coming,
>   sitting on a donkey's colt."*

¹⁶His disciples didn't realize at the time that this was a fulfillment of prophecy. But after Jesus entered into his glory, they remembered that these Scriptures had come true before their eyes.

¹⁷Those in the crowd who had seen Jesus call Lazarus back to life were telling others all about it. ¹⁸That was the main reason so many went out to meet him—because they had heard about this mighty miracle. ¹⁹Then the Pharisees said to each other, "We've lost. Look, the whole world has gone after him!"

JESUS PREDICTS HIS DEATH

²⁰Some Greeks who had come to Jerusalem to attend the Passover ²¹paid a visit to Philip, who was from Bethsaida in Galilee. They said, "Sir, we want to meet Jesus." ²²Philip told Andrew about it, and they went together to ask Jesus.

²³Jesus replied, "The time has come for the Son of Man to enter into his glory. ²⁴The truth is, a kernel of wheat must be planted in the soil. Unless it dies it will be alone—a single seed. But its death will produce many new kernels—a plentiful harvest of new lives. ²⁵Those who love their life in this world will lose it. Those who despise their life in this world will keep it for eternal life. ²⁶All those who want to be my disciples must come and follow me, because my servants must be where I am. And if they follow me, the Father will honor them. ²⁷Now my soul is deeply troubled. Should I pray, 'Father, save me from what lies ahead'? But that is the very reason why I came! ²⁸Father, bring glory to your name."

Then a voice spoke from heaven, saying, "I have already brought it glory, and I will do it again." ²⁹When the crowd heard the voice, some thought it was thunder, while others declared an angel had spoken to him.

³⁰Then Jesus told them, "The voice was for your benefit, not mine. ³¹The time of judgment for the world has come, when the prince of this world* will be cast out. ³²And when I am lifted up on the cross,* I will draw everyone to myself." ³³He said this to indicate how he was going to die.

³⁴"Die?" asked the crowd. "We understood

12:5 Greek *300 denarii.* A denarius was equivalent to a full day's wage.　12:9 Greek *Jewish people;* also in 12:11.　12:13a Greek *Hosanna,* an exclamation of praise that literally means "save now."　12:13b Ps 118:25-26; Zeph 3:15.　12:15a Greek *daughter of Zion.*　12:15b Zech 9:9.　12:31 *The prince of this world* is a name for Satan.　12:32 Greek *lifted up from the earth.*

from Scripture that the Messiah would live forever. Why are you saying the Son of Man will die? Who is this Son of Man you are talking about?"

[35]Jesus replied, "My light will shine out for you just a little while longer. Walk in it while you can, so you will not stumble when the darkness falls. If you walk in the darkness, you cannot see where you are going. [36]Believe in the light while there is still time; then you will become children of the light." After saying these things, Jesus went away and was hidden from them.

THE UNBELIEF OF THE PEOPLE

[37]But despite all the miraculous signs he had done, most of the people did not believe in him. [38]This is exactly what Isaiah the prophet had predicted:

"Lord, who has believed our message?
    To whom will the Lord reveal his saving
      power?"*

[39]But the people couldn't believe, for as Isaiah also said,

[40] "The Lord has blinded their eyes
    and hardened their hearts—
so their eyes cannot see,
    and their hearts cannot understand,
and they cannot turn to me
    and let me heal them."*

[41]Isaiah was referring to Jesus when he made this prediction, because he was given a vision of the Messiah's glory. [42]Many people, including some of the Jewish leaders, believed in him. But they wouldn't admit it to anyone because of their fear that the Pharisees would expel them from the synagogue. [43]For they loved human praise more than the praise of God.

[44]Jesus shouted to the crowds, "If you trust me, you are really trusting God who sent me. [45]For when you see me, you are seeing the one who sent me. [46]I have come as a light to shine in this dark world, so that all who put their trust in me will no longer remain in the darkness. [47]If anyone hears me and doesn't obey me, I am not his judge—for I have come to save the world and not to judge it. [48]But all who reject me and my message will be judged at the day of judgment by the truth I have spoken. [49]I don't speak on my own authority. The Father who sent me gave me his own instructions as to what I should say. [50]And I know his instructions lead to eternal life; so I say whatever the Father tells me to say!"

JESUS WASHES HIS DISCIPLES' FEET

13 Before the Passover celebration, Jesus knew that his hour had come to leave this world and return to his Father. He now showed the disciples the full extent of his love.* [2]It was time for supper, and the Devil had already enticed Judas, son of Simon Iscariot, to carry out his plan to betray Jesus. [3]Jesus knew that the Father had given him authority over everything and that he had come from God and would return to God. [4]So he got up from the table, took off his robe, wrapped a towel around his waist, [5]and poured water into a basin. Then he began to wash the disciples' feet and to wipe them with the towel he had around him.

[6]When he came to Simon Peter, Peter said to him, "Lord, why are you going to wash my feet?"

[7]Jesus replied, "You don't understand now why I am doing it; someday you will."

[8]"No," Peter protested, "you will never wash my feet!"

Jesus replied, "But if I don't wash you, you won't belong to me."

[9]Simon Peter exclaimed, "Then wash my hands and head as well, Lord, not just my feet!"

[10]Jesus replied, "A person who has bathed all over does not need to wash, except for the feet,* to be entirely clean. And you are clean,

---

12:38 Isa 53:1.   12:40 Isa 6:10.   13:1 Or *He loved his disciples to the very end.*   13:10 Some manuscripts do not include *except for the feet.*

but that isn't true of everyone here." [11]For Jesus knew who would betray him. That is what he meant when he said, "Not all of you are clean."

[12]After washing their feet, he put on his robe again and sat down and asked, "Do you understand what I was doing? [13]You call me 'Teacher' and 'Lord,' and you are right, because it is true. [14]And since I, the Lord and Teacher, have washed your feet, you ought to wash each other's feet. [15]I have given you an example to follow. Do as I have done to you. [16]How true it is that a servant is not greater than the master. Nor are messengers more important than the one who sends them. [17]You know these things—now do them! That is the path of blessing.

JESUS PREDICTS HIS BETRAYAL

[18]"I am not saying these things to all of you; I know so well each one of you I chose. The Scriptures declare, 'The one who shares my food has turned against me,'* and this will soon come true. [19]I tell you this now, so that when it happens you will believe I am the Messiah. [20]Truly, anyone who welcomes my messenger is welcoming me, and anyone who welcomes me is welcoming the Father who sent me."

[21]Now Jesus was in great anguish of spirit, and he exclaimed, "The truth is, one of you will betray me!"

[22]The disciples looked at each other, wondering whom he could mean. [23]One of Jesus' disciples, the one Jesus loved, was sitting next to Jesus at the table.* [24]Simon Peter motioned to him to ask who would do this terrible thing. [25]Leaning toward Jesus, he asked, "Lord, who is it?"

[26]Jesus said, "It is the one to whom I give the bread dipped in the sauce." And when he had dipped it, he gave it to Judas, son of Simon Iscariot. [27]As soon as Judas had eaten the bread, Satan entered into him. Then Jesus told him, "Hurry. Do it now." [28]None of the others

at the table knew what Jesus meant. [29]Since Judas was their treasurer, some thought Jesus was telling him to go and pay for the food or to give some money to the poor. [30]So Judas left at once, going out into the night.

JESUS PREDICTS PETER'S DENIAL

[31]As soon as Judas left the room, Jesus said, "The time has come for me, the Son of Man, to enter into my glory, and God will receive glory because of all that happens to me. [32]And God will bring* me into my glory very soon. [33]Dear children, how brief are these moments before I must go away and leave you! Then, though you search for me, you cannot come to me—just as I told the Jewish leaders. [34]So now I am giving you a new commandment: Love each other. Just as I have loved you, you should love each other. [35]Your love for one another will prove to the world that you are my disciples."

[36]Simon Peter said, "Lord, where are you going?"

And Jesus replied, "You can't go with me now, but you will follow me later."

[37]"But why can't I come now, Lord?" he asked. "I am ready to die for you."

[38]Jesus answered, "Die for me? No, before the rooster crows tomorrow morning, you will deny three times that you even know me.

JESUS, THE WAY TO THE FATHER

14 "Don't be troubled. You trust God, now trust in me. [2]There are many rooms in my Father's home, and I am going to prepare a place for you. If this were not so, I would tell you plainly. [3]When everything is ready, I will come and get you, so that you will always be with me where I am. [4]And you know where I am going and how to get there."

[5]"No, we don't know, Lord," Thomas said. "We haven't any idea where you are going, so how can we know the way?"

[6]Jesus told him, "I am the way, the truth,

13:18 Ps 41:9.   13:23 Greek *was reclining on Jesus' bosom.* The "disciple whom Jesus loved" was probably John.   13:32 Some manuscripts read *And if God is glorified in him [the Son of Man], God will bring.*

My Daily Worship

— *October 20* —

THE SERVANT-SAVIOR

JOHN 13:1–14:31

And since I, the Lord and Teacher, have washed your feet, you ought to wash each other's feet.
I have given you an example to follow. Do as I have done to you (13:14–15).

[i reflect]

The senior pastor was only months into his tenure at his new church in the Midwest when church members made an astonishing discovery. Following a special dramatic presentation in the sanctuary, participants began the laborious process of putting the large room back in order for the next service. Although the church employed several full-time custodians, the new pastor rolled up his sleeves and began to move furniture and vacuum the carpet. Church members exchanged stunned glances.

We are often surprised when our leaders take on the role of servants. We live in a culture in which being a member of a certain group, as the credit card commercial boasts, "has its privileges." We have become accustomed to leaders who would rather ascend to a position of status than stoop to serve others.

Today's key passage reflects the opposite principle. Washing the feet of houseguests was a job assigned to the lowliest servant, and the disciples were astounded when Jesus himself took on that humble task. Scripture tells us that Peter protested vigorously. Jesus had a point to make, however, and he taught his followers what it meant to be a servant-leader not by preaching but by practice.

"A servant is not greater than the master" (13:16). When we seek to model ourselves after the One we worship, we need to start from the ground up, and that means serving others in the most humble of ways. Oswald Chambers put it this way, "Towels and dishes and sandals, all the ordinary sordid things of our lives, reveal more quickly than anything what we are made of. It takes God Almighty in us to do the meanest duty as it ought to be done."

Throughout the day look for practical, unexpected ways in which you can serve others with the caring and compassion of Christ. Don't seek the credit, but rather do it to become more like the Master.

[i pray]

Lord, I realize that I've been careless in the way I treat those who work under me. If I'm honest,
I enjoy the perks that come with my position more than I do the responsibility
to model servanthood. Help me learn to exhibit authentic humility.

[i respond]

Think of all the ways that Christ has served you in recent days. Select one of those ways and do that for another person—whether it's someone you know or not. If the person asks, tell him or her that you are serving because of what your Master has done for you.

and the life. No one can come to the Father except through me. [7]If you had known who I am, then you would have known who my Father is.* From now on you know him and have seen him!"

[8]Philip said, "Lord, show us the Father and we will be satisfied."

[9]Jesus replied, "Philip, don't you even yet know who I am, even after all the time I have been with you? Anyone who has seen me has seen the Father! So why are you asking to see him? [10]Don't you believe that I am in the Father and the Father is in me? The words I say are not my own, but my Father who lives in me does his work through me. [11]Just believe that I am in the Father and the Father is in me. Or at least believe because of what you have seen me do.

> *Unless there is within us that which is above us, we shall soon yield to that which is around us.*
>
> P. T. FORSYTH

[12]"The truth is, anyone who believes in me will do the same works I have done, and even greater works, because I am going to be with the Father. [13]You can ask for anything in my name, and I will do it, because the work of the Son brings glory to the Father. [14]Yes, ask anything in my name, and I will do it!

JESUS PROMISES THE HOLY SPIRIT

[15]"If you love me, obey my commandments. [16]And I will ask the Father, and he will give you another Counselor,* who will never leave you. [17]He is the Holy Spirit, who leads into all truth. The world at large cannot receive him,

because it isn't looking for him and doesn't recognize him. But you do, because he lives with you now and later will be in you. [18]No, I will not abandon you as orphans—I will come to you. [19]In just a little while the world will not see me again, but you will. For I will live again, and you will, too. [20]When I am raised to life again, you will know that I am in my Father, and you are in me, and I am in you. [21]Those who obey my commandments are the ones who love me. And because they love me, my Father will love them, and I will love them. And I will reveal myself to each one of them."

[22]Judas (not Judas Iscariot, but the other disciple with that name) said to him, "Lord, why are you going to reveal yourself only to us and not to the world at large?"

[23]Jesus replied, "All those who love me will do what I say. My Father will love them, and we will come to them and live with them. [24]Anyone who doesn't love me will not do what I say. And remember, my words are not my own. This message is from the Father who sent me. [25]I am telling you these things now while I am still with you. [26]But when the Father sends the Counselor as my representative— and by the Counselor I mean the Holy Spirit— he will teach you everything and will remind you of everything I myself have told you.

[27]"I am leaving you with a gift—peace of mind and heart. And the peace I give isn't like the peace the world gives. So don't be troubled or afraid. [28]Remember what I told you: I am going away, but I will come back to you again. If you really love me, you will be very happy for me, because now I can go to the Father, who is greater than I am. [29]I have told you these things before they happen so that you will believe when they do happen.

[30]"I don't have much more time to talk to you, because the prince of this world approaches. He has no power over me, [31]but I will do what the Father requires of me, so that the world will know that I love the Father. Come, let's be going.

14:7 Some manuscripts read *If you really have known me, you will know who my Father is.* **14:16** Or *Comforter,* or *Encourager,* or *Advocate.* Greek *Paraclete;* also in 14:26.

JESUS, THE TRUE VINE

15 "I am the true vine, and my Father is the gardener. [2]He cuts off every branch that doesn't produce fruit, and he prunes the branches that do bear fruit so they will produce even more. [3]You have already been pruned for greater fruitfulness by the message I have given you. [4]Remain in me, and I will remain in you. For a branch cannot produce fruit if it is severed from the vine, and you cannot be fruitful apart from me.

[5]"Yes, I am the vine; you are the branches. Those who remain in me, and I in them, will produce much fruit. For apart from me you can do nothing. [6]Anyone who parts from me is thrown away like a useless branch and withers. Such branches are gathered into a pile to be burned. [7]But if you stay joined to me and my words remain in you, you may ask any request you like, and it will be granted! [8]My true disciples produce much fruit. This brings great glory to my Father.

[9]"I have loved you even as the Father has loved me. Remain in my love. [10]When you obey me, you remain in my love, just as I obey my Father and remain in his love. [11]I have told you this so that you will be filled with my joy. Yes, your joy will overflow! [12]I command you to love each other in the same way that I love you. [13]And here is how to measure it—the greatest love is shown when people lay down their lives for their friends. [14]You are my friends if you obey me. [15]I no longer call you servants, because a master doesn't confide in his servants. Now you are my friends, since I have told you everything the Father told me. [16]You didn't choose me. I chose you. I appointed you to go and produce fruit that will last, so that the Father will give you whatever you ask for, using my name. [17]I command you to love each other.

THE WORLD'S HATRED

[18]"When the world hates you, remember it hated me before it hated you. [19]The world would love you if you belonged to it, but you don't. I chose you to come out of the world,

SPIRIT, HOLY SPIRIT

Spirit, Holy Spirit—Hebrew *ru-ach* "breath, wind, spirit"; *ru-ach go-desh* "spirit of holiness"; Greek *pneu-ma* "breath, wind, spirit"; *to pneu-ma to ha-gi-on* "the Holy Spirit."

"Always be joyful," writes Paul. "Keep on praying. No matter what happens, always be thankful, for this is God's will for you who belong to Christ Jesus." Immediately he adds, "Do not stifle the Holy Spirit" (1 Thessalonians 5:16–19). Maintaining a worshipful lifestyle depends on being open to the work of the Spirit. The Holy Spirit puts Jesus' words into our thoughts (John 14:26) and prompts us to acknowledge him as our Lord (1 Corinthians 12:3). No action of worship is more basic than this, to declare, "Jesus Christ is Lord!"

In our desire not to stifle the Spirit in our worship, we might confuse the motivation of our own spirit with the prompting of the Spirit of God. One criterion always helps us here: Does our act of worship glorify Christ, or call attention to us? Sometimes we just need to go for it, and let God sort it out. Better, perhaps, to err on the side of daring than on the side of caution. "Don't take your Holy Spirit from me" (Psalm 51:11).

and so it hates you. [20]Do you remember what I told you? 'A servant is not greater than the master.' Since they persecuted me, naturally they will persecute you. And if they had listened to me, they would listen to you! [21]The people of the world will hate you because you belong to me, for they don't know God who sent me. [22]They would not be guilty if I had not come and spoken to them. But now they have no excuse for their sin. [23]Anyone who hates me hates my Father, too. ²⁴If I hadn't done such miraculous signs among them that no one else could do, they would not be counted guilty. But as it is, they saw all that I did and yet hated both of us—me and my Father. ²⁵This has fulfilled what the Scriptures said: 'They hated me without cause.'*

²⁶"But I will send you the Counselor*—the Spirit of truth. He will come to you from the Father and will tell you all about me. ²⁷And you must also tell others about me because you have been with me from the beginning.

16 "I have told you these things so that you won't fall away. ²For you will be expelled from the synagogues, and the time is coming when those who kill you will think they are doing God a service. ³This is because they have never known the Father or me. ⁴Yes, I'm telling you these things now, so that when they happen, you will remember I warned you. I didn't tell you earlier because I was going to be with you for a while longer.

THE WORK OF THE HOLY SPIRIT

⁵"But now I am going away to the one who sent me, and none of you has asked me where I am going. ⁶Instead, you are very sad. ⁷But it is actually best for you that I go away, because if I don't, the Counselor* won't come. If I do go away, he will come because I will send him to you. ⁸And when he comes, he will convince the world of its sin, and of God's righteousness, and of the coming judgment. ⁹The world's sin is unbelief in me. ¹⁰Righteousness is available because I go to the Father, and you will see me no more. ¹¹Judgment will come because the prince of this world has already been judged.

¹²"Oh, there is so much more I want to tell you, but you can't bear it now. ¹³When the Spirit of truth comes, he will guide you into all truth. He will not be presenting his own ideas; he will be telling you what he has heard. He will tell you about the future. ¹⁴He will

bring me glory by revealing to you whatever he receives from me. ¹⁵All that the Father has is mine; this is what I mean when I say that the Spirit will reveal to you whatever he receives from me.

SADNESS WILL BE TURNED TO JOY

¹⁶"In just a little while I will be gone, and you won't see me anymore. Then, just a little while after that, you will see me again."

¹⁷The disciples asked each other, "What does he mean when he says, 'You won't see me, and then you will see me'? And what does he mean when he says, 'I am going to the Father'? ¹⁸And what does he mean by 'a little while'? We don't understand."

¹⁹Jesus realized they wanted to ask him, so he said, "Are you asking yourselves what I meant? I said in just a little while I will be gone, and you won't see me anymore. Then, just a little while after that, you will see me again. ²⁰Truly, you will weep and mourn over what is going to happen to me, but the world will rejoice. You will grieve, but your grief will suddenly turn to wonderful joy when you see me again. ²¹It will be like a woman experiencing the pains of labor. When her child is born, her anguish gives place to joy because she has brought a new person into the world. ²²You have sorrow now, but I will see you again; then you will rejoice, and no one can rob you of that joy. ²³At that time you won't need to ask me for anything. The truth is, you can go directly to the Father and ask him, and he will grant your request because you use my name. ²⁴You haven't done this before. Ask, using my name, and you will receive, and you will have abundant joy.

²⁵"I have spoken of these matters in parables, but the time will come when this will not be necessary, and I will tell you plainly all about the Father. ²⁶Then you will ask in my name. I'm not saying I will ask the Father on your behalf, ²⁷for the Father himself loves you

---

15:25 Pss 35:19; 69:4. 15:26 Or *Comforter,* or *Encourager,* or *Advocate.* Greek *Paraclete.* 16:7 Or *Comforter,* or *Encourager,* or *Advocate.* Greek *Paraclete.*

— *October 21* —

BELONGING TO EACH OTHER

JOHN 15:1–17:26

I am praying not only for these disciples but also for all who will ever believe in me
because of their testimony. My prayer for all of them is that they will be one,
just as you and I are one, Father—that just as you are in me and I am in you,
so they will be in us, and the world will believe you sent me (17:20–21).

[i reflect]

In a *Peanuts* cartoon strip that appeared some years ago, Charlie Brown sighed: "I love humanity; it's just people I can't stand!"

If we're honest with ourselves, we sometimes feel the same way. As followers of Christ we know that we are to love one another as he first loved us, but that doesn't mean we will always like each other very much. The necessity of the body of Christ remaining united is a theme that runs throughout the Bible, yet it is perhaps one of the most difficult goals for us to achieve.

Dietrich Bonhoeffer describes the vital importance of believers working and worshiping together for a common cause: "Christianity means community through Jesus Christ and in Jesus Christ. No Christian community is more or less than this. Whether it be a brief, single encounter or the daily fellowship of years, Christian community is only this. We belong to one another only through and in Jesus Christ. What does this mean? It means, first, that a Christian needs others because of Jesus Christ. It means, second, that a Christian comes to others only through Jesus Christ. It means, third, that in Jesus Christ we have been chosen from eternity, accepted in time, and united for eternity."

Are you ever tempted to think that you can go it alone without the fellowship of other Christians? Jesus' prayer for his disciples was also a prayer for us—we who would place our faith in him in the centuries that followed his life on this earth. He stressed again and again his passionate desire that we "be one" even as he and his Father are one. When we gather together, he has promised to be in our midst. God's union with us allows us unity with each other.

As you worship God now, imagine the countless other believers who also are bowing before him. Pray for the unity of believers both in your community and around the world.

[i pray]

Lord, you know there are certain people I simply don't like very much, and yet they are part of your
family. Give me grace to embrace them with your love as a witness to the watching world.

[i respond]

What steps can you take to help unify the church where you worship? Ask God to show you simple ways that you can encourage and strengthen others who are part of the body of Christ.

dearly because you love me and believe that I came from God. ²⁸Yes, I came from the Father into the world, and I will leave the world and return to the Father."

²⁹Then his disciples said, "At last you are speaking plainly and not in parables. ³⁰Now we understand that you know everything and don't need anyone to tell you anything.* From this we believe that you came from God."

³¹Jesus asked, "Do you finally believe? ³²But the time is coming—in fact, it is already here—when you will be scattered, each one going his own way, leaving me alone. Yet I am not alone because the Father is with me. ³³I have told you all this so that you may have peace in me. Here on earth you will have many trials and sorrows. But take heart, because I have overcome the world."

THE PRAYER OF JESUS

17 When Jesus had finished saying all these things, he looked up to heaven and said, "Father, the time has come. Glorify your Son so he can give glory back to you. ²For you have given him authority over everyone in all the earth. He gives eternal life to each one you have given him. ³And this is the way to have eternal life—to know you, the only true God, and Jesus Christ, the one you sent to earth. ⁴I brought glory to you here on earth by doing everything you told me to do. ⁵And now, Father, bring me into the glory we shared before the world began.

⁶"I have told these men about you. They were in the world, but then you gave them to me. Actually, they were always yours, and you gave them to me; and they have kept your word. ⁷Now they know that everything I have is a gift from you, ⁸for I have passed on to them the words you gave me; and they accepted them and know that I came from you, and they believe you sent me.

⁹"My prayer is not for the world, but for those you have given me, because they belong to you. ¹⁰And all of them, since they are mine, belong to you; and you have given them back to me, so they are my glory! ¹¹Now I am departing the world; I am leaving them behind and coming to you. Holy Father, keep them and care for them—all those you have given me—so that they will be united just as we are. ¹²During my time here, I have kept them safe.* I guarded them so that not one was lost, except the one headed for destruction, as the Scriptures foretold.

¹³"And now I am coming to you. I have told them many things while I was with them so they would be filled with my joy. ¹⁴I have given them your word. And the world hates them because they do not belong to the world, just as I do not. ¹⁵I'm not asking you to take them out of the world, but to keep them safe from the evil one. ¹⁶They are not part of this world any more than I am. ¹⁷Make them pure and holy by teaching them your words of truth. ¹⁸As you sent me into the world, I am sending them into the world. ¹⁹And I give myself entirely to you so they also might be entirely yours.

²⁰"I am praying not only for these disciples but also for all who will ever believe in me because of their testimony. ²¹My prayer for all of them is that they will be one, just as you and I are one, Father—that just as you are in me and I am in you, so they will be in us, and the world will believe you sent me.

²²"I have given them the glory you gave me, so that they may be one, as we are—²³I in them and you in me, all being perfected into one. Then the world will know that you sent me and will understand that you love them as much as you love me. ²⁴Father, I want these whom you've given me to be with me, so they can see my glory. You gave me the glory because you loved me even before the world began!

²⁵"O righteous Father, the world doesn't know you, but I do; and these disciples know you sent me. ²⁶And I have revealed you to them and will keep on revealing you. I will do this so that your love for me may be in them and I in them."

16:30 Or *don't need that anyone should ask you anything.* 17:12 Greek *I have kept in your name those whom you have given me.*

JESUS IS BETRAYED AND ARRESTED

18 After saying these things, Jesus crossed the Kidron Valley with his disciples and entered a grove of olive trees. ²Judas, the betrayer, knew this place, because Jesus had gone there many times with his disciples. ³The leading priests and Pharisees had given Judas a battalion of Roman soldiers and Temple guards to accompany him. Now with blazing torches, lanterns, and weapons, they arrived at the olive grove.

⁴Jesus fully realized all that was going to happen to him. Stepping forward to meet them, he asked, "Whom are you looking for?"

⁵"Jesus of Nazareth," they replied.

"I am he,"* Jesus said. Judas was standing there with them when Jesus identified himself. ⁶And as he said, "I am he," they all fell backward to the ground! ⁷Once more he asked them, "Whom are you searching for?"

And again they replied, "Jesus of Nazareth."

⁸"I told you that I am he," Jesus said. "And since I am the one you want, let these others go." ⁹He did this to fulfill his own statement: "I have not lost a single one of those you gave me."*

¹⁰Then Simon Peter drew a sword and slashed off the right ear of Malchus, the high priest's servant. ¹¹But Jesus said to Peter, "Put your sword back into its sheath. Shall I not drink from the cup the Father has given me?"

ANNAS QUESTIONS JESUS

¹²So the soldiers, their commanding officer, and the Temple guards arrested Jesus and tied him up. ¹³First they took him to Annas, the father-in-law of Caiaphas, the high priest that year. ¹⁴Caiaphas was the one who had told the other Jewish leaders, "Better that one should die for all."

PETER'S FIRST DENIAL

¹⁵Simon Peter followed along behind, as did another of the disciples. That other disciple was acquainted with the high priest, so he was allowed to enter the courtyard with Jesus.

¹⁶Peter stood outside the gate. Then the other disciple spoke to the woman watching at the gate, and she let Peter in. ¹⁷The woman asked Peter, "Aren't you one of Jesus' disciples?"

"No," he said, "I am not."

¹⁸The guards and the household servants were standing around a charcoal fire they had made because it was cold. And Peter stood there with them, warming himself.

THE HIGH PRIEST QUESTIONS JESUS

¹⁹Inside, the high priest began asking Jesus about his followers and what he had been teaching them. ²⁰Jesus replied, "What I teach is widely known, because I have preached regularly in the synagogues and the Temple. I have been heard by people* everywhere, and I teach nothing in private that I have not said in public. ²¹Why are you asking me this question? Ask those who heard me. They know what I said."

²²One of the Temple guards standing there struck Jesus on the face. "Is that the way to answer the high priest?" he demanded.

²³Jesus replied, "If I said anything wrong, you must give evidence for it. Should you hit a man for telling the truth?"

²⁴Then Annas bound Jesus and sent him to Caiaphas, the high priest.

PETER'S SECOND AND THIRD DENIALS

²⁵Meanwhile, as Simon Peter was standing by the fire, they asked him again, "Aren't you one of his disciples?"

"I am not," he said.

²⁶But one of the household servants of the high priest, a relative of the man whose ear Peter had cut off, asked, "Didn't I see you out there in the olive grove with Jesus?" ²⁷Again Peter denied it. And immediately a rooster crowed.

JESUS' TRIAL BEFORE PILATE

²⁸Jesus' trial before Caiaphas ended in the early hours of the morning. Then he was

18:5 Greek *I am;* also in 18:6, 8. 18:9 See John 6:39 and 17:12. 18:20 Greek *Jewish people;* also in 18:38.

taken to the headquarters of the Roman governor. His accusers didn't go in themselves because it would defile them, and they wouldn't be allowed to celebrate the Passover feast. ²⁹So Pilate, the governor, went out to them and asked, "What is your charge against this man?"

³⁰"We wouldn't have handed him over to you if he weren't a criminal!" they retorted.

³¹"Then take him away and judge him by your own laws," Pilate told them.

"Only the Romans are permitted to execute someone," the Jewish leaders replied. ³²This fulfilled Jesus' prediction about the way he would die.*

³³Then Pilate went back inside and called for Jesus to be brought to him. "Are you the King of the Jews?" he asked him.

³⁴Jesus replied, "Is this your own question, or did others tell you about me?"

³⁵"Am I a Jew?" Pilate asked. "Your own people and their leading priests brought you here. Why? What have you done?"

³⁶Then Jesus answered, "I am not an earthly king. If I were, my followers would have fought when I was arrested by the Jewish leaders. But my Kingdom is not of this world."

³⁷Pilate replied, "You are a king then?"

"You say that I am a king, and you are right," Jesus said. "I was born for that purpose. And I came to bring truth to the world. All who love the truth recognize that what I say is true."

³⁸"What is truth?" Pilate asked. Then he went out again to the people and told them, "He is not guilty of any crime. ³⁹But you have a custom of asking me to release someone from prison each year at Passover. So if you want me to, I'll release the King of the Jews."

⁴⁰But they shouted back, "No! Not this man, but Barabbas!" (Barabbas was a criminal.)

JESUS SENTENCED TO DEATH

19 Then Pilate had Jesus flogged with a lead-tipped whip. ²The soldiers made a crown of long, sharp thorns and put it on his head, and they put a royal purple robe on him. ³"Hail! King of the Jews!" they mocked, and they hit him with their fists.

⁴Pilate went outside again and said to the people, "I am going to bring him out to you now, but understand clearly that I find him not guilty." ⁵Then Jesus came out wearing the crown of thorns and the purple robe. And Pilate said, "Here is the man!"

⁶When they saw him, the leading priests and Temple guards began shouting, "Crucify! Crucify!"

"You crucify him," Pilate said. "I find him not guilty."

⁷The Jewish leaders replied, "By our laws he ought to die because he called himself the Son of God."

⁸When Pilate heard this, he was more frightened than ever. ⁹He took Jesus back into the headquarters again and asked him, "Where are you from?" But Jesus gave no answer. ¹⁰"You won't talk to me?" Pilate demanded. "Don't you realize that I have the power to release you or to crucify you?"

¹¹Then Jesus said, "You would have no power over me at all unless it were given to you from above. So the one who brought me to you has the greater sin."

¹²Then Pilate tried to release him, but the Jewish leaders told him, "If you release this man, you are not a friend of Caesar. Anyone who declares himself a king is a rebel against Caesar."

¹³When they said this, Pilate brought Jesus out to them again. Then Pilate sat down on the judgment seat on the platform that is called the Stone Pavement (in Hebrew, *Gabbatha*). ¹⁴It was now about noon of the day of preparation for the Passover. And Pilate said to the people,* "Here is your king!"

¹⁵"Away with him," they yelled. "Away with him—crucify him!"

"What? Crucify your king?" Pilate asked.

"We have no king but Caesar," the leading priests shouted back.

18:32 See John 12:32-33. 19:14 Greek *Jewish people*; also in 19:20.

My Daily Worship

— *October 22* —

THE CROSS AND THE CROWN

JOHN 18:1 – 19:42

The soldiers made a crown of long, sharp thorns and put it on his head,
and they put a royal purple robe on him. "Hail! King of the Jews!"
they mocked, and they hit him with their fists (19:2–3).

[i reflect]

Ironic, isn't it? Just a few days before this pummeling by the soldiers, Jesus had been hailed by the people as the king of Israel. Now he was once again being hailed as a king, but this time by men intent on mocking, humiliating, and physically abusing him.

It is painful to read of the torture that Christ received. The One we worship was subjected to a twisted form of veneration. The soldiers were ordered only to flog Jesus, but their cruelty went beyond carrying out that court-ordered punishment. They chose instead to "worship" him by placing a painful crown on his bloody head and a purple robe on his battered body, all the while taunting and mocking his identity.

Satan counterfeits every good gift that God has given us. We have the capacity to worship Christ in gratitude and reverence, yet we also live in a world that continues to mock his name and those who bear it.

The bloody crown of briers that Jesus wore for our sake was not a symbol of defeat, however. Tertullian, an ancient church father, explained it this way: "Jesus was not greeted in heaven as the King of Glory until he had been condemned to the cross as King of the Jews. The Father first made him a little lower than the angels for a time and then crowned him with glory and honor. If you owe your own head to him for these things, repay it if you can; he presented his for yours."

How can we possibly repay the One who has the very universe at his disposal? We can give him nothing that he does not already possess—nothing, that is, except our hearts. Reflect today on the sacrifice of the One who bore both the cross and the crown for you.

[i pray]

It causes me pain, Lord, to think of the way you were treated in your final moments on earth.
You deserved reverence but received ridicule instead. Forgive us, Lord,
when we fail to give you the worship of which you are worthy.

[i respond]

Write down all the words you typically associate with cross and with crown. Using these words, construct a word poem. If you want, write it in the shape of a cross or a crown.

[16]Then Pilate gave Jesus to them to be crucified.

THE CRUCIFIXION

So they took Jesus and led him away. [17]Carrying the cross by himself, Jesus went to the place called Skull Hill (in Hebrew, *Golgotha*). [18]There they crucified him. There were two others crucified with him, one on either side, with Jesus between them. [19]And Pilate posted a sign over him that read, "Jesus of Nazareth, the King of the Jews." [20]The place where Jesus was crucified was near the city; and the sign was written in Hebrew, Latin, and Greek, so that many people could read it.

[21]Then the leading priests said to Pilate, "Change it from 'The King of the Jews' to 'He said, I am King of the Jews.'"

[22]Pilate replied, "What I have written, I have written. It stays exactly as it is."

[23]When the soldiers had crucified Jesus, they divided his clothes among the four of them. They also took his robe, but it was seamless, woven in one piece from the top. [24]So they said, "Let's not tear it but throw dice* to see who gets it." This fulfilled the Scripture that says, "They divided my clothes among themselves and threw dice for my robe."* So that is what they did.

[25]Standing near the cross were Jesus' mother, and his mother's sister, Mary (the wife of Clopas), and Mary Magdalene. [26]When Jesus saw his mother standing there beside the disciple he loved, he said to her, "Woman, he is your son." [27]And he said to this disciple, "She is your mother." And from then on this disciple took her into his home.

THE DEATH OF JESUS

[28]Jesus knew that everything was now finished, and to fulfill the Scriptures he said, "I am thirsty."* [29]A jar of sour wine was sitting there, so they soaked a sponge in it, put it on a hyssop branch, and held it up to his lips. [30]When Jesus had tasted it, he said, "It is finished!" Then he bowed his head and gave up his spirit.

[31]The Jewish leaders didn't want the victims hanging there the next day, which was the Sabbath (and a very special Sabbath at that, because it was the Passover), so they asked Pilate to hasten their deaths by ordering that their legs be broken. Then their bodies could be taken down. [32]So the soldiers came and broke the legs of the two men crucified with Jesus. [33]But when they came to Jesus, they saw that he was dead already, so they didn't break his legs. [34]One of the soldiers, however, pierced his side with a spear, and blood and water flowed out. [35]This report is from an eyewitness giving an accurate account; it is presented so that you also can believe. [36]These things happened in fulfillment of the Scriptures that say, "Not one of his bones will be broken,"* [37]and "They will look on him whom they pierced."*

THE BURIAL OF JESUS

[38]Afterward Joseph of Arimathea, who had been a secret disciple of Jesus (because he feared the Jewish leaders), asked Pilate for permission to take Jesus' body down. When Pilate gave him permission, he came and took the body away. [39]Nicodemus, the man who had come to Jesus at night, also came, bringing about seventy-five pounds* of embalming ointment made from myrrh and aloes. [40]Together they wrapped Jesus' body in a long linen cloth with the spices, as is the Jewish custom of burial. [41]The place of crucifixion was near a garden, where there was a new tomb, never used before. [42]And so, because it was the day of preparation before the Passover and since the tomb was close at hand, they laid Jesus there.

THE RESURRECTION

20 Early Sunday morning,* while it was still dark, Mary Magdalene came to the tomb and found that the stone had been

---

19:24a Greek *cast lots.*   19:24b Ps 22:18.   19:28 See Pss 22:15; 69:21.   19:36 Exod 12:46; Num 9:12; Ps 34:20.   19:37 Zech 12:10.
19:39 Greek *100 litras* [32.7 kilograms].   20:1 Greek *On the first day of the week.*

rolled away from the entrance. ²She ran and found Simon Peter and the other disciple, the one whom Jesus loved. She said, "They have taken the Lord's body out of the tomb, and I don't know where they have put him!"

³Peter and the other disciple ran to the tomb to see. ⁴The other disciple outran Peter and got there first. ⁵He stooped and looked in and saw the linen cloth lying there, but he didn't go in. ⁶Then Simon Peter arrived and went inside. He also noticed the linen wrappings lying there, ⁷while the cloth that had covered Jesus' head was folded up and lying to the side. ⁸Then the other disciple also went in, and he saw and believed—⁹for until then they hadn't realized that the Scriptures said he would rise from the dead. ¹⁰Then they went home.

JESUS APPEARS TO MARY MAGDALENE

¹¹Mary was standing outside the tomb crying, and as she wept, she stooped and looked in. ¹²She saw two white-robed angels sitting at the head and foot of the place where the body of Jesus had been lying. ¹³"Why are you crying?" the angels asked her.

"Because they have taken away my Lord," she replied, "and I don't know where they have put him."

¹⁴She glanced over her shoulder and saw someone standing behind her. It was Jesus, but she didn't recognize him. ¹⁵"Why are you crying?" Jesus asked her. "Who are you looking for?"

She thought he was the gardener. "Sir," she said, "if you have taken him away, tell me where you have put him, and I will go and get him."

¹⁶"Mary!" Jesus said.

She turned toward him and exclaimed, "Teacher!"*

¹⁷"Don't cling to me," Jesus said, "for I haven't yet ascended to the Father. But go find my brothers and tell them that I am ascending to my Father and your Father, my God and your God."

¹⁸Mary Magdalene found the disciples and told them, "I have seen the Lord!" Then she gave them his message.

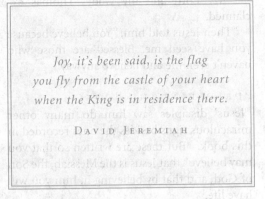

Joy, it's been said, is the flag you fly from the castle of your heart when the King is in residence there.

DAVID JEREMIAH

JESUS APPEARS TO HIS DISCIPLES

¹⁹That evening, on the first day of the week, the disciples were meeting behind locked doors because they were afraid of the Jewish leaders. Suddenly, Jesus was standing there among them! "Peace be with you," he said. ²⁰As he spoke, he held out his hands for them to see, and he showed them his side. They were filled with joy when they saw their Lord! ²¹He spoke to them again and said, "Peace be with you. As the Father has sent me, so I send you." ²²Then he breathed on them and said to them, "Receive the Holy Spirit. ²³If you forgive anyone's sins, they are forgiven. If you refuse to forgive them, they are unforgiven."

JESUS APPEARS TO THOMAS

²⁴One of the disciples, Thomas (nicknamed the Twin*), was not with the others when Jesus came. ²⁵They told him, "We have seen the Lord!" But he replied, "I won't believe it unless I see the nail wounds in his hands, put my fingers into them, and place my hand into the wound in his side."

²⁶Eight days later the disciples were together again, and this time Thomas was with them. The doors were locked; but suddenly, as before, Jesus was standing among them. He said, "Peace be with you." ²⁷Then he said to

20:16 Greek *and said in Hebrew, "Rabboni," which means "Teacher."* 20:24 Greek *the one who was called Didymus.*

Thomas, "Put your finger here and see my hands. Put your hand into the wound in my side. Don't be faithless any longer. Believe!"

[28]"My Lord and my God!" Thomas exclaimed.

[29]Then Jesus told him, "You believe because you have seen me. Blessed are those who haven't seen me and believe anyway."

PURPOSE OF THE BOOK

[30]Jesus' disciples saw him do many other miraculous signs besides the ones recorded in this book. [31]But these are written so that you may believe* that Jesus is the Messiah, the Son of God, and that by believing in him you will have life.

JESUS APPEARS TO SEVEN DISCIPLES

21 Later Jesus appeared again to the disciples beside the Sea of Galilee.* This is how it happened. [2]Several of the disciples were there—Simon Peter, Thomas (nicknamed the Twin*), Nathanael from Cana in Galilee, the sons of Zebedee, and two other disciples.

[3]Simon Peter said, "I'm going fishing."

"We'll come, too," they all said. So they went out in the boat, but they caught nothing all night.

[4]At dawn the disciples saw Jesus standing on the beach, but they couldn't see who he was. [5]He called out, "Friends, have you caught any fish?"

"No," they replied.

[6]Then he said, "Throw out your net on the right-hand side of the boat, and you'll get plenty of fish!" So they did, and they couldn't draw in the net because there were so many fish in it.

[7]Then the disciple whom Jesus loved said to Peter, "It is the Lord!" When Simon Peter heard that it was the Lord, he put on his tunic (for he had stripped for work), jumped into the water, and swam ashore. [8]The others stayed with the boat and pulled the loaded net to the shore, for they were only out about three hundred feet.* [9]When they got there, they saw that a charcoal fire was burning and fish were frying over it, and there was bread.

[10]"Bring some of the fish you've just caught," Jesus said. [11]So Simon Peter went aboard and dragged the net to the shore. There were 153 large fish, and yet the net hadn't torn.

[12]"Now come and have some breakfast!" Jesus said. And no one dared ask him if he really was the Lord because they were sure of it. [13]Then Jesus served them the bread and the fish. [14]This was the third time Jesus had appeared to his disciples since he had been raised from the dead.

JESUS CHALLENGES PETER

[15]After breakfast Jesus said to Simon Peter, "Simon son of John, do you love me more than these?"

"Yes, Lord," Peter replied, "you know I love you."

"Then feed my lambs," Jesus told him.

[16]Jesus repeated the question: "Simon son of John, do you love me?"

"Yes, Lord," Peter said, "you know I love you."

"Then take care of my sheep," Jesus said.

[17]Once more he asked him, "Simon son of John, do you love me?"

Peter was grieved that Jesus asked the question a third time. He said, "Lord, you know everything. You know I love you."

Jesus said, "Then feed my sheep. [18]The truth is, when you were young, you were able to do as you liked and go wherever you wanted to. But when you are old, you will stretch out your hands, and others will direct you and take you where you don't want to go." [19]Jesus said this to let him know what kind of death he would die to glorify God. Then Jesus told him, "Follow me."

[20]Peter turned around and saw the disciple Jesus loved following them—the one who had leaned over to Jesus during supper and asked, "Lord, who among us will betray you?" [21]Peter asked Jesus, "What about him, Lord?"

My Daily Worship

— *October 23* —

THE GOD OF THE SECOND CHANCE

JOHN 20:1–21:25

Once more he asked him, "Simon son of John, do you love me?" Peter was grieved that
Jesus asked the question a third time. He said, "Lord, you know everything.
You know I love you." Jesus said, "Then feed my sheep" (21:17).

[i reflect]

The story of Peter's failure is well known. Despite Peter's confident statement that he was willing to die for Jesus (13:37), he instead denied three times that he even knew the Lord whom he professed to love.

The account of Peter's restoration in today's passage is highly significant. Three times Peter had denied Christ and three times he was given the opportunity to reaffirm his love. Jesus was not only Peter's master, but he also was a master teacher. A good teacher usually knows whether his or her students will pass a test. The purpose of the test is so that the students will know whether they have mastered the subject.

In Peter's case, his teacher was not only fully human but also divine. Jesus had predicted how Peter would perform in the crisis that led to the cross. Now he offered Peter the chance to retake the exam. A second chance.

In *A Heart for the Master*, co-authors Gordon and Gail MacDonald tell the story of Aba Mios, who was asked by a soldier whether God would forgive him. "After instructing him at some length, the old man asked him: 'Tell me, my son, if your cloak were torn, would you throw it away?' 'Oh, no!' the soldier replied. 'I would mend it and wear it again.' The old man said to him, 'Well, if you care for your cloak, will not God show mercy to his own creature?'"

The point is well made. If we as flawed human beings take care to mend and repair that which has been torn, would God not want to see his broken ones restored?

We serve the God of the second chance. Each of us, like Peter, is offered the opportunity to pour our brokenness at the feet of the One who was himself broken for our sake. Repentance is one of the truest forms of worship, for it has the power to remove any barrier of sin that separates us from the Savior. Take a moment to thank him for that privilege today.

[i pray]

Forgive me, Lord, for the ways in which I have behaved as if I don't even know you. Thank you for offering me a second chance to express my love through service to others in your name.

[i respond]

Think of a relationship or a situation where you would love to have a second chance. Ask Jesus to provide that opportunity for you; then follow it through with either a phone call or a letter asking forgiveness or healing in that situation.

²²Jesus replied, "If I want him to remain alive until I return, what is that to you? You follow me." ²³So the rumor spread among the community of believers* that that disciple wouldn't die. But that isn't what Jesus said at all. He only said, "If I want him to remain alive until I return, what is that to you?"

CONCLUSION

²⁴This is that disciple who saw these events and recorded them here. And we all know that his account of these things is accurate.

²⁵And I suppose that if all the other things Jesus did were written down, the whole world could not contain the books.

21:23 Greek *the brothers.*

Acts

They worshiped together at the Temple each day, met in homes for the Lord's Supper,

and shared their meals with great joy and generosity—all the while praising

God and enjoying the goodwill of all the people (2:46–47).

A Community of Worshipers

What is the purpose of the church?

It's a good question . . . and also an important one. Why *do* Christian congregations exist? Why do we have choirs and candles? Bus ministries and Bible studies? Is our mission primarily to build special buildings where we can retreat for once-a-week religious programs and services? Or is it something more?

The book of Acts takes us back to our roots—the birth of the church—picking up where the Gospels stop. Following his death, burial, and resurrection, Jesus Christ gathers his followers and outlines their mission: "But when the Holy Spirit has come upon you, you will receive power and will tell people about me everywhere—in Jerusalem, throughout Judea, in Samaria, and to the ends of the earth" (1:8).

In short, the people of God have an urgent message to take to their neighbors and to the nations. It's the good news that Jesus Christ is Lord, that he is the answer to the deepest needs of the human heart. It's the promise that he is coming back. Those first-century followers took this news and told it, and—in the process—turned the world upside down (Acts 17:6).

Acts is an "up close and personal" look at church life as God intended. It reveals a community of transformed individuals knitted together into a spiritual family. Together they learned what it means to love and serve Christ. Together they made an eternal difference by reaching out in every imaginable direction with the life-changing gospel.

Acts reminds us that this is our purpose, too: to band together with others whose lives have been transformed by Christ and share his love everywhere! When you think about it, our mission is to gather worshipers for that ultimate worship service in heaven (as described in Revelation 7:9)—"a vast crowd, too great to count, from every nation and tribe and people and language, standing in front of the throne and before the Lamb."

Worship Moments

- Conviction and true worship is brought about through the power of the Holy Spirit (2:17).

- The church worshiped together at the Temple daily, and grew in numbers (2:46).

- Stephen, full of the Holy Spirit, saw the heavens opened and Jesus at the right hand of God (7:56).

- Even in prison, Paul and Silas worshiped, praying and singing hymns to God (16:25).

- God's purpose was for all nations to seek after him, the one true God deserving our worship (17:27).

THE PROMISE OF THE HOLY SPIRIT

1 Dear Theophilus:

In my first book* I told you about everything Jesus began to do and teach ²until the day he ascended to heaven after giving his chosen apostles further instructions from the Holy Spirit. ³During the forty days after his crucifixion, he appeared to the apostles from time to time and proved to them in many ways that he was actually alive. On these occasions he talked to them about the Kingdom of God.

⁴In one of these meetings as he was eating a meal with them, he told them, "Do not leave Jerusalem until the Father sends you what he promised. Remember, I have told you about this before. ⁵John baptized with* water, but in just a few days you will be baptized with the Holy Spirit."

THE ASCENSION OF JESUS

⁶When the apostles were with Jesus, they kept asking him, "Lord, are you going to free Israel now and restore our kingdom?"

⁷"The Father sets those dates," he replied, "and they are not for you to know. ⁸But when the Holy Spirit has come upon you, you will receive power and will tell people about me everywhere—in Jerusalem, throughout Judea, in Samaria, and to the ends of the earth."

⁹It was not long after he said this that he was taken up into the sky while they were watching, and he disappeared into a cloud. ¹⁰As they were straining their eyes to see him, two white-robed men suddenly stood there among them. ¹¹They said, "Men of Galilee, why are you standing here staring at the sky? Jesus has been taken away from you into heaven. And someday, just as you saw him go, he will return!"

MATTHIAS REPLACES JUDAS

¹²The apostles were at the Mount of Olives when this happened, so they walked the half mile* back to Jerusalem. ¹³Then they went to the upstairs room of the house where they were staying. Here is the list of those who were present:

Peter,
John,
James,
Andrew,
Philip,
Thomas,
Bartholomew,
Matthew,
James (son of Alphaeus),
Simon (the Zealot),
and Judas (son of James).

¹⁴They all met together continually for prayer, along with Mary the mother of Jesus, several other women, and the brothers of Jesus.

¹⁵During this time, on a day when about 120 believers* were present, Peter stood up and addressed them as follows:

¹⁶"Brothers, it was necessary for the Scriptures to be fulfilled concerning Judas, who guided the Temple police to arrest Jesus. This was predicted long ago by the Holy Spirit, speaking through King David. ¹⁷Judas was one of us, chosen to share in the ministry with us."

¹⁸(Judas bought a field with the money he received for his treachery, and falling there, he burst open, spilling out his intestines. ¹⁹The news of his death spread rapidly among all the people of Jerusalem, and they gave the place the Aramaic name *Akeldama*, which means "Field of Blood.")

²⁰Peter continued, "This was predicted in the book of Psalms, where it says, 'Let his home become desolate, with no one living in it.' And again, 'Let his position be given to someone else.'*

²¹"So now we must choose another man to take Judas's place. It must be someone who has been with us all the time that we were with the Lord Jesus—²²from the time he was

---

1:1 The reference is to the book of Luke.   1:5 Or *in;* also in 1:5b.   1:12 Greek *a Sabbath day's journey.*   1:15 Greek *brothers.*
1:20 Pss 69:25; 109:8.

My Daily Worship

— *October 24* —

THE STILL SOURCE OF MOVEMENT

ACTS 1:1–2:47

They all met together continually for prayer, along with Mary the mother of Jesus, several other women, and the brothers of Jesus (1:14).

[i reflect]

Jeremiah Lanphier, a businessman recently appointed as a missionary to New York City, wondered how best to begin his new work. After praying about it, he decided to put up copies of a handbill advertising a prayer meeting to be held every Wednesday at noon. The line at the top of the handbill asked, "How often shall I pray?"

On the first day of the prayer meeting, September 23, 1857, Lanphier was ready and waiting at noon. Five minutes passed, and nobody showed up. Fifteen minutes: still nobody. Lanphier was starting to get discouraged. Finally at 12:30 Lanphier heard footsteps on the stairs as the first of six people entered the room to pray.

The next week, forty intercessors showed up. Then more. Soon Lanphier decided to make the prayer meeting daily instead of weekly. Within six months, ten thousand businesspeople were meeting daily for prayer in New York City alone. The practice quickly spread to other cities.

This prayer movement set off one of the greatest revivals in American history. According to research by Edwin Orr, one million Americans were converted in 1858 and 1859, out of a national population of 30 million.

Great acts of God arise out of the prayers of his people the way great symphonies arise out of the ready silence of musicians.

That's the way it was with the early Christians after the ascension of Jesus. They spent their time praying together, as today's passage indicates. So the Spirit descended upon them. So they were sent out. So that group of 120 believers (not much larger than the size of the average local church in America) lit the world on fire.

Do we ask ourselves, how often shall I pray? Today, make it your practice to pray as often as you can. Choose some device—such as a stop sign, or weather report on the radio—as a signal to pray.

[i pray]

*Come, for you are yourself the desire that is within me. Come, my breath and
my life. Come, the consolation of my humble soul. Come, my joy,
my glory, my endless delight (prayer of Symeon, 949–1022).*

[i respond]

Find others with whom to pray this week. Maybe your church has a prayer meeting. Maybe your small group could get together. Maybe you could call some friends. Whatever—just pray. And expect God to act.

baptized by John until the day he was taken from us into heaven. Whoever is chosen will join us as a witness of Jesus' resurrection."

²³So they nominated two men: Joseph called Barsabbas (also known as Justus) and Matthias. ²⁴Then they all prayed for the right man to be chosen. "O Lord," they said, "you know every heart. Show us which of these men you have chosen ²⁵as an apostle to replace Judas the traitor in this ministry, for he has deserted us and gone where he belongs." ²⁶Then they cast lots, and in this way Matthias was chosen and became an apostle with the other eleven.

THE HOLY SPIRIT COMES

2 On the day of Pentecost, seven weeks after Jesus' resurrection,* the believers were meeting together in one place. ²Suddenly, there was a sound from heaven like the roaring of a mighty windstorm in the skies above them, and it filled the house where they were meeting. ³Then, what looked like flames or tongues of fire appeared and settled on each of them. ⁴And everyone present was filled with the Holy Spirit and began speaking in other languages,* as the Holy Spirit gave them this ability.

⁵Godly Jews from many nations were living in Jerusalem at that time. ⁶When they heard this sound, they came running to see what it was all about, and they were bewildered to hear their own languages being spoken by the believers.

⁷They were beside themselves with wonder. "How can this be?" they exclaimed. "These people are all from Galilee, ⁸and yet we hear them speaking the languages of the lands where we were born! ⁹Here we are—Parthians, Medes, Elamites, people from Mesopotamia, Judea, Cappadocia, Pontus, the province of Asia, ¹⁰Phrygia, Pamphylia, Egypt, and the areas of Libya toward Cyrene, visitors from Rome (both Jews and converts to Judaism), ¹¹Cretans, and Arabians. And we all

hear these people speaking in our own languages about the wonderful things God has done!" ¹²They stood there amazed and perplexed. "What can this mean?" they asked each other. ¹³But others in the crowd were mocking. "They're drunk, that's all!" they said.

PETER PREACHES TO A CROWD

¹⁴Then Peter stepped forward with the eleven other apostles and shouted to the crowd, "Listen carefully, all of you, fellow Jews and residents of Jerusalem! Make no mistake about this. ¹⁵Some of you are saying these people are drunk. It isn't true! It's much too early for that. People don't get drunk by nine o'clock in the morning. ¹⁶No, what you see this morning was predicted centuries ago by the prophet Joel:

¹⁷ 'In the last days, God said,
   I will pour out my Spirit upon all people.
Your sons and daughters will prophesy,
   your young men will see visions,
   and your old men will dream dreams.
¹⁸ In those days I will pour out my Spirit
   upon all my servants, men and women alike,
   and they will prophesy.
¹⁹ And I will cause wonders in the heavens above
   and signs on the earth below—
   blood and fire and clouds of smoke.
²⁰ The sun will be turned into darkness,
   and the moon will turn bloodred,
   before that great and glorious day of the Lord arrives.
²¹ And anyone who calls on the name of the Lord
   will be saved.'*

²²"People of Israel, listen! God publicly endorsed Jesus of Nazareth by doing wonderful miracles, wonders, and signs through him, as you well know. ²³But you followed God's

---

2:1 Greek *When the day of Pentecost arrived.* This annual celebration came 50 days after the Passover ceremonies. See Lev 23:16.
2:4 Or *in other tongues.* **2:17-21** Joel 2:28-32.

prearranged plan. With the help of lawless Gentiles, you nailed him to the cross and murdered him. [24]However, God released him from the horrors of death and raised him back to life again, for death could not keep him in its grip. [25]King David said this about him:

'I know the Lord is always with me.
I will not be shaken, for he is right beside me.
[26] No wonder my heart is filled with joy, and my mouth shouts his praises!
My body rests in hope.
[27] For you will not leave my soul among the dead*
or allow your Holy One to rot in the grave.
[28] You have shown me the way of life, and you will give me wonderful joy in your presence.'*

[29]"Dear brothers, think about this! David wasn't referring to himself when he spoke these words I have quoted, for he died and was buried, and his tomb is still here among us. [30]But he was a prophet, and he knew God had promised with an oath that one of David's own descendants would sit on David's throne as the Messiah. [31]David was looking into the future and predicting the Messiah's resurrection. He was saying that the Messiah would not be left among the dead and that his body would not rot in the grave.

[32]"This prophecy was speaking of Jesus, whom God raised from the dead, and we all are witnesses of this. [33]Now he sits on the throne of highest honor in heaven, at God's right hand. And the Father, as he had promised, gave him the Holy Spirit to pour out upon us, just as you see and hear today. [34]For David himself never ascended into heaven, yet he said,

'The LORD said to my Lord,
Sit in honor at my right hand
[35]   until I humble your enemies,

making them a footstool under your feet.'*

[36]So let it be clearly known by everyone in Israel that God has made this Jesus whom you crucified to be both Lord and Messiah!"

[37]Peter's words convicted them deeply, and they said to him and to the other apostles, "Brothers, what should we do?"

[38]Peter replied, "Each of you must turn from your sins and turn to God, and be baptized in the name of Jesus Christ for the forgiveness of your sins. Then you will receive the gift of the Holy Spirit. [39]This promise is to you and to your children, and even to the Gentiles*—all who have been called by the Lord our God." [40]Then Peter continued preaching for a long time, strongly urging all his listeners, "Save yourselves from this generation that has gone astray!"

[41]Those who believed what Peter said were baptized and added to the church—about three thousand in all. [42]They joined with the other believers and devoted themselves to the apostles' teaching and fellowship, sharing in the Lord's Supper and in prayer.

THE BELIEVERS MEET TOGETHER

[43]A deep sense of awe came over them all, and the apostles performed many miraculous signs and wonders. [44]And all the believers met together constantly and shared everything they had. [45]They sold their possessions and shared the proceeds with those in need. [46]They worshiped together at the Temple each day, met in homes for the Lord's Supper, and shared their meals with great joy and generosity—[47]all the while praising God and enjoying the goodwill of all the people. And each day the Lord added to their group those who were being saved.

PETER HEALS A CRIPPLED BEGGAR

3 Peter and John went to the Temple one afternoon to take part in the three o'clock

---

2:27 Greek in Hades; also in 2:31.   2:25-28 Ps 16:8-11.   2:34-35 Ps 110:1.   2:39 Greek to those far away.

prayer service. [2]As they approached the Temple, a man lame from birth was being carried in. Each day he was put beside the Temple gate, the one called the Beautiful Gate, so he could beg from the people going into the Temple. [3]When he saw Peter and John about to enter, he asked them for some money.

[4]Peter and John looked at him intently, and Peter said, "Look at us!" [5]The lame man looked at them eagerly, expecting a gift. [6]But Peter said, "I don't have any money for you. But I'll give you what I have. In the name of Jesus Christ of Nazareth, get up and walk!"

[7]Then Peter took the lame man by the right hand and helped him up. And as he did, the man's feet and anklebones were healed and strengthened. [8]He jumped up, stood on his feet, and began to walk! Then, walking, leaping, and praising God, he went into the Temple with them.

[9]All the people saw him walking and heard him praising God. [10]When they realized he was the lame beggar they had seen so often at the Beautiful Gate, they were absolutely astounded! [11]They all rushed out to Solomon's Colonnade, where he was holding tightly to Peter and John. Everyone stood there in awe of the wonderful thing that had happened.

PETER PREACHES IN THE TEMPLE

[12]Peter saw his opportunity and addressed the crowd. "People of Israel," he said, "what is so astounding about this? And why look at us as though we had made this man walk by our own power and godliness? [13]For it is the God of Abraham, the God of Isaac, the God of Jacob, the God of all our ancestors who has brought glory to his servant Jesus by doing this. This is the same Jesus whom you handed over and rejected before Pilate, despite Pilate's decision to release him. [14]You rejected this holy, righteous one and instead demanded the release of a murderer. [15]You killed the author of life, but God raised him to life. And we are witnesses of this fact!

[16]"The name of Jesus has healed this man—

and you know how lame he was before. Faith in Jesus' name has caused this healing before your very eyes.

[17]"Friends,* I realize that what you did to Jesus was done in ignorance; and the same can be said of your leaders. [18]But God was fulfilling what all the prophets had declared about the Messiah beforehand—that he must suffer all these things. [19]Now turn from your sins and turn to God, so you can be cleansed of your sins. [20]Then wonderful times of refreshment will come from the presence of the Lord, and he will send Jesus your Messiah to you again. [21]For he must remain in heaven until the time for the final restoration of all things, as God promised long ago through his prophets. [22]Moses said, 'The Lord your God will raise up a Prophet like me from among your own people. Listen carefully to everything he tells you.'* [23]Then Moses said, 'Anyone who will not listen to that Prophet will be cut off from God's people and utterly destroyed.'*

[24]"Starting with Samuel, every prophet spoke about what is happening today. [25]You are the children of those prophets, and you are included in the covenant God promised to your ancestors. For God said to Abraham, 'Through your descendants all the families on earth will be blessed.'* [26]When God raised up his servant, he sent him first to you people of Israel, to bless you by turning each of you back from your sinful ways."

PETER AND JOHN BEFORE THE COUNCIL

4 While Peter and John were speaking to the people, the leading priests, the captain of the Temple guard, and some of the Sadducees came over to them. [2]They were very disturbed that Peter and John were claiming, on the authority of Jesus, that there is a resurrection of the dead. [3]They arrested them and, since it was already evening, jailed them until morning. [4]But many of the people

---

3:17 Greek *Brothers.* 3:22 Deut 18:15. 3:23 Deut 18:19; Lev 23:29. 3:25 Gen 22:18.

My Daily Worship

— *October 25* —

ON LIFE ROW

ACTS 3:1–5:16

Turn from your sins and turn to God,
so you can be cleansed of your sins (3:19).

[i reflect]

On June 13, 1983, Karla Faye Tucker and her boyfriend, Danny Garrett, both high on drugs, snuck into an apartment, intent on stealing a motorcycle. But something went terribly wrong, and the pair ended up murdering two occupants of the apartment.

Seven years later, Karla was on Death Row inside Mountain View Prison, Gatesville, Texas. The preaching of prison ministers had started to get through to her, so one night she snuck a Bible back to her cell and started reading. Soon she found herself on the floor, crying and asking God to forgive her.

Later, she recalled, "I knew that no matter what I had done, I was loved, just like that, just like I was. That's when the whole weight of what I did fell on me. I realized for the first time that I had brutally murdered two people and there were people out there hurting because of me. Yet God was saying, 'I love you.' . . . At that moment, he reached down inside of me and ripped out that violence at the very roots and poured himself in."

It takes the grace of God to let us see our sins for the slop pail they are. We may not be murderers like Tucker, but we've done plenty to color our cheeks with shame blushes. How wonderful if the grace of God has also helped us make the U-turn of repentance and God has cleansed us of our sins! Peter exhorted the crowd at Pentecost (and us, too) to "turn from your sins and turn to God," and find refreshment.

Let us be earnest seekers after holiness as well as ones who authentically and persistently urge others to join us on what Karla Faye Tucker called "Life Row."

Thank God right now that he has caused you to repent.

[i pray]

I naturally want to minimize my sins, God, but don't let me get away with it.
Show my sins to me as you see them, that is, as they are in their true
horror. Help me run away from evil—straight into your arms.

[i respond]

How good are you at telling the story of how you found God and turned away from your previous worldly life? As an act of worship, practice telling the story with a friend, so that you will be ready when you meet a fellow sinner who needs to turn toward forgiveness.

other relatives of the high priest. [7]They brought in the two disciples and demanded, "By what power, or in whose name, have you done this?"

[8]Then Peter, filled with the Holy Spirit, said to them, "Leaders and elders of our nation, [9]are we being questioned because we've done a good deed for a crippled man? Do you want to know how he was healed? [10]Let me clearly state to you and to all the people of Israel that he was healed in the name and power of Jesus Christ from Nazareth, the man you crucified, but whom God raised from the dead. [11]For Jesus is the one referred to in the Scriptures, where it says,

'The stone that you builders rejected
    has now become the cornerstone.'*

[12]There is salvation in no one else! There is no other name in all of heaven for people to call on to save them."

[13]The members of the council were amazed when they saw the boldness of Peter and John, for they could see that they were ordinary men who had had no special training. They also recognized them as men who had been with Jesus. [14]But since the man who had been healed was standing right there among them, the council had nothing to say. [15]So they sent Peter and John out of the council chamber* and conferred among themselves.

[16]"What should we do with these men?" they asked each other. "We can't deny they have done a miraculous sign, and everybody in Jerusalem knows about it. [17]But perhaps we can stop them from spreading their propaganda. We'll warn them not to speak to anyone in Jesus' name again." [18]So they called the apostles back in and told them never again to speak or teach about Jesus.

[19]But Peter and John replied, "Do you think God wants us to obey you rather than him? [20]We cannot stop telling about the wonderful things we have seen and heard."

[21]The council then threatened them further,

who heard their message believed it, so that the number of believers totaled about five thousand men, not counting women and children.*

[5]The next day the council of all the rulers and elders and teachers of religious law met in Jerusalem. [6]Annas the high priest was there, along with Caiaphas, John, Alexander, and

4:4 Greek *5,000 adult males.*   4:11 Ps 118:22.   4:15 Greek *the Sanhedrin.*

but they finally let them go because they didn't know how to punish them without starting a riot. For everyone was praising God ²²for this miraculous sign—the healing of a man who had been lame for more than forty years.

THE BELIEVERS PRAY FOR COURAGE

²³As soon as they were freed, Peter and John found the other believers and told them what the leading priests and elders had said. ²⁴Then all the believers were united as they lifted their voices in prayer: "O Sovereign Lord, Creator of heaven and earth, the sea, and everything in them—²⁵you spoke long ago by the Holy Spirit through our ancestor King David, your servant, saying,

'Why did the nations rage?
  Why did the people waste their time
    with futile plans?
²⁶ The kings of the earth prepared for battle;
    the rulers gathered together
  against the Lord
    and against his Messiah.'*

²⁷"That is what has happened here in this city! For Herod Antipas, Pontius Pilate the governor, the Gentiles, and the people of Israel were all united against Jesus, your holy servant, whom you anointed. ²⁸In fact, everything they did occurred according to your eternal will and plan. ²⁹And now, O Lord, hear their threats, and give your servants great boldness in their preaching. ³⁰Send your healing power; may miraculous signs and wonders be done through the name of your holy servant Jesus." ³¹After this prayer, the building where they were meeting shook, and they were all filled with the Holy Spirit. And they preached God's message with boldness.

THE BELIEVERS SHARE THEIR POSSESSIONS

³²All the believers were of one heart and mind, and they felt that what they owned was not their own; they shared everything they had. ³³And the apostles gave powerful witness to the resurrection of the Lord Jesus, and God's great favor was upon them all. ³⁴There was no poverty among them, because people who owned land or houses sold them ³⁵and brought the money to the apostles to give to others in need.

³⁶For instance, there was Joseph, the one the apostles nicknamed Barnabas (which means "Son of Encouragement"). He was from the tribe of Levi and came from the island of Cyprus. ³⁷He sold a field he owned and brought the money to the apostles for those in need.

ANANIAS AND SAPPHIRA

5 There was also a man named Ananias who, with his wife, Sapphira, sold some property. ²He brought part of the money to the apostles, but he claimed it was the full amount. His wife had agreed to this deception.

³Then Peter said, "Ananias, why has Satan filled your heart? You lied to the Holy Spirit, and you kept some of the money for yourself. ⁴The property was yours to sell or not sell, as you wished. And after selling it, the money was yours to give away. How could you do a thing like this? You weren't lying to us but to God."

⁵As soon as Ananias heard these words, he fell to the floor and died. Everyone who heard about it was terrified. ⁶Then some young men wrapped him in a sheet and took him out and buried him.

⁷About three hours later his wife came in, not knowing what had happened. ⁸Peter asked her, "Was this the price you and your husband received for your land?"

"Yes," she replied, "that was the price."

⁹And Peter said, "How could the two of you even think of doing a thing like this—conspiring together to test the Spirit of the Lord? Just outside that door are the young men who

4:25-26 Ps 2:1-2.

buried your husband, and they will carry you out, too."

[10]Instantly, she fell to the floor and died. When the young men came in and saw that she was dead, they carried her out and buried her beside her husband. [11]Great fear gripped the entire church and all others who heard what had happened.

THE APOSTLES HEAL MANY

[12]Meanwhile, the apostles were performing many miraculous signs and wonders among the people. And the believers were meeting regularly at the Temple in the area known as Solomon's Colonnade. [13]No one else dared to join them, though everyone had high regard for them. [14]And more and more people believed and were brought to the Lord— crowds of both men and women. [15]As a result of the apostles' work, sick people were brought out into the streets on beds and mats so that Peter's shadow might fall across some of them as he went by. [16]Crowds came in from the villages around Jerusalem, bringing their sick and those possessed by evil spirits, and they were all healed.

THE APOSTLES MEET OPPOSITION

[17]The high priest and his friends, who were Sadducees, reacted with violent jealousy. [18]They arrested the apostles and put them in the jail. [19]But an angel of the Lord came at night, opened the gates of the jail, and brought them out. Then he told them, [20]"Go to the Temple and give the people this message of life!" [21]So the apostles entered the Temple about daybreak and immediately began teaching.

When the high priest and his officials arrived, they convened the high council,* along with all the elders of Israel. Then they sent for the apostles to be brought for trial. [22]But when the Temple guards went to the jail, the men were gone. So they returned to the council and reported, [23]"The jail was locked,

with the guards standing outside, but when we opened the gates, no one was there!"

[24]When the captain of the Temple guard and the leading priests heard this, they were perplexed, wondering where it would all end. [25]Then someone arrived with the news that the men they had jailed were out in the Temple, teaching the people.

[26]The captain went with his Temple guards and arrested them, but without violence, for they were afraid the people would kill them if they treated the apostles roughly. [27]Then they brought the apostles in before the council. [28]"Didn't we tell you never again to teach in this man's name?" the high priest demanded. "Instead, you have filled all Jerusalem with your teaching about Jesus, and you intend to blame us for his death!"

[29]But Peter and the apostles replied, "We must obey God rather than human authority. [30]The God of our ancestors raised Jesus from the dead after you killed him by crucifying him. [31]Then God put him in the place of honor at his right hand as Prince and Savior. He did this to give the people of Israel an opportunity to turn from their sins and turn to God so their sins would be forgiven. [32]We are witnesses of these things and so is the Holy Spirit, who is given by God to those who obey him."

[33]At this, the high council was furious and decided to kill them. [34]But one member had a different perspective. He was a Pharisee named Gamaliel, who was an expert on religious law and was very popular with the people. He stood up and ordered that the apostles be sent outside the council chamber for a while. [35]Then he addressed his colleagues as follows: "Men of Israel, take care what you are planning to do to these men! [36]Some time ago there was that fellow Theudas, who pretended to be someone great. About four hundred others joined him, but he was killed, and his followers went their various ways. The whole movement came to nothing. [37]After him, at the time of the census, there was Judas of

5:21 Greek *Sanhedrin;* also in 5:27, 41.

Galilee. He got some people to follow him, but he was killed, too, and all his followers were scattered.

[38]"So my advice is, leave these men alone. If they are teaching and doing these things merely on their own, it will soon be overthrown. [39]But if it is of God, you will not be able to stop them. You may even find yourselves fighting against God."

[40]The council accepted his advice. They called in the apostles and had them flogged. Then they ordered them never again to speak in the name of Jesus, and they let them go. [41]The apostles left the high council rejoicing that God had counted them worthy to suffer dishonor for the name of Jesus. [42]And every day, in the Temple and in their homes,* they continued to teach and preach this message: "The Messiah you are looking for is Jesus."

SEVEN MEN CHOSEN TO SERVE

6 But as the believers* rapidly multiplied, there were rumblings of discontent. Those who spoke Greek complained against those who spoke Hebrew, saying that their widows were being discriminated against in the daily distribution of food. [2]So the Twelve called a meeting of all the believers.

"We apostles should spend our time preaching and teaching the word of God, not administering a food program," they said. [3]"Now look around among yourselves, brothers, and select seven men who are well respected and are full of the Holy Spirit and wisdom. We will put them in charge of this business. [4]Then we can spend our time in prayer and preaching and teaching the word."

[5]This idea pleased the whole group, and they chose the following: Stephen (a man full of faith and the Holy Spirit), Philip, Procorus, Nicanor, Timon, Parmenas, and Nicolas of Antioch (a Gentile convert to the Jewish faith, who had now become a Christian). [6]These seven were presented to the apostles, who prayed for them as they laid their hands on them.

[7]God's message was preached in ever-widening circles. The number of believers greatly increased in Jerusalem, and many of the Jewish priests were converted, too.

> *God wants worshipers before workers; indeed the only acceptable workers are those who have learned the lost art of worship.*
>
> A.W. TOZER

STEPHEN IS ARRESTED

[8]Stephen, a man full of God's grace and power, performed amazing miracles and signs among the people. [9]But one day some men from the Synagogue of Freed Slaves, as it was called, started to debate with him. They were Jews from Cyrene, Alexandria, Cilicia, and the province of Asia. [10]None of them was able to stand against the wisdom and Spirit by which Stephen spoke.

[11]So they persuaded some men to lie about Stephen, saying, "We heard him blaspheme Moses, and even God." [12]Naturally, this roused the crowds, the elders, and the teachers of religious law. So they arrested Stephen and brought him before the high council.* [13]The lying witnesses said, "This man is always speaking against the Temple and against the law of Moses. [14]We have heard him say that this Jesus of Nazareth will destroy the Temple and change the customs Moses handed down to us." [15]At this point everyone in the council stared at Stephen because his face became as bright as an angel's.

STEPHEN ADDRESSES THE COUNCIL

7 Then the high priest asked Stephen, "Are these accusations true?"

5:42 Greek *from house to house.*   **6:1** Greek *disciples;* also in 6:2, 7.   **6:12** Greek *Sanhedrin;* also in 6:15.

²This was Stephen's reply: "Brothers and honorable fathers, listen to me. Our glorious God appeared to our ancestor Abraham in Mesopotamia before he moved to Haran.* ³God told him, 'Leave your native land and your relatives, and come to the land that I will show you.'* ⁴So Abraham left the land of the Chaldeans and lived in Haran until his father died. Then God brought him here to the land where you now live. ⁵But God gave him no inheritance here, not even one square foot of land. God did promise, however, that eventually the whole country would belong to Abraham and his descendants—though he had no children yet. ⁶But God also told him that his descendants would live in a foreign country where they would be mistreated as slaves for four hundred years. ⁷'But I will punish the nation that enslaves them,' God told him, 'and in the end they will come out and worship me in this place.'* ⁸God also gave Abraham the covenant of circumcision at that time. And so Isaac, Abraham's son, was circumcised when he was eight days old. Isaac became the father of Jacob, and Jacob was the father of the twelve patriarchs of the Jewish nation.

⁹"These sons of Jacob were very jealous of their brother Joseph, and they sold him to be a slave in Egypt. But God was with him ¹⁰and delivered him from his anguish. And God gave him favor before Pharaoh, king of Egypt. God also gave Joseph unusual wisdom, so that Pharaoh appointed him governor over all of Egypt and put him in charge of all the affairs of the palace.

¹¹"But a famine came upon Egypt and Canaan. There was great misery for our ancestors, as they ran out of food. ¹²Jacob heard that there was still grain in Egypt, so he sent his sons* to buy some. ¹³The second time they went, Joseph revealed his identity to his brothers, and they were introduced to Pharaoh. ¹⁴Then Joseph sent for his father, Jacob, and all his relatives to come to Egypt,

seventy-five persons in all. ¹⁵So Jacob went to Egypt. He died there, as did all his sons. ¹⁶All of them were taken to Shechem and buried in the tomb Abraham had bought from the sons of Hamor in Shechem.

¹⁷"As the time drew near when God would fulfill his promise to Abraham, the number of our people in Egypt greatly increased. ¹⁸But then a new king came to the throne of Egypt who knew nothing about Joseph. ¹⁹This king plotted against our people and forced parents to abandon their newborn babies so they would die.

²⁰"At that time Moses was born—a beautiful child in God's eyes. His parents cared for him at home for three months. ²¹When at last they had to abandon him, Pharaoh's daughter found him and raised him as her own son. ²²Moses was taught all the wisdom of the Egyptians, and he became mighty in both speech and action.

²³"One day when he was forty years old, he decided to visit his relatives, the people of Israel. ²⁴During this visit, he saw an Egyptian mistreating a man of Israel. So Moses came to his defense and avenged him, killing the Egyptian. ²⁵Moses assumed his brothers would realize that God had sent him to rescue them, but they didn't.

²⁶"The next day he visited them again and saw two men of Israel fighting. He tried to be a peacemaker. 'Men,' he said, 'you are brothers. Why are you hurting each other?'

²⁷"But the man in the wrong pushed Moses aside and told him to mind his own business. 'Who made you a ruler and judge over us?' he asked. ²⁸'Are you going to kill me as you killed that Egyptian yesterday?' ²⁹When Moses heard that, he fled the country and lived as a foreigner in the land of Midian, where his two sons were born.

³⁰"Forty years later, in the desert near Mount Sinai, an angel appeared to Moses in the flame of a burning bush. ³¹Moses saw it and wondered what it was. As he went to see,

---

7:2 *Mesopotamia* was the region now called Iraq. *Haran* was a city in what is now called Syria. 7:3 Gen 12:1. 7:5-7 Gen 12:7; 15:13-14; Exod 3:12. 7:12 Greek *our fathers;* also in 7:15.

My Daily Worship

— *October 26* —

A WINDOW TO HEAVEN

ACTS 5:17–7:60

Stephen, full of the Holy Spirit, gazed steadily upward into heaven and saw the glory of God, and he saw Jesus standing in the place of honor at God's right hand (7:55).

[i reflect]

In her book *A Window to Heaven*, pediatric oncologist Diane Komp tells of sitting with a couple during their last moments with their seven-year-old daughter, a victim of leukemia. "Before she died," Komp recalls of little Anna, "She mustered the final energy to sit up in her hospital bed and say: 'The angels—they're so beautiful! Mommy, can you see them? Do you hear their singing? I've never heard such beautiful singing!' Then she laid back on her pillow and died."

A number of times in Scripture we read how certain persons were privileged to see angels of God. One familiar example is that of the Bethlehem shepherds who witnessed a heavenly host praising God for the birth of the Savior. In such a case, the angels would appear suddenly—or perhaps they were always there and what occurred suddenly was the granting to some fortunate human the ability to see them.

Stephen, the first Christian martyr, was even more fortunate. Before dying, he saw a vision of the glory of God and of Jesus at his right hand. And as if Stephen were reflecting some of the light of heaven streaming down, "his face became as bright as an angel's" (Acts 6:15). Perhaps Stephen's countenance was like that of Moses, who had to wear a veil to hide the glow of his face after meeting with God (Exodus 34:29–35).

What would it be like to live with our spirits wide open to supernatural realities? Would it make us bold in testifying of Jesus, as Stephen was before the Sanhedrin? Would our faces betray the experience with a heaven-lit glow? Would we tune our voices to the singing of the angels?

Today, picture Jesus, not as the dusty itinerant rabbi he once was, but as the Son of Man in heaven that he now is, with face shining, eyes blazing, voice thundering (Revelation 1:13–16). Worship this glorious Lord.

[i pray]

I want to see you, Lord, every minute, every day. You are the light that draws me, yours the glory I want to reflect. Bathe me in the glow of your presence.

[i respond]

To the best of your ability, describe heaven and what (and who) you will encounter there to another person. Tell them about the glorious King you will serve for all eternity.

the voice of the Lord called out to him, [32]"I am the God of your ancestors—the God of Abraham, Isaac, and Jacob.' Moses shook with terror and dared not look.

[33]"And the Lord said to him, 'Take off your sandals, for you are standing on holy ground. [34]You can be sure that I have seen the misery of my people in Egypt. I have heard their cries. So I have come to rescue them. Now go, for I will send you to Egypt.'* [35]And so God sent back the same man his people had previously rejected by demanding, 'Who made you a ruler and judge over us?' Through the angel who appeared to him in the burning bush, Moses was sent to be their ruler and savior. [36]And by means of many miraculous signs and wonders, he led them out of Egypt, through the Red Sea, and back and forth through the wilderness for forty years.

[37]"Moses himself told the people of Israel, 'God will raise up a Prophet like me from among your own people.'* [38]Moses was with the assembly of God's people in the wilderness. He was the mediator between the people of Israel and the angel who gave him life-giving words on Mount Sinai to pass on to us.

[39]"But our ancestors rejected Moses and wanted to return to Egypt. [40]They told Aaron, 'Make us some gods who can lead us, for we don't know what has become of this Moses, who brought us out of Egypt.' [41]So they made an idol shaped like a calf, and they sacrificed to it and rejoiced in this thing they had made. [42]Then God turned away from them and gave them up to serve the sun, moon, and stars as their gods! In the book of the prophets it is written,

'Was it to me you were bringing sacrifices
    during those forty years in the
        wilderness, Israel?
[43] No, your real interest was in your pagan
        gods—
    the shrine of Molech,
    the star god Rephan,

and the images you made to worship
    them.
So I will send you into captivity
    far away in Babylon.'*

[44]"Our ancestors carried the Tabernacle* with them through the wilderness. It was constructed in exact accordance with the plan shown to Moses by God. [45]Years later, when Joshua led the battles against the Gentile nations that God drove out of this land, the Tabernacle was taken with them into their new territory. And it was used there until the time of King David.

[46]"David found favor with God and asked for the privilege of building a permanent Temple for the God of Jacob.* [47]But it was Solomon who actually built it. [48]However, the Most High doesn't live in temples made by human hands. As the prophet says,

[49] 'Heaven is my throne,
    and the earth is my footstool.
Could you ever build me a temple as good
        as that?'
    asks the Lord.
'Could you build a dwelling place for me?
[50]   Didn't I make everything in heaven and
        earth?'*

[51]"You stubborn people! You are heathen at heart and deaf to the truth. Must you forever resist the Holy Spirit? But your ancestors did, and so do you! [52]Name one prophet your ancestors didn't persecute! They even killed the ones who predicted the coming of the Righteous One—the Messiah whom you betrayed and murdered. [53]You deliberately disobeyed God's law, though you received it from the hands of angels.*"

[54]The Jewish leaders were infuriated by Stephen's accusation, and they shook their fists in rage.* [55]But Stephen, full of the Holy Spirit, gazed steadily upward into heaven and

---

7:31-34 Exod 3:5-10. 7:37 Deut 18:15. 7:42-43 Amos 5:25-27. 7:44 Greek *the tent of witness.* 7:46 Some manuscripts read *the house of Jacob.* 7:49-50 Isa 66:1-2. 7:53 Greek *received the Law as it was ordained by angels.* 7:54 Greek *they were grinding their teeth against him.*

saw the glory of God, and he saw Jesus standing in the place of honor at God's right hand. [56]And he told them, "Look, I see the heavens opened and the Son of Man standing in the place of honor at God's right hand!"

[57]Then they put their hands over their ears, and drowning out his voice with their shouts, they rushed at him. [58]They dragged him out of the city and began to stone him. The official witnesses took off their coats and laid them at the feet of a young man named Saul.*

[59]And as they stoned him, Stephen prayed, "Lord Jesus, receive my spirit." [60]And he fell to his knees, shouting, "Lord, don't charge them with this sin!" And with that, he died.

8 Saul was one of the official witnesses at the killing of Stephen.

PERSECUTION SCATTERS THE BELIEVERS

A great wave of persecution began that day, sweeping over the church in Jerusalem, and all the believers except the apostles fled into Judea and Samaria. [2](Some godly men came and buried Stephen with loud weeping.) [3]Saul was going everywhere to devastate the church. He went from house to house, dragging out both men and women to throw them into jail.

PHILIP PREACHES IN SAMARIA

[4]But the believers who had fled Jerusalem went everywhere preaching the Good News about Jesus. [5]Philip, for example, went to the city of Samaria and told the people there about the Messiah. [6]Crowds listened intently to what he had to say because of the miracles he did. [7]Many evil spirits were cast out, screaming as they left their victims. And many who had been paralyzed or lame were healed. [8]So there was great joy in that city.

[9]A man named Simon had been a sorcerer there for many years, claiming to be someone great. [10]The Samaritan people, from the least to the greatest, often spoke of him as "the Great One—the Power of God." [11]He was very

influential because of the magic he performed. [12]But now the people believed Philip's message of Good News concerning the Kingdom of God and the name of Jesus Christ. As a result, many men and women were baptized. [13]Then Simon himself believed and was baptized. He began following Philip wherever he went, and he was amazed by the great miracles and signs Philip performed.

[14]When the apostles back in Jerusalem heard that the people of Samaria had accepted God's message, they sent Peter and John there. [15]As soon as they arrived, they prayed for these new Christians to receive the Holy Spirit. [16]The Holy Spirit had not yet come upon any of them, for they had only been baptized in the name of the Lord Jesus. [17]Then Peter and John laid their hands upon these believers, and they received the Holy Spirit.

[18]When Simon saw that the Holy Spirit was given when the apostles placed their hands upon people's heads, he offered money to buy this power. [19]"Let me have this power, too," he exclaimed, "so that when I lay my hands on people, they will receive the Holy Spirit!"

[20]But Peter replied, "May your money perish with you for thinking God's gift can be bought! [21]You can have no part in this, for your heart is not right before God. [22]Turn from your wickedness and pray to the Lord. Perhaps he will forgive your evil thoughts, [23]for I can see that you are full of bitterness and held captive by sin."

[24]"Pray to the Lord for me," Simon exclaimed, "that these terrible things won't happen to me!"

[25]After testifying and preaching the word of the Lord in Samaria, Peter and John returned to Jerusalem. And they stopped in many Samaritan villages along the way to preach the Good News to them, too.

PHILIP AND THE ETHIOPIAN EUNUCH

[26]As for Philip, an angel of the Lord said to him, "Go south* down the desert road that

7:58 Saul is later called Paul; see 13:9. **8:26** Or Go at noon.

runs from Jerusalem to Gaza." [27]So he did, and he met the treasurer of Ethiopia, a eunuch of great authority under the queen of Ethiopia.* The eunuch had gone to Jerusalem to worship, [28]and he was now returning. Seated in his carriage, he was reading aloud from the book of the prophet Isaiah.

[29]The Holy Spirit said to Philip, "Go over and walk along beside the carriage."

[30]Philip ran over and heard the man reading from the prophet Isaiah; so he asked, "Do you understand what you are reading?"

[31]The man replied, "How can I, when there is no one to instruct me?" And he begged Philip to come up into the carriage and sit with him. [32]The passage of Scripture he had been reading was this:

"He was led as a sheep to the slaughter.
   And as a lamb is silent before the
      shearers,
   he did not open his mouth.
[33] He was humiliated and received no justice.
   Who can speak of his descendants?
   For his life was taken from the earth."*

[34]The eunuch asked Philip, "Was Isaiah talking about himself or someone else?" [35]So Philip began with this same Scripture and then used many others to tell him the Good News about Jesus.

[36]As they rode along, they came to some water, and the eunuch said, "Look! There's some water! Why can't I be baptized?"* [38]He ordered the carriage to stop, and they went down into the water, and Philip baptized him. [39]When they came up out of the water, the Spirit of the Lord caught Philip away. The eunuch never saw him again but went on his way rejoicing. [40]Meanwhile, Philip found himself farther north at the city of Azotus! He preached the Good News there and in every city along the way until he came to Caesarea.

SAUL'S CONVERSION

9 Meanwhile, Saul was uttering threats with every breath. He was eager to destroy the Lord's followers,* so he went to the high priest. [2]He requested letters addressed to the synagogues in Damascus, asking their cooperation in the arrest of any followers of the Way he found there. He wanted to bring them— both men and women—back to Jerusalem in chains.

[3]As he was nearing Damascus on this mission, a brilliant light from heaven suddenly beamed down upon him! [4]He fell to the ground and heard a voice saying to him, "Saul! Saul! Why are you persecuting me?"

[5]"Who are you, sir?" Saul asked.

And the voice replied, "I am Jesus, the one you are persecuting! [6]Now get up and go into the city, and you will be told what you are to do."

[7]The men with Saul stood speechless with surprise, for they heard the sound of someone's voice, but they saw no one! [8]As Saul picked himself up off the ground, he found that he was blind. [9]So his companions led him by the hand to Damascus. He remained there blind for three days. And all that time he went without food and water.

[10]Now there was a believer* in Damascus named Ananias. The Lord spoke to him in a vision, calling, "Ananias!"

"Yes, Lord!" he replied.

[11]The Lord said, "Go over to Straight Street, to the house of Judas. When you arrive, ask for Saul of Tarsus. He is praying to me right now. [12]I have shown him a vision of a man named Ananias coming in and laying his hands on him so that he can see again."

[13]"But Lord," exclaimed Ananias, "I've heard about the terrible things this man has done to the believers in Jerusalem! [14]And we hear that he is authorized by the leading priests to arrest every believer in Damascus."

[15]But the Lord said, "Go and do what I say.

8:27 Greek *under the Candace, the queen of Ethiopia.*   8:32-33 Isa 53:7-8.   8:36 Some manuscripts add verse 37, *"You can," Philip answered, "if you believe with all your heart." And the eunuch replied, "I believe that Jesus Christ is the Son of God."*   9:1 Greek *disciples.* 9:10 Greek *disciple;* also in 9:36.

My Daily Worship

— *October 27* —

GOING SOUTH

ACTS 8:1–9:43

*As for Philip, an angel of the Lord said to him, "Go south down the
desert road that runs from Jerusalem to Gaza" (8:26).*

[i reflect]

An expert in psychology and religion, Henri Nouwen spent many years teaching at Yale and Harvard. But then in 1985 he wrote the following words in his journal.

> I want to cry out loudly to my colleagues and students: "Do not serve Harvard, but God and his beloved, Jesus Christ, and speak words of hope to those who suffer from loneliness, depression, and spiritual poverty. But I myself have come to the painful discovery that when I am chained by ambition it is hard for me to see those who are chained by poverty. Therefore this is not a time to play the prophet, but a time to listen more carefully to the voice of God calling within me."

In response to the voice of God, Nouwen left Harvard for Toronto to care for mentally retarded persons in a household connected with the l'Arche federation. Later, in a moving speech at Harvard, Nouwen reported that the apparent demotion of working with a severely handicapped young man had given him "a whole new understanding of God's love."

Perhaps the apostle Philip thought it a demotion when the Lord told him to head for Gaza. After all, Philip had been leading a wildly successful ministry in Samaria. Now God wanted him to talk to a single foreigner standing in the desert? But he obeyed the Lord and wound up sending an enthusiastic new believer back to Ethiopia (Nubia), further extending the infant church.

As with Philip and Henri Nouwen, God's call on us may not meet our expectations. Whether prestigious or obscure, publicly successful or personally humbling, our ministry is the right one if God has called us to it. We are his to direct. Faithfulness is what matters most in a minister.

Banishing your pride, ask God to confirm that you are doing the right ministry or to redirect you toward another that he would rather you do. Then sit with the palms of your hands facing upward, in the receiving position, and listen for God to speak.

[i pray]

*I want to help build your kingdom, Lord; that's all. Send me where you will.
Assign me the task of your choice. I will do it.*

[i respond]

God often uses other people to affirm our place in ministry. Ask at least three people who know you well as to whether you are serving God in the right place.

For Saul is my chosen instrument to take my message to the Gentiles and to kings, as well as to the people of Israel. [16]And I will show him how much he must suffer for me."

[17]So Ananias went and found Saul. He laid his hands on him and said, "Brother Saul, the Lord Jesus, who appeared to you on the road, has sent me so that you may get your sight back and be filled with the Holy Spirit." [18]Instantly something like scales fell from Saul's eyes, and he regained his sight. Then he got up and was baptized. [19]Afterward he ate some food and was strengthened.

SAUL IN DAMASCUS AND JERUSALEM

Saul stayed with the believers* in Damascus for a few days. [20]And immediately he began preaching about Jesus in the synagogues, saying, "He is indeed the Son of God!"

[21]All who heard him were amazed. "Isn't this the same man who persecuted Jesus' followers with such devastation in Jerusalem?" they asked. "And we understand that he came here to arrest them and take them in chains to the leading priests."

[22]Saul's preaching became more and more powerful, and the Jews in Damascus couldn't refute his proofs that Jesus was indeed the Messiah. [23]After a while the Jewish leaders decided to kill him. [24]But Saul was told about their plot, and that they were watching for him day and night at the city gate so they could murder him. [25]So during the night, some of the other believers* let him down in a large basket through an opening in the city wall.

[26]When Saul arrived in Jerusalem, he tried to meet with the believers, but they were all afraid of him. They thought he was only pretending to be a believer! [27]Then Barnabas brought him to the apostles and told them how Saul had seen the Lord on the way to Damascus. Barnabas also told them what the Lord had said to Saul and how he boldly preached in the name of Jesus in Damascus.

[28]Then the apostles accepted Saul, and after that he was constantly with them in Jerusalem, preaching boldly in the name of the Lord. [29]He debated with some Greek-speaking Jews, but they plotted to murder him. [30]When the believers* heard about it, however, they took him to Caesarea and sent him on to his hometown of Tarsus.

[31]The church then had peace throughout Judea, Galilee, and Samaria, and it grew in strength and numbers. The believers were walking in the fear of the Lord and in the comfort of the Holy Spirit.

PETER HEALS AENEAS AND RAISES DORCAS

[32]Peter traveled from place to place to visit the believers, and in his travels he came to the Lord's people in the town of Lydda. [33]There he met a man named Aeneas, who had been paralyzed and bedridden for eight years. [34]Peter said to him, "Aeneas, Jesus Christ heals you! Get up and make your bed!" And he was healed instantly. [35]Then the whole population of Lydda and Sharon turned to the Lord when they saw Aeneas walking around.

[36]There was a believer in Joppa named Tabitha (which in Greek is Dorcas*). She was always doing kind things for others and helping the poor. [37]About this time she became ill and died. Her friends prepared her for burial and laid her in an upstairs room. [38]But they had heard that Peter was nearby at Lydda, so they sent two men to beg him, "Please come as soon as possible!"

[39]So Peter returned with them; and as soon as he arrived, they took him to the upstairs room. The room was filled with widows who were weeping and showing him the coats and other garments Dorcas had made for them. [40]But Peter asked them all to leave the room; then he knelt and prayed. Turning to the body he said, "Get up, Tabitha." And she opened her eyes! When she saw Peter, she sat up! [41]He gave her his hand and helped her up. Then he

9:19 Greek *disciples;* also in 9:26.   9:25 Greek *his disciples.*   9:30 Greek *brothers.*   9:36 The names *Tabitha* in Aramaic and *Dorcas* in Greek both mean "gazelle."

called in the widows and all the believers, and he showed them that she was alive.

⁴²The news raced through the whole town, and many believed in the Lord. ⁴³And Peter stayed a long time in Joppa, living with Simon, a leatherworker.

CORNELIUS CALLS FOR PETER

10 In Caesarea there lived a Roman army officer named Cornelius, who was a captain of the Italian Regiment. ²He was a devout man who feared the God of Israel, as did his entire household. He gave generously to charity and was a man who regularly prayed to God. ³One afternoon about three o'clock, he had a vision in which he saw an angel of God coming toward him. "Cornelius!" the angel said.

⁴Cornelius stared at him in terror. "What is it, sir?" he asked the angel.

And the angel replied, "Your prayers and gifts to the poor have not gone unnoticed by God! ⁵Now send some men down to Joppa to find a man named Simon Peter. ⁶He is staying with Simon, a leatherworker who lives near the shore. Ask him to come and visit you."

⁷As soon as the angel was gone, Cornelius called two of his household servants and a devout soldier, one of his personal attendants. ⁸He told them what had happened and sent them off to Joppa.

PETER VISITS CORNELIUS

⁹The next day as Cornelius's messengers were nearing the city, Peter went up to the flat roof to pray. It was about noon, ¹⁰and he was hungry. But while lunch was being prepared, he fell into a trance. ¹¹He saw the sky open, and something like a large sheet was let down by its four corners. ¹²In the sheet were all sorts of animals, reptiles, and birds. ¹³Then a voice said to him, "Get up, Peter; kill and eat them."

¹⁴"Never, Lord," Peter declared. "I have never in all my life eaten anything forbidden by our Jewish laws.*"

¹⁵The voice spoke again, "If God says something is acceptable, don't say it isn't."* ¹⁶The same vision was repeated three times. Then the sheet was pulled up again to heaven.

¹⁷Peter was very perplexed. What could the vision mean? Just then the men sent by Cornelius found the house and stood outside at the gate. ¹⁸They asked if this was the place where Simon Peter was staying. ¹⁹Meanwhile, as Peter was puzzling over the vision, the Holy Spirit said to him, "Three men have come looking for you. ²⁰Go down and go with them without hesitation. All is well, for I have sent them."

²¹So Peter went down and said, "I'm the man you are looking for. Why have you come?"

²²They said, "We were sent by Cornelius, a Roman officer. He is a devout man who fears the God of Israel and is well respected by all the Jews. A holy angel instructed him to send for you so you can go to his house and give him a message." ²³So Peter invited the men to be his guests for the night. The next day he went with them, accompanied by some other believers* from Joppa.

²⁴They arrived in Caesarea the following day. Cornelius was waiting for him and had called together his relatives and close friends to meet Peter. ²⁵As Peter entered his home, Cornelius fell to the floor before him in worship. ²⁶But Peter pulled him up and said, "Stand up! I'm a human being like you!" ²⁷So Cornelius got up, and they talked together and went inside where the others were assembled.

²⁸Peter told them, "You know it is against the Jewish laws for me to come into a Gentile home like this. But God has shown me that I should never think of anyone as impure. ²⁹So I came as soon as I was sent for. Now tell me why you sent for me."

³⁰Cornelius replied, "Four days ago I was praying in my house at three o'clock in the afternoon. Suddenly, a man in dazzling clothes was standing in front of me. ³¹He told me, 'Cornelius, your prayers have been heard,

---

10:14 Greek *anything common and unclean.*　10:15 Greek *"What God calls clean you must not call unclean."*　10:23 Greek *brothers.*

and your gifts to the poor have been noticed by God! ³²Now send some men to Joppa and summon Simon Peter. He is staying in the home of Simon, a leatherworker who lives near the shore.' ³³So I sent for you at once, and it was good of you to come. Now here we are, waiting before God to hear the message the Lord has given you."

THE GENTILES HEAR THE GOOD NEWS

³⁴Then Peter replied, "I see very clearly that God doesn't show partiality. ³⁵In every nation he accepts those who fear him and do what is right. ³⁶I'm sure you have heard about the Good News for the people of Israel—that there is peace with God through Jesus Christ, who is Lord of all. ³⁷You know what happened all through Judea, beginning in Galilee after John the Baptist began preaching. ³⁸And no doubt you know that God anointed Jesus of Nazareth with the Holy Spirit and with power. Then Jesus went around doing good and healing all who were oppressed by the Devil, for God was with him.

³⁹"And we apostles are witnesses of all he did throughout Israel and in Jerusalem. They put him to death by crucifying him, ⁴⁰but God raised him to life three days later. Then God allowed him to appear, ⁴¹not to the general public,* but to us whom God had chosen beforehand to be his witnesses. We were those who ate and drank with him after he rose from the dead. ⁴²And he ordered us to preach everywhere and to testify that Jesus is ordained of God to be the judge of all—the living and the dead. ⁴³He is the one all the prophets testified about, saying that everyone who believes in him will have their sins forgiven through his name."

THE GENTILES RECEIVE THE HOLY SPIRIT

⁴⁴Even as Peter was saying these things, the Holy Spirit fell upon all who had heard the message. ⁴⁵The Jewish believers who came with Peter were amazed that the gift of the Holy Spirit had been poured out upon the Gentiles, too. ⁴⁶And there could be no doubt about it, for they heard them speaking in tongues and praising God.

Then Peter asked, ⁴⁷"Can anyone object to their being baptized, now that they have received the Holy Spirit just as we did?" ⁴⁸So he gave orders for them to be baptized in the name of Jesus Christ. Afterward Cornelius asked him to stay with them for several days.

PETER EXPLAINS HIS ACTIONS

11 Soon the news reached the apostles and other believers* in Judea that the Gentiles had received the word of God. ²But when Peter arrived back in Jerusalem, some of the Jewish believers* criticized him. ³"You entered the home of Gentiles* and even ate with them!" they said.

⁴Then Peter told them exactly what had happened. ⁵"One day in Joppa," he said, "while I was praying, I went into a trance and saw a vision. Something like a large sheet was let down by its four corners from the sky. And it came right down to me. ⁶When I looked inside the sheet, I saw all sorts of small animals, wild animals, reptiles, and birds that we are not allowed to eat. ⁷And I heard a voice say, 'Get up, Peter; kill and eat them.'

⁸" 'Never, Lord,' I replied. 'I have never eaten anything forbidden by our Jewish laws.*'

⁹"But the voice from heaven came again, 'If God says something is acceptable, don't say it isn't.'*

¹⁰"This happened three times before the sheet and all it contained was pulled back up to heaven. ¹¹Just then three men who had been sent from Caesarea arrived at the house where I was staying. ¹²The Holy Spirit told me to go with them and not to worry about their being Gentiles. These six brothers here accompanied me, and we soon arrived at the home of the man who had sent for us. ¹³He told us how

10:41 Greek *the people.* 11:1 Greek *brothers.* 11:2 Greek *those of the circumcision.* 11:3 Greek *of uncircumcised men.* 11:8 Greek *anything common or unclean.* 11:9 Greek *'What God calls clean you must not call unclean.'*

My Daily Worship

— *October 28* —

GOD IN MOTION

ACTS 10:1–12:25

When he arrived and saw this proof of God's favor, he was filled with joy,
and he encouraged the believers to stay true to the Lord (11:23).

[i reflect]

We all encounter ideas that are difficult to understand. For the earliest Christians (all of them Jews), one such idea was that God might accept Gentiles on an equal footing with Jews through faith in Christ. That's why leaders of the mother church in Jerusalem sent Barnabas to verify reports of Gentiles becoming followers of Jesus. A fortunate choice, Barnabas. When this good man saw that God had indeed been moving among Gentiles in Antioch, he rejoiced in the work and did his little bit to push it along, encouraging all "the believers to stay true to the Lord."

We have our own ideas of what the church should be, and sometimes the movement of God in the world surprises us. G. K. Chesterton was right: "The greatest of all illusions is the illusion of familiarity." How do we feel when a celebrity who has political views opposed to our own is born again—and doesn't change her politics? How do we feel when we hear of growth in a church movement that includes some secondary doctrinal beliefs that make us uncomfortable? The point is not that others are right and we are wrong. The point is that God may be moving among others even though they are different from and (amazing!) no more perfect than us.

The earth is the Lord's, and he ranges about it freely, acting in ways we could not always predict. Let us not be worried by this but instead open our eyes and our minds to what God might be doing. We have to "test the spirits," of course, but God wants us to cheer on his every work in the world.

Rejoice today in the work that the Lord is doing in your community. As you do errands or commute to work, pray for the congregations of the churches you pass along the way.

[i pray]

Holy Spirit, you are the wind that turns over leaves here, there, and all over the forest.
Blow, blow, blow! Move through my community, my church, my soul,
so that I might encourage others involved in your work.

[i respond]

Sometime in the next month, worship with a friend from another church—either attend theirs, or invite that person to attend your congregation. Celebrate the Lord together, sharing your common bond in him.

an angel had appeared to him in his home and had told him, 'Send messengers to Joppa to find Simon Peter. [14]He will tell you how you and all your household will be saved!'

[15]"Well, I began telling them the Good News, but just as I was getting started, the Holy Spirit fell on them, just as he fell on us at the beginning. [16]Then I thought of the Lord's words when he said, 'John baptized with* water, but you will be baptized with the Holy Spirit.' [17]And since God gave these Gentiles the same gift he gave us when we believed in the Lord Jesus Christ, who was I to argue?"

[18]When the others heard this, all their objections were answered and they began praising God. They said, "God has also given the Gentiles the privilege of turning from sin and receiving eternal life."

THE CHURCH IN ANTIOCH OF SYRIA

[19]Meanwhile, the believers who had fled from Jerusalem during the persecution after Stephen's death traveled as far as Phoenicia, Cyprus, and Antioch of Syria. They preached the Good News, but only to Jews. [20]However, some of the believers who went to Antioch from Cyprus and Cyrene began preaching to Gentiles* about the Lord Jesus. [21]The power of the Lord was upon them, and large numbers of these Gentiles believed and turned to the Lord.

[22]When the church at Jerusalem heard what had happened, they sent Barnabas to Antioch. [23]When he arrived and saw this proof of God's favor, he was filled with joy, and he encouraged the believers to stay true to the Lord. [24]Barnabas was a good man, full of the Holy Spirit and strong in faith. And large numbers of people were brought to the Lord.

[25]Then Barnabas went on to Tarsus to find Saul. [26]When he found him, he brought him back to Antioch. Both of them stayed there with the church for a full year, teaching great numbers of people. (It was there at Antioch that the believers* were first called Christians.)

[27]During this time, some prophets traveled from Jerusalem to Antioch. [28]One of them named Agabus stood up in one of the meetings to predict by the Spirit that a great famine was coming upon the entire Roman world. (This was fulfilled during the reign of Claudius.) [29]So the believers in Antioch decided to send relief to the brothers and sisters* in Judea, everyone giving as much as they could. [30]This they did, entrusting their gifts to Barnabas and Saul to take to the elders of the church in Jerusalem.

JAMES IS KILLED AND PETER IS IMPRISONED

12 About that time King Herod Agrippa* began to persecute some believers in the church. [2]He had the apostle James (John's brother) killed with a sword. [3]When Herod saw how much this pleased the Jewish leaders, he arrested Peter during the Passover celebration* [4]and imprisoned him, placing him under the guard of four squads of four soldiers each. Herod's intention was to bring Peter out for public trial after the Passover. [5]But while Peter was in prison, the church prayed very earnestly for him.

PETER'S MIRACULOUS ESCAPE FROM PRISON

[6]The night before Peter was to be placed on trial, he was asleep, chained between two soldiers, with others standing guard at the prison gate. [7]Suddenly, there was a bright light in the cell, and an angel of the Lord stood before Peter. The angel tapped him on the side to awaken him and said, "Quick! Get up!" And the chains fell off his wrists. [8]Then the angel told him, "Get dressed and put on your sandals." And he did. "Now put on your coat and follow me," the angel ordered.

11:16 Or *in;* also in 11:16b. **11:20** Greek *the Greeks;* other manuscripts read *the Hellenists.* **11:26** Greek *disciples;* also in 11:29. **11:29** Greek *the brothers.* **12:1** Greek *Herod the king.* He was the nephew of Herod Antipas and a grandson of Herod the Great. **12:3** Greek *the days of unleavened bread.*

⁹So Peter left the cell, following the angel. But all the time he thought it was a vision. He didn't realize it was really happening. ¹⁰They passed the first and second guard posts and came to the iron gate to the street, and this opened to them all by itself. So they passed through and started walking down the street, and then the angel suddenly left him.

¹¹Peter finally realized what had happened. "It's really true!" he said to himself. "The Lord has sent his angel and saved me from Herod and from what the Jews were hoping to do to me!"

¹²After a little thought, he went to the home of Mary, the mother of John Mark, where many were gathered for prayer. ¹³He knocked at the door in the gate, and a servant girl named Rhoda came to open it. ¹⁴When she recognized Peter's voice, she was so overjoyed that, instead of opening the door, she ran back inside and told everyone, "Peter is standing at the door!"

¹⁵"You're out of your mind," they said. When she insisted, they decided, "It must be his angel."

¹⁶Meanwhile, Peter continued knocking. When they finally went out and opened the door, they were amazed. ¹⁷He motioned for them to quiet down and told them what had happened and how the Lord had led him out of jail. "Tell James and the other brothers what happened," he said. And then he went to another place.

¹⁸At dawn, there was a great commotion among the soldiers about what had happened to Peter. ¹⁹Herod Agrippa ordered a thorough search for him. When he couldn't be found, Herod interrogated the guards and sentenced them to death. Afterward Herod left Judea to stay in Caesarea for a while.

THE DEATH OF HEROD AGRIPPA

²⁰Now Herod was very angry with the people of Tyre and Sidon. So they sent a delegation to make peace with him because their cities were dependent upon Herod's country for their food. They made friends with Blastus, Herod's personal assistant, ²¹and an appointment with Herod was granted. When the day arrived, Herod put on his royal robes, sat on his throne, and made a speech to them. ²²The people gave him a great ovation, shouting, "It is the voice of a god, not of a man!"

²³Instantly, an angel of the Lord struck Herod with a sickness, because he accepted the people's worship instead of giving the glory to God. So he was consumed with worms and died.

²⁴But God's Good News was spreading rapidly, and there were many new believers.

²⁵When Barnabas and Saul had finished their mission in Jerusalem, they returned to Antioch, taking John Mark with them.

BARNABAS AND SAUL ARE SENT OUT

13 Among the prophets and teachers of the church at Antioch of Syria were Barnabas, Simeon (called "the black man"*), Lucius (from Cyrene), Manaen (the childhood companion of King Herod Antipas*), and Saul. ²One day as these men were worshiping the Lord and fasting, the Holy Spirit said, "Dedicate Barnabas and Saul for the special work I have for them." ³So after more fasting and prayer, the men laid their hands on them and sent them on their way.

PAUL'S FIRST MISSIONARY JOURNEY

⁴Sent out by the Holy Spirit, Saul and Barnabas went down to the seaport of Seleucia and then sailed for the island of Cyprus. ⁵There, in the town of Salamis, they went to the Jewish synagogues and preached the word of God. (John Mark went with them as their assistant.)

⁶Afterward they preached from town to town across the entire island until finally they reached Paphos, where they met a Jewish sorcerer, a false prophet named Bar-Jesus. ⁷He

13:1a Greek *who was called Niger.*   13:1b Greek *Herod the tetrarch.*

had attached himself to the governor, Sergius Paulus, a man of considerable insight and understanding. The governor invited Barnabas and Saul to visit him, for he wanted to hear the word of God. ⁸But Elymas, the sorcerer (as his name means in Greek), interfered and urged the governor to pay no attention to what Saul and Barnabas said. He was trying to turn the governor away from the Christian faith.

⁹Then Saul, also known as Paul, filled with the Holy Spirit, looked the sorcerer in the eye and said, ¹⁰"You son of the Devil, full of every sort of trickery and villainy, enemy of all that is good, will you never stop perverting the true ways of the Lord? ¹¹And now the Lord has laid his hand of punishment upon you, and you will be stricken awhile with blindness." Instantly mist and darkness fell upon him, and he began wandering around begging for someone to take his hand and lead him. ¹²When the governor saw what had happened, he believed and was astonished at what he learned about the Lord.

PAUL PREACHES IN ANTIOCH OF PISIDIA

¹³Now Paul and those with him left Paphos by ship for Pamphylia,* landing at the port town of Perga. There John Mark left them and returned to Jerusalem. ¹⁴But Barnabas and Paul traveled inland to Antioch of Pisidia.*

On the Sabbath they went to the synagogue for the services. ¹⁵After the usual readings from the books of Moses and from the Prophets, those in charge of the service sent them this message: "Brothers, if you have any word of encouragement for us, come and give it!"

¹⁶So Paul stood, lifted his hand to quiet them, and started speaking. "People of Israel," he said, "and you devout Gentiles who fear the God of Israel, listen to me.

¹⁷"The God of this nation of Israel chose our ancestors and made them prosper in Egypt. Then he powerfully led them out of their slavery. ¹⁸He put up with them* through forty years of wandering around in the wilderness. ¹⁹Then he destroyed seven nations in Canaan and gave their land to Israel as an inheritance. ²⁰All this took about 450 years. After that, judges ruled until the time of Samuel the prophet. ²¹Then the people begged for a king, and God gave them Saul son of Kish, a man of the tribe of Benjamin, who reigned for forty years. ²²But God removed him from the kingship and replaced him with David, a man about whom God said, 'David son of Jesse is a man after my own heart, for he will do everything I want him to.'*

²³"And it is one of King David's descendants, Jesus, who is God's promised Savior of Israel! ²⁴But before he came, John the Baptist preached the need for everyone in Israel to turn from sin and turn to God and be baptized. ²⁵As John was finishing his ministry he asked, 'Do you think I am the Messiah? No! But he is coming soon—and I am not even worthy to be his slave.*'

²⁶"Brothers—you sons of Abraham, and also all of you devout Gentiles who fear the God of Israel—this salvation is for us! ²⁷The people in Jerusalem and their leaders fulfilled prophecy by condemning Jesus to death. They didn't recognize him or realize that he is the one the prophets had written about, though they hear the prophets' words read every Sabbath. ²⁸They found no just cause to execute him, but they asked Pilate to have him killed anyway.

²⁹"When they had fulfilled all the prophecies concerning his death, they took him down from the cross and placed him in a tomb. ³⁰But God raised him from the dead! ³¹And he appeared over a period of many days to those who had gone with him from Galilee to Jerusalem—these are his witnesses to the people of Israel.

³²"And now Barnabas and I are here to bring you this Good News. God's promise to our

13:13-14 *Pamphylia* and *Pisidia* were districts in the land now called Turkey.   **13:18** Other manuscripts read *He cared for them;* compare Deut 1:31.   **13:22** 1 Sam 13:14.   **13:25** Greek *to untie his sandals.*

My Daily Worship

— October 29 —

DANCING YOUR WAY TO HEAVEN

ACTS 13:1–15:21

The believers were filled with joy and with the Holy Spirit (13:52).

[i reflect]

As a seminary student, when burdened by the constant pressure of his studies, W. A. Criswell would sometimes pause to pray, read a passage from the Bile, or sing a cheerful gospel song. On one occasion, right before midterm exams, Criswell began singing, not out of discouragement but from pure joy, the old gospel tune, "It Pays to Serve Jesus."

Years later, preaching at the First Baptist Church in Richmond, Virginia, a fellow pastor spoke to him after the service, tears in his eyes: "Dr. Criswell, years ago when I was a student at Southern Seminary, God used you to change my life. The heavy class load had worn me down. My bags were packed. My resignation letter was written. I was heading for the door, when suddenly I heard a voice begin to sing just outside my room in Mullins Hall."

The young man was forever changed as he heard the unrestrained joy as Criswell sang, "It pays to serve Jesus, it pays every day. . . .Though the pathway to glory may sometimes be drear, you'll he happy each step of the way."

The new converts in Antioch of Pisidia (today's central Turkey) had that kind of joy. The apostles who had brought them the gospel, Paul and Barnabas, were chased out of town. But the local Christians were not discouraged; they were "filled with joy and the Holy Spirit."

What does it take to possess a joy that bubbles up despite trouble and travail? A fixation on God and the salvation he grants through his Son. We each can be like David dancing before the ark of God if we are forgiven in Christ and have the Holy Spirit living within us.

How long has it been since you felt joy? If it has been a while, might there be a problem in your relationship with God? If you do have joy, find some way to express it today—pray, sing a song, or just cheer out of the sheer joy of knowing that God is with you always.

[i pray]

While all around me others are engaged in the pursuit of happiness, I'm aiming higher, Lord. Let me share in the mood of heaven. Let me have joy.

[i respond]

Celebrate God's presence in your life by reading a familiar psalm, such as Psalm 98, 100, 103, or another favorite. Underline the many reasons you have to be joyful because of God's loving presence in your life.

ancestors has come true in our own time, [33]in that God raised Jesus. This is what the second psalm is talking about when it says concerning Jesus,

'You are my Son.
Today I have become your Father.*'

[34]For God had promised to raise him from the dead, never again to die. This is stated in the Scripture that says, 'I will give you the sacred blessings I promised to David.'* [35]Another psalm explains more fully, saying, 'You will not allow your Holy One to rot in the grave.'* [36]Now this is not a reference to David, for after David had served his generation according to the will of God, he died and was buried, and his body decayed. [37]No, it was a reference to someone else—someone whom God raised and whose body did not decay.

[38]"Brothers, listen! In this man Jesus there is forgiveness for your sins. [39]Everyone who believes in him is freed from all guilt and declared right with God—something the Jewish law could never do. [40]Be careful! Don't let the prophets' words apply to you. For they said,

[41] 'Look, you mockers,
be amazed and die!
For I am doing something in your own day,
something you wouldn't believe
even if someone told you about it.'* "

[42]As Paul and Barnabas left the synagogue that day, the people asked them to return again and speak about these things the next week. [43]Many Jews and godly converts to Judaism who worshiped at the synagogue followed Paul and Barnabas, and the two men urged them, "By God's grace, remain faithful."

PAUL TURNS TO THE GENTILES

[44]The following week almost the entire city turned out to hear them preach the word of the Lord. [45]But when the Jewish leaders saw the crowds, they were jealous; so they slandered Paul and argued against whatever he said.

[46]Then Paul and Barnabas spoke out boldly and declared, "It was necessary that this Good News from God be given first to you Jews. But since you have rejected it and judged yourselves unworthy of eternal life—well, we will offer it to Gentiles. [47]For this is as the Lord commanded us when he said,

'I have made you a light to the Gentiles,
to bring salvation to the farthest corners
of the earth.'* "

[48]When the Gentiles heard this, they were very glad and thanked the Lord for his message; and all who were appointed to eternal life became believers. [49]So the Lord's message spread throughout that region.

[50]Then the Jewish leaders stirred up both the influential religious women and the leaders of the city, and they incited a mob against Paul and Barnabas and ran them out of town. [51]But they shook off the dust of their feet against them and went to the city of Iconium. [52]And the believers* were filled with joy and with the Holy Spirit.

PAUL AND BARNABAS IN ICONIUM

14 In Iconium,* Paul and Barnabas went together to the synagogue and preached with such power that a great number of both Jews and Gentiles believed. [2]But the Jews who spurned God's message stirred up distrust among the Gentiles against Paul and Barnabas, saying all sorts of evil things about them. [3]The apostles stayed there a long time, preaching boldly about the grace of the Lord. The Lord proved their message was true by giving them power to do miraculous signs and wonders. [4]But the people of the city were divided in their opinion about them. Some sided with the Jews, and some with the apostles.

13:33 Or *Today I reveal you as my Son.* Ps 2:7.   13:34 Isa 55:3.   13:35 Ps 16:10.   13:41 Hab 1:5.   13:47 Isa 49:6.   13:52 Greek *the disciples.*   14:1 *Iconium,* as well as *Lystra* and *Derbe* (14:6), were cities in the land now called Turkey.

⁵A mob of Gentiles and Jews, along with their leaders, decided to attack and stone them. ⁶When the apostles learned of it, they fled for their lives. They went to the region of Lycaonia, to the cities of Lystra and Derbe and the surrounding area, ⁷and they preached the Good News there.

> *Missions is not the ultimate goal of the church. Worship is. Missions exists because worship doesn't.*
>
> JOHN PIPER

PAUL AND BARNABAS IN LYSTRA AND DERBE

⁸While they were at Lystra, Paul and Barnabas came upon a man with crippled feet. He had been that way from birth, so he had never walked. ⁹He was listening as Paul preached, and Paul noticed him and realized he had faith to be healed. ¹⁰So Paul called to him in a loud voice, "Stand up!" And the man jumped to his feet and started walking.

¹¹When the listening crowd saw what Paul had done, they shouted in their local dialect, "These men are gods in human bodies!" ¹²They decided that Barnabas was the Greek god Zeus and that Paul, because he was the chief speaker, was Hermes. ¹³The temple of Zeus was located on the outskirts of the city. The priest of the temple and the crowd brought oxen and wreaths of flowers, and they prepared to sacrifice to the apostles at the city gates.

¹⁴But when Barnabas and Paul heard what was happening, they tore their clothing in dismay and ran out among the people, shouting, ¹⁵"Friends,* why are you doing this? We are merely human beings like yourselves! We have come to bring you the Good News that you should turn from these worthless things to the living God, who made heaven and earth, the sea, and everything in them. ¹⁶In earlier days he permitted all the nations to go their own ways, ¹⁷but he never left himself without a witness. There were always his reminders, such as sending you rain and good crops and giving you food and joyful hearts." ¹⁸But even so, Paul and Barnabas could scarcely restrain the people from sacrificing to them.

¹⁹Now some Jews arrived from Antioch and Iconium and turned the crowds into a murderous mob. They stoned Paul and dragged him out of the city, apparently dead. ²⁰But as the believers* stood around him, he got up and went back into the city. The next day he left with Barnabas for Derbe.

PAUL AND BARNABAS RETURN TO ANTIOCH OF SYRIA

²¹After preaching the Good News in Derbe and making many disciples, Paul and Barnabas returned again to Lystra, Iconium, and Antioch of Pisidia, ²²where they strengthened the believers. They encouraged them to continue in the faith, reminding them that they must enter into the Kingdom of God through many tribulations. ²³Paul and Barnabas also appointed elders in every church and prayed for them with fasting, turning them over to the care of the Lord, in whom they had come to trust. ²⁴Then they traveled back through Pisidia to Pamphylia. ²⁵They preached again in Perga, then went on to Attalia.

²⁶Finally, they returned by ship to Antioch of Syria, where their journey had begun and where they had been committed to the grace of God for the work they had now completed. ²⁷Upon arriving in Antioch, they called the church together and reported about their trip, telling all that God had done and how he had opened the door of faith to the Gentiles, too. ²⁸And they stayed there with the believers in Antioch for a long time.

14:15 Greek *Men.* 14:20 Greek *disciples;* also in 14:22, 28.

The Council at Jerusalem

15 While Paul and Barnabas were at Antioch of Syria, some men from Judea arrived and began to teach the Christians*: "Unless you keep the ancient Jewish custom of circumcision taught by Moses, you cannot be saved." ²Paul and Barnabas, disagreeing with them, argued forcefully and at length. Finally, Paul and Barnabas were sent to Jerusalem, accompanied by some local believers, to talk to the apostles and elders about this question. ³The church sent the delegates to Jerusalem, and they stopped along the way in Phoenicia and Samaria to visit the believers.* They told them—much to everyone's joy—that the Gentiles, too, were being converted.

⁴When they arrived in Jerusalem, Paul and Barnabas were welcomed by the whole church, including the apostles and elders. They reported on what God had been doing through their ministry. ⁵But then some of the men who had been Pharisees before their conversion stood up and declared that all Gentile converts must be circumcised and be required to follow the law of Moses.

⁶So the apostles and church elders got together to decide this question. ⁷At the meeting, after a long discussion, Peter stood and addressed them as follows: "Brothers, you all know that God chose me from among you some time ago to preach to the Gentiles so that they could hear the Good News and believe. ⁸God, who knows people's hearts, confirmed that he accepts Gentiles by giving them the Holy Spirit, just as he gave him to us. ⁹He made no distinction between us and them, for he also cleansed their hearts through faith. ¹⁰Why are you now questioning God's way by burdening the Gentile believers* with a yoke that neither we nor our ancestors were able to bear? ¹¹We believe that we are all saved the same way, by the special favor of the Lord Jesus."

¹²There was no further discussion, and everyone listened as Barnabas and Paul told about the miraculous signs and wonders God had done through them among the Gentiles.

¹³When they had finished, James stood and said, "Brothers, listen to me. ¹⁴Peter* has told you about the time God first visited the Gentiles to take from them a people for himself. ¹⁵And this conversion of Gentiles agrees with what the prophets predicted. For instance, it is written:

¹⁶ 'Afterward I will return,
　and I will restore the fallen kingdom of David.
From the ruins I will rebuild it,
　and I will restore it,
¹⁷ so that the rest of humanity might find the Lord,
　including the Gentiles—
　all those I have called to be mine.
This is what the Lord says,
¹⁸　he who made these things known long ago.'*

¹⁹And so my judgment is that we should stop troubling the Gentiles who turn to God, ²⁰except that we should write to them and tell them to abstain from eating meat sacrificed to idols, from sexual immorality, and from consuming blood or eating the meat of strangled animals. ²¹For these laws of Moses have been preached in Jewish synagogues in every city on every Sabbath for many generations."

The Letter for Gentile Believers

²²Then the apostles and elders and the whole church in Jerusalem chose delegates, and they sent them to Antioch of Syria with Paul and Barnabas to report on this decision. The men chosen were two of the church leaders*—Judas (also called Barsabbas) and Silas. ²³This is the letter they took along with them:

"This letter is from the apostles and elders, your brothers in Jerusalem. It is written to

---

15:1 Greek *brothers;* also in 15:32, 33.　**15:3** Greek *brothers;* also in 15:23, 36, 40.　**15:10** Greek *disciples.*　**15:14** Greek *Simon.*
15:16-18 Amos 9:11-12; Isa 45:21.　**15:22** Greek *were leaders among the brothers.*

the Gentile believers in Antioch, Syria, and Cilicia. Greetings!

²⁴"We understand that some men from here have troubled you and upset you with their teaching, but they had no such instructions from us. ²⁵So it seemed good to us, having unanimously agreed on our decision, to send you these official representatives, along with our beloved Barnabas and Paul, ²⁶who have risked their lives for the sake of our Lord Jesus Christ. ²⁷So we are sending Judas and Silas to tell you what we have decided concerning your question.

²⁸"For it seemed good to the Holy Spirit and to us to lay no greater burden on you than these requirements: ²⁹You must abstain from eating food offered to idols, from consuming blood or eating the meat of strangled animals, and from sexual immorality. If you do this, you will do well. Farewell."

³⁰The four messengers went at once to Antioch, where they called a general meeting of the Christians and delivered the letter. ³¹And there was great joy throughout the church that day as they read this encouraging message.

³²Then Judas and Silas, both being prophets, spoke extensively to the Christians, encouraging and strengthening their faith. ³³They stayed for a while, and then Judas and Silas were sent back to Jerusalem, with the blessings of the Christians, to those who had sent them.* ³⁵Paul and Barnabas stayed in Antioch to assist many others who were teaching and preaching the word of the Lord there.

PAUL AND BARNABAS SEPARATE

³⁶After some time Paul said to Barnabas, "Let's return to each city where we previously preached the word of the Lord, to see how the new believers are getting along." ³⁷Barnabas

agreed and wanted to take along John Mark. ³⁸But Paul disagreed strongly, since John Mark had deserted them in Pamphylia and had not shared in their work. ³⁹Their disagreement over this was so sharp that they separated. Barnabas took John Mark with him and sailed for Cyprus. ⁴⁰Paul chose Silas, and the believers sent them off, entrusting them to the Lord's grace. ⁴¹So they traveled throughout Syria and Cilicia to strengthen the churches there.

PAUL'S SECOND MISSIONARY JOURNEY

16 Paul and Silas went first to Derbe and then on to Lystra. There they met Timothy, a young disciple whose mother was a Jewish believer, but whose father was a Greek. ²Timothy was well thought of by the believers* in Lystra and Iconium, ³so Paul wanted him to join them on their journey. In deference to the Jews of the area, he arranged for Timothy to be circumcised before they left, for everyone knew that his father was a Greek. ⁴Then they went from town to town, explaining the decision regarding the commandments that were to be obeyed, as decided by the apostles and elders in Jerusalem. ⁵So the churches were strengthened in their faith and grew daily in numbers.

A CALL FROM MACEDONIA

⁶Next Paul and Silas traveled through the area of Phrygia and Galatia, because the Holy Spirit had told them not to go into the province of Asia at that time. ⁷Then coming to the borders of Mysia, they headed for the province of Bithynia,* but again the Spirit of Jesus did not let them go. ⁸So instead, they went on through Mysia to the city of Troas.

⁹That night Paul had a vision. He saw a man from Macedonia in northern Greece, pleading with him, "Come over here and help us." ¹⁰So we* decided to leave for Macedonia at once,

---

15:33 Some manuscripts add verse 34, *But Silas decided to stay there.* **16:2** Greek *brothers;* also in 16:40. **16:6-7** *Phrygia, Galatia, Asia, Mysia,* and *Bithynia* were all districts in the land now called Turkey. **16:10** Luke, the writer of this book, here joined Paul and accompanied him on his journey.

for we could only conclude that God was calling us to preach the Good News there.

LYDIA OF PHILIPPI BELIEVES IN JESUS

[11]We boarded a boat at Troas and sailed straight across to the island of Samothrace, and the next day we landed at Neapolis. [12]From there we reached Philippi, a major city of the district of Macedonia and a Roman colony; we stayed there several days.

[13]On the Sabbath we went a little way outside the city to a riverbank, where we supposed that some people met for prayer, and we sat down to speak with some women who had come together. [14]One of them was Lydia from Thyatira, a merchant of expensive purple cloth. She was a worshiper of God. As she listened to us, the Lord opened her heart, and she accepted what Paul was saying. [15]She was baptized along with other members of her household, and she asked us to be her guests. "If you agree that I am faithful to the Lord," she said, "come and stay at my home." And she urged us until we did.

PAUL AND SILAS IN PRISON

[16]One day as we were going down to the place of prayer, we met a demon-possessed slave girl. She was a fortune-teller who earned a lot of money for her masters. [17]She followed along behind us shouting, "These men are servants of the Most High God, and they have come to tell you how to be saved."

[18]This went on day after day until Paul got so exasperated that he turned and spoke to the demon within her. "I command you in the name of Jesus Christ to come out of her," he said. And instantly it left her.

[19]Her masters' hopes of wealth were now shattered, so they grabbed Paul and Silas and dragged them before the authorities at the marketplace. [20]"The whole city is in an uproar because of these Jews!" they shouted. [21]"They are teaching the people to do things that are against Roman customs."

[22]A mob quickly formed against Paul and Silas, and the city officials ordered them stripped and beaten with wooden rods. [23]They were severely beaten, and then they were thrown into prison. The jailer was ordered to make sure they didn't escape. [24]So he took no chances but put them into the inner dungeon and clamped their feet in the stocks.

[25]Around midnight, Paul and Silas were praying and singing hymns to God, and the other prisoners were listening. [26]Suddenly, there was a great earthquake, and the prison was shaken to its foundations. All the doors flew open, and the chains of every prisoner fell off! [27]The jailer woke up to see the prison doors wide open. He assumed the prisoners had escaped, so he drew his sword to kill himself. [28]But Paul shouted to him, "Don't do it! We are all here!"

[29]Trembling with fear, the jailer called for lights and ran to the dungeon and fell down before Paul and Silas. [30]He brought them out and asked, "Sirs, what must I do to be saved?"

[31]They replied, "Believe on the Lord Jesus and you will be saved, along with your entire household." [32]Then they shared the word of the Lord with him and all who lived in his household. [33]That same hour the jailer washed their wounds, and he and everyone in his household were immediately baptized. [34]Then he brought them into his house and set a meal before them. He and his entire household rejoiced because they all believed in God.

[35]The next morning the city officials sent the police to tell the jailer, "Let those men go!" [36]So the jailer told Paul, "You and Silas are free to leave. Go in peace."

[37]But Paul replied, "They have publicly beaten us without trial and jailed us—and we are Roman citizens. So now they want us to leave secretly? Certainly not! Let them come themselves to release us!"

[38]When the police made their report, the city officials were alarmed to learn that Paul and Silas were Roman citizens. [39]They came to the jail and apologized to them. Then they brought them out and begged them to leave the city. [40]Paul and Silas then returned to the

My Daily Worship

AUDIENCE OF ONE

ACTS 15:22–17:34

Around midnight, Paul and Silas were praying and singing hymns to God,
and the other prisoners were listening (16:25).

[i reflect]

Jerome Hines (1921–2003) thrilled audiences in opera houses around the world when he sang the bass lead in such operas as *Boris Godunov* and *Faust.* He also became a Christian in young adulthood. In his autobiography, *This Is My Story, This Is My Song,* Hines recalled the first time he sang for a Christian gathering, at a Salvation Army meeting in London:

It was announced that we would have a solo. I started to get up from my chair, but the officer in charge introduced a lady officer from another corps who arose and began to sing.

"Why," I thought, "do they let her sing? What a terrible sound. It's strange that they'd let her sing, knowing there's a Metropolitan Opera singer on the program."

Then my attention was caught by the radiant, beautiful look on her face and the impact of the words she was singing struck me. She sang with such dedication and sincerity that I began to forget the unpleasant scratch of her voice.

"Lord," I whispered, "it may sound bad to me, but I'll bet that is beautiful music to your ears."

We do not make our joyful noise to the Lord because the sound of our voice is a treat for God. We do not necessarily sing praises because we're feeling happy. Like Paul and Silas in prison, things may not be going well for us. And if others are listening who might be blessed by our singing (like the other prisoners in the jail or Jerome Hines at the Salvation Army gathering), that's great; but if not, we sing anyway. We sing because we have an audience of one, and he has filled our hearts with a joy that *must* come out.

Stand up right now and sing! It doesn't matter what—your audience of one does not care.

[i pray]

I will sing unto you, Lord, making a joyful noise unto the rock of my salvation. I will come
before your presence with thanksgiving and make a joyful noise unto you with psalms.

[i respond]

Whether singing along to a CD, using a songbook, or singing favorite songs from memory, spend some time vocalizing your praise to God. Make it a time when you forget your present troubles and just enjoy sweet communion with your Lord.

home of Lydia, where they met with the believers and encouraged them once more before leaving town.

PAUL PREACHES IN THESSALONICA

17 Now Paul and Silas traveled through the towns of Amphipolis and Apollonia and came to Thessalonica, where there was a Jewish synagogue. [2]As was Paul's custom, he went to the synagogue service, and for three Sabbaths in a row he interpreted the Scriptures to the people. [3]He was explaining and proving the prophecies about the sufferings of the Messiah and his rising from the dead. He said, "This Jesus I'm telling you about is the Messiah." [4]Some who listened were persuaded and became converts, including a large number of godly Greek men and also many important women of the city.*

[5]But the Jewish leaders were jealous, so they gathered some worthless fellows from the streets to form a mob and start a riot. They attacked the home of Jason, searching for Paul and Silas so they could drag them out to the crowd.* [6]Not finding them there, they dragged out Jason and some of the other believers* instead and took them before the city council. "Paul and Silas have turned the rest of the world upside down, and now they are here disturbing our city," they shouted. [7]"And Jason has let them into his home. They are all guilty of treason against Caesar, for they profess allegiance to another king, Jesus."

[8]The people of the city, as well as the city officials, were thrown into turmoil by these reports. [9]But the officials released Jason and the other believers after they had posted bail.

PAUL AND SILAS IN BEREA

[10]That very night the believers sent Paul and Silas to Berea. When they arrived there, they went to the synagogue. [11]And the people of Berea were more open-minded than those in Thessalonica, and they listened eagerly to Paul's message. They searched the Scriptures day after day to check up on Paul and Silas, to see if they were really teaching the truth. [12]As a result, many Jews believed, as did some of the prominent Greek women and many men.

[13]But when some Jews in Thessalonica learned that Paul was preaching the word of God in Berea, they went there and stirred up trouble. [14]The believers acted at once, sending Paul on to the coast, while Silas and Timothy remained behind. [15]Those escorting Paul went with him to Athens; then they returned to Berea with a message for Silas and Timothy to hurry and join him.

PAUL PREACHES IN ATHENS

[16]While Paul was waiting for them in Athens, he was deeply troubled by all the idols he saw everywhere in the city. [17]He went to the synagogue to debate with the Jews and the God-fearing Gentiles, and he spoke daily in the public square to all who happened to be there.

[18]He also had a debate with some of the Epicurean and Stoic philosophers. When he told them about Jesus and his resurrection, they said, "This babbler has picked up some strange ideas." Others said, "He's pushing some foreign religion."

[19]Then they took him to the Council of Philosophers.* "Come and tell us more about this new religion," they said. [20]"You are saying some rather startling things, and we want to know what it's all about." [21](It should be explained that all the Athenians as well as the foreigners in Athens seemed to spend all their time discussing the latest ideas.)

[22]So Paul, standing before the Council,* addressed them as follows: "Men of Athens, I notice that you are very religious, [23]for as I was walking along I saw your many altars. And one of them had this inscription on it—'To an Unknown God.' You have been worshiping him without knowing who he is, and now I wish to tell you about him.

[24]"He is the God who made the world and

17:4 Some manuscripts read *many of the wives of the leading men.*   17:5 Or *the city council.*   17:6 Greek *brothers;* also in 17:10, 14.
17:19 Greek *the Areopagus.*   17:22 Or *in the middle of Mars Hill;* Greek reads *in the middle of the Areopagus.*

everything in it. Since he is Lord of heaven and earth, he doesn't live in man-made temples, [25]and human hands can't serve his needs—for he has no needs. He himself gives life and breath to everything, and he satisfies every need there is. [26]From one man he created all the nations throughout the whole earth. He decided beforehand which should rise and fall, and he determined their boundaries.

[27]"His purpose in all of this was that the nations should seek after God and perhaps feel their way toward him and find him—though he is not far from any one of us. [28]For in him we live and move and exist. As one of your own poets says, 'We are his offspring.' [29]And since this is true, we shouldn't think of God as an idol designed by craftsmen from gold or silver or stone. [30]God overlooked people's former ignorance about these things, but now he commands everyone everywhere to turn away from idols and turn to him.* [31]For he has set a day for judging the world with justice by the man he has appointed, and he proved to everyone who this is by raising him from the dead."

[32]When they heard Paul speak of the resurrection of a person who had been dead, some laughed, but others said, "We want to hear more about this later." [33]That ended Paul's discussion with them, [34]but some joined him and became believers. Among them were Dionysius, a member of the Council,* a woman named Damaris, and others.

PAUL MEETS PRISCILLA AND AQUILA IN CORINTH

18 Then Paul left Athens and went to Corinth.* [2]There he became acquainted with a Jew named Aquila, born in Pontus, who had recently arrived from Italy with his wife, Priscilla. They had been expelled from Italy as a result of Claudius Caesar's order to deport all Jews from Rome. [3]Paul lived and worked with them, for they were tentmakers* just as he was.

Words of Worship

CELEBRATE

Celebrate, Celebration—Hebrew *'a-* "to do, observe"; *cha-* "keep a festival"; Greek *-ro* "rejoice, be glad."

The word "celebration" invokes images of partying: balloons, singing, sweets, games, special hats, or costumes. When the Lord gave the Israelites a calendar of three annual festivals, he ordered the people to "celebrate" them. By this, he simply meant to *observe* or *keep* them. But the partying aspect wasn't absent! At the festivals the people gathered to eat together, enjoy each other's company, take part in special events, and rejoice in the Lord and his saving deeds. Biblical worship is celebration—even partying—and God commands it.

When we can't worship with brothers and sisters in the faith, we feel left out of the party, like the psalm writer who wistfully recalls the singing of the festival crowds—"it was the sound of a great celebration!" (Psalm 42:4). As Christians, we have much to celebrate. God reaches out in love to restore those who have fallen away from his presence. He brought us to himself, and he is bringing others. He's like the father Jesus told about, who joyfully welcomed back his wayward son and then threw a party—because, as he said, "we had to celebrate this happy day" (Luke 15:32).

---

[4]Each Sabbath found Paul at the synagogue, trying to convince the Jews and Greeks alike. [5]And after Silas and Timothy came down from Macedonia, Paul spent his full time preaching and testifying to the Jews, telling them, "The Messiah you are looking for is

---

17:30 Greek *everywhere to repent.* 17:34 Greek *an Areopagite.* 18:1 *Athens* and *Corinth* were major cities in Achaia, the region on the southern end of the Greek peninsula. 18:3 Or *leatherworkers.*

Jesus." ⁶But when the Jews opposed him and insulted him, Paul shook the dust from his robe and said, "Your blood be upon your own heads—I am innocent. From now on I will go to the Gentiles."

⁷After that he stayed with Titius Justus, a Gentile who worshiped God and lived next door to the synagogue. ⁸Crispus, the leader of the synagogue, and all his household believed in the Lord. Many others in Corinth also became believers and were baptized.

⁹One night the Lord spoke to Paul in a vision and told him, "Don't be afraid! Speak out! Don't be silent! ¹⁰For I am with you, and no one will harm you because many people here in this city belong to me." ¹¹So Paul stayed there for the next year and a half, teaching the word of God.

¹²But when Gallio became governor of Achaia, some Jews rose in concerted action against Paul and brought him before the governor for judgment. ¹³They accused Paul of "persuading people to worship God in ways that are contrary to the law." ¹⁴But just as Paul started to make his defense, Gallio turned to Paul's accusers and said, "Listen, you Jews, if this were a case involving some wrongdoing or a serious crime, I would be obliged to listen to you. ¹⁵But since it is merely a question of words and names and your Jewish laws, you take care of it. I refuse to judge such matters." ¹⁶And he drove them out of the courtroom. ¹⁷The mob had grabbed Sosthenes, the leader of the synagogue, and had beaten him right there in the courtroom. But Gallio paid no attention.

PAUL RETURNS TO ANTIOCH OF SYRIA

¹⁸Paul stayed in Corinth for some time after that and then said good-bye to the brothers and sisters* and sailed for the coast of Syria, taking Priscilla and Aquila with him. (Earlier, at Cenchrea, Paul had shaved his head according to Jewish custom, for he had taken a vow.)

¹⁹When they arrived at the port of Ephesus, Paul left the others behind. But while he was there, he went to the synagogue to debate with the Jews. ²⁰They asked him to stay longer, but he declined. ²¹So he left, saying, "I will come back later,* God willing." Then he set sail from Ephesus. ²²The next stop was at the port of Caesarea. From there he went up and visited the church at Jerusalem* and then went back to Antioch.

²³After spending some time in Antioch, Paul went back to Galatia and Phrygia, visiting all the believers,* encouraging them and helping them to grow in the Lord.

APOLLOS INSTRUCTED AT EPHESUS

²⁴Meanwhile, a Jew named Apollos, an eloquent speaker who knew the Scriptures well, had just arrived in Ephesus from Alexandria in Egypt. ²⁵He had been taught the way of the Lord and talked to others with great enthusiasm and accuracy about Jesus. However, he knew only about John's baptism. ²⁶When Priscilla and Aquila heard him preaching boldly in the synagogue, they took him aside and explained the way of God more accurately.

²⁷Apollos had been thinking about going to Achaia, and the brothers and sisters in Ephesus encouraged him in this. They wrote to the believers in Achaia, asking them to welcome him. When he arrived there, he proved to be of great benefit to those who, by God's grace, had believed. ²⁸He refuted all the Jews with powerful arguments in public debate. Using the Scriptures, he explained to them, "The Messiah you are looking for is Jesus."

PAUL'S THIRD MISSIONARY JOURNEY

19 While Apollos was in Corinth, Paul traveled through the interior provinces. Finally, he came to Ephesus, where he found several believers.* ²"Did you receive the

---

18:18 Greek *brothers;* also in 18:27. 18:21 Some manuscripts read *"I must by all means be at Jerusalem for the upcoming festival, but I will come back later."* 18:22 Greek *the church.* 18:23 Greek *disciples;* also in 18:27. 19:1 Greek *disciples;* also in 19:9, 30.

Holy Spirit when you believed?" he asked them.

"No," they replied, "we don't know what you mean. We haven't even heard that there is a Holy Spirit."

³"Then what baptism did you experience?" he asked.

And they replied, "The baptism of John."

⁴Paul said, "John's baptism was to demonstrate a desire to turn from sin and turn to God. John himself told the people to believe in Jesus, the one John said would come later."

⁵As soon as they heard this, they were baptized in the name of the Lord Jesus. ⁶Then when Paul laid his hands on them, the Holy Spirit came on them, and they spoke in other tongues and prophesied. ⁷There were about twelve men in all.

PAUL MINISTERS IN EPHESUS

⁸Then Paul went to the synagogue and preached boldly for the next three months, arguing persuasively about the Kingdom of God. ⁹But some rejected his message and publicly spoke against the Way, so Paul left the synagogue and took the believers with him. Then he began preaching daily at the lecture hall of Tyrannus. ¹⁰This went on for the next two years, so that people throughout the province of Asia—both Jews and Greeks—heard the Lord's message.

¹¹God gave Paul the power to do unusual miracles, ¹²so that even when handkerchiefs or cloths that had touched his skin were placed on sick people, they were healed of their diseases, and any evil spirits within them came out.

¹³A team of Jews who were traveling from town to town casting out evil spirits tried to use the name of the Lord Jesus. The incantation they used was this: "I command you by Jesus, whom Paul preaches, to come out!" ¹⁴Seven sons of Sceva, a leading priest, were doing this. ¹⁵But when they tried it on a man possessed by an evil spirit, the spirit replied, "I

know Jesus, and I know Paul. But who are you!" ¹⁶And he leaped on them and attacked them with such violence that they fled from the house, naked and badly injured.

¹⁷The story of what happened spread quickly all through Ephesus, to Jews and Greeks alike. A solemn fear descended on the city, and the name of the Lord Jesus was greatly honored. ¹⁸Many who became believers confessed their sinful practices. ¹⁹A number of them who had been practicing magic brought their incantation books and burned them at a public bonfire. The value of the books was several million dollars.* ²⁰So the message about the Lord spread widely and had a powerful effect.

THE RIOT IN EPHESUS

²¹Afterward Paul felt impelled by the Holy Spirit* to go over to Macedonia and Achaia before returning to Jerusalem. "And after that," he said, "I must go on to Rome!" ²²He sent his two assistants, Timothy and Erastus, on ahead to Macedonia while he stayed awhile longer in the province of Asia.

²³But about that time, serious trouble developed in Ephesus concerning the Way. ²⁴It began with Demetrius, a silversmith who had a large business manufacturing silver shrines of the Greek goddess Artemis.* He kept many craftsmen busy. ²⁵He called the craftsmen together, along with others employed in related trades, and addressed them as follows:

"Gentlemen, you know that our wealth comes from this business. ²⁶As you have seen and heard, this man Paul has persuaded many people that handmade gods aren't gods at all. And this is happening not only here in Ephesus but throughout the entire province! ²⁷Of course, I'm not just talking about the loss of public respect for our business. I'm also concerned that the temple of the great goddess Artemis will lose its influence and that Artemis—this magnificent goddess worshiped throughout the province of Asia and

19:19 Greek 50,000 pieces of silver, each of which was the equivalent of a day's wage. 19:21 Or purposed in his spirit. 19:24 Artemis is otherwise known as Diana.

all around the world—will be robbed of her prestige!"

²⁸At this their anger boiled, and they began shouting, "Great is Artemis of the Ephesians!" ²⁹A crowd began to gather, and soon the city was filled with confusion. Everyone rushed to the amphitheater, dragging along Gaius and Aristarchus, who were Paul's traveling companions from Macedonia. ³⁰Paul wanted to go in, but the believers wouldn't let him. ³¹Some of the officials of the province, friends of Paul, also sent a message to him, begging him not to risk his life by entering the amphitheater.

³²Inside, the people were all shouting, some one thing and some another. Everything was in confusion. In fact, most of them didn't even know why they were there. ³³Alexander was thrust forward by some of the Jews, who encouraged him to explain the situation. He motioned for silence and tried to speak in defense. ³⁴But when the crowd realized he was a Jew, they started shouting again and kept it up for two hours: "Great is Artemis of the Ephesians! Great is Artemis of the Ephesians!"

³⁵At last the mayor was able to quiet them down enough to speak. "Citizens of Ephesus," he said. "Everyone knows that Ephesus is the official guardian of the temple of the great Artemis, whose image fell down to us from heaven. ³⁶Since this is an indisputable fact, you shouldn't be disturbed, no matter what is said. Don't do anything rash. ³⁷You have brought these men here, but they have stolen nothing from the temple and have not spoken against our goddess. ³⁸If Demetrius and the craftsmen have a case against them, the courts are in session and the judges can take the case at once. Let them go through legal channels. ³⁹And if there are complaints about other matters, they can be settled in a legal assembly. ⁴⁰I am afraid we are in danger of being charged with rioting by the Roman government, since there is no cause for all this commotion. And if Rome demands an explanation, we won't know what to say." ⁴¹Then he dismissed them, and they dispersed.

PAUL GOES TO MACEDONIA AND GREECE

20 When it was all over, Paul sent for the believers* and encouraged them. Then he said good-bye and left for Macedonia. ²Along the way, he encouraged the believers in all the towns he passed through. Then he traveled down to Greece, ³where he stayed for three months. He was preparing to sail back to Syria when he discovered a plot by some Jews against his life, so he decided to return through Macedonia.

⁴Several men were traveling with him. They were Sopater of Berea, the son of Pyrrhus; Aristarchus and Secundus, from Thessalonica; Gaius, from Derbe; Timothy; and Tychicus and Trophimus, who were from the province of Asia. ⁵They went ahead and waited for us at Troas. ⁶As soon as the Passover season* ended, we boarded a ship at Philippi in Macedonia and five days later arrived in Troas, where we stayed a week.

PAUL'S FINAL VISIT TO TROAS

⁷On the first day of the week, we gathered to observe the Lord's Supper.* Paul was preaching; and since he was leaving the next day, he talked until midnight. ⁸The upstairs room where we met was lighted with many flickering lamps. ⁹As Paul spoke on and on, a young man named Eutychus, sitting on the windowsill, became very drowsy. Finally, he sank into a deep sleep and fell three stories to his death below. ¹⁰Paul went down, bent over him, and took him into his arms. "Don't worry," he said, "he's alive!" ¹¹Then they all went back upstairs and ate the Lord's Supper together.* And Paul continued talking to them until dawn; then he left. ¹²Meanwhile, the young man was taken home unhurt, and everyone was greatly relieved.

PAUL MEETS THE EPHESIAN ELDERS

¹³Paul went by land to Assos, where he had arranged for us to join him, and we went on

---

20:1 Greek *disciples.* 20:6 Greek *the days of unleavened bread.* 20:7 Greek *to break bread.* 20:11 Greek *broke the bread.*

My Daily Worship

— *October 31* —

LIFTING UP THE DOWN-AND-OUT

ACTS 18:1–20:38

I have been a constant example of how you can help the poor by working hard. You should remember the words of the Lord Jesus: "It is more blessed to give than to receive" (20:35).

[i reflect]

Where do we direct our eyes? Do we look upward in envy at those who have more than us—and then climb to get where they are? Or do we look downward in compassion at those who are less fortunate and so stoop to give them a hand?

The apostle Paul chose to look downward. He knew a trade—tentmaking—and he put it to good use by earning enough money, not only to support himself (thereby relieving fledgling congregations of that responsibility), but also to give to the poor. Said Paul, "I have been a constant example of how you can help the poor by working hard." He makes a good model for us, embodying as he did the spirit of generosity that permeates the teachings of Jesus.

While many today are frankly fascinated by the lifestyles of the rich and famous, others are following the example of the apostle Paul by caring for the poor. Mary Jo Copeland is one such.

Copeland grew up in a desperately poor home, then married and raised twelve children of her own amid difficult circumstances. But she could not ignore those still needier than herself. In 1985 she started a ministry to the homeless in the Twin Cities called Sharing and Caring Hands. Tireless in her efforts, Copeland has built a complex of services that today gives shelter, hot meals, bus tokens, showers, clothing, medical and dental care, legal aid, counseling, and referrals to more than one thousand persons a day. The "Mother Teresa of Minneapolis" is known for personally washing the filthy, blistered feet of the street persons who come her way.

Mary Jo Copeland saw the poor and didn't look away. Let us, likewise, give to and get involved in the lives of the poor. A blessing awaits us when we do.

As an act of worship today, donate a bag of clothing to a local charity or buy a bag of groceries for the local food pantry.

[i pray]

Forgive me, Lord, for the times I have been focused on accumulating when you would rather I had been disbursing. The poor have a constant friend in you. From now on, may I earn the title "friend of the poor" too.

[i respond]

Get in your car and drive to a poor section of your city. Pray for the needy ones you see and pray for creative options to lighten the burden of the poor.

ahead by ship. ¹⁴He joined us there and we sailed together to Mitylene. ¹⁵The next day we passed the island of Kios. The following day, we crossed to the island of Samos. And a day later we arrived at Miletus.

¹⁶Paul had decided against stopping at Ephesus this time because he didn't want to spend further time in the province of Asia. He was hurrying to get to Jerusalem, if possible, for the Festival of Pentecost. ¹⁷But when we landed at Miletus, he sent a message to the elders of the church at Ephesus, asking them to come down to meet him.

¹⁸When they arrived he declared, "You know that from the day I set foot in the province of Asia until now ¹⁹I have done the Lord's work humbly—yes, and with tears. I have endured the trials that came to me from the plots of the Jews. ²⁰Yet I never shrank from telling you the truth, either publicly or in your homes. ²¹I have had one message for Jews and Gentiles alike—the necessity of turning from sin and turning to God, and of faith in our Lord Jesus.

²²"And now I am going to Jerusalem, drawn there irresistibly by the Holy Spirit,* not knowing what awaits me, ²³except that the Holy Spirit has told me in city after city that jail and suffering lie ahead. ²⁴But my life is worth nothing unless I use it for doing the work assigned me by the Lord Jesus—the work of telling others the Good News about God's wonderful kindness and love.

²⁵"And now I know that none of you to whom I have preached the Kingdom will ever see me again. ²⁶Let me say plainly that I have been faithful. No one's damnation can be blamed on me,* ²⁷for I didn't shrink from declaring all that God wants for you.

²⁸"And now beware! Be sure that you feed and shepherd God's flock—his church, purchased with his blood—over whom the Holy Spirit has appointed you as elders.* ²⁹I know full well that false teachers, like vicious wolves, will come in among you after I leave, not sparing the flock. ³⁰Even some of you will distort the truth in order to draw a following. ³¹Watch out! Remember the three years I was with you—my constant watch and care over you night and day, and my many tears for you.

³²"And now I entrust you to God and the word of his grace—his message that is able to build you up and give you an inheritance with all those he has set apart for himself.

³³"I have never coveted anyone's money or fine clothing. ³⁴You know that these hands of mine have worked to pay my own way, and I have even supplied the needs of those who were with me. ³⁵And I have been a constant example of how you can help the poor by working hard. You should remember the words of the Lord Jesus: 'It is more blessed to give than to receive.'"

³⁶When he had finished speaking, he knelt and prayed with them. ³⁷They wept aloud as they embraced him in farewell, ³⁸sad most of all because he had said that they would never see him again. Then they accompanied him down to the ship.

PAUL'S JOURNEY TO JERUSALEM

21 After saying farewell to the Ephesian elders, we sailed straight to the island of Cos. The next day we reached Rhodes and then went to Patara. ²There we boarded a ship sailing for the Syrian province of Phoenicia. ³We sighted the island of Cyprus, passed it on our left, and landed at the harbor of Tyre, in Syria, where the ship was to unload. ⁴We went ashore, found the local believers,* and stayed with them a week. These disciples prophesied through the Holy Spirit that Paul should not go on to Jerusalem. ⁵When we returned to the ship at the end of the week, the entire congregation, including wives and children, came down to the shore with us. There we knelt, prayed, ⁶and said our farewells. Then we went aboard, and they returned home.

⁷The next stop after leaving Tyre was Ptolemais, where we greeted the brothers and sisters* but stayed only one day. ⁸Then we

---

20:22 Or *by my spirit,* or *by an inner compulsion;* Greek reads *by the spirit.*   20:26 Greek *I am innocent of the blood of all.*   20:28 Greek *overseers.*   21:4 Greek *disciples;* also in 21:16.   21:7 Greek *brothers;* also in 21:17.

went on to Caesarea and stayed at the home of Philip the Evangelist, one of the seven men who had been chosen to distribute food. ⁹He had four unmarried daughters who had the gift of prophecy.

¹⁰During our stay of several days, a man named Agabus, who also had the gift of prophecy, arrived from Judea. ¹¹When he visited us, he took Paul's belt and bound his own feet and hands with it. Then he said, "The Holy Spirit declares, 'So shall the owner of this belt be bound by the Jewish leaders in Jerusalem and turned over to the Romans.' " ¹²When we heard this, we who were traveling with him, as well as the local believers, begged Paul not to go on to Jerusalem.

¹³But he said, "Why all this weeping? You are breaking my heart! For I am ready not only to be jailed at Jerusalem but also to die for the sake of the Lord Jesus." ¹⁴When it was clear that we couldn't persuade him, we gave up and said, "The will of the Lord be done."

PAUL ARRIVES AT JERUSALEM

¹⁵Shortly afterward we packed our things and left for Jerusalem. ¹⁶Some believers from Caesarea accompanied us, and they took us to the home of Mnason, a man originally from Cyprus and one of the early disciples. ¹⁷All the brothers and sisters in Jerusalem welcomed us cordially.

¹⁸The next day Paul went in with us to meet with James, and all the elders of the Jerusalem church were present. ¹⁹After greetings were exchanged, Paul gave a detailed account of the things God had accomplished among the Gentiles through his ministry.

²⁰After hearing this, they praised God. But then they said, "You know, dear brother, how many thousands of Jews have also believed, and they all take the law of Moses very seriously. ²¹Our Jewish Christians here at Jerusalem have been told that you are teaching all the Jews living in the Gentile world to turn their backs on the laws of Moses. They say that you teach people not to circumcise their

children or follow other Jewish customs. ²²Now what can be done? For they will certainly hear that you have come.

²³"Here's our suggestion. We have four men here who have taken a vow and are preparing to shave their heads. ²⁴Go with them to the Temple and join them in the purification ceremony, and pay for them to have their heads shaved. Then everyone will know that the rumors are all false and that you yourself observe the Jewish laws.

²⁵"As for the Gentile Christians, all we ask of them is what we already told them in a letter: They should not eat food offered to idols, nor consume blood, nor eat meat from strangled animals, and they should stay away from all sexual immorality."

PAUL IS ARRESTED

²⁶So Paul agreed to their request, and the next day he went through the purification ritual with the men and went to the Temple. Then he publicly announced the date when their vows would end and sacrifices would be offered for each of them.

²⁷The seven days were almost ended when some Jews from the province of Asia saw Paul in the Temple and roused a mob against him. They grabbed him, ²⁸yelling, "Men of Israel! Help! This is the man who teaches against our people and tells everybody to disobey the Jewish laws. He speaks against the Temple— and he even defiles it by bringing Gentiles in!" ²⁹(For earlier that day they had seen him in the city with Trophimus, a Gentile from Ephesus,* and they assumed Paul had taken him into the Temple.)

³⁰The whole population of the city was rocked by these accusations, and a great riot followed. Paul was dragged out of the Temple, and immediately the gates were closed behind him. ³¹As they were trying to kill him, word reached the commander of the Roman regiment that all Jerusalem was in an uproar. ³²He immediately called out his soldiers and officers and ran down among the crowd. When

21:29 Greek *Trophimus, the Ephesian.*

the mob saw the commander and the troops coming, they stopped beating Paul. ³³The commander arrested him and ordered him bound with two chains. Then he asked the crowd who he was and what he had done. ³⁴Some shouted one thing and some another. He couldn't find out the truth in all the uproar and confusion, so he ordered Paul to be taken to the fortress. ³⁵As they reached the stairs, the mob grew so violent the soldiers had to lift Paul to their shoulders to protect him. ³⁶And the crowd followed behind shouting, "Kill him, kill him!"

PAUL SPEAKS TO THE CROWD

³⁷As Paul was about to be taken inside, he said to the commander, "May I have a word with you?"

"Do you know Greek?" the commander asked, surprised. ³⁸"Aren't you the Egyptian who led a rebellion some time ago and took four thousand members of the Assassins out into the desert?"

³⁹"No," Paul replied, "I am a Jew from Tarsus in Cilicia, which is an important city. Please, let me talk to these people." ⁴⁰The commander agreed, so Paul stood on the stairs and motioned to the people to be quiet. Soon a deep silence enveloped the crowd, and he addressed them in their own language, Aramaic.*

22 "Brothers and esteemed fathers," Paul said, "listen to me as I offer my defense." ²When they heard him speaking in their own language,* the silence was even greater. ³"I am a Jew, born in Tarsus, a city in Cilicia, and I was brought up and educated here in Jerusalem under Gamaliel. At his feet I learned to follow our Jewish laws and customs very carefully. I became very zealous to honor God in everything I did, just as all of you are today. ⁴And I persecuted the followers of the Way, hounding some to death, binding and delivering both men and women to prison. ⁵The high priest and the whole council of leaders can testify that this is so. For I received letters from them to our Jewish brothers in Damascus, authorizing me to bring the Christians from there to Jerusalem, in chains, to be punished.

⁶"As I was on the road, nearing Damascus, about noon a very bright light from heaven suddenly shone around me. ⁷I fell to the ground and heard a voice saying to me, 'Saul, Saul, why are you persecuting me?'

⁸"'Who are you, sir?' I asked. And he replied, 'I am Jesus of Nazareth, the one you are persecuting.' ⁹The people with me saw the light but didn't hear the voice.

¹⁰"I said, 'What shall I do, Lord?' And the Lord told me, 'Get up and go into Damascus, and there you will be told all that you are to do.'

¹¹"I was blinded by the intense light and had to be led into Damascus by my companions. ¹²A man named Ananias lived there. He was a godly man in his devotion to the law, and he was well thought of by all the Jews of Damascus. ¹³He came to me and stood beside me and said, 'Brother Saul, receive your sight.' And that very hour I could see him!

¹⁴"Then he told me, 'The God of our ancestors has chosen you to know his will and to see the Righteous One and hear him speak. ¹⁵You are to take his message everywhere, telling the whole world what you have seen and heard. ¹⁶And now, why delay? Get up and be baptized, and have your sins washed away, calling on the name of the Lord.'

¹⁷"One day after I returned to Jerusalem, I was praying in the Temple, and I fell into a trance. ¹⁸I saw a vision of Jesus saying to me, 'Hurry! Leave Jerusalem, for the people here won't believe you when you give them your testimony about me.'

¹⁹"'But Lord,' I argued, 'they certainly know that I imprisoned and beat those in every synagogue who believed on you. ²⁰And when your witness Stephen was killed, I was standing there agreeing. I kept the coats they laid aside as they stoned him.'

21:40 Or *Hebrew.* 22:2 Greek *in Aramaic.*

My Daily Worship

— *November 1* —

TRUTH BE TOLD

ACTS 21:1 – 23:35

"Brothers and esteemed fathers," Paul said, "listen to me as I offer my defense" (22:1).

[i reflect]

As a young woman, Rebecca Manley Pippert was talking with a new acquaintance on the campus of the University of California, Berkeley. The conversation turned to God, and Becky began going on and on about her Christian faith. Meanwhile, the other woman fell silent.

Finally Becky interrupted herself and said, "Look, I feel really bad. I am very excited about who God is and what he's done in my life. But I hate it when people push 'religion' on me. So if I'm coming on too strong, will you just tell me?"

The other woman said, "I never knew Christians were aware that we hate being recipients of a running monologue."

"Listen," Becky responded, "most Christians I know are very hesitant to share their faith *precisely* because they're afraid they'll offend."

"But as long as you let people know that you're aware of where they're coming from, you can say anything you want!"

And thus an unbeliever gave Becky—and now us—a lesson in how to do evangelism. We need to be respectful to unbelievers, certainly, but there's an interchange of ideas going on out there all the time; we don't have to be ashamed to put in our comments about Christ. Who knows? God may use our words to revolutionize the life of another.

The apostle Paul found himself in a tricky position when he was mistakenly accused of violating temple protocol. But caught in the spotlight, he used the occasion to boldly, yet respectfully, tell his own story of encountering Christ. We can do the same whenever we've got spoken or unspoken permission from another to share what's closest to our heart.

You can honor him today by sharing with someone your own encounter with the One you worship.

[i pray]

May I become so transparent, Lord, that people will see you living inside me. Then it will be the most natural thing in the world to confirm with my lips what others already see in my life.

[i respond]

If you have never done so, write down your own personal testimony. Be sure to include how God has revealed himself to you through the years and how he has worked in your life. Let others know who it is you worship, and why.

[21]"But the Lord said to me, 'Leave Jerusalem, for I will send you far away to the Gentiles!' "

[22]The crowd listened until Paul came to that word; then with one voice they shouted, "Away with such a fellow! Kill him! He isn't fit to live!" [23]They yelled, threw off their coats, and tossed handfuls of dust into the air.

PAUL REVEALS HIS ROMAN CITIZENSHIP

[24]The commander brought Paul inside and ordered him lashed with whips to make him confess his crime. He wanted to find out why the crowd had become so furious. [25]As they tied Paul down to lash him, Paul said to the officer standing there, "Is it legal for you to whip a Roman citizen who hasn't even been tried?"

[26]The officer went to the commander and asked, "What are you doing? This man is a Roman citizen!"

[27]So the commander went over and asked Paul, "Tell me, are you a Roman citizen?"

"Yes, I certainly am," Paul replied.

[28]"I am, too," the commander muttered, "and it cost me plenty!"

"But I am a citizen by birth!"

[29]The soldiers who were about to interrogate Paul quickly withdrew when they heard he was a Roman citizen, and the commander was frightened because he had ordered him bound and whipped.

PAUL BEFORE THE HIGH COUNCIL

[30]The next day the commander freed Paul from his chains and ordered the leading priests into session with the Jewish high council.* He had Paul brought in before them to try to find out what the trouble was all about.

23 Gazing intently at the high council,* Paul began: "Brothers, I have always lived before God in all good conscience!"

[2]Instantly Ananias the high priest commanded those close to Paul to slap him on the mouth. [3]But Paul said to him, "God will slap you, you whitewashed wall! What kind of judge are you to break the law yourself by ordering me struck like that?"

[4]Those standing near Paul said to him, "Is that the way to talk to God's high priest?"

[5]"I'm sorry, brothers. I didn't realize he was the high priest," Paul replied, "for the Scriptures say, 'Do not speak evil of anyone who rules over you.'*"

[6]Paul realized that some members of the high council were Sadducees and some were Pharisees, so he shouted, "Brothers, I am a Pharisee, as were all my ancestors! And I am on trial because my hope is in the resurrection of the dead!"

[7]This divided the council—the Pharisees against the Sadducees—[8]for the Sadducees say there is no resurrection or angels or spirits, but the Pharisees believe in all of these. [9]So a great clamor arose. Some of the teachers of religious law who were Pharisees jumped up to argue that Paul was all right. "We see nothing wrong with him," they shouted. "Perhaps a spirit or an angel spoke to him." [10]The shouting grew louder and louder, and the men were tugging at Paul from both sides, pulling him this way and that. Finally, the commander, fearing they would tear him apart, ordered his soldiers to take him away from them and bring him back to the fortress.

[11]That night the Lord appeared to Paul and said, "Be encouraged, Paul. Just as you have told the people about me here in Jerusalem, you must preach the Good News in Rome."

THE PLAN TO KILL PAUL

[12]The next morning a group of Jews got together and bound themselves with an oath to neither eat nor drink until they had killed Paul. [13]There were more than forty of them. [14]They went to the leading priests and other leaders and told them what they had done. "We have bound ourselves under oath to neither eat nor drink until we have killed Paul. [15]You and the high council should tell the commander to bring Paul back to the council

---

22:30 Greek *Sanhedrin.* **23:1** Greek *Sanhedrin;* also in 23:6, 15, 20, 28. **23:5** Exod 22:28.

Words of Worship

KING, KINGDOM

King, Kingdom—Hebrew *-lech* "king"; *ma-le-* "reign, kingdom"; *mam-la-* "kingdom"; Greek *ba-si-l* "king"; *ba-si- -a* "kingdom."

The Bible tells of a time when Israel had no king, "so the people did whatever seemed right in their own eyes" (Judges 21:25). It was an era of violence and moral confusion, not unlike our own time, with its slogan, "Do your own thing." When spiritual anchoring and authority are neglected, peoples' lives are broken by self-centered acts and short-sighted choices. And everyone pays the price of the chaos that follows.

Christian worshipers understand that our relationship with God is not a democracy, but the kingdom Jesus proclaimed (Mark 1:14–15). The principles of life in God's kingdom aren't just the feeble suggestions of a meddlesome uncle. As our covenant-giver, God is our authority, and his way is the only way to a blessed life. His Word in Christ is the foundation of our universe (Hebrews 1:3). The biblical worshiper's first affirmation is, "The LORD is king!" (Psalm 93:1). For everyone enslaved by self-rule, deluded by the false promise of "having it your way," the proclamation of the rule of God and of his Messiah is good news. "The LORD is king! Let the earth rejoice!" (Psalm 97:1).

again," they requested. "Pretend you want to examine his case more fully. We will kill him on the way."

[16]But Paul's nephew heard of their plan and went to the fortress and told Paul. [17]Paul called one of the officers and said, "Take this young man to the commander. He has something important to tell him."

[18]So the officer did, explaining, "Paul, the prisoner, called me over and asked me to bring this young man to you because he has something to tell you."

[19]The commander took him by the arm, led him aside, and asked, "What is it you want to tell me?"

[20]Paul's nephew told him, "Some Jews are going to ask you to bring Paul before the Jewish high council tomorrow, pretending they want to get some more information. [21]But don't do it! There are more than forty men hiding along the way ready to jump him and kill him. They have vowed not to eat or drink until they kill him. They are ready, expecting you to agree to their request."

[22]"Don't let a soul know you told me this," the commander warned the young man as he sent him away.

PAUL IS SENT TO CAESAREA

[23]Then the commander called two of his officers and ordered, "Get two hundred soldiers ready to leave for Caesarea at nine o'clock tonight. Also take two hundred spearmen and seventy horsemen. [24]Provide horses for Paul to ride, and get him safely to Governor Felix." [25]Then he wrote this letter to the governor:

[26]"From Claudius Lysias, to his Excellency, Governor Felix. Greetings! [27]This man was seized by some Jews, and they were about to kill him when I arrived with the troops. When I learned that he was a Roman citizen, I removed him to safety. [28]Then I took him to their high council to try to find out what he had done. [29]I soon discovered it was something regarding their religious law—certainly nothing worthy of imprisonment or death. [30]But when I was informed of a plot to kill him, I immediately sent him on to you. I have told his accusers to bring their charges before you."

[31]So that night, as ordered, the soldiers took Paul as far as Antipatris. [32]They returned to the fortress the next morning, while the

horsemen took him on to Caesarea. [33]When they arrived in Caesarea, they presented Paul and the letter to Governor Felix. [34]He read it and then asked Paul what province he was from. "Cilicia," Paul answered.

[35]"I will hear your case myself when your accusers arrive," the governor told him. Then the governor ordered him kept in the prison at Herod's headquarters.

PAUL APPEARS BEFORE FELIX

24 Five days later Ananias, the high priest, arrived with some of the Jewish leaders and the lawyer* Tertullus, to press charges against Paul. [2]When Paul was called in, Tertullus laid charges against Paul in the following address to the governor:

"Your Excellency, you have given peace to us Jews and have enacted reforms for us. [3]And for all of this we are very grateful to you. [4]But lest I bore you, kindly give me your attention for only a moment as I briefly outline our case against this man. [5]For we have found him to be a troublemaker, a man who is constantly inciting the Jews throughout the world to riots and rebellions against the Roman government. He is a ringleader of the sect known as the Nazarenes. [6]Moreover he was trying to defile the Temple when we arrested him.* [8]You can find out the truth of our accusations by examining him yourself." [9]Then the other Jews chimed in, declaring that everything Tertullus said was true.

[10]Now it was Paul's turn. The governor motioned for him to rise and speak. Paul said, "I know, sir, that you have been a judge of Jewish affairs for many years, and this gives me confidence as I make my defense. [11]You can quickly discover that it was no more than twelve days ago that I arrived in Jerusalem to worship at the Temple. [12]I didn't argue with anyone in the Temple, nor did I incite a riot in any synagogue or on the streets of the city. [13]These men certainly cannot prove the things they accuse me of doing.

[14]"But I admit that I follow the Way, which they call a sect. I worship the God of our ancestors, and I firmly believe the Jewish law and everything written in the books of prophecy. [15]I have hope in God, just as these men do, that he will raise both the righteous and the ungodly. [16]Because of this, I always try to maintain a clear conscience before God and everyone else.

[17]"After several years away, I returned to Jerusalem with money to aid my people and to offer sacrifices to God. [18]My accusers saw me in the Temple as I was completing a purification ritual. There was no crowd around me and no rioting. [19]But some Jews from the province of Asia were there—and they ought to be here to bring charges if they have anything against me! [20]Ask these men here what wrongdoing the Jewish high council* found in me, [21]except for one thing I said when I shouted out, 'I am on trial before you today because I believe in the resurrection of the dead!'"

[22]Felix, who was quite familiar with the Way, adjourned the hearing and said, "Wait until Lysias, the garrison commander, arrives. Then I will decide the case." [23]He ordered an officer to keep Paul in custody but to give him some freedom and allow his friends to visit him and take care of his needs.

[24]A few days later Felix came with his wife, Drusilla, who was Jewish. Sending for Paul, they listened as he told them about faith in Christ Jesus. [25]As he reasoned with them about righteousness and self-control and the judgment to come, Felix was terrified. "Go away for now," he replied. "When it is more convenient, I'll call for you again." [26]He also hoped that Paul would bribe him, so he sent for him quite often and talked with him.

[27]Two years went by in this way; then Felix was succeeded by Porcius Festus. And because Felix wanted to gain favor with the Jewish leaders, he left Paul in prison.

24:1 Greek *some elders and an orator.* **24:6** Some manuscripts add *We would have judged him by our law, [7]but Lysias, the commander of the garrison, came and took him violently away from us, [8]commanding his accusers to come before you.* **24:20** Greek *Sanhedrin.*

PAUL APPEARS BEFORE FESTUS

25 Three days after Festus arrived in Caesarea to take over his new responsibilities, he left for Jerusalem, [2]where the leading priests and other Jewish leaders met with him and made their accusations against Paul. [3]They asked Festus as a favor to transfer Paul to Jerusalem. (Their plan was to waylay and kill him.) [4]But Festus replied that Paul was at Caesarea and he himself would be returning there soon. [5]So he said, "Those of you in authority can return with me. If Paul has done anything wrong, you can make your accusations."

[6]Eight or ten days later he returned to Caesarea, and on the following day Paul's trial began. [7]On Paul's arrival in court, the Jewish leaders from Jerusalem gathered around and made many serious accusations they couldn't prove. [8]Paul denied the charges. "I am not guilty," he said. "I have committed no crime against the Jewish laws or the Temple or the Roman government."

[9]Then Festus, wanting to please the Jews, asked him, "Are you willing to go to Jerusalem and stand trial before me there?"

[10]But Paul replied, "No! This is the official Roman court, so I ought to be tried right here. You know very well I am not guilty. [11]If I have done something worthy of death, I don't refuse to die. But if I am innocent, neither you nor anyone else has a right to turn me over to these men to kill me. I appeal to Caesar!"

[12]Festus conferred with his advisers and then replied, "Very well! You have appealed to Caesar, and to Caesar you shall go!"

[13]A few days later King Agrippa arrived with his sister, Bernice,* to pay their respects to Festus. [14]During their stay of several days, Festus discussed Paul's case with the king. "There is a prisoner here," he told him, "whose case was left for me by Felix. [15]When I was in Jerusalem, the leading priests and other Jewish leaders pressed charges against him and asked me to sentence him. [16]Of course, I quickly pointed out to them that Roman law

> *We worship whom we trust,*
> *and we trust whom we know.*
>
> DAVID JEREMIAH

does not convict people without a trial. They are given an opportunity to defend themselves face to face with their accusers.

[17]"When they came here for the trial, I called the case the very next day and ordered Paul brought in. [18]But the accusations made against him weren't at all what I expected. [19]It was something about their religion and about someone called Jesus who died, but whom Paul insists is alive. [20]I was perplexed as to how to conduct an investigation of this kind, and I asked him whether he would be willing to stand trial on these charges in Jerusalem. [21]But Paul appealed to the emperor. So I ordered him back to jail until I could arrange to send him to Caesar."

[22]"I'd like to hear the man myself," Agrippa said.

And Festus replied, "You shall—tomorrow!"

PAUL SPEAKS TO AGRIPPA

[23]So the next day Agrippa and Bernice arrived at the auditorium with great pomp, accompanied by military officers and prominent men of the city. Festus ordered that Paul be brought in. [24]Then Festus said, "King Agrippa and all present, this is the man whose death is demanded both by the local Jews and by those in Jerusalem. [25]But in my opinion he has done nothing worthy of death. However, he appealed his case to the emperor, and I decided to send him. [26]But what shall I write

25:13 Greek *Agrippa the king and Bernice arrived.*

the emperor? For there is no real charge against him. So I have brought him before all of you, and especially you, King Agrippa, so that after we examine him, I might have something to write. ²⁷For it doesn't seem reasonable to send a prisoner to the emperor without specifying the charges against him!"

26

Then Agrippa said to Paul, "You may speak in your defense."

So Paul, with a gesture of his hand, started his defense: ²"I am fortunate, King Agrippa, that you are the one hearing my defense against all these accusations made by the Jewish leaders, ³for I know you are an expert on Jewish customs and controversies. Now please listen to me patiently!

⁴"As the Jewish leaders are well aware, I was given a thorough Jewish training from my earliest childhood among my own people and in Jerusalem. ⁵If they would admit it, they know that I have been a member of the Pharisees, the strictest sect of our religion. ⁶Now I am on trial because I am looking forward to the fulfillment of God's promise made to our ancestors. ⁷In fact, that is why the twelve tribes of Israel worship God night and day, and they share the same hope I have. Yet, O king, they say it is wrong for me to have this hope! ⁸Why does it seem incredible to any of you that God can raise the dead?

⁹"I used to believe that I ought to do everything I could to oppose the followers of Jesus of Nazareth.* ¹⁰Authorized by the leading priests, I caused many of the believers in Jerusalem to be sent to prison. And I cast my vote against them when they were condemned to death. ¹¹Many times I had them whipped in the synagogues to try to get them to curse Christ. I was so violently opposed to them that I even hounded them in distant cities of foreign lands.

¹²"One day I was on such a mission to Damascus, armed with the authority and commission of the leading priests. ¹³About noon, Your Majesty, a light from heaven brighter than the sun shone down on me and my companions. ¹⁴We all fell down, and I heard a voice saying to me in Aramaic,* 'Saul, Saul, why are you persecuting me? It is hard for you to fight against my will.*'

¹⁵"'Who are you, sir?' I asked.

"And the Lord replied, 'I am Jesus, the one you are persecuting. ¹⁶Now stand up! For I have appeared to you to appoint you as my servant and my witness. You are to tell the world about this experience and about other times I will appear to you. ¹⁷And I will protect you from both your own people and the Gentiles. Yes, I am going to send you to the Gentiles, ¹⁸to open their eyes so they may turn from darkness to light, and from the power of Satan to God. Then they will receive forgiveness for their sins and be given a place among God's people, who are set apart by faith in me.'

¹⁹"And so, O King Agrippa, I was not disobedient to that vision from heaven. ²⁰I preached first to those in Damascus, then in Jerusalem and throughout all Judea, and also to the Gentiles, that all must turn from their sins and turn to God—and prove they have changed by the good things they do. ²¹Some Jews arrested me in the Temple for preaching this, and they tried to kill me. ²²But God protected me so that I am still alive today to tell these facts to everyone, from the least to the greatest. I teach nothing except what the prophets and Moses said would happen— ²³that the Messiah would suffer and be the first to rise from the dead as a light to Jews and Gentiles alike."

²⁴Suddenly, Festus shouted, "Paul, you are insane. Too much study has made you crazy!"

²⁵But Paul replied, "I am not insane, Most Excellent Festus. I am speaking the sober truth. ²⁶And King Agrippa knows about these things. I speak frankly, for I am sure these events are all familiar to him, for they were not done in a corner! ²⁷King Agrippa, do you believe the prophets? I know you do—"

26:9 Greek oppose the name of Jesus the Nazarene. **26:14a** Or Hebrew. **26:14b** Greek It is hard for you to kick against the oxgoads.

My Daily Worship

— *November 2* —

LOONEY FOR JESUS

ACTS 24:1—26:32

Suddenly, Festus shouted, "Paul, you are insane.
Too much study has made you crazy!" (26:24).

[i reflect]

Reports filtering out of North Korea suggest that incarcerated Christians in this officially atheistic society have been treated more harshly than other prisoners. U.S. State Department reports frequently accuse North Korea of torturing and executing Christians because of their faith. One former North Korean prison guard also testified that "those believing in God were regarded as insane." In this, North Korea stole a page from the former Soviet Union, which for decades committed Christians to insane asylums, where they were subjected to cruel and unnecessary "treatments."

We are fortunate to live in a society in which Christian faith is not equated with lunacy. Or at least not seriously. Some may still shout, "You've got to be nuts!" when we testify of the Lord.

That's the sort of reaction Paul got while giving his defense before a pair of local rulers, Festus and Agrippa. When Paul got to the part of the story where Jesus rises from the dead, Festus blurted out his views on Paul's mental health, and the proceedings came to a crashing halt. Perhaps it was experiences like this that led Paul to write about how God's wisdom seems foolish to the world (1 Corinthians 1:18–25).

It all has to do with the trend of one's thinking. Academics tell us that we all have mental "paradigms," or sets of assumptions about reality. It takes a powerful exposure to new truth to cause a "paradigm shift." In fact, it takes the Holy Spirit to shift a person from worldly-mindedness to heavenly-mindedness. When others think we're crazy for believing as we do, our response should be to pray that God will enable them to believe "crazily" in Jesus too (Acts 26:29).

Be "looney" for Jesus today. Express your worship and faith in him by reaching out to a hurting friend, reconciling a broken relationship, forgiving an enemy.

[i pray]

I believe all the "insane" stuff about you, Lord—the conception without intercourse, the lake used
as a sidewalk, the lunchbox feeding a crowd, the devils in a pig stampede, the corpse who
got up and walked, everything. Thank you for making me one of your "loonies"!

[i respond]

Apologetics isn't saying you're sorry; it's defending the faith. Read a book on how to answer Christianity's critics, or read a classic book of apologetics such as Mere Christianity by C. S. Lewis, to better prepare yourself to explain why worshiping Jesus makes sense.

[28]Agrippa interrupted him. "Do you think you can make me a Christian so quickly?"*

[29]Paul replied, "Whether quickly or not, I pray to God that both you and everyone here in this audience might become the same as I am, except for these chains."

[30]Then the king, the governor, Bernice, and all the others stood and left. [31]As they talked it over they agreed, "This man hasn't done anything worthy of death or imprisonment." [32]And Agrippa said to Festus, "He could be set free if he hadn't appealed to Caesar!"

PAUL SAILS FOR ROME

27 When the time came, we set sail for Italy. Paul and several other prisoners were placed in the custody of an army officer named Julius, a captain of the Imperial Regiment. [2]And Aristarchus, a Macedonian from Thessalonica, was also with us. We left on a boat whose home port was Adramyttium; it was scheduled to make several stops at ports along the coast of the province of Asia.

[3]The next day when we docked at Sidon, Julius was very kind to Paul and let him go ashore to visit with friends so they could provide for his needs. [4]Putting out to sea from there, we encountered headwinds that made it difficult to keep the ship on course, so we sailed north of Cyprus between the island and the mainland. [5]We passed along the coast of the provinces of Cilicia and Pamphylia, landing at Myra, in the province of Lycia. [6]There the officer found an Egyptian ship from Alexandria that was bound for Italy, and he put us on board.

[7]We had several days of rough sailing, and after great difficulty we finally neared Cnidus. But the wind was against us, so we sailed down to the leeward side of Crete, past the cape of Salmone. [8]We struggled along the coast with great difficulty and finally arrived at Fair Havens, near the city of Lasea. [9]We had lost a lot of time. The weather was becoming

dangerous for long voyages by then because it was so late in the fall,* and Paul spoke to the ship's officers about it.

[10]"Sirs," he said, "I believe there is trouble ahead if we go on—shipwreck, loss of cargo, injuries, and danger to our lives." [11]But the officer in charge of the prisoners listened more to the ship's captain and the owner than to Paul. [12]And since Fair Havens was an exposed harbor—a poor place to spend the winter—most of the crew wanted to go to Phoenix, farther up the coast of Crete, and spend the winter there. Phoenix was a good harbor with only a southwest and northwest exposure.

THE STORM AT SEA

[13]When a light wind began blowing from the south, the sailors thought they could make it. So they pulled up anchor and sailed along close to shore. [14]But the weather changed abruptly, and a wind of typhoon strength (a "northeaster," they called it) caught the ship and blew it out to sea. [15]They couldn't turn the ship into the wind, so they gave up and let it run before the gale.

[16]We sailed behind a small island named Cauda,* where with great difficulty we hoisted aboard the lifeboat that was being towed behind us. [17]Then we banded the ship with ropes to strengthen the hull. The sailors were afraid of being driven across to the sandbars of Syrtis off the African coast, so they lowered the sea anchor and were thus driven before the wind.

[18]The next day, as gale-force winds continued to batter the ship, the crew began throwing the cargo overboard. [19]The following day they even threw out the ship's equipment and anything else they could lay their hands on. [20]The terrible storm raged unabated for many days, blotting out the sun and the stars, until at last all hope was gone.

[21]No one had eaten for a long time. Finally, Paul called the crew together and said, "Men, you should have listened to me in the first

---

26:28 Or "A little more, and your arguments would make me a Christian." **27:9** Greek because the fast was now already gone by. This fast happened on the Day of Atonement (Yom Kippur), which occurred in late September or early October. **27:16** Some manuscripts read Clauda

place and not left Fair Havens. You would have avoided all this injury and loss. ²²But take courage! None of you will lose your lives, even though the ship will go down. ²³For last night an angel of the God to whom I belong and whom I serve stood beside me, ²⁴and he said, 'Don't be afraid, Paul, for you will surely stand trial before Caesar! What's more, God in his goodness has granted safety to everyone sailing with you.' ²⁵So take courage! For I believe God. It will be just as he said. ²⁶But we will be shipwrecked on an island."

THE SHIPWRECK

²⁷About midnight on the fourteenth night of the storm, as we were being driven across the Sea of Adria,* the sailors sensed land was near. ²⁸They took soundings and found the water was only 120 feet deep. A little later they sounded again and found only 90 feet.* ²⁹At this rate they were afraid we would soon be driven against the rocks along the shore, so they threw out four anchors from the stern and prayed for daylight. ³⁰Then the sailors tried to abandon the ship; they lowered the lifeboat as though they were going to put out anchors from the prow. ³¹But Paul said to the commanding officer and the soldiers, "You will all die unless the sailors stay aboard." ³²So the soldiers cut the ropes and let the boat fall off.

³³As the darkness gave way to the early morning light, Paul begged everyone to eat. "You haven't touched food for two weeks," he said. ³⁴"Please eat something now for your own good. For not a hair of your heads will perish." ³⁵Then he took some bread, gave thanks to God before them all, and broke off a piece and ate it. ³⁶Then everyone was encouraged, ³⁷and all 276 of us began eating—for that is the number we had aboard. ³⁸After eating, the crew lightened the ship further by throwing the cargo of wheat overboard.

³⁹When morning dawned, they didn't recognize the coastline, but they saw a bay with a beach and wondered if they could get between the rocks and get the ship safely to shore. ⁴⁰So they cut off the anchors and left them in the sea. Then they lowered the rudders, raised the foresail, and headed toward shore. ⁴¹But the ship hit a shoal and ran aground. The bow of the ship stuck fast, while the stern was repeatedly smashed by the force of the waves and began to break apart.

⁴²The soldiers wanted to kill the prisoners to make sure they didn't swim ashore and escape. ⁴³But the commanding officer wanted to spare Paul, so he didn't let them carry out their plan. Then he ordered all who could swim to jump overboard first and make for land, ⁴⁴and he told the others to try for it on planks and debris from the broken ship. So everyone escaped safely ashore!

PAUL ON THE ISLAND OF MALTA

28 Once we were safe on shore, we learned that we were on the island of Malta. ²The people of the island were very kind to us. It was cold and rainy, so they built a fire on the shore to welcome us and warm us.

³As Paul gathered an armful of sticks and was laying them on the fire, a poisonous snake, driven out by the heat, fastened itself onto his hand. ⁴The people of the island saw it hanging there and said to each other, "A murderer, no doubt! Though he escaped the sea, justice will not permit him to live." ⁵But Paul shook off the snake into the fire and was unharmed. ⁶The people waited for him to swell up or suddenly drop dead. But when they had waited a long time and saw no harm come to him, they changed their minds and decided he was a god.

⁷Near the shore where we landed was an estate belonging to Publius, the chief official of the island. He welcomed us courteously and fed us for three days. ⁸As it happened, Publius's father was ill with fever and dysentery. Paul went in and prayed for him, and laying his hands on him, he healed him. ⁹Then all

27:27 The *Sea of Adria* is in the central Mediterranean; it is not to be confused with the Adriatic Sea. 27:28 Greek *20 fathoms . . . 15 fathoms* [37 meters . . . 27 meters].

the other sick people on the island came and were cured. [10]As a result we were showered with honors, and when the time came to sail, people put on board all sorts of things we would need for the trip.

PAUL ARRIVES AT ROME

[11]It was three months after the shipwreck that we set sail on another ship that had wintered at the island—an Alexandrian ship with the twin gods* as its figurehead. [12]Our first stop was Syracuse,* where we stayed three days. [13]From there we sailed across to Rhegium.* A day later a south wind began blowing, so the following day we sailed up the coast to Puteoli. [14]There we found some believers,* who invited us to stay with them seven days. And so we came to Rome.

[15]The brothers and sisters* in Rome had heard we were coming, and they came to meet us at the Forum* on the Appian Way. Others joined us at The Three Taverns.* When Paul saw them, he thanked God and took courage.

[16]When we arrived in Rome, Paul was permitted to have his own private lodging, though he was guarded by a soldier.

PAUL PREACHES AT ROME UNDER GUARD

[17]Three days after Paul's arrival, he called together the local Jewish leaders. He said to them, "Brothers, I was arrested in Jerusalem and handed over to the Roman government, even though I had done nothing against our people or the customs of our ancestors. [18]The Romans tried me and wanted to release me, for they found no cause for the death sentence. [19]But when the Jewish leaders protested the decision, I felt it necessary to appeal to Caesar, even though I had no desire to press charges against my own people. [20]I asked you to come here today so we could get acquainted and so I could tell you that I am bound with this chain because I believe that the hope

of Israel—the Messiah—has already come."

[21]They replied, "We have heard nothing against you. We have had no letters from Judea or reports from anyone who has arrived here. [22]But we want to hear what you believe, for the only thing we know about these Christians* is that they are denounced everywhere."

[23]So a time was set, and on that day a large number of people came to Paul's house. He told them about the Kingdom of God and taught them about Jesus from the Scriptures—from the five books of Moses and the books of the prophets. He began lecturing in the morning and went on into the evening. [24]Some believed and some didn't. [25]But after they had argued back and forth among themselves, they left with this final word from Paul: "The Holy Spirit was right when he said to our ancestors through Isaiah the prophet,

[26] 'Go and say to my people,
  You will hear my words,
    but you will not understand;
  you will see what I do,
    but you will not perceive its meaning.
[27] For the hearts of these people are
      hardened,
    and their ears cannot hear,
    and they have closed their eyes—
  so their eyes cannot see,
    and their ears cannot hear,
    and their hearts cannot understand,
  and they cannot turn to me
    and let me heal them.'*

[28]So I want you to realize that this salvation from God is also available to the Gentiles, and they will accept it."*

[30]For the next two years, Paul lived in his own rented house.* He welcomed all who visited him, [31]proclaiming the Kingdom of God with all boldness and teaching about the Lord Jesus Christ. And no one tried to stop him.

28:11 The *twin gods* were the Roman gods Castor and Pollux. **28:12** *Syracuse* was on the island of Sicily. **28:13** *Rhegium* was on the southern tip of Italy. **28:14** Greek *brothers*. **28:15a** Greek *brothers*. **28:15b** The *Forum* was about 43 miles (70 kilometers) from Rome. **28:15c** *The Three Taverns* was about 35 miles (57 kilometers) from Rome. **28:22** Greek *this sect*. **28:26-27** Isa 6:9-10. **28:28** Some manuscripts add verse 29, *And when he had said these words, the Jews departed, greatly disagreeing with each other.* **28:30** Or *at his own expense*.

My Daily Worship

— *November 3* —

CHANGE OF ITINERARY

ACTS 27:1–28:31

I asked you to come here today so . . . I could tell you that I am bound
with this chain because I believe that the hope of Israel—
the Messiah—has already come (28:20).

[*i reflect*]

Dayna Curry and Heather Mercer were young Americans who wanted to tell people about Jesus. They went to Afghanistan as missionaries at a time when the extremist Muslim Taliban ruled much of the nation. So on August 3, 2001, after showing a film about Jesus in a Kabul home, the two young women were picked up by Taliban operatives and thrown into prison.

But a strange thing happened. Instead of putting an end to the women's Christian influence, their imprisonment multiplied it. As they state in *Prisoners of Hope,* while in prison, Curry and Mercer were able to live closer to Afghan women (other prisoners) than they ever had before. And following their rescue by American troops, their media popularity enabled them to tell about the love of God to many in the United States who otherwise would never have heard of them.

In a similar situation, the apostle Paul may have been disappointed to see his plans to minister in Rome seemingly derailed when he was arrested in Jerusalem and then spent years incarcerated in Caesarea. But he wound up in Rome eventually anyway, arriving on a different timetable, with a different set of people to witness to, and with a more poignant testimony to give. As he told the Jewish leaders of Rome, he was in chains for the sake of the Messiah.

One way to look at an unexpected turn of events is to become angry and fearful. Another is to assume that God has something better (though not necessarily easier) in mind for us and to look for the opportunities he is putting in our way. If our desire is to live for him, he will make it happen in the way that best suits his purposes.

What particular person or circumstance do you feel is "in your way"? Confess those thoughts to God now and ask that he help you to submit to his timetable, his purposes, for his glory.

[*i pray*]

I will make my plans, Father, but I won't object if you remake them. A change of
itinerary to my life journey? That's okay. Tell me where, and I will go.

[*i respond*]

What decisions lie in front of you? Make a list of the important decisions that you will face in the next month, next year, or next five years. Commit these decisions to God as an act of worship.

Romans

So now we can rejoice in our wonderful new relationship with God—all because of what our Lord Jesus Christ has done for us in making us friends of God (5:11).

Getting Right and Doing Right

To most people the words "righteous" and "righteousness" are complicated, seldom-used theological terms. Yet they contain (and convey) an essential truth: *Before we can ever "do right" in the sight of God, we first have to "be right" with him.*

This, at its essence, is the message of the New Testament book (or letter) called "Romans." Here is the apostle Paul's masterpiece, his systematic outline of the Christian faith. Paul begins his presentation (and outlines all that he wants to say) with this stunning sentence: "Through Christ, God has given us the privilege and authority to tell Gentiles everywhere what God has done for them, so that they will believe and obey him, bringing glory to his name" (1:5).

The first eleven chapters of Romans explain all that God has done. Though we are rebellious creatures who resent God and reject his rule, God nevertheless sent his Son, Jesus, to pay the ultimate penalty (that is, death) for our sins. Christ is the Savior of the world, our only hope for a restored relationship with the Creator.

The last five chapters of Romans unpack the implications of this remarkable offer of mercy and grace, showing those who *do* receive them how to live in light of the new life they've been given.

Here, then, is a concise course in "righteousness"—in becoming a devoted follower of Christ. Here is the explanation of how to bring glory to God's name: Believe the breathtaking news of the gospel. Embrace Jesus. Trust fully in him. Romans assures us there is no other way to get right with God. We become God's friends only by putting our faith in Jesus.

But that's only the beginning. A life of worship involves not just *being right* with God, but also *doing right*. Faith involves obedience—leaving old habits, walking away from wrong attitudes and actions, and going in new directions. Let Romans show you how!

Worship Moments

- Faith is the key to worshiping and glorifying God. Abraham's faith did not waver and he brought glory to God. Faith begins by confessing with our mouth and believing in our heart that Jesus is Lord (4:20; 10:9).

- The Holy Spirit empowered the worship of the early church, for "all who are led by the Spirit of God are children of God" (8:14).

- Worship was done in community: "All of you can join together with one voice, giving praise and glory to God" (15:6).

GREETINGS FROM PAUL

1 This letter is from Paul, Jesus Christ's slave, chosen by God to be an apostle and sent out to preach his Good News. [2]This Good News was promised long ago by God through his prophets in the holy Scriptures. [3]It is the Good News about his Son, Jesus, who came as a man, born into King David's royal family line. [4]And Jesus Christ our Lord was shown to be the Son of God when God powerfully raised him from the dead by means of the Holy Spirit.* [5]Through Christ, God has given us the privilege and authority to tell Gentiles everywhere what God has done for them, so that they will believe and obey him, bringing glory to his name.

[6]You are among those who have been called to belong to Jesus Christ, [7]dear friends in Rome. God loves you dearly, and he has called you to be his very own people.

May grace and peace be yours from God our Father and the Lord Jesus Christ.

GOD'S GOOD NEWS

[8]Let me say first of all that your faith in God is becoming known throughout the world. How I thank God through Jesus Christ for each one of you. [9]God knows how often I pray for you. Day and night I bring you and your needs in prayer to God, whom I serve with all my heart* by telling others the Good News about his Son.

[10]One of the things I always pray for is the opportunity, God willing, to come at last to see you. [11]For I long to visit you so I can share a spiritual blessing with you that will help you grow strong in the Lord. [12]I'm eager to encourage you in your faith, but I also want to be encouraged by yours. In this way, each of us will be a blessing to the other.

[13]I want you to know, dear brothers and sisters,* that I planned many times to visit you, but I was prevented until now. I want to work among you and see good results, just as I have done among other Gentiles. [14]For I have a great sense of obligation to people in our culture and to people in other cultures,* to the educated and uneducated alike. [15]So I am eager to come to you in Rome, too, to preach God's Good News.

[16]For I am not ashamed of this Good News about Christ. It is the power of God at work, saving everyone who believes—Jews first and also Gentiles. [17]This Good News tells us how God makes us right in his sight. This is accomplished from start to finish by faith. As the Scriptures say, "It is through faith that a righteous person has life."*

GOD'S ANGER AT SIN

[18]But God shows his anger from heaven against all sinful, wicked people who push the truth away from themselves.* [19]For the truth about God is known to them instinctively.* God has put this knowledge in their hearts. [20]From the time the world was created, people have seen the earth and sky and all that God made. They can clearly see his invisible qualities—his eternal power and divine nature. So they have no excuse whatsoever for not knowing God.

[21]Yes, they knew God, but they wouldn't worship him as God or even give him thanks. And they began to think up foolish ideas of what God was like. The result was that their minds became dark and confused. [22]Claiming to be wise, they became utter fools instead. [23]And instead of worshiping the glorious, ever-living God, they worshiped idols made to look like mere people, or birds and animals and snakes.

[24]So God let them go ahead and do whatever shameful things their hearts desired. As a result, they did vile and degrading things with each other's bodies. [25]Instead of believing what they knew was the truth about God, they deliberately chose to believe lies. So they worshiped the things God made but not the Creator himself, who is to be praised forever. Amen.

1:4 Or the Spirit of holiness. 1:9 Or in my spirit. 1:13 Greek brothers. 1:14 Greek to Greeks and to barbarians. 1:17 Hab 2:4.
1:18 Or who prevent the truth from being known. 1:19 Greek is manifest in them.

[26]That is why God abandoned them to their shameful desires. Even the women turned against the natural way to have sex and instead indulged in sex with each other. [27]And the men, instead of having normal sexual relationships with women, burned with lust for each other. Men did shameful things with other men and, as a result, suffered within themselves the penalty they so richly deserved.

[28]When they refused to acknowledge God, he abandoned them to their evil minds and let them do things that should never be done. [29]Their lives became full of every kind of wickedness, sin, greed, hate, envy, murder, fighting, deception, malicious behavior, and gossip. [30]They are backstabbers, haters of God, insolent, proud, and boastful. They are forever inventing new ways of sinning and are disobedient to their parents. [31]They refuse to understand, break their promises, and are heartless and unforgiving. [32]They are fully aware of God's death penalty for those who do these things, yet they go right ahead and do them anyway. And, worse yet, they encourage others to do them, too.

GOD'S JUDGMENT OF SIN

2 You may be saying, "What terrible people you have been talking about!" But you are just as bad, and you have no excuse! When you say they are wicked and should be punished, you are condemning yourself, for you do these very same things. [2]And we know that God, in his justice, will punish anyone who does such things. [3]Do you think that God will judge and condemn others for doing them and not judge you when you do them, too? [4]Don't you realize how kind, tolerant, and patient God is with you? Or don't you care? Can't you see how kind he has been in giving you time to turn from your sin?

[5]But no, you won't listen. So you are storing up terrible punishment for yourself because of your stubbornness in refusing to turn from your sin. For there is going to come a day of judgment when God, the just judge of all the world, [6]will judge all people according to what they have done. [7]He will give eternal life to those who persist in doing what is good, seeking after the glory and honor and immortality that God offers. [8]But he will pour out his anger and wrath on those who live for themselves, who refuse to obey the truth and practice evil deeds. [9]There will be trouble and calamity for everyone who keeps on sinning—for the Jew first and also for the Gentile. [10]But there will be glory and honor and peace from God for all who do good—for the Jew first and also for the Gentile. [11]For God does not show favoritism.

[12]God will punish the Gentiles when they sin, even though they never had God's written law. And he will punish the Jews when they sin, for they do have the law. [13]For it is not merely knowing the law that brings God's approval. Those who obey the law will be declared right in God's sight. [14]Even when Gentiles, who do not have God's written law, instinctively follow what the law says, they show that in their hearts they know right from wrong. [15]They demonstrate that God's law is written within them, for their own consciences either accuse them or tell them they are doing what is right. [16]The day will surely come when God, by Jesus Christ, will judge everyone's secret life. This is my message.

THE JEWS AND THE LAW

[17]If you are a Jew, you are relying on God's law for your special relationship with him. You boast that all is well between yourself and God. [18]Yes, you know what he wants; you know right from wrong because you have been taught his law. [19]You are convinced that you are a guide for the blind and a beacon light for people who are lost in darkness without God. [20]You think you can instruct the ignorant and teach children the ways of God. For you are certain that in God's law you have complete knowledge and truth.

[21]Well then, if you teach others, why don't you teach yourself? You tell others not to steal, but do you steal? [22]You say it is wrong to com-

My Daily Worship

— *November 4* —

A SILENCE THAT SPEAKS VOLUMES

ROMANS 1:1–3:20

From the time the world was created, people have seen the earth and sky and all that God made.
They can clearly see his invisible qualities—his eternal power and divine nature.
So they have no excuse whatsoever for not knowing God (1:20).

[i reflect]

The sun rises in the east, sets in the west. Summer follows spring, which follows winter, which follows autumn, which follows summer. Orion, Pleiades, and Ursa Major move in their bejeweled glory across the night sky in the same pattern, night after night, millennium after millennium. The tide ebbs and flows, ebbs and flows.

All of creation bears witness to its Creator. If you had never read a Bible, attended a church service, or heard the term "general revelation," you would still know that this world was planned and placed here by an Intelligent Designer. As Psalm 19:1–2 puts it: "The heavens tell of the glory of God. The skies display his marvelous craftsmanship. Day after day they continue to speak; night after night they make him known."

Today's passage makes the case more emphatically. Paul stated that all people everywhere can look at this marvelous planet and the skies above it and know that it must have been created by Someone. Furthermore, we can discern some traits about that Someone, namely, that he is powerful, orderly, beautiful, and creative. These qualities are mirrored, if rather imperfectly, in his Creation. No, nature alone cannot impart the whole gospel to us, but it can and does point unmistakably to its origin.

Ralph Waldo Emerson wrote, "If the stars should appear just one night in a thousand years, how would men believe and adore!" As you consider the majesty and beauty of the cosmos, pause to praise and adore its Artist.

Spend a few moments today in God's creation—whether it's at a nearby park, a conservatory, or just in your backyard. Worship the Creator of all that you see.

[i pray]

Lord of Creation, you are a God of beauty, order, creativity, and complexity. As I daily experience
the splendor of sunrise and sunset, butterflies and rainbows, waterfalls and whales,
help me see beyond their natural magnificence and into your supernatural
benevolence. Thank you for giving us such a marvelous world to enjoy.

[i respond]

As soon as possible—today, if you can—set aside some time to think of and list what kinds of natural phenomena you can readily observe where you live (for example, mountains, seashores, eagles, canyons, snowfalls, dolphins, fields of wheat). What attributes of God can you discern simply by looking at his creation? Now look at people and ask the same question.

mit adultery, but do you do it? You condemn idolatry, but do you steal from pagan temples? [23]You are so proud of knowing the law, but you dishonor God by breaking it. [24]No wonder the Scriptures say, "The world blasphemes the name of God because of you."*

[25]The Jewish ceremony of circumcision is worth something only if you obey God's law. But if you don't obey God's law, you are no better off than an uncircumcised Gentile. [26]And if the Gentiles obey God's law, won't God give them all the rights and honors of being his own people? [27]In fact, uncircumcised Gentiles who keep God's law will be much better off than you Jews who are circumcised and know so much about God's law but don't obey it.

[28]For you are not a true Jew just because you were born of Jewish parents or because you have gone through the Jewish ceremony of circumcision. [29]No, a true Jew is one whose heart is right with God. And true circumcision is not a cutting of the body but a change of heart produced by God's Spirit. Whoever has that kind of change seeks praise from God, not from people.

GOD REMAINS FAITHFUL

3 Then what's the advantage of being a Jew? Is there any value in the Jewish ceremony of circumcision? [2]Yes, being a Jew has many advantages. First of all, the Jews were entrusted with the whole revelation of God.*

[3]True, some of them were unfaithful; but just because they broke their promises, does that mean God will break his promises? [4]Of course not! Though everyone else in the world is a liar, God is true. As the Scriptures say, "He will be proved right in what he says, and he will win his case in court."*

[5]"But," some say, "our sins serve a good purpose, for people will see God's goodness when he declares us sinners to be innocent. Isn't it unfair, then, for God to punish us?" (That is actually the way some people talk.) [6]Of course not! If God is not just, how is he qualified

---

Words of Worship

GIFTS OF THE SPIRIT

Gifts of the Spirit—Greek *cha-**ris**-ma-ta* "graces, favors"; ***do**-ma* "gift."

In the New Testament, gifts of the Spirit to the worshiper are usually designated as *charismata* of the Holy Spirit, though the term *doma* is used once (Ephesians 4:11) to refer to the ministry offices given by the ascended Christ.

The Lord gives each believer the resources with which to worship him. The New Testament lists these gifts in several places (Romans 12:6–8; 1 Corinthians 12:8–10, 28; Ephesians 4:11–12). These lists are not a complete catalog. Whatever contributes to God's glory and helps us, and others, to approach him in prayer and praise might be called a gift of the Holy Spirit.

Some gifts are more obvious than others. Those who teach, lead worship, or bring a wise and perceptive word from the Lord seem to occupy center stage. Others exercise their gifts behind the scenes, as diligent administrators, willing helpers, generous contributors. But all gifts are meant to build up Christ's body to which we belong. If we're inclined to envy the gifts of others because of their prominence, we do well to recall Paul's words: "Now there are different kinds of spiritual gifts, but it is the same Holy Spirit who is the source of them all" (1 Corinthians 12:4).

---

to judge the world? [7]"But," some might still argue, "how can God judge and condemn me as a sinner if my dishonesty highlights his truthfulness and brings him more glory?" [8]If

2:24 Isa 52:5. **3:2** Greek *the oracles of God.* **3:4** Ps 51:4.

you follow that kind of thinking, however, you might as well say that the more we sin the better it is! Those who say such things deserve to be condemned, yet some slander me by saying this is what I preach!

ALL PEOPLE ARE SINNERS

[9]Well then, are we Jews better than others?* No, not at all, for we have already shown that all people, whether Jews or Gentiles, are under the power of sin. [10]As the Scriptures say,

"No one is good—
  not even one.
[11] No one has real understanding;
  no one is seeking God.
[12] All have turned away from God;
  all have gone wrong.
No one does good,
  not even one."*
[13] "Their talk is foul, like the stench from an
    open grave.
  Their speech is filled with lies."
"The poison of a deadly snake drips from
    their lips."*
[14]   "Their mouths are full of cursing and
    bitterness."*
[15] "They are quick to commit murder.
[16]   Wherever they go, destruction and
    misery follow them.
[17] They do not know what true peace is."*
[18]   "They have no fear of God to restrain
    them."*

[19]Obviously, the law applies to those to whom it was given, for its purpose is to keep people from having excuses and to bring the entire world into judgment before God. [20]For no one can ever be made right in God's sight by doing what his law commands. For the more we know God's law, the clearer it becomes that we aren't obeying it.

CHRIST TOOK OUR PUNISHMENT

[21]But now God has shown us a different way of being right in his sight—not by obeying the law but by the way promised in the Scriptures long ago. [22]We are made right in God's sight when we trust in Jesus Christ to take away our sins. And we all can be saved in this same way, no matter who we are or what we have done.

[23]For all have sinned; all fall short of God's glorious standard. [24]Yet now God in his gracious kindness declares us not guilty. He has done this through Christ Jesus, who has freed us by taking away our sins. [25]For God sent Jesus to take the punishment for our sins and to satisfy God's anger against us. We are made right with God when we believe that Jesus shed his blood, sacrificing his life for us. God was being entirely fair and just when he did not punish those who sinned in former times. [26]And he is entirely fair and just in this present time when he declares sinners to be right in his sight because they believe in Jesus.

[27]Can we boast, then, that we have done anything to be accepted by God? No, because our acquittal is not based on our good deeds. It is based on our faith. [28]So we are made right with God through faith and not by obeying the law.

[29]After all, God is not the God of the Jews only, is he? Isn't he also the God of the Gentiles? Of course he is. [30]There is only one God, and there is only one way of being accepted by him. He makes people right with himself only by faith, whether they are Jews or Gentiles. [31]Well then, if we emphasize faith, does this mean that we can forget about the law? Of course not! In fact, only when we have faith do we truly fulfill the law.

THE FAITH OF ABRAHAM

4 Abraham was, humanly speaking, the founder of our Jewish nation. What were his experiences concerning this question of being saved by faith? [2]Was it because of his good deeds that God accepted him? If so, he would have had something to boast about. But from God's point of view Abraham had no basis at all for pride. [3]For the Scriptures tell

3:9 Greek *Are we better?* **3:10-12** Pss 14:1-3; 53:1-3. **3:13** Pss 5:9; 140:3. **3:14** Ps 10:7. **3:15-17** Isa 59:7-8. **3:18** Ps 36:1.

us, "Abraham believed God, so God declared him to be righteous."*

⁴When people work, their wages are not a gift. Workers earn what they receive. ⁵But people are declared righteous because of their faith, not because of their work.

⁶King David spoke of this, describing the happiness of an undeserving sinner who is declared to be righteous:

⁷ "Oh, what joy for those whose
disobedience is forgiven,
whose sins are put out of sight.
⁸ Yes, what joy for those
whose sin is no longer counted against
them by the Lord."*

⁹Now then, is this blessing only for the Jews, or is it for Gentiles, too? Well, what about Abraham? We have been saying he was declared righteous by God because of his faith. ¹⁰But how did his faith help him? Was he declared righteous only after he had been circumcised, or was it before he was circumcised? The answer is that God accepted him first, and then he was circumcised later!

¹¹The circumcision ceremony was a sign that Abraham already had faith and that God had already accepted him and declared him to be righteous—even before he was circumcised. So Abraham is the spiritual father of those who have faith but have not been circumcised. They are made right with God by faith. ¹²And Abraham is also the spiritual father of those who have been circumcised, but only if they have the same kind of faith Abraham had before he was circumcised.

¹³It is clear, then, that God's promise to give the whole earth to Abraham and his descendants was not based on obedience to God's law, but on the new relationship with God that comes by faith. ¹⁴So if you claim that God's promise is for those who obey God's law and think they are "good enough" in God's sight, then you are saying that faith is useless. And in that case, the promise is also

meaningless. ¹⁵But the law brings punishment on those who try to obey it. (The only way to avoid breaking the law is to have no law to break!)

¹⁶So that's why faith is the key! God's promise is given to us as a free gift. And we are certain to receive it, whether or not we follow Jewish customs, if we have faith like Abraham's. For Abraham is the father of all who believe. ¹⁷That is what the Scriptures mean when God told him, "I have made you the father of many nations."* This happened because Abraham believed in the God who brings the dead back to life and who brings into existence what didn't exist before.

¹⁸When God promised Abraham that he would become the father of many nations, Abraham believed him. God had also said, "Your descendants will be as numerous as the stars,"* even though such a promise seemed utterly impossible! ¹⁹And Abraham's faith did not weaken, even though he knew that he was too old to be a father at the age of one hundred and that Sarah, his wife, had never been able to have children.

²⁰Abraham never wavered in believing God's promise. In fact, his faith grew stronger, and in this he brought glory to God. ²¹He was absolutely convinced that God was able to do anything he promised. ²²And because of Abraham's faith, God declared him to be righteous.

²³Now this wonderful truth—that God declared him to be righteous—wasn't just for Abraham's benefit. ²⁴It was for us, too, assuring us that God will also declare us to be righteous if we believe in God, who brought Jesus our Lord back from the dead. ²⁵He was handed over to die because of our sins, and he was raised from the dead to make us right with God.

FAITH BRINGS JOY

5 Therefore, since we have been made right in God's sight by faith, we have peace with

4:3 Gen 15:6. 4:7-8 Ps 32:1-2. 4:17 Gen 17:5. 4:18 Gen 15:5.

My Daily Worship

— *November 5* —

FROM ENEMIES TO FRIENDS

ROMANS 3:21–5:21

For since we were restored to friendship with God by the death of his Son while we were still his enemies, we will certainly be delivered from eternal punishment by his life (5:10).

[i reflect]

In C. S. Lewis's *The Lion, the Witch and the Wardrobe*, in the Chronicles of Narnia series, a boy named Edmund commits a terrible act of treachery and is thus condemned to die by the laws of Narnia. According to this law—the Deep Magic from the Dawn of Time—all traitors are the rightful property of the evil White Witch. But Aslan, the great lion, frees Edmund by dying in his place. The Witch exults, believing she now has Narnia in her unchallenged grip. The next morning, however, Aslan comes back to life. He explains to Edmund's sister Susan that although the Witch knew the Deep Magic, there is an even Deeper Magic she doesn't know: when an innocent, willing victim is killed in place of a traitor, death itself begins to work backwards. The Deeper Magic from Before the Dawn of Time is a law of sacrifice, atonement, and redemption.

What Lewis illustrates in his masterful children's tale is what Paul says in Romans 5:6–10 happened in reality in the life, atoning death, and resurrection of Jesus. Sinful humanity stood justly condemned before a holy God. Lawbreakers all, we deserved judgment and condemnation, but an innocent Substitute took our place and gave us the opportunity to be redeemed from the penalty of the law.

From enemies to friends, from estranged to reconciled, from orphans to beloved children—the grace of God manifested in the cross of Christ has accomplished this amazing transformation in us and for us. Can we respond with anything less than total gratitude to God for all he has done?

Reflect for a few moments on your life prior to meeting Jesus. What did it mean for you to be an enemy of God at that time? Thank God right now that you no longer are condemned, but that you stand before him as a friend.

[i pray]

Lord, I cannot begin to understand the kind of love you have shown me—sending your own beloved Son to die in my place when I was lost from you and, in fact, was an enemy toward you. I have never seen or heard of a love like that anywhere else, and I don't begin to grasp its fullness and depth. Help me enjoy and appreciate the love you have for me, your former enemy, now your friend.

[i respond]

If you haven't read it already, get a copy of Corrie ten Boom's *The Hiding Place*. Read it with an eye for the reconciling work of Jesus in Corrie's life as she responded to her enemies. Think of that person with whom you need to reconcile and forgive. Ask God to give you that ability.

God because of what Jesus Christ our Lord has done for us. [2]Because of our faith, Christ has brought us into this place of highest privilege where we now stand, and we confidently and joyfully look forward to sharing God's glory.

[3]We can rejoice, too, when we run into problems and trials, for we know that they are good for us—they help us learn to endure. [4]And endurance develops strength of character in us, and character strengthens our confident expectation of salvation. [5]And this expectation will not disappoint us. For we know how dearly God loves us, because he has given us the Holy Spirit to fill our hearts with his love.

[6]When we were utterly helpless, Christ came at just the right time and died for us sinners. [7]Now, no one is likely to die for a good person, though someone might be willing to die for a person who is especially good. [8]But God showed his great love for us by sending Christ to die for us while we were still sinners. [9]And since we have been made right in God's sight by the blood of Christ, he will certainly save us from God's judgment. [10]For since we were restored to friendship with God by the death of his Son while we were still his enemies, we will certainly be delivered from eternal punishment by his life. [11]So now we can rejoice in our wonderful new relationship with God—all because of what our Lord Jesus Christ has done for us in making us friends of God.

Adam and Christ Contrasted

[12]When Adam sinned, sin entered the entire human race. Adam's sin brought death, so death spread to everyone, for everyone sinned. [13]Yes, people sinned even before the law was given. And though there was no law to break, since it had not yet been given, [14]they all died anyway—even though they did not disobey an explicit commandment of God, as Adam did. What a contrast between Adam and Christ, who was yet to come! [15]And what a difference between our sin and God's generous gift of forgiveness. For this one man,

Adam, brought death to many through his sin. But this other man, Jesus Christ, brought forgiveness to many through God's bountiful gift. [16]And the result of God's gracious gift is very different from the result of that one man's sin. For Adam's sin led to condemnation, but we have the free gift of being accepted by God, even though we are guilty of many sins. [17]The sin of this one man, Adam, caused death to rule over us, but all who receive God's wonderful, gracious gift of righteousness will live in triumph over sin and death through this one man, Jesus Christ.

[18]Yes, Adam's one sin brought condemnation upon everyone, but Christ's one act of righteousness makes all people right in God's sight and gives them life. [19]Because one person disobeyed God, many people became sinners. But because one other person obeyed God, many people will be made right in God's sight.

[20]God's law was given so that all people could see how sinful they were. But as people sinned more and more, God's wonderful kindness became more abundant. [21]So just as sin ruled over all people and brought them to death, now God's wonderful kindness rules instead, giving us right standing with God and resulting in eternal life through Jesus Christ our Lord.

Sin's Power Is Broken

6 Well then, should we keep on sinning so that God can show us more and more kindness and forgiveness? [2]Of course not! Since we have died to sin, how can we continue to live in it? [3]Or have you forgotten that when we became Christians and were baptized to become one with Christ Jesus, we died with him? [4]For we died and were buried with Christ by baptism. And just as Christ was raised from the dead by the glorious power of the Father, now we also may live new lives.

[5]Since we have been united with him in his death, we will also be raised as he was. [6]Our old sinful selves were crucified with Christ so that sin might lose its power in our lives. We

are no longer slaves to sin. [7]For when we died with Christ we were set free from the power of sin. [8]And since we died with Christ, we know we will also share his new life. [9]We are sure of this because Christ rose from the dead, and he will never die again. Death no longer has any power over him. [10]He died once to defeat sin, and now he lives for the glory of God. [11]So you should consider yourselves dead to sin and able to live for the glory of God through Christ Jesus.

[12]Do not let sin control the way you live;* do not give in to its lustful desires. [13]Do not let any part of your body become a tool of wickedness, to be used for sinning. Instead, give yourselves completely to God since you have been given new life. And use your whole body as a tool to do what is right for the glory of God. [14]Sin is no longer your master, for you are no longer subject to the law, which enslaves you to sin. Instead, you are free by God's grace.

FREEDOM TO OBEY GOD

[15]So since God's grace has set us free from the law, does this mean we can go on sinning? Of course not! [16]Don't you realize that whatever you choose to obey becomes your master? You can choose sin, which leads to death, or you can choose to obey God and receive his approval. [17]Thank God! Once you were slaves of sin, but now you have obeyed with all your heart the new teaching God has given you. [18]Now you are free from sin, your old master, and you have become slaves to your new master, righteousness.

[19]I speak this way, using the illustration of slaves and masters, because it is easy to understand. Before, you let yourselves be slaves of impurity and lawlessness. Now you must choose to be slaves of righteousness so that you will become holy. [20]In those days, when you were slaves of sin, you weren't concerned with doing what was right. [21]And what was the result? It was not good, since now you are ashamed of the things you used to do, things that end in eternal doom. [22]But now you are free from the power of sin and have become slaves of God. Now you do those things that lead to holiness and result in eternal life. [23]For the wages of sin is death, but the free gift of God is eternal life through Christ Jesus our Lord.

NO LONGER BOUND TO THE LAW

7 Now, dear brothers and sisters*—you who are familiar with the law—don't you know that the law applies only to a person who is still living? [2]Let me illustrate. When a woman marries, the law binds her to her husband as long as he is alive. But if he dies, the laws of marriage no longer apply to her. [3]So while her husband is alive, she would be committing adultery if she married another man. But if her husband dies, she is free from that law and does not commit adultery when she remarries.

[4]So this is the point: The law no longer holds you in its power, because you died to its power when you died with Christ on the cross. And now you are united with the one who was raised from the dead. As a result, you can produce good fruit, that is, good deeds for God. [5]When we were controlled by our old nature, sinful desires were at work within us, and the law aroused these evil desires that produced sinful deeds, resulting in death. [6]But now we have been released from the law, for we died with Christ, and we are no longer captive to its power. Now we can really serve God, not in the old way by obeying the letter of the law, but in the new way, by the Spirit.

GOD'S LAW REVEALS OUR SIN

[7]Well then, am I suggesting that the law of God is evil? Of course not! The law is not sinful, but it was the law that showed me my sin. I would never have known that coveting is wrong if the law had not said, "Do not covet."* [8]But sin took advantage of this law and aroused all kinds of forbidden desires

6:12 Or *Do not let sin reign in your body, which is subject to death.* 7:1 Greek *brothers.* 7:7 Exod 20:17; Deut 5:21.

within me! If there were no law, sin would not have that power.

[9]I felt fine when I did not understand what the law demanded. But when I learned the truth, I realized I had broken the law and was a sinner, doomed to die. [10]So the good law, which was supposed to show me the way of life, instead gave me the death penalty. [11]Sin took advantage of the law and fooled me; it took the good law and used it to make me guilty of death. [12]But still, the law itself is holy and right and good.

[13]But how can that be? Did the law, which is good, cause my doom? Of course not! Sin used what was good to bring about my condemnation. So we can see how terrible sin really is. It uses God's good commandment for its own evil purposes.

Struggling with Sin

[14]The law is good, then. The trouble is not with the law but with me, because I am sold into slavery, with sin as my master. [15]I don't understand myself at all, for I really want to do what is right, but I don't do it. Instead, I do the very thing I hate. [16]I know perfectly well that what I am doing is wrong, and my bad conscience shows that I agree that the law is good. [17]But I can't help myself, because it is sin inside me that makes me do these evil things.

[18]I know I am rotten through and through so far as my old sinful nature is concerned. No matter which way I turn, I can't make myself do right. I want to, but I can't. [19]When I want to do good, I don't. And when I try not to do wrong, I do it anyway. [20]But if I am doing what I don't want to do, I am not really the one doing it; the sin within me is doing it.

[21]It seems to be a fact of life that when I want to do what is right, I inevitably do what is wrong. [22]I love God's law with all my heart. [23]But there is another law at work within me that is at war with my mind. This law wins the fight and makes me a slave to the sin that is still within me. [24]Oh, what a miserable person

I am! Who will free me from this life that is dominated by sin?* [25]Thank God! The answer is in Jesus Christ our Lord. So you see how it is: In my mind I really want to obey God's law, but because of my sinful nature I am a slave to sin.

Life in the Spirit

8 So now there is no condemnation for those who belong to Christ Jesus. [2]For the power* of the life-giving Spirit has freed you* through Christ Jesus from the power of sin that leads to death. [3]The law of Moses could not save us, because of our sinful nature. But God put into effect a different plan to save us. He sent his own Son in a human body like ours, except that ours are sinful. God destroyed sin's control over us by giving his Son as a sacrifice for our sins. [4]He did this so that the requirement of the law would be fully accomplished for us* who no longer follow our sinful nature but instead follow the Spirit.

[5]Those who are dominated by the sinful nature think about sinful things, but those who are controlled by the Holy Spirit think about things that please the Spirit. [6]If your sinful nature controls your mind, there is death. But if the Holy Spirit controls your mind, there is life and peace. [7]For the sinful nature is always hostile to God. It never did obey God's laws, and it never will. [8]That's why those who are still under the control of their sinful nature can never please God.

[9]But you are not controlled by your sinful nature. You are controlled by the Spirit if you have the Spirit of God living in you. (And remember that those who do not have the Spirit of Christ living in them are not Christians at all.) [10]Since Christ lives within you, even though your body will die because of sin, your spirit is alive* because you have been made right with God. [11]The Spirit of God, who raised Jesus from the dead, lives in you. And just as he raised Christ from the

---

7:24 Greek *from this body of death?* 8:2a Greek *the law;* also in 8:2b. 8:2b Some manuscripts read *me.* 8:4 Or *accomplished by us.*
8:10 Or *the Spirit will bring you eternal life.*

My Daily Worship

— *November 6* —

LOOKING FROM THE OUTSIDE IN

ROMANS 6:1–8:17

Oh, what a miserable person I am! Who will free me
from this life that is dominated by sin? (7:24).

[i reflect]

Have you ever seen a snakeskin without a snake in it? Snakes cast off their skin every so often by a process known as molting. Sometimes you can find a complete skin whose owner has slithered off in its brand-new covering. Wouldn't that be wonderful—to be able to shed your external shell like that and start over in a brand new one? Just one problem: the snake that molts and leaves behind its old skin *is still a snake.*

When we try to reinvent ourselves—through exercise, meditation, twelve-step programs, or any other form of self-help—we can end up just like our reptilian friends. We may look better, dress better, talk better, and even think and feel better, but still end up just slightly modified versions of the same old persons we were before. We need help from something (or Someone) outside of ourselves.

That was Paul's dilemma in Romans 7:24–25. He tried to make himself better by obedience to the Law; he probably tried as hard as anyone ever has. And he failed miserably. That's why he cried out in this passage, "Oh, what a miserable person I am! Who will free me from this life that is dominated by sin?" Paul had given his best effort at remaking himself and it had ended in despair. He was like the snake that shed its skin only to realize it was still a snake. That despair then drove him straight to the grace of God as manifested in Jesus Christ.

Bono, lead singer of the band U2, recently said: "The most powerful idea that's entered the world in the last few thousand years—the idea of grace—is the reason I would like to be a Christian. Though . . . I sometimes feel more like a fan, rather than actually in the band. I can't live up to it. But the reason I would like to is the idea of grace. It's really powerful."

Has that powerful grace changed you in ways you could never change on your own? In what significant ways has God changed you since you became a Christian? Have you thanked him for what he's done—and is doing—in you, with you, for you, and through you? Take a few moments to thank God for helping you "shed your skin" and put on the new one he alone provides.

[i pray]

Father, thank you for changing me from the outside in. Thank you for delivering me from my old
way of life and clothing me in your righteousness. Help me live in a manner that reflects
well on you and gives you honor and glory, in gratitude for all you've done for me.

[i respond]

List the specific "snake skins" you have shed in the last week, the last month, or the last year or two. Ask God to show you what "skins" still need to be shed.

dead, he will give life to your mortal body by this same Spirit living within you.

[12]So, dear brothers and sisters,* you have no obligation whatsoever to do what your sinful nature urges you to do. [13]For if you keep on following it, you will perish. But if through the power of the Holy Spirit you turn from it* and its evil deeds, you will live. [14]For all who are led by the Spirit of God are children* of God.

[15]So you should not be like cowering, fearful slaves. You should behave instead like God's very own children, adopted into his family* —calling him "Father, dear Father."* [16]For his Holy Spirit speaks to us deep in our hearts and tells us that we are God's children. [17]And since we are his children, we will share his treasures—for everything God gives to his Son, Christ, is ours, too. But if we are to share his glory, we must also share his suffering.

THE FUTURE GLORY

[18]Yet what we suffer now is nothing compared to the glory he will give us later. [19]For all creation is waiting eagerly for that future day when God will reveal who his children really are. [20]Against its will, everything on earth was subjected to God's curse. [21]All creation anticipates the day when it will join God's children in glorious freedom from death and decay. [22]For we know that all creation has been groaning as in the pains of childbirth right up to the present time. [23]And even we Christians, although we have the Holy Spirit within us as a foretaste of future glory, also groan to be released from pain and suffering. We, too, wait anxiously for that day when God will give us our full rights as his children,* including the new bodies he has promised us. [24]Now that we are saved, we eagerly look forward to this freedom. For if you already have something, you don't need to hope for it. [25]But if we look forward to something we don't have yet, we must wait patiently and confidently.

[26]And the Holy Spirit helps us in our distress. For we don't even know what we should pray for, nor how we should pray. But the Holy Spirit prays for us with groanings that cannot be expressed in words. [27]And the Father who knows all hearts knows what the Spirit is saying, for the Spirit pleads for us believers in harmony with God's own will. [28]And we know that God causes everything to work together* for the good of those who love God and are called according to his purpose for them. [29]For God knew his people in advance, and he chose them to become like his Son, so that his Son would be the firstborn, with many brothers and sisters. [30]And having chosen them, he called them to come to him. And he gave them right standing with himself, and he promised them his glory.

NOTHING CAN SEPARATE US FROM GOD'S LOVE

[31]What can we say about such wonderful things as these? If God is for us, who can ever be against us? [32]Since God did not spare even his own Son but gave him up for us all, won't God, who gave us Christ, also give us everything else?

[33]Who dares accuse us whom God has chosen for his own? Will God? No! He is the one who has given us right standing with himself. [34]Who then will condemn us? Will Christ Jesus? No, for he is the one who died for us and was raised to life for us and is sitting at the place of highest honor next to God, pleading for us.

[35]Can anything ever separate us from Christ's love? Does it mean he no longer loves us if we have trouble or calamity, or are persecuted, or are hungry or cold or in danger or threatened with death? [36](Even the Scriptures say, "For your sake we are killed every day; we are being slaughtered like sheep."*) [37]No, despite all these things, overwhelming victory is ours through Christ, who loved us.

8:12 Greek *brothers;* also in 8:29.   **8:13** Greek *put it to death.*   **8:14** Greek *sons;* also in 8:19.   **8:15a** Greek *You received a spirit of sonship.* **8:15b** Greek *"Abba, Father." Abba* is an Aramaic term for "father."   **8:23** Greek *wait anxiously for sonship.*   **8:28** Some manuscripts read *And we know that everything works together.*   **8:36** Ps 44:22.

My Daily Worship

— *November 7* —

THE OTHER SIDE OF THE DARKNESS
ROMANS 8:18–10:21

And I am convinced that nothing can ever separate us from his love. Death can't, and life can't. The angels can't, and the demons can't. Our fears for today, our worries about tomorrow, and even the powers of hell can't keep God's love away (8:38).

[i reflect]

Do you sometimes find yourself in circumstances that cause you to question whether or not God really loves you? A divorce, a death in the family, financial difficulties, a rebellious child, illness or injury—all these can make us wonder if God has lost our address.

Yet Paul assures us that regardless of the crisis or calamity, we can never be lost to God's love. *Nothing can separate us from his love.* Nothing.

Why then does God allow us to undergo such difficulties and such pains? Often, the best answer is, we just don't know. His ways are not always our ways, and his thoughts are not always our thoughts (Isaiah 55:8–9). Perhaps an even tougher question is: *Why does he love us so tenaciously in the first place?* Again, it's hard to fathom that a holy God could love sinful men and women. Max Lucado writes:

> We are his idea. We are his. His face. His eyes. His hands. His touch. We are his. Look deeply into the face of every human being on earth, and you will see his likeness. Though some appear to be distant relatives, they are not. God has no cousins, only children. We are, incredibly, the body of Christ. And though we may not act like our Father, there is no greater truth than this: We are his. Unalterably. He loves us. Undyingly. Nothing can separate us from the love of Christ.

It's natural to question his love when times are tough. It is supernatural to see through the pain and discern the face of a loving Father.

An old Puritan prayer says, "My Father, I trust thee, even when I do not understand thee." Make that your prayer in the dark places.

[i pray]

Father, sometimes I wonder about the difficulties and the trials in my life and the lives of others. Help me to see through the pain and the suffering to your never-failing love for me. Amen.

[i respond]

If you are going through a difficult time right now, seek out counsel from another Christian who has gone through something similar. If you have come through a valley and are now enjoying God's peace and blessing, look for someone else who is struggling right now and see if God might want to use you as an instrument of his grace, mercy, and healing.

[38]And I am convinced that nothing can ever separate us from his love. Death can't, and life can't. The angels can't, and the demons can't. Our fears for today, our worries about tomorrow, and even the powers of hell can't keep God's love away. [39]Whether we are high above the sky or in the deepest ocean, nothing in all creation will ever be able to separate us from the love of God that is revealed in Christ Jesus our Lord.

GOD'S SELECTION OF ISRAEL

9 In the presence of Christ, I speak with utter truthfulness—I do not lie—and my conscience and the Holy Spirit confirm that what I am saying is true. [2]My heart is filled with bitter sorrow and unending grief [3]for my people, my Jewish brothers and sisters.* I would be willing to be forever cursed—cut off from Christ!—if that would save them. [4]They are the people of Israel, chosen to be God's special children.* God revealed his glory to them. He made covenants with them and gave his law to them. They have the privilege of worshiping him and receiving his wonderful promises. [5]Their ancestors were great people of God, and Christ himself was a Jew as far as his human nature is concerned. And he is God, who rules over everything and is worthy of eternal praise! Amen.*

[6]Well then, has God failed to fulfill his promise to the Jews? No, for not everyone born into a Jewish family is truly a Jew! [7]Just the fact that they are descendants of Abraham doesn't make them truly Abraham's children. For the Scriptures say, "Isaac is the son through whom your descendants will be counted,"* though Abraham had other children, too. [8]This means that Abraham's physical descendants are not necessarily children of God. It is the children of the promise who are considered to be Abraham's children. [9]For God had promised, "Next year I will return, and Sarah will have a son."*

[10]This son was our ancestor Isaac. When he grew up, he married Rebekah, who gave birth to twins. [11]But before they were born, before they had done anything good or bad, she received a message from God. (This message proves that God chooses according to his own plan, [12]not according to our good or bad works.) She was told, "The descendants of your older son will serve the descendants of your younger son."* [13]In the words of the Scriptures, "I loved Jacob, but I rejected Esau."*

[14]What can we say? Was God being unfair? Of course not! [15]For God said to Moses,

"I will show mercy to anyone I choose,
    and I will show compassion to anyone I
    choose."*

[16]So receiving God's promise is not up to us. We can't get it by choosing it or working hard for it. God will show mercy to anyone he chooses.

[17]For the Scriptures say that God told Pharaoh, "I have appointed you for the very purpose of displaying my power in you, and so that my fame might spread throughout the earth."* [18]So you see, God shows mercy to some just because he wants to, and he chooses to make some people refuse to listen.

[19]Well then, you might say, "Why does God blame people for not listening? Haven't they simply done what he made them do?"

[20]No, don't say that. Who are you, a mere human being, to criticize God? Should the thing that was created say to the one who made it, "Why have you made me like this?" [21]When a potter makes jars out of clay, doesn't he have a right to use the same lump of clay to make one jar for decoration and another to throw garbage into? [22]God has every right to exercise his judgment and his power, but he also has the right to be very patient with those who are the objects of his judgment and are fit only for destruction. [23]He also has the right to pour out the riches of his glory upon those he prepared to be the objects of his mercy—

9:3 Greek *my brothers.* **9:4** Greek *chosen for sonship.* **9:5** Or *May God, who rules over everything, be praised forever. Amen.* **9:7** Gen 21:12. **9:9** Gen 18:10, 14. **9:12** Gen 25:23. **9:13** Mal 1:2-3. **9:15** Exod 33:19. **9:17** Exod 9:16.

[24]even upon us, whom he selected, both from the Jews and from the Gentiles.

[25]Concerning the Gentiles, God says in the prophecy of Hosea,

"Those who were not my people,
 I will now call my people.
And I will love those
 whom I did not love before."*

[26]And,

"Once they were told,
 'You are not my people.'
But now he will say,
 'You are children of the living God.'* "

[27]Concerning Israel, Isaiah the prophet cried out,

"Though the people of Israel are as
 numerous as the sand on the seashore,
 only a small number will be saved.
[28] For the Lord will carry out his sentence
 upon the earth
 quickly and with finality."*

[29]And Isaiah said in another place,

"If the Lord Almighty
 had not spared a few of us,
we would have been wiped out
 as completely as Sodom and Gomorrah."*

ISRAEL'S UNBELIEF

[30]Well then, what shall we say about these things? Just this: The Gentiles have been made right with God by faith, even though they were not seeking him. [31]But the Jews, who tried so hard to get right with God by keeping the law, never succeeded. [32]Why not? Because they were trying to get right with God by keeping the law and being good instead of by depending on faith. They stumbled over the great rock in their path. [33]God warned them of this in the Scriptures when he said,

"I am placing a stone in Jerusalem* that
 causes people to stumble,
 and a rock that makes them fall.*
But anyone who believes in him
 will not be disappointed.*"

10 Dear brothers and sisters,* the longing of my heart and my prayer to God is that the Jewish people might be saved. [2]I know what enthusiasm they have for God, but it is misdirected zeal. [3]For they don't understand God's way of making people right with himself. Instead, they are clinging to their own way of getting right with God by trying to keep the law. They won't go along with God's way. [4]For Christ has accomplished the whole purpose* of the law. All who believe in him are made right with God.

SALVATION IS FOR EVERYONE

[5]For Moses wrote that the law's way of making a person right with God requires obedience to all of its commands.* [6]But the way of getting right with God through faith says, "You don't need to go to heaven" (to find Christ and bring him down to help you). [7]And it says, "You don't need to go to the place of the dead" (to bring Christ back to life again). [8]Salvation that comes from trusting Christ— which is the message we preach—is already within easy reach. In fact, the Scriptures say, "The message is close at hand; it is on your lips and in your heart."*

[9]For if you confess with your mouth that Jesus is Lord and believe in your heart that God raised him from the dead, you will be saved. [10]For it is by believing in your heart that you are made right with God, and it is by confessing with your mouth that you are saved. [11]As the Scriptures tell us, "Anyone who believes in him will not be disappointed.*"

9:25 Hos 2:23. 9:26 Greek *You are sons of the living God.* Hos 1:10. 9:27-28 Isa 10:22-23. 9:29 Isa 1:9. 9:33a Greek *in Zion.*
9:33b Isa 8:14. 9:33c Or *will not be put to shame.* Isa 28:16. 10:1 Greek *Brothers.* 10:4 Or *the end.* 10:5 Lev 18:5. 10:6-8 Deut 30:12-14.
10:11 Or *will not be put to shame.* Isa 28:16.

[12]Jew and Gentile are the same in this respect. They all have the same Lord, who generously gives his riches to all who ask for them. [13]For "Anyone who calls on the name of the Lord will be saved."*

[14]But how can they call on him to save them unless they believe in him? And how can they believe in him if they have never heard about him? And how can they hear about him unless someone tells them? [15]And how will anyone go and tell them without being sent? That is what the Scriptures mean when they say, "How beautiful are the feet of those who bring good news!"*

> Our ordinary abilities will never worship God unless they are transformed by the indwelling Son of God.
>
> OSWALD CHAMBERS

[16]But not everyone welcomes the Good News, for Isaiah the prophet said, "Lord, who has believed our message?"* [17]Yet faith comes from listening to this message of good news— the Good News about Christ.

[18]But what about the Jews? Have they actually heard the message? Yes, they have:

"The message of God's creation has gone
out to everyone,
and its words to all the world."*

[19]But did the people of Israel really understand? Yes, they did, for even in the time of Moses, God had said,

"I will rouse your jealousy by blessing
other nations.

I will make you angry by blessing the
foolish Gentiles."*

[20]And later Isaiah spoke boldly for God:

"I was found by people
who were not looking for me.
I showed myself to those
who were not asking for me."*

[21]But regarding Israel, God said,

"All day long I opened my arms to them,
but they kept disobeying me and
arguing with me."*

GOD'S MERCY ON ISRAEL

11 I ask, then, has God rejected his people, the Jews? Of course not! Remember that I myself am a Jew, a descendant of Abraham and a member of the tribe of Benjamin.

[2]No, God has not rejected his own people, whom he chose from the very beginning. Do you remember what the Scriptures say about this? Elijah the prophet complained to God about the people of Israel and said, [3]"Lord, they have killed your prophets and torn down your altars. I alone am left, and now they are trying to kill me, too."*

[4]And do you remember God's reply? He said, "You are not the only one left. I have seven thousand others who have never bowed down to Baal!"*

[5]It is the same today, for not all the Jews have turned away from God. A few* are being saved as a result of God's kindness in choosing them. [6]And if they are saved by God's kindness, then it is not by their good works. For in that case, God's wonderful kindness would not be what it really is—free and undeserved.

[7]So this is the situation: Most of the Jews have not found the favor of God they are looking for so earnestly. A few have—the ones

10:13 Joel 2:32. 10:15 Isa 52:7. 10:16 Isa 53:1. 10:18 Ps 19:4. 10:19 Deut 32:21. 10:20 Isa 65:1. 10:21 Isa 65:2. 11:3 1 Kgs 19:10, 14. 11:4 1 Kgs 19:18. 11:5 Greek *A remnant.*

God has chosen—but the rest were made unresponsive. [8]As the Scriptures say,

"God has put them into a deep sleep.
To this very day he has shut their eyes so
   they do not see,
   and closed their ears so they do not
      hear."*

[9]David spoke of this same thing when he said,

"Let their bountiful table become a snare,
   a trap that makes them think all is well.
   Let their blessings cause them to
      stumble.
[10] Let their eyes go blind so they cannot see,
   and let their backs grow weaker and
      weaker."*

[11]Did God's people stumble and fall beyond recovery? Of course not! His purpose was to make his salvation available to the Gentiles, and then the Jews would be jealous and want it for themselves. [12]Now if the Gentiles were enriched because the Jews turned down God's offer of salvation, think how much greater a blessing the world will share when the Jews finally accept it.

[13]I am saying all of this especially for you Gentiles. God has appointed me as the apostle to the Gentiles. I lay great stress on this, [14]for I want to find a way to make the Jews want what you Gentiles have, and in that way I might save some of them. [15]For since the Jews' rejection meant that God offered salvation to the rest of the world, how much more wonderful their acceptance will be. It will be life for those who were dead! [16]And since Abraham and the other patriarchs were holy, their children will also be holy.* For if the roots of the tree are holy, the branches will be, too.

[17]But some of these branches from Abraham's tree, some of the Jews, have been broken off. And you Gentiles, who were branches from a wild olive tree, were grafted in. So now you also receive the blessing God has promised Abraham and his children, sharing in God's rich nourishment of his special olive tree. [18]But you must be careful not to brag about being grafted in to replace the branches that were broken off. Remember, you are just a branch, not the root.

[19]"Well," you may say, "those branches were broken off to make room for me." [20]Yes, but remember—those branches, the Jews, were broken off because they didn't believe God, and you are there because you do believe. Don't think highly of yourself, but fear what could happen. [21]For if God did not spare the branches he put there in the first place, he won't spare you either.

[22]Notice how God is both kind and severe. He is severe to those who disobeyed, but kind to you as you continue to trust in his kindness. But if you stop trusting, you also will be cut off. [23]And if the Jews turn from their unbelief, God will graft them back into the tree again. He has the power to do it.

[24]For if God was willing to take you who were, by nature, branches from a wild olive tree and graft you into his own good tree—a very unusual thing to do—he will be far more eager to graft the Jews back into the tree where they belong.

GOD'S MERCY IS FOR EVERYONE

[25]I want you to understand this mystery, dear brothers and sisters,* so that you will not feel proud and start bragging. Some of the Jews have hard hearts, but this will last only until the complete number of Gentiles comes to Christ. [26]And so all Israel will be saved. Do you remember what the prophets said about this?

"A Deliverer will come from Jerusalem,*
   and he will turn Israel* from all
      ungodliness.
[27] And then I will keep my covenant with
      them
   and take away their sins."*

11:8 Deut 29:4; Isa 29:10. **11:9-10** Ps 69:22-23. **11:16** Greek *If the dough offered as firstfruits is holy, so is the whole lump.* **11:25** Greek *brothers.* **11:26a** Greek *from Zion.* **11:26b** Greek *Jacob.* **11:26-27** Isa 59:20-21.

²⁸Many of the Jews are now enemies of the Good News. But this has been to your benefit, for God has given his gifts to you Gentiles. Yet the Jews are still his chosen people because of his promises to Abraham, Isaac, and Jacob. ²⁹For God's gifts and his call can never be withdrawn. ³⁰Once, you Gentiles were rebels against God, but when the Jews refused his mercy, God was merciful to you instead. ³¹And now, in the same way, the Jews are the rebels, and God's mercy has come to you. But someday they,* too, will share in God's mercy. ³²For God has imprisoned all people in their own disobedience so he could have mercy on everyone.

³³Oh, what a wonderful God we have! How great are his riches and wisdom and knowledge! How impossible it is for us to understand his decisions and his methods! ³⁴For who can know what the Lord is thinking? Who knows enough to be his counselor?* ³⁵And who could ever give him so much that he would have to pay it back? ³⁶For everything comes from him; everything exists by his power and is intended for his glory. To him be glory evermore. Amen.

A LIVING SACRIFICE TO GOD

12 And so, dear brothers and sisters,* I plead with you to give your bodies to God. Let them be a living and holy sacrifice— the kind he will accept. When you think of what he has done for you, is this too much to ask? ²Don't copy the behavior and customs of this world, but let God transform you into a new person by changing the way you think. Then you will know what God wants you to do, and you will know how good and pleasing and perfect his will really is.

³As God's messenger, I give each of you this warning: Be honest in your estimate of yourselves, measuring your value by how much faith God has given you. ⁴Just as our bodies have many parts and each part has a special function, ⁵so it is with Christ's body. We are all parts of his one body, and each of us has different work to do. And since we are all one body in Christ, we belong to each other, and each of us needs all the others.

⁶God has given each of us the ability to do certain things well. So if God has given you the ability to prophesy, speak out when you have faith that God is speaking through you. ⁷If your gift is that of serving others, serve them well. If you are a teacher, do a good job of teaching. ⁸If your gift is to encourage others, do it! If you have money, share it generously. If God has given you leadership ability, take the responsibility seriously. And if you have a gift for showing kindness to others, do it gladly.

⁹Don't just pretend that you love others. Really love them. Hate what is wrong. Stand on the side of the good. ¹⁰Love each other with genuine affection,* and take delight in honoring each other. ¹¹Never be lazy in your work, but serve the Lord enthusiastically.

¹²Be glad for all God is planning for you. Be patient in trouble, and always be prayerful. ¹³When God's children are in need, be the one to help them out. And get into the habit of inviting guests home for dinner or, if they need lodging, for the night.

¹⁴If people persecute you because you are a Christian, don't curse them; pray that God will bless them. ¹⁵When others are happy, be happy with them. If they are sad, share their sorrow. ¹⁶Live in harmony with each other. Don't try to act important, but enjoy the company of ordinary people. And don't think you know it all!

¹⁷Never pay back evil for evil to anyone. Do things in such a way that everyone can see you are honorable. ¹⁸Do your part to live in peace with everyone, as much as possible. ¹⁹Dear friends, never avenge yourselves. Leave that to God. For it is written,

"I will take vengeance;
    I will repay those who deserve it,"*
    says the Lord.

11:31 Some manuscripts read *But now they;* other manuscripts read *But they.* 11:34 See Isa 40:13. 12:1 Greek *brothers.* 12:10 Greek *with brotherly love.* 12:19 Deut 32:35.

My Daily Worship

— *November 8* —

ALL I KNOW

ROMANS 11:1–13:14

And so, dear brothers and sisters, I plead with you to give your bodies to God. Let them
be a living and holy sacrifice—the kind he will accept. When you think of
what he has done for you, is this too much to ask? (12:1).

[i reflect]

Can you picture an Old Testament worship service? Imagine:
- The splendor of the Temple
- Priests dressed in strange garb
- A gold-plated altar
- Fire, smoke, and sacrificial animals being led, uncomprehending, to their deaths

Now think about a worship service under the New Covenant:
- Buildings become irrelevant (John 4:19–24);
- No "priestly" dress code is prescribed—in fact, the whole idea of a separate priesthood is superceded by the reality of the priesthood of all believers (1 Peter 2:4–10);
- The system of animal sacrifice is done away with in view of the sufficiency and finality of the sacrifice of Jesus on the cross (Hebrews 9).

If there is no Temple and there are no priests offering animal sacrifices for the people, and if in fact we as Christians are, in Peter's words, "a kingdom of priests," what exactly are we to offer to the Lord in worship? Paul puts it quite plainly in Romans 12:1—we are to offer our bodies as a "living and holy sacrifice." In other words, we are to offer *ourselves*, our hearts, minds, bodies, wills—our total selves. Our forebears used to offer *animal* sacrifices for *sin*; now we offer *ourselves* for *holiness*. The animals went *unknowingly*; we go *knowing* what we're doing.

Worship is not for wimps. It is an all-encompassing, all-engaging, all-consuming offering of ourselves before our triune God. As St. Chrysostom wrote, "Let us give the first-fruit of our hands, feet, mouth, and all other parts to God. Such a sacrifice is well-pleasing."

That may sound overwhelming, but "when you think of what he has done for you, is this too much to ask?" Think of your hands, your feet, your mouth—use them today as an act of sacrifice to the Lord.

[i pray]

Father, offering all I know of myself to all I know of you seems so lofty, so out of reach for me. I'm
no spiritual giant, no mystic. I feel as though I am in the kindergarten of spirituality, and this is
a graduate-level requirement. Please lead me along gently, keeping the steps short and
simple, or I will get lost and left behind. Bring me by your grace to that point where
I can truly offer myself as a living and holy sacrifice—the kind you will accept.

[i respond]

What are the areas in your life in which you have the hardest time submitting yourself to the Lordship of Christ? Make a list of those and take them openly and honestly to the Lord in prayer.

[20]Instead, do what the Scriptures say:

> "If your enemies are hungry, feed them.
> If they are thirsty, give them something to drink,
>> and they will be ashamed of what they have done to you."*

[21]Don't let evil get the best of you, but conquer evil by doing good.

RESPECT FOR AUTHORITY

13 Obey the government, for God is the one who put it there. All governments have been placed in power by God. [2]So those who refuse to obey the laws of the land are refusing to obey God, and punishment will follow. [3]For the authorities do not frighten people who are doing right, but they frighten those who do wrong. So do what they say, and you will get along well. [4]The authorities are sent by God to help you. But if you are doing something wrong, of course you should be afraid, for you will be punished. The authorities are established by God for that very purpose, to punish those who do wrong. [5]So you must obey the government for two reasons: to keep from being punished and to keep a clear conscience.

[6]Pay your taxes, too, for these same reasons. For government workers need to be paid so they can keep on doing the work God intended them to do. [7]Give to everyone what you owe them: Pay your taxes and import duties, and give respect and honor to all to whom it is due.

LOVE FULFILLS GOD'S REQUIREMENTS

[8]Pay all your debts, except the debt of love for others. You can never finish paying that! If you love your neighbor, you will fulfill all the requirements of God's law. [9]For the commandments against adultery and murder and stealing and coveting—and any other com- mandment—are all summed up in this one commandment: "Love your neighbor as your-self."* [10]Love does no wrong to anyone, so love satisfies all of God's requirements.

[11]Another reason for right living is that you know how late it is; time is running out. Wake up, for the coming of our salvation is nearer now than when we first believed. [12]The night is almost gone; the day of salvation will soon be here. So don't live in darkness. Get rid of your evil deeds. Shed them like dirty clothes. Clothe yourselves with the armor of right liv- ing, as those who live in the light. [13]We should be decent and true in everything we do, so that everyone can approve of our behavior. Don't participate in wild parties and getting drunk, or in adultery and immoral living, or in fighting and jealousy. [14]But let the Lord Jesus Christ take control of you, and don't think of ways to indulge your evil desires.

THE DANGER OF CRITICISM

14 Accept Christians who are weak in faith, and don't argue with them about what they think is right or wrong. [2]For instance, one person believes it is all right to eat anything. But another believer who has a sensitive conscience will eat only vegetables. [3]Those who think it is all right to eat anything must not look down on those who won't. And those who won't eat certain foods must not condemn those who do, for God has accepted them. [4]Who are you to condemn God's ser- vants? They are responsible to the Lord, so let him tell them whether they are right or wrong. The Lord's power will help them do as they should.

[5]In the same way, some think one day is more holy than another day, while others think every day is alike. Each person should have a personal conviction about this matter. [6]Those who have a special day for worshiping the Lord are trying to honor him. Those who eat all kinds of food do so to honor the Lord, since they give thanks to God before eating.

12:20 Greek *and you will heap burning coals on their heads.* Prov 25:21-22.   **13:9** Lev 19:18.

And those who won't eat everything also want to please the Lord and give thanks to God. [7]For we are not our own masters when we live or when we die. [8]While we live, we live to please the Lord. And when we die, we go to be with the Lord. So in life and in death, we belong to the Lord. [9]Christ died and rose again for this very purpose, so that he might be Lord of those who are alive and of those who have died.

[10]So why do you condemn another Christian*? Why do you look down on another Christian? Remember, each of us will stand personally before the judgment seat of God. [11]For the Scriptures say,

> " 'As surely as I live,' says the Lord,
> 'every knee will bow to me
>   and every tongue will confess allegiance
>   to God.' "*

[12]Yes, each of us will have to give a personal account to God. [13]So don't condemn each other anymore. Decide instead to live in such a way that you will not put an obstacle in another Christian's path.

[14]I know and am perfectly sure on the authority of the Lord Jesus that no food, in and of itself, is wrong to eat. But if someone believes it is wrong, then for that person it is wrong. [15]And if another Christian is distressed by what you eat, you are not acting in love if you eat it. Don't let your eating ruin someone for whom Christ died. [16]Then you will not be condemned for doing something you know is all right.

[17]For the Kingdom of God is not a matter of what we eat or drink, but of living a life of goodness and peace and joy in the Holy Spirit. [18]If you serve Christ with this attitude, you will please God. And other people will approve of you, too. [19]So then, let us aim for harmony in the church and try to build each other up.

[20]Don't tear apart the work of God over what you eat. Remember, there is nothing wrong with these things in themselves. But it is wrong to eat anything if it makes another person stumble. [21]Don't eat meat or drink wine or do anything else if it might cause another Christian to stumble. [22]You may have the faith to believe that there is nothing wrong with what you are doing, but keep it between yourself and God. Blessed are those who do not condemn themselves by doing something they know is all right. [23]But if people have doubts about whether they should eat something, they shouldn't eat it. They would be condemned for not acting in faith before God. If you do anything you believe is not right, you are sinning.

LIVING TO PLEASE OTHERS

15 We may know that these things make no difference, but we cannot just go ahead and do them to please ourselves. We must be considerate of the doubts and fears of those who think these things are wrong. [2]We should please others. If we do what helps them, we will build them up in the Lord. [3]For even Christ didn't please himself. As the Scriptures say, "Those who insult you are also insulting me."* [4]Such things were written in the Scriptures long ago to teach us. They give us hope and encouragement as we wait patiently for God's promises.

[5]May God, who gives this patience and encouragement, help you live in complete harmony with each other—each with the attitude of Christ Jesus toward the other. [6]Then all of you can join together with one voice, giving praise and glory to God, the Father of our Lord Jesus Christ.

[7]So accept each other just as Christ has accepted you; then God will be glorified. [8]Remember that Christ came as a servant to the Jews to show that God is true to the promises he made to their ancestors. [9]And he came so the Gentiles might also give glory to God for his mercies to them. That is what the psalmist meant when he wrote:

14:10 Greek *your brother;* also in 14:10b, 13, 15, 21. **14:11** Isa 45:23. **15:3** Ps 69:9.

"I will praise you among the Gentiles;
   I will sing praises to your name."*

¹⁰And in another place it is written,

"Rejoice, O you Gentiles,
   along with his people, the Jews."*

¹¹And yet again,

"Praise the Lord, all you Gentiles;
   praise him, all you people of the earth."*

¹²And the prophet Isaiah said,

"The heir to David's throne* will come,
   and he will rule over the Gentiles.
They will place their hopes on him."*

¹³So I pray that God, who gives you hope, will keep you happy and full of peace as you believe in him. May you overflow with hope through the power of the Holy Spirit.

PAUL'S REASON FOR WRITING

¹⁴I am fully convinced, dear brothers and sisters,* that you are full of goodness. You know these things so well that you are able to teach others all about them. ¹⁵Even so, I have been bold enough to emphasize some of these points, knowing that all you need is this reminder from me. For I am, by God's grace, ¹⁶a special messenger from Christ Jesus to you Gentiles. I bring you the Good News and offer you up as a fragrant sacrifice to God so that you might be pure and pleasing to him by the Holy Spirit. ¹⁷So it is right for me to be enthusiastic about all Christ Jesus has done through me in my service to God. ¹⁸I dare not boast of anything else. I have brought the Gentiles to God by my message and by the way I lived before them. ¹⁹I have won them over by the miracles done through me as signs from God—all by the power of God's Spirit. In this way, I have fully presented the Good News of Christ all the way from Jerusalem clear over into Illyricum.*

²⁰My ambition has always been to preach the Good News where the name of Christ has never been heard, rather than where a church has already been started by someone else. ²¹I have been following the plan spoken of in the Scriptures, where it says,

"Those who have never been told about
   him will see,
   and those who have never heard of him
   will understand."*

²²In fact, my visit to you has been delayed so long because I have been preaching in these places.

PAUL'S TRAVEL PLANS

²³But now I have finished my work in these regions, and after all these long years of waiting, I am eager to visit you. ²⁴I am planning to go to Spain, and when I do, I will stop off in Rome. And after I have enjoyed your fellowship for a little while, you can send me on my way again.

²⁵But before I come, I must go down to Jerusalem to take a gift to the Christians there. ²⁶For you see, the believers in Greece* have eagerly taken up an offering for the Christians in Jerusalem, who are going through such hard times. ²⁷They were very glad to do this because they feel they owe a real debt to them. Since the Gentiles received the wonderful spiritual blessings of the Good News from the Jewish Christians, they feel the least they can do in return is help them financially. ²⁸As soon as I have delivered this money and completed this good deed of theirs, I will come to see you on my way to Spain. ²⁹And I am sure that when I come, Christ will give me a great blessing for you.

³⁰Dear brothers and sisters, I urge you in the

15:9 Ps 18:49. 15:10 Deut 32:43. 15:11 Ps 117:1. 15:12a Greek *The root of Jesse.* 15:12b Isa 11:10. 15:14 Greek *brothers;* also in 15:30. 15:19 *Illyricum* was a region northeast of Italy. 15:21 Isa 52:15. 15:26 Greek *Macedonia and Achaia,* the northern and southern regions of Greece.

My Daily Worship

— *November 9* —

WITH ONE VOICE

ROMANS 14:1–16:27

May God, who gives this patience and encouragement, help you live in complete harmony with each other—each with the attitude of Christ Jesus toward the other. Then all of you can join together with one voice, giving praise and glory to God, the Father of our Lord Jesus Christ (15:5–6).

[i reflect]

You've heard it before: a duet, a trio, a quartet, or even a whole choir that just can't quite find the right notes, can't quite blend their voices into that harmony they were aiming for. Or maybe they weren't even close. Either way, it is a very unpleasant, uncomfortable experience for the listeners. The song can't end fast enough.

God must feel something like that when we squabble in our churches over issues that, more often than not, are not really all that important. Instead of being "in complete harmony with each other" (Romans 15:5) and "join[ing] together with one voice, giving praise and glory to God" (v. 6), we warble off in our own key, our own pitch, our own melody, our own tempo. Individually, it might sound fine. But when it's time to blend together with other believers, it's dissonant and discordant. Worse, it's unworthy of our magnificent Lord.

Coming together as Christians means not only accepting Jesus' view on the authority of Scripture, the nature of heaven, and the reality of the resurrection. It also means adopting the attitude of love toward other Christians that Jesus has for us. Only then, can we truly join together in praising him "with one voice." As George Washington Carver wrote, "How far you go in life depends on your being tender with the young, compassionate with the aged, sympathetic with the striving, and tolerant of the weak and the strong. Because someday in life you will have been all of these."

Are there people you have a hard time being considerate of, "accept[ing them] just as Christ has accepted you" (Romans 15:7)? Do you tend to focus on the things that divide and distract from God and his glory? Pray today that he will give you "the attitude of Christ Jesus toward the other" so that you will be better able, both individually and corporately, to praise God with one voice.

[i pray]

Lord, you know how prone I am to want to have things my own way, regardless of the affect it may have on others. Help me keep my eyes on Jesus, remembering that "even Christ didn't please himself."

[i respond]

Make it a priority this week to contact a person in your life who requires a large amount of grace for you to deal with. Take that person for coffee, or write them a note of encouragement. Look for the common bonds that you share rather than the discordant chords.

name of our Lord Jesus Christ to join me in my struggle by praying to God for me. Do this because of your love for me, given to you by the Holy Spirit. [31]Pray that I will be rescued from those in Judea who refuse to obey God. Pray also that the Christians there will be willing to accept the donation I am bringing them. [32]Then, by the will of God, I will be able to come to you with a happy heart, and we will be an encouragement to each other.

[33]And now may God, who gives us his peace, be with you all. Amen.

PAUL GREETS HIS FRIENDS

16 Our sister Phoebe, a deacon in the church in Cenchrea, will be coming to see you soon. [2]Receive her in the Lord, as one who is worthy of high honor. Help her in every way you can, for she has helped many in their needs, including me.

[3]Greet Priscilla and Aquila. They have been co-workers in my ministry for Christ Jesus. [4]In fact, they risked their lives for me. I am not the only one who is thankful to them; so are all the Gentile churches. [5]Please give my greetings to the church that meets in their home.

Greet my dear friend Epenetus. He was the very first person to become a Christian in the province of Asia. [6]Give my greetings to Mary, who has worked so hard for your benefit. [7]Then there are Andronicus and Junia,* my relatives,* who were in prison with me. They are respected among the apostles and became Christians before I did. Please give them my greetings. [8]Say hello to Ampliatus, whom I love as one of the Lord's own children, [9]and Urbanus, our co-worker in Christ, and beloved Stachys.

[10]Give my greetings to Apelles, a good man whom Christ approves. And give my best regards to the members of the household of Aristobulus. [11]Greet Herodion, my relative.* Greet the Christians in the household of Narcissus. [12]Say hello to Tryphena and Tryphosa, the Lord's workers, and to dear Persis, who has worked so hard for the Lord. [13]Greet Rufus, whom the Lord picked out to be his very own; and also his dear mother, who has been a mother to me.

[14]And please give my greetings to Asyncritus, Phlegon, Hermes, Patrobas, Hermas, and the brothers and sisters* who are with them. [15]Give my greetings to Philologus, Julia, Nereus and his sister, and to Olympas and all the other believers who are with them. [16]Greet each other in Christian love.* All the churches of Christ send you their greetings.

PAUL'S FINAL INSTRUCTIONS

[17]And now I make one more appeal, my dear brothers and sisters. Watch out for people who cause divisions and upset people's faith by teaching things that are contrary to what you have been taught. Stay away from them. [18]Such people are not serving Christ our Lord; they are serving their own personal interests. By smooth talk and glowing words they deceive innocent people. [19]But everyone knows that you are obedient to the Lord. This makes me very happy. I want you to see clearly what is right and to stay innocent of any wrong. [20]The God of peace will soon crush Satan under your feet. May the grace of our Lord Jesus Christ be with you.

[21]Timothy, my fellow worker, and Lucius, Jason, and Sosipater, my relatives, send you their good wishes.

[22]I, Tertius, the one who is writing this letter for Paul, send my greetings, too, as a Christian brother.

[23]Gaius says hello to you. I am his guest, and the church meets here in his home. Erastus, the city treasurer, sends you his greetings, and so does Quartus, a Christian brother.*

[25]God is able to make you strong, just as the Good News says. It is the message about Jesus Christ and his plan for you Gentiles, a plan kept secret from the beginning of time. [26]But

---

16:7a Or *Junias;* some manuscripts read *Julia.* 16:7b Or *compatriots;* also in 16:21. 16:11 Or *compatriot.* 16:14 Greek *brothers;* also in 16:17. 16:16 Greek *with a sacred kiss.* 16:23 Some manuscripts add verse 24, *May the grace of our Lord Jesus Christ be with you all. Amen.*

now as the prophets* foretold and as the eternal God has commanded, this message is made known to all Gentiles everywhere, so that they might believe and obey Christ. ²⁷To God, who alone is wise, be the glory forever through Jesus Christ. Amen.

16:26 Greek *the prophetic writings.*

1 Corinthians

Whatever you do, you must do all for the glory of God (10:31).

The Messy Marvel

Radically changed people, joyfully sharing a common life in Christ, partnering together to offer hope and help to a dying world—it's a powerful message of spiritual deliverance packaged with desperately needed physical assistance. No doubt about it, when it's "right," the church is an absolute marvel. People are helped. Christians are fulfilled. Most importantly, God is glorified.

Unfortunately, the people of God often get off track. We forget our mission, or become divided. We squabble and focus on trivial things. We drift into immorality. When we are "wrong," the church is an absolute mess. God gets a "black eye," and we reap the scorn of a mocking world.

First Corinthians is the apostle Paul's letter to a church in chaos—a church that has gone wrong. It's an instruction manual for how a messed-up congregation, full of petty and immature individuals, can get back on track.

A lot of practical wisdom is offered here, food for thought for those who want to honor God both individually and corporately. In this interesting peek into first-century church life, we find instructions about how to live a pure life in the midst of an impure culture, how to deal with division and immorality in the church, how to handle disputes between believers, as well as specific instructions about the Lord's Supper and corporate worship. Ironic, isn't it? The modern church struggles with many of the very same problems! King Solomon was right—there really is nothing new under the sun.

Here then is an ancient and timeless guide for learning to live in unity and love with other believers, so that the world is compelled to see the power and majesty of God. When the people of God live for the glory of God, God's glory shines even brighter in a dark world, drawing others to worship him.

Let 1 Corinthians show you the way from mess to marvel.

Worship Moments

- Those who had the Spirit could understand the things of Christ. All believers are individually a "temple of God," with the Spirit of God living in each of them (2:15; 3:16).

- Worship in the early church and celebrating the festivals required purity and truth (5:8).

- Paul warned that our worship should not give offense to weaker members of the church (10:32).

- The Lord's Supper was part of the early church's worship, and was taken seriously (11:27–30).

GREETINGS FROM PAUL

1 This letter is from Paul, chosen by the will of God to be an apostle of Christ Jesus, and from our brother Sosthenes.

[2]We are writing to the church of God in Corinth, you who have been called by God to be his own holy people. He made you holy by means of Christ Jesus, just as he did all Christians everywhere—whoever calls upon the name of Jesus Christ, our Lord and theirs.

[3]May God our Father and the Lord Jesus Christ give you his grace and peace.

PAUL GIVES THANKS TO GOD

[4]I can never stop thanking God for all the generous gifts he has given you, now that you belong to Christ Jesus. [5]He has enriched your church with the gifts of eloquence and every kind of knowledge. [6]This shows that what I told you about Christ is true. [7]Now you have every spiritual gift you need as you eagerly wait for the return of our Lord Jesus Christ. [8]He will keep you strong right up to the end, and he will keep you free from all blame on the great day when our Lord Jesus Christ returns. [9]God will surely do this for you, for he always does just what he says, and he is the one who invited you into this wonderful friendship with his Son, Jesus Christ our Lord.

DIVISIONS IN THE CHURCH

[10]Now, dear brothers and sisters,* I appeal to you by the authority of the Lord Jesus Christ to stop arguing among yourselves. Let there be real harmony so there won't be divisions in the church. I plead with you to be of one mind, united in thought and purpose. [11]For some members of Chloe's household have told me about your arguments, dear brothers and sisters. [12]Some of you are saying, "I am a follower of Paul." Others are saying, "I follow Apollos," or "I follow Peter,*" or "I follow only Christ." [13]Can Christ be divided into pieces?

Was I, Paul, crucified for you? Were any of you baptized in the name of Paul? [14]I thank God that I did not baptize any of you except Crispus and Gaius, [15]for now no one can say they were baptized in my name. [16](Oh yes, I also baptized the household of Stephanas. I don't remember baptizing anyone else.) [17]For Christ didn't send me to baptize, but to preach the Good News—and not with clever speeches and high-sounding ideas, for fear that the cross of Christ would lose its power.

THE WISDOM OF GOD

[18]I know very well how foolish the message of the cross sounds to those who are on the road to destruction. But we who are being saved recognize this message as the very power of God. [19]As the Scriptures say,

> "I will destroy human wisdom
> and discard their most brilliant ideas."*

[20]So where does this leave the philosophers, the scholars, and the world's brilliant debaters? God has made them all look foolish and has shown their wisdom to be useless nonsense. [21]Since God in his wisdom saw to it that the world would never find him through human wisdom, he has used our foolish preaching to save all who believe. [22]God's way seems foolish to the Jews because they want a sign from heaven to prove it is true. And it is foolish to the Greeks because they believe only what agrees with their own wisdom. [23]So when we preach that Christ was crucified, the Jews are offended, and the Gentiles say it's all nonsense. [24]But to those called by God to salvation, both Jews and Gentiles,* Christ is the mighty power of God and the wonderful wisdom of God. [25]This "foolish" plan of God is far wiser than the wisest of human plans, and God's weakness is far stronger than the greatest of human strength.

[26]Remember, dear brothers and sisters, that few of you were wise in the world's eyes, or powerful, or wealthy when God called you. [27]Instead, God deliberately chose things the world considers foolish in order to shame those who think they are wise. And he chose

---

1:10 Greek *brothers*; also in 1:11, 26. 1:12 Greek *Cephas*. 1:19 Isa 29:14. 1:24 Greek *Greeks*.

those who are powerless to shame those who are powerful. ²⁸God chose things despised by the world, things counted as nothing at all, and used them to bring to nothing what the world considers important, ²⁹so that no one can ever boast in the presence of God.

³⁰God alone made it possible for you to be in Christ Jesus. For our benefit God made Christ to be wisdom itself. He is the one who made us acceptable to God. He made us pure and holy, and he gave himself to purchase our freedom. ³¹As the Scriptures say,

"The person who wishes to boast
should boast only of what the Lord has done."*

PAUL PREACHES WISDOM

2 Dear brothers and sisters,* when I first came to you I didn't use lofty words and brilliant ideas to tell you God's message.* ²For I decided to concentrate only on Jesus Christ and his death on the cross. ³I came to you in weakness—timid and trembling. ⁴And my message and my preaching were very plain. I did not use wise and persuasive speeches, but the Holy Spirit was powerful among you. ⁵I did this so that you might trust the power of God rather than human wisdom.

⁶Yet when I am among mature Christians, I do speak with words of wisdom, but not the kind of wisdom that belongs to this world, and not the kind that appeals to the rulers of this world, who are being brought to nothing. ⁷No, the wisdom we speak of is the secret wisdom of God,* which was hidden in former times, though he made it for our benefit before the world began. ⁸But the rulers of this world have not understood it; if they had, they would never have crucified our glorious Lord. ⁹That is what the Scriptures mean when they say,

"No eye has seen, no ear has heard,
and no mind has imagined

what God has prepared
for those who love him."*

¹⁰But we know these things because God has revealed them to us by his Spirit, and his Spirit searches out everything and shows us even God's deep secrets. ¹¹No one can know what anyone else is really thinking except that person alone, and no one can know God's thoughts except God's own Spirit. ¹²And God has actually given us his Spirit (not the world's spirit) so we can know the wonderful things God has freely given us. ¹³When we tell you this, we do not use words of human wisdom. We speak words given to us by the Spirit, using the Spirit's words to explain spiritual truths.* ¹⁴But people who aren't Christians can't understand these truths from God's Spirit. It all sounds foolish to them because only those who have the Spirit can understand what the Spirit means. ¹⁵We who have the Spirit understand these things, but others can't understand us at all. ¹⁶How could they? For,

"Who can know what the Lord is thinking?
Who can give him counsel?"*

But we can understand these things, for we have the mind of Christ.

PAUL AND APOLLOS, SERVANTS OF CHRIST

3 Dear brothers and sisters,* when I was with you I couldn't talk to you as I would to mature Christians. I had to talk as though you belonged to this world or as though you were infants in the Christian life.* ²I had to feed you with milk and not with solid food, because you couldn't handle anything stronger. And you still aren't ready, ³for you are still controlled by your own sinful desires. You are jealous of one another and quarrel with each other. Doesn't that prove you are

1:31 Jer 9:24. 2:1a Greek Brothers. 2:1b Greek mystery; other manuscripts read testimony. 2:7 Greek we speak God's wisdom in a mystery. 2:9 Isa 64:4. 2:13 Or explaining spiritual truths in spiritual language, or explaining spiritual truths to spiritual people. 2:16 Isa 40:13. 3:1a Greek Brothers. 3:1b Greek in Christ.

My Daily Worship

— November 10 —

THE FOOLISH PLAN OF GOD

1 CORINTHIANS 1:1–3:23

So when we preach that Christ was crucified, the Jews are offended, and the Gentiles say
it's all nonsense. But to those called by God to salvation, both Jews and Gentiles, Christ
is the mighty power of God and the wonderful wisdom of God. This "foolish" plan
of God is far wiser than the wisest of human plans, and God's weakness
is far stronger than the greatest of human strength (1:23–25).

[i reflect]

Perhaps you've heard the haunting Christmas song which imagines Joseph surveying the Bethlehem stable on that first Christmas night and wondering why. Why him, a simple man of trade? Why a stable? Why a baby? Why an ordinary girl? The chorus ends, "Now I'm not one to second guess what angels have to say, but this is such a strange way to save the world."

Strange indeed. Jesus, the baby "savior," grows up in obscurity, not even making a public splash until he's thirty. And even then, his ministry is a mixed bag. He gathers far more enemies than followers, until his surprising words and unpredictable actions at last earn him a date with the executioner. When rich friends put his battered body in a grave, what has he got to show for his three plus years of effort? A ragtag group of frightened men and a few weeping women.

The whole thing is odd, bizarre beyond words. But it gets even more strange. The grave can't hold Christ. He emerges from the tomb, gives his followers new hope, eternal hope, and then departs. Before he goes he commissions them, a motley crew of messed-up misfits, to take the message of his life and death and resurrection to the whole world. He calls them to live sacrificially and to overcome evil with good. They do just t hat, turning "the world upside down" (Acts 17:6).

Today, rejoice that you are part of this amazing and strange story. Think of the "odd" events God used to save you. Imagine how he might want to use you to pull someone else into his forever family.

[i pray]

Why me, Lord? Why do you love me so? How could you ever use me to touch others?
But you do love me, and you can and will use me. Your power is made perfect
in my weakness. Thank you for letting me be part of your "foolish" plan.

[i respond]

Make a list of all the questions you have about God's "foolish" plan. Share it with someone you consider a "wise" Christian. Together, celebrate that God is "far wiser than the wisest of human plans."

controlled by your own desires? You are acting like people who don't belong to the Lord. [4]When one of you says, "I am a follower of Paul," and another says, "I prefer Apollos," aren't you acting like those who are not Christians?*

[5]Who is Apollos, and who is Paul, that we should be the cause of such quarrels? Why, we're only servants. Through us God caused you to believe. Each of us did the work the Lord gave us. [6]My job was to plant the seed in your hearts, and Apollos watered it, but it was God, not we, who made it grow. [7]The ones who do the planting or watering aren't important, but God is important because he is the one who makes the seed grow. [8]The one who plants and the one who waters work as a team with the same purpose. Yet they will be rewarded individually, according to their own hard work. [9]We work together as partners who belong to God. You are God's field, God's building—not ours.

[10]Because of God's special favor to me, I have laid the foundation like an expert builder. Now others are building on it. But whoever is building on this foundation must be very careful. [11]For no one can lay any other foundation than the one we already have— Jesus Christ. [12]Now anyone who builds on that foundation may use gold, silver, jewels, wood, hay, or straw. [13]But there is going to come a time of testing at the judgment day to see what kind of work each builder has done. Everyone's work will be put through the fire to see whether or not it keeps its value. [14]If the work survives the fire, that builder will receive a reward. [15]But if the work is burned up, the builder will suffer great loss. The builders themselves will be saved, but like someone escaping through a wall of flames.

[16]Don't you realize that all of you together are the temple of God and that the Spirit of God lives in* you? [17]God will bring ruin upon anyone who ruins this temple. For God's temple is holy, and you Christians are that temple.

[18]Stop fooling yourselves. If you think you

Words of Worship

FEAST, FESTIVAL

Feast, Festival—Hebrew *chag* "feast, festival"; Greek *he-or-te* "feast, festival"; *he-or-ta-zo* "observe a festival"; *ga-mos* "wedding banquet."

The Lord commanded Israel to observe three annual festivals: Unleavened Bread (Passover), Harvest (Pentecost), and Shelters (Deuteronomy 16:16). Sometimes the festivals are called *feasts*, since the people gathered for special meals. In addition, occasions like weddings called for feasting. During such festive times the ordinary routine of life gave way to celebration. Life moved to a higher plane of enjoying the Lord's goodness and blessing.

In this sense, our worship of God is always a festival! It can't be tedious or dull. But our entire life in Christ is a celebration. Paul compares it to a feast, when he says, "Let us celebrate the festival, not by eating the old bread of wickedness and evil, but by eating the new bread of purity and truth" (1 Corinthians 5:8). Jesus attended a festival, and at its climax, he told his people where true life could be found: "If you are thirsty, come to me!" (John 7:37). He compared the kingdom of God to a wedding feast (Matthew 22:2). And when his purpose for us is fulfilled, it will be like being invited to his own marriage feast, "the wedding feast of the Lamb" (Revelation 19:9).

are wise by this world's standards, you will have to become a fool so you can become wise by God's standards. [19]For the wisdom of this world is foolishness to God. As the Scriptures say,

3:4 Greek *aren't you merely human?* **3:16** Or *among.*

"God catches those who think they are wise
in their own cleverness."*

20And again,

"The Lord knows the thoughts of the wise,
that they are worthless."*

21So don't take pride in following a particular leader. Everything belongs to you: 22Paul and Apollos and Peter*; the whole world and life and death; the present and the future. Everything belongs to you, 23and you belong to Christ, and Christ belongs to God.

PAUL AND THE CORINTHIANS

4 So look at Apollos and me as mere servants of Christ who have been put in charge of explaining God's secrets. 2Now, a person who is put in charge as a manager must be faithful. 3What about me? Have I been faithful? Well, it matters very little what you or anyone else thinks. I don't even trust my own judgment on this point. 4My conscience is clear, but that isn't what matters. It is the Lord himself who will examine me and decide.

5So be careful not to jump to conclusions before the Lord returns as to whether or not someone is faithful. When the Lord comes, he will bring our deepest secrets to light and will reveal our private motives. And then God will give to everyone whatever praise is due.

6Dear brothers and sisters,* I have used Apollos and myself to illustrate what I've been saying. If you pay attention to the Scriptures,* you won't brag about one of your leaders at the expense of another. 7What makes you better than anyone else? What do you have that God hasn't given you? And if all you have is from God, why boast as though you have accomplished something on your own?

8You think you already have everything you need! You are already rich! Without us you have become kings! I wish you really were on your thrones already, for then we would be reigning with you! 9But sometimes I think God has put us apostles on display, like prisoners of war at the end of a victor's parade, condemned to die. We have become a spectacle to the entire world—to people and angels alike.

10Our dedication to Christ makes us look like fools, but you are so wise! We are weak, but you are so powerful! You are well thought of, but we are laughed at. 11To this very hour we go hungry and thirsty, without enough clothes to keep us warm. We have endured many beatings, and we have no homes of our own. 12We have worked wearily with our own hands to earn our living. We bless those who curse us. We are patient with those who abuse us. 13We respond gently when evil things are said about us. Yet we are treated like the world's garbage, like everybody's trash—right up to the present moment.

14I am not writing these things to shame you, but to warn you as my beloved children. 15For even if you had ten thousand others to teach you about Christ, you have only one spiritual father. For I became your father in Christ Jesus when I preached the Good News to you. 16So I ask you to follow my example and do as I do.

17That is the very reason I am sending Timothy—to help you do this. For he is my beloved and trustworthy child in the Lord. He will remind you of what I teach about Christ Jesus in all the churches wherever I go.

18I know that some of you have become arrogant, thinking I will never visit you again. 19But I will come—and soon—if the Lord will let me, and then I'll find out whether these arrogant people are just big talkers or whether they really have God's power. 20For the Kingdom of God is not just fancy talk; it is living by God's power. 21Which do you choose? Should I come with punishment and scolding, or should I come with quiet love and gentleness?

3:19 Job 5:13. 3:20 Ps 94:11. 3:22 Greek *Cephas*. 4:6a Greek *Brothers*. 4:6b Or *You must learn not to go beyond "what is written,"* so that.

PAUL CONDEMNS SPIRITUAL PRIDE

5 I can hardly believe the report about the sexual immorality going on among you, something so evil that even the pagans don't do it. I am told that you have a man in your church who is living in sin with his father's wife. [2]And you are so proud of yourselves! Why aren't you mourning in sorrow and shame? And why haven't you removed this man from your fellowship?

[3]Even though I am not there with you in person, I am with you in the Spirit.* Concerning the one who has done this, I have already passed judgment [4]in the name of the Lord Jesus. You are to call a meeting of the church,* and I will be there in spirit, and the power of the Lord Jesus will be with you as you meet. [5]Then you must cast this man out of the church and into Satan's hands, so that his sinful nature will be destroyed* and he himself* will be saved when the Lord returns.

[6]How terrible that you should boast about your spirituality, and yet you let this sort of thing go on. Don't you realize that if even one person is allowed to go on sinning, soon all will be affected? [7]Remove this wicked person from among you so that you can stay pure.* Christ, our Passover Lamb, has been sacrificed for us. [8]So let us celebrate the festival, not by eating the old bread* of wickedness and evil, but by eating the new bread* of purity and truth.

[9]When I wrote to you before, I told you not to associate with people who indulge in sexual sin. [10]But I wasn't talking about unbelievers who indulge in sexual sin, or who are greedy or are swindlers or idol worshipers. You would have to leave this world to avoid people like that. [11]What I meant was that you are not to associate with anyone who claims to be a Christian* yet indulges in sexual sin, or is greedy, or worships idols, or is abusive, or a drunkard, or a swindler. Don't even eat with such people.

[12]It isn't my responsibility to judge outsiders, but it certainly is your job to judge those inside the church who are sinning in these ways. [13]God will judge those on the outside; but as the Scriptures say, "You must remove the evil person from among you."*

AVOIDING LAWSUITS WITH CHRISTIANS

6 When you have something against another Christian, why do you file a lawsuit and ask a secular court to decide the matter, instead of taking it to other Christians to decide who is right? [2]Don't you know that someday we Christians are going to judge the world? And since you are going to judge the world, can't you decide these little things among yourselves? [3]Don't you realize that we Christians will judge angels? So you should surely be able to resolve ordinary disagreements here on earth. [4]If you have legal disputes about such matters, why do you go to outside judges who are not respected by the church? [5]I am saying this to shame you. Isn't there anyone in all the church who is wise enough to decide these arguments? [6]But instead, one Christian* sues another—right in front of unbelievers!

[7]To have such lawsuits at all is a real defeat for you. Why not just accept the injustice and leave it at that? Why not let yourselves be cheated? [8]But instead, you yourselves are the ones who do wrong and cheat even your own Christian brothers and sisters.*

AVOIDING SEXUAL SIN

[9]Don't you know that those who do wrong will have no share in the Kingdom of God? Don't fool yourselves. Those who indulge in sexual sin, who are idol worshipers, adulterers, male prostitutes, homosexuals, [10]thieves,

---

5:3 Or *in spirit.* **5:4** Or *In the name of the Lord Jesus, you are to call a meeting of the church.* **5:5a** Or *so that he will die;* Greek reads *for the destruction of the flesh.* **5:5b** Greek *and the spirit.* **5:6-7** Greek *Don't you realize that even a little leaven spreads quickly through the whole batch of dough? [7]Purge out the old leaven so that you can be a new batch of dough, just as you are already unleavened.* **5:8a** Greek *not with old leaven.* **5:8b** Greek *but with unleavened [bread].* **5:11** Greek *a brother.* **5:13** Deut 17:7. **6:6** Greek *one brother.* **6:8** Greek *brothers.*

My Daily Worship

— *November 11* —

POWER IN THE BLOOD

1 CORINTHIANS 4:1—6:20

Christ, our Passover Lamb, has been sacrificed for us (5:7).

[i reflect]

The old Isaac Watts hymn, "Not All the Blood of Beasts," is a great worship song about Christ, our Passover Lamb. The first two stanzas go like this:

Not all the blood of beasts
On Jewish altars slain,
Could give the guilty conscience peace,
Or wash away the stain.
But Christ, the heavenly Lamb,
Takes all our sins away;
A sacrifice of nobler name
And richer blood than they.

Passover's origins are found at the end of the Jews' 400-year period of Egyptian bondage (about 1440 B.C., see Exodus 1:13). Under the leadership of Moses, the Jews watched God bring a series of ever-worsening plagues on their oppressors. Finally, each Hebrew family was instructed to take an unblemished male lamb, slaughter it, and sprinkle its blood above the doorframe of their home. They were then to eat a meal of roasted lamb and unleavened bread and prepare to depart. As judgment fell upon Egypt, those "under the blood" were spared. Death "passed over" their houses. But in every home not covered by the blood of a Passover lamb, the oldest son (and animal) died.

This is nothing less than a preview of the gospel—a sneak peek at the one who would come almost fifteen centuries later, and about whom John the Baptizer would proclaim, "Look! There is the Lamb of God who takes away the sin of the world!" (John 1:29)

Here then is one more reason to worship: Christ died on our behalf. He poured out his blood, his life, so that our lives might be spared. And if he died for you, is it asking too much today that you be willing to live for him?

[i pray]

Lord Jesus, thank you for your great sacrifice on my behalf. By your death, I find life. Grant me the strength to live purely and wholly for you this day. I want to be a living sacrifice for you.

[i respond]

Get an older hymnal and read some of the other classic hymns that speak of the blood of Christ: "There Is a Fountain," "Are You Washed in the Blood?", "At the Cross," "Nothing But the Blood." What do these old hymns add to your understanding of Christ's sacrifice for you?

greedy people, drunkards, abusers, and swindlers—none of these will have a share in the Kingdom of God. [11]There was a time when some of you were just like that, but now your sins have been washed away,* and you have been set apart for God. You have been made right with God because of what the Lord Jesus Christ and the Spirit of our God have done for you.

[12]You may say, "I am allowed to do anything." But I reply, "Not everything is good for you." And even though "I am allowed to do anything," I must not become a slave to anything. [13]You say, "Food is for the stomach, and the stomach is for food." This is true, though someday God will do away with both of them. But our bodies were not made for sexual immorality. They were made for the Lord, and the Lord cares about our bodies. [14]And God will raise our bodies from the dead by his marvelous power, just as he raised our Lord from the dead. [15]Don't you realize that your bodies are actually parts of Christ? Should a man take his body, which belongs to Christ, and join it to a prostitute? Never! [16]And don't you know that if a man joins himself to a prostitute, he becomes one body with her? For the Scriptures say, "The two are united into one."* [17]But the person who is joined to the Lord becomes one spirit with him.

[18]Run away from sexual sin! No other sin so clearly affects the body as this one does. For sexual immorality is a sin against your own body. [19]Or don't you know that your body is the temple of the Holy Spirit, who lives in you and was given to you by God? You do not belong to yourself, [20]for God bought you with a high price. So you must honor God with your body.

INSTRUCTION ON MARRIAGE

7 Now about the questions you asked in your letter. Yes, it is good to live a celibate life. [2]But because there is so much sexual immorality, each man should have his own wife, and each woman should have her own husband.

[3]The husband should not deprive his wife of sexual intimacy, which is her right as a married woman, nor should the wife deprive her husband. [4]The wife gives authority over her body to her husband, and the husband also gives authority over his body to his wife. [5]So do not deprive each other of sexual relations. The only exception to this rule would be the agreement of both husband and wife to refrain from sexual intimacy for a limited time, so they can give themselves more completely to prayer. Afterward they should come together again so that Satan won't be able to tempt them because of their lack of self-control. [6]This is only my suggestion. It's not meant to be an absolute rule. [7]I wish everyone could get along without marrying, just as I do. But we are not all the same. God gives some the gift of marriage, and to others he gives the gift of singleness.

[8]Now I say to those who aren't married and to widows—it's better to stay unmarried, just as I am. [9]But if they can't control themselves, they should go ahead and marry. It's better to marry than to burn with lust.

[10]Now, for those who are married I have a command that comes not from me, but from the Lord.* A wife must not leave her husband. [11]But if she does leave him, let her remain single or else go back to him. And the husband must not leave his wife.

[12]Now, I will speak to the rest of you, though I do not have a direct command from the Lord. If a Christian man* has a wife who is an unbeliever and she is willing to continue living with him, he must not leave her. [13]And if a Christian woman has a husband who is an unbeliever, and he is willing to continue living with her, she must not leave him. [14]For the Christian wife brings holiness to her marriage, and the Christian husband brings holiness to his marriage. Otherwise, your children would not have a godly influence, but now they are set apart for him. [15](But if the husband or wife who isn't a Christian insists on

6:11 Or *you have been cleansed.* 6:16 Gen 2:24. 7:10 See Matt 5:32; 19:9; Mark 10:11-12; Luke 16:18. 7:12 Greek *a brother.*

leaving, let them go. In such cases the Christian husband or wife is not required to stay with them, for God wants his children to live in peace.) [16]You wives must remember that your husbands might be converted because of you. And you husbands must remember that your wives might be converted because of you.

[17]You must accept whatever situation the Lord has put you in, and continue on as you were when God first called you. This is my rule for all the churches. [18]For instance, a man who was circumcised before he became a believer should not try to reverse it. And the man who was uncircumcised when he became a believer should not be circumcised now. [19]For it makes no difference whether or not a man has been circumcised. The important thing is to keep God's commandments.

[20]You should continue on as you were when God called you. [21]Are you a slave? Don't let that worry you—but if you get a chance to be free, take it. [22]And remember, if you were a slave when the Lord called you, the Lord has now set you free from the awful power of sin. And if you were free when the Lord called you, you are now a slave of Christ. [23]God purchased you at a high price. Don't be enslaved by the world.* [24]So, dear brothers and sisters,* whatever situation you were in when you became a believer, stay there in your new relationship with God.

[25]Now, about the young women who are not yet married. I do not have a command from the Lord for them. But the Lord in his kindness has given me wisdom that can be trusted, and I will share it with you. [26]Because of the present crisis,* I think it is best to remain just as you are. [27]If you have a wife, do not end the marriage. If you do not have a wife, do not get married. [28]But if you do get married, it is not a sin. And if a young woman gets married, it is not a sin. However, I am trying to spare you the extra problems that come with marriage.

[29]Now let me say this, dear brothers and sis-ters: The time that remains is very short, so husbands should not let marriage be their major concern. [30]Happiness or sadness or wealth should not keep anyone from doing God's work. [31]Those in frequent contact with the things of the world should make good use of them without becoming attached to them, for this world and all it contains will pass away. [32]In everything you do, I want you to be free from the concerns of this life. An unmarried man can spend his time doing the Lord's work and thinking how to please him. [33]But a married man can't do that so well. He has to think about his earthly responsibilities and how to please his wife. [34]His interests are divided. In the same way, a woman who is no longer married or has never been married can be more devoted to the Lord in body and in spirit, while the married woman must be concerned about her earthly responsibilities and how to please her husband.

[35]I am saying this for your benefit, not to place restrictions on you. I want you to do whatever will help you serve the Lord best, with as few distractions as possible. [36]But if a man thinks he ought to marry his fiancée because he has trouble controlling his passions and time is passing, it is all right; it is not a sin. Let them marry. [37]But if he has decided firmly not to marry and there is no urgency and he can control his passion, he does well not to marry. [38]So the person who marries does well, and the person who doesn't marry does even better.

[39]A wife is married to her husband as long as he lives. If her husband dies, she is free to marry whomever she wishes, but this must be a marriage acceptable to the Lord.* [40]But in my opinion it will be better for her if she doesn't marry again, and I think I am giving you counsel from God's Spirit when I say this.

FOOD SACRIFICED TO IDOLS

8 Now let's talk about food that has been sacrificed to idols. You think that every-

---

7:23 Greek *don't become slaves of people.* **7:24** Greek *brothers;* also in 7:29. **7:26** Or *pressures of life.* **7:39** Or *but only to a Christian;* Greek reads *but only in the Lord.*

one should agree with your perfect knowledge. While knowledge may make us feel important, it is love that really builds up the church. [2]Anyone who claims to know all the answers doesn't really know very much. [3]But the person who loves God is the one God knows and cares for.

[4]So now, what about it? Should we eat meat that has been sacrificed to idols? Well, we all know that an idol is not really a god and that there is only one God and no other. [5]According to some people, there are many so-called gods and many lords, both in heaven and on earth. [6]But we know that there is only one God, the Father, who created everything, and we exist for him. And there is only one Lord, Jesus Christ, through whom God made everything and through whom we have been given life.

[7]However, not all Christians realize this. Some are accustomed to thinking of idols as being real, so when they eat food that has been offered to idols, they think of it as the worship of real gods, and their weak consciences are violated. [8]It's true that we can't win God's approval by what we eat. We don't miss out on anything if we don't eat it, and we don't gain anything if we do. [9]But you must be careful with this freedom of yours. Do not cause a brother or sister with a weaker conscience to stumble.

[10]You see, this is what can happen: Weak Christians who think it is wrong to eat this food will see you eating in the temple of an idol. You know there's nothing wrong with it, but they will be encouraged to violate their conscience by eating food that has been dedicated to the idol. [11]So because of your superior knowledge, a weak Christian,* for whom Christ died, will be destroyed. [12]And you are sinning against Christ when you sin against other Christians* by encouraging them to do something they believe is wrong. [13]If what I eat is going to make another Christian sin, I will never eat meat again as long as I live—for

I don't want to make another Christian stumble.

PAUL GIVES UP HIS RIGHTS

9 Do I not have as much freedom as anyone else?* Am I not an apostle? Haven't I seen Jesus our Lord with my own eyes? Isn't it because of my hard work that you are in the Lord? [2]Even if others think I am not an apostle, I certainly am to you, for you are living proof that I am the Lord's apostle.

[3]This is my answer to those who question my authority as an apostle.* [4]Don't we have the right to live in your homes and share your meals? [5]Don't we have the right to bring a Christian wife* along with us as the other disciples and the Lord's brothers and Peter* do? [6]Or is it only Barnabas and I who have to work to support ourselves? [7]What soldier has to pay his own expenses? And have you ever heard of a farmer who harvests his crop and doesn't have the right to eat some of it? What shepherd takes care of a flock of sheep and isn't allowed to drink some of the milk? [8]And this isn't merely human opinion. Doesn't God's law say the same thing? [9]For the law of Moses says, "Do not keep an ox from eating as it treads out the grain."* Do you suppose God was thinking only about oxen when he said this? [10]Wasn't he also speaking to us? Of course he was. Just as farm workers who plow fields and thresh the grain expect a share of the harvest, Christian workers should be paid by those they serve.

[11]We have planted good spiritual seed among you. Is it too much to ask, in return, for mere food and clothing? [12]If you support others who preach to you, shouldn't we have an even greater right to be supported? Yet we have never used this right. We would rather put up with anything than put an obstacle in the way of the Good News about Christ.

[13]Don't you know that those who work in the Temple get their meals from the food brought to the Temple as offerings? And those

8:11 Greek brother; also in 8:13. 8:12 Greek brothers. 9:1 Greek Am I not free? 9:3 Greek those who examine me. 9:5a Greek a sister, a wife. 9:5b Greek Cephas. 9:9 Deut 25:4.

My Daily Worship

— November 12 —

KEEP YOUR EYES ON THE PRIZE

1 CORINTHIANS 7:1–9:27

Remember that in a race everyone runs, but only one person gets the prize.
You also must run in such a way that you will win (9:24).

[i reflect]

Those who watched the 1976 Summer Olympics may remember (with a little prompting) the exploits of a Japanese gymnast named Shun Fujimoto. In his quest for the men's all-around gold medal, the 26 year-old shattered his right knee in the floor exercises. Yet, amazingly, he continued to compete, even in what many regard as the most grueling event of all—the rings. Onlookers were stunned by his flawless routine and flabbergasted when he "nailed" a perfect triple somersault twist dismount, landing squarely on his devastated knee.

Interviewed later about his feat, Fujimoto said: "Yes, the pain shot through me like a knife. It brought tears to my eyes. But now I have a gold medal and the pain is gone."

It is this mindset that Christians need to embrace and live out—a dogged determination to suffer and persevere for the faith. An absolute refusal to cut corners or "cheat" in any way. A never-say-die commitment to go the distance for Christ, no matter what that requires. A disciplined and long-term pursuit of the highest prize of all—our Lord and Savior examining our lives (2 Corinthians 5:10) and saying, "Well done, my good and faithful servant. You have been faithful"(Matthew 25:21). As today's text teaches, we must all "run in such a way that [we] will win."

What do you see when you look at your life today? Laziness? Half-heartedness? A spiritual commitment that comes and goes? A tendency to throw in the towel at the first little bit of discomfort? A lifestyle of self-indulgence, or one of self-denial?

No athlete becomes a champion through ordinary effort. He or she takes home the top prize by putting forth extraordinary effort. And if they're willing to go to such lengths for a medal or trophy, for short-lived athletic glory, how much more committed should we be to receive eternal spiritual glory?

As you go through your day, imagine the errands, tasks, and work you do as "running the race" for Christ. Commit your best efforts to him as your act of worship.

[i pray]

Lord, you are worthy. You deserve all that I am, and all that I have. And yet far too often, my commitment fades and my devotion wanes. Forgive me. Fill me again with a passion for you and with the self-control I need to stay single-minded and focused on what really matters.

[i respond]

Spend some time thinking carefully about your life: your regular activities, your thoughts and dreams, your use of time and energy and money. What do these "bits of evidence" suggest about what you prize most, about the prize in life you are seeking?

who serve at the altar get a share of the sacrificial offerings. ¹⁴In the same way, the Lord gave orders that those who preach the Good News should be supported by those who benefit from it. ¹⁵Yet I have never used any of these rights. And I am not writing this to suggest that I would like to start now. In fact, I would rather die than lose my distinction of preaching without charge. ¹⁶For preaching the Good News is not something I can boast about. I am compelled by God to do it. How terrible for me if I didn't do it!

¹⁷If I were doing this of my own free will, then I would deserve payment. But God has chosen me and given me this sacred trust, and I have no choice. ¹⁸What then is my pay? It is the satisfaction I get from preaching the Good News without expense to anyone, never demanding my rights as a preacher.

¹⁹This means I am not bound to obey people just because they pay me, yet I have become a servant of everyone so that I can bring them to Christ. ²⁰When I am with the Jews, I become one of them so that I can bring them to Christ. When I am with those who follow the Jewish laws, I do the same, even though I am not subject to the law, so that I can bring them to Christ. ²¹When I am with the Gentiles who do not have the Jewish law,* I fit in with them as much as I can. In this way, I gain their confidence and bring them to Christ. But I do not discard the law of God; I obey the law of Christ.

²²When I am with those who are oppressed, I share their oppression so that I might bring them to Christ. Yes, I try to find common ground with everyone so that I might bring them to Christ. ²³I do all this to spread the Good News, and in doing so I enjoy its blessings.

²⁴Remember that in a race everyone runs, but only one person gets the prize. You also must run in such a way that you will win. ²⁵All athletes practice strict self-control. They do it to win a prize that will fade away, but we do it

for an eternal prize. ²⁶So I run straight to the goal with purpose in every step. I am not like a boxer who misses his punches.* ²⁷I discipline my body like an athlete, training it to do what it should. Otherwise, I fear that after preaching to others I myself might be disqualified.

WARNINGS AGAINST IDOLATRY

10 I don't want you to forget, dear brothers and sisters,* what happened to our ancestors in the wilderness long ago. God guided all of them by sending a cloud that moved along ahead of them, and he brought them all safely through the waters of the sea on dry ground. ²As followers of Moses, they were all baptized in the cloud and the sea. ³And all of them ate the same miraculous* food, ⁴and all of them drank the same miraculous water. For they all drank from the miraculous rock that traveled with them, and that rock was Christ. ⁵Yet after all this, God was not pleased with most of them, and he destroyed them in the wilderness.

⁶These events happened as a warning to us, so that we would not crave evil things as they did ⁷or worship idols as some of them did. For the Scriptures say, "The people celebrated with feasting and drinking, and they indulged themselves in pagan revelry."* ⁸And we must not engage in sexual immorality as some of them did, causing 23,000 of them to die in one day. ⁹Nor should we put Christ* to the test, as some of them did and then died from snakebites. ¹⁰And don't grumble as some of them did, for that is why God sent his angel of death to destroy them. ¹¹All these events happened to them as examples for us. They were written down to warn us, who live at the time when this age is drawing to a close.

¹²If you think you are standing strong, be careful, for you, too, may fall into the same sin. ¹³But remember that the temptations that come into your life are no different from what others experience. And God is faithful. He will keep the temptation from becoming so strong

---

9:21 Greek *those without the law.* **9:26** Or *I am not just shadowboxing.* **10:1** Greek *brothers.* **10:3** Greek *spiritual;* also in 10:4. **10:7** Exod 32:6. **10:9** Some manuscripts read *the Lord.*

My Daily Worship

— *November 13* —

LOVE CONQUERS ALL

1 CORINTHIANS 10:1–12:31

But remember that the temptations that come into your life are no different from what others experience. And God is faithful. He will keep the temptation from becoming so strong that you can't stand up against it. When you are tempted, he will show you a way out so that you will not give in to it (10:13).

[i reflect]

The 1983 hit movie *Mr. Mom* is about a husband who gets laid-off at work and becomes a stay-at-home Dad, while the mother of the family's young children reenters the workplace. It's a funny film that also contains a powerful lesson about temptation.

The scene comes at the end of the movie. Due to a whole series of misunderstandings, the stressed-out husband and wife are barely speaking. To make matters worse, both are being seduced—she by her annoying boss, he by a sultry neighbor. Jack, the husband, is clearly torn. Given the sad state of his marriage, the forbidden fruit is very tantalizing. The grass on the other side of the marital fence definitely looks greener. But after wrestling with his options he stares at his reflection in the bathroom mirror and says soberly, "You're not going to do anything, because, you, my friend, are in love with your wife." What a powerful truth! It is love, and nothing else, that gives us true power to resist temptation.

Notice that the Bible assures us that temptations *will* come. They are a fact of life in a fallen world. Notice also that we're not unique in the kinds of temptations we experience. Others wrestle with the same kinds of mess. Notice that the Scriptures pledge that God is faithful. He will never allow a temptation so strong that we are unable to resist. Notice finally that in every inducement to evil, God will show us a way out, a way of escape.

The best escape, as we've already noted, is love. When we love Christ above all else, when he is the greatest desire of our lives and the one we want most to please, it becomes so much easier to say no to sin.

Ask God to deepen your love for him, so that sin seems less tantalizing and more shocking and illogical. Turn temptations today into occasions for worship. See each refusal to sin as building a little altar to honor God.

[i pray]

Father, thank you for your faithfulness. Thank you for the absolute assurance that I do not have to yield to sin. No temptation is that strong. Increase my love for you until it is higher and deeper than the most alluring enticements of the evil one.

[i respond]

Memorize the words of 1 Corinthians 10:13 as another weapon in your battle against temptations. Spend time in thanksgiving that God is faithful, that he will keep the temptation from overwhelming you, and that he will show you a way out.

that you can't stand up against it. When you are tempted, he will show you a way out so that you will not give in to it.

[14]So, my dear friends, flee from the worship of idols. [15]You are reasonable people. Decide for yourselves if what I am about to say is true. [16]When we bless the cup at the Lord's Table, aren't we sharing in the benefits of the blood of Christ? And when we break the loaf of bread, aren't we sharing in the benefits of the body of Christ? [17]And we all eat from one loaf, showing that we are one body. [18]And think about the nation of Israel; all who eat the sacrifices are united by that act.

[19]What am I trying to say? Am I saying that the idols to whom the pagans bring sacrifices are real gods and that these sacrifices are of some value? [20]No, not at all. What I am saying is that these sacrifices are offered to demons, not to God. And I don't want any of you to be partners with demons. [21]You cannot drink from the cup of the Lord and from the cup of demons, too. You cannot eat at the Lord's Table and at the table of demons, too. [22]What? Do you dare to rouse the Lord's jealousy as Israel did? Do you think we are stronger than he is?

[23]You say, "I am allowed to do anything"— but not everything is helpful. You say, "I am allowed to do anything"—but not everything is beneficial. [24]Don't think only of your own good. Think of other Christians and what is best for them.

[25]Here's what you should do. You may eat any meat that is sold in the marketplace. Don't ask whether or not it was offered to idols, and then your conscience won't be bothered. [26]For "the earth is the Lord's, and everything in it."*

[27]If someone who isn't a Christian asks you home for dinner, go ahead; accept the invitation if you want to. Eat whatever is offered to you and don't ask any questions about it. Your conscience should not be bothered by this. [28]But suppose someone warns you that this meat has been offered to an idol. Don't eat it,

out of consideration for the conscience of the one who told you. [29]It might not be a matter of conscience for you, but it is for the other person.

Now, why should my freedom be limited by what someone else thinks? [30]If I can thank God for the food and enjoy it, why should I be condemned for eating it? [31]Whatever you eat or drink or whatever you do, you must do all for the glory of God. [32]Don't give offense to Jews or Gentiles or the church of God. [33]That is the plan I follow, too. I try to please everyone in everything I do. I don't just do what I like or what is best for me, but what is best for them so they may be saved.

11 And you should follow my example, just as I follow Christ's.

INSTRUCTIONS FOR PUBLIC WORSHIP

[2]I am so glad, dear friends, that you always keep me in your thoughts and you are following the Christian teaching I passed on to you. [3]But there is one thing I want you to know: A man is responsible to Christ, a woman is responsible to her husband, and Christ is responsible to God. [4]A man dishonors Christ* if he covers his head while praying or prophesying. [5]But a woman dishonors her husband* if she prays or prophesies without a covering on her head, for this is the same as shaving her head. [6]Yes, if she refuses to wear a head covering, she should cut off all her hair. And since it is shameful for a woman to have her hair cut or her head shaved, then she should wear a covering.* [7]A man should not wear anything on his head when worshiping, for man is God's glory, made in God's own image, but woman is the glory of man. [8]For the first man didn't come from woman, but the first woman came from man. [9]And man was not made for woman's benefit, but woman was made for man. [10]So a woman should wear a covering on her head as a sign of authority because the angels are watching.

10:26 Ps 24:1. **11:4** Greek *his head.* **11:5** Greek *her head.* **11:6** Or *then she should have long hair.*

¹¹But in relationships among the Lord's people, women are not independent of men, and men are not independent of women. ¹²For although the first woman came from man, all men have been born from women ever since, and everything comes from God.

¹³What do you think about this? Is it right for a woman to pray to God in public without covering her head? ¹⁴Isn't it obvious that it's disgraceful for a man to have long hair? ¹⁵And isn't it obvious that long hair is a woman's pride and joy? For it has been given to her as a covering. ¹⁶But if anyone wants to argue about this, all I can say is that we have no other custom than this, and all the churches of God feel the same way about it.

ORDER AT THE LORD'S SUPPER

¹⁷But now when I mention this next issue, I cannot praise you. For it sounds as if more harm than good is done when you meet together. ¹⁸First of all, I hear that there are divisions among you when you meet as a church, and to some extent I believe it. ¹⁹But, of course, there must be divisions among you so that those of you who are right will be recognized!

²⁰It's not the Lord's Supper you are concerned about when you come together. ²¹For I am told that some of you hurry to eat your own meal without sharing with others. As a result, some go hungry while others get drunk. ²²What? Is this really true? Don't you have your own homes for eating and drinking? Or do you really want to disgrace the church of God and shame the poor? What am I supposed to say about these things? Do you want me to praise you? Well, I certainly do not!

²³For this is what the Lord himself said, and I pass it on to you just as I received it. On the night when he was betrayed, the Lord Jesus took a loaf of bread, ²⁴and when he had given thanks, he broke it and said, "This is my body, which is given* for you. Do this in remem-brance of me." ²⁵In the same way, he took the cup of wine after supper, saying, "This cup is the new covenant between God and you, sealed by the shedding of my blood. Do this in remembrance of me as often as you drink it." ²⁶For every time you eat this bread and drink this cup, you are announcing the Lord's death until he comes again.

²⁷So if anyone eats this bread or drinks this cup of the Lord unworthily, that person is guilty of sinning against the body and the blood of the Lord. ²⁸That is why you should examine yourself before eating the bread and drinking from the cup. ²⁹For if you eat the bread or drink the cup unworthily, not honoring the body of Christ,* you are eating and drinking God's judgment upon yourself. ³⁰That is why many of you are weak and sick and some have even died.

³¹But if we examine ourselves, we will not be examined by God and judged in this way. ³²But when we are judged and disciplined by the Lord, we will not be condemned with the world. ³³So, dear brothers and sisters,* when you gather for the Lord's Supper, wait for each other. ³⁴If you are really hungry, eat at home so you won't bring judgment upon yourselves when you meet together.

I'll give you instructions about the other matters after I arrive.

SPIRITUAL GIFTS

12 And now, dear brothers and sisters,* I will write about the special abilities the Holy Spirit gives to each of us, for I must correct your misunderstandings about them. ²You know that when you were still pagans you were led astray and swept along in worshiping speechless idols. ³So I want you to know how to discern what is truly from God: No one speaking by the Spirit of God can curse Jesus, and no one is able to say, "Jesus is Lord," except by the Holy Spirit.

⁴Now there are different kinds of spiritual gifts, but it is the same Holy Spirit who is the

---

11:24 Some manuscripts read *broken*.   11:29 Greek *the body*; some manuscripts read *the Lord's body*.   11:33 Greek *brothers*.
12:1 Greek *brothers*.

source of them all. ⁵There are different kinds of service in the church, but it is the same Lord we are serving. ⁶There are different ways God works in our lives, but it is the same God who does the work through all of us. ⁷A spiritual gift is given to each of us as a means of helping the entire church.

⁸To one person the Spirit gives the ability to give wise advice; to another he gives the gift of special knowledge. ⁹The Spirit gives special faith to another, and to someone else he gives the power to heal the sick. ¹⁰He gives one person the power to perform miracles, and to another the ability to prophesy. He gives someone else the ability to know whether it is really the Spirit of God or another spirit that is speaking. Still another person is given the ability to speak in unknown languages,* and another is given the ability to interpret what is being said. ¹¹It is the one and only Holy Spirit who distributes these gifts. He alone decides which gift each person should have.

ONE BODY WITH MANY PARTS

¹²The human body has many parts, but the many parts make up only one body. So it is with the body of Christ. ¹³Some of us are Jews, some are Gentiles, some are slaves, and some are free. But we have all been baptized into Christ's body by one Spirit, and we have all received the same Spirit.*

¹⁴Yes, the body has many different parts, not just one part. ¹⁵If the foot says, "I am not a part of the body because I am not a hand," that does not make it any less a part of the body. ¹⁶And if the ear says, "I am not part of the body because I am only an ear and not an eye," would that make it any less a part of the body? ¹⁷Suppose the whole body were an eye—then how would you hear? Or if your whole body were just one big ear, how could you smell anything?

¹⁸But God made our bodies with many parts, and he has put each part just where he wants it. ¹⁹What a strange thing a body would be if it had only one part! ²⁰Yes, there are many parts, but only one body. ²¹The eye can never say to the hand, "I don't need you." The head can't say to the feet, "I don't need you."

²²In fact, some of the parts that seem weakest and least important are really the most necessary. ²³And the parts we regard as less honorable are those we clothe with the greatest care. So we carefully protect from the eyes of others those parts that should not be seen, ²⁴while other parts do not require this special care. So God has put the body together in such a way that extra honor and care are given to those parts that have less dignity. ²⁵This makes for harmony among the members, so that all the members care for each other equally. ²⁶If one part suffers, all the parts suffer with it, and if one part is honored, all the parts are glad.

²⁷Now all of you together are Christ's body, and each one of you is a separate and necessary part of it. ²⁸Here is a list of some of the members that God has placed in the body of Christ:

first are apostles,
second are prophets,
third are teachers,
then those who do miracles,
those who have the gift of healing,
those who can help others,
those who can get others to work together,
those who speak in unknown languages.

²⁹Is everyone an apostle? Of course not. Is everyone a prophet? No. Are all teachers? Does everyone have the power to do miracles? ³⁰Does everyone have the gift of healing? Of course not. Does God give all of us the ability to speak in unknown languages? Can everyone interpret unknown languages? No! ³¹And in any event, you should desire the most helpful gifts.

LOVE IS THE GREATEST

First, however, let me tell you about something else that is better than any of them!

12:10 Or *in tongues;* also in 12:28, 30. **12:13** Greek *we were all given one Spirit to drink.*

13

If I could speak in any language in heaven or on earth* but didn't love others, I would only be making meaningless noise like a loud gong or a clanging cymbal. ²If I had the gift of prophecy, and if I knew all the mysteries of the future and knew everything about everything, but didn't love others, what good would I be? And if I had the gift of faith so that I could speak to a mountain and make it move, without love I would be no good to anybody. ³If I gave everything I have to the poor and even sacrificed my body, I could boast about it;* but if I didn't love others, I would be of no value whatsoever.

⁴Love is patient and kind. Love is not jealous or boastful or proud ⁵or rude. Love does not demand its own way. Love is not irritable, and it keeps no record of when it has been wronged. ⁶It is never glad about injustice but rejoices whenever the truth wins out. ⁷Love never gives up, never loses faith, is always hopeful, and endures through every circumstance.

⁸Love will last forever, but prophecy and speaking in unknown languages* and special knowledge will all disappear. ⁹Now we know only a little, and even the gift of prophecy reveals little! ¹⁰But when the end comes, these special gifts will all disappear.

¹¹It's like this: When I was a child, I spoke and thought and reasoned as a child does. But when I grew up, I put away childish things. ¹²Now we see things imperfectly as in a poor mirror, but then we will see everything with perfect clarity.* All that I know now is partial and incomplete, but then I will know everything completely, just as God knows me now.

¹³There are three things that will endure—faith, hope, and love—and the greatest of these is love.

THE GIFTS OF TONGUES AND PROPHECY

14

Let love be your highest goal, but also desire the special abilities the Spirit gives, especially the gift of prophecy. ²For if your gift is the ability to speak in tongues,* you will be talking to God but not to people, since they won't be able to understand you. You will be speaking by the power of the Spirit, but it will all be mysterious. ³But one who prophesies is helping others grow in the Lord, encouraging and comforting them. ⁴A person who speaks in tongues is strengthened personally in the Lord, but one who speaks a word of prophecy strengthens the entire church.

⁵I wish you all had the gift of speaking in tongues, but even more I wish you were all able to prophesy. For prophecy is a greater and more useful gift than speaking in tongues, unless someone interprets what you are saying so that the whole church can get some good out of it.

⁶Dear brothers and sisters,* if I should come to you talking in an unknown language,* how would that help you? But if I bring you some revelation or some special knowledge or some prophecy or some teaching—that is what will help you. ⁷Even musical instruments like the flute or the harp, though they are lifeless, are examples of the need for speaking in plain language. For no one will recognize the melody unless the notes are played clearly. ⁸And if the bugler doesn't sound a clear call, how will the soldiers know they are being called to battle? ⁹And it's the same for you. If you talk to people in a language they don't understand, how will they know what you mean? You might as well be talking to an empty room.

¹⁰There are so many different languages in the world, and all are excellent for those who understand them, ¹¹but to me they mean nothing. I will not understand people who speak those languages, and they will not understand me. ¹²Since you are so eager to have spiritual gifts, ask God for those that will be of real help to the whole church.

13:1 Greek *in tongues of people and angels.* 13:3 Some manuscripts read *and even gave my body to be burned.* 13:8 Or *in tongues.* 13:12 Greek *see face to face.* 14:2 Or *in unknown languages;* also in 14:4, 5, 13, 14, 18, 22, 28, 39. 14:6a Greek *brothers;* also in 14:20, 26, 39. 14:6b Or *in tongues;* also in 14:19, 23, 26, 27.

¹³So anyone who has the gift of speaking in tongues should pray also for the gift of interpretation in order to tell people plainly what has been said. ¹⁴For if I pray in tongues, my spirit is praying, but I don't understand what I am saying.

¹⁵Well then, what shall I do? I will do both. I will pray in the spirit,* and I will pray in words I understand. I will sing in the spirit, and I will sing in words I understand. ¹⁶For if you praise God only in the spirit, how can those who don't understand you praise God along with you? How can they join you in giving thanks when they don't understand what you are saying? ¹⁷You will be giving thanks very nicely, no doubt, but it doesn't help the other people present.

¹⁸I thank God that I speak in tongues more than all of you. ¹⁹But in a church meeting I would much rather speak five understandable words that will help others than ten thousand words in an unknown language.

²⁰Dear brothers and sisters, don't be childish in your understanding of these things. Be innocent as babies when it comes to evil, but be mature and wise in understanding matters of this kind. ²¹It is written in the Scriptures,*

"I will speak to my own people
   through unknown languages
   and through the lips of foreigners.
But even then, they will not listen to me,"*
   says the Lord.

²²So you see that speaking in tongues is a sign, not for believers, but for unbelievers; prophecy, however, is for the benefit of believers, not unbelievers. ²³Even so, if unbelievers or people who don't understand these things come into your meeting and hear everyone talking in an unknown language, they will think you are crazy. ²⁴But if all of you are prophesying, and unbelievers or people who don't understand these things come into your meeting, they will be convicted of sin, and

they will be condemned by what you say. ²⁵As they listen, their secret thoughts will be laid bare, and they will fall down on their knees and worship God, declaring, "God is really here among you."

A CALL TO ORDERLY WORSHIP

²⁶Well, my brothers and sisters, let's summarize what I am saying. When you meet, one will sing, another will teach, another will tell some special revelation God has given, one will speak in an unknown language, while another will interpret what is said. But everything that is done must be useful to all and build them up in the Lord. ²⁷No more than two or three should speak in an unknown language. They must speak one at a time, and someone must be ready to interpret what they are saying. ²⁸But if no one is present who can interpret, they must be silent in your church meeting and speak in tongues to God privately.

²⁹Let two or three prophesy, and let the others evaluate what is said. ³⁰But if someone is prophesying and another person receives a revelation from the Lord, the one who is speaking must stop. ³¹In this way, all who prophesy will have a turn to speak, one after the other, so that everyone will learn and be encouraged. ³²Remember that people who prophesy are in control of their spirit and can wait their turn. ³³For God is not a God of disorder but of peace, as in all the other churches.*

³⁴Women should be silent during the church meetings. It is not proper for them to speak. They should be submissive, just as the law says. ³⁵If they have any questions to ask, let them ask their husbands at home, for it is improper for women to speak in church meetings.*

³⁶Do you think that the knowledge of God's word begins and ends with you Corinthians? Well, you are mistaken! ³⁷If you claim to be a prophet or think you are very spiritual, you should recognize that what I am saying is a com-

---

14:15 Or *in the Spirit;* also in 14:15b, 16.   14:21a Greek *in the law.*   14:21b Isa 28:11-12.   14:33 The phrase *as in all the other churches* could be joined to the beginning of 14:34.   14:35 Some manuscripts place verses 34-35 after 14:40.

My Daily Worship

— November 14 —

ALL YOU NEED IS LOVE
1 CORINTHIANS 13:1–16:24

Love never gives up, never loses faith, is always hopeful, and endures
through every circumstance. Love will last forever (13:7–8).

[i reflect]

The final verse of the grand old hymn "The Love of God" says:

Could we with ink the ocean fill, and were the skies of parchment made,
Were every stalk on earth a quill, and every man a scribe by trade,
To write the love of God above would drain the ocean dry.
Nor could the scroll contain the whole, though stretched from sky to sky.

Here is a brilliant and beautiful combination of theology and poetry! God's love is wondrous. As today's passage teaches, God's love never gives up, never loses faith. His love endures. No wonder the apostle Paul prayed for his Ephesian brothers and sisters in the faith: "May your roots go down deep into the soil of God's marvelous love. And may you have the power to understand, as all God's people should, how wide, how long, how high, and how deep his love really is. May you experience the love of Christ, though it is so great you will never fully understand it" (Ephesians 3:17–19).

God's stunning love alone has the power to change us. No strings. No conditions. No getting our acts together first. He doesn't love us *because* of anything. He doesn't love us *if* we measure up to certain standards. He just sets his perfect affection on us—or, we could say, he sets us permanently in the warmth of his absolute care and favor. Max Lucado writes in his book *A Love Worth Giving*, "God loves you simply because he has chosen to do so. He loves you when you don't feel lovely. He loves you when no one else loves you. Others may abandon you, divorce you, and ignore you, but God will love you. Always. No matter what."

No matter what. It is this immense and endless love that liberates us from our prisons of fear and self-protection, with the result being that we find a new capacity to love others. Spend some time meditating on God's great love for you. Then, in the overflow of that love, share it with someone.

[i pray]

Lord Jesus, thank you for your amazing love. I do not understand it, and I certainly
do not deserve it. But I welcome it, and ask you to transform me as
I come to experience your affection more and more.

[i respond]

It's an old exercise, but a good one. Read 1 Corinthians 13 and substitute your name every place you see the word "love." Is this accurate? Where do you fall short? How can living like this be a lifestyle of worship?

mand from the Lord himself. [38]But if you do not recognize this, you will not be recognized.*

[39]So, dear brothers and sisters, be eager to prophesy, and don't forbid speaking in tongues. [40]But be sure that everything is done properly and in order.

THE RESURRECTION OF CHRIST

15 Now let me remind you, dear brothers and sisters,* of the Good News I preached to you before. You welcomed it then and still do now, for your faith is built on this wonderful message. [2]And it is this Good News that saves you if you firmly believe it—unless, of course, you believed something that was never true in the first place.

[3]I passed on to you what was most important and what had also been passed on to me—that Christ died for our sins, just as the Scriptures said. [4]He was buried, and he was raised from the dead on the third day, as the Scriptures said. [5]He was seen by Peter* and then by the twelve apostles. [6]After that, he was seen by more than five hundred of his followers* at one time, most of whom are still alive, though some have died by now. [7]Then he was seen by James and later by all the apostles. [8]Last of all, I saw him, too, long after the others, as though I had been born at the wrong time. [9]For I am the least of all the apostles, and I am not worthy to be called an apostle after the way I persecuted the church of God.

[10]But whatever I am now, it is all because God poured out his special favor on me—and not without results. For I have worked harder than all the other apostles, yet it was not I but God who was working through me by his grace. [11]So it makes no difference whether I preach or they preach. The important thing is that you believed what we preached to you.

THE RESURRECTION OF THE DEAD

[12]But tell me this—since we preach that Christ rose from the dead, why are some of you say-ing there will be no resurrection of the dead? [13]For if there is no resurrection of the dead, then Christ has not been raised either. [14]And if Christ was not raised, then all our preaching is useless, and your trust in God is useless. [15]And we apostles would all be lying about God, for we have said that God raised Christ from the grave, but that can't be true if there is no resurrection of the dead. [16]If there is no resurrection of the dead, then Christ has not been raised. [17]And if Christ has not been raised, then your faith is useless, and you are still under condemnation for your sins. [18]In that case, all who have died believing in Christ have perished! [19]And if we have hope in Christ only for this life, we are the most miserable people in the world.

[20]But the fact is that Christ has been raised from the dead. He has become the first of a great harvest of those who will be raised to life again.

[21]So you see, just as death came into the world through a man, Adam, now the resurrection from the dead has begun through another man, Christ. [22]Everyone dies because all of us are related to Adam, the first man. But all who are related to Christ, the other man, will be given new life. [23]But there is an order to this resurrection: Christ was raised first; then when Christ comes back, all his people will be raised.

[24]After that the end will come, when he will turn the Kingdom over to God the Father, having put down all enemies of every kind.* [25]For Christ must reign until he humbles all his enemies beneath his feet. [26]And the last enemy to be destroyed is death. [27]For the Scriptures say, "God has given him authority over all things."* (Of course, when it says "authority over all things," it does not include God himself, who gave Christ his authority.) [28]Then, when he has conquered all things, the Son will present himself to God, so that God, who gave his Son authority over all things, will be utterly supreme over everything everywhere.

14:38 Some manuscripts read *If you are ignorant of this, stay in your ignorance.*   **15:1** Greek *brothers;* also in 15:31, 50, 58.
15:5 Greek *Cephas.*   **15:6** Greek *the brothers.*   **15:24** Greek *every ruler and every authority and power.*   **15:27** Ps 8:6.

²⁹If the dead will not be raised, then what point is there in people being baptized for those who are dead? Why do it unless the dead will someday rise again?

³⁰And why should we ourselves be continually risking our lives, facing death hour by hour? ³¹For I swear, dear brothers and sisters, I face death daily. This is as certain as my pride in what the Lord Jesus Christ has done in you. ³²And what value was there in fighting wild beasts—those men of Ephesus*—if there will be no resurrection from the dead? If there is no resurrection,

> *We are always in the presence of God. We never leave church. There is never a nonsacred moment!*
>
> MAX LUCADO

"Let's feast and get drunk, for tomorrow we die!"*

³³Don't be fooled by those who say such things, for "bad company corrupts good character." ³⁴Come to your senses and stop sinning. For to your shame I say that some of you don't even know God.

THE RESURRECTION BODY

³⁵But someone may ask, "How will the dead be raised? What kind of bodies will they have?" ³⁶What a foolish question! When you put a seed into the ground, it doesn't grow into a plant unless it dies first. ³⁷And what you put in the ground is not the plant that will grow, but only a dry little seed of wheat or whatever it is you are planting. ³⁸Then God gives it a new body—just the kind he wants it to have. A different kind of plant grows from each kind of

seed. ³⁹And just as there are different kinds of seeds and plants, so also there are different kinds of flesh—whether of humans, animals, birds, or fish.

⁴⁰There are bodies in the heavens, and there are bodies on earth. The glory of the heavenly bodies is different from the beauty of the earthly bodies. ⁴¹The sun has one kind of glory, while the moon and stars each have another kind. And even the stars differ from each other in their beauty and brightness.

⁴²It is the same way for the resurrection of the dead. Our earthly bodies, which die and decay, will be different when they are resurrected, for they will never die. ⁴³Our bodies now disappoint us, but when they are raised, they will be full of glory. They are weak now, but when they are raised, they will be full of power. ⁴⁴They are natural human bodies now, but when they are raised, they will be spiritual bodies. For just as there are natural bodies, so also there are spiritual bodies.

⁴⁵The Scriptures tell us, "The first man, Adam, became a living person."* But the last Adam—that is, Christ—is a life-giving Spirit. ⁴⁶What came first was the natural body, then the spiritual body comes later. ⁴⁷Adam, the first man, was made from the dust of the earth, while Christ, the second man, came from heaven. ⁴⁸Every human being has an earthly body just like Adam's, but our heavenly bodies will be just like Christ's. ⁴⁹Just as we are now like Adam, the man of the earth, so we will someday be like Christ, the man from heaven.

⁵⁰What I am saying, dear brothers and sisters, is that flesh and blood cannot inherit the Kingdom of God. These perishable bodies of ours are not able to live forever.

⁵¹But let me tell you a wonderful secret God has revealed to us. Not all of us will die, but we will all be transformed. ⁵²It will happen in a moment, in the blinking of an eye, when the last trumpet is blown. For when the trumpet sounds, the Christians who have died* will be raised with transformed bodies. And then we

---

15:32a Greek *fighting wild beasts in Ephesus.* 15:32b Isa 22:13. 15:45 Gen 2:7. 15:52 Greek *the dead.*

who are living will be transformed so that we will never die. ⁵³For our perishable earthly bodies must be transformed into heavenly bodies that will never die.

⁵⁴When this happens—when our perishable earthly bodies have been transformed into heavenly bodies that will never die—then at last the Scriptures will come true:

"Death is swallowed up in victory.*
⁵⁵ O death, where is your victory?
O death, where is your sting?"*

⁵⁶For sin is the sting that results in death, and the law gives sin its power. ⁵⁷How we thank God, who gives us victory over sin and death through Jesus Christ our Lord!

⁵⁸So, my dear brothers and sisters, be strong and steady, always enthusiastic about the Lord's work, for you know that nothing you do for the Lord is ever useless.

THE COLLECTION FOR JERUSALEM

16 Now about the money being collected for the Christians in Jerusalem: You should follow the same procedures I gave to the churches in Galatia. ²On every Lord's Day,* each of you should put aside some amount of money in relation to what you have earned and save it for this offering. Don't wait until I get there and then try to collect it all at once. ³When I come I will write letters of recommendation for the messengers you choose to deliver your gift to Jerusalem. ⁴And if it seems appropriate for me also to go along, then we can travel together.

PAUL'S FINAL INSTRUCTIONS

⁵I am coming to visit you after I have been to Macedonia, for I am planning to travel through Macedonia. ⁶It could be that I will stay awhile with you, perhaps all winter, and then you can send me on my way to the next

destination. ⁷This time I don't want to make just a short visit and then go right on. I want to come and stay awhile, if the Lord will let me. ⁸In the meantime, I will be staying here at Ephesus until the Festival of Pentecost, ⁹for there is a wide-open door for a great work here, and many people are responding. But there are many who oppose me.

¹⁰When Timothy comes, treat him with respect. He is doing the Lord's work, just as I am. ¹¹Don't let anyone despise him. Send him on his way with your blessings when he returns to me. I am looking forward to seeing him soon, along with the other brothers.

¹²Now about our brother Apollos—I urged him to join the other brothers when they visit you, but he was not willing to come right now. He will be seeing you later, when the time is right.

¹³Be on guard. Stand true to what you believe. Be courageous. Be strong. ¹⁴And everything you do must be done with love.

¹⁵You know that Stephanas and his household were the first to become Christians in Greece,* and they are spending their lives in service to other Christians. I urge you, dear brothers and sisters,* ¹⁶to respect them fully and others like them who serve with such real devotion. ¹⁷I am so glad that Stephanas, Fortunatus, and Achaicus have come here. They have been making up for the help you weren't here to give me. ¹⁸They have been a wonderful encouragement to me, as they have been to you, too. You must give proper honor to all who serve so well.

PAUL'S FINAL GREETINGS

¹⁹The churches here in the province of Asia* greet you heartily in the Lord, along with Aquila and Priscilla and all the others who gather in their home for church meetings.

15:54 Isa 25:8. 15:55 Hos 13:14. 16:2 Greek *every first day of the week*. 16:15a Greek *were the firstfruits in Achaia,* the southern region of the Greek peninsula. 16:15b Greek *brothers;* also in 16:20. 16:19 *Asia* was a Roman province in what is now western Turkey.

²⁰All the brothers and sisters here have asked me to greet you for them. Greet each other in Christian love.*

²¹Here is my greeting, which I write with my own hand—PAUL.

²²If anyone does not love the Lord, that person is cursed. Our Lord, come!"

²³May the grace of the Lord Jesus be with you.

²⁴My love to all of you in Christ Jesus.*

16:20 Greek with a sacred kiss. 16:22 From Aramaic, Marana tha. 16:24 Some manuscripts add Amen.

1523

2 Corinthians

For our present troubles are quite small and won't last very long.

Yet they produce for us an immeasurably great glory that will last forever! (4:17).

Worship Is Worth It

Why devote your life to loving and serving Christ? History shows that those who take God seriously end up either misunderstood or mocked. The Bible promises that if we become wild-eyed worshipers, at best we'll be avoided; at worst, attacked. Who needs the hassle? Isn't it a waste to give everything you've got to advance the invisible kingdom of a King you've never seen?

Not if you ask the apostle Paul. Not when you understand 2 Corinthians.

Second Corinthians is the great missionary's most personal letter. It was written to an immature church that had been questioning the apostle's motives and his authority—in short his whole ministry. The result is a remarkable peek into the heart of a man whose one aim in life was to please Jesus (5:9).

Paul's experience as a servant of Christ was anything but easy. Consider his testimony:

"We were crushed and completely overwhelmed, and we thought we would never live through it" (1:8).

"We get knocked down, but we get up again and keep going" (4:9).

"We serve God whether people honor us or despise us, whether they slander us or praise us" (6:8).

"I have lived with weariness and pain and sleepless nights. Often I have been hungry and thirsty and have gone without food" (11:27).

Yet through each trial Paul continued to honor God. As he said, "Since I know it is all for Christ's good, I am quite content with my weaknesses and with insults, hardships, persecutions, and calamities" (12:10).

The message of 2 Corinthians is that we can live like Paul did. We are new creatures (5:17) who will one day stand before Christ (5:10). If we continue to give of ourselves, our time, our efforts, and our resources to God, we will bring him the glory he deserves, and we will share in that glory. Clearly, a life of worship is infinitely worth it!

Worship Moments

- Recognizing who we are leads to true worship. Paul said, "We are the temple of the living God" (6:16).

- Worship in the early church involved dedication and humility. "Their first action was to dedicate themselves to the Lord and to us for whatever directions God might give them" (8:5).

- The early Christians worshiped and glorified God through their generous giving and obedience to the gospel (9:13).

GREETINGS FROM PAUL

1 This letter is from Paul, appointed by God to be an apostle of Christ Jesus, and from our dear brother Timothy.

We are writing to God's church in Corinth and to all the Christians throughout Greece.* ²May God our Father and the Lord Jesus Christ give you his grace and peace.

GOD OFFERS COMFORT TO ALL

³All praise to the God and Father of our Lord Jesus Christ. He is the source* of every mercy and the God who comforts us. ⁴He comforts us in all our troubles so that we can comfort others. When others are troubled, we will be able to give them the same comfort God has given us. ⁵You can be sure that the more we suffer for Christ, the more God will shower us with his comfort through Christ. ⁶So when we are weighed down with troubles, it is for your benefit and salvation! For when God comforts us, it is so that we, in turn, can be an encouragement to you. Then you can patiently endure the same things we suffer. ⁷We are confident that as you share in suffering, you will also share God's comfort.

⁸I think you ought to know, dear brothers and sisters,* about the trouble we went through in the province of Asia. We were crushed and completely overwhelmed, and we thought we would never live through it. ⁹In fact, we expected to die. But as a result, we learned not to rely on ourselves, but on God who can raise the dead. ¹⁰And he did deliver us from mortal danger. And we are confident that he will continue to deliver us. ¹¹He will rescue us because you are helping by praying for us. As a result, many will give thanks to God because so many people's prayers for our safety have been answered.

PAUL'S CHANGE OF PLANS

¹²We can say with confidence and a clear conscience that we have been honest* and sincere in all our dealings. We have depended on God's grace, not on our own earthly wisdom. That is how we have acted toward everyone, and especially toward you. ¹³My letters have been straightforward, and there is nothing written between the lines and nothing you can't understand. I hope someday you will fully understand us, ¹⁴even if you don't fully understand us now. Then on the day when our Lord Jesus comes back again, you will be proud of us in the same way we are proud of you.

¹⁵Since I was so sure of your understanding and trust, I wanted to give you a double blessing. ¹⁶I wanted to stop and see you on my way to Macedonia and again on my return trip. Then you could send me on my way to Judea.

¹⁷You may be asking why I changed my plan. Hadn't I made up my mind yet? Or am I like people of the world who say yes when they really mean no? ¹⁸As surely as God is true, I am not that sort of person. My yes means yes ¹⁹because Jesus Christ, the Son of God, never wavers between yes and no. He is the one whom Timothy, Silas,* and I preached to you, and he is the divine Yes—God's affirmation. ²⁰For all of God's promises have been fulfilled in him. That is why we say "Amen" when we give glory to God through Christ. ²¹It is God who gives us, along with you, the ability to stand firm for Christ.* He has commissioned us, ²²and he has identified us as his own by placing the Holy Spirit in our hearts as the first installment of everything he will give us.

²³Now I call upon God as my witness that I am telling the truth. The reason I didn't return to Corinth was to spare you from a severe rebuke. ²⁴But that does not mean we want to tell you exactly how to put your faith into practice.* We want to work together with you so you will be full of joy as you stand firm in your faith.

2 So I said to myself, "No, I won't do it. I won't make them unhappy with another painful visit." ²For if I cause you pain and

1:1 Greek *Achaia*, the southern region of the Greek peninsula. 1:3 Greek *the Father*. 1:8 Greek *brothers*. 1:12 Some manuscripts read *holy*. 1:19 Greek *Silvanus*. 1:21 Or *who has identified us and you as genuine Christians*. 1:24 Greek *want to lord it over your faith*.

make you sad, who is going to make me glad? ³That is why I wrote as I did in my last letter, so that when I do come, I will not be made sad by the very ones who ought to give me the greatest joy. Surely you know that my happiness depends on your happiness. ⁴How painful it was to write that letter! Heartbroken, I cried over it. I didn't want to hurt you, but I wanted you to know how very much I love you.

FORGIVENESS FOR THE SINNER

⁵I am not overstating it when I say that the man who caused all the trouble hurt your entire church more than he hurt me. ⁶He was punished enough when most of you were united in your judgment against him. ⁷Now it is time to forgive him and comfort him. Otherwise he may become so discouraged that he won't be able to recover. ⁸Now show him that you still love him.

⁹I wrote to you as I did to find out how far you would go in obeying me. ¹⁰When you forgive this man, I forgive him, too. And when I forgive him (for whatever is to be forgiven), I do so with Christ's authority for your benefit, ¹¹so that Satan will not outsmart us. For we are very familiar with his evil schemes.

MINISTERS OF THE NEW COVENANT

¹²Well, when I came to the city of Troas to preach the Good News of Christ, the Lord gave me tremendous opportunities. ¹³But I couldn't rest because my dear brother Titus hadn't yet arrived with a report from you. So I said good-bye and went on to Macedonia to find him.

¹⁴But thanks be to God, who made us his captives and leads us along in Christ's triumphal procession. Now wherever we go he uses us to tell others about the Lord and to spread the Good News like a sweet perfume. ¹⁵Our lives are a fragrance presented by Christ to God. But this fragrance is perceived differently by those being saved and by those per-

ishing. ¹⁶To those who are perishing we are a fearful smell of death and doom. But to those who are being saved we are a life-giving perfume. And who is adequate for such a task as this? ¹⁷You see, we are not like those hucksters—and there are many of them—who preach just to make money. We preach God's message with sincerity and with Christ's authority. And we know that the God who sent us is watching us.

3 Are we beginning again to tell you how good we are? Some people need to bring letters of recommendation with them or ask you to write letters of recommendation for them. ²But the only letter of recommendation we need is you yourselves! Your lives are a letter written in our* hearts, and everyone can read it and recognize our good work among you. ³Clearly, you are a letter from Christ prepared by us. It is written not with pen and ink, but with the Spirit of the living God. It is carved not on stone, but on human hearts.

⁴We are confident of all this because of our great trust in God through Christ. ⁵It is not that we think we can do anything of lasting value by ourselves. Our only power and success come from God. ⁶He is the one who has enabled us to represent his new covenant. This is a covenant, not of written laws, but of the Spirit. The old way ends in death; in the new way, the Holy Spirit gives life.

THE GLORY OF THE NEW COVENANT

⁷That old system of law etched in stone led to death, yet it began with such glory that the people of Israel could not bear to look at Moses' face. For his face shone with the glory of God, even though the brightness was already fading away. ⁸Shouldn't we expect far greater glory when the Holy Spirit is giving life? ⁹If the old covenant, which brings condemnation, was glorious, how much more glorious is the new covenant, which makes us right with God! ¹⁰In fact, that first glory was

3:2 Some manuscripts read *your*.

My Daily Worship

— *November 15* —

THE GOD OF ALL COMFORT

2 CORINTHIANS 1:1–3:18

All praise to the God and Father of our Lord Jesus Christ. He is the source
of every mercy and the God who comforts us (1:3).

[i reflect]

As human beings, we like our comforts. Consider these comments given to the staff of the Bridger Wilderness Area:

- "Too many bugs and leeches and spiders and spider webs. Please spray the wilderness to rid the areas of these pests."
- "Chair lifts need to be in some places so that we can get to wonderful views without having to hike to them."
- "Escalators would help on steep uphill sections."

When Scripture speaks of comfort, it is not referring to the satisfaction we find in plush surroundings. Rather, today's passage teaches us about the true nature of comfort—the sort of solace and consolation that can only come from God himself.

Like the loving parent that he is, God models comfort for us, so that we in turn can reach out to others with the compassion of Christ. He never promises to remove all difficulties from our lives, but rather to give us the consolation and encouragement we need to endure them.

Human comfort often comes in the form of a hug or the offer of a hand to hold. Scripture teaches us that God is our refuge, and that his everlasting arms are under us (Deuteronomy 33:27). When we "hold" others in their times of sorrow through words of solace or acts of kindness, God redeems our troubles by allowing them to be used for his purposes.

Karen Mains, author of *Comforting One Another*, puts it this way: "When we hold [others] in their hour of deepest need, we lift them up. Like a bruised and frightened bird cupped in a woman's hand and then lofted into the air for flight, . . . we offer them up to God. When we are held by those who understand the sacramentality of this embrace, we in our turn are offered up to him. And those who witness lifting up are also lifted."

Worship flows freely from the heart that has received divine comfort. How has God embraced you in comfort? Extend that to a family or friend who is in need of encouragement today.

[i pray]

Lord, teach me to comfort others in the same way that you have sent solace my way in the past.
I want to learn to extend your arms of comfort to a hurting world.

[i respond]

Take a few moments to list the ways you have personally received consolation. What was most helpful—phone calls, notes, practical acts of mercy? Share that particular means with someone you know who is hurting.

not glorious at all compared with the overwhelming glory of the new covenant. [11]So if the old covenant, which has been set aside, was full of glory, then the new covenant, which remains forever, has far greater glory.

[12]Since this new covenant gives us such confidence, we can be very bold. [13]We are not like Moses, who put a veil over his face so the people of Israel would not see the glory fading away. [14]But the people's minds were hardened, and even to this day whenever the old covenant is being read, a veil covers their minds so they cannot understand the truth. And this veil can be removed only by believing in Christ. [15]Yes, even today when they read Moses' writings, their hearts are covered with that veil, and they do not understand.

[16]But whenever anyone turns to the Lord, then the veil is taken away. [17]Now, the Lord is the Spirit, and wherever the Spirit of the Lord is, he gives freedom. [18]And all of us have had that veil removed so that we can be mirrors that brightly reflect* the glory of the Lord. And as the Spirit of the Lord works within us, we become more and more like him and reflect his glory even more.

TREASURE IN PERISHABLE CONTAINERS

4 And so, since God in his mercy has given us this wonderful ministry, we never give up. [2]We reject all shameful and underhanded methods. We do not try to trick anyone, and we do not distort the word of God. We tell the truth before God, and all who are honest know that.

[3]If the Good News we preach is veiled from anyone, it is a sign that they are perishing. [4]Satan, the god of this evil world, has blinded the minds of those who don't believe, so they are unable to see the glorious light of the Good News that is shining upon them. They don't understand the message we preach about the glory of Christ, who is the exact likeness of God.

[5]We don't go around preaching about ourselves; we preach Christ Jesus, the Lord. All we say about ourselves is that we are your servants because of what Jesus has done for us. [6]For God, who said, "Let there be light in the darkness," has made us understand that this light is the brightness of the glory of God that is seen in the face of Jesus Christ.

[7]But this precious treasure—this light and power that now shine within us—is held in perishable containers, that is, in our weak bodies.* So everyone can see that our glorious power is from God and is not our own.

[8]We are pressed on every side by troubles, but we are not crushed and broken. We are perplexed, but we don't give up and quit. [9]We are hunted down, but God never abandons us. We get knocked down, but we get up again and keep going. [10]Through suffering, these bodies of ours constantly share in the death of Jesus so that the life of Jesus may also be seen in our bodies.

[11]Yes, we live under constant danger of death because we serve Jesus, so that the life of Jesus will be obvious in our dying bodies. [12]So we live in the face of death, but it has resulted in eternal life for you.

[13]But we continue to preach because we have the same kind of faith the psalmist had when he said, "I believed in God, and so I speak."* [14]We know that the same God who raised our Lord Jesus will also raise us with Jesus and present us to himself along with you. [15]All of these things are for your benefit. And as God's grace brings more and more people to Christ, there will be great thanksgiving, and God will receive more and more glory.

[16]That is why we never give up. Though our bodies are dying, our spirits are* being renewed every day. [17]For our present troubles are quite small and won't last very long. Yet they produce for us an immeasurably great glory that will last forever! [18]So we don't look at the troubles we can see right now; rather,

---

3:18 Or *so that we can see in a mirror.*   **4:7** Greek *But we have this treasure in earthen vessels.*   **4:13** Ps 116:10.   **4:16** Greek *our inner being is.*

My Daily Worship

— *November 16* —

NEVER GIVE UP OR GIVE IN
2 CORINTHIANS 4:1–7:16

And so, since God in his mercy has given us this wonderful ministry, we never give up (4:1).

[i reflect]

The story is told of a famous speech Winston Churchill once delivered at Harrow, his former prep school. Churchill is often quoted as having stated, "Never give up. Never give up. Never give up!"

What Churchill actually said was this: "Never give in, never give in, never, never, never, never—in nothing, great or small, large or petty—never give in, except to convictions of honor and good sense."

Giving up or giving in—is there a difference? Let's face it, sometimes it feels like the same thing. We try to serve others only to have our motives misunderstood or our methods questioned. We volunteer months of free time only to have our efforts go unnoticed and unappreciated. We suggest needed change only to face so much resistance that our resolve crumbles and we give in to the naysayers.

Ministry is tough, and at times we honestly wonder whether it is worth it.

That's when the words of the apostle Paul serve to strengthen our spirit just as Churchill stiffened the spines of the young men at Harrow. "We never give up," urges Paul, "since God in his mercy has given us this wonderful ministry."

Do you notice the descriptor used here? This is a *wonderful* ministry, Paul reminds us—one that you are privileged to have because it was given to you by God himself. It is a magnificent extension of God's mercy that he allows us to minister to others in the name of his own son.

What about the work God has given you to do? Are you tempted to give up in discouragement or give in to doubt? Take heart from the Scriptures and set aside any thought of quitting. Remember that "this light and power that now shine within us . . . is from God and is not our own" (4:7).

Allow God's light and power to shine through you today in the attitude and way you serve others. Rejoice in the *wonderful* ministry to which he has called you.

[i pray]

Lord, thank you for this wonderful ministry you have called me to in my home,
my neighborhood, at church, and at work. Help me to see that wherever
you have placed me, I am to persevere for your honor and glory.

[i respond]

Where has God called you to minister? Think of all the places in which you serve others. Evaluate your "discouragement" level in each one. Consider one or two ideas you can adopt that will help you persevere.

we look forward to what we have not yet seen. For the troubles we see will soon be over, but the joys to come will last forever.

NEW BODIES

5 For we know that when this earthly tent we live in is taken down—when we die and leave these bodies—we will have a home in heaven, an eternal body made for us by God himself and not by human hands. [2]We grow weary in our present bodies, and we long for the day when we will put on our heavenly bodies like new clothing. [3]For we will not be spirits without bodies, but we will put on new heavenly bodies. [4]Our dying bodies make us groan and sigh, but it's not that we want to die and have no bodies at all. We want to slip into our new bodies so that these dying bodies will be swallowed up by everlasting life. [5]God himself has prepared us for this, and as a guarantee he has given us his Holy Spirit.

[6]So we are always confident, even though we know that as long as we live in these bodies we are not at home with the Lord. [7]That is why we live by believing and not by seeing. [8]Yes, we are fully confident, and we would rather be away from these bodies, for then we will be at home with the Lord. [9]So our aim is to please him always, whether we are here in this body or away from this body. [10]For we must all stand before Christ to be judged. We will each receive whatever we deserve for the good or evil we have done in our bodies.

WE ARE GOD'S AMBASSADORS

[11]It is because we know this solemn fear of the Lord that we work so hard to persuade others. God knows we are sincere, and I hope you know this, too. [12]Are we trying to pat ourselves on the back again? No, we are giving you a reason to be proud of us, so you can answer those who brag about having a spectacular ministry rather than having a sincere heart before God. [13]If it seems that we are crazy, it is to bring glory to God. And if we are in our right minds, it is for your benefit. [14]Whatever we do, it is because Christ's love controls us.* Since we believe that Christ died for everyone, we also believe that we have all died to the old life we used to live.* [15]He died for everyone so that those who receive his new life will no longer live to please themselves. Instead, they will live to please Christ, who died and was raised for them.

[16]So we have stopped evaluating others by what the world thinks about them. Once I mistakenly thought of Christ that way, as though he were merely a human being. How differently I think about him now! [17]What this means is that those who become Christians become new persons. They are not the same anymore, for the old life is gone. A new life has begun!

[18]All this newness of life is from God, who brought us back to himself through what Christ did. And God has given us the task of reconciling people to him. [19]For God was in Christ, reconciling the world to himself, no longer counting people's sins against them. This is the wonderful message he has given us to tell others. [20]We are Christ's ambassadors, and God is using us to speak to you. We urge you, as though Christ himself were here pleading with you, "Be reconciled to God!" [21]For God made Christ, who never sinned, to be the offering for our sin, so that we could be made right with God through Christ.

6 As God's partners,* we beg you not to reject this marvelous message of God's great kindness. [2]For God says,

"At just the right time, I heard you.
    On the day of salvation, I helped you."*

Indeed, God is ready to help you right now. Today is the day of salvation.

PAUL'S HARDSHIPS

[3]We try to live in such a way that no one will be hindered from finding the Lord by the way

---

5:14a Or *urges us on.*   **5:14b** Greek *Since one died on behalf of all, then all died.*   **6:1** Or *As we work together.*   **6:2** Isa 49:8.

Words of Worship

COUNSELOR

Counselor—Greek *pa-ra-kle-tos* "helper, intercessor."

Christian worship is about Christ. When we come to the Father in prayer and personal adoration, we come through Jesus Christ. We come in thanksgiving for what God has done for us, reconciling us to himself through the death of his Son (2 Corinthians 5:18–19). We come to God through Christ because "the Son reflects God's own glory, and everything about him reflects God exactly. He sustains the universe by the mighty power of his command" (Hebrews 1:3).

But we don't have Jesus with us in the flesh. He's with us now through the Holy Spirit, who reminds us of what Jesus taught about the God we worship. Jesus promised, "I will send you the Counselor—the Spirit of truth. He will come to you from the Father and will tell you all about me" (John 15:26). The Greek word for "counselor" refers to someone we can call upon to advise us and intercede for us. Worship celebrates Christ because he has asked for this Counselor to be with us, to help us remember who Jesus is. And, he promised, this Counselor will never leave us (John 14:16).

we act, and so no one can find fault with our ministry. ⁴In everything we do we try to show that we are true ministers of God. We patiently endure troubles and hardships and calamities of every kind. ⁵We have been beaten, been put in jail, faced angry mobs, worked to exhaustion, endured sleepless nights, and gone without food. ⁶We have proved ourselves by our purity, our under-standing, our patience, our kindness, our sincere love, and the power of the Holy Spirit.* ⁷We have faithfully preached the truth. God's power has been working in us. We have righteousness as our weapon, both to attack and to defend ourselves. ⁸We serve God whether people honor us or despise us, whether they slander us or praise us. We are honest, but they call us impostors. ⁹We are well known, but we are treated as unknown. We live close to death, but here we are, still alive. We have been beaten within an inch of our lives. ¹⁰Our hearts ache, but we always have joy. We are poor, but we give spiritual riches to others. We own nothing, and yet we have everything.

¹¹Oh, dear Corinthian friends! We have spoken honestly with you. Our hearts are open to you. ¹²If there is a problem between us, it is not because of a lack of love on our part, but because you have withheld your love from us. ¹³I am talking now as I would to my own children. Open your hearts to us!

THE TEMPLE OF THE LIVING GOD

¹⁴Don't team up with those who are unbelievers. How can goodness be a partner with wicked-ness? How can light live with darkness? ¹⁵What harmony can there be between Christ and the Devil*? How can a believer be a partner with an unbeliever? ¹⁶And what union can there be between God's temple and idols? For we are the temple of the living God. As God said:

"I will live in them
　　and walk among them.
I will be their God,
　　and they will be my people.*
¹⁷ Therefore, come out from them
　　and separate yourselves from them, says
　　　the Lord.
Don't touch their filthy things,
　　and I will welcome you.*
¹⁸ And I will be your Father,
　　and you will be my sons and daughters,
　　　says the Lord Almighty.*"

6:6 Or *the holiness of spirit.*　**6:15** Greek *and Beliar.*　**6:16** Lev 26:12; Ezek 37:27.　**6:17** Isa 52:11; Ezek 20:34.　**6:18** 2 Sam 7:14.

7 Because we have these promises, dear friends, let us cleanse ourselves from everything that can defile our body or spirit. And let us work toward complete purity because we fear God.

PAUL'S JOY AT THE CHURCH'S REPENTANCE

² Please open your hearts to us. We have not done wrong to anyone. We have not led anyone astray. We have not taken advantage of anyone. ³ I'm not saying this to condemn you, for I said before that you are in our hearts forever. We live or die together with you. ⁴ I have the highest confidence in you, and my pride in you is great. You have greatly encouraged me; you have made me happy despite all our troubles.

⁵ When we arrived in Macedonia there was no rest for us. Outside there was conflict from every direction, and inside there was fear. ⁶ But God, who encourages those who are discouraged, encouraged us by the arrival of Titus. ⁷ His presence was a joy, but so was the news he brought of the encouragement he received from you. When he told me how much you were looking forward to my visit, and how sorry you were about what had happened, and how loyal your love is for me, I was filled with joy!

⁸ I am no longer sorry that I sent that letter to you, though I was sorry for a time, for I know that it was painful to you for a little while. ⁹ Now I am glad I sent it, not because it hurt you, but because the pain caused you to have remorse and change your ways. It was the kind of sorrow God wants his people to have, so you were not harmed by us in any way. ¹⁰ For God can use sorrow in our lives to help us turn away from sin and seek salvation. We will never regret that kind of sorrow. But sorrow without repentance is the kind that results in death.

¹¹ Just see what this godly sorrow produced in you! Such earnestness, such concern to clear yourselves, such indignation, such alarm, such longing to see me, such zeal, and such a readiness to punish the wrongdoer. You showed that you have done everything you could to make things right. ¹² My purpose was not to write about who did the wrong or who was wronged. I wrote to you so that in the sight of God you could show how much you really do care for us. ¹³ We have been encouraged by this.

In addition to our own encouragement, we were especially delighted to see how happy Titus was at the way you welcomed him and set his mind at ease. ¹⁴ I had told him how proud I was of you—and you didn't disappoint me. I have always told you the truth, and now my boasting to Titus has also proved true! ¹⁵ Now he cares for you more than ever when he remembers the way you listened to him and welcomed him with such respect and deep concern. ¹⁶ I am very happy now because I have complete confidence in you.

A CALL TO GENEROUS GIVING

8 Now I want to tell you, dear brothers and sisters,* what God in his kindness has done for the churches in Macedonia. ² Though they have been going through much trouble and hard times, their wonderful joy and deep poverty have overflowed in rich generosity. ³ For I can testify that they gave not only what they could afford but far more. And they did it of their own free will. ⁴ They begged us again and again for the gracious privilege of sharing in the gift for the Christians in Jerusalem. ⁵ Best of all, they went beyond our highest hopes, for their first action was to dedicate themselves to the Lord and to us for whatever directions God might give them.

⁶ So we have urged Titus, who encouraged your giving in the first place, to return to you and encourage you to complete your share in this ministry of giving. ⁷ Since you excel in so many ways—you have so much faith, such gifted speakers, such knowledge, such enthusiasm, and such love for us*—now I want you

---

8:1 Greek *brothers.*   **8:7** Some manuscripts read *love from us to you.*

> The worship most acceptable
> to God comes from a thankful
> and cheerful heart.
>
> PLUTARCH

to excel also in this gracious ministry of giving. [8]I am not saying you must do it, even though the other churches are eager to do it. This is one way to prove your love is real.

[9]You know how full of love and kindness our Lord Jesus Christ was. Though he was very rich, yet for your sakes he became poor, so that by his poverty he could make you rich.

[10]I suggest that you finish what you started a year ago, for you were the first to propose this idea, and you were the first to begin doing something about it. [11]Now you should carry this project through to completion just as enthusiastically as you began it. Give whatever you can according to what you have. [12]If you are really eager to give, it isn't important how much you are able to give. God wants you to give what you have, not what you don't have. [13]Of course, I don't mean you should give so much that you suffer from having too little. I only mean that there should be some equality. [14]Right now you have plenty and can help them. Then at some other time they can share with you when you need it. In this way, everyone's needs will be met. [15]Do you remember what the Scriptures say about this? "Those who gathered a lot had nothing left over, and those who gathered only a little had enough."*

TITUS AND HIS COMPANIONS

[16]I am thankful to God that he has given Titus the same enthusiasm for you that I have. [17]He welcomed our request that he visit you again. In fact, he himself was eager to go and see you. [18]We are also sending another brother with Titus. He is highly praised in all the churches as a preacher of the Good News. [19]He was appointed by the churches to accompany us as we take the offering to Jerusalem*—a service that glorifies the Lord and shows our eagerness to help. [20]By traveling together we will guard against any suspicion, for we are anxious that no one should find fault with the way we are handling this generous gift. [21]We are careful to be honorable before the Lord, but we also want everyone else to know we are honorable.

[22]And we are also sending with them another brother who has been thoroughly tested and has shown how earnest he is on many occasions. He is now even more enthusiastic because of his increased confidence in you. [23]If anyone asks about Titus, say that he is my partner who works with me to help you. And these brothers are representatives* of the churches. They are splendid examples of those who bring glory to Christ. [24]So show them your love, and prove to all the churches that our boasting about you is justified.

THE COLLECTION FOR
CHRISTIANS IN JERUSALEM

9 I really don't need to write to you about this gift for the Christians in Jerusalem.* [2]For I know how eager you are to help, and I have been boasting to our friends in Macedonia that you Christians in Greece* were ready to send an offering a year ago. In fact, it was your enthusiasm that stirred up many of them to begin helping. [3]But I am sending these brothers just to be sure that you really are ready, as I told them you would be, with your money all collected. I don't want it to turn out that I was wrong in my boasting about you. [4]I would be humiliated—and so would you—if some Macedonian Christians came with me, only to find that you still

8:15 Exod 16:18. 8:19 See 1 Cor 16:3-4. 8:23 Greek *apostles*. 9:1 Greek *about the offering for the saints*. 9:2 Greek *Achaia*, the southern region of the Greek peninsula.

weren't ready after all I had told them! ⁵So I thought I should send these brothers ahead of me to make sure the gift you promised is ready. But I want it to be a willing gift, not one given under pressure.

⁶Remember this—a farmer who plants only a few seeds will get a small crop. But the one who plants generously will get a generous crop. ⁷You must each make up your own mind as to how much you should give. Don't give reluctantly or in response to pressure. For God loves the person who gives cheerfully. ⁸And God will generously provide all you need. Then you will always have everything you need and plenty left over to share with others. ⁹As the Scriptures say,

"Godly people give generously to the poor.
    Their good deeds will never be
        forgotten."*

¹⁰For God is the one who gives seed to the farmer and then bread to eat. In the same way, he will give you many opportunities to do good, and he will produce a great harvest of generosity* in you.

¹¹Yes, you will be enriched so that you can give even more generously. And when we take your gifts to those who need them, they will break out in thanksgiving to God. ¹²So two good things will happen—the needs of the Christians in Jerusalem will be met, and they will joyfully express their thanksgiving to God. ¹³You will be glorifying God through your generous gifts. For your generosity to them will prove that you are obedient to the Good News of Christ. ¹⁴And they will pray for you with deep affection because of the wonderful grace of God shown through you.

¹⁵Thank God for his Son—a gift too wonderful for words!*

PAUL DEFENDS HIS AUTHORITY

10 Now I, Paul, plead with you. I plead with the gentleness and kindness that Christ himself would use, even though some of you say I am bold in my letters but timid in person. ²I hope it won't be necessary, but when I come I may have to be very bold with those who think we act from purely human motives. ³We are human, but we don't wage war with human plans and methods. ⁴We use God's mighty weapons, not mere worldly weapons, to knock down the Devil's strongholds. ⁵With these weapons we break down every proud argument that keeps people from knowing God. With these weapons we conquer their rebellious ideas, and we teach them to obey Christ. ⁶And we will punish those who remained disobedient after the rest of you became loyal and obedient.

⁷The trouble with you is that you make your decisions on the basis of appearance.* You must recognize that we belong to Christ just as much as those who proudly declare that they belong to Christ. ⁸I may seem to be boasting too much about the authority given to us by the Lord. But this authority is to build you up, not to tear you down. And I will not be put to shame by having my work among you destroyed.

⁹Now this is not just an attempt to frighten you by my letters. ¹⁰For some say, "Don't worry about Paul. His letters are demanding and forceful, but in person he is weak, and his speeches are really bad!" ¹¹The ones who say this must realize that we will be just as demanding and forceful in person as we are in our letters.

¹²Oh, don't worry; I wouldn't dare say that I am as wonderful as these other men who tell you how important they are! But they are only comparing themselves with each other, and measuring themselves by themselves. What foolishness!

¹³But we will not boast of authority we do not have. Our goal is to stay within the boundaries of God's plan for us, and this plan includes our working there with you. ¹⁴We are not going too far when we claim authority over you, for we were the first to travel all the

9:9 Ps 112:9.   9:10 Greek *righteousness*.   9:15 Greek *Thank God for his indescribable gift*.   10:7 Or *Look at the obvious facts*.

My Daily Worship

— *November 17* —

A HARVEST OF GENEROSITY
2 CORINTHIANS 8:1–10:18

For God is the one who gives seed to the farmer and then bread to eat.
In the same way, he will give you many opportunities to do good,
and he will produce a great harvest of generosity in you (9:10).

[i reflect]

John Wesley practiced what he preached when it came to giving. Wesley limited his expenditures by not buying the kinds of things generally considered essential for a man in his station of life. In 1776 the English tax commissioners inspected his return and wrote back, "[We] cannot doubt but you have plate for which you have hitherto neglected to make entry."

They assumed that a man of his prominence certainly had silver dinnerware in his house, and they wanted him to pay the proper tax on it. Wesley wrote back, "I have two silver spoons at London and two at Bristol. This is all the plate I have at present, and I shall not buy any more while so many round me want bread."

Today's passage teaches that God himself is the source and supply of every blessing we have, including the material ones. We are not to keep what we are given for ourselves alone, but rather we're to use our resources wisely so that a "harvest of generosity" will be produced from which we can bless others.

When we donate to charity or write a check to support our local church, we are not simply fulfilling a religious obligation. God does not desire our sacrifices but rather our hearts. According to Paul's second letter to the Corinthian church, giving is not only an act of worship itself but also results in worship. Those who benefit from our giving "will break out in thanksgiving to God."

Oswald Chambers put it this way: "Worship is giving God the best that he has given you. Be careful what you do with the best you have. Whenever you get a blessing from God, give it back to him as a love gift. Take time to meditate before God and offer the blessing back to him in a deliberate act of worship."

Offer your blessings back to God as a love gift today.

[i pray]

Lord, too often I view the giving of my tithes and offerings as an obligation rather than an
act of love. Help me to glorify you through giving generously out of a thankful heart.

[i respond]

Have a "pre-thanksgiving" dinner this week. Set aside one meal where you as a family can name the many blessings that God has given to you, and then "break out in thanksgiving." Use songs, psalms, or prayers to express your gratitude.

way to you with the Good News of Christ. [15]Nor do we claim credit for the work someone else has done. Instead, we hope that your faith will grow and that our work among you will be greatly enlarged. [16]Then we will be able to go and preach the Good News in other places that are far beyond you, where no one else is working. Then there will be no question about being in someone else's territory. [17]As the Scriptures say,

"The person who wishes to boast
     should boast only of what the Lord has
     done."*

[18]When people boast about themselves, it doesn't count for much. But when the Lord commends someone, that's different!

PAUL AND THE FALSE APOSTLES

11 I hope you will be patient with me as I keep on talking like a fool. Please bear with me. [2]I am jealous for you with the jealousy of God himself. For I promised you as a pure bride* to one husband, Christ. [3]But I fear that somehow you will be led away from your pure and simple devotion to Christ, just as Eve was deceived by the serpent. [4]You seem to believe whatever anyone tells you, even if they preach about a different Jesus than the one we preach, or a different Spirit than the one you received, or a different kind of gospel than the one you believed. [5]But I don't think I am inferior to these "super apostles." [6]I may not be a trained speaker, but I know what I am talking about. I think you realize this by now, for we have proved it again and again.

[7]Did I do wrong when I humbled myself and honored you by preaching God's Good News to you without expecting anything in return? [8]I "robbed" other churches by accepting their contributions so I could serve you at no cost. [9]And when I was with you and didn't have enough to live on, I did not ask you to help me. For the brothers who came from Macedonia brought me another gift. I have never yet asked you for any support, and I never will. [10]As surely as the truth of Christ is in me, I will never stop boasting about this all over Greece.* [11]Why? Because I don't love you? God knows I do.

[12]But I will continue doing this to cut the ground out from under the feet of those who boast that their work is just like ours. [13]These people are false apostles. They have fooled you by disguising themselves as apostles of Christ. [14]But I am not surprised! Even Satan can disguise himself as an angel of light. [15]So it is no wonder his servants can also do it by pretending to be godly ministers. In the end they will get every bit of punishment their wicked deeds deserve.

PAUL'S MANY TRIALS

[16]Once again, don't think that I have lost my wits to talk like this. But even if you do, listen to me, as you would to a foolish person, while I also boast a little. [17]Such bragging is not something the Lord wants, but I am acting like a fool. [18]And since others boast about their human achievements, I will, too. [19]After all, you, who think you are so wise, enjoy listening to fools! [20]You put up with it when they make you their slaves, take everything you have, take advantage of you, put on airs, and slap you in the face. [21]I'm ashamed to say that we were not strong enough to do that!

But whatever they dare to boast about—I'm talking like a fool again—I can boast about it, too. [22]They say they are Hebrews, do they? So am I. And they say they are Israelites? So am I. And they are descendants of Abraham? So am I. [23]They say they serve Christ? I know I sound like a madman, but I have served him far more! I have worked harder, been put in jail more often, been whipped times without number, and faced death again and again. [24]Five different times the Jews gave me thirty-nine lashes. [25]Three times I was beaten with rods. Once I was stoned. Three times I was shipwrecked. Once I spent a whole night and

10:17 Jer 9:24. 11:2 Greek *a virgin.* 11:10 Greek *Achaia.*

My Daily Worship

— *November 18* —

THANKFUL FOR THE THORNS

2 CORINTHIANS 11:1–13:13

I have received wonderful revelations from God. But to keep me from
getting puffed up, I was given a thorn in my flesh, a messenger from
Satan to torment me and keep me from getting proud (12:7).

[i reflect]

Max Lucado wrote, "God never promises to remove us from our struggles. He does promise, however, to change the way we look at them." Paul's famous "thorn in the flesh" provides a perfect illustration for this principle.

Many have speculated as to the nature of Paul's thorn. It could have been a chronic physical condition, such as failing eyesight, or even a person or group of people who were opposed to his ministry (see 2 Corinthians 11:32–33). Whether Paul was dealing with an illness that was a physical disability or a person who became a psychological liability, it seems clear that his focus was not on what his thorn was, but rather on why God had allowed it.

How can it be possible to not only accept our human frailties but also literally to praise God because of them? Rather than bemoan his plight, Paul instead was able to "boast" about his weaknesses because he recognized that his condition provided a showcase for God's divine power to be displayed through his life.

Do you have a thorn or two in your garden of relationships, or perhaps a physical weakness that never seems to improve? Take your cue from Paul and respond by thanking God for your thorn. In Ephesians 5:20, Paul puts it very plainly: " Always give thanks for everything to God the Father in the name of our Lord Jesus Christ."

Bible teacher Beth Moore has said that whether or not God chooses to remove a thorn depends on the point. He may choose to demonstrate his supremacy—that he can do it, or to demonstrate his sufficiency—that he can get you through it. Regardless of how God answers our plea for help, our choice is clear: we can praise him for the grace that allows his power to work through us.

Thank him today for your "thorn."

[i pray]

Lord, you know what my thorn is, and you know that I have pleaded with you to
take it from me. Regardless of how you choose to answer my prayer,
I thank you for your presence and power in my life.

[i respond]

Jot down a few of the thorns you are experiencing now, as well as some you have experienced in the past. Next to each one, write either "supremacy" or "sufficiency," depending on how God has worked in each circumstance. Praise him for his power—then and now.

a day adrift at sea. [26]I have traveled many weary miles. I have faced danger from flooded rivers and from robbers. I have faced danger from my own people, the Jews, as well as from the Gentiles. I have faced danger in the cities, in the deserts, and on the stormy seas. And I have faced danger from men who claim to be Christians but are not.* [27]I have lived with weariness and pain and sleepless nights. Often I have been hungry and thirsty and have gone without food. Often I have shivered with cold, without enough clothing to keep me warm.

[28]Then, besides all this, I have the daily burden of how the churches are getting along. [29]Who is weak without my feeling that weakness? Who is led astray, and I do not burn with anger?

[30]If I must boast, I would rather boast about the things that show how weak I am. [31]God, the Father of our Lord Jesus, who is to be praised forever, knows I tell the truth. [32]When I was in Damascus, the governor under King Aretas kept guards at the city gates to catch me. [33]But I was lowered in a basket through a window in the city wall, and that's how I got away!

PAUL'S VISION AND HIS THORN IN THE FLESH

12 This boasting is all so foolish, but let me go on. Let me tell about the visions and revelations I received from the Lord. [2]I* was caught up into the third heaven fourteen years ago. [3]Whether my body was there or just my spirit, I don't know; only God knows. [4]But I do know that I* was caught up into paradise and heard things so astounding that they cannot be told. [5]That experience is something worth boasting about, but I am not going to do it. I am going to boast only about my weaknesses. [6]I have plenty to boast about and would be no fool in doing it, because I would be telling the truth. But I won't do it. I don't want anyone to think more highly of me than

what they can actually see in my life and my message, [7]even though I have received wonderful revelations from God. But to keep me from getting puffed up, I was given a thorn in my flesh, a messenger from Satan to torment me and keep me from getting proud.

[8]Three different times I begged the Lord to take it away. [9]Each time he said, "My gracious favor is all you need. My power works best in your weakness." So now I am glad to boast about my weaknesses, so that the power of Christ may work through me. [10]Since I know it is all for Christ's good, I am quite content with my weaknesses and with insults, hardships, persecutions, and calamities. For when I am weak, then I am strong.

PAUL'S CONCERN FOR THE CORINTHIANS

[11]You have made me act like a fool—boasting like this. You ought to be writing commendations for me, for I am not at all inferior to these "super apostles," even though I am nothing at all. [12]When I was with you, I certainly gave you every proof that I am truly an apostle, sent to you by God himself. For I patiently did many signs and wonders and miracles among you. [13]The only thing I didn't do, which I do in the other churches, was to become a burden to you. Please forgive me for this wrong!

[14]Now I am coming to you for the third time, and I will not be a burden to you. I don't want what you have; I want you. And anyway, little children don't pay for their parents' food. It's the other way around; parents supply food for their children. [15]I will gladly spend myself and all I have for your spiritual good, even though it seems that the more I love you, the less you love me.

[16]Some of you admit I was not a burden to you. But they still think I was sneaky and took advantage of you by trickery. [17]But how? Did any of the men I sent to you take advantage of you? [18]When I urged Titus to visit you and sent our other brother with him, did Titus

11:26 Greek *from false brothers.* 12:2 Greek *I know a man in Christ who.* 12:4 Greek *he.*

take advantage of you? No, of course not! For we both have the same Spirit and walk in each other's steps, doing things the same way.

[19]Perhaps you think we are saying all this just to defend ourselves. That isn't it at all. We tell you this as Christ's servants, and we know that God is listening. Everything we do, dear friends, is for your benefit. [20]For I am afraid that when I come to visit you I won't like what I find, and then you won't like my response. I am afraid that I will find quarreling, jealousy, outbursts of anger, selfishness, backstabbing, gossip, conceit, and disorderly behavior. [21]Yes, I am afraid that when I come, God will humble me again because of you. And I will have to grieve because many of you who sinned earlier have not repented of your impurity, sexual immorality, and eagerness for lustful pleasure.

PAUL'S FINAL ADVICE

13 This is the third time I am coming to visit you. As the Scriptures say, "The facts of every case must be established by the testimony of two or three witnesses."* [2]I have already warned those who had been sinning when I was there on my second visit. Now I again warn them and all others, just as I did before, that this next time I will not spare them.

[3]I will give you all the proof you want that Christ speaks through me. Christ is not weak in his dealings with you; he is a mighty power among you. [4]Although he died on the cross in weakness, he now lives by the mighty power of God. We, too, are weak, but we live in him and have God's power—the power we use in dealing with you.

[5]Examine yourselves to see if your faith is really genuine. Test yourselves. If you cannot tell that Jesus Christ is among you,* it means you have failed the test. [6]I hope you recognize that we have passed the test and are approved by God.

[7]We pray to God that you will not do anything wrong. We pray this, not to show that our ministry to you has been successful, but because we want you to do right even if we ourselves seem to have failed. [8]Our responsibility is never to oppose the truth, but to stand for the truth at all times. [9]We are glad to be weak, if you are really strong. What we pray for is your restoration to maturity.

[10]I am writing this to you before I come, hoping that I won't need to deal harshly with you when I do come. For I want to use the authority the Lord has given me to build you up, not to tear you down.

PAUL'S FINAL GREETINGS

[11]Dear brothers and sisters,* I close my letter with these last words: Rejoice. Change your ways. Encourage each other. Live in harmony and peace. Then the God of love and peace will be with you.

[12]Greet each other in Christian love.* All the Christians here send you their greetings.

[13]May the grace of our Lord Jesus Christ, the love of God, and the fellowship of the Holy Spirit be with you all.*

13:1 Deut 19:15. 13:5 Or *in you.* 13:11 Greek *Brothers.* 13:12 Greek *with a sacred kiss.* 13:12-13 Some English versions divide verse 12 into verses 12 and 13, and then verse 13 becomes verse 14.

Galatians

Because you Gentiles have become his children, God has sent the Spirit of his Son into your hearts, and now you can call God your dear Father (4:6).

The Gift of Worship

Not many people, given a chance for a life-saving operation, would make the bad choice to die slowly in excruciating pain. Paul's appeal to the Christians in Galatia is something akin to shaking sense into a person whose choices are clearly heading in the wrong direction. It's taking by the shoulders a blindfolded weirdo walking onto the track in the middle of the Indianapolis 500 and tearing off his blindfold. "Don't be so clueless!" the rescuer warns.

Paul's advice to the Galatians, and to us, comes almost as a no-brainer. Christ has set us free. Why retreat into slavery? Christ has made us a new creation. Why continue with the old? There's no future there at all. What sensible person would give up the best in favor of nothing?

Paul might well have written: Look at how your worship is going, you idiots! (Okay, a nicer term, miscreants). You are sick with worry when you come to worship, and sicker when you leave. Your focus on the law only reminds you how far short you fall of God's expectations. Your future is miserable, your life is sullen, your spirit subdued. Hel-lo-o!

Christ alone satisfies all the requirements of the law. There is nothing more we can do. By grace, because of his great love, God includes us in the family. Status, background, gender, or wealth—these matter nothing. Your acceptance of God's gift—new life in Christ—is all God sees. That should make worship something to be happy about.

Paul offers no advice on how to worship in this short letter. But he gives very good reasons why we can worship joyfully. Our freedom was promised to Abraham, secured by Christ's obedience, and preached by Paul and the apostles. Accept no substitutes, he urges. Instead, celebrate this wonderful gift. Show the world how important your new life is by expressing the fruits of the Spirit. In worship, let your gift of freedom ring.

Worship Moments

- Worship celebrates spiritual life that no longer requires maximum self-effort. Life is God's gift, anchored in Christ's resurrection, guaranteed by God's love (2:20).

- Worship celebrates freedom from God's judgment. Under the law, sin requires justice; because God himself in Christ has satisfied that justice, the law no longer presents a barrier to fellowship with God (3:10–13).

- Worship celebrates the family of faith, a family whose most important mark is belonging to Christ. In Christ, all nations meet, all people rejoice together (3:26–28).

GREETINGS FROM PAUL

1 This letter is from Paul, an apostle. I was not appointed by any group or by human authority. My call is from Jesus Christ himself and from God the Father, who raised Jesus from the dead.

²All the brothers and sisters* here join me in sending greetings to the churches of Galatia.

³May grace and peace be yours from God our Father and from the Lord Jesus Christ. ⁴He died for our sins, just as God our Father planned, in order to rescue us from this evil world in which we live. ⁵That is why all glory belongs to God through all the ages of eternity. Amen.

THERE IS ONLY ONE GOOD NEWS

⁶I am shocked that you are turning away so soon from God, who in his love and mercy called you to share the eternal life he gives through Christ. You are already following a different way ⁷that pretends to be the Good News but is not the Good News at all. You are being fooled by those who twist and change the truth concerning Christ.

⁸Let God's curse fall on anyone, including myself, who preaches any other message than the one we told you about. Even if an angel comes from heaven and preaches any other message, let him be forever cursed. ⁹I will say it again: If anyone preaches any other gospel than the one you welcomed, let God's curse fall upon that person.

¹⁰Obviously, I'm not trying to be a people pleaser! No, I am trying to please God. If I were still trying to please people, I would not be Christ's servant.

PAUL'S MESSAGE COMES FROM CHRIST

¹¹Dear brothers and sisters, I solemnly assure you that the Good News of salvation which I preach is not based on mere human reasoning or logic. ¹²For my message came by a direct revelation from Jesus Christ himself. No one else taught me.

¹³You know what I was like when I followed the Jewish religion—how I violently persecuted the Christians.* I did my best to get rid of them. ¹⁴I was one of the most religious Jews of my own age, and I tried as hard as possible to follow all the old traditions of my religion.

¹⁵But then something happened! For it pleased God in his kindness to choose me and call me, even before I was born! What undeserved mercy! ¹⁶Then he revealed his Son to me* so that I could proclaim the Good News about Jesus to the Gentiles. When all this happened to me, I did not rush out to consult with anyone else; ¹⁷nor did I go up to Jerusalem to consult with those who were apostles before I was. No, I went away into Arabia and later returned to the city of Damascus. ¹⁸It was not until three years later that I finally went to Jerusalem for a visit with Peter* and stayed there with him for fifteen days. ¹⁹And the only other apostle I met at that time was James, our Lord's brother. ²⁰You must believe what I am saying, for I declare before God that I am not lying. ²¹Then after this visit, I went north into the provinces of Syria and Cilicia. ²²And still the Christians in the churches in Judea didn't know me personally. ²³All they knew was that people were saying, "The one who used to persecute us now preaches the very faith he tried to destroy!" ²⁴And they gave glory to God because of me.

THE APOSTLES ACCEPT PAUL

2 Then fourteen years later I went back to Jerusalem again, this time with Barnabas; and Titus came along, too. ²I went there because God revealed to me that I should go. While I was there I talked privately with the leaders of the church. I wanted them to understand what I had been preaching to the Gentiles. I wanted to make sure they did not disagree, or my ministry would have been useless. ³And they did agree. They did not even demand that my companion Titus be circumcised, though he was a Gentile.*

1:2 Greek *brothers*; also in 1:11. **1:13** Greek *the church of God.* **1:16** Or *in me.* **1:18** Greek *Cephas.* **2:3** Greek *a Greek.*

⁴Even that question wouldn't have come up except for some so-called Christians there—false ones, really*—who came to spy on us and see our freedom in Christ Jesus. They wanted to force us, like slaves, to follow their Jewish regulations. ⁵But we refused to listen to them for a single moment. We wanted to preserve the truth of the Good News for you.

⁶And the leaders of the church who were there had nothing to add to what I was preaching. (By the way, their reputation as great leaders made no difference to me, for God has no favorites.) ⁷They saw that God had given me the responsibility of preaching the Good News to the Gentiles, just as he had given Peter the responsibility of preaching to the Jews. ⁸For the same God who worked through Peter for the benefit of the Jews worked through me for the benefit of the Gentiles. ⁹In fact, James, Peter,* and John, who were known as pillars of the church, recognized the gift God had given me, and they accepted Barnabas and me as their co-workers. They encouraged us to keep preaching to the Gentiles, while they continued their work with the Jews. ¹⁰The only thing they suggested was that we remember to help the poor, and I have certainly been eager to do that.

PAUL CONFRONTS PETER

¹¹But when Peter came to Antioch, I had to oppose him publicly, speaking strongly against what he was doing, for it was very wrong. ¹²When he first arrived, he ate with the Gentile Christians, who don't bother with circumcision. But afterward, when some Jewish friends of James came, Peter wouldn't eat with the Gentiles anymore because he was afraid of what these legalists would say. ¹³Then the other Jewish Christians followed Peter's hypocrisy, and even Barnabas was influenced to join them in their hypocrisy.

¹⁴When I saw that they were not following the truth of the Good News, I said to Peter in front of all the others, "Since you, a Jew by birth, have discarded the Jewish laws and are living like a Gentile, why are you trying to make these Gentiles obey the Jewish laws you abandoned? ¹⁵You and I are Jews by birth, not 'sinners' like the Gentiles. ¹⁶And yet we Jewish Christians know that we become right with God, not by doing what the law commands, but by faith in Jesus Christ. So we have believed in Christ Jesus, that we might be accepted by God because of our faith in Christ—and not because we have obeyed the law. For no one will ever be saved by obeying the law."*

¹⁷But what if we seek to be made right with God through faith in Christ and then find out that we are still sinners? Has Christ led us into sin? Of course not! ¹⁸Rather, I make myself guilty if I rebuild the old system I already tore down. ¹⁹For when I tried to keep the law, I realized I could never earn God's approval. So I died to the law so that I might live for God. I have been crucified with Christ. ²⁰I myself no longer live, but Christ lives in me. So I live my life in this earthly body by trusting in the Son of God, who loved me and gave himself for me. ²¹I am not one of those who treats the grace of God as meaningless. For if we could be saved by keeping the law, then there was no need for Christ to die.

THE LAW AND FAITH IN CHRIST

3 Oh, foolish Galatians! What magician has cast an evil spell on you? For you used to see the meaning of Jesus Christ's death as clearly as though I had shown you a signboard with a picture of Christ dying on the cross. ²Let me ask you this one question: Did you receive the Holy Spirit by keeping the law? Of course not, for the Holy Spirit came upon you only after you believed the message you heard about Christ. ³Have you lost your senses? After starting your Christian lives in the Spirit, why are you now trying to become perfect by your own human effort? ⁴You have suffered so much for the Good News. Surely it was not in

2:4 Greek *some false brothers.* 2:9 Greek *Cephas;* also in 2:11, 14. 2:16 Some translators hold that the quotation extends through verse 14; others through verse 16; and still others through verse 21.

My Daily Worship

— *November 19* —

THE GOD WHO CHANGES LIVES

GALATIANS 1:1–2:21

All they knew was that people were saying, "The one who used to persecute us now preaches the very faith he tried to destroy!" And they gave glory to God because of me (1:23–24).

[i reflect]

Lee Strobel, who was at one-time a staunch atheist, now serves as a pastor. When asked to describe the difference God made in his life, he shared the following story:

> My daughter Allison was five years old when I became a follower of Jesus, and all she had known in those five years was a dad who was profane and angry. I remember I came home one night and kicked a hole in the living room wall just out of anger with life. I am ashamed to think of the times Allison hid in her room to get away from me. Five months after I gave my life to Jesus Christ, that little girl went to my wife and said, 'Mommy, I want God to do for me what he's done for Daddy.' God changed my family. He changed my world. He changed my eternity.

We worship a God who has the power to change human lives. The same resurrection power that raised Jesus from the dead can also transform those who are spiritually dead into fully awakened followers of Christ. As today's passage illustrates, God did it with Paul, a persecutor-turned-preacher. He did it with Lee Strobel, who once profaned the very gospel he now proclaims. No one is beyond the reach of God's grace.

If you struggle with feelings of self-defeat or failure, thinking you lack the ability to make a new start, take heart from the fact that this same life-changing power is available to you as well. The most powerful testimony on earth is that of a transformed life. Perhaps one day those who know you will respond the way the Judean Christians did who witnessed the change in Paul: *"They gave glory to God because of me."*

Today, each time you turn on a light, radio, or any electrical appliance, thank God for the life-changing power he has made available to you.

[i pray]

Lord, I believe the power to change lies in my relationship with Jesus Christ, the one true God. Bring glory to yourself through me, Father. Help me to become like the One I worship.

[i respond]

Divide a piece of paper into two columns. Title one side before, and the other column after. List the traits you saw in yourself before you knew Christ, and then the ones after you've known him. Thank God for the changes he has made in your life already.

vain, was it? Are you now going to just throw it all away?

[5]I ask you again, does God give you the Holy Spirit and work miracles among you because you obey the law of Moses? Of course not! It is because you believe the message you heard about Christ.

[6]In the same way, "Abraham believed God, so God declared him righteous because of his faith."* [7]The real children of Abraham, then, are all those who put their faith in God.

[8]What's more, the Scriptures looked forward to this time when God would accept the Gentiles, too, on the basis of their faith. God promised this good news to Abraham long ago when he said, "All nations will be blessed through you."* [9]And so it is: All who put their faith in Christ share the same blessing Abraham received because of his faith.

[10]But those who depend on the law to make them right with God are under his curse, for the Scriptures say, "Cursed is everyone who does not observe and obey all these commands that are written in God's Book of the Law."* [11]Consequently, it is clear that no one can ever be right with God by trying to keep the law. For the Scriptures say, "It is through faith that a righteous person has life."* [12]How different from this way of faith is the way of law, which says, "If you wish to find life by obeying the law, you must obey all of its commands."* [13]But Christ has rescued us from the curse pronounced by the law. When he was hung on the cross, he took upon himself the curse for our wrongdoing. For it is written in the Scriptures, "Cursed is everyone who is hung on a tree."* [14]Through the work of Christ Jesus, God has blessed the Gentiles with the same blessing he promised to Abraham, and we Christians receive the promised Holy Spirit through faith.

THE LAW AND GOD'S PROMISES

[15]Dear brothers and sisters,* here's an example from everyday life. Just as no one can set aside

or amend an irrevocable agreement, so it is in this case. [16]God gave the promise to Abraham and his child.* And notice that it doesn't say the promise was to his children,* as if it meant many descendants. But the promise was to his child—and that, of course, means Christ. [17]This is what I am trying to say: The agreement God made with Abraham could not be canceled 430 years later when God gave the law to Moses. God would be breaking his promise. [18]For if the inheritance could be received only by keeping the law, then it would not be the result of accepting God's promise. But God gave it to Abraham as a promise.

[19]Well then, why was the law given? It was given to show people how guilty they are. But this system of law was to last only until the coming of the child to whom God's promise was made. And there is this further difference. God gave his laws to angels to give to Moses, who was the mediator between God and the people. [20]Now a mediator is needed if two people enter into an agreement, but God acted on his own when he made his promise to Abraham.

[21]Well then, is there a conflict between God's law and God's promises? Absolutely not! If the law could have given us new life, we could have been made right with God by obeying it. [22]But the Scriptures have declared that we are all prisoners of sin, so the only way to receive God's promise is to believe in Jesus Christ.

[23]Until faith in Christ was shown to us as the way of becoming right with God, we were guarded by the law. We were kept in protective custody, so to speak, until we could put our faith in the coming Savior.

GOD'S CHILDREN THROUGH FAITH

[24]Let me put it another way. The law was our guardian and teacher to lead us until Christ came. So now, through faith in Christ, we are

---

3:6 Gen 15:6. **3:8** Gen 12:3; 18:18; 22:18. **3:10** Deut 27:26. **3:11** Hab 2:4. **3:12** Lev 18:5. **3:13** Deut 21:23. **3:15** Greek *Brothers.* **3:16a** Greek *seed;* also in 3:16c, 19. See Gen 12:7. **3:16b** Greek *seeds.*

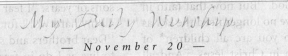

My Daily Worship

— *November 20* —

AIMING AT HEAVEN

GALATIANS 3:1—4:31

And now that you have found God (or should I say, now that God has found you),
why do you want to go back again and become slaves once more to
the weak and useless spiritual powers of this world? (4:9).

[i reflect]

C. S. Lewis, a former agnostic who became one of the twentieth century's foremost apologists for Christianity, once wrote: "Aim at heaven, and you will get earth thrown in. Aim at earth, and you will get neither one."

Where we look can make all the difference. We know that's true about non-Christians, who spend their time and energy chasing after success, material possessions, and wealth, yet miss out on eternal life. But Christians can also fall into this same trap.

In today's passage, the apostle Paul was writing to Christians—the very ones who should be enjoying the benefits and privileges of their faith. Instead, however, they are returning to their old ways—placing themselves once again in bondage to works and religious rituals.

The temptation to place our trust in our own achievements and earning our way to heaven still marks our world. Worship should be a celebration of the glorious status we have in Christ, whose sacrificial death for us on the cross paid the penalty for our sins once and for all. Our old nature, however, resists this freedom and at times beckons us to return to the way of life we left behind.

Cyprian explained it this way: "Don't look to things behind us that the devil calls us back to. Instead, look to things ahead of us that Christ calls us to. Let us lift our eyes up to heaven, lest the earth deceive us with its delights and enticements."

Worship allows us to fix our focus not on the things we can see around us, but on the unseen realities of the spiritual world. Meditate on the glorious inheritance that is waiting for you in eternity. Take aim at heaven; your faith has already shown you the way.

[i pray]

Your Word teaches me that I am justified in your sight not by works but by faith in Christ alone.
I understand that truth, Lord, yet I still catch myself focusing too much on my own
achievements. Help me live within eternity's value system and not that of this world.

[i respond]

Sit down with a friend this week who knows you well. Ask that friend to point out the areas, if any, where you tend to be "legalistic." Spend time praying with that friend for God to free you from these bonds.

made right with God. [25]But now that faith in Christ has come, we no longer need the law as our guardian. [26]So you are all children* of God through faith in Christ Jesus. [27]And all who have been united with Christ in baptism have been made like him. [28]There is no longer Jew or Gentile,* slave or free, male or female. For you are all Christians—you are one in Christ Jesus. [29]And now that you belong to Christ, you are the true children of Abraham. You are his heirs, and now all the promises God gave to him belong to you.

4 Think of it this way. If a father dies and leaves great wealth for his young children, those children are not much better off than slaves until they grow up, even though they actually own everything their father had. [2]They have to obey their guardians until they reach whatever age their father set.

[3]And that's the way it was with us before Christ came. We were slaves to the spiritual powers of this world. [4]But when the right time came, God sent his Son, born of a woman, subject to the law. [5]God sent him to buy freedom for us who were slaves to the law, so that he could adopt us as his very own children.* [6]And because you Gentiles have become his children, God has sent the Spirit of his Son into your hearts, and now you can call God your dear Father.* [7]Now you are no longer a slave but God's own child.* And since you are his child, everything he has belongs to you.

PAUL'S CONCERN FOR THE GALATIANS

[8]Before you Gentiles knew God, you were slaves to so-called gods that do not even exist. [9]And now that you have found God (or should I say, now that God has found you), why do you want to go back again and become slaves once more to the weak and useless spiritual powers of this world? [10]You are trying to find favor with God by what you do or don't do on certain days or months or sea-

sons or years. [11]I fear for you. I am afraid that all my hard work for you was worth nothing. [12]Dear brothers and sisters,* I plead with you to live as I do in freedom from these things, for I have become like you Gentiles were—free from the law.

You did not mistreat me when I first preached to you. [13]Surely you remember that I was sick when I first brought you the Good News of Christ. [14]But even though my sickness was revolting to you, you did not reject me and turn me away. No, you took me in and cared for me as though I were an angel from God or even Christ Jesus himself. [15]Where is that joyful spirit we felt together then? In those days, I know you would gladly have taken out your own eyes and given them to me if it had been possible. [16]Have I now become your enemy because I am telling you the truth?

[17]Those false teachers who are so anxious to win your favor are not doing it for your good. They are trying to shut you off from me so that you will pay more attention to them. [18]Now it's wonderful if you are eager to do good, and especially when I am not with you. [19]But oh, my dear children! I feel as if I am going through labor pains for you again, and they will continue until Christ is fully developed in your lives. [20]How I wish I were there with you right now, so that I could be more gentle with you. But at this distance I frankly don't know what else to do.

ABRAHAM'S TWO CHILDREN

[21]Listen to me, you who want to live under the law. Do you know what the law really says? [22]The Scriptures say that Abraham had two sons, one from his slave-wife and one from his freeborn wife.* [23]The son of the slave-wife was born in a human attempt to bring about the fulfillment of God's promise. But the son of the freeborn wife was born as God's own fulfillment of his promise.

[24]Now these two women serve as an illustra-

3:26 Greek sons. 3:28 Greek Jew or Greek. 4:5 Greek sons; also in 4:6. 4:6 Greek into your hearts, crying, "Abba, Father." Abba is an Aramaic term for "father." 4:7 Greek son; also in 4:7b. 4:12 Greek brothers; also in 4:28, 31. 4:22 See Gen 16:15; 21:2-3.

tion of God's two covenants. Hagar, the slave-wife, represents Mount Sinai where people first became enslaved to the law. [25]And now Jerusalem is just like Mount Sinai in Arabia, because she and her children live in slavery. [26]But Sarah, the free woman, represents the heavenly Jerusalem. And she is our mother. [27]That is what Isaiah meant when he prophesied,

"Rejoice, O childless woman!
Break forth into loud and joyful song,
    even though you never gave birth to a
        child.
For the woman who could bear no
        children
    now has more than all the other
        women!"*

[28]And you, dear brothers and sisters, are children of the promise, just like Isaac. [29]And we who are born of the Holy Spirit are persecuted by those who want us to keep the law, just as Isaac, the child of promise, was persecuted by Ishmael, the son of the slave-wife. [30]But what do the Scriptures say about that? "Get rid of the slave and her son, for the son of the slave woman will not share the family inheritance with the free woman's son."* [31]So, dear brothers and sisters, we are not children of the slave woman, obligated to the law. We are children of the free woman, acceptable to God because of our faith.

FREEDOM IN CHRIST

5 So Christ has really set us free. Now make sure that you stay free, and don't get tied up again in slavery to the law.

[2]Listen! I, Paul, tell you this: If you are counting on circumcision to make you right with God, then Christ cannot help you. [3]I'll say it again. If you are trying to find favor with God by being circumcised, you must obey all of the regulations in the whole law of Moses. [4]For if you are trying to make yourselves right

with God by keeping the law, you have been cut off from Christ! You have fallen away from God's grace.

[5]But we who live by the Spirit eagerly wait to receive everything promised to us who are right with God through faith. [6]For when we place our faith in Christ Jesus, it makes no difference to God whether we are circumcised or not circumcised. What is important is faith expressing itself in love.

[7]You were getting along so well. Who has interfered with you to hold you back from following the truth? [8]It certainly isn't God, for he is the one who called you to freedom. [9]But it takes only one wrong person among you to infect all the others—a little yeast spreads quickly through the whole batch of dough! [10]I am trusting the Lord to bring you back to believing as I do about these things. God will judge that person, whoever it is, who has been troubling and confusing you.

[11]Dear brothers and sisters,* if I were still preaching that you must be circumcised—as some say I do—why would the Jews persecute me? The fact that I am still being persecuted proves that I am still preaching salvation through the cross of Christ alone. [12]I only wish that those troublemakers who want to mutilate you by circumcision would mutilate themselves.*

[13]For you have been called to live in freedom—not freedom to satisfy your sinful nature, but freedom to serve one another in love. [14]For the whole law can be summed up in this one command: "Love your neighbor as yourself."* [15]But if instead of showing love among yourselves you are always biting and devouring one another, watch out! Beware of destroying one another.

LIVING BY THE SPIRIT'S POWER

[16]So I advise you to live according to your new life in the Holy Spirit. Then you won't be doing what your sinful nature craves. [17]The old sinful nature loves to do evil, which is just opposite from what the Holy Spirit wants.

4:27 Isa 54:1. 4:30 Gen 21:10. 5:11 Greek *Brothers*. 5:12 Or *castrate themselves;* Greek reads *cut themselves off.* 5:14 Lev 19:18.

And the Spirit gives us desires that are opposite from what the sinful nature desires. These two forces are constantly fighting each other, and your choices are never free from this conflict. [18]But when you are directed by the Holy Spirit, you are no longer subject to the law.

[19]When you follow the desires of your sinful nature, your lives will produce these evil results: sexual immorality, impure thoughts, eagerness for lustful pleasure, [20]idolatry, participation in demonic activities, hostility, quarreling, jealousy, outbursts of anger, selfish ambition, divisions, the feeling that everyone is wrong except those in your own little group, [21]envy, drunkenness, wild parties, and other kinds of sin. Let me tell you again, as I have before, that anyone living that sort of life will not inherit the Kingdom of God.

[22]But when the Holy Spirit controls our lives, he will produce this kind of fruit in us: love, joy, peace, patience, kindness, goodness, faithfulness, [23]gentleness, and self-control. Here there is no conflict with the law.

[24]Those who belong to Christ Jesus have nailed the passions and desires of their sinful nature to his cross and crucified them there. [25]If we are living now by the Holy Spirit, let us follow the Holy Spirit's leading in every part of our lives. [26]Let us not become conceited, or irritate one another, or be jealous of one another.

We Reap What We Sow

6 Dear brothers and sisters, if another Christian* is overcome by some sin, you who are godly should gently and humbly help that person back onto the right path. And be careful not to fall into the same temptation yourself. [2]Share each other's troubles and problems, and in this way obey the law of Christ. [3]If you think you are too important to help someone in need, you are only fooling yourself. You are really a nobody.

[4]Be sure to do what you should, for then you will enjoy the personal satisfaction of having done your work well, and you won't need to compare yourself to anyone else. [5]For we are each responsible for our own conduct.

[6]Those who are taught the word of God should help their teachers by paying them.

[7]Don't be misled. Remember that you can't ignore God and get away with it. You will always reap what you sow! [8]Those who live only to satisfy their own sinful desires will harvest the consequences of decay and death. But those who live to please the Spirit will harvest everlasting life from the Spirit. [9]So don't get tired of doing what is good. Don't get discouraged and give up, for we will reap a harvest of blessing at the appropriate time. [10]Whenever we have the opportunity, we should do good to everyone, especially to our Christian brothers and sisters.

Paul's Final Advice

[11]Notice what large letters I use as I write these closing words in my own handwriting. [12]Those who are trying to force you to be circumcised are doing it for just one reason. They don't want to be persecuted for teaching that the cross of Christ alone can save. [13]And even those who advocate circumcision don't really keep the whole law. They only want you to be circumcised so they can brag about it and claim you as their disciples.

[14]As for me, God forbid that I should boast about anything except the cross of our Lord Jesus Christ. Because of that cross,* my interest in this world died long ago, and the world's interest in me is also long dead. [15]It doesn't make any difference now whether we have been circumcised or not. What counts is whether we really have been changed into new and different people. [16]May God's mercy and peace be upon all those who live by this principle. They are the new people of God.*

[17]From now on, don't let anyone trouble me with these things. For I bear on my body the scars that show I belong to Jesus.

[18]My dear brothers and sisters,* may the grace of our Lord Jesus Christ be with you all. Amen.

6:1 Greek Brothers, if a man.　6:14 Or Because of him.　6:16 Greek the Israel of God.　6:18 Greek Brothers.

My Daily Worship

— *November 21* —

BE A BURDEN-BEARER
GALATIANS 5:1–6:18

Share each other's troubles and problems, and in this way obey the law of Christ (6:2).

[i reflect]

In his book *When You Can't Come Back*, former major league pitcher Dave Dravecky comments, "In America, Christians pray for the burden of suffering to be lifted from their backs. In the rest of the world Christians pray for stronger backs so they can bear their suffering."

No one enjoys suffering, and it's quite natural to ask God to remove our burdens from us. Do we recognize the presence of divine intervention, however, when others come along to share our pain?

The apostle Paul instructed the Galatians to share each other's loads, for in this way they would be fulfilling the law of Christ. Bearing one another's burdens is not an option for believers; it is a command. Shared joy is doubled joy; shared sorrow is halved-sorrow.

How can we learn to be more sensitive when it comes to sharing the needs of others? It begins with listening to quiet instructions from the Father who cares for his children. We hear his voice when we worship—when we deliberately set aside time to communicate with him on the most intimate of levels. Scripture is clear that God intends for us to care for one another.

Lactantius, one of the early church fathers, explains this principle: "He has given us the affection of compassion so that we can protect lives by helping one another. If we are created by one God, descended from one man, and, therefore, are thus connected by the law of kinship, we should love everyone. Our frailty is prone to many accidents and inconveniences. Expect that what you see happening to someone else may also happen to you. You will be excited to help someone if you shall assume the mind of those who, being placed in danger, beg for your help."

Dave Dravecky was right: we need to pray for stronger backs—backs fit to bear the burdens of a world needing to know of the strength we find in Christ.

Help carry the burden for someone else today. Take time to listen to a friend who is hurting. Visit a church member in the hospital. Encourage a young person struggling with school.

[i pray]

Lord, I admit that most of the time my greatest concern is for my own comfort or that of those I love. Please help me hear your voice when you can use me to share the load of someone who lacks the support system that I enjoy.

[i respond]

Visit a friend or family member who is experiencing a difficult time. Take your calendar and schedule in specific times where you can assist them in carrying their burden.

Ephesians

May you experience the love of Christ, though it is so great you will never fully understand it.
Then you will be filled with the fullness of life and power that comes from God (3:19).

The Right Response

Paul celebrates the embrace of God in this powerful letter to the church at Ephesus. At one time excluded from God's family, we are now brothers and sisters with all God's people. Once dead in spirit, we live. Once captured by passions and the sedatives of sin, we have the Spirit of God leading us forward. It's a complete change of course, and all God's doing. We don't deserve a bit of it.

The letter contains a wonderful description of the church. In it, Paul affirms the character of the body of believers: in Christ, we have been showered with God's kindness (1:3–8), chosen for greatness (1:9–12), marked by the Spirit (1:13–14), and freed from sin's curse and bondage (2:1–10). In response, we need to be "filled by Christ" (1:23), to become "members of God's family" (2:19), to be filled with "mighty inner strength through his Holy Spirit" (3:16), so that we can ultimately become "in every way like Christ" (4:15).

All this divine action puts worship in its proper light. We praise God because his power has made the difference between life and death, hope and bleakness, love and bitterness. We sing because God invites us into the "choir." We pray because the many thank-yous for his gifts just keep on coming.

Filled with life, God's people need no special command to worship—it's the normal response. We find encouragement here, but no command. You don't order a thirsty person to drink—just bring the water. Worship is what the new people of God do. In worship we connect with the One whose gifts are beyond belief.

As you read through Ephesians, look for the many reasons we have to worship the One who gives so much, over and above, life, hope, love. Then as your response, worship. It's so natural, so right.

Worship Moments

- A well-known praise song is taken from 1:18: *"Open the eyes of my heart, Lord."* To see what? The hope at the center of God's good news. Spiritual truth is God-given, not innate or hard-wired.

- Praise God for life (2:4–5). What a gift: life in His Spirit. Worship is our essential vitamin for spiritual growth. We cannot be strong in Christ if we resist or ignore worship.

- Worship purges the heart of bitterness and rage (4:31–32). In worship God heals us. Rage becomes kindness.

GREETINGS FROM PAUL

1 This letter is from Paul, chosen by God to be an apostle of Christ Jesus.

It is written to God's holy people in Ephesus,* who are faithful followers of Christ Jesus.

[2]May grace and peace be yours, sent to you from God our Father and Jesus Christ our Lord.

SPIRITUAL BLESSINGS

[3]How we praise God, the Father of our Lord Jesus Christ, who has blessed us with every spiritual blessing in the heavenly realms because we belong to Christ. [4]Long ago, even before he made the world, God loved us and chose us in Christ to be holy and without fault in his eyes. [5]His unchanging plan has always been to adopt us into his own family by bringing us to himself through Jesus Christ. And this gave him great pleasure.

[6]So we praise God for the wonderful kindness he has poured out on us because we belong to his dearly loved Son. [7]He is so rich in kindness that he purchased our freedom through the blood of his Son, and our sins are forgiven. [8]He has showered his kindness on us, along with all wisdom and understanding.

[9]God's secret plan has now been revealed to us; it is a plan centered on Christ, designed long ago according to his good pleasure. [10]And this is his plan: At the right time he will bring everything together under the authority of Christ—everything in heaven and on earth. [11]Furthermore, because of Christ, we have received an inheritance from God,* for he chose us from the beginning, and all things happen just as he decided long ago. [12]God's purpose was that we who were the first to trust in Christ should praise our glorious God. [13]And now you also have heard the truth, the Good News that God saves you. And when you believed in Christ, he identified you as his own by giving you the Holy Spirit, whom he

promised long ago. [14]The Spirit is God's guarantee that he will give us everything he promised and that he has purchased us to be his own people. This is just one more reason for us to praise our glorious God.

PAUL'S PRAYER FOR SPIRITUAL WISDOM

[15]Ever since I first heard of your strong faith in the Lord Jesus and your love for Christians everywhere, [16]I have never stopped thanking God for you. I pray for you constantly, [17]asking God, the glorious Father of our Lord Jesus Christ, to give you spiritual wisdom and understanding, so that you might grow in your knowledge of God. [18]I pray that your hearts will be flooded with light so that you can understand the wonderful future he has promised to those he called. I want you to realize what a rich and glorious inheritance he has given to his people.*

[19]I pray that you will begin to understand the incredible greatness of his power for us who believe him. This is the same mighty power [20]that raised Christ from the dead and seated him in the place of honor at God's right hand in the heavenly realms. [21]Now he is far above any ruler or authority or power or leader or anything else in this world or in the world to come. [22]And God has put all things under the authority of Christ, and he gave him this authority for the benefit of the church. [23]And the church is his body; it is filled by Christ, who fills everything everywhere with his presence.

MADE ALIVE WITH CHRIST

2 Once you were dead, doomed forever because of your many sins. [2]You used to live just like the rest of the world, full of sin, obeying Satan, the mighty prince of the power of the air. He is the spirit at work in the hearts of those who refuse to obey God. [3]All of us used to live that way, following the passions and desires of our evil nature. We were born

---

1:1 Some manuscripts do not include *in Ephesus.* 1:11 Or *we have become God's inheritance.* 1:18 Or *realize how much God has been honored by acquiring his people.*

with an evil nature, and we were under God's anger just like everyone else.

⁴But God is so rich in mercy, and he loved us so very much, ⁵that even while we were dead because of our sins, he gave us life when he raised Christ from the dead. (It is only by God's special favor that you have been saved!) ⁶For he raised us from the dead along with Christ, and we are seated with him in the heavenly realms—all because we are one with Christ Jesus. ⁷And so God can always point to us as examples of the incredible wealth of his favor and kindness toward us, as shown in all he has done for us through Christ Jesus.

⁸God saved you by his special favor when you believed. And you can't take credit for this; it is a gift from God. ⁹Salvation is not a reward for the good things we have done, so none of us can boast about it. ¹⁰For we are God's masterpiece. He has created us anew in Christ Jesus, so that we can do the good things he planned for us long ago.

ONENESS AND PEACE IN CHRIST

¹¹Don't forget that you Gentiles used to be outsiders by birth. You were called "the uncircumcised ones" by the Jews, who were proud of their circumcision, even though it affected only their bodies and not their hearts. ¹²In those days you were living apart from Christ. You were excluded from God's people, Israel, and you did not know the promises God had made to them. You lived in this world without God and without hope. ¹³But now you belong to Christ Jesus. Though you once were far away from God, now you have been brought near to him because of the blood of Christ.

¹⁴For Christ himself has made peace between us Jews and you Gentiles by making us all one people. He has broken down the wall of hostility that used to separate us. ¹⁵By his death he ended the whole system of Jewish law that excluded the Gentiles. His purpose was to make peace between Jews and Gentiles by creating in himself one new person from the two groups. ¹⁶Together as one body, Christ reconciled both groups to God by means of his death, and our hostility toward each other was put to death. ¹⁷He has brought this Good News of peace to you Gentiles who were far away from him, and to us Jews who were near. ¹⁸Now all of us, both Jews and Gentiles, may come to the Father through the same Holy Spirit because of what Christ has done for us.

A TEMPLE FOR THE LORD

¹⁹So now you Gentiles are no longer strangers and foreigners. You are citizens along with all of God's holy people. You are members of God's family. ²⁰We are his house, built on the foundation of the apostles and the prophets. And the cornerstone is Christ Jesus himself. ²¹We who believe are carefully joined together, becoming a holy temple for the Lord. ²²Through him you Gentiles are also joined together as part of this dwelling where God lives by his Spirit.

GOD'S SECRET PLAN REVEALED

3 I, Paul, am a prisoner of Christ Jesus because of my preaching to you Gentiles. ²As you already know, God has given me this special ministry of announcing his favor to you Gentiles. ³As I briefly mentioned earlier in this letter, God himself revealed his secret plan to me. ⁴As you read what I have written, you will understand what I know about this plan regarding Christ. ⁵God did not reveal it to previous generations, but now he has revealed it by the Holy Spirit to his holy apostles and prophets.

⁶And this is the secret plan: The Gentiles have an equal share with the Jews in all the riches inherited by God's children. Both groups have believed the Good News, and both are part of the same body and enjoy together the promise of blessings through Christ Jesus. ⁷By God's special favor and mighty power, I have been given the wonderful privilege of serving him by spreading this Good News.

⁸Just think! Though I did nothing to deserve it, and though I am the least deserving

My Daily Worship

— *November 22* —

ADOPTED BY GOD

EPHESIANS 1:1–2:22

His unchanging plan has always been to adopt us into his own family by bringing us to himself through Jesus Christ. And this gave him great pleasure. So we praise God for the wonderful kindness he has poured out on us because we belong to his dearly loved Son (1:5–6).

[i reflect]

In her autobiographical book *Amazed by Grace*, author Lucinda Secrest McDowell relates the story of the adoption of her oldest three children, whose biological mother had died of cancer some years before. To her surprise, each of the children was given a newly revised birth certificate with her name on the line for "mother" as well as her place of residence at the time of their births. Even though Cindy was living elsewhere in the United States during the years when the children were born in Seattle, that did not alter the fact that she was now, legally and in every other way, their mother. God had brought them together and made them a family.

Today's passage brings the wonderful news that those who belong to Christ have been spiritually adopted into God's own family. Where we were born and into what circumstances no longer matters, for God has chosen us to be his own. Our advocate, Jesus Christ, provided the way and the means for our adoption to take place. No wonder we are given the right to call God our "dear Father" (Galatians 4:6)!

Our status as children of God gives us both the right and the privilege to lay claim to "every spiritual blessing in the heavenly realms." Notice the passionate praise in this passage. "How we praise God, the Father of our Lord Jesus Christ," Paul writes in Ephesians 1:3, and again in verse 6, "We praise God for the wonderful kindness he has poured out on us."

Just as an adoptive father or mother becomes a parent by choice, God draws us into his spiritual family. Let that reality take root in your life: you are God's beloved child, and as his heir you stand to receive an eternal inheritance one day. Need a copy of your "birth certificate"? You're holding it in your hands!

Celebrate your birthright as God's adopted child today.

[i pray]

What a privilege you have given me, that I can call you Father! I can never thank you enough for adopting me into your heavenly family, and giving me every spiritual blessing in Christ.

[i respond]

Read Ephesians 1–2 again. List all the privileges you have as a child of God that you find in these two passages. Give thanks to your Father for what he has given to you.

Christian there is, I was chosen for this special joy of telling the Gentiles about the endless treasures available to them in Christ. [9]I was chosen to explain to everyone this plan that God, the Creator of all things, had kept secret from the beginning.

[10]God's purpose was to show his wisdom in all its rich variety to all the rulers and authorities in the heavenly realms. They will see this when Jews and Gentiles are joined together in his church. [11]This was his plan from all eternity, and it has now been carried out through Christ Jesus our Lord.

[12]Because of Christ and our faith in him, we can now come fearlessly into God's presence, assured of his glad welcome. [13]So please don't despair because of what they are doing to me here. It is for you that I am suffering, so you should feel honored and encouraged.

PAUL'S PRAYER FOR SPIRITUAL EMPOWERING

[14]When I think of the wisdom and scope of God's plan, I fall to my knees and pray to the Father,* [15]the Creator of everything in heaven and on earth. [16]I pray that from his glorious, unlimited resources he will give you mighty inner strength through his Holy Spirit. [17]And I pray that Christ will be more and more at home in your hearts as you trust in him. May your roots go down deep into the soil of God's marvelous love. [18]And may you have the power to understand, as all God's people should, how wide, how long, how high, and how deep his love really is. [19]May you experience the love of Christ, though it is so great you will never fully understand it. Then you will be filled with the fullness of life and power that comes from God.

[20]Now glory be to God! By his mighty power at work within us, he is able to accomplish infinitely more than we would ever dare to ask or hope. [21]May he be given glory in the church and in Christ Jesus forever and ever through endless ages. Amen.

UNITY IN THE BODY

4 Therefore I, a prisoner for serving the Lord, beg you to lead a life worthy of your calling, for you have been called by God. [2]Be humble and gentle. Be patient with each other, making allowance for each other's faults because of your love. [3]Always keep yourselves united in the Holy Spirit, and bind yourselves together with peace.

[4]We are all one body, we have the same Spirit, and we have all been called to the same glorious future. [5]There is only one Lord, one faith, one baptism, [6]and there is only one God and Father, who is over us all and in us all and living through us all. [7]However, he has given each one of us a special gift according to the generosity of Christ. [8]That is why the Scriptures say,

"When he ascended to the heights,
he led a crowd of captives
and gave gifts to his people."*

[9]Notice that it says "he ascended." This means that Christ first came down to the lowly world in which we live.* [10]The same one who came down is the one who ascended higher than all the heavens, so that his rule might fill the entire universe.

[11]He is the one who gave these gifts to the church: the apostles, the prophets, the evangelists, and the pastors and teachers. [12]Their responsibility is to equip God's people to do his work and build up the church, the body of Christ, [13]until we come to such unity in our faith and knowledge of God's Son that we will be mature and full grown in the Lord, measuring up to the full stature of Christ.

[14]Then we will no longer be like children, forever changing our minds about what we believe because someone has told us something different or because someone has cleverly lied to us and made the lie sound like the truth. [15]Instead, we will hold to the truth in love, becoming more and more in every way like Christ, who is the head of his body, the

3:14 Some manuscripts read *the Father of our Lord Jesus Christ.* 4:8 Ps 68:18. 4:9 Or *to the lowest parts of the earth.*

My Daily Worship

— *November 23* —

BIND US TOGETHER

EPHESIANS 3:1–4:32

We are all one body, we have the same Spirit, and we have
all been called to the same glorious future (4:4).

[i reflect]

There is one word—one beautiful word—that sums up the principle described in the verse above: *unity*. This passage in Ephesians specifies three reasons that we should exhibit unity as believers in Christ. We are (1) one body, (2) with one Spirit, (3) destined for one common future. What reasons could possibly exist that would divide us?

Many things divide us, unfortunately. We are born with a sin nature, and even those who sincerely profess a common faith in Christ can still find themselves at odds over differences in doctrine or practice. One of the greatest privileges we have as believers is that of worship itself, yet disagreements over worship styles or musical preferences have often caused serious division within the body. America's great seventeenth-century theologian and preacher Jonathan Edwards lived in an era when some people considered any songs but the Psalms the "devil's music." Edwards found himself the object of criticism when he endorsed the hymns of Isaac Watts and Charles Wesley.

Little wonder, then, that Paul urged the Ephesians to "always keep yourselves united in the Holy Spirit, and bind yourselves together with peace" (4:3). Saint Chrysostom explained it this way: "What is the 'unity of Spirit?' In the human body there is a spirit that holds all the different parts together. It is the same here. The Spirit was given to unite those separated by race and manners. For young and old, rich and poor, children and youth, women and men, every soul becomes more completely one than in the human body. This spiritual relationship is far greater than the other natural one and the perfection of the union is even more complete in its simplicity. How is this unity maintained? 'In the bond of peace.'"

A simple worship chorus pleads, "Bind us together, Lord, bind us together, with chords that cannot be broken." Let's not debate its use but, rather, live by its truth.

Spend time praying for "chords that cannot be broken" in your own church, your ministry, and among believers in your community.

[i pray]

Blessed be the ties that bind, Father. Cause me to look for the blessings of unity with other believers. Thank you for the Holy Spirit that binds us together with peace.

[i respond]

Form a bond with someone in your local congregation with whom you have few common interests. Mentor a young person. Visit a shut-in. Spend time with someone whose interests are varied from yours. Use those times as opportunities to praise God for the ties that bind.

church. [16]Under his direction, the whole body is fitted together perfectly. As each part does its own special work, it helps the other parts grow, so that the whole body is healthy and growing and full of love.

LIVING AS CHILDREN OF LIGHT

[17]With the Lord's authority let me say this: Live no longer as the ungodly* do, for they are hopelessly confused. [18]Their closed minds are full of darkness; they are far away from the life of God because they have shut their minds and hardened their hearts against him. [19]They don't care anymore about right and wrong, and they have given themselves over to immoral ways. Their lives are filled with all kinds of impurity and greed.

[20]But that isn't what you were taught when you learned about Christ. [21]Since you have heard all about him and have learned the truth that is in Jesus, [22]throw off your old evil nature and your former way of life, which is rotten through and through, full of lust and deception. [23]Instead, there must be a spiritual renewal of your thoughts and attitudes. [24]You must display a new nature because you are a new person, created in God's likeness—righteous, holy, and true.

[25]So put away all falsehood and "tell your neighbor the truth"* because we belong to each other. [26]And "don't sin by letting anger gain control over you."* Don't let the sun go down while you are still angry, [27]for anger gives a mighty foothold to the Devil.

[28]If you are a thief, stop stealing. Begin using your hands for honest work, and then give generously to others in need. [29]Don't use foul or abusive language. Let everything you say be good and helpful, so that your words will be an encouragement to those who hear them.

[30]And do not bring sorrow to God's Holy Spirit by the way you live. Remember, he is the one who has identified you as his own, guaranteeing that you will be saved on the day of redemption.

[31]Get rid of all bitterness, rage, anger, harsh words, and slander, as well as all types of malicious behavior. [32]Instead, be kind to each other, tenderhearted, forgiving one another, just as God through Christ has forgiven you.

LIVING IN THE LIGHT

5 Follow God's example in everything you do, because you are his dear children. [2]Live a life filled with love for others, following the example of Christ, who loved you and gave himself as a sacrifice to take away your sins. And God was pleased, because that sacrifice was like sweet perfume to him.

[3]Let there be no sexual immorality, impurity, or greed among you. Such sins have no place among God's people. [4]Obscene stories, foolish talk, and coarse jokes—these are not for you. Instead, let there be thankfulness to God. [5]You can be sure that no immoral, impure, or greedy person will inherit the Kingdom of Christ and of God. For a greedy person is really an idolater who worships the things of this world. [6]Don't be fooled by those who try to excuse these sins, for the terrible anger of God comes upon all those who disobey him. [7]Don't participate in the things these people do. [8]For though your hearts were once full of darkness, now you are full of light from the Lord, and your behavior should show it! [9]For this light within you produces only what is good and right and true.

[10]Try to find out what is pleasing to the Lord. [11]Take no part in the worthless deeds of evil and darkness; instead, rebuke and expose them. [12]It is shameful even to talk about the things that ungodly people do in secret. [13]But when the light shines on them, it becomes clear how evil these things are. [14]And where your light shines, it will expose their evil deeds. This is why it is said,

"Awake, O sleeper,
rise up from the dead,
and Christ will give you light."

4:17 Greek *Gentiles.* 4:25 Zech 8:16. 4:26 Ps 4:4.

My Daily Worship

— *November 24* —

EYES WIDE OPEN

EPHESIANS 5:1–6:24

Pray at all times and on every occasion in the power of the Holy Spirit. Stay alert
and be persistent in your prayers for all Christians everywhere (6:18).

[i reflect]

The late songwriter and Christian recording artist Keith Green was known for his passion for missions and ministry. A song called "Make My Life a Prayer to You" contained his plea to the God whom Keith loved so much that his life contain no empty words, no white lies, no token prayers, and no compromise.

In the letter to the Ephesians, Paul is instructing believers to pray continually, at all times, and on every occasion. Live constantly in a spirit of worship, he urges us. Stay fully alert; pray with unrelenting faith. It's almost as if he's saying, "Pray with the eyes of your heart wide open!"

Cyprian, one of the leaders of the church during the fourth century, reaffirmed this teaching. "When we pray, beloved, we should be alert and earnest with our whole heart, intent on our prayers. Let all worldly thoughts pass away. Don't let the soul think about anything but the object of its prayer. Don't allow God's enemy to approach your heart at that time. For, frequently, he sneaks up on us and calls our prayers away from God so that we have one thing on our heart and another in our voice. You may appear watchful, but your heart is asleep. Instead, your heart should be watchful even when your eyes are closed in prayer."

As we learn to be continually watchful in prayer, offering up each anxious thought and every situation to his sovereignty, we will find that Keith Green's plea of making our lives a prayer has been realized. Even when asleep, our hearts are awake to his will. Our very lives have become a prayer to God.

Find different times of the day to pray than is your usual habit. Spend time in prayer before you enter your place of work, or right before the children get home. Let this break in routine refresh your prayer life and keep you alert.

[i pray]

Lord, I want my life to become a prayer to you. Teach me what it means
to have the eyes of my heart fully awakened to your will.

[i respond]

In what areas of your prayer life would you most like to see improvement? The acrostic ACTS can remind us to include each of these elements as we pray throughout the day: Adoration, Confession, Thanksgiving, and Supplication.

LIVING BY THE SPIRIT'S POWER

[15]So be careful how you live, not as fools but as those who are wise. [16]Make the most of every opportunity for doing good in these evil days. [17]Don't act thoughtlessly, but try to understand what the Lord wants you to do. [18]Don't be drunk with wine, because that will ruin your life. Instead, let the Holy Spirit fill and control you. [19]Then you will sing psalms and hymns and spiritual songs among yourselves, making music to the Lord in your hearts. [20]And you will always give thanks for everything to God the Father in the name of our Lord Jesus Christ.

SPIRIT-GUIDED RELATIONSHIPS: WIVES AND HUSBANDS

[21]And further, you will submit to one another out of reverence for Christ. [22]You wives will submit to your husbands as you do to the Lord. [23]For a husband is the head of his wife as Christ is the head of his body, the church; he gave his life to be her Savior. [24]As the church submits to Christ, so you wives must submit to your husbands in everything.

[25]And you husbands must love your wives with the same love Christ showed the church. He gave up his life for her [26]to make her holy and clean, washed by baptism and God's word.* [27]He did this to present her to himself as a glorious church without a spot or wrinkle or any other blemish. Instead, she will be holy and without fault. [28]In the same way, husbands ought to love their wives as they love their own bodies. For a man is actually loving himself when he loves his wife. [29]No one hates his own body but lovingly cares for it, just as Christ cares for his body, which is the church. [30]And we are his body.

[31]As the Scriptures say, "A man leaves his father and mother and is joined to his wife, and the two are united into one."* [32]This is a great mystery, but it is an illustration of the way Christ and the church are one. [33]So again I say, each man must love his wife as he loves himself, and the wife must respect her husband.

CHILDREN AND PARENTS

6 Children, obey your parents because you belong to the Lord, for this is the right thing to do. [2]"Honor your father and mother." This is the first of the Ten Commandments that ends with a promise. [3]And this is the promise: If you honor your father and mother, "you will live a long life, full of blessing."*

[4]And now a word to you fathers. Don't make your children angry by the way you treat them. Rather, bring them up with the discipline and instruction approved by the Lord.

SLAVES AND MASTERS

[5]Slaves, obey your earthly masters with deep respect and fear. Serve them sincerely as you would serve Christ. [6]Work hard, but not just to please your masters when they are watching. As slaves of Christ, do the will of God with all your heart. [7]Work with enthusiasm, as though you were working for the Lord rather than for people. [8]Remember that the Lord will reward each one of us for the good we do, whether we are slaves or free.

[9]And in the same way, you masters must treat your slaves right. Don't threaten them; remember, you both have the same Master in heaven, and he has no favorites.

THE WHOLE ARMOR OF GOD

[10]A final word: Be strong with the Lord's mighty power. [11]Put on all of God's armor so that you will be able to stand firm against all strategies and tricks of the Devil. [12]For we are not fighting against people made of flesh and blood, but against the evil rulers and authorities of the unseen world, against those mighty powers of darkness who rule this world, and against wicked spirits in the heavenly realms.

[13]Use every piece of God's armor to resist the enemy in the time of evil, so that after the battle you will still be standing firm. [14]Stand your ground, putting on the sturdy belt of truth and the body armor of God's righteous-

5:26 Greek *having cleansed her by the washing of water with the word.*   5:31 Gen 2:24.   6:2-3 Exod 20:12; Deut 5:16.

ness. [15]For shoes, put on the peace that comes from the Good News, so that you will be fully prepared.* [16]In every battle you will need faith as your shield to stop the fiery arrows aimed at you by Satan.* [17]Put on salvation as your helmet, and take the sword of the Spirit, which is the word of God. [18]Pray at all times and on every occasion in the power of the Holy Spirit. Stay alert and be persistent in your prayers for all Christians everywhere.

[19]And pray for me, too. Ask God to give me the right words as I boldly explain God's secret plan that the Good News is for the Gentiles, too.* [20]I am in chains now for preaching this message as God's ambassador.

But pray that I will keep on speaking boldly for him, as I should.

FINAL GREETINGS

[21]Tychicus, a much loved brother and faithful helper in the Lord's work, will tell you all about how I am getting along. [22]I am sending him to you for just this purpose. He will let you know how we are, and he will encourage you.

[23]May God give you peace, dear brothers and sisters,* and love with faith, from God the Father and the Lord Jesus Christ. [24]May God's grace be upon all who love our Lord Jesus Christ with an undying love.

6:15 Or For shoes, put on the readiness to preach the Good News of peace with God.   6:16 Greek by the evil one.   6:19 Greek explain the mystery of the gospel.   6:23 Greek brothers.

Philippians

At the name of Jesus every knee will bow, . . . and every tongue

will confess that Jesus Christ is Lord (2:10–11).

Joyful Worship

Paul had good reason to feel as if his life were crumbling beneath him. He had prison to endure, loneliness, and a nagging sense that heaven would be postponed too long. Other missionaries were working his territory with mixed motives; some wannabes were actually subverting the church with legalism and ritual. Paul had reason for fatigue and bitterness.

Yet, he emerges from his very bad day with remarkable vibrancy. He climbs above every cloud and rides out the storm with a song. Look at Paul's first-person action verbs, and you will see an individual whose life compass is fixed firmly Jesus-ward. Examples: "I give thanks; I am sure; I love you; I pray; I live in eager expectation and hope; I am convinced; I never get tired; I hope; how grateful I am; how I praise the Lord."

The seven secrets of success and the power of positive thinking seem wrapped up in this one person whose spirit soars when it should be flat. What's his game?

Paul tells only his life passions here, not his life story. Yet we know that Paul's extraordinary journey began with a vision on the Damascus Road and grew into a close relationship with the living Christ. Intimacy with Christ such as he experienced is nourished in worship—prayer, praise, meditation, song—renewed in worship, and grounded in worship. Paul offers no worship instruction here, but everywhere he points to the living Savior who made himself nothing, obeyed God unto death, and now accepts the confession of every tongue and the prayer on every bent knee.

Join with Paul as you read through Philippians in joyful worship.

Worship Moments

- Worship unifies. To worship is to take the eye off worry, jealousy, and anger. It is to unite with different people around a common Savior, and to find strength together (1:27).

- Love and common purpose are the keynotes for Christian community. In worship we discover and practice this relationship of mutual concern and support (2:1).

- Worship is the reminder that the "here and now" is not forever. Jesus welcomes us now to eternal life, then to heaven (3:20).

- Getting strength from God to do what needs to be done comes in time set apart to magnify God in prayer, praise, and song (4:13).

GREETINGS FROM PAUL

1 This letter is from Paul and Timothy, slaves of Christ Jesus.

It is written to all of God's people in Philippi, who believe in Christ Jesus, and to the elders* and deacons.

[2]May God our Father and the Lord Jesus Christ give you grace and peace.

PAUL'S THANKSGIVING AND PRAYER

[3]Every time I think of you, I give thanks to my God. [4]I always pray for you, and I make my requests with a heart full of joy [5]because you have been my partners in spreading the Good News about Christ from the time you first heard it until now. [6]And I am sure that God, who began the good work within you, will continue his work until it is finally finished on that day when Christ Jesus comes back again.

[7]It is right that I should feel as I do about all of you, for you have a very special place in my heart. We have shared together the blessings of God, both when I was in prison and when I was out, defending the truth and telling others the Good News. [8]God knows how much I love you and long for you with the tender compassion of Christ Jesus. [9]I pray that your love for each other will overflow more and more, and that you will keep on growing in your knowledge and understanding. [10]For I want you to understand what really matters, so that you may live pure and blameless lives until Christ returns. [11]May you always be filled with the fruit of your salvation*—those good things that are produced in your life by Jesus Christ—for this will bring much glory and praise to God.

PAUL'S JOY THAT CHRIST IS PREACHED

[12]And I want you to know, dear brothers and sisters,* that everything that has happened to me here has helped to spread the Good News. [13]For everyone here, including all the soldiers in the palace guard, knows that I am in chains because of Christ. [14]And because of my imprisonment, many of the Christians* here have gained confidence and become more bold in telling others about Christ.

[15]Some are preaching out of jealousy and rivalry. But others preach about Christ with pure motives. [16]They preach because they love me, for they know the Lord brought me here to defend the Good News. [17]Those others do not have pure motives as they preach about Christ. They preach with selfish ambition, not sincerely, intending to make my chains more painful to me. [18]But whether or not their motives are pure, the fact remains that the message about Christ is being preached, so I rejoice. And I will continue to rejoice. [19]For I know that as you pray for me and as the Spirit of Jesus Christ helps me, this will all turn out for my deliverance.

PAUL'S LIFE FOR CHRIST

[20]For I live in eager expectation and hope that I will never do anything that causes me shame, but that I will always be bold for Christ, as I have been in the past, and that my life will always honor Christ, whether I live or I die. [21]For to me, living is for Christ, and dying is even better. [22]Yet if I live, that means fruitful service for Christ. I really don't know which is better. [23]I'm torn between two desires: Sometimes I want to live, and sometimes I long to go and be with Christ. That would be far better for me, [24]but it is better for you that I live.

[25]I am convinced of this, so I will continue with you so that you will grow and experience the joy of your faith. [26]Then when I return to you, you will have even more reason to boast about what Christ Jesus has done for me.

LIVE AS CITIZENS OF HEAVEN

[27]But whatever happens to me, you must live in a manner worthy of the Good News about Christ, as citizens of heaven. Then, whether I come and see you again or only hear about you, I will know that you are standing side by

1:1 Greek *overseers.* 1:11 Greek *the fruit of righteousness.* 1:12 Greek *brothers.* 1:14 Greek *brothers in the Lord.*

side, fighting together for the Good News. [28]Don't be intimidated by your enemies. This will be a sign to them that they are going to be destroyed, but that you are going to be saved, even by God himself. [29]For you have been given not only the privilege of trusting in Christ but also the privilege of suffering for him. [30]We are in this fight together. You have seen me suffer for him in the past, and you know that I am still in the midst of this great struggle.

UNITY THROUGH HUMILITY

2 Is there any encouragement from belonging to Christ? Any comfort from his love? Any fellowship together in the Spirit? Are your hearts tender and sympathetic? [2]Then make me truly happy by agreeing wholeheartedly with each other, loving one another, and working together with one heart and purpose.

[3]Don't be selfish; don't live to make a good impression on others. Be humble, thinking of others as better than yourself. [4]Don't think only about your own affairs, but be interested in others, too, and what they are doing.

CHRIST'S HUMILITY AND EXALTATION

[5]Your attitude should be the same that Christ Jesus had. [6]Though he was God, he did not demand and cling to his rights as God. [7]He made himself nothing;* he took the humble position of a slave and appeared in human form.* [8]And in human form he obediently humbled himself even further by dying a criminal's death on a cross. [9]Because of this, God raised him up to the heights of heaven and gave him a name that is above every other name, [10]so that at the name of Jesus every knee will bow, in heaven and on earth and under the earth, [11]and every tongue will confess that Jesus Christ is Lord, to the glory of God the Father.

SHINE BRIGHTLY FOR CHRIST

[12]Dearest friends, you were always so careful to follow my instructions when I was with you.

And now that I am away you must be even more careful to put into action God's saving work in your lives, obeying God with deep reverence and fear. [13]For God is working in you, giving you the desire to obey him and the power to do what pleases him.

[14]In everything you do, stay away from complaining and arguing, [15]so that no one can speak a word of blame against you. You are to live clean, innocent lives as children of God in a dark world full of crooked and perverse people. Let your lives shine brightly before them. [16]Hold tightly to the word of life, so that when Christ returns, I will be proud that I did not lose the race and that my work was not useless. [17]But even if my life is to be poured out like a drink offering to complete the sacrifice of your faithful service (that is, if I am to die for you), I will rejoice, and I want to share my joy with all of you. [18]And you should be happy about this and rejoice with me.

PAUL COMMENDS TIMOTHY

[19]If the Lord Jesus is willing, I hope to send Timothy to you soon. Then when he comes back, he can cheer me up by telling me how you are getting along. [20]I have no one else like Timothy, who genuinely cares about your welfare. [21]All the others care only for themselves and not for what matters to Jesus Christ. [22]But you know how Timothy has proved himself. Like a son with his father, he has helped me in preaching the Good News. [23]I hope to send him to you just as soon as I find out what is going to happen to me here. [24]And I have confidence from the Lord that I myself will come to see you soon.

PAUL COMMENDS EPAPHRODITUS

[25]Meanwhile, I thought I should send Epaphroditus back to you. He is a true brother, a faithful worker, and a courageous soldier. And he was your messenger to help me in my need. [26]Now I am sending him home again, for he has been longing to see you, and

2:7a Or *He laid aside his mighty power and glory.* **2:7b** Greek *and was born in the likeness of men and was found in appearance as a man.*

My Daily Worship

— November 25 —

A GROWING APPRECIATION!

PHILIPPIANS 1:1–2:30

I pray that your love for each other will overflow more and more, and that you will keep on growing in your knowledge and understanding (1:9).

[i reflect]

Remember thinking:

- Your college roommate was a real loser . . . and she became your best friend!
- The salesman had nothing to offer . . . but you bought and the product was amazing!
- The restaurant looked like a hole in the wall . . . but served reasonably priced gourmet meals.
- Your neighbor was pretentious . . . but he turned out to be a down-to-earth guy.
- The women's Bible study was filled with cliques. . . and they warmly embraced and accepted you.

First impressions can indeed be misleading. When you take the time to know someone deeply, that relationship changes your attitudes about the other person or product or place. It also changes you. That's why the apostle Paul let the Christians in Philippi know that he was praying that their knowledge of God would increase. He knew that as we grow In our awareness of our heavenly Father we come to a deeper appreciation of his glory and greatness. The more we appreciate him the more we want to please him. As a result our lives, relationships, and choices are positively impacted.

Origen, an early church father, put it this way: "If we look at the names by which the Son of God is called, we will understand how many of these good things he is." Study the Person of Christ and all his many attributes, and there is no doubt that you will be changed.

Celebrate as many attributes of Christ as you can think of in the next five minutes. Use these names and attributes throughout the day to worship him.

[i pray]

Lord, I'm excited that you want to grow my life from the inside out. Help me be aware of the choices I make today that will facilitate that growth or detract from it. Amen.

[i respond]

Make a growth chart of your relationship with God. Write in categories, such as prayer, meditation, praise, thanksgiving, Bible study/reading. Assess yourself in each category and determine in which area you need the most growth.

he was very distressed that you heard he was ill. [27]And he surely was ill; in fact, he almost died. But God had mercy on him—and also on me, so that I would not have such unbearable sorrow.

[28]So I am all the more anxious to send him back to you, for I know you will be glad to see him, and that will lighten all my cares. [29]Welcome him with Christian love* and with great joy, and be sure to honor people like him. [30]For he risked his life for the work of Christ, and he was at the point of death while trying to do for me the things you couldn't do because you were far away.

THE PRICELESS GAIN OF KNOWING CHRIST

3 Whatever happens, dear brothers and sisters,* may the Lord give you joy. I never get tired of telling you this. I am doing this for your own good.

[2]Watch out for those dogs, those wicked men and their evil deeds, those mutilators who say you must be circumcised to be saved. [3]For we who worship God in the Spirit* are the only ones who are truly circumcised. We put no confidence in human effort. Instead, we boast about what Christ Jesus has done for us.

[4]Yet I could have confidence in myself if anyone could. If others have reason for confidence in their own efforts, I have even more! [5]For I was circumcised when I was eight days old, having been born into a pure-blooded Jewish family that is a branch of the tribe of Benjamin. So I am a real Jew if there ever was one! What's more, I was a member of the Pharisees, who demand the strictest obedience to the Jewish law. [6]And zealous? Yes, in fact, I harshly persecuted the church. And I obeyed the Jewish law so carefully that I was never accused of any fault.

[7]I once thought all these things were so very important, but now I consider them worthless because of what Christ has done.

[8]Yes, everything else is worthless when compared with the priceless gain of knowing Christ Jesus my Lord. I have discarded everything else, counting it all as garbage, so that I may have Christ [9]and become one with him. I no longer count on my own goodness or my ability to obey God's law, but I trust Christ to save me. For God's way of making us right with himself depends on faith. [10]As a result, I can really know Christ and experience the mighty power that raised him from the dead. I can learn what it means to suffer with him, sharing in his death, [11]so that, somehow, I can experience the resurrection from the dead!

PRESSING TOWARD THE GOAL

[12]I don't mean to say that I have already achieved these things or that I have already reached perfection! But I keep working toward that day when I will finally be all that Christ Jesus saved me for and wants me to be. [13]No, dear brothers and sisters, I am still not all I should be,* but I am focusing all my energies on this one thing: Forgetting the past and looking forward to what lies ahead, [14]I strain to reach the end of the race and receive the prize for which God, through Christ Jesus, is calling us up to heaven.*

[15]I hope all of you who are mature Christians will agree on these things. If you disagree on some point, I believe God will make it plain to you. [16]But we must be sure to obey the truth we have learned already.

[17]Dear brothers and sisters, pattern your lives after mine, and learn from those who follow our example. [18]For I have told you often before, and I say it again with tears in my eyes, that there are many whose conduct shows they are really enemies of the cross of Christ. [19]Their future is eternal destruction. Their god is their appetite, they brag about shameful things, and all they think about is this life here on earth. [20]But we are citizens of heaven, where the Lord Jesus Christ lives. And we are

---

2:29 Greek *in the Lord.*   3:1 Greek *brothers;* also in 3:13, 17.   3:3 Or *in spirit;* some manuscripts read *worship by the Spirit of God.*
3:13 Some manuscripts read *I am not all I should be.*   3:14 Or *from heaven.*

My Daily Worship

— *November 26* —

TOWERING ABOVE THE TRASH

PHILIPPIANS 3:1–4:23

*Yes, everything else is worthless when compared to the priceless gain of knowing
Christ Jesus my Lord. I have discarded everything else, counting it all
garbage, so that I may have Christ and become one with him (3:8–9).*

[i reflect]

Thousands who travel by cruise ships through the Inside Passage of Alaska annually journey inland to visit the old gold rush town of Nome. But few visitors would label it an attractive tourist spot. Garbage lines the streets. Due to harsh winters, permafrost, and limited landfill area, litter is left in front of many houses. Wrecked cars and broken down snowmobiles sit and rust on grassless front yards. Abandoned appliances, outgrown toys, and assorted refuse contribute to the unsightly landscape until the winter snows blanket them.

Amid the debris and litter that has come to define Nome's landscape is the community's Christian radio station that broadcasts biblical teaching, praise and worship songs, as well as Russian programs (that are heard 150 miles to the west in Siberia). KICY's transmitter tower stands 250 feet in the air pointing toward the One in whose name they broadcast daily. The contrast between the garbage on the ground and the tower in the air is striking.

According to what Paul is saying in this verse, our firsthand knowledge of Jesus elevates us to a level of living that towers over everything else in this world. We have a choice each day to preoccupy ourselves with the "garbage" of this world—career advancement, material possessions and wealth, pleasure, family life—or we can reach upward to what truly counts: a relationship with Christ.

All our other pursuits (including job, education, family life, hobbies, and future plans) are like the litter in Nome. They may represent valid experiences and meaningful accomplishments, but they are an eyesore in contrast to the beautiful relationship the Lord has invited us to experience with him.

Charles Wesley wrote passionately, "Thou, O Christ, art all I want, more than all in Thee I find."

Take out the garbage today—remove all the litter that is preventing you from living for Jesus today.

[i pray]

*Lord, I'm ashamed to admit it, but you already know it's true. I am more apt to focus
on the routines and relationships that characterize my life than to look up in
your direction to remember what's really important. Forgive me, Father.
Cause me to remember where my worth really lies. Amen.*

[i respond]

Make a sign that reads "All for the burning." Tape it to the garbage can you use the most in your home (most likely the one in the kitchen). Each time you go to throw something away, allow the sign to remind you that all is trash except for your relationship with Jesus.

eagerly waiting for him to return as our Savior. [21]He will take these weak mortal bodies of ours and change them into glorious bodies like his own, using the same mighty power that he will use to conquer everything, everywhere.

4 Dear brothers and sisters,* I love you and long to see you, for you are my joy and the reward for my work. So please stay true to the Lord, my dear friends.

PAUL'S FINAL THOUGHTS

[2]And now I want to plead with those two women, Euodia and Syntyche. Please, because you belong to the Lord, settle your disagreement. [3]And I ask you, my true teammate,* to help these women, for they worked hard with me in telling others the Good News. And they worked with Clement and the rest of my coworkers, whose names are written in the Book of Life.

[4]Always be full of joy in the Lord. I say it again—rejoice! [5]Let everyone see that you are considerate in all you do. Remember, the Lord is coming soon.

[6]Don't worry about anything; instead, pray about everything. Tell God what you need, and thank him for all he has done. [7]If you do this, you will experience God's peace, which is far more wonderful than the human mind can understand. His peace will guard your hearts and minds as you live in Christ Jesus.

[8]And now, dear brothers and sisters, let me say one more thing as I close this letter. Fix your thoughts on what is true and honorable and right. Think about things that are pure and lovely and admirable. Think about things that are excellent and worthy of praise. [9]Keep putting into practice all you learned from me and heard from me and saw me doing, and the God of peace will be with you.

PAUL'S THANKS FOR THEIR GIFTS

[10]How grateful I am, and how I praise the Lord that you are concerned about me again. I know you have always been concerned for me, but for a while you didn't have the chance to help me. [11]Not that I was ever in need, for I have learned how to get along happily whether I have much or little. [12]I know how to live on almost nothing or with everything. I have learned the secret of living in every situation, whether it is with a full stomach or empty, with plenty or little. [13]For I can do everything with the help of Christ who gives me the strength I need. [14]But even so, you have done well to share with me in my present difficulty.

[15]As you know, you Philippians were the only ones who gave me financial help when I brought you the Good News and then traveled on from Macedonia. No other church did this. [16]Even when I was in Thessalonica you sent help more than once. [17]I don't say this because I want a gift from you. What I want is for you to receive a well-earned reward because of your kindness.

[18]At the moment I have all I need—more than I need! I am generously supplied with the gifts you sent me with Epaphroditus. They are a sweet-smelling sacrifice that is acceptable to God and pleases him. [19]And this same God who takes care of me will supply all your needs from his glorious riches, which have been given to us in Christ Jesus. [20]Now glory be to God our Father forever and ever. Amen.

PAUL'S FINAL GREETINGS

[21]Give my greetings to all the Christians there. The brothers who are with me here send you their greetings. [22]And all the other Christians send their greetings, too, especially those who work in Caesar's palace.

[23]May the grace of the Lord Jesus Christ be with your spirit.

4:1 Greek brothers; also in 4:8.   4:3 Greek true yokefellow, or loyal Syzygus.

Colossians

For God in all his fullness was pleased to live in Christ, and by him God reconciled

everything to himself. He made peace with everything in heaven and

on earth by means of his blood on the cross (1:19–20).

The Only Way to Worship

What is worthy of your worship? High-minded solid citizens of all ages have worshiped rocks, ironwork, statues, and prophets with a message from God—or sometimes with just a severely super-charged idea of the self. Finding something to worship is not difficult. Candidates line up. Religious movements supply many options.

Paul writes this letter to Christians at Colosse to spare them the really bad mistake of worship wrongly directly. A person who wakes up to discover that the little god of stone is worthless is a person whose soul is scarred and whose heart may harden to the truth. And the truth is so full of wonder—it is so good!—that no one should be diverted by little gods. Yet we are.

With a strong love for his readers, Paul warns against "empty philosophy and high-sounding nonsense that come from human thinking" (2:8). He pleads with the church not to be preoccupied with worshiping angels (2:18), and goes on to explain that worship is not the work of the flesh (2:20–23) or restricted to a certain group of people (3:11).

All these worship options are many ways to penetrate the divine mystery and harness its power. Yet each, sadly, distracts us into a cul-de-sac away from the flow of God's action in the world.

The truth is that God created the world, lost it to sin, then won it back and made us part of his family again through the work of Christ. Because Christ was God's way of provision, he is the *only* way. The heart of God, the power and purpose of God, is found in Jesus Christ.

Today a mood of secularism offers powerful substitutes for needs that only God can meet. Paul's letter to Colosse reminds us: not many ways, not human ways, but God's way—Jesus. Worship him.

Worship Moments

- Worshiping the results of good thinking turns a God-given capacity into a terrible distraction (2:8).

- Rules and rituals help us keep peace and celebrate our common bonds. Keep useful rules and rituals properly focused. Keep Christ supreme (2:16–17).

- Proper relationships reduce stress and create communities capable of cooperation and worship. Trust God with your life, and praise God for each day's opportunities (3:18–4:1).

- Worship involves music, recitation, and instruction designed to foster gratitude to God. Each component is to be focused on exploring and adopting the Words of Christ (3:16).

GREETINGS FROM PAUL

1 This letter is from Paul, chosen by God to be an apostle of Christ Jesus, and from our brother Timothy.

[2] It is written to God's holy people in the city of Colosse, who are faithful brothers and sisters* in Christ.

May God our Father give you grace and peace.

PAUL'S THANKSGIVING AND PRAYER

[3] We always pray for you, and we give thanks to God the Father of our Lord Jesus Christ, [4] for we have heard that you trust in Christ Jesus and that you love all of God's people. [5] You do this because you are looking forward to the joys of heaven—as you have been ever since you first heard the truth of the Good News. [6] This same Good News that came to you is going out all over the world. It is changing lives everywhere, just as it changed yours that very first day you heard and understood the truth about God's great kindness to sinners.

[7] Epaphras, our much loved co-worker, was the one who brought you the Good News. He is Christ's faithful servant, and he is helping us in your place.* [8] He is the one who told us about the great love for others that the Holy Spirit has given you.

[9] So we have continued praying for you ever since we first heard about you. We ask God to give you a complete understanding of what he wants to do in your lives, and we ask him to make you wise with spiritual wisdom. [10] Then the way you live will always honor and please the Lord, and you will continually do good, kind things for others. All the while, you will learn to know God better and better.

[11] We also pray that you will be strengthened with his glorious power so that you will have all the patience and endurance you need. May you be filled with joy, [12] always thanking the Father, who has enabled you to share the inheritance that belongs to God's holy people, who live in the light. [13] For he has rescued us from the one who rules in the kingdom of darkness, and he has brought us into the Kingdom of his dear Son. [14] God has purchased our freedom with his blood* and has forgiven all our sins.

CHRIST IS SUPREME

[15] Christ is the visible image of the invisible God. He existed before God made anything at all and is supreme over all creation.* [16] Christ is the one through whom God created everything in heaven and earth. He made the things we can see and the things we can't see—kings, kingdoms, rulers, and authorities. Everything has been created through him and for him. [17] He existed before everything else began, and he holds all creation together.

[18] Christ is the head of the church, which is his body. He is the first of all who will rise from the dead,* so he is first in everything. [19] For God in all his fullness was pleased to live in Christ, [20] and by him God reconciled everything to himself. He made peace with everything in heaven and on earth by means of his blood on the cross. [21] This includes you who were once so far away from God. You were his enemies, separated from him by your evil thoughts and actions, [22] yet now he has brought you back as his friends. He has done this through his death on the cross in his own human body. As a result, he has brought you into the very presence of God, and you are holy and blameless as you stand before him without a single fault. [23] But you must continue to believe this truth and stand in it firmly. Don't drift away from the assurance you received when you heard the Good News. The Good News has been preached all over the world, and I, Paul, have been appointed by God to proclaim it.

1:2 Greek *faithful brothers.* 1:7 Greek *he is ministering on your behalf;* other manuscripts read *he is ministering on our behalf.* 1:14 Some manuscripts do not include *with his blood.* 1:15 Greek *He is the firstborn of all creation.* 1:18 Greek *He is the beginning, the firstborn from the dead.*

My Daily Worship

— *November 27* —

ENEMIES NO LONGER

COLOSSIANS 1:1–2:23

You were his enemies, separated from him by your evil thoughts and actions,
yet now he has brought you back as his friends (1:21–22).

[i reflect]

When Wayne Messmer was shot in the throat by a teenage thug in April 1994, he thought his career was over. In addition to singing the national anthem at various sporting events, the Chicago businessman had made his living as a motivational speaker. Doctors doubted if Wayne would speak again (let alone sing) if he survived.

Miraculously Mr. Star Spangled Banner was at the mike six months later honoring America at the start of the Chicago Blackhawks game. What was an even greater miracle was Wayne's decision to seek out his assailant to offer forgiveness. Driving to the Galesburg Correctional Center, this Christian celebrity extended his hand to James Hampton and said, "I bid you peace."

Amazing? Yes. Yet that is exactly the action God has taken in response to our malicious thoughts and behavior. The offended holy One, with every reason to consider us his enemies, has welcomed us as his friends. It's more than a truce. The lines of separation have been erased. Relationship exists where once there was alienation and condemnation. That's how Paul describes God's disposition towards us in this verse. In his infinite mercy, God has drawn us to himself as friends.

It's totally unexpected and undeserved. Songwriter Stephen Curtis Chapman wrote about this incredible truth, "In the gospel, we discover we are far worse off than we thought, and far more loved than we dreamed." Apart from that love, there is no way that our sin could be removed or forgiven—or that we could offer that same love and forgiveness to another.

You are God's friend. Celebrate that truth today by renewing that friendship. Spend time with him. Talk to him. Share with him your gratitude for all he has done for you.

[i pray]

Heavenly Father, how can I say thanks for all you've done for me? I don't deserve
the friendship you hold out to me. But the offer is too wonderful
to hold at arms length. Help me embrace it with both arms.

[i respond]

Finish this statement, "Because God is my friend, I have . . ." Share your thoughts with one of your close friends. Together, rejoice in the gift of friendship.

PAUL'S WORK FOR THE CHURCH

²⁴I am glad when I suffer for you in my body, for I am completing what remains of Christ's sufferings for his body, the church. ²⁵God has given me the responsibility of serving his church by proclaiming his message in all its fullness to you Gentiles. ²⁶This message was kept secret for centuries and generations past, but now it has been revealed to his own holy people. ²⁷For it has pleased God to tell his people that the riches and glory of Christ are for you Gentiles, too. For this is the secret: Christ lives in you, and this is your assurance that you will share in his glory.

²⁸So everywhere we go, we tell everyone about Christ. We warn them and teach them with all the wisdom God has given us, for we want to present them to God, perfect* in their relationship to Christ. ²⁹I work very hard at this, as I depend on Christ's mighty power that works within me.

2 I want you to know how much I have agonized for you and for the church at Laodicea, and for many other friends who have never known me personally. ²My goal is that they will be encouraged and knit together by strong ties of love. I want them to have full confidence because they have complete understanding of God's secret plan, which is Christ himself. ³In him lie hidden all the treasures of wisdom and knowledge.

⁴I am telling you this so that no one will be able to deceive you with persuasive arguments. ⁵For though I am far away from you, my heart is with you. And I am very happy because you are living as you should and because of your strong faith in Christ.

FREEDOM FROM RULES AND NEW LIFE IN CHRIST

⁶And now, just as you accepted Christ Jesus as your Lord, you must continue to live in obedience to him. ⁷Let your roots grow down into him and draw up nourishment from him, so you will grow in faith, strong and vigorous in the truth you were taught. Let your lives overflow with thanksgiving for all he has done.

⁸Don't let anyone lead you astray with empty philosophy and high-sounding nonsense that come from human thinking and from the evil powers of this world,* and not from Christ. ⁹For in Christ the fullness of God lives in a human body,* ¹⁰and you are complete through your union with Christ. He is the Lord over every ruler and authority in the universe.

¹¹When you came to Christ, you were "circumcised," but not by a physical procedure. It was a spiritual procedure—the cutting away of your sinful nature. ¹²For you were buried with Christ when you were baptized. And with him you were raised to a new life because you trusted the mighty power of God, who raised Christ from the dead.

¹³You were dead because of your sins and because your sinful nature was not yet cut away. Then God made you alive with Christ. He forgave all our sins. ¹⁴He canceled the record that contained the charges against us. He took it and destroyed it by nailing it to Christ's cross. ¹⁵In this way, God disarmed the evil rulers and authorities. He shamed them publicly by his victory over them on the cross of Christ.

¹⁶So don't let anyone condemn you for what you eat or drink, or for not celebrating certain holy days or new-moon ceremonies or Sabbaths. ¹⁷For these rules were only shadows of the real thing, Christ himself. ¹⁸Don't let anyone condemn you by insisting on self-denial. And don't let anyone say you must worship angels, even though they say they have had visions about this. These people claim to be so humble, but their sinful minds have made them proud. ¹⁹But they are not connected to Christ, the head of the body. For we are joined together in his body by his strong sinews, and we grow only as we get our nourishment and strength from God.

²⁰You have died with Christ, and he has set

1:28 Or *mature.*   **2:8** Or *from the basic principles of this world;* also in 2:20.   **2:9** Greek *in him dwells all the fullness of the Godhead bodily.*

My Daily Worship
— November 28 —

A Stadium Choir
Colossians 3:1 – 4:18

Let the words of Christ, in all their richness, live in your hearts and make you wise.
Use his words to teach and counsel each other. Sing psalms and hymns
and spiritual songs to God with thankful hearts (3:16).

[i reflect]

For the last decade of the twentieth century, an amazing phenomenon occurred in sports stadiums across the United States. Hundreds of thousands of men gathered to do something other than cheer on their favorite team. They were cheering their Creator with Christian music. The Promise Keepers movement saw arenas and stadiums packed to capacity with men acknowledging their need for God. The two-day events were filled with testimonies, biblical teaching, and extended times of singing.

What occurred during those events is exactly what Paul describes in this letter to the Colossian Christians—the rich words of Christ so embedded in the soul that they find expression in psalms, hymns, and spiritual songs. With tears rolling down their up-turned faces, big burly men sang "O For a Thousand Tongues to Sing" and "Amazing Grace." But they also sang lyrics they had learned for the first time—songs like "Open the Eyes of My Heart" and "Give Thanks." It's an awesome sound.

Even if you never attended a Promise Keeper event, you can experience the power of praise music in your personal time of worship at home. Go ahead and crank up your CD player with your favorite album of Christian music. Close your eyes and close out the demands of your calendar and "to do" list. Sing along. Open your Bible and let the words of God take root in your heart.

[i pray]

Jesus, thanks for the wonderful gift of lyrics and music. I want to worship you today
with an open heart and an open mouth. Accept my vocal offering
(even if it's somewhat out of tune) as my gift of love.

[i respond]

If you haven't treated yourself recently, make a trip to your local Christian bookstore and buy a new praise and worship CD or tape. As you drive home, crank it up and sing along, giving the anxieties of your day to the Lord.

you free from the evil powers of this world. So why do you keep on following rules of the world, such as, ²¹"Don't handle, don't eat, don't touch." ²²Such rules are mere human teaching about things that are gone as soon as we use them. ²³These rules may seem wise because they require strong devotion, humility, and severe bodily discipline. But they have no effect when it comes to conquering a person's evil thoughts and desires.

Living the New Life

3 Since you have been raised to new life with Christ, set your sights on the realities of heaven, where Christ sits at God's right hand in the place of honor and power. ²Let heaven fill your thoughts. Do not think only about things down here on earth. ³For you died when Christ died, and your real life is hidden with Christ in God. ⁴And when Christ, who is your* real life, is revealed to the whole world, you will share in all his glory.

⁵So put to death the sinful, earthly things lurking within you. Have nothing to do with sexual sin, impurity, lust, and shameful desires. Don't be greedy for the good things of this life, for that is idolatry. ⁶God's terrible anger will come upon those who do such things. ⁷You used to do them when your life was still part of this world. ⁸But now is the time to get rid of anger, rage, malicious behavior, slander, and dirty language. ⁹Don't lie to each other, for you have stripped off your old evil nature and all its wicked deeds. ¹⁰In its place you have clothed yourselves with a brand-new nature that is continually being renewed as you learn more and more about Christ, who created this new nature within you. ¹¹In this new life, it doesn't matter if you are a Jew or a Gentile,* circumcised or uncircumcised, barbaric, uncivilized,* slave, or free. Christ is all that matters, and he lives in all of us.

¹²Since God chose you to be the holy people whom he loves, you must clothe yourselves with tenderhearted mercy, kindness, humility, gentleness, and patience. ¹³You must make allowance for each other's faults and forgive the person who offends you. Remember, the Lord forgave you, so you must forgive others. ¹⁴And the most important piece of clothing you must wear is love. Love is what binds us all together in perfect harmony. ¹⁵And let the peace that comes from Christ rule in your hearts. For as members of one body you are all called to live in peace. And always be thankful.

¹⁶Let the words of Christ, in all their richness, live in your hearts and make you wise. Use his words to teach and counsel each other. Sing psalms and hymns and spiritual songs to God with thankful hearts. ¹⁷And whatever you do or say, let it be as a representative of the Lord Jesus, all the while giving thanks through him to God the Father.

Instructions for Christian Households

¹⁸You wives must submit to your husbands, as is fitting for those who belong to the Lord. ¹⁹And you husbands must love your wives and never treat them harshly.

²⁰You children must always obey your parents, for this is what pleases the Lord. ²¹Fathers, don't aggravate your children. If you do, they will become discouraged and quit trying.

²²You slaves must obey your earthly masters in everything you do. Try to please them all the time, not just when they are watching you. Obey them willingly because of your reverent fear of the Lord. ²³Work hard and cheerfully at whatever you do, as though you were working for the Lord rather than for people. ²⁴Remember that the Lord will give you an inheritance as your reward, and the Master you are serving is Christ. ²⁵But if you do what is wrong, you will be paid back for the wrong you have done. For God has no favorites who can get away with evil.

3:4 Some manuscripts read *our.* 3:11a Greek *Greek.* 3:11b Greek *Barbarian, Scythian.*

4 You slave owners must be just and fair to your slaves. Remember that you also have a Master—in heaven.

AN ENCOURAGEMENT FOR PRAYER

²Devote yourselves to prayer with an alert mind and a thankful heart. ³Don't forget to pray for us, too, that God will give us many opportunities to preach about his secret plan—that Christ is also for you Gentiles. That is why I am here in chains. ⁴Pray that I will proclaim this message as clearly as I should.

⁵Live wisely among those who are not Christians, and make the most of every opportunity. ⁶Let your conversation be gracious and effective so that you will have the right answer for everyone.

PAUL'S FINAL INSTRUCTIONS AND GREETINGS

⁷Tychicus, a much loved brother, will tell you how I am getting along. He is a faithful helper who serves the Lord with me. ⁸I have sent him on this special trip to let you know how we are doing and to encourage you. ⁹I am also sending Onesimus, a faithful and much loved brother, one of your own people. He and Tychicus will give you all the latest news.

¹⁰Aristarchus, who is in prison with me, sends you his greetings, and so does Mark, Barnabas's cousin. And as you were instructed before, make Mark welcome if he comes your way. ¹¹Jesus (the one we call Justus) also sends his greetings. These are the only Jewish Christians among my co-workers; they are working with me here for the Kingdom of God. And what a comfort they have been!

¹²Epaphras, from your city, a servant of Christ Jesus, sends you his greetings. He always prays earnestly for you, asking God to make you strong and perfect, fully confident of the whole will of God. ¹³I can assure you that he has agonized for you and also for the Christians in Laodicea and Hierapolis.

¹⁴Dear Doctor Luke sends his greetings, and so does Demas. ¹⁵Please give my greetings to our Christian brothers and sisters* at Laodicea, and to Nympha and those who meet in her house.

¹⁶After you have read this letter, pass it on to the church at Laodicea so they can read it, too. And you should read the letter I wrote to them. ¹⁷And say to Archippus, "Be sure to carry out the work the Lord gave you."

¹⁸Here is my greeting in my own handwriting—PAUL.

Remember my chains.

May the grace of God be with you.

4:15 Greek *brothers*.

1 & 2 Thessalonians

But you aren't in the dark about these things, dear brothers and sisters, and you won't be surprised when the day of the Lord comes like a thief. For you are all children of the light and of the day. . . . So encourage each other and build each other up (1 Thessalonians 5:4–5, 11).

Keeping the Faith

To the young church of mostly new believers, in the very large city of Thessalonica in Macedonia, Paul writes two passionate letters of appeal. *Keep your unity, your love, your eagerness to serve the Lord Jesus,* he urges. First like a mother, then like a father, Paul reminds these people of his love for them. Like a good parent, he shares his spiritual concern over their future. He asks them to do three things.

First, remember the truth. Paul had taught them well, though his visit was brief. If new believers forget the truth, all is lost. Live as they had been taught (1 Thessalonians 4:1–2), and keep from false claims that can shake the faith (2 Thessalonians 2:2).

Second, build up this new community Christ has created, the church. Don't tolerate slackers, but don't reject them either. Build each other up.

Third, be watchful for the consummation, the final days, the Lord's coming in judgment and triumph. A "man of lawlessness" is hell-bent on spiritual destruction. False prophets claim to offer divine insight. An era of rebellion will tempt believers to cave in and give up. Be smart and steady, Paul writes.

None of these counter-strategies—truth-keeping, church-building, steadiness under fire—can happen without the Christian community's center holding strong. Paul did not have to say it. Everywhere he points to it: worship together, pray, sing, and teach the Word; grow in the knowledge of God; let the Spirit of God deepen your faith.

Christians cannot build the church when worship is pencilled lightly on the calendar. Strong people and churches know worship is priority one, the center. In worship, darkness gets pushed back as the brilliance of God's truth captures the heart. For this Paul prays. These children of light, newborns in the life of God, will have to carry on when Paul is gone.

Worship Moments

- Love is overture and response, initiative and reception. It is the keynote, the bedrock, of all personal relationships for the Christian (1 Thessalonians 3:12).

- Christian life cannot stagnate. God wills for spiritual progress in his people, for worship to be increasingly focused on the glory that others cannot see (1 Thessalonians 4:1–3).

- God actively strengthens us for witness and service. This strengthening occurs in corporate and personal worship, in sharing life with other believers, in centering our ambitions and energies on God's glory (2 Thessalonians 2:16–17).

Greetings from Paul

1 This letter is from Paul, Silas,* and Timothy.

It is written to the church in Thessalonica, you who belong to God the Father and the Lord Jesus Christ.

May his grace and peace be yours.

The Faith of the Thessalonian Believers

2 We always thank God for all of you and pray for you constantly. 3 As we talk to our God and Father about you, we think of your faithful work, your loving deeds, and your continual anticipation of the return of our Lord Jesus Christ.

4 We know that God loves you, dear brothers and sisters,* and that he chose you to be his own people. 5 For when we brought you the Good News, it was not only with words but also with power, for the Holy Spirit gave you full assurance that what we said was true. And you know that the way we lived among you was further proof of the truth of our message. 6 So you received the message with joy from the Holy Spirit in spite of the severe suffering it brought you. In this way, you imitated both us and the Lord. 7 As a result, you yourselves became an example to all the Christians in Greece.* 8 And now the word of the Lord is ringing out from you to people everywhere, even beyond Greece, for wherever we go we find people telling us about your faith in God. We don't need to tell them about it, 9 for they themselves keep talking about the wonderful welcome you gave us and how you turned away from idols to serve the true and living God. 10 And they speak of how you are looking forward to the coming of God's Son from heaven—Jesus, whom God raised from the dead. He is the one who has rescued us from the terrors of the coming judgment.

Paul Remembers His Visit

2 You yourselves know, dear brothers and sisters,* that our visit to you was not a failure. 2 You know how badly we had been treated at Philippi just before we came to you and how much we suffered there. Yet our God gave us the courage to declare his Good News to you boldly, even though we were surrounded by many who opposed us. 3 So you can see that we were not preaching with any deceit or impure purposes or trickery.

4 For we speak as messengers who have been approved by God to be entrusted with the Good News. Our purpose is to please God, not people. He is the one who examines the motives of our hearts. 5 Never once did we try to win you with flattery, as you very well know. And God is our witness that we were not just pretending to be your friends so you would give us money! 6 As for praise, we have never asked for it from you or anyone else. 7 As apostles of Christ we certainly had a right to make some demands of you, but we were as gentle among you as a mother* feeding and caring for her own children. 8 We loved you so much that we gave you not only God's Good News but our own lives, too.

9 Don't you remember, dear brothers and sisters, how hard we worked among you? Night and day we toiled to earn a living so that our expenses would not be a burden to anyone there as we preached God's Good News among you. 10 You yourselves are our witnesses—and so is God—that we were pure and honest and faultless toward all of you believers. 11 And you know that we treated each of you as a father treats his own children. 12 We pleaded with you, encouraged you, and urged you to live your lives in a way that God would consider worthy. For he called you into his Kingdom to share his glory.

13 And we will never stop thanking God that when we preached his message to you, you didn't think of the words we spoke as being just our own. You accepted what we said as the very word of God—which, of course, it was. And this word continues to work in you who believe.

1:1 Greek *Silvanus*. 1:4 Greek *brothers*. 1:7 Greek *Macedonia and Achaia*, the northern and southern regions of Greece; also in 1:8. 2:1 Greek *brothers*; also in 2:9, 14, 17. 2:7 Some manuscripts read *we were as infants among you; we were as a mother*.

[14]And then, dear brothers and sisters, you suffered persecution from your own countrymen. In this way, you imitated the believers in God's churches in Judea who, because of their belief in Christ Jesus, suffered from their own people, the Jews. [15]For some of the Jews had killed their own prophets, and some even killed the Lord Jesus. Now they have persecuted us and driven us out. They displease God and oppose everyone [16]by trying to keep us from preaching the Good News to the Gentiles, for fear some might be saved. By doing this, they continue to pile up their sins. But the anger of God has caught up with them at last.

TIMOTHY'S GOOD REPORT ABOUT THE CHURCH

[17]Dear brothers and sisters, after we were separated from you for a little while (though our hearts never left you), we tried very hard to come back because of our intense longing to see you again. [18]We wanted very much to come, and I, Paul, tried again and again, but Satan prevented us. [19]After all, what gives us hope and joy, and what is our proud reward and crown? It is you! Yes, you will bring us much joy as we stand together before our Lord Jesus when he comes back again. [20]For you are our pride and joy.

3 Finally, when we could stand it no longer, we decided that I should stay alone in Athens, [2]and we sent Timothy to visit you. He is our co-worker for God and our brother in proclaiming the Good News of Christ. We sent him to strengthen you, to encourage you in your faith, [3]and to keep you from becoming disturbed by the troubles you were going through. But, of course, you know that such troubles are going to happen to us Christians. [4]Even while we were with you, we warned you that troubles would soon come—and they did, as you well know. [5]That is why, when I could bear it no longer,

I sent Timothy to find out whether your faith was still strong. I was afraid that the Tempter had gotten the best of you and that all our work had been useless. [6]Now Timothy has just returned, bringing the good news that your faith and love are as strong as ever. He reports that you remember our visit with joy and that you want to see us just as much as we want to see you. [7]So we have been greatly comforted, dear brothers and sisters,* in all of our own crushing troubles and suffering, because you have remained strong in your faith. [8]It gives us new life, knowing you remain strong in the Lord.

[9]How we thank God for you! Because of you we have great joy in the presence of God. [10]Night and day we pray earnestly for you, asking God to let us see you again to fill up anything that may still be missing in your faith.

[11]May God himself, our Father, and our Lord Jesus make it possible for us to come to you very soon. [12]And may the Lord make your love grow and overflow to each other and to everyone else, just as our love overflows toward you. [13]As a result, Christ will make your hearts strong, blameless, and holy when you stand before God our Father on that day when our Lord Jesus comes with all those who belong to him.

LIVE TO PLEASE GOD

4 Finally, dear brothers and sisters,* we urge you in the name of the Lord Jesus to live in a way that pleases God, as we have taught you. You are doing this already, and we encourage you to do so more and more. [2]For you remember what we taught you in the name of the Lord Jesus. [3]God wants you to be holy, so you should keep clear of all sexual sin. [4]Then each of you will control your body* and live in holiness and honor—[5]not in lustful passion as the pagans do, in their ignorance of God and his ways.

[6]Never cheat a Christian brother in this matter by taking his wife, for the Lord avenges

3:7 Greek *brothers.* 4:1 Greek *brothers;* also in 4:10, 13. 4:4 Or *will know how to take a wife for himself;* Greek reads *will know how to possess his own vessel.*

My Daily Worship

MORE THAN MERE WORDS

1 THESSALONIANS 1:1–3:13

For when we brought you the Good News, it was not only with words but also with power,
for the Holy Spirit gave you full assurance that what we said was true (1:5).

[i reflect]

In 1992 a community choir from Magadan, Siberia traveled to California on a tour. It was one of the first cultural exchanges following the fall of communism. In addition to performing Russian folk songs, the chorus also sang eastern European hymns that they had only recently learned. Because of the oppressive regime under which they had lived, the choir had never heard the rich songs of their nation's previous Christian heritage. These anthems had been locked in vaults for over seven decades.

As they stood before their American audiences, it was obvious the musicians had learned the music well. Their performance was technically correct. But their faces did not reflect the joy of faith the hymn's lyrics suggested. For the atheistic choir, the words wed to the melodies were only words. It was clear that they didn't believe the truth they were singing about.

That isn't only true of Siberian singers; we see that all around us. It's easy to say the right words or mouth worshipful lyrics without meaning what we say. Talk is cheap, right? As Paul writes these words to the Thessalonians, he is aware that words of faith don't always translate into lives of faith. His desire for them (and God's desire for us) is that Bible reading or Scripture memory not be an end in itself. What matters is the impact those words have on our life by putting them into practice.

As Billy Graham once observed, "Like Joseph storing up grain during the years of plenty to be used during the years of famine that lay ahead, we may store up the truths of God's Word in our hearts as much as possible, so that we are prepared for whatever suffering we are called upon to endure."

Store up God's powerful truths in your heart today. Read aloud this passage or another one that addresses your situation and circumstances. Speak powerfully and with expression.

[i pray]

Lord, please remind me today as I hold the Bible in my hands that I am really holding a book with
the spiritual power of several sticks of dynamite. I want the power of your life-transforming
truth to explode in my life. For today, I long to live out the words I read. Amen.

[i respond]

One of the songs performed at the Magadan choir concert was "How Great Thou Art." Find the family hymnal (or search on the Internet) and read through the lyrics of this wonderful hymn. Pray for those in Russia that they may not only hear these words, but also live in the truth of this hymn.

all such sins, as we have solemnly warned you before. [7]God has called us to be holy, not to live impure lives. [8]Anyone who refuses to live by these rules is not disobeying human rules but is rejecting God, who gives his Holy Spirit to you.

[9]But I don't need to write to you about the Christian love* that should be shown among God's people. For God himself has taught you to love one another. [10]Indeed, your love is already strong toward all the Christians* in all of Macedonia. Even so, dear brothers and sisters, we beg you to love them more and more. [11]This should be your ambition: to live a quiet life, minding your own business and working with your hands, just as we commanded you before. [12]As a result, people who are not Christians will respect the way you live, and you will not need to depend on others to meet your financial needs.

THE HOPE OF THE RESURRECTION

[13]And now, brothers and sisters, I want you to know what will happen to the Christians who have died so you will not be full of sorrow like people who have no hope. [14]For since we believe that Jesus died and was raised to life again, we also believe that when Jesus comes, God will bring back with Jesus all the Christians who have died.

[15]I can tell you this directly from the Lord: We who are still living when the Lord returns will not rise to meet him ahead of those who are in their graves. [16]For the Lord himself will come down from heaven with a commanding shout, with the call of the archangel, and with the trumpet call of God. First, all the Christians who have died will rise from their graves. [17]Then, together with them, we who are still alive and remain on the earth will be caught up in the clouds to meet the Lord in the air and remain with him forever. [18]So comfort and encourage each other with these words.

5 I really don't need to write to you about how and when all this will happen, dear brothers and sisters.* [2]For you know quite well that the day of the Lord will come unexpectedly, like a thief in the night. [3]When people are saying, "All is well; everything is peaceful and secure," then disaster will fall upon them as suddenly as a woman's birth pains begin when her child is about to be born. And there will be no escape.

[4]But you aren't in the dark about these things, dear brothers and sisters, and you won't be surprised when the day of the Lord comes like a thief. [5]For you are all children of the light and of the day; we don't belong to darkness and night. [6]So be on your guard, not asleep like the others. Stay alert and be sober. [7]Night is the time for sleep and the time when people get drunk. [8]But let us who live in the light think clearly, protected by the body armor of faith and love, and wearing as our helmet the confidence of our salvation. [9]For God decided to save us through our Lord Jesus Christ, not to pour out his anger on us. [10]He died for us so that we can live with him forever, whether we are dead or alive at the time of his return. [11]So encourage each other and build each other up, just as you are already doing.

PAUL'S FINAL ADVICE

[12]Dear brothers and sisters, honor those who are your leaders in the Lord's work. They work hard among you and warn you against all that is wrong. [13]Think highly of them and give them your wholehearted love because of their work. And remember to live peaceably with each other.

[14]Brothers and sisters, we urge you to warn those who are lazy. Encourage those who are timid. Take tender care of those who are weak. Be patient with everyone.

[15]See that no one pays back evil for evil, but always try to do good to each other and to everyone else.

[16]Always be joyful. [17]Keep on praying. [18]No

4:9 Greek *brotherly love.*   **4:10** Greek *the brothers.*   **5:1** Greek *brothers*; also in 5:4, 12, 14, 25, 26, 27.

My Daily Worship

— *November 30* —

THANKFUL, NO MATTER WHAT

1 THESSALONIANS 4:1–5:28

No matter what happens, always be thankful, for this is God's will
for you who belong to Christ Jesus (5:18).

[i reflect]

Fanny Jane Crosby was born in 1820. Shortly after she was born, the family doctor made a tragic mistake. Instead of irrigating her infant eyes with prescribed drops, he inadvertently used a toxic substance. The result? Fanny was blind for life. Amazingly, she lived without resentment or bitterness. This gifted poet, who penned several thousand poems that were set to music, was known for her cheerful outlook and her customary greeting: "God bless your dear soul." Her remarkable hymns are a chronicle of gratitude for God's blessings she experienced in her 95 years.

Although Christians still sing several of her well-known hymns a century after her death, one song in particular has universal appeal. The first stanza begins with these words: "To God be the glory, great things he has done." Isn't that something? How could Fanny attest to God's goodness when she was the victim of such a horrendous injustice? Obviously, she had reached the spiritual destination Paul held out as a worthy goal for all believers (including us). In spite of unpredictable circumstances, the apostle calls us to express our gratitude. He says it's God's will.

The tragic events that we are exposed to in an imperfect world are not necessarily the will of the Lord. But he does will that our response to those events be sprinkled with thanksgiving, knowing that he is still in control. That's not an easy assignment. To do this, we need to make time for God during each day. Laying our concerns at the Lord's feet, with thanksgiving, reminds us that someone greater than us is concerned about what we are going through.

Respond to God in praise every hour—no matter what has gone on before nor what you will be facing in the hour ahead. Model today what Paul encouraged believers to do centuries ago, "always be thankful."

[i pray]

O Lord, forgive me for thinking my life is bad when I consider the plight of someone like Fanny
Crosby. Help me respond today to the difficulties of my life in a way that honors you.

[i respond]

Resist the temptation to close your eyes to God's goodness because of any hurt feelings you are nursing. On a sheet of paper, list the blessings of your life that you tend to overlook. Start with sight. Include the ability to breathe or walk. How about having enough to eat? You've got the idea. Now keep adding to the list.

matter what happens, always be thankful, for this is God's will for you who belong to Christ Jesus.

[19] Do not stifle the Holy Spirit. [20] Do not scoff at prophecies, [21] but test everything that is said. Hold on to what is good. [22] Keep away from every kind of evil.

PAUL'S FINAL GREETINGS

[23] Now may the God of peace make you holy in every way, and may your whole spirit and soul and body be kept blameless until that day when our Lord Jesus Christ comes again. [24] God, who calls you, is faithful; he will do this.

[25] Dear brothers and sisters, pray for us.

[26] Greet all the brothers and sisters in Christian love.*

[27] I command you in the name of the Lord to read this letter to all the brothers and sisters.

[28] And may the grace of our Lord Jesus Christ be with all of you.

GREETINGS FROM PAUL

1 This letter is from Paul, Silas,* and Timothy.

It is written to the church in Thessalonica, you who belong to God our Father and the Lord Jesus Christ.

²May God our Father and the Lord Jesus Christ give you grace and peace.

ENCOURAGEMENT DURING PERSECUTION

³Dear brothers and sisters,* we always thank God for you, as is right, for we are thankful that your faith is flourishing and you are all growing in love for each other. ⁴We proudly tell God's other churches about your endurance and faithfulness in all the persecutions and hardships you are suffering. ⁵But God will use this persecution to show his justice. For he will make you worthy of his Kingdom, for which you are suffering, ⁶and in his justice he will punish those who persecute you. ⁷And God will provide rest for you who are being persecuted and also for us when the Lord Jesus appears from heaven. He will come with his mighty angels, ⁸in flaming fire, bringing judgment on those who don't know God and on those who refuse to obey the Good News of our Lord Jesus. ⁹They will be punished with everlasting destruction, forever separated from the Lord and from his glorious power ¹⁰when he comes to receive glory and praise from his holy people. And you will be among those praising him on that day, for you believed what we testified about him.

¹¹And so we keep on praying for you, that our God will make you worthy of the life to which he called you. And we pray that God, by his power, will fulfill all your good intentions and faithful deeds. ¹²Then everyone will give honor to the name of our Lord Jesus because of you, and you will be honored along with him. This is all made possible because of the undeserved favor of our God and Lord, Jesus Christ.*

EVENTS PRIOR TO THE LORD'S SECOND COMING

2 And now, brothers and sisters,* let us tell you about the coming again of our Lord Jesus Christ and how we will be gathered together to meet him. ²Please don't be so easily shaken and troubled by those who say that the day of the Lord has already begun. Even if they claim to have had a vision, a revelation, or a letter supposedly from us, don't believe them. ³Don't be fooled by what they say.

For that day will not come until there is a great rebellion against God and the man of lawlessness is revealed—the one who brings destruction.* ⁴He will exalt himself and defy every god there is and tear down every object of adoration and worship. He will position himself in the temple of God, claiming that he himself is God. ⁵Don't you remember that I told you this when I was with you? ⁶And you know what is holding him back, for he can be revealed only when his time comes.

⁷For this lawlessness is already at work secretly, and it will remain secret until the one who is holding it back steps out of the way. ⁸Then the man of lawlessness will be revealed, whom the Lord Jesus will consume with the breath of his mouth and destroy by the splendor of his coming. ⁹This evil man will come to do the work of Satan with counterfeit power and signs and miracles. ¹⁰He will use every kind of wicked deception to fool those who are on their way to destruction because they refuse to believe the truth that would save them. ¹¹So God will send great deception upon them, and they will believe all these lies. ¹²Then they will be condemned for not believing the truth and for enjoying the evil they do.

BELIEVERS SHOULD STAND FIRM

¹³As for us, we always thank God for you, dear brothers and sisters loved by the Lord. We are thankful that God chose you to be among the first* to experience salvation, a salvation that came through the Spirit who makes you holy

---

1:1 Greek *Silvanus.* 1:3 Greek *Brothers.* 1:12 Or *of our God and the Lord Jesus Christ.* 2:1 Greek *brothers;* also in 2:13, 15. 2:3 Greek *the son of destruction.* 2:13 Some manuscripts read *God chose you from the very beginning.*

and by your belief in the truth. [14]He called you to salvation when we told you the Good News; now you can share in the glory of our Lord Jesus Christ.

[15]With all these things in mind, dear brothers and sisters, stand firm and keep a strong grip on everything we taught you both in person and by letter.

[16]May our Lord Jesus Christ and God our Father, who loved us and in his special favor gave us everlasting comfort and good hope, [17]comfort your hearts and give you strength in every good thing you do and say.

PAUL'S REQUEST FOR PRAYER

3 Finally, dear brothers and sisters,* I ask you to pray for us. Pray first that the Lord's message will spread rapidly and be honored wherever it goes, just as when it came to you. [2]Pray, too, that we will be saved from wicked and evil people, for not everyone believes in the Lord. [3]But the Lord is faithful; he will make you strong and guard you from the evil one.* [4]And we are confident in the Lord that you are practicing the things we commanded you, and that you always will. [5]May the Lord bring you into an ever deeper understanding of the love of God and the endurance that comes from Christ.

AN EXHORTATION TO PROPER LIVING

[6]And now, dear brothers and sisters, we give you this command with the authority of our Lord Jesus Christ: Stay away from any Christian* who lives in idleness and doesn't follow the tradition of hard work we gave you. [7]For you know that you ought to follow our example. We were never lazy when we were with you. [8]We never accepted food from anyone without paying for it. We worked hard day and night so that we would not be a burden to any of you. [9]It wasn't that we didn't have the right to ask you to feed us, but we wanted to give you an example to follow. [10]Even while we were with you, we gave you this rule: "Whoever does not work should not eat."

[11]Yet we hear that some of you are living idle lives, refusing to work and wasting time meddling in other people's business. [12]In the name of the Lord Jesus Christ, we appeal to such people—no, we command them: Settle down and get to work. Earn your own living. [13]And I say to the rest of you, dear brothers and sisters, never get tired of doing good.

[14]Take note of those who refuse to obey what we say in this letter. Stay away from them so they will be ashamed. [15]Don't think of them as enemies, but speak to them as you would to a Christian who needs to be warned.

PAUL'S FINAL GREETINGS

[16]May the Lord of peace himself always give you his peace no matter what happens. The Lord be with you all.

[17]Now here is my greeting, which I write with my own hand—PAUL. I do this at the end of all my letters to prove that they really are from me.

[18]May the grace of our Lord Jesus Christ be with you all.

3:1 Greek *brothers;* also in 3:6, 13. 3:3 Or *from evil.* 3:6 Greek *brother;* also in 3:15.

My Daily Worship

— *December 1* —

A DAILY DRESS REHEARSAL

2 THESSALONIANS 1:1–3:18

And you will be among those praising him on that day,
for you believed what we testified about him (1:10).

[i reflect]

For years Jerome Hines was a bass soloist with the Metropolitan Opera. His renditions of classic arias brought audiences to their feet in applause. It was obvious to all who heard him that he had a musical gift. But being endowed with an exceptional ability did not relieve Jerome Hines from the need of rehearsing.

When the well-known Presbyterian pastor Dr. John A. Huffman, Jr. invited Jerome to sing at a special occasion at his church, the opera star stayed in the Huffman home. Early Sunday morning Jerome could be heard throughout the house as he warmed up his voice with melodic scales, and then rehearsed the song he was to perform later that day. Although he was a gifted singer, rehearsing was a prerequisite.

In much the same way, we have been "gifted" with salvation. It's a gift God gave us when we believed what we heard about Jesus. And we exercise our gift of salvation by spending time with the Lord each day and obeying his Word. Doing our spiritual "scales" helps us fine-tune our understanding of what the Lord has done for us.

In the words of Karl Barth, worship is "the most momentous, the most urgent, the most glorious action that can take place in human life." That's because it gets us ready for what's to come. Just like an opera singer spends time practicing his arias as a way of anticipating his performance, our personal worship time is a dress rehearsal for "that day" Paul talks about in this verse. Praising God now gets us in tune for the future performance we will offer to an audience of One.

Rehearse today the many blessings you received when you exercised your gift of salvation.

[i pray]

Lord Jesus, help me see what I do each day in your presence as a dress rehearsal for the day when I will fall on my face before you and, with all the saints of all the ages, worship you in person.

[i respond]

Who first told you about Jesus? Was it a Christian parent? Grandparent? Perhaps a Sunday school teacher or a pastor? If they are still living, write them a note or send an E-mail, thanking them for making sure you heard the Word.

1 & 2 Timothy

Work hard so God can approve you. Be a good worker, one who does not need to be ashamed and who correctly explains the word of truth (2 Timothy 2:15).

Grounded in the Truth

Paul, the great missionary to the Gentile world, writes twice to Timothy, his envoy and spokesperson, with words to encourage true worship and avoid the pitfalls of distraction, arrogance, and false teaching.

All Christians need these warnings. Since God's good news spreads through words—communication tools easily abused—Paul urges that words spoken for God be true, grounded in the Scriptures, and filled with love. Such words must sometimes be strong and corrective, but never belligerent or domineering.

All Christians are called to ministry. God fashions vastly different roles for his people but we all have this focus: Jesus the Savior of all is our only hope. Some may trumpet this central truth through a career in business, others in trades or professions. All carry the responsibility to share this hope truthfully with the world around them.

Parts of these two letters are quoted in youth rallies and retirement prayer groups alike, as Paul talks about hope for all ages. On the other hand, parts of these letters have caused well-meaning Christians much difficulty. Do women have a role in preaching and teaching? Much depends on the context and breadth of Paul's instruction. Is the "rule of silence" (1 Timothy 2:12) directed at a particular problem in the local church, or does the rule apply to all churches of all times? Matters such as these are to be settled by considering the Bible's entire teaching. Then worship can proceed with peace, joy, and power.

If you are called to lead the church in worship, then follow Paul's advice to Timothy: Be a good worker; explain the word of truth correctly with confidence so that God will make oak trees out of seedlings despite the troubles you face along the way. Paul urged Timothy to stay faithful, to not be afraid, and to encourage the people—advice for all time to leaders of the worshiping church.

Worship Moments

- Much time can be wasted on matters not central to spiritual growth. Center worship on the center: Jesus, the hope of everyone (1 Timothy 1:4).

- Hard feelings that settle into hatred make a mockery of worship. Reconcile with people we have offended (1 Timothy 2:8).

- Truth is found in Scripture, which must be read often and taught faithfully. Worship is instructional (2 Timothy 3:16).

- Not every listener will follow the truth. Some reject Jesus' words; some will reject ours. Worshiping people patiently urge all to join in. Stragglers and naysayers should never discourage or stop our worship (2 Timothy 4:3–4).

GREETINGS FROM PAUL

1 This letter is from Paul, an apostle of Christ Jesus, appointed by the command of God our Savior and by Christ Jesus our hope.

[2]It is written to Timothy, my true child in the faith.

May God our Father and Christ Jesus our Lord give you grace, mercy, and peace.

WARNINGS AGAINST FALSE TEACHINGS

[3]When I left for Macedonia, I urged you to stay there in Ephesus and stop those who are teaching wrong doctrine. [4]Don't let people waste time in endless speculation over myths and spiritual pedigrees.* For these things only cause arguments; they don't help people live a life of faith in God.* [5]The purpose of my instruction is that all the Christians there would be filled with love that comes from a pure heart, a clear conscience, and sincere faith.

[6]But some teachers have missed this whole point. They have turned away from these things and spend their time arguing and talking foolishness. [7]They want to be known as teachers of the law of Moses, but they don't know what they are talking about, even though they seem so confident. [8]We know these laws are good when they are used as God intended. [9]But they were not made for people who do what is right. They are for people who are disobedient and rebellious, who are ungodly and sinful, who consider nothing sacred and defile what is holy, who murder their father or mother or other people. [10]These laws are for people who are sexually immoral, for homosexuals and slave traders, for liars and oath breakers, and for those who do anything else that contradicts the right teaching [11]that comes from the glorious Good News entrusted to me by our blessed God.

PAUL'S GRATITUDE FOR GOD'S MERCY

[12]How thankful I am to Christ Jesus our Lord for considering me trustworthy and appoint-

ing me to serve him, [13]even though I used to scoff at the name of Christ. I hunted down his people, harming them in every way I could. But God had mercy on me because I did it in ignorance and unbelief. [14]Oh, how kind and gracious the Lord was! He filled me completely with faith and the love of Christ Jesus.

[15]This is a true saying, and everyone should believe it: Christ Jesus came into the world to save sinners—and I was the worst of them all. [16]But that is why God had mercy on me, so that Christ Jesus could use me as a prime example of his great patience with even the worst sinners. Then others will realize that they, too, can believe in him and receive eternal life. [17]Glory and honor to God forever and ever. He is the eternal King, the unseen one who never dies; he alone is God. Amen.

TIMOTHY'S RESPONSIBILITY

[18]Timothy, my son, here are my instructions for you, based on the prophetic words spoken about you earlier. May they give you the confidence to fight well in the Lord's battles. [19]Cling tightly to your faith in Christ, and always keep your conscience clear. For some people have deliberately violated their consciences; as a result, their faith has been shipwrecked. [20]Hymenaeus and Alexander are two examples of this. I turned them over to Satan so they would learn not to blaspheme God.

INSTRUCTIONS ABOUT WORSHIP

2 I urge you, first of all, to pray for all people. As you make your requests, plead for God's mercy upon them, and give thanks. [2]Pray this way for kings and all others who are in authority, so that we can live in peace and quietness, in godliness and dignity. [3]This is good and pleases God our Savior, [4]for he wants everyone to be saved and to understand the truth. [5]For there is only one God and one Mediator who can reconcile God and people. He is the man Christ Jesus. [6]He gave his life to purchase freedom for everyone. This is the

---

1:4a Greek *in myths and endless genealogies, which cause speculation.*   1:4b Greek *a stewardship of God in faith.*

message that God gave to the world at the proper time. ⁷And I have been chosen—this is the absolute truth—as a preacher and apostle to teach the Gentiles about faith and truth.

⁸So wherever you assemble, I want men to pray with holy hands lifted up to God, free from anger and controversy. ⁹And I want women to be modest in their appearance. They should wear decent and appropriate clothing and not draw attention to themselves by the way they fix their hair or by wearing gold or pearls or expensive clothes. ¹⁰For women who claim to be devoted to God should make themselves attractive by the good things they do.

¹¹Women should listen and learn quietly and submissively. ¹²I do not let women teach men or have authority over them. Let them listen quietly. ¹³For God made Adam first, and afterward he made Eve. ¹⁴And it was the woman, not Adam, who was deceived by Satan, and sin was the result. ¹⁵But women will be saved through childbearing* and by continuing to live in faith, love, holiness, and modesty.

LEADERS IN THE CHURCH

3 It is a true saying that if someone wants to be an elder,* he desires an honorable responsibility. ²For an elder must be a man whose life cannot be spoken against. He must be faithful to his wife.* He must exhibit self-control, live wisely, and have a good reputation. He must enjoy having guests in his home and must be able to teach. ³He must not be a heavy drinker or be violent. He must be gentle, peace loving, and not one who loves money. ⁴He must manage his own family well, with children who respect and obey him. ⁵For if a man cannot manage his own household, how can he take care of God's church?

⁶An elder must not be a new Christian, because he might be proud of being chosen

so soon, and the Devil will use that pride to make him fall.* ⁷Also, people outside the church must speak well of him so that he will not fall into the Devil's trap and be disgraced.

⁸In the same way, deacons must be people who are respected and have integrity. They must not be heavy drinkers and must not be greedy for money. ⁹They must be committed to the revealed truths of the Christian faith and must live with a clear conscience. ¹⁰Before they are appointed as deacons, they should be given other responsibilities in the church as a test of their character and ability. If they do well, then they may serve as deacons.

¹¹In the same way, their wives* must be respected and must not speak evil of others. They must exercise self-control and be faithful in everything they do.

¹²A deacon must be faithful to his wife, and he must manage his children and household well. ¹³Those who do well as deacons will be rewarded with respect from others and will have increased confidence in their faith in Christ Jesus.

THE TRUTHS OF OUR FAITH

¹⁴I am writing these things to you now, even though I hope to be with you soon, ¹⁵so that if I can't come for a while, you will know how people must conduct themselves in the household of God. This is the church of the living God, which is the pillar and support of the truth.

¹⁶Without question, this is the great mystery of our faith:

Christ* appeared in the flesh
    and was shown to be righteous by the
        Spirit.*
He was seen by angels
    and was announced to the nations.
He was believed on in the world
    and was taken up into heaven.*

2:15 Or *will be saved by accepting their role as mothers,* or *will be saved by the birth of the Child.* 3:1 Greek *overseer;* also in 3:2. 3:2 Greek *be the husband of one wife;* also in 3:12. 3:6 Or *he might fall into the same judgment as the Devil.* 3:11 Or *the women deacons.* The Greek word can be translated *women* or *wives.* 3:16a Greek *Who;* some manuscripts read *God.* 3:16b Or *in his spirit.* 3:16c Greek *in glory.*

My Daily Worship

— *December 2* —

HATCHET MAN OR HALO-WEARER?

1 TIMOTHY 1:1–3:16

This is a true saying, and everyone should believe it: Christ Jesus came into the world
to save sinners—and I was the worst of them all (1:15).

[i reflect]

Chuck Colson has become an authoritative moral voice among Christians in America. Thousands of Christians read his column in Christian magazines and listen to his daily radio commentaries. His leadership of a ministry to those behind bars means his growing constituency includes converted prisoners and their families. But Chuck Colson has not always been a Christian leader or viewed as a moral voice.

When Richard Nixon occupied the White House, Colson was his chief counsel. He was also the President's pawn. Known as the "hatchet man," Colson was called on to do what the Chief Executive didn't relish. He had a reputation for dirty tricks and deception. But that changed when Colson accepted Jesus as his Lord and Savior. When news of Colson's conversion to Christianity leaked to the press in 1973, the *Boston Globe* reported, "If Mr. Colson can repent of his sins, there just has to be hope for everybody."

That's the picture we have of the apostle Paul in this passage. Aware of his sinful past, the apostle calls attention to it. Lest we think of him as some larger-than-life saint, he reminds us of his true identity—the worst sinner of them all. But we are grateful that Jesus came into the world to do God's bidding for him. He came to reach out to the Pauls and Chucks of a fallen planet. Except for his grace, we *all* would still be lost in our sins and trapped in reputations we well deserve.

When is the last time you really pondered what God did to free you from your sin? Take time right now to compose a mental picture of your life "before" and "after" meeting Christ. Then worship the One who "came into the world to save sinners."

[i pray]

Lord Jesus, thank you for coming into the world to save sinners, and that includes me.
Even though I accept your forgiveness, I know how much I am prone to wander
from your plan for my life. Keep me headed in your direction.

[i respond]

If you haven't read Chuck Colson's biography *Born Again*, check it out of the local public library or your church library. Let his story inspire you to continue to pray for those who don't know Christ yet.

WARNINGS AGAINST FALSE TEACHERS

4 Now the Holy Spirit tells us clearly that in the last times some will turn away from what we believe; they will follow lying spirits and teachings that come from demons. ²These teachers are hypocrites and liars. They pretend to be religious, but their consciences are dead.*

³They will say it is wrong to be married and wrong to eat certain foods. But God created those foods to be eaten with thanksgiving by people who know and believe the truth. ⁴Since everything God created is good, we should not reject any of it. We may receive it gladly, with thankful hearts. ⁵For we know it is made holy by the word of God and prayer.

A GOOD SERVANT OF CHRIST JESUS

⁶If you explain this to the brothers and sisters,* you will be doing your duty as a worthy servant of Christ Jesus, one who is fed by the message of faith and the true teaching you have followed. ⁷Do not waste time arguing over godless ideas and old wives' tales. Spend your time and energy in training yourself for spiritual fitness. ⁸Physical exercise has some value, but spiritual exercise is much more important, for it promises a reward in both this life and the next. ⁹This is true, and everyone should accept it. ¹⁰We work hard and suffer much* in order that people will believe the truth, for our hope is in the living God, who is the Savior of all people, and particularly of those who believe.

¹¹Teach these things and insist that everyone learn them. ¹²Don't let anyone think less of you because you are young. Be an example to all believers in what you teach, in the way you live, in your love, your faith, and your purity. ¹³Until I get there, focus on reading the Scriptures to the church, encouraging the believers, and teaching them. ¹⁴Do not neglect the spiritual gift you

received through the prophecies spoken to you when the elders of the church laid their hands on you. ¹⁵Give your complete attention to these matters. Throw yourself into your tasks so that everyone will see your progress. ¹⁶Keep a close watch on yourself and on your teaching. Stay true to what is right, and God will save you and those who hear you.

5 Never speak harshly to an older man,* but appeal to him respectfully as though he were your own father. Talk to the younger men as you would to your own brothers. ²Treat the older women as you would your mother, and treat the younger women with all purity as your own sisters.

ADVICE ABOUT WIDOWS, ELDERS, AND SLAVES

³The church should care for any widow who has no one else to care for her. ⁴But if she has children or grandchildren, their first responsibility is to show godliness at home and repay their parents by taking care of them. This is something that pleases God very much.

⁵But a woman who is a true widow, one who is truly alone in this world, has placed her hope in God. Night and day she asks God for help and spends much time in prayer. ⁶But the widow who lives only for pleasure is spiritually dead. ⁷Give these instructions to the church so that the widows you support* will not be criticized.

⁸But those who won't care for their own relatives, especially those living in the same household, have denied what we believe. Such people are worse than unbelievers.

⁹A widow who is put on the list for support must be a woman who is at least sixty years old and was faithful to her husband.* ¹⁰She must be well respected by everyone because of the good she has done. Has she brought up her children well? Has she been kind to strangers? Has she served other Christians humbly?* Has she helped those who are in

---

4:2 Greek *are seared.* **4:6** Greek *brothers.* **4:10** Some manuscripts read *and strive.* **5:1** Or *an elder.* **5:7** Or *so the church;* Greek reads *so they.* **5:9** Greek *was the wife of one man.* **5:10** Greek *Has she washed the feet of saints?*

My Daily Worship

— *December 3* —

A STANDING OVATION
FIT FOR A KING

1 TIMOTHY 4:1–6:21

For at the right time Christ will be revealed from heaven by the blessed and almighty God,
the King of kings and Lord of lords. He alone can never die, and he lives in light
so brilliant that no human can approach him (6:15–16).

[i reflect]

George Frederic Handel wrote his masterpiece oratorio *Messiah* in a mere three weeks. He wrote nonstop as if driven by a power greater than himself night and day. He neglected food, sleep, and friends in order to accomplish what he viewed as a God-given goal. Picture the composer seated at his piano with sheets of music strewn around him. No doubt tears were streaming down his face. Handel, having encountered the majesty of a holy God while composing music for the Scriptural lyrics, said "I do believe I have seen all of Heaven before me, and the great God Himself."

When the composer introduced his oratorio to a London audience, King George was in attendance. Unable to restrain himself, when the orchestra and choir sang the "Hallelujah Chorus," the king stood to his feet in adoration of God because he knew his position paled in contrast to the King of kings. Since then, audiences have followed the monarch's example and continue to stand whenever that familiar chorus is sung. Based on what the apostle writes in today's passage, kings, princes, and citizens of *all* nations will have an opportunity to pay homage to the Messiah in person when he returns to earth someday.

At the same time, Paul reminds us in the next verse that God's holiness is so brilliant that no one can approach him. We need to remember that the only means we have to come and worship before the Lord of lords, and King of kings, is through his Son, Jesus Christ. Only he is able to stand before God, totally pure and blameless. Only through his work on the Cross are we able to come near.

Today, as you prayerfully worship, adopt a different posture. Stand in homage to the King of kings, or bow down in humbleness before his brilliant light. Because of Christ, you can do both.

[i pray]

Lord Jesus, I can hardly wait to see you in person. You are the source of my life and my joy.
As I read your Word, I find myself identifying with what Handel said. It is as if
I have a peek into your very presence. Even so, come quickly.

[i respond]

Do you have a copy of Handel's *Messiah?* If not, it would be a nice addition to your musical collection. Play it on your audio system on Sunday mornings as you get ready for church. You can also listen on-line by typing in "Hallelujah Chorus" on your Internet search engine.

trouble? Has she always been ready to do good?

[11]The younger widows should not be on the list, because their physical desires will over-power their devotion to Christ and they will want to remarry. [12]Then they would be guilty of breaking their previous pledge. [13]Besides, they are likely to become lazy and spend their time gossiping from house to house, getting into other people's business and saying things they shouldn't. [14]So I advise these younger widows to marry again, have children, and take care of their own homes. Then the enemy will not be able to say anything against them. [15]For I am afraid that some of them have already gone astray and now follow Satan.

[16]If a Christian woman has relatives who are widows, she must take care of them and not put the responsibility on the church. Then the church can care for widows who are truly alone.

[17]Elders who do their work well should be paid well,* especially those who work hard at both preaching and teaching. [18]For the Scripture says, "Do not keep an ox from eating as it treads out the grain." And in another place, "Those who work deserve their pay!"*

[19]Do not listen to complaints against an elder unless there are two or three witnesses to accuse him. [20]Anyone who sins should be rebuked in front of the whole church so that others will have a proper fear of God.

[21]I solemnly command you in the presence of God and Christ Jesus and the holy angels to obey these instructions without taking sides or showing special favor to anyone. [22]Never be in a hurry about appointing an elder. Do not participate in the sins of others. Keep yourself pure.

[23]Don't drink only water. You ought to drink a little wine for the sake of your stomach because you are sick so often.

[24]Remember that some people lead sinful lives, and everyone knows they will be judged. But there are others whose sin will not be revealed until later. [25]In the same way, every-one knows how much good some people do, but there are others whose good deeds won't be known until later.

6 Christians who are slaves should give their masters full respect so that the name of God and his teaching will not be shamed. [2]If your master is a Christian, that is no excuse for being disrespectful. You should work all the harder because you are helping another believer* by your efforts.

FALSE TEACHING AND TRUE RICHES

Teach these truths, Timothy, and encourage everyone to obey them. [3]Some false teachers may deny these things, but these are the sound, wholesome teachings of the Lord Jesus Christ, and they are the foundation for a godly life. [4]Anyone who teaches anything different is both conceited and ignorant. Such a person has an unhealthy desire to quibble over the meaning of words. This stirs up argu-ments ending in jealousy, fighting, slander, and evil suspicions. [5]These people always cause trouble. Their minds are corrupt, and they don't tell the truth. To them religion is just a way to get rich.

[6]Yet true religion with contentment is great wealth. [7]After all, we didn't bring anything with us when we came into the world, and we certainly cannot carry anything with us when we die. [8]So if we have enough food and cloth-ing, let us be content. [9]But people who long to be rich fall into temptation and are trapped by many foolish and harmful desires that plunge them into ruin and destruction. [10]For the love of money is at the root of all kinds of evil. And some people, craving money, have wandered from the faith and pierced themselves with many sorrows.

PAUL'S FINAL INSTRUCTIONS

[11]But you, Timothy, belong to God; so run from all these evil things, and follow what is right and good. Pursue a godly life, along with

5:17 Greek *should be worthy of double honor.* 5:18 Deut 25:4; Luke 10:7. 6:2 Greek *a brother.*

faith, love, perseverance, and gentleness. [12]Fight the good fight for what we believe. Hold tightly to the eternal life that God has given you, which you have confessed so well before many witnesses. [13]And I command you before God, who gives life to all, and before Christ Jesus, who gave a good testimony before Pontius Pilate, [14]that you obey his commands with all purity. Then no one can find fault with you from now until our Lord Jesus Christ returns. [15]For at the right time Christ will be revealed from heaven by the blessed and only almighty God, the King of kings and Lord of lords. [16]He alone can never die, and he lives in light so brilliant that no human can approach him. No one has ever seen him, nor ever will. To him be honor and power forever. Amen.

[17]Tell those who are rich in this world not to be proud and not to trust in their money, which will soon be gone. But their trust should be in the living God, who richly gives us all we need for our enjoyment. [18]Tell them to use their money to do good. They should be rich in good works and should give generously to those in need, always being ready to share with others whatever God has given them. [19]By doing this they will be storing up their treasure as a good foundation for the future so that they may take hold of real life.

[20]Timothy, guard what God has entrusted to you. Avoid godless, foolish discussions with those who oppose you with their so-called knowledge. [21]Some people have wandered from the faith by following such foolishness.

May God's grace be with you all.

GREETINGS FROM PAUL

1 This letter is from Paul, an apostle of Christ Jesus by God's will, sent out to tell others about the life he has promised through faith in Christ Jesus.

²It is written to Timothy, my dear son.

May God our Father and Christ Jesus our Lord give you grace, mercy, and peace.

ENCOURAGEMENT TO BE FAITHFUL

³Timothy, I thank God for you. He is the God I serve with a clear conscience, just as my ancestors did. Night and day I constantly remember you in my prayers. ⁴I long to see you again, for I remember your tears as we parted. And I will be filled with joy when we are together again.

⁵I know that you sincerely trust the Lord, for you have the faith of your mother, Eunice, and your grandmother, Lois. ⁶This is why I remind you to fan into flames the spiritual gift God gave you when I laid my hands on you. ⁷For God has not given us a spirit of fear and timidity, but of power, love, and self-discipline. ⁸So you must never be ashamed to tell others about our Lord. And don't be ashamed of me, either, even though I'm in prison for Christ. With the strength God gives you, be ready to suffer with me for the proclamation of the Good News.

⁹It is God who saved us and chose us to live a holy life. He did this not because we deserved it, but because that was his plan long before the world began—to show his love and kindness to us through Christ Jesus. ¹⁰And now he has made all of this plain to us by the coming of Christ Jesus, our Savior, who broke the power of death and showed us the way to everlasting life through the Good News. ¹¹And God chose me to be a preacher, an apostle, and a teacher of this Good News.

¹²And that is why I am suffering here in prison. But I am not ashamed of it, for I know the one in whom I trust, and I am sure that he is able to guard what I have entrusted to him* until the day of his return.

¹³Hold on to the pattern of right teaching you learned from me. And remember to live in the faith and love that you have in Christ Jesus. ¹⁴With the help of the Holy Spirit who lives within us, carefully guard what has been entrusted to you.

¹⁵As you know, all the Christians who came here from the province of Asia have deserted me; even Phygelus and Hermogenes are gone. ¹⁶May the Lord show special kindness to Onesiphorus and all his family because he often visited and encouraged me. He was never ashamed of me because I was in prison. ¹⁷When he came to Rome, he searched everywhere until he found me. ¹⁸May the Lord show him special kindness on the day of Christ's return. And you know how much he helped me at Ephesus.

A GOOD SOLDIER OF CHRIST JESUS

2 Timothy, my dear son, be strong with the special favor God gives you in Christ Jesus. ²You have heard me teach many things that have been confirmed by many reliable witnesses. Teach these great truths to trustworthy people who are able to pass them on to others.

³Endure suffering along with me, as a good soldier of Christ Jesus. ⁴And as Christ's soldier, do not let yourself become tied up in the affairs of this life, for then you cannot satisfy the one who has enlisted you in his army. ⁵Follow the Lord's rules for doing his work, just as an athlete either follows the rules or is disqualified and wins no prize. ⁶Hardworking farmers are the first to enjoy the fruit of their labor. ⁷Think about what I am saying. The Lord will give you understanding in all these things.

⁸Never forget that Jesus Christ was a man born into King David's family and that he was raised from the dead. This is the Good News I preach. ⁹And because I preach this Good News, I am suffering and have been chained

1:12 Or what has been entrusted to me.

My Daily Worship

— *December 4* —

RUNNING WITH A PURE HEART

2 TIMOTHY 1:1–2:26

*Run from anything that stimulates youthful lust. Follow anything that makes you want
to do right. Pursue faith and love and peace, and enjoy the companionship
of those who call on the Lord with pure hearts (2:22).*

[i reflect]

Eric Liddell's God-honoring life is the basis for the movie, "Chariots of Fire," that won the Academy Award for best picture in 1981. The movie tells the story of this sprinter from Scotland who loved to run almost as much as he loved his Lord. Eric qualifies to be part of Great Britain's team in the 1924 Paris Olympics. When he discovers that his qualifying event at the Games is scheduled for Sunday, Eric is faced with a issue of conscience.

Given his personal interpretation of the fourth commandment, he does not feel the personal liberty to compete on the Lord's Day. In the film version, Eric's decision to give up his spot on the Olympic team rather than dishonor the Lord is unexpectedly rewarded. A teammate, who already has won a medal, offers to let Eric take his place in another event that will be held midweek. Gratefully, Eric accepts the offer, and wins the race! Here is a godly athlete who not only runs around a track but also runs toward God, determined to keep his heart pure and his relationship with his Lord unblemished.

That determination is what Paul has in mind when he refers to pursuing faith and love and peace. Paul uses words such as "run," "follow anything," "pursue." Our faith is one of action, not passivity. It means legging it out on a daily basis with our eyes focused on pleasing God. It also involved running in stride with those who (like us) are committed to lives of purity.

Run toward God. Confess whatever is causing you to stumble and falter. Use the times when you wash your hands today as a reminder to purify your heart as well through personal confession.

[i pray]

*Lord, the life of Eric Liddell inspires me. I want to be capable of standing up for what
I believe in, even if it means giving up something I've lived for all my life. Give me
the desire to remain pure in heart and to keep short accounts with you.*

[i respond]

Running from sin requires lacing up your spiritual shoes each day. Why not leave a pair of running shoes by the front door this week as a silent reminder to be proactive in running toward faith, love, and peace.

like a criminal. But the word of God cannot be chained. [10]I am willing to endure anything if it will bring salvation and eternal glory in Christ Jesus to those God has chosen.

[11]This is a true saying:

If we die with him,
    we will also live with him.
[12] If we endure hardship,
    we will reign with him.
If we deny him,
    he will deny us.
[13] If we are unfaithful,
    he remains faithful,
    for he cannot deny himself.

AN APPROVED WORKER

[14]Remind everyone of these things, and command them in God's name to stop fighting over words. Such arguments are useless, and they can ruin those who hear them. [15]Work hard so God can approve you. Be a good worker, one who does not need to be ashamed and who correctly explains the word of truth. [16]Avoid godless, foolish discussions that lead to more and more ungodliness. [17]This kind of talk spreads like cancer. Hymenaeus and Philetus are examples of this. [18]They have left the path of truth, preaching the lie that the resurrection of the dead has already occurred; and they have undermined the faith of some.

[19]But God's truth stands firm like a foundation stone with this inscription: "The Lord knows those who are his,"* and "Those who claim they belong to the Lord must turn away from all wickedness."*

[20]In a wealthy home some utensils are made of gold and silver, and some are made of wood and clay. The expensive utensils are used for special occasions, and the cheap ones are for everyday use. [21]If you keep yourself pure, you will be a utensil God can use for his purpose. Your life will be clean, and you will be ready for the Master to use you for every good work.

[22]Run from anything that stimulates youthful lust. Follow anything that makes you want to do right. Pursue faith and love and peace, and enjoy the companionship of those who call on the Lord with pure hearts.

[23]Again I say, don't get involved in foolish, ignorant arguments that only start fights. [24]The Lord's servants must not quarrel but must be kind to everyone. They must be able to teach effectively and be patient with difficult people. [25]They should gently teach those who oppose the truth. Perhaps God will change those people's hearts, and they will believe the truth. [26]Then they will come to their senses and escape from the Devil's trap. For they have been held captive by him to do whatever he wants.

THE DANGERS OF THE LAST DAYS

3 You should also know this, Timothy, that in the last days there will be very difficult times. [2]For people will love only themselves and their money. They will be boastful and proud, scoffing at God, disobedient to their parents, and ungrateful. They will consider nothing sacred. [3]They will be unloving and unforgiving; they will slander others and have no self-control; they will be cruel and have no interest in what is good. [4]They will betray their friends, be reckless, be puffed up with pride, and love pleasure rather than God. [5]They will act as if they are religious, but they will reject the power that could make them godly. You must stay away from people like that.

[6]They are the kind who work their way into people's homes and win the confidence of* vulnerable women who are burdened with the guilt of sin and controlled by many desires. [7]Such women are forever following new teachings, but they never understand the truth. [8]And these teachers fight the truth just as Jannes and Jambres fought against Moses. Their minds are depraved, and their faith is counterfeit. [9]But they won't get away with this for long. Someday everyone will recognize

2:19a Num 16:5. 2:19b See Isa 52:11. 3:6 Greek *and take captive.*

My Daily Worship

— December 5 —

THE JOY OF WAITING

2 TIMOTHY 3:1–4:22

And now the prize awaits me—the crown of righteousness that the Lord, the righteous Judge
will give me on that great day of his return. And the prize is not just for me
but for all who eagerly look forward to his glorious return (4:8).

[i reflect]

Dietrich Bonhoeffer was a Lutheran pastor in Germany during the days of the Third Reich. He was arrested for his part in a Christian resistance movement. A month before the Allied forces freed Germany the 39-year-old pastor was executed. Some months before his death, Bonhoeffer's fiancée surprised him with a visit. He pleaded with her not to come unannounced again. For him, the ability to anticipate a longed-for reunion was a gift too precious to be denied.

Isn't that something? When you stop and think about it, you can understand his logic. Put yourself in that Nazi cell and feel the prisoner's longing for the day to come when he could look his loved one in the face. In the same way, as Paul neared the end of his life, he began to think of being in the presence of Jesus. This passage reveals his longing for the day of his reunion with the Lord, while calling us to anticipate when we, too, will stand before the Lover of our souls.

In all honesty, how eagerly are you looking forward to Jesus' glorious return? No doubt your life is filled with busyness and "to do" lists. You're used to thinking about upcoming goals and deadlines. But how much do you think about the Second Coming? This is a worthy aim in our daily personal worship times. The more we anticipate what is to come, the greater our satisfaction and fulfillment when we see Christ. You can count on that!

With eyes closed in a totally quiet room, picture the Lord returning for you. Visualize his smiling face. Feel his arms reaching out to embrace you. Imagine the words he will speak to you as he places "the crown of righteousness" on your head.

[i pray]

Jesus, I can't wait to see you. Like the old gospel song says, "It will be worth it all."
Forgive me, my Lord, for getting so uptight over the stresses of this world
that I forget it's but a dress rehearsal of what's still to come.

[i respond]

Perhaps you need to anticipate eternity more than you do. Try writing the word "HEAVEN" on an index card. Write "HE'S COMING SOON" on another one. Spell "KEEP LOOKING UP" on a third. Place one of these cards on your fridge, another one on your bathroom mirror, and the third on the dashboard of your car.

what fools they are, just as happened with Jannes and Jambres.

PAUL'S CHARGE TO TIMOTHY

[10]But you know what I teach, Timothy, and how I live, and what my purpose in life is. You know my faith and how long I have suffered. You know my love and my patient endurance. [11]You know how much persecution and suffering I have endured. You know all about how I was persecuted in Antioch, Iconium, and Lystra—but the Lord delivered me from all of it. [12]Yes, and everyone who wants to live a godly life in Christ Jesus will suffer persecution. [13]But evil people and impostors will flourish. They will go on deceiving others, and they themselves will be deceived.

[14]But you must remain faithful to the things you have been taught. You know they are true, for you know you can trust those who taught you. [15]You have been taught the holy Scriptures from childhood, and they have given you the wisdom to receive the salvation that comes by trusting in Christ Jesus. [16]All Scripture is inspired by God and is useful to teach us what is true and to make us realize what is wrong in our lives. It straightens us out and teaches us to do what is right. [17]It is God's way of preparing us in every way, fully equipped for every good thing God wants us to do.

4 And so I solemnly urge you before God and before Christ Jesus—who will someday judge the living and the dead when he appears to set up his Kingdom: [2]Preach the word of God. Be persistent, whether the time is favorable or not. Patiently correct, rebuke, and encourage your people with good teaching.

[3]For a time is coming when people will no longer listen to right teaching. They will follow their own desires and will look for teachers who will tell them whatever they want to hear. [4]They will reject the truth and follow strange myths.

[5]But you should keep a clear mind in every situation. Don't be afraid of suffering for the Lord. Work at bringing others to Christ. Complete the ministry God has given you.

PAUL'S FINAL WORDS

[6]As for me, my life has already been poured out as an offering to God. The time of my death is near. [7]I have fought a good fight, I have finished the race, and I have remained faithful. [8]And now the prize awaits me—the crown of righteousness that the Lord, the righteous Judge, will give me on that great day of his return. And the prize is not just for me but for all who eagerly look forward to his glorious return.

[9]Please come as soon as you can. [10]Demas has deserted me because he loves the things of this life and has gone to Thessalonica. Crescens has gone to Galatia, and Titus has gone to Dalmatia. [11]Only Luke is with me. Bring Mark with you when you come, for he will be helpful to me. [12]I sent Tychicus to Ephesus. [13]When you come, be sure to bring the coat I left with Carpus at Troas. Also bring my books, and especially my papers.*

[14]Alexander the coppersmith has done me much harm, but the Lord will judge him for what he has done. [15]Be careful of him, for he fought against everything we said.

[16]The first time I was brought before the judge, no one was with me. Everyone had abandoned me. I hope it will not be counted against them. [17]But the Lord stood with me and gave me strength, that I might preach the Good News in all its fullness for all the Gentiles to hear. And he saved me from certain death.* [18]Yes, and the Lord will deliver me from every evil attack and will bring me safely to his heavenly Kingdom. To God be the glory forever and ever. Amen.

PAUL'S FINAL GREETINGS

[19]Give my greetings to Priscilla and Aquila and those living at the household of Onesiphorus.

4:13 Greek *especially the parchments.* 4:17 Greek *from the mouth of a lion.*

²⁰Erastus stayed at Corinth, and I left Trophimus sick at Miletus.

²¹Hurry so you can get here before winter. Eubulus sends you greetings, and so do Pudens, Linus, Claudia, and all the brothers and sisters.*

²²May the Lord be with your spirit. Grace be with you all.

4:21 Greek *brothers.*

Titus

But then God our Savior showed us his kindness and love. He saved us,
not because of the good things we did, but because of his mercy (3:4–5).

Worship and Do Good

I f Paul's short letter to Titus had fallen into the hands of Cretan newspaper reporters, headlines and lawsuits surely would have out-numbered sermons and converts there. Rarely does Paul speak so clearly about the moral depravity of the people he wishes to serve. Paul affirms without a wink that the popular take on Cretans is true. Titus has his work cut out for him.

That explains the emphasis in this letter on moral instruction and "doing good"—a reminder to all Christians that worship and life form a common thread. We cannot raise hell during the week, then politely file into a church seat on Sunday and expect God's help and power. "Do good, live well, learn, and practice the virtues" is to be Titus's consistent message to this new church. Show in life the evidence of God's truth that you celebrate in worship.

Why? Because social patterns are hard to break. Christians are susceptible to the winds of culture and may bend to pressure. Should that happen, the church is no longer distinctive. Worship becomes pointless, for the reality of God has been submerged in the pattern of behavior common to every street corner. The light fades; people shuffle away. Weeds invade the flowers. Preaching becomes insipid, singing is perfunctory, and praying is daydreaming.

Live with joy and discipline, preach with stamina and truthfulness, Paul urges Titus. It's good advice for us as well. In that way, our worship and our life will grow together in the knowledge and love of God.

Worship Moments

- Hypocrites tell you one thing on Sunday and rob you on Monday. Such people play at worship, thinking they can use a God-event to disguise their real commitment: me, mine, and myself (1:16).

- Worship anticipates eternity. It looks beyond the present to that moment when Jesus comes again (2:13).

- Worship leaders cannot run from the moral failure of others. It must be confronted. Learning this skill requires mentoring, but the difficulty of confrontation (and its frequent backlash of criticism) cannot be ignored (2:15).

GREETINGS FROM PAUL

1 This letter is from Paul, a slave of God and an apostle of Jesus Christ. I have been sent to bring faith to those God has chosen and to teach them to know the truth that shows them how to live godly lives. [2]This truth gives them the confidence of eternal life, which God promised them before the world began—and he cannot lie. [3]And now at the right time he has revealed this Good News, and we announce it to everyone. It is by the command of God our Savior that I have been trusted to do this work for him.

[4]This letter is written to Titus, my true child in the faith that we share.

May God the Father and Christ Jesus our Savior give you grace and peace.

TITUS'S WORK IN CRETE

[5]I left you on the island of Crete so you could complete our work there and appoint elders in each town as I instructed you. [6]An elder must be well thought of for his good life. He must be faithful to his wife,* and his children must be believers who are not wild or rebellious. [7]An elder* must live a blameless life because he is God's minister. He must not be arrogant or quick-tempered; he must not be a heavy drinker, violent, or greedy for money. [8]He must enjoy having guests in his home and must love all that is good. He must live wisely and be fair. He must live a devout and disciplined life. [9]He must have a strong and steadfast belief in the trustworthy message he was taught; then he will be able to encourage others with right teaching and show those who oppose it where they are wrong.

[10]For there are many who rebel against right teaching; they engage in useless talk and deceive people. This is especially true of those who insist on circumcision for salvation. [11]They must be silenced. By their wrong teaching, they have already turned whole families away from the truth. Such teachers only want your money. [12]One of their own men, a prophet from Crete, has said about them,

"The people of Crete are all liars; they are cruel animals and lazy gluttons." [13]This is true. So rebuke them as sternly as necessary to make them strong in the faith. [14]They must stop listening to Jewish myths and the commands of people who have turned their backs on the truth.

[15]Everything is pure to those whose hearts are pure. But nothing is pure to those who are corrupt and unbelieving, because their minds and consciences are defiled. [16]Such people claim they know God, but they deny him by the way they live. They are despicable and disobedient, worthless for doing anything good.

PROMOTE RIGHT TEACHING

2 But as for you, promote the kind of living that reflects right teaching. [2]Teach the older men to exercise self-control, to be worthy of respect, and to live wisely. They must have strong faith and be filled with love and patience.

[3]Similarly, teach the older women to live in a way that is appropriate for someone serving the Lord. They must not go around speaking evil of others and must not be heavy drinkers. Instead, they should teach others what is good. [4]These older women must train the younger women to love their husbands and their children, [5]to live wisely and be pure, to take care of their homes, to do good, and to be submissive to their husbands. Then they will not bring shame on the word of God.

[6]In the same way, encourage the young men to live wisely in all they do. [7]And you yourself must be an example to them by doing good deeds of every kind. Let everything you do reflect the integrity and seriousness of your teaching. [8]Let your teaching be so correct that it can't be criticized. Then those who want to argue will be ashamed because they won't have anything bad to say about us.

[9]Slaves must obey their masters and do their best to please them. They must not talk back [10]or steal, but they must show themselves to be

---

1:6 Or *have only one wife,* or *be married only once;* Greek reads *be the husband of one wife.* 1:7 Greek *overseer.*

entirely trustworthy and good. Then they will make the teaching about God our Savior attractive in every way.

[11]For the grace of God has been revealed, bringing salvation to all people. [12]And we are instructed to turn from godless living and sinful pleasures. We should live in this evil world with self-control, right conduct, and devotion to God, [13]while we look forward to that wonderful event when the glory of our great God and Savior, Jesus Christ, will be revealed. [14]He gave his life to free us from every kind of sin, to cleanse us, and to make us his very own people, totally committed to doing what is right. [15]You must teach these things and encourage your people to do them, correcting them when necessary. You have the authority to do this, so don't let anyone ignore you or disregard what you say.

Do What Is Good

3 Remind your people to submit to the government and its officers. They should be obedient, always ready to do what is good. [2]They must not speak evil of anyone, and they must avoid quarreling. Instead, they should be gentle and show true humility to everyone.

[3]Once we, too, were foolish and disobedient. We were misled by others and became slaves to many wicked desires and evil pleasures. Our lives were full of evil and envy. We hated others, and they hated us.

[4]But then God our Savior showed us his kindness and love. [5]He saved us, not because of the good things we did, but because of his mercy. He washed away our sins and gave us a new life through the Holy Spirit.* [6]He gener-ously poured out the Spirit upon us because of what Jesus Christ our Savior did. [7]He declared us not guilty because of his great kindness. And now we know that we will inherit eternal life. [8]These things I have told you are all true. I want you to insist on them so that everyone who trusts in God will be careful to do good deeds all the time. These things are good and beneficial for everyone.

Paul's Final Remarks and Greetings

[9]Do not get involved in foolish discussions about spiritual pedigrees* or in quarrels and fights about obedience to Jewish laws. These kinds of things are useless and a waste of time. [10]If anyone is causing divisions among you, give a first and second warning. After that, have nothing more to do with that person. [11]For people like that have turned away from the truth. They are sinning, and they condemn themselves.

[12]I am planning to send either Artemas or Tychicus to you. As soon as one of them arrives, do your best to meet me at Nicopolis as quickly as you can, for I have decided to stay there for the winter. [13]Do everything you can to help Zenas the lawyer and Apollos with their trip. See that they are given everything they need. [14]For our people should not have unproductive lives. They must learn to do good by helping others who have urgent needs.

[15]Everybody here sends greetings. Please give my greetings to all of the believers who love us.

May God's grace be with you all.

3:5 Greek *He saved us through the washing of regeneration and renewing of the Holy Spirit.*   3:9 Greek *discussions and genealogies.*

My Daily Worship

— *December 6* —

LIVING OUR WORSHIP

TITUS 1:1—3:15

Remind your people to submit to the government and its officers. They should be obedient, always ready to do what is good. They must not speak evil of anyone, and they must avoid quarreling. Instead, they should be gentle and show true humility to everyone (3:1–2).

[i reflect]

It's said that the following statement was on the wall of Gandhi's home, "When you are in the right, you can afford to keep your temper; when you are in the wrong, you cannot afford to lose it." Today's passage in Titus reminds us that the reverence we hold for God should extend to the way we treat other people.

If we worship the Lord faithfully on Sunday but behave contentiously on Monday, we are not allowing our faith to filter our conduct. A follower of Christ is not usually recognized by his or her worship style, but rather by his or her behavior towards others. It's pleasant to praise God when those around us behave agreeably; the real test of character, however, comes when we rub shoulders with those who are difficult.

Therese of Lisieux once wrote about a difficult person in her life:

> There is one sister in the community who has the knack of rubbing me up the wrong way at every turn; her tricks of manner, her tricks of speech, her character, strike me as unlovable. But then, . . . God must love her dearly, so I wasn't going to let this natural antipathy get the best of me. I reminded myself that charity isn't a matter of fine sentiments; it means doing things. So I determined to treat this sister as if she were the person I loved best in the world. Every time I met her, I used to pray for her, offering to God all her virtues and her merits. I felt certain that Jesus would like me to do that.

In his letter to Titus, the apostle Paul instructs believers not to let these occasional feelings of discomfort towards others—even those in the Christian community—get the best of us. Instead our lives are to be characterized by a submissive, obedient spirit towards those in authority, and gentle humility towards everyone else. Jesus, quite certainly, would like us to do that.

Today, as an act of worship, pray specifically for your employer or someone in authority over you. Treat them with added respect, as if they were the people you love best in the world.

[i pray]

Lord, you know there are people in my life who I find very difficult to relate to. Grant me the grace to not quarrel but, rather, to demonstrate a gentle spirit of compassion towards them.

[i respond]

What practical things can you do today to live out your faith as you relate to those with whom you live or work? Choose a project that you can adopt for the next month or so.

Philemon

I, Paul, write this in my own handwriting: "I will repay it."
And I won't mention that you owe me your very soul! (19).

Passing On the Faith

It's easy today for a Christian to forget that the person who introduced him or her to faith, who brought the new convert into the worshiping family of God, is actually a lifetime VIP. Here, in the context of asking his friend Philemon to forgive and restore the renegade (now Christian brother) Onesimus, Paul mentions the unmentionable: "You owe *me* your life in faith! God used *me* to show his love to you." That creates a relationship that should never be broken, and a debt that can never be repaid, except to pass it on.

Next time at a worship service, take note of the people around you. Who has been your teacher, your prayer partner, your encourager? Who has given to you generously or helped you sort out a tangled problem? Who has forgiven a wrong and shown you the mercy of God? These people are not casual passers-by; they are family in Christ. You owe them your soul, as Paul reminded Philemon of his spiritual debt.

In this short letter, Paul shows that in the worshiping community, social differences give way to God-centered relationships. The slave Onesimus is now a brother. This radical redrawing of persons is possible only because God saves us, changes us, and then works in us to reflect his own character. And all of this change is mediated mostly through people—the great VIPs of our lives, those wonderful caring people who worship God with you, past and present.

You are family. Pass it on.

Worship Moments

- Worship leaders do well to note that Paul identified himself not as a "reverend" or bishop (or guitarist or lead vocalist), but as a prisoner (1).

- Focus on the richness and miracle of others' spiritual lives, not on the hurts, disappointments, or blemishes (4–5).

- We need to find ways to provide encouragement and refreshment to others—in song, word, or prayer (7).

- Worship breaks social barriers and creates wonderful new possibilities for diverse people to show the miracle of God's salvation (16).

My Daily Worship

— *December 7* —

GENEROUS FAITH

PHILEMON 1–25

You are generous because of your faith. And I am praying that you will really put your
generosity to work, for in so doing you will come to an understanding
of all the good things we can do for Christ (6).

[i reflect]

In 1908, explorer Ernest Shackleton led an expedition to Antarctica to reach the South Pole. They came close, but just ninety-seven miles short of the pole, they had to turn back. On the return trip, food supplies had dwindled save for one last ration of hardtack that was given to each man. In his diary, Shackleton recorded that some men consumed their ration immediately; others, however, stowed it away, saving it for a last moment of hungry desperation.

Shackleton was almost asleep when he noticed one of his most trusted men sitting up in his sleeping bag, looking to see if anyone was watching. Shackleton's heart sank as he watched the man reach over to the food sack of the man next to him—until he realized that the man was actually putting his own hardtack into the other's food sack!

Such acts of generosity stir our emotions. It is what Paul was writing about to his friend Philemon, "I myself have gained much joy and comfort from your love, my brother, because your kindness has so often refreshed the hearts of God's people" (v. 7). Every good deed becomes an act of worship, for in serving others, we serve Christ.

Paul encouraged Philemon to extend that same kindness to his runaway slave, not because "you were forced to do it but because you wanted to" (v. 14). Paul was confident that Philemon would do all he asked and even more, because now Onesimus was part of the family of God.

Our generous giving not only is an outward demonstration of our faith, but it also brings glory to the One we worship. It is, in fact, an act of worship. Do you give generously of your time and talents? Do you give freely from your abundance to build up the body of Christ?

Look for opportunities to give generously today—whether it's monetary or material, your talents or your time. Give out of your faith and love for God.

[i pray]

Lord, I confess that often I am not generous with my time or money.
I do not trust you to provide, but depend on my own efforts.
Help me to trust you with my life so that I may give more to others.

[i respond]

In what area is it hardest for you to give generously—time, talents, money? Ask your pastor or a close friend for suggestions on how you can make changes in that area. Then donate generously for Christ.

GREETINGS FROM PAUL

This letter is from Paul, in prison for preaching the Good News about Christ Jesus, and from our brother Timothy.

It is written to Philemon, our much loved co-worker, ²and to our sister Apphia and to Archippus, a fellow soldier of the cross. I am also writing to the church that meets in your house.

³May God our Father and the Lord Jesus Christ give you grace and peace.

PAUL'S THANKSGIVING AND PRAYER

⁴I always thank God when I pray for you, Philemon, ⁵because I keep hearing of your trust in the Lord Jesus and your love for all of God's people. ⁶You are generous because of your faith. And I am praying that you will really put your generosity to work, for in so doing you will come to an understanding of all the good things we can do for Christ. ⁷I myself have gained much joy and comfort from your love, my brother, because your kindness has so often refreshed the hearts of God's people.

PAUL'S APPEAL FOR ONESIMUS

⁸That is why I am boldly asking a favor of you. I could demand it in the name of Christ because it is the right thing for you to do, ⁹but because of our love, I prefer just to ask you. So take this as a request from your friend Paul, an old man, now in prison for the sake of Christ Jesus.

¹⁰My plea is that you show kindness to Onesimus. I think of him as my own son because he became a believer as a result of my ministry here in prison. ¹¹Onesimus* hasn't been of much use to you in the past, but now he is very useful to both of us. ¹²I am sending him back to you, and with him comes my own heart.

¹³I really wanted to keep him here with me while I am in these chains for preaching the Good News, and he would have helped me on your behalf. ¹⁴But I didn't want to do anything without your consent. And I didn't want you to help because you were forced to do it but because you wanted to. ¹⁵Perhaps you could think of it this way: Onesimus ran away for a little while so you could have him back forever. ¹⁶He is no longer just a slave; he is a beloved brother, especially to me. Now he will mean much more to you, both as a slave and as a brother in the Lord.

¹⁷So if you consider me your partner, give him the same welcome you would give me if I were coming. ¹⁸If he has harmed you in any way or stolen anything from you, charge me for it. ¹⁹I, Paul, write this in my own handwriting: "I will repay it." And I won't mention that you owe me your very soul!

²⁰Yes, dear brother, please do me this favor for the Lord's sake. Give me this encouragement in Christ. ²¹I am confident as I write this letter that you will do what I ask and even more!

²²Please keep a guest room ready for me, for I am hoping that God will answer your prayers and let me return to you soon.

PAUL'S FINAL GREETINGS

²³Epaphras, my fellow prisoner in Christ Jesus, sends you his greetings. ²⁴So do Mark, Aristarchus, Demas, and Luke, my co-workers.

²⁵The grace of the Lord Jesus Christ be with your spirit.

---

11 *Onesimus* means "useful."

Hebrews

So let us come boldly to the throne of our gracious God. There we will receive

his mercy, and we will find grace to help us when we need it (4:16).

The Call to Worship

The book of Hebrews celebrates the continuity and discontinuity of the Old Testament and the New Testament. One almighty God speaks in both testaments urging people to accept his mercy and pledging his fidelity to the promise to save us. One God speaks in various ways. One God warns against unbelief.

The same God puts aside the sacrificial system of the Old Testament when the Son of God, Jesus, comes to make full and final payment for sin. Finding God now is not a repeat of Old Testament forms, but the acceptance of God's Word written in our hearts in the new and living way. This new way is typified by faith, it keeps a keen focus on Jesus, and it perseveres despite setbacks and struggles. New Testament believers follow God so closely that opponents can do nothing to thwart that steady march.

Yet there are warnings: don't give up, don't look back, don't neglect celebrating God's mercy together, don't abuse the love of God or fall into unbelief. Keep your eyes on Jesus. In that sense, the book of Hebrews is like a prayer to continue praying, a song repeated one more time, hands high in praise.

The call to worship pulsates through these thirteen chapters. Worship sustains us through trials and trouble. Worship exalts Jesus as the author and finisher of faith. Worship is our drawing near to the God who feels our pain and leads us throughout life to a new city in heaven, our home.

Worship Moments

- Unbelief is the enemy of worship. In our faith, spirit, and integrity, we need to keep worship strong (3:19; 4:3).

- As we grow in faith, we will mature in worship style and format (6:1).

- God does not cherish the worshiper who merely goes through motions. God wants your heart (8:10).

- Holding tightly to our faith and finding encouragement are reasons to consistently meet together in worship (10:24–25).

- When times get hard and we feel God has checked out, look at Jesus. Follow his lead (12:2).

JESUS CHRIST IS GOD'S SON

1 Long ago God spoke many times and in many ways to our ancestors through the prophets. [2]But now in these final days, he has spoken to us through his Son. God promised everything to the Son as an inheritance, and through the Son he made the universe and everything in it. [3]The Son reflects God's own glory, and everything about him represents God exactly. He sustains the universe by the mighty power of his command. After he died to cleanse us from the stain of sin, he sat down in the place of honor at the right hand of the majestic God of heaven.

CHRIST IS GREATER THAN THE ANGELS

[4]This shows that God's Son is far greater than the angels, just as the name God gave him is far greater than their names. [5]For God never said to any angel what he said to Jesus:

"You are my Son.
    Today I have become your Father.*"

And again God said,

"I will be his Father,
    and he will be my Son."*

[6]And then, when he presented his honored* Son to the world, God said, "Let all the angels of God worship him."* [7]God calls his angels

"messengers swift as the wind,
    and servants made of flaming fire."*

[8]But to his Son he says,

"Your throne, O God, endures forever and
        ever.
    Your royal power is expressed in
        righteousness.
[9] You love what is right and hate what is
        wrong.

Therefore God, your God, has anointed
        you,
    pouring out the oil of joy on you more
        than on anyone else."*

[10]And,

"Lord, in the beginning you laid the
        foundation of the earth,
    and the heavens are the work of your
        hands.
[11] Even they will perish, but you remain
        forever.
    They will wear out like old clothing.
[12] You will roll them up like an old coat.
    They will fade away like old clothing.
But you are always the same;
    you will never grow old."*

[13]And God never said to an angel, as he did to his Son,

"Sit in honor at my right hand
    until I humble your enemies,
        making them a footstool under your feet."*

[14]But angels are only servants. They are spirits sent from God to care for those who will receive salvation.

A WARNING AGAINST DRIFTING AWAY

2 So we must listen very carefully to the truth we have heard, or we may drift away from it. [2]The message God delivered through angels has always proved true, and the people were punished for every violation of the law and every act of disobedience. [3]What makes us think that we can escape if we are indifferent to this great salvation that was announced by the Lord Jesus himself? It was passed on* to us by those who heard him speak, [4]and God verified the message by signs and wonders and various miracles and by giving gifts of the Holy Spirit whenever he chose to do so.

1:5a Or *Today I reveal you as my Son.* Ps 2:7.   1:5b 2 Sam 7:14.   1:6a Greek *firstborn.*   1:6b Deut 32:43.   1:7 Ps 104:4.   1:8-9 Ps 45:6-7. 1:10-12 Ps 102:25-27.   1:13 Ps 110:1.   2:3 Or *and confirmed.*

My Daily Worship

— *December 8* —

THE ESSENCE OF EMPATHY

HEBREWS 1:1–3:19

Since he himself has gone through suffering and temptation,
he is able to help us when we are being tempted (2:18).

[i reflect]

How often have you heard someone say, "Oh, how awful. I know *exactly* how you feel."

But it's not true. You know that this person does not even know *approximately* how you feel, much less *exactly*. Their presumption only adds to the pain. No one could possibly know.

Then there is Jesus.

He is the Son of God, the high and lofty One, seated at the right hand of the Father Almighty, who became a human being. The impossible is true. There *is* One who knows exactly how you feel.

The letter to the Hebrews is the Epistle of Empathy, good news of the most personal nature. "It was necessary for Jesus to be in every respect like us, his brothers and sisters, so that he could be our merciful and faithful High Priest before God. He then could offer a sacrifice that would take away the sins of the people" (2:17).

We read as well, "This High Priest of ours understands our weaknesses, for he faced all of the same temptations we do, yet he did not sin" (4:15). Consider Jesus' life: the forty days in the wilderness, the three years of struggle in ministry, the prayers in the Garden of Gethsemane. He faced physical suffering, mental anguish, emotional upheaval, loss, abandonment, as well as being tempted to grab the glory, to rush ahead of the Father's plan, to give up entirely.

"In every respect like us"—not in some respects, in *every* respect. He does not understand approximately how we feel, but exactly. His identification with us is complete.

What will you do with this truth? Hebrews offers us an invitation as well as encouragement: "So let us come boldly to the throne of our gracious God. There we will receive his mercy, and we will find grace to help us when we need it" (4:16).

Come boldly before his throne right now. Tell him what you have not revealed to anyone. He knows. Exactly.

[i pray]

Lord Jesus, you alone know my struggles and my temptations. I thank you that you
came to earth in human form and I ask for the mercy and grace I need.

[i respond]

Write down the three most difficult problems and temptations you are facing this week. What parallel situations can you see in Jesus' life on earth? Write those down as well, and be confident of his grace and mercy.

JESUS, THE MAN

[5]And furthermore, the future world we are talking about will not be controlled by angels. [6]For somewhere in the Scriptures it says,

"What is man that you should think of him,
    and the son of man* that you should
        care for him?
[7] For a little while you made him lower than
        the angels,
    and you crowned him with glory and
        honor.*
[8] You gave him authority over all things."*

Now when it says "all things," it means nothing is left out. But we have not yet seen all of this happen. [9]What we do see is Jesus, who "for a little while was made lower than the angels" and now is "crowned with glory and honor" because he suffered death for us. Yes, by God's grace, Jesus tasted death for everyone in all the world. [10]And it was only right that God—who made everything and for whom everything was made—should bring his many children into glory. Through the suffering of Jesus, God made him a perfect leader, one fit to bring them into their salvation.

[11]So now Jesus and the ones he makes holy have the same Father. That is why Jesus is not ashamed to call them his brothers and sisters.* [12]For he said to God,

"I will declare the wonder of your name to
    my brothers and sisters.*
I will praise you among all your people."

[13]He also said, "I will put my trust in him." And in the same context he said, "Here I am— together with the children God has given me."*

[14]Because God's children are human beings—made of flesh and blood—Jesus also became flesh and blood by being born in human form. For only as a human being could he die, and only by dying could he break the power of the Devil, who had the power of death. [15]Only in this way could he deliver those who have lived all their lives as slaves to the fear of dying.

[16]We all know that Jesus came to help the descendants of Abraham, not to help the angels. [17]Therefore, it was necessary for Jesus to be in every respect like us, his brothers and sisters, so that he could be our merciful and faithful High Priest before God. He then could offer a sacrifice that would take away the sins of the people. [18]Since he himself has gone through suffering and temptation, he is able to help us when we are being tempted.

JESUS IS GREATER THAN MOSES

3 And so, dear brothers and sisters who belong to God* and are bound for heaven, think about this Jesus whom we declare to be God's Messenger and High Priest. [2]For he was faithful to God, who appointed him, just as Moses served faithfully and was entrusted with God's entire house. [3]But Jesus deserves far more glory than Moses, just as a person who builds a fine house deserves more praise than the house itself. [4]For every house has a builder, but God is the one who made everything.

[5]Moses was certainly faithful in God's house, but only as a servant. His work was an illustration of the truths God would reveal later. [6]But Christ, the faithful Son, was in charge of the entire household. And we are God's household, if we keep up our courage and remain confident in our hope in Christ. [7]That is why the Holy Spirit says,

"Today you must listen to his voice.
[8] Don't harden your hearts against him
        as Israel did when they rebelled,
    when they tested God's patience in the
        wilderness.
[9] There your ancestors tried my patience,
    even though they saw my miracles for
        forty years.

2:6 Or Son of Man. 2:7 Some manuscripts add You put him in charge of everything you made. 2:6-8 Ps 8:4-6. 2:11 Greek his brothers; also in 2:17. 2:12 Greek my brothers. Ps 22:22. 2:13 Isa 8:17-18. 3:1 Greek And so, holy brothers.

¹⁰ So I was angry with them, and I said,
　'Their hearts always turn away from me.
　They refuse to do what I tell them.'
¹¹ So in my anger I made a vow:
　'They will never enter my place of rest.'"*

¹²Be careful then, dear brothers and sisters.* Make sure that your own hearts are not evil and unbelieving, turning you away from the living God. ¹³You must warn each other every day, as long as it is called "today," so that none of you will be deceived by sin and hardened against God. ¹⁴For if we are faithful to the end, trusting God just as firmly as when we first believed, we will share in all that belongs to Christ. ¹⁵But never forget the warning:

"Today you must listen to his voice.
　Don't harden your hearts against him
　as Israel did when they rebelled."*

¹⁶And who were those people who rebelled against God, even though they heard his voice? Weren't they the ones Moses led out of Egypt? ¹⁷And who made God angry for forty years? Wasn't it the people who sinned, whose bodies fell in the wilderness? ¹⁸And to whom was God speaking when he vowed that they would never enter his place of rest? He was speaking to those who disobeyed him. ¹⁹So we see that they were not allowed to enter his rest because of their unbelief.

PROMISED REST FOR GOD'S PEOPLE

4 God's promise of entering his place of rest still stands, so we ought to tremble with fear that some of you might fail to get there. ²For this Good News—that God has prepared a place of rest—has been announced to us just as it was to them. But it did them no good because they didn't believe what God told them.* ³For only we who believe can enter his place of rest. As for those who didn't believe, God said,

"In my anger I made a vow:
　'They will never enter my place of rest,'"*

even though his place of rest has been ready since he made the world. ⁴We know it is ready because the Scriptures mention the seventh day, saying, "On the seventh day God rested from all his work."* ⁵But in the other passage God said, "They will never enter my place of rest."* ⁶So God's rest is there for people to enter. But those who formerly heard the Good News failed to enter because they disobeyed God. ⁷So God set another time for entering his place of rest, and that time is today. God announced this through David a long time later in the words already quoted:

"Today you must listen to his voice.
　Don't harden your hearts against him."*

⁸This new place of rest was not the land of Canaan, where Joshua led them. If it had been, God would not have spoken later about another day of rest. ⁹So there is a special rest* still waiting for the people of God. ¹⁰For all who enter into God's rest will find rest from their labors, just as God rested after creating the world. ¹¹Let us do our best to enter that place of rest. For anyone who disobeys God, as the people of Israel did, will fall.

¹²For the word of God is full of living power. It is sharper than the sharpest knife, cutting deep into our innermost thoughts and desires. It exposes us for what we really are. ¹³Nothing in all creation can hide from him. Everything is naked and exposed before his eyes. This is the God to whom we must explain all that we have done.

CHRIST IS OUR HIGH PRIEST

¹⁴That is why we have a great High Priest who has gone to heaven, Jesus the Son of God. Let us cling to him and never stop trusting him. ¹⁵This High Priest of ours understands our

3:7-11 Ps 95:7-11.　3:12 Greek brothers.　3:15 Ps 95:7-8.　4:2 Some manuscripts read they didn't share the faith of those who listened [to God].　4:3 Ps 95:11.　4:4 Gen 2:2.　4:5 Ps 95:11.　4:7 Ps 95:7-8.　4:9 Or Sabbath rest.

weaknesses, for he faced all of the same temptations we do, yet he did not sin. [16]So let us come boldly to the throne of our gracious God. There we will receive his mercy, and we will find grace to help us when we need it.

5 Now a high priest is a man chosen to represent other human beings in their dealings with God. He presents their gifts to God and offers their sacrifices for sins. [2]And because he is human, he is able to deal gently with the people, though they are ignorant and wayward. For he is subject to the same weaknesses they have. [3]That is why he has to offer sacrifices, both for their sins and for his own sins. [4]And no one can become a high priest simply because he wants such an honor. He has to be called by God for this work, just as Aaron was.

[5]That is why Christ did not exalt himself to become High Priest. No, he was chosen by God, who said to him,

"You are my Son.
 Today I have become your Father.*"

[6]And in another passage God said to him,

"You are a priest forever
 in the line of Melchizedek."*

[7]While Jesus was here on earth, he offered prayers and pleadings, with a loud cry and tears, to the one who could deliver him out of death. And God heard his prayers because of his reverence for God. [8]So even though Jesus was God's Son, he learned obedience from the things he suffered. [9]In this way, God qualified him as a perfect High Priest, and he became the source of eternal salvation for all those who obey him. [10]And God designated him to be a High Priest in the line of Melchizedek.

A CALL TO SPIRITUAL GROWTH

[11]There is so much more we would like to say about this. But you don't seem to listen, so it's hard to make you understand. [12]You have been Christians a long time now, and you ought to be teaching others. Instead, you need someone to teach you again the basic things a beginner must learn about the Scriptures.* You are like babies who drink only milk and cannot eat solid food. [13]And a person who is living on milk isn't very far along in the Christian life and doesn't know much about doing what is right. [14]Solid food is for those who are mature, who have trained themselves to recognize the difference between right and wrong and then do what is right.

6 So let us stop going over the basics of Christianity* again and again. Let us go on instead and become mature in our understanding. Surely we don't need to start all over again with the importance of turning away from evil deeds and placing our faith in God. [2]You don't need further instruction about baptisms, the laying on of hands, the resurrection of the dead, and eternal judgment. [3]And so, God willing, we will move forward to further understanding.

[4]For it is impossible to restore to repentance those who were once enlightened—those who have experienced the good things of heaven and shared in the Holy Spirit, [5]who have tasted the goodness of the word of God and the power of the age to come—[6]and who then turn away from God. It is impossible to bring such people to repentance again because they are nailing the Son of God to the cross again by rejecting him, holding him up to public shame.

[7]When the ground soaks up the rain that falls on it and bears a good crop for the farmer, it has the blessing of God. [8]But if a field bears thistles and thorns, it is useless. The farmer will condemn that field and burn it.

[9]Dear friends, even though we are talking like this, we really don't believe that it applies to you. We are confident that you are meant for better things, things that come with salvation. [10]For God is not unfair. He will not

5:5 Or *Today I reveal you as my Son*. Ps 2:7.   5:6 Ps 110:4.   5:12 Or *about the oracles of God*.   6:1 Or *the basics about Christ*.

My Daily Worship

— *December 9* —

CUTTING DEEP, CUTTING TRUE
HEBREWS 4:1–6:20

For the word of God is full of living power. It is sharper than the sharpest knife, cutting deep into our innermost thoughts and desires. It exposes us for what we really are (4:12).

[i reflect]

"Then the lion said—but I don't know if it spoke—'You will have to let me undress you.' I was afraid of his claws, I can tell you, but I was pretty nearly desperate now. So I just lay flat down on my back to let him do it."

The speaker is Eustace, a boy whose greed turned him into a dragon, in *The Voyage of the Dawn Treader*. The lion, Aslan, is the Christ-figure in C. S. Lewis's series The Chronicles of Narnia.

Eustace continues: "The very first tear he made was so deep that I thought it had gone right into my heart. And when he began pulling the skin off, it hurt worse than anything I've ever felt. The only thing that made me able to bear it was just the pleasure of feeling the stuff peel off. . . . And there was I as smooth and soft as a peeled switch and smaller than I had been."

The Word was made flesh. The Word cuts through flesh, through the façade, through the falsehood. Nothing is safe from the sharp knife of Christ, but nothing is truly safe without it; the frightening claws of Narnia's Aslan are both the ultimate weapon against the dragon hide and the only tool to give Eustace new skin, new life.

The Scriptures can cut our hearts to the quick, but the wounds are not malicious. Rather, the knife of God's Word slices through and slices away our own malice, our own layers of sin and excuses. The knife is the sharpest, used by the only surgeon able to do the job.

Do you shrink from the knife of the Word? Only Aslan's claws could cut through to a new life for Eustace. Only God's Word cuts deep but cuts true in our lives.

Take a few moments to reflect on what areas of your life you most need the sharp edge of God's Word applied. Prayerfully give him your consent and your thanks.

[i pray]

God, I acknowledge that layers cover me and keep me from the life you want me to live.
Wield the knife of your Word. Cut through and cut away what you hate,
so that healing and new growth can start.

[i respond]

Read Hebrews 4:12–13 in at least two other translations. Note the imagery and word pictures used to express the sharpness of God's Word (such as "two-edged sword," "piercing"). Thank God for the power and effectiveness of Scripture.

Words of Worship

MAJESTY

Majesty—Hebrew *ge-'* "majesty"; *ha-dar* "splendor, honor"; Greek *me-ga-lo- -ne* "greatness."

Our personal worship results in intimate moments with the Lord. He says, "I live in that high and holy place with those whose spirits are contrite and humble" (Isaiah 57:15). Throughout Scripture he speaks tenderly to those who are his. Yet the Bible reveals another side of God's presence: his awesome and overwhelming dignity. "He is robed in majesty. Indeed, the LORD is robed in majesty and armed with strength" (Psalm 93:1). His presence is like a fire that overwhelms those who oppose him (Psalm 97:3). As the writer of Hebrews reminds us, "It is a terrible thing to fall into the hands of the living God" (Hebrews 10:31).

God is our tender, compassionate friend. He is also our majestic and powerful Judge. To worship him rightly is to perform a balancing act, holding both aspects of his presence in our vision. In Jesus Christ we can do this, for both sides of God are revealed in him. "All glory to him, who alone is God our Savior, through Jesus Christ our Lord. Yes, glory, majesty, power, and authority belong to him, in the beginning, now, and forevermore. Amen" (Jude 25).

indifferent. Instead, you will follow the example of those who are going to inherit God's promises because of their faith and patience.

GOD'S PROMISES BRING HOPE

[13]For example, there was God's promise to Abraham. Since there was no one greater to swear by, God took an oath in his own name, saying:

[14] "I will certainly bless you richly,
    and I will multiply your descendants
        into countless millions."*

[15]Then Abraham waited patiently, and he received what God had promised.
    [16]When people take an oath, they call on someone greater than themselves to hold them to it. And without any question that oath is binding. [17]God also bound himself with an oath, so that those who received the promise could be perfectly sure that he would never change his mind. [18]So God has given us both his promise and his oath. These two things are unchangeable because it is impossible for God to lie. Therefore, we who have fled to him for refuge can take new courage, for we can hold on to his promise with confidence.
    [19]This confidence is like a strong and trustworthy anchor for our souls. It leads us through the curtain of heaven into God's inner sanctuary. [20]Jesus has already gone in there for us. He has become our eternal High Priest in the line of Melchizedek.

MELCHIZEDEK IS COMPARED TO ABRAHAM

7 This Melchizedek was king of the city of Salem and also a priest of God Most High. When Abraham was returning home after winning a great battle against many kings, Melchizedek met him and blessed him. [2]Then Abraham took a tenth of all he had won in the battle and gave it to Melchizedek. His name means "king of justice." He is also "king

forget how hard you have worked for him and how you have shown your love to him by caring for other Christians, as you still do. [11]Our great desire is that you will keep right on loving others as long as life lasts, in order to make certain that what you hope for will come true. [12]Then you will not become spiritually dull and

6:14 Gen 22:17.

of peace" because *Salem* means "peace." [3]There is no record of his father or mother or any of his ancestors—no beginning or end to his life. He remains a priest forever, resembling the Son of God.

[4]Consider then how great this Melchizedek was. Even Abraham, the great patriarch of Israel, recognized how great Melchizedek was by giving him a tenth of what he had taken in battle. [5]Now the priests, who are descendants of Levi, are commanded in the law of Moses to collect a tithe from all the people, even though they are their own relatives.* [6]But Melchizedek, who was not even related to Levi, collected a tenth from Abraham. And Melchizedek placed a blessing upon Abraham, the one who had already received the promises of God. [7]And without question, the person who has the power to bless is always greater than the person who is blessed.

[8]In the case of Jewish priests, tithes are paid to men who will die. But Melchizedek is greater than they are, because we are told that he lives on. [9]In addition, we might even say that Levi's descendants, the ones who collect the tithe, paid a tithe to Melchizedek through their ancestor Abraham. [10]For although Levi wasn't born yet, the seed from which he came was in Abraham's loins when Melchizedek collected the tithe from him.

[11]And finally, if the priesthood of Levi could have achieved God's purposes—and it was that priesthood on which the law was based— why did God need to send a different priest from the line of Melchizedek, instead of from the line of Levi and Aaron?*

[12]And when the priesthood is changed, the law must also be changed to permit it. [13]For the one we are talking about belongs to a different tribe, whose members do not serve at the altar. [14]What I mean is, our Lord came from the tribe of Judah, and Moses never mentioned Judah in connection with the priesthood.

CHRIST IS LIKE MELCHIZEDEK

[15]The change in God's law is even more evident from the fact that a different priest, who is like Melchizedek, has now come. [16]He became a priest, not by meeting the old requirement of belonging to the tribe of Levi, but by the power of a life that cannot be destroyed. [17]And the psalmist pointed this out when he said of Christ,

"You are a priest forever
    in the line of Melchizedek."*

[18]Yes, the old requirement about the priesthood was set aside because it was weak and useless. [19]For the law made nothing perfect, and now a better hope has taken its place. And that is how we draw near to God.

[20]God took an oath that Christ would always be a priest, but he never did this for any other priest. [21]Only to Jesus did he say,

"The Lord has taken an oath
    and will not break his vow:
    'You are a priest forever.'"*

[22]Because of God's oath, it is Jesus who guarantees the effectiveness of this better covenant.

[23]Another difference is that there were many priests under the old system. When one priest died, another had to take his place. [24]But Jesus remains a priest forever; his priesthood will never end. [25]Therefore he is able, once and forever, to save* everyone who comes to God through him. He lives forever to plead with God on their behalf.

[26]He is the kind of high priest we need because he is holy and blameless, unstained by sin. He has now been set apart from sinners, and he has been given the highest place of honor in heaven. [27]He does not need to offer sacrifices every day like the other high priests. They did this for their own sins first and then for the sins of the people. But Jesus did this

---

7:5 Greek *their brothers, who are descendants of Abraham.* 7:11 Greek *according to the order of Aaron.* 7:17 Ps 110:4. 7:21 Ps 110:4.
7:25 Or *able to save completely.*

once for all when he sacrificed himself on the cross. [28]Those who were high priests under the law of Moses were limited by human weakness. But after the law was given, God appointed his Son with an oath, and his Son has been made perfect forever.

CHRIST IS OUR HIGH PRIEST

8 Here is the main point: Our High Priest sat down in the place of highest honor in heaven, at God's right hand. [2]There he ministers in the sacred tent, the true place of worship that was built by the Lord and not by human hands.

[3]And since every high priest is required to offer gifts and sacrifices, our High Priest must make an offering, too. [4]If he were here on earth, he would not even be a priest, since there already are priests who offer the gifts required by the law of Moses. [5]They serve in a place of worship that is only a copy, a shadow of the real one in heaven. For when Moses was getting ready to build the Tabernacle, God gave him this warning: "Be sure that you make everything according to the design I have shown you here on the mountain."* [6]But our High Priest has been given a ministry that is far superior to the ministry of those who serve under the old laws, for he is the one who guarantees for us a better covenant with God, based on better promises.

[7]If the first covenant had been faultless, there would have been no need for a second covenant to replace it. [8]But God himself found fault with the old one when he said:

"The day will come, says the Lord,
    when I will make a new covenant
    with the people of Israel and Judah.
[9] This covenant will not be like the one
    I made with their ancestors
when I took them by the hand
    and led them out of the land of Egypt.
They did not remain faithful to my
    covenant,

so I turned my back on them, says the
    Lord.
[10] But this is the new covenant I will make
    with the people of Israel on that day,
    says the Lord:
I will put my laws in their minds
    so they will understand them,
and I will write them on their hearts
    so they will obey them.
I will be their God,
    and they will be my people.
[11] And they will not need to teach their
    neighbors,
    nor will they need to teach their family,
    saying, 'You should know the Lord.'
For everyone, from the least to the greatest,
    will already know me.
[12] And I will forgive their wrongdoings,
    and I will never again remember their
    sins."*

[13]When God speaks of a new covenant, it means he has made the first one obsolete. It is now out of date and ready to be put aside.

OLD RULES ABOUT WORSHIP

9 Now in that first covenant between God and Israel, there were regulations for worship and a sacred tent here on earth. [2]There were two rooms in this tent. In the first room were a lampstand, a table, and loaves of holy bread on the table. This was called the Holy Place. [3]Then there was a curtain, and behind the curtain was the second room called the Most Holy Place. [4]In that room were a gold incense altar and a wooden chest called the Ark of the Covenant, which was covered with gold on all sides. Inside the Ark were a gold jar containing some manna, Aaron's staff that sprouted leaves, and the stone tablets of the covenant with the Ten Commandments written on them. [5]The glorious cherubim were above the Ark. Their wings were stretched out over the Ark's cover, the place of atonement. But we cannot explain all of these things now.

8:5 Exod 25:40; 26:30. **8:8-12** Jer 31:31-34.

My Daily Worship

— *December 10* —

PERFECTLY CLEAR, CLEARLY PERFECT

HEBREWS 7:1–9:28

Just think how much more the blood of Christ will purify our hearts from deeds that lead
to death so that we can worship the living God. For by the power of the eternal Spirit,
Christ offered himself to God as a perfect sacrifice for our sins (9:14).

[i reflect]

The perfect gift. A perfect 4.0 grade point average. The perfect match. A perfect 10 from the Olympic judges. A perfect fit. A perfect score. All of these may be uncommon, but are not impossible.

She had tormented herself with trying to be perfect for as long as she could remember. The oldest daughter of alcoholics, Christy had felt the responsibility for—what was it?—oh, yes, for everything. Perfectionism, with its illusion of control, was how she coped.

"If I could just be the best little girl there ever was" changed to "If I could just get all A's." Then it became "If I could just be the perfect wife" and "If I could just work harder and be the Employee of the Year instead of just the Month." And on and on, through all the roles in her life.

She had started going to Al-Anon, and she found it helpful. One slogan caught her ear—"Progress, not perfection"—but she had many years of habitual thinking to conquer. Even at church, pleas for perfection caught her ear. *Didn't Saint Paul exhort, "Be ye perfect"? OK, so I'll be the perfect Christian,* she promised herself.

Then during a Communion Service, Christy heard words she had heard before but had never really absorbed: "He stretched out his arms upon the cross, and offered himself, in obedience to your will, a perfect sacrifice for the whole world."

It had been done already. Perfection had been reached. As Augustine wrote, "For God, in his goodness, has given us any holiness that we might have." Tears of relief joined tears of gratitude running down her cheeks. Jesus was the perfect sacrifice for the whole world, and for her.

He is also the perfect sacrifice for you. Allow that truth today to release you from the tyranny of "perfection." Lift up a praise of thanksgiving for his holiness.

[i pray]

Lord Jesus, you alone are the perfect One, the perfect sacrifice. Forgive me for
presuming to think I could add anything to your sacrifice on the cross.
I am grateful with all my heart for your offering of yourself.

[i respond]

Memorize Hebrews 9:14: "For by the power of the eternal Spirit, Christ offered himself to God as a perfect sacrifice for our sins." In the next few days, share what this verse means to you with another person.

⁶When these things were all in place, the priests went in and out of the first room* regularly as they performed their religious duties. ⁷But only the high priest goes into the Most Holy Place, and only once a year, and always with blood, which he offers to God to cover his own sins and the sins the people have committed in ignorance. ⁸By these regulations the Holy Spirit revealed that the Most Holy Place was not open to the people as long as the first room and the entire system it represents were still in use.

⁹This is an illustration pointing to the present time. For the gifts and sacrifices that the priests offer are not able to cleanse the consciences of the people who bring them. ¹⁰For that old system deals only with food and drink and ritual washing—external regulations that are in effect only until their limitations can be corrected.

CHRIST IS THE PERFECT SACRIFICE

¹¹So Christ has now become the High Priest over all the good things that have come. He has entered that great, perfect sanctuary in heaven, not made by human hands and not part of this created world. ¹²Once for all time he took blood into that Most Holy Place, but not the blood of goats and calves. He took his own blood, and with it he secured our salvation forever.

¹³Under the old system, the blood of goats and bulls and the ashes of a young cow could cleanse people's bodies from ritual defilement. ¹⁴Just think how much more the blood of Christ will purify our hearts from deeds that lead to death so that we can worship the living God. For by the power of the eternal Spirit, Christ offered himself to God as a perfect sacrifice for our sins. ¹⁵That is why he is the one who mediates the new covenant between God and people, so that all who are invited can receive the eternal inheritance God has promised them. For Christ died to set them free from the penalty of the sins they had committed under that first covenant.

¹⁶Now when someone dies and leaves a will, no one gets anything until it is proved that the person who wrote the will* is dead.* ¹⁷The will goes into effect only after the death of the person who wrote it. While the person is still alive, no one can use the will to get any of the things promised to them.

¹⁸That is why blood was required under the first covenant as a proof of death. ¹⁹For after Moses had given the people all of God's laws, he took the blood of calves and goats, along with water, and sprinkled both the book of God's laws and all the people, using branches of hyssop bushes and scarlet wool. ²⁰Then he said, "This blood confirms the covenant God has made with you."* ²¹And in the same way, he sprinkled blood on the sacred tent and on everything used for worship. ²²In fact, we can say that according to the law of Moses, nearly everything was purified by sprinkling with blood. Without the shedding of blood, there is no forgiveness of sins.

²³That is why the earthly tent and everything in it—which were copies of things in heaven—had to be purified by the blood of animals. But the real things in heaven had to be purified with far better sacrifices than the blood of animals.

²⁴For Christ has entered into heaven itself to appear now before God as our Advocate.* He did not go into the earthly place of worship, for that was merely a copy of the real Temple in heaven. ²⁵Nor did he enter heaven to offer himself again and again, like the earthly high priest who enters the Most Holy Place year after year to offer the blood of an animal. ²⁶If that had been necessary, he would have had to die again and again, ever since the world began. But no! He came once for all time, at the end of the age, to remove the power of sin forever by his sacrificial death for us.

²⁷And just as it is destined that each person dies only once and after that comes judgment,

---

9:6 Greek *first tent;* also in 9:8. 9:16a Or *covenant.* 9:16b Or *Now when someone makes a covenant, it is necessary to ratify it with the death of a sacrifice.* 9:20 Exod 24:8. 9:24 Greek *on our behalf.*

28so also Christ died only once as a sacrifice to take away the sins of many people. He will come again but not to deal with our sins again. This time he will bring salvation to all those who are eagerly waiting for him.

CHRIST'S SACRIFICE ONCE FOR ALL

10 The old system in the law of Moses was only a shadow of the things to come, not the reality of the good things Christ has done for us. The sacrifices under the old system were repeated again and again, year after year, but they were never able to provide perfect cleansing for those who came to worship. 2If they could have provided perfect cleansing, the sacrifices would have stopped, for the worshipers would have been purified once for all time, and their feelings of guilt would have disappeared.

3But just the opposite happened. Those yearly sacrifices reminded them of their sins year after year. 4For it is not possible for the blood of bulls and goats to take away sins. 5That is why Christ, when he came into the world, said,

"You did not want animal sacrifices and
    grain offerings.
    But you have given me a body so that I
        may obey you.
6 No, you were not pleased with animals
        burned on the altar
    or with other offerings for sin.
7 Then I said, 'Look, I have come to do your
        will, O God—
    just as it is written about me in the
        Scriptures.'"*

8Christ said, "You did not want animal sacrifices or grain offerings or animals burned on the altar or other offerings for sin, nor were you pleased with them" (though they are required by the law of Moses). 9Then he added, "Look, I have come to do your will." He can-

cels the first covenant in order to establish the second. 10And what God wants is for us to be made holy by the sacrifice of the body of Jesus Christ once for all time.

11Under the old covenant, the priest stands before the altar day after day, offering sacrifices that can never take away sins. 12But our High Priest offered himself to God as one sacrifice for sins, good for all time. Then he sat down at the place of highest honor at God's right hand. 13There he waits until his enemies are humbled as a footstool under his feet. 14For by that one offering he perfected forever all those whom he is making holy.

15And the Holy Spirit also testifies that this is so. First he says,

16 "This is the new covenant I will make
        with my people on that day, says the
        Lord:
    I will put my laws in their hearts
        so they will understand them,
    and I will write them on their minds
        so they will obey them."

17Then he adds,

    "I will never again remember
        their sins and lawless deeds."*

18Now when sins have been forgiven, there is no need to offer any more sacrifices.

A CALL TO PERSEVERE

19And so, dear brothers and sisters,* we can boldly enter heaven's Most Holy Place because of the blood of Jesus. 20This is the new, life-giving way that Christ has opened up for us through the sacred curtain, by means of his death for us.* 21And since we have a great High Priest who rules over God's people, 22let us go right into the presence of God, with true hearts fully trusting him. For our evil consciences have been sprinkled with Christ's blood to make us

10:5-7 Ps 40:6-8. 10:16-17 Jer 31:33-34. 10:19 Greek brothers. 10:20 Greek his flesh.

clean, and our bodies have been washed with pure water.

²³Without wavering, let us hold tightly to the hope we say we have, for God can be trusted to keep his promise. ²⁴Think of ways to encourage one another to outbursts of love and good deeds. ²⁵And let us not neglect our meeting together, as some people do, but encourage and warn each other, especially now that the day of his coming back again is drawing near.

²⁶Dear friends, if we deliberately continue sinning after we have received a full knowledge of the truth, there is no other sacrifice that will cover these sins. ²⁷There will be nothing to look forward to but the terrible expectation of God's judgment and the raging fire that will consume his enemies. ²⁸Anyone who refused to obey the law of Moses was put to death without mercy on the testimony of two or three witnesses. ²⁹Think how much more terrible the punishment will be for those who have trampled on the Son of God and have treated the blood of the covenant as if it were common and unholy. Such people have insulted and enraged the Holy Spirit who brings God's mercy to his people.

³⁰For we know the one who said,

"I will take vengeance.
I will repay those who deserve it."

He also said,

"The Lord will judge his own people."*

³¹It is a terrible thing to fall into the hands of the living God.

³²Don't ever forget those early days when you first learned about Christ. Remember how you remained faithful even though it meant terrible suffering. ³³Sometimes you were exposed to public ridicule and were beaten, and sometimes you helped others who were suffering the same things. ³⁴You suffered along with those who were thrown into jail.

When all you owned was taken from you, you accepted it with joy. You knew you had better things waiting for you in eternity.

³⁵Do not throw away this confident trust in the Lord, no matter what happens. Remember the great reward it brings you! ³⁶Patient endurance is what you need now, so you will continue to do God's will. Then you will receive all that he has promised.

³⁷ "For in just a little while,
    the Coming One will come and not
       delay.
³⁸ And a righteous person will live by faith.
    But I will have no pleasure in anyone
       who turns away."*

³⁹But we are not like those who turn their backs on God and seal their fate. We have faith that assures our salvation.

GREAT EXAMPLES OF FAITH

11 What is faith? It is the confident assurance that what we hope for is going to happen. It is the evidence of things we cannot yet see. ²God gave his approval to people in days of old because of their faith.

³By faith we understand that the entire universe was formed at God's command, that what we now see did not come from anything that can be seen.

⁴It was by faith that Abel brought a more acceptable offering to God than Cain did. God accepted Abel's offering to show that he was a righteous man. And although Abel is long dead, he still speaks to us because of his faith.

⁵It was by faith that Enoch was taken up to heaven without dying—"suddenly he disappeared because God took him."* But before he was taken up, he was approved as pleasing to God. ⁶So, you see, it is impossible to please God without faith. Anyone who wants to come to him must believe that there is a God and that he rewards those who sincerely seek him.

10:30 Deut 32:35-36.   10:37-38 Hab 2:3-4.   11:5 Gen 5:24.

My Daily Worship

— December 11 —

ALL, ALL IS WELL

HEBREWS 10:1–11:40

Do not throw away this confident trust in the Lord, no matter what happens. Remember the
great reward it brings you! Patient endurance is what you need now, so you will continue
to do God's will. Then you will receive all that he has promised (10:35–36).

[i reflect]

Confident trust, patient endurance. Chapters 10 and 11 of the letter to the Hebrews form a kind of "Guide to the Care and Feeding of Faith." Faith is defined indirectly, as in today's verses, and then directly in Hebrews 11:1: "What is faith? It is the confident assurance that what we hope for is going to happen. It is the evidence of things we cannot yet see."

Then there is the Hall of Fame of Faith, examples of those Old Testament heroes through the centuries who placed their faith in God. People who were rewarded with prosperity, military victories, political gain, public acclaim, narrow escapes from death, as well as loneliness, humiliation, imprisonment, torture, and violent death. The rewards vary; the reason is constant—their faith.

In recent centuries the same extremes of faith's rewards are evident. Highly visible public figures and survivors of certain death have equal billing along with the martyred missionaries and anonymous students mocked for their beliefs in today's Faith Hall of Fame.

Little is known about Mary Bowley Peters; a highly visible public figure she was not. The wife of an Anglican rector in Gloucestershire, England, in the early 1800s, she may have been constrained by the expectations of society. Still, she wrote *The World's History from the Creation to the Accession of Queen Victoria* (in seven volumes) and more than twenty hymns. Only forty-three when she died, her living out of her faith encourages us to do the same.

Consider the words of the final verse of her best-known hymn, "Through the Love of God Our Savior":

We expect a bright tomorrow, All will be well;
Faith can sing, through days of sorrow, All, all is well;
On our Father's love relying, Jesus ev'ry need supplying,
Or in living or in dying, All must be well.

Reflect on your favorite inductee in the Hall of Faith—whether it is a biblical person or historical one. What about that person's faith walk encourages you? Use that person as a model for your own journey.

[i pray]

Holy Lord, I am overwhelmed by your care and your love for me. I am grateful
for the examples of faithful people and place my faith in you, certain
of a reward from your hand, whatever form it takes.

[i respond]

In a hymnal or on the Internet, look up the hymn "Through the Love of God Our Savior" and read or sing it through. Write a fourth verse expressing your thanks for faith's rewards, no matter what.

[7]It was by faith that Noah built an ark to save his family from the flood. He obeyed God, who warned him about something that had never happened before. By his faith he condemned the rest of the world and was made right in God's sight.

[8]It was by faith that Abraham obeyed when God called him to leave home and go to another land that God would give him as his inheritance. He went without knowing where he was going. [9]And even when he reached the land God promised him, he lived there by faith—for he was like a foreigner, living in a tent. And so did Isaac and Jacob, to whom God gave the same promise. [10]Abraham did this because he was confidently looking forward to a city with eternal foundations, a city designed and built by God.

[11]It was by faith that Sarah together with Abraham was able to have a child, even though they were too old and Sarah was barren. Abraham believed that God would keep his promise.* [12]And so a whole nation came from this one man, Abraham, who was too old to have any children—a nation with so many people that, like the stars of the sky and the sand on the seashore, there is no way to count them.

[13]All these faithful ones died without receiving what God had promised them, but they saw it all from a distance and welcomed the promises of God. They agreed that they were no more than foreigners and nomads here on earth. [14]And obviously people who talk like that are looking forward to a country they can call their own. [15]If they had meant the country they came from, they would have found a way to go back. [16]But they were looking for a better place, a heavenly homeland. That is why God is not ashamed to be called their God, for he has prepared a heavenly city for them.

[17]It was by faith that Abraham offered Isaac as a sacrifice when God was testing him. Abraham, who had received God's promises, was ready to sacrifice his only son, Isaac,

[18]though God had promised him, "Isaac is the son through whom your descendants will be counted."* [19]Abraham assumed that if Isaac died, God was able to bring him back to life again. And in a sense, Abraham did receive his son back from the dead.

[20]It was by faith that Isaac blessed his two sons, Jacob and Esau. He had confidence in what God was going to do in the future.

[21]It was by faith that Jacob, when he was old and dying, blessed each of Joseph's sons and bowed in worship as he leaned on his staff.

> *For years, the church has emphasized evangelism, teaching, fellowship, missions, and service to society to the neglect of the very source of its power—worship.*
>
> ROBERT E. WEBBER

[22]And it was by faith that Joseph, when he was about to die, confidently spoke of God's bringing the people of Israel out of Egypt. He was so sure of it that he commanded them to carry his bones with them when they left!

[23]It was by faith that Moses' parents hid him for three months. They saw that God had given them an unusual child, and they were not afraid of what the king might do.

[24]It was by faith that Moses, when he grew up, refused to be treated as the son of Pharaoh's daughter. [25]He chose to share the oppression of God's people instead of enjoying the fleeting pleasures of sin. [26]He thought it was better to suffer for the sake of the Messiah than to own the treasures of Egypt, for he was looking ahead to the great reward that God would give him. [27]It was by faith that Moses left the land of Egypt. He was not afraid of the king. Moses kept right on going because he kept his eyes on the one who is

11:11 Some manuscripts read *It was by faith that Sarah was able to have a child, even though she was too old and barren. Sarah believed that God would keep his promise.* 11:18 Gen 21:12.

invisible. ²⁸It was by faith that Moses commanded the people of Israel to keep the Passover and to sprinkle blood on the doorposts so that the angel of death would not kill their firstborn sons.

²⁹It was by faith that the people of Israel went right through the Red Sea as though they were on dry ground. But when the Egyptians followed, they were all drowned.

³⁰It was by faith that the people of Israel marched around Jericho seven days, and the walls came crashing down.

³¹It was by faith that Rahab the prostitute did not die with all the others in her city who refused to obey God. For she had given a friendly welcome to the spies.

³²Well, how much more do I need to say? It would take too long to recount the stories of the faith of Gideon, Barak, Samson, Jephthah, David, Samuel, and all the prophets. ³³By faith these people overthrew kingdoms, ruled with justice, and received what God had promised them. They shut the mouths of lions, ³⁴quenched the flames of fire, and escaped death by the edge of the sword. Their weakness was turned to strength. They became strong in battle and put whole armies to flight. ³⁵Women received their loved ones back again from death.

But others trusted God and were tortured, preferring to die rather than turn from God and be free. They placed their hope in the resurrection to a better life. ³⁶Some were mocked, and their backs were cut open with whips. Others were chained in dungeons. ³⁷Some died by stoning, and some were sawed in half; others were killed with the sword. Some went about in skins of sheep and goats, hungry and oppressed and mistreated. ³⁸They were too good for this world. They wandered over deserts and mountains, hiding in caves and holes in the ground.

³⁹All of these people we have mentioned received God's approval because of their faith, yet none of them received all that God had promised. ⁴⁰For God had far better things in mind for us that would also benefit them, for they can't receive the prize at the end of the race until we finish the race.*

GOD'S DISCIPLINE PROVES HIS LOVE

12 Therefore, since we are surrounded by such a huge crowd of witnesses to the life of faith, let us strip off every weight that slows us down, especially the sin that so easily hinders our progress. And let us run with endurance the race that God has set before us. ²We do this by keeping our eyes on Jesus, on whom our faith depends from start to finish.* He was willing to die a shameful death on the cross because of the joy he knew would be his afterward. Now he is seated in the place of highest honor beside God's throne in heaven. ³Think about all he endured when sinful people did such terrible things to him, so that you don't become weary and give up. ⁴After all, you have not yet given your lives in your struggle against sin.

⁵And have you entirely forgotten the encouraging words God spoke to you, his children? He said,

"My child, don't ignore it when the Lord
    disciplines you,
  and don't be discouraged when he
    corrects you.
⁶ For the Lord disciplines those he loves,
  and he punishes those he accepts as his
    children."*

⁷As you endure this divine discipline, remember that God is treating you as his own children. Who ever heard of a child who was never disciplined? ⁸If God doesn't discipline you as he does all of his children, it means that you are illegitimate and are not really his children after all. ⁹Since we respect our earthly fathers who disciplined us, should we not all the more cheerfully submit to the discipline of our heavenly Father and live forever*?

11:40 Greek *for us, for they apart from us can't finish.* **12:2** Or *Jesus, the Originator and Perfecter of our faith.* **12:5-6** Prov 3:11-12. **12:9** Or *really live.*

[10]For our earthly fathers disciplined us for a few years, doing the best they knew how. But God's discipline is always right and good for us because it means we will share in his holiness. [11]No discipline is enjoyable while it is happening—it is painful! But afterward there will be a quiet harvest of right living for those who are trained in this way.

[12]So take a new grip with your tired hands and stand firm on your shaky legs. [13]Mark out a straight path for your feet. Then those who follow you, though they are weak and lame, will not stumble and fall but will become strong.

A Call to Listen to God

[14]Try to live in peace with everyone, and seek to live a clean and holy life, for those who are not holy will not see the Lord. [15]Look after each other so that none of you will miss out on the special favor of God. Watch out that no bitter root of unbelief rises up among you, for whenever it springs up, many are corrupted by its poison. [16]Make sure that no one is immoral or godless like Esau. He traded his birthright as the oldest son for a single meal. [17]And afterward, when he wanted his father's blessing, he was rejected. It was too late for repentance, even though he wept bitter tears.

[18]You have not come to a physical mountain, to a place of flaming fire, darkness, gloom, and whirlwind, as the Israelites did at Mount Sinai when God gave them his laws. [19]For they heard an awesome trumpet blast and a voice with a message so terrible that they begged God to stop speaking. [20]They staggered back under God's command: "If even an animal touches the mountain, it must be stoned to death."* [21]Moses himself was so frightened at the sight that he said, "I am terrified and trembling."*

[22]No, you have come to Mount Zion, to the city of the living God, the heavenly Jerusalem, and to thousands of angels in joyful assembly. [23]You have come to the assembly of God's firstborn children, whose names are written in heaven. You have come to God himself, who is the judge of all people. And you have come to the spirits of the redeemed in heaven who have now been made perfect. [24]You have come to Jesus, the one who mediates the new covenant between God and people, and to the sprinkled blood, which graciously forgives instead of crying out for vengeance as the blood of Abel did.

[25]See to it that you obey God, the one who is speaking to you. For if the people of Israel did not escape when they refused to listen to Moses, the earthly messenger, how terrible our danger if we reject the One who speaks to us from heaven! [26]When God spoke from Mount Sinai his voice shook the earth, but now he makes another promise: "Once again I will shake not only the earth but the heavens also."* [27]This means that the things on earth will be shaken, so that only eternal things will be left.

[28]Since we are receiving a Kingdom that cannot be destroyed, let us be thankful and please God by worshiping him with holy fear and awe. [29]For our God is a consuming fire.

Concluding Words

13 Continue to love each other with true Christian love.* [2]Don't forget to show hospitality to strangers, for some who have done this have entertained angels without realizing it! [3]Don't forget about those in prison. Suffer with them as though you were there yourself. Share the sorrow of those being mistreated, as though you feel their pain in your own bodies.

[4]Give honor to marriage, and remain faithful to one another in marriage. God will surely judge people who are immoral and those who commit adultery.

[5]Stay away from the love of money; be satisfied with what you have. For God has said,

"I will never fail you.
    I will never forsake you."*

12:20 Exod 19:13. **12:21** Deut 9:19. **12:26** Hag 2:6. **13:1** Greek *with brotherly love*. **13:5** Deut 31:6, 8.

My Daily Worship

— *December 12* —

ONE AND THE SAME

HEBREWS 12:1—13:25

Jesus Christ is the same yesterday, today, and forever (13:8).

[i reflect]

Is this ever different, Jeff thinks. *It's nothing like our old church. Just like Chicago is nothing like the last city.*

Jeff and his family have moved around the country. A lot. He is sick of it. They are visiting another new church.

"Could this place get any older?" he whispers to his mother. She shrugs; she is sick of change, too. They find some seats and look around. Finally, their eyes focus on the large lettering above the altar: "Jesus Christ is the same yesterday, and today, and forever." They gulp. They blink. They close their eyes and thank the changeless One.

Moody Memorial Church was completed in 1925, itself a product of great change. Started as a Sunday school by the evangelist Dwight L. Moody, it was organized as a church in 1864, but burned in the Great Chicago Fire of 1871. The words of Hebrews 13:8 echo in the hearts and minds of all worshipers there. Limitations of time and geography vanish in this verse. The verb tense is past, present, and future.

The truth reaches back to the second century, to Saint Irenaeus, who reaches out to us: "For although the languages of the world differ, the significance of the faith is one and the same. For the churches which have been planted in Germany do not believe or hand down anything different, nor do those in Spain, nor those in France, nor those in the East, nor those in Egypt, nor those in Libya, nor those which have been established in the central regions of the world. . . . The preaching of the truth shines everywhere. . . . For the faith is always one and the same." Jesus and his truth transcends geography, race, age, and time. That same incomparable Savior is ours.

Today as you experience changes in the world and in your life, rest in the One who remains wonderfully the same. Praise his changeless name.

[i pray]

Christ Jesus, I rejoice that you are the same for all people, of all times, and in all places. I rest in your eternal changelessness. I praise and glorify your eternal holiness.

[i respond]

Choose one attribute of God (for example, his love, power, holiness). Write down the ways God has demonstrated that particular attribute at different times in your life.

[6]That is why we can say with confidence,

"The Lord is my helper,
   so I will not be afraid.
   What can mere mortals do to me?"*

[7]Remember your leaders who first taught you the word of God. Think of all the good that has come from their lives, and trust the Lord as they do.

[8]Jesus Christ is the same yesterday, today, and forever. [9]So do not be attracted by strange, new ideas. Your spiritual strength comes from God's special favor, not from ceremonial rules about food, which don't help those who follow them.

[10]We have an altar from which the priests in the Temple on earth have no right to eat. [11]Under the system of Jewish laws, the high priest brought the blood of animals into the Holy Place as a sacrifice for sin, but the bodies of the animals were burned outside the camp. [12]So also Jesus suffered and died outside the city gates in order to make his people holy by shedding his own blood. [13]So let us go out to him outside the camp and bear the disgrace he bore. [14]For this world is not our home; we are looking forward to our city in heaven, which is yet to come.

[15]With Jesus' help, let us continually offer our sacrifice of praise to God by proclaiming the glory of his name. [16]Don't forget to do good and to share what you have with those in need, for such sacrifices are very pleasing to God.

[17]Obey your spiritual leaders and do what they say. Their work is to watch over your souls, and they know they are accountable to God. Give them reason to do this joyfully and not with sorrow. That would certainly not be for your benefit.

[18]Pray for us, for our conscience is clear and we want to live honorably in everything we do. [19]I especially need your prayers right now so that I can come back to you soon.

[20-21]And now, may the God of peace, who brought again from the dead our Lord Jesus, equip you with all you need for doing his will. May he produce in you, through the power of Jesus Christ, all that is pleasing to him. Jesus is the great Shepherd of the sheep by an everlasting covenant, signed with his blood. To him be glory forever and ever. Amen.

[22]I urge you, dear brothers and sisters,* please listen carefully to what I have said in this brief letter.

[23]I want you to know that our brother Timothy is now out of jail. If he comes here soon, I will bring him with me to see you.

[24]Give my greetings to all your leaders and to the other believers there. The Christians from Italy send you their greetings.

[25]May God's grace be with you all.

13:6 Ps 118:6. 13:22 Greek *brothers.*

James

*It isn't enough just to have faith. Faith that doesn't show itself
by good deeds isn't faith at all—it is dead and useless (2:17).*

Real Worship in Actions

At first glance, you might expect James to be seated in the last row, near the door, fidgeting throughout worship, eager to get outside and back to work. A no-frills worshiper.

Perhaps that impression comes from his outdoor metaphors and his consistent call to living out in deed the faith we profess in praise and worship.

Actually, James is a careful worshiper—careful to reckon the importance of prayer, of integrity, of faith. James may be sick and tired of people who talk the talk, then falter. James loves to give his heart to God, then his energy, his simplicity, his real world. All of it is God's, or none of it.

No author among the Bible writers is so crisply critical of "faith alone" as James. If you go to worship with James, be prepared for a service project afterward. The faith he celebrates in worship begs for application. For James, the last words of worship are always, "Now go out to love and serve the Lord." The proof of faith's reality is Monday's agenda.

You might expect a driven personality to lie behind this short book, as if the Christian earns God's favor with merit badges and service sign-ups. Not so. This compassionate pastor simply won't tolerate hungry orphans and forgotten shut-ins. He won't make excuses for slackers, and he's done with words untested in life. Real faith is alive and expressive. Real faith moves up and onward. The sweetness of worship is like the team meeting before the game. Now go play with all your heart!

To follow James is to practice and demonstrate, to testify by loving service and consistent regard for others, to show discipline at those junctions of life when most people lay on their horns. The real worshiper takes that God-focus of praise into the street, where critics wait to howl "Hypocrite!" and offers those guys a hand and a smile. Faith like that conquers the world.

Worship Moments

- Worship should have no favorites based on wealth, prestige, or status. No royalty, no major honors. Just people together in praise and service (2:1–3).

- For those who doubt, James has simple advice: instead of withdrawing from worship, *do it*. Find God pro-actively (4:8, 10).

- Prayer counts. But the context of prayer counts too. Prayer is never just a string of words, but an expression of your commitment (5:16).

GREETINGS FROM JAMES

1 This letter is from James, a slave of God and of the Lord Jesus Christ.

It is written to Jewish Christians scattered among the nations.*

Greetings!

FAITH AND ENDURANCE

²Dear brothers and sisters,* whenever trouble comes your way, let it be an opportunity for joy. ³For when your faith is tested, your endurance has a chance to grow. ⁴So let it grow, for when your endurance is fully developed, you will be strong in character and ready for anything.

⁵If you need wisdom—if you want to know what God wants you to do—ask him, and he will gladly tell you. He will not resent your asking. ⁶But when you ask him, be sure that you really expect him to answer, for a doubtful mind is as unsettled as a wave of the sea that is driven and tossed by the wind. ⁷People like that should not expect to receive anything from the Lord. ⁸They can't make up their minds. They waver back and forth in everything they do.

⁹Christians who are* poor should be glad, for God has honored them. ¹⁰And those who are rich should be glad, for God has humbled them. They will fade away like a flower in the field. ¹¹The hot sun rises and dries up the grass; the flower withers, and its beauty fades away. So also, wealthy people will fade away with all of their achievements.

¹²God blesses the people who patiently endure testing. Afterward they will receive the crown of life that God has promised to those who love him. ¹³And remember, no one who wants to do wrong should ever say, "God is tempting me." God is never tempted to do wrong, and he never tempts anyone else either. ¹⁴Temptation comes from the lure of our own evil desires. ¹⁵These evil desires lead to evil actions, and evil actions lead to death. ¹⁶So don't be misled, my dear brothers and sisters.

¹⁷Whatever is good and perfect comes to us from God above, who created all heaven's lights.* Unlike them, he never changes or casts shifting shadows. ¹⁸In his goodness he chose to make us his own children by giving us his true word. And we, out of all creation, became his choice possession.

LISTENING AND DOING

¹⁹My dear brothers and sisters, be quick to listen, slow to speak, and slow to get angry. ²⁰Your anger can never make things right in God's sight.

²¹So get rid of all the filth and evil in your lives, and humbly accept the message God has planted in your hearts, for it is strong enough to save your souls.

²²And remember, it is a message to obey, not just to listen to. If you don't obey, you are only fooling yourself. ²³For if you just listen and don't obey, it is like looking at your face in a mirror but doing nothing to improve your appearance. ²⁴You see yourself, walk away, and forget what you look like. ²⁵But if you keep looking steadily into God's perfect law—the law that sets you free—and if you do what it says and don't forget what you heard, then God will bless you for doing it.

²⁶If you claim to be religious but don't control your tongue, you are just fooling yourself, and your religion is worthless. ²⁷Pure and lasting religion in the sight of God our Father means that we must care for orphans and widows in their troubles, and refuse to let the world corrupt us.

A WARNING AGAINST PREJUDICE

2 My dear brothers and sisters,* how can you claim that you have faith in our glorious Lord Jesus Christ if you favor some people more than others?

²For instance, suppose someone comes into your meeting* dressed in fancy clothes and expensive jewelry, and another comes in who is poor and dressed in shabby clothes. ³If you

---

1:1 Greek *To the twelve tribes in the dispersion.* **1:2** Greek *brothers;* also in 1:16, 19. **1:9** Greek *The brother who is.* **1:17** Greek *from above, from the Father of lights.* **2:1** Greek *brothers;* also in 2:5, 14. **2:2** Greek *synagogue.*

My Daily Worship

ASKED AND ANSWERED

JAMES 1:1 – 2:26

But when you ask him, be sure that you really expect him to answer, for a doubtful mind is as unsettled as a wave of the sea that is driven and tossed by the wind (1:6).

[i reflect]

In the 1880s, George and Sarah Clarke opened the Pacific Garden Mission of Chicago—a ministry to homeless alcoholics and downtrodden men—with little more than their personal funds and faith that God would provide. As the ministry expanded, expenses grew and the couple's resources dwindled. Eventually, the day came when they could not pay the rent. With only 24 hours to pay the rent or lose the lease, the couple began to pray.

Throughout the night, the Clarkes prayed for God's guidance and provision. They reminded him of the souls being saved. They asked why their work—God's work—was in such straits. But they were determined to trust God, so stayed before the throne of grace in simple faith until dawn. When they emerged from their house, the couple discovered their lawn was covered in white—mushrooms of the very best quality! The Clarkes gathered the mushrooms and carted them to the chefs of the Palmer House, a famed hotel in Chicago. The receipts for the mushrooms were enough to pay the rent, with enough left over to meet other ministry expenses.

The Clarke's faith-filled prayers exemplify exactly what today's passage exhorts believers to do: pray believing that God will answer. As Clement wrote, "The all-merciful and giving Father lovingly gives good things to those who come to him with a trusting mind."

People of prayer are people who pray *before* things gets desperate. Before the well runs dry, the doorways are blocked, or every other remedy has been tried twice. People of prayer come before the throne of grace, like the Clarkes, trusting, believing, anticipating. They come, not out of their own selfish desires or thoughtless request. But they confident that God will align their desires with his purposes.

So go to God's throne in prayer. Be confident that he will hear you. Be ready to receive his answer. He is waiting to listen and to act.

Name what you need most from God right now. Ask that your desires will become his.

[i pray]

O God, I thank you for the privilege and power of prayer. May you strengthen me to come to you boldly and come to you always.

[i respond]

This week, read through the book of Nehemiah for a model on praying in faith and expectation. Note all the on which Nehemiah turns to God in prayer. Note also any parallels to your own prayer life.

give special attention and a good seat to the rich person, but you say to the poor one, "You can stand over there, or else sit on the floor"—well, [4]doesn't this discrimination show that you are guided by wrong motives?

[5]Listen to me, dear brothers and sisters. Hasn't God chosen the poor in this world to be rich in faith? Aren't they the ones who will inherit the Kingdom he promised to those who love him? [6]And yet, you insult the poor man! Isn't it the rich who oppress you and drag you into court? [7]Aren't they the ones who slander Jesus Christ, whose noble name you bear?

[8]Yes indeed, it is good when you truly obey our Lord's royal command found in the Scriptures: "Love your neighbor as yourself."* [9]But if you pay special attention to the rich, you are committing a sin, for you are guilty of breaking that law.

[10]And the person who keeps all of the laws except one is as guilty as the person who has broken all of God's laws. [11]For the same God who said, "Do not commit adultery," also said, "Do not murder."* So if you murder someone, you have broken the entire law, even if you do not commit adultery.

[12]So whenever you speak, or whatever you do, remember that you will be judged by the law of love, the law that set you free. [13]For there will be no mercy for you if you have not been merciful to others. But if you have been merciful, then God's mercy toward you will win out over his judgment against you.

Faith without Good Deeds Is Dead

[14]Dear brothers and sisters, what's the use of saying you have faith if you don't prove it by your actions? That kind of faith can't save anyone. [15]Suppose you see a brother or sister who needs food or clothing, [16]and you say, "Well, good-bye and God bless you; stay warm and eat well"—but then you don't give that person any food or clothing. What good does that do?

[17]So you see, it isn't enough just to have faith. Faith that doesn't show itself by good deeds is no faith at all—it is dead and useless.

[18]Now someone may argue, "Some people have faith; others have good deeds." I say, "I can't see your faith if you don't have good deeds, but I will show you my faith through my good deeds."

[19]Do you still think it's enough just to believe that there is one God? Well, even the demons believe this, and they tremble in terror! [20]Fool! When will you ever learn that faith that does not result in good deeds is useless?

[21]Don't you remember that our ancestor Abraham was declared right with God because of what he did when he offered his son Isaac on the altar? [22]You see, he was trusting God so much that he was willing to do whatever God told him to do. His faith was made complete by what he did—by his actions. [23]And so it happened just as the Scriptures say: "Abraham believed God, so God declared him to be righteous."* He was even called "the friend of God."* [24]So you see, we are made right with God by what we do, not by faith alone.

[25]Rahab the prostitute is another example of this. She was made right with God by her actions—when she hid those messengers and sent them safely away by a different road. [26]Just as the body is dead without a spirit, so also faith is dead without good deeds.

Controlling the Tongue

3 Dear brothers and sisters,* not many of you should become teachers in the church, for we who teach will be judged by God with greater strictness.

[2]We all make many mistakes, but those who control their tongues can also control themselves in every other way. [3]We can make a large horse turn around and go wherever we want by means of a small bit in its mouth. [4]And a tiny rudder makes a huge ship turn wherever the pilot wants it to go, even though the winds

---

2:8 Lev 19:18.   2:11 Exod 20:13-14; Deut 5:17-18.   2:23a Gen 15:6.   2:23b See Isa 41:8.   3:1 Greek *brothers*; also in 3:10.

are strong. [5]So also, the tongue is a small thing, but what enormous damage it can do. A tiny spark can set a great forest on fire. [6]And the tongue is a flame of fire. It is full of wickedness that can ruin your whole life. It can turn the entire course of your life into a blazing flame of destruction, for it is set on fire by hell itself.

[7]People can tame all kinds of animals and birds and reptiles and fish, [8]but no one can tame the tongue. It is an uncontrollable evil, full of deadly poison. [9]Sometimes it praises our Lord and Father, and sometimes it breaks out into curses against those who have been made in the image of God. [10]And so blessing and cursing come pouring out of the same mouth. Surely, my brothers and sisters, this is not right! [11]Does a spring of water bubble out with both fresh water and bitter water? [12]Can you pick olives from a fig tree or figs from a grapevine? No, and you can't draw fresh water from a salty pool.

TRUE WISDOM COMES FROM GOD

[13]If you are wise and understand God's ways, live a life of steady goodness so that only good deeds will pour forth. And if you don't brag about the good you do, then you will be truly wise! [14]But if you are bitterly jealous and there is selfish ambition in your hearts, don't brag about being wise. That is the worst kind of lie. [15]For jealousy and selfishness are not God's kind of wisdom. Such things are earthly, unspiritual, and motivated by the Devil. [16]For wherever there is jealousy and selfish ambition, there you will find disorder and every kind of evil.

[17]But the wisdom that comes from heaven is first of all pure. It is also peace loving, gentle at all times, and willing to yield to others. It is full of mercy and good deeds. It shows no partiality and is always sincere. [18]And those who are peacemakers will plant seeds of peace and reap a harvest of goodness.

DRAWING CLOSE TO GOD

4 What is causing the quarrels and fights among you? Isn't it the whole army of evil desires at war within you? [2]You want what you don't have, so you scheme and kill to get it. You are jealous for what others have, and you can't possess it, so you fight and quarrel to take it away from them. And yet the reason you don't have what you want is that you don't ask God for it. [3]And even when you do ask, you don't get it because your whole motive is wrong—you want only what will give you pleasure.

[4]You adulterers! Don't you realize that friendship with this world makes you an enemy of God? I say it again, that if your aim is to enjoy this world, you can't be a friend of God. [5]What do you think the Scriptures mean when they say that the Holy Spirit, whom God has placed within us, jealously longs for us to be faithful*? [6]He gives us more and more strength to stand against such evil desires. As the Scriptures say,

"God sets himself against the proud,
    but he shows favor to the humble."*

[7]So humble yourselves before God. Resist the Devil, and he will flee from you. [8]Draw close to God, and God will draw close to you. Wash your hands, you sinners; purify your hearts, you hypocrites. [9]Let there be tears for the wrong things you have done. Let there be sorrow and deep grief. Let there be sadness instead of laughter, and gloom instead of joy. [10]When you bow down before the Lord and admit your dependence on him, he will lift you up and give you honor.

WARNING AGAINST JUDGING OTHERS

[11]Don't speak evil against each other, my dear brothers and sisters.* If you criticize each other and condemn each other, then you are criticizing and condemning God's law. But

4:5 Or *the spirit that God placed within us tends to envy,* or *the Holy Spirit, whom God has placed within us, opposes our envy.* 4:6 Prov 3:34. 4:11 Greek *brothers.*

you are not a judge who can decide whether the law is right or wrong. Your job is to obey it. [12]God alone, who made the law, can rightly judge among us. He alone has the power to save or to destroy. So what right do you have to condemn your neighbor?

WARNING ABOUT SELF-CONFIDENCE

[13]Look here, you people who say, "Today or tomorrow we are going to a certain town and will stay there a year. We will do business there and make a profit." [14]How do you know what will happen tomorrow? For your life is like the morning fog—it's here a little while, then it's gone. [15]What you ought to say is, "If the Lord wants us to, we will live and do this or that." [16]Otherwise you will be boasting about your own plans, and all such boasting is evil.

[17]Remember, it is sin to know what you ought to do and then not do it.

WARNING TO THE RICH

5 Look here, you rich people, weep and groan with anguish because of all the terrible troubles ahead of you. [2]Your wealth is rotting away, and your fine clothes are moth-eaten rags. [3]Your gold and silver have become worthless. The very wealth you were counting on will eat away your flesh in hell.* This treasure you have accumulated will stand as evidence against you on the day of judgment. [4]For listen! Hear the cries of the field workers whom you have cheated of their pay. The wages you held back cry out against you. The cries of the reapers have reached the ears of the Lord Almighty.

[5]You have spent your years on earth in luxury, satisfying your every whim. Now your hearts are nice and fat, ready for the slaughter. [6]You have condemned and killed good people who had no power to defend themselves against you.

PATIENCE IN SUFFERING

[7]Dear brothers and sisters,* you must be patient as you wait for the Lord's return. Consider the farmers who eagerly look for the rains in the fall and in the spring. They patiently wait for the precious harvest to ripen. [8]You, too, must be patient. And take courage, for the coming of the Lord is near.

[9]Don't grumble about each other, my brothers and sisters, or God will judge you. For look! The great Judge is coming. He is standing at the door!

[10]For examples of patience in suffering, dear brothers and sisters, look at the prophets who spoke in the name of the Lord. [11]We give great honor to those who endure under suffering. Job is an example of a man who endured patiently. From his experience we see how the Lord's plan finally ended in good, for he is full of tenderness and mercy.

[12]But most of all, my brothers and sisters, never take an oath, by heaven or earth or anything else. Just say a simple yes or no, so that you will not sin and be condemned for it.

THE POWER OF PRAYER

[13]Are any among you suffering? They should keep on praying about it. And those who have reason to be thankful should continually sing praises to the Lord.

[14]Are any among you sick? They should call for the elders of the church and have them pray over them, anointing them with oil in the name of the Lord. [15]And their prayer offered in faith will heal the sick, and the Lord will make them well. And anyone who has committed sins will be forgiven.

[16]Confess your sins to each other and pray for each other so that you may be healed. The earnest prayer of a righteous person has great

5:3 Or *will eat your flesh like fire.*   5:7 Greek *brothers;* also in 5:9, 10, 12, 19.

My Daily Worship

TAKE COURAGE FROM HIM

JAMES 3:1–5:20

And take courage, for the coming of the Lord is near (5:8).

[i reflect]

Surely there are better ways to celebrate a saint's life than by getting drunk, hanging shamrocks, and turning rivers green. Saint Patrick was not even Irish.

Pirates kidnapped and took this sixteen-year-old British boy to Ireland. Sold into slavery, he was sustained by his faith in Christ. Six years later he escaped to England, but God called him back to Ireland to spread the gospel. Patrick became a missionary to Ireland around A.D. 400.

"Take courage," God told him, for his life was under constant threat as he traveled the entire island. But the former slave convinced nearly the entire population to become slaves of Christ.

Scholars are uncertain whether he wrote "Saint Patrick's Breastplate," but the prayer was composed around the time that he lived and certainly is in keeping with his trust in the Trinity and in Christ's protection. One translation begins: "I arise today through a mighty strength, the invocation of the Trinity." It continues: "Christ be with me, Christ within me, Christ behind me, Christ before me, Christ beside me, Christ to win me, Christ to comfort and restore me. Christ beneath me, Christ above me, Christ in quiet, Christ in danger, Christ in hearts of all that love me, Christ in mouth of friend and stranger."

Lean into the Lord Christ. Know that he is all around you. Praise his name for the courage and protection he offers.

Before you leave your quiet time, bind yourself to Christ by reading aloud the prayer of Saint Patrick written above.

[i pray]

Lord Christ, I thank you that you are with me, within me, behind me, before me, beside me, beneath me, and above me. Give me your courage and protection as I serve you wherever you lead me.

[i respond]

In a reference book or on the Internet, look up the full text of "Saint Patrick's Breastplate," which begins with, "I arise today. . . ." Read through it and write down all the words that communicate Christ's power and protection.

power and wonderful results. ¹⁷Elijah was as human as we are, and yet when he prayed earnestly that no rain would fall, none fell for the next three and a half years! ¹⁸Then he prayed for rain, and down it poured. The grass turned green, and the crops began to grow again.

RESTORE WANDERING BELIEVERS

¹⁹My dear brothers and sisters, if anyone among you wanders away from the truth and is brought back again, ²⁰you can be sure that the one who brings that person back will save that sinner from death and bring about the forgiveness of many sins.

1 & 2 Peter

All honor to the God and Father of our Lord Jesus Christ, for it is by his boundless mercy that God has given us the privilege of being born again (1 Peter 1:3).

Now Is the Time to Worship

Peter wastes no words. Immediately his two letters launch into praise and worship. In a natural response to God's love, the words of praise and thanks flow. When you open these books, the choir director is ready with hands up to direct. There's only a brief introduction before the chorus begins.

So why waste time if time is precious? Peter understands that Jesus has begun a new era, the last period of human history. God's great judgment is coming, and after that a new heaven and new earth. While time allows, let praises ring!

Yet Peter's eyes are not blind to lurking trouble. He knows how difficult unity can be. There are so many reasons to split apart, so many aggravations, so much petty jealousy. And if fractious worshipers are not trouble enough, false teachers roam about bending truth, teaching an audience-friendlier version of God's truth (if that can be!), a no-fault faith. Peter urges God's people to cling together, keep away from error. Embrace the truth; exclude the lie.

Peter's faith is filled with hope. He knows where Project Earth is headed. He worships the One whose design is unfolding, who saves us from ruin, who leads us to renewal. Worship directed toward God's future is worship that survives the worst the world can offer. The fire of God's love shines bright against the flicker of oppression his people endure along the way.

Keep this in mind, Peter writes. Regular worship is our best way of doing that—worship rising in crescendo until that day of God's fury and grace.

Worship Moments

- Christian worship needs leaders, but all believers—leader and newcomer—are priests in God's temple. The Holy Spirit has come to everyone (1 Peter 2:9)

- Suffering can revive and deepen our worship, as we commit our pain to God, for his glory (1 Peter 4:1).

- God calls and chooses us (other Bible versions use the term "election"). Should that mean pacifism in the face of God's all-powerful will, or praise for God's loving favor (2 Peter 1:10)?

- Worship of God flows from one aeon to the next. Whatever else happens, that part only gets better (2 Peter 3:13).

GREETINGS FROM PETER

1 This letter is from Peter, an apostle of Jesus Christ.

I am writing to God's chosen people who are living as foreigners in the lands of Pontus, Galatia, Cappadocia, the province of Asia, and Bithynia. ²God the Father chose you long ago, and the Spirit has made you holy. As a result, you have obeyed Jesus Christ and are cleansed by his blood.

May you have more and more of God's special favor and wonderful peace.

THE HOPE OF ETERNAL LIFE

³All honor to the God and Father of our Lord Jesus Christ, for it is by his boundless mercy that God has given us the privilege of being born again. Now we live with a wonderful expectation because Jesus Christ rose again from the dead. ⁴For God has reserved a priceless inheritance for his children. It is kept in heaven for you, pure and undefiled, beyond the reach of change and decay. ⁵And God, in his mighty power, will protect you until you receive this salvation, because you are trusting him. It will be revealed on the last day for all to see. ⁶So be truly glad!* There is wonderful joy ahead, even though it is necessary for you to endure many trials for a while.

⁷These trials are only to test your faith, to show that it is strong and pure. It is being tested as fire tests and purifies gold—and your faith is far more precious to God than mere gold. So if your faith remains strong after being tried by fiery trials, it will bring you much praise and glory and honor on the day when Jesus Christ is revealed to the whole world.

⁸You love him even though you have never seen him. Though you do not see him, you trust him; and even now you are happy with a glorious, inexpressible joy. ⁹Your reward for trusting him will be the salvation of your souls.

¹⁰This salvation was something the prophets wanted to know more about. They prophesied about this gracious salvation prepared for you, even though they had many questions as to what it all could mean. ¹¹They wondered what the Spirit of Christ within them was talking about when he told them in advance about Christ's suffering and his great glory afterward. They wondered when and to whom all this would happen.

¹²They were told that these things would not happen during their lifetime, but many years later, during yours. And now this Good News has been announced by those who preached to you in the power of the Holy Spirit sent from heaven. It is all so wonderful that even the angels are eagerly watching these things happen.

A CALL TO HOLY LIVING

¹³So think clearly and exercise self-control. Look forward to the special blessings that will come to you at the return of Jesus Christ. ¹⁴Obey God because you are his children. Don't slip back into your old ways of doing evil; you didn't know any better then. ¹⁵But now you must be holy in everything you do, just as God—who chose you to be his children—is holy. ¹⁶For he himself has said, "You must be holy because I am holy."*

¹⁷And remember that the heavenly Father to whom you pray has no favorites when he judges. He will judge or reward you according to what you do. So you must live in reverent fear of him during your time as foreigners here on earth. ¹⁸For you know that God paid a ransom to save you from the empty life you inherited from your ancestors. And the ransom he paid was not mere gold or silver. ¹⁹He paid for you with the precious lifeblood of Christ, the sinless, spotless Lamb of God. ²⁰God chose him for this purpose long before the world began, but now in these final days, he was sent to the earth for all to see. And he did this for you.

²¹Through Christ you have come to trust in God. And because God raised Christ from the dead and gave him great glory, your faith and

---

1:6 Or *So you are truly glad.*   **1:16** Lev 11:44-45; 19:2; 20:7.

My Daily Worship

O GRACIOUS LIGHT

1 PETER 1:1—2:25

You are a kingdom of priests, God's holy nation, his very own possession.
This is so you can show others the goodness of God, for he called
you out of the darkness into his wonderful light (2:9).

[i reflect]

The flames leaped higher, yet still he sang with joy and with the confidence that God was with him, onlookers said.

In the third century, the Emperor Diocletian's reign claimed yet another martyr. The bishop and theologian Athenogenes was burned alive, along with ten of his students. But the beautiful song that he sang as he entered the flames lives in our liturgy today. Called the *Phos Hilaron* in its original Greek, it praises God's "wonderful light," about which Peter wrote in today's passage.

Ever since Athenogenes' death, the hymn attributed to him has been used in the Orthodox tradition as part of its evening vespers liturgy. It was not translated into English until the 1600s but soon became part of Anglican and later Roman Catholic vespers services. Sung or read aloud, the beauty and brilliance of God's wonderful light shines through:

"O Gracious Light,/Pure brightness of the everliving Father in heaven,/O Jesus Christ, holy and blessed!

"Now as we come to the setting of the sun,/And our eyes behold the vesper light,/We sing your praises, O God: Father, Son, and Holy Spirit.

"You are worthy at all times to be praised by happy voices,/O Son of God, O Giver of life,/And to be glorified through all the worlds."

God has called us out of darkness into his wonderful light. Consider the brightness of his ways. Close your eyes and imagine the purity of the flame of his love for the world, his love for you.

Jesus *is* a gracious light. You were called into this light, "so you can show others the goodness of God." Show his goodness today by doing an unexpected kindness toward a family member, friend, or co-worker.

[i pray]

Jesus Christ, you are the Light of the world. The brilliance of your love and purity overwhelm me.
I thank you that you have called me out of darkness into your wonderful light.

[i respond]

Celebrate the wonderful light of Christ this evening by having your own vespers service. Read 1 Peter 2:4–10 again, then read "O Gracious Light" aloud as a prayer of praise.

hope can be placed confidently in God. ²²Now you can have sincere love for each other as brothers and sisters* because you were cleansed from your sins when you accepted the truth of the Good News. So see to it that you really do love each other intensely with all your hearts.*

²³For you have been born again. Your new life did not come from your earthly parents because the life they gave you will end in death. But this new life will last forever because it comes from the eternal, living word of God. ²⁴As the prophet says,

> "People are like grass that dies away;
>   their beauty fades as quickly as the
>   beauty of wildflowers.
> The grass withers,
>   and the flowers fall away.
> ²⁵ But the word of the Lord will last
>   forever."*

And that word is the Good News that was preached to you.

2 So get rid of all malicious behavior and deceit. Don't just pretend to be good! Be done with hypocrisy and jealousy and backstabbing. ²You must crave pure spiritual milk so that you can grow into the fullness of your salvation. Cry out for this nourishment as a baby cries for milk, ³now that you have had a taste of the Lord's kindness.

LIVING STONES FOR GOD'S HOUSE

⁴Come to Christ, who is the living cornerstone of God's temple. He was rejected by the people, but he is precious to God who chose him. ⁵And now God is building you, as living stones, into his spiritual temple. What's more, you are God's holy priests, who offer the spiritual sacrifices that please him because of Jesus Christ. ⁶As the Scriptures express it,

> "I am placing a stone in Jerusalem,*
>   a chosen cornerstone,
> and anyone who believes in him
>   will never be disappointed.*"

⁷Yes, he is very precious to you who believe. But for those who reject him,

> "The stone that was rejected by the builders
>   has now become the cornerstone."*

⁸And the Scriptures also say,

> "He is the stone that makes people stumble,
>   the rock that will make them fall."*

They stumble because they do not listen to God's word or obey it, and so they meet the fate that has been planned for them.

⁹But you are not like that, for you are a chosen people. You are a kingdom of priests, God's holy nation, his very own possession. This is so you can show others the goodness of God, for he called you out of the darkness into his wonderful light.

> ¹⁰ "Once you were not a people;
>   now you are the people of God.
> Once you received none of God's mercy;
>   now you have received his mercy."*

¹¹Dear brothers and sisters, you are foreigners and aliens here. So I warn you to keep away from evil desires because they fight against your very souls. ¹²Be careful how you live among your unbelieving neighbors. Even if they accuse you of doing wrong, they will see your honorable behavior, and they will believe and give honor to God when he comes to judge the world.*

RESPECTING PEOPLE IN AUTHORITY

¹³For the Lord's sake, accept all authority—the king as head of state, ¹⁴and the officials he has

---

1:22a Greek *can have brotherly love.*   1:22b Some manuscripts read *with a pure heart.*   1:24-25 Isa 40:6-8.   2:6a Greek *in Zion.*
2:6b Or *will never be put to shame.* Isa 28:16.   2:7 Ps 118:22.   2:8 Isa 8:14.   2:10 Hos 1:6, 9; 2:23.   2:12 Or *on the day of visitation.*

appointed. For the king has sent them to punish all who do wrong and to honor those who do right.

[15]It is God's will that your good lives should silence those who make foolish accusations against you. [16]You are not slaves; you are free. But your freedom is not an excuse to do evil. You are free to live as God's slaves. [17]Show respect for everyone. Love your Christian brothers and sisters.* Fear God. Show respect for the king.

SLAVES

[18]You who are slaves must accept the authority of your masters. Do whatever they tell you—not only if they are kind and reasonable, but even if they are harsh. [19]For God is pleased with you when, for the sake of your conscience, you patiently endure unfair treatment. [20]Of course, you get no credit for being patient if you are beaten for doing wrong. But if you suffer for doing right and are patient beneath the blows, God is pleased with you.

[21]This suffering is all part of what God has called you to. Christ, who suffered for you, is your example. Follow in his steps. [22]He never sinned, and he never deceived anyone. [23]He did not retaliate when he was insulted. When he suffered, he did not threaten to get even. He left his case in the hands of God, who always judges fairly. [24]He personally carried away our sins in his own body on the cross so we can be dead to sin and live for what is right. You have been healed by his wounds! [25]Once you were wandering like lost sheep. But now you have turned to your Shepherd, the Guardian of your souls.

WIVES

3 In the same way, you wives must accept the authority of your husbands, even those who refuse to accept the Good News. Your godly lives will speak to them better than any words. They will be won over [2]by watching your pure, godly behavior.

[3]Don't be concerned about the outward beauty that depends on fancy hairstyles, expensive jewelry, or beautiful clothes. [4]You should be known for the beauty that comes from within, the unfading beauty of a gentle and quiet spirit, which is so precious to God. [5]That is the way the holy women of old made themselves beautiful. They trusted God and accepted the authority of their husbands. [6]For instance, Sarah obeyed her husband, Abraham, when she called him her master. You are her daughters when you do what is right without fear of what your husbands might do.

HUSBANDS

[7]In the same way, you husbands must give honor to your wives. Treat her with understanding as you live together. She may be weaker than you are, but she is your equal partner in God's gift of new life. If you don't treat her as you should, your prayers will not be heard.

ALL CHRISTIANS

[8]Finally, all of you should be of one mind, full of sympathy toward each other, loving one another with tender hearts and humble minds. [9]Don't repay evil for evil. Don't retaliate when people say unkind things about you. Instead, pay them back with a blessing. That is what God wants you to do, and he will bless you for it. [10]For the Scriptures say,

"If you want a happy life and good days,
    keep your tongue from speaking evil,
    and keep your lips from telling lies.
[11] Turn away from evil and do good.
    Work hard at living in peace with others.
[12] The eyes of the Lord watch over those who
    do right,
    and his ears are open to their prayers.
But the Lord turns his face
    against those who do evil."*

SUFFERING FOR DOING GOOD

[13]Now, who will want to harm you if you are eager to do good? [14]But even if you suffer for doing what is right, God will reward you

2:17 Greek *Love the brotherhood.* 3:10-12 Ps 34:12-16.

for it. So don't be afraid and don't worry. [15]Instead, you must worship Christ as Lord of your life. And if you are asked about your Christian hope, always be ready to explain it. [16]But you must do this in a gentle and respectful way. Keep your conscience clear. Then if people speak evil against you, they will be ashamed when they see what a good life you live because you belong to Christ. [17]Remember, it is better to suffer for doing good, if that is what God wants, than to suffer for doing wrong!

[18]Christ also suffered when he died for our sins once for all time. He never sinned, but he died for sinners that he might bring us safely home to God. He suffered physical death, but he was raised to life in the Spirit.*

[19]So he went and preached to the spirits in prison—[20]those who disobeyed God long ago when God waited patiently while Noah was building his boat. Only eight people were saved from drowning in that terrible flood.* [21]And this is a picture of baptism, which now saves you by the power of Jesus Christ's resurrection. Baptism is not a removal of dirt from your body; it is an appeal to God from* a clean conscience.

[22]Now Christ has gone to heaven. He is seated in the place of honor next to God, and all the angels and authorities and powers are bowing before him.

LIVING FOR GOD

4 So then, since Christ suffered physical pain, you must arm yourselves with the same attitude he had, and be ready to suffer, too. For if you are willing to suffer for Christ, you have decided to stop sinning. [2]And you won't spend the rest of your life chasing after evil desires, but you will be anxious to do the will of God. [3]You have had enough in the past of the evil things that godless people enjoy— their immorality and lust, their feasting and drunkenness and wild parties, and their terrible worship of idols.

[4]Of course, your former friends are very surprised when you no longer join them in the wicked things they do, and they say evil things about you. [5]But just remember that they will have to face God, who will judge everyone, both the living and the dead. [6]That is why the Good News was preached even to those who have died—so that although their bodies were punished with death, they could still live in the spirit as God does.

[7]The end of the world is coming soon. Therefore, be earnest and disciplined in your prayers. [8]Most important of all, continue to show deep love for each other, for love covers a multitude of sins. [9]Cheerfully share your home with those who need a meal or a place to stay.

[10]God has given gifts to each of you from his great variety of spiritual gifts. Manage them well so that God's generosity can flow through you. [11]Are you called to be a speaker? Then speak as though God himself were speaking through you. Are you called to help others? Do it with all the strength and energy that God supplies. Then God will be given glory in everything through Jesus Christ. All glory and power belong to him forever and ever. Amen.

SUFFERING FOR BEING A CHRISTIAN

[12]Dear friends, don't be surprised at the fiery trials you are going through, as if something strange were happening to you. [13]Instead, be very glad—because these trials will make you partners with Christ in his suffering, and afterward you will have the wonderful joy of sharing his glory when it is displayed to all the world.

[14]Be happy if you are insulted for being a Christian, for then the glorious Spirit of God will come upon you. [15]If you suffer, however, it must not be for murder, stealing, making trouble, or prying into other people's affairs. [16]But it is no shame to suffer for being a Christian. Praise God for the privilege of being called by his wonderful name! [17]For the time has come for judgment, and it must begin first

3:18 Or *spirit.*   **3:20** Greek *saved through water.*   **3:21** Or *for.*

My Daily Worship

— December 16 —

SEE HIM IN THE CLOUDS

1 PETER 3:1–5:14

So humble yourselves under the mighty power of God, and in his good time he will honor you.
Give all your worries and cares to God, for he cares about what happens to you (5:6–7).

[i reflect]

In some places the sun always shines, or nearly so. In other places, the weather seems to change significantly by the hour. Some places have only one season. Others have only two seasons: the rainy season and the rainier season.

But there is no place on earth where the clouds of bad times signal God's absence.

"In the Bible clouds are always associated with God," wrote Oswald Chambers in *My Utmost for His Highest.* "Clouds are the sorrows, sufferings, or providential circumstances, within or without our personal lives, which actually seem to contradict the sovereignty of God. Yet it is through these very clouds that the Spirit of God is teaching us how to walk by faith. They are a sign that God is there."

The very clouds that we think push out the sunshine of his care are, in his forecast for our lives, his means of arrival. As meteorologists can sometimes be surprised by the significance or timing of the weather, we are sometimes way off in our interpretations and predictions of what—and Who—the clouds bring.

Steven Curtis Chapman, inspired by Chambers, wrote "Sometimes He Comes in the Clouds." Though "his face cannot be found" and the sky is all manner of dastardly colors, it is only at that time our faith can grow. Sometimes he does come in the clouds, in the rain, "and we question the pain."

Yet he *was* there. *Is* there. *In* the rain and the pain, not despite it. In the words of Peter's letter, "in his good time he will honor you." Ready to restore, support, strengthen. Time will show us, in the words of Chapman's song, "He was right there with us."

The clouds come. But rejoice and thank God, who not only allows them but also accompanies them.

Spend some time looking at the clouds today. Let them cause you to worship God's constant care.

[i pray]

Heavenly Father, you are God of the heavens, God of the clouds. I am grateful for your care, grateful for your presence in the clouds of my life. Help me to trust your care and your timing.

[i respond]

Watch for the next time there are distinct cloud formations. Observe them and imagine what weather—rain, snow, hail—they may bring. Pray in thanks to God for recent cloudy times and how he was "right there with you."

among God's own children. And if even we Christians must be judged, what terrible fate awaits those who have never believed God's Good News? [18]And

"If the righteous are barely saved,
what chance will the godless and sinners have?"*

[19]So if you are suffering according to God's will, keep on doing what is right, and trust yourself to the God who made you, for he will never fail you.

ADVICE FOR ELDERS AND YOUNG MEN

5 And now, a word to you who are elders in the churches. I, too, am an elder and a witness to the sufferings of Christ. And I, too, will share his glory and his honor when he returns. As a fellow elder, this is my appeal to you: [2]Care for the flock of God entrusted to you. Watch over it willingly, not grudgingly— not for what you will get out of it, but because you are eager to serve God. [3]Don't lord it over the people assigned to your care, but lead them by your good example. [4]And when the head Shepherd comes, your reward will be a never-ending share in his glory and honor.

[5]You younger men, accept the authority of the elders. And all of you, serve each other in humility, for

"God sets himself against the proud,
but he shows favor to the humble."*

[6]So humble yourselves under the mighty power of God, and in his good time he will honor you. [7]Give all your worries and cares to God, for he cares about what happens to you.

[8]Be careful! Watch out for attacks from the Devil, your great enemy. He prowls around like a roaring lion, looking for some victim to devour. [9]Take a firm stand against him, and be strong in your faith. Remember that your Christian brothers and sisters* all over the world are going through the same kind of suffering you are.

[10]In his kindness God called you to his eternal glory by means of Jesus Christ. After you have suffered a little while, he will restore, support, and strengthen you, and he will place you on a firm foundation. [11]All power is his forever and ever. Amen.

PETER'S FINAL GREETINGS

[12]I have written this short letter to you with the help of Silas,* whom I consider a faithful brother. My purpose in writing is to encourage you and assure you that the grace of God is with you no matter what happens.

[13]Your sister church here in Rome* sends you greetings, and so does my son Mark. [14]Greet each other in Christian love.*

Peace be to all of you who are in Christ.

4:18 Prov 11:31.   **5:5** Prov 3:34.   **5:9** Greek *your brothers.*   **5:12** Greek *Silvanus.*   **5:13** Greek *The elect one in Babylon.* Babylon was probably a code name for Rome.   **5:14** Greek *with a kiss of love.*

— *December 17* —

MAKE EVERY EFFORT TO REMEMBER

2 PETER 1:1–2:22

So make every effort to apply the benefits of these promises to your life. Then your faith
will produce a life of moral excellence. . . . But those who fail to develop these virtues
are blind or, at least, very shortsighted. They have already forgotten that
God has cleansed them from their old life of sin (1:5, 9).

[i reflect]

She walks into the kitchen to get something. Problem is, nearly ten seconds have elapsed, and she has no idea what she wanted.

Alzheimer's patient? Possibly, but more likely it's a middle-aged woman with middle-aged memory challenges and thirty things on her mind. And she never was good at multi-tasking.

Our walk with God often encounters memory challenges. We forget that his promises to care for us are not conditional. We quickly forget that prayer really does work, that, as Peter expresses it, God has cleansed us from our old life of sin.

The apostle James also exhorts us to remember better: "For if you just listen and don't obey, it is like looking at your face in a mirror but doing nothing to improve your appearance. You see yourself, walk away, and forget what you look like. But if you keep looking steadily into God's perfect law—the law that sets you free—and if you do what it says and don't forget what you heard, then God will bless you for doing it" (James 1:23–25).

Charles Wesley, cofounder of the Methodist movement with his brother John, could relate. Sure, he wrote an unbelievable number of upbeat hymns that we still enjoy today, but he was also a poet. One that was never set to music is "Times Without Number Have I Pray'd," with its theme of relapsing—a forgetting, intentionally or not, of what life in Christ means:

"Times without number have I pray'd, 'This only once forgive';
Relapsing, when Thy hand was stay'd, and suffer'd me to live:—

"Yet now the kingdom of Thy peace, Lord, to my heart restore;
Forgive my vain repentances, and bid me sin no more."

Return to God. Remember. And worship him today with gratitude for your new life.

[i pray]

Lord God, forgive me when I fail to remember what life in your name means. Help me with
my spiritual memory lapses and to live in obedience to your call.

[i respond]

Using the theme of forgetting and remembering, write your own poem about "applying the benefits of God's promises" and living a life that demonstrates that God has "cleansed you from your old life of sin."

GREETINGS FROM PETER

1 This letter is from Simon* Peter, a slave and apostle of Jesus Christ.

I am writing to all of you who share the same precious faith we have, faith given to us by Jesus Christ, our God and Savior, who makes us right with God.

²May God bless you with his special favor and wonderful peace as you come to know Jesus, our God and Lord,* better and better.

GROWING IN THE KNOWLEDGE OF GOD

³As we know Jesus better, his divine power gives us everything we need for living a godly life. He has called us to receive his own glory and goodness! ⁴And by that same mighty power, he has given us all of his rich and wonderful promises. He has promised that you will escape the decadence all around you caused by evil desires and that you will share in his divine nature.

⁵So make every effort to apply the benefits of these promises to your life. Then your faith will produce a life of moral excellence. A life of moral excellence leads to knowing God better. ⁶Knowing God leads to self-control. Self-control leads to patient endurance, and patient endurance leads to godliness. ⁷Godliness leads to love for other Christians,* and finally you will grow to have genuine love for everyone. ⁸The more you grow like this, the more you will become productive and useful in your knowledge of our Lord Jesus Christ. ⁹But those who fail to develop these virtues are blind or, at least, very short-sighted. They have already forgotten that God has cleansed them from their old life of sin.

¹⁰So, dear brothers and sisters,* work hard to prove that you really are among those God has called and chosen. Doing this, you will never stumble or fall away. ¹¹And God will open wide the gates of heaven for you to enter into the eternal Kingdom of our Lord and Savior Jesus Christ.

PAYING ATTENTION TO SCRIPTURE

¹²I plan to keep on reminding you of these things—even though you already know them and are standing firm in the truth. ¹³Yes, I believe I should keep on reminding you of these things as long as I live. ¹⁴But the Lord Jesus Christ has shown me that my days here on earth are numbered and I am soon to die.* ¹⁵So I will work hard to make these things clear to you. I want you to remember them long after I am gone.

¹⁶For we were not making up clever stories when we told you about the power of our Lord Jesus Christ and his coming again. We have seen his majestic splendor with our own eyes. ¹⁷And he received honor and glory from God the Father when God's glorious, majestic voice called down from heaven, "This is my beloved Son; I am fully pleased with him." ¹⁸We ourselves heard the voice when we were there with him on the holy mountain.

¹⁹Because of that, we have even greater confidence in the message proclaimed by the prophets. Pay close attention to what they wrote, for their words are like a light shining in a dark place—until the day Christ appears and his brilliant light shines in your hearts.* ²⁰Above all, you must understand that no prophecy in Scripture ever came from the prophets themselves* ²¹or because they wanted to prophesy. It was the Holy Spirit who moved the prophets to speak from God.

THE DANGER OF FALSE TEACHERS

2 But there were also false prophets in Israel, just as there will be false teachers among you. They will cleverly teach their destructive heresies about God and even turn against their Master who bought them. Theirs will be a swift and terrible end. ²Many will fol-

---

1:1 Greek *Simeon.* 1:2 Or *come to know God and Jesus our Lord.* 1:7 Greek *brotherly love.* 1:10 Greek *brothers.* 1:14 Greek *I must soon put off this earthly tent.* 1:19 Or *until the day dawns and the morning star rises in your hearts.* 1:20 Or *is a matter of one's own interpretation.*

My Daily Worship

— December 18 —

THE PICTURE OF PATIENCE

2 PETER 3:1–18

The Lord isn't really being slow about his promise to return, as some people think.
No, he is being patient for your sake. He does not want anyone to perish,
so he is giving more time for everyone to repent (3:9).

[i reflect]

"What's wrong with that idiot! Where are the police when you need them?!" we yell in traffic, wishing for instant justice for a reckless driver. Waiting isn't easy, especially when we witness or *experience* injustice. Politicians, police, and other authorities all seem to move slowly, if at all, especially dealing with *our* problems.

And when we learn of tragic national and world events, injustice on an international scale, our impatience moves to a higher level. "Where is God?" we ask. "What's he waiting for? Why doesn't he step in and end all of this?" God's patience does not seem to us to be one of his better attributes.

Yet where would we be if God were not patient with *all* sinners, including ourselves? Clearly, the Bible teaches us that the world as we know it will come to an end. Today's passage speaks of the character of a patient God who is not willing to see anyone perish in the destruction to come. His Word provides ample warning, and his own compassion holds the tribulation to come at bay to allow "more time for everyone to repent."

The fact that we worship a patient, longsuffering God should give us cause for rejoicing every day of our lives. It is still not too late to embrace the Savior who came "to seek and to save those . . . who are lost" (Luke 19:10). An old hymn called "Rescue the Perishing" written over a hundred years ago puts it this way: "Though they are slighting him, still he is waiting/Waiting the penitent child to receive."

This is good news—*very* good news. Peter cautions us that the day of the Lord is coming when the heavens and the earth will be consumed by fire and the ungodly will perish. But it is not here yet because of God's compassion for those he created and his wonderful patience.

As you read today's headlines or listen to the news, thank God for his merciful patience and his perfect timing.

[i pray]

Forgive me, Lord, for my complacency. I live on a planet I know will be destroyed one day, and yet I hesitate to tell others the way of escape. Give me your compassion for a dying world.

[i respond]

Let the picture of a patient God renew your commitment to pray for friends or family members who have not yet come into the kingdom. Bring those names to the One who is waiting.

low their evil teaching and shameful immorality. And because of them, Christ and his true way will be slandered. [3]In their greed they will make up clever lies to get hold of your money. But God condemned them long ago, and their destruction is on the way.

[4]For God did not spare even the angels when they sinned; he threw them into hell,* in gloomy caves* and darkness until the judgment day. [5]And God did not spare the ancient world—except for Noah and his family of seven. Noah warned the world of God's righteous judgment. Then God destroyed the whole world of ungodly people with a vast flood. [6]Later, he turned the cities of Sodom and Gomorrah into heaps of ashes and swept them off the face of the earth. He made them an example of what will happen to ungodly people. [7]But at the same time, God rescued Lot out of Sodom because he was a good man who was sick of all the immorality and wickedness around him. [8]Yes, he was a righteous man who was distressed by the wickedness he saw and heard day after day.

[9]So you see, the Lord knows how to rescue godly people from their trials, even while punishing the wicked right up until the day of judgment. [10]He is especially hard on those who follow their own evil, lustful desires and who despise authority. These people are proud and arrogant, daring even to scoff at the glorious ones* without so much as trembling. [11]But the angels, even though they are far greater in power and strength than these false teachers, never speak out disrespectfully against* the glorious ones.

[12]These false teachers are like unthinking animals, creatures of instinct, who are born to be caught and killed. They laugh at the terrifying powers they know so little about, and they will be destroyed along with them. [13]Their destruction is their reward for the harm they have done. They love to indulge in evil pleasures in broad daylight. They are a disgrace and a stain among you. They revel in deceitfulness while they feast with you. [14]They commit adultery with their eyes, and their lust is never satisfied. They make a game of luring unstable people into sin. They train themselves to be greedy; they are doomed and cursed. [15]They have wandered off the right road and followed the way of Balaam son of Beor,* who loved to earn money by doing wrong. [16]But Balaam was stopped from his mad course when his donkey rebuked him with a human voice.

[17]These people are as useless as dried-up springs of water or as clouds blown away by the wind—promising much and delivering nothing. They are doomed to blackest darkness. [18]They brag about themselves with empty, foolish boasting. With lustful desire as their bait, they lure back into sin those who have just escaped from such wicked living. [19]They promise freedom, but they themselves are slaves to sin and corruption. For you are a slave to whatever controls you. [20]And when people escape from the wicked ways of the world by learning about our Lord and Savior Jesus Christ and then get tangled up with sin and become its slave again, they are worse off than before. [21]It would be better if they had never known the right way to live than to know it and then reject the holy commandments that were given to them. [22]They make these proverbs come true: "A dog returns to its vomit,"* and "A washed pig returns to the mud."

THE DAY OF THE LORD IS COMING

3 This is my second letter to you, dear friends, and in both of them I have tried to stimulate your wholesome thinking and refresh your memory. [2]I want you to remember and understand what the holy prophets said long ago and what our Lord and Savior commanded through your apostles.

[3]First, I want to remind you that in the last days there will be scoffers who will laugh at the truth and do every evil thing they desire.

2:4a Greek *Tartaros*.   2:4b Some manuscripts read *chains of gloom*.   2:10 *The glorious ones* are probably evil angels; also in 2:11.
2:11 Greek *never bring blasphemous judgment from the Lord against*.   2:15 Other manuscripts read *Bosor*.   2:22 Prov 26:11.

⁴This will be their argument: "Jesus promised to come back, did he? Then where is he? Why, as far back as anyone can remember, everything has remained exactly the same since the world was first created."

⁵They deliberately forget that God made the heavens by the word of his command, and he brought the earth up from the water and surrounded it with water. ⁶Then he used the water to destroy the world with a mighty flood. ⁷And God has also commanded that the heavens and the earth will be consumed by fire on the day of judgment, when ungodly people will perish.

⁸But you must not forget, dear friends, that a day is like a thousand years to the Lord, and a thousand years is like a day. ⁹The Lord isn't really being slow about his promise to return, as some people think. No, he is being patient for your sake. He does not want anyone to perish, so he is giving more time for everyone to repent. ¹⁰But the day of the Lord will come as unexpectedly as a thief. Then the heavens will pass away with a terrible noise, and everything in them will disappear in fire, and the earth and everything on it will be exposed to judgment.*

¹¹Since everything around us is going to melt away, what holy, godly lives you should be living! ¹²You should look forward to that day and hurry it along—the day when God will set the heavens on fire and the elements will melt away in the flames. ¹³But we are looking forward to the new heavens and new earth he has promised, a world where everyone is right with God.

¹⁴And so, dear friends, while you are waiting for these things to happen, make every effort to live a pure and blameless life. And be at peace with God.

¹⁵And remember, the Lord is waiting so that people have time to be saved. This is just as our beloved brother Paul wrote to you with the wisdom God gave him—¹⁶speaking of these things in all of his letters. Some of his comments are hard to understand, and those who are ignorant and unstable have twisted his letters around to mean something quite different from what he meant, just as they do the other parts of Scripture—and the result is disaster for them.

PETER'S FINAL WORDS

¹⁷I am warning you ahead of time, dear friends, so that you can watch out and not be carried away by the errors of these wicked people. I don't want you to lose your own secure footing. ¹⁸But grow in the special favor and knowledge of our Lord and Savior Jesus Christ.

To him be all glory and honor, both now and forevermore. Amen.

3:10 Some manuscripts read *will be burned up.*

1, 2 & 3 John

Dear friends, let us continue to love one another, for love comes from God.
Anyone who loves is born of God and knows God (1 John 4:7).

Walk in Light and Love

Light and darkness tell of God's work on earth. To the former belong love, life, fellowship, and truth. To the latter, false faith, distrust, greed, and pride. The lighted path makes the trek more vulnerable to attack from roadside thugs, but less vulnerable to tripping over rocks. Children of light trade a certain distance from the world's strategies in favor of certain clarity about God's purposes. Worship is the common practice of light-seeking people. The elder apostle John writes in simple hues: do good, not evil; follow truth, not falsity; love each other when the more common way is exploitation; show hospitality to strangers when the norm is a locked gate. In these ways bring God's light to bear among the shadows.

At the very center of this worshiping community, however, is the confession that Jesus Christ is the Son of God. John has strong words for those who deny that Jesus is the Christ, saying that these people have no place in the community of faith (1 John 2:19, 22). True worship exalts Jesus as Lord of all and points people to the truth (3 John 1:3–4), to love (2 John 1:5–6), and to the light (1 John 1:7).

Is worship, then, a light-only operation? No, some worship acknowledges the shadows, as the worship we do at funerals and on Good Friday. Minor chords remind us that God's promises are yet to be fully realized. That said, Christians are children of light. They love light. They move towards it, knowing it points ever to God. In song, praise, quiet meditation, thoughtful sermon, steady testimony, and faith-filled prayer, Christians are light-responsive people. We seek it; we want it. We praise the God of light and life.

Worship Moments

- Confession of sin brings integrity to worship. In many liturgies, confession precedes praise. True worship does not neglect cleaning out our hearts as we prepare to enter God's presence (1 John 1:9).

- John said there is either love or hate; truth or lies. Worship has no locker for storing up hate, no library for the collection of lies (1 John 2:9–10).

- Worship changes everything. The light of praise shines in the market, at the office, in the classroom. Worshipers rearrange everything to catch the light of God's glory and love (1 John 3:18–19).

- Worship embraces the stranger, not foolishly, but consistently, as if God himself has sent the visitor. What part of our corporate worship says "Come in, be with us"? (3 John 1:5–8).

INTRODUCTION

1 The one who existed from the beginning* is the one we have heard and seen. We saw him with our own eyes and touched him with our own hands. He is Jesus Christ, the Word of life. ²This one who is life from God was shown to us, and we have seen him. And now we testify and announce to you that he is the one who is eternal life. He was with the Father, and then he was shown to us. ³We are telling you about what we ourselves have actually seen and heard, so that you may have fellowship with us. And our fellowship is with the Father and with his Son, Jesus Christ.

⁴We are writing these things so that our* joy will be complete.

LIVING IN THE LIGHT

⁵This is the message he has given us to announce to you: God is light and there is no darkness in him at all. ⁶So we are lying if we say we have fellowship with God but go on living in spiritual darkness. We are not living in the truth. ⁷But if we are living in the light of God's presence, just as Christ is, then we have fellowship with each other, and the blood of Jesus, his Son, cleanses us from every sin.

⁸If we say we have no sin, we are only fooling ourselves and refusing to accept the truth. ⁹But if we confess our sins to him, he is faithful and just to forgive us and to cleanse us from every wrong. ¹⁰If we claim we have not sinned, we are calling God a liar and showing that his word has no place in our hearts.

2 My dear children, I am writing this to you so that you will not sin. But if you do sin, there is someone to plead for you before the Father. He is Jesus Christ, the one who pleases God completely.* ²He is the sacrifice for our sins. He takes away not only our sins but the sins of all the world.

³And how can we be sure that we belong to him? By obeying his commandments. ⁴If someone says, "I belong to God," but doesn't obey God's commandments, that person is a liar and does not live in the truth. ⁵But those who obey God's word really do love him. That is the way to know whether or not we live in him. ⁶Those who say they live in God should live their lives as Christ did.

A NEW COMMANDMENT

⁷Dear friends, I am not writing a new commandment, for it is an old one you have always had, right from the beginning. This commandment—to love one another—is the same message you heard before. ⁸Yet it is also new. This commandment is true in Christ and is true among you, because the darkness is disappearing and the true light is already shining.

⁹If anyone says, "I am living in the light," but hates a Christian brother or sister,* that person is still living in darkness. ¹⁰Anyone who loves other Christians* is living in the light and does not cause anyone to stumble. ¹¹Anyone who hates a Christian brother or sister is living and walking in darkness. Such a person is lost, having been blinded by the darkness.

¹²I am writing to you, my dear children, because your sins have been forgiven because of Jesus.

¹³I am writing to you who are mature because you know Christ, the one who is from the beginning.

I am writing to you who are young because you have won your battle with Satan.

¹⁴I have written to you, children, because you have known the Father.

I have written to you who are mature because you know Christ, the one who is from the beginning.

I have written to you who are young because you are strong with God's word

---

1:1 Greek *What was from the beginning.* 1:4 Some manuscripts read *your.* 2:1 Greek *Jesus Christ, the righteous.* 2:9 Greek *his brother;* also in 2:11. 2:10 Greek *his brother.*

living in your hearts, and you have won your battle with Satan.

[15] Stop loving this evil world and all that it offers you, for when you love the world, you show that you do not have the love of the Father in you. [16] For the world offers only the lust for physical pleasure, the lust for everything we see, and pride in our possessions. These are not from the Father. They are from this evil world. [17] And this world is fading away, along with everything it craves. But if you do the will of God, you will live forever.

[18] Dear children, the last hour is here. You have heard that the Antichrist is coming, and already many such antichrists have appeared. From this we know that the end of the world has come. [19] These people left our churches because they never really belonged with us; otherwise they would have stayed with us. When they left us, it proved that they do not belong with us. [20] But you are not like that, for the Holy Spirit has come upon you,* and all of you know the truth. [21] So I am writing to you not because you don't know the truth but because you know the difference between truth and falsehood. [22] And who is the great liar? The one who says that Jesus is not the Christ. Such people are antichrists, for they have denied the Father and the Son. [23] Anyone who denies the Son doesn't have the Father either. But anyone who confesses the Son has the Father also.

[24] So you must remain faithful to what you have been taught from the beginning. If you do, you will continue to live in fellowship with the Son and with the Father. [25] And in this fellowship we enjoy the eternal life he promised us.

[26] I have written these things to you because you need to be aware of those who want to lead you astray. [27] But you have received the Holy Spirit,* and he lives within you, so you don't need anyone to teach you what is true. For the Spirit teaches you all things, and what he teaches is true—it is not a lie. So continue in what he has taught you, and continue to live in Christ.

[28] And now, dear children, continue to live in fellowship with Christ so that when he returns, you will be full of courage and not shrink back from him in shame. [29] Since we know that God is always right, we also know that all who do what is right are his children.

LIVING AS CHILDREN OF GOD

3 See how very much our heavenly Father loves us, for he allows us to be called his children, and we really are! But the people who belong to this world don't know God, so they don't understand that we are his children. [2] Yes, dear friends, we are already God's children, and we can't even imagine what we will be like when Christ returns. But we do know that when he comes we will be like him, for we will see him as he really is. [3] And all who believe this will keep themselves pure, just as Christ is pure.

[4] Those who sin are opposed to the law of God, for all sin opposes the law of God. [5] And you know that Jesus came to take away our sins, for there is no sin in him. [6] So if we continue to live in him, we won't sin either. But those who keep on sinning have never known him or understood who he is.

[7] Dear children, don't let anyone deceive you about this: When people do what is right, it is because they are righteous, even as Christ is righteous. [8] But when people keep on sinning, it shows they belong to the Devil, who has been sinning since the beginning. But the Son of God came to destroy these works of the Devil. [9] Those who have been born into God's family do not sin, because God's life is in them. So they can't keep on sinning, because they have been born of God. [10] So now we can tell who are children of God and who are children of the Devil. Anyone who does not obey God's commands and does not love other Christians* does not belong to God.

2:20 Greek But you have an anointing from the Holy One. 2:27 Greek the anointing. 3:10 Greek his brother.

My Daily Worship

— *December 19* —

SHOWERS OF BLESSING

1 J O H N 1 : 1 – 3 : 2 4

*But if we confess our sins to him, he is faithful and just to forgive us and to cleanse us from
every wrong. If we claim we have not sinned, we are calling God a liar and
showing that his word has no place in our hearts (1:9–10).*

[i reflect]

Military personnel who were stationed in Iraq during the spring of 2003 were heard to comment that one of the things they most looked forward to, after weeks of enduring the dust and dirt of the battlefield, was a shower. Imagine the layers of grit and desert grime washing away under the steady stream of refreshing and restoring water.

In the same way, God has provided a way for us to be cleansed spiritually as well. Today's passage teaches one of the most important principles in all of Scripture, that of confessing our sins. Confession has been described as agreeing with God about the things we have done that violate his commandments and his will for us. No human intermediary is necessary. God knows every secret of the human heart, and he stands ready to forgive us. There is only one condition: we must confess.

Sin separates us from the One who longs to enjoy unbroken fellowship with us. When Adam and Eve first sinned in the Garden of Eden, their disobedience and deceit caused them to hide from the Lord. It's often been noted that the first recorded question in the history of the universe was not, "God, where are you?" but rather, "Adam, where are you?"

No one can hide from God. The early church father Lactantius wrote, "Let us cleanse our consciences which are open to the eyes of God. Remember that we are being watched at every moment by the One who will be both Judge and Witness."

God observes us through eyes of love, much like a father who carefully watches to see if his child will own up to wrongdoing. Have your times of personal worship felt lifeless and dry? If your actions or attitudes have erected a barrier between you and your Lord, confession will knock it down. A heavenly shower of blessing awaits you.

Spend time in confession now. Imagine the cleansing waters of God's forgiveness washing away the grit of sin.

[i pray]

*God, I confess that there are areas of my life I wish that you couldn't see.
I know I can hide nothing from you—not even myself. Forgive me,
Father, and cleanse me from all that offends your holiness.*

[i respond]

Using a pencil, write down the sins that you need to confess. Don't forget about the subtle sins of pride, jealousy, self-pity, or gossiping. As you confess each one to God, erase that sin from your paper.

LOVE ONE ANOTHER

[11]This is the message we have heard from the beginning: We should love one another. [12]We must not be like Cain, who belonged to the evil one and killed his brother. And why did he kill him? Because Cain had been doing what was evil, and his brother had been doing what was right. [13]So don't be surprised, dear brothers and sisters,* if the world hates you.

[14]If we love our Christian brothers and sisters, it proves that we have passed from death to eternal life. But a person who has no love is still dead. [15]Anyone who hates another Christian* is really a murderer at heart. And you know that murderers don't have eternal life within them. [16]We know what real love is because Christ gave up his life for us. And so we also ought to give up our lives for our Christian brothers and sisters. [17]But if anyone has enough money to live well and sees a brother or sister in need and refuses to help— how can God's love be in that person?

[18]Dear children, let us stop just saying we love each other; let us really show it by our actions. [19]It is by our actions that we know we are living in the truth, so we will be confident when we stand before the Lord, [20]even if our hearts condemn us. For God is greater than our hearts, and he knows everything.

[21]Dear friends, if our conscience is clear, we can come to God with bold confidence. [22]And we will receive whatever we request because we obey him and do the things that please him. [23]And this is his commandment: We must believe in the name of his Son, Jesus Christ, and love one another, just as he commanded us. [24]Those who obey God's commandments live in fellowship with him, and he with them. And we know he lives in us because the Holy Spirit lives in us.

DISCERNING FALSE PROPHETS

4 Dear friends, do not believe everyone who claims to speak by the Spirit. You must test them to see if the spirit they have comes from God. For there are many false prophets in the world. [2]This is the way to find out if they have the Spirit of God: If a prophet acknowledges that Jesus Christ became a human being, that person has the Spirit of God. [3]If a prophet does not acknowledge Jesus, that person is not from God. Such a person has the spirit of the Antichrist. You have heard that he is going to come into the world, and he is already here.

[4]But you belong to God, my dear children. You have already won your fight with these false prophets, because the Spirit who lives in you is greater than the spirit who lives in the world. [5]These people belong to this world, so they speak from the world's viewpoint, and the world listens to them. [6]But we belong to God; that is why those who know God listen to us. If they do not belong to God, they do not listen to us. That is how we know if someone has the Spirit of truth or the spirit of deception.

LOVING ONE ANOTHER

[7]Dear friends, let us continue to love one another, for love comes from God. Anyone who loves is born of God and knows God. [8]But anyone who does not love does not know God—for God is love.

[9]God showed how much he loved us by sending his only Son into the world so that we might have eternal life through him. [10]This is real love. It is not that we loved God, but that he loved us and sent his Son as a sacrifice to take away our sins.

[11]Dear friends, since God loved us that much, we surely ought to love each other. [12]No one has ever seen God. But if we love each other, God lives in us, and his love has been brought to full expression through us.

[13]And God has given us his Spirit as proof that we live in him and he in us. [14]Furthermore, we have seen with our own eyes and now testify that the Father sent his Son to be the Savior of the world. [15]All who proclaim that Jesus is the Son of God have God living in

---

3:13 Greek *brothers;* also in 3:14, 16. **3:15** Greek *his brother.*

My Daily Worship

— *December 20* —

LOVE IS NOT OPTIONAL
1 JOHN 4:1–5:21

If someone says, "I love God," but hates a Christian brother or sister, that person is a liar;
for if we don't love people we can see, how can we love God, whom we have not seen? (4:20).

[i reflect]

Pastor Mike, a New England pastor, was preaching a series of sermons one winter on what it means to truly love God. When he polled his congregation, most responded that they demonstrated their love for God through faithful church attendance, tithing, and service on various committees. An elderly woman, however, rose to her feet a bit unsteadily. "I am here this morning," she said quietly, "because my friend was willing to drive me. We were able to get out of my driveway because a neighbor came over to shovel the snow. My home has heat because the church paid my bill. I don't need to ask what it means for people to love God, because I have already seen it."

Today's passage stresses again and again the importance of loving one another, "for love comes from God." If loving others were a simple matter, though, perhaps so much of this letter from John wouldn't be devoted to the subject. G. K. Chesterton wryly observed, "The Bible tells us to love our neighbors, and also to love our enemies; probably because they are generally the same people."

Let's face it: not everyone is easy to get along with, including ourselves! Scripture provides a powerful reason for loving others, however. If we say we love God, then he commands us to love the other members of our family in Christ. It is not optional.

C. S. Lewis explains how the commandments to love God and love people complement one another. "When I have learned to love God better than my earthly dearest, I shall love my earthly dearest better than I do now. Insofar as I learn to love my earthly dearest at the expense of God and instead of God, I shall be moving toward the state in which I shall not love my earthly dearest at all. When first things are put first, second things are not suppressed but increased."

Name the person who is the most difficult for you to love right now. As an act of worship to the One who is love, show your love to that person today in a tangible, concrete way.

[i pray]

Lord, you know that there are others who claim the name of Christ who I simply
don't like very much. Teach me how to love them not with my feelings
but with my faith. Let me do it out of an overflow of love for you.

[i respond]

The real test of our love for God is how you treat the people who you are in contact with daily. Make a list of those people; then assess how well you show God's love to them. For those, where you might get a below average rating, think of one or two ways you can show God's love to that person.

them, and they live in God. [16]We know how much God loves us, and we have put our trust in him.

God is love, and all who live in love live in God, and God lives in them. [17]And as we live in God, our love grows more perfect. So we will not be afraid on the day of judgment, but we can face him with confidence because we are like Christ here in this world.

[18]Such love has no fear because perfect love expels all fear. If we are afraid, it is for fear of judgment, and this shows that his love has not been perfected in us. [19]We love each other* as a result of his loving us first.

[20]If someone says, "I love God," but hates a Christian brother or sister,* that person is a liar; for if we don't love people we can see, how can we love God, whom we have not seen? [21]And God himself has commanded that we must love not only him but our Christian brothers and sisters, too.

FAITH IN THE SON OF GOD

5 Everyone who believes that Jesus is the Christ is a child of God. And everyone who loves the Father loves his children, too. [2]We know we love God's children if we love God and obey his commandments. [3]Loving God means keeping his commandments, and really, that isn't difficult. [4]For every child of God defeats this evil world by trusting Christ to give the victory. [5]And the ones who win this battle against the world are the ones who believe that Jesus is the Son of God.

[6]And Jesus Christ was revealed as God's Son by his baptism in water and by shedding his blood on the cross*—not by water only, but by water and blood. And the Spirit also gives us the testimony that this is true. [7]So we have these three witnesses*—[8]the Spirit, the water, and the blood—and all three agree. [9]Since we

believe human testimony, surely we can believe the testimony that comes from God. And God has testified about his Son. [10]All who believe in the Son of God know that this is true. Those who don't believe this are actually calling God a liar because they don't believe what God has testified about his Son.

[11]And this is what God has testified: He has given us eternal life, and this life is in his Son. [12]So whoever has God's Son has life; whoever does not have his Son does not have life.

CONCLUSION

[13]I write this to you who believe in the Son of God, so that you may know you have eternal life. [14]And we can be confident that he will listen to us whenever we ask him for anything in line with his will. [15]And if we know he is listening when we make our requests, we can be sure that he will give us what we ask for.

[16]If you see a Christian brother or sister* sinning in a way that does not lead to death, you should pray, and God will give that person life. But there is a sin that leads to death, and I am not saying you should pray for those who commit it. [17]Every wrong is sin, but not all sin leads to death.

[18]We know that those who have become part of God's family do not make a practice of sinning, for God's Son holds them securely, and the evil one cannot get his hands on them. [19]We know that we are children of God and that the world around us is under the power and control of the evil one. [20]And we know that the Son of God has come, and he has given us understanding so that we can know the true God. And now we are in God because we are in his Son, Jesus Christ. He is the only true God, and he is eternal life.

[21]Dear children, keep away from anything that might take God's place in your hearts.*

4:19 Or We love him; Greek reads We love. 4:20 Greek brother; also in 4:21. 5:6 Greek This is he who came by water and blood. 5:7 Some very late manuscripts add in heaven—the Father, the Word, and the Holy Spirit, and these three are one. And we have three witnesses on earth. 5:16 Greek your brother. 5:21 Greek keep yourselves from idols.

My Daily Worship

— *December 21* —

WATCHING AND WORKING
2 JOHN 1–13

Watch out, so that you do not lose the prize for which we have been working so hard.
Be diligent so that you will receive your full reward (8).

[i reflect]

The infamous criminal Willie Sutton was once asked why he robbed banks. His reply? "Because that's where the money is."

A similar reasoning motivates our enemy. Why does Satan work so hard at deceiving believers in Jesus? Why, in every generation, does he continually unleash legions of false teachers on the church? Answer: Because that's where the worship is. The devil hates to see God honored. He will do anything to stop this. In fact, he would really like to steal this affection for himself.

Like so many of the New Testament letters, 2 John warns believers to watch out. We have to pay attention and be on our guard. Otherwise we can get sloppy in our lives. Without vigilance and diligence, we can get off track and shift our focus and affection to unworthy things. Suddenly we find ourselves valuing that which is not God.

The point? A fully devoted life of worship encompasses more than just attending praise services. Worship is more than singing exuberantly and praying fervently. Worship involves *watching*. We have to be alert to the schemes of the enemy. Like a cosmic terrorist, he is always looking for an opening. Therefore we cannot afford to be careless. Worship involves watching, and watching requires *work*.

When you get a valuable new possession—a car, a piece of jewelry, a laptop computer, etc.—you fuss over it carefully. You insure it. You lock it up. You go to great lengths to protect it. How much more should we work to guard our worship of the one true God from the one who would like to steal it away!

Spend time reflecting on today's verse. Memorize it as a way to guard against becoming lazy in your worship and faith.

[i pray]

Lord God, remind me today (and everyday) that I have an enemy who wants to steal my affection from you by deceiving me. Make me watchful. Give me a diligent heart, so that I might enjoy the great reward of knowing and serving you.

[i respond]

At your church, sign up for a Bible study course or join a small group that is examining what Christians believe. Understanding the historic Christian faith is the best way to guard against false teaching and counterfeit belief systems.

GREETINGS

This letter is from John the Elder.*

It is written to the chosen lady and to her children,* whom I love in the truth, as does everyone else who knows God's truth—²the truth that lives in us and will be in our hearts forever.

³May grace, mercy, and peace, which come from God our Father and from Jesus Christ his Son, be with us who live in truth and love.

LIVE IN THE TRUTH

⁴How happy I was to meet some of your children and find them living in the truth, just as we have been commanded by the Father.

⁵And now I want to urge you, dear lady, that we should love one another. This is not a new commandment, but one we had from the beginning. ⁶Love means doing what God has commanded us, and he has commanded us to love one another, just as you heard from the beginning.

⁷Many deceivers have gone out into the world. They do not believe that Jesus Christ came to earth in a real body. Such a person is a deceiver and an antichrist. ⁸Watch out, so that you do not lose the prize for which we* have been working so hard. Be diligent so that you will receive your full reward. ⁹For if you wander beyond the teaching of Christ, you will not have fellowship with God. But if you continue in the teaching of Christ, you will have fellowship with both the Father and the Son.

¹⁰If someone comes to your meeting and does not teach the truth about Christ, don't invite him into your house or encourage him in any way. ¹¹Anyone who encourages him becomes a partner in his evil work.

CONCLUSION

¹²Well, I have much more to say to you, but I don't want to say it in a letter. For I hope to visit you soon and to talk with you face to face. Then our joy will be complete.

¹³Greetings from the children of your sister,* chosen by God.

1a Greek *From the elder.* 1b Or *the church God has chosen and her members,* or *the chosen Kyria and her children.* 8 Some manuscripts read *you.* 13 Or *from the members of your sister church.*

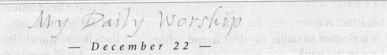

— *December 22* —

NEIGHBORHOOD WATCH

3 JOHN 1–15

*Some of the brothers recently returned and made me very happy by telling me
about your faithfulness and that you are living in the truth (3).*

[i reflect]

A disturbing number of modern Christians do not understand (or else they simply do not embrace) the concept of biblical community. They prefer to view the faith as a private, personal matter. Engaging others, being a vital member of a church, sharing life as a body of believers (see 1 Corinthians 12)—all this is seen as optional, certainly unnecessary, and possibly even undesirable.

This was never God's intent. The Bible both describes and proscribes a kind of spiritual existence in which people of faith live and serve together (Acts 2:42–47). Third John is such an example. It's essentially a postcard—a window into true spiritual friendship. It depicts believers not just co-existing but co-laboring in a great cause. And why? Because we need each other. God purposely designed us to be interdependent. Left alone we are vulnerable and incomplete. Even worse, we may forget what's true, stop doing what's important, and stop ordering our lives and activities around the One who is worthy of all that we are and have.

The great nineteenth-century preacher Charles Spurgeon observed: "Communion is strength; solitude is weakness. Alone, the free old beech yields to the blast and lies prone on the meadow. In the forest, supporting each other, the trees laugh at the hurricane. The sheep of Jesus flock together. The social element is the genius of Christianity."

Check your own habits of interaction with other believers. Are you deeply involved in your church? Do you attend? Participate? Serve? Give? Do you have Christian friends who continually motivate you to love Christ better and better?

Practice Christian community today. Call one or two friends and spend time in prayer, Bible reading, or encouraging one another.

[i pray]

Lord, forgive me for thinking I can live independently from the rest of your body, the church. Cause my personal worship to instill within me a hunger for corporate worship with the people of God. Remind me in newer and deeper ways that the best worship is worship in community.

[i respond]

If you are not an official member of a local body of believers, join *this week*. Go against the flow of a culture that abhors commitment. Your actions will not only honor God and fill you with a renewed sense of mission, but they will greatly encourage whatever congregation you join.

GREETINGS

This letter is from John the Elder.*

It is written to Gaius, my dear friend, whom I love in the truth.

[2] Dear friend, I am praying that all is well with you and that your body is as healthy as I know your soul is. [3] Some of the brothers recently returned and made me very happy by telling me about your faithfulness and that you are living in the truth. [4] I could have no greater joy than to hear that my children live in the truth.

CARING FOR THE LORD'S WORKERS

[5] Dear friend, you are doing a good work for God when you take care of the traveling teachers* who are passing through, even though they are strangers to you. [6] They have told the church here of your friendship and your loving deeds. You do well to send them on their way in a manner that pleases God. [7] For they are traveling for the Lord* and accept nothing from those who are not Christians.* [8] So we ourselves should support them so that we may become partners with them for the truth.

[9] I sent a brief letter to the church about this, but Diotrephes, who loves to be the leader, does not acknowledge our authority. [10] When I come, I will report some of the things he is doing and the wicked things he is saying about us. He not only refuses to welcome the traveling teachers, he also tells others not to help them. And when they do help, he puts them out of the church.

[11] Dear friend, don't let this bad example influence you. Follow only what is good. Remember that those who do good prove that they are God's children, and those who do evil prove that they do not know God. [12] But everyone speaks highly of Demetrius, even truth itself. We ourselves can say the same for him, and you know we speak the truth.

CONCLUSION

[13] I have much to tell you, but I don't want to do it in a letter. [14] For I hope to see you soon, and then we will talk face to face.

[15] May God's peace be with you.

Your friends here send you their greetings. Please give my personal greetings to each of our friends there.

---

1 Greek *From the elder.* 5 Greek *the brothers;* also in verse 10. 7a Greek *the Name.* 7b Greek *from Gentiles.*

Jude

But you, dear friends, must continue to build your lives on the foundation of your holy faith. And continue to pray as you are directed by the Holy Spirit (20).

Building Up the Body

It is such a paradox that worship should attract phonies and con artists. These people should be somewhere else—the carnival, the wharf, the alley—where prey is easy. Yet it happens sometimes that powerful personalities with noble voices and proven success strategies turn God's people away from worship toward something quite different, usually feathering the leader's bank account and always netting headlines.

Jude warns against leaders who bend the path to God. He cites the biblical record to warn that these enemies of faith are not so ugly and transparent as their evil might suggest. Even the worst of them all has the respect of the angels.

Jude's solution: Build yourself up, get strong, know God's will, stay focused. Jude's advice is always in the plural: God's people hang together, need each other, grow to delight in each other's company. So Jude advises to grow up, steadily, in God's love revealed in Jesus Christ. This is the way of eternal life.

Then, as if offering a delicious dessert after a spartan meal, Jude provides us with one of the Bible's most cited blessings. It points surely to God, who has our destiny in his hands. It looks to a future of great wonder and richness. It distinguishes God as the only source of truth, God's Word as the only way of life, God's Son as the Lord of all.

Pronounce this doxology to each other at the close of worship. It is a gift to encourage the weary and strengthen the frail. God has done it. God is able.

Worship Moments

- Worship, like salvation, is a shared experience. The church is composed of believers around the world, small groups of whom meet regularly to praise and pray (3).

- False worship is typified by a denial of Jesus and an unbounded freedom to try anything in the name of religion (4).

- God's Spirit is present in worship. We should be able to detect the absence of God's Spirit in false worship. Be alert (19).

- Not all who doubt or give in to temptation are enemies. Doubters and moral weaklings need our help, not shunning. Be merciful (22–23).

- Worship is entering God's glorious presence, majesty, and power (24–25).

GREETINGS FROM JUDE

This letter is from Jude, a slave of Jesus Christ and a brother of James.

I am writing to all who are called to live in the love of God the Father and the care of Jesus Christ.

²May you receive more and more of God's mercy, peace, and love.

THE DANGER OF FALSE TEACHERS

³Dearly loved friends, I had been eagerly planning to write to you about the salvation we all share. But now I find that I must write about something else, urging you to defend the truth of the Good News.* God gave this unchanging truth once for all time to his holy people. ⁴I say this because some godless people have wormed their way in among you, saying that God's forgiveness allows us to live immoral lives. The fate of such people was determined long ago, for they have turned against our only Master and Lord, Jesus Christ.

⁵I must remind you—and you know it well—that even though the Lord* rescued the whole nation of Israel from Egypt, he later destroyed every one of those who did not remain faithful. ⁶And I remind you of the angels who did not stay within the limits of authority God gave them but left the place where they belonged. God has kept them chained in prisons of darkness, waiting for the day of judgment. ⁷And don't forget the cities of Sodom and Gomorrah and their neighboring towns, which were filled with sexual immorality and every kind of sexual perversion. Those cities were destroyed by fire and are a warning of the eternal fire that will punish all who are evil.

⁸Yet these false teachers, who claim authority from their dreams, live immoral lives, defy authority, and scoff at the power of the glorious ones.* ⁹But even Michael, one of the mightiest of the angels, did not dare accuse Satan of blasphemy, but simply said, "The Lord rebuke you." (This took place when Michael was arguing with Satan about Moses' body.) ¹⁰But these people mock and curse the things they do not understand. Like animals, they do whatever their instincts tell them, and they bring about their own destruction. ¹¹How terrible it will be for them! For they follow the evil example of Cain, who killed his brother. Like Balaam, they will do anything for money. And like Korah, they will perish because of their rebellion.

¹²When these people join you in fellowship meals celebrating the love of the Lord, they are like dangerous reefs that can shipwreck you.* They are shameless in the way they care only about themselves. They are like clouds blowing over dry land without giving rain, promising much but producing nothing. They are like trees without fruit at harvesttime. They are not only dead but doubly dead, for they have been pulled out by the roots. ¹³They are like wild waves of the sea, churning up the dirty foam of their shameful deeds. They are wandering stars, heading for everlasting gloom and darkness.

¹⁴Now Enoch, who lived seven generations after Adam, prophesied about these people. He said,

"Look, the Lord is coming
  with thousands of his holy ones.
¹⁵ He will bring the people of the world
  to judgment.
He will convict the ungodly of all the evil
  things
  they have done in rebellion
and of all the insults that godless sinners
  have spoken against him."*

¹⁶These people are grumblers and complainers, doing whatever evil they feel like. They are loudmouthed braggarts, and they flatter others to get favors in return.

---

3 Greek *to contend for the faith.* 5 Some manuscripts read *Jesus.* 8 *The glorious ones* are probably evil angels. 12 Or *they are contaminants among you,* or *they are stains.* 14-15 The quotation comes from the Apocrypha: Enoch 1:9.

— *December 23* —

BE A LIFEGUARD

JUDE 1–25

Show mercy to those whose faith is wavering. Rescue others by snatching them from the flames of judgment. There are still others to whom you need to show mercy, but be careful that you aren't contaminated by their sins (22–23).

[i reflect]

The beach is a beautiful place, and also a dangerous one. Every summer we hear grim stories of shark attacks or tragic tales of swimmers being pulled out to sea by strong undertows. Perhaps you've even experienced the phenomenon of dozing off on a raft, only to wake up and find that you've drifted. The wind and waves have gently pushed and pulled you far from where you began your floating.

That's a good metaphor for life. The world is beautiful, and dangerous! Our enemy can be more vicious and deadly than the giant shark of the movie *Jaws*. And if he doesn't attack us in overt ways, then through more subtle means he tries to get us to drift away from God and from what is true. Many times the process is imperceptible. It happens so gradually that we don't even notice— until we "wake up," far from where we need to be.

This short New Testament letter warns readers about the enemy and his diabolical tactics. Not only are we urged to pay attention to our own safety, we are also called to look out for others. To be *lifeguards,* in the most critical sense of the term. Cyprian put it this way, "Considering his love and mercy, we shouldn't be bitter, cruel, or inhuman toward believers." We are called to rescue, show mercy, and help "those whose faith is wavering."

A big part of what it means to worship God is to care for his people. By protecting those who are called to worship him, we enhance his glory and the honor due his name. Today, make it your goal to throw a lifeline to someone in trouble. Be a prayer warrior. Speak words of encouragement. Pull someone toward the safety of Christ our Rock.

[i pray]

Lord Jesus, thank you for rescuing me—for opening my eyes to who you are and why you are worthy of my worship. Give me a heart of compassion so that I might do the same for others.

[i respond]

Re-read the short book of Jude. Memorize the final verse of this letter (v. 25).

A CALL TO REMAIN FAITHFUL

[17]But you, my dear friends, must remember what the apostles of our Lord Jesus Christ told you, [18]that in the last times there would be scoffers whose purpose in life is to enjoy themselves in every evil way imaginable. [19]Now they are here, and they are the ones who are creating divisions among you. They live by natural instinct because they do not have God's Spirit living in them.

[20]But you, dear friends, must continue to build your lives on the foundation of your holy faith. And continue to pray as you are directed by the Holy Spirit.* [21]Live in such a way that God's love can bless you as you wait for the eternal life that our Lord Jesus Christ in his mercy is going to give you. [22]Show mercy to those whose faith is wavering. [23]Rescue others by snatching them from the flames of judgment. There are still others to whom you need to show mercy, but be careful that you aren't contaminated by their sins.*

A PRAYER OF PRAISE

[24]And now, all glory to God, who is able to keep you from stumbling, and who will bring you into his glorious presence innocent of sin and with great joy. [25]All glory to him, who alone is God our Savior, through Jesus Christ our Lord. Yes, glory, majesty, power, and authority belong to him, in the beginning, now, and forevermore. Amen.

20 Greek *Pray in the Holy Spirit.*   **23** Greek *mercy, hating even the clothing stained by the flesh.*

Revelation

Praise our God, all his servants, from the least to the greatest, all who fear him (19:5).

The Final Victory

Some claim this last book of the Bible is the most obtuse, its language beyond comprehension. Surely its differing interpretations have caused division in the church, and its central message has been obscured by efforts to find in its roaring symbols keys to the future.

But read this book as a whole, and the overwhelming response is to kneel in worship before the mighty God whose plan is good and just, who defeats evil and death, and who welcomes his people into paradise that never ends. God be praised!

Everywhere in Revelation, worship is the keynote. In song, word, and deed, God is the focus and God's people are the chorus. And everywhere is an unavoidable warning: outside the chorus are those whose doom is sure.

Revelation, like the Psalms, is a book of praise, thanksgiving, and gratitude. While news headlines daily tout the powerful over the weak and focus attention on the cruel over the humble, the real news behind the news is God's triumph over every evil. God can do it, and he will. His people shout their praise, some with voices cracked in pain. Scars cover these singers. Yet hope sees past the lash and fire. A dinner table is set for the guests at God's banquet. Outside, stylish jingles speak of titillation and thin glamour. But the pure, sweet song never ends for the chorus at the table of God.

Worship points to this: the kingdom of God—promised long ago, shown by Jesus, preached by many witnesses—is coming. Its approach will be cataclysmic and its power will be overwhelming. Evil will resist and fall. The river of life will wash the ancient pain away. In this new era, Jesus is the Morning Star, the theme of every song.

Anybody want to sing?

Worship Moments

- The famous letters to seven churches warn of superficial worship and fateful compromise. Keep faith growing and love expanding, the warnings urge (2:4).

- God loves all people. In the heavenly chorus stand people from everywhere. Let the church on earth reflect God's welcome to all (7:9).

- These singers keep their soulful chorus through loss and death. Nothing quenches their song of praise and rejoicing (12:11).

- All of heaven's inhabitants fall on their faces in worship of our Lord God Almighty, the Lamb of God, who will reign forever and ever (7:11; 11:16–17).

PROLOGUE

1 This is a revelation from* Jesus Christ, which God gave him concerning the events that will happen soon. An angel was sent to God's servant John so that John could share the revelation with God's other servants. [2]John faithfully reported the word of God and the testimony of Jesus Christ—everything he saw.

[3]God blesses the one who reads this prophecy to the church, and he blesses all who listen to it and obey what it says. For the time is near when these things will happen.

JOHN'S GREETING TO THE SEVEN CHURCHES

[4]This letter is from John to the seven churches in the province of Asia. Grace and peace from the one who is, who always was, and who is still to come; from the sevenfold Spirit* before his throne; [5]and from Jesus Christ, who is the faithful witness to these things, the first to rise from the dead, and the commander of all the rulers of the world.

All praise to him who loves us and has freed us from our sins by shedding his blood for us. [6]He has made us his Kingdom and his priests who serve before God his Father. Give to him everlasting glory! He rules forever and ever! Amen!

[7]Look! He comes with the clouds of heaven. And everyone will see him—even those who pierced him. And all the nations of the earth will weep because of him. Yes! Amen!

[8]"I am the Alpha and the Omega—the beginning and the end," says the Lord God. "I am the one who is, who always was, and who is still to come, the Almighty One."

VISION OF THE SON OF MAN

[9]I am John, your brother. In Jesus we are partners in suffering and in the Kingdom and in patient endurance. I was exiled to the island of Patmos for preaching the word of God and speaking about Jesus. [10]It was the Lord's Day,

and I was worshiping in the Spirit.* Suddenly, I heard a loud voice behind me, a voice that sounded like a trumpet blast. [11]It said, "Write down what you see, and send it to the seven churches: Ephesus, Smyrna, Pergamum, Thyatira, Sardis, Philadelphia, and Laodicea."

[12]When I turned to see who was speaking to me, I saw seven gold lampstands. [13]And standing in the middle of the lampstands was the Son of Man.* He was wearing a long robe with a gold sash across his chest. [14]His head and his hair were white like wool, as white as snow. And his eyes were bright like flames of fire. [15]His feet were as bright as bronze refined in a furnace, and his voice thundered like mighty ocean waves. [16]He held seven stars in his right hand, and a sharp two-edged sword came from his mouth. And his face was as bright as the sun in all its brilliance.

[17]When I saw him, I fell at his feet as dead. But he laid his right hand on me and said, "Don't be afraid! I am the First and the Last. [18]I am the living one who died. Look, I am alive forever and ever! And I hold the keys of death and the grave.* [19]Write down what you have seen—both the things that are now happening and the things that will happen later. [20]This is the meaning of the seven stars you saw in my right hand and the seven gold lampstands: The seven stars are the angels of* the seven churches, and the seven lampstands are the seven churches.

THE MESSAGE TO THE CHURCH IN EPHESUS

2 "Write this letter to the angel of* the church in Ephesus. This is the message from the one who holds the seven stars in his right hand, the one who walks among the seven gold lampstands:

[2]"I know all the things you do. I have seen your hard work and your patient endurance. I know you don't tolerate evil people. You have examined the claims of

---

1:1 Or *of.* 1:4 Greek *the seven spirits.* 1:10 Or *in spirit.* 1:13 Or *one who looked like a man;* Greek reads *one like a son of man.* See Dan 7:13. 1:18 Greek *and Hades.* 1:20 Or *the messengers for.* 2:1 Or *the messenger for;* also in 2:8, 12, 18.

My Daily Worship

— *December 24* —

IT'S WORTH IT!

REVELATION 1:1—2:29

Don't be afraid of what you are about to suffer. The Devil will throw some of you into prison and put you to the test. You will be persecuted for "ten days." Remain faithful even when facing death, and I will give you the crown of life (2:10).

[i reflect]

The young mother-to-be watches as her schoolgirl figure changes before her eyes. Morning sickness, weight gain, stretch marks, the agony of labor—is motherhood worth all this trouble? Ask her as she lies there smiling through the tears at the miracle of her newborn child.

The football player endures grueling two-a-day practices in the 90-degree heat of late summer. He then plays all season long through countless aches and pains. Why? What's the point? Ask him as he hoists the championship trophy above his head in front of thousands of screaming fans.

Painful preparation is not limited to the maternity ward or the football field. We are in a contest of eternal proportions. Everything—everything!—is on the line. We can find comfort and new strength by remembering that God is watching. He sees. He keeps records. And he has pledged to reward faithfulness. This is what he promised the Christians in the ancient church at Smyrna (in what is now modern-day Turkey). It is also what he guarantees us (Ephesians 6:8). We *will* one day enjoy glory, but first we must pass the test. And that test involves suffering.

When you endure, when you continue to enthrone God in your heart and life, no matter what, then you will one day be crowned with glory by the glorious One who owns all glory. In short, it pays to walk with God. It will be worth it. You watch. You wait. You'll see.

In the words from the liturgy of St. Mark, "Preserve us in our pilgrimage through this life from hurt and danger, and grant that we may finish our lives as Christians who are well-pleasing to you and free from sin and that we may have our portion and lot with all your saints . . . ."

Today make it your goal to cling fiercely and stubbornly to God. Instead of letting suffering and trials drive a wedge between you and the Lord, let your troubles be an opportunity to praise him.

[i pray]

Father, I need fresh strength. I need a second wind. I need the courage to push on and not quit. Give me the grace to see that the temporary suffering I face will result in eternal glory, for me, but more importantly, for You.

[i respond]

Get a Bible concordance and look up every reference to "rewards" or "crowns" in the New Testament. What does your study reveal to you?

those who say they are apostles but are not. You have discovered they are liars. ³You have patiently suffered for me without quitting. ⁴But I have this complaint against you. You don't love me or each other as you did at first! ⁵Look how far you have fallen from your first love! Turn back to me again and work as you did at first. If you don't, I will come and remove your lampstand from its place among the churches. ⁶But there is this about you that is good: You hate the deeds of the immoral Nicolaitans, just as I do.

⁷"Anyone who is willing to hear should listen to the Spirit and understand what the Spirit is saying to the churches. Everyone who is victorious will eat from the tree of life in the paradise of God.

The Message to the Church in Smyrna

⁸"Write this letter to the angel of the church in Smyrna. This is the message from the one who is the First and the Last, who died and is alive:

⁹"I know about your suffering and your poverty—but you are rich! I know the slander of those opposing you. They say they are Jews, but they really aren't because theirs is a synagogue of Satan. ¹⁰Don't be afraid of what you are about to suffer. The Devil will throw some of you into prison and put you to the test. You will be persecuted for 'ten days.' Remain faithful even when facing death, and I will give you the crown of life.

¹¹"Anyone who is willing to hear should listen to the Spirit and understand what the Spirit is saying to the churches. Whoever is victorious will not be hurt by the second death.

The Message to the Church in Pergamum

¹²"Write this letter to the angel of the church in Pergamum. This is the message from the one who has a sharp two-edged sword:

¹³"I know that you live in the city where that great throne of Satan is located, and yet you have remained loyal to me. And you refused to deny me even when Antipas, my faithful witness, was martyred among you by Satan's followers. ¹⁴And yet I have a few complaints against you. You tolerate some among you who are like Balaam, who showed Balak how to trip up the people of Israel. He taught them to worship idols by eating food offered to idols and by committing sexual sin. ¹⁵In the same way, you have some Nicolaitans among you—people who follow the same teaching and commit the same sins. ¹⁶Repent, or I will come to you suddenly and fight against them with the sword of my mouth.

¹⁷"Anyone who is willing to hear should listen to the Spirit and understand what the Spirit is saying to the churches. Everyone who is victorious will eat of the manna that has been hidden away in heaven. And I will give to each one a white stone, and on the stone will be engraved a new name that no one knows except the one who receives it.

The Message to the Church in Thyatira

¹⁸"Write this letter to the angel of the church in Thyatira. This is the message from the Son of God, whose eyes are bright like flames of fire, whose feet are like polished bronze:

¹⁹"I know all the things you do—your love, your faith, your service, and your patient endurance. And I can see your constant improvement in all these things. ²⁰But I have this complaint against you. You are permitting that woman—that Jezebel who calls herself a prophet—to lead my servants astray. She is encouraging them to worship idols, eat food offered to idols, and commit sexual sin. ²¹I gave her time to repent, but she would not turn away from her immorality. ²²Therefore, I will throw

her upon a sickbed, and she will suffer greatly with all who commit adultery with her, unless they turn away from all their evil deeds. ²³I will strike her children dead. And all the churches will know that I am the one who searches out the thoughts and intentions of every person. And I will give to each of you whatever you deserve. ²⁴But I also have a message for the rest of you in Thyatira who have not followed this false teaching ('deeper truths,' as they call them—depths of Satan, really). I will ask nothing more of you ²⁵except that you hold tightly to what you have until I come.

²⁶"To all who are victorious, who obey me to the very end, I will give authority over all the nations. ²⁷They will rule the nations with an iron rod and smash them like clay pots. ²⁸They will have the same authority I received from my Father, and I will also give them the morning star! ²⁹Anyone who is willing to hear should listen to the Spirit and understand what the Spirit is saying to the churches.

THE MESSAGE TO THE CHURCH IN SARDIS

3 "Write this letter to the angel of* the church in Sardis. This is the message from the one who has the sevenfold Spirit* of God and the seven stars:

"I know all the things you do, and that you have a reputation for being alive—but you are dead. ²Now wake up! Strengthen what little remains, for even what is left is at the point of death. Your deeds are far from right in the sight of God. ³Go back to what you heard and believed at first; hold to it firmly and turn to me again. Unless you do, I will come upon you suddenly, as unexpected as a thief.

⁴"Yet even in Sardis there are some who have not soiled their garments with evil deeds. They will walk with me in white, for they are worthy. ⁵All who are victorious will be clothed in white. I will never erase their names from the Book of Life, but I will announce before my Father and his angels that they are mine. ⁶Anyone who is willing to hear should listen to the Spirit and understand what the Spirit is saying to the churches.

THE MESSAGE TO THE CHURCH IN PHILADELPHIA

⁷"Write this letter to the angel of the church in Philadelphia. This is the message from the one who is holy and true. He is the one who has the key of David. He opens doors, and no one can shut them; he shuts doors, and no one can open them.

⁸"I know all the things you do, and I have opened a door for you that no one can shut. You have little strength, yet you obeyed my word and did not deny me. ⁹Look! I will force those who belong to Satan—those liars who say they are Jews but are not—to come and bow down at your feet. They will acknowledge that you are the ones I love.

¹⁰"Because you have obeyed my command to persevere, I will protect you from the great time of testing that will come upon the whole world to test those who belong to this world. ¹¹Look, I am coming quickly. Hold on to what you have, so that no one will take away your crown. ¹²All who are victorious will become pillars in the Temple of my God, and they will never have to leave it. And I will write my God's name on them, and they will be citizens in the city of my God—the new Jerusalem that comes down from heaven from my God. And they will have my new name inscribed upon them. ¹³Anyone who is willing to hear should listen to the Spirit and understand what the Spirit is saying to the churches.

3:1a Or the messenger for; also in 3:7, 14. 3:1b Greek the seven spirits.

The Message to the Church in Laodicea

[14]"Write this letter to the angel of the church in Laodicea. This is the message from the one who is the Amen—the faithful and true witness, the ruler* of God's creation:

[15]"I know all the things you do, that you are neither hot nor cold. I wish you were one or the other! [16]But since you are like lukewarm water, I will spit you out of my mouth! [17]You say, 'I am rich. I have everything I want. I don't need a thing!' And you don't realize that you are wretched and miserable and poor and blind and naked. [18]I advise you to buy gold from me—gold that has been purified by fire. Then you will be rich. And also buy white garments so you will not be shamed by your nakedness. And buy ointment for your eyes so you will be able to see. [19]I am the one who corrects and disciplines everyone I love. Be diligent and turn from your indifference.

[20]"Look! Here I stand at the door and knock. If you hear me calling and open the door, I will come in, and we will share a meal as friends. [21]I will invite everyone who is victorious to sit with me on my throne, just as I was victorious and sat with my Father on his throne. [22]Anyone who is willing to hear should listen to the Spirit and understand what the Spirit is saying to the churches."

Worship in Heaven

4 Then as I looked, I saw a door standing open in heaven, and the same voice I had heard before spoke to me with the sound of a mighty trumpet blast. The voice said, "Come up here, and I will show you what must happen after these things." [2]And instantly I was in the Spirit,* and I saw a throne in heaven and someone sitting on it! [3]The one sitting on the throne was as brilliant as gemstones—jasper and carnelian. And the glow of an emerald circled his throne like a rainbow. [4]Twenty-four thrones surrounded him, and twenty-four elders sat on them. They were all clothed in white and had gold crowns on their heads. [5]And from the throne came flashes of lightning and the rumble of thunder. And in front of the throne were seven lampstands with burning flames. They are the seven spirits* of God. [6]In front of the throne was a shiny sea of glass, sparkling like crystal.

In the center and around the throne were four living beings, each covered with eyes, front and back. [7]The first of these living beings had the form of a lion; the second looked like an ox; the third had a human face; and the fourth had the form of an eagle with wings spread out as though in flight. [8]Each of these living beings had six wings, and their wings were covered with eyes, inside and out. Day after day and night after night they keep on saying,

"Holy, holy, holy is the Lord God
    Almighty—
  the one who always was, who is, and
  who is still to come."

[9]Whenever the living beings give glory and honor and thanks to the one sitting on the throne, the one who lives forever and ever, [10]the twenty-four elders fall down and worship the one who lives forever and ever. And they lay their crowns before the throne and say,

[11] "You are worthy, O Lord our God,
  to receive glory and honor and power.
For you created everything,
  and it is for your pleasure that they exist
  and were created."

The Lamb Opens the Scroll

5 And I saw a scroll in the right hand of the one who was sitting on the throne. There was writing on the inside and the outside of the scroll, and it was sealed with seven seals.

3:14 Or *the source.* **4:2** Or *in spirit.* **4:5** See 1:4 and 3:1, where the same expression is translated *the sevenfold Spirit.*

My Daily Worship

— *December 25* —

STANDING AT THE DOOR

REVELATION 3:1—5:14

Look! Here I stand at the door and knock. If you hear me calling and open the door,
I will come in, and we will share a meal as friends (3:20).

[i reflect]

Before he died on July 28, 1982 in a tragic plane crash, Keith Green was, arguably, the biggest name in contemporary Christian music. He had the heart of a David and the prophetic message of a John the Baptist. His song, "You Love the World," written from Christ's point of view to his followers, is typical of Keith's radical, in-your-face style. Consider some of the lyrics: "You prefer the light of your TV, you love the world, and you're avoiding me." Jesus goes on to ask if it is right to ignore him after "I gave my blood to save your life."

Hard-hitting words, but certainly nothing new. The message of these uncomfortable lyrics is the same message we find in Revelation 3:20. Speaking to and through the apostle John, Jesus describes himself as being at a "door," knocking, and desiring to come in.

Christians typically use this verse in evangelism, urging unbelievers to "open their hearts to Jesus." While it is certainly true that Christ wants non-Christians to receive him in faith (John 1:12), this particular verse is actually addressed to Christians! A group of believers in Laodicea (modern-day Turkey) had become spiritually indifferent. They were going through the motions of Christianity, but in their attitudes and by their actions, they had actually shut Christ out of their lives—like a lot of modern-day Christians have done.

Sometimes we marginalize Christ, even on this day as we celebrate his birth. Seeing him as helpless baby, we leave him in the manger instead of worshiping him as Lord of lords and King of kings.

Examine your heart today. Have you shoved Christ over into the margins of your life? Has he become a bit player in the drama of your life? He wants to be central in your thoughts and plans. He wants to fellowship with you and be your closest friend. Are you letting him?

The baby grew to a man. Faithful to his plan, he died and rose again, for you. Now he stands at the door. Open your life to Christ today. Re-read the familiar Christmas story in Luke 2, but this time worship him as the Savior that he is.

[i pray]

Lord Jesus, forgive me for the assorted ways and the many times I have locked you out
of my thoughts and denied you access to my actions. Today, in a fresh new way, I want
you to be at home in the center of my life. I want you to govern me, lead me,
guide me, and change me. Please come and fellowship with me.

[i respond]

At dinner, set an extra place setting for Jesus. Expect his presence at your celebration today. Remember he promised! "If you hear me calling and open the door, I will come in, and we will share a meal as friends."

²And I saw a strong angel, who shouted with a loud voice: "Who is worthy to break the seals on this scroll and unroll it?" ³But no one in heaven or on earth or under the earth was able to open the scroll and read it.

⁴Then I wept because no one could be found who was worthy to open the scroll and read it. ⁵But one of the twenty-four elders said to me, "Stop weeping! Look, the Lion of the tribe of Judah, the heir to David's throne,* has conquered. He is worthy to open the scroll and break its seven seals."

⁶I looked and I saw a Lamb that had been killed but was now standing between the throne and the four living beings and among the twenty-four elders. He had seven horns and seven eyes, which are the seven spirits* of God that are sent out into every part of the earth. ⁷He stepped forward and took the scroll from the right hand of the one sitting on the throne. ⁸And as he took the scroll, the four living beings and the twenty-four elders fell down before the Lamb. Each one had a harp, and they held gold bowls filled with incense— the prayers of God's people!

⁹And they sang a new song with these words:

"You are worthy to take the scroll
and break its seals and open it.
For you were killed, and your blood has
ransomed people for God
from every tribe and language and
people and nation.
¹⁰ And you have caused them to become
God's Kingdom and his priests.
And they will reign* on the earth."

¹¹Then I looked again, and I heard the singing of thousands and millions of angels around the throne and the living beings and the elders. ¹²And they sang in a mighty chorus:

"The Lamb is worthy—the Lamb who was
killed.

He is worthy to receive power and riches
and wisdom and strength
and honor and glory and blessing."

¹³And then I heard every creature in heaven and on earth and under the earth and in the sea. They also sang:

"Blessing and honor and glory and power
belong to the one sitting on the throne
and to the Lamb forever and ever."

¹⁴And the four living beings said, "Amen!" And the twenty-four elders fell down and worshiped God and the Lamb.

THE LAMB BREAKS THE FIRST SIX SEALS

6 As I watched, the Lamb broke the first of the seven seals on the scroll. Then one of the four living beings called out with a voice that sounded like thunder, "Come!" ²I looked up and saw a white horse. Its rider carried a bow, and a crown was placed on his head. He rode out to win many battles and gain the victory.

³When the Lamb broke the second seal, I heard the second living being say, "Come!" ⁴And another horse appeared, a red one. Its rider was given a mighty sword and the authority to remove peace from the earth. And there was war and slaughter everywhere.

⁵When the Lamb broke the third seal, I heard the third living being say, "Come!" And I looked up and saw a black horse, and its rider was holding a pair of scales in his hand. ⁶And a voice from among the four living beings said, "A loaf of wheat bread or three loaves of barley for a day's pay.* And don't waste* the olive oil and wine."

⁷And when the Lamb broke the fourth seal, I heard the fourth living being say, "Come!" ⁸And I looked up and saw a horse whose color was pale green like a corpse. And Death was the name of its rider, who was followed

---

5:5 Greek *the root of David.* **5:6** See note on 4:5. **5:10** Some manuscripts read *they are reigning.* **6:6a** Greek *A choinix of wheat for a denarius, and 3 choinix of barley for a denarius.* **6:6b** Or *hurt.*

Words of Worship

LAMB

Lamb—Hebrew *seh*; *ke-ves*; Greek *am-nos*; *ar-ni-on*. Also Hebrew *pe-sach* "passover sacrifice" is sometimes translated "lamb."

Animal sacrifices were a major component of the rites of Israelite worship, and the lamb was an animal often sacrificed. Worshipers believed the sacrificial victim, which they provided at some cost to themselves, would please the Lord. The animal consumed on the altar's fires atoned for the people's sin and guilt, as God had directed. During the exodus from Egypt, the blood of a lamb marked the Israelites' homes, sparing them from the wrath of the Lord against their oppressors (Exodus 12:21–23).

In the New Testament, this powerful symbolism expresses Jesus' victory over evil in delivering us from sin through his death. Christ is called "our Passover Lamb" (1 Corinthians 5:7), the one "who takes away the sin of the world" (John 1:29). The victim becomes the victor, for the Lamb is also the conquering Lion of Judah (Revelation 5:5–6). As the Lamb, Christ receives the high praises of heaven and earth: "The Lamb is worthy—the Lamb who was killed. He is worthy to receive power and riches and wisdom and strength and honor and glory and blessing!" (Revelation 5:12).

around by the Grave.* They were given authority over one-fourth of the earth, to kill with the sword and famine and disease* and wild animals.

⁹And when the Lamb broke the fifth seal, I saw under the altar the souls of all who had been martyred for the word of God and for being faithful in their witness. ¹⁰They called loudly to the Lord and said, "O Sovereign Lord, holy and true, how long will it be before you judge the people who belong to this world for what they have done to us? When will you avenge our blood against these people?" ¹¹Then a white robe was given to each of them. And they were told to rest a little longer until the full number of their brothers and sisters* —their fellow servants of Jesus—had been martyred.

¹²I watched as the Lamb broke the sixth seal, and there was a great earthquake. The sun became as dark as black cloth, and the moon became as red as blood. ¹³Then the stars of the sky fell to the earth like green figs falling from trees shaken by mighty winds. ¹⁴And the sky was rolled up like a scroll and taken away. And all of the mountains and all of the islands disappeared. ¹⁵Then the kings of the earth, the rulers, the generals, the wealthy people, the people with great power, and every slave and every free person—all hid themselves in the caves and among the rocks of the mountains. ¹⁶And they cried to the mountains and the rocks, "Fall on us and hide us from the face of the one who sits on the throne and from the wrath of the Lamb. ¹⁷For the great day of their wrath has come, and who will be able to survive?"

GOD'S PEOPLE WILL BE PRESERVED

7 Then I saw four angels standing at the four corners of the earth, holding back the four winds from blowing upon the earth. Not a leaf rustled in the trees, and the sea became as smooth as glass. ²And I saw another angel coming from the east, carrying the seal of the living God. And he shouted out to those four angels who had been given power to injure land and sea, ³"Wait! Don't hurt the land or the sea or the trees until we have placed the seal of God on the foreheads of his servants."

6:8a Greek *by Hades.* 6:8b Greek *death.* 6:11 Greek *their brothers.*

⁴And I heard how many were marked with the seal of God. There were 144,000 who were sealed from all the tribes of Israel:

⁵	from Judah	12,000
	from Reuben	12,000
	from Gad	12,000
⁶	from Asher	12,000
	from Naphtali	12,000
	from Manasseh	12,000
⁷	from Simeon	12,000
	from Levi	12,000
	from Issachar	12,000
⁸	from Zebulun	12,000
	from Joseph	12,000
	from Benjamin	12,000

PRAISE FROM THE GREAT MULTITUDE

⁹After this I saw a vast crowd, too great to count, from every nation and tribe and people and language, standing in front of the throne and before the Lamb. They were clothed in white and held palm branches in their hands. ¹⁰And they were shouting with a mighty shout, "Salvation comes from our God on the throne and from the Lamb!"

¹¹And all the angels were standing around the throne and around the elders and the four living beings. And they fell face down before the throne and worshiped God. ¹²They said,

> "Amen! Blessing and glory and
> wisdom
> and thanksgiving and honor and power
> and strength
> belong to our God forever and forever.
> Amen!"

¹³Then one of the twenty-four elders asked me, "Who are these who are clothed in white? Where do they come from?"

¹⁴And I said to him, "Sir, you are the one who knows."

Then he said to me, "These are the ones coming out of the great tribulation. They washed their robes in the blood of the Lamb and made them white. ¹⁵That is why they are standing in front of the throne of God, serv-ing him day and night in his Temple. And he who sits on the throne will live among them and shelter them. ¹⁶They will never again be hungry or thirsty, and they will be fully protected from the scorching noontime heat. ¹⁷For the Lamb who stands in front of the throne will be their Shepherd. He will lead them to the springs of life-giving water. And God will wipe away all their tears."

THE LAMB BREAKS THE SEVENTH SEAL

8 When the Lamb broke the seventh seal, there was silence throughout heaven for about half an hour. ²And I saw the seven angels who stand before God, and they were given seven trumpets.

³Then another angel with a gold incense burner came and stood at the altar. And a great quantity of incense was given to him to mix with the prayers of God's people, to be offered on the gold altar before the throne. ⁴The smoke of the incense, mixed with the prayers of the saints, ascended up to God from the altar where the angel had poured them out. ⁵Then the angel filled the incense burner with fire from the altar and threw it down upon the earth; and thunder crashed, lightning flashed, and there was a terrible earthquake.

THE FIRST FOUR TRUMPETS

⁶Then the seven angels with the seven trumpets prepared to blow their mighty blasts.

⁷The first angel blew his trumpet, and hail and fire mixed with blood were thrown down upon the earth, and one-third of the earth was set on fire. One-third of the trees were burned, and all the grass was burned.

⁸Then the second angel blew his trumpet, and a great mountain of fire was thrown into the sea. And one-third of the water in the sea became blood. ⁹And one-third of all things living in the sea died. And one-third of all the ships on the sea were destroyed.

¹⁰Then the third angel blew his trumpet, and a great flaming star fell out of the sky,

My Daily Worship

— December 26 —

THE SWEET SMELL OF PRAYER

REVELATION 6:1–8:5

Then another angel with a gold incense burner came and stood at the altar. And a great quantity of incense was given to him to mix with the prayers of God's people, to be offered on the gold altar before the throne. The smoke of the incense, mixed with the prayers of the saints, ascended up to God from the altar where the angel had poured them out (8:3–4).

[i reflect]

Surveys show that an overwhelming majority of people pray. Believe it or not, even many self-described atheists admit to sending an occasional spiritual smoke signal toward heaven. Yet to a large number prayer feels like nothing more than religious self-talk, mixing up a lot of God-words and aiming them God-ward, all in the elaborate attempt to trick ourselves into feeling better about our lives.

Does God hear our prayers? Does prayer make a real difference? "I felt like my prayers were falling on deaf ears, or bouncing off the ceiling," is a common complaint. Perhaps you've felt this, or *said* this yourself. So what can we conclude? Is prayer nothing more than superstition? Is it merely a fancy kind of religious mumbo-jumbo, a silly exercise in wishful thinking?

Look again at the passage above. Notice the prayers of the saints mixed with incense and ascending into the very presence of God. Not sweet-smelling incense alone, not mere religious ritual, but sacrifice permeated by prayer. Desperate cries. Longings for God. Fervent expressions of love and trust. No wonder the Scripture says: "The LORD . . . delights in the prayers of the upright" (Proverbs 15:8).

Writer Howard Macy puts it this way: "Prayer has less to do with getting things than with knowing God. It is more concerned with loving God than with lists of prayer requests. Asking for assistance and knowing God are related, of course, but coming into intimacy with the Holy One is the principal purpose and context of prayer."

Today, if your heart is right, your prayers will be too. By communing with God and leaning on him as you work and play and rest, you *are* worshiping. Make it your practice to do so throughout the day.

[i pray]

Teach me, O Lord, how to make my entire life a continual prayer service. Help me to develop the discipline of communing with you, or, as one old saint put it, "practicing your presence."

[i respond]

Buy the short book *The Practice of the Presence of God* by Brother Lawrence. It will take you an hour or so to read. It will take you a lifetime to digest.

burning like a torch. It fell upon one-third of the rivers and on the springs of water. ¹¹The name of the star was Bitterness.* It made one-third of the water bitter, and many people died because the water was so bitter.

¹²Then the fourth angel blew his trumpet, and one-third of the sun was struck, and one-third of the moon, and one-third of the stars, and they became dark. And one-third of the day was dark and one-third of the night also.

¹³Then I looked up. And I heard a single eagle crying loudly as it flew through the air, "Terror, terror, terror to all who belong to this world because of what will happen when the last three angels blow their trumpets."

THE FIFTH TRUMPET BRINGS THE FIRST TERROR

9 Then the fifth angel blew his trumpet, and I saw a star that had fallen to earth from the sky, and he was given the key to the shaft of the bottomless pit. ²When he opened it, smoke poured out as though from a huge furnace, and the sunlight and air were darkened by the smoke.

³Then locusts came from the smoke and descended on the earth, and they were given power to sting like scorpions. ⁴They were told not to hurt the grass or plants or trees but to attack all the people who did not have the seal of God on their foreheads. ⁵They were told not to kill them but to torture them for five months with agony like the pain of scorpion stings. ⁶In those days people will seek death but will not find it. They will long to die, but death will flee away!

⁷The locusts looked like horses armed for battle. They had gold crowns on their heads, and they had human faces. ⁸Their hair was long like the hair of a woman, and their teeth were like the teeth of a lion. ⁹They had armor made of iron, and their wings roared like an army of chariots rushing into battle. ¹⁰They had tails that stung like scorpions, with power to torture people. This power was given to

them for five months. ¹¹Their king is the angel from the bottomless pit; his name in Hebrew is *Abaddon,* and in Greek, *Apollyon*—the Destroyer.

¹²The first terror is past, but look, two more terrors are coming!

> *If you don't worship . . .*
> *you'll never experience God.*
>
> DAVID JEREMIAH

THE SIXTH TRUMPET BRINGS THE SECOND TERROR

¹³Then the sixth angel blew his trumpet, and I heard a voice speaking from the four horns of the gold altar that stands in the presence of God. ¹⁴And the voice spoke to the sixth angel who held the trumpet: "Release the four angels who are bound at the great Euphrates River." ¹⁵And the four angels who had been prepared for this hour and day and month and year were turned loose to kill one-third of all the people on earth. ¹⁶They led an army of 200 million mounted troops—I heard an announcement of how many there were.

¹⁷And in my vision, I saw the horses and the riders sitting on them. The riders wore armor that was fiery red and sky blue and yellow. The horses' heads were like the heads of lions, and fire and smoke and burning sulfur billowed from their mouths. ¹⁸One-third of all the people on earth were killed by these three plagues—by the fire and the smoke and burning sulfur that came from the mouths of the horses. ¹⁹Their power was in their mouths, but also in their tails. For their tails had heads like snakes, with the power to injure people.

²⁰But the people who did not die in these

8:11 Greek *Wormwood.*

plagues still refused to turn from their evil deeds. They continued to worship demons and idols made of gold, silver, bronze, stone, and wood—idols that neither see nor hear nor walk! [21]And they did not repent of their murders or their witchcraft or their immorality or their thefts.

THE ANGEL AND THE SMALL SCROLL

10 Then I saw another mighty angel coming down from heaven, surrounded by a cloud, with a rainbow over his head. His face shone like the sun, and his feet were like pillars of fire. [2]And in his hand was a small scroll, which he had unrolled. He stood with his right foot on the sea and his left foot on the land. [3]And he gave a great shout, like the roar of a lion. And when he shouted, the seven thunders answered.

[4]When the seven thunders spoke, I was about to write. But a voice from heaven called to me: "Keep secret what the seven thunders said. Do not write it down."

[5]Then the mighty angel standing on the sea and on the land lifted his right hand to heaven. [6]And he swore an oath in the name of the one who lives forever and ever, who created heaven and everything in it, the earth and everything in it, and the sea and everything in it. He said, "God will wait no longer. [7]But when the seventh angel blows his trumpet, God's mysterious plan will be fulfilled. It will happen just as he announced it to his servants the prophets."

[8]Then the voice from heaven called to me again: "Go and take the unrolled scroll from the angel who is standing on the sea and on the land."

[9]So I approached him and asked him to give me the little scroll. "Yes, take it and eat it," he said. "At first it will taste like honey, but when you swallow it, it will make your stomach sour!" [10]So I took the little scroll from the hands of the angel, and I ate it! It was sweet in my mouth, but it made my stomach sour. [11]Then he said to me, "You must prophesy again about many peoples, nations, languages, and kings."

THE TWO WITNESSES

11 Then I was given a measuring stick, and I was told, "Go and measure the Temple of God and the altar, and count the number of worshipers. [2]But do not measure the outer courtyard, for it has been turned over to the nations. They will trample the holy city for 42 months. [3]And I will give power to my two witnesses, and they will be clothed in sackcloth and will prophesy during those 1,260 days."

[4]These two prophets are the two olive trees and the two lampstands that stand before the Lord of all the earth. [5]If anyone tries to harm them, fire flashes from the mouths of the prophets and consumes their enemies. This is how anyone who tries to harm them must die. [6]They have power to shut the skies so that no rain will fall for as long as they prophesy. And they have the power to turn the rivers and oceans into blood, and to send every kind of plague upon the earth as often as they wish.

[7]When they complete their testimony, the beast that comes up out of the bottomless pit will declare war against them. He will conquer them and kill them. [8]And their bodies will lie in the main street of Jerusalem,* the city which is called "Sodom" and "Egypt," the city where their Lord was crucified. [9]And for three and a half days, all peoples, tribes, languages, and nations will come to stare at their bodies. No one will be allowed to bury them. [10]All the people who belong to this world will give presents to each other to celebrate the death of the two prophets who had tormented them. [11]But after three and a half days, the spirit of life from God entered them, and they stood up! And terror struck all who were staring at them. [12]Then a loud voice shouted from

11:8 Greek *the great city.*

heaven, "Come up here!" And they rose to heaven in a cloud as their enemies watched.

¹³And in the same hour there was a terrible earthquake that destroyed a tenth of the city. Seven thousand people died in that earthquake. And everyone who did not die was terrified and gave glory to the God of heaven.

¹⁴The second terror is past, but look, now the third terror is coming quickly.

THE SEVENTH TRUMPET BRINGS THE THIRD TERROR

¹⁵Then the seventh angel blew his trumpet, and there were loud voices shouting in heaven: "The whole world has now become the Kingdom of our Lord and of his Christ, and he will reign forever and ever."

¹⁶And the twenty-four elders sitting on their thrones before God fell on their faces and worshiped him. ¹⁷And they said,

"We give thanks to you, Lord God
 Almighty,
 the one who is and who always was,
 for now you have assumed your great
  power
 and have begun to reign.
¹⁸ The nations were angry with you,
 but now the time of your wrath has
  come.
It is time to judge the dead and reward
 your servants.
You will reward your prophets and your
 holy people,
 all who fear your name, from the least to
  the greatest.
And you will destroy all who have caused
 destruction on the earth."

¹⁹Then, in heaven, the Temple of God was opened and the Ark of his covenant could be seen inside the Temple. Lightning flashed, thunder crashed and roared; there was a great hailstorm, and the world was shaken by a mighty earthquake.

12:10 Greek *brothers*.

THE WOMAN AND THE DRAGON

12 Then I witnessed in heaven an event of great significance. I saw a woman clothed with the sun, with the moon beneath her feet, and a crown of twelve stars on her head. ²She was pregnant, and she cried out in the pain of labor as she awaited her delivery.

³Suddenly, I witnessed in heaven another significant event. I saw a large red dragon with seven heads and ten horns, with seven crowns on his heads. ⁴His tail dragged down one-third of the stars, which he threw to the earth. He stood before the woman as she was about to give birth to her child, ready to devour the baby as soon as it was born.

⁵She gave birth to a boy who was to rule all nations with an iron rod. And the child was snatched away from the dragon and was caught up to God and to his throne. ⁶And the woman fled into the wilderness, where God had prepared a place to give her care for 1,260 days.

⁷Then there was war in heaven. Michael and the angels under his command fought the dragon and his angels. ⁸And the dragon lost the battle and was forced out of heaven. ⁹This great dragon—the ancient serpent called the Devil, or Satan, the one deceiving the whole world—was thrown down to the earth with all his angels.

¹⁰Then I heard a loud voice shouting across the heavens,

"It has happened at last—the salvation and power and kingdom of our God, and the authority of his Christ! For the Accuser has been thrown down to earth—the one who accused our brothers and sisters* before our God day and night. ¹¹And they have defeated him because of the blood of the Lamb and because of their testimony. And they were not afraid to die. ¹²Rejoice, O heavens! And you who live in the heavens, rejoice! But terror will come on the earth and the sea. For the Devil has come

My Daily Worship

— *December 27* —

No Dispute

REVELATION 8:6–11:19

And the twenty-four elders sitting on their thrones before God fell on their faces and worshiped him. And they said, "We give thanks to you, Lord God Almighty, the one who is and who always was, for now you have assumed your great power and have begun to reign" (11:16–17).

[i reflect]

So much about the book of Revelation is disputed. What is the purpose of this odd series of visions? How literally should we interpret all the imagery in the book? When will the events prophesied in these twenty-two chapters take place?

But so much about Revelation is *not* disputed. There is no disputing its claims of Who is in charge. Time and time again, the curtains of heaven are pulled back, so to speak, to reveal Almighty God on his throne, reigning over the heavens and ruling over human affairs.

The creatures and inhabitants of heaven have no confusion about worship. Interestingly, everyone and everything is described in terms of where it is in relation to the triune God. The elders are described as being "before God" or "before the throne" (4:10). Millions of angels are shown to be singing wildly and dipping and wheeling "around the throne" (5:11). Countless other creatures are revealed to be "standing in front of the throne and before the Lamb" (7:9). God is the worthy one, the celebrated one. The Lord is central. He is lifted up. Exalted. Adored. Honored. *He* is the focal point.

Scholars will be disputing the finer points of theology from now till kingdom come. Far wiser to follow the example of Augustine, "Let others wrangle; I will wonder."

Will you do that today? Wonder at all these breathtaking peeks into eternity? Wonder at a God who holds time in his hands and who has the whole cosmos on a perfect schedule? Wonder at the opportunity to know the Creator—who desires to make his home in you and to reign over your heart with perfect love and mercy?

Wonder.

[i pray]

I love you, Lord. And I praise you for the undeniable truth that you reign. Those with the best view of reality, the best seats in the universe, have the clearest priorities. They understand that you are worthy. And they order their existence around you. Teach me to do the same.

[i respond]

In your family hymnal or on the Internet, look for the words to hymns or praise songs that celebrate the glory of God, such as "Majesty," "All Hail the Power," or "My God Reigns." Let the lyrics of these songs lift your eyes heavenward.

Words of Worship

CONFESS

Confess, Confession—Hebrew *ho-dah* "confess, acknowledge"; Greek *ho-mo-lo-ge-o* "confess"; *ex-o-mo-lo-ge-o* "confess, acknowledge."

To confess means to agree with God's judgment about who we are. Usually we understand this negatively—we agree that we have been disobedient and turned away from God. That's a good move, because acknowledging our shortcomings is the first step toward the healing of our brokenness. The Bible promises that those who confess their sin will receive God's mercy (Proverbs 28:13). John assures us, "But if we confess our sins to him, he is faithful and just to forgive us and to cleanse us from every wrong" (1 John 1:9).

But Biblical confession has another side. To confess means to acknowledge that we are God's servants, and his Son is our Lord. Paul says, "If you confess with your mouth that Jesus is Lord and believe in your heart that God raised him from the dead, you will be saved" (Romans 10:9). Eventually, he adds, every tongue will have to make this confession, bringing glory to the Father (Philippians 2:11). Confessing our sins may be saying something negative about us, but it leads to something positive: we agree that we belong to Christ the Lord. In our worship life, we need to do both kinds of confessing.

down to you in great anger, and he knows that he has little time."

¹³And when the dragon realized that he had been thrown down to the earth, he pursued the woman who had given birth to the child. ¹⁴But she was given two wings like those of a great eagle. This allowed her to fly to a place prepared for her in the wilderness, where she would be cared for and protected from the dragon* for a time, times, and half a time. ¹⁵Then the dragon tried to drown the woman with a flood of water that flowed from its mouth. ¹⁶But the earth helped her by opening its mouth and swallowing the river that gushed out from the mouth of the dragon. ¹⁷Then the dragon became angry at the woman, and he declared war against the rest of her children—all who keep God's commandments and confess that they belong to Jesus.

THE BEAST OUT OF THE SEA

¹⁸Then he stood* waiting on the shore of the sea.

13 And now in my vision I saw a beast rising up out of the sea. It had seven heads and ten horns, with ten crowns on its horns. And written on each head were names that blasphemed God. ²This beast looked like a leopard, but it had bear's feet and a lion's mouth! And the dragon gave him his own power and throne and great authority.

³I saw that one of the heads of the beast seemed wounded beyond recovery—but the fatal wound was healed! All the world marveled at this miracle and followed the beast in awe. ⁴They worshiped the dragon for giving the beast such power, and they worshiped the beast. "Is there anyone as great as the beast?" they exclaimed. "Who is able to fight against him?"

⁵Then the beast was allowed to speak great blasphemies against God. And he was given authority to do what he wanted for forty-two months. ⁶And he spoke terrible words of blasphemy against God, slandering his name and all who live in heaven, who are his temple. ⁷And the beast was allowed to wage war

12:14 Greek *the serpent;* also in 12:15. See 12:9.   **12:18** Some manuscripts read *Then I stood,* and some translations put this entire sentence into 13:1.

My Daily Worship

— *December 28* —

THE LANGUAGE OF HEAVEN

REVELATION 12:1–14:20

This great choir sang a wonderful new song in front of the throne of God and before the four living beings and the twenty-four elders. And no one could learn this song except those 144,000 who had been redeemed from the earth (14:3).

[i reflect]

Author Simone Weil observed that the only two things that can pierce the human heart are beauty and affliction. Perhaps she forgot a third item. What about *music*?

Try to imagine a world filled with random, jarring noises but no notes or melodious tunes. Not a single choir. No violin concertos or chirping birds. No pianos or three-part harmony. It's hard to fathom, isn't it? How grim. What an ugly thought!

Thankfully, we do enjoy God's gift of music. In the verse above we are reminded that heaven is filled with gorgeous, otherworldly praise music. Anthems, hymns, and songs, forever new, that will absolutely take your breath away. Angelic choruses that fill heaven with joy and gladness.

God is good enough to give us little previews of this on earth, here in this life. You've had the experience. You hear a new song that sets your toe a-tapping. It puts a bounce in your step and a smile on your face that lasts all day. Or you hear an instrumental arrangement or a beautiful solo and for some inexplicable reason, tears fill your eyes. What can this mean?

Frederick Buechner in his book *Whistling in the Dark: A Doubter's Dictionary* counsels: "Whenever you find tears in your eyes, especially unexpected tears, it is well to pay the closest attention. They are not only telling you something about the secret of who you are, but more often than not God is speaking to you through them of the mystery of where you have come from and is summoning you to where, if your soul is to be saved, you should go to next."

Today, why not surround yourself with praise music? Turn off the news or sports radio and let music fill your day. Be transported into the presence of God and then try to keep from singing.

[i pray]

Father in heaven, you are worthy. Thank you for the gift of music with which to exalt and honor you. Let my whole life be a song of praise to you, and let today be a new song, or at least a beautiful new verse.

[i respond]

Try your hand at writing a simple praise chorus. If you are "musically challenged," then try to set new words to an old, familiar tune.

against God's holy people and to overcome them. And he was given authority to rule over every tribe and people and language and nation. [8]And all the people who belong to this world worshiped the beast. They are the ones whose names were not written in the Book of Life, which belongs to the Lamb who was killed before the world was made.

[9]Anyone who is willing to hear should listen and understand. [10]The people who are destined for prison will be arrested and taken away. Those who are destined for death will be killed. But do not be dismayed, for here is your opportunity to have endurance and faith.

THE BEAST OUT OF THE EARTH

[11]Then I saw another beast come up out of the earth. He had two horns like those of a lamb, and he spoke with the voice of a dragon. [12]He exercised all the authority of the first beast. And he required all the earth and those who belong to this world to worship the first beast, whose death-wound had been healed. [13]He did astounding miracles, such as making fire flash down to earth from heaven while everyone was watching. [14]And with all the miracles he was allowed to perform on behalf of the first beast, he deceived all the people who belong to this world. He ordered the people of the world to make a great statue of the first beast, who was fatally wounded and then came back to life. [15]He was permitted to give life to this statue so that it could speak. Then the statue commanded that anyone refusing to worship it must die.

[16]He required everyone—great and small, rich and poor, slave and free—to be given a mark on the right hand or on the forehead. [17]And no one could buy or sell anything without that mark, which was either the name of the beast or the number representing his name. [18]Wisdom is needed to understand this. Let the one who has understanding solve the number of the beast, for it is the number of a man.* His number is 666.*

THE LAMB AND THE 144,000

14 Then I saw the Lamb standing on Mount Zion, and with him were 144,000 who had his name and his Father's name written on their foreheads. [2]And I heard a sound from heaven like the roaring of a great waterfall or the rolling of mighty thunder. It was like the sound of many harpists playing together.

[3]This great choir sang a wonderful new song in front of the throne of God and before the four living beings and the twenty-four elders. And no one could learn this song except those 144,000 who had been redeemed from the earth. [4]For they are spiritually undefiled, pure as virgins,* following the Lamb wherever he goes. They have been purchased from among the people on the earth as a special offering* to God and to the Lamb. [5]No falsehood can be charged against them; they are blameless.

THE THREE ANGELS

[6]And I saw another angel flying through the heavens, carrying the everlasting Good News to preach to the people who belong to this world—to every nation, tribe, language, and people. [7]"Fear God," he shouted. "Give glory to him. For the time has come when he will sit as judge. Worship him who made heaven and earth, the sea, and all the springs of water."

[8]Then another angel followed him through the skies, shouting, "Babylon is fallen—that great city is fallen—because she seduced the nations of the world and made them drink the wine of her passionate immorality."

[9]Then a third angel followed them, shouting, "Anyone who worships the beast and his statue or who accepts his mark on the forehead or the hand [10]must drink the wine of God's wrath. It is poured out undiluted into God's cup of wrath. And they will be tormented with fire and burning sulfur in the presence of the holy angels and the Lamb. [11]The smoke of their torment rises forever and ever, and they will have no relief day or night,

---

13:18a Or *of humanity.* 13:18b Some manuscripts read *616.* 14:4a Greek *they are virgins who have not defiled themselves with women.* 14:4b Greek *as firstfruits.*

for they have worshiped the beast and his statue and have accepted the mark of his name. [12]Let this encourage God's holy people to endure persecution patiently and remain firm to the end, obeying his commands and trusting in Jesus."

[13]And I heard a voice from heaven saying, "Write this down: Blessed are those who die in the Lord from now on. Yes, says the Spirit, they are blessed indeed, for they will rest from all their toils and trials; for their good deeds follow them!"

THE HARVEST OF THE EARTH

[14]Then I saw the Son of Man* sitting on a white cloud. He had a gold crown on his head and a sharp sickle in his hand.

[15]Then an angel came from the Temple and called out in a loud voice to the one sitting on the cloud, "Use the sickle, for the time has come for you to harvest; the crop is ripe on the earth." [16]So the one sitting on the cloud swung his sickle over the earth, and the whole earth was harvested.

[17]After that, another angel came from the Temple in heaven, and he also had a sharp sickle. [18]Then another angel, who has power to destroy the world with fire, shouted to the angel with the sickle, "Use your sickle now to gather the clusters of grapes from the vines of the earth, for they are fully ripe for judgment." [19]So the angel swung his sickle on the earth and loaded the grapes into the great winepress of God's wrath. [20]And the grapes were trodden in the winepress outside the city, and blood flowed from the winepress in a stream about 180 miles* long and as high as a horse's bridle.

THE SONG OF MOSES AND OF THE LAMB

15 Then I saw in heaven another significant event, and it was great and marvelous. Seven angels were holding the seven last plagues, which would bring God's wrath to completion. [2]I saw before me what seemed to be a crystal sea mixed with fire. And on it stood all the people who had been victorious over the beast and his statue and the number representing his name. They were all holding harps that God had given them. [3]And they were singing the song of Moses, the servant of God, and the song of the Lamb:

"Great and marvelous are your actions,
  Lord God Almighty.
Just and true are your ways,
  O King of the nations.*
[4] Who will not fear, O Lord, and glorify
  your name?
  For you alone are holy.
All nations will come and worship before
  you,
  for your righteous deeds have been
  revealed."

THE SEVEN BOWLS OF THE SEVEN PLAGUES

[5]Then I looked and saw that the Temple in heaven, God's Tabernacle, was thrown wide open! [6]The seven angels who were holding the bowls of the seven plagues came from the Temple, clothed in spotless white linen* with gold belts across their chests. [7]And one of the four living beings handed each of the seven angels a gold bowl filled with the terrible wrath of God, who lives forever and forever. [8]The Temple was filled with smoke from God's glory and power. No one could enter the Temple until the seven angels had completed pouring out the seven plagues.

16 Then I heard a mighty voice shouting from the Temple to the seven angels, "Now go your ways and empty out the seven bowls of God's wrath on the earth."

[2]So the first angel left the Temple and poured out his bowl over the earth, and horrible, malignant sores broke out on everyone who had the mark of the beast and who worshiped his statue.

14:14 Or *one who looked like a man;* Greek reads *one like a son of man.* **14:20** Greek *1,600 stadia* [296 kilometers]. **15:3** Some manuscripts read *King of the ages;* other manuscripts read *King of the saints.* **15:6** Some manuscripts read *in bright and sparkling stone.*

³Then the second angel poured out his bowl on the sea, and it became like the blood of a corpse. And everything in the sea died.

⁴Then the third angel poured out his bowl on the rivers and springs, and they became blood. ⁵And I heard the angel who had authority over all water saying, "You are just in sending this judgment, O Holy One, who is and who always was. ⁶For your holy people and your prophets have been killed, and their blood was poured out on the earth. So you have given their murderers blood to drink. It is their just reward." ⁷And I heard a voice from the altar saying, "Yes, Lord God Almighty, your punishments are true and just."

⁸Then the fourth angel poured out his bowl on the sun, causing it to scorch everyone with its fire. ⁹Everyone was burned by this blast of heat, and they cursed the name of God, who sent all of these plagues. They did not repent and give him glory.

¹⁰Then the fifth angel poured out his bowl on the throne of the beast, and his kingdom was plunged into darkness. And his subjects ground their teeth in anguish, ¹¹and they cursed the God of heaven for their pains and sores. But they refused to repent of all their evil deeds.

¹²Then the sixth angel poured out his bowl on the great Euphrates River, and it dried up so that the kings from the east could march their armies westward without hindrance. ¹³And I saw three evil spirits that looked like frogs leap from the mouth of the dragon, the beast, and the false prophet. ¹⁴These miracle-working demons caused all the rulers of the world to gather for battle against the Lord on that great judgment day of God Almighty.

¹⁵"Take note: I will come as unexpectedly as a thief! Blessed are all who are watching for me, who keep their robes ready so they will not need to walk naked and ashamed."

¹⁶And they gathered all the rulers and their armies to a place called *Armageddon* in Hebrew.

¹⁷Then the seventh angel poured out his bowl into the air. And a mighty shout came from the throne of the Temple in heaven, saying, "It is finished!" ¹⁸Then the thunder crashed and rolled, and lightning flashed. And there was an earthquake greater than ever before in human history. ¹⁹The great city of Babylon split into three pieces, and cities around the world fell into heaps of rubble. And so God remembered all of Babylon's sins, and he made her drink the cup that was filled with the wine of his fierce wrath. ²⁰And every island disappeared, and all the mountains were leveled. ²¹There was a terrible hailstorm, and hailstones weighing seventy-five pounds* fell from the sky onto the people below. They cursed God because of the hailstorm, which was a very terrible plague.

THE GREAT PROSTITUTE

17 One of the seven angels who had poured out the seven bowls came over and spoke to me. "Come with me," he said, "and I will show you the judgment that is going to come on the great prostitute, who sits on many waters. ²The rulers of the world have had immoral relations with her, and the people who belong to this world have been made drunk by the wine of her immorality."

³So the angel took me in spirit* into the wilderness. There I saw a woman sitting on a scarlet beast that had seven heads and ten horns, written all over with blasphemies against God. ⁴The woman wore purple and scarlet clothing and beautiful jewelry made of gold and precious gems and pearls. She held in her hand a gold goblet full of obscenities and the impurities of her immorality. ⁵A mysterious name was written on her forehead: "Babylon the Great, Mother of All Prostitutes and Obscenities in the World." ⁶I could see that she was drunk—drunk with the blood of God's holy people who were witnesses for Jesus. I stared at her completely amazed.

⁷"Why are you so amazed?" the angel asked.

16:21 Greek *1 talent* [34 kilograms].   17:3 Or *in the Spirit*.

My Daily Worship

CAUGHT OFF GUARD?

REVELATION 15:1–17:18

Take note: I will come as unexpectedly as a thief! Blessed are all who are watching for me,
who keep their robes ready so they will not need to walk naked and ashamed (16:15).

[i reflect]

A television commercial features excited workers throwing an all-out party to celebrate the company president going away on business, only to find out that he had cancelled his trip and would be arriving at the office any minute. An old cartoon features an obviously angry boss standing over the desk of a clearly surprised employee. The employer is saying, "Why aren't you working!?" And the reply of the underling? "Because I didn't know you were here!"

Anyone who's ever held a job smiles at these glimpses of office humor. Funny how a person's efficiency increases when the boss is in the building. (Similar to the way we become *extremely* conscious of the speed limit when we spot a police car on the side of the highway up ahead!)

Revelation 16:15 echoes a theme found throughout the New Testament. It is imperative that Christians live faithfully because Jesus Christ could return at any moment. We cannot afford to slack off or get sloppy in our faith. In fact, we are warned to faithfully watch and wait—even as we work hard and serve well. We are to "keep our robes ready"—which we might interpret as keeping our lives ready, our hearts right, our souls full of love and worship and anticipation for the Lord's coming. In one of his letters, the apostle John puts it this way, "And now, dear children, continue to live in fellowship with Christ, so that when he returns, you will be full of courage and not shrink back from him in shame" (1 John 2:28).

As Dwight L. Moody wrote, "The moment a person takes hold of the truth that Jesus Christ is coming back again to receive his friends to himself, this world loses it hold upon him. Gas stocks, stocks in banks and in railroads are of much less consequence. The heart is free to look for the blessed appearing of our Lord, who at his coming will take us into his blessed kingdom."

What's the status of your heart today? Is your heart free to look for the blessed appearing of Christ, or does this world still have a hold on you? Take a few minutes to reflect on your readiness to receive Jesus.

[i pray]

Lord, thank you for the reminder that your return is imminent. Forgive me for fudging in my faith—
cutting corners, rationalizing, taking questionable liberties. Renew my heart and my
passion to live and serve with excellence as I watch for your coming.

[i respond]

Are you kind of fuzzy about what the Bible teaches regarding the return of Christ? Ask your pastor or small group leader to recommend a good resource.

"I will tell you the mystery of this woman and of the beast with seven heads and ten horns. ⁸The beast you saw was alive but isn't now. And yet he will soon come up out of the bottomless pit and go to eternal destruction. And the people who belong to this world, whose names were not written in the Book of Life from before the world began, will be amazed at the reappearance of this beast who had died.

⁹"And now understand this: The seven heads of the beast represent the seven hills of the city where this woman rules. They also represent seven kings. ¹⁰Five kings have already fallen, the sixth now reigns, and the seventh is yet to come, but his reign will be brief. ¹¹The scarlet beast that was alive and then died is the eighth king. He is like the other seven, and he, too, will go to his doom. ¹²His ten horns are ten kings who have not yet risen to power; they will be appointed to their kingdoms for one brief moment to reign with the beast. ¹³They will all agree to give their power and authority to him. ¹⁴Together they will wage war against the Lamb, but the Lamb will defeat them because he is Lord over all lords and King over all kings, and his people are the called and chosen and faithful ones."

¹⁵And the angel said to me, "The waters where the prostitute is sitting represent masses of people of every nation and language. ¹⁶The scarlet beast and his ten horns—which represent ten kings who will reign with him—all hate the prostitute. They will strip her naked, eat her flesh, and burn her remains with fire. ¹⁷For God has put a plan into their minds, a plan that will carry out his purposes. They will mutually agree to give their authority to the scarlet beast, and so the words of God will be fulfilled. ¹⁸And this woman you saw in your vision represents the great city that rules over the kings of the earth."

The Fall of Babylon

18 After all this I saw another angel come down from heaven with great authority, and the earth grew bright with his splendor. ²He gave a mighty shout, "Babylon is fallen—that great city is fallen! She has become the hideout of demons and evil spirits, a nest for filthy buzzards, and a den for dreadful beasts. ³For all the nations have drunk the wine of her passionate immorality. The rulers of the world have committed adultery with her, and merchants throughout the world have grown rich as a result of her luxurious living."

⁴Then I heard another voice calling from heaven, "Come away from her, my people. Do not take part in her sins, or you will be punished with her. ⁵For her sins are piled as high as heaven, and God is ready to judge her for her evil deeds. ⁶Do to her as she has done to your people. Give her a double penalty for all her evil deeds. She brewed a cup of terror for others, so give her twice as much as she gave out. ⁷She has lived in luxury and pleasure, so match it now with torments and sorrows. She boasts, 'I am queen on my throne. I am no helpless widow. I will not experience sorrow.' ⁸Therefore, the sorrows of death and mourning and famine will overtake her in a single day. She will be utterly consumed by fire, for the Lord God who judges her is mighty."

⁹And the rulers of the world who took part in her immoral acts and enjoyed her great luxury will mourn for her as they see the smoke rising from her charred remains. ¹⁰They will stand at a distance, terrified by her great torment. They will cry out, "How terrible, how terrible for Babylon, that great city! In one single moment God's judgment came on her."

¹¹The merchants of the world will weep and mourn for her, for there is no one left to buy their goods. ¹²She bought great quantities of gold, silver, jewels, pearls, fine linen, purple dye, silk, scarlet cloth, every kind of perfumed wood, ivory goods, objects made of expensive wood, bronze, iron, and marble. ¹³She also bought cinnamon, spice, incense, myrrh, frankincense, wine, olive oil, fine flour, wheat, cattle, sheep, horses, chariots, and slaves—yes, she even traded in human lives.

¹⁴"All the fancy things you loved so much are gone," they cry. "The luxuries and splendor that you prized so much will never be yours again. They are gone forever."

¹⁵The merchants who became wealthy by selling her these things will stand at a distance, terrified by her great torment. They will weep and cry. ¹⁶"How terrible, how terrible for that great city! She was so beautiful—like a woman clothed in finest purple and scarlet linens, decked out with gold and precious stones and pearls! ¹⁷And in one single moment all the wealth of the city is gone!"

And all the shipowners and captains of the merchant ships and their crews will stand at a distance. ¹⁸They will weep as they watch the smoke ascend, and they will say, "Where in all the world is there another city like this?" ¹⁹And they will throw dust on their heads to show their great sorrow. And they will say, "How terrible, how terrible for the great city! She made us all rich from her great wealth. And now in a single hour it is all gone."

²⁰But you, O heaven, rejoice over her fate. And you also rejoice, O holy people of God and apostles and prophets! For at last God has judged her on your behalf.

²¹Then a mighty angel picked up a boulder as large as a great millstone. He threw it into the ocean and shouted, "Babylon, the great city, will be thrown down as violently as I have thrown away this stone, and she will disappear forever. ²²Never again will the sound of music be heard there—no more harps, songs, flutes, or trumpets. There will be no industry of any kind, and no more milling of grain. ²³Her nights will be dark, without a single lamp. There will be no happy voices of brides and grooms. This will happen because her merchants, who were the greatest in the world, deceived the nations with her sorceries. ²⁴In her streets the blood of the prophets was spilled. She was the one who slaughtered God's people all over the world."

SONGS OF VICTORY IN HEAVEN

19 After this, I heard the sound of a vast crowd in heaven shouting, "Hallelujah! Salvation is from our God. Glory and power belong to him alone. ²His judgments are just and true. He has punished the great prostitute who corrupted the earth with her immorality, and he has avenged the murder of his servants." ³Again and again their voices rang, "Hallelujah! The smoke from that city ascends forever and forever!"

⁴Then the twenty-four elders and the four living beings fell down and worshiped God, who was sitting on the throne. They cried out, "Amen! Hallelujah!"

⁵And from the throne came a voice that said, "Praise our God, all his servants, from the least to the greatest, all who fear him."

⁶Then I heard again what sounded like the shout of a huge crowd, or the roar of mighty ocean waves, or the crash of loud thunder: "Hallelujah! For the Lord our God, the Almighty, reigns. ⁷Let us be glad and rejoice and honor him. For the time has come for the wedding feast of the Lamb, and his bride has prepared herself. ⁸She is permitted to wear the finest white linen." (Fine linen represents the good deeds done by the people of God.)

⁹And the angel said, "Write this: Blessed are those who are invited to the wedding feast of the Lamb." And he added, "These are true words that come from God."

¹⁰Then I fell down at his feet to worship him, but he said, "No, don't worship me. For I am a servant of God, just like you and other brothers and sisters* who testify of their faith in Jesus. Worship God. For the essence of prophecy is to give a clear witness for Jesus.*"

THE RIDER ON THE WHITE HORSE

¹¹Then I saw heaven opened, and a white horse was standing there. And the one sitting on the horse was named Faithful and True. For he judges fairly and then goes to war. ¹²His eyes were bright like flames of fire, and on his head

---

19:10a Greek *brothers.* **19:10b** Or *is the message confirmed by Jesus.*

were many crowns. A name was written on him, and only he knew what it meant. ¹³He was clothed with a robe dipped in blood, and his title was the Word of God. ¹⁴The armies of heaven, dressed in pure white linen, followed him on white horses. ¹⁵From his mouth came a sharp sword, and with it he struck down the nations. He ruled them with an iron rod, and he trod the winepress of the fierce wrath of almighty God. ¹⁶On his robe and thigh was written this title: King of kings and Lord of lords.

¹⁷Then I saw an angel standing in the sun, shouting to the vultures flying high in the sky: "Come! Gather together for the great banquet God has prepared. ¹⁸Come and eat the flesh of kings, captains, and strong warriors; of horses and their riders; and of all humanity, both free and slave, small and great."

¹⁹Then I saw the beast gathering the kings of the earth and their armies in order to fight against the one sitting on the horse and his army. ²⁰And the beast was captured, and with him the false prophet who did mighty miracles on behalf of the beast—miracles that deceived all who had accepted the mark of the beast and who worshiped his statue. Both the beast and his false prophet were thrown alive into the lake of fire that burns with sulfur. ²¹Their entire army was killed by the sharp sword that came out of the mouth of the one riding the white horse. And all the vultures of the sky gorged themselves on the dead bodies.

THE THOUSAND YEARS

20 Then I saw an angel come down from heaven with the key to the bottomless pit and a heavy chain in his hand. ²He seized the dragon—that old serpent, the Devil, Satan—and bound him in chains for a thousand years. ³The angel threw him into the bottomless pit, which he then shut and locked so Satan could not deceive the nations anymore until the thousand years were finished. Afterward he would be released again for a little while.

⁴Then I saw thrones, and the people sitting on them had been given the authority to judge. And I saw the souls of those who had been beheaded for their testimony about Jesus, for proclaiming the word of God. And I saw the souls of those who had not worshiped the beast or his statue, nor accepted his mark on their forehead or their hands. They came to life again, and they reigned with Christ for a thousand years. ⁵This is the first resurrection. (The rest of the dead did not come back to life until the thousand years had ended.) ⁶Blessed and holy are those who share in the first resurrection. For them the second death holds no power, but they will be priests of God and of Christ and will reign with him a thousand years.

THE DEFEAT OF SATAN

⁷When the thousand years end, Satan will be let out of his prison. ⁸He will go out to deceive the nations from every corner of the earth, which are called Gog and Magog. He will gather them together for battle—a mighty host, as numberless as sand along the shore. ⁹And I saw them as they went up on the broad plain of the earth and surrounded God's people and the beloved city. But fire from heaven came down on the attacking armies and consumed them.

¹⁰Then the Devil, who betrayed them, was thrown into the lake of fire that burns with sulfur, joining the beast and the false prophet. There they will be tormented day and night forever and ever.

THE FINAL JUDGMENT

¹¹And I saw a great white throne, and I saw the one who was sitting on it. The earth and sky fled from his presence, but they found no place to hide. ¹²I saw the dead, both great and small, standing before God's throne. And the books were opened, including the Book of Life. And the dead were judged according to the things written in the books, according to what they had done. ¹³The sea gave up the dead in it, and death and the

My Daily Worship

— December 30 —

THE ROAR OF THE CROWD
REVELATION 18:1–20:15

Then I heard again what sounded like the shout of a huge crowd, or the roar of mighty ocean waves, or the crash of loud thunder: "Hallelujah! For the Lord our God, the Almighty, reigns" (19:6).

[i reflect]

Kevin is forty-three and a believer in Jesus Christ. He leads a men's group, works as an accountant, is a husband, and the father of two teenagers. Yesterday (that is, Saturday), he went to watch his alma mater play a big conference basketball game. Talk about exciting! Down by 18 points at halftime, his team came roaring back to win in double-overtime. Kevin was ecstatic. He behaved like a wild man, jumping up and down, even high-fiving total strangers!

Today at church, as the worship team sings songs about the greatness of God and the wonder of his love, Kevin barely sings. During one especially upbeat chorus, a group of college students begins to clap enthusiastically. Kevin contemplates joining in, but then feels sheepish, so he shoves his hands in his pockets.

Question #1: Why do so many Christians get so excited about so many things, yet remain unexcited when celebrating their faith?

Question #2: Why shouldn't our weekly church services be as thrilling as a great sporting event?

What the apostle John saw in his visions of heaven was anything but tame. Loud worship. Wild celebration. Unbridled joy.

Consider the words of Jim Cymbala from his book *Fresh Wind, Fresh Fire*: "If we don't want to experience God's closeness here on earth, why would we want to go to heaven anyway? He is the center of everything there. If we don't enjoy being in his presence here and now, then heaven would not be heaven for us. Why would he send anyone there who doesn't long for him passionately here on earth?"

What are your expectations for worship—personal and corporate—this week? Remember—wherever you worship, you will be in the presence of great God Almighty. What will you do differently to lose yourself in reverence and praise?

Stand up and shout. Clap your hands. Raise your arms in praise. Do something to express your excitement of being in God's presence.

[i pray]

Lord, forgive me for the times I get overly excited at superficial stuff and act ho-hum about the things that matter most. Give me eyes to see you as you really are, and the courage to care less about what others think. I want my whole life to roar with praise for you!

[i respond]

Watch a few minutes of a live (or televised) sporting event. What can you learn about worship from watching the fans (the "fanatics") in attendance?

> *In the process of being worshiped . . .*
> *God communicates*
> *his presence to men.*
>
> C. S. LEWIS

grave* gave up the dead in them. They were all judged according to their deeds. ¹⁴And death and the grave were thrown into the lake of fire. This is the second death—the lake of fire. ¹⁵And anyone whose name was not found recorded in the Book of Life was thrown into the lake of fire.

THE NEW JERUSALEM

21 Then I saw a new heaven and a new earth, for the old heaven and the old earth had disappeared. And the sea was also gone. ²And I saw the holy city, the new Jerusalem, coming down from God out of heaven like a beautiful bride prepared for her husband.

³I heard a loud shout from the throne, saying, "Look, the home of God is now among his people! He will live with them, and they will be his people. God himself will be with them.* ⁴He will remove all of their sorrows, and there will be no more death or sorrow or crying or pain. For the old world and its evils are gone forever."

⁵And the one sitting on the throne said, "Look, I am making all things new!" And then he said to me, "Write this down, for what I tell you is trustworthy and true." ⁶And he also said, "It is finished! I am the Alpha and the Omega—the Beginning and the End. To all who are thirsty I will give the springs of the water of life without charge! ⁷All who are victorious will inherit all these blessings, and I

will be their God, and they will be my children. ⁸But cowards who turn away from me, and unbelievers, and the corrupt, and murderers, and the immoral, and those who practice witchcraft, and idol worshipers, and all liars—their doom is in the lake that burns with fire and sulfur. This is the second death."

⁹Then one of the seven angels who held the seven bowls containing the seven last plagues came and said to me, "Come with me! I will show you the bride, the wife of the Lamb."

¹⁰So he took me in spirit* to a great, high mountain, and he showed me the holy city, Jerusalem, descending out of heaven from God. ¹¹It was filled with the glory of God and sparkled like a precious gem, crystal clear like jasper. ¹²Its walls were broad and high, with twelve gates guarded by twelve angels. And the names of the twelve tribes of Israel were written on the gates. ¹³There were three gates on each side—east, north, south, and west. ¹⁴The wall of the city had twelve foundation stones, and on them were written the names of the twelve apostles of the Lamb.

¹⁵The angel who talked to me held in his hand a gold measuring stick to measure the city, its gates, and its wall. ¹⁶When he measured it, he found it was a square, as wide as it was long. In fact, it was in the form of a cube, for its length and width and height were each 1,400 miles.* ¹⁷Then he measured the walls and found them to be 216 feet thick* (the angel used a standard human measure).

¹⁸The wall was made of jasper, and the city was pure gold, as clear as glass. ¹⁹The wall of the city was built on foundation stones inlaid with twelve gems: the first was jasper, the second sapphire, the third agate, the fourth emerald, ²⁰the fifth onyx, the sixth carnelian, the seventh chrysolite, the eighth beryl, the ninth topaz, the tenth chrysoprase, the eleventh jacinth, the twelfth amethyst.

²¹The twelve gates were made of pearls—each gate from a single pearl! And the main street was pure gold, as clear as glass.

20:13 Greek *and Hades; also in* 20:14. 21:3 Some manuscripts read *God himself will be with them, their God.* 21:10 Or *in the Spirit.* 21:16 Greek *12,000 stadia* [2,220 kilometers]. 21:17 Greek *144 cubits* [65 meters].

My Daily Worship

— December 31 —

OPEN AT LAST

REVELATION 21:1 – 22:21

He who is the faithful witness to all these things says, "Yes, I am coming soon!"
Amen! Come, Lord Jesus! (22:20).

[i reflect]

In his wonderfully rich sermon "The Weight of Glory," C. S. Lewis addresses the inconsolable longing of the human heart for heaven. He observes: "At present we are on the outside of the world, the wrong side of the door. We discern the freshness and purity of morning, but they do not make us fresh and pure. We cannot mingle with the splendours we see. But all the leaves of the New Testament are rustling with the rumour that it will not always be so. Some day, God willing, we shall get *in*."

This is precisely what we discover in Revelation 21 and 22. The gates to Paradise are opened. The curse of Eden is broken. "There will be no more death or sorrow or crying or pain. For the old world and its evils are gone forever" (21:4). All things are restored. John's finite, stunned mind scrambles feverishly to come up with adequate words to describe all that he sees unfolded before him. But not even an unabridged thesaurus can do eternity justice.

Beauty, purity, newness. Heaven is a marvel—exquisite wonders and infinite mysteries. But chief among them all is the promise that we "will see his face" (22:4). No wonder John cries out at the end of his book, "Amen! Come, Lord Jesus!" This is the cry of every worshiper. This is the deepest desire of our hearts—to be swept up into perfect intimacy with God. This is the great hope of the believer. Only this promise can sustain us in a fallen world. Lewis puts it this way, "The door on which we have been knocking all our lives will open at last."

Today, let the reality of heaven give you a newer, truer perspective on this world.

[i pray]

Come, Lord Jesus! Only you can fill the deep needs of my soul. Only you can satisfy
the hunger of my heart. You alone are worthy. Again, I present myself
to you—all that I am, all that I have. Be glorified in me. Amen!

[i respond]

Take a brief inventory of your soul. What attitudes, actions, possessions, relationships, etc. obscure the reality of eternity in your life? What is the Spirit of God prompting you to discard, initiate, or rearrange so that Christ is preeminent in your heart?

[22]No temple could be seen in the city, for the Lord God Almighty and the Lamb are its temple. [23]And the city has no need of sun or moon, for the glory of God illuminates the city, and the Lamb is its light. [24]The nations of the earth will walk in its light, and the rulers of the world will come and bring their glory to it. [25]Its gates never close at the end of day because there is no night. [26]And all the nations will bring their glory and honor into the city. [27]Nothing evil will be allowed to enter—no one who practices shameful idolatry and dishonesty—but only those whose names are written in the Lamb's Book of Life.

22 And the angel showed me a pure river with the water of life, clear as crystal, flowing from the throne of God and of the Lamb, [2]coursing down the center of the main street. On each side of the river grew a tree of life, bearing twelve crops of fruit,* with a fresh crop each month. The leaves were used for medicine to heal the nations.

[3]No longer will anything be cursed. For the throne of God and of the Lamb will be there, and his servants will worship him. [4]And they will see his face, and his name will be written on their foreheads. [5]And there will be no night there—no need for lamps or sun—for the Lord God will shine on them. And they will reign forever and ever.

[6]Then the angel said to me, "These words are trustworthy and true: 'The Lord God, who tells his prophets what the future holds, has sent his angel to tell you what will happen soon.'"

JESUS IS COMING

[7]"Look, I am coming soon! Blessed are those who obey the prophecy written in this scroll."

[8]I, John, am the one who saw and heard all these things. And when I saw and heard these things, I fell down to worship the angel who showed them to me. [9]But again he said, "No, don't worship me. I am a servant of God, just like you and your brothers the prophets, as well as all who obey what is written in this scroll. Worship God!"

[10]Then he instructed me, "Do not seal up the prophetic words you have written, for the time is near. [11]Let the one who is doing wrong continue to do wrong; the one who is vile, continue to be vile; the one who is good, continue to do good; and the one who is holy, continue in holiness."

[12]"See, I am coming soon, and my reward is with me, to repay all according to their deeds. [13]I am the Alpha and the Omega, the First and the Last, the Beginning and the End."

[14]Blessed are those who wash their robes so they can enter through the gates of the city and eat the fruit from the tree of life. [15]Outside the city are the dogs—the sorcerers, the sexually immoral, the murderers, the idol worshipers, and all who love to live a lie.

[16]"I, Jesus, have sent my angel to give you this message for the churches. I am both the source of David and the heir to his throne.* I am the bright morning star."

[17]The Spirit and the bride say, "Come." Let each one who hears them say, "Come." Let the thirsty ones come—anyone who wants to. Let them come and drink the water of life without charge. [18]And I solemnly declare to everyone who hears the prophetic words of this book: If anyone adds anything to what is written here, God will add to that person the plagues described in this book. [19]And if anyone removes any of the words of this prophetic book, God will remove that person's share in the tree of life and in the holy city that are described in this book.

[20]He who is the faithful witness to all these things says, "Yes, I am coming soon!"

Amen! Come, Lord Jesus!

[21]The grace of the Lord Jesus be with you all.

22:2 Or *12 kinds of fruit.* 22:16 Greek *I am the root and offspring of David.*

Words of Worship Index

Worship Quotes Author Index